THE BANTAM NEW COLLEGE DICTIONARY SERIES

John C. Traupman, Author

JOHN C. TRAUPMAN received his B.A. in German and in Latin at Moravian College and his M.A. and Ph.D. in Classics at Princeton University. He is chairman of the Department of Classical Languages at St. Joseph's University (Philadelphia). He served as president of the Philadelphia Classical Society, of the Pennsylvania Classical Association, and of the Classical and Modern Language League. He has published widely in learned journals and is the author of *The New College Latin & English Dictionary* (Bantam Books, 1966) and an associate editor of *The Scribner-Bantam English Dictionary* (Scribner's, 1977; Bantam Books, 1979).

Edwin B. Williams, General Editor

EDWIN B. WILLIAMS (1891–1975), A.B., A.M., Ph.D., Doct. d'Univ., LL.D., L.H.D., was chairman of the Department of Romance Languages, dean of the Graduate School, and provost of the University of Pennsylvania. He was a member of the American Philosophical Society and the Hispanic Society of America. Among his many lexicographical works are *The Williams Spanish and English Dictionary* (Scribner's, formerly Holt) and *The Bantam New College Spanish and English Dictionary*. He created and coordinated the Bantam series of original dictionaries—English, French, German, Italian, Latin, and Spanish.

Webster's
GERMAN & ENGLISH
Dictionary

By John C. Traupman, Ph.D.

St. Joseph's University, Philadelphia

CASTLE BOOKS
A Division of BOOK SALES, INC.
110 Enterprise Avenue Secaucus, N.J. 07094

ISBN: 0-89009-330-X

CONTENTS

I wish to express my appreciation to the many persons on whose help I relied in researching and compiling this Dictionary. I am particularly indebted to Edwin B. Williams, Walter D. Glanze, Donald Reis, Rudolf Pillwein, and Helmut Kreitz.

J. C. T.

HOW TO USE THIS DICTIONARY

HINWEISE FÜR DEN BENUTZER

All entry words are treated in a fixed order according to the parts of speech and the functions of verbs. On the German-English side: past participle, adjective, adverb, pronoun, preposition, conjunction, interjection, transitive verb, reflexive verb, reciprocal verb, intransitive verb, impersonal verb, auxiliary verb, substantive; on the English-German side: adjective, substantive, pronoun, adverb, preposition, conjunction, transitive verb, intransitive verb, auxiliary verb, impersonal verb, interjection.

Alle Stichwörter werden in einheitlicher Reihenfolge gemäß der Wortart und der Verbfunktion behandelt. Im deutsch-englischen Teil: Partizip Perfekt, Adjektiv, Adverb, Pronomen, Präposition, Konjunktion, Interjektion, transitives Verb, reflexives Verb, reziprokes Verb, intransitives Verb, unpersönliches Verb, Hilfsverb, Substantiv; im englisch-deutschen Teil: Adjektiv, Substantiv, Pronomen, Adverb, Präposition, Konjunktion, transitives Verb, intransitives Verb, Hilfsverb, unpersönliches Verb, Interjektion.

The order of meanings within an entry is as follows: first, the more general meanings; second, the meanings with usage labels; third, the meanings with subject labels in alphabetical order; fourth, illustrative phrases in alphabetical order.

Die verschiedenen Bedeutungen sind innerhalb eines Stichwortartikels in folgender Anordnung gegeben: zuerst die allgemeinen Bedeutungen; dann die Bedeutungen mit Bezeichnung der Sprachgebrauchsebene; dann die Bedeutungen mit Bezeichnung des Sachgebietes, in alphabetischer Reihenfolge; zuletzt die Anwendungsbeispiele, in alphabetischer Reihenfolge.

Subject and usage labels (printed in roman and in parentheses) refer to the preceding entry word or illustrative phrase in the source language (printed in boldface), e.g.,

Die Bezeichnungen der Sprachgebrauchsebene und des Sachgebiets (in Antiqua und in Klammern) beziehen sich auf das vorangehende Stichwort oder Anwendungsbeispiel in der Ausgangssprache (halbfett gedruckt), z.B.

mund'tot *adj*—**j-n m. machen** (fig) silence s.o.
Pinke ['pɪŋkə] *f* (—;) (coll) dough

Words in parentheses and in roman coming after a meaning serve to clarify that meaning, e.g.,

Kursiv gedruckte Wörter in Klammern, die nach einer Bedeutung stehen, sollen diese Bedeutung illustrieren, z.B.

überschau'en *tr* look over, survey; overlook (*a scene*)

Words in parenthese and in roman type coming after or before a meaning are optional additions to the word in the target language, e.g.,	In Antiqua gedruckte Wörter in Klammern, die nach oder vor einer Bedeutung stehen, sind wahlfreie Erweiterungen des Wortes der Zielsprache, z.B.

Tanne ['tanə] *f* (–;–n) fir (tree)
Pap′rikaschote *f* (green) pepper

Meaning discriminations are given in the source language and are in italics, e.g.,	Bedeutungsdifferenzierungen sind in der Ausgangssprache angegeben und kursiv gedruckt, z.B.

überrei′zen *tr* overexcite; (*Augen, Nerven*) strain
earn [ʌrn] *tr* (*money*) verdienen; (*interest*) einbringen

Since vocabulary entries are not determined on the basis of etymology, homographs are listed as a single entry.	Da die Etymologie bei der Anführung der Stichwörter unberücksichtigt bleibt, sind gleichgeschriebene Wörter als ein und dasselbe Stichwort verzeichnet.

The entry word is represented within the entry by its initial letter followed by a period (if the entry word contains more than three letters), provided the form is identical. The same applies to a word that follows the parallels. The entry word is not abbreviated within the entry when associated with suspension points, e.g.,	Innerhalb eines Stichwortartikels wird das Stichwort (wenn es mehr als drei Buchstaben enthält) durch seinen Anfangsbuchstaben und einen Punkt angegeben, vorausgesetzt, daß die betreffende Form mit dem Stichwort identisch ist. Das Gleiche gilt für ein Wort, das nach den Vertikalstrichen steht. Wenn ein Stichwort innerhalb eines Stichwortartikels in Verbindung mit Auslassungspunkten angegeben ist, wird es nicht abgekürzt, z.B.

weder . . . noch

Parallels are used (a) to separate parts of speech, (b) to separate transitive, reflexive, reciprocal, intransitive, impersonal, and auxiliary verbs, (c) to separate verbs taking HABEN from those taking SEIN, (d) to indicate a change in pronunciation of the entry word, depending on the meaning, e.g.,	Es ist der Zweck der Vertikalstriche, (a) Wortarten voneinander zu trennen, (b) transitive, reflexive, reziproke, intransitive, unpersönliche Verben und Hilfsverben zu trennen, (c) Verben mit dem Hilfsverb HABEN von Verben mit dem Hilfsverb SEIN zu trennen, (d) verschiedene Aussprachen des Stichwortes je nach Bedeutung anzuzeigen, z.B.

bow [baʊ] *s* Verbeugung *f;* (naut) Bug *m* . . .
‖ [bo] *s* (*weapon*) Bogen *m;* . . .

(e) to show change from a strong verb to a weak verb and vice versa, (f) to show a change in the case governed by	(e) den Wechsel von einem starken zu einem schwachen Verb und umgekehrt anzuzeigen, (f) den Wechsel in einem

viii

a preposition where the entry word is a preposition, (g) to show a shift of accent, e.g.,	von einer Präposition regierten Fall anzuzeigen, wo das Stichwort selbst eine Präposition ist, (g) unterschiedliche Stellungen des Akzents anzuzeigen, z.B.

ü′bergießen *tr* . . . ‖ übergie′ßen *tr* . . .

The centered period in the English word on the German-English side marks the point at which the following letters are dropped before irregular plural endings are added. The centered period in the entry word on the English-German side marks the point at which the following letters are dropped before irregular plural endings are added to nouns and inflections are added to verbs. The centered period in the phonetic spelling indicates diaeresis, e.g.,	Der auf Mitte stehende Punkt im Stichwort des deutsch-englischen Teils zeigt die Stelle an, wo die nachfolgenden Buchstaben abzutrennen sind, bevor unregelmäßige Pluralendungen angefügt werden können. Der auf Mitte stehende Punkt im Stichwort des englisch-deutschen Teils zeigt die Stelle an, wo die nachfolgenden Buchstaben abzutrennen sind, bevor unregelmäßige Pluralendungen an Hauptwörter and Flexionen an Verben angefügt werden können. Der auf Mitte stehende Punkt in der Lautschrift zeigt Diärese an, z.B.

befähigt [bə′fe·ɪçt]

On the German-English and the English-German side, in the case of a transitive verb, the meaning discrimination in parentheses before the target word is always the object of the verb. On the German-English side, in the case of an intransitive verb, the meaning discrimination in parentheses before the target word is always the subject of the verb. On the English-German side, the suggested subject of a verb is prefaced by the words "said of".	Im deutsch-englischen und im englisch-deutschen Teil ist die bei transitiven Verben in Klammern vor dem Wort in der Zielsprache angegebene Bedeutungsdifferenzierung immer das Objekt des Verbs. Im deutsch-englischen Teil ist bei intransitiven Verben die vor dem Wort in der Zielsprache angegebene Bedeutungsdifferenzierung immer das Subjekt des Verbs. Im englisch-deutschen Teil stehen vor dem beabsichtigten Subjekt eines Verbs die Worte "said of."

Inflections are generally not shown for compound entry words, since the inflections have been shown where the components are entry words. However, when the last component of a compound noun on the German-English side has various inflections depending on meaning, the inflection is shown for the compound, e.g.,	Bei zusammengesetzten Stichwörtern ist die Flexion im Allgemeinen nicht angegeben, da sie unter den als Stichwörter angeführten Teilen des Kompositums angegeben ist. Falls jedoch der letzte Teil eines deutschen Kompositums je nach der Bedeutung verschieden flektiert wird, ist die Flexion für das Kompositum angegeben, z.B.

Ton′band *n* (–[e]s;=er) . . .

German verbs are regarded as reflexive regardless of whether the reflexive pronoun is the direct or indirect object of the verb.	Deutsche Verben gelten als reflexiv ohne Rücksicht darauf, ob das Reflexivpronomen das direkte oder indirekte Objekt des Verbs ist.

On the English-German side, when the pronunciation of an entry word is not given, stress in the entry word is shown as follows: a high-set primary stress mark ′ follows the syllable that receives the primary stress, and a high-set secondary stress mark ′ follows the syllable that receives the secondary stress. When the pronunciation of an entry word *is* provided [given in brackets], a high-set primary stress mark ' *precedes* the syllable that receives the primary stress, and a *low*-set secondary stress mark ˌ *precedes* the syllable that receives the secondary stress.

On the German-English side, when the pronunciation of an entry word is not given, a high-set primary stress mark ′ follows the syllable of the entry word that receives the primary stress. When the pronunciation of the entry *is* provided [given in brackets], a high-set primary stress mark ' *precedes* the syllable that receives the primary stress. (Because opinions on the system of secondary stress in German differ widely, secondary stress marks are not employed in this Dictionary.)

Wo die Aussprache des Stichwortes im englisch-deutschen Teil nicht angegeben ist, wird die Betonung des Stichwortes folgendermaßen angedeutet: Das stärkere, obere graphische Zeichen ′ steht nach der Silbe mit dem Haupttonakzent, und das schwächere, obere Zeichen ′ steht nach der Silbe mit dem Nebentonakzent. Wo hingegen die Aussprache des Stichwortes im englisch-deutschen Teil [in eckigen Klammern] angegeben ist, steht das stärkere, obere Zeichen ' *vor* der Silbe mit dem Haupttonakzent und das schwächere, *untere* Zeichen ˌ *vor* der Silbe mit dem Nebentonakzent.

Wo die Aussprache das Stichwortes im deutsch-englischen Teil nicht angegeben ist, steht das starke Zeichen ′ nach der Stichwortsilbe mit dem Haupttonakzent. Wo hingegen die Aussprache des Stichwortes im deutsch-englischen Teil [in eckigen Klammern] angegeben ist, steht das starke Zeichen ' *vor* der Silbe mit dem Haupttonakzent. (Wegen der widersprüchlichen Theorien, die die Frage des Nebentonakzents im Deutschen umgeben, wendet dieses Wörterbuch keine Nebentonakzente für die deutschen Wörter an.)

Proper nouns and general abbreviations are listed in their alphabetical position in the main body of the Dictionary.

Eigennamen und allgemeine Abkürzungen sind in den beiden Hauptteilen des Wörterbuches in alphabetischer Reihenfolge angegeben.

This Dictionary contains approximately 75,000 "entries." As entries are counted (a) nonindented boldface headwords and (b) elements that could have been set nonindented as separate headwords, too, but that for reasons of style and typography are grouped under the nonindented headwords, namely, separate parts of speech and boldface idioms and phrases.

Dieses Wörterbuch enthält ungefähr 75.000 "Stichwörter." Die folgenden Elemente gelten als Stichwörter: (a) die nicht eingerückten fettgedruckten Wörter am Anfang eines Stichwortartikels und (b) Elemente, die man auf dieselbe Weise hatte drucken können, die aber aus Stil– und Typographiegründen eingerückt wurden, nämlich die unterschiedlichen Wortarten und die fettgedruckten Redewendungen.

PART ONE

German-English

GERMAN—ENGLISH

A

A, a [ɑ] *invar n* A, a; (mus) A; **das A und O** the beginning and the end; (*das Wichtigste*) the most important thing

Aal [ɑl] *m* (**-[e]s;-e**) eel; (nav) torpedo

aal'glatt' *adj* (fig) sly as a fox

Aas [ɑs] *n* (**-es;-e**) carrion; (sl) louse

ab [ap] *adv* off; away; down; on, e.g., **von heute ab** from today on; (theat) exit, exeunt, e.g., **Hamlet ab** exit Hamlet; **ab und zu** now and then || *prep* (*dat*) from, e.g., **ab Frankfurt** from Frankfurt; minus, e.g., **ab Skonto** minus discount

ab'ändern *tr* alter; (*völlig*) change; (*mildern*) modify; (parl) amend

Ab'änderung *f* (**-;-en**) alteration; change; modification; (parl) amendment

Ab'änderungsantrag *m* (parl) (proposed) amendment

ab'arbeiten *tr* work off || *ref* work hard

Ab'art *f* variety, type

ab'arten *intr* (SEIN) deviate from type

Ab'bau *m* (**-[e]s;**) demolition; reduction; cutback; layoff; (chem) decomposition; (min) exploitation

ab'bauen *tr* demolish; (*Maschinen, Fabriken*) dismantle; (*Steuern, Preise, Truppen*) reduce; (*Zelt*) take down; (*Lager*) break; (*Angestellte*) lay off; (chem) decompose; (min) work, exploit

ab'beißen §53 *tr* bite off || *intr* take a bite

ab'bekommen §99 *tr* (*seinen Teil*) get; (*Schmutz*) get out; (*Deckel*) get off; **du wirst was a.!** you're going to get it!

ab'berufen §122 *tr* (dipl) recall

ab'bestellen *tr* cancel

ab'betteln *tr*—**die ganze Straße a.** beg up and down the street; **j-m etw a.** chisel s.th. from s.o.

ab'biegen §57 *tr* bend, twist off; (*Gefahr*) avert; (*Plan*) thwart; **das Gespräch a.** change the subject || *intr* (SEIN) branch off; (fig) get off the track; **in e-e Seitenstraße a.** turn down a side street; **nach links a.** turn left; **von e-r Straße a.** turn off a road

Ab'bild *n* picture, image

ab'bilden *tr* represent

Ab'bildung *f* (**-;-en**) illustration, figure

ab'binden §59 *tr* untie; (*Kalb*) wean; (*Arm*) apply a tourniquet to; (surg) tie off || *intr* (*Zement*) set

Ab'bitte *f* apology; **A. tun wegen** apologize for

ab'bitten §60 *tr* apologize for || *intr* apologize

ab'blasen §61 *tr* blow off; (fig) call off || *intr* (mil) sound the retreat

ab'blättern *intr* (SEIN) shed leaves; (*Farben, Haut*) flake, peel

ab'blenden *tr* dim; (cin) fade out; (phot) stop down || *intr* (aut) dim the lights; (nav) darken ship; (phot) stop down the lens

Ab'blendlicht *n* (aut) low-beam lights

ab'blitzen *intr* (SEIN) be unsuccessful; **j-n a. lassen** snub s.o.

ab'blühen *intr* stop blooming || *intr* (SEIN) fade

ab'böschen *tr* slope; (*Mauer*) batter

ab'brausen *tr* hose down || *ref* shower off || *intr* (SEIN) (coll) roar off

ab'brechen §64 *tr* break off; (*Belagerung*) raise; (*Gebäude*) demolish; (*Zelt*) take down; (sport) call; **das Lager a.** break camp || *intr* (SEIN) (& fig) break off

ab'bremsen *tr* slow down; (*Streik*) prevent; (*Motoren*) (aer) rev || *intr* put on the brakes; (aer) fishtail

ab'brennen §97 *tr* burn off; (*Feuerwerk*) set off; (*Geschütz*) fire; (chem) distil out; (metal) refine; (naut) bream; **ich bin vollkommen abgebrannt** (coll) I'm dead broke || *intr* (SEIN) burn down

ab'bringen §65 *tr* (*Fleck*) remove; (*gestrandetes Schiff*) refloat; **davon a. zu** (*inf*) dissuade from (*ger*); **vom rechten Weg a.** lead astray; **vom Thema a.** throw off; **von der Spur a.** throw off the scent; **von e-r Gewohnheit a.** break of the habit

ab'bröckeln *intr* crumble; (*Farbe*) peel (off); (*Preis, Aktie*) go slowly down; (*Mitglieder*) fall off

Ab'bruch *m* (*e-s Zweiges, der Beziehungen*) breaking off; (*e-s Gebäudes*) demolition; (*Schaden*) damage; **A. des Spiels** (sport) calling of the game; **A. tun** (*dat*) harm, spoil; **auf A. verkaufen** sell at demolition value; (*Maschinen*) sell for junk

ab'brühen *tr* (culin) scald

ab'brummen *tr* (*Strafe*) (coll) serve, do || *intr* (SEIN) (coll) clear out

ab'buchen *tr* (*abschreiben*) write off; (acct) debit

ab'bürsten *tr* brush off

ab'büßen *tr* atone for; **e-e Strafe a.** serve time; **er hat es schwer a. müssen** (coll) he had to pay for it dearly

Abc [abeˈtse] *n* (**-;-**) ABC's

Abc'-Schütze *m* (**-n;-n**) pupil

ab'danken *tr* dismiss; (*pensionieren*)

A, a　　　　3　　　　**abdanken**

retire || *intr* resign; (*Herrscher*) ab-
dicate; (mil) get a discharge
ab'decken *tr* uncover; (*Tisch*) clear;
(*Bett*) turn down; (*Vieh*) skin; (*e-e
Schuld*) pay back; (mil) camouflage;
(phot) mask
ab'dichten *tr* seal (off); (*Loch*) plug
up; (*mit weichem Material*) pack;
(naut) caulk
ab'dienen *tr* (*Schuld*) work off; (mil)
serve (*one's term*)
ab'drehen *tr* twist off; (*Gas, Licht,
Wasser*) turn off || *intr* turn away
ab'dreschen §67 *tr* thrash
Ab'druck *m* (-s;-e) reprint; offprint;
copy; (*Abguß*) casting; (phot, typ)
proof || *m* (-s;-̈e) impression, im-
print
ab'drucken *tr* print
ab'drücken *tr* (*abformen*) mold; (*Gewehr*) fire; (*Pfeil*) shoot; (*umarmen*)
hug; **den Hahn a.** pull the trigger ||
ref leave an impression || *intr* pull
the trigger
ab'duschen *ref* shower off
Abend ['ɑbənt] *m* (-s;-e) evening;
am A. in the evening; **bunter A.** social; (telv) variety show; **des Abends**
in the evening(s); **zu A. essen** eat
dinner
A'bendblatt *n* evening paper
A'bendbrot *n* supper, dinner
A'benddämmerung *f* twilight, dusk
A'bendessen *n* supper, dinner
abendfüllend ['ɑbəntfylənt] *adj* full-
length (*movie*)
A'bendgesellschaft *f* party (*in the
evening*)
A'bendland *n* West, Occident
abendländisch ['ɑbəntlɛndɪʃ] *adj* occi-
dental
a'bendlich *adj* evening || *adv* evenings
A'bendmahl *n* supper; **das Heilige A.**
Holy Communion
abends ['ɑbənts] *adv* in the evening
Abenteuer ['ɑbəntɔɪ·ər] *s* (-s;-) adventure; **galantes A.** (love) affair
a'benteuerlich *adj* adventurous; (*Unternehmen*) risky
aber ['ɑbər] *adv* yet, however; (before
adjectives and adverbs) really, indeed; **a. und abermals** over and
over again; **hundert und a. hundert**
hundreds and hundreds of || *conj*
but || *interj*—aber, aber! now, now!
|| **Aber** *n* (-s;-s) but; **hier gibt es
kein A.!** no ifs and buts
A'berglaube *m* superstition
abergläubisch ['ɑbərglɔɪbɪʃ] *adj* superstitious
ab'erkennen §97 *tr*—**j-m etw a.** deny
s.o. s.th.; (jur) dispossess s.o. of s.th.
Ab'erkennung *f* (-;-en) denial; (jur)
dispossession
abermalig ['ɑbərmɑlɪç] *adj* repeated
abermals ['ɑbərmɑls] *adv* once more
ab'ernten *tr* reap, harvest
ab'fahren §71 *tr* cart away; (*Strecke*)
cover; (*Straße*) wear out; (*Reifen*)
wear down || *intr* (SEIN) depart;
drive off
Ab'fahrt *f* departure
Ab'fall *m* (*der Blätter*) falling; (*Bö-

schung*) steep slope; (*von e-m Glauben*) falling away; (*von e-r Partei*)
defection; (*Sinken*) drop, decrease;
Abfälle garbage, trash; chips, shavings
ab'fallen §72 *intr* (SEIN) fall off; (*von
e-r Partei*) defect; (*vom Glauben*)
fall away; (*abnehmen*) decrease,
fail; (*Kunden*) stay away; (sport)
fall behind; **a. gegen** compare badly
with; **es wird etw für dich a.** there'll
be s.th. in it for you; **körperlich a.**
lose weight; **steil a.** drop away
abfällig ['ɑpfɛlɪç] *adj* disparaging
Ab'fallprodukt *n* by-product
ab'fangen §73 *tr* catch; (*Angriff*) foil;
(*Brief*) intercept; (aer) pull out of a
dive; (*U-Boot*) (nav) trim; (sport)
catch (up with); **j-m die Kunden a.**
steal s.o.'s customers
ab'färben *intr* (*Farben*) run; (*Stoff*)
fade; **a. auf** (*acc*) stain; (fig) rub
off on
ab'fassen *tr* compose, draft; (*erwischen*) catch
Ab'fassung *f* (-;-en) wording; composition
ab'faulen *intr* (SEIN) rot away
ab'fegen *tr* sweep off, whisk off
abfertigen ['ɑpfɛrtɪgən] *tr* get ready
for sending off; (*Gepäck*) check;
(*Zöllgüter*) clear; (*Kunden*) wait on;
(*abweisen*) snub; (*verwaltungsmä-
ßig*) (adm) process;
Ab'fertigung *f* (-;-en) dispatch; snub;
zollamtliche A. clearance
ab'feuern *tr* fire; (rok) launch
ab'finden §59 *tr* (*Gläubiger*) satisfy;
(*Partner*) buy off; (*entschädigen*)
(*für*) compensate (for) || *ref*—**sich a.
lassen** settle for a lump-sum payment; **sich a. mit** put up with; come
to terms with
Ab'findung *f* (-;-en) satisfaction;
lump-sum settlement
Ab'findungsvertrag *m* lump-sum settlement
abflachen ['ɑpflɑxən] *tr* level; (*ab-
schrägen*) bevel || *ref* flatten out
abflauen ['ɑpflɑu·ən] *intr* (SEIN) slack
off; (*Interesse*) flag; (*Preis*) go
down; (st. exch.) ease off
ab'fliegen §57 *intr* (SEIN) take off
ab'fließen §76 *intr* (SEIN) flow off,
drain off
Ab'flug *m* takeoff, departure
Ab'fluß *m* discharge; drain, gutter,
gully; **See ohne A.** lake without outlet
Ab'flußrinne *f* drainage ditch
Ab'flußrohr *n* drainpipe; soil pipe;
(*vom Dach*) downspout
ab'fordern *tr*—**j-m etw a.** demand s.th.
from s.o.
ab'fragen *tr*—**j-n etw a.** question s.o.
about s.th.; quiz s.o. on s.th.
ab'fressen §70 *tr* eat up; crop, chew
off; (*Metall*) corrode
ab'frieren §77 *intr* (SEIN) be nipped by
the frost; **abgefroren** frostbitten
Abfuhr ['ɑpfur] *f* (-;-en) removal;
(*Abweisung*) (coll) cold shoulder,
snub

ab'führen *tr* lead away; *(festnehmen)* arrest; (fencing) defeat ‖ *intr* cause the bowels to move

Abführmittel ['apfʏrmɪtəl] *n* laxative

ab'füllen *tr (Wein, Bier)* bottle

Ab'gabe *f (Auslieferung)* delivery; *(Verkauf)* sale; *(Steuer)* tax; *(Zoll)* duty; *(der Wahlstimme)* casting; *(e-s Urteils)* pronouncing; *(e-r Meinung)* expressing; (fb) pass; **Abgaben** taxes, fees

ab'gabenfrei *adj* tax-free, duty-free

abgabenpflichtig ['apgabənpflɪçtɪç] *adj* taxable, subject to duty

Ab'gang *m* departure; *(von e-m Amt)* retirement; *(von der Schule)* dropping out; graduation; *(Verlust)* loss; *(Abnahme)* decrease; (gym) finish; (pathol) discharge; (pathol) miscarriage; (theat) exit; **guten A. haben** sell well

abgängig ['apgɛŋɪç] *adj* lost, missing; (com) marketable

Ab'gangsprüfung *f* final examination

Ab'gangspunkt *m* point of departure

Ab'gas *n* (aut) exhaust; (indust) waste gas

ab'geben §80 *tr (Paß)* hand over; *(Gepäck)* check; *(abliefern)* deliver; *(Schulheft)* hand in; *(Urteil)* pass; *(Meinung)* express; *(Gutachten)* give; *(Amt)* lay down; *(gute Ernte)* yield; *(Schuß)* fire; *(Wahlstimme)* cast; *(Waren)* sell, let go; *(sich eignen als)* act as, serve as; be cut out to be; (elec) deliver; (fb) pass; (phys) give off; **e-e Offerte a.** (jur) make an offer; **e-n Narren a.** play the fool; **er würde e-n guten Vater a.** he would make a good father; **j-m eins a.** (coll) let s.o. have it; **j-m von etw a.** share s.th. with s.o. ‖ *ref*—**sich a. mit** bother with; associate with; spend time on

abgebrannt ['apgəbrant] *adj* (coll) broke

abgebrüht ['apgəbryt] *adj* (fig) hardened

abgedroschen ['apgədrɔʃən] *adj* trite, hackneyed; *(Witz)* stale

abgefeimt ['apgəfaɪmt] *adj* cunning; out-and-out

abgegriffen ['apgəgrɪfən] *adj* well-thumbed

abgehackt ['apgəhakt] *adj* jerky

abgehärmt ['apgəhɛrmt] *adj* careworn, drawn

ab'gehen §82 *intr* (SEIN) leave, depart; *(Brief)* go off; *(Knopf)* come off; *(Schuß)* go off; *(Farbe)* fade; *(Seitenweg)* branch off; *(vom Gesprächsgegenstand)* digress, go off; *(vom rechten Wege)* stray; *(aus e-m Amt)* resign, retire; *(von der Bühne)* retire; *(von der Schule)* drop out; graduate; (com) sell; (theat) exit; **bei Barzahlung gehen fünf Prozent ab** you get a five-percent reduction for paying cash; **davon kann ich nicht a.** I must insist on it; **er geht mir sehr ab** I miss him a lot; **nicht a. von** stick to; **reißend a.** sell like hotcakes; ‖ *ref*—**sich** [dat] **nichts a.**

lassen deny oneself nothing ‖ *impers* —**es geht ihm nichts ab** he lacks for nothing; **es gehen mir zehn Dollar ab** I am ten dollars short; **es ist alles glatt abgegangen** everything went well

ab'gehend *adj (Post, Beamte)* outgoing; *(Zug)* departing

abgekämpft ['apgəkɛmpft] *adj* exhausted

abgekartet ['apgəkartət] *adj (Spiel)* fixed; **abgekartete Sache** put-up job

abgeklappert ['apgəklapərt] *adj* hackneyed

abgeklärt ['apgəklert] *adj* mellow, wise

abgelebt ['apgəlept] *adj* decrepit

abgelegen ['apgəlegen] *adj* out-of-the-way, outlying

ab'gelten §83 *tr* meet, satisfy

abgemacht ['apgəmaxt] *adj* settled ‖ *interj* agreed!

abgemagert ['apgəmagərt] *adj* emaciated

abgemessen ['apgəmesən] *adj* measured; *(genau)* exact; *(Rede)* deliberate; *(Person)* stiff, formal

abgeneigt ['apgənaɪkt] *adj* reluctant; *(dat)* averse to; **ich bin durchaus nicht a.** (coll) I don't mind if I do

Ab'geneigtheit *f* (–;) aversion

abgenutzt ['apgənutst] *adj* worn out

Abgeordnete ['apgə·ɔrdnətə] §5 *mf* delegate; (pol) representative; deputy *(member of the Bundestag)*; (Brit) Member of Parliament

Ab'geordnetenhaus *n* House of Representatives; (Brit) House of Commons

abgerissen ['apgərɪsən] *adj* torn; *(zerlumpt)* ragged; *(ohne Zusammenhang)* incoherent, disconnected

Abgesandte ['apgəzantə] §5 *mf* envoy

abgeschieden ['apgəʃidən] *adj* secluded; *(verstorben)* deceased, late

Ab'geschiedenheit *f* (–;) seclusion

abgeschliffen ['apgəʃlɪfən] *adj* polished

abgeschlossen ['apgəʃlɔsən] *adj* isolated; *(Leben)* secluded; *(Ausbildung)* completed

abgeschmackt ['apgəʃmakt] *adj* tactless, tasteless; (fig) insipid

abgesehen ['apgəze·ən] *adj*—**a. davon, daß** not to mention that; **a. von** aside from, except for

abgespannt ['apgəʃpant] *adj* tired out

abgestanden ['apgəʃtandən] *adj* stale

abgestorben ['apgəʃtɔrbən] *adj (Pflanze, Gewebe)* dead; *(Glied)* numb

abgestumpft ['apgəʃtumpft] *adj* blunt; *(Kegel)* truncated; (fig) dull; **(gegen)** indifferent (to)

abgetakelt ['apgətakəlt] *adj (Person)* seedy; *(Schiff)* unrigged

abgetan ['apgətan] *adj* settled

abgetragen ['apgətragən] *adj* threadbare

abgetreten ['apgətretən] *adj* worn-down

ab'gewinnen §52 *tr* win; **e-r Sache Geschmack a.** acquire a taste for s.th.; **e-r Sache Vergnügen a.** derive pleas-

ure from s.th.; **j-m e-n Vorteil a.**
gain an advantage over s.o.
abgewirtschaftet [ˈapgəvɪrtʃaftət] *adj*
run-down
ab'gewöhnen *tr*—**ich kann es mir nicht
a.** I can't get it out of my system;
j-m etw a. break s.o. of s.th.
abgezehrt [ˈapgətsert] *adj* emaciated
ab'gießen §76 *tr* pour off; (*Statue*)
cast; (chem) decant; (culin) strain
off
Ab'glanz *m* reflection
ab'gleiten §86 *intr* (SEIN) slip off; (**an**
dat) glance off (*s.th.*); (aer, aut)
skid; (st. exch.) decline
Ab'gott *m* idol
Abgötterei [apgœtəˈraɪ] *f* (-;-en) idolatry; **A. treiben** worship idols; **mit
j-m A. treiben** idolize s.o.
abgöttisch [ˈapgœtɪʃ] *adj* idolatrous ||
adv—**a. lieben** idolize
Ab'gottschlange *f* boa constrictor
ab'graben §87 *tr* (*Bach*) divert; (*Feld*)
drain; (*Hügel*) level
ab'grämen *ref* eat one's heart out
ab'grasen *tr* (*Wiese*) graze on; (fig)
scour, search
ab'greifen §88 *tr* wear out (*by constant handling*); (*Buch*) thumb
ab'grenzen *tr* mark off, demarcate; delimit; (fig) differentiate
Ab'grund *m* abyss; precipice
abgründig [ˈapgrʏndɪç] *adj* precipitous; (fig) deep, unfathomable
ab'gucken *tr* (coll) copy, crib; (coll)
pick up a habit from || *intr* (coll)
copy, crib
Ab'guß *m* (sculp) cast; **A. in Gips**
plaster cast
ab'hacken *tr* chop off; (*Baum*) chop
down
ab'haken *tr* unhook, undo; (*in e-r
Liste*) check off; (telp) take off (*the
receiver*)
ab'halftern *tr* unharness; (fig) sack
ab'halten §90 *tr* hold off; (*Vorlesung*)
give; (*Regen*) keep out; (*Versammlung, Parade*) hold; (**von**) keep
(from)
Ab'haltung *f* (-;-en) hindrance; (*e-r
Versammlung*) holding; (*e-s Festes*)
celebration
ab'handeln *tr* (*Thema*) treat; (*erörtern*) discuss; **er läßt sich nichts a.**
he won't come down (*in price*); **etw
vom Preise a.** get s.th. off the price
(*by bargaining*)
abhanden [apˈhandən] *adv*—**a. kommen** get lost; **a. sein** be missing
Ab'handlung *f* (-;-en) essay; (*Vortrag
in e-m gelehrten Verein*) paper;
(*Doktorarbeit*) thesis, dissertation;
(*mündlich*) discourse, discussion
Ab'hang *m* slope
ab'hängen *tr* (*vom Haken*) take off;
(*e-n Verfolger*) shake off; (rr) un-
couple || *intr* (telp) hang up; **a. von**
depend on; be subject to (*s.o.'s approval*)
abhängig [ˈaphɛŋɪç] *adj* (*Stellung*) subordinate; (*Satz*) dependent; (*Rede*)
indirect; (*Kasus*) oblique; (**von**) dependent (on), contingent (upon)

Ab'hängigkeit *f* (-;-en) dependence;
(gram) subordination; **gegenseitige
A.** interdependence
ab'härmen *ref* pine away; **sich a. wegen** (or **über** *acc*) fret about
ab'härten *tr* harden; (**gegen**) inure (to)
|| *ref* (**gegen**) become hardened (to)
ab'hauen §93 *tr* cut off; chop off ||
§109 *intr* (SEIN) (coll) scram, get lost
ab'häuten *tr* skin, flay
ab'heben §94 *tr* lift off; (*Rahm*) skim;
(*Geld*) withdraw; (*Dividende*) col-
lect; (*Haut*) (surg) strip off || *ref* be-
come airborne; (**von**) contrast (with)
Ab'hebung *f* (-;-en) lifting; (*vom
Bankkonto*) withdrawal; (cards) cutting
Ab'hebungsformular *n* withdrawal slip
ab'heften *tr* (*Briefe*) file; (sew) tack
ab'heilen *intr* (HABEN & SEIN) heal up
ab'helfen §96 *intr* (*dat*) (*e-m Unrecht*)
redress; (*e-r Schwierigkeit*) remove;
(*e-m Mangel*) relieve; **dem ist nicht
abzuhelfen** that can't be helped
ab'hetzen *tr* drive hard, work to death;
(hunt) hunt down || *ref* rush; tire
oneself out
Ab'hilfe *f* remedy, redress; **A. schaffen** take remedial measures; **A.
schaffen für** remedy, redress
ab'hobeln *tr* plane (down)
abhold [ˈaphɔlt] *adj* (*dat*) ill-disposed
(towards), averse (to)
Abholdienst [ˈapholdinst] *m* pickup
service
ab'holen *tr* fetch, call for, pick up
ab'holzen *tr* clear (of trees), deforest
Abhörapparat [ˈaphøraparɑt] *m* (mil,
nav) listening device
ab'horchen *tr* overhear; (med) sound;
(rad, telp) monitor
ab'hören *tr* overhear, eavesdrop on;
(*Studenten*) quiz; (*Schallplatte, Tonband*) listen to; (mil) intercept;
(telp) monitor
Ab'hörgerät *n* bugging device
Ab'hörraum *m* (rad, telv) control
room
Ab'irrung *f* (-;-en) deviation; (opt)
aberration
Abitur [abɪˈtur] *n* (-s;-e) final examination (*at end of junior college*);
das A. bestehen graduate
Abiturient –**in** [abɪturiˈent(ɪn)] §7 *mf*
graduate (*of a junior college*)
Abitur'zeugnis *n* diploma (*from senior
high school or junior college*)
ab'jagen *tr* drive hard; **j-m etw a.** re-
cover s.th. from s.o. || *ref* run one's
head off
abkanzeln [ˈapkantsəln] *tr* (coll) give
(*s.o.*) a good talking to
ab'kauen *tr* chew off || *ref*—**sich** [*dat*]
die Nägel a. bite one's nails
ab'kaufen *tr*—**j-m etw a.** buy s.th.
from s.o.
Abkehr [ˈapker] *f* (-;) turning away;
estrangement; (*Verzicht*) renunciation
ab'kehren *tr* turn away, avert; (*mit
dem Besen*) sweep off || *ref* turn
away; become estranged
ab'klappern *tr* (coll) scour, search

ab'klatschen *tr* imitate slavishly; make an exact copy of; *(beim Tanzen)* cut in on; (typ) pull *(a proof)*

ab'klingen §142 *intr* (SEIN) *(Farbe)* fade; *(Töne)* die away; *(Schmerz)* ease off

ab'klopfen *tr* beat off, knock off; *(Teppich)* beat; (med) tap, percuss ‖ *intr* stop the music *(with the rap of the baton)*

ab'knabbern *tr* (coll) nibble off

ab'knallen *tr* fire off; (sl) bump off

ab'knicken *tr* snap off ‖ *intr* (SEIN) snap off

ab'knipsen *tr* pinch off, snip off; *(Film)* use up

ab'knöpfen *tr* unbutton; **j-m Geld a.** squeeze money out of s.o.

ab'knutschen *tr* (coll) pet

ab'kochen *tr* boil; *(Obst)* stew; *(Milch)* scald ‖ *intr* cook out

ab'kommandieren *tr* detach, detail

ab'kommen §99 *intr* (SEIN) **(von)** get away (from); *(Mode)* go out of style; (naut) become afloat (again); **auf zwei Tage a.** get away for two days; **gut** (or **schlecht**) **a.** (sport) get off to a good (or bad) start; **hoch** (or **tief**) **a.** aim too high (or low); **vom Kurs a.** go off course; **vom Boden a.** become airborne; **vom Thema a.** get off the subject; **vom Wege a.** lose one's way, stray; **von der Wahrheit a.** deviate from the truth; **von e-r Ansicht a.** change one's views ‖ **Abkommen** *n* (–s;–) (com, pol) agreement; (jur) settlement

abkömmlich ['apkœmlıç] *adj*—**a. sein** be able to get away

Abkömmling ['apkœmlıŋ] *m* (–s;–e) descendant, scion

ab'koppeln *tr* uncouple

ab'kratzen *tr* scratch off; *(Schuhe)* scuff up ‖ *intr* (sterben) (sl) croak; *(abhauen)* (sl) beat it; **kratz ab!** drop dead!

ab'kriegen *tr* (coll) get off or out

ab'kühlen *tr*, *ref* & *intr* cool off

Abkunft ['apkunft] *f* (–;) lineage

ab'kürzen *tr* shorten; *(Inhalt)* abridge; *(Wort)* abbreviate; (math) reduce

Ab'kürzung *f* (–;–en) shortening; abridgement; abbreviation; *(kürzerer Weg)* shortcut

ab'küssen *tr* smother with kisses

ab'laden §103 *tr* unload; *(Schutt)* dump

Ab'ladeplatz *m* dump; (mil) unloading point

Ab'lage *f* *(für Kleider)* cloakroom; *(Lagerhaus)* depot, warehouse; *(abgelegte Akten)* files; (mil) dump

ab'lagern *tr* *(Wein, usw.)* age; (geol) deposit ‖ *ref* (geol) be deposited ‖ *intr*—**a. lassen** age, season

Ab'laß *m* (–lasses;–lässe) outlet, drain; (com) deduction; (eccl) indulgence

ab'lassen §104 *tr* leave off; *(Bier)* tap; *(Dampf)* let off; *(Teich, Faß)* drain; *(Waren)* sell; **etw vom Preise a.** knock s.th. off the price; **j-m etw billig a.** (com) let s.o. have s.th. cheaply ‖ *intr* desist, stop; **a. von** let go of, give up

Ablativ ['ablatif] *m* (–s;–e) ablative

Ab'lauf *m* overflow; *(e-r Frist, e-s Vertrags)* expiration; *(der Ereignisse)* course; (sport) start

ab'laufen §105 *tr* *(Strecke)* run; *(Stadt)* scour; *(Schuhe)* wear out; **j-m den Rang a.** get the better of s.o.; outrun s.o. ‖ *intr* (SEIN) run away; *(Zeit)* expire; *(ausfallen)* turn out; (com) fall due; (sport) start

Ab'laut *m* ablaut

Ab'leben *n* demise, decease

ab'lecken *tr* lick (off)

ab'legen *tr* *(Last, Waffen)* lay down; *(ausziehen)* take off; *(Schwert)* lay aside; *(die alte Haut)* slough; *(Karten)* discard; *(Akten, Dokumente)* file; *(Briefe)* sort; *(Namen)* drop, stop using; *(Sorgen, Kummer)* put away; *(Prüfung, Gelübde, Eid)* take; *(Predigt)* deliver; *(Gewohnheit)* give up; *(Rechenschaft)* render, give; **Bekenntnis a.** make a confession; **die Maske a.** (fig) throw off all disguise; **die Trauer a.** come out of mourning; **ein volles Geständnis a.** come clean; **Probe a.** furnish proof; **seine Fehler a.** mend one's ways; **Zeugnis a.** (für or gegen) testify (for or against) ‖ *intr* take off one's coat or hat and coat); **bitte, legen Sie ab!** please take your things off

Ab'leger *m* (–s;–) (bot) shoot; (com) subsidiary; (hort) slip, cutting

ab'lehnen *tr* refuse, turn down; *(Antrag)* reject; *(Zeugen)* challenge; *(Erbschaft)* renounce; **durch Abstimmung a.** vote down

ab'lehnend *adj* negative

Ab'lehnung *f* (–;–en) refusal

ab'leiern *tr* recite mechanically

ab'leisten *tr* *(Eid)* take; **den Militärdienst a.** (mil) serve one's time

ab'leiten *tr* lead away; *(Herkunft)* trace back; *(Fluß, Blitz)* divert; *(Wasser)* drain off; *(Wärme)* conduct; (chem) derive; (elec) shunt; (gram, math) derive; **abgeleitetes Wort** derivative ‖ *ref* **(aus, von)** be derived (from)

Ab'leitung *f* (–;–en) *(e-s Flusses)* diversion; *(des Wassers)* drainage; (elec, phys) conduction; (gram, math) derivation; (phys) convection

ab'lenken *tr* turn away, divert; *(Gefahr, Verdacht)* ward off; (fencing) parry; (opt, phys) deflect

Ab'lenkung *f* (–;–en) diversion; distraction; (opt) refraction

ab'lernen *tr*—**j-m etw a.** learn s.th. from s.o.

ab'lesen §107 *tr* read off; *(Zähler)* read; *(Obst)* pick; **es j-m vom Gesicht a., daß** tell by looking at s.o. that

ab'leugnen *tr* deny, disown; *(Glauben)* renounce

Ab'leugnung *f* (–;–en) denial, disavowal

ab'liefern *tr* deliver, hand over, surrender

Ab'lieferung *f* (–;–en) delivery; *(der Schußwaffen)* surrender

ab'liegen §108 *intr* (*Wein*) mature; (*Obst*) ripen ‖ *intr* (SEIN) be remote
ab'löschen *tr* extinguish; (*Stahl*) temper; (*Tinte*) blot; (*Kalk*) slake
ab'lösen *tr* loosen, detach; (*Posten*) relieve; (*Schuld*) discharge; (*Pfand*) redeem; (*Haut*) peel off ‖ *ref* (*bei*) take turns (at)
Ab'lösung *f* (-;-en) loosening; relief; discharge
ab'machen *tr* undo, untie; (*erledigen*) settle, arrange; (*Vertrag*) conclude; (*Rechnung*) close
Ab'machung *f* (-;-en) settlement
abmagern ['apmɑgərn] *intr* (SEIN) grow thin, thin down
Ab'magerung *f* (-;) emaciation
ab'mähen *tr* mow
ab'malen *tr* portray; (fig) depict
Ab'marsch *m* departure
ab'marschieren *intr* (SEIN) march off
Ab'mattung *f* (-;) fatigue
ab'melden *tr* (*Besuch*) (coll) call off; **der ist bei mir abgemeldet** (coll) I've had it with him; **j–n bei der Polizei a.** give notice to the police that s.o. is leaving town ‖ *ref* (mil) report off duty
ab'messen §70 *tr* measure (off); (*Worte*) weigh; (*Land*) survey
ab'montieren *tr* dismantle; (*Geschütz*) disassemble; (*Reifen*) take off ‖ *ref* (aer) (coll) disintegrate in the air
ab'mühen *ref* exert oneself, slave
ab'murksen *tr* (sl) do in
ab'nagen *tr* gnaw (off); (*Knochen*) pick
Ab'nahme *f* (-;-n) (*Verminderung*) (**an** *dat*) reduction (in), drop (in); (*des Gewichts*) loss; (*des Mondes*) waning; (*des Tages*) shortening; (*e-s Eides*) administering; (*e-r Rechnung*) auditing; (indust) final inspection; (surg) amputation; **A. der Geschäfte** decline in business; **A. e-r Parade** reviewing of the troops; **A. finden** be sold; **in A. geraten** decline, wane
ab'nehmen §116 *tr* take off, remove; (*Wäsche*) take down; (*Schnurrbart*) shave off; (*wegnehmen*) take away; (*Hörer*) lift, unhook; (*Strom*) use; (*Obst*) pick; (*Eid*) administer; (*Waren*) purchase; (*Rechnung*) audit; (*prüfen*) inspect and pass; (*Verband*) remove; (phot) take; (surg) amputate; **aus Berichten a.** gather from reports; **das kann ich dir nicht a.** I can't accept what you are saying; **die Parade a.** inspect the troops; **j–m die Arbeit a.** take the work off s.o.'s shoulders; **j–m die Beichte a.** hear s.o.'s confession; **j–m die Maske a.** unmask s.o., expose s.o.; **j–m die Verantwortung a.** relieve s.o. of responsibility; **j–m ein Versprechen a.** make s.o. make a promise; **j–m zuviel a.** charge s.o. too much ‖ *intr* diminish; (*Preise*) drop; (*Wasser*) recede; (*Kräfte*) fail; (*Mond*) be on the wane; **an Dicke a.** taper; **an Gewicht a.** lose weight; **an Kräften a.** lose strength ‖ **Abnehmen**

n (-s;) decrease; **im A. sein** be on the decrease
Ab'nehmer **–in** §6 *mf* buyer, consumer; (*Kunde*) customer; (*Hehler*) fence
Ab'neigung *f* (-;-en) (**gegen, vor** *dat*) aversion (to, for), dislike (of)
abnorm [ap'nɔrm] *adj* abnormal
Abnormität [apnɔrmɪ'tet] *f* (-;-en) abnormity, monstrosity
ab'nötigen *tr* (*dat*) extort (from)
ab'nutzen, ab'nützen *tr* wear out ‖ *ref* wear out, become worn out
Ab'nutzung *f* (-;-en) wear and tear; (*Abrieb*) abrasion; (mil) attrition
Ab'öl *n* (-s;-e) used oil
Abonnement [abɔn(ə)'mã] *n* (-s;-s) (**auf** *acc*) subscription (to)
Abonnements'karte *f* commutation ticket
Abonnent **–in** [abɔ'nɛnt(ɪn)] §7 *mf* subscriber
abonnieren [abɔ'nirən] *tr* subscribe to; **abonniert sein auf** (*acc*) have a subscription to ‖ *intr* (**auf** *acc*) subscribe (to)
ab'ordnen *tr* delegate, deputize
Ab'ordnung *f* (-;-en) delegation
Abort [a'bɔrt] *m* (-s;-e) toilet ‖ [a'bɔrt] *m* (-s;-e) abortion
ab'passen *tr* measure, fit; (*abwarten*) watch for; (*auflauern*) waylay
ab'pfeifen §88 *tr* (sport) stop
ab'pflücken *tr* pluck (off)
ab'placken, ab'plagen *ref* work oneself to death, slave
ab'platzen *intr* (SEIN) come loose
Abprall ['apral] *m* rebound; (*Geschoß*) richochet
ab'prallen *intr* (SEIN) rebound; ricochet
ab'pressen *tr* extort
ab'putzen *tr* clean (off); (*polieren*) polish; (*Mauer*) roughcast, plaster
ab'raten §63 *intr*—**j–m von etw a.** advise s.o. against s.th.
Ab'raum *m* (-es;) rubble; (min) overburden
ab'räumen *tr* clear away; (*Tisch*) clear
ab'reagieren *tr* (*Spannung, Erregung*) work off ‖ *ref* (coll) calm down
ab'rechnen *tr* subtract; (*Spesen*) account for; (com) deduct ‖ *intr* settle accounts
Ab'rechnung *f* (-;-en) (*von Konten*) settlement; (*Abzug*) deduction; **A. halten** balance accounts
Ab'rede *f* agreement, arrangement; **in A. stellen** deny
ab'reden *intr*—**j–m von etw a.** dissuade s.o. from s.th.
ab'reiben *tr* rub off; (*Körper*) rub down
Ab'reise *f* departure
ab'reisen *intr* (SEIN) (**nach**) depart (for)
ab'reißen §53 *tr* tear off; (*Haus*) tear down; (*Kleid*) wear out ‖ *intr* (SEIN) tear off
ab'richten *tr* (*Tier*) train; (*Pferd*) break in; (*Brett*) dress
Ab'richter **–in** §6 *mf* trainer
ab'riegeln *tr* (*Tür*) bolt; (mil) seal off

ab'ringen §142 *tr*—j-m etw a. wrest
s.th. from s.o.
ab'rinnen §121 *intr* (SEIN) run off, run
down
Ab'riß *m* summary, outline; (*Skizze*)
sketch
ab'rollen *tr* & *ref* unroll, unwind ||
intr (SEIN) unroll, unwind
ab'rücken *tr* push away, move back ||
intr (SEIN) clear out; (fig) dissociate
oneself; (mil) march off
Ab'ruf *m* recall; **auf A.** on call
ab'rufen §122 *tr* call away; (*Zug*) call
out, announce
ab'runden *tr* round off
ab'rupfen *tr* pluck (off)
ab'rüsten *tr* & *intr* disarm
Ab'rüstung *f* (-;) disarmament
ab'rutschen *intr* (SEIN) slip (off)
absacken ['apzakən] *intr* (SEIN) sink;
(*Flugzeug*) pancake
Ab'sage *f* cancellation; (*Ablehnung*)
refusal
ab'sagen *tr* cancel || *intr* decline; (*dat*)
renounce, repudiate
ab'sägen *tr* saw off
ab'sahnen *tr* (& fig) skim (off)
Ab'satz *m* stop, pause, break; (*Zeilen-
einrückung*) indentation; (*Abschnitt*)
paragraph; (*des Schuhes*) heel; (*der
Treppen*) landing; (*Vertrieb*) market,
sale(s); **ohne A.** without a break
ab'satzfähig *adj* marketable
Ab'satzgebiet *n* territory (*of a salesman*)
Ab'satzmarkt *m* (com) outlet
Ab'satzstockung *f* slump in sales
ab'saugen *tr* suck off; (*Teppich*) vacuum
Ab'saugventilator *m* exhaust fan
ab'schaben *tr* scrape off
ab'schaffen *tr* abolish, do away with;
(*Mißbrauch*) redress; (*Diener*) dismiss
ab'schälen *tr* peel
ab'schalten *tr* switch off
ab'schätzen *tr* (*Wert*) estimate; (*für
die Steuer*) assess, appraise
abschätzig ['apʃetsɪç] *adj* disparaging
Ab'schaum *m* (-[e]s;) (& fig) scum
ab'scheiden §112 *tr* part, sever;
(physiol) excrete; (physiol) secrete ||
intr (SEIN) pass away, pass on
Ab'scheu *m* (-[e]s;) (**vor** *dat*, **gegen**)
abhorrence (of), disgust (at)
ab'scheuern *tr* scrub off, scour; (*Haut*)
scrape; (*abnutzen*) wear out
abscheu'lich *adj* atrocious
ab'schicken *tr* send away; (*Post*) mail
ab'schieben §130 *tr* shove off; deport
Abschied ['apʃit] *m* (-[e]s;-e) (*Weggang*) departure; (*Entlassung*) dismissal; (mil) discharge; **A. nehmen
von** take leave of; (*e-m Amt*) resign,
retire from
Ab'schiedsfeier *f* farewell party
Ab'schiedsrede *f* valediction
Ab'schiedsschmaus *m* farewell dinner
ab'schießen §76 *tr* (*Gewehr*) fire,
shoot; (*Flugzeug*) shoot down; (*Panzer*) knock out; (rok) launch; **j-n a.**
bring about s.o.'s downfall
ab'schinden §167 *tr* skin || *ref* slave

ab'schirmen *tr* screen (off); (**gegen**)
guard (against)
ab'schlachten *tr* butcher; (fig) massacre
Ab'schlag *m* discount; (golf) tee shot;
auf A. in part payment, on account
ab'schlagen §132 *tr* knock off; (*Baum*)
fell; (*Angriff*) repel; (*Bitte*) refuse;
das Wasser a. pass water || *intr*
(golf) tee off
abschlägig ['apʃlegɪç] *adj* negative;
a. bescheiden turn down
Ab'schlagszahlung *f* installment
ab'schleifen §88 *tr* grind off; (fig) re-
fine, polish || *ref* become refined
ab'schleppen *tr* drag away, tow away
Ab'schleppwagen *m* tow truck
ab'schleudern *tr* fling off, catapult
ab'schließen §76 *tr* lock (up); (*Straße*)
close off; (*Rechnung*) close, settle;
(*Bücher*) balance; (*Vertrag*) conclude; (*Rede*) wind up; (*Wette*)
wager || *ref* seclude oneself, shut one-
self off || *intr* conclude
ab'schließend *adj* definitive; (*Worte*)
concluding || *adv* definitively;
(*schließlich*) in conclusion
Ab'schluß *m* completion; (*e-s Vertrags*) conclusion; (*Geschäft*) transaction, deal; (*Verkauf*) sale; (*Rech-
nungs-, Konto-, Buch-*) closing;
(mach) seal
ab'schmeicheln *tr*—j-m etw a. coax
s.th. out of s.o.
ab'schmelzen §133 *tr* (*Erz*) smelt;
(*Schnee*) melt || *intr* (SEIN) melt
ab'schmieren *tr* copy carelessly; (coll)
beat up; (aut) lubricate || *intr* (SEIN)
(aer) (coll) crash
ab'schnallen *tr* unbuckle, unstrap
ab'schnappen *intr* (SEIN) (coll) stop
dead; (coll) die
ab'schneiden §106 *tr* cut (off); (*Hecke*)
trim; **den Weg. a.** take a shortcut;
j-m das Wort a. cut s.o. short; **j-n
die Ehre a.** steal s.o.'s good name ||
intr—**gut a.** do well
Ab'schnitt *m* cut, cutting; (*Teilstück*)
part, section; (*im Scheckbuch*) stub;
(*Kapitel*) section, paragraph; (math)
segment; (mil) sector
ab'schnüren *tr* untie; (surg) ligature;
j-m den Atem a. choke s.o.
ab'schöpfen *tr* skim off
ab'schrägen *tr* & *ref* slant, slope
ab'schrauben *tr* unscrew
ab'schrecken §134 *tr* scare off; (*abbringen*) deter
ab'schreiben §62 *tr* copy; (*Schularbeit*)
crib; (*uneinbringliche Forderung*)
write off; (*Literaturwerk*) plagiarize;
(*Wert*) depreciate || *intr* send a re-
fusal
Ab'schreiber **-in** §6 *mf* plagiarist
Ab'schreibung *f* (-;-en) write-off
ab'schreiten §86 *tr* pace off; (mil) review; **die Front a.** review the troops
Ab'schrift *f* copy, transcript; (com,
jur) duplicate
ab'schriftlich *adj* & *adv* in duplicate
ab'schuften *ref* work oneself to death
ab'schürfen *ref*—**sich** [*dat*] **die Haut
a.** skin oneself

Ab'schürfung f (-;-en) abrasion
Ab'schuß m (e-r Waffe) firing; (e-r Rakete) launching; (e-s Panzers) knocking out; (e-s Flugzeugs) downing, kill; (hunt) kill
abschüssig ['apʃysɪç] adj sloping; (steil) steep
Ab'schußrampe f launch pad
ab'schütteln tr shake off
ab'schwächen tr weaken; (vermindern) diminish, reduce; (Farben) tone down || ref (Preis) decline
ab'schweifen intr (SEIN) stray, digress
Ab'schweifung f (-;-en) digression
ab'schwellen §119 intr (SEIN) go down; (Lärm, Gesang) die down
ab'schwenken intr (SEIN) swerve
ab'schwören intr (dat) (dem Glauben) deny; (dem Trunk) swear off
ab'segeln intr (SEIN) set sail
absehbar ['apzebar] adj foreseeable
ab'sehen §138 tr foresee; **es abgesehen haben auf** (acc) be out to get || intr—a. **von** disregard; refrain from
ab'seifen tr soap down
abseits ['apzaɪts] adv aside; (sport) offside || prep (genit) off
ab'senden §140 tr send (off), dispatch; (Post) mail; (befördern) forward
Ab'sender –in §6 mf sender, dispatcher
Ab'sendung f (-;-en) sending, dispatching; mailing, shipping
ab'sengen tr singe off
Absentismus [apzɛn'tɪsmus] m (-;) absenteeism
ab'setzen tr (Betrag) deduct; (Last) set down; (entwöhnen) wean; (Beamten) remove; (König) depose; (Fallschirmtruppen, Passagiere) drop; (com) sell; (typ) set up || ref settle, set; (mil) disengage || intr stop, pause
Absetzung f (-;-en) dismissal
Ab'sicht f intention, purpose; **in der A.** with the intention; **mit A.** on purpose; **ohne A.** unintentionally
ab'sichtlich adj intentional || adv on purpose, intentionally
ab'sitzen §144 tr (Strafzeit) serve, do || intr (SEIN) (vom Pferde) dismount; **a. lassen** (chem) let settle
absolut [apzɔ'lut] adj
absolvieren [apzɔl'virən] tr absolve; (Studien) finish; (Hochschule) graduate from; (Prüfung) pass
abson'derlich adj peculiar, strange
ab'sondern tr separate, segregate; (Kranken) isolate; (physiol) secrete || ref keep aloof
absorbieren [apzɔr'birən] tr absorb
ab'speisen tr feed; **j-n mit schönen Worten a.** put s.o. off with polite words
abspenstig ['apʃpɛnstɪç] adj—a. **machen** lure away; **j-m a. werden** desert s.o.
ab'sperren tr shut off, block off; (Tür) lock; (Strom) cut off; (Gas) turn off
ab'spielen tr play through to the end; (Schallplatte, Tonband) play; (Tonbandaufnahme) play back || ref take place
ab'sprechen §64 tr dispute, deny; (ab-

machen) arrange; **j-m das Recht a. zu** (inf) dispute s.o.'s right to (inf)
ab'sprechend adj (Urteil) unfavorable; (Kritik) adverse; (tadelnd) disparaging
ab'springen §142 intr (SEIN) jump down, jump off; (Ball) rebound; (Glasur) chip; (abschweifen) digress; (aer) bail out, jump; **a. von** quit, desert
Ab'sprung m jump; (ins Wasser) dive; (des Balles) rebound
ab'spulen tr unwind, unreel
ab'spülen tr rinse (off)
ab'stammen intr (SEIN) (von) be descended (from); (von) be derived (from)
Abstammung f (-;-en) descent, extraction; (gram) derivation
Ab'stand m distance; (räumlich und zeitlich) interval; **A. nehmen von** refrain from; **A. zahlen** pay compensation
abstatten ['apʃtatən] tr (Besuch) pay; (Bericht) file; (Dank) give, return
ab'stauben tr dust off; (sl) swipe
ab'stechen §64 tr (töten) stab; (Rasen) cut; (Hochofen) tap; (Karten) trump || intr—**gegen** (or **von**) etwa a. contrast with s.th.
Ab'stecher m (-s;-) side trip; (Umweg) detour; (fig) digression
ab'stecken tr (Haar) unpin, let down; (Kleid) pin, fit; (surv) mark off
ab'stehen §146 intr (entfernt sein) (von) be, stand away (from); (Ohren, usw.) stick out || intr (HABEN & SEIN) (von) refrain (from)
ab'steigen §148 intr (SEIN) get down, descend; **in e-m Gasthof a.** stay at a hotel
ab'stellen tr (Last) put down; (Radio, Gas, usw.) turn off; (Motor) switch off; (Auto) park; (Mißstand) redress; (mil) detach, assign; **a. auf** (acc) gear to
Ab'stellraum m storage room
ab'stempeln tr stamp
ab'sterben §149 intr (SEIN) die off; (Pflanzen) wither; (Glieder) get numb
Abstieg ['apʃtik] m (-[e]s;) descent
ab'stimmen tr tune; (com) balance; **a. auf** (acc) (fig) atune (to) || intr (über acc) vote (on)
Abstinenzler –in [apstɪ'nɛntslər(ɪn)] §6 mf teetotaler
ab'stoppen tr stop; (sport) clock
ab'stoßen §150 tr push off; (Waren) get rid of, sell; (Schulden) pay off; (Geweih) shed; (fig) disgust, sicken; (phys) repel || ref—sich [dat] **die Hörner a.** (fig) sow one's wild oats || intr (SEIN) shove off
ab'stoßend adj repulsive
abstrakt [ap'strakt] adj abstract
ab'streichen tr (abwischen) wipe off; (Rasiermesser) strop; (abhaken) check off; (bact) swab; (com) deduct
ab'streifen tr (Handschuh, usw.) take off; (Haut) slough off; (Gewohnheit) break || intr (SEIN) deviate, stray
ab'streiten §86 tr contest, dispute

Ab'strich *m* (*beim Schreiben*) down-stroke; (*Abzug*) cut; (bact) swab

ab'stufen *tr* (*Gelände*) terrace; (*Farben*) shade off

abstumpfen ['apstumpfən] *tr* blunt

Ab'sturz *m* fall; (*Abhang*) precipice; (aer) crash

abstürzen *intr* (SEIN) fall down; (aer) crash

ab'suchen *tr* (*Gebiet*) scour, comb

Ab·szeß [ap'stsɛs] *m* (–szesses; –szesse) abscess

Abt [apt] *m* (–[e]s;⁼e) abbot

ab'takeln *tr* unrig; (coll) sack, fire

ab'tasten *tr* probe; (rad) scan

Abtei [ap'taɪ] *f* (–;–en) abbey

Ab'teil *m* compartment

ab'teilen *tr* divide, partition

Ab'teilung *f* (–;–en) department, division; (*im Krankenhaus*) ward; (arti) battery; (mil) detachment, unit

Ab'teilungsleiter –*in* §6 *mf* department head, section head

Ab'teilungszeichen *n* hyphen

Äbtissin [ɛp'tɪsɪn] *f* (–;–nen) abbess

ab'tönen *tr* tone down, shade off

ab'töten *tr* (*Bakterien*) kill; (*das Fleisch*) mortify

Abtrag ['aptrɑk] *m* (–[e]s;⁼e)—j-m A. leisten compensate s.o.; j-m A. tun hurt s.o.

ab'tragen §132 *tr* carry away; (*Gebäude*) raze; (*Kleid*) wear out; (*Schuld*) pay

abträglich ['aptreklɪç] *adj* detrimental

ab'treiben §62 *tr* drive away; (*Leibesfrucht*) abort ‖ *intr* (SEIN) drift away; **vom Kurs a.** drift off course

Ab'treibung *f* (–;–en) abortion

ab'trennen *tr* separate, detach; (*Glied*) sever; (*Genähtes*) unstitch

ab'treten §152 *tr* wear out (*by walking*); (*aufgeben*) cede, turn over ‖ *intr* (SEIN) retire, resign; (theat) exit

Ab'treter *m* (–s;–) doormat

Ab'tretung *f* (–;–en) (*von Grundeigentum*) transfer; (pol) cession

ab'trocknen *tr* dry ‖ *intr* (SEIN) dry

ab'tropfen *intr* (SEIN) trickle, drip

ab'trudeln *intr* (SEIN) go into a tailspin; (coll) toddle off, saunter off

abtrünnig ['aptrynɪç] *adj* unfaithful; (eccl) apostate; **a. werden** defect

Ab'trünnigkeit *f* (–;) desertion, defection; (eccl) apostasy

ab'tun §154 *tr* (*ablegen*) take off; (*beiseite schieben*) get rid of; (*töten*) kill; (*erledigen*) settle; **a. als** dismiss as; **kurz a.** make short work of; **mit e-m Achselzucken a.** shrug off

ab'urteilen *tr* pass final judgment on

ab'verlangen *tr*—j-m etw **a.** demand s.th. of s.o.

ab'wägen §156 *tr* weigh

ab'wälzen *tr* roll away; (*Schuld*) shift

ab'wandeln *tr* (*Thema*) vary; (*Hauptwort*) (gram) decline; (*Zeitwort*) (gram) conjugate

ab'wandern *intr* (SEIN) wander off; (*Bevölkerung*) migrate; (*Arbeitskräfte*) drift away

Ab'wanderung *f* (–;–en) exodus, migration

Ab'wandlung *f* (–;–en) variation; (*e-s Hauptwortes*) declension; (*e-s Zeitwortes*) conjugation

ab'warten *tr* wait for; (*Anweisung*) await; **das bleibt abzuwarten!** that remains to be seen! **s-e Zeit a.** bide one's time ‖ *intr* wait and see

abwärts ['apverts] *adv* down, downwards; **mit ihm geht es a.** (coll) he's going downhill

ab'waschen §158 *tr* wash (off)

ab'wechseln *tr* & *intr* alternate

ab'wechselnd *adj* alternate

Ab'wechs(e)lung *f* (–;–en) variation; (*Mannigfaltigkeit*) variety; (*Zerstreuung*) diversion, entertainment

Ab'weg *m* wrong way; **auf Abwege führen** mislead; **auf Abwege geraten** go wrong

Ab'wehr *f* (–;–en) defense; (*e-s Stoßes, usw.*) warding off; (mil) counter-espionage service

ab'wehren *tr* ward off, avert

ab'weichen §85 *intr* (SEIN) deviate, diverge; (*verschieden sein*) differ

Ab'weichung *f* (–;–en) deviation; difference; (math) divergence

ab'weiden *tr* graze on

ab'weisen §118 *tr* refuse, turn down; (*Angriff*) repel; (*Berufung*) deny

ab'weisend *adj* (gegen) unfriendly (to)

Ab'weisung *f* (–;–en) refusal; (jur) denial; (mil) repulse

ab'wenden *tr* turn away, turn aside; (*Augen*) avert; (*Aufmerksamkeit*) divert; (*Krieg, Gefahr*) prevent ‖ §140 & 120 *ref* (**von**) turn away (from)

ab'werfen §160 *tr* throw off; (*Bomben*) drop; (*Blätter, Geweih*) shed; (*Gewinn*) bring in, yield; (*Zinsen*) bear; (*Karten*) discard; (*Joch*) shake off

ab'werten *tr* devaluate

Ab'wertung *f* (–;–en) devaluation

abwesend ['apvezənt] *adj* absent, missing; (fig) absent-minded

Ab'wesenheit *f* (–;) absence; (fig) absent-mindedness

ab'wickeln *tr* unwind, unroll; (*Geschäfte*) transact; (*Schulden*) settle; (*Aktiengesellschaft*) liquidate ‖ *ref* unwind; (fig) develop **sich gut a.** (com) turn out well

ab'wiegen §57 *tr* weigh

ab'wischen *tr* wipe off, wipe clean

Abwurf ['apvurf] *m* drop(ping); (*Bomben*) release; (*Ertrag*) yield

ab'würgen *tr* wring the neck of; (aut) stall

ab'zahlen *tr* pay off

ab'zählen *tr* count off

Ab'zahlung *f* (–;–en) payment in installments; (*Rate*) installment; **auf A.** on terms

Ab'zahlungsgeschäft *n* deferred-payment system

ab'zapfen *tr* (*Bier*) tap; (*Blut*) draw

Ab'zehrung *f* emaciation; consumption

Ab'zeichen *n* distinguishing mark; badge; (mil) decoration

ab'zeichnen *tr* copy, draw, sketch;

(*Dokument*) initial || *ref* become apparent; (**gegen**) stand out (against)
Ab'ziehbild *n* decal
ab'ziehen §163 *tr* pull off; (*Kunden*) lure away; (*Reifen*) take off; (*Bett*) strip; (*vom Preise*) deduct, knock off; (*vervielfältigen*) run off; (*Abziehbild*) transfer; (*Schlüssel vom Loch*) take out; (*Rasiermesser*) strop; (*Wein*) draw; (*Truppen*) withdraw; (*Aufmerksamkeit*) divert; (arith) deduct; (phot) print; (typ) pull || *intr* (SEIN) depart; (*abmarschieren*) march off; (*Rauch*) disperse
Ab'zug *m* (*e-r Summe*) deduction; (*Rabatt*) rebate, allowance; (*Skonto*) discount; (*am Gewehr*) trigger; (*Weggang*) departure; (*für Wasser*) outlet; (*für Rauch*) escape; (mil) withdrawal; (phot) print; (typ) proof sheet
abzüglich ['aptsyklɪç] *prep* (*genit* or *acc*) less, minus
Ab'zugsbogen *m* proof sheet
Ab'zugspapier *n* duplicating paper; (phot) printing paper
Ab'zugsrohr *n* drainpipe
ab'zweigen *tr* divert || *intr* (SEIN) branch off
ach [ax] *interj* oh!; ah!; **ach so!** oh, I see!; **ach was!** nonsense!; **ach wo!** of course not!
Achse ['aksə] *f* (-;-n) axis; (*am Wagen*) axle; (mach) shaft; **auf der A.** on the move; **per A.** by truck; by rail
Achsel ['aksəl] *f* (-;-n) shoulder; **auf die leichte A. nehmen** make light of; **mit den Achseln zucken** shrug one's shoulders; **über die Achseln ansehen** look down on
Ach'selbein *n* shoulder blade
Ach'selgrube *f*, **Ach'selhöhle** *f* armpit
Ach'selträger -in §6 *mf* opportunist
acht [axt] *adj* eight; **alle a. Tage** once a week; **in a. Tagen** within a week; **über a. Tage** a week from today || **Acht** *f* (-;-en) eight || *f* (-;) (*Bann*) outlawry; (*Obacht*) care, attention; **in die A. erklären** outlaw; (fig) ostracize; **sich in a. nehmen vor** (*dat*) watch out for
achtbar ['axtbɑr] *adj* respectable
achte ['axtə] §9 *adj & pron* eight
achteckig ['axtekɪç] *adj* octagonal
Achtel ['axtəl] *n* (-s;-) eighth (*part*)
achten ['axtən] *tr* (*beachten*) respect; (*schätzen*) esteem; (*erachten*) consider || *intr*—**a. auf** (*acc*) pay attention to; **a. darauf, daß** see to it that
ächten ['ɛçtən] *tr* outlaw, proscribe; (*gesellschaftlich*) ostracize
ach'tenswert *adj* respectable
achter(n) ['axtər(n)] *adv* aft, astern
acht'geben §80 *intr* (**auf** *acc*) pay attention (*to*); **gib acht!** watch out!
acht'los *adj* careless
Acht'losigkeit *f* (-;) carelessness
acht'sam *adj* ['axtzɑm] cautious; (**auf** *acc*) attentive (to); (**auf** *acc*) careful (of)
Acht'samkeit *f* (-;) carefulness

achttägig ['axttegɪç] *adj* eight-day; eight-day old; one-week
Ach'tung *f* (-;) attention; (**vor** *dat*) respect (for); **A.!** watch out!; (mil) attention!
ach'tungsvoll *adj* respectful; (*als Briefschluß*) Yours truly
acht'zehn *adj & pron* eighteen || **Achtzehn** *f* (-;-en) eighteen
acht'zehnte §9 *adj & pron* eighteenth
achtzig ['axtsɪç] *adj* eighty
achtziger ['axtsɪgər] *invar adj* of the eighties; **die a. Jahre** the eighties || **Achtziger** -in §6 *mf* octogenarian
achtzigste ['axtsɪçstə] §9 *adj* eightieth
ächzen ['ɛçtsən] *intr* groan, moan
Acker ['akər] *m* (-s;—) soil, (arable) land, field; (*Maß*) acre
Ackerbau (**Ak'kerbau**) *m* farming
ackerbautreibend ['akərbautraɪbənt] *adj* agricultural
Ackerbestellung (**Ak'kerbestellung**) *f* cultivation, tilling
Ackerland (**Ak'kerland**) *n* arable land
ackern ['akərn] *tr & intr* plow
addieren [a'dirən] *tr & intr* add
Addiermaschine [a'dirmaʃinə] *f* adding machine
Addition [adɪ'tsjon] *f* (-;-en) addition
ade [a'de] *interj* farewell!; bye-bye!
Adel ['adəl] *m* (-s;) nobility, noble birth; (*edle Gesinnung*) noble-mindedness
ad(e)lig ['ad(ə)lɪç] *adj* noble, titled; nobleman's || **Ad(e)lige** §5 *m* nobleman || §5 *f* noblewoman
A'delsstand *m* nobility
Ader ['adər] *f* (-;-n) vein
adieu [a'djø] *interj* adieu!
Adjektiv ['atjektif] *n* (-s;-e) adjective
Adjutant -in [atjʊ'tant(ɪn)] §7 *mf* adjutant; (*e-s Generals*) aide(-de-camp)
Adler ['adlər] *m* (-s;-) eagle
Ad'lernase *f* aquiline nose
Admiral [atmɪ'rɑl] *m* (-[e]s;-e) admiral
Admiralität [atmɪralɪ'tet] *f* (-;) admiralty
adoptieren [adɔp'tirən] *tr* adopt
Adoption [adɔp'tsjon] *f* (-;-en) adoption
Adoptiv- [adɔp'tif] *comb. fm.* adoptive
Adressat -in [adrɛ'sat(ɪn)] §7 *mf* addressee; (*e-r Warensendung*) consignee
Adresse [a'drɛsə] *f* (-;-n) address; **an die falsche A. kommen** (fig) bark up the wrong tree; **per A.** care of
adressieren [adrə'sirən] *tr* address; (*Waren*) consign
adrett [a'drɛt] *adj* smart, neat
Advent [at'vɛnt] *m* (-s;-e) Advent
Adverb [at'vɛrp] *n* (-[e]s;-ien [-ɪ.ən]) adverb
Advokat -in [atvɔ'kat(ɪn)] §7 *mf* lawyer
Affäre [a'fɛrə] *f* (-;-n) affair
Affe ['afə] *m* (-n;-n) ape, monkey; **e-n Affen haben** (sl) be drunk
Affekt [a'fɛkt] *m* (-[e]s;-e) emotion; (*Leidenschaft*) passion
affektiert [afɛk'tirt] *adj* affected

Affektiert'heit *f* (**-;-en**) affectation
äffen ['ɛfən] *tr* ape, mimic
Af'fenliebe *f* doting
Af'fenpossen *pl* monkeyshines
Af'fenschande *f* crying shame
Af'fentheater *n* farce, joke
affig ['afɪç] *adj* affected; (*geckenhaft*) foppish
Äffin ['ɛfɪn] *f* (**-;-nen**) female ape, female monkey
Afrika ['afrɪka] *n* (**-s;**) Africa
afrikanisch [afrɪ'kanɪʃ] *adj* African
After ['aftər] *m* (**-s;-**) anus
AG, A.G., A.-G. *abbr* (**Aktiengesellschaft**) stock company
ägäisch [ɛ'ge·ɪʃ] *adj* Aegean
Agende [a'gɛndə] *f* (**-;-n**) memo pad
Agent -in [a'gɛnt(ɪn)] §7 *mf* agent, representative; (*Geheim-*) secret agent
Agentur [agɛn'tur] *f* (**-;-en**) agency
aggressiv [agrɛ'sif] *adj* aggressive
Ägide [ɛ'gidə] *f* (**-;-n**) aegis
Agio ['aʒi·o] *n* (**-s;-s**) premium
Agitation [agɪta'tsjon] *f* (**-;-en**) agitation, rabble-rousing
Agi·tator [agɪ'tatər] *m* (**-s;-tatoren** [ta'torən] (**& mach**) agitator
agitatorisch [agɪta'torɪʃ] *adj* inflammatory
agitieren [agɪ'tirən] *intr* agitate
Agraffe [a'grafə] *f* (**-;-n**) clasp
agrarisch [a'grarɪʃ] *adj* agrarian
Ägypten [ɛ'gyptən] *n* (**-s;**) Egypt
Ägypter -in [ɛ'gyptər(ɪn)] §6 *mf* Egyptian
ägyptisch [ɛ'gyptɪʃ] *adj* Egyptian
ah [a] *interj* ah!
Ahle ['alə] *f* (**-;-n**) awl, punch
Ahn [an] *m* (**-(e)s & -en;-en**) ancestor
ahnden ['andən] *tr* (*strafen*) punish; (*rächen*) avenge
Ahn'dung *f* (**-;**) revenge
ähneln ['enəln] *intr* (*dat*) resemble
ahnen ['anən] *tr* have a premonition of, suspect; (*erfassen*) divine
Ah'nentafel *f* family tree
ähnlich ['enlɪç] *adj* alike; (*dat*) similar (to), analogous (to): **das sieht ihm ä.** that's just like him; **j–m ä sehen** look like s.o.
Ähn'lichkeit *f* (**-;-en**) (*mit*) resemblance (to)
Ah'nung ['anuŋ] *f* (**-;-en**) (*Vorgefühl*) presentiment, hunch; (*böse*) misgiving; (*Argwohn*) suspicion; **keine A. haben** have no idea
ah'nungslos *adj* unsuspecting
ah'nungsvoll *adj* full of misgivings
Ahorn ['ahɔrn] *m* (**-[e]s;-e**) maple
Ähre ['erə] *f* (**-;-n**) (*Korn*) ear; (*e–r Blume*) spike; **Ähren lesen** glean
Ais ['a·ɪs] *n* (**-;-**) (**mus**) A sharp
Akade·mie [akadə'mi] *f* (**-;-mien** ['mi·ən]) academy; university
Akademiker -in [aka'demɪkər(ɪn)] §6 *mf* university graduate
akademisch [aka'demɪʃ] *adj* academic; university
Akazie [a'katsjə] *f* (**-;-n**) acacia
akklimatisieren [aklɪmatɪ'zirən] *tr* acclimate || *ref* become acclimated
Akkord [a'kɔrt] *m* (**-[e]s;-e**) chord;

(*Vereinbarung*) accord; (**com**) settlement; **im A. arbeiten** do piecework
Akkord'arbeit *f* piecework
Akkordeon [a'kɔrde·ən] *n* (**-s;-s**) accordion
akkreditieren [akrɛdɪ'tirən] *tr* accredit; open an account for
Akkreditiv [akrɛdɪ'tif] *n* (**-[e]s;-e**) (*Beglaubigungsschreiben*) credentials; (**com**) letter of credit
Akkumula·tor [akumu'latər] *m* (**-s; -toren** ['torən]) storage battery
akkurat [aku'rat] *adj* accurate
Akkusativ ['akuzatif] *m* (**-[e]s;-e**) accusative (case)
Akrobat [akro'bat] §7 *m* acrobat
Akrobatik [akro'batɪk] *f* (**-;**) acrobatics
Akrobatin [akro'batɪn] §7 *f* acrobat
Akt [akt] *m* (**-[e]s;-e**) act, action; (*paint*) nude; (**theat**) act
Akte ['aktə] *f* (**-;-n**) document; record, file; (**jur**) instrument; **zu den Akten legen** file; (**fig**) shelve
Ak'tendeckel *m* file folder
Ak'tenklammer *f* paper clip
Ak'tenmappe *f* brief case, portfolio
ak'tenmäßig *adj* documentary
Ak'tenschrank *m* file cabinet
Ak'tentasche *f* brief case
Ak'tenzeichen *n* file number
Aktie ['aktsjə] *f* (**-;-n**) stock
Ak'tienbesitzer -in §6 *mf* stockholder
Ak'tienbörse *f* stock exchange
Ak'tiengesellschaft *f* corporation
Ak'tieninhaber -in §6 *mf* stockholder
Ak'tienmakler -in §6 *mf* stockbroker
Ak'tienmarkt *m* stock market
Ak'tienschein *m* stock certificate
Aktion [ak'tsjon] *f* (**-;-en**) action; (*Unternehmung*) campaign, drive; (*polizeiliche*) raid; (**mil**) operation; **Aktionen** activity
Aktionär -in [aktsjo'ner(ɪn)] §8 *mf* stockholder
aktiv [ak'tif] *adj* active; (*Bilanz*) favorable; (**chem**) activated; (**gram**) active; **a. werden** become a member (*of a student club*) || **Aktiv** *n* (**-s;**) (**gram**) active voice
Aktiva [ak'tiva] *pl* assets; **A. und Passiva** assets and liabilities
Aktiv'posten *m* asset
aktuell [aktu'ɛl] *adj* current, topical || **Aktuelle** *pl* (**journ**) newsbriefs
Akustik [a'kustɪk] *f* (**-;**) acoustics
akustisch [a'kustɪʃ] *adj* acoustic(al)
akut [a'kut] *adj* acute
Akzent [ak'tsɛnt] *m* (**-[e]s;-e**) accent (mark); (*Nachdruck*) emphasis; (**phonet**) stress
akzentuieren [aktsɛntu'irən] *tr* accent; (**fig**) stress, accentuate
akzeptieren [aktsɛp'tirən] *tr* accept
Alabaster [ala'bastər] *m* (**-s;**) alabaster
Alarm [a'larm] *m* (**-[e]s;-e**) alarm; **A. blasen** (or **schlagen**) (**mil & fig**) sound the alarm; **blinder A.** false alarm
Alarm'anlage *f* alarm system; warning system (*in civil defense*)
alarm'bereit *adj* on the alert

Alarm'bereitschaft *f* (state of) readiness; **in A.** on the alert
alarmieren [alar'mirən] *tr* alert; alarm
Alaun [a'laun] *m* (-s;-e) alum
Alaun'stift *m* steptic pencil
Albanien [al'banjən] *n* (-s;) Albania
albanisch [al'banɪʃ] *adj* Albanian
albern ['albərn] *adj* silly
Al·bum ['album] *n* (-s;-ben [bən]) album
Alchimist [alçɪ'mɪst] §7 *m* alchemist
Alge ['algə] *f* (-;-n) alga; seaweed
Algebra ['algebra] *f* (-;) algebra
algebraisch [alge'bra·ɪʃ] *adj* algebraic
Algerien [al'gerjən] *n* (-s;) Algeria
algerisch [al'gerɪʃ] *adj* Algerian
Algier ['alʒir] *n* (-s;) Algiers
Alibi ['alɪbɪ] *n* (-s;-s) alibi
Alimente [alɪ'mɛntə] *pl* child support
alimentieren [alɪmɛn'tirən] *tr* pay alimony to; (*Kind*) support
Alkohol ['alkəhol] *m* (-s;-e) alcohol
al'koholfrei *adj* non-alcoholic
Alkoholiker –in [alkə'holɪkər(ɪn)] §6 *mf* alcoholic
alkoholisch [alkə'holɪʃ] *adj* alcoholic
all [al] *adj* all; (*jeder*) every; (*jeder beliebige*) any; **alle beide** both (of them); **alles Gute!** take care!; (*im Brief*) best wishes; **alle zehn Minuten** every ten minutes; **alle zwei Tage** every other day; **auf alle Fälle** in any case || *indef pron* each, each one; everyone, everything; all; **aller und jeder** each and every one; **in allem** all told; **vor allem** above all, first of all
alle ['alə] *adv* all gone; **a. machen** finish off; **a. sein** be all gone; **a. werden** run low
Allee [a'le] *f* (-;-n) (tree-lined) avenue; (tree-lined) walk
Allego·rie [alegə'ri] *f* (-;-rien ['ri·ən]) allegory
allegorisch [ale'gorɪʃ] *adj* allegoric(al)
allein [a'laɪn] *adj* alone || *adv* alone; only; however; no fewer than, no less than; **schon a. der Gedanke** the mere thought
Allein'berechtigung *f* exclusive right
Allein'flug *m* solo flight
Allein'handel *m* monopoly
Allein'herrschaft *f* autocracy
Allein'herrscher –in §6 *mf* autocrat
allei'nig *adj* (*ausschließlich*) sole, exclusive; (*einzig*) only
allein'stehend *adj* alone in the world; (*unverheiratet*) single; (*Gebäude*) detached
Allein'verkauf *m*, **Allein'vertrieb** *m* franchise
al'lemal *adv* every time; **ein für a.** once and for all
al'lenfalls *adv* if need be; (*vielleicht*) possibly; (*höchstens*) at most
allenthalben ['alənt'halbən] *adv* everywhere
al'lerart *invar adj* all kinds of
al'lerbe'ste §9 *adj* very best; **aufs a.** in the best possible manner
al'lerdings' *adv* (*gewiß*) certainly (*strong affirmative answer*); (*zugestehend*) admittedly, I must admit

al'lerer'ste §9 *adj* very first, first ... of all
Aller·gie [alɛr'gi] (-;-gien ['gi·ən]) allergy
allergisch [a'lɛrgɪʃ] *adj* allergic
al'lerhand' *invar adj* all kinds of; (*viel*) a lot of || *indef pron* —**das ist a.!** that's great!; **das ist doch a.!** the nerve!
Allerhei'ligen *invar n* All Saints' Day
allerlei ['alər'laɪ] *invar adj* all kinds of || **Allerlei** *n* (-s;-s) hotchpotch; (mus) medley
al'lerlet'zte §9 *adj* very last, last of all; latest
allerliebste ['alər'lipstə] §9 *adj* dearest ... of all; (*Kind*) sweet
al'lermei'ste §9 *adj* most; **am allermeisten** most of all; chiefly
al'lernäch'ste §9 *adj* very next
al'lerneu'este §9 *adj* latest, newest
Allersee'len *invar n* All Souls' Day
allesamt [alə'zamt] *adv* all together
al'lezeit *adv* always
Allge'genwart *f* omnipresence
all'gemein *adj* general, universal
All'gemeinheit *f* universality; (*Öffentlichkeit*) public
Allheil'mittel *n* cure-all
Allianz [alɪ'ants] *f* (-;-en) alliance
alliieren [alɪ'irən] *ref*—**sich a. mit** ally oneself with
alliiert [alɪ'irt] *adj* allied || **Alliierte** §5 *mf* ally
alljähr'lich *adj* annual, yearly
All'macht *f* omnipotence
allmäch'tig *adj* omnipotent, almighty
allmählich [al'melɪç] *adj* gradual
allnächt'lich *adj* nightly
allseitig ['alzaɪtɪç] *adj* all-round || *adv* from all sides, on all sides
All'tag *m* daily routine
alltäg'lich *adj* daily; (fig) everyday
all'tags *adv* daily; (*wochentags*) weekdays
All'tags– *comb.fm.* everyday; (fig) commonplace
All'tagsmensch *m* common man
All'tagswort *n* (-[e]s;̈er) household word
allwissend [al'vɪsənt] *adj* omniscient
allwö'chentlich *adj & adv* weekly
allzu– *comb.fm.* all too
all'zumal *adv* one and all, all together
all'zusammen *adv* all together
Alm [alm] *f* (-;-en) Alpine meadow
Almanach ['almanax] *m* (-[e]s;-e) almanac
Almosen ['almozen] *n* (-s;-) alms
Alp [alp] *m* (-[e]s;-e) elf, goblin; (*Alptraum*) nightmare
Alp'druck *m* (-[e]s;), **Alp'drücken** *n* (-s;) nightmare
Alpen ['alpən] *pl* Alps
Alphabet [alfa'bet] *n* (-[e]s;-e) alphabet
alphabetisch [alfa'betɪʃ] *adj* alphabetical
alpin [al'pin] *adj* alpine
als [als] *adv* as, like || *conj* than; when, as; but, except; **als ob** as if
alsbald' *adv* presently, immediately
alsdann' *adv* then, thereupon

also ['alzo] *adv* so, thus; therefore, consequently; **na a.!** well then!

alt [alt] *adj* (**älter** ['ɛltər], **älteste** ['ɛltəstə] §9) *adj* old; (*bejahrt*) aged; (*gebraucht*) second-hand; (*abgestanden*) stale; (*antik*) antique; (*Sprache*) ancient || **Alt** *m* (-[e]s;-e) contralto || **Alte** §5 *m* (coll) old man; **die Alten** the ancients; **mein Alter** (coll) my husband || **Alte** §5 *f* (coll) old woman; **meine Alte** (coll) my wife

Altan [al'tan] *m* (-[e]s;-e), **Altane** [al'tanə] *f* (-;-n) balcony, gallery

Altar [al'tar] *m* (-[e]s;-̈e) altar

alt'bewährt *adj* long-standing

Alt'eisen *n* scrap iron

Alt'eisenhändler *m* junk dealer

Alter ['altər] *n* (-s;-) age; (*Greisen-*) old age; (*Zeit-*) epoch; (*Dienst-*) seniority; **er ist in meinem A.** he is my age; **im A. von** at the age of; **mittleren Alters** middle-aged

altern ['altərn] *intr* (SEIN) age

Alternative [alterna'tivə] *f* (-;-n) alternative

Al'tersgrenze *f* age limit; (*für Beamte*) retirement age

Al'tersheim *n* home for the aged

Al'tersrente *f* old-age pension

al'tersschwach *adj* decrepit; senile

Al'tersschwäche *f* (feebleness of) old age

Al'tersversorgungskasse *f* old-age pension fund

Altertum ['altərtum] *n* (-s;) antiquity

altertümlich ['altərtymlıç] *adj* ancient; (*Möbel*) antique; (*veraltet*) archaic

Al'tertumsforscher -in §6 *mf* archaeologist; (*Antiquar*) antiquarian

Al'tertumskunde *f*, **Al'tertumswissenschaft** *f* study of antiquity; classical studies

althergebracht ['alt'hergəbraxt] *adj* long-standing, traditional

alther'kömmlich *adj* ancient, traditional

Altist [al'tıst] §7 *m* alto (*singer*)

Altistin [al'tıstın] §7 *f* contralto (*female singer*)

alt'klug *adj* precocious

ältlich ['ɛltlıç] *adj* elderly

Alt'meister *m* past master; (sport) exchampion

alt'modisch *adj* old-fashioned

Alt'stadt *f* old (part of the) city

Alt'stadtsanierung *f* urban renewal

Alt'stimme *f* alto; contralto (*female voice*)

altväterlich ['altfetərlıç], **altväterisch** ['altfetərıʃ] *adj* old-fashioned; old-time

Alt'warenhändler -in §6 *mf* second-hand dealer

Altweibersommer [alt'vaɪbərzəmər] *m* Indian summer; (*Spinnweb*) gossamer

Aluminium [alu'minjum] *n* (-s;) aluminum

am [am] *contr* **an dem**

amalgamieren [amalga'mirən] *tr* amalgamate

Amateur [ama'tør] *m* (-s;-e) amateur

Amazone [ama'tsonə] *f* (-;-n) Amazon

Am·boß ['ambɔs] *m* (-bosses;-bosse) anvil

ambulant [ambu'lant] *adj* ambulatory || *adv*—**a. Behandelte** out-patient

Ambulanz [ambu'lants] *f* (-;-en) out-patient clinic; (*Krankenwagen*) ambulance

Ameise ['amaɪzə] *f* (-;-n) ant

Amerika [a'merıka] *n* (-s;) America

Amerikaner -in [amerı'kanər(ın)] §6 *mf* American

amerikanisch [amerı'kanıʃ] *adj* American

Ami ['ami] *m* (-s;-s) (sl) Yank || *f* (-;-s) American cigarette

Amme ['amə] *f* (-;-n) nurse, wet-nurse

Amnes·tie [amnes'ti] *f* (-;-tien ['ti·ən]) amnesty

amnestieren [amnes'tirən] *tr* pardon

A·mor ['amɔr] (-s;-moren ['morən]) (myth) Cupid

Amortisation [amətıza'tsjon] *f* (-;-en) amortization

Amortisations'kasse *f* sinking fund

amortisieren [amərtı'zirən] *tr* amortize

Ampel ['ampəl] *f* (-;-n) hanging lamp; (*Verkehrs-*) traffic light

Ampere [am'per] *n* (-s;-) ampere

Amphibie [am'fibjə] *f* (-;-n) amphibian

Amphi'bienpanzerwagen *m* amphibious tank

Amphitheater [am'fite·atər] *n* (-s;-) amphitheater

Ampulle [am'pulə] *f* (-;-n) phial

Amputation [amputa'tsjon] *f* (-;-en) amputation

amputieren [ampu'tirən] *tr* amputate

Amputierte [ampu'tirtə] §5 *mf* amputee

Amsel ['amzəl] *f* (-;-n) blackbird

Amt [amt] *n* (-[e]s;-̈er) office; (*Pflicht*) duty, function; (dipl) post; (eccl) divine service; (telp) exchange

amtieren [am'tirən] *intr* be in office, hold office; (eccl) officiate

amt'lich *adj* official

Amts- *comb.fm.* official, of (an) office

Amts'antritt *m* inauguration

Amts'befugnis *f* competence

Amts'bereich *m* jurisdiction

Amts'bewerber -in §6 *mf* office seeker

Amts'bezirk *m* jurisdiction

Amts'blatt *n* official bulletin

Amts'eid *m* oath of office

Amts'enthebung *f* dismissal

Amts'führung *f* administration

amts'gemäß *adj* official || *adv* officially

Amts'gericht *n* district court

Amts'gerichtsrat *m* (official rank of) district-court judge

Amts'geschäfte *pl* official duties

Amts'gewalt *f* (official) authority

Amts'handlung *f* official act

Amts'niederlegung *f* resignation

Amts'schimmel *m* bureaucracy; (coll) red tape

Amts'siegel *n* seal of office

Amts'sprache *f* official language; (coll) officialese, gobbledygook

Amts'tracht *f* robes

Amts'träger –in §6 *mf* officeholder

Amts'verletzung *f* misconduct in office

Amts'weg *m*—auf dem Amtswege through official channels

Amts'zeichen *n* (telp) dial tone

Amulett [amu'let] *n* (–[e]s;–e) amulet

amüsant [amy'zant] *adj* amusing

amüsieren [amy'zirən] *tr* amuse, entertain || *ref* amuse oneself; (*sich gut unterhalten*) enjoy oneself

an [an] *adv* on; onward || *prep* (*dat*) at, against, on, upon, by, to; (*Grad, Maß*) in; **an sich** per se; **an und für sich** properly speaking; **es ist an dir zu** (*inf*) it's up to you to (*inf*) || *prep* (*acc*) at, on, upon, against, to

analog [ana'lok] *adj* analogous

Analo·gie [analə'gi] *f* (–;–gien ['gi·ən]) analogy

Analphabet –in [analfa'bet(ɪn) §7 *mf* illiterate

Analphabetentum [analfa'betəntum] *n* (–s;), Analphabetismus [analfabe-'tɪsmus] *m* (–;) illiteracy

analphabetisch [analfa'betɪʃ] *adj* illiterate

Analyse [ana'lyzə] *f* (–;–n) analysis; (gram) parsing; **durch A.** analytically

analysieren [analy'zirən] *tr* analyze; (gram) parse

Analy·sis [a'nalyzɪs] *f* (–;–sen [ana-'lyzən]) (math) analysis

Analytiker –in [ana'lytɪkər(ɪn)] §6 *mf* analyst

analytisch [ana'lytɪʃ] *adj* analytic(al)

Anämie [anɛ'mi] *f* (–;) anemia

anämisch [an'emɪʃ] *adj* anemic

Ananas ['ananas] *f* (–;–se) pineapple

Anarchie [anar'çi] *f* (–;) anarchy

anästhesieren [anɛstɛ'zirən] *tr* anesthetize

Anästheti·kum [anɛs'tetɪkum] *n* (–s; –ka [ka]) anesthetic

an'atmen *tr* breathe on

Anato·mie [anatə'mi] *f* (–;–mien ['mi·ən]) anatomy

anatomisch [ana'tomɪʃ] *adj* anatomical

an'backen §50 *tr* bake gently || *intr* (HABEN & SEIN) cake on

an'bahnen *tr* pave the way for

anbandeln ['anbandəln] *intr*—a. mit flirt with

An'bau *m* (–[e]s;) cultivation || *m* (–[e]s;–bauten) annex, new wing

an'bauen *tr* cultivate; (*Gebäudeteil*) add on

An'baufläche *f* (arable) acreage

An'baumöbel *pl* sectional furniture

An'beginn *m* outset

an'behalten §90 *tr* keep (*garment*) on

anbei [an'baɪ] *adv* enclosed (herewith)

an'beißen §53 *tr* bite into, take the first bite of || *intr* nibble at the bait; (fig) bite

an'belangen *tr*—was mich anbelangt as far as I am concerned, as for me

an'bellen *tr* bark at

anberaumen ['anbəraumən] *tr* schedule

an'beten *tr* (& fig) worship

An'betracht *m*—in A. (*genit*) in consideration of, in view of

an'betteln *tr* bum, chisel

An'betung *f* (–;) worship

an'betungswürdig *adj* adorable

an'bieten §58 *tr* offer || *ref* offer one's services

an'binden §59 *tr* tie (up) || *intr*—mit j–m a. pick a quarrel with s.o.

an'blasen §61 *tr* blow at, blow on

An'blick *m* look, view, sight

an'blicken *tr* look at; (*besehen*) view; (*mustern*) eye

an'blinzeln *tr* wink at

an'brechen §64 *tr* (*Vorräte*) break into; (*Flasche, Kiste*) open || *intr* (SEIN) (*Tag*) dawn; (*Nacht*) come on

an'brennen §97 *tr* light || *intr* (SEIN) catch fire; (*Speise*) burn

an'bringen §65 *tr* bring, fetch; (*befestigen*) (an *acc*) attach (to): (*Bitte*) make; (*Klage*) lodge; (*Geld*) invest; (*Tochter*) marry off; (*Waren*) sell, get rid of; (*Bemerkung*) insert; (*Licht, Lampe*) install; (*Geld*) (coll) blow

An'bruch *m* break; **bei A. der Nacht** at nightfall; **bei A. des Tages** at daybreak

an'brüllen *tr* roar at

Andacht ['andaxt] *f* (–;–en) devotion; (*Gottesdienst*) devotions

andächtig ['andɛçtɪç] *adj* devout

an'dauern *intr* continue, last; (*hartnäckig sein*) persist

An'denken *n* (–s;–) remembrance; souvenir; **zum A. an** (*acc*) in remembrance of

andere ['andərə] §9 *adj* & *pron* other; (*folgend*) next; **ein anderer** another; another one; **kein anderer** no one else

ändern ['ɛndərn] *tr* change; (*Wortlaut*) modify || *ref* change

andernfalls ['andərn'fals] *adv* (or) else

anders ['andərs] *adj* else; (*als*) different (from); **a. werden** change || *adv* otherwise differently

an'dersartig *adj* of a different kind

anderseits ['andər'zaɪts] *adv* on the other hand

an'derswo' *adv* somewhere else

anderthalb ['andərt'halp] *invar adj* one and a half

Än'derung *f* (–;–n) change, variation; modification

Än'derungsantrag *m* amendment

anderwärts ['andər'verts] *adv* elsewhere

anderweitig ['andər'vaɪtɪç] *adj* other, further || *adv* otherwise; elsewhere

an'deuten *tr* indicate, suggest; (*anspielen*) hint at, allude to; (*zu verstehen geben*) imply, intimate

an'deutungsweise *adv* by way of suggestion

an'dichten *tr*—j–m etw a. impute s.th. to s.o.

An'drang *m* rush; crowd; heavy traffic; (*von Arbeit*) pressure

an'drehen *tr* turn on; j–m etw a. palm s.th. off on s.o.

an'drohen tr—j-m etw a. threaten s.o. with s.th.

an'drücken tr—etw a. an (acc) press s.th. against

an'eignen ref—sich [dat] a. appropriate; (Gewohnheit) acquire; (Meinungen) adopt; (Sprache) master; (widerrechtlich) appropriate, usurp

aneinan'der adv together

aneinan'dergeraten §63 intr (SEIN) come to blows

Anekdote [anɛk'dotə] f (-;-n) anecdote

an'ekeln tr disgust, nauseate

an'empfehlen §147 tr recommend

An'erbieten n (-s;-) offer, proposal

an'erkennbar adj recognizable

an'erkennen §97 tr (als) recognize (as); (als) acknowledge (as); (Schuld) admit; (billigen) approve; (lobend) appreciate; (Anspruch) allow; **nicht a.** repudiate, disown; (sport) disallow

An'erkennung f (-;-en) acknowledgement; recognition; appreciation; admission; **lobende A.** honorable mention

anfachen ['anfaxən] tr (Feuer) fan; (Gefühle) inflame; (Haß) stir up

an'fahren §71 tr (herbeibringen) carry, convey; (anstoßen) run into; (fig) snap at; (naut) run afoul of ‖ intr (SEIN) drive up; (losfahren) start off

An'fall m attack

an'fallen §72 tr attack, assail ‖ intr (SEIN) accumulate, accrue

anfällig ['anfɛlɪç] adj (für) susceptible (to)

An'fang m beginning, start; **von A. an** from the very beginning

an'fangen §73 tr & intr begin, start

Anfänger –in ['anfɛŋər(ɪn)] §6 mf beginner; (Neuling) novice

anfänglich ['anfɛŋlɪç] adj initial

an'fangs adv at the start, initially

An'fangsbuchstabe m initial (letter)

An'fangsgründe pl rudiments, elements

an'fassen tr take hold of; (behandeln) handle, touch ‖ intr lend a hand

an'faulen intr (SEIN) begin to rot

anfechtbar ['anfɛçtbɑr] adj debatable, questionable; (jur) contestable

an'fechten §74 tr (Richtigkeit) contest; (beunruhigen) trouble; (jur) challenge

An'fechtung f (-;-en) (eccl) temptation; (jur) challenge

an'fertigen tr make, manufacture

an'feuchten tr moisten, wet

an'feuern tr inflame; (sport) cheer

an'flehen tr implore

an'fliegen §57 tr (aer) approach

An'flug m (Anzeichen) suggestion, trace; (oberflächliche Kenntnis) smattering; (dünner Überzug) film; **A. von Bart** down; **leichter A. von** slight case of

an'fordern tr call for, demand; (mil) requisition

an'fragen intr (über acc, wegen, nach) ask (about s.th.); (bei) inquire (of s.o.)

an'fressen §70 tr gnaw; (Metall) corrode

anfreunden ['anfrɔɪndən] ref (mit) make friends (with)

an'frieren §77 intr (SEIN) begin to freeze; **a. an** (acc) freeze onto

an'fügen tr (an acc) join (to)

an'fühlen tr & ref feel

Anfuhr ['anfur] f (-;-en) delivery

an'führen tr lead; (Worte) quote; (Grund) adduce; (täuschen) take in, fool; (mil) lead, command

An'führer –in §6 mf leader; (mil) commander; (pol) boss

An'führung f quotation

An'führungszeichen n quotation mark

an'füllen tr & ref fill up

An'gabe f (Erklärung) statement; (beim Zollamt) declaration; (coll) showing off; **Angaben** data; directions; **nähere Angaben machen** give particulars; **wer hat die A.?** whose serve is it?

an'geben §80 tr (mitteilen) state; (bestimmen) appoint; (anzeigen) inform against; (vorgeben) pretend; (Preis) quote ‖ intr (coll) show off; (cards) deal first; (tennis) serve

An'geber –in §6 mf informer; (Prahler) show-off

angeblich ['angeplɪç] adj alleged

an'geboren adj innate, natural

An'gebot n offer; (bei Auktionen) bid; **A. und Nachfrage** supply and demand

angebracht ['angəbraxt] adj advisable; **es für a. halten zu** (inf) see fit to (inf); **gut a.** appropriate; **schlecht a.** ill-timed

angegossen ['angəgɔsən] adj—**wie a. sitzen** fit like a glove

angeheiratet ['angəhaɪratət] adj related by marriage

angeheitert ['angəhaɪtərt] adj tipsy

an'gehen §82 tr charge, attack; (Problem) tackle; **das geht dich gar nichts an** that's none of your business; **j-n um etw a.** approach s.o. for s.th. ‖ intr (SEIN) begin; (zulässig sein) be allowable; (leidlich sein) be tolerable; **das geht nicht an** that won't do

an'gehend adj future, prospective

an'gehören intr (dat) be a member (of)

Angehörige ['angəhørɪgə] §5 mf member; **nächste Angehörigen** next of kin; **seine Angehörigen** his relatives

Angeklagte ['angəklɑktə] §5 mf defendant; (wenn verhaftet) suspect

Angel ['aŋəl] f (-;-n) fishing tackle; (e-r Tür) hinge; **aus den Angeln heben** (& fig) unhinge

an'gelangen intr (SEIN) (an dat, bei) arrive (at)

an'gelegen adj—**sich** [dat] **etw a. sein lassen** make s.th. one's business

An'gelegenheit f (-;-en) affair, business

angelehnt ['angəlent] adj ajar

An'gelgerät n fishing tackle

An'gelhaken m fish(ing) hook

angeln ['aŋəln] intr (nach) fish (for)

An'gelpunkt m pivot, central point

An'gelrute f fishing rod

angelsächsisch ['aŋəlzɛksɪʃ] *adj* Anglo-Saxon
An'gelschnur *f* fishing line
angemessen ['angəmɛsən] *adj* suitable (*ausreichend*) adequate; (*annehmbar*) reasonable; (*Benehmen*) proper; (*dat*) in keeping (with); **für a. halten** think fit
angenehm ['angənem] *adj* pleasant; **sehr a!** pleased to meet you!
angeregt ['angərɛkt] *adj* lively
angeschlagen ['angəʃlagən] *adj* chipped; (*Boxer*) groggy; (mil) hard-hit
angesehen ['angəze-ən] *adj* respected; (*ausgezeichnet*) distinguished
An'gesicht *n* countenance, face; **von A.** by sight
an'gesichts *prep* (*genit*) in the presence of; (fig) in view of
angestammt ['angəʃtamt] *adj* hereditary
Angestellte ['angəʃtɛltə] §5 *mf* employee; **die Angestellten** the staff
angetan ['angətɑn] (**mit**) clad (in); **a. sein von** have a liking for; **ganz danach a. zu** (*inf*) very likely to (*inf*)
angetrunken ['angətruŋkən] *adj* tipsy
angewandt ['angəvant] *adj* applied
angewiesen ['angəvizən] *adj*—**a. sein auf** (*acc*) have to rely on
an'gewöhnen *tr*—**j-m etw a.** accustom s.o. to s.th.
An'gewohnheit *f* (–;–en) habit
an'gleichen §85 *tr* adapt, adjust
Angler –in ['aŋlər(ɪn)] §6 *mf* fisher
an'gliedern *tr* link, attach; (*Gesellschaft*) affiliate
an'greifen §88 *tr* (*anfassen*) handle; (*Vorräte*) draw on, dip into; (*Körper*) affect; (mil) attack
an'greifend *adj* aggressive, offensive
An'greifer –in §6 *mf* aggressor
an'grenzen *intr* (**an** *acc*) be adjacent (to), border (on)
An'griff *m* attack
An'griffskrieg *m* war of aggression
an'griffslustig *adj* aggressive
Angst [aŋst] *f* (–;¨e) fear, anxiety
ängstigen ['ɛŋstɪgən] *tr* alarm || *ref* (**vor**) be afraid (of); (**um**) be alarmed (about)
ängstlich ['ɛŋstlɪç] *adj* uneasy, jittery; (*besorgt*) anxious; (*sorgfältig*) scrupulous; (*schüchtern*) timid
Angst'zustände *pl* jitters
an'haben §89 *tr* have on; **j-m etw a.** have s.th. on. s.o.; **j-m etw a. können** be able to harm s.o.
an'haften *intr* (*dat*) stick (to)
an'haken *tr* check off; (**an** *acc*) hook (onto)
an'halten §90 *tr* stop; (*Atem, Ton*) hold; || *intr* stop; (*andauern*) continue, last
an'haltend *adj* continuous
An'halter *m*—**per A. fahren** hitch-hike
An'haltspunkt *m* clue, lead
An'hang *m* (–[e]s;¨e) appendix; (*Gefolgschaft*) following; (jur) codicil
an'hängen §92 & §109 *tr* (*Hörer*) hang up; (*hinzufügen*) add on; **j-m e-e Krankheit a.** infect s.o. with a disease; **j-m e-n Prozeß a.** bring suit

against s.o.; **j-m etw a.** pin s.th. on s.o. || §92 *intr* (**an** *dat*) adhere (to)
An'hänger –in §6 *mf* follower || *m* (*Schmuck*) pendant; (aut) trailer
anhänglich ['anhɛŋlɪç] *adj* (**an** *acc*) attached (to), devoted (to)
Anhängsel ['anhɛŋzəl] *m* (–s;–) appendage, adjunct
an'hauchen *tr* breathe on
an'häufen *tr & ref* pile up
An'häufung *f* (–;–en) accumulation
an'heben §94 *tr* lift (up); (*Lied*) strike up; (aut) jack up
an'heften *tr* fasten; (*annähen*) stitch
an'heilen *tr & intr* heal up
anheim'fallen §72 *intr* (SEIN) (*dat*) devolve (upon)
anheim'stellen *tr* (*dat*) leave (to)
An'höhe *f* rise, hill
an'hören *tr* listen to, hear || *ref* —**sich gut a.** sound good
Anilin [anɪ'lin] *n* (–s;) aniline
Animier'dame *f* B-girl
animieren [anɪ'mirən] *tr* encourage
Anis [a'nis] *m* (–es;–e) anise
an'kämpfen *intr* (**gegen**) struggle (against)
An'kauf *m* purchase
an'kaufen *tr* purchase
Anker ['aŋkər] *m* (–s;–) anchor; (elec) armature; **vor A. gehen** drop anchor
ankern ['aŋkərn] *intr* anchor
an'ketten *tr* (**an** *acc*) chain (to)
An'klage *f* accusation, charge; (jur) indictment; **A. erheben** prefer charges; **die A. vertreten** be counsel for the prosecution; **unter A. stellen** indict
an'klagen *tr* (**wegen**) accuse (of), charge (with), indict (for)
An'kläger –in §6 *mf* accuser; (jur) prosecutor
An'klageschrift *f* (bill of) indictment
an'klammern *tr* (**an** *acc*) clip (to) || *ref* (**an** *acc*) cling (to)
An'klang *m* (**an** *acc*) reminiscence (of), trace (of); **A. finden** be well received, catch on
an'kleben *tr* (**an** *acc*) paste (on), stick (on) || *intr* (HABEN & SEIN) stick
an'kleiden *tr & ref* dress
an'klingeln *tr* ring, call up || *intr*— **bei j-m a.** ring s.o.'s doorbell
an'klopfen *intr* (**an** *acc*) knock (on)
an'knipsen *tr* switch on
an'knüpfen *tr* tie, attach; (*Gespräch*) start || *intr* (**an** *acc*) link up (with)
an'kommen §99 *intr* (SEIN) (**in** *dat*) arrive (at); (**bei**) be well received (by); (**bei**) get a job (with); **es darauf a. lassen** take one's chances; **es kommt ganz darauf an, ob** it (all) depends on whether
Ankömmling ['ankœmlɪŋ] *m* (–s;–e) newcomer, arrival
an'kündigen *tr* announce, proclaim; **j-m etw a.** notify s.o. of s.th.
An'kündigung *f* (–;–en) announcement
Ankunft ['ankunft] *f* (–;¨e) arrival
an'kurbeln *tr* crank up; **die Wirtschaft a.** prime the economy
an'lachen *tr* laugh at
An'lage *f* (*Anordnung*) plan, layout;

(*Bau*) construction; (*Errichtung*) installation; (*Fabrik*) plant, works; (*Garten*) park, grounds; (*Fähigkeit*) ability, aptitude (*im Brief*) enclosure; **in der A.** enclosed
An'lagekapital *n* invested capital; permanent assets
an'langen *tr*—**was mich anlangt** as far as I'm concerned ‖ *intr* (SEIN) arrive
An·laß ['anlas] *m* (-lasses;-lässe) occasion; (*Grund*) reason, motive; **A. geben zu** give rise to; **ohne allen A.** without any reason
an'lassen §104 *tr* (*Kleid*) keep on; (*Motor*) start (up); (*Wasser*) turn on; (*Pumpe*) prime; (*Stahl*) temper; **j-n hart a.** rebuke s.o. sharply ‖ *ref* **sich gut a.** shape up
Anlasser ['anlasər] *m* (-s;-) starter
anläßlich ['anleslɪç] *prep* (*genit*) on the occasion of
An'lauf *m* run, start
an'laufen §105 *tr* run at; (*Hafen*) put into ‖ *intr* (SEIN) (*Motor*) start up; (*Brille*) fog up; (*Metall*) tarnish; (*anwachsen*) accumulate; (*Schulden*) mount up; (*Film*) start, come on; **angelaufen kommen** come running up; **ins Rollen a.** (fig) get rolling; **rot a.** blush
an'legen *tr* (an *acc*) put (on), lay (on); (*Garten; Geld*) lay out; (*Kapital*) invest; (*Leitung*) install; (*Verband*) apply; (*Kolonie*) found ‖ *ref*—**sich a. mit** have a run-in with ‖ *intr* put ashore; moor
An'legeplatz *m* pier
an'lehnen *tr* (an *acc*) lean (against); (*Tür*) leave ajar ‖ *ref* (an *acc*) lean (against); (fig) be based (on), rely (on)
Anleihe ['anlaɪ·ə] *f* (-;-n) loan
an'leiten *tr* (zu) guide (to); **a. in** (*dat*) instruct in
An'leitung *f* (-;-en) guidance; (*Lehre*) instruction
an'lernen *tr* train, break in
an'liegen §108 *intr* (*passen*) fit; (an *dat*) lie near, be adjacent (to); **eng a.** fit tight; **j-m a.** pester s.o. ‖ **Anliegen** *n* (-s;-) request; **ein A. an j-n haben** have a request to make of s.o.
an'liegend *adj* adjacent; (*Kleid*) tight-fitting; (*im Brief*) enclosed
an'locken *tr* lure (on)
an'machen *tr* (*Licht*) switch on; (*Feuer*) light; (*zubereiten*) prepare; (an *acc*) attach (to)
an'malen *tr* paint
an'marschieren *intr* (SEIN) approach
anmaßen ['anmasən] *ref*—**sich** [*dat*] **etw a.** usurp s.th.; **sich** [*dat*] **a., etw zu sein** pretend to be s.th.
an'maßend *adj* arrogant
An'meldeformular *n* registration form
an'melden *tr* announce; report; (*Anspruch, Berufung*) file; (*Konkurs*) declare; (*Patent*) apply for; (educ) register; (sport) enter ‖ *ref* (bei) make an appointment (with); (zu) enroll (in); (mil) report in
an'merken *tr* note down; **j-m etw a.** notice s.th. in s.o.

an'messen §70 *tr*—**j-m etw a.** measure s.o. for s.th.
An'mut *f* (-;) charm, attractiveness
an'mutig *adj* charming
an'nageln *tr* (an *acc*) nail (to)
an'nähen *tr* (an *acc*) sew on (to)
annähernd ['anne·ərnt] *adj* approximate
An'näherung *f* (-;-en) approach
An'näherungsversuch *m* (romantic) pass; attempt at reconciliation
an'näherungsweise *adv* approximately
An'nahme *f* (-;-n) acceptance; (*Vermutung*) assumption
annehmbar ['annembar] *adj* acceptable
an'nehmen §116 *tr* accept, take; (*vermuten*) assume, suppose, guess; (*Glauben*) embrace; (*Gewohnheit*) acquire; (*Gesetz*) pass; (*Kind*) adopt; (*Arbeiter*) hire; (*Farbe, Gestalt*) take on; (*Titel*) assume; **etw als erwiesen a.** take s.th. for granted ‖ *ref* (*genit*) take care of
annektieren [anek'tirən] *tr* annex
Annexion [ane·ksjon] *f* (-;-en) annexation
Annonce [a'nõsə] *f* (-;-n) advertisement
annoncieren [anɔ'sirən] *tr* advertise
anöden [a'nødən] *tr* bore to death
anonym [ano'nym] *adj* anonymous
an'ordnen *tr* arrange; (*befehlen*) order
an'packen *tr* grab hold of, seize; (*Problem*) tackle
an'passen *tr* fit; (*Worte*) adapt; ‖ *ref* (dat or an *acc*) adapt oneself (to)
an'passungsfähig *adj* adaptable
an'pflanzen *tr* plant, cultivate
an'pflaumen *tr* (coll) kid
anpöbeln ['anpøbəln] *tr* mob
an'pochen *tr* (an *acc*) knock (on)
An'prall *m* impact; (*e-s Angriffs*) brunt
an'prallen *intr* (SEIN) (gegen, an *acc*) collide (with), run (into)
an'preisen *tr* praise; **j-m etw a.** recommend s.th. to s.o.
An'probe *f* fitting, trying on
an'probieren *tr* try on
an'pumpen *tr*—**j-n a. um** hit s.o. for
an'quatschen *tr* talk the ears off
an'raten §63 *tr* advise, recommend
an'rechnen *tr* charge; **hoch a.** appreciate; **j-m etw a.** charge s.o. for s.th.
An'recht *n* (auf *acc*) right (to)
An'rede *f* address
an'reden *tr* address, speak to
an'regen *tr* stimulate; suggest
An'reiz *m* incentive
an'reizen *tr* stimulate; spur on
an'rennen §97 *intr* (SEIN) (gegen) run (into); **angerannt kommen** come running
an'richten *tr* (*Schaden*) cause, do; (culin) prepare
anrüchig ['anrʏçɪç] *adj* disreputable
an'rücken *intr* SEIN) approach
An'ruf *m* (telephone) call
an'rufen §122 *tr* call; (*Gott*) invoke; (*Schiff*) hail; (jur) appeal to; (mil) challenge; (telp) call up
an'rühren *tr* touch; (*Thema*) touch on; (*mischen*) stir
An'sage *f* announcement

an'sagen *tr* announce; (*Trumpf*) declare

An'sager –in §6 *mf* announcer

an'sammeln *tr* gather; (*anhäufen*) amass; (*Truppen*) concentrate || *ref* gather; (*Zinsen*) accumulate

ansässig ['anzɛsɪç] *adj* residing; **a. werden** (or **sich a. machen**) settle || **Ansässige** §5 *mf* resident

An'satz *m* start; (*Mundstück*) mouthpiece; (*Spur*) trace; (*in e-r Rechnung*) charge; (*Schätzung*) estimate; (geol) deposit; (mach) attachment; (math) statement

an'saugen §125 *tr* suck in; (*Pumpe*) prime

an'schaffen *tr* procure; (*kaufen*) get, purchase; **Kinder a.** (coll) have kids

an'schalten *tr* switch on

an'schauen *tr* look at

an'schaulich *adj* graphic

An'schauung *f* outlook, opinion; (*Vorstellung*) perception; (*Auffassung*) conception; (*Erkenntnis*) intuition; (*Betrachtung*) contemplation

An'schauungsbild *n* mental image

An'schauungsmaterial *n* visual aids

An'schein *m* appearance

an'scheinend *adj* apparent, seeming

an'scheinlich *adv* apparently

an'schicken *ref* get ready

an'schieben §130 *tr* give (*s.th.*) a push

anschirren ['anʃɪrən] *tr* harness

An'schlag *m* (**an** *acc*, **gegen**) striking (against); (*Anprall*) impact; (*Attentat*) attempt; (*Bekanntmachung*) notice; (*e-r Uhr*) stroke; (*e-r Taste*) hitting; (*Berechnung*) calculation; (*e-s Gewehrs*) firing position; (*Komplott*) plot; (mach) stop (*for arresting motion*); (mus) touch; (tennis) serve; **A. spielen** play tag

An'schlagbrett *n* bulletin board

an'schlagen §132 *tr* (**an** *acc*) fasten (to); (*Plakat*) post; (*Gewehr*) level; (*Tasse, usw.*) chip; (*Taste*) hit; (*einschätzen*) estimate; (*Gegner*) (box) have in trouble; **e-n anderen Ton a.** (fig) change one's tune || *ref* bump oneself || *intr* (*Wellen*) (**an** *acc*) beat against); (*Hund*) let out a bark; (*Arznei*) work

An'schlagzettel *m* notice; poster

an'schließen §76 *tr* padlock; (*anketten*) chain; (*verbinden*) connect; (*anfügen*) join; (com) affiliate; (elec) plug in || *ref* (*dat*, **an** *acc*) join, side with ||*intr* (*Kleid*) be tight

an'schließend *adj* (**an** *acc*) subsequent (to); adjacent (to) || *adv* next, then

An'schluß *m* connection; (pol) annexation, union; **sie sucht A.** (coll) she is looking for a man

An'schlußbahn *f* (rr) branch line

An'schlußdose *f* (elec) receptacle

An'schlußschnur *f* (elec) cord

An'schlußzug *m* connection, connecting train

an'schmachten *tr* make eyes at

an'schmiegen *ref* (**an** *acc*) nestle up (to); (*Kleid*) (**an** *acc*) cling (to)

anschmiegsam ['anʃmikzɑm] *adj* accommodating; cuddly

an'schmieren *tr* smear; (coll) bamboozle

an'schnallen *tr* buckle || *ref* fasten one's seat belt

an'schnauzen *tr* snap at, bawl out

an'schneiden §106 *tr* cut into; (*Thema*) take up

An'schnitt *m* first cut

an'schrauben *tr* (**an** *acc*) screw on (to)

an'schreiben §62 *tr* write down; (*Spielstand*) mark; (*dat*) charge (to): (com) write to; **etw a. lassen** buy s.th. on credit

An'schreiber –in §6 *mf* scorekeeper

An'schreibetafel *f* scoreboard

an'schreien §135 *tr* yell at

An'schrift *f* address

An'schriftenmaschine *f* addressograph

anschuldigen ['anʃuldɪgən] *tr* accuse

an'schwärzen *tr* blacken, disparage

an'schwellen *tr* cause to swell; (*Unkosten, usw.*) swell || §119 *intr* (SEIN) swell up, puff up; increase

an'schwemmen *tr* wash (*s.th.*) ashore; (geol) deposit

an'sehen §138 *tr* look at; (fig) regard || **Ansehen** *n* (**-s;-**) appearance; (*Achtung*) reputation; (*Geltung*) prestige, authority; **von A.** by sight; of high repute

ansehnlich ['anzenlɪç] *adj* good-looking; (*beträchtlich*) considerable; (*eindrucksvoll*) imposing

An'sehung *f* (**-;**)—**in A.** (*genit*) in consideration of

anseilen ['anzaɪlən] *tr* rope together

an'setzen *tr* (**an** *acc*) put (on), apply (to): (*zum Kochen*) put on; (*Frist, Preis*) set; (*abschätzen*) rate; (*berechnen*) charge; (*Knospen*) put forth || *intr* begin; (*fett werden*) get fat

An'sicht *f* view; (*Meinung*) opinion; **zur A.** on approval

an'sichtig *adj*—**a. werden** (*genit*) catch sight of

An'sichtspostkarte *f* picture postcard

An'sichtssache *f* matter of opinion

An'sichtsseite *f* frontal view, façade

An'sichtssendung *f* article(s) sent on approval

ansiedeln *tr* & *ref* settle

An'siedler –in §6 *mf* settler

An'siedlung *f* (**-;-en**) settlement

An'sinnen *n* (**-s;-**) unreasonable demand

an'spannen *tr* stretch; (*Pferd*) hitch up; (fig) exert, strain

An'spannung *f* (**-;-en**) exertion, strain

an'speien §135 *tr* spit on

an'spielen *tr* (cards) lead with || *intr* (**auf** *acc*) allude (to); (mus) start playing; (sport) kick off, serve, break

An'spielung *f* (**-;-en**) allusion, hint

an'spitzen *tr* sharpen (*to a point*)

An'sporn *m* spur, stimulus

an'spornen *tr* spur

An'sprache *f* (**an** *acc*) address (to); **e-e A. halten** deliver an address

an'sprechen §64 *tr* speak to, address; (*Ziel, Punkt*) make out; **a. als** regard as; **j-n a. um** ask s.o. for || *intr* (*dat*) appeal to, interest; (**auf** *acc*) respond (to)

an'sprechend *adj* appealing
an'springen §142 *tr* leap at ‖ *intr*
(SEIN) (*Motor*) start (up); **angesprun-**
gen kommen come skipping along
an'spritzen *tr* sprinkle, squirt
An'spruch *m* claim; **A. haben auf** (*acc*)
be entitled to; **A. machen** (or **er-**
heben) **auf** (*acc*), **in A. nehmen** demand, require, claim; **große An-**
sprüche stellen ask too much
an'spruchslos *adj* unpretentious
an'spruchsvoll *adj* pretentious; (*wäh-*
lerisch) choosey, hard to please
an'spucken *tr* spit on
an'spülen *tr* wash ashore; (geol) deposit
an'stacheln *tr* goad on
Anstalt ['an∫talt] *f* (–;–en) institution,
establishment; **Anstalten treffen zu**
make preparations for
An'stand *m* (*Schicklichkeit*) decency;
(*Bedenken*) hesitation; (*Einwendung*)
objection; (hunt) blind
anständig ['an∫tendıç] *adj* decent
An'standsbesuch *m* formal call
An'standsdame *f* chaperone
An'standsgefühl *n* tact
an'standshalber *adv* out of politeness,
out of human decency
an'standslos *adv* without fuss
an'starren *tr* stare at, gaze at
anstatt [an'∫tat] *prep* (genit) instead of
an'stauen *tr* dam up ‖ *ref* pile up
an'staunen *tr* gaze at (*in astonishment*)
an'stecken *tr* stick on; (*Ring*) put on;
(*anzünden*) set on fire; (*Zigarette,*
Feuer) light; (pathol) infect ‖ *ref*
become infected
an'steckend *adj* infectious; (*durch Be-*
rührung) contagious
An'steckung *f* (–;–en) infection; (*durch*
Berührung) contagion
an'stehen §146 *intr* (**nach**) line up
(for): (*zögern*) hesitate; **j–m gut a.**
fit s.o. well, become s.o.
an'steigen §148 *intr* (SEIN) rise, ascend; (*zunehmen*) increase, mount
up
an'stellen *tr* (**an** *acc*) place (against);
(*beschäftigen*) hire; (*Versuch, usw.*)
(*Vergleich*) draw; (*Heizung, Radio*)
turn on ‖ *ref* (**nach**) line up (for);
sich a., als ob act as if; stell dich
nicht so dumm an! don't play dumb!
anstellig ['an∫telıç] *adj* skillful
An'stellung *f* (–;–en) hiring; job
an'steuern *tr* steer for
Anstieg ['an∫tik] *m* (–[e]s;–e) rise;
(*e–s Weges*) grade
an'stieren *tr* stare at, glower at
an'stiften *tr* instigate
An'stifter –in §6 *mf* instigator
an'stimmen *tr* (*Lied*) strike up; (*Ge-*
heul) let out
An'stoß *m* impact; (*Antrieb*) impulse;
(*Ärgernis*) offense; (sport) kickoff;
den A. geben zu start
an'stoßen §150 *tr* bump against; (*Ball*)
kick off; (*Wagen*) give a push; (*mit*
dem Ellbogen) nudge, poke ‖ *intr*
clink glasses; **a. an** (*acc*) adjoin; **bei**
j–m a. shock s.o.; **mit den Gläsern a.**
clink glasses; **mit der Zunge a.** lisp ‖

intr (SEIN)—**mit dem Kopf a. an**
(*acc*) bump one's head against
an'stoßend *adj* adjoining
anstößig ['an∫tøsıç] *adj* shocking
an'strahlen *tr* beam on; (fig) beam at;
(*mit Scheinwerfern*) floodlight
an'streben *tr* strive for
an'streichen §85 *tr* paint; (*Fehler*)
underline; (*anhaken*) check off
An'streicher *m* house painter
an'streifen *tr* brush against, graze
an'strengen *tr* exert; (*Geist*) tax; **e–n**
Prozeß a. file suit ‖ *intr* be a strain
an'strengend *adj* strenuous, trying
An'strengung *f* (–;–en) exertion, effort
An'strich *m* (*Farbe*) paint; (*Überzug*)
coat (*of paint*); (fig) tinge
An'sturm *m* assault, charge
antarktisch [ant'arktı∫] *adj* antarctic
an'tasten *tr* touch, finger
An'teil *m* share, portion; (*Quote*)
quota; (st. exch.) share; **A. nehmen**
an (*dat*) take part in; (fig) sympathize with
an'teilmäßig *adj* proportional
An'teilnahme *f* (–;) (**an** *dat*) participation (in); (*Mitleid*) sympathy
Antenne [an'tenə] *f* (–;–n) antenna,
aerial; (ent) antenna, feeler
Antibioti·kum [antıbı'otıkum] *n* (–s;
–ka [ka]) antibiotic
antik [an'tik] *adj* ancient; classical ‖
Antike *f* (–;–n) (classical) antiquity;
(*Kunstwerk*) antique
Anti'kenhändler –in §6 *mf* antique
dealer
Antilope [antı'lopə] *f* (–;–n) antelope
Antipa·thie [antıpa'ti] *f* (–;–thien
['ti·ən]) antipathy
an'tippen *tr & intr* tap
Antiqua [an'tikva] *f* (–;) roman (type)
Antiquar –in [antı'kvar(ın)] §8 *mf*
antique dealer; second-hand book-
dealer
Antiquariat [antıkva'rjat] *n* (–[e]s;–e)
second-hand bookstore
antiquarisch [antı'kvarı∫] *adj* second-
hand
Antiquität [antıkvı'tet] *f* (–;–en) antique
Antlitz ['antlıts] *m* (–es;–e) (Bib, poet)
countenance
Antrag ['antrak] *m* (–[e]s;–̈e) (*Ange-*
bot) offer; (*Vorschlag*) proposal;
(*Gesuch*) application; (pol) motion
an'tragen §132 *tr* offer; (*vorschlagen*)
propose ‖ *intr*—**a. auf** (*acc*) make a
motion for; propose, suggest
An'tragsformular *n* application form
Antragsteller –in ['antrak∫telər(–ın)]
§6 *mf* applicant; (parl) mover
an'treffen §151 *tr* meet; find at home
an'treiben §62 *tr* drive on, urge on;
(*Schiff*) propel; (*anreizen*) egg on ‖
intr (SEIN) wash ashore
an'treten §152 *tr* (*Amt, Erbschaft*) enter (upon); (*Reise*) set out on; (*Mo-*
torrad) start up ‖ *intr* (SEIN) take
one's place; (mil) fall in; (sport)
enter
An'trieb *m* (–s;–e) (*Beweggrund*) motive; (*Anreiz*) incentive; (mech)
drive, impetus; **aus eigenem A.** on

one's own initiative; **neuen A. verleihen** (*dat*) give fresh impetus to
An'tritt *m* (-[e]s;-e) beginning, start;
(*e-s Amtes*) entrance upon
an'tun §154 *tr* (*Kleid*) put on; **j-m
etw a.** do s.th. to s.o.
Antwort ['antvɔrt] *f* (-;-en) answer
antworten ['antvɔrtən] *intr* (**auf** *acc*)
reply (to), answer; **j-m a.** answer s.o.
an'vertrauen *tr* entrust; (*mitteilen*)
tell, confide
an'verwandt *adj* related ‖ **Anver-
wandte** §5 *mf* relative
an'wachsen §155 *intr* (SEIN) begin to
grow; grow together; (*Wurzel schlagen*) take root; (*zunehmen*) increase
Anwalt ['anvalt] *m* (-[e]s;-̈e) attorney
An'waltschaft *f* legal profession, bar
an'wandeln *tr*—**mich wandelte die Lust
an zu** (*inf*) I got a yen to (*inf*); **was
wandelte dich an?** what got into
you?
An'wandlung *f* (-;-en) impulse, sudden feeling; (*von Zorn*) fit
An'wärter –in §6 *mf* candidate; (mil)
cadet, officer candidate
Anwartschaft ['anvartʃaft] *f* (-;) expectancy; (*Aussicht*) prospect
an'wehen *tr* blow on ‖ *intr* (SEIN)
drift
an'weisen §118 *tr* (*beauftragen*) instruct; (*zuteilen*) assign; (*Geld*) remit
An'weisung *f* (-;-en) instruction; assignment; (fin) money order
anwendbar ['anventbar] *adj* (**auf** *acc*)
applicable (to); (**für, zu**) that can be
used (for)
an'wenden §140 *tr* (**auf** *acc*) apply
(to); (**für, zu**) use (for)
An'wendung *f* (-;-en) application;
use
an'werben §149 *tr* recruit
an'werfen §160 *tr* (*Motor*) start up
An'wesen *n* estate, property; presence
anwesend ['anvezənt] *adj* present ‖
Anwesende §5 *mf* person present;
verehrte Anwesende! ladies and
gentlemen!
An'wesenheit *f* (-;) presence
an'wurzeln *ref* & *intr* (SEIN) take root;
wie angewurzelt rooted to the spot
An'zahl *f* (-;) number, quantity
an'zahlen *tr* pay down ‖ *intr* make a
down payment
an'zapfen *tr* tap
An'zeichen *n* indication, sign; (*Vorbe-
deutung*) omen; (pathol) symptom
Anzeige ['antsaɪgə] *f* (-;-n) (*Ankündigung*) announcement, notice; (*Reklame*) ad; (med) advice; **kleine
Anzeigen** classified ads
an'zeigen *tr* announce; notify; (*Symp-
tome, Fieber*) show, indicate; (*bei
der Polizei*) report, inform against;
(*inserieren*) advertise
An'zeigenvermittlung *f* advertising
agency
an'zetteln *tr* (*Verschwörung*) hatch
an'ziehen §163 *tr* pull; (& fig) attract;
(*Kleid*) put on; (*e-e Person*) dress;
(*Riemen, Schraube*) tighten; (*Bremse*)
apply; (*Beispiele, Quellen*) quote ‖

intr pull, start pulling; (*Preis*) go up;
(chess) go first
An'ziehung *f* (-;-en) attraction; (*Zitat*)
quotation
An'ziehungskraft *f* appeal; (& phys)
attraction; (astr) gravitation
An'zug *m* suit; (mil) uniform; **in A.
sein** (*Armee*) be approaching;
(*Sturm*) be gathering; (*Gefahr*) be
imminent
anzüglich ['antsylɪç] *adj* offensive; **a.
werden** become personal
an'zünden *tr* set on fire; (*Feuer*) light
an'zweifeln *tr* doubt, question
apart [a'part] *adj* charming; (coll)
cute
Apathie [apa'ti] *f* (-;) apathy
apathisch [a'patɪʃ] *adj* apathetic
Apfel ['apfəl] *m* (-s;-̈) apple
Ap'felkompott *n* stewed apples
Ap'felmus *n* applesauce
Ap'felsaft *m* apple juice
Apfelsine [apfəl'zinə] *f* (-;-n) orange
Ap'feltorte *f* apple tart; **gedeckte A.**
apple pie
Ap'felwein *m* cider
Apostel [a'pɔstəl] *m* (-s;-) apostle
Apostroph [apɔ'strof] *m* (-[e]s;-e)
apostrophe
Apotheke [apɔ'tekə] *f* (-;-n) phar-
macy
Apotheker –in [apɔ'tekər(ɪn)] §6 *mf*
druggist
Apothe'kerwaren *pl* drugs
Apparat [apa'rat] *m* (-[e]s;-e) ap-
paratus, device; (phot) camera; (rad,
telv) set; (telp) telephone; **am A.!**
speaking
Appell [a'pɛl] *m* (-[e]s;-e) appeal;
(mil) roll call; (mil) inspection
appellieren [apɛ'lirən] *intr* (& jur)
(**an** *acc*) appeal (to)
Appetit [ape'tit] *m* (-[e]s;-e) appetite
Appetit'brötchen *n* canapé
appetit'lich *adj* appetizing; (*Mädchen*)
attractive
applaudieren [aplau'dirən] *tr* & *intr*
applaud
Applaus [a'plaus] *m* (-es;-e) applause
Appretur [aprɛ'tur] *f* (-;-en) (tex)
finish
Aprikose [aprɪ'kozə] *f* (-;-n) apricot
April [a'prɪl] *m* (-[s];-e) April
Aquarell [akva'rɛl] *n* (-[e]s;-e) water-
color; watercolor painting
Aqua·rium [a'kvarjum] *n* (-s;-rien
[rɪ-ən]) aquarium
Äqua·tor [ɛ'kvatər] *m* (-s;-toren
['torən]) equator
Ära ['era] *f* (-;Ären ['erən]) era
Araber –in ['arabər(ɪn)] §6 *mf* Arab
Arabien [a'rabjən] *n* (-s;) Arabia
arabisch [a'rabɪʃ] *adj* Arabian; (*Zif-
fer*) Arabic
Arbeit ['arbaɪt] *f* (-;-en) work
arbeiten ['arbaɪtən] *tr* & *intr* work
Arbeiter ['arbaɪtər] *m* (-s;-) worker;
A. und Unternehmer *pl* labor and
management
Ar'beiterausstand *m* walkout, strike
Ar'beitergewerkschaft *f* labor union
Arbeiterin ['arbaɪtərɪn] *f* (-;-nen)
working woman, working girl

Ar'beiterschaft *f* (–;) working class
Arbeitertum ['arbaɪtərtum] *n* (–s;) working class, workers
Ar'beitgeber –in §6 *mf* employer
Ar'beitnehmer –in §6 *mf* employee
arbeitsam ['arbaɪtzam] *adj* industrious
Ar'beitsanzug *m* overalls; (mil) fatigue clothes, fatigues
Ar'beitseinkommen *n* earned income
Ar'beitseinstellung *f* work stoppage
ar'beitsfähig *adj* fit for work
Ar'beitsgang *m* process; operation (*single step of a process*)
Ar'beitsgemeinschaft *f* team; (educ) workshop
Ar'beitsgerät *n* equipment, tools
Ar'beitskommando *n* (mil) work detail
Ar'beitskraft *f* labor force; **Arbeitskräfte** personnel
Ar'beitsleistung *f* (work) quota; (*e-r Maschine, Fabrik*) output
Ar'beitslohn *m* wages, pay
ar'beitslos *adj* unemployed
Ar'beitslosenunterstützung *f* unemployment compensation
Ar'beitslosigkeit *f* unemployment
Ar'beitsmarkt *m* labor market
Ar'beitsminister *m* secretary of labor
Ar'beitsministerium *n* department of labor
Ar'beitsnachweis *m*, **Ar'beitsnachweisstelle** *f* employment agency
Ar'beitsniederlegung *f* walkout, strike
ar'beitsparend *adj* labor-saving
Ar'beitspause *f* break, rest period
Arbeitspferd *n* (& *fig*) workhorse
Ar'beitsplatz *m* job, place of employment
Ar'beitsrecht *n* labor law
ar'beitsscheu *adj* work-shy, lazy
Ar'beitsschicht *f* shift
Ar'beitsstätte *f* place of employment; workshop; yard
Ar'beitsstelle *f* job, position
Ar'beitstag *m* workday
Ar'beitsvermittlung *f* employment agency
Ar'beitsversäumnis *n* absenteeism
Ar'beitszeug *n* tools
Ar'beitszimmer *n* study; workroom
archaisch [ar'ça·ɪʃ] *adj* archaic
Archäologe [arçɛ·ɔ'logə] *m* (–n;–n) archaeologist
Archäologie [arçɛ·ɔlɔ'gi] *f* (–;) archaeology
Archäologin [arçɛ·ɔ'logɪn] *f* (–;–nen) archaeologist
archäologisch [arçɛ·ɔ'logɪʃ] *adj* archaeological
Architekt –in [arçɪ'tɛkt(ɪn)] §7 *mf* architect
Architektur [arçɪtɛk'tur] *f* (–;–en) architecture
Ar·chiv [ar'çif] *n* (–[e]s;–chive ['çivə]) archives; (*für Zeitungen*) morgue
Areal [arɛ'al] *n* (–s;–e) area
Are·na [a'rena] *f* (–;–nen [nən]) arena
arg [ark] *adj* (**ärger** ['ɛrgər]; **ärgste** ['ɛrkstə] §9) bad, evil, wicked; (coll) awful; (*schlimm*) grave; (*Raucher*)

heavy ‖ **Arg** *n* (–s;) malice, cunning ‖ **Arge** §5 *m* Evil One ‖ §5 *n* evil
Argentinien [argɛn'tinjən] *n* (–s;) Argentina
Argentinier –in [argɛn'tinjər(ɪn)] §6 *mf* Argentinean
Ärger ['ɛrgər] *m* (–s;) irritation; **mit j–m Ä. haben** have trouble with s.o.
är'gerlich *adj* (**auf** *acc* or **über** *acc*) annoyed (at); irritating, annoying
ärgern ['ɛrgərn] *tr* annoy ‖ *ref* (**über** *acc*) be annoyed (at)
Ärgernis ['ɛrgərnɪs] *n* (–ses;–se) scandal, offense; (*Mißstand*) nuisance
Arg'list *f* craft, cunning
arg'listig *adj* crafty, cunning
arg'los *adj* guileless; (*nichtsahnend*) unsuspecting
Argwohn ['arkvon] *m* (–s;) suspicion
argwöhnen ['arkvønən] *tr* suspect
argwöhnisch ['arkvønɪʃ] *adj* suspicious
Arie ['arjə] *f* (–;–n) aria
Arier –in ['arjər(ɪn)] §6 Aryan
arisch ['arɪʃ] *adj* Aryan
Aristokrat [arɪstɔ'krat] *m* (–en;–en) aristocrat
Aristokra·tie [arɪstɔkra'ti] *f* (–;–tien ['ti·ən]) aristocracy
Aristokratin [arɪstɔ'kratɪn] *f* (–;–nen) aristocrat
Arithmetik [arɪt'metɪk] *f* (–;) arithmetic
Arktis ['arktɪs] *f* (–;) Arctic
arktisch ['arktɪʃ] *adj* arctic
arm [*arm*] *adj* (**ärmer** ['ɛrmər], **ärmste** ['ɛrmstə] §9 (**an** *dat*) poor in) ‖ **Arm** *m* (–[e]s;–e) arm; (*e-s Flusses*) branch
Armatur [arma'tur] *f* (–;–en) armature; **Armaturen** fittings, mountings
Armatu'renbrett *n* instrument panel; (aut) dashboard
Arm'band *n* (–[e]s;–̈er) bracelet; watchband; (*Armabzeichen*) brassard
Arm'banduhr *f* wrist watch
Arm'binde *f* brassard; (med) sling
Ar·mee [ar'me] *f* (–;–meen ['me·ən]) army
Ärmel ['ɛrməl] *m* (–s;–) sleeve
Är'melaufschlag *m* cuff
Är'melkanal *m* English Channel
är'mellos *adj* sleeveless
Armen– [armən] *comb.fm.* for the poor
Ar'menhaus *n* poorhouse
Armenien [ar'menjən] *n* (–s;) Armenia
armenisch [ar'menɪʃ] *adj* Armenian
Ar'menpflege *f* public assistance
Ar'menunterstützung *f* public assistance, welfare
Ar'menviertel *n* slums
Armesün'dermiene *f* hangdog look
Arm'lehne *f* arm, armrest
Arm'leuchter *m* candelabrum
ärmlich ['ɛrmlɪç] *adj* poor, humble
arm'selig *adj* poor, wretched; (*kläglich*) paltry
Armut ['armut] *f* (–;) poverty
Arm'zeichen *n* semaphore
Aro·ma [a'roma] *n* (–s;–men [mən], –mata [mata]) aroma
aromatisch [arɔ'matɪʃ] *adj* aromatic
Arrest [a'rɛst] *m* (–[e]s;–e) arrest;

(*in der Schule*) detention; (jur) impounding, seizure

Arsch [arʃ] *m* (**-es;-͞e**) (sl) ass

Arsch'backe *f* (sl) buttock

Arsch'kriecher *m* (sl) brown-noser

Arsch'lecker *m* (sl) brown-noser

Arsen [ar'zen] *n* (**-s;**) arsenic

Arsenal [arze'nɑl] (**-s;-e**) arsenal

Art [art] *f* (**-;-en**) sort, kind; nature; (*Rasse*) race, breed; species; (*Weise*) manner; (*Verfahren*) procedure; (*Muster*) model; **das ist keine Art!** that's no way to behave!

art'eigen *adj* true to type

arten ['artən] *intr* (SEIN)—**a. nach** take after

Arterie [ar'terjə] *f* (**-;-n**) artery

artig ['artıç] *adj* (*brav*) good, well-behaved; (*höflich*) polite

Artikel [ar'tikəl] (**-s;-**) (com, gram, journ) article

Artillerie [artılə'ri] *f* (**-;**) artillery

Artillerie'aufklärer *m* artillery spotter

Artischocke [artı'ʃokə] *f* (**-;-n**) artichoke

Artist **-in** [ar'tıst(ın)] §7 *mf* artist; (*beim Zirkus*) performer

Arznei [arts'naı] *f* (**-;-en**) medicine, medication, drug

Arznei'kraut *n* herb, medicinal plant

Arznei'kunde *f*, **Arznei'kunst** *f* pharmaceutics; pharmacology

Arznei'mittel *n* medication

Arzt [artst] *m* (**-[e]s;-͞e**) doctor

Ärztin ['ertstın] *f* (**-;-nen**) doctor

ärztlich ['ertstlıç] *adj* medical

As [as] *n* (**Asses; Asse**) ace ‖ *n* (**-;-**) (mus) A flat

Asbest [as'best] *m* (**-[e]s;-e**) asbestos

asch'bleich *adj* ashen, pale

Asche ['aʃə] *f* (**-;-n**) ash(es), cinders

Aschen- *comb.fm.* ash; cinder; funerary

A'schenbahn *f* cinder track

A'schenbecher *m* ashtray

Aschenbrödel ['aʃənbrødəl] *n* (**-s;-**) Cinderella; drudge

Aschermittwoch [aʃər'mıtvɔx] *m* (**-s; -e**) Ash Wednesday

asch'fahl *adj* ashen, pale

äsen ['ezen] *intr* graze, feed

asiatisch [azı'atıʃ] *adj* Asiatic

Asien ['ɑzjən] *n* (**-s;**) Asia

Asket [as'ket] *m* (**-en;-en**) ascetic

asketisch [as'ketıʃ] *adj* ascetic

Asphalt [as'falt] *m* (**-[e]s;**) asphalt

asphaltieren [asfal'tirən] *tr* asphalt

Asphalt'pappe *f* tar paper

aß[as] *pret* of **essen**

Assistent **-in** [asıs'tent(ın)] §7 *mf* assistant

Assistenz [asıs'tents] *f* (**-;-en**) assistance

Assistenz'arzt *m*, **Assistenz'ärztin** *f* intern

Ast [ast] *m* (**-es;-͞e**) bough, branch; (*im Holz*) knot, knob

ästhetisch [es'tetıʃ] *adj* esthetic(al)

Asthma ['astma] *n* (**-s;**) asthma

ast'rein *adj* free of knots; **nicht ganz a.** (coll) not quite kosher

Astrologe [astro'logə] *m* (**-n;-n**) astrologer

Astrologie [astrolo'gi] *f* (**-;**) astrology

Astronaut [astro'naut] *m* (**-en;-en**) astronaut

Astronom [astro'nom] *m* (**-en;-en**) astronomer

Astronomie [astrono'mi] (**-;**) astronomy

astronomisch [astro'nomıʃ] *adj* astronomic(al)

Astrophysik [astrofY'zik] *f* (**-;**) astrophysics

Asyl [a'zyl] *n* (**-[e]s;-e**) asylum, sanctuary; (*Obdach*) shelter; **ohne A.** homeless

Atelier [ate'lje] *n* (**-s;-s**) studio

Atem ['atəm] *m* (**-s;**) breath

A'tembeklemmung *f* shortness of breath

A'temholen *n* (**-s;**) respiration

a'temlos *adj* breathless

A'temnot *f* breathing difficulty

A'tempause *f* breathing spell

a'temraubend *adj* breath-taking

A'temzug *m* breath

Atheismus [ate'ısmʊs] *m* (**-;**) atheism

Atheist **-in** [ate'ıst(ın)] §7 *mf* atheist

Äther ['etər] *m* (**-s;**) ether

Athlet [at'let] *m* (**-en;-en**) athlete

Athletik [at'letık] *f* (**-;**) athletics

Athletin [at'letın] *f* (**-;-nen**) athlete

athletisch [at'letıʃ] *adj* athletic

Atlantik [at'lantık] *m* (**-s;**) Atlantic

At·las ['atlas] *m* (**-';**) (myth) Atlas ‖ *m* (**-lasses; -lanten** ['lantən] & **-lasse**) atlas ‖ *m* (**- & -lasses;-lasse**) satin

atmen ['atmən] *tr & intr* breathe

Atmosphäre [atmo'sferə] *f* (**-;-n**) (& fig) atmosphere

atmosphärisch [atmo'sferıʃ] *adj* atmospheric; **atmosphärische Störungen** (rad) static

At'mung *f* (**-;**) breathing

Atom [a'tom] *n* (**-s;-e**) atom

Atom- *comb. fm.* atom, atomic

Atom'abfall *m* fallout; atomic waste

atomar [ato'mar] *adj* atomic

Atom'bau *m* atomic structure

atom'betrieben *adj* atomic-powered

Atom'bombe *f* atomic bomb

Atom'bombenversuch *m* atomic test

Atom'-Epoche *f* atomic age

Atom'kern *m* atomic nucleus

Atom'müll *m* atomic waste

Atom'regen *m* fallout

Atom'schutt *m* atomic waste

ätsch [etʃ] *interj* (to express gloating) serves you right!, good for you!

Attentat [aten'tat] *n* (**-s;-e**) attempt (*on s.o.'s life*); assassination

Attentäter **-in** [aten'tetər(ın)] §6 *mf* assailant, would-be assassin; assassin

Attest [a'test] *n* (**-es;-e**) certificate

attestieren [ates'tirən] *tr* attest (to)

Attrappe [a'trapə] *f* (**-;-n**) dummy

Attribut [atrı'but] *n* (**-[e]s;-e**) attribute; (gram) attributive

atzen ['atsən] *tr* feed

ätzen ['etsən] *tr* corrode; (med) cauterize (typ) etch

ät'zend *adj* corrosive; caustic

Au [au] *f* (**-;-en**) (poet) mead, meadow

au *interj* ow!, ouch!; oh!

Aubergine [ɔber'ʒin(ə)] *f* (-;-n) egg-plant

auch [aux] *adv* also, too; (*selbst*) even

Audienz [au'djents] *f* (-;-en) audience; (jur) hearing

auf [auf] *adv* up; **auf und ab** up and down; **von Kind auf** from childhood on || *prep* (*dat*) on, upon; **auf der ganzen Welt** in the whole world; **auf der Universität** at the university || *prep* (*acc*) on; up; to; **auf den Bahnhof gehen** go to the station; **auf deutsch** in German; **drei aufs Dutzend** three to a dozen; **es geht auf vier Uhr zu** it's going on four; **Monat auf Monat verging** month after month passed || *interj* get up! || **Auf** *n*—**das Auf und Nieder** the ups and downs

auf'arbeiten *tr* (*Rückstände*) catch up on; (*verbrauchen*) use up; (*erneuern*) renovate; (mach) recondition || *ref* work one's way up

auf'atmen *intr* breathe a sigh of relief

aufbahren ['aufbarən] *tr* lay out

Auf'bau *m* (-[e]s;) construction; structure; organization; (*Anlage*) arrangement, setup; (chem) synthesis || *m* (-[e]s;-ten) structure; (aer) framework; (aut) body; (naut) superstructure

auf'bauen *tr* erect; (*Organization*) establish; (chem) synthesize; (mach) assemble || *ref*—**er baute sich vor mir auf** he planted himself in front of me; **sich** [*dat*] **e-e Existenz a.** make a life for oneself

auf'bäumen *ref* rear; (fig) rebel

auf'bauschen *tr* puff up; (fig) exaggerate

auf'begehren *intr* flare up; (**gegen**) protest (against), rebel (against)

auf'behalten §90 *tr* keep on; keep open

auf'bekommen §99 *tr* (*Tür*) get open; (*Knoten*) loosen; (*Hausaufgabe*) be assigned

auf'bereiten *tr* prepare, process

auf'bessern *tr* (*Gehalt*) improve, raise

auf'bewahren *tr* keep, store; **das Gepäck a. lassen** check one's baggage

auf'bieten §58 *tr* summon; (*Brautpaar*) announce the banns of; (mil) call up

auf'binden §58 *tr* tie up; (*lösen*) untie; **j-m etw a.** put s.th. over on s.o.

auf'blähen *tr* inflate, distend

auf'blasen §61 *tr* inflate || *ref* get puffed up

auf'bleiben §62 *intr* (SEIN) (*Tür*) stay open; (*wachen*) stay up

auf'blenden *intr* turn on the high beam

auf'blicken *intr* glance up

auf'blitzen *intr* (HABEN & SEIN) flash

auf'blühen *intr* (SEIN) begin to bloom

auf'bocken *tr* (aut) jack up

auf'brauchen *tr* use up

auf'brausen *intr* (HABEN & SEIN) bubble, seethe; (*Wind*) roar; (fig) flare up

auf'brausend *adj* effervescent; irascible

auf'brechen §64 *tr* break up; break open; (hunt) eviscerate || *intr* (SEIN)

burst open; (*fortgehen*) (**nach**) set out (for)

auf'bringen §65 *tr* bring up; (*Geld, Truppen*) raise; (*Schiff*) capture; (*Kraft*) gather; (*Mut*) get up; (*erzürnen*) infuriate

Auf'bruch *m* departure

auf'brühen *tr* bring to a boil

auf'bügeln *tr* iron, press; refresh (*one's knowledge of s.th.*)

aufbürden ['aufbʏrdən] *tr*—**j-m etw a.** saddle s.o. with s.th.

auf'decken *tr* uncover; (*Bett*) turn down; (*Tischtuch*) spread

auf'drängen *tr* force open; **j-m etw a.** force s.th. on s.o.

auf'drehen *tr* turn up; (*Uhr*) wind; (*Hahn*) turn on; (*Schraube*) unscrew; (*Strick*) untwist || *intr* (*Wagen*) increase speed; (coll) step on it, get a move on

auf'dringlich *adj* pushy; (*Farben*) gaudy

Auf'druck *m* print, imprint

auf'drücken *tr* impress, imprint, affix; (*öffnen*) squeeze open

aufeinan'der *adv* one after the other

Aufeinan'derfolge *f* succession; series

aufeinan'derfolgen *intr* (SEIN) follow one another

aufeinan'derfolgend *adj* successive

Aufenthalt ['aufenthalt] *m* (-[e]s;-e) holdup, delay; **ohne A.** nonstop

Auf'enthaltsgenehmigung *f* residence permit

Auf'enthaltsort *m* (*Wohnsitz*) residence; (*Verbleib*) whereabouts

Auf'enthaltsraum *m* lounge

auf'erlegen *tr* impose || *ref*—**sich** [*dat*] **die Pflicht a. zu** (*inf*) make it one's duty to (*inf*); **sich** [*dat*] **Zwang a. müssen** have to restrain oneself

auf'erstehen §146 *intr* (SEIN) rise (from the dead)

Auf'erstehung *f* (-;) resurrection

auf'erwecken *tr* raise from the dead

auf'erziehen §163 *tr* bring up, raise

auf'essen §70 *tr* eat up

auf'fädeln *tr* (*Perlen*) string

auf'fahren §71 *tr* (*Fahrzeuge*) park; (*Geschütze*) bring up; (*Wein, Speisen*) serve up || *intr* (SEIN) rise, mount; (*im Auto*) pull up; (*in Erregung*) jump (up); (arti) move into position; **a. auf** (*acc*) run into

Auf'fahrt *f* ascent; (*Zufahrt*) driveway

auf'fallen §72 *intr* (SEIN) be conspicuous; **j-m a.** strike s.o.

auf'fallend, auf'fällig *adj* striking; noticeable; (*Farben*) loud, gaudy

auf'fangen §73 *tr* (*Ball, Worte*) catch; (*Briefe, Nachrichten*) intercept

auf'fassen *tr* comprehend; (*deuten*) interpret; (*Perlen*) string

Auf'fassung *f* (-;-en) understanding; interpretation; (*Meinung*) view

auf'finden §59 *tr* find (*after searching*)

auf'fliegen §57 *intr* (SEIN) fly up; (*Tür*) fly open; (*scheitern*) fail; **a. lassen** break up (*e.g., a gang*)

auf'fordern *tr* call upon, ask

Auf'forderung *f* (-;-en) invitation; (jur) summons

auf'frischen *tr* freshen up, touch up

auf'führen *tr* (*Bau*) erect; (*Schauspiel*) present; (*eintragen*) enter; (*Zeugen*) produce; (*anführen*) cite; (mil) post; **einzeln a.** itemize || *ref* behave, act

Auf'führung *f* (–;–en) erection; performance; entry; specification; behavior

auf'füllen *tr* fill up

Auf'gabe *f* task, job; (*e-s Briefes*) mailing; (*des Gepäcks*) checking; (*e-r Bestellung*) placing; (*e-s Amtes, e-s Geschäfts*) giving up; (educ) homework; (jur) waiver; (math) problem; (mil) assignment

auf'gabeln *tr* (& coll) pick up

Auf'gang *m* ascent; (*Treppe*) stairs; (astr) rising

auf'geben §80 *tr* give up; (*Amt*) resign; (*Post*) mail; (*Gepäck*) check in; (*Anzeige*) place; (*Preis*) quote; (*Arbeit*) assign; (*Telegramm*) send

auf'geblasen *adj* (fig) uppity

Auf'gebot *n* public notice; (eccl) banns; (mil) call-up

auf'gebracht *adj* angry, irate

auf'gedonnert *adj* (coll) dolled up

auf'gehen §82 *intr* (SEIN) rise; (*Tür*) open; (*Pflanzen*) come up; (arith) go into; **genau a.** come out exactly

auf'geklärt *adj* enlightened

auf'geknöpft *adj* (coll) chatty

auf'gekratzt *adj* (coll) chipper

Auf'geld *n* surcharge; premium

auf'gelegt *adj* (**zu**) disposed (to)

auf'geräumt *adj* (fig) good-humored

auf'geschlossen *adj* open-minded; (**für**) receptive (to)

auf'geschmissen *adj* (coll) stuck

auf'gestaut *adj* pent-up

auf'geweckt *adj* smart, bright

auf'geworfen *adj* (*Lippen*) pouting; (*Nase*) turned-up

auf'gießen §76 *tr* (**auf** *acc*) pour (on); (*Tee, Kaffee*) make, brew

auf'graben §87 *tr* dig up

auf'greifen §88 *tr* pick up; (*Dieb*) catch; (fig) take up

auf'haben §98 *tr* (*Hut*) have on; (*Tür, Mund*) have open; (*Aufgabe*) have to do

auf'hacken *tr* hoe up

auf'haken *tr* unhook

auf'halten §90 *tr* hold up; (*Tür*) hold open; (*anhalten*) stop, delay || *ref* stay; (*wohnen*) live; **sich über etw a.** find fault with s.th.

Auf'hängeleine *f* clothesline

auf'hängen §92 *tr* hang up; **j-m etw a.** push s.th. on s.o.; (*Wertloses*) palm s.th. off on s.o.

auf'häufen *tr* & *ref* pile up

auf'heben §94 *tr* lift up, pick up; (*bewahren*) preserve; (*ungültig machen*) cancel; (*Gesetz*) repeal; (*ausgleichen*) cancel out, offset; (*Strafe, Belagerung*) lift; **gut aufgehoben sein** be in good hands

auf'heitern *tr* cheer up || *ref* cheer up; (*Gesicht*) brighten; (*Wetter*) clear up

auf'hellen *ref* & *intr* brighten

auf'hetzen *tr* incite, egg on

auf'holen *tr* hoist; (*Verspätung*) make up for || *intr* catch up

auf'horchen *intr* prick up one's ears

auf'hören *intr* stop, quit

auf'jauchzen *intr* shout for joy

auf'kaufen *tr* buy up; (*Markt*) corner

auf'klären *tr* clear up; enlighten; (mil) reconnoitre || *ref* clear up; (*Gesicht*) light up, brighten

Auf'klärer *m* (–s;–) (aer) reconnaissance plane; (mil) scout

Auf'klärung *f* (–;–en) explanation; enlightenment; (mil) reconnaissance

Auf'klärungsbuch *n* sex-education book

Auf'klärungsspähtrupp *m* reconnaissance patrol

auf'kleben *tr* (**auf** *acc*) paste (onto)

auf'klinken *tr* unlatch

auf'knacken *tr* crack open

auf'knöpfen *tr* unbutton

auf'knüpfen *tr* (*lösen*) untie; (*hängen*) (coll) string up

auf'kochen *tr* & *intr* boil

auf'kommen §99 *intr* (SEIN) come up, rise; (*Gedanke*) occur; (*Mode*) come into fashion; (*Schiff*) appear on the horizon; **a. für** answer for; (*Kosten*) defray; **a. gegen** stand up against, cope with; **a. von** recover from || **Aufkommen** *n* (–s;) rise; recovery

auf'krempeln *tr* roll up

auf'kreuzen *intr* (coll) show up

auf'kriegen *tr see* aufbekommen

auf'lachen *intr* burst out laughing

auf'laden §103 *tr* load up; (*Batterie*) charge || *ref*—**sich** [*dat*] **etw a.** saddle oneself with s.th.

Auf'lage *f* edition, printing; (*e-r Zeitung*) circulation; (*Steuer*) tax; (*Stütze*) rest, support

auf'lassen §104 *tr* leave open; (*Fabrik, Bergwerk*) abandon

auf'lauern *intr* (*dat*) lie in wait (for)

Auf'lauf *m* gathering, crowd; (*Tumult*) riot; (com) accumulation; (culin) soufflé

auf'laufen §105 *intr* (SEIN) rise; (*anwachsen*) accrue; (*Schiff*) get stranded; (*Panzer*) get stuck

auf'leben *intr* (SEIN) revive

auf'lecken *tr* lick up

auf'legen *tr* (**auf** *acc*) put (on); (*Steuer*) impose; (*Hörer*) hang up; (*Buch*) publish; (*Karten*) lay on the table; (*Liste*) make available for inspection; (*Anleihe*) float; (*Faß Bier*) put on || *intr* (telp) hang up

auf'lehnen *tr* (**auf** *acc*) lean (on) || *ref* (**auf** *acc*) lean (on); (**gegen**) rebel (against)

Auf'lehnung *f* (–;–en) rebellion; resistance

auf'lesen §107 *tr* pick up, gather

auf'liegen §108 *intr* (**auf** *dat*) lie (on); (*zur Ansicht*) be displayed

auf'lockern *tr* loosen; (*Eintönigkeit, Vortrag*) break (up)

auf'lösbar *adj* soluble; solvable

auf'lösen *tr* untie; (*öffnen*) loosen; (*entwirren*) disentangle; (*Versammlung*) break up; (*Heer*) disband; (*Ehe*) dissolve; (*Verbindung*) sever; (*Firma*) liquidate; (*Rätsel*) solve;

(*zerlegen*) break down; dissolve; (*entziffern*) decode; **ganz aufgelöst** all out of breath

Auf′lösung *f* (–;–en) solution; disentanglement; (*e–r Versammlung, Ehe*) breakup; (*Zerfall*) disintegration; (*von Beziehungen*) severance; (com) liquidation

auf′machen *tr* open (up); (*Geschäft*) open; (*Dampf*) get up; (coll) do up (e.g., big, tastefully) ‖ *ref* (*Wind*) rise; (**nach**) set out (for)

Auf′machung *f* (–;–en) layout, format; (*Kleidung*) outfit

Auf′marsch *m* parade; (mil) concentration; (*zum Gefecht*) (mil) deployment

auf′marschieren *intr* (SEIN) parade; (*strategisch*) assemble; (*taktisch*) deploy

auf′merken *tr* (**auf** *acc*) pay attention (to)

aufmerksam [′aufmɛrkzɑm] *adj* (**auf** *acc*) attentive (to)

Auf′merksamkeit *f* (–;) attention

auf′möbeln *tr* (coll) dress up; (*anherrschen*) (sl) chew out; (*aufmuntern*) (coll) pep up ‖ *ref* (coll) doll up

auf′muntern *tr* cheer up

Auf′nahme *f* (–;–n) taking up; (*Empfang*) reception (*Zulassung*) admission; (*von Beziehungen*) establishment; (*Inventur*) stock-taking; (electron) recording; (phot) photograph

Auf′nahmeapparat *m* camera; recorder

Auf′nahmegerät *n* camera; recorder

Auf′nahmeprüfung *f* entrance exam

auf′nehmen §116 *tr* take up; (*erfassen*) grasp; (*Diktat*) take down; (*Gast*) receive; (*Inventar*) take; (*Geld*) borrow; (*Anleihe*) float; (*Spur*) pick up; (*Beziehungen*) establish; (*eintragen*) enter; (*durch*) *Tonband, Schallplatte*) record; (geog) map out; (phot) take

auf′opfern *tr* offer up, sacrifice

auf′päpeln *tr* spoon-feed

auf′passen *intr* pay attention; look out; **paß auf!** watch out!

auf′pflanzen *tr* set up; (*Seitengewehr*) fix

auf′platzen *intr* (SEIN) burst (open)

auf′polieren *tr* polish up

auf′prägen *tr* (**auf** *acc*) (& fig) impress (on)

auf′prallen *intr* (**auf** *acc*) crash (into)

auf′pumpen *tr* pump up

auf′putschen *tr* incite; (coll) pep up

auf′putzen *tr* dress up; clean up ‖ *ref* dress up

auf′raffen *tr* pick up ‖ *ref* stand up; (fig) pull oneself together

auf′ragen *intr* tower, stand high

auf′räumen *tr* (*Zimmer*) straighten up; (*wegräumen*) clear away ‖ *intra—a.* **mit** do away with, get rid of

Auf′räumungsarbeiten *pl* clearance

auf′rechnen *tr* add up; (acct) balance

auf′recht *adj* upright, erect

auf′rechterhalten §90 *tr* maintain

auf′regen *tr* excite, stir up; (*unruhig machen*) disturb, upset

Auf′regung *f* (–;–en) excitement

auf′reiben §62 *tr* rub off; (*wundreiben*) rub sore; (*vertilgen*) destroy; (*Heer*) grind up; (*Kräfte*) sap; (*Nerven*) fray ‖ *ref* worry onself to death

auf′reibend *adj* wearing, exhausting

auf′reihen *tr* string, thread

auf′reißen §53 *tr* tear open; (*Straße*) tear up; (*Tür*) fling open; (*Augen*) open wide; (*zeichnen*) sketch ‖ *intr* (SEIN) split open, crack

auf′reizen *tr* provoke, incite; (*stark erregen*) excite

auf′reizend *adj* provoking, annoying; (*Rede*) inflammatory; (*Anblick*) sexy

auf′richten *tr* erect, set up; (*trösten*) comfort ‖ *ref* sit up

auf′richtig *adj* upright, sincere

Auf′richtigkeit *f* sincerity

auf′riegeln *tr* unbolt

Auf′riß *m* front view

auf′rollen *tr* roll up; (*entfalten*) unroll

auf′rücken *intr* (SEIN) advance; (**zu**) be promoted (to)

Auf′ruf *m* (*Aufschrei*) outcry; (*Aufforderung*) call; (mil) call-up

auf′rufen §122 *tr* call on; (*appellieren an*) appeal to; (*Banknoten*) call in

Auf′ruhr *m* uproar; (*Tumult*) riot

auf′rühren *tr* stir up

aufrührerisch [′aufryːrərɪʃ] *adj* inflammatory, rebellious; (mil) mutinous

auf′runden *tr* round out

auf′rüsten *tr* & *intr* arm; rearm

Auf′rüstung *f* (–;–en) rearmament

auf′rütteln *tr* wake up (*by shaking*)

auf′sagen *tr* recite; (*ein Ende machen mit*) terminate

auf′sammeln *tr* gather up

aufsässig [′aufzɛsɪç] *adj* hostile; (*widerspenstig*) rebellious

Auf′satz *m* superstructure; (*auf dem Tische*) centerpiece; (*Schularbeit*) essay, composition; (*in der Zeitung*) article; (golf) tee; (mil) gun sight

auf′saugen §125 *tr* suck up; absorb

auf′schauen *intr* look up

auf′scheuchen *tr* scare up

auf′scheuern *tr* scrape

auf′schichten *tr* stack (up), pile (up)

auf′schieben §130 *tr* push up; (*Tür*) push open; (*verschieben*) postpone

auf′schießen §76 *intr* (SEIN) shoot up

Auf′schlag *m* (**auf** *acc*) striking (upon), impact (on); (*an Kleidung*) cuff, lapel; (*Steuer–*) surtax; (*Preis–*) price hike; (tennis) service, serve

auf′schlagen §132 *tr* (*öffnen*) open; (*Ei*) crack; (*Karte, Ärmel*) turn up; (*Zelt*) pitch; (*Wohnung*) take up; (*Preis*) raise; (*Knie, usw.*) bruise; (*Ball*) serve ‖ *intr* (SEIN) (*Tür*) fly open; (*Flugzeug*) crash; (*Ball*) bounce; (tennis) serve

auf′schließen §76 *tr* unlock, open ‖ *ref* (*dat*) pour out one's heart (to) ‖ *intr* (mil) close ranks

auf′schlitzen *tr* slit open

Auf′schluß *m* information; (chem) decomposition

auf′schlußreich *adj* informative

auf′schnallen *tr* buckle; unbuckle

auf′schnappen *tr* snap up; (*Nachricht*) pick up

Auf′schneidemaschine *f* meat slicer
auf′schneiden §106 *tr* cut open; (*Fleisch*) slice ‖ *intr* (coll) talk big
Auf′schneider *m* boaster
Auf′schnitt *m*—**kalter A.** cold cuts
auf′schnüren *tr* untie, undo
auf′schrauben *tr* unscrew; (**auf** *acc*) screw (on)
auf′schrecken §134 *tr* startle; (*Wild*) scare up ‖ *intr* (SEIN) be startled
Auf′schrei *m* scream, yell; (fig) outcry
auf′schreiben §62 *tr* write down
auf′schreien §135 *intr* scream, yell
Auf′schrift *f* inscription; (*Anschrift*) address; (*e-r Flasche*) label
Auf′schub *m* deferment, postponement; (*Verzögerung*) delay; (jur) stay
auf′schürfen *tr* scrape; (*Bein*) skin
auf′schwellen §119 *intr* (SEIN) swell up; (*Fluß*) rise
auf′schwemmen *tr* bloat
auf′schwingen §142 *ref* (& fig) soar; **sich a., etw zu tun** bring oneself to do s.th.
Auf′schwung *m* (& fig) upswing
auf′sehen §138 *intr* look up ‖ **Aufsehen** *n* (-s;) sensation, stir
auf′sehenerregend *adj* sensational
Auf′seher –**in** §6 *mf* supervisor; (*im Museum*) guard; (*im Geschäft*) floorwalker
auf′sein §139 *intr* (SEIN) be up; (*Tür*) be open
auf′setzen *tr* put on; (*aufrichten*) set up; (*schriftlich*) compose, draft ‖ *ref* sit up ‖ *intr* (aer) touch down; (rok) splash down
Auf′sicht *f* inspection, supervision
Auf′sichtsbeamte *m*, **Auf′sichtsbeamtin** *f* inspector, supervisor
Auf′sichtsbehörde *f* control board
Auf′sichtsdame *f* floorwalker
Auf′sichtsherr *m* floorwalker
Auf′sichtsrat *m* board of trustees; (*Mitglied*) trustee
auf′sitzen §144 *intr* (SEIN) sit up; (**auf** *dat*) sit (on), rest (on); **j–m a.** be taken in by s.o.; **j–n a. lassen** stand s.o. up
auf′spannen *tr* stretch, spread; (*Regenschirm*) open
auf′sparen *tr* save (up)
auf′speichern *tr* store (up)
auf′sperren *tr* unlock; (*Augen, Tür*) open wide
auf′spielen *tr* strike up ‖ *ref* (**mit**) show off (with) ‖ *intr* play dance music
auf′spießen *tr* spear, pierce
auf′sprengen *tr* force open; (*mit Sprengstoff*) blow up
auf′springen §142 *intr* (SEIN) jump up; (*Tür*) fly open; (*Ball*) bounce; (*Haut*) chap, crack
auf′spritzen *tr* (*Farbe*) spray on; (sl) shoot up ‖ *intr* (SEIN) squirt up
auf′sprudeln *intr* (SEIN) bubble (up)
auf′spulen *tr* wind up
auf′spüren *tr* track down, ferret out
auf′stacheln *tr* goad; (fig) stir up
auf′stampfen *intr*—**mit dem Fuß a.** stamp one's foot
Auf′stand *m* insurrection, uprising

aufständisch [′aufʃtɛndɪʃ] *adj* insurgent ‖ **Aufständischen** *pl* insurgents
auf′stapeln *tr* stack up, pile up
auf′stechen §64 *tr* puncture; (surg) lance
auf′stecken *tr* (*Flagge*) plant; (*Haar*) pin up; (coll) give up; **j–m ein Licht a.** enlighten s.o.
auf′stehen §146 *intr* (HABEN) stand open ‖ *intr* (SEIN) stand up, get up; (*gegen*) revolt (against)
auf′steigen §148 *intr* (SEIN) climb; (*Reiter*) mount; (*Rauch*) rise; (*Gewitter*) come up; (*Tränen*) well up; **a. auf** (*acc*) get on
auf′stellen *tr* set up, put up; (*Beispiel*) set; (*Behauptung*) make; (*Wachposten*) post; (*Bauten*) erect; (*Leiter*) raise (*Waren*) display; (*Maschine*) assemble; (*als Kandidaten*) nominate; (*Regel, Problem*) state; (*Lehre*) propound; (*Rekord*) set; (*Liste*) make out; (*Rechnung*) draw up, make out; (*Stühle*) arrange; (*Falle*) set; (*Bedingungen, Grundsätze*) lay down; (*Beweis*) furnish ‖ *ref* station oneself
Auf′stellung *f* (-;-en) erection; assertion; list, schedule; (mil) formation; (pol) nomination; (sport) lineup
auf′stemmen *tr* pry open ‖ *ref* prop oneself up
Auf′stieg *m* climb; (*Steigung*) slope; (fig) advancement
auf′stöbern *tr* ferret out; (fig) unearth
auf′stoßen §150 *tr* push open ‖ *ref*—**sich** [*dat*] **das Knie a.** skin one's knee ‖ *intr* (HABEN) (sl) belch ‖ *intr* (HABEN & SEIN) bump, touch; (*Schiff*) touch bottom ‖ *intr* (SEIN)—**j–m a.** strike s.o., cross s.o.'s mind
auf′streichen §85 *tr* (*Butter*) spread
auf′streuen *tr* (**auf** *acc*) sprinkle (on)
Auf′strich *m* upstroke; (*auf Brot*) spread
auf′stützen *tr* prop up
auf′suchen *tr* search for; (*nachschlagen*) look up; (*Ort*) visit; (*aufsammeln*) pick up; (*Arzt*) go to see
Auf′takt *m* upbeat; (fig) prelude
auf′tauchen *intr* (SEIN) turn up, appear; (*Frage*) crop up; (*U-Boot*) surface; (*Gerücht*) arise
auf′tauen *tr* & *intr* (SEIN) thaw
auf′teilen *tr* divide up
Auftrag [′auftrɑk] *m* (-[e]s;ː̈e) (*Anweisung*) orders, instructions; (*Bestellung*) order, commission; (*Sendung*) mission; **in A. von** on behalf of
auf′tragen §132 *tr* instruct, order; (*Speise*) serve; (*Farben, Butter*) put on; (*Kleidungsstück*) wear out; (surv) plot; **j–m etw a.** impose s.th. on s.o. ‖ *intr*—**dick** (or **stark**) **a.** (sl) put it on thick
Auf′traggeber –**in** §6 *mf* employer; (*Besteller*) client, customer
Auf′tragsformular *n* order blank
auf′tragsgemäß, auf′trag(s)mäßig *adv* as ordered, according to instructions
auf′treffen §151 *intr* (SEIN) strike
Auf′treffpunkt *m* point of impact
auf′treiben §62 *tr* (*Staub; Geld*) raise;

(*Wild*) flush; (*aufblähen*) distend; (*Teig*) cause to rise

auf′trennen *tr* rip, undo, unstitch

auf′treten §152 *tr* (*Tür*) kick open ‖ *intr* (SEIN) step, tread; (*erscheinen*) appear; (*handeln*) act, behave; (*eintreten*) occur, crop up; (pathol) break out; (theat) enter ‖ **Auftreten** *n* (−s;) appearance; occurrence; behavior; **sicheres A.** poise

Auf′trieb *m* drive; buoyancy; (aer & fig) lift; (agr) cattle drive; **j−m A. geben** encourage s.o.

Auf′tritt *m* (*Streit*) scene, row; (theat) entrance (*of an actor*); (theat) scene

auf′trumpfen *intr* play a higher trump; **gegen j−n a.** go to s.o. better

auf′tun §154 *tr & ref* open

auf′türmen *tr & intr* pile up

auf′wachen *intr* (SEIN) awaken, wake up

auf′wachsen §155 *intr* (SEIN) grow up

auf′wallen *intr* (SEIN) boil, seethe; (fig) surge, rise up

Auf′wallung *f* (−;−en) (fig) outburst

Aufwand [′aufvant] *m* (−[e]s;−e) (an *dat*) expenditure (of); (*Prunk*) show

auf′wärmen *tr* warm up; (fig) drag up

Auf′wartefrau *f* cleaning woman

auf′warten *intr* (*dat*) wait on; **a. mit** oblige with, offer

Auf′wärter −in §6 *mf* attendant ‖ *f* cleaning woman

aufwärts [′aufverts] *adv* upward(s)

Auf′wärtshaken *m* (box) uppercut

Auf′wartung *f* (−;) attendance; (*bei Tisch*) service; (*Besuch*) call; **j−m seine A. machen** pay one's respects to s.o.

Aufwasch [′aufvaʃ] *m* (−es;) washing; dirty dishes

auf′waschen §158 *tr & intr* wash up

auf′wecken *tr* wake (up)

auf′weichen *tr* soften; soak ‖ *intr* (SEIN) become soft; become sodden

auf′weisen §118 *tr* produce, show

auf′wenden §140 *tr* spend, expend; **Mühe a.** take pains

auf′werfen §160 *tr* throw up; (*Tür*) fling open; (*Graben*) dig; (*Frage*) raise ‖ *ref*—**sich a. zu** set oneself up as

auf′wickeln *tr* wind up; (*Haar*) curl; (*loswickeln*) unwind

aufwiegeln [′aufvigəln] *tr* instigate

Aufwiegler −in [′aufviglər(ɪn)] §6 *mf* instigator

aufwieglerisch [′aufwiglərɪʃ] *adj* inflammatory

Auf′wind *m* updraft

auf′winden §59 *tr* wind up; (*Anker*) weigh ‖ *ref* coil up

auf′wirbeln *tr* (*Staub*) raise; **viel Staub a.** (coll) make quite a stir

auf′wischen *tr* wipe up

auf′wühlen *tr* dig up; (*Wasser*) churn up; (fig) stir up

auf′zählen *tr* enumerate, itemize

auf′zäumen *tr* bridle

auf′zehren *tr* consume

auf′zeichnen *tr* make a sketch of; (*notieren*) write down, record

aufzeigen *tr* point out

auf′ziehen §163 *tr* pull up; (*öffnen*) pull open; (*Uhr*) wind; (*Saite*) put on; (*Perlen*) string; (*Kind*) bring up; (*Tier*) breed; (*Pflanzen*) grow; (*Flagge, Segel*) hoist; (*Anker*) weigh; (*Veranstaltung*) arrange, organize; (coll) kid ‖ *intr* (SEIN) approach, pull up

Auf′zucht *f* breeding, raising

Auf′zug *m* elevator; (*e−r Uhr*) winder; (*Aufmarsch*) parade , procession; (gym) chin-up; (theat) act

auf′zwingen §142 *tr*—**j−m etw a.** force s.th. on s.o.; **j−m seinen Willen a.** impose one's will on s.o.

Augapfel [′aukapfəl] *m* eyeball; (fig) apple of the eye

Auge [′augə] *n* (−s;−n) eye; (*auf Würfeln*) dot; (hort) bud; (typ) face

äugeln [′ɔɪgəln] *intr*.—**ä. mit** wink at

Augen− [augən] *comb.fm.* eye, of the eye(s), in the eye(s); visual; (anat) ocular, optic(al)

Au′genblick *m* moment, instant

au′genblicklich *adj* momentary; (*sofortig*) immediate, instantaneous

Au′genblicksmensch *m* hedonist; impulsive person

Au′genbraue *f* eyebrow

Au′genbrauenstift *m* eyebrow pencil

au′genfällig *adj* conspicuous, obvious

Au′genhöhle *f* eye socket

Au′genlicht *n* eyesight

Au′genlid *n* eyelid

Au′genmaß *n* sense of proportion; **ein gutes A. haben** have a keen eye; **nach dem A.** by eye

Au′genmerk *n* attention

Au′gennerv *m* optic nerve

Au′genschein *m* inspection; (*Anschein*) appearances; **in A. nehmen** inspect

au′genscheinlich *adj* obvious

Au′genstern *n* pupil; iris

Au′gentäuschung *f* optical illusion

Au′gentrost *m* sight for sore eyes

Au′genwasser *n* eyewash

Au′genweide *f* sight for sore eyes

Au′genwimper *f* eyelash

Au′genwinkel *m* corner of the eye

Au′genzeuge *m*, **Au′genzeugin** *f* eyewitness

−äugig [ɔɪgɪç] *comb.fm.* −eyed

August [au′gust] *m* (−[e]s & −;−e) August

Auktion [auk′tsjon] *f* (−;−en) auction

Auktio·nator [auktsjo′nɑtor] *m* (−s; −natoren [na′torən]) auctioneeer

auktionieren [auktsjo′nirən] *tr* auction off, put up for auction

Au·la [′aula] *f* (−;−s & −len [lən]) auditorium

aus [aus] *adv* out; **von ... aus** from, e.g., **vom Fenster aus** from the window ‖ *prep* (*dat*) out of, from; because of

aus′arbeiten *tr* elaborate; finish ‖ *ref* work out, take physical exercise

Aus′arbeitung *f* (−;−en) elaboration; (*schriftlich*) composition; (*körperlich*) workout; (tech) finish

aus′arten *intr* (SEIN) get out of hand; (in *acc*) degenerate (into)

aus′atmen *tr* exhale

aus'baden *tr* (coll) take the rap for
aus'baggern *tr* dredge
Aus'bau *m* (-[e]s;) completion; expansion, development
aus'bauen *tr* complete; (*erweitern*) expand, develop
aus'bedingen *tr* stipulate
aus'bessern *tr* repair; (*Kleid*) mend; (*Bild*) retouch
aus'beulen *tr* take the dents out of
Aus'beute *f* (*Ertrag*) output; (*Gewinn*) profit, gain
ausbeuten ['ausbɔıtən] *tr* exploit
aus'biegen §57 *tr* bend out || *intr* (SEIN) curve; (*dat*, **vor** *dat*) make way (for)
aus'bilden *tr* develop; (*lehren*) train, educate; (mil) drill || *ref* train
Aus'bilder *m* (mil) drill instructor
aus'bitten §60 *ref*—**sich** [*dat*] **etw a.** ask for s.th.; insist on s.th.
aus'bleiben §62 *intr* (SEIN) stay out; stay away; be missing
aus'bleichen §85 *tr* & *intr* (SEIN) bleach; fade
aus'blenden *tr* (cin, rad) fade-out
Aus'blick *m* (**auf** *acc*) view (of); (fig) outlook
aus'bohren *tr* bore (out), drill (out)
aus'borgen *ref*—**sich** [dat] **etw a. von** borrow s.th. from
aus'brechen §64 *tr* break off || *intr* (SEIN) (aus) break out (of)
aus'breiten *tr* & *ref* spread; extend
aus'brennen §97 *tr* burn out, gut; (*Sonne*) parch; (med) cauterize || *intr* (SEIN) burn out; (*Haus*) be gutted
Aus'bruch *m* outbreak; (*e-s Vulkans*) eruption; (*e-s Gefangenen*) break-out; (*des Gelächters*) outburst
aus'brüten *tr* incubate; hatch
Ausbuchtung ['ausbuxtuŋ] *f* (-;-en) bulge
ausbuddeln ['ausbudəln] *tr* (coll) dig out
aus'bügeln *tr* iron out
Aus'bund *m* (**von**) very embodiment (of)
ausbürgern ['ausbʏrgərn] *tr* expatriate
aus'bürsten *tr* brush out
Aus'dauer *f* perseverance
aus'dauern *intr* persevere, persist
aus'dauernd *adj* persevering; (bot) perennial
aus'dehnen *tr* & *ref* stretch, expand; (*Organ*) dilate
aus'denken §66 *tr* think out; think up; **nicht auszudenken** inconceivable
aus'deuten *tr* interpret, explain
aus'dienen *intr* serve one's time
aus'dorren *intr* (SEIN) dry up; wither
aus'dörren *tr* dry up, parch
aus'drehen *tr* turn out; turn off
Aus'druck *m* expression
aus'drücken *tr* squeeze out; (fig) express
ausdrücklich ['ausdrʏklıç] *adj* express, explicit
aus'druckslos *adj* expressionless
aus'drucksvoll *adj* expressive
Aus'drucksweise *f* way of speaking
aus'dünsten *tr* exhale, give off || *intr* evaporate; (*schwitzen*) sweat

auseinan'der *adv* apart; separately
auseinan'derfallen §72 *intr* (SEIN) fall apart
auseinan'dergehen §82 *intr* (SEIN) part; (*Versammlung*) break up; (*Meinungen*) differ; (*Wege*) branch off; (*auseinanderfallen*) come apart
auseinan'derhalten §90 *tr* keep apart
auseinan'derlaufen §105 *intr* (SEIN) (*Menge*) disperse; (*Wege*) diverge
auseinan'dernehmen §116 *tr* take apart
auseinan'dersetzen *tr* explain || *ref*—**sich mit etw a.** come to grips with s.th.; **sich mit j-m a.** have it out with s.o.; (*gütlich*) come to an understanding with s.o.
Auseinan'dersetzung *f* explanation; (*Erörterung*) discussion, controversy; (*Übereinkommen*) arrangement
aus'erkoren *adj* chosen; predestined
aus'erlesen *adj* choice || §107 *tr* choose, select
aus'ersehen §138 *tr* destine
aus'erwählen *tr* pick out, choose
aus'fahren §71 *tr* (*Straße, Gleis*) wear out; (aer) let down; **den Motor a.** (coll) open it up; **die Kurve a.** not cut the corner || *intr* (SEIN) drive out; (naut) put to sea; (rr) pull out
Aus'fahrt *f* departure; exit; (*Spazierfahrt*) ride, drive; (*Torweg*) gateway
Aus'fall *m* falling out; (*Ergebnis*) result; (*Verlust*) loss; (fencing) lunge; (mach) breakdown; (mil) sally
aus'fallen §72 *intr* (SEIN) fall out; (*nicht stattfinden*) fail to take place; (*ausgelassen werden*) be omitted; (*versagen*) go out of commission; (*Ergebnis*) turn out; (mil) sortie
aus'fallend *adj* aggressive, insulting
aus'fechten §74 *tr* (*Kampf*) fight; (*Streit*) settle (by fighting)
aus'fegen *tr* sweep (out)
aus'fertigen *tr* finish; (*Paß*) issue; (*Scheck*) write out; (*Schriftstück*) draw up, draft; **doppelt a.** draw up in duplicate
aus'findig *adj*—**a. machen** find out; (*aufspüren*) trace
aus'fliegen §57 *intr* (SEIN) fly out; (*wegfliegen*) fly away; (*von Hause wegziehen*) leave home; go on a trip
aus'fließen §76 *intr* (SEIN) flow out
Aus'flucht *f* evasion; **Ausflüchte machen** dodge, beat around the bush
aus'fluchten *tr* align
Aus'flug *m* trip, outing
Ausflügler ['ausflyglər] *m* (-s;-) tourist, vacationer
Aus'fluß *m* outflow; (*Eiter*) discharge; (*Ergebnis*) outcome; (*Mündung*) outlet
aus'folgen *tr* hand over
aus'forschen *tr* investigate; sound out
aus'fragen *tr* interrogate, quiz
aus'fressen §70 *tr* empty (by eating); (chem) corrode; (geol) erode; **was hast du denn ausgefressen?** (coll) what were you up to?
Ausfuhr ['ausfur] *f* (-;-en) export
Aus'fuhrabgabe *f* export duty
ausführbar ['ausfyrbar] *adj* feasible

aus'führen *tr* carry out; export, ship; (*Auftrag*) fill; (*darlegen*) explain

Aus'fuhrhändler –in §6 *mf* exporter

ausführlich ['ausfyrlıç] *adj* detailed || *adv* in detail, in full

Aus'führung *f* (–;–en) carrying out, performance; (*Qualität*) workmanship; (*Darlegung*) explanation; (*e–s Gesetzes, Befehls*) implementation; (*Fertigstellung*) completion; (*e–s Verbrechens*) perpetrations; (*typ*) type, model; copy

Aus'fuhrwaren *pl* exports

aus'füllen *tr* fill out; (*Zeit*) occupy; (*Lücke; Stellung*) fill

Aus'gabe *f* (*Verteilung*) distribution; (*von Geldern*) expenditure; (*von Briefen*) delivery; (*e–s Buches*) edition; (*von Aktien*) issue

Aus'gang *m* exit; (*Auslaß*) outlet; (*Ergebnis*) result; (*Ende*) close, end; (aer) gate

Aus'gangspunkt *m* starting point

Aus'gangssprache *f* source language

aus'geben §80 *tr* give out, distribute; (*Aktien; Befehl*) issue; (*Geld*) spend; (*Briefe*) deliver; (*Karten*) deal || *ref*—sich a. für pass oneself off as

ausgebeult ['ausgəbɔɪlt] *adj* baggy

Aus'geburt *f* figment

aus'gedehnt *adj* extensive

aus'gedient *adj* retired; (educ) emeritus

aus'gefallen *adj* (fig) eccentric, odd

aus'gefeilt *adj* (fig) flawless

aus'geglichen *adj* (*Person*) well-balanced; (*Styl*) balanced

aus'gehen §82 *intr* (SEIN) go out; (*Vorräte, Geld, Geduld*) run out; (*Haar*) fall out; (*Farbe*) fade: a. auf (*acc*) aim at, be bent on; a von proceed from; die Sache ging von ihm aus it was his idea; frei a. get off scot-free; gut a. turn out well; leer a. come away empty-handed; wenn wir davon a., daß going on the assumption that

Aus'gehverbot *n* curfew

aus'gekocht *adj* (*Lügner*) out-and-out; (*Verbrecher*) hardened

aus'gelassen *adj* boisterous

aus'geleiert *adj* trite; worn-out; (*Gewinde*) stripped

aus'gemacht *adj* settled; downright

ausgenommen *prep* (*acc*) except; niemand a. bar none

aus'gepicht *adj* inveterate

aus'gerechnet *adv* just, of all ...; a. Sie! you of all people!

aus'geschlossen *adj* out of the question, impossible

Ausgesiedelte ['ausgəzidəltə] §5 *mf* evacuee, displaced person

aus'gestalten *tr* make arrangements for

aus'gesucht *adj* choice

aus'gezeichnet *adj* excellent

ausgiebig ['ausgibıç] *adj* abundant; (*ergiebig*) productive

aus'gießen §76 *tr* pour out, pour away

Aus'gleich *m* (–s;–e) (*Ersatz*) compensation; (*Vergleich*) compromise; (acct) settlement; (tennis) deuce

aus'gleichen §85 *tr* level, smooth out; (*Konten*) balance; (*Verlust*) compensate for || *ref* cancel one another out

Ausgleichs– *comb.fm.* balancing, compensating

Aus'gleichung *f* (–;–en) equalization; settlement; compensation

aus'gleiten §86 *intr* (SEIN) slip

aus'graben §87 *tr* dig out, dig up; (*Leiche*) exhume; (archeol) excavate

aus'greifen §88 *intr* reach out; weit ausgreifend far-reaching

Ausguck ['ausguk] *m* (–s;–e) lookout

aus'gucken *intr* (nach) be on the lookout (for)

Aus'guß *m* sink; (*Tülle*) spout, nozzle

aus'haken *tr* unhook

aus'halten §90 *tr* endure, stand || *intr* persevere, stick it out

aus'handeln *tr* get by bargaining

aushändigen ['aushɛndıgən] *tr* hand over, surrender

Aus'hang *m* notice, shingle

Aus'hängeschild *n* (–[e]s;–er) sign board, shingle; (fig) front, cover

aus'harren *intr* hold out, last

aus'hauchen *tr* breathe out, exhale

aus'heben §94 *tr* lift out; (*Tür*) lift off its hinges; (*Truppen*) recruit

aushecken ['aushɛkən] *tr* (fig) hatch

aus'heilen *tr* heal completely || *intr* (SEIN) heal up

aus'helfen §96 *intr* (*dat*) help out

Aus'hilfe *f* (temporary) help; (temporary) helper; makeshift

Aushilfs– *comb.fm.* temporary, emergency

Aus'hilfsarbeit *f* part-time work

Aus'hilfslehrer –in §6 *mf* substitute teacher

aus'hilfsweise *adv* temporarily

aus'höhlen *tr* hollow out

aus'holen *tr* (*ausfragen*) sound out || *intr* (*beim Schwimmen*) stroke; mit dem Arm a. raise the arm (*before striking*); weit a. start from the beginning

aus'horchen *tr* sound out, pump

aus'hülsen *tr* (*Bohnen, usw.*) shell

aus'hungern *tr* starve (out)

aus'husten *tr* cough up

aus'kehlen *tr* groove

Aus'kehlung *f* (–;–en) groove

aus'kehren *tr* sweep (out)

aus'kennen §97 *ref* know one's way; (in e–m Fach) be well versed

Aus'klang *m* end, close

aus'klappen *tr* pull out (*a fold-away bed*)

aus'kleiden *tr* line, panel; (*ausziehen*) undress || *ref* undress

aus'klopfen *tr* beat the dust out of

ausklügeln ['ausklygəln] *tr* figure out (ingeniously)

aus'kneifen §88 *intr* (SEIN) beat it

aus'knipsen *tr* (coll) switch off

ausknobeln ['ausknobəln] *tr* figure out

aus'kochen *tr* boil out; boil clean

aus'kommen §99 *intr* (SEIN) come out, get out; (*ausreichen*) manage || Auskommen *n* (–s;) livelihood

auskömmlich ['auskœmlıç] *adj* adequate

aus'kosten *tr* relish

aus'kramen ['auskramən] *tr* (*aus Schubladen*) drag out; (fig) show off

aus′kratzen *tr* scratch out; (surg) curette

aus′kriechen §102 *intr* (SEIN) be hatched

aus′kugeln *ref*—**sich** [*dat*] **den Arm a.** dislocate the shoulder

aus′kundschaften *tr* explore; (mil) scout

Auskunft [′auskʊnft] *f* (–;ᵘᵉe) information, piece of information

Auskunftei [aʊskʊnf′taɪ] *f* (–;–en) private detective agency

Aus′kunftschalter *m* information desk

aus′kuppeln *tr* uncouple; (*die Kupplung*) release ‖ *intr* disengage the clutch

aus′lachen *tr* laugh at ‖ *ref* have a good laugh

aus′laden §103 *tr* unload; (*Gast*) put off ‖ *intr* project, jut out ‖ **Ausladen** *n* (–s;) unloading; projection

Aus′lage *f* (*von Geld*) outlay; (*Unkosten*) expenses; (*von Waren*) display; (*Schaufenster*) display window

Aus′land *n* foreign country, foreign countries; **im A. leben** live abroad; **ins A. gehen** go abroad

Ausländer –**in** [′aʊslɛndər(ɪn)] §6 *mf* foreigner, alien

aus′ländisch *adj* foreign, alien

Auslands– *comb.fm.* foreign

Aus·laß [′aʊslas] *m* (–lasses;–lässe) outlet

aus′lassen §104 *tr* let out; (*weglassen*) omit; (*Wut*) (**an** *dat*) vent (on) ‖ *ref* express one′s opinion

Aus′lassung *f* omission; (*Bemerkung*) remark

Aus′lassungszeichen *n* (gram) apostrophe; (typ) caret

Aus′lauf *m* sailing; room to run

aus′laufen §105 *intr* (SEIN) run out; (*Schiff*) put out to sea; (*Farbe*) run; **a. in** (*acc*) end in; (*Straße*) run into

Aus′läufer *m* (geol)) spur; (hort) runner

aus′leben *tr* live out ‖ *ref* make the most of one′s life ‖ *intr* die

aus′lecken *tr* lick clean

aus′leeren *tr* empty ‖ *ref* have a bowel movement

aus′legen *tr* lay out; (*Waren*) display; (*erklären*) construe; (*Geld*) advance; (*Fußboden*) cover (*with carpeting*); (*Minen*) lay; (*Schlinge*) set; **falsch a.** misconstrue, misinterpret

Aus′leger –**in** §6 *mf* interpreter ‖ *m* outrigger; (*e–s Krans*) boom

aus′leihen §81 *tr* lend (out) ‖ *ref*—**sich** [*dat*] **etw a.** borrow s.th.

aus′lernen *intr* finish one′s apprenticeship; **man lernt nie aus** one never stops learning

Aus′lese *f* pick, choice

aus′lesen §107 *tr* pick out; (*Buch*) finish reading

aus′liefern *tr* deliver, turn over; (*verteilen*) distribute; (*Verbrecher*) extradite; **j–m ausgeliefert sein** be at s.o.′s mercy

aus′liegen §108 *intr* (SEIN) be on display

aus′löffeln *tr* spoon out; **etw. zu ha-** ben have to face the consequences of s.th.

aus′löschen *tr* (*Feuer*) extinguish; (*Licht*) put out; (*Schreiben*) erase

aus′losen *tr* draw lots for

aus′lösen *tr* loosen, release; (*Gefangegen*) ransom; (*Pfand*) redeem

Aus′löser *m* (–s;–) release

aus′loten *tr* (naut & fig) plumb

aus′lüften *tr* air, ventilate

aus′machen *tr* (*Feuer*) put out; (*sichten*) make out; (*betragen*) amount to; (*Fleck*) remove; (*Licht*) turn out; (*bilden*) constitute; (*vereinbaren*) agree upon; **es macht nichts aus** it doesn′t matter

aus′malen *tr* paint ‖ *ref*—**sich** [*dat*] **etw a.** picture s.th.

aus′marschieren *intr* (SEIN) march out

Aus′maß *n* measurement; dimensions; **in großem A.** on a large scale; (fig) to a great extent

ausmergeln [′aʊsmergərln] *tr* exhaust

ausmerzen [′aʊsmertsən] *tr* reject; (*ausrotten*) eradicate

aus′messen §70 *tr* measure; survey

aus′misten *tr* (*Stall*) clean; (fig) clean up

aus′mustern *tr* discard; (mil) discharge

Aus′nahme *f* (–;–n) exception

Aus′nahmezustand *m* state of emergency

aus′nahmslos *adj* & *adv* without exception

aus′nahmsweise *adv* by way of exception

aus′nehmen §116 *tr* take out; (*Fisch, Huhn*) clean; (*ausschließen*) exclude; (sl) clean out (of money) ‖ *ref*—**sich gut a.** look good

aus′nutzen, aus′nützen *tr* utilize; (*Gelegenheit*) take advantage of

aus′packen *tr* unpack; (*Geheimnis*) disclose ‖ *intr* (coll) unburden oneself, open up

aus′pfeifen §88 *tr* hiss (off the stage)

aus′plappern *tr* blurt out, blab out

aus′plaudern *tr* blab out

aus′plündern *tr* ransack; (coll) clean out (of money)

aus′polstern *tr* stuff, pad

aus′posaunen *tr* (coll) broadcast

aus′probieren *tr* try out, test

Aus′puff *m* (–[e]s;–e) exhaust

Aus′puffleitung *f* (aut) manifold

Aus′puffrohr *n* exhaust pipe

Aus′pufftopf *m* (aut) muffler

aus′pumpen *tr* pump out; **ausgepumpt** (coll) exhausted

aus′putzen *tr* (*reinigen*) clean out; (*schmücken*) adorn ‖ *ref* dress up

aus′quartieren *tr* put out (*of s.o.′s room*)

aus′radieren *tr* erase

aus′rangieren *tr* (coll) scrap

aus′rauben *tr* rob, ransack

aus′räumen *tr* (*Schrank*) clear out; (*Möbel*) remove; (med) clean out

aus′rechnen *tr* figure out

aus′recken *tr* stretch ‖ *ref*—**sich** [*dat*] **den Hals a.** crane one′s neck

Aus′rede *f* evasion, excuse

aus′reden *tr*—**j–m etw a.** talk s.o. out

of s.th. || *ref* make excuses || *intr* finish speaking
aus′reiben §62 *tr* rub out; (mach) ream
aus′reichen *tr* suffice, be enough
aus′reichend *adj* sufficient
Aus′reise *f* departure; way out
aus′reißen §53 *tr* tear out || *ref*—**er reißt sich** [*dat*] **dabei kein Bein aus** he's not exactly killing himself || *intr* (SEIN) run away
Aus′reißer *m* runaway
aus′renken *tr* dislocate
aus′richten *tr* straighten; (*in e-e Linie bringen*) align; (*vollbringen*) accomplish; (*Botschaft, Gruß*) convey
aus′roden *tr* root out; (*Wald*) clear
aus′rollen *tr* roll out || *intr* (SEIN) (aer) taxi to a standstill
ausrotten [′ausrɔtən] *tr* root out; (*Volk, Tierrasse*) exterminate; (*Übel*) eradicate
aus′rücken *tr* (*Kupplung*) disengage || *intr* (SEIN) march off; run away
Aus′ruf *m* outcry; (*öffentlich*) proclamation; (*gram*) interjection
aus′rufen §122 *tr* call out; exclaim; **a. als** (or **zum**) proclaim
Aus′rufungszeichen *n* exclamation point
aus′ruhen *ref* & *intr* rest
aus′rupfen *tr* pluck
aus′rüsten *tr* equip, fit out; arm
aus′rutschen *intr* (SEIN) slip (out)
Aus′saat *f* sowing; (& fig) seed(s)
aus′säen *tr* sow; (fig) disseminate
Aus′sage *f* statement; (gram) predicate; (jur) affidavit
aus′sagen *tr* state || *intr* give evidence, make a statement
Aus′sagesatz *m* declarative sentence
Aus′sageweise *f* (gram) mood
Aus′satz *m* leprosy
Aussätzige [′ausztsɪgə] §5 *mf* leper
aus′saugen §125 *tr* suck dry; (fig) bleed white
Aus′sauger –**in** §6 *mf* (coll) bloodsucker
aus′schalten *tr* (*Licht, Radio, Fernseher*) turn off; (fig) shut out
Aus′schalter *m* circuit breaker
Aus′schank *m* sale of alcoholic drinks; (*Kneipe*) bar, taproom
aus′scharren *tr* dig up
Aus′schau *f*—**A. halten nach** be on the lookout for
aus′schauen *intr*—**a. nach** look out for; look like; **gut schaust du aus!** what a mess you are!
aus′scheiden §112 *tr* eliminate; (physiol) excrete, secrete || *intr* (SEIN) retire, resign; (sport) drop out; **das scheidet aus!** that's out!
Aus′scheidung *f* (–;–en) elimination; retirement; (physiol) excretion, secretion
Aus′scheidungskampf *m* elimination bout
aus′schelten §83 *tr* scold, berate
aus′schenken *tr* pour (*drinks*)
aus′scheren *intr* (aus) veer away (from)
aus′schiffen *tr* disembark; (*Ladung*) unload || *ref* disembark
aus′schimpfen *tr* scold, take to task

aus′schirren *tr* unharness
aus′schlachten *tr* cut up; (*Flugzeuge, usw.*) cannibalize; (*ausnutzen*) make the most of
aus′schlafen §131 *tr* sleep off || *ref* & *intr* get enough sleep
Aus′schlag *m* rash; (*e–s Zeigers*) deflection; **den A. geben** turn the scales
aus′schlagen §132 *tr* knock out; (*Feuer*) beat out; (*Metall*) hammer out; (*Innenraum*) line; (*Angebot*) refuse || *intr* bud; sprout; (*Pferd*) kick; (*Pendel*) swing; (*Zeiger*) move || *intr* (SEIN) turn out
aus′schlaggebend *adj* decisive
aus′schließen §76 *tr* lock out; (*von der Schule*) expel; (*ausscheiden*) exclude; (sport) disqualify
aus′schließlich *adj* exclusive, sole || *adv* exclusively, only || *prep* (genit) exclusive of
aus′schlürfen *tr* sip
aus′schmieren *tr* grease; (**mit**) smear (with); (fig) pull a fast one on; (mas) point
aus′schmücken *tr* adorn, decorate; (*Geschichte*) embellish
aus′schnaufen *intr* get one's wind
aus′schneiden §106 *tr* cut out; **tief ausgeschnitten** low-cut, low-necked
Aus′schnitt *m* cut; (*Zeitungs–*) clipping; (*Kleid–*) neckline; (*literarisch*) extract; (geom) sector
aus′schreiben §62 *tr* write out (in full); finish writing; (*ankündigen*) announce; (*Formular*) fill out; (*Rezept*) make out
aus′schreiten §86 *tr* pace off || *intr* (SEIN) walk briskly
Aus′schreitung *f* (–;–en) excess
Aus′schuß *m* waste, scrap; (*Komitee*) committee
Aus′schußware *f* (indust) reject
aus′schütten *tr* pour out, spill; (*Dividende*) pay || *ref*—**sich vor Lachen a.** split one's sides laughing
aus′schwärmen *intr* (SEIN) swarm out; (*Truppen*) deploy
aus′schwatzen *tr* blab out, blurt out
aus′schweifend *adj* (*Phantasie*) wild; (*liederlich*) wild, dissolute
Aus′schweifung *f* (–;–en) excess; curve; digression
aus′schwemmen *tr* rinse out; wash out
aus′schwenken *tr* rinse
aus′schwitzen *tr* sweat out; exude
aus′sehen §138 *intr* look; **nach j–m a.** look out for s.o.; **nach Regen a.** look like rain; **wie sieht er aus?** what does he look like? || **Aussehen** *n* (–s;) look(s); appearance(s)
außen [′ausən] *adv* outside; **nach a.** out(wards)
außen–, Außen– *comb.fm.* external; outer; exterior; outdoor; foreign
Au′ßenaufnahme *f* (phot) outdoor shot
Au′ßenbahn *f* (sport) outside lane
aus′senden §140 *tr* send out
Au′ßenfläche *f* outer surface
Au′ßenminister *m* Secretary of State; (Brit) Foreign Secretary
Au′ßenpolitik *f* foreign policy
Au′ßenseite *f* outside

Außenseiter ['aʊsənzaɪtər] m (-s;-) dark horse, long shot; (*Einzelgänger*) loner; (*Nichtfachmann*) layman

Außenstände ['aʊsənʃtendə] pl accounts receivable

Au'ßenstelle f branch office

außer ['aʊsər] prep (genit)—a. Landes abroad || prep (dat) outside, out of; except, but; besides, in addition to; a. Hause not at home; a. sich sein be beside oneself

au'ßeramtlich adj unofficial, private

außerdem ['aʊsərdem] adv also, besides; moreover, furthermore

au'ßerdienstlich adj unofficial, private; (mil) off duty

äußere ['ɔɪsərə] §9 adj outer, exterior, external || **Äußere** §5 n exterior

au'ßerehelich adj extra-marital; (*Kind*) illegitimate

au'ßergewöhnlich adj extraordinary

außerhalb ['aʊsərhalp] prep (genit) outside, out of

äußerlich ['ɔɪsərlɪç] adj external, outward; (*oberflächlich*) superficial

Äu'ßerlichkeit f superficiality; (*Formalität*) formality; **Äußerlichkeiten** externals; formalities

äußern ['ɔɪsərn] tr express || ref (über acc) express one's views (about); (in dat) be manifested (in)

au'ßerordentlich adj extraordinary; **außerordentlicher Professor** associate professor

äußerst ['ɔɪsərst] adj outermost; (fig) extreme, utmost || adv extremely, highly || **Äußerste** §5 n extremity, extreme(s); **aufs Ä.** to the utmost; **bis zum Äußersten** to extremes; to the bitter end

außerstande ['aʊsərʃandə] adj unable

Äu'ßerung f (-;-en) (*Ausdruck*) expression; (*Bemerkung*) remark

aus'setzen tr set out, put out; (an der Küste) maroon; (*Kind; dem Wetter*) expose; (*Boot*) lower; (*Wachen*) post; (*Belohnung*) hold out, promise; (*Tätigkeit*) discontinue; **auszusetzen haben an** (dat) find fault with || intr stop, halt

Aus'sicht f (auf acc) view (of); (fig) (auf acc) hope (of); **in A. nehmen** consider, plan

aus'sichtslos adj hopeless

Aus'sichtspunkt m vantage point

aus'sichtsreich adj promising

Aus'sichtsturm m lookout tower

aussichtsvoll adj promising

aus'sieben tr sift out; (fig) screen

aus'siedeln tr evacuate by force

Aus'siedlung f (-;-en) forced evacuation

aus'sinnen §121 tr think up, devise

aussöhnen ['aʊszønən] tr reconcile

aus'sondern tr (trennen) separate; (auswählen) single out; (physiol) excrete

aus'spähen tr spy out || intr (nach) keep a lookout (for), reconnoiter

aus'spannen tr stretch; extend; (*Zugtiere*) unhitch || intr relax

Aus'spannung f (-;) relaxation

aus'speien §135 tr spit out

aus'sperren tr lock out, shut out

aus'spielen tr (*Karten*) lead with; (*Preis*) play for || intr lead off

aus'spionieren tr spy out

Aus'sprache f pronunciation; (*Erörterung*) discussion, talk

aus'sprechen §64 tr pronounce; (*deutlich*) articulate; (*ausdrücken*) express || ref (über acc) speak one's mind (about); (für; gegen) declare oneself (for; against); **sich mit j-m über etw a.** talk s.th. over with s.o. || intr finish speaking

Aus'spruch m statement

aus'spülen tr rinse

aus'spüren tr trace (down)

aus'staffieren tr fit out, furnish

aus'stampfen tr stamp out

Aus'stand m walkout

aus'ständig adj on strike, striking; (fin) in arrears, outstanding

ausstatten ['aʊsʃtatən] tr furnish, equip; (*Tochter*) give a dowry to

Aus'stattung f (-;-en) furnishings; equipment; trousseau

aus'stechen §64 tr cut out; (*Auge*) poke out; (fig) outdo

aus'stehen §146 tr endure, stand || intr still be expected, be overdue

aus'steigen §148 intr (SEIN) get out, get off

aus'stellen tr exhibit; (*Wache*) post; (*Quittung, Scheck*) make out; (*Paß*) issue

Aus'stellung f (-;-en) exhibit; issuance; criticism

Aus'stelungsdatum n date of issue

aus'sterben §149 intr (SEIN) die out

Aus'steuer f hope chest, dowry

aus'stopfen tr stuff, pad

Aus'stoß m (indust) output

aus'stoßen §150 tr knock out; (*vertreiben*) eject; (*Seufzer, Schrei, Fluch*) utter; (*Torpedo*) launch; (math) eliminate; (phonet) elide; (phys) emit

Aus'stoßrohr n torpedo tube

Aus'stoßung f (-;-en) ejection; utterance; (gram) elision

Aus'stoßzahlen pl (indust) production figures

aus'strahlen tr & intr radiate

aus'strecken tr & ref stretch out

aus'streichen §85 tr cross out; (*glätten*) smooth out; (*Bratpfanne*) grease

aus'streuen tr strew, scatter, spread

aus'strömen tr & intr (SEIN) pour out

aus'studieren tr study thoroughly

aus'suchen tr pick out

Aus'tausch m exchange

aus'tauschbar adj exchangeable; interchangeable

aus'tauschen tr exchange; interchange

Aus'tauschstoff m substitute

Aus'tauschstück n spare part

aus'teilen tr distribute, deal out

Auster ['aʊstər] f (-;-n) oyster

aus'tilgen tr exterminate, wipe out

aus'toben tr give vent to || ref (*Person*) let one's hair down; (*Kinder*) raise a rumpus; (*Gewitter*) stop raging

aus'tollen ref make a racket

Austrag ['aʊstrak] m (-[e]s;)—**bis zum A. der Sache** until the matter is decided; **zum A. bringen** bring to a head; (jur) settle; **zum A. kommen** come up for a decision

aus'tragen §132 *tr* carry out; (*Briefe*) deliver; (*Kleider*) wear out; (*Meisterschaft*) decide; (*Klatschereien*) spread; (acct) cancel

Aus'träger *m* deliveryman

Australien [aʊs'trɑljən] *n* (–s;) Australia

Australier –**in** [aʊs'trɑljər(ɪn)] §6 *mf* Australian

aus'treiben §62 *tr* drive out; exorcise

aus'treten §152 *tr* (*Feuer*) tread out; (*Schuhe, Treppen*) wear out || *intr* (SEIN) step out; (*Blut*) come out; (coll) go to the bathroom; **a. aus** leave (*school, a company, club*)

aus'trinken §143 *tr* drink up, drain

Aus'tritt *m* withdrawal

aus'trocknen *tr* & *intr* (SEIN) dry up

aus'tüfteln *tr* puzzle out

aus'üben *tr* (*Aufsicht, Macht*) exercise; (*Beruf*) practice; (*Pflicht*) carry out; (*Einfluß, Druck*) exert; (*Verbrechen*) commit; **ausübende Gewalt** executive power

Aus'verkauf *m* clearance sale

aus'verkaufen *tr* sell out; close out

aus'wachsen §155 *tr* outgrow

Aus'wahl *f* choice, selection

aus'wählen *tr* select, pick out

Aus'wanderer –**in** §6 *mf* emigrant

aus'wandern *intr* (SEIN) emigrate

auswärtig ['aʊsvertɪç] *adj* out-of-town; (*ausländisch*) foreign

auswärts ['aʊsverts] *adv* outward(s); out, away from home; (*außer der Stadt*) out of town; (*im Ausland*) abroad

Aus'wärtsspiel *n* away game

aus'wechselbar *adj* interchangeable

aus'wechseln *tr* exchange, interchange; (*ersetzen*) replace

Aus'weg *m* way out; escape

Ausweich– *comb.fm.* evasive; alternate; substitute; emergency; reserve

aus'weichen §85 *intr* (SEIN) (*dat*) make way (for), get out of the way (of); (*dat*) evade; **a. auf** (*acc*) switch to

aus'weichend *adj* evasive

Aus'weichklausel *f* escape clause

Aus'weichlager *n* emergency store

Aus'weichstelle *f* passing zone

Aus'weichstraße *f* bypass

Aus'weichziel *n* secondary target

aus'weinen *ref* have a good cry || *intr* stop crying

Ausweis ['aʊsvaɪs] *m* (–s;–e) identification (card); (com) statement

aus'weisen §118 *tr* expel; (*aus Besitz*) evict; (*verbannen*) banish, deport; (*zeigen*) show || *ref* prove one's identity

Aus'weispapiere *pl* identification papers

Aus'weisung *f* (–;–en) expulsion; eviction; deportation

aus'weiten *tr* & *ref* widen, expand

auswendig ['aʊsvendɪç] *adj* outer || *adv* outside; outwardly; by heart

aus'werfen §160 *tr* throw out; (*Graben*) dig; (*Summe*) allocate; (*Lava*) eject; (*Blut, Schleim*) spit up; (angl) cast

aus'werten *tr* evaluate; (*ausnützen*) utilize; (*Statistik*) interpret

aus'wickeln *tr* unwrap

aus'wiegen §57 *tr* weigh out

aus'wirken *tr* knead || *ref* take effect; **sich a. auf** (*acc*) affect; **sich** [*dat*] **etw bei j–m a.** obtain s.th. from s.o.

Aus'wirkung *f* (–;–en) effect

aus'wischen *tr* wipe out; wipe clean; **j–m eins a.** play a dirty joke on s.o.

aus'wittern *tr* season || *intr* weather

aus'wringen §142 *tr* wring out

Aus'wuchs *m* outgrowth; (pathol) tumor

Aus'wurf *m* throwing out; (fig) scum; (mach) ejection

aus'zacken *tr* indent; (*wellenförmig*) scallop

aus'zahlen *tr* pay out; pay off || *ref*— **es zahlt sich nicht aus** it doesn't pay

aus'zählen *tr* count out

aus'zanken *tr* scold

aus'zehren *tr* consume, waste

Aus'zehrung *f* (–;) consumption

aus'zeichnen *tr* mark, tag; (*ehren*) honor; (fig) distinguish

Aus'zeichnung *f* (–;–en) labeling; decoration, honor; distinction

aus'ziehen §163 *tr* pull out; (*Kleid*) take off; (*Stelle*) excerpt; (*Zeichnung*) ink in; (chem) extract || *ref* undress || *intr* (SEIN) set out; (*aus e–r Wohnung*) move out

aus'zischen *tr* hiss off the stage

Aus'zug *m* departure; moving; excerpt; (*Abriß*) summary; (Bib) Exodus; (chem) extract; (com) statement

aus'zugsweise *adv* in summary form

aus'zupfen *tr* pluck out

authentisch [aʊ'tentɪʃ] *adj* authentic

Auto ['aʊto] *n* (–s;–s) auto(mobile)

Au'tobahn *f* superhighway

Au'tobus *m* bus

Autodidakt [aʊtodɪ'dakt] *m* (–en;–en) self-educated person

Au'todroschke *f* taxi

Au'tofahrer –**in** §6 *mf* motorist

Au'tofahrschule *f* driving school

Au'tofahrt *f* car ride, drive

Au'tofalle *f* speed trap

Autogramm [aʊto'gram] *n* (–[e]s;–e) autograph

Autogramm'jäger –**in** §6 *mf* autograph hound

Au'tokino *n* drive-in movie

Au'tokolonne *f* motorcade

Autokrat [aʊto'krat] *m* (–en;–en) autocrat

autokratisch [aʊto'kratɪʃ] *adj* autocratic

Automat [aʊto'mat] *m* (–en;–en) vending machine; (*Musik–*) jukebox; (*Spiel–*) slot machine

Automa'tenrestaurant *n* automat

automatisch [aʊto'matɪʃ] *adj* automatic

Automobil [aʊtomo'bil] *n* (–[e]s;–e) automobile

autonom [aʊto'nom] *adj* autonomous

Autonomie [aʊtono'mi] *f* (–;) autonomy

Au·tor ['aʊtor] *m* (–s;–toren ['torən]) author

Autoreparatur'werkstatt *f* auto repair shop, garage
Autorin [auˈtorɪn] *f* (–;–nen) authoress
autorisieren [autorɪˈzirən] *tr* authorize
autoritär [autorɪˈter] *adj* authoritarian
Autorität [autorɪˈtet] *f* (–;–en) authority
Au'toschlosser *m* automobile mechanic
Au'toschuppen *m* carport

Au'tounfall *m* automobile accident
avancieren [avãˈsirən] *intr* (SEIN) advance; (zu) be promoted (to)
avisieren [avɪˈzirən] *tr* advise, notify
Axt [akst] *f* (–;ːe) ax
Azalee [atsaˈleˑə] *f* (–;–n) azalea
Azetat [atseˈtat] *n* (–[e]s;–e) acetate
Azeton [atseˈton] *n* (–s;) acetone
Azetylen [atsetyˈlen] *n* (–s;) acetylene
azurn [aˈtsurn] *adj* azure, sky-blue

B

B, b [*be*] *invar n* B, b; (mus) B flat
babbeln [ˈbabəln] *intr* babble
Baby [ˈbebi] *n* (–s;–s) baby
Babysitter [ˈbebɪzitər] *m* (–s;–) baby-sitter
Bach [bax] *m* (–[e]s;ːe) brook, creek
Backe [ˈbakə] *f* (–;–n) cheek; jaw (*of a vise*); (mach) die
backen [ˈbakən] §50 (& *pret* **backte**) *tr* bake; (*in der Pfanne*) fry ‖ (*pret* **backte**; *pp* **gebacken**) *intr* bake ‖ §109 *intr* (HABEN & SEIN) cake; stick
Backenbart (**Bak'kenbart**) *m* side whiskers
Backenstreich (**Bak'kenstreich**) *m* slap
Backenzahn (**Bak'kenzahn**) *m* molar; **kleiner** (or **vorderer**) **B.** bicuspid
Bäcker [ˈbɛckər] *m* (–s;–) baker
Bäckerei [bɛkəˈraɪ] *f* (–;–en) bakery
Back'fett *n* shortening
Back'fisch *m* fried fish; (fig) teenager
Back'fischalter *n* teens (*of girls*)
Back'form *f* cake pan
Back'hähnchen *n* fried chicken
Back'hendel *n* (Aust) fried chicken
Back'huhn *n* fried chicken
Back'obst *n* dried fruit
Back'ofen *m* baking oven
Back'pfeife *f* slap in the face, smack
Back'pflaume *f* prune
Back'pulver *n* baking powder
Back'stein *m* brick
Back'trog *m* kneading trough
Back'waren *pl* baked goods
Back'werk *n* pastries
Bad [bat] *n* (–[e]s;ːer) bath; bathroom; (*Badeort*) spa
Ba'deanstalt *f* public baths; public pool
Ba'deanzug *m* swim suit
Ba'dehaube *f* bathing cap
Ba'dehose *f* bathing trunks
Ba'dekappe *f* bathing cap
Ba'demantel *m* bathrobe
baden [ˈbadən] *tr & ref* bathe ‖ *intr* take a bath; **b. gehen** go swimming
Ba'deort *m* bathing resort; spa
Ba'destrand *m* bathing beach
Ba'detuch *n* bath towel
Ba'dewanne *f* bathtub
Badende [ˈbadəndə] §5 *mf* bather
Ba'dewärter –n §6 *mf* lifeguard; bathhouse attendant
Ba'dezimmer *n* bathroom
baff [baf] *adj* dumbfounded

Bagage [baˈgaʒə] *f* (–;) (fig) rabble; (mil) baggage
Bagatelle [bagaˈtɛlə] *f* (–;–n) trifle
Bagatel'lesache *f* petty offense
bagatellisieren [bagatɛlɪˈzirən] *tr* minimize, make light of
Bagger [ˈbagər] *m* (–s;–) dredge
baggern [ˈbagərn] *tr & intr* dredge
bähen [ˈbeˑən] *intr* bleat
Bahn [ban] *f* (–;–en) way, path; (aer) runway; (astr) orbit; (aut) lane; (rr) railroad; (sport) course, track; (*Eis–*) (sport) rink; **auf die schiefe B. geraten** go astray; **B. brechen** (*dat*) pave the way (for); **mit der B. fahren** travel by train
bahn'brechend *adj* pioneering, epoch-making
Bahn'brecher –in §6 *mf* pioneer
Bahn'damm *m* railroad embankment
bahnen [ˈbanən] *tr*—e–n Weg. b. clear a path, open up a path
Bahn'fahrt *f* train trip
bahn'frei *adj* free on board, f.o.b.
Bahn'hof *m* railroad station
Bahn'hofshalle *f* concourse
Bahn'hofsvorsteher *m* stationmaster
Bahn'linie *f* railroad line
Bahn'schranke *f* (rr) barrier
Bahn'steig *m* (rr) platform
Bahn'strecke *f* (rr) line, track
Bahn'übergang *m* railroad crossing
Bahn'wärter *m* (rr) signalman
Bahre [ˈbarə] *f* (–;–n) stretcher; bier
Bahr'tuch *n* pall
Bai [baɪ] *f* (–;–en) bay
Baiser [beˈze] *m & n* (–s;–s) meringue cookie
Baisse [ˈbesə] *f* (–;–n) (com) slump
Bais'sestimmung *f* downward trend
Baissier [besˈje] *m* (–s;–s) (st.exch.) bear
Bajonett [bajoˈnɛt] *n* (–s;–e) bayonet
Bake [ˈbakə] *f* (–;–n) beacon
Bakterie [bakˈterjə] *f* (–;–n) bacterium
Bakte'rienforscher –in §6 *mf* bacteriologist
Bakte'rienkunde *f* bacteriology
Balance [baˈlãsə] *f* (–;–n) balance
balancieren [balãˈsirən] *tr & intr* balance
bald [balt] *adv* (**eher** [ˈeˑər]; **eheste** [ˈeˑəstə] §9 soon; (*beinahe*) nearly
baldig [ˈbaldɪç] *adj* speedy; (*Antwort*) early

baldigst ['baldɪgst] *adv* very soon; at the earliest possible moment

Balg [balk] *m* (-[e]s;⁀e) skin, pelt; (*Hülse*) shell, husk; **Bälge** bellows; **j-m den B. abziehen** fleece s.o. ‖ *m* & *n* (-[e]s;⁀er) (coll) brat

balgen ['balgən] *ref* roll around, romp; (*raufen*) scuffle ‖ **Balgen** *m* (-s;-) (phot) bellows

Balgerei [balgə'raɪ] *f* (-;-en) scuffle

Balken ['balkən] *m* (-s;-) beam, rafter

Bal'kenwerk *n* framework

Balkon [bal'kon] *m* (-s;-e) balcony

Ball [bal] *m* (-[e]s;⁀e) ball; (*Tanz*) ball

Ballade [ba'ladə] *f* (-;-n) ballad

Ballast ['balast] *m* (-[e]s;-e) ballast; (fig) drag; (coll) padding

ballen ['balən] *tr*—**die Faust b.** clench one's fist ‖ *ref* form a cluster ‖ **Ballen** *m* (-s;-) (anat) ball; (com) bale; (pathol) bunion

ballern ['balərn] *intr* (coll) bang away

Ballett [ba'lɛt] *n* (-[e]s;-e) ballet

Ballistik [ba'lɪstɪk] *f* (-;) ballistics

Ballon [ba'lon] *m* (-s;-s) balloon

Ball'saal *m* ballroom

Ball'schläger *m* (sport) bat

Ball'spiel *n* ball game

Bal'lung *f* (-;-en) (mil) massing (of troops)

Balsam ['balzɑm] *m* (-s;-e) balm, balsam; (fig) balm

balsamieren [balza'mirən] *tr* embalm

balzen ['baltsən] *intr* perform a mating dance

Bambus ['bambʊs] *m* (-;- & -ses;-se) bamboo

Bam'busrohr *n* bamboo, bamboo cane

banal [ba'nal] *adj* banal

Banane [ba'nɑnə] *f* (-;-n) banana

Banause [ba'nauzə] *f* (-n;-n) philistine

banausisch [ba'nauzɪʃ] *adj* narrow-minded

Band [bant] *m* (-[e]s;⁀e) volume; (*Einband*) binding ‖ *n* (-[e]s;-e) bond, tie; **Bande** chains, shackles ‖ *n* [-[e]s;⁀er] (*e-s Hutes, usw.*) band; (*Bindfaden*) string; (*zum Schmuck*) ribbon; tape; (anat) ligament; (electron) recording tape; (rad) band; **am laufenden B.** continuously

Bandage [ban'daʒə] *f* (-;-n) bandage

bandagieren [banda'ʒirən] *tr* bandage

Bande ['bandə] *f* (-;-n) band, gang, crew; (billiards) cushion

Ban'denkrieg *m* guerilla war(fare)

Ban'denmitglied *n* gangster; (mil) guerilla

Ban'denunwesen *n* gangsterism; partisan activities

bändigen ['bɛndɪgən] *tr* tame; (fig) subdue, overcome, master

Bandit [ban'dit] *m* (-en;-en) bandit

Band'maß *n* tape measure

Band'säge *f* band saw

Band'scheibe *f* (anat) disk

Band'scheibenquetschung *f* slipped disk

Band'wurm *m* tapeworm

bang(e) [baŋ(ə)] *adj* scared, anxious; (*Gefühl*) disquieting; **j-m b. machen** scare s.o. ‖ **Bange** *f* (-;) fear

Bangigkeit ['baŋɪçkaɪt] *f* (-;) fear

Bank [baŋk] *f* (-;⁀e) bench; pew; (geol) layer, bed ‖ *f* (-;-en) bank

Bank'anweisung *f* check

Bank'ausweis *m* bank statement

Bank'einlage *f* bank deposit

Bankett [baŋ'kɛt] *n* (-s;-e) banquet

bank'fähig *adj* negotiable

Bank'guthaben *n* bank balance

Bank'halter **-in** §6 *mf* banker (*in games*)

Bankier [baŋ'je] *m* (-s;-s) banker

Bank'konto *n* bank account

bank'mäßig *adj* by check

bankrott [baŋ'rɔt] *adj* bankrupt ‖ *m* (-[e]s;-e) bankruptcy

Bank'verkehr *m* banking (*activity*)

Bank'wesen *n* banking

Bann [ban] *m* (-[e]s;-e) ban; (*Zauber*) spell; (eccl) excommunication

bannen ['banən] *tr* banish; (*Geister*) exorcize; (eccl) excommunicate

Banner ['banər] *n* (-s;-) banner; standard

Ban'nerträger *m* standard-bearer

Bann'fluch *m* anathema

Bann'kreis *m* spell; **in j-s B. geraten** come under s.o.'s spell

Bann'meile *f* (fig) city limits

Bann'ware *f* contraband

bar [bar] *adj* bare; (*rein*) pure, sheer; (fin) cash ‖ *adv* cash ‖ *prep* (*genit*) devoid of, lacking ‖ **Bar** *f* (-;-s) bar, taproom

Bär [ber] *m* (-en;-en) bear; (astr) Dipper; **j-m e-n B. aufbinden** tell s.o. a fish story

Bar- *comb.fm.* cash

Baracke [ba'rakə] *f* (-;-n) barrack; (wooden) hut

Barbar **-in** [bar'bar(ɪn)] §7 *mf* barbarian

Barbarei [barba'raɪ] *f* (-;-en) barbarism; (*Grausamkeit*) barbarity

barbarisch [bar'barɪʃ] *adj* barbarous; barbaric, primitive

bärbeißig ['berbaɪsɪç] *adj* surly

Bar'bestand *m* cash on hand

Bar'betrag *m* amount in cash

Barbier [bar'bir] *m* (-s;-e) barber

barbieren [bar'birən] *tr* shave; (fig) fleece

Barett [ba'ret] *n* (-[e]s;-e) beret

barfuß ['barfus] *adv* barefoot

barfüßig ['barfysɪç] *adj* barefooted

barg [bark] *pret* of **bergen**

Bar'geld *n* cash

barhäuptig ['barhɔɪptɪç] *adj* bareheaded

Bar'hocker *m* bar stool

Bariton ['barɪton] *m* (-s;-e) baritone

Barkasse [bar'kasə] *f* (-;-n) launch

Bärme ['bermə] *f* (-;) yeast, leaven

barmherzig [barm'hertsɪç] *adj* merciful

Bar'mittel *pl* cash

barock [ba'rɔk] *adj* baroque ‖ **Barock** *m* & *n* (-s;) baroque; baroque period

Barometer [barə'metər] *n* (-s;-) barometer

Baron [ba'ron] *m* (-s;-e) baron

Baronin [ba'ronɪn] *f* (-;-nen) baroness

Barre ['barə] *f* (-;-n) bar
Barren ['barən] *m* (-s;-) bar; ingot; (gym) parallel bars
Barriere [bar'jerə] *f* (-;-n) barrier
barsch [barʃ] *adj* gruff, rude || **Barsch** *m* (-es;-e) (ichth) perch
Barschaft ['barʃaft] *f* (-;) cash
barst [barst] *pret* of **bersten**
Bart [bart] *m* (-[e]s;ː) beard; (e-r *Katze*) whiskers; (e-s *Fisches*) barb; **der B. ist ab!** the jig is up!; **sich** [*dat*] **e-n B. wachsen lassen** grow a beard
bärtig ['bertıç] *adj* bearded
bart'los *adj* beardless
Bar'verlust *m* straight loss
Basalt [ba'zalt] *m* (-[e]s;-e) basalt
Basar [ba'zar] *m* (-s;-e) bazaar
Ba·sis ['bazıs] *f* (-;-sen [zən]) basis; (archit, math, mil) base
Baß [bas] *m* (**Basses;Bässe**) (mus) bass
Baß'geige *f* bass viol, contrabass
Bassin [ba'sɛ̃] *n* (-s;-s) reservoir; swimming pool; (naut) dock, basin
Baß'schlüssel *m* bass clef
Baß'stimme *f* bass (voice), basso
basta ['basta] *interj*—**und damit b.!** and that's that!
Bastard ['bastart] *m* (-[e]s;-e) bastard; (bot) hybrid
Bastei [bas'taı] *f* (-;-en) bastion
basteln ['bastəln] *intr* tinker
Bast'ler –in §6 *mf* hobbyist
bat [bat] *pret* of **bitten**
Bataillon [batal'jon] *n* (-s;-e) battalion
Batte·rie [batə'ri] *f* (-;-rien ['ri·ən] battery
Bau [bau] *m* (-[e]s;) erection, construction, building; (*Bauart*) structure, design; (*Körper–*) build; **er ist beim Bau** he is in the building trade; **er ist vom Bau** (coll) he's in the racket; **im Bau** under construction || *m* (-[e]s;-ten) building; **auf dem Bau** at the construction site || *m* (-[e]s;-e) burrow, hole; (min) mine **–bau** *m comb.fm.* –construction, –building; –culture; –mining
Bau'abnahme *f* building inspection
Bau'arbeiter *m* construction worker
Bau'art *f* build; structure; type, model
Bauch [baux] *m* (-[e]s;ː) belly, stomach; (*Leib*) bowels; (coll) pot-belly
Bauch– *comb.fm.* abdominal
bauchig ['bauxıç] *adj* bulging; convex
Bauch'klatscher *m* belly flop
Bauch'laden *m* vendor's tray
Bauch'landung *f* belly-landing
Bauch'redner –in §6 *mf* ventriloquist
Bauch'speicheldrüse *f* pancreas
Bauch'weh *n* stomach ache, bellyache
bauen ['bau·ən] *tr* build; erect; make, manufacture; (*ackern*) till; (*anbauen*) grow || *intr* build; (**an** *dat*) work (at); (**auf** *acc*) depend (on), trust
Bauer ['bau·ər] *m* (-s & -n;-n) farmer; (cards) jack; (chess) pawn || *m* (-s;-) builder || *m & n* (-s;-) birdcage
Bäuerchen ['bɔı·ərçən] *n* (-s;-) small farmer; (baby's) burp

Bäuerin ['bɔı·ərın] *f* (-;-nen) farmer's wife
bäuerisch ['bɔı·ərıʃ] *adj* boorish
Bau'erlaubnis *f* building permit
bäuerlich ['bɔı·ərlıç] *adj* rural
Bau'ernbursche *m* country lad
Bau'erndirne *f* country girl
Bauernfänger ['bau·ərnfɛŋər] *m* (-s;-) confidence man
Bau'erngut *n,* **Bau'ernhof** *m* farm
Bau'fach *n* architecture
bau'fällig *adj* dilapidated
Bau'genehmigung *f* building permit
Bau'gerüst *n* scaffold(ing)
Bau'gewerbe *n* building trade
Bau'gewerkschule *f* school of architecture and civil engineering
Bau'grundstück *n* building site
Bau'holz *n* lumber
Bau'kasten *m* building set
Bau'kunst *f* architecture
bau'lich *adj* architectural; structural; **in gutem baulichen Zustand** in good repair
Baum [baum] *m* (-[e]s;ː) tree; (mach) shaft, axle; (naut) boom
Bau'meister *m* building contractor, builder; architect
baumeln ['bauməln] *intr* dangle
bäumen ['bɔımən] *ref* rear
Baum'garten *m* orchard
Baum'grenze *f* timber line
Baum'krone *f* treetop
Baum'schere *f* pruning shears
Baum'schule *f* nursery (*of saplings*)
Baum'stamm *m* tree trunk
baum'stark' *adj* strong as an ox
Bau'muster *n* model (number)
Baum'wolle *f* cotton
Baum'wollkapsel *f* cotton boll
Baum'wollsamt *m* velveteen
Bau'plan *m* ground plan
Bau'platz *m* building lot
Bau'rat *m* (-[e]s;ː) building inspector
Bausch [bauʃ] *m* (-[e]s;ː) pad, wad; (e-s *Segels*) bulge, belly; **in B. und Bogen** wholesale
bauschen ['bauʃən] *tr, ref & intr* bulge, swell
bauschig ['bauʃıç] *adj* puffy; baggy
Bau'schule *f* school of architecture and civil engineering
Bau'sparkasse *f* building and loan association
Bau'stahl *m* structural steel
Bau'stein *m* building stone; brick
Bau'stelle *f* building site; road construction
Bau'stoff *m* building material
Bau'techniker *m* construction engineer
Bau'unternehmer *m* contractor
Bau'unternehmung *f* building firm, building contractors
Bau'werk *n* building, edifice
Bau'wesen *n* building industry
Bau'zaun *m* hoarding
Bau'zeichnung *f* blueprint
Bayer –in ['baı·ər(ın)] §6 *mf* Bavarian
bayerisch ['baı·ərıʃ] *adj* Bavarian
Bayern ['baı·ərn] *n* (-s;) Bavaria
Bazillenträger [ba'tsıləntregər] *m* germ carrier

Bazil·lus [ba'tsɪlʊs] *m* (-;-len [lən]) bacillus

be- [bə] *insep pref*

beabsichtigen [bə'apzɪçtɪgən] *tr* intend; (mit) mean (by)

beach'ten *tr* pay attention to; (*merken*) note, notice; (*befolgen*) observe; (*berücksichtigen*) consider

beach'tenswert *adj* noteworthy

Beach'tung *f* (-;) attention; notice; observance; consideration

Beamte [bə'amtə] *m* (-n;-n) official

Beam'tenherrschaft *f* bureaucracy

Beam'tenlaufbahn *f* civil service career

Beamtentum [bə'amtəntum] *n* (-[e]s;) officialdom, bureaucracy

Beamtin [bə'amtɪn] *f* (-;-nen) official

beäng'stigen *tr* make anxious, alarm

beanspruchen [bə'anʃpruxən] *tr* claim; (*Zeit, Raum*) require; **zu stark beansprucht werden** be worked too hard

beanstanden [bə'anʃtandən] *tr* object to, find fault with; (*Waren*) reject; (*Wahl*) contest; (*Recht*) challenge

Bean'standung *f* (-;-en) objection; complaint

bean'tragen *tr* propose; (**bei**) apply for (to)

beant'worten *tr* answer

Beant'wortung *f* (-;-en) answer

bear'beiten *tr* work; (*Land*) cultivate; (*Buch, Text*) revise; (*Wörterbuch*) compile; (*für die Bühne*) adapt; (*ein Manuskript*) prepare; (*Thema; Kunden*) work on; (*Person*) try to influence; (chem) treat; (*Auftrag*) (com) handle; (*Fall*) (jur) handle; (metal) machine, tool; (mus) arrange

bearg'wöhnen *tr* be suspicious of

beaufsichtigen [bə'aufzɪçtɪgən] *tr* supervise; (*Arbeiten*) superintend; (*Kinder*) look after; (educ) proctor; **streng b.** keep a sharp eye on

beauf'tragen *tr* commission, appoint; (mit) entrust (with)

Beauftragte [bə'auftrɑktə] §5 *mf* representative; (com) agent

bebau'en *tr* cultivate; (*Gelände*) build up

beben ['bebən] *intr* (**vor**) tremble (with), shake (with); (*Erde*) quake

bebrillt [bə'brɪlt] *adj* bespectacled

Becher ['beçər] *m* (-s;-) cup, mug

bechern ['beçərn] *intr* (coll) booze

Becken ['bɛkən] *n* (-s;-) basin, bowl; (anat) pelvis; (mus) cymbal

bedacht [bə'daxt] *adj* (**auf** *acc*) intent (on); **auf alles b. sein** think of everything; **darauf b. sein zu** (*inf*) be anxious to (*inf*) ‖ **Bedacht** *m*—**B. nehmen auf** (*acc*) take into consideration; **mit B.** deliberately; with caution

bedächtig [bə'dɛçtɪç], **bedachtsam** [bə'daxtzam] *adj* cautious, deliberate

bedan'ken *ref*—**ich würde mich bestens b., wenn** (iron) I would be most indignant if; **sich b. bei j-m für** thank s.o. for

Bedarf [bə'darf] *m* (-[e]s;) demand; requirement; (**an** *dat*) need (of); **bei B.** if required; **den B. decken** meet the demand; **nach B.** as required;

seinen B. decken an (*dat*) get one's supply of

Bedarfs'artikel *pl* needs, supplies

Bedarfs'fall *m*—**im B.** in case of need

Bedarfs'güter *pl* consumer goods

Bedarfs'haltestelle *f* optional bus or trolley stop

Bedarfs'träger *m* consumer

bedauerlich [bə'dau·ərlɪç] *adj* regrettable

bedau'erlicherweise *adv* unfortunately

bedauern [bə'dau·ərn] *tr* pity, feel sorry for; regret, deplore ‖ **Bedauern** *n* (-s;) (**über** *acc*) regret (over); (*Mitleid*) (mit) pity (for)

bedau'ernswert *adj* pitiful, pitiable

bedecken (bedek'ken) *tr* cover; **bedeckt** overcast

Bedeckung (Bedek'kung) *f* (-;-en) cover; escort; (mil) escort; (nav) convoy

beden'ken §66 *tr* consider; (*beachten*) bear in mind; (*im Testament*) provide for ‖ *ref* deliberate, think a matter over; **sich e-s anderen b.** change one's mind ‖ **Bedenken** *n* (-s;-) (*Erwägung*) consideration, reflection; (*Einwand*) objection, (*Zweifel*) doubt, scruple

bedenk'lich *adj* (*ernst*) serious, critical; (*gefährlich*) risky; (*heikel*) ticklish; (*Charakter*) questionable

bedeu'ten *tr* mean; **das hat nichts zu b.** that doesn't matter; **j-m b., daß** make it clear to s.o. that

bedeu'tend *adj* important; (*beträchtlich*) considerable

bedeutsam [bə'dɔɪtzam] *adj* significant; (*Blick*) meaningful

Bedeu'tung *f* (-;-en) meaning; (*Wichtigkeit*) importance

bedeu'tungsvoll *adj* significant

bedie'nen *tr* wait on, serve; (*Maschine*) operate ‖ *ref* (*genit*) make use of; **bedienen Sie sich** help yourself ‖ *intr* wait on people; (cards) follow suit

Bedie'nung *f* (-;) service; servants; waitresses

Bedienungs- *comb.fm.* control

Bedie'nungsanweisung *f* instructions

Bedie'nungsmannshaft *f* gun crew

bedingen [bə'dɪŋən] *tr* condition, stipulate; (*in sich schließen*) imply; **bedingt** conditioned, conditional

bedin'gungsweise *adv* conditionally

bedrän'gen *tr* press hard; (*beunruhigen*) pester; **bedrängte Lage** state of distress; **bedrängte Verhältnisse** financial difficulties

Bedrängnis [bə'drɛŋnɪs] *f* (-;-se) distress; **in ärgster B.** in dire straits

bedro'hen *tr* threaten, menace

bedroh'lich *adj* threatening

bedrucken (bedruk'ken) *tr* print on; (*Stoff*) print

bedrücken (bedrük'ken) *tr* oppress

bedür'fen §69 *intr* (*genit*) require

Bedürfnis [bə'dʏrfnɪs] *n* (-ses;-se) need, requirement; (*Wunsch*) desire; **Bedürfnisse** necessities; **das dringende B. haben zu** (*inf*) have the urge to (*inf*)

Bedürf'nisanstalt *f* comfort station
bedürf'nislos *adj* having few needs
bedürftig [bə'dʏrftɪç] *adj* needy; **b. sein** (*genit*) be in need of
Beefsteak ['bifstek] *n* (-s;-s) steak; **Deutsches B.** hamburger
beehren [bə'erən] *tr* honor ‖ *ref*— **sich b. zu** (*inf*) have the honor of (*ger*)
beei'len *ref* hurry (up)
beein'drucken *tr* impress
beeinflussen [bə'aɪnflusən] *tr* influence
Beein'flussung *f* (-;) (*genit*) influence (on), effect (on); (*pol*) lobbying
beeinträchtigen [bə'aɪntreçtɪgən] *tr* (*Ruf*) damage; (*Wert*) detract from; (*Rechte*) encroach upon; (*Aussichten*) hurt, spoil
been'den, been'digen *tr* end, conclude; (*Arbeit*) complete
beengen [bə'ɛŋən] *tr* confine, cramp; **sich beengt fühlen** feel cramped; (fig) feel restricted
beer'ben *tr*—**j-n b.** inherit s.o.'s estate
beerdigen [bə'erdɪgən] *tr* bury, inter
Beer'digung *f* (-;-en) burial
Beere ['berə] *f* (-;-n) berry
Beet [bet] *n* (-[e]s;-e) (agr) bed
befähigen [bə'fe·ɪgən] *tr* enable, qualify
befähigt [bə'fe·ɪçt] *adj* able, capable
Befä'higung *f* (-;-en) qualification; (*Fähigkeit*) ability
befahl [bə'fɑl] *pret* of **befehlen**
befahrbar [bə'fɑrbɑr] *adj* (*Weg*) passable; (*Wasser*) navigable
befah'ren §71 *tr* travel; (*Meer*) sail; (*Fluß*) navigate; (*Küste*) sail along; (*Schacht*) go down into
befal'len §72 *tr* strike, attack; infest
befan'gen *adj* embarrassed; (*schüchtern*) shy; (*voreingenommen*) prejudiced; (*parteiisch*) partial
befas'sen *tr* touch, handle ‖ *ref*—**sich b. mit** concern oneself with
befehden [bəfedən] *tr* make war on
Befehl [bə'fel] *m* (-s;-e) order, command; **auf B.** (*genit*) by order of
befeh'len §51 *tr* order, command; **was b. Sie?** what is your pleasure?
befehligen [bə'felɪgən] *tr* command, be in command of
Befehls'form *f* imperative mood
Befehlshaber [bə'felshɑbər] *m* (-s;-) (mil) commanding officer; (nav) commander in chief; **oberster B.** supreme commander
befehlshaberisch [bə'felshɑbərɪʃ] *adj* imperious
Befehls'stelle *f* command post
befe'stigen *tr* (**an** *dat*) fasten (to), attach (to); (mil) fortify
Befe'stigung *f* (-;-en) fortification
befeuchten [bə'fɔɪçtən] *tr* moisten, wet
befeu'ern *tr* (aer, naut) mark with lights; (mil) fire on, shoot at
befin'den §59 *tr* deem ‖ *ref* be, feel ‖ **Befinden** *n* (-s;) judgment, view; (state of) health; **je nach B.** according to taste
befindlich [bə'fɪntlɪç] *adj* present, to

be found; **all die im Hafen befindlichen Schiffe** the ships (present) in the harbor; **b. sein** happen to be
beflecken (beflek'ken) *tr* stain, taint
beflissen [bə'flɪsən] *adj* (*genit*) keen (on), interested (in) ‖ **Beflissene** §5 *mf* (*genit*) student (of)
befohlen [bə'folən] *pp* of **befehlen**
befol'gen *tr* obey, comply with
Befol'gung *f* (-;) observance
beför'dern *tr* ship; (*spedieren*) forward; (*im Rang*) promote; (*fördern*) further
Beför'derungsmittel *n* means of transportation
befra'gen *tr* question, interrogate; poll; (*um Rat*) consult
befrakt [bə'frakt] *adj* in tails
befrei'en *tr* free; liberate; (*vom Militärdienst*) exempt; (*von e-r Aufgabe*) excuse; (*von Sorgen, e-r Last*) relieve
Befrei'ung *f* (-;-en) freeing; liberation; exemption; rescue
befremden [bə'frɛmdən] *tr* surprise, astonish; strike as odd ‖ **Befremden** *n* (-s;) surprise, astonishment
befreunden [bə'frɔɪndən] *ref*—**sich mit etw b.** reconcile oneself to s.th.; **sich mit j-m b.** make friends with s.o.
befrieden [bə'fridən] *tr* pacify
befriedigen [bə'fridɪgən] *tr* satisfy
befrie'digend *adj* satisfactory
befristen [bə'frɪstən] *tr* set a time limit on
Befri'stung *f* (-;-en) time limit
befruchten [bə'fruxtən] *tr* (*Land*) make fertile; (*schwängern*) impregnate; (*Ei*) fertilize; **künstlich b.** inseminate; (bot) pollinate
befugt [bə'fukt] *adj* authorized
befüh'len *tr* feel, touch
Befund' *m* (-[e]s;-e) findings, facts
befürch'ten *tr* fear, be afraid of
Befürch'tung *f* (-;-en) apprehension
befürworten [bə'fyrvɔrtən] *tr* support; (*anraten*) recommend
begabt [bə'gɑpt] *adj* gifted, talented
Bega'bung *f* (-;-en) aptitude; (natural) gift, talent
Bega'bungsprüfung *f* intelligence test
begann [bə'gan] *pret* of **beginnen**
begatten [bə'gatən] *tr* mate with ‖ *ref* copulate, mate
bege'ben §80 *tr* (*Anleihen*) float, place; (*Wertpapiere*) sell ‖ *ref* go; occur; **es begab sich** (Bib) it came to pass; **sich an die Arbeit b.** set to work; **sich auf die Flucht b.** take to flight; **sich auf die Reise b.** set out on a trip; **sich b.** (*genit*) renounce; **sich in Gefahr b.** expose oneself to danger
Bege'benheit *f* (-;-en) event, incident
begegnen [bə'gegnən] *intr* (SEIN) (*dat*) meet, come upon; (*Schwierigkeiten, Feind*) encounter; (*Gefahr*) face
bege'hen §82 *tr* walk on; walk along; (*Verbrechen, Irrtum*) commit; (*Fest*) celebrate
Begehr [bə'ger] *m & n* (-s;) desire; request; (econ) demand
begehren [bə'gerən] *tr* wish for; crave;

(Bib) covet; **etw von j–m b.** ask s.o. for s.th. ‖ *intr* **(nach)** yearn (for)

begeh'renswert *adj* desirable

begehr'lich *adj* covetous

begehrt [bə'gert] *adj* in demand

begeistert [bə'gaɪstərt] *adj* enthusiastic

Begei'sterung *f* (–;) enthusiasm

Begier [bə'gir] *f* (–;) var of **Begierde**

Begierde [bə'girdə] *f* (–;–n) desire; (fleshly) appetite; eagerness; craving

begierig [bə'giriç] *adj* eager; (*Augen*) hungry; **(nach, auf** *acc*) desirous (of); **b. zu** (*inf*) eager to (*inf*)

begie'ßen §76 *tr* water; (culin) baste; **das wollen wir b.** we want to celebrate it (*by drinking*)

Beginn [bə'gɪn] *m* (–[e]s;) beginning; (*Ursprung*) origin

beginnen [bə'gɪnən] §52 *tr & intr* begin

beglaubigen [bə'glaubɪgən] *tr* certify, authenticate; (*Gesandten*) accredit

Beglau'bigung *f* (–;) authentication; accreditation

Beglau'bigungsschreiben *n* (dipl) credentials

beglei'chen §85 *tr* balance; (*Rechnung*) pay in full; (*Streit*) settle

begleiten [bə'glaɪtən] *tr* accompany; escort; see (*e.g., off, home*); **hinaus b.** see to the door

Beglei'ter –in §6 *mf* companion

Begleit'erscheinung *f* concomitant

Begleit'musik *f* background music

Begleit'schreiben *s* covering letter

Beglei'tung *f* (–;–en) company; escort; (*Gefolge*) retinue; (mus) accompaniment

beglück'wünschen *tr* **(zu)** congratulate (on)

Beglück'wünschung *f* (–;–en) congratulation

begnadet [bə'gnɑdət] *adj* highly gifted

begnadigen [bə'gnɑdɪgən] *tr* pardon; (pol) grant amnesty to

Begna'digung *f* (–;–en) pardon; amnesty

begnügen [bə'gnygən] *ref* **(mit)** content oneself (with), be satisfied (with)

begonnen [bə'gɔnən] *pp* of **beginnen**

begra'ben §87 *tr* bury

Begräbnis [bə'grepnis] *n* (–ses;–se) burial; funeral

Begräb'nisfeier *f* funeral

Begräb'nisstätte *f* burial place

begradigen [bə'grɑdɪgən] *tr* straighten; (tech) align

begrei'fen §88 *tr* touch, handle; (*verstehen*) grasp; (*enthalten*) comprise

begreif'lich *adj* understandable

begreif'licherweise *adv* understandably

begren'zen *tr* bound; limit, restrict

Begren'zung *f* (–;–en) limitation

Begriff [bə'grɪf] *m* (–[e]s;–e) idea, notion; (*Ausdruck*) term; (philos) concept; **im B. sein zu** (*inf*) be on the point of (*ger*)

begriffen [bə'grɪfən] *adj*—**b. sein in** (*dat*) be in the process of

begrün'den *tr* found, establish; (*Behauptung*) substantiate, prove

Begrün'der –in §6 *mf* founder

Begrün'dung *f* (–;–en) establishment; proof; (*Grund*) ground, reason

begrüßen *tr* greet; welcome

begünstigen [bə'gʏnstɪgən] *tr* favor; (*fördern*) promote, support; (jur) aid and abet

Begün'stiger *m* (–s;–) accessory after the fact

Begünstigte [bə'gʏnstɪçtə] §5 *mf* (ins) beneficiary

Begün'stigung *f* (–;–en) promotion, encouragement; support, backing; (jur) aiding and abetting

begut'achten *tr* give an expert opinion on; **b. lassen** obtain expert opinion on

begütert [bə'gytərt] *adj* well-to-do

begütigen [bə'gytɪgən] *tr* appease

behaart [bə'hɑrt] *adj* hairy

behäbig [bə'hebɪç] *adj* comfort-loving; (*beleibt*) portly

behaftet [bə'haftət] *adj* afflicted

behagen [bə'hagən] *intr* (*dat*) please, suit ‖ **Behagen** *n* (–s;) pleasure

behaglich [bə'haklɪç] *adj* pleasant; (*traulich*) snug, cozy

behal'ten §90 *tr* keep, retain; **Recht b.** turn out to be right

Behälter [bə'heltər] *m* (–s;–) container; box; (*für Öl, usw.*) tank

behan'deln *tr* treat; deal with; handle

behän'gen §92 *tr* hang; deck out

beharren [bə'harən] *intr* remain (unchanged); (**in** *dat*) persevere (in); (**auf** *dat*) persist (in), stick (to)

beharrlich [bə'harlɪç] *adj* steadfast

behau'en §93 *tr* hew

behaupten [bə'hauptən] *tr* declare, assert; (*festhalten*) maintain, retain; allege ‖ *ref* stand one's ground; (*Preise*) remain steady

behausen [bə'hauzən] *tr* lodge, house

Behau'sung *f* (–;–en) dwelling

behe'ben §94 *tr* (*Schwierigkeiten*) remove; (*Zweifel*) dispel; (*Schaden*) repair; (*Lage*) remedy; (*Geld*) withdraw; (*Schmerzen*) eliminate

beheimatet [bə'haɪmatət] *adj*—**b. sein in** (*dat*) reside in; come from

Behelf [bə'helf] *m* (–[e]s;–e) expedient; makeshift

behel'fen §96 *ref* **(mit)** make do (with)

Behelfs– *comb.fm.* temporary

behelfs'mäßig *adj* temporary, makeshift

behelligen [bə'helɪgən] *tr* bother

Behel'ligung *f* (–;–en) bother, trouble

behende [bə'hendə] *adj* agile, quick; (*gewandt*) handy; (*geistig*) smart

beherbergen [bə'herbergən] *tr* take in, put up (*as guest*)

beherr'schen *tr* (*Land*) rule; (*Sprache*) master; (*Gefühle*) control; (*überragen*) tower over; **den Luftraum b.** (mil) have air supremacy

Beherr'scher –in §6 *mf* ruler ‖ *m* master ‖ *f* mistress

beherzigen [bə'hertsɪgən] *tr* take to heart, remember

beherzt [bə'hertst] *adj* courageous

behe'xen *tr* bewitch; (fig) captivate

behilflich [bə'hɪlflɪç] *adj* helpful

behin'dern *tr* hinder; hamper; block

behor'chen *tr* overhear

Behörde [bə'hørdə] *f* (-;-n) authority, board; *die Behörden* the authorities
behördlich [bə'hørtlɪç] *adj* official
behü′ten *tr* (**vor** *dat*) protect (against); **Gott behüte!** God forbid!
behutsam [bə'hutsɑm] *adj* wary
bei [baɪ] *prep* (*dat*) (*Ort*) by, beside, at, with, in; (*in Anschriften*) in care of, c/o; (*Zeit, Umstände*) at, by, during, on; (*Zustände, Eigenschaften*) at, while, in; **bei mir haben** have on me; **bei meiner Ehre** upon my honor; **bei Schiller** in the works of Schiller; **bei uns** at our house; **bei weitem** by far
bei′behalten §90 *tr* retain, keep
Bei′blatt *n* supplement
bei′bringen §65 *tr* obtain, procure; (*Beweise, Zeugen*) produce; (*Arznei, Gift*) administer; (*Wunde, Niederlage, Schlag, Verluste*) inflict; **j—m die Nachricht schonend b.** break the news gently to s.o.; **j—m etw b.** teach s.o. s.th., make s.th. clear to s.o.
Beichte ['baɪçtə] *f* (-;-n) confession
beichten ['baɪçtən] *tr* (eccl) confess
Beicht′kind *n* (eccl) penitent
Beicht′stuhl *m* (eccl) confessional
beide ['baɪdə] *adj* both; two ‖ *pron* both; two; **keiner von beiden** neither of them
beiderlei ['baɪdər'laɪ] *invar adj* both kinds of
beiderseitig ['baɪdər'zaɪtɪç] *adj* bilateral; (*gemeinsam*) mutual
beiderseits ['baɪdər'zaɪts] *adv* on both sides; mutually, reciprocally ‖ *prep* (*genit*) on both sides of
beieinan′der *adv* together; **gut b. sein** (coll) be in good shape
Bei′fahrer **-in** §6 *mf* relief driver; passenger (*next to the driver*)
Bei′fall *m* approval; applause
bei′fällig *adj* approving; (*Bericht*) favorable ‖ *adv* approvingly
Bei′fallklatschen *n* clapping, applause
Bei′fallsgeschrei *n* loud cheering
Bei′fallsruf *m* cheer
Bei′film *m* (cin) second feature
bei′folgend *adj* enclosed
bei′fügen *tr* add; (*e—m Brief*) enclose
bei′fügend *adj* (gram) attributive
Bei′fügung *f* (-;-en) addition; enclosure; (gram) attributive
Bei′gabe *f* extra; funerary gift
bei′geben §80 *tr* add; assign ‖ *intr* give in; **klein b.** knuckle under
Bei′geschmack *m* taste, flavor; tinge
Bei′hilfe *f* aid; (*Stipendium*) grant; (*Unterstützung*) subsidy; allowance; (jur) aiding and abetting
bei′kommen § 99 *intr* (SEIN) (*dat*) get the better of; (*dat*) reach; *e—r Schwierigkeit*) overcome
Beil [baɪl] *n* (-[e]s;-e) hatchet
Bei′lage *f* (*im Brief*) enclosure; (*e—r Zeitung*) supplement; **Fleisch mit B.** meat and vegetables
beiläufig ['baɪlɔɪfɪç] *adj* incidental; casual ‖ *adv* by the way, incidentally; **b. erwähnen** mention in passing
bei′legen *tr* add; (*Titel*) confer; (*Wichtigkeit*) attach; (*Streit*) settle; **etw**

e—m Brief b. enclose s.th. in a letter ‖ *intr* heave to
Bei′leid *n* (-s;) condolence(s)
bei′liegen §108 *intr*—**e—m Brief b.** be enclosed in a letter; **j—m b.** lie with s.o
beim *abbr* **bei dem**
bei′messen §70 *tr* attribute, impute
bei′mischen *tr* mix in
Bein [baɪn] *n* (-[e]s;-e) leg; (*Knochen*) bone; (fig) foot; **j—m ein B. stellen** trip s.o.
beinahe ['baɪnɑ•ə], [baɪ'nɑ•e] *adv* almost, nearly
Bei′name *m* appellation; (*Spitzname*) nickname
Bein′bruch *m* fracture, broken leg
Bein′schiene *f* (surg) splint; (sport) shin guard
Bein′schützer *m* (sport) shin guard
Bein′stellen *n* (sport) tripping
bei′ordnen *tr* assign, appoint (*s.o.*) as assistant; (*dat*) place (*s.th.*) on a level (with)
beipflichten ['baɪpflɪçtən] *intr* (*dat*) agree with (*s.o.*), agree to (*s.th.*)
Bei′programm *n* (cin) second feature
Bei′rat *m* (-s;ꞏe) adviser, counselor; (*Körperschaft*) advisory board
beir′ren *tr* mislead
beisammen [baɪ'zamən] *adv* together
Beisam′mensein *n* (-s;) being together; gathering, reunion; **geselliges B.** social; informal reception
Bei′satz *m* addition; (*bei Legierung*) alloy; (gram) appositive
Bei′schlaf *m* sexual intercourse
bei′schließen §76 *tr* enclose
Bei′schluß *m*—**unter B. von allen Dokumenten** with all documents attached
bei′schreiben §62 *tr* write in the margin; add as a postscript
Bei′schrift *f* postscript
Bei′sein *n* (-s;) presence
beisei′te *adv* aside; **b. schaffen** remove; (coll) do (*s.o.*) in
bei′setzen *tr* bury, inter
Bei′sitzer *m* associate judge
Bei′spiel *n* example; **zum B.** for example
bei′spielhaft *adj* exemplary
bei′spiellos *adj* unparalleled
bei′spielsweise *adv* by way of example
bei′springen §142 *intr* (*dat*) come to the aid of
beißen ['baɪsən] §53 *tr & intr* bite
bei′ßend *adj* biting; stinging, pungent, acrid; sarcastic; (*Reue*) bitter
Beiß′korb *m* muzzle
Beiß′zahn *m* (anat) incisor
Beiß′zange *f* pincers, nippers
Bei′stand *m* aid, support; (*Person*) assistant
bei′stehen §146 *intr* (*dat*) stand by, back, support
Bei′steuer *f* contribution
bei′steuern *tr* contribute
bei′stimmen *intr* (*dat*) agree with
Bei′stimmung *f* (-;) approval
Bei′strich *m* comma
Beitrag ['baɪtrɑk] *m* (-[e]s;ꞏe) contribution; (*e—s Mitglieds*) dues

bei'tragen §132 *tr* & *intr* contribute
bei'treiben §62 *tr* collect; (*Abgaben*) exact; (mil) commandeer, requisition
bei'treten §152 *intr* (SEIN) (*dat*) join; (*j–s Meinung*) concur in
Bei'tritt *m* joining; concurrence
Bei'wagen *m* (aut) sidecar
Bei'werk *n* (-[e]s;) accessories
bei'wohnen *intr* (*dat*) attend; (*e–m Ereignis*) be witness to; (*j–m*) have intercourse with (*s.o.*)
Bei'wort *n* (-[e]s;⸚er) epithet; (gram) adjective
Beize ['baɪtsə] *f* (-;-n) corrosive; (wood) stain; (*Falken–*) falconry; (culin) marinade
beizeiten [baɪ'tsaɪtən] *adv* on time; (*frühzeitig*) early
beizen ['baɪtsən] *tr* (*ätzen*) corrode; (*Holz*) stain; (*Wunde*) cauterize; (hunt) go hawking
bejahen [bə'jɑ·ən] *tr* say 'yes' to
beja'hend *adj* affirmative
bejahrt [bə'jɑrt] *adj* aged
bekämp'fen *tr* fight, oppose
bekannt [bə'kant] *adj* known; familiar; (*berühmt*) well-known ‖ **Bekannte** §5 *mf* acquaintance
Bekannt'gabe *f* announcement
bekannt'geben §80 *tr* announce
bekannt'lich *adv* as is well known
bekannt'machen *tr* announce; (*Gesetz*) promulgate
Bekannt'machung *f* (-;-en) publication, announcement; (*Plakat*) poster
Bekannt'schaft *f* (-;) acquaintance; (coll) acquaintances
bekeh'ren *tr* convert ‖ *ref* (zu) become a convert (to)
Bekehrte [bə'kertə] §5 *mf* convert
beken'nen §97 *tr* (*Sünde*) confess; (*zugestehen*) admit; **Farbe b.** follow suit; (fig) put one's cards on the table ‖ *ref*—**sich schuldig b.** plead guilty; **sich zu e–r Religion b.** profess a religion; **sich zu e–r Tat b.** own up to a deed; **sich zu j–m b.** stand by s.o., believe in s.o.
Bekennt'nis *n* (eccl) confession; (*Konfession*) denomination
bekla'gen *tr* deplore; (*Tod*) mourn ‖ *ref* (über *acc*) complain (about), find fault (with)
bekla'genswert *adj* deplorable
Beklagte [bə'klɑktə] §5 *mf* defendant
beklat'schen *tr* applaud
bekle'ben *tr* paste; (*mit Etiketten*) label; **e–e Mauer mit Plakaten b.** paste posters on a wall
beklei'den *tr* clothe, dress; (*Mauer*) face, cover; (*Amt*) hold
beklem'men *tr* stifle, oppress
Beklem'mung *f* (-;-en) worry, anxiety; **Beklemmungen** claustrophobia
beklommen [bə'klɔmən] *adj* uneasy
bekom'men §99 *tr* get; obtain; receive; (*Schnupfen*) catch; (*Risse*) develop ‖ *intr* (*dat*) do good; **j–m schlecht b.** do s.o. harm; **wohl bekomm's!** to your health!
bekömmlich [bə'kœmlɪç] *adj* digestible; (*gesund*) healthful; (*zuträglich*) wholesome

beköstigen [bə'kœstɪgən] *tr* board, feed ‖ *ref*—**sich selbst b.** do one's own cooking
bekräf'tigen *tr* (*Vorschlag*) support; (*bestätigen*) substantiate; **mit e–m Eid b.** seal with an oath
bekrän'zen *tr* wreath, crown
bekreu'zen, bekreu'zigen *ref* cross oneself, make the sign of the cross
bekrie'gen *tr* make war on
bekrit'teln *tr* criticize, pick at
bekrit'zeln *tr* scribble on, doodle on
beküm'mern *tr* worry, trouble ‖ *ref* (um) concern onself· (with), bother (about)
beküm'mert *adj* (über *acc*) worried (about)
bekunden [bə'kundən] *tr* manifest, show; (*öffentlich*) state publicly
bela'den §103 *tr* load; (fig) burden
Belag [bə'lɑk] *m* (-[e]s;⸚) covering; coat(ing); flooring; layer; surface
bela'gern *tr* besiege, beleaguer
Bela'gerung *f* (-;-en) siege
Belang [bə'laŋ] *m* (-[e]s;e) importance, consequence; **Belange** interests
belan'gen *tr* (jur) sue; **was mich belangt** as far as I am concerned
belang'los *adj* unimportant
bela'sten *tr* load (down); (*Grundstück*) encumber; (fig) burden; (acct) charge; (jur) incriminate
belästigen [bə'lɛstɪgən] *tr* annoy, bother; (*mit Fragen*) pester; (*unabsichtlich*) inconvenience
Bela'stung *f* (-;-en) load; encumbrance; (fig) burden; (acct) debit; **die Zeiten größter B.** the peak hours
Bela'stungsprobe *f* (fig) acid test
Bela'stungszeuge *m* witness for the prosecution
belau'fen §105 *ref*—**sich b. auf** (*acc*) amount to, come to
belau'schen *tr* overhear
bele'ben *tr* animate; (*Getränk*) spike; **wieder b.** revive
belebt [bə'lept] *adj* animated, lively
Bele'bungsmittel *n* stimulant
Beleg [bə'lek] *m* (-s;-e) (*Beweisstück*) evidence; (*Unterlage*) voucher; (*Beispiel*) example; (jur) exhibit
bele'gen *tr* cover; (*Platz*) take, occupy; (*bemannen*) man; (*beweisen*) verify; (*Vorlesung*) register for; **ein Brötchen mit Schinken b.** make a ham sandwich; **mit Beispielen b.** exemplify; **mit Fliesen b.** tile; **mit Steuern b.** tax; **mit Teppichen b.** carpet ‖ *ref* become coated
Beleg'schaft *f* (-;-en) crew; personnel; shift
Beleg'schein *m* voucher; receipt
Beleg'stelle *f* reference
belegt [bə'lekt] *adj* (*Platz*) reserved; (*Zunge*) coated; (*Stimme*) husky; (telp) busy; **belegtes Brot** sandwich
beleh'ren *tr* instruct ‖ *ref*—**sich b. lassen** listen to reason
beleh'rend *adj* instructive
Beleh'rung *f* (-;-en) instruction; (*Lehre*) lesson; (*Rat*) advice; **zu Ihrer B.** for your information

beleibt [bə'laɪpt] *adj* stout
beleidigen [bə'laɪdɪgən] *tr* offend
belei'digend *adj* offensive
bele'sen *adj* well-read
beleuch'ten *tr* light (up), illuminate; (fig) throw light on
Beleuch'ter *m* (aer) pathfinder; (theat) juicer
Beleuch'tung *f* (-;-en) lighting, illumination; (fig) elucidation
Beleuch'tungskörper *m* lighting fixture
Belgien ['bɛlgjən] *n* (-s;) Belgium
Belgier **-in** ['bɛlgjər(ɪn)] §6 *mf* Belgian
belgisch ['bɛlgɪʃ] *adj* Belgian
belichten [bə'lɪçtən] *tr* (phot) expose
Belich'tung *f* (-;-en) exposure
belie'ben *intr* please || *impers* (*dat*)— wenn es Ihnen beliebt if you please || **Belieben** *n* (-s;) liking; es steht in Ihrem B. it's up to you; nach B. as you like
beliebig [bə'libɪç] *adj* any (you please) || *adv* as … as you please
beliebt [bə'lipt] *adj* favorite; (bei) popular (with)
Beliebt'heit *f* (-;) popularity
belie'fern *tr* supply, furnish
bellen ['bɛlən] *intr* bark
belob(ig)en [bə'lob(ɪg)ən] *tr* praise; commend; (mil) cite
beloh'nen *tr* reward
belü'gen §111 *tr* lie to, deceive
belustigen [bə'lustɪgən] *tr* amuse
bemächtigen [bə'mɛçtɪgən] *intr* (*genit*) seize, get hold of; (mil) seize
bemä'keln *tr* criticize, carp at
bema'len *tr* paint; decorate
bemängeln [bə'mɛŋəln] *tr* criticize
bemannen [bə'manən] *tr* man
Beman'nung *f* (-;-en) (nav) crew
bemänteln [bə'mɛntəln] *tr* gloss over; (*Fehler, Fehltritt*) cover up
bemei'stern *tr* master || *ref* control oneself; (*genit*) get hold of
bemerk'bar *adj* perceptible
bemer'ken *tr* notice; (*äußern*) remark
bemer'kenswert *adj* remarkable
Bemer'kung *f* (-;-en) note; remark
bemes'sen §70 *tr* measure; proportion
bemit'leiden *tr* pity, feel sorry for
bemittelt [bə'mɪtəlt] *adj* well-to-do
bemogeln [bə'mogəln] *tr* cheat
bemü'hen *tr* trouble, bother; **bemüht sein zu** (*inf*) take pains to (*inf*) || *ref* bother, exert oneself; **sich für j-n b.** intervene for s.o.; **sich um etw b.** make an effort to obtain s.th.; **sich um j-n b.** attend to s.o.; **sich zu j-m b.** go to s.o.
Bemü'hung *f* (-;-en) bother; effort
bemüßigt [bə'mysɪçt] *adj*—**sich b. fühlen zu** (*inf*) feel obliged to (*inf*)
bemu'stern *tr*—**ein Angebot b.** (com) send samples of an offer
bemuttern [bə'mutərn] *tr* mother
benachbart [bə'naxbart] *adj* neighboring; (*Fachgebiet*) related, allied
benachrichtigen [bə'naxrɪçtɪgən] *tr* notify; put on notice
Benach'richtigung *f* (-;-en) notification; notice
benachteiligen [bə'naxtaɪlɪgən] *tr* place at a disadvantage, handicap; discriminate against
benebelt [bə'nebəlt] *adj* covered in mist; (fig) groggy
benedeien [bene'daɪ•ən] *tr* bless
beneh'men §116 *tr*—**j-m etw b.** take s.th. away from s.o. || *ref* behave || **Benehmen** *n* (-s;) behavior
beneiden [bə'naɪdən] *tr*—**j-n um etw b.** begrudge s.o. s.th.
benei'denswert *adj* enviable
benen'nen §97 *tr* name, term
Bengel ['bɛŋəl] *m* (-s;-) rascal
benommen [bə'nɔmən] *adj* dazed
benö'tigen *tr* need
benutz'bar *adj* usable
benut'zen, benüt'zen *tr* use, make use of
Benut'zerkarte *f* library card
Benzin [bɛnt'sin] *n* (-s;-e) gasoline
Benzin'behälter *m* gas tank
beobachten [bə'obaxtən] *tr* observe; (*polizeilich*) keep under surveillance; (med) keep under observation
Beob'achtung *f* (-;-en) observation; (*e-s Gesetzes*) observance
beor'dern *tr* order (*to go to a place*)
bepacken (**bepak'ken**) *tr* load (down)
bepflan'zen *tr* plant
bequem [bə'kvem] *adj* comfortable; cozy; (*Stellung*) soft; (*Raten, Lösung*) easy; (*faul*) lazy; **b. zur Hand haben** have handy
berappen [bə'rapən] *tr* (coll) shell out
bera'ten §63 *tr* (über *acc*) advise (on); discuss || *ref* & *intr* (über *acc*) confer (about), deliberate (on)
bera'tend *adj* advisory, consulting
beratschlagen [bə'rat/lagən] *intr* (über *acc*) consult (on); **mit j-m b.** consult s.o., confer with s.o.
berat'schlagend *adj* advisory
Bera'tung *f* (-;-en) advice; (jur, med) consultation; **in B. sein** be under consideration
Bera'tungsstelle *f* counseling center
berau'ben *tr* (*genit*) rob (of); (*genit*) dispossess (of); (*genit*) deprive (of); (*genit*) bereave (of)
berech'nen *tr* calculate, figure out; (*schätzen*) estimate; (com) charge
berech'nend *adj* calculating
Berech'nung *f* (-;-en) calculation
berechtigen [bə'rɛçtɪgən] *tr* authorize; justify, warrant; (zu) entitle (to)
Berech'tigung *f* (-;-en) right, authorization; justification; (zu) title (to)
bereden [bə'redən] *tr* talk over, discuss; **j-n zu etw b.** talk s.o. into s.th. || *ref*—**sich mit j-m über etw b.** confer with s.o. on s.th.
beredsam [bə'retzam] *adj* eloquent
beredt [bə'ret] *adj* eloquent
Bereich *m* & *n* (-[e]s;-e) region; range; (fig) field, sphere; **es fällt nicht in meinen B.** it's not within my province
bereichern [bə'raɪçərn] *tr* enrich
berei'fen *tr* cover with frost; (aut) put tires on
berei'nigen *tr* (*Streit, Konto*) settle; (*Mißverständnis*) clear up
berei'sen *tr* tour

bereit [bə'raɪt] *adj* ready
bereiten [bə'raɪtən] *tr* prepare; (*Kaffee*) make; (*Freude*) give
Bereit'schaft *f* (-;) readiness; team, squad; (mil) alert
bereit'stellen *tr* make available
Berei'tung *f* (-;-en) preparation; (*Herstellung*) manufacture
bereit'willig *adj* ready, willing
bereu'en *tr* rue, regret
Berg [bɛrk] *m* (-[e]s;-e) mountain; (*Hügel*) hill; **über alle Berge sein** be off and away; **zu Berge stehen** stand on end
bergab' *adv* downhill, down the mountain
bergauf' *adv* uphill; up the mountain
Berg'bahn *f* mountain railroad
Berg'bau *m* (-[e]s;) mining
Berg'bewohner –in §6 *mf* mountaineer
bergen ['bɛrgən] §54 *tr* rescue; (*enthalten*) hold; (*Gefahr*) involve; (*Segel*) take in; (naut) salvage; (poet) conceal; (rok) recover || *ref*—**in sich b.** involve
bergig ['bɛrgɪç] *adj* mountainous
Berg'kessel *m* gorge
Berg'kette *f* mountain range
Berg'kluft *f* ravine, gully
Berg'kristall *m* rock crystal, quartz
Berg'land *n* hill country
Berg'mann *m* (-[e]s;-leute) miner
Berg'predigt *f* Sermon on the Mount
Berg'recht *n* mining law
Berg'rücken *m* ridge
Berg'rutsch *m* landslide
Berg'schlucht *f* gorge, ravine
Berg'spitze *f* mountain peak
Berg'steiger –in §6 *mf* mountain climber
Berg'steigerei *f* mountain climbing
Berg'sturz *m* landslide
Ber'gung *f* (-;-en) rescue; (naut) salvage; (rok) recovery
Ber'gungsarbeiten *pl* salvage operations
Ber'gungsschiff *n* salvage vessel; (rok) recovery ship
Berg'wacht *f* mountain rescue service
Berg'werk *n* mine
Berg'wesen *n* mining
Bericht [bə'rɪçt] *m* (-[e]s;-e) report
berichten [bə'rɪçtən] *tr & intr* report
Berichterstatter –in [bə'rɪçter/tatər (ɪn)] §6 *mf* reporter; correspondent; (rad) commentator
Bericht'erstattung *f* (-;) reporting
berichtigen [bə'rɪçtɪgən] *tr* rectify; (*Text*) emend; (*Schuld*) pay off
berie'chen §102 *tr* sniff at; (fig) size up || *recip* (coll) sound each other out
Berlin [bɛr'lin] *n* (-s;) Berlin
Bernstein ['bɛrn/taɪn] *m* amber
bersten ['bɛrstən] §55 *intr* (SEIN) (**vor** *dat*) burst (with)
berüchtigt [bə'rʏçtɪçt] *adj* notorious
berücken (berük'ken) *tr* captivate
berücksichtigen [bə'rʏkzɪçtɪgən] *tr* (*erwägen*) consider; (*in Betracht ziehen*) make allowance for
Berück'sichtigung *f* (-;-en) consideration

Beruf' *m* (-[e]s;-e) vocation; profession; (*Gewerbe*) trade; (*Tätigkeit*) occupation; (*Laufbahn*) career
beru'fen *adj* called; authorized || §122 *tr* call; (*ernennen*) appoint; (*Geister*) conjure up || *ref*—**sich auf ein Gesetz b.** quote a law (*in support*); **sich auf j-n b.** use s.o.'s name as a reference
beruf'lich *adj* professional; vocational
Berufs– *comb.fm.* professional; vocational
Berufs'diplomat *m* career diplomat
Berufs'genossenschaft *f* professional association; trade association
Berufs'heer *n* regular army
Berufs'schule *f* vocational school
Berufs'sportler –in §6 *mf* professional
berufs'tätig *adj* working
Beru'fung *f* (-;-en) call; vocation; appointment; (jur) appeal; **B. einlegen** (jur) appeal; **unter B. auf** (*acc*) referring to
Beru'fungsgericht *n* appellate court
beru'hen *intr* (**auf** *dat*) be based (on); (**auf** *dat*) be due (to); **e-e Sache auf sich b. lassen** let a matter rest
beruhigen [bə'ru·ɪgən] *tr* calm; appease
beru'higend *adj* soothing; reassuring
Beru'higung *f* (-;) calming; appeasement, pacification; reassurance; (*der Lage*) stabilization; **zu meiner großen B.** much to my relief
Beru'higungsmittel *n* sedative
berühmt [bə'rymt] *adj* (**wegen**) famous (for)
Berühmt'heit *f* (-;-en) renown; (*berühmte Persönlichkeit*) celebrity
berüh'ren *tr* touch; (*erwähnen*) touch on; (*wirken auf*) affect; (*Zug*) pass through || *ref* come in contact, meet
Berüh'rung *f* (-;-en) touch; contact
besä'en *tr* sow; (*bestreuen*) strew; **mit Sternen besät** star-spangled
besa'gen *tr* say; (*bedeuten*) mean
besagt [bə'zakt] *adj* aforesaid
besänftigen [bə'zɛnftɪgən] *tr* calm; appease || *ref* calm down
Besatz' *m* trimming
Besat'zung *f* (-;-en) garrison; occupation; army of occupation; (aer, nav) crew
Besat'zungsarmee *f* army of occupation
Besat'zungsbehörde *f* military government
besau'fen §124 *ref* (coll) get drunk
beschä'digen *tr* damage || *ref* injure oneself
beschaf'fen *adj*—**ich bin eben so b.** that's the way I am; **übel b. sein** be in bad shape || *tr* get, procure; (*Geld*) raise
Beschaf'fenheit *f* (-;-en) quality, property; (*Zustand*) state; (*Art*) nature; (*Anlage*) design
Beschaf'fung *f* (-;-en) procuring; (*Erwerb*) acquisition
beschäftigen [bə'/ɛftɪgən] *tr* occupy; keep busy; (*anstellen*) employ; **beschäftigt sein bei** work for (*a company*); **beschäftigt sein mit** be busy with

beschä′men *tr* shame, make ashamed; beschämt sein be ashamed
Beschau′ *f* inspection
beschau′en *tr* look at; inspect
beschau′lich *adj* contemplative
Bescheid [bə′ʃaɪt] *m* (-[e]s;–e) answer; (*Anweisung*) instructions, directions; (*Auskunft*) information; (jur) decision; **B. hinterlassen bei** leave word with; **B. wissen** be well-informed; **j–m B. geben** (or sagen) give s.o. information or directions
beschei′den *adj* modest; (*Preise*) moderate; (*Auswahl*) limited; (*einfach*) simple, plain ‖ §112 *tr* inform; (*beordern*) order, direct; (*vorladen*) summon; (*zuteilen*) allot; **abschlägig b.** turn down; **es ist mir beschieden** it fell to my lot ‖ *ref* be satisfied
Beschei′denheit *f* (-;) modesty
bescheinigen [bə′ʃaɪnɪgən] *tr* (*Empfang*) acknowledge; (*bezeugen*) certify
Beschei′nigung *f* (-;–en) acknowledgement; certification; (*Schein*) certificate; (*im Brief*) to whom it may concern
beschei′ßen §53 *tr* (sl) cheat
beschen′ken *tr*—j–n b. mit present s.o. with
bescheren [bə′ʃerən] *tr* give gifts to
Besche′rung *f* (-;–en) distribution of gifts (*especially at Christmas*); **e–e schöne B.** (coll) a nice mess
beschicken (beschik′ken) *tr* (*mit Waren*) supply; (*Messe*) exhibit at, send exhibits to; (*Kongreß*) send delegates to; (*Hochofen*) feed, charge
beschie′ßen §76 *tr* shoot up; (mil, phys) bombard
beschimp′fen *tr* insult, call (*s.o.*) names
beschir′men *tr* shield, protect
beschla′fen *tr* (*e–e Frau*) sleep with; (*e–e Sache*) sleep on
Beschlag′ *m* (-s;–e) hardware; (*Huf–*) horse shoes; (*auf Fensterscheiben*) steam, vapor; (*Überzug*) thin coating; **in B. nehmen** confiscate; (*Schiff*) seize; (*Gehalt*) attach
beschla′gen *adj*—b. in (*dat*) well-versed in ‖ §132 *tr* cover, coat; (*Metallverzierungen*) fit, mount; (*Pferd*) shoe ‖ *ref & intr* steam up; (*Mauer*) sweat; (*Metall*) oxidize
beschlagnahmen [bə′ʃlaknɑmən] *tr* confiscate; (*Schuldnervermögen*) attach; (mil) requisition; (naut) seize
beschlei′chen §85 *tr* stalk, creep up on
beschleunigen [bə′ʃlɔɪnɪgən] *tr* accelerate, speed up
Beschleu′niger *m* (-s;–) accelerator
beschlie′ßen §76 *tr* end, wind up; (*sich entschließen*) decide
Beschluß′ *m* conclusion; decision; resolution; (jur) order; **unter B.** under lock and key; **zum B.** in conclusion
beschluß′fähig *adj*—b. sein have a quorum; **beschlußfähige Anzahl** quorum
beschmie′ren *tr* smear, coat; grease
beschmut′zen *tr* soil, dirty

beschnei′den §106 *tr* clip, trim; (fig) curtail; (surg) circumcise
beschneit [bə′ʃnaɪt] *adj* snow-covered
beschönigen [bə′ʃønɪgən] *tr* (*Fehler*) whitewash, cover up, gloss over
beschrän′ken *tr* limit
beschränkt′ *adj* limited; (*Verhältnisse*) straitened; (*geistig*) dense
beschrei′ben §62 *tr* describe; use up (*in writing*)
Beschrei′bung *f* (-;–en) description
beschrei′ten §86 *tr* walk on; **den Rechtsweg b.** take legal action
beschriften [bə′ʃrɪftən] *tr* inscribe; (*Kisten*) mark; (*mit Etikett*) label
Beschrif′tung *f* (-;–en) inscription; lettering; (*erläuternde*) caption
beschuldigen [bə′ʃuldɪgən] *tr* (*genit*) accuse (of), charge (with)
beschummeln [bə′ʃuməln] *tr* (coll) (um) cheat (out of)
Beschuß′ *m* test firing
beschüt′zen *tr* protect, defend
beschwat′zen *tr* gossip about; **j–n dazu b. zu** (*inf*) talk s.o. into (*ger*)
Beschwerde [bə′ʃverdə] *f* (-;–n) trouble; (*Klage, Krankheit*) complaint
beschweren [bə′ʃverən] *tr* burden ‖ *ref* (über *acc*) complain (about)
beschwer′lich *adj* troublesome
beschwichtigen [bə′ʃvɪçtɪgən] *tr* appease; (*Hunger*) satisfy; (*Gewissen*) soothe
beschwin′deln *tr* (um) swindle (out of)
beschwingt [bə′ʃvɪŋt] *adj* lively
beschwipst [bə′ʃvɪpst] *adj* tipsy, high
beschwö′ren *tr* swear to; (*Geister*) conjure up; (*bitten*) implore, entreat
Beschwö′rungsformel *f* incantation
beseelen [bə′zelən] *tr* inspire, animate
beseelt′ *adj* animated; (*von Hoffnungen*) filled; (*Spiel*) inspired
bese′hen §138 *tr* look at; inspect
beseitigen [bə′zaɪtɪgən] *tr* eliminate, remove, clear away; (*Übel, Fehler*) redress; (*Schwierigkeit*) overcome; (*töten*) do away with; (pol) purge
Besen [′bezən] *m* (-s;–) broom
Be′senstiel *m* broomstick
besessen [bə′zesən] *adj* (von) obsessed (by); (*vom Teufel*) possessed
Beses′senheit *f* (-;–en) obsession; (*vom Teufel*) possession
beset′zen *tr* occupy; (*mit Juwelen*) set off; (*Amt, Rolle*) fill; (*Hut*) trim
besetzt′ *adj* (*Platz, Abort*) occupied; (*Stelle*) filled; (*Kleid*) trimmed, set off; (telp) busy
Besetzt′zeichen *n* (telp) busy signal
Beset′zung *f* (-;–en) decoration; (*e–r Stelle*) filling; (mil) occupation; (theat) cast
besichtigen [bə′zɪçtɪgən] *tr* view; tour; inspect; (mil) inspect, review
Besich′tigung *f* (-;–en) sightseeing; inspection; (mil) inspection, review
besie′deln *tr* colonize; populate
besie′geln *tr* seal
besie′gen *tr* defeat; (*Widerstand*) overcome; (*Gefühle*) master
besin′nen §121 *ref* consider; think (of); **sich anders b.** change

one's mind; **sich e–s Besseren b.** think better of it

besinn'lich *adj* reflective

Besin'nung *f* (–;) consciousness; reflection; **j–n zur B. bringen** bring s.o. to his senses

besin'nungslos *adj* unconscious; (*unüberlegt*) senseless

Besitz' *m* (–es;–e) possession; **in B. nehmen** take possession of

bestiz'anzeigend *adj* possessive

besit'zen §144 *tr* own, possess

Besit'zer –in §6 *mf* possessor, owner

Besitz'ergreifung *f* (–;–en) occupancy; seizure

Besitz'stand *m* ownership; (fin) assets

Besitztum [bə'zɪtstum] *n* (–s;–er) possession

Besit'zung *f* (–;–en) possession, property; (*Landgut*) estate

besoffen [bə'zɔfən] *adj* (coll) soused

besohlen [bə'zolən] *tr* sole

besolden [bə'zɔldən] *tr* pay

Besol'dung *f* (–;–en) pay, salary

beson'dere §9 *adj* particular, special

Beson'derheit *f* (–;–en) peculiarity; (com) specialty

beson'ders *adv* especially; separately

besonnen [bə'zɔnən] *adj* prudent; (*bedacht*) considerate; level-headed

besor'gen *tr* take care of; (*beschaffen*) procure, get; (*befürchten*) fear

Besorgnis [bə'zɔrknɪs] *f* (–;–se) concern; (*Furcht*) fear

besorg'niserregend *adj* alarming

besorgt [bə'zɔrkt] *adj* (**um**) worried (about), anxious (for)

Besor'gung *f* (–;–en) care; procurement; (*Auftrag*) errand; **Besorgungen machen** run errands

bespre'chen §64 *tr* discuss; (*Buch*) review; **e–e Schallplatte b.** make a recording ‖ *ref* confer

Bespre'cher –in §6 *mf* reviewer, critic

bespren'gen *tr* sprinkle

besprit'zen *tr* splash; spray

besser ['bɛsər] *adj & adv* better

bessern ['bɛsərn] *tr* better, improve ‖ *ref* improve

Bes'serung *f* (–;–en) improvement; **baldige B.** speedy recovery

Bes'serungsanstalt *f* reform school

Bestand' *m* (–[e]s;–e) existence; (*Vorrat*) stock, inventory; (*Kassen–*) cash on hand; (*Baum–*) stand; **B. an** (*dat*) number of; **B. an kampffähigen Truppen** effective strength; **B. haben, von B. sein** have endurance, be lasting

bestän'dig *adj* constant, steady

Bestands'aufnahme *f* inventory

Bestand'teil *m* component; ingredient

bestär'ken *tr* strengthen, fortify

bestätigen [bə'ʃtetɪgən] *tr* confirm; (*Zeugnis*) corroborate; (*Empfang*) acknowledge; (*Vertrag*) ratify ‖ *ref* prove true, come true

bestatten [bə'ʃtatən] *tr* bury, inter

Bestat'tungsinstitut *n* funeral home

bestau'ben, bestäuben (bə'ʃtɔɪbən) *tr* cover with dust; sprinkle; (bot) pollinate

beste ['bɛstə] §9 *adj* best; **am besten**

best (of all); **auf dem besten Weg sein zu** be well on the way to; **aufs b.** in the best way; **der erste b.** anybody

beste'chen §64 *tr* bribe; (fig) impress

beste'chend *adj* fascinating, charming

bestech'lich *adj* open to bribery

Beste'chung *f* (–;) bribery

Beste'chungsgeld *n* bribe

Besteck [bə'ʃtɛk] *n* (–[e]s;–e) kit; (*Tisch–*) single service; (aer, naut) reckoning, position; (med) set of instruments

bestecken (bestek'ken) *tr* stick; (culin) garnish

beste'hen §146 *tr* undergo; (*Prüfung*) pass ‖ *intr* exist, be; (**gegen**) hold one's own (against); (*in e–r Prüfung*) pass; **b. auf** (*dat*) insist on; **b. aus** consist of; **b. in** (*dat*) consist in

beste'hend *adj* existing, extant; present

besteh'len §147 *tr* (**um**) rob (of)

bestei'gen §148 *tr* climb; (*Schiff*) board; (*Pferd*) mount; (*Thron*) ascend

Bestell'buch *n* order book

bestel'len *tr* order; (*Zimmer*) reserve; (*Zeitung*) subscribe to; (*ernennen*) appoint; (*Briefe*) deliver; (*Feld*) till; (*kommen lassen*) send for

Bestell'zettel *m* order slip

be'stenfalls *adv* at best

besteu'ern *tr* tax

bestialisch [bɛst'jɑlɪʃ] *adj* beastly

Bestie ['bɛstjə] *f* (–;–n) beast

bestim'men *tr* determine; (*Zeit, Preis*) set; (*ernennen*) appoint; (*Begriff*) define; (gram) modify; (math) find; **j–n b. zu** (or **für**) destine s.o. for; talk s.o. into ‖ *intr* decree; **b. in** (*dat*) have a say in; **b. über** (*acc*) dispose of

bestimmt' *adj* determined; definite; particular ‖ *adv* definitely

Bestim'mung *f* (–;–en) determination; (*e–r Zeit, e–s Preises*) setting; destination; mission, goal; (*e–s Begriffs*) definition; (*Schicksal*) fate; (*Vorschrift*) regulation; (*e–s Vertrags*) provision; (gram) modifier; **mit B. nach** (naut) heading for; **seiner B. übergeben** dedicate, open

bestra'fen *tr* punish

bestrah'len *tr* irradiate; (med) give radiation treatment to

bestre'ben *ref* strive, endeavor ‖ **Bestreben** *n* (–s;) tendency

Bestre'bung *f* (–;–en) effort

bestrei'chen §85 *tr* spread; (*mit Feuer*) rake; **mit Butter b.** butter

bestrei'ken *tr* strike

bestrei'ten §86 *tr* contest; fight; (*Ausgaben*) defray; (*Recht*) challenge; (*leugnen*) deny; **e–e Unterhaltung allein b.** do all the talking

bestreu'en *tr* (**mit**) strew (with)

bestricken (bestrik'ken) *tr* (fig) charm

bestücken [bə'ʃtʏkən] *tr* arm, equip

bestür'men *tr* storm; (fig) bombard

Bestür'mung *f* (–;–en) storming

bestür'zen *tr* dismay

Besuch [bə'zux] *m* (–[e]s;–e) visit; (*Besucher*) visitor(s), company;

(*genit*) visit (to); **auf B. gehen** pay a visit

besu′chen *tr* visit; (*Gasthaus, usw.*) frequent; (*Schule, Versammlung*) attend; (*Kino*) go to

Besu′cher **–in** §6 *mf* visitor, caller

Besuchs′zeit *f* visiting hours

besudeln *tr* soil, stain

betagt [bə'takt] *adj* advanced in years

beta′sten *tr* finger, touch, handle

betätigen [bə'tɛtɪgən] *tr* set in operation; (*Maschine*) operate; (*Bremse*) apply || *ref*—**sich nützlich b.** make oneself useful; **sich politisch b.** be active in politics

betäuben [bə'tɔɪbən] *tr* deafen; stun; (*Schmerz*) deaden; (*durch Rauschgift*) drug, dope; (*med*) anesthetize

Betäu′bungsmittel *n* drug; painkiller; (*med*) anesthetic

Bete ['betə] *f* (**–;–n**) beet

beteiligen [bə'taɪlɪgən] *tr* (**an** *dat*, **bei**) give (*s.o.*) a share (in) || *ref* (**an** *dat*) participate (in)

Betei′ligung *f* (**–;–en**) participation; (*Teilhaberschaft*) partnership; (*Teilnehmerzahl*) attendance

beten ['betən] *tr & intr* pray

beteuern [bə'tɔɪ·ərn] *tr* affirm

betiteln [bə'titəln] *tr* entitle

Beton [be'ton] *m* (**–s;**) concrete

betonen [bə'tonən] *tr* (*Silbe*) stress, accent; (*nachdrücklich*) emphasize

betonieren [bəto'nirən] *tr* cement

Betonmisch′maschine *f* cement mixer

betören [bə'tørən] *tr* infatuate

Betracht′ *m* (**–[e]s;**) consideration; **außer B. lassen** rule out; **es kommt nicht in B.** it is out of the question; **in B. ziehen** take into account, consider

betrachten [bə'traxtən] *tr* look at; consider

beträchtlich [bə'trɛçtlɪç] *adj* considerable

Betrach′tung *f* (**–;–en**) observation; consideration; meditation; **Betrachtungen anstellen über** (*acc*) reflect on

Betrag [bə'trak] *m* (**–[e]s;̈e**) amount; **über den B. von** in the amount of

betra′gen §132 *tr* amount to || *ref* behave || **Betragen** *n* (**–s;**) behavior

betrau′en *tr* entrust

betrau′ern *tr* mourn for

Betreff [bə'trɛf] *m* (**–[e]s;**) (*am Briefanfang*) re; **in B.** (*genit*) in regard to

betref′fen §151 *tr* befall; (*berühren*) affect, hit; (*angehen*) concern; **betrifft** (*acc*) re; **was das betrifft** as far that is concerned; **was mich betrifft** I for one

betreffs [bə'trɛfs] *prep* (*genit*) concerning

betrei′ben §62 *tr* carry on; (*leiten*) manage; (*Beruf*) practice; (*Studien*) pursue; (*Maschine*) operate

betre′ten *adj* embarrassed || §152 *tr* step on; set foot on or in; (*Raum*) enter; (*unbefugt*) trespass on

betreuen [bə'trɔɪ·ən] *tr* look after

Betrieb [bə'trip] *m* (**–s;–e**) operation,

running; (*Unternehmen*) business; (*Anlage*) plant; (*Werkstatt*) workshop; (*fig*) rush, bustle; **aus dem B. ziehen** take out of service; **außer B.** out of order; **großer B.** hustle and bustle; **in vollem B.** in full swing

betriebsam [bə'tripzam] *adj* enterprising, active

Betrieb′samkeit *f* (**–;**) hustle

betriebs′fähig *adj* in working order

betriebs′fertig *adj* ready for use

Betriebs′ingenieur *m* production engineer

Betriebs′kosten *pl* operating costs

Betriebs′leiter *m* superintendent

Betriebs′material *n* (**rr**) rolling stock

Betriebs′prüfer **–in** §6 *mf* auditor

Betriebs′ruhe *f*—**heute B.** (public sign) closed today

Betriebs′stoff *m* fuel

Betriebs′störung *f* breakdown

Betriebs′wirtschaft *f* industrial management

betrin′ken §143 *ref* get drunk

betroffen [bə'trɔfən] *adj* shocked, stunned; (*heimgesucht*) afflicted

betrü′ben *tr* sadden, distress

betrüb′lich *adj* sad, distressing

betrübt [bə'trypt] *adj* sad, sorrowful

Betrug [bə'truk] *m* (**–[e]s;**) fraud, swindle; **frommer B.** white lie

betrü′gen §111 *tr* cheat, swindle

Betrügerei [bətrygə'raɪ] *f* (**–;–en**) deceit, cheating

betrü′gerisch *adj* deceitful; fraudulent

betrunken [bə'trʊŋkən] *adj* drunk

Bett [bɛt] *n* (**–[e]s;–en**) bed

Bett′decke *f* bedspread

Bettelei [bɛtə'laɪ] *f* (**–;**) begging

betteln ['bɛtəln] *intr* (**um**) beg (for)

betten ['bɛtən] *tr* put to bed || *ref* make onself a bed; bed down

Bett′genosse *m* bedfellow

Bett′gestell *n* bedstead

Bett′himmel *m* canopy (*over a bed*)

bettlägerig ['bɛtlegərɪç] *adj* bedridden

Bett′laken *n* bed sheet

Bettler **–in** ['bɛtlər(ɪn)] §6 *mf* beggar

Bett′stelle *f* bedstead

Bettuch (**Bett′tuch**) *n* sheet

Bet′tung *f* (**–;**) bedding; (*mil*) emplacement; (**rr**) bed

Bett′vorleger *m* bedside rug

Bett′wäsche *f* bed linen

Bett′zeug *n* bedding

betupfen [bə'tʊpfən] *tr* dab (at); (*surg*) swab

beugen ['bɔɪgən] *tr* bend; (*fig*) humble; (*gram*) inflect || *ref* bend; bow

Beu′gung *f* (**–;–en**) bending; bowing; (*gram*) inflection

Beule ['bɔɪlə] *f* (**–;–n**) lump; (*Geschwür*) boil; (*kleiner Blechschaden*) dent

beunruhigen [bə'ʊnru·ɪgən] *tr* make uneasy, worry, disturb

Beun′ruhigung *f* (**–;–en**) anxiety, uneasiness; disturbance

beurkunden [bə'urkʊndən] *tr* authenticate

beurlauben [bə'urlaʊbən] *tr* grant leave of absence to; (*vom Amt*) suspend; (*mil*) furlough; **sich b. lassen**

ask for time off ‖ *ref* **(bei)** take one's leave (of)
beur'teilen *tr* evaluate; **(nach)** judge (by); **falsch b.** misjudge
Beute ['bɔɪtə] *f* (-;) booty, loot; **zur B. fallen** (*dat*) fall prey to
Beutel ['bɔɪtəl] *m* (-s;-) bag, pouch; purse; (billiards) pocket
beu'telig *adj* baggy
Beu'tezug *m* raid
bevölkern [be'fœlkərn] *tr* populate
Bevöl'kerung *f* (-;-en) population
bevollmächtigen [be'fɔlmɛçtɪgən] *tr* authorize; (jur) give (*s.o.*) power of attorney
Bevoll'mächtigte §5 *mf* authorized agent; proxy; (pol) plenipotentiary
bevor [bə'for] *conj* before; **bevor . . . nicht** until
bevormunden [be'formundən] *tr* treat in a patronizing manner
bevor'raten *tr* stock; stockpile
bevorrechtet [bə'fɔrrɛçtət] *adj* privileged
bevor'stehen §146 *intr* be imminent, be on hand; **bevorstehend** forthcoming; **j-m b.** be in store for s.o.
bevorzugen [bə'fortsugən] *tr* prefer
bevor'zugt *adj* preferential; high-priority; privileged; favorite
bewa'chen *tr* guard, watch over
bewach'sen §155 *tr* overgrow, cover
Bewa'chung *f* (-;-en) guard, custody
bewaff'nen *tr* arm
Bewaff'nung *f* (-;) armament, arms
Bewahr'anstalt *f* detention home
bewah'ren *tr* keep, preserve; **(vor** *dat***)** save (from), protect (against)
bewäh'ren *tr* prove ‖ *ref* prove one's worth; **sich nicht b.** prove a failure
Bewah'rer –in §6 *mf* keeper
bewahrheiten [bə'varhaɪtən] *tr* verify ‖ *ref* come true
bewährt [bə'vert] *adj* tried, trustworthy
Bewah'rung *f* (-;) preservation
Bewäh'rung *f* (-;-en) testing, trial; (jur) probation
Bewäh'rungsfrist *f* (jur) probation; **j-m B. zubilligen** put s.o. on probation
Bewäh'rungsprobe *f* test
bewaldet [bə'valdət] *adj* woody
bewältigen [bə'vɛltɪgən] *tr* (*Hindernis*) overcome; (*Lehrstoff*) master
bewandert [bə'vandərt] *adj* experienced
Bewandtnis [bə'vantnɪs] *f* (-;) circumstances, situation
bewäs'sern *tr* water, irrigate
bewegen [bə'vegən] *tr* move, stir ‖ *ref* move, stir; (*von der Stelle*) budge; (*Temperatur*) vary; (*exerzieren*) take exercise; (astr) revolve ‖ §56 *tr* prompt, induce
Beweg'grund *m* motive; incentive
beweg'lich *adj* movable; (*behend*) agile; (*Geist*) versatile; (*Zunge*) glib
Beweg'lichkeit *f* (-;) mobility; agility; versatility
bewegt [bə'vekt] *adj* agitated; (*ergreifend*) stirring; (*Stimme*) trembling; (*Unterhaltung*) lively; (*Leben*) eventful; (*unruhig*) turbulent
Bewe'gung *f* (-;-en) movement; mo-

tion; move; (*Gebärde*) gesture; (fig) emotion; **in B. setzen** set in motion
Bewe'gungsfreiheit *f* room to move; (fig) leeway, freedom of action
bewe'gungslos *adj* motionless
beweh'ren *tr* arm; (*Beton*) reinforce
beweihräuchern [bə'vaɪrɔɪçərn] *tr* (fig) flatter; (eccl) incense
bewei'nen *tr* mourn, shed tears over
Beweis [bə'vaɪs] *m* (-es;-e) **(für)** proof (of), evidence (of)
beweisen [be'vaɪzən] §118 *tr* prove, demonstrate; (*bestätigen*) substantiate
Beweis'führung *f* argumentation
Beweis'grund *m* argument
Beweis'kraft *f* cogency, force
beweis'kräftig *adj* convincing
Beweis'last *f* burden of proof
Beweis'stück *n* exhibit
bewen'den *intr*—**es dabei b. lassen** leave it at that ‖ **Bewenden** *n*—**damit hat es sein B.** there the matter rests
bewer'ben §149 *ref*—**sich b. um** apply for; (*kandidieren*) run for; (*Vertrag*) bid for; (*Preis*) compete for; (*Frau*) court
Bewer'ber –in §6 *mf* applicant; candidate; bidder; competitor ‖ *m* suitor
Bewer'bungsformular *n* application form
Bewer'bungsschreiben *n* written application
bewer'fen §160 *tr* pelt; (*Mauer*) plaster
bewerkstelligen [bə'verk/tɛlɪgən] *tr* manage, bring off
bewer'ten *tr* **(auf** *acc***)** value (at), appraise (at); **b. mit fünf Punkten** give five points to (*e.g., a performance*); **zu hoch b.** overrate
Bewer'tung *f* (-;-en) valuation
bewilligen [bə'vɪlɪgən] *tr* approve, grant
Bewil'ligung *f* (-;-en) approval; permit
bewillkommnen [bə'vɪlkɔmnən] *tr* welcome
bewir'ken *tr* cause, occasion, effect
bewir'ten *tr* entertain
bewirt'schaften *tr* (*Acker*) cultivate; (*Betrieb*) manage; (*Mangelware*) ration
Bewir'tung *f* (-;) hospitality
bewitzeln [bə'vɪtsəln] *tr* poke fun at
bewog [bə'vok] *pret* of **bewegen**
bewogen [bə'vogən] *pp* of **bewegen**
bewoh'nen *tr* inhabit, occupy
Bewoh'ner –in §6 *mf* (*e-s Landes*) inhabitant; (*e-s Hauses*) occupant
bewölken [bə'vœlkən] *tr* cloud ‖ *ref* cloud over, get cloudy
bewölkt' *adj* cloudy, overcast
Bewöl'kung *f* (-;) clouds
bewun'dern *tr* admire
bewun'dernswert, bewun'dernswürdig *adj* admirable
bewußt [bə'vust] *adj* conscious; **die bewußte Sache** the matter in question
bewußt'los *adj* unconscious
Bewußt'sein *n* consciousness; **bei B. sein** be conscious
Bewußt'seinsspaltung *f* schizophrenia
bezah'len *tr* pay; (*Gekauftes*) pay for

Bezah'lung _f_ (-;-en) payment; (_Lohn_) pay

bezäh'men _tr_ tame; (fig) control

bezau'bern _tr_ bewitch; (fig) fascinate

bezeich'nen _tr_ (_zeichnen_) mark; (_bedeuten_) signify; (_benennen_) designate; (_kennzeichnen_) characterize; (_zeigen_) point out

bezeich'nend _adj_ characteristic

Bezeich'nung _f_ (-;-en) marking, mark; (_Name_) name; (_Ausdruck_) term

bezei'gen _tr_ show, manifest, express

bezeu'gen _tr_ attest; (jur) testify to

bezichtigen [bə'tsɪçtɪgən] _tr_ accuse

bezieh'bar _adj_ (_Ware_) obtainable; (_Wohnung_) ready for occupancy; (_auf_ _acc_) referable (to)

bezie'hen §163 _tr_ (_Polstermöbel_) cover; (_Wohnung_) move into; (_Universität_) go to; (_geliefert bekommen_) get; (_Gehalt_) draw; (_auf_ _acc_) relate (to), refer (to); **das Bett frisch b.** change the bed linens; **die Stellung b.** (mil) occupy the position; **die Wache b.** (mil) go on guard duty || _ref_ become overcast; **sich auf j-n b.** use s.o.'s name as a reference

Bezie'hung _f_ (-;-en) relation, connection, respect; **in B. auf** (_acc_) in respect to; **in guten Beziehungen stehen zu** be on good terms with

bezie'hungslos _adj_ unrelated; irrelevant

Bezie'hungssatz _m_ relative clause

bezie'hungsweise _adv_ respectively

Bezie'hungswort _n_ [-[e]s; ̈-er) (gram) antecedent

beziffern [bə'tsɪfərn] _tr_ (**auf** _acc_) estimate (at) || _ref_—**sich b. auf** (_acc_) amount to, number

Bezirk [bə'tsɪrk] _m_ (-s;-e) district, ward, precinct; (_Bereich_) sphere

Bezug' _m_ (-[e]s; ̈-e) cover, case; (_von_ _Waren_) purchase; (_von Zeitungen_) subscription; (_Auftrag_) order; **Bezüge** earnings; **B. nehmen auf** (_acc_) refer to; **in B. auf** (_acc_) in reference to

bezüglich [bə'tsyklɪç] _adj_ (**auf** _acc_) relative (to); **bezügliches Fürwort** relative pronoun || _prep_ (_genit_) concerning, as to, with regard to

Bezugnahme [bə'tsuknɑmə] _f_—**unter B. auf** (_acc_) with reference to

Bezugs'anweisung _f_ delivery order

bezugs'berechtigt _adj_ entitled to receive || **Bezugsberechtigte** §5 _mf_ (ins) beneficiary

bezwecken [bə'tsvɛkən] _tr_ aim at, have in mind; (**mit**) intend (by)

bezwei'feln _tr_ doubt, question

bezwin'gen §142 _tr_ conquer; (fig) control, master

Bibel ['bibəl] _f_ (-;-n) Bible

Bi'belforscher -in §6 _mf_ Jehovah's Witness

Biber ['bibər] _m_ (-s;-) beaver

Bibliothek [bɪblɪ·ɔ'tek] _f_ (-;-en) library

Bibliothekar -in [bɪblɪ·ɔte'kar(ɪn)] §8 _mf_ librarian

biblisch ['biblɪʃ] _adj_ biblical

bieder ['bidər] _adj_ honest; (_leichtgläubig_) gullible

Bie'dermann _m_ (-[e]s; ̈-er) honest man

biegen ['bigən] §57 _tr_ bend; (gram) inflect || _ref_—**sich vor Lachen b.** double up with laughter || _intr_ (SEIN) bend; **um die Ecke b.** go around the corner

biegsam ['bikzɑm] _adj_ flexible

Bie'gung _f_ (-;-en) bend, bending; (gram) inflection

Biene ['binə] _f_ (-;-n) bee

Bie'nenfleiß _m_—**mit B. arbeiten** work like a bee

Bie'nenhaus _n_ beehive

Bie'nenkorb _m_ beehive

Bie'nenstich _m_ bee sting; (culin) almond pastry

Bie'nenstock _m_ beehive

Bie'nenzucht _f_ beekeeping

Bier [bir] _n_ (-[e]s;-e) beer

bie'ten ['bitən] §58 _tr_ offer; **b. auf** (_acc_) bid for || _ref_ present itself; **das läßt er sich nicht b.** he won't stand for it

Bigamie [bɪga'mi] _f_ (-;) bigamy

bigott [bɪ'gɔt] _adj_ bigoted

Bigotterie [bɪgɔtə'ri] _f_ (-;) bigotry

Bilanz [bɪ'lants] _f_ (_acct_) balance; (acct) balance sheet

Bilanz'abteilung _f_ auditing department

bilanzieren [bɪlan'tsirən] _intr_ balance

Bild [bɪlt] _n_ (-es;-er) picture; image; (_Bildnis_) portrait; (_in e-m Buch_) illustration; (_Vorstellung_) idea; (rhet) metaphor, figure of speech; **im Bilde sein** be in the know

Bild'band _m_ (-[e]s; ̈-e) picture book || _n_ (-[e]s; ̈-er) (telv) video tape

Bild'bandgerät _n_ video tape recorder

Bild'betrachter _m_ slide viewer

Bildchen ['bɪltçən] _n_ (-s;-) small picture; (cin) frame

Bild'einstellung _f_ (-;-en) focusing

bilden ['bɪldən] _tr_ form, fashion, create; (_entwerfen_) design; (_gründen_) establish; (_Geist_) educate, develop; (_Gruppe_) constitute || _ref_ form, be produced; develop; educate oneself

bil'dend _adj_ instructive; **bildende Künste** fine arts, plastic arts

bil'derreich _adj_ (_Buch_) richly illustrated; (_Sprache_) picturesque, ornate

Bil'derschrift _f_ picture writing

Bil'dersprache _f_ imagery

Bil'derstürmer _m_ iconoclast

Bild'frequenz _f_ camera speed

Bild'funk _m_ television

bild'haft _adj_ pictorial; graphic

Bildhauer ['bɪlthaʊ·ər] _m_ (-s;-) sculptor

Bildhauerei ['bɪlthaʊ·əraɪ] _f_ (-;) sculpture

Bildhauerin ['bɪlthaʊ·ərɪn] _f_ (-;-nen) sculptress

bild'hübsch _adj_ pretty as a picture

Bild'karte _f_ photographic map; (cards) face card

bild'lich _adj_ pictorial; figurative

Bildner -in ['bɪldnər(ɪn)] §6 _mf_ sculptor || _m_ (fig) molder || _f_ sculptress

Bildnis ['bɪltnɪs] _n_ (-ses;-se) portrait

Bild'röhre _f_ picture tube, TV tube

bildsam ['bɪltzɑm] _adj_ plastic; (fig) pliant

Bild'säule f statue
Bild'schirm m television screen
bild'schön adj very beautiful
Bild'schriftzeichen n hieroglyph
Bild'seite f head, obverse
Bild'signal n video signal
Bild'stock m wayside shrine
Bild'streifen m filmstrip; (journ) comic strip
Bild'sucher m (phot) viewfinder
Bild'teppich m tapestry
Bild'ton'kamera f sound-film camera
Bil'dung f (-;-en) formation; shape; education, culture
Bil'dungsanstalt f educational institution
Bild'werfer m projector
Bild'werk n sculpture; imagery
Billard ['bɪljart] n (-s;) billiards
Bil'lardkugel f billiard ball
Bil'lardloch n pocket
Bil'lardstab, Bil'lardstock m cue
Billett [bɪl'jɛt] m (-s;-e) ticket
Billett'ausgabe f, **Billett'schalter** m ticket office; (theat) box office
billig ['bɪlɪç] adj cheap; (Preis) low; (Ausrede, Trost) poor
billigen ['bɪlɪgən] tr approve
Bil'ligung f (-;) approval
Billion [bɪl'jon] f (-;-en) trillion; (Brit) billion
bimbam ['bɪm'bam] interj ding-dong || **Bimbam** m—heiliger B.! holy smokes!
bimmeln ['bɪməln] intr (coll) jingle; (telp) ring
Bimsstein ['bɪms/taɪn] m (-s;-e) pumice stone
Binde ['bɪndə] f (-;-n) band; (Krawatte) tie; (Armschlinge) sling; (für Frauen) sanitary napkin; (med) bandage
Bin'deglied n link; (fig) bond, tie
binden ['bɪndən] §59 tr bind, tie
Bin'destrich m hyphen; **mit B. schreiben** hyphenate
Bin'dewort n (-[e]s;-er) conjunction
Bind'faden m string, twine; **es regnet Bindfäden** it's raining cats and dogs
Bin'dung f (-;-en) binding; tie, bond; obligation; (mus) ligature
binnen ['bɪnən] prep (genit & dat) within; **b. kurzem** before long
Binnen- comb.fm. inner; internal; inland; domestic, home
Bin'nengewässer n inland water
Bin'nenhandel m domestic trade
Bin'nenland n inland; interior; **im B.** inland
Binse ['bɪnzə] f (-;-n) rush, reed; **in die Binsen gehen** (coll) go to pot
Bin'senwahrheit f truism
Biochemie [bi·oçe'mi] f (-;) biochemistry
Biogra·phie [bi·ogra'fi] (-;-phien ['fi·ən] biography
biographisch [bi·o'grafɪ/] adj biographic(al)
Biologie [bi·olo'gi] f (-;) biology
biologisch [bi·o'logɪ/] adj biological
Biophysik [bi·ofy'zik] f (-;) biophysics
Birke ['bɪrkə] f (-;-n) birch
Birma ['bɪrma] n (-s;) Burma

Birne ['bɪrnə] f (-;-n) pear; (elec) bulb; (Kopf) (sl) bean
bis [bɪs] prep (acc) (zeitlich) till, until; (örtlich) up to, to; **bis an** (acc) up to; **bis auf** (acc) except for; **bis nach** as far as || conj until, till
Bisamratte ['bizamratə] f (-;-n) muskrat
Bischof ['bɪ/ɔf] m (-;-e) bishop
bischöflich ['bɪ/øflɪç] adj episcopal
Bi'schofsamt n episcopate
Bi'schofsmütze f miter
Bi'schofssitz m episcopal see
Bi'schofsstab m crosier
bisher [bɪs'her] adv till now
bisherig [bɪs'herɪç] adj former, previous; (Präsident) outgoing
Biskuit [bɪs'kvit] m & n (-[e]s;-e) biscuit
bislang' adv till now
biß [bɪs] pret of **beißen** || **Biß** m (Bisses; Bisse) bite; sting
bißchen ['bɪsçən] n (also used as invar adj & adv) bit, little bit
Bissen ['bɪsən] m (-s;-) bit, morsel
bissig ['bɪsɪç] adj biting, snappish
Bistum ['bɪstum] n (-s;-er) bishopric
bisweilen [bɪs'vaɪlən] adv sometimes
Bitte ['bɪtə] f (-;-n) request; **e-e B. einlegen bei** intercede with
bitten ['bɪtən] §60 tr ask || intr **b. für** intercede for; **b. um** ask for; **wie bitte?** I beg your pardon? || interj please!; you are welcome!
bitter ['bɪtər] adj bitter
bit'terböse adj (coll) furious
Bit'terkeit f (-;) bitterness
bit'terlich adv bitterly; deeply
Bit'tersalz n Epsom salts
Bittgang ['bɪtgaŋ] m (-[e]s;-e) (eccl) procession
Bittsteller ['bɪt/tɛlər] m (-s;-) petitioner, suppliant
Biwak ['bivak] n (-s;-s) bivouac
biwakieren [biva'kirən] intr bivouac
bizarr [bi'tsar] adj bizarre
blähen ['ble·ən] tr inflate, distend || ref swell || intr cause gas
blaken ['blakən] intr smolder
Blamage [bla'maʒə] f (-;-n) disgrace
blamieren [bla'mirən] tr embarrass || ref make a fool of oneself
blank [blaŋk] adj bright; (Schuh) shiny; (bloß) bare; (Schwert) drawn; (sl) broke; **blanke Waffe** side arms; **b. ziehen** draw one's sword
Blankett [blaŋ'kɛt] n (-s;-e) blank
blanko ['blaŋko] adv—**b. lassen** leave blank; **b. verkaufen** sell short
Blan'koscheck m blank check
Blan'kovollmacht f blanket authority
Blank'vers m blank verse
Bläschen ['blɛsçən] n (-s;-) small blister; small bubble
Blase ['blazə] f (-;-n) blister; bubble; (coll) gang; (anat) bladder; **Blasen werfen** (Farbe) blister; **Blasen ziehen** (Haut) blister
Bla'sebalg m pair of bellows
blasen ['blazən] tr blow; (Instrument) play || intr blow
Bla'senleiden n bladder trouble
Bläser ['blezər] m (-s;-) blower

blasiert [bla'zirt] *adj* blasé
blasig ['blɑzɪç] *adj* blistery; bubbly
Blas'instrument *n* wind instrument
Blasphe•mie [blasfe'mi] *f* (–;–mien ['mi•ən]) blasphemy
blasphemieren [blasfe'mirən] *intr* blaspheme
Blas'rohr *n* blowpipe; peashooter
blaß [blas] *adj* pale; keine blasse Ahnung not the foggiest notion
Blässe ['blɛsə] *f* (–;) paleness, pallor
Blatt [blat] *n* (–s;–er) leaf; (*Papier–*) sheet; (*Gras–*) blade
Blatter ['blatər] *f* (–;–n) pustule; die Blattern smallpox
blätterig ['blɛtərɪç] *adj* leafy; scaly
blättern ['blɛtərn] *intr*—in e–m Buch b. page through a book
Blat'ternarbe *f* pockmark
Blät'terwerk *n* foliage
Blatt'gold *n* gold leaf, gold foil
Blatt'laus *f* aphid
Blatt'pflanze *f* house plant
blättrig ['blɛtrɪç] *adj var* of blätterig
Blatt'zinn *n* tin foil
blau [blau] *adj* (& *fig*) blue; (coll) drunk; blaues Auge black eye; keinen blauen Dunst haben (coll) not have the foggiest notion; mit e–m blauen Auge davonkommen (coll) get off easy ‖ Blau *n* (–s;–s) blue; blueness
blau'äugig *adj* blue-eyed
Blau'beere *f* blueberry
Bläue ['blɔɪ•ə] *f* (–;) blue; blueness
bläuen ['blɔɪ•ən] *tr* dye blue
bläulich ['blɔɪlɪç] *adj* bluish
blau'machen *intr* (coll) take off from work
Blech [blɛç] *n* (–[e]s;–e) sheet metal; (sl) baloney; (mus) brass
Blech'büchse *f* tin can
blechen ['blɛçən] *tr* (coll) pay out ‖ *intr* (coll) cough up the dough
Blech'instrument *n* brass instrument
blecken ['blɛkən] *tr*—die Zähnen b. bare one's teeth
Blei [blaɪ] *n* (–[e]s;) lead
Bleibe ['blaɪbə] *f* (–;–n) place to stay
bleiben ['blaɪbən] §62 *intr* (SEIN) remain, stay; am Leben b. survive; bei etw b. stick to s.th.; dabei bleibt es! that's final!; für sich b. keep to oneself; sich [dat] gleich b. never change; und wo bleibe ich? (coll) and where do I come in?
blei'bend *adj* lasting, permanent
bleich [blaɪç] *adj* pale ‖ Bleiche *f* (–;) bleaching; paleness
blei'chen *tr* bleach; make pale ‖ *intr* (SEIN) bleach; (*verblassen*) fade
Bleich'gesicht *n* paleface
Bleich'mittel *n* bleach
bleiern ['blaɪ•ərn] *adj* leaden
Blei'soldat *m* tin soldier
Blei'stift *m* pencil
Bleistiftspitzer ['blaɪʃtɪft/pɪtsər] *m* (–s;–) pencil sharpener
Blende ['blɛndə] *f* (–;–n) window blind; shutter; (phot) diaphragm
blen'den *tr* blind; (*bezaubern*) dazzle
blen'dend *adj* fabulous
Blen'der *m* (–s;–) (coll) fourflusher

Blendling ['blɛntlɪŋ] *m* (–s;–e) (*Mischling*) mongrel; (bot) hybrid
Blick [blɪk] *m* (–[e]s;–e) glance, look; (auf *acc*) view (of)
blicken (blik'ken) *intr* (auf *acc*, nach) glance (at), look (at); sich b. lassen show one's face
Blick'fang *m* (coll) eye catcher
blieb [blip] *pret* of bleiben
blies [blis] *pret* of blasen
blind [blɪnt] *adj* (für, gegen) blind (to); (*Spiegel*) clouded; (*trübe*) dull; (*Alarm*) false; (*Patrone*) blank; blinder Passagier stowaway
Blind'band *m* (–[e]s;–e) (typ) dummy
Blind'boden *m* subfloor
Blind'darm *m* appendix
Blind'darmentzündung *f* appendicitis
Blind'darmoperation *f* appendectomy
Blin'denheim *n* home for the blind
Blin'denhund *m* Seeing-Eye dog
Blin'denschrift *f* braille
Blind'flug *m* blind flying
Blind'gänger *m* (mil) dud
Blind'landung *f* instrument landing
blindlings ['blɪntlɪŋs] *adv* blindly
Blind'schreiben *n* touch typing
blinken ['blɪŋkən] *intr* blink, twinkle; (*Sonne*) shine; (mil) signal
Blin'ker *m*, Blink'licht *n* (aut) blinker
blinzeln ['blɪntsəln] *intr* blink, wink
Blitz [blɪts] *m* (–es;–e) lightning; (fig & phot) flash
Blitz'ableiter *m* lightning rod
blitz'blank' *adj* shining; spick and span
Blitz'krieg *m* blitzkrieg
Blitz'licht *n* (phot) flash
Blitz'lichtaufnahme *f* (phot) flash shot
Blitz'lichtbirne *f* (phot) flash bulb
Blitz'lichtgerät *n* flash gun
Blitz'lichtröhre *f* (phot) electronic flash, flash tube
Blitz'schlag *m* stroke of lightning
blitz'schnell' *adj* quick as lightning
Blitz'strahl *m* flash of lightning
Block [blɔk] *m* (–s;–e) block, log; (*Stück Seife*) cake; (*von Schokolade*) bar; (*von Löschpapier*) pad; (geol) boulder; (metal) ingot; (pol) bloc
Blockade [blɔ'kɑdə] *f* (–;–n) blockade
Blocka'debrecher *m* blockade runner
blocken (blok'ken) *tr* (sport) block
Block'haus *n* log cabin
blockieren [blɔ'kirən] *tr* block up; (mil) blockade
Block'kalender *m* tear-off calendar
Block'schrift *f* block letters
blöd(e) ['blød(ə)] *adj* stupid, idiotic; feeble-minded; (*schüchtern*) shy
Blöd'heit *f* (–;) stupidity, idiocy
Blö'digkeit *f* (–;) shyness
Blöd'sinn *m* idiocy; nonsense
blöd'sinnig *adj* idiotic ‖ *adv* idiotically; (*sehr*) (coll) awfully
blöken ['bløkən] *intr* bleat; (*Kuh*) moo
blond [blɔnt] *adj* blond, fair ‖ Blonde §5 *m* blond ‖ *f* blonde
blondieren [blɔn'dirən] *tr* bleach
Blondine [blɔn'dinə] *f* (–;–n) blonde
bloß [blos] *adj* bare; (*nichts als*) mere ‖ *adv* only; barely
Blöße ['bløsə] *f* bareness; nakedness; (fig) weak point

bloß'legen *tr* lay bare
bloß'stellen *tr* expose
blühen ['bly·ən] *intr* blossom, bloom; (*Backen*) be rosy; (fig) flourish
Blume ['blumə] *f* (-;-n) flower; (*des Weins*) bouquet; (*des Biers*) head
Blu'menbeet *n* flower bed
Blu'menblatt *n* petal
Blu'mengewinde *n* garland, festoon
Blu'menhändler –in §6 *mf* florist
Blu'menkelch *m* calyx
Blu'menkohl *m* cauliflower
Blu'menstaub *m* pollen
Blu'mentopf *m* flowerpot
Bluse ['bluzə] *f* (-;-n) blouse
Blut [blut] *n* (-[e]s;) blood; **bis aufs B.** almost to death; **B. lecken** taste blood; **heißes B.** hot temper
Blut'andrang *m* (pathol) congestion
blut'arm *adj* anemic
Blut'armut *f* anemia
Blut'bahn *f* bloodstream
Blut'bild *n* blood count
blut'dürstig *adj* bloodthirsty
Blüte ['blytə] *f* (-;-n) blossom, flower, bloom; (fig) prime
Blut'egel *m* leech
bluten ['blutən] *intr* bleed
Blü'tenblatt *n* petal
Blü'tenstaub *m* pollen
Blu'terguß *m* bruise
Blu'terkrankheit *f* hemophilia
Blü'tezeit *f* blooming period; (fig) heyday
Blut'farbstoff *m* hemoglobin
Blut'gerinnsel *n* blood clot
Blut'hund *m* bloodhound
blutig ['blutıç] *adj* bloody
blut'jung' *adj* very young, green
Blut'körperchen *n* corpuscle
Blut'kreislauf *m* blood circulation
blut'leer, blut'los *adj* bloodless
Blut'pfropfen *m* blood clot
Blut'probe *f* blood test
Blut'rache *f* blood feud
Blut'rausch *m* mania to kill
blutrünstig ['blutrynstıç] *adj* gory
Blut'sauger *m* bloodsucker, leech
Blut'schande *f* incest
blutschänderisch ['blutʃendərıʃ] *adj* incestuous
Blut'spender –in §6 *mf* blood donor
blut'stillend *adj* coagulant
Blut'sturz *m* hemorrhage
Bluts'verwandte §5 *mf* blood relation
Blut'übertragung *f* blood transfusion
blut'unterlaufen *adj* bloodshot
Blut'vergießen *n* (-s;) bloodshed
blut'voll *adj* lively, vivid
Blut'wasser *n* lymph
Blut'zeuge *m*, **Blut'zeugin** *f* martyr
Bö [bø] *f* (-;-en) gust, squall
Bob [bɔb] *m* (-s;-s) bobsled
Bock [bɔk] *m* (-[e]s; ̈e) buck; ram; he-goat; (*Kutsch*-) driver's seat; (tech) horse; **B. springen** play leapfrog; **e–n B. schießen** pull a boner
bockbeinig ['bɔkbaınıç] *adj* stubborn
bocken ['bɔkən] *intr* buck; (*sich aufbäumen*) rear; (*ausschlagen*) kick; (*brunsten*) be in heat; (aut) hesitate
bockig ['bɔkıç] *adj* thickheaded
Bock'sprung *m* caper; leapfrog

Boden ['bodən] *m* (-s; ̈) (*Erd*-) ground, soil; (*Meeres*-) bottom; (*Fuß*-) floor; (*Dach*-) attic; (*Trocken*-) loft; **B. fassen** get a firm footing; **zu B. drücken** crush
Bo'denertrag *m* (agr) yield
Bo'denfenster *n* dormer window
Bo'denfläche *f* floor space; (agr) acreage
Bo'denfliese *f* floor tile
Bodenfräse ['bodənfrezə] *f* (-;-n) Rotortiller
Bo'denhaftung *f* roadability
Bo'denkammer *f* attic
bo'denlos *adj* bottomless; (fig) unmitigated
Bo'denmannschaft *f* (aer) ground crew
Bo'denreform *f* agrarian reform
Bo'densatz *m* grounds, sediment
Bodenschätze ['bodən'ʃɛtsə] *pl* mineral resources
Bo'densee *m* (-s;) Lake Constance
bo'denständig *adj* native, indigenous
bog [bok] *pret* of **biegen**
Bogen ['bogən] *m* (-s; ̈) bow; (*Kurve*) curve; (*Papier*-) sheet; (*beim Schilaufen*) turn; (*beim Eislaufen*) circle; (archit) arch; (math) arc; **den B. raushaben** have the hang of it; **den B. überspannen** (fig) go too far; **e–n großen B. um j–n machen** give s.o. wide berth
Bo'genfenster *n* bow window
bo'genförmig *adj* arched
Bo'gengang *m* arcade; archway
Bo'genschießen *n* (-s;) archery
Bo'genschütze *m* archer
Bo'gensehne *f* bowstring
Bohle ['bolə] *f* (-;-n) plank
Böhme ['bømə] *m* (-n;-n) Bohemian
Böhmen ['bømən] *n* (-s;) Bohemia
Bohne ['bonə] *f* (-;-n) bean; **blaue Bohnen** bullets; **grüne Bohnen** string beans
Boh'nermasse *f* polish; floor polish
bohnern ['bonərn] *tr* wax, polish
Boh'nerwachs *n* floor wax
Bohr– [bor] *comb.fm.* drill, drilling, bore, boring
bohren ['borən] *tr* drill, bore
Bohrer *m* (-s;-) drill; (ent) borer
Bohr'insel *f* offshore drilling platform
Bohr'presse *f* drill press
Bohr'turm *m* derrick
böig ['bø·ıç] *adj* gusty; (aer) bumpy
Boje ['bojə] *f* (-;-n) buoy
Böller ['bœlər] *m* (-s;-) mortar
böllern ['bœlərn] *intr* fire a mortar
Bollwerk ['bɔlverk] *n* (-s;-e) bulwark
Bolzen ['bɔltsən] *m* (-s;-) bolt; dowel
Bombardement [bɔmbardə'mã] *n* (-s; -s) bombardment
bombardieren [bɔmbar'dirən] *tr* bombard
Bombe ['bɔmbə] *f* (-;-n) bomb, bombshell; (coll) smash hit
Bomben– *comb.fm.* bomb, bombing; huge
Bom'benabwurf *m* bombing; **gezielter B.** precision bombing
Bom'benerfolg *m* (theat) smash hit
bom'benfest *adj* bombproof
Bom'benflugzeug *m* bomber

Bom'bengeschäft n (coll) gold mine
Bom'benpunktzielwurf m precision bombing
Bom'benreihenwurf m stick bombing
Bom'bensache f (coll) humdinger
Bom'benschacht m bomb bay
Bom'benschütze m bombardier
Bom'bentrichter m bomb crater
Bom'benzielanflug m bombing run
Bom'benzielgerät n bombsight
Bon [bõ] m (-s;-s) sales slip; (*Gutschein*) credit note
Bonbon [bõ'bõ] m & n (-s;-s) piece of candy; **Bonbons** candy
Bonbonniere [bõbɔnɪ'ɛrə] f (-;-n) box of candy
Bonze ['bɔntsə] m (-;-n) (coll) big shot, bigwig; (pol) boss
Boot [bot] n (-[e]s;-e) boat
Boots'mann m (-es;-leute) boatswain; (nav) petty officer
Bord [bɔrt] m (-es;e) edge; bookshelf; (naut) board, side; **an B.** aboard, on board; **von B. gehen** leave the ship
Bordell [bɔr'dɛl] n (-s;-e) brothel
Bord'karte f boarding pass
Bord'schütze m aerial gunner
Bord'schwelle f curb
Bord'stein m curb
Bord'waffen pl (aer, mil) armament
Bord'wand f ship's side
Borg [bɔrk] m (-s;) borrowing; **auf B.** on credit; on loan
borgen ['bɔrgən] tr (**von, bei**) borrow (from); loan out, lend
Borke ['bɔrkə] f (-;-n) bark
Born [bɔrn] m (-es; -e) (poet) fountain
borniert [bɔr'nirt] adj narrow-minded
Borsäure ['bɔrzɔɪrə] f (-;) boric acid
Börse ['bœrzə] f (-;-n) purse; stock exchange
Bör'senkurs m market price; quotation
Bör'senmakler **-in** §6 mf stockbroker
Bör'senmarkt m stockmarket
Bör'sennotierung f (st.exch.) quotation
Bör'senpapiere pl stocks, shares, securities
Borste ['bɔrstə] f (-;-n) bristle
borstig ['bɔrstɪç] adj birstly; (fig) crusty
Borte ['bɔrtə] f (-;-n) trim; braid; (*Saum*) hem
bös [bøs] var of **böse**
bös'artig adj nasty; (*Tier*) vicious; (pathol) malignant
Böschung ['bœʃʊŋ] f (-;-en) slope; (*e-s Flusses*) bank; (rr) embankment
böse ['bøzə] adj bad, evil, nasty; angry || **Böse** §5 mf wicked person || m devil || n evil; harm
Bösewicht ['bøzəvɪçt] m (-s;-e) villain
boshaft ['boshaft] adj malicious; wicked; (*tückisch*) spiteful
bossieren [bɔ'sirən] tr emboss
bös'willig adj malicious, willful
bot [bot] pret of **bieten**
Botanik [bɔ'tanɪk] f (-;) botany
Botaniker **-in** §6 mf botanist
botanisch [bɔ'tanɪʃ] adj botanic(al)
Bote ['botə] m (-n;-n) messenger
Bo'tengang m errand
Botin ['botɪn] f (-;-nen) messenger

Bot'schaft f (-;-en) message, news; (*Amt*) embassy; (*Auftrag*) mission
Botschafter **-in** ['botʃaftər(ɪn)] §6 ambassador
Bottich ['bɔtɪç] m (-s;-e) tub; vat
Bouillon (bʊl'jõ] f (-;-s) bouillon
Bowle ['bolə] f (-;-n) punch
boxen ['bɔksən] tr & intr box
Bo'xer m (-s;-) boxer
Box'kampf m boxing match
Boykott [bɔɪ'kɔt] m (-s;-e) boycott
boykottieren [bɔɪkɔ'tirən] tr boycott
brach [brax] pret of **brechen** || adj fallow
brachte ['braxtə] pret of **bringen**
brackig ['brakɪç] adj brackish
Branche ['brãʃə] f (-;-n) line of business; (com) branch
Brand [brant] m (-[e]s;ː̈e) burning; fire; (coll) thirst; (agr) blight; (pathol) gangrene **in B. geraten** catch fire; **in B. setzen** (or **stecken**) set on fire
Brand'blase f blister
Brand'bombe f incendiary bomb ·
Brand'brief m urgent letter
Brand'direktor m fire chief
branden ['brandən] intr surge, break
Brand'fackel f firebrand
brandig ['brandɪç] adj (agr) blighted; (pathol) gangrenous
Brand'mal n brand; (fig) moral stigma
brand'marken tr stigmatize
Brand'mauer f fire wall
brandschatzen ['brantʃatsən] tr sack
Brand'stifter **-in** §6 mf arsonist
Bran'dung f (-;) breakers
Bran'dungswelle f breaker
Brand'wunde f burn
Brand'zeichen n brand
brannte ['brantə] pret of **brennen**
Branntwein ['brantvaɪn] m brandy
Brasilien [bra'ziljən] n (-s;) Brazil
Bratapfel ['bratapfəl] m baked apple
braten ['bratən] §63 tr & intr roast; (*im Ofen*) bake; (*auf dem Rost*) broil, grill; (*in der Pfanne*) fry || **Braten** m (-s;-) roast
Bra'tensoße f gravy
Brat'fisch m fried fish
Brat'huhn n broiler
Brat'kartoffeln pl fried potatoes
Brat'pfanne f frying pan, skillet
Bratsche ['bratʃə] f (-;-n) viola
Bräu [brɔɪ] m & n (-[e]s;-e) brew
Brauch [braux] m (-[e]s;ː̈e) custom
brauchbar ['brauxbar] adj useful
brauchen ['brauxən] tr need; (*Zeit*) take; (*gebrauchen*) use
Brauchtum ['brauxtum] n (-s;) tradition
Braue ['brau·ə] f (-;-n) eyebrow
brauen ['brau·ən] tr brew
Brau'er m (-s;-) brewer
Brauerei [brau·ə'raɪ] f (-;-en), **Brau'-haus** n brewery
braun [braun] adj brown; (*Pferd*) bay
Bräune ['brɔɪnə] f (-;) brown; sun tan; (pathol) diphtheria
bräunen ['brɔɪnən] tr tan; (culin) brown || ref & intr tan
bräunlich ['brɔɪnlɪç] adj brownish
Braus [braus] m (-es;) noise; revelry

Brause ['brauzə] f (-;-n) soda, soft drink; (*Duschbad*) shower; (*an Gieß-kannen*) nozzle
Brau'sebad n shower
Brau'sekopf m hothead
Brau'selimonade f soda, soft drink
brau'sen tr spray, water || intr bubble; (*toben*) roar || intr (SEIN) rush
Braut [braut] f (-;-̈e) fiancée; bride
Braut'ausstattung f trousseau
Braut'führer m usher
Bräutigam ['brɔɪtɪgam] m (-s;-e) fiancé; bridegroom
Braut'jungfer f (-;-n) bridesmaid; er-ste B. maid of honor
Braut'kleid n bridal gown
Braut'leute pl engaged couple
bräutlich ['brɔɪtlɪç] adj bridal; nuptial
Braut'schatz m dowry
Braut'werber **-in** §6 mf matchmaker
Braut'werbung f courting
Braut'zeit f period of engagement
Braut'zeuge m best man
brav [braf] adj well-mannered, good, honest
Brav'heit f good behavior
Bravour [bra'vur] f (-;) bravado
Brech'eisen n crowbar, jimmy
brechen ['breçən] §64 tr break; (*Papier*) fold; (*Steine*) quarry; (*Blumen*) pick; (coll) vomit; (opt) refract; **die Ehe b.** commit adultery || ref break; (opt) be refracted || intr (SEIN) break; (coll) vomit
Brech'reiz m nausea
Brech'stange f crowbar
Bre'chung f (-;-en) (opt) refraction
Brei [braɪ] m (-s;-e) paste; pap, gruel; **zu B. schlagen** beat to a pulp
breit [braɪt] adj broad, wide
breitbeinig ['braɪtbaɪnɪç] adv with legs outspread
breit'drücken tr flatten (out)
Brei'te f (-;-n) width; latitude
Brei'tengrad m degree of latitude
breit'machen ref take up (too much) room; (fig) throw one's weight around
breit'schlagen §132 tr (coll) persuade
breitschulterig ['braɪtʃultərɪç] adj broad-shouldered
breitspurig ['braɪtʃpurɪç] adj (coll) pompous; (rr) broad-gauge
breit'treten §152 tr belabor
Breit'wand f (cin) wide screen
Bremsbelag ['bremsbəlak] m brake lining
Bremse ['bremzə] f (-;-n) brake; (ent) horsefly
bremsen ['bremzən] tr brake; (fig) curb; (atom phys) slow down || intr brake
Brem'ser m (-s;-) brakeman
Brems'flüssigkeit f brake fluid
Brems'fußhebel m brake pedal
Brems'klotz m wheel chock
Bremsleuchte ['bremslɔɪçtə] f, **Brems'-licht** n (aut) brake light
Brems'rakete f (rok) retrorocket
Brems'schuh m brake shoe
brems'sicher adj skidproof
Brems'spur f skid mark
Brems'wagen m (rr) caboose

Brems'weg m braking distance
Brennapparat ['brenaparat] m still
brennbar ['brenbar] adj inflammable, combustible
brennen §97 tr burn; (*Branntwein*) distil; (*Kaffee*) roast; (*Haar*) curl; (*Ziegel*) fire || intr burn; smart
Bren'ner m (-s;-) burner; distiller
Brennerei [brenə'raɪ] f (-;-en) distillery
Brenn'holz n firewood
Brenn'material n fuel
Brenn'ofen m kiln
Brenn'punkt m focus; **im B. stehen** be the focal point
Brenn'schere f curler
Brenn'schluß m (rok) burnout
Brenn'spiegel m concave mirror
Brenn'stoff m fuel
brenzlig ['brentslɪç] adj (*Geruch*) burnt; (*Situation*) precarious
Bresche ['breʃə] f (-;-n) breach; e-e B. schlagen make a breach
Brett [bret] n (-[e]s;-er) board; plank; (*für Bücher, Geschirr*) shelf; **Bretter** (coll) skis; (theat) stage; **Schwarzes B.** bulletin board
Bret'terbude f shack
Bret'terverschlag m wooden partition
Brett'säge f ripsaw
Brezel ['bretsəl] f (-;-n) pretzel
Brief [brif] m (-[e]s;-e) letter; **Briefe wechseln** correspond
Brief'ausgabe f mail delivery
Briefbeschwerer ['brifbəʃverər] m (-s;-) paperweight
Brief'bestellung f mail delivery
Brief'beutel m mail bag
Brief'bogen m piece of notepaper
Brief'bote m mailman, postman
Briefchen ['brifçən] n (-s;-) note; **B. Streichhölzer** book of matches
Brief'einwurf m slot in a mailbox; letterdrop; mailbox
Brief'fach n pigeonhole; post-office box
Brief'freund **-in** §8 mf pen pal
Brief'hülle f envelope
Brief'kasten m mailbox
Brief'klammer f paper clip
Brief'kopf m letterhead
Brief'kurs m (st.exch.) selling price
brief'lich adj written; **brieflicher Verkehr** correspondence || adv by letter
Brief'mappe f folder
Brief'marke f postage stamp
Brief'markenautomat m stamp machine
Brief'ordner m ring binder
Brief'papier n stationery; note paper
Brief'porto n postage
Brief'post f first-class mail
Brief'schaften pl correspondence
Brief'stempel m postmark
Brief'tasche f billfold, wallet
Brief'taube f carrier pigeon
Brief'träger m mailman, postman
Brief'umschlag m envelope
Brief'verkehr m correspondence
Brief'waage f postage scales
Brief'wahl f absentee ballot
Brief'wechsel m correspondence
brief [brit] pret of **braten**

Brigade [brɪ'gɑdə] *f* (-;-n) brigade
Briga'degeneral *m* brigadier general; (Brit) brigadier
Brikett [brɪ'kɛt] *n* (-[e]s;-s) briquette
brillant [brɪl'jant] *adj* brilliant || **Brillant** *m* (-en;-en) precious stone (esp. diamond)
Brille ['brɪlə] *f* (-;-n) eyeglasses; (*für Pferde*) blinkers; (*Toilettenring*) toilet seat; **B. mit doppeltem Brennpunkt** bifocals
Bril'lenbügel *m* sidepiece (*of glasses*)
Bril'lenfassung *f* eyeglass frame
Bril'lenschlange *f* cobra
bringen ['brɪŋən] §65 *tr* bring, take; **an sich b.** acquire; **es mit sich b., daß** bring it about that; **es zu etw b.** achieve s.th.; **etw hinter sich b.** get s.th. over and done with; **etw über sich** (or **übers Herz**) **b.** be able to bear s.th.; **j-n auf etw b.** put s.o. on to s.th.; **j-n außer sich b.** enrage s.o.; **j-n dazu b. zu** (*inf*) get s.o. to (*inf*); **j-m um etw b.** deprive s.o. of s.th.; **j-n zum Lachen b.** make s.o. laugh; **unter die Leute b.** circulate
brisant [brɪ'zant] *adj* high-explosive
Brise ['brizə] *f* (-;-n) breeze
Britannien [brɪ'tanjən] *n* (-s;) Britain
Brite ['brɪtə] *m* (-n;-n) Briton, Britisher; **die Briten** the British
Britin ['brɪtɪn] *f* (-;-nen) Briton, British woman
britisch ['brɪtɪʃ] *adj* British
Broché [brɔ'ʃe] *n* (-s;) broché; brocaded fabric
Bröckchen ['brœkçən] *n* (-s;-) bit; morsel, crumb; fragment
bröck(e)lig ['brœk(ə)lɪç] *adj* crumbly
bröckeln ['brœkəln] *tr & intr* crumble
brocken ['brɔkən] *tr*—**Brot in die Suppe b.** break bread into the soup || **Brocken** *m* (-s;-) piece, bit; lump; **Brocken** *pl* scraps, bits and pieces; **harter B.** (coll) tough job
brockenweise (brok'kenweise) *adv* bit by bit
brodeln ['brodəln] *intr* bubble, simmer
Brokat [brɔ'kat] *m* (-s;-e) brocade
Brombeere ['brɔmberə] *f* (-;-n) blackberry
Bromid [brɔ'mit] *n* (-[e]s;-e) bromide
Bronchitis [brɔn'çitɪs] *f* (-;) bronchitis
Bronze ['brɔsə] *f* (-;-n) bronze
Brosche ['brɔʃə] *f* (-;-n) brooch
broschieren [brɔ'ʃirən] *tr* stitch; brocade; **broschiert** with stapled binding
Broschüre [brɔ'ʃyrə] *f* (-;-n) brochure
Brösel ['brøzəl] *m* (-s;-) crumb
Brot [brot] *n* (-[e]s;-e) bread; loaf; **geröstetes B.** toast
Brot'aufstrich *m* spread
Brötchen ['brøtçən] *n* (-s;-) roll
Brot'erwerb *m* livelihood, living
Brot'geber *m*, **Brot'herr** *m* employer
Brot'kasten *m* breadbox
brot'los *adj* unemployed; unprofitable
Brot'neid *m* professional jealousy
Brot'röster *m* (-s;-) toaster
Brot'schnitte *f* slice of bread
Brot'studium *n* bread-and-butter courses
Brot'zeit *f* breakfast

Bruch [brux] *m* (-[e]s;ᵘe) breaking; break, crack; breakage; (aer) crash; (geol) fault; (math) fraction; (min) quarry; (pathol) hernia; (surg) fracture; **B. machen** crash-land; **in die Brüche gehen** go to pot; **zu B. gehen** break || [brux] *m & n* (-s;ᵘe) bog
Bruch'band *n* (-s;ᵘer) (surg) truss
Bruch'bude *f* shanty
brüchig ['bryçɪç] *adj* fragile, brittle
Bruch'landung *f* crash landing
Bruch'rechnung *f* fractions
Bruch'stück *n* fragment, chip; **Bruchstücke** (fig) scraps, snatches
bruch'stückhaft *adj* fragmentary
Bruch'teil *m* fraction; **im B. e-r Sekunde** in a split second
Bruch'zahl *f* fractional number
Brücke ['brykə] *f* (-;-n) bridge; (*Teppich*) small (narrow) rug; (gym) backbend
Brückenkopf (Brük'kenkopf) *m* bridgehead
Brückenpfeiler (Brük'kenpfeiler) *m* pier of a bridge
Brückenwaage (Brük'kenwaage) *f* platform scale
Brückenzoll (Brük'kenzoll) *m* bridge toll
Bruder ['brudər] *m* (-sᵘ) brother; (*Genosse*) companion; (eccl) lay brother
brüderlich ['brydərlɪç] *adj* brotherly
Brüderschaft ['brydərʃaft] *f* (-;-en) brotherhood; fraternity
Brühe ['bry.ə] *f* (-;-n) broth; (*Fleisch-*) gravy; **in der B. stecken** be in a jam
brühen ['bry.ən] *tr* boil; scald
brüh'heiß' *adj* piping hot
Brüh'kartoffeln *pl* potatoes boiled in broth
Brüh'würfel *m* bouillon cube
brüllen ['brylən] *tr & intr* roar, bellow; (*Sturm*) howl; (*Ochse*) low; **b. vor Lachen** roar with laughter
Brummbär ['brumber] *m* (-en;-en) grouch
brummen ['brumən] *tr* mumble; grumble; growl || *intr* mumble; grumble; growl; (*summen*) buzz, hum; (*Orgel*) boom; (*im Gefängnis*) do time, do a stretch
brummig ['brumɪç] *adj* grouchy
brünett [bry'nɛt] *adj* brunet(te) || **Brünette** §5 brunette
Brunft [brunft] *f* (-;) rut
Brunft'zeit *f* rutting season
Brunnen ['brunən] *m* (-s;-) well; (*Spring-*) spring
Brunnenkresse ['brunənkrɛsə] *f* (-;-n) watercress
Brunst [brunst] *f* (-;) rut, heat; (fig) ardor, passion
brunsten ['brunstən] *intr* be in heat
brünstig ['brynstɪç] *adj* in heat; (fig) passionate
brüsk [brusk] *adj* brusque
brüskieren [brys'kirən] *tr* snub
Brust [brust] *f* (-;ᵘ) breast, chest
Brust'bein *n* breastbone, sternum
Brust'bild *n* portrait; (sculp) bust
brüsten ['brystən] *ref* show off

Brust'fellentzündung *f* pleurisy
Brust'kasten *m,* **Brust'korb** *m* thorax
Brust'schwimmen *n* breast stroke
Brust'stück *n* (culin) brisket
Brust'ton *m* —im **B.** der Überzeugung with utter conviction
Brust'umfang *m* chest measurement; (*bei Frauen*) bust measurement
Brü'stung *f* (–;–en) balustrade
Brust'warze *f* nipple
Brust'wehr *f* breastwork
Brut [brut] *f* (–;–en) brood; (pej) scum
brutal [bru'tal] *adj* brutal
Brut'apparat *m,* **Brut'ofen** *m* incubator
brüten ['brytən] *tr* hatch; (fig) plan ‖ *intr* incubate; **b. auf** (*dat*) (fig) sit on; **b. über** (*dat*) brood over; pore over
brutto ['bruto] *adj* (com) gross
Brut'tosozialprodukt *n* gross national product
Bube ['bubə] *m* (–n;–n) boy; (*Schurke*) rascal; (cards) jack
Bu'benstreich *m,* **Bu'benstück** *n* prank; dirty trick
bübisch ['bybɪʃ] *adj* rascally
Buch [bux] *n* (–[e]s;⁼er) book; (cards) straight
Buch'besprechung *f* book review
Buchbinderei ['buxbɪndəraɪ] *f* (–;–en) bookbindery; (*Gewerbe*) bookbinding
Buch'binderleinwand *f* buckram
Buch'deckel *m* book cover
Buch'drama *n* closet drama
Buch'druck *m* printing, typography
Buch'drucker *m* printer
Buch'druckerei *f* print shop; (*Gewerbe*) printing
Buche ['buxə] *f* (–;–n) beech
Buchecker ['buxɛkər] *f* (–;–n) beechnut
buchen ['buxən] *tr* book, reserve; (com) enter
Bücher– [byçər] *comb.fm.* book
Bü'cherabschluß *m* balancing of books
Bücherausgabe *f* circulation desk
Bü'cherbrett *n* bookshelf
Bücherei [byçə'raɪ] *f* (–;–en) library
Bü'cherfreund *m* bibliophile
Bü'chergestell *n* bookrack, bookcase
Bü'cherregal *n* bookshelf; bookcase
Bü'cherrevision *f* audit
Bü'cherrevisor *m* auditor; accountant
Bü'cherschrank *m* bookcase
Bü'cherstütze *f* book end
Buch'führung *f* bookkeeping, accounting
Buch'halter –in §6 *mf* bookkeeper
Buch'haltung *f* bookkeeping; accounting department
Buch'händler –in §6 *mf* book dealer
Buch'handlung *f* bookstore
Büchlein ['byçlaɪn] *n* (–s;–) booklet
Buch'macher *m* bookmaker
Buch'prüfer –in §6 *mf* auditor
Buchsbaum ['buksbaum] *m* boxwood
Buchse ['buksə] *f* (–;–n) (mach) bushing
Büchse ['byksə] *f* (–;–n) box, case; (*Dose*) can; (*Gewhr*) rifle
Büch'senfleisch *n* canned meat

Büch'senöffner *m* can opener
Buchstabe ['buxʃtabə] *m* (–n;–n) letter
buchstabieren [buxʃta'birən] *tr & intr* spell
buchstäblich ['buxʃtepliç] *adj* literal
Bucht [buxt] *f* (–;–en) bay
Buch'umschlag *m* book jacket
Bu'chung *f* (–;–en) booking; (acct) entry
Buckel ['bukəl] *m* (–s;–) hump; (coll) back; **B. haben** be hunchback; **e–n B. machen** arch its back
buck(e)lig ['buk(ə)liç] *adj* hunchbacked ‖ **Buck(e)lige** §5 *mf* hunchback
bücken ['bykən] *tr & ref* bow (down)
Bückling ['byklɪŋ] *m* (–s;–e) bow
Bude ['budə] *f* (–;–n) booth, stall; (coll) shanty; (coll) hole in the wall
Budget [by'dʒe] *n* (–s;–s) budget
Büfett [by'fe], [by'fet] *n* (–s;–s) buffet, sideboard; counter; (*Schanktisch*) bar; **kaltes B.** cold buffet
Büffel ['byfəl] *m* (–s;–) buffalo
Büffelei [byfə'laɪ] *f* (–;–en) cramming
büffeln ['byfəln] *intr* (für) cram (for)
Bug [buk] *m* (–[e]s;–e) (aer) nose; (naut) bow; (zool) shoulder, withers
Bügel ['bygəl] *m* (–s;–) handle; (*Kleider–*) coat hanger; (*Steig–*) stirrup; (*e–r Säge*) frame
Bü'gelbrett *n* ironing board
Bü'geleisen *n* iron, flatiron
Bü'gelfalte *f* crease
bü'gelfrei *adj* drip-dry
bügeln ['bygəln] *tr* iron, press
Bü'gelsäge *f* hacksaw
bugsieren [buk'sirən] *tr* tow
Buhldirne ['buldɪrnə] *f* (–;–n) bawd
buhlen ['bulən] *intr* have an affair; **um j–s Gunst b.** curry favor with s.o.
Bühne ['bynə] *f* (–;–n) stage; platform
Büh'nenanweisung *f* stage direction
Büh'nenaussprache *f* standard pronunciation
Büh'nenausstattung *f,* **Büh'nenbild** *n* set
Büh'nenbildner –in §6 *mf* stage designer
Büh'nendeutsch *n* standard German
Büh'nendichter –in §6 *mf* playwright
Büh'nendichtung *f* drama, play
Büh'nenkünstler *m* actor
Büh'nenkünstlerin *f* actress
Büh'nenleiter –in §6 *mf* stage manager
Büh'nenstück *n* play, stage play
buk [buk] *pret* of **backen**
Bukarest ['bukarɛst] *n* (–s;) Bucharest
Bulette [bu'letə] *f* (–;–n) meatball
Bulgarien [bul'garjən] *n* (–s;) Bulgaria
Bullauge ['bulaugə] *n* (–s;–en) porthole
Bulldogge ['buldɔgə] *f* (–;–n) bulldog
Bulle ['bulə] *m* (–n;–n) bull; brawny fellow; (sl) cop ‖ *f* (–;–n) (eccl) bull
bullern ['bulərn] *intr* bubble, boil; (*Feuer*) roar; (*Sturm*) rage
Bummel ['buməl] *m* (–s;) stroll
Bummelei [bumə'laɪ] *f* (–;–en) dawdling; loafing; sloppiness
bummelig ['buməliç] *adj* slow; sloppy
bummeln ['buməln] *intr* loaf; dawdle; (*Autos*) crawl ‖ *intr* (SEIN) stroll

Bum′melstreik *m* slowdown
Bum′melzug *m* (coll) slow train, local
Bummler [′bumlər] *m* (-s;-) loafer, bum; slowpoke; gadabout
Bums [bums] *m* (-es;-e) thud, thump, bang ‖ *interj* boom!; bang!
bumsen [′bumsən] *intr* thud, thump, bump; (sl) have intercourse
Bums′lokal *n* (coll) dive, joint
Bund [bunt] *m* (-[e]s;ː) union, federation; (*Schlüssel*-) ring; (*Rand an Hose*) waistband; (*Ehe*-) bond; (mach) flange; (mus) fret; (pol) federal government; **im Bunde mit** with the cooperation of ‖ *n* (-[e]s;- & -e) bunch, bundle
Bündel [′byndəl] *n* (-s;-) bunch, bundle; (phys) beam
Bundes- *comb.fm.* federal
Bun′desgenosse *m* ally, confederate
Bun′desgerichtshof *m* federal supreme court
Bun′deslade *f* ark of the covenant
bun′desstaatlich *adj* state; federal
Bun′destag *m* lower house
bündig [′byndıç] *adj* binding; (*überzeugend*) convincing; (*treffend*) succint; **b. liegen** be flush
Bündnis [′byntnıs] *n* (-ses;-se) agreement, pact, alliance
Bunker [′buŋkər] *m* (-;-) bin; (agr) silo; (aer) air-raid shelter; (mil) bunker; (nav) submarine pen
bunt [bunt] *adj* colored; (*mehrfarbig*) multicolored; (*gefleckt*) dappled; (*gemischt*) varied, motley; (*Farbe*) bright, gay; (*Wiese*) gay with flowers; **bunter Abend** variety show; **buntes Durcheinander** complete muddle
Bunt′metall *n* nonferrous metal
Bunt′stift *m* colored pencil, crayon
Bürde [′byrdə] *f* (-;-n) burden
Burg [burk] *f* (-;-en) fortress, stronghold; citadel; castle
Bürge [′byrgə] *m* (-;-n) bondsman, guarantor, surety; **B. sein für** (or **als B. haften für**) stand surety for (*s.o.*); vouch for (*s.th.*)
bürgen [′byrgən] *intr*—**b. für** put up bail for (*s.o.*); vouch for (*s.th.*)
Bürger **-in** [′byrgər(ın)] §6 *mf* citizen; member of the middle class; commoner
Bür′gerkrieg *m* civil war
bür′gerlich *adj* civic; civil; middle-class; (*nicht überfeinert*) plain
Bür′germeister *m* mayor
Bür′gerrecht *n* civil rights
Bür′gerschaft *f* (-;) citizens

Bür′gersteig *m* sidewalk
Bürgschaft [′byrkʃaft] *f* (-;-en) security, guarantee; (jur) bail; **gegen B. freilassen** release on bail
Büro [by′ro] *n* (-s;-s) office
Büro′angestellte §5 *mf* clerk
Büro′bedarf *m* office supplies
Büro′klammer *f* paper clip
Büro′kraft *f* office worker; **Bürokräfte** office personnel
Bürokrat [byro′krat] *m* (-en;-en) bureaucrat
Bürokra·tie [byrokra′ti] *f* (-;-tien [′ti-ən]) bureaucracy; (fig) red tape
bürokratisch [byro′kratıʃ] *adj* bureaucratic
Bursch(e) [′burʃ(ə)] *m* (-[e]n;-[e]n) boy, fellow; (mil) orderly; **ein übler B.** a bad egg
burschikos [burʃı′kos] *adj* tomboyish; devil-may-care
Bürste [′byrstə] *f* (-;-n) brush; (coll) crewcut
bürsten [′byrstən] *tr* brush
Bürzel [′byrtsəl] *m* (-s;-) rump (*of bird*)
Bus [bus] *m* (-ses;-se) bus
Busch [buʃ] *m* (-es;ː e) bush; forest
Büschel [′byʃəl] *m* & *n* clump, bunch, cluster; (*Haar*-) tuft; (elec) brush
Busch′holz *n* brushwood
buschig [′buʃıç] *adj* bushy; shaggy
Busch′klepper *m* bushwacker
Busch′messer *n* machete
Busch′werk *n* bushes, brush
Busen [′buzən] *m* (-s;-) bosom, breast; (*Bucht*) bay, gulf; (fig) bosom
Bussard [′busart] *m* (-s;-e) buzzard
Buße [′busə] *f* (-n;-n) penance; (*Sühne*) atonement; (*Strafgeld*) fine
büßen [′bysən] *tr* atone for, pay for
Büßer **-in** [′bysər(ın)] §6 *mf* penitent
Busserl [′busərl] *n* (-s;-n) kiss
buß′fertig *adj* repentant
Bussole [bu′solə] *f* (-;-n) compass
Büste [′bystə] *f* (-;-n) bust
Bü′stenhalter *m* brassière, bra
Bütte [′bytə] *f* (-;-n) tub; vat
Butter [′butər] *f* (-;) butter
But′terbrot *n* bread and butter
But′terdose *f* butter dish
But′termilch *f* buttermilk
buttern [′butərn] butter ‖ *intr* make butter
byzantinisch [bytsan′tinıʃ] *adj* Byzantine
Byzanz [by′tsants] *n* (-′;) Byzantium
bzw. *abbr* (**beziehungsweise**) respectively

C

C, c [tze] *invar n* C, c;(meteor) centigrade; (mus) C
Café [ka′fe] *n* (-s;-s) café; coffee shop
Camping [′kempıŋ] *n* (-s;-s) camping
Canaille [ka′naljə] *f* (-;-n) scoundrel
Cäsar [′tsezar] *m* (-s;) Caesar
Cellist **-in** [tʃɛ′lıst(ın)] §7 *mf* cellist

Cello [′tʃɛlo] *n* (-s;-s) cello
Cellophan [tsɛlo′fan] *n* (-s;) cellophane
Celsius [′tsɛlzjus] centigrade
Cembalo [′tʃɛmbalo] *n* (-s;-s) harpsichord
Ces [tsɛs] *n* (-;-) (mus) C flat

Champagner [ʃamˈpanjər] *m* (-s;-) champagne
Champignon [ˈʃampɪnjɔ̃] *m* (-s;-s) mushroom
Chance [ˈʃansə] *f* (-;-n) chance
Chaos [ˈkɑ·ɔs] *n* (-;) chaos
chaotisch [kaˈotɪʃ] *adj* chaotic
Charak·ter [kaˈraktər] *m* (-s;-tere [ˈterə]) character; (mil) honorary rank
Charak'terbild *n* character sketch
Charak'tereigenschaft *f* trait
charak'terfest *adj* of a strong character
charakterisieren [karaktɛrɪˈzirən] *tr* characterize
Charakteristik [karaktɛˈrɪstɪk] *f* (-; -en) characterization
Charakteristi·kum [karaktɛˈrɪstɪkum] *n* [-s;-ka [ka]) characteristic
charakteristisch [karaktɛˈrɪstɪʃ] *adj* (für) characteristic (of)
charak'terlich *adj* of character || *adv* in character
charak'terlos *adj* wishy-washy
Charak'terzug *m* characteristic, trait
Charge [ˈʃarʒə] *f* (-;-n) (metal) charge; (mil) rank; **Chargen** (mil) non-coms
charmant [ʃarˈmant] *adj* charming
Charme [ʃarm] *m* (-s;) charm, grace
Chas·sis [ʃaˈsi] *n* (-sis [ˈsi[s]]; -sis [ˈsis]) chassis
Chaus·see [ʃɔˈse] *f* (-;-seen [ˈse·ən]) highway
Chef [ʃɛf] *m* (-s;-s) chief, head; (com) boss; (culin) chef; **C. des Generalstabs** chief of staff; **C. des Heeresjustizwesens** judge advocate general
Chemie [çɛˈmi] *f* (-;) chemistry; **technische C.** chemical engineering
Chemie'faser *f* synthetic fiber
Chemikalien [çemɪˈkaljən] *pl* chemicals
Chemiker **-in** [ˈçemɪkər(ɪn)] §6 *mf* chemist; student of chemistry
chemisch [ˈçemɪʃ] *adj* chemical; **chemische Reinigung** dry cleaning
Chemotechniker **-in** [çemoˈtɛçnɪkər(ɪn)] §6 *mf* chemical engineer
Chiffre [ˈʃɪfər] *f* (-;-n) cipher; code; (in Anzeigen) box number
Chif'freschrift *f* code
chiffrieren [ʃɪˈfrirən] *tr* code
China [ˈçina] *n* (-s;) China
Chinese [çɪˈnezə] *m* (-n;-n;), **Chinesin** [çɪˈnezɪn] *f* (-;-nen) Chinese
chinesisch [çɪˈnezɪʃ] *adj* Chinese
Chinin [çɪˈnin] *n* (-s;) quinine
Chirurg [çɪˈrurg] *m* (-en;-en) surgeon
Chirurgie [çɪrurˈgi] *f* (-;) surgery
chirurgisch [çɪˈrurgɪʃ] *adj* surgical
Chlor [klor] *n* (-s;) chlorine
chloren [ˈklorən] *tr* chlorinate
Chlorid [kloˈrit] *n* (-[e]s;-e) chloride
Chloroform [kloroˈfɔrm] *n* (-s;) chloroform

chloroformieren [klɔrɔfɔrˈmirən] *tr* chloroform
Cholera [ˈkolɛra] *f* (-;) cholera
cholerisch [koˈlerɪʃ] *adj* choleric
Chor [kor] *m* (-s;ᵉe) choir; chorus
Choral [koˈral] *m* (-s;ᵉe) Gregorian chant; (Prot) hymn
Chor'altar *m* high altar
Chor'anlage *f* (archit) choir
Chor'bühne *f* choir loft
Choreograph **-in** [kɔre·ɔˈgraf(ɪn)] §7 *mf* choreographer
Chor'hemd *n* surplice
Chor'stuhl *m* choir stall
Christ [krɪst] *m* (-s;) Christ || *m* (-en; -en) Christian
Christ'abend *m* Christmas Eve
Christ'baum *m* Christmas tree
Chri'stenheit *f* (-;) Christendom
Christentum [ˈkrɪstəntum] *n* (-s;) Christianity
Christin [ˈkrɪstɪn] *f* (-;-nen) Christian
Christ'kind *m* Christ child
christ'lich *adj* Christian
Christ'nacht *f* Holy Night
Chri·stus [ˈkrɪstus] *m* (-sti [sti];) Christ; **nach Christi Geburt** A.D.; **vor Christus** B.C.
Chri'stusbild *n* crucifix; picture of Christ
Chrom [krom] *n* (-s;) chromium, chrome
chromatisch [krɔˈmatɪʃ] *adj* chromatic
Chromosom [kromɔˈzom] *n* (-s;-en) chromosome
Chronik [ˈkronɪk] *f* (-;-en) chronicle
chronisch [ˈkronɪʃ] *adj* chronic
Chronist **-in** [kroˈnɪst(ɪn)] §7 *mf* chronicler
Chronolo·gie [kronɔlɔˈgi] *f* (-;-gien [ˈgi·ən]) chronology
chronologisch [kronɔˈlogɪʃ] *adj* chronological
circa [ˈtsɪrka] *adv* approximately
Cis [tsɪs] *n* (-;-) (mus) C sharp
Clique [ˈklɪkə] *f* (-;-n) clique
Cocktail [ˈkɔktel] *m* (-s;-s) cocktail
Conferencier [kɔ̃feraˈsje] *m* (-s;-s) master of ceremony
Couch [kautʃ] *f* (-;-es) couch
Countdown [ˈkauntdaun] *m* (-s;-s) (rok) countdown
Couplet [kuˈple] *n* (-s;-s) song (in a musical)
Coupon [kuˈpõ] *m* (-s;-s) coupon
Courage [kuˈraʒə] *f* (-;) courage
Courtage [kurˈtaʒə] *f* (-;-n) brokerage
Cousin [kuˈzɛ̃] *m* (-s;-s) cousin
Cousine [kuˈzinə] *f* (-;-n) cousin
Cowboy [ˈkaubɔɪ] *m* (-s;-s) cowboy
creme [krem] *adj* cream-colored || **Creme** [ˈkrem(ə)] *f* (-;) cream; custard
Crew [kru] *f* (-;) crew; (nav) cadets (of the same year)
Cut [kœt] *m* (-s;-s) cutaway

D

D, d [de] *invar n* D, d; (mus) D
da [dɑ] *adv* there; then; in that case,
 da und da at such and such a place;
 wieder da back again ‖ *conj* since,
 because; when
dabei [da'baɪ] *adv* nearby; besides,
 moreover; at that; at the same time;
 (*trotzdem*) yet; **d. bleiben** stick to
 one's point; **d. sein** be present, take
 part; **d. sein zu** (*inf*) be on the point
 of (*ger*); **es ist nichts d.** there's nothing to it
da capo [da'kɑpo] *interj* encore!
Dach [dax] *n* (-[e]s;ˑˑer) roof; (fig)
 shelter; **unter D. und Fach** under
 cover
Dach'boden *m* attic
Dach'decker *m* roofer
Dach'fenster *n* dormer window; sky-
 light
Dach'first *m* ridge of a roof
Dach'geschoß *n* top floor
Dach'gesellschaft *f* holding company
Dach'kammer *f* attic room
Dach'luke *f* skylight
Dach'organisation *f* parent company
Dach'pappe *f* roofing paper
Dach'pfanne *f* roof tile
Dach'rinne *f* rain gutter; eaves
Dach'röhre *f* downspout
Dachs [daks] *m* (-es;-e) badger; **ein
 frecher D.** a young whippersnapper
Dachs'hund *m* dachshund
Dach'sparren *m* rafter
Dach'stube *f* attic, garret
Dach'stuhl *m* roof framework
dachte ['daxtə] *pret of* **denken**
Dach'traufe *f* rain gutter
Dach'werk *n* roof
Dach'ziegel *m* roof tile
dadurch [da'durç] *adv* through it;
 thereby; by this means; **dadurch, daß**
 by (*ger*)
dafür [da'fyr] *adv* for it or them; in
 its place; that's why; therefore
Dafür'halten *n*—**nach meinem D.** in
 my opinion
dagegen [da'gegən] *adv* against it or
 them; in exchange for it or them; in
 comparison; on the other hand; **etw
 d. haben** have an objection; **ich bin
 d.** I'm against it
daheim [da'haɪm] *adv* at home
daher [da'her] *adv* from there; therefore; (bei *Verben der Bewegung*)
 along ‖ ['daher] *adv* that's why
dahin [da'hɪn] *adv* there, to that place;
 (*vergangen*) gone; (bei *Verben der
 Bewegung*) along; **bis d.** that far, up
 to there; until then; **es steht mir
 bis d.** I'm fed up with it
da'hinauf *adv* up there
da'hinaus *adv* out there
dahin'geben §80 *tr* give away; give up
dahin'gehen §82 *intr* (SEIN) walk along;
 pass; (*sterben*) pass away; **dahinge-
 hend, daß** to the effect that
dahingestellt [da'hɪngəʃtɛlt] *adj*—**d.**

 sein lassen, ob leave the question
 open whether
dahin'leben *intr* exist from day to day
dahin'raffen *tr* carry off
dahin'scheiden §112 *intr* (SEIN) pass on
dahin'schwinden *intr* (SEIN) dwindle
 away; fade away; pine away
dahin'stehen §146 *impers*—**es steht dahin** it is uncertain
dahin'ten *adv* back there
dahin'ter *adv* behind it or them
dahinterher' *adv*—**d. sein, daß** be insistent that
dahin'terkommen §99 *intr* (SEIN) find
 out about it; get behind the truth
 of it
dahin'tersetzen *tr* put (*s.o.*) to work
 on it
dahin'welken §113 *intr* (SEIN) fade
 away
dahin'ziehen §163 *intr* (SEIN) move
 along
Dakapo [da'kɑpo] *n* (-s;-s) encore
da'lassen §104 *tr* leave behind
dalli ['dalɪ] *interj*—**mach d.!** step on
 it!
damalig ['dɑmɑlɪç] *adj* of that time
damals ['dɑmɑls] *adv* then, at that
 time
Damast [da'mast] *m* (-es;-e) damask
Dame ['dɑmə] *f* (-;-n) lady; (*beim
 Tanz*) partner; (cards, chess) queen;
 (checkers) king; **e-e D. machen**
 crown a checker; **meine D.!** madam!;
 meine Damen und Herrn! ladies and
 gentlemen!
Da'mebrett *n* checkerboard
Da'menbinde *f* sanitary napkin
Da'mendoppelspiel *n* (tennis) women's
 doubles
Da'meneinzelspiel *n* (tennis) women's
 singles
Da'mengesellschaft *f* hen party
da'menhaft *adj* ladylike
Da'menhemd *n* chemise
Da'menschneider -in §6 *mf* dressmaker
Da'menwäsche *f* lingerie
Da'mespiel *n* checkers
damisch ['dɑmɪʃ] *adj* dopey
damit [da'mɪt] *adv* with it or them;
 by it; thereby; **d. hat's noch Zeit**
 that can wait; **es ist nichts d.** it is
 useless ‖ *conj* in order that, to
dämlich ['demlɪç] *adj* dopey
Damm [dam] *m* (-[e]s;ˑˑe) dam; dike;
 embankment; causeway; breakwater;
 pier; (fig) barrier; (anat) perineum;
 auf dem D. sein feel up to it; **wieder
 auf dem D. sein** be on one's feet
 again
Dämmer ['demər] *m* (-s;) (poet) twilight
dämmerig ['demərɪç] *adj* dusky, dim
Däm'merlicht *n* dusk, twilight
dämmern ['demərn] *intr* dawn, grow
 light; (*am Abend*) grow dark, become twilight

Däm'merung ƒ (-;-en) (*Morgenrot*) dawn; (*am Abend*) dusk, twilight
Dämmplatte ['dɛmplatə] ƒ acoustical tile
Dämmstoff ['dɛmʃtɔf] m insulation
Damm'weg m causeway
Dämon ['dɛmən] m (-s; **Dämonen** [dɛ'monən] demon
dämonisch [dɛ'monɪʃ] adj demoniacal
Dampf [dampf] m (-[e]s;⁼e) steam; vapor; (*Angst*) (coll) fear; (*Hunger*) (coll) hunger; (vet) broken wind; **D. dahinter machen** (coll) step on it
dampfen ['dampfən] intr steam ‖ intr (SEIN) steam along, steam away
dämpfen ['dɛmpfən] tr (*dünsten*) steam; (*Lärm*) muffle; (*Farben, Gefühle, Lichter*) subdue; (*Stoß*) absorb; (*Begeisterung*) dampen; **mit gedämpfter Stimme** under one's breath
Dampfer ['dampfər] m (-s;-) steamer
Dämpfer ['dɛmpfər] m (-s;-) (culin) steamer, boiler; (mach) baffle; (mus) mute; (*beim Klavier*) (mus) damper; **e-n D. aufsetzen** (dat) put a damper on
Dampf'heizung ƒ steam heat
Dampf'kessel m steam boiler, boiler
Dampf'maschine ƒ steam engine
Dampf'schiffahrtslinie ƒ steamship line
Dämp'fungsfläche ƒ (aer) stabilizer
Dampf'walze ƒ steam roller
Damspiel ['damʃpil] n var of **Damespiel**
danach [da'nɑx] adv after it or them; accordingly; according to it or them; afterwards; **d. fragen** ask about it; **d. streben** strive for it; **d. sieht er auch aus** that's just what he looks like
Däne ['dɛnə] m (-n;-n) Dane
daneben [da'nebən] adv next to it or them ‖ adv in addition
dane'bengehen §82 intr (SEIN) go amiss
dane'benhauen intr miss; (fig) be wrong
Dänemark ['dɛnəmark] n (-s;) Denmark
dang [daŋ] pret of **dingen**
daniederliegen [da'nidərligən] §108 intr (fig) be down; **d. an** (dat) be laid up with
Dänin ['dɛnɪn] ƒ (-;-nen) Dane
dänisch ['dɛnɪʃ] adj Danish
dank [daŋk] prep (dat) thanks to ‖ **Dank** m [-[e]s;) thanks; gratitude; **Gott sei D.!** thank God!, thank heaven!
dankbar ['daŋkbar] adj thankful; (*lohnend*) rewarding, profitable
Dank'barkeit ƒ (-;) gratitude
danken ['daŋkən] intr (dat) thank; **danke!** thanks!; (*bei Ablehnung*) no, thanks!; **danke schön!** thank you!; **nichts zu d.!** you are welcome!
dan'kenswert adj meritorious; rewarding
dank'sagen intr return thanks
Danksagung ['daŋkzɑguŋ] ƒ (-;) thanksgiving
Dank'sagungstag m Thanksgiving Day

Dank'schreiben n letter of thanks
dann [dan] adv then; **d. und wann** now and then
dannen ['danən] adv—**von d.** away
daran [da'ran] adv on, at, by, in, onto it or them; **das ist alles d.!** that's great!; **er ist gut d.** he's well off; **er tut gut d. zu** (inf) he does well to (inf); **es ist nichts d.** there's nothing to it; **ich will wissen, wie ich d. bin** I want to know where I stand; **jetzt bin ich d.** it's my turn; **nahe d. sein zu** (inf) be on the point of (ger); **was liegt d.?** what does it matter?
daran'gehen §82 intr (SEIN) go about it; **d. gehen zu** (inf) proceed to (inf)
daran'setzen tr—**alles d. zu** (inf) do one's level best to (inf)
darauf [da'rauf] adv on it or them; after that; **d. kommt es an** that's what matters; **gerade d. zu** straight towards; **gleich d.** immediately afterwards; **ich lasse es d. ankommen** I'll risk it
daraufhin [darauf'hɪn] adv thereupon
daraus [da'raus] adv of it, from it; from that; from them; hence; **d. wird nichts!** nothing doing!; **es wird nichts d.** nothing will come of it
darben ['darbən] intr live in poverty
darbieten ['darbitən] §58 tr present
Dar'bietung ƒ (-;-en) presentation; (theat) performance
dar'bringen §65 tr present, offer
Dardanellen [darda'nɛlən] pl Dardanelles
darein [da'raɪn] adv into it or them
darein'reden intr interrupt; **er redet mir in alles d.** he interferes in all that I do
darin [da'rɪn] adv in it or them
dar'legen tr explain; state
Dar'legung ƒ (-;-en) explanation
Darlehen [da'darle(ə)n] n (-s;-) loan
Dar'leh(e)nskasse ƒ loan association
Darm [darm] m (-[e]s;⁼e) intestine, gut; (*Wursthaut*) skin
Darm- comb.fm. intestinal
Darm'entzündung ƒ enteritis
Darm'fäule ƒ dysentery
dar'stellen tr describe; show, depict, portray; represent; mean; plot, chart; (indust) produce; (theat) play the part of
Dar'steller -in §6 mf performer
Dar'stellung ƒ (-;-en) representation; portrayal; account, version; (indust) production; (theat) performance
dar'tun §154 tr prove; demonstrate
darüber [da'rybər] adv over it or them; (*querüber*) across it; (*betreffs*) about that; **d. hinaus** beyond it; moreover; **ich bin d. hinweg** I've gotten over it
darum [da'rum] adv around it or them; (*deshalb*) therefore; **er weiß d.** he's aware of it; **es ist mir nur d. zu tun, daß** all I ask is that
darunter [da'runtər] adv below it or them; among them; (*weniger*) less; **d. leiden** suffer from it; **zehn Jahre und d.** ten years and under
das [das] §1 def art the ‖ §1 dem adj & dem pron this, that; **das und das**

such and such || §11 *rel pron* which, that, who

da'sein §139 *intr* (SEIN) be there; be present; exist; **es ist schon alles mal dagewesen** there's nothing new under the sun; **noch nie dagewesen** unprecedented || **Dasein** *n* (-s;) being, existence, life

Da'seinsberechtigung *f* raison d'être

daselbst [da'zɛlpst] *adv* just there; ibidem; **wohnhaft d.** address as above

dasjenige ['dasjenɪgə] §4,3 *dem adj* that || **dem** *pron* the one

daß [das] *conj* that; **daß du nicht vergißt!** be sure not to forget!; **daß er doch käme!** I wish he'd come; **es sei denn, daß** unless

dasselbe [das'zɛlbə] §4,3 *dem adj* & *dem pron* the same

da'stehen §146 *intr* stand there; **einzig d.** be unrivaled; **gut d.** be well-off; **wie stehe ich nun da!** how foolish I look now!

Daten ['dɑtən] *pl* data

Da'tenverarbeitung *f* data processing

datieren [da'tirən] *tr* & *intr* date

Dativ ['dɑtif] *m* (-s;-e) dative (case)

dato ['dɑto] *adv*—**bis d.** to date

Dattel ['datəl] *f* (-;-n) (bot) date

Da-tum ['dɑtum] *n* (-s;-ten [tən]) date; **Daten** data, facts; **heutigen Datums** of today; **neueren Datums** of recent date; **welches D. haben wir heute?** what's today's date?

Daube ['daubə] *f* (-;-n) (barrel) stave

Dauer ['dau-ər] *f* (-;) length, duration; permanence; **auf die D.** in the long run; **für die D. von** for a period of; **von D. sein** last, endure

Dau'erauftrag *m* standing order

Dau'erbelastung *f* constant load

Dau'erertrag *m* constant yield

Dau'erfeuer *n* (mil) automatic fire

Dau'erflug *m* endurance flight

Dau'ergeschwindigkeit *f* cruising speed

dau'erhaft *adj* lasting, durable; (*Farbe*) fast

Dau'erkarte *f* season ticket; (rr) commutation ticket

Dau'erlauf *m* (long-distance) jogging

dauern ['dau-ərn] *tr*—**er dauert mich** I feel sorry for him || *intr* last, continue; **die Fahrt dauert fünf Stunden** the trip takes five hours; **es wird nicht lange d., dann** it won't be long before; **lange d.** take a long time

Dau'erplisseé *n* permanent pleat

Dau'erprobe *f* endurance test

Dau'erschmierung *f* self-lubrication

Dau'erstellung *f* permanent job

Dau'erton *m* (telp) dial tone

Dau'erversuch *m* endurance test

Dau'erwelle *f* permanent wave

Dau'erwirkung *f* lasting effect

Dau'erwurst *f* hard salami

Dau'erzustand *m* permanent condition; **zum D. werden** get to be a regular thing

Daumen ['daumən] *m* (-s;-) thumb; **D. halten!** keep your fingers crossed!; **die D. drehen** twiddle one's thumbs; **über den D. peilen** (or **schätzen**) give a rough estimate of

Dau'menabdruck *m* thumb print

Dau'menindex *m* thumb index

Daune ['daunə] *f* (-;-n) downy feather; **Daunen** down

Dau'nenbett *n* feather bed

Davit ['devɪt] *m* (-s;-s) (naut) davit

davon [da'fɔn] *adv* of it or them; from it or them; about it or them; away

davon'kommen §99 *intr* (SEIN) escape

davon'laufen §105 *intr* (SEIN) run away; || **Davonlaufen** *n*—**es ist zum D.** (coll) it's enough to drive you insane

davon'machen *ref* take off, go away

davon'tragen §132 *tr* carry off; win

davor [da'for] *adv* in front of it or them; of it or them; from it or them

dawider [da'vidər] *adv* against it

dazu [da'tsu] *adv* thereto; to it or them; in addition to that; for that purpose; about it or them; with it or them

dazu'gehörig *adj* belonging to it; proper, appropriate

da'zumal *adv* at that time

dazu'tun §154 *tr* add || **Dazutun** *n*—**ohne sein D.** without any effort on his part

dazwischen [da'tsvɪʃən] *adv* in between; among them

dazwi'schenfahren §71 *intr* (SEIN) jump in to intervene

dazwi'schenfunken *intr* (coll) butt in

dazwi'schenkommen §99 *intr* (SEIN) intervene

Dazwischenkunft [da'tsvɪʃənkunft] *f* (-;) intervention

dazwi'schentreten §152 *intr* (SEIN) intervene

Debatte [dɛ'batə] *f* (-;-n) debate, discussion; **zur D. stehen** be under discussion; **zur D. stellen** open to discussion

debattieren [dɛba'tirən] *tr* & *intr* debate, discuss

Debet ['debɛt] *n* (-s;) debit; **im D. stehen** be on the debit side

Debüt [dɛ'by] *n* (-s;-s) debut

Debütantin [dɛby'tantɪn] *f* (-;-nen) debutante

debütieren [dɛby'tierən] *intr* make one's debut

Dechant [dɛ'çant] *m* (-en;-en) (educ; R.C.) dean

dechiffrieren [dɛʃɪf'rirən] *tr* decipher

Deck [dɛk] *n* (-s;-s) deck

Deck'anstrich *m* final coat

Deck'bett *n* feather bed

Deck'blatt *n* overlay

Decke ['dɛkə] *f* (-;-n) cover, covering; (*Bett*-) blanket; (*Tisch*-) tablecloth; (*Zimmer*-) ceiling; (*Schicht*) layer; **mit j-m unter e-r D.** be in cahoots with s.o.; **sich nach der D. strecken** make the best of it

Deckel ['dɛkəl] *m* (-s;-) lid, cap; (*Buch*-) cover; **j-m eins auf den D. geben** (coll) chew s.o. out

decken ['dɛkən] *tr* cover; (*Tisch*) set; **das Tor d.** guard the goal || *ref* coincide || *intr* cover

Deckenbeleuchtung (**Dek'kenbeleuchtung**) *f* (-;) ceiling lighting

Deckenlicht (Dek'kenlicht) n ceiling light; skylight; (aut) dome light
Deck'farbe f one-coat paint
Deck'konto n secret account
Deck'mantel m pretext, pretense
Deck'name m pseudonym; alias; (mil) code name, cover name
Deck'offizier m (nav) warrant officer
Deck'plane f awning; tarpaulin
Deckung (Dek'kung) f (-;-en) covering; protection; roofing; (box) defense; (com) security, surety; collateral
deckungsgleich (dek'kungsgleich) adj congruent
defekt [de'fɛkt] adj defective || **Defekt** m (-[e]s;-e) defect
defensiv [defen'zif] adj defensive || **Defensive** [defen'zivə] f (-;-n) defensive
definieren [defɪ'nirən] tr define
definitiv [defɪnɪ'tif] adj (endgültig) definitive; (bestimmt) definite
Defizit ['defɪtsɪt] n (-s;-e) deficit
Degen ['degən] m (-s;-) sword; (poet) warrior; (typ) compositor
degradieren [degra'dirən] tr demote
Degradie'rung f (-;-en) demotion
dehnbar ['denbɑr] adj elastic; (Metall) ductile; (fig) vague, loose
dehnen ['denən] tr stretch; extend; expand; (Worte) drawl out; (Vokal) lengthen; (mus) sustain || ref stretch out; expand
Deh'nung f (-;-en) extension; expansion; dilation; (ling) lengthening
Deich [daɪç] m (-[e]s;-e) dike; (Damm) bank, embankment
Deichsel ['daɪksəl] f (-;-n) pole
deichseln ['daɪksəln] tr (coll) manage
dein [daɪn] §2 poss adj your, thy
deinerseits ['daɪnər'zaɪts] adv on your part
deinesgleichen ['daɪnəs'glaɪçən] invar pron your own kin, your equals, the likes of you
deinethalben ['daɪnət'halbən], **deinetwegen** ['daɪnət'vegən], **deinetwillen** ['daɪnət'vɪlən] adv for your sake; because of you, on your account
deinige ['daɪnɪgə] poss pron yours
Dekan [de'kɑn] m (-s;-e) dean
deklamieren [dekla'mirən] tr & intr declaim; recite
Deklination [deklɪna'tsjon] f (-;-en) declension
deklinieren [deklɪ'nirən] tr decline
dekolletiert [dekɔle'tirt] adj low-necked; (Dame) bare-necked
Dekorateur [dekɔra'tør] m (-s;-e) decorator, interior decorator
Dekoration [dekɔra'tsjon] f (-;-en) decoration; (theat) scenery
dekorieren [dekɔ'rirən] tr decorate
Dekret [de'kret] n (-[e]s;-e) decree
delikat [delɪ'kat] adj delicate; (lecker) delicious
Delikt [de'lɪkt] n (-[e]s;-e) offense
Delle ['dɛlə] f (-;-n) dent; dip
Delphin [del'fin] m (-s;-e) dolphin
Delta ['delta] n (-s;-s) delta
dem [dɛm] §1 def art, dem adj & dem pron || §11 rel pron

Demagoge [dema'gogə] m (-n;-n) demagogue
Dementi [de'mɛnti] n (-s;-s) official denial
dementieren [demɛn'tirən] tr deny (officially)
dem'entsprechend adj corresponding || adv correspondingly, accordingly
dem'gegenüber adv in contrast
dem'gemäß adv accordingly
dem'nach adv therefore; accordingly
dem'nächst adv soon, before long; (theat) (public sign) coming soon
demobilisieren [demɔbɪlɪ'zirən] tr & intr demobilize
Demokrat [demɔ'krat] m (-en;-en) democrat
Demokra·tie [demɔkra'ti] f (-;-tien ['ti·ən]) democracy
Demokratin [demɔ'kratɪn] f (-;-nen) democrat
demokratisch [demɔ'kratɪʃ] adj democratic
demolieren [demɔ'lirən] tr demolish
Demonstrant –in [demɔn'strant(ɪn)] §7 mf demonstrator
demonstrieren [demɔn'strirən] tr & intr demonstrate
Demontage [demɔn'taʒə] f (-;) dismantling
demontieren [demɔn'tirən] tr dismantle
demselben [dɛm'zɛlbən] §4,3 dem adj & dem pron
Demut ['demut] f (-;) humility
demütig ['demytɪç] adj humble
demütigen ['demytɪgən] tr humble; (beschämen) humiliate
De'mütigung f (-;-en) humiliation
de'mutsvoll adj submissive
dem'zufolge adv accordingly
den [dɛn] §1 def art, dem adj & dem pron || §11 rel pron whom
denen ['denən] §11 rel pron to whom
Denkarbeit ['deŋkarbaɪt] f (-;) brainwork
Denkart ['deŋkart] f var of **Denkungsart**
Denkaufgabe ['deŋkaufgabə] f brain twister, problem
denkbar ['deŋkbar] adj conceivable; (vorstellbar) imaginable
denken ['deŋkən] §66 tr think, consider; **was d. Sie zu tun?** what do you intend to do? || ref—**bei sich** (or **für sich**) **d.** think to oneself; **denke dir e-e Zahl** think of a number; **d. Sie sich in ihre Lage** imagine yourself in her place; **sich** [dat] **etw d.** imagine s.th.; **was denkst du dir eigentlich?** what do you think you're doing? || intr think; **das gibt mir zu d.** that set me thinking; **d. an** (acc) think about
denk'faul adj mentally lazy
Denk'fehler m fallacy, false reasoning
Denk'mal n (-s;-e & ⸚er) monument
Denk'schrift f (pol) memorandum
Denkungsart ['deŋkuŋsart] f way of thinking, mentality
Denk'weise f way of thinking, mentality
denk'würdig adj memorable

Denk'zettel *m—j—m* e-n D. geben teach s.o. a lesson

denn [dɛn] *adv* then; es sei denn, daß unless || *conj* for

dennoch ['dɛnɔx] *adv* nevertheless, all the same, (but) still

Dentist –in [dɛn'tɪst(ɪn)] §7 *mf* dentist

Denunziant –in [dɛnʊn'tsjant(ɪn)] §7 *mf* informer

denunzieren [dɛnʊn'tsirən] *tr* denounce

Depesche [de'pɛʃə] *f* (–;–n) dispatch

De·ponens [de'ponɛns] *n* (–;–ponenzien [pə'nɛntsjən]) (gram) deponent

deponieren [depo'nirən] *tr* (com) deposit

deportieren [depɔr'tirən] *tr* deport

Depot [de'po] *n* (–s;–s) depot; warehouse; storage; safe; safe deposit

Depp [dɛp] *m* (–s;–e) (coll) dope

Depression [dɛprɛ'sjon] *f* (–;–en) depression

der [dɛr] §1 *def art* the || §1 *dem adj* & *dem pron* this, that; der und der such and such, so and so || §11 *rel pron* who, which, that; (to) whom

der'art *adv* so, in such a way; (coll) that

der'artig *adj* such, of that kind

derb [dɛrp] *adj* coarse; tough; rude

Derb'heit *f* (–;–en) coarseness; toughness; crude joke

dereinst' *adv* some day

deren ['derən] §11 *rel pron* whose

derenthalben ['derənt'halbən], **derentwegen** ['derənt'vegən], **derentwillen** ['derənt'vɪlən] *adv* for her sake, for their sake

dergestalt ['dergə'ʃtalt] *adv* so

dergleichen ['der'glaiçən] *invar dem adj* such; similar; of that kind || *invar dem pron* such a thing; und d. and the like; und d. mehr and so on

derjenige ['derjenɪgə] §4,3 *dem adj* that || *dem pron* the one; he

dermaßen [der'masən] *adv* so, in such a way

derselbe [der'zɛlbə] §4,3 *dem adj* & *dem pron* the same

derweilen ['der'vailən] *adv* meanwhile

derzeit ['der'tsait] *adv* at present

derzeitig ['der'tsaitɪç] *adj* present; then, of that time

des [dɛs] *n* (–;–) (mus) D flat

Desaster [de'zastər] *n* (–s;–) disaster

Deserteur [dezɛr'tør] *m* (–s;–e) deserter

desertieren [dezɛr'tirən] *intr* (SEIN) desert

desgleichen ['dɛs'glaiçən] *invar dem pron* such a thing || *invar rel pron* the likes of which || *adv* likewise

deshalb ['dɛshalp] *adv* therefore

Desinfektion [dɛsɪnfɛk'tsjon] *f* (–;–en) disinfection

Desinfektions'mittel *n* disinfectant

desinfizieren [dɛsɪnfɪ'tsirən] *tr* disinfect

Despot [dɛs'pot] *m* (–en;–en) despot

despotisch [dɛs'potɪʃ] *adj* despotic

Dessin [de'sɛ̃] *n* (–s;–s) design

destillieren [dɛstɪ'lirən] *tr* distill

desto ['dɛsto] *adv* the; d. besser the better, all the better

deswegen ['dɛs'vegən] *adv* therefore

Detail [de'tai(l)] *n* (–s;–s) detail; (com) retail

Detail'geschäft *n* retail store

Detail'händler –in §6 *mf* retail dealer

detaillieren [dɛta'jirən] *tr* relate in detail; specify; itemize

Detek·tiv [detɛk'tif] *m* (–s;–tive ['tivə]) private investigator; (coll) private eye

detonieren [deto'nirən] *intr* detonate; etw. d. lassen detonate s.th.

deuchte ['dɔiçtə] *pret* of dünken

Deutelei [dɔitə'lai] *f* (–;–en) quibble

deuteln ['dɔitəln] *intr* (an dat) quibble (about), split hairs (over)

deuten ['dɔitən] *tr* interpret; falsch d. misinterpret || *intr* (auf acc) (& fig) point (to)

deutlich ['dɔitlɪç] *adj* clear, distinct

deutsch [dɔitʃ] *adj* German || **Deutsche** §5 *mf* German

Deu'tung *f* (–;–en) interpretation

Devise [de'vizə] *f* (–;–n) motto; **Devisen** foreign currency

Devi'senbestand *m* foreign-currency reserve

Devi'senbilanz *f* balance of payments

Devi'senkurs *m* rate of exchange

Dezember [de'tsɛmbər] *m* (–s;–) December

dezent [de'tsɛnt] *adj* unobtrusive; (Licht, Musik) soft; (anständig) decent

Dezernat [detsɛr'nat] *n* (–[e]s;–e) (administrative) department

dezimal [detsɪ'mal] *adj* decimal || **Dezimale** [detsɪ'malə] *f* (–;–n) decimal

Dezimal'bruch *m* decimal fraction

Dezimal'zahl *f* decimal

dezimieren [detsɪ'mirən] *tr* decimate

Dia ['di·a] *n* (–s;–s) (coll) slide

Diadem [di·a'dem] *n* (–s;–e) diadem

Diagnose [di·a'gnozə] *f* (–;–n) diagnosis

diagnostizieren [di·agnɔstɪ'tsirən] *tr* diagnose

diagonal [di·ago'nal] *adj* diagonal || **Diagonale** *f* (–;–n) diagonal

Diagramm [di·a'gram] *n* (–[e]s;e) diagram; graph

Diakon [di·a'kon] *m* (–s;–e & –en;–en) deacon

Dialekt [di·a'lɛkt] *m* (–[e]s;–e) dialect

dialektisch [di·a'lɛktɪʃ] *adj* dialectical

Dialog [di·a'lok] *m* (–s;–e) dialogue

Diamant [di·a'mant] *m* (–en;–en) diamond

Diaposi·tiv [di·apɔzɪ'tif] *n* (–s;–tive ['tivə]) slide, transparency

Diät [dɪ'et] *f* (–;–en) diet (under medical supervision); **Diäten** daily allowance; diät leben be on a diet

Diät– *comb.fm.* dietary

diätetisch [dɪe'tetɪʃ] *adj* dietetic

dich [dɪç] §11 *pers pron* you, thee || *reflex pron* yourself, thyself

dicht [dɪçt] *adj* dense; thick; heavy; leakproof; tight || **Dichte** ['dɪçtə] *f* (–;–en) density

dichten ['dıçtən] *tr* tighten; caulk; compose, write ‖ *intr* write poetry

Dichter ['dıçtər] *m* (-s;-) (important) writer; poet

Dichterin ['dıçtərın] *f* (-;-nen) poetess

dichterisch ['dıçtərıʃ] *adj* poetic(al)

dicht'gedrängt *adj* tightly packed

dicht'halten §90 *intr* keep mum

Dicht'heit *f* (-;), **Dich'tigkeit** *f* (-;) density; compactness; tightness

Dich'kunst *f* poetry

dicht'machen *tr* (coll) close up

Dich'tung *f* (-;-en) gasket; packing; imagination; fiction; poetry; poem;

Dich'tungsring *m*, **Dich'tungsscheibe** *f* washer; gasket

dick [dık] *adj* thick; fat; big; (*Luft, Freunde*) close; **dicke Luft!** (coll) cheese it!; **sich d. tun** talk big ‖ **Dicke** *f* (-;) thickness, stoutness

Dick'darm *m* (anat) colon

dickfellig ['dıkfelıç] *adj* thick-skinned

dick'flüssig *adj* viscous

Dickicht ['dıkıçt] *n* (-[e]s;-e) thicket

Dick'kopf *m* thick head

dickköpfig ['dıkkœpfıç] *adj* thick-headed

dickleibig ['dıklaıbıç] *adj* stout, fat

Dick'schädel *m* thick head

dick'schädelig ['dıkʃedəlıç] *adj* thick-headed

die [di] §1 *def art* the ‖ §1 *dem adj* & *dem pron* this, that; **die und die** such and such ‖ §11 *rel pron* who, which, that

Dieb [dip] *m* (-[e]s;-e) thief

Dieberei [dibə'raı] *f* (-;-en) thievery; (*Diebstahl*) theft

Diebesbande ['dibəsbandə] *f* pack of thieves

Diebin ['dibın] *f* (-;-nen) thief

diebisch ['dibıʃ] *adj* thievish ‖ *adv*— **sich d. freuen** be tickled pink

Diebstahl ['dip/tal] *m* (-[e]s;-̈) theft, larceny; **leichter D.** petty larceny; **schwerer D.** grand larceny

diejenige ['dijenıgə] §4,3 *dem adj* that ‖ *dem pron* the one; she

Diele ['dilə] *f* (-;-n) floorboard; (*breiter Flur*) entrance hall; **Dielen** flooring

dienen ['dinən] *intr* (*dat*) serve; **damit ist mir nicht gedient** that doesn't help me any; **womit kann ich d.?** may I help you?

Diener –in ['dinər(ın)] §6 *mf* servant

die'nerhaft *adj* servile

dienern ['dinərn] *intr* bow and scrape

Die'nerschaft *f* (-;) domestics, help

dienlich ['dinlıç] *adj* useful

Dienst [dinst] *m* (-es;-e) service; job; employment; (adm, mil) grade; **außer D.** retired; **im. D.** on duty; **j-m e-n D. tun** do s.o. a favor

Dienstag ['dinstak] *m* (-[e]s;-e) Tuesday

Dienst'alter *n* seniority

dienstbar ['dinstbar] *adj* subservient

Dienst'barkeit *f* (-;) servitude, bondage; (jur) easement

dienst'beflissen *adj* eager to serve ‖ *adv* eagerly

Dienst'bote *m* servant, domestic

Dienst'boteneingang *m* service entrance

Dienst'eid *m* oath of office

dienst'eifrig *adj* eager to serve ‖ *adv* eagerly

Dienst'einteilung *f* work schedule; (mil) duty roster

Dienst'fahrt *f* official trip

dienst'frei *adj*—**d. haben** be off duty

Dienst'gebrauch *m*—**nur zum D.** for official use only

Dienst'gespräch *n* business call

Dienst'grad *m* (mil) rank, grade; (nav) rating

dienst'habend *adj* on duty

Dienst'herr *m* employer; (hist) lord

Dienst'leistung *f* service

dienst'lich *adj* official ‖ *adv* officially; on official business

Dienst'mädchen *n* maid

Dienst'pflicht *f* official duty; compulsory military service

Dienst'plan *m* work schedule; (mil) duty roster

Dienst'sache *f* official business

dienst'tauglich *adj* fit for active service

diensttuend ['dinsttu·ənt] *adj* on duty; active; in charge

Dienst'weg *m* official channels

Dienst'wohnung *f* official residence

dies [dis] *dem adj* & *dem pron* var of **dieses**

diese ['dizə] §3 *dem adj* this ‖ *dem pron* this one

dieselbe [di'zelbə] §4,3 *dem adj* & *dem pron* the same

Dieselmotor ['dizəlmotor] *m* diesel engine

dieser ['dizər] §3 *dem adj* this ‖ *dem pron* this one

dieses ['dizəs] §3 *dem adj* this ‖ *dem pron* this one

diesig ['dizıç] *adj* hazy, misty

dies'jährig *adj* this year's

dies'mal *adv* this time

diesseits ['diszaıts] *prep* (*genit*) on this side of

Dietrich ['ditrıç] *m* (-s;-e) skeleton key; (*Einbrecherwerkzeug*) picklock

Differential [dıferən'tsjal] *n* (-s;-e) (aut, math) differential

Differential– *comb.fm.* (econ, elec, mach, math, phys) differential

Differenz [dıfe'rents] *f* (-;-en) difference

Diktaphon [dıkta'fon] *n* (-[e]s;-e) dictaphone

Diktat [dık'tat] *n* (-s;-e) dictation; **nach D. schreiben** take dictation

Dik·tator [dık'tator] *m* (-s;-tatoren) [ta'torən]) dictator

diktatorisch [dıkta'toriʃ] *adj* dictatorial

Diktatur [dıkta'tur] *f* (-;-en) dictatorship

diktieren [dık'tirən] *tr* & *intr* dictate

Dilettant –in [dıle'tant(ın)] §7 *mf* dilettante, amateur

Diner [dı'ne] *n* (-s;-s) dinner

Ding [dıŋ] *n* (-[e]s;-e) thing; **ein D. drehen** (coll) pull a job

dingen ['dıŋən] §109 & §142 *tr* hire

ding'fest *adj*—**j-n d. machen** arrest s.o.
ding'lich *adj* real
Dings [dɪŋs] *n* (-s;) (coll) thing, doodad, thingamajig
Dings'bums *m* & *n* (-;) var of **Dingsda**
Dings'da *mfn* (-s;) what-d'ye-call-it
Diözese [dɪ·ø'tsezə] *f* (-;-n) diocese
Diphtherie [dɪfte'ri] *f* (-;) diphtheria
Dipl.-Ing. *abbr* (**Diplom-Ingenieur**) engineer holding a degree
Diplom [dɪ'plom] *n* (-s;-e) diploma
Diplom- *comb.fm.* holding a degree
Diplomat [dɪplɔ'mat] *m* (-en;-en) diplomat
Diplomatie [dɪplɔma'ti] *f* (-;) diplomacy
Diplomatin [dɪplɔ'matɪn] *f* (-;-nen) diplomat
diplomatisch [dɪplɔ'matɪʃ] *adj* diplomatic
dir [dir] §11 *pers pron* to or for you, to or for thee ‖ *reflex pron* to or for yourself, to or for thyself
direkt [dɪ'rɛkt] *adj* direct
Direktion [dɪrɛk'tsjon] *f* (-;) direction; (*Verwaltung*) management
Direk•tor [dɪ'rɛktɔr] *m* (-s;-toren ['torən]) director; (*e-r Bank*) president; (*e-r Schule*) principal; (*e-s Gefängnisses*) warden
Direktorat [dɪrɛktɔ'rat] *n* (-[e]s;-e) directorship
Direktorin [dɪrɛk'torɪn] *f* (-;-nen) director; (educ) principal
Direkto•rium [dɪrɛk'torɪ·um] *n* (-s; -rien [rɪ·ən]) board of directors; executive committee
Direktrice [dɪrɛk'trisə] *f* (-;-n) directress, manager
Dirigent –in [dɪrɪ'gɛnt(ɪn)] §7 *mf* (mus) conductor
dirigieren [dɪrɪ'girən] *tr* direct, manage; (mus) conduct
Dirnd(e)l ['dɪrndəl] *n* (-s;-) girl; (*Tracht*) dirndle
Dirne ['dɪrnə] *f* (-;-n) girl; (pej) prostitute
Dis [dɪs] *n* (-;-) D sharp
disharmonisch [dɪshar'monɪʃ] *adj* discordant
Diskont [dɪs'kɔnt] *m* (-[e]s;-e) discount
diskontieren [dɪskɔn'tirən] *tr* discount
Diskothek [dɪskɔ'tek] *f* (-;-en) discotheque
diskret [dɪs'kret] *adj* discreet
Diskretion [dɪskre'tsjon] *f* (-;-en) discretion
Diskussion [dɪsku'sjon] *f* (-;-en) discussion
diskutieren [dɪsku'tirən] *tr* discuss ‖ *intr*—**d. über** (*acc*) discuss
disponieren [dɪspɔ'nirən] *intr* (**über** *acc*) dispose (of)
Disposition [dɪspɔzɪ'tsjon] *f* (-;-en) disposition; arrangement; disposal
Distanz [dɪs'tants] *f* (-;-en) distance
distanzieren [dɪstan'tsirən] *tr* (**mit**) beat (by, *e.g., one meter*) ‖ *ref* (**von**) dissociate oneself (from)
distanziert' *adj* (fig) detached
Distel ['dɪstəl] *f* (-;-n) thistle
Dis'telfink *m* goldfinch

Distrikt [dɪs'trɪkt] *m* (-[e]s;-e) district
Disziplin [dɪstsɪ'plin] *f* (-;-en) discipline
disziplinarisch [dɪstsɪplɪ'narɪʃ] *adj* disciplinary
dito ['dito] *adv* ditto ‖ **Dito** *n* (-s;-s) ditto
Dividend [dɪvɪ'dɛnt] *m* (-en;-en), **Dividende** [dɪvɪ'dɛndə] *f* (-;-n) dividend
dividieren [dɪvɪ'dirən] *tr* divide
Division [dɪvɪ'zjon] *f* (-;-en) division
Diwan ['divan] *m* (-s;-e) divan
D-Mark ['demark] *f* (-;-) mark (*monetary unit of West Germany*)
doch [dɔx] *adv* yet; of course
Docht [dɔxt] *m* (-[e]s;-e) wick
Dock [dɔk] *n* (-[e]s;-s & -e) dock
docken ['dɔkən] *tr* & *intr* (naut, rok) dock
Dogge ['dɔgə] *f* (-;-n) mastiff; **deutsche D.** Great Dane
Dog•ma ['dɔgma] *n* (-s;-men [mən]) dogma
Dohle ['dolə] *f* (-;-n) jackdaw
Dok•tor ['dɔktɔr] *m* (-s;-toren ['torən]) doctor
Dok'torarbeit *f* dissertation
Dok'torvater *m* adviser (*for a doctoral dissertation*)
Dokument [dɔku'mɛnt] *n* (-[e]s;-e) document; (jur) instrument, deed
Dokumentarfilm [dɔkumen'tarfɪlm] *m* documentary
dokumentarisch [dɔkumen'tarɪʃ] *adj* documentary
Dolch [dɔlç] *m* (-[e]s;-e) dagger
Dolch'stoß *m* (pol) stab in the back
Dollar ['dɔlar] *m* (-s;-) dollar
dolmetschen ['dɔlmetʃən] *tr* & *intr* interpret
Dol'metscher –in §6 *mf* interpreter
Dom [dom] *m* (-[e]s;-e) cathedral; dome
Domäne [dɔ'menə] *f* (-;-n) domain
Domino ['domino] *n* (-s;-s) domino
Donau ['donau] *f* (-;) Danube
Donner ['dɔnər] *m* (-s;-) thunder
Don'nerkeil *m* thunderbolt
donnern ['dɔnərn] *intr* thunder
Don'nerschlag *m* clap of thunder
Don'nerstag *m* (-[e]s;-e) Thursday
Don'nerwetter *n* thunderstorm; **zum D.!** confound it! ‖ *interj* geez!
doof [dof] *adj* (coll) goofy
dopen ['dopən] *tr* dope (*a racehorse*)
Doppel ['dɔpəl] *n* (-s;-) duplicate; (tennis) doubles
Doppel- *comb.fm.* double, two, bi-, twin
Dop'pelbelichtung *f* double exposure
Dop'pelbild *n* (telv) ghost
Dop'pelbruch *m* compound fracture
Dop'pelehe *f* bigamy
Dop'pelgänger *m* double; second self
Dop'pellaut *m* diphthong
doppeln ['dɔpəln] *tr* double
Dop'pelprogramm *n* double feature
Dop'pelpunkt *m* (typ) colon
doppelreihig ['dɔpəlraɪ·ɪç] *adj* double-breasted
Dop'pelrendezvous *n* double date

dop'pelseitig *adj* reversible; (*Lunge-nentzündung*) double

Dop'pelsinn *m* double entendre

dop'pelsinnig *adj* ambiguous

Dop'pelspiel *n* (fig) double-dealing; (sport) double-header; (tennis) doubles

doppelt ['dɔpəlt] *adj* double; **doppelter Boden** false bottom; **ein doppeltes Spiel spielen mit** doublecross; **in doppelter Ausführung** in duplicate || *adv* twice; **ein Buch d. haben** have two copies of a book

Dop'pelverdiener **-in** §6 *mf* moonlighter

Dop'pelvokal *m* diphthong

doppelzüngig ['dɔpəltsyŋɪç] *adj* two-faced

Dorf [dɔrf] *n* (-[e]s;⸚er) village

Dorf'bewohner **-in** §6 *mf* villager

Dörfchen ['dœrfçən] *n* (-s;-) hamlet

Dorn [dɔrn] *m* (-[e]s;-en) thorn; tongue (*of a buckle*); (mach) pin; (sport) spike

Dorn'busch *m* briar, bramble

dornig ['dɔrnɪç] *adj* thorny

Dornröschen ['dɔrnrøsçən] *n* (-s;) Sleeping Beauty

Dörr- [dœr] *comb.fm.* dried

dorren ['dɔrən] *intr* (SEIN) dry (up)

dörren ['dœrən] *tr* dry

Dorschlebertran ['dɔrʃlebərtran] *m* (-[e]s;) cod-liver oil

dort [dɔrt] *adv* there, over there

dort'her *adv* from there

dort'hin *adv* there, to that place

dor'tig *adj* in that place, there

Dose ['dozə] *f* (-;-n) can; box

dösen ['døzən] *intr* doze

Do'senöffner *m* can opener

dosieren [do'zirən] *tr* prescribe (the correct dosage of)

Dosie'rung *f* (-;-en) dosage

Do·sis ['dozɪs] *f* (-;-sen [zən]) dose

dotieren [do'tirən] *tr* endow; **ein Preis mit 100 Mark dotiert** a prize worth 100 marks

Dotter ['dɔtər] *m & n* (-s;-) yolk

Double ['dubəl] *m & n* (-s;-s) (cin, theat) stand-in

Dozent **-in** [do'tsɛnt(ɪn)] §7 (university) instructor, lecturer

Drache ['draxə] *m* (-n;-n) dragon; (*böses Weib*) battle-ax

Drachen ['draxən] *m* (-s;-) kite

Dra'chenfliegen *n* (-s;) hang gliding

Draht [drat] *m* (-[e]s;⸚e) wire; **auf D. sein** (coll) be on the beam

drahten ['dratən] *tr* telegraph, wire

draht'haarig *adj* wire-haired

Draht'hindernis *n* (mil) wire entanglement, barbed wire

drahtig ['dratɪç] *adj* wiry

draht'los *adj* wireless

Draht'seil *n* cable

Draht'seilbahn *f* cable car, funicular

Draht'zaun *m* wire fence

drall [dral] *adj* plump; (*Faden*) sturdy || **Drall** *m* (-s;-e) rifling

Dra·ma ['drama] *n* (-s;-men [mən]) drama

Dramatiker **-in** [dra'matikər(ɪn)] §6 *mf* dramatist, playwright

dramatisch [dra'matɪʃ] *adj* dramatic

dran [dran] *adv* var of **daran**

drang [draŋ] *pret* of **dringen** || **Drang** *m* (-[e]s;⸚e) pressure; urge

drängeln ['drɛŋəln] *tr & intr* shove

drängen ['drɛŋən] *tr & intr* push, shove; (*drücken*) press || *ref* crowd, crowd together; force one's way

Drangsal ['draŋzal] *f* (-;-e) distress, anguish; hardship

drangsalieren [draŋza'lirən] *tr* vex

drastisch ['drastɪʃ] *adj* drastic

drauf [drauf] *adv* var of **darauf**

Drauf'gänger *m* (-s;-) go-getter

drauf'gehen §82 *intr* (SEIN) (coll) go down the drain

drauflos' *adv*—**d. arbeiten an** (*dat*) work away at

drauflos'gehen §82 *intr* (SEIN)—**d. auf** (*acc*) make straight for

drauflos'reden *intr* ramble on

drauflos'schlagen §132 *intr* (**auf** *acc*) let fly (at)

draußen ['drausən] *adv* outside; out of doors; (*in der Fremde*) abroad

drechseln ['drɛksəln] *tr* work (*on a lathe*); (fig) embellish

Dreck [drɛk] *m* (-[e]s;) dirt; mud; excrement; (*Abfälle*) trash

dreckig ['drɛkɪç] *adj* dirty; muddy

Dreh- [dre] *comb.fm.* revolving, rotary

Dreh'arbeiten *pl* (cin) shooting

Dreh'aufzug *m* dumb waiter

Dreh'bank *f* (-;⸚e) lathe

drehbar ['drebar] *adj* revolving

Dreh'buch *n* (mov) script, scenario

drehen ['dre·ən] *tr* turn; (*Zigaretten*) roll; (coll) wangle; (cin) shoot || *ref* turn; rotate

Dreh'kreuz *n* turnstile

Dreh'orgel *f* hurdy-gurdy

Dreh'orgelspieler *m* organ grinder

Dreh'punkt *m* fulcrum; (fig) pivotal point

Dreh'scheibe *f* potter's wheel; (rr) turntable

Dreh'stuhl *m* swivel chair

Dre'hung *f* (-;-en) turn

Dreh'zahl *f* revolutions per minute

Dreh'zahlmesser *m* tachometer

drei [drai] *adj & pron* three || **Drei** *f* (-;-en) three; (educ) C

dreidimensional ['draidɪmɛnzjɔnal] *adj* three-dimensional

Dreieck ['drai·ɛk] *n* (-[e]s;-e) triangle

drei'eckig *adj* triangular

drei'fach *adj* threefold, triple

dreifältig ['draifɛltɪç] *adj* threefold, triple

Dreifaltigkeit [drai'faltɪçkait] *f* (-;) Trinity

Drei'fuß *m* tripod

Dreikäsehoch [drai'kezəhoç] *m* (-s;-) (coll) shrimp, runt

drei'mal *adv* three times, thrice

Drei'rad *n* tricycle

Drei'sprung *m* hop, step, and jump

dreißig ['draisɪç] *adj & pron* thirty || **Dreißig** *f* (-;- & -en) thirty

dreißiger ['draisɪgər] *invar adj* of the thirties, in the thirties

dreißigste ['draisɪçstə] §9 *adj & pron* thirtieth

dreist [draɪst] *adj* brazen, bold
dreistimmig ['draɪ∫tɪmɪç] *adj* for three voices
drei'zehn *adj & pron* thirteen || **Dreizehn** *f* (-;-) thirteen
drei'zehnte §9 *adj & pron* thirteenth
dreschen ['drε∫ən] §67 *tr* thresh; (coll) thrash
Dresch'flegel *m* flail
Dresch'tenne *f* threshing floor
dressieren [drε'sirən] *tr* train; (*Pferd*) break in
Dressur [drε'sur] *f* (-;) training
dribbeln ['drɪbəln] *intr* (sport) dribble
drillen ['drɪlən] *tr* drill; train
Drillich ['drɪlɪç] *m* (-s;-e) denim
Dril'lichanzug *m* dungarees; (mil) fatigue uniform, fatigues
Dril lichhosen *pl* dungarees, jeans
Drilling ['drɪlɪŋ] *m* (-s;-e) triplet
drin [drɪn] *adv* var of **darin**
dringen ['drɪŋən] §142 *intr* (auf *acc*) press (for), insist (on); (in *acc*) pressure, urge || *intr* (SEIN) (aus) break forth (from); (**durch**) penetrate, pierce; (**durch**) force one's way (through); (in *acc*) penetrate (into), get (into); **in die Öffentlichkeit d.** leak out; **in j-n d.** press the point with s.o.; **d. bis zu** get as far as
drin'gend *adj* urgent; (*Gefahr*) imminent; (*Verdacht*) strong
dring'lich *adj* urgent
Dring'lichkeit *f* (-;-en) urgency; priority
Drink [drɪŋk] *m* (-s;-s) alcoholic drink
drinnen ['drɪnən] *adv* inside
dritt [drɪt] *adv*—**zu d.** the three of
dritte ['drɪtə] §9 *adj & pron* third; **ein Dritter** a disinterested person; (com, jur) a third party
Drittel ['drɪtəl] *n* (-s;-) third (*part*)
drittens ['drɪtəns] *adv* thirdly
dritt'letzt *adj* third from last
droben ['drobən] *adv* above; up there
Droge ['drogə] *f* (-;-n) drug
Droge·rie [drogə'ri] *f* (-;-rien ['ri·ən]) drugstore
Drogist –**in** [dro'gɪst(ɪn)] §7 *mf* druggist
Droh'brief *m* threatening letter
drohen ['dro·ən] *intr* (dat) threaten
dro'hend *adj* threatening; impending
Drohne ['dronə] *f* (-;-n) drone
dröhnen ['drønən] *intr* boom, roar; (*Kopf, Motor*) throb
Dro'hung *f* (-;-en) threat
drollig ['drolɪç] *adj* amusing, funny
Dromedar [dromε'dar] *n* (-s;-e) dromedary
drosch [dro∫] *pret* of **dreschen**
Droschke ['dro∫kə] *f* (-;-n) cab, hackney; taxi
Drosch'kenkutscher *m* coachman
Drossel ['drosəl] *f* (-;-n) thrush; (aut) throttle
Dros'selhebel *m* (aut) throttle
drosseln ['drosəln] *tr* (coll) curb, cut; (aut) throttle; (elec) choke
drüben ['drybən] *adv* over there
Druck [druk] *m* (-[e]s;-̈e) (& fig) pressure; (*der Hand*) squeeze; (phys)

compression, pressure || *m* (-[e]s-e) printing; print, type; (tex) print
Druck'anzug *m* (aer) pressurized suit
Druck'bogen *m* (printed) sheet
druck'dicnt *adj* pressurized
Drückeberger ['drʏkəbergər] *m* (-s;-) shirker; absentee; (mil) goldbrick
drucken ['drukən] *tr* print
drücken ['drʏkən] *tr* press; squeeze; imprint; (*Preise*) lower; (cards) discard; **die Stimmung d.** be a kill-joy; **j–m die Hand d.** shake hands with s.o. || *intr* (*Schuh*) pinch
Druck'entlastung *f* decompression
Drucker ['drukər] *m* (-s;-) printer
Drücker ['drʏkər] *m* (-s;-) push button; (*e–s Schlosses*) latch, latch key; (*e–s Gewehrs*) trigger
Druckerei [drukə'raɪ] *f* (-;-en) print shop, press
Druckerschwärze (**Druk'kerschwärze**) *f* printer's ink
Druck'fehler *m* misprint
druck'fertig *adj* ready for the press
druck'fest *adj* pressurized
Druck'kabine *f* pressurized cabin
Druck'knopf *m* push button; (*am Kleid*) snap
Druck'knopfbetätigung *f* push-button control
Druck'luft *f* compressed air
Druckluft– *comb.fm.* pneumatic, air
Druck'luftbremse *f* air brake
Druck'lufthammer *m* jackhammer
Druck'messer *m* pressure gauge
Druck'sache *f* printed matter; **Drucksachen** (com) literature
Druck'schrift *f* type; block letters; publication, printed work; leaflet
drucksen ['druksən] *intr* hem and haw
drum [drum] *adv* var of **darum**
Drüse ['dryzə] *f* (-;-n) gland
Drüsen– *comb.fm.* glandular
Dschungel ['d͡ʒuŋəl] *m* (-s;-) jungle
du [du] §11 *per pron* you, thou
Dübel ['dybəl] *m* (-s;-) dowel
Dublette [du'blεtə] *f* (-;-n) duplicate; imitation stone
ducken ['dukən] *tr* (den *Kopf*) duck; (coll) take down a peg or two || *ref* duck
Duckmäuser ['dukmɔɪzər] *m* (-s;-) pussyfoot
dudeln ['dudəln] *tr* hum || *intr* hum, drone; (mus) play the bagpipe
Dudelsack ['dudəlzak] *m* bagpipe
Duell [du'εl] *n* (-s;-e) duel
duellieren [du·ə'lirən] *recip* duel
Duett [du'εt] *n* (-[e]s;-e) duet
Duft [duft] *m* (-[e]s;-̈e) fragrance
duften ['duftən] *intr* be fragrant
duf'tend *adj* fragrant
duftig ['duftɪç] *adj* flimsy, dainty
dulden ['duldən] *tr* (ertragen) bear; (leiden) suffer; (zulassen) tolerate || *intr* suffer
duldsam ['duldzam] *adj* tolerant
Duld'samkeit *f* (-;) tolerance
dumm [dum] *adj* stupid, dumb; foolish
Dumm'heit *f* (-;-en) stupidity; foolishness; (*Streich*) foolish prank
Dumm'kopf *m* dunderhead
dumpf [dumpf] *adj* dull, muffled;

(*schwül*) muggy; (*moderig*) musty, moldy; (*Ahnung*) vague

dumpfig ['dʊmpfɪç] *adj* musty, moldy; muggy

Düne ['dynə] *f* (-;-n) sand dune

Dung [dʊŋ] *m* (-[e]s;) dung; (*künstlicher*) fertilizer

düngen ['dyŋən] *tr* manure; fertilize

Dünger ['dyŋər] *m* (-s;) var of **Dung**

dunkel ['dʊŋkəl] *adj* dark; vague; obscure || **Dunkel** *n* (-s;) darkness

Dünkel ['dyŋkəl] *m* (-s;) conceit

dün'kelhaft *adj* conceited

Dun'kelheit *f* (-;) darkness; obscurity

Dun'kelkammer *f* (phot) darkroom

Dun'kelmann *m* (-[e]s;∸er) shady character

dünn [dyn] *adj* thin

Dunst [dʊnst] *m* (-es;∸e) vapor, mist, haze; (*Rauch*) smoke; (*Dampf*) steam; **in D. und Rauch aufgehen** (fig) go up in smoke; **sich in (blauen) D. auflösen** vanish in thin air

dünsten ['dynstən] *tr & intr* stew; steam

dunstig ['dʊnstɪç] *adj* steamy; (*Wetter*) misty, hazy

Duplikat [dʊplɪ'kɑt] *n* (-[e]s;-e) duplicate; copy

Dur [dur] *invar n* (mus) major

durch [dʊrç] *adv* throughout; **d. und d.** through and through || *prep* (*acc*) through, by, by means of

durch'arbeiten *tr* work through || *ref* (durch) work one's way (through); elbow one's way (through)

durchaus' *adv* throughout; entirely; quite, absolutely; **d. nicht** by no means

durch'backen §50 *tr* bake through and through

durch'blättern *tr* thumb through

durch'bleuen *tr* beat up

Durch'blick *m* vista

durch'blicken *intr* be apparent; (durch) look (through); **d. lassen** intimate

durchblutet [dʊrç'blutət] *adj* supplied with blood

durch'bohren *tr* bore through || **durchboh'ren** *tr* pierce

durch'braten §63 *tr* roast thoroughly

durchbre'chen §64 *tr* break through; (*Vorschriften*) violate; (mil) breach || **durch'brechen** *tr* cut (*a hole*); break in half || *intr* (SEIN) break through

durch'brennen §97 *tr* burn through; (*e-e Sicherung*) blow || *intr* (SEIN) run away; (*Sicherung*) blow

durch'bringen §65 *tr* get through; (*Gesetz*) pass; (*Geld*) spend; (med) pull (*a patient*) through || *ref* support oneself; **sich ehrlich d.** make an honest living

Durch'bruch *m* breakthrough; (*Öffnung*) breach, gap; (*der Zähne*) cutting

durch'denken §66 *tr* think through || **durchden'ken** *tr* think out, think over

durch'drängen *ref* push one's way through

durch'drehen *tr* grind; (*Wäsche*) put

through the wringer || *intr* (SEIN) (coll) go mad

durchdrin'gen §142 *tr* penetrate; pervade, imbue || **durch'dringen** *intr* (SEIN) get through; penetrate

durch'drucken *tr* (parl) push through

durchdrungen [dʊrç'drʊŋən] *adj* imbued

durchei'len *tr* rush through || **durch'eilen** *intr* (SEIN) (durch) rush through

durcheinan'der *adj & adv* in confusion || **Durcheinander** *n* (-s;-) mess, muddle

durcheinan'derbringen §65 *tr* muddle

durcheinan'dergeraten §63 *intr* (SEIN) get mixed up

durcheinan'derlaufen §105 *intr* (SEIN) mill about

durcheinan'derreden *intr* speak all at once

durcheinan'derwerfen §160 *tr* throw into confusion, turn upside down

durchfah'ren §71 *tr* travel through; (*Gedanke, Schreck*) strike || **durch'fahren** §71 *intr* (SEIN) go through without stopping

Durch'fahrt *f* passage; **keine D.!** no thoroughfare

Durch'fahrtshöhe *f* clearance

Durch'fall *m* diarrhea; (coll) flop; (educ) flunk, failure

durch'fallen §72 *intr* (SEIN) fall through; (educ) flunk; (theat) flop

durch'fechten §74 *tr* fight through

durch'finden §59 *ref* find one's way

durchflech'ten *tr* interweave

durchfor'schen *tr* examine, make an exhaustive study of

Durchfor'schung *f* exploration; search; thorough research

durch'fressen §70 *tr* eat through; corrode || *ref* (bei) sponge (on); (durch) work one's way (through)

Durchfuhr ['dʊrçfur] *f* (-;-en) transit

durchführbar ['dʊrçfyrbɑr] *adj* feasible

durch'führen *tr* lead through or across; (*Auftrag*) carry out; (*Gesetz*) enforce

Durch'gang *m* passage; aisle; (fig) transition; (astr, com) transit; **D. verboten!** no thoroughfare, no trespassing

Durch'gänger *m* (-s;-) runaway

Durch'gangslager *n* transit camp

Durch'gangsverkehr *m* through traffic

Durch'gangszug *m* through train

durch'geben §80 *tr* pass on

durch'gebraten *adj* (culin) well done

durch'gehen §82 *tr* (SEIN) go through; (*durchlesen*) go over || *intr* (SEIN) go through; (*Pferd*) bolt; (*heimlich davonlaufen*) run away; abscond; (*Vorschlag*) pass

durch'gehend(s) *adv* generally; (*durchaus*) throughout

durchgeistigt [dʊrç'gaɪstɪçt] *adj* highly intellectual

durch'greifen §88 *intr* reach through; (fig) take drastic measures

durch'greifend *adj* vigorous; drastic

durch'halten §90 *tr* keep up || *intr* hold out, stick it out

durch'hauen §93 *tr* chop through;

knock a hole through; (coll) thrash, beat
durch′hecheln tr (coll) run down
durch′helfen §96 intr (dat) (durch) help (through) ‖ ref ′get by, manage
durch′kämmen tr (& fig) comb through
durch′kochen tr boil thoroughly
durch′kommen §99 intr (SEIN) come through; (durch Krankheit) pull through; (sich durchhelfen) get by; (educ) pass
durchkreu′zen tr cross; (durchstreichen) cross out; (fig) frustrate
Durch·laß ['durçlas] m (–lasses;–lässe) passage; outlet; culvert
durch′lassen §104 tr let through, let pass; (Licht) transmit; (educ) pass
durchlässig ['durçlesıç] adj permeable
Durch′laßschein m pass
durchlau′fen §105 tr run through; look through; (Schule) go through; **seine Bahn d.** run its course ‖ **durch′laufen** §105 ref—sich [dat] **die Schuhe d.** wear out one's shoes ‖ §105 intr (SEIN) run through
durchle′ben tr live through
durch′lesen §107 tr read over, peruse
durchleuch′ten tr illuminate; (Gesicht) light up; (Ei) test; X-ray
durch′liegen §108 ref develop bedsores ‖ **Durchliegen** n (–s;) bedsores
durchlo′chen tr punch
durch′löchern tr perforate; pierce; (mit Kugeln) riddle
durch′machen tr go through, undergo
Durch′marsch m marching through; (coll) diarrhea, runs
Durch′messer m diameter
durchnäs′sen tr soak, drench
durch′nehmen §116 tr (in der Klasse) do, have
durch′pausen tr trace
durch′peitschen tr whip soundly; (Gesetzentwurf) rush through
durchque′ren tr cross, traverse
durch′rechnen tr check, go over
Durch′reise f passage; **auf seiner D.** on his way through
durch′reisen intr (SEIN) travel through
Durch′reisende §5 mf transient, transit passenger
durch′reißen §53 tr tear in half ‖ intr (SEIN) tear, break, snap
Durch′sage f special announcement
durch′sagen tr announce
durchschau′en tr (fig) see through ‖ **durch′schauen** intr look through
durch′scheinen §128 intr shine through; show through; be seen
durch′scheuern tr rub through
durchschie′ßen §76 tr shoot through, riddle; (typ) lead ‖ **durch′schießen** §76 intr (durch) shoot (through) ‖ intr (SEIN) dash through
Durch′schlag m carbon copy; (Sieb) (large) strainer, separator; (elec) breakdown; (tech) punch
durchschla′gen §132 tr penetrate ‖ **durch′schlagen** §132 tr knock a hole through; (Holz) split; (Fensterscheibe) smash; (Nagel) drive through; (Kartoffeln, Früchte) strain; (mit Kohlepapier) make a carbon copy of

‖ ref fight one's way through; (sich durchhelfen) manage ‖ intr come through; penetrate; take effect; show up ‖ intr (SEIN) (Sicherung) blow
durch′schlagend adj effective; striking
Durch′schlagpapier n carbon paper
durch′schleichen §85 ref & intr (SEIN) creep through
durchschleu′sen tr pass (a ship) through a lock; (Passagiere, Rekruten, usw.) process; (fig) sneak (s.o.) through
durch′schneiden §106 tr cut through; cut in half ‖ **durchschnei′den** §106 tr cut through, cut across ‖ ref cross, intersect
Durch′schnitt m cutting through; average; cross section; **der große D. der Menschen** the majority of people; **im D.** on an average
durch′schnittlich adj average ‖ adv on the average
Durchschnitts– comb.fm. average; mean
Durch′schnittsmensch m average person
durch′schreiben §62 tr make a carbon copy of
durch′sehen §138 tr look over, examine; (flüchtig anschauen) scan; (Papiere, Post) check ‖ intr see through
durch′seihen tr filter; percolate
durchset′zen tr intersperse; penetrate ‖ **durch′setzen** tr carry through; **d., daß** bring it about that, succeed in (ger) ‖ ref get one's way
Durch′sicht f examination, inspection; (auf acc) view (of)
durch′sichtig adj transparent; clear
durch′sickern intr (SEIN) seep out; (Wahrheit, Gerücht) leak out
durch′sieben tr sift
durch′sprechen §64 tr talk over
durchste′chen §64 tr pierce ‖ **durch′stechen** §64 tr (Nadel) stick through
durch′stehen §146 tr go through
durchstö′bern tr rummage through
durch′stoßen §150 tr push (s.th.) through; (Tür) knock down; (Scheibe) smash in; (Ellbogen) wear through; (mil) penetrate ‖ **durchsto′ßen** §150 tr break through ‖ **durch′stoßen** §150 intr (SEIN) break through
durchstrei′chen §85 tr roam through ‖ **durch′streichen** §85 tr cross out
durchstrei′fen tr wander through
durchsu′chen tr go through, search
durch′treten §152 tr (Sohle) wear a hole in; (Gashebel) floor ‖ intr (SEIN) go through, pass through
durchtrieben [durç′tribən] adj sly
durchwa′chen tr remain awake through
durchwach′sen adj gristly
durch′wählen tr & intr dial direct
durchwan′dern tr travel or walk through ‖ **durch′wandern** intr (SEIN) (durch) walk (through), hike (through)
durchwe′ben tr interweave
durch′weg(s) adv throughout
durchwei′chen, durch′weichen tr soak
durchwüh′len tr burrow through; (Ge-

päck, Schränke) rummage through ||
durch'wühlen *ref* burrow through;
(fig) work one's way through
durch'wursteln *ref* muddle through
durchzie'hen §163 *tr* pass through,
cross; (*Zimmer*) permeate, fill;
streak; (sew) interweave || **durch'-**
ziehen §163 *tr* pull through || *intr*
(SEIN) pass through; flow through
durchzucken (durchzuk'ken) *tr* flash
through the mind of
Durch'zug *m* passage; (*Luftzug*) draft
durch'zwängen *tr* force through || *ref*
squeeze through
dürfen ['dʏrfən] §69 *aux* be allowed;
be likely; **darf ich?** may I?; **ich darf**
nicht I must not; **man darf wohl er-**
warten it is to be expected
durfte ['dʊrftə] *pret* of **dürfen**
dürftig ['dʏrftɪç] *adj* needy; poor,
wretched, miserable, scanty
dürr [dʏr] *adj* dry; (*Boden*) arid, barren; (*Holz*) dead, dry; (*Mensch*)
skinny || **Dürre** ['dʏrə] *f* (–;) dry-
ness; barrenness; leanness; drought
Durst [dʊrst] *m* (–[e]s;) (**nach**) thirst
(for); **D. haben** be thirsty

dursten ['dʊrstən], **dürsten** ['dʏr-
stən] *intr* be thirsty; (**nach**) thirst
(for)
durstig ['dʊrstɪç] *adj* thirsty
Dusche ['duʃə] *f* (–;–n) shower
duschen ['duʃən] *intr* take a shower
Düse ['dyzə] *f* (–;–n) nozzle, jet
Dusel ['duzəl] *m* (–s;–) (coll) fluke
Düsen– *comb.fm.* jet
Dü'senantrieb *m* jet propulsion
Dü'senjäger *m* jet fighter
düster ['dystər] *adj* gloomy; sad; dark
|| **Düster** *n* (–s;) gloom; darkness
Dutzend ['dʊtsənt] *n* (–s;– & –e) dozen
dut'zendmal *adv* a dozen times
dut'zendweise *adv* by the dozen
Duzbruder ['dʊtsbrudər] *m* buddy
duzen ['dʊtsən] *tr* say **du** to, be on in-
timate terms with
Dynamik [dʏ'namɪk] *f* (–s;) dynamics
dynamisch [dʏ'namɪʃ] *adj* dynamic
Dynamit [dʏna'mit] *n* (–s;–e) dyna-
mite
Dynamo ['dynamo] *m* (–s;–s) dynamo
Dyna•stie [dʏnas'ti] *f* (–;–stien
['sti•ən] dynasty
D'-Zug *m* through train, express

E

E, e [e] *invar n* E, e; (mus) E
Ebbe ['ɛbə] *f* (–;–n) ebb tide
eben ['ebən] *adj* even, level, flat; **zu**
ebener Erde on the ground floor ||
adv just; a moment ago; exactly
|| *interj* exactly!; that's right!
E'benbild *n* image, exact likeness
ebenbürtig ['ebənbʏrtɪç] *adj* of equal
rank, equal
ebenda ['ebən'da] *adv* right there;
(*beim Zitieren*) ibidem
ebendersel'be §4,3 *adj* self-same
ebendes'wegen *adv* for that very reason
Ebene ['ebənə] *f* (–;–n) plain; (fig)
level; (geom) plane
e'benerdig *adj* ground-floor
e'benfalls *adv* likewise, too
E'benholz *n* ebony
E'benmaß *n* right proportions
e'benmäßig *adj* well-proportioned
e'benso *adv* just as; likewise
e'bensogut *adv* just as well
e'bensoviel *adv* just as much
e'bensowenig *adv* just as little
Eber ['ebər] *m* (–s;–) boar
E'beresche *f* mountain ash
ebnen ['ebnən] *tr* level, even; smooth
Echo ['ɛço] *n* (–s;–s) echo
echoen ['ɛço•ən] *intr* echo
echt [ɛçt] *adj* genuine, real, true
Eck [ɛk] *n* (–[e]s;–e) corner; end
Eck– *comb.fm.* corner; end
Ecke ['ɛkə] *f* (–;–n) corner; edge
Ecker ['ɛkər] *f* (–;–n) beechnut
eckig ['ɛkɪç] *adj* angular; (fig) awkward; **eckige Klammer** bracket
Eck'stein *m* cornerstone; (cards) dia-
monds

Eck'stoß *m* (fb) corner kick
Eck'zahn *m* canine tooth
Eclair [ɛ'kler] *n* (–s;–s) éclair
edel ['edəl] *adj* noble; (*Metall*) pre-
cious; (*Pferd*) thoroughbred; **edle**
Teile vital organs
e'deldenkend *adj* noble-minded
e'delgesinnt *adj* noble-minded
E'del•mann *m* (–[e]s;–leute) noble
e'delmütig *adj* noble-minded
E'delstahl *m* high-grade steel
E'delstein *m* precious stone, gem
E'delweiß *n* (–[e]s;–e) edelweiss
Edikt [ɛ'dɪkt] *n* (–[e]s;–e) edict
Edle ['edlə] §5 *mf* noble
Efeu ['efɔɪ] *m* (–s;–e) ivy
Effekt [ɛ'fɛkt] *m* (–[e]s;–e) effect
Effekten [ɛ'fɛktən] *pl* property; ef-
fects; (fin) securities, stocks
Effek'tenmakler –in §6 *mf* stock broker
Effekthascherei [ɛfɛkthaʃə'raɪ] *f* (–;)
showiness
effektiv [ɛfɛk'tif] *adj* effective; (*wirk-*
lich) actual
Effektiv'lohn *m* take-home pay
Effet [ɛ'fe] *n* (–s;) spin, English
egal [ɛ'gal] *adj* equal; all the same
Egge ['ɛgə] *f* (–;–n) harrow
eggen ['ɛgən] *tr* harrow
Ego ['ego] *n* (–s;) ego
Egoismus [ego'ɪsmʊs] *m* (–;) egoism
Egoist –in [ego'ɪst(ɪn)] §7 *mf* egoist
egoistisch [ego'ɪstɪʃ] *adj* egoistic
Egotist –in [ego'tɪst(ɪn)] §7 *mf* egotist
eh [e] *adv* (Aust) anyhow, anyway
ehe ['e•ə] *conj* before || **Ehe** *f* (–;–n)
marriage; matrimony
E'hebrecher *m* (–s;–) adulterer

E'hebrecherin *f* (–;–nen) adulteress
e'hebrecherisch *adj* adulterous
E'hebruch *m* adultery, infidelity
ehedem ['eˑəˈdem] *adv* formerly
E'hefrau *f* wife
E'hegatte *m* spouse
E'hegattin *f* spouse
E'hegelöbnis *n* marriage vow
E'hehälfte *f* (coll) better half
E'heleute *pl* married couple
e'helich *adj* marital; (*Kind*) legitimate
e'helos *adj* unmarried, single
E'helosigkeit *f* (–;) celibacy
ehemalig ['eˑəmɑlɪç] *adj* former; ex–; (*verstorben*) late
ehemals ['eˑəmɑls] *adv* formerly
E'hemann *m* husband
E'hepaar *n* married couple
eher ['eˑər] *adv* sooner; rather
E'hering *m* wedding band
ehern ['eˑərn] *adj* brass; (fig) unshakable
E'hescheidung *f* divorce
E'hescheidungsklage *f* divorce suit
E'heschließung *f* marriage
E'hestand *m* married state, wedlock
ehestens ['eˑəstəns] *adv* at the earliest; as soon as possible
E'hestifter –in §6 *mf* matchmaker
E'heversprechen *n* promise of marriage
Ehrabschneider –in ['erapʃnaɪdər(ɪn)] §6 *mf* slanderer
ehrbar ['erbɑr] *adj* honorable, respectable
Ehr'barkeit *f* (–;) respectability
Ehre ['erə] *f* (–;–n) honor; glory
ehren ['erən] *tr* honor; **Sehr geehrter Herr** Dear Sir
eh'renamtlich *adj* honorary
Eh'rendoktor *m* honorary doctor
Eh'renerklärung *f* apology
eh'renhaft *adj* honorable
ehrenhalber ['erənhalbər] *invar adj—* **Doktor e.** Doctor honoris causa
Eh'renmitglied *n* honorary member
Eh'renrechte *pl*—**bürgerliche E.** civil rights
Eh'rensache *f* point of honor
eh'renvoll *adj* honorable, respectable
eh'renwert *adj* honorable
Eh'renwort *n* word of honor; **auf E. entlassen** put on parole
ehrerbietig ['ererbitɪç] *adj* respectful, reverent, deferential
Ehrerbietung ['ererbituŋ] *f* (–;), **Ehrfurcht** ['erfurçt] *f* (–;) respect, reverence; (**vor** *dat*) awe (of)
ehrfürchtig ['erfyrçtɪç], **ehrfurchtsvoll** ['erfurçtsfəl] *adj* respectful
Ehr'gefühl *n* sense of honor
Ehr'geiz *m* ambition
ehr'geizig *adj* ambitious
ehrlich ['erlɪç] *adj* honest; sincere; fair; **j–n e. machen** restore s.o.'s good name
Ehr'lichkeit *f* (–;) honesty; candor
ehr'los *adj* dishonorable; (*Frau*) of easy virtue; infamous
Ehr'losigkeit *f* (–;) dishonesty; infamy
ehrsam ['erzɑm] *adj* respectable
Ehr'sucht *f* (–;) ambition
ehr'süchtig *adj* ambitious

Ehr'verlust *m* loss of civil rights
ehr'würdig *adj* venerable; (eccl) reverend
ei [aɪ] *interj* oh!; ah!; **ei,ei!** oho!; **ei je!** oh dear!; **ei was!** nonsense! || **Ei** *n* (–[e]s;–er) egg
Eiche ['aɪçə] *f* (–;–n) oak
Eichel ['aɪçəl] *f* (–;–n) acorn; (cards) club
eichen ['aɪçən] *adj* oak || *tr* gauge
Ei'chenlaub *n* oak leaf cluster
Eichhörnchen ['aɪçhœrnçən] *n* (–s;–), **Eichkätzchen** ['aɪçkɛtsçən] *n* (–s;–) squirrel
Eichmaß ['aɪçmɑs] *n* gauge; standard
Eid [aɪt] *m* (–[e]s;–e) oath
Eid'bruch *m* perjury
eid'brüchig *adj* perjured
Eidechse ['aɪdɛksə] *f* (–;–n) lizard
Eiderdaunen ['aɪdərdaunən] *pl* eider down
eidesstattlich ['aɪdəsʃtatlɪç] *adj* in lieu of an oath, solemn
eid'lich *adj* sworn || *adv* under oath
Ei'dotter *m* egg yolk
Ei'erkrem *f* custard
Ei'erkuchen *m* omelet; pancake
Ei'erlandung *f* three-point landing
Ei'erlikör *m* eggnog
Ei'erschale *f* eggshell
Ei'erstock *m* ovary
Eifer ['aɪfər] *m* (–;) zeal, eagerness
Eiferer –in ['aɪfərər(ɪn)] §6 *mf* zealot
Ei'fersucht *f* jealousy
ei'fersüchtig *adj* (**auf** *acc*) jealous (of)
eifrig ['aɪfrɪç] *adj* zealous; ardent
Ei'gelb *n* (–[e]s;–e) egg yolk
eigen ['aɪgən] *adj* own; of (my, your, etc.) own; (*dat*) peculiar (to), characteristic (of) || *invar pron—etw* **mein e. nennen** call s.th. my own
ei'genartig *adj* peculiar; odd, queer
Eigenbrötler ['aɪgənbrøtlər] *m* (–s;–) (coll) lone wolf, loner; crank
Ei'gengewicht *n* dead weight
eigenhändig ['aɪgənhɛndɪç] *adj & adv* with or in one's own hand
Ei'genheit *f* (–;–en) peculiarity
Ei'genliebe *f* self-love, egotism
Ei'genlob *n* self-praise
ei'genmächtig *adj* arbitrary, highhanded
Ei'genname *m* proper name
Ei'gennutz *m* self-interest
ei'gennützig *adj* selfish
eigens ['aɪgəns] *adv* expressly
Ei'genschaft *f* (–;–en) quality, property; **in seiner E. als** in his capacity as
Ei'genschaftswort *n* (–[e]s;⁼er) adjective
Ei'gensinn *m* stubbornness
ei'gensinnig *adj* stubborn
eigentlich ['aɪgəntlɪç] *adj* actual || *adv* actually, really
Eigentum ['aɪgəntum] *n* (–[e]s;⁼er) property, possession; ownership
Eigentümer –in ['aɪgəntymər(ɪn)] §6 *mf* (legal) owner || *m* proprietor || *f* proprietress
eigentümlich ['aɪgəntymlɪç] *adj* odd; (*dat*) peculiar (to)
Ei'gentümlichkeit *f* (–;–en) peculiarity

Ei'gentumsrecht *n* ownership, title
Ei'genwechsel *m* promissory note
ei'genwillig *adj* independent; (*Stil*) original
eignen ['aɪgnən] *ref* (**für**) be suited (to); (**als**) be suitable (as); (**zu**) be cut out (for)
Eig'nung *f* (**-;-en**) qualification, aptitude
Ei'gnungsprüfung *f* aptitude test
Eilbrief ['aɪlbrif] *m* special delivery
Eile ['aɪlə] *f* (**-;**) hurry; **E. haben** or **in E. sein** be in a hurry
eilen ['aɪlən] *ref* hurry (up) || *intr* be urgent || *intr* (SEIN) hurry; **eilt!** (*Briefaufschrift*) urgent! || *impers—* **es eilt mir nicht damit** I'm in no hurry about it
eilends ['aɪlənts] *adv* hurriedly
Eilgut ['aɪlgut] *n* express freight
eilig ['aɪlɪç] *adj* quick, hurried; urgent || *adv* hurriedly; **es e. haben** be in a hurry
Eilpost ['aɪlpɔst] *f* special delivery
Eilzug ['aɪltsuk] *m* (rr) limited
Eimer ['aɪmər] *m* (**-s;-**) bucket, pail
ein [aɪn] §2,1 *indef art* a, an || §2,1 *num adj* one || *adv* in; **ein und aus in** and out; **nicht ein und aus wissen** not know which way to turn || **einer** *indef pron* & *num pron* see **einer**
ein-, Ein- *comb.fm.* one-, single
einan'der *invar recip pron* each other; (*unter mehreren*) one another
ein'arbeiten *tr* train (for a job); (**in** (*acc*) work (into) || *ref* (**in** *acc*) become familiar (with), get the hang (of)
einarmig ['aɪnarmɪç] *adj* one-armed
einäschern ['aɪnɛʃərn] *tr* reduce to ashes, incinerate; (*Leiche*) cremate
ein'atmen *tr* & *intr* inhale
ein'äugig *adj* one-eyed
einbahnig ['aɪnbɑnɪç] *adj* single-lane; single-line; one-way
Ein'bahnstraße *f* one-way street
ein'balsamieren *tr* embalm
Ein'band *m* (**-[e]s;-̈e**) binding; cover
ein'bauen *tr* build in, install
einbegriffen ['aɪnbəgrɪfən] *adj* included. inclusive
ein'behalten §90 *tr* retain; (*Lohn*) withhold
ein'berufen §122 *tr* call, convene; (mil) call up, draft || **Einberufene** §5 *mf* draftee
Ein'berufung *f* (**-;-en**) (mil) induction
ein'betten *tr* embed
ein'beziehen §163 *tr* include
ein'bilden *ref—***sich** [*dat*] **etw e.** imagine s.th.
ein'binden §59 *tr* (bb) bind
ein'blenden *tr* (cin) fade in
Ein'blick *m* view; (fig) insight
ein'brechen §64 *tr* break in || *intr* (SEIN) collapse; (*Nacht*) fall; (*Kälte*) set in; (*Dieb*) break in
Ein'brecher –**in** §6 *mf* burglar
ein'bringen §65 *tr* bring in; earn; yield
Ein'bruch *m* break-in, burglary; invasion; **E. der Nacht** nightfall
Ein'bruchsdiebstahl *m* burglary
ein'bruchssicher *adj* burglarproof

einbürgern ['aɪnbyrgərn] *tr* naturalize || *ref* (fig) take root, become accepted
Ein'bürgerung *f* (**-;**) naturalization
Ein'buße *f* loss, forfeiture
ein'büßen *tr* lose, forfeit
ein'dämmen *tr* check, contain
ein'decken *tr* cover || *ref* (**mit**) stock up (on)
Eindecker ['aɪndɛkər] *m* (**-s;-**) monoplane
ein'deutig *adj* unequivocal, clear
eindeutschen ['aɪndɔɪtʃən] *tr* Germanize
ein'drängen *ref* squeeze in; interfere
ein'dringen §142 *intr* (SEIN) penetrate, come in; **e. auf** (*acc*) crowd in on; **e. in** (*acc*) rush into; penetrate; infiltrate; (mil) invade
ein'dringlich *adj* urgent
Eindringling ['aɪndrɪŋlɪŋ] *m* (**-s;-e**) intruder, interloper; gate-crasher
Ein'druck *m* imprint; impression
ein'drücken *tr* press in; crash, flatten; imprint; (*Fenster*) smash in
Ein'druckskunst *f* impressionism
ein'drucksvoll *adj* impressive
ein'engen *tr* narrow; (fig) limit
einer ['aɪnər] §2,4 *indef pron* & *num pron* one || **Einer** *m* (**-s;-**) (math) unit
einerlei ['aɪnərlaɪ] *invar adj* (*nur attributiv*) one kind of; (*nur prädikativ*) all the same || **Einerlei** *n* (**-;**) monotony
einerseits ['aɪnərzaɪts], **einesteils** ['aɪnəstaɪls] *adv* on the one hand
ein'fach *adj* single; simple || *adv* simply
einfädeln ['aɪnfedəln] *tr* thread; (fig) engineer
ein'fahren §71 *tr* (*Auto*) break in; (*Ernte*) bring in; (aer) retract || *ref* get driving experience; **die Sache hat sich gut eingefahren** it's off to a good start || *intr* (SEIN) drive in; (rr) arrive
Ein'fahrt *f* entrance; gateway
Ein'fall *m* inroad; (fig) idea; (mil) invasion
ein'fallen §72 *intr* (SEIN) fall in; cave in. collapse; (*in die Rede*) butt in; join in; **e. in** (*acc*) invade; **j-m e.** occur to s.o.; **sich** [*dat*] **etw e. lassen** take s.th. into one's head: think up s.th.; **sich** [*dat*] **nicht e. lassen** not dream of; **was fällt dir ein?** what's the idea?
ein'fallslos *adj* unimaginative
ein'fallsreich *adj* imaginative
Ein'falt *f* simplicity; simple-mindedness
einfältig ['aɪnfɛltɪç] *adj* (pej) simple
Ein'faltspinsel *m* sucker, simpleton
ein'farbig *adj* one-colored; plain
ein'fassen *tr* edge, trim; (*einschließen*) enclose; (*Edelstein*) set
Ein'fassung *f* (**-;-en**) border; mounting
ein'fetten *tr* grease
ein'finden §59 *ref* show up
ein'flechten *tr* plait; (*Haar*) braid; (fig) insert
ein'fliegen §57 *tr* (*Truppen*) fly in;

(Flugzeug) flight-test ‖ *intr* (SEIN) fly in

ein'fließen §76 *intr* (SEIN) flow in; **e. in** *(acc)* flow into; **einige Bemerkungen e. lassen** slip in a few remarks

ein'flößen *tr* infuse, instill

Ein'fluß *m* influx; (fig) influence

ein'flußreich *adj* influential

ein'förmig *adj* monotonous

einfried(ig)en ['aɪnfrid(ɪg)ən] *tr* enclose, fence in

ein'frieren §77 *tr* (& fin) freeze ‖ *intr* (SEIN) freeze (up) ‖ **Einfrieren** *n* (-s;) (fin) freeze

ein'fügen *tr* insert, fit ‖ *ref* fit in; **(in** *acc)* adapt oneself (to)

ein'fühlen *ref* (in *acc*) relate (to)

Einfuhr ['aɪnfur] *f* (-;-en) importation; **Einfuhren** imports

ein'führen *tr* import; introduce; *(in ein Amt)* install

Ein'führung *f* (-;-en) introduction

Ein'fuhrwaren *pl* imports

Ein'fuhrzoll *m* import duty

ein'füllen *tr*—**e. in** *(acc)* pour into

Ein'gabe *f* petition; application

Ein'gang *m* entrance; entry; beginning; introduction; *(von Waren)* arrival; **Eingänge** (com) incoming goods; incoming mail; (fin) receipts

ein'geben §80 *tr* suggest, prompt; (med) administer, give

eingebildet ['aɪngəbɪldət] *adj* imaginary; self-conceited

eingeboren ['aɪngəborən] *adj* native; only-begotten; *(Eigenschaft)* innate ‖ **Eingeborene** §5 *mf* native

Ein'gebung *f* (-:-en) suggestion; *(höhere)* inspiration

eingedenk ['aɪngədɛŋk] *adj (genit)* mindful (of)

ein'gefallen *adj (Backen, Augen)* sunken

eingefleischt ['aɪngəflaɪʃt] *adj* inveterate

ein'gefroren *adj* icebound

ein'gehen §82 *tr* (HABEN & SEIN) enter into; *(Verpflichtungen)* incur; *(Wette, Geschäft)* make; *(Chance)* take; *(Versicherung)* take out; **e-n Vergleich e.** come to an agreement ‖ *intr* (SEIN) come in; arrive; *(aufhören)* come to an end; fizzle out; *(Stoff)* shrink; (bot, zool) die off; (com) close down; **e. auf** *(acc)* go into, consider; consent to; **e. lassen** drop, discontinue; **es geht mir nicht ein, daß** I can't accept the fact that

ein'gehend *adj* thorough

eingelegt ['aɪngəlegt] *adj* inlaid

Eingemachte ['aɪngəmaxtə] §5 *n* (-n;) preserves

eingemeinden ['aɪngəmaɪndən] *tr (Vorort)* incorporate

eingenommen ['aɪngənəmən] *adj* prejudiced; **von sich e.** self-conceited

eingeschnappt ['aɪngəʃnapt] *adj* (coll) peeved

eingeschneit ['aɪngəʃnaɪt] *adj* snowed in

Eingesessene ['aɪngəzɛsənə] §5 *mf* resident

Ein'geständis *n* (-ses;-se) confession

ein'gestehen §146 *tr* confess, admit

Eingeweide ['aɪngəvaɪdə] *pl* viscera; intestines; *(von Vieh)* entrails

Eingeweihte ['aɪngəvaɪtə] §5 *mf* insider

ein'gewöhnen *tr* (in *acc*) accustom (to) ‖ *ref* (in *acc*) become accustomed (to)

eingewurzelt ['aɪngəvurtsəlt] *adj* deeprooted

ein'gießen §76 *tr* pour in, pour out

eingleisig ['aɪnglaɪzɪç] *adj* single-track

ein'gliedern *tr* integrate; annex

ein'graben §87 *tr* bury; engrave ‖ *ref* burrow; (mil) dig in

ein'greifen §88 *intr* take action; interfere; *(in j-s Rechte)* encroach; (mach) mesh, be in gear ‖ **Eingreifen** *n* (-s;) interference; (mach) meshing

Ein'griff *m* interference; encroachment; (mach) meshing; (surg) operation

ein'hacken *tr*—**e. auf** *(acc)* peck at; (fig) pick at

ein'haken *tr* (in *acc*) hook (into) ‖ *ref* —**sich bei j-m e.** link arms with s.o. ‖ *intr* (fig) cut in

Ein'halt *m* (-[e]s;) stop, halt; **E. gebieten** *(dat)* put a stop to

ein'halten §90 *tr* stick to; *(Verabredung)* keep; *(Zahlungen)* keep up; **die Zeit e.** be punctual ‖ *intr* stop

ein'händigen *tr* hand over

ein'hängen §92 *tr (Türe)* hang; **(in** *acc)* hook (into); (telp) hang up ‖ *ref*—**sich bei j-m e.** link arms with s.o. ‖ *intr* (telp) hang up

ein'heften *tr* sew in; baste on

ein'heimisch *adj* domestic; local; homegrown; **e. in** *(dat)* native to

einheimsen ['aɪnhaɪmzən] *tr* reap

Einheit ['aɪnhaɪt] *f* (-;-en) oneness, unity; (math, mil) unit

ein'heitlich *adj* uniform

Einheits– *comb.fm.* standard, uniform; unit; united

ein'heizen *intr* start a fire; **j-m tüchtig e.** (fig) burn s.o. up

einhellig ['aɪnhɛlɪç] *adj* unanimous

ein'holen *tr* bring in; *(Flagge)* hawl down; *(Segel)* hawl down; *(im Wettein'holen* *tr* bring in; *(Flagge, Segel)* lower, hawl down; *(im Wettlauf)* catch up with; *(Erkundigungen lauf)* catch up with; *(Erkundigungen)* make; *(Rat, Nachricht, Erlaubnis)* get; *(Verlust)* make good; *(abholen und geleiten)* escort; *(Schiff, Tau)* tow in ‖ *intr* shop

Ein'horn *n* (myth) unicorn

ein'hüllen *tr* wrap up; enclose

einig ['aɪnɪç] *adj* united; of one mind; **sich** *[dat]* **e. sein** be in agreement

einige ['aɪnɪgə] §9 *indef adj & indef pron* some

einigen ['aɪnɪgən] *tr* unite ‖ *ref* come to terms, agree

einigermaßen ['aɪnɪgərmɑsən] *adv* to some extent; *(ziemlich)* somewhat

ei'niggehen §82 *intr* (SEIN) concur

Ei'nigkeit *f* (-;) unity; harmony; agreement

Ei′nigung *f* (–;–en) unification; agreement, understanding

ein′impfen *tr*—j–m Impfstoff e. inoculate s.o. with vaccine; j–m e., daß (fig) drive it into s.o. that

ein′jagen *tr* (*dat*) put (*e.g., a scare*) into

ein′jährig *adj* one-year-old; (bot) annual

ein′kassieren *tr* collect

Ein′kauf *m* purchase; **Einkäufe machen** go shopping

ein′kaufen *tr* purchase; **e. gehen** go shopping

Ein′käufer –in §6 *mf* shopper

Ein′kaufspreis *m* purchase price

Ein′kehr *f*—E. **bei sich halten** search one's conscience; **E. halten** stop off

ein′kehren *intr* (SEIN) stay overnight; (*im Gasthaus*) stop off, stay

ein′keilen *tr* wedge in

ein′kerben *tr* notch, cut a notch in

einkerkern ['aɪnkɛrkərn] *tr* imprison

einkesseln ['aɪnkesəln) *tr* encircle

ein′klagen *tr* sue for (*a bad debt*)

ein′klammern *tr* bracket, put in parentheses

Ein′klang *m* unison; accord

Ein′klebebuch *n* scrap book

ein′kleben *tr* (in *acc*) paste (into)

ein′kleiden *tr* clothe; vest; (mil) issue uniforms to

ein′klemmen *tr* jam in, squeeze in

ein′klinken *tr* & *intr* engage, catch

ein′knicken *tr* fold

ein′kochen *tr* thicken (*by boiling*); can || *intr* thicken

ein′kommen §99 *intr* (SEIN)—**bei j–m um etw e.** apply to s.o. for s.th. || **Einkommen** *n* (–s;) income, revenue

Ein′kommensteuer *f* income tax

Ein′kommensteuererklärung *f* income-tax return

Ein′kommenstufe *f* income bracket

ein′kreisen *tr* encircle

Einkünfte ['aɪnkynftə] *pl* revenue

ein′kuppeln *tr* let out the clutch

ein′laden §103 *tr* load; invite

Ein′ladung *f* (–;–en) invitation

Ein′lage *f* (–;–n) (*im Brief*) enclosure; (*im Schuh*) insole; arch support; (*Zwischenfutter*) padding; (*Kapital–*) investment; (*Sparkassen–*) deposit; (*beim Spiel*) bet; (culin) solids (*in soup*); (dent) temporary filling; (mus) musical extra

ein′lagern *tr* store, store up

Ein·laß ['aɪnlas] *m* (–lasses;) admission; admittance; (tech) intake

ein′lassen §104 *tr* let it, admit; (tech) (in *acc*) sink (into) || *ref* (auf *acc*, in *acc*) let oneself get involved (in)

Ein′laßkarte *f* admission ticket

Ein′lauf *m* incoming mail; (*e–s Schiffes*) arrival; **j–m e–n E. machen** give s.o. an enema

ein′laufen §105 *intr* (SEIN) come in, arrive; (*Stoff*) shrink; **das Badewasser e. lassen** run the bath; **j–m das Haus e.** keep running to s.o.'s house || *ref* warm up (*by running*)

ein′leben *ref* (in *acc*) accustom oneself (to)

Ein′legearbeit *f* inlaid work

Ein′legebrett *n* (*e–s Tisches*) leaf

ein′legen *tr* put in; (*Fleisch, Gurken*) pickle; (*Geld*) deposit; (*in e–n Brief*) enclose; (*Film, Kassette*) insert; (*Veto*) interpose; (*Beschwerde*) lodge; (*Protest*) enter; (*Berufung*) (jur) file; **Busse e.** put on extra buses

ein′leiten *tr* introduce; (*Buch*) write a preface to; (*beginnen, eröffnen*) start, open; **ein Verfahren e. gegen** institute proceedings against s.o.

Ein′leitung *f* (–;–en) introduction; initiation

ein′lenken *intr* (fig) give in

ein′leuchten *intr* be evident; (coll) sink in

ein′liefern *tr* deliver; (*ins Gefängnis*) put, commit; **ins Krankenhaus e.** take to the hospital

ein′lösen *tr* ransom; redeem; (*Scheck*) cash

ein′machen *tr* can, preserve

ein′mal *adv* once; (*künftig*) one day; **auf e.** suddenly; all at the same time; **einmal...einmal** now...now; **nicht e.** (unstressed) not even; (stressed) not even once

Ein′maleins′ *n* multiplication table

ein′malig *adj* unique

Einmann– *comb.fm.* one-man

Ein′marsch *m* entry

ein′marschieren *intr* (SEIN) march in

ein′mauern *tr* wall in

ein′mengen *ref*, **ein′mischen** *ref* (in *acc*) meddle (with), interfere (with)

Ein′mischung *f* (–;–en) interference

einmotorig ['aɪnmə'torɪç] *adj* single-engine

einmummen ['aɪnmumən] *ref* bundle up

ein′münden *intr* (in *acc*) empty (into); (*Straßen*) run (into)

Ein′mündung *f* (–;–en) (*e–s Flusses*) mouth; (*e–r Straße*) junction

ein′mütig *adj* unanimous

ein′nähen *tr* sew in; (*Kleid*) take in

Ein′nahme *f* (–;–n) taking; capture; (fin) receipts; **Einnahmen** income

ein′nehmen §116 *tr* take; capture; (*Essen*) eat; (*Geld*) earn; (*Steuern*) collect; (*Stellung*) fill; (sew) take in; **e–e Haltung e.** assume an attitude; **e–e hervorragende Stelle e.** rank high; **j–n für sich e.** captivate s.o.; **j–n gegen sich e.** prejudice s.o. against oneself; **seinen Platz e.** take one's seat

ein′nicken *intr* (SEIN) doze off

ein′nisten *ref* (in *dat*) settle (in); (fig) find a home (at)

Ein′öde *f* desert, wilderness

ein′ordnen *tr* put in its place; file; classify || *ref* fit into place; (*sich anstellen*) get in line; **sich rechts** (or **links**) **e.** get into the right (or left) lane

ein′packen *tr* pack up

ein′passen *tr* (in *acc*) fit (into)

ein′pauken *tr*—j–m etw e. drum s.th. into s.o.'s head

ein′pferchen *tr* pen up; (fig) crowd together

ein'pflanzen *tr* plant; implant
ein'pökeln *tr* pickle; salt
ein'prägen *tr* imprint, impress
ein'quartieren *tr* billet, quarter
ein'rahmen *tr* frame
ein'rammen *tr* ram in, drive in
ein'räumen *tr* (*Recht, Kredit*) grant; (*zugeben*) concede, admit; **e. in** (*acc*) put into
ein'rechnen *tr* include, comprise
Ein'rede *f* objection; (jur) plea
ein'reden *tr*—**j-m etw e.** talk s.o. into s.th; **das lasse ich mir nicht e.** I can't believe that || *intr*—**auf j-n e.** badger s.o.
ein'reiben §62 *tr* rub
ein'reichen *tr* hand in, file; (*Rechnung*) present; (*Abschied*) tender; (*Gesuch*) submit; (*Beschwerde, Klage*) file
ein'reihen *tr* file; rank; enroll; (*Bücher*) shelve || *ref* fall into place; fall in line
ein'reihig *adj* single-breasted
Ein'reise *f* entry
ein'reißen §53 *tr* tear; demolish || *intr* (SEIN) tear; (fig) spread
ein'renken *tr* (*Knochen*) set; (fig) set right
ein'richten *tr* arrange; establish; (*Wohnung*) furnish; (surg) set || *ref* settle down; economize, make ends meet; (**auf** *acc*) make arrangements (for); (**nach**) adapt oneself (to)
Ein'richtung *f* (–;–en) setup; establishment; furniture; equipment
Ein'richtungsgegenstand *m* piece of furniture, piece of equipment
ein'rosten *intr* (SEIN) get rusty
ein'rücken *tr* (*Zeile*) indent; (*Anzeige*) put in || *intr* (SEIN) march in; **in j-s Stelle e.** succeed s.o.; **zum Militär e.** enter military service
Ein'rückung *f* (–;–en) indentation
ein'rühren *tr* (in *acc*) stir (into)
eins [aɪns] *pron* one; one o'clock; **es ist mir eins** it's all the same to me || **Eins** *f* (–;–en) one; (*auf Würfeln*) ace; (educ) A
einsam ['aɪnzam] *adj* lonely, lonesome
ein'sammlen *tr* gather; (*Geld*) collect
Ein'satz *m* insert, insertion; (*Wette*) bet; (*Risiko*) risk; (*Verwendung*) use; (*für Flaschen*) deposit; (aer) sortie; (mil) action; (mus) starting in, entry; **im E. stehen** be in action; **im vollen E.** in full operation; **unter E. seines Lebens** at the risk of one's life; **zum E. bringen** employ, use; (*Maschinen*) put into operation; (*Polizei*) call out; (mil) throw into action
ein'satzbereit *adj* combat-ready
Ein'satzstück *n* insert
ein'saugen *tr* suck in; (fig) imbibe
ein'säumen *tr* (sew) hem
ein'schalten *tr* insert; (elec) switch on, turn on || *ref* intervene
ein'schärfen *tr*—**j-m etw e.** impress s.th. on s.o.
ein'schätzen *tr* appraise, value
ein'schenken *tr* pour
ein'schicken *tr* send in
ein'schieben §130 *tr* push in; insert

ein'schießen §76 *tr* (*Gewehr*) test; (*Geld*) contribute; (*Brot in den Ofen*) shove; (fb) score || *ref* (**auf** *acc*) zero in (on)
ein'schiffen *tr* & *intr* embark
Ein'schiffung *f* (–;–en) embarkation
ein'schlafen §131 *intr* (SEIN) fall asleep; (*Glied*) go to sleep
ein'schläf(e)rig *adj* single (bed)
einschläfern ['aɪnʃlɛfərn] *tr* lull to sleep; (vet) put to sleep
Ein'schlag *m* striking; impact; explosion; (*Umschlag*) wrapper; (fig) admixture, element; (golf) putt; (sew) tuck; (tex) weft, woof
ein'schlagen §132 *tr* (*Nagel*) drive in; (*zerbrechen*) smash, bash in; (*einwickeln*) wrap; (*Weg*) take; (*Laufbahn*) enter upon; (*Pflanzen*) stick in the ground; (golf) putt; **die Richtung e. nach** go in the direction of || *intr* (*Blitz*) strike; (*Erfolg haben*) be a success; **nicht e.** fail
einschlägig ['aɪnʃlɛgɪç] *adj* relevant
Ein'schlagpapier *n* wrapping paper
ein'schleichen §85 *ref* (**in** *acc*) creep (into), slip (into); (**in j–s Gunst**) worm one's way
ein'schleppen *tr* tow in; (*e–e Krankheit*) bring in (*from abroad*)
ein'schleusen *tr* (*Schmuggelwaren*) sneak in; (*Spionen*) plant
ein'schließen §76 *tr* lock up; (*in e–m Brief*) enclose; (fig) include; (mil) encircle, surround
ein'schließlich *adv* inclusive(ly) || *prep* (*genit*) inclusive of
ein'schlummern *intr* (SEIN) doze off
Ein'schluß *m* encirclement; **mit E.** (*genit*) including
ein'schmeicheln *ref* (**bei**) ingratiate oneself (with)
ein'schmeichelnd *adj* ingratiating
ein'schmuggeln *tr* smuggle in
ein'schnappen *intr* (SEIN) snap shut; (fig) take offense
ein'schneidend *adj* (fig) incisive
Ein'schnitt *m* cut, incision; (*Kerbe*) notch; (geol) gorge; (pros) caesura
ein'schnüren *tr* tie up; pinch
ein'schränken *tr* (**auf** *acc*) restrict (to), confine (to); (*Ausgaben*) cut; (*Behauptung*) qualify || *ref* economize
Ein'schränkung *f* (–;–en) restriction; **ohne jede E.** without reservation
Ein'schreibebrief *m* registered letter
ein'schreiben §62 *tr* enroll; (*Brief*) register; (*eintragen*) enter; **e–n Brief e. lassen** send a letter by registered mail || *ref* register
ein'schreiten §86 *intr* (SEIN) step in, intervene; (**gegen**) take action (against)
ein'schrumpfen *intr* (SEIN) shrivel up
ein'schüchtern *tr* intimidate, overawe
Ein'schüchterung *f* (–;) intimidation
ein'schulen *tr* enroll in school
Ein'schuß *m* hit (*of a bullet*)
ein'schütten *tr* pour in
ein'segnen *tr* (*neues Gebäude*) consecrate; (*konfirmieren*) confirm
ein'sehen §138 *tr* inspect; (*Akten*) consult; (fig) realize; (mil) observe ||

Einsehen n—**ein E. haben** show (some) consideration
ein′seifen tr soap; (coll) softsoap
ein′seitig adj one-sided
ein′senden §140 tr send in, submit
Ein′sender −in §6 mf sender
ein′senken tr (in acc) sink (into)
ein′setzen tr insert, put in; (Geld) bet; (Leben) risk; (Polizei) call out; (Truppen) commit; (Kräfte) muster; (Einfluß) use; (Beamten) install; (ernennen) appoint; (einpflanzen) plant; (Artillerie, Tanks, Bomber) employ; (Edelsteine) mount || ref (für) stand up (for) || intr set in, begin; (mus) come in
Ein′sicht f inspection; (fig) insight
ein′sichtig adj understanding
ein′sichtsvoll adj understanding
ein′sickern intr (SEIN) seep in; (mil) infiltrate
Einsiedelei [aɪnzidə′laɪ] f (−;−en) hermitage
Einsiedler −in [′aɪnzidlər(ɪn)] §6 mf hermit, recluse
einsilbig [′aɪnzɪlbɪç] adj monosyllabic; (fig) taciturn
ein′sinken §143 intr (SEIN) sink in; (Erdboden) subside
ein′sparen tr economize on, save
ein′sperren tr lock up
ein′springen §142 intr (SEIN) jump in; (für) substitute (for); (tech) catch
ein′spritzen tr inject
Ein′spritzung f (−;−en) injection
Ein′spruch m objection; (jur) appeal
einspurig [′aɪnʃpurɪç] adj single-track
einst [aɪnst] adv once; (künftig) someday; **e. wie jezt** (now) as ever
Ein′stand m (tennis) deuce
ein′stecken tr insert, put in; stick in, pocket; (Schwert) sheathe; (hinnehmen) take; (coll) lock up, jail
ein′stehen §146 intr (SEIN) (für) vouch (for), stand up (for); **für die Folgen e.** take the responsibility
ein′steigen §148 intr (SEIN) get in; **alle e.!** all aboard!
Ein′steigkarte f (aer) boarding pass
Ein′steigloch n manhole
einstellbar [′aɪnstɛlbɑr] adj adjustable
ein′stellen tr put in; (Arbeiter) hire; (Gerät) set, adjust; (beenden) stop, quit; (Sender) tune in on; (Fernglas, Kamera) focus; **die Arbeit e.** go on strike; **etw bei j–m e.** leave s.th. at s.o.'s house; **in die Garage e.** put into the garage; **zum Heeresdienst e.** induct || ref show up, turn up; **sich e. auf** (acc) attune oneself to
Ein′stellung f (−;−en) adjustment; setting; focusing; stoppage; (der Feindseligkeiten, Zahlungen) suspension; hiring; (aut) timing; (mil) induction; **E. des Feuers** cease-fire; **geistige E.** mental attitude
einstig [′aɪnstɪç] adj former; (verstorben) late; (künftig) future
ein′stimmen intr join in; **e. in** (acc) agree to, consent to
einstimmig [′aɪnʃtɪmɪç] adj unanimous
ein′studieren tr study; rehearse
ein′stufen tr classify

ein′stürmen intr (SEIN) (auf acc) rush (at); (mil) charge
Ein′sturz m (−es;) collapse
ein′stürzen intr (SEIN) collapse; **e. auf** (acc) (fig) overwhelm
einstweilen [′aɪnstvaɪlən] adv for the present; temporarily
einstweilig [′aɪnstvaɪlɪç] adj temporary
Ein′tänzer m gigolo
ein′tauschen tr trade in; **e. gegen** exchange for
ein′teilen tr divide; (austeilen) distribute; (einstufen) classify; (Geld, Zeit) budget; (Arbeit) plan
eintönig [′aɪntønɪç] adj monotonous
Ein′tönigkeit f (−;) monotony
Ein′topf m, **Ein′topfgericht** n one-dish meal
Ein′tracht f (−;) harmony, unity
einträchtig [′aɪntrɛçtɪç] adj harmonious
Eintrag [′aɪntrɑk] m (−[e]s;⸚e) entry; **E. tun** (dat) hurt
ein′tragen §132 tr enter, register; (Gewinn) bring in, yield; **j–m etw e.** bring down s.th. on s.o. || ref register
einträglich [′aɪntreklɪç] adj profitable, lucrative
Ein′tragung f (−;−en) entry
ein′treffen §151 intr (SEIN) arrive; (in Erfüllung gehen) come true
ein′treiben §62 tr drive in; (Geld) collect || intr (SEIN) drift in, sail in
ein′treten §152 tr smash in || ref—**sich** [dat] **e–n Nagel e.** step on a nail || intr (SEIN) enter; (geschehen) occur; (Fieber) develop; (Fall, Not) arise; (Dunkelheit) fall; **e. für** stand up for, champion; **e. in** (acc) join, enter
Ein′tritt m (−s;) entry; (Einlaß) admittance; (Anfang) beginning, onset; (rok) re-entry; **E. frei** free admission; **E. verboten** no admittance
Ein′trittsgeld n admission fee
Ein′trittskarte f admission ticket
ein′trocknen intr (SEIN) dry up
ein′trüben ref become overcast
ein′tunken tr (in acc) dip (into)
ein′üben tr practice; train, coach
ein′verleiben tr incorporate
Einvernahme [′aɪnfernɑmə] f (−;−n) interrogation
Ein′vernehmen n (−s;) agreement; **sich mit j–m ins E. setzen** try to come to an understanding with s.o.
einverstanden [′aɪnferʃtɑndən] adj in agreement || interj agreed!
Ein′verständnis n agreement; approval
ein′wachsen tr wax || intr (SEIN) (in acc) grow (into)
Ein′wand m (−s;⸚e) objection
Ein′wanderer −in §6 mf immigrant
ein′wandern intr (SEIN) immigrate
Ein′wanderung f (−;) immigration
ein′wandfrei adj unobjectionable; (tadellos) flawless; (Alibi, Zustand) perfect; (Quelle) unimpeachable
einwärts [′aɪnverts] adv inward(s)
Einweg- comb.fm. disposable
ein′weichen tr soak
ein′weihen tr consecrate, dedicate; **e. in** (acc) initiate into; let in on

Ein'weihung *f* (−;−en) dedication; initiation
ein'weisen §118 *tr* install; (*Verkehr*) direct; **e. in** (*acc*) assign to; **j–n in seine Pflichten e.** brief s.o. in his duties; **j–n ins Krankenhaus e.** have s.o. admitted to the hospital
ein'wenden §140 *tr*—**etw e. gegen** raise an objection to; **nichts einzuwenden haben gegen** have no objections to
Ein'wendung *f* (−;−en) objection
ein'werfen §160 *tr* throw in; (*Fenster*) smash; (*Brief*) mail; (*Münze*) insert; (fig) interject
ein'wickeln *tr* wrap (up); (fig) trick
ein'willigen *intr* (**in** *acc*) agree (to)
ein'wirken *intr* (**auf** *acc*) have an effect (on), exercise infuence (**on**)
Ein'wirkung *f* (−;−en) effect, influence
Ein'wohner **–in** §6 *mf* inhabitant
Ein'wurf *m* (*Schlitz*) slot; (*e–r Münze*) insertion; (*Einwand*) objection
ein'wurzeln *ref* take root
Ein'zahl *f* (−;) singular
ein'zahlen *tr* pay in; (**in** *e–e Kasse*) deposit
Ein'zahlung *f* (−;−en) payment; deposit
Ein'zahlungsschein *m* deposit slip
einzäunen ['aɪntsɔɪnən] *tr* fence in
Einzel ['aɪntsəl] *n* (−s;−) singles
Einzel– *comb.fm.* individual; single; isolated; detailed; retail
Ein'zelbild *n* (cin) frame; (phot) still
Ein'zelfall *m* individual case
Ein'zelgänger *m* (coll) lone wolf
Ein'zelhaft *f* solitary confinement
Ein'zelhandel *m* retail trade
Ein'zelheit *f* (−;−en) item; detail, particular; **wegen näherer Einzelheiten** for further particulars
einzellig ['aɪntsɛlɪç] *adj* single-cell
einzeln ['aɪntsəln] *adj* single; particular, individual; separate
Ein'zelperson *f* individual
Ein'zelspiel *n* singles (match)
Ein'zelwesen *n* individual
Ein'zelzimmer *n* single room; (*im Krankenhaus*) private room
ein'ziehen §163 *tr* draw in; retract; (*Flagge*) hawl down; (*Segel*) take in; (*Münzen*) call in; (*eintreiben*) collect; (mil) draft || *intr* (SEIN) move in; **e. in** (*acc*) enter; penetrate
einzig ['aɪntsɪç] *adj* & *adv* only; **e. darstellen** be unique || *indef pron*— **ein einziger** one only; **kein einziger** not a single one
ein'zigartig *adj* unique; extraordinary
Ein'zug *m* entry; moving in; (*Beginn*) start; (tvp) indentation; **seinen E. halten** make one's entry
ein'zwängen *tr* (**in** *acc*) squeeze (into)
Eis [aɪs] *n* (−es;) ice; (*Speise–*) ice cream || ['eˑɪs] *n* (−;−s) (mus) E sharp
Eis'bahn *f* ice-skating rink
Eis'bär *m* polar bear
Eis'bein *n* (culin) pigs feet
Eis'berg *m* iceberg
Eis'beutel *m* (med) ice pack
Eis'blume *f* window frost
Eis'creme *f* ice cream
Eis'diehle *f* ice cream parlor

Eisen ['aɪzən] *n* (−s;−) iron; **altes E.** scrap iron; **heißes E.** (fig) hot potato; **zum alten E. werfen** (fig) scrap
Ei'senbahn *f* railroad; **mit der E.** by train, by rail
Ei'senbahndamm *m* railroad embankment
Ei'senbahner *m* (−s;−) railroader
Ei'senbahnknotenpunkt *m* railroad junction
Ei'senblech *n* sheet iron
Ei'senerz *n* iron ore
Ei'senhütte *f* ironworks
Ei'senwaren *pl* hardware, ironware
Ei'senwarenhandlung *f* hardware store
Ei'senzeit *f* iron age
eisern ['aɪzərn] *adj* iron; (*Fleiß*) unflagging; (*Rationen*) emergency
Eis'glätte *f* icy road conditions
eis'grau *adj* hoary
eisig ['aɪsɪç] *adj* icy; icy-cold
Eis'kappe *f* ice cap
Eis'kunstlauf *m* figure skating
Eis'lauf *m* ice skating
Eis'laufbahn *f* ice-skating rink
eis'laufen §105 *intr* (SEIN) ice-skate
Eis'läufer **–in** §6 *mf* skater
Eis'meer *n*—**Nördliches E.** Arctic Ocean; **Südliches E.** Antarctic Ocean
Eis'pickel *m* ice axe
Eis'schnellauf *m* speed skating
Eis'scholle *f* ice floe
Eis'schrank *m* icebox
Eis'vogel *m* kingfisher
Eis'würfel *m* ice cube
Eis'würfelschale *f* ice-cube tray
Eis'zapfen *m* icicle
Eis'zeit *f* ice age, glacial period
eitel ['aɪtəl] *adj* (*nutzlos*) vain, empty; (*selbstgefällig*) vain; || *invar adj* pure || *adv* merely
Ei'telkeit *f* (−;) vanity
Eiter ['aɪtər] *m* (−s;) pus
Ei'terbeule *f* boil, abscess
eitern ['aɪtərn] *intr* fester, suppurate
Ei'terung *f* (−;−en) festering
eitrig ['aɪtrɪç] *adj* pussy
Ei'weiß *n* (−es;−e) egg white; albumen
Ekel ['ekəl] *m* (−s;) (**vor** *dat*) disgust (at) || *n* (−s;) (coll) pest
ekelerregend ['ekəleregənt] *adj* sickening, nauseating
e'kelhaft *adj* disgusting
ekeln ['ekəln] *impers*—**es eket mir** or **mich** I am disgusted || *ref* (**vor** *dat*) feel disgusted (at)
eklig ['eklɪç] *adj* disgusting, revolting; nasty, beastly
Ekzem [ek'tsem] *n* (−s;−e) eczema
elastisch [ɛ'lastɪʃ] *adj* elastic
Elch [ɛlç] *m* (−[e]s;−e) elk, moose
Elefant [ɛlɛ'fant] *m* (−en;−en) elephant
Elefan'tentreiber *m* mahout
Elefan'tenzahn *m* elephant's tusk
elegant [ɛlɛ'gant] *adj* elegant
Eleganz [ɛlɛ'gants] *f* (−;) elegance
Elektriker [ɛ'lɛktrɪkər] *m* (−s;−) electrician
elektrisch [ɛ'lɛktrɪʃ] *adj* electric(al)
elektrisieren [ɛlɛktrɪ'ziɾən] *tr* electrify
Elektrolyse [ɛlɛktro'lyzə] *f* (−;−) electricity

Elektrizitäts– *comb.fm.* electric, electro–

Elektro– [ɛlɛktrə] *comb.fm.* electrical, electro–

Elektrode [ɛlɛk'trodə] *f* (–;–n) electrode

Elek'trogerät *n* electrical appliance

Elektrizität [ɛlɛktrɪtsɪ'tet] *f* (–;) electricity

Elek·tron [ɛ'lɛktrən] *n* (–s;–tronen ['tronən]) electron

Elektronen– [ɛlɛktronən–] *comb.fm.* electronic

Elektronik [ɛlɛk'tronɪk] *f* (–;) electronics

Elektrotechnik *f* (–;) electrical engineering

Elektrotech'niker *m* (–s;–) electrical engineer

Element [ɛlɛ'mɛnt] *n* (–[e]s;–e) element; (elec) cell

elementar [ɛlɛmɛn'tar] *adj* elementary

Elementar'buch *n* primer

Elen ['elɛn] *m & n* (–s;–) elk

elend ['elənt] *adj* miserable ‖ **Elend** *n* (–[e]s;) misery; extreme poverty; **das graue E.** the blues

E'lendsviertel *n* slums

elf [ɛlf] *adj & pron* eleven ‖ **Elf** *f* (–;–en) eleven

Elfe ['ɛlfə] *m* (–n;–n), *f* (–;–n) elf

Elfenbein ['ɛlfənbaɪn] *n* (–s;) ivory

elfte ['ɛlftə] §9 *adj & pron* eleventh

Elftel ['ɛlftəl] *n* (–s;–) eleventh (*part*)

Elite [ɛ'litə] *f* (–;) elite, flower

Ellbogen ['ɛlbogən] *m* (–s;–) elbow

Ell'bogenfreiheit *f* elbowroom

Elsaß ['ɛlzas] *n* (–;) Elsace

elsässisch ['ɛlzɛsɪʃ] *adj* Alsatian

Elster ['ɛlstər] *f* (–;–n) magpie

elterlich ['ɛltərlɪç] *adj* parental

Eltern ['ɛltərn] *pl* parents; **nicht von schlechtern E.** (coll) terrific

El'ternbeirat *m* Parent-Teacher Association

El'ternhaus *n* home

el'ternlos *adj* orphaned; **elternlose Zeugung** spontaneous generation

El'ternschaft *f* parenthood

El'ternteil *m* parent

Email [ɛ'maj] *n* (–s;), **Emaille** [ɛ'maljə] *f* (–;) enamel

Email'geschirr *n* enamelware

Email'lack *m* enamel paint

emaillieren [ɛma(l)'jirən] *tr* enamel

Email'waren *pl* enamelware

emanzipieren [ɛmantsɪ'pirən] *tr* emancipate

Embargo [ɛm'bargo] *n* (–s;–s) embargo

Embo·lie [ɛmbə'li] *f* (–;–lien ['li·ən]) embolism

Embry·o ['ɛmbry·o] *m* (–s;–onen ['onən]) embryo

Emigrant –in [ɛmɪ'grant(ɪn)] §7 *mf* emigrant

Emission [ɛmɪ'sjon] *f* (–;–en) emission; (fin) issuance; (rad) broadcasting

empfahl [ɛm'pfal] *pret* of **empfehlen**

Empfang [ɛm'pfaŋ] *m* (–[e]s;–̈e) reception; (*Erhalten*) receipt; (*im Hotel*) reception desk

empfangen [ɛm'pfaŋən] §73 *tr* receive; (*Kind*) conceive

Empfänger –in (ɛm'pfɛŋər(ɪn)] §6 *mf* receiver, recipient; addressee

empfänglich [ɛm'pfɛŋlɪç] *adj* (für) susceptible (to)

Empfängnis [ɛm'pfɛŋnɪs] *f* (–;) conception

empfäng'nisverhütend *adj* contraceptive; **empfängnisverhütendes Mittel** contraceptive

Empfäng'nisverhütung *f* contraception

Empfangs'chef *m* desk clerk

Empfangs'dame *f* receptionist; (*im Restaurant*) hostess

Empfangs'schein *m* (com) receipt

empfehlen [ɛm'pfelən] §147 *tr* recommend; **e. Sie mich** (*dat*) remember me to ‖ *ref* say goodbye

empfeh'lenswert *adj* commendable

Empfeh'lung *f* (–;–en) recommendation; (*Gruß*) compliments

empfinden [ɛm'pfɪndən] §59 *tr* feel

empfindlich [ɛm'pfɪntlɪç] *adj* sensitive; delicate, touchy; (*Kälte*) bitter; (gegen) susceptible (to)

Empfind'lichkeit *f* (–;–en) sensitivity, touchiness; susceptibility

empfindsam [ɛm'pfɪntzam] *adj* sensitive, touchy; sentimental

Empfind'samkeit *f* (–;–en) sensibility; sentimentality

Empfin'dung *f* (–;–en) sensation; feeling, sentiment

empfin'dunglos *adj* numb; (fig) callous

Empfin'dungswort *n* (gram) interjection

Emphysem [ɛmfy'zem] *n* (–s;) emphysema

empor [ɛm'por] *adv* up, upwards

empören [ɛm'pørən] *tr* anger, shock ‖ *ref* rebel, revolt; (mil) mutiny

empor'fahren §71 *intr* (SEIN) jump up

empor'kommen §99 *intr* (SEIN) rise up; (*in der Welt*) get ahead

Emporkömmling [ɛm'porkœmlɪŋ] *m* (–s;–e) upstart, parvenu

empor'ragen *intr* tower, rise

empor'steigen §148 *intr* (SEIN) rise

empor'streben *intr* (SEIN) rise, soar; (fig) aspire

Empö'rung *f* (–;–en) revolt; (über *acc*) indignation (at)

emsig ['ɛmzɪç] *adj* industrious, busy

Em'sigkeit *f* (–;) industry; activity

End– [ɛnt] *comb.fm.* final, ultimate

Ende ['ɛndə] *n* (–s;–n) end; ending; outcome; **letzten Endes** in the final analysis; **zu E. gehen** end; **zu E. sein** be over

enden ['ɛndən] *tr & intr* end; **nicht e. wollend** unending

End'ergebnis *n* final result, upshot

End'gerade *f* (–;) home stretch

end'gültig *adj* final, definitive

endigen ['ɛndɪgən] *tr & intr* end; **e. auf** (*acc*) (gram) terminate in

Endivie [ɛn'divjə] *f* (–;–n) endive

End'lauf *m* (sport) final heat

end'lich *adj* final; limited, finite ‖ *adv* finally, at last

end'los *adj* endless

End'runde *f* final round, finals

End'station ƒ final stop, terminus
End'summe ƒ sum total
End'termin m final date; closing date
En'dung ƒ (-;-en) ending
Ener·gie [ɛnɛr'gi] ƒ (-;-gien ['gi·ən])
energy
energisch [ɛ'nɛrgiʃ] adj energetic
eng [ɛŋ] adj narrow; tight; (Freunde)
close; (innig) intimate; im engeren
Sinne strictly speaking
engagieren [ãga'zirən] tr engage, hire
|| ref commit oneself
Enge ['ɛŋə] ƒ (-;-n) narrowness; tight-
ness; (Meer-) strait; (fig) tight spot
Engel ['ɛŋəl] m (-s;-) angel
en'gelhaft adj angelic
eng'herzig adj stingy; petty
England ['ɛŋlant] n (-s;) England
Engländer ['ɛŋlɛndər] m (-s;-) Eng-
lishman; die E. the English
Engländerin ['ɛŋlɛndərɪn] ƒ (-;-nen)
Englishwoman
englisch ['ɛŋlɪʃ] adj English
Eng'paß m pass, defile; (fig) bottleneck
engros [ã'gro] adv wholesale
engstirnig ['ɛŋʃtɪrnɪç] adj narrow-
minded
Enkel ['ɛŋkəl] m (-s;-) grandson
Enkelin ['ɛŋkəlɪn] ƒ (-;-nen) grand-
daughter
En'kelkind n grandchild
enorm [ɛ'nɔrm] adj enormous
Ensemble [ã'sãbl(ə)] n (-s;-s) (mus)
ensemble; (theat) company, cast
ent- [ɛnt] insep pref
entarten [ɛnt'artən] intr (SEIN) degenerate
entartet [ɛnt'artət] adj degenerate;
(fig) decadent
entäu'ßern ref (genit) divest oneself of
entbehren [ɛnt'berən] tr lack, miss;
do without; spare; dispense with
entbehr'lich adj dispensable; needless,
superfluous
Entbeh'rung ƒ (-;-en) privation, need
entbin'den §59 tr release, absolve;
(Frau) deliver || intr give birth
Entbin'dung ƒ (-;-en) dispensation;
(Niederkünft) delivery, childbirth
Entbin'dungsanstalt ƒ maternity hospital
entblät'tern tr defoliate || ref defoliate;
(coll) strip
entblößen [ɛnt'bløsən] tr bare; un-
cover; (mil) expose || ref strip; re-
move one's hat
entbren'nen §97 intr (SEIN) flare up
entdecken (entdek'ken) tr discover ||
ref—sich j-m e. confide in s.o.
Entdeckung (Entdek'kung) ƒ (-;-en)
discovery
Ente ['ɛntə] ƒ (-;-n) duck; (coll) hoax
enteh'ren tr dishonor; (Mädchen) violate, deflower
enteh'rend adj disgraceful
Enteh'rung ƒ (-;-en) disgrace; rape
enteig'nen tr dispossess
enteisen [ɛnt'aizən] tr defrost; deice
enter'ben tr disinherit
Enterich ['ɛntərɪç] m (-s;-e) drake
entern ['ɛntərn] tr (naut) board
entfachen [ɛnt'faxən] tr kindle; (fig)
provoke

entfah'ren §71 intr (SEIN) (dat) slip
out (on)
entfal'len §72 intr (SEIN) (dat) slip
(from); auf j-n e. fall to s.o.'s share;
entfällt not applicable
entfal'ten tr unfold; display; (mil) de-
ploy || ref unfold; develop
entfernen [ɛnt'fɛrnən] tr remove || ref
withdraw, move away; deviate
entfernt [ɛnt'fɛrnt] adj distant; nicht
weit davon e. zu (inf) far from (ger)
Entfer'nung ƒ (-;-en) removal; range;
distance; absence
Entfer'nungsmesser m (phot) range
finder
entfes'seln tr unleash
entflam'men tr inflame || intr (SEIN)
ignite; flash; (fig) flare up
entflech'ten tr disentangle; (Kartell)
-break up; (mil) disengage
entflie'hen §75 intr (SEIN) flee, escape;
(Zeit) fly
entfremden [ɛnt'frɛmdən] tr alienate
enfrosten [ɛnt'frɔstən] tr defrost
entfüh'ren tr abduct; kidnap; (Flugzeug) hijack; (hum) steal
Entfüh'rer -in §6 mƒ abductor, kidnaper; (aer) hijacker
Entfüh'rung ƒ (-;-en) abduction; kidnaping; (aer) hijacking
entge'gen prep (dat) contrary to; in the
direction of, towards
entge'gengehen §82 intr (SEIN) (dat)
go to meet; (dat) face, confront
entge'gengesetzt adj contrary, opposite
entge'genhalten §90 tr hold out; point
out, say in answer
entge'genkommen §99 intr (SEIN) (dat)
approach; (dat) come to meet; (dat)
meet halfway || Entgegenkommen n
(-s;) courtesy
entge'genkommend adj on-coming;
(fig) accommodating
entge'genlaufen §105 intr (SEIN) (dat)
run towards; (dat) run counter to
entge'gennehmen §116 tr accept, receive
entge'gensehen §138 intr (dat) look forward to; (dat) await; (dat) face
entge'gensetzen tr put up, offer
entge'genstehen §146 intr (dat) oppose
entge'genstellen tr set in opposition ||
ref (dat) oppose, resist
entge'genstrecken tr (dat) stretch out
(toward)
entge'gentreten §152 intr (SEIN) (dat)
walk toward; (fig) (dat) confront
entgegnen [ɛnt'gegnən] tr & intr reply
Entgeg'nung ƒ (-;-en) reply
entge'hen §82 intr (SEIN) (dat) escape,
elude; sich [dat] etw e. lassen let
s.th. slip by
Entgelt [ɛnt'gɛlt] n (-[e]s;) compensation, payment
entgel'ten §83 tr pay for
entgeistert [ɛnt'gaistərt] adj aghast
entgleisen [ɛnt'glaizən] intr (SEIN)
jump the track; (fig) make a slip
Entglei'sung ƒ (-;-en) derailment;
(fig) slip
entglei'ten §86 intr (SEIN) (dat) slip
away (from)
entgräten [ɛnt'gretən] tr bone (a fish)

enthaaren [ɛnt'hɑrən] *tr* remove the hair from
Enthaa'rungsmittel *n* hair remover
enthal'ten §90 *tr* contain; comprise || *ref* (*genit*) refrain (from); **sich der Stimme e.** (parl) abstain
enthaltsam [ɛnt'haltzɑm] *adj* abstinent
Enthalt'samkeit *f* (–;) abstinence
Enthal'tung *f* (–;–en) abstention
enthär'ten *tr* (*Wasser*) soften
enthaupten [ɛnt'haʊptən] *tr* behead
enthäuten [ɛnt'hɔɪtən] *tr* skin
enthe'ben §94 *tr* (*genit*) exempt (from), relieve (of); (*e–s Amtes*) remove (*from office*)
enthei'ligen *tr* desecrate, profane
enthül'len *tr* unveil; reveal, expose
Enthül'lung *f* (–;–en) unveiling; (fig) exposé
enthül'sen *tr* shell; (*Mais*) husk
Enthusiasmus [ɛntʊzi'asmʊs] *m* (–;) enthusiasm
enthusiastisch [ɛntʊzi'astɪʃ] *adj* enthusiastic
entjungfern [ɛnt'jʊŋfərn] *tr* deflower
entkei'men *tr* sterilize; (*Milch*) pasteurize || *intr* (SEIN) sprout
entkernen [ɛnt'kɛrnən] *tr* (*Obst*) pit
entklei'den *tr* undress; (*genit*) strip (of), divest (of) || *ref* undress
Entklei'dungsnummer *f* striptease act
Entklei'dungsrevué *f* striptease show
entkom'men §99 *intr* (SEIN) (*dat*) escape (from) || **Entkommen** *n* (–s;) escape
entkor'ken *tr* uncork, open
entkräften [ɛnt'krɛftən] *tr* weaken; (*Argument*) refute
entla'den §103 *tr* unload; (*Batterie*) discharge || *ref* (*Gewehr*) go off; (*Sturm*) break; (elec) discharge; **sein Zorn entlud sich** he vented his anger
Entla'dung *f* (–;–en) unloading; discharge; explosion; **zur E. bringen** detonate
entlang' *adv* along || *prep* (*dat* or *acc* or *an dat*; or after *genit* or *dat*) along
entlarven [ɛnt'larfən] *tr* expose
entlas'sen §104 *tr* dismiss, fire; set free; (mil) discharge
Entlas'sungspapiere *pl* discharge papers
entla'sten *tr* unburden; (**von**) relieve (of); (jur) exonerate
Entla'stungsstraße *f* bypass
Entla'stungszeuge *m* witness for the defense
entlauben [ɛnt'laʊbən] *tr* defoliate
entlaubt' *adj* leafless
entlau'fen §105 *intr* (SEIN) (*dat*) run away (from); (*mit e–m Liebhaber*) elope
entlausen [ɛnt'laʊzən] *tr* delouse
entledigen [ɛnt'ledɪgən] *tr* (*genit*) release (from) || *ref* (*genit*) get rid (of), rid oneself (of)
entlee'ren *tr* empty; drain
entle'gen *adj* distant, remote
entleh'nen *tr* borrow
entlei'hen §81 *tr* borrow
entlo'ben *ref* break the engagement
entlocken (**entlok'ken**) *tr* elicit
entloh'nen *tr* pay, pay off
entlüf'ten *tr* ventilate

entmannen [ɛnt'manən] *tr* castrate
entmilitarisieren [ɛntmɪlɪtarɪ'zirən] *tr* demilitarize
entmutigen [ɛnt'mutɪgən] *tr* discourage
entneh'men §116 *tr* (*dat*) take (from); (*Geld*) (**aus**) withdraw (from); (*dat* or **aus**) infer (from), gather (from)
entnerven [ɛnt'nɛrfən] *tr* enervate
entpuppen [ɛnt'pʊpən] *ref* emerge from the cocoon; **sich e. als** (fig) turn out to be
enträtseln [ɛnt'rɛtsəln] *tr* solve; (*Schriftzeichen*) decipher
entrei'ßen §53 *tr* (*dat*) wrest (from)
entrich'ten *tr* pay
entrin'nen §121 *intr* (SEIN) escape (from)
entrol'len *tr* unroll; unfurl || *ref* unroll || *intr* (SEIN) roll down
entrüsten [ɛnt'rʏstən] *tr* anger || *ref*— **sich e. über** (*acc*) become incensed at; be shocked at
Entrü'stung *f* (–;) anger, indignation
entsa'gen *intr* (*dat*) renounce, forego; **dem Thron e.** abdicate
Entsatz' *m* (–es;) (mil) relief
entschä'digen *tr*. compensate; reimburse
Entschä'digung *f* (–;) compensation
Entschä'digungsanspruch *m* damage claim
entschär'fen *tr* defuse
Entscheid [ɛnt'ʃaɪt] *m* (–[e]s;–e) (jur) decision
entschei'den §112 *tr, ref* & *intr* decide
entschei'dend *adj* decisive
Entschei'dung *f* (–;–en) decision
Entschei'dungsbefugnis *f* jurisdiction
Entschei'dungskampf *m* (sport) finals
Entschei'dungsspiel *n* (cards) rubber game; (sport) finals
Entschei'dungsstunde *f* moment of truth
entschei'dungsvoll *adj* critical
entschieden [ɛnt'ʃidən] *adj* decided; decisive; firm, resolute
entschla'fen §131 *intr* (SEIN) fall asleep; (*sterben*) pass away, die
entschlei'ern *tr* unveil; (fig) reveal
entschlie'ßen §76 *ref* (**zu**) decide (on)
Entschlie'ßung *f* (–;–en) (parl) resolution
entschlossen [ɛnt'ʃlɔsən] *adj* resolute
entschlüp'fen *intr* (SEIN) (*dat*) slip away (from); (*dat*) slip out (on)
Entschluß' *m* resolve, decision
entschlüs'seln *tr* decipher
Entschluß'kraft *f* will power
entschulden [ɛnt'ʃʊldən] *tr* free of debt
entschuldigen [ɛnt'ʃʊldɪgən] *tr* excuse; exculpate || *ref* apologize; **es läßt sich e.** it's excusable; **sich e. lassen** beg to be excused; **sich mit Unwissenheit e.** plead ignorance
entschul'digend *adj* apologetic
Entschul'digung *f* (–;–en) excuse; apology; **ich bitte um E.** I beg your pardon
Entschul'digungsgrund *m* excuse
entseelt [ɛnt'zelt] *adj* lifeless, dead
entsen'den §140 *tr* send off
entset'zen *tr* horrify; (mil) relieve ||

ref (über *acc*) be horrified (at) || **Entsetzen** *n* (-s;) horror
entsetz'lich *adj* horrible, appalling || *adv* (coll) awfully
Entset'zung *f* (-;) dismissal; (mil) relief
entsi'chern *tr* take (*a gun*) off safety
entsie'geln *tr* unseal
entsin'nen §121 *ref* (*genit*) recall
entspan'nen *tr* & *ref* relax
Entspan'nung *f* (-;) relaxation; (pol) detente
entspre'chen §64 *intr* (*dat*) correspond (to); (*dat*) meet, suit; (*dat*) be equivalent (to); (*dat*) answer (*a description*)
entspre'chend *adj* corresponding; adequate; equivalent || *adv* accordingly || *prep* (*dat*) according to
entsprin'gen §142 *intr* (SEIN) rise, originate; (*entlaufen*) escape
entstaatlichen [ɛnt'ʃtatlɪçən] *tr* free from state control, denationalize
entstam'men *intr* (SEIN) (*dat*) descend (from), originate (from)
entste'hen §146 *intr* (SEIN) originate
Entste'hung *f* (-;) origin
entstel'len *tr* disfigure; deface; (*Tatsachen*) distort
enttäu'schen *tr* disappoint
entthronen [ɛnt'tronən] *tr* dethrone
entvölkern [ɛnt'fœlkərn] *tr* depopulate
entwach'sen §155 *intr* (SEIN) (*dat*) outgrow
entwaff'nen *tr* disarm
entwar'nen *intr* sound the all-clear
entwäs'sern *tr* drain; dehydrate
entweder [ɛnt'vedər] *conj*—**entweder ... oder** either ... or
entwei'chen §85 *intr* (SEIN) escape
entwei'hen *tr* desecrate, profane
entwen'den *tr* steal
entwer'fen §160 *tr* sketch; draft
entwer'ten *tr* (*Geld*) depreciate; (*Briefmarke*) cancel; (*Karten*) punch
entwickeln (**entwik'keln**) *tr* develop; evolve; (mil) deploy || *ref* develop
Entwick'lung *f* (-;-en) development; evolution; (mil) deployment
Entwick'lungsland *n* developing country
Entwick'lungslehre *f* theory of evolution
entwin'den §59 *tr* (*dat*) wrest (from) || *ref* extricate oneself
entwirren [ɛnt'vɪrən] *tr* & *ref* unravel
entwi'schen *intr* (SEIN) escape; (*dat* or *aus*) slip away (from)
entwöhnen [ɛnt'vønən] *tr* wean; **j—n e.** (*genit*) break s.o. of || *ref* (*genit*) give up
Entwurf' *m* (-s;⁻e) sketch; draft
entwur'zeln *tr* uproot
entzau'bern *tr* disenchant
entzie'hen §163 *tr* (*dat*) withdraw (from), take away (from); (chem) extract; **j—m das Wort e.** (parl) rule s.o. out of order || *ref* (*dat*) shirk, elude
Entzie'hungsanstalt *f* rehabilitation center
entziffern [ɛnt'tsɪfərn] *tr* decipher
entzücken (**entzük'ken**) *tr* delight

Entzückung (**Entzük'kung**) *f* (-;-en) delight, rapture
Entzug' *m* (-[e]s;) deprivation
entzündbar [ɛnt'tsʏntbar] *adj* inflammable
entzün'den *tr* set on fire; (fig) inflame || *ref* catch fire; (pathol) become inflamed
Entzün'dung *f* (-;) kindling; (pathol) inflammation
entzwei' *adv* in two, apart
entzwei'brechen §64 *tr* & *intr* break in two, snap
entzweien [ɛnt'tsvaɪ·ən] *tr* divide
Enzykli·ka [ɛn'tsʏklɪka] *f* (-;-ken [kən]) encyclicle
Enzyklopä·die [ɛntsʏklopɛ'di] *f* (-;-dien ['di·ən]) encyclopedia
Enzym [ɛn'tsym] *n* (-[e]s;-e) enzyme
Epaulette [ɛpɔ'lɛtə] *f* (-;-n) epaulet
ephemer [ɛfɛ'mer] *adj* ephemeral
Epide·mie [ɛpɪdɛ'mi] *f* (-;-mien ['mi·ən] epidemic
epidemisch [ɛpɪ'demɪʃ] *adj* epidemic
Epigramm [ɛpɪ'gram] *n* (-s;-e) epigram
Epik ['epɪk] *f* (-;) epic poetry
Epilog [ɛpɪ'lok] *m* (-s;-e) epilogue
episch ['epɪʃ] *adj* epic
Episode [ɛpɪ'zodə] *f* (-;-n) episode
Epoche [ɛ'pɔxə] *f* (-;-n) epoch
Epos ['epɔs] *n* (-; **Epen** ['epən]) epic
Equipage [ɛk(v)ɪ'paʒə] *f* (-;-n) carriage; (naut) crew; (sport) team
Equipe [ɛ'k(v)ɪp(ə)] *f* (-;-n) team; group
er [er] §11 *pers pron* he; it
er- [ɛr] *insep pref*
erach'ten *tr* think || **Erachten** *n* (-s;) opinion; **meines Erachtens** in my opinion
erar'beiten *tr* acquire (*by working*)
Erb- [ɛrp] *comb.fm.* hereditary
Erb'anfall *m* inheritance
Erb'anlage *f* (biol) gene
erbarmen [ɛr'barmən] *tr* move to pity || *ref* (*genit*) pity; **erbarme Dich unser** have mercy on us || **Erbarmen** *n* (-s;) pity, mercy
erbar'menswert, erbar'menswürdig *adj* pitiable
erbärmlich [ɛr'bɛrmlɪç] *adj* pitiful; wretched, miserable || *adv* awfully
erbar'mungslos *adj* pitiless
erbau'en *tr* erect; (fig) edify || *ref* (**an** *dat*) be edified (by)
Erbau'er *m* (-s;-) builder
erbau'lich *adj* edifying
Erbau'ung *f* (-;) building; edification
Erbau'ungsbuch *n* book of devotions
erb'berechtigt *adj* eligible as heir
Erbe ['ɛrbə] *m* (-n;-n) heir; **ohne Leibliche Erben** without issue || *n* (-s;) inheritance, heritage; **väterliches E.** patrimony
erbe'ben *intr* (SEIN) tremble
erb'eigen *adj* hereditary
erben ['ɛrbən] *tr* inherit
erbet'teln *tr* get (by begging)
erbeuten [ɛr'bɔɪtən] *tr* capture
Erb'feind *m* traditional enemy
Erb'folge *f* succession
erbie'ten §58 *ref* volunteer

Erbin ['ɛrbɪn] f (–;–nen) heiress
erbit'ten §60 ref—sich [dat] etw e. ask for s.th., request s.th.
erbittern [ɛr'bɪtərn] tr embitter
Erb'krankheit f hereditary disease
erblassen [ɛr'blasən] intr (SEIN) turn pale
Erblasser –in ['ɛrplasər(ɪn)] §6 mf testator
erbleichen [ɛr'blaɪçən] §85 & §109 intr (SEIN) turn pale; (poet) die
erb'lich adj hereditary
Erb'lichkeit f (–;) heredity
erblicken (erblik'ken) tr spot, see
erblinden [ɛr'blɪndən] intr (SEIN) go blind
Erblin'dung f (–;) loss of sight
Erb'onkel m (coll) rich uncle
erbre'chen §64 tr break open || ref vomit
erbrin'gen §65 tr produce
Erb'schaft f (–;–en) inheritance
Erbse ['ɛrpsə] f (–;–n) pea
Erb'stück n heirloom
Erb'sünde f original sin
Erb'tante f (coll) rich aunt
Erb'teil m share (in an inheritance)
Erd– [ert] comb.fm. earth, of the earth; geo–; ground
Erd'anschluß m (elec) ground
Erd'arbeiten pl excavation work
Erd'bahn f orbit of the earth
Erd'ball m globe
Erd'beben n (–s;–) earthquake
Erd'bebenmesser m seismograph
Erd'beere f strawberry
Erd'boden m ground, earth; dem E. gleichmachen raze (to the ground)
Erde ['erdə] f (–;–n) earth; ground, soil, land; (elec) ground wire; zu ebener E. on the ground floor
erden ['erdən] tr (elec) ground
erden'ken §66 tr think up
erdenk'lich adj imaginable
Erd'gas n natural gas
Erd'geschoß n ground floor
erdich'ten tr fabricate, think up
Erdich'tung f (–;–en) fabrication
erdig ['erdɪç] adj earthy
Erd'innere §5 n interior of the earth
Erd'klumpen m clod
Erd'kreis m earth, world
Erd'kugel f globe, sphere; world
Erd'kunde f geography
Erd'leitung f (elec) ground wire
Erd'nuß f peanut
Erd'nußbutter f peanut butter
Erd'öl n petroleum, oil; auf E. stoßen strike oil
erdolchen [ɛr'dɔlçən] tr stab
Erd'reich n soil
erdreisten [ɛr'draɪstən] ref have the nerve, have the audacity
Erd'rinde f crust of the earth
erdros'seln tr strangle
erdrücken (erdrük'ken) tr crush to death
erdrückend (erdrük'kend) adj overwhelming
Erd'rutsch m land slide
Erd'schicht f stratum
Erd'spalte f fissure; chasm
Erd'teil m continent

erdul'den tr suffer
ereifern [ɛr'aɪfərn] ref get excited
ereignen [ɛr'aɪgnən] ref happen, occur
Ereignis [ɛr'aɪgnɪs] n (–ses;–se) event, occurrence
ereig'nislos adj uneventful
ereig'nisvoll adj eventful
Erektion [erek'tsjon] f (–;–en) erection
Eremit [ere'mit] m (–en;–en) hermit
erer'ben tr inherit
erfah'ren adj experienced || §71 tr find out; (erleben) experience; (Pflege) receive
Erfah'rung f (–;–en) experience
erfas'sen tr grasp; understand; include; register, list
erfin'den §59 tr invent
Erfin'der –in §6 mf inventor
erfinderisch [ɛr'fɪndərɪʃ] adj inventive
Erfin'dung f (–;–en) invention
Erfin'dungsgabe f inventiveness
erfle'hen tr obtain (by entreaty)
Erfolg [ɛr'fɔlk] m (–[e]s;–e) success; (Wirkung) result
erfol'gen intr (SEIN) ensue; occur
erfolg'los adj unsuccessful || adv in vain
erfolg'reich adj successful
Erfolgs'mensch m go-getter
erfolg'versprechend adj promising
erforderlich [ɛr'fɔrdərlɪç] adj required, necessary
erfor'derlichenfalls adv if need be
erfordern [ɛr'fɔrdərn] tr require
Erfordernis [ɛr'fɔrdərnɪs] n (–ses;–se) requirement; exigency
erfor'schen tr investigate; (Land) explore
Erfor'scher –in §6 mf explorer
Erfor'schung f (–;–en) investigation; exploration
erfra'gen tr ask for; find out
erfreu'en tr delight || ref (an dat) be delighted (at); sich e. (genit) enjoy
erfreulich [ɛr'frɔɪlɪç] adj delightful; (Nachricht) welcome, good
erfreut [ɛr'frɔɪt] adj (über acc) glad (about); e. zu (inf) pleased to (inf)
erfrie'ren §77 intr (SEIN) freeze to death; (Pflanzen) freeze
Erfrie'rung f (–;–en) frostbite
erfrischen [ɛr'frɪʃən] tr refresh
Erfri'schung f (–;–en) refreshment
erfül'len tr fill; fulfill; (Aufgabe) perform; (Bitte) comply with; (Hoffnungen) live up to || ref materialize
Erfül'lung f (–;) fulfillment; accomplishment; in E. gehen come true
erfunden [ɛr'fundən] adj made-up
ergänzen [ɛr'gɛntsən] tr complete; complement; (Statue) restore
ergän'zend adj complementary
ergattern [ɛr'gatərn] tr (coll) dig up
ergau'nern tr—etw von j–m e. cheat s.o. out of s.th.
erge'ben adj devoted || §80 tr yield; amount to; show || ref surrender; (dat) devote oneself (to); (aus) result (from); sich dem Trunk e. take to drinking; sich e. in (acc) resign oneself to
Erge'benheit f (–;) devotion; resignation

ergebenst [ɛr'gebənst] *adv* respectfully
Ergebnis [ɛr'gepnɪs] *n* (-ses;-se) result, outcome; (*Punktzahl*) score
Erge'bung *f* (-;) submission, resignation; (mil) surrender
erge'hen §82 *intr* (SEIN) come out, be published; **e. lassen** issue, publish; **etw über sich e. lassen** put up with s.th.; **Gnade vor Recht e. lassen** show leniency || *ref* take a stroll; **sich e. in** (*acc*) indulge in; **sich e. über** (*acc*) expatiate on || *impers*—**es ist ihm gut ergangen** things went well for him || **Ergehen** *n* (-s;) state of health
ergiebig [ɛr'gibɪç] *adj* productive, fertile; rich, abundant
ergie'ßen §76 *ref* flow; pour out
ergötzen [ɛr'gœtsən] *tr* amuse || *ref* (**an** *dat*) take delight (in)
ergötz'lich *adj* delightful
ergrau'en *intr* (SEIN) turn gray
ergrei'fen §88 *tr* seize; (*Verbrecher*) apprehend; (*Gemüt*) move; (*Beruf, Waffen*) take up; (*Maßnahmen*) take
Ergrei'fung *f* (-;) seizure
ergriffen [ɛr'grɪfən] *adj* moved; **e. von** seized with
Ergrif'fenheit *f* (-;) emotion
ergrün'den *tr* get to the bottom of
Erguß' *m* discharge; (fig) flood of words
erha'ben *adj* elevated, lofty; **erhabene Arbeit** relief work; **e. sein über** (*acc*) be above
Erhalt' *m* (-es;) receipt
erhal'ten §90 *tr* get, receive; keep, keep up, maintain; conserve; (*Familie*) support; (*Gesundheit*) preserve; **Betrag dankend e.** (*stamped on bills*) paid; **gut e.** well preserved; **noch e. sein** survive || *ref* survive; (**von**) subsist (on)
erhältlich [ɛr'hɛltɪç] *adj* obtainable
Erhal'tung *f* (-;) preservation; maintenance; support; (*der Energie, usw.*) conservation
erhän'gen *tr* hang
erhär'ten *tr* harden; (fig) substantiate || *intr* (SEIN) harden
erha'schen *tr* catch; **e-n Blick von ihr e.** catch her eye
erhe'ben §94 *tr* raise; (*erhöhen*) elevate; (*preisen*) exalt; (*Steuern*) collect; (*Anklage*) bring; (math) raise || *ref* get up, rise, start; arise
erheblich [ɛr'heplɪç] *adj* considerable
Erhe'bung *f* (-;-en) elevation; promotion; uprising, revolt; **Erhebungen machen** make inquiries
erheitern [ɛr'haɪtərn] *tr* amuse || *ref* cheer up
erhellen [ɛr'hɛlən] *tr* light up; (fig) shed light on || *ref* grow light(er); light up || *impers*—**es erhellt** it appears
erhitzen [ɛr'hɪtsən] *tr* heat; (fig) inflame || *ref* grow hot; get angry
erhöhen [ɛr'hø·ən] *tr* raise; (fig) heighten || *ref* increase; be enhanced
Erhö'hung *f* (-;-en) rise
erho'len *ref* recover; relax
Erho'lung *f* (-;-en) recovery; relaxation; recreation

erho'lungsbedürftig *adj* in need of rest
Erho'lungsheim *n* convalescent home
erhö'ren *tr* (*Gebet*) hear; (*Bitte*) grant
erinnerlich [ɛr'ɪnərlɪç] *adj*—**das ist mir nicht e.** it slipped my mind; **soviel mir e. ist** as far as I can remember
erinnern [ɛr'ɪnərn] *tr* (**an** *acc*) remind (of) || *ref* (**an** *acc*) remember
Erin'nerung *f* (-;-en) recollection, remembrance; (*Mahnung*) reminder; **zur E. an** (*acc*) in memory of
Erin'nerungsvermögen *n* memory
erkalten [ɛr'kaltən] *intr* (SEIN) cool off; (fig) grow cool
erkälten [ɛr'kɛltən] *ref* catch cold
Erkäl'tung *f* (-;-en) cold
erkennbar [ɛr'kɛnbɑr] *adj* recognizable
erkennen [ɛr'kenən] §97 *tr* make out; recognize; detect; realize; **j-n e. für** (com) credit s.o. with; **sich zu e. geben** disclose one's identity; **zu e. geben, daß** indicate that || *intr*—**auf e-e Geldstrafe e.** impose a fine; **gegen j-n e.** judge against s.o.
erkenntlich [ɛr'kɛntlɪç] *adj* grateful
Erkennt'lichkeit *f* (-;) gratitude
Erkenntnis [ɛr'kɛntnɪs] *f* (-;-se) insight, judgment, realization, knowledge; (philos) cognition || *n* (-ses; -se) decision, finding
Erker ['ɛrkər] *m* (-s;-) (archit) oriel
Er'kerfenster *n* bay window
erklären [ɛr'klɛrən] *tr* explain, account for; (*aussprechen*) state
Erklä'rer **-in** §6 *mf* commentator
erklär'lich *adj* explicable
Erklä'rung *f* (-;-en) explanation; statement; commentary; (jur) deposition
erklin'gen §142 *intr* (SEIN) sound; (*widerhallen*) resound
erkor (ɛr'kor] *pret* of **erkiesen**
erkoren [ɛr'korən] *adj* chosen
erkranken [ɛr'kraŋkən] *intr* (SEIN) get sick; (*Pflanzen*) become diseased
erkühnen [ɛr'kynən] *ref* dare, venture
erkunden [ɛr'kundən] *tr & intr* reconnoiter
erkundigen [ɛr'kundɪgən] *ref* inquire
Erkun'digung *f* (-;-en) inquiry
Erkun'dung *f* (-;) reconnaissance
erlahmen [ɛr'lɑmən] *intr* (SEIN) tire; (*Kraft*) give out
erlangen [ɛr'laŋən] *tr* reach; (*sich verschaffen*) get; **wieder e.** recover
Er·laß [ɛr'las] *m* (-lasses;-lässe) remission; exemption; edict, order
erlas'sen §104 *tr* release; (*Schulden*) cancel; (*Strafe*) remit; (*Sünden*) pardon; (*Verordnung*) issue; **e. Sie es mir zu** (*inf*) allow me not to (*inf*), don't ask me to (*inf*)
erläßlich [ɛr'leslɪç] *adj* pardonable
erlauben [ɛr'laubən] *tr* allow || *ref*—**sich** [*dat*] **e. zu** (*inf*) take the liberty to (*inf*); **sich** [*dat*] **nicht e.** not be able to afford
Erlaubnis [ɛr'laupnɪs] *f* (-;-se) permission
Erlaub'nisschein *m* permit, license
erlaucht [ɛr'lauxt] *adj* illustrious
erläutern [ɛr'lɔɪtərn] *tr* explain
Erläu'terung *f* (-;-en) explanation

Erle ['ɛrlə] *f* (-;-n) (bot) alder
erle'ben *tr* live to see; experience
Erlebnis [ɛr'lepnɪs] *n* (-ses;-se) experience, adventure; occurrence
erledigen [ɛr'ledɪgən] *tr* settle; (*Post, Einkäufe, Gesuch*) attend to, take care of; **j-n e.** (coll) do s.o. in
erledigt [ɛr'ledɪçt] *adj* (& fig) finished; (*Stellung*) open; (coll) bushed
erle'gen *tr* pay down; (*töten*) kill
erleichtern [ɛr'laiçtərn] *tr* lighten; make easy; (*Not*) relieve, ease
Erleich'terung *f* (-;) alleviation
erlei'den §106 *tr* suffer
erler'nen *tr* learn
erle'sen *adj* choice || §107 *tr* choose
erleuch'ten *tr* light up; enlighten
erlie'gen §108 *intr* (SEIN) (*dat*) succumb (to), fall victim (to)
erlogen [ɛr'logən] *adj* false
Erlös [ɛr'løs] *m* (-es;) proceeds
erlosch [ɛr'loʃ] *pret* of **erlöschen**
erloschen [ɛr'loʃən] *pp* of **erlöschen**
erlöschen [ɛr'lœʃən] §110 *intr* (SEIN) go out; (*Vertrag*) expire; (fig) become extinct
erlö'sen *tr* redeem; free; get (*by sale*)
Erlö'ser *m* (-s;-) deliverer; (relig) Redeemer
Erlö'sung *f* (-;) redemption
ermächtigen [ɛr'mɛçtɪgən] *tr* authorize
Ermäch'tigung *f* (-;-en) authorization
ermah'nen *tr* admonish
Ermah'nung *f* (-;-en) admonition
ermangeln [ɛr'maŋəln] *intr* (*genit*) lack; **es an nichts e. lassen** spare no pains; **nicht e. zu** (*inf*) not fail to (*inf*)
Erman'gelung *f*—**in E.** (*genit*) in default of
ermä'ßigen *tr* reduce
ermatten [ɛr'matən] *tr* tire || *intr* (SEIN) tire; grow weak; slacken
Ermat'tung *f* (-;) fatigue
ermes'sen §70 *tr* judge, estimate; realize; **e. aus** infer from || **Ermessen** *n* (-s;) judgment, opinion; **nach freiem E.** at one's discretion
ermitteln [ɛr'mɪtəln] *tr* ascertain || *intr* conduct an investigation
Ermitt'lung *f* (-;-en) ascertainment; **Ermittlungen** investigation
Ermitt'lungsausschuß *m* fact-finding committee
Ermitt'lungsbeamte *m* investigator
Ermitt'lungsverfahren *n* judicial inquiry
ermöglichen [ɛr'møklɪçən] *tr* enable, make possible
ermorden [ɛr'mordən] *tr* murder
ermüden [ɛr'mydən] *tr* tire || *intr* (SEIN) tire, get tired
Ermü'dung *f* (-;) fatigue
ermuntern [ɛr'muntərn] *tr* cheer up; encourage || *ref* cheer up
Ermun'terung *f* (-;) encouragement
ermutigen [ɛr'mutɪgən] *tr* encourage
ernäh'ren *tr* nourish; (fig) support
Ernäh'rer –**in** §6 *mf* supporter
Ernäh'rung *f* (-;) nourishment; support; (physiol) nutrition
ernen'nen §97 *tr* nominate, appoint
erneuern [ɛr'nɔi·ərn] *tr* renew; renovate; (*Gemälde*) restore; (*Öl*) change; (*Reifen*) retread; (mach) replace
erneu'ert *adj* repeated || *adv* anew
Erneu'erung *f* (-;-en) renewal; renovation; restoration; replacement
erniedrigen [ɛr'nidrɪgən] *tr* lower; (*demütigen*) humble; (*im Rang*) degrade || *ref* humble oneself; debase oneself
ernst [ɛrnst] *adj* earnest; serious || **Ernst** *m* (-[e]s;) seriousness; **im E.** in earnest
Ernst'fall *m*—**im E.** in case of emergency; (mil) in case of war
ernst'haft *adj* earnest, serious
ernst'lich *adj* earnest; serious
Ernte ['ɛrntə] *f* (-;-n) harvest; crop
ernten ['ɛrntən] *tr* reap, harvest
ernüch'tern *tr* sober; disallusion || *ref* sober up; be disillusioned
Ero'berer –**in** §6 *mf* conqueror
erobern [ɛr'obərn] *tr* conquer
Ero'berung *f* (-;-en) conquest
eröff'nen *tr* open; (*feierlich*) inaugurate; disclose || *ref* open; present itself; **sich j-m e.** unburden oneself to s.o.
Eröff'nung *f* (-;-en) (grand) opening; inauguration; announcement
erörtern [ɛr'œrtərn] *tr* discuss
erotisch [ɛ'rotɪʃ] *adj* erotic
Erpel ['ɛrpəl] *m* (-s;-) drake
erpicht [ɛr'pɪçt] *adj*—**e. auf** (*acc*) keen on, dead set on, hell bent on
erpres'sen *tr* extort; (*Person*) blackmail
Erpres'sung *f* (-;-en) extortion; blackmail
erpro'ben *tr* test, try out
erquicken [ɛr'kvɪkən] *tr* refresh
erquick'lich *adj* refreshing; agreeable
erra'ten §63 *tr* guess
errech'nen *tr* calculate
erregbar [ɛr'rekbɑr] *adj* excitable; irritable
erregen [ɛr'regən] *tr* excite; cause || *ref* get excited, get worked up
Erre'gung *f* (-;) excitation; agitation; excitment; **E. öffentlichen Ärgernisses** disorderly conduct
erreichbar [ɛr'raiçbɑr] *adj* reachable; available
errei'chen *tr* reach, attain; get to; (*Zug, Bus*) catch; **e., daß** bring it about that
erret'ten *tr* save, rescue
Erret'tung *f* (-;-en) rescue; (relig) Salvation
errich'ten *tr* erect; found
errin'gen §142 *tr* get; attain, achieve
errö'ten *intr* (SEIN) redden; blush
Errungenschaft [ɛr'ruŋən/aft] *f* (-; -en) achievement; acquisition
Ersatz' *m* (-es;) substitute; replacement; compensation; (mil) recruitment
Ersatz– *comb.fm.* substitute, replacement; spare; alternative; recruiting
Ersatz'mann *m* substitute; alternate
Ersatz'stück *n*, **Ersatz'teil** *n* spare part, spare
erschaf'fen §126 *tr* create
Erschaf'fer –**in** §6 *mf* creator
Erschaf'fung *f* (-;-en) creation

erschal'len §127 *intr* (SEIN) begin to sound; ring out; resound

erschau'ern *intr* shudder

erschei'nen §128 *intr* (SEIN) appear; (*Buch*) come out, be published

Erschei'nung *f* (-;-en) appearance; apparition; phenomenon

erschie'ßen §76 *tr* shoot (dead)

Erschie'ßung *f* (-;-en) shooting, execution

Erschie'ßungskommando *n* .firing squad

erschlaffen [ɛr'ʃlafən] *tr* relax; enervate || *intr* (SEIN) relax; weaken

erschla'gen §132 *tr* slay; **wie e.** dead tired

erschlie'ßen §76 *tr* open up; develop; **e. aus** infer from; derive from || *ref* —**sich j-m e.** unburden oneself to s.o.

erschöp'fen *tr* exhaust; (fig) deplete

erschrak [ɛr'ʃrak] *pret* of **erschrecken**

erschrecken (erschrek'ken) *tr* startle; shock || *ref* get scared || §134 *intr* (SEIN) be startled

erschreckend (erschrek'kend) *adj* terrifying; alarming; dreadful

erschüt'ten *tr* shake; upset; move deeply

Erschüt'terung *f* (-;-en) tremor; vibration; deep feeling; concussion

erschweren [ɛr'ʃverən] *tr* make more difficult; hamper, impede

erschwin'deln *tr*—**etw von j-m e.** cheat s.o. out of s.th.

erschwin'gen §142 *tr* afford

erschwing'lich *adj* within one's means

erse'hen §138 *tr* (aus) gather (from)

erseh'nen *tr* long for

ersetzbar [ɛr'zetsbar] *adj* replaceable

erset'zen *tr* replace; (*Schaden*) compensate for; (*Kräfte*) renew; **j-m etw e.** reimburse s.o. for s.th.; **sie ersetzte ihm die Eltern** she was mother and father to him

ersetz'lich *adj* replaceable

ersicht'lich *adj* evident

ersin'nen §121 *tr* think up

erspa'ren *tr* save

Ersparnis [ɛr'ʃparnɪs] *f* (-;-se) (an *dat*) saving (in)

ersprießlich [ɛr'ʃprisliç] *adj* useful

erst [ɛrst] *adv* first; at first; just; only; not until; **e. recht** really; **e. recht nicht** most certainly not

erstar'ren *intr* (SEIN) grow stiff; (*Finger*) grow numb; (*Blut*) congeal; (*Zement*) set; (fig) run cold; **vor Schreck e.** be paralyzed with fear

erstatten [ɛr'ʃtatən] *tr* refund, repay; (*Bericht*) file; **Meldung e.** report

Erstat'tung *f* (-;-en) refund; reimbursement; compensation

Erst'aufführung *f* primiere

erstau'nen *tr* astonish || *intr* (SEIN) (über *acc*) be astonished (at) || Erstaunen *n* (-s;) astonishment; **in E. setzen** astonish

erstaun'lich *adj* astonishing

Erst'ausfertigung *f* original

erste ['ɛrstə] §9 *adj* first; **der erste beste** the first that comes along; **fürs e.** for the time being; **zum ersten, zum zweiten, zum dritten** going, going, gone

erste'chen §64 *tr* stab

erste'hen §146 *tr* buy, get || *intr* (SEIN) rise; (*Städte*) spring up

erstei'gen §148 *tr* climb

erstel'len *tr* provide, supply; erect

erstens ['ɛrstəns] *adv* first; in the first place

erst'geboren *adj* first-born

ersticken [ɛr'ʃtikən] *tr* choke, stifle, smother; **im Keim e.** nip in the bud || *intr* (SEIN) choke; **in Arbeit e.** be snowed under

erstklassig ['ɛrstklasiç] *adj* first-class

Erstling ['ɛrstlɪŋ] *m* (-s;-e) first-born child; (fig) first fruits

Erstlings– *comb.fm.* first

Erst'lingsausstattung *f* layette

erstmalig ['ɛrstmaliç] *adj* first

erstre'ben *tr* strive for

erstrecken (erstrek'ken) *ref* extend

ersu'chen *tr* request, ask

ertappen [ɛr'tapən] *tr* surprise, catch

ertei'len *tr* give; confer; (*Auftrag*) place; (*Audienz, Patent*) grant

ertö'nen *intr* (SEIN) sound; resound

ertö'ten *tr* (fig) stifle

Ertrag [ɛr'trak] *m* (-[e]s;–e) yield; proceeds; produce

ertra'gen §132 *tr* stand, bear

erträglich [ɛr'trekliç] *adj* bearable

ertränken [ɛr'treŋkən] *tr* drown

erträu'men *tr* dream of

ertrin'ken §143 *intr* (SEIN) drown

ertüchtigen [ɛr'tʏçtigən] *tr* train

erübrigen [ɛr'ybrigən] *tr* save; (*Zeit*) spare || *ref* be superfluous

erwa'chen *intr* (SEIN) wake up

erwach'sen *adj* adult || §155 *intr* (SEIN) grow, grow up; arise || **Erwachsene** §5 *mf* adult, grown-up

erwä'gen §156 *tr* weigh, consider

Erwä'gung *f* (-;-en) consideration

erwäh'len *tr* choose

erwäh'nen *tr* mention

erwäh'nenswert *adj* worth mentioning

Erwäh'nung *f* (-;) mention

erwär'men *tr* warm, warm up

erwar'ten *tr* expect, await; **etw zu e. haben** be in for s.th.

Erwar'tung *f* (-;-en) expectation

erwar'tungsvoll *adj* expectant

erwecken (erwek'ken) *tr* wake; (*Hoffnungen*) raise; (*Gefühle*) awaken; **den Anschein e.** give the impression

erweh'ren *ref* (genit) ward off; (genit) refrain from; (*der Tränen*) hold back

erwei'chen *tr* soften; (fig) move, touch; **sich e. lassen** relent

erwei'sen §118 *tr* prove; show; (*Achtung*) show; (*Dienst*) render; (*Ehre, Gunst*) do || *ref*—**sich e. als** prove

erweitern [ɛr'vaitərn] *tr* & *ref* widen; (*vermehren*) increase; extend, expand

Erwerb [ɛr'verp] *m* (-[e]s;-e) acquisition; (*Verdienst*) earnings; (*Unterhalt*) living

erwer'ben §149 *tr* acquire; gain; (*verdienen*) earn; (*kaufen*) purchase

erwerbs'behindert *adj* disabled

Erwerbs'betrieb *m* business enterprise

erwerbs'fähig *adj* capable of earning a living

erwerbs'los *adj* unemployed

Erwerbs'quelle *f* source of income
Erwerbs'sinn *m* acquisitiveness
erwerbs'tätig *adj* gainfully employed
erwerbs'unfähig *adj* unable to earn a living
Erwerbs'zweig *m* line of business
Erwer'bung *f* (-;-en) acquisition
erwidern [ɛr'vidərn] *tr* reply; reciprocate, return
Erwi'derung *f* (-;-en) reply; return; retaliation
erwir'ken *tr* secure, obtain
erwi'schen *tr* catch; **ihn hat's erwischt!** (coll) he's had it!
erwünscht [ɛr'vyn∫t] *adj* desired; welcome; (*wünschenswert*) desirable
erwür'gen *tr* strangle
Erz [ɛrts] *n* (-es;-e) ore; brass; bronze
Erz–, erz– *comb.fm.* ore; bronze; utterly; (fig) arch–
erzählen [ɛr'tselən] *tr* tell, narrate
Erzäh'lung *f* (-;-en) story, narrative
Erz'bischof *m* archbishop
Erz'engel *m* archangel
erzeu'gen *tr* beget; manufacture; produce; generate
Erzeugnis [ɛr'tsɔɪknɪs] *n* (-ses;-se) product; produce
Erzeu'gung *f* (-;-en) production; manufacture
erzie'hen §163 *tr* bring up, rear; (*geistig*) educate
Erzieher [ɛr'tsi·ər] *m* (-s;-) educator; private tutor
Erzieherin [ɛr'tsi·ərɪn] *f* (-;-nen) educator; governess
erzieherisch [ɛr'tsi·ərɪ∫] *adj* educational, pedagogical
Erzie'hung *f* (-;) upbringing; education; (*Lebensart*) breeding
Erzie'hungslehre *f* (educ) education
Erzie'hungswesen *n* educational system
erzie'len *tr* achieve, reach; (*Gewinn*) realize; (sport) score
Erz'lager *n* ore deposit
Erz'probe *f* assay
erzür'nen *tr* anger ‖ *ref* get angry
erzwin'gen §142 *tr* force; wring, obtain by force; (*Gehorsam*) exact
es [ɛs] *adv* (as expletive) there; **es gibt** there is, there are ‖ §11 *pers pron* it; he; she ‖ **Es** *n* (-;-) (mus) E flat; (psychol) id
Esche ['ɛ∫ə] *f* (-;-n) ash tree
Esel ['ezəl] *m* (-s;-) donkey, ass
Eselei [ezə'laɪ] *f* (-;-en) foolish act, foolish remark
E'selsbrücke *f* (educ) pony
E'selsohr *n* dog's-ear
eskalieren [ɛska'lirən] *tr* & *intr* escalate
Eskimo ['ɛskɪmo] *m* (-s;-s) Eskimo
Espe ['ɛspə] *f* (-;-n) (bot) aspen
eßbar ['ɛsbɑr] *adj* edible, eatable
Eßbesteck ['ɛsbə∫tɛk] *n* knife, fork, and spoon
Esse ['ɛsə] *f* (-;-n) chimney; forge
essen ['ɛsən] §70 *tr* & *intr* eat; **zu Mittag e.** eat lunch ‖ **Essen** *n* (-s;) eating; food, meal
Essenz [ɛ'sɛnts] *f* (-;-en) essence
Eßgeschirr ['ɛsgə∫ɪr] *n* (-s;) tableware; table service; (mil) mess kit

Eßgier ['ɛsgir] *f* (-;) gluttony
Essig ['ɛsɪç] *m* (-s;-e) vinegar
Es'siggurke *f* pickle, gherkin
Es'sigsäure *f* acetic acid
Eßlöffel ['ɛslœfəl] *m* (-s;-) tablespoon
Eßnapf ['ɛsnapf] *m* dinner pail
Eßsaal ['ɛszɑl] *m* dining room
Eßstäbchen ['ɛs∫tɛpçən] *n* chopstick
Eßwaren ['ɛsvɑrən] *pl* food, victuals
Eßzimmer ['ɛstsɪmər] *n* (-s;-) dining room
Estland ['ɛstlant] *n* (-s;) Estonia
Estrade [ɛs'trɑdə] *f* (-;-n) dais
etablieren [eta'blirən] *tr* establish
Etablissement [etablɪs(ə)'mã] *n* (-s;-s) establishment
Etage [ɛ'taʒə] *f* (-;-n) floor, story
Eta'genbett *n* bunk bed
Eta'genwohnung *f* apartment
Etappe [ɛ'tapə] *f* (-;-n) (*Teilstrecke*) leg, stage; (mil) rear eschelon, rear
Etat [ɛ'ta] *m* (-s;-s) budget
Etats'jahr *n* fiscal year
etepetete [etəpɛ'tetə] *adj* overly particular
Ethik ['etɪk] *f* (-;) ethics
ethisch ['etɪ∫] *adj* ethical
ethnisch ['ɛtnɪ∫] *adj* ethnic
Ethnologie [ɛtnɔlɔ'gi] *f* (-;) ethnology
Etikett [ɛtɪ'kɛt] *n* (-s;-e) tab, label
Etikette [ɛtɪ'ketə] *f* (-;) etiquette
etikettieren [ɛtɪke'tirən] *tr* label
etliche ['ɛtlɪçə] *adj* & *pron* a few
Etui [ɛ'tvi] *n* (-s;-s) case (*for spectacles, cigarettes, etc.*)
etwa ['ɛtva] *adv* about, around; perhaps; by chance; for example
etwaig [ɛt'va·ɪç] *adj* eventual
etwas ['ɛtvas] *adj* some, a little ‖ *adv* somewhat ‖ *pron* something; anything ‖ **Etwas** *n*—**ein gewißes E.** a certain something
euch [ɔɪç] *pers pron* you; to you ‖ *reflex pron* yourselves
euer ['ɔɪ·ər] *adj* your
Eukalyp·tus [ɔɪka'lʏptʊs] *m* (-;- & –ten) eucalyptus
Eule ['ɔɪlə] *f* (-;-n) owl
Euphorie [ɔɪfɔ'ri] *f* (-;) euphoria
euphorisch [ɔɪ'forɪ∫] *adj* euphoric
eurige ['ɔɪrɪgə] §2,5 *pron* yours
Europa [ɔɪ'ropa] *n* (-s;) Europe
Europäer –in [ɔɪrɔ'pe·ər(ɪn)] §6 *mf* European
europäisch [ɔɪrɔ'pe·ɪ∫] *adj* European
Euter ['ɔɪtər] *n* (-s;-) udder
evakuieren [ɛvaku'irən] *tr* evacuate
evangelisch [ɛvan'gelɪ∫] *adj* evangelical; Protestant
Evangelist [ɛvange'lɪst] *m* (-en;-en) Evangelist
Evange·lium [ɛvan'geljʊm] *n* (-s;-lien [ljən]) gospel
eventuell [ɛventu'ɛl] *adj* eventual ‖ *adv* possibly
ewig ['eviç] *adj* eternal; perpetual
E'wigkeit *f* (-;-en) eternity
e'wiglich *adv* forever
exakt [ɛ'ksakt] *adj* exact
Exa·men [ɛ'ksamən] *n* (-s;-s & –mina [mɪna]) examination
examinieren [ɛksami'nirən] *tr* examine
exekutiv [ɛksekʊ'tif] *adj* executive

Exempel [ε'ksεmpəl] *n* (−s;−) example; ein E. statuieren an (*dat*) make an example of
Exemplar [εksεm'plɑr] *n* (−s;−e) sample, specimen; (*e−s Buches*) copy
exerzieren [εksεr'tsirən] *tr & intr* exercise
Exil [ε'ksil] *n* (−s;−e) exile
Existenz [εksı'stεnts] *f* (−;−en) existence; livelihood; personality
Existenz'minimum *n* living wage
existieren [εksıs'tirən] *intr* exist
exklusiv [εkslu'zif] *adj* exclusive
Exkommunikation [εkskɔmunıka'tsjon] *f* (−;−en) excommunication
exkommunizieren [εkskɔmunı'tsirən] *tr* excommunicate
Exkrement [εkskrε'mεnt] *n* (−[e]s;−e) excrement
exmittieren [εksmı'tirən] *tr* evict
exotisch [ε'ksotıʃ] *adj* exotic
expedieren [εkspε'dirən] *tr* send, ship
Expedition [εkspεdı'tsjon] *f* (−;−en) forwarding; (mil) expedition
Experiment [εkspεrı'mεnt] *n* (−[e]s;−e) experiment
experimentieren [εkspεrımεn'tirən] *intr* experiment

explodieren [εksplɔ'dirən] *intr* (SEIN) explode; blow up
Explosion [εksplɔ'zjon] *f* (−;−en) explosion
exponieren [εkspɔ'nirən] *tr* expose; (*darlegen*) expound, set forth
Export [εks'pɔrt] *m* (−[e]s;−e) export
exportieren [εkspɔr'tirən] *tr* export
Ex-preß [εks'prεs] *m* (−presses; −presse) express
Expreß'zug *m* express train
extra ['εkstrɑ] *adv* extra; (coll) on purpose, for spite
Ex'trablatt *n* (journ) extra
extrahieren [εkstra'hirən] *tr* extract
Extrakt [εks'trakt] *m* (−[e]s;−e) extract; (*aus Büchern*) excerpt
extravagant [εkstrava'gant] *adj* luxurious; wild, fantastic
Extravaganz [εkstrava'gants] *f* (−;−en) luxury
extrem [εks'trem] *adj* extreme ‖ **Extrem** *n* (−s;−e) extreme
Exzellenz [εkstsε'lεnts] *f* (−;−en) Excellency
exzentrisch [εks'tsεntrıʃ] *adj* eccentric
Ex-zeß [εks'tsεs] *m* (−zesses;−zesse) excess

F

F, f [εf] *invar n* F, f; (mus) F
Fabel ['fɑbəl] *f* (−;−n) fable; story; (*e−s Dramas*) plot
fa'belhaft *adj* fabulous
fabeln ['fɑbəln] *intr* tell stories
Fabrik [fa'brik] *f* (−;−en) factory, mill
Fabrik'anlage *f* manufacturing plant
Fabrikant −in [fabrı'kant(ın)] §7 *mf* manufacturer, maker
Fabrikat [fabrı'kɑt] *n* (−[e]s;−e) product; brand, make
Fabrikation [fabrıka'tsjon] *f* (−;) manufacture, manufacturing
Fabrikations'fehler *m* flaw, defect
Fabrikations'nummer *f* serial number
Fabrik'marke *f* trademark
fabrik'mäßig *adj* mass
Fabrik'nummer *f* serial number
Fabrik'waren *pl* manufactured goods
Fabrik'zeichen *n* trademark
fabrizieren [fabrı'tsirən] *tr* manufacture
fabulieren [fabu'lirən] *tr* make up ‖ *intr* tell yarns
fabulös [fabu'løs] *adj* fabulous
Facette [fa'sεtə] *f* (−;−n) facet
Fach [fax] *n* (−[e]s;=er) compartment; (*im Schreibtisch*) pigeonhole; (*Bücherbrett*) shelf; (*fig*) field, department; line, business; (educ) subject; vom F. sein be an expert
Fach'arbeiter −in §6 *mf* specialist
Fach'arzt *m*, **Fach'ärztin** *f* (med) specialist
Fach'ausbildung *f* professional training
Fach'ausdruck *m* technical term

fächeln ['fεçəln] *tr* fan
Fächer ['fεçər] *m* (−s;−) fan
Fä'cherpalme *f* palmetto
Fach'gebiet *n* field, line; department
Fach'gelehrte §5 *mf* expert
fach'gemäß *adj* expert, professional
Fach'genosse *m* colleague
Fach'kenntnisse *pl* specialized knowledge
Fach'kreis *m* experts, specialists
fach'kundig *adj* expert, experienced
fach'lich *adj* professional; technical, specialized
Fach'mann *m* (−es;=er & −leute) expert, specialist
fachmännisch ['faxmεnıʃ] *adj* expert
Fach'schule *f* vocational school
Fachsimpelei [faxzımpə'laı] *f* (−;−en) shoptalk
fachsimpeln ['faxzımpəln] *intr* talk shop
Fach'werk *n* framework; specialized book
Fach'zeitschrift *f* technical journal
Fackel ['fakəl] *f* (−;−n) torch
fackeln ['fakəln] *intr* flare; (fig) hesitate, dilly-dally
Fackelschein (Fak'kelschein) *m* torchlight
Fackelzug (Fak'kelzug) *m* torchlight procession
fade ['fɑdə] *adj* stale; (fig) dull
Faden ['fɑdən] *m* (−s;=) (& fig) thread; filament; (naut) fathom; keinen guten F. lassen an (*dat*) tear apart
Fa'denkreuz *n* crosshairs
Fa'dennudeln *pl* vermicelli

fadenscheinig [ˈfɑdənʃaınıç] *adj* threadbare
Fagott [faˈgɔt] *n* (-[e]s;-e) bassoon
fähig [ˈfeˑıç] *adj* capable, able
Fä'higkeit *f* (-;-en) ability; talent
fahl [fɑl] *adj* pale; faded, washed-out
fahnden [ˈfɑndən] *intr* (**nach**) search (for), hunt (for)
Fahn'dung *f* (-;-en) search, hunt
Fahne [ˈfɑnə] *f* (-;-n) flag; pennant; (mil) colors; (typ) galley proof
Fah'nenabzug *m* galley proof
Fah'neneid *m* (mil) swearing in
Fah'nenflucht *f* desertion
fah'nenflüchtig *adj*—**f. werden** desert || **Fahnenflüchtige** §5 *mf* deserter
Fah'nenmast *m* flagpole
Fah'nenträger –**in** §6 *mf* standard bearer
Fähnrich [ˈfenrıç] *m* (-s;-e) officer cadet; **F. zur See** midshipman
Fahrbahn [ˈfɑrban] *f* (traffic) lane
fahrbar [ˈfɑrbar] *adj* passable; navigable; mobile
fahrbereit [ˈfɑrbərait] *adj* in running order
Fahr'bereitschaft *f* (-;-en) motor pool
Fähre [ˈferə] *f* (-;-n) ferry
fahren [ˈfɑrən] §71 *tr* haul; (*lenken*) drive; (*Boot*) sail || *intr* (SEIN) go; travel, drive; ride; **es fuhr mir durch den Sinn** it flashed across my mind; **f. lassen** (*a boat, train*); let go; (fig) abandon, renounce; **gut f. bei** do well in; **mit der Hand f. über** (*acc*) run one's hand over; **rechts f.** (public sign) keep right; **was ist in ihn gefahren?** what's gotten into him?
fah'renlassen §104 *tr* let go of
Fah'rer –**in** §6 *mf* driver
Fah'rerflucht *f* hit-and-run case
Fahrgast [ˈfɑrgast] *m* passenger
Fahrgeld [ˈfɑrgelt] *n* fare
Fahrgelegenheit [ˈfɑrgələgənhait] *f* transportation (facilities)
Fahrgestell [ˈfɑrgəʃtel] *n* (-[e]s;-e) (aer) landing gear; (aut) chassis
fahrig [ˈfɑrıç] *adj* fidgety
Fahrkarte [ˈfɑrkartə] *f* ticket
Fahr'kartenausgabe *f*, **Fahr'kartenschalter** *m* ticket window
fahrlässig [ˈfɑrlesıç] *adj* negligent; **fahrlässige Tötung** involuntary manslaughter
Fahr'lässigkeit *f* (-;) negligence
Fahrlehrer –**in** [ˈfɑrlerər(ın)] §6 *mf* driving instructor
Fahrnis [ˈfɑrnıs] *f* (-;-se) movables
Fährnis [ˈfernıs] *f* (-;-se) (poet) danger
Fahrplan [ˈfɑrplan] *m* schedule
fahr'planmäßig *adj* scheduled || *adv* on schedule, on time
Fahrpreis [ˈfɑrprais] *m* fare
Fahrprüfung [ˈfɑrpryfuŋ] *f* driver's test
Fahrrad [ˈfɑrrad] *n* bicycle
Fahrrinne [ˈfɑrrınə] *f* channel
Fahrschein [ˈfɑrʃain] *m* ticket
Fahrstuhl [ˈfɑrʃtul] *m* elevator; (med) wheel chair
Fahr'stuhlführer –**in** §6 *mf* elevator operator

Fahr'stuhlschacht *m* elevator shaft
Fahrstunde [ˈfɑrʃtundə] *f* driving lesson
Fahrt [fɑrt] *f* (-;-en) ride, drive; trip; **auf F. gehen** go hiking; **F. verlieren** lose speed; **freie F. haben** have the green light; **in F. kommen** pick up speed; (fig) swing into action; **in F. sein** (coll) be keyed up; (coll) be on the warpath; (naut) be under way
Fährte [ˈfertə] *f* (-;-n) track, scent
Fahrt'unterbrechung *f* (-;-en) stopover
Fahrwasser [ˈfɑrvasər] *n* navigable water; (& fig) wake
Fahrwerk [ˈfɑrverk] *n* see **Fahrgestell**
Fahrzeug [ˈfɑrtsɔik] *n* vehicle; vessel, craft
Fahr'zeugpark *m* (aut) fleet; (rr) rolling stock
fair [fer] *adj* fair
Fairneß [ˈfernes] *f* (-;) fairness
Fäkalien [feˈkaljən] *pl* feces
faktisch [ˈfaktıʃ] *adj* actual, factual
Fak·tor [ˈfaktər] *m* (-s;-toren [ˈtorən]) factor; foreman; (com) agent
Faktu·ra [fakˈtura] *f* (-;-ren [rən]) invoice
Fakultät [fakulˈtet] *f* (-;-en) (educ) department, school
falb [falp] *adj* claybank (*horse*)
Falke [ˈfalkə] *m* (-;-n) falcon; (pol) hawk
Fal'kenjagd *f* falconry
Falkner [ˈfalknər] *m* (-s;-) falconer
Fall [fal] *m* (-[e]s;Ꞌe) fall, drop; downfall; case; **auf alle Fälle** in any case; **auf keinen F.** in no case; **auf jeden F.** in any case; **gesetzt den F.** supposing; **im besten F.** at best; **im schlimmsten F.** if worst comes to worst; **von F. zu F.** according to circumstances; **zu F. bringen**; (fig) ruin; (parl) defeat; **zu F. kommen** (fig) collapse
Fall'brücke *f* drawbridge
Falle [ˈfalə] *f* (-;-n) (& fig) trap; (fig) pitfall; (*Bett*) (coll) sack
fallen [ˈfalən] §72 *intr* (SEIN) fall, drop; (*Schuß*) be heard; (mil) fall in battle; **j–m ins Wort f.** interrupt s.o. || **Fallen** *n* (-s;) fall, drop; (fig) downfall
fällen [ˈfelən] *tr* (*Bäume*) fell; (*Urteil*) pass; (chem) precipitate
Fallensteller [ˈfalənʃtelər] *m* (-s;-) trapper
Fall'grube *f* trap, pit; (fig) pitfall
fällig [ˈfelıç] *adj* due; payable
Fäl'ligkeit *f* (-;-en) due date
Fall'obst *n* windfall
Fall'rohr *n* soil pipe; (*e–r Dachrinne*) down spout
falls [fals] *conj* in case, if
Fall'schirm *m* parachute
Fall'schirmabsprung *m* parachute jump
Fall'schirmjäger *m* paratrooper
Fall'schirmspringer –**in** §6 *mf* parachutist, sky diver
Fall'strick *m* snare
Fall'sucht *f* (pathol) epilepsy
fall'süchtig *adj* (pathol) epileptic
Fall'tür *f* trapdoor

falsch 90 Fasttag

falsch [falʃ] *adj* false; (*verkehrt*) wrong; (*unecht*) counterfeit; **falsches Spiel** double-dealing || *adv* wrongly; **f. gehen** (horol) be off; **f. schreiben** misspell; **f. schwören** perjure oneself; **f. singen** sing off key; **f. spielen** cheat; **f. verbunden** wrong number || **Falsch** *m*—**ohne F.** without guile

fälschen ['fɛlʃən] *tr* falsify; (*Geld*) counterfeit; (*Urkunde*) forge

Fäl'scher –**in** §6 *mf* forger; counterfeiter

Falsch'geld *n* counterfeit money

Falsch'heit *f* (–;–en) falsity; deceitfulness

fälschlich ['fɛlʃlɪç] *adv* falsely

Falsch'münzer *m* counterfeiter

Falsch'spieler –**in** §6 *mf* card sharp

Fäl'schung *f* (–;–en) falsification; forgery; fake

Faltboot ['faltbot] *n* collapsible boat

Falte ['faltə] *f* (–;–n) fold; (*Plissee*) pleat, crease; (*Runzel*) wrinkle

fälteln ['fɛltəln] *tr* pleat

falten ['faltən] *tr* fold; wrinkle

Fal'tenrock *m* pleated skirt

Falter ['faltər] *m* (–s;–) butterfly; (*Nacht-*) moth

faltig ['faltıç] *adj* creased; wrinkled

Falz [falts] *m* (–es;–e) fold; (*Kerbe*) notch; (carp) rabbet

familiär [famı'ljer] *adj* intimate; familiar

Familie [fa'miljə] *f* (–;–n) family

Fami'lienangehörige §5 *mf* member of the family

Fami'lienanschluß *m*—**F. haben** live as one of the family

Fami'lienname *m* last name

Fami'lienstand *m* marital status

Fami'lienstück *n* family heirloom

Fami'lienzuwachs *m* addition to the family

famos [fa'mos] *adj* excellent, swell

Fan [fɛn] *m* (–s;–s) (sport) fan

Fanatiker –**in** [fa'natıkər(ın)] §6 *mf* fanatic; (sport) fan

fanatisch [fa'natıʃ] *adj* fanatic

fand [fant] *pret* of **finden**

Fanfare [fan'farə] *f* (–;–n) (mus) fanfare

Fang [faŋ] *m* (–[e]s;–e) capture; (*Fisch-*) haul, catch; (*Falle*) trap; (*Kralle*) claw

Fang'arm *m* tentacle

Fang'eisen *n* steel trap

fangen ['faŋən] §73 *tr* catch; trap; (*Ohrfeige*) get || *ref* get caught || **Fangen** *n*—**F. spielen** play catch

Fang'frage *f* loaded question

Fang'messer *n* hunting knife

Fang'zahn *m* fang; tusk

Farb– [farp] *comb.fm.* color

Farb'abzug *m* (phot) color print

Farb'aufnahme *f* color photograph

Farb'band *n* (–[e]s;–er) typewriter ribbon

Farbe ['farbə] *f* (–;–n) color; dye; (*zum Malen*) paint; (*Gesichts-*) complexion; (cards) suit; **F. bekennen** folow suit; (fig) lay one's cards on the table

färben ['fɛrbən] *tr* color, dye, tint ||

ref take on color; change color; **sich rot f.** turn red; blush

far'benprächtig *adj* colorful

Fär'ber –**in** §6 *mf* dyer

Farb'fernsehen *n* color television

Farb'film *m* color film

farbig ['farbıç] *adj* colored; colorful

Farb'kissen *n* ink pad

Farb'körper *m* pigment

farb'los *adj* colorless

Farb'spritzpistole *f* paint sprayer

Farb'stift *m* colored pencil; crayon

Farb'stoff *m* dye

Farb'ton *m* tone, hue, shade

Fär'bung *f* (–;–en) coloring; hue

Farm [farm] *f* (–;–en) farm

Farmer –**in** ['farmər(ın)] §6 *mf* farmer

Farn [farn] *m* (–[e]s;–e) fern

Farn'kraut *n* fern

Fasan [fa'zan] *m* (–s;–e & –en) pheasant

Fasching ['faʃıŋ] *m* (–s;) carnival

Faschismus [fa'ʃısmus] *m* (–;) fascism

Faschist –**in** [fa'ʃıst(ın)] §7 *mf* fascist

Faselei [fazə'laı] *f* (–;–en) drivel

Faselhans ['fazəlhans] *m* (–';–e & –e) blabberer; scatterbrain

faseln ['fazəln] *intr* talk nonsense

Faser ['fazər] *f* (–;–n) fiber; (*im Holz*) grain; (*Fädchen*) thread, string

Fa'serholzplatte *f* fiberboard

fasern ['fazərn] *tr* unravel || *ref* fray || *intr* unravel

Fa'serschreiber *m* felt pen

Faß [fas] *n* (Fasses;Fässer) barrel, keg; (*Bütte*) vat, tub

Fassade [fa'sadə] *f* (–;–n) façade

faßbar ['fasbar] *adj* comprehensible

Faß'bier *n* draft beer

fassen ['fasən] *tr* (*packen*) seize; (*erwischen*) apprehend; (*begreifen*) grasp; (*Edelstein*) mount; (*enthalten können*) hold, seat; (*Essen*) (mil) draw; **e–n Gedanken f.** form an idea; **in Worte f.** put into words; **j–n bei der Ehre f.** appeal to s.o.'s honor; **Tritt fassen** fall in step || *ref* get hold of oneself; **in sich f.** include; **sich f. an** (*acc*) put one's hand to, touch; **sich in Geduld f.** exercise patience; **sich kurz f.** be brief || *intr* take hold; (*nach*) grab (for); **es ist nicht zu f.** it is incomprehensible

Faß'hahn *m* tap, faucet

faß'lich *adj* conceivable

Fasson [fa'son] *f* (–;–en) style, cut

Fas'sung *f* (–;–en) composure; (*schriftlich*) draft; (*für Edelsteine*) setting, mounting; (*Brillenrand*) frame; (*Wortlaut*) wording; (*Lesart*) version; (elec) socket; **aus der F. bringen** upset; **außer F. sein** be beside onself

Fas'sungskraft *f* comprehension

fas'sungslos *adj* disconcerted, shaken

Fas'sungsvermögen *n* capacity; (*geistliches*) (powers of) comprehension

fast [fast] *adv* almost, nearly

fasten ['fastən] *intr* fast || **Fasten** *n* (–s;) fasting

Fa'stenzeit *f* Lent, Lenten season

Fast'nacht *f* carnival

Fast'tag *m* day of fasting, fast day

faszinieren [fastsɪ'nirən] *tr* fascinate
fatal [fa'tɑl] *adj* disastrous; (*unange-nehm*) unpleasant
fauchen ['fauxən] *intr* hiss; (*Person*) snarl; (*Katze*) spit
faul [faul] *adj* rotten; lazy; bad, nasty; (*verdächtig*) fishy; (*Ausrede, Witz*) lame, poor; (sport) foul || **Faul** *n* (-s;-s) (sport) foul
Fäule ['fɔɪlə] *f* (-;) rot, decay
faulen ['faulən] *intr* rot, decay
faulenzen ['faulɛntsən] *intr* loaf
Faulenzer ['faulɛntsər] *m* (-s;-) loaf-er; (*Liegestuhl*) chaise longue; (*Li-nienblatt*) ruled sheet of paper
Faul'heit *f* (-;) laziness
faulig ['faulɪç] *adj* rotten, putrid
Fäulnis ['fɔɪlnɪs] *f* (-;) rot; **in F. übergehen** begin to rot
Faul'pelz *m* (coll) loafer
Faust [faust] *f* (-;ⁿe) fist; **auf eigene F.** on one's own
faust'dick' *adj* (coll) whopping
Faust'handschuh *m* mitten
Faust'kampf *m* boxing match
Fäustling ['fɔɪstlɪŋ] *m* (-[e]s;-e) mitten
Faust'schlag *m* punch, blow
Favorit –in [favo'rit(ɪn)] §7 *mf* favo-rite
Faxen ['faksən] *pl* antics; faces; **F. machen** fool around; make a fuss; **F. schneiden** make faces
Fazit ['fatsɪt] *n* (-s;-e & -s) result; **das F. ziehen** sum it up
Feber ['febər] *m* (-[s];-) (Aust) Feb-ruary
Februar ['febru·ar] *m* (-[s];-e) Feb-ruary
fechten ['fɛçtən] §74 *intr* fence; fight; (*betteln*) beg
Feder ['fedər] *f* (-;-n) feather; pen; quill; (mach) spring; **F. und Nut** (carp) tongue and groove
Fe'derball *m* shuttlecock
Fe'derballspiel *n* badminton
Fe'derbett *n* feather bed
Fe'derbusch *m* plume
Fe'derdecke *f* feather quilt
Federfuchser ['fedərfuksər] *m* (-s;-) scribbler; hack writer
fe'derführend *adj* in charge
Fe'dergewicht *n* featherweight division
Federgewichtler ['fedərgəvɪçtlər] *m* (-s;-) featherweight (boxer)
Fe'derhubtor *n* overhead door
Fe'derkernmatratze *f* innerspring mat-tress
Fe'derkiel *m* quill
Fe'derkraft *f* springiness; tension
Fe'derkrieg *m* paper war, war of words
fe'derleicht' *adj* light as a feather
Fe'derlesen *n*—**ohne viel Federlesen(s)** without much ado
Fe'dermesser *n* penknife
federn ['fedərn] *tr* fit with springs || *intr* be springy; (*Vogel*) moult; (gym) bounce
Fe'derring *m* lock washer
Fe'derstrich *m* stroke of the pen
Fe'derung *f* (-;) (aut) suspension
Fe'derzug *m* stroke of the pen
Fee [fe] *f* (-;**Feen** ['fe·ən]) fairy

Feg(e)feuer ['feg(ə)fɔɪ·ər] *n* (-s;) purgatory
fegen ['fegən] *tr* sweep; (*Laub*) tear off || *intr* (SEIN) tear along
Fehde ['fedə] *f* (-;-n) feud
Feh'dehandschuh *m* gauntlet
fehl [fel] *adj*—**f. am Ort** out of place || **Fehl** *m* (-[e]s;-e) blemish; fault
fehl– *comb.fm.* wide of the mark; mis–, incorrectly, wrongly || **Fehl–** *comb. fm.* missing; vain, unsuccessful; in-correct, wrong; faulty; negative
Fehl'anzeige *f* negative report
Fehl'ball *m* (tennis) fault
fehlbar ['felbar] *adj* fallible
Fehl'betrag *m* shortage, deficit
Fehl'bitte *f* vain request; **e–e F. tun** meet with a refusal
fehlen ['felən] *tr* miss || *intr* be absent; be missing; be lacking; fail, be un-successful; sin, err; (*dat*) miss, e.g., **er fehlt mir sehr** I miss him very much; (*dat*) lack, e.g., **ihm fehlt die Zeit** he lacks the time; **was fehlt Ihnen?** what's wrong with you? || *impers*—**es fehlte nicht viel, und ich wäre gefallen** I came close to falling
Fehler ['felər] *m* (-s;-) mistake, error; flaw, imperfection; blunder
feh'lerfrei *adj* faultless, flawless
feh'lerhaft *adj* faulty
feh'lerlos *adj* faultless, flawless
Fehl'geburt *f* miscarriage
fehl'gehen §82 *intr* (SEIN) go wrong; (*Schuß*) miss
Fehl'gewicht *n* short weight
fehl'greifen §88 *intr* miss one's hold; (fig) make a mistake
Fehl'griff *m* mistake, blunder
Fehl'leistung *f* (Freudian) slip
fehl'leiten *tr* (& fig) misdirect
Fehl'schlag *m* miss; failure, disappoint-ment; (baseball) foul
Fehl'schluß *m* false inference; fallacy
Fehl'spruch *m* miscarriage of justice
Fehl'start *m* false start
Fehl'tritt *m* false step; (fig) slip
Fehl'wurf *m* (*beim Würfeln*) crap
fehl'zünden *intr* backfire
feien ['faɪ·ən] *tr*—**gefeit sein gegen** be immune to; **j–n f. gegen** make s.o. immune to
Feier ['faɪ·ər] *f* (-;-n) celebration; ceremony
Fei'erabend *m* closing time
fei'erlich *adj* solemn
Fei'erlichkeit *f* (-;-en) solemnity; **Feierlichkeiten** festivities; ceremo-nies
feiern ['faɪ·ərn] *tr* celebrate, observe; honor || *intr* rest from work
Fei'erstunde *f* commemorative cere-mony
Fei'ertag *m* holiday; holy day
feig [faɪk] *adj* cowardly
feige ['faɪgə] *adj* cowardly || **Feige** *f* (-;-n) fig
Feig'heit *f* (-;) cowardice
feig'herzig *adj* faint-hearted
Feigling ['faɪklɪŋ] *m* (-s;-e) coward
feil [faɪl] *adj* for sale
feil'bieten §58 *tr* offer for sale
Feile ['faɪlə] *f* (-;-n) file

feilen ['faɪlən] *tr* file
feilschen ['faɪlʃən] *intr* (**um**) haggle (over), dicker (about)
Feilspäne ['faɪlʃpenə] *pl* filings
fein [faɪn] *adj* fine; delicate; fancy
feind [faɪnt] *adj* hostile || **Feind** *m* (-[e]s;-e) enemy, foe
Feind– *comb.fm.* enemy, hostile; against the enemy
Feind'fahrt *f* (nav) operation against the enemy
Feind'flug *m* (aer) combat mission
Feindin ['faɪndɪn] *f* (-;-nen) enemy
feind'lich *adj* hostile
Feind'schaft *f* (-;-en) enmity
feind'selig *adj* hostile
Feind'seligkeit *f* (-;-en) hostility, animosity; hostile action
fein'fühlend, fein'fühlig *adj* sensitive
Fein'gefühl *n* sensitivity
Fein'heit *f* (-;-en) fineness, fine quality; delicacy; subtlety
Fein'mechanik *f* precision engineering
Feinschmecker ['faɪnʃmɛkər] *m* (-s;-) gourmet, epicure
fein'sinnig *adj* sensitive; subtle
feist [faɪst] *adj* fat, plump
Feld [fɛlt] *n* (-[e]s;-er) field; panel, compartment; (checkers, chess) square; **auf dem Felde** in the field(s); **auf freiem Felde** in the open; **aufs F. gehen** go to (work in) the fields; **das F. behaupten** stand one's ground; **ins F. ziehen** take the field
Feld'bau *m* agriculture
Feld'becher *m* collapsible drinking cup
Feld'bett *n* army cot; camping cot
Feld'blume *f* wild flower
Feld'bluse *f* army jacket
feld'dienstfähig *adj* fit for active duty
Feld'flasche *f* canteen
Feld'geistliche *m* (-n;-n) army chaplain
Feld'gendarm *m* military police
Feld'gendarmerie *f* military police
Feld'geschrei *n* battle cry
Feld'geschütz *n* field gun, field piece
Feld'herr *m* general; commander in chief
Feld'lager *n* bivouac, camp
Feld'lazarett *n* evacuation hospital
Feld'lerche *f* skylark
Feld'marschall *m* field marshal
feld'marschmäßig *adj* with full field pack
Feld'messer *m* surveyor
Feld'meßkunst *f* (-;) surveying
Feld'mütze *f* (mil) overseas cap
Feld'postamt *n* army post office
Feld'schlacht *f* battle
Feld'stecher *m* field glasses
Feldwebel ['fɛltvebəl] *m* (-s;-) sergeant
Feld'zeichen *n* ensign, standard
Feld'zug *m* campaign
Felge ['fɛlgə] *f* (-;-n) rim
Fell [fɛl] *n* (-[e]s;-e) pelt, skin; fur; **ein dickes F. haben** be thick-skinned
Fels [fɛls] *m* (-es & -en;-en) rock; cliff; **zackige Felsen** crags
Fels'block *m* boulder
Felsen ['fɛlzən] *m* (-s;-) rock; cliff
fel'senfest *adj* firm as a rock

Fel'sengebirge *n* Rocky Mountains
Fel'senklippe *f* cliff
Fel'senriff *n* reef
felsig ['fɛlzɪç] *adj* rocky
Fenster ['fɛnstər] *n* (-s;-) window
Fen'sterbrett *n* window sill
Fen'sterflügel *m* casement
Fen'sterladen *m* window shutter
Fen'sterleder *n* chamois
Fen'sterplatz *m* (rr) window seat
Fen'sterrahmen *m* window frame; sash
Fen'sterrosette *f* rose window
Fen'sterscheibe *f* windowpane
Ferien ['ferjən] *pl* vacation; (parl) recess
Fe'rienreisende §5 *mf* vacationer
Fe'rienstimmung *f* holiday spirit
Ferkel ['fɛrkəl] *n* (-s;-) piglet
Ferkelei [fɛrkə'laɪ] *f* (-;-en) obscenity
fern [fɛrn] *adj* far, distant; (*entlegen*) remote; (*weit fort*) far away
Fern'amt *n* long-distance exchange
Fern'anruf *m* long-distance call
Fern'aufklärung *f* long-range reconnaissance
Fern'bedienung *f* remote control
fern'bleiben §62 *intr* (SEIN) (*dat*) stay away (from) || **Fernbleiben** *n* (-s;) absence; absenteeism
Fern'blick *m* distant view, vista
Ferne ['fɛrnə] *f* (-;-n) distance
ferner ['fɛrnər] *adj* remote, distant || *adv* further; moreover
Fern'fahrer *m* long-distance trucker
Fern'fahrt *f* long-distance trip
Fern'gang *m* (aut) overdrive
Fern'geschoß *n* long-range missile
Fern'geschütz *n* long-range gun
Fern'gespräch *n* long-distance call; toll call
Fern'glas *n* binoculars
fern'halten §90 *tr* & *ref* keep away
Fern'heizung *f* heating from a central heating plant
Fern'kursus *m* correspondence course
Fern'laster *m* long-distance truck
fern'lenken *tr* guide by remote control
Fern'lenkrakete *f* guided missile
Fern'lenkung *f* (-;-en) remote control
Fern'lenkwaffe *f* guided missile
Fern'licht *n* (aut) high beam
fern'liegen §108 *impers*—**es liegt mir fern zu** (*inf*) I'm far from (*ger*)
Fernmelde– [fɛrnmɛldə] *comb.fm.* communications, signal
Fern'meldetruppen *pl* signal corps
Fern'meldewesen *n* telecommunications system
fern'mündlich *adj* & *adv* by telephone
Fern'objektiv *n* telephoto lens
Fernost– *comb.fm.* Far Eastern
fern'östlich *adj* Far Eastern
Fern'rohr *n* telescope
Fern'rohraufsatz *m* telescopic gun sight
Fern'ruf *m* telephone call; telephone number
Fern'schnellzug *m* long-distance express
Fern'schreiber *m* teletype, telex
Fernseh– [fɛrnze] *comb.fm.* television
Fern'sehansager –**in** §6 *mf* television announcer
Fern'sehapparat *m* television set

Fern′sehbildröhre *f* picture tube
fern′sehen §138 *intr* watch television ‖ **Fernsehen** *n* (-s;) television
Fern′seher *m* (-s;-) television set; television viewer
Fern′sehgerät *n* television set
Fern′sehkanal *m* television channel
Fern′sehschau *f* television show
Fern′sehsendung *f* telecast
Fern′sehteilnehmer -in §6 *mf* televiewer
Fern′sehübertragung *f* telecast
Fern′sicht *f* view, vista; panorama
fern′sichtig *adj* far-sighted
Fernsprech- [fɛrnʃprɛç] *comb.fm.* telephone
Fern′sprechauftragsdienst *m* answering service
Fern′sprechautomat *m* pay phone
Fern′sprecher *m* telephone
Fern′sprechzelle *f* telephone booth
fern′stehen §146 *intr* (*dat*) have no personal contact (with); (*dat*) not be close (to)
Fern′stehende §5 *mf* outsider; disinterested observer
fern′steuern *tr* guide by remote control
Fern′studium *n* correspondence course
Ferse [′fɛrzə] *f* (-;-n) heel
Fer′sengeld *n*—**F. geben** take to one's heels
fertig [′fɛrtɪç] *adj* finished; ready; (*kaputt*) ruined, done for
fertig-, Fertig- *comb.fm.* final; finished; finishing; prefabricated
fer′tigbringen §65 *tr* finish, get done; bring about; **es glatt f. zu** (*inf*) be capable of (*ger*); **es nicht f., ihm das zu sagen** not have the heart to tell him that
fertigen [′fɛrtɪgən] *tr* manufacture
Fer′tigkeit *f* (-;-en) skill
Fer′tigrasen *m* sod
fer′tigstellen *tr* complete; get ready
Fer′tigung *f* (-;-en) manufacture, production; copy, draft
Fes [fɛs] *n* (mus) F flat
fesch [fɛʃ] *adj* smart, chic
Fessel [′fɛsəl] *f* (-;-n) fetter, bond; (anat) ankle; (vet) fetlock
Fes′selballon *m* captive balloon
fesseln [′fɛsəln] *tr* chain, tie; (*bezaubern*) captivate, arrest; (mil) contain; **ans Bett gefesselt** confined to bed, bedridden
fes′selnd *adj* fascinating, gripping; (*Personalität*) magnetic
fest [fɛst] *adj* firm; solid; tight; stationary; steady; (*Preis, Kost, Einkommen, Gehalt*) fixed; (*Schlaf*) sound; (mil) fortified; **feste Straße** improved road ‖ **Fest** *n* (-es;-e) feast; festival
fest′backen *intr* (SEIN) cake (on)
fest′besoldet *adj* with a fixed salary
fest′binden §59 *tr* (**an** *dat*) tie (to)
Fest′essen *n* banquet
fest′fahren §71 *tr* run aground ‖ *ref* come to a standstill
fest′halten §90 *tr* hold on to ‖ *ref* (**an** *dat*) cling (to), hold (on)
festigen [′fɛstɪgən] *tr* strengthen; consolidate ‖ *ref* grow stronger

Fe′stigkeit *f* (-;-en) firmness; steadiness; strength
Fe′stigung *f* (-;) strengthening; consolidation; stabilization
Fest′land *n* continent
fest′legen *tr* fix, determine, set; (*Anordnung*) lay down; (fin, naut) tie up; **j-n f. auf** (*acc*) pin s.o. down on ‖ *ref* (**auf** *acc*) commit oneself (to)
fest′lich *adj* festive
Fest′lichkeit *f* (-;-en) festivity
fest′liegen §108 *intr* be stranded
fest′machen *tr* fix; (fig) settle ‖ *intr* (naut) moor
Fest′mahl *n* feast
Fest′nahme *f* (-;-n) arrest
fest′nehmen §116 *tr* arrest, apprehend
Fest′rede *f* ceremonial speech
Fest′saal *m* grand hall, banquet hall
fest′schnallen *tr* buckle up ‖ *ref* fasten one's seat belt
Fest′schrift *f* homage volume
fest′setzen *tr* fix, set ‖ *ref* settle down (*in a town, etc.*)
fest′sitzen *intr* fit tight; be stuck
Fest′spiel *n* play for a festive occasion; **Festspiele** (mus, theat) festival
fest′stehen §146 *intr* stand firm; (*Tatsache*) be certain ‖ *impers*—**es steht fest** it is a fact
fest′stehend *adj* stationary; (*Achse*) fixed; (*Tatsache*) established
feststellbar [′fɛstʃtɛlbɑr] ascertainable
Fest′stellbremse *f* hand brake
fest′stellen *tr* ascertain; (*unbeweglich machen*) lock, secure; (*Tatbestand*) find out, establish; (*angeben*) state; (*Schaden*) assess; (*Kurs*) (fin) set, fix
Fest′stellschraube *f* set screw
Fest′tag *m* feastday; holiday
Fe′stung *f* (-;-en) fortress
Fe′stungsgraben *m* moat
Fest′wagen *m* float
Fest′wert *m* standard value; (math, phys) constant
Fest′wiese *f* fairground
fest′ziehen §163 *tr* pull tight
Fest′zug *m* procession
Fetisch [′fetɪʃ] *m* (-[e]s;-e) fetish
fett [fɛt] *adj* fat; (*Boden, Milch, Gemisch*) rich; (*Zeiten, Leben*) of plenty ‖ **Fett** *n* (-[e]s;-e) fat; (*Schmalz*) lard; (*Pflanzen-*) shortening; (*Schmier-*) grease
Fett′auge *n* speck of fat
Fett′druck *m* boldface type
fetten [′fɛtən] *tr* grease, lubricate
Fett′fleck *m* grease spot
fettig [′fɛtɪç] *adj* fatty, greasy, oily
Fett′kloß *m* (coll) fatso
Fett′kohle *f* bituminous coal
fettleibig [′fɛtlaɪbɪç] *adj* stout
Fettnäpfchen [′fɛtnɛpfçən] *n*—**bei j-m ins F. treten** hurt s.o.'s feelings; **ins F. treten** put one's foot in it
Fett′presse *f* (aut) grease gun
Fett′spritze *f* (aut) grease gun
Fett′sucht *f* obesity
Fett′wanst *m* (sl) fatso
Fetzen [′fɛtsən] *m* (-s;-) rag; bit, scrap; (Aust) dishcloth; **daß die F. fliegen** violently
feucht [fɔɪçt] *adj* moist, damp, humid

feuchten ['fɔɪçtən] *tr* moisten, dampen
Feuch'tigkeit *f* (-;) moisture, dampness, humidity
feudal [fɔɪ'dɑl] *adj* feudal; (fig) magnificent
Feudalismus [fɔɪdɑ'lɪsmʊs] *m* (-;) feudalism
Feuer ['fɔɪ·ər] *n* (-s;-) fire
Feu'eralarm *m* fire alarm
Feu'eralarmübung *f* fire drill
feu'erbeständig *adj* fireproof
Feu'erbestattung *f* cremation
Feu'erbrand *m* firebrand
Feu'ereifer *m* enthusiasm, zeal
Feu'ereinstellung *f* cease-fire
feu'erfest *adj* fireproof
Feu'erfliege *f* firefly
feu'erflüssig *adj* molten
feu'ergefährlich *adj* inflammable
Feu'erhahn *m* hydrant, fireplug
Feu'erhaken *m* poker
Feu'erherd *m* fireplace
Feu'erkampf *m* fire fight, gun battle
Feu'erkraft *f* (mil) fire power
Feu'erleiter *f* fire ladder; (*Nottreppe*) fire escape
Feu'erlinie *f* firing line
Feu'erlöscher *m* fire extinguisher
Feu'ermelder *m* fire alarm
Feu'ermeldung *f* fire alarm
feuern ['fɔɪ·ərn] *tr* fire; (coll) fire, sack || *intr* fire, shoot
Feu'erprobe *f* ordeal by fire; acid test
Feu'ersalve *f* fusillade
Feu'erschneise *f* firebreak
Feu'erspritze *f* fire engine
Feu'erstein *m* flint
Feu'ertaufe *f* baptism of fire
Feu'erversicherung *f* fire insurance
Feu'erwache *f* firehouse
Feu'erwalze *f* (mil) creeping barrage
Feu'erwehr *f* fire department
Feu'erwehrmann *m* (-[e]s;-̈er & -leute) fireman
Feu'erwerk *n* fireworks
Feu'erwerkskörper *m* firecracker
Feu'erzange *f* fire tongs
Feu'erzeug *n* cigarette lighter
Feu'erzeugbenzin *n* lighter fluid
feurig ['fɔɪrɪç] *adj* fiery; ardent
Fiasko [fɪ'asko] *n* (-s;-s) fiasco
Fibel ['fibəl] *f* (-;-n) primer; (archeol) fibula
Fiber ['fibər] *f* (-;-n) fiber
Fichte ['fɪçtə] *f* (-;-n) spruce; pine
Fich'tennadel *f* pine needle
fidel [fɪ'del] *adj* jolly, cheerful
Fieber ['fibər] *n* (-s;-) fever; das F. messen take the temperature
fie'berhaft *adj* feverish
fieberig ['fibərɪç] *adj* feverish
fie'berkrank *adj* running a fever
fiebern ['fibərn] *intr* be feverish
Fie'berphantasie *f* delirium
Fie'bertabelle *f* temperature chart
Fiedel ['fidəl] *f* (-;-n) fiddle
Fie'delbogen *m* fiddlestick
fiel [fil] *pret* of fallen
Figur [fɪ'gur] *f* (-;-en) figure; (cards) face card
figürlich [fɪ'gyrlɪç] *adj* figurative
fiktiv [fɪk'tif] *adj* fictitious
Filet [fɪ'le] *n* (-s;-s) (culin) fillet

Filiale [fɪl'jɑlə] *f* (-;-n) branch
Filia'lengeschäft *n* chain store
Filigran [fɪlɪ'grɑn] *n* (-s;-e), Fili-gran'arbeit *f* filigree
Film [fɪlm] *m* (-s;-e) film; (cin) movie
Film'atelier *n* motion-picture studio
Film'empfindlichkeit *f* film speed
Film'kulisse *f* (cin) movie set
Film'leinwand *f* movie screen
Film'probe *f* screen test
Film'regisseur *m* (cin) director
Film'wesen *n* motion-picture industry
Filter ['fɪltər] *m & n* (-s;-) filter
Fil'teranlage *f* filtration plant
Fil'terkaffee *m* drip-grind coffee
Fil'termundstück *n* filter tip
filtern ['fɪltərn] *tr* filter, strain
filtrieren [fɪl'trirən] *tr* filter
Filz [fɪlts] *m* (-es;-e) felt; (coll) miser, skinflint
Filz'schreiber *m* felt pen
Fimmel ['fɪməl] *m* (-s;-) craze, fad
-fimmel *m comb.fm.* mania for
Finanz [fɪ'nants] *f* (-;-en) finance
Finanz- *comb.fm.* financial, fiscal
Finanz'amt *n* internal revenue service
Finanz'ausschuß *m* (adm) ways and means committee
Finanzen [fɪ'nantsən] *pl* finances
finanziell [fɪnan'tsjɛl] *adj* financial
finanzieren [fɪnan'tsirən] *tr* finance
Finanz'minister *m* secretary of the treasury
Finanz'ministerium *n* treasury department
Finanz'wesen *n* finances
Finanz'wirtschaft *f* public finances
Findelkind ['fɪndəlkɪnt] *n* foundling
finden ['fɪndən] §59 *tr* find; f. Sie nicht? don't you think so? || *ref* be found; ach, das wird sich schon f. oh, we'll see about that; es fanden sich there were; es findet sich it happens, it turns out; sich f. in (*acc*) resign oneself to; sie haben sich gefunden they were united || *intr* find one's way
findig ['fɪndɪç] *adj* resourceful
Findling ['fɪntlɪŋ] *m* (-s;-e) foundling; (geol) boulder
fing [fɪŋ] *pret* of fangen
Finger ['fɪŋər] *m* (-s;-) finger
Fin'gerabdruck *m* fingerprint
fin'gerfertig *adj* deft
Fin'gerhut *m* thimble; (bot) foxglove
fingern ['fɪŋərn] *tr* finger
Fin'gerspitze *f* finger tip; bis in die Fingerspitzen through and through
Fin'gerspitzengefühl *n* sensitivity
Fin'gersprache *f* sign language
Fingerzeig ['fɪŋərtsaɪk] *m* (-s;-e) hint
fingieren [fɪŋ'girən] *tr* feign
fingiert [fɪŋ'girt] *adj* fictitious
Fink [fɪŋk] *m* (-en;-en) finch
Finne ['fɪnə] *m* (-n;-n) Finn || *f* (-; -n) fin; (*Ausschlag*) pimple
Fin'nenausschlag *m* acne
Finnin ['fɪnɪn] *f* (-;-nen) Finn
finnisch ['fɪnɪʃ] *adj* Finnish
Finnland ['fɪnlant] *n* (-s;) Finland
finster ['fɪnstər] *adj* dark; gloomy
Finsternis ['fɪnstərnɪs] *f* (-;) darkness; gloom

Finte ['fɪntə] ƒ (-;-n) feint; trick
Firlefanz ['fɪrləfants] m (-es;) junk;
F. treiben fool around
Fir·ma ['fɪrma] ƒ (-;-men [mən]) firm
Firmament [fɪrma'mɛnt] n (-[e]s;-e)
firmament
firmen ['fɪrmən] tr (Cath) confirm
Fir'menschild n (com) name plate
Fir'menwert m (com) good will
Firmling ['fɪrmlɪŋ] m (-s;-e) (Cath)
person to be confirmed
Fir'mung ƒ (-;-en) (Cath) confirma-
tion
Fir·nis ['fɪrnɪs] m (-ses;-se) varnish;
mit F. streichen varnish
firnissen ['fɪrnɪsən] tr varnish
First [fɪrst] m (-es;-e) (archit) ridge
(of roof); (poet) mountain ridge
Fis [fɪs] n (-;-) (mus) F sharp
Fisch [fɪʃ] m (-es;-e) fish
fischen ['fɪʃən] tr fish for, catch ‖ intr
(nach) fish (for)
Fi'scher m (-s;-) fisherman
Fischerei [fɪʃə'raɪ] ƒ (-;-en) fishing;
fishery; fishing trade
Fi'schergerät n fishing tackle
Fisch'fang m catch, haul
Fisch'gräte ƒ fishbone
Fisch'grätenmuster n (tex) herringbone
Fisch'händler –in §6 mƒ fishmonger
fischig ['fɪʃɪç] adj fishy
Fisch'kunde ƒ ichthyology
Fisch'laich m spawn, fish eggs
Fisch'otter m & ƒ otter
Fisch'rogen m roe
Fisch'schuppe ƒ scale (of a fish)
Fisch'zug m (& fig) catch
fiskalisch [fɪs'kɑlɪʃ] adj fiscal
Fis·kus ['fɪskus] m (-;-kusse & –ken
[kən]) treasury
Fistelstimme ['fɪstəlʃtɪmə] ƒ falsetto
Fittich ['fɪtɪç] m (-es;-e) (poet) wing
fix [fɪks] adj (Idee, Preis) fixed;
(flink) smart, sharp; **fix und fertig**
all set; all in; done for; **fix und
fertig mit** through with; **mach fix!**
make it snappy!
fixen ['fɪksən] intr sell short
fixieren [fɪ'ksirən] tr fix, decide upon;
stare fixedly at; (phot) fix
Fixier'mittel n (phot) fixer
flach [flax] adj flat, level; shallow;
(Relief) low; (fig) dull
Fläche ['flɛçə] ƒ (-;-n) surface; plain;
expanse; facet; (geom) area
Flä'cheninhalt m (geom) area
Flä'chenraum m surface area
flach'fallen §72 intr (SEIN) (coll) fall
flat, flop
Flach'heit ƒ (-;) flatness; shallowness
Flach'land n lowland
Flach'relief n low relief, bas-relief
Flach'rennen n flat racing
Flachs [flaks] m (-es;-e) flax
flachsen ['flaksən] intr (coll) kid
flächse(r)n ['flɛksə(r)n] adj flaxen
Flach'zange ƒ pliers
flackern ['flakərn] intr flicker; (Stim-
me) quaver, shake
Flagge ['flagə] ƒ (-;-n) flag (esp. for
signaling or identification)
Flag'genmast m flagpole
Flag'genstange ƒ flagstaff

Flagg'schiff n flagship
Flak [flak] abbr (**Flugzeugabwehr-
kanone**) anti-aircraft gun
Flak'feuer n flak
Flakon [fla'kõ] m & n (-s;-s) perfume
bottle
Flamme ['flamə] ƒ (-;-n) flame
flammen ['flamən] intr blaze; be in
flames
flam'mend adj passionate
Fla'mmenwerfer m flame thrower
Flandern ['flandərn] n (-s;) Flanders
flandrisch ['flandrɪʃ] adj Flemish
Flanell [fla'nɛl] m (-s;-e) flannel
Flanke ['flaŋkə] ƒ (-;-n) flank
Flan'kenfeuer n (mil) enfilade; **mit F.
bestreichen** enfilade
flankieren [flaŋ'kirən] tr flank
Flansch [flanʃ] m (-es;-e) flange
Flasche ['flaʃə] ƒ (-;-n) bottle; (coll)
flop; (mach) pulley
Fla'schengranate ƒ Molotov cocktail
Fla'schenzug m block and tackle; (coll)
pulley
Flaschner ['flaʃnər] m (-s;-) plumber
flatterhaft ['flatərhaft] adj fickle
flattern ['flatərn] intr flutter, flap
flau [flau] adj stale; (schwach) feeble,
faint; (fade) dull, lifeless; (com)
slack; (phot) overexposed; **mir ist
f.** (im Magen) I feel queezy
Flaum [flaum] m (-[e]s;) down; (am
Gesicht, am Pfirsich) fuzz
flaumig ['flaumɪç] adj downy, fluffy
Flause ['flauzə] ƒ (-;-n) fib; **Flausen**
funny ideas, nonsense
Flaute ['flautə] ƒ (-;-n) (com) slack
period; (naut) dead calm
fläzen ['flɛtsən] ref sprawl out
Flechse ['flɛksə] ƒ (-;-n) (dial) sinew,
tendon
Flechte ['flɛçtə] ƒ (-;-n) plait; (bot)
lichen; (pathol) ringworm
flechten ['flɛçtən] §74 tr braid, plait;
(Körbe) weave
Fleck [flɛk] m (-[e]s;-e & –en) spot;
blemish; (Flicken, Landstück) patch
Flecken ['flɛkən] m (-s;-) spot; piece
of land; (Markt–) market town
fleckenlos [flɛk'kenlos] adj spotless
Fleck'fieber n spotted fever
fleckig ['flɛkɪç] adj spotty; splotchy
fleddern ['flɛdərn] tr (sl) rob
Fledermaus ['fledərmaus] ƒ bat
Flegel ['flegəl] m (-s;-) flail; (coll)
lout, boor
Flegelei [flegə'laɪ] ƒ (-;) rudeness
fle'gelhaft adj uncouth, boorish
Fle'geljahre pl awkward age
flehen ['fle·ən] intr plea; **zu j-m f.**
implore s.o. ‖ **Flehen** n (-s;-) sup-
plication
Fleisch [flaɪʃ] n (-es;) flesh; meat;
sich ins eigene F. schneiden cut one's
own throat; **wildes F.** proud flesh
Fleisch'bank ƒ (-;-̈e) meat counter
Fleisch'beil n cleaver
Fleisch'beschau ƒ meat inspection
Fleisch'brühe ƒ broth
Flei'scher m (-s;-) butcher
Flei'scheslust ƒ (-;) lust
Fleisch'farbe ƒ flesh color
fleisch'fressend adj carnivorous

Fleisch'hacker (-s;-) *m*, **Fleisch'hauer** *m* (-s;-) butcher
fleischig ['flaɪʃɪç] *adj* fleshy; meaty
fleisch'lich *adj* carnal
Fleisch'markt *m* meat market
Fleisch'pastete *f* meat pie
Fleisch'saft *m* meat juice, gravy
Fleisch'salat *m* diced-meat salad
Fleisch'speise *f* meat course
Fleisch'spieß *m* skewer
Fleischwerdung ['flaɪʃverduŋ] *f* (-;) incarnation
Fleisch'wolf *m* meat grinder
Fleisch'wunde *f* flesh wound, laceration
Fleisch'wurst *f* pork sausage
Fleiß [flaɪs] *m* (-es;) diligence, industry; **mit F.** intentionally
fleißig ['flaɪsɪç] *adj* diligent, hard-working
flektieren [flɛk'tirən] *tr* inflect
fletschen ['flɛtʃən] *tr* bare (*teeth*)
Flexion [flɛk'sjon] *f* (-;-en) (gram) inflection
flicken ['flɪkən] *tr* patch, repair || **Flicken** *m* (-s;-) patch
Flick'schuster *m* cobbler
Flick'werk *n* patchwork; hotchpotch; (*Pfuscherei*) bungling job
Flick'zeug *n* repair kit
Flieder ['flidər] *m* (-s;-) lilac
Fliege ['fligə] *f* (-;-n) fly; (coll) bow tie
fliegen ['fligən] §57 *tr* fly, pilot || *intr* (SEIN) fly; (coll) get sacked; **in die Luft f.** blow up
Flie'genfenster *n* window screen
Flie'gengewicht *n* flyweight division
Fliegengewichtler ['fligəngəvɪçtlər] *m* (-s;-) flyweight (boxer)
Flie'gengitter *n* screen
Flie'genklappe *f*, **Flie'genklatsche** *f* fly swatter
Flie'genpilz *m* toadstool
Flie'ger *m* (-s;-) flyer
Flieger- *comb.fm.* air-force; air, aerial; flying; airman's
Flie'gerabwehr *f* anti-aircraft defense
Flie'geralarm *m* air-raid alarm
Flie'gerangriff *m* air raid
Flie'gerheld *m* (aer) ace
Flie'gerhorst *m* air base
Flie'gerin *f* (-;-nen) flyer
Flie'gerschaden *m* air-raid damage
fliehen ['fli-ən] §75 *tr* run away from; avoid || *intr* (SEIN) flee
Flieh'kraft *f* (-;) centrifugal force
Fliese ['flizə] *f* (-;-n) tile
Flie'senleger *m* tiler, tile man
Fließband ['flisbant] *n* (-[e]s;ᵂer) assembly line
fließen ['flisən] §76 *intr* (SEIN) flow
flie'ßend *adj* (*Wasser*) running; (fig) fluent
Fließheck ['flishɛk] *n* (aut) fastback
Fließpapier ['flispapir] *n* blotting paper
flimmern ['flɪmərn] *intr* glimmer; glisten, shimmer; flicker
flink [flɪŋk] *adj* nimble, quick; **mach mal f.!** get a move on!
Flinte ['flɪntə] *f* (-;-n) shotgun; gun
Flin'tenlauf *m* gun barrel

flirren ['flɪrən] *intr* shimmer
Flirt [flɪrt] *m* (-s;-s) flirtation; boyfriend, girlfriend
flirten ['flɪrtən] *intr* flirt
Flitter ['flɪtər] *m* (-s;-) sequins; (*Scheinglanz*) flashiness
Flit'terglanz *m* flashiness
Flit'tergold *m* gold tinsel
Flit'terkram *m* trinkets
Flit'terstaat *m* flashy clothes
Flit'terwochen *pl* honeymoon
flitzen ['flɪtsən] *intr* (SEIN) flit
flocht [flɔxt] *pret of* **flechten**
Flocke ['flɔkə] *f* (-;-n) flake; tuft
flog [flok] *pret of* **fliegen**
floh [flo] *pret of* **fliehen** || **Floh** *m* (-s;ᵂe) flea; **j-m e-n F. ins Ohr setzen** put a bug in s.o.'s ear
Floh'hüpfspiel *n* tiddlywinks
Flor [flor] *m* (-s;-e) bloom || *m* (-s;-e & ᵂe) gauze; (tex) nap, pile
Flor'band *n* (-[e]s;ᵂer) crepe; mourning band
Florett [flo'rɛt] *n* (-s;-e) foil
florieren [flo'rirən] *intr* flourish
Floskel ['flɔskəl] *f* (-;-n) rhetorical ornament, flowery phrase
Floß [flos] *n* (-es;ᵂe) raft
Flosse ['flɔsə] *f* (-;-n) fin; (aer) stabilizer
flößen ['fløsən] *tr* float
Flöte ['fløtə] *f* (-;-n) flute; (cards) flush
flöten ['fløtən] *tr* play on the flute || *intr* play the flute; **f. gehen** (fig) go to the dogs
flott [flɔt] *adj* afloat; brisk, lively; gay; chic, dashing
Flotte ['flɔtə] *f* (-;-n) fleet
Flot'tenstützpunkt *m* naval base
flott'gehend *adj* (com) brisk, lively
Flottille [flɔ'tɪljə] *f* (-;-n) flotilla
flott'machen *tr* set afloat; (fig) get going again
Flöz [fløts] *n* (-es;-e) (min) seam
Fluch [flux] *m* (-[e]s;ᵂe) curse
fluchen ['fluxən] *intr* curse
Flucht [fluxt] *f* (-;-en) flight; escape; straight line, alignment; (*Häuser-*) row; (*Spielraum*) space, leeway; (*Zimmer-*) suite; **außerhalb der F. out of line**; **in die F. schlagen** put to flight
flüchten ['flʏçtən] *ref* (an *acc*, in *acc*) take refuge (in), have recourse (to) || *intr* (SEIN) flee; escape; (vor *dat*) run away (from)
flüchtig ['flʏçtɪç] *adj* fugitive; fleeting; cursory, superficial; hurried; (chem) volatile; **f. sein** be on the run; **f. werden** escape, flee
Flüch'tigkeitsfehler *m* oversight, slip
Flüchtling ['flʏçtlɪŋ] *m* (-s;-) fugitive; refugee
Flücht'lingslager *n* refugee camp
Flug [fluk] *m* (-[e]s;ᵂe) flight
Flug'abwehr *f* anti-aircraft defense
Flugabwehr- *comb.fm.* anti-aircraft
Flug'anschluß *m* plane connection
Flug'aufgabe *f*, **Flug'auftrag** *m* (aer) mission
Flug'bahn *f* line of flight; trajectory
Flug'blatt *n* leaflet, flyer

Flügel ['flygəl] *m* (**-s;-**) wing; (*e–r Doppeltür*) leaf; (mus) grand piano
Flü'geladjutant *m* aide-de-camp
Flü'gelfenster *n* casement window
Flü'gelmutter *f* wing nut
Flü'gelschlag *m* flap of the wings
Flü'gelschraube *f* thumb screw
Flü'geschraubenmutter *f* wing nut
Flü'geltür *f* folding door
Flug'gast *m* (aer) passenger
flügge ['flYgə] *adj* (*Vogel*) fledged (fig) ready to go on one's own
Flug'gesellschaft *f* airline company
Flug'hafen *m* airport
Flug'hafenbefeuerung *f* airport lights
Flug'kapitän *m* captain, pilot
Flug'karte *f* plane ticket; aeronautical chart
flug'klar *adj* ready for take-off
Flug'körper *m* missile; space vehicle
Flug'leitung *f* air-traffic control
Flug'linie *f* air route; airline
Flug'meldesystem *n* air-raid warning system
Flug'motor *m* aircraft engine
Flug'ortung *f* (aer) navigation
Flug'plan *m* flight schedule
Flug'platz *m* airfield, airport
Flug'post *f* air mail
Flug'preis *m* air fare
flugs [fluks] *adv* quickly; at once
Flug'schein *m* plane ticket
Flug'schneise *f* air lane
Flug'schrift *f* pamphlet
Flug'strecke *f* flying distance
Flug'stützpunkt *m* air base
flug'tauglich, flug'tüchtig *adj* airworthy
Flug'techniker –in §6 *mf* aeronautical engineer
Flug'verbot *n* (aer) grounding
Flug'verkehr *m* air traffic
Flug'wesen *n* aviation; aeronautics
Flug'wetter *n* flying weather
Flug'zeug *n* airplane, aircraft
Flug'zeugabwehrgeschütz *n*, Flug'zeugabwehrkanone *f* anti-aircraft gun
Flug'zeugführer *m* pilot; zweiter F. copilot, second officer
Flug'zeugführerschein *m* pilot's license
Flug'zeuggeschwader *n* wing (*consisting of 3 squadrons of 9 planes each*)
Flug'zeugkreuzer *m*, Flug'zeugmutterschiff *n* seaplane tender, seaplane carrier
Flug'zeugrumpf *m* fuselage
Flug'zeugstaffel *f* squadron (*consisting of 9 planes*)
Flug'zeugträger *m* aircraft carrier
Flug'zeugwerk *n* aircraft factory
Flunder ['flundər] *f* (**-;-n**) flounder
Flunkerer ['fluŋkərər] *m* (**-s;-**) fibber
flunkern ['fluŋkərn] *intr* fib
Flunsch [flunʃ] *m* (**-es;-e**) face; e-n F. ziehen (or machen) make a face
Fluor ['flu·ər] *n* (**-s;**) fluorine
Fluoreszenz [flu·ɔres'tsɛnts] *f* (**-;**) fluorescence; fluorescent light
Fluorid [flu·ɔ'rit] *n* (**-[e]s;-e**) fluoride
Flur [flur] *m* (**-[e]s;-e**) entrance hall; hallway || *f* (**-;-en**) open farmland; meadow; community farmland

Flur'garderobe *f* hallway closet
Fluß [flus] *m* (**Flusses; Flüsse**) river; flow; (metal) fusion; (phys) flux
flußab'wärts *adv* downstream
flußauf'wärts *adv* upstream
Fluß'bett *n* riverbed, channel
Flüßchen ['flYsçən] *n* (**-s;-**) rivulet
flüssig ['flYsiç] *adj* liquid; fluid; (*Gelder*) ready; f. machen convert into cash || *adv* fluently
Flüs'sigkeit *f* (**-;-en**) liquid, fluid; (fig) fluency; (fin) liquidity
Flüs'sigkeitsmaß *n* liquid measure
Fluß'pferd *n* hypopotamus
flüstern ['flYstərn] *tr & intr* whisper
Flü'sterparole *f* rumor
Flut [flut] *f* (**-;-en**) flood; waters; high tide
fluten ['flutən] *tr* flood || *intr* (SEIN) flow, pour
Flut'grenze *f* high-water mark
Flut'licht *n* floodlight
Flut'linie *f* high-water mark
Flut'wasser *n* tidewater
Flut'welle *f* tidal wave
Flut'zeit *f* flood tide, high tide
focht [foxt] *pret* of fechten
Focksegel ['fɔkzegəl] *n* (**-s;-**) foresail
fohlen ['folən] *intr* foal || **Fohlen** *n* (**-s;-**) foal
Folge ['fɔlgə] *f* (**-;-n**) sequence; consequence; succession; series; (*e–s Romans*) continuation; (*e–r Zeitschrift*) number; die Folgen tragen take the consequences; in der F. subsequently
folgen ['fɔlgən] *intr* (*dat*) obey || *intr* (SEIN) (*dat*) follow; (*dat*) succeed; (aus) ensue (from)
folgendermaßen ['fɔlgəndərmasən] *adv* in the following manner, as follows
fol'genschwer *adj* momentous, grave
fol'gerichtig *adj* logical, consistent
folgern ['fɔlgərn] *tr* infer, conclude
Fol'gerung *f* (**-;-en**) inference, conclusion
Fol'gesatz *m* (gram) result clause
fol'gewidrig *adj* inconsistent
Fol'gezeit *f*—in der F. in subsequent times
folglich ['fɔlkliç] *adv* consequently
folgsam ['fɔlkzam] *adj* obedient
Foliant [fol'jant] *m* (**-en;-en**) folio
Folie ['foljə] *f* (**-;-n**) (metal) foil
Folter ['fɔltər] *f* (**-;-n**) torture; rack; auf die F. spannen put to the rack; (fig) keep in suspense
Fol'terbank *f* (**-;⁻e**) rack
foltern ['fɔltərn] *tr* torture
Fol'terqual *f* torture
Fol'terverhör *n* third degree
Fön [føn] *m* (**-[e]s;-e**) hand hairdryer
Fond [fõ] *m* (**-s;-s**) background; rear, back; (culin) gravy
Fonds [fõ] *m* **-s** [fõs];**-s** [fõs]) fund
Fontäne [fon'tɛnə] *f* (**-;-n**) fountain
foppen ['fɔpən] *tr* tease; bamboozle
Fopperei [fɔpə'raɪ] *f* (**-;-en**) teasing
forcieren [fɔr'sirən] *tr* force; speed up
Förderband ['fœdərbant] *n* (**-;⁻er**) conveyor belt

För'derer m (-s;-) promoter; patron
för'derlich adj useful; (dat) conducive
(to)
fordern ['fɔrdərn] tr demand; (Recht)
claim; (zum Zweikampf) challenge;
(vor Gericht) summon
fördern ['fœrdərn] tr promote, back;
(Kohle) produce; **förderndes Mitglied** social member; **zutage f.** bring
to light
For'derung f (-;-en) demand, claim;
debt; (zum Zweikampf) challenge
För'derung f (-;-en) promotion; support; encouragement; (min) output
Forelle [fɔ'rɛlə] f (-;-n) trout
Forke ['fɔrkə] f (-;-n) pitchfork
Form [fɔrm] f (-;-en) form; shape;
mold; condition; (gram) voice; **die
F. wahren** keep up appearances
formal [fɔr'mɑl] adj formal
Formalität [fɔrmalɪ'tet] f (-;-en) formality
Format [fɔr'mɑt] n (-[e]s;-e) size,
format; distinction, stature
Formel ['fɔrməl] f (-;-n) formula
for'melhaft adj (Wendung, Gebet) set
formell [fɔr'mɛl] adj formal
formen ['fɔrmən] tr form, shape, mold
For'menlehre f morphology
Form'fehler m defect; flaw; (jur) irregularity
formieren [fɔr'mirən] tr & ref line up
-förmig ['fœrmɪç] comb.fm. -shaped
förmlich ['fœrmlɪç] adj formal || adv
virtually; literally; formally
form'los adj shapeless; informal; unconventional; rude; (chem) amor-
phous
form'schön adj well-shaped, beautiful
Formular [fɔrmu'lar] n (-s;-e) form,
blank
formulieren [fɔrmu'lirən] tr formulate; word, phrase
Formulie'rung f (-;-en) formulation;
wording
form'vollendet adj perfectly shaped
forsch [fɔrʃ] adj dashing || adv briskly
forschen ['fɔrʃən] intr do research;
(nach) search (for)
For'scher –in §6 mf researcher; scholar; explorer
For'schung f (-;-en) research
For'schungsanstalt f research center
Forst [fɔrst] m (-[e]s;-e) forest
Förster ['fœrstər] m (-s;-) forester;
forest ranger
Forst'fach n forestry
Forst'mann m (-es;-leute) forester
Forst'revier n forest range
Forst'wesen n, **Forst'wirtschaft** f forestry
fort [fɔrt] adv away; gone, lost; (weiter) on; (vorwärts) forward; **ich muß
f.** I must be off; **in e-m f.** continu-
ously; **und so f.** and so forth || **Fort**
[fɔr] n (-s;-s) (mil) fort
fortan' adv from now on, henceforth
Fort'bestand m continued existence
fort'bestehen §146 intr continue
fort'bewegen §56 tr move along || ref
get about
fort'bilden ref continue one's studies
Fort'bildung f continuing education

fort'bleiben §62 intr (SEIN) stay away
Fort'dauer f continuance
fort'dauern intr continue; last
fort'fahren §71 tr hawl away; continue
(to say); **f. zu** (inf) continue to (inf),
go on (ger) || intr continue, go on ||
intr (SEIN) drive off, leave
Fort'fall m omission; discontinuation;
in F. kommen be discontinued
fort'fallen §72 intr (SEIN) drop out; be
omitted; be discontinued
fort'führen tr lead away; continue;
(Geschäft) carry on; (Linie) extend
Fort'gang m departure; continuation;
progress
fort'gehen §82 intr (SEIN) go away
fort'geschritten adj advanced; late
fort'gesetzt adj incessant
fort'kommen §99 intr (SEIN) go on,
make progress; get away; **in der
Welt f.** get ahead in the world ||
Fortkommen n (-s;) progress
fort'lassen §104 tr allow to go; omit
fort'laufen §105 intr (SEIN) run away
fort'laufend adj continuing; (Nummer)
consecutive
fort'leben intr live on
fort'pflanzen tr propagate; spread ||
ref reproduce; propagate; spread
Fort'pflanzung f (-;) propagation
fort'reißen §53 tr tear away; **j–n mit
sich f.** sweep s.o. off his feet; **sich f.
lassen** be caried away
fort'schaffen tr remove
fort'scheren ref (coll) scram
fort'schreiten §86 intr (SEIN) progress,
advance
Fort'schritt m progress; improvement
fort'schrittlich adj progressive
fort'setzen tr continue; resume
Fort'setzung f (-;-en) continuation;
sequel; installment; **F. folgt** to be
continued
fort'während adj continual; lasting,
permanent || adv all the time, always
Fossil [fɔ'sil] n (-s;-ien [jən]) fossil
foul [faul] adj foul, dirty || **Foul** n
(-s;-) (sport) foul; **ein F. begehen
an** (dat) commit a foul against
foulen ['faulən] tr (sport) foul
Foyer [fwa'je] n (-s;-s) foyer; (im
Hotel) lobby
Fracht [fraxt] f (-;-en) freight, cargo
Fracht'brief m bill of lading
Frachter ['fraxtər] m (-s;-) freighter
Fracht'gut n freight, goods
Fracht'raum m cargo compartment;
cargo capacity
Fracht'stück n package
Frack [frak] m (-[e]s;ːe & -s) tails
Frack'schoß m coattail
Frage ['frɑgə] f (-;-n) question; **außer
F. stehen** be out of the question;
e–e F. stellen ask a question; **in F.
stellen** call in question; **kommt nicht
in F.!** nothing doing!
Fra'gebogen m questionnaire
fragen ['frɑgən] tr ask; **j–n f. nach**
ask s.o. about; **j–n nach der Zeit f.**
ask s.o. the time; **j–n f. um** ask s.o.
for || ref wonder || impers ref—**es
fragt sich, ob** the question is whether
|| intr ask

Fra'gesatz *m* interrogative sentence; **abhängiger F.** indirect question

Fragesteller ['fragəʃtɛlər] *m* (-s;-) questioner

Fra'gewort *n* (-es;-̈er) interrogative

Fra'gezeichen *n* question mark

fraglich ['fraklɪç] *adj* questionable

fraglos ['fraklos] *adv* unquestionably

Fragment [frag'ment] *n* (-[e]s;-e) fragment

frag'würdig *adj* questionable

Fraktion [frak'tsjon] *f* (-;-en) (chem) fraction; (pol) faction

fraktionell [fraktsə'nɛl] *adj* factional

Fraktur [frak'tur] *f* (-;-en) fracture; Gothic type, Gothic lettering; **mit j-m F. reden** talk turkey with s.o.

frank [fraŋk] *adv*—**f. und frei** quite frankly

Franke ['fraŋkə] *m* (-n;-n) Franconian; (hist) Frank

Franken ['fraŋkən] *m* (-[e]s;-) (Swiss) franc || *n* (-s;) Franconia

frankieren [fraŋ'kirən] *tr* frank, put postage on

Fränkin ['frɛŋkɪn] *f* (-;-nen) Frank

franko ['fraŋko] *adv* postage paid; **f. Berlin** freight paid to Berlin; **f. verzollt** free of freight and duty

Frank'reich *n* (-s;) France

Franse ['franzə] *f* (-;-n) fringe

fransen ['franzən] *intr* fray

Franzband ['frantsbant] *m* (-[e]s;-̈e) leather binding

Franz'branntwein *m* rubbing alcohol

Franzose [fran'tsozə] *m* (-n;-n) Frenchman; **die Franzosen** the French

Französin [fran'tsøzɪn] *f* (-;-nen) Frenchwoman

französisch [fran'tsøzɪʃ] *adj* French

frappant [fra'pant] *adj* striking

frappieren [fra'pirən] *tr* strike, astonish; (*Wein*) put on ice

fräsen ['frezən] *tr* mill

fraß [fras] *pret* of **fressen** || **Fraß** *m* (-es;) fodder, food; (pel) garbage

Fratz [frats] *m* (-es;-e) brat

Fratze ['fratsə] *f* (-;-n) grimace; (coll) face; **e-e F. schneiden** make a face

frat'zenhaft *adj* grotesque

Frau [frau] *f* (-;-en) woman; lady; wife; (*vor Namen*) Mrs; **zur F. geben** give in marriage

Frauen- *comb.fm.* of women

Frau'enarzt *m*, **Frau'enärztin** *f* gynecologist

Frau'enheld *m* ladykiller

Frau'enkirche *f* Church of Our Lady

Frau'enkleidung *f* women's wear

Frau'enklinik *f* women's hospital

Frau'enleiden *n* gynecological disorder

Frau'enzimmer *n* (pej) woman, female

Fräulein ['frɔɪlaɪn] *n* (-s;-) young lady; (*vor Namen*) Miss

frau'lich *adj* womanly

frech [frɛç] *adj* brazen; fresh, smart

Frech'dachs *m* smart aleck

Frech'heit *f* (-;-en) impudence

Fregatte [frɛ'gatə] *f* (-;-n) frigate

frei [fraɪ] *adj* free; (*Feld*) open; (*offen*) frank; **auf freien Fuß setzen** release; **auf freier Strecke** (rr) outside the station; **die freien Berufe** the professions; **freie Fahrt** (public sign) resume speed; **freies Spiel haben** have a free hand; **frei werden** (chem) be released; **ich bin so frei** thank you, I will have some; **sich frei machen** take off one's clothes || **Freie** §5 *n*—**im Freien** out of doors; **ins Freie** out of doors, into the open

Frei'bad *n* outdoor swimming pool

Frei'bank *f* (-;-̈e) cheap-meat counter

frei'beruflich *adj* freelance

Frei'betrag *m* allowable deduction

Frei'brief *m* charter; (fig) license

Freier ['fraɪ-ər] *m* (-s;-) suitor

Frei'frau *f* baroness

Frei'gabe *f* release

frei'geben §80 *tr* release; **für den Verkehr f.** open to traffic || *intr*—**j-m f. give** s.o. (*time*) off

freigebig ['fraɪgebɪç] *adj* generous

Frei'gebigkeit *f* (-;) generosity

Frei'geist *m* freethinker

frei'geistig *adj* open-minded

frei'gestellt *adj* optional

frei'haben *intr* be off

Frei'hafen *m* free port

frei'halten §90 *tr* keep open; **j-n f.** pay the tab for s.o.

Frei'heit *f* (-;-en) freedom; **dichterische F.** poetic license

Frei'heitskrieg *m* war of liberation

Frei'heitsstrafe *f* imprisonment

Frei'herr *m* baron

Frei'karte *f* free ticket; (theat) complimentary ticket

Frei'korps *n* volunteer corps

frei'lassen §104 *tr* release, set free

Frei'lauf *m* coasting

frei'legen *tr* lay open, expose

frei'lich *adv* of course

Freilicht- *comb.fm.* open-air

frei'machen *tr* (*Platz*) vacate; (*Straße*) clear; (*Brief*) stamp; **den Arm f.** roll up one's sleeves || *ref* undress

Frei'marke *f* postage stamp

Frei'maurer *m* Freemason

Frei'maurerei *f* freemasonry

Frei'mut *m* frankness

frei'mütig *adj* frank, outspoken

frei'schaffend *adj* freelance

Frei'sinn *m* (pol) liberalism

frei'sinnig *adj* (pol) liberal

frei'sprechen §64 *tr* acquit

Frei'spruch *m* acquittal

frei'stehen §146 *intr*—**es steht Ihnen frei zu** (*inf*) you are free to (*inf*)

frei'stehend *adj* free-standing; (*Gebäude*) detached

Frei'stelle *f* scholarship

frei'stellen *tr* exempt; **j-m etw f.** leave it to s.o.'s discretion

Frei'stoß *m* (fb) free kick

Frei'tag *m* Friday

Frei'tod *m* suicide

Frei'treppe *f* outdoor stairway

Frei'wild *n* (& fig) fair game

frei'willig *adj* voluntary || **Freiwillige** §5 *mf* (& mil) volunteer

Frei'zeichen *n* (telp) dial tone

Frei'zeit *f* spare time, leisure

Frei'zeitgestaltung *f* planning one's leisure time

freizügig ['fraɪtsygɪç] *adj* unhampered

fremd [frɛmt] *adj* foreign; strange; someone else's; (*Name*) assumed
fremd'artig *adj* strange, odd
Fremde ['frɛmdə] §5 *mf* foreigner; stranger || *f*—aus der F. from abroad; in der F. far from home; in die F. gehen go far from home; go abroad
Frem'denbuch *n* visitors' book
Frem'denführer –in §6 *mf* tour guide; (*Buch*) guidebook
Frem'denheim *n* boarding house
Frem'denlegion *f* foreign legion
Frem'denverkehr *m* tourism
Frem'denzimmer *n* guest room; spare room
Fremd'herrschaft *f* foreign domination
Fremd'körper *m* foreign body; (pol) alien element
fremdländisch ['frɛmtlɛndɪʃ] *adj* foreign
Fremdling ['frɛmtlɪŋ] *m* (–s;–) stranger
Fremd'sprache *f* foreign language
Fremd'wort *n* (–es;–̈er) foreign word
frequentieren [frɛkvɛn'tirən] *tr* frequent
Frequenz [frɛ'kvɛnts] *f* (–;–en) frequency; (*Besucherzahl*) attendance
Freske ['frɛskə] *f* (–;–n), **Fres·ko** ['frɛsko] *n* (–s;–ken [kən]) fresco
Freßbeutel ['frɛsbɔɪtəl] *m* feed bag
Fresse ['frɛsə] *f* (–;–n) (sl) puss
fressen ['frɛsən] §70 *tr* (*von Tieren*) eat; feed on; (sl) devour; (*ätzen*) corrode, pit; (tech) freeze || *ref*—sich satt f. stuff oneself || *intr* (sl) eat; (an *dat*) gnaw (at)
Fresserei [frɛsə'raɪ] *f* (–;) gluttony
Freude ['frɔɪdə] *f* (–;–n) joy, pleasure
Freu'denbotschaft *f* glad tidings
Freu'denfeier *f*, **Freu'denfest** *n* celebration, happy occasion
Freu'denhaus *n* brothel
Freu'denmädchen *n* prostitute
freudig ['frɔɪdɪç] *adj* joyful, happy
freud'los *adj* joyless, sad
freuen ['frɔɪ·ən] *tr* please || *ref* be happy; (an *dat*) be delighted (by); (auf *acc*) look forward (to); (über *acc*) be glad (about) || *impers*—es freut mich I am glad
Freund [frɔɪnt] *m* (–[e]s;–e) friend; boyfriend; F. der Musik music lover
Freundin ['frɔɪndɪn] *f* (–;–nen) friend; girlfriend
freund'lich *adj* friendly; cheerful
Freund'lichkeit *f* (–;) friendliness
Freund'schaft *f* (–;–en) friendship
Frevel ['frefəl] *m* (–s;–) outrage; crime; sacrilege
fre'velhaft *adj* wicked
freveln ['frefəln] *intr* commit an outrage; am Gesetz f. violate the law
Fre'veltat *f* outrage
Friede ['fridə] *m* (–ns;), **Frieden** ['fridən] *m* (–s;) peace
Frie'densrichter *m* justice of the peace
Frie'densschluß *m* conclusion of peace
Frie'densstifter –in §6 *mf* peacemaker
Frie'densverhandlungen *pl* peace negotiations
Frie'densvertrag *m* peace treaty

friedfertig ['fritfɛrtɪç] *adj* peaceable
Friedhof ['frithof] *m* cemetery
friedlich ['fritlɪç] *adj* peaceful
friedliebend ['fritlibənt] *adj* peaceloving
frieren ['frirən] §77 *intr* be cold; freeze || *impers*—es friert mich I'm freezing
Fries [fris] *m* (–es;–e) frieze
Frikadelle [frɪka'dɛlə] *f* (–;–n) meatball
frisch [frɪʃ] *adj* fresh; (*kühl*) cool; (*munter*) brisk || *adv* freshly; f. gestrichen (public sign) wet paint; f. zu! on with it! || **Frische** *f* (–;) freshness; coolness; briskness
Frisch'haltepackung *f* vacuum package
Friseur [frɪ'zør] *m* (–s;–e) barber
Friseur'laden *m* barbershop
Friseur'sessel *m* barber chair
Friseuse [frɪ'zøzə] *f* (–;–n) hairdresser
frisieren [frɪ'zirən] *tr* (*Dokumente*) doctor; (aut) soup up; j–m die Haare f. do s.o.'s hair
Frisier'haube *f* hair dryer; hair net
Frisier'kommode *f*, **Frisier'tisch** *m* dresser
Frist [frɪst] *f* (–;–en) time, period, term; (com, jur) grace; die F. einhalten meet the deadline
fristen ['frɪstən] *tr*—das Leben f. eke out a living
Frisur [frɪ'zur] *f* (–;–en) hairstyle
frivol [frɪ'vol] *adj* frivolous
froh [fro] *adj* glad, happy, joyful
froh'gelaunt *adj* cheerful
fröhlich ['frølɪç] *adj* gay, merry
froh'locken *intr* rejoice
Froh'sinn *m* good humor
fromm [frɔm] *adj* pious, devout
Frömmelei [frœmə'laɪ] *f* (–;–en) sanctimoniousness; sanctimonious act
frommen ['frɔmən] *intr* (dat) profit
Frömmigkeit ['frœmɪçkaɪt] *f* (–;) piety
Frömmler –in ['frœmlər–ɪn] §6 *mf* hypocrite
Fron [fron] *f* (–;) drudgery; (hist) forced labor
frönen ['frønən] *intr* (dat) gratify
Fron'leichnam *m* Corpus Christi
Front [frɔnt] *f* (–;–en) (& mil) front
Front'abschnitt *m* (mil) sector
fror [fror] *pret* of **frieren**
Frosch [frɔʃ] *m* (–es;–̈e) frog; (*Feuerwerkkörper*) firecracker; sei kein F.! don't be a party pooper
Frost [frɔst] *m* (–es;–̈e) frost
Frost'beule *f* chilblain
frösteln ['frœstəln] *intr* feel chilly
Frosterfach ['frɔstərfax] *n* freezer compartment (*of refrigerator*)
frostig ['frɔstɪç] *adj* frosty; chilly
Frost'schutzmittel *n* antifreeze
Frottee [frɔ'te] *m* & *n* (–s;–s) terry cloth
frottieren [frɔ'tirən] *tr* rub down
Frottier'tuch *n* Turkish towel
Frucht [fruxt] *f* (–;–̈e) fruit; foetus
fruchtbar ['fruxtbar] *adj* fruitful
frucht'bringend *adj* productive
Früch'tebecher *m* fruit cup (*as dessert*)
fruchten ['fruxtən] *intr* bear fruit; have effect; be of use

Frucht'folge f rotation of crops
Frucht'knoten m (bot) pistil
frucht'los adj fruitless
Frucht'saft m fruit juice
Frucht'wechsel m rotation of crops
frugal [fru'gɑl] adj frugal
früh [fry] adj early || adv early; in the morning; **von f. bis spät** from morning till night || **Frühe** f (-;) early morning; **in aller F.** very early
früher ['fry·ər] adj earlier; former || adv earlier; sooner; formerly
frühestens ['fry·əstəns] adv at the earliest
Früh'geburt f premature birth
Früh'jahr n, **Frühling** ['frylɪŋ] m (-s; -e) spring
Früh'lingsmüdigkeit f spring fever
früh'reif adj precocious
Früh'schoppen m eye opener (beer, wine)
Früh'stück n breakfast; **zweites F.** lunch
frühstücken ['fryʃtykən] intr eat breakfast
früh'zeitig adj & adv (too) early
Fuchs [fuks] m (-es;ꞏe) fox; (Pferd) sorrel, chestnut; (educ) freshman
Fuchsie ['fuksjə] f (-;-n) fuchsia
fuchsig ['fuksɪç] adj red; (fig) furious, wild
Fuchs'jagd f fox hunt(ing)
fuchs'rot' adj sorrel
Fuchs'schwanz m foxtail; (bot) amaranth; (carp) hand saw (with tapered blade)
fuchs'teufelswild' adj hopping mad
Fuge ['fugə] f (-;-n) joint; (mus) fugue; **aus allen Fugen gehen** come apart; go to pieces, go to pot
fügen ['fygən] tr join; (verhängen) decree; (carp) joint || ref give in; **es fügte sich** it so happened
fügsam ['fykzɑm] adj compliant; (Haar) manageable
Fü'gung f (-;-en) (gram) construction; **F. des Himmels, F. Gottes** divine providence; **F. des Schicksals** stroke of fate; **göttliche F.** divine providence
fühlbar ['fylbɑr] adj tangible; noticeable; **sich f. machen** make itself felt
fühlen ['fylən] tr feel, touch; sense || ref feel; feel big || intr—**f. mit** feel for (s.o.); **f. nach** feel for, grope for
-fühlig [fylɪç] comb.fm. -feeling
Füh'lung f (-;) touch, contact; **F. nehmen mit** get in touch with
fuhr [fur] pret of **fahren**
Fuhre ['furə] f (-;-n) wagon load
führen ['fyrən] tr lead; guide; (Artikel) carry, sell; (Besprechungen) hold, conduct; (Bücher) keep; (Geschäft) run, manage; (Krieg) carry on; (Sprache) use; (Titel) bear; (Truppen) command; (Waffe) wield; (Fahrzeug) drive; (aer) pilot; **den Beweis f.** prove; **de Aufsicht f. über** (acc) superintend; **j-m den Haushalt f.** keep house for s.o. || ref conduct oneself || intr lead; (sport) be in the lead
Füh'rer -in §6 mf leader, guide; (aer)

pilot; (aut) driver; (com) manager; (sport) captain
Füh'rerschaft f (-;) leadership
Füh'rerschein m driver's license
Füh'rerscheinentzug m suspension of driver's license
Führhund ['fyrhunt] m Seeing Eye dog
Fuhr'park m (aut) fleet
Füh'rung f (-;-en) guidance; leadership; management; guided tour; behavior; (mil) command; (sport) lead
Füh'rungskraft f executive; **die Führungskräfte** management; (pol) authorities; **untere F.** junior executive
Füh'rungsschicht f (com) management
Füh'rungsspitze f top echelon
Fuhr'unternehmen n trucking
Fuhr'werk n cart, wagon; vehicle
Füllbleistift ['fylblaiʃtɪft] m mechanical pencil
Fülle ['fylə] f (-;) fullness; abundance, wealth; (Körper-) plumpness
füllen ['fylən] tr fill || ref fill up || **Füllen** n (-s;-) foal, colt, filly
Fül'ler m (-s;-) fountain pen
Füll'federhalter m fountain pen
Füll'horn n cornucopia
Füllsel ['fylzəl] n (-s;-) stopgap; (beim Schreiben) padding; (culin) stuffing
Fül'lung f (-;-en) (Zahn-) filling; (Tür-) panel; (culin) stuffing
Fund [funt] m (-[e]s;-e) find; discovery
Fundament [funda'ment] n (-[e]s;-e) foundation
fundamental [fundamen'tɑl] adj fundamental
Fund'büro n lost-and-found department
Fund'grube f (fig) mine, storehouse
fundieren [fun'dirən] tr lay the foundations of; found; establish; (Schuld) fund; **fundiertes Einkommen** unearned income; **gut fundiert** well-established
fünf [fynf] adj & pron five || **Fünf** f (-;-en) five
Fünf'eck n pentagon
fünfte ['fynftə] §9 adj & pron fifth
Fünftel ['fynftəl] n (-s;-) fifth (part)
fünf'zehn adj & pron fifteen || **Fünfzehn** f (-;-en) fifteen
fünf'zehnte §9 adj & pron fifteenth
Fünf'zehntel n (-s;-) fifteenth (part)
fünfzig ['fynfzɪç] adj fifty
fünf'ziger invar adj of the fifties; **die f. Jahre** the fifties
fünfzigste ['fynftsɪçstə] §9 adj & pron fiftieth
fungieren [fuŋ'girən] intr function; **f. als** function as, act as
Funk [funk] m (-s;) radio
Funk'amateur m (rad) ham
Funk'bastler -in §6 mf (rad) ham
Fünkchen ['fyŋkçən] n (-s;-) small spark; **kein F.** (fig) not an ounce
Funke ['fuŋkə] m (-ns;-n), **Funken** ['fuŋkən] m (-s;-) spark
funkeln ['fuŋkəln] intr sparkle; (Sterne) twinkle
fun'kelnagelneu' adj brand-new

funken [ˈfuŋkən] *tr* radio, broadcast ‖ *intr* spark
Fun'ker *m* (-s;-) radio operator
Funk'feuer *n* (aer) radio beacon
Funk'leitstrahl *m* radio beam
Funk'meßanlage *f* radar installation
Funk'meßgerät *n* radar
Funk'netz *n* radio network
Funk'peilung *f* radio direction finding
Funk'spruch *m* radiogram
Funk'streifenwagen *m* squad car
Funktionär –in [fuŋktsjəˈnɛr(ɪn)] §8 *mf* functionary
für [fyr] *prep* (*acc*) for ‖ **Für** *n*—das **Für und Wider** the pros and cons
Für'bitte *f* intercession
Furche [ˈfurçə] *f* (-;-n) furrow; (*Runzel*) wrinkle; (*Wagenspur*) rut
furchen [ˈfurçən] *tr* furrow; wrinkle
Furcht [furçt] *f* (-;) fear, dread
furchtbar [ˈfurçtbɑr] *adj* terrible
fürchten [ˈfʏrçtən] *tr* fear, be afraid of ‖ *ref* (**vor** *dat*) be afraid (of)
fürchterlich [ˈfʏrçtərlɪç] *adj* terrible, awful
furcht'erregend *adj* awe-inspiring
furcht'los *adj* fearless
furchtsam [ˈfurçtzɑm] *adj* timid, shy
Furie [ˈfurjə] *f* (-;-n) (myth) Fury
Furnier [furˈnir] *n* (-s;-e) veneer
Furore [fuˈrorə] *f* (-;) & *n* (-s;) stir; **F. machen** cause a stir, be a big hit
Für'sorge *f* care; welfare
Für'sorgeamt *n* welfare department
Fürsorger –in [ˈfʏrzɔrgər(ɪn)] §6 *mf* social worker; welfare officer
fürsorglich [ˈfʏrzɔrklɪç] *adj* thoughtful
Für'sprache *f* intercession; **F. einlegen** intercede
Für'sprecher –in §6 *mf* intercessor
Fürst [fʏrst] *m* (-en;-en) prince
Fürstentum [ˈfʏrstəntum] *n* (-s;-er) principality
Fürstin [ˈfʏrstɪn] *f* (-;-nen) princess
fürst'lich *adj* princely
Furt [furt] *f* (-;-en) ford
Furunkel [fuˈrunkəl] *m* (-s;-) boil
Für'wort *n* (-[e]s;-er) pronoun

Furz [furts] *m* (-es;-e) (vulg) fart
Fusel [ˈfuzəl] *m* (-s;) (coll) booze
Fusion [fuˈsjon] *f* (-;-en) (com) merger
Fuß [fus] *m* (-es;-e) foot; **auf freien Fuß setzen** set free; **zu Fuß** on foot; **zu Fuß gehen** walk
Fuß'abdruck *m* footprint
Fuß'ball *m* soccer; football
Fuß'bank *f* (-;-e) footstool
Fuß'bekleidung *f* footwear
Fuß'boden *m* floor; flooring
Fussel [ˈfusəl] *f* (-;-n) fuzz
fußen [ˈfusən] *intr*—**f. auf** (*dat*) be based on; rely on
Fuß'fall *m* prostration
fuß'fällig *adv* on one's knees
fuß'frei *adj* ankle-length
Fuß'freiheit *f* leg room
Fuß'gänger *m* (-s;-) pedestrian
Fuß'gelenk *n* ankle joint
Fuß'gestell *n* pedestal
–**füßig** [fysɪç] *comb.fm.* –footed
Fuß'knöchel *m* ankle
Fuß'leiste *f* baseboard, washboard
Füßling [ˈfyslɪŋ] *m* (-s;-e) foot (*of stocking, sock, etc.*)
Fuß'note *f* footnote
Fuß'pfad *m* footpath
Fuß'pilz *m* athlete's foot
Fuß'spur *f* footprint(s)
Fuß'stapfe *f* footstep
Fuß'steg *m* footbridge; footpath
Fuß'steig *m* footpath; sidewalk
Fuß'tritt *m* step; (*Stoß*) kick
futsch [futʃ] *adj* (coll) gone; (coll) ruined
Futter [ˈfutər] *n* (-s;) fodder, feed; (*e-s Mantels*) lining
Futteral [futəˈral] *n* (-s;-e) case
Fut'terkrippe *f* crib; (sl) gravy train
Fut'terkrippensystem *n* (pol) spoils system
futtern [ˈfutərn] *intr* (coll) eat heartily
füttern [ˈfytərn] *tr* feed; (*Kleid, Mantel, Pelz*) line
Fut'terneid *m* jealousy
Fut'terstoff *m* lining
Fut'tertrog *m* feed trough

G

G, g [ge] *invar n* G, g; (mus) G
gab [gɑp] *pret of* **geben**
Gabardine [gabarˈdinə] *m* (-s;-) (tex) gabardine
Gabe [ˈgɑbə] *f* (-;-n) gift; donation; talent; (med) dose; **milde G.** alms
Gabel [ˈgɑbəl] *f* (-;-n) fork; (arti) bracket; (telp) cradle
Ga'belbein *n* wishbone
Ga'belbissen *m* tidbit
Ga'belfrühstück *n* brunch
gabelig [ˈgɑbəlɪç] *adj* forked
gabeln [ˈgɑbəln] *tr* pick up with a fork ‖ *ref* divide, branch off
Ga'belstapler *m* forklift
Ga'belung *f* (-;-en) fork (*in the road*)

gackeln [ˈgakəln], **gackern** [ˈgakərn], **gacksen** [ˈgaksən] *intr* cackle, cluck
Gage [ˈgaʒə] *f* (-;-n) salary, pay
gähnen [ˈgenən] *intr* yawn
gaffen [ˈgafən] *intr* gape; stare
Gala [ˈgala] *invar f* gala, Sunday best
galant [gaˈlant] *adj* courteous; **galantes Abenteuer** love affair
Galante·rie [galantəˈri] *f* (-;-rien [ˈri·ən]) courtesy; flattering word
Gala·xis [gaˈlaksɪs] *f* (-;-xien [ksjən]) galaxy
Galeere [gaˈlerə] *f* (-;-n) galley
Gale·rie [galəˈri] *f* (-;-rien [ˈri·ən]) gallery
Galgen [ˈgalgən] *m* (-s;-) gallows

Gal'genfrist *f* (coll) brief respite
Gal'genhumor *m* grim humor
Gal'genstrick *m*, **Gal'genvogel** *m* (coll) good-for-nothing
gälisch ['gɛlɪʃ] *adj* Gaelic
Galle ['galə] *f* (-;) gall, bile; (fig) bitterness
Gal·lenblase *f* gall bladder
Gal'lenstein *m* gallstone
Gallert ['galərt] *n* (-[e]s;-e), **Gallerte** [ga'lɛrtə] *f* (-;-n) gelatine; jelly
gallig ['galɪç] *adj* bitter; grouchy
Gallone [ga'lonə] *f* (-;-n) gallon
Galopp [ga'lɔp] *m* (-[e]s;-s & -e) gallop; **im G. reiten** gallop; **in gestrecktem G.** at full gallop; **in kurzem G.** at a canter
galoppieren [galə'pirən] *intr* (SEIN) gallop
galt [galt] *pret* of **gelten**
galvanisieren [galvanɪ'zirən] *tr* galvanize; electroplate
Gambe ['gambə] *f* (-;-n) bass viol
gammeln ['gaməln] *intr* bum around
Gammler ['gamlər] *m* (-s;-) hippie
Gamsbart ['gamsbart] *m* goatee
gang [gaŋ] *adj*—**g. und gäbe** customary ‖ **Gang** *m* (-[e]s;ᴗ̈) walk, gait; (*e-r Maschine*) running, operation; (*im Hause*) hallway; (*zwischen Reihen*) aisle; (*Botengang*) errand; (*Röhre*) conduit; (*e-r Schraube*) thread; (anat) duct, canal; (aut) gear; (box) round; (culin) course; (min) vein, lode; (min) gallery; (mus) run; **außer G. setzen** stop; (aut) put in neutral; **erster G.** low gear; **es ist etw im G.** there is s.th. afoot; **im G. sein** be in operation; be in progress; **in G. bringen** (or **setzen**) set in motion; **in vollem G.** in full swing
Gang'art *f* gait
gangbar ['gaŋbar] *adj* passable; (*Münze*) current; (com) marketable
Gängelband ['gɛŋəlbant] *n*—**am G. führen** (fig) lead by the nose, dominate
-gänger [gɛŋər] *comb.fm.*, e.g., **Fußgänger** pedestrian
gängig ['gɛŋɪç] *adj* see **gangbar**
Gang'schaltung *f* (aut) gear shift
Gangster ['gɛŋstər] *m* (-s;-s) gangster
Ganove [ga'novə] *m* (-;-n) crook
Gans [gans] *f* (-;ᴗ̈e) goose
Gänseblümchen ['gɛnzəblymçən] *n* (-s;-) daisy
Gänsehaut ['gɛnzəhaut] *f* (coll) goose flesh, goose pimples
Gänseklein ['gɛnzəklaɪn] *n* (-s;) (culin) giblets
Gänsemarsch ['gɛnzəmarʃ] *m* single file
Gänserich ['gɛnzərɪç] *m* (-s;-e) gander
ganz [gants] *adj* whole; all; total; intact; **im ganzen** in all ‖ *adv* entirely, quite; **g. und gar** completely; **g. und gar nicht** not at all ‖ **Ganze** §5 *n* whole; **aufs G. gehen** go all the way
Ganz'aufnahme *f* full-length photograph
Gänze ['gɛntsə] *f* (-;)—**in G.** in its entirety; **zur G.** entirely
Ganz'fabrikat *n* finished product

Ganz'leinenband *m* (-[e]s;ᴗ̈e) cloth-bound volume
gänzlich ['gɛntslɪç] *adj* entire, total
ganz'seitig *adj* full-page
ganz'tägig *adj* full-time
gar [gar] *adj* (culin) well done; (metal) refined ‖ *adv* quite, very; (*sogar*) even; **gar nicht** not at all
Garage [ga'raʒə] *f* (-;-n) garage
Garan·tie [garan'ti] *f* (-;-tien ['ti·ən]) guarantee
garantieren [garan'tirən] *tr* guarantee ‖ *intr*—**g. dafür, daß** guarantee that
Garaus ['garaus] *m* (-;) finishing blow
Garbe ['garbə] *f* (-;-n) sheaf, shock
Garde ['gardə] *f* (-;-n) guard
Gardenie [gar'denjə] *f* (-;-n) gardenia
Garderobe [gardə'robə] *f* (-;-n) wardrobe; (*Kleiderablage*) cloakroom; (theat) dressing room
Gardero'benmarke *f* hat or coat check
Gardero'benständer *m* coatrack, hatrack
Garderobiere [gardərə'bjerə] *f* (-;-n) cloakroom attendant
Gardine [gar'dinə] *f* (-;-n) curtain
Gardi'nenhalter *m* tieback
Gardi'nenpredigt *f* (coll) dressing down
Gardi'nenstange *f* curtain rod
gären ['gerən] §78 *intr* ferment; bubble
Gärmittel ['germɪtəl] *n* ferment; leaven
Garn [garn] *n* (-[e]s;-e) yarn; thread; snare; (fig) trap; (fig) yarn
Garnele [gar'nelə] *f* (-;-n) shrimp
garnieren [gar'nirən] *tr* garnish; trim
Garnison [garnɪ'zon] *f* (-;-en) garrison
Garnitur [garnɪ'tur] *f* (-;-en) trimming; set (*of matching objects*); (mach) fittings, mountings; (mil) uniform
garstig ['garstɪç] *adj* ugly; nasty
Garten ['gartən] *m* (-s;ᴗ̈) garden
Gar'tenanlage *f* gardens, grounds
Gar'tenarbeit *f* gardening
Gar'tenarchitekt *m* landscape gardener
Gar'tenbau *m* gardening; horticulture
Gar'tenlaube *f* arbor
Gar'tenmesser *n* pruning knife
Gärtner ['gertnər] *m* (-s;-) gardener
Gärtnerei [gertnə'raɪ] *f* (-;-en) gardening; truck farm; nursery
Gä'rung *f* (-;) fermentation
Gas [gas] *n* (-es;-e) gas; **Gas geben** step on the gas
Gas'anstalt *f* gasworks
gas'artig *adj* gaseous
Gas'behälter *m* gas tank
gas'förmig *adj* gaseous
Gas'hebel *m* (aut) accelerator
Gas'heizung *f* gas heat(ing)
Gas'herd *m* gas range
Gas'krieg *m* chemical warfare
Gas'leitung *f* gas main
Gas'messer *m* gas meter
Gasse ['gasə] *f* (-;-n) side street; **über die G. verkaufen** sell takeouts
Gas'sendirne *f* streetwalker
Gas'senhauer *m* popular song
Gas'senjunge *m* urchin

Gast [gast] *m* (-[e]s;⁼e) guest; boarder; (com) customer; (theat) guest performer; **zu Gast bitten** invite

Gästebuch ['gɛstəbux] *n* guest book; visitors' book

Gast'freund *m* guest

gast'freundlich *adj* hospitable

Gast'freundschaft *f* hospitality

Gast'geber *m* host

Gast'geberin *f* hostess

Gast'haus *n*, **Gast'hof** *m* inn

Gast'hörer –in §6 *mf* (educ) auditor

gastieren [gas'tirən] *intr* (telv, theat) appear as a guest

gast'lich *adj* hospitable

Gast'mahl *n* feast; banquet

Gast'professor *m* visiting professor

Gast'rolle *f* guest performance; **e–e G. geben** pay a flying visit

Gast'spiel *n* (theat) guest performance

Gast'stätte *f* restaurant

Gast'stube *f* dining room

Gast'wirt *m* innkeeper

Gast'wirtschaft *f* restaurant

Gas'uhr *f* gas meter

Gas'werk *n* gas works

Gas'zähler *m* gas meter

Gatte ['gatə] *m* (-n;-n) husband; **Gatten** married couple

Gatter ['gatər] *n* (-s;-) grating; latticework; iron gate

Gattin ['gatın] *f* (-;-nen) wife

Gattung ['gatuŋ] *f* (-;-en) kind, type, species; family; (biol) genus

Gat'tungsname *m* generic name; (gram) common noun

Gau [gau] *m* (-[e]s;-e) district

Gaukelbild ['gaukəlbılt] *n* illusion

gaukeln ['gaukəln] *intr* flit, flutter; perform hocus-pocus

Gau'kelspiel *n*, **Gau'kelwerk** *n* sleight of hand; delusion

Gaul [gaul] *m* (-[e]s;⁼e) horse; nag

Gaumen ['gaumən] *m* (-s;-) palate

Gauner ['gaunər] *m* (-s;-) rogue; swindler

Gaunerei [gaunə'rai] *f* (-;-en) swindling, cheating

gaunern ['gaunərn] *intr* swindle

Gau'nersprache *f* thieves' slang

Gaze ['gazə] *f* (-;-n) gauze; cheesecloth

Gazelle [ga'tsɛlə] *f* (-;-n) gazelle

Geächtete [gə'ɛçtətə] §5 *mf* outlaw

Geächze [gə'ɛçtsə] *n* (-s;) moaning

geartet [gə'artət] *adj*—**anders g. sein** be of a different disposition

Gebäck [gə'bɛk] *n* (-s;) baked goods, cookies

geballt [gə'balt] *adj* concentrated; dense; (*Schnee*) hardened; (*Faust*) clenched; (*Stil*) succinct

gebannt [gə'bant] *adj* spellbound

gebar [gə'bar] *pret* of **gebären**

Gebärde [gə'bɛrdə] *f* (-;-n) gesture

gebärden [gə'bɛrdən] *ref* behave

Gebär'denspiel *n* gesticulation

gebaren [gə'barən] *ref* behave, act ‖ **Gebaren** *n* (-s;) behavior

gebären [gə'bɛrən] §79 *tr* bear ‖ **Gebären** *n* (-s;) childbirth; labor

Gebär'mutter *f* (anat) uterus

Gebär'mutterkappe *f* diaphragm

Gebäude [gə'bɔɪdə] *n* (-s;-) building

gebefreudig ['gebəfrɔɪdıç] *adj* openhanded

Gebein [gə'bain] *n* (-[e]s;-e) bones; **Gebeine** bones; mortal remains

Gebell [gə'bɛl] *n* (-[e]s;), **Gebelle** [gə'bɛlə] *n* (-s;) barking

geben ['gebən] §80 *tr* give; yield; (*Gelegenheit*) afford; (*Laut*) utter; (*Karten*) deal; **Feuer g.** give (*s.o.*) a light; (mil) open fire; **viel g. auf** (*acc*) set great store by; **von sich g.** utter; throw up; (*Rede*) deliver; (chem) give off ‖ *ref* give; (*Kopfweh, usw.*) get better; **sich g. als** pretend to be; **sich gefangen g.** surrender ‖ *impers*—**es gibt** there is, there are; **es wird Regen geben** it's going to rain

Ge'ber –in §6 *mf* giver, donor

Gebet [gə'bet] *n* (-[e]s;-e) prayer

gebeten [gə'betən] *pp* of **bitten**

Gebiet [gə'bit] *n* (-[e]s;-e) district, territory; (*Fläche*) area; (*Fach*) line; (*Bereich*) field, sphere

gebieten [gə'bitən] §58 *tr* (*Stillschweigen*) impose; (*Ehrfurcht*) command; (*verlangen*) demand; **j–m g., etw zu tun** order s.o. to do s.th. ‖ *intr* (*über acc*) have control (over); (*dat*) control

Gebieter [gə'bitər] *m* (-s;-) master; ruler; commander; governor

Gebieterin [gə'bitərın] *f* (-;-nen) mistress; (*des Hauses*) lady

gebieterisch [gə'bitərıʃ] *adj* imperious

Gebilde [gə'bıldə] *n* (-s;-) shape, form; structure; (geol) formation

gebildet [gə'bıldət] *adj* educated

Gebirge [gə'bırgə] *n* (-s;-) mountain range, mountains; **festes G.** bedrock

gebirgig [gə'bırgıç] *adj* mountainous

Gebirgs– [gəbırks] *comb.fm.* mountain

Gebirgs'bewohner –in §6 *mf* mountaineer

Gebirgs'kamm *m*, **Gebirgs'rücken** *m* mountain ridge

Gebirgs'zug *m* mountain range

Ge·biß [gə'bıs] *n* (-bisses;-bisse) teeth; false teeth; (*am Zaum*) bit

gebissen [gə'bısən] *pp* of **beißen**

Gebläse [gə'blɛzə] *n* (-s;-) bellows; blower; (aut) supercharger

geblieben [gə'blibən] *pp* of **bleiben**

Geblök [gə'bløk] *n* (-[e]s;) bleating

geblümt [gə'blymt] *adj* flowered

Geblüt [gə'blyt] *n* (-[e]s;) (& fig) blood

geboren [gə'borən] *pp* of **gebären** ‖ *adj* born; native; **geborene** nee

geborgen [gə'bɔrgən] *pp* of **bergen** ‖ *adj* safe

Gebor'genheit *f* (-;) safety, security

geborsten [gə'bɔrstən] *pp* of **bersten**

Gebot [gə'bot] *n* (-[e]s;-e) order, command; commandment; (*Angebot*) bid

geboten [gə'botən] *pp* of **bieten** ‖ *adj* requisite; **dringend g.** imperative

Gebr. *abbr.* (**Gebrüder**) Brothers

gebracht [gə'braxt] *pp* of **bringen**

gebrannt [gə'brant] *pp* of **brennen**

Gebräu [gə'brɔɪ] n (-[e]s;-e) brew
Gebrauch [gə'braux] m (-s;-̈e) use; usage; (Sitte) custom
gebrauchen [gə'brauxen] tr use, employ
gebräuchlich [gə'brɔɪçlɪç] adj usual; in use; (gemein) common
Gebrauchs'anweisung f directions
gebrauchs'fertig adj ready for use; (Kaffee, usw.) instant
Gebrauchs'graphik f commercial art
Gebrauchs'gut n commodity
Gebrauchs'muster n registered pattern
gebraucht [gə'brauxt] adj second-hand
Gebraucht'wagen m used car
Gebrechen [gə'breçən] n (-s;-) physical disability, infirmity
gebrech'lich adj frail, weak; rickety
gebrochen [gə'brɔxən] pp of brechen
Gebrüder [gə'brydər] pl brothers
Gebrüll [gə'bryl] n (-[e]s;) roaring; bellowing; lowing
Gebühr [gə'byr] f (-;-en) charge, fee; due, what is due; nach G. deservedly; über G. excessively; zu ermäßigter G. at a reduced rate
gebühren [gə'byrən] intr (dat) be due to || impers ref—es gebührt sich it is proper
gebüh'rend adj due; (entsprechend) appropriate || adv duly
gebüh'renfrei adj free of charge
gebüh'renpflichtig adj chargeable
gebunden [gə'bundən] pp of binden || adj bound; (Hitze) latent; (Preise) controlled; (Kapital) tied-up; g. an (acc) (chem) combined with; gebundene Rede verse
Geburt [gə'burt] f (-;-en) birth
Gebur'tenbeschränkung f birth control
Gebur'tenregelung f birth control
Gebur'tenrückgang m decline in births
gebürtig [gə'byrtɪç] adj native
Geburts'anzeige f announcement of birth; registration of birth
Geburts'fehler n congenital defect
Geburts'helfer –in §6 mf obstetrician || f midwife
Geburts'hilfe f obstetrics
Geburts'mal n birth mark
Geburts'recht n birthright
Geburts'schein m birth certificate
Geburts'tag m birthday
Geburts'tagskind n person celebrating his or her birthday
Geburts'wehen pl labor pains
Geburts'zange f forceps
Gebüsch [gə'byʃ] n (-es;-e) thicket, underbrush; clump of bushes
Geck [gek] m (-en;-en) dude
geckenhaft [gek'kenhaft) adj flashy
gedacht [gə'daxt] pp of denken
Gedächtnis [gə'deçtnɪs] n (-ses;) memory; aus dem G. by heart; im G. behalten bear in mind; zum G. (genit or an acc) in memory of
Gedächt'nisfehler m lapse of memory
Gedächt'nisrede f memorial address
gedämpft [gə'dempft] adj muffled; hushed, quiet; (Licht, Stimme) subdued; (culin) stewed
Gedanke [gə'daŋkə] m (-ns;-n) thought; notion, idea; etw in Ge-

danken tun do s.th. absent-mindedly; in Gedanken sein be preoccupied; sich [dat] Gedanken machen über (acc) worry about
Gedan'kenblitz m (iron) brain wave
Gedan'kenfolge f, Gedan'kengang m train of thought
gedan'kenlos adj thoughtless; absent-minded; irresponsible
Gedan'kenpunkt m suspension point
Gedan'kenstrich m (typ) dash
Gedan'kenübertragung f telepathy
gedank'lich adj mental; intellectual
Gedärme [gə'dermə] pl intestines
Gedeck [gə'dek] n (-[e]s;-e) cover; table setting; menu
gedeihen [gə'daɪ.ən] §81 intr (SEIN) thrive; succeed || Gedeihen n (-s;) prosperity; success
Gedenk- [gədeŋk] comb.fm. memorial; commemorative
gedenken [gə'deŋkən] §66 intr (genit) think of, be mindful of; remember; mention; g. zu (inf) intend to (inf) || Gedenken n (-s;) memory
gedeucht [gə'dɔɪçt] pp of dünken
Gedicht [gə'dɪçt] n (-[e]s;-e) poem; (fig) dream
gediegen [gə'digən] adj (Gold) solid; (Silber) sterling; (Arbeit) excellent; (Kenntnisse) thorough; (Möbel) solidly made; (Charakter) sterling; (coll) very funny
gedieh [gə'di] pret of gedeihen
gediehen [gə'dɪ.ən] pp of gedeihen
Gedränge [gə'dreŋə] n (-s;-) pushing; crowd; difficulties; (fb) scrimmage
gedrängt [gə'dreŋt] adj crowded, packed; (Sprache) concise
gedroschen [gə'drɔʃən] pp of dreschen
gedrückt [gə'drykt] adj depressed
gedrungen [gə'druŋən] pp of dringen || adj compact; stocky; squat; (Sprache) concise
Geduld [gə'dult] f (-;) patience
gedulden [gə'duldən] ref wait (patiently)
geduldig [gə'duldɪç] adj patient
Geduld'spiel n puzzle
gedungen [gə'duŋən] pp of dingen
gedunsen [gə'dunzən] adj bloated
gedurft [gə'durft] pp of dürfen
geehrt [gə'ert] adj—Sehr geehrte Herren! Dear Sirs; Sehr geehrter Herr X! Dear Mr. X
geeignet [gə'aɪgnət] adj suitable, right; qualified; appropriate
Gefahr [gə'far] f (-;-en) danger; (Wagnis) risk; G. laufen zu (inf) run the risk of (ger)
gefährden [gə'ferdən] tr jeopardize
gefährlich [gə'ferlɪç] adj dangerous
gefahr'los adj safe
Gefährt [gə'fert] n (-[e]s;-e) carriage
Gefährte [gə'fertə] m (-n;-n), Gefährtin [gə'fertɪn] f (-;-nen) companion; spouse
Gefälle [gə'felə] n (-s;-) pitch; slope
gefallen [gə'falən] adj fallen; (mil) killed in action || §72 ref—sich g. in (dat) take pleasure in || intr please; das gefällt mir I like this; das lasse ich mir nicht g. I won't stand for

this || **Gefallen** *m* (-;-) favor || *n* (-s;) (**an** *dat*) pleasure (in); **j-m etw zu G. tun** do s.th. to please s.o.; **nach G.** as one pleases; at one's descretion

gefällig [gə'fɛlɪç] *adj* pleasing; obliging; kind; **j-m g. sein** do s.o. a favor; **Kaffee g.?** would you care for coffee?; **was ist g.?** what can I do for you?; **würden Sie so g. sein zu** (*inf*)? would you be so kind as to (*inf*)?

Gefäl'ligkeit *f* (-;-en) favor

gefälligst [gə'fɛlɪçst] *adv* if you please; please

gefangen [gə'faŋən] *pp of* **fangen** || *adj* captive; **g. nehmen** take prisoner || **Gefangene** §5 *mf* captive, prisoner

Gefan'genenlager *n* prison camp; (mil) prisoner-of-war camp

Gefan'gennahme *f* (-;) capture; arrest

gefan'gennehmen §116 *tr* take prisoner

Gefan'genschaft *f* (-;) captivity; imprisonment; **in G. geraten** be taken prisoner

gefan'gensetzen *tr* imprison

Gefängnis [gə'fɛŋnɪs] *n* (-ses;-se) prison, jail; imprisonment

Gefäng'nisdirektor *m* warden

Gefäng'nisstrafe *f* prison term

Gefäng'niswärter –in §6 *mf* guard

Gefäß [gə'fes] *n* (-es;-e) vessel; jar

gefaßt [gə'fast] *adj* calm, composed; **g. auf** (*acc*) ready for

Gefecht [gə'fɛçt] *n* (-[e]s;-e) fight, battle, action

Gefechts'auftrag *m* (mil) objective

Gefechts'kopf *m* warhead

Gefechts'lage *f* tactical situation

Gefechts'stand *m* command post

gefeit [gə'faɪt] *adj* (**gegen**) immune (from), proof (against)

Gefieder [gə'fidər] *n* (-s;-) plumage

gefleckt [gə'flɛkt] *adj* spotted

geflissentlich [gə'flɪsəntlɪç] *adj* intentional, willful

geflochten [gə'flɔxtən] *pp of* **flechten**

geflogen [gə'flogən] *pp of* **fliegen**

geflohen [gə'flo·ən] *pp of* **fliehen**

geflossen [gə'flɔsən] *pp of* **fließen**

Geflügel [gə'flygəl] *n* (-s;) fowl; (*Federvieh*) poultry

Geflü'gelmagen *m* gizzard

Geflunker [gə'fluŋkər] *m* (-s;) (coll) fibbing

Geflüster [gə'flystər] *n* (-s;) whisper

Gefolge [gə'fɔlgə] *n* (-s;-) retinue; **in seinem G.** in its wake

Gefolgschaft [gə'fɔlkʃaft] *f* (-;-en) allegiance; following

gefräßig [gə'fresɪç] *adj* gluttonous

Gefrä'ßigkeit *f* (-;) gluttony

Gefreite [gə'fraɪtə] §5 *m* private first class; lance corporal (Brit)

gefressen [gə'fresən] *pp of* **fressen**

Gefrieranlage [gə'friranlagə] *f* **Gefrierapparat** [gə'friraparat] *m* freezer

gefrieren [gə'frirən] §77 *intr* (SEIN) freeze

Gefrie'rer *m* (-s;-) freezer; deepfreeze

Gefrier'fach *n* freezing compartment

Gefrier'punkt *m* freezing point

Gefrier'schutz *m,* **Gefrier'schutzmittel** *n* antifreeze

gefroren [gə'frorən] *pp of* **frieren** || **Gefrorene** §5 *n* ice cream

Gefüge [gə'fygə] *n* (-s;-) structure, make-up; arrangement; texture

gefügig [gə'fygɪç] *adj* pliant, pliable

Gefühl [gə'fyl] *n* (-[e]s;-e) feeling; feel; touch; sense; sensation

gefühl'los *adj* numb; callous

gefühls-, Gefühls- [gəfyls] *comb.fm.* of the emotions; emotional; sentimental; (anat) sensory

gefühls'betont *adj* emotional

Gefühlsduselei [gə'fylsduzəlaɪ] *f* (-;) sentimentalism, mawkishness

gefühls'selig *adj* mawkish

gefühl'voll *adj* sensitive; tender-hearted || *adv* with feeling

gefunden [gə'fundən] *pp of* **finden**

gefurcht [gə'furçt] *adj* furrowed

gegangen [gə'gaŋən] *pp of* **gehen**

gegeben [gə'gebən] *pp of* **geben** || *adj* given; (*Umstände*) existing; **gegebene Methode** best approach; **zu gegebener Zeit** at the proper time

gege'benfalls *adv* if necessary

gegen ['gegən] *prep* (*acc*) towards; against; about, approximately; compared with; contrary to; in exchange for

gegen-, Gegen- *comb.fm.* anti-; counter-; contrary; opposite; back; in return

Ge'genantwort *f* rejoinder

Ge'genbeschuldigung *f* countercharge

Ge'genbild *n* counterpart

Gegend ['gegənt] *f* (-;-en) neighborhood, vicinity; region, district

gegeneinan'der *adv* against one another; towards one another

Ge'gengerade *f* back stretch

Ge'gengewicht *n* counterbalance; (am Rad) (aut) weight; **das G. halten** (*dat*) counterbalance

Ge'gengift *n* antidote

Ge'genkandidat –in §7 *mf* rival candidate

Ge'genklage *f* countercharge; counterclaim

Ge'genmittel *n* (**gegen**) remedy (for), antidote (against)

Ge'genrede *f* reply, rejoinder

Ge'gensatz *m* contrast; opposite, antithesis; (*Widerspruch*) opposition

gegensätzlich ['gegənzɛtslɪç] *adj* contrary, opposite, antithetical

Ge'genschlag *m* counterplot

ge'genseitig *adj* mutual, reciprocal

Ge'genstand *m* object, thing; subject

gegenständlich ['gegənʃtɛntlɪç] *adj* objective; (fa) representational; (log) concrete

ge'genstandslos *adj* baseless; without purpose; irrelevant; (fa) non-representational

Ge'genstoß *m* (box) counterpunch; (mil) counterthrust

Ge'genstück *n* counterpart

Ge'genteil *n* contrary, opposite; **im G.** on the contrary

ge'genteilig *adj* contrary, opposite

gegenü'ber *prep* (*dat*) opposite to; across from; with regard to; compared with

gegenü'berstellen tr (dat) place opposite to; (dat) confront with; (dat) contrast with

Gegenü'berstellung f confrontation; comparison; (auf e-r Wache) line-up

Gegenwart ['gegənvart] f (-;) present; present time; (gram) present tense

gegenwärtig ['gegənvertiç] adj present, current || adv at present; nowadays

Ge'genwehr f defense, resistance

Ge'genwind m head wind

Ge'genwirkung f (auf acc) reaction (to)

ge'genzeichnen tr countersign

Ge'genzug m countermove

geglichen [gə'gliçən] pp of gleichen

geglitten [gə'glitən] pp of gleiten

Gegner –in ['gegnər(in)] §6 mf opponent, rival || m (mil) enemy

gegnerisch ['gegnəriʃ] adj adverse; antagonistic; opposing; (mil) enemy

gegolten [gə'gəltən] pp of gelten

gegoren [gə'gorən] pp of gären

gegossen [gə'gosən] pp of gießen

gegriffen [gə'grifən] pp of greifen

Gehabe [gə'habə] n (-s;) affectation

gehaben [gə'habən] ref fare; **gehab dich nicht so!** stop putting on!; **gehab dich wohl!** farewell!

Gehackte [gə'haktə] §5 n hamburger

Gehalt [gə'halt] m (-[e]s;-e) contents; capacity; standard; **G. an** (dat) percentage of || n (-[e]s;–er) salary

Gehalts'stufe f salary bracket

Gehalts'zulage f increment, raise

gehalt'voll adj substantial; profound

Gehänge [gə'heŋə] n (-s;-) slope; pendant; festoon; (e-s Degens) belt

gehangen [gə'haŋən] pp of hängen

gehässig [gə'hesiç] adj spiteful, nasty

Gehäuse [gə'hɔɪzə] n (-s;-) case, box; housing; (e-r Schnecke) shell; (e-s Apfels) core

Gehege [gə'hegə] n (-s;-) enclosure

geheim [gə'haɪm] adj secret; **streng g.** top-secret

geheim'halten §90 tr keep secret

Geheimnis [gə'haɪmnis] n (-ses;-se) secret, mystery

geheim'nisvoll adj mysterious

Geheim'schrift f code; coded message

Geheim'tinte f invisible ink

Geheim'vorbehalt m mental reservation

Geheiß [gə'haɪs] n (-es;) bidding

gehen ['ge·ən] §82 intr (SEIN) go; walk; leave; (Teig) rise; (Maschine) work; (Uhr) go; (Ware) sell; (Wind) blow; **das geht nicht** that will not do; **das geht schon** it will be all right; **sich g. lassen** take it easy; **wieviel Zoll g. auf einen Fuß?** how many inches make a foot? || impers—**es geht mir gut** I am doing well; **es geht nichts über** (acc) there is nothing like; **es geht um...** is at stake; **wie geht es Ihnen?** how are you?

geheuer [gə'hɔɪ·ər] adj—**mir war nicht recht g. zumute** I didn't feel quite at ease; **nicht g.** spooky; suspicious; risky

Geheul [gə'hɔɪl] n (-s;) howling; loud sobbing

Gehilfe [gə'hilfə] m (-n;-n), **Gehilfin** [gə'hilfin] f (-;-nen) assistant

Gehirn [gə'hirn] n (-[e]s;-e) brains, mind; (anat) brain; **sein G. anstrengen** rack one's brain

Gehirn– comb.fm. brain; cerebral

Gehirn'erschütterung f concussion

Gehirn'schlag m (pathol) stroke

Gehirn'wäsche f brainwashing

gehoben [gə'hobən] pp of heben || adj (Stellung) high; (Stil) lofty; **gehobene Stimmung** high spirits

Gehöft [gə'hœft] n (-[e]s;-e) farm

geholfen [gə'hɔlfən] pp of helfen

Gehölz [gə'hœlts] n (-es;-e) grove; thicket

Gehör [gə'hør] n (-s;) hearing; ear

Gehör– comb.fm. of hearing; auditory

gehorchen [gə'hɔrçən] intr (dat) obey

gehören [gə'hørən] ref be proper, be right || intr (dat or zu) belong to; (in acc) go into, belong in

gehörig [gə'høriç] adj proper, due; (dat or zu) belonging to || adv properly; duly; thoroughly

Gehörn [gə'hørn] n (-s;-e) horns; **Gehörne** sets of horns

gehorsam [gə'horzam] adj obedient || adv obediently; **gehorsamst** respectfully || **Gehorsam** m (-s;) obedience

Gehor'samverweigerung f disobedience

gehren [gerən] tr (carp) miter

Gehrlade ['gerladə] f (-;-n) miter box

Gehrock ['gerɔk] m Prince Albert

Geh'rung f—**auf G., nach der G.** on the slant; **auf G. verbinden** miter

Geh'rungslade f (-;-n) miter box

Gehsteig ['ge/taɪk] m sidewalk

Gehweg ['gewek] m sidewalk; footpath

Gehwerk ['geverk] n clockwork, works

Geier ['gaɪ·ər] m (-s;-) vulture; **zum Geier!** what the devil!

Geifer ['gaɪfər] m (-s;) drivel; froth, slaver, foam; (fig) venom

geifern ['gaɪfərn] intr slaver

Geige ['gaɪgə] f (-;-n) violin, fiddle

geigen ['gaɪgən] intr play the violin

Gei'genbogen m bow, fiddlestick

Gei'genharz n rosin

Gei'ger –in §6 mf violinist

geil [gaɪl] adj lustful; in heat; (Boden) rich; (üppig) luxuriant

Geisel ['gaɪzəl] f (-;-n) hostage

Geiser ['gaɪzər] m (-s;-) geyser

Geiß [gaɪs] f (-;-en) she-goat

Geißel ['gaɪsəl] f (-;-n) scourge

geißeln ['gaɪsəln] tr scourge; (fig) castigate

Geist [gaɪst] m (-es;-er) spirit; (Gespenst) ghost; (Verstand) mind, intellect; **im Geiste** in one's imagination; in spirit

Gei'sterbeschwörung f (-;) necromancy

Gei'sterstadt f ghost town

Gei'sterstunde f witching hour

geistes– [gaɪstəs] comb.fm. spiritually; mentally, intellectually || **Geistes–** comb.fm. spiritual; mental, intellectual

gei'stesabwesend adj absent-minded

Gei'stesanlagen pl natural gift

Gei'stesarbeit f brainwork

Gei'stesarmut f dullness, stupidity

Gei'stesblitz *m* brain wave; aphorism
Gei'stesflug *m* flight of the imagination
Gei'stesfreiheit *f* intellectual freedom
Gei'stesfrucht *f* brainchild
Gei'stesgegenwart *f* presence of mind
gei'stesgegenwärtig *adj* mentally alert
geistesgestört ['gaɪstəsgəʃtørt] *adj* mentally disturbed
Gei'steshaltung *f* mentality
gei'steskrank *adj* insane
gei'stesschwach *adj* feeble-minded
Gei'stesstörung *f* mental disorder
Gei'stes- und Natur'wissenschaften *pl* arts and sciences
Gei'stesverfassung *f* frame of mind
gei'stesverwandt *adj* (mit) spiritually akin (to); (mit) congenial (with)
Gei'stesverwirrung *f* derangement
Gei'steswissenschaften *pl* humanities
gei'steswissenschaftlich *adj* humanistic
Gei'steszustand *m* state of mind
geistig ['gaɪstɪç] *adj* mental, intellectual; spiritual
geist'lich *adj* spiritual; (*Orden*) religious; (*kirchlich*) sacred, ecclesiastical; **der geistliche Stand** holy orders; the clergy || **Geistliche §5** *m* clergyman
Geist'lichkeit *f* (-;) clergy
geist'los *adj* spiritless; dull; stupid
geist'reich *adj* witty; ingenious
Geiz [gaɪts] *m* (-es;) stinginess; avarice
geizen ['gaɪtsən] *intr*—g. mit be sparing with; nicht g. mit show freely
Geiz'hals *m* (coll) tightwad
geizig ['gaɪtsɪç] *adj* stingy, miserly
Geiz'kragen *m* (coll) tightwad
Gejammer [gə'jamər] *n* (-s;) wailing
gekannt [gə'kant] *pp* of kennen
Geklapper [gə'klapər] *n* (-s;) rattling
Geklatsche [gə'klatʃə] *n* (-s;) clapping; gossiping
Geklirr [gə'klɪr] *n* (-[e]s;) rattling
geklommen [gə'klɔmən] *pp* of klimmen
geklungen [gə'kluŋən] *pp* of klingen
gekniffen [gə'knɪfən] *pp* of kneifen
gekonnt [gə'kɔnt] *pp* of können
Gekreisch [gə'kraɪʃ] *n* (-es;) screaming; screeching
Gekritzel [gə'krɪtsəl] *n* (-s;) scribbling
gekrochen [gə'krɔxən] *pp* of kriechen
Gekröse [gə'krøzə] *n* (-s;) tripe
gekünstelt [gə'kynstəlt] *adj* affected
Gelächter [gə'leçtər] *n* (-s;) laughter
Gelage [gə'lagə] *n* (-s;) carousing
Gelände [gə'lendə] *n* (-s;-) terrain; site, lot; (educ) campus; (golf) fairway
Gelän'delauf *m* crosscountry running
Gelän'depunkt *m* landmark
Geländer [gə'lendər] *n* (-s;-) railing; guardrail; banister; parapet
gelang [gə'laŋ] *pret* of gelingen
gelangen [gə'laŋən] *intr* (SEIN) (an *acc*, in *acc*, zu) attain, reach
gelassen [gə'lasən] *pp* of lassen || *adj* composed, calm
Gelatine [ʒɛla'tinə] *f* (-;) gelatin
geläufig [gə'lɔɪfɪç] *adj* fluent; (*gemein*) common; (*Zunge*) glib

gelaunt [gə'launt] *adj*—gut gelaunt in good humor; zu etw g. sein be in the mood for s.th.
Geläut [gə'lɔɪt] *n* (-es;), **Geläute** [gə'lɔɪtə] *n* (-s;) ringing; chimes
gelb [gelp] *adj* yellow || **Gelb** *n* (-s;) yellow
gelb'lich *adj* yellowish
Gelb'sucht *f* jaundice
Geld [gelt] *n* (-[e]s;) money; bares G. cash
Geld- *comb.fm.* money, financial
-geld *n comb.fm.* money; fee(s); tax, toll; allowance
Geld'anlage *f* investment
Geld'anleihe *f* loan
Geld'anweisung *f* money order; draft
Geld'ausgabe *f* expense; expenditure
Geld'beutel *m* pocketbook
Geld'bewilligung *f* (parl) appropriation
Geld'buße *f* fine
Geld'einlage *f* deposit
Geld'einwurf *m* coin slot
Geld'entwertung *f* inflation
Geld'erwerb *m* moneymaking
Geld'geber *m* investor; mortgagee
Geld'gier *f* avarice
Geld'mittel *pl* funds, resources
Geld'onkel *m* sugar daddy
Geld'schein *m* bank note, bill
Geld'schrank *m* safe
Geld'schublade *f* till (*of cash register*)
Geld'sendung *f* remittance
Geld'sorte *f* (fin) denomination
Geld'spende *f* contribution, donation
Geld'strafe *f* fine
Geld'stück *n* coin
Geld'überhang *m* surplus (of money)
Geld'währung *f* currency; monetary standard
Geld'wechsel *m* money exchange
Geld'wesen *n* financial system, finance
Gelee [ʒɛ'le] *m & n* (-s;-s) jelly
gelegen [gə'legən] *pp* of liegen || *adj* located; convenient; opportune; du kommst mir gerade g. you're just the person I wanted to see; es kommt mir gerade gelegen that suits me just fine; mir ist daran g. zu (*inf*) I'm anxious to (*inf*); was ist daran g.? what of it?
Gele'genheit *f* (-;-en) occasion; opportunity, chance; (com) bargain
Gelegenheits- *comb.fm.* occasional
Gele'genheitsarbeit *f* odd job
Gele'genheitskauf *m* good bargain
gele'gentlich *adj* occasional; casual; chance || *adv* occasionally || *prep* (*genit*) on the occasion of
gelehrig [gə'lerɪç] *adj* teachable; intelligent
gelehrsam [gə'lerzam] *adj* erudite
gelehrt [gə'lert] *adj* learned, erudite || **Gelehrte §5** *mf* scholar
Geleise [gə'laɪzə] *n* (-s;-) rut; (rr) track; totes G. blind alley, deadlock
Geleit [gə'laɪt] *n* (-[e]s;) escort; freies (or sicheres) G. safe-conduct; j-m das G. geben escort s.o., accompany s.o.; zum G. forward
geleiten [gə'laɪtən] *tr* escort, accompany; j-n zur Tür g. see s.o. to the door

Geleit′zug m convoy
Geleit′zugsicherung f convoy escort
Gelenk [gə′lɛŋk] n (-[e]s;-e) joint
Gelenk′entzündung f arthritis
gelenkig [gə′lɛŋkɪç] adj jointed; flexible; agile
gelernt [gə′lɛrnt] adj skilled
Gelichter [gə′lɪçtər] n (-s;) riffraff
Geliebte [gə′liptə] §6 mf beloved, sweetheart
geliehen [gə′li·ən] pp of **leihen**
gelieren [ʒɛ′lirən] intr jell, gel
gelinde [gə′lɪndə] adj soft; gentle, mild ‖ adv gently, mildly; **g. gesagt** to put it mildly
gelingen [gə′lɪŋən] §142 intr (SEIN) succeed ‖ impers (SEIN)—**es gelingt mir** I succeed ‖ **Gelingen** n (-s;) success
gelitten [gə′lɪtən] pp of **leiden**
gell [gɛl] adj shrill ‖ interj say!
gellen [′gɛlən] intr ring out; yell
gel′lend adj shrill, piercing
geloben [gə′lobən] tr solemnly promise, vow; **take the vow of** ‖ **ref—sich** [dat] **g. vow** to oneself
gelogen [gə′logən] pp of **lügen**
gelt [gɛlt] interj say!
gelten [′gɛltən] §83 tr **be worth**; **wenig g.** mean little ‖ intr be valid; (*Münze*) be legal tender; (*Gesetz*) be in force; (*Grund*) hold true; (*Regel*) apply; (*Mittel*) be allowable; (*beim Spiel*) count; **g. als** or **für** have the force of; be ranked as; pass for, be considered; **g. lassen** acknowledge as correct; **j—m g. be aimed at s.o.** ‖ impers—**es gilt** (*acc*) be at stake; be a matter of; be worth (*s.th.*); **es gilt mir gleich, ob** it's all the same to me whether; **es gilt zu** (*inf*) it is necessary to (*inf*); **jetzt gilt's!** here goes!
Gel′tung f (-;) validity; value, importance; **zur G. bringen** make the most of; **zur G. kommen** show off well
Gel′tungsbedürfnis n need for recognition
Gelübde [gə′lypdə] n (-s;-) vow
gelungen [gə′luŋən] pp of **gelingen** ‖ adj successful; (*Wendung*) well-turned; funny
Gelüst [gə′lyst] n (-[e]s;-e) desire
gelüsten [gə′lystən] impers—**es gelüstet mich nach** I could go for
gemach [gə′max] adv slowly, by degrees ‖ **Gemach** n (-[e]s;-̈er) room; apartment; chamber
gemächlich [gə′mɛçlɪç] adj leisurely; comfortable
Gemahl [gə′mal] m (-[e]s;-e) husband
Gemahlin [gə′malɪn] f (-;-nen) wife
Gemälde [gə′mɛldə] n (-s;-) painting
gemäß [gə′mes] prep (*dat*) according to
gemäßigt [gə′mesɪçt] adj moderate
gemein [gə′main] adj common; mean, vile; **sich g. machen mit** associate with ‖ **Gemeine** §5 m (mil) private
Gemeinde [gə′maində] f (-;-n) community; municipality; (eccl) parish
Gemein′deabgaben pl local taxes
Gemein′deanleihen pl municipal bonds

Gemein′dehaus n town hall
gemein′frei adj in the public domain
gemein′gefährlich adj constituting a public danger, dangerous
gemein′gültig adj generally accepted
Gemein′heit f (-;-en) meanness; dirty trick; vulgarity
gemein′hin adv commonly, usually
Gemein′kosten pl overhead
Gemein′nutz m public interest
gemein′nützig adj non-profit
Gemein′platz m platitude
gemeinsam [gə′mainzam] adj common, joint; mutual
Gemein′schaft f (-;-en) community; close association
gemein′schaftlich adj common, joint; mutual
Gemein′schaftsanschluß m (telp) party line
Gemein′schaftsarbeit f teamwork
Gemein′schaftsgeist m esprit de corps
Gemein′sinn m public spirit
gemein′verständlich adj popular; **g. darstellen** popularize
Gemein′wesen n community
Gemein′wohl n commonweal
Gemenge [gə′mɛŋə] n (-s;-) mixture; (*Kampfgewühl*) scuffle, melee
gemessen [gə′mɛsən] pp of **messen** ‖ adj deliberate; precise; dignified; **g. an** (*dat*) compared with
Gemetzel [gə′mɛtsəl] n (-s;-) massacre
gemieden [gə′midən] pp of **meiden**
Gemisch [gə′mɪʃ] n (-es;-e) mixture
Gemischt′warenhandlung f general store
Gemme [′gɛmə] f (-;-n) gem
gemocht [gə′məxt] pp of **mögen**
gemolken [gə′məlkən] pp of **melken**
Gemse [′gɛmzə] f (-;-n) chamois
Gemunkel [gə′muŋkəl] n (-s;-) gossip, whispering
Gemurmel [gə′murməl] n (-s;) murmur
Gemüse [gə′myzə] n (-s;-) vegetable; vegetables
Gemü′sebau m (-[e]s;) vegetable gardening
Gemü′sekonserven pl canned vegetables
gemüßigt [gə′mysɪçt] adj—**sich g. fühlen** feel compelled
gemußt [gə′must] pp of **müssen**
Gemüt [gə′myt] n (-[e]s;-er) mind; disposition; person, soul; warmth of feeling; **j—m etw zu Gemüte führen** bring s.th. home to s.o.
gemütlich [gə′mytlɪç] adj good-natured, easy-going; (*Wohnung*) cosy
Gemüt′lichkeit f (-;) easy-going nature; cosiness
Gemüts′art f disposition, nature
Gemüts′bewegung f emotion
gemüts′krank adj melancholy
Gemüts′mensch m warm-hearted person
Gemüts′ruhe f—**in (aller) G.** in peace and quiet
Gemüts′stimmung f mood
Gemüts′verfassung f state of mind
Gemüts′zustand m frame of mind

gemüt'voll *adj* emotional
gen [gɛn] *prep (acc)* (poet) towards ‖
Gen [gen] *n* (-s;-e) (biol) gene
genannt [gə'nant] *pp* of **nennen**
genau [gə'nau] *adj* exact; fussy
genau'genommen *adv* strictly speaking
Genau'igkeit *f* (-;) exactness, accuracy; meticulousness
Gendarm [ʒã'darm] *m* (-en;-en) policeman
Gendarme·rie [ʒãdarmə'ri] *f* (-;-rien ['ri·ən]) rural police; rural police station
Genealo·gie [genɛ·alɔ'gi] *f* (-;-gien ['gi·ən]) genealogy
genehm [gə'nem] *adj* agreeable; acceptable; *(dat)* convenient (for)
genehmigen [gə'nemɪgən] *tr* grant; approve; **sich** [*dat*] **etw g.** (coll) treat oneself to s.th.; **genehmigt O.K.**
Geneh'migung *f* (-;-en) grant; approval; permission; permit
geneigt [gə'naɪkt] *adj* sloping; (**zu**) inclined (to); *(dat)* well-disposed (towards)
Geneigt'heit *f* inclination; good will
General [genɛ'ral] *m* (-[e]s;-e & -e) general
General'feldmarschall *m* field marshal
General'inspekteur *m* chief of the joint chiefs of staff
Generalität [generali'tet] *f* (-;) body of generals
General'konsul *m* consul general
General'leutnant *m* lieutenant general; (aer) air marshal
General'major *m* major general
General'nenner *m* common denominator
General'probe *f* dress rehearsal
General'stabskarte *f* strategic map
General'vollmacht *f* full power of attorney
Generation [genɛra'tsjon] *f* (-;-en) generation
generell [genɛ'rel] *adj* general, blanket
genesen [gə'nezən] §84 *intr* (SEIN) convalesce; (**von**) recover (from)
Gene'sung *f* (-;-en) convalescence
Gene'sungsheim *n* convalescent home
genetisch [ge'netɪʃ] *adj* genetic
Genf [genf] *n* (-s;) Geneva
Gen'forscher -in §6 *mf* genetic engineer
Gen'forschung *f* (-;) genetic engineering
genial [ge'njal] *adj* brilliant, gifted
Genick [gə'nɪk] *n* (-s;-e) nape of the neck
Genick'bruch *m* broken neck
Genick'schlag *m* (box) rabbit punch
Genie [ʒe'ni] *n* (-s;-s) (man of) genius
genieren [ge'nirən] *tr* bother; embarrass ‖ *ref* feel embarrassed
genießbar [gə'nisbar] *adj* edible; drinkable; (fig) agreeable
genießen [gə'nisən] §76 *tr* enjoy; eat; drink
Genie'streich *m* stroke of genius
Genitalien [geni'taljən] *pl* genitals
Geni·tiv ['genitif] *m* (-s;-tive ['tivə]) genitive
genommen [gə'nɔmən] *pp* of **nehmen**

genoß [gə'nɔs] *pret* of **genießen**
Genosse [gə'nɔsə] *m* (-n;-n) companion, buddy; (pol) comrade
-genosse *m comb.fm.* fellow-, -mate
Genos'senschaft *f* (-;-en) association; coöperative
Genossin [gə'nɔsɪn] *f* (-;-nen) companion, buddy; (pol) comrade
genug [gə'nuk] *invar adj & adv* enough
Genüge [gə'nygə] *f—j—m* **G. tun** give s.o. satisfaction; **zur G.** enough; only too well
genügen [gə'nygən] *intr* suffice, do ‖ *ref—sich* [*dat*] **g. lassen an** *(dat)* be content with
genü'gend *adj* sufficient
genügsam [gə'nykzam] *adj* easily satisfied; frugal
genug'tun §154 *intr* *(dat)* satisfy
Genugtuung [gə'nuktu·uŋ] *f* (-;) satisfaction
Ge·nuß [gə'nus] *m* (-nusses;-nüsse) enjoyment; pleasure; *(Nutznießung)* use; *(von Speisen)* consumption
Genuß'mittel *n* semi-luxury *(as coffee, tobacco, etc.)*
genuß'reich *adj* thoroughly enjoyable
genuß'süchtig *adj* pleasure-seeking
Geographie [ge·ɔgra'fi] *f* (-;) geography
geographisch [ge·ɔ'grafɪʃ] *adj* geographical
Geologe [ge·ɔ'logə] *m* (-n;-n) geologist
Geologie [ge·ɔlɔ'gi] *f* (-;) geology
Geometer [ge·ɔ'metər] *m* (-s;-) surveyor
Geometrie [ge·ɔme'tri] *f* (-;) geometry
Geophysik [ge·ɔfy'zik] *f* (-;) geophysics
Geopolitik [ge·ɔpɔli'tik] *f* (-;) geopolitics
Georgine [ge·ɔr'ginə] *f* (-;-n) dahlia
Gepäck [gə'pek] *n* (-[e]s;) luggage
Gepäck'abfertigung *f* luggage check-in; luggage counter
Gepäck'ablage *f* luggage rack
Gepäck'anhänger *m* tag; luggage trailer
Gepäck'aufbewahrung *f* baggage room
Gepäck'netz *n* baggage rack *(net type)*
Gepäck'raum *m* luggage compartment
Gepäck'schein *m* luggage check
Gepäck'träger *m* porter; (aut) roof rack
Gepäck'wagen *m* (rr) baggage car
gepanzert [gə'pantsərt] *adj* armored
gepfeffert [gə'pfefərt] *adj* peppered; *(Worte)* sharp; *(Preis)* exorbitant
Gepfeife [gə'pfaɪfə] *n* (-s;) whistling
gepfiffen [gə'pfɪfən] *pp* of **pfeifen**
gepflogen [gə'pflogən] *pp* of **pflegen**
Gepflo'genheit *f* (-;-en) custom, practice
Geplänkel [gə'pleŋkəl] *n* (-s;) skirmish; (fig) exchange of words
Geplapper [gə'plapər] *n* (-s;) jabber
Geplärr [gə'pler] *n* (-s;) bawling
Geplauder [gə'plaudər] *n* (-s;) small talk, chat
Gepolter [gə'pɔltər] *n* (-s;) rumbling
Gepräge [gə'pregə] *n* (-s;) impression; stamp, character
Gepränge [gə'preŋə] *n* (-s;) pomp

gepriesen [gə'prizən] *pp* of **preisen**
gequollen [gə'kvɔlən] *pp* of **quellen**
gerade [gə'radə] *adj* straight; even; direct; (*Haltung*) erect; (*aufrichtig*) straightforward || *adv* straight; exactly; just; just now || **Gerade** *f* (−**n**; −**n**) straight line; straightaway; (box) straight; **rechte G.** straight right
gerade(n)wegs [gə'radə(n)veks] *adv* immediately, straightaway
geradezu' *adv* downright
Geranie [ge'ranjə] *f* (−;−**n**) geranium
gerannt [gə'rant] *pp* of **rennen**
Gerassel [gə'rasəl] *n* (−**s**;) clanking
Gerät [gə'ret] *n* (−[e]**s**;−**e**) device, instrument; tool; (rad, telv) set
geraten [gə'ratən] *pp* of **raten** || *adj* successful; (*ratsam*) advisable || §63 *intr* (SEIN) (*gut, schlecht, usw.*) turn out; **außer sich g.** be beside oneself; **g. an** (*acc*) come by; **g. auf** (*acc*) get into; get on to; **g. hinter** (*acc*) get behind; find out about; **g. in** (*acc*) get into, fall into; **g. nach** take after; **g. über** (*acc*) come across; **in Bewegung g.** begin to move; **in Brand g.** catch fire; **ins Schleudern g.** begin to skid; **ins Stocken g.** come to a standstill
Gerä'teschuppen *m* tool shed
Geratewohl [gə'ratəvol] *n* (−**s**;)—**aufs G.** at random
geraum [gə'raum] *adj* considerable
geräumig [gə'rɔɪmɪç] *adj* spacious
Geräusch [gə'rɔɪʃ] *n* (−[e]**s**;−**e**) noise
gerben ['gerbən] *tr* tan
Gerberei [gerbə'raɪ] *f* (−;−**en**) tannery
gerecht [gə'reçt] *adj* just, fair; justified; **g. werden** (*dat*) do justice to
Gerech'tigkeit *f* (−;) justice; fairness
Gerede [gə'redə] *n* (−**s**;) talk; hearsay
gereichen [gə'raɪçən] *intr*—**es gereicht ihm zur Ehre** it does him justice; **es gereicht ihm zum Vorteil** it is to his advantage; **es gereicht mir zur Freude** it gives me pleasure
gereizt [gə'raɪtst] *adj* irritable; irritated
gereuen [gə'rɔɪ-ən] *tr* cause (*s.o.*) regret || *ref*—**sich keine Mühe g. lassen** spare no trouble || *impers*—**es gereut mich** I regret
Geriatrie [geri·a'tri] *f* (−;) geriatrics
Gericht [gə'rɪçt] *n* (−[e]**s**;−**e**) court; courthouse; judgment; (culin) dish; **das Jüngste G.** the Last Judgment
gericht'lich *adj* legal, judicial, court
Gerichtsbarkeit [gə'rɪçtsbarkaɪt] *f* (−;) jurisdiction
Gerichts'bote *m* (jur) bailiff
Gerichts'hof *m* law court; **Oberster G.** Supreme Court
Gerichts'medizin *f* forensic medicine
Gerichts'saal *m* courtroom
Gerichts'schreiber **−in** §6 *mf* (jur) clerk
Gerichts'stand *m* (jur) venue
Gerichts'verhandlung *f* hearing; trial
Gerichts'vollzieher *m* (jur) marshal
Gerichts'wesen *n* judicial system
gerieben [gə'ribən] *pp* of **reiben** || *adj* cunning, smart
Geriesel [gə'rizəl] *n* (−**s**;) purling
gering [gə'rɪŋ] *adj* slight, trifling;

small; (*niedrig*) low; (*ärmlich*) poor; (*minderwertig*) inferior; **nicht im geringsten** not in the least
gering'achten *tr* think little of
gering'fügig *adj* insignificant
gering'schätzen *tr* look down on
Gering'schätzung *f* contempt, disdain
gerinnen [gə'rɪnən] §121 *intr* coagulate, clot; (*Milch*) curdle
Gerinnsel [gə'rɪnzəl] *n* (−**s**;−) clot
Gerippe [gə'rɪpə] *n* (−**s**;−) skeleton; (*Gerüst*) framework
gerippt [gə'rɪpt] *adj* ribbed; (*Säule*) fluted; (*Stoff*) corded
gerissen [gə'rɪsən] *pp* of **reißen** || *adj* sly
geritten [gə'rɪtən] *pp* of **reiten**
gern(e) ['gern(ə)] *adv* gladly; **g. haben** or **mögen** like; **ich rauche g.** I like to smoke
gerochen [gə'rɔxən] *pp* of **riechen**
Geröll [gə'rœl] *n* (−**s**;) pebbles
geronnen [gə'rɔnən] *pp* of **gerinnen** & **rinnen**
Gerste ['gerstə] *f* (−;−**n**) barley
Ger'stenkorn *n* grain of barley; (pathol) sty
Gerte ['gertə] *f* (−;−**n**) switch, rod
Geruch [gə'rux] *m* (−[e]**s**;⁻**e**) smell
geruch'los *adj* odorless
Gerücht [gə'ryçt] *m* (−[e]**s**;−**e**) rumor
geruhen [gə'ru-ən] *intr* deign
geruhsam [gə'ruzam] *adj* quiet; relaxed
Gerümpel [gə'rympəl] *n* (−**s**;) junk
gerungen [gə'ruŋən] *pp* of **ringen**
Gerüst [gə'ryst] *n* (−**s**;−**e**) scaffold; (*Tragewerk*) frame; (fig) outline
Ges [ges] *n* (−;−) (mus) G flat
gesamt [gə'zamt] *adj* entire, total
gesamt−, Gesamt− *comb.fm.* total, overall; all−; joint; collective
gesandt [gə'zant] *pp* of **senden**
Gesand'te §5 *mf* envoy
Gesandt'schaft *f* (−;−**en**) legation
Gesang [gə'zaŋ] *m* (−[e]**s**;⁻**e**) singing; song; (lit) canto
Gesang'verein *m* glee club
Gesäß [gə'zes] *n* (−**es**;−**e**) buttocks; (coll) behind
Geschäft [gə'ʃeft] *n* (−[e]**s**;−**e**) business; deal, bargain; shop, store
Geschäftemacherei [gə'ʃeftəmaxəraɪ] *f* (−;) commercialism
geschäftig [gə'ʃetɪç] *adj* busy
Geschäf'tigkeit *f* (−;) hustle, bustle
geschäft'lich *adj* business || *adv* on business
Geschäfts'abschluß *m* contract; deal
Geschäfts'aufsicht *f* receivership
Geschäfts'bedingungen *pl* terms
geschäfts'führend *adj* managing; executive; **geschäftsführende Regierung** caretaker government
Geschäfts'führer **−in** §6 *mf* manager
Geschäfts'haus *n* firm; office building
Geschäfts'inhaber **−in** §6 *mf* proprietor
geschäfts'kundig *adj* with business experience
Geschäfts'lokal *n* business premises; (*Laden*) shop; (*Büro*) office
Geschäfts'mann *m* (−[e]**s**;−**leute**) businessman

geschäfts'mäßig *adj* business-like
Geschäfts'ordnung *f* rules of procedure; zur G.! point of order!
Geschäfts'reise *f* business trip
Geschäfts'schluß *m* closing time
Geschäfts'stelle *f* office; branch
Geschäfts'träger *m* agent, representative; (pol) chargé d'affaires
geschäfts'tüchtig *adj* sharp
Geschäfts'verbindung *f* business connections
Geschäfts'verkehr *m* business transactions
Geschäfts'viertel *n* business district
Geschäfts'wert *m* (com) good will
Geschäfts'zweig *m* line of business
geschah [gə'ʃɑ] *pret* of geschehen
geschehen [gə'ʃe·ən] §138 *intr* (SEIN) happen; take place; be done; das geschieht dir recht! serves you right! || Geschehen *n* (-s;) events
Geschehnis [gə'ʃenɪs] *n* (-ses;-se) event
gescheit [gə'ʃaɪt] *adj* clever; bright; sensible; er ist wohl nicht ganz g. he's not all there
Geschenk [gə'ʃɛŋk] *n* (-[e]s;-e) gift
Geschichte [gə'ʃɪçtə] *f* (-;-n) story; history; (coll) affair, thing
geschicht'lich *adj* historical
Geschichts'forscher -in §6 *mf*, Geschichts'schreiber -in §6 *mf* historian
Geschick [gə'ʃɪk] *n* (-[e]s;-e) fate, destiny; dexterity, skill
Geschick'lichkeit *f* (-;) skillfulness
geschickt [gə'ʃɪkt] *adj* skillful
geschieden [gə'ʃidən] *pp* of scheiden
geschienen [gə'ʃinən] *pp* of scheinen
Geschirr [gə'ʃɪr] *n* (-[e]s;-e) dishes; china; pot; (e-s Pferdes) harness
Geschirr'schrank *m* kitchen cabinet
Geschirrspülmaschine [gə'ʃɪrʃpylmaʃinə] *f* dishwasher
Geschirr'tuch *n* dishtowel
geschissen [gə'ʃɪsən] *pp* of scheißen
Geschlecht [gə'ʃlɛçt] *n* (-[e]s;-er) sex; race; family, line; generation; (gram) gender
geschlecht'lich *adj* sexual
Geschlechts'krankheit *f* venereal disease
Geschlechts'teile *pl* genitals
Geschlechts'trieb *m* sexual instinct
Geschlechts'verkehr *m* intercourse
Geschlechts'wort *n* (-[e]s;-̈) (gram) article
geschlichen [gə'ʃlɪçən] *pp* of schleichen
geschliffen [gə'ʃlɪfən] *pp* of schleifen || *adj* (Glas) cut; (fig) polished
geschlissen [gə'ʃlɪsən] *pp* of schleißen
geschlossen [gə'ʃlɔsən] *pp* of schließen || *adj* closed; enclosed; (Front) united; (Gesellschaft) private; (ling) close; (telv) closed-circuit || *adv* unanimously; g. hinter j-m stehen be solidly behind s.o.
geschlungen [gə'ʃluŋən] *pp* of schlingen
Geschmack [gə'ʃmak] *m* (-s;-̈e & -̈er) taste
Geschmacks'richtung *f* vogue

geschmeidig [ge'ʃmaɪdɪç] *adj* pliant; flexible; lithe; (Haar) manageable
Geschmeiß [gə'ʃmaɪs] *n* (-es;) vermin; rabble
geschmissen [gə'ʃmɪsən] *pp* of schmeißen
geschmolzen [gə'ʃmɔltsən] *pp* of schmelzen
Geschnatter [gə'ʃnatər] *n* (-s;) cackle
geschniegelt [gə'ʃnigəlt] *adj* spruce
geschnitten [gə'ʃnɪtən] *pp* of schneiden
geschnoben [gə'ʃnobən] *pp* of schnauben
geschoben [gə'ʃobən] *pp* of schieben
gescholten [gə'ʃɔltən] *pp* of schelten
Geschöpf [gə'ʃœpf] *n* (-[e]s;-e) creature
geschoren [gə'ʃorən] *pp* of scheren
Ge-schoß [gə'ʃɔs] *n* (-schosses; -schosse) shot; missile; shell; floor, story
Geschoß'bahn *f* trajectory
geschossen [gə'ʃɔsən] *pp* of schießen
geschraubt [gə'ʃraubt] *adj* affected; (Stil) stilted
Geschrei [gə'ʃraɪ] *n* (-[e]s;-e) shouting
Geschreibsel [gə'ʃraɪpsəl] *n* (-s;) scribbling, scrawl
geschrieben [gə'ʃribən] *pp* of schreiben
geschrieen [gə'ʃri·ən] *pp* of schreien
geschritten [gə'ʃrɪtən] *pp* of schreiten
geschunden [gə'ʃundən] *pp* of schinden
Geschütz [gə'ʃyts] *n* (-es;-e) gun
Geschütz'bedienung *f* gun crew
Geschütz'legierung *f* gun metal
Geschütz'stand *m* gun emplacement
Geschwader [gə'ʃvadər] *n* (-s;-) (aer) group (consisting of 27 aircraft); (nav) squadron
Geschwätz [gə'ʃvɛts] *n* (-es;) chatter
geschweige [gə'ʃvaɪgə]—g. denn let alone, much less
geschwiegen [gə'ʃvigən] *pp* of schweigen
geschwind [gə'ʃvɪnt] *adj* quick
Geschwin'digkeit *f* (-;-en) speed; velocity; mit der G. von at the rate of
Geschwin'digkeitsbegrenzung *f* speed limit
Geschwin'digkeitsmesser *m* speedometer
Geschwind'schritt *m* (mil) double time
Geschwister [gə'ʃvɪstər] *pl* brother and sister, brothers, sisters, brothers and sisters; siblings
geschwollen [gə'ʃvolən] *pp* of schwellen || *adj* turgid
geschwommen [gə'ʃvomən] *pp* of schwimmen
geschworen [gə'ʃvorən] *pp* of schwören || Geschworene §5 *mf* juror; die Geschworenen the jury
Geschwo'renengericht *n* jury
Geschwulst [gə'ʃvulst] *f* (-;-̈e) swelling; tumor
geschwunden [gə'ʃvundən] *pp* of schwinden
geschwungen [gə'ʃvuŋən] *pp* of schwingen
Geschwür [gə'ʃvyr] *n* (-s;-e) ulcer

Geselle [gə'zɛlə] *m* (−n;−n) journeyman; companion; lad, fellow

gesellen [gə'zɛlən] *ref*—**sich zu j−m g.** join s.o.

gesellig [gə'zɛlɪç] *adj* gregarious, sociable

Gesell'schaft *f* (−;−en) society; company; (pej) bunch; (com) company; **j−m G. leisten** keep s.o. company

Gesell'schafter −in §6 *mf* companion; shareholder; (com) partner

gesell'schaftlich *adj* social

Gesell'schaftsspiel *n* party game

Gesell'schaftswissenschaft *f* social science; sociology

gesessen [gə'zɛsən] *pp* of **sitzen**

Gesetz [gə'zɛts] *n* (−es;−e) law

Gesetz'buch *n* legal code

Gesetz'entwurf *m* (parl) bill

Gesetzes− [gəzɛtsəs] *comb.fm.* legal, of law, of the law

Geset'zesantrag *m*, **Geset'zesvorlage** *f* (parl) bill

gesetz'gebend *adj* legislative

Gesetz'geber −in §6 *mf* legislator

Gesetz'gebung *f* (−;) legislation

gesetz'lich *adj* legal

gesetz'los *adj* lawless

gesetz'mäßig *adj* legal; legitimate

Gesetz'sammlung *f* code of laws

gesetzt [gə'zɛtst] *adj* sedate; (*Alter*) mature; **g. den Fall, daß** assuming that ‖ *adv* in a dignified manner

gesetz'widrig *adj* illegal, unlawful

Gesicht [gə'zɪçt] *n* (−[e]s;−er) face; sight; eyesight; (*Aussehen*) look

Gesichts'farbe *f* complexion

Gesichts'kreis *m* horizon; outlook

Gesichts'punkt *m* point of view, angle

Gesichts'spannung *f* face lift

Gesichts'zug *m* feature

Gesims [gə'zɪms] *n* (−es;−e) molding

Gesindel [gə'zɪndəl] *n* (−s;) rabble; **lichtscheues G.** shady characters

gesinnt [gə'zɪnt] *adj* disposed; −minded

Gesinnung [gə'zɪnʊŋ] *f* (−;−en) mind; character; convictions

gesin'nungslos *adj* without definite convictions

gesin'nungsmäßig *adv* according to one's convictions

gesin'nungstreu, gesin'nungstüchtig *adj* staunch

gesittet [gə'zɪtət] *adj* polite; civilized

gesoffen [gə'zɔfən] *pp* of **saufen**

gesogen [gə'zogən] *pp* of **saugen**

gesonnen [gə'zɔnən] *pp* of **sinnen** ‖ *adj*—**g. sein zu** (*inf*) have a mind to (*inf*), be inclined to (*inf*)

gesotten [gə'zɔtən] *pp* of **sieden**

Gespann [gə'ʃpan] *n* (−[e]s;−e) team; pair, combination

gespannt [gə'ʃpant] *adj* stretched; tense; (*Aufmerksamkeit*) close; (*Beziehungen*) strained; **ich bin g.** (coll) I wonder, I am anxious to know

Gespenst [gə'ʃpɛnst] *n* (−[e]s;−er) ghost, specter

gespen'sterhaft *adj* ghostly; spooky

gespenstisch [gə'ʃpɛnstɪʃ] *adj* ghostly

gespie(e)n [gə'ʃpi(ə)n] *pp* of **speien**

Gespiele [gə'ʃpilə] *m* (−n;−n), **Gespielin** [gə'ʃpilɪn] *f* (−;−nen) playmate

Gespinst [gə'ʃpɪnst] *n* (−es;−e) yarn; (*Gewebe*) web

gesponnen [gə'ʃpɔnən] *pp* of **spinnen**

Gespött [gə'ʃpœt] *n* (−[e]s;) ridicule; laughing stock

Gespräch [gə'ʃprɛç] *n* (−[e]s;−e) conversation; (telp) call; **Gespräche** (pol) talks; **G. mit Voranmeldung** person-to-person call

gesprächig [gə'ʃprɛçɪç] *adj* talkative

gespreizt [gə'ʃpraɪtst] *adj* outspread; affected ‖ *adv*—**g. tun** act big

gesprenkelt [gə'ʃprɛŋkəlt] *adj* spotted

gesprochen [gə'ʃprɔçən] *pp* of **sprechen**

gesprossen [gə'ʃprɔsən] *pp* of **sprießen**

gesprungen [gə'ʃprʊŋən] *pp* of **springen**

Gestade [gə'ʃtadə] *n* (−s;−) (river) bank; (sea)shore

Gestalt [gə'ʃtalt] *f* (−;−en) shape; figure; (*Wuchs*) stature

gestalten [gə'ʃtaltən] *tr* shape; form; arrange ‖ *ref* take shape; turn out

Gestal'tung *f* (−;−en) formation; development; arrangement; design

gestanden [gə'ʃtandən] *pp* of **stehen**

geständig [gə'ʃtɛndɪç] *adj*—**g. sein** admit one's guilt

Geständnis [gə'ʃtɛntnɪs] *n* (−ses;−se) confession, admission

Gestank [gə'ʃtaŋk] *m* (−[e]s;) stench

Gestapo [gə'ʃtapo] *f* (−;) (Geheime Staatspolizei) secret state police

gestatten [gə'ʃtatən] *tr* permit, allow

Geste ['gɛstə] *f* (−;−n) gesture

gestehen [gə'ʃte·ən] §146 *tr* admit

Gestein [gə'ʃtaɪn] *n* (−[e]s;−e) rock

Gestell [gə'ʃtɛl] *n* (−[e]s;−e) frame; rack; mounting; (coll) beanpole

Gestel'lungsbefehl *m* (mil) induction orders

gestern ['gɛstərn] *adv* yesterday; **g. abend** last evening, last night

gestiefelt [gə'ʃtifəlt] *adj* in boots

gestiegen [gə'ʃtigən] *pp* of **steigen**

gestikulieren [gɛstiku'lirən] *intr* gesticulate

Gestirn [gə'ʃtɪrn] *n* (−[e]s;−e) star; (*Sternbild*) constellation

gestirnt [gə'ʃtɪrnt] *adj* starry

gestoben [gə'ʃtobən] *pp* of **stieben**

Gestöber [gə'ʃtøbər] *n* (−s;−) snow flurry

gestochen [gə'ʃtɔxən] *pp* of **stechen**

gestohlen [gə'ʃtolən] *pp* of **stehlen**

gestorben [gə'ʃtɔrbən] *pp* of **sterben**

gestoßen [gə'ʃtosən] *pp* of **stoßen**

Gesträuch [gə'ʃtrɔɪç] *n* (−[e]s;) bushes, shrubbery

gestreift [gə'ʃtraɪft] *adj* striped

gestrichen [gə'ʃtrɪçən] *pp* of **streichen**

gestrig ['gɛstrɪç] *adj* yesterday's

gestritten [gə'ʃtrɪtən] *pp* of **streiten**

Gestrüpp [gə'ʃtrʏp] *n* (−[e]s;) underbrush

gestunken [gə'ʃtʊŋkən] *pp* of **stinken**

Gestüt [gə'ʃtyt] *n* (−[e]s;−e) stud farm

Gestüt'hengst *m* stallion, studhorse

Gesuch [gə'zux] *n* (−[e]s;−e) request; application; (jur) petition

gesucht [gə'zuxt] *adj* wanted; in demand; studied; (*Vergleich*) farfetched

Gesudel [gə'zudəl] *n* (−s;) messy job

Gesumme [gə'zumə] *n* (-s;) humming
gesund [gə'zunt] *adj* healthy; sound;
wholesome; **g. werden** get well
Gesund'beter -in §6 *mf* faith healer
Gesund'brunnen *m* mineral spring
gesunden [gə'zundən] *intr* (SEIN) get
well again, recover
Gesund'heit *f* (-;) health; **auf Ihre G.!**
to your health!; **G.!** (God) bless you!
Gesund'heitslehre *f* hygiene
Gesund'heitspflege *f* hygiene
Gesund'heitsrücksichten *pl*—**aus G.**
for reasons of health
Gesund'heitswesen *n* public health
gesungen [gə'zuŋən] *pp* of **singen**
gesunken [gə'zuŋkən] *pp* of **sinken**
Getäfel [gə'tɛfəl] *n* (-s;) wainscoting
getä'felt *adj* inlaid
getan [gə'tan] *pp* of **tun**
Getöse [gə'tøzə] *n* (-s;) din, noise
getragen [gə'tragən] *pp* of **tragen** || *adj*
solemn
Getrampel [gə'trampəl] *n* (-s;) trample
Getränk [gə'treŋk] *n* (-[e]s;-e) drink
getrauen [gə'trau-ən] *ref* dare
Getreide [gə'traɪdə] *n* (-s;-) grain
Getrei'deboden *m* granary
Getrei'despeicher *m* grain elevator
getreu [gə'trɔɪ] *adj* faithful, true
getreu'lich *adv* faithfully
Getriebe [gə'tribə] *n* (-s;-) hustle and
bustle; (adm) machinery; (aut) transmission
getrieben [gə'tribən] *pp* of **treiben**
getroffen [gə'trɔmən] *pp* of **treffen**
getrogen [gə'trogən] *pp* of **trügen**
getrost [gə'trost] *adj* confident
getrunken [gə'truŋkən] *pp* of **trinken**
Getto ['geto] *n* (-s;-s) ghetto
Getue [gə'tu-ə] *n* (-s;) fuss
Getümmel [gə'tʏməl] *n* (-s;) turmoil
getupft [gə'tupft] *adj* polka-dot
Geviert [gə'firt] *n* (-[e]s;-e) square
Gewächs [gə'veks] *n* (-es;-e) growth;
plant
gewachsen [gə'vaksən] *adj*—**g. sein**
(*dat*) be equal to, be up to
Gewächs'haus *n* greenhouse, hothouse
gewagt [gə'vakt] *adj* risky; off-color
gewählt [gə'velt] *adj* choice; refined
gewahr [gə'var] *adj*—**g. werden** (*genit*)
become aware of
Gewähr [gə'ver] *f* (-;) guarantee
gewahren [gə'varən] *tr* notice
gewähren [gə'verən] *tr* grant
gewähr'leisten *tr* guarantee, ensure
Gewähr'leistung *f* (-;-en) guarantee
Gewahrsam [gə'varzam] *m* (-[e]s;)
safekeeping, custody || *n* (-[e]s;-e)
prison
Gewährs'mann *m* (-[e]s;̈-er & -leute)
informant, source
Gewährs'pflicht *f* warranty
Gewalt [gə'valt] *f* (-;-en) force; violence; authority; (*Aufsicht*) control
Gewalt'haber *m* (-s;-) ruler; tyrant
Gewalt'herrschaft *f* tyranny
Gewalt'herrscher *m* tyrant
gewal'tig *adj* powerful; huge; (coll)
awful || *adv* terribly
Gewalt'kur *f* drastic measure; (coll)
crash program
gewalt'los *adj* nonviolent

Gewalt'marsch *m* forced march
Gewalt'mensch *m* brute, tyrant
gewaltsam [gə'valtzam] *adj* violent;
forcible; drastic || *adv* by force
Gewalt'samkeit *f* (-;) violence
Gewalt'streich *m* bold stroke
Gewalt'tat *f* act of violence
gewalt'tätig *adj* violent, brutal
Gewalt'verbrechen *n* felony
Gewalt'verbrecher -in §6 *mf* felon
Gewand [gə'vant] *n* (-[e]s;̈-er) robe;
appearance, guise; (eccl) vestment
gewandt [gə'vant] *pp* of **wenden** || *adj*
agile; clever
gewann [gə'van] *pret* of **gewinnen**
gewärtig [gə'vertɪç] *adj*—**g. sein**
(*genit*) be prepared for
Gewäsch [gə'veʃ] *n* (-es;) nonsense
Gewässer [gə'vesər] *n* (-s;-) body of
water; waters
Gewebe [gə'vebə] *n* (-s;-) tissue; (tex)
fabric
geweckt [gə'vekt] *adj* bright, sharp
Gewehr [gə'ver] *n* (-[e]s;-e) rifle
Geweih [gə'vaɪ] *n* (-[e]s;-e) antlers
Gewerbe [gə'verbə] *n* (-s;-) trade,
business; calling, profession; industry
Gewer'bebetrieb *m* business enterprise
Gewer'beschule *f* trade school
gewerblich [gə'verplɪç] *adj* industrial;
commercial, business
gebwerbs'mäßig *adj* professional
Gewerkschaft [gə'verkʃaft] *f* (-;-en)
labor union
gewerk'schaftlich *adj* union || *adv*—
sich g. organisieren unionize
Gewerk'schaftsbeitrag *m* union dues
gewesen [gə'vezən] *pp* of **sein**
gewichen [gə'vɪçən] *pp* of **weichen**
Gewicht [gə'vɪçt] *n* (-[e]s;-e) (& fig)
weight
gewichtig [gə'vɪçtɪç] *adj* weighty
gewiegt [gə'vigt] *adj* experienced,
smart, shrewd
gewiesen [gə'vizən] *pp* of **weisen**
gewillt [gə'vɪlt] *adj* willing
Gewimmel [gə'vɪməl] *n* (-s;) swarm;
(*Menschen*-) throng
Gewimmer [gə'vɪmər] *n* (-s;) whim-
pering; whining
Gewinde [gə'vɪndə] *n* (-s;-) thread
(*of a screw*); (*Kranz*) garland; skein
Gewinn [gə'vɪn] *m* (-[e]s;-e) win-
nings; profit; (*Vorteil*) advantage
Gewinn'anteil *m* dividend
Gewinn'aufschlag *m* (com) markup
Gewinn'beteiligung *f* profit sharing
gewinn'bringend *adj* profitable
gewinnen [gə'vɪnən] §121 *tr* win, gain;
reach || *intr* win; make a profit;
improve; **g. an** (*dat*) gain in; **g. von**
or **durch** profit by
gewin'nend *adj* engaging
Gewinn'spanne *f* margin of profit
Gewinn'sucht *f* greed; profiteering
Gewinsel [gə'vɪnzəl] *n* (-s;) whim-
pering
Gewirr [gə'vɪr] *n* (-[e]s;-e) tangle;
entanglement; maze
gewiß [gə'vɪs] *adj* sure, certain || *adv*
certainly; **aber g.!** of course!
Gewissen [gə'vɪsən] *n* (-s;-) conscience

gewis'senhaft adj conscientious
gewis'senlos adj unscrupulous
Gewis'sensbisse pl pangs of conscience
Gewis'sensnot f moral dilemma
gewis'sermaßen adv to some extent; so to speak
Gewiß'heit f (-;-en) certainty
gewiß'lich adv certainly
Gewitter [gə'vɪtər] n (-s;-) thunderstorm
gewittern [gə'vɪtərn] impers—es gewittert a storm is brewing
Gewit'terregen m thundershower
gewitzigt [gə'vɪtsɪçt] adj—g. sein to have learned from experience
gewitzt [gə'vɪtst] adj bright, smart
gewoben [gə'vobən] pp of weben
gewogen [gə'vogən] pp of wägen & wiegen || adj well disposed
Gewo'genheit f (-;) favorable attitude
gewöhnen [gə'vønən] tr (an acc) accustom (to) || ref (an acc) get used (to)
Gewohnheit [gə'vonhaɪt] f (-;-en) habit, custom
gewohn'heitsmäßig adj habitual
Gewohn'heitsmensch m creature of habit
gewöhnlich [gə'vønlɪç] adj usual; normal; common, ordinary
gewohnt [gə'vont] adj usual; g. sein (acc) be used to
Gewölbe [gə'vœlbə] n (-s;-) vault; arch
gewölbt [gə'vœlpt] adj vaulted
Gewölk [ge'vœlk] n (-[e]s;) clouds
gewonnen [gə'vonən] pp of gewinnen
geworben [gə'vorbən] pp of werben
geworden [gə'vordən] pp of werden
geworfen [gə'vorfən] pp of werfen
gewrungen [gə'vruŋən] pp of wringen
Gewühl [gə'vyl] n (-[e]s;) milling crowd
gewunden [gə'vundən] pp of winden
gewürfelt [gə'vyrfəlt] adj checkered
Gewürm [gə'vyrm] n (-[e]s;) vermin
Gewürz [gə'vyrts] n (-[e]s;-e) spice
Gewürz'nelke f clove
gewußt [gə'vust] pp of wissen
Geysir ['gaɪzɪr] m (-s;-) geyser
gezackt [gə'tsakt] adj jagged; (bot) serrated
gezähnt [gə'tsent] adj toothed; (Rand) perforated; (bot) dentated
Gezänk [gə'tsɛŋk] n (-[e]s;) squabbling
Gezeiten [gə'tsaɪtən] pl tides
Gezeiten- comb.fm. tidal
Gezeter [gə'tsetər] n (-s;) yelling
geziehen [gə'tsi-ən] pp of zeihen
geziemen [gə'tsimən] intr (dat) be proper for || impers ref—es geziemt sich für j–n it is right for s.o.
geziert [gə'tsirt] adj affected, phoney
Gezisch [gə'tsɪʃ] n (-es;) hissing
gezogen [gə'tsogən] pp of ziehen
Gezücht [gə'tsyçt] n (-[e]s;-e) riffraff
Gezwitscher [gə'tsvɪtʃər] n (-s;) chirping
gezwungen [gə'tsvuŋən] pp of zwingen || adj forced; (Stil) labored || adv stiffly
Gicht [gɪçt] f (-;-en) gout

Giebel ['gibəl] m (-s;-) gable
Gier [gir] f (-;) greed
gierig ['girɪç] adj (nach) greedy (for)
Gießbach ['gisbax] m torrent
gießen ['gisən] §76 tr pour; (Blumen, usw.) water; (metal) cast, found || impers—es gießt it is pouring
Gießer ['gisər] m (-s;-) foundryman
Gießerei [gisə'raɪ] f (-;-en) foundry
Gieß'form f casting mold; (typ) matrix
Gieß'kanne f sprinkling can
Gift [gɪft] n (-[e]s;-e) poison
giftig ['gɪftɪç] adj poisonous; malicious
Gigant [gɪ'gant] m (-en;-en) giant
Gilde ['gɪldə] f (-;-n) guild
Gimpel ['gɪmpəl] m (-s;-) (coll) sucker
ging [gɪŋ] pret of gehen
Gipfel ['gɪpfəl] m (-s;-) top; peak
Gip'felkonferenz f summit meeting
Gips [gɪps] m (-es;-e) gypsum; plaster of Paris; (surg) cast
Gips'arbeit f plastering
Gips'diele f plasterboard
gipsen ['gɪpsən] tr plaster
Gips'verband m (surg) cast
Giraffe [gɪ'rafə] f (-;-n) giraffe
girieren [ʒɪ'rirən] tr endorse
Girlande [gɪr'landə] f (-;-n) garland
Giro ['ʒiro] n (-s;-s) endorsement
girren ['gɪrən] intr coo
Gis [gɪs] n (-;-) (mus) G sharp
Gischt [gɪʃt] m (-es;) foam; spray
Gitarre [gɪ'tarə] f (-;-n) guitar
Gitter ['gɪtər] n (-s;-) grating, grille; bars; lattice; railing; trellis; (electron) grid
Git'terbett n baby crib
Git'ternetz n grid (on map)
Git'tertor n wrought-iron gate
Git'terwerk n latticework
Glacéhandschuhe [gla'sehantʃu·ə] pl (& fig) kid gloves
Gladi·ator [gladɪ'atər] m (-s;-atoren [a'torən]) gladiator
Glanz [glants] m (-es;) shine; polish; luster; brilliance
glänzen ['glentsən] tr polish || intr shine; durch Abwesenheit g. be conspicuous by one's absence
glän'zend adj bright; glossy; polished; (fig) splendid, brilliant
Glanz'leder n patent leather
Glanz'licht n (paint) highlight
glanz'los adj dull; lackluster
Glanz'punkt m highlight
Glanz'stück n master stroke
glanz'voll adj brilliant, splendid
Glanz'zeit f heyday, golden age
Glas [glas] n (-es;-er) glass
Glaser ['glazər] m (-s;-) glazier
gläsern ['glezərn] adj glass; glassy
Glas'hütte f glassworks
glasieren [gla'zirən] tr glaze; (Kuchen) frost, ice
glasig ['glazɪç] adj glassy; vitreous
Glas'jalousie f jalousie window
Glas'scheibe f pane of glass
Glasur [gla'zur] f (-;-en) enamel (on pots); glaze; (culin) icing
glatt [glat] adj smooth; (eben) even; (poliert) glossy; (schlüpfrig) slippery; (Absage) flat; (Lüge) downright || adv smoothly; directly; entirely

Glätte ['glɛtə] ƒ (-;) smoothness; slipperiness; (*Politur*) polish

Glatt'eis n sheet of ice; **bei G. fahren** drive in icy conditions

glätten ['glɛtən] tr smooth; smooth out || ref smooth out; become calm

glatt'streichen §85 tr smooth out

glatt'weg adv outright, point-blank

glattzüngig ['glattsYŋɪç] adj smooth-talking

Glatze ['glatsə] ƒ (-;-n) bald head

glatz'köpfig adj baldheaded

Glaube ['glaubə] m (-ns;), **Glauben** ['glaubən] m (-s;) belief; faith

glauben ['glaubən] tr believe; (*annehmen*) suppose || intr (*dat*) believe; **g. an** (*acc*) believe in; **j-m aufs Wort glauben** take s.o.'s word

Glau'bensbekenntnis n profession of faith; creed

Glau'benslehre ƒ Christian doctrine

Glau'benssatz m dogma

gläubig ['glɔɪbɪç] adj believing || **Gläubige** §5 mƒ believer || **Gläubiger –in** §6 mƒ creditor

glaublich ['glaupliç] adj credible

glaub'würdig adj credible; reliable; plausible

Glaukom [glau'kom] n (-s;-e) glaucoma

gleich [glaɪç] adj (*dat*) like; (**an** *dat*) equal (in); **es ist mir ganz g.** it's all the same to me || adv equally; immediately

gleichaltrig ['glaɪçaltrɪç] adj of the same age

gleich'artig adj similar, homogeneous

gleich'bedeutend adj synonymous

Gleich'berechtigung ƒ (pol) equality

gleichen ['glaɪçən] §85 intr (*dat*) resemble, look like, be like

glei'chermaßen adv equally, likewise

gleich'falls adv likewise; as well

gleich'förmig adj uniform; regular; monotonous

gleich'gesinnt adj like-minded

Gleich'gewicht n equilibrium

gleich'gültig adj indifferent; **es ist mir g.** it's all the same to me

Gleich'heit ƒ (-;-en) equality; (*Ähnlichkeit*) likeness

Gleich'klang m consonance; unison

gleich'kommen §99 intr (SEIN) (*dat*) equal; (*dat*) be tantamount to

gleich'laufend adj (mit) parallel (to)

gleich'machen tr make equal; standardize: **dem Erdboden g. raze**

Gleich'maß n regularity; evenness; balance, equilibrium; proportion

gleich'mäßig adj symmetrical; regular

Gleich'mut m equanimity, calmness

gleich'mütig adj calm

gleichnamig ['glaɪçnamɪç] adj of the same name; (phys) like

Gleichnis ['glaɪçnɪs] n (-ses;-se) parable; figure of speech; simile

Gleich'richter m (elec) rectifier

gleichsam ['glaɪçzam] adv so to speak; more or less, practically

gleichschenklig ['glaɪç/eŋklɪç] adj isosceles

Gleich'schritt m—im G. in cadence; **im G. marsch!** forward, march!

gleich'seitig adj equilateral

gleich'setzen tr (*dat* or **mit**) equate (with)

Gleich'setzung ƒ (-;), **Gleich'stellung** ƒ (-;) equalization

Gleich'strom m direct current

gleich'tun §154 tr—es j-m g. emulate s.o.

Glei'chung ƒ (-;-en) (math) equation

gleichviel' adv—g. wer not matter who

gleich'wertig adj evenly matched

gleichwohl' adv nevertheless

gleich'zeitig adj simultaneous

gleich'ziehen §163 intr (**mit**) catch up (with or to)

Gleis [glaɪs] n (-es;-e) (rr) track

Gleitboot ['glaɪtbot] n hydrofoil

gleiten ['glaɪtən] §86 intr (SEIN) glide; slip, slide

Gleitfläche ['glaɪtfleçə] ƒ (aer) hydroplane

Gleitflugzeug ['glaɪtfluktsɔɪk] n (aer) glider

Gleitschutz– comb.fm. skid-proof

Gleit'zeit ƒ flexitime

Gletscher ['glɛt/ər] m (-s;-) glacier

glich [glɪç] pret of **gleichen**

Glied [glit] n (-[e]s;-er) limb; member; joint; link; (anat) penis; (log, math) term; (mil) rank, file

glie'derlahm adj paralyzed

gliedern ['glidərn] tr arrange; plan; divide, break down || ref (**in** *acc*) consist of

Glie'derung ƒ (-;-en) arrangement; construction; division; organization

Gliedmaßen ['glitmasən] pl limbs

glimmen ['glɪmən] intr §136 & §109 intr glimmer; glow

Glim'mer m (-s;) glimmer; (min) mica

glimpflich ['glɪmpfliç] adj gentle; (*Strafe*) light, lenient

glitschen ['glɪt/ən] intr (SEIN) slip

glitschig ['glɪt/ɪç] adj slippery

glitt [glɪt] pret of **gleiten**

glit'zern ['glɪtsərn] intr glitter

global [glo'bal] adj global

Glo-bus ['globus] m (-bus & -busses; -busse & -ben [bən]) globe

Glöckchen ['glœkçən] n (-s;-) small bell

Glocke ['glɔkə] ƒ (-;-n) bell; (e-s *Rocks*) flare

Glockenspiel (**Glok'kenspiel**) n carillon

Glockenstube (**Glok'kenstube**) ƒ, **Glockenturm** (**Glok'kenturm**) m belfry

Glockenzug (**Glok'kenzug**) m bell rope

Glöckner ['glœknər] m (-s;-) bell ringer; sexton

glomm [glɔm] pret of **glimmen**

Glorie ['glorjə] ƒ (-;-n) glory

Glo'rienschein m halo

glorreich ['glorraɪç] adj glorious

glotzäugig ['glɔtsɔɪgɪç] adj popeyed

glotzen ['glɔtsən] intr stare, goggle

Glück [glyk] n (-[e]s;) luck; fortune; happiness; **auf gut G.** at random; **zum G.** luckily

glucken ['glukən] intr cluck

glücken ['glykən] intr (SEIN) succeed || impers—**es glückt mir** I succeed

gluckern ['glukərn] intr gurgle

glück'lich *adj* lucky, fortunate; happy; (*günstig*) auspicious
glück'licherweise *adv* fortunately
glück'selig *adj* blissful; blessed; joyful
Glück'seligkeit *f* (-;) bliss; joy
glucksen ['gluksən] *intr* gurgle; chuckle
Glücks'fall *m* stroke of luck; windfall
Glücks'güter *pl* earthly possessions
Glücks'hafen *m* raffle drum
Glücks'pilz *m* (coll) lucky dog
Glücks'spiel *n* game of chance
Glücks'topf *m* grab bag
glück'verheißend *adj* auspicious
Glück'wunsch *m* good wishes, congratulations
Glück'wunschkarte *f* greeting card
Glühbirne ['glybɪrnə] *f* light bulb
glühen ['gly·ən] *tr* make red-hot; (metal) anneal || *intr* glow
glü'hendheiß' *adj* red-hot
Glühfaden ['glyfɑdən] *m* filament
Glühwurm ['glyvurm] *m* firefly
Glut [glut] *f* (-;) embers; fire; scorching heat; (fig) ardor
Glyzerin [glytsə'rin] *n* (-s;) glycerine
GmbH *abbr* (Gesellschaft mit beschränkter Haftung) Inc.; Ltd. (Brit)
Gnade ['gnɑdə] *f* (-;-n) grace; favor; mercy; **von eigenen Gnaden** self-styled
Gna'denbeweis *m* token of favor
Gna'denbrot *n*—**bei j-m das G. essen** to live on s.o.'s charity
Gna'denfrist *f* grace, e.g., **e-e G. von zwei Monaten** two months' grace
Gna'dengesuch *n* plea for mercy
Gna'denstoß *m* coup de grâce, death-blow
gnädig ['gnedɪç] *adj* gracious, kind; merciful; **gnädige Frau** madam; **Sehr verehrte gnädige Frau** Dear Madam
Gold [gɔlt] *n* (-[e]s;) gold
Gold'blech *n* gold foil
Gold'fink *m* (orn) goldfinch
goldig ['gɔldɪç] *adj* (coll) cute
Gold'plombe *f* (dent) gold filling
Gold'schmied *m* goldsmith
Gold'schnitt *m* gilt edging
Golf [gɔlf] *m* (-[e]s;-e) gulf; bay || *n* (-s;) golf
Golf'platz *m* golf course
Golf'schläger *m* golf club
Gondel ['gɔndəl] *f* (-;-n) gondola
Gon'delführer *m* gondolier
gönnen ['gœnən] *tr* not begrudge; allow; **j-m etw nicht g.** begrudge s.o. s.th.
Gön'ner –in §6 *mf* patron
gön'nerhaft *adj* patronizing
Gön'nerschaft *f* (-;) patronage
gor [gor] *pret* of gären
Gorilla [gə'rɪla] *m* (-s;-s) gorilla
goß [gɔs] *pret* of gießen
Gosse ['gɔsə] *f* (-;-n) gutter
Gote ['gotə] *m* (-n;-n) Goth
gotisch ['gotiʃ] *adj* Gothic
Gott [gɔt] *m* (-[e]s;-er) god; God
gottbegnadet ['gɔtbəgnɑdət] *adj* gifted
gott'ergeben *adj* resigned to God's will
Got'tesdienst *m* divine service; Mass
got'tesfürchtig *adj* God-fearing
Got'tesgabe *f* godsend

got'teslästerlich *adj* blasphemous
Got'teslästerung *f* blasphemy
Got'tesurteil *n* ordeal
gott'gefällig *adj* pleasing to God
Gott'heit *f* (-;-en) deity, divinity
Göttin ['gœtɪn] *f* (-;-nen) goddess
göttlich ['gœtlɪç] *adj* godlike, divine; (fig) heavenly
gottlob' *interj* thank goodness!
Gott'mensch *m* God incarnate
gott'selig *adj* godly
gott'verlassen *adj* godforsaken
Götze ['gœtsə] *m* (-n;-n) idol
Göt'zenbild *n* idol
Göt'zendiener –in §6 *mf* idolater
Göt'zendienst *m* idolatry
Gouvernante [guvɛr'nantə] *f* (-;-n) governess
Gouverneur [guvɛr'nør] *m* (-s;-e) governor
Grab [grɑp] *n* (-[e]s;-er) grave; tomb
graben ['grɑbən] §87 *tr* dig; burrow || Graben *m* (-s;-) ditch; trench; moat
Grab'geläute *n* death knell
Grab'gesang *m* funeral dirge
Grab'hügel *m* burial mound
Grab'inschrift *f* epitaph
Grab'mal *n* tombstone; tomb, sepulcher
Grab'stätte *f* burial place
Grab'stelle *f* burial plot
Grad [grɑt] *m* (-[e]s;-e) degree; grade; (mil) rank
grade ['grɑdə] *adv* var of gerade
Grad'einteilung *f* gradation
Grad'messer *m* graduated scale; (fig) yardstick
grad'weise *adv* by degrees
Graf [grɑf] *m* (-en;-en) count; earl (Brit)
Gräfin ['grefɪn] *f* (-;-nen) countess
gräflich ['grefliç] *adj* count's; earl's
Graf'schaft *f* (-;-en) county
gram [grɑm] *adj*—**j-m g. sein** be cross with s.o. || Gram *m* (-[e]s;) grief
grämen ['gremən] *tr* sadden, distress || *ref* (über *acc*) grieve (over)
grämlich ['gremlɪç] *adj* glum; crabby
Gramm [grɑm] *n* (-s;- & -e) gram
Grammatik [gra'matɪk] *f* (-;-en) grammar
grammatisch [gra'matiʃ] *adj* grammatical
Gran [grɑn] *n* (-[e]s;) (fig) bit, jot
Granat [gra'nɑt] *m* (-[e]s;-e) garnet
Granat'apfel *m* pomegranate
Granate [gra'nɑtə] *f* (-;-n) (arti) shell; (mil) grenade
Granat'feuer *n* shelling
Granat'hülse *f* shell case
Granat'splitter *m* shrapnel
Granat'werfer *m* (mil) mortar
grandios [grandi'os] *adj* grandiose
Granit [gra'nit] *m* (-[e]s;-e) granite
Graphik ['grafɪk] *f* (-;-en) graphic arts; print; engraving; woodcut
graphisch ['grafiʃ] *adj* graphic
Graphit [gra'fit] *m* (-[e]s;) graphite
Gras [grɑs] *n* (-es;-er) grass
grasen ['grɑzən] *intr* graze
Gras'halm *m* blade of grass
Grashüpfer ['grɑshypfer] *m* (-s;-) grasshopper

grasig 118 Großmut

grasig ['grɑːzɪç] adj grassy
Gras'mäher m lawn mower; grass cutter
Gras'mähmaschine f lawn mower
Gras'narbe f sod, turf
grassieren [gra'siːrən] intr rage
gräßlich ['grɛslɪç] adj grisly
Gras'weide f pasture
Grat [grɑːt] m (-[e]s;-e) ridge; edge
Gräte ['grɛːtə] f (-;-n) fishbone
Gratifikation [gratɪfɪkaˈtsjoːn] f (-;-en) bonus
grätig ['grɛːtɪç] adj full of fishbones; (mürrisch) crabby
gratis ['grɑːtɪs] adv gratis; **g. und franko** (coll) for free
Gratulation [gratulaˈtsjoːn] f (-;-en) congratulations
gratulieren [gratuˈliːrən] intr—j-m g. zu congratulate s.o. on
grau [grau] adj gray; (Vorzeit) remote ‖ **Grau** n (- & -s;-s) gray
Grau'bär m grizzly bear
grauen ['grau·ən] intr dawn ‖ impers —es graut day is breaking; **es graut mir vor** (dat) I shudder at ‖ **Grauen** n (-s;) (vor dat) horror (of)
grau'enhaft, grau'envoll adj horrible
gräulich ['grɔɪlɪç] adj grayish
Graupe ['graupə] f (-;-n) peeled barley
graupeln ['graupəln] impers—es graupelt it is sleeting ‖ **Graupeln** pl sleet
Graus [graus] m (-es;) dread, horror
grausam ['grauzɑm] adj cruel; (coll) awful
Grau'schimmel m gray horse
grausen ['grauzən] impers—es graust mir vor (dat) I shudder at
grausig ['grauzɪç] adj gruesome
Graveur [gra'vøːr] m (-s;-e) engraver
gravieren [gra'viːrən] tr engrave
gravie'rend adj aggravating
gravitätisch [graviˈtɛːtɪʃ] adj stately
Grazie ['grɑːtsjə] f (-;-n) grace, charm
graziös [gra'tsjøːs] adj graceful
Greif [graif] m (-[e]s;-e) griffin
greifbar ['graifbɑr] adj tangible; at hand
greifen ['graifən] §88 tr grasp; seize; (Note) strike ‖ intr (Anker) catch; (Zahnrad) engage; **ans Herz g.** touch deeply; **an j-s Ehre g.** attack s.o.'s honor; **g. in** (acc) reach into; **g. nach** reach for; try to seize; **g. zu** reach for; (fig) resort to; **um sich g.** grope about; (Feuer) spread; **zu den Waffen g.** take up arms
Greis [grais] m (-es;-e) old man
Grei'senalter n old age
grei'senhaft adj aged; senile
Greisin ['graizɪn] f (-;-nen) old lady
grell [grɛl] adj (Ton) shrill; (Farbe, Kleider) flashy; (Licht) glaring
Gre·mium ['greːmjum] n (-s;-mien [mjən]) group, body; committee; corporation
Grenze ['grɛntsə] f (-;-n) boundary; frontier; borderline; limit
grenzen ['grɛntsən] intr (**an** acc) adjoin, border (on); (fig) verge (on)
gren'zenlos adj limitless
Grenz'fall m borderline case

Grenz'linie f boundary line
Grenz'sperre f ban on border traffic; frontier barricade
Grenz'stein m boundary stone
Greuel ['grɔɪ·əl] m (-s;-) abhorrence; horror, abomination
Greu'eltat f atrocity
greulich ['grɔɪlɪç] adj horrible
Griebs ['grips] m (-es;-e) core
Grieche ['griːçə] m (-n;-n) Greek
Grie'chenland n (-s;) Greece
Griechin ['griːçɪn] f (-;-nen) Greek
griechisch ['griːçɪʃ] adj Greek
Griesgram ['griːsgrɑm] m (-[e]s;-e) (coll) grouch
Grieß [griːs] m (-es;-e) grit; gravel
Grieß'mehl n farina
griff [grɪf] pret of **greifen** ‖ **Griff** m (-[e]s;-e) grip; handle; hilt; (mus) touch
Grill [grɪl] m (-s;-s) grill; broiler
Grille ['grɪlə] f (-;-n) cricket; (fig) whim
grillen ['grɪlən] tr grill; broil
gril'lenhaft adj whimsical
Grimasse [grɪ'masə] f (-;-n) grimace
Grimm [grɪm] m (-[e]s;) anger, fury
grimmig ['grɪmɪç] adj furious
Grind [grɪnt] m (-[e]s;-e) scab
grinsen ['grɪnzən] intr grin
Grippe ['grɪpə] f (-;) grippe
grob [grop] adj coarse, rough; crude
Grobian ['grobjan] m (-s;-e) boor
gröblich ['grøplɪç] adj gross
grölen ['grøːlən] intr shout raucously
Groll [grɔl] m (-[e]s;) resentment
grollen ['grɔlən] intr rumble; (über acc) be resentful (about); **j-m g.** have a grudge against s.o.
Grönland ['grønlant] n (-s;) Greenland
Gros [groːs] n (-ses;-) gross ‖ [gro] n (-;-) bulk; (mil) main forces
Groschen ['grɔʃən] m (-s;-) (Aust) penny (one hundredth of a shilling)
groß [groːs] adj big, large; tall; great
groß'artig adj grand; magnificent
Groß'aufnahme f (phot) close-up
groß'äugig adj wide-eyed
Groß'betrieb m big company
Großbritan'nien n Great Britain
Größe ['grøːsə] f (-;-n) size, greatness; celebrity; (astr) magnitude; (math) quantity
Groß'eltern pl grandparents
Groß'enkel m great-grandson
Groß'enkelin f great-granddaughter
großenteils ['groːsəntails] adv largely
Größenwahn ['grøːsənvan] f megalomania
Groß'grundbesitz m large estate
Groß'handel m wholesale trade; **im G. kaufen** buy wholesale
Großhandels- comb.fm. wholesale
Groß'händler -in §6 mf wholesaler
Groß'handlung f (-;-en) wholesale business
groß'herzig adj big-hearted
Grossist [grɔ'sɪst] m (-en;-en) wholesaler
groß'jährig adj of legal age
Groß'maul n bigmouth
Groß'mut m magnanimity

groß'mütig *adj* big-hearted
Groß'mutter *f* grandmother
Groß'onkel *m* great-uncle
Groß'schreibung *f* capitalization
Groß'segel *n* main sail
Groß'sprecher *m* braggart
großspurig ['groſ/puriç] *adj* pompous
Groß'stadt *f* large city (*with over 100,000 inhabitants*)
Großstädter ['gros/tɛtər] *m* (*-s;-*) (coll) city slicker
Groß'tat *f* achievement
Groß'teil *m* major part
größtenteils ['grøstəntaıls] *adv* mainly
groß'tun §154 *intr* brag; put on the dog
Groß'vater *m* grandfather
Groß'wild *n* big game
groß'ziehen §163 *tr* bring up, raise
großzügig ['grostsygıç] *adj* broad-minded, liberal; generous; large-scale
grotesk [gro'tɛsk] *adj* grotesque
Grotte ['grotə] *f* (*-;-n*) grotto
grub [grup] *pret* of **graben**
Grübchen ['grypçən] *n* (*-s;-*) dimple
Grube ['grubə] *f* (*-;-n*) pit; mine
Grübelei [grybə'laı] *f* (*-;-en*) brooding
grübeln ['grybəln] *intr* brood
Gruben– [grubən] *comb.fm.* mine, miner's
Gruft [gruft] *f* (*-;-̈e*) tomb, vault
grün [gryn] *adj* green; **Grüne Minna** (sl) paddy wagon ‖ **Grün** *n* (*-s;*) green
Grün'anlage *f* public park
Grund [grunt] *m* (*-[e]s;-̈e*) ground; land; bottom; foundation, basis; cause, ground; **auf G. von** on the strength of; **G. und Boden** property; **im Grunde genommen** after all; **in G. und Boden** outright
–grund *m* *comb.fm.* bottom of; –ground; grounds for, reasons for
Grund'anstrich *m* first coat
Grund'ausbildung *f* (mil) basic training
Grund'bedeutung *f* primary meaning
Grund'begriff *m* fundamental principle
Grund'besitz *m* real estate
Grund'buch *n* land register
grund'ehr'lich *adj* thoroughly honest
gründen ['gryndən] *tr* found; **g. auf** (*acc*) base on ‖ *ref* (**auf** *acc*) be based (on)
Gründer –in ['gryndər(ın)] §6 *mf* founder
grund'falsch' *adj* absolutely false
Grund'farbe *f* primary color
Grund'fläche *f* area; (geom) base
grundieren [grun'dirən] *tr* prime; size
Grundier'farbe *f* primer coat
Grundier'schicht *f* primer coat
Grund'kapital *n* capital stock
Grund'lage *f* basis, foundation
grund'legend *adj* basic, fundamental
Grund'legung *f* founding, foundation
gründlich ['gryntlıç] *adj* thorough
Grund'linie *f* (geom) base; **Grundlinien** basic features, outlines
Gründon'nerstag *m* Holy Thursday
Grund'riß *m* floor plan; outline

Grund'satz *m* principle
grundsätzlich ['gruntzɛtslıç] *adj* basic ‖ *adv* as a matter of principle
Grund'schule *f* primary school
Grund'stein *m* cornerstone
Grund'stellung *f* position of attention; **die G. einnehmen** come to attention
Grund'steuer *f* real-estate tax
Grund'stoff *m* raw material; (chem) element
Grund'strich *m* downstroke
Grund'stück *n* lot, property
Grund'ton *m* (fig) prevailing mood; (mus) keynote; (paint) ground shade
Grün'dung *f* (*-;-en*) foundation
grund'verschie'den *adj* entirely different
Grund'wasserspiegel *m* water table
Grund'zahl *f* cardinal number
Grund'zug *m* main feature; **Grundzüge** fundamentals, essentials
Grüne ['grynə] *n*—**ins G.** into the country
grün'lich *adj* greenish
Grün'schnabel *m* know-it-all
Grünspan ['grynſpan] *m* (*-[e]s;*) verdigris
Grün'streifen *m* grass strip; (*auf der Autobahn*) median strip
grunzen ['gruntsən] *tr & intr* grunt
Gruppe ['grupə] *f* (*-;-n*) group; (mil) squad
Grup'penführer *m* group leader; (hist) lieutenant general (*of S.S. troops*); (mil) squad leader
gruppieren [gru'pirən] *tr & ref* group
Gruppie'rung *f* (*-;-en*) grouping
gruselig ['gruzəlıç] *adj* creepy
gruseln ['gruzəln] *intr*—**j–n g. machen** give s.o. the creeps ‖ *ref* have a creepy feeling ‖ *impers*—**es gruselt mir** (or **mich**) it gives me the creeps
Gruß [grus] *m* (*-es;-̈e*) greeting, salute; greetings, regards; **mit freundlichem Gruß, Ihr** ... Sincerely yours
grüßen ['grysən] *tr* greet; salute, **grüß Gott!** hello!; **j–n g. lassen** send best regards to s.o.
Grütze ['grytsə] *f* (*-;-n*) groats; (coll) brains
gucken ['gukən] *intr* look; peep
Guck'loch *n* peephole
Guerilla [gɛ'rılja] *m* (*-s;-s*) guerilla
Gulasch ['gulaſ] *n* (*-[e]s;*) goulash
gültig ['gyltıç] *adj* valid; legal
Gummi ['gumi] *m & n* (*-s;-s*) gum; rubber
gum'miartig *adj* gummy; rubbery
Gum'miband *n* (*-[e]s;-̈er*) rubber band; elastic
Gum'mibaum *m* rubber plant
Gum'mibonbon *m & n* gumdrop
gummieren [gu'mirən] *tr* gum; rubberize
Gum'miknüppel *m* truncheon; billy club
Gummilinse *f* (phot) zoom lens
Gum'mimantel *m* mackintosh
Gum'mireifen *m* tire
Gum'mischuhe *pl* rubbers
Gum'mizelle *f* padded cell
Gunst [gunst] *f* (*-;*) favor, goodwill; kindness, good turn

Gunst'bezeigung _f_ expression of good-will
günstig ['gynstıç] _adj_ favorable; _(Bedingungen)_ easy
Günstling ['gynstlıŋ] _m_ (-s;-e) favorite; (pej) minion
Gurgel ['gurgəl] _f_ (-;-n) gullet
gurgeln ['gurgəln] _intr_ gurgle; gargle
Gurke ['gurkə] _f_ (-;-n) cucumber
Gurt [gurt] _m_ (-[e]s;-e) belt, strap
Gürtel ['gyrtəl] _m_ (-s;-) girdle; belt; (geog) zone
gürten ['gyrtən] _tr_ gird
Guß [gus] _m_ (**Gusses; Güsse**) gush; _(Regen)_ downpour; _(Gießen)_ casting; (culin) icing; (typ) font
gut [gut] _adj_ good; **es ist schon gut** it's all right; **mach's gut!** so long! ‖ _adv_ well ‖ **Gut** _n_ (-[e]s;ẞer) good; possessions; estate; (com) commodity; **Güter** goods; assets
Gut'achten _n_ (-s;-) expert opinion
gut'artig _adj_ good-natured; (pathol) benign
gut'aussehend _adj_ good-looking
Gut'dünken _n_ (-s;) judgment; discretion; **nach G.** at will, as one pleases; (culin) to taste
Gute ['gutə] §5 _n_ good; **alles G.!** best of everything!; **sein Gutes haben** have its good points
Güte ['gytə] _f_ (-;) goodness
Güter- [gytər] _comb.fm._ freight; property; (com) of goods
Gü'terabfertigung _f_ freight office
Gü'terbahnhof _m_ (rr) freight yard
gut'erhalten _adj_ in good condition

Gü'terwagen _m_ freight car; **geschlossener G.** boxcar; **offener G.** gondola car
Gü'terzug _m_ freight train
gut'gelaunt _adj_ good-humored
gut'gesinnt _adj_ well-disposed
gut'haben §89 _tr_ have to one's credit ‖ **Guthaben** _n_ (-s;-) credit balance
gut'heißen §95 _tr_ approve of
gut'herzig _adj_ good-hearted
gütig ['gytıç] _adj_ kind, good
gütlich ['gytlıç] _adj_ amicable
gut'machen _tr_—**wieder g.** make good for
gut'mütig _adj_ good-natured
gut'sagen _intr_—**für j-n g.** vouch for s.o.
Gut'schein _m_ coupon; credit note
gut'schreiben §62 _tr_—**j-m e-n Betrag g.** credit s.o. with a sum
Gut'schrift _f_ credit entry; credit item
Gut'schriftsanzeige _f_ credit note
Guts'herr _m_ landowner
gut'tun §154 _intr_ do good; behave
gut'willig _adj_ willing, obliging
Gymnasiast –in [gym'nazjast(ın)] §7 _mf_ high school student
Gymna·sium [gym'nazjum] _n_ (-s;-sien [zjən]) high school _(with academic course)_
Gymnastik [gym'nastık] _f_ (-;) gymnastics
Gynäkologe [gynɛkə'logə] _m_ (-n;-n), **Gynakologin** [gynɛkə'logın] _f_ (-;nen) gynecologist
Gynäkologie [gynɛkələ'gi] _f_ (-;) gynecology

H

H, h [hɑ] _invar n_ H, h; (mus) B
Haar [hɑr] _n_ (-[e]s;-e) hair; (tex) nap, pile; **aufs H.** exactly; **um ein H.** by a hair's breadth
Haar'büschel _n_ tuft of hair
haaren ['hɑrən] _intr_ lose hair
Haarfärbmittel ['hɑrferpmıtəl] _n_ hair dye
Haar'feder _f_ hairspring
haar'genau' _adj_ exact, precise
haarig ['hɑrıç] _adj_ hairy
haar'klein _adj_ (coll) in detail
Haar'locke _f_ lock of hair
Haar'nadel _f_ hairpin
haar'scharf' _adj_ razor-sharp
Haar'schneider _m_ barber
Haar'schnitt _m_ haircut
Haar'spange _f_ barrette
Haarspray ['hɑrspre] _m_ (-s;-s) hair spray
haar'sträubend _adj_ hair-raising
Haar'teil _m_ hair piece
Haar'tolle _f_ loose curl
Haar'tracht _f_ hairdo
Haar'trockner _m_, **Haar'trockenhaube** _f_ hair dryer
Haar'wäsche _f_ shampoo
Haar'wasser _n_ hair tonic

Haar'wickler _m_ curler; hair roller
Haar'zwange _f_ tweezers
Hab [hap] _invar n_—**Hab und Gut** possessions
Habe ['habə] _f_ (-;) possessions
haben ['habən] §89 _tr & aux_ have ‖ **Haben** _n_ (-s;) credit side
Habe'nichts _m_ (-es;-e) have-not
Hab'gier _f_ greed, avarice
hab'haft _adj_—**h. werden** _(genit)_ get hold of; _(Diebes)_ apprehend
Habicht ['habıçt] _m_ (-[e]s;-e) hawk
Ha'bichtsnase _f_ aquiline nose
Habilitation [habılıta'tsjon] _f_ (-;-en) accreditation as a university lecturer
habilitieren [habılı'tirən] _ref_ be accredited as a university lecturer
Hab'seligkeiten _pl_ belongings
Hab'sucht _f_ greed, avarice
hab'süchtig _adj_ greedy, avaricious
Hackbeil ['hakbaıl] _n_ cleaver
Hacke ['hakə] _f_ (-;-n) heel; hoe; pick; pickax; hatchet; mattock
hacken ['hakən] _tr_ hack, chop; peck ‖ _intr_ (nach) peck (at)
Häckerling ['hɛkərlıŋ] _m_ (-s;) chaff
Hackfleisch ['hakflaıʃ] _n_ ground meat
Häcksel ['hɛksəl] _n_ (-s;) chaff

Hader ['hɑdər] *m* (**-s;** **-n**) rag strife ‖ *m* (**-s;**

hadern ['hɑdərn] *intr* quarrel
Hafen ['hɑfən] *m* (**-s;⸗**) harbor; port; (fig) haven
Ha'fenamt *n* port authority
Ha'fenanlagen *pl* docks
Ha'fenarbeiter *m* longshoreman
Ha'fendamm *m* jetty, mole
Ha'fensperre *f* blockade
Ha'fenstadt *f* seaport
Ha'fenviertel *n* dock area, waterfront
Hafer ['hɑfər] *m* (**-s;-**) oats; **ihn sticht der H.** he's feeling his oats
Ha'fergrütze *f*, **Ha'fermehl** *n* oatmeal
Hafner ['hɑfnər] *m* (**-s;-**) potter
Haft [haft] *f* (**-;**) arrest; custody; imprisonment; **in H.** under arrest; in custody; **in** prison
haftbar ['haftbɑr] *adj* (jur) liable
Haft'befehl *m* warrant for arrest
haften ['haftən] *intr* (**an** *dat*) cling (to), stick (to); **h. für** vouch for; (jur) be held liable for; (jur) put up bail for
Haft'fähigkeit *f*, **Haft'festigkeit** *f* adhesion
Häftling ['heftlɪŋ] *m* (**-s;-e**) prisoner
Haft'lokal *n* (mil) guardhouse
Haft'pflicht *f* liability
haft'pflichtig *adj* (**für**) liable (for)
Haft'pflichtversicherung *f* liability insurance
Haft'richter *m* (jur) magistrate
Haft'schale *f* contact lens
Haf'tung *f* (**-;-en**) liability
Hag [hɑk] *m* (**-[e]s;-e**) enclosure; (*Hain*) grove; (*Buschwerk*) bushes
Hagedorn ['hɑgədɔrn] *m* hawthorn
Hagel ['hɑgəl] *m* (**-s;**) hail
Ha'gelkorn *n* hailstone
hageln ['hɑgəln] *intr* (SEIN) (fig) rain down ‖ *impers*—**es hagelt** it is hailing
Ha'gelschauer *m* hailstorm
hager ['hɑgər] *adj* gaunt, haggard
Hagestolz ['hɑgəʃtɔlts] *m* (**-es;-e**) confirmed bachelor
Häher ['he·ər] *m* (**-s;-**) (orn) jay
Hahn [hɑn] *m* (**-[e]s;⸗e**) rooster; (*Wasser-*) faucet; **den H. spannen** cock the gun; **H. im Korbe sein** rule the roost
Hähnchen ['hençən] *n* (**-s;-**) young rooster
Hah'nenkamm *m* cockscomb
Hah'nenkampf *m* cock fight
Hah'nenschrei *m* crow of the cock
Hahnrei ['hɑnraɪ] *m* (**-s;-e**) cuckold
Hai [haɪ] *m* (**-[e]s;-e**), **Hai'fisch** *m* shark
Hain [haɪn] *m* (**-[e]s;-e**) grove
Haiti [ha'iti] *n* (**-s;**) Haiti
Häkelarbeit ['hekəlarbaɪt] *f* crocheting
häkeln ['hekəln] *tr & intr* crochet ‖ **Häkeln** *n* (**-s;**) crocheting
Haken ['hɑkən] *m* (**-s;-**) hook; (*Spange*) clasp; (fig) snag, hitch
Ha'kenkreuz *n* swastika
Ha'kennase *f* hooknose
halb [halp] *adj & adv* half
halb-, Halb- *comb.fm.* half-, semi-
Halb'blut *n* half-breed

-halber [halbər] *comb.fm.* for the sake of; owing to
halb'fett *adj* (typ) bold
Halb'franzband *m* (bb) half leather
halb'gar *adj* (culin) (medium) rare
Halb'gott *m* demigod
Halbheit ['halphaɪt] *f* (**-;**) half-
Halb'kugel *f* hemisphere
halbieren [hal'biran] *tr* halve, bisect
Halb'insel *f* peninsula
Halb'kettenfahrzeug *n* half-track
Halb'kugel *f* hemisphere
halb'lang *adj* half-length; **halblange Ärmel** half sleeves
halb'laut *adj* low ‖ *adv* in a low voice
Halb'leiter *m* (elec) semiconductor
halb'mast *adv* at half-mast; **auf h. at** half-mast
Halb'messer *m* radius
halbpart ['halppart] *adv*—**mit j-m h. machen** go fifty-fifty with s.o.
Halb'schuh *m* low shoe
Halb'schwergewicht *n* light-heavyweight division
Halb'schwergewichtler *m* light-heavyweight
halb'stündig *adj* half-hour
halb'stündlich *adj* half-hourly ‖ *adv* every half hour
Halb'vers *m* hemistich
halbwegs ['halbveks] *adv* halfway
Halb'welt *f* demimonde
halbwüchsig ['halpvyksıç] *adj* teenage ‖ **Halbwüchsige §5** *mf* teenager
Halb'zug *m* (mil) section
Halde ['haldə] *f* (**-;-n**) slope; (*Schutt-*) slag pile
half [half] *pret* of **helfen**
Hälfte ['helftə] *f* (**-;-n**) half
Halfter ['halftər] *f* (**-;-n**) holster ‖ *n* (**-s;-**) halter
Hall [hal] *m* (**-[e]s;-e**) sound; clang
Halle ['halə] *f* (**-;-n**) hall; (*e-s Hotels*) lobby; (aer) hangar; (rr) concourse
hallen ['halən] *intr* sound, resound
Hal'lenbad *n* indoor pool
Hallo [ha'lo] *n* (**-s;**) hullabaloo ‖ *interj* (to attract attention) hey!; (telp) hello
Halm [halm] *m* (**-[e]s;-e**) stem, stalk; blade (*of grass*)
Hals [hals] *m* (**-es;⸗e**) neck; throat; **H. über Kopf** head over heels
Hals'abschneider *m* cutthroat
hals'abschneiderisch *adj* cutthroat
Hals'ader *f* jugular vein
Hals'ausschnitt *m* neckline, neck
Hals'band *n* (**-[e]s;⸗er**) necklace, choker; (*e-s Hundes*) collar
halsbrecherisch ['halsbreçərıʃ] *adj* breakneck
Hals'entzündung *f* sore throat
Hals'kette *f* necklace, chain
Hals'kragen *m* collar
Hals'krause *f* frilled collar
hals'starrig *adj* stubborn
Hals'weh *n* sore throat
halt [halt] *adv* just, simply ‖ *interj* stop!; (mil) halt! ‖ **Halt** *m* (**-[e]s; -e**) hold; foothold; support; stability; stop, halt
haltbar ['haltbɑr] *adj* durable; tenable

halten ['haltən] §90 *tr* hold; keep; detain; (*Rede*) deliver; (*Vorlesung*) give; (*feiern*) celebrate; **es h. mit** do with; **have an affair with; etw auf sich h.** have self-respect; **j-n h. für** take s.o. for; **viel h. von** think highly of || *ref* keep, last; hold ones own; **an sich h.** restrain oneself; **auf sich h.** be particular about one's appearance; **sich an etw h.** (fig) stick to s.th.; **sich an j-n h.** hold s.o. liable; **sich gesund h.** keep healthy; **sich links h.** keep to the left || *intr* stop; last; **h. auf** (*acc*) pay attention to; **h. nach** head for; **h. zu** stick by; **was das Zeug hält** with might and main

Hal′ter *m* (–s;–) holder; rack; owner

Hal′teriemen *m* strap (*on bus or trolley*)

Hal′testelle *f* bus stop, trolley stop; (rr) stop

Hal′teverbot *n* (public sign) no stopping

–haltig [haltɪç] *comb.fm.* containing

halt′los *adj* without support; helpless; unprincipled

halt′machen *intr* stop, halt

Hal′tung *f* (–;–en) pose, posture; attitude

Halte′zeichen *n* stop sign

Halunke [ha'luŋkə] *m* (–;–n) rascal

hämisch ['hemɪʃ] *adj* spiteful, malicious

Hammel ['haməl] *m* (–s;–e & ∺) wether; (coll) mutton-head; (culin) mutton

Ham′melkeule *f* leg of mutton

Hammer ['hamər] *m* (–s;∺) hammer; gavel; **unter den H. kommen** be auctioned off

hämmern ['hemərn] *tr & intr* hammer

Hämorrhoiden [hemɔrə'idən] *pl* hemorroids, piles

Hampelmann ['hampəlman] *m* (–[e]s; ∺er) jumping jack

hamstern ['hamstərn] *tr* hoard

Hand [hant] *f* (–;∺e) hand; **an H. von** with the help of; **auf eigene H.** of one's own accord; **aus erster H.** (*bei Verkauf*) one-owner; **aus erster H. haben** hear first-hand; **aus erster H. kaufen** buy directly; **bei der H.** at hand, handy; **die letzte H.** finishing touches; **die öffentliche H.** the state, public authorities; **es liegt auf der H.** it is obvious; **H. ans Werk legen** get down to work; **H. aufs Herz!** cross my heart!; **Hände hoch!** hands up!; **H. und Fuß haben** make sense; **in die H.** (or **Hände**) **bekommen** get one's hands on; **j–m an die H. gehen** lend s.o. a hand; **j–m die H. drücken** shake hands with s.o.; **j–m etw an (die) H. geben** quote s.o. a price on s.th.; **j–m zur H. gehen** lend s.o. a hand; **unter der H.** underhandedly; unofficially; **von der H. weisen** reject; **zu Händen Herrn X** Attention Mr. X; **zur H.** at hand, handy

Hand′arbeit *f* manual labor; needlework

Hand′aufheben *n,* **Hand′aufhebung** *f* show of hands

Hand′ausgabe *f* abridged edition

Hand′bedienung *f* manual control

Hand′betrieb *m*—**mit** (or **für**) **H.** hand-operated

Hand′bibliothek *f* reference library

hand′breit *adj* wide as a hand || **Hand′breit** *f* (–;–) hand's breadth

Hand′bremse *f* (aut) hand brake

Hand′buch *n* handbook, manual

Händedruck ['hendədrʊk] *m* handshake

Händeklatschen ['hendəklat ʃən] *n* clapping

Handel ['handəl] *m* (–s;∺) trade; deal, bargain; business; affair; **e–n H. eingehen** conclude a deal; **e–n H. treiben** carry on business; **H. und Gewerbe** trade and industry; **Händel suchen** pick a quarrel; **im H. sein** be on the market; **in den H. bringen** put on the market

–handel *m comb.fm.* –trade, –business

handeln ['handəln] *intr* act; take action; proceed; **gegen das Gesetz h.** go against the law; **gut an j–m h.** treat s.o. well; **h. über** (*acc*) or **von** deal with; **h. mit** do business with; **im großen h.** do wholesale business || *impers ref*—**es handelt sich um** it is a matter of; **darum handelt es sich nicht** that's not the point

Han′delsabkommen *n* trade agreement

Han′delsartikel *m* commodity

Han′delsbetrieb *m* commercial enterprise; business; firm

Han′delsbilanz *f* balance of trade; **aktive H.** favorable balance of trade

Han′delsdampfer *m* (naut) merchantman

han′delseinig *adj*—**h. werden mit** come to terms with

Han′delsgärtner *m* truck farmer

Han′delskammer *f* chamber of commerce

Han′delsmarine *f* merchant marine

Han′delsmarke *f* trademark

Han′delsminister *m* secretary of commerce

Han′delsministerium *n* department of commerce

Han′delsplatz *m* trade center

Han′delsschiff *n* merchantman

Han′delssperre *f* trade embargo

händelsüchtig ['hendəlzʏçtɪç] *adj* quarrelsome

Han′delsvertrag *m* commercial treaty

Han′delswert *m* trade-in value

Han′delszeichen *n* trademark

Hand′exemplar *n* desk copy

Hand′fertigkeit *f* manual dexterity

Hand′fessel *f* handcuff

hand′fest *adj* sturdy; well-founded

Hand′fläche *f* palm of the hand

Hand′geld *n* advance payment; deposit

Hand′gelenk *n* wrist; **aus** (or **mit**) **dem H.** (coll) easy as pie

hand′gemein *adj*—**h. werden** come to blows

Hand′gemenge *n* scuffle

Hand′gepäck *n* hand luggage

Hand′gepäckschließfach *n* locker

Hand′granate *f* hand grenade

hand′greiflich *adj* tangible; obvious;

j–m etw h. machen make s.th. clear to s.o.; **h. werden** come to blows
Hand′griff *m* grip; handle; **keinen H. tun** not lift a finger
Hand′habe *f* (–;–n) handle; pretext; occasion; **er hat keine H. gegen mich** he has nothing on me
hand′haben *tr* handle; (*Maschine*) operate; (*Rechtspflege*) administer; (fig) manage
–händig [hendɪç] *comb.fm.* –handed
Hand′karren *m* hand cart, push cart
Hand′koffer *m* suitcase; attaché case
Handlanger [′hantlaŋər] *m* (–s;–) handyman; (pej) underling
Händler –in [′hendlər(ɪn)] §6 *mf* dealer, merchant; storekeeper
Hand′lesekunst *f* palmistry
Hand′leserin *f* (–;–nen) palm reader
hand′lich *adj* handy
Hand′lung *f* (–;–en) shop; act, action
–handlung *f comb.fm.* business; shop
Hand′lungsgehilfe *m* clerk, salesman
Hand′lungsweise *f* conduct
Hand′pflege *f* manicure
Hand′pflegerin *f* (–;–nen) manicurist
Hand′rücken *m* back of the hand
Hand′schaltung *f* manual shift
Hand′schelle *f* handcuff
Hand′schlag *m* handshake
Hand′schreiben *n* hand-written letter
Hand′schrift *f* handwriting; manuscript; (sl) slap, box on the ear
Hand′schriftenkunde *f* paleography
hand′schriftlich *adj* hand-written
Hand′schuh *m* glove
Hand′schuhfach *n* (aut) glove compartment
Hand′streich *m* (mil) raid
Hand′tasche *f* handbag, purse
Hand′tuch *n* towel; **schmales H.** (sl) beanpole
Hand′tuchhalter *m* towel rack
Hand′umdrehen *n*—**im. H.** in a jiffy
Hand′voll *f* (–;–) handful
Hand′werk *n* craft, trade; **j–m ins H. pfuschen** (sl) stick one's nose in s.o. eise's business
Hand′werker *m* craftsman
Hand′werkszeug *n* tool kit
Hand′wörterbuch *n* pocket dictionary
Hand′wurzel *f* wrist
Hand′zettel *m* handbill
hanebüchen [′hanəbyçən] *adj* (coll) incredible; (coll) monstrous
Hanf [hanf] *m* (–[e]s;) hemp
Hang [haŋ] *m* (–[e]s;∺) slope; hillside; (fig) inclination, tendency
Hangar [′haŋɡar] *m* (–s;–s) hangar
Hängebacken [′heŋəbakən] *pl* jowls
Hängebauch [′heŋəbaux] *m* potbelly
Hängebrücke [′heŋəbrykə] *f* suspension bridge
Hängematte [′heŋəmatə] *f* hammock
hängen [′heŋən] *tr* hang ‖ *ref*—**sich an j–n h.** hang on to s.o.; **sich ans Telephon h.** be on the telephone ‖ §92 *intr* hang; cling, stick
hän′genbleiben §62 *intr* (SEIN) stick; be detained, get stuck; **(an** *dat*) get caught (on); (educ) stay behind
Hans [hans] *m* (–′ & –ens;) Johnny, Jack

Hans′dampf *m* (–[e]s;–e) busybody; **H. in allen Gassen** jack-of-all trades
Hänselei [henzə′laɪ] *f* (–;–en) teasing
hänseln [′henzəln] *tr* tease
Hans′narr *m* fool
Hans′wurst *m* (–es;–e & ∺e) clown
Hantel [′hantəl] *f* (–;–n) dumbell
hantieren [han′tirən] *intr* (an *acc*) be busy (with); **mit etw h.** handle s.th.
hapern [′hapərn] *impers*—**bei mir hapert es an** (*dat*) (or mit) I am short of; **bei mir hapert es in** (*dat*) (or mit) I am weak in; **damit hapert's** that's the hitch
Happen [′hapən] *m* (–s;–) morsel; mouthful; (fig) good opportunity; **fetter H.** (coll) big hawl
happig [′hapɪç] *adj* greedy; (*Preis*) steep
Härchen [′herçən] *n* (–s;–) tiny hair
Harem [′harem] *m* (–s;–s) harem
Häre·sie [here′zi] *f* (–;–sien [′zi·ən]) heresy
Häretiker [hɛ′retɪkər] *m* (–s;–) heretic
Harfe [′harfə] *f* (–;–n) harp
Harke [′harkə] *f* (–;–n) rake
harken [′harkən] *tr & intr* rake
Harm [harm] *m* (–[e]s;) harm; grief
härmen [′hermən] *ref* (**um**) grieve (over)
harm′los *adj* harmless
Harmo·nie [harmə′ni] *f* (–;–nien [′ni·ən]) harmony
harmonieren [harmə′nirən] *intr* harmonize
Harmoni·ka [har′monɪka] *f* (–;–kas & –ken [kən]) accordion; harmonica
harmonisch [har′monɪʃ] *adj* harmonious
Harn [harn] *m* (–[e]s;–e) urine; **H. lassen** pass water
Harn′blase *f* (anat) bladder
harnen [′harnən] *intr* urinate
Harn′glas *n* urinal
Harn′grieß *m* (pathol) gravel
Harnisch [′harnɪʃ] *m* (–es;–e) armor; **in H. geraten über** (*acc*) fly into a rage over; **j–n in H. bringen** get s.o. hopping mad
Harn′leiter *m* (anat) ureter; (surg) catheter
Harn′röhre *f* urethra
harn′treibend *adj* diuretic
Harpune [har′punə] *f* (–;–n) harpoon
harpunieren [harpu′nirən] *tr* harpoon
harren [′harən] *intr* tarry; hope; (*genit* or **auf** *acc*) wait (for)
harsch [harʃ] *adj* harsh ‖ **Harsch** *m* (–es;), **Harsch′schnee** *m* crushed snow
hart [hart] *adj* hard; severe ‖ *adv*— **h. an** (*dat*) close to, hard by
Härte [′hertə] *f* (–;) hardness; severity
härten [′hertən] *tr, ref & intr* harden
Hart′faserplatte *f* fiber board
Hart′geld *n* coins
hartgesotten [′hartɡəzɔtən] *adj* hard-boiled; (*Verbrecher*) hardened
hart′herzig *adj* hard-hearted
hart′köpfig *adj* thick-headed
hart′leibig *adj* constipated
Hart′leibigkeit *f* (–;) constipation
hart′löten *tr* braze

hartnäckig ['hartnɛkıç] *adj* stubborn
Hart'platz *m* (tennis) hard court
Harz Lharts] *n* (-es;-e) resin; rosin
harzig [hartsıç] *adj* resinous
Hasardspiel [ha'zartʃpil] *n* gambling game; gamble
haschen ['haʃən] *tr* snatch, grab ‖ *intr* (**nach**) try to catch, snatch (at)
Hase ['hazə] *m* (-n;-n) hare; **alter H.** old-timer, veteran
Ha'selnuß ['hazəlnus] *f* hazelnut
Hasenfuß *m* (coll) coward
Ha'senherz *n* (coll) yellow belly
Ha'senmaus *f* chinchilla
Hasenpanier ['hazənpanir] *n—das* **H. ergreifen** take to ones heels
ha'senrein *adj—nicht ganz* **h.** (fig) a bit fishy, rather shady
Ha'senscharte *f* harelip
Haspe ['haspə] *f* (-;-n) hasp
Haspel ['haspəl] *f* (-;-n) & *m* (-s;-) reel, spool; winch, windlass
haspeln ['haspəln] *tr* reel, spool
Haß *m* (**Hasses**;) hatred
hassen ['hasən] *tr* hate
has'senswert, has'senswürdig *adj* hateful
häßlich ['hɛslıç] *adj* ugly; nasty
Hast [hast] *f* (-;) haste
hasten ['hastən] *intr* be in a hurry, act quickly ‖ *intr* (SEIN) hasten, rush
hastig ['hastıç] *adj* hasty
hätscheln ['hɛtʃəln] *tr* caress, cuddle; (*verzärteln*) coddle, spoil
hatte ['hatə] *pret of* **haben**
Haube ['haubə] *f* (-;-n) cap; (aer) cowling; (aut) hood; (orn) crest
Haubitze [hau'bıtsə] *f* (-;-n) howitzer
Hauch [haux] *m* (-[e]s;-e) breath; breeze; (*Schicht*) thin layer; (*Spur*) trace
hauch'dünn' *adj* paper-thin
hauchen ['hauxən] *tr* whisper; (ling) aspirate ‖ *intr* breathe
Hauch'laut *m* (ling) aspirate
Haue ['hau·ə] *f* (-;-n) hoe; adze; **H. kriegen** get a spanking
hauen ['hau·ən] §93 *tr* hack, cut; strike; (*Baum*) fell; (*Stein*) hew ‖ §109 *tr* beat (up) ‖ *intr—h.* **nach** lash out at; **um sich h.** flail
Hauer ['hau·ər] *m* (-s;-) tusk
häufeln ['hɔıfəln] *tr* hill
häufen ['hɔıfən] *tr & ref* pile up
Haufen ['haufən] *m* (-s;-) pile, heap
Hau'fenwolke *f* cumulus cloud
häufig ['hɔıfıç] *adj* frequent ‖ *adv* frequently
Häu'figkeit *f* (-;) frequency
Häu'fung *f* (-;-en) accumulation
Haupt [haupt] *n* (-[e]s;⁀er) head; top; chief, leader **aufs H. schlagen** vanquish
Haupt- *comb.fm.* head; chief; major; most important; prime; primary, leading
Haupt'altar *m* high altar
haupt'amtlich *adj* full-time
Haupt'bahnhof *m* main train station
Haupt'darsteller *m* leading man
Haupt'darstellerin *f* leading lady
Häuptel ['hɔıptəl] *n* (-s;-) head
Haupt'fach *n* (educ) major

Haupt'farbe *f* primary color
Haupt'feldwebel *m* first sergeant
Haupt'film *m* (cin) feature
Haupt'gefreite §5 *m* private first class; lance corporal (Brit); seaman; airman second class
Haupt'geschäftsstelle *f* head office
Haupt'gewinn *m* first price
Haupt'haar *n* hair (*on the head*)
Häuptling ['hɔıptlıŋ] *m* (-s;-e) chief
häuptlings ['hɔıptlıŋs] *adv* head first
Haupt'linie *f* (rr) trunk line
Haupt'mann *m* (-[e]s;-leute) captain
Haupt'masse *f* bulk
Haupt'mast *m* mainmast
Hauptnenner ['hauptnenər] *m* (-s;-) (math) common denominator
Haupt'probe *f* dress rehearsal
Haupt'quartier *n* headquarters; **Großes H.** general headquarters
Haupt'rolle *f* leading role, lead
Haupt'sache *f* main thing; (jur) point at issue
haupt'sächlich *adj* main, principal
Haupt'satz *m* (gram) main clause; (phys) principle, law
Haupt'schalter *m* master switch
Haupt'schiff *n* (archit) nave
Haupt'schlagader *f* aorta
Haupt'schlüssel *m* master key, pass key
Haupt'schriftleiter *m* editor in chief
Haupt'spaß *m* great fun; great joke
Haupt'stadt *f* capital
Haupt'straße *f* main street; highway
Haupt'strecke *f* (rr) main line
Haupt'stütze *f* mainstay
Haupt'ton *m* primary accent
Haupt'treffer *m* first prize; jackpot
Haupt'verkehr *m* peak-hour traffic
Haupt'verkehrsstraße *f* main artery
Haupt'verkehrszeit *f* rush hour
Haupt'wort *n* (-[e]s;⁀er) noun
Haus [haus] *n* (-es;⁀er) house; **ein großes H. führen** do a lot of entertaining; **H. und Hof** house and home; **öffentliches H.** brothel; **nach Hause** home; **sich zu Hause fühlen** feel at home; **von zu Hause** from home
Haus'angestellte §5 *mf* domestic
Haus'apotheke *f* medicine cabinet
Haus'arbeit *f* housework; (educ) homework
Haus'arzt *m* family doctor
Haus'aufgabe *f* homework
haus'backen *adj* homemade; (*Frau*) plain; (fig) provincial
Haus'bedarf *m* household needs; **für den H.** for the home
Haus'brand *m* domestic fuel
Haus'bursche *m* porter
Haus'diener *m* porter
hausen ['hauzən] *intr* reside; (coll) make a mess; **schlimm h.** wreak havoc
Häuserblock ['hɔızərblɔk] *m* block of houses
Häusermakler **-in** ['hɔızərmaklər(ın)] §6 *mf* realtor
Haus'flur *m* entrance hall; hallway
Haus'frau *f* housewife; landlady
Haus'freund *m* friend of the family; (coll) wife's lover

Haus′gebrauch *m* family custom; household use
Haus′gehilfin *f* domestic
Haus′genosse *m*, **Haus′genossin** *f* occupant of the same house
Haus′gesinde *n* domestics
Haus′glocke *f* doorbell
Haus′halt *m* household; budget; **den H. führen** keep house
haus′halten §90 *intr* keep house; economize
Haushälter –in [′haʊshɛltər(ɪn)] §6 *mf* housekeeper
haushälterisch [′haʊshɛltərɪʃ] *adj* economical
Haus′haltsausschuß *m* ways and means committee
Haus′haltsgerät *n* household utensil
Haus′haltsjahr *n* fiscal year
Haus′haltsplan *m* budget
Haus′haltung *f* housekeeping; household; family budget; management
Haus′haltungslehre *f* home economics
Haus′herr *m* master of the house; landlord
Haus′herrin *f* lady of the house; landlady
haus′hoch′ *adj* very high; vast
Haus′hofmeister *m* steward
hausieren [haʊ′zirən] *intr*—**mit etw h.** peddle s.th.; go around telling everyone about s.th.
Hausierer [haʊ′zirər] *m* (-s;-) door-to-door salesman
Haus′lehrer –in §6 *mf* private tutor
häuslich [′hɔɪslɪç] *adj* home, domestic; homey; thrifty
Häus′lichkeit *f* (-;) family life; home
Haus′mädchen *n* maid
Haus′meister *m* caretaker, janitor
Haus′mittel *n* home remedy
Haus′mutter *f* mother of the family
Haus′pflege *f* home nursing
Haus′schlüssel *m* front-door key
Haus′schuh *m* slipper
Hausse [′hose] *f* (-;-n) (econ, st. exch.) boom
Haus′sespekulant *m* (st. exch.) bull
Haussier [hos′je] *m* (-s;-) (st. exch.) bull
haussieren [ho′sirən] *tr* (fin) raise ‖ *intr* (fin) go up, rise
Haus′stand *m* household
Haus′suchungsbefehl *m* search warrant
Haus′tier *n* domestic animal; pet
Haus′vater *m* father of the family
Haus′verwalter *m* superintendent
Haus′wesen *n* household
Haus′wirt *m* landlord
Haus′wirtin *f* landlady
Haus′wirtschaft *f* housekeeping
haus′wirtschaftlich *adj* domestic; household
Haus′wirtschaftslehre *f* home economics
Haus′zins *m* house rent
Haut [haʊt] *f* (-;ːe) skin; hide; **aus der H. fahren** fly off the handle
Haut′abschürfung *f* skin abrasion
Haut′arzt *m* dermatologist
Haut′ausschlag *m* rash
Häutchen [′hɔɪtçən] (-s;-) membrane; pellicle; film

häuten [′hɔɪtən] *tr* skin ‖ *ref* slough the skin
haut′eng *adj* skin-tight
Haut′farbe *f* complexion
Haut′plastik *f* skin graft
Haut′reizung *f* skin irritation
Haut′transplantation *f*, **Haut′verpflanzung** *f* skin grafting
havariert [hava′rirt] *adj* damaged
H′-Bombe *f* H-bomb
Hebamme [′hepamə] *f* (-;-n) midwife
Hebebaum [′hebəbaum] *m* lever
Hebebühne [′hebəbynə] *f* car lift
Hebeeisen [′hebə·aɪzən] *n* crowbar
Hebel [′hebəl] *m* (-s;-) lever
heben [′hebən] §94 *tr* lift, raise; (*steigern*) increase; (*fördern*) further; (aut) jack up ‖ *ref* rise
Heber [′hebər] *m* (-s;-) siphon; (aut) jack
Hebeschiff [′hebəʃɪf] *n* salvage ship
Hebräer –in [hɛ′bre·ər(ɪn)] §6 *mf* Hebrew
hebräisch [hɛ′bre·ɪʃ] *adj* Hebrew
He′bung *f* (-;-en) lifting; increase; improvement; (mus, pros) stress
Hecht [hɛçt] *m* (-[e]s;-e) (ichth) pike
hechten [′hɛçtən] *intr* dive
Hecht′sprung *m* flying leap; jacknife dive
Heck [hɛk] *n* (-[e]s;-e & -s) stern; (aer) tail; (aut) rear
Heck′antrieb *m* (aut) rear drive
Hecke [′hɛkə] *f* (-;-n) hedge; brood, hatch
hecken [′hɛkən] *tr* & *intr* breed
Heckenhüpfen (Hek′kenhüpfen) *n* (-s;) (aer) hedgehopping
Heckenschütze (Hek′kenschütze) *m* sniper
Heck′fenster *n* (aut) rear window
Heck′licht *n* (aer, aut) tail light
Heck′motor *m* rear engine
Heck′pfennig *m* lucky penny
Heck′schütze *m* (aer) tail gunner
heda [′hedɑ] *interj* hey there!
Heer [her] *n* (-[e]s;-e) army; host
Heeres– [herəs] *comb.fm.* army
Hee′resbericht *m* official army communiqué
Hee′resdienst *m* military service
Hee′resdienstvorschriften *pl* army regulations
Hee′resgeistliche §5 *m* army chaplain
Hee′resmacht *f* armed forces; army
Hee′reszug *m* (mil) campaign
Heer′lager *n* army camp; (pol) faction
Heer′schar *f* host, legion
Heer′zug *m* (mil) campaign
Hefe [′hefə] *f* (-;-n) yeast; dregs
He′feteig *m* leavened dough
Heft [hɛft] *n* (-[e]s;-e) haft, handle; notebook; (e–r Zeitschrift) issue
heften [′hɛftən] *tr* fasten together; sew, stitch; tack, baste; (Blick) fix ‖ *ref* (an acc) stick close (to)
heftig [′hɛftɪç] *adj* violent; (Regen) heavy; (Fieber) high; **h. werden** lose one's temper
Heft′klammer *f* paper clip; staple
Heft′maschine *f* stapler
Heft′stich *m* (sew) tack
Heft′zwecke *f* thumbtack

hegen ['heːgən] *tr* (*Wild*) preserve; (*Zweifel, Gedanken*) have; **h. und pflegen** lavish care on
Hehl [heːl] *n* (-[e]s;) secret
hehlen ['heːlən] *intr* receive stolen goods
Heh'ler –**in** §6 *mf* fence
hehr [heːr] *adj* sublime, noble
Heide ['haɪdə] *m* (-n;-n) heathen; (Bib) gentile || *f* (-;-n) heath
Hei'dekraut *n* heather
Heidelbeere ['haɪdəlbeːrə] *f* blueberry
Hei'denangst *f* (coll) jitters
Hei'dengeld *n* (coll) piles of money
Hei'denlärm *m* hullabaloo
hei'denmäßig *adv*—**h. viel** tremendous amount of
Hei'denspaß *m* (coll) great fun
Heidentum ['haɪdəntum] *n* (-s;) heathendom
heidi [haɪ'di] *adj* gone; lost; **h. gehen** get lost; be all gone || *interj* quick!
Heidin ['haɪdɪn] *f* (-;-nen) heathen
heidnisch ['haɪdnɪʃ] *adj* heathen
heikel ['haɪkəl] *adj* particular, fastidious; (*Sache*) ticklish
heil [haɪl] *adj* safe, sound; undamaged || **Heil** *n* (-[e]s;) welfare, benefit; salvation || **Heil** *interj* hail!
Heiland ['haɪlant] *m* (-[e]s;) Saviour
Heil'anstalt *f* sanitarium
Heil'bad *n* spa
heilbar ['haɪlbɑr] *adj* curable
heil'bringend *adj* beneficial, healthful
Heilbutt ['haɪlbut] *m* (-[e]s;-e) (ichth) halibut
heilen ['haɪlən] *tr* heal || *intr* (HABEN & SEIN) heal
Heil'gehilfe *m* male nurse
Heil'gymnastik *f* physical therapy
heilig ['haɪlɪç] *adj* holy, sacred || **Heilige** §5 *mf* saint
Hei'ligabend *m* Christmas Eve
heiligen ['haɪlɪgən] *tr* hallow
Hei'ligenschein *m* halo
Hei'ligkeit *f* (-;) holiness, sanctity
hei'ligsprechen §64 *tr* canonize
Heiligtum ['haɪlɪçtum] *n* (-[e]s;-er) sanctuary; shrine; sacred relic
Hei'ligung *f* (-;) sanctification
Heil'kraft *f* healing power
Heil'kraut *n* medicinal herb
Heil'kunde *f* medical science
heil'los *adj* wicked; (coll) awful
Heil'mittel *n* remedy; medicine
Heil'mittellehre *f* pharmacology
heilsam ['haɪlzɑm] *adj* healthful
Heils'armee *f* Salvation Army
Heil'stätte *f* sanitarium
Hei'lung *f* (-;-en) cure
heim [haɪm] *adv* home || **Heim** *n* (-[e]s;-e) home; (*Alters-*) old-age home
Heimat ['haɪmɑt] *f* (-;-en) home; hometown; homeland
hei'matlich *adj* native
hei'matlos *adj* homeless
Hei'matort *m* hometown, home village
Hei'matstadt *f* hometown, native city
heim'begeben §80 *ref* head home
Heimchen ['haɪmçən] *n* (-s;-) cricket
Heim'computer *m* home computer
Heim'fahrt *f* homeward journey

heim'finden §59 *intr* find one's way home
Heim'gang *m* going home; passing on
heimisch ['haɪmɪʃ] *adj* local; locally-produced; domestic; **heimische Sprache** vernacular; **h. werden** settle down; become established; **sich h. fühlen** feel at home
Heimkehr ['haɪmkeːr] *f* (-;) homecoming
heim'kehren *intr* (SEIN) return home
Heim'kunft *f* homecoming
heim'leuchten *intr* (sl) (*dat*) tell (*s.o.*) where to get off
heim'lich *adj* secret
Heim'lichkeit *f* (-;-en) secrecy; (*Geheimnis*) secret
Heim'reise *f* homeward journey
heim'suchen *tr* afflict, plague
Heim'tücke *f* treachery
heim'tückisch *adj* treacherous
heimwärts ['haɪmverts] *adv* homeward
Heim'weh *n* homesickness; nostalgia
heim'zahlen *tr*—**j-m etw h.** (coll) pay s.o. back for s.th.
Heini ['haɪni] *m* (-s;) Harry; guy
Heinzelmännchen ['haɪntsəlmɛnçən] *pl* (myth) little people
Heirat ['haɪrɑt] *f* (-;-en) marriage
heiraten ['haɪrɑtən] *tr & intr* marry
Hei'ratsantrag *m* marriage proposal
hei'ratsfähig *adj* marriageable
Hei'ratsgut *n* dowry
Hei'ratskandidat *m* eligible bachelor
Hei'ratsurkunde *f* marriage certificate
Hei'ratsvermittler –**in** §6 *mf* marriage broker
heischen ['haɪʃən] *tr* demand; beg
heiser ['haɪzər] *adj* hoarse
heiß [haɪs] *adj* hot; (fig) ardent
heißen ['haɪsən] §95 *tr* call; ask, bid; mean || *intr* be called; **das heißt** that is, i.e.; **wie h. Sie?** what is your name?
heiß'geliebt *adj* beloved
heiter ['haɪtər] *adj* cheerful; hilarious; serene; (*Wetter*) clear
Heiz– [haɪts] *comb.fm.* heating
Heiz'anlage *f* heating system
Heiz'apparat *m* heater
heizen ['haɪtsən] *tr* heat; **den Ofen mit Kohle h.** burn coal in the stove || *intr* give off heat; heat; turn on the heating; light the fire (or stove)
Hei'zer *m* (-s;) boilerman; (naut) stoker; (rr) fireman
Heiz'faden *m* (elec) filament
Heiz'kissen *n* heating pad
Heiz'körper *m* radiator; heater
Heiz'material *n* fuel
Heiz'platte *f* hot plate
Heiz'raum *m* boiler room
Heiz'schlange *f* heating coil
Hei'zung *f* (-;) heating; (coll) central heating; radiator
Hei'zungskessel *m* boiler
Hei'zungsrohr *n* radiator pipe
Held [hɛlt] *m* (-en;-en) hero
Hel'denalter *n* heroic age
Hel'dendenkmal *n* epic
Hel'dengedicht *n* epic
Hel'dengeist *m* heroism
hel'denhaft *adj* heroic
Hel'denmut *m* heroism

hel'denmütig *adj* heroic
Hel'dentat *f* heroic deed, exploit
Heldentum ['hɛldəntum] *n* (-[e]s;) heroism
Heldin ['hɛldɪn] *f* (-;-nen) heroine
helfen ['hɛlfən] *intr* (*dat*) help; **es hilft nichts** it's of no use
Hel'fer –in §6 *mf* helper
Hel'fershelfer *m* accomplice
Helikopter [helɪ'kɔptər] *m* (-s;-) helicopter
hell [hɛl] *adj* clear; bright; lucid; (*Haar*) fair; (*Bier*) light; (*Wahnsinn, usw.*) sheer ‖ **Helle** §5 *f* brightness; lightness; clarity ‖ *n* light; **ein Helles** a glass of light beer
hellenisch [hɛ'lenɪʃ] *adj* Hellenic
Heller ['hɛlər] *m* (-s;-) penny
hellhörig ['hɛlhørɪç] *adj* having sharp ears; **h. werden** prick up one's ears
hellicht ['hɛlɪçt] *adj*—**hellichter Tag** broad daylight
Hel'ligkeit *f* (-;-en) brightness; (astr) magnitude
hell'sehen §138 *intr* be clairvoyant ‖ **Hellsehen** *n* (-s;) clairvoyance
Hell'seher –in §6 *mf* clairvoyant; (coll) mind reader
hell'sichtig *adj* clear-sighted
hell'wach' *adj* wide awake
Helm [hɛlm] *m* (-[e]s;-e) helmet; (archit) dome, spire; (naut) helm
Helm'busch *m* crest, plume
Hemd [hɛmt] *n* (-[e]s;-en) shirt
Hemd'brust *f* dickey, shirt front
Hemd'hose *f* union suit
hemmen ['hɛmən] *tr* slow up; stop; **gehemmt** inhibited
Hemmnis ['hɛmnɪs] *n* (-ses;-se) hindrance
Hemmschuh ['hɛmʃu] *m* (fig) hindrance; (rr) brake
Hem'mung *f* (-;-en) inhibition
hem'mungslos *adj* uninhibited
Hengst [hɛŋst] *m* (-es;-e) stallion
Henkel ['hɛŋkəl] *m* (-s;-) handle
henken ['hɛŋkən] *tr* hang (*s.o.*)
Henker ['hɛŋkər] *m* (-s;-) hangman
Henne ['hɛnə] *f* (-;-n) hen
her [her] *adv* hither, here; ago
herab [he'rap] *adv* down, downwards
herab- *comb.fm.* down; down here
herab'drücken *tr* press down; force down; **die Kurse h.** bear the market
herab'lassen §104 *ref* condescend
Herab'lassung *f* (-;) condescension
herab'sehen §138 *intr* (**auf** *acc*) look down (on)
herab'setzen *tr* put down; reduce; belittle, disparage
herab'steigen §148 *intr* (SEIN) climb down; (*vom Pferd*) dismount
herab'würdigen *tr* demean
Heraldik [he'raldɪk] *f* (-;) heraldry
heran [he'ran] *adv* near; up
heran'arbeiten *ref* (**an** *acc*) work one's way (towards)
heran'bilden *tr* (**zu**) train (as)
heran'brechen §64 *intr* (SEIN) (*Tag*) dawn, break; (*Nacht*) fall, come on
heran'gehen §82 *intr* (SEIN) go close; **h. an** (*acc*) approach, go up to
heran'kommen §99 *intr* (SEIN) come

near; **h. an** (*acc*) approach; get at; **h. bis an** (*acc*) reach as far as
heran'machen *ref*—**h. an** (*acc*) apply oneself to; approach
heran'nahen *intr* (SEIN) approach
heran'wachsen §155 *intr* (SEIN) (**zu**) grow up (to be)
heran'wagen *ref* (**an** *acc*) dare to approach
heran'ziehen §163 *tr* pull closer; call on for help; (*Quellen*) consult; (*zur Beratung*) call in; (*Pflanzen*) grow; (*Nachwuchs*) train ‖ *intr* (SEIN) approach
herauf [he'rauf] *adv* up, up here; upstairs
herauf'arbeiten *ref* work one's way up
herauf'bemühen *ref* take the trouble to come up (or upstairs)
herauf'beschwören §137 *tr* conjure up; (*verursachen*) bring on, provoke
herauf'kommen §99 *intr* (SEIN) come up
herauf'setzen *tr* raise, increase
herauf'steigen §148 *intr* (SEIN) climb up; (*Tag*) dawn
herauf'ziehen §163 *tr* pull up ‖ *intr* (SEIN) move upstairs; (*Sturm*) come up
heraus [he'raus] *adv* out, out here
heraus'bekommen §99 *tr* (**aus**) get out (of); (*Wort*) utter; (*Geld*) get back in change; (*Problem*) figure out
heraus'bringen §65 *tr* bring out; (*Wort*) utter; (*Lösung*) work out; (*Buch*) publish; (*Fabrikat*) bring out
heraus'drücken *tr* squeeze out; (*die Brust*) throw out
heraus'fahren §71 *intr* (SEIN) drive out; (*aus dem Bett*) jump out; (*Bemerkung*) slip out
heraus'finden §59 *tr* find out ‖ *ref* (**aus**) find one's way out (of)
heraus'fordern *tr* challenge, call on
heraus'fordernd *adj* defiant ‖ *adv* defiantly; **sich h. anziehen** dress provocatively
Heraus'forderung *f* (-;-en) challenge
heraus'fühlen *tr* sense
Heraus'gabe *f* surrender; (*e-s Buches*) publication; (jur) restitution
heraus'geben §80 *tr* surrender; give back; (*Buch*) publish ‖ *intr* (*dat*) give (*s.o.*) his change; **h. auf** (*acc*) give change for
Heraus'geber *m* publisher; (*Redakteur*) editor
heraus'greifen §88 *tr* single out
heraus'haben §89 *tr* have (*s.th.*) figured out; **er hat den Bogen heraus** (coll) he has the knack of it
heraus'halten §90 *tr* hold out ‖ *ref* (**aus**) keep out (of)
heraus'hängen §92 *tr* & *intr* hang out
heraus'kommen §99 *intr* (SEIN) come out
heraus'lesen §107 *tr* pick out; deduce; **zu viel aus e-m Gedicht h.** read too much into a poem
heraus'machen *tr* (*Fleck*) get out ‖ *ref* (*Kinder*) turn out well; (*Geschäft*) make out well
heraus'nehmen §116 *tr* take out ‖ *ref*

—**sich** [*dat*] **zu viel** (or **Freiheiten**) **h.** take liberties
heraus′platzen *intr* (SEIN)—**mit etw h.** blurt out s.th.
heraus′putzen *ref* dress up
heraus′reden *ref* (**aus**) talk one's way out (of)
heraus′rücken *tr* move out (here); (coll) (*Geld*) shell out ‖ *intr* (SEIN) —**mit dem Geld h.** shell out money; **mit der Sprache h.** reveal it, admit it
heraus′schälen *ref* become apparent
heraus′stehen §146 *intr* protrude
heraus′steigen §148 *intr* (SEIN) (**aus**) climb out (of), step out (of)
heraus′stellen *tr* put out; **groß h.** give a big build-up to; **klar h.** present clearly ‖ *ref* emerge, come to light; **sich h. als** prove to be
heraus′streichen §85 *tr* delete; (fig) praise
heraus′suchen *tr* pick out
heraus′treten §152 *intr* (SEIN) come out, step out; bulge, protrude
heraus′winden §59 *ref* extricate oneself
heraus′wirtschaften *tr* manage to save; (*Profit*) manage to make
heraus′ziehen §163 *tr* pull out
herb [herp] *adj* harsh; (*sauer*) sour; (*zusammenziehend*) tangy; (*Wein*) dry; (*Worte*) bitter; (*Schönheit*) austere ‖ **Herbe** *f* (−;) harshness; tang; bitterness; austerity
herbei′ *adv* here (*toward the speaker*)
herbei– *comb.fm.* up, along, here (*toward the speaker*)
herbei′bringen §65 *tr* bring along
herbei′eilen *intr* (SEIN) hurry here
herbei′führen *tr* bring here; cause
herbei′kommen §99 *intr* (SEIN) come up
herbei′lassen §104 *ref* condescend
herbei′rufen §122 *tr* call over; summon
herbei′schaffen *tr* bring here; procure; (*Geld*) raise
herbei′sehnen *tr* long for
herbei′strömen *intr* (SEIN) come flocking, flock
herbei′winken *tr* beckon (*s.o.*) to come over
herbei′wünschen *tr* long for, wish for
Herberge [′hɛrbɛrgə] *f* (−;−n) lodging, shelter; hostel; (obs) inn
her′beten *tr* say mechanically
Herb′heit *f* (−;), **Her′bigkeit** *f* (−;) harshness; tang; bitterness; austerity
her′bringen §65 *tr* bring here
Herbst [herpst] *m* (−es;−e) autumn
herbst′lich *adj* autumn, fall
Herd [hert] *m* (−[e]s;−e) hearth, fireplace; home; kitchen range; center
Herde [′hɛrdə] *f* (−;−n) herd, flock
herein [hɛ′raɪn] *adv* in, in here; **h.!** come in!
herein– *comb.fm.* in, in here (*toward the speaker*)
herein′bemühen *tr* ask (*s.o.*) to come in ‖ *ref* trouble oneself to come in
herein′bitten §60 *tr* invite in
Herein′fall *m* disappointment, letdown
herein′fallen §72 *intr* (SEIN) fall in; **h. auf** (*acc*) fall for; **h. in** (*acc*) fall into

herein′legen *tr* fool, take in
herein′platzen *intr* (SEIN) burst in
her′fallen §72 *intr* (SEIN)—**h. über** (*acc*) fall upon, attack
her′finden §59 *ref* & *intr* find one's way here
Her′gang *m* background details
her′geben §80 *tr* hand over; give up ‖ *ref*—**sich h. zu** be a party to
her′halten §90 *tr* hold out, extend ‖ *intr*—**h. müssen** (*Person*) be the victim; (*Sache*) have to do (*as a makeshift*)
Hering [′herɪŋ] *m* (−s;−e) herring; **sitzen wie die Heringe** be packed in like sardines
her′kommen §99 *intr* (SEIN) come here; (*Wort*) originate; **wo kommst du denn her?** where have you come from? ‖ **Herkommen** *n* (−s;−) origin; custom, tradition, convention
herkömmlich [′hɛrkœmlɪç] *adj* customary, usual; traditional, conventional
Herkunft [′herkunft] *f* (−;) origin; birth, family
her′laufen §105 *intr* (SEIN) walk here; **hinter j-m h.** follow s.o.
her′leiten *tr* derive; deduce, infer
Her′leitung *f* (−;−en) derivation
her′machen *tr*—**viel h. von** make a fuss over ‖ *ref*—**sich h. über** (*acc*) attack; (fig) tackle
Hermelin [hɛrmə′lin] *m* (−s;−e) ermine ‖ *n* (−s;−e) (zool) ermine
hermetisch [hɛr′metɪʃ] *adj* hermetic
hernach′ *adv* afterwards
her′nehmen §116 *tr* get; **j-n scharf h.** give s.o. a good talking-to
hernie′der *adv* down, down here
Heroin [hero′in] *n* (−s;) (pharm) heroin
Heroine [hero′inə] *f* (−;−n) heroine
heroisch [he′ro·ɪʃ] *adj* heroic
Heroismus [hero′ɪsmus] *m* (−;) heroism
Herold [′herɔlt] *m* (−[e]s;−e) herald
Heros [′herɔs] *m* (−; **Heroen** [he′ro·ən]) hero
Herr [hɛr] *m* (−n;−en) lord; master; gentleman; (*als Anrede*) Sir; (*vor Eigennamen*) Mr.; (*Gott*) Lord; **meine Herren!** gentlemen!
her′reichen *tr* hand, pass
Herren– [′hɛrən] *comb.fm.* man's, men's; gentlemen's
Her′renabend *m* stag party
Her′renbegleitung *f*—**in H.** accompanied by a gentleman
Her′rendoppel(spiel) *n* (tennis) men's doubles
Her′reneinzel(spiel) *n* (tennis) men's singles
Her′renfahrer *m* (aut) owner-driver
Her′renfriseur *m* barber
Her′rengesellschaft *f* male company; stag party
Her′rengröße *f* men's size
Her′rengut *n* domain, manor
Her′renhaus *n* mansion; House of Lords
Her′renhof *m* manor
Her′renleben *n* life of Riley

her'renlos *adj* ownerless
Her'renmensch *m* born leader
Her'renschnitt *m* woman's very short hairstyle
Her'renzimmer *n* study
Herr'gott *m* Lord, Lord God
her'richten *tr* arrange; get ready
Herrin ['herɪn] *f* (-;-nen) lady
herrisch ['herɪʃ] *adj* masterful
herr'lich *adj* splendid
Herr'lichkeit *f* (-;-en) splendor
Herr'schaft *f* (-;-en) rule, domination; mastery; control; lord, master; estate; **meine Herrschaften!** ladies and gentlemen!
herr'schaftlich *adj* ruler's; gentleman's; high-class
herrschen ['herʃən] *intr* rule; prevail; exist
Herr'scher –in §6 *mf* ruler
Herrschsucht ['herʃzuçt] *f* (-;) thirst for power; bossiness
herrsch'süchtig *adj* power-hungry; autocratic; domineering
her'rühren *intr*—**h. von** come from, originate with
her'sagen *tr* recite, say
her'schaffen *tr* get (here)
her'stammen *intr*—**h. von** come from, be descended from; (gram) be derived from
her'stellen *tr* put here; (*erzeugen*) produce; **fabrikmäßig h.** mass-produce; **Verbindung h.** establish contact; (telp) put a call through
Her'steller *m* (-s;-) manufacturer
Her'stellung *f* (-;-en) production
Her'stellungsbetrieb *m* factory
Her'stellungsverfahren *n* manufacturing process
herüber [he'rybər] *adv* over, over here, in this direction (*toward the speaker*)
herum [he'rum] *adv* around; about
herum'bringen §65 *tr* bring around; (*Zeit*) spend
herum'drehen *tr, ref & intr* turn around
herum'fragen *intr* make inquiries
herumfuchteln [he'rumfuxtəln] *intr*— **mit den Händen h.** wave one's hands about
herum'führen *tr* show around
herum'greifen §88 *intr*—**h. um** reach around
herum'hacken *intr*—**h. auf** (*dat*) pick on, criticize
herum'kauen *intr* (**an** *dat,* **auf** *dat*) chew away (on)
herum'kommen §99 *intr* (SEIN) get around; **h. um** get around; evade
herum'lungern *intr* loaf around
herum'reiten §86 *intr* (SEIN) ride around; **h. auf** (*dat*) harp on (*s.th.*); pick on (*s.o.*)
herum'schnüffeln *intr* snoop around
herum'streichen §85 *intr* (SEIN) prowl about
herum'streiten §86 *ref* squabble
herum'treiben §62 *tr* drive around ‖ *ref* roam around, knock about
Herum'treiber *m* (-s;-) loafer, tramp
herum'ziehen §163 *tr* pull around; **h. um** draw (*s.th.*) around ‖ *ref*—**sich h. um** surround ‖ *intr* (SEIN) wander

around; run around; **h. um** march around
herunter [he'runtər] *adv* down, down here (*towards the speaker*); downstairs; **den Berg h.** down the mountain; **ins Tal h.** down into the valley
herun'terbringen §65 *tr* bring down; (fig) lower, reduce
herun'tergehen §82 *intr* (SEIN) go down; (*Preis, Temperatur*) fall, drop
herun'terhandeln *tr* (*Preis*) beat down
herun'terhauen §93 *tr* chop off; (*Brief*) dash off; **j–m eins h.** clout s.o.
herun'terkommen §99 *intr* (SEIN) come down; come downstairs; deteriorate
herun'terlassen §104 *tr* let down, lower
herun'terleiern *tr* drone
herun'terlesen §107 *tr* (*Liste*) read down; rattle off
herun'termachen *tr* take down; turn down; (coll) chew out; (coll) pan
herun'terschießen §76 *tr* shoot down
herun'tersein §139 *intr* (SEIN) be run-down
herun'terwirtschaften *tr* ruin (*through mismanagement*)
herun'terwürgen *tr* choke down
hervor [her'for] *adv* out; forth
hervor'bringen §65 *tr* bring out; engender, produce; (*Wort*) utter
hervor'dringen §142 *intr* (SEIN) emerge
hervor'gehen §82 *intr* (SEIN)—**h. aus** come from; emerge from; to have been trained at
hervor'heben §94 *tr* highlight
hervor'holen *tr* produce
hervor'kommen §99 *intr* (SEIN) come out
hervor'lugen *intr* peep out
hervor'ragen *intr* jut out; be prominent; **h. über** (*acc*) tower over
hervor'ragend *adj* prominent
hervor'rufen §122 *tr* evoke, cause; (*Schauspieler*) recall
hervor'stechen §64 *intr* stick out; be conspicuous; be prominent
hervor'treten §152 *intr* (SEIN) emerge; come to the fore; become apparent; (*Augen*) bulge; (*Ader*) protrude
hervor'tun §154 *ref* distinguish oneself
hervor'wagen *ref* dare to come out; **sich mit e–r Antwort h.** venture an answer
hervor'zaubern *tr* produce by magic; **ein Essen h.** whip up a meal
Herweg ['hervek] *m* way here; way home
Herz [herts] *n* (-ens;-en) heart; (*als Anrede*) darling; (cards) heart(s); **ich bringe es nicht übers H. zu** (*inf*) I haven't the heart to (*inf*); **sich** [*dat*] **ein H. fassen** get up the courage; **seinem Herzen Luft machen** give vent to one's feelings
Herz– *comb.fm.* heart, cardiac
Herz'anfall *m* heart attack
Herz'beschwerden *pl* heart trouble
Herz'blume *f* (bot) bleeding heart
herzen ['hertsən] *tr* hug, embrace
Her'zensgrund *m* bottom of one's heart
her'zensgut *adj* good-hearted

Her′zenslust *f*—**nach H.** to one's heart's content

herz′ergreifend *adj* moving, touching

Herz′geräusch *n* heart murmur

herz′haft *adj* hearty

herzig [′hɛrtsɪç] *adj* sweet, cute

–herzig *comb.fm.* –hearted

Herzinfarkt [′hɛrtsɪnfarkt] *m* (–[e]s; –e) cardiac infarction

herz′innig *adj* heartfelt

herz′inniglich *adv* sincerely

Herz′klappe *f* cardiac valve

Herz′klopfen *n* palpitations

Herz′kollaps *m* heart failure

herz′lich *adj* cordial; sincere ‖ *adv* very; **h. wenige** precious few

herz′los *adj* heartless

Herzog [′hɛrtsɔk] *m* (–[e]s; ̈e) duke

Herzogin [′hɛrtsɔgɪn] *f* (–; –nen) duchess

Herzogtum [′hɛrtsɔktum] *n* (–[e]s; ̈er) dukedom; duchy

Herz′schlag *m* heartbeat; heart failure

Herz′stück *n* heart, central point

Herz′verpflanzung *f* heart transplant

Herz′weh *n* (& fig) heartache

Hetzblatt [′hɛtsblat] *n* scandal sheet

Hetze [′hɛtsə] *f* (–; –n) hunting; hurry, rush; vicious campaign; baiting

hetzen [′hɛtsən] *tr* hunt; bait; rush; (fig) hound; **e-n Hund auf j-n h.** sic a dog on s.o. ‖ *ref* rush ‖ *intr* stir up trouble; **h. gegen** conduct a vicious campaign against ‖ *intr* (SEIN) race, dash

Het′zer –in §6 *mf* agitator

Hetz′hund *m* hound, hunting dog

Hetz′jagd *f* hunt; baiting; hurry

Hetz′rede *f* inflammatory speech

Heu [hɔɪ] *n* (–[e]s;) hay

Heu′boden *m* hayloft

Heuchelei [hɔɪçə′laɪ] *f* (–; –en) hypocrisy; piece of hypocrisy

heucheln [′hɔɪçəln] *tr* feign ‖ *intr* be hypocritical

Heuch′ler –in §6 *mf* hypocrite

heuchlerisch [′hɔɪçlərɪʃ] *adj* hypocritical

heuen [′hɔɪ·ən] *intr* make hay

heuer [′hɔɪ·ər] *adv* this year

heuern [′hɔɪ·ərn] *tr* hire

Heu′fieber *n* hayfever

Heu′gabel *f* pitchfork

heulen [′hɔɪlən] *intr* bawl; (*Wind*) howl

heurig [′hɔɪrɪç] *adj* this year's ‖ **Heurige** §5 *m* new wine

Heu′schnupfen *m* (–s;) hayfever

Heuschober [′hɔɪʃobər] *m* (–s; –) haystack

Heu′schrecke *f* (–; –n) locust

heute [′hɔɪtə] *adv* today; **h. abend** this evening; **h. früh** (or **h. morgen**) this morning; **h. vor acht Tagen** a week ago today; **h. in acht Tagen** today a week

heutig [′hɔɪtɪç] *adj* today's; present-day; **am heutigen Tage** (or **der heutige Tag** or **mit dem heutigen Tag**) today

heutzutage [′hɔɪttsutɑgə] *adv* nowadays

Hexe [′hɛksə] *f* (–; –n) witch; hag

hexen [′hɛksən] *intr* practice witchcraft

He′xenkessel *m* chaos, inferno

He′xenmeister *m* wizard; sorcerer

He′xenschuß *m* lumbago

Hexerei [hɛksə′raɪ] *f* (–;) witchcraft

Hiatus [hɪ′ɑtus] *m* (–;–) (& pros) hiatus

Hibis·kus [hɪ′bɪskus] *m* (–;–ken [kən]) hibiscus

hieb [hip] *pret* of **hauen** ‖ **Hieb** *m* (–[e]s;–e) blow, stroke; **Hiebe** thrashing

hieb′–undstich′fest *adj* (fig) watertight

Hieb′wunde *f* gash

hielt [hilt] *pret* of **halten**

hier [hir] *adv* here

hieran′ *adv* at (by, in, on, to) it or them

Hierar·chie [hɪ·erar′çi] *f* (–;–chien [′çi·ən]) hierarchy

hierauf′ *adv* on it, on them; then

hieraus′ *adv* out of it (or them); from this (or these)

hierbei′ *adv* near here; here; in this case; in connection with this

hierdurch′ *adv* through it (or them); through here; hereby

hierfür′ *adv* for it (or them)

hierge′gen *adv* against it

hierher′ *adv* hither, here

hier′herum *adv* around here

hierhin′ *adv* here; **bis h.** up to here

hierin′ *adv* herein, in this

hiermit′ *adv* herewith, with it

hiernach′ *adv* after this, then; about this; according to this

Hieroglyphe [hɪ·ero′glyfə] *f* (–;–n) hieroglyph

hierorts [′hirɔrts] *adv* in this town

hierü′ber *adv* over it (or them); about it (or this)

hierzu′ *adv* to it; in addition to it; concerning this

hiesig [′hizɪç] *adj* local

hieß [his] *pret* of **heißen**

Hilfe [′hɪlfə] *f* (–;–n) help, aid; **zu H. nehmen** make use of

Hil′feleistung *f* assistance

Hil′feruf *m* cry for help

hilf′los *adj* helpless

hilf′reich *adj* helpful

Hilfs– [hɪlfs] *comb.fm.* auxiliary

Hilfs′arbeiter –in §6 *mf* unskilled laborer

Hilfs′arzt *m*, **Hilf′ärztin** *f* intern

hilfs′bedürftig *adj* needy

hilfs′bereit *adj* ready to help

Hilfs′dienst *m* help, assistance

Hilfs′gerät *n* labor-saving device

Hilfs′kraft *f* assistant, helper; (mach) auxiliary power

Hilfs′kraftbremse *f* power brake

Hilfs′kraftlenkung *f* power steering

Hilfs′lehrer –in §6 *mf* student teacher

Hilfs′maschine *f* auxiliary engine

Hilfs′mittel *n* aid, device; remedy; financial aid

Hilfs′quellen *pl* material; sources

Hilfs′rakete *f* booster rocket

Hilfs′schule *f* school for the mentally slow

Hilfs'truppen *pl* auxiliaries

Hilfs'werk *n* welfare organization

Hilfs'zeitwort *n* (-[e]s;⁼er) (gram) auxiliary (verb)

Himbeere ['hɪmberə] *f* (-;-n) raspberry

Himmel ['hɪməl] *m* (-s;-) sky, skies; heaven(s); firmament; (eccl) baldachin; **ach du lieber H.!** good heavens!; **aus heiterem H.** out of the blue; **in den H. heben** praise to the skies

himmelan' *adv* skywards; heavenwards

him'melangst *invar adj*—**mir wird h.** I feel frightened to death

Him'melbett *n* canopy bed

him'melblau *adj* sky-blue

Him'melfahrt *f* ascension; assumption

Him'melfahrtstag *m* Ascension Day

Him'melreich *n* kingdom of heaven

Himmels– *comb.fm.* celestial

him'melschreiend *adj* atrocious

Him'melsgegend *f* region of the sky; point of the compass

Him'melskörper *m* celestial body

Him'melsrichtung *f* point of the compass; direction

Him'melsschrift *f* skywriting

Him'melswagen *m* (astr) Great Bear

Him'melszelt *n* canopy of heaven

himmelwärts ['hɪməlverts] *adv* skywards; heavenwards

himmlisch ['hɪmlɪʃ] *adj* heavenly, celestial; divine; (coll) gorgeous

hin [hɪn] *adv* there (*away from the speaker*); **ganz hin** (coll) bushed; (coll) quite carried away; **hin ist hin** what's done is done; **hin und her** up and down, back and forth; **hin und wieder** now and then; **vor sich hin** to oneself

hinab' *adv* down

hinan' *adv* up; **bis an etw h.** up to s.th., as far as s.th.

hinauf' *adv* up, up there; upstairs; **den Fluß h.** up the river

hinauf'reichen *tr* hand (*s.th.*) up ‖ *intr* reach up

hinauf'schrauben *tr* (Preis) jack up

hinauf'setzen *tr* raise, increase

hinauf'steigen §148 *tr* (SEIN) (Treppe, Berg) climb ‖ *intr* (SEIN) climb up; (Temperatur) rise

hinaus' *adv* out, out there; **auf viele Jahre h.** for many years to come

hinaus'beißen §53 *tr* (coll) edge out

hinaus'gehen §82 *intr* (SEIN) go out; **h. auf** (acc) look out over; lead to; drive at, imply; **h. über** (acc) exceed

hinaus'kommen §99 *intr* (SEIN) come out; **es kommt auf eins** (or **aufs gleiche**) **hinaus** it amounts to the same thing; **h. über** (acc) get beyond

hinaus'laufen §105 *intr* (SEIN) run out; **es läuft aufs eins** (or **aufs gleiche**) **hinaus** it amounts to the same thing

hinaus'schieben §130 *tr* push out; (Termin, usw.) postpone

hinaus'werfen §160 *tr* throw out; fire

hinaus'wollen §162 *intr* want to go out; **h. auf** (acc) be driving at; **hoch h.** aim high, be ambitious

hinaus'ziehen §163 *tr* prolong ‖ *ref*

take longer than expected ‖ *intr* (SEIN) go out; move out

Hin'blick *m*—**im H. auf** (acc) in view of

hin'bringen §65 *tr* bring (there); take (there); (Zeit) pass

hinderlich ['hɪndərlɪç] *adj* in the way

hindern ['hɪndərn] *tr* block; **h. an** (dat) prevent from (ger)

Hindernis ['hɪndərnɪs] *n* (-ses;-se) hindrance; obstacle

Hin'dernisbahn *f* obstacle course

Hin'dernislauf *m* (sport) hurdles

Hin'dernisrennen *n* steeplechase; hurdles

hin'deuten *intr* (auf acc) point (to)

hindurch' *adv* through; **den ganzen Sommer h.** throughout the summer

hinein' *adv* in, in there

hinein'arbeiten *ref*—**sich h. in** (acc) work one's way into

hinein'denken §66 *ref*—**sich h. in** (acc) imagine oneself in

hinein'geraten §63 *intr* (SEIN)—**h. in** (acc) get into, fall into

hinein'leben *intr*—**in den Tag h.** live for the moment

hinein'tun §154 *tr* put in

Hin'fahrt *f* journey there, out-bound passage

hin'fallen §72 *intr* (SEIN) fall down

hinfällig ['hɪnfɛlɪç] *adj* frail; (Gesetz) invalid

hinfort' *adv* henceforth

hing [hɪŋ] *pret* of **hängen**

Hin'gabe *f* (an acc) devotion (to)

hin'geben §80 *tr* give up ‖ *ref* (dat) abandon oneself (to)

Hin'gebung *f* (-;) devotion

hinge'gen *adv* on the other hand

hin'gehen §82 *intr* (SEIN) go there; pass

hin'halten §90 *tr* hold out; (Person) keep waiting, string along; **den Kopf h.** (fig) take the rap

hinken ['hɪŋkən] *intr* limp; **der Vergleich hinkt** that's a poor comparison ‖ *intr* (SEIN) limp

hin'länglich *adj* sufficient

hin'legen *tr* put down ‖ *ref* lie down

hin'nehmen §116 *tr* accept; take, put up with

hin'raffen *tr* snatch away

hin'reichen *tr* (dat) pass to, hand to ‖ *intr* reach; suffice

hin'reißen §53 *tr* enchant, carry away

hin'richten *tr* execute; **h. auf** (acc) direct towards

Hin'richtung *f* (-;-en) execution

Hin'richtungsbefehl *m* death warrant

hin'setzen *tr* put down ‖ *ref* sit down

Hin'sicht *f* respect, way; **in H. auf** (acc) regarding, in regard to

hin'sichtlich *prep* (genit) regarding

hin'stellen *tr* put there; put down

hintan'setzen, hintan'stellen *tr* put last, consider last

hinten ['hɪntən] *adv* at the back, in the rear; **h. im Zimmer** at the back of the room; **nach h.** to the rear; backwards; **von h.** from the rear

hinter ['hɪntər] *prep* (dat) behind; **j–m her sein** be after s.o. ‖ *prep* (acc) behind; **h. etw kommen** find out about s.th., get to the bottom of s.th.

Hin'terachse *f* rear axle

Hin'terbacke *f* buttock

Hin'terbein *n* hind leg; **sich auf die Hinterbeine setzen** strain oneself

Hinterbliebene ['hɪntərblibənə] §5 *mf* survivor (*of a deceased*); **H.** *pl* next-of-kin

hinterbrin'gen §65 *tr*—j-m etw h. let s.o. in on s.th.

Hin'terdeck *n* quarter deck

hinterdrein [hɪntər'draɪn] *adv* after; subsequently, afterwards

hin'tere §9 *adj* back, rear ‖ **Hintere** §5 *m* (coll) behind

hintereinan'der *adv* one behind the other; in succession; one after the other

Hin'terfuß *m* hind foot

Hin'tergaumen *m* soft palate, velum

Hin'tergedanke *m* ulterior motive

hinterge'hen §82 *tr* deceive

Hin'tergrund *m* background

Hin'terhalt *m* ambush

hinterhältig ['hɪntərhɛltɪç] *adj* underhanded

Hin'terhand *f* hind quarters (*of horse*)

Hin'terhaus *n* rear building

hinterher' *adv* behind; afterwards

Hin'terhof *m* backyard

Hin'terkopf *m* back of the head

Hin'terland *n* hinterland

hinterlas'sen §104 *tr* leave behind

Hinterlas'senschaft *f* (–;–en) inheritance

Hin'terlauf *m* hind leg

hinterle'gen *tr* deposit

Hinterle'gung *f* (–;–en) deposit

Hin'terlist *f* deceit; trick, ruse

Hin'termann *m* (–[e]s;–er) instigator; wheeler-dealer; (pol) backer

Hintern ['hɪntərn] *m* (–s;–) (coll) behind

Hin'terradantrieb *m* rear-wheel drive

hinterrücks ['hɪntərrʏks] *adv* from behind; (fig) behind one's back

Hin'tertreffen *n*—ins **H. geraten** fall behind; **im H. sein** be at a disadvantage

hintertrei'ben §62 *tr* frustrate

Hintertrei'bung *f* (–;–en) frustration

Hin'tertreppe *f* backstairs

Hin'tertür *f* backdoor

Hinterwäldler ['hɪntərvɛltlər] *m* (–s;–) hillbilly

hin'terwäldlerisch *adj* hillbilly

hinterzie'hen §163 *tr* evade

Hinterzie'hung *f* (–;) tax evasion

hinü'ber *adv* over, over there; across

hinun'ter *adv* down

hinun'tergehen §82 *tr* (SEIN) (*Treppe*) go down ‖ *intr* (SEIN) go down

hinweg [hɪn'vɛk] *adv* away; **über etw h.** over s.th., across s.th. ‖ **Hinweg** ['hɪnvɛk] *m* way there

hinweg'kommen §99 *intr* (SEIN)—**h. über** (*acc*) get over

hinweg'sehen §138 *intr*—**h. über** (*acc*) look over; overlook, ignore

hinweg'setzen *ref*—**sich h. über** (*acc*) ignore, disregard

hinweg'täuschen *tr* mislead, blind

Hinweis ['hɪnvaɪs] *m* (–es;–e) reference; hint; announcement

hin'weisen §118 *tr*—j-n **h. auf** (*acc*) point s.th. out to s.o. ‖ *intr*—**h. auf** (*acc*) point to; point out

hin'werfen §160 *tr* throw down; (coll) dash off, jot down

hin'wirken *intr*—**h. auf** (*acc*) work toward(s)

hin'ziehen §163 *tr* attract protract ‖ *ref* drag on; **sich h. an** (*dat*) run along; **sich h. bis zu** extend to

hin'zielen *intr*—**h. auf** (*acc*) aim at

hinzu' *adv* there, thither; in addition

hinzu'fügen *tr* add

hinzu'kommen §99 *intr* (SEIN) come (upon the scene); be added; **es kamen noch andere Gründe hinzu** besides, there were other reasons

hinzu'setzen *tr* add

hinzu'treten §152 *intr* (SEIN) (**zu**) walk up (to); **es traten noch andere Gründe hinzu** besides, there were other reasons

hinzu'tun §154 *tr* add

hinzu'ziehen §163 *tr* (*Arzt*) call in

Hirn [hɪrn] *n* (–[e]s;–e) brain; brains; **sein H. anstrengen** rack one's brains

Hirn– *comb.fm.* brain; cerebral; intellectual

Hirn'anhang *m* pituitary gland

Hirn'gespinst *n* figment of the imagination

Hirn'hautentzündung *f* meningitis

hirn'los *adj* brainless

Hirn'rinde *f* (anat) cortex

Hirn'schale *f* cranium

hirn'verbrannt *adj* (coll) crazy

Hirsch [hɪrʃ] *m* (–es;–e) deer, stag

Hirsch'fänger *m* hunting knife

Hirsch'kalb *n* fawn, doe

Hirsch'kuh *f* hind

Hirsch'leder *n* deerskin, buckskin

Hirt [hɪrt] *m* (–en;–en) shepherd

–hirte [hɪrtə] *m* (–n;–n) –herd

Hir'tenbrief *m* (eccl) pastoral letter

Hirtin ['hɪrtɪn] *f* (–;–nen) shepherdess

His [hɪs] *n* (–;) (mus) B sharp

hissen ['hɪsən] *tr* hoist

Historie [hɪs'torjə] *f* (–;–n) history; story

Historiker –**in** [hɪs'torɪkər(ɪn)] §6 *mf* historian

historisch [hɪs'torɪʃ] *adj* historical

Hitze ['hɪtsə] *f* (–;–n) heat

hit'zebeständig *adj* heat-resistant

Hit'zeferien *pl* school holiday (*because of hot weather*)

Hit'zeschild *m* (rok) heat shield

Hit'zewelle *f* heat wave

hitzig ['hɪtsɪç] *adj* hot-tempered

Hitz'kopf *m* hothead

hitz'köpfig *adj* hot-headed

Hitz'schlag *m* heatstroke

hob [hop] *pret* of **heben**

Hobel ['hobəl] *m* (–s;–) (carp) plane

Ho'belbank *f* carpenter's bench

hobeln ['hobəln] *tr* (carp) plane

hoch [hox], (**hohe** ['ho·ə] §9) *adj* (**höher** ['hø·ər]; **höchste** ['høçstə] §9) high; noble; (*Alter*) advanced; **das ist mir zu h.** that's beyond me; **hohes Gericht!** your honor!; members of the jury!; **in höchster Not** in dire need ‖ *adv* high; highly, very; (math) to the ... power ‖ **Hoch** *n* (-s;-s) (*Trinkspruch, Heilruf*) cheer; (meteor) high

hoch– *comb.fm.* up; upwards; highly, very; high, as high as

hoch'achten *tr* esteem

Hoch'actung *f* (-;) esteem; **mit vorzüglicher H., Ihr ... or Ihre ...** Very truly yours, Respectfully yours

hoch'achtungsvoll *adj* respectful ‖ **adv —h., Ihr ... or Ihre ...** Very truly yours, Respectfully yours

Hoch'amt *n* (eccl) High Mass

Hoch'antenne *f* outdoor antenna

hoch'arbeiten *ref* work one's way up

hoch'aufgeschossen *adj* tall, lanky

Hoch'bahn *f* el, elevated train

Hoch'bauingenieur *m* structural engineer

hoch'bäumen *ref* rear up

Hoch'behälter *m* water tower; reservoir

Hochbeiner ['hoxbaɪnər] *m* (-s;-) (ent) daddy-long-legs

hoch'beinig *adj* long-legged

hoch'betagt *adj* advanced in years

Hoch'betrieb *m* bustle, big rush

Hoch'blüte *f* high bloom; (fig) heyday

hoch'bringen §65 *tr* restore to health; (*Geschäft*) put on its feet; **es h.** (sport) get a high score

Hoch'burg *f* fortress, citadel

hoch'denkend *adj* noble-minded

hoch'deutsch *adj* High German

Hoch'druck *m* high pressure; (fig) great pressure; (meteor) high; **mit H.** (fig) full blast

Hoch'druckgebiet *n* (meteor) high, high-pressure area

Hoch'ebene *f* plateau

hoch'fahrend *adj* high-handed

hoch'fein *adj* very refined; high-grade

Hoch'flut *m* high tide; (fig) deluge

Hoch'form *f* top form

hochfrequent ['hoxfrɛkvɛnt] *adj* high-frequency

Hoch'frequenz *f* high-frequency

Hoch'frisur *f* upsweep

Hoch'gefühl *n* elation

hoch'gemut *adj* cheerful

Hoch'genuß *m* great pleasure

Hoch'gericht *n* place of execution

hoch'gesinnt *adj* noble-minded

hoch'gespannt *adj* (*Hoffnungen*) high; (elec) high-voltage

hoch'gestellt *adj* high-ranking

Hoch'glanz *m* high polish, high gloss

Hoch'haus *n* high rise (building)

hoch'herzig *adj* generous

hoch'jagen *tr* (*Wild*) ferret out; (*Motor*) race; (coll) blow up

hochkant ['hoxkant] *adv* on end

Hoch'konjunktur *f* (econ) boom

Hoch'land *n* highlands; plateau

Hoch'leistung *f* (-;-en) high output; (sport) first-class performance

Hochleistungs– *comb.fm.* high-powered; high-capacity; high-speed; heavy-duty

Hoch'mut *m* haughtiness, pride

hoch'mütig *adj* haughty, proud

hochnäsig ['hoxnɛzɪç] *adj* snooty

Hoch'ofen *m* blast furnace

hoch'ragend *adj* towering

hoch'rappeln *ref* (coll) get on one's feet again, pick up again

hoch'rollen *tr* roll up

Hoch'ruf *m* cheer

Hoch'saison *f* height of the season

Hoch'schule *f* university, academy

Hoch'schüler –in §6 *mf* university student

Hoch'seefischerei *f* deep-sea fishing

hoch'selig *adj* late, of blessed memory

Hoch'spannung *f* high voltage

Hoch'spannungsleitung *f* high-tension line

hoch'spielen *tr* play up; put into the limelight

Hoch'sprache *f* standard language; (die) **deutsche H.** standard German

höchst *adv* see **hoch**

Höchst– *comb.fm.* maximum, top

Hochstapelei [hoxʃtapə'laɪ] *f* (-;) false pretenses; fraud

Hochstapler ['hoxʃtaplər] *m* (-s;) confidence man; imposter, swindler

Hoch'start *m* (sport) standing start

Höchst'belastung *f* (-;-en) maximum load; (elec) peak load

höchstens ['høçstəns] *adv* at best, at the very most

Höchst'form *f* (sport) top form

Höchst'frequenz *f* ultrahigh frequency

Höchst'geschwindigkeit *f* top speed; **zulässige H.** speed limit

Höchst'leistung *f* (-;-en) maximum output; highest achievement; (sport) record

Hoch'straße *f* overpass

Hoch'ton *m* (ling) primary stress

hoch'tönend *adj* bombastic

hochtourig ['hoxturɪç] *adj* high-revving

hoch'trabend *adj* pompous

Hoch'–und Tief'bau *m* (-[e]s;) civil engineering

hoch'verdient *adj* of great merit

Hoch'verrat *m* high treason

Hoch'verräter –in §6 *mf* traitor

Hoch'wasser *n* flood(s); **der Fluß führt H.** the river is swollen

hoch'wertig *adj* high-quality

Hoch'wild *n* big game

Hoch'würden *pl* (*als Anrede*) Reverend; **Seine H. ...** the Reverend ...

Hoch'zeit *f* wedding

hoch'zeitlich *adj* bridal; nuptial

Hoch'zeitsfeier *f* wedding ceremony; wedding reception

Hoch'zeitspaar *n* newly-weds

Hoch'zeitsreise *f* honeymoon

Hocke ['hokə] *f* (-;-n) crouch

hocken ['hokən] *ref* & *intr* squat; (coll) sit down

Hocker ['hokər] *m* (-s;-) stool

Höcker ['hœkər] *m* (-s;-) hump; bump

höckerig ['hœkərɪç] *adj* hunchbacked; (*Weg*) bumpy

Hockey ['hoki] *n* (-s;) hockey

Ho'ckeyschläger *m* hockey stick

Hode ['hodə] *f* (-;-n) testicle

Ho'densack *m* (anat) scrotum

Hof [hof] *m* (-[e]s;∹e) courtyard;

yard; barnyard; (*e–s Königs*) court; (astr) halo; corona; **e–m Mädchen den Hof machen** court a girl
Hoffart ['hɔfart] *f* (–;) haughtiness
hoffärtig ['hɔfertɪç] *adj* haughty
hoffen ['hɔfən] *tr*—**das Beste h.** hope for the best || *intr* (**auf** *acc*) hope (for); **auf j–n h.** put one's hopes in s.o
hoffentlich ['hɔfəntlɪç] *adv* as I hope; **h. kommt er bald** I hope he comes soon
Hoffnung ['hɔfnʊŋ] *f* (–;–en) hope
hoff'nungslos *adj* hopeless
hoff'nungsvoll *adj* hopeful; promising
Hof'hund *m* watchdog
hofieren [hɔ'firən] *tr* court
höfisch ['høfɪʃ] *adj* court, courtly
höflich ['høflɪç] *adj* polite, courteous
Höf'lichkeit *f* (–;–en) politeness, courtesy
Höf'lichkeitsformel *f* complimentary close (*in a letter*)
Höfling ['høflɪŋ] *m* (–[e]s;–e) courtier
Hof'meister *m* steward; tutor
Hof'narr *m* court jester
Hof'staat *m* royal household; retinue
hohe ['ho·ə] *adj* see **hoch**
Höhe ['hø·ə] *f* (–;–en) height; altitude; (*Anhöhe*) hill; (mus) pitch; **auf der H.** in good shape; **das ist die H.!** that's the limit!; **in der H.** von in the amount of; **in die H.** up; **in die H. fahren** jump up; **wieder in die H. bringen** (com) put back on its feet
Hoheit ['hohaɪt] *f* (–;–en) sovereignty; (*als Titel*) Highness
Ho'heitsbereich *m* (pol), **Ho'heitsgebiet** *n* (pol) territory
Ho'heitsgewässer *pl* territorial waters
Ho'heitsrechte *pl* sovereign rights
ho'heitsvoll *adj* regal, majestic
Ho'heitszeichen *n* national emblem
Hö'henmesser *m* altimeter
Hö'henruder *n* (aer) elevator
Hö'hensonne *f* ultra-violet lamp
Hö'henstrahlen *pl* cosmic rays
Hö'henzug *m* mountain range
Ho'hepriester *m* high priest
Hö'hepunkt *m* climax; height, acme
höher ['hø·ər] *adj* see **hoch**
hohl [hol] *adj* hollow
Höhle ['hølə] *f* (–;–n) cave; grotto; lair, den; hollow, cavity; socket
Höh'lenmensch *m* caveman
hohl'geschliffen *adj* hollow-ground
Hohl'heit *f* (–;) hollowness
Hohl'maß *n* dry measure; liquid measure
Hohl'raum *m* hollow, cavity
Hohl'saum *m* hemstitch
Hohl'weg *m* defile, narrow pass
Hohn [hon] *m* (–[e]s;) scorn; sarcasm; **etw j–m Hohn tun** do s.th. in defiance of s.o.
höhnen ['hønən] *intr* jeer; sneer
höhnisch ['hønɪʃ] *adj* scornful
hohn'sprechen §64 *intr* (*dat*) treat with scorn; defy; make a mockery of
Höker –in ['høkər(ɪn)] §6 *mf* huckster
hold [hɔlt] *adj* kindly; lovely, sweet
hold'selig *adj* lovely, sweet

holen ['holən] *tr* fetch; get; (*Atem, Luft*) draw; **h. lassen** send for; **sich** [*dat*] **etw h.** (coll) catch s.th.
Holland ['hɔlant] *n* (–s;) Holland
Holländer ['hɔlendər] *m* (–s;–) Dutchman
Holländerin ['hɔlendərɪn] *f* (–;–nen) Dutch woman
holländisch ['hɔlendɪʃ] *adj* Dutch
Hölle ['hœlə] *f* (–;) hell
Höl'lenangst *f* mortal fear
höllisch ['hœlɪʃ] *adj* hellish
Holm [hɔlm] *m* (–[e]s;–e) islet; (*Stiel*) handle; (aer) spar; (gym) parallel bar
holp(e)rig ['hɔlp(ə)rɪç] *adj* bumpy
holpern ['hɔlpərn] *intr* jolt, bump along; (*beim Lesen*) stumble
Holunder [hɔ'lundər] *m* (–s;–) (bot) elder
Holz [hɔlts] *n* (–es;̈er) wood; lumber; timber, trees; **ins H. gehen** go into the woods
Holz'apfel *m* crab apple
Holz'arbeit *f* woodwork; lumbering
Holz'arbeiter *m* woodworker; lumberjack
holz'artig *adj* woody
Holz'blasinstrumente *pl* wood winds
Holz'brei *m* wood pulp
holzen ['hɔltsən] *tr* fell; deforest; (coll) spank || *intr* cut wood
hölzern ['hœltsərn] *adj* wooden; (fig) clumsy
Holzfäller ['hɔltsfelər] *m* (–s;–) lumberjack, logger
Holz'faser *f* wood fiber; wood pulp; grain; **gegen die H.** against the grain
Holz'faserstoff *m* wood pulp
Holzhacker ['hɔltshakər] *m* (–s;–), **Holzhauer** ['hɔltshau·ər] *m* (–s;–) lumberjack; wood chopper
holzig ['hɔltsɪç] *adj* woody, wooded; (*Gemüse*) stringy
Holz'knecht *m* lumberjack
Holz'kohle *f* charcoal
Holz'nagel *m* wooden peg
Holz'platz *m* lumber yard
holz'reich *adj* wooded
Holz'schnitt *m* woodcut; wood engraving
Holz'schuh *m* wooden shoe
Holz'schuppen *m* woodshed
Holz'wolle *f* excelsior
Homi-lie [hɔmɪ'li] *f* (–;–lien ['li·ən]) homily
homogen [hɔmɔ'gen] *adj* homogeneous
Homosexualität [hɔmɔzeksu·alɪ'tet] *f* (–;) homosexuality
homosexuell [hɔmɔzeksu'el] *adj* homosexual || **Homosexuelle** §5 *mf* homosexual
Honig ['honɪç] *m* (–s;) honey
Ho'nigkuchen *m* gingerbread
ho'nigsüß *adj* sweet as honey
Ho'nigwabe *f* honeycomb
Honorar [hɔnɔ'rar] *n* (–s;–e) fee
Honoratioren [hɔnɔratsɪ'orən] *pl* dignitaries
honorieren [hɔnɔ'rirən] *tr* give an honorarium to; pay royalties to; (*Scheck*) honor
Hopfen ['hɔpfən] *m* (–s;) hops

hopp [hɔp] *interj* up!; quick!; **hopp, los!** get going!

hoppla ['hɔpla] *interj* whoops!; **jetzt aber h.!** come on!; look sharp!

hops [hɔps] *adj*—**h. gehen** go to pot; **h. sein** be done for

hopsasa ['hɔpsasa] *interj* upsy-daisy

hopsen ['hɔpsən] *intr* (SEIN) hop

Hop'ser *m* (-s;-) hop

Hörapparat ['høraparat] *m* hearing aid

hörbar ['hørbar] *adj* audible

hörbehindert ['hørbəhındərt] *adj* hard of hearing

Hörbericht ['hørbərıçt] *m* radio report; radio commentary

horchen ['hɔrçən] *intr* listen; eavesdrop

Hor'cher –in §6 *mf* eavesdropper

Horch'gerät *n* sound detector; (nav) hydrophone

Horch'posten *m* (mil) listening post

Horde ['hɔrdə] *f* (-;-n) horde

hören ['hørən] *tr* hear; listen to; (*Vorlesung*) attend || *intr* hear; **h. auf** (*acc*) pay attention to, obey

Hö'rer *m* (-s;-) listener; member of an audience; student; (telp) receiver

Hö'rerbrief *m* letter from a listener

Hö'rerkreis *m* listeners

Hö'rerschaft *f* (-;-en) audience; (educ) enrollment

Hör'folge *f* radio serial

Hör'gerät *n* hearing aid

hörig ['hørıç] *adj* in bondage || **Hörige** §5 *mf* serf, thrall

Horizont [hɔrı'tsɔnt] *m* (-[e]s;-e) horizon

horizontal [hɔrıtsɔn'tal] *adj* horizontal || **Horizontale** §5 *f* horizontal line

Horn [hɔrn] *n* (-[e]s;ᵗer) horn; (mil) bugle; (mus) horn, French horn

Hörnchen ['hœrnçən] *n* (-s;-) crescent roll

Horn'haut *f* (anat) cornea

Hornisse [hɔr'nısə] *f* (-;-n) hornet

Hornist [hɔr'nıst] *m* (-en;-en) bugler

Horn'ochse *f* (coll) dumb ox

Horoskop [hɔrɔ'skop] *n* (-[e]s;-e) horoscope

horrend [hɔ'rent] *adj* (coll) terrible

Hör'rohr *n* stethescope

Hör'saal *m* lecture room

Hör'spiel *n* radio play

Horst [hɔrst] *m* (-[e]s;-e) (eagle's) nest

Hort [hɔrt] *m* (-[e]s;-e) hoard, treasure; (place of) refuge; protector

Hör'weite *f*—**in H.** within earshot

Hose ['hozə] *f* (-;-n), **Hosen** ['hozən] *pl* pants, trousers; (*Unterhose*) shorts; panties; **sich auf die Hosen setzen** buckle down

Ho'senboden *m* seat (of trousers)

Ho'senklappe *f*, **Ho'senlatz** *m* fly

Ho'senrolle *f* (theat) male role

Ho'senträger *pl* suspenders

Hospitant [hɔspı'tant] *m* (-en;-en) (educ) auditor

hospitieren [hɔspı'tirən] *intr* (educ) audit a course

Hospiz [hɔs'pits] *n* (-es;-e) hospice

Hostie ['hɔstjə] *f* (-;-n) host, wafer

Hotel [hɔ'tɛl] *n* (-s;-s) hotel

Hotel'boy *m* bellboy, bellhop

Hotel'diener *m* hotel porter

Hotel'fach *n*, **Hotel'gewerbe** *n* hotel business

Hub [hup] *m* (-[e]s;ᵗe) (mach) stroke

hübsch [hүpʃ] *adj* pretty; handsome; (coll) good-sized

Hubschrauber ['hupʃraubər] *m* (-s;-) helicopter

huckepack ['hukəpak] *adv* piggyback

hudeln ['hudəln] *intr* be sloppy

Huf [huf] *m* (-[e]s;-e) hoof

Huf'eisen *n* horseshoe

Huf'schlag *m* hoofbeat

Hüfte ['hүftə] *f* (-;-n) hip; **die Arme in die Hüften gestemmt** with arms akimbo

Hüft'gelenk *n* hip joint

Hüft'gürtel *m*, **Hüft'halter** *m* garter belt

Hügel ['hygəl] *m* (-s;-) hill; mound

hügelab' *adv* downhill

hügelauf' *adv* uphill

hügelig ['hygəlıç] *adj* hilly

Huhn [hun] *n* (-[e]s;ᵗer) fowl; hen, chicken

Hühnchen ['hynçən] *n* (-s;-) young chicken; **ein H. zu rupfen haben mit** (fig) have a bone to pick with

Hüh'nerauge *n* (pathol) corn

Hüh'nerdraht *m* chicken wire

Hüh'nerhund *m* bird dog

Huld [hult] *f* (-;) grace, favor

huldigen ['huldıgən] *intr* (*dat*) pay homage to

Hul'digung *f* (-;) homage

Hul'digungseid *m* oath of allegiance

huld'reich, huld'voll *adj* gracious

Hülle ['hүlə] *f* (-;-n) cover; case; wrapper; envelope; (*e-s Buches*) jacket; (fig) cloak; **in H. und Fülle** in abundance; **sterbliche H.** mortal remains

hüllen ['hүlən] *tr* cover; veil; wrap

Hülse ['hүlzə] *f* (-;-n) pod, hull; cartridge case, shell case

Hül'senfrucht *f* legume

human [hu'man] *adj* humane

humanistisch [huma'nıstıʃ] *adj* humanistic; classical

humanitär [humanı'ter] *adj* humanitarian

Humanität [humanı'tet] *f* (-;) humanity; humaneness

Humanitäts'duselei *f* sentimental humanitarianism

Humanitäts'verbrechen *n* crime against humanity

Hummel ['huməl] *f* (-;-n) bumblebee

Hummer ['humər] *m* (-s;-) lobster

Humor [hu'mor] *m* (-s;) humor

humoristisch [humɔ'rıstıʃ] *adj* humorous

humpeln ['humpəln] *intr* (SEIN) hobble

Hund [hunt] *m* (-[e]s;-e) dog

Hündchen ['hyntçən] *n* (-s;-) small dog; puppy

Hun'deangst *f*—**e-e H. haben** (coll) be scared stiff

Hun'dearbeit *f* drudgery

Hun'dehütte *f* doghouse

Hun'dekälte *f* severe cold

Hun'demarke *f* dog tag
hun'demü'de *adj* (coll) dog-tired
hundert ['hʊndərt] *invar adj & pron* hundred ‖ **Hundert** *n* (-s;-e) hundred; **drei von H.** three percent; **im H.** by the hundred ‖ *f* (-;-en) hundred
hun'dertfach *adj* hundredfold
Hundertjahr'feier *f* centennial
Hun'dertsatz *m* percentage
hundertste ['hʊndərtstə] §9 *adj & pron* hundredth
Hun'deschau *f* dog show
Hun'dezwinger *m* dog kennel
Hündin ['hʏndɪn] *f* (-;-nen) bitch
hündisch ['hʏndɪʃ] *adj* (*Benehmen*) servile; (*Angst*) deadly
hunds'gemein *adj* beastly
hunds'miserabel *adj* (sl) lousy
Hunds'stern *m* Dog Star
Hunds'tage *pl* dog days
Hüne ['hynə] *m* (-n;-n) giant
hü'nenhaft *adj* gigantic
Hunger ['hʊŋər] *m* (-s;) hunger; **H. haben** be hungry
Hun'gerkur *f* starvation diet
Hun'gerlohn *m* starvation wages
hungern ['hʊŋərn] *intr* be hungry; go without food; **h. nach** yearn for ‖ *impers*—**es hungert mich** I am hungry
Hun'gersnot *f* famine
Hun'gertod *m* death from starvation
Hun'gertuch *n*—**am H. nagen** go hungry; live in poverty
hungrig ['hʊŋrɪç] *adj* hungry; (*Jahre*) lean
Hunne ['hʊnə] *m* (-n;-n) (hist) Hun
Hupe ['hupə] *f* (-;-n) (aut) horn
hupen ['hupən] *intr* blow the horn
hüpfen ['hʏpfən], **hupfen** ['hʊpfən] *intr* (SEIN) hop, jump
Hürde ['hʏrdə] *f* (-;-n) hurdle
Hure ['hurə] *f* (-;-n) whore
huren ['hurən] *intr* whore around
hurtig ['hʊrtɪç] *adj* nimble, swift
huschen ['huʃən] *intr* (SEIN) scurry
hüsteln ['hʏstəln] *intr* clear the throat
husten ['hustən] *tr* cough up ‖ *intr* cough; **h. auf** (*acc*) (coll) not give a rap about

Hut [hut] *m* (-[e]s;ːe) hat ‖ *f* (-;) protection, care; **auf der Hut sein** be on guard
hüten ['hytən] *tr* guard, protect; tend; **das Bett h.** be confined to bed; **das Haus h.** stay indoors; **Kinder h.** baby-sit ‖ *ref* (**vor** *dat*) be on guard (against), beware (of); **ich werde mich schön h.** (coll) I'll do no such thing
Hü'ter –**in** §6 *mf* guardian
Hut'krempe *f* brim of a hat
hut'los *adj* hatless
Hütte ['hʏtə] *f* (-;-n) hut; cabin; doghouse; glassworks; (Bib) tabernacle; (metal) foundry
Hüt'tenkunde *f*, **Hüt'tenwesen** *n* metallurgy
Hyäne [hy'enə] *f* (-;-n) hyena
Hyazinthe [hya'tsɪntə] *f* (-;-n) hyacinth
Hydrant [hy'drant] *m* (-en;-en) hydrant
Hydraulik [hy'draulɪk] *f* (-;) hydraulics; hydraulic system
hydraulisch [hy'draulɪʃ] *adj* hydraulic
hydrieren [hy'drirən] *tr* hydrogenate
Hygiene [hy'gjenə] *f* (-;) hygiene
hygienisch [hy'gjenɪʃ] *adj* hygienic
Hymne ['hymnə] *f* (-;-n) hymn; anthem
Hyperbel [hy'perbəl] *f* (-;-n) (geom) hyperbola; (rhet) hyperbole
Hypnose [hyp'nozə] *f* (-;-n) hypnosis
hypnotisch [hyp'notɪʃ] *adj* hypnotic
Hypothese [hflpə'tezə] *f* (-;-n) hypothesis
Hypochonder [hypə'xɔndər] *m* (-s;-) hypochondriac
Hypothek [hypə'tek] *f* (-;-en) mortgage
Hypothe'kengläubiger *m* mortgagee
Hypothe'kenschuldner *m* mortgagor
Hypothese [hypə'tezə] *f* (-;-n) hypothesis
hypothetisch [hypə'tetɪʃ] *adj* hypothetical
Hysterektomie [hysterektə'mi] *f* (-;) hysterectomy
Hysterie [hyste'ri] *f* (-;) hysteria
hysterisch [hys'terɪʃ] *adj* hysterical

I

I, i [i] *invar n* I, i
iah ['i'a] *interj* heehaw!
iahen ['i'a·ən] *intr* heehaw, bray
iberisch [i'berɪʃ] *adj* Iberian
ich [ɪç] §11 *pers pron* I
ichbezogen ['ɪçbətsogən] *adj* self-centered, egocentric
Ich'sucht *f* egotism
ideal [ide'al] *adj* ideal ‖ **Ideal** *n* (-s; -e) deal
idealisieren [ide·alɪ'zirən] *tr* idealize
Idealismus [ide·a'lɪsmʊs] *m* (-;) idealism
Idealist –**in** [ide·a'lɪst(ɪn)] §7 *mf* idealist

idealistisch [ide·a'lɪstɪʃ] *adj* idealistic
I·dee [ɪ'de] *f* (-;-deen ['de·ən]) idea
Iden ['idən] *pl* Ides
identifizieren [ɪdɛntɪfɪ'tsirən] *tr* identify ‖ *ref*—**i. mit** identify with
identisch [ɪ'dɛntɪʃ] *adj* identical
Identität [ɪdɛntɪ'tet] *f* (-;-en) identity
Ideolo·gie [ide·ɔlə'gi] *f* (-;-gien ['gi·ən]) ideology
Idiom [ɪ'djom] *n* (-s;-e) idiom, dialect, language
idiomatisch [ɪdjə'matɪʃ] *adj* idiomatic
Idiosynkra·sie [ɪdjəzʏnkra'zi] *f* (-; -sien ['zi·ən]) idiosyncrasy
Idiot [ɪ'djot] *m* (-en;-en) idiot

Idio·tie [ɪdjə'ti] *f* (–;–tien ['ti·ən]) idiocy
Idiotin [ɪdjotɪn] *f* (–;–nen) idiot
Idol [ɪ'dol] *n* (–s;–e) idol
idyllisch [ɪ'dYlɪʃ] *adj* idyllic
Igel ['igəl] *m* (–s;–) hedgehog
Ignorant [ɪgnə'rant] *m* (–en;–en) ignoramus
ignorieren [ɪgnə'rirən] *tr* ignore
ihm [im] §11 *pers pron* (dative of **er** and **es**) (to) him; (to) it
ihn [in] §11 *pers pron* (accusative of **er**) him
ihnen ['inən] §11 *pers pron* (dative of **sie**) (to) them ‖ **Ihnen** §11 *pers pron* (dative of **Sie**) (to) you
ihr [ir] §2,2 *poss adj* her; their ‖ §11 *pers pron* (dative of **sie**) (to) her ‖ **Ihr** §2,2 *poss adj* your
ihrerseits ['irərzaɪts] *adv* on her (or their) part; **Ihrerseits** on your part
ihresgleichen ['irəs'glaɪçən] *pron* the likes of her (or them); her (or their) equal(s); **Ihresgleichen** the likes of you; your equal(s)
ihrethalben ['irət'halbən] *adv* var of **ihretwegen**
ihretwegen ['irət'vegen] *adv* because of her (or them); for her (or their) sake; **Ihretwegen** because of you, for your sake
ihretwillen ['irət'vɪlən] *adv* var of **ihretwegen**
ihrige ['irɪgə] §2,5 *poss pron* hers; theirs; **Ihrige** yours
Ikone [ɪ'konə] *f* (–;–n) icon
illegal [ɪle'gal] *adj* illegal
illegitim [ɪlegɪ'tim] *adj* illegitimate
illuminieren [ɪlumɪ'nirən] *tr* illuminate
Illusion [ɪlu'zjon] *f* (–;–en) illusion
illustrieren [ɪlus'trirən] *tr* illustrate
Illustrierte [ɪlus'trirtə] §5 *f* (illustrated) magazine
Iltis ['ɪltɪs] *m* (–ses;–se) polecat
im [ɪm] *contr* in dem
Image ['ɪmɪdʒ] *n* (–s;–s) (fig) image
imaginär [ɪmagɪ'ner] *adj* imaginary
Im·biß ['ɪmbɪs] *m* (–bisses;–bisse) snack
Im'bißhalle *f* luncheonette
Im'bißstube *f* snack bar
Imi·tator [ɪmɪ'tɑtər] *m* (–s;–tatoren [ta'torən]) imitator; impersonator
Imker ['ɪmkər] *m* (–s;–) beekeeper
immateriell [ɪmate'rjel] *adj* immaterial, spiritual
immatrikulieren [ɪmatrɪku'lirən] *tr & intr* register; **sich i. lassen** get registered
immens [ɪ'mens] *adj* immense
immer ['ɪmər] *adv* always; **auf i. und ewig** for ever and ever; **für i.** for good; **i. langsam!** steady now!; **i. mehr** more and more; **i. wieder** again and again; **noch i.** still; **nur i. zu!** keep trying!; **was auch i.** whatever
immerdar' *adv* (Lit) forever
immerfort' *adv* all the time
im'mergrün *adj* evergreen ‖ **Immergrün** *n* (–s;–e) evergreen
immerhin' *adv* after all, anyhow
immerwäh'rend *adj* perpetual
immerzu' *adv* all the time, constantly

Immobilien [ɪmə'biljen] *pl* real estate
Immobi'lienmakler –**in** §6 *mf* real-estate broker
immun [ɪ'mun] *adj* (**gegen**) immune (to)
immunisieren [ɪmunɪ'zirən] *tr* immunize
Imperativ [ɪmpera'tif] *m* (–s;–e) (gram) imperative
Imperfek·tum [ɪmper'fektum] *n* (–s; –ta [ta]) (gram) imperfect
Imperialismus [ɪmperɪ·a'lɪsmus] *m* (–;) imperialism
impfen ['ɪmpfen] *tr* vaccinate; inoculate
Impfling ['ɪmpflɪŋ] *m* (–s;–e) person to be vaccinated or inoculated
Impf'schein *m* vaccination certificate
Impf'stoff *m* vaccine
Imp'fung *f* (–;–en) vaccination; inoculation
imponieren [ɪmpə'nirən] *intr* (*dat*) impress
Import [ɪm'pɔrt] *m* (–[e]s;–e) import
importieren [ɪmpɔr'tirən] *tr* import
imposant [ɪmpɔ'zant] *adj* imposing
imprägnieren [ɪmpreg'nirən] *tr* waterproof; creosote
Impresario [ɪmpre'zarjo] *m* (–s;–s) agent, business manager
Impres·sum [ɪm'presum] *n* (–s;–sen [sən]) (journ) masthead
imstande [ɪm'ʃtandə] *adv*—**i. sein zu** (*inf*) be in a position to (*inf*)
in [ɪn] *prep* (*position*) (*dat*) in, at; (*direction*) (acc) in, into
Inangriffnahme [ɪn'angrɪfnamə] *f* (–;) starting; putting into action
Inanspruchnahme [ɪn'anʃpruxnamə] *f* (–;) laying claim; demands; utilization
In'begriff *m* essence; embodiment
in'begriffen *adj* included
Inbrunst ['ɪnbrunst] *f* (–;) ardor
inbrünstig ['ɪnbrYnstɪç] *adj* ardent
indem [ɪn'dem] *conj* while, as; by (*ger*)
Inder –**in** ['ɪndər(ɪn)] §6 *mf* Indian (*inhabitant of India*)
indes [ɪn'des], **indessen** [ɪn'desən] *adv* meanwhile; however ‖ *conj* while; whereas
Indianer –**in** [ɪn'djɑnər(ɪn)] §6 *mf* Indian (*of North America*)
Indien ['ɪndjən] *n* (–s;) India
Indio ['ɪndɪ·o] *m* (–s;–s) Indian (*of Central or South America*)
indisch ['ɪndɪʃ] *adj* Indian
indiskret [ɪndɪs'kret] *adj* indiscreet
indiskutabel [ɪndɪsku'tabəl] *adj* out of the question
individuell [ɪndɪvɪdu'el] *adj* individual
Individu·um [ɪndɪ'vidu·um] *n* (–s;–en [ən]) individual; (pej) character
Indizienbeweis [ɪn'ditsjənbəvaɪs] *m* (piece of) circumstantial evidence
Indossament [ɪndɔsa'ment] *n* (–[e]s; –e) indorsement
Indossant [ɪndɔ'sant] *m* (–en;–en) indorser
indossieren [ɪndɔ'sirən] *tr* indorse
industrialisieren [ɪndustrɪ·alɪ'zirən] *tr* industrialize

Indus·trie [ɪndʊs'tri] *f* (–;–**trien** ['triən]) industry
Industrie'anlage *f* industrial plant
Industrie'betrieb *m* industrial establishment
Industrie'kapitän *m* tycoon
industriell [ɪndʊstrɪ'ɛl] *adj* industrial || **Industrielle** §5 *m* industrialist
ineinan'der *adv* into one another; **i. übergehen** merge
ineinan'derfügen *tr* dovetail
ineinan'dergreifen §88 *intr* mesh
ineinan'derpassen *intr* dovetail
infam [ɪn'fam] *adv* (coll) frightfully
Infante·rie [ɪnfantə'ri] *f* (–;–**rien** ['riən]) infantry
Infanterist [ɪnfantə'rɪst] *m* (–en;–en) infantryman
infantil [ɪnfan'til] *adj* infantile
Infektion [ɪnfɛk'tsjon] *f* (–;–en) infection
Infini·tiv [ɪnfɪnɪ'tif] *m* (–s;–**tive** ['tivə]) infinitive
infizieren [ɪnfɪ'tsirən] *tr* infect
infolge [ɪn'fɔlgə] *prep* (genit) in consequence of, owing to; according to
infolgedes'sen *adv* consequently
Information [ɪnfɔrma'tsjon] *f* (–;–en) (piece of) information
informieren [ɪnfɔr'mirən] *tr* inform
infrarot [ɪnfra'rot] *adj* infrared || **Infrarot** *n* (–s;–) infrared
Ingenieur [ɪnʒen'jør] *m* (–s;–e) engineer
Ingenieur'bau *m* (–[e]s;) civil engineering
Ingenieur'wesen *n* engineering
ingeniös [ɪnge'njøs] *adj* ingenious
Ingrimm ['ɪngrɪm] *m* inner rage
Ingwer ['ɪŋvər] *m* (–s;) ginger
Ing'werplätzchen *n* gingersnap
Inhaber –in ['ɪnhabər(ɪn)] §6 *mf* owner; bearer; occupant; holder
inhaftieren [ɪnhaf'tirən] *tr* arrest
Inhalierapparat [ɪnha'liraparat] *m* (med) inhalator
inhalieren [ɪnha'lirən] *tr & intr* inhale
Inhalt ['ɪnhalt] *m* (–[e]s;–e) contents; subject matter; (geom) area; volume
In'haltsangabe *f* summary; list of contents
in'haltsarm, in'haltsleer *adj* empty
in'haltsreich *adj* substantive; (Leben) full
in'haltsschwer *adj* pregnant with meaning; momentous
In'haltsverzeichnis *n* table of contents
in'haltsvoll *adj* full of meaning
inhibieren [ɪnhɪ'birən] *tr* inhibit
Initiative [ɪnɪtsja'tivə] *f* (–;–en) initiative
Injektion [ɪnjɛk'tsjon] *f* (–;–en) injection
Injektions'nadel *f* hypodermic needle
injizieren [ɪnjɪ'tsirən] *tr* inject
Inkasso [ɪn'kaso] *n* (–s;–s) bill collecting
Inkas'sobeamte *m* bill collector
inklusive [ɪnklu'zivə] *adj* inclusive || *prep* (genit) including
inkonsequent ['ɪnkɔnzɛkvɛnt] *adj* inconsistent; illogical
Inkraft'treten *n* going into effect

In'land *n* (–[e]s;) home country; interior
Inländer –in ['ɪnlɛndər(ɪn)] §6 *mf* native
inländisch ['ɪnlɛndɪʃ] *adj* home, domestic; inland
In'landspost *f* domestic mail
Inlett ['ɪnlɛt] *n* (–[e]s;–e) bedtick
in'liegend *adj* enclosed
inmit'ten *prep* (genit) in the middle of, among
innehaben ['ɪnəhabən] §89 *tr* (Amt) hold; (Wohnung) occupy, own
innehalten ['ɪnəhaltən] §90 *intr* stop
innen ['ɪnən] *adv* inside; indoors; **nach i.** inwards; **tief i.** deep down
Innen– *comb.fm.* inner, internal; inside, interior; home, domestic
In'nenarchitekt –in §7 *mf* interior decorator
In'nenaufnahme *f* (phot) indoor shot
In'nenhof *m* quadrangle
In'nenleben *n* inner life
In'nenminister *m* Secretary of the Interior; Secretary of State for Home Affairs (Brit)
In'nenpolitik *f* domestic policy
In'nenraum *m* interior (of building)
In'nenstadt *f* center of town, inner city
inner– [ɪnər] *comb.fm.* internal; intra-
innere ['ɪnərə] §9 *adj* inner, internal; inside; inward; domestic || **Innere** §5 *n* inside, interior
in'nerhalb *adv* on the inside; **i. von** within || *prep* (genit) inside, within
in'nerlich *adj* inner, inward || *adv* inwardly; mentally, emotionally
In'nerlichkeit *f* (–;–en) introspection; inner quality
innerste ['ɪnərstə] §9 *adj* innermost
innesein ['ɪnəzaɪn] §139 *intr* (SEIN) (genit) be aware of
innewerden ['ɪnəverdən] §159 *intr* (SEIN) (genit) become aware of
innig ['ɪnɪç] *adj* close; deep, heartfelt || *adv* deeply
In'nigkeit *f* (–;) intimacy; deep feeling; tender affection
Innung ['ɪnʊŋ] *f* (–;–en) guild
inoffiziell ['ɪnɔfɪtsjel] *adj* unofficial
ins *contr* in das
Insasse ['ɪnzasə] *m* (–n;–n), **Insassin** ['ɪnsasɪn] *f* (–;–nen) occupant; (e–s Gefängnisses) inmate; (e–s Autos) passenger
insbesondere [ɪnsbə'zɔndərə] *adv* in particular, especially
In'schrift *f* inscription
Insekt [ɪn'zɛkt] *n* (–[e]s;–en) insect
Insek'tenbekämpfungsmittel *n* insecticide
Insek'tenkunde *f* entomology
Insek'tenstich *m* insect bite
Insektizid [ɪnzɛktɪ'tsit] *n* (–[e]s;–e) insecticide
Insel ['ɪnzəl] *f* (–;–n) island
Inserat [ɪnzə'rat] *n* (–es;–e) classified advertisement, ad
inserieren [ɪnzə'rirən] *tr* insert || *intr* (in dat) advertise (in)
insgeheim [ɪnsgə'haɪm] *adv* secretly
insgemein [ɪnsgə'maɪn] *adv* as a whole; in general, generally

insgesamt [ɪnsgə'zamt] *adv* in a body, as a unit; in all, altogether

inso'fern *adv* to this extent || **insofern'** *conj* in so far as

insoweit' *adv* & *conj* var of **insofern**

Inspek•tor [ɪn'spɛktər] *m* (-s;-toren ['torən]) inspector

inspirieren [ɪnspɪ'rirən] *tr* inspire

inspizieren [ɪnspɪ'tsirən] *tr* inspect

Installation [ɪnstala'tsjon] *f* (-;-en) installation

installieren [ɪnsta'lirən] *tr* install

instand [ɪn'ʃtant] *adv*—**i. halten** keep in good condition; **i. setzen** repair

Instand'haltung *f* upkeep, maintenance

inständig [ɪn'ʃtɛndɪç] *adj* insistent

Instand'setzung *f* repair, renovation

Instanz [ɪn'stants] *f* (-;-en) (adm) authority; **e–e höhere I. anrufen** appeal to a higher court; **Gericht der ersten I.** court of primary jurisdiction; **Gericht der zweiten I.** court of appeal; **höchste I.** court of final appeal

Institut [ɪnstɪ'tut] *n* (-[e]s;-e) institute

instruieren [ɪnstru'irən] *tr* instruct

Instruktion [ɪnstruk'tsjon] *f* (-;-en) instruction

Instrument [ɪnstru'mɛnt] *n* (-[e]s;-e) instrument

Instrumentalist –in [ɪnstrumenta'lɪst (ɪn)] §7 *mf* instrumentalist

Insulaner –in [ɪnzu'lɑnər(ɪn)] §6 *mf* islander

insular [ɪnzu'lɑr] *adj* insular

Insulin [ɪnzu'lin] *n* (-s;) insulin

inszenieren [ɪnstsɛ'nirən] *tr* stage

Intellekt [ɪntɛ'lɛkt] *m* (-[e]s;) intellect

intellektuell [ɪntɛlɛktu'ɛl] *adj* intellectual || **Intellektuelle** §5 *mf* intellectual

intelligent [ɪntɛlɪ'gɛnt] *adj* intelligent

Intelligenzler [ɪntɛlɪ'gɛntslər] *m* (-s;-) (pej) egghead

Intendant [ɪntɛn'dant] *m* (-en;-en) (theat) director

intensiv [ɪntɛn'zif] *adj* intense; intensive

–intensiv *comb.fm.*, e.g., **lohnintensive Güter** goods of which wages constitute a high proportion of the cost

interessant [ɪntɛrɛ'sant] *adj* interesting

Interesse [ɪntɛ'rɛsə] *n* (-s;-n) (an *dat*, für) interest (in)

interes'selos *adj* uninterested

Interes'sengemeinschaft *f* community of interest; (com) syndicate

Interessent –in [ɪntɛrɛ'sɛnt(ɪn)] §7 *mf* interested party

interessieren [ɪntɛrɛ'sirən] *tr* (für) interest (in) || *ref*—**sich i. für** be interested in

interimistisch [ɪntɛrɪ'mɪstɪʃ] *adj* provisional

intern [ɪn'tɛrn] *adj* internal

Internat [ɪntɛr'nat] *n* (-[e]s;-e) boarding school

international [ɪntɛrnatsjɔ'nal] *adj* international

Internat(s)'schüler –in §6 *mf*, **Interne** [ɪn'tɛrnə] §5 *mf* boarding student

internieren [ɪntɛr'nirən] *tr* intern

Internist –in [ɪntɛr'nɪst(ɪn)] §7 *mf* (med) internist

Interpret [ɪntɛr'pret] *m* (-en;-en) interpreter; exponent

interpunktieren [ɪntɛrpuŋk'tirən] *tr* punctuate

Interpunktion [ɪntɛrpuŋk'tsjon] *f* (-; -en) punctuation

Interpunktions'zeichen *n* punctuation mark

Intervall [ɪntɛr'val] *n* (-s;-e) interval

intervenieren [ɪntɛrvɛ'nirən] *intr* intervene

Interview ['ɪntɛrvju] *n* (-s;-s) interview

interviewen [ɪntɛr'vju·ən] *tr* interview

intim [ɪn'tim] *adj* intimate

Intimität [ɪntɪmɪ'tet] *f* (-;-en) intimacy

intolerant [ɪntɔlɛ'rant] *adj* intolerant

intonieren [ɪntɔ'nirən] *tr* intone

intransitiv ['ɪntransɪtif] *adj* intransitive

intravenös [ɪntravɛ'nøs] *adj* intravenous

intrigant [ɪntrɪ'gant] *adj* intriguing, scheming || **Intragant** –in §7 *mf* intriguer, schemer

Intrige [ɪn'trigə] *f* (-;-n) intrigue

introspektiv [ɪntrɔspɛk'tif] *adj* introspective

Introvertierte [ɪntrɔvɛr'tirtə] §5 *mf* introvert

invalide [ɪnva'lidə] *adj* disabled || **Invalide** §5 *mf* invalid

Invalidität [ɪnvalɪdɪ'tet] *f* (-;) disability

Invasion [ɪnva'zjon] *f* (-;-en) invasion

Inventar [ɪnvɛn'tar] *n* (-s;-e) inventory

Inventur [ɪnvɛn'tur] *f* (-;-en) stock taking; **I. machen** take stock

inwärts ['ɪnvɛrts] *adv* inwards

inwendig ['ɪnvɛndɪç] *adj* inward, inner

inwiefern' *adv* how far; in what way

inwieweit' *adv* var of **inwiefern**

In'zucht *f* inbreeding

inzwi'schen *adv* meanwhile

Ion [ɪ'on] *n* (-s;-en) (phys) ion

ionisieren [ɪ·ɔnɪ'zirən] *tr* ionize

Irak [ɪ'rak] *m* (-s;) Iraq

Iraker –in [ɪ'rakər(ɪn)] §6 *mf* Iraqi

irakisch [ɪ'rakɪʃ] *adj* Iraqi

Iran [ɪ'ran] *n* (-s;) Iran

Iraner –in [ɪ'ranər(ɪn)] §6 *mf* Iranian

iranisch [ɪ'ranɪʃ] *adj* Iranian

irden ['ɪrdən] *adj* earthen

irdisch ['ɪrdɪʃ] *adj* earthly, worldly || **Irdische** §5 *n* earthly nature

Ire ['ɪrə] *m* (-n;-n) Irishman; **die Iren** the Irish

irgend ['ɪrgənt] *adv*—**i. etwas** something, anything; **i. jemand** someone, anyone; **nur i.** possibly

ir'gendein *adj* some, any || **ingendeiner** *indef pron* someone, anyone

ir'gendeinmal *adv* at some time or other

ir'gendwann *adv* at some time or other

ir'gendwelcher *adj* any; any kind of

ir'gendwer *indef pron* someone

ir'gendwie *adv* somehow or other

ir'gendwo *adv* somewhere or other; anywhere

ir'gendwoher *adv* from somewhere or other
ir'gendwohin *adv* somewhere or other
Irin ['irin] *f* (–;–nen) Irish woman
Iris ['iris] *f* (–;–) (anat, bot) iris
irisch ['iriʃ] *adj* Irish
Irland ['irlant] *n* (–s;) Ireland
Iro·nie [iro'ni] *f* (–;–nien ['ni·ən]) irony
ironisch [i'roniʃ] *adj* ironic(al)
irre ['irə] *adj* stray; confused; mad; **i. werden** go astray; get confused; **i. werden an** (*dat*) lose faith in || **Irre** §5 *mf* lunatic || *f* maze; wrong track; **in die I. führen** put on the wrong track; **in die I. gehen** go astray
ir'refahren §71 *intr* (SEIN) lose one's way, go wrong
ir'reführen *tr* mislead
ir'regehen §82 *intr* (SEIN) lose one's way; (fig) go wrong
ir'remachen *tr* confuse; **j–n i. an** (*dat*) make s.o. lose faith in
irren ['irən] *intr* go astray; err || *ref* (in *dat*) be mistaken (about); **sich in der Straße i.** take the wrong road; **sich in der Zeit i.** misjudge the time
Ir'renanstalt *f*, Ir'renhaus *n* insane asylum
Ir'renhäusler ['irənhɔizlər] *m* (–s;–) inmate of an insane asylum
ir'rereden *intr* rave; talk deliriously
Irrfahrt ['irfart] *f* odyssey
Irrgang ['irgaŋ] *m* winding path
Irrgarten ['irgartən] *m* labyrinth
Irrglaube ['irglaubə] *m* heresy
irrgläubig ['irglɔibiç] *adj* heretical
irrig ['iriç] *adj* mistaken
Irri·gator [iri'gatər] *m* (–s;–gatoren [ga·torən]) douche

irritieren [iri'tirən] *tr* irritate; (coll) confuse
Irrlehre ['irlerə] *f* false doctrine
Irrlicht ['irliçt] *n* jack-o'-lantern
Irrsinn ['irzin] *m* insanity
irr'sinnig *adj* insane
Irrtum ['irtum] *n* (–s;–er) error
irrtümlich ['irtymliç] *adj* erroneous
Irrweg ['irvek] *m* wrong track
Irrwisch ['irviʃ] *m* (–es;–e) jack-o'-lantern; (coll) fireball
Islam [is'lam] *m* (–s;) Islam
Island ['islant] *n* (–s;) Iceland
Iso·lator [izo'latər] *m* (–s;–latoren [la'torən]) (elec) insulator
Isolier– [izolir] *comb.fm.* isolation; insulating; insulated
Isolier'band *n* (–[e]s;–er) friction tape
isolieren [izo'lirən] *tr* (*Kranke*) isolate; (*abdichten*) insulate
Isolier'haft *f* solitary confinement
Insolier'station *f* isolation ward
Isolie'rung *f* (–;–en) isolation; (elec) insulation
Isotop [izo'top] *n* (–[e]s;–e) isotope
Israel ['isra·εl] *n* (– & –s;) Israel
Israeli [isra'eli] *m* (–s;–s) Israeli
israelisch [isra'eliʃ] *adj* Israeli
Israelit –in [isra·ε'lit(in)] §7 *mf* Israelite
israelitisch [isra·ε'litiʃ] *adj* Israelite
Ist– [ist] *comb.fm.* actual
Ist–'Bestand *m* actual stock; (fin) actual balance; (mil) actual stockpile
Ist–'Stand *m*, Ist–'Stärke *f* (mil) effective strength
Italien [i'taljən] *n* (–s;) Italy
Italiener –in [ital'jenər(in)] §6 *mf* Italian
italienisch [ital'jeniʃ] *adj* Italian

J

J, j [jɔt] *invar n* J, j
ja [ja] *adv* yes; indeed, certainly; of course || **Ja** *n* (–s;–s) yes
Jacht [jaxt] *f* (–;–en) yacht
Jacke ['jakə] *f* (–;–n) jacket, coat
Jackenkleid (Jak'kenkleid) *n* lady's two-piece suit
Jackett [ʒa'kɛt] *n* (–s;–s) jacket
Jagd [jakt] *f* (–;–en) hunt(ing); **auf die J. gehen** go hunting; **J. machen auf** (*acc*) hunt for
Jagd'abschirmung *f* (aer) fighter screen
Jagd'aufseher *m* gamewarden
jagdbar ['jaktbar] *adj* in season, fair (*game*)
Jagd'bomber *m* (aer) fighter-bomber
Jagd'flieger *m* fighter pilot
Jagd'flugzeug *n* (aer) fighter plane
Jagd'gehege *n* game preserve
Jagd'geleit *n* (aer) fighter escort
Jagd'hund *m* hunting dog, hound
Jagd'rennen *n* steeplechase
Jagd'revier *n* hunting ground
Jagd'schein *m* hunting license

Jagd'schutz *m* (aer) fighter protection
Jagd'verband *m* (aer) fighter unit
Jagd'wild *n* game; game bird
jagen ['jagən] *tr* hunt; pursue; chase; (fig) follow close on; **in die Luft j.** blow up || *intr* go hunting; **j. nach** pursue || *intr* (SEIN) rush
Jäger ['jegər] *m* (–s;–) hunter; (aer) fighter plane; (mil) rifleman
Jägerei [jegə'rai] *f* (–;) hunting
Jä'gerlatein *n* (coll) fish story
Jaguar ['jagu·ar] *m* (–s;–s) jaguar
jäh [je] *adj* sudden; steep || **Jähe** *f* (–;) suddenness; steepness
jählings ['jeliŋs] *adv* suddenly; steeply
Jahr [jar] *n* (–[e]s;–e) year
jahraus' *adv*—j. jahrein year in year out, year after year
Jahr'buch *n* almanac; yearbook; annual
jahrelang ['jarəlaŋ] *adj* long-standing || *adv* for years
jähren ['jerən] *ref* be a year ago
Jahres– [jarəs] *comb.fm.* annual, yearly, of the year

Jah'resfeier *f* anniversary
Jah'resfrist *f* period of a year
Jah'resrente *f* annuity
Jah'restag *m* anniversary
Jah'reszahl *f* date, year
Jah'reszeit *f* season
jah'reszeitlich *adj* seasonal
Jahr'gang *m* age group; class, year; crop; vintage; **er gehört zu meinem J.** he was born in the same year as I
Jahrhun'dert *n* century
–jährig [jɛrɪç] *comb.fm.* –year-old
jährlich ['jerlɪç] *adj* yearly, annual
Jahr'markt *m* fair
Jahr'marktplatz *m* fairground
Jahrtau'send *n* millennium
Jahrzehnt [jɑr'tsent] *n* (–[e]s;–e) decade
Jäh'zorn *m* fit of anger; hot temper
jäh'zornig *adj* quick-tempered
Jalou·sie [ʒalu'zi] *f* (–;–sien ['zi·ən]) louvre; Venetian blind
Jammer ['jamər] *m* (–s;) misery; wailing; **es ist ein J., daß** it's a pity that
Jam'merlappen *m* (pej) jellyfish
jämmerlich ['jemərlɪç] *adj* miserable; pitiful; *(Anblick)* sorry
jammern ['jamərn] *tr* move to pity || *intr* **(über** *acc,* **um)** moan (about); **j. nach** (or **um)** whimper for
jam'merschade *adj* deplorable
Jänner ['jɛnər] *m* (–s & –;–) (Aust) January
Januar ['janu·ɑr] *m* (–s & –;–e) January
Japan ['japan] *n* (–s;) Japan
Japaner **–in** [ja'panər(ɪn)] §6 *mf* Japanese
japanisch [ja'panɪʃ] *adj* Japanese
jappen ['japən] *intr* pant, gasp
Jasager ['jɑzagər] *m* (–s;–) yes-man
jäten ['jetən] *tr* weed; **das Unkraut j.** pull out weeds || *intr* weed
Jauche ['jauxə] *f* (–;–n) liquid manure; (sl) slop
jauchen ['jauxən] *tr* manure
Jau'chegrube *f* cesspool
jauchzen ['jauxtsən] *intr* rejoice; **vor Freude j.** shout for joy || **Jauchzen** *n* (–s;) jubilation
Jauch'zer *m* (–s;–) shout of joy
jawohl [ja'vol] *interj* yes, indeed!
Ja'wort *n* (–[e]s;) consent
Jazz [dʒez], [jats] *m* (–;) jazz
je [je] *adv* ever; **denn je** than ever; **je länger, je** (or **desto) besser** the longer the better; **je nach** according to, depending on; **je nachdem, ob** according to whether; **je Pfund** per pound; **je zwei** two each; two by two, in twos; **seit je** always
Jeans [dʒinz] *pl* jeans
jedenfalls ['jedənfals] *adv* at any rate; **ich j.** I for one
jeder ['jedər] §3 *indef adj* each, every || *indef pron* each one, everyone
jederlei ['jedər'laɪ] *invar adj* every kind of
je'dermann *indef pron* everyone, everybody
je'derzeit *adv* at all times, at any time
je'desmal *adv* each time, every time
jedoch [jɛ'dɔx] *adv* however

jeglicher ['jeklɪçər] §3 *indef adj* each, every || *indef pron* each one, everyone
je'her *adv*—**von j.** since time immemorial
Jelän'gerjelie'ber *m* & *n* honeysuckle
jemals ['jemals] *adv* ever
jemand ['jemant] *indef pron* someone, somebody; anyone, anybody
jener ['jenər] §3 *dem adj* that || *dem pron* that one
jenseitig ['jenzaɪtɪç] *adj* opposite, beyond, otherworldly
jenseits ['jenzaɪts] *prep (genit)* on the other side of; beyond || **Jenseits** *n* (–;) beyond
jetzig ['jetsɪç] *adj* present, current
jetzt [jetst] *adv* now
jeweilig ['jevaɪlɪç] *adj* at that time
jeweils ['jevaɪls] *adv* at that time
jiddisch ['jɪdɪʃ] *adj* Yiddish
Joch [jɔx] *n* (–[e]s;–e) yoke; yoke of oxen; *(e–r Brücke)* span; *(e–s Berges)* saddleback
Joch'bein *n* cheekbone
Joch'brücke *f* pile bridge
Jockei ['dʒɔki] *m* (–s;–s) jockey
Jod [jot] *n* (–s;) iodine
jodeln ['jodəln] *intr* yodel
Jodler **–in** ['jodlər(ɪn)] §6 *mf* yodeler || *m* yodel
Jodtinktur ['jottɪŋktur] *f* (–;) (pharm) iodine
Johannisbeere [jo'hanɪsberə] *f* currant
johlen ['jolən] *intr* yell, boo
jonglieren [ʒɔŋ'(g)lirən] *tr* & *intr* juggle
Journalist **–in** [ʒurna'lɪst(ɪn)] §7 *mf* journalist
jovial [jo'vjal] *adj* jovial
Jubel ['jubəl] *m* (–s;) jubilation
Ju'belfeier *f*, **Ju'belfest** *n* jubilee
Ju'beljahr *n* jubilee year
jubeln ['jubəln] *intr* rejoice; shout for joy
Jubilä·um [jubɪ'le·um] *n* (–s;–en [ən]) jubilee
juche [jux'he] *interj* hurray!
juchei [jux'haɪ] *interj* hurray!
juchzen ['juxtsən] *intr* shout for joy
jucken ['jukən] *tr* itch; scratch || *ref* scratch || *intr* itch || *impers*—**es juckt mich** I feel itchy; **es juckt mir** (or **mich) in den Fingern zu** *(inf)* I am itching to *(inf)*; **es juckt sie in den Beinen** she is itching to dance
Jude ['judə] *m* (–n;–n) Jew
Ju'denschaft *f* (–;) Jewry
Ju'denstern *m* star of David
Judentum ['judəntum] *n* (–s;) Judaism; **das J.** the Jews
Jüdin ['jydɪn] *f* (–;–nen) Jewish woman
jüdisch ['jydɪʃ] *adj* Jewish
Jugend ['jugənt] *f* (–;) youth
Ju'gendalter *n* youth; adolescence
Ju'gendgericht *n* juvenile court
Ju'gendherberge *f* youth hostel
Ju'gendkriminalität *f* juvenile delinquency
jugendlich ['jugəntlɪç] *adj* youthful || **Jugendliche** §5 *mf* youth, teenager
Ju'gendliebe *f* puppy love
Ju'gendstrich *m* youthful prank

Jugoslawien [jugɔ'slavjən] *n* (-s;) Yugoslavia
jugoslawisch [jugɔ'slavɪʃ] *adj* Yugoslav
Juli ['juli] *m* (-[s];-s) July
jung [juŋ] *adj* (jünger ['jyŋər]; jüngste ['jyŋstə] §9) young; (*Erbsen*) green; (*Wein*) new ‖ **Junge** §5 *m* boy ‖ *n* newly born; young
jungen ['juŋən] *intr* produce young
jun'genhaft *adj* boyish
Jünger ['jyŋər] *m* (-s;-) disciple
Jungfer ['juŋfər] *f* (-;-n) maiden; virgin
jüngeferlich ['jyŋfərlɪç] *adj* maidenly
Jung'fernfahrt *f* maiden voyage
Jung'fernhäutchen *n* hymen
Jung'fernkranz *m* bridal wreath
Jung'fernschaft *f* virginity
Jung'frau *f* virgin
jungfräulich ['juŋfrɔɪlɪç] *adj* maidenly; virgin
Jung'fräulichkeit *f* virginity
Jung'geselle *m* bachelor
Jung'gesellenstand *m* bachelorhood
Jung'gesellin *f* single girl
Jüngling ['jyŋlɪŋ] *m* (-s;-e) young man
jüngst [jyŋst] *adv* recently
jüng'ste *adj* see **jung**

Juni ['juni] *m* (-[s];-s) June
Junker ['juŋkər] *m* (-s;-) young nobleman; nobleman
Jura ['jura] *pl*—J. studieren study law
Jurist -in [ju'rɪst(ɪn)] §7 *mf* lawyer; (educ) law student
Juristerei [jurɪstə'raɪ] *f* (-;) jurisprudence
juristisch [ju'rɪstɪʃ] *adj* legal, law; juristische Person legal entity, corporation
just [just] *adv* just, precisely
justieren [jus'tirən] *tr* adjust
Justiz [jus'tits] *f* (-;) justice; administration of justice
Justiz'irrtum *m* miscarriage of justice
Justiz'minister *m* minister of justice; attorney general; Lord Chancellor (Brit)
Jutesack ['jutəzak] *m* gunnysack
Juwel [ju'vel] *n* (-s;-en) jewel, gem; Juwelen jewelry
Juwe'lenkästchen *n* jewel box
Juwelier -in [juvɛ'lir(ɪn)] §6 *mf* jeweler
Juwelier'waren *pl* jewelry
Jux [juks] *m* (-es;-e) spoof, joke; aus Jux as a joke; sich [*dat*] e-n Jux mit j-m machen play a joke on s.o.

K

K, k [ka] *invar n* K, k
Kabale [ka'balə] *f* (-;-n) intrigue
Kabarett [kaba'rɛt] *n* (-[e]s;-e) cabaret; floor show; (*drehbare Platte*) lazy Suzan
Kabel ['kabəl] *n* (-s;-) cable
Ka'belgramm *n* (-es;-e) cablegram
Kabeljau ['kabəljau] *m* (-s;-e) codfish
kabeln ['kabəln] *tr* cable
Kabine [ka'binə] *f* (-;-n) cabin; booth; (aer) cockpit
Kabinett [kabɪ'nɛt] *n* (-s;-e) closet; small room; (& pol) cabinet
Kabriolett [kabrɪɔ'lɛt] *n* (-[e]s;-e) (aut) convertible
Kachel ['kaxəl] *f* (-;-n) glazed tile
kacken ['kakən] *intr* (sl) defecate
Kadaver [ka'davər] *m* (-s;-) cadaver
Kada'vergehorsam *m* blind obedience
Kadenz [ka'dɛnts] *f* (-;-en) cadence
Kader ['kadər] *m* (-s;-) cadre
Kadett [ka'dɛt] *m* (-en;-en) cadet
Käfer ['kefər] *m* (-s;-) beetle
Kaffee ['kafe] *m* (-s;-s) coffee
Kaf'feebohne *f* coffee bean
Kaf'feeklatsch *m* coffee klatsch
Kaf'feemaschine *f* coffee maker
Kaf'feepflanzung *f*, Kaf'feeplantage *f* coffee plantation
Kaf'feesatz *m* coffee grounds
Kaf'feetante *f* coffee fiend
Käfig ['kefɪç] *m* (-[e]s;-e) cage
kahl [kal] *adj* bald; (*Baum*) bare; (*Landschaft*) bleak, barren
kahl'köpfig *adj* bald-headed
Kahm [kam] *m* (-[e]s;-e) mold; scum

kahmig ['kamɪç] *adj* moldy; scummy
Kahn [kan] *m* (-[e]s;ᵘe) boat; barge
Kai [kaɪ], [ke] *m* (-s;-s) quay, wharf
Kaiser ['kaɪzər] *m* (-s;-) emperor
Kaiserin ['kaɪzərɪn] *f* (-;-nen) empress
kai'serlich *adj* imperial
Kai'serreich *n*, Kaisertum ['kaɪzərtum] *n* (-[e]s;ᵘer) empire
Kai'serschnitt *m* Caesarian operation
Kai'serzeit *f* (*hist*) Empire
Kajüte [ka'jytə] *f* (-;-n) (naut) cabin
Kajü'tenjunge *m* cabin boy
Kajü'tentreppe *f* (naut) companionway
Kakao [ka'ka·ɔ] *m* (-s;-) cocoa; j-n durch den K. ziehen pull s.o.'s leg
Kaktee [kak'te·ə] *f* (-;-n), Kaktus ['kaktus] *m* (-;-se) cactus
Kalauer ['kalau·ər] *m* (-s;-) pun
Kalb [kalp] *n* (-[e]s;ᵘer) calf
Kalbe ['kalbə] *f* (-;-n) heifer
kalbern ['kalbərn] *intr* be silly
Kalb'fell *n* calfskin
Kalb'fleisch *n* veal
Kalbs'braten *m* roast veal
Kalbs'kotelett *n* veal cutlet
Kalbs'schnitzel *n* veal cutlet
Kaleidoskop [kalaɪdɔ'skop] *n* (-s;-e) kaleidoscope
Kalender [ka'lɛndər] *m* (-s;-) calendar
Kali ['kalɪ] *n* (-s;) potash
Kaliber [ka'libər] *n* (-s;-) caliber
kalibrieren [kalɪ'brirən] *tr* calibrate; gauge
Kaliko ['kalɪko] *m* (-s;-s) calico
Kalium ['kaljum] *n* (-s;) potassium

Kalk [kalk] *m* (–[e]s;–e) lime; calcium
kalken ['kalkən] *tr* whitewash; lime
kalkig ['kalkıç] *adj* limy
Kalk'ofen *m* limekiln
Kalk'stein *m* limestone
Kalk'steinbruch *m* limestone quarry
Kalkül [kal'kyl] *m & n* (–s;–e) calculation; (math) calculus
kalkulieren [kalku'lirən] *tr* calculate
Kal·mar ['kalmar] *m* (–s;–mare ['marə]) squid
Kalo·rie [kalɔ'ri] *f* (–;–rien ['ri·ən]) calorie
Kalotte [ka'lɔtə] *f* (–;–n) skullcap
kalt [kalt] *adj* (**kälter** ['kɛltər]; **kälteste** ['kɛltəstə] §9) cold
kaltblütig ['kaltblytıç] *adj* cold-blooded
Kälte ['kɛltə] *f* (–;) cold, coldness
käl'tebeständig *adj* cold-resistant
Käl'tegrad *m* degree below freezing
kälten ['kɛltən] *tr* chill
Käl'tewelle *f* (meteor) cold wave
Kalt'front *f* cold front
kalt'herzig *adj* cold-hearted
kalt'machen *tr* (sl) bump off
kaltschnäuzig ['kalt/nɔıtsıç] *adj* (coll) callous; (coll) cool, unflappable
kalt'stellen *tr* render harmless
kam [kam] *pret* of **kommen**
Kambodscha [kam'bɔtʒa] *n* (–s;) Cambodia
kambodschanisch [kambɔ'dʒanı/] *adj* Cambodian
Kamel [ka'mel] *n* (–[e]s;–e) camel
Kamel'garn *n* mohair
Kamera ['kamɛra] *f* (–;–s) camera
Kamerad [kamə'rat] *m* (–en;–en), **Kameradin** [kamə'radın] *f* (–;–nen) comrade
Kamerad'schaft ((–;–en) comradeship
Kamin [ka'min] *m* (–s;–e) chimney; fireplace
Kamin'platte *f* hearthstone
Kamin'sims *n* mantelpiece
Kamm [kam] *m* (–[e]s;–e) comb; (*e–s Gebirges*) ridge; (*e–r Welle*) crest
kämmen ['kɛmən] *tr* comb; (*Wolle*) card
Kammer ['kamər] *f* (–;–n) chamber; (adm) board; (anat) ventricle
Kam'merdiener *m* valet
Kämmerer ['kɛmərər] *m* (–s;–) chamberlain; (*Schatzmeister*) treasurer
Kam'mermusik *f* chamber music
Kamm'garn *n* (tex) worsted
Kamm'rad *n* cogwheel
Kampagne [kam'panjə] *f* (–;–n) campaign
Kämpe ['kɛmpə] *m* (–n;–n) warrior
Kampf [kampf] *m* (–[e]s;–e) fight
Kampf'bahn *f* (sport) stadium, arena
kämpfen ['kɛmpfən] *tr & intr* fight
Kampfer ['kampfər] *m* (–s;) camphor
Kämpfer **–in** ['kɛmpfər(ın)] §6 *mf* fighter
kämpferisch ['kɛmpfərı/] *adj* fighting
kampf'erprobt *adj* battle-tested
kampf'fähig *adj* fit to fight; (mil) fit for active service
Kampf'hahn *m* gamecock; (fig) scrapper
Kampf'handlung *f* (mil) action

Kampf'müdigkeit *f* combat fatigue
Kampf'parole *f* (pol) campaign slogan
Kampf'platz *m* battleground
Kampf'raum *m* battle zone
Kampf'richter *m* referee, umpire
Kampf'schwimmer *m* (nav) frogman
Kampf'spiel *n* (sport) competition
Kampf'staffel *f* tactical squadron
kampf'unfähig *adj* disabled; **k. machen** put out of action
Kampf'veranstalter *m* (sport) promotor
Kampf'verband *m* combat unit
Kampf'wert *m* fighting efficiency
Kampf'ziel *n* (mil) objective
kampieren [kam'pirən] *intr* camp
Kanada ['kanada] *n* (–s;) Canada
Kanadier **–in** [ka'nadjər(ın)] §6 *mf* Canadian || *m* canoe
kanadisch [ka'nadı/] *adj* Canadian
Kanaille [ka'naljə] *f* (–;–n) bum; (*Pöbel*) riffraff
Kanal [ka'nal] *m* (–s;–e) canal; (*für Abwasser*) drain, sewer; (agr) irrigation ditch; (anat, elec) duct; (geol, telv) channel
Kanalisation [kanalıza'tsjon] *f* (–;) drainage; sewerage system
Kanalräumer [ka'nalrɔımər] *m* (–s;–) sewer worker
Kanal'wähler *m* (telv) channel selector
Kanapee ['kanape] *n* (–s;–s) sofa
Kanarienvogel [ka'narjənfogəl] *m* canary
Kandare [kan'darə] *f* (–;–n) bit, curb; **j–n an die K. nehmen** take s.o. in hand
Kanda'renkette *f* curb chain
Kandelaber [kandɛ'labər] *m* (–s;–) candelabrum
Kandidat **–in** [kandı'dat(ın)] §7 *mf* candidate
Kandidatur [kandıda'tur] *f* (–;–en) candidacy
kandideln [kan'didəln] *ref* get drunk
kandidieren [kandı'dirən] *intr* be a candidate, run for office
Kandis ['kandıs] *m* (–;) rock candy
Kaneel [ka'nel] *m* (–s;–e) cinnamon
Känguruh ['kɛnguru] *n* (–s;–s) kangaroo
Kaninchen [ka'nınçən] *n* (–s;–) rabbit
Kanister [ka'nıstər] *m* (–s;–) canister
Kanne ['kanə] *f* (–;–n) can; pot; jug
Kannelüre [kanə'lyrə] *f* (–;–n) (archit) flute
Kannibale [kanı'balə] *m* (–n;–n), **Kannibalin** [kanı'balın] *f* (–;–nen) cannibal
kannte ['kantə] *pret* of **kennen**
Ka·non ['kanɔn] *m* (–s;–s) (*Maßstab; Gebet bei der Messe*) canon; (mus) round || *m* (–s;–nones ['nonəs] canon (*of Canon Law*)
Kanone [ka'nonə] *f* (–;–n) (arti) gun; (hist) canon; (coll) expert; **unter aller K.** indescribably bad
Kano'nenboot *n* gunboat
Kano'nenrohr *n* gun barrel; **heiliges K.!** holy smokes!
kanonisieren [kanɔnı'zirən] *tr* canonize
Kante ['kantə] *f* (–;–n) edge

kanten ['kantən] *tr* set on edge; (*beim Schifahren*) cant ‖ **Kanten** *m* (-s;-) end of a loaf, crust
Kanthaken ['kanthakən] *m* grappling hook
kantig ['kantıç] *adj* angular; squared
Kantine [kan'tinə] *f* (-;-n) canteen; (mil) post exchange
Kanton [kan'ton] *m* (-s;-e) canton
Kan·tor ['kantər] *m* (-s;-toren ['torən]) choir master; organist
Kanu [ka'nu] *n* (-s;-s) canoe
Kanzel ['kantsəl] *f* (-;-n) pulpit; (aer) cockpit
Kanzlei [kants'laı] *f* (-;-en) office; chancellery
Kanzlei'papier *n* official foolscap
Kanzlei'sprache *f* legal jargon
Kanzler ['kantslər] *m* (-s;-) chancellor
Kap [kap] *n* (-s;-s) cape, headland
Kapaun [ka'paun] *m* (-s;-e) capon
Kapazität [kapatsı'tet] *f* (-;-en) capacity; (*Könner*) authority
Kapelle [ka'pɛlə] *f* (-;-n) chapel; (mus) band
Kapell'meister *m* band leader; orchestra conductor
kapern ['kapərn] *tr* capture; (coll) nab
kapieren [ka'pirən] *tr* get, understand ‖ *intr* get it; **kapiert?** got it?
kapital [kapı'tal] *adj* excellent ‖ **Kapital** *n* (-s;-e & -ien [jən]) (fin) capital; **K. schlagen aus** capitalize on; **K. und Zinsen** principal and interest
Kapital'anlage *f* investment
Kapital'ertragssteuer *f* tax on unearned income
kapitalisieren [kapıtalı'zirən] *tr* (fin) capitalize
Kapitalismus [kapıta'lısmus] *m* (-s;) capitalism
Kapitalist –**in** [kapıta'lıst(ın)] *m* §7 capitalist
Kapital'verbrechen *n* capital offense
Kapitän [kapı'ten] *m* (-s;-e) captain, skipper; **K. zur See** (nav) captain
Kapitän'leutnant *m* (nav) lieutenant
Kapitel [ka'pıtəl] *n* (-s;-) chapter
Kapitell [kapı'tel] *n* (-s;-e) (archit) capital
kapitulieren [kapıtu'lirən] *intr* capitulate, surrender; reenlist
Kaplan [ka'plan] *m* (-s;⸚e) chaplain; (R.C.) assistant (pastor)
Kapo ['kapo] *m* (-s;-s) prisoner overseer; (mil) (coll) N.C.O.
Kappe ['kapə] *f* (-;-n) cap; hood, cover; **etw auf seine eigene K. nehmen** take the responsibility for s.th.
Käppi ['kɛpı] *n* (-s;-s) garrison cap
Kaprice [ka'prisə] *f* (-;-n) caprice
Kapriole [kaprı'olə] *f* (-;-n) caper
kaprizieren [kaprı'tsirən] *ref*—**sich k. auf** (*acc*) be dead set on
kapriziös [kaprı'tsjøs] *adj* capricious
Kapsel ['kapsəl] *f* (-;-n) capsule; (*e–r Flasche*) cap; (*e–s Sprengkörpers*) detonator
kaputt [ka'put] *adj* (sl) broken; (sl) ruined; (sl) exhausted; (sl) dead
kaputt'gehen §82 *intr* (SEIN) get ruined
kaputt'machen *tr* ruin

Kapuze [ka'putsə] *f* (-;-n) hood; (eccl) cowl
Kapuziner [kapu'tsinər] *m* (-s;-) Capuchin
Kapuzi'nerkresse *f* Nasturtium
Karabiner [kara'binər] *m* (-s;-) carbine
Karabi'nerhaken *m* snap
Karaffe [ka'rafə] *f* (-;-n) carafe
Karambolage [karambo'laʒə] *f* (-;-n) (coll) collision
karambolieren [karambo'lirən] *intr* (coll) collide
Karamelle [kara'mɛlə] *f* (-;-n) caramel
Karat [ka'rat] *n* (-[e]s;) carat
–**karätig** [karetıç] *comb.fm.* –*carat*
Karawane [kara'vanə] *f* (-;-n) caravan
Karbid [kar'bit] *n* (-[e]s;-e) carbide
Karbolsäure [kar'bolzɔırə] *f* (-;) carbolic acid
Karbon [kar'bon] *n* (-s;) (geol) carbon
Karbunkel [kar'buŋkəl] *n* (-s;-) carbuncle
Kardinal– [kardınal] *comb.fm.* cardinal, principal ‖ **Kardinal** *m* (-s;⸚e) (eccl, orn) cardinal
Karenzzeit [ka'rentstsaıt] *f* (ins) waiting period
Karfreitag [kar'fraıtak] *m* Good Friday
karg [kark] *adj* (**karger** & **kärger** ['kɛrgər]; **kargste** & **kärgste** ['kɛrstə] §9) (*ärmlich*) meager; (*Boden*) poor; (*Landschaft*) bleak
kargen ['kargən] *intr* be sparing
Karg'heit *f* (-;) bleakness; meagerness; frugality
kärglich ['kɛrlıç] *adj* meager, poor
kariert [ka'rirt] *adj* checked, squared
Karikatur [karıka'tur] *f* (-;-en) caricature; cartoon
karikieren [karı'kirən] *tr* caricature
Karl [karl] *m* (-s;) Charles; **Karl der Große** Charlemagne
Karmeliter [karmɛ'litər] *m* (-s;-) Carmelite Friar
Karmelitin [karmɛ'litın] *f* (-;-nen) Carmelite nun
karmesinrot [karmɛ'zinrot], **karminrot** [kar'minrot] *adj* crimson
Karneval ['karnəval] *m* (-s;-s & -e) carnival
Karnickel [kar'nıkəl] *n* (-s;-) (coll) rabbit; (*Sündenbock*) (coll) scapegoat; (*Einfaltspinsel*) simpleton
Karo ['karə] *n* (-s;-s) diamond; check, square; (cards) diamond(s)
Karosse [ka'rɔsə] *f* (-;-n) state carriage
Karosse·rie [karɔsə'ri] *f* (-;-rien ['ri·ən] (aut) body
Karotte [ka'rɔtə] *f* (-;-n) carrot
Karpfen ['karpfən] *m* (-s;-) carp
Karre ['karə] *f* (-;-n), **Karren** ['karən] *m* (-s;-) cart; wheelbarrow; **die alte K.** the old rattletrap
Karriere [ka'rjerə] *f* (-;-n) career; gallop; **K. machen** get ahead
Karte ['kartə] *f* (-;-n) card; ticket; (*Landkarte*) map; (*Speise*–) menu
Kartei [kar'taı] *f* (-;-en) card file
Kartei'karte *f* index card

Kartell [kar'tɛl] *n* (-s;-e) cartel
Kar'tenkunststück *n* card trick
Kartenlegerin ['kartənlegərın] *f* (-; -nen) fortuneteller
Kar'tenstelle *f* ration board
Kartoffel [kar'tɔfəl] *f* (-;-n) potato
Kartof'felbrei *m* mashed potatoes
Kartoffelpuffer [kar'tɔfəlpufər] *m* (-s; -) potato pancake
Karton [kar'ton] *m* (-s;-s) cardboard; carton; (paint) cartoon
Kartonage [kartɔ'naʒə] *f* (-;-n) cardboard box
kartoniert [kartɔ'nirt] *adj* (bb) softcover
Karton'papier *n* (thin) cardboard
Kartothek [kartɔ'tek] *f* (-;-en) card index; card filing system
Kartothek'ausgabe *f* loose-leaf edition
Karussell [karu'sɛl] *n* (-s;-e) merry-go-round
Karwoche ['karvɔxə] *f* Holy Week
Karzer ['kartsər] *m* (-s;-) (educ) detention room; **K. bekommen** get a detention
Kaschmir ['kaʃmɪr] *m* (-s;-e) cashmere
Käse ['kezə] *m* (-s;-) cheese; (sl) baloney
Kaserne [ka'zɛrnə] *f* (-;-n) barracks
käsig ['kezɪç] *adj* cheesy; (*Gesichtsfarbe*) pasty
Kasino [ka'zino] *n* (-s;-s) casino; (mil) officer's mess
Kas'pisches Meer' ['kaspɪ/əs] *n* Caspian Sea
Kassa ['kasa] *f—***per K. in cash**
Kassa- *comb.fm.* cash, spot
Kasse ['kasə] *f* (-;-n) money box; till; cash register; cashiers desk; (*Bargeld*) cash; (adm) finance department; (educ) bursars office; (sport) ticket window; (theat) box office; **gegen** (or **per**) **K.** cash, for cash; **gut bei K. sein** (coll) be flush
Kas'senabschluß *m* balancing of accounts
Kas'senbeamte *m* cashier; teller
Kas'senbeleg *m* sales slip
Kas'senbestand *m* cash on hand
Kas'senerfolg *m* (theat) hit
Kas'senführer -in §6 *mf* cashier
Kas'senschalter *m* teller's window
Kas'senschrank *m* safe
Kas'senzettel *m* sales slip
Kasserolle [kasə'rɔlə] *f* (-;-n) casserole
Kassette [ka'sɛtə] *f* (-;-n) base, box; (cin, phot) cassette
kassieren [ka'sirən] *tr* (*Geld*) take in; get; (*Urteil*) annul; (coll) confiscate; (coll) arrest; (mil) break
Kassie'rer -in §6 *mf* cashier; teller
Kastagnette [kastan'jetə] *f* (-;-n) castanet
Kastanie [kas'tanjə] *f* (-;-n) chestnut
Kästchen ['kɛstçən] *n* (-s;-) case, box
Kaste ['kastə] *f* (-;-n) caste
kasteien [kas'taɪ·ən] *tr & ref* mortify; **sein Leib k.** mortify the flesh
Kastell [kas'tɛl] *n* (-s;-e) small fort
Kasten ['kastən] *m* (-s;ᵘ & -) chest, case, box; cupboard, cabinet; (*Auto*)

(coll) crate; (*Boot*) (coll) tub; (*Gefängnis*) (coll) jug
Ka'stengeist *m* snobbishness
Ka'stenwagen *m* (aut) panel truck; (rr) boxcar
Ka'stenwesen *n* caste system
Kastrat [kas'trat] *m* (-en;-en) eunuch
kastrieren [kas'trirən] *tr* castrate
Katakomben [kata'kɔmbən] *pl* catacombs
Katalog [kata'lok] *m* (-[e]s;-e) catalogue
katalogisieren [katalɔgɪ'zirən] *tr* catalogue
Katapult [kata'pult] *m & n* (-[e]s;-e) catapult
katapultieren [katapul'tirən] *tr* catapult
Katarakt [kata'rakt] *m* (-[e]s;-e) cataract, rapids; (pathol) cataract
Katasteramt [ka'tastəramt] *n* land-registry office
katastrophal [katastrɔ'fal] *adj* catastrophic, disastrous
Katastrophe [kata'strofə] *f* (-;-n) catastrophe, disaster
Katastro'phengebiet *m* disaster area
Katego·rie [katego'ri] *f* (-;-rien ['ri·ən] category
kategorisch [katɛ'gorɪ/] *adj* categorical
Kater ['katər] *m* (-s;-) tomcat; (coll) hangover
Katheder [ka'tedər] *n & m* (-s;-) teacher's desk
Kathe'derblüte *f* teacher's blunder
Kathedrale [katɛ'dralə] *f* (-;-n) cathedral
Kathode [ka'todə] *f* (-;-n) cathode
Katholik -in [katɔ'lik(ɪn)] §7 *mf* Catholic
katholisch [ka'tolɪ/] *adj* Catholic
Kattun [ka'tun] *m* (-s;-e) calico
Kätzchen ['kɛtsçən] *n* (-s;-) kitten
Katze ['katsə] *f* (-;-n) cat; **für die K.** (coll) for the birds
kat'zenartig *adj* cat-like, feline
Kat'zenauge *n* reflector
Kat'zenbuckel *m* cat's arched back; **vor j-m K. machen** lick s.o.'s boots
kat'zenfreundlich *adj* overfriendly
Kat'zenjammer *m* hangover; blues
Kat'zenkopf *m* (coll) cobblestone; (box) rabbit punch
Kat'zensprung *m* stone's throw
Kauderwelsch ['kaudərvɛl/] *n* (-es;) gibberish
kauen ['kau·ən] *tr* chew
kauern ['kau·ərn] *ref & intr* cower
Kauf [kauf] *m* (-[e]s;ᵘe) purchase; **in K. nehmen** (fig) take, put up with; **leichten Kaufes davonkommen** get off cheaply; **zum K. stehen** be for sale
Kauf'auftrag *m* (com) order
kaufen ['kaufən] *tr* purchase, buy
Käufer -in ['kɔɪfər(ın)] §6 *mf* buyer
Kauf'haus *n* department store
Kauf'kraft *f* purchasing power
käuflich ['kɔɪflɪç] *adj* for sale; (*bestechlich*) open to bribes
Kauf'mann *m* (-[e]s;-leute) businessman; salesman

kaufmännisch ['kaufmɛnɪʃ] *adj* commercial, business
Kauf'mannsdeutsch *n* business German
Kauf'zwang *m* obligation to buy
Kaugummi ['kaugumɪ] *m* chewing gum
kaukasisch [kau'kazɪʃ] *adj* Caucasian
Kaulquappe ['kaulkvapə] *f* (-;-n) tadpole, polliwog
kaum [kaum] *adv* hardly, scarcely
Kautabak ['kautabak] *m* chewing tobacco
Kaution [kau'tsjon] *f* (-;-en) (jur) bond; (*Bürgschaft*) (jur) bail; **gegen K. on bail**
Kautschuk ['kautʃuk] *m* (-s;-e) rubber
Kauz [kauts] *m* (-es;-e) owl; (sl) crackpot
Kavalier [kava'lir] *m* (-s;-e) cavalier; gentleman; beau
Kavalkade [kaval'kadə] *f* (-;-n) cavalcade
Kavalle•rie [kavalə'ri] *f* (-;-rien ['ri-ən]) cavalry
Kavallerist [kavalə'rɪst] *m* (-en;-en) cavalryman, trooper
Kaviar ['kavjar] *m* (-[e]s;-e) caviar
keck [kɛk] *adj* bold; impudent; cheeky
Kegel ['kegəl] *m* (-s;-) tenpin; (geom) cone; **K. schieben** bowl
Ke'gelbahn *f* bowling alley
kegeln ['kegəln] *intr* bowl
Keg'ler –in §6 *mf* bowler
Kehle ['kelə] *f* (-;-n) throat
kehlig ['kelɪç] *adj* throaty
Kehlkopf ['kelkɔpf] *m* larynx
Kehl'kopfentzündung *f* laryngitis
Kehre ['kerə] *f* (-;-n) turn, bend
kehren ['kerən] *tr* sweep; (*wenden*) turn; **alles zum besten k.** make the best of it; **j-m den Rücken k.** turn one's back on s.o. || *ref* turn; **in sich gekehrt sein** be lost in thought; **sich an nichts k.** not care about anything; **sich k. an** (*acc*) heed || *intr* sweep
Kehricht ['kerɪçt] *m & n* (-[e]s;) sweepings: trash, rubbish
Keh'richteimer *m* trash can
Keh'richtschaufel *f* dustpan
Kehr'maschine *f* street cleaner
Kehr'reim *m* refrain, chorus
Kehr'seite *f* reverse; (fig) seamy side
kehrtmachen ['kertmaxən] *intr* turn around; (mil) about-face
Kehrt'wendung *f* about-face
keifen ['kaifən] *intr* nag
Keiferei [kaifə'rai] *f* (-;-en) nagging; squabble
Keil [kail] *m* (-[e]s;-e) wedge
keilen ['kailən] *tr* wedge; (*coll*) recruit || *recip* scrap
Keilerei [kailə'rai] *f* (-;-en) scrap
keil'förmig *adj* wedge-shaped; tapered
Keil'hammer *m* sledgehammer
Keil'hose *f* tapered trousers
Keil'schrift *f* cuneiform writing
Keim [kaim] *m* (-[e]s;-e) germ; embryo; (fig) seeds; (bot) bud, sprout; **im K. ersticken** nip in the bud; **im K. vorhanden** at an embryonic stage; **Keime treiben** germinate
keimen ['kaimən] *intr* germinate;

sprout || **Keimen** *n*—**zum K. bringen** cause to germinate
keim'frei *adj* germ-free, sterile
Keimling ['kaimlɪŋ] *m* (-s;-e) embryo; sprout; seedling
keimtötend ['kaimtøtənt] *adj* germicidal; antiseptic, sterilizing
Keim'zelle *f* germ cell, sex cell
kein [kain] §2,2 *adj* no, not any
keiner ['kainər] §2,4 *indef pron* none; no one, nobody, not one; **k. von beiden** neither of them
keinerlei ['kainər'lai] *invar adj* no... of any kind, no...whatsoever
keineswegs ['kainəs'veks] *adv* by no means, not at all
Keks [keks] *m & n* (-es;-e) biscuit, cracker; cookie
Kelch [kɛlç] *m* (-[e]s;-e) cup; (bot) calyx; (eccl) chalice
Kelch'blatt *n* (bot) sepal
Kelle ['kɛlə] *f* (-;-n) ladle; (hort, mas) trowel
Keller ['kɛlər] *m* (-s;-) cellar
Kel'lergeschoß *n* basement
Kel'lergewölbe *n* underground vault
Kellner ['kɛlnər] *m* (-s;-) waiter
Kellnerin ['kɛlnərɪn] *f* (-;-nen) waitress
Kelte ['kɛltə] *m* (-n;-n) Celt
Kelter ['kɛltər] *f* (-;-n) wine press
keltern ['kɛltərn] *tr* press
Keltin ['kɛltɪn] *f* (-;-nen) Celt
keltisch ['kɛltɪʃ] *adj* Celtic
kennbar ['kɛnbar] *adj* recognizable
kennen ['kɛnən] §97 *tr* be acquainted with, know
ken'nenlernen *tr* get to know, meet
Ken'ner –in §6 *mf* expert
Ken'nerblick *m* knowing glance
Ken'ner –in §6 *mf* expert
Kennkarte ['kɛnkartə] *f* identity card
kenntlich ['kɛntlɪç] *adj* identifiable, recognizable; conspicuous
Kenntnis ['kɛntnɪs] *f* (-;-se) knowledge; **gute Kenntnisse haben in** (*dat*) be well versed in; **j-n von etw in K. setzen** apprise s.o. of s.th.; **Kenntnisse** knowledge; skills; know-how; **oberflächliche Kenntnisse** a smattering; **von etw K. nehmen** take note of s.th.; **zur K. nehmen** take note of s.th.
Kennwort ['kɛnvɔrt] *n* (-[e]s;-er) code word; (mil) password
Kennzeichen ['kɛntsaiçən] *n* distinguishing mark; hallmark; criterion; (aer) marking; (aut) license number
kennzeichnen ['kɛntsaiçnən] *tr* characterize; identify; brand
Kennziffer ['kɛntsɪfər] *f* code number
kentern ['kɛntərn] *intr* (SEIN) capsize
Keramik [ke'ramɪk] *f* (-;) ceramics; pottery
keramisch [ke'ramɪʃ] *adj* ceramic
Kerbe ['kɛrbə] *f* (-;-n) notch, groove
kerben ['kɛrbən] *tr* notch, nick; make a groove in; serrate
Kerbholz ['kɛrbhɔlts] *n*—**etw auf dem K. haben** have a crime chalked up against one
Kerbtier ['kɛrptir] *n* insect
Kerker ['kɛrkər] *m* (-s;-) jail

Kerl [kɛrl] *m* (-s;-e) fellow, guy; (*Mädchen*) lass

Kern [kɛrn] *m* (-[e]s;-e) kernel; (*im Obst*) pit, stone, pip; hard core; (*e-s Problems*) crux; (phys) nucleus

Kern- *comb.fm.* core; central, basic; through and through; (phys) nuclear

Kern'aufbau *m* nuclear structure

kern'deutsch' *adj* German through and through

Kern'energie *f* nuclear energy

Kern'fächer *pl* core curriculum

kern'gesund' *adj* perfectly sound

Kern'holz *n* heartwood

kernig ['kɛrnɪç] *adj* full of seeds; robust, vigorous

kern'los *adj* seedless

Kern'physik *f* nuclear physics

Kern'punkt *m* gist, crux; focal point

Kern'schußweite *f*—**auf K.** at point-blank range

Kern'spaltung *f* nuclear fission

Kern'truppen *pl* crack troops

Kern'verschmelzung *f* nuclear fusion

Kern'waffe *f* nuclear weapon

Kerosin [kɛro'zin] *n* (-s;) kerosene

Kerze ['kɛrtsə] *f* (-;-n) candle; (aut) plug

ker'zengera'de *adj* straight as an arrow || *adv* bolt upright

Kessel ['kɛsəl] *m* (-s;-) kettle; cauldron; boiler; (geog) basin-shaped valley; (mil) pocket

Kes'selpauke *f* kettledrum

Kes'selraum *m* boiler room

Kes'selschmied *m* boilermaker

Kes'selwagen *m* (aut) tank truck; (rr) tank car

Kette ['kɛtə] *f* (-;-n) chain; (*e-s Panzers*) track

ketten ['kɛtən] *tr* (**an** *acc*) chain (to)

Ket'tengeschäft *n* chain store

Ket'tenglied *n* chain link

Ket'tenhund *m* watch dog

Ket'tenrad *n* sprocket

Ket'tenraucher –**in** §6 *mf* chain smoker

Ket'tenstich *m* chain stitch, lock stitch

Ketzer –**in** ['kɛtsər(ɪn)] §6 *mf* heretic

Ketzerei [kɛtsə'raɪ] *f* (-;-en) heresy

ketzerisch ['kɛtsərɪʃ] *adj* heretical

keuchen ['kɔɪçən] *intr* pant, gasp

Keuch'husten *m* (-s;) whooping cough

Keule ['kɔɪlə] *f* (-;-n) club; (culin) leg, drumstick

keusch [kɔɪʃ] *adj* chaste

Keusch'heit *f* (-;) chastity

KG *abbr* (**Kommanditgesellschaft**) Ltd.

Khaki ['kɑki] *m* (-s;) (tex) khaki

kichern ['kɪçərn] *intr* giggle

kicken ['kɪkən] *tr* (fb) kick

Kicker ['kɪkər] *m* (-s;-) soccer player

Kiebitz ['kibɪts] *m* (-[e]s;-e) (orn) lapwing; (*Zugucker*) kibitzer

kiebitzen ['kibɪtsən] *intr* kibitz

Kiefer ['kifər] *m* (-s;-) jaw(bone) || *f* (-;-n) pine; **gemeine K.** Scotch pine

Kiel [kil] *m* (-[e]s;-e) (*Feder*) quill; (naut) keel

Kiel'raum *m* hold

Kiel'wasser *n* wake

Kieme ['kimə] *f* (-;-n) gill

Kien ['kin] *m* (-[e]s;-e) pine cone

Kien'span *m* pine torch

Kiepe ['kipə] *f* (-;-n) basket (*carried on one's back*)

Kies [kis] *m* (-es;-e) gravel

Kiesel ['kizəl] *m* (-s;-) pebble

Kilo ['kilo] *n* (-s;-s & -) kilogram

Kilogramm [kɪlo'gram] *n* (-s;-e & -) kilogram

Kilometer [kɪlo'metər] *m* & *n* (-s;-) kilometer

Kilome'terfresser *m* (coll) speedster

Kilowatt [kɪlo'vat] *n* (-s;-) kilowatt

Kimm [kɪm] *m* (-es;-e) horizon || *f* (-;-e) (naut) bilge

Kimme ['kɪmə] *f* (-;-n) notch; groove; (*e-s Gewehrs*) sight

Kind [kɪnt] *n* (-[e]s;-er) child; baby

Kinder- [kɪndər] *comb.fm.* child's, children's

Kin'derarzt *m*, **Kin'derärztin** *f* pediatrician

Kinderei [kɪndə'raɪ] *f* (-;-en) childish behavior, childish prank

Kin'derfrau *f* nursemaid

Kin'derfräulein *n* governess

Kin'derfürsorge *f* child welfare

Kin'dergarten *m* nursery school, playschool

Kin'dergärtnerin *f* nursery school attendant

Kin'dergeld *n* see **Kinderzulage**

Kin'derheilkunde *f* pediatrics

Kin'derheim *n* children's home

Kin'derhort *m* day nursery

Kin'derlähmung *f* polio

kin'derleicht *adj* easy as pie

Kin'derlied *n* nursery rhyme

kin'derlos *adj* childless

Kin'dermädchen *n* nursemaid

Kin'derpuder *m* baby powder

Kin'derreim *m* nursery rhyme

Kin'derschreck *m* bogeyman

Kin'dersportwagen *m* stroller

Kin'derstube *f* nursery; (*Erziehung*) upbringing

Kin'derstuhl *m* highchair

Kin'derwagen *m* baby carriage

Kin'derzulage *f* family allowance (*paid by the employer*)

Kin'desalter *n* childhood; infancy

Kin'desannahme *f* adoption

Kin'desbeine *pl*—**von Kindesbeinen an** from childhood on

Kin'desentführer –**in** §6 *mf* kidnaper

Kin'desentführung *f*, **Kin'desraub** *m* kidnaping

Kind'heit *f* (-;) childhood

kindisch ['kɪndɪʃ] *adj* childish

kindlich ['kɪntlɪç] *adj* childlike

Kinetik [kɪ'netɪk] *f* (-;) kinetics

kinetisch [kɪ'netɪʃ] *adj* kinetic

Kinkerlitzchen ['kɪŋkərlɪtsçən] *pl* trifles; gimmicks

Kinn [kɪn] *n* (-[e]s;-e) chin

Kinn'backen *m* jawbone

Kinn'haken *m* (box) uppercut

Kinn'kette *f* curb chain

Kino ['kino] *n* (-s;-s) movie theater

Ki'nobesucher –**in** §6 *mf* moviegoer

Ki'nokamera *f* movie camera

Ki'nokasse *f* box office

Kiosk [kɪ'ɔsk] *m* (-[e]s;-e) stand

Kipfel ['kɪpfəl] *n* (-s;-) (Aust) (culin) crescent roll

Kippe ['kɪpə] *f* (-;-n) edge; *(Zigarettenstummel)* butt; **auf der K. stehen** stand on edge; (fig) be touch and go
kippen ['kɪpən] *tr* tilt, tip over; dump || *intr* (SEIN) tilt; overturn
Kipper ['kɪpər] *m* (-s;-) dump truck
Kirche ['kɪrçə] *f* (-;-n) church
Kirchen– [kɪrçən] *comb.fm.* church, ecclesiastical
Kir'chenbann *m* excommunication; **in den K. tun** excommunicate
Kir'chenbau *m* (-[e]s;) building of churches || *m* (-[e]s;-ten) church
Kir'chenbesuch *m* church attendance
Kir'chenbuch *n* parish register
Kir'chendiener *m* sacristan, sexton
Kir'chengut *n* church property
Kir'chenlied *n* hymn
Kir'chenschändung *f* desecration of a church
Kir'chenschiff *n* (archit) nave
Kir'chenspaltung *f* schism
Kir'chenstaat *m* Papal States
Kir'chenstuhl *m* pew
Kir'chentag *m* Church congress
Kirchgang ['kɪrçgaŋ] *m* going to church
Kirch'gänger –in §6 *mf* church-goer
Kirch'hof *m* churchyard
kirch'lich *adj* church, ecclesiastical
Kirch'spiel *n* parish
Kirch'turm *m* steeple
Kirch'turmpolitik *f* (pej) parochialism
Kirch'turmspitze *f* spire
Kirchweih ['kɪrçvaɪ] *f* (-;-en) church picnic
Kirch'weihe *f* dedication of a church
Kirch'weihfest *n* church picnic
Kirsch [kɪrʃ] *m* (-es;-) cherry brandy
Kirsche ['kɪrʃə] *f* (-;-n) cherry
Kirsch'wasser *n* cherry brandy
Kissen ['kɪsən] *n* (-s;-) cushion, pillow; *(Polster)* pad
Kis'senbezug *m* pillowcase
Kiste ['kɪstə] *f* (-;-n) box, crate, case; (aer) crate; (aut) rattletrap; (naut) tub
Kitsch [kɪtʃ] *m* (-es;) kitsch
kitschig ['kɪtʃɪç] *adj* trashy; mawkish
Kitt [kɪt] *m* (-[e]s;-e) putty; cement; **der ganze Kitt** the whole caboodle
Kittchen ['kɪtçən] *n* (-s;-) (coll) jail
Kittel ['kɪtəl] *m* (-s;-) smock, coat; *(Aust)* skirt
Kit'telkleid *n* house dress
kitten ['kɪtən] *tr* putty; cement, glue; (fig) patch up
Kitzel ['kɪtsəl] *m* (-s;) tickle; (fig) itch
kitzeln ['kɪtsəln] *tr* tickle
kitzlig ['kɪtslɪç] *adj* ticklish
Kladderadatsch [kladəra'datʃ] *m* (-es;) crash, bang; mess, muddle
klaffen ['klafən] *intr* gape, yawn
kläffen ['klɛfən] *intr* yelp
Klafter ['klaftər] *f* (-; & -n), *m & n* (-s;-) fathom; *(Holz–)* cord
klagbar ['klakbar] *adj* (jur) actionable
Klage ['klaɡə] *f* (-;-n) complaint; (jur) (civil) suit
Kla'gelied *n* dirge, threnody
klagen ['klaɡən] *tr—j-m seinen Kummer k.** pour out one's troubles to s.o.

|| *intr* complain; **auf Scheidung k.** sue for divorce; **k. über** (*acc*) complain about; **k. um** lament
Kläger –in ['klegər(ɪn)] §6 *mf* (jur) plaintiff
Kla'geweib *n* hired mourner
kläglich ['kleklɪç] *adj* plaintive, pitiful; *(Zustand)* sorry; *(Ergebnis, Ende)* miserable
klaglos ['klaklos] *adv* uncomplainingly
klamm [klam] *adj* *(erstarrt)* numb; *(feuchtkalt)* clammy; **k. an Geld** (coll) short of dough || **Klamm** *f* (-;-en) gorge
Klammer ['klamər] *f* (-;-n) clamp; clip; paper clip; *(Schließe)* clasp; clothespin; hair clip, bobby pin; **eckige K.** bracket; **runde K.** parenthesis
klammern ['klamərn] *tr* clamp; clasp || *ref—sich k. an* (*acc*) cling to
Klamotte [kla'mɔtə] *f* (-;-n)—**alte K.** oldy; (aer, aut) old crate; **Klamotten** things, clothes
Klampfe ['klampfə] *f* (-;-n) guitar
klang [klaŋ] *pret* of **klingen** || **Klang** *m* (-[e]s;⁻e) tone, sound
Klang'farbe *f* timbre
klang'getreu *adj* high-fidelity
Klang'regler *m* (rad) tone-control knob
Klang'taste *f* tone-control push button
klang'voll *adj* sonorous
Klappe ['klapə] *f* (-;-n) flap; *(Mund)* (sl) trap; (anat, mach) valve; **in die K. gehen** (sl) hit the sack
klappen ['klapən] *tr* flip || *intr* flap, fold || *impers—es klappt* (coll) it clicks, it turns out well
Klapper ['klapər] *f* (-;-n) rattle
klap'perdürr' *adj* skinny
Klap'pergestell *n* (coll) beanpole; *(Kiste)* (coll) rattletrap
klappern ['klapərn] *intr* rattle, clatter; *(Zähne)* chatter
Klap'perschlange *f* rattlesnake
Klap'perstorch *m* stork
Klappflügel ['klapflyɡəl] *m* (aer) folding wing *(of carrier plane)*
Klappmesser ['klapmɛsər] *n* jackknife
klapprig ['klaprɪç] *adj* rickety
Klappstuhl ['klapʃtul] *m* folding chair
Klapptisch ['klaptɪʃ] *m* drop-leaf table
Klapptür ['klaptyr] *f* trap door
Klaps [klaps] *m* (-es;-e) smack, slap; **e-n K. kriegen** (sl) go nuts
klapsen ['klapsən] *tr* smack, slap
Klaps'mühle *f* (coll) booby hatch
klar [klar] *adj* clear; **klar zum Start** ready for take-off
Kläranlage ['kleranlaɡə] *f* sewage-disposal plant
klären ['klerən] *tr* clear; *(Mißverständnis)* clear up || *ref* become clear
Klar'heit *f* (-;) clearness, clarity
Klarinette [klarɪ'nɛtə] *f* (-;-n) clarinet
klar'legen, klar'stellen *tr* clear up
Klärung ['kleruŋ] *f* (-;) clarification
Klasse ['klasə] *f* (-;-n) class; (educ) grade, class
Klas'senarbeit *f* test
Klas'senaufsatz *m* composition *(written in class)*
klas'senbewußt *adj* class-conscious

Klas'seneinteilung *f* classification
Klas'senkamerad –in §7 *mf* classmate
Klas'sentreffen *n* (–s;–) class reunion
klassifizieren [klasɪfɪ'tsirən] *tr* classify
Klassifizie'rung *f* (–;–en) classification
–klassig [klasɪç] *comb.fm.* –class,
–grade
Klassik ['klasɪk] *f* (–;) classical antiquity, classical period
Klas'siker –in §6 *mf* classical author
klassisch ['klasɪʃ] *adj* classic(al)
Klatsch [klatʃ] *m* (–es;) clap; gossip
Klatsch'base *f* gossipmonger; tattletale
Klatsch'blatt *n* scandal sheet
Klatsche ['klatʃə] *f* (–;–n) fly swatter; tattletale; (educ) pony
klatschen ['klatʃən] *tr* smack, slap; **dem Lehrer etw k.** tattletale to the teacher about s.th.; **j–m Beifall k.** applaud s.o. ‖ *intr* clap; (*Regen*) patter; (fig) gossip; **in die Hände (or mit den Händen) k.** clap the hands
Klatscherei [klatʃə'raɪ] *f* (–;–en) gossip
klatsch'naß' *adj* soaking wet
Klatsch'spalte *f* glossip column
klauben ['klaubən] *tr* pick
Klaue ['klau·ə] *f* (–;–n) claw, talon; (*Spalthuf*) hoof; (coll) scrawl
klauen ['klau·ən] *tr* (coll) snitch
Klause ['klauzə] *f* (–;–n) hermitage; (*Schlucht*) (coll) den, pad
Klausel ['klauzəl] *f* (–;–n) clause; (*Abmachung*) stipulation
Klausner ['klauznər] *m* (–s;–) hermit
Klausur [klau'zur] *f* (–;–en) seclusion; (educ) final examination
Klausur'arbeit *f* final examination
Klaviatur [klavja'tur] *f* (–;–en) keyboard
Klavier [kla'vir] *n* (–[e]s;–e) piano
Klavier'auszug *m* piano score
Klebemittel ['klebəmɪtəl] *n* (–s;–) adhesive, glue
kleben ['klebən] *tr & intr* stick
Kleberolle ['klebərɔlə] *f* roll of gummed tape
Klebestreifen ['klebə/traɪfən] *m* adhesive tape; Scotch tape (*trademark*)
Klebezettel ['klebətsetəl] *m* label, sticker
klebrig ['klebrɪç] *adj* sticky
Klebstoff ['klep/tɔf] *m* adhesive
Klecks [kleks] *m* (–es;–e) stain; dab
klecksen ['kleksən] *tr* splash ‖ *intr* make blotches
Kleckser –in ['kleksər(ɪn)] §6 *mf* scribbler; dauber
Klee [kle] *m* (–s;) clover
Klee'blatt *n* cloverleaf; (fig) trio
Kleid [klaɪt] *n* (–[e]s;–er) garment; dress; robe; **Kleider** clothes
kleiden ['klaɪdən] *tr* dress; **j–n gut k.** look good on s.o.
Klei'derablage *f* cloakroom; (*Kleiderständer*) clothes rack
Klei'derbestand *m* wardrobe
Klei'derbügel *m* coat hanger
Klei'dersack *m* (mil) duffle bag
Klei'derschrank *m* clothes closet
Klei'derständer *m* clothes rack
kleidsam ['klaɪtzɑm] *adj* well-fitting, becoming

Klei'dung *f* (–;) clothing
Kleie ['klaɪ·ə] *f* (–;–n) bran
klein [klaɪn] *adj* small, little; short; ein k. wenig a little bit ‖ **Kleine** §5 *m* little boy ‖ *f* little girl ‖ *n* little one
Klein'anzeigen *pl* classified ads
Klein'arbeit *f* detailed work
Klein'asien *n* Asia Minor
Klein'bahn *f* narrow-gauge railroad
Klein'bauer *m* small farmer
Klein'betrieb *m* small business
Kleinbild– *comb.fm.* (phot) 35mm
klein'bürgerlich *adj* lower middle-class
Klein'geld *n* change
klein'gläubig *adj* of little faith
Klein'handel *m* retail business
Klein'händler –in §6 *mf* retailer
Klein'hirn *n* (anat) cerebellum
Klein'holz *n* kindling; **K. aus j–m machen** (coll) beat s.o. to a pulp
Klei'nigkeit *f* small object; trifle, minor detail; small matter
Klei'nigkeitskrämer *m* fusspot
kleinkalibrig ['klaɪnkalibrɪç] *adj* smallbore
Klein'kind *n* infant
Klein'kinderbewahranstalt *f* day care center
Klein'kram *m* odds and ends; details
klein'laut *adj* subdued
klein'lich *adj* stingy; (*Betrag*) paltry; (*engstirnig*) narrow-minded, pedantic
Klein'mut *m* despondency; faintheartedness
klein'mütig *adj* despondent; fainthearted
Klei·nod ['klaɪnot] *n* (–[e]s;–node & –nodien ['nodjən] jewel, gem
klein'schneiden §106 *tr* chop up
Klein'schreibmaschine *f* portable typewriter
Kleister ['klaɪstər] *m* (–s;–) paste
Klemme ['klemə] *f* (–;–n) clamp, clip; (coll) tight spot, fix; (elec) terminal; (surg) clamp
klemmen ['klemən] *tr* tuck, put; (*stehlen*) pinch, swipe ‖ *ref—sich [dat]* **den Finger k.** smash one's finger; **sich hinter die Arbeit k.** get down to business; **sich k. hinter** (*acc*) get after ‖ *intr* be stuck
Klempner ['klempnər] *m* (–s;–) tinsmith; plumber
Klempnerei [klempnə'raɪ] *f* (–;) plumbing
Kleptomane [klepto'manə] §5 *mf* kleptomaniac
klerikal [klerɪ'kal] *adj* clerical
Kleriker ['klerɪkər] *m* (–s;–) clergyman, priest
Klerus ['klerus] *m* (–;) clergy
Klette ['kletə] *f* (–;–n) (bot) burr; (coll) pain in the neck
Klet'tergarten *m* training area (*for mountain climbing*)
klettern ['kletərn] *intr* (SEIN) climb
Klet'terpflanze *f* (bot) creeper
Klet'terrose *f* rambler
Klet'tertour *f* climbing expedition
Klient [klɪ'ent] *m* (–en;–en) client
Klientel [klɪ·en'tel] *f* (–;–en) clientele (*of a lawyer*)

Klientin [klɪ'entɪn] f (-;-nen) client
Klima ['klima] n (-s;-s) climate
Kli'maanlage f air conditioner
kli'magerecht adj air-conditioned
klimatisch [klɪ'matɪʃ] adj climatic
klimatisieren [klɪmatɪ'zirən] tr air-condition
Klimatisie'rung f (-;) air conditioning
Klimbim [klɪm'bɪm] m (-s;) (coll) junk; (coll) racket; (coll) fuss
klimmen ['klɪmən] §164 intr (SEIN) climb
klimpern ['klɪmpərn] intr jingle; (auf der Gitarre) strum; **mit den Wimpern k.** flutter one's eyelashes
Klinge ['klɪŋə] f (-;-n) blade; sword, saber; **über die K. springen lassen** put to the sword
Klingel ['klɪŋəl] f (-;-n) bell
Klin'gelbeutel m collection basket
Klin'gelknopf m doorbell button
klingeln ['klɪŋəln] intr ring, tinkle; (Vers, Reim) jingle || impers—es **klingelt** the doorbell is ringing; there goes the (school) bell; the phone is ringing
kling'klang interj ding-dong!
Klinik ['klinɪk] f (-;-en) teaching hospital (of a university); private hospital; nursing home
klinisch ['klinɪʃ] adj clinical; hospital
Klinke ['klɪŋkə] f (-;-n) door handle; (telp) jack; **Klinken putzen** beg or peddle from door to door
Klippe ['klɪpə] f (-;-n) rock, reef
klirren ['klɪrən] intr rattle, clang; (Gläser) clink; (Waffen) clash
Klischee [klɪ'ʃe] n (-s;-s) cliché
Klistier [klɪs'tir] n (-s;-e) enema
klistieren [klɪs'tirən] tr give an enema to
klitschig ['klɪtʃɪç] adj doughy
Klo [klo] n (-s;-s) (coll) john
Kloake [klo'akə] f (-;-n) sewer
Kloben ['klobən] m (-s;-) pulley; (Holz) block; (Schraubenstock) vise
klobig ['klobɪç] adj clumsy; bulky
klomm [klɔm] pret of **klimmen**
klopfen ['klɔpfən] tr (Nagel) drive; (Teppich) beat; (Fleisch) pound || intr (Herz) beat, pound; (Motor) ping; **j–m auf die Schulter k.** pat s.o. on the back || impers—es **klopft** s.o. is knocking
klopffest ['klɔpffest] adj antiknock
Klöppel ['klœpəl] m (-s;-) bobbin; (e–r Glocke) clapper; (mus) mallet
klöppeln ['klœpəln] tr make (lace) with bobbins
Klops [klɔps] m (-es;-e) meatball
Klosett [klo'zɛt] n (-s;-e & -s) (flush) toilet
Klosett'becken n toilet bowl
Klosett'brille f toilet seat
Klosett'deckel m toilet-seat lid
Klosett'papier n toilet paper
Kloß [klos] m (-es;-e) dumpling; **e–n K. im Hals haben** have a lump in one's throat
Kloster ['klostər] n (-s;-) monastery; convent
Kloster– comb.fm. monastic
Klo'sterbruder m lay brother, friar

Klo'sterfrau f nun
klösterlich ['kløstərlɪç] adj monastic
Klotz [klɔts] m (-es;-e) block; toy building block; (coll) blockhead; **ein K. am Bein** (coll) a drag; **wie ein K.** schlafen sleep like a log
klotzig ['klɔtsɪç] adj clumsy; uncouth || adv—k. reich filthy rich
Klub [klup] m (-s;-s) club
Klub'jacke f blazer
Klub'sessel m easy chair
Kluft [kluft] f (-;-e) gorge, ravine; (fig) gulf; (poet) chasm || f (-;-en) outfit, uniform
klug [kluk] adj (klüger ['klʏgər]; klügste ['klʏgstə] §9) clever, bright; wise; **aus Schaden k. werden** learn the hard way; **nicht k. werden können aus** be unable to figure out
klügeln ['klʏgəln] intr quibble
Klug'heit f (-;) cleverness; intelligence; wisdom
klüglich ['klʏklɪç] adv wisely
Klug'redner m wise guy, know-it-all
Klumpen ['klumpən] m (-s;-) lump, clod; (Haufen) heap; (min) nugget
Klumpfuß ['klumpfus] m clubfoot
klumpig ['klumpɪç] adj lumpy
Klüngel ['klʏŋəl] m (-s;-) clique
knabbern ['knabərn] intr nibble
Knabe ['knabə] m (-n;-n) boy
Kna'benalter n boyhood
kna'benhaft adj boyish
knack [knak] interj crack!; snap!; click!
knacken ['knakən] tr crack || intr crack; (Schloß) click; (Feuer) crackle
Knacks [knaks] m (-es;-e) crack; snap; click; **e–n K. kriegen** get a crack; **e–n K. weg haben** be badly hit; **sich [dat] e–n K. holen** suffer a blow
Knack'wurst f pork sausage; smoked sausage
Knall [knal] m (-[e]s;-e) crack, bang; **K. und Fall** on the spot, at once
Knallblättchen ['knalblɛtçən] n (-s;-) cap (for a toy pistol)
Knall'bonbon m & n noise maker
Knall'büchse f popgun
Knall'dämpfer m silencer
Knall'effekt m big surprise
knall'rot adj fiery red
knapp [knap] adj (eng) close, tight; (Mehrheit) bare; (Zeit) short; (Stil) concise; **k. werden** run short, run low
Knappe ['knapə] m (-n;-n) (hist) squire; (min) miner
Knapp'heit f (-;) closeness, tightness; shortage; conciseness
Knapp'schaft f (-;-en) miner's union
Knapp'schaftskasse f miner's insurance
knarren ['knarən] intr creek
Knaster ['knastər] m (-s;-) tobacco
knattern ['knatərn] intr crackle; (Maschinengewehr) rattle || intr (SEIN) put-put along
Knäuel ['knɔɪ·əl] m & n (-s;-) (Garn–) ball; (Menschen–) throng
Knauf [knauf] m (-[e]s;-e) knob
Knauser –in ['knauzər(ɪn)] §6 mf tightwad

Knauserei [knauzə'raɪ] f (-;) stinginess
knauserig ['knauzərɪç] adj stingy
knausern ['knauzərn] intr be stingy
knautschen ['knautʃən] tr crumple || intr crumple; (coll) wimper
Knebel ['knebəl] m (-s;-) gag
Kne'belbart m handlebar moustache
knebeln ['knebəln] tr gag; (fig) muzzle
Kne'belpresse f tourniquet
Kne'belung f—K. der Presse muzzling of the press
Knecht [knɛçt] m (-[e]s;-e) servant; farmhand; serf; slave
knechten ['knɛçtən] tr enslave; oppress
knechtisch ['knɛçtɪʃ] adj servile
Knecht'schaft f (-;) servitude
kneifen ['knaɪfən] §88 & §109 tr pinch || §88 intr (Kleid) be too tight; back out, back down; (fencing) retreat; **k. vor** (dat) shirk, dodge
Kneifzange ['knaɪftsaŋə] f (pair of) pincers
Kneipe ['knaɪpə] f (-;-n) saloon
kneipen ['knaɪpən] intr (coll) booze
Knei'penwirt m saloon keeper
Kneiperei [knaɪpə'raɪ] f (-;-en) drinking bout
kneten ['knetən] tr knead; massage
Knick [knɪk] m (-[e]s;-e) bend; (Bruch) break; (Falte) fold, crease
knicken ['knɪkən] tr bend; break; fold; (Hoffnungen) dash || intr (SEIN) snap
Knicker ['knɪkər] m (-s;-) tightwad
Knicks [knɪks] m (-es;-e) curtsy
knicksen ['knɪksən] intr curtsy
Knie [kni] n (-s;- ['kni·ə]) knee
Knie'beuge f knee bend
Knie'beugung f genuflection
knie'fällig adj on one's knees
knie'frei adj above-the-knee
Knie'freiheit f legroom
Knie'kehle f hollow of the knee
knien ['kni·ən] intr kneel
Knie'scheibe f kneecap
Knie'schützer m (sport) kneepad
kniff [knɪf] pret of kneifen || **Kniff** m (-[e]s;-e) crease, fold; (Kunstgriff) knack
kniff(e)lig ['knɪf(ə)lɪç] adj tricky
kniffen ['knɪfən] tr crease, fold
Knigge ['knɪgə] m (-;) (fig) Emily Post
knipsen ['knɪpsən] tr (Karte) punch; (phot) snap || intr snap a picture; **mit den Fingern k.** snap one's fingers
Knirps [knɪrps] m (-es;-e) (coll) shrimp
knirschen ['knɪrʃən] intr crunch; **mit den Zähnen k.** gnash one's teeth
knistern ['knɪstərn] intr crackle; (Seide) rustle
knitterfest ['knɪtərfɛst] adj wrinkleproof
knittern ['knɪtərn] tr wrinkle; crumple
knobeln ['knobəln] intr play dice; **an e-m Problem k.** puzzle over a problem
Knoblauch ['knoblaux] m (-[e]s;) garlic
Knöchel ['knœçəl] m (-s;-) knuckle, joint; ankle
Knochen ['knɔxən] m (-s;-) bone

Kno'chenbruch m fracture
Kno'chengerüst n skeleton
Kno'chenmark n marrow
Kno'chenmühle f (coll) sweat shop
knöchern ['knœçərn] adj bone; bony
knochig ['knɔxɪç] adj bony
Knödel ['knødəl] m (-s;-) dumpling; **e-n K. im Hals haben** have a lump in one's throat
Knolle ['knɔlə] f (coll) bulbous nose; (bot) tuber
Knollen ['knɔlən] m (-s;-) lump; (coll) bulbous nose
knollig ['knɔlɪç] adj bulbous
Knopf [knɔpf] m (-[e]s;̈-e) button; knob; (e-r Stechnadel) head; **alter K.** old fogey
knöpfen ['knœpfən] tr button
Knopf'loch n buttonhole
knorke ['knɔrkə] adj (coll) super
Knorpel ['knɔrpəl] m (-s;-) cartilage
Knorren ['knɔrən] m (-s;-) knot, gnarl
knorrig ['knɔrɪç] adj gnarled, knotty
Knospe ['knɔspə] f (-;-n) bud
knospen ['knɔspən] intr bud
knoten ['knotən] tr & intr knot || **Knoten** m (-s;-) knot; (Schwierigkeit) snag; (Haarfrisur) chignon; (Seemeile) knot; (astr, med, phys) node; (theat) plot
Kno'tenpunkt m intersection, interchange; (rr) junction
knotig ['knotɪç] adj knotty
Knuff [knuf] m (-[e]s;̈-e) (coll) poke
knuffen ['knufən] tr (coll) poke
knüllen ['knYlən] tr crumple
Knüller ['knYlər] m (-s;-) (coll) hit
knüpfen ['knYpfən] tr tie, knot; (Teppich) weave; (Bündnis) form; (befestigen) fasten; **k. an** (acc) tie in with || ref—sich k. an (acc) be tied in with
Knüppel ['knYpəl] m (-s;-) cudgel; (e-s Polizisten) blackjack; (aer) control stick
knurren ['knurən] intr growl, snarl; (Magen) rumble; (fig) grumble
knurrig ['knurɪç] adj grumpy
knusprig ['knusprɪç] adj crisp; (Mädchen) attractive
Knute ['knutə] f (-;-n) whip; (Gewalt) power; (Gewaltherrschaft) tyranny
knutschen ['knutʃən] tr, recip & intr (coll) neck, pet
Knüttel ['knYtəl] m (-s;-) cudgel
Knüt'telvers m doggerel
k.o. ['ka'o] adj knocked out || adv—**k.o. schlagen** knock out || **K.O.** m (-[s];-s) knockout
Koalition [kɔ·alɪ'tsjon] f (-;-en) coalition
Kobalt ['kobalt] n (-es;) cobalt
Koben ['kobən] m (-s;-) pigsty
Kobold ['kobɔlt] m (-[e]s;-e) goblin
Kobolz [kɔ'bɔlts] m—e-n K. schießen do a somersault
Koch [kɔx] m (-[e]s;̈-e) cook
Koch'buch n cookbook
kochen ['kɔxən] tr & intr cook; boil
Kocher ['kɔxər] m (-s;-) cooker; boiler

Köcher ['kœçər] *m* (-s;-) quiver; golf bag
Koch'fett *n* shortening
Koch'geschirr *n* (mil) mess kit
Koch'herd *m* kitchen range
Köchin ['kœçɪn] *f* (-;-nen) cook
Koch'löffel *m* wooden spoon
Koch'salz *n* table salt
Köder ['kødər] *m* (-s;-) bait; lure
ködern ['kødərn] *tr* bait; lure
Kodex ['kodɛks] *m* (-es;-e) codex; (jur) code
kodifizieren [kodɪfɪ'tsirən] *tr* codify
Koffein [kɔfɛ'in] *n* (-s;) caffeine
Koffer ['kɔfər] *m* (-s;-) suitcase; trunk; case (*for portable items*)
Kof'ferfernseher *m* portable television
Kof'fergerät *n* (rad, telv) portable set
Kof'ferraum *m* (aut) trunk
Kof'ferschreibmaschine *f* portable typewriter
Kognak ['kɔnjak] *m* (-s;-s) cognac
Kohl [kol] *m* (-s;) cabbage; nonsense
Kohle ['kolə] *f* (-;-n) coal; (*Holzkohle*) charcoal
Kohlehydrat ['koləhydrɑt] *n* (-[e]s; -e) carbohydrate
kohlen ['kolən] *tr & intr* carbonize
Koh'lenbergbau *m* coal mining
Koh'lenbergwerk *n* coal mine
Koh'lendioxyd *n* carbon dioxide
Koh'lenoxyd *n* carbon monoxide
Koh'lenrevier *n* coal field
Koh'lensäure *f* carbonic acid
Koh'lenstoff *m* carbon
Koh'lenwagen *m* coal truck; (rr) coal car
Koh'lepapier *n* carbon paper
Koh'leskizze *f* charcoal sketch
kohl'ra'benschwarz' *adj* jet black
Koitus ['ko·ɪtus] *m* (-;) coitus
Koje ['kojə] *f* (-;-n) bunk, berth
Kojote [kɔ'jotə] *m* (-;-n) coyote
Kokain [koka'in] *n* (-s;) cocaine
Kokerei [kokə'raɪ] *f* (-;-en) coking plant
kokett [ko'kɛt] *adj* flirtatious || Kokette *f* (-;-n) flirt
kokettieren [kokɛ'tirən] *intr* flirt
Kokon [ko'kõ] *m* (-s;-s) cocoon
Kokosnuß ['kokɔsnus] *f* coconut
Kokospalme ['kokɔspalmə] *f* coconut palm, coconut tree
Koks [koks] *m* (-es;-e) coke; (coll) nonsense; (*Geld*) (coll) dough
Kolben ['kɔlbən] *m* (-s;-) butt; (*Keule*) mace; (*Löt-*) soldering iron; (aut) piston; (chem) flask; (culin) cob; (elec) bulb
Kol'benhub *m* piston stroke
Kol'benring *m* piston ring
Kol'benstange *f* piston rod
Kolchose [kɔl'çozə] *f* (-;-n) collective farm
Kolibri ['kolɪbrɪ] *m* (-s;-s) humming bird
Kolik ['kolɪk] *f* (-;-en) colic
Kolkrabe ['kɔlkrabə] *m* (-n;-n) raven
Kollaborateur [kɔlabɔra'tør] *m* (-s;-) collaborator (*with the enemy*)
kollaborieren [kɔlabɔ'rirən] *intr* collaborate
Kollaps [kɔ'laps] *m* (-es;-e) collapse

kollationieren [kɔlatsjɔ'nirən] *tr* collate
Kol·leg [kɔ'lek] *n* (-s;-s & -legien ['legjən]) lecture; course of lectures; theological college
Kollege [kɔ'legə] *m* (-n;-n) colleague
Kolleg'heft *n* lecture notes
Kollegin [kɔ'legɪn] *f* (-;-nen) colleague
Kollekte [kɔ'lɛktə] *f* (-;-n) collection; (eccl) collect
Kollektion [kɔlɛk'tsjon] *f* (-;-en) collection
kollektiv [kɔlɛk'tif] *adj* collective || Kollektiv *n* (-s;-e) collective
Koller ['kɔlər] *m* (-s;) rage, temper
kollern ['kɔlərn] *ref* roll about; (*vor Lachen*) double over || *intr* (*Puter*) gobble; (*Magen*) rumble || *intr* (SEIN) roll
kollidieren [kɔlɪ'dirən] *intr* (SEIN) collide
Kollier [kɔ'lir] *n* (-s;-s) necklace
Kollision [kɔlɪ'zjon] *f* (-;-en) collision
Köln [kœln] *n* (-s;) Cologne
Kölnischwasser [kœlnɪʃ'vasər] *n* cologne
kolonial [kolo'njal] *adj* colonial
Kolonial'waren *pl* groceries
Kolonial'warengeschäft *n* grocery store
Kolo·nie [kolo'ni] *f* (-;-nien ['ni·ən]) colony
Kolonnade [kolo'nadə] *f* (-;-n) colonnade
Kolonne [kɔ'lɔnə] *f* (-;-n) column; (mil) convoy (*of vehicles*)
kolorieren [kolo'rirən] *tr* color
Kolorit [kolo'rit] *n* (-[e]s;-e) coloring
Ko·loß [kɔ'lɔs] *m* (-losses;-losse) colossus; giant
kolossal [kolo'sal] *adj* colossal
Kolportage [kɔlpɔr'taʒə] *f* (-;-n) trashy literature; spreading of rumors
kolportieren [kɔlpɔr'tirən] *tr* peddle; (*Gerüchte*) spread
Kolumnist –in [kolum'nɪst(ɪn)] §7 *mf* columnist
Kombi ['kɔmbi] *m* (-s;-s) (coll) station wagon
Kombination [kɔmbɪna'tsjon] *f* (-; -en) combination; (*Flieger-*) flying suit; (*e-s Monteurs*) coveralls; sport suit; reasoning, deduction; conjecture
kombinieren [kɔmbɪ'nirən] *tr* combine || *intr* reason
Kom'biwagen *m* station wagon
Kombüse [kɔm'byzə] *f* (-;-n) (naut) galley, kitchen
Komik ['komɪk] *f* (-;) humor
Komiker ['komɪkər] *m* (-s;-) comedian
Komikerin ['komɪkərɪn] *f* (-;-nen) comedienne
komisch ['komɪʃ] *adj* funny
Komitee [komɪ'te] *n* (-s;-s) committee
Komma ['koma] *n* (-s;-s) comma; (*Dezimalzeichen*) decimal point
Kommandant [koman'dant] *m* (-en; -en) commanding officer; commandant

Kommandantur [kɔmandan'tur] *f* (-; -en) headquarters

Kommandeur [kɔman'dør] *m* (-s;-e) commanding officer, commander

kommandieren [kɔman'dirən] *tr* command, order; be in command of; (mil) detail; (mil) detach || *intr* command, be in command

Kommanditgesellschaft [kɔman'ditgəzɛlʃaft] *f* limited partnership; **K. auf Aktien** partnership limited by shares

Kommando [kɔ'mando] *n* (-s;-s) command, order; (mil) command; (mil) detachment, detail; **K. zurück!** as you were!

Komman'dobrücke *f* (nav) bridge

Komman'doraum *m* control room

Komman'dostab *m* baton

Komman'dostand *m*, **Komman'dostelle** *f* command post; (nav) bridge

Komman'dotruppe *f* commando unit

Komman'doturm *m* conning tower; control tower (*of an aircraft carrier*)

kommen ['kɔmən] §99 *intr* (SEIN) come; (*geschehen*) happen; **auf etw** [*acc*] **k.** hit on s.th.; **auf jeden k. drei Mark** each one gets three marks; **das kommt bloß daher, daß** that's entirely due to; **dazu k.** get around to it; get hold of it; **hinter etw** [*acc*] **k.** find s.th. out; **j-m grob k.** be rude to s.o.; **k. lassen** send for; **nichts k. lassen auf** (*acc*) defend; **so weit k., daß** reach the point where; **ums Leben k.** lose one's life; **wenn Sie mir so k.** if you talk like that to me; **weit k.** get far; **wieder zu sich k.** come to, regain consciousness; **wie kam er denn dazu?** how come he did it? **wie komme ich zum Bahnhof?** how do I get to the train station?

Kommentar [kɔmɛn'tar] *m* (-s;-e) commentary; **kein K.!** no comment!

Kommen·tator [kɔmɛn'tator] *m* (-s; -tatoren [ta'torən]) commentator

kommentieren [kɔmɛn'tirən] *tr* comment on

Kommers [kɔ'mɛrs] *m* (-es;-e) drinking party

Kommers'buch *n* students' song book

kommerziell [kɔmɛr'tsjɛl] *adj* commercial

Kommilitone [kɔmɪlɪ'tonə] *m* (-n;-n) fellow student

Kom·mis [kɔ'mi] *m* (-mis ['mis]; -mis ['mis]) clerk

Kom·miß [kɔ'mɪs] *m* (-misses;) (coll) army; (coll) army life

Kommissar [kɔmɪ'sar] *m* (-s;-e) commissioner; (pol) commissar

kommissarisch [kɔmɪ'sarɪʃ] *adj* provisional, temporary

Kommission [kɔmɪ'sjon] *f* (-;-en) commission, board; **in K.** (com) on consignment; **on a commission basis**

Kommissionär [kɔmɪsjɔ'ner] *m* (-s;-e) agent; wholesale bookseller

Kommissions'gebühr *f* (com) commission

kommissions'weise *adv* on a commission basis

Kommiß'stiefel *m* army boot

kommod [kɔ'mot] *adj* comfortable

Kommode [kɔ'modə] *f* (-;-n) bureau, chest of drawers

kommunal [kɔmu'nal] *adj* municipal, local

Kommunal'politik *f* local politics

Kommune [kɔ'munə] *f* (-;-n) municipality; **die K.** the Commies

Kommunikant -in [kɔmuni'kant(ɪn)] §7 *mf* communicant

Kommunion [kɔmu'njon] *f* (-;-en) Communion

Kommuniqué [kɔmyni'ke] *n* (-s;-s) communiqué

Kommunismus [kɔmu'nɪsmus] *m* (-;) communism

Kommunist -in [kɔmu'nɪst(ɪn)] §7 *mf* communist

kommunistisch [kɔmu'nɪstɪʃ] *adj* communist(ic)

Komödiant [kɔmø'djant] *m* (-en;-en) comedian; (pej) ham

Komödie [kɔ'mødjə] *f* (-;-n) comedy; **K. spielen** (coll) put on an act

Kompagnon [kɔmpan'jõ] *m* (-s;-s) (business) partner; associate

kompakt [kɔm'pakt] *adj* compact

Kompa·nie [kɔmpa'ni] *f* (-;-nien ['ni·ən]) company

Kompanie'chef *m* company commander

komparativ [kɔmpara'tif] *adj* comparative || **Komparativ** *m* (-s;-e) comparative

Komparse [kɔm'parzə] *m* (-n;-n) (theat) extra

Kom·paß ['kɔmpas] *m* (-passes; -passe) compass

Kompen·dium [kɔm'pɛndjum] *n* (-s; -dien [djən]) compendium

Kompensation [kɔmpɛnza'tsjon] *f* (-; -en) compensation

kompensieren [kɔmpɛn'zirən] *tr* compensate for, offset

Kompetenz [kɔmpe'tɛnts] *f* (-;-en) (jur) jurisdiction

komplementär [kɔmplemɛn'ter] *adj* complementary

Komplet [kɔ̃'ple] *n* (-s;-s) dress with matching coat

komplett [kɔm'plet] *adj* complete; everything included

komplex [kɔm'plɛks] *adj* complex || **Komplex** *m* (-es;-e) complex

Komplice [kɔm'plitsə] *m* (-n;-n) accomplice

komplizieren [kɔmplɪ'tsirən] *tr* complicate

Komplott [kɔm'plɔt] *n* (-[e]s;-e) plot

Komponente [kɔmpo'nɛntə] *f* (-;-n) component

komponieren [kɔmpo'nirən] *tr* compose

Komponist -in [kɔmpo'nɪst(ɪn)] §7 *mf* composer

Komposition [kɔmpozɪ'tsjon] *f* (-;-en) composition

Komposi·tum [kɔm'pozɪtum] *n* (-s; -ta [ta] & -ten [tən]) compound (word)

Kompott [kɔm'pɔt] *n* (-[e]s;-e) stewed fruit

Kompres·sor [kɔm'prɛsɔr] *m* (–s; –soren ['sorən]) compressor; (aut) supercharger

komprimieren [kɔmprɪ'mirən] *tr* compress

Kompro·miß [kɔmprɔ'mɪs] *m* (–misses; –misse) compromise

kompromittieren [kɔmprɔmɪ'tirən] *tr* compromise

kondensieren [kɔndɛn'zirən] *tr, ref & intr* (SEIN) condense

Kondensmilch [kɔn'dɛnsmɪlç] *f* evaporated milk

Kondens'streifen [kɔn'dɛnsʃtraɪfən] *m* contrail

Konditorei [kɔndɪtɔ'raɪ] *f* (–;–en) pastry shop

Konfekt [kɔn'fɛkt] *n* (–[e]s;) candy, chocolates; fancy cookies

Konfektion [kɔnfɛk'tsjon] *f* (–;) readymade clothes; manufacture of readymade clothes

Konfektionär [kɔnfɛktsjɔ'ner] *m* (–s; –e) clothing manufacturer; clothing retailer

konfektionieren [kɔnfɛktsjɔ'nirən] *tr* manufacture (*clothes*)

Konferenz [kɔnfɛ'rɛnts] *f* (–;–en) conference

konferieren [kɔnfɛ'rirən] *intr* confer, hold a conference

Konfession [kɔnfɛ'sjon] *f* (–;–en) religious denomination; (eccl) confession; confession of faith, creed

konfessionell [kɔnfɛsjɔ'nɛl] *adj* denominational

konfessions'los *adj* nondenominational

Konfessions'schule *f* denominational school, parochial school

konfirmieren [kɔnfɪr'mirən] *tr* (eccl) (Prot) confirm

konfiszieren [kɔnfɪs'tsirən] *tr* confiscate

Konfitüre [kɔnfɪ'tyrə] *f* (–;–n) jam

Konflikt [kɔn'flɪkt] *m* (–[e]s;–e) conflict

konform [kɔn'fɔrm] *adj* concurring; mit j–m k. gehen agree with s.o.

Konfrontation [kɔnfrɔnta'tsjon] *f* (–; –en) confrontation

konfrontieren [kɔnfrɔn'tirən] *tr* confront

konfus [kɔn'fus] *adj* confused, puzzled

Kongruenz [kɔngru'ɛnts] *f* (–;) (geom) congruence; (gram) agreement

König ['kønɪç] *m* (–[e]s;–e) king

Königin ['kønɪgɪn] *f* (–;–nen) queen

kö'niglich *adj* kingly, royal

Kö'nigreich *n* kingdom

Kö'nigsadler *m* golden eagle

Kö'nigsrose *f* (bot) peony

Kö'nigsschlange *f* boa constrictor

kö'nigstreu *adj* royalist

Kö'nigswürde *f* kingship

Königtum ['kønɪçtum] *n* (–s;) royalty, kinship; monarchy

konisch ['konɪʃ] *adj* conical

konjugieren [kɔnju'girən] *tr* conjugate

Konjunktion [kɔnjuŋk'tsjon] *f* (–;–en) conjunction

Konjunktiv [kɔnjuŋk'tif] *m* (–s;–e) subjunctive mood

Konjunktur [kɔnjuŋk'tur] *f* (–;–en) economic situation; business trend; (*Hochstand*) boom

konkav [kɔn'kaf] *adj* concave

konkret [kɔn'kret] *adj* concrete

Konkurrent –in [kɔnku'rɛnt(ɪn)] §7 *mf* competitor

Konkurrenz [kɔnku'rɛnts] *f* (–;–en) competition; K. machen (*dat*) compete with

konkurrenz'fähig *adj* competitive

konkurrieren [kɔnku'rirən] *intr* compete

Konkurs [kɔn'kurs] *m* (–es;–e) bankruptcy; in K. gehen (or geraten) go bankrupt; K. anmelden declare bankruptcy

Konkurs'masse *f* bankrupt company's assets

können ['kœnən] §100 *tr* able to do; know; ich kann nichts dafür I can't help it || *intr*—ich kann nicht hinein I can't get in || *mod aux* be able to; know how to; be allowed; das kann sein that may be; ich kann nicht sehen I can't see || Können *n* (–s;) ability

Könner ['kœnər] *m* (–s;–) expert

konnte ['kɔntə] *pret* of können

konsequent [kɔnze'kvɛnt] *adj* consistent

Konsequenz [kɔnze'kvɛnts] *f* (–;–en) consistency; (*Folge*) consequence

konservativ [kɔnzɛrva'tif] *adj* conservative

Konservato·rium [kɔnzɛrva'torjum] *n* (–s;–rien [rjən]) conservatory

Konserve [kɔn'zɛrvə] *f* (–;–n) canned food

Konser'venbüchse *f*, **Konser'vendose** *f* can

Konser'venfabrik *f* cannery

Konser'venöffner *m* can opener

konservieren [kɔnzɛr'virən] *tr* preserve

Konservie'rung *f* (–;) preservation

Konsisto·rium [kɔnzɪs'torjum] *n* (–s; –rien [rjən]) (eccl) consistory

Konsole [kɔn'zolə] *f* (–;–n) bracket; (archit) console

konsolidieren [kɔnzɔlɪ'dirən] *tr* consolidate

Konsonant [kɔnzɔ'nant] *m* (–en;–en) consonant

Konsorte [kɔn'zɔrtə] *m* (–n;–n) (pej) accomplice; (fin) member of a syndicate

Konsor·tium [kɔn'zɔrtjum] *n* (–s;–tien [tjən]) (fin) syndicate

konstant [kɔn'stant] *adj* constant || **Konstante** §5 *f* (math, phys) constant

konstatieren [kɔnsta'tirən] *tr* ascertain; state; (med) diagnose

konsterniert [kɔnster'nirt] *adj* stunned

konstituieren [kɔnstɪtu'irən] *tr* constitute || *ref* be established; sich als Ausschuß k. form a committee of the whole

konstitutionell [kɔnstɪtutsjɔ'nɛl] *adj* constitutional

konstruieren [kɔnstru'irən] *tr* construct; (*entwerfen*) design; (gram) construe

Konsul ['kɔnzul] *m* (–s;–n) consul

konsularisch [kɔnzu'larɪʃ] *adj* consular

Konsulat [kɔnzu'lat] *n* (-[e]s;-e) consulate; (hist) consulship

Konsulent –in [kɔnzu'lɛnt(ɪn)] §7 *mf* (jur) counsel

konsultieren [kɔnzul'tirən] *tr* consult

Konsum [kɔn'zum] *m* (-s;-s) cooperative store; (com) consumption

Konsument –in [kɔnzu'mɛnt(ɪn)] §7 *mf* consumer

Konsum'güter *pl* consumer goods

konsumieren [kɔnzu'mirən] *tr* consume

Konsum'verein *m* cooperative society

Kontakt [kɔn'takt] *m* (-[e]s;-e) contact

Kontakt'glas *n*, **Kontakt'schale** *f* contact lens

Konteradmiral ['kɔntəratmɪral] *m* rear admiral

Konterfei [kɔntər'faɪ] *n* (-s;-e) portrait, likeness

kontern ['kɔntərn] *tr* counter

Kontinent ['kɔntɪnənt] *m* (-[e]s;-e) continent

Kontingent [kɔntɪŋ'gɛnt] *n* (-[e]s;-e) quota; (mil) contingent

Kon·to ['kɔnto] *n* (-s;-s & -ten [tən]) account

Kon'toauszug *m* bank statement

Kontor [kɔn'tor] *n* (-s;-e) (com) office

Kontorist –in [kɔntə'rɪst(ɪn)] §7 *mf* clerk (*in an office*)

Kontrahent [kɔntra'hɛnt] *m* (-en;-en) contracting party; dueller

kontrahieren [kɔntra'hirən] *tr* & *intr* contract

Kontrakt [kɔn'trakt] *m* (-[e]s;-e) contract

Kontrapunkt ['kɔntrapuŋkt] *m* (mus) counterpoint

konträr [kɔn'trer] *adj* contrary

Kontrast [kɔn'trast] *m* (-[e]s;-e) contrast

konstrastieren [kɔntras'tirən] *intr* contrast

Kontrast'regelung *f* (telv) contrast button

Kontroll– [kɔn'trɔl] *comb.fm.* checking; control

Kontroll'abschnitt *m* stub (*of ticket*)

Kontrolle [kɔn'trɔlə] *f* (-;-n) control; check, inspection

Kontrolleur [kɔntrɔ'lør] *m* (-s;-e) inspector, supervisor; (aer) air-traffic controller; (indust) timekeeper

kontrollieren [kɔntrɔ'lirən] *tr* control; check, inspect; (*Bücher*) audit

Kontroll'kasse *f* cash register

Kontroll'leuchte *f* (aut) warning light (*on dashboard*)

Kontroll'turm *m* (aer) control tower

Kontroverse [kɔntrə'vɛrzə] *f* (-;-n) controversy

Kontur [kɔn'tur] *f* (-;-en) contour

Konvent [kɔn'vɛnt] *m* (-[e]s;-e) convent; monastery; (*Versammlung*) convention

Konvention [kɔnvɛn'tsjon] *f* (-;-en) convention

konventionell [kɔnvɛntsjɔ'nɛl] *adj* conventional

Konversation [kɔnvɛrza'tsjon] *f* (-;-en) conversation

Konversations'lexikon *n* encyclopedia; **wandelndes K.** (coll) walking encyclopedia

konvertieren [kɔnvɛr'tirən] *tr* convert || *intr* be converted

Konvertit –in [kɔnvɛr'tit(ɪn)] §7 *mf* convert

konvex [kɔn'vɛks] *adj* convex

Konvikt [kɔn'vɪkt] *n* (-s;-e) minor seminary

Konvoi ['kɔnvɔɪ] *m* (-s;-s) convoy

Konvolut [kɔnvɔ'lut] *n* (-[e]s;-e) bundle, roll

Konzentration [kɔntsɛntra'tsjon] *f* (-; -en) concentration

Konzentrations'lager *n* concentration camp

konzentrieren [kɔntsɛn'trirən] *tr* & *ref* (auf *acc*) concentrate (*on*)

konzentrisch [kɔn'tsɛntrɪʃ] *adj* concentric

Konzept [kɔn'tsɛpt] *n* (-[e]s;-e) rough draft; **aus dem K. bringen** confuse, throw off; **aus dem K. kommen** lose one's train of thought

Konzept'papier *n* scribbling paper

Konzern [kɔn'tsɛrn] *m* (-s;-e) (com) combine

Konzert [kɔn'tsɛrt] *n* (-[e]s;-e) concert

Konzert'flügel *m* grand piano

Konzession [kɔntsɛ'sjon] *f* (-;-en) concession; license

konzessionieren [kɔntsɛsjɔ'nirən] *tr* (com) license

Kon·zil [kɔn'tsil] *n* (-[e]s;-e & -zilien ['tsiljən]) (eccl) council

konziliant [kɔntsɪ'ljant] *adj* conciliatory; understanding

konzipieren [kɔntsɪ'pirən] *tr* conceive

koordinieren [kɔ·ɔrdɪ'nirən] *tr* coordinate

Kopf [kɔpf] *m* (-es;⸚e) head; **aus dem Kopfe** by heart; **j-m über den K. wachsen** be taller than s.o.; (fig) be too much for s.o.; **mit dem K. voran** head first; **seinen eigenen K. haben** have a mind of one's own; **seinen K. lassen müssen** lose one's life

Kopf'bedeckung *f* headgear, head wear

Kopf'brett *n* headboard

köpfen ['kœpfən] *tr* behead; (*Baum*) top; (fb) head

Kopf'ende *n* head (*of bed, etc.*)

Kopf'geld *n* reward (*for capture of criminal*)

Kopf'haut *f* scalp

Kopf'hörer *m* headset, earphones

–köpfig [kœpfɪç] *comb.fm.* –headed; –man

Kopf'kissen *n* pillow

Kopf'kissenbezug *m* pillowcase

kopf'lastig *adj* top-heavy

Kopf'lehne *f* headrest

Kopf'rechnen *n* (-s;) mental arithmetic

Kopf'salat *m* head lettuce

kopf'scheu *adj* (*Pferd*) nervous; (*Person*) shy; **k. werden** become alarmed

Kopf'schmerzen *pl* headache

Kopf'schuppen *pl* dandruff

Kopf'sprung *m* dive; **e–n K. machen** dive

Kopf'stand *m* handstand; **e–n K. machen (aer)** nose over

Kopf'stärke *f* (mil) strength

kopf'stehen §146 *intr* stand on one's head; (fig) be upside down

Kopf'steinpflaster *n* cobblestones

Kopf'steuer *f* poll tax

Kopf'stimme *f* falsetto

Kopf'stoß *m* butt; (fb) header

Kopf'tuch *n* kerchief, babushka

kopfü'ber *adv* head over heels

kopfun'ter *adv*—**kopfüber k.** head over heels

Kopf'weh *n* headache

Kopf'wellenknall *m* sonic boom

Ko·pie [kɔ'pi] *f* (–;–**pien** ['pi·ən]) copy, duplicate; (phot) print

kopieren [kɔ'pirən] *tr* copy; (phot) print

Kopier'maschine *f* copier, photocopying machine

Kopier'papier *n* tracing paper; carbon paper; (phot) printing paper

Kopier'stift *m* indelible pencil

Koppel ['kɔpəl] *f* (–;–n) leash; (*Gehege*) enclosure, paddock || *n* (–s;–) (mil) belt

koppeln ['kɔpəln] *tr* tie together, yoke; (fig) tie in; (elec) connect; (rad, rr) couple; (rok) dock || **Koppeln** *n* (–s;) (aer, naut) dead reckoning; (rok) docking

Kopplungsgeschäft ['kɔpluŋsgəʃɛft] *n* package deal

Koralle [kɔ'ralə] *f* (–;–n) coral

Korb [kɔrp] *m* (–[e]s;–̈e) basket; **j–m den K. geben** (fig) give s.o. the brush-off

Korb'ball *m* basketball

Körbchen ['kœrpçən] *n* (–s;–) little basket; (*e–s Büstenhalters*) cup

Korb'flasche *f* demijohn

Korb'geflecht *n* wickerwork

Korb'möbel *pl* wicker furniture

Korb'weide *f* (bot) osier

Kordel ['kɔrdəl] *f* (–;–n) cord

Kordon [kɔr'dõ] *m* (–s;–s) cordon; (*Ordensband*) ribbon

Korea [kɔ're·a] *n* (–s;) Korea

koreanisch [kɔre'anɪ] *adj* Korean

Korinthe [kɔ'rɪntə] *f* (–;–n) currant

Kork [kɔrk] *m* (–[e]s;–e) cork

Korken ['kɔrkən] *m* (–s;–) cork, stopper

Korkenzieher ['kɔrkəntsi·ər] *m* (–s;–) corkscrew

Korn [kɔrn] *n* (–[e]s;–̈er) grain; seed; (*am Gewehr*) bead; (*Getreide*) rye; (*e–r Münze*) fineness; (phot) graininess; **j–n aufs K. nehmen** draw a bead on s.o.

Korn'ähre *f* ear of grain

Korn'branntwein *m* whiskey

Kornett [kɔr'nɛt] *n* (–[e]s;–e) (mus) cornet

körnig ['kœrnɪç] *adj* granular

Korn'kammer *f* granary; (fig) breadbasket

koronar [kɔrə'nar] *adj* coronary

Körper ['kœrpər] *m* (–s;–) body; (geom, phys) solid

Kör'perbau *m* (–[e]s;) build, physique

kör'perbehindert *adj* physically handicapped

Kör'perbeschaffenheit *f* constitution

Körperchen ['kœrpərçən] *n* (–s;–) corpuscle

Kör'perfülle *f* plumpness, corpulence

Kör'pergeruch *m* body odor

Kör'perhaltung *f* posture, bearing

Kör'perkraft *f* physical strength

kör'perlich *adj* physical; (*stofflich*) corporeal

Kör'perpflege *f* personal hygiene

Kör'perpuder *m* talcum powder

Kör'perschaft *f* (–;–en) body (*of persons*); corporation

Kör'perverletzung *f* bodily injury

Korporation [kɔrpɔra'tsjon] *f* (–;–en) corporation

Korps [kor] *n* (– [kors];– [kors]) corps

Korps'geist *m* esprit de corps

Korps'student *m* member of a fraternity

korrekt [kɔ'rɛkt] *adj* correct, proper

Korrek·tor [kɔ'rɛktər] *m* (–s;–**toren** ['torən]) proofreader

Korrektur [kɔrɛk'tur] *f* (–;–en) correction; proofreading

Korrektur'bogen *m* page proof

Korrektur'fahne *f* galley proof

Korrelat [kɔrɛ'lat] *n* (–[e]s;–e) correlative

Korrespondent –in [kɔrɛspɔn'dɛnt(ɪn)] §7 *mf* correspondent

Korrespondenz [kɔrɛspɔn'dɛnts] *f* (–;–en) correspondence

Korrespondenz'karte *f* (Aust) postcard

Korridor ['kɔrɪdor] *m* (–s;–e) corridor

korrigieren [kɔrɪ'girən] *tr* correct

korrodieren [kɔrɔ'dirən] *tr & intr* corrode

Korse ['kɔrzə] *m* (–n;–n) Corsican

Korsett [kɔr'zɛt] *n* (–[e]s;–e & –s) corset

Korsika ['kɔrzika] *n* (–s;) Corsica

Korvette [kɔr'vɛtə] *f* (–;–n) corvette

Kosak [kɔ'zak] *m* (–en;–en) Cossack

K.-o.-Schlag [ka'oʃlak] *m* knockout punch

kosen ['kozən] *tr* fondle, caress

Kosename ['kozənamə] *m* pet name

Kosmetik [kɔs'metɪk] *f* (–;) beauty treatment; **chirugische K.** cosmetic surgery, plastic surgery

Kosme'tikartikel *m* cosmetic

Kosmeti·kum [kɔs'metɪkʊm] *n* (–s;–**ka** [ka]) cosmetic

kosmisch ['kɔzmɪʃ] *adj* cosmic

kosmopolitisch [kɔsmɔpɔ'litɪʃ] *adj* cosmopolitan

Kosmos ['kɔsmɔs] *m* (–;) cosmos

Kost [kɔst] *f* (–;) food, board

kostbar ['kɔstbar] *adj* valuable; costly

Kost'barkeit *f* (–;–en) costliness; (fig) precious thing

kosten [kɔstən] *tr* cost; taste, sip || **Kosten** *pl* costs; **auf K.** (*genit*) at the expense of; **auf seine K. kommen** get one's money's worth; **sich in K. stürzen** go to great expense

Ko'stenanschlag *m* estimate

Ko'stenaufwand *m* expenditure, outlay

Ko'stenberechnung *f* cost accounting

Ko'stenersatz m, **Ko'stenerstattung** f
reimbursement of expenses
ko'stenlos adj free of charge
Ko'stenvoranschlag m estimate
Kost'gänger –in §6 mf boarder
köstlich ['kœstlıç] adj delicious; delightful ‖ adv—**sich k. amüsieren**
have a grand time
Kost'probe f sample (to taste)
kostspielig ['kost/piliç] adj expensive
Kostüm [kɔs'tym] n (-s;-e) costume;
woman's suit; fancy dress
kostümieren [kɔsty'mirən] tr & ref
dress up
Kostüm'probe f dress rehearsal
Kot [kot] m (-[e]s;) mud, dirt; (tierischer) dirt, dung; excrement
Kotelett [kɔtə'lɛt] n (-[e]s;-e & -s)
pork chop; cutlet
Köter ['køtər] m (-s;-) mut, mongrel
Kot'flügel m (aut) fender
kotig ['kotıç] adj muddy, dirty
kotzen ['kɔtsən] intr (sl) puke ‖ **Kot-**
zen n—**es ist zum K.** it's enough to
make you throw up
Krabbe ['krabə] f (-;-n) crab; shrimp;
(niedliches Kind) little darling
krabbeln ['krabəln] tr & intr tickle ‖
intr (SEIN) crawl
Krach [krax] m (-[e]s;-s & -e) crash,
bang; (Lärm) racket; (Streit) row;
(fin) crash; **K. machen** kick up a row
krachen ['kraxən] intr crash, crack
krächzen ['krɛçtsən] intr croak, caw
kraft [kraft] prep (genit) by virtue of
‖ **Kraft** f (-;⁼e) strength, power,
force; **außer K. setzen** repeal; **in K.
sein** be in force; **in K. treten** come
into force
Kraft'anlage f (elec) power plant
Kraft'anstrengung f strenuous effort
Kraft'aufwand m effort
Kraft'ausdruck m swear word; **Kraft-**
ausdrücke strong language
Kraft'brühe f concentrated broth
Kraft'fahrer –in §6 mf motorist
Kraft'fahrzeug n motor vehicle
kräftig ['krɛftıç] adj strong, powerful;
(Speise) nutritious ‖ adv hard; heart-
ily
kräftigen ['krɛftıgən] tr strengthen
Kraft'leistung f feat of strength
kraft'los adj powerless; weak
Kraft'meier m (coll) bully; (coll) mus-
cle man
Kraft'probe f test of strength
Kraft'protz m (coll) powerhouse
Kraft'rad n motorcycle
Kraft'stoff m fuel
Kraft'stoffleitung f fuel line
kraftstrotzend ['kraft/trɔtsənt] adj
strapping
Kraft'übertragung f (aut) transmission
Kraft'wagen m motor vehicle
Kraft'werk n generating plant
Kraft'wort n (-[e]s;⁼er) swear word
Kragen ['kragən] m (-s;-) collar
Krähe ['kre·ə] f (-;-n) crow
krähen ['kre·ən] intr crow
Krähenfüße ['kre·ənfysə] pl crow's
feet (wrinkles)
Krakeel [kra'kel] m (-s;-e) (coll)
rumpus; (lauter Streit) brawl

krakeelen [kra'kelən] intr (coll) kick
up a storm
Kralle ['kralə] f (-;-n) claw
Kram [kram] m (-[e]s;) (coll) things,
stuff; (coll) business, affairs
kramen ['kramən] intr rummage
Krämer –in ['kremər(ın)] §6 mf shopkeeper ‖ m (pej) philistine
Krä'merseele f philistine
Kram'laden m general store
Krampe ['krampə] f (-;-n) staple
Krampf [krampf] m (-[e]s;⁼e) cramp,
spasm; convulsion; (Unsinn) nonsense
Krampf'ader f varicose vein
krampf'artig adj spasmodic
krampf'haft adj convulsive
Kran [kran] m (-[e]s;⁼e & -e) (mach)
crane
Kranich ['kranıç] m (-s;-e) (orn)
crane
krank [kraŋk] adj sick, ill ‖ **Kranke**
§5 mf patient
-krank comb.fm. suffering from
kränkeln ['krɛŋkəln] intr be sickly
kranken ['kraŋkən] intr—**k. an** (dat)
suffer from
kränken ['krɛŋkən] tr hurt, offend ‖
ref (über acc) feel hurt (at)
Kran'kenanstalt f hospital
Kran'kenbahre f stretcher
Kran'kenbett n sickbed
Kran'kenfahrstuhl m wheel chair
Kran'kengeld n sick benefit
Kran'kenhaus n hospital; **ins K. ein-**
weisen hospitalize
Kran'kenkasse f medical insurance
plan
Kran'kenlager n sickbed
Kran'kenpflege f nursing
Kran'kenpfleger –in §6 mf nurse
Kran'kenrevier n (mil) sick quarters;
(nav) sick bay
Kran'kensaal m hospital ward
Kran'kenschwester f nurse
Kran'kenstube f infirmary
Kran'kenstuhl m wheel chair
Kran'kenurlaub m sick leave
Kran'kenversicherung f health insur-
ance
Kran'kenwagen m ambulance
krank'feiern intr (coll) play sick
krank'haft adj morbid, pathological
Krank'heit f (-;-en) sickness, disease
Krank'heitsbericht m medical bulletin
Krank'heitserscheinung f symptom
kränklich ['krɛŋklıç] adj sickly
Kränk'lichkeit f (-;) poor health
Kränkung ['krɛŋkuŋ] f (-;-en) offense
Kran'wagen m (aut) wrecker, tow
truck
Kranz [krants] m (-[e]s;⁼e) wreath
Kränzchen ['krɛntsçən] n (-s;-) small
wreath; ladies' circle; informal dance
kränzen ['krɛntsən] tr wreathe
Krapfen ['krapfən] m (-s;-) doughnut
kraß [kras] adj crass, gross
Krater ['kratər] m (-s;-) crater
Kratzbürste ['kratsbʏrstə] f wire
brush; (fig) stand-offish woman
Krätze ['krɛtsə] f (-;) itch, scabies
kratzen ['kratsən] tr & intr scratch
Krat'zer m (-s;-) scratch; scraper

krauen ['krau·ən] *tr* scratch gently
kraus [kraus] *adj* (*Haar*) frizzy; (*Gedanken*) confused; **die Stirn k. ziehen** knit one's brows
Krause ['krauzə] *f* (-;-n) ruffle
kräuseln ['krɔızəln] *tr* & *ref* curl
Krau'seminze *f* (bot) spearmint
Kraus'haar *n* frizz
Kraut [kraut] *n* (-[e]s;-er) herb, plant; leafy top; (*Kohl*) cabbage; **ins K. schießen** run wild
Krawall [kra'val] *m* (-[e]s;-e) riot; (coll) rumpus
Krawatte [kra'vatə] *f* (-;-n) necktie
Krawat'tenhalter *m* tie clip
kraxeln ['kraksəln] *intr* (SEIN) climb
Kreatur [krɛ·a'tur] *f* (-;-en) creature
Krebs [kreps] *m* (-es;-e) crawfish, crab; (pathol) cancer
krebs'artig *adj* (pathol) cancerous
Kredenz [kre'dɛnts] *f* (-;-en) buffet, credenza, sideboard
kredenzen [kre'dɛntsən] *tr* (*Wein*) serve
Kredit [kre'dit] *m* (-[e]s;-e) credit
Kredit'bank *f* commercial bank
kreditieren [kredi'tirən] *tr* credit ǁ *intr* give credit
Kredit'karte *f* credit card
Kredit'würdigkeit *f* trustworthiness; (com) credit rating
Kreide ['kraidə] *f* (-;-n) chalk, piece of chalk, crayon
kreieren [kre'irən] *tr* create
Kreis [krais] *m* (-es;-e) circle; (*Bereich*) field; (*Bezirk*) district; (adm) county; (elec) circuit
Kreis'abschnitt *m* segment
Kreis'amt *n* district office
Kreis'ausschnitt *m* sector
Kreis'bahn *f* orbit
Kreis'bogen *m* (geom) arc
kreischen ['krai∫ən] *intr* shriek
Kreisel ['kraizəl] *m* (-s;-) gyroscope; top (*toy*)
Krei'selbewegung *f* gyration
Krei'selhorizont *m* artificial horizon
kreiseln ['kraizəln] *intr* spin, rotate, gyrate; spin the top
Krei'selpumpe *f* centrifugal pump
kreisen ['kraizən] *intr* circle; revolve; (*Blut*) circulate
kreis'förmig *adj* circular
Kreis'lauf *m* circulation; cycle
Kreis'laufsstörung *f* circulatory disorder
kreis'rund *adj* circular
Kreis'säge *f* circular saw, buzz saw
kreißen ['kraisən] *intr* be in labor
Kreißsaal ['kraiszɑl] *m* delivery room
Kreis'stadt *f* (rural) county seat
Kreis'umfang *m* circumference
Kreis'verkehr *m* traffic circle
Krem [krem] *f* (-;-s) & *m* (-s;-s) cream
Kreml ['kreməl] *m* (-[e]s;) Kremlin
Krempe ['krɛmpə] *f* (-;-n) brim, rim
Krempel ['krɛmpəl] *m* (-s;) (coll) stuff, junk ǁ *f* (-;-n) (tex) card
Kren [kren] *m* (-[e]s;) horseradish
krepieren [kre'pirən] *intr* (SEIN) (*Tiere*) die; (*Granate*) explode, burst; (sl) kick the bucket

Krepp [krep] *m* (-s;-s) crepe
Kreta ['kreta] *n* (-s;) Crete
Kretonne [kre'tɔnə] *f* (-;-n) cretonne
kreuz [krɔits] *adv*—**k. und quer** crisscross ǁ **Kreuz** *n* (-es;-e) cross; (anat) small of the back; (cards) club(s)
Kreuz'abnahme *f* deposition
Kreuz'band *n* (-[e]s;-er) mailing wrapper (*for newspapers, etc.*)
kreuz'brav' *adj* (coll) very honest; (coll) very well-behaved
kreuzen ['krɔitsən] *tr* cross ǁ *recip* cross; interbreed ǁ *intr* cruise
Kreuzer ['krɔitsər] *m* (-s;-) penny; (nav) cruiser
Kreuz'fahrer *m* crusader
Kreuz'fahrt *f* cruise; (hist) crusade
Kreuz'feuer *n* crossfire
kreuz'fidel' *adj* very cheerful
Kreuz'gang *m* (archit) cloister(s)
kreuzigen ['krɔitsigən] *tr* crucify
Kreu'zigung *f* (-;-en) crucifixion
Kreuz'otter *f* adder
Kreuz'ritter *m* crusader; Knight of the Teutonic Order
Kreuz'schiff *m* transept (*of church*)
Kreuz'schlitzschraubenzieher *m* Phillips screwdriver
Kreu'zung *f* (-;-en) intersection; crossbreeding; hybrid; (rr) crossing
Kreuz'verhör *n* cross-examination; **j-n ins K. nehmen** cross-examine s.o.
Kreuz'verweis *m* cross reference
Kreuz'weg *m* crossroad; (eccl) stations of the cross
Kreuz'worträtsel *n* crossword puzzle
Kreuz'zeichen *n* (eccl) sign of the cross; (typ) dagger
Kreuz'zug *m* crusade
kribbelig ['kribəliç] *adj* irritable; (*nervös*) edgy, on edge
kribbeln ['kribəln] *intr* tickle
kriechen ['kriçən] §102 *intr* (SEIN) creep, crawl
kriecherisch ['kriçəri∫] *adj* fawning
Kriechtier ['kriçtir] *n* reptile
Krieg [krik] *m* (-[e]s;-e) war
kriegen ['krigən] *tr* (coll) get, catch
Krie'ger *m* (-s;-) warrior
kriegerisch ['krigəri∫] *adj* warlike; (*Person*) belligerent
krieg'führend *adj* warring
Kriegs'akademie *f* war college
Kriegs'bemalung *f* war paint
Kriegs'berichter *m*, **Kriegs'berichterstatter** *m* war correspondent
Kriegs'dienst *m* military service
Kriegs'dienstverweigerer *m* conscientious objector
Kriegs'einsatz *m* (mil) action
Kriegs'entschädigung *f* reparations
Kriegs'fall *m*—**im K.** in case of war
Kriegs'flotte *f* fleet; naval force
Kriegs'fuß *m*—**mit j-m auf K. stehen** be at loggerheads with s.o.
Kriegs'gebiet *n* war zone
Kriegs'gefangene §5 *mf* prisoner of war
Kriegs'gericht *n* court martial
Kriegsgewinnler ['kriksgəvinlər] *m* (-s;-) war profiteer
Kriegs'hafen *m* naval base
Kriegs'hetzer *m* warmonger

Kriegs'kamerad *m* fellow soldier
Kriegs'lazarett *n* base hospital
Kriegs'list *f* stratagem
Kriegs'marine *f* navy
Kriegs'ministerium *n* war department
Kriegs'opfer *n* war victim
Kriegs'pfad *m* warpath
Kriegs'rat *m* council of war
Kriegs'recht *n* martial law
Kriegs'rüstung *f* arming for war; war production
Kriegs'schauplatz *m* theater of war
Kriegs'schuld *f* war debt; war guilt
Kriegs'teilnehmer *m* combatant; (*ehemaliger*) ex-serviceman, veteran
Kriegs'verbrechen *n* war crime
Kriegs'versehrte §5 *m* disabled veteran
kriegs'verwendungsfähig *adj* fit for active duty
Kriegs'wesen *n* warfare, war
Kriegs'zug *m* (mil) campaign
Kriegs'zustand *m* state of war
Krim [krɪm] *f* (–;) Crimea
Krimi ['krimi] *m* (–s;–s) & (–;–) (coll) murder mystery; (telv) thriller
kriminal [krɪmɪ'nal] *adj* criminal
Kriminal– *comb.fm.* criminal, crime
Kriminal'beamte *m* criminal investigator
Kriminal'roman *m* detective novel
Kriminal'stück *n* (telv) thriller
kriminell [krɪmɪ'nel] *adj* criminal ||
Kriminelle §5 *mf* criminal
Krimskrams ['krɪmskrams] *m* (–es;) (coll) junk
Kripo ['kripo] *abbr* (**Kriminalpolizei**) crime squad
Krippe ['krɪpə] *f* (–;–n) crib, manger; day nursery (*for infants up to 3 years*)
Krise ['krizə] *f* (–;–n) crisis
kriseln ['krizəln] *impers*—**es kriselt** there's a crisis, trouble is brewing
Kristall [krɪs'tal] *m* (–s;–e) crystal
Kristalleuchter (**Kristall'leuchter**) *m* crystal chandelier
Kristall'glas *n* crystal
kristallisieren [krɪstalɪ'zirən] *ref* & *intr* crystallize
Kristall'zucker *m* granulated sugar
Krite·rium [krɪ'terjum] *n* (–s;–rien [rjən]) criterion
Kritik [krɪ'tik] *f* (–;–en) criticism; critique; **unter aller K.** abominable
Kritikaster [krɪtɪ'kaster] *m* (–s;–) (pej) faultfinder
Kritiker –**in** ['kritɪkər(ɪn)] §6 *mf* critic; reviewer
kritik'los *adj* uncritical
kritisch ['kritɪʃ] *adj* critical
kritisieren [krɪtɪ'zirən] *tr* criticize; (*werten*) review
Krittelei [krɪtə'laɪ] *f* (–;–en) faultfinding; petty criticism
kritteln ['krɪtəln] *intr* (**an** *dat*) find fault (with), grumble (about)
Kritzelei [krɪtsə'laɪ] *f* (–;–en) scribbling, scrawling; scribble, scrawl
kritzeln ['krɪtsəln] *tr* & *intr* scribble
kroch [krɔx] *pret* of **kriechen**
Krokodil [krɔko'dil] *n* (–[e]s;–e) crocodile
Krokus ['krokʊs] *m* (–;– & –se) crocus

Krone ['kronə] *f* (–;–n) crown
krönen ['krønən] *tr* crown
Kronerbe ['kronɛrbə] *m*, **Kronerbin** ['kronɛrbɪn] *f* heir apparent
Kronleuchter ['kronlɔɪçtər] *m* chandelier
Kronprinz ['kronprɪnts] *m* crown prince
Kronprinzessin ['kronprɪntsesɪn] *f* crown princess
Krö'nung *f* (–;–en) coronation
Kropf [krɔpf] *m* (–[e]s;ːe) crop (*of bird*); (pathol) goiter
Kröte ['krøtə] *f* (–;–n) toad; **Kröten** (coll) coins, coppers
Krücke ['krʏkə] *f* (–;–n) crutch
Krückstock ['krʏkʃtɔk] *m* walking stick
Krug [kruk] *m* (–[e]s;ːe) jar, jug; mug; pitcher; (*Wirtshaus*) tavern
Krume ['krumə] *f* (–;–n) crumb; topsoil
Krümel ['kryməl] *m* (–s;–) crumb
krümeln ['kryməln] *tr* & *intr* crumble
krumm [krʊm] *adj* (**krummer** & **krümmer** ['krʏmər]; **krummste** & **krümmste** ['krʏmstə] §9) bent, stooping; crooked
krumm'beinig *adj* bowlegged
krümmen ['krʏmən] *tr* bend, curve || *ref* (*vor Schmerzen*) writhe; (*vor Lachen*) double up; (*Wurm*) wriggle; (*Holz*) warp; (*Fluß, Straße*) wind
Krümmer ['krʏmər] *m* (–s;–) (tech) elbow
krumm'nehmen §116 *tr* (coll) take the wrong way, take amiss
Krumm'stab *m* (eccl) crozier
Krüm'mung *f* (–;–en) bend, curve; winding
krumpeln ['krʊmpəln] *tr* & *intr* (coll) crumple, crease
Krüppel ['krʏpəl] *m* (–s;–) cripple; **zum K. machen** cripple
krüp'pelhaft *adj* deformed
krüp'pelig *adj* crippled; stunted
Kruste ['krustə] *f* (–;–n) crust
Kru'stentier *n* crustacean
krustig ['krustɪç] *adj* crusty
Kruzifix [krutsɪ'fiks] *n* (–es;–e) crucifix
Kryp·ta ['krypta] *f* (–;–ten [tən]) crypt
Kübel ['kybəl] *m* (–s;–) tub; bucket
Kü'belwagen *m* jeep
kubieren [ku'birən] *tr* (math) cube
Kubik– [kubik] *comb.fm.* cubic
Kubik'maß *n* cubic measure
kubisch ['kubɪʃ] *adj* cubic
Kubismus [ku'bɪsmus] *m* (–;) cubism
Küche ['kʏçə] *f* (–;–n) kitchen; (culin) cuisine
Kuchen ['kuxən] *m* (–s;–) cake, pie
Ku'chenblech *n* cookie sheet
Küchenchef *m* chef
Kü'chendienst *m* (mil) K.P.
Ku'chenform *f* cake pan
Kü'chengerät *n* kitchen utensil
Kü'chengeschirr *n* kitchen utensils
Kü'chenherd *m* kitchen range, stove
Kü'chenmaschine *f* electric kitchen appliance
Kü'chenmeister *m* chef

Kü'chenzettel *m* menu
Küchlein ['kyçlaɪn] *n* (**-s;-**) chick; (culin) small cake
Kuckuck ['kʊkʊk] *m* (-s;-e) cuckoo; **zum K.** gehen (coll) go to hell
Kufe ['kufə] *f* (-;-n) vat; (*Schlitten-*) runner
Küfer ['kyfər] *m* (-s;-) cooper
Kugel ['kugəl] *f* (-;-n) ball; sphere; (*Geschoß*) bullet; (sport) shot
ku'gelfest *adj* bulletproof
ku'gelförmig *adj* spherical
Ku'gelgelenk *n* (mach) ball-and-socket joint; (anat) socket joint
Ku'gellager *n* ball bearing
kugeln ['kugəln] *tr* roll ‖ *ref* roll around; **sich vor Lachen k.** double over with laughter ‖ *intr* (SEIN) roll
Ku'gelregen *m* hail of bullets
ku'gelrund' *adj* round; (coll) tubby
Ku'gelschreiber *m* ball-point pen
Ku'gelstoßen *n* (sport) shot put
Kuh [ku] *f* (-;̈e) cow
Kuh'dorf *n* hick town
Kuh'fladen *m* cow dung
Kuh'handel *m* (pol) horse trading
Kuh'haut *f* cowhide; **das geht auf keine K.** but that's a long story
kühl [kyl] *adj* cool
Kühl'anlage *f* refrigerator; cooling system; cold storage (room)
Kühle ['kylə] *f* (-;) cool, coolness
kühlen ['kylən] *tr* cool; (*Wein*) chill
Küh'ler *m* (-s;-) cooler; (aut) radiator
Küh'lerverschluß *m* radiator cap
Kühl'mittel *n* coolant
Kühl'schrank *m* refrigerator
Kühl'truhe *f* freezer
Kühl'wagen *m* refrigerator truck; (rr) refrigerator car
Kuh'magd *f* milkmaid
Kuh'mist *m* cow dung
kühn [kyn] *adj* bold, daring
Kühn'heit *f* (-;) boldness, daring
Kuhpocken ['kupəkən] *pl* cowpox
Kuh'stall *m* cowshed, cow barn
Kujon [kʊ'jon] *m* (-s;-e) (pej) louse
kujonieren [kʊjo'nirən] *tr* bully
Küken ['kykən] *n* (-s;-) chick
Kukuruz ['kukʊrʊts] *m* (-es;) (Aust) corn
kulant [kʊ'lant] *adj* obliging; generous
Kuli ['kulɪ] *m* (-s;-s) coolie
kulinarisch [kʊlɪ'narɪʃ] *adj* culinary
Kulisse [kʊ'lɪsə] *f* (-;-n) (theat) wing; **hinter den Kulissen** behind the scenes; **Kulissen** scenery
Kulis'senfieber *n* stage fright
kullern ['kʊlərn] *intr* (SEIN) roll
kulminieren [kʊlmɪ'nirən] *intr* culminate
Kult [kʊlt] *m* (-[e]s;-e) cult
kultivieren [kʊltɪ'virən] *tr* cultivate
Kultur [kʊl'tur] *f* (-;-en) culture, civilization; (agr) cultivation; (bact, chem) culture
Kultur'austausch *m* cultural exchange
kulturell [kʊltʊ'rel] *adj* cultural
Kultur'erbe *n* cultural heritage
Kultur'film *m* educational film
Kultur'geschichte *f* history of civilization; cultural history
Kultur'volk *n* civilized people

Kul·tus ['kʊltʊs] *m* (-;-te [tə]) cult
Kümmel ['kʏməl] *m* (-s;-) caraway seed; caraway brandy
Küm'melbrot *n* seeded rye bread
Kummer ['kʊmər] *m* (-s;) grief, sorrow; worry, concern, trouble; **j-m großen K.** bereiten cause s.o. a lot of worry; **sich** [*dat*] **K. machen über** (*acc*) worry about
kümmerlich ['kʏmərlɪç] *adj* wretched; (*dürftig*) needy
Kümmerling ['kʏmərlɪŋ] *m* (-s;-e) stunted animal; stunted plant
kümmern ['kʏmərn] *tr* trouble, worry; concern ‖ *ref*—**sich k. um** worry about; take care of; **sich nicht k. um** not bother about; neglect
Kümmernis ['kʏmərnɪs] *f* (-;-se) worry, trouble
kum'mervoll *adj* grief-stricken
Kumpan [kʊm'pan] *m* (-s;-e) companion; buddy
Kumpel ['kʊmpəl] *m* (-s;-) buddy, sidekick; (min) miner
kund [kʊnt] *adj* known
kündbar ['kʏntbar] *adj* (*Vertrag*) terminable; (fin) redeemable
Kunde ['kʊndə] *m* (-n;-n) customer; **übler K.** (fig) tough customer ‖ *f* (-;) news, information; lore
-kunde *f* *comb.fm.* –ology; –graphy; science of; guide to, study of
Kun'dendienst *m* customer service; warranty service
Kun'denkreis *m* clientele
kund'geben §80 *tr* make known, announce
Kundgebung ['kʊntgebʊŋ] *f* (-;-en) manifestation; (pol) rally
kundig ['kʊndɪç] *adj* well-informed; **k. sein** (*genit*) know
-kundig *comb.fm.* well versed in; able to
kündigen ['kʏndɪgən] *tr* (*Vertrag*) give notice to terminate; (*Wohnung*) give notice to vacate; (*Stellung*) give notice of quitting; (*Kapital*) call in; (*Hypothek*) foreclose on; **j-n fristlos k.** (coll) sack s.o. ‖ *intr* (*dat*) given notice to, release
Kün'digung *f* (-;-en) (*seitens des Arbeitnehmers*) resignation; (*seitens des Arbeitgebers*) notice (*of termination*); **mit monatlicher K.** subject to a month's notice
Kün'digungsfrist *f* period of notice
kund'machen *tr* make known, announce
Kund'machung *f* (-;-en) announcement
Kund'schaft *f* (-;) clientele, customer(s); (mil) reconnaissance
kundschaften ['kʊntʃaftən] *intr* go on reconnaissance, scout
Kund'schafter *m* (-s;-) scout, spy
kund'tun §154 *tr* make known, announce
kund'werden §159 *intr* (SEIN) become known
künftig ['kʏnftɪç] *adj* future, to come, next ‖ *adv* in the future, from now on
künf'tighin' *adv* from now on, hereafter

Kunst [kʊnst] ƒ (-;-̈e) art; skill; **das ist keine K.** it's easy
Kunstbanause ['kʊnstbanaʊzə] m (-n; -n) philistine
Kunst′dünger m chemical fertilizer
Künstelei [kʏnstə'laɪ] ƒ (-;-en) affectation
Kunst′faser ƒ synthetic fiber
Kunst′fehler m—**ärztlicher K.** malpractice
kunst′fertig adj skillful, skilled
Kunst′flieger m stunt pilot
Kunst′flug m stunt flying
Kunst′freund –in §8 mƒ art lover; patron of the arts
Kunst′gegenstand m objet d'art
kunst′gerecht adj skillful; expert
Kunst′gewerbe n arts and crafts
Kunst′glied n artificial limb
Kunst′griff m trick
Kunst′händler –in §6 mƒ art dealer
Kunst′kenner –in §6 mƒ art connoisseur
Kunst′laufen n figure skating
Künstler –in ['kʏnstlər(ɪn)] §6 mƒ artist; performer
künstlerisch ['kʏnstlərɪʃ] adj artistic
künstlich ['kʏnstlɪç] adj artificial; (chem) synthetic
Kunst′liebhaber –in §6 mƒ art lover
kunst′los adj unaffected
Kunst′maler –in §6 mƒ painter, artist
Kunst′pause ƒ pause for effect
kunst′reich adj ingenious
Kunst′reiter m equestrian
Kunst′seide ƒ rayon
Kunst′springen n (sport) diving
Kunst′stoff m plastic material; synthetic material; (tex) synthetic fiber
Kunststoff– comb.fm. plastic; plastics
Kunst′stopfen n invisible mending
Kunst′stück n trick, feat
Kunst′tischler m cabinet maker
Kunstverständige ['kʊnstferʃtɛndɪgə] §5 mƒ art expert
kunst′voll adj elaborate, ornate
Kunst′werk n work of art
kunterbunt ['kʊntərbʊnt] adj chaotic
Kupfer ['kʊpfər] n (-s;) copper
kupfern ['kʊpfərn] adj copper
kupieren [kʊ'pirən] tr (Schwanz, Ohren) cut off; (Spielkarten) cut; (Fahrkarten) punch
Kuppe ['kʊpə] ƒ (-;-n) top, summit
Kuppel ['kʊpəl] ƒ (-;-n) cupola
Kuppelei [kʊpə'laɪ] ƒ (-;) procuring
kuppeln ['kʊpəln] tr couple, connect ‖ intr be a pimp; be a procuress; (aut) operate the clutch
Kuppler ['kʊplər] m (-s;-) pimp
Kupplerin ['kʊplərɪn] ƒ (-;-nen) procuress
Kupplung ['kʊplʊŋ] ƒ (-;-en) (aut) clutch; (rr) coupling
Kur [kur] ƒ (-;-en) cure (at a spa); **j-n in die Kur nehmen** give s.o. a talking to
Kuratel [kura'tel] ƒ (-;) guardianship; **j-n unter K. stellen** appoint a guardian for s.o.
Ku·rator [kʊ'ratər] m (-s;-ratoren [ra'torən]) (e-s Museums) curator; (educ) trustee; (jur) guardian

Kurato·rium [kura'torjum] n (-s;-rien [rjən]) (educ) board of trustees
Kurbel ['kurbəl] ƒ (-;-n) crank, handle, winch
Kurbelei [kurbə'laɪ] ƒ (-;-en) shooting a film; (aer) dogfight
Kur′belgehäuse n (aut) crankcase
kurbeln ['kurbəln] tr crank; (Film) shoot ‖ intr engage in a dogfight
Kur′belstange ƒ (mach) connecting rod
Kur′belwelle ƒ (mach) crankshaft
Kürbis ['kʏrbɪs] m (-ses;-se) pumpkin; (Kopf) (sl) bean
küren ['kyrən] §165 & §109 tr elect
Kurfürst ['kurfʏrst] m (-en;-en) elector (of the Holy Roman Empire)
Kur′haus n spa; hotel
Kurie ['kurjə] ƒ (-;-n) (eccl) curia
Kurier [ku'rir] m (-s;-e) courier
kurieren [ku'rirən] tr cure
kurios [ku'rjos] adj odd, curious
Kuriosität [kurjozɪ'tet] ƒ (-;-en) quaintness; curio, curiosity
Kur′ort m health resort, spa
Kurpfuscher ['kurpfuʃər] m (-s;-) quack
Kurrentschrift [ku'rɛntʃrɪft] ƒ cursive script
Kurs [kurs] m (-es;-e) (educ) course; (fin) rate of exchange; (fin) circulation; (naut) course; (st. exch.) price; **außer K. setzen** take out of circulation; **hoch im K. stehen** be at a premium; (fig) rate high; **zum Kurse von** at the rate of
Kurs′bericht m (st. exch.) market report
Kurs′buch n (rr) timetable
Kürschner ['kʏrʃnər] m (-s;-) furrier
Kurs′entwicklung ƒ price trend
Kurs′gewinn m (st. exch.) gain
kursieren [kur'zirən] intr circulate
Kursive [kur'zivə] ƒ (-;), **Kursivschrift** [kur'zifʃrɪft] ƒ (-;) italics
Kurs′stand m (st. exch.) price level
Kur·sus ['kurzus] m (-;-se [zə]) (educ) course
Kurs′veränderung ƒ (fin) change in exchange rates; (naut) change of course; (pol) change of policy; (st. exch.) price change
Kurs′wert m (st. exch.) market value
Kurve ['kurvə] ƒ (-;-n) curve; **in die K. gehen** (aer) bank
kurz [kurts] adj (kürzer ['kʏrtsər]; kürzeste ['kʏrtsəstə] §9) short, brief; **auf das kürzeste** very briefly; **binnen kurzem** within a short time; **in kurzem** before long; **k. und gut** in a word; **seit kurzem** for the last few days or weeks; **über k. oder lang** sooner or later; **zu k. kommen** (coll) get the short end of it ‖ adv shortly; briefly; curtly
kurzatmig ['kurtsatmɪç] adj short-winded; (Pferd) broken-winded
Kürze ['kʏrtsə] ƒ (-;) shortness; brevity; **in K.** shortly; briefly
kürzen ['kʏrtsən] tr shorten; (Gehalt) cut; (math) reduce
kurzerhand′ adv offhand
Kurz′fassung ƒ abridged version
Kurz′film m (cin) short

kurzfristig ['kʊrtsfrɪstɪç] *adj* short-term
Kurz'geschichte *f* short story
kurzlebig ['kʊrtslebɪç] *adj* short-lived
kürzlich ['kʏrtslɪç] *adj* lately, recently
Kurz'meldung *f* news flash
Kurz'nachrichten *pl* news summary
kurz'schließen §76 *tr* short-circuit
Kurz'schluß *m* short circuit
Kurz'schlußbrücke *f* (elec) jumper
Kurz'schrift *f* shorthand
kurz'sichtig *adj* near-sighted; (fig) short-sighted
Kurz'streckenlauf *m* sprint
Kurz'streckenläufer –in §6 *mf* sprinter
kurzum' *adv* in short, in a word
Kür'zung *f* (–;–en) reduction; curtailment; (*e–s Buches*) abridgment
Kurz'waren *pl* sewing supplies
kurz'weg *adv* bluntly, flatly
Kurzweil ['kʊrtsvaɪl] *f* (–;) pastime
kurzweilig ['kʊrtsvaɪlɪç] *adj* amusing
kusch [kʊʃ] *interj* lie down! (*to a dog*)
kuschen ['kʊʃən] *ref* lie down; crouch || *intr* lie down; crouch, cringe; (*Person*) knuckle under, submit
Kusine [kʊ'zinə] *f* (–;–n) female cousin
Kuß [kʊs] *m* (**Kusses; Küsse**) kiss; **kalter K.** popsicle

küssen ['kʏsən] *tr & intr* kiss
Kuß'hand *f*—j–m **e–e K. zuwerfen** throw s.o. a kiss; **mit K.** with pleasure
Küste ['kʏstə] *f* (–;–n) coast, shore
Kü'stenfahrer *m* coasting vessel
Kü'stenfischerei *f* inshore fishing
Kü'stengewässer *n* coastal waters
Kü'stenlinie *f* coastline, shoreline
kü'stennah *adj* offshore; coastal
Kü'stenschiffahrt *f* coastal shipping
Kü'stenstreife *f* shore patrol
Küster ['kʏstər] *m* (–s;–) sexton
Kustos ['kʊstɔs] *m* (–; **Kustoden** [kʊs'todən]) custodian
Kutsche ['kʊtʃə] *f* (–;–n) coach
Kut'scher *m* (–s;–) coachman
kutschieren [kʊ'tʃirən] *intr* drive a coach || *intr* (SEIN) ride in a coach
Kutte ['kʊtə] *f* (–;–n) (eccl) cowl
Kutteln ['kʊtəln] *pl* tripe
Kutter ['kʊtər] *m* (–s;–) (naut) cutter
Kuvert [kʊ'vɛrt] *n* (–s;–s) & (–[e]s;–n) envelope; table setting
kuvertieren [kʊvɛr'tirən] *tr* put into an envelope
Kux [kʊks] *m* (–es;–e) mining share
Kyklon [ky'klon] *m* (–s;–e) cyclone
Kyniker ['kynɪkər] *m* (–s;–) (philos) cynic

L

L, l [ɛl] *invar n* L, l
laben ['labən] *tr* refresh
Labial [la'bjal] *m* (–s;–e) labial
labil [la'bil] *adj* unstable
Labor [la'bor] *n* (–s;–s) (coll) lab
Laborant [labɔ'rant] (–ɪn)] §7 *mf* laboratory technician
Laborato•rium [labɔra'torjʊm] *n* (–s; **rien** [rjən]) laboratory
laborieren [labɔ'rirən] *intr* experiment; **l. an** (*dat*) suffer from
Labsal ['lapzal] *n* (–[e]s;–e) refreshment
La'bung *f* (–;–en) refreshment
Labyrinth [laby'rɪnt] *n* (–[e]s;–e) labyrinth
Lache ['laxə] *f* (–;–n) puddle, pool; laugh; **e–e gellende L. anschlagen** break out in laughter
lächeln ['lɛçəln] *intr* (**über** *acc*) smile (at) || **Lächeln** *n* (–s;) smile; **höhnisches L.** sneer
lachen ['laxən] *intr* laugh; **daß ich nicht lache!** don't make me laugh! || **Lachen** *n* (–s;) laugh, laughter; **du hast gut L.!** you can laugh!
lächerlich ['lɛçərlɪç] *adj* ridiculous; **l. machen** ridicule; **sich l. machen** make a fool of oneself
lachhaft ['laxhaft] *adj* ridiculous
Lachkrampf ['laxkrampf] *m* fit of laughter
Lachs [laks] *m* (–es;–e) salmon
Lachsalve ['laxzalvə] *f* (–;–n) peal of laughter

Lachs'schinken *m* raw, lightly smoked ham
Lack [lak] *m* (–[e]s;–e) lacquer, varnish
Lackel ['lakəl] *m* (–s;–) (coll) dope
lackieren [la'kirən] *tr* lacquer, varnish; (*Autos*) paint
Lack'leder *n* patent leather
Lackmuspapier ['lakmʊspapir] *n* litmus paper
Lack'schuhe *pl* patent-leather shoes
Lade ['ladə] *f* (–;–n) box, case; (*Schublade*) drawer
La'dearbeiter *m* loader
La'debaum *m* derrick
La'defähigkeit *f* loading capacity
La'dehemmung *f* jamming (*of a gun*); **L. haben** jam
La'deklappe *f* tailgate
La'delüke *f* (naut) hatch
laden ['ladən] §103 *tr* load; (*Gast*) invite; (elec) charge; (jur) summon; **geladen sein** (coll) be burned up || **Laden** *m* (–s;⁼) store, shop; (*Fenster-*) shutter; **den L. schmeißen** pull it off, lick it
La'dendieb *m*, **La'dendiebin** *f* shoplifter
La'dendiebstahl *m* shoplifting
La'denhüter *m* drug on the market
La'deninhaber –in §6 *mf* shopkeeper
La'denkasse *f* till
Lä'denmädchen *n* salesgirl
La'denpreis *m* retail price
La'denschluß *m* closing time

La'denschwengel *m* (pej) stupid shop clerk
La'dentisch *m* counter
La'derampe *f* loading platform
La'deschein *m* bill of lading
La'destock *m* ramrod
La'destreifen *m* cartridge clip
La'dung *f* (-;-en) loading; load; (*Güter*) freight; (elec) charge; (jur) summons; (mil) charge; (naut) cargo
Lafette [la'fɛtə] *f* (-;-n) gun mount
Laffe ['lafə] *m* (-n;-n) jazzy dresser
lag [lɑk] *pret* of **liegen**
Lage ['lɑgə] *f* (-;-n) site, location; situation; (*Zustand*) condition, state; (*Haltung*) posture; (*Schicht*) layer, deposit; (*Salve*) volley; (*Bier*) round; (bb) quire; (mil) position; (mus) pitch; **mißliche L.** predicament; **versetzen Sie sich in meine L.** put yourself in my position
Lager ['lɑgər] *n* (-s;-) bed; (*e-s Wildes*) lair; (*Stapelplatz*) dump; (*Partei*) side, camp; (*von Waffen*) cache; (*Vorrat*) stock; (*Warenlager*) stockroom; (geol) stratum, vein; (mach) bearing; (mil) camp; **auf L.** in stock; (fig) up one's sleeve; **ein L. halten von** keep stock of
La'geraufnahme *f* inventory
La'gerbier *n* lager beer
La'gerfähigkeit *f* shelf life
La'gerfeuer *n* campfire
La'gergebühr *f* storage charges
La'gerhalter *m* stock clerk
La'gerhaus *n* warehouse
Lagerist -in [lɑgə'rɪst(ɪn)] §7 *mf* warehouse clerk
La'gerleben *n* camp life
lagern ['lɑgərn] *tr* lay down; (*Waren*) stock, store; (*altern*) season; (mach) mount on bearings ‖ *ref* lie down, rest ‖ *intr* lie down, rest; (*Waren*) be stored; (*Wein*) season; (geol) be deposited; (mil) camp
La'gerort *m*, **La'gerplatz** *m* resting place; (*Stapelplatz*) dump; (mil) camp site
La'gerraum *m* storeroom, stockroom
La'gerstand *m* stock on hand, inventory
La'gerstätte *f*, **La'gerstelle** *f* resting place; (geol) deposit; (mil) camp site
La'gerung *f* (-;-en) storage; (*Alterung*) seasoning; (geol) stratification
La'gervorrat *m* stock, supply
Lagune [la'gunə] *f* (-;-n) lagoon
lahm [lɑm] *adj* lame; paralyzed ‖ **Lahme** §5 *mf* paralytic
lahmen ['lɑmən] *intr* be lame, limp
lähmen ['lɛmən] *tr* paralyze; (*Verkehr*) tie up; (fig) cripple
lahm'legen *tr* cripple, paralyze; (mil) neutralize
Läh'mung *f* (-;-en) paralysis
Laib [laɪp] *m* (-[e]s;-e) loaf
Laich [laɪç] *m* (-[e]s;-e) spawn
laichen ['laɪçən] *intr* spawn
Laie ['laɪ·ə] *m* (-n;-n) layman; **Laien** laity
Lai'enbruder *m* lay brother
lai'enhaft *adj* layman's
Lakai [la'kaɪ] *m* (-en;-en) lackey

Lake ['lɑkə] *f* (-;-n) brine, pickle
Laken ['lɑkən] *n* (-s;-) sheet
lakonisch [la'konɪʃ] *adj* laconic
Lakritze [la'krɪtsə] *f* (-;-n) licorice
Lakune [la'kunə] *f* (-;-n) lacuna
lallen ['lalən] *tr & intr* stammer
lamellenförmig [la'mɛlənfœrmɪç] *adj* laminate
lamentieren [lamɛn'tirən] *intr* wail
Lametta [la'mɛta] *n* (-s;) tinsel
Lamm [lam] *n* (-[e]s;-̈er) lamb
Lamm'braten *m* roast lamb
Lämmerwolke ['lɛmərvɔlkə] *f* cirrus
Lamm'fleisch *n* (culin) lamb
lamm'fromm' *adj* meek as a lamb
Lampe ['lampə] *f* (-;-n) lamp; light
Lam'penfieber *n* stage fright
Lam'penschirm *m* lamp shade
Lampion [lam'pjõ] *m* (-s;-s) Chinese lantern
lancieren [lã'sirən] *tr* launch, promote; (*Kandidaten*) (pol) groom
Land [lant] *n* (-[e]s;-̈er & -e) land; (*Ackerboden*) ground, soil; (*Staat*) country; (*Provinz*) state; (*Gegensatz: Stadt*) country; **ans L.** ashore; **auf dem Lande** in the country; **aufs L.** into the country; **aus aller Herren Ländern** from everywhere; **außer Landes gehen** go abroad; **zu Lande** by land
Land'arbeiter *m* farm hand
Land'armee *f* land forces
Land'bau *m* farming, agriculture
Land'besitz *m* landed property
Land'besitzer *m* §6 *mf* landowner
Landebahn ['landəban] *f* runway
Landedeck ['landədɛk] *n* flight deck
Land'edel·mann *m* (-es;-leute) country gentleman
Landefeuer ['landəfɔɪ·ər] *n* runway lights
land'einwärts *adv* inland
Landekopf ['landəkɔpf] *m* beachhead
landen ['landən] *tr & intr* (SEIN) land
Land'enge *f* isthmus, neck of land
Landeplatz ['landəplats] *m* wharf; (aer) landing field
Länderei [lɛndə'raɪ] *f* (-;-en) or **Ländereien** *pl* lands, estates
Länderkunde ['lɛndərkundə] *f* geography
Landes– [landəs] *comb.fm.* national, native, of the land
Lan'desaufnahme *f* land survey
Lan'desbank *f* national bank
Lan'desbeschreibung *f* topography
lan'deseigen *adj* state-owned
Lan'deserzeugnis *n* domestic product
Lan'desfarben *pl* national colors
Lan'desfürst *m* sovereign
Lan'desgesetz *n* law of the land
Lan'desherr *m* sovereign
Lan'desherrschaft *f*, **Lan'deshoheit** *f* sovereignty
Lan'dessprache *f* vernacular
Lan'destracht *f* national costume
Lan'destrauer *f* public mourning
lan'desüblich *adj* customary
Lan'desvater *m* sovereign
Lan'desverrat *m* high treason
Lan'desverräter -in §6 *mf* traitor
Lan'desverteidigung *f* national defense

Land'flucht f rural exodus
land'flüchtig adj exiled, fugitive
Land'friedensbruch m disturbance of the peace
Land'gericht n district court, superior court
Land'gewinnung f land reclamation
Land'gut n country estate
Land'haus n country house
Land'jäger m rural policeman; (culin) sausage
Land'junker m country squire
Land'karte f map
Land'kreis m rural district
land·läufig adj customary
Ländler ['lɛntlər] m (-s;-) waltz
Land'leute pl country folk
ländlich ['lɛntlɪç] adj rural, rustic
Land'luft f country air
Land'macht f land forces
Land'mann m (-[e]s;-leute) farmer
Land'marke f landmark (for travelers and sailors)
Land'maschinen pl farm machinery
Land'messer m surveyor
Land'partie f outing, picnic
Land'plage f nation-wide plague; (coll) big nuisance
Land'rat m regional governor
Land'ratte f (fig) landlubber
Land'recht n common law
Land'regen m steady rain
Land'rücken m ridge
Land'schaft f (-;-en) landscape, scenery; (Bezirk) district, region
land'schaftlich adj scenic; regional
Landser ['lantsər] m (-s;-) G.I.
Lands'knecht m mercenary
Lands'mann m (-[e]s;-leute) fellow countryman
Land'spitze f promontory
Land'straße f highway
Land'streicher m (-s;-) tramp, hobo
Land'strich m tract of land
Land'sturm m home guard
Land'tag m state assembly
landumschlossen ['lantʊmʃlɔsən] adj landlocked
Lan'dung f (-;-en) landing
Lan'dungsboot n landing craft
Lan'dungsbrücke f jetty, pier
Lan'dungsgestell n landing gear
Lan'dungssteg m gangplank
Land'vermessung f surveying
Land'volk n country folk
Land'weg m overland route
Land'wehr f militia, home guard
Land'wirt m farmer
Land'wirtschaft f agriculture; **L. betreiben** farm
land'wirtschaftlich adj farm, agricultural
Land'zunge f spit of land
lang [laŋ] adj (**länger** ['lɛŋər]; **längste** ['lɛŋstə] §9) long; (Person) tall || adv—**die ganze Woche l.** all week; **e–e Stunde l.** for an hour
langatmig ['laŋatmɪç] adj long-winded
lang'beinig adj long-legged
lange ['laŋə] adv long, a long time; **es ist noch l. nicht fertig** it is far from ready; **schon l. her** long ago; **schon l. her, daß** a long time since;

so l. bis until; **so l. wie** as long as; **wie l.?** how long?
Länge ['lɛŋə] f (-;-n) length; long syllable; (geog) longitude; (pros) quantity; **auf die L.** in the long run; **der L. nach** lengthwise; **in die L. ziehen** drag out
langen ['laŋən] tr reach, hand; **j–m eine l.** (coll) give s.o. a smack || intr be enough; **l. nach** reach for || impers—**es langt mir** I have enough; **jetzt langt's mir aber!** I've had it!
Län'gengrad m degree of longitude
Län'genkreis m meridian
Län'genmaß n linear measure
Lan'geweile f boredom; **sich** [dat] **die L. vertreiben** (coll) kill time
Lang'finger m pickpocket
langfingerig ['laŋfɪŋərɪç] adj (fig) thievish
langfristig ['laŋfrɪstɪç] adj long-term
lang'jährig adj long-standing
Lang'lauf m crosscountry skiing
langlebig ['laŋlebɪç] adj long-lived
Lang'lebigkeit f (-;) longevity
lang'legen ref lie down, stretch out
länglich ['lɛŋlɪç] adj oblong
läng'lichrund adj oval, elliptical
Lang'mut f patience
lang'mütig adj patient
Lang'mütigkeit f patience
längs [lɛŋs] prep (genit or dat) along
langsam ['laŋzam] adj slow
Lang'spielplatte f long-playing record
längst [lɛŋst] adv long since, long ago
längstens ['lɛŋstəns] adv at the latest; (höchstens) at the most
Langstrecken– comb.fm. long-range; (sport) long-distance
langweilen ['laŋvaɪlən] tr bore || ref feel bored
Lang'weiler m (-s;-) slowpoke
langweilig ['laŋvaɪlɪç] adj boring
langwierig ['laŋvirɪç] adj lengthy
Lanolin [lano'lin] n (-s;) lanolin
Lanze ['lantsə] f (-;-n) lance, spear
Lan'zenstechen n (-s;) jousting
Lanzette [lan'tsetə] f (-;-n) lancet
Lappalie [la'paljə] f (-;-n) trifle
Lappen ['lapən] m (-s;-) rag; wash-rag; (Flicken) patch; (anat) lobe
läppisch ['lɛpɪʃ] adj silly, trifling
Lappland ['laplant] n (-s;) Lapland
Lärche ['lɛrçə] f (-;-n) (bot) larch
Lärm [lɛrm] m (-[e]s;) noise; **L. schlagen** (fig) make a fuss
lärmen ['lɛrmən] intr make noise
lär'mend adj noisy
Larve ['larfə] f (-;-n) mask; larva
las [las] pret of **lesen**
lasch [laʃ] adj limp; (Speise) insipid
Lasche ['laʃə] f (-;-n) (Klappe) flap; (Schuh–) tongue; (rr) fishplate
lasieren [la'zirən] tr glaze
lassen ['lasən] §104 tr let; (erlauben) allow; (bewirken) have, make; leave (behind, undone, open, etc.); **den Film entwickeln l.** have the film developed; **etw fallen l.** drop s.th.; **ich kann es nicht l.** I can't help it; **j–n warten l.** keep s.o. waiting; **kommen l.** send for; **laß den Lärm!** stop

the noise!; **laß es!** cut it out!; **laßt uns gehen** let us go; **sein Leben l.** lose one's life; **sein Leben l. für** sacrifice one's life for ‖ *ref*—**das läßt sich denken** I can imagine; **das läßt sich hören!** now you're talking!; **es läßt sich nicht beschreiben** it defies description; **es läßt sich nicht leugnen, daß** it cannot be denied that; **sich** [*dat*] **Zeit l.** take one's time

lässig ['lɛsɪç] *adj* (*faul*) lazy; (*träge*) sluggish; (*nachlässig*) remiss

Läs'sigkeit *f* (-;) laziness; negligence

läßlich ['lɛslɪç] *adj* venial

Last [last] *f* (-;-en) load, weight; (*Bürde*) burden; (*Hypotek*) encumbrance; (aer, naut) cargo, freight; **j-m etw zur L. legen** blame s.o. for s.th.; **L. der Beweise** weight of evidence; **ruhende L.** dead weight; **zur L. fallen** (*dat*) become a burden for

Last'auto *n* truck

lasten ['lastən] *intr* (**auf** *dat*) weigh (on)

la'stenfrei *adj* unencumbered

La'stensegler *m* transport glider

Laster ['lastər] *m* (-s;-) (coll) truck ‖ *n* (-s;-) vice

Lästerer –in ['lɛstərər(ɪn)] §6 *mf* slanderer; blasphemer

la'sterhaft *adj* vicious

La'sterleben *n* life of vice

lästerlich ['lɛstərlɪç] *adj* slanderous; blasphemous

Lästermaul ['lɛstərmaʊl] *n* scandalmonger

lästern ['lɛstərn] *tr* slander; blaspheme

Lä'sterung *f* (-;-en) slander; blasphemy

lästig ['lɛstɪç] *adj* troublesome; **j-m l. fallen** bother s.o.

Last'kahn *m* barge

Last'kraftwagen *m* truck

Last'schrift *f* (acct) debit

Last'tier *n* beast of burden

Last'träger *m* porter

Last'wagen *m* truck

Last'zug *m* tractor-trailer (*consisting of several trailers*)

Lasur [la'zur] *f* (-;) glaze

Latein [la'taɪn] *n* (-s;) Latin

lateinisch [la'taɪnɪʃ] *adj* Latin

Laterne [la'tɛrnə] *f* (-;-n) lantern; lamp

Latrine [la'trinə] *f* (-;-n) latrine

Latri'nenparole *f* scuttlebut

Latsche ['latʃə] *f* (-;-n) (coll) slipper ‖ ['latʃə] *f* (-;-n) (bot) dwarf pine

latschen ['latʃən] *intr* (SEIN) shuffle along

Latte ['latə] *f* (-;-n) lath

Lat'tenkiste *f* crate

Lat'tenzaun *m* picket fence

Lattich ['latɪç] *m* (-[e]s;-e) lettuce

Latz [lats] *m* (-es;̈e) bib; (*Klappe*) flap; (*Schürzchen*) pinafore

Lätzchen ['lɛtsçən] *n* (-s;-) bib

lau [laʊ] *adj* lukewarm; (*Wetter*) mild; (fig) half-hearted

Laub [laʊp] *n* (-[e]s;) foliage

Laub'baum *m* deciduous tree

Laube ['laʊbə] *f* (-;-n) arbor; (*Säulen-*

gang) portico; (*Bogengang*) arcade; (theat) box

Lau'bengang *m* arcade

Laub'säge *f* fret saw

Laub'sägearbeit *f* fretwork

Laub'werk *n* foliage

Lauer ['laʊ·ər] *f* (-;) ambush; **auf der L. liegen** lie in wait

lauern ['laʊ·ərn] *intr* lurk; **l. auf** (*acc*) lie in wait for, watch for

lau'ernd *adj* (*Blick*) wary; (*Gefahr*) lurking

Lauf [laʊf] *m* (-[e]s;̈e) running; run; (*e-s Flusses*) course; (*Strömung*) current; (*Wettlauf*) race; (*e-s Gewehrs*) barrel; (astr) path, orbit; **den Dingen freien L. lassen** let things take their course; **im Laufe der Zeit** in the course of time; **im vollen Laufe** at full speed

Lauf'bahn *f* career; (astr) orbit; (sport) lane

Lauf'bursche *m* errand boy; office boy

laufen ['laʊfən] §105 *intr* (SEIN) run; (*zu Fuß gehen*) walk; (*leck sein*) leak; (*Zeit*) pass; **die Dinge l. lassen** let things slide; **j-n l. lassen** let s.o. go; (*straflos*) let s.o. off

lau'fend *adj* (*ständig*) steady; (*Jahr, Preis*) current; (*Nummern*) consecutive; (*Wartung, Geschäft*) routine; (*Meter, usw.*) running; **auf dem laufenden** up to date; **laufendes Band** conveyor belt; assembly line

Läufer ['lɔɪfər] *m* (-s;-) runner; (*Teppich*) runner; (chess) bishop; (fb) halfback; (mach) rotor; (mus) run

Lauferei [laʊfə'raɪ] *f* (-;-en) running around

Lauf'feuer *n* (-s;) wildfire

Lauf'fläche *f* tread (*on tire*)

Lauf'gewicht *n* sliding weight

Lauf'gitter *n* playpen

Lauf'graben *m* trench

läufig ['lɔɪfɪç] *adj* in heat

Läu'figkeit *f* (-;) heat

Lauf'junge *m* errand boy; office boy

Lauf'kran *m* (mach) traveling crane

Lauf'kunde *m* chance customer

Lauf'masche *f* run (*in stocking*)

lauf'maschenfrei *adj* runproof

Lauf'paß *m* (coll) walking papers; (coll) brush-off

Lauf'planke *f* gangplank

Lauf'rad *n* (*e-r Turbine*) rotor; (aer) landing wheel

Lauf'schritt *m* double-quick time

Lauf'steg *m* footbridge

Laufställchen ['laʊfʃtɛlçən] *n* (-s;-) playpen

Lauf'zeit *f* rutting season; (*e-s Vertrags*) term; (cin) running time; (mach) (service) life

Lauge ['laʊgə] *f* (-;-n) lye; (*Salzlauge*) brine; (*Seifenlauge*) suds

Lau'gensalz *n* alkali

lau'gensalzig *adj* alkaline

Laune ['laʊnə] *f* (-;-n) mood, humor; (*Grille*) whim

lau'nenhaft *adj* capricious

launig ['laʊnɪç] *adj* humorous, witty

lau'nisch *adj* moody

Laus [laʊs] *f* (-;̈e) louse

Laus'bub m rascal

lauschen ['lauʃən] intr listen; eavesdrop; **l. auf** (acc) listen to

Lau'scher –in §6 mf eavesdropper

lauschig ['lauʃɪç] adj cosy, peaceful

Lau'sebengel m, **Lau'sejunge** m, **Lau'sekerl** m (coll) rascal, brat

lausen ['lauzən] tr pick lice from; **ich denke, mich laust der Affe** (coll) I couldn't believe my eyes

lausig ['lauzɪç] adj lousy

laut [laut] adj loud; (lärmend) noisy; **l. werden** become public; **l. werden lassen** divulge || prep (genit & dat) according to; (com) as per; **l. Bericht** according to the report || **Laut** m (–[e]s;–e) sound

Laute ['lautə] f (–;–n) lute

lauten ['lautən] intr sound; (Worte) read, go, say; **das Urteil lautet auf Tod** the sentence is death

läuten ['lɔɪtən] tr & intr ring, toll || impers—**es läutet** the bell is ringing || **Läuten** n (–s;) toll

lauter ['lautər] adj pure; (aufrecht) sincere || invar adj (nichts als) nothing but

Lau'terkeit f (–;) purity; sincerity

läutern ['lɔɪtərn] tr purify; (Metall, Zucker) refine; (veredeln) ennoble

Laut'gesetz n phonetic law

Laut'lehre f phonetics, phonology

laut'lich adj phonetic

laut'los adj soundless

Laut'malerei f onomatopoeia

Laut'schrift f phonetic spelling

Laut'sprecher m loudspeaker

Laut'sprecheranlage f public address system

Laut'sprecherwagen m sound truck

Laut'stärke f volume

Laut'stärkeregler m volume control

Laut'system n phonetic system

Laut'zeichen n phonetic symbol

lau'warm adj lukewarm

Lava ['lava] f (–;) lava

Lavendel [la'vɛndəl] m (–s;) (bot) lavender

laven'delfarben adj lavender

lavieren [la'virən] intr (fig) maneuver; (naut) tack

Lawine [la'vinə] f (–;–n) avalanche

lax [laks] adj lax

Lax'heit f (–;) laxity

Laxiermittel [la'ksɪrmɪtəl] n laxative

Layout ['le·aut] n (–s;–s) layout

Lazarett [latsa'rɛt] n (–[e]s;–e) (mil) hospital

Lebedame ['lebədamə] f woman of leisure

Lebehoch [lebə'hox] n (–s;–s) cheer; toast; **ein dreimaliges L.** three cheers

Lebemann ['lebəman] m playboy

leben ['lebən] tr & intr live || **Leben** n (–s;–) life; existence; **am L. bleiben** survive; **am L. erhalten** keep alive; **ins L. rufen** bring into being; **sein L. lang** all his life; **ums L. kommen** lose one's life

lebendig [le'bɛndɪç] adj living, alive; (lebhaft) lively; (Darstellung) vivid

Le'bensalter n age, period of life

Le'bensanschauung f outlook on life

Le'bensart f manners

Le'bensaufgabe f mission in life

Le'bensbaum m (bot) arbor vitae

Le'bensbedingungen pl living conditions

Le'bensbeschreibung f biography

Le'bensdauer f life span

Le'benserwartung f life expectancy

le'bensfähig adj viable

Le'bensfrage f vital question

Le'bensgefahr f mortal danger

le'bensgefährlich adj perilous

Le'bensgefährte m, **Le'bensgefährtin** f life companion, spouse

le'bensgroß adj life-size

Le'benshaltung f standard of living

Le'benshaltungskosten pl cost of living

Le'bensinteressen pl vital interests

Le'benskraft f vitality

Le'benskünstler m—**er ist ein L.** nothing can get him down

lebenslänglich ['lebənslɛŋlɪç] adj life

Le'benslauf m curriculum vitae

Le'bensmittel pl groceries

Le'bensmittelgeschäft n grocery store

Le'bensmittelkarte f food ration card

Le'bensmittellieferant m caterer

le'bensmüde adj weary of life

le'bensnotwendig adj vital, essential

Le'bensprozeß m vital function

Le'bensstandard m standard of living

Le'bensstellung f lifetime job; tenure

Le'bensstil m life style

Le'bensunterhalt m livelihood

le'bensuntüchtig adj impractical

Le'bensversicherung f life insurance

Le'benswandel m conduct; life

Le'bensweise f way of life

Le'bensweisheit f worldly wisdom

le'benswichtig adj vital, essential

Le'benszeichen n sign of life

Le'benszeit f lifetime; **auf L.** for life

Leber ['lebər] f (–;–n) liver; **frei von der L. weg reden** speak frankly

Le'berfleck m mole

Leberkäs ['lebərkes] m (–es;) meat loaf (made with liver)

Le'bertran m cod-liver oil

Lebewesen ['lebəvezən] n living being

Lebewohl [lebə'vol] n (–[e]s;–e) farewell

lebhaft ['lephaft] adj lively; full of life; (Farbe) bright; (Straße) busy; (Börse) brisk; (Interesse) keen

Lebkuchen ['lepkuxən] m gingerbread

leblos ['leplos] adj lifeless

Lebtag ['leptak] m—**mein L.** in all my life

Lebzeiten ['leptsaɪtən] pl—**zu meinen L.** in my lifetime

lechzen ['lɛçtsən] intr (nach) thirst (for)

leck [lɛk] adj leaky || **Leck** n (–[e]s;–e) leak; **ein L. bekommen** spring a leak

lecken ['lɛkən] tr lick || intr leak; (naut) have sprung a leak

lecker ['lɛkər] adj dainty; (köstlich) delicious

Leckerbissen (**Lek'kerbissen**) m delicacy, dainty

Leckerei [lɛkə'raɪ] f (–;–en) daintiness; sweets

leckerhaft (**lek'kerhaft**) adj dainty

Leckermaul (Lek'kermaul) *n*—ein L.
sein have a sweet tooth
Leder ['leder] *n* (-s;) leather
ledern ['ledərn] *adj* leather; (fig) dull,
boring
ledig ['ledıç] *adj* single; (*Kind*) illegitimate; l. (*genit*) free of; **lediger
Stand** single state; celibacy
le'diglich *adv* merely, only
leer [ler] *adj* empty, void; (fig) vain ||
Leere *f* (-;) emptiness, void; vacuum
|| *n*—**der Schlag ging ins L.** the blow
missed; **ins L. starren** stare into
space
leeren ['lerən] *tr* empty
Leer'gut *n* empties (*bottles, cases*)
Leer'lauf *m* (aut) idling, idle; (*Gang*)
(aut) neutral
leer'laufen §105 *intr* (SEIN) idle
leer'stehend *adj* unoccupied, vacant
Leer'taste *f* (typ) space bar
legal [le'gal] *adj* legal
legalisieren [legalı'zirən] *tr* legalize
Legat [le'gat] *m* (-en;-en) legate || *n*
(-[e]s;-e) legacy, bequest
legen ['legən] *tr* lay, put; **auf die Kette
l.** chain, tie up; **j-m ans Herz l.** recommend warmly to s.o.; **Nachdruck
l. auf** (*acc*) emphasize; **Wert l. auf**
(*acc*) attach importance to || *ref* lie
down; go to bed; (*Wind*) die down;
**die Krankheit hat sich ihm auf die
Lungen gelegt** his sickness affected
his lungs
legendär [legen'der] *adj* legendary
Legende [le'gendə] *f* (-;-n) legend
legieren [le'girən] *tr* alloy
Legie'rung *f* (-;-en) alloy
Legion [le'gjon] *f* (-;-en) legion
Legionär [legjo'ner] *m* (-s;-e) legionnaire, legionary
legislativ [legısla'tif] *adj* legislative ||
Legislative [legısla'tivə] *f* (-;-n)
legislature
Legis·lator [legıs'latər] *m* (-s;-latoren
[la'torən]) legislator
Legislatur [legısla'tur] *f* (-;-en) legis-
ature
legitim [legı'tim] *adj* legitimate
Legitimation [legıtıma'tsjon] *f* (-;-en)
proof of identity
legitimieren [legıtı'mirən] *tr* legitimize;
(*berechtigen*) authorize || *ref* prove
one's identity
Lehen ['le·ən] *n* (-s;-) (hist) fief
Le'hensherr *m* liege lord
Le'hens·mann *m* (-[e]s;-leute) vassal
Lehm [lem] *m* (-[e]s;-e) clay, loam
lehmig ['lemıç] *adj* clayey, loamy
Lehne ['lenə] *f* (-;-n) support; (*e-s
Stuhls*) arm, back; (*Abhang*) slope
lehnen ['lenən] *tr, ref & intr* lean
Lehnsessel ['lenzesəl] *m*, **Lehnstuhl**
['len∫tul] *m* armchair, easy chair
Lehn'wort ['lenvort] *n* (-[e]s;ːer)
loan word
Lehramt ['leramt] *n* teaching profes-
sion; professorship
Lehranstalt ['leran∫talt] *f* educational
institution
Lehrbrief ['lerbrif] *m* apprentice's di-
ploma
Lehrbube ['lerbubə] *m* apprentice

Lehrbuch ['lerbux] *n* textbook
Lehrbursche ['lerbur∫ə] *m* apprentice
Lehre ['lerə] *f* (-;-n) doctrine, teaching; (*Wissenschaft*) science; (*Theorie*) theory; (*Unterweisung*) instruction; (*Warnung*) lesson; (*e-r Fabel*)
moral; (*Richtschnur*) rule, precept;
(*e-s Lehrlings*) apprenticeship; (tech)
gauge; **in der L. sein** be serving
one's apprenticeship
lehren ['lerən] *tr* teach, instruct
Lehrer –in ['lerər(ın)] §6 *mf* teacher
Leh'rerbildungsanstalt *f* teacher's college
Leh'rerkollegium *n* teaching staff
Lehrfach ['lerfax] *n* subject
Lehrfilm ['lerfılm] *m* educational film
Lehrgang ['lergaŋ] *m* (educ) course
Lehrgedicht ['lergədıçt] *n* didactic
poem
Lehrgegenstand ['lergegən/tant] *m*
(educ) subject
Lehrgeld ['lergelt] *n*—L. **zahlen** (fig)
learn the hard way
lehrhaft ['lerhaft] *adj* didactic
Lehrjunge ['lerjuŋə] *m* apprentice
Lehrkörper ['lerkørpər] *m* teaching
staff; faculty (*of a university*)
Lehrling ['lerlıŋ] *m* (-s;-e) apprentice
Lehrmädchen ['lermetçən] *n* girl ap-
prentice
Lehrmeister ['lermaıstər] *m* master,
teacher, instructor
Lehrmittel ['lermıtəl] *n* teaching aid
Lehrplan ['lerplan] *m* curriculum
lehrreich ['lerraıç] *adj* instructive
Lehrsaal ['lerzal] *m* lecture hall
Lehrsatz ['lerzats] *m* (eccl) dogma;
(math) theorem
Lehrspruch ['ler∫prux] *m* maxim
Lehrstelle ['ler∫telə] *f* position as an
apprentice
Lehrstoff ['ler∫tof] *m* subject matter
Lehrstuhl ['ler∫tul] *m* (educ) chair
Lehrstunde ['ler∫tundə] *f* lesson
Lehrzeit ['lertsaıt] *f* apprenticeship
Leib [laıp] *m* (-[e]s;-er) body;
(*Bauch*) belly, abdomen; (*Taille*)
waist; (*Mutterleib*) womb; **am gan-
zen L. zittern** tremble all over; **bleib
mir nur damit vom Leibe!** (coll)
don't bother me with that: **e-n harten
L. haben** be constipated; **gesegneten
Leibes** with child; **L. und Leben** life
and limb; **mit L. und Seele** through
and through; **sich** [*dat*] **j-n vom
Leibe halten** keep s.o. at arm's
length; **zu Leibe gehen** (*dat*) tackle
(*s.th.*), attack (*s.o.*)
Leib'arzt *m* personal physician
Leib'binde *f* sash
Leibchen ['laıpçən] *n* (-s;-) bodice;
vest
leib'eigen *adj* in bondage |; **Leibeigene**
§5 *mf* serf
Leib'eigenschaft *f* (-;) serfdom, bond-
age
Lei'besbeschaffenheit *f* (-;-en) con-
stitution
Lei'beserbe *m* (-n;-n) offspring
Lei'beserziehung *f* physical education
Lei'besfrucht *f* fetus
Lei'beskräfte *pl*—aus **Leibeskräften**

schreien scream at the top of one's lungs
Lei'besübungen pl physical education
Lei'besvisitation f body search
Leib'garde f bodyguard
Leibgardist ['laɪpgardɪst] m (-en;-en) bodyguard
Leib'gericht n favorite dish
leibhaft(ig) ['laɪphaft(ɪç)] adj incarnate, real
leib'lich adj bodily, corporal; **leiblicher Vetter** first cousin; **sein leiblicher Sohn** his own son
Leib'rente f annuity for life
Leib'schmerzen pl, **Leib'schneiden** n abdominal pains
Leibstandarte ['laɪpʃtandartə] f (-;-n) (hist) SS bodyguard
Leib'wache f bodyguard
Leib'wäsche f underwear
Leiche ['laɪçə] f (-;-n) corpse, body; carcass; (dial) funeral
Leichenbegängnis ['laɪçənbəgɛŋnɪs] n (-ses;-se) funeral, interment
Leichenbeschauer ['laɪçənbəʃaʊ·ər] m (-s;-) coroner
Leichenbestatter ['laɪçənbəʃtatər] m (-s;-) undertaker
Lei'chenbittermiene f woe-begone look
Leichenfledderer ['laɪçənfledərər] m (-s;-) body stripper
Lei'chengift n ptomaine poison
lei'chenhaft adj corpse-like
Lei'chenhalle f mortuary
Lei'chenöffnung f autopsy
Lei'chenräuber m body snatcher
Lei'chenrede f eulogy
Lei'chenschau f post mortem
Lei'chenschauhaus m morgue
Lei'chenstarre f rigor mortis
Lei'chenträger m pallbearer
Lei'chentuch n shroud
Lei'chenverbrennung f cremation
Lei'chenwagen m hearse
Lei'chenzug m funeral cortege
Leichnam ['laɪçnam] m (-[e]s;-e) corpse
leicht [laɪçt] adj light; (nicht schwierig) easy; (gering) slight; **leichten Herzens** light-heartedly
Leicht'atletik f track and field
Leicht'bauweise f lightweight construction
Leicht'benzin n cleaning fluid
leichtbeschwingt ['laɪçtbəʃvɪŋt] adj gay
leicht'blütig adj light-hearted
leicht'entzündlich adj highly flammable
Leichter ['laɪçtər] m (-s;-) (naut) lighter
leicht'fertig adj frivolous, flippant; careless
leicht'flüchtig adj highly volatile
leicht'flüssig adj thin
Leicht'gewicht n lightweight division
Leichtgewichtler ['laɪçtgəvɪçtlər] m (-s;-) lightweight boxer
leicht'gläubig adj gullible
leicht'hin' adv lightly, casually
Leich'tigkeit f (-;) ease
leichtlebig ['laɪçtlebɪç] adj easygoing
Leicht'sinn m frivolity, irresponsibility;

(Sorglosigkeit) carelessness; (Unbedachtsamkeit) imprudence
leicht'sinnig adj frivolous, irresponsible
leicht'verdaulich adj easy to digest
leicht'verderblich adj perishable
leid [laɪt] adj—er tut mir l. I feel sorry for him; **es tut mir l., daß I am sorry that; es ist (or tut) mir l. um** I feel sorry for, I regret; **ich bin es l.** I'm fed up with it ‖ **Leid** n (-[e]s;) (Betrübnis) sorrow; (Schaden) harm; (Unrecht) wrong; **j-m ein L. antun** harm s.o.
Leideform ['laɪdəfɔrm] f (gram) passive voice
leiden ['laɪdən] §106 tr suffer; (ertragen) stand ‖ intr (an dat) suffer (from) ‖ **Leiden** n (-s;-) suffering; (Krankheit) ailment
Lei'denschaft f (-;-en) passion
lei'denschaftlich adj passionate
lei'denschaftslos adj dispassionate
Lei'densgefährte m, **Lei'densgefährtin** f fellow sufferer
Lei'densgeschichte f tale of woe; (relig) Passion
Lei'densweg m way of the cross
leider ['laɪdər] adv unfortunately
leiderfüllt ['laɪtərfʏlt] adj sorrowful
leidig ['laɪdɪç] adj tiresome
leidlich ['laɪtlɪç] adv tolerable; (halbwegs gut) passable ‖ adv so-so
leidtragend ['laɪttragənt] adj in mourning ‖ **Leidtragende** §5 mf mourner; **er ist der L. dabei** he is the one that suffers for it
Leid'wesen n—**zu meinem L.** to my regret
Leier ['laɪ·ər] f (-;-n) (mus) lyre
Lei'erkasten m hand organ, hurdygurdy
Lei'ermann m (-[e]s;⸚er) organ grinder
leiern ['laɪ·ərn] tr (winden) crank; (Gebete, Verse) drone ‖ intr drone
Leih- [laɪ] comb.fm. loan, rental
Leih'amt n, **Leih'anstalt** f loan office
Leih'bibliothek f rental library
leihen ['laɪ·ən] tr lend, loan out; (entleihen) (von) borrow (from)
Leih'gebühr f rental fee
Leih'haus n pawnshop
Leim [laɪm] m (-[e]s;-e) glue; birdlime; **aus dem L. gehen** fall apart; **j-m auf den L. gehen** be taken in by s.o.
leimen ['laɪmən] tr glue; (betrügen) take in, fool
Leim'farbe f distemper
leimig ['laɪmɪç] adj gluey
Lein [laɪn] m (-[e]s;-e) flax
Leine ['laɪnə] f (-;-n) line, cord; (Hunde-) leash
Leinen ['laɪnən] n (-s;-) linen
Lei'neneinband m (-[e]s;⸚e) (bb) cloth binding
Lei'nenschuh m sneaker, canvas shoe
Lei'nenzeug n linen fabric
Lein'öl n linseed oil
Lein'tuch n sheet
Lein'wand f linen cloth; canvas; (cin) screen
leise ['laɪzə] adj soft, low; (sanft) gentle; (gering) faint; (Schlaf) light

lei′sestellen tr (rad) turn down
Lei′setreter m (-s;-) pussyfoot
Leiste [′laɪstə] f (-;-n) (Rand) border; (anat) groin; (carp) molding
leisten [′laɪstən] tr do, perform, accomplish; (Dienst) render; (Eid) take; (Abbitte, Hilfe, Widerstand) offer; **Bürgschaft l. für** put up bail for; **Folge l.** (dat), **Gehorsam l.** (dat) obey; **Genüge l.** (dat) satisfy; **j-m Gesellschaft l.** keep s.o. company; **sich** [dat] **etw l. können** be able to afford s.th. || **Leisten** m (-s;-) last; **alles über e-n L. schlagen** (fig) be undiscriminating
Lei′stenbruch m hernia, rupture
Lei′stung f (-;-en) performance; efficiency; ability; feat, achievement; (Ergebnis) result; (Erzeugung) production; (Abgabe, Ausstoß) output; (Beitrag) contribution; (Dienstleistungen) services rendered; (elec) power, wattage; (indust) output, production; (insur) benefits; (mach) capacity
Lei′stungsanreiz m incentive
lei′stungsfähig adj (Person) efficient; (Motor) powerful; (Fabrik) productive; (phys) efficient
Lei′stungsfähigkeit f efficiency; proficiency; (e-s Autos) performance; (e-s Motors) power; (mach) output
lei′stungsgerecht adj based on merit
Lei′stungsgrenze f peak of performance
Leis′tungslohn m pay based on performance
Lei′stungszulage f bonus
Leit- [laɪt] comb.fm. leading, dominant, guiding
Leit′artikel m editorial
Leit′bild n (good) example, ideal
leiten [′laɪtən] tr lead, guide; (Verkehr) route; (Betrieb) direct, run; (Versammlung) preside over; (arti) direct; (elec, mus, phys) conduct
Lei′ter m (-s;-) leader; director; (educ) principal; (elec, mus) conductor || f (-;-n) ladder
Lei′terin f (-;-nen) leader; director
Leit′faden m manual, guide
Leit′fähigkeit f conductivity
Leit′gedanke m main idea, main theme
Leit′hammel m (fig) boss, leader
Leit′motiv n keynote; (mus) leitmotiv
Leit′satz m basic point
Leit′spruch m motto
Leit′stelle f head office
Leit′stern m polestar, lodestar
Lei′tung f (-;-en) direction, guidance; (Beaufsichtigung) management; (Rohr) pipeline; (für Gas, Wasser) main; (elec) lead; (phys) conduction; (telp) line; **e-e lange L. haben** be rather dense; **L. besetzt!** line is busy!
Lei′tungsdraht m (elec) lead
Lei′tungsmast m telephone pole
Lei′tungsnetz n (elec) power lines
Lei′tungsrohr n pipe, main
Lei′tungsvermögen n conductivity
Lei′tungswasser n tap water
Leit′werk n (aer) tail assembly
Leit′zahl f code number

Lektion [lɛk′tsjon] f (-;-en) lesson; (fig) lecture, rebuke
Lek·tor [′lɛktɔr] m (-s;-toren [′torən]) lecturer; (e-s Verlags) reader
Lektüre [lɛk′tyrə] f (-;) reading matter, literature
Lende [′lɛndə] f (-;-n) loin; (Hüfte) hip
Len′denbraten m roast loin, sirloin
len′denlahm adj stiff; (Ausrede) lame
Len′denschurz m loincloth
Len′denstück n tenderloin, sirloin
lenkbar [′lɛŋkbar] adj manageable; steerable, maneuverable; **lenkbares Luftschiff** dirigible
lenken [′lɛŋkən] tr guide, control; (Wagen) drive; (wenden) turn; (steuern) steer; **Aufmerksamkeit l. auf** (acc) call attention to
Len′ker –in §6 mf ruler; (aut) driver
Lenkrad [′lɛŋkrat] n steering wheel
Lenksäule [′lɛŋkzɔɪlə] f steering column
Lenkstange [′lɛŋkʃtaŋə] f handlebar; (aut) connecting rod
Len′kung f (-;-en) guidance, control; (aut) steering mechanism
Lenz [lɛnts] m (-es;-e) (fig) prime of life; (poet) spring
Lenz′pumpe f bilge pump
Lepra [′lepra] f (-;) leprosy
Lerche [′lɛrçə] f (-;-n) (orn) lark
lernbegierig [′lɛrnbəgiriç] adj eager to learn, studious
lernen [′lɛrnən] tr & intr learn; study
Lesart [′lezart] f version
lesbar [′lezbar] adj legible; readable
Lesbierin [′lɛsbɪ·ərɪn] f (-;-nen) lesbian
lesbisch [′lɛsbɪʃ] adj lesbian; **lesbische Liebe** lesbianism
Lese [′lezə] f (-;-n) gathering, picking; (Wein–) vintage
Lese- [lezə] comb.fm. reading; lecture
Le′sebrille f reading glasses
Le′sebuch n reader
Le′sehalle f reading room
lesen [′lezən] §107 tr read; gather; (Messe) say || intr read; lecture; **l. über** (acc) lecture on
le′senswert adj worth reading
Le′seprobe f specimen from a book; (theat) reading rehearsal
Le′ser –in §6 mf reader; picker
Le′seratte f (coll) bookworm
le′serlich adj legible
Le′serzuschrift f letter to the editor
Le′sestoff m reading matter
Le′sezeichen n bookmark
Le′sung f (-;-en) reading
Lette [′lɛtə] m (-n;-n), **Lettin** [′lɛtɪn] f (-;-nen) Latvian
lettisch [′lɛtɪʃ] adj Latvian
Lettland [′lɛtlant] n (-[e]s;) Latvia
letzte [′lɛtstə] §9 adj last; (endgültig) final, ultimate; (neueste) latest; (Ausweg) last; **bis ins l.** to the last detail; **in den letzten Jahren** in recent years; **in der letzten Zeit** lately; **letzten Endes** in the final analysis || **Letzte** §5 pron last, last one; **am Letzten** on the last of the month; **sein Letztes hergeben** do one's ut-

most; **zu guter Letzt** finally, last but not least
letztens ['lɛtstəns] *adv* lately
letztere ['lɛtstərə] §5 *mfn* latter
letzthin [lɛtst'hɪn] *adv* lately
letztlich ['lɛtstlɪç] *adv* lately, recently; in the final analysis
letztwillig ['lɛtstvɪlɪç] *adj* testamentary
Leucht– [lɔɪçt] *comb.fm.* luminous; illuminating
Leucht'bombe *f* flare bomb
Leuchte ['lɔɪçtə] *f* (–;–n) light, lamp; lantern; (fig) luminary
leuchten ['lɔɪçtən] *intr* shine
leuch'tend *adj* shining, bright; luminous
Leuchter ['lɔɪçtər] *m* (–s;–) candlestick; chandelier
Leucht'farbe *f* luminous paint
Leucht'feuer *n* (aer) flare; (naut) beacon
Leucht'käfer *m* lightning bug
Leucht'körper *m* light bulb; light fixture
Leucht'kugel *n* tracer bullet; flare
Leucht'pistole *f* Very pistol
Leucht'rakete *f* (aer) flare
Leucht'reklame *f* neon sign
Leucht'röhre *f* fluorescent lamp
Leucht'spurgeschoß *n* tracer bullet
Leucht'turm *m* lighthouse
Leucht'zifferblatt *n* luminous dial
leugnen ['lɔɪgnən] *tr* deny; disclaim
Leukoplast [lɔɪkə'plast] *n* (–[e]s;–e) adhesive tape
Leumund ['lɔɪmʊnt] *m* (–[e]s;) reputation
Leu'mundszeugnis *n* character reference
Leute ['lɔɪtə] *pl* people, persons, men; (*Dienstleute*) servants
Leu'teschinder *m* oppressor; slave driver
Leutnant ['lɔɪtnant] *m* (–s;–s) lieutenant
Leut'priester *m* secular priest
leut'selig *adj* affable
Lexikograph [lɛksɪkə'graf] *m* (–en;–en) lexicographer
Lexikon ['lɛksɪkɔn] *n* (–s;–s) encyclopedia
Libanon ['libanɔn] *n* (–s;) Lebanon
Libelle [lɪ'bɛlə] *f* (–;–n) dragonfly; (carp) level
liberal [libe'ral] *adj* liberal
Liberalismus [lɪbera'lɪsmʊs] *m* (–s;) liberalism
Libyen ['liby·ən] *n* (–s;) Libya
licht [lɪçt] *adj* light, bright; (*durchsichtig*) clear || **Licht** *n* (–[e]s;–er) light; (*Kerze*) candle
licht'beständig *adj* non-fading
Licht'bild *n* photograph
Licht'bildervortrag *m* illustrated lecture
licht'blau *adj* light-blue
Licht'blick *m* (fig) bright spot
Licht'bogen *m* (elec) arc
Licht'bogenschweißung *f* arc welding
Licht'brechung *f* (–;–en) refraction of light
Licht'druck *m* phototype
licht'durchlässig *adj* translucent

licht'echt *adj* non-fading
licht'empfindlich *adj* sensitized; **l. machen** sensitize
Licht'empfindlichkeit *f* (phot) speed
lichten ['lɪçtən] *tr* clear; thin; (*Anker*) weigh
lichterloh ['lɪçtərlo] *adv* ablaze; **l. brennen** be ablaze
Licht'hof *m* (archit) light well, inner court; (phot) halo
Licht'kegel *m* beam of light
Licht'maschine *f* generator, dynamo
Licht'pause *f* blueprint
Licht'punkt *m* (fig) ray of hope
Licht'schacht *m* light well
Licht'schalter *m* light switch
licht'scheu *adj*—**lichtscheues Gesindel** shady characters
Licht'schirm *m* lamp shade
Licht'seite *f* (fig) bright side
Licht'spiele *pl*, **Licht'spielhaus** *n*, **Licht'spieltheater** *n* movie theater
licht'stark *adj* (*Objektiv*) high-powered; (phot) high-speed
Lich'tung *f* (–;–en) clearing
Lid [lit] *n* (–[e]s;–er) eyelid
Lid'schatten *m* eye shadow
lieb [lip] *adj* dear; (*nett*) nice; **der liebe Gott** the good Lord; **es ist mir l., daß** I am glad that; **seien Sie so l. und** please; **sich lieb Kind machen bei** ingratiate oneself with
lieb'äugeln *intr*—**l. mit** (& *fig*) flirt with
Liebchen ['lipçən] *n* (–s;–) darling
Liebe ['libə] *f* (–;) (zu) love (*for, of*)
liebedienerisch ['libədinərɪʃ] *adj* fawning
Liebelei [libə'laɪ] *f* (–;–en) flirtation
lieben ['libən] *tr* love, be fond of
lie'bend *adj* loving || *adv*—**l. gern** gladly || **Liebende** §5 *mf* lover
lie'benswert *adj* lovable
lie'benswürdig *adj* lovable; charming; **das ist sehr l. von Ihnen** that's very kind of you
lieber ['libər] *adv* rather, sooner; **l. haben** prefer
Liebes– [libəs] *comb.fm.* love, of love
Lie'besdienst *m* favor, good turn
Lie'beserlebnis *n* romance
Lie'besgabe *f* charitable gift
Lie'beshandel *m* love affair
Lie'besmahl *n* love feast
Lie'besmühe *f*—**verlorene L.** wasted effort
Lie'bespaar *n* couple (of lovers)
Lie'bespfand *n* token of love
Lie'bestrank *m* love potion
Lie'beswerben *n* advances
lie'bevoll *adj* loving, affectionate
Lieb'frauenkirche *f* Church of Our Lady
lieb'gewinnen §121 *tr* grow fond of
lieb'haben §89 *tr* love, be fond of
Liebhaber ['liphabər] *m* (–s;–) lover, beau; amateur; fan, buff; **erster L.** leading man
lieb'kosen *tr* caress, fondle
lieb'lich *adj* lovely, sweet; charming
Liebling ['liplɪŋ] *m* (–s;–e) darling; (*Haustier*) pet; (*Günstling*) favorite
Lieblings– *comb.fm.* favorite

Lieb'lingsgedanke *m* pet idea
Lieb'lingswunsch *m* dearest wish
lieb'los *adj* unkind
lieb'reich *adj* kind, affectionate
Lieb'reiz *m* charm, attractiveness
lieb'reizend *adj* charming
Lieb'schaft *f* (-;-en) love affair
liebste ['lipstə] §9 *adj* favorite; **am liebsten trinke ich Wein** I like wine best of all
Lied [lit] *n* (-[e]s;-er) song; **er weiß ein L. davon zu singen** he can tell you all about it; **geistliches L.** hymn
liederlich ['lidərlɪç] *adj* dissolute; (*unordentlich*) disorderly
lief [lif] *pret* of **laufen**
Lieferant –in [lifə'rant(ɪn)] §7 *mf* supplier; (*Verteiler*) distributor; (*von Lebensmitteln*) caterer
Lieferauto ['lifərauto] *n* delivery truck
lieferbar ['lifərbar] *adj* available, deliverable
Liefergebühr ['lifərgə'byr] *f* delivery charge
liefern ['lifərn] *tr* deliver; (*beschaffen*) supply, furnish; (*Ertrag*) yield; **ich bin geliefert** (coll) I'm done for
Lieferschein ['lifərʃain] *m* delivery receipt
Lie'ferung *f* (-;-en) delivery, shipment; supply; (*e-s Werkes*) installment, number; **zahlbar bei L.** cash on delivery
Lieferwagen ['lifərvagən] *m* delivery truck
Liege ['ligə] *f* (-;-n) couch
Lie'gekur *f* rest cure
liegen ['ligən] §108 *intr* lie, be situated; **gut auf der Straße l.** hug the road; **l. an** (*dat*) lie near; (fig) be due to; **wie die Sache jetzt liegt** as matters now stand || *impers*—**es liegt an ihm zu** (*inf*) it's up to him to (*inf*); **es liegt auf der Hand** it is obvious; **es liegt mir nichts daran** it doesn't matter to me; **es liegt mir (sehr viel) daran** it matters (a great deal) to me
lie'genbleiben §62 *intr* (SEIN) stay in bed; (*Waren*) remain unsold; (*stekkenbleiben*) have a breakdown; (*Arbeit*) be left undone
lie'genlassen §104 *tr* let lie; leave alone; (*Arbeit*) leave undone
Lie'genschaft *f* (-;-en) real estate
Lie'gestuhl *m* deck chair
Lie'gestütz *m* (gym) pushup
lieh [li] *pret* of **leihen**
ließ [lis] *pret* of **lassen**
Li·ga ['liga] *f* (-;-gen [gən)] league
Liguster [li'gustər] *m* (-s;-) privet
liieren [li'irən] *ref*—**sich l. mit** ally oneself with
Likör [li'kør] *m* (-s;-e) liqueur
lila ['lila] *adj* lilac
Lilie ['liljə] *f* (-;-n) lily
Limonade [limo'nadə] *f* (-;-n) soft drink, soda
lind [lɪnt] *adj* mild, gentle
Linde ['lɪndə] *f* (-;-n) (bot) linden
lindern ['lɪndərn] *tr* alleviate; (*Übel*) mitigate; (*mildern*) soften

Lindwurm ['lɪntvʊrm] *m* dragon
Lineal [line'al] *n* (-s;-e) ruler
Linguist –in [lɪŋgu'ist(ɪn)] §7 *mf* linguist
Linie ['linjə] *f* (-;-n) line; **auf gleicher L. mit** on a level with; **in erster L.** in the first place
Li'nienpapier *n* lined paper
Li'nienrichter *m* (sport) linesman
Li'nienschiff *n* ship of the line
li'nientreu *adj*—**l. sein** follow the party line
linieren [li'nirən] *tr* line, rule
linke ['lɪŋkə] §9 *adj* left; (*Seite*) wrong, reverse || §5 **Linke** *m* (box) left || §5 *f* left side; left hand; **die L.** (pol) the left
linkisch ['lɪŋkɪʃ] *adj* clumsy, awkward
links [lɪŋks] *adv* left; to the left; on the left; (*verkehrt*) inside out; **l. liegenlassen** bypass, ignore; **links um!** left, face!
links'drehend *adj* counterclockwise
linksgängig ['lɪŋksgɛŋɪç] *adj* counterclockwise
Linkshänder ['lɪŋkshɛndər] *m* (-s;-) left-hander
links'läufig *adj* counterclockwise
links'stehend *adj* (pol) leftist
Linnen ['lɪnən] *n* (-s;) linen
Linse ['lɪnzə] *f* (-;-n) (bot) lentil; (opt) lens
Lippe ['lɪpə] *f* (-;-n) lip; **e-e L. riskieren** (fig) speak out of turn
Lip'penbekenntnis *n* lip service
Lip'penlaut *m* labial
Lip'penstift *m* lipstick
liquid [li'kvit] *adj* (*Geldmittel*) liquid; (*Gesellschaft*) solvent
Liquidation [likvida'tsjon] *f* (-;-en) liquidation; (*Kostenrechnung*) bill
liquidieren [likvi'dirən] *tr* liquidate; (*Geschäft*) wind up; (*Honorar*) charge
lispeln ['lɪspəln] *tr & intr* lisp; (*flüstern*) whisper
Lissabon [lɪsa'bɔn] *n* (-s;) Lisbon
List [lɪst] *f* (-;-en) cunning; trick
Liste ['lɪstə] *f* (-;-n) list; **schwarze L.** blacklist
Li'stenwahl *f* block voting
listig ['lɪstɪç] *adj* cunning, sly
Litanei [lita'nai] *f* (-;-en) litany
Litauen ['litau·ən] *n* (-s;) Lithuania
litauisch ['litau·iʃ] *adj* Lithuanian
Liter ['litər] *m & n* (-s;-) liter
literarisch [litə'rariʃ] *adj* literary
Literatur [litera'tur] *f* (-;-en) literature
Litfaßsäule ['lɪtfaszɔilə] *f* advertising pillar
Liturgie [litur'gi] *f* (-;-gien ['gi·ən]) liturgy
Litze ['lɪtsə] *f* (-;-n) cord; (elec) strand
Li·vree [li'vre] *f* (-;-vreen ['vre·ən]) uniform, livery
Lizenz [li'tsents] *f* (-;-en) license
Lob [lop] *n* (-[e]s;) praise
loben ['lobən] §109 *tr* praise
lo'benswert *adj* praiseworthy
Lobhudelei [lophudə'lai] *f* (-;-en) flattery

lob'hudeln *tr* heap praise on
löblich ['løplɪç] *adj* commendable
lob'preisen *tr* extol, praise
Lob'rede *f* panegyric
Loch [lɔx] *n* (-es;̈er) hole
Loch'bohrer *m* auger
lochen ['lɔxən] *tr* punch, perforate
Locher ['lɔxər] *m* (-s;-) punch
löcherig ['lœçərɪç] *adj* full of holes
Loch'karte *f* punch card
Lo'chung *f* (-;-en) perforation
Locke ['lɔkə] *f* (-;-n) lock, curl
locken ['lɔkən] *tr* allure, entice; decoy; (*Hund*) whistle to
locker ['lɔkər] *adj* loose; (*nicht straff*)
  slack; spongy; (*moralisch*) loose
lockern ['lɔkərn] *tr* loosen
lockig ['lɔkɪç] *adj* curly, curled
Lock'mittel *n*, **Lock'speise** *f* (& fig)
  bait
Lockspitzel ['lɔkʃpɪtsəl] *m* stoolpigeon
Lo'ckung *f* (-;-en) allurement
Lock'vogel *m* (& fig) decoy
Loden ['lodən] *m* (-s;-) coarse woolen
  cloth
lodern ['lodərn] *intr* blaze; (fig) glow
Löffel ['lœfəl] *m* (-s;-) spoon; (culin)
  spoonful; (coll & hunt) ear; **über
  den L. balbieren** hoodwink
Löf'felbagger *m* power shovel
löffeln ['lœfəln] *tr* spoon out
log [lok] *pret* of **lügen**
Logbuch ['lɔkbux] *n* logbook
Loge ['loʒə] *f* (-;-n) (*der Freimau-
  rer*) lodge; (theat) box
Lo'genbruder *m* freemason
Logierbesuch [lɔ'ʒirbəzux] *m* house-
  guest(s)
logieren [lɔ'ʒirən] *intr* (**bei**) stay (*with*)
Logik ['logɪk] *f* (-;) logic
Logis [lɔ'ʒi] *invar n* lodgings
logisch ['logɪʃ] *adj* logical
Lohe ['lo·ə] *f* (-;-n) blaze, flame
Lohgerber ['logerbər] *m* (-s;-) tanner
Lohn [lon] *m* (-[e]s;̈e) pay, wages;
  (fig) reward
Lohn'abbau *m* wage cut
lohnen ['lonən] *tr* compensate, reward;
  (*Arbeiter*) pay; **j-m etw l.** reward
  s.o. for s.th. || *ref* pay, be worth-
  while
löhnen ['lønən] *tr* pay, pay wages to
Lohn'erhöhung *f* raise, wage increase
Lohn'gefälle *n* wage differential
Lohn'herr *m* employer
lohn'intensiv *adj* with high labor costs
Lohn'liste *f* payroll
Lohn'satz *m* pay rate
Lohn'stopp *m* wage freeze
Lohn'tag *m* payday
Lohn'tüte *f* pay envelope
Löh'nung *f* (-;-en) payment
lokal [lɔ'kal] *adj* local || **Lokal** *n*
  (-[e]s;-e) locality, premises; (*Wirts-
  haus*) restaurant, pub, inn
lokalisieren [lɔkalɪ'zirən] *tr* localize
Lokalität [lɔkalɪ'tet] *f* (-;-en) locality
Lokomotive [lɔkɔmo'tivə] *f* (-;-n) lo-
  comotive
Lokomotiv'führer *m* (rr) engineer
Lokus ['lokus] *m* (-;-se) (coll) john
Lorbeer ['lɔrbər] *m* (-s;-en) laurel

los [los] *adj* loose; **es ist etw los** there
  is s.th. going on; **es ist nichts los**
  there is nothing going on; **etw los
  haben** have s.th. on the ball; **j-n**
  (or **etw**) **los sein** be rid of s.o. (or
  s.th.); **los!** go on!, scram!; (*sprich!*)
  fire away!; (*mach schnell!*) let's go!;
  (sport) play ball!; **mit ihm ist nicht
  viel los** he's no great shakes; **was
  ist los?** what's the matter? || **Los** *n*
  (-[e]s;-e) lot; (*Lotterie-*) ticket;
  (*Anteil*) lot, portion; (*Schicksal*)
  fate; **das Große Los** first prize; **das
  Los ziehen** draw lots; **die Lose sind
  gefallen** the die is cast
los- *comb.fm.* un-, e.g., **losmachen**
  undo
los'arbeiten *tr* extricate || *ref* get
  loose, extricate oneself || *intr* (**auf**
  acc) work away (*at*)
lösbar ['løsbar] *adj* solvable
los'binden §59 *tr* loosen, untie
los'brechen §64 *tr* break off || *intr*
  (SEIN) break loose
Löschblatt ['lœʃblat] *n* blotter
Löscheimer ['lœʃaɪmər] *m* fire bucket
löschen ['lœʃən] *tr* put out; (*Durst*)
  quench; (*Schuld*) cancel; (*Schrift*)
  blot; (*Bandaufnahme*) erase; (*Firma*)
  liquidate; (*Hypotek*) pay off; (naut)
  unload
Lö'scher *m* (-s;-) blotter; (*Feuer-*)
  fire extinguisher
Löschgerät ['lœʃgəret] *n* fire extinguisher
Löschmannschaft ['lœʃmanʃaft] *f* fire
  brigade
Löschpapier ['lœʃpapir] *n* blotting
  paper
Lö'schung *f* (-;-en) extinction; (*Tilgung*) cancellation; (naut) unloading
los'drehen *tr* unscrew, twist off
los'drücken *tr* fire || *intr* pull the
  trigger
lose ['lozə] §9 *adj* loose
Lösegeld ['løzəgelt] *n* ransom
loseisen ['losaɪzən] *tr*—**Geld l. von**
  wangle money out of; **j-n l. aus** get
  s.o. out of; **j-n l. von** get s.o. away
  from || *ref* (**von**) worm one's way
  (*out of*)
losen ['lozən] *intr* draw lots
lösen ['løzən] *tr* loosen, untie; (*abtrennen*) sever; (*Bremse*) release;
  (*Fahrkarte*) buy; (*loskaufen*) ransom;
  (*lossprechen*) absolve; (*Rätsel*) solve;
  (*Schuß*) fire; (*Verlobung*) break off
  || *ref* come loose, come undone; dis-
  solve; (*sich befreien*) free oneself
los'fahren §71 *intr* (SEIN) drive off; **l.
  auf** (*acc*) head for; rush at; attack
  (verbally)
los'gehen §82 *intr* (SEIN) (coll) begin;
  (*Gewehr*) go off; (*sich lösen*) come
  loose; **auf j-n l.** attack s.o.
los'haken *tr* unhook
los'kaufen *tr* ransom
los'ketten *tr* unchain
los'kommen §99 *intr* (SEIN) come loose,
  come off; **ich komme nicht davon
  los** I can't get over it; **l. von** get
  away from; get rid of
los'lachen *intr* burst out laughing

los′lassen §104 *tr* let go; release; **den Hund l. auf** (*acc*) sic the dog on
los′legen *intr* (coll) start up, let fly; (*reden*) (coll) open up; **leg los!** (*coll*) fire away!
löslich [ˈløslɪç] *adj* soluble
los′lösen *tr* detach
los′machen *tr* undo, untie; (*freimachen*) free ‖ *ref* disengage onself
los′platzen *intr* (SEIN) burst out laughing; **l. mit** blurt out
los′reißen §53 *tr* & *ref* break loose
los′sagen *ref*—**sich l. von** renounce
los′schlagen §132 *tr* knock off; (*verkaufen*) dispose of, sell cheaply ‖ *intr* open the attack; **l. auf** (*acc*) let fly at
los′schnallen *tr* unbuckle
los′schrauben *tr* unscrew
los′sprechen §64 *tr* absolve
los′steuern *intr*—**l. auf** (*acc*) head for
Lo′sung *f* (–;–en) (*Kot*) dung; (mil) password; (pol) slogan
Lö′sung *f* (–;–en) solution
Lö′sungsmittel *n* solvent; thinner
los′werden §159 *tr* (SEIN) get rid of
los′ziehen §163 *intr* (SEIN) set out, march away; **l. auf** (*acc*) talk about, run down
Lot [lot] *n* (–[e]s;–e) plummet; plumb line; (*Lötmetall*) solder; (geom) perpendicular; **im Lot** perpendicular; (fig) in order; **ins Lot bringen** (fig) set right
Löteisen [ˈløtaɪzən] *n* soldering iron
loten [ˈlotən] *tr* (naut) plumb ‖ *intr* (naut) take soundings
löten [ˈløtən] *tr* solder
Lötkolben [ˈløtkɔlbən] *m* soldering iron
Lötlampe [ˈløtlampə] *f* blowtorch
Lötmetall [ˈløtmɛtal] *n* solder
lot′recht *adj* perpendicular
Lotse [ˈlotsə] *m* (–n;–n) (aer) air traffic controller; (naut) pilot
lotsen [ˈlotsən] *tr* (*Flugzeuge*) guide in; (naut) pilot
Lotte·rie [lɔtəˈri] *f* (–;–rien [ˈri·ən]) lottery, sweepstakes
Lotterie′los *n* lottery ticket
lotterig [ˈlɔtərɪç] *adj* sloppy
Lotterleben [ˈlɔtərlebən] *n* dissolute life
Lotto [ˈlɔto] n (–s;–s) state-owned numbers game
Löwe [ˈløvə] *m* (–n;–n) lion
Lö′wenanteil *m* lion's share
Lö′wenbändiger –in §6 *mf* lion tamer
Lö′wengrube *f* lion's den
Lö′wenmaul *n* (bot) snapdragon
Lö′wenzahn *m* (bot) dandelion
Löwin [ˈløvɪn] *f* (–;–nen) lioness
loyal [lɔ·aˈjal] *adj* loyal
Luchs [luks] *m* (–es;–e) lynx
Lücke [ˈlʏkə] *f* (–;–n) gap, hole; (*Mangel*) deficiency; (*im Gesetz*) loophole; (*Zwischenraum*) interval; **auf L. stehend** staggered
Lückenbüßer [ˈlʏkənbysər] *m* (–s;–) stop-gap
lückenhaft (lük′kenhaft) *adj* defective, fragmentary
Luder [ˈludər] *n* (–s;–) carrion; (coll)

cad; (*Weibsbild*) slut; **das arme L.!** the poor thing!; **dummes L.!** fathead!
Lu′derleben *n* dissolute life
ludern [ˈludərn] *intr* lead a dissolute life
Luft [luft] *f* (–;–̈e) air; (*Atem*) breath; (*Brise*) breeze; **die L. ist rein** the coast is clear; **es ist dicke L.** there is trouble brewing; **es liegt etw in der L.** (fig) there's s.th. in the air; **frische L. schöpfen** get a breath of fresh air; **in die L. fliegen** be blown up; **in die L. gehen** blow one's top; **in die L. sprengen** blow up; **j–n an die L. setzen** give s.o. the air; **nach L. schnappen** gasp for breath; **seinem Zorn L. machen** give vent to one's anger; **tief L. holen** take a deep breath
Luft′alarm *m* air-raid alarm
Luft′angriff *m* air raid
Luft′ansicht *f* aerial view
Luft′aufklärung *f* air reconnaissance
Luft′bild *n* aerial photograph
Luft′bremse *f* air brake
Luft′brücke *f* airlift
Lüftchen [ˈlʏftçən] *n* (–s;–) gentle breeze
luft′dicht′ *adj* airtight
Luft′druck *m* atmospheric pressure; (*e–r Explosion*) blast; (aut) air pressure
Luft′druckbremse *f* air brake
Luft′druckmesser *m* barometer
Luft′druckprüfer *m* tire gauge
Luft′düse *f* air nozzle, air jet
lüften [ˈlʏftən] *tr* air, ventilate; **den Hut l.** tip one's hat
Luft′fahrt *f* aviation
Luft′fahrzeug *n* aircraft
Luft′flotte *f* air force
luft′förmig *adj* gaseous
Luft′hafen *m* airport
Luft′heizung *f* hot-air heating
Luft′herrschaft *f* air supremacy
Luft′hülle *f* atmosphere
luftig [ˈluftɪç] *adj* airy; (*windig*) windy; (*Person*) flighty; (*Kleidung*) loosely woven, light
Luftikus [ˈluftɪkus] *m* (–;–se) light-headed person
Luft′klappe *f* air valve
luft′krank *adj* airsick
Luft′kurort *m* mountain resort
Luft′landetruppen *pl* airborne troops
luft′leer *adj* vacuous; **luftleerer Raum** vacuum
Luft′linie *f* beeline; **fünfzig Kilometer L.** 50 kilometers as the crow flies
Luft′loch *n* vent; (aer) air pocket
Luft′parade *f* flyover
Luft′post *f* airmail
Luft′raum *m* atmosphere; air space
Luft′reifen *m* tire
Luft′reklame *f* sky writing
Luft′röhre *f* (anat) windpipe
Luft′schiff *n* airship
Luft′schiffahrt *f* aviation
Luft′schloß *n* castle in the air
Luft′schutz *m* air-raid protection
Luft′schutzkeller *m* air-raid shelter
Luft′schutzwart *m* air-raid warden
Luft′spiegelung *f* mirage

Luft'sprung m caper
Luft'streitkräfte pl air force
Luft'strom m air current
Luft'strudel m (aer) wash
Luft'stützpunkt m air base
luft'tüchtig adj air-worthy
Lüf'tung f (-;) airing, ventilation
Luft'veränderung f change of climate
Luft'verkehrsgesellschaft f, Luft'ver-
 kehrslinie f airline
Luft'vermessung f aerial survey
Luft'verpestung f (-;), Luft'ver-
 schmutzung f (-;), Luft'verunreini-
 gung f (-;) air pollution
Luft'waffe f air force
Luft'warnung f air-raid warning
Luft'weg m air route; auf dem Luft-
 wege by air
Luft'widerstand m (phys) air resistance
Luft'zug m draft
Lug [luk] m (-[e]s;) lie; Lug und Trug
 pack of lies
Lüge ['lygə] f (-;-n) lie; fromme L.
 white lie; j-n Lügen strafen prove
 s.o. a liar
lugen ['lugən] intr peep
lügen ['lygən] §111 tr—das Blaue vom
 Himmel herunter l. lie like mad ||
 intr lie, tell a lie
Lügendetek·tor ['lygəndetektɔr] m (-s;
 -toren ['torən]) lie detector
Lü'gengeschichte f cock-and-bull story
Lü'gengespinst n, Lü'gengewebe n tissue of lies
lü'genhaft adj (Person) dishonest, ly-
 ing; (Nachricht) untrue
Lügner –in ['lygnər(ın)] §6 mf liar
lügnerisch ['lygnərɪʃ] adj dishonest
Luke ['lukə] f (-;-n) (am Dach) dormer window; (naut) hatch
Lümmel ['lʏməl] m (-s;-) lout
Lump [lump] m (-en;-en) scoundrel
lumpen ['lumpən] intr lead a wild life;
 sich nicht l. lassen (coll) be gener-
 ous || Lumpen m (-s;-) rag
Lum'pengeld n measly sum; für ein L.
 dirtcheap
Lum'pengesindel n mob, rabble
Lum'penhändler m ragman
Lum'penkerl m (coll) bum
Lum'penpack n rabble, riffraff
Lumperei [lumpə'raɪ] f (-;-en) shady
 deal; dirty trick; (Kleinigkeit) trifle
lumpig ['lumpɪç] adj ragged; shabby

Lunge ['luŋə] f (-;-n) lung
Lungen– comb.fm. pulmonary
Lun'genentzündung f pneumonia
Lun'genflügel m lung
lun'genkrank adj consumptive || Lun-
 genkranke §5 mf consumptive
Lun'genschwindsucht f tuberculosis
lungern ['luŋərn] intr (HABEN & SEIN)
 loiter about, lounge about
Lunte ['luntə] f (-;-n) fuse; L. riechen
 smell a rat
Lupe ['lupə] f (-;-n) magnifying glass;
 unter die L. nehmen examine closely
lüpfen ['lʏpfən] tr lift gently
Lust [lust] f (-;-̈e) pleasure; (Verlangen) desire; (Wollust) lust; L.
 haben zu (inf) feel like (ger); mit
 L. und Liebe with heart and soul
Lust'barkeit f (-;-en) amusement, entertainment
Lüster ['lʏstər] m (-s;-) luster
lüstern ['lʏstərn] adj (nach) desirous
 (of); lustful; (Bilder, Späße) lewd
Lü'sternheit f (-;) greediness; lustful-
 ness; lewdness
Lust'fahrt f pleasure ride
lustig ['lustɪç] adv gay, jolly; (belu-
 stigend) amusing; du bist vielleicht
 l.! you must be joking!; l. sein have
 a gay time; sich l. machen über
 (acc) poke fun at
Lüstling ['lʏstlɪŋ] m (-s;-e) lecher
lust'los adj listless; (Börse) inactive
Lustmolch ['lustmɔlç] m (-[e]s;-e)
 sex fiend
Lust'mord m sex murder
Lust'reise f pleasure trip
Lust'seuche f venereal disease
Lust'spiel n comedy
lust'wandeln intr (SEIN) stroll
Lutheraner –in [lutə'ranər(ın)] §6 mf
 Lutheran
lutherisch ['lutərɪʃ] adj Lutheran
lutschen ['lutʃən] tr & intr suck
Lut'scher m (-s;-) nipple, pacifier
Luxus ['luksus] m (-;) luxury
Lu'xusausgabe f deluxe edition
Luzerne [lu'tsernə] f (-;-n) alfalfa
Lymphe ['lʏmfə] f (-;-n) lymph
lynchen ['lʏnçən] tr lynch
Lyrik ['lyrɪk] f (-;) lyric poetry
lyrisch ['lyrɪʃ] adj lyric(al)
Lyze·um [ly'tse·um] n (-s;-en [ən])
 girls' high school

M

M, m [ɛm] invar n M, m
M abbr (Mark) (fin) mark
Maar [mar] n (-[e]s;-e) crater lake
Maat [mat] m (-[e]s;-e) (naut) mate
Machart ['maxart] f make, type
Mache ['maxə] f (-;) (coll) make-believe; er hat es schon in der M. he is
 working on it
machen ['maxən] tr make; (tun) do;
 (bewirken) produce; (verursachen)
 cause; (Prüfung, Reise, Spaziergang)
take; (Begriff) form; (Besuch) pay;
(Freude) give; (Holz) chop; (Konkurrenz) offer; das macht mir zu
schaffen that causes me trouble; das
macht nichts it doesn't matter; never
mind; das macht Spaß that's fun;
Dummheiten m. behave foolishly;
Ernst m. be in earnest; gemacht!
right!; O.K.!; Geschäfte m. do business; Geschichten m. make a fuss;
Hochzeit m. get married; ich mache

Spaß I'm joking; **mach dir nichts daraus!** don't worry about it; **mach's gut!** so long!; **wieviel macht es?** how much is it? || *ref* make progress, do all right; **sich auf den Weg m.** set out; **sich** [*dat*] **etw m.** lassen have s.th. made to order; **sich m.** an (*acc*) get down to; **sich** [*dat*] **nichts daraus m.** not care for (or about) || *intr*—laß **mich nur m.**! just leave it to me; **mach, daß . . .**! see to it that . . .!; **m.** in (*dat*) deal in; dabble in; **mach schon** (or zu)! get going!; **nichts zu m!** (coll) nothing doing! no dice!

Machenschaften ['maxənʃaftən] *pl* intrigues

Macher ['maxər] *m* (-s;-) instigator; (coll) big shot

Macht [maxt] *f* (-;⁻e) might, power; (*Kraft*) force, strength; **aus eigener M.** on one's own responsibility; **an der Macht** in power; **an die M. kommen** come to power

Macht'ausgleich *m* balance of power

Macht'befugnis *f* authority

Machthaber ['maxthabər] *m* (-s;-) ruler; dictator

machthaberisch ['maxthabərɪʃ] *adj* dictatorial

mächtig ['mɛçtɪç] *adj* mighty, powerful; (*riesig*) huge

macht'los *adj* powerless

Macht'losigkeit *f* (-;) impotence

Macht'politik *f* power politics

Macht'vollkommenheit *f* absolute power; **aus eigener M.** on one's own authority

Macht'wort *n* (-[e]s;⁻e)—**ein M. sprechen** put one's foot down

Machwerk ['maxverk] *n* bad job

Mädchen ['mɛtçən] *n* (-s;-) girl; maid

mäd'chenhaft *adj* girlish; maidenly

Mäd'chenhandel *m* white slavery

Mäd'chenname *m* maiden name; girl's name

Made ['madə] *f* (-;-n) maggot

Mädel ['medəl] *n* (-s;-) (coll) girl

madig ['madɪç] *adj* wormy

Magazin [maga'tsin] *n* (-s;-e) warehouse; (*Zeitschrift; Fernsehprogramm; am Gewehr*) magazine

Magd [makt] *f* (-;⁻e) maid; (poet) maiden

Magen ['magən] *m* (-s;⁻ & -) stomach; **auf nüchternen M.** on an empty stomach

Ma'genbeschwerden *pl* stomach trouble

Ma'gengrube *f* pit of the stomach

Ma'gensaft *m* gastric juice

Ma'genweh *n* stomach ache

mager ['magər] *adj* lean; (*Ernte*) poor

Magie [ma'gi] *f* (-;) magic

Magier -in ['magjər(ɪn)] §6 *mf* magician

magisch ['magɪʃ] *adj* magic(al)

Magister [ma'gɪstər] *m* (-s;-) school teacher; **M. der freien Künste** Master of Arts

Magistrat [magɪs'trat] *m* (-[e]s;⁻e) city council; (hist) magistracy

Magnat [mag'nat] *m* (-en;-en) magnate

Magnet [mag'net] *m* (-[e]s;-e) or (-en;-en) magnet

magnetisch [mag'netɪʃ] *adj* magnetic

magnetisieren [magnetɪ'zirən] *tr* magnetize

Magnetismus [magne'tɪsmʊs] *m* (-;) magnetism

Mahagoni [maha'goni] *n* (-s;) mahogony

Mahd [mat] *f* (-;-en) mowing

Mähdrescher ['medrɛʃər] *m* (agr) combine

mähen ['me·ən] *tr* mow; (*Getreide*) reap

Mä'her *m* (-s;-) mower; reaper

Mahl [mal] *n* (-[e]s;⁻er) meal

mahlen ['malən] (*pp* **gemahlen**) *tr* grind || *intr* spin

Mahl'zahn *m* molar

Mahl'zeit *f* meal; **prost M.!** that's a nice mess!

Mähmaschine ['memaʃinə] *f* reaper; (*Rasen-*) lawn mower

Mähne ['menə] *f* (-;-n) mane

mahnen ['manən] *tr* (**an** *acc*) remind (of); (**an** *acc*) warn (about or of)

Mahnmal ['manmal] *n* (-s;-e) monument

Mah'nung *f* (-;-en) admonition; (com) reminder, notice

Mähre ['merə] *f* (-;-n) old nag

Mähren ['merən] *n* (-s;) Moravia

Mai [maɪ] *m* (-[e]s;-e) May

Mai'baum *m* maypole

Mai'blume *f* lily of the valley

Maid [maɪt] *f* (-;-en) (poet) maiden

Mai'glöckchen *n* lily of the valley

Mai'käfer *m* June bug

Mailand ['maɪlant] *n* (-[e]s;) Milan

Mais [maɪs] *m* (-es;) Indian corn

Maische ['maɪʃə] *f* (-;) mash

Mais'hülse *f* corn husk

Mais'kolben *m* corncob

Majestät [majɛs'tet] *f* (-;-en) majesty

majestätisch [majɛs'tetɪʃ] *adj* majestic

Major [ma'jor] *m* (-s;-e) major

Majoran [majo'ran] *m* (-s;-e) marjoram

majorenn [majo'rɛn] *adj* of age

Majorität [majorɪ'tet] *f* (-;-en) majority

Makel ['makəl] *m* (-s;-) spot, stain

Mäkelei [mekə'laɪ] *f* (-;-en) carping

mäkelig ['mekəlɪç] *adj* critical; (*im Essen*) picky

ma'kellos *adj* spotless; (fig) impeccable

mäkeln ['mekəln] *intr* (**an** *dat*) carp (at), find fault (with)

Makkaroni [maka'roni] *pl* macaroni

Makler -in ['maklər(ɪn)] §6 *mf* agent, broker

Mäkler -in ['meklər(ɪn)] §6 *mf* faultfinder

Mak'lergebühr *f* brokerage

Makrele [ma'krelə] *f* (-;-n) mackerel

Makrone [ma'kronə] *f* (-;-n) macaroon

Makulatur [makʊla'tur] *f* (-;) waste

mal [mal] *adv* (coll) once; (arith) times; **komm mal her!** come here once!; **zwei mal drei** two times three; **zwei mal Spinat** two (orders of) spinach ‖ **Mal** *n* (-[e]s;-e) mark, sign; (*Mutter-*) birthmark, mole; (*Fleck*) stain; time; **dieses Mal** this time; **manches liebe Mal** many a time; **mit e-m Male** all at once

Malbuch ['mɑlbux] *n* coloring book

malen ['mɑlən] *tr & intr* paint

Ma'ler –**in** §6 *mf* painter

Malerei [mɑlə'raɪ] *f* (-;-en) painting

malerisch ['mɑlərɪʃ] *adj* picturesque

Ma'lerleinwand *f* canvas

Malkunst ['mɑlkunst] *f* art of painting

Malstrom ['mɑlʃtrom] *m* maelstrom

malträtieren [maltre'tirən] *tr* maltreat

Malve ['mɑlvə] *f* (-;-n) mallow

Malz [malts] *n* (-es;) malt

Malz'bonbon *m* cough drop

Mal'zeichen *n* multiplication sign

Mama [mɑ'mɑ], ['mɑmɑ] *f* (-;-s) mom, ma

Mamsell [mam'zel] *f* (-;-en) miss; (*Wirtschafterin*) housekeeper

man [man] *indef pron* one, they, people, you; **man hat mir gesagt** I have been told

manch [manç] *invar adj*—**manch ein** many a ‖ **mancher** §3 *adj* many a; **manche** *pl* some, several ‖ *pron* many a person; many a thing

mancherlei ['mançərlaɪ] *invar adj* all sorts of, various

Manchester [man'ʃestər] *m* (-s;) corduroy

manch'mal *adv* sometimes

Mandant –**in** [man'dant(ɪn)] §7 *mf* client

Mandarine [manda'rinə] *f* (-;-n) tangerine

Mandat [man'dɑt] *n* (-[e]s;-e) mandate

mandatieren [manda'tirən] *tr* mandate

Mandel ['mandəl] *f* (-;-n) almond; (*15 Stück*) fifteen; (anat) tonsil

Man'delentzündung *f* tonsilitis

Mandoline [mandɔ'linə] *f* (-;-n) mandolin

Mandschurei [mantʃu'raɪ] *f* (-;) Manchuria

Mangan [maŋ'gan] *n* (-s;) manganese

Mangel ['maŋəl] *m* (-s;⸚) lack, deficiency; (*Knappheit*) shortage; (*Fehler*) shortcoming; **aus M. an** (*dat*) for lack of; **M. haben an** (*dat*) be deficient in; **M. leiden an** (*dat*) be short of ‖ *f* (-;-n) mangle

Mangel- *comb.fm.* in short supply

Man'gelberuf *m* undermanned profession

man'gelhaft *adj* defective; faulty; unsatisfactory, deficient

Man'gelkrankheit *f* nutritional deficiency

mangeln ['maŋəln] *tr* (*Wäsche*) mangle ‖ *intr* (**an** *dat*) be short of, lack ‖ *impers*—**es mangelt mir an** (*dat*) I lack

Mängelrüge ['meŋəlrygə] *f* (-;-n) (com) complaint (*about a shipment*)

mangels ['maŋəls] *prep* (*genit*) for want of, for lack of

Ma·nie [ma'ni] *f* (-;-nien ['ni·ən]) mania

Manier [ma'nir] *f* (-;-en) manner

maniert [manɪ'rirt] *adj* affected

Manieriert'heit *f* (-;-en) mannerism

manier'lich *adj* mannerly, polite

Manifest [manɪ'fest] *n* (-es;-e) (aer, naut) manifest; (pol) manifesto

Maniküre [manɪ'kyrə] *f* (-;-n) manicure; manicurist

maniküren [manɪ'kyrən] *tr* manicure

manipulieren [manɪpu'lirən] *tr* manipulate

manisch ['manɪʃ] *adj* maniacal

Manko ['maŋko] *n* (-s;-s) deficit; (com) shortage

Mann [man] *m* (-[e]s;⸚er) man; (*Gatte*) husband; **an den M. bringen** manage to get rid of; **der M. aus dem Volke** the man in the street; **seinen M. stehen** hold one's own

mannbar ['manbar] *adj* marriageable

Mann'barkeit *f* (-;) puberty; marriageable age (*of girls*)

Männchen ['mençən] *n* (-s;-) little man; (*Ehemann*) hubby; (zool) male; **M. machen** sit on its hind legs

Männerchor ['menərkor] *m* men's choir

Mannesalter ['manəsaltər] *n* manhood

Manneszucht ['manəstsuxt] *f* discipline

mann'haft *adj* manly, valiant

mannigfaltig ['manɪçfaltɪç] *adj* manifold

Man'nigfaltigkeit *f* (-;) diversity

männlich ['menlɪç] *adj* male; (fig) manly; (gram) masculine

Männ'lichkeit *f* (-;) manhood; virility

Mannsbild ['mansbɪlt] *n* (pej) man

Mann'schaft *f* (-;-en) crew; (sport) team, squad; **Mannschaften** (mil) enlisted men

Mann'schaftsführer –**in** §6 *mf* (sport) captain

Mann'schaftswagen *m* (mil) personnel carrier

Mannsleute ['manslɔɪtə] *pl* menfolk

mannstoll ['manstɔl] *adj* man-crazy

Manns'tollheit *f* (-;) nymphomania

Mann'weib *n* mannish woman

Manometer [manə'metər] *n* pressure gauge

Manöver [ma'nøvər] *n* (-s;-) maneuver

manövrieren [manøvri'rən] *intr* maneuver

manövrier'fähig *adj* maneuverable

Mansarde [man'zardə] *f* (-;-n) attic

manschen ['manʃən] *tr & intr* splash

Manschette [man'ʃetə] *f* (-;-n) cuff

Manschet'tenknopf *m* cuff link

Mantel ['mantəl] *m* (-s;⸚) overcoat; (*Fahrrad-*) tire; (*e-s Kabels*) sheathing; (*Geschoß-*) jacket, case; (geol, orn) mantle

manuell [manu'el] *adj* manual

Manufaktur [manufak'tur] *f* (-;-en) manufacture

Manufaktur'waren *pl* manufactured goods

Manuskript [manu'skrɪpt] *n* (-[e]s;-e) manuscript

Mappe ['mapə] *f* (-;-n) briefcase; (*Aktendeckel*) folder

Märchen ['merçən] *n* (-s;-) fairy tale

mär'chenhaft *adj* legendary; (fig) fabulous

Mär'chenland *n* fairyland
Marchese [mar'kezə] *m* (-;-n) marquis
Marder ['mardər] *m* (-s;-) marten; (fig) thief
Margarine [marga'rinə] *f* (-;) margarine
Marienbild [ma'ri·ənbɪlt] *n* image of the Virgin
Marienfäden [ma'ri·ənfedən] *pl* gossamer(s)
Marienglas [ma'ri·ənglas] *n* mica
Marienkäfer [ma'ri·ənkefər] *m* ladybug
Marine [ma'rinə] *f* (-;-n) (*Kriegs-*) navy; (*Handels-*) merchant marine
mari'neblau *adj* navy-blue
Mari'neflugzeug *n* seaplane
Mari'neinfanterie *f* marines
Mari'neminister *m* secretary of the navy
Mari'neoffizier –**in** §6 *mf* naval officer
Mari'nesoldat *m* marine
marinieren [marɪ'nirən] *tr* marinate
Marionette [marɪ·ə'netə] *f* (-;-n) puppet
Marionet'tentheater *n* puppet show
Mark [mark] *f* (-;-) (fin) mark; (hist) borderland, march || *n* (-[e]s;) marrow; (*im Holz*) pith; **bis ins M.** to the quick; **er hat M.** (fig) he has guts; **j–m durch M. und Bein gehen** (fig) go right through s.o.
markant [mar'kant] *adj* (*einprägsam*) marked; (*außergewöhnlich*) striking; (*Geländepunkt*) prominent
Marke ['markə] *f* (-;-n) mark; (*Brief-*) stamp; (*Handelszeichen*) trademark; (*Sorte*) brand; (*Fabrikat*) make; (*Spiel-*) counter
mark'erschütternd *adj* piercing
Marketenderei [markətendə'raɪ] *f* (-; -en) post exchange, PX
Marketing ['markɪtɪŋ] *n* (-s;) (com) marketing
markieren [mar'kirən] *tr* mark; (*spielen*) pretend to be
Markise [mar'kizə] *f* (-;-n) awning
Mark'stein *m* landmark
Markt [markt] *m* (-[e]s;ᵘe) market; (*Jahrmarkt*) fair
Markt'bude *f* booth, stall
markten ['marktən] *intr* (**um**) bargain (for)
markt'fähig *adj* marketable
Markt'flecken *m* market town
marktgängig ['marktgeŋɪç] *adj* marketable
Markt'platz *m* market place
Markt'schreier *m* quack
Marmelade [marmə'ladə] *f* (-;-n) jam
Marmor ['marmɔr] *m* (-s;-e) marble
Mar'morbruch *m* marble quarry
marmorn ['marmɔrn] *adj* marble
marode [ma'rodə] *adj* (coll) tired out
Marodeur [marə'dør] *m* (-s;-e) marauder
marodieren [marə'dirən] *intr* maraud
Marone [ma'ronə] *f* (-;-n) chestnut
Maroquin [marə'kɛ̃] *m* (-s;) morocco
Marotte [ma'rotə] *f* (-;-n) whim
marsch [marʃ] *interj* march!; be off!; **m., m.!** on the double || **Marsch** *m* (-es; ᵘe) march; **in M. setzen** get

going; **j–m den M. blasen** (coll) chew s.o. out; (**sich**) **in M. setzen** set out
Marschall ['marʃal] *m* (-s;ᵘe) marshal
Mar'schallstab *m* marshal's baton
Marsch'gepäck *n* full field pack
marschieren [mar'ʃirən] *intr* (SEIN) march
Marsch'kompanie *f* replacement company
Marsch'lied *n* marching song
Marsch'verpflegung *f* field rations
Marter ['martər] *f* (-;-n) torture
martern ['martərn] *tr* torture, torment
Mar'terpfahl *m* stake
Märtyrer –**in** ['mertyrər(ɪn)] §6 *mf* martyr
Märtyrertum ['mertyrərtum] *n* (-s;) martyrdom
März [merts] *m* (-[es];-e) March
Masche ['maʃə] *f* (-;-n) mesh; stitch; (fig) trick
Ma'schendraht *m* chicken wire; screen; wire mesh
ma'schenfest *adj* runproof
Maschine [ma'ʃinə] *f* (-;-n) machine; (aer) airplane
maschinell [maʃɪ'nel] *adj* mechanical || *adv* by machine
Maschi'nenantrieb *m*—**mit M.** machine-driven
Maschi'nenbau *m* (-[e]s;) mechanical engineering
Maschi'nengewehr *n* machine gun
Maschi'nengewehrschütze *m* machine gunner
maschi'nenmäßig *adj* mechanical
Maschi'nenpistole *f* tommy gun
Maschi'nenschaden *m* engine trouble
Maschi'nenschlosser *m* machinist
maschi'nenschreiben *tr* type || **Maschinenschreiben** *n* (-s;-) typing; typewritten letter
Maschi'nenschrift *f* typescript
Maschi'nensprache *f* computer language
Maschinerie [maʃɪnə'ri] *f* (-;) (& fig) machinery
Maschinist –**in** [maʃɪ'nɪst(ɪn)] §7 *mf* machinist
Masern ['mazərn] *pl* measles
Maserung ['mazəruŋ] *f* (-;) grain (*in wood*)
Maske ['maskə] *f* (-;-n) mask; (fig) disguise; (theat) make-up
Ma'skenball *m* masquerade
Maskerade [maskə'radə] *f* (-;-n) masquerade
maskieren [mas'kirən] *tr* mask
Maskotte [mas'kotə] *f* (-;-n) mascot
maskulin [masku'lin] *adj* masculine
Maskuli·num [masku'linum] *n* (-s;-na [na]) masculine noun
maß [mas] *pret of* **messen** || **Maß** *n* (-es;-e) measure; (*Messung*) measurement; (*Ausdehnung*) extent, dimension; (*Verhältnis*) rate, proportion; (*Grad*) degree; (*Mäßigung*) moderation; **das Maß ist voll!** I've had it!; **das Maß überschreiten** go too far; **er hat sein gerütteltes Maß an Kummer gehabt** he had his full share of trouble; **in gewissem Maße** to a certain extent; **in hohem Maße**

highly; **j-m Maß nehmen zu** take
s.o.'s measurements for; **Maß halten**
observe moderation; **mit Maße in**
moderation; **nach Maß angefertigt**
custom-made; **ohne Maß und Ziel**
without limit; **weder Maß noch Ziel**
kennen know no bounds; **zweierlei**
Maß double standard || *f* (-;- & -e)
quart (*of beer*), stein
massakrieren [masa'kɾirən] *tr* massacre
Maß'anzug *m* tailor-made suit
Maß'arbeit *f* work made to order
Masse ['masə] *f* (-;-n) mass; bulk;
(*Menge*) volume; (*Volk*) crowd;
(*Hinterlassenschaft*) estate; (elec)
ground; **die breite M.** the masses;
the rank and file; **e-e Masse...**(coll)
lots of
Maß'einheit *f* unit of measure
Masseleisen ['masəlaɪzən] *n* pigiron
Massen– *comb.fm.* mass, bulk, wholesale
Mas'senabsatz *m* wholesale selling
Mas'senangriff *m* mass attack
Mas'senanziehung *f* gravitation
mas'senhaft *adj* in large quantities
Maß'gabe *f*—**mit der M., daß** with the
understanding that; **nach M.** (*genit*)
in proportion to; according to; (jur)
as provided in
maß'gebend, maßgeblich ['masgeplɪç]
adj standard; authoritative; (*Kreise*)
leading, influential; **das ist nicht**
maßgebend für that is no criterion
for
maß'gerecht *adj* to scale
maß'halten §90 *intr* observe moderation
maß'haltig *adj* precise
massieren [ma'sirən] *tr* massage;
(*Truppen*) mass
massig ['masɪç] *adj* bulky; solid; (*Per-
son*) stout || *adv*—**m. viel** (coll) very
much
mäßig ['mesɪç] *adj* moderate; frugal;
(*Leistung*) mediocre
mäßigen ['mesɪgən] *tr* moderate, tone
down || *ref* control oneself
Mä'ßigkeit *f* moderation; frugality;
temperance
Mä'ßigung *f* (-;) moderation
massiv [ma'sif] *adj* massive; solid
Maß'krug *m* beer mug, stein
Maß'liebchen *n* daisy
maß'los *adj* immoderate || *adv* ex-
tremely
Maß'nahme *f* (-;-n), **Maß'regel** *f* (-;
-n) measure, step, move
maß'regeln *tr* reprimand
Maß'schneider *m* custom tailor
Maß'stab *m* ruler; (fig) yardstick,
standard; (*auf Landkarten*) scale;
jeden M. verlieren lose all sense of
proportion
maß'voll *adj* moderate; (*Benehmen*)
discreet
Mast [mast] *m* (-es;-en & -e) pole;
(naut) mast || *f* (-;) (*Schweinfutter*)
mast
Mast'baum *m* (naut) mast
Mast'darm *m* rectum
mästen ['mestən] *tr* fatten

Mast'korb *m* masthead, crow's nest
Material [materɪ'al] *n* (-s;-ien [ɪ·ən])
material
Materialismus [materɪ·a'lɪsmʊs] *m*
(-;) materialism
materialistisch [materɪ·a'lɪstɪʃ] *adj*
materialistic
Material'waren *pl* (Aust) medical sup-
plies
Materie [ma'terɪ·ə] *f* (-;-n) matter
materiell [materɪ'el] *adj* material;
(*Schwierigkeiten*) financial; (*Recht*)
substantive
Mathe ['matə] *f* (-;) (coll) math
Mathematik [matema'tik] *f* (-;)
mathematics
Mathematiker –in [mate'matɪkər(ɪn)]
§6 *mf* mathematician
mathematisch [mate'matɪʃ] *adj* mathe-
matical
Matratze [ma'tratsə] *f* (-;-n) mattress
Mätresse [me'tresə] *f* (-;-n) mistress
Matrize [ma'tritsə] *f* (-;-n) stencil;
(*Stempel*) die, matrix
Matrone [ma'tronə] *f* (-;-n) matron
matro'nenhaft *adj* matronly
Matrose [ma'trozə] *m* (-n;-n) sailor
Matro'senanzug *m* sailor's uniform
Matro'senjacke *f* (nav) peacoat
Matsch [matʃ] *m* (-es;) (*Brei*) mush;
(*Schlamm*) mud; (*halbgetauter*
Schnee) slush
matschig ['matʃɪç] *adj* mushy; muddy;
slushy
matt [mat] *adj* dull; weak; limp; (*Glas,*
Birne) frosted; (*Börse*) slack; (*er-*
schöpft) exhausted; (*Kugel*) spent;
(*Licht*) dim; (*Metall*) tarnished;
(phot) matt; **m. machen** dull; tarnish;
m. setzen checkmate
Matte ['matə] *f* (-;-n) mat; (*Wiese*)
Alpine meadow; (poet) mead
Matt'glas *n* frosted glass
Matt'gold *n* dull gold
Matt'heit *f* dullness; fatigue
matt'herzig *adj* faint-hearted
Mat'tigkeit *f* (-;) fatigue
Matura [ma'tura] *f* (-;) (Aust) final
examination (*before graduation*)
Mätzchen ['metsçən] *n* (-s;-) trick; **M.**
machen play tricks; put on airs
Mauer ['mau·ər] *f* (-;-n) wall
Mau'erblümchen *n* (fig) wallflower
Mau'erkalk *m* mortar
mauern ['mau·ərn] *tr* build (*in stone*
or brick)
Mau'erstein *m* brick
Mau'erwerk *n* brickwork; masonry
Mau'erziegel *m* brick
Maul [maul] *n* (-[e]s;-er) mouth;
maw; **halt's M.!** (sl) shut up!
Maul'affe *m* gaping fool
Maul'beerbaum *m* mulberry tree
Maul'beere *f* mulberry
maulen ['maulən] *intr* gripe
Maul'esel *m* mule
maul'faul *adj* too lazy to talk
Maul'held *m* braggart
Maul'korb *m* muzzle
Maul'schelle *f* slap in the face
Maul'sperre *f* lock jaw
Maul'tier *n* mule
Maul'trommel *f* Jew's-harp

Maul'– und Klau'enseuche *f* hoof and mouth disease
Maul'werk *n*—**ein großes M. haben** have the gift of gab
Maul'wurf *m* (zool) mole
Maul'wurfshaufen *m*, **Maul'wurfshügel** *m* molehill
Maure ['maurə] *m* (–n;–n) Moor
Maurer ['maurər] *m* (–s;–) mason; bricklayer
Mau'rerkelle *f* trowel
Mau'rerpolier *m* bricklayer foreman
Maus [maus] *f* (–;̈e) mouse
Mäuschen ['mɔɪsçən] *n* (–s;–) little mouse; (fig) pet, darling; wench
Mau'sefalle *f* mousetrap
mausen ['mauzən] *tr* pilfer, swipe ‖ *intr* catch mice
Mauser ['mauzər] *f* (–;) molting season; **in der M. sein** be molting
mausern ['mauzərn] *ref* molt
mau'setot' *adj* dead as a doornail
mausig ['mauzɪç] *adj*—**sich m. machen** put on airs, be stuck-up
Mauso•leum [mauzɔ'le•um] *n* (–s; –leen ['le•ən]) mausoleum
Maxime [ma'ksimə] *f* (–;–n) maxim
Mayonnaise [majɔ'nezə] *f* (–;) mayonnaise
Mechanik [mɛ'çanɪk] *f* (–;–en) mechanics; (*Triebwerk*) mechanism
Mechaniker [mɛ'çanɪkər] *m* (–s;–) mechanic
mechanisch [mɛ'çanɪʃ] *adj* mechanical; power—
mechanisieren [meçanɪ'zirən] *tr* mechanize
Mechanis•mus [meça'nɪsmus] *m* (–; –men [mən]) mechanism; (*Uhrwerk*) works
Meckerer ['mɛkərər] *m* (–s;–) (coll) grumbler
meckern ['mɛkərn] *intr* bleat; (coll) grumble
Medaille [mɛ'daljə] *f* (–;–n) medal
Medaillon [medal'jõ] *n* (–s;–s) medallion; locket
Medikament [medɪka'mɛnt] *n* (–s;–e) medication
Meditation [medɪta'tsjon] *f* (–;–en) meditation
meditieren [medɪ'tirən] *intr* meditate
Medizin [medɪ'tsin] *f* (–;–en) medicine
Medizinalassistant [medɪtsɪ'nalasɪstant(ɪn)] §7 *mf* intern
Medizinalbeamte [medɪtsɪ'nalbə•amtə] *m* health officer
Medizinalbehörde[medɪtsɪ'nalbəhørdə] *f* board of health
Mediziner –in [medɪ'tsinər(ɪn)] §6 *mf* physician; medical student
medizinisch [medɪ'tsinɪʃ] *adj* medical, medicinal; medicated; **medizinische Fakultät** medical school
Meer [mer] *n* (–[e]s;–e) sea; **am Meere** at the seashore; **übers M.** overseas
Meer'busen *m* bay, gulf
Meer'enge *f* straits
Meeres– [merəs] *comb.fm.* sea, marine
Mee'resarm *m* inlet
Mee'resboden *m* bottom of the sea
Mee'resbucht *f* bay

Mee'resgrund *m* bottom of the sea
Mee'reshöhe *f* sea level
Mee'resküste *f* seacoast
Mee'resleuchten *n* phosphorescence
Mee'resspiegel *m* sea level
meer'grün *adj* sea-green
Meer'rettich *m* horseradish
Meer'schaum *m* meerschaum
Meer'schwein *n* porpoise
Meer'schweinchen *n* guinea pig
Meer'ungeheuer *n* sea monster
Meer'weib *n* mermaid
Mehl [mel] *n* (–[e]s;) (*grobes*) meal; (*feines*) flour; (*Staub*) dust, powder
Mehl'kloß *m* dumpling
Mehl'speise *f* pastry; pudding
Mehl'suppe *f* gruel
Mehl'tau *m* mildew
mehr [mer] *invar adj & adv* more; **immer m.** more and more; **kein Wort m.!** not another word!; **m. oder weniger** more or less, give or take; **nicht m.** no more, no longer; **nie m.** never again ‖ **Mehr** *n* (–s;) majority; (*Zuwachs*) increase; (*Überschuß*) surplus
Mehr'arbeit *f* extra work; (*Überstunden*) overtime
Mehr'aufwand *m*, **Mehr'ausgabe** *f* additional expenditure
Mehr'betrag *m* surplus; extra charge
mehr'deutig *adj* ambiguous
mehren ['merən] *tr & ref* increase
mehrere ['merərə] *adj & pron* several
mehr'fach *adj* manifold; repeated, multiple
mehr'farbig *adj* multicolored
Mehr'gebot *n* higher bid
Mehr'gepäck *n* excess luggage
Mehr'gewicht *n* excess weight
Mehr'heit *f* (–;–en) majority; (pol) plurality
Mehr'heitsbeschluß *m*, **Mehr'heitsentscheidung** *f* plurality vote
mehr'jährig *adj* (bot) perennial
Mehr'kosten *pl* extra charges
Mehr'ladegewehr *n* repeater
Mehr'leistung *f* increased performance; (ins) extended benefits
mehrmalig ['mermalɪç] *adj* repeated
mehrmals ['mermals] *adv* several times, on several occasions; repeatedly
Mehr'porto *n* additional postage
Mehr'preis *m* extra charge
mehr'seitig *adj* multilateral; many-sided; (*Brief*) of many pages
mehrsilbig ['merzɪlbɪç] *adj* polysyllabic
mehrsprachig ['merʃpraxɪç] *adj* polyglot
mehrstöckig ['merʃtœkɪç] *adj* multistory
mehrstufig ['merʃtufɪç] *adj* multistage
Meh'rung *f* (–;) increase, multiplication
Mehr'verbrauch *m* increased consumption
Mehr'wertsteuer *f* added value tax
Mehr'zahl *f* majority; (gram) plural
meiden ['maɪdən] §112 *tr* avoid, shun
Meier ['maɪ•ər] *m* (–s;–) tenant farmer; dairy farmer
Meierei [maɪ•ə'raɪ] *f* (–;–en) dairy

Mei′ergut *n*, **Mei′erhof** *m* dairy farm
Meile [′maɪlə] *f* (-;-n) mile
mei′lenweit *adj* extending for miles, miles and miles of ‖ *adv* far away; **m. auseinander** miles apart
Mei′lenzahl *f* mileage
mein [maɪn] §2,2 *poss adj* my ‖ §2,4,5 *pron* mine; **das Meine** my share; my due; **die Meinen** my family
Meineid [′maɪnaɪt] *m* (-[e]s;) perjury; **e-n M.** schwören (or **leisten**) commit perjury
meineidig [′maɪnaɪdɪç] *adj* perjured; **m. werden** perjure oneself
meinen [′maɪnən] *tr* think; (*im Sinne haben*) mean, intend; **das will ich m.** I should think so; **die Sonne meint es heute gut** the sun is very warm today; **es ehrlich m.** have honorable intentions; **es gut m.** mean well; **ich meinte dich im Recht** I thought you were in the right; **m. Sie das ernst** (or **im Ernst**)? do you really mean it?; **was m. Sie damit?** what do you mean by that?; **was m. Sie dazu?** what do you think of that? ‖ *intr* think; **m. Sie?** do you think so?; **m. Sie nicht auch?** don't you agree?; **wie m. Sie?** I beg your pardon?
meinerseits [′maɪnər′zaɪts] *adv* for my part
meinesgleichen [′maɪnəs′glaɪçən] *pron* people like me, the likes of me
meinethlben [′maɪnət′halbən], **meinetwegen** [′maɪnət′vegən] *adv* for my sake, on my account; for all I care
meinetwillen [′maɪnət′vɪlən] *adv*—**um m.** for my sake, on my behalf
meinige [′maɪnɪgə] §2,5 *pron* mine
Mei′nung *f* (-;-en) opinion; **anderer M. mit j-m sein über** (*acc*) disagree with s.o. about; **der M. sein** be of the opinion; **geteilter M. sein** be of two minds; **j-m die** (or **seine**) **M. sagen** give s.o. a piece of one's mind; **meiner M. nach** in my opinion; **vorgefaßte M.** preconceived idea
Mei′nungsäußerung *f* expression of opinion
Mei′nungsaustausch *m* exchange of views
Mei′nungsbefragung *f*, **Mei′nungsforschung** *f* public opinion poll
Mei′nungsumfrage *f* public opinion poll
Mei′nungsverschiedenheit *f* difference of opinion, disagreement
Meise [′maɪzə] *f* (-;-n) titmouse
Meißel [′maɪsəl] *m* (-s;-) chisel
meißeln [′maɪsəln] *tr* & *intr* chisel
meist [maɪst] *adj* most; **am meisten** most; **das meiste** the most; **die meisten Menschen** most people; **die meiste Zeit** most of the time; **die meiste Zeit des Jahres** most of the year ‖ *adv* usually, generally
Meist′begünstigungsklausel *f* most-favored nation clause
Meist′bietende §5 *mf* highest bidder
meistens [′maɪstəns] *adv* mostly
Meister [′maɪstər] *m* (-s;-) master; boss; (*im Betrieb*) foreman; (sport) champion
mei′sterhaft *adj* masterly

Meisterin [′maɪstərɪn] *f* (-;-nen) master's wife; (sport) champion
mei′sterlich *adj* masterly
meistern [′maɪstərn] *tr* master
Mei′sterschaft *f* (-;-en) mastery; (sport) championship
Mei′sterstück *n*, **Mei′sterwerk** *n* masterpiece
Mei′sterzug *m* master stroke
Melancholie [melaŋkɔ′li] *f* (-;) melancholy
melancholisch [melaŋ′kolɪʃ] *adj* melancholy
Melasse [me′lasə] *f* (-;-n) molasses
Meldeamt [′meldə·amt] *n.* **Meldebüro** [′meldəbyro] *n* registration office
Meldefahrer [′meldəfarər] *m* (mil) dispatch rider
Meldegänger [′meldəgeŋər] *m* (mil) messenger, runner
melden [′meldən] *tr* report; (*polizeilich*) turn (*s.o.*) in; **den Empfang m.** (*genit*) acknowledge the receipt of; **er hat nichts zu m.** he has nothing to say in the matter; **gemeldet werden zu** (sport) be entered in; **j-m m. lassen, daß** send s.o. word that ‖ *ref* report; (*Alter*) begin to show; (*Gläubiger*) come forward; (*Kind*) cry; (*Magen*) growl; (*polizeilich*) register; (*Winter*) set in; (telp) answer; **sich auf e-e Anzeige m.** answer an ad; **sich krank m.** (mil) go on sick call; **sich m. zu** apply for; (*freiwillig*) volunteer for; (mil) enlist in; (sport) enter; **sich zum Dienst m.** (mil) report for duty; **sich zum Wort m.** ask to speak; (*in der Schule*) hold up the hand
Mel′der *m* (-s;-) (mil) runner
Meldezettel [′meldətsetəl] *m* registration form
Mel′dung *f* (-;-en) report; message, notification; (*Bewerbung*) application
Melkeimer [′melkaɪmər] *m* milk pail
melken [′melkən] §113 *tr* milk
Melo·die [melo′di] *f* (-;-dien [′di·ən]) melody
melodisch [me′lodɪʃ] *adj* melodious
Melone [me′lonə] *f* (-;-n) melon; (coll) derby
Meltau [′meltau] *m* (-[e]s;) honeydew
Membran [mem′bran] *f* (-;-en), **Membrane** [mem′branə] *f* (-;-n) membrane
Memme [′memə] *f* (-;-n) coward
Memoiren [memo′arən] *pl* memoirs
memorieren [memo′rirən] *tr* memorize
Menge [′meŋə] *f* (-;-n) quantity, amount; crowd; **e-e M.** a lot of
mengen [′meŋən] *tr* mix ‖ *ref* (*acc*) mingle (with); (**in** *acc*) meddle (in)
Men′genlehre *f* (math) theory of sets
men′genmäßig *adj* quantitative
Mengsel [′meŋzəl] *n* (-s;-) hodgepodge
Mennige [′menɪgə] *f* (-;) rust-preventive paint
Mensch [menʃ] *m* (-en;-en) human being, man; person, individual; **die Menschen** the people; **kein M.** no one ‖ *n* (-es; -er) hussy, slut

Menschen– [mɛnʃən] *comb.fm.* man, of men; human
Men'schenalter *n* generation, age
Men'schenfeind –in §8 *mf* misanthropist
Men'schenfresser *m* cannibal
Men'schenfreund –in §8 *mf* philanthropist
men'schenfreundlich *adj* philanthropic, humanitarian
Men'schengedenken *n*—seit M. since time immemorial
Men'schengeschlecht *n* mankind
Men'schengewühl *n* milling crowd
Men'schenglück *n* human happiness
Men'schenhandel *m* slave trade
Men'schenhaß *m* misanthropy
Men'schenjagd *f* manhunt
Men'schenkenner –in §6 *mf* judge of human nature
Men'schenkind *n* human being; **armes M.** poor soul
men'schenleer *adj* deserted
Men'schenliebe *f* philanthropy
Men'schenmaterial *n* manpower
men'schenmöglich *adj* humanly possible
Men'schrenraub *m* kidnaping
Men'schenräuber –in §6 *mf* kidnaper
Men'schenrechte *pl* human rights
men'schenscheu *adj* shy, unsociable
Men'schenschinder *m* oppressor, slave driver
Men'schenschlag *m* race
Men'schenseele *f* human soul; **keine M.** not a living soul
Men'schenskind *interj* man alive!
Men'schensohn *m* (Bib) Son of man
men'schenunwürdig *adj* degrading
Men'schenverächter –in §6 *mf* cynic
Men'schenverstand *m*—guter M. common sense
Men'schenwürde *f* human dignity
men'schenwürdig *adj* decent
Mensch'heit *f* (–;) mankind, humanity
mensch'lich *adj* human; (*human*) humane
Mensch'lichkeit *f* (–;) humanity
Menschwerdung ['mɛnʃverduŋ] *f* (–;) incarnation
Menstruation [mɛntru·a'tsjon] *f* (–;–en) menstruation
Mensur [mɛn'zur] *f* (–;–en) measure; (*Meßglas*) measuring glass; students' duel
Mentalität [mɛntalɪtet] *f* (–;) mentality
Menuett [menu'ɛt] *n* (–[e]s;–e) minuet
Meridian [merɪ'djan] *m* (–s;–e) (astr) meridian
merkbar ['mɛrkbar] *adj* noticeable
Merkblatt ['mɛrkblat] *n* instruction sheet
Merkbuch ['mɛrkbux] *n* notebook
merken ['mɛrkən] *tr* notice; realize; etw m. lassen show s.th., betray s.th.; man merkte es sofort an ihrem Ausdruck, daß one noticed immediately by her expression that || *ref*—m. Sie sich [*dat*], was ich sage! mark my word!; sich [*dat*] etw m. bear s.th. in mind; sich [*dat*] nichts m. lassen not give oneself away || *intr*—m. auf (*acc*) pay attention to, heed
merk'lich *adj* noticeable

Merkmal ['mɛrkmal] *n* (–[e]s;–e) mark, feature, characteristic
Merkur [mɛr'kur] *m* & *n* (–s;) mercury
Merk'wort *n* (–[e]s;–er) catchword; (theat) cue
merk'würdig *adj* remarkable; (*seltsam*) curious, strange
merkwürdigerweise ['mɛrkvyrdɪgər-vaɪzə] *adv* strange to say
Merk'würdigkeit *f* (–;–en) strange thing
Merk'zeichen *n* mark
meschugge [me'ʃugə] *adj* (coll) nuts
Mesner ['mɛsnər] *m* (–s;–) sexton
Meß– [mes] *comb.fm.* measuring; (eccl) mass
Meß'band *n* (–[e]s;–er) measuring tape
meßbar ['mɛsbar] *adj* measurable
Meß'buch *n* (relig) missal
Meß'diener *m* acolyte
Messe ['mɛsə] *f* (–;–n) fair; (eccl) mass; (nav) officers' mess
messen ['mɛsən] §70 *tr* measure; (*Zeit*) time, clock; (*mustern*) size up || *ref* —sich m. mit cope with; (*geistig*) match wits with; sich nicht m. können mit be no match for || *intr* measure
Messer ['mɛsər] *m* (–s;–) gauge; meter || *n* (–s;–) knife; (surg) scalpel; bis aufs M. to the death
Mes'serheld *m* (coll) cutthroat
mes'serscharf' *adj* razor-sharp
Mes'serschmied *m* cutler
Messerschmiedewaren ['mɛsərʃmidəva-rən] *pl* cutlery
Mes'serschneide *f* knife edge
Meß'gewand *n* (eccl) vestment; chasuble
Meß'hemd *n* (eccl) alb
Messias [mɛ'si·as] *invar m* Messiah
Messing ['mɛsɪŋ] *n* (–s;) brass
messingen ['mɛsɪŋən] *adj* brass
Meß'opfer *n* sacrifice of the mass
Mes'sung *f* (–;–en) measurement
Metall [me'tal] *n* (–s;–e) metal
Metall'baukasten *m* erector set
metallen [me'talən], **metallisch** [me-'talɪʃ] *adj* metallic
Metall'säge *f* hacksaw
Metallurgie [metalur'gi] *f* (–;) metallurgy
metall'verarbeitend *adj* metal-processing
Metall'waren *pl* hardware
Metapher [me'tafər] *f* (–;–n) metaphor
Meteor [mete'or] *m* (–s;–e) meteor
Meteorloge [mɛtɛ·ɔrɔ'logə] *m* (–n;–n) meteorologist
Meteorologie [mɛtɛ·ɔrɔlɔ'gi] *f* (–;) meteorolgy
Meteorologin [mɛtɛ·ɔrɔ'login] *f* (–;–nen) meteorologist
meteorologisch [mɛtɛ·ɔrɔ'logɪʃ] *adj* meteorological
Meteor'stein *m* meteorite, aerolite
Meter ['metər] *m* & *n* (–s;–) meter
Me'termaß *n* tape measure
Methode [me'todə] *f* (–;–n) method
methodisch [me'todɪʃ] *adj* methodical
Metrik ['metrɪk] *f* (–;) metrics
metrisch ['metrɪʃ] *adj* metrical

Metropole [metrɔ'polə] ƒ (-;-n) metropolis
Mette ['metə] ƒ (-;-n) matins
Mettwurst ['metvurst] ƒ soft sausage
Metzelei [metsə'laɪ] ƒ (-;-en) massacre, slaughter
metzeln ['metsəln] tr massacre
Metzger ['metsgər] m (-s;-) butcher
Metzgerei [metsgə'raɪ] ƒ (-;-en) butcher shop
Meuchelmord ['mɔɪçəlmɔrt] m assassination
Meuchelmörder –in ['mɔɪçəlmœrdər (ɪn)] §6 mƒ assassin
meucheln ['mɔɪçəln] tr murder
meuchlerisch ['mɔɪçlərɪʃ] adj murderous
meuchlings ['mɔɪçlɪŋs] adv treacherously
Meute ['mɔɪtə] ƒ (-;-n) pack (of hounds); (fig) horde, gang
Meuterei [mɔɪtə'raɪ] ƒ (-;-en) mutiny
meuterisch ['mɔɪtərɪʃ] adj mutinous
meutern ['mɔɪtərn] intr mutiny
Mexikaner –in [meksɪ'kɑnər(ɪn)] §6 mƒ Mexican
mexikanisch [meksɪ'kɑnɪʃ] adj Mexican
Mexiko ['meksɪko] n (-s;) Mexico
miauen [mɪ'au·ən] intr meow
mich [mɪç] §11 pers pron me ‖ §11 reflex pron myself
mied [mit] pret of **meiden**
Mieder ['midər] n (-s;-) bodice
Mie'derwaren pl foundation garments
Mief [mif] n (-s;) foul air
Miene ['minə] ƒ (-;-n) mien; facial expression; **M. machen zu** (inf) make a move to (inf); **ohne die M. zu verziehen** without flinching
mies [mis] adj (coll) miserable, lousy
Mies'macher m (-s;-) alarmist
Miet– [mit] comb.fm. rental, rented; rent
Miet'auto n rented car
Miete ['mitə] ƒ (-;-n) rent; (Zins) rental; (Erd–) pit (for storing vegetables); **in M. geben** rent out; **in M. nehmen** rent; **kalte M.** rent not including heat; **zur M. wohnen** live in a rented apartment (or home)
mieten ['mitən] tr rent, hire; (Flugzeug) charter
Miet'entschädigung ƒ allowance for house rent
Mie'ter –in §6 mƒ tenant
Miet'ertrag m rent, rental
Miet'kontrakt m lease
Mietling ['mitlɪŋ] m (-s;-e) hireling
Miets'haus n apartment building
Miets'kaserne ƒ tenement house
Miet'vertrag m lease
Miet'wagen m rented car
Miet'wohung ƒ apartment
Miet'zins m rent
Mieze ['mitsə] ƒ (-;-n) pussy
Migräne [mɪ'grenə] ƒ (-;-n) migraine
Mikrobe [mɪ'krobə] ƒ (-;-n) microbe
Mikrofilm ['mikrɔfɪlm] m microfilm
Mikrophon [mɪkrɔ'fon] n (-s;-e) microphone
Mikroskop [mɪkrɔ'skop] n (-s;-e) microscope

mikroskopisch [mɪkrɔ'skopɪʃ] adj microscopic
Milbe ['mɪlbə] ƒ (-;-n) (ent) mite
Milch [mɪlç] ƒ (-;) milk
Milch'bart m sissy
Milch'brot n, **Milch'brötchen** n French roll
Milch'bruder m foster brother
Milch'drüse ƒ mammary gland
Milch'eimer m milk pail
Milch'geschäft n creamery, dairy
Milch'glas m milk glass
milchig ['mɪlçɪç] adj milky
Milch'mädchen n milkmaid
Milch'mädchenrechnung ƒ oversimplification
Milch'mixgetränk n milkshake
Milch'pulver n powdered milk
Milch'reis m rice pudding
Milch'schwester ƒ foster sister
Milch'straße ƒ Milky Way
Milch'tüte ƒ carton of milk
Milch'wirtschaft ƒ dairy
Milchzähne ['mɪlçtsenə] pl baby teeth
mild [mɪlt] adj mild; (nicht streng) lenient; (Stiftung) charitable; (Wein) smooth; (Lächeln) faint ‖ **Milde** ƒ (-;) mildness; leniency; kindness
mildern ['mɪldərn] tr soften, alleviate; **mildernde Umstände** extenuating circumstances
Mil'derung ƒ (-;) softening, alleviation, mitigation
mild'herzig, mild'tätig adj charitable
Militär [mɪlɪ'ter] n (-s;) military, army; **zum M. gehen** join the army ‖ m (-s;-s) professional soldier
Militär'dienst m military service
Militär'geistliche §5 m chaplain
Militär'gericht n military court
militärisch [mɪlɪ'terɪʃ] adj military
Militarismus [mɪlɪta'rɪsmus] m (-;) militarism
Miliz [mɪ'lɪts] ƒ (-;) militia
Miliz'soldat m militiaman
Milliardär –in [mɪljar'der(ɪn)] §8 mƒ multimillionaire
Milliarde [mɪl'jardə] ƒ (-;-n) billion
Milligramm [mɪlɪ'gram] n milligram
Millimeter [mɪlɪ'metər] n & m millimeter
Millime'terpapier n graph paper
Million [mɪl'jon] ƒ (-;-en) million
Millionär –in [mɪljɔ'ner(ɪn)] §8 mƒ millionaire
millionste [mɪl'jonstə] §9 adj & pron millionth
Milz [mɪlts] ƒ (-;) spleen
Mime ['mimə] m (-n;-n) mime
Mimiker –in ['mimɪkər(ɪn)] §6 mƒ mimic
Mimose [mɪ'mozə] ƒ (-;-n) mimosa
minder ['mɪndər] adj lesser, smaller; (geringer) minor, inferior ‖ adv less; **m. gut** inferior; **nicht m.** likewise
min'derbedeutend adj less important
min'derbegabt adj less talented
min'derbemittelt adj of moderate means
Min'derbetrag m shortage, deficit
Min'derheit ƒ (-;-en) minority
min'derjährig adj underage ‖ **Minderjährige** §5 mƒ minor

mindern ['mɪndərn] *tr* lessen, diminish
Min'derung *f* (-;-en) diminution
min'derwertig *adj* inferior
Min'derwertigkeit *f* inferiority
Min'derwertigkeitskomplex *m* inferiority complex
Min'derzahl *f* minority
Mindest– [mɪndəest] *comb.fm.* minimum
mindeste ['mɪndəstə] §9 *adj* least; (*kleinste*) smallest; **nicht die mindesten Aussichten** not the slightest chance; **nicht im mindesten** not in the least; **zum mindesten** at the very least
mindestens ['mɪndəstəns] *adv* at least
Min'destgebot *n* lowest bid
Min'destlohn *m* minimum wage
Mine ['minə] *f* (-;-n) (*im Bleistift*) lead; (mil, min) mine; **alle Minen springen lassen** (fig) pull out all the stops
Minenleger ['minənlegər] *m* (-s;-) minelayer
Minenräumboot ['minənrɔɪmbot] *n* minesweeper
Mineral [minə'ral] *n* (-s;-e & -ien [jən]) mineral
mineralisch [minə'ralɪʃ] *adj* mineral
Mineralogie [minəralo'gi] *f* (-;) mineralogy
Miniatur [minja'tur] *f* (-;-en) miniature
minieren [mi'nirən] *tr* (fig) undermine; (mil) mine
minimal [mini'mal] *adj* minimal
Minirock ['minirɔk] *m* miniskirt
Minister [mi'nɪstər] *m* (-s;-) minister, secretary
Ministe•rium [minɪs'terjum] *n* (-s; -rien [rjən]) ministry, department
Mini'sterpräsident *m* prime minister
Mini'sterrat *m* (-[e]s;-̈e) cabinet
Ministrant [minɪs'trant] *m* (-en;-en) altar boy, acolyte
Minne ['minə] *f* (-;) (obs) love
Min'nesänger *m* minnesinger; troubadour
minorenn [mino'rɛn] *adj* underage
minus ['minus] *adv* minus || **Minus** *n* (-;-) minus; (com) deficit
Minute [mi'nutə] *f* (-;-n) minute
Minu'tenzeiger *m* minute hand
-minutig [minutɪç] *comb.fm.* -minute
Minze ['mɪntsə] *f* (-;-n) (bot) mint
mir [mir] §11 *pers pron* me, to me, for me; **mir ist kalt** I am cold; **mir nichts, dir nichts** suddenly; **von mir aus** for all I care || §11 *reflex pron* myself, to myself, for myself
Mirabelle [mira'bɛlə] *f* (-;-n) yellow plum
Mirakel [mi'rakəl] *n* (-s;-) miracle
Mira'kelspiel *n* miracle play
Mischehe ['mɪʃe•ə] *f* mixed marriage
mischen ['mɪʃən] *tr* mix, blend; (cards) shuffle
Mischling ['mɪʃlɪŋ] *m* (-es;-e) halfbreed; mongrel
Mischmasch ['mɪʃmaʃ] *m* (-es;-e) hodgepodge
Mischpult ['mɪʃpult] *n* (rad, telv) master console

Mischrasse ['mɪʃrasə] *f* cross-breed
Mi'schung *f* (-;-en) mixture, blend
Misere [mi'zerə] *f* (-;-n) misery
Miß–, miß– [mɪs] *comb.fm.* mis-, dis-, amiss; bad, wrong, false
mißach'ten *tr* disregard; (*geringschätzen*) slight
mißartet [mɪs'artət] *adj* degenerate
miß'behagen *intr* (*dat*) displeasure || **Mißbehagen** *n* (-s;) displeasure
miß'bilden *tr* misshape, deform
Miß'bildung *f* (-;-en) deformity
miß'billigen *tr* disapprove
Miß'billigung *f* (-;-en) disapproval
Miß'brauch *m* abuse; (*falsche Anwendung*) misuse
mißbrau'chen *tr* abuse; misuse
mißbräuchlich ['mɪsbrɔɪçlɪç] *adj* improper
mißdeu'ten *tr* misinterpret
missen ['mɪsən] *tr* miss; do without
Miß'erfolg *m* failure, flop
Miß'ernte *f* bad harvest
Missetat ['mɪsətat] *f* misdeed; (*Verstoß*) offense; (*Verbrechen*) felony; (*Sünde*) sin
Missetäter –in ['mɪsətetər(ɪn)] §6 *mf* wrongdoer; offender; felon; sinner
mißfal'len §72 *intr* (*dat*) displease || **Mißfallen** *n* (-s;) displeasure
miß'fällig *adj* displeasing; (*anstößig*) shocking; (*verächtlich*) disparaging
miß'farben, miß'farbig *adj* discolored
Miß'geburt *f* freak
mißgelaunt ['mɪsgəlaunt] *adj* in bad humor, sour
Miß'geschick *n* (-s;) mishap; misfortune
Miß'gestalt *f* deformity; monster
miß'gestaltet *adj* deformed, misshapen
mißgestimmt ['mɪsgəʃtɪmt] *adj* grumpy
mißglücken (**mißglük'ken**) *intr* (SEIN) fail, not succeed
mißgön'nen *tr* begrudge
Miß'griff *m* mistake
Miß'gunst *f* grudge, jealousy
mißhan'deln *tr* mistreat
Miß'heirat *f* mismarriage
Mißhelligkeit ['mɪshɛlɪçkaɪt] *f* (-;-en) friction, disagreement
Mission [mi'sjon] *f* (-;-en) mission
Missionar [mɪsjo'nar] *m*, **Missionär** [mɪsjo'ner] *m* (-s;-e) missionary
Miß'klang *m* dissonance; (fig) sour note
Miß'kredit *m* discredit, disrepute
mißlang [mɪs'laŋ] *pret* of **mißlingen**
miß'lich *adj* awkward; (*gefährlich*) dangerous; (*bedenklich*) critical
miß'liebig *adj* unpopular
mißlingen [mɪs'lɪŋən] §142 *intr* (SEIN) go wrong, misfire, prove a failure || **Mißlingen** *n* (-s;) failure
Miß'mut *m* bad humor; discontent
miß'mutig *adj* sullen; discontented
mißra'ten §63 *intr* (SEIN) go wrong, misfire; **mißratene Kinder** spoiled children
Miß'stand *m* bad state of affairs; **Mißstände abschaffen** remedy abuses
Miß'stimmung *f* dissension; (*Mißmut*) bad humor
Miß'ton *m* dissonance; (fig) sour note

mißtrau′en *intr* (*dat*) mistrust, distrust || **Miß′trauen** *n* (–s;) mistrust
mißtrauisch [′mɪstrau·ɪʃ] *adj* distrustful
Miß′vergnügen *n* displeasure
miß′vergnügt *adj* cross; discontented
Miß′verhältnis *n* disproportion
Miß′verständnis *n* misunderstanding
miß′verstehen §146 *tr* & *intr* misunderstand
Miß′wirtschaft *f* mismanagement
Mist [mɪst] *m* (–es;) dung, manure; (*Schmutz*) dirt; (fig) mess, nonsense; **M. machen** (coll) blow the job; (*Spaß machen*) (coll) horse around; **viel M. verzapfen** talk a lot of nonsense
Mist′beet *n* hotbed
Mistel [′mɪstəl] *f* (–;–n) mistletoe
misten [′mɪstən] *tr* (*Stall*) muck; (*Acker*) fertilize
Mist′fink *m* (coll) dirty brat
Mist′haufen *m* manure pile
mistig [′mɪstɪç] *adj* dirty; (*sehr unangenehm*) very unpleasant
mit [mɪt] *adv* along; also, likewise; simultaneously || *prep* (*dat*) with; **mit 18 Jahren** at the age of eighteen
Mit′angeklagte §5 *mf* codefendant
Mit′arbeit *f* cooperation, collaboration
mit′arbeiten *intr* cooperate, collaborate; **m. an** (*dat*) contribute to
Mit′arbeiter –in §6 *mf* co-worker
Mit′arbeiterstab *m* staff
mit′bekommen §99 *tr* receive when leaving; (*verstehen*) get, catch
mit′benutzen *tr* use jointly
Mit′bestimmung *f* share in decision making
mit′bewerben *ref* (um) compete (for)
Mit′bewerber –in §6 *mf* competitor
mit′bringen §65 *tr* bring along
Mitbringsel [′mɪtbrɪŋzəl] *n* (–s;–) little present
Mit′bürger –in §6 *mf* fellow citizen
Mit′eigentümer –in §6 *mf* co-owner
miteinan′der *adv* together
mit′empfinden §59 *tr* sympathize with
Mit′erbe *m.* **Mit′erbin** *f* coheir
Mitesser [′mɪtɛsər] *m* (–s;–) pimple, blackhead
mit′fahren §71 *intr* (SEIN) ride along; **j–n m. lassen** give s.o. a lift
mit′fühlen *tr* share, sympathize with
mit′fühlend *adj* sympathetic
mit′gehen §82 *intr* (SEIN) (mit) go along (with)
Mit′gift *f* dowry
Mit′giftjäger *m* fortune hunter
Mit′glied *n* member; **M. auf Lebenszeit** life member
Mit′gliederversammlung *f* general meeting
Mit′gliederzahl *f* membership
Mit′gliedsbeitrag *m* dues
Mit′gliedschaft *f* (–;–en) membership
Mit′gliedskarte *f* membership card
Mit′gliedstaat *m* member nation
Mit′haftung *f* joint liability
mit′halten §90 *intr* be one of a party; **ich halte mit** I'll join you
mit′helfen §96 *intr* help along, pitch in

Mit′helfer –in §6 *mf* assistant
Mit′herausgeber –in §6 *mf* coeditor
Mit′hilfe *f* assistance
mithin′ *adv* consequently
mit′hören *tr* listen in on; (*zufällig*) overhear; (rad, telp) monitor
Mit′inhaber –in §6 *mf* copartner
Mit′kämpfer –in §6 *mf* fellow fighter
mit′klingen §142 *intr* resonate
mit′kommen §99 *intr* (SEIN) come along; (fig) keep up
mit′kriegen *tr* (coll) see **mitbekommen**
Mit′läufer –in §6 *mf* (pol) fellow traveler
Mit′laut *m* consonant
Mit′leid *n* compassion, pity
Mit′leidenschaft *f*—**j–n in M. ziehen** affect s.o.
mit′leidig *adj* compassionate; pitiful
Mit′leidsbezeigung *f* condolences
mit′leidslos *adj* pitiless
mit′leidsvoll *adj* full of pity
mit′machen *tr* participate in, join in on; (*ertragen*) suffer, endure
Mit′mensch *m* fellow man
mit′nehmen §116 *tr* take along; (*erschöpfen*) wear out, exhaust; (*abholen*) pick up; (*Ort, Museum*) visit, take in; **j–n arg m.** treat s.o. roughly
mitnichten [mɪt′nɪçtən] *adv* by no means, not at all
mit′rechnen *tr* include || *intr* count
mit′reden *tr*—**ein Wort mitzureden haben bei** have a say in || *intr* join in a conversation
Mit′reisende §5 *mf* travel companion
mit′reißen §53 *tr* (& fig) carry away
mit′reißend *adj* stirring
mitsamt [mɪt′zamt] *prep* (*dat*) together with
mit′schreiben §62 *intr* take notes
Mit′schuld *f* (an *dat*) complicity in
mit′schuldig *adj* (an *dat*) accessory (to) || **Mitschuldige** §5 *mf* accomplice
Mit′schüler –in §6 *mf* schoolmate
mit′singen §142 *intr* sing along
mit′spielen *intr* play along; (fig) be involved; **j–m arg** (or **übel**) **m.** play s.o. dirty
Mit′spieler –in §6 *mf* partner
Mit′spracherecht *n* right to share in decision making
mit′sprechen §64 *tr* say with (*s.o.*) || *intr* be involved; (*an e–r Entscheidung beteiligt sein*) share in decision making
Mit′tag *m* noon; (poet) South; **M. machen** stop for lunch; **zu M. essen** eat lunch
Mittag– *comb.fm.* midday, noon; lunch
Mit′tagbrot *n,* **Mit′tagessen** *n* lunch
mit′täglich *adj* midday, noontime
mittags [′mɪtaks] *adv* at noon
Mit′tagskreis *m,* **Mit′tagslinie** *f* meridian
Mit′tagsruhe *f* siesta
Mit′tagsstunde *f* noon; lunch hour
Mit′tagstisch *m* lunch table; lunch; **gut bürglicher M.** good home cooking
Mit′tagszeit *f* noontime; lunch time
Mit′täter –in §6 *mf* accomplice
Mit′täterschaft *f* complicity

Mitte ['mɪtə] ƒ (-;-n) middle, midst; (*Mittelpunkt*) center; **ab durch die M.!** (coll) scram!; **aus unserer M.** from among us; **die goldene M.** the golden mean; **die richtige M.** treffen hit a happy medium; **er ist M. Vierzig** he is in his mid-forties; **in die M.** nehmen take by both arms; (sport) sandwich in; **j–m um die M.** fassen put one's arms around s.o.'s waist

mit'teilbar *adj* communicable

mit'teilen *tr* tell; (*im Vertrauen*) intimate; **ich muß Ihnen leider m.,** **daß** I regret to inform you that

mitteilsam ['mɪttaɪlzɑm] *adj* communicative

Mit'teilung ƒ (-;-en) communication; information; (*amtliche*) communiqué; (*an die Presse*) release

mittel ['mɪtəl] *adj* medium, average || **Mittel** *n* (-s;-) middle; means; (*Heil–*) remedy; (*Maßnahme*) measure; (*Ausweg*) expedient; (*Durchschnitt*) average; (math) mean; (phys) medium; **im M.** on the average; **ins M. treten** (or **sich ins M. legen**) intervene, intercede; **letztes M.** last resort; **mit allen Mitteln** by every means; **Mittel** *pl* resources, means; funds; **M. und Wege** ways and means; **M. zum Zweck** means to an end; **sicheres M.** reliable method

Mit'telalter *n* Middle Ages

mittelalterlich ['mɪtəlaltərlɪç] *adj* medieval

Mit'telamerika *n* Central America

mittelbar ['mɪtəlbɑr] *adj* indirect

Mit'telgang *m* center aisle

Mit'telgebirge *n* highlands

Mit'telgewicht *n* (box) middleweight class

Mittelgewichtler ['mɪtəlgəvɪçtlər] *m* (-s;-) middleweight boxer

Mit'telgröße ƒ medium size

mit'telhochdeutsch *adj* Middle High German || **Mittelhochdeutsch** *n* (-es;) Middle High German

Mit'tellage ƒ central position; (mus) middle range

mittelländisch ['mɪtəllɛndɪʃ] *adj* Mediterranean

Mit'telläufer *m* (fb) center halfback

mit'tellos *adj* penniless, destitute

Mit'telmaß *n* medium; balance; average

mitt'telmäßig *adj* medium, mediocre; (*leidlich*) indifferent, so–so

Mit'telmäßigkeit ƒ mediocrity

Mit'telmast *m* mainmast

Mit'telmeer *n* Mediterranean

Mit'telohr *n* middle ear

Mit'telpreis *m* average price

Mit'telpunkt *m* center

mittels ['mɪtəls] *prep* (*genit*) by means of

Mit'telschiff *n* (archit) nave

Mit'telschule ƒ secondary school

Mit'tels·mann *m* (-[e]s;ᵉer & –leute) go-between; (com) middleman

Mit'telsorte ƒ medium quality

Mit'telsperson ƒ see **Mittelsmann**

Mit'telstand *m* middle class

Mit'telstürmer *m* (fb) center forward

Mit'telweg *m* middle course; **der goldene M.** the golden mean; **e–n M.** einschlagen steer a middle course

Mit'telwort *n* (-[e]s;ᵉer) (gram) participle

mitten ['mɪtən] *adv*—**m. am Tage** in broad daylight; **m. auf dem Wege** well on the way; **m. auf der Straße;** right in the middle of the street; **m. aus** from the midst of, from among; **m. darin** right in the very center (of it, of them); **m. entzwei brechen** break right in two; **m. im Winter** in the dead of winter; **m. in der Luft** in midair; **m. ins zwanzigste Jahrhundert** well into the twentieth century

Mitternacht ['mɪtərnaxt] ƒ midnight

mitternächtig ['mɪtərneçtɪç], **mitternächtlich** ['mɪtərneçtlɪç] *adj* midnight

Mittler –in ['mɪtlər(ɪn)] §6 *mƒ* mediator; (com) middleman

mittlere ['mɪtlərə] §9 *adj* middle, central; (*durchschnittlich*) average; (*mittelmäßig*) medium; (math) mean; **der Mittlere Osten** the Middle East; **in mittleren Jahren sein** be middleaged; **von mittlerer Größe** medium-sized

mitt'lerweile *adv* in the meantime

mittschiffs ['mɪtʃɪfs] *adv* amidships

Mittwoch ['mɪtvɔx] *m* (-[e]s;-e) Wednesday

mitun'ter *adv* now and then

mit'unterzeichnen *tr* & *intr* countersign

mit'verantwortlich *adj* jointly responsible

Mit'verantwortung ƒ joint responsibility

Mit'verschworene §5 *mƒ* co-conspirator

Mit'welt ƒ present generation; our (his, etc.) contemporaries

mit'wirken *intr* (**an** *dat* or **bei**) cooperate (in)

Mit'wirkung ƒ cooperation

Mit'wissen *n*—**ohne mein M.** without my knowledge

Mitwisser –in ['mtvɪsər(ɪn)] §6 *mƒ* accessory; one in the know

mit'zählen *tr* include || *intr* count along

mixen ['mɪksən] *tr* mix

Mixgetränk ['mɪksgətreŋk] *n* mixed drink

Mixtur [mɪks'tur] ƒ (-;-en) mixture

Möbel ['møbəl] *n* (-s;-) piece of furniture; **Möbel** *pl* furniture

Mö'belstück *n* piece of furniture

Möbeltransporteur ['møbəltranspɔrtør] *m* (-s;-e) mover

Mö'belwagen *m* moving van

mobil [mo'bil] *adj* movable; (*flink*) chipper; (mil) mobile

Mobiliar [mobɪ'ljar] *n* (-[e]s;) furniture

Mobilien [mo'biljən] *pl* movables

mobilisieren [mobɪlɪ'zirən] *tr* mobilize

Mobilisierung [mobɪlɪ'ziruŋ] ƒ (-;) mobilization

mobil'machen *tr* mobilize
Mobilmachung [mɔ'bilmaxʊŋ] *f* (-;) mobilization
möblieren [mø'blirən] *tr* furnish; **möbliert wohnen** (coll) live in a furnished room; **neu m.** refurnish
mochte ['mɔxtə] *pret* of **mögen**
Mode ['modə] *f* (-;-n) fashion, style
Mo'debild *n* fashion plate
Modell [mɔ'dɛl] *n* (-[e]s;-e) model; (*Muster*) pattern; (fig) prototype; **M. stehen zu** (*dat*) model for
modellieren [mɔdɛ'lirən] *tr* fashion, shape
Modell'puppe *f* mannequin
modeln ['modəln] *tr* fashion, shape; (**nach**) model (on) || *ref*—**zu alt sein, um sich m. zu lassen** be too old to change
Mo'dengeschäft *n* dress shop
Mo'denschau *f* fashion show
Mo'denzeitung *f* fashion magazine
Moder ['modər] *m* (-;) mold; mustiness; (*Schlamm*) mud
Mo'derduft *m*, **Mo'dergeruch** *m* musty smell
moderig ['modərɪç] *adj* moldy, musty
modern [mɔ'dɛrn] *adj* modern || ['modərn] *intr* rot, decay || **Modern** *n* (-s;) decay
modernisieren [mɔdɛrnɪ'zirən] *tr* modernize; bring up to date
Mo'deschmuck *m* costume jewelry
Mo'deschriftsteller **–in** §6 *mf* popular writer
Mo'dewaren *pl* (com) novelties
modifizieren [mɔdɪfɪ'tsirən] *tr* modify
modisch ['modɪʃ] *adj* fashionable
Modistin [mɔ'dɪstɪn] *f* (-;-nen) milliner
modrig ['modrɪç] *adj* moldy
modulieren [mɔdu'lirən] *tr* modulate; (*Stimme*) inflect
Mo•dus ['modʊs] *m* (-;-di [di]) mode, manner; (gram) mood
mogeln ['mogəln] *intr* cheat || **Mogeln** *n* (-s;) cheating
mögen ['møgən] §114 *tr* like, care for; **ich mag lieber** I prefer || *mod aux* may; can; care to; **er mag nicht nach Hause gehen** he doesn't care to go home; **ich möchte lieber bleiben** I'd rather stay; **ich möchte wissen** I should like to know; **mag kommen was da will** come what may; **wer mag das nur sein?** who can that be?; **wie mag das geschehen sein?** how could this have happened?
möglich ['møklɪç] *adj* possible; (*ausführbar*) feasible; **sein möglichstes tun** do one's utmost || **Mögliche** §5 *n* possibility; **er muß alles Mögliche bedenken** he must consider every possibility; **im Rahmen des Möglichen** within the realm of possibility
möglichenfalls ['møklɪçənfals], **möglicherweise** ['møklɪçərvaɪzə] *adv* possibly, if possible
Mög'lichkeit *f* (-;-en) possibility; potentiality; **ist es die M.!** well, I never!; **finanzielle Möglichkeiten** financial means; **nach M.** as far as possible

möglichst ['møklɪçst] *adv* as ... as possible
Mohn [mon] *m* (-[e]s;-e) poppyseed; (bot) poppy
Mohn'samen *m* poppyseed
Mohr [mor] *m* (-en;-en) Moor
Möhre ['mørə] *f* (-;-n) carrot
Mohr'rübe *f* carrot
Mokka ['mɔka] *m* (-s;-s) mocha (*coffee*)
Molch [mɔlç] *m* (-[e]s;-e) salamander
Mole ['molə] *f* (-;-n) mole, breakwater
Molekül [mɔlɛ'kyl] *n* (-s;-e) molecule
molekular [mɔleku'lar] *adj* molecular
Molke ['mɔlkə] *f* (-;) whey
Molkerei [mɔlkə'raɪ] *f* (-;-en) dairy
Moll [mɔl] *invar n* (mus) minor
mollig ['mɔlɪç] *adj* plump; (*Frau*) buxom; (*behaglich*) snug, cozy
Moll'tonart *f* (mus) minor key
Moment [mo'mɛnt] *m* (-[e]s;-e) moment || *n* (-[e]s;-e) momentum; (*Antrieb*) impulse, impetus; (*Faktor*) factor, point; (*Beweggrund*) motive
momentan [momɛn'tan] *adj* momentary
Moment'aufnahme *f* snapshot; (*Bewegungsaufnahme*) action shot
Monarch [mo'narç] *m* (-en;-en) monarch
Monar•chie [monar'çi] *f* (-;-chien ['çi•ən]) monarchy
Monat ['monat] *m* (-[e]s;-e) month
monatelang ['monatəlaŋ] *adj* lasting for months || *adv* for months
mo'natlich *adj* monthly
Mo'natsbinde *f* sanitary napkin
Mo'natsfluß *m* menstruation
mo'natsweise *adv* monthly
Mönch [mœnç] *m* (-[e]s;-e) monk, friar
Mönchs'kappe *f* monk's cowl
Mönchs'kloster *n* monastery
Mönchs'kutte *f* monk's habit
Mönchs'orden *m* monastic order
Mönchs'wesen *n* monasticism
Mond [mont] *m* (-[e]s;-e) moon; **abnehmender M.** waning moon; **zunehmender M.** waxing moon
mondän [mon'dɛn] *adj* sophisticated
Mond'fähre *f* (rok) lunar lander
Mond'finsternis *f* lunar eclipse
mond'hell' *adj* moonlit
Mond'jahr *n* lunar year
Mond'kalb *n* (fig) born fool
Mond'schein *m* moonlight
Mond'sichel *f* crescent moon
Mond'sucht *f* lunacy; somnambulism
mond'süchtig *adj* moonstruck
Moneten [mo'netən] *pl* (coll) dough
monieren [mo'nirən] *tr* criticize; remind
Monogramm [mono'gram] *n* (-s;-e) monogram
Monolog [mono'lok] *m* (-s;-e) monologue
Monopol [mono'pol] *n* (-s;-e) monopoly
monopolisieren [monopolɪ'zirən] *tr* monopolize
monoton [mono'ton] *adj* monotonous
Monotonie [monɔtɔ'ni] *f* (-;) monotony

Monsterfilm ['mɔnstərfɪlm] *m* (cin) spectacular
Monstranz [mɔn'strants] *f* (-;-en) monstrance
monströs [mɔn'strøs] *adj* monstrous
Monstrosität [mɔnstrɔzɪ'tet] *f* (-;-en) monstrosity
Mon·strum ['mɔnstrum] *n* (-;-stra [stra]) monster
Monsun [mɔ'zun] *m* (-s;-e) monsoon
Montag ['mɔntɑk] *m* (-[e]s;-e) Monday
Montage [mɔn'tɑʒə] *f* (-;-n) mounting, fitting; (mach) assembly
Monta'gebahn *f*, **Monta'geband** *n* assembly line
Monta'gehalle *f* assembly room
montags ['mɔntɑks] *adv* Mondays
Montan– [mɔntɑn] *comb.fm.* mining
Monteur [mɔn'tør] *m* (-s;-e) assembly-man, mechanic
Monteur'anzug *m* coveralls
montieren [mɔn'tirən] *tr* mount, fit; (*zusammenbauen*) assemble; (*einrichten*) install; (*aufstellen*) set up
Montur [mɔn'tur] *f* (-;-en) uniform
Moor [mor] *n* (-[e]s;-e) swamp
Moor'bad *n* mud bath
moorig ['morɪç] *adj* swampy
Moos [mos] *n* (-es;) moss; (*Geld*) (coll) dough
Mop [mɔp] *m* (-s;-s) mop
Moped ['mopɛd] *n* (-s;-s) motor bike, moped
moppen ['mɔpən] *tr* mop
mopsen ['mɔpsən] *tr* (coll) swipe || *ref* be bored stiff; be upset
Moral [mo'rɑl] *f* (-;) morality; (*Nutzwendung*) moral; (mil) morale
moralisch [mo'rɑlɪʃ] *adj* moral
moralisieren [mɔralɪ'zirən] *intr* moralize
Moralität [mɔralɪ'tet] *f* (-;) morality
Morast [mo'rast] *m* (-es;-e & -̈e) mire; morass, quagmire
Mord [mɔrt] *m* (-[e]s;-e) murder
Mord'anschlag *m* murder attempt; (pol) assassination attempt
Mord'brennerei *f* arson and murder
Mord'bube *m* murderer, assassin
morden ['mɔrdən] *tr* & *intr* murder
Mörder –in ['mœrdər(ɪn)] §6 murderer
möderisch ['mœrdərɪʃ] *adj* murderous; (coll) awful, terrible
mord'gierig *adj* bloodthirsty
Mord'kommission *f* homicide squad
mord'lustig *adj* bloodthirsty
Mords– [mɔrts] *comb.fm.* huge; terrible, awful; fantastic, incredible
Mords'angst *f* mortal fear
Mords'geschichte *f* tall story
Mords'geschrei *n* loud shouting
Mords'kerl *m* (coll) great guy
mords'mäßig *adv* (coll) awfully
Mords'spektakel *n* awful din
Mord'tat *f* murder
Mord'waffe *f* murder weapon
Mores ['morɛs] *pl*—**j-n M. lehren** teach s.o. manners
morgen ['mɔrgən] *adv* tomorrow; **m. abend** tomorrow evening (or night); **m. früh** tomorrow morning; **m. in**

acht Tagen (or **über acht Tage**) a week from tomorrow; **m. mittag** tomorrow noon || **Morgen** *m* (-s;-) morning; acre; **des Morgens** in the morning || *n* (-;) tomorrow
Mor'genblatt *n* morning paper
Mor'gendämmerung *f* dawn, daybreak
mor'gendlich *adj* morning
Mor'gengabe *f* wedding present
Mor'gengrauen *n* dawn, daybreak
Mor'genland *n* Orient
Morgenländer –in ['mɔrgənlendər(ɪn)] §6 *mf* Oriental
Mor'genrock *m* house robe
Mor'genrot *n*, **Mor'genröte** *f* dawn, sunrise; (fig) dawn, beginning
morgens ['mɔrgəns] *adv* in the morning
Mor'genstern *m* morning star
Mor'genstunde *f* morning hour
Mor'genzeitung *f* morning paper
morgig ['mɔrgɪç] *adj* tomorrow's
Morphium ['mɔrfjum] *n* (-s;) morphine
morsch [mɔrʃ] *adj* rotten; (*baufällig*) dilapidated; (*brüchig*) brittle; (fig) decadent
Morsealphabet ['mɔrzə·alfabet] *n* Morse code
Mörser ['mœrzər] *m* (-s;-) (& mil) mortar
Mör'serkeule *f* pestle
Mörtel ['mœrtəl] *m* (-s;-) mortar; plaster; **mit M. bewerfen** roughcast
Mör'telkelle *f* trowel
Mör'teltrog *m* hod
Mosaik [mɔzɑ'ik] *n* (-s;-en) mosaic
mosaisch [mo'zɑ·ɪʃ] *adj* Mosaic
Moschee [mo'ʃe] *f* (-;-n) mosque
Moskau ['mɔskau] *n* (-s;) Moscow
Moslem ['mɔsləm] *m* (-s;-s) Moslem
moslemisch [mɔs'lemɪʃ] *adj* Moslem
Most [mɔst] *m* (-es;-e) must, grape juice; new wine
Mostrich ['mɔstrɪç] *m* (-[e]s;-e) mustard
Motel [mo'tel] *n* (-s;-s) motel
Motiv [mo'tif] *n* (-[e]s;-e) (*Beweggrund*) motive; (mus, paint) motif
motivieren [mɔti'virən] *tr* justify
Mo·tor ['motər], [mo'tor] *m* (-s; -toren ['torən] & -tore ['torə]) motor
Mo'tordefekt *m* motor trouble
Mo'torhaube *f* (aer) cowl; (aut) hood
–motorig [motorɪç] *comb.fm.* –motor, –engine
Mo'torpanne *f* (aut) breakdown
Mo'torpflug *m* tractor plow
Mo'torrad *n* motorcycle
Mo'torradfahrer –in §6 *mf* motorcyclist
Mo'torrasenmäher *m* power mower
Mo'torroller *m* motor scooter
Mo'torsäge *f* power saw
Mo'torschaden *m* engine trouble
Motte ['mɔtə] *f* (-;-n) moth
mot'tenfest *adj* mothproof
Mot'tenkugel *f* mothball
Motto ['mɔto] *n* (-s;-s) motto
moussieren [mu'sirən] *intr* fizz; (*Wein*) sparkle
Möwe ['møvə] *f* (-;-n) sea gull

Mucke ['mʊkə] *f* (–;–n) whim; (dial) gnat; **Mucken haben** have moods
Mücke ['mʏkə] *f* (–;–n) gnat; mosquito; (dial) fly
Mucker ['mʊkər] *m* (–s;–) hypocrite; bigot; grouch; (coll) awkward guy
Muckerei [mʊkə'raɪ] *f* (–;) hypocrisy
muckerhaft ['mʊkərhaft] *adj* hypocritical, bigoted
Mucks [mʊks] *m* (–es;–e) faint sound; **keinen M. mehr!** not another sound!
mucksen ['mʊksən] *ref* & *intr* stir, say a word; **nicht gemuckst!** stay pat!
müde ['mydə] *adj* tired; **zum Umfallen m.** ready to drop
Mü'digkeit *f* (–;) weariness
Muff [mʊf] *m* (–[e]s;–e) (*Handwärmer*) muff; (*Schimmel*) mold; musty smell
Muffe ['mʊfə] *f* (–;–n) (mach) sleeve
muffeln ['mʊfəln] *intr* sulk, be grouchy; (*anhaltend kauen*) munch; mumble
muffig ['mʊfɪç] *adj* musty; (*Person*) sulky; (*Luft*) stale, frowzy
Mühe ['my·ə] *f* (–;–n) trouble, pains; (*Anstrengung*) effort; **geben Sie sich keine M.!** don't bother; **j–m M. machen** cause s.o. trouble; **mit M.** with difficulty; **mit M. und Not** barely; **nicht der M. wert** not worthwhile; **sich** [*dat*] **große M. machen** go to great pains; **verlorene M.** wasted effort
mü'helos *adj* easy, effortless
muhen ['mu·ən] *intr* moo, low
mühen ['my·ən] *ref* take pains
mü'hevoll *adj* hard, troublesome
Mühewaltung ['my·əvaltʊŋ] *f* (–;) trouble, efforts; **für Ihre M. dankend, verbleiben wir** ... thanking you for your cooperation, we remain ...
Mühle ['mylə] *f* (–;–n) mill
Mühlrad ['mylrat] *n* water wheel
Mühlstein ['mylʃtaɪn] *m* millstone
Muhme ['mumə] *f* (–;–n) aunt; cousin
Mühsal ['myzal] *f* (–;–e) trouble
mühsam ['myzam] *adj* wearisome; (*Leben*) hard; (*Arbeit*) painstaking || *adv* with effort, with difficulty
mühselig ['myzelɪç] *adj* (*Arbeit*) hard; (*Leben*) miserable, tough
Mulatte [mu'latə] *m* (–n;–n), **Mulattin** [mu'latɪn] *f* (–;–nen) mulatto
Mulde ['mʊldə] *f* (–;–n) trough; (geol) depression, basin
Mull [mʊl] *m* (–[e]s;) gauze
Müll [myl] *m* (–[e]s;) dust, ashes; (*Abfälle*) trash, garbage
Müll'abfuhr *f* garbage disposal
Müll'abfuhrwagen *m* garbage truck
Müll'eimer *m* trash can, garbage can
Müller ['mylər] *m* (–s;–) miller
Müllerin ['mylərɪn] *f* (–;–nen) miller's wife; miller's daughter
Müll'fahrer *m* garbage man
Müll'haufen *m* scrap heap
Müll'platz *m* garbage dump
Müll'schaufel *f* dustpan
Mulm [mʊlm] *m* (–[e]s;) rotten wood
mul'mig *adj* rotten; dusty; (*Luft*) sticky; (*Lage*) ticklish

Multiplikation [mʊltɪplɪka'tsjon] *f* (–;) multiplication
multiplizieren [mʊltɪplɪ'tsirən] *tr* multiply
Mumie ['mumjə] *f* (–;–n) mummy
Mumm [mʊm] *m* (–s;) (coll) drive, grit
Mummelgreis ['mumalɡraɪs] *m* (coll) old fogey
mummeln ['mumaln] *tr* & *intr* mumble
Mund [mʊnt] *m* (–[e];–er) mouth; **den M. aufreißen** brag; **den M. halten** shut up; **den M. vollnehmen** talk big; **e–n losen M. haben** answer back; **sich** [*dat*] **den Mund verbrennen** put one's foot into it; **wie auf den M. geschlagen** dumbfounded
Mund'art *f* dialect
Mündel ['mʏndəl] *m* & *n* (–s;–) & *f* (–;–n) ward
Mündelgelder ['mʏndəlɡeldər] *pl* trustfund
mün'delsicher *adj* gilt-edged; absolutely safe
munden ['mundən] *intr* taste good
münden ['mʏndən] *intr*—m. **in** (*acc*) empty into, flow into
mund'faul *adj* too lazy to talk
mund'gerecht *adj* palatable
Mund'geruch *m* halitosis
Mund'harmonika *f* mouth organ
Mund'höhle *f* oral cavity
mündig ['mʏndɪç] *adj* of age
Mün'digkeit *f* (–;) majority, full age
mündlich ['mʏntlɪç] *adj* oral, verbal
Mund'pflege *f* oral hygiene
Mund'sperre *f* lockjaw
Mund'stück *n* mouthpiece; (*Zigaretten*–) tip; (*Düse*) nozzle
mund'tot *adj*—j–n m. **machen** (fig) silence s.o.
Mund'tuch *n* table napkin
Mün'dung *f* (*e–s Flusses*) mouth; (*e–r Feuerwaffe*) muzzle
Mün'dungsfeuer *n* muzzle flash
Mün'dungsweite *f* (arti) bore
Mund'vorrat *m* provisions
Mund'wasser *n* mouthwash
Mund'werk *n* (fig) mouth, tongue
Mund'winkel *m* corner of the mouth
Munition [munɪ'tsjon] *f* (–;) ammunition
Munitions'lager *n* ammunition dump
munkeln ['muŋkəln] *tr* & *intr* whisper
Münster ['mʏnstər] *m* (–s;–) cathedral
munter ['muntər] *adj* awake; (*lebhaft*) lively; (*rüstig*) vigorous; gay
Münz– [mʏnts] *comb.fm.* monetary; of the mint; coin; coinage; coin-operated
Münz'anstalt *f* mint
Münze ['mʏntsə] *f* (–;–n) coin; change; (*Münzanstalt*) mint; (*Denkmünze*) medal; **bare M.** hard cash; **für bare Münze nehmen** take at face value
Münz'einheit *f* monetary unit
Münz'einwurf *m* coin slot
münzen ['mʏntsən] *tr* coin, mint; **das ist auf ihn gemünzt** that is meant for him || **Münzen** *n* (–s;) mintage, coinage
Münz'fälscher *m* counterfeiter
Münz'fernsprecher *m* public telephone

Münz'kunde *f* numismatics
Münz'wesen *n* monetary system
Münz'wissenschaft *f* numismatics
mürb [mʏrp], **mürbe** ['mʏrbə] *adj*
(*Fleisch*) tender; (*sehr reif*) mellow;
(*gut durchgekocht*) well done; (*Gebäck*) crisp and flaky; (*brüchig*)
brittle; (*erschöpft*) worn out; (mil)
demoralized; **j–n mürbe machen** (fig)
break s.o. down; **mürbe werden**
soften, give in
Murks [mʊrks] *m* (**–es;**) bungling job
murksen ['mʊrksən] *intr* bungle
Murmel ['mʊrməl] *f* (**–;–n**) marble
murmeln ['mʊrməln] *tr* & *intr* murmur
Mur'meltier *n* ground hog, woodchuck
murren ['mʊrən] *intr* grumble
mürrisch ['mʏrɪʃ] *adj* grouchy, crabby
Mus [mus] *n* (**–es;–e**) purée; sauce
Muschel ['mʊʃəl] *f* (**–;–n**) mussel;
(*Schale*) shell; (anat) concha
Muse ['muzə] *f* (**–;–n**) (myth) Muse
Muse·um [mʊ'ze·um] *n* (**–s;–en**) museum
Musik [mʊ'zik] *f* (**–;**) music
Musikalien [muzɪ'kaljən] *pl* music
book
musikalisch [muzɪ'kalɪʃ] *adj* musical
Musikant [muzɪ'kant] *m* (**–en;–en**)
musician
Musikan'tenknochen *m* funny bone
Musik'automat *m*, **Musikbox** ['mjuzɪkbɔks] *f* (**–;–en**) juke box
Musiker –in ['muzɪkər(ɪn)] §6 *mf*
musician
Musik'hochschule *f* conservatory
Musik'kapelle *f* band
Musik'korps *n* military band
Musik'pavillon *m* bandstand
Musik'schrank *m*, **Musik'truhe** *f* radiophonograph console
Musi·kus ['muzɪkus] *m* (**–;–zi** [tsi])
(hum) musician
Musik'wissenschaft *f* musicology
musisch ['muzɪʃ] *adj* artistic
musizieren [muzɪ'tsirən] *intr* play
music
Muskat [mʊs'kat] *m* (**–[e]s;–e**) nutmeg
Muskateller [muska'tɛlər] *m* (**–s;**)
muscatel
Muskat'nuß *f* nutmeg
Muskel ['mʊskəl] *m* (**–s;–n**) muscle
Mus'kelkater *m* (coll) charley horse
Mus'kelkraft *f* brawn
Mus'kelriß *m* torn muscle
Mus'kelschwund *m* muscular distrophy
Mus'kelzerrung *f* pulled muscle
Muskete [mʊs'ketə] *f* (**–;–n**) musket
Muskulatur [muskula'tur] *f* (**–;–en**)
muscles, muscular system
muskulös [mʊsku'løs] *adj* muscular
Muß [mʊs] *invar n* must, necessity
Muße ['musə] *f* (**–;**) leisure; **mit M.**
at leisure
Muß'ehe *f* shotgun wedding
Musselin [mʊsə'lin] *m* (**–s;–e**) muslin
müssen ['mʏsən] *intr*—**ich muß nach
Hause** I must go home || *mod aux*—
ich muß (*inf*) I must (*inf*), I have to
(*inf*); **ich muß nicht** I don't have to;
muß das wirklich sein? is it really
neecessary?; **sie hätten hier sein m.**

they ought to have been here; **sie
müssen bald kommen** they are bound
to come soon
müßig ['mysɪç] *adj* idle; (*unnütz*) unprofitable; (*zwecklos*) useless; (*überflüssig*) superfluous
Mü'ßiggang *m* idleness
Müßiggänger *m* loafer
mußte ['mustə] *pret* of **müssen**
Muster ['mustər] *n* (**–s;–**) pattern;
(*Probestück*) sample; (*Vorbild*) example, model; **das M. e–r Hausfrau**
a model housewife; **nach dem M.
von** along the lines of; **sich** [*dat*]
ein M. nehmen an (*dat*) model oneself on
Mu'sterbeispiel *n* typical example
Mu'sterbild *n* ideal, paragon
Mu'stergatte *m* model husband
Mu'stergattin *f* model wife
mu'stergültig *adj* model, ideal
Mu'stergut *n* model farm
mu'sterhaft *adj* model, ideal
Mu'sterknabe *m* (pej) sissy
Mu'sterkollektion *f* (kit of) samples
mustern ['mustərn] *tr* examine, eye,
size up; (mil) inspect, review
Mu'sterprozeß *m* test case
Mu'sterschüler –in §6 *mf* model pupil
Mu'sterstück *n* specimen, sample
Mu'sterstudent –in §7 *mf* model student
Mu'sterung *f* (**–;–en**) inspection; examination; (mil) review
Mu'sterungsbescheid *m* induction ŋotice
Mu'sterungskommission *f* draft board
Mu'sterwerk *n* standard work
Mu'sterwort *n* (**–[e]s;–er**) (gram) paradigm
Mut [mut] *m* (**–[e]s;**) courage; **den
Mut sinken lassen** lose heart; **guten
Mutes sein** feel encouraged; **j–m
den Mut nehmen** discourage s.o.;
nur Mut! cheer up!
Mutation [muta'tsjon] *f* (**–;–en**) (biol)
mutation, sport
Mütchen ['mytçən] *n*—**sein M. kühlen
an** (*dat*) take it out on
mutieren [mu'tirən] *intr* (*Stimme*)
change
mutig ['mutɪç] *adj* courageous, brave
–mütig [mytɪç] *comb.fm.* **–minded,
–feeling**
mut'los *adj* discouraged
Mut'losigkeit *f* (**–;**) discouragement
mutmaßen ['mutmasən] *tr* suppose,
conjecture
mutmaßlich ['mutmaslɪç] *adj* supposed, alleged; **mutmaßlicher Erbe**
heir presumptive || *adv* presumably
Mut'maßung *f* (**–;–en**) conjecture,
guesswork; **Mutmaßungen anstellen**
conjecture
Mutter ['mutər] *f* (**–;–̈**) mother; **werdende M.** expectant mother || *f* (**–;–n**) nut
Mut'terboden *m* rich soil
Mütterchen ['mytərçən] *n* (**–s;–**)
mummy; little old lady
Mut'tererde *f* rich soil; native soil
Mut'terfürsorge *f* maternity welfare
Mut'terkuchen *m* (anat) placenta

Mut'terleib *m* womb
Mütterlich ['mʏtərlıç] *adj* motherly, maternal; **m. verwandt** related on the mother's side
mut'terlos *adj* motherless
Mut'termal *n* birthmark
Mut'terpferd *n* mare
Mut'terschaf *n* ewe
Mut'terschaft *f* (–;) motherhood, maternity
Mut'terschlüssel *m* (mach) wrench
mut'terseelenallein' *adj* all alone
Muttersöhnchen ['mutərzønçən] *n* (–s;–) mamma's boy
Mut'tersprache *f* mother tongue
Mut'terstelle *f*—**bei j–m die M. vertreten** be a mother to s.o.
Mut'terstute *f* mare
Mut'tertier *n* (zool) dam
Mut'terwitz *m* common sense
Mutti ['muti] *f* (–;–s) (coll) mom
mut'voll *adj* courageous
Mut'wille *m* mischievousness

mut'willig *adj* mischievous, willful
Mütze ['mʏtsə] *f* (–;–n) cap
Myriade [mʏrı'adə] *f* (–;–n) myriad
Myrrhe ['mʏrə] *f* (–;–n) myrrh
Myrte ['mʏrtə] *f* (–;–n) myrtle
Mysterienspiel [mʏs'terjənʃpil] *n* (theat) mystery play
mysteriös [mʏstɛ'rjøs] *adj* mysterious
Myste·rium [mʏs'terjum] *n* (–s;–rien [rjən]) mystery
mystifizieren [mʏstıfı'tsirən] *tr* mystify; (*täuschen*) hoax
Mystik ['mʏstık] *f* (–;) mysticism
My'stiker –**in** §6 *mf* mystic
mystisch ['mʏstıʃ] *adj* mystic(al)
Mythe ['mʏtə] *f* (–;–n) myth
mythisch ['mʏtıʃ] *adj* mythical
Mytholo·gie [mʏtəlɔ'gi] *f* (–;–gien ['gi·ən]) mythology
mythologisch [mʏtɔ'logıʃ] *adj* mythological
My·thus ['mʏtus] *m* (–;–then [tən]) myth

N

N, n [ɛn] *invar n* N, n
na [na] *interj* well!; **na also!** there you are!; **na, so was!** don't tell me!; **na, und ob!** I'll say!; **na, warte!** just you wait!
Nabe ['nabə] *f* (–;–n) hub
Nabel ['nabəl] *m* (–s;–) navel
Na'belschnur *f* umbilical cord
nach [nax] *adv* after; **n. und n.** little by little; **n. wie vor** now as ever || *prep* (*dat*) (*Zeit*) after; (*Reihenfolge*) after, behind; (*Ziel, Richtung*) to, towards, for; (*Art, Maß, Vorbild, Richtschnur*) according to, after
Nach–, nach– *comb.fm.* subsequent, additional; supplementary; post–; over, over again, re–; after
nach'äffen *tr* ape, imitate
nachahmen ['naxamən] *tr* imitate, copy
Nach'ahmer –**in** §6 *mf* imitator
Nach'ahmung *f* (–;–en) imitation, copy
nach'arbeiten *tr* copy; (*ausbessern*) touch up; (*Versäumtes*) make up for
nach'arten *intr* (SEIN) (*dat*) take after
Nachbar ['naxbar] *m* (–s & –n;–n), **Nachbarin** ['naxbarın] *f* (–;–nen) neighbor
nach'barlich *adj* neighborly; neighboring
Nach'barschaft *f* (–;–en) neighborhood; **gute N. halten** be on friendly terms with neighbors
Nach'bau *m* (–s;) imitation, duplication; licensed manufacture; **unerlaubter N.** illegal manufacture
Nach'behandlung *f* (med) follow-up treatment
nach'bestellen *tr* reorder, order more of
Nach'bestellung *f* (–;–en) repeat order
nach'beten *tr* & *intr* repeat mechanically

nach'bezahlen *tr* pay afterwards; pay the rest of || *intr* pay afterwards
Nach'bild *n* copy
nach'bilden *tr* copy
Nach'bildung *f* (–;–en) copying; (*Kopie*) copy, reproduction; (*Modell*) mock-up; (*Attrappe*) dummy
nach'bleiben §62 *intr* (SEIN) remain behind; (educ) stay in; **hinter j–m n.** lag behind s.o.
nach'blicken *intr* (*dat*) look after
nach'brennen §97 *intr* smolder || **Nachbrennen** *n* (–s;) (rok) afterburn
Nach'brenner *m* (aer) afterburner
nach'datieren *tr* postdate
nachdem [nax'dem] *adv* afterwards; **je n.** as the case may be, it all depends || *conj* after, when; **je n.** according to how, depending on how
nach'denken §66 *intr* think it over; **n. über** (*acc*) think over, reflect on || **Nachdenken** *n* (–s;) reflection; **bei weiterem N.** on second thought
nach'denklich *adj* reflective, thoughtful; (*Buch*) thought-provoking; (*abwesend*) lost in thought
Nach'dichtung *f* (–;–en) free poetical rendering
nach'drängen *intr* (SEIN) (*dat*) crowd after; pursue
nach'dringen §142 *intr* be in hot pursuit; (*dat*) pursue
Nach'druck *m* (*Betonung*) stress, emphasis; energy; (*Raubdruck*) pirated edition; (typ) reprint; **mit N.** emphatically; **N. verboten** all rights reserved
nach'drucken *tr* reprint
nach'drücklich *adj* emphatic; **n. betonen** emphasize
nach'dunkeln *intr* get darker
nach'eifern *intr* (*dat*) emulate

nach'eilen *intr* (SEIN) (*dat*) hasten after, rush after

nacheinan'der *adv* one after another

nach'empfinden §59 *tr* have a feeling for; **j-m etw n.** sympathize with s.o. about s.th.

Nachen ['naxən] *m* (–s;–) (poet) boat

nach'erzählen *tr* repeat, retell

Nachfahr ['naxfar] *m* (–s;–en) descendant

nach'fahren §71 *intr* (SEIN) (*dat*) drive after, follow

nach'fassen *tr* (mil) get a second helping of || *intr* (econ) do a follow-up

Nach'folge *f* succession

nach'folgen *intr* (*dat*) succeed, follow; follow in the footsteps of

nach'folgend *adj* following, subsequent

Nach'folger –in §6 *mf* follower; successor

nach'fordern *tr* charge extra; claim subsequently

nach'forschen *intr* (*dat*) investigate

Nach'frage *f* inquiry; (com) demand

nach'fragen *intr* (nach) ask (about)

Nach'frist *f* time extension

nach'fühlen *tr*—**j-m etw n.** sympathize with s.o. about s.th.

nach'füllen *tr* refill, fill up

nach'geben §80 *tr* give later; (*beim Essen*) give another helping of; **j-m nichts an Eifer n.** not be outdone by s.o. in zeal || *intr* give way, give; (*schlaff werden*) slacken, give; (*dat*) give in to, yield to

nach'geboren *adj* younger; posthumous

Nach'gebühr *f* postage due

nach'gehen §82 *intr* (SEIN) (*dat*) follow; (*Geschäften*) attend to; (*untersuchen*) investigate, check on

nachgemacht ['naxgəmaxt] *adj* false, imitation; (*künstlich*) artificial

nachgeordnet ['naxgə·ɔrdnət] *adj* subordinate

nach'gerade *adv* by now; (*allmählich*) gradually; (*wirklich*) really

Nach'geschmack *m* aftertaste, bad taste

nachgewiesenermaßen ['naxgəvizənərmasən] *adv* as has been shown (or proved)

nachgiebig ['naxgibɪç] *adj* elastic, yielding, compliant; (*nachsichtig*) indulgent; (st. exch.) declining

nach'gießen §76 *tr* fill up, refill || *intr* add more

nach'glühen *tr* (tech) temper || *intr* smolder

nach'grübeln *intr* (*dat* or **über** *acc*) mull (over), ponder (on)

Nach'hall *m* echo, reverberation

nach'hallen *intr* echo, reverberate

nachhaltig ['naxhaltɪç] *adj* lasting

nach'hängen §92 *intr* (*dat*) give free rein to || *impers*—**es hängt mir nach** I still feel the effects of it

nach'helfen §96 *intr* (*dat*) help along

nach'her *adv* afterwards, later, then; **bis n.!** so long!

nachherig ['naxherɪç] *adj* later

Nach'hilfe *f* assistance, help

Nach'hilfelehrer –in §6 *mf* tutor

Nach'hilfestunde *f* tutoring lesson

Nach'hilfeunterricht *m* tutoring

nach'hinken *intr* (*dat*) lag behind

Nachholbedarf ['naxholbədarf] *m* backlog of unsatisfied demands

nach holen *tr* make up for

Nach'hut *f* (mil) rear guard

nach'jagen *tr*—**j-m etw n.** send s.th. after s.o. || *intr* (SEIN) (*dat*) pursue

Nach'klang *m* echo; (fig) reminiscence

nach'klingen §142 *intr* reecho, resound

Nachkomme ['naxkɔmə] *m* (–n;–n) offspring, descendant

nach'kommen §99 *intr* (SEIN) (*dat*) follow; join (*s.o.*) later; (*Vorschriften, e–m Gesetz*) obey; (*e–m Versprechen*) keep; (*e–r Pflicht*) live up to

Nach'kommenschaft *f* (–;) posterity

Nachkömmling ['naxkœmlɪŋ] *m* (–s; –e) offspring, descendant

Nach·laß ['naxlas] *m* (–lasses;–lässe) remission; (*am Preis*) reduction; (*Erbschaft*) estate; **literarischer N.** unpublished works

nach'lassen §104 *tr* leave behind; (*lockern*) slacken; **j-m 15% vom Preise n.** give s.o. a fifteen percent reduction in price || *intr* (*sich lockern*) slacken; (*sich vermindern*) diminish; (*milder werden*) relent; (*Regen*) let up; (*Kräfte*) give out; (*Wind, Sturm*) die down; (*schlechter werden*) get worse

Nach'laßgericht *n* probate court

nach'lässig *adj* careless, negligent

Nach'lässigkeit *f* carelessness, negligence

nach'laufen §105 *intr* (SEIN) (*dat*) run after, pursue

nach'leben *intr* (*dat*) live up to || **Nachleben** *n* afterlife

Nach'lese *f* gleanings

nach'lesen §107 *tr* glean; (*Stelle im Buch*) reread, look up

nach'liefern *tr* deliver subsequently

nach'machen *tr* imitate; (*fälschen*) counterfeit; **j-m alles n.** imitate s.o. in everything

nach'malen *tr* copy

nachmalig ['naxmalɪç] *adj* later

nachmals ['naxmals] *adv* afterwards

nach'messen §70 *tr* measure again

Nach'mittag *m* afternoon

nach'mittags *adv* in the afternoon

Nach'mittagsvorstellung *f* matinée

Nach'nahme *f* (–;) C.O.D.

Nach'name *m* last name, family name

nach'plappern *tr* repeat mechanically

Nach'porto *n* postage due

nachprüfbar ['naxpryfbar] *adj* verifiable

nach'prüfen *tr* verify, check out

nach'rechnen *tr* (acct) check

Nach'rede *f* epilogue; **j-n in üble N. bringen** bring s.o. into bad repute; **üble N.** slander; **üble N. verbreiten** spread nasty rumors

nach'reden *tr*—**j-m etw n.** say s.th. behind s.o.'s back

Nachricht ['naxrɪçt] *f* (–;–en) news; (*Bericht*) report; (*kurzer Bericht*) notice; (*Auskunft*) information; **e–e N. verbreiten** spread the news; **geben Sie mir von Zeit zu Zeit N.!** keep me advised; **Nachrichten** (rad, telv) news, news report; **Nachrichten einholen** make inquiries; **Nachrichten einziehen** gather information; **zur N.!** for your information

Nach'richtenabteilung *f* (mil) intelligence section

Nach'richtenagentur *f* news agency

Nach'richtenbüro *n* news room; news agency

Nach'richtendienst *m* news service; (mil) army intelligence

Nach'richtensatellit *m* communications satellite

Nach'richtensendung *f* newscast

Nach'richtenwesen *n* communications

nach'rücken *intr* (SEIN) (im *Rang*) move up; (mil) (*dat*) follow up; **j–m n.** move up into s.o.'s position

Nach'ruf *m* obituary

nach'rufen §122 *tr* (*dat*) call after

Nach'ruhm *m* posthumous fame

nach'rühmen *tr*—**j-m etw n.** say s.th. nice about s.o.

nach'sagen *tr*—**j-m etw n.** repeat s.th. after s.o.; say s.th behind s.o.'s back; **das lasse ich mir nicht n.** I won't let that be said of me

Nach'satz *m* concluding clause

nach'schaffen *tr* replace

nach'schauen *intr* (*dat*) gaze after

nach'schicken *tr* forward

Nachschlagebuch ['nɑxʃlɑgəbux] *n* reference book

nach'schlagen §132 *tr* look up; (*Buch*) consult || *intr* (box) counter

Nachschlagewerk ['nɑxʃlɑgəvɛrk] *n* reference work

Nach'schlüssel *m* skeleton key

nach'schreiben §62 *tr* copy; take down from dictation

Nach'schrift *f* postscript

Nach'schub *m* (mil) supply, fresh supplies; (mil) supply lines

Nach'schublinie *f* (mil) supply line

Nach'schubstützpunkt *m* (mil) supply base

Nach'schubweg *m* supply line

nach'sehen §138 *tr* (*nachschlagen*) look up; (*nachprüfen*) check; (acct) audit; (mach) overhaul; **j-m vieles n.** overlook much in s.o. || *intr* (*dat*) gaze after || **Nachsehen** *n*—**das N. haben** get the short end

nach'senden §140 *tr* send after, forward

nach'setzen *intr* (*dat*) run after

Nach'sicht *f* patience; **mit j-m N. üben** have patience with s.o.

nach'sichtig, nach'sichtsvoll *adj* lenient, considerate

Nach'silbe *f* suffix

nach'sinnen §121 *intr* (**über** *acc*) reflect (on), muse (over)

nach'sitzen *intr* be kept in after school

Nach'sommer *m* Indian summer

Nach'speise *f* dessert

Nach'spiel *n* (fig) sequel

nach'spüren *intr* (*dat*) track down

nächst [nɛçst] *prep* (*dat*) next to

nächst'beste §9 *adj* second-best

nächstdem' *adv* thereupon

nächste ['nɛçstə] §9 *adj* (*super* of

nahe) next; (*Weg*) shortest; (*Beziehungen*) closest || **Nächste** §5 *mf* neighbor, fellow man, fellow creature

nach'stehen §146 *intr* (*dat*) be inferior to

nach'stehend *adj* following || *adv* (mentioned) below

nach'stellen *tr* (*Schraube*) reset, adjust; (*Uhr*) set back || *intr* (*dat*) be after; (*e–m Mädchen*) run after

Nach'stellung *f* (–;–en) persecution; ambush; (gram) postposition

nächsten ['nɛçstən] *adv* one of these days, before long; next time

Näch'stenliebe *f* charity

nächst'liegend *adj* nearest

nach'stöbern *intr* rummage about

nach'stoßen §150 *intr* (SEIN) (*dat*) (mil) follow up

nach'streben *intr* (*dat*) strive after; (*e–r Person*) emulate

nach'strömen, nach'strümen, nach'stürzen *intr* (SEIN) (*dat*) crowd after

nach'suchen *tr* search for || *intr*—**n. um** apply for

Nach'suchung *f* (–;–en) search, inquiry; petition

Nacht [nɑxt] *f* (–;ꞏe) night; **bei N. und Nebel** under cover of night

Nacht'ausgabe *f* final (edition)

Nacht'teil *m* disadvantage

nach'teilig *adj* disadvantageous

Nacht'essen *n* supper

Nacht'eule *f* night owl

Nacht'falter *m* (ent) moth

Nacht'geschirr *n* chamber pot

Nacht'gleiche *f* equinox

Nacht'hemd *n* nightgown

Nachtigall ['nɑxtɪgal] *f* (–;–n) nightingale

nächtigen ['nɛçtɪgən] *intr* pass the night

Nacht'tisch *m* dessert

Nacht'klub *m,* **Nacht'lokal** *n* nightclub

Nacht'lager *n* accommodations for the night

nächtlich ['nɛçtlɪç] *adj* night, nightly

Nacht'mal *n* supper

Nacht'musik *f* serenade

nach'tönen *intr* resound; (*Note*) linger

Nacht'quartier *n* accommodations for the night

Nachtrag ['nɑxtrak] *m* (–[e]s;ꞏe) supplement, addition

nach'tragen §132 *tr* add; **j-m etw n.** carry s.th. after s.o.; (fig) hold s.th. against s.o.

nachträgerisch ['nɑxtregərɪʃ] *adj* resentful, vindictive

nachträglich ['nɑxtreklɪç] *adj* supplementary; (*später*) subsequent

Nachtrags– *comb.fm.* supplementary

Nach'trupp *m* (–s;) rear guard

nachts [nɑxts] *adv* at night

Nacht'schicht *f* night shift

nacht'schlafend *adj*—**bei** (or **zu**) **nacht schlafender Zeit** late at night

Nacht'schwärmer –in §6 *mf* reveler

Nacht'tisch *m* night table

Nacht'topf *m* chamber pot

nach'tun §154 *tr*—**j-m etw n.** imitate s.o. in s.th.

Nacht'wache *f* night watch, vigil

Nacht'wächter *m* night watchman

Nachtwandler –in ['naxtvandlər(ɪn)] §6 *mf* sleepwalker, somnambulist
Nacht'zeug *n* overnight things
Nach'urlaub *m* extended leave
nach'wachsen §155 *intr* (SEIN) grow again
Nach'wahl *f* special election
Nachwehen ['naxve·ən] *pl* afterpains; (fig) painful consequences
nach'weinen *tr*—keine Tränen n. (*dat*) waste no tears over ‖ *intr* (*dat*) cry over
Nachweis ['naxvaɪs] *m* (–es;–e) proof; den N. bringen (or führen) furnish proof
nach'weisbar *adj* demonstrable
nach'weisen §118 *tr* point, show; (*beweisen*) prove; (*begründen*) substantiate; (*verweisen*) refer to
nach'weislich *adj* demonstrable
Nach'welt *f* posterity
nach'wiegen §57 *tr* verify the weight of
nach'wirken *intr* have an aftereffect
Nach'wirkung *f* (–;–en) aftereffect
Nach'wort *n* (–[e]s;–e) epilogue
Nach'wuchs *m* younger generation; younger set; children
nach'zahlen *tr* & *intr* pay extra
nach'zählen *tr* count over, check
nach'zeichnen *tr* draw a copy of ‖ *intr* copy
nach'ziehen §163 *tr* drag; tow; (*Linien*) trace; (*Schraube*) tighten ‖ *intr* (SEIN) (*dat*) follow after
nach'zoteln *intr* (SEIN) (coll) trot after
Nachzügler –in ['naxtsyklər(ɪn)] §6 *mf* straggler; latecomer
Nackedei ['nakədaɪ] *m* (–[e]s;–e) naked child; nude
Nacken ['nakən] *m* (–s;–) nape of the neck
nackend ['nakənt] *adj* var of **nackt**
Nackenschlag (Nak'kenschlag) *m* rabbit punch; (fig) hard blow
–nackig [nakɪç] *comb.fm.* –necked
nackt [nakt] *adj* nude, bare; (*Tatsache*) hard; sich n. ausziehen strip bare
Nackt'heit *f* (–;) nudity, nakedness
Nadel ['nadəl] *f* (–;–n) needle; pin; wie auf Nadeln sitzen be on pins and needles
Na'delbaum *m* coniferous tree
Na'delkissen *n* pin cushion
Nadelöhr ['nadəlør] *n* (–s;–e) eye of a needle
Na'delstich *m* pinprick; (sew) stitch
Nagel ['nagəl] *m* (–s;–̈) nail; an den N. hängen (fig) shelve; an den Nägeln kauen bite one's nails
Na'gelhaut *f* cuticle
nageln ['nagəln] *tr* & *intr* nail
na'gelneu *adj* brand-new
nagen ['nagən] *tr* gnaw; das Fleisch vom Knochen n. pick the meat off the bone ‖ *intr* (an *dat*) gnaw (at), nibble (at); (fig) (an *dat*) rankle
Nagetier ['nagətir] *n* rodent
Nah– [na] *comb.fm.* close-range, short-range
Näh– [ne] *comb.fm.* sewing, needle-work
Näh'arbeit *f* sewing, needlework
Nah'aufnahme *f* (phot) close-up

nahe ['na·ə] *adj* (**näher** ['ne·ər]; **nächste** ['neçstə] §9) near, close; nearby; (*bevorstehend*) forthcoming; (*Gefahr*) imminent ‖ *adv*—j–m zu n. treten hurt s.o.'s feelings; n. an. (*dat* or *acc*), n. bei close to; n. daran sein zu (*inf*) be on the point of (*ger*)
Nähe ['ne·ə] *f* (–;–n) nearness; vicinity; in der N. close by
na'hebei *adv* nearby
na'hebringen §65 *tr* drive home
na'hegehen §82 *intr* (SEIN) (*dat*) affect, touch, grieve
na'hekommen §99 *intr* (SEIN) approach; (*dat*) come near to; der Wahrheit n. get at the truth
na'helegen *tr* suggest
na'heliegen §108 *intr* be close by; be obvious; be easy
na'heliegend *adj* obvious
nahen ['na·ən] *ref* & *intr* (SEIN) approach; (*dat*) draw near to
nähen ['ne·ən] *tr* & *intr* sew, stitch
näher ['ne·ər] *adj* (*comp* of **nahe**) nearer; bei näherer Betrachtung upon further consideration ‖ *adv* closer; immer n. kommen close in; treten Sie n.! this way, please! ‖ Nähere §5 *n* details, particulars; das N. auseinandersetzen explain fully; Näheres erfahren learn further particulars; sich des Näheren entsinnen remember all particulars; wenn Sie Näheres wissen wollen if you want details
Näherin ['ne·ərɪn] *f* (–;–nen) seamstress
nähern ['ne·ərn] *ref* approach; (*dat*) draw near to, approach
Nä'herungswert *m* approximate value
na'hestehen §146 *intr* (*dat*) share the view of
na'hetreten §152 *intr* (SEIN) (*dat*) come into close contact with
na'hezu *adv* almost, nearly
Näh'garn *n* thread
Nah'kampf *m* hand-to-hand fighting; (box) in-fighting
nahm [nam] *pret* of **nehmen**
Näh'maschine *f* sewing machine
–nahme [namə] *f* (–;–n) *comb.fm.* taking
Nähr– [ner] *comb.fm.* nutritive
Nähr'boden *m* rich soil; (fig) breeding ground; (biol) culture medium
nähren ['nerən] *tr* nourish, feed; (*Kind*) nurse ‖ *ref* make a living; sich n. von subsist on ‖ *intr* be nutritious
nahrhaft ['narhaft] *adj* nourishing, nutritious, nutritive
Nähr'mittel *pl* (*Teigwaren*) noodles; (*Hülsenfrüchte*) beans and peas
Nahrung ['narʊŋ] *f* (–;) nourishment; (*Kost*) diet; (*Unterhalt*) livelihood
Nah'rungsmittel *pl* food
Nah'rungsmittelvergiftung *f* food poisoning
Nah'rungssorgen *pl* difficulty in making ends meet
Nähr'wert *m* nutritive value
Näh'stube *f* sewing room
Naht [nat] *f* (–;–̈e) seam

Nah'verkehr m local traffic
Näh'zeug n sewing kit
naiv [na'if] adj naive
Name ['namə] m (-ns;-n), **Namen** ['namən] m (-s;-) name
na'menlos adj nameless; (unsäglich) indescribable
namens ['naməns] adv named, called || prep (genit) in the name of, on behalf of
Na'mensschild n nameplate
Na'menstag m name day
Na'mensvetter m namesake
namentlich ['naməntlıç] adj—namentliche Abstimmung roll-call vote || adv by name, individually; (besonders) especially
Na'menverzeichnis n index of names; nomenclature
namhaft ['namhaft] adj distinguished; (beträchtlich) considerable; **n. machen** name, specify
nämlich ['nemlıç] adv namely, that is; (coll) you know, you see
nannte ['nantə] pret of **nennen**
nanu [na'nu] interj gee!
Napf [napf] m (-es;̈-e) bowl
Narbe ['narbə] f (-;-n) scar; (des Leders) grain; (agr) topsoil
narbig ['narbıç] adj scarred
Narkose [nar'kozə] f (-;-n) anesthesia
Narkoti·kum [nar'kotıkʊm] n (-s;-ka [ka]) narcotic, dope
narkotisch [nar'kotıʃ] adj narcotic
Narr [nar] m (-en;-en) fool; (hist) jester; **j-n zum Narren halten** make a fool of s.o.
Närrchen ['nerçən] n (-s;-) silly little goose
narren ['narən] tr make a fool of
Narrenfest ['narənfest] n masquerade
Narrenhaus ['narənhaʊs] n madhouse
Narrenkappe ['narənkapə] f cap and bells
narrensicher ['narənzıçər] adj (coll) foolproof
Narren(s)possen ['narən(s)pɔsən] pl horseplay; **laß die N.!** stop horsing around!
Narr'heit f (-;-en) folly
närrisch ['nerıʃ] adj foolish; (verrückt) crazy; (Kauz) eccentric; **n. sein auf** (acc) be crazy about
Narzisse [nar'tsısə] f (-;-n) (bot) narcissus; **gelbe N.** daffodil
naschen ['naʃən] tr nibble at || intr (an dat, von) nibble (on); **gern n.** have a sweet tooth
Näscher –in ['neʃər(ın)] §6 mf nibbler
Näscherei [neʃə'raı] f (-;-en) snack
naschhaft ['naʃhaft] adj sweet-toothed
Naschkatze ['naʃkatsə] f nibbler
Naschmaul ['naʃmaʊl] n nibbler
Naschwerk ['naʃverk] n sweets, tidbits
Nase ['nazə] f (-;-n) nose; **auf der N. liegen** be laid up in bed; **aufgeworfene N.** turned-up nose; **das sticht ihm in die N.** it annoys him; he's itching to have it; **daß du die N. im Gesicht behältst!** keep your shirt on!; **dem Kind die N. putzen** wipe the child's nose; **die N. läuft ihm blau an** his nose is getting red; **die N. rüm-**

pfen über (acc) turn up one's nose at; **die N. voll haben von** be fed up with; **e-e tüchtige N. voll bekommen** get chewed out; **faß dich an deine eigene N.!** mind your own business!; **feine N. für** flair for; **immer der N. nach!** follow your nose!; **in der N. bohren** poke one's nose; **j-m e-e lange N. machen** thumb one's nose at s.o.; **j-m e-e N. drehen** outwit s.o.; **j-m die Würmer aus der N. ziehen** worm it out of s.o.; **j-m etw auf die N. binden** divulge s.th. to s.o.; **j-m in die N. fahren** (or **steigen**) annoy s.o.; **j-n an der N. herumführen** lead s.o. by the nose; **man kann es ihm an der N. ansehen** it's written all over his face; **mit langer N. abziehen** be the loser; **pro N.** per head; **sich** [dat] **die N. begießen** wet one's whistle
näseln ['nezəln] intr speak through the nose || **Näseln** n (-s;) nasal twang
nä'selnd adj nasal
Na'senbein n nasal bone
Na'senbluten n (-s;) nosebleed
na'senlang adv—**alle n.** constantly
Na'senlänge f—**um e-e N.** by a nose
Na'senlaut m (phonet) nasal
Na'senloch n nostril
Na'senrücken m bridge of the nose
Na'senschleim m mucus
Na'senschleimhaut f mucous membrane
Nasenspray ['nazənspre] m (-s;-s) nose spray
Na'sentropfen m nose drop
na'seweis adj fresh, wise || **Naseweis** m (-es;-e) wise guy
Na'seweisheit f freshness
nasführen ['nasfyrən] tr lead by the nose; (foppen) fool
Nashorn ['nashɔrn] n (-[e]s;̈-er) rhinoceros
naß [nas] adj (nasser ['nasər] or nässer ['nesər]; nasseste ['nasəstə] or nässeste ['nesəstə] §9) wet; (feucht) moist || **Naß** n (Nasses;) (poet) liquid
Nassauer ['nasaʊ·ər] m (-s;-) sponger, chiseler
nassauern ['nasaʊ·ərn] intr (coll) sponge
Nässe ['nesə] f (-;) wetness; moisture
nässen ['nesən] tr wet; moisten || intr ooze
naß'forsch adj rash, bold
naß'kalt adj raw, cold and damp
Nation [na'tsjon] f (-;-en) nation
national [natsjo'nal] adj national
National'hymne f national anthem
nationalisieren [natsjonalı'zirən] tr nationalize
Nationalismus [natsjona'lısmʊs] m (-;) nationalism
Nationalität [natsjonalı'tet] f (-;-en) nationality; ethnic minority
National'sozialismus m national socialism, Nazism
National'sozialist –in §7 mf national socialist, Nazi
National'tracht f national costume
Nativität [natıvı'tet] f (-;-en) horoscope

Natrium ['nɑtrɪ·ʊm] *n* (–s;) sodium
Natter ['natər] *f* (–;-n) adder, viper
Natur [na'tur] *f* (–;-en) nature; (*Körperbeschaffenheit*) constitution; (*Gemütsart*) disposition; (*Art*) character; (*Person*) creature; **von N.** by nature
Natura [na'tura] *f*—**in N.** in kind
Naturalien [natu'raljən] *pl* produce
naturalisieren [naturalɪ'zirən] *tr* naturalize || *ref*—**sich n.** lassen become naturalized
Natur'anlage *f* disposition
Natur'arzt *m* naturopath
Naturell [natu'rɛl] *n* (–[e]s;-e) nature, temperament
Natur'erscheinung *f* phenomenon
Natur'forscher –**in** §6 *mf* naturalist
Natur'gabe *f* natural gift, talent
natur'gemäß *adv* naturally
Natur'geschichte *f* natural history
Natur'gesetz *n* natural law
natur'getreu *adj* life-like
Natur'kunde *f*, **Natur'lehre** *f* natural science
natürlich [na'tyrlɪç] *adj* natural; (*echt*) real; (*ungezwungen*) natural; das geht aber nicht mit natürlichen Dingen zu there is s.th. fishy about it; das geht ganz n. zu there is nothing strange about it || *adv* naturally, of course
Natur'mensch *m* primitive man; nature enthusiast
Natur'philosoph *m* natural philosopher
Natur'recht *n* natural right
Natur'schutz *m* preservation of natural beauty
Natur'schutzgebiet *n* wildlife preserve
Natur'schutzpark *m* national park
Natur'spiel *n* freak of nature
Natur'theater *n* outdoor theater
Natur'trieb *m* instinct
Natur'verehrung *f* natural religion
Natur'volk *n* primitive people
natur'widrig *adj* contrary to nature
Natur'wissenschaft *f* natural science
Natur'wissenschaftler –**in** §6 *mf* scientist
naturwüchsig [na'turvyksɪç] *adj* unspoiled by civilization
Natur'zustand *m* natural state
nautisch ['naʊtɪʃ] *adj* nautical
Navigation [navɪga'tsjon] *f* (–;) navigation
navigieren [navɪ'girən] *intr* navigate
Nazi ['nɑtsi] *m* (–s;-s) Nazi
Nazismus [na'tsɪmʊs] *m* (–;) Nazism
nazistisch [na'tsɪstɪʃ] *adj* Nazi
Nebel ['nebəl] *m* (–s;–) fog, mist; (*Dunst*) haze
Ne'belbank *f* (–;ᵘe) fog bank
Ne'belfeld *n* patch of fog
Ne'belferne *f* hazy distance; (fig) dim future
Ne'belfleck *m* (astr) nebula
ne'belhaft *adj* foggy, hazy; (*Ferne*) dim
Ne'belhorn *n* foghorn
nebeln ['nebəln] *intr* be foggy
Ne'belscheinwerfer *m* (aut) fog light
Ne'belschicht *f* fog bank
Ne'belschirm *m* smoke screen
Ne'belvorhang *m* smoke screen
neben ['nebən] *prep* (*dat & acc*) by,

beside; side by side with, alongside, close to, next to; (*verglichen mit*) compared with; (*außer*) besides, aside from; in addition to; extra
Neben– *comb.fm.* secondary, accessory, by-, side-, subordinate
Ne'benabsicht *f* ulterior motive
Ne'benaltar *m* side altar
Ne'benamt *n* additional duties
nebenan' *adv* close by; next-door
Ne'benanschluß *m* (telp) extension; (telp) party line
Ne'benarbeit *f* extra work
Ne'benarm *m* tributary, branch
Ne'benausgaben *pl* incidentals, extras
Ne'benausgang *m* side exit
Ne'benbahn *f* (rr) branch line
Ne'benbedeutung *f* (–;-en) secondary meaning
nebenbei' *adv* close by; (*außerdem*) besides, on the side; (*beiläufig*) incidentally
Ne'benberuf *m* sideline, side job
ne'benberuflich *adj* sideline, spare-time
Ne'benbeschäftigung *f* sideline
Nebenbuhler –**in** ['nebənbulər(ɪn)] §6 *mf* competitor, rival
ne'benbuhlerisch *adj* rival
Ne'benbending *n* secondary matter
nebeneinan'der *adv* side by side; neck and neck; (*gleichzeitig*) simultaneously; **n. bestehen** coexist
Nebeneinan'derleben *n* coexistence
nebeneinan'derstellen *tr* juxtapose
Ne'beneingang *m* side entrance
Ne'beneinkünfte *pl*, **Ne'beneinnahmen** *pl* extra income
Ne'benerzeugnis *n* by-product
Ne'benfach *n* (educ) minor; **als N. studieren** minor in
Ne'benflügel *m* (archit) wing
Ne'benfluß *m* tributary
Ne'benfrage *f* side issue
Ne'benfrau *f* concubine
Ne'bengang *m* side aisle
Ne'bengasse *f* side street, alley
Ne'bengebäude *n* annex, wing
Ne'bengedanke *m* ulterior motive
Ne'bengericht *n* side dish
Ne'bengeschäft *n* (com) branch
Ne'bengleis *n* (rr) siding, sidetrack
Ne'benhandlung *f* (–;-en) subplot
nebenher' *adv* on the side; besides; along
nebenhin' *adv* incidentally, by the way
Ne'benkosten *pl* incidentals, extras
Ne'benlinie *f* (rr) branch line
Ne'benmann *m* (–[e]s;ᵘer) neighbor
Ne'benprodukt *n* by-product
Ne'benpunkt *m* minor point
Ne'benrolle *f* supporting role
Ne'bensache *f* side issue
ne'bensächlich *adj* subordinate; incidental; (*unwesentlich*) unimportant
Ne'bensächlichkeit *f* unimportance; triviality
Ne'bensatz *m* subordinate clause
Ne'benschaltung *f* (–;-en) (elec) shunt
Ne'benschluß *m* (elec) shunt
Ne'benspesen *pl* additional charges
ne'benstehend *adj* marginal, in the margin || **Nebenstehende** §5 *mf* bystander

Ne'benstelle f branch; (telp) extension
Ne'benstraße f side street
Ne'bentisch m next table
Ne'bentür f side door
Ne'benverdienst m extra pay; side job
Ne'benvorstellung f side show
Ne'benweg m side road
Ne'benwirkung f (-;-en) side effect
Ne'benzimmer n adjoining room
Ne'benzweck m secondary aim
neblig ['nebliç] adj foggy, misty
nebst [nepst] prep (dat) including
necken ['nɛkən] tr & recip tease, kid
Neckerei [nɛkə'raɪ] f (-;-en) teasing
neckisch ['nɛkɪʃ] adj fond of teasing; (coll) cute
nee [ne] adv (dial) no
Neffe ['nɛfə] m (-n;-n) nephew
Negation [nega'tsjon] f (-;-en) negation
negativ [nega'tif] adj negative || **Negativ** n (-s;-e) negative
Neger –in ['negər(ɪn)] §6 mf black, Negro
Negligé [negli'ʒe] n (-s;-s) negligee
nehmen ['nemən] §116 tr take; (weg-) take away; (anstellen) take on, hire; (Anwalt) retain; (Hindernis) clear, take; (Kurve) negotiate; (Schaden) suffer; **Anfang n.** begin; **Anstand n.** hesitate; **an sich n.** pocket, misappropriate; collect; retrieve; **Anstoß n. an** (dat) take offense at; **auf sich n.** assume, take upon oneself; **das Wort n.** begin to speak; **den Mund voll n.** (coll) talk big; **die Folgen auf sich n.** bear the consequences; **ein Ende n.** come to an end; **ein gutes Ende n.** turn out all right; **er versteht es, die Kunden richtig zu n.** he knows how to handle customers; **etw genau n.** take s.th. literally; **ich lasse es mir nicht n. zu** (inf) I insist on (ger); **im Grunde genommen** basically; **in Angriff n.** begin; **in Arbeit n.** start making; **in die Hand n.** pick up; (fig) take in hand; **j-m etw n.** take s.th. away from s.o.; deprive s.o. of s.th.; **kein Ende n.** go on endlessly; **man nehme zwei Eier, usw.** (im Kochbuch) take two eggs, etc.; **n. Sie bitte Platz!** please sit down; **n. wir den Fall, daß** let's suppose that; **Rücksicht n. auf** (acc) show consideration for; **sich** [dat] **das Leben n.** take one's life; **sich** [dat] **nichts von seinen Rechten n.** lassen insist on one's rights; **streng genommen** strictly speaking; **Stunden n.** take lessons; **Urlaub n.** take a vacation; (mil) go on furlough; **wie man's nimmt** it all depends; **zu Hilfe n.** use; **zur Ehe n.** marry; **zu sich** [dat] **n.** put into one's pocket; (Speise) eat; (Kind) take charge of
Neid [naɪt] m (-es;) envy; **blasser** (or **gelber**) **N.** pure envy; **vor N. vergehen** die of envy
neiden ['naɪdən] tr—**j-m etw n.** envy s.o. for s.th.
Neid'hammel m envious person
nei'dig adj (dial) var of **neidisch**
neidisch ['naɪdɪʃ] adj (**auf** acc) envious (of)

neid'los adj free of envy
Neid'nagel m hangnail
Neige ['naɪgə] f (-;-n) slope; (Abnahme) decline; (Überbleibsel) sediment, dregs; **zur N. gehen** (Geld, Vorräte) run low; (Sonne) go down; (Tag, Jahr) draw to a close
neigen ['naɪgən] tr incline, bend; **geneigt** sloping; (fig) friendly, favorable || ref (**vor** dat) bow (to); (Abhang) slope; **sich zum Ende n.** draw to a close || intr—**n. zu** be inclined to
Nei'gung f (-;-en) slope, incline; (des Hauptes) bowing; (e-s Schiffes) list; (in der Straße) dip; (Gefälle) gradient; (Hang) inclination; (Anlage) tendency; (Vorliebe) taste, liking; (Zuneigung) affection; **e-e N. nach rechts haben** lean towards the right; **N. fassen zu** take (a fancy) to
nein [naɪn] adv no || **Nein** n (-s;) no
Nein'stimme f (parl) nay
Nekrolog [nekro'lok] m (-[e]s;-e) obituary
Nektar ['nektar] m (-s;) nectar
Nelke ['nɛlkə] f (-;-n) carnation; (Gewürz) clove
Nel'kenöl n oil of cloves
Nel'kenpfeffer m allspice
Nemesis ['nemezɪs] f (-;) Nemesis
nennbar ['nɛnbar] adj mentionable
nennen ['nɛnən] §97 tr name, call; (erwähnen) mention; (benennen) term || ref be called, be named
nen'nenswert adj worth mentioning
Nenner ['nɛnər] m (-s;-) (math) denominator; **auf e-n gemeinsamen N. bringen** reduce to a common denominator
Nennform ['nɛnfɔrm] f (gram) infinitive
Nenngeld ['nɛngelt] n entry fee
Nen'nung f (-;) naming; mentioning
Nennwert ['nɛnvert] m face value
Neologis•mus [ne.ɔlɔ'gismus] m (-; -men [mən]) neologism
Neon ['ne.ɔn] n (-s;) neon
Ne'onlicht n neon light
Nepotismus [nepo'tismus] m (-;) nepotism
neppen ['nɛpən] tr (coll) gyp, clip
Nepplokal ['nɛplɔkal] n (sl) clip joint
Neptun [nɛp'tun] m (-s;) Neptune
Nerv [nɛrf] m (-s;-en) nerve; **die Nerven behalten** keep cool; **die Nerven verlieren** lose one's head; **j-m auf die Nerven gehen** get on s.o.'s nerves; **mit den Nerven herunter sein** be a nervous wreck
Nerven-, nerven- [nɛrfən] comb.fm. nervous, neuro–, of nerves
Ner'venarzt m, **Ner'venärztin** f neurologist
ner'venaufreibend adj nerve-racking
Ner'venberuhigungsmittel n sedative
Ner'venbündel n (fig) bundle of nerves
Ner'venentzündung f neuritis
Ner'venfaser f nerve fiber
Ner'venheilanstalt f mental institution
Ner'venheilkunde f neurology
Ner'venkitzel m thrill, suspense
Ner'venknoten m ganglion
ner'venkrank adj neurotic

Ner′venkrieg *m* war of nerves
Ner′venlehre *f* neurology
Ner′vensäge *f* (coll) pain in the neck
Ner′venschmerz *m* neuralgia
Ner′venschwäche *f* nervousness
Ner′venzentrum *n* (fig) nerve center
Ner′venzusammenbruch *m* nervous breakdown
nervig [′nɛrvɪç], [′nɛrfɪç] *adj* sinewy
nervös [nɛr′vøs] *adj* nervous
Nervosität [nɛrvɔzɪ′tɛt] *f* (–;) nervousness
Nerz [nɛrts] *m* (–es;–e) (zool) mink
Nerz′mantel *m* mink coat
Nessel [′nɛsəl] *f* (–;–n) nettle; **sich in die Nesseln setzen** (fig) get oneself into hot water
Nest [nɛst] *n.* (–es;–er) nest; (*Schlupfwinkel*) hideout; small town; dead town; (*Bett*) (coll) bed
nesteln [′nɛstəln] *tr* lace, tie ‖ *intr* —n. an (*dat*) fiddle with, fuss with
Nesthäkchen [′nɛsthɛkçən] *n* (–s;–), Nestküken [′nɛstkykən] *n* (–s;–) baby (*of the family*)
nett [nɛt] *adj* nice; (*sauber*) neat; (*niedlich*) cute; **das kann ja n. werden!** (iron) that's going to be just dandy!
netto [′nɛto] *adv* net; clear
Net′togewicht *n* net weight
Net′togewinn *m* clear profit
Net′tolohn *m* take-home pay
Net′topreis *m* net price
Netz [nɛts] *n* (–es;–e) net; network; grid
netzen [′nɛtsən] *tr* wet, moisten
Netz′haut *f* retina
Netz′werk *n* netting, webbing
neu [nɔɪ] *adj* new; (*frisch*) fresh; (*unlängst geschehen*) recent; **aufs neue** anew; **neuere Geschichte** modern history; **neuere Sprachen** modern languages; **von neuem** all over again ‖ *adv* newly; recently; anew; afresh ‖ **Neue** §5 *mf* newcomer ‖ §5 *n*— **was gibt es Neues?** what's new?
Neu-, neu- *comb.fm.* new-, newly; re-; neo-
Neu′anlage *f* new installation; (fin) reinvestment
Neu′anschaffung *f* recent acquisition
neu′artig *adj* novel; modern
Neu′aufführung *f* (–;–en) (theat) revival
Neu′ausgabe *f* new edition, republication; (*Neudruck*) reprint
Neu′bau *m* (–[e]s;–bauten) new building
neu′bearbeiten *tr* revise
Neubelebung [′nɔɪbələbuŋ] *f* (–;–en) revival
Neu′bildung *f* (–;–en) new growth; (gram) neologism
Neu′druck *m* reprint
neuerdings [′nɔɪ·ərdɪŋs] *adv* recently; (*vom neuem*) anew
Neuerer –in [′nɔɪ·ərər(ɪn)] §6 *mf* innovator
Neuerung [′nɔɪ·əruŋ] *f* (–;–en) innovation
neuestens [′nɔɪ·əstəns] *adv* recently
Neu′fassung *f* revision

Neufundland [nɔɪ′funtlant] *n* (–s;) Newfoundland
neu′gebacken *adj* fresh-baked; brand-new
neu′geboren *adj* new-born
neu′gestalten *tr* reorganize
Neu′gier *f*, Neugierde [′nɔɪgɪrdə] *f* (–;) curiosity, inquisitiveness
neu′gierig *adj* curious, nosey
Neu′gründung *f* (–;–en) reestablishment
Neu′gruppierung *f* (–;–en) regrouping; reshuffling
Neu′heit *f* (–;–en) novelty
neu′hochdeutsch *adj* modern High German
Neu′igkeit *f* (–;–en) news, piece of news
Neu′jahr *n* New Year
Neu′land *n* virgin soil; (fig) new ground
neu′lich *adv* lately
Neuling [′nɔɪlɪŋ] *m* (–[e]s;–e) beginner
neu′modisch *adj* fashionable; newfangled
neun [nɔɪn] *invar adj & pron* nine ‖ Neun *f* (–;–en) nine
Neunmalkluge [′nɔɪnmalklugə] §5 *mf* wiseacre
neunte [′nɔɪntə] §9 *adj & pron* ninth
Neuntel [′nɔɪntəl] *n* (–s;–) ninth
neun′zehn *invar adj & pron* nineteen ‖ Neunzehn *f* (–;–en) nineteen
neun′zehnte §9 *adj & pron* nineteenth
neunzig [′nɔɪntsɪç] *invar adj & pron* ninety ‖ Neunzig *f* (–;–en) ninety
neunziger [′nɔɪntsɪgər] *invar adj* of the nineties; **die n. Jahre** the nineties ‖ Neunziger –in §6 *mf* nonagenarian
neunzigste [′nɔɪntsɪçstə] §9 *adj & pron* ninetieth
Neu′ordnung *f* (–;–en) reorganization
Neural·gie [nɔɪral′gi] *f* (–;–gien [′gi·ən]) neuralgia
Neu′regelung *f* (–;–en) rearrangement
Neu·ron [′nɔɪrɔn] *n* (–;–ronen [′ronən]) neuron
Neurose [nɔɪ′rozə] *f* (–;–n) neurosis
Neurotiker –in [nɔɪ′rotɪkər(ɪn)] §6 *mf* neurotic
neurotisch [nɔɪ′rotɪʃ] *adj* neurotic
Neusee′land *n* (–s;) New Zealand
Neu′silber *n* German silver
Neusprachler –in [′nɔɪ/praxlər(ɪn)] §6 *mf* modern-language teacher
Neu′stadt *f* new section of town
Neu′steinzeit *f* neolithic age
neu′steinzeitlich *adj* neolithic
neutral [nɔɪ′tral] *adj* neutral
neutralisieren [nɔɪtralɪ′zirən] *tr* neutralize
Neutralität [nɔɪtralɪ′tɛt] *f* (–;) neutrality
Neu·tron [′nɔɪtrɔn] *n* (–;–tronen [′tronən]) neutron
Neu·trum [′nɔɪtrum] *n* (–s;–tra [tra] & –tren [trən]) (gram) neuter
neuvermählt [′nɔɪfermɛlt] *adj* newly married ‖ Neuvermählte §5 *pl* newlyweds
Neu′zeit *f* recent times
Nibelung [′nibəluŋ] *m* (–s;) (myth)

(King) Nibelung ‖ *m* (-en;-en)
Nibelung

nicht [nɪçt] *adv* not; **auch...nicht** not
...either; **n. doch!** please don't; **n.
einmal** not even, not so much as; **n.
mehr** no longer, no more; **n. um die
Welt** not for the world; **n. wahr?**
isn't it so?, no?, right?

Nicht-, nicht- *comb.fm.* in-, im-, un-,
non-

Nicht'achtung *f* disregard, disrespect;
N. des Gerichts contempt of court

nicht'amtlich *adj* unofficial

Nicht'angriffspakt *m* nonaggression
pact

Nicht'annahme *f* nonacceptance

Nichte ['nɪçtə] *f* (-;-n) niece

Nicht'einmischung *f* noninterference

Nicht'eisenmetall *n* nonferrous metal

nichtig ['nɪçtɪç] *adj* invalid; void;
(*eitel*) vain; (*vergänglich*) transitory;
für n. erklären annul

Nich'tigkeit *f* (-;-en) invalidity; futility; (*Kleinigkeit*) trifle; **Nichtigkeiten**
trivia

Nich'tigkeitserklärung *f* annulment

Nicht'kämpfer *m* noncombatant

nicht'öffentlich *adj* private; (*Sitzung*)
closed

nicht'rostend *adj* rustproof; (*Stahl*)
stainless

nichts [nɪçts] *indef pron* nothing; **gar
n.** nothing at all; **n. als** nothing but;
n. mehr davon! not another word
about it!; **n. und wieder n.** absolutely
nothing; **soviel wie n.** next to nothing;
um n. for nothing, to no avail; **weiter
n.?** is that all?; **wenn es weiter n. ist!**
if it's nothing worse than that ‖
Nichts *n* (-s;) nothingness; nonentity;
(*Leere*) void; (*Kleinigkeit*) trifle; **vor
dem N. stehen** be faced with utter
ruin

nichtsdestowe'niger *adv* nevertheless

Nichts'könner *m* incompetent person;
ignoramus

Nichts'nutz *m* good-for-nothing

nichts'nutzig *adj* good-for-nothing

nichts'sagend *adj* insignificant; (*Antwort*) vague; noncommittal; (*Gesicht*) vacuous; (*Redensart*) trite

Nichts'tuer –in §6 *mf* loafer

Nichts'wisser –in §6 *mf* ignoramus

nichts'würdig *adj* contemptible

Nicht'zutreffende §5 *n*—**Nichtzutref-
fendes streichen!** delete if not applicable

Nickel ['nɪkəl] *n* (-;-) (metal) nickel

nicken ['nɪkən] *intr* nod; (*schlummern*)
nap

Nickerchen ['nɪkərçən] *n* (-s;-) nap

nie [ni] *adv* never, at no time

nieder ['nidər] *adj* low; (*gemein*) base
‖ *adv* down

nie'derbrechen §64 *tr & intr* (SEIN)
break down

nie'derbrennen §97 *tr & intr* (SEIN)
burn down

nie'derdeutsch *adj* Low German ‖
Niederdeutsch *n* Low German ‖
Niederdeutsche §5 *mf* North German

nie'derdonnern *tr* (coll) shout down ‖
intr go (or come) crashing down

Nie'derdruck *m* low pressure

nie'derdrücken *tr* press down (fig)
weigh down; (*unterdrücken*) oppress;
(*entmutigen*) depress

nie'derfallen §72 *intr* (SEIN) fall down

Nie'derfrequenz *f* low frequency; audio
frequency

Nie'dergang *m* descent; (*der Sonne*)
setting; (fig) decline, fall

nie'dergehen §82 *intr* (SEIN) go down;
(*Flugzeug*) land; (*Regen*) fall; (*Vorhang*) drop

nie'dergeschlagen *adj* dejected

nie'derhalten §90 *tr* hold down, keep
down

nie'derholen *tr* lower, haul down

Nie'derholz *n* underbrush

nie'derkämpfen *tr* (& fig) overcome

nie'derkommen §99 *intr* (SEIN) (**mit**)
give birth (to)

Niederkunft ['nidərkunft] *f* (-;) confinement, childbirth

Nie'derlage *f* defeat; (*Lager*) warehouse; (*Filiale*) branch

Niederlande, die ['nidərlandə] *pl* The
Netherlands, Holland

Niederländer ['nidərlɛndər] *m* (-s;-)
Dutchman

niederländisch ['nidərlɛndɪʃ] *adj* Dutch

nie'derlassen §104 *tr* let down ‖ *ref*
sit down, recline; (*Wohnsitz nehmen*)
settle; (*ein Geschäft eröffnen*) set
oneself up in business; (*Vogel, Flugzeug*) land

Nie'derlassung *f* (-;-en) settlement,
colony; establishment; (*e-r Bank*)
branch; (com) plant

nie'derlegen *tr* lay down, put down;
(*Amt*) resign; (*Geschäft*) give up;
(*Krone*) abdicate; (*schriftlich*) set
down in writing; **die Arbeit n.** go on
strike ‖ *ref* lie down; go to bed

nie'dermachen *tr* butcher, massacre

nie'dermähen *tr* mow down

nie'dermetzeln *tr* butcher, massacre

Nie'derschlag *m* (*Bodensatz*) sediment;
(box) knockdown; (chem) precipi-
tate; (meteor) precipitation; **radioaktiver N.** fallout

nie'derschlagen §132 *tr* knock down;
(*Augen*) cast down; (*Aufstand*) put
down; (*vertuschen*) hush up; (*Verfahren*) quash; (*Forderung*) waive;
(*Hoffnungen*) dash; (chem) precipitate

nie'derschmettern *tr* knock to the
ground; (fig) crush

nie'derschreiben §62 *tr* write down

nie'dersetzen *tr* set down ‖ *ref* sit down

nie'dersinken §143 *intr* (SEIN) sink
down

nie'derstimmen *tr* vote down

Nie'dertracht *f* nastiness, meanness

nie'derträchtig *adj* nasty; underhand

Nie'derung *f* (-;-en) low ground, depression

niederwärts ['nidərverts] *adv* downward

nie'derwerfen §160 *tr* knock down;
(*Aufstand*) put down ‖ *ref* fall down

Nie'derwild *n* small game

niedlich ['nitlɪç] *adj* nice, cute

Niednagel ['nitnagəl] *m* hangnail

niedrig ['nidrɪç] *adj* low; (*Herkunft*) humble; (*gemein*) mean, base

niemals ['nimɑls] *adv* never

niemand ['nimant] *indef pron* no one, nobody

Nie'mandsland *n* no man's land

Niere ['nirə] *f* (−;−n) kidney; **das geht mir an die Nieren** (fig) that cuts me deep

nieseln ['nizəln] *impers*—**es nieselt** it is drizzling

Nie'selregen *m* drizzle

niesen ['nizən] *intr* sneeze

Niet [nit] *m* (−[e]s;−e) rivet

Niete ['nitə] *f* (−;−n) rivet; (*in der Lotterie*) blank; (*Versager*) flop

nieten ['nitən] *tr* rivet

niet-' und na'gelfest *adj* nailed down

Nihilismus [nihi'lɪsmɪs] *m* (−;) nihilism

Nikotin [nikə'tin] *n* (−s;) nicotine

nikotin'arm *adj* low in nicotine

Nil [nil] *m* (−s;) Nile

Nil'pferd *n* hippopotamus

Nimbus ['nimbus] *m* (−;−se) halo; aura; (*Ansehen*) prestige; (meteor) nimbus

nimmer ['nimər] *adv* never; (dial) no more

nim'mermehr *adv* never more; by no means

Nippel ['nipəl] *m* (−s;−) (mach) nipple

nippen ['nipən] *tr & intr* sip

Nippsachen ['nipzaxən] *pl* knicknacks

nirgends ['nirgənts] *adv* nowhere

nirgendwo ['nirgəntvo] *adv* nowhere

Nische ['niʃə] *f* (−;−n) niche

nisten ['nistən] *intr* nest

Nitrat [ni'trat] *n* (−[e]s;−e) nitrate

Nitrid [ni'trit] *n* (−[e]s;−e) nitride

Nitroglyzerin [nitroglytsə'rin] *n* (−s;) nitroglycerin

Niveau [ni'vo] *n* (−s;−s) level; **N. haben** have class; **unter dem N. sein** be substandard

Niveau'übergang *m* (rr) grade crossing

nivellieren [nive'lirən] *tr* level

nix [niks] *indef pron* (dial) nothing ‖ **Nix** *m* (−[e]s;−e) water sprite

Nixe ['niksə] *f* (−;−n) water nymph

nobel ['nobəl] *adj* noble; elegant; (*freigebig*) generous

noch [nɔx] *adv* still, yet; even; else; **heute n.** this very day; **n. besser** even bettter; **n. dazu** over and above that; **n. einer** one more, still another; **n. einmal** once more; **n. einmal so viel** twice as much; **n. etwas** one more thing; **n. etwas?** anything else?; **n. heute** even today; **n. immer** still; **n. nicht** not yet; **n. nie** never before; **n. und n.** (coll) over and over; **sei es n. so klein** now matter how small it is; **was denn n. alles?** what next? **wer kommt n.?** who else is coming?

noch'mal *adv* once more

nochmalig ['nɔxmaliç] *adj* repeated

nochmals ['nɔxmals] *adv* once more

Nocke ['nɔkə] *f* (−;−n) (mach) cam

Nockenwelle (Nok'kenwelle) *f* camshaft

Nockerl ['nɔkərl] *n* (−s;− & −n) (Aust) dumpling

Nomade [nɔ'madə] *m* (−n;−n) nomad

nominell [nɔmi'nɛl] *adj* nominal

nominieren [nɔmi'nirən] *tr* nominate

Nonne ['nɔnə] *f* (−;−n) nun

Non'nenkloster *n* convent

Noppe ['nɔpə] *f* (−;−n) (tex) nap

Nord [nɔrt] *m* (−[e]s;) North; (poet) north wind

Norden ['nɔrdən] *m* (−s;) North; **im N. von** north of

nordisch ['nɔrdɪʃ] *adj* northern; (*Rasse*) Nordic; (*skandinavisch*) Norse

nördlich ['nœrtlɪç] *adj* northern

Nord'licht *n* northern lights

nordwärts ['nɔrtverts] *adv* northward

Nörgelei [nœrgə'lai] *f* (−;−en) griping

nörgelig ['nœrgəliç] *adj* nagging

nörgeln ['nœrgəln] *intr*—**n. an** (*dat*) gripe about, kick about

Norm [nɔrm] *f* (−;−en) norm, standard

normal [nɔr'mal] *adj* normal, standard

normalisieren [nɔrmali'zirən] *tr* normalize

Normal'zeit *f* standard time

Normanne [nɔr'manə] *m* (−n;−n) Norman

normen ['nɔrmən], **normieren** [nɔr'mirən] *tr* normalize, standardize

Norwegen ['nɔrvegən] *n* (−s;) Norway

Norweger –in ['nɔrvegər(in)] §6 *mf* Norwegian

norwegisch ['nɔrvegɪʃ] *adj* Norwegian

Not [not] *f* (−;⸚e) need, want; (*Notlage*) necessity; (*Gefahr*) distress; (*Dringlichkeit*) emergency; **es hat keine Not** there's no hurry about it; **es tut not** it is necessary; **in der Not** in a pinch; **in Not geraten** fall upon hard times; **j–m große Not machen** give s.o. a lot of trouble; **j–m seine Not klagen** cry on s.o.'s shoulders; **mit knapper Not** narrowly; **mit Not** scarcely; **Not haben zu** (*inf*) be scarcely able to (*inf*); **Not leiden** suffer want; **ohne Not** needlessly; **seine liebe Not haben mit** have a lot of trouble with; **sie haben Not auszukommen** they have difficulty making ends meet; **zur Not** if need be, in a pinch

Nota ['nota] *f* (−;−s) note; **etw in N. geben** place an order for s.th.; **etw in N. nehmen** make a note of s.th.

Notar –in [nɔ'tar(in)] §8 *mf* notary public

Notariat ⎸nɔta'rjat] *n* (−[e]s;−e) notary office

notariell [nɔta'rjɛl] *adv*—**n. beglaubigen** notarize

Not'ausgang *m* emergency exit

Not'ausstieg *m* escape hatch

Not'behelf *m* makeshift, stopgap

Not'bremse *f* (rr) emergency brake

Not'durft ['notdurft] *f* (−;) want; necessities of life; **seine N. verrichten** relieve oneself

not'dürftig *adj* scanty, poor; hard up; (*behelfsmäßig*) temporary

Note ['notə] *f* (−;−n) note; (*Banknote*) bill; (*Eigenart*) trait; (educ) mark; (mus) note; **in Noten setzen** set to music; **nach Noten** (fig) thoroughly; **persönliche Note** personal

touch; **wie nach Noten** like clock-work
No'tenblatt n sheet music
No'tenbuch n, **No'tenheft** n music book
No'tenlinie f (mus) line
No'tenschlüssel m (mus) clef
No'tenständer m music stand
No'tensystem n (mus) staff
Not'fall m emergency
notfalls ['notfals] adv if necessary
notgedrungen ['notgədruŋən] adj compulsory || adv of necessity
notieren [nɔ'tirən] tr note down; jot down; (Preise) quote
Notie'rung f (–;-en) noting; (st. exch.) quotation
nötig ['nøtɪç] adj necessary; **das habe ich nicht n.!** I don't have to stand for that!; **n. haben** need
nötigen ['nøtɪgən] tr urge; (zwingen) force || ref—**lassen Sie sich nicht n.!** don't wait to be asked; **sich genötigt sehen zu** (inf) feel compelled to (inf)
nö'tigenfalls adv in case of need
Nö'tigung f (–;) compulsion; urgent request; (jur) duress
Notiz [nɔ'tits] f (–;-en) notice; (Vermerk) note, memorandum; **keine N. nehmen von** take no notice of; **sich** [dat] **Notizen machen** jot down notes
Notiz'block m scratch pad
Not'lage f predicament; emergency
Not'landung f emergency landing
Not'lüge f white lie
Not'maßnahme f emergency measure
Not'nagel m (fig) stopgap
notorisch [nɔ'torɪʃ] adj notorious
Not'pfennig m savings; **sich e-n N. aufsparen** save up for a rainy day
Not'ruf m (telp) emergency
Not'signal n distress signal
Not'stand m state of emergency
Not'standsgebiet n disaster area
Not'treppe f fire escape
Not'wehr f—**aus N.** in self-defense
notwendig ['notvendɪç] adj necessary
Not'wendigkeit f (–;-en) necessity
Not'zeichen n distress signal
Not'zucht f rape
not'züchtigen tr rape, ravish
Nougat ['nugat] m & n (–s;-s) nougat
Novelle [nɔ'vɛlə] f (–;-n) short story; (parl) amendment, rider
November [nɔ'vɛmbər] m (–s;–) November
Novität [nɔvɪ'tet] f (–;-en) novelty
Novize [nɔ'vitsə] m (–n;-n), **Novizin** [nɔ'vitsɪn] f (–;-nen), novice
Noviziat [nɔvɪ'tsjat] n (–[e]s;-e) novitiate
Nu [nu] invar m—**im Nu** in a jiffy
Nuance [ny'ãsə] f (–;-n) nuance
nüchtern ['nyçtərn] adj fasting; not having had breakfast; (Magen) empty; (nicht betrunken) sober; (leidenschaftslos) cool; (geistlos) dry, dull; (unsentimental) matter-of-fact
Nudel ['nudəl] f (–;-n) noodle; **e-e komische N.** (coll) a funny person
Nu'delholz n rolling pin

nudeln ['nudəln] tr force-feed
Nugat ['nugat] m (–s;-s) nougat
nuklear [nukle'ar] adj nuclear
Nukle·on ['nukle·ɔn] n (–s;-onen ['onən]) nucleon
null [nul] adj null; **n. und nichtig** null and void; **n. und nichtig machen** annul || **Null** f (–;-en) naught; zero; (fig) nobody; **in N. Komma nichts** in less than no time, in no time
Null'punkt m zero; freezing point; **auf dem N. angekommen sein** hit bottom
Numera·le [nume'ralə] n (–s;-lien ljən] & –lia [lja]) numeral
numerieren [nume'rirən] tr number; **numerierten Platz** reserved seat
numerisch [nu'merɪʃ] adj numerical
Nummer ['numər] f (–;-n) number; (Größe) size; (e-r Zeitung) issue; **auf N. Sicher sitzen** (sl) be in jail; **bei j-m e-e gute N. haben** (coll) be in good with s.o.; **e-e bloße N.** a mere figurehead; **er ist e-e N.** he's quite a character; **laufende N.** serial number; **N. besetzt!** line is busy!
Num'mernfolge f numerical order
Num'mernscheibe f (telp) dial
Num'mernschild n (aut) license plate
nun [nun] adv now; **nun?** well?; **nun aber** now; **nun also!** well now!; **nun gut!** all right then!; **nun und nimmer(mehr)** never more; **von nun ab** from now on; **wenn er nun käme?** what if he came?
nun'mehr' adv now; from now on
nur [nur] adv only, merely, but; (lauter) nothing but; **nicht nur ... sondern auch** not only ... but also; **nur daß** except that; **nur eben** scarcely; (zeitlich) a moment ago; **nur zu!** go to it!; **wenn nur** if only, provided that
Nürnberg ['nyrnberk] n (–s;) Nuremberg
nuscheln ['nuʃəln] intr (coll) mumble
Nuß [nus] f (–; Nüsse) nut
nuß'braun adj nut-brown; (Augen) hazel
Nuß'kern m kernel
Nußknacker ['nusknakər] m (–s;–) nutcracker
Nuß'schale f nutshell
Nüster ['nystər] f (–;-n) nostril
Nut [nut] f (–;-en), **Nute** ['nutə] f (–;-n) groove, rabbet
Nutte ['nutə] f (–;-n) whore
nutz [nuts] adj useful; **zu nichts n. sein** be good for nothing || **Nutz** m (–es;) use; benefit; profit; **zu j-s N. und Frommen** for s.o.'s benefit
Nutz'anwendung f utilization
nutzbar ['nutsbar] adj useful; **sich** [dat] **etw n. machen** utilize s.th.
nutz'bringend adj useful, profitable
nütze ['nytsə] adj useful; **nichts n.** of no use; **zu nichts n. sein** be good for nothing
Nutz'effekt m efficiency
nutzen ['nutsən], **nützen** ['nytsən] tr make use of; **das kann mir viel** (**wenig, nichts**) **n.** this can do me much (little, no) good; **was nützt das**

alles? what's the good of all this? ||
intr do good || *impers*—es **nützt
nichts** it's no use || **Nutzen** *m* (-s;-)
use; benefit; (*Gewinn*) profit; (*Vor-
teil*) advantage; **von N. sein** be of use
Nutz′fahrzeug *n* commercial vehicle
Nutz′garten *m* vegetable garden
Nutz′holz *n* lumber
Nutz′leistung *f* (mech) output

nützlich ['nʏtslɪç] *adj* useful
nutz′los *adj* useless
Nutz′losigkeit *f* (-;) uselessness
Nutz′schwelle *f* break-even point
Nut′zung *f* (-;) use
Nylon ['naɪlon] *n* (-s;) nylon
Nymphe ['nʏmfə] *f* (-;-n) nymph
Nymphomanin [nʏmfɔ'manɪn] *f* (-;
-nen) nymphomaniac

O

O, o [o] *invar n* O, o
Oase [ɔ'ɑzə] *f* (-;-n) oasis
ob [ɔp] *prep* (*dat*) above; (*genit*) on
account of || *conj* whether; **als ob**
as if; **na ob!** rather!; **und ob!** and
how!
Obacht ['obaxt] *f* (-;)—**in O. nehmen**
take care of; **O.!** watch out!; **O.
geben auf** (*acc*) pay attention to;
take care of
Obdach ['ɔpdax] *n* (-[e]s;) shelter
ob′dachlos *adj* homeless
Obduktion [ɔpduk'tsjon] *f* (-;-en)
autopsy
obduzieren [ɔpdu'tsirən] *tr* perform
an autopsy on
O-Beine ['obaɪnə] *pl* bow legs
O′-beinig *adj* bowlegged
Obelisk [obe'lɪsk] *m* (-en;-en) obelisk
oben ['obən] *adv* above; (*in der Höhe*)
up; (*im Himmelsraum*) on high; (*im
Hause*) upstairs; (*auf der Spitze*) at
the top; (*auf der Oberfläche*) on the
surface; (*Aufschrift auf Kisten*) this
side up; **da o.** up there; **nach o.
gehen** go up, go upstairs; **o. am
Tische sitzen** sit at the head of the
table; **o. auf** (*dat*) at the top of, on
the top of; **von o.** from above; **von
o. bis unten** from top to bottom;
from head to foot; **von o. herab** (fig)
condescendingly; **wie o. angegeben**
as stated above
obenan′ *adv* at the top, at the head
obenauf′ *adv* on top; **immer o. sein**
be always in top spirits
obendrein [obən'draɪn] *adv* on top of
it, into the bargain
o′benerwähnt, o′bengennant *adj* above-
mentioned
o′bengesteuert *adj* (aut) overhead
obenhin′ *adv* superficially; perfunctorily
obenhinaus′ *adv*—**o. wollen** have big
ideas
o′ben-oh′ne *adj* (coll) topless
o′benstehend *adj* given above
Ober ['obər] *m* (-s;-) (coll) waiter;
Herr O.! waiter!
Ober- *comb.fm.* upper, higher; superior; chief, supreme, head; southern
O′berägypten *n* Upper Egypt
O′berarm *m* upper arm
O′beraufseher *m* inspector general;
superintendent
O′beraufsicht *f* superintendence

O′berbau *m* (-[e]s;-ten) superstructure
O′berbefehl *m* supreme command; **O.
führen** have supreme command
O′berbefehlshaber *m* commander in
chief
O′berbegriff *m* wider concept
O′berdeck *n* upper deck
O′berdeckomnibus *m* double-decker
bus
o′berdeutsch *adj* of southern Germany
obere ['obərə] §9 *adj* higher, upper;
chief, superior; supreme || **Obere** §5
m (eccl) father superior || *n* top
o′berfaul *adj* (fig) fishy
O′berfeldwebel *m* sergeant first class
O′berfläche *f* surface
o′berflächlich *adj* superficial
O′bergefreite §5 *m* corporal
O′bergeschoß *n* upper floor
O′bergewalt *f* supreme authority
o′berhalb *prep* (*genit*) above
O′berhand *f* (fig) upper hand; **die O.
gewinnen über** (*acc*) get the better
of
O′berhaupt *n* head, chief
O′berhaus *n* upper house
O′berhaut *f* epidermis
O′berhemd *n* shirt, dress shirt
O′berherr *m* sovereign
O′berherrschaft *f* sovereignty; suprem-
acy
O′berhirte *m* prelate
O′berhofmeister *m* Lord Chamberlain
O′berhoheit *f* supreme authority
Oberin ['obərɪn] *f* (-;-nen) mother
superior; (med) head nurse
O′beringenieur *m* chief engineer
o′berirdisch *adj* above-ground; over-
head
O′berkellner *m* head waiter
O′berkiefer *m* upper jaw
O′berkleidung *f* outer wear
O′berkommando *n* general headquar-
ters
O′berkörper *m* upper part of the body
O′berland *n* highlands
Oberländer -in ['obərlɛndər(ɪn)] §6
mf highlander
o′berlastig *adj* top-heavy
O′berleder *n* uppers
O′berlehrer -in §6 *mf* secondary school
teacher, high school teacher
O′berleitung *f* supervision; (elec) over-
head line (*of trolley, etc.*)
O′berleutnant *m* first lieutenant

O'berlicht *n* skylight
O'berliga *f* (sport) upper division
O'berlippe *f* upper lip
O'berpostamt *n* general post office
O'berprima *f* senior class
Obers ['obərs] *m* (-;) (Aust) cream
O'berschenkel *m* thigh
O'berschicht *f* upper layer; (*der Be-völkerung*) upper classes; **geistige O.** intelligentsia
O'berschule *f* high school
O'berschwester *f* (med) head nurse
O'berseite *f* topside, right side
Oberst ['obərst] *m* (-en;-en) colonel
O'berstaatsanwalt *m* attorney general
oberste ['obərstə] §9 *adj* (*super* of *obere*) uppermost, highest, top ‖ Oberste §5 *mf* senior, chief
O'berstimme *f* treble, soprano
O'berstleutnant *m* lieutenant colonel
O'berstock *m* upper floor
O'berwasser *n*—**O. haben** (fig) have the upper hand
O'berwelt *f* upper world
O'berwerk *n* upper manual (*of organ*)
obgleich' *conj* though, although
Ob'hut *f* (-;) care, protection
obig ['obiç] *adj* above, above-mentioned
Objekt [ɔp'jɛkt] *n* (-[e]s;-e) object
objektiv [ɔpjɛk'tif] *adj* objective; (*un-parteiisch*) impartial ‖ **Objektiv** *n* (-s;-e) objective lens
Objektivität [ɔpjɛktɪvɪ'tet] *f* (-;) objectivity; impartiality
Objekt'träger *m* slide (*of microscope*)
Oblate [ɔ'blatə] *f* (-;-n) wafer; (eccl) host
obliegen [ɔp'ligən] §108 *intr* (*dat*) apply oneself to, devote oneself to; (*dat*) be incumbent upon ‖ *impers*—es obliegt mir zu (*inf*) it's up to me to (*inf*)
Ob'liegenheit *f* (-;-en) obligation
obligat [ɔblɪ'gat] *adj* obligatory; (*uner-läßlich*) indispensable; (*unvermeid-lich*) inevitable
Obligation [ɔblɪga'tsjon] *f* (-;-en) bond; obligation
obligatorisch [ɔblɪga'torɪʃ] *adj* obligatory
Ob·mann ['ɔpman] *m* (-[e]s;⸚er & -leute) chairman; (jur) foreman
Oboe [ɔ'bo·ə] *f* (-;-n) oboe
Obrigkeit ['obrɪçkaɪt] *f* (-;-en) authority; (coll) authorities
o'brigkeitlich *adj* government(al)
obschon' *conj* though, although
Observato·rium [ɔpzɛrva'torjʊm] *n* (-s;-rien) [rjən]) observatory
obsiegen ['ɔpzigən] *intr* be victorious; (*dat*) triumph over
obskur [ɔps'kur] *adj* obscure
Obst [ɔpst] *n* (-es;) (*certain kinds of*) fruit (*mainly central-European, e.g., apples, plums; but not bananas, oranges*); **O. und Südfrüchte** European and (sub)tropical fruit
Obst'garten *m* orchard
Obst'kern *m* stone; seed, pip
Obstruktion [ɔpstruk'tsjon] *f* (-;-en) obstruction; (pol) filibuster; **O. treiben** filibuster

obszön [ɔps'tsøn] *adj* obscene
Obszönität [ɔpstsønɪ'tet] *f* (-;-en) obscenity
ob'walten, obwal'ten *intr* exist; prevail; hold sway
obwohl' *conj* though, although
Ochse ['ɔksə] *m* (-n;-n) ox
ochsen ['ɔksən] *intr* (educ) cram
O'chsenfleisch *n* beef
O'chsenfrosch *m* bullfrog
öde ['ødə] *adj* bleak ‖ öde *f* (-;-n) wasteland; (fig) bleakness
Ödem [ø'dem] *n* (-s;-e) edema
oder ['odər] *conj* or
Öd·land ['øtlant] *n* (-[e]s;-ländereien [lɛndə'rai·ən]) wasteland
Ofen ['ofən] *m* (-s;⸚) stove; (*Back-*) oven; (*Hoch-*) furnace; (*Brenn-, Dürr-*) kiln
O'fenklappe *f* damper
O'fenrohr *n* stovepipe
O'fenröhre *f* warming oven
offen ['ɔfən] *adj* open; (*öffentlich*) public; (fig) frank, open
offenbar ['ɔfənbar] *adj* obvious, manifest
offenbaren [ɔfən'barən] *tr* reveal
Offenba'rung *f* (-;-en) revelation
Of'fenheit *f* (-;) openness
of'fenherzig *adj* forthright; (*Kleid*) (hum) low-cut
of'fenkundig *adj* well-known; (*offen-sichtlich*) obvious; (*Beweis*) clear
of'fensichtlich *adj* obvious
offensiv [ɔfɛn'zif] *adj* offensive ‖ Offensive [ɔfɛn'zivə] *f* (-;-n) offensive
öffentlich ['œfəntlɪç] *adj* public; (*Dienst*) civil; **öffentliches Haus** brothel
Öf'fentlichkeit *f* (-;) public; publicity; **an die Ö. treten** appear in public; **im Licht der Ö.** in the limelight; **in aller Ö.** in public; **sich in die Ö. flüchten** rush into print
offerieren [ɔfə'rirən] *tr.* offer
Offerte [ɔ'fɛrtə] *f* (-;-n) offer
Offerto·rium [ɔfɛr'torjʊm] *n* (-s;-rien [rjən]) offertory
Offiziant [ɔfi'tsjant] *m* (-en;-en) officiating priest
offiziell [ɔfi'tsjɛl] *adj* official
Offizier -in [ɔfi'tsir(ɪn)] §6 *mf* officer
Offiziers'anwärter -in §6 *mf* officer candidate
Offiziers'bursche *m* orderly
Offiziers'deck *n* quarter deck
Offiziers'kasino *n* officers' club
Offiziers'patent *n* officer's commission
Offizin [ɔfi'tsin] *f* (-;-en) drugstore; (*Druckerei*) print shop, press
offiziös [ɔfi'tsjøs] *adj* semiofficial
öffnen ['œfnən] *tr* & *ref* open
Öff'ner *m* (-s;-) opener
Öff'nung *f* (-;-en) opening
oft [ɔft], öfter(s) ['œftər(s)] *adv* often
oftmals ['ɔftmals] *adv* often(times)
oh [o] *interj* oh!, O!
Oheim ['ohaɪm] *m* (-s;-e) uncle
Ohm [om] *m* (-s;-e) (poet) uncle ‖ *n* (-s;-) (elec) ohm
ohne ['onə] *prep* (*acc*) without; **o. daß** (*ind*) without (*ger*); **o. mich!** count

me out!; **o. weiteres** right off; **o. zu**
(*inf*) without (*ger*)
ohnedies' *adv* anyhow, in any case
ohneglei'chen *adj* unequaled
ohnehin' *adv* anyhow, as it is
Ohnmacht ['onmaxt] *f* (–;) faint, unconsciousness; helplessness; **in O.**
fallen (or **sinken**) faint, pass out
ohnmächtig ['onmeçtiç] *adj* unconscious; helpless; **o. werden** faint
Ohr [or] *n* (–[e]s;–en) ear; (*im Buch*)
dog-ear; **die Ohren spitzen** prick up
the ears; **es dick hinter den Ohren**
haben be sly; **ganz Ohr sein** be all
ears; **j–m in den Ohren liegen** keep
dinning it into s.o.'s ears; **j–n hinter**
die Ohren hauen box s.o.'s ears; **j–n**
übers Ohr hauen cheat s.o.; **sich aufs**
Ohr legen take a nap; **zum e–n Ohr**
hinein, zum anderen wieder hinaus
in one ear and out the other
Öhr [ør] *n* (–(e)s;–e) eye (*of needle*);
ax hole, hammer hole
ohrenbetäubend *adj* earsplitting
Oh'renklingen *n* ringing in the ears
Oh'rensausen *n* buzzing in the ear
Oh'renschmalz *n* earwax
Oh'renschmaus *m* treat for the ears
Ohrenschützer *m* earmuff
Ohr'feige *f* (–;–n) box on the ear
ohrfeigen ['orfaigən] *tr* box on the ear
Ohrläppchen ['orlɛpçən] *n* (–s;–) ear-
lobe
Ohr'muschel *f* auricle
okkult [ɔ'kult] *adj* occult
Ökologie [økɔlɔ'gi] *f* (–;) ecology
ökologisch [øko'logiʃ] *adj* ecological
Ökonom [øko'nom] *m* (–en;–en) economist
ökono·mie [økɔnɔ'mi] (–;–mien ['mi·
ən]) economy; economics
ökonomisch [økɔ'nomiʃ] *adj* economical
Oktav [ɔk'taf] *n* (–s;–e) octavo
Oktave [ɔk'tavə] *f* (–;–n) octave
Oktober [ɔk'tobər] *m* (–s;–) October
oktroyieren [ɔktrwa'jirən] *tr* impose
Okular [ɔku'lar] *n* (–s;–e) eyepiece
okulieren [ɔku'lirən] *tr* inoculate
Ökumene [øku'menə] *f* (–;) ecume-
nism
ökumenisch [øku'meniʃ] *adj* ecumeni-
cal
Okzident ['ɔktsidɛnt] *m* (–s;) Occident
Öl [øl] *n* (–[e]s;–e) oil; **Öl ins Feuer**
gießen (fig) add fuel to the fire
öl'baum *m* olive tree
öl'berg *m* Mount of Olives
Oleander [ɔle'andər] *m* (–s;–) oleander
ölen ['ølən] *tr* oil; (mach) lubricate
öl'götze *m* (coll) dummy, lout
öl'heizung *f* oil heat
ölig ['øliç] *adj* oily
Oligar·chie [ɔligar'çi] *f* (–;–chien**
['çi·ən]) oligarchy
Olive [ɔ'livə] *f* (–;–n) olive
Oli'venöl *n* olive oil
öl'leitung *f* pipeline
öl'quelle *f* oil well
öl'schlick *m* oil slick
öl'stand *m* (aut) oil level
öl'standanzeiger *m* oil gauge

öl'standmesser *m* (aut) oil gauge; dip
stick
ö'lung *f* (–;–en) oiling; anointing; **die**
Letzte Ö. extreme unction
Olymp [ɔ'lymp] *m* (–s;) Mt. Olympus
Olmypiade [ɔlym'pjɑdə] *f* (–;–n) olym-
piad
olympisch [ɔ'lympiʃ] *adj* Olympian;
Olympic; **die Olympischen Spiele** the
Olympics
öl'zweig *m* olive branch
Oma ['oma] *f* (–;–s) (coll) grandma
Omelett [ɔm(ə)'lɛt] *n* (–[e]s;–e & –s)
omelette
O·men ['omɛn] *n* (–s;–mina [mina])
omen
ominös [ɔmi'nøs] *adj* ominous
Omnibus ['ɔmnibus] *m* (ses;–se) bus
Onanie [ɔna'ni] *f* (–;) masturbation
ondulieren [ɔndu'lirən] *tr* (*Haar*) wave
Onkel ['ɔŋkəl] *m* (–s;– & –s) uncle;
der große O. (coll) the big toe
Opa ['opa] *m* (–s;–s) (coll) grandpa
Oper ['opər] *f* (–;–n) opera
Operateur [ɔpera'tør] *m* (–s;–s) operator; (cin) projectionist; (surg) operating surgeon
Operation [ɔpera'tsjon] *f* (–;–en) operation
Operations'gebiet *n* theater of opera-
tions
Operations'saal *m* operating room
operativ [ɔpera'tif] *adj* surgical; operational, strategic
operieren [ɔpe'rirən] *tr* operate on;
sich o. lassen undergo an operation
O'pernglas *n*, **O'perngucker** *m* opera
glasses
O'pernhaus *n* opera house, opera
Opfer ['ɔpfər] *n* (–s;–) sacrifice; victim; **zum O. fallen** (*dat*) fall victim
to
op'ferfreudig *adj* self-sacrificing
Op'fergabe *f* offering
Op'ferkasten *m* poor box
Op'ferlamm *n* sacrificial lamb; Lamb
of God; (fig) victim
Op'fermut *m* spirit of sacrifice
opfern ['ɔpfərn] *tr* sacrifice, offer up
Op'ferstock *m* poor box
Op'fertier *n* victim
Op'fertod *m* sacrifice of one's life
Op'fertrank *m* libation
Op'ferung *f* (–;–en) offering, sacrifice
op'ferwillig *adj* willing to make sacri-
fices
opponieren [ɔpo'nirən] *intr* (*dat*) oppose
opportun [ɔpor'tun] *adj* opportune
optieren [ɔp'tirən] *intr*—**o. für** opt for
Optik ['ɔptik] *f* (–;) optics
Optiker –in ['ɔptikər(in)] §6 *mf* optician
optimistisch [ɔpti'mistiʃ] *adj* optimistic
optisch ['ɔptiʃ] *adj* optic(al)
Orakel [ɔ'rakəl] *n* (–s;–) oracle
ora'kelhaft *adj* oracular
orange [ɔ'rãʒə] *adj* orange ‖ **Orange**
f (–;–n) orange
oran'genfarben, oran'genfarbig *adj* or-
ange-colored
oratorisch [ɔra'toriʃ] *adj* oratorical

Orchester [ɔr'kɛstər] *n* (-s;-) orchestra
orchestral [ɔrçɛs'trɑl] *adj* orchestral
orchestrieren [ɔrkɛs'trirən] *tr* orchestrate
Orchidee [ɔrçɪ'de·ə] *f* (-;-n) orchid
Orden ['ɔrdən] *m* (-s;-) medal, decoration; (eccl) order
Or'densband *n* (-[e]s;⸗er) ribbon
Or'densbruder *m* monk, friar
Or'denskleid *n* (eccl) habit
Or'densschwester *f* nun, sister
ordentlich ['ɔrdəntlıç] *adj* orderly;
(*aufgeräumt*) tidy; (*anständig*) decent, respectable; (*regelrecht*) regular; (*tüchtig*) sound; (*Frühstück*)
solid; (*Mitglied*) active; (*Professor*)
full; **e-e ordentliche Leistung** a
pretty good job; **in ordentlichem
Zustand** in good condition || *adv*
thoroughly, properly; (*sehr*) (coll)
awfully, very; really
Order ['ɔrdər] *f* (-;-n) (com, mil) order
ordinär [ɔrdı'nɛr] *adj* ordinary; vulgar; rude
Ordina·rius [ɔrdı'nɑrjʊs] *m* (-;-rien
[rjən]) professor; (eccl) ordinary
Ordinär'preis *m* retail price
ordinieren [ɔrdı'nirən] *tr* ordain ||
intr (med) have office hours
ordnen ['ɔrdnən] *tr* arrange; (*regeln*)
put in order; (*säubern*) tidy up
Ord'nung *f* (-;-en) order, arrangement;
classification; system; class; rank;
regulation; (mil) formation; **aus der
O. bringen** disturb; **in bester O.** in
tiptop shape; **in O. bringen** set in
order; **in O. sein** be all right; **nicht
in O. sein** be out of order; be wrong;
be out of sorts
ord'nungsgemäß *adv* duly
Ord'nungsliebe *f* tidiness, orderliness
ord'nungsmäßig *adj* orderly, regular ||
adv duly
Ord'nungsruf *m* (parl) call to order
Ord'nungssinn *m* sense of order
Ord'nungsstrafe *f* fine
ord'nungswidrig *adj* irregular, illegal
Ord'nungszahl *f* ordinal number
Ordonnanz [ɔrdɔ'nants] *f* (-;-en) (mil)
orderly
Organ [ɔr'gɑn] *n* (-s;-e) organ
Organisation [ɔrganıza'tsjon] *f* (-;-en)
organization
organisch [ɔr'gɑnıʃ] *adj* organic; (*Ge-
webe*) structural || *adv* organically
organisieren [ɔrganı'zirən] *tr* organize;
(mil) scrounge || *ref* unionize; **or-
ganisierter Arbeiter** union worker
Organis·mus [ɔrga'nısmʊs] *m* (-;-men
[mən]) organism
Organist –in [ɔrga'nıst(ın)] §7 *mf*
organist
Orgas·mus [ɔr'gasmʊs] *m* (-;-men
[mən]) orgasm
Orgel ['ɔrgəl] *f* (-;-n) organ
Or'gelzug *m* organ stop
Orgie ['ɔrgjə] *f* (-;-n) orgy
Orient ['orjɛnt] *m* (-s;) Orient
Orientale [ɔrjɛn'tɑlə] *m* (-n;-n) Ori-
entalin [ɔrjɛn'tɑlın] *f* (-;-nen) Ori-
ental
orientalisch [ɔrjɛn'tɑlıʃ] *adj* oriental

orientieren [ɔrjɛn'tirən] *tr* orient; (fig)
inform, instruct; (mil) brief
Orientie'rung *f* (-;-en) orientation; in-
formation, instruction; **die O. ver-
lieren** lose one's bearings
Orientie'rungssinn *m* sense of direction
original [ɔrıgı'nɑl] *adj* original ||
Original *n* (-s;-e) original; (typ)
copy
Original'ausgabe *f* first edition
Originalität [ɔrıgınalı'tet] *f* (-;) originality
Original'sendung *f* live broadcast
originell [ɔrıgı'nɛl] *adj* original
Orkan [ɔr'kɑn] *m* (-[e]s;-e) hurricane
Ornament [ɔrna'mɛnt] *n* (-[e]s;-e)
ornament
Ornat [ɔr'nɑt] *m* (-[e]s;-e) robes
Ort [ɔrt] *m* (-[e]s;-e) place, spot;
(*örtlichkeit*) locality; (*Dorf*) village;
am Ort sein be appropriate; **an
allen Orten** everywhere; **an Ort und
Stelle** on the spot; **an Ort und Stelle
gelangen** reach one's destination;
höheren Ortes at higher levels; **Ort
der Handlung** scene of action; **vor
Ort** on location; **vor Ort arbeiten**
(min) work at the face || *m* (-[e]s;
⸗er) position, locus
Örtchen ['œrtçən] *n* (-s;-) toilet
orten ['ɔrtən] *tr* get the bearing on,
locate || *intr* take a bearing
orthodox [ɔrtɔ'dɔks] *adj* orthodox
Orthographie [ɔrtɔgra'fi] *f* (-;) orthography
Orthopäde [ɔrtɔ'pɛdə] *m* (-n;-n),
Orthopädin [ɔrtɔ'pɛdın] *f* (-;-nen)
orthopedist
orthopädisch [ɔrtɔ'pɛdıʃ] *adj* ortho-
pedic
örtlich ['œrtlıç] *adj* local, topical
Ört'lichkeit *f* (-;-en) locality
Orts-, orts- [ɔrts] *comb.fm.* local
Orts'amt *n* (telp) local exchange
Orts'angabe *f* address
orts'ansässig *adj* resident || **Ortsan-
sässige §5** *mf* resident
Orts'behörde *f* local authorities
Orts'beschreibung *f* topography
Ort'schaft *f* (-;-en) place; (*Dorf*) vil-
lage
orts'fremd *adj* nonlocal, out-of-town
Orts'gespräch *n* (telp) local call
Orts'kenntnis *f* familiarity with a place
orts'kundig *adj* familiar with the lo-
cality
Orts'name *m* place name
Orts'sinn *m* sense of direction
Orts'veränderung *f* change of scenery
Orts'verkehr *m* local traffic
Orts'zeit *f* local time
Orts'zustellung *f* local delivery
Or'tung *f* (-;-en) (aer, naut) taking of
bearings, navigation
Öse ['øzə] *f* (-;-n) loop, eye; (*des
Schuhes*) eyelet
Ost [ɔst] *m* (-es;-e) East; (poet) east
wind
Ost- *comb.fm.* eastern, East
Osten ['ɔstən] *m* (-s;) East; **der Ferne
O.** the Far East; **der Nahe O.** the
Near East; **nach O.** eastward
ostentativ [ɔstɛnta'tif] *adj* ostentatious

Oster– [ostər] *comb.fm.* Easter
O'sterei *n* Easter egg
O'sterfest *n* Easter
O'sterhase *m* Easter bunny
O'sterlamm *m* paschal lamb
Ostern ['ostərn] *n* (–;–) & *pl* Easter
Österreich ['østəraɪç] *n* (–s;) Austria
Österreicher –in ['østəraɪçər(ɪn)] §6 *mf* Austrian
österreichisch ['østəraɪçɪʃ] *adj* Austrian
O'sterzeit *f* Eastertide
Ost'front *f* eastern front
Ost'gote *m* Ostrogoth
östlich ['œstlɪç] *adj* eastern, easterly; Oriental; ö. von east of
Ost'mark *f* East-German mark
Ost'see *f* Baltic Sea
ostwärts ['ostverts] *adv* eastward

Otter ['otər] *m* (–s;–) otter ‖ *f* (–;–n) (*Schlange*) adder
Ouvertüre [ʊver'tyrə] *f* (–;–n) (mus) overture
oval [o'val] *adj* oval ‖ Oval *n* (–s;–e) oval
Ovar [o'var] *n* (–s;–e & –ien [jən]) ovary
Overall ['ovərol] *m* (–s;–s) overalls
Oxyd [o'ksyt] *n* (–[e]s;–e) oxide
Oxydation [oksyda'tsjon] *f* (–;) oxidation
oxydieren [oksy'dirən] *tr & intr* (SEIN) oxidize
Ozean ['otsɛ·an] *m* (–s;–e) ocean; der Große (or Stille) O. the Pacific
Ozeanographie [otsɛ·anɔgra'fi] *f* (–;) oceanography
Ozon [o'tson] *n* (–s;) ozone

P

P, p [pe] *invar n* P, p
paar [par] *adj* even ‖ *invar adj*—ein p. a couple of, a few ‖ Paar *n* (–[e]s; –e) pair, couple; zu Paaren treiben rout
paaren ['parən] *tr* match, mate ‖ *ref* mate
paarig ['parɪç] *adj* in pairs
paar'laufen §105 *intr* (SEIN) skate as a couple
paar'mal *adv*—ein p. a couple of times
Paa'rung *f* (–;) pairing, matching; (*Begattung*) mating
Paa'rungszeit *f* mating season
paar'weise *adv* in pairs, two by two
Pacht [paxt] *f* (–;–en) lease; (*Geld*) rent; in P. geben lease out; in P. nehmen lease, rent
Pacht'brief *m* lease
pachten ['paxtən] *tr* take a lease on
Pächter –in ['peçtər(ɪn)] §6 *mf* tenant
Pacht'ertrag *m*, Pacht'geld *n* rent
Pacht'gut *n*, Pacht'hof *m* leased farm
Pacht'kontrakt *m* lease
Pach'tung *f* (–;–en) leasing; leasehold
Pacht'vertrag *m* lease
Pacht'zeit *f* term of lease
Pacht'zins *m* rent
Pack [pak] *m* (–[e]s;–e & ⁼e) pack; (*Paket*) parcel; (*Ballen*) bale; ein P. Spielkarten a pack of cards ‖ *n* (–[e]s;) rabble; ein P. von Lügnern a pack of liars
Päckchen ['pɛkçən] *n* (–s;–) small package; (*Zigaretten–*) pack
packen ['pakən] *tr* pack, pack up; (*fassen*) seize, grab; (fig) grip, thrill; pack dich! scram! ‖ Packen *m* (–s;–) pack; (*Ballen*) bale ‖ *n* (–s;) packing
Pack'esel *m* (fig) drudge
Pack'papier *n* wrapping paper
Pack'pferd *n* packhorse
Pack'tier *n* pack animal
Packung (Pak'kung) *f* (–;–en) packing; (*Paket*) packet; P. Zigaretten pack of cigarettes

Pack'wagen *m* (rr) baggage car
Pädadoge [pɛda'gogə] *m* (–n;–n) pedagogue
Pädagogik [pɛda'gogɪk] *f* (–;) pedagogy
pädagogisch [pɛda'gogɪʃ] *adj* pedagogical, educational
Paddel ['padəl] *n* (–s;–) paddle
Pad'delboot *n* canoe
paddeln ['padəln] *intr* paddle, canoe
Pädiatrie [pɛdɪ·a'tri] *f* (–;) pediatrics
paff [paf] *interj* bang!
paffen ['pafən] *tr & intr* puff
Page ['paʒə] *m* (–n;–n) page
Pa'genfrisur *f*, Pa'genkopf *m* pageboy
Pagode [pa'godə] *f* (–;–n) pagoda
Pair [per] *m* (–s;–s) peer
Pak [pak] *f* (–;– & –s) (Panzerabwehrkanone) antitank gun
Paket [pa'ket] *n* (–[e]s;–e) parcel; (*Bücher–*, *Post–*) bundle
Paket'adresse *f* gummed label
Paket'post *f* parcel post
Pakt [pakt] *m* (–[e]s;–e) pact
paktieren [pak'tirən] *intr* make a pact
Paläontologie [palɛ·ɔntɔlɔ'gi] *f* (–;) paleontology
Palast [pa'last] *m* (–es;⁼e) palace
palast'artig *adj* palatial
Palästina [pale'stina] *n* (–s;) Palestine
Palette [pa'lɛtə] *f* (–;–n) palette
Palisade [palɪ'zadə] *f* (–;–n) palisade
Palme ['palmə] *f* (–;–n) palm tree; palm branch; j–n auf die P. bringen (coll) drive s.o. up the wall
Palm'wedel *m*, Palm'zweig *m* palm branch
Pampelmuse ['pampəlmuzə] *f* (–;–n) grapefruit
Pamphlet [pam'flet] *n* (–[e]s;–e) lampoon
Panama ['panama] *n* (–s;) Panama
Paneel [pa'nel] *n* (–s;–e) panel
paneelieren [pane'lirən] *tr* panel
Panier [pa'nir] *n* (–s;–e) slogan
panieren [pa'nirən] *tr* (culin) bread

Panik ['pɑnɪk] *f* (–;) panic
panisch ['pɑnɪʃ] *adj* panic-stricken
Panne ['pɑnə] *f* (–;–n) breakdown; (*Reifenpanne*) blowout; (fig) mishap
Panora·ma [panɔ'rɑma] *n* (–s;–men [mən]) panorama
panschen ['pɑnʃən] *tr* adulterate, water down ‖ *intr* splash about; mix
Panther ['pɑntər] *m* (–s;–) panther
Pantine [pan'tinə] *f* (–;–n) clog
Pantoffel [pan'tɔfəl] *m* (–s;–n) slipper; **unter dem P. stehen** be henpecked
Pantof'felheld *m* henpecked husband
Panzer ['pantsər] *m* (–s;–) armor; armor plating; (mil) tank; (zool) shell
Pan'zerabwehrkanone *f* antitank gun
pan'zerbrechend *adj* armor-piercing
Pan'zerfalle *f* tank trap
Pan'zerfaust *f* bazooka
Pan'zergeschoß *n*, **Pan'zergranate** *f* armor-piercing shell
Pan'zerhandschuh *m* gauntlet
Pan'zerhemd *n* coat of mail
Pan'zerkreuzer *m* battle cruiser
panzern ['pantsərn] *tr* armor ‖ *ref* arm oneself
Pan'zerschrank *m* safe
Panzerspähwagen ['pantsər/pevagən] *m* (mil) armored car
Pan'zersperre *f* antitank obstacle
Pan'zerung *f* (–;–en) armor plating
Pan'zerwagen *m* armored car
Papagei [papa'gai] *m* (–en;–en) & (–[e]s;–e) parrot
Papier [pa'pir] *n* (–[e]s;–e) paper
Papier'bogen *m* sheet of paper
Papier'brei *m* paper pulp
papieren [pa'pirən] *adj* paper
Papier'fabrik *f* paper mill
Papier'format *n* size of paper
Papier'korb *m* wastebasket
Papier'krieg *m* (fig) red tape
Papier'mühle *f* paper mill
Papier'schlange *f* paper streamer
Papier'tüte *f* paper bag
Papier'waren *pl* stationery
Papp [pap] *m* (–[e]s;–e) (*Brei*) pap; (*Kleister*) paste
Papp– [pap] *comb.fm.* sticky; cardboard
Papp'band *m* (–[e]s;–̈e) paperback
Papp'deckel *m* piece of cardboard
Pappe ['papə] *f* (–;) cardboard
Pappel ['papəl] *f* (–;–n) poplar
päppeln ['pepəln] *tr* feed lovingly
pappen ['papən] *tr* paste, glue ‖ *intr* stick
Pap'penstiel *m* (coll) trifle; **das ist keinen P. wert** (coll) this isn't worth a thing
papperlapapp [papərla'pap] *interj* nonsense!
pap'pig *adj* sticky
Papp'karton *m*, **Papp'schachtel** *f* cardboard box, cardboard carton
Papp'schnee *m* sticky snow (*for skiing*)
Paprika ['paprika] *m* (–s;) paprika
Pap'rikaschote *f* (green) pepper
Papst [papst] *m* (–es;–̈e) pope
päpstlich ['pepstliç] *adj* papal
Papsttum ['papsttum] *n* (–s;) papacy
Papy·rus [pa'pyrus] *m* (–;–ri) [ri]) papyrus

Parabel [pa'rabəl] *f* (–;–n) parable; (geom) parabola
Parade [pa'radə] *f* (–;–n) parade; (fencing) parry; (mil) review; (fb) save
Para'deanzug *m* (mil) dress uniform
Paradeiser [para'daizər] *m* (–s;–) (Aust) tomato
Para'depferd *n* (fig) show-off
Para'deplatz *m* parade ground
Para'deschritt *m* goose step
paradieren [para'dirən] *intr* parade; (fig) show off
Paradies [para'dis] *n* (–es;–e) paradise
Paradies'apfel *m* tomato
paradox [para'dɔks] *adj* paradoxical ‖ **Paradox** *n* (–es;–e) paradox
Paraffin [para'fin] *n* (–s;–e) paraffin
Paragraph [para'graf] *m* (–en & –s; –en) paragraph; (jur) section
parallel [para'lel] *adj* parallel ‖ **Parallele** *f* (–;–n) parallel
Paralyse [para'lyzə] *f* (–;–n) paralysis
paralysieren [paraly'zirən] *tr* paralyze
Paralytiker –in [para'lytɪkər(ɪn)] §6 *mf* paralytic
Paranuß ['paranus] *f* Brazil nut
Parasit [para'zit] *m* (–en;–en) parasite
parat [pa'rat] *adj* ready
Pardon [par'dɔ̃] *m* (–s;) pardon; **keinen P. geben** (mil) given no quarter
Parenthese [parɛn'tezə] *f* (–;–n) parenthesis
Parfüm [par'fym] *n* (–[e]s;–e) perfume
Parfüme·rie [parfymə'ri] *f* (–;–rien ['ri·ən]) perfume shop
parfümieren [parfy'mirən] *tr* perfume
pari ['pari] *adv* at par ‖ **Pari** *m* (– [s];) par; **auf P.** at par
Paria ['parja] *m* (–s;–s) pariah
parieren [pa'rirən] *tr* (*Pferd*) rein in; (*Hieb*) parry ‖ *intr* (dat) obey
Pa'rikurs *m* (com) parity
Paris [pa'ris] *n* (–;) Paris
Pariser –in [pa'rizər(ɪn)] §6 *mf* Parisian
Parität [pari'tet] *f* (–;) equality; (fin, st. exch.) parity
paritätisch [pari'tetɪʃ] *adj* on a footing of equality
Park [park] *m* (–s;–s & –e) park
Park'anlage *f* park; **Parkanlagen** grounds
parken ['parkən] *tr & intr* park
Parkett [par'ket] *n* (–[e]s;–e) (*Fußboden*) parquet; (theat) parquet
Parkett'fußboden *m* parquet flooring
Park'licht *n* parking light
Park'platz *m* parking lot
Park'platzwärter *m* parking lot attendant
Park'uhr *f* parking meter
Parlament [parla'mɛnt] *n* (–[e]s;–e) parliament
Parlamentär [parlamɛn'ter] *m* (–s;–e) truce negotiator
parlamentarisch [parlamɛn'tarɪʃ] *adj* parliamentary
parlamentieren [parlamɛn'tirən] *intr* (coll) parley
Paro·die [parɔ'di] *f* (–;–dien ['di·ən]) parody
parodieren [parɔ'dirən] *tr* parody

Parole [pa'rolə] *f* (-;-n) (mil) password; (pol) slogan
Partei [par'taɪ] *f* (-;-en) party; (*Mieter*) tenant(s); (jur, pol) party; (sport) side; **j–s P. ergreifen** or **P. nehmen für j–n** side with s.o.
Partei'bonze *m* (pol) party boss
Partei'gänger –in §6 *mf* (pol) party sympathizer
Partei'genosse *m*, **Partei'genossin** *f* party member
Partei'grundsatz *m* party plank
parteiisch [par'taɪ·ɪʃ] *adj* partial, biased; (pol) partisan
partei'lich *adj* partisan
Partei'lichkeit *f* (-;) partiality
partei'los *adj* (pol) independent ‖ **Parteilose** §5 *mf* independent
Partei'losigkeit *f* (-;) impartiality; political independence
Partei'nahme *f* (-;) taking sides
Partei'programm *n* party platform
Partei'tag *m* party rally
Partei'zugehörigkeit *f* party affiliation
Parterre [par'ter] *n* (-s;-s) ground floor; (theat) parterre
Par·tie [par'ti] *f* (-;-tien ['ti-ən]) part; (*Gesellschaft*) party; (*Spiel*) game; (*Ausflug*) outing; (com) lot; (theat) role; **e–e gute P. machen** (coll) marry rich; **ich bin mit von der P.!** count me in!
partiell [par'tsjɛl] *adj* partial ‖ *adv* partly, partially
Partikel [par'tikəl] *f* (-;-n) particle
Partisan –in [partɪ'zɑn(ɪn)] §7 *mf* partisan
Partitur [partɪ'tur] *f* (-;-en) (mus) score
Partizip [partɪ'tsip] *n* (-s;-ien [jən]) participle
Partner –in ['partnər(ɪn)] §6 *mf* partner
Part'nerschaft *f* (-;-en) partnership
Parzelle [par'tsɛlə] *f* (-;-n) lot
parzellieren [partsɛ'lirən] *tr* parcel out, allot
paschen ['paʃən] *tr* smuggle ‖ *intr* smuggle; (*würfeln*) play dice
Paß [pas] *m* (**Passes; Pässe**) pass; passport; (geog) mountain pass
passabel [pa'sabəl] *adj* tolerable
Passage [pa'sɑʒə] *f* (-;-n) passage; (mus) run
Passagier [pasa'ʒir] *m* (-s;-e) passenger; **blinder P.** stowaway
Passagier'dampfer *m* passenger liner
Passagier'gut *n* luggage
Passah ['pasa] *n* (-s;), **Pas'sahfest** *n* Passover
Paß'amt *n* passport office
Passant –in [pa'sant(ɪn)] §7 *mf* passer-by
Paß'ball *m* (sport) pass
Paß'bild *n* passport photograph
passen ['pasən] *ref* be proper ‖ *intr* fit; (*dat*) suit; (cards, fb) pass; **p. auf** (*acc*) watch for, wait for; **p. zu** suit, fit; **sie p. zueinander** they are a good match
pas'send *adj* suitable; convenient; (*Kleidungsstück*) matching; **für p. halten** think it proper

Paß'form *f*—**e–e gute P. haben** be form-fitting
passierbar [pa'sirbar] *adj* passable
passieren [pa'sirən] *tr* pass, cross; (culin) sift, sieve ‖ *intr* (SEIN) happen
Passier'schein *m* pass, permit
Passion [pa'sjon] *f* (-;-en) passion
passioniert [pasjo'nirt] *adj* ardent
Passions'spiel *n* passion play
passiv [pa'sif] *adj* passive; (*Handelsbilanz*) unfavorable; **passives Wahlrecht** eligibility ‖ **Passiv** *n* (-s;-e) (gram) passive
Passiva [pa'siva] *pl*, **Passiven** [pa'sivən] *pl* debts, liabilities
Paß'kontrolle *f* passport inspection
Paste ['pastə] *f* (-;-n) paste
Pastell [pa'stɛl] *n* (-s;-e) pastel; crayon
pastell'farben *adj* pastel
Pastell'stift *m* crayon
Pastete [pas'tetə] *f* (-;-n) meat pie, fish pie
pasteurisieren [pastœrɪ'zirən] *tr* pasteurize
Pastille [pa'stɪlə] *f* (-;-n) lozenge
Pa·stor ['pastər] *m* (-s;-storen ['torən]) pastor, minister, vicar
Pate ['patə] *m* (-n;-n) godfather ‖ *f* (-;-n) godmother
Pa'tenkind *n* godchild
patent [pa'tent] *adj* neat; smart; **ein patenter Kerl** quite a fellow ‖ **Patent** *n* (-[e]s;-e) patent; (mil) commission; **P. angemeldet** patent pending
Patent'amt *n* patent office
patentieren [paten'tirən] *tr* patent
Pater ['patər] *m* (-s; **Patres** ['patres]) (eccl) Father
pathetisch [pa'tetɪʃ] *adj* impassioned; solemn
Pathologe [pato'logə] *m* (-n;-n) pathologist
Pathologie [patolo'gi] *f* (-;) pathology
Pathologin [pato'login] *f* (-;-nen) pathologist
Patient –in [pa'tsjɛnt(ɪn)] §7 *mf* patient
Patin ['patɪn] *f* (-;-nen) godmother
Patriarch [patrɪ'arç] *m* (-en;-en) patriarch
Patriot –in [patrɪ'ot(ɪn)] §7 *mf* patriot
patriotisch [patrɪ'otɪʃ] *adj* patriotic
Patrize [pa'tritsə] *f* (-;-n) die, stamp
Patrizier –in [pa'tritsjər(ɪn)] §6 *mf* patrician
Patron [pa'tron] *m* (-s;-e) patron; (pej) guy
Patronat [patro'nat] *n* (-[e]s;-e) patronage
Patrone [pa'tronə] *f* (-;-n) cartridge
Patro'nengurt *m* cartridge belt
Patro'nenhülse *f* cartridge case
Patronin [pa'tronɪn] *f* (-;-nen) patroness
Patrouille [pa'truljə] *f* (-;-n) patrol
patrouillieren [patru'ljirən] *tr & intr* patrol
Patsche ['patʃə] *f* (-;-en) (*Pfütze*) puddle; (coll) jam, scrape; **in der P. lassen** leave in a lurch; **in e–e P. geraten** get into a jam

patschen ['patʃən] *tr* slap || *intr* splash; **in die Hände p.** clap hands
patsch'naß' *adj* soaking wet
patzig ['patsɪç] *adj* snappy, sassy
Pauke ['paukə] *f* (-;-n) kettledrum; **j-m e-e P. halten** give s.o. a lecture
pauken ['paukən] *tr* (educ) cram || *intr* beat the kettledrum; (educ) cram
Pau'ker *m* (-s;-) (coll) martinet
pausbackig ['pausbakɪç], **pausbäckig** ['pausbekɪç] *adj* chubby-faced
pauschal [pau'ʃal] *adj* (*Summe*) flat
Pauschal'betrag *m* flat rate
Pauscha•le [pau'ʃalə] *n* (-s;-lien [ljən]) lump sum
Pauschal'preis *m* package price
Pauschal'reise *f* all-inclusive tour
Pauschal'summe *f* flat sum
Pause ['pauzə] *f* (-;-n) pause; (*Pauszeichnung*) tracing; (educ) recess, break; (mus) rest; (theat) intermission; **e-e P. machen** take a break
pausen ['pauzən] *tr* trace
pau'senlos *adj* continuous
Pau'senzeichen *n* (rad) station identification
pausieren [pau'zirən] *intr* pause; rest
Pauspapier ['pauzpapir] *n* tracing paper
Pavian ['pavjan] *m* (-s;-e) baboon
Pavillon ['pavɪljõ] *m* (-s;-s) pavilion
Pazifik [pa'tsifɪk] *m* (-s;) Pacific
pazifisch [pa'tsifɪʃ] *adj* Pacific
Pazifist –in [patsɪ'fɪst(ɪn)] §7 *mf* pacifist
Pech [peç] *n* (-[e]s;-e) pitch; **P. haben** (coll) have tough luck
Pech'fackel *f* torch
Pech'kohle *f* bituminous coal
pech'ra'benschwarz' *adj* pitch-black
pech'schwarz' *adj* pitch-dark
Pech'strähne *f* streak of bad luck
Pech'vogel *m* (coll) unlucky fellow
Pedal [pe'dal] *n* (-s;-e) pedal
Pedant [pe'dant] *m* (-en;-en) pedant
pedantisch [pe'dantɪʃ] *adj* pedantic
Pegel ['pegəl] *m* (-s;-) water gauge
Pe'gelstand *m* water level
Peil– [paɪl] *comb.fm.* direction-finding, sounding
peilen ['paɪlən] *tr* take the bearings of; (*Tiefe*) sound; **über den Daumen p.** (coll) estimate roughly || *intr* take bearings
Pei'lung *f* (-;-en) bearings; taking of bearings; sounding
Pein [paɪn] *f* (-;) pain, torment
peinigen ['paɪnɪgən] *tr* torment
pein'lich *adj* painful; embarrassing; (*genau*) painstaking; (*sorgfältig*) scrupulous || *adv* scrupulously; carefully
Peitsche ['paɪtʃə] *f* (-;-n) whip; **mit der P. knallen** crack the whip
peitschen ['paɪtʃən] *tr* whip
Peit'schenhieb *m* whiplash
Peit'schenknall *m* crack of the whip
Pelerine [pelə'rinə] *f* (-;-n) cape
Pelikan ['pelɪkan] *m* (-s;-e) pelican
Pelle ['pelə] *f* (-;-n) peel, skin
pellen ['pelən] *tr* peel, skin
Pellkartoffeln ['pelkartɔfəln] *pl* potatoes in their jackets

Pelz [pelts] *m* (-es;-e) fur; (*Fell*) pelt; fur coat
Pelz'besatz *m* fur trimming
Pelz'futter *n* fur lining
Pelz'händler –in §6 *mf* furrier
pel'zig *adj* furry; (*Gefühl im Mund*) cottony
Pelz'tier *n* fur-bearing animal
Pelz'tierjäger *m* trapper
Pelz'werk *n* furs
Pendel ['pendəl] *n* (-s;-) pendulum
pendeln ['pendəln] *intr* swing, oscillate; (*zwischen zwei Orten*) commute
Pen'deltür *f* swinging door
Pen'delverkehr *m* commuter traffic; shuttle service
Pen'delzug *m* shuttle train
Pendler ['pentlər] *m* (-s;-) commuter
Penizillin [penɪtsɪ'lin] *n* (-s;) penicillin
Pension [pen'zjon] *f* (-;-en) pension, retirement pay; (*Fremdenhaus*) boarding house; (*Unterkunft und Verpflegung*) room and board; (*Pensionat*) girls' boarding school; **in P. gehen** go on pension
Pensionär [penzjo'ner] *m* (-s;-e) pensioner; boarder
Pensionat [penzjo'nat] *n* (-[e]s;-e) girls boarding school
pensionieren [penzjo'nirən] *tr* put on pension; (mil) retire on half pay; **sich p. lassen** retire
Pensions'kasse *f* pension fund
Pensions'preis *m* price of room and board
Pen•sum ['penzum] *n* (-s;-sen [zən] & –sa [za]) task, assignment; quota
per [per] *prep* (*acc*) per, by, with; (*zeitlich*) by, until; **per Adresse** care of, c/o; **per sofort** at once
perfekt [per'fekt] *adj* perfect; concluded || **Perfekt** *n* (-[e]s;-e) perfect
Pergament [perga'ment] *n* (-[e]s;-e) parchment
Periode [per'jodə] *f* (-;-n) period
periodisch [per'jodɪʃ] *adj* periodic
Periphe•rie [perɪfe'ri] *f* (-;-rien ['ri•ən]) periphery
Periskop [perɪ'skop] *n* (-s;-e) periscope
Perle ['perlə] *f* (-;-n) pearl; (*aus Glas*) bead; (*Tropfen*) drop, bead; (*Bläschen*) bubble; (fig) gem
perlen ['perlən] *intr* sparkle
Per'lenauster *f* pearl oyster
Per'lenkette *f*, **Per'lenschnur** *f* pearl necklace, string of pearls
Perlhuhn ['perlhun] *n* guinea fowl
perlig ['perlɪç] *adj* pearly
Perl'muschel *f* pearl oyster
Perlmutt ['perlmut] *n* (-s;), **Perl'mutter** *f* mother of pearl
perplex [per'pleks] *adj* perplexed
Persenning [per'zenɪŋ] *f* (-;-en) tarpaulin
Persien ['perzjən] *n* (-s;) Persia
persisch [perzɪʃ] *adj* Persian
Person [per'zon] *f* (-;-en) person; (theat) character; **ich für meine P.** I for one; **klein von P.** small of stature
Personal [perzo'nal] *n* (-s;) personnel
Personal'akte *f* personal file, dossier

Personal'angaben *pl* personal data
Personal'aufzug *m* passenger elevator
Personal'ausweis *m* identity card
Personal'chef *m* personnel manager
Personalien [pɛrzɔ'naljən] *pl* personal data, particulars
Personal'pronomen *n* personal pronoun
Perso'nengedächtnis *n* good memory for names
Perso'nenkraftwagen *m* passenger car
Perso'nenschaden *m* personal injury
Perso'nenverzeichnis *n* list of persons; (theat) dramatis personae, cast
Perso'nenwagen *m* passenger car
Perso'nenzug *m* passenger train; (rr) local
personifizieren [pɛrzɔnifɪ'tsirən] *tr* personify
persönlich [pɛr'zønlɪç] *adj* personal ‖ *adv* personally, in person
Persön'lichkeit *f* (-;-en) personality
Perspektiv [pɛrspɛk'tif] *n* (-s;-e) telescope
Perücke [pɛ'rʏkə] *f* (-;-n) wig
pervers [pɛr'vɛrs] *adj* perverse
pessimistisch [pɛsɪ'mɪstɪʃ] *adj* pessimistic
Pest [pɛst] *f* (-;) plague
pest'artig *adj* pestilential
Pestilenz [pɛstɪ'lɛnts] *f* (-;-en) pestilence
Petersilie [pɛtər'ziljə] *f* (-;) parsley
Petroleum [pɛ'trolɛ·ʊm] *n* (-s;) petroleum
Petschaft ['pɛtʃaft] *n* (-s;-e) seal
Petting ['pɛtɪŋ] *n* (-s;) petting
petto ['pɛto]—in p. haben have in reserve; (coll) have up one's sleeve
Petunie [pɛ'tunjə] *f* (-;-n) petunia
Petze ['pɛtsə] *f* (-;-n) tattletale
petzen ['pɛtsən] *intr* tattle, squeal
Pfad [pfɑt] *m* (-[e]s;-e) path, track
Pfadfinder ['pfɑtfɪndər] *m* (-s;-) boy scout
Pfadfinderin ['pfɑtfɪndərɪn] *f* (-;-nen) girl scout
Pfaffe ['pfafə] *m* (-n;-n) (pej) priest
Pfahl [pfɑl] *m* (-[e]s;ꞏe) stake; post
Pfahl'bau *m* (-[e]s;-bauten) lake dwelling
Pfahl'werk *n* palisade, stockade
Pfahl'wurzel *f* taproot
Pfahl'zaun *m* palisade, stockade
Pfälzer –in ['pfɛltsər(ɪn)] §6 *mf* inhabitant of the Palatinate
Pfand [pfant] *n* (-[e]s;ꞏer) pledge; deposit; (Bürgschaft) security, pawn (auf Immobilien) mortgage; zum Pfande geben (or setzen) pawn, mortgage
pfändbar ['pfɛntbɑr] *adj* (jur) attachable
Pfand'brief *m* mortgage papers
pfänden ['pfɛndən] *tr* attach, impound
Pfand'geber *m* mortgagor
Pfand'gläubiger *m* mortgagee
Pfand'haus *n*, Pfand'leihe *f* pawnshop
Pfand'leiher –in §6 *mf* pawnbroker
Pfand'recht *n* lien
Pfand'schein *m* pawn ticket
Pfand'schuldner *m* mortgagor
Pfän'dung *f* (-;-en) attachment, confiscation

Pfanne ['pfanə] *f* (-;-n) pan; (anat) socket; etw auf der P. haben (fig) have s.th. up one's sleeve; in die P. hauen (fig) make mincemeat of
Pfan'nenstiel *m* panhandle
Pfann'kuchen *m* pancake; Berliner P. doughnut
Pfarr– [pfar] *comb.fm.* parish, parochial
Pfarr'amt *n* rectory
Pfarr'bezirk *m* parish
Pfarr'dorf *n* parish seat
Pfarre ['pfarə] *f* (-;-n) parish; (Pfarrhaus) rectory
Pfarrei [pfa'raɪ] *f* (-;-en) parish; (Pfarrhaus) rectory
Pfarrer ['pfarər] *m* (-s;-) pastor
Pfarr'gemeinde *f* parish
Pfarr'haus *n* rectory
Pfarr'kind *n* parishioner
Pfarr'kirche *f* parish church
Pfarr'schule *f* parochial school
Pfau [pfaʊ] *m* (-[e]s;-en) peacock
Pfau'enhenne *f* peahen
Pfeffer ['pfɛfər] *m* (-s;) pepper
pfefferig ['pfɛfərɪç] *adj* peppery
Pfef'ferkorn *n* peppercorn
Pfef'ferkuchen *m* gingerbread
Pfef'ferminze *f* (bot) peppermint
Pfef'ferminzplätzchen *n* peppermint cookie
pfeffern ['pfɛfərn] *tr* pepper
Pfef'fernuß *f* ginger nut
Pfeife ['pfaɪfə] *f* (-;-n) whistle; (Orgel–) pipe; (zum Rauchen) (tobacco) pipe
pfeifen ['pfaɪfən] *tr* whistle; ich pfeife ihm was he can whistle for it ‖ *intr* whistle; (Schiedsrichter) blow the whistle; (Maus) squeak; (Vogel) sing; (dat) whistle for or to; auf dem letzten Loche p. be on one's last legs; ich pfeife darauf! I couldn't care less!
Pfei'fenkopf *m* pipe bowl
Pfei'fenrohr *n* pipestem
Pfei'fer –in §6 *mf* whistler; (mus) piper, fife player
Pfeif'kessel *m*, Pfeif'topf *m* whistling kettle
Pfeil [pfaɪl] *m* (-[e]s;-e) arrow, dart; P. und Bogen bow and arrow
Pfei'ler *m* (-s;-) (& fig) pillar; (e-r Brücke) pier
pfeil'gera'de *adj* straight as an arrow
pfeil'schnell' *adj* swift as an arrow ‖ *adv* like a shot
Pfeil'schütze *m* archer
Pfeil'spitze *f* arrowhead
Pfennig ['pfɛnɪç] *m* (-[e]s;-e & -) pfennig, penny (one hundredth of a mark)
Pfennigfuchser ['pfɛnɪçfʊksər] *m* (-s; -) penny pincher
Pferch [pfɛrç] *m* (-[e]s;-e) fold, pen
pferchen ['pfɛrçən] *tr* herd together, pen in
Pferd [pfert] *n* (-[e]s;-e) horse; zu Pferde on horseback
Pferde– [pferdə] *comb.fm.* horse
Pfer'deapfel *m* horse manure
Pfer'debremse *f* horsefly
Pfer'dedecke *f* horse blanket

Pfer'defuß m (*Kennzeichen des Teu-fels*) cloven hoof; (pathol) clubfoot
Pfer'degeschirr n harness
Pfer'degespann n team of horses
Pfer'deknecht m groom
Pfer'dekoppel f corral
Pfer'delänge f (*beim Rennen*) length
Pfer'derennbahn f race track
Pfer'derennen n horse racing
Pfer'destärke f horsepower
Pfer'dezucht f horse breeding
pfiff [pfɪf] *pret* of **pfeifen** ‖ **Pfiff** m (-[e]s;-e) whistle; **den P. heraus-haben** (fig) know the ropes
Pfifferling ['pfɪfərlɪŋ] m (-s;-e) (bot) chanterelle; **keinen P. wert** not worth a thing
pfiffig ['pfɪfɪç] *adj* shrewd, sharp
Pfiffikus ['pfɪfɪkʊs] m (-;-), (-ses;-se) (coll) sly fox
Pfingsten ['pfɪŋstən] n (-s;) Pentecost
Pfingst'rose f (bot) peony
Pfingst'son'ntag m Whitsunday
Pfirsich ['pfɪrzɪç] m (-[e]s;-e) peach
Pflanze ['pflantsə] f (-;-n) plant
pflanzen ['pflantsən] *tr* plant
Pflan'zenfaser f vegetable fiber
Pflan'zenfett n vegetable shortening
pflan'zenfressend *adj* herbivorous
Pflan'zenkost f vegetable diet
Pflan'zenkunde f botany
Pflan'zenleben n plant life, vegetation
Pflan'zenlehre f botany
Pflan'zenöl n vegetable oil
Pflan'zenreich n vegetable kingdom
Pflan'zensaft m sap, juice
Pflan'zenschutzmittel n pesticide
Pflan'zenwelt f flora
Pflan'zer -in §6 *mf* planter
pflanz'lich *adj* vegetable
Pflanz'schule f, **Pflanz'stätte** f nursery; (fig) hotbed
Pflan'zung f (-;-en) plantation
Pflaster ['pflastər] n (-s;-) pavement; (*Fleck*) patch; (med) Band-Aid; **als P.** (fig) in compensation; **ein teueres P.** (fig) an expensive place; **P. treten** (fig) pound the sidewalks
Pflasterer ['pflastərər] m (-s;-) paver
pfla'stermüde *adj* tired of walking the streets
pflastern ['pflastərn] *tr* pave
Pfla'sterstein m paving stone; (*Kopf-stein*) cobblestone
Pfla'stertreter m (-s;-) loafer
Pfla'sterung f (-;) paving
Pflaume ['pflaumə] f (-;-n) plum; (*spitze Bermerkung*) dig
pflaumen ['pflaumən] *intr* (coll) tease
pflau'menweich *adj* (fig) spineless
Pflege ['pfle:gə] f (-;-n) care; (*e-s Kranken*) nursing; (*Wartung*) tend-ing; (*e-s Gartens, der Künste*) culti-vation; **gute P. haben** be well cared for; **in P. nehmen** take charge of
Pflegebefohlene ['pfle:gəbəfo:lənə] §5 *mf* charge; fosterchild
Pfle'geeltern *pl* foster parents
Pfle'geheim n nursing home
Pfle'gekind n foster child
pflegen ['pfle:gən] *tr* take care of, look after; (*Kranken*) nurse; (*Garten, Kunst*) cultivate; (*Freundschaft*) fos-

ter; **Geselligkeit p.** lead an active social life; **Umgang p. mit** associate with ‖ *intr*—**p. zu** (*inf*) be wont to (*inf*), be in the habit of (*ger*); **sein Vater pflegte zu sagen** his father used to say; **sie pflegt morgens zeitig aufzustehen** she usually gets up early in the morning ‖ *intr* (*pp* **gepflegt** & **gepflogen**) (*genit*) carry on; **der Liebe p.** enjoy the pleasures of love; **der Ruhe p.** take a rest; **Rats p. mit** consult with
Pfle'ger -in §6 *mf* nurse; (jur) guardian
Pfle'gesohn m foster son
Pfle'gestelle f foster home
Pfle'getocher f foster daughter
Pfle'gevater m foster father
pfleglich ['pfle:klɪç] *adj* careful
Pflegling ['pfle:klɪŋ] m (-s;-e) foster child; (*Pflegebefohlener*) charge
Pflegschaft ['pfle:kʃaft] f (-;-en) (jur) guardianship
Pflicht [pflɪçt] f (-;-en) duty; **sich seiner P. entziehen** evade one's duty
pflicht'bewußt *adj* conscientious
Pflicht'bewußtsein n conscientiousness
Pflicht'eifer m zeal
pflicht'eifrig *adj* zealous
Pflicht'erfüllung f performance of duty
Pflicht'fach n (educ) required course
Pflicht'gefühl n sense of duty
pflicht'gemäß *adj* dutiful
-pflichtig [pflɪçtɪç] *comb.fm.* obli-gated, e.g., **schulpflichtig** obligated to attend school
pflicht'schuldig *adj* duty-bound
pflicht'treu *adj* dutiful, loyal
pflicht'vergessen *adj* forgetful of one's duty; (*untreu*) disloyal
Pflicht'vergessenheit f dereliction of duty; disloyalty
Pflicht'verletzung f, **Pflicht'versäum-nis** n neglect of duty
Pflock [pflɔk] m (-[e]s;-e) peg; **e-n P. zurückstecken** (fig) come down a peg
pflog [pflo:k] *pret* of **pflegen**
pflücken ['pflʏkən] *tr* pluck, pick
Pflug [pflu:k] m (-[e]s;-e) plow
pflügen ['pfly:gən] *tr* & *intr* plow
Pflug'schar f plowshare
Pforte ['pfɔrtə] f (-;-n) gate
Pförtner -in ['pfœrtnər(ɪn)] §6 *mf* gatekeeper ‖ m doorman; (anat) pylorus
Pfosten ['pfɔstən] m (-s;-) post; (carp) jamb
Pfote ['pfo:tə] f (-;-n) paw; **j-m eins auf die Pfoten geben** rap s.o.'s knuckles
Pfriem [pfri:m] m (-[e]s;-e) awl
Pfropf [pfrɔpf] m (-[e]s;-e) stopper, plug, cork
pfropfen ['pfrɔpfən] *tr* cork, plug; (*stopfen*) cram; (hort) graft ‖ **Pfrop-fen** m (-s;-) stopper, plug, cork
Pfrop'fenzieher m corkscrew
Pfropf'reis n (hort) graft
Pfründe ['pfrʏndə] f (-;-n) benefice; (*ohne Seelsorge*) sinecure; **fette P.** (fig) cushy, well-paying job
Pfuhl [pfu:l] m (-[e]s;-e) pool, puddle; (fig) pit

Pfühl [pfyl] *m* (-[e]s;-e) (poet) cushion
pfui ['pfu·i] *interj* phooey!; **p. über
dich!** shame on you!
Pfund [pfunt] *n* (-[e]s;-e) pound
pfundig ['pfundıç] *adj* (coll) great
-pfündig [pfʏndıç] *comb.fm.* -pound
Pfundskerl ['pfuntskɛrl] *m* (coll) great
  guy
pfund'weise *adv* by the pound
Pfuscharbeit ['pfuʃarbaɪt] *f* bungling
pfuschen ['pfuʃən] *tr & intr* bungle;
  j-m ins Handwerk p. meddle in s.o.'s
  business
Pfuscherei [pfuʃə'raɪ] f (-;-en) bungling
Pfütze ['pfʏtsə] *f* (-;-n) puddle
Phänomen [fɛnɔ'men] *n* (-s;-e) phenomenon
phänomenal [fɛnɔmɛ'nal] *adj* phenomenal
Phanta·sie [fanta'zi] *f* (-;-sien ['zi·
  ən]) imagination
Phantasie'gebilde *n* daydream
phantasieren [fanta'zirən] *intr* daydream; (mus) improvise; (pathol) be
  delirious
phantasie'voll *adj* imaginative
Phantast –in [fan'tast(ın)] §7 *mf*
  visionary
phantastisch [fan'tastıʃ] *adj* fantastic
Phantom [fan'tom] *n* (-s;-e) phantom
Pharisäer [farı'ze·ər] *m* (-s;-) Pharisee; (fig) pharisee
pharmazeutisch [farma'tsɔɪtıʃ] *adj*
  pharmaceutical
Pharmazie [farma'tsi] *f* (-;) pharmacy
Phase ['fazə] *f* (-;-n) phase
Philantrop –in [fılan'trop(ın)] §7 *mf*
  philanthropist
philanthropisch [fılan'tropıʃ] *adj* philanthropic
Philister [fı'lıstər] *m* (-s;-) Philistine
Phiole [fı'olə] *f* (-;-n) vial, phial
Philologe [fılɔ'logə] *m* (-n;-n) philologist
Philologie [fılɔlɔ'gi] *f* (-;) philology
Philologin [fılɔ'logın] *f* (-;-nen) philologist
Philosoph [fılɔ'zof] *m* (-en;-en) philos-
  opher
Philoso·phie [fılɔzɔ'fi] *f* (-;-fien ['fi·
  ən]) philosophy
philosophieren [fılɔzɔ'firən] *intr* phi-
  losophize
philosophisch [fılɔ'zofıʃ] *adj* philo-
  sophic(al)
Phlegma ['flɛgma] *n* (-s;) indolence
Phonetik [fɔ'netık] *f* (-;) phonetics
phonetisch [fɔ'netıʃ] *adj* phonetic
Phönix ['fønıks] *m* (-[e]s;-e) phoenix
Phönizien [fø'nitsjən] *n* (-s;) Phoenicia
Phönizier –in [fø'nitsjər[ın]] §6 *mf*
  Phoenician
Phosphor ['fɔsfɔr] *m* (-s;) phosphorus
phos'phorig *adj* phosphorous
Photo ['foto] *n* (-s;-) photo
Pho'toapparat *m* camera
photogen [fɔtɔ'gen] *adj* photogenic
Photograph [fɔtɔ'graf] *m* (-en;-en)
  photographer
Photogra·phie [fɔtɔgra'fi] *f* (-;-fien
  ['fi·ən]) photography

photographieren [fɔtɔgra'firən] *tr &
intr* photograph; **sich p. lassen** have
  one's photograph taken
Photographin [fɔtɔ'grafın] *f* (-;-nen)
  photographer
photographisch [fɔtɔ'grafıʃ] *adj* photographic
Photokopie' *f* photocopy
photokopie'ren *tr* photocopy
Pho'tozelle *f* photoelectric cell
Phrase ['frazə] *f* (-;-n) phrase; (fig)
  platitude; **das sind nur Phrasen** that's
  just talk
phra'senhaft *adj* empty, trite; windy
Physik [fʏ'zik] *f* (-;) physics
physikalisch [fʏzı'kalıʃ] *adj* physical
Physiker –in ['fʏsıkər(ın)] §6 *mf*
  physicist
Physiogno·mie [fʏzjɔgnɔ'mi] *f* (-;
  -mien ['mi·ən]) physiognomy
Physiologie [fʏzjɔlɔ'gi] *f* (-;) physiology
physiologisch [fʏzjɔ'logıʃ] *adj* physiological
physisch ['fʏzıʃ] *adj* physical
Pianino [pı·a'nino] *n* (-s;-s) small
  upright piano
Pianist –in [pı·a'nıst(ın)] §7 *mf* pianist
picheln ['pıçəln] *tr & intr* tipple
pichen ['pıçən] *tr* pitch, cover with
  pitch
Pichler –in ['pıçlər(ın)] §6 *mf* tippler
Picke ['pıkə] *f* (-;-n) pickax
Pickel ['pıkəl] *m* (-s;-) pimple;
  (*Picke*) pickax; (*Eispicke*) ice ax
Pickelhaube (Pik'kelhaube) *f* spiked
  helmet
Pickelhering (Pik'kelhering) *m* pickled
  herring
pickelig (pik'kelig) *adj* pimply
picken ['pıkən] *tr & intr* peck
picklig ['pıklıç] *adj* var of **pickelig**
Picknick ['pıknık] *n* (-s;-s) picnic
pieken ['pikən] *tr* sting; (coll) prick
piekfein ['pik'faın] *adj* tiptop
pieksauber ['pik'zaubər] *adj* spick and
  span
piepen ['pipən] *intr* chirp; (*Maus*)
  squeal; **bei dir piept's wohl?** are
  you quite all there? || **Piepen** *n*—
  das ist zum P.! that's ridiculous
Pier [pir] *m* (-s;-e) pier
piesacken ['pizakən] *tr* (coll) pester
Pietät [pı·ɛ'tet] *f* (-;) piety
pietät'los *adj* irreverent
pietät'voll *adj* reverent(ial)
Pigment [pıg'ment] *n* (-[e]s;-e) pigment
Pik [pik], [pık] *m* (-s;-s & -e) (*Berg-
spitze*) peak || *m* (-s;-e) (coll)
  grudge; **e-n Pik auf j-n haben** hold
  a grudge against s.o. || *n* (-s;-e)
  (cards) spade(s)
pikant [pı'kant] *adj* piquant, pungent;
  (*Bermerkung*) suggestive
Pikante·rie [pıkantə'ri] *f* (-;-rien
  ['ri·ən]) piquancy; spicy story, suggestive remark
Pike ['pikə] *f* (-;-n) pike, spear; **von
der P. auf dienen** (fig) rise through
  the ranks
pikiert [pı'kirt] *adj* (**über** *acc*) piqued
  (at)

Pikkolo ['pɪkɔlo] *m* (-s;-s) apprentice waiter; (mus) piccolo
Pik'koloflöte *f* (mus) piccolo
Pilger ['pɪlgər] *m* (-s;-) pilgrim
Pil'gerfahrt *f* pilgrimage
Pilgerin ['pɪlgərɪn] *f* (-;-nen) pilgrim
pilgern ['pɪlgərn] *intr* (SEIN) go on a pilgrimage, make a pilgrimage
Pille ['pɪlə] *f* (-;-n) pill; **P. danach** morning-after pill
Pilot -in [pɪ'lot(ɪn)] §7 *mf* pilot
Pilz [pɪlts] *m* (-es;-e) fungus; mushroom
pimp(e)lig ['pɪmp(ə)lɪç] *adj* sickly, delicate; (*verweichlicht*) effeminate
Pinguin [pɪŋgu'in] *m* (-s;-e) penguin
Pinie ['pinjə] *f* (-;-n) umbrella pine
Pinke ['pɪŋkə] *f* (-;) (coll) dough
Pinkel ['pɪŋkəl] *m* (-s;-) (coll) dude
pinkeln ['pɪŋkəln] *intr* (sl) pee
Pinne ['pɪnə] *f* (-;-n) pin; tack; (naut) tiller
Pinscher ['pɪnʃər] *m* (-s;-) terrier
Pinsel ['pɪnzəl] *m* (-s;-) brush; (fig) simpleton, dope
Pinselei [pɪnzə'laɪ] *f* (-;-en) daubing; (*schlechte Malerei*) daub
pinseln ['pɪnzəln] *tr & intr* paint
Pinzette [pɪn'tsetə] *f* (-;-n) pair of tweezers, tweezers
Pionier [pɪ·ɔ'nir] *m* (-s;-e) (fig) pioneer; (mil) engineer
Pionier'arbeit *f* (fig) spadework
Pionier'truppe *f* (mil) engineers
Pirat [pɪ'rat] *m* (-en;-en) pirate
Piraterie [pɪratə'ri] *f* (-;) piracy
Pirol [pɪ'rol] *m* (-s;-e) oriole
Pirsch [pɪrʃ] *f* (-;) hunt
pirschen ['pɪrʃən] *intr* stalk game
Pirsch'jagd *f* hunt
Pistazie [pɪs'tatsjə] *f* (-;-n) pistachio
Piste ['pɪstə] *f* (-;-n) beaten track; ski run; toboggan run; (aer) runway
Pistole [pɪs'tolə] *f* (-;-n) pistol
Pisto'lentasche *f* holster
pitsch(e)naß ['pɪtʃ(ə)'nas] *adj* soaked to the skin
pittoresk [pɪtɔ'resk] *adj* picturesque
Pkw., PKW *abbr* (**Personenkraftwagen**) passenger car
placieren [pla'sirən] *tr* place
placken ['plakən] *tr* pester, plague || *ref* toil, drudge
Plackerei [plakə'raɪ] *f* (-;) drudgery
plädieren [plɛ'dirən] *intr* plead
Plädoyer [pledwa'je] *n* (-s;-s) plea
Plage ['plagə] *f* (-;-n) trouble, bother; torment; (*Seuche*) plague
Pla'gegeist *m* pest, pain in the neck
plagen ['plagən] *tr* trouble, bother; (*mit Fragen, usw.*) pester
Plagiat [pla'gjat] *n* (-[e]s;-e) plagiarism
Pla'giator [pla'gjatɔr] *m* (-s;-giatoren [gja'torən]) plagiarist
Plakat [pla'kat] *n* (-[e]s;-e) poster
Plakat'träger *m* sandwich man
Plakette [pla'ketə] *f* (-;-n) plaque
plan [plan] *adj* plain, clear; (*eben*) level || **Plan** *m* (-[e]s;-̈e) plan; (*Stadt-*) map; (poet) battlefield; **auf den P. treten** appear on the scene
Plane ['planə] *f* (-;-n) tarpaulin

Plänemacher ['plenəmaxər] *m* (-s;-) schemer
planen ['planən] *tr* plan
Pläneschmied ['plenəʃmit] *m* schemer
Planet [pla'net] *m* (-en;-en) planet
Planeta·rium [plane'tarjum] *n* (-s; -rien [rjən]) planetarium
Planeten- [planetən] *comb.fm.* planetary
Plane'tenbahn *f* planetary orbit
plan'gemäß *adv* according to plan
planieren [pla'nirən] *tr* level, grade
Planier'raupe *f* bulldozer
Planimetrie [planime'tri] *f* (-;) plane geometry
Planke ['plaŋkə] *f* (-;-n) plank
Plänkelei [pleŋkə'laɪ] *f* (-;-en) skirmish, skirmishing
plänkeln ['pleŋkəln] *intr* skirmish
plan'los *adj* aimless; indiscriminate
plan'mäßig *adj* systematic; fixed, regular; (*Verkehr*) scheduled || *adv* according to plan
planschen ['planʃən] *intr* splash
Plantage [plan'taʒə] *f* (-;-n) plantation
Pla'nung *f* (-;) planning
plan'voll *adj* systematic, methodical
Plan'wagen *m* covered wagon
Plan'wirtschaft *f* planned economy
Plapperei [plapə'raɪ] *f* (-;) chatter
Plappermaul ['plapərmaul] *n* chatterbox
plappern ['plapərn] *intr* chatter; prattle
plärren ['plerən] *intr* (coll) bawl
Plas·ma ['plasma] *n* (-s;-men [mən]) plasma
Plastik ['plastɪk] *f* (-;-en) (*Bildwerk*) sculpture; (surg) plastic surgery || *n* (-s;) plastic
plastisch ['plastɪʃ] *adj* plastic; (*anschaulich*) graphic
Platane [pla'tanə] *f* (-;-n) sycamore
Plateau [pla'to] *n* (-s;-s) plateau
Plateau'schuhe *pl* platform shoes
Platin [pla'tin] *n* (-s;) platinum
platin'blond *adj* platinum-blonde
Platoniker [pla'tonɪkər] *m* (-s;-) Platonist
platonisch [pla'tonɪʃ] *adj* Platonic
plätschern ['pletʃərn] *intr* splash; (*Bach*) babble
platt [plat] *adj* flat; (*nichtssagend*) trite; (coll) flabbergasted
Plättbrett ['pletbret] *n* ironing board
platt'deutsch *adj* Low German
Platte ['platə] *f* (-;-n) plate; top, surface; slab; (*Präsentierteller*) tray; (*Speise*) dish; (fig) pate, bean; (mus) record; (phot) plate
Plätteisen ['pletaɪzən] *n* flatiron
plätten ['pletən] *tr & intr* iron
Plat'tenjockey *m* disc jockey
Plat'tenspieler *m* record player
Plat'tenteller *m* turntable
Plat'tenwechsler *m* record changer
Platt'form *f* platform
Platt'fuß *m* (aut) flat; **Plattfüße** flat feet
platt'füßig *adj* flat-footed
Platt'heit *f* (-;-en) flatness; (fig) banality

plattieren [pla'tirən] *tr* plate
Plättwäsche ['plɛtvɛʃə] *f* ironing
Platz [plats] *m* (-es;⁼e) place; spot; locality; square; (*Sitz*) seat; (*Raum*) room, space; (*Stellung*) position; (sport) ground, field; (tennis) court; **auf die Plätze, fertig, los!** on your marks, get set, go! **fester P.** (mil) fortified position; **freier P.** open space; **immer auf dem Platze sein** be always on the alert; **nicht am P. sein** be out of place; be irrelevant; **P. da!** make way; **P. greifen** (fig) take effect, gain ground; **P. machen** make room; **P. nehmen** sit down; **seinen P. behaupten** stand one's ground
Platz'anweiser –in §6 *mf* usher
Plätzchen ['plɛtsçən] *n* (-s;-) little place; little square; (*Süßware*) candy wafer; (*Gebäck*) cookie, cracker
platzen ['platsən] *intr* (SEIN) burst; split; crack; (*Granate*) explode; (*Luftreifen*) blow out; (fig) come to nothing; **da platzte ihm endlich der Kragen** he finally blew his top; **der Wechsel ist geplatzt** the check bounced
Platz'karte *f* reserved-seat ticket
Platz'kommandant *m* commandant
Platz'konzert *n* open-air concert
Platz'patrone *f* blank cartridge; **mit Platzpatronen schießen** fire blanks
Platz'regen *m* cloudburst
Platz'runde *f* (aer) circuit of a field
Platz'wechsel *m* change of place; (sport) change in lineup
Platz'wette *f* betting on a horse to finish in first, second, or third place, bet to place
Plauderei [plaudə'raɪ] *f* (-;-en) chat; small talk
Plau'derer –in §6 *mf* talker, chatterer
plaudern ['plaudərn] *intr* chat, chatter; **aus der Schule p.** tell tales out of school
Plaudertasche ['plaudərtaʃə] *f* chatterbox
Plauderton ['plaudərton] *m* conversational tone
plausibel [plau'zibəl] *adj* plausible
plauz [plauts] *interj* crash!
pleite ['plaɪtə] *adj* (coll) broke ‖ *adv* —**p. gehen** go broke ‖ **Pleite** *f* (-;) (coll) bankruptcy; **P. machen** (coll) go broke
Plenarsitzung [ple'narzɪtsuŋ] *f* (-;-en) plenary session
Plenum ['plenum] *n* (-s;) plenary session
Pleuelstange ['plɔɪ.əlʃtaŋə] *f* (mach) connecting rod
Plexiglas ['plɛksɪglas] *n* (-es;) plexiglass
Plinse ['plɪnzə] *f* (-;-n) pancake; fritter
Plissee [plɪ'se] *n* (-s;-s) pleat
Plissee'rock *m* pleated skirt
plissieren [plɪ'sirən] *tr* pleat
Plombe ['plɔmbə] *f* (-;-n) lead seal; (dent) filling
plombieren [plɔm'birən] *tr* seal with lead; (dent) fill

plötzlich ['plœtslɪç] *adj* sudden ‖ *adv* suddenly, all of a sudden
plump [plump] *adj* (*unförmig*) shapeless; (*schwerfällig*) heavy, slow; (*derb*) coarse; (*unbeholfen*) ungainly; (*taktlos*) tactless, blunt
plumps [plumps] *interj* plop! thump!
plumpsen ['plumpsən] *intr* (HABEN & SEIN) plop, flop
Plunder ['plundər] *m* (-s;) junk
plündern ['plyndərn] *tr & intr* plunder
Plural ['plural] *m* (-s;-e) plural
plus [plus] *adv* plus ‖ **Plus** *n* (-;-) plus; (*Überschuß*) surplus; (*Vorteil*) advantage, edge
Plus'pol *m* (elec) positive pole
Plutokrat [pluto'krat] *m* (-en;-en) plutocrat
Plutonium [plu'tonjum] *n* (-s;) plutonium
pneumatisch [pnɔɪ'matɪʃ] *adj* pneumatic
Pöbel ['pøbəl] *m* (-s;) mob, rabble
pö'belhaft *adj* rude, rowdy
Pö'belherrschaft *f* mob rule
pochen ['pɔxən] *tr* (min) crush ‖ *intr* knock; (*Herz*) pound; **p. an** (*dat*) knock on; **p. auf** (*acc*) pound on; (fig) insist on
Pochmüle ['pɔxmylə] *f*, **Pochwerk** ['pɔxvɛrk] *n* crushing mill
Pocke ['pɔkə] *f* (-;-n) pockmark; **Pokken** (pathol) smallpox
Pockennarbe [**Pok'kennarbe**] *f* pockmark
pockennarbig (**pok'kennarbig**) *adj* pockmarked
Podest [po'dɛst] *m & n* (-es;-e) pedestal; (*Treppenabsatz*) landing; podium
Po·dium ['podjum] *n* (-s;-dien [djən]) podium, platform
Poesie [po.e'zi] *f* (-;) poetry
Poet [po'et] *m* (-en;-en) poet
Poetik [po'etɪk] *f* (-;) poetics
poetisch [po'etɪʃ] *adj* poetic
Pointe [po'ɛ̃tə] *f* (-;) point (*of joke*)
Pokal [po'kal] *m* (-s;-e) goblet; (sport) cup
Pökel ['pøkəl] *m* (-s;) brine
Pö'kelfleisch *n* salted meat
Pö'kelhering *m* pickled herring
pökeln ['pøkəln] *tr* pickle, salt
Poker ['pokər] *n* (-s;) poker
Pol [pol] *m* (-s;-e) pole
Polar- [polar] *comb.fm.* polar
polarisieren [polarɪ'zirən] *tr* polarize
Polarität [polarɪ'tɛt] *f* (-;-en) polarity
Polar'kreis *m* polar circle; **nördlicher P.** Arctic Circle; **südlicher P.** Antarctic Circle
Polar'licht *n* polar lights
Polar'stern *m* polestar
Polar'zone *f* frigid zone
Pole ['polə] *m* (-n;-n) Pole
Polemik [po'lemɪk] *f* (-;) polemics
polemisch [po'lemɪʃ] *adj* polemical
Polen ['polən] *n* (-s;) Poland
Police [po'lisə] *f* (-;-n) (ins) policy
Polier [po'lir] *m* (-s;-e) foreman
polieren [po'lirən] *tr* polish
Polin ['polɪn] *f* (-;-nen) Pole
Politik [poli'tik] *f* (-;-en) policy; (*Staatsangelegenheiten*) politics

Politiker –in [pɔ'lɪtɪkər(ɪn)] §6 *mf* politician
Politi·kum [pɔ'lɪtɪkʊm] *n* (–s;–ka [ka]) political issue, political matter
politisch [pɔ'lɪtɪʃ] *adj* political
politisieren [pɔlɪtɪ'zirən] *intr* talk politics
Politur [pɔlɪ'tur] *f* (–;–en) polish
Polizei [pɔlɪ'tsaɪ] *f* (–;) police
Polizei'aufgebot *n* posse
Polizei'aufsicht *f*—unter P. stehen have to report periodically to the police
Polizei'beamte §5 *m* police officer
Polizei'büro *n*, Polizei'dienststelle *f* police station
Polizei'knüppel *m* billy club
Polizei'kommissar *m* police commissioner
polizei'lich *adj* police
Polizei'präsident *m* chief of police
Polizei'revier *n* police station
Polizei'spion *m*, Polizei'spitzel *m* stoolpigeon
Polizei'streife *f* raid; police patrol
Polizei'streifenwagen *m* squad car
Polizei'stunde *f* closing time; curfew
Polizei'wache *f* police station
polizei'widrig *adj* against police regulations
Polizist [pɔlɪ'tsɪst] *m* (–en;–en) policeman
Polizistin [pɔlɪ'tsɪstɪn] *f* (–;–nen) policewoman
Polizze [pɔ'lɪtsə] *f* (–;–n) (Aust) insurance policy
Polka ['pɔlka] *f* (–;–s) polka
polnisch ['pɔlnɪʃ] *adj* Polish
Polo ['polo] *n* (–s;) (sport) polo
Polster ['pɔlstər] *m & n* (–s;–) cushion
Pol'stergarnitur *f* living-room suite
Pol'stermöbel *pl* upholstered furniture
polstern ['pɔlstərn] *tr* upholster
Pol'stersessel *m* upholstered chair
Pol'sterstuhl *m* padded chair
Pol'sterung *f* (–;) padding, stuffing
Polterabend ['pɔltərabənt] *m* eve of the wedding day
Poltergeist ['pɔltərgaɪst] *m* poltergeist
poltern ['pɔltərn] *intr* make noise; (*rumpeln*) rumble; (*zanken*) bluster
Polyp [pɔ'lyp] *m* (–en;–en) (pathol, zool) polyp; (*Polizist*) (sl) cop
Polytechni·kum [pɔly'tɛçnɪkʊm] *n* (–s; –ka [ka]) polytechnic institute
Pomade [pɔ'mɑdə] *f* (–;–n) pomade
Pomeranze [pɔmə'rantsə] *f* (–;–n) bitter orange
Pommern ['pɔmərn] *n* (–s;) Pomerania
Pommes frites [pɔm'frɪt] *pl* French fries
Pomp [pɔmp] *m* (–es;) pomp
Pompadour ['pɔmpadur] *m* (–s;–e & –s) lady's string-drawn bag
pomp'haft, pompös [pɔm'pøs] *adj* pompous
pontifikal [pɔntɪfɪ'kal] *adj* pontifical
Pontifikat [pɔntɪfɪ'kat] *n* (–s;) pontificate
Pontius ['pɔntsjʊs] *m*—von P. zu Pilatus geschickt werden (coll) get the run-around
Pony ['pɔnɪ] *m* (–s;–s) (*Damenfrisur*) pony ǁ *n* (–s;–s) (*Pferd*) pony

Popo [pɔ'po] *m* (–s;–s) (coll) backside
populär [pɔpu'ler] *adj* popular
Popularität [pɔpularɪ'tet] *f* (–;) popularity
Pore ['porə] *f* (–;–n) pore
porig ['porɪç] *adj* porous
Pornofilm ['pɔrnofɪlm] *m* (coll) smoker, pornographic movie
Pornoladen ['pɔrnoladən] *m* (coll) porn shop
Pornographie [pɔrnɔgra'fi] *f* (–;) pornography
poros [pɔ'ros] *adj* porous
Porphyr ['pɔrfyr] *m* (–s;) porphyry
Porree ['pɔre] *m* (–s;–s) (bot) leek
Portal [pɔr'tal] *n* (–s;–e) portal
Portemonnaie [pɔrtmɔ'ne] *n* (–s;–s) wallet
Portier [pɔr'tje] *m* (–s;–s) doorman
Portion [pɔr'tsjon] *f* (–;–en) portion; (culin) serving, helping; halbe P. (coll) half pint; zwei Portionen Kaffee two cups of coffee
Por·to ['pɔrto] *n* (–s;–ti [ti]) postage
Por'togebühren *pl* postage
Por'tokasse *f* petty cash
Porträt [pɔr'tret] *n* (–s;–s), (–[e]s;–e) portrait
porträtieren [pɔrtre'tirən] *tr* portray
Portugal ['pɔrtugal] *n* (–s;) Portugal
Portugiese [pɔrtu'gizə] *m* (–n;–n), Portugiesin [pɔrtu'gizɪn] *f* (–;–nen) Portuguese
portugiesisch [pɔrtu'gizɪʃ] *adj* Portuguese
Porzellan [pɔrtsə'lan] *n* (–s;–e) porcelain; china; Meißener Porzellan Dresden china
Porzellan'brennerei *f* porcelain factory
Posament [pɔza'mɛnt] *n* (–[e]s;–en) trimming, lace
Posaune [pɔ'zaʊnə] *f* (–;–n) trombone
posaunen [pɔ'zaʊnən] *intr* play the trombone
Pose ['pozə] *f* (–;–n) pose
posieren [pɔ'zirən] *intr* pose
Position [pɔzɪ'tsjon] *f* (–;–en) position
Positions'lampe *f* Positions'licht *n* (aer, naut) navigation light
positiv [pɔzɪ'tif] *adj* (*bejahend*) affirmative; (*Kritik*) favorable; (elec, math, med) positive ǁ *adv* in the affirmative; (coll) for certain ǁ Positiv *m* (–s;–e) (gram) positive degree ǁ *n* (–s;–e) (mus) small organ; (phot) positive
Positur [pɔzɪ'tur] *f* (–;–en) posture, attitude; sich in P. setzen (or stellen or werfen) strike a pose
Posse ['pɔsə] *f* (–;–n) (theat) farce
Possen ['pɔsən] *m* (–s;–) trick, practical joke; j–m e–n P. spielen play a practical joke on s.o.; laß die P.! cut out the nonsense; P. treiben (or reißen) crack jokes
pos'senhaft *adj* farcical, comical
Possenreißer ['pɔsənraɪsər] *m* (–s;–) joker
Pos'senspiel *n* farce, burlesque
possierlich [pɔ'sirlɪç] *adj* funny
Post [pɔst] *f* (–;–en) mail; (*Postgebäude*) post office
postalisch [pɔs'talɪʃ] *adj* postal

Postament [pɔsta'mɛnt] *n* (-[e]s;-e) pedestal
Post'amt *n* post office
Post'anweisung *f* money order
Post'auto *n* mail truck
Post'beamte *m* postal clerk
Post'beutel *m* mailbag
Post'bote *m* mailman
Post'direktor *m* postmaster
Posten ['pɔstən] *m* (-s;-) post; (*Stellung*) position; (acct) entry, item; (com) line, lot; (mil) guard, sentinel; **auf dem P. sein** (fig) be on guard; **auf verlorenem P. kämpfen** (coll) play a losing game; **nicht recht auf dem P. sein** be out of sorts; **P. aufstellen** post sentries; **P. stehen** stand guard; **ruhiger P.** (mil) soft job
Po'stenjäger –in §6 *mf* job hunter
Po'stenkette *f* line of outposts
Post'fach *n* post-office box
Post'gebühr *f* postage
posthum [pɔst'hum] *adj* posthumous
postieren [pɔs'tirən] *tr* post, place
Postille [pɔs'tilə] *f* (-;-n) devotional book
Post'karte *f* post card
Post'kasten *m* mail box
Post'kutsche *f* stagecoach
post'lagernd *adj* general-delivery || *adv* general delivery
Postleitzahl ['pɔstlaɪttsal] *f* zip code
Post'minister *m* postmaster general
Post'nachnahme *f* (-;-n) C.O.D.
Post'sack *m* mailbag
Post'schalter *m* post-office window
Post'scheck *m* postal check
Postschließfach ['pɔst/lisfax] *n* post-office box
Postskript [pɔst'skript] *n* (-[e]s;-e) postscript
Post'stempel *m* postmark
Post'überweisung *f* money order
post'wendend *adj* & *adv* by return mail
Post'wertzeichen *n* postage stamp
Post'wesen *n* postal system
potent [pɔ'tɛnt] *adj* potent
Potential [pɔtɛn'tsjal] *n* (-s;-e) potential
Potenz [pɔ'tɛnts] *f* (-;-en) potency; (math) power; **dritte P.** (math) cube; **zweite P.** (math) square
potenzieren [pɔtɛn'tsirən] *tr* raise to a higher power; (fig) intensify
Pottasche ['pɔta/ə] *f* (-;) potash
Pottwal ['pɔtval] *m* sperm whale
potz [pɔts] *interj*—**p. Blitz!** holy smoke!
potztau'send *interj* holy smoke!
poussieren [pʊ'sirən] *tr* (coll) flirt with; (coll) butter up || *intr* flirt
Pracht [praxt] *f* (-;) splendor, magnificence
Pracht'ausgabe *f* deluxe edition
Pracht'exemplar *n* beauty, beaut
prächtig ['prɛçtɪç] *adj* splendid
Pracht'kerl *m* (coll) great guy
Pracht'stück *n* (coll) beauty, beaut
pracht'voll *adj* gorgeous
Pracht'zimmer *n* stateroom (*in palace*)
Prädikat [predɪ'kat] *n* (-[e]s;-e) title; (educ) mark, grade; (gram) predicate

Prädikatsnomen [predɪ'katsnomən] *n* (-s;-s) (gram) complement
Präfix [prɛ'fɪks] *n* (-es;-e) prefix
Prag [prak] *n* (-s;) Prague
Prägeanstalt ['pregə·anstalt] *f* mint
prägen ['pregən] *tr* stamp, coin || *ref* —**das hat sich mir tief in das Gedächtnis geprägt** that made a lasting impression on me
Prä'gestempel *m* (mach) die
pragmatisch [prag'matɪ/] *adj* pragmatic
prägnant [prɛ'gnant] *adj* pithy, terse
Prä'gung *f* (-;-en) coining, minting; (fig) coinage
prahlen ['pralən] *intr* (**mit**) brag (about); (**mit**) show off (with)
Prah'ler *m* (-s;-) braggart; show-off
Prahlerei [pralə'raɪ] *f* (-;-en) bragging, boasting; (*Prunken*) showing off
Prah'lerin *f* (-;-nen) braggart; show-off
prahlerisch ['pralərɪ/] *adj* bragging
Prahlhans ['pralhans] *m* (-es;-̈e) braggart
Prahm [pram] *m* (-[e]s;-e) flat-bottomed lighter
Praktik ['praktɪk] *f* (-;-en) practice; (*Kniff*) trick
Praktikant –in [praktɪ'kant(ɪn)] §7 *mf* student in on-the-job training
Praktiker ['praktɪkər] *m* (-s;-) practical person
Prakti·kum ['praktɪkʊm] *n* (-s;-ka [ka]) practical training
Praktikus ['praktɪkʊs] *m* (-;-se) old hand
praktisch ['praktɪ/] *adj* practical; **praktischer Arzt** general practitioner
praktizieren [praktɪ'tsirən] *tr* practice; **etw in die Tasche p.** manage to slip s.th. into the pocket
Prälat [prɛ'lat] *m* (-en;-en) prelate
Praline [pra'linə] *f* (-;-n) chocolate
prall [pral] *adj* (*straff*) tight; (*Brüste*) full; (*Backen*) chubby; (*Arme, Beine*) shapely; (*Sonne*) blazing || **Prall** *m* (-[e]s;-e) impact; collision
prallen ['pralən] *intr* (SEIN) bounce, rebound; (*Sonne*) beat down
Prämie ['premjə] *f* (-;-n) award, prize; premium; bonus
prämiieren [premi'irən] *tr* award a prize to
prangen ['praŋən] *intr* shine; look beautiful
Pranger ['praŋər] *m* (-s;-) pillory
Pranke ['praŋkə] *f* (-;-n) claw
pränumerando [prɛnumə'rando] *adv* in advance, beforehand
Präparat [prɛpa'rat] *n* (-[e]s;-e) preparation
präparieren [prɛpa'rirən] *tr* prepare
Präposition [prɛpɔzi'tsjon] *f* (-;-en) preposition
Prä·rie [prɛ'ri] *f* (-;-rien ['ri·ən]) prairie
Präsens ['prezɛns] *n* (-; **Präsentia** [prɛ'zɛntsi·a]) (gram) present
präsent [prɛ'zɛnt] *adj* present || **Präsent** *n* (-s;-e) present, gift
präsentieren [prezɛn'tirən] *tr* present
Präsentier'teller *m* tray

Präsenzstärke [prɛ'zɛnts/tɛrkə] *f* effective strength
Präservativ [prɛzɛrva'tif] *m* (-s;-e) prophylactic, condom
Präsident [prɛzɪ'dɛnt] *m* (-en;-en) president
Präsidenten– [prɛzɪdɛntən] *comb.fm.* presidential
Präsident'schaft *f* (-;-en) presidency
präsidieren [prɛzɪ'dirən] *intr* preside
Präsi·dium [prɛ'zidjʊm] *n* (-s;-dien [djən]) presidency; chairmanship
prasseln ['prasəln] *intr* crackle; (*Regen*) patter
prassen ['prasən] *intr* lead a dissipated life
Prasserei [prasə'raɪ] *f* (-;) luxurious living, high life
Prätendent [prɛtɛn'dɛnt] *m* (-en;-en) (**auf** *acc*) pretender (to)
Pra·xis ['praksɪs] *f* (-;-xen [ksən]) practice; experience; doctor's office; law office; (jur) clientele; (med) patients
Präzedenzfall [prɛtsɛ'dɛntsfal] *m* precedent
präzis [prɛ'tsis] *adj* precise
Präzision [prɛtsɪ'zjon] *f* (-;) precision
predigen ['predɪgən] *tr* & *intr* preach
Prediger ['predɪgər] *m* (-s;-) preacher
Predigt ['predɪçt] *f* (-;-en) sermon
Preis [praɪs] *m* (-es;-e) price, rate, cost; (poet) praise, glory; **äußerster P.** (coll) rock-bottom price; **um jeden P.** (fig) at all costs; **um keinen P.** (fig) on no account; **zum P. von** at the rate of
Preis'aufgabe *f* project in a competition
Preis'aufschlag *m* extra charge
Preis'ausschreiben *n* competition
Preisdrückerei ['praɪsdrʏkəraɪ] *f* (-; -en) price cutting
Preiselbeere ['praɪzəlberə] *f* cranberry
preisen ['praɪzən] *tr* praise
Preis'ermäßigung *f* price reduction
Preis'frage *f* question in a competition; question of price (coll) sixty-four-dollar question
Preis'gabe *f* abandonment, surrender
preis'geben §80 *tr* abandon, surrender; (*Geheimnis*) betray; **j–n dem Spott p.** hold s.o. up to ridicule
preisgekrönt ['praɪsgəkrønt] *adj* prize-winning
Preis'gericht *n* jury
Preis'grenze *f* price limit; **obere P.** ceiling; **untere P.** minimum price
preis'günstig *adj* worth the money
Preis'lage *f* price range
Preis'niveau *n* price level
Preis'notierung *f* rate of exchange
Preis'richter *m* judge (*in competition*)
Preis'schießen *n* shooting competition
Preis'schild *n* price tag
Preis'schlager *m* bargain price
Preis'schrift *f* prize-winning essay
Preis'stopp *m* price freezing
Preis'sturz *m* drop in prices
Preis'träger –in §6 *mf* prize winner
Preistreiberei [praɪstraɪbə'raɪ] *f* (-;) price rigging
Preis'überwachung *f* price control

Preis'verzeichnis *n* price list
preis'wert, preis'würdig *adj* worth the money, reasonable
Preis'zuschlag *m* markup
prekär [pre'ker] *adj* precarious
Prellbock ['prɛlbɔk] *m* (rr) buffer
prellen ['prɛlən] *tr* bump; bounce; toss up (*in a blanket*); (**um**) cheat (out of) || *ref—sich* [*dat*] **den Arm p.** bruise one's arm
Prel'ler *m* (-s;-) bump; ricochet; bilker, cheat
Prellerei [prɛlə'raɪ] *f* (-;-en) (act of) cheating
Prell'schuß *m* ricochet
Prell'stein *m* curbstone
Prel'lung *f* (-;-en) bruise
Premier [prə'mje] *m* (-s;-s) premier
Premiere [prə'mjerə] *f* (-;-n) (theat) premiere, first night, opening
Premier'minister *m* prime minister
Presbyterianer –in [presbʏtə'rjanər (ɪn)] §6 *mf* Presbyterian
presbyterianisch [presbʏtə'rjanɪʃ] *adj* Presbyterian
preschen ['preʃən] *intr* charge
pressant [prɛ'sant] *adj* pressing
Presse ['presə] *f* (-;-n) (& journ) press; (educ) cram class
Pres'seagentur *f* press agency
Pres'seamt *n* public-relations office
Pres'seausweis *m* press card
Pres'sebericht *m* press report
Pres'sechef *m* press secretary
Pres'sekonferenz *f* press conference
Pres'semeldung *f* news item
Pres'sestelle *f* public-relations office
Pres'severtreter *m* reporter; public-relations officer
Preßkohle ['preskolə] *f* briquette
Preßluft ['presluft] *f* compressed air
Preß'lufthammer *m* jackhammer
Preuße ['prɔɪsə] *m* (-n;-n) Prussian
Preußen ['prɔɪsən] *n* (-s;) Prussia
Preußin ['prɔɪsɪn] *f* (-;-nen) Prussian
preußisch ['prɔɪsɪʃ] *adj* Prussian
prickeln ['prɪkəln] *intr* tingle
Priem [prim] *m* (-[e]s;-e) plug (*of tobacco*)
priemen ['primən] *intr* chew tobacco
pries [pris] *pret* of **preisen**
Priester ['pristər] *m* (-s;-) priest
Prie'steramt *n* priesthood
Priesterin ['pristərɪn] *f* (-;-nen) priestess
prie'sterlich *adj* priestly
Prie'sterrock *m* cassock
Priestertum ['pristərtum] *n* (-s;) priesthood
Prie'sterweihe *f* (eccl) ordination
prima ['prima] *invar adj* first-class; terrific, swell
primär [prɪ'mer] *adj* primary || *adv* primarily
Primat [prɪ'mat] *m* & *n* (-[e]s;-e) primacy, priority || *m* (-en;-en) primate
Primel ['priməl] *f* (-;-n) primrose
primitiv [primɪ'tif] *adj* primitive
Prinz [prɪnts] *m* (-en;-en) prince
Prinzessin [prɪn'tsɛsɪn] *f* (-;-nen) princess
Prinz'gemahl *m* prince consort

Prin·zip [prɪn'tsip] *n* (**-s;-zipien** ['tsipjən]) principle
prinzipiell [prɪntsɪ'pjɛl] *adj* in principle, fundamentally
Prinzi'pienreiter *m* (coll) pedant
prinz'lich *adj* princely
Pri·or ['pri·ɔr] *m* (**-s;-oren** ['orən]) (eccl) prior
Priorität [prɪ·ɔrɪ'tet] *f* (**-;-en**) priority
Prise ['prizə] *f* (**-;-n**) pinch (*of salt, etc.*); (nav) prize
Pris·ma ['prɪsma] *n* (**-s;-men** [mɛn]) prism
privat [prɪ'vat] *adj* private; personal
Privat'adresse *f*, **Privat'anschrift** *f* home address
Privat'dozent -in §7 *mf* non-salaried university lecturer
Privat'druck *m* private printing
Privat'eigentum *n* private property
Privat'gespräch *n* (telp) personal call
privatim [prɪ'vatɪm] *adv* privately; confidentially
privatisieren [prɪvatɪ'zirən] *intr* be financially independent
Privat'lehrer -in §6 *mf* tutor
Privat'recht *n* civil law
privat'rechtlich *adj* (jur) civil
Privi·leg [prɪvɪ'lek] *n* (**-[e]s;-legien** ['legjən]) privilege
privilegiert [prɪvɪle'girt] *adj* privileged
probat [pro'bat] *adj* tried, tested
Probe ['probə] *f* (**-;-n**) (*Versuch*) trial, experiment; (*Prüfung*) test; (*Muster*) sample; (*Beweis*) proof; (theat) rehearsal; **auf die P. stellen** put to the test; **auf** (or **zur**) **P.** on approval
Pro'beabdruck *m*, **Pro'beabzug** *m* (typ) proof
Pro'bebild *n* (phot) proof
Pro'bebogen *m* proof sheet
Pro'bedruck *m* (typ) proof
Pro'befahrt *f* road test, trial run
Pro'beflug *m* test flight
Pro'belauf *m* trial run; dry run
Pro'besendung *f* sample sent on approval
Pro'bestück *n* sample, specimen
pro'beweise *adv* on trial; on approval
Pro'bezeit *f* probation period
probieren [pro'birən] *tr* try out, test; try, taste; (metal) assay
Probier'glas *n* test tube
Probier'stein *m* touch-stone
Problem [pro'blem] *n* (**-s;-e**) problem
Produkt [pro'dʊkt] *n* (**-[e]s;-e**) product; (*des Bodens*) produce
Produktion [prodʊk'tsjon] *f* (**-;-en**) production; (indust) output
produktiv [prodʊk'tif] *adj* productive
Produ₂ent [produ'tsɛnt] *m* (**-en;-en**) (& cin) producer
produzieren [produ'tsirən] *tr* produce || *ref* perform; (pej) show off
profan [pro'fan] *adj* profane
profanieren [profa'nirən] *tr* profane
Profession [profe'sjon] *f* (**-;-en**) profession
Professional [profesjə'nal] *m* (**-s;-e**) (sport) professional
professionell [profesjə'nɛl] *adj* professional
Profes·sor [pro'fɛsɔr] *m* (**-s;-soren**

['sorən]), **Professorin** [profɛ'sorɪn] *f* (**-;-nen**) professor; **außerordentlicher P.** associate professor; **ordentlicher P.** full professor
Professur [profe'sur] *f* (**-;-en**) professorship
Profi ['profi] *m* (**-s;-s**) (coll) pro
Profil [pro'fil] *n* (**-s;-e**) profile; (aut) tread; **im P.** in profile
profiliert [profi'lirt] *adj* outstanding
Profit [pro'fit] *m* (**-[e]s;-e**) profit
profitabel [profi'tabəl] *adj* profitable
Profit'gier *f* profiteering
profitieren [profi'tirən] *tr & intr* profit
Prognose [pro'gnozə] *f* (**-;-n**) (med) prognosis; (meteor) forecast
Programm [pro'gram] *n* (**-s;-e**) program; (pol) platform
programmieren [progra'mirən] *tr* (data proc) program
Projekt [pro'jɛkt] *n* (**-[e]s;-e**) project
Projektil [projɛk'til] *n* (**-s;-e**) projectile
Projektion [projɛk'tsjon] *f* (**-;-en**) projection
Projektions'apparat *m*, **Projektions' gerät** *n*, **Projek·tor** [pro'jɛktɔr] *m* (**-s;-toren** ['torən]) projector
projizieren [projɪ'tsirən] *tr* project
proklamieren [prokla'mirən] *tr* proclaim
Prokura [pro'kura] *f* (**-;**) power of attorney; **per P.** by proxy
Prolet [pro'let] *m* (**-en;-en**) (pej) cad
Proletariat [proleta'rjat] *n* (**-[e]s;-e**) proletariat
Proletarier -in [prole'tarjər(ɪn)] §6 *mf* proletarian
proletarisch [prole'tarɪʃ] *adj* proletarian
Prolog [pro'lok] *m* (**-[e]s;-e**) prologue
prolongieren [proloŋ'girən] *tr* extend; (cin) hold over
Promenade [promə'nadə] *f* (**-;-n**) avenue; (*Spaziergang*) promenade
promenieren [promə'nirən] *intr* stroll
prominent [promɪ'nɛnt] *adj* prominent
Promotion [promo'tsjon] *f* (**-;-en**) awarding of the doctor's degree
promovieren [promo'virən] *intr* attain a doctor's degree
prompt [prompt] *adj* prompt, quick
Prono·men [pro'nomən] *n* (**-s;-mina** [mɪna]) pronoun
Propaganda [propa'ganda] *f* (**-;**) propaganda
propagieren [propa'girən] *tr* propagate
Propeller [pro'pɛlər] *m* (**-s;-**) propeller
Prophet [pro'fet] *m* (**-en;-en**) prophet
Prophetin [pro'fetɪn] *f* (**-;-nen**) prophetess
prophetisch [pro'fetɪʃ] *adj* prophetic
prophezeien [profɛ'tsaɪ·ən] *tr* prophesy
Prophezei'ung *f* (**-;-en**) prophecy
Proportion [propor'tsjon] *f* (**-;-en**) proportion
proportional [proportsjo'nal] *adj* proportional
proportioniert [proportsjo'nirt] *adj* proportionate
Propst [propst] *m* (**-es;̈-e**) provost

Prosa ['proza] f (-;) prose
prosaisch [prɔ'za·ɪʃ] adj prosaic
prosit ['prozɪt] interj to your health!
|| Prosit n (-s;-s) toast
Prospekt [prɔ'spɛkt] m (-[e]s;-e)
prospect, view; brochure, folder
prostituieren [prɔstɪtu'irən] tr prostitute
Prostituierte [prɔstɪtu'irtə] §5 f prostitute
protegieren [protə'girən] tr patronize;
(schützen) protect
Protektion [prɔtek'tsjon] f (-;) pull,
connections
Protest [prɔ'test] m (-es;-e) protest
Protestant -in [protes'tant(ɪn)] §7 mf
Protestant
protestantisch [protes'tantɪʃ] adj Protestant
protestieren [protes'tirən] tr & intr
protest
Protokoll [protɔ'kɔl] n (-s;-e) protocol; record, minutes; P. führen take
the minutes; zu P. nehmen take down
Protokoll'führer -in §6 mf recording
secretary; (jur) clerk
protokollieren [protɔkɔ'lirən] tr record
Pro·ton ['proton] n (-s;-tonen
['tonən]) (phys) proton
Protz [prɔts] m (-en;-en) show-off
protzen ['prɔtsən] intr show off
prot'zenhaft, protzig ['prɔtsɪç] adj
show-offish
Prozedur [protse'dur] f (-;-en) procedure; (jur) proceeding
Prozent [prɔ'tsɛnt] n (-[e]s;-e) percent
Prozent'satz m percentage
Pro·zeß [prɔ'tsɛs] m (-zesses;-zesse)
process; (jur) case, suit; (jur) proceedings; e-en P. anstrengen (or
führen) gegen sue; kurzen P. machen
mit make short work of
Prozeß'akten pl (jur) record
Prozeß'führer -in §6 mf litigant
prozessieren [protse'sirən] intr go to
court; p. gegen sue
Prozession [protse'sjon] f (-;-en) procession
Prozeß'kosten pl (jur) court costs
Prozeß'vollmacht f power of attorney
prüde ['prydə] adj prudish
prüfen ['pryfən] tr test; (nachprüfen)
check, verify; (untersuchen) examine;
(kosten) taste; (acct) audit
Prüfer -in §6 mf examiner; (acct) auditor
Prüfling ['pryflɪŋ] m (-s;-e) examinee
Prüfstein ['pryfʃtaɪn] m touchstone
Prü'fung f (-;-en) test; examination;
check, verification; (acct) audit; (jur)
review
Prü'fungsarbeit f test paper
Prü'fungsausschuß m, Prü'fungskom-
mission f examining board
Prügel ['prygəl] m (-s;-) stick, cudgel;
Prügel pl whipping
Prügelei [prygə'laɪ] f (-;-en) brawl;
free-for-all
Prü'gelknabe m whipping boy, scape-
goat
prügeln ['prygəln] tr beat, whip || ref
have a fight

Prü'gelstrafe f corporal punishment
Prunk [pruŋk] m (-[e]s;) pomp, show
prunken ['pruŋkən] intr show off
Prunk'gemach n stateroom
prunk'haft adj showy
Prunk'sucht f ostentatiousness
prunk'süchtig adj ostentatious
prunk'voll adj gorgeous
Prunk'zimmer n stateroom
prusten ['prustən] intr snort
Psalm [psalm] m (-s;-en) psalm
Psalter ['psaltər] m (-s;-) psalter
Pseudonym [psɔɪdɔ'nym] n (-s;-e)
pseudonym
Psychiater (psʏçɪ'atər] m (-s;-) psychiatrist
Psychiatrie [psʏçɪ·a'tri] f (-;) psychiatry
psychiatrisch [psʏçɪ'atrɪʃ] adj psychi-
atric
psychisch ['psʏçɪʃ] adj psychic(al)
Psychoanalyse [psʏçɔ·ana'lyzə] f (-;)
psychoanalysis
Psychoanalytiker -in [psʏçɔ·ana'lytɪ-
kər(ɪn)] §6 mf psychoanalyst
Psychologe [psʏçɔ'logə] m (-n;-n) psychologist
Psychologie [psʏçɔlɔ'gi] f (-;) psychology
Psychologin [psʏçɔ'logɪn] f (-;-nen)
psychologist
psychologisch [psʏçɔ'logɪʃ] adj psy-
chological
Psychopath -in [psʏçɔ'pat(ɪn)] §7 mf
psychopath
Psychose [psʏ'çozə] f (-;-n) psychosis
Psychotherapie [psʏçɔtera'pi] f (-;)
psychotherapy
Pubertät [pubɛr'tet] f (-;) puberty
publik [pub'lik] adj public
Publi·kum ['publɪkum] n (-s;-ka
[ka]) public; (theat) audience
publizieren [publɪ'tsirən] tr publish
Publizist -in [publɪ'tsɪst(ɪn)] §7 mf
(journ) writer on public affairs;
teacher or student of journalism
Publizität [publɪtsɪ'tet] f (-;) publicity
Pudel ['pudəl] m (-s;-) poodle; des
Pudels Kern (fig) gist of the matter
Pu'delmütze f fur cap; woolen cap
pu'delnaß' adj (coll) soaking wet
Puder ['pudər] m (-s;) powder
Pu'derdose f powder box; compact
Pu'derquaste f powder puff
Pu'derzucker m powdered sugar
Puff [puf] m (-[e]s;=e & -e) (Stoß)
poke; (Knall) pop; (Bausch) puff;
|| m (-s;-s) (coll) brothel
Puff'ärmel m puffed sleeve
puffen ['pufən] tr poke; (coll) prod ||
intr puff; (knallen) pop, bang away
Puffer ['pufər] m (-s;-) buffer; pop-
gun; (culin) potato pancake
Puf'ferbatterie f booster battery
Puf'ferstaat m buffer state
Puff'mais m popcorn
Puff'reis m (-es;) puffed rice
Pulli ['puli] m (-s;-s) (coll) sweater
Pullover [pu'lovər] m (-s;-) sweater
Puls [puls] m (-es;-e) pulse
Puls'ader f artery
pulsieren [pul'zirən] intr pulsate
Puls'schlag m pulse beat

Pult [pʊlt] *n* (-[e]s;-e) desk
Pulver ['pʊlfər] *n* (-s;-) powder;
(*Schieß-*) gunpowder; (coll) dough
pul'verig *adj* powdery
pulverisieren [pʊlfərɪ'zirən] *tr* pulverize
Pul'verschnee *m* powdery snow
Pummel ['pʊməl] *m* (-s;-) butterball
(*chubby child*)
pummelig ['pʊməlɪç] *adj* (coll) chubby
Pump [pʊmp] *m*—**auf P.** (coll) on tick
Pumpe ['pʊmpə] *f* (-;-n) pump
pumpen ['pʊmpən] *tr* pump; (coll) give
on tick; (coll) get on tick || *intr*
pump
Pum'penschwengel *m* pump handle
Pumpernickel ['pʊmpərnɪkəl] *m* (-s;
-) pumpernickel
Pump'hosen *f* pair of knickerbockers
Punkt [pʊŋkt] *m* (-[e]s;-e) point;
(*Tüpfelchen*) dot; (*Stelle*) spot; (*Einzelheit*) item; (gram) period; **der tote
P.** a deadlock; **dunkler P.** (fig) skeleton in the closet; **nach Punkten siegen** win on points; **P. sechs Uhr** at
six o'clock sharp; **springender P.**
crux; **strittiger P.** point at issue;
wunder P. (fig) sore spot
Punkt'gleichheit *f* (sport) tie
punktieren [pʊŋk'tirən] *tr* dot, stipple;
punktierte Linie dotted line
pünktlich ['pʏŋktlɪç] *adj* punctual
Punkt'sieg *m* (box) winning on points
punktum ['pʊŋktum] *interj*—**und damit p.!** and that's it!; period!
Punkt'zahl *f* (sport) score
Punsch [pʊnʃ] *m* (-es;) punch (*drink*)
Punze ['pʊntsə] *f* (-;-n) punch, stamp
pun⁊en ['pʊntsən] *tr* punch, stamp
Pupille [pʊ'pɪlə] *f* (-;-n) (anat) pupil
Puppe ['pʊpə] *f* (-;-n) doll; puppet;
(*Schneider-*) dummy; (zool) pupa
Pup'penspiel *n* puppet show
Pup'penwagen *m* doll carriage
pur [pur] *adj* pure, sheer

Püree [pʏ're] *n* (-s;-s) mashed potatoes; puree
purgieren [pʊr'girən] *tr* & *intr* purge
Purpur ['pʊrpur] *m* (-s;) purple
pur'purfarben *adj* purple
purpurn [pʊrpʊrn] *adj* purple
Purzelbaum ['pʊrtsəlbaum] *m* somersault; **e-en P. schlagen** do a somersault
purzeln ['pʊrtsəln] *intr* (SEIN) tumble
pusselig ['pʊsəlɪç] *adj* fussy
Puste ['pʊstə] *f* (-;) (coll) breath
Pustel ['pʊstəl] *f* (-;-n) pustule
pusten ['pʊstən] *tr*—**ich puste dir was!**
(coll) you may whistle for it! || *intr*
puff, pant
Pu'sterohr *n* peashooter
Pute ['pʊtə] *f* (-;-n) turkey (hen)
Puter ['pʊtər] *m* (-s;-) turkey (cock)
Putsch [pʊtʃ] *m* (-es;-e) putsch, uprising
Putz [pʊts] *m* (-es;) finery; trimming;
ornaments; plaster
putzen ['pʊtsən] *tr* (*reinigen*) clean;
(*Schuhe*) polish; (*Zähne*) brush; (*Person*) dress; (*schmücken*) adorn || *ref*
dress; **sich** [*dat*] **die Nase p.** blow
one's nose
Put'zer *m* (-s;-) cleaner; (mil) orderly
Putzerei [pʊtsə'raɪ] *f* (-;-en) (Aust)
dry cleaner's; (Aust) laundry
Putz'frau *f* cleaning woman
putzig ['pʊtsɪç] *adj* funny
Putz'lappen *m* cleaning cloth
Putz'mittel *n* cleaning agent
Putz'wolle *f* cotton waste
Putz'zeug *n* cleaning things
Pygmäe [pʏg'me·ə] *m* (-n;-n) pygmy
Pyjama [pɪ'dʒama] *m* (-s;-s) pajamas
Pyramide [pʏra'midə] *f* (-;-n) pyramid; (mil) stack
Pyrenäen [pʏrə'ne·ən] *pl* Pyrenees
Pyrotechnik [pʏrə'teçnɪk] *f* (-;) pyrotechnics
Pythonschlange ['pytən/laŋə] *f* python

Q

Q, q [ku] *invar n* Q, q
quabbelig ['kvabəlɪç] *adj* flabby; quivering, jelly-like
quabbeln ['kvabəln] *intr* quiver
Quackelei [kvakə'laɪ] *f* (-;-en) silly
talk; (*unnützes Zeug*) rubbish
Quacksalber ['kvakzalbər] *m* (-s;-)
quack
Quader ['kvadər] *m* (-s;-) ashlar
Quadrant [kva'drant] *m* (-en;-en)
quadrant
Quadrat [kva'drat] *n* (-[e]s;-e)
square; **e-e Zahl ins Q. erheben**
square a number; **zwei Fuß im Q.**
two feet square
quadratisch [kva'dratɪʃ] *adj* square;
quadratic
Quadrat'meter *n* square meter
Quadrat'wurzel *f* square root
quadrieren [kva'drirən] *tr* square

quaken ['kvakən] *intr* (*Ente*) quack;
(*Frosch*) croak
quäken ['kvekən] *intr* bawl
Qual [kval] *f* (-;-en) torment, agony
quälen ['kvelən] *tr* torment; worry;
(*ständig bedrängen*) pester || *ref*—
sich mit e-r Arbeit q. slave at a job;
sich umsonst q. labor in vain; **sich
zu Tode q.** worry oneself to death
Quälgeist ['kvelgaɪst] *m* pest
Qualifikation [kvalɪfɪka'tsjon] *f* (-;
-en) qualification
qualifizieren [kvalɪfɪ'tsirən] *tr* & *ref*
(zu) qualify (for)
Qualität [kvalɪ'tet] *f* (-;-en) quality
Qualitäts- *comb.fm.* high-quality, highgrade, quality
Qualle ['kvalə] *f* (-;-n) jellyfish
Qualm [kvalm] *m* (-[e]s;) smoke;
vapor

qualmen ['kvalmən] *tr* smoke ‖ *intr* smoke; (coll) smoke like a chimney
qual'mig *adj* smoky
qual'voll *adj* agonizing
Quantentheorie ['kvantəntɛ·ɔri] *f* quantum theory
Quantität [kvantɪ'tɛt] *f* (–;–en) quantity
Quan·tum ['kvantʊm] *n* (–s;–ten [tən]) quantum; quantity; (*Anteil*) portion
Quappe ['kvapə] *f* (–;–n) tadpole
Quarantäne [kvaran'tɛnə] *f* (–;–n) quarantine
Quark [kvark] *m* (–[e]s;) curds; cottage cheese; (fig) nonsense
Quark'käse *m* cottage cheese
quarren ['kvarən] *intr* (*Frosch*) croak; (fig) groan
Quart [kvart] *n* (–s;–e) quart; quarto ‖ *f* (–;–en) (mus) fourth
Quartal [kvar'tal] *n* (–s;–e) quarter (*of a year*)
Quartals'abrechnung *f* (fin) quarterly statement
Quartals'säufer *m* periodic drunkard
Quart'band *m* (–[e]s;–e) quarto volume
Quarte ['kvartə] *f* (–;–n) (mus) fourth
Quartett [kvar'tɛt] *n* (–[e]s;–e) quartet
Quart'format *n* quarto
Quartier [kvar'tir] *n* (–s;–e) (*Stadtviertel*) quarter; (*Unterkunft*) quarters; (mil) quarters, billet
Quartier'meister *m* (mil) quartermaster
Quarz [kvarts] *m* (–es;–e) quartz
quasseln ['kvasəln] *tr* (coll) talk ‖ *intr* talk nonsense
Quast [kvast] *m* (–[e]s;–e) brush
Quaste ['kvastə] *f* (–;–n) tassel
Quatsch [kvatʃ] *m* (–es;) (coll) baloney
quatschen ['kvatʃən] *intr* chatter; talk nonsense; (*durch Schlamm*) slog
Quecksilber ['kvɛkzɪlbər] *n* mercury
queck'silbrig *adj* fidgety
Quell [kvɛl] *m* (–[e]s;–e) (poet) var of **Quelle**
Quelle ['kvɛlə] *f* (–;–n) fountainhead; source; spring
quellen ['kvɛlən] §119 *tr* cause to swell; soak ‖ *intr* (SEIN) spring, gush; (*Tränen*) well up; (*anschwellen*) swell; **ihm quollen die Augen fast aus dem Kopf** his eyes almost popped out
Quel'lenangabe *f* citation; bibliography
quel'lenmäßig *adj* according to the best authorities, authentic
Quel'lenmaterial *n* source material
Quel'lenstudium *n* original research

Quell'fluß *m* source
Quell'gebiet *n* headwaters
Quell'wasser *n* spring water
Quengelei [kvɛŋə'laɪ] *f* (–;–en) nagging
quengeln ['kvɛŋəln] *intr* nag
quer [kver] *adj* cross, transverse ‖ *adv* crosswise; **q. über** (*acc*) across
Quer'balken *m* crossbeam
Quere ['kverə] *f* (–;) diagonal direction; **j–m in die Q. kommen** run across s.o.; (fig) disturb s.o.
queren ['kverən] *tr* traverse, cross
querfeldein' *adv* cross-country
Quer'kopf *m* contrary person
quer'köpfig *adj* contrary
Quer'pfeife *f* (mus) fife
Quer'ruder *n* (aer) aileron
Quer'schiff *n* (archit) transept
Quer'schläger *m* ricochet
Quer'schnitt *m* cross section
Quer'treiber *m* schemer, plotter
querü'ber *adv* straight across
Querulant –in [kveru'lant(ɪn)] §7 *mf* grumbler, grouch
Quetsche ['kvɛtʃə] *f* (–;–n) squeezer; (pej) joint
quetschen ['kvɛtʃən] *tr* squeeze, pinch; bruise; (*zerquetschen*) crush, mash
Quetsch'kartoffeln *pl* mashed potatoes
Quet'schung *f* (–;–en) bruise, contusion
Quetsch'wunde *f* bruise
quick [kvɪk] *adj* brisk, lively
quick'lebendig *adj* (coll) very lively
quieken ['kvikən] *intr* squeal, squeak
quietschen ['kvitʃən] *intr* (*Tür*) creak; (*Ferkel*) squeal; (*Bremsen*) screetch
Quintessenz ['kvɪntɛsɛnts] *f* (–;) quintessence
Quintett [kvɪn'tɛt] *n* (–[e]s;–e) quintet
Quirl [kvɪrl] *m* (–[e]s;–e) (fig) fidgeter; (culin) whisk, mixer
quirlen ['kvɪrlən] *tr* beat, mix
quitt [kvɪt] *adj* even, square
Quitte ['kvɪtə] *f* (–;–n) quince
quittieren [kvɪ'tirən] *tr* give a receipt for; (*aufgeben*) quit
Quit'tung *f* (–;–en) receipt
Quiz [kvɪs] *n* (–;–) quiz
quoll [kvɔl] *pret* of **quellen**
Quotation [kvota'tsjon] *f* (–;–en) (st. exch.) quotation
Quote ['kvotə] *f* (–;–en) quota
Quotient [kvo'tsjent] *m* (–en;–en) quotient
quotieren [kvo'tirən] *tr* quote

R

R, r [ɛr] *invar n* R, r
Rabatt [ra'bat] *m* (–[e]s;–e) reduction, discount
Rabatt'marke *f* trading stamp
Rabatz [ra'bats] *m*—**R. machen** (coll) raise Cain
Rab·bi ['rabi] *m* (–[s];–s & –binen

['binən]), **Rabbiner** [ra'binər] *m* (–s;–) rabbi
Rabe ['rabə] *m* (–n;–n) raven; **weißer R.** (fig) rare bird
Ra'benaas *n* (coll) beast
Ra'benmutter *f* hard-hearted mother
ra'benschwarz' *adj* jet-black

rabiat [ra'bjɑt] *adj* rabid, raving
Rache ['raxə] *f* (–;) revenge
Rachen ['raxən] *m* (–s;–) throat; mouth; (fig) jaws
rächen ['rɛçən] *tr* avenge ‖ *ref* (an *dat*) avenge oneself (on)
Ra'chenhöhle *f* pharynx
Ra'chenkatarrh *m* sore throat
Rä'cher –in §6 *mf* avenger
Rachgier ['raxgir] *f* revengefulness
rach'gierig, rach'süchtig *adj* vengeful
Rad [rɑt] *n* (–[e]s;=er) wheel; bike; ein Rad schlagen turn a cartwheel; (Pfau) fan the tail
Radar ['radɑr], [ra'dɑr] *n* (–s;) radar
Ra'dargerät *n* radar
Ra'darschirm *m* radarscope
Radau [ra'dau] *m* (–s;–) (coll) row
Radau'macher *m* rowdy
Rädchen ['rɛtçən] *n* (–s;–) little wheel
Rad'dampfer *m* river boat
radebrechen ['radəbrɛçən] §64 *tr* murder (*a language*)
radeln ['radəln] *intr* (SEIN) (coll) ride a bike
Rädelsführer ['rɛdəlsfyrər] *m* ringleader
rädern ['rɛdərn] *tr* torture; wie gerädert sein (coll) be bushed
Räderwerk ['rɛdərvɛrk] *n* gears; (fig) clockwork
rad'fahren §71 *intr* (SEIN) ride a bicycle
radieren [ra'dirən] *tr* erase; etch
Radie'rer *m* (–s;–) eraser; etcher
Radier'gummi *m* eraser
Radier'kunst *f* art of etching
Radier'messer *n* scraper, eraser
Radie'rung *f* (–;–en) erasure; etching
Radieschen [ra'disçən] *n* (–s;–) radish
radikal [radi'kɑl] *adj* radical ‖ Radikale §5 *mf* radical, extremist
Radio ['radjo] *n* (–s;–s) radio; im R. on the radio; R. hören listen to the radio
Ra'dioamateur *m* (rad) ham
Ra'dioapparat *m*, Ra'diogerät *n* radio set
Radiologe [radjo'logə] *m* (–n;–n) radiologist
Radiologie [radjolo'gi] *f* (–;) radiology
Ra'dioröhre *f* radio tube
Ra'diosender *m* radio transmitter
Radium ['radium] *n* (–s;) radium
Ra·dius ['radjus] *m* (–;–dien [djən]) radius
Rad'kappe *f* hubcap
Rad'kranz *m* rim
Radler –in ['radlər(ɪn)] §6 *mf* cyclist
Rad'nabe *f* hub
Rad'rennen *n* bicycle race
–rädrig [redriç] *comb.fm.* –wheeled
rad'schlagen §132 *intr* turn a cartwheel
Rad'spur *f* rut, track
Rad'stand *m* wheelbase
Rad'zahn *m* cog
raffen ['rafən] *tr* snatch up, gather up; (sew) take up
Raffgier ['rafgir] *f* rapacity
raffgierig ['rafgiriç] *adj* rapacious
Raffine·rie [rafinə'ri] *f* (–;–rien ['ri·ən]) refinery
raffinieren [rafi'nirən] *tr* refine

raffiniert [rafi'nirt] *adj* refined; (fig) shrewd, cunning
Raffzahn ['raftsɑn] *m* canine tooth
ragen ['ragən] *intr* tower, loom
Ragout [ra'gu] *n* (–s;–s) (culin) stew
Rahe ['ra·ə] *f* (–;–n) (naut) yard
Rahm [ram] *m* (–[e]s;) cream
Rahmen ['ramən] *m* (–s;–) frame; (Gefüge) framework; (Bereich) scope, limits; (fig) setting; (aut) chassis; aus dem R. fallen be out of place; e–n R. abgeben für form a setting for; im R. (genit) in the course of; im R. von (or genit) within the scope of; within the framework of
Rah'menerzählung *f* story within a story
rahmig ['ramiç] *adj* creamy
Rakete [ra'ketə] *f* (–;–n) rocket
Rake'tenabschußrampe *f* launch pad
Rake'tenbunker *m* silo
Rake'tenstart *m* rocket launch
Rake'tenwerfer *m* rocket launcher
Rake'tenwesen *n* rocketry
Rakett [ra'kɛt] *n* (–[e]s;–e & –s) (tennis) racket
Rammbär ['rambɛr] *m*, Rammbock ['rambɔk] *m*, Ramme ['ramə] *f* (–;–n) rammer; pile driver
rammeln ['raməln] *tr* shove; (zusammenpressen) pack; (belegen) copulate with ‖ *intr* copulate
rammen ['ramən] *tr* ram; (Beton) tamp
Rampe ['rampə] *f* (–;–n) ramp; (rok) launch pad; (rr) platform; (theat) apron
Ram'penlicht *n* footlights; (fig) limelight
Ramsch [ramʃ] *m* (–es;) odds and ends; junk; (com) rummage
Ramsch'verkauf *m* rummage sale
Ramsch'waren *pl* junk
Rand [rant] *m* (–[e]s;=er) edge, border; (e–s Druckseite) margin; am Rande bemerken note in passing; außer R. und Band completely out of control; bis zum Rande to the brim; e–n R. hinterlassen leave a ring (e.g., from a wet glass); Ränder unter den Augen circles under the eyes
Rand'auslöser *m* (typ) margin release
Rand'bemerkung *f* marginal note; (fig) snide remark
rändeln ['rɛndəln], rändern ['rɛndərn] *tr* border, edge; (Münzen) mill
Rand'gebiet *n* borderland; (e–r Stadt) outskirts
rand'los *adj* rimless
Rand'staat *m* border state
Ranft [ranft] *m* (–[e]s;=e) crust
rang [ran] *pret* of ringen ‖ Rang *m* (–[e]s;=e) rank; (theat) balcony; j–m den R. ablaufen (fig) run rings around s.o.
Rang'abzeichen *n* insignia of rank
Rang'älteste §5 *mf* ranking officer
Range ['ranə] *m* (–n;–n) & *f* (–;–n) brat
Rangier'bahnhof *m* (rr) marshaling yard
rangieren [rã'ʒirən] *tr* rank; (rr) shunt, switch ‖ *intr* rank

Rang'ordnung f order of precedence
Rang'stufe f rank
rank [raŋk] adj slender
Ranke ['raŋkə] f (-;-n) tendril
Ränke ['reŋkə] pl schemes; **R. schmieden** scheme
ranken ['raŋkən] ref & intr creep, climb; **sich r. um** wind around
rän'kevoll adj scheming
rann [ran] pret of **rinnen**
rannte ['rantə] pret of **rennen**
Ranzen ['rantsən] m (-s;-) knapsack; school bag; (Bauch) belly; (mil) field pack
ranzig ['rantsɪç] adj rancid
rapid [ra'pit], **rapide** [ra'pidə] adj rapid
Rappe ['rapə] m (-n;-n) black horse
rar [rar] adj rare, scarce
Rarität [rarɪ'tet] f (-;-en) rarity
rasant [ra'zant] adj grazing, pointblank (fire); (fig) impetuous
Rasanz [ra'zants] f (-;) flat trajectory; (fig) impetuosity
rasch [raʃ] adj quick; (hastig) hasty
rascheln ['raʃəln] intr rustle
Rasch'heit f (-;) haste, speed
rasen ['razən] intr rage, rave ‖ intr (SEIN) rush; (aut) speed ‖ **Rasen** m (-s;-) lawn, grass
ra'send adj raging, raving; wild, mad; (Hunger) ravenous; (Wut) towering; (Tempo) break-neck; **r. werden** see red
Ra'sendecke f turf
Ra'senmäher m lawn mower
Ra'senplatz m lawn
Ra'sensprenger m lawn sprinkler
Raserei [razə'raɪ] f (-;) rage, madness; (aut) reckless driving
Rasier- [razir] comb.fm. shaving, razor
Rasier'apparat m safety razor
rasieren [ra'zirən] tr & ref shave
Rasier'klinge f razor blade
Rasier'messer n straight razor
Rasier'napf m shaving mug
Rasier'pinsel m shaving brush
Rasier'wasser n after-shave lotion
Rasier'zeug n shaving outfit
Raspel ['raspəl] f (-;-n) rasp; (culin) grater
raspeln ['raspəln] tr rasp; grate
Rasse ['rasə] f (-;-n) race; (Zucht) breed, blood, stock; (fig) good breeding
Rassel ['rasəl] f (-;-n) rattle
rasseln ['rasəln] intr rattle; **durchs Examen r.** (coll) flunk the exam
Rassen- [rasən] comb.fm. racial
Ras'senfrage f racial problem
Ras'senhaß m racism, race hatred
Ras'senkreuzung f miscegenation; crossbreeding
Ras'senkunde f ethnology
ras'senmäßig adj racial
Ras'senmerkmal n racial characteristic
Ras'sentrennung f segregation
Ras'senunruhen pl racial disorders
Ras'sepferd n thoroughbred (horse)
ras'serein adj racially pure; thoroughbred
Ras'sevieh n purebred cattle

rassig ['rasɪç] adj racy; thoroughbred
rassisch ['rasɪʃ] adj racial
Rast [rast] f (-;-en) rest; station, stage; (mach) notch, groove; (mil) halt; **e-e R. machen** take a rest
rasten ['rastən] intr rest; (mil) halt
rast'los adj restless
Rast'losigkeit f (-;) restlessness
Rast'platz m, **Rast'stätte** f resting place
Rast'tag m day of rest
Rasur [ra'zur] f (-;-en) shave
Rat [rat] m (-[e]s; **Ratschläge** ['ratʃlegə]) advice, piece of advice, counsel; (Beratung) deliberation; (Ausweg) means, solution; **auf e-n Rat hören** listen to reason; **sich** [dat] **keinen Rat mehr wissen** be at one's wits' end; **zu Rate ziehen** consult (a person, dictionary, etc.) ‖ m (-[e]s; ¨e) council, board; (Person) councilor, alderman; advisor; (jur) counsel
Rate ['ratə] f (-;-n) installment; **auf Raten** on the installment plan
raten ['ratən] §63 tr guess; (Rätsel) solve; **das will ich dir nicht geraten haben!** you had better not!; **geraten!** you guessed it!; **j-m etw r.** advise s.o. about s.th.; **komm nicht wieder. das rate ich dir!** take my advice and don't come back! ‖ intr guess; give advice; (dat) advise; **gut r.** take a good guess; **hin und her r.** make random guesses; **j-m gut r.** give s.o. good advice; **j-m zu etw r.** recommend s.th. to s.o. ‖ **Raten** n (-s;) guesswork; advice
ra'tenweise adv by installments
Ra'tenzahlung f payment in installments; **auf R.** on the installment plan
Räterepublik ['retərepublik] f Soviet Union, Soviet Republic
Rat'geber -in §6 mf adviser, counselor
Rat'haus n city hall
ratifizieren [ratɪfɪ'tsirən] tr ratify
Ratifizie'rung f (-;-en) ratification
Ration [ra'tsjon] f (-;-en) ration
rational [ratsjo'nal] adj rational
rationalisieren [ratsjonalɪ'zirən] tr streamline (operations in industry)
rationell [ratsjo'nel] adj rational
rationieren [ratsjo'nirən] tr ration
rätlich ['retlɪç] adj advisable
rat'los adj helpless, perplexed
ratsam ['ratzam] adj advisable
Ratsche ['ratʃə] f (-;-n) rattle; (coll) chatterbox; (tech) ratchet
ratschen ['ratʃən] intr make noise with a rattle; (coll) chat
Rat'schlag m advice, piece of advice
rat'schlagen §132 intr deliberate, consult
Rat'schluß m decision, decree, resolution
Rätsel ['retsəl] n (-s;-) puzzle; (fig) riddle, enigma, mystery
rät'selhaft adj puzzling; mysterious
Ratte ['ratə] f (-;-n) rat
Rat'tenschwanz m rat tail; (fig) tangle; (coll) whole string (of questions, etc.); (Haarzopf) (coll) pigtail
rattern ['ratərn] intr rattle
ratzekahl ['ratsə'kal] adj (Person)

completely bald; (*Landschaft*) completely barren || *adv* completely
Raub [raup] *m* (-[e]s;) robbery; plunder; (*Beute*) prey, spoils; **zum Raube fallen** fall prey, fall victim
Raub– comb.fm. predatory, rapacious
Raub'bau *m* (-[e]s;) excessive exploitation (*of natural resources*)
rauben ['raubən] *tr—j—m etw r.* rob s.o. of s.th.; **e–m Mädchen die Unschuld r.** seduce a girl; **e–n Kuß r.** steal a kiss || *intr* rob
Räuber ['rɔɪbər] *m* (-s;-) robber; **R. und Gendarm spielen** play cops and robbers
Räu'berbande *f* gang of robbers
Räu'berhauptmann *m* gang leader
räuberisch ['rɔɪbərɪʃ] *adj* predatory
Raub'fisch *m* predatory fish
Raub'gesindel *n* gang of robbers
Raub'lust *f* rapacity
raub'gierig *adj* rapacious
Raub'lust *f* rapacity
Raub'mord *m* murder with robbery
Raub'mörder *m* robber and murderer
Raub'schiff *n* corsair, pirate ship
Raub'tier *n* beast of prey
Raub'überfall *m* holdup, robbery
Raub'vogel *m* bird of prey
Raub'zug *m* plundering raid
Rauch [raux] *m* (-[e]s;) smoke
rauchen ['rauxən] *tr & intr* smoke
Raucher ['rauxər] *m* (-s;-) smoker
Räucher– [rɔɪxər] *comb.fm.* smoked
Rau'cherabteil *n* smoking section
Räu'cherfaß *n* (eccl) censer
Räu'cherhering *m* smoked herring
Rau'cherhusten *m* cigarette cough
Räu'cherkammer *f* smokehouse
räuchern ['rɔɪxərn] *tr* smoke, cure; (*desinzieren*) fumigate
Räu'cherschinken *m* smoked ham
Räu'cherung *f* (-;) smoking; fumigation
Rau'cherwagen *m* (rr) smoker
Rauch'fahne *f* trail of smoke
Rauch'fang *m* (*über dem Herd*) hood; (*im Schornstein*) flue
Rauch'fleisch *n* smoked meat
rauchig ['rauxɪç] *adj* smoky
rauch'los *adj* smokeless
Rauch'schleier *m* (mil) smoke screen
Rauch'waren *pl* (*Pelze*) furs; (*Tabakwaren*) tobacco supplies
Räude ['rɔɪdə] *f* (-;) mange
räudig ['rɔɪdɪç] *adj* mangy; **räudiges Schaf** (fig) black sheep
Raufbold ['raufbɔlt] *m* (-[e]s;-e) roughneck, bully
Raufe ['raufə] *f* (-;-n) hayrack
raufen ['raufən] *tr* tear, pull out || *recip & intr* fight, brawl, scuffle
Rauferei [raufə'raɪ] *f* (-;-en) fight, scuffle
Rauf'handel *m* fight, scuffle
rauf'lustig *adj* scrappy, belligerent
rauh [rau] *adj* rough; (*Hals*) hoarse; (*Behandlung*) harsh; **rauhe Wirklichkeit** hard facts
Rauh'bein *n* (fig) roughneck, churl
rauh'beinig *adj* tough, churlish
Rau'heit *f* (-;) roughness; hoarseness
rauhen ['rau·ən] *tr* roughen

Rauh'futter *n* roughage
rauh'haarig *adj* shaggy, hirsute
Rauh'reif *m* hoarfrost
Raum [raum] *m* (-[e]s;ˉe) room, space; (*Zimmer*) room; (*Bereich*) area; (*e–s Schiffes*) hold; **am Rande R. lassen** (typ) leave a margin; **freier R.** open space; **gebt R.!** make way! **luftleerer R.** vacuum; **R. bieten für** accommodate; **R. einnehmen** take up space; **R. geben** (*dat*) give way to; comply with
Raum'anzug *m* space suit
Räumboot ['rɔɪmbot] *n* minesweeper
Raum'dichte *f* (phys) density by volume
räumen ['rɔɪmən] *tr* clear; (*Wohnung*) vacate; (*Minen*) sweep; (mil) evacuate; **den Saal r.** clear the room; **das Lager r.** (com) clear out the stock; **j–n aus dem Wege r.** (fig) finish s.o. off
Raum'ersparnis *f* economy of space; **der R. wegen** to save space
Raum'fahrer *m* spaceman
Raum'fahrt *f* space travel
Raum'flug *m* space flight
Raum'gestaltung *f* interior decorating
Raum'inhalt *m* volume, capacity
Raum'kunst *f* interior decorating
Raum'lehre *f* geometry
räumlich ['rɔɪmlɪç] *adj* spatial
Räum'lichkeit *f* (-;-en) room
Raum'mangel *m* lack of space
Raum'medizin *f* space medicine
Raum'meter *n* cubic meter
Raum'schiff *n* space ship
Raum'schiffart *f* space travel
Raum'schiffkapsel *f* space capsule
Raum'sonde *f* unmanned space explorer
Raum'ton *m* stereophonic sound
Räu'mung *f* (-;-en) clearing, removal; (com) clearance; (mil) evacuation
Räu'mungsausverkauf *m* clearance sale
Räu'mungsbefehl *m* eviction notice; (mil) evacuation order
raunen ['raunən] *tr & intr* whisper
raunzen ['rauntsən] *intr* grumble
Raupe ['raupə] *f* (-;-n) (ent, mach) caterpillar
Rau'penfahrzeug *n* full-track vehicle
Rau'penkette *f* caterpillar track
Rau'penschlepper *m* caterpillar tractor
Rausch [rauʃ] *m* (-es;-e) drunkenness; (fig) intoxication, ecstasy; **e–n R. haben** be drunk; **sich** [*dat*] **e–n R. antrinken** get drunk
rauschen ['rauʃən] *intr* (*Blätter, Seide*) rustle; (*Bach*) murmur; (*Brandung, Sturm*) roar || *intr* (SEIN) strut; rush
rau'schend *adj* rustling; (*Fest*) uproarious; (*Beifall*) thunderous
Rausch'gift *n* drug, dope
Rausch'gifthandel *m* drug traffic
Rausch'giftschieber **–in** §6 *mf* pusher
Rausch'giftsucht *f* drug addiction
Rausch'giftsüchtige §5 *mf* dope addict
Rausch'gold *n* tinsel
räuspern ['rɔɪspərn] *ref* clear one's throat
Rausschmeißer ['rausʃmaɪsər] *m* (-s;-) (coll) bouncer

Raute ['rautə] *f* (-;-n) (cards) diamond; (geom) rhombus

Rayon [rɛ'jõ] *m* (-s;-s) (*Bezirk*) district, region; (*im Warenhaus*) department

Raz·zia ['ratsja] *f* (-;-zien [tsjən]) police raid

Reagenzglas [rɛ·a'gɛntsglas] *n* test tube

reagieren [rɛ·a'girən] *intr* (auf *acc*) react (to)

Reaktion [rɛ·ak'tsjon] *f* (-;-en) reaction

reaktionär [rɛ·aktsjə'nɛr] *adj* reactionary || **Reaktionär** *m* (-s;-e) reactionary

Reak·tor [rɛ'aktɔr] *m* (-s;-toren [-'torən]) (phys) reactor

real [rɛ'al] *adj* real

Real'gymnasium *n* high school (*where modern languages, mathematics, or sciences are stressed*)

Realien [rɛ'aljən] *pl* real facts, realities; exact sciences

realisieren [rɛ·alɪ'zirən] *tr* realize

Realist **-in** [rɛ·a'lɪst(ɪn)] §7 *mf* realist

realistisch [rɛ·a'lɪstɪʃ] *adj* realistic

Realität [rɛ·alɪ'tɛt] *f* (-;-en) reality; **Realitäten** real property

Real'lexikon *n* encyclopedia

Real'lohn *m* purchasing power of wages

Real'schule *f* non-classical secondary school

Rebe ['rebə] *f* (-;-n) vine; tendril

Rebell [rɛ'bɛl] *m* (-en;-en) rebel

rebellieren [rɛbɛ'lirən] *intr* rebel

Rebellin [rɛ'bɛlɪn] *f* (-;-nen) rebel

Rebellion [rɛbɛl'jon] *f* (-;-en) rebellion

rebellisch [rɛ'bɛlɪʃ] *adj* rebellious

Re'bensaft *m* (poet) juice of the grape

Rebhuhn ['rephun] *n* partridge

Rebstock ['repʃtɔk] *m* vine

rechen ['rɛçən] *tr* rake || **Rechen** *m* (-s;-) rake; grate

Re'chenaufgabe *f* arithmetic problem

Re'chenautomat *m* computer

Re'chenbrett *n* abacus

Re'chenbuch *n* arithmetic book

Re'chenexemplar *n* arithmetic problem

Re'chenkunst *f* arithmetic

Re'chenmaschine *f* calculator

Re'chenpfennig *m* counter

Re'chenschaft *f* (-;) account; **j-n zur R. ziehen** call s.o. to account

Re'chenschaftsbericht *m* report

Re'chenschieber *m* slide rule

rechnen ['rɛçnən] *tr* reckon, calculate, figure out || *intr* reckon; calculate; **falsch r.** miscalculate; **r. auf** (*acc*) count on; **r. mit** be prepared for; expect; take into account; **r. zu** be counted among || **Rechnen** *n* (-s;) arithmetic; calculation

Rech'ner *m* (-s;-) calculator, computer; **er ist ein guter R.** he is good at numbers

rechnerisch ['rɛçnərɪʃ] *adj* arithmetical

Rech'nung *f* (-;-en) calculation; account; bill; (*Warenrechnung*) invoice; (*im Restaurant*) check; **auf j-s R. setzen** (or **stellen**) charge to s.o.'s account; **auf R. kaufen** buy on credit; **auf seine R. kaufen** get one's money's worth; **außer R. lassen** overlook; **das geht auf meine R.** this is on me; **die R. begleichen** settle an account (or bill); **j-m in R. stellen** charge to s.o.'s account; **in R. ziehen** take into account; **R. tragen** (*dat*) make allowance for

Rech'nungsabschluß *m* closing of accounts

Rech'nungsauszug *m* (com) statement

Rech'nungsführer **-in** §6 *mf* accountant

Rech'nungsführung *f* accounting

Rech'nungsjahr *n* fiscal year

Rech'nungsprüfer **-in** §6 *mf* auditor

Rech'nungswesen *n* accounting

recht [rɛçt] *adj* right; (*richtig*) correct; (*echt*) real; (*gerecht*) all right, right; (*geziemend*) suitable, proper; **es ist mir nicht r.** I don't like it; **es ist schon r.** that's all right; **mir soll's r. sein** I don't mind; **zur rechten Zeit** at the right moment || *adv* right; quite; (*sehr*) very; **das kommt mir gerade r.** that comes in handy; **erst r.** all the more; **es j-m r. machen** please s.o.; **es geschieht ihm r.** it serves him right; **j-m r. geben** agree with s.o.; **nun erst r. nicht** now less than ever; **r. daran tun zu** (*inf*) do right to (*inf*); **r. haben** be right || **Recht** *n* (-[e]s;-e) right; (*Vorrecht*) privilege; (jur) law; **alle Rechte vorbehalten** all rights reserved; **die Rechte studieren** study law; **mit R.** with good reason; **R. sprechen** dispense justice; **sich** [*dat*] **selbst R. verschaffen** take the law into one's hands; **von Rechts wegen** by rights; **wieder zu seinem Rechte kommen** come into one's own again; **zu R. bestehen** be justified || **Rechte** §5 *mf* right person; **an den Rechten kommen** meet one's match; **du bist mir der R.!** you're a fine fellow! || *f* right hand; (box) right; **die R.** (pol) the right || *n* right; **er dünkt sich** [*dat*] **was Rechtes** he thinks he's somebody; **nach dem Rechten sehen** look after things

Recht'eck *n* rectangle, oblong

recht'eckig *adj* rectangular

recht'fertigen *tr* justify, vindicate

Recht'fertigung *f* (-;-en) justification

recht'gläubig *adj* orthodox

rechthaberisch ['rɛçthabərɪʃ] *adj* dogmatic

recht'lich *adj* legal, lawful; (*ehrlich*) honest, honorable

Recht'lichkeit *f* (-;) legality; (*Redlichkeit*) honesty

recht'los *adj* without rights

recht'mäßig *adj* legal; legitimate

Recht'mäßigkeit *f* (-;) legality; legitimacy

rechts [rɛçts] *adv* on the right; right, to the right

Rechts- *comb.fm.* legal

Rechts'angelegenheit *f* legal matter

Rechts'anspruch *m* legal claim

Rechts'anwalt *m* lawyer, attorney

Rechtsausdruck 225 **Reflexbewegung**

Rechts'ausdruck *m* legal term
Rechts'auskunft *f* legal advice
Rechts'außen *m* (-;-) (fb) right wing
Rechts'beistand *m* legal adviser
recht'schaffen *adj* honest
Recht'schaffenheit *f* (-;) honesty
Recht'schreibung *f* orthography
Rechts'fall *m* case, legal case
Rechts'gang *m* legal procedure
Rechts'gefühl sense of justice
Rechts'gelehrsamkeit *f* jurisprudence
Rechts'grund *m* legal grounds; (*An-spruch*) title, claim
rechts'gültig *adj* legal, valid
Rechts'gültigkeit *f* legality
Rechts'gutachten *n* legal opinion
Rechts'handel *m* lawsuit
rechtshändig ['rɛçtshɛndɪç] *adj* right-handed
rechts'herum *adv* clockwise
Rechts'kraft *f* legal force
rechts'kräftig *adj* valid
Rechts'lage *f* legal status
Rechts'lehre *f* jurisprudence
Rechts'mittel *n* legal remedy
Rechts'pflege *f* administration of justice
Recht'sprechung *f* (-;) administration of justice; die R. (coll) the judiciary
Rechts'schutz *m* legal protection
Rechts'spruch *m* verdict
Rechts'streit *m* legal dispute; pending case; difference of opinion in the interpretation of the law
rechtsum' *interj* (mil) right face!
rechts'ungültig *adj* illegal, invalid
rechts'verbindlich *adj* legally binding
Rechtsverdreher –in ['rɛçtsfɛrdre·ər(ɪn)] §6 *mf* pettifogger
Rechts'verletzung *f* (-;-en) violation of the law; infringement of another's rights
Rechts'weg *m* recourse to the law; auf dem Rechtswege by the courts; den R. beschreiten take legal action
Rechts'wissenschaft *f* jurisprudence
Reck [rɛk] *n* (-[e]s;-e) horizontal bar
recken ['rɛkən] *tr* stretch; den Hals r. crane one's neck
Redakteur [redak'tør] *m* (-s;-e) editor
Redaktion [redak'tsjon] *f* (-;-en) editorship; (*Arbeitskräfte*) editorial staff; (*Arbeitsraum*) editorial office
redaktionell [redaktsjo'nɛl] *adj* editorial
Redaktions'schluß *m* press time, deadline
Rede ['redə] *f* (-;-n) speech; (*Ge-spräch*) conversation; (*Gerücht*) rumor; das ist nicht der R. wert that is not worth mentioning; davon kann keine R. sein that's out of the question; die in R. stehende Person the person in question; e-e R. halten give a speech; es geht die R., daß it is rumored that; gebundene R. verse; gehobene R. lofty language; j-m in die R. fallen interrupt s.o.; j-m R. und Antwort stehen explain oneself to s.o.; j-n zur R. stellen take s.o. to task; keine R.! absolutely not!; lose Reden führen engage in loose talk; ungebundene R. prose

Re'defigur *f* figure of speech
Re'defluß *m* flow of words
Re'defreiheit *f* freedom of speech
Re'degabe *f* eloquence, fluency
re'degewandt *adj* fluent; (iron) glib
Re'degewandtheit *f* fluency, eloquence
Re'dekunst *f* eloquence
reden ['redən] *tr* speak, talk ‖ ref— mit sich r. lassen listen to reason; sich heiser r. talk oneself hoarse; von sich r. machen cause a lot of talk ‖ *intr* speak, talk; converse; du hast gut r.! it's easy for you to talk; j-m ins Gewissen r. appeal to s.o.'s conscience; j-m nach dem Munde r. humor s.o.; mit j-m deutsch r. (fig) talk turkey to s.o.
Re'densart *f* phrase, expression; idiom
Rederei [redə'raɪ] *f* (-;-en) empty talk
Re'deschwall *m* verbosity
Re'deteil *m* part of speech
Re'deweise *f* style of speaking
Re'dewendung *f* phrase, expression
redigieren [redi'girən] *tr* edit
redlich ['retlɪç] *adj* upright, honest ‖ *adv*—es r. meinen mean well; sich r. bemühen make an honest effort
Red'lichkeit *f* (-;) honesty, integrity
Redner –in ['rednər(ɪn)] §6 *mf* speaker
Red'nerbühne *f* podium, platform
Red'nergabe *f* (gift of) eloquence
rednerisch ['rednərɪʃ] *adj* rhetorical
Redoute [rɛ'dutə] *f* (-;-n) masquerade; (mil) redoubt
redselig ['retzelɪç] *adj* talkative
Reduktion [reduk'tsjon] *f* (-;-en) reduction
reduplizieren [reduplɪ'tsirən] *tr* reduplicate
reduzieren [redu'tsirən] *tr* (auf *acc*) reduce (to)
Reede ['redə] *f* (-;-n) (naut) roadstead
Reeder ['redər] *m* (-s;-) shipowner
Reederei [redə'raɪ] *f* (-;-en) shipping company; shipping business
reell [re'ɛl] *adj* honest; (*Preis*) fair; (*Geschäft*) sound ‖ *adv*—r. bedient werden get one's money's worth
Reep [rep] *n* (-[e]s;-e) (naut) rope
Referat [refə'rat] *n* (-[e]s;-e) report; (*Vortrag*) paper; ein R. halten give a paper
Referendar [referen'dar] *m* (-s;-e) junior lawyer; in-service teacher
Referent –in [refe'rent(ɪn)] §7 *mf* reader of a paper; (*Berichterstatter*) reporter; (*Gutachter*) official adviser
Referenz [refe'rents] *f* (-;-en) reference; j-n als R. angeben give s.o. as a reference; über gute Referenzen verfügen have good references
referieren [refe'rirən] *intr* (über *acc*) give a report (on); (über *acc*) read a paper (on)
reffen ['rɛfən] *tr* (naut) reef
reflektieren [reflɛk'tirən] *tr* reflect ‖ *intr* reflect; r. auf (*acc*) reflect on; (com) think of buying
Reflek·tor [rɛ'flɛktɔr] *m* (-s;-toren) ['torən]) reflector
Reflex [rɛ'flɛks] *m* (-es;-e) reflex
Reflex'bewegung *f* reflex action

Reflexion [rɛflɛ'ksjon] ƒ (-;-en) reflection
reflexiv [rɛflɛ'ksif] *adj* reflexive
Reform [rɛ'fɔrm] ƒ (-;-en) reform
Reformation [rɛfɔrma'tsjon] ƒ (-;-en) reformation
Refor·mator [rɛfɔr'matɔr] *m* (-s; [ma'torən]) reformer
Reform'haus *n* health-food store
reformieren [rɛfɔr'mirən] *tr* reform
Reform'kost ƒ health food
Refrain [rə'frɛ̃] *m* (-s;-s) refrain; **den R. mitsingen** join in the refrain
Regal [rɛ'gal] *n* (-s;-e) shelf
Regat·ta [rɛ'gata] ƒ (-;-ten [tən]) regatta
rege ['rega] *adj* brisk, lively
Regel ['regəl] ƒ (-;-n) rule, regulation; (pathol) menstruation; **in der R. as a rule**
re'gellos *adj* irregular; disorderly
Re'gellosigkeit ƒ (-;-en) irregularity
re'gelmäßig *adj* regular
Re'gelmäßigkeit ƒ regularity
regeln ['regəln] *tr* regulate; arrange; control
re'gelrecht *adj* regular; downright
Re'gelung ƒ (-;-en) regulation; control
re'gelwidrig *adj* against the rules; (sport) foul
regen ['regən] *tr & ref* move, stir ‖ **Regen** *m* (-s;-) rain; **vom R. unter die Traufe kommen** jump out of the frying pan into the fire
re'genarm *adj* rainless, dry
Re'genbö ƒ rain squall
Re'genbogen *m* rainbow
Re'genbogenhaut ƒ (anat) iris
re'gendicht *adj* rainproof
Re'genfall *m* rainfall
re'genfest *adj* rainproof
Re'genguß *m* downpour
Re'genhaut ƒ oilskin coat
Re'genmantel *m* raincoat
Re'genmenge ƒ amount of rainfall
Re'genmesser *m* rain gauge
Re'genpfeifer *m* (orn) plover
Re'genschauer *m* shower
Re'genschirm *m* umbrella
Regent –in [rɛ'gɛnt(ɪn)] §7 *mƒ* regent
Re'gentag *m* rainy day
Re'gentropfen *m* raindrop
Re'genumhang *m* cape
Re'genwetter *n* rainy weather
Re'genwurm *m* earthworm
Re'genzeit ƒ rainy season
Re·gie [rɛ'ʒi] ƒ (-;-gien ['ʒi·ən]) management, administration; (com) state monopoly; (cin, theat) direction
Regie'assistent –in §7 *mƒ* (cin, theat) assistant director
Regie'pult *n* (rad) control console
Regie'raum *m* (rad) control room
regieren [rɛ'girən] *tr* govern, rule; (gram) govern, take ‖ *intr* reign; (fig) predominate
Regie'rung ƒ (-;-en) government, rule; administration; reign
Regie'rungsanleihe ƒ government loan
Regie'rungsantritt *m* accession
Regie'rungsbeamte §5 *m* government official
Regie'rungssitz *m* seat of government

Regie'rungszeit ƒ reign; administration
Regime [rɛ'ʒim] *n* (-s;-s) regime
Regiment [rɛgɪ'mɛnt] *n* (-[e]s;-e) rule, government ‖ *n* (-[e]s;-er) (mil) regiment
Regiments– *comb.fm.* regimental
Regiments'kommandeur *m* regimental commander
Region [rɛ'gjon] ƒ (-;-en) region
regional [rɛgjɔ'nal] *adj* regional
Regisseur [rɛʒɪ'sør] *m* (-s;-e) (cin, theat) director
Register [rɛ'gɪstər] *n* (-s;-) file clerk; (*Inhaltsverzeichnis*) index; (*Orgel–*) stop
Regi·strator [rɛgɪs'tratɔr] *m* (-s; –stratoren [stra'torən]) registrar
Registratur [rɛgɪstra'tur] ƒ (-;-en) filing; filing cabinet
registrieren [rɛgɪs'trirən] *tr* register; (*Betrag*) ring up
Registrier'kasse ƒ cash register
Registrie'rung ƒ (-;-en) registration
Reglement [reglə'mã] *n* (-s;-s) regulation(s), rule(s)
Regler ['reglər] *m* (-s;-) regulator; (mach) governor
reglos ['reklos] *adj* motionless
regnen ['regnən] *impers*—**es regnet** it is raining; **es regnet Bindfäden** it's raining cats and dogs; **es regnete Püffe** blows came thick and fast
regnerisch ['regnərɪʃ] *adj* rainy
Re·greß [rɛ'grɛs] *m* (-gresses;-gresse) recourse, remedy; **R. nehmen zu** have recourse to
regsam ['rekzam] *adj* lively; quick
regulär [regu'ler] *adj* regular
regulierbar [regu'lirbar] *adj* adjustable
regulieren [regu'lirən] *tr* regulate; adjust
Regung ['regʊŋ] ƒ (-;-en) motion, stirring; emotion; impulse
Reh [re] *n* (-[e]s;-e) deer
rehabilitieren [rɛhabɪlɪ'tirən] *tr* rehabilitate
Rehabilitie'rung ƒ (-;-en) rehabilitation
Reh'bock *m* roebuck
Reh'braten *m* roast venison
Reh'kalb *n* fawn
Reh'keule ƒ leg of venison
Rehkitz ['rekɪts] *n* (-es;-e) fawn
Reh'leder *n* doeskin
Reibahle ['raɪpalə] ƒ (-;-n) reamer
Reibe ['raɪbə] ƒ (-;-n) (coll) grater
Reibeisen ['raɪpaɪzən] *n* (culin) grater
reiben ['raɪbən] §62 *tr* rub; grate; grind ‖ *ref*—**sich r. an** (*dat*) take offense at ‖ *intr* rub
Reiberei [raɪbə'raɪ] ƒ (-;-en) (coll) friction, squabble
Rei'bung ƒ (-;-en) friction
rei'bungslos *adj* frictionless; (fig) smooth
reich [raɪç] *adj* wealthy; (an *dat*) rich (in); (*Fang*) big; (*Phantasie*) fertile; (*Mahlzeit*) lavish ‖ **Reich** *n* (-[e]s; –e) empire, realm; kingdom
reichen ['raɪçən] *tr* reach; hand, pass ‖ *intr* reach, extend; do, manage; **das reicht!** that will do!
reich'haltig *adj* rich; abundant

reich'lich adj plentiful, abundant || adv pretty, fairly
Reichs'kanzlei f chancellery
Reichs'kanzler m chancellor
Reichs'mark f reichsmark
Reichts'tag m (hist) diet; (hist) Reichstag (lower house)
Reichtum ['raiçtum] n (-s;ﬂer) riches
Reich'weite f reach, range
reif [raif] adj ripe; (fig) mature || **Reif** m (-[e]s;) frost
Reife ['raifə] f (-;) ripeness; (fig) maturity
reifen ['raifən] intr (SEIN) ripen; mature || impers—es **reift** there is frost || **Reifen** m (-s;-) tire; hoop
Rei'fendruckmesser m tire gauge
Rei'fenpanne f, **Rei'fenschaden** m flat tire, blowout
Rei'feprüfung f final examination (as prerequisite for entering university)
Rei'fezeugnis n high school diploma
reif'lich adj careful
Reigen ['raigən] m (-s;-) square dance
Reihe ['rai·ə] f (-;-n) row, string; set, series; rank, file; turn; **an der R. sein** be next; **an die R. kommen** get one's turn; **aus der R. tanzen** (fig) go one's own way; **die R. ist an mir** it's my turn; **nach der R.** in succession
reihen ['rai·ən] tr range, rank; (Perlen) string
Rei'hendorf n one-street village
Rei'henfabrikation f assembly-line production
Rei'henfolge f succession, sequence
Rei'henhaus n row house
Rei'henschaltung f (elec) series connection
reih'enweise adv in rows
Reiher ['rai·ər] m (-s;-) heron
Reim [raim] m (-[e]s;-e) rhyme
reimen ['raimən] tr (auf acc) make rhyme (with) || ref rhyme; (fig) make sense; (auf acc) rhyme (with) || intr rhyme
reim'los adj unrhymed, blank
rein [rain] adj pure; (sauber) clean; (klar) clear; (Gewinn) net; (Wahrheit) simple; (Wahnsinn) sheer, absolute; **etw ins reine bringen** clear up s.th.; **etw ins reine schreiben** write (or type) a final copy of s.th.; **mit j-m ins reine kommen** come to an understanding with s.o. || adv quite, downright; **r. alles** almost everything || **Rein** f (-;-en) pan
Reindl ['raindəl] n (-s;- & -n) pan
Rei'nemachen n (-s;) housecleaning
Rein'ertrag m clear profit
Rein'fall m flop, disappointment
Rein'gewicht n net weight
Rein'gewinn m net profit
Rein'heit f (-;) purity; cleanness
reinigen ['rainigən] tr clean, cleanse; (fig) purify, refine
Rei'nigung f (-;-en) cleaning; purification; dry cleaning
Rei'nigungsanstalt f dry cleaner's
Rei'nigungsmittel n cleaning agent
Reinmachefrau ['rainmaxəfrau] f cleaning woman
Rein'schrift f final copy

reinweg ['rain'vɛk] adv (coll) flatly, absolutely
rein'wollen adj all-wool
Reis [rais] m (-es;) rice || n (-es;-er) twig; (fig) scion
Reis'brei m rice pudding
Reise ['raizə] f (-;-n) trip, tour; (aer) flight; (naut) voyage; **auf der R.** while traveling; **auf Reisen sein** be traveling
Rei'sebericht m travelogue
Rei'sebeschreibung f travel book
Rei'sebüro n travel agency
rei'sefertig adj ready to leave
Rei'seführer m guidebook
Rei'segefährte m, **Rei'segefährtin** f travel companion
Rei'segenehmigung f travel permit
Rei'segepäck n luggage; (rr) baggage
Rei'segesellschaft f tour operator(s); travel group
Rei'sehandbuch n guidebook
Rei'seleiter –in §6 mf courier, guide
rei'selustig adj fond of traveling
reisen ['raizən] intr (SEIN) travel
Reisende ['raizəndə] §5 mf traveler
Rei'sepaß m passport
Rei'seplan m itinerary
Rei'seprospekt m travel folder
Rei'seroute f itinerary
Rei'sescheck m traveler's check
Rei'seschreibmaschine f portable typewriter
Rei'sespesen pl travel expenses
Rei'setasche f overnight bag, flight bag
Rei'seziel n destination
Reisig ['raiziç] n (-s;) brushwood
Rei'sigbündel n faggot
Reisige ['raizigə] §5 m cavalryman
Reißaus [rais'aus] n—**R. nehmen** (coll) take to one's heels
Reißbrett ['raisbret] n drawing board
reißen ['raisən] §53 tr tear, rip; (ziehen) pull, yank; (wegschnappen) wrest, snatch || intr tear; pull, tug; break, snap; (sich spalten) split, burst; **das reißt ins Geld** this is running into money; **mir reißt die Geduld** I am losing all patience || ref—**an sich r.** seize; (com) monopolize; **die Führung an sich r.** take the lead; **sich an e-m Nagel r.** scratch oneself on a nail; **sich um etw r.** scramble for s.th. || **Reißen** n (-s;) tearing; bursting; sharp pains; rheumatism
rei'ßend adj rapid; (Schmerz) sharp; (Tier) rapacious; **reißenden Absatz finden** (coll) sell like hotcakes
Reißer ['raisər] m (-s;-) bestseller; (cin) box-office hit; (com) good seller
Reißfeder ['raisfedər] f drawing pen
Reißleine ['raislainə] f rip cord
Reißnagel ['raisnagəl] m thumbtack
Reißschiene ['rais/inə] f T-square
Reißverschluß ['raisfer/lus] m zipper
Reißzahn ['raistsan] m canine tooth
Reißzeug ['raistsɔik] n mechanical-drawing tools
Reißzwecke ['raistsvɛkə] f thumbtack
Reit– [rait] comb.fm. riding
Reit'anzug m riding habit

Reit'bahn f riding ring
reiten ['raɪtən] §86 tr ride; **e–n Weg r.** ride along a road; **ihn reitet der Teufel** (coll) he is full of the devil; **krumme Touren r.** (coll) pull shady deals; **Prinzipien r.** (fig) stick rigidly to principles; **über den Haufen r.** knock down || intr (SEIN) go horseback riding; **geritten kommen** come on horseback; **vor Anker r.** ride at anchor
Rei'ter –in §6 mf rider
Rei'terstandbild n equestrian statue
Reit'gerte f riding crop
Reit'hose f riding breeches
Reit'knecht m groom
Reit'kunst f horsemanship
Reit'peitsche f riding crop
Reit'pferd n saddle horse
Reit'schule f riding academy
Reit'stiefel m riding boot
Reit'weg m bridle path
Reiz [raɪts] m (–es;–e) charm, appeal; (Erregung) irritation; (physiol, psychol) stimulus; **e–n R. ausüben auf** (acc) attract; **sie läßt ihre Reize spielen** she turns on the charm
reizbar ['raɪtsbar] adj irritable; (empfindlich) sensitive, touchy
reizen ['raɪtsən] tr (entzünden, ärgern) irritate; (locken) allure; (anziehen) attract; (anregen) excite, stimulate; (aufreizen) provoke; (Appetit) whet || intr (cards) bid || impers—**es reizt mich zu** (inf) I'm itching to (inf)
rei'zend adj charming; cute, sweet; (pathol) irritating
Reiz'entzug m sensory deprivation
Reiz'husten m (–s;) constant cough
reiz'los adj unattractive; (Kost) bland
Reiz'mittel n stimulant; (fig) incentive
Reiz'stoff m irritant
Rei'zung f (–;–en) irritation; (Lockung) allurement; (Anregung) stimulation; (Aufreizung) provocation
reiz'voll adj charming, attractive; fascinating; (verlockend) tempting
rekeln ['rekəln] ref (coll) lounge
Reklamation [reklama'tsjon] f (–;–en) complaint, protest
Reklame [re'klamə] f (–;–n) advertisement, ad; publicity; **R. machen für** advertise
Rekla'mebüro n advertising agency
Rekla'mefeldzug m advertising campaign
reklamieren [rekla'mirən] tr claim || intr (gegen) protest (against); (wegen) complain (about)
rekognoszieren [rekɔs'tsirən] tr & intr reconnoiter
Rekonvaleszent –in [rekɔnvales'tsent (ɪn)] §7 mf convalescent
Rekonvaleszenz [rekɔnvales'tsents] f (–;) convalescence
Rekord [re'kɔrt] m (–[e]s;–e) record
Rekord'ernte f bumper crop, record crop
Rekordler –in [re'kɔrtlər(ɪn)] §6 mf (coll) record holder
Rekord'versuch m attempt to break the record

Rekrut [re'krut] m (–en;–en) recruit
Rekru'tenausbildung f basic training
Rekru'tenaushebung f recruitment
rekrutieren [rekru'tirən] tr recruit || ref—**sich r. aus** be recruited from
Rek·tor ['rektɔr] m (–s;–toren ['torən]) principal; (e–r Universität) president
Relais [rə'le] n (–lais ['le(s)];–lais ['les]) relay
relativ [rela'tif] adj relative
Relegation [relega'tsjon] f (–;–en) expulsion
relegieren [rele'girən] tr expel
Relief [re'ljef] n (–s;–s & –e) relief
Religion [relɪ'gjon] f (–;–en) religion
Religions'ausübung f practice of religion
Religions'bekenntnis n religious denomination
religiös [relɪ'gjøs] adj religious
Reling ['relɪŋ] f (–s;–s) (naut) rail
Reliquie [re'likvjə] f (–;–n) relic
Reli'quienschrein m reliquary
remis [rə'mi] adj (cards) tied || **Remis** n (–;–) (chess) tie, draw
remittieren [remɪ'tirən] tr (Geld) remit; (Waren) return || intr (Fieber) go down
rempeln ['rempəln] tr bump, jostle || intr (fb) block
Remter ['remtər] m (–s;–) refectory; assembly hall
Ren [ren] (–s;–e) reindeer
Renaissance [rene'sãs] f (–;–n) renaissance
Rendite [ren'ditə] f (–;–n) return
Renn– [ren] comb.fm. race, racing
Renn'bahn f race track; (aut) speedway
Renn'boot n racing boat
rennen ['renən] §97 tr run; **j–m den Degen durch den Leib r.** run s.o. through with a sword; **über den Haufen r.** run over; **zu Boden r.** knock down || intr (SEIN) run; race || **Rennen** n (–s;–) running; race; (Einzelrennen) heat; **das R. machen** win the race; **totes R.** dead heat, tie
Ren'ner m (–s;–) (good) race horse
Renn'fahrer m (aut) race driver
Renn'pferd n race horse
Renn'platz m race track; (aut) speedway
Renn'rad n racing bicycle, racer
Renn'sport m racing
Renn'strecke f race track; distance (to be raced); (aut) speedway
Renn'wagen m racing car, racer
Renommee [reno'me] n (–s;–s) reputation
renommieren [reno'mirən] intr (mit) brag (about), boast (about)
renommiert' adj (wegen) renowned (for)
Renommist [reno'mɪst] m (–en;–en) braggart
renovieren [reno'virən] tr renovate; redecorate
rentabel [ren'tabəl] adj profitable
Rentabilität [rentabilɪ'tet] f (–;–en) (e–r Investition) return; (fin) productiveness

Rente ['rɛntə] *f* (–;–n) income, revenue; pension; annuity
Ren'tenbrief *m* annuity bond
Ren'tenempfänger –**in** §6 *mf* pensioner
Rentier [rɛn'tje] *m* (–s;–s) person of independent means ‖ ['rentir] *n* (–s; –s;) reindeer
rentieren [rɛn'tirən] *ref* pay
Rentner –**in** ['rɛntnər(ɪn)] §6 *mf* person on pension
Reparatur [rɛpara'tur] *f* (–;–en) repair
Reparatur'werkstatt *f* repair shop; (aut) garage
reparieren [repa'rirən] *tr* repair, fix
Reportage [repɔr'taʒə] *f* (–;–n) report; coverage
Reporter –**in** [re'pɔrtər(ɪn)] §6 *mf* reporter
Repräsentant –**in** [reprɛzɛn'tant(ɪn)] §7 *mf* representative
repräsentieren [reprɛzɛn'tirən] *tr* represent ‖ *intr* be a socialite
Repressalie [repre'saljə] *f* (–;–n) reprisal
Reprise [re'prizə] *f* (–;–n) (cin) rerun; (mus) repeat; (theat) revival
reproduzieren [reprodu'tsirən] *tr* reproduce
Reptil [rep'til] *n* (–s;–ien [jən] & –e) reptile
Republik [repu'blik] *f* (–;–en) republic
Republikaner –**in** [republi'kanər(ɪn)] §6 *mf* republican
republikanisch [republi'kanɪʃ] *adj* republican
Requisit [rekvi'zit] *n* (–[e]s;–en) requisite; **Requisiten** (theat) props
Reservat [rezer'vat] *n* (–[e]s;–e) reservation
Reserve [re'zervə] *f* (–;–n) reserve
Reser'vebank *f* (–;–̈e) (sport) bench
Reser'vereifen *m* spare tire
Reser'veteil *m* spare part
Reser'vetruppen *pl* (mil) reserves
reservieren [rezer'virən] *tr* reserve
Reservie'rung *f* (–;–en) reservation
Residenz [rezi'dɛnts] *f* (–;–en) residence
Residenz'stadt *f* capital
residieren [rezi'dirən] *intr* reside
resignieren [rezɪg'nirən] *intr* resign
Respekt [re'spɛkt] *m* (–[e]s;) respect
respektabel [rɛspɛk'tabəl] *adj* respectable
respektieren [rɛspɛk'tirən] *tr* respect
respekt'los *adj* disrespectful
respekt'voll *adj* respectful
Ressort [rɛ'sor] *n* (–s;–s) department
Rest [rest] *m* (–es;–e & –er) rest; (*Stoff–*) remnant; (*Zahlungs–*) balance; (*Bodensatz*) residue; (math) remainder; **irdische** (or **sterbliche**) **Reste** earthly (or mortal) remains; **j–m den R. geben** (coll) finish s.o. off
Rest'auflage *f* remainders
Restaurant [rɛstɔ'rɑ̃] *n* (–s;–s) restaurant
Restauration [rɛstaura'tsjon] *f* (–;–en) restoration; (Aust) restaurant
Rest'bestand *m* remainder
Rest'betrag *m* balance, remainder
Re'steverkauf *m* remnant sale

rest'lich *adj* remaining
rest'los *adj* complete
Resultat [rezul'tat] *n* (–[e]s;–e) result; upshot; (sport) score
retten ['retən] *tr* save, rescue
Ret'ter *m* (–s;–) rescuer; (*Heiland*) Savior
Ret'tung *f* (–;–en) rescue; salvation
Ret'tungsaktion *f* rescue operation
Ret'tungsboot *n* lifeboat
Ret'tungsfloß *n* life raft
Ret'tungsgürtel *m* life preserver
Ret'tungsleine *f* life line
ret'tungslos *adj* irretrievable
Ret'tungsmannschaft *f* rescue party
Ret'tungsring *m* life preserver
Ret'tungsstation *f* first-aid station
retuschieren [retu'ʃirən] *tr* retouch
Reue ['rɔɪ·ə] *f* (–;) remorse
reu'elos *adj* remorseless, impenitent
reuen ['rɔɪ·ən] *tr*—**die Tat reut mich** I regret having done it; **die Zeit reut mich** I regret wasting the time ‖ *impers*—**es reut mich, daß** I regret that, I am sorry that
reu'evoll *adj* repentant, contrite
Reugeld ['rɔɪgelt] *n* forfeit
reumütig ['rɔɪmytɪç] *adj* repentant
Revanche [re'vɑ̃ʃə] *f* (–;) revenge
Revan'chekrieg *m* punitive wår
revan'chelustig *adj* vengeful
Revan'chepartie *f* (sport) return game
revanchieren [revɑ̃'ʃirən] *ref* (an *dat*) take revenge (on); **sich für e–en Dienst r.** return a favor
Revers [re'vers] *m* (–es;–e) (*e–r Münze*) reverse; (*Erklärung*) statement ‖ (re'ver] *m* (Aust) & *n* (–;–) lapel; cuff
revidieren [revi'dirən] *tr* revise; (*nachprüfen*) check; (com) audit
Revier [re'vir] *n* (–s;–e) district; quarter; hunting ground; police station; (mil) sick quarters
Revier'stube *f* (mil) sickroom
Revision [revi'zjon] *f* (–;–en) revision; (com) audit; (jur) appeal
Re•visor [re'vizɔr] *m* (–s;–visoren [vi'zorən]) reviser; (com) auditor
Revolte [re'vɔltə] *f* (–;–n) revolt
revoltieren [revɔl'tirən] *intr* revolt
Revolution [revɔlu'tsjon] *f* (–;–en) revolution
revolutionär [revɔlutsjɔ'ner] *adj* revolutionary ‖ **Revolutionär** –**in** §8 *mf* revolutionary
Revolver [re'vɔlvər] *m* (–s;–) revolver
Revol'verblatt *n* (coll) scandal sheet
Revol'verschnauze *f* (coll) lip, sass
Re•vue [re'vy] *f* (–;–vuen ['vy·ən]) review; (theat) revue
Rezensent –**in** [retsen'zent(ɪn)] §7 *mf* reviewer, critic
rezensieren [retsen'zirən] *tr* review
Rezension [retsen'zjon] *f* (–;–en) review
Rezept [re'tsept] *n* (–[e]s;–e) (culin) recipe; (med) prescription
rezitieren [retsi'tirən] *tr* recite
Rhabarber [ra'barbər] *m* (–s;) rhubarb
Rhapso•die [rapso'di] *f* (–;–dien ['di·ən]) rhapsody

Rhein [raɪn] *m* (-[e]s;) Rhine
Rhesusfaktor ['rezʊsfaktɔr] *m* (-s;) Rh factor
Rhetorik [re'torɪk] *f* (-;) rhetoric
rhetorisch [re'torɪʃ] *adj* rhetorical
rheumatisch [rɔɪ'matɪʃ] *adj* rheumatic
Rheumatismus [rɔɪma'tɪsmʊs] *m* (-;) rheumatism
rhythmisch ['rʏtmɪʃ] *adj* rhythmical
Rhyth·mus ['rʏtmʊs] *m* (-;-men [mən]) rhythm
Richtbeil ['rɪçtbaɪl] *n* executioner's ax
Richtblei ['rɪçtblaɪ] *n* plummet
richten ['rɪçtən] *tr* arrange, adjust; put in order; (*lenken*) direct; (*Waffe, Fernrohr*) (*auf acc*) point (at), aim (at); (*Bitte, Brief, Frage, Rede*) (*an acc*) address (to); (*Augenmerk, Streben*) (*auf acc*) concentrate (on), focus (on); (*Bett*) make; (*Essen*) prepare; (*ausbessern*) fix; (*gerade biegen*) straighten; (*jur*) judge, sentence; (*mil*) dress; **zugrunde r.** ruin || *ref* (*auf acc*, *gegen*) be directed (at); **das richtet sich ganz danach, ob** it all depends on whether; **sich** [*dat*] **die Haare r.** do one's hair; **sich r. nach** follow the example of; **sich selbst r.** commit suicide || *intr* judge, sit in judgment
Rich'ter *m* (-s;-) judge
Rich'teramt *n* judgeship
Rich'terin *f* (-;-nen) judge
Rich'terkollegium *n* (jur) bench
rich'terlich *adj* judicial
Rich'terspruch *m* judgment; sentence
Rich'terstand *m* judiciary
Rich'terstuhl *m* tribunal, bench
richtig ['rɪçtɪç] *adj* right, correct; (*echt*) real, genuine; (*genau*) exact; (*Zeit*) proper || *adv* right, really, downright; **die Uhr geht r.** the clock keeps good time; **und r., da kam sie!** and sure enough, there she was!
rich'tiggehend *adj* (*Uhr*) keeping good time; (fig) regular
Rich'tigkeit *f* (-;) correctness; accuracy
rich'tigstellen *tr* rectify
Richtlinien ['rɪçtlinjən] *pl* guidelines
Richtlot ['rɪçtlot] *n* plumbline
Richtmaß ['rɪçtmas] *n* standard, gauge
Richtplatz ['rɪçtplats] *m* place of execution
Richtpreis ['rɪçtpraɪs] *n* standard price
Richtschnur ['rɪçtʃnur] *f* plumbline; (fig) guiding principle
Richtschwert ['rɪçtʃvert] *n* executioner's sword
Richtstätte ['rɪçtʃtɛtə] *f* place of execution
Rich'tung *f* (-;-en) direction; (*Weg*) course; (*Entwicklung*) trend; (*Einstellung*) slant, view
Rich'tungsanzeiger *m* (aut) direction signal
Richtwaage ['rɪçtvagə] *f* level
rieb [rip] *pret* of reiben
riechen ['riçən] §102 *tr* smell; (fig) stand; **kein Pulver r. können** have no guts || *intr* smell; **r. an** (*dat*) sniff at; **r. nach** smell of
Riechsalz ['riçzalts] *n* smelling salts

rief [rif] *pret* of rufen
Riefe ['rifə] *f* (-;-n) groove; (archit) flute
Riege ['rigə] *f* (-;-n) (gym) squad
Riegel ['rigəl] *m* (-s;-) bolt; (*Seife*) cake; (*Schokolade*) bar
riegeln ['rigəln] *tr* bolt, bar
Riemen ['rimən] *m* (-s;-) strap; (*Leib-, Trieb-*) belt; (*Ruder*) oar; (*e-s Gewehrs*) sling
Rie'menscheibe *f* pulley
Ries [ris] *n* (-es;-e) ream (*of one thousand sheets*)
Riese ['rizə] *m* (-;-n) giant
rieseln ['rizəln] *intr* (HABEN & SEIN) trickle; (*Bach*) purl || *impers*—es **rieselt** it is drizzling
Rie'selregen *m* drizzle
Rie'senbomber *m* superbomber
Rie'senerfolg *m* smash hit
rie'sengroß *adj* gigantic
rie'senhaft *adj* gigantic
Rie'senrad *n* Ferris wheel
Rie'senschlange *f* boa constrictor
Rie'sentanne *f* (bot) sequoia
riesig ['rizɪç] *adj* gigantic, huge || *adv* (coll) awfully
Riesin ['rizin] *f* (-;-nen) giant
riet [rit] *pret* of raten
Riff [rɪf] *n* (-[e]s;-e) reef
Rille ['rɪlə] *f* (-;-n) groove; small furrow; (archit) flute
Rimesse [rɪ'mesə] *f* (-;-n) (com) remittance
Rind [rɪnt] *n* (-[e]s;-er) head of cattle; **Rinder** cattle
Rinde ['rɪndə] *f* (-;-n) rind; (*Baum-*) bark; (*Brot-*) crust; (anat) cortex
Rin'derbraten *m* roast beef
Rin'derbremse *f* horsefly
Rin'derherde *f* herd of cattle
Rin'derhirt *m* cowboy
Rind'fleisch *n* beef
Rinds'leder *n* cowhide
Rinds'lendenstück *n* rump steak, tenderloin
Rinds'rückenstück *n* sirloin of beef
Rind'vieh *n* cattle; (sl) idiot
Ring [rɪŋ] *m* (-[e]s;-e) ring; (*Kreis*) circle; (*Kettenglied*) link; (*Kartell*) combine; (astr) halo
Ringel ['rɪŋəl] *m* (-s;) small ring; (*Locke*) ringlet, curl
Rin'gelblume *f* marigold
ringeln ['rɪŋəln] *tr* & *ref* curl
Rin'gelreihen *m* ring-around-the-rosy
Rin'gelspiel *n* merry-go-round
ringen ['rɪŋən] §142 *tr* wrestle; (*Wäsche, Hände*) wring; (*herauswinden*) wrest || *intr* wrestle; (fig) struggle
Rin'ger –in §6 *mf* wrestler
Ring'kampf *m* wrestling match
Ring'mauer *f* town wall, city wall
Ring'richter *m* (box) referee
rings [rɪŋs] *adv* around; **r. um** all around
Ring'schlüssel *m* socket wrench
rings'herum', rings'um', rings'umher' *adv* all around
Rinne ['rɪnə] *f* (-;-n) groove; (*Strombett*) channel; (*Leitung*) duct; (*Gosse*) gutter; (*Erdfurche*) furrow

rinnen ['rɪnən] §121 *intr* (SEIN) run, flow; trickle ‖ *intr* (HABEN) leak
Rinnsal ['rɪnzɑl] *n* (-[e]s;-e) little stream
Rinn'stein *m* gutter; (*Ausgußbecken*) sink; (*unterirdisch*) culvert
Rippchen ['rɪpçən] *n* (-s;-) cutlet
Rippe ['rɪpə] *f* (-;-n) rib; (*Schokolade*) bar; (archit) groin
rippen ['rɪpən] *tr* rib, flute
Rip'penfellentzündung *f* pleurisy
Rip'penstoß *m* nudge (in the ribs)
Rip'penstück *n* loin end
Risi·ko ['rizɪko] *n* (-s;-s & -ken [kən]) risk; **ein R. eingehen** take a risk
riskant [rɪs'kant] *adj* risky
riskieren [rɪs'kirən] *tr* risk
riß [rɪs] *pret* of **reißen** ‖ **Riß** *m* (**Risses; Risse**) tear, rip; (*Bruch*) fracture; (*Lücke*) gap; (*Kratzer*) scratch; (*Spalt*) split, cleft; (*Spaltung*) fissure; (*Sprung*) crack; (*Zeichnung*) sketch; (eccl) schism; (geol) crevasse
rissig ['rɪsɪç] *adj* torn; cracked; split; (*Haut*) chapped
Rist [rɪst] *m* (-es;-e) wrist; (*des Fußes*) instep
ritt [rɪt] *pret* of **reiten** ‖ **Ritt** *m* (-[e]s; -e) ride
Ritter ['rɪtər] *m* (-s;-) knight; cavalier; **zum R. schlagen** knight
Rit'tergut *n* manor
Rit'terkreuz *n* (mil) Knight's Cross (*of the Iron Cross*)
rit'terlich *adj* knightly; (fig) chivalrous
Rit'terlichkeit *f* (-;) chivalry
Rit'terzeit *f* age of chivalry
rittlings ['rɪtlɪŋs] *adv*—**r. auf** (*dat* or *acc*) astride
Ritual [rɪtu'ɑl] *n* (-s;-e & -ien [jən]) ritual
rituell [rɪtu'el] *adj* ritual
Ri·tus ['ritus] *m* (-;-ten [tən]) rite
Ritz [rɪts] *m* (-es;-e), **Ritze** ['rɪtsə] *f* (-;-en) crack, crevice; (*Schlitz*) slit; (*Schramme*) scratch
ritzen ['rɪtsən] *tr* scratch; (*Glas*) cut
Rivale [rɪ'vɑlə] *m* (-n;-n), **Rivalin** [rɪ'vɑlɪn] *f* (-;-nen) rival
rivalisieren [rɪvɑlɪ'zirən] *intr* be in rivalry; **r. mit** rival
Rivalität [rɪvɑlɪ'tet] *f* (-;-en) rivalry
Rizinusöl ['ritsɪnusøl] *n* castor oil
Robbe ['rɔbə] *f* (-;-n) seal
robben ['rɔbən] *intr* (HABEN & SEIN) (mil) crawl (*using one's elbows*)
Rob'benfang *m* seal hunt
Robe ['robə] *f* (-;-n) robe, gown
Roboter ['robɔtər] *m* (-s;-) robot
robust [ro'bust] *adj* robust
roch [rɔx] *pret* of **riechen**
röcheln ['rœçəln] *tr* gasp out ‖ *intr* rattle (*in one's throat*)
rochieren [rɔ'ʃirən] *intr* (chess) castle
Rock [rɔk] *m* (-[e]s;⁻e) skirt; jacket
Rock'schoß *m* coattail
Rodel ['rodəl] *m* (-s;-) & *f* (-;-n) toboggan; (*mit Steuerung*) bobsled
Ro'delbahn *f* toboggan slide
rodeln ['rodəln] *intr* (HABEN & SEIN) toboggan
Ro'delschlitten *m* toboggan; bobsled

roden ['rodən] *tr* root out; (*Wald*) clear; (*Land*) make arable
Rogen ['rogən] *m* (-s;) roe, spawn
Roggen ['rɔgən] *m* (-s;) rye
roh [ro] *adj* raw; crude; (*Steine*) unhewn; (*Dielen*) bare; (fig) uncouth, brutal
Roh'bau *m* (-[e]s;-ten) rough brickwork
Roh'diamant *m* uncut diamond
Roh'einnahme *f* gross receipts
Roh'eisen *n* pig iron
Roh'heit *f* (-;) rawness, raw state; crudeness; brutality
Roh'entwurf *m* rough sketch
Roh'gewicht *n* gross weight
Roh'gewinn *m* gross profit
Roh'gummi *m* crude rubber
Roh'haut *f* rawhide
Roh'kost *f* uncooked vegetarian food
Rohling ['rolɪŋ] *m* (-s;-e) blank; slug; (fig) thug, hoodlum
Roh'material *n* raw material
Roh'öl *n* crude oil
Rohr [ror] *n* (-[e]s;-e) reed, cane; (*Röhre*) pipe, tube; (*Kanal*) duct, channel; (*Gewehrlauf*) barrel
Rohr'anschluß *m* pipe joint
Rohr'bogen *m* elbow
Röhre ['rørə] *f* (-;-n) tube, pipe; (electron) tube
Röh'renblitz *m* electronic flash
Röh'renblitzgerät *n* electronic flash unit
Rohr'leger *m* pipe fitter
Rohr'leitung *f* pipeline, main
Rohr'schäftung *f* sleeve joint
Rohr'schelle *f* pipe clamp
Rohr'zange *f* pipe wrench
Rohr'zucker *m* cane sugar
Roh'stoff *m* raw material
Rolladen (**Roll'laden**) *m* sliding shutter; sliding cover
Rollbahn ['rɔlbɑn] *f* (aer) runway; (mil) road leading up to the front
Röllchen ['rœlçən] *n* (-s;-) caster
Rolldach ['rɔldɑx] *n* (aut) sun roof
Rolle ['rɔlə] *f* (-;-n) roll; (*Walze*) roller; (*Flaschenzug*) pulley; (*Spule*) spool, reel; (*unter Möbeln*) caster; (*Mangel*) mangle; (*Liste*) list, register; (theat) role; **aus der R. fallen** (fig) misbehave; **spielt keine R.!** never mind!, forget it!
rollen ['rɔlən] *tr* roll; (*auf Rädern*) wheel; (*Wäsche*) mangle; ‖ *ref* curl up ‖ *intr* (HABEN & SEIN) roll; (*Flugzeug*) taxi; (*Geschütze*) roar ‖ **Rollen** *n*—ins. **R. kommen** get going
Rol'lenbesetzung *f* (theat) cast
Rol'lenlager *n* roller bearing
Rol'lenzug *m* block and tackle
Rol'ler *m* (-s;-) scooter; motor scooter
Roll'feld *n* (aer) runway
Roll'kragen *m* turtleneck
Roll'mops *m* pickled herring
Rollo ['rɔlo] *n* (-s;-s) (coll) blind, shade
Roll'schuh *m* roller skate; **R. laufen** roller-skate
Roll'schuhbahn *f* roller-skating rink
Roll'stuhl *m* wheelchair
Roll'treppe *f* escalator

Roll'wagen *m* truck
Rom [rom] *n* (-s;) Rome
Roman [rɔ'mɑn] *m* (-s;-e) novel
Roman'folge *f* serial
roman'haft *adj* fictional
romanisch [rɔ'mɑnıʃ] *adj* (*Sprache*) Romance; (archit) Romanesque
Romanist **-in** [rɔma'nıst(ın)] §7 *mf* scholar of Romance languages
Roman'schriftsteller **-in** §6 *mf* novelist
Romantik [rɔ'mɑntık] *f* (-;) Romanticism
romantisch [rɔ'mɑntıʃ] *adj* romantic
Romanze [rɔ'mantsə] (-;-n) romance
Römer **-in** ['rǿmər(ın)] §6 *mf* Roman
römisch ['rǿmıʃ] *adj* Roman
rö'misch-katho'lisch *adj* Roman Catholic
röntgen ['rœntgən] *tr* x-ray
Rönt'genapparat *m* x-ray machine
Rönt'genarzt *m*, **Rönt'genärztin** *f* radiologist
Rönt'genaufnahme *f*, **Rönt'genbild** *n* x-ray
Rönt'genstrahlen *pl* x-rays
rosa ['roza] *adj* pink || **Rosa** *n* (-s;- & -s) pink
Rose ['rozə] *f* (-;-n) rose
Ro'senkohl *m* Brussels sprouts
Ro'senkranz *m* (eccl) rosary
ro'senrot *adj* rosy, rose-colored
Ro'senstock *m* rosebush
rosig ['rozıç] *adj* (& fig) rosy; (*Laune*) happy
Rosine [rɔ'zine] *f* (-;-n) raisin
Roß [rɔs] *n* (**Rosses; Rosse**) horse; (sl) jerk; (poet) steed
Rost [rɔst] *m* (-es;) rust; mildew || *m* (-es;-e) grate; grill; **auf dem R. braten** grill
Rost'braten *m* roast beef
Röstbrot ['rǿstbrot] *n* toast
rosten ['rɔstən] *intr* rust
rösten ['rǿstən] *tr* (*auf dem Rost*) grill; (*in der Pfanne*) roast; (*Brot*) toast; (*Mais*) pop; (*Kaffee*) roast
Rö'ster *m* (-s;-) roaster; toaster
Rost'fleck *m* rust stain
rost'frei *adj* rust-proof; (*Stahl*) stainless
rostig ['rɔstıç] *adj* rusty, corroded
rot [rot] *adj* (**röter** ['rǿtər]; **röteste** ['rǿtəstə] §9) red || **Rot** *n* (-es;) red; (*Schminke*) rouge
Rotation [rɔta'tsion] *f* (-;-en) rotation
Rotations'maschine *f* rotary press
rotbäckig ['rotbɛkıç] *adj* red-cheeked
Rot'dorn *m* (bot) pink hawthorn
Röte ['rǿtə] *f* (-;) red(ness); blush
Röteln ['rǿtəln] *pl* German measles
rotieren [rɔ'tirən] *intr* rotate
Rotkäppchen ['rotkɛpçən] *n* (-s;) Little Red Riding Hood
Rotkehlchen ['rotkɛlçən] *n* (-s;-) robin
rötlich ['rǿtlıç] *adj* reddish
Ro·tor ['rotɔr] *m* (-s;-toren ['torən]) (aer) rotor; (elec) armature
Rot'schimmel *m* roan (*horse*)
Rot'tanne *f* spruce
Rotte ['rɔtə] *f* (-;-n) gang, mob
Rotz [rɔts] *m* (-es;-e) (sl) snot
rot'zig *adj* (sl) snotty

Rouleau [ru'lo] *n* (-s;-s) window shade
Route ['rutə] *f* (-;-n) route
Routine [ru'tinə] *f* (-;) routine; practice, experience
routiniert [ruti'nirt] *adj* experienced
Rübe ['rybə] *f* (-;-n) beet; **gelbe R.** carrot; **weiße R.** turnip
Rubin [ru'bin] *m* (-s;-e) ruby
Rubrik [ru'brik] *f* (-;-en) rubric; heading; (*Spalte*) column
ruchbar ['ruxbar] *adj* known, public
ruchlos ['ruxlos] *adj* wicked
Ruck [ruk] *m* (-[e]s;-e) jerk; yank; jolt; **auf e-n R.** at once; **mit e-m R.** in one quick move
Rück-, rück- [ryk] *comb.fm.* re-, back, rear; return
Rück'ansicht *f* rear view
Rück'antwort *f* reply; **Postkarte mit R.** prepaid reply postcard
rück'bezüglich *adj* (gram) reflexive
Rück'bleibsel *n* remainder
rücken ['rykən] *tr* move, shove || *intr* (SEIN) move; (*Platz machen*) move over; (*marschieren*) march; **höher r.** be promoted; **näher r.** approach || **Rücken** *m* (-s;-) back; (*Rückseite*) rear; (*der Nase*) bridge
Rückendeckung (**Rük'kendeckung**) *f* (fig) backing, support
Rückenlehne (**Rük'kenlehne**) *f* back rest
Rückenmark (**Rük'kenmark**) *n* spinal cord
Rückenschwimmen (**Rük'kenschwimmen**) *n* backstroke
Rückenwind (**Rük'kenwind**) *m* tail wind
Rückenwirbel (**Rük'kenwirbel**) *m* (anat) vertebra
rück'erstatten *tr* reimburse, refund
Rück'fahrkarte *f*, **Rück'fahrschein** *m* round-trip ticket
Rück'fahrt *f* return trip
Rück'fall *m* relapse
rück'fällig *adj* habitual, relapsing
rück'federnd *adj* resilient
Rück'flug *m* return flight
Rück'frage *f* further question
Rück'führung *f* repatriation
Rück'gabe *f* return, restitution
Rück'gang *m* return; regression; (*der Preise*) drop; (econ) recession
rückgängig ['rykgɛnıç] *adj* retrogressive; dropping; **r. machen** cancel
rück'gewinnen §121 *tr* recover
Rück'grat *n* backbone, spine
Rück'griff *m* (auf *acc*) recourse (to)
Rück'halt *m* backing; (mil) reserves; **e-n R. an j-m haben** have s.o.'s backing; **ohne R.** without reservation
rück'haltlos *adj* frank, unreserved || *adv* without reserve
Rück'handschlag *m* (tennis) back-hand stroke
Rück'kauf *m* repurchase
Rück'kehr *f* return; (fig) comeback
Rück'kopplung *f* (electron) feedback
Rück'lage *f* reserves, savings
Rück'lauf *m* reverse; (mil) recoil
Rück'läufer *m* letter returned to sender
rückläufig ['rykløıfıç] *adj* retrograde

Rück′licht n (aut) taillight
rücklings ['rʏklɪŋs] adv backwards
Rück′nahme f withdrawal, taking back
Rück′porto n return postage
Rück′prall m bounce, rebound, recoil
Rück′reise f return trip
Ruck′sack m knapsack
Rück′schau m—**R. halten auf** (acc) look back on
Rück′schlag m back stroke; (e–s Balles) bounce; (fig) setback
Rück′schluß m conclusion, inference
Rück′schritt m backward step; (fig) falling off, retrogression
Rück′seite f back; reverse; wrong side
Rück′sicht f regard, respect, consideration; **aus R. auf** (acc) out of consideration for; **in** (or **mit**) **R. auf** (acc) in regard to; **ohne R. auf** (acc) irrespective of; **R. nehmen auf** (acc) take into account, show consideration for
rück′sichtlich prep (genit) considering
rück′sichtslos adj inconsiderate; reckless; ruthless
rück′sichtsvoll adj considerate
Rück′sitz m (aut) rear seat
Rück′spiegel m (aut) rear-view mirror
Rück′spiel n return match
Rück′sprache f discussion; conference; **R. nehmen mit** consult with
Rück′stand m arrears; (Satz) sediment; (Rest) remainder; (von Aufträgen, usw.) backlog; (chem) residue
rück′ständig adj behind, in arrears; (Geld) outstanding; (Raten) delinquent; (altmodisch) backward
Rück′stau m back-up water
Rück′stelltaste f backspace key
Rück′stoß m repulsion; recoil, kick
Rückstrahler ['rʏkstralər] m (-s;-) reflector
Rück′strahlung f reflection
Rück′tritt m resignation
Rück′trittbremse f coaster brake
Rück′umschlag m return envelope
rückwärts ['rʏkverts] adv backward(s)
Rück′wärtsgang m (aut) reverse
Rück′weg m way back, return
ruck′weise adv by fits and starts
rück′wirken intr react
rück′wirkend adj retroactive
Rück′wirkung f (-;-en) reaction; repercussion
rück′zahlen tr repay, refund
Rück′zug m withdrawal; retreat; **zum R. blasen** sound the retreat
Rück′zugsgefecht n running fight
rüde ['rydə] adj rude, coarse ‖ **Rüde** m (-n;-n) male (wolf, fox, etc.)
Rudel ['rudəl] n (-s;-) herd; flock; (von Wölfen, U-Booten) wolf pack
Ruder ['rudər] n (-s;-) (aer, naut) rudder; (naut) oar
Ru′derblatt n blade of an oar
Ru′derboot n rowboat
Ru′derer –in §6 mf rower
Ru′derklampe f oarlock
rudern ['rudərn] tr & intr row
Ru′derschlag m stroke of the oar
Ru′dersport m (sport) crew
Ruf [ruf] m (-[e]s;-e) call; shout, yell; (Berufung) vocation; (Nach-

rede) reputation; appointment; (com) credit
rufen ['rufən] §122 tr call; shout; **r. lassen** send for ‖ intr call; shout
Ruf′mord m character assassination
Ruf′name m first name
Ruf′nummer f telephone number
Ruf′weite f—**in R.** within earshot
Ruf′zeichen n (rad) station identification; (telp) call sign
Rüge ['rygə] f (-;-n) reprimand
rügen ['rygən] tr reprimand
Ruhe ['ru·ə] f (-;) rest; quiet, calm; (Frieden) peace; (Stille) silence; **immer mit der R.!** (coll) take it easy!
ru′hebedürftig adj in need of rest
Ru′hegehalt n pension
Ru′hekur f rest cure
ru′helos adj restless
ruhen ['ru·ən] intr rest; sleep
Ru′hepause f pause, break
Ru′heplatz m resting place
Ru′hestand m retirement
Rü′hestätte f resting place
Ru′hestörer –in §6 mf disturber of the peace
Ru′hetag m day of rest, day off
Ru′hezeit f leisure
ruhig ['ru·ɪç] adj still, quiet; calm
Ruhm [rum] m (-[e]s;) glory, fame
rühmen ['rymən] tr praise ‖ ref (genit) boast (about)
rühmlich ['rymlɪç] adj praiseworthy
ruhm′los adj inglorious
ruhmredig ['rumredɪç] adj vainglorious
ruhm′reich adj glorious
ruhm′voll adj famous, glorious
ruhm′würdig adj praiseworthy
Ruhr [rur] f (-;) dysentery; **Ruhr** (river)
Rührei ['ryraɪ] n scrambled egg
rühren ['ryrən] tr stir; touch, move; (Trommel) beat; **alle Kräfte r.** exert every effort ‖ ref stir, move; get a move on; **rührt euch!** (mil) at ease! ‖ intr stir, move; **r. an** (acc) touch; (fig) mention; **r. von** originate in
rührig ['ryrɪç] adj active; agile
Rührlöffel ['ryrlœfəl] m ladle
rührselig ['ryrzelɪç] adj sentimental
Rührstück ['ryr/tʏk] n soap opera
Rüh′rung f (-;-en) emotion
Ruin [ru'in] m (-s;) ruin; decay
Ruine [ru'inə] f (-;-n) ruins; (fig) wreck
rui′nenhaft adj ruinous
ruinieren [ru·ɪ'nirən] tr ruin
Rülps [rʏlps] m (-es;-e) belch
rülpsen ['rʏlpsən] intr belch
Rülp′ser m (-s;-) belch
Rum [rum] m (-s;-s) rum
Rumäne [ru'menə] m (-n;-n) Rumanian
Rumänien [ru'menjən] n (-s;) Rumania
Rumänin [ru'menɪn] f (-;-nen) Rumanian
rumänisch [ru'menɪʃ] adj Rumanian
Rummel ['ruməl] m (-s;) junk; racket; hustle and bustle; **auf den R. gehen** go to the fair; **den ganzen R. kaufen** (coll) buy the works
Rum′melplatz m amusement park, fair
Rumor [ru'mor] m (-s;) noise, racket

Rumpel ['rumpəl] *f* (-;-n) scrub board
Rum'pelkammer *f* storage room, junk room
Rum'pelkasten *m* (aut) jalopy
rumpeln ['rumpəln] *tr* (*Wäsche*) scrub || *intr* rumble, rattle
Rumpf [rumpf] *m* (-[e]s;ᵇe) trunk, body; torso; (aer) fuselage; (naut) hull
rümpfen ['rʏmpfən] *tr*—die Nase r. über (*acc*) turn up one's nose at
rund [runt] *adj* round; (*Absage*) flat || *adv* around; about, approximately; r. um around
Rund'blick *m* panorama
Rund'brief *m* circular letter
Runde ['rundə] *f* (-;-n) round; (box) round; (*beim Rennsport*) lap
runden ['rundən] *tr* make round; round off || *ref* become round
Rund'erlaß *m* circular
rund'erneuern *tr* (aut) retread; **runderneuerter Reifen** *m* retread
Rund'fahrt *f* sightseeing tour
Rund'flug *m* (aer) circuit
Rund'frage *f* questionnaire, poll
Rund'funk *m* radio; **im R.** on the radio
Rund'funkansage *f* radio announcement
Rund'funkansager –in §6 *mf* radio announcer
Rund'funkgerät *n* radio set
Rund'funkgesellschaft *f* broadcasting company
Rund'funkhörer –in §6 *mf* listener
Rund'funknetz *n* radio network
Rund'funksender *m* broadcasting station
Rund'funksendung *f* radio broadcast
Rund'funksprecher –in §6 *mf* announcer
Rund'funkwerbung *f* (rad) commercial
Rund'gang *m* tour; stroll
rund'heraus' *adv* plainly, flatly
rundherum' *adv* all around
rund'lich *adj* round; (*dick*) plump
Rund'reise *f* sightseeing tour
Rund'schau *f* panorama; (journ) news in brief
Rund'schreiben *n* circular letter
rundweg ['runt'vɛk] *adv* bluntly, flatly

Runzel ['runtsəl] *f* (-;-n) wrinkle
runzelig ['runtseliç] *adj* wrinkled
runzeln ['runtsəln] *tr* wrinkle; **die Brauen r.** knit one's brows; **die Stirn r.** frown || *ref* wrinkle
Rüpel ['rypəl] *m* (-s;-) boor
rü'pelhaft *adj* rude, boorish
rupfen ['rupfən] *tr* pluck; (fig) fleece
ruppig ['rupiç] *adj* shabby; (fig) rude
Ruprecht ['rupreçt] *m* (-s;)—**Knecht R.** Santa Claus
Ruß [rus] *m* (-es;) soot
Russe ['rusə] *m* (-n;-n) Russian
Rüssel ['rysəl] *m* (-s;-) snout; (*Elephanten-*) trunk; (coll) snoot; (ent) proboscis
rußig ['rusiç] *adj* sooty
Russin ['rusin] *f* (-;-nen) Russian
russisch ['rusiʃ] *adj* Russian
Rußland ['ruslant] *n* (-s;) Russia
Rüst- [rʏst] *comb.fm.* scaffolding; armament, munition
rüsten ['rʏstən] *tr* arm, equip; prepare || *ref* get ready || *intr* (**zu**) get ready (for); **zum Krieg r.** mobilize
Rüster ['rʏstər] *f* (-;-n) elm
rüstig ['rʏstiç] *adj* vigorous; alert
Rüst'kammer *f* armory, arsenal
Rü'stung *f* (-;-en) preparation; equipment; armament; mobilization; armor; implements; (archit) scaffolding
Rü'stungsbetrieb *m* munitions factory
Rü'stungsfertigung *f* war production
Rü'stungsindustrie *f* war industry
Rü'stungskontrolle *f* arms control
Rü'stungsmaterial *n* war materiel
Rü'stungsstand *m* state of preparedness
Rüst'zeug *n* kit; (fig) knowledge
Rute ['rutə] *f* (-;-n) rod; twig; tail; (anat) penis
Rutsch [rutʃ] *m* (-es;-e) slip, slide
Rutsch'bahn *f* slide; chute
Rutsche ['rutʃə] *f* (-;-n) slide; chute
rutschen ['rutʃən] *intr* (SEIN) slip, slide; (aut) skid
rutschig ['rutʃiç] *adj* slippery
rütteln ['rʏtəln] *tr* shake; jolt; (*Getreide*) winnow; (*aus dem Schlafe*) rouse || *intr*—**r. an** (*acc*) cause to rattle; (fig) try to undermine

S

S, s [ɛs] *invar n* S, s
SA *abbr* (mil) (*Sturmabteilung*) storm troopers
Saal [zal] *m* (-[e]s; **Säle** ['zɛlə]) hall
Saat [zat] *f* (-;-en) seed; (*Säen*) sowing; (*Getreide auf dem Halm*) crop(s); **die S. bestellen** sow
Saat'bestellung *f* sowing
Saat'kartoffel *f* seed potato
Sabbat ['zabat] *m* (-s;-e) Sabbath
Sabberei [zabə'raɪ] *f* (-;-en) drooling; (*Geschwätz*) drivel
sabbern ['zabərn] *intr* drool, drivel

Säbel ['zebəl] *m* (-s;) saber; **mit dem S. rasseln** (pol) rattle the saber
sä'belbeinig *adj* bowlegged
säbeln ['zebəln] *tr* (coll) hack
Sä'belrasseln *n* (pol) saber rattling
Sabotage [zabo'taʒə] *f* (-;-n) sabotage
Saboteur [zabo'tør] *m* (-s;-e) saboteur
sabotieren [zabo'tirən] *tr* sabotage
Saccharin [zaxa'rin] *n* (-s;) saccharin
Sach- [zax] *comb.fm.* of facts, factual
Sach'anlagevermögen *n* tangible fixed assets
Sach'bearbeiter –in §6 *mf* specialist

Sach'beschädigung *f* property damage
Sach'bezüge *pl* compensation in kind
Sach'buch *n* nonfiction (work)
Sach'darstellung *f* statement of facts
sach'dienlich *adj* relevant, pertinent
Sache ['zaxə] *f* (-;-n) thing, matter;
cause; (jur) case; **bei der S.** sein be
on the ball; **beschlossene S.** foregone
conclusion; **die S. der Freiheit** the
cause of freedom; **große S.** big affair; **gute S.** good cause; **heikle S.**
delicate point; **in eigner S.** on one's
own behalf; **in Sachen X gegen Y**
(jur) in the case of X versus Y;
meine sieben Sachen all my belongings; **nicht bei der S. sein** not be with
it; **nicht zur S. gehörig** irrelevant;
von der S. abkommen get off the
subject; **zur S.!** come to the point!
(parl) question!
sach'gemäß *adj* proper, pertinent ‖ *adv*
in a suitable manner
Sach'kenner –in §6 *mf* expert
Sach'kenntnis *f*, Sach'kunde *f* expertise
sach'kundig *adj* expert ‖ Sach'kundige
§5 *mf* expert
Sach'lage *f* state of affairs, circumstances
Sach'leistung *f* payment in kind
sach'lich *adj* (*treffend*) to the point;
(*gegenständlich*) objective; (*tatsächlich*) factual; (*unparteiisch*) impartial; (*nüchtern*) matter-of-fact ‖ *adv*
to the point
sächlich ['zɛçlɪç] *adj* (gram) neuter
Sach'lichkeit *f* (-;) objectivity; reality;
impartiality; matter-of-factness
Sach'register *n* index
Sach'schaden *m* property damage
Sach'schadenersatz *m* indemnity (*for
property damage*)
Sachse ['zaksə] *m* (-n;-n) Saxon
Sachsen ['zaksən] *n* (-s;) Saxony
sächsisch ['zɛksɪʃ] *adj* Saxon
sacht(e) ['zaxt(ə)] *adj* soft, gentle;
(*langsam*) slow ‖ *adv* gingerly; **immer sacht!** easy does it!
Sach'verhalt *m* facts of the case
Sach'vermögen *n* real property
sach'verständig *adj* experienced ‖
Sachverständige §5 *mf* expert
Sach'wert *m* actual value; **Sachwerte**
material assets
Sach'wörterbuch *n* encyclopedia
Sack [zak] *m* (-[e]s;⁼e) sack, bag;
pocket; **j–n in den S. stecken** (coll)
be way above s.o.; **mit S. und Pack**
bag and baggage
Säckel ['zɛkəl] *m* (-s;–) little bag;
pocket; purse
sacken ['zakən] *tr* bag ‖ *ref* be baggy
‖ *intr* (SEIN) sag; (archit) settle;
(naut) founder
Sack'gasse *f* blind alley, dead end;
(fig) stalemate, dead end
Sack'leinwand *f* burlap
Sack'pfeife *f* bagpipe
Sack'tuch *n* handkerchief
Sadist –in [za'dɪst(ɪn)] §7 *mf* sadist
sadistisch [za'dɪstɪʃ] *adj* sadistic
säen ['zɛ·ən] *tr* & *intr* sow
Saffian ['zafjɑn] *m* (-s;) morocco

Safran ['zafrɑn] *m* (-s;–e) saffron
Saft [zaft] *m* (-[e]s;⁼e) juice; sap;
(culin) gravy
saftig ['zaftɪç] *adj* juicy; (*Witze*) spicy
saft'los *adj* juiceless; (fig) wishy-washy
saft'reich *adj* juicy, succulent
Sage ['zagə] *f* (-;-n) legend, saga
Säge ['zegə] *f* (-;-n) saw
Sä'geblatt *n* saw blade
Sä'gebock *m* sawhorse, sawbuck
Sä'gefisch *m* sawfish
Sä'gemehl *n* sawdust
sagen ['zagən] *tr* say; (*mitteilen*) tell;
das hat nichts zu s. that's neither
here nor there; **das will nicht s.** that
is not to say; **gesagt, getan** no sooner
said than done; **j–m s. lassen** send
s.o. word; **laß dir gesagt sein** let it
be a warning to you; **sich** [*dat*]
nichts s. lassen not listen to reason
sägen ['zegən] *tr* saw ‖ *intr* saw; (coll)
snore, cut wood
sa'genhaft *adj* legendary
Sägespäne ['zegəʃpenə] *pl* sawdust
Sä'gewerk *n* sawmill
sah [za] *pret* of **sehen**
Sahne ['zanə] *f* (-;) cream
Saison [sɛ'zõ] *f* (-;-s) season
Saison– *comb.fm.* seasonal
saison'bedingt, saison'mäßig *adj* sea-
sonal
Saite ['zaɪtə] *f* (-;-n) string, chord
Sai'teninstrument *n* string instrument
Sakko ['zako] *m* & *n* (-s;-s) suit coat
Sak'koanzug *m* sport suit
Sakrament [zakra'mɛnt] *n* (-[e]s;-e)
sacrament; **das S. des Altars** the
Eucharist ‖ *interj* (sl) dammit!
Sakrileg [zakri'lek] *n* (-s;-e) sacrilege
Sakristan [zakrɪs'tan] *m* (-s;-e) sac-
ristan
Sakristei [zakrɪs'taɪ] *f* (-;-en) sacristy
Säkular– [zekular] *comb.fm.* secular;
centennial
säkularisieren [zekularɪ'zirən] *tr* secu-
larize
Salami [za'lami] *f* (-;-s) salami
Salat [za'lat] *m* (-[e]s;-e) salad; let-
tuce; **gemischter S.** tossed salad
Salat'soße *f* salad dressing
salbadern [zal'badərn] *intr* talk hypo-
critically, put on the dog
Salbe ['zalbə] *f* (-;-n) salve
salben ['zalbən] *tr* put salve on; anoint
Sal'bung *f* (-;-en) anointing
sal'bungsvoll *adj* unctuous
saldieren [zal'dirən] *tr* (com) balance
Sal·do ['zaldo] *m* (-s;-s & di [di])
(acct) balance; **e–n S. aufstellen** (or
ziehen) strike a balance; **e–n S. ausweisen** show a balance
Saline [za'linə] *f* (-;-n) saltworks
Salmiak [zal'mjak] *m* (-s;) ammonium
chloride, sal ammoniac
Salmiak'geist *m* ammonia
Salon [za'lõ] *m* (-s;-s) salon; parlor,
living room
salon'fähig *adj* (*Aussehen*) presentable;
(*Ausdruck*) fit for polite company
Salon'held *m*, Salon'löwe *m* ladies' man
salopp [za'lɔp] *adj* sloppy; (*ungezwungen*) casual
Salpeter [zal'petər] *m* (-s;) saltpeter

salpeterig [zal'petərıç] *adj* nitrous
Salpe'tersäure *f* nitric acid
Salto ['zalto] *m* (-s;-s) somersault
Salut [za'lut] *m* (-[e]s;-e) salute; S.
  schießen fire a salute
salutieren [zalu'tirən] *tr & intr* salute
Salve ['zalvə] *f* (-;-n) volley, salvo
Salz [zalts] *n* (-es;-e) salt
Salz'bergwerk *n* salt mine
Salz'brühe *f* brine
salzen ['zaltsən] *tr* salt
Salz'faß *n* salt shaker
Salz'fleisch *n* salted meat
Salz'gurke *f* pickle
salz'haltig *adj* saline
Salz'hering *m* pickled herring
salzig ['zaltsıç] *adj* salty; saline
Salz'kartoffeln *pl* boiled potatoes
Salz'lake *f* brine
Salz'säure *f* hydrochloric acid, muriatic
  acid
Salz'sole *f* brine
Salz'werk *n* salt works
Samariter –in [zama'ritər(ın)] §6 *mf*
  Samaritan
Same ['zamə] *m* (-ns;-n), Samen
  ['zamən] *m* (-s;-) seed; (biol) semen
Sa'menkorn *n* grain of seed
Sa'menstaub *m* pollen
Samentierchen ['zaməntirçən] *n* (-s;-)
  spermatozoon
sämig ['zemıç] *adj* (culin) thick,
  creamy
Sämischleder ['zemı/ledər] *n* chamois
Sämling ['zemlıŋ] *m* (-s;-e) seedling
Sammel– [zaməl] *comb.fm.* collecting,
  collective
Sam'melbatterie *f* storage battery
Sam'melbecken *n* reservoir; storage
  tank
Sam'melbegriff *m* collective noun
Sam'melbüchse *f* poor box
Sam'mellinse *f* convex lens
sammeln ['zaməln] *tr* gather; collect;
  (*Aufmerksamkeit, Truppen*) concen-
  trate || *ref* gather; compose oneself;
  sich wieder s. (mil) reassemble
Sam'melname *m* collective noun
Sam'melplatz *m* collecting point; meet-
  ing place; (mil) rendezvous
Sam'melverbindung *f* conference call
Sam'melwerk *n* compilation
Sammler ['zamlər] *m* (-s;-) collector;
  compiler; (elec) storage cell
Samm'lung *f* (-;-en) collection; (*Zu-
  sammenstellung*) compilation; (*Fas-
  sung*) composure; concentration
Samstag ['zamstak] *m* (-[e]s;-e) Sat-
  urday
samt [zamt] *adv*—s. und sonders each
  and everyone, without exception ||
  prep (*dat*) together with || Samt *m*
  (-[e]s;-e) velvet
samt'artig *adj* velvety
sämtlich ['zemtlıç] *adj* all, complete ||
  adv all together
Sanato·rium [zana'torjum] *n* (-s;-rien
  [rjən]) sanitarium
Sand [zant] *m* (-[e]s;-e) sand; im
  Sande verlaufen (fig) peter out
Sandale [zan'dalə] *f* (-;-n) sandal
Sand'bahn *f* (sport) dirt track
Sand'bank *f* (-;ᵕe) sandbank

Sand'boden *m* sandy soil
Sand'düne *f* sand dune
Sand'grube *f* sand pit
sandig ['zandıç] *adj* sandy
Sand'kasten *m* sand box
Sand'korn *n* grain of sand
Sand'mann *m* (-[e]s;) (*fig*) sandman
Sand'papier *n* sandpaper; mit S. ab-
  schleifen sand, sandpaper
Sand'sack *m* sandbag
Sand'stein *m* sandstone
Sand'steingebäude *n* brownstone
sand'strahlen *tr* sandblast
Sand'sturmgebiet *n* dust bowl
sandte ['zantə] *pret* of senden
Sand'torte *f* sponge cake
Sand'uhr *f* hour glass
Sand'wüste *f* sandy desert
sanft [zanft] *adj* soft, gentle
Sänfte ['zɛnftə] *f* (-;-n) sedan chair
Sanft'mut *f* gentleness, meekness
sanft'mütig *adj* gentle, meek, mild
sang [zaŋ] *pret* of singen || Sang *m*
  (-[e]s;ᵕe) song; mit S. und Klang
  (fig) with great fanfare
sang–'und klang'los *adv* unceremoni-
  ously
Sänger ['zɛŋər] *m* (-s;-) singer
Sän'gerchor *m* glee club
Sängerin ['zɛŋərin] *f* (-;-nen) singer
Sanguiniker [zaŋ'gwinıkər] *m* (-s;-)
  optimist
sanguinisch [zaŋ'gwinı/] *adj* sanguine
sanieren [za'nirən] *tr* cure; improve
  the sanitary conditions of; disinfect;
  (fin) put on a firm basis
Sanie'rung *f* (-;-en) restoration; reorganization
sanitär [zanı'ter] *adj* sanitary
Sanitäter [zanı'tetər] *m* (-s;-) first-
  aid-man; (mil) medic
Sanitäts– [zanıtets] *comb.fm.* first-aid,
  medical
Sanitäts'korps *n* army medical corps
Sanitäts'soldat *m* medic
Sanitäts'wache *f* first-aid station
Sanitäts'wagen *m* ambulance
Sanitäts'zug *m* hospital train
sank [zaŋk] *pret* of sinken
Sanka ['zaŋka] *m* (-s;-s) (Sanitäts-
  kraftwagen) field ambulance
Sankt [zaŋkt] *invar mf* Saint
Sanktion [zaŋk'tsjon] *f* (-;-en) sanc-
  tion
sanktionieren [zaŋktsjə'nirən] *tr* sanc-
  tion
sann [zan] *pret* of sinnen
Saphir ['zafır] *m* (-s;-e) sapphire
Sardelle [zar'dɛlə] *f* (-;-n) anchovy
Sardine [zar'dinə] *f* (-;-n) sardine
Sardinien [zar'dinjən] *n* (-s;) Sardinia
sardinisch [zar'dinı/] *adj* Sardinian
Sarg [zark] *m* (-[e]s;ᵕe) coffin
Sarg'tuch *n* pall
Sarkasmus [zar'kasmus] *m* (-;) sar-
  casm
sarkastisch [zar'kastı/] *adj* sarcastic
Sarkophag [zarkə'fak] *m* (-s;-e) sar-
  cophagus
saß [zas] *pret* of sitzen
Satan ['zatan] *m* (-s;-e) Satan

satanisch [za'tɑnɪʃ] *adj* satanic(al)
Satellit [zate'lit] *m* (**-en;-en**) satellite
Satin [sa'tẽ] *m* (**-s;-s**) satin
Satire [za'tirə] *f* (**-;-n**) satire
Satiriker **-in** [za'tirɪkər(ɪn)] §6 *mf* satirist
satirisch [za'tirɪʃ] *adj* satirical
satt [zat] *adj* satisfied; satiated; (*Farben*) deep, rich; (chem) saturated; **etw s. bekommen** (or **haben**) be fed up with s.th.; **ich bin s.** I've had enough; **sich s. essen** eat one's fill
Sattel ['zatəl] *m* (**-s;⸚**) saddle
sat'telfest *adj* (fig) well-versed
Sat'telgurt *m* girth
satteln ['zatəln] *tr* saddle
Sat'telschlepper *m* semi-trailer
Sat'teltasche *f* saddlebag
Satt'heit *f* (**-;**) saturation; (*der Farben*) richness
sättigen ['zetɪgən] *tr* satisfy, satiate; saturate
Sät'tigung *f* (**-;**) satiation; saturation
Sattler ['zatlər] *m* (**-s;-**) harness maker
sattsam ['zatzɑm] *adv* sufficiently
saturieren [zatu'rirən] *tr* saturate
Satz [zats] *m* (**-es;⸚e**) sentence; clause; phrase; (*Behauptung*) proposition; (*Bodensatz*) grounds; sediment; (*Betrag*) amount; (*Tarif*) rate; (*Gebühr*) fee; (*Garnitur*) set; (*Sprung*) leap; (*Wette*) stake; (*Menge*) batch; (math) theorem; (mus) movement; (tennis) set; (typ) typesetting, composition; **e-en S. machen** jump; **e-n S. aufstellen** down an article of faith; **einfacher S.** simple sentence; **hauptwörtlicher S.** substantive clause; **in S. gehen** go to press; **verkürzter S.** phrase; **zum S. von** at the rate of; **zusammengesetzter S.** compound sentence
Satz'aussage *f* gram) predicate
Satz'bau *m* (**-[e]s;**) (gram) construction
Satz'gefüge *n* complex sentence
Satz'gegenstand *m* (gram) subject
Satz'lehre *f* syntax
Satz'teil *m* (gram) part of speech
Sat'zung *f* (**-;-en**) rule, regulation; (*Vereins-*) bylaw; statute
sat'zungsgemäß, sat'zungsmäßig *adj* statutory, according to the bylaws
Satz'zeichen *n* punctuation mark
Sau [zau] *f* (**-;⸚e**) sow; (pej) pig; **wie e-e gesengte Sau fahren** drive like a maniac
Sau'arbeit *f* (coll) sloppy work; (coll) tough job; (coll) dirty job
sauber ['zaubər] *adj* clean; exact
säuberlich ['zɔɪbərlɪç] *adj* clean, neat; (*anständig*) decent
sau'bermachen *tr* clean, clean up
säubern ['zɔɪbərn] *tr* clean; (*freimachen*) clear; (*Buch*) expurgate; (mil) mop up; (pol) purge
Säu'berungsaktion *f* (mil) mopping-up operation; (pol) purge
Sau'borste *f* hog bristle
Sauce ['zosə] *f* (**-;-n**) sauce; gravy; (*Salat-*) dressing
sau'dumm' *adj* (coll) awfully dumb
sauer ['zau-ər] *adj* sour

Sau'erbraten *m* braised beef soaked in vinegar
Sauerei [zau-ə'raɪ] *f* (**-;-en**) filth, filthy joke
Sau'erkohl *m*, **Sau'erkraut** *n* sauerkraut
säuerlich ['zɔɪ-ərlɪç] *adj* sourish, acidulous; (*Lächeln*) forced
säuern ['zɔɪ-ərn] *tr* sour; (*Teig*) leaven || *intr* turn sour, acidify
Sau'erstoff *m* (**-[e]s;**) oxygen
Sau'erstoffflasche *f* oxygen tank
Sau'erteig *m* leaven
Sau'ertopf *m* (coll) sourpuss
Sau'erwasser *n* sparkling water
Saufaus ['zaufaus] *m* (**-;-**), **Saufbold** ['zaufbɔlt] *m* (**-[e]s;-e**), **Saufbruder** ['zaufbrudər] *m* (coll) booze hound
saufen ['zaufən] §124 *tr* drink, guzzle || *intr* drink; (sl) booze
Säufer **-in** ['zɔɪfər(ɪn)] §6 *mf* drunkard
Saufgelage ['zaufgəlɑgə] *n* booze party
Sau'fraß *m* terrible food, slop
Säugamme ['zɔɪkamə] *f* wet nurse
saugen ['zaugən] §109 & §125 *tr* suck || *ref*—**sich** [*dat*] **etw aus den Fingern s.** invent s.th., make up s.th.
säugen ['zɔɪgən] *tr* suckle, nurse
Sauger ['zaugər] *m* (**-s;-**) sucker; nipple; pacifier
Säuger ['zɔɪgər] *m* (**-s;-**), **Säugetier** ['zɔɪgətir] *n* mammal
Saug'flasche *f* baby bottle
Säugling ['zɔɪklɪŋ] *m* (**-s;-e**) baby
Säug'lingsausstattung *f* layette
Säug'lingsheim *n* nursery
Sau'glück *n* (coll) dumb luck
Saug'napf *m* suction cup
Saug'pumpe *f* suction pump
Saug'watte *f* absorbent cotton
Saug'wirkung *f* suction
Sau'hund *m* (sl) louse, dirty dog
Sau'igel *m* (sl) dirty guy
sauigeln ['zau-igəln] *intr* (sl) tell dirty jokes
Sau'kerl *m* (sl) cad, skunk
Säule ['zɔɪlə] *f* (**-;-n**) column; (& fig) pillar; (elec) dry battery; (phys) pile
Säu'lenfuß *m* base of a column
Säu'lengang *m* colonnade, peristyle
Säu'lenhalle *f* portico. gallery
Säu'lenkapitell *n*, **Säu'lenknauf** *m*, **Säu'lenknopf** *m* (archit) capital
Säu'lenschaft *m* shaft of a column
Säu'lenvorbau *m* portico, (front) porch
Saum [zaum] *m* (**-[e]s;⸚e**) seam, hem; (*Rand*) border; (*e-r Stadt*) outskirts
säumen ['zɔɪmən] *tr* hem; border; (*Straßen*) line || *intr* tarry
Sau'mensch *n* (vulg) slut
säumig ['zɔɪmɪç] *adj* tardy
Säumnis ['zɔɪmnɪs] *f* (**-;-nisse**) dilatoriness; (*Verzug*) delay; (*Nichterfüllung*) default
Saum'pfad *m* mule track
Saum'tier *n* beast of burden
Sau'pech *n* (coll) rotten luck
Säure ['zɔɪrə] *f* (**-;-n**) sourness, acidity; tartness; (chem) acid
Sauregur'kenzeit *f* slack season
Säu'remesser *m* (aut) battery tester
Saures ['zaurəs] *n*—**gib ihm S.** (coll) give it to 'im!

Saus [zaʊs] *m*—**in S. und Braus leben**
live high

säuseln [ˈzɔɪzəln] *intr* rustle; **mit
säuselnder Stimme** in whispers

sausen [ˈzaʊsən] *intr* (*Wind, Kugel*)
whistle; (*Wasser*) gush || *intr* (SEIN)
rush, whiz || *impers*—**mir saust es in
den Ohren** my ears are ringing ||
Sausen *n* (**-s;**) rush and roar; humming, ringing (*in the ears*)

Sau'stall *m* pigsty; (fig) terrible mess

Sau'wetter *n* (coll) nasty weather

Sau'wirtschaft *f* (coll) helluva mess

sau'wohl' *adj* (coll) in great shape

Saxophon [zaksɔˈfoːn] *n* (**-s;-e**) saxophone

Schabe [ˈʃaːbə] *f* (**-;-n**) cockroach

Schabeisen [ˈʃaːpaɪzən] *n* scraper

schaben [ˈʃaːbən] *tr* scrape; grate, rasp

Scha'ber *m* (**-s;-**) scraper

Schabernack [ˈʃaːbərnak] *m* (**-[e]s;-e**)
practical joke

schäbig [ˈʃɛːbɪç] *adj* shabby; (fig) mean

Schablone [ʃaˈbloːnə] *f* (**-;-n**) (*Muster*) pattern, model; (*Matrize*) stencil; (*mechanische Arbeit*) routine;
nach der S. mechanically

schablo'nenhaft, schablo'nenmäßig *adj*
mechanical; (*Arbeit*) routine

Schach [ʃax] *n* (**-[e]s;**) chess; **in S.
halten** (fig) keep in check; **S. bieten**
(*or* **geben**) check; (fig) defy; **S. dem
König!** check!

Schach'brett *n* chessboard

Schacher [ˈʃaxər] *m* (**-s;**) haggling; **S.
treiben** haggle, huckster

Schach'feld *n* (chess) square

Schach'figur *f* chessman; (fig) pawn

schach'matt' *adj* checkmated; (fig) beat

Schach'partie *f*, **Schach'spiel** *n* game
of chess

Schacht [ʃaxt] *m* (**-[e]s;ːe**) shaft;
manhole

Schacht'deckel *m* manhole cover

Schachtel [ˈʃaxtəl] *f* (**-;-n**) box; (*von
Zigaretten*) pack; (fig) frump

Schach'zug *m* (chess & fig) move

schade [ˈʃaːdə] *adj* too bad

Schädel [ˈʃɛːdəl] *m* (**-s;-**) skull; **mir
brummt** (*or* **dröhnt**) **der S.** my head
is throbbing

Schä'delbruch *m*, **Schä'delfraktur** *f*
skull fracture

Schä'delhaut *f* scalp

Schä'delknochen *m* cranium

Schä'dellehre *f* phrenology

schaden [ˈʃaːdən] *intr* do harm; (*dat*)
harm, damage; **das wird ihr nichts s.**
it serves her right; **ein Versuch kann
nichts s.** there's no harm in trying ||
impers—**es schadet nichts** it doesn't
matter || **Schaden** *m* (**-s;ː**) damage,
injury; (*Verlust*) loss; (*Nachteil*) disadvantage; **er will deinen S. nicht** he
means you no harm; **j-m S. zufügen**
inflict loss on s.o.; (coll) give s.o.
a black eye; **mit S. verkaufen** sell at
a loss; **S. nehmen** come to grief; **zu
meinem S.** to my detriment

Scha'denersatz *m* compensation, damages; (*Wiedergutmachen*) reparation;
S. leisten pay damages; make amends

Scha'denersatzklage *f* damage suit

Scha'denfreude *f* gloating

scha'denfroh *adj* gloating, malicious

Scha'denversicherung *f* comprehensive
insurance

schadhaft [ˈʃaːthaft] *adj* damaged;
(*Material*) faulty; (*Zähne*) decayed;
(*baufällig*) dilapidated

schädigen [ˈʃɛːdɪgən] *tr* inflict financial damage on; (*benachteiligen*)
wrong; (*Ruf*) damage; (*Rechte*) infringe on

Schä'digung *f* (**-;**) damage

schädlich [ˈʃɛːtlɪç] *adj* harmful; (*nachteilig*) detrimental; (*verderblich*)
noxious; (*Speise*) unwholesome

Schädling [ˈʃɛːtlɪŋ] *m* (**-s;-e**) (*Person*)
parasite; (ent) pest; **Schädlinge** vermin

Schäd'lingsbekämpfung *f* pest control

schadlos [ˈʃaːtloːs] *adj*—**sich an j-m s.
halten** make s.o. pay (*for an injury
done to oneself*); **sich für etw s.
halten** compensate oneself for s.th.,
make up for s.th.

Schaf [ʃaːf] *n* (**-[e]s;-e**) sheep; (fig)
blockhead, dope

Schaf'bock *m* ram

Schäfchen [ˈʃɛːfçən] *n* (**-s;-**) lamb;
(*Wolken*) fleecy clouds

Schäf'chenwolke *f* fleecy cloud

Schäfer [ˈʃɛːfər] *m* (**-s;-**) shepherd

Schä'ferhund *m* sheep dog; **deutscher
S.** German shepherd

Schaf'fell *n* sheepskin

schaffen [ˈʃafən] §109 *tr* do; get; put;
manage, manage to do; (*erreichen*)
accomplish; (*liefern*) supply; (*er-
schaffen*) bring, cause; (*wegbringen*)
take; **auf die Seite s.** put aside; (*betrügerisch*) embezzle; **ich schaffe es
noch, daß** I'll see to it that; **Rat s.**
know what to do; **vom Halse s.** get
off one's neck || §126 *tr* create; pro-
duce; **wie geschaffen sein für** cut out
for || §109 *intr* do; (*arbeiten*) work;
j-m viel zu s. machen cause s.o. a
lot of trouble; **sich zu s. machen** be
busy, putter around

schaf'fend *adj* working; (*schöpferisch*)
creative; (*produktiv*) productive

Schaf'fensdrang *m* creative urge

Schaf'fenskraft *f* creative power

Schaffner [ˈʃafnər] *m* (**-s;-**) (rr) conductor

Schaf'fung *f* (**-;-en**) creation

Schaf'hirt *m* shepherd

Schaf'pelz *m* sheepskin coat

Schaf'pferch *m* sheepfold

Schafs'kopf *m* (sl) mutton-head

Schaf'stall *m* sheepfold

Schaft [ʃaft] *m* (**-[e]s;ːe**) shaft; (*e-r
Feder*) stem; (*e-s Gewehrs*) stock;
(*e-s Ankers*) shank; (bot) stem, stalk

Schaft'stiefel *m* high boot

Schaf'zucht *f* sheep raising

Schakal [ʃaˈkal] *m* (**-s;-e**) jackal

schäkern [ˈʃɛːkərn] *intr* joke around;
flirt

schal [ʃaːl] *adj* stale; insipid; (fig) flat
|| **Schal** *m* (**-s;-e & -s**) scarf; shawl

Schale [ˈʃaːlə] *f* (**-;-n**) bowl; (*Tasse*)
cup; (*von Obst*) peel, skin; (*Hülse*)
shell; (*Schote*) pod; (*Rinde*) bark;

(*Waagschale*) scale; (zool) shell; **sich in S. werfen** (coll) doll up

schälen ['ʃɛlən] *tr* peel; (*Mais*) husk; (*Baumrinde*) bark || *ref* peel off

Scha'lentier *n* (zool) crustacean

Schalk [ʃalk] *m* (-[e]s;-e & ⸚e) rogue

schalk'haft *adj* roguish

Schall [ʃal] *m* (-[e]s;-e & ⸚e) sound; (*Klang*) ring; (*Lärm*) noise

Schall'boden *m* sounding board

Schall'dämpfer *m* (*an Schußwaffen*) silencer; (aut) muffler; (mus) soft pedal

schall'dicht *adj* soundproof

Schall'dose *f* (electron) pickup

Schall'druck *m* sonic boom

Schallehre (Schall'lehre) *f* acoustics

schallen ['ʃalən] *intr* sound, resound

Schall'grenze *f* sound barrier

Schall'mauer *f* sound barrier

Schall'meßgerät *n* sonar

Schall'pegel *m* sound level

Schall'platte *f* phonograph record

Schall'plattenaufnahme *f* recording

Schall'wand *f* baffle

Schall'welle *f* sound wave

Schalotte [ʃaˈlɔtə] *f* (-;-n) (bot) scallion

schalt [ʃalt] *pret* of **schelten**

Schalt- *comb.fm.* switch; connecting; breaking; shifting

Schalt'bild *n* circuit diagram

Schalt'brett *n* switchboard; control panel; (aut) dashboard

Schalt'dose *f* switch box

schalten ['ʃaltən] *tr* switch; (*anlassen*) start; (*Gang*) (aut) shift || *intr* switch; (*regieren*) be in command; (aut) shift gears; **s. und walten mit** do as one pleases with

Schal'ter *m* (-s;-) switch; (*Ausschalter*) circuit breaker; (*für Kundenverkehr*) window, ticket window

Schal'terdeckel *m* switch plate

Schalt'hebel *m* (aut) gearshift; (elec) switch lever

Schalt'jahr *n* leap year

Schalt'kasten *m* switch box

Schalt'pult *n* (rad, telv) control desk

Schalt'tafel *f* switchboard, instrument panel; (aut) dashboard

Schalt'uhr *f* timer

Schal'tung *f* (-;-en) switching; (elec) connection; (elec) circuit

Schaluppe [ʃaˈlupə] *f* (-;-n) sloop

Scham [ʃam] *f* (-;) shame; (anat) genitals

Scham'bein *n* (anat) pubis

schämen ['ʃɛmən] *ref* (**über** *acc*) feel ashamed (of)

Scham'gefühl *n* sense of shame

Scham'haar *n* pubic hair

scham'haft *adj* modest, bashful

scham'los *adj* shameless

Schampun [ʃamˈpun] *n* (-s;-s) shampoo

schampunieren [ʃampuˈnirən] *tr* shampoo

scham'rot *adj* blushing; **s. werden** blush

Scham'teile *pl* genitals

Schand- [ʃant] *comb.fm.* of shame

schandbar ['ʃantbar] *adj* shameful; infamous

Schande ['ʃandə] *f* (-;) shame, disgrace

schänden ['ʃɛndən] *tr* disgrace; (*entweihen*) desecrate; (*Mädchen*) rape

Schän'der *m* (-s;-) violator; rapist

Schand'fleck *m* stain; (fig) blemish; (fig) good-for-nothing; **der S. der Familie** the disgrace of the family

schändlich ['ʃɛntlɪç] *adj* shameful, disgraceful; scandalous || *adv* (coll) awfully

Schand'mal *n* stigma

Schand'tat *f* shameful deed, crime

Schän'dung *f* (-;-en) desecration; disfigurement; rape

Schank [ʃaŋk] *m* (-[e]s;⸚e) bar, saloon

Schank'bier *n* draft beer

Schank'erlaubnis *f*, **Schank'gerechtigkeit** *f*, **Schank'konzession** *f* liquor license

Schank'stätte *f* bar, tavern

Schank'tisch *m* bar

Schank'wirt *m* bartender

Schank'wirtschaft *f* bar, saloon

Schanzarbeit ['ʃantsarbaɪt] *f* earthwork; **Schanzarbeiten** entrenchments

Schanze ['ʃantsə] *f* (-;-n) entrenchments, trenches; (naut) quarter-deck; (sport) take-off ramp (*of ski jump*)

Schanz'gerät *n* entrenching tool

Schar [ʃar] *f* (-;-en) group, bunch; crowd; (*von Vögeln*) flock, flight

Scharade [ʃaˈradə] *f* (-;-n) charade

scharen ['ʃarən] *ref* (**um**) gather (around)

scharf [ʃarf] *adj* (**schärfer** ['ʃɛrfər]; **schärfste** ['ʃɛrfstə] §9) sharp; (*Tempo*) fast; (*Bemerkung*) cutting; (*Blick*) hard; (*Brille*) strong; (*Fernrohr*) powerful; (*Geruch*) pungent; (*Munition*) live; (*Pfeffer, Senf*) hot; (*streng*) severe; (*genau*) exact; (*Ton*) shrill; (*wahrnehmend*) keen; **s. machen** sharpen; **s. sein auf** (*acc*) be keen on || *adv* hard; fast; **j-n s. nehmen** be very strict with s.o.; **s. ansehen** look hard at; **s. geladen** loaded; **s. schießen** shoot with live ammunition; **s. umreißen** define clearly

Scharf'blick *m* (fig) sharp eye

Schärfe ['ʃɛrfə] *f* (-;-n) sharpness; keenness; pungency; severity; accuracy

Scharf'einstellung *f* (phot) focusing

schärfen ['ʃɛrfən] *tr* sharpen, whet; make pointy; (fig) intensify

scharf'kantig *adj* sharp-edged

scharf'machen *tr* stir up; (*Bomben*) arm; (*Zünder*) activate

Scharf'macher *m* demagogue, agitator

Scharf'richter *m* executioner

Scharf'schütze *m* (mil) sharpshooter

scharf'sichtig *adj* sharp-eyed; (fig) clear-sighted

Scharf'sinn *m* sagacity, acumen

scharf'sinnig *adj* sharp, sagacious

Scharlach ['ʃarlax] *m* (-s;-e) scarlet; (pathol) scarlet fever

schar'lachfarben *adj* scarlet

schar'lachrot *adj* scarlet

Scharlatan ['ʃarlatan] *m* (-s;-e) charlatan, quack

scharmant [ʃar'mant] *adj* charming
Scharmützel [ʃar'mʏtsəl] *n* (–s;–) skirmish
Scharnier [ʃar'nir] *n* (–s;–e) hinge; joint
Schärpe ['ʃɛrpə] *f* (–;–n) sash
Scharre ['ʃarə] *f* (–;–n) scraper
Scharreisen ['ʃaraɪzən] *n* scraper
scharren ['ʃarən] *tr* scrape, paw || *intr* scrape; (**an** *acc*) scratch (on); **auf den Boden s.** paw the ground; **mit den Füßen** scrape the feet (*in disapproval*)
Scharte ['ʃartə] *f* (–;–n) nick, dent; (*Kerbe*) notch; (*Kratzer*) scratch; (*Riß*) crack; (*Bergsattel*) gap; (fig) mistake; **e–e S. auswetzen** (fig) make amends
Scharteke [ʃar'tekə] *f* (–;–n) worthless old book; (fig) frump
schartig ['ʃartɪç] *adj* jagged; notched
Schatten ['ʃatən] *m* (–s;–) shade; shadow; **in den S. stellen** throw into the shade
Schat′tenbild *n* silhouette; (fig) phantom
Schat′tendasein *n* shadowy existence
Schat′tengestalt *f* shadowy figure
schat′tenhaft *adj* shadowy
Schat′tenriß *m* silhouette
Schat′tenseite *f* shady side; dark side; (fig) seamy side
schattieren [ʃa'tirən] *tr* shade; (*schraffieren*) hatch; (*abtönen*) tint
Schattie′rung *f* (–;–en) shading; (*Farbton*) shade, tint
schattig ['ʃatɪç] *adj* shadowy; shady
Schatulle [ʃa'tulə] *f* (–;–n) cash box; (*für Schmuck*) jewelry box; (hist) private funds (*of a prince*)
Schatz [ʃats] *m* (–es;–̈e) treasure; (*Vorrat*) store; (fig) sweetheart
Schatz′amt *n* treasury department
Schatz′anweisung *f* treasury bond
schätzbar ['ʃɛtsbar] *adj* valuable
schätzen ['ʃɛtsən] *tr* (*Grundstücke, Häuser, Schaden*) estimate, appraise; (*urteilen, vermuten*) guess; (*achten*) esteem, value; (*würdigen*) appreciate; **er schätzte mich auf 20 Jahre** he took me for 20 years old; **zu hoch s.** overestimate, overrate; **zu s. wissen** appreciate || *ref*—**sich** [*dat*] **es zu Ehre s.** consider it an honor; **sich glücklich s.** consider oneself lucky || *recip*—**sie s. sich nicht** there's no love lost between them
schät′zenswert *adj* valuable
Schät′zer –**in** §6 *mf* appraiser; (*zur Besteuerung*) assessor
Schatz′kammer *m* treasury; (fig) storehouse
Schatz′meister –**in** §6 *mf* treasurer
Schät′zung *f* (–;–en) estimate; (*Meinung*) estimation; (*Hochachtung*) esteem; (*Hochschätzung*) appreciation; (*zur Besteuerung*) assessment
schät′zungsweise *adv* approximately
Schät′zungswert *m* estimated value; assessed value; (*des Schadens*) appraisal
Schatz′wechsel *m* treasury bill
Schau [ʃau] *f* (–;–en) view; (*Ausstel-*

lung) exhibition, show; (mil) review; (telv) show; **zur S. stehen** be on display; **zur S. stellen** put on display; **zur S. tragen** feign
Schau′bild *n* diagram, chart
Schauder ['ʃaudər] *m* (–s;–) shudder, shiver; (*Schrecken*) horror, terror
schauderbar ['ʃaudərbar] *adj* terrible
schau′dererregend *adj* horrifying
schau′derhaft *adj* horrible, awful
schaudern ['ʃaudərn] *intr* (**vor** *dat*) shudder (at) || *impers*—**es schaudert mich** I shudder
schauen ['ʃau·ən] *tr* look at; (*beobachten*) observe || *intr* look
Schauer ['ʃau·ər] *m* (–s;–) shower, downpour; (*Schauder*) shudder, chill; thrill; (*Anfall*) fit, attack; **einzelne S.** scattered showers
Schau′erdrama *n* (theat) thriller
schau′erlich *adj* dreadful, horrible
schauern ['ʃau·ərn] *intr* shudder || *impers*—**es schauert** it is pouring; **es schauert mich** (or **mir**) **vor** (*dat*) I shudder at; I shiver with
Schau′erroman *m* thriller
Schaufel ['ʃaufəl] *f* (–;–n) shovel; scoop; (*Rad–*) paddle; (*Turbinen–*) blade, vane
schaufeln ['ʃaufəln] *tr* shovel; (*Grab*) dig || *intr* shovel
Schau′felrad *n* paddle wheel
Schau′fenster *n* display window; **die S. ansehen** go window-shopping
Schau′fensterauslage *f* window display
Schau′fensterbummel *m* window-shopping
Schau′fensterdekoration *f* window dressing
Schau′fliegen *n* stunt flying
Schau′flug *m* air show
Schau′gepränge *n* pageantry
Schau′gerüst *n* grandstand
Schau′kampf *m* (box) exhibition fight
Schau′kasten *m* showcase
Schaukel ['ʃaukəl] *f* (–;–n) swing
Schau′kelbrett *n* seesaw
schaukeln ['ʃaukəln] *tr* swing; rock || *intr* swing; rock; sway
Schau′kelpferd *n* rocking horse
Schau′kelreck *n* trapeze
Schau′kelstuhl *m* rocking chair
Schau′loch *n* peephole
Schaum [ʃaum] *m* (–[e]s;–̈e) foam, froth; (*Abschaum*) scum; (*Geifer*) slaver; **zu S. schlagen** whip; **zu S. werden** (fig) come to nothing
Schaum′bad *n* bubble bath
schäumen ['ʃɔɪmən] *intr* foam; (*Wein*) sparkle; (*aus Wut*) fume, boil
Schaum′gummi *n* & *m* foam rubber
Schaum′haube *f* head (*on beer*)
schaumig ['ʃaumɪç] *adj* foamy
Schaum′krone *f* whitecap (*on wave*)
Schau′modell *n* mock-up
Schaum′wein *m* sparkling wine
Schau′platz *m* scene, theater
Schau′prozeß *m* mock trial
schaurig ['ʃaurɪç] *adj* horrible
Schau′spiel *n* play, drama; spectacle
Schau′spieler *m* actor
Schau′spielerin *f* actress
schau′spielerisch *adj* theatrical

schauspielern ['ʃauʃpilərn] *intr* act; (*schwindeln*) act, make believe
Schau'spielhaus *n* theater
Schau'spielkunst *f* dramatic art
Schau'stück *n* show piece; (*Muster*) sample
Scheck [ʃɛk] *m* (-s;-s & -e) check; **e-n S. ausstellen an** (*acc*) **über** (*acc*) write out a check to (*s.o.*) in the amount of; **e-n S. einlösen** cash a check; **e-n S. sperren lassen** stop payment on a check; **offener S.** blank check
Scheck'abschnitt *m* check stub
Scheck'formular *n* blank check
Scheck'heft *n* check book
scheckig ['ʃɛkɪç] *adj* dappled
Scheck'konto *n* checking account
scheel [ʃel] *adj* squinting; squint-eyed; (fig) envious, jealous
Scheffel ['ʃɛfəl] *m* (-s;-) bushel
scheffeln ['ʃɛfəln] *tr* amass
Scheibe ['ʃaɪbə] *f* (-;-n) disk; sheet; plate; (*Glas-*) pane; (*Honig-*) honeycomb; (*Ziel*) target; (*Schnitte*) slice; (astr) orb, disk; (mach) washer; (telp) dial
Schei'benbremse *f* disk brake
Schei'benkönig *m* top marksman
Schei'benschießen *n* target practice
Schei'benwäscher *m* windshield washer
Schei'benwischer *m* windshield wiper
Scheide ['ʃaɪdə] *f* (-;-n) sheath; border, boundary; (anat) vagina
Schei'debrief *m* farewell letter
Schei'degruß *m* goodbye
scheiden ['ʃaɪdən] §112 *tr* separate, divide; (*zerlegen*) decompose; (*Ehe*) dissolve; (*Eheleute*) divorce; (chem) analyze; (chem) refine ‖ *ref* part; **sich s. lassen** get a divorce ‖ *intr* (SEIN) part; depart; (*aus dem Amt*) resign, retire
schei'dend *adj* (*Tag*) closing; (*Sonne*) setting
Schei'dewand *f* partition
Schei'deweg *m* fork, crossroad; (fig) moment of decision
Schei'dung *f* (-;-en) separation; (*Ehe-*) divorce
Schein [ʃaɪn] *m* (-[e]s;-e) shine; (*Licht*) light; (*Schimmer*) gleam, glitter; (*Strahl*) flash; (*Erscheinung*) appearance; (*Anschein*) pretense, show; (*Urkunde*) certificate, papers, license, ticket; (*Geldschein*) bill; (*Quittung*) receipt; **dem Scheine nach** apparently; **den äußeren S. wahren** save face; **sich** [*dat*] **den S. geben** make believe; **zum S.** pro forma
Schein- *comb.fm.* sham, mock, make-believe
scheinbar ['ʃaɪnbar] *adj* seeming, apparent; likely; (*vorgeblich*) make-believe
Schein'bild *n* illusion; phantom
scheinen ['ʃaɪnən] §128 *intr* shine; seem, appear ‖ *impers—es scheint* it seems
Schein'grund *n* pretext
schein'heilig *adj* sanctimonious, hypocritical
Schein'tod *m* suspended animation

Schein'werfer *m* flashlight; (aer) beacon; (aut) headlight
Scheit [ʃaɪt] *n* (-[e]s;-e) piece of chopped wood; **Holz in Scheite hakken** chop wood
Scheitel ['ʃaɪtəl] *m* (-s;-) apex, top; top of the head; (*des Haares*) part; **e-n S. ziehen** make a part
scheiteln ['ʃaɪtəln] *tr & ref* part
Schei'telpunkt *m* (fig) summit; (astr) zenith; (math) vertex
Schei'telwinkel *m* opposite angle
Scheiterhaufen ['ʃaɪtərhaufən] *m* funeral pile; **auf dem S. sterben** die at the stake
scheitern ['ʃaɪtərn] *intr* (SEIN) run aground, be wrecked; (*Plan*) miscarry ‖ **Scheitern** *n* (-s;) shipwreck; (fig) failure
Schelle ['ʃɛlə] *f* (-;-n) bell; (*Fessel*) handcuff; (*Ohrfeige*) box on the ear
schellen ['ʃɛlən] *tr & intr* ring
Schel'lenkappe *f* cap and bells
Schellfisch ['ʃɛlfɪʃ] *m* haddock
Schelm [ʃɛlm] *m* (-[e]s;-e) rogue; (Lit) knave; **armer S.** poor devil
Schel'menstreich *m* prank
schelmisch ['ʃɛlmɪʃ] *adj* roguish, impish
Schelte ['ʃɛltə] *f* (-;-n) scolding
schelten ['ʃɛltən] *tr & intr* scold
Scheltwort ['ʃɛltvɔrt] *n* (-[e]s;-e & ⸚er) abusive word; word of reproof
Sche·ma ['ʃema] *n* (-s;-s & -mata [mata] & -men [mən]) scheme; diagram; (*Muster*) pattern, design
Schemel ['ʃeməl] *m* (-s;-) stool
Schemen ['ʃemən] *m* (-s;-) phantom, shadow
sche'menhaft *adj* shadowy
Schenk [ʃɛŋk] *m* (-en;-en) bartender
Schenke ['ʃɛŋkə] *f* (-;-n) bar, tavern
Schenkel ['ʃɛŋkəl] *m* (-s;-) thigh; (*e-s Winkels*) side; (*e-r Schere*) blade; (*e-s Zirkels*) leg
schenken ['ʃɛŋkən] *tr* give, offer; pour (out); (*Aufmerksamkeit*) pay; (*Schuld*) remit; **das ist geschenkt** that's dirt cheap; **das kann ich mir s.** I can pass that up; **das kannst du dir s.!** keep it to yourself! **j-m Beifall s.** applaud s.o.; **j-m das Leben s.** grant s.o. pardon
Schenk'stube *f* taproom, barroom
Schenk'tisch *m* bar
Schen'kung *f* (-;-en) donation
Schenk'wirt *m* bartender
scheppern ['ʃɛpərn] *intr* (coll) rattle
Scherbe ['ʃɛrbə] *f* (-;-n), **Scherben** ['ʃɛrbən] *m* (-s;-) broken piece; potsherd; **in Scherben gehen** go to pieces
Scher'bengericht *n* ostracism
Scherbett [ʃɛr'bɛt] *m* (-[e]s;-e) sherbe(r)t
Schere ['ʃerə] *f* (-;-n) (pair of) scissors; shears; (*Draht-*) cutter; (zool) claw
scheren ['ʃerən] *tr* bother; **was schert dich das?** what's that to you? ‖ §129 *tr* cut, clip, trim; (*Schafe*) shear; ‖ §109 *ref—scher dich ins Bett!* off to bed with you!; **scher dich zum Teu-**

fel! the devil with you!; **sich um etw s.** trouble oneself about s.th.
Schererei [ʃerə'raɪ] f (-;-en) trouble
Scherflein ['ʃerflaɪn] n (-s;-) bit; **sein S. beitragen** contribute one's bit
Scherz [ʃerts] m (-es;-e) joke; **im** (or **zum**) **S.** for fun; **S. treiben mit** make fun of
scherzen ['ʃertsən] intr joke, kid
scherz'haft adj joking, humorous
Scherz'name m nickname
scherz'weise adv in jest, as a joke
scheu [ʃɔɪ] adj shy; **s. machen** frighten; startle ‖ **Scheu** f (-;) shyness
Scheuche ['ʃɔɪçə] f (-;-n) scarecrow
scheuchen ['ʃɔɪçən] tr scare (away)
scheuen ['ʃɔɪ·ən] tr shun; shrink from; fear; (Mühen, Kosten) spare; **ohne die Kosten zu s.** regardless of expenses ‖ ref (vor dat) be afraid (of); **ich s. mich zu** (inf) I am reluctant to (inf) ‖ intr—**s. vor** (dat) shy at
Scheuer ['ʃɔɪ·ər] f (-;-n) barn
Scheu'erbürste f scrub brush
Scheu'erfrau f scrubwoman
Scheu'erlappen m scrub rag
scheuern ['ʃɔɪ·ərn] tr scrub, scour; (reiben) rub
Scheu'erpulver n scouring powder
Scheu'klappe f blinder (for horses)
Scheune ['ʃɔɪnə] f (-;-n) barn
Scheu'nendrescher m—**er ißt wie ein S.** (coll) he eats like a horse
Scheusal ['ʃɔɪzal] n (-s;-e) monster
scheußlich ['ʃɔɪslɪç] adj dreadful, atrocious; (coll) awful, rotten
Scheuß'lichkeit f (-;-en) hideousness; (Tat) atrocity
Schi [ʃi] m (-s;- & -er) ski; **Schi fahren** (or **laufen**) ski
Schicht [ʃɪçt] f (-;-en) layer, film; (Farb-) coat; (Arbeiter-) shift; (Gesellschafts-) class; (geol) stratum; (phot) emulsion; **Leute aus allen Schichten** people from all walks of life; **S. machen** (coll) knock off from work
Schicht'arbeit f shift work
schichten ['ʃɪçtən] tr arrange in layers; laminate; (Holz) stack (up); (in Klassen einteilen) classify; (geol) stratify; (Ladung) (naut) stow
Schich'tenaufbau m, **Schich'tenbildung** f (geol) stratification
-schichtig [ʃɪçtɪç] comb.fm. -layer, -ply
Schicht'linie f contour
Schicht'linienplan m contour map
Schicht'meister m shift foreman
schicht'weise adv in layers; in shifts
schick [ʃɪk] adj chic, swank ‖ **Schick** m (-[e]s;) stylishness; (Geschick) skill; (Geschmack) tact, taste; **S. haben für** have a knack for
schicken ['ʃɪkən] tr send ‖ ref—**sich s. für** (or **zu**) be suitable for; **sich s. in** (acc) adapt oneself to; resign oneself to ‖ intr—**nach j-m s.** send for s.o. ‖ impers—**es schickt sich** it is proper; (sich ereignen) come to pass
schick'lich adj proper; decent
Schick'lichkeit f (-;) propriety

Schick'lichkeitsgefühl n sense of propriety
Schicksal ['ʃɪkzal] n (-[e]s;-e) destiny, fate
Schick'salsgefährte m fellow sufferer
Schick'salsglaube m fatalism
Schick'salsgöttinnen pl (myth) Fates
Schick'salsschlag m stroke of fate
Schickung (Schik'kung) f (-;-en) (divine) dispensation
Schiebe– [ʃibə] comb.fm. sliding, push
Schie'beleiter f extension ladder
schieben ['ʃibən] §130 tr push, shove; traffic in; **auf die lange Bank s.** put off; **e-e ruhige Kugel s.** have a cushy job; **Kegel s.** bowl; **Wache s.** (mil) pull guard duty ‖ ref move, shuffle ‖ intr shuffle along; profiteer
Schieber ['ʃibər] m (-s;-) slide valve; (Riegel) bolt; (am Schornstein) damper; (fig) racketeer
Schie'bergeschäft f (com) racket
Schiebertum ['ʃibərtum] n (-s;) (com) racketeering
Schie'betür f sliding door
schied [ʃit] pret of **scheiden**
Schieds– [ʃits] comb.fm. of arbitration
Schieds'gericht n board of arbitration; **an ein S. verweisen** refer to arbitration
Schieds'mann m (-[e]s;-̈er) arbitrator
Schieds'richter m arbitrator; (sport) referee, umpire
schieds'richterlich adj of an arbitration board ‖ adv by arbitration
Schieds'spruch m decision; **e-n S. fällen** render a decision
schief [ʃif] adj (abfallend) slanting; (krumm) crooked; (einseitig) lopsided; (geneigt) inclined; (Winkel) oblique; (falsch) false, wrong; **auf die schiefe Ebene geraten** (fig) go downhill; **schiefe Lage** (fig) tight spot; **schiefes Licht** (fig) bad light ‖ adv at an angle; awry; obliquely; wrong; **s. ansehen** look askance at; **s. halten** tip, tilt; **s. nehmen** take amiss
Schiefer ['ʃifər] m (-s;-) slate; (Splitter) splinter
Schie'ferbruch m slate quarry
Schie'feröl n shale oil
Schie'fertafel f (educ) slate
schief'gehen §82 intr (SEIN) go wrong
schief'treten §152 tr—**die Abstätze s.** wear down the heels
schieläugig ['ʃilɔɪɡɪç] adj squint-eyed; cross-eyed
schielen ['ʃilən] intr squint; **s. nach** squint at; leer at
schie'lend adj squinting; cross-eyed; furtive
schien [ʃin] pret of **scheinen**
Schienbein ['ʃinbaɪn] n shinbone, tibia
Schien'beinschützer m shinguard
Schiene ['ʃinə] f (-;-n) (rr) rail, track; (surg) splint; **aus den Schienen springen** jump the track
schienen ['ʃinən] tr put in splints
Schie'nenbahn f track, rails; streetcar; railroad
Schie'nenfahrzeug n rail car
Schie'nengleis n track

schier [ʃir] *adj* sheer || *adv* almost
Schierling [ˈʃirlɪŋ] *m* (-s;-e) (bot) hemlock
Schieß- [ʃis] *comb.fm.* shooting
Schieß'baumwolle *f* guncotton
Schieß'bedarf *m* ammunition
Schieß'bude *f* shooting gallery
Schieß'eisen *n* (hum) shooting iron
schießen [ˈʃisən] §76 *tr* shoot, fire; **e-n Bock s.** (coll) pull a boner; **ein Tor s.** make a goal || *intr* (**auf** *acc*) shoot (at); **aus dem Hinterhalt s.** snipe; **gut s.** be a good shot; **scharf s.** shoot with live ammunition || *intr* (SEIN) shoot up; spurt; zig, fly; **das Blut schoß ihm ins Gesicht** his face got red; **in Samen s.** go to seed; **ins Kraut s.** sprout || **Schießen** *n* (-s;) shooting; **das ist ja zum s.!** (coll) that's a riot!
Schießerei [ʃisəˈraɪ] *f* (-;-en) gun fight; pointless firing
Schieß'gewehr *n* firearm
Schieß'hund *m* (hunt) pointer
Schieß'lehre *f* ballistics
Schieß'platz *m* firing range
Schieß'prügel *m* (hum) shooting iron
Schieß'pulver *n* gunpowder
Schieß'scharte *f* loophole
Schieß'scheibe *f* target
Schieß'stand *m* shooting gallery; (mil) firing range, rifle range
Schieß'übung *f* firing practice
Schi'fahrer **-in** §6 *mf* skier
Schiff [ʃɪf] *n* (-[e]s;-e) ship; (archit) nave; (typ) galley
Schiffahrt (**Schiff'fahrt**) *f* navigation
Schiffahrtslinie (**Schiff'fahrtslinie**) *f* steamship line
Schiffahrtsweg (**Schiff'fahrtsweg**) *m* shipping lane
schiffbar [ˈʃɪfbɑr] *adj* navigable
Schiff'bau *m* (-[e]s;) shipbuilding
Schiff'bruch *m* shipwreck
schiff'brüchig *adj* shipwrecked
Schiff'brücke *f* pontoon bridge; (naut) bridge
Schiffchen [ˈʃɪfçən] *n* (-s;-) little ship; (mil) overseas cap; (tex) shuttle
schiffen [ˈʃɪfən] *intr* (vulg) pee || *impers*—**es schifft** (vulg) it's pouring
Schiffer [ˈʃɪfər] *m* (-s;-) seaman; skipper; (*Schiffsführer*) navigator
Schif'ferklavier *n* (coll) concertina
Schiffs'journal *n* log, logbook
Schiffs'junge *m* cabin boy
Schiffs'küche *f* galley
Schiffs'ladung *f* cargo
Schiffs'luke *f* hatch
Schiffs'mannschaft *f* crew
Schiffs'ortung *f* dead reckoning
Schiffs'raum *m* hold; tonnage
Schiffs'rumpf *m* hull
Schiffs'schraube *f* propeller
Schiffs'tau *n* hawser
Schiffs'taufe *f* christening of a ship
Schiffs'werft *f* shipyard, dockyard
Schiffs'winde *f* winch, capstan
Schiffs'zimmermann *m* ship's carpenter; (*bei e-r Werft*) shipwright
Schikane [ʃɪˈkɑnə] *f* (-;-n) chicanery; **mit allen Schikanen** with all the frills; (aut) fully loaded

schikanieren [ʃɪkaˈnirən] *tr* harass
schikanös [ʃɪkaˈnøs] *adj* annoying
Schi'langlauf *m* cross-country skiing
Schi'lauf *m* skiing
schi'laufen §105 *intr* (SEIN) ski || **Schilaufen** *n* (-s;) skiing
Schi'läufer **-in** §6 *mf* skier
Schild [ʃɪlt] *m* (-[e]s;-e) shield; (heral) coat of arms; **etw im Schilde führen** have s.th. up one's sleeve || *n* (-[e]s;-er) sign; road sign; nameplate; (*e-s Arztes, usw.*) shingle; (*Etikett*) label; (*Mützenschirm*) visor, shade
Schild'bürger *m* (fig) dunce
Schild'bürgerstreich *m* boner
Schild'drüse *f* thyroid gland
Schilderhaus [ˈʃɪldərhaus] *n* sentry box
Schil'dermaler *m* sign painter
schildern [ˈʃɪldərn] *tr* depict, describe
Schil'derung *f* (-;-en) description
Schild'kröte *f* tortoise, turtle
Schildpatt [ˈʃɪltpat] *n* (-[e]s;) tortoise shell, turtle shell
Schilf [ʃɪlf] *n* (-[e]s;-e) reed
Schilf'rohr *n* reed
Schi'lift *m* ski lift
Schiller [ˈʃɪlər] *m* (-s;) luster; iridescence
schillern [ˈʃɪlərn] *intr* be iridescent
Schil'lerwein *m* bright-red wine
Schilling [ˈʃɪlɪŋ] *m* (-s;- & -e) shilling; (Aust) schilling
Schimäre [ʃɪˈmɛrə] *f* (-;-n) chimera
Schimmel [ˈʃɪməl] *m* (-s;-) white horse; mildew, mold
schimmelig [ˈʃɪməlɪç] *adj* moldy
schimmeln [ˈʃɪməln] *intr* (HABEN & SEIN) get moldy
Schimmer [ˈʃɪmər] *m* (-s;) glimmer
schimmern [ˈʃɪmərn] *intr* glimmer
schimmlig [ˈʃɪmlɪç] *adj* moldy
Schimpanse [ʃɪmˈpanzə] *m* (-n;-n) chimpanzee
Schimpf [ʃɪmpf] *m* (-[e]s;-e) insult, abuse
schimpfen [ˈʃɪmpfən] *tr* scold, abuse || *intr* be abusive; (**über** *acc* or **auf** *acc*) curse (at), swear (at)
schimpf'lich *adj* disgraceful
Schimpf'name *m* nickname; **j-m Schimpfnamen geben** call s.o. names
Schimpf'wort *n* (-[e]s;-e & ⸚er) swear word
Schindaas [ˈʃɪntɑs] *n* carrion
Schindel [ˈʃɪndəl] *f* (-;-n) shingle
schindeln [ˈʃɪndəln] *tr* shingle
schinden [ˈʃɪndən] §167 *tr* skin; torment; oppress; exploit; **Eindruck s.** try to make an impression; **Eintrittsgeld s.** crash the gate; **Zeilen s.** pad the writing; **Zigaretten s.** bum cigarettes || *ref* break one's back
Schin'der *m* (-s;-) slave driver
Schinderei [ʃɪndəˈraɪ] *f* (-;-en) drudgery, grind
Schindluder [ˈʃɪntludər] *n* carrion; **mit j-m S. treiben** treat s.o. outrageously
Schindmähre [ˈʃɪntmɛrə] *f* old nag
Schinken [ˈʃɪŋkən] *m* (-s;-) ham; (hum) tome; (hum) huge painting
Schinnen [ˈʃɪnən] *pl* dandruff

Schippe [ˈʃɪpə] *f* (–;–n) shovel, scoop; (cards) spade(s); **e–e S. machen** (or **ziehen**) pout; **j–n auf die S. nehmen** (coll) pull s.o.'s leg

schippen [ˈʃɪpən] *tr & intr* shovel

Schirm [ʃɪrm] *m* (–[e]s;–e) screen; umbrella; x-ray screen; lampshade; visor; (fig) protection, shelter; (hunt) blind

Schirm'bild *n* x-ray

Schirm'bildaufnahme *f* x-ray

Schirm'dach *n* lean-to

schirmen [ˈʃɪrmən] *tr* protect

Schirm'futteral *n* umbrella case

Schirm'herr *m* protector, patron

Schirm'herrin *f* protectress, patroness

Schirm'herrschaft *f* protectorate; patronage

Schirm'ständer *m* umbrella stand

Schir'mung *f* (–;–en) (elec) shielding

schirren [ˈʃɪrən] *tr* harness

Schis•ma [ˈʃɪsma] *n* (–;–mata [mata] & –men [mən] schism

Schi'sprung *m* ski jump

Schi'stock *m* ski pole

schizophren [sçɪtsɔˈfren] *adj* schizophrenic

Schizophrenie [sçɪtsɔfreˈni] *f* (–;) schizophrenia

schlabbern [ˈʃlabərn] *tr* lap up ‖ *intr* (*geifern*) slobber; (fig) babble

Schlacht [ʃlaxt] *f* (–;–en) battle; **die S. bei** the battle of

schlachten [ˈʃlaxtən] *tr* slaughter

Schlach'tenbummler *m* camp follower; (sport) fan

Schlächter [ˈʃlɛçtər] *m* (–s;–) butcher

Schlacht'feld *n* battlefield

Schlacht'flieger *m* combat pilot; close-support fighter

Schlacht'geschrei *n* battle cry

Schlacht'haus *n* slaughterhouse

Schlacht'kreuzer *m* heavy cruiser

Schlacht'opfer *n* sacrifice; (fig) victim

Schlacht'ordnung *f* battle array

Schlacht'roß *n* (hist) charger

Schlacht'ruf *m* battle cry

Schlacht'schiff *n* battleship

Schlach'tung *f* (–;–en) slaughter

Schlacke [ˈʃlakə] *f* (–;–n) cinder; lava; (metal) slag, dross

schlackig [ˈʃlakɪç] *adj* sloppy (*weather*)

Schlaf [ʃlaf] *m* (–[e]s;) sleep

Schlaf'abteil *n* sleeping compartment

Schlaf'anzug *m* pajamas

Schläfchen [ˈʃlɛfçən] *n* (–s;–) nap; **ein S. machen** take a nap

Schläfe [ˈʃlɛfə] *f* (–;–n) temple

schlafen [ˈʃlafən] §131 *tr* sleep ‖ *intr* sleep; **sich s. legen** go to bed

Schla'fenszeit *f* bedtime

Schläfer –in [ˈʃlefər(ɪn)] §6 *mf* sleeper

schläfern [ˈʃlefərn] *impers*—**es schläfert mich** I'm sleepy

schlaff [ʃlaf] *adj* slack; limp; flabby; (*locker*) loose

Schlaf'gelegenheit *f* sleeping accommodations

Schlaf'kammer *f* bedroom

Schlaf'krankheit *f* sleeping sickness

schlaf'los *adj* sleepless

Schlaf'losigkeit *f* (–;) sleeplessness

Schlaf'mittel *n* sleeping pill

Schlaf'mütze *f* nightcap; (fig) sleepyhead

schläfrig [ˈʃlefrɪç] *adj* sleepy, drowsy

Schläf'rigkeit *f* (–;) sleepiness, drowsiness

Schlaf'rock *m* housecoat

Schlaf'saal *m* dormitory

Schlaf'sack *m* sleeping bag

Schlaf'stätte *f*, **Schlaf'stelle** *f* place to sleep

Schlaf'stube *f* bedroom

Schlaf'trunk *m* (hum) nightcap

schlaf'trunken *adj* still half-asleep

Schlaf'wagen *m* (rr) sleeping car

schlaf'wandeln *intr* (SEIN) walk in one's sleep

Schlafwandler –in [ˈʃlafvandlər(ɪn)] §6 *mf* sleepwalker

Schlaf'zimmer *n* bedroom

Schlag [ʃlak] *m* (–[e]s;–̈e) blow; stroke; (*Puls–*) beat; (*Faust–*) punch; (*Hand–*) slap; (*Donner–*) clap; (*Tauben–*) loft; (*Art, Sorte*) kind, sort, breed; (*e–s Taues*) coil; (*der Vögel*) song; (*vom Pferd*) kick; (*e–r Kutsche*) door; (*Holz–*) cut; (*Pendel*) swing; (agr) field; (elec) shock; (mil) scoop, ladleful; (pathol) stroke; **ein S. ins Wasser** a vain attempt; **Leute seines Schlages** the likes of him; **S. zwölf Uhr** at the stroke of twelve; **von gutem S.** of the right sort

Schlag'ader *f* artery

Schlag'anfall *m* (pathol) stroke

schlag'artig *adj* sudden, surprise; (*heftig*) violent ‖ *adv* all of a sudden; with a bang

Schlag'baum *m* barrier

Schlag'besen *m* eggbeater

Schlag'bolzen *m* firing pin

Schlägel [ˈʃlegəl] *m* (–s;–) sledge hammer

schlagen [ˈʃlagən] §132 *tr* hit; strike; beat; (*besiegen*) defeat; (*strafen*) spank; (*Alarm*) sound; (*Brücke*) build; (*Eier*) beat; (*Geld*) coin; (*Holz*) fell; (*Saiten*) strike; (*Schlacht*) fight; **die Augen zu Boden s.** cast down the eyes; **durch ein Sieb s.** strain, sift; **e–e geschlagene Stunde** (coll) a solid hour; **in die Flucht s.** put to flight; **in Fesseln s.** put in chains; **in Papier s.** wrap in paper; **Wurzel s.** take root; **zu Boden s.** knock down ‖ *ref* come to blows; fight a duel; fence; **sich gut s.** stand one's ground; **sich s. zu** side with; **um sich s.** flail about ‖ *intr* strike; beat; (*Pferd*) kick; (*Vogel*) sing; **mit den Flügeln s.** flap the wings; **nach j–m s.** take a swing at s.o.; (fig) be like s.o., take after s.o.

schla'gend *adj* striking, impressive; convincing; **schlagende Verbindung** dueling fraternity; **schlagende Wetter** firedamp

Schla'ger *m* (–s;–) (*tolle Sache*) hot item; (mus, theat) hit

Schläger [ˈʃlegər] *m* (–s;–) beater; hitter; batter; baseball bat; golf club; tennis racket; eggbeater; mallet; (*Singvogel*) warbler; (*Raufbold*) bully

Schlägerei [ʃlɛgəˈraɪ] f (–;–en) fight, fighting; brawl

Schla'gerpreis m rock-bottom price

Schla'gersänger –in §6 mf pop singer

schlag'fertig adj quick with an answer; (Antwort) ready

Schlag'holz n club, bat

Schlag'instrument n percussion instrument

Schlag'kraft f striking power

schlag'kräftig adj (Armee) powerful; (Beweis) conclusive

Schlag'licht n strong light; glare

Schlag'loch n pothole

Schlag'mal n (baseball) home plate

Schlag'ring m brass knuckles

Schlag'sahne f whipped cream

Schlag'schatten m deep shadow

Schlag'seite f (naut) list; S. haben have a list; (hum) be drunk

Schlag'uhr f striking clock

Schlag'weite f striking distance

Schlag'welle f breaker, comber

Schlag'wetter pl (min) firedamp

Schlag'wort n (–[e]s;⁼er & –e) slogan; key word, subject (in cataloguing); (Phrasendrescherei) claptrap

Schlag'wörterkatalog m (libr) subject index

Schlag'zeile f headline

Schlag'zeug n percussion instruments

Schlaks [ʃlaks] m (–es;–e) lanky person

schlaksig [ˈʃlaksɪç] adj lanky

Schlamassel [ʃlaˈmasəl] m & n (–s;–) (coll) jam, pickle, mess

Schlamm [ʃlam] m (–[e]s;–e) mud, slime; (im Motor) sludge; (fig) mire

Schlamm'bad n mud bath

schlämmen [ˈʃlɛmən] tr dredge; (metal) wash

schlammig [ˈʃlamɪç] adj muddy

Schlampe [ˈʃlampə] f (–;–n) frump; (sl) slut

Schlamperei [ʃlampəˈraɪ] f (–;–en) slovenliness; untidiness, mess

schlampig [ˈʃlampɪç] adj sloppy

schlang [ʃlaŋ] pret of schlingen

Schlange [ˈʃlaŋə] f (–;–n) snake; queue, waiting line; (Wasserschlauch) hose; Schlange stehen nach line up for

schlängeln [ˈʃlɛŋəln] ref wind; (Fluß) meander; (sich krümmen) squirm; wriggle; (fig) worm one's way

Schlan'genbeschwörer –in §6 mf snake charmer

Schlan'genlinie f wavy line

schlank [ʃlaŋk] adj slender, slim; im schlanken Trabe at a fast clip

Schlank'heit f (–;) slenderness

Schlank'heitskur f—e–e S. machen diet

schlankweg [ˈʃlaŋkvɛk] adv flatly; downright

schlapp [ʃlap] adj slack, limp; flabby; (müde) washed out || Schlappe f (–;–n) setback; (Verlust) loss

schlappen [ˈʃlapən] intr flap; shuffle along || Schlappen m (–s;–) slipper

schlappern [ˈʃlapərn] tr lap up

schlapp'machen intr (zusammenbrechen) collapse; (ohnmächtig werden) faint; (nicht durchhalten) call it quits

Schlapp'schwanz m (coll) weakling, sissy; (Feigling) coward

Schlaraffenland [ʃlaˈrafənlant] n paradise

Schlaraffenleben [ʃlaˈrafənlebən] n life of Riley

schlau [ʃlau] adj sly; clever

Schlauch [ʃlaux] m (–[e]s;⁼e) hose; tube; (fig) souse; (aut) inner tube; (educ) pony

Schlauch'boot n rubber dinghy

schlauchen [ˈʃlauxən] tr drive hard; (mil) drill mercilessly

Schlauch'ventil n (aut) valve

Schläue [ˈʃlɔɪ·ə] f (–;) slyness

schlau'erweise adv prudently

Schlaufe [ˈʃlaufə] f (–;–n) loop

Schlau'kopf m, Schlau'meier m sly fox

schlecht [ʃlɛçt] adj bad, poor; mir wird s. I'm getting sick; schlechter werden get worse; s. werden go bad || adv poorly; die Uhr geht s. the clock is off; s. daran sein be badly off; s. und recht somehow; s. zu sprechen sein auf (acc) have it in for

schlechterdings [ˈʃlɛçtərdɪŋs] adv utterly, absolutely

schlecht'gelaunt adj in a bad mood

schlecht'hin' adv simply, downright

schlecht'machen tr talk behind the back of

schlechtweg [ˈʃlɛçtvɛk] adv simply, downright

schlecken [ˈʃlɛkən] tr lick || intr eat sweets, nibble

Schleckerei [ʃlɛkəˈraɪ] f (–;–en) sweets

schleckern [ˈʃlɛkərn] intr have a sweet tooth || impers—mich schleckert es nach I have a yen for

Schlegel [ˈʃlegəl] m (–s;–) sledge hammer; (Holz–) mallet; (culin) leg; (mus) drumstick

schleichen [ˈʃlaɪçən] §85 ref & intr (SEIN) sneak

schlei'chend adj creeping; furtive; (Krankheit) lingering; (Gift) slow

Schlei'cher m (–s;–) sneak, hypocrite

Schleicherei [ʃlaɪçəˈraɪ] f (–;–en) sneaking; underhand dealing

Schleich'gut n contraband

Schleich'handel m underhand dealing; smuggling; black-marketing

Schleich'weg m secret path; auf Schleichwegen in a roundabout way

Schleier [ˈʃlaɪ·ər] m (–s;–) veil; haze; gauze

schlei'erhaft adj hazy; mysterious; (fig) veiled; das ist mir s. I don't know what to make of it

Schleif– [ʃlaif] comb.fm. sliding, grinding, abrasive

Schleif'bürste f (elec) brush

Schleife [ˈʃlaifə] f (–;–n) (am Kleid, im Haar) bow; (in Schnüren) slipknot; (e–r Straße) hairpin curve; (e–s Flusses) bend; (Wende–) loop; (mit langen Bändern) streamer; (Rutschbahn) slide, chute; (aer) loop

schleifen [ˈʃlaifən] tr drag; (Kleid) trail along; demolish; raze; (mus) slur || §88 tr grind; whet; polish; (Glas, Edelstein) cut; (mil) drill hard || §109 intr drag, trail

Schleif'mit'tel n abrasive
Schleif'papier n sandpaper
Schleif'rad n emery wheel
Schleif'stein m whetstone
Schleim [ʃlaɪm] m (-[e]s;-e) slime; mucus, phlegm
Schleim'haut f mucous membrane
schleimig ['ʃlaɪmɪç] adj slimy; mucous
schleißen ['ʃlaɪsən] §53 tr split; slit; (Federkiele) strip || intr wear out
Schlemm [ʃlɛm] m (-s;-e) (cards) slam
schlemmen ['ʃlɛmən] intr carouse; gorge oneself; live high
Schlem'mer –in §6 mf glutton, guzzler; gourmet
schlem'merhaft adj gluttonous; (üppig) plentiful, luxurious
Schlem'merlokal n gourmet restaurant
Schlempe ['ʃlɛmpə] f (-;-n) slop
schlendern ['ʃlɛndərn] intr (SEIN) stroll
Schlendrian ['ʃlɛndrɪ·an] m (-s;) routine
schlenkern ['ʃlɛŋkərn] tr dangle, swing || intr dangle; **mit den Armen s.** swing the arms
Schlepp– [ʃlɛp] comb.fm. towing, drag
Schlepp'dampfer m tugboat
Schlepp'dienst m towing service
Schleppe ['ʃlɛpə] f (-;-n) train
schleppen ['ʃlɛpən] tr drag; lug, tote; (aer, naut) tow || ref drag along; **sich mit etw s.** be burdened with s.th.
Schlep'penkleid n dress with a train
Schlep'per m (-s;-) hauler; tractor; tugboat; tender, lighter
Schlepp'fischerei f trawling
Schlepp'netz n dragnet, dredge; trawling net
Schlepp'netzboot n trawler
Schlepp'schiff n tugboat
Schlepp'tau n towline; **ins S. nehmen** take in tow
Schleuder ['ʃlɔɪdər] f (-;-n) sling, slingshot; (aer) catapult; (mach) centrifuge
schleudern ['ʃlɔɪdərn] tr fling; sling; (aer) catapult || intr (aut) skid; (com) undersell
Schleu'derpreis m cutrate price
Schleu'dersitz m (aer) ejection seat
schleunig ['ʃlɔɪnɪç] adj speedy || adv in all haste; (sofort) at once
schleunigst ['ʃlɔɪnɪçst] adv as soon as possible; right away
Schleuse ['ʃlɔɪzə] f (-;-n) lock, sluice, sluice way; drain, sewer
schleusen ['ʃlɔɪzən] tr (fig) maneuver
schlich [ʃlɪç] pret of **schleichen** || **Schlich** [ʃlɪç] m (-[e]s;-e) trick; **alle Schliche kennen** know all the ropes; **j-m auf die Schliche** (or **hinter j-s Schliche**) **kommen** be on to s.o.
schlicht [ʃlɪçt] adj smooth; plain
schlichten ['ʃlɪçtən] tr smooth; (fig) settle, arbitrate
Schlich'ter –in §6 mf arbitrator
Schlich'tung f (-;-en) arbitration; settlement
schlief [ʃlif] pret of **schlafen**
Schleiße ['ʃlisə] f (-;-n) clasp; pin
schließen ['ʃlisən] §76 tr shut, close; lock; end, conclude; (Betrieb) shut

down; (Bücher) balance; (Konto; Klammer) close; (Bündnis) form; (Frieden; Rede) conclude; (Kompromiß) reach; (Heirat) form; (Geschäft, Handel) strike; (Versammlung) adjourn; (Wette) make; (Reihen) (mil) close; **ans Herz s.** press to one's heart; **aus etw. s., daß** conclude from s.th. that; **den Zug s.** (mil) bring up the rear; **e-n Vergleich s.** come to an agreement; **ins Herz s.** take a liking to; **kurz s.** (elec) short || ref shut, close; **in sich s.** comprise, include; (bedeuten) imply; (umfassen) involve; **von sich auf andere s.** judge others by oneself || intr shut, close; end
Schließ'fach n post office box; safe-deposit box
schließlich ['ʃlislɪç] adj final, eventual || adv finally
schliff [ʃlɪf] pp of **schleifen** || **Schliff** m (-[e]s;-e) polish; (e-s Diamanten) cut; (fig) polish; (mil) rigorous training
schlimm [ʃlɪm] adj bad; (bedenklich) serious; (traurig) sad; (wund) sore; (eklig) nasty; **am schlimmsten** worst; **immer schlimmer** worse and worse; **s. daran sein** be badly off
schlimmstenfalls ['ʃlɪmstənfals] adv at worst
Schlinge ['ʃlɪŋə] f (-;-n) loop; coil; (fig) trap, difficulty; (bot) tendril; (hunt) snare; (surg) sling; **in die S. gehen** (fig) fall into a trap
Schlingel ['ʃlɪŋəl] m (-s;-) rascal; **fauler S.** lazybones
schlingen ['ʃlɪŋən] §142 tr tie; twist; wind; wrap; gulp || ref wind, coil; climb, creep || intr gulp down food
Schlingerbewegung ['ʃlɪŋərbəvegʊŋ] f (naut) roll
schlingern ['ʃlɪŋərn] intr (naut) roll
Schlinggewächs ['ʃlɪŋgəvɛks] n, **Schlingpflanze** ['ʃlɪŋpflantsə] f climber
Schlips [ʃlɪps] m (-es;-e) necktie
Schlitten ['ʃlɪtən] m (-s;-) sled; (an der Schreibmaschine) carriage
schlit'tenfahren §71 intr go sleigh riding; **mit j-m s.** make life miserable for s.o.
schlittern ['ʃlɪtərn] intr (HABEN & SEIN) slide; (Wagen) skid
Schlittschuh ['ʃlɪtʃu] m ice skate; **S. laufen** skate, go ice-skating
Schlitt'schuhläufer –in §6 mf ice skater
Schlitz [ʃlɪts] m (-es;-e) slit, slot; (Hosen–) fly
schlitz'äugig adj slit-eyed, sloe-eyed
schlitzen ['ʃlɪtsən] tr slit; rip
Schloß [ʃlɔs] n (Schlosses; Schlösser) castle; country mansion; lock; snap, clasp; **hinter S. und Riegel** behind bars; **unter S. und Riegel** under lock and key
Schloße ['ʃlosə] f (-;-n) hailstone
Schlosser ['ʃlɔsər] m (-s;-) mechanic; locksmith
Schloß'graben m moat
Schlot [ʃlot] m (-[e]s;-e & ˵e) chimney, smokestack; (fig) louse

Schlot'baron m (coll) tycoon
Schlot'feger m chimney sweep
schlotterig ['ʃlɔtərɪç] adj loose, dangling; wobbly; (liederlich) slovenly
schlottern ['ʃlɔtərn] intr fit loosely; (baumeln) dangle; (zittern) tremble; (wackeln) wobble
Schlucht [ʃluçt] f (-;-en) gorge; ravine
schluchzen ['ʃluxtsən] intr sob
Schluck [ʃluk] m (-[e]s;-e) gulp; sip
Schluck'auf m (-s;) hiccups
schlucken ['ʃlukən] tr & intr gulp
Schlucker ['ʃlukər] m (-s;-)—armer S. (coll) poor devil
schlucksen ['ʃluksən] intr have the hiccups
schluderig ['ʃludərɪç] adj slipshod
schludern ['ʃludərn] intr do slipshod work
Schlummer ['ʃlumər] m (-s;) slumber
Schlum'merlied n lullaby
schlummern ['ʃlumərn] intr slumber
schlum'mernd adj latent
Schlum'merrolle f cushion
Schlund [ʃlunt] m (-[e]s;-e) gullet; pharynx; (e-s Vulcans) crater; (fig) abyss
Schlund'röhre f esophagus
Schlupf [ʃlupf] m (-[e]s;ːe) hole; (elec, mach) slip
schlüpfen ['ʃlʏpfən] intr (SEIN) slip; sneak
Schlüp'fer m (-s;-) (pair of) panties; (pair of) bloomers
Schlupf'jacke f sweater
Schlupf'loch n hiding place; loophole
schlüpfrig ['ʃlʏpfrɪç] adj slippery; (obszön) off-color
Schlupf'winkel m hiding place; haunt
schlurfen ['ʃlurfən] intr (SEIN) shuffle
schlürfen ['ʃlʏrfən] tr slurp; lap up
Schluß [ʃlus] m (Schlusses; Schlüsse) end, close; (Ablauf) expiration; (Folgerung) conclusion; **S. damit!** time!; cut it out!; **S. folgt** to be concluded; **S. machen mit** put an end to; knock off from (work); break up with (s.o.); **zum S.** in conclusion
Schluß'effekt m upshot
Schlüssel ['ʃlʏsəl] m (-s;-) key; wrench; quota; code key; (fig) key, clue
Schlüs'selbein n collarbone, clavicle
Schlüs'selblume f cowslip; **helle S.** primrose
Schlüs'selbrett n keyboard
Schlüs'selbund m bunch of keys
schlüs'selfertig adj ready for occupancy
Schlüs'selloch n keyhole
Schluß'ergebnis n final result
Schluß'folge f, **Schluß'folgerung** f conclusion, deduction
Schluß'formel f complimentary close
schlüssig ['ʃlʏsɪç] adj determined; logical; (Beweis) conclusive; **sich** [dat] **noch nicht s. sein, ob** be undecided whether
Schluß'licht n (aut) taillight
Schluß'linie f (typ) dash
Schluß'rennen n (sport) final heat
Schluß'runde f (sport) finals
Schluß'schein m sales agreement

Schluß'verkauf m clearance sale
Schmach [ʃmax] f (-;) disgrace, shame; insult; humiliation
schmachten ['ʃmaxtən] intr (vor dat) languish (with); **s. nach** long for
Schmachtfetzen ['ʃmaxtfetsən] m sentimental song or book; melodrama
schmächtig ['ʃmeçtɪç] adj scrawny
Schmachtriemen ['ʃmaxtrimən] m— **den S. enger schnallen** (fig) tighten one's belt
schmach'voll adj disgraceful; humiliating
schmackhaft ['ʃmakhaft] adj tasty
schmähen ['ʃme·ən] tr revile, abuse; speak ill of
schmählich ['ʃmelɪç] adj disgraceful, scandalous; humiliating
Schmährede ['ʃmeredə] f abuse; diatribe
Schmähschrift ['ʃmeʃrɪft] f libel
schmähsüchtig ['ʃmezʏçtɪç] adj abusive
Schmä'hung f (-;-en) abuse; slander
schmal [ʃmal] adj narrow; slim; meager
schmälern ['ʃmelərn] tr curtail; belittle
Schmal'spurbahn f narrow-gauge railroad
Schmalz [ʃmalts] n (-[e]s;) lard, grease; (fig) schmaltz
schmalzen ['ʃmaltsən] tr lard, grease
schmalzig ['ʃmaltsɪç] adj greasy; fatty; (fig) schmaltzy
schmarotzen [ʃma'rɔtsən] intr (bei) sponge (on)
Schmarot'zer m (-s;-) sponger; (zool) parasite
schmarotzerisch [ʃma'rɔtsərɪʃ] adj sponging; (zool) parasitic(al)
Schmarre ['ʃmarə] f (-;-n) scar; scratch
schmarrig ['ʃmarɪç] adj scary
Schmatz [ʃmats] m (-es;-e) hearty kiss
schmatzen ['ʃmatsən] tr (coll) kiss loudly ‖ intr smack one's lips
Schmaus [ʃmaus] m (-es;ːe) feast; treat
schmausen ['ʃmauzən] intr (von) feast (on)
schmecken ['ʃmekən] tr taste, sample; (fig) stand ‖ intr taste good; **s. nach** taste like
Schmeichelei [ʃmaɪçə'laɪ] f (-;-en) flattery; coaxing
schmeichelhaft ['ʃmaɪçəlhaft] adj flattering
schmeicheln ['ʃmaɪçəln] ref—**sich** [dat] **s. zu** (inf) pride oneself on (ger) ‖ intr be flattering; (dat) flatter
Schmeich'ler –in §6 mf flatterer
schmeichlerisch ['ʃmaɪçlərɪʃ] adj flattering; complimentary; fawning
schmeißen ['ʃmaɪsən] §53 tr (coll) throw; (coll) manage; **e-e Runde Bier s.** set up a round of beer ‖ ref—**mit Geld um sich s.** throw money around
Schmelz [ʃmelts] m (-es;-e) enamel; glaze; melodious ring; (fig) bloom
schmelzen ['ʃmeltsən] §133 tr melt; smelt ‖ intr (SEIN) melt; (fig) soften

schmel'zend adj mellow; melodious
Schmelzerei [ʃmɛltsə'raɪ] f (-;-en) foundry
schmelz'flüssig adj molten
Schmelz'hütte f foundry
Schmelz'käse m soft cheese
Schmelz'ofen m smelting furnace
Schmelz'punkt m melting point
Schmelz'tiegel m crucible, melting pot
Schmer [ʃmer] m & n (-s;) fat, grease
Schmer'bauch m (coll) potbelly
Schmerz [ʃmerts] m (-es;-en) pain, ache; **mit Schmerzen** (coll) anxiously, impatiently
schmerzen ['ʃmertsən] tr & intr hurt
schmer'zend adj aching, sore
Schmer'zensgeld n damages (*for pain or anguish*)
Schmer'zenskind n problem child
schmerz'haft adj painful, aching
schmerz'lich adj painful, severe
schmerz'lindernd adj soothing
schmerz'los adj painless
Schmerz'schwelle f threshold of pain
Schmetterling ['ʃmetərlɪŋ] m (-s;-e) butterfly
Schmet'terlingsstil m (sport) butterfly
schmettern ['ʃmetərn] tr smash; **zu Boden s.** knock down || intr (*Trompete*) blare; (*Vogel*) warble
Schmied [ʃmit] m (-[e]s;-e) smith
Schmiede ['ʃmidə] f (-;-n) forge; blacksmith shop
Schmie'deeisen n wrought iron
Schmie'dehammer m sledge hammer
schmieden ['ʃmidən] tr forge; hammer; (*Pläne, usw.*) devise, concoct
schmiegen ['ʃmigən] tr—**das Kinn (or die Wange) in die Hand s.** prop one's chin (or cheek) in one's hand || ref (an acc) snuggle up (to); **sich s. und biegen vor** (dat) bow and scrape before
schmiegsam ['ʃmikzam] adj flexible
Schmier– [ʃmir] comb.fm. grease, lubricating; smearing
Schmiere ['ʃmirə] f (-;-n) grease; lubricant; salve; (*Schmutz*) muck; (fig) mess; (fig) spanking; (theat) barnstormers; **S. stehen** be the lookout man
schmieren ['ʃmirən] tr grease, lubricate; smear; (*Butter*) spread; (*Brot*) butter; (*bestechen*) bribe; **j-m e-e s.** (coll) paste s.o.; **wie geschmiert** like greased lightning || ref—**sich** [dat] **die Kehle s.** (coll) wet one's whistle || intr scribble
Schmie'renkomödiant –in §7 mf (theat) barnstormer, ham
Schmiererei [ʃmirə'raɪ] f (-;-en) greasing; smearing; scribbling
Schmier'fink m scrawler; (*Schmutzkerl*) dirty fellow
Schmier'geld n (coll) bribe; (coll) hush money; (pol) slush fund
schmierig ['ʃmirɪç] adj smeary, greasy; oily; (*Geschäfte*) dirty
Schmier'käse m cheese spread
Schmier'mittel n lubricant
Schmier'pistole f, **Schmier'presse** f grease gun
Schmie'rung f (-;-en) lubrication

Schminke ['ʃmɪŋkə] f (-;-n) rouge; make-up
schminken ['ʃmɪŋkən] tr apply make-up to; rouge; **die Lippen s.** put on lipstick || ref put on make-up
Schminkunterlage ['ʃmɪŋkuntərlagə] f base
Schmirgel ['ʃmɪrgəl] m (-s;) emery
Schmir'gelleinen n, **Schmir'gelleinwand** f emery cloth
Schmir'gelpapier n emery paper
Schmir'gelscheibe f emery wheel
Schmiß [ʃmɪs] m (Schmisses; Schmisse) (coll) stroke, blow; (coll) gash; (coll) dueling scar; (coll) zip
schmissig ['ʃmɪsɪç] adj (coll) snazzy
schmollen ['ʃmɔlən] intr pout, sulk
schmolz [ʃmɔlts] pret of **schmelzen**
Schmorbraten ['ʃmorbratən] m braised meat
schmoren ['ʃmorən] tr braise, stew || intr (fig) swelter; **laß ihn s.!** let him stew!
schmuck [ʃmʊk] adj nice, cute; smart, dapper; (*sauber*) neat || **Schmuck** m (-[e]s;) ornament; decoration; trimmings; trinket(s); jewelry
schmücken ['ʃmykən] tr adorn; decorate, trim; (*Aufsatz*) embellish || ref spruce up, dress up
Schmuck'kästchen n jewel box
schmuck'los adj unadorned, plain
Schmuck'waren pl jewelry
Schmuddel ['ʃmʊdəl] m (-s;-) slob
schmuddelig ['ʃmʊdəlɪç] adj dirty
Schmuggel ['ʃmʊgəl] m (-s;), **Schmuggelei** [ʃmʊgə'laɪ] f (-;-en) smuggling
schmuggeln ['ʃmʊgəln] tr & intr smuggle
Schmug'gelware f contraband
Schmuggler –in ['ʃmʊglər(ɪn)] §6 mf smuggler
schmunzeln ['ʃmʊntsəln] intr grin || **Schmunzeln** n (-s;) big grin
Schmutz [ʃmʊts] m (-es;) dirt, filth; (*Zote*) smut
schmutzen ['ʃmʊtsən] tr & intr soil
Schmutz'fink m (coll) slob
Schmutz'fleck m stain, smudge, blotch
schmut'zig adj dirty
Schnabel ['ʃnabəl] m (-s;ː) beak, bill; **halt den S.!** (sl) shut up!
Schna'belhieb m peck
schnäbeln ['ʃnebəln] tr & intr peck; (fig) kiss
Schnalle ['ʃnalə] f (-;-n) buckle; (vulg) whore
schnallen ['ʃnalən] tr buckle, fasten
schnalzen ['ʃnaltsən] intr—**mit den Fingern s.** snap one's fingers; **mit der Zunge s.** click one's tongue
schnapp [ʃnap] interj snap!
schnappen ['ʃnapən] tr grab; (*Dieb*) nab || intr snap; **ins Schloß s.** snap shut; **mit den Fingern s.** snap one's fingers; **nach Luft s.** gasp for air; **s. nach** snap at
Schnapp'messer n jackknife
Schnapp'schuß m (phot) snapshot
Schnaps [ʃnaps] m (-es;ː e) hard liquor
Schnaps'brennerei f distillery
Schnaps'bruder m (coll) booze hound

Schnaps'idee f (coll) crazy idea
schnarchen ['ʃnarçən] intr snore
Schnarre ['ʃnarə] f (-;-n) rattle
schnarren ['ʃnarən] intr rattle; (Säge) buzz; (Insekten) drone, buzz
schnattern ['ʃnatərn] intr (Enten) cackle; (Zähne) chatter; (fig) gab
schnauben ['ʃnaubən] intr pant, puff; (Pferd) snort; **nach Rache s.** breathe revenge; **vor Wut s.** fume with rage ‖ ref blow one's nose
schnaufen ['ʃnaufən] intr pant; wheeze
Schnau'fer m (-s;-) (coll) deep breath
Schnauzbart ['ʃnautsbart] m mustache
Schnauze ['ʃnautsə] f (-;-n) snout, muzzle; spout; (sl) snoot; (sl) big mouth
Schnauzer ['ʃnautsər] m (-s;-) schnauzer
schnauzig ['ʃnautsɪç] adj rude
Schnecke ['ʃnɛkə] f (-;-n) snail; (Nacht-) slug; (e-r Säule) volute; spiral; (anat) cochlea; (mach) worm; (e-r Violine) (mus) scroll
Schneckenhaus (Schnek'kenhaus) n snail shell
Schneckentempo (Schnek'kentempo) n (fig) snail's pace
Schnee [ʃne] m (-s;) snow; whipped egg white
Schnee'besen m eggbeater
Schnee'brett n snow slide, avalanche
Schnee'brille f snow goggles
Schnee'decke f blanket of snow
Schnee'flocke f snowflake
Schnee'gestöber n snow flurry
schneeig ['ʃne·ɪç] adj snowy
Schnee'matsch m slush
Schnee'pflug m snowplow
Schnee'schaufel f, **Schnee'schippe** f snow shovel
Schnee'schläger m eggbeater
Schnee'schmelze f thaw
Schnee'treiben n blizzard
schneeverweht ['ʃnefɛrvet] adj snowbound
Schnee'verwehung f snowdrift
Schnee'wehe f snowdrift
Schneewittchen ['ʃnevɪtçən] n (-s;) Snow White
Schneid [ʃnaɪt] m (-[e]s;) (coll) pluck; (Mut) (coll) guts
Schneid'brenner m cutting torch
Schneide ['ʃnaɪdə] f (-;-n) (cutting) edge; (e-s Hobels) blade; **auf des Messers S.** (fig) on the razor's edge
Schnei'debrett n cutting board
Schnei'demaschine f cutter, slicer
Schnei'demühle f sawmill
schneiden ['ʃnaɪdən] §106 tr cut; (Baum) prune; (Fingernägel) pare; (Hecke) trim; (nicht grüßen) snub; (surg) operate on; (tennis) slice; **Gesichter s.** make faces; **klein s.** cut up ‖ ref (fig) be mistaken; (fig) be disappointed; (math) intersect; **sich in den Finger s.** cut one's finger ‖ intr cut
Schnei'der (-s;-) m cutter; tailor
Schneiderei [ʃnaɪdə'raɪ] f (-;-en) tailoring; (Werkstatt) tailorshop
Schnei'derin f (-;-nen) dressmaker

schneidern ['ʃnaɪdərn] tr make ‖ intr do tailoring; be a dressmaker
Schnei'derpuppe f dummy
Schnei'dezahn m incisor
schneidig ['ʃnaɪdɪç] adj sharp-edged; energetic; smart, sharp
schneien ['ʃnaɪ·ən] impers—es schneit it is snowing
Schneise ['ʃnaɪzə] f (-;-n) lane (between rows of trees)
schnell [ʃnɛl] adj fast, quick
Schnellauf (Schnell'lauf) m race; sprint; speed skating
Schnell'bahn f high-speed railroad
Schnelle ['ʃnɛlə] f (-;-n) speed; (Strom-) rapids; **auf die S.** (coll) in a hurry, very briefly
schnellen ['ʃnɛlən] tr let fly ‖ intr (SEIN) spring, jump up; (Preise) shoot up; **mit dem Finger s.** snap one's fingers
Schnell'gang m (aut) overdrive
Schnellhefter ['ʃnɛlhɛftər] m (-s;-) folder, file
Schnell'imbiß m snack
Schnell'kraft f elasticity
schnellstens ['ʃnɛlstəns] adv as fast as possible
Schnell'verfahren n quick process; (jur) summary proceeding
Schnell'zug m express train
Schneppe ['ʃnɛpə] f (-;-n) spout; (sl) prostitute
schneuzen ['ʃnɔɪtsən] ref blow one's nose
schniegeln ['ʃnigəln] ref dress up; **geschniegelt und gebügelt** dressed to kill
schnipfeln ['ʃnɪpfəln] tr & intr snip
Schnippchen ['ʃnɪpçən] n—j-m ein S. schlagen (coll) pull a fast one on s.o.; outwit s.o.
Schnippel ['ʃnɪpəl] m & n (-s;-) chip
schnippeln ['ʃnɪpəln] tr & intr snip
schnippen ['ʃnɪpən] intr—mit den Fingern s. (coll) snap one's fingers
schnippisch ['ʃnɪpɪʃ] adj fresh ‖ adv pertly; **s. erwidern** snap back
schnitt [ʃnɪt] pret of schneiden ‖ Schnitt m (-[e]s;-e) cut, incision; (Kerbe) notch; (Schnitte) slice; (Quer-) profile, cross section; (Durch-) average; (e-s Anzuges) cut, style; (Gewinn) cut; (agr) reaping; (bb) edge; (cin) editing; (geom) intersection; **weicher Schnitt** (cin) dissolve
Schnitt'ansicht f sectional view
Schnitt'ball m (tennis) slice
Schnitt'blumen pl cut flowers
Schnitt'bohnen pl string beans
Schnittchen ['ʃnɪtçən] n (-s;-) thin slice; sandwich
Schnitte ['ʃnɪtə] f (-;-n) slice
Schnit'ter -in §6 mf reaper, mower
Schnitt'fläche f (geom) plane
Schnitt'holz n lumber
schnittig ['ʃnɪtɪç] adj smart-looking; (aut) streamlined
Schnitt'lauch ['ʃnɪtlaux] m (-[e]s;) (bot) chive
Schnitt'linie f (geom) secant
Schnitt'meister m (cin) editor

Schnitt′muster n pattern (*of dress, etc.*)
Schnitt′punkt m intersection
Schnitt′waren pl dry goods
Schnitt′wunde f cut, gash
Schnitz [ʃnɪts] m (-es;-e) cut; slice; chop; chip
Schnitzel [ʃnɪtsəl] n (-s;-) chip; slice; shred; (*Abfälle*) parings; (culin) cutlet
schnitzeln [ʃnɪtsəln] tr cut up; shred; (*Holz*) whittle
schnitzen [ʃnɪtsən] tr carve
Schnit′zer m (-s;-) carver; (*Fehler*) blunder; **grober S.** boner
Schnitzerei [ʃnɪtsəˈraɪ] f (-;-en) wood carving, carved work
schnob [ʃnop] pret of **schnauben**
schnodderig [ʃnɔdərɪç] adj brash
schnöde [ʃnøːdə] adj vile; disdainful; (*Gewinn*) filthy
Schnorchel [ʃnɔrçəl] m (-s;-) snorkel
Schnörkel [ʃnœrkəl] m (-s;-) (*beim Schreiben*) flourish; (fig) frills; (archit) scroll
schnorren [ʃnɔrən] tr (coll) chisel, bum ‖ intr (coll) sponge, chisel
Schnösel [ʃnøːzəl] m (-s;-) wise guy
schnüffeln [ʃnʏfəln] intr snoop around; (**an** dat) sniff (at)
Schnüff′ler –in §6 mf (coll) snoop
Schnuller [ʃnʊlər] m (-s;-) pacifier
Schnultze [ʃnʊltsə] f (-;-n) (coll) tear-jerker
schnultzig [ʃnʊltsɪç] adj (coll) corny, mawkish
schnupfen [ʃnʊpfən] tr snuff ‖ intr take snuff ‖ **Schnupfen** m (-s;-) cold; **den S. bekommen** catch a cold
Schnupftabak [ʃnʊpftabak] m snuff
schnuppe [ʃnʊpə] adj—**das ist mir s.** it's all the same to me ‖ **Schnuppe** f (-;-n) shooting star; (e-r Kerze) snuff
Schnur [ʃnur] f (-;ːe & -en) string; (*Band*) braid; (elec) flexible cord; **nach der S.** regularly
Schnürband [ʃnʏrbant] n (-[e]s;ːer) shoestring; corset lace
Schnürchen [ʃnʏrçən] n (-s;-) string; **etw am S. haben** have at one's fingertips; **wie am S.** like clockwork
schnüren [ʃnʏrən] tr tie; lace; (*Perlen*) string ‖ ref put on a corset
schnur′gerade adj straight ‖ adv straight, as the crow flies
schnurr [ʃnur] interj purr!; buzz!
Schnurrbart [ʃnurbart] m mustache
schnurren [ʃnurən] intr (*Katze*) purr; (*Rad*) whir; (*Maschine*) hum; (*schnorren*) sponge, chisel
schnurrig [ʃnurɪç] adj funny; queer
Schnürschuh [ʃnʏrʃu] m oxford shoe
Schnürsenkel [ʃnʏrzɛŋkəl] m shoestring
schnurstracks [ʃnurˈtraks] adv right away; directly; **s. entgegengesetzt** diametrically opposite; **s. losgehen auf** (acc) make a beeline for
schob [ʃop] pret of **schieben**
Schober [ʃobər] m (-s;-) stack
Schock [ʃɔk] m (-[e]s;-s) shock ‖ n (-[e]s;-e) threescore
schockant [ʃɔˈkant] adj shocking

schockieren [ʃɔˈkirən] tr shock
schofel [ʃofəl] adj mean; miserable; (*schäbig*) shabby; (*geizig*) stingy
Schöffe [ʃœfə] m (-n;-n) juror
Schokolade [ʃokɔˈladə] f (-;-n) chocolate
schokoladen [ʃokɔˈladən] adj chocolate
Schokola′dentafel f chocolate bar
scholl [ʃɔl] pret of **schallen**
Scholle [ʃɔlə] f (-;-n) clod; sod; stratum; ice floe; (ichth) sole; **heimatliche S.** native soil
schon [ʃon] adv already; as early as; yet, as yet; (*sogar*) even; (*bloß*) the bare, the mere; **ich komme s.!** all right, I'm coming!; **s. am folgenden Tage** on the very next day; **s. der Gedanke** the mere thought; **s. früher** before now; **s. gut!** all right!; **s. immer** always; **s. lange** long since, for a long time; **s. wieder** again
schön [ʃøn] adj beautiful; nice; (*Künste*) fine; (*Mann*) handsome; (*Summe*) nice round; (*Geschlecht*) fair; **schönen Dank!** many thanks!; **schönen Gruß an** (acc) best regards to ‖ adv nicely; **der Hund macht s.** the dog sits up and begs; **s. warm** nice and warm
schonen [ʃonən] tr spare; take it easy on; treat with consideration ‖ ref take care of oneself
scho′nend adj careful; considerate
schön′färben tr gloss over
Schon′frist f period of grace
Schon′gang m (aut) overdrive
Schön′heit f (-;-en) beauty
Schön′heitsfehler m flaw
Schön′heitskönigin f beauty queen
Schön′heitspflege f beauty treatment
schön′tun §154 intr (dat) flatter; (dat) flirt (with)
Scho′nung f (-;-en) care, careful treatment; mercy; consideration; tree nursery; wild-game preserve
scho′nungslos adj unsparing; merciless; relentless
scho′nungsvoll adj considerate
Schon′zeit f (hunt) closed season
Schopf [ʃɔpf] m (-[e]s;ːe) tuft of hair; (orn) crest
schöpfen [ʃœpfən] tr draw; bail; scoop, ladle; (*frische Luft*) breathe; (*Mut*) take; **Verdacht s.** become suspicious; **wieder Atem** (or **Luft**) **s.** (fig) breathe freely again
Schöp′fer m (-s;-) creator; author; composer; painter; sculptor; dipper, ladle
schöpferisch [ʃœpfərɪʃ] adj creative
Schöp′ferkraft f creative power
Schöpf′kelle f scoop
Schöpf′löffel m ladle
Schöp′fung f (-;-en) creation
Schoppen [ʃɔpən] m (-s;-) pint; glass of beer, glass of wine
schor [ʃor] pret of **scheren**
Schorf [ʃɔrf] m (-[e]s;-e) scab
Schornstein [ʃɔrnʃtaɪn] m chimney; smokestack
Schorn′steinfeger m chimney sweeper
Schoß [ʃos] m (**Schosses; Schosse**)

sprout ‖ [ʃos] *m* (-es;⸚e) lap; womb; (fig) bosom; **die Hände in den S. legen** cross one's arms; (fig) be idle

Schößling ['ʃœslɪŋ] *m* (-s;-e) shoot

Schote ['ʃotə] *f* (-;-n) pod, shell

Schotte ['ʃotə] *m* (-n;-n) Scotchman ‖ *f* (-;-n) (naut) bulkhead

Schotter ['ʃotər] *m* (-s;-) gravel; macadam, crushed stone; (rr) ballast

Schottin ['ʃotɪn] *f* (-;-nen) Scotchwoman

schottisch ['ʃotɪʃ] *adj* Scotch

schraffieren [ʃra'firən] *tr* hatch

schräg [ʃrek] *adj* oblique; (*abfallend*) slanting, sloping; diagonal ‖ *adv* obliquely; **s. gegenüber von** diagonally across from; **s. geneigt** sloping

Schräg'linie *f* diagonal

schrak [ʃrak] *pret* of **schrecken**

Schramme ['ʃramə] *f* (-;-n) scratch, abrasion; scar

schrammen ['ʃramən] *tr* scratch; skin

Schrank [ʃraŋk] *m* (-[e]s;⸚e) closet

Schranke ['ʃraŋkə] *f* (-;-n) barrier; (fig) bounds, limit; (jur) bar; (rr) gate; (sport) starting gate

schran'kenlos *adj* boundless; exaggerated

Schran'kenwärter *m* (rr) signalman

Schrank'fach *n* compartment

Schrank'koffer *m* wardrobe trunk

Schrapnell [ʃrap'nɛl] *n* (-s;-e & -s) shrapnel, piece of shrapnel

Schraubdeckel ['ʃraupdɛkəl] *m* screw-on cap

Schraube ['ʃraubə] *f* (-;-n) screw; bolt; (aer, naut) propeller

schrauben ['ʃraubən] *tr* screw; **in die Höhe s.** raise ‖ *ref*—**sich in die Höhe s.** circle higher and higher

Schrau'benflügel *m* propeller blade

Schrau'bengang *m*, **Schrau'bengewinde** *n* thread (of a screw)

Schrau'benmutter *f* (-;-n) nut

Schrau'benschlüssel *m* wrench; **verstellbarer S.** monkey wrench

Schrau'benstrahl *m*, **Schrau'benstrom** *m* (aer) slipstream

Schraubenzieher ['ʃraubəntsi·ər] *m* (-s;-) screwdriver

Schraubstock ['ʃraupʃtɔk] *m* vice

Schrebergarten ['ʃrebərgartən] *m* garden plot (*at edge of town*)

Schreck [ʃrek] *m* (-[e]s;-e) var of **Schrecken**

Schreck'bild *n* frightful sight; boogeyman

schrecken ['ʃrekən] *tr* frighten, scare ‖ **Schrecken** *m* (-s;-) fright, fear

Schreckensbotschaft (**Schrek'kensbotschaft**) *f* alarming news

Schreckensherrschaft (**Schrek'kensherrschaft**) *f* reign of terror

Schreckenskammer (**Schrek'kenskammer**) *f* chamber of horrors

Schreckensregiment (**Schrek'kensregiment**) *n* reign of teror, terrorism

Schreckenstat (**Schrek'kenstat**) *f* atrocity

schreck'haft *adj* timid

schreck'lich *adj* frightful, terrible

Schrecknis ['ʃrɛknɪs] *n* (-ses;-se) horror

Schreck'schuß *m* warning shot

Schreck'sekunde *f* reaction time

Schrei [ʃraɪ] *m* (-[e]s;-e) cry, shout; **letzter S.** latest fashion

Schreib- [ʃraɪp] *comb.fm.* writing

Schreib'art *f* style; spelling

Schreib'bedarf *m* stationery

Schreib'block *m* writing pad, note pad

schreiben ['ʃraɪbən] §62 *tr* write; spell; type; **ins Konzept s.** make a rough draft of; **ins reine s.** make a clean copy; **Noten s.** copy music ‖ *ref* spell one's name ‖ *intr* write; spell; type ‖ **Schreiben** *n* (-s;-) writing; (com) letter

Schrei'ber *m* (-s;-) writer; clerk; recording instrument, recorder

schreib'faul *adj* too lazy to write

Schreib'feder *f* pen

Schreib'fehler *m* slip of the pen

Schreib'heft *n* copybook, exercise book

Schreib'mappe *f* portfolio

Schreib'maschine *f* typewriter; **mit der S. geschrieben** typed; **S. schreiben** type

Schreib'maschinenfarbband *n* (-[e]s; ⸚er) typewriter ribbon

Schreib'maschinenschreiber –in §6 *mf* typist

Schreib'maschinenschrift *f* typescript

Schreib'materialien *pl*, **Schreib'papier** *n* stationery

Schreib'schrift *f* (typ) script

Schreib'stube *f* (mil) orderly room

Schreib'tisch *m* desk

Schrei'bung *f* (-;-en) spelling

Schreib'unterlage *f* desk pad

Schreib'waren *pl* stationery

Schreib'warenhandlung *f* stationery store

Schreibweise *f* style; spelling

Schreib'zeug *n* writing materials

schreien ['ʃraɪ·ən] §135 *tr* cry, shout, scream, howl ‖ *ref*—**sich heiser s.** shout oneself hoarse; **sich tot s.** yell one's lungs out ‖ *intr* cry, shout, scream, howl; (*Esel*) bray; (*Eule*) screech; (*Schwein*) squeal; **s. nach** clamor for; **s. über** (*acc*) cry out against; **s. vor** (*dat*) shout for (*joy*); cry out in (*pain*); roar with (*laughter*) ‖ **Schreien** *n* (-s;) shouting; **das ist zum S.!** that's a scream!

schrei'end *adj* shrill; (*Farbe*) loud; (*Unrecht*) flagrant

Schrei'hals *m* (coll) crybaby

Schrei'krampf *m* crying fit

Schrein [ʃraɪn] *m* (-[e]s;-e) reliquary

Schreiner ['ʃraɪnər] *m* (-s;-) carpenter; cabinetmaker

schreiten ['ʃraɪtən] §86 *intr* (SEIN) step; stride; **zur Abstimmung s.** proceed to vote; **zur Tat s.** proceed to act

schrie [ʃri] *pret* of **schreien**

schrieb [ʃrip] *pret* of **schreiben**

Schrift [ʃrɪft] *f* (-;-en) writing; handwriting; letter, character; document; book; publication; periodical; (*auf Münzen*) legend; (typ) type, font; **die Heilige S.** Holy Scripture; **nach der S. sprechen** speak standard German

Schrift′art f type, font
Schrift′auslegung f exegesis
Schrift′bild n type face
Schrift′deutsch n literary German
Schrift′führer −in §6 mf secretary
Schrift′leiter −in §6 mf editor
schrift′lich adj written || adv in writing; s. **wiedergeben** transcribe
Schrift′satz m (jur) brief; (typ) composition
Schrift′setzer m typesetter
Schrift′sprache f literary language
Schriftsteller −in [′ʃrɪftʃtelər(ɪn)] §6 mf writer, author
Schrift′stück n piece of writing; document
Schrifttum [′ʃrɪfttum] n (−s;) literature
Schrift′verkehr m, **Schrift′wechsel** m correspondence
Schrift′zeichen n letter, character
schrill [ʃrɪl] adj shrill
schrillen [′ʃrɪlən] intr ring loudly
schritt [ʃrɪt] pret of **schreiten** || **Schritt** m (−[e]s;−e) step; pace; stride; (e−r Hose) crotch; (fig) step
Schritt′macher m pacemaker
schritt′weise adv gradually; step by step
schroff [ʃrɔf] adj steep; rugged; rude, uncouth; rough, harsh; (Ablehnung, Widerspruch) flat
schröpfen [′ʃrœpfən] tr (fig) milk, fleece; (med) bleed, cup
Schrot [ʃrot] m & n (−[e]s;−e) scrap; (Getreide) crushed grain, grits; (zum Schießen) buckshot
Schrot′brot n whole grain bread
Schrot′flinte f shotgun
Schrot′korn n, **Schrot′kugel** f pellet
Schrott [ʃrɔt] m (−[e]s;) scrap metal
Schrott′platz m junk yard
schrubben [′ʃrubən] tr scrub
Schrulle [′ʃrulə] f (−;−n) (coll) nutty idea
schrul′lenhaft, schrullig [′ʃrulɪç] adj whimsical
schrumpelig [′ʃrumpəlɪç] adj crumpled; wrinkled, shriveled
schrumpeln [′ʃrumpəln] intr shrivel
schrumpfen [′ʃrumpfən] intr (SEIN) shrink; shrivel; (pathol) atrophy
Schub [ʃup] m (−[e]s;−e) shove, push; batch; (phys) thrust
Schub′fach n drawer
Schub′karre f, **Schub′karren** m wheelbarrow
Schub′kasten m drawer
Schub′kraft f thrust
Schub′lade f drawer
Schub′leistung f thrust
Schubs [ʃups] m (−es;−e) (coll) shove
schubsen [′ʃupsən] tr & intr shove
Schub′stange f (aut) connecting rod
schüchtern [′ʃʏçtərn] adj shy, bashful
schuf [ʃuf] pret of **schaffen**
Schuft [ʃuft] m (−[e]s;−e) cad
schuften [′ʃuftən] intr drudge, slave
Schufterei [ʃuftəˈraɪ] f (−;) drudgery; (Schuftigkeit) meanness
schuftig [′ʃuftɪç] adj (fig) rotten
Schuh [ʃu] m (−[e]s;−e) shoe; boot
Schuh′band n (−[e]s;−er) shoestring

Schuhflicker [′ʃuflɪkər] m (−s;−) shoe repairman, shoemaker
Schuh′krem m shoe polish
Schuh′laden m shoe store
Schuh′leisten m last
Schuh′löffel m shoehorn
Schuh′macher m shoemaker
Schuhplattler [′ʃuplatlər] m (−s;−) Bavarian folk dance
Schuh′putzer m shoeshine boy
Schuh′sohle f sole
Schuhspanner [′ʃuʃpanər] m (−s;−) shoetree
Schuh′werk n footwear
Schuh′wichse f shoe polish
Schuh′zeug n footwear
Schul− [ʃul] comb.fm. school
Schul′amt n school board
Schul′arbeit f homework; (Aust) classroom work
Schul′aufsicht f school board
Schul′bank f (−;−e) school desk
Schul′behörde f school board; board of education
Schul′beispiel n (fig) test case
Schul′besuch m attendance at school
Schul′bildung f schooling, education
schuld [ʃult] adj at fault, to blame || **Schuld** f (−;−en) debt; fault; guilt
schuld′bewußt adj conscious of one's guilt
schulden [′ʃuldən] tr owe
schuld′haft adj culpable || **Schuld′haft** f imprisonment for debt
Schul′diener m school janitor
schuldig [′ʃuldɪç] adj guilty; responsible; j−m etw s. sein owe s.o. s.th. || **Schuldige** §5 mf culprit; guilty party
Schul′digkeit f (−;−en) duty, obligation; seine S. tun do one's duty
Schul′direktor −in §7 mf principal
schuld′los adj innocent
Schuld′losigkeit f (−;) innocence
Schuldner −in [′ʃuldnər(ɪn)] §6 mf debtor
Schuld′schein m promissory note, IOU
Schuld′spruch m verdict of guilty
Schuld′verschreibung f promissory note, IOU; (Obligation) bond
Schule [′ʃulə] f (−;−n) school; auf der S. in school; S. machen (fig) set a precedent; von der S. abgehen quit school
schulen [′ʃulən] tr train; (pol) indoctrinate
Schüler [′ʃylər] m (−s;−) pupil (in grammar school or high school); trainee; (Jünger) disciple
Schü′leraustausch m student exchange
Schülerin [′ʃylərɪn] f (−;−nen) pupil
Schul′film m educational film
Schul′flug m training flight
schul′frei adj−schulfreier **Tag** holiday; s. haben have off
Schul′gelände n school grounds; campus
Schul′geld n tuition
Schul′gelehrsamkeit f book learning
Schul′hof m schoolyard, playground
Schul′kamerad m school chum
Schul′lehrer −in §6 mf schoolteacher
Schul′mappe f schoolbag
Schul′meister m schoolmaster; pedant
schul′meistern intr criticize

Schul'ordnung *f* school regulation
Schul'pflicht *f* compulsory school attendance
schul'pflichtig *adj* of school age; **schulpflichtiges Alter** school age
Schul'plan *m* curriculum
Schul'ranzen *m* schoolbag
Schul'rat *m* (-[e]s;ⁿe) (educ) superintendent
Schul'reise *f* field trip
Schul'schiff *n* training ship
Schul'schluß *m* close of school
Schul'schwester *f* teaching nun
Schul'stunde *f* lesson, period
Schul'tasche *f* schoolbag
Schulter ['ʃʊltər] *f* (-;-n) shoulder
Schul'terblatt *n* shoulder blade
schul'terfrei *adj* off-the-shoulder; (*trägerfrei*) strapless
schultern ['ʃʊltərn] *tr* shoulder
Schul'terstück *n* epaulet
Schul'unterricht *m* instruction; schooling; **im S.** in school
Schul'wesen *n* school system
Schul'zeugnis *n* report card
Schul'zimmer *n* classroom
Schul'zwang *m* compulsory education
schummeln ['ʃʊməln] *intr* (coll) cheat
schund [ʃʊnt] *pret* of **schinden** ‖ **Schund** *m* (-[e]s;) junk, trash
Schund'literatur *f* trashy literature
Schund'roman *m* dime novel
Schupo ['ʃupo] *m* (-s;-s) (**Schutzpolizist**) policeman, copy ‖ *f* (-;) (**Schutzpolizei**) police
Schuppe [ʃupə] *f* (-;-n) scale; **Schuppen** dandruff
schuppen ['ʃupən] *tr* scale; scrape ‖ **Schuppen** *m* (-s;-) shed; (aer) hangar; (aut) garage
schuppig ['ʃupɪç] *adj* scaly, flaky
Schups [ʃups] *m* (-es;-e) shove
schupsen ['ʃupsən] *tr* shove
Schüreisen ['ʃyraɪzən] *n* poker
schüren ['ʃyrən] *tr* poke, stir; (fig) stir up, foment
schürfen ['ʃyrfən] *tr* scratch, scrape; dig for ‖ *intr* (**nach**) prospect (for)
schurigeln ['ʃurigəln] *tr* (coll) bully
Schurke ['ʃurkə] *m* (-n;-n) bum, punk
Schur'kenstreich *m*, **Schur'kentat** *f*, **Schurkerei** [ʃurkə'raɪ] *f* (-;-en) mean trick
schurkisch ['ʃurkɪʃ] *adj* mean, lowdown
Schürze ['ʃyrtsə] *f* (-;-n) apron
schürzen ['ʃyrtsən] *tr* tuck up; tie
Schür'zenband *n* (-[e]s;ⁿer) apron
Schür'zenjäger *m* skirt chaser, wolf
Schuß [ʃus] *m* (**Schusses**; **Schüsse**) shot; (*Ladung*) round; (*Schußwunde*) gunshot wound; (*rasche Bewegung*) rush; (*Brot*) batch; (bot) shoot; (culin) dash; (sport) shot; **blinder S.** blank; **e-n S. abgeben** fire a shot; **ein S. ins Blaue** a wild shot; **ein S. ins Schwarze** a bull's-eye; **im S. haben** have under control; **im vollen S.** in full swing; **in S. bekommen** get going; **in S. bringen** get (*s.th.*) going; **j-m vor den S. kommen** come within s.o.'s range; (fig) come across s.o.; **scharfer S.**

live round; **weit vom S.** out of harm's way
Schüssel ['ʃysəl] *f* (-;-n) bowl; (fig) dish
schuß'fest, schuß'sicher *adj* bulletproof
Schuß'waffe *f* firearm
Schuß'weite *f* range
Schuster ['ʃustər] *m* (-s;-) shoemaker; (fig) bungler
schustern ['ʃustərn] *intr* bungle
Schutt [ʃut] *m* (-es;) rubbish; rubble
Schutt'abladeplatz *m* dump
Schüttboden ['ʃytbodən] *m* granary
Schüttelfrost ['ʃytəlfrost] *m* shivers
schütteln ['ʃytəln] *tr* shake; **j-m die Hand s.** shake hands with s.o.
schütten ['ʃytən] *tr* pour, spill ‖ *impers* —**es schüttet** it is pouring
Schutz [ʃuts] *m* (-es;) protection, defense; (*Obdach*) shelter; (*Deckung*) cover; (*Schirm*) screen; (*Schutzgeleit*) safeguard; **zu S. und Trutz** defensive and offensive
Schutz'brille *f* safety goggles
Schütze ['ʃytsə] *m* (-n;-n) marksman, shot; (astr) Sagittarius; (mil) rifleman ‖ *f* (-;-n) sluice gate
schützen ['ʃytsən] *tr* (**gegen**) protect (against), defend (against); (**vor** *dat*) preserve (from) ‖ **Schützen** *m* (-s;-) tex) shuttle
schüt'zend *adj* protective; tutelary
Schutz'engel *m* guardian angle
Schüt'zengraben *m* (mil) foxhole
Schüt'zenkompanie *f* rifle company
Schüt'zenkönig *m* crack shot
Schüt'zenloch *n* (mil) foxhole
Schüt'zenmine *f* anti-personnel mine
Schutz'geleit *n* escort; safe conduct; (aer) air cover; (nav) convoy
Schutz'glocke *f* (aer) umbrella
Schutz'gott *m*, **Schutz'göttin** *f* tutelary deity
Schutz'haft *f* protective custody
Schutzheilige §5 *mf* patron saint
Schutz'herr *m* protector; patron
Schutz'herrin *f* protectress; patroness
Schutz'impfung *f* immunization
Schutz'insel *f* traffic island
Schützling ['ʃytslɪŋ] *m* (-s;-e) ward
schutz'los *adj* defenseless
Schutz'mann *m* (-[e]s;ⁿer & -leute) policeman
Schutz'marke *f* trademark
Schutz'mittel *n* preservative; preventive
Schutz'patron -**in** §8 *mf* patron saint
Schutz'polizei *f* police
Schutz'polizist *m* policeman, cop
Schutz'scheibe *f* (aut) windshield
Schutz'staffel *f* SS troops
Schutz'umschlag *m* dust jacket
Schutz-'und-Trutz-'Bündnis *f* defensive and offensive alliance
Schutz'waffe *f* defensive weapon
Schutz'zoll *m* protective tariff
Schwabe ['ʃvabə] *m* (-n;-n) Swabian
Schwaben ['ʃvabən] *n* (-s;) Swabia
Schwäbin ['ʃvebɪn] *f* (-;-nen) Swabian
schwäbisch ['ʃvebɪʃ] *adj* Swabian; **das Schwäbische Meer** Lake Constance
schwach [ʃvax] *adj* (**schwächer** ['ʃveçər]; **schwächste** ['ʃveçstə] §9)

weak; (*Hoffnung, Ton, Licht*) faint; (*unzureichend*) scanty; sparse; (*armselig*) poor

Schwäche ['ʃvɛçə] *f* (-;-n) weakness

Schwach'kopf *m* dunce; sap, dope

schwächlich ['ʃvɛçlɪç] *adj* feeble, delicate

Schwächling ['ʃvɛçlɪŋ] *m* (-s;-e) weakling

schwach'sinnig *adj* feeble-minded ‖ **Schwachsinnige** §5 *mf* dimwit, moron

Schwach'strom *m* low-voltage current

Schwaden ['ʃvɑdən] *m* (-s;-) swath; cloud (*of smoke, etc.*)

Schwadron [ʃva'dron] *f* (-;-en) squadron

schwadronieren [ʃvadrɔ'nirən] *intr* (coll) brag

schwafeln ['ʃvɑfəln] *intr* talk nonsense

Schwager ['ʃvɑgər] *m* (-s;⁼) brother-in-law

Schwägerin ['ʃvɛgərɪn] *f* (-;-nen) sister-in-law

Schwalbe ['ʃvalbə] *f* (-;-n) swallow

Schwal'bennest *n* (aer) gun turret

Schwal'benschwanz *m* (*Frack*) tails; (carp) dovetail

Schwall [ʃval] *m* (-[e]s;-e) flood; (*von Worten*) torrent

schwamm [ʃvam] *pret of* **schwimmen** ‖ **Schwamm** *m* (-[e]s;⁼e) sponge; mushroom; fungus; dry rot; **S. darüber!** skip it!

schwammig ['ʃvamɪç] *adj* spongy

Schwan [ʃvɑn] *m* (-[e]s;⁼e) swan

schwand [ʃvant] *pret of* **schwinden**

schwang [ʃvaŋ] *pret of* **schwingen**

schwanger ['ʃvaŋər] *adj* pregnant

schwängern ['ʃvɛŋərn] *tr* make pregnant; (fig) impregnate

Schwan'gerschaft *f* (-;-en) pregnancy

Schwan'gerschaftsverhütung *f* contraception

schwank [ʃvaŋk] *adj* flexible; unsteady ‖ **Schwank** *m* (-[e]s;⁼e) prank; joke; funny story; (theat) farce

schwanken ['ʃvaŋkən] *intr* stagger; (*schaukeln*) rock; (*schlingern*) roll; (*stampfen*) pitch; (*Flamme*) flicker; (*pendeln*) oscillate; (*vibrieren*) vibrate; (*wellenartig*) undulate; (*zittern*) shake; (*Preise*) fluctuate; (*zögern*) vacillate, hesitate

Schwanz [ʃvants] *m* (-es;⁼e) tail; (*Gefolge*) train; (*vulg*) pecker; **kein S.** not a living soul; **mit dem S. wedeln** (or **wippen**) wag its tail

schwänzeln ['ʃvɛntsəln] *intr* wag its tail; **s. um** fawn on

schwänzen ['ʃvɛntsən] *tr*—**die Schule s.** play hooky from school; **e-e Stunde s.** cut a class ‖ *intr* play hooky

schwappen ['ʃvapən] *intr* slosh around; **s. über** (*acc*) spill over

schwapps [ʃvaps] *interj* slap!; splash!

Schwäre ['ʃvɛrə] *f* (-;-n) abscess

schwären ['ʃvɛrən] *intr* fester

Schwarm [ʃvarm] *m* (-[e]s;⁼e) swarm; flock, herd; (*von Fischen*) school; (fig) idol; (fig) craze; (aer) flight of five aircraft; **sie ist mein S.** (coll) I have a crush on her

schwärmen ['ʃvɛrmən] *intr* swarm; stray; daydream; go out on the town; **s. für** (or **über** *acc* or **von**) rave about

Schwär'mer *m* (-s;-) enthusiast; reveler; daydreamer; firecracker; (religious) fanatic; (ent) hawk moth

Schwärmerei [ʃvɛrmə'raɪ] *f* (-;-en) enthusiasm; daydreaming; revelry; fanaticism

schwärmerisch ['ʃvɛrmərɪʃ] *adj* enthusiastic; gushy; fanatic; fanciful

Schwarte ['ʃvartə] *f* (-;-n) rind, skin; (coll) old book

schwarz [ʃvarts] *adj* black; dark; (*ungesetzlich*) illegal; (*schmutzig*) dirty; (*düster*) gloomy; (*von der Sonne*) tanned; **schwarze Kunst** black magic; **schwarzes Brett** bulletin board ‖ *adv* illegally

Schwarz'arbeit *f* moonlighting; non-union work; illicit work

Schwarz'brenner *m* moonshiner

Schwärze ['ʃvɛrtsə] *f* (-;-n) blackness; darkness; printer's ink

schwärzen ['ʃvɛrtsən] *tr* darken; blacken

schwarz'fahren §71 *intr* (SEIN) drive without a license; ride without a ticket

Schwarz'fahrer –**in** §6 *mf* unlicensed driver; rider without a ticket

Schwarz'fahrt *f* joy ride; ride without a ticket

Schwarz'handel *m* black-marketing

Schwarz'händler –**in** §6 *mf* black marketeer; (*mit Eintrittskarten*) scalper

schwärzlich ['ʃvɛrtslɪç] *adj* blackish

Schwarz'markt *m* black market

Schwarz'seher –**in** §6 *mf* pessimist

Schwarz'sender *m* illegal transmitter

schwatzen ['ʃvatsən], **schwätzen** ['ʃvɛtsən] *tr* (coll) talk ‖ *intr* (coll) yap, talk nonsense; (coll) gossip

Schwät'zer –**in** §6 *mf* windbag; gossip

schwatz'haft *adj* talkative

Schwatz'maul *n* blabber mouth

Schwebe ['ʃvebə] *f* (-;) suspense; **in der S. sein** be undecided; be pending

Schwe'bebahn *f* cablecar

Schwe'beflug *m* hovering, soaring

schweben ['ʃvebən] *intr* (HABEN & SEIN) be suspended, hang; float; (*Hubschrauber*) hover; (*Segelflugzeug*) soar; glide; (fig) waver, be undecided; **in Gefahr s.** be in danger; **in Ungewißheit s.** be in suspense

Schwede ['ʃvedə] *m* (-n;-n) Swede

Schweden ['ʃvedən] *n* (-s;) Sweden

Schwedin ['ʃvedɪn] *f* (-;-nen) Swede

schwedisch ['ʃvedɪʃ] *adj* Swedish

Schwefel ['ʃvefəl] *m* (-s;) sulfur

Schwe'felsäure *f* sulfuric acid

Schweif [ʃvaɪf] *m* (-[e]s;-e) tail; (fig) train

schweifen ['ʃvaɪfən] *tr* curve; (*spülen*) rinse ‖ *intr* (SEIN) roam, wander

Schweigegeld ['ʃvaɪgəgɛlt] *n* hush money

schweigen ['ʃvaɪgən] §148 *intr* be silent, keep silent; (*aufhören*) stop; **ganz zu s. von** to say nothing of; **s. zu** make no reply to

schwei'gend adj silent || adv in silence
schweigsam ['ʃvaɪkzəm] adj taciturn
Schwein [ʃvaɪn] n (-[e]s;-e) pig, hog;
  S. haben be lucky, have luck
Schwei'nebraten m roast pork
Schwei'nefleisch n pork
Schwei'nehund m (pej) filthy swine
Schwei'nekoben m pigsty, pig pen
Schweinerei [ʃvaɪnə'raɪ] f (-;-en)
  mess; dirty business
Schwei'nerippchen pl pork chops
Schwei'newirtschaft f dirty mess
Schweins'kotelett n pork chop
Schweiß [ʃvaɪs] m (-es;) perspiration
schweißen ['ʃvaɪsən] tr weld || intr
  begin to melt, fuse; (hunt) bleed
Schwei'ßer -in §6 mf welder
Schweißfüße ['ʃvaɪsfysə] pl sweaty
  feet
schweißig ['ʃvaɪsɪç] adj sweaty; (hunt)
  bloody
Schweiß'perle f bead of sweat
Schweiz [ʃvaɪts] f (-;)—**die S.** Switzerland
Schwei'zer m Swiss; dairyman
schweizerisch ['ʃvaɪtsərɪʃ] adj Swiss
schwelen ['ʃvelən] intr smolder
schwelgen ['ʃvelɡən] intr feast; **s. in**
  (dat) (fig) revel in; wallow in
Schwelgerei [ʃvelɡə'raɪ] f (-;-en)
  feasting, carousing
schwelgerisch ['ʃvelɡərɪʃ] adj riotous;
  luxurious
Schwelle ['ʃvelə] f (-;-n) sill; door-
  step; (fig) verge; (psychol) threshold; (rr) railroad tie
schwellen ['ʃvelən] §119 tr swell || intr
  (SEIN) swell; (Wasser) rise; (anwachsen) increase
Schwel'lung f (-;-en) swelling
Schwemme ['ʃvemə] f (-;-n) watering
  place; (coll) taproom; (com) glut
schwemmen ['ʃvemən] tr wash off,
  rinse; (Vieh) water; (Holz) float
Schwengel ['ʃveŋəl] m (-s;-) pump
  handle; (e-r Glocke) hammer
schwenkbar ['ʃveŋkbar] adj rotating
schwenken ['ʃveŋkən] tr swing; shake;
  (drohend) brandish; (Hut) wave;
  (spülen) rinse || intr (SEIN) turn;
  swivel, pivot; (Geschütz) traverse;
  (mil) wheel; (pol) change sides
Schwen'kung f (-;-en) turn; wheeling;
  traversing; (fig) change of mind
schwer [ʃver] adj heavy; difficult,
  hard; serious; (schwerfällig) ponderous; (Strafe) severe; (Wein) strong;
  (Speise) rich; (unbeholfen) clumsy;
  (Kompanie) heavy-weapons; **drei
  Pfund s. sein** weigh three pounds;
  schweres Geld bezahlen pay a stiff
  price || adv hard; with difficulty;
  (coll) very
Schwere ['ʃverə] f (-;) weight; seriousness; (des Weines) body; difficulty;
  significance; (phys) gravity
schwe'relos adj weightless
schwer'fällig adj heavy; clumsy, slow
Schwer'gewicht n heavyweight class;
  (Nachdruck) emphasis
Schwergewichtler -in ['ʃverɡəvɪçtlər
  (ɪn)] §6 mf (sport) heavyweight
schwer'hörig adj hard of hearing

Schwer'industrie f heavy industry
Schwer'kraft f gravity
schwer'lich adv hardly
Schwer'mut f melancholy, depression
schwer'mütig adj melancholy, de-
  pressed
schwer'nehmen §116 tr take hard
Schwer'punkt m center of gravity; cru-
  cial point, focal point
Schwert [ʃvert] n (-[e]s;-er) sword
Schwer'verbrecher -in §6 mf felon
schwer'verdient adj hard-earned
schwer'wiegend adj weighty
Schwester ['ʃvestər] f (-;-n) sister;
  nurse; nun
Schwe'sterhelferin f nurse's aide
schwieg [ʃvik] pret of schweigen
Schwieger– [ʃviɡər] comb.fm. -in-law
Schwie'germutter f mother-in-law
Schwie'gersohn m son-in-law
Schwie'gertochter f daughter-in-law
Schwie'gervater m father-in-law
Schwiele ['ʃvilə] f (-;-n) callus
schwielig ['ʃvilɪç] adj callous
schwierig ['ʃvirɪç] adj hard, difficult
Schwie'rigkeit f (-;-en) difficulty
Schwimm– [ʃvim] comb.fm. swimming
Schwimm'anstalt f, **Schwimm'bad** n,
  Schwimm'bassin n, **Schwimm'becken**
  n swimming pool
schwimmen ['ʃvimən] §136 intr (HA-
  BEN & SEIN) swim; float
Schwimm'gürtel m life belt
Schwimm'haut f web
Schwimm'hose f bathing trunks
Schwimm'kraft f buoyancy
Schwimm'panzer m amphibious tank
Schwimm'weste f life jacket
Schwindel ['ʃvindəl] m (-s;-) dizzi-
  ness; swindle, gyp; (Unsinn) bunk;
  (pathol) vertigo; **der ganze S.** the
  whole caboodle
Schwin'delanfall m dizzy spell
Schwin'delfirma f fly-by-night
schwin'delhaft adj fraudulent, bogus
schwindelig ['ʃvindəlɪç] adj dizzy
schwindeln ['ʃvindəln] tr swindle ||
  intr fib || impers—**mir schwindelt**
  I feel dizzy
Schwin'delunternehmen n fly-by-night
schwinden ['ʃvindən] §59 intr (SEIN)
  dwindle; decline; (Farbe) fade
Schwind'ler -in §6 mf swindler; fibber
schwindlig ['ʃvɪntlɪç] adj dizzy
Schwindsucht ['ʃvɪntzuçt] f tuberculosis
Schwinge ['ʃviŋə] f (-;-n) wing; fan;
  winnow; (poet) pinion
schwingen ['ʃviŋən] §142 tr swing;
  wave; brandish; (agr) winnow; (tex)
  swingle || ref vault; soar || intr swing;
  sway; oscillate; vibrate
Schwin'ger m (-s;-) oscillator; (box)
  haymaker
Schwin'gung f (-;-en) oscillation; vibration; swinging
Schwips [ʃvips] m—**e-n S. haben** (coll)
  be tight, be tipsy
schwirren ['ʃvirən] intr (HABEN &
  SEIN) whiz, whir; buzz; (Gerüchte)
  fly
Schwitzbad ['ʃvitsbat] n Turkish bath
schwitzen ['ʃvitsən] tr & intr sweat

schwoll [ʃvɔl] *pret* of schwellen
schwor [ʃvor] *pret* of schwören
schwören ['ʃvøːrən] §137 *tr & intr* swear; auf j-n (or etw) s. swear by s.o. (or s.th.)
schwul [ʃvul] *adj* (vulg) homosexual
schwül [ʃvyl] *adj* sultry, muggy
Schwulität [ʃvuliˈtɛt] *f* (-;-en) trouble
Schwulst [ʃvulst] *m* (-es;⸚e) bombast
schwülstig ['ʃvylstiç] *adj* bombastic
schwummerig ['ʃvuməriç] *adj* (coll) shaky
Schwund [ʃvunt] *m* (-[e]s;) dwindling; shrinkage; loss; leakage; (*des Haares*) falling out; (rad) fading; (pathol) atrophy
Schwung [ʃvuŋ] *m* (-[e]s;⸚e) swing; vault; (*Tatkraft*) zip, go; (*der Phantasie*) flight; in S. bringen start; S. bekommen gather momentum
schwung'haft *adj* brisk, lively
Schwung'kraft *f* centrifugal force; (fig) zip, pep; (phys) momentum
Schwung'rad *n* (mach) flywheel
schwung'voll *adj* enthusiastic, lively
schwur [ʃvur] *pret* of schwören ‖ Schwur *m* (-[e]s;⸚e) oath
Schwur'gericht *n* jury
sechs [zɛks] *invar adj & pron* six ‖ Sechs *f* (-;-en) six
Sechs'eck *n* hexagon
Sechser ['zɛksər] *m* (-s;-) six; (*in der Lotterie*) jackpot
Sechsta'gerennen *n* six-day bicycle race
sechste ['zɛkstə] §9 *adj & pron* sixth
Sechstel ['zɛkstəl] *n* (-s;-) sixth
sech'zehn *invar adj & pron* sixteen ‖ Sech'zehn *f* (-;-en) sixteen
sech'zehnte §9 *adj & pron* sixteenth
Sech'zehntel *n* (-s;-) sixteenth
sechzig ['zɛçtsiç] *invar adj & pron* sixty ‖ Sechzig *f* (-;-en) sixty
sechziger ['zɛçtsiɡər] *invar adj* of the sixties; die s. Jahre the sixties ‖ Sechziger *m* (-s;-) sexagenarian
sechzigste ['zɛçtsiçstə] §9 *adj & pron* sixtieth
See [ze] *m* (Sees; Seen ['ze·ən] lake ‖ *f* (See; Seen ['ze·ən]) sea; ocean; an der See at the seashore; an die See gehen go to the seashore; auf See at sea; in See gehen (or stechen) put out to sea; in See sein be in open water; Kapitän zur See navy captain; zur See gehen go to sea
See'bad *n* seashore resort
See'bär *m* (fig) sea dog
see'fähig *adj* seaworthy
See'fahrer *m* seafarer
See'fahrt *f* seafaring; voyage
see'fest *adj* seaworthy; s. werden get one's sea legs
See'gang *m*—hoher (or schwerer or starker) S. heavy seas
See'hafen *m* seaport
See'handel *m* maritime trade
See'hund *m* (zool) seal
See'jungfer *f*, See'jungfrau *f* mermaid
See'kadett *m* naval cadet
See'karte *f* (naut) chart
see'krank *adj* seasick
See'krebs *m* lobster
Seele ['zelə] *f* (-;-n) soul; mind; (*Ein-*

wohner) inhabitant, soul; (*e-s Geschützes*) bore; (*e-s Kabels*) core
See'lenangst *f* mortal fear
See'lenfriede *m* peace of mind
See'lenheil *n* salvation
See'lennot *f* mental distress
See'lenpein *f*, See'lenqual *f* mental anguish
See'lenruhe *f* peace of mind; composure
see'lensgut *adj* good-hearted
seelisch ['zeliʃ] *adj* mental, psychic
Seel'sorge *f* (-;) ministry
Seel'sorger *m* (-s;-) minister, pastor
See'macht *f* sea power
See'mann *m* (-[e]s;-leute) seaman
See'meile *f* nautical mile
See'möwe *f* sea gull
See'not *f* (naut) distress
See'ratte *f* (fig) old salt
See'raub *m* piracy
See'räuber *m* pirate; corsair
See'räuberei *f* piracy
See'recht *n* maritime law
See'reise *f* voyage; cruise
See'sperre *f* naval blockade
See'stadt *f* seaport town; coastal town
See'straße *f* shipping lane
See'streitkräfte *pl* naval forces
See'tang *m* seaweed
see'tüchtig *adj* seaworthy
See'warte *f* oceanographic institute
See'weg *m* sea route; auf dem S. by sea
See'wesen *n* naval affairs
Segel ['zeɡəl] *n* (-s;-) sail
Se'gelboot *n* sailboat; (sport) yacht
Se'gelfliegen *n* gliding
Se'gelflieger *-in* §6 *mf* glider pilot
Se'gelflug *m* glide, gliding
Se'gelflugzeug *n* glider
Se'gelleinwand *f* sailcloth, canvas
segeln ['zeɡəln] *intr* (HABEN & SEIN) sail; (aer) glide
Se'gelschiff *n* sailing vessel
Se'gelsport *m* sailing
Se'geltuch *n* sailcloth, canvas
Se'geltuchhülle *f*, Se'geltuchplane *f* tarpaulin
Segen ['zeɡən] *m* (-s;-) blessing
se'gensreich *adj* blessed, blissful
Segler ['zeɡlər] *m* (-s;-) yachtsman; (aer) glider; (naut) sailing vessel
segnen ['zeɡnən] *tr* bless
Seh- [ze] *comb.fm.* visual, of vision
sehen ['ze·ən] §138 *tr* see ‖ *intr* see; look; s. auf (*acc*) look at; take care of; face (*a direction*); s. nach look for, look around for; schlecht s. have poor eyes ‖ Sehen *n* (-s;) sight; eyesight, vision; vom S. by sight
se'henswert *adj* worth seeing
Se'henswürdigkeit *f* object of interest; Sehenswürdigkeiten sights
Seher ['ze·ər] *m* (-s;-) seer, prophet
Se'hergabe *f* gift of prophecy
Seh'feld *n* field of vision
Seh'kraft *f* eyesight
Sehne ['zenə] *f* (-;-n) tendon, sinew; (*Bogen-*) string; (geom) secant
sehnen ['zenən] *ref*—sich s. nach long for, crave ‖ Sehnen *n* (-s;) longing
Seh'nerv *m* optic nerve

sehnig ['zenɪç] *adj* sinewy; (*Fleisch*) stringy
sehnlich ['zenlɪç] *adj* longing; ardent
Sehnsucht ['zenzʊçt] *f* (-;) yearning
sehr [zer] *adv* very; very much
Seh'rohr *n* periscope
Seh'vermögen *n* sight, vision
Seh'weite *f* visual range; **in S.** within sight
seicht [zaɪçt] *adj* (& fig) shallow
Seide ['zaɪdə] *f* (-;-n) silk
seiden ['zaɪdən] *adj* silk, silky
Sei'denatlas *m* satin
Sei'denpapier *n* tissue paper
Sei'denraupe *f* silkworm
Sei'denspinnerei *f* silk mill
Sei'denstoff *m* silk cloth
seidig ['zaɪdɪç] *adj* silky
Seife ['zaɪfə] *f* (-;-n) soap
Sei'fenblase *f* soap bubble
Sei'fenbrühe *f* soapsuds
Sei'fenflocken *pl* soap flakes
Sei'fenlauge *f* soapsuds
Sei'fenpulver *n* soap powder
Sei'fenschale *f* soap dish
Sei'fenschaum *m* lather
seifig ['zaɪfɪç] *adj* soapy
seihen ['zaɪ·ən] *tr* strain, filter
Sei'her *m* (-s;-) strainer, filter
Seil [zaɪl] *n* (-[e]s;-e) rope; cable
Seil'bahn *f* cable railway; cable car
seil'springen *intr* jump rope
Seil'tänzer -in §6 *mf* ropewalker
sein [zaɪn] §139 *intr* (SEIN) be; exist; **es ist mir, als wenn** I feel as if; **es sei denn, daß** unless; **lassen Sie das s.!** stop it!; **wenn dem so ist** if that is the case; **wie dem auch sein mag** however that may be || *aux* (to form compound past tenses of intransitive verbs of motion, change of condition, etc.) have, e.g., **ich bin gegangen** I have gone, I went || §2.2 *poss adj* his; its; one's; her || §2,4,5 *poss pron* his; hers; **die Seinen** his family; **er hat das Seine getan** he did his share; **jedem das Seine** to each his own || **Sein** *n* (-s;) being; existence; reality
seinerseits ['zaɪnər'zaɪts] *adv* for his part
seinerzeit ['zaɪnər'tsaɪt] *adv* in its time; in those days; in due time
seinesgleichen ['zaɪnəs'glaɪçən] *pron* people like him, the likes of him
seinethalben ['zaɪnət'halbən], **seinetwegen** ['zaɪnət'vegən] *adv* for his sake; on his account; (*von ihm aus*) for all he cares
seinetwillen ['zaɪnət'vɪlən] *adv*—**um s.** for his sake, on his behalf
Seinige ['zaɪnɪgə] §2,5 *pron* his; **das S.** his property, his own; his due; his share; **die Seinigen** his family
seit [zaɪt] *prep* (*dat*) since, for; **s. e-m Jahr** for one year; **s. einiger Zeit** for some time past; **s. kurzem** lately; **s. langem** for a long time; **s. wann** since when || *conj* since
seitdem [zaɪt'dem] *adv* since that time || *conj* since
Seite ['zaɪtə] *f* (-;-n) side; page; direction; (*Quelle*) source; (mil) flank
Sei'tenansicht *f* side view, profile

Sei'tenbau *m* (-[e]s;-ten) annex
Sei'tenblick *m* side glance
Sei'tenflosse *f* (aer) horizontal stabilizer
Sei'tenflügel *m* (archit) wing
Sei'tengang *m* side aisle
Sei'tengeleise *n* sidetrack
Sei'tenhieb *m* snide remark, dig
sei'tenlang *adj* pages of
Sei'tenriß *m* profile
sei'tens *prep* (*genit*) on the part of
Sei'tenschiff *n* (archit) aisle
Sei'tenschwimmen *n* sidestroke
Sei'tensprung *m* (fig) escapade
Sei'tenstück *n* (fig) counterpart
Sei'tenwind *m* cross wind
seither [zaɪt'her] *adv* since then
-seitig [zaɪtɪç] *comb.fm.* -sided
seit'lich *adj* lateral
seitwärts ['zaɪtverts] *adv* sideways, sidewards; aside
Sekretär -in [zekre'ter(ɪn)] §8 *mf* secretary
Sekt [zekt] *m* (-[e]s;-e) champagne
Sekte ['zektə] *f* (-;-n) sect
Sek·tor ['zektɔr] *m* (-s;-toren ['torən]) sector; (fig) field
Sekundant [zekun'dant] *m* (-en;-en) (box) second
sekundär [zekun'der] *adj* secondary
Sekunde [ze'kundə] *f* (-;-n) second
Sekun'denbruchteil *m* split second
Sekun'denzeiger *m* second hand
Sekurit [zeku'rit] *n* (-s;) safety glass
selber ['zelbər] *invar pron* (coll) var of **selbst**
selbst [zelpst] *invar pron* self; in person, personally; (*sogar*) even; by oneself; **ich s.** I myself; **von s.** voluntarily; spontaneously; automatically || *adv* even; **s. ich** even I; **s. wenn** even if, even when
Selbst'achtung *f* self-respect
selbständig ['zelpʃtendɪç] *adj* independent
Selbst'bedienung *f* self-service
Selbst'beherrschung *f* self-control
Selbst'beobachtung *f* introspection
Selbst'bestimmung *f* self-determination
Selbst'betrug *m* self-deception
selbst'bewußt *adj* self-confident
Selbst'binder *m* necktie; (agr) combine
Selbst'erhaltung *f* self-preservation
selbst'gebacken *adj* homemade
selbst'gefällig *adj* complacent, smug
Selbst'gefühl *n* self-confidence
selbst'gemacht *adj* homemade
selbst'gerecht *adj* self-righteous
Selbst'gespräch *n* soliloquy
selbst'gezogen *adj* home-grown
selbst'herrlich *adj* high-handed
Selbst'herrschaft *f* autocracy
Selbst'herrscher *m* autocrat
Selbst'kosten *pl* production costs
Selbst'kostenpreis *m* factory price; **zum S. abgeben** sell at cost
Selbstlader ['zelpstladər] *m* (-s;-) automatic (weapon)
Selbst'laut *m* vowel
selbst'los *adj* unselfish
Selbst'mord *m* suicide
selbst'sicher *adj* self-confident
Selbst'steuer *n* automatic pilot

Selbst'sucht f egotism, selfishness
selbst'süchtig adj egotistical
selbst'tätig adj automatic
Selbst'täuschung f self-deception
Selbstüberhebung ['zɛlpstybərhebuŋ] f (–;) self-conceit, presumption
Selbst'verbrennung f spontaneous combustion; self-immolation
Selbst'verlag m—im **S.** printed privately
Selbst'verleugnung f self-denial
Selbst'versorger m (–s;–) self-supporter
selbst'verständlich adj obvious; natural || adv of course
Selbst'verständlichkeit f foregone conclusion, matter of course
Selbst'verteidigung f self-defense
Selbst'vertrauen n self-confidence
Selbst'verwaltung f autonomy
Selbst'wähler m (–s;–) dial telephone
Selbst'zucht f self-discipline
selbst'zufrieden adj self-satisfied
Selbst'zufriedenheit f self-satisfaction
Selbst'zweck m end in itself
selig ['zelıç] adj blessed; (verstorben) late; (fig) ecstatic; (fig) tipsy; **seligen Angedenkens** of blessed memory; **s. werden** attain salvation, be saved
Se'ligkeit f (–;) happiness; salvation
Se'ligpreisung f (Bib) beatitude
se'ligsprechen §64 tr beatify
Sellerie ['zɛləri] m (–s;) & f (–;) celery (bulb)
selten ['zɛltən] adj rare, scarce || adv seldom, rarely
Selterswasser ['zɛltərsvasər] n seltzer, soda water
seltsam ['zɛltzam] adj odd, strange
Semester [ze'mɛstər] n (–s;–) semester
Semikolon ['zɛmıkolən] n semicolon
Seminar [zɛmı'nɑr] n (–s;–e) seminary; (educ) seminar
Seminarist [zɛmına'rıst] m (–en;–en) seminarian
semitisch [ze'mıtı ʃ] adj Semitic
Semmel ['zɛməl] f (–;–n) roll
Senat [ze'nat] m (–[e]s;–e) senate
Se-nator [ze'natər] m (–s;–natoren [na'torən]) senator
Sende– [zɛndə] comb.fm. transmitting, transmitter, broadcasting
senden ['zɛndən] tr & intr transmit, broadcast; telecast || §120 & §140 tr send || intr—**s. nach** send for
Sen'der m (–s;–) (rad, telv) transmitter; (rad) broadcasting station
Sen'deraum m broadcasting studio
Sen'dezeichen n station identification
Sen'dezeit f air time
Sen'dung f (–;–en) sending; (fig) mission; (com) shipment; (rad) broadcast; (telv) telecast
Senf [zɛnf] m (–[e]s;–e) mustard
sengen ['zɛŋən] tr singe, scorch
seng(e)rig ['zɛŋ(ə)rıç] adj burnt; (fig) suspicious, fishy
senil [ze'nil] adj senile
Senilität [zɛnılı'tet] f (–;) senility
senior ['zɛnjor] adj senior
Senkblei ['zɛŋkblaı] n plummet; (naut) sounding lead
Senke ['zɛŋkə] f (–;–n) depression
senken ['zɛŋkən] tr lower; sink; (Kopf)

bow || ref sink, settle; dip, slope; (Mauer) sag
Senkfüße ['zɛŋkfysə] pl flat feet, fallen arches
Senk'fußeinlage f arch support
Senkgrube ['zɛŋkgrubə] f cesspool
Senkkasten ['zɛŋkkastən] m caisson
senkrecht ['zɛŋkreçt] adj vertical; (geom) perpendicular
Sen'kung f (–;–en) sinking; depression; dip, slope; sag; (der Preise) lowering
Sensation [zɛnza'tsjon] f (–;–en) sensation
sensationell [zɛnzatsjə'nɛl] adj sensational
Sensations'blatt n (pej) scandal sheet
Sensations'lust f sensationalism
Sensations'meldung f, **Sensations'nachricht** f (journ) scoop
Sensations'presse f yellow journalism
Sense ['zɛnzə] f (–;–n) scythe
sensibel [zɛn'zibəl] adj sensitive; (Nerven) sensory
Sensibilität [zɛnzıbılı'tet] f (–;) sensitivity, sensitiveness
sentimental [zɛntımen'tal] adj sentimental
separat [zɛpa'rat] adj separate
September [zɛp'tɛmbər] m (–[s];) September
Serenade [zɛre'nadə] f (–;–n) serenade
Serie ['zɛrjə] f (–;–n) series; line
Se'rienanfertigung f, **Se'rienbau** m, **Se'rienfabrikation** f, **Se'rienherstellung** f mass production
se'rienmäßig adj—**serienmäßige Herstellung** mass production || adv—**s. herstellen** mass-produce
Se'riennummer f serial number
Se'rienproduktion f mass production
seriös [zɛ'rjøs] adj serious; reliable
Se-rum ['zerum] n (–s;–ren [rən] & –ra [ra]) serum
Service ['zørvıs] m (Services ['zørvıs(əs)];) (Kundendienst) service || [zer'vis] n (Services [zer'vis]; **Service** [zer'vis(ə)]) (Tafelgeschirr) service
Servierbrett [zɛr'virbrɛt] n tray
servieren [zɛr'virən] tr serve; **es ist serviert!** dinner is ready! || intr wait at table
Serviertisch [zɛr'virtı ʃ] m sideboard
Servierwagen [zɛr'virvagən] m serving cart
Serviette [zɛr'vjɛtə] f (–;–n) napkin
Servo– [zɛrvə] comb.fm. booster, auxiliary, servo, power, automatic
Ser'vobremsen pl power brakes
Ser'vokupplung f automatic transmission
Ser'volenkung f power steering
Servus ['zɛrvʊs] interj (Aust) hello!; (coll) so long!
Sessel ['zɛsəl] m (–s;–) easy chair
Ses'sellift m chair lift
seßhaft ['zɛshaft] adj settled; **sich s. machen** settle down
Setzei ['zɛtsaı] n fried egg
setzen ['zɛtsən] tr set, put, place; seat; (beim Spiel) bet; (Denkmal) erect; (Frist) fix; (Junge) breed; (Fische) stock; (Pflanzen) plant; (mus) com-

pose; (typ) set ‖ *ref* sit down; (*Kaffee*) settle ‖ *intr* set type; **s. auf** (*acc*) bet on ‖ *intr* (SEIN)—**s. über** (*acc*) jump over
Set'zer *m* (-s;-) typesetter, compositor
Setz'fehler *m* typographical error
Seuche ['zɔɪçə] *f* (-;-n) epidemic
seufzen ['zɔɪftsən] *intr* sigh
Seuf'zer *m* (-s;-) sigh
Sex [zɛks] *m* (-es;) sex
Sex-Appeal ['zɛks ə'pil] *m* (-s;) sex appeal
Sex'-Bombe *f* (coll) sex pot
Sexual– [zɛksʊal] *comb.fm.* sex
sexuell [zɛksʊ 'ɛl] *adj* sexual
Sexus ['zɛksʊs] *m* (-;-) sex
sezieren [zɛ'tsirən] *tr* dissect
Shampoo [ʃam'pu] *n* (-s;-s) shampoo
Sibirien [zɪ'birjən] *n* (-s;) Siberia
sich [zɪç] §11 *reflex pron* oneself; himself; herself; itself; themselves; **an (und für) s.** in itself; **außer s. sein** be beside oneself ‖ *recip pron* each other, one another
Sichel ['zɪçəl] *f* (-;-n) sickle
sicher ['zɪçər] *adj* sure; positive; reliable; (**vor** *dat*) safe (from), secure (from) ‖ *adv* surely, certainly
Si'cherheit *f* (-;-en) safety, security; (*Gewißheit*) certainty; (*Zuverlässigkeit*) reliability; (*im Auftreten*) assurance; (com) security; (jur) bail
Si'cherheitsgurt *m*, **Si'cherheitsgürtel** *m* (aer, aut) seat belt
Si'cherheitsnadel *f* safety pin
Si'cherheitspolizei *f* security police
Si'cherheitsspielraum *m* margin of safety, leeway
si'cherlich *adv* surely, certainly
sichern ['zɪçərn] *tr* secure; fasten; guarantee; (*Gewehr*) put on safety
Si'cherstellung *f* safekeeping; guarantee
Si'cherung *f* (-;-en) protection; guarantee; (*an Schußwaffe*) safety catch; (elec) fuse; **durchgebrannte S.** blown fuse
Si'cherungskasten *m* fuse box
Sicht [zɪçt] *f* (-;) sight; (*Aussicht*) view; (*Sichtigkeit*) visibility; **auf kurze S.** short-range; **auf S.** at sight
sichtbar ['zɪçtbar] *adj* visible
sichten ['zɪçtən] *tr* sight; (fig) sift
sichtig ['zɪçtɪç] *adj* clear
sicht'lich *adj* visible
Sicht'vermerk *m* visa
sickern ['zɪkərn] *intr* (HABEN & SEIN) trickle, seep, leak
sie [zi] §11 *pers pron* she, her; it; they, them ‖ §11 **Sie** *pers pron* you
Sieb [zip] *n* (-[e]s;-e) sieve, colander; screen; (rad) filter
sieben ['zibən] *invar adj & pron* seven ‖ *tr* sift, strain; (fig) screen; (rad) filter ‖ **Sieben** *f* (-;-en) seven
siebente ['zibəntə] §9 *adj & pron* seventh
Siebentel ['zibəntəl] *n* (-s;-) seventh
siebte ['ziptə] §9 *adj & pron* seventh
Siebtel ['ziptəl] *n* (-s;-) seventh
siebzehn ['ziptsen] *invar adj & pron* seventeen ‖ **Siebenzehn** *f* (-;-en) seventeen

siebzehnte ['ziptsentə] §9 *adj & pron* seventeenth
Siebzehntel ['ziptsentəl] *n* (-s;-) seventeenth
siebzig ['ziptsɪç] *invar adj & pron* seventy ‖ **Siebzig** *f* (-;-en) seventy
siebziger ['ziptsɪgər] *invar adj* of the seventies; **die s. Jahre** the seventies ‖ **Siebziger** *m* (-s;-) septuagenarian
siebzigste ['ziptsɪçstə] §9 *adj & pron* seventieth
siech [ziç] *adj* sickly
siechen ['ziçən] *intr* be sickly
Siechtum ['ziçtum] *n* (-s;) lingering illness
siedeheiß ['zidə'hais] *adj* piping hot
siedeln ['zidəln] *intr* settle
sieden ['zidən] §141 *tr & intr* boil
Siedepunkt ['zidəpuŋkt] *m* boiling point
Siedler –in ['zidlər(ɪn)] §6 *mf* settler
Sied'lerstelle *f* homestead
Sied'lung *f* (-;-en) settlement; colony; housing development
Sieg [zik] *m* (-[e]s;-e) victory
Siegel ['zigəl] *n* (-s;-) seal
siegeln ['zigəln] *tr* seal
Sie'gelring *m* signet ring
siegen ['zigən] *intr* win, be victorious
Sie'ger –in §6 *mf* winner, victor; **zweiter Sieger** runner-up
Sieges– [zigəs] *comb.fm.* victory, of victory, triumphal
Sie'gesbogen *m* triumphal arch
sieg'reich *adj* victorious
Signal [zɪg'nal] *n* (-s;-e) signal
signalisieren [zɪgnalɪ'zirən] *tr* signal
Silbe ['zɪlbə] *f* (-;-n) syllable
Sil'bentrennung *f* syllabification
Silber ['zɪlbər] *n* (-s;) silver
silbern ['zɪlbərn] *adj* silver, silvery
Sil'berzeug *n* silver, silverware
Silhouette [zɪlʊ'ɛtə] *f* (-;-n) silhouette
Silo ['zilo] *m* (-s;-s) silo
Silvester [zɪl'vɛstər] *m* (-s;-), **Silve'sterabend** *m* New Year's Eve
simpel ['zɪmpəl] *adj* simple ‖ **Simpel** *m* (-s;-) simpleton
Sims [zɪms] *m & n* (-es;-e) ledge; (*Fenster–*) sill; (*Kamin–*) mantelpiece
Simulant –in [zɪmʊ'lant(ɪn)] §7 *mf* faker; (mil) goldbrick
simulieren [zɪmʊ'lirən] *tr* simulate, fake ‖ *intr* loaf
simultan [zɪmʊl'tan] *adj* simultaneous
Sinfo·nie [zɪnfo'ni] *f* (-;-nien ['ni·ən]) symphony
singen ['zɪŋən] §142 *tr & intr* sing
Singsang ['zɪŋzaŋ] *m* (-[e]s;) singsong
Sing'spiel *n* musical comedy, musical
Sing'stimme *f* vocal part
Singular ['zɪŋgʊlar] *m* (-s;-e) singular
sinken ['zɪŋkən] §143 *intr* (SEIN) sink slump, sag; (*Preise*) drop; **s. lassen** lower; (*Mut*) lose
Sinn [zɪn] *m* (-[e]s;-e) sense; mind; meaning; liking, taste
Sinn'bild *n* emblem, symbol
sinn'bildlich *adj* symbolic(al) ‖ *adv* symbolically; **s. darstellen** symbolize
sinnen ['zɪnən] §121 *tr* plan; plot ‖ *intr* (**auf** *acc*) plan, plot; (**über** *acc*)

think (about) || **Sinnen** *n* (–s;) reflection, meditation, reverie
sin'nend *adj* pensive, reflective
Sin'nenlust *f* sensuality
Sin'nenmensch *m* sensualist
Sin'nenwelt *f* material world
Sin'nesänderung *f* change of mind
Sin'nesart *f* character, disposition
Sin'nestäuschung *f* illusion, hallucination, mirage
sinn'lich *adj* sensual; material
sinn'los *adj* senseless
sinn'reich *adj* ingenious, bright
sinn'verwandt *adj* synonymous
sinn'voll *adj* meaningful; sensible
Sintflut ['zɪntflut] *f* deluge, flood
Sippe ['zɪpə] *f* (–;–n) kin; clan
Sipp'schaft *f* (–;–en) clique, set
Sirup ['zirup] *m* (–s;–e) syrup
Sitte ['zɪtə] *f* (–;–n) custom; habit; usage; **die Sitten** the morals
Sit'tenbild *n*, **Sit'tengemälde** *n* description of the manners (*of an age*)
Sit'tengesetz *n* moral law
Sit'tenlehre *f* ethics
sit'tenlos *adj* immoral
Sit'tenpolizei *f* vice squad
sit'tenrein *adj* chaste
Sit'tenrichter *m* censor
sit'tenstreng *adj* puritanical, prudish
Sittich ['zɪtiç] *m* (–s;–e) parakeet
sittlich ['zɪtlɪç] *adj* moral, ethical
Sittlichkeit *f* (–;) morality
Sitt'lichkeitsverbrechen *n* indecent assault
sittsam ['zɪtzam] *adj* modest, decent
Situation [zɪtʊ·aˈtsjon] *f* (–;–en) situation
situiert [zɪtuˈirt] *adj*—**gut s.** well-to-do
Sitz [zɪts] *m* (–es;–e) seat; residence; (*e–s Kleides*) fit; (eccl) see
sitzen ['zɪtsən] §144 *intr* sit; dwell; (*Vögel*) perch; (*Kleider*) fit; (*Hieb*) hit home; (coll) be in jail
sit'zenbleiben §62 *intr* (SEIN) remain seated; (*beim Tanzen*) be a wallflower; (*bei der Heirat*) remain unmarried; (educ) stay behind, flunk
sit'zenlassen §104 *tr* leave, abandon; (*Mädchen*) jilt
Sitz'gelegenheit *f* seating accommodation
Sitz'ordnung *f* seating arrangement
Sitz'platz *m* seat
Sitz'streik *m* sit-down strike
Sit'zung *f* (–;–en) session
Sit'zungsbericht *m* minutes
Sit'zungsperiode *f* session; (jur) term
Sizilien [zɪˈtsiljən] *n* (–s;) Sicily
Ska·la ['skala] *f* (–;–len [lən]) scale
Skandal [skanˈdal] *m* (–s;–e) scandal
skandalös [skandaˈløs] *adj* scandalous
Skandinavien [skandɪˈnavjən] *n* (–s;) Scandinavia
Skelett [skɛˈlet] *n* (–[e]s;–e) skeleton
Skepsis ['skepsɪs] *f* (–;) skepticism
Skeptiker –in ['skɛptɪkər(ɪn)] §6 *mf* skeptic
skeptisch ['skeptɪʃ] *adj* skeptical
Ski [ʃi] *m* (–s; **Skier** ['ʃi·ər]) ski
Skizze ['skɪtsə] *f* (–;–n) sketch
skizzieren [skɪˈtsirən] *tr & intr* sketch
Sklave ['sklavə] *m* (–n;–n) slave

Sklaverei [sklavəˈraɪ] *f* (–;) slavery
sklavisch ['sklavɪʃ] *adj* slavish
Skonto ['skɔnto] *m & n* (–s;–s) discount
Skrupel ['skrupəl] *m* (–s;–) scruple
skru'pellos *adj* unscrupulous
skrupulös [skrupuˈløs] *adj* scrupulous
Skulptur [skʊlpˈtur] *f* (–;–en) sculpture
Slalom ['slalom] *m & n* (–s;–s) slalom
Slawe ['slavə] *m* (–n;–n), **Slawin** ['slavɪn] *f* (–;–nen) Slav
slawisch ['slavɪʃ] *adj* Slavic
Smaragd [smaˈrakt] *m* (–[e]s;–e) emerald
Smoking ['smokɪŋ] *m* (–s;–s) tuxedo
so [zo] *adv* so; this way, thus; **so ein** such a; **so oder so** by hook or by crook; **so...wie** as...as
sobald' *conj* as soon as
Socke ['zɔkə] *f* (–;–n) sock
Sockenhalter (**Sok'kenhalter**) *m* garter
Soda ['zoda] *f* (–;) & *n* (–s;) soda
sodann' *adv* then
Sodbrennen ['zotbrɛnən] *n* (–s;) heartburn
soeben [zoˈebən] *adv* just now, just
Sofa ['zofa] *n* (–s;–s) sofa
sofern' *conj* provided, if
soff [zɔf] *pret* of **saufen**
sofort' *adv* at once, right away
sofortig [zoˈfɔrtɪç] *adj* immediate
sog [zok] *pret* of **saugen** || **Sog** *m* (–[e]s;) suction; undertow; (aer) wash
sogar' *adv* even
so'genannt *adj* so-called; would-be
sogleich' *adv* at once, right away
Sohle ['zolə] *f* (–;–n) sole; bottom
Sohn [zon] *m* (–[e]s;–e) son
solan'ge *conj* as long as
solch [zɔlç] *adj* such
Sold [zɔlt] *m* (–[e]s;–e) pay
Soldat [zɔlˈdat] *m* (–en;–en) soldier
Söldner ['zœldnər] *m* (–s;–) mercenary
Sole ['zolə] *f* (–;–n) brine
solid [zoˈlit] *adj* solid; sound; reliable; steady; respectable; (*Preis*) reasonable; (com) sound, solvent
solide [zoˈlidə] *adj* var of **solid**
Solist –in [zoˈlɪst(ɪn)] §7 *mf* soloist
Soll [zɔl] *n* (–s;–e) quota; (acct) debit side; **S. und Haben** debit and credit
Soll– *comb.fm.* estimated; debit
sollen ['zɔlən] §145 *mod* (*inf*) be obliged to (*inf*), have to (*inf*); (*inf*) be supposed to (*inf*); (*inf*) be said to (*inf*)
Soll'wert *m* face value
solo ['zolo] *adv* (mus) solo || **So·lo** *n* (–s;–s & –li [li]) solo
somit' *adv* so, consequently
Sommer ['zɔmər] *m* (–s;–) summer
Som'merfrische *f* health resort; **in die S. fahren** go to the country
Sommerfrischler ['zɔmərfrɪʃlər] *m* (–s;–) vacationer
som'merlich *adj* summery
Som'mersprosse *f* freckle
sonach' *adv* consequently, so
Sonate [zoˈnatə] *f* (–;–n) sonata
Sonde ['zɔndə] *f* (–;–n) probe
Sonder– [zɔndər] *comb.fm.* special, extra; separate

sonderbar ['zɔndərbɑr] *adj* strange, odd; peculiar

son'derlich *adj* special, particular

Sonderling ['zɔndərlɪŋ] *m* (-s;-e) odd person, strange character

sondern ['zɔndərn] *tr* separate; sever; part; sort out; classify ‖ *conj* but

Son'derrecht *n* privilege

Son'derung *f* (-;-en) separation; sorting, sifting; classifying

Son'derverband *m* (mil) task force

Son'derzug *m* (rr) special

sondieren [zɔn'dirən] *tr* probe; (fig) sound out; (naut) sound

Sonnabend ['zɔnɑbənt] *m* (-s;-e) Saturday

Sonne ['zɔnə] *f* (-;-n) sun

sonnen ['zɔnən] *tr* sun ‖ *ref* sun oneself

Son'nenaufgang *m* sunrise

Son'nenbad *n* sun bath

Son'nenblende *f* (aut) sun visor; (phot) lens shade

Sonnenbrand *m* sunburn

Son'nenbräune *f* suntan

Son'nenbrille *f* (pair of) sun glasses

Son'nendach *n* awning

Son'nenenergie *f* solar energy

Son'nenfinsternis *f* eclipse of the sun

Son'nenfleck *m* sunspot

Son'nenjahr *n* solar year

son'nenklar' *adj* sunny; (fig) clear as day

Son'nenlicht *n* sunlight

Son'nenschein *m* sunshine

Son'nenschirm *m* parasol

Son'nensegel *n* awning

Son'nenseite *f* sunny side

Son'nenstich *m* sunstroke

Son'nenstrahl *m* sunbeam

Son'nensystem *n* solar system

Son'nenuhr *f* sundial

Son'nenuntergang *m* sunset

son'nenverbrannt *adj* sunburnt, tanned

Son'nenwende *f* solstice

sonnig ['zɔnɪç] *adj* sunny

Sonntag ['zɔntak] *m* (-s;-e) Sunday

sonn'tags *adv* on Sundays

Sonn'tagsfahrer –in §6 *mf* Sunday driver

Sonn'tagskind *n* person born under a lucky star

Sonn'tagsstaat *m* Sunday clothes

sonor [zɔ'nor] *adj* sonorous

sonst [zɔnst] *adv* otherwise; else; (*ehemals*) formerly; **s. etw** something else; **s. keiner** no one else; **s. nichts** nothing else; **s. noch was?** anything else?; **wie s.** as usual; **wie s. was** (coll) like anything

sonstig ['zɔnstɪç] *adj* other

sonst'wer *pron* someone else

sonst'wie *adv* in some other way

sonst'wo *adv* somewhere else

Sopran [zɔ'prɑn] *m* (-s;-e) soprano; treble

Sopranist –in [zɔprɑ'nɪst(ɪn)] §7 *mf* soprano

Sorge ['zɔrgə] *f* (-;-n) care; worry; **außer S. sein** be at ease; **keine S.!** don't worry; **sich** [*dat*] **Sorgen machen über** (*acc*) or **um** be worried about

sorgen ['zɔrgən] *intr*—**dafür s., daß** take care that, see to it that; **s. für** take care of ‖ *ref* be uneasy; **sich s. über** (*acc*) grieve over; **sich s. um** be worried about

sor'genfrei *adj* carefree; untroubled

Sor'genkind *n* problem child

sor'genlos *adj* carefree

sor'genvoll *adj* uneasy, anxious

Sor'gerecht *n* (**für**) custody (of)

Sorgfalt ['zɔrkfalt] *f* (-;) care, carefulness; accuracy

sorgfältig ['zɔrkfeltɪç] *adj* careful

sorglich ['zɔrklɪç] *adj* careful

sorglos ['zɔrklos] *adj* careless; thoughtless; carefree

sorgsam ['zɔrkzɑm] *adj* careful; cautious

Sorte ['zɔrtə] *f* (-;-n) sort, kind

sortieren [zɔr'tirən] *tr* sort out

Sortiment [zɔrtɪ'ment] *n* (-[e]s;-e) assortment

Soße ['zosə] *f* (-;-n) sauce; gravy

sott [zɔt] *pret* of **sieden**

Souffleur [zu'flør] *m* (-s;-s), **Souffleuse** [zu'fløzə] *f* (-;-n) prompter

soufflieren [zu'flirən] *intr* (*dat*) prompt

Soutane [zu'tɑnə] *f* (-;-n) cassock

Souvenir [zuvə'nir] *n* (-s;-s) souvenir

souverän [zuvə'ren] *adj* sovereign ‖ **Souverän** *m* (-s;-e) sovereign

Souveränität [zuvɛrɛni'tet] *f* (-;) sovereignty

soviel' *adv* so much; **noch einmal s.** twice as much ‖ *conj* as far as

soweit' *conj* as far as

sowie' *conj* as well as

sowieso' *adv* in any case, anyhow

Sowjet [zɔv'jet] *m* (-s;-s) Soviet

sowjetisch [zɔv'jetɪʃ] *adj* Soviet

sowohl' *conj*—**sowohl...als auch** as well as, both...and

sozial [zo'tsjal] *adj* social

Sozial'fürsorge *f* social welfare

sozialisieren [zotsjalɪ'zirən] *tr* nationalize

Sozialismus [zotsja'lɪsmus] *m* (-;) socialism

Sozialist –in [zotsja'lɪst(ɪn)] §7 *mf* socialist

sozialistisch [zotsja'lɪstɪʃ] *adj* socialistic

Sozial'wissenschaft *f* social science

Soziologie [zotsjolɔ'gi] *f* (-;) sociology

Sozius ['zotsjus] *m* (-;-se) associate, partner; (*auf dem Motorrad*) rider

sozusa'gen *adv* so to speak, as it were

Spachtel ['ʃpaxtəl] *m* (-s;-) & *f* (-;-n) spatula; putty knife

Spach'telmesser *n* putty knife

Spagat [ʃpa'gat] *m* (-[e]s;-e) (gym) split; (dial) string

spähen ['ʃpe-ən] *intr* peer; spy

Spä'her *m* (-s;-) lookout; (mil) scout

Spä'herblick *m* searching glance

Spähtrupp ['ʃpetrup] *m* reconnaissance squad

Späh'wagen *m* reconnaissance car

Spalier [ʃpa'lir] *n* (-s;-e) trellis; double line (*of people*)

Spalt [ʃpalt] *m* (-[e]s;-e) split; crack; slit; (geol) cleft

Spalte ['ʃpaltə] ƒ (-;-n) split; crack; slit; (typ) column

spalten ['ʃpaltən] tr (pp **gespaltet** or **gespalten**) split; slit; crack; (Holz) chop

Spal'tung ƒ (-;-en) split; (der Meinungen) division; (chem) decomposition; (eccl) schism; (phys) fission

Span [ʃpan] m (-[e]s;-̈e) chip; splinter; **Späne** shavings

Span'ferkel n suckling pig

Spange ['ʃpaŋə] ƒ (-;-n) clasp; hair clip; (Schnalle) buckle

Spanien ['ʃpanjən] n (-s;) Spain

Spanier -in ['ʃpanjər(ɪn)] §6 mƒ Spaniard

spanisch ['ʃpanɪʃ] adj Spanish; **das kommt mir s. vor** (coll) that's Greek to me; **spanischer Pfeffer** paprika; **spanische Wand** folding screen

spann [ʃpan] pret of **spinnen** ‖ **Spann** m (-s;-e) instep

Spanne ['ʃpanə] ƒ (-;-n) span; (com) margin

spannen ['ʃpanən] tr stretch; strain; make tense; (Bogen) bend; (Feder) tighten; (Flinte) cock; (Erwartungen) raise; (Pferde) hitch; **straff s.** tighten; ‖ intr be (too) tight; **s. auf** (acc) wait eagerly for; listen closely to

span'nend adj tight; exciting

Spann'kraft ƒ tension; elasticity; (fig) resiliency

spann'kräftig adj elastic

Span'nung ƒ (-;-en) stress; strain; pressure; close attention; suspense; excitement; strained relations; (elec) voltage

Spar- [ʃpar] comb.fm. savings

Spar'buch n bank book, pass book

Spar'büchse ƒ piggy bank

sparen ['ʃparən] tr & intr save

Spar'flamme ƒ pilot light

Spargel ['ʃpargəl] m (-s;-) asparagus

Spar'kasse ƒ savings bank

Spar'konto n savings account

spärlich ['ʃperlɪç] adj scanty; scarce; sparse; frugal; (Haar) thin ‖ adv poorly; scantily; sparsely

Sparren ['ʃparən] m (-s;-) rafter

sparsam ['ʃparzam] adj thrifty

Spaß [ʃpas] m (-es;-̈e) joke; fun; **aus S. in fun; S. beiseite!** all joking aside; **S. haben an** (dat) enjoy; **S. machen** be joking; be fun; **viel S.!** have fun!; **zum S.** for fun

spaß'haft, spaßig ['ʃpasɪç] adj funny, facetious

Spaß'macher m joker

Spaßverderber ['ʃpasverderbər] m (-s;-) (coll) kill-joy

Spaß'vogel m joker

spät [ʃpet] adj late; **wie s. ist es?** what time is it? ‖ adv late

Spaten ['ʃpatən] m (-s;-) spade

später ['ʃpetər] adv later

späterhin' adv later on

spätestens ['ʃpetəstəns] adv at the latest

Spät'jahr n autumn, fall

Spatz [ʃpats] m (-es & -en;-en) sparrow

spazieren [ʃpa'tsirən] intr (SEIN) stroll, take a walk

spazie'renfahren §71 intr (SEIN) go for a drive

spazie'renführen tr walk (e.g., a dog)

spazie'rengehen §82 intr (SEIN) go for a walk

Spazier'fahrt ƒ drive

Spazier'gang m stroll, walk; **e-n S. machen** take a walk

Spazier'gänger -in §6 mƒ stroller

Spazier'weg m walk

Specht [ʃpeçt] m (-[e]s;-e) woodpecker

Speck [ʃpek] m (-[e]s;) fat; bacon; (beim Wal) blubber

Speck'bauch m (coll) potbelly

speckig ['ʃpekɪç] adj greasy, dirty

spedieren [ʃpe'dirən] tr dispatch, ship

Spediteur [ʃpedɪ'tør] m (-s;-e) shipper; furniture mover

Spedition [ʃpedɪ'tsjon] ƒ (-;-en) shipment; moving company, movers

Speer [ʃper] m (-[e]s;-e) spear; (sport) javelin

Speiche ['ʃpaɪçə] ƒ (-;-n) spoke

Speichel ['ʃpaɪçəl] m (-s;) saliva

Spei'chellecker m brown-noser

speicheln ['ʃpaɪçəln] intr drool

Speicher ['ʃpaɪçər] m (-s;-) warehouse; grain elevator; attic, loft

speichern ['ʃpaɪçərn] tr store

speien ['ʃpaɪ·ən] §135 tr vomit; spit; (Feuer) belch; (Wasser) spurt ‖ intr vomit, throw up; spit

Speise ['ʃpaɪzə] ƒ (-;-n) food; meal; (Gericht) dish

Spei'seeis n ice cream

Spei'sekammer ƒ pantry

Spei'sekarte ƒ menu

speisen ['ʃpaɪzən] tr feed; (fig) supply ‖ intr eat; **auswärts s.** dine out

Spei'senfolge ƒ menu

Spei'sereste pl leftovers

Spei'serohr n (mach) feed pipe

Spei'seröhre ƒ esophagus

Spei'sesaal m dining room

Spei'seschrank m cupboard

Spei'sewagen m (rr) diner

Spei'sezimmer n dining room

Spektakel [ʃpek'takəl] m (-s;-) noise, racket

Spekulant -in [ʃpeku'lant(ɪn)] §7 mƒ speculator

Spekulation [ʃpekula'tsjon] f (-;-en) speculation; venture

spekulieren [ʃpeku'lirən] intr speculate, reflect; (fin) speculate

Spelunke [ʃpe'luŋkə] ƒ (-;-n) (coll) drive, joint

Spende ['ʃpendə] ƒ (-;-n) donation

spenden ['ʃpendən] tr give; donate; (Sakramente) administer; (Lob) bestow; **j-m Trost s.** comfort s.o.

spendieren [ʃpen'dirən] tr—**j-m etw s.** treat s.o. to s.th.

Sperling ['ʃperlɪŋ] m (-s;-e) sparrow

Sperr- [ʃper] comb.fm. barrage; barred

Sperr'baum m barrier, bar

Sperre ['ʃperə] ƒ (-;-n) shutting; close; blockade; embargo; barricade; catch; lock; (rr) gate

sperren ['ʃperən] tr shut; (Gas, Licht) cut off; (Straße) block off; cordon off; (*blockieren*) blockade; (*mit Schloß*) lock; (*verriegeln*) bolt; (*Konto, Gelder*) freeze; (*Scheck*) stop payment on; (*verbieten*) stop; (sport) block; (sport) suspend; (typ) space || *intr* jam, be stuck

Sperr′feuer *n* barrage

Sperr′gebiet *n* restricted area

Sperr′holz *n* plywood

sperrig [′ʃpɛrɪç] *adj* bulky

Sperr′sitz *m* (*im Kino*) rear seat; (*im Zirkus*) front seat

Sperr′stunde *f* closing time; curfew

Sper′rung *f* (-;-en) stoppage; blocking; blockade; embargo; suspension (*of telephone service, etc.*)

Spesen [′ʃpezən] *pl* costs, expenses

Spezi [′ʃpetsi] *m* (-s;-s) (coll) buddy

spezial [ʃpɛ′tsjal] *adj* special

Spezial′arzt *m*, **Spezial′ärztin** *f* specialist

Spezial′fach *n* specialty

Spezial′geschäft *n* specialty shop

spezialisieren [ʃpɛtsjalɪ′zirən] *ref* (*auf acc*) specialize (in)

Spezialist –in [ʃpɛtsja′lɪst(ɪn)] §7 *mf* specialist

Spezialität [ʃpɛtsjalɪ′tet] *f* (-;-en) specialty

speziell [ʃpɛ′tsjɛl] *adj* special

spezifisch [ʃpɛ′tsifɪʃ] *adj* specific

Sphäre [′sferə] *f* (-;-n) sphere

sphärisch [′sferɪʃ] *adj* spherical

Spickaal [′ʃpɪkal] *m* smoked eel

spicken [′ʃpɪkən] *tr* lard; (fig) bribe

spie [ʃpi] *pret* of **speien**

Spiegel [′ʃpigəl] *m* (-s;-) mirror

Spie′gelbild *n* reflection (*in mirror*)

spie′gelblank′ *adj* spick and span

Spie′gelei *n* fried egg

spie′gelglatt′ *adj* glassy

spiegeln [′ʃpigəln] *tr* reflect; mirror || *ref* be reflected || *intr* shine

Spiel [ʃpil] *n* (-[e]s;-e) game; play; set (*of chessmen or checkers*); (cards) deck; (mach) play; (mus) playing; (sport) match; (theat) acting, performance; **auf dem S. stehen** be at stake; **aufs S. setzen** risk; **bei etw im S. sein** be at the bottom of s.th.; **leichtes S. haben mit** have an easy time with; **S. der Natur** freak of nature

Spiel′art *f* (biol) variety

Spiel′automat *m* slot machine

Spiel′bank *f* (-;-en) gambling table; gambling casino

Spiel′dose *f* music box

spielen [′ʃpilən] *tr & intr* play

Spielerei [ʃpilə′raɪ] *f* (-;-en) fooling around; child's play

Spiel′ergebnis *n* (sport) score

spielerisch [′ʃpilərɪʃ] *adj* playful

Spiel′feld *n* (sport) playing field

Spiel′film *m* feature film

Spiel′folge *f* program

Spiel′gefährte *m*, **Spiel′gefährtin** *f* playmate

Spiel′karten *pl* (playing) cards

Spiel′leiter *m* (cin, theat) director

Spiel′marke *f* chip, counter

Spiel′plan *m* program

Spiel′platz *m* playground; playing field

Spiel′raum *m* (fig) elbowroom; (mach) play

Spiel′sachen *pl* toys

Spiel′tisch *m* gambling table

Spiel′verderber *m* kill-joy

Spiel′verlängerung *f* overtime

Spiel′waren *pl* toys

Spiel′zeug *n* toy(s)

Spieß [ʃpis] *m* (-es;-e) spear, pike; (sl) top kick; (culin) spit; **den S. umdrehen gegen** turn the tables on

Spieß′bürger *m* Philistine, lowbrow

spieß′bürgerlich *adj* narrow-minded

spießen [′ʃpisən] *tr* spear; spit

Spie′ßer *m* (-s;-) Philistine, lowbrow

Spieß′gesell *m* accomplice

Spießruten [′ʃpisrutən] *pl*—**S. laufen** run the gauntlet

spinal [ʃpɪ′nal] *adj* spinal; **spinale Kinderlähmung** infantile paralysis

Spinat [ʃpɪ′nat] *m* (-[e]s;-e) spinach

Spind [ʃpɪnt] *m & n* (-[e]s;-e) wardrobe; (mil) locker

Spindel [′ʃpɪndəl] *f* (-;-n) spindle; (*Spinnrocken*) distaff

spin′deldürr′ *adj* skinny, scrawny

Spinne [′ʃpɪnə] *f* (-;-n) spider

spinnen [′ʃpɪnən] *tr* spin; **Ränke s.** hatch plots || *intr* purr; (*im Gefängnis sitzen*) do time; (sl) be looney

Spin′nengewebe *n* spider web

Spin′ner *m* (-s;-) spinner; (sl) nut

Spinnerei [ʃpɪnə′raɪ] *f* (-;-en) spinning; spinning mill

Spinn′faden *m* spider thread; **Spinnfäden** gossamer

Spinn′gewebe *n* (-s;-) cobweb

Spinn′rad *n* spinning wheel

Spinn′webe *f* (-;-n) (Aust) cobweb

Spion [ʃpɪ′on] *m* (-[e]s;-e) spy

Spionage [ʃpɪ·ɔ′naʒə] *f* (-;) spying, espionage

Spiona′geabwehr *f* counterintelligence

spionieren [ʃpɪ·ɔ′nirən] *intr* spy

Spirale [ʃpɪ′ralə] *f* (-;-n) spiral

Spirituosen [ʃpɪrɪtu′ozən] *pl* liquor

Spiritus [′ʃpɪrɪtus] *m* (-;-se) alcohol

Spital [ʃpɪ′tal] *n* (-s;ˍer) hospital

spitz [ʃpɪts] *adj* pointed; sharp; (*Winkel*) acute

Spitz′bart *m* goatee

Spitz′bube *m* rascal; thief; swindler

Spitze [′ʃpɪtsə] *f* (-;-n) point; tip; top, summit; (tex) lace; **an der S. liegen** be in the lead; **auf die S. treiben** carry to extremes

Spitzel [′ʃpɪtsəl] *m* (-s;-) spy; stool pigeon; plain-clothes man

spitzen [′ʃpɪtsən] *tr* point; sharpen; (*Ohren*) prick up; **den Mund s.** purse the lips || *ref*—**sich s. auf** (*acc*) look look forward to || *intr* be on one's toes

Spitzen– *comb.fm.* top; peak; leading; topnotch; maximum; (tex) lace

Spit′zenform *f* (sport) top form

Spit′zenleistung *f* top performance

Spit′zenmarke *f* (com) top brand

Spit′zer *m* (-s;-) pencil sharpener

spitz′findig *adj* subtle; sharp

Spitz′hacke *f*, **Spitz′haue** *f* pickax

spitzig [′ʃpɪtsɪç] *adj* pointed; (& fig) sharp

Spitz'marke f (typ) heading
Spitz'name m nickname; pet name
Spitz'nase f pointed nose
spleißen ['ʃplaɪsən] §53 tr splice
spliß [ʃplɪs] pret of **spleißen**
Splitter ['ʃplɪtər] m (-s;-) splinter; chip; fragment
split'ternackt' adj stark-naked
Split'terpartei f splinter party
split'tersicher adj shatterproof
spontan [ʃpɔn'tan] adj spontaneous
Spore ['ʃporə] f (-;-n) spore
Sporn [ʃpɔrn] m (-[e]s; **Sporen** ['ʃporən]) spur; (fig) stimulus; (aer) tail skid; (naut) ram
spornen ['ʃpɔrnən] tr spur
Sport [ʃpɔrt] m (-[e]s;-e) sport(s); **S. ausüben** (or **treiben**) play sports
Sport'freund –in §8 mf sports fan
Sport'hose f shorts, trunks
Sport'jacke f sport jacket, blazer
Sport'kleidung f sportswear
Sportler –in ['ʃpɔrtlər(ɪn)] §6 mf athlete
sport'lich adj sportsmanlike; (Figur) athletic; (Kleidung) sport
Sport'wagen m sports car; (Kinderwagen) stroller
Sport'wart m trainer
Spott [ʃpɔt] m (-[e]s;) mockery; scorn
Spott'bild n caricature
spott'bil'lig adj dirt-cheap
Spott'drossel f mockingbird
Spöttelei [ʃpœtə'laɪ] f (-;-en) mockery
spotten ['ʃpɔtən] intr (über acc) scoff (at), ridicule; **das spottet jeder Beschreibung** that defies description
Spötterei [ʃpœtə'raɪ] f (-;-en) mockery
Spott'gebot n (com) ridiculous offer
spöttisch ['ʃpœtɪʃ] adj mocking, satirical; sneering
Spott'name m nickname
Spott'schrift f satire
sprach [ʃprax] pret of **sprechen**
Sprach– comb.fm. speech; grammatical; linguistic; philological
Sprache ['ʃpraxə] f (-;-n) language, tongue; speech; diction; style; idiom
Sprach'eigenheit f, **Sprach'eigentümlichkeit** f idiom, idiomatic expression
Sprach'fehler m speech defect
Sprach'forschung f linguistics
Sprach'führer m phrase book
Sprach'gebrauch m usage
Sprach'gefühl n feeling for a language
sprach'gewandt adj fluent
sprach'kundig adj proficient in languages
Sprach'lehre f grammar
Sprach'lehrer –in §6 mf language teacher
sprach'lich adj grammatical; linguistic
sprach'los adj speechless
Sprach'rohr n megaphone; (fig) mouthpiece
Sprach'schatz m vocabulary
Sprach'störung f speech defect
Sprach'wissenschaft f philology; linguistics
sprang [ʃpraŋ] pret of **springen**
Sprech– [ʃprɛç] comb.fm. speaking
Sprech'art f way of speaking

Sprech'bühne f legitimate theater
sprechen ['ʃprɛçən] §64 tr speak; talk; (Gebet) say; (Urteil) pronounce; speak to, see || intr (über acc, von) speak (about), talk (about); **er ist nicht zu s.** he's not available
Spre'cher –in §6 mf speaker, talker
Sprech'fehler m slip of the tongue
Sprech'funkgerät n walkie-talkie
Sprech'probe f audition
Sprech'sprache f spoken language
Sprech'stunde f office hours
Sprech'stundenhilfe f receptionist
Sprech'zimmer n office (of doctor, etc.)
Spreize ['ʃpraɪtsə] f (-;-n) prop, strut; (gym) split
spreizen ['ʃpraɪtsən] tr spread, stretch out || ref sprawl out; (fig) (mit) boast (of); **sich s. gegen** resist
Spreng– [ʃprɛŋ] comb.fm. high-explosive
Sprengel ['ʃprɛŋəl] m (-s;-) diocese; parish
sprengen ['ʃprɛŋən] tr break, burst; (mit Sprengstoff) blow up; (Tür) force; (Versammlung) break up; (Mine) set off; (bespritzen) sprinkle; (Garten) water || intr (SEIN) gallop
Spreng'kommando n bomb disposal unit
Spreng'kopf m warhead
Spreng'körper m, **Spreng'stoff** m explosive
Spreng'wagen m sprinkling truck
Sprenkel ['ʃprɛŋkəl] m (-s;-) speck
sprenkeln ['ʃprɛŋkəln] tr speckle
Spreu [ʃprɔɪ] f (-;) chaff
Sprichwort ['ʃprɪçvɔrt] n (-[e]s;ˮer) proverb, saying
sprichwörtlich ['ʃprɪçvœrtlɪç] adj proverbial
sprießen ['ʃprisən] §76 intr (SEIN) sprout
Springbrunnen ['ʃprɪŋbrʊnən] m (-s;-) fountain
springen ['ʃprɪŋən] §142 intr (SEIN) jump; dive; burst; (Eis) crack; (coll) rush, hurry
Sprin'ger m (-s;-) jumper; (chess) knight; (sport) diver
Spring'insfeld m (-[e]s;-e) (coll) live wire
Spring'kraft f (& fig) resiliency
Spring'seil n jumping rope
Sprint [ʃprɪnt] m (-s;-s) sprint
Sprit [ʃprit] m (-[e]s;-e) alcohol; (coll) gasoline
Spritze ['ʃprɪtsə] f (-;-n) squirt; (Feuerwehr) fire engine; (med) injection, shot; (med) syringe
spritzen ['ʃprɪtsən] tr squirt; splash; (sprühen) spray; (sprengen) sprinkle; (Wein) mix with soda water; (med) inject || intr spurt, spout || impers—**es spritzt** it is drizzling || intr (SEIN) dash, flit
Spritz'tour f (coll) side trip
spröde ['ʃprødə] adj brittle; (Haut) chapped; (fig) prudish, coy
sproß [ʃprɔs] pret of **sprießen** || **Sproß** m (Sprosses; Sprosse) offspring, descendant; (bot) shoot

Sprosse ['ʃprɔsə] f (-;-n) rung; prong
sprossen ['ʃprɔsən] intr (HABEN & SEIN) sprout
Sprößling ['ʃprœslɪŋ] m (-s;-e) offspring, descendant; (bot) sprout
Spruch [ʃprux] m (-[e]s;ꞋꞋe) saying; motto; text, passage; (jur) sentence; (jur) verdict; **e-n S. fällen** give the verdict
Spruch'band n (-[e]s;ꞋꞋer) banderole
Sprudel ['ʃprudəl] m (-s;-) mineral water
sprudeln ['ʃprudəln] intr bubble
sprühen ['ʃpry·ən] tr emit ‖ intr spray; sparkle; (fig) flash ‖ impers— **es sprüht** it is drizzling
Sprüh'regen m drizzle
Sprüh'teufel m (coll) spitfire
Sprung [ʃprʊŋ] m (-[e]s;ꞋꞋe) jump; crack; (sport) dive
Sprung'brett m diving board; (fig) stepping stone
Spucke ['ʃpʊkə] f (-;) (coll) spit
spucken ['ʃpʊkən] tr spit ‖ intr spit; (Motor) sputter
Spuk [ʃpuk] m (-[e]s;-e) ghost, spook; (Lärm) racket; (Alptraum) nightmare
spuken ['ʃpukən] intr linger on ‖ impers—**es spukt hier** this place is haunted
spuk'haft adj spooky
Spülabort ['ʃpylabɔrt] m flush toilet
Spül'becken n sink
Spule ['ʃpulə] f (-;-n) spool, reel; (elec) coil
Spüle ['ʃpylə] f (-;-n) wash basin
spulen ['ʃpulən] tr reel, wind
spülen ['ʃpylən] tr wash, rinse; (Abort) flush; **an Land s.** wash ashore ‖ intr flush the toilet; undulate
Spü'ler m (-s;-) dishwasher
Spülicht ['spylɪçt] n (-[e]s;-e) dishwater; swill, slop
Spül'maschine f dishwasher
Spül'mittel n detergent
Spülwasser n dishwater
Spund [ʃpʊnt] m (-[e]s;ꞋꞋe) bung, plug; (carp) feather, tongue
Spur [ʃpur] f (-;-en) trace; track, rut; (hunt) scent; **S. Salz** pinch of salt
spürbar ['ʃpyrbɑr] adj perceptible
spüren ['ʃpyrən] tr trace; track, trail; (fühlen) feel; (wahrnehmen) perceive
spur'los adj trackless ‖ adv without a trace
Spür'nase f (coll) good nose
Spür'sinn m flair
Spur'weite f (aut) tread; (rr) gauge
sputen ['sputən] ref hurry up
SS ['ɛs'ɛs] f (-;) (Schutzstaffel) S.S.
Staat [ʃtat] m (-[e]s;-en) state; government; (Aufwand) show; (Putz) finery
Staats- comb.fm. state; government; national; public; political
Staatsangehörigkeit ['ʃtatsangəhøriçkaɪt] f (-;) nationality
Staats'anwalt m district attorney
Staats'bauten pl public works
Staats'beamte m civil servant

Staats'bürger –in §6 mf citizen
Staats'bürgerkunde f civics
Staats'bürgerschaft f citizenship
Staats'dienst m civil service
staats'eigen adj state-owned
Staats'feind m public enemy
staats'feindlich adj subversive
Staats'form f form of government
Staats'gewalt f supreme power
Staats'hoheit f sovereignty
staats'klug adj politic, diplomatic
Staats'klugheit f statecraft
Staats'kunst f statesmanship
Staats'mann m (-[e]s;ꞋꞋer) statesman
staats'männisch adj statesmanlike
Staats'oberhaupt n head of state
Staats'papiere pl government bonds
Staats'recht n public law
Staats'streich m coup d'état
Staats'wirtschaft f political economy
Staats'wissenschaft f political science
Stab [ʃtap] m (-[e]s;ꞋꞋe) staff; rod; bar; (e-r Jalousie) slat; (eccl) crozier; (mil) staff; (mil) headquarters; (mus, sport) baton
stab'hochspringen §142 intr (SEIN) pole-vault
stabil [ʃta'bil] adj stable, steady
stabilisieren [ʃtabɪlɪ'zirən] tr stabilize
stach [ʃtax] pret of **stechen**
Stachel ['ʃtaxəl] m (-s;-n) prick; quill; (bot) thorn; (ent) sting
Sta'chelbeere f gooseeberry
Sta'cheldraht m barbed wire
stachelig ['ʃtaxəlɪç] adj prickly; (& fig) thorny
Sta'chelschwein n porcupine
Sta·dion ['ʃtadjɔn] n (-s;-dien [djən]) stadium
Sta·dium ['ʃtadjʊm] n (-s;-dien [djən]) stage
Stadt [ʃtat] f (-;ꞋꞋe) city, town
Städtchen ['ʃtɛtçən] n (-s;-) town
Städtebau ['ʃtɛtəbau] m (-[e]s;) city planning
Stadt'gemeinde f township
Stadt'gespräch n talk of the town
städtisch ['ʃtɛtɪʃ] adj municipal
Stadt'plan m map of the city
Stadt'rand m outskirts
Stadt'rat m (-[e]s;ꞋꞋe) city council; (Person) city councilor
Stadt'teil m **Stadt'viertel** n quarter (of the city)
Stafette [ʃta'fetə] f (-;-n) courier; (sport) relay
Staffel ['ʃtafəl] f (-;-n) step, rung; (Stufe) degree; (aer) squadron (of nine aircraft); (sport) relay team
Staffelei [ʃtafə'laɪ] f (-;-en) easel
Staf'felkeil m (aer) V-formation
Staf'fellauf m relay race
staffeln ['ʃtafəln] tr graduate; (Arbeitszeit, usw.) stagger
stahl [ʃtal] pret of **stehlen** ‖ **Stahl** m (-[e]s;ꞋꞋe) steel
Stahl'beton m reinforced concrete
stählen ['ʃtelən] tr temper; (fig) steel
Stahl'kammer f steel vault
Stahlspäne ['ʃtalʃpenə] pl steel wool
stak [ʃtak] pret of **stecken**
Stalag ['ʃtalak] n (-s;-s) (Stammlager) main camp (for P.O.W.'s)

Stall [ʃtal] *m* (-[e]s;-ᵉe) stable; shed
Stall'knecht *m* groom
Stamm [ʃtam] *m* (-[e]s;-ᵉe) stem;
stalk; trunk; stock, race; tribe; breed
Stamm'aktie *f* common stock
Stamm'baum *m* family tree; pedigree
stammeln ['ʃtaməln] *tr & intr* stammer
Stamm'eltern *pl* ancestors
stammen ['ʃtamən] *intr* (SEIN) (aus,
von) come (from); (von) date
(from); (gram) (von) be derived
(from)
Stamm'gast *m* regular customer
stämmig ['ʃtemɪç] *adj* stocky; husky
Stamm'kneipe *f* favorite bar
Stamm'kunde *m*, Stamm'kundin *f* regular customer
Stamm'personal *n* skeleton staff
Stamm'tisch *m* reserved table
Stammutter (Stamm'mutter) *f* ances-
tress
Stamm'vater *m* ancestor
stampfen ['ʃtampfən] *tr* tamp, pound;
(*Kartoffeln*) mash; (*Boden*) paw ||
intr stamp the ground; (*durch
Schnee*) trudge; (naut) pitch
stand [ʃtant] *pret* of stehen || Stand *m*
(-[e]s;-ᵉe) stand; footing, foothold;
level, height; condition; status, rank;
class, caste; booth; profession; trade;
(sport) score; seinen S. behaupten
hold one's ground
Standard ['ʃtandart] *m* (-s;-s) standard
Standarte [ʃtan'dartə] *f* (-;-n) banner;
standard
Stand'bild *n* statue
Ständchen ['ʃtentçən] *n* (-s;-) serenade; j-m ein S. bringen serenade
s.o.
Ständer ['ʃtendər] *m* (-s;-) stand,
rack; pillar; stud; (mach) column
Stan'desamt *n* bureau of vital statistics
stan'desamtlich *adj & adv* before a
civil magistrate
stan'desgemäß *adj* according to rank
Stan'desperson *f* dignitary
stand'fest *adj* stable, steady, sturdy
stand'haft *adj* steadfast
stand'halten §90 *intr* hold out; (*dat*)
withstand
ständig ['ʃtendɪç] *adj* permanent;
steady, constant
Stand'licht *n* parking light
Stand'ort *m* position; station; (mil)
base; (mil) garrison
Stand'pauke *f* (coll) lecture
Stand'punkt *m* standpoint
Stand'recht *n* martial law
Stand'uhr *f* grandfather's clock
Stange ['ʃtaŋə] *f* (-;-n) pole; rod, bar;
perch, roost; e-e S. Zigaretten a carton of cigarettes; von der S. readymade (*clothes*)
stank [ʃtaŋk] *pret* of stinken
stänkern ['ʃteŋkərn] *intr* (coll) stink;
(coll) make trouble
Stanniol [ʃta'njol] *n* (-s;-e), Stanniol'papier *n* tinfoil
Stanze ['ʃtantsə] *f* (-;-n) stanza;
punch, die, stamp
stanzen ['ʃtantsən] *tr* (mach) punch
Stapel ['ʃtapəl] *m* (-s;-) stack; depot;

stock; (naut) slip; (tex) staple; auf
S. liegen be in drydock; vom S.
laufen lassen launch
Sta'pellauf *m* launching
stapeln ['ʃtapəln] *tr* stack, pile up
Sta'pelplatz *m* lumberyard; depot
stapfen ['ʃtapfən] *intr* (SEIN) slog
Star [ʃtar] *m* (-[e]s;-e) (orn) starling;
(pathol) cataract; grauer S. cataract;
grüner S. glaucoma || *m* (-s;-s) (cin,
theat) star
starb [ʃtarp] *pret* of sterben
stark [ʃtark] *adj* (stärker ['ʃterkər];
stärkste ['ʃterkstə] §9) strong; stout;
(*Erkältung*) bad; (*Familie*) big;
(*Kälte*) severe; (*Frost, Verkehr*)
heavy; (*Wind*) high; (*Stunde*) full ||
adv much; hard; very
Stärke ['ʃterkə] *f* (-;-n) strength;
force; stoutness; thickness; might;
violence; intensity; (*Anzahl*) number; (fig) forte; (chem) starch
stärken ['ʃterkən] *tr* strengthen;
(*Wäsche*) starch || *ref* take some
refreshment
Stark'strom *m* high-voltage current
Stär'kung *f* (-;-en) strengthening; refreshment; (*Imbiß*) snack
starr [ʃtar] *adj* stiff, rigid; fixed; inflexible; obstinate; dumbfounded;
numb || *adv*—s. ansehen stare at
starren ['ʃtarən] *intr* (auf *acc*) stare
(at); s. von be covered with
Starr'kopf *m* stubborn fellow
starr'köpfig *adj* stubborn
Starr'krampf *m* (-es;) tetanus
Starr'sinn *m* (-[e]s;) stubbornness
Start [ʃtart] *m* (-[e]s;-s & -e) start;
(aer) take-off; (rok) launching
Start'bahn *f* (aer) runway
starten ['ʃtartən] *tr* start; launch ||
intr (SEIN) start; (aer) take off; (rok)
lift off, be launched
Start'rampe *f* (rok) launch pad
Station [ʃta'tsjon] *f* (-;-en) station;
(med) ward; freie S. free room and
board
statisch ['ʃtatɪʃ] *adj* static
Statist –in [ʃta'tɪst(ɪn)] §7 *mf* (cin)
extra; (theat) supernumerary
Statistik [ʃta'tɪstɪk] *f* (-;-en) statistic;
(*Wissenschaft*) statistics
statistisch [ʃta'tɪstɪʃ] *adj* statistical
Stativ [ʃta'tif] *n* (-s;-e) stand; (phot)
tripod
statt [ʃtat] *prep* (genit) instead of; s.
zu (*inf*) instead of (*ger*) || Statt *f*
(-;) place, stead; an Kindes S. annehmen adopt
Stätte ['ʃtetə] *f* (-;-n) place, spot;
(*Wohnung*) abode; room
statt'finden §59 *intr* take place
statt'haft *adj* admissible; legal
Statthalter ['ʃtathaltər] *m* (-s;-) governor
statt'lich *adj* stately; imposing
Statue ['ʃtatu·ə] *f* (-;-n) statue
statuieren [ʃtatu'irən] *tr* establish; ein
Exempel s. an (*dat*) make an example of
Statur [ʃta'tur] *f* (-;-en) stature
Statut [ʃta'tut] *n* (-[e]s;-en) statute;
Statuten bylaws

Stau [ʃtaʊ] *m* (–[e]s;–e) dammed-up water; updraft; (aut) tie-up

Staub [ʃtaʊp] *m* (–[e]s;) dust

Stau'becken *n* reservoir

stauben ['ʃtaʊbən] *intr* make dust

stäuben ['ʃtɔɪbən] *tr* dust; sprinkle, powder; (*Flüssigkeit*) spray ‖ *intr* make dust; throw off spray

staubig ['ʃtaʊbɪç] *adj* dusty

staub'saugen *tr & intr* vacuum

Staub'sauger *m* vacuum cleaner

Staub'wedel *m* feather duster

Staub'zucker *m* powdered sugar

stauchen ['ʃtaʊçən] *tr* knock, jolt; compress; (sl) chew out

Stau'damm *m* dam

Staude ['ʃtaʊdə] *f* (–;–n) perennial

stauen ['ʃtaʊ·ən] *tr* dam up; (*Waren*) stow away; (*Blut*) stanch ‖ *ref* be blocked, jam up

Stau'er *m* (–s;–) stevedore

staunen ['ʃtaʊnən] *intr* (**über** *acc*) be astonished (at) ‖ **Staunen** *n* (–s;) astonishment

stau'nenswert *adj* astonishing

Staupe ['ʃtaʊpə] *f* (–;) (vet) distemper

Stau'see *m* reservoir

Stau'ung *f* (–;–en) damming up; blockage; (*Engpaß*) bottleneck; (*Verkehrs-*) jam-up; (pathol) congestion

stechen ['ʃtɛçən] §64 *tr* prick; sting, bite; (*mit e-r Waffe*) stab; (*Torf*) cut; (*Star*) remove; (*Kontrolluhr*) punch; (*Wein*) draw; (*Näherei*) stitch; (*gravieren*) engrave; (cards) trump; (cards) take (*a trick*) ‖ *intr* sting, bite; (*Sonne*) be hot; (cards) be trump; **j–m in die Augen s.** catch s.o.'s eye ‖ *impers*—**es sticht mich in der Brust** I have a sharp pain in my chest

ste'chend *adj* (*Blick*) piercing; (*Geruch*) strong; (*Schmerz*) sharp, stabbing

Stech'karte *f* timecard

Stech'schritt *m* goosestep

Stech'uhr *f* time clock

Steckbrief ['ʃtɛkbrif] *m* warrant for arrest

steck'brieflich *adv*—**s. verfolgen** put out a "wanted" notice for

Steckdose ['ʃtɛkdozə] *f* (elec) outlet

stecken ['ʃtɛkən] *tr & intr* stick ‖ **Stecken** *m* (–s;–) stick

steckenbleiben (stek'kenbleiben) §62 *intr* (SEIN) get stuck

Steckenpferd (Stek'kenpferd) hobbyhorse; (fig) hobby

Stecker (Stek'ker) *m* (–s;–) (elec) plug

Steck'kontakt *m* (elec) plug

Steck'nadel *f* pin

Steg [ʃtek] *m* (–[e]s;–e) footpath; footbridge; (*e-r Brille, Geige*) bridge; (*Landungs-*) jetty; (naut) gangplank

Steg'reif *m*—**aus dem S.** extempore

stehen ['ʃte·ən] §146 *tr*—**e-m Maler Modell s.** sit for a painter; **Schlange s.** stand in line; **Schmiere s.** (coll) be a lookout; **Wache s.** stand guard ‖ *intr* (HABEN & SEIN) stand; stop; be; (gram) occur, be used; (*Kleider*) fit; **das steht bei Ihnen** that depends

on you; **gut s.** (*dat*) fit, suit; **gut s. mit** be on good terms with; **wie steht's?** (coll) how is it going?

ste'henbleiben §62 *intr* (SEIN) stop

ste'henlassen §104 *tr* leave standing; (*nicht anrühren*) leave alone; (*Fehler*) leave uncorrected; (*vergessen*) forget; (culin) allow to stand or cool

Ste'her *m* (–s;–) long-distance cyclist

Stehlampe ['ʃtelampə] *f* floor lamp

Stehleiter ['ʃtelaɪtər] *f* stepladder

stehlen ['ʃtelən] §147 *tr & intr* steal

Stehplatz ['ʃteplats] *m* standing room

steif [ʃtaɪf] *adj* stiff; rigid; (*Lächeln*) forced; (*förmlich*) formal; (*starr*) numb

steifen ['ʃtaɪfən] *tr* stiffen; (*Wäsche*) starch

Steig [ʃtaɪk] *m* (–[e]s;–e) path

Steig'bügel *m* stirrup

steigen ['ʃtaɪgən] §148 *tr* (*Treppen*) climb ‖ *intr* (SEIN) climb; rise; go up; (*Nebel*) lift; (*Blut in den Kopf*) rush ‖ **Steigen** *n* (–s;) rise; increase

steigern ['ʃtaɪgərn] *tr* raise, increase; (*verstärken*) enhance; (gram) compare ‖ *ref* increase, go up

Stei'gerung *f* (–;–en) rising; increase; intensification; (gram) comparison

Stei'gerungsgrad *m* (gram) degree of comparison

Stei'gung *f* (–;–en) rise; (*Hang*) slope; (*e-s Propellers*) pitch

steil [ʃtaɪl] *adj* steep

Stein [ʃtaɪn] *m* (–[e]s;–e) stone; rock; (horol) jewel; (pathol) stone

stein'alt' *adj* old as the hills

Stein'bruch *m* quarry

Stein'druck *m* lithography; (*Bild*) lithograph

steinern ['ʃtaɪnərn] *adj* stone

Stein'gut *n* earthenware

steinig ['ʃtaɪnɪç] *adj* stony, rocky

steinigen ['ʃtaɪnɪgən] *tr* stone

Stein'kohle *f* hard coal

Stein'metz *m* stonemason

stein'reich' *adj* (coll) filthy rich

Stein'salz *n* rock salt

Stein'schlag *m* (public sign) falling rocks

Stein'wurf *m* stone's throw

Stein'zeit *f* stone age

Steiß [ʃtaɪs] *m* (–es;–e) buttocks

Stelldichein ['ʃtɛldɪçaɪn] *n* (–[s]; –[s]) (coll) date

Stelle ['ʃtɛlə] *f* (–;–n) place, spot; position; job; agency, department; quotation; (math) digit; **an S. von** in place of; **auf der S.** on the spot; **auf der S. treten** (fig & mil) mark time; **freie** (or **offene**) **S.** opening; **zur S. sein** be on hand

stellen ['ʃtɛlən] *tr* put, place; set; stand; (*ein–*) regulate, adjust; (*anordnen*) fix, arrange; (*Frage*) ask; (*Horoskop*) cast; (*Diagnose*) give; (*Falle, Wecker*) set; (*Kaution*) put up; (*Zeugen*) produce; **e–n Antrag s.** make a motion; **in Dienst s.** appoint; put into service ‖ *ref* place oneself, stand; give oneself up; **der Preis stellt sich auf...** the price is...; **sich s., als ob** act as if

Stel'lenangebot *n* help wanted
Stel'lenbewerber –in §6 *mf* applicant
Stel'lengesuch *n* situation wanted
Stel'lenjagd *f* job hunting
Stel'lennachweis *m*, **Stel'lenvermitt-lungsbüro** *n* employment agency
stel'lenweise *adv* here and there
–stellig [ʃtɛlɪç] *comb.fm.* –digit
Stell'schraube *f* set screw
Stel'lung *f* (–;–en) position; situation; job; standing; status; rank; posture; (mil) line, position; (mil) emplacement; **S. nehmen zu** express one's opinion on; (*erklären*) explain; (*beantworten*) answer
Stel'lungnahme *f* (–;–n) attitude, point of view; (*Erklärung*) comment; (*Gutachten*) opinion; (*Bericht*) report; (*Beantwortung*) answer; (*Entscheid*) decision; **sich** [*dat*] **e–e S. vorbehalten** not commit oneself
Stel'lungsgesuch *n* (job) application
stel'lungslos *adj* jobless
stell'vertretend *adj* acting
Stell'vertreter –in §6 *mf* representative; deputy; proxy; substitute
Stell'vertretung *f* (–;–en) representation; substitution; **in S.** by proxy
Stelzbein [ʃtɛltsbaɪn] *n* wooden leg
Stelze [ʃtɛltsə] *f* (–;–n) stilt
stelzen [ʃtɛltsən] *intr* (SEIN) stride
Stemmeisen [ʃtɛmaɪzən] *n* crowbar
stemmen [ʃtɛmən] *tr* support; (*Gewicht*) lift; (*Loch*) chisel || *ref*—**sich s. gegen** oppose
Stempel [ʃtɛmpəl] *m* (–s;–) stamp; prop; (*Kolben*) piston; (bot) pistil
Stem'pelkissen *n* ink pad, stamp pad
stempeln [ʃtɛmpəln] *tr* stamp || *intr*—**s. gehen** (coll) collect unemployment insurance
Stengel [ʃtɛŋəl] *m* (–s;–) stalk
Steno [ʃteno] *f* (–;) stenography
Stenograph [ʃtenoˈgraf] *m* (–en;–en) stenographer
Stenographie [ʃtenograˈfi] *f* (–;) stenography, shorthand
stenographieren [ʃtenogrˈfirən] *tr* take down in shorthand || *intr* do shorthand
Stenographin [ʃtenoˈgrafɪn] *f* (–;–nen) stenographer
Stenotypistin [ʃtenotyˈpɪstɪn] *f* (–;–nen) stenographer
Step [ʃtɛp] *m* (–s;–) tap dance; **S. tanzen** tap-dance
Steppdecke [ʃtɛpdɛkə] *f* comforter
Steppe [ʃtɛpə] *f* (–;–n) steppe
steppen [ʃtɛpən] *tr* quilt || *intr* tap-dance || **Steppen** *n* (–s;) tap-dancing
Sterbe– [ʃtɛrbə] *comb.fm.* dying, death
Ster'befall *m* death
Ster'begeld *n* death benefit
Ster'behilfe *f* euthanasia
sterben [ʃtɛrbən] §149 *intr* (SEIN) (**an** *dat*) die (of)
sterb'lich *adj* mortal || *adv*—**s. verliebt in** (*acc*) head over heals in love with
Sterb'lichkeit *f* (–;) mortality
Sterb'lichkeitsziffer *f* death rate
stereotyp [stereɔˈtyp] *adj* stereotyped
steril [ʃteˈril] *adj* sterile
sterilisieren [ʃterɪlɪˈzirən] *tr* sterilize

Stern [ʃtɛrn] *m* (–[e]s;–e) star; (typ) asterisk
Stern'bild *n* constellation
Stern'blume *f* aster
Sterndeuter [ʃtɛrndɔɪtər] *m* (–s;–) astrologer
Sterndeuterei [ʃtɛrndɔɪtəˈraɪ] *f* (–;) astrology
Ster'nenbanner *n* Stars and Stripes
stern'ha'gelvoll' *adj* (sl) dead drunk
stern'hell' *adj* starlit
Stern'himmel *m* starry sky
Stern'kunde *f* astronomy
Stern'schuppe *f* shooting star
Stern'warte *f* observatory
stet [ʃtet], **stetig** [ʃtetɪç] *adj* steady
stets [ʃtets] *adv* constantly, always
Steuer [ʃtɔɪ·ər] *f* (–;–n) tax; duty || *n* (–s;–) rudder, helm; (aer) controls; (aut) steering wheel; **am S.** at the helm; (aut) behind the wheel
Steu'eramt *n* tax office
Steu'erbord *n* (naut) starboard
Steu'ererhebung *f* levy of taxes
Steu'ererklärung *f* tax return
Steu'erflosse *f* vertical stabilizer
Steu'erhinterziehung *f* tax evasion
Steu'erjahr *n* fiscal year
Steu'erknüppel *m* control stick
Steu'er·mann *m* (–[e]s;–er & –leute) helmsman
steuern [ʃtɔɪ·ərn] *tr* steer; control; regulate; (aer, naut) pilot; (aut) drive || *intr* (*dat*) curb, check
steu'erpflichtig *adj* taxable; dutiable
Steu'errad *n* steering wheel
Steu'erruder *n* rudder, helm
Steu'ersatz *m* tax rate
Steu'ersäule *f* (aer) control column; (aut) steering column
Steu'erstufe *f* tax bracket
Steu'erung *f* (–;–en) steering; (*Bekämpfung*) control; (*Verhinderung*) prevention; (aer) piloting; (aut) steering mechanism
Steu'erveranlagung *f* tax assessment
Steu'erwerk *n* (aer) controls
Steu'erzahler –in §6 *mf* tax payer
Steu'erzuschlag *m* surtax
Steven [ʃtevən] *m* (–s;–) (naut) stem
Stewar·deß [ˈst(j)u·ərdɛs] *f* (–;–dessen [dɛsən]) (aer) stewardess
stibitzen [ʃtiˈbɪtsən] *tr* snitch
Stich [ʃtɪç] *m* (–[e]s;–e) prick; (*Messer–*) stab; (*Insekten–*) sting, bite; (*Stoß*) thrust; (*Seitenstechen*) sharp pain; (*Kupfer–*) engraving; (cards) trick; (naut) knot; (sew) stitch; **im S. lassen** abandon
Stichelei [ʃtɪçəˈlaɪ] *f* (–;–en) taunt
sticheln [ʃtɪçəln] *intr*—**gegen j–n s.** (fig) needle s.o.
Stich'flamme *f* flash
stich'haltig *adj* valid, sound
Stich'probe *f* spot check
Stich'tag *m* effective date; due date
Stich'wahl *f* run-off election
Stich'wort *n* (–[e]s;–er) key word; dictionary entry || *n* (–[e]s;–e) (theat) cue
Stich'wunde *f* stab wound
sticken [ʃtɪkən] *tr* embroider || *intr* embroider

Stickerei [ʃtɪkə'raɪ] f (-;-en) embroidery
Stick'husten m whooping cough
stickig ['ʃtɪkɪç] adj stuffy, close
Stick'stoff m nitrogen
stieben ['ʃtibən] §130 intr (HABEN & SEIN) fly; (Menge) disperse
Stief [ʃtif] comb.fm. step–
Stief'bruder m stepbrother
Stiefel ['ʃtifəl] m (-s;-) boot
Stie'felknecht m bootjack
Stief'mutter f stepmother
Stief'mütterchen n (bot) pansy
Stief'vater m stepfather
stieg [ʃtik] pret of steigen
Stiege ['ʃtigə] f (-;-n) staircase
Stiel [ʃtil] m (-[e]s;-e) handle; (bot) stalk
stier [ʃtir] adj staring, glassy || **Stier** m (-[e]s;-e) bull; (astr) Taurus
stieren ['ʃtirən] intr (auf acc) stare (at)
Stier'kampf m bullfight
stieß [ʃtis] pret of stoßen
Stift [ʃtɪft] m (-[e]s;-e) pin; peg; pencil; crayon; (Zwecke) tack; (coll) apprentice || n (-[e]s;-e & -er) charitable foundation or institution
stiften ['ʃtɪftən] tr (gründen) found; (spenden) donate; (verursachen) cause; (Unruhe) stir up; (Frieden) make; (Brand) start; (e-e Runde Bier) set up
Stif'ter –in §6 mf founder; donor; (fig) author, cause
Stif'tung f (-;-en) foundation; donation; grant; **fromme S.** religious establishment; **milde S.** charitable institution
Stif'tungsfest n founder's day
Stil [ʃtil] m (-[e]s;-e) style
stil'gerecht adj in good taste
stilisieren [ʃtili'zirən] tr word
stilistisch [ʃti'lɪstɪʃ] adj stylistic
still [ʃtɪl] adj still; calm; silent; (com) slack; **im stillen** in secret; **Stiller Ozean** Pacific Ocean || **Stille** f (-;) stillness; silence
still'bleiben §62 intr (SEIN) keep still
Stilleben (Still'leben) n still life
stillegen (still'legen) tr (Betrieb) shut down; (Verkehr) stop; (Schiff) put into mothballs
stillen ['ʃtɪlən] tr still; (Hunger) appease; (Durst) quench; (Blut) stanch; (Begierde) gratify
stilliegen (still'liegen) §108 intr lie still; (Betrieb) lie idle; (Verkehr) be at a standstill
still'schweigen §148 intr be silent; **s. zu** acquiesce in || **Stillschweigen** n (-s;) silence; secrecy
still'schweigend adj silent; (fig) tacit
Still'stand m standstill; (Sackgasse) stalemate, deadlock
still'stehen §146 intr stand still; (Betrieb) be idle; (mil) stand at attention; **stillgestanden!** (mil) attention!
Stil'möbel pl period furniture
stil'voll adj stylish
Stimm– [ʃtɪm] comb.fm. vocal; voting
Stimm'abgabe f vote, voting
Stimm'band n (-[e]s;-er) vocal cord

Stimm'block m (parl) bloc
Stimm'bruch m change of voice
Stimme ['ʃtɪmə] f (-;-n) voice; vote
stimmen ['ʃtɪmən] tr make feel (happy, etc.); (mus) tune || intr be right; vote; (mus) be in tune
Stim'menrutsch m (pol) landslide
Stimm'enthaltung f abstention
Stimm'gabel f tuning fork
Stimm'recht n right to vote, suffrage
Stim'mung f (-;-en) tone; (Laune) mood; (mil) morale; (mus) tuning; (st.exch.) trend
stim'mungsvoll adj cheerful
Stimm'zettel m ballot
stinken ['ʃtɪŋkən] §143 intr stink
Stink'tier n skunk
Stipen·dium [ʃtɪ'pɛndjʊm] n (-s;-dien [djən]) scholarship, grant
stippen ['ʃtɪpən] tr (coll) dunk
Stippvisite ['ʃtɪpvɪzitə] f (-;-n) short visit
Stirn [ʃtɪrn] f (-;-en), **Stirne** ['ʃtɪrnə] f (-;-n) forehead, brow; (fig) insolence, gall; **die S. runzeln** frown
Stirn'runzeln n (-s;) frown(ing)
stob [ʃtop] pret of stieben
stöbern ['ʃtøbərn] tr (Wild) flush; (aus dem Bett) yank || intr poke around; browse; (Schnee) drift
stochern ['ʃtoxərn] intr poke around; **im Essen s.** pick at one's food; **im Feuer s.** stoke the fire; **in den Zähnen s.** pick one's teeth
Stock [ʃtok] m (-[e]s;-e) stick; cane; wand; baton; stem; vine; tree stump; cleaning rod; beehive; massif; story, floor; **im ersten S.** on the second floor
Stock-, stock- comb.fm. thoroughly
stock'blind' adj stone-blind
stock'dun'kel adj pitch-dark
Stöckel ['ʃtœkəl] m (-s;-) high heel
stocken ['ʃtokən] intr stop; (Geschäft) slack off; (Blut) coagulate; (in der Rede) get stuck; (Milch) curdle; (Stimme) falter; (schimmeln) get moldy; (Unterhandlungen) become deadlocked; (Verkehr) get tied up; (zögern) hesitate || **Stocken** n (-s;) stopping; hesitation; **ins S. bringen** tie up
stock'fin'ster adj pitch-black
Stock'fleck m mildew
stock'fleckig adj mildewy
stockig ['ʃtokɪç] adj moldy
–stöckig [ʃtœkɪç] comb.fm. –story
stock'nüch'tern adj dead-sober
stock'steif' adj stiff as a board
stock'taub' adj stone-deaf
Stockung (Stok'kung) f (-;-en) stoppage; (des Verkehrs) congestion; (des Blutes) congestion; (Unterbrechung) interruption; (Verlangsamung) slowdown; (Zeitverlust) delay; (Pause) pause; (Zögern) hesitation; (der Unterhandlungen) deadlock
Stock'werk n story, floor
Stoff [ʃtof] m (-[e]s;-e) stuff, matter; fabric, material; cloth; subject, topic; (chem) substance
stoff'lich adj material
Stoff'rest m (tex) remnant

Stoff'wechsel *m* metabolism
stöhnen ['ʃtønən] *intr* groan, moan
Stolle ['ʃtɔlə] *f* (-;-n) fruit cake
Stollen ['ʃtɔlən] *m* (-s;-) fruit cake;
tunnel; (*Pfosten*) post; (*Stütze*) prop
stolpern ['ʃtɔlpərn] *intr* (SEIN) stumble, trip
stolz [ʃtɔlts] *adj* (auf *acc*) proud (of)
‖ **Stolz** *m* (-es;) pride
stolzieren [ʃtɔl'tsirən] *intr* (SEIN) strut;
(*Pferd*) prance
stopfen ['ʃtɔpfən] *tr* stuff, cram;
(*Pfeife*) fill; (*Strumpf*) darn; (mus)
mute; **j-m den Mund s.** shut s.o. up
‖ *intr* be filling; cause constipation
Stopf'garn *n* darning yarn
Stoppel ['ʃtɔpəl] *f* (-;-n) stubble
stoppelig ['ʃtɔpəlɪç] *adj* stubbly
stoppeln ['ʃtɔpəln] *tr* glean; (fig) patch
stoppen ['ʃtɔpən] *tr* stop; clock, time
‖ *intr* stop
Stopp'licht *n* tail light; stoplight
Stopp'uhr *f* stopwatch
Stöpsel ['ʃtœsəl] *m* (-s;-) stopper,
cork; (coll) squirt; (elec) plug
stöpseln ['ʃtœpsəln] *tr* plug; cork
Storch [ʃtɔrç] *m* (-[e]s;ꞏe) stork
stören ['ʃtørən] *tr* disturb, bother;
(*Pläne*) cross; (*Vergnügen*) spoil;
(mil) harass; (rad) jam
Störenfried ['ʃtørənfrit] *m* (-[e]s;-e)
pain in the neck
störrig ['ʃtœrɪç], **störrisch** ['ʃtœrɪʃ]
adj stubborn
Stö'rung *f* (-;-en) disturbance, trouble;
breakdown; interruption; annoyance;
intrusion; (rad) static; (rad) jamming
Stoß [ʃtos] *m* (-es;ꞏe) push, shove;
hit, blow; nudge, poke; (*Einschlag*)
impact; (*Erschütterung*) shock;
(*Fecht-*) pass; (*Feuer-*) burst (*of
fire*); (*Fuß-*) kick; (*Haufen*) pile,
bundle; (*Rück-*) recoil; (*Saum*)
seam, hem; (*Schwimm-*) stroke;
(*Trompeten-*) blast; (*Wind-*) gust;
(mil) thrust; (orn) tail
Stoß'dämpfer *m* shock absorber
Stößel ['ʃtøsəl] *m* (-s;-) pestle
stoßen ['ʃtosən] §150 *tr* push, shove;
hit, knock; kick; punch; jab, nudge,
poke; ram; pound; pulverize; oust ‖
ref bump oneself; **sich s. an** (*dat*)
take offense at; take exception to ‖
intr kick; (*mit den Hörnen*) butt;
(*Gewehr*) recoil, kick; (*Wagen*) jolt
(*Schiff*) toss; **in die Trompete s.**
blow the trumpet; **s. auf** (*acc*) swoop
down on ‖ *intr* (SEIN)—**s. an** (*acc*)
bump against; adjoin; be next-door
to; **s. auf** (*acc*) run into; come across;
(naut) dash against; **s. durch** (mil)
smash through; **vom Lande s.** shove
off; **zu j-m s.** side with s.o.
Stoß'stange *f* (aut) bumper
Stoß'trupp *m* assault party; **Stoßtruppen** shock troops; commandos, rangers
Stoß'zahn *m* tusk
stottern ['ʃtɔtərn] *tr* stutter, stammer
‖ *intr* stutter, stammer; (aut) sputter
stracks [ʃtraks] *adv* immediately; (*geradeaus*) straight ahead
Straf- [ʃtraf] *comb.fm.* penal; criminal

Straf'anstalt *f* penal institution
Straf'arbeit *f* (educ) extra work
Straf'aufschub *m* reprieve
strafbar ['ʃtrafbar] *adj* punishable
Strafe ['ʃtrafə] *f* (-;-n) punishment;
penalty; (*Geld-*) fine; **bei S. von**
under pain of; **zur S.** as punishment
strafen ['ʃtrafən] *tr* punish
straff [ʃtraf] *adj* tight; (*Seil*) taut;
(*gespannt*) tense; (*aufrecht*) erect;
(fig) strict; **s. spannen** tighten
straf'fällig *adj* punishable; culpable
Straf'geld *n* fine
Straf'gesetzbuch *n* penal code
sträflich ['ʃtreflɪç] *adj* culpable
Sträfling ['ʃtreflɪŋ] *m* (-s;-e) convict
straf'los *adj* unpunished
Straf'porto *n* postage due
Straf'predigt *f* talking-to, lecture
Straf'raum *m* (sport) penalty box
Straf'recht *n* criminal law
Straf'stoß *m* (sport) penalty kick
Straf'umwandlung *f* (jur) commutation
Straf'verfahren *n* criminal proceedings
Strahl [ʃtral] *m* (-[e]s;-en) ray; beam;
flash; jet; (geom) radius
Strahl'antrieb *m* jet propulsion
strahlen ['ʃtralən] *intr* beam, shine
Strahl'motor *m*, **Strahl'triebwerk** *n* jet
engine
Strah'lung *f* (-;-en) radiation
Strähne ['ʃtrenə] *f* (-;-n) strand; lock;
hank, skein
strähnig ['ʃtrenɪç] *adj* wispy
stramm [ʃtram] *adj* tight; (*kräftig*)
strapping; (*Zucht*) strict; (*Arbeit*)
hard; (*Soldat*) smart; (*Mädel*) buxom
‖ *adv*—**s. stehen** stand at attention
stramm'ziehen §163 *tr* draw tight
strampeln ['ʃtrampəln] *intr* kick
Strand [ʃtrant] *m* (-[e]s;ꞏe) beach,
seashore, shore
stranden ['ʃtrandən] *intr* (SEIN) be
beached, run aground. be stranded
Strand'gut *n* flotsam, jetsam
Strand'gutjäger **-in** §6 *mf* beachcomber
Strand'korb *m* hooded beach chair
Strand'schirm *m* beach umbrella
Strang [ʃtraŋ] *m* (-[e]s;ꞏe) rope;
(*Strähne*) hank; (*Zugseil*) trace; (rr)
track; **wenn alle Stränge reißen** (fig)
if worse comes to worst
Strapaze [ʃtra'patsə] *f* (-;-n) fatigue;
exertion, strain
strapazieren [ʃtrapa'tsirən] *tr* tire out;
(*Kleider*) wear hard
strapazier'fähig *adj* heavy-duty
strapaziös [ʃtrapa'tsjøs] *adj* tiring
Straße ['ʃtrasə] *f* (-;-n) street; road,
highway; (*Meerenge*) strait
Stra'ßenanzug *m* business suit
Stra'ßenbahn *f* streetcar, trolley; trolley line
Stra'ßenbahnwagen *m* streetcar
Stra'ßendirne *f* streetwalker
Stra'ßengraben *m* ditch, gutter
Stra'ßenhändler **-in** §6 *mf* street vendor
Stra'ßenjunge *m* urchin
Stra'ßenkarte *f* street map
Stra'ßenkreuzung *f* intersection
Stra'ßenlage *f* (aut) roadability
Stra'ßenrennen *n* drag race

Stra′ßenrinne *f* gutter
Stra′ßenschild *n* street sign
Stra′ßensperrung *f* (public sign) road closed
Stra′ßenstreife *f* highway patrol
strategisch [ʃtra′tegɪʃ] *adj* strategic
sträuben [′ʃtrɔɪbən] *tr* ruffle ‖ *ref* bristle, stand on end; **sich s. gegen** resist, struggle against
Strauch [ʃtraux] *m* (–[e]s;–er) shrub
straucheln [′ʃtrauxəln] *intr* (SEIN) stumble, trip; (fig) go wrong
Strauß [ʃtraus] *m* (–[e]s;–e) bouquet ‖ *m* (–[e]s;–e) ostrich
Strebe [′ʃtrebə] *f* (–;–n) prop, strut
Stre′bebogen *m* flying buttress
streben [′ʃtrebən] *intr* (**nach**) strive (after); (**nach**) tend (toward) ‖ **Streben** *n* (–s;–) striving; pursuit; (*Hang*) tendency; (*Anstrengung*) endeavor
Stre′ber *m* (–s;–) go-getter, eager beaver; social climber; (*in der Schule*) grind
strebsam [′ʃtrepzam] *adj* zealous
Streb′samkeit *f* (–;) zeal; industry
Strecke [′ʃtrɛkə] *f* (–;–n) stretch; extent; distance; stage, leg; (geom) straight line; (hunt) bag; (rr) section; **zur S. bringen** catch up with; (box) defeat; (hunt) bag
strecken [′ʃtrɛkən] *tr* stretch; (*Metalle*) laminate; (*Wein*) dilute; (fig) make last; **die Waffen s.** lay down one's arms ‖ *ref* stretch (oneself)
Streich [ʃtraɪç] *m* (–[e]s;–e) blow; (fig) trick, prank
streicheln [′ʃtraɪçəln] *tr* stroke; pat
streichen [′ʃtraɪçən] §85 *tr* stroke; (*Butter, usw.*) spread; (*an–*) paint; (*Geige*) play; (*Messer*) whet; (*Rasiermesser*) strop; (*Streichholz*) strike; (*Flagge, Segel*) lower; (*Ärmel*) roll down; (*Ziegel*) make; (*mit Ruten*) flog; delete; (sport) scratch ‖ *intr*—**mit der Hand s. über** (*acc*) pass one's hand over ‖ *intr* (SEIN) stretch, extend; wander; pass, move; rush
Streich′holz *n* match
Streich′holzbrief *m* matchbook
Streich′instrument *n* stringed instrument
Streich′orchester *n* string band
Streich′riemen *m* razor strop
Streif [straɪf] *m* (–[e]s;–e) streak, stripe; strip
Streif′band *n* (–[e]s;–er) wrapper
Streife [′ʃtraɪfə] *f* (–;–n) raid; (*Runde*) beat; (mil) patrol
streifen [′ʃtraɪfən] *tr* stripe; streak; graze; skim over; (*abziehen*) strip; (*grenzen an*) verge on; (*Thema*) touch on ‖ *intr* (SEIN) roam; (mil) patrol; **s. an** (*acc*) brush against; (fig) verge on; **s. über** (*acc*) scan ‖ **Streifen** *m* (–s;–) stripe; streak; strip; slip; (cin) movie
Strei′fendienst *m* patrol duty
Strei′fenwagen *m* patrol car, squad car
streifig [′ʃtraɪfɪç] *adj* striped
Streif′licht *n* flash, streak of light; **S. werfen auf** (*acc*) shed light on
Streif′wunde *f* scratch

Streif′zug *m* exploratory trip, looksee
Streik [ʃtraɪk] *m* (–[e]s;–s) strike, walkout; **wilder S.** wildcat strike
streiken [′ʃtraɪkən] *intr* go on strike
Strei′kende §5 *mf* striker
Streik′posten *m* picket; **S. stehen** picket
Streit [ʃtraɪt] *m* (–[e]s;–e) fight; argument, quarrel; (jur) litigation
Streit′axt *f* battle-ax; **die S. begraben** (fig) bury the hatchet
streitbar [′ʃtraɪtbar] *adj* belligerent
streiten [′ʃtraɪtən] §86 *recip* & *intr* quarrel
Streit′frage *f* point at issue
streitig [′ʃtraɪtɪç] *adj* controversial; at issue
Streit′kräfte *pl* (mil) forces, troops
streitlustig *adj* belligerent, scrappy
Streit′objekt *n* bone of contention
Streit′punkt *m* issue, point at issue
streit′süchtig *adj* quarrelsome
streng [ʃtrɛŋ] *adj* severe, stern; austere; strict; (*Geschmack*) sharp ‖ **Strenge** *f* (–;) severity, sternness; austerity; strictness; sharpness
streng′genommen *adv* strictly speaking
streng′gläubig *adj* orthodox
Streu [ʃtrɔɪ] *f* (–;–en) straw bed
Streu′büchse *f* shaker
streuen [′ʃtrɔɪ·ən] *tr* strew, sprinkle; (*ausbreiten*) spread; (*verbreiten*) scatter ‖ *intr* spread, scatter
strich [ʃtrɪç] *pret of* **streichen** ‖ **Strich** *m* (–[e]s;–e) stroke; line; (*Streif*) stripe; (*Landstrich*) tract; (carp) grain; (tex) nap; (typ) dash; **auf den S. gehen** walk the streets (*as prostitute*); **gegen den S. gehen** go against the grain; (fig) rub the wrong way
Strich′mädchen *n* streetwalker
Strich′punkt *m* semicolon
Strich′regen *m* local shower
strich′weise *adv* here and there
Strick [ʃtrɪk] *m* (–[e]s;–e) rope, cord; (fig) rogue, good-for-nothing
stricken [′ʃtrɪkən] *tr* & *intr* knit
Strick′garn *n* knitting yarn
Strick′jacke *f* cardigan
Strick′kleid *n* knitted dress
Strick′leiter *f* rope ladder
Strick′waren *pl* knitwear
Strick′zeug *n* knitting things
Striemen [′ʃtrimən] *m* (–s;–) stripe, streak; (*in der Haut*) weal
Strippe [′ʃtrɪpə] *f* (–;–n) string; strap; shoestring; (telp) line
stritt [ʃtrɪt] *pret of* **streiten**
strittig [′ʃtrɪtɪç] *adj* controversial
Stroh [ʃtro] *n* (–[e]s;) straw
Stroh′dach *n* thatched roof
Stroh′halm *m* straw; drinking straw
Stroh′mann *m* (–[e]s;–er) scarecrow; (cards) dummy
Stroh′puppe *f* scarecrow
Stroh′sack *m* straw mattress; **heiliger S.!** holy smokes!
Strolch [ʃtrɔlç] *m* (–[e]s;–e) bum
strolchen [′ʃtrɔlçən] *intr* bum around
Strom [ʃtrom] *m* (–[e]s;–e) river; stream; (*von Worten*) torrent; (& elec) current

stromab′wärts *adv* downstream
stromauf′wärts *adv* upstream
Strom′ausfall *m* (elec) power failure
strömen [′ʃtrømən] *intr* (HABEN & SEIN) stream; (*Regen*) pour (down)
Stro′mer *m* (-s;-) (coll) tramp
Strom′kreis *m* (elec) circuit
strom′linienförmig *adj* streamlined
Strom′richter *m* (elec) converter
Strom′schnelle *f* rapids
Strom′spannung *f* voltage
Strom′stärke *f* (elec) amperage
Strö′mung *f* (-;-en) current; trend
Strom′unterbrecher *m* circuit breaker
Strom′wandler *m* (elec) transformer
Strom′zähler *m* electric meter
Strophe [′ʃtrofə] *f* (-;-n) stanza
strotzen [′ʃtrɔtsən] *intr*—s. **von** or **vor** (*dat*) abound in, teem with
Strudel [′ʃtrudəl] *m* (-s;-) eddy, whirl-pool; (fig) maelstrom; (culin) strudel
strudeln [′ʃtrudəln] *intr* eddy, whirl
Struktur [ʃtrʊk′tur] *f* (-;-en) structure; (tex) texture
Strumpf [ʃtrʊmpf] *m* (-[e]s;ˮe) stocking
Strumpf′band *n* (-[e]s;ˮer), **Strumpf-halter** *m* garter
Strumpf′waren *pl* hosiery
struppig [′ʃtrʊpɪç] *adj* shaggy, unkempt
Stube [′ʃtubə] *f* (-;-n) room
Stu′benmädchen *n* chambermaid
stu′benrein *adj* housebroken
Stubsnase [′ʃtupsnazə] *f* snub nose
Stuck [ʃtʊk] *m* (-[e]s;) stucco
Stück [ʃtʏk] *n* (-[e]s;-e) piece; lot; plot; stretch distance; (*Butter*) pat; (*Zucker*) lump; (*Seife*) cake; (*Vieh*) head; (mus) piece, number; (theat) play, show; **pro S.** apiece
stückeln [′ʃtʏkəln] *tr* cut or break into small pieces; piece together
stück′weise *adv* piecemeal
Stück′werk *n* patchwork
Student [ʃtu′dɛnt] *m* (-en;-en) college student
Studen′tenheim *n* dormitory
Studen′tenverbindung *f* fraternity
Studentin [ʃtu′dɛntɪn] *f* (-;-nen) college student, coed
Studie [′ʃtudjə] *f* (-;-n) (Lit) essay; (paint) study, sketch
Stu′diengang *m* (educ) course
Stu′dienplan *m* curriculum
Stu′dienrat *m* (-[e]s;ˮe) high school teacher
Stu′dienreferendar –**in** §8 *mf* practice teacher
Stu′dienreise *f* (educ) field trip
studieren [ʃtu′dirən] *tr* & *intr* study (*at college*); examine
studiert [ʃtu′dirt] *adj* college-educated; (*gekünstelt*) affected
Studier′zimmer *n* study
Stu·dium [′ʃtudjʊm] *n* (-s;-dien [djən]) study (*at college*); studies
Stufe [′ʃtufə] *f* (-;-n) step, stair; (*e-r Leiter*) rung; (*Grad*) degree; (*Niveau*) level; stage; (mus) interval
Stu′fenfolge *f* graduation; succession
Stu′fenleiter *f* stepladder; (fig) gamut
stu′fenweise *adv* by degrees

Stuhl [ʃtul] *m* (-[e]s;ˮe) chair; (*Stuhlgang*) stool, feces; **der Heilige S.** the Holy See
Stuhl′bein *n* leg of a chair
Stuhl′drang *m* urgent call of nature
Stuhl′gang *m* stool, feces; **S. haben** have a bowel movement
Stuhl′lehne *f* back of a chair
Stulpe [′ʃtʊlpə] *f* (-;-n) cuff
Stülpnase [′ʃtʏlpnazə] *f* snub nose
stumm [ʃtʊm] *adj* dumb, mute; (*schweigend*) silent; (gram) mute
Stummel [′ʃtuməl] *m* (-s;-) (*e-s Armes, Baumes, e-r Zigarette*) stump
Stümper [′ʃtʏmpər] *m* (-s;-) bungler
Stümperei [ʃtʏmpə′raɪ] *f* (-;-en) bungling
stüm′perhaft *adj* bungling
stümpern [′ʃtʏmpərn] *tr* & *intr* bungle
stumpf [ʃtumpf] *adj* blunt; (& fig) obtuse ‖ **Stumpf** *m* (-[e]s;ˮe) stump
Stumpf′sinn *m* apathy, dullness
stumpf′sinnig *adj* dull, stupid
Stunde [′ʃtundə] *f* (-;-n) hour; (educ) class, lesson, period
stunden [′ʃtundən] *tr* grant postponement of
Stun′dengeld *n* tutoring fee
Stun′dengeschwindigkeit *f* miles per hour
Stun′denkilometer *pl* kilometers per hour
stun′denlang *adv* for hours
Stun′denlohn *m* hourly wage(s)
Stun′denplan *m* roster, schedule
stun′denweise *adv* by the hour
Stun′denzeiger *m* hour hand
–**ständig** [ʃtʏndɪç] *comb fm.* –hour
stündlich [′ʃtʏntlɪç] *adj* hourly
Stun′dung *f* (-;-en) period of grace
Stunk [ʃtʊŋk] *m* (-[e]s;) stink; **S. machen** (sl) raise a stink
Stups [ʃtups] *m* (-es;-e) nudge
stupsen [′ʃtupsən] *tr* nudge
Stups′nase *f* snub nose
stur [ʃtur] *adj* stubborn; (*Blick*) fixed
Sturm [ʃtʊrm] *m* (-[e]s;ˮe) storm; gale
Sturm′abteilung *f* storm troopers
stürmen [′ʃtʏrmən] *tr* storm ‖ *intr* rage, roar ‖ *intr* (SEIN) rush ‖ *impers*—**es stürmt** it is stormy
Stürmer [′ʃtʏrmər] *m* (-s;-) (fb) forward
stürmisch [′ʃtʏrmɪʃ] *adj* stormy; impetuous ‖ *adv*—**nicht so s.!** not so fast!
Sturm′schritt *m* (mil) double time
Sturm′trupp *m* assault party
Sturm′welle *f* (mil) assault wave
Sturm′wind *m* gale, hurricane
Sturz [ʃtʊrts] *m* (-es;ˮe) fall, sudden drop; overthrow; collapse; (archit) lintel; (aut) camber; (com) slump
Sturz′bach *m* torrent
Sturz′bomber *m* dive bomber
Stürze [′ʃtʏrtsə] *f* (-;-n) lid
stürzen [′ʃtʏrtsən] *tr* throw down; upset, overturn; overthrow; (*tauchen*) plunge; **nicht s.!** this side up! ‖ *ref* rush; plunge ‖ *intr* (SEIN) fall, tumble; rush; (*Tränen*) pour; (aer) dive
Sturz′flug *m* (aer) dive
Sturz′helm *m* crash helmet

Sturz'regen *m* downpour
Sturz'see *f* heavy seas
Stute ['ʃtutə] *f* (-;-n) mare
Stütze ['ʃtʏtsə] *f* (-;-n) support, prop; (fig) help, support
stutzen ['ʃtutsən] *tr* cut short; (*Flügel*) clip; (*Bäume*) prune; (*Ohren*) crop; (*Bart*) trim ‖ *intr* stop short; be startled; (*Pferd*) shy
stützen ['ʃtʏtsən] *tr* support; prop; shore up; (fig) support ‖ *ref*—**sich s. auf** (*acc*) lean on; (fig) depend on
Stutzer ['ʃtutsər] *m* (-s;-) car coat; (coll) snazzy dresser
Stutz'flügel *m* baby grand piano
stutzig ['ʃtutsɪç] *adj* suspicious
Stütz'pfeiler *m* abutment
Stütz'punkt *m* footing; (mil) base; (phys) fulcrum
Subjekt [zup'jɛkt] *n* (-[e]s;-e) (coll) guy, character; (gram) subject
subjektiv [zupjɛk'tif] *adj* subjective
Substantiv [zupstan'tif] *n* (-[e]s;-e) (gram) substantive, noun
Substanz [zup'stants] *f* (-;-en) substance
subtil [zup'til] *adj* subtle
subtrahieren [zuptra'hirən] *tr* subtract
Subtraktion [zuptrak'tsjon] *f* (-;-en) subtraction
Subvention [zupvɛn'tsjon] *f* (-;-en) subsidy
Such- [zux] *comb.fm.* search
Such'anzeige *f* want ad
Such'büro *n*, **Such'dienst** *m* missing-persons bureau
Suche ['zuxə] *f* (-;-en) search; **auf der S. nach** in search of, in quest of
suchen ['zuxən] *tr* search for, look for; (*erstreben*) seek; want, desire; (*in der Zeitung*) advertise for; (*Gefahr*) court; **das Weite s.** run away ‖ *intr* search; **nach etw s.** look for s.th.
Sucht [zuxt] *f* (-;⁻e) passion, mania; (*nach*) addition (to)
süchtig ['zʏçtɪç] *adj* addicted ‖ **Süchtige §5** *mf* addict
Sud [zut] *m* (-[e]s;-e) brewing; brew
Süd [zyt] *m* (-[e]s;) south
sudelhaft ['zudəlhaft], **sudelig** ['zudəlɪç] *adj* slovenly, sloppy
sudeln ['zudəln] *tr & intr* mess up
Süden ['zydən] *m* (-s;) south
Sudeten [zu'detən] *pl* Sudeten mountains (*along northern border of Czechoslovakia*)
Süd'früchte *pl* (*tropical and subtropical*) fruit (*e.g., bananas, oranges*)
süd'lich *adj* south, southern, southerly; **s. von** south of ‖ *adv* south
Südost' *m*, **Südo'sten** *m* southeast
südöst' lich *adj* southeast(ern)
Süd'pol *m* (-s;) South Pole
südwärts ['zytvɛrts] *adv* southward
Südwest' *m*, **Südwe'sten** *m* southwest
süffig ['zʏfɪç] *adj* tasty
suggerieren [zugɛ'rirən] *tr* suggest
suggestiv [zugɛs'tif] *adj* suggestive
Suggestiv'frage *f* leading question
suhlen ['zulən] *ref* wallow
Sühne ['zynə] *f* (-;) atonement
sühnen ['zynən] *tr* atone for, expiate
Sülze ['zʏltsə] *f* (-;-n) jellied meat

summarisch [zu'marɪʃ] *adj* summary
Summe ['zumə] *f* (-;-n) sum, total
summen ['zumən] *tr* hum ‖ *intr* hum; buzz
Sum'mer *m* (-s;-) buzzer
summieren [zu'mirən] *tr* sum up, total ‖ *ref* run up, pile up
Summton ['zumton] *m* (telp) dial tone
Sumpf [zumpf] *m* (-[e]s;⁻e) swamp
sumpfig ['zumpfɪç] *adj* swampy, marshy
Sünde ['zʏndə] *f* (-;-n) sin
Sün'denbock *m* scapegoat
Sün'denerlaß *m* absolution
Sün'denfall *m* original sin
Sün'der *m* (-s;-) sinner
Sünd'flut ['zʏntflut] *f* Deluge
sünd'haft, sündig ['zʏndɪç] *adj* sinful
sündigen ['zʏndɪgən] *intr* sin
Superlativ ['zuperlatif] *m* (-s;-e) (gram) superlative
Su'permarkt *m* supermarket
Suppe ['zupə] *f* (-;-n) soup
Sup'penschüssel *f* tureen
surren ['zurən] *intr* buzz
Surrogat [zuro'gat] *n* (-[e]s;-e) substitute
suspendieren [zuspɛn'dirən] *tr* suspend
süß [zys] *adj* sweet ‖ **Süße** *f* (-;) sweetness
süßen ['zysən] *tr* sweeten
Sü'ßigkeit *f* (-;-en) sweetness; **Süßigkeiten** sweets, candy
Süß'kartoffel *f* sweet potato
süß'lich *adj* sweetish; (fig) mawkish
Süß'stoff *m* artificial sweetener
Süß'waren *pl* sweets, candy
Süß'wasser *n* fresh water
Symbol [zʏm'bol] *n* (-s;-e) symbol
Symbolik [zʏm'bolɪk] *f* (-;) symbolism
symbolisch [zʏm'bolɪʃ] *adj* symbolic(al)
Symme·trie [zʏmɛ'tri] *f* (-;-trien) ['tri·ən]) symmetry
symmetrisch [zʏ'metrɪʃ] *adj* symmetrical
Sympa·thie [zʏmpa'ti] *f* (-;-thien) ['ti·ən]) liking
sympathisch [zʏm'patɪʃ] *adj* likeable; **er ist mir s.** I like him
sympathisieren [zʏmpatɪ'zirən] *intr*—**s. mit** sympathize with; like
Sympho·nie [zʏmfo'ni] *f* (-;-nien) ['ni·ən]) symphony
Symptom [zʏmp'tom] *n* (-s;-e) symptom
symptomatisch [zʏmptə'matɪʃ] *adj* (*für*) symptomatic (of)
Synagoge [zyna'gogə] *f* (-;-n) synagogue
synchronisieren [zʏnkrɔnɪ'zirən] *tr* synchronize
Syndikat [zʏndɪ'kat] *n* (-[e]s;-e) syndicate
Syndi·kus ['zʏndɪkus] *m* (-;-kusse & -ki [ki]) corporation lawyer
synonym [zyno'nym] *adj* synonymous ‖ **Synonym** *n* (-s;-e) synonym
Syntax ['zʏntaks] *f* (-;) syntax
synthetisch [zʏn'tetɪʃ] *adj* synthetic
Syrien ['zyrjən] *n* (-s;) Syria

System [zɪs'tem] n (-s;-e) system
systematisch [zɪste'matɪʃ] adj systematic
Szene ['stsenə] f (-;-n) scene; in S.

setzen stage; sich in S. setzen put on
an act
Sze'nenaufnahme f (cin) take
Szenerie [stenə'ri] f (-;) scenery

T

T, t [te] invar n T, t
Tabak [ta'bak], ['tɑbak] m (-[e]s;-e)
tobacco
Tabaks'beutel m tobacco pouch
Tabak'trafik f (Aust) cigar store
Tabak'waren pl tobacco products
tabellarisch [tabɛ'lɑrɪʃ] adj tabular
tabellarisieren [tabɛlɑrɪ'zirən] tr tabulate
Tabelle [ta'bɛlə] f (-;-n) table, chart;
graph
Tabernakel [tabɛr'nɑkəl] m & n (-s;-)
tabernacle
Tablett [ta'blɛt] n (-[e]s;-e) tray
Tablette [ta'bletə] f (-;-n) tablet, pill
tabu [ta'bu] adj taboo ‖ Tabu n (-s;
-s) taboo
Tachometer [taxɔ'metər] n speedometer
Tadel ['tɑdəl] m (-s;-) scolding;
(Schuld) blame; (educ) demerit
ta'dellos adj blameless; flawless
tadeln ['tɑdəln] tr scold, reprimand;
blame, find fault with
Tafel ['tɑfəl] f (-;-n) (Tisch, Diagramm) table; (Anschlag-) billboard;
(Glas-) pane; (Holz-, Schalt-) panel;
(Mahlzeit) meal, dinner; (Metall-)
sheet, plate; (Platte) slab; (Schiefer-)
slate; (Schreib-) tablet; (Schokolade)
bar; (Wand-) blackboard; bei T. at
dinner; die T. decken set the table;
offene T. halten have open house
Ta'felaufsatz m centerpiece
Ta'felbesteck n knife, fork, and spoon
ta'felförmig adj tabular
Ta'felgeschirr n table service
Ta'felland n tableland, plateau
Ta'felmusik f dinner music
tafeln ['tɑfəln] intr dine, feast
täfeln ['tefəln] tr (Wand) wainscot,
panel; (Fußboden) parquet
Ta'felöl n salad oil
Ta'felservice n tableware
Tä'felung f (-;-en) inlay; paneling
Taft [taft] m (-[e]s;-e) taffeta
Tag [tak] m (-[e]s;-e) day; daylight;
am Tage by day; am Tage nach the
day after; an den Tag bringen bring
to light; bei Tage by day, in the daytime; den ganzen Tag all day long;
e-n Tag um den andern every other
day; e-s Tages someday; es wird Tag
day is breaking; guten Tag! hello!;
how do you do?; (bei Verabschiedung) good day!; goodby!; Tag der
offenen Tür open house; unter Tage
(min) underground, below the surface
tagaus', tagein' adv day in and day out
Tage- [tɑgə] comb.fm. day-, daily

Ta'geblatt n daily, daily paper
Ta'gebuch n diary, journal
Ta'gegeld n per diem allowance
ta'gelang adv for days
Ta'gelohn m daily wage
Tagelöhner –in ['tɑgəlønər(ɪn)] §6 mf
day laborer
tagen ['tɑgən] intr dawn; (beraten)
meet; (jur) be in session
Ta'gesanbruch m daybreak
Ta'gesangriff m (aer) daylight raid
Ta'gesbefehl m (mil) order of the day
Ta'gesbericht m daily report
Ta'geseinnahme f daily receipts
Ta'gesgespräch n topic of the day
ta'geshell' adj as light as day
Ta'geskasse f (theat) box office
Ta'gesleistung f daily output
Ta'geslicht n daylight
Ta'geslichtaufnahme f (phot) daylight
shot
Ta'gesordnung f agenda; (coll) order
of the day
Ta'gespreis m market price
Ta'gespresse f daily press
Ta'gesschau f (telv) news
Ta'geszeit f time of day; daytime; zu
jeder T. at any hour
Ta'geszeitung f daily paper
ta'geweise adv by the day
Ta'gewerk n day's work
–tägig [tegɪç] comb.fm. –day
täglich ['teklɪç] adj daily
tags [taks] adv—t. darauf the follow-
ing day; t. zuvor the day before
Tag'schicht f day shift
tags'über adv during the day, in the
daytime
Tagung ['tɑguŋ] f (-;-en) convention,
conference, meeting
Ta'gungsort m meeting place
Taifun [taɪ'fun] m (-s;-e) typhoon
Taille ['taljə] f (-;-n) waist; (Mieder) bodice
Takel ['tɑkəl] n (-s;-) tackle
Takelage [takə'lɑʒə] f (-;-n) rigging
takeln ['tɑkəln] tr rig
Ta'kelwerk n var of Takelage
Takt [takt] m (-[e]s;-e) tact; (mach)
stroke; (mus) time, beat; (mus) bar;
den T. schlagen mark time; im T. in
time; in step; T. halten mark time
takt'fest adj keeping good time; (fig)
reliable
Taktik ['taktɪk] f (-;-en) (& fig)
tactics
Tak'tiker m (-s;-) tactician
taktisch ['taktɪʃ] adj tactical
takt'los adj tactless
Takt'messer m metronome
Takt'stock m baton

Takt'strich *m* (mus) bar
takt'voll *adj* tactful
Tal [tɑl] *n* (-[e]s;-̈er) valley
Talar [ta'lɑr] *m* (-s;-e) robe, gown
Tal'boden *m* valley floor
Talent [ta'lent] *n* (-[e]s;-e) talent
talentiert [talen'tirt] *adj* talented
Tal'fahrt *f* descent
Talg [talk] *m* (-[e]s;-e) suet; tallow
Talg'kerze *f*, **Talg'licht** *n* tallow candle
Talisman ['tɑlɪsman] *m* (-s;-e) talisman
Talk(um)puder ['talk(ʊm)pudər] *m* talcum powder
Talmi ['talmi] *n* (-s;) (fig) imitation
Tal'sperre *f* dam
Tamburin [tambʊ'rin] *n* (-s;-e) tambourine
Tampon [tã'põ] *m* (-s;-s) (med) tampon
Tamtam [tam'tam] *n* (-s;-s) gong; (fig) fanfare, drum beating
Tand [tant] *m* (-[e]s;) trifle; bauble
tändeln ['tendəln] *intr* trifle; flirt
Tang [taŋ] *m* (-[e]s;-e) seaweed
Tangente [taŋ'gentə] *f* (-;-n) (geom) tangent
tangieren [taŋ'girən] *tr* concern
Tango ['taŋgo] *m* (-s;-s) tango
Tank [taŋk] *m* (-[e]s;-e & -s) tank
tanken ['taŋkən] *intr* get gas; refuel
Tan'ker *m*, **Tank'schiff** *n* tanker
Tank'stelle *f* gas (or service) station
Tank'wagen *m* tank truck; (rr) tank car
Tankwart ['taŋkvart] *m* (-[e]s;-e) gas station attendant
Tanne ['tanə] *f* (-;-n) fir (tree)
Tan'nenbaum *m* fir tree
Tan'nenzapfen *m* fir cone
Tante ['tantə] *f* (-;-n) aunt; **T. Meyer** (coll) john
Tantieme [tã'tjemə] *f* (-;-n) dividend; (com) royalty
Tanz [tants] *m* (-es;-̈e) dance
Tanz'bein *n*—**das T. schwingen** (coll) cut a rug
Tanz'diele *f* dance hall
tänzeln ['tentsəln] *intr* (HABEN & SEIN) skip about; (*Pferd*) prance
tanzen ['tantsən] *tr* & *intr* dance
Tänzer –in ['tentsər(ɪn)] §6 *mf* dancer
Tanz'fläche *f* dance floor
Tanz'kapelle *f* dance band
Tanz'lokal *n* dance hall
Tanz'saal *m* ballroom
Tanz'schritt *m* dance step
Tanz'stunde *f* dancing lesson
Tapete [ta'petə] *f* (-;-n) wallpaper
Tape'tenpapier *n* wallpaper (*in rolls*)
Tape'tentür *f* wallpapered door
Tapezierarbeit [tapε'tsirarbaɪt] *f* paperhanging
tapezieren [tapε'tsirən] *tr* wallpaper
Tapezie'rer *m* (-s;-) paperhanger
tapfer ['tapfər] *adj* brave, valiant
Ta'pferkeit *f* (-;) bravery, valor
tappen ['tapən] *intr* (HABEN & SEIN) grope about; **t. nach** grope for
täppisch ['tεpɪʃ] *adj* clumsy
tapsen ['tapsən] *intr* (SEIN) clump along

Tara ['tɑra] *f* (-;) (com) tare
Tarif [ta'rif] *m* (-s;-e) tariff; price list; wage scale; postal rates
Tarif'lohn *m* standard wages
Tarif'verhandlung *f* collective bargaining
Tarif'vertrag *m* wage agreement
Tarn– [tarn] *comb.fm.* camouflage
tarnen ['tarnən] *tr* camouflage
Tarn'kappe *f* (myth) magic cap (*rendering wearer invisible*)
Tar'nung *f* (-;) camouflage
Tasche ['taʃə] *f* (-;-n) pocket; handbag; pocketbook; schoolbag; flight bag; pouch; briefcase
Ta'schenausgabe *f* pocket edition
Ta'schenbuch *n* paperback
Ta'schendieb *m* pickpocket
Ta'schendiebstahl *m* pickpocketing
Ta'schengeld *n* pocket money
Ta'schenlampe *f* flashlight
Ta'schenmesser *n* pocketknife
Ta'schenrechner *m* pocket calculator
Ta'schenspieler –in §6 *mf* magician
Ta'schenspielerei *f* sleight of hand
Ta'schentuch *n* handkerchief
Ta'schenuhr *f* pocket watch
Ta'schenwörterbuch *n* pocket dictionary
Tasse ['tasə] *f* (-;-n) cup
Tastatur [tasta'tur] *f* (-;-en) keyboard
Taste ['tastə] *f* (-;-n) key
tasten ['tastən] *tr* feel, touch; (telg) send ‖ *ref* feel one's way ‖ *intr* (**nach**) grope (for)
Tastsinn ['tastzɪn] *m* sense of touch
tat [tɑt] *pret of* **tun** ‖ **Tat** *f* (-;-en) deed, act; (*Verbrechen*) crime; **auf frischer Tat ertappen** catch redhanded; **in der Tat** in fact; **in die Tat umsetzen** implement
Tat'bestand *m* facts of the case
Tat'bestandsaufnahme *f* factual statement
tatenlos ['tɑtənlos] *adj* inactive
Ta'tenlosigkeit *f* (-;) inactivity
Täter –in ['tetər(ɪn)] §6 *mf* doer, perpetrator; culprit
Tat'form *f* (gram) active voice
tätig ['tetɪç] *adj* active; busy; **t. sein bei** be employed by
tätigen ['tetɪgən] *tr* conclude
Tä'tigkeit *f* (-;-en) activity; occupation, job, profession
Tä'tigkeitsbericht *m* progress report
Tä'tigkeitsfeld *n* field, line
Tä'tigung *f* (-;-en) transaction
Tat'kraft *f* energy, strength; vigor
tat'kräftig *adj* energetic; vigorous
tätlich ['tetlɪç] *adj* violent; **tätliche Beleidigung** (jur) assault and battery; **t. werden gegen** assault ‖ *adv* —**t. beleidigen** (jur) assault
Tät'lichkeit *f* (-;-en) (act of) violence; **es kam zu Tätlichkeiten** it came to blows
Tat'ort *m* scene of the crime
tätowieren [tεtɔ'virən] *tr* tattoo
Tätowie'rung *f* (-;-en) tattoo
Tat'sache *f* fact
Tat'sachenbericht *m* factual report
tat'sächlich *adj* actual, real, factual
tätscheln ['tet/əln] *tr* pet, stroke

Tatterich ['tatərɪç] *m* (-s;) shakes
Tatze ['tatsə] *f* (-;-n) paw
Tau [tau] *m* (-[e]s;) dew ‖ *n* (-[e]s;
-e) rope; (naut) hawser
taub [taup] *adj* deaf; (*betäubt*) numb;
(*unfruchtbar*) barren; (*Gestein*) not
containing ore; (*Nuß*) hollow; (*Ei*)
unfertile; (*Hafer*) wild; **t. gegen** deaf
to; **t. vor Kälte** numb with cold
Taube ['taubə] *f* (-;-n) pigeon; (pol)
dove
Tau'benhaus *n*, **Tau'benschlag** *m* dovecote
Taub'heit *f* (-;) deafness; numbness
taub'stumm *adj* deaf and dumb ‖ **Taub-
stumme §5** *mf* deaf-mute
Tauchboot ['tauxbot] *n* submarine
tauchen ['tauxən] *tr* dip, duck, immerse ‖ *intr* (HABEN & SEIN) dive,
plunge; (naut) submerge, dive
Tau'cher -in §6 *mf* (& orn) diver
Tau'cheranzug *m* diving suit
Tau'chergerät *n* aqualung
Tau'cherglocke *f* diving bell
Tauch'krankheit *f* bends
Tauch'schwimmer *m* (nav) frogman
tauen ['tau·ən] *tr* thaw, melt; (*schlep-
pen*) tow ‖ *intr* (HABEN & SEIN) thaw
‖ *impers*—**es taut** dew is falling ‖
impers (HABEN & SEIN)—**es taut** it is
thawing ‖ **Tauen** *n* (-s;) thaw
Tauf- [tauf] *comb.fm.* baptismal
Tauf'becken *n* baptismal font
Tauf'buch *n* parish register
Taufe ['taufə] *f* (-;-n) baptism, chris-
tening
taufen ['taufən] *tr* baptize, christen
Täufer ['tɔɪfər] *m*—**Johannes der T.**
John the Baptizer
Täufling ['tɔɪflɪŋ] *m* (-s;-e) child (or
person) to be baptized
Tauf'name *m* Christian name
Tauf'pate *m* godfather
Tauf'patin *f* godmother
Tauf'schein *m* baptismal certificate
taugen ['taugən] *intr* be of use; **zu
etw t.** be good for s.th.
Taugenichts ['taugənɪçts] *m* (-es;-e)
good-for-nothing
tauglich ['tauklɪç] *adj* (**für, zu**) good
(for), fit (for), suitable (for); (mil)
able-bodied; **t. zu** (*inf*) able to (*inf*)
Taumel ['tauməl] *m* (-s;) giddiness;
(*Überschwang*) ecstasy
taumelig ['tauməlɪç] *adj* giddy; reeling
taumeln ['tauməln] *intr* (SEIN) reel,
stagger; be giddy; be ecstatic
Tausch [tauʃ] *m* (-es;-e) exchange
tauschen ['tauʃən] *tr* (**gegen**) exchange
(for) ‖ *intr*—**mit j-m t.** exchange
places with s.o.
täuschen ['tɔɪʃən] *tr* deceive, fool;
(*betrügen*) cheat; (*Erwartungen*) disappoint ‖ *ref* be mistaken
täu'schend *adj* deceptive, illusory;
(*Ähnlichkeit*) striking
Tausch/geschäft *n* exchange, swap
Tausch/handel *m* barter; **T. treiben**
barter
Täu'schung *f* (-;-en) deception, deceit;
fraud; **optische T.** optical illusion
Täu'schungsangriff *m* (mil) feint attack
Täu'schungsmanöver *n* feint

Tausch'wert *m* trade-in value
tausend ['tauzənt] *invar adj* & *pron*
thousand ‖ **Tausend** *m*—**ei der T.!**
(or **potz T.!**) holy smokes! ‖ *f* (-;
-en) thousand ‖ *n* (-s;-e) thousand
Tau'sendfuß *m*, **Tausendfüß(l)er** ['tau-
zəntfys(l)ər] *m* (-s;-) centipede
tausendste ['tauzəntstə] **§9** *adj* & *pron*
thousandth
Tausendstel ['tauzəntstəl] *n* (-s;-)
thousandth
Tau'tropfen *m* dewdrop
Tau'werk *n* (naut) rigging
Tau'wetter *n* thaw
Tau'ziehen *n* tug of war
Taxameter [taksa'metər] *m* taxi meter
Taxe ['taksə] *f* (-;-n) tax; (*Schätzung*)
appraisal; (*Gebühr*) fee; (*Taxi*) taxi
Taxi ['taksi] *n* (-s;-s) taxi, cab
taxieren [ta'ksirən] *tr* appraise; rate
Taxifahrer -in §6 *mf* taxi driver
Ta'xistand *m* taxi stand
Taxus ['taksus] *m* (-;-) (bot) yew
Team [tim] *n* (-s;-s) team
Technik ['tɛçnɪk] *f* (-;-en) technique;
workmanship; technology
Tech'niker -in §6 *mf* technician; engi-
neer
Techni-kum ['tɛçnɪkum] *n* (-s;-ka
[ka] & -ken [kən]) technical school;
school of engineering
technisch ['tɛçnɪʃ] *adj* technical; **tech-
nische Angelegenheit** technicality;
technische Hochschule technical in-
stitute
Technologie [tɛçnɔlɔ'gi] *f* (-;) tech-
nology
technologisch [tɛçnɔ'logɪʃ] *adj* techno-
logical
Tee [te] *m* (-s;-s) tea
Tee'gebäck *n* tea biscuit, cookie
Tee'kanne *f* teapot
Tee'kessel *m* teakettle
Tee'löffel *m* teaspoon; teaspoonful
Teenager ['tinedʒər] *m* (-s;-) teenager
Teer [ter] *m* (-[e]s;-e) tar
Teer'decke *f* tar surface, blacktop
teeren ['terən] *tr* tar
Teer'pappe *f* tar paper
Tee'satz *m* tealeaves
Teich [taɪç] *m* (-[e]s;-e) pond, pool
Teig [taɪk] *m* (-[e]s;-e) dough
teigig ['taɪgɪç] *adj* doughy
Teig'mulde *f* kneading trough
Teig'waren *pl* noodles; pastries
Teil [taɪl] *m* & *n* (-[e]s;-e) part;
piece; portion; (*Abschnitt*) section;
(jur) party; **der dritte T. von** one
third of; **edle Teile des Körpers** vital
parts; **zu gleichen Teilen** fifty-fifty;
zum größten T. for the most part;
zum T. partly, in part
Teil- *comb.fm.* partial
teilbar ['taɪlbar] *adj* divisible
Teilchen ['taɪlçən] *n* (-s;-) particle
teilen ['taɪlən] *tr* divide; (**mit**) share
(with) ‖ *ref* (*Weg*) divide; (*An-
sichten*) differ; **sich t. in** (*acc*) share
teil'haben §89 *intr* (**an** *dat*) participate
(in), share (in)
Teilhaber -in ['taɪlhabər(ɪn)] **§6** *mf*
participant; (com) partner
Teil'haberschaft *f* (-;-en) partnership

–teilig [taɪlɪç] *comb.fm.* –piece
Teil'nahme *f* (–;) participation; sympathy; interest
teilnahmslos ['taɪlnɑmslɔs] *adj* indifferent; apathetic
Teil'nahmslosigkeit *f* (–;) indifference; apathy
teilnahmsvoll ['taɪlnɑmsfɔl] *adj* sympathetic; (*besorgt*) solicitous
teil'nehmen §116 *intr* (**an** *dat*) participate (in), take part (in); (**an** *dat*) attend; (fig) (**an** *dat*) sympathize (with)
Teil'nehmer –in §6 *mf* participant; (*Mitglied*) member; (sport) competitor; (telp) customer, party
teils [taɪls] *adv* partly
Teil'strecke *f* section, stage
Tei'lung *f* (–;–en) division; partition; separation; (*Grade*) graduation, scale; (*Anteile*) sharing
teil'weise *adv* partly
Teil'zahlung *f* partial payment; **auf T. kaufen** buy on the installment plan
Teint [tẽ] *m* (–s;–s) complexion
Telefon [tɛlɛ'fɔn] *n* (–s;–e) telephone
Telegramm [tɛlɛ'gram] *n* (–s;–e) telegram
Telegraph [tɛlɛ'graf] *m* (–en;–en) telegraph
Telegra'phenstange *f* telegraph pole
telegraphieren [tɛlɛgra'firən] *tr* & *intr* telegraph; (*nach Übersee*) cable
Teleobjektiv ['tɛlɛ·ɔbjɛktif] *n* telephoto lens
Telephon [tɛlɛ'fɔn] *n* (–s;–e) telephone, phone; **ans T. gehen** answer the phone
Telephon'anruf *m* telephone call
Telephon'anschluß *m* telephone connection
Telephon'gespräch *n* telephone call
Telephon'hörer *m* receiver
telephonieren [tɛlɛfɔ'nirən] *intr* telephone; **mit j–m t.** phone s.o.
telephonisch [tɛlɛ'fɔnɪʃ] *adj* telephone || *adv* by telephone
Telephonist –in [tɛlɛfɔ'nɪst(ɪn)] §7 *mf* telephone operator
Telephon'vermittlung *f* telephone exchange
Telephon'zelle *f* telephone booth
Telephon'zentrale *f* telephone exchange
Teleskop [tɛlɛ'skɔp] *n* (–s;–e) telescope
Television [tɛlɛvɪ'zjɔn] *f* (–;) television
Teller ['tɛlər] *m* (–s;–) plate
Tel'lereisen *n* trap
Tel'lermine *f* antitank mine
Tel'lertuch *n* dishtowel
Tempel ['tɛmpəl] *m* (–s;–) temple
Temperament [tɛmpəra'mɛnt] *n* (–[e]s;–e) temperament; enthusiasm; **er hat kein T.** he has no life in him; **hitziges T.** hot temper
temperament'los *adj* lifeless, boring
temperament'voll *adj* lively, vivacious
Temperatur [tɛmpəra'tur] *f* (–;–en) temperature
Temperenzler [tɛmpɛ'rɛntslər] *m* (–s;–) teetotaler
temperieren [tɛmpɛ'rirən] *tr* temper; cool; air-condition; (mus) temper

Tem·po ['tɛmpo] *n* (–s;–s & *pl* [pi]) tempo; speed; (mus) movement
Tem·pus ['tɛmpʊs] *n* (–; –pora [pɔra]) (gram) tense
Tendenz [tɛn'dɛnts] *f* (–;–en) tendency
Tender ['tɛndər] *m* (–s;–) (nav, rr) tender
Tenne ['tɛnə] *f* (–;–n) threshing floor
Tennis ['tɛnɪs] *n* (–;) tennis
Ten'nisplatz *m* tennis court
Ten'nisschläger *m* tennis racket
Ten'nistournier *n* tennis tournament
Tenor ['tɛnɔr] *m* (–s;) (*Wortlaut*) tenor, purport || [tɛ'nor] *m* (–[e]s; ⁼e) tenor
Teppich ['tɛpɪç] *m* (–s;–e) rug, carpet
Teppichkehrmaschine ['tɛpɪçkermaʃinə] *f* carpet sweeper
Termin [tɛr'min] *m* (–s;–e) date, time, day; deadline; (com) due date; **er hat heute T.** he is to appear in court today; **äußerster T.** deadline
termin'gemäß *adv* on time, punctually
Termin'geschäft *n* futures
Termin'kalender *m* appointment book; (jur) court calendar
Terminolo·gie [tɛrmɪnɔlə'gi] *f* (–; –gien ['gi·ən]) terminology
termin'weise *adv* (com) on time
Terpentin [tɛrpɛn'tin] *m* (–s;) terpentine
Terrain [tɛ'rẽ] *n* (–s;–s) ground; (*Grundstück*) lot; (mil) terrain; **T. gewinnen** (fig & mil) gain ground
Terrasse [tɛ'rasə] *f* (–;–n) terrace
terras'senförmig *adj* terraced
Terrine [tɛ'rinə] *f* (–;–n) tureen
Territo·rium [tɛrɪ'torjum] *n* (–s;–rien [rjən]) territory
Terror ['tɛrɔr] *m* (–s;) terror
terrorisieren [tɛrɔrɪ'zirən] *tr* terrorize
Terrorist –in [tɛrə'rɪst(ɪn)] §7 *mf* terrorist
Terz [tɛrts] *f* (–;–en) (mus) third
Terzett [tɛr'tsɛt] *n* (–[e]s;–e) trio
Test [tɛst] *m* (–[e]s;–e & –s) test
Testament [tɛsta'mɛnt] *n* (–[e]s;–e) will; (eccl) Testament
testamentarisch [tɛstamɛn'tarɪʃ] *adj* testamentary || *adv* by will; **t. bestimmen** will
Testaments'vollstrecker –in §6 *mf* executor
testen ['tɛstən] *tr* test
teuer ['tɔɪ·ər] *adj* dear, expensive; (*Preis*) high
Teu'erung *f* (–;–en) rise in price
Teu'erungswelle *f* rise in prices
Teu'erungszulage *f* cost-of-living increase
Teufel ['tɔɪfəl] *m* (–s;–) devil; **des Teufels sein** be mad; **wer zum T.?** who the devil?
Teufelei [tɔɪfə'laɪ] *f* (–;–en) deviltry
Teufelsbanner ['tɔɪfəlsbanər] *m* (–s;–) exorcist
Teu'felskerl *m* helluva fellow
teuflisch ['tɔɪflɪʃ] *adj* devilish
Teutone [tɔɪ'tonə] *m* (–n;–n) Teuton
teutonisch [tɔɪ'tonɪʃ] *adj* Teutonic
Text [tɛkst] *m* (–[e]s;–e) text, words; (cin) script; (mus) libretto; (typ) double pica; **aus dem T. kommen**

lose the train of thought; **j—m den T. lesen** give s.o. a lecture
Text'buch n (mus) libretto
Texter –in ['tɛkstər(ɪn)] §6 mf ad writer, ad man; (mus) lyricist
Textil– [tɛkstil] comb.fm. textile
Textilien [tɛks'tiljən] pl, **Textil'waren** pl textiles
text'lich adj textual
Theater [te'ɑtər] n (–s;–) theater; **T. machen** (fig) make a fuss; **T. spielen** (fig) make believe, put on
Thea'terbesucher –in §6 mf theatergoer
Thea'terdichter –in §6 mf playwright
Thea'terkarte f theater ticket
Thea'terkasse f box office
Thea'terprobe f rehearsal
Thea'terstück n play
Thea'terzettel m program
theatralisch [te·a'trɑlɪʃ] adj theater; (fig) theatrical
Theke ['tekə] f (–;–n) counter; bar
The·ma ['tema] n (–s;–men [mən] & –mata [mɑta]) theme, subject
Theologe [tɛ·ɔ'logə] m (–n;–n) theologian
Theologie [tɛ·ɔlɔ'gi] f (–;) theology
theologisch [tɛ·ɔ'logɪʃ] adj theological
theoretisch [tɛ·ɔ'retɪʃ] adj theoretic(al)
Theo·rie [tɛ·ɔ'ri] f (–;–rien ['ri·ən]) theory
Thera·pie [tɛra'pi] f (–;–pien ['pi·ən]) therapy
Thermalbad [tɛr'mɑlbɑt] n thermal bath
Thermometer [tɛrmɔ'metər] n thermometer
Thermome'terstand m thermometer reading
Thermosflasche ['tɛrmɔsflɑʃə] f thermos bottle
Thermostat [tɛrmɔ'stɑt] m (–[e]s;–e) & (–en;–en) thermostat
These ['tezə] f (–;–n) thesis
Thrombose [trɔm'bozə] f (–;–n) thrombosis
Thron [tron] m (–[e]s;–e) throne
Thron'besteigung f accession to the throne
Thron'bewerber m pretender to the throne
Thron'folge f succession to the throne
Thron'folger m successor to the throne
Thron'himmel m canopy, baldachin
Thron'räuber m usurper
Thunfisch ['tunfɪʃ] m tuna
Tick [tɪk] m (–[e]s;–s & –e) tic; (fig) eccentricity; **e–n T. auf j–n haben** have a grudge against s.o.; **e–n T. haben** (coll) be balmy
ticken ['tɪkən] intr tick
ticktack ['tɪk'tɑk] adv ticktock ‖ **Ticktack** n (–s;) ticktock
tief [tif] adj deep; profound; (niedrig) low; (Schlaf) sound; (Farbe) dark; (äußerst) extreme; **aus tiefstem Herzen** from the bottom of one's heart; **im tiefsten Winter** in the dead of winter ‖ adv deeply; **zu t. singen** be flat ‖ **Tief** n (–[e]s;–e) (meteor) low
Tief'angriff m low-level attack

Tief'bau m (–[e]s;) underground engineering; underground work
tief'betrübt adj deeply grieved
Tief'druckgebiet n (meteor) low
Tiefe ['tifə] f (–;–n) depth; profundity
Tief'ebene f lowlands, plain
teif'empfunden adj heartfelt
Tie'fenanzeiger m (naut) depth gauge
Tie'fenschärfe f (phot) depth of field
Tief'flug m low-level flight
Tief'gang m (fig) depth; (naut) draft
tief'gekühlt adj deep-freeze
tief'greifend adj far-reaching; radical; deep-seated
Tief'kühlschrank m deep freeze
Tief'land n lowlands
tief'liegend adj low-lying; deep-seated; (Augen) sunken
Tief'punkt m (& fig) low point
Tief'schlag m (box) low blow
Tiefsee– [tifze] comb.fm. deep-sea
tief'sinnig adj pensive; melancholy
Tief'stand m low level
Tiegel ['tigəl] m (–s;–) saucepan; (zum Schmelzen) crucible; (typ) platen
Tier [tir] n (–[e]s;–e) animal; (& fig) beast; **großes** (or **hohes**) **T.** (coll) big shot, big wheel
Tier'art f species (of animal)
Tier'arzt m veterinarian
Tier'bändiger –in §6 mf wild-animal tamer
Tier'garten m zoo
Tier'heilkunde f veterinary medicine
tierisch ['tirɪʃ] adj animal (fig) brutish, bestial
Tier'kreis m zodiac
Tier'kreiszeichen n sign of the zodiac
Tier'quälerei f cruelty to animals
Tier'reich n animal kingdom
Tier'schutzverein m society for the prevention of cruelty to animals
Tier'wärter m keeper (at zoo)
Tier'welt f animal kingdom
Tiger ['tigər] m (–s;–) tiger
Tigerin ['tigərɪn] f (–;–nen) tigress
tilgen ['tɪlgən] tr wipe out; (ausrotten) eradicate; (Schuld) pay off; (Sünden) expiate; (streichen) delete
Til'gung f (–;–en) eradication, extinction; payment; deletion
Til'gungsfonds m sinking fund
Tingeltangel ['tɪŋəltaŋəl] m & n (–s;–) honky-tonk
Tinktur [tɪŋk'tur] f (–;–en) tincture
Tinte ['tɪntə] f (–;–n) ink; **in der T. sitzen** (coll) be in a pickle
Tin'tenfaß n inkwell
Tin'tenfisch m cuttlefish
Tin'tenfleck m, **Tin'tenklecks** m ink spot
Tin'tenstift m indelible pencil
Tip [tɪp] m (–s;–s) tip, hint
Tippelbruder ['tɪpəlbrudər] m tramp
tippeln ['tɪpəl] intr (SEIN) (coll) tramp; (coll) toddle
tippen ['tɪpən] tr type ‖ intr type; tap; (wetten) bet; **an j–n nicht t. können** not be able to come near s.o. (in performance); **daran kannst du nicht t.** that's beyond your reach; **t. auf** (acc) predict ‖ ref—**sich an die Stirn t.** tap one's forehead

Tippfehler ['tɪpfelər] *m* typographical error
Tippfräulein ['tɪpfrɔɪlaɪn] *n* (coll) typist
tipptopp ['tɪp'tɔp] *adj* tiptop
Tirol [tɪ'rol] *n* (-s;) Tyrol
Tiroler –in [tɪ'rolər(ɪn)] §6 *mf* Tyrolean
tirolerisch [tɪ'rolərɪʃ] *adj* Tyrolean
Tisch [tɪʃ] *m* (-es;-e) table; (*Mahlzeit*) meal, dinner, supper; **bei T.** during the meal; **nach T.** after the meal; **reinen T. machen** make a clean sweep of it; **unter den T. fallen** be ignored; **vom grünen T.** arm-chair; bureaucratic; **vor T.** before the meal; **zu T., bitte!** dinner is ready
Tisch'aufsatz *m* centerpiece
Tisch'besen *m* crumb brush
Tisch'besteck *n* knife, fork, and spoon
Tisch'blatt *n* leaf of a table
Tisch'decke *f* tablecloth
Tisch'gast *m* dinner guest
Tisch'gebet *n*—**T. sprechen** say grace
Tisch'gesellschaft *f* dinner party
Tisch'glocke *f* dinner bell
Tisch'karte *f* name plate
Tisch'lampe *f* table lamp; desk lamp
Tischler ['tɪʃlər] *m* (-s;-) cabinet maker
Tisch'platte *f* table top
Tisch'rede *f* after-dinner speech
Tisch'tennis *n* Ping-Pong
Tisch'tuch *n* tablecloth
Tisch'zeit *f* mealtime, dinner time
Tisch'zeug *n* table linen and tableware
Titan [tɪ'tan] *m* (-en;-en) Titan ‖ *n* (-s;) (chem) titanium
titanisch [tɪ'tanɪʃ] *adj* titanic
Titel ['titəl] *m* (-s;-) title; (*Anspruch*) claim; **e–n T. innehaben** (sport) hold a title
Ti'telbild *n* frontispiece; (*e–r Illustrierten*) cover picture
Ti'telblatt *n* title page
Ti'telkampf *m* (box) title bout
Ti'telrolle *f* title role
titulieren [tɪtu'lirən] *tr* title
Toast [tost] *m* (-es;-e & -s) toast
toasten ['tostən] *tr* (*Brot*) toast ‖ *intr* propose a toast, drink a toast; **auf j–n t.** toast s.o.
toben ['tobən] *intr* rage; (*Kinder*) raise a racket ‖ **Toben** *n* (-s;) rage, raging; racket, noise
Tob'sucht *f* frenzy, madness
tob'süchtig *adj* raving, mad; frantic
Tochter ['tɔxtər] *f* (-;=) daughter
Toch'terfirma *f*, **Toch'tergesellschaft** *f* (com) subsidiary, affiliate
Tod [tot] *m* (-es;-e) death; (jur) decease; **des Todes sein** be a dead man; **sich** [*dat*] **den Tod holen** catch a death of a cold
tod'ernst' *adj* dead serious
Todes– [todəs] *comb.fm.* of death; deadly
To'desanzeige *f* obituary
To'desfall *m* death
To'desgefahr *f* mortal danger
To'deskampf *m* death struggle
To'deskandidat *m* one at death's door
To'desstoß *m* coup de grâce

To'desstrafe *f* death penalty; **bei T. on** pain of death
To'destag *m* anniversary of death
To'desursache *f* cause of death
To'desurteil *n* death sentence
Tod'feind –in §8 *mf* mortal enemy
todgeweiht ['totgəvaɪt] *adj* doomed
tödlich ['tøtlɪç] *adj* deadly, fatal
tod'mü'de *adj* dead tired
tod'schick' *adj* (coll) very chic
tod'si'cher *adj* (coll) dead sure
Tod'sünde *f* mortal sin
Toilette [twa'letə] *f* (-;-n) toilet
Toilet'tentisch *m* dressing table
tolerant [tɔle'rant] *adj* (**gegen**) tolerant (toward)
Toleranz [tɔle'rants] *f* (-;-en) toleration; (mach) tolerance
tolerieren [tɔle'rirən] *tr* tolerate
toll [tɔl] *adj* mad, crazy; fantastic, terrific; **das wird noch toller kommen** the worst is yet to come; **er ist nicht so t.** (coll) he's not so hot; **es zu t. treiben** carry it a bit too far; **t. nach** crazy about
tollen ['tɔlən] *intr* (HABEN & SEIN) romp about
Toll'haus *n* (fig) bedlam
Toll'heit *f* (-;) madness
Toll'kopf *m* (coll) crackpot
toll'kühn *adj* foolhardy, rash
Toll'wut *f* rabies
Tolpatsch ['tɔlpatʃ] *m* (-es;-e), **Tölpel** ['tœlpəl] *m* (-s;-) (coll) clumsy ox
töl'pelhaft *adj* clumsy
Tomate [to'matə] *f* (-;-n) tomato
Ton [ton] *m* (-[e]s;-e) tone; sound; tint, shade; (*Betonung*) accent, stress; (fig) fashion; **den Ton angeben** (fig) set the tone; (mus) give the keynote; **e–n anderen Ton anschlagen** change one's tune; **große Töne reden** talk big; **guter Ton** (fig) good taste; **hast du Töne!** can you beat that! ‖ *m* (-s;-e) clay
Ton'abnehmer *m* (electron) pickup
ton'angebend *adj* leading
Ton'arm *m* pickup arm
Ton'art *f* type of clay; (mus) key
Ton'atelier *n* (cin) sound studio
Ton'band *n* (-[e]s;=er) (cin) sound track; (electron) tape
Ton'bandgerät *n* tape recorder
tönen ['tønən] *tr* tint, shade ‖ *intr* sound; (*läuten*) ring
tönern ['tønərn] *adj* clay, of clay
Ton'fall *m* intonation, accent
Ton'farbe *f* timbre
Ton'film *m* sound film
Ton'folge *f* melody
Ton'frequenz *f* audio frequency
Ton'geschirr *n* earthenware
Ton'höhe *f*, **Ton'lage** *f* pitch
Ton'leiter *f* (mus) scale
ton'los *adj* voiceless; unstressed
Ton'malerei *f* onomotopoeia
Ton'meister *m* sound engineer
Tonnage [tɔ'naʒə] *f* (-;-n) (naut) tonnage
Tonne ['tɔnə] *f* (-;-n) barrel; ton
Ton'silbe *f* accented syllable
Ton'spur *f* groove (*of record*)
Ton'streifen *m* (cin) sound track

Tonsur [tɔn'zur] *f* (–;–en) tonsure
Ton'taube *f* clay pigeon
Ton'taubenschießen *n* trapshooting
Tö'nung *f* (–;–en) tint; (phot) tone
Ton'verstärker *m* amplifier
Ton'waren *pl* earthenware
Topas [to'pɑs] *m* (–es;–e) topaz
Topf [tɔpf] *m* (–[e]s;̈–e) pot
Topf'blume *f* potted flower
Töpfer ['tœpfər] *m* (–s;–) potter
Töpferei [tœpfə'raɪ] *f* (–;–en) potter's shop
Töp'ferscheibe *f* potter's wheel
Töp'ferwaren *pl* pottery
Topf'lappen *m* potholder
Topf'pflanze *f* potted plant
Topp [tɔp] *m* (–s;–e) (naut) masthead ‖ **topp** *interj* it's a deal
Tor [tor] *m* (–en;–en) fool ‖ *n* (–[e]s; –e) gate; gateway; (sport) goal
Torbogen *m* archway
Torf [tɔrf] *m* (–[e]s;) peat
Tor'flügel *m* door (*of double door*)
Torf'moos *n* peat moss
Tor'heit *f* (–;–en) foolishness, folly
Tor'hüter *m* gatekeeper; (sport) goalie
töricht ['tørɪçt] *adj* foolish, silly
Törin ['tørɪn] *f* (–;–nen) fool
torkeln ['tɔrkəln] *intr* (HABEN & SEIN) (coll) stagger
Tor'latte *f* (sport) crossbar
Tor'lauf *m* slalom
Tor'linie *f* (sport) goal line
Tornister [tɔr'nɪstər] *m* (–s;–) knapsack; school bag; (mil) field pack
torpedieren [tɔrpɛ'dirən] *tr* torpedo
Torpedo [tɔr'pedo] *m* (–s;–s) torpedo
Tor'pfosten *m* doorpost; (fb) goal post
Tor'schluß *m*—**kurz vor T.** (fig) at the eleventh hour
Torte ['tɔrtə] *f* (–;–n) cake; pie
Tortur [tɔr'tur] *f* (–;–en) torture
Tor'wächter *m*, **Torwart** ['torvart] *m* (–[e]s;–e) (sport) goalie
Tor'weg *m* gateway
tosen ['tozən] *intr* (HABEN & SEIN) rage, roar ‖ **Tosen** *n* (–s;) rage, roar
tot [tot] *adj* dead; (*Kapital*) idle; (*Wasser*) stagnant; **toter Punkt** dead center; (fig) snag; **totes Rennen** dead heat; **tote Zeit** dead season
total [to'tɑl] *adj* total; all-out
totalitär [totalɪ'ter] *adj* totalitarian
tot'arbeiten *ref* work oneself to death
Tote ['totə] §5 *mf* dead person
töten ['tøtən] *tr* kill; (*Nerv*) deaden
To'tenacker *m* churchyard
To'tenbett *n* deathbed
to'tenblaß' *adj* deathly pale
To'tenblässe *f* deathly pallor
to'tenbleich' *adj* deathly pale
To'tengräber *m* gravedigger
To'tengruft *f* crypt
To'tenhemd *n* shroud, winding sheet
To'tenklage *f* lament
To'tenkopf *m* skull
To'tenkranz *m* funeral wreath
To'tenmaske *f* death mask
To'tenmesse *f* requiem
To'tenreich *n* (myth) underworld
To'tenschau *f* coroner's inquest
To'tenschein *m* death certificate
To'tenstadt *f* necropolis

To'tenstarre *f* rigor mortis
To'tenstille *f* dead silence
To'tenwache *f* wake
tot'geboren *adj* stillborn
Tot'geburt *f* stillbirth
tot'lachen *ref* die laughing
Toto ['toto] *m* (–s;–s) football pool
tot'schießen §76 *tr* shoot dead
Tot'schlag *m* manslaughter
tot'schlagen §132 *tr* strike dead; (*Zeit*) kill
tot'schweigen §148 *tr* hush up; keep under wraps ‖ *intr* hush up
tot'stellen *ref* feign death, play dead
tot'treten §152 *tr* trample to death
Tö'tung *f* (–;–en) killing
Tour [tur] *f* (–;–en) tour; turn; (*Umdrehung*) revolution; **auf die krumme T.** by hook or by crook; **auf die langsame T.** very leisurely; **auf höchsten Touren** at full spead; (fig) full blast; **auf Touren bringen** (aut) rev up; **auf Touren kommen** pick up speed; (fig) get worked up; **auf Touren sein** (coll) be in good shape
Tou'renzahl *f* revolutions per minute
Tourismus [tu'rɪsmʊs] *m* (–;) tourism
Tourist [tu'rɪst] *m* (–en;–en) tourist
Touri'stenverkehr *m*, **Touristik** [tu'rɪstɪk] *f* (–;) tourism
Touristin [tu'rɪstɪn] *f* (–;–nen) tourist
Tour·nee [tur'ne] *f* (–;–neen ['ne·ən]) (mus, theat) tour
Trab [trɑp] *m* (–[e]s;) trot; **im T.** at a trot
Trabant [tra'bant] *m* (–en;–en) satellite
traben ['trɑbən] *intr* (HABEN & SEIN) trot
Tra'ber *m* (–s;–) trotter
Tra'berwagen *m* sulky
Trab'rennen *n* harness racing
Tracht [traxt] *f* (–;–en) costume; (*Last*) load; (*Ertrag*) yield
trachten ['traxtən] *intr*—**t. nach** strive for; **t. zu** (*inf*) endeavor to (*inf*)
trächtig ['treçtɪç] *adj* pregnant
Tradition [tradɪ'tsjon] *f* (–;–en) tradition
traditionell [tradɪtsjo'nel] *adj* traditional
traf [trɑf] *pret of* **treffen**
Trafik [tra'fɪk] *f* (–;–en) (Aust) cigar store
träg [trek] *adj var of* **träge**
Tragbahre ['trɑkbɑrə] *f* (–;–n) stretcher, litter
Trag'balken ['trɑkbalkən] *m* supporting beam; girder; joist
Tragband ['trɑkbant] *n* (–[e]s;̈–er) strap; shoulder strap
tragbar ['trɑkbɑr] *adj* portable; (*Kleid*) wearable; (fig) bearable
Trage ['trɑgə] *f* (–;–n) litter
träge ['tregə] *adj* lazy; slow; inert
tragen ['trɑgən] §132 *tr* carry; bear; endure; support; (*Kleider*) wear, have on; (*hervorbringen*) produce, yield; (*Bedenken*) have; (*Folgen*) take; (*Risiko*) run; (*Zinsen*) yield; **bei sich t.** have on one's person; **getragen sein von** be based on; **zur Schau t.** show off ‖ *ref* dress; **sich**

gut t. wear well ‖ *intr* (*Stimme*) carry; (*Schußwaffe*) have a range; (*Baum, Feld*) bear, yield; (*Eis*) be thick enough

Träger ['trɛgər] *m* (-s;-) carrier; porter; (*Inhaber*) bearer; shoulder strap; (archit) girder, beam

Trä'gerflugzeug *n* carrier plane

trä'gerlos *adj* strapless

tragfähig ['trɑkfe·ɪç] *adj* strong enough, capable of carrying; **tragfähige Grundlage** (fig) sound basis

Trag'fähigkeit *f* (-;-en) capacity, load limit; (naut) tonnage

Tragfläche ['trɑkflɛçə] *f,* **Tragflügel** ['trɑkflygəl] *m* airfoil

Träg'heit ['trɛkhaɪt] *f* (-;) laziness; (phys) inertia

Traghimmel ['trɑkhɪməl] *m* canopy

Tragik ['trɑgɪk] *f* (-;) tragedy

tragisch ['trɑgɪʃ] *adj* tragic

Tragödie [tra'gødjə] *f* (-;-n) tragedy

Tragriemen ['trɑkrimən] *m* strap

Tragsessel ['trɑkzɛsəl] *m* sedan chair

Tragtasche ['trɑktaʃə] *f* shopping bag

Tragtier ['trɑktir] *n* pack animal

Tragweite ['trɑkvaɪtə] *f* range; (*Bedeutung*) significance, moment

Tragwerk ['trɑkvɛrk] *n* (aer) airfoil

Trainer ['trɛnər] *m* (-s;-) coach

trainieren [trɛ'nirən] *tr & intr* train; coach

Training ['trɛnɪŋ] *n* (-s;) training

Trai'ningsanzug *m* sweat suit

traktieren [trak'tirən] *tr* treat; treat roughly

Trak·tor ['traktɔr] *m* (-s;-toren ['torən]) tractor

trällern ['trɛlərn] *tr & intr* hum

trampeln ['trampəln] *tr* trample

Tram/pelpfad *m* beaten path

Tran [trɑn] *m* (-[e]s;-e) whale oil; **im T. sein** be drowsy; be under the influence of alcohol

tranchieren [trɑ̃'ʃirən] *tr* carve

Träne ['trɛnə] *f* (-;-n) tear

tränen ['trɛnən] *intr* water

Trä'nengas *n* tear gas

trank [traŋk] *pret* of **trinken** ‖ **Trank** *m* [-[e]s;ˀe) drink, beverage; potion

Tränke ['trɛŋkə] *f* (-;-n) watering hole

tränken ['trɛŋkən] *tr* give (*s.o.*) a drink; (*Tiere*) water; soak

Transfor·mator [transfɔr'matɔr] *m* (-s; -matoren [ma'torən] transformer

transformieren [transfɔr'mirən] *tr* transform; step up; step down

Transfusion [transfu'zjon] *f* (-;-en) transfusion

Tran·sistor [tran'zɪstɔr] *m* (-s;-sistoren [zɪs'torən]) transistor

transitiv [tranzi'tif] *adj* transitive

Transmission [transmɪ'sjon] *f* (-;-en) transmission

transparent [transpa'rɛnt] *adj* transparent ‖ **Transparent** *n* (-[e]s;-e) transparency; (*Spruchband*) banderol

transpirieren [transpɪ'rirən] *intr* perspire

Transplantation [transplanta'tsjon] *f* (-;-en) (surg) transplant

Transport [trans'pɔrt] *m* (-[e]s;-e) transportation

transportabel [transpɔr'tabəl] *adj* transportable

Transporter [trans'pɔrtər] *m* (-s;-) troopship; transport plane

transport/fähig *adj* transportable

transportieren [transpɔr'tirən] *tr* transport, ship

Transport/unternehmen *n* carrier

Trapez [tra'pets] *n* (-es;-e) trapeze; (geom) trapezoid

trappeln ['trapəln] *intr* (SEIN) clatter; (*Kinder*) patter

Trassant [tra'sant] *m* (-en;-en) (fin) drawer

Trassat [tra'sat] *m* (-en;-en) drawee

trassieren [tra'sirən] *tr* trace, lay out; **e-n Wechsel t. auf** (*acc*) write out a check to

trat [trɑt] *pret* of **treten**

Tratsch [trɑtʃ] *m* (-es;) gossip

tratschen ['trɑtʃən] *intr* gossip

Tratte ['trɑtə] *f* (-;-n) (fin) draft

Trau- [trau] *comb.fm.* wedding, marriage

Traube ['traubə] *f* (-;-n) grape; bunch of grapes; (fig) bunch

Trau'bensaft *m* grape juice

Trau'benzucker *m* glucose

trauen ['trau·ən] *tr* (*Brautpaar*) marry; **sich t. lassen** get married ‖ *ref* dare ‖ *intr* (*dat*) trust (in), have confidence (in)

Trauer ['trau·ər] *f* (-;) grief, sorrow; mourning; (*Trauerkleidung*) mourning clothes; **T. anlegen** put on mourning clothes; **T. haben** be in mourning

Trau'eranzeige *f* obituary

Trau'erbotschaft *f* sad news

Trau'erfall *m* death

Trau'erfeier *f* funeral ceremony

Trau'erflor *m* mourning crepe

Trau'ergefolge *n,* **Trau'ergeleit** *n* funeral procession

Trau'ergottesdienst *m* funeral service

Trau'erkloß *m* (coll) sad sack

Trau'ermarsch *m* funeral march

trauern ['trau·ərn] *intr* (**um**) mourn (for); (**um**) wear mourning (for)

Trau'erspiel *n* tragedy

Trau'erweide *f* weeping willow

Trau'erzug *m* funeral cortege

Traufe ['traufə] *f* (-;-e) eaves

träufeln ['trɔɪfəln] *tr & intr* drip

Trauf'rinne *f* rain gutter

Trauf'röhre *f* rain pipe

traulich ['traulɪç] *adj* intimate; cozy

Traum [traum] *m* (-[e]s;ˀe) dream; (fig) daydream, reverie

Traum'bild *n* vision, phantom

Traum'deuter **–in** §6 *mf* interpreter of dreams

träumen ['trɔɪmən] *tr & intr* dream

Träu'mer *m* (-s;-) dreamer

Träumerei [trɔɪmə'raɪ] *f* (-;-en) dreaming; daydream

Träumerin ['trɔɪmərɪn] *f* (-;-nen) dreamer

träumerisch ['trɔɪmərɪʃ] *adj* dreamy; absent-minded

Traum'gesicht *n* vision, phantom

traum'haft *adj* dream-like

traurig ['traurɪç] *adj* sad

Trau'ring *m* wedding ring (or band)

Trau'schein m marriage certificate
traut [traut] adj dear; cozy; intimate
Trau'ung f (-;-en) marriage ceremony; **kirchliche T.** church wedding; **standesamtliche T.** civil ceremony
Trau'zeuge m best man
Trecker ['trɛkər] m (-s;-) tractor
Treff [trɛf] n (-s;-s) (cards) club(s)
treffen ['trɛfən] §151 tr hit; (begegnen) meet; (betreffen) concern || ref meet; assemble; **sich t. mit** meet with || intr hit home; (box) land, connect || **Treffen** n (-s;-) meeting; (mil) encounter; (sport) meet
tref'fend adj pertinent; to the point; (Ähnlichkeit) striking
Tref'fer m (-s;-) hit; winner; prize
treff'lich adj excellent
Treff'punkt m rendezvous, meeting place
Treib- [traip] comb.fm. moving; driving
treiben ['traibən] §62 tr drive; propel; chase, expel; (Beruf) pursue; (Blätter, Blüten) put forth; (Geschäft) run, carry on; (Metall) work; (Musik, Sport) go in for; (Sprachen) study; (Pflanzen) force; **es zu weit t.** go too far; **was treibst du denn?** (coll) what are you doing? || intr blossom; sprout; (Teig) ferment || intr (SEIN) drift, float || **Treiben** n (-s;) doings, activity; drifting, floating
Treib'haus n hothouse
Treib'holz n driftwood
Treib'kraft f driving force
Treib'mine f floating mine
Treib'rakete f booster rocket
Treib'riemen m drive belt
Treib'sand m drifting sand; quicksand
Treib'stange f connecting rod
Treib'stoff m fuel; propellant
Treib'stoffbehälter m fuel tank
trennbar ['trɛnbɑr] adj separable
trennen ['trɛnən] tr separate; sever; (Naht) undo; (Ehe) dissolve; (elec, telp) cut off || ref part; separate; (Weg) branch off
Tren'nung f (-;-en) separation; parting; dissolution
Tren'nungsstrich m dividing line; hyphen
Trense ['trɛnzə] f (-;-n) snaffle
Treppe ['trɛpə] f (-;-n) stairs, stairway; flight of stairs; **die T. hinauffallen** (coll) be kicked upstairs; **zwei Treppen hoch wohnen** live two flights up
Trep'penabsatz m landing
Trep'penflucht f flight of stairs
Trep'pengeländer n banister
Trep'penhaus n staircase
Trep'penläufer m stair carpet
Trep'penstufe f step, stair
Tresor [trɛ'zor] m (-s;-e) safe; vault
Tresse ['trɛsə] f (-;-n) (mil) stripe
treten ['tretən] §152 tr tread; tread on; trample; (Fußhebel) work; (Orgel) pump; **mit Füßen t.** (fig) trample under foot || intr (SEIN) step, walk; tread; **an j-s Stelle t.** succeed s.o.; **auf der Stelle t.** (mil) mark time; **in**

Kraft t. go into effect; **j-m zu nahe t.** offend s.o.; **t. in** (acc) enter (into)
Tretmühle ['tretmylə] f treadmill
treu [trɔɪ] adj loyal, faithful, true
Treu'bruch m breach of faith
Treue ['trɔɪ·ə] f (-;) loyalty, fidelity; allegiance; **j-m die T. halten** remain loyal to s.o.
Treu'eid m oath of allegiance
Treu'hand f (jur) trust
Treuhänder -in ['trɔɪhɛndər(ɪn)] §6 mf trustee
Treu'handfonds m trust fund
treu'herzig adj trusting; sincere
treu'los adj unfaithful; (gegen) disloyal (to)
Tribüne [trɪ'bynə] f (-;-n) rostrum; (mil) reviewing stand; (sport) grandstand
Tribut [trɪ'but] m (-[e]s;-e) tribute
Trichter ['trɪçtər] m (-s;-) funnel; (Bomben-) crater, pothole; (mus) bell (of wind instrument); **auf den T. kommen** (coll) catch on
Trick [trɪk] m (-s;-s & -e) trick
Trick'film m animated cartoon
trieb [trip] pret of **treiben** || **Trieb** m (-[e]s;-e) sprout, shoot; urge, drive; instinct
Trieb'feder f (horol) mainspring
Trieb'kraft f motive power
trieb'mäßig adj instinctive
Trieb'werk n motor, engine
triefäugig ['trifɔɪgɪç] adj bleary-eyed
triefen ['trifən] §153 intr drip; (Augen) water; (Nase) run
triezen ['tritsən] tr (coll) tease
Trift [trɪft] f (-;-en) pasture land; cattle track; log-running
triftig ['trɪftɪç] adj cogent; valid
Trigonometrie [trɪgɔnəme'tri] f (-;) trigonometry
Trikot [trɪ'ko] m & n (-s;-s) knitted cloth; (sport) trunks, tights
Triller ['trɪlər] m (-s;-) trill; (mus) quaver
trillern ['trɪlərn] intr trill; (Vogel) warble
Tril'lerpfeife f whistle
Trink- [trɪŋk] comb.fm. drinking
trinkbar ['trɪŋkbɑr] adj drinkable
Trink'becher m drinking cup
trinken ['trɪŋkən] §143 tr & intr drink
Trin'ker -in §6 mf drinker
trink'fest adj able to hold one's liquor
Trink'gelage n drinking party
Trink'geld n tip, gratuity
Trink'glas n drinking glass
Trink'halm m straw
Trink'spruch m toast
Trink'wasser n drinking water
Trio ['tri·o] n (-s;-s) trio
trippeln ['trɪpəln] intr (SEIN) patter
Tripper ['trɪpər] m (-s;) gonorrhea
trist [trɪst] adj dreary
tritt [trɪt] pret of **treten** || m (-[e]s; -e) step; kick; pace; footstep; footprint; small stepladder; pedal; **j-m e-n T. versetzen** give s.o. a kick
Tritt'brett n running board
Tritt'leiter f stepladder
Triumph [trɪ'umf] m (-[e]s;-e) triumph

Triumph'bogen *m* triumphal arch
triumphieren [trɪ·um'firən] *intr* triumph
Triumph'zug *m* triumphal procession
trocken ['trɔkən] *adj* dry; arid; **trockenes Brot** plain bread
Trockenbagger (**Trok'kenbagger**) *m* (mach) excavator
Trockendock (**Trok'kendock**) *n* drydock
Trockenei (**Trok'kenei**) *n* dehydrated eggs
Trockeneis (**Trok'keneis**) *n* dry ice
Trockenhaube (**Trok'kenhaube**) *f* hair drier
Trockenheit (**Trok'kenheit**) *f* (-;) dryness, aridity
trockenlegen (**trok'kenlegen**) *tr* (*Sumpf*) drain; (*Säugling*) change (the diapers of)
Trockenmaß (**Trok'kenmaß**) *n* dry measure
Trockenmilch (**Trok'kenmilch**) *f* powdered milk
Trockenschleuder (**Trok'kenschleuder**) *f* spin-drier, clothes drier
Trockenübung (**Trok'kenübung**) *f* dry run
trocknen ['trɔknən] *tr* dry || *intr* (SEIN) dry, dry up
Troddel ['trɔdəl] *f* (-;-n) tassel
Trödel ['trødəl] *m* (-s;) secondhand goods; old clothes; junk; (fig) nuisance, waste of time
Trö'delkram *m* junk
trödeln ['trødəln] *intr* waste time
Tröd'ler –in §6 *mf* secondhand dealer
troff [trɔf] *pret* of **triefen**
trog [trok] *pret* of **trügen**   **Trog** *m* (-[e]s;⁼e) trough
Trommel ['trɔməl] *f* (-;-n) drum
Trom'melfell *n* drumhead; (anat) eardrum
trommeln ['trɔməln] *tr & intr* drum
Trom'melschlag *m* drumbeat
Trom'melschlegel *m*, **Trom'melstock** *m* drumstick
Trom'melwirbel *m* drum roll
Trommler ['trɔmlər] *m* (-s;-) drummer
Trompete [trɔm'petə] *f* (-;-n) trumpet
trompeten [trɔm'petən] *intr* blow the trumpet; (*Elefant*) trumpet
Trompe'ter –in §6 *mf* trumpeter
Tropen ['tropən] *pl* tropics
Tropf [trɔpf] *m* (-[e]s;⁼e) simpleton; **armer T.** poor devil
tröpfeln ['trœpfəln] *tr & intr* drip || *intr* (SEIN) trickle || *impers*—**es tröpfelt** it is sprinkling
tropfen ['trɔpfən] *tr & intr* drip || *intr* (SEIN) trickle || **Tropfen** *m* (-s;-) drop; **ein T. auf den heißen Stein** a drop in the bucket
trop'fenweise *adv* drop by drop
Trophäe [tro'fe·ə] *f* (-;-n) trophy
tropisch ['tropɪʃ] *adj* tropical
Troß [trɔs] *m* (**Trosses; Trosse**) (coll) load, baggage; (coll) hangers-on
Trosse ['trɔsə] *f* (-;-n) cable; (naut) hawser
Trost [trost] *m* (-es;) consolation, comfort; **geringer T.** cold comfort;

wohl nicht bei T. sein not be all there
trösten ['trøstən] *tr* console, comfort || *ref* cheer up; feel consoled
tröstlich ['trøstlɪç] *adj* comforting
trost'los *adj* disconsolate; bleak
Trost'preis *m* consolation prize
trost'reich *adj* comforting
Trö'stung *f* (-;-en) consolation
Trott [trɔt] *m* (-[e]s;⁼e) trot; (coll) routine
Trottel ['trɔtəl] *m* (-s;-) (coll) dope
trotten ['trɔtən] *intr* (SEIN) trot
Trottoir [trɔ'twar] *n* (-s;-e & -s) sidewalk
trotz [trɔts] *prep* (*genit*) in spite of; **t. alledem** for all that || **Trotz** *m* (-es;) defiance; **j-m T. bieten** defy s.o.
trotz'dem *adv* nevertheless || *conj* although
trotzen ['trɔtsən] *intr* be stubborn; (*schmollen*) sulk; (*dat*) defy
trotzig ['trɔtsɪç] *adj* defiant; sulky; obstinate
Trotz'kopf *m* defiant child (or adult)
trüb [tryp], **trübe** ['trybə] *adj* turbid, muddy; (*Wetter*) dreary; (*glanzlos*) dull; (*Erfahrung*) sad
Trubel ['trubəl] *m* (-s;) bustle
trüben ['trybən] *tr* make turbid, muddy; dim; dull; disturb, trouble (*Freude, Stimmung*) spoil || *ref* grow cloudy; become muddy; become strained
Trübsal ['trypzal] *f* (-;-en) distress, misery; **T. blasen** be in the dumps
trüb'selig *adj* gloomy, sad
Trüb'sinn *m* (-[e]s;) gloom
trüb'sinnig *adj* gloomy
Trü'bung *f* (-;) muddiness; blurring
trudeln ['trudəln] *intr* go into a spin || **Trudeln** *n* (-s;) spin; **ins T. kommen** (aer) go into a spin
trug [truk] *pret* of **tragen** || **Trug** *m* (-[e]s;) deceit, fraud; delusion
Trug'bild *n* phantom; illusion
trügen ['trygən] §111 *tr & intr* deceive
trügerisch ['trygərɪʃ] *adj* deceptive, illusory; (*verräterisch*) treacherous
Trug'schluß *m* fallacy
Truhe ['tru·ə] *f* (-;-n) trunk, chest
Trulle ['trulə] *f* (-;-n) slut
Trümmer ['trʏmər] *pl* ruins; rubble
Trumpf [trumpf] *m* (-[e]s;⁼e) trump
Trunk [truŋk] *m* (-[e]s;⁼e) drinking; **im T.** when drunk
trunken ['truŋkən] *adj* drunk; **t. vor** (*dat*) elated with
Trunkenbold ['truŋkənbɔlt] *m* (-[e]s; -e) drunkard
Trun'kenheit *f* (-;) drunkenness; **T. am Steuer** (jur) drunken driving
trunk'süchtig *adj* alcoholic || **Trunksüchtige** §5 *mf* alcoholic
Trupp [trup] *m* (-s;-s) troop, gang; (mil) detail, detachment
Truppe ['trupə] *f* (-;-n) (mil) troop; (theat) troupe; **Truppen** (mil) troops
Trup'peneinheit *f* unit
Trup'penersatz *m* reserves
Trup'pengattung *f* branch of service
Trup'penschau *f* (mil) review, parade

Trup'pentransporter m (aer) troop car-
rier; (nav) troopship
Trüp'penübung f field exercise
Trup'penverband m unit; task force
Trup'penverbandplatz m (mil) first-aid
station
Trust [trʊst] m (-[e]s;-e & -s) (com)
trust
Truthahn ['truthɑn] m turkey (cock)
Truthenne ['truthɛnə] f turkey (hen)
trutzig ['trʊtsɪç] adj defiant
Tscheche ['tʃɛçə] m (-n;-n), **Tschechin**
['tʃɛçɪn] f (-;-nen) Czech
tschechisch ['tʃɛçɪʃ] adj Czech
Tschechoslowakei [tʃɛçəsləva'kaɪ] f
(-;)—**die T.** Czechoslovakia
Tube ['tubə] f (-;-n) tube; **auf die T.
drücken** (aut) step on it
Tuberkulose [tubɛrkʊ'lozə] f (-;)
tuberculosis
Tuch [tux] n (-[e]s;-e) cloth; fabric
‖ n (-[e]s;-̈er) kerchief; shawl; scarf
tuchen ['tuxən] adj cloth, fabric
Tuch'fühlung f—**T. haben mit** (mil)
stand shoulder to shoulder with; **T.
halten mit** keep in close touch with
Tuch'seite f right side (of cloth)
tüchtig ['tʏçtɪç] adj able, capable, efficient; sound, thorough; excellent;
good; (Trinker) hard; **t. in** (dat)
good at; **t. zu** qualified for ‖ adv
very much; hard; soundly, through-
ly; (sl) awfully
Tüch'tigkeit f (-;) ability, efficiency;
soundness, thoroughness; excellency
Tuch'waren pl dry goods
Tücke ['tʏkə] f (-;-n) malice; **mit List
und T.** by cleverness
tückisch ['tʏkɪʃ] adj insidious
tüfteln ['tʏftəln] intr—**t. an** (dat) (coll)
puzzle over
Tugend ['tugənt] f (-;-en) virtue
Tugendbold ['tugəntbɔlt] m (-[e]s;-e)
(pej) paragon of virtue
tu'gendhaft adj virtuous
Tulpe ['tʊlpə] f (-;-n) tulip
tummeln ['tuməln] tr (Pferd) exercise
‖ ref hurry; (Kinder) romp about
Tum'melplatz m playground; (fig)
arena
Tümmler ['tʏmlər] m (-s;-) dolphin;
(Taube) tumbler
Tumor ['tumər] m (-s; **Tumoren**
[tu'morən]) tumor
Tümpel ['tʏmpəl] m (-s;-) pond
Tumult [tu'mʊlt] m (-[e]s;-e) uproar;
uprising
tun [tun] §154 tr do; make; take; **dazu
tun** add to it; **e-n Zug tun** take a
swig; **es zu tun bekommen mit** have
trouble with; **j-n in ein Internat tun**
send s.o. to a boarding school ‖ intr
do; be busy; **alle Hände voll zu tun
haben** have one's hands full; **es ist
mir darum zu tun** I am anxious about
it; **groß tun** talk big; **mir ist sehr
darum zu tun zu** (inf) it is very important for me to (inf); **nur so tun,
als ob** pretend that; **spröde tun** be
prudish; **stolz tun** be proud; **weh tun**
hurt; **zu t. haben** be busy; have one's
work cut out; **zu tun haben mit** have
trouble with ‖ impers—**es tut mir**

leid I am sorry; **es tut nichts** it
doesn't matter ‖ **Tun** n (-s;) doings;
action; **Tun und Treiben** doings
Tünche ['tʏnçə] f (-;-n) whitewash
tünchen ['tʏnçən] tr whitewash
Tunichtgut ['tunɪçtgut] m (- & -[e]s;
-e) good-for-nothing
Tunke ['tuŋkə] f (-;-n) sauce; gravy
tunken ['tuŋkən] tr dip, dunk
tunlichst ['tunlɪçst] adv—**das wirst du
t. bleiben lassen** you had better leave
it alone
Tunnel ['tunəl] m (-s;- & -s) tunnel
Tüpfchen ['tʏpfçən] n (-s;-) dot
Tüpfel ['tʏpfəl] m & n (-s;-) dot
tupfen ['tupfən] tr dab; dot ‖ **Tupfen**
m (-s;-) dot, spot
Tür [tyr] f (-;-en) door
Tür'angel f door hinge
Tür'anschlag m doorstop
Turbine [tur'binə] f (-;-n) turbine
Turboprop ['turbəprɔp] m (-s;-s)
turboprop
Tür'drücker m latch
Tür'flügel m door (of double door)
Tür'griff m door handle; door knob
Türke ['tʏrkə] m (-n;-n) Turk
Türkei [tʏr'kaɪ] f (-;)—**die T.** Turkey
Türkin ['tʏrkɪn] f (-;-nen) Turk
Türkis [tʏr'kis] m (-es;-e) turquoise
türkisch ['tʏrkɪʃ] adj Turkish
türkisen [tʏr'kizən] adj turquoise
Tür'klingel f doorbell
Tür'klinke f door handle
Turm [turm] m (-[e]s;-̈e) tower;
steeple; turret; (chess) castle
Türmchen ['tʏrmçən] n (-s;-) turret
türmen ['tʏrmən] tr & ref pile up ‖
intr (SEIN) run away, bolt
turm'hoch' adj towering ‖ adv (by) far
Turm'spitze f spire
Turm'springen n high diving
Turn– [turn] comb.fm. gymnastic, gym,
athletic
turnen ['turnən] intr do exercises ‖
Turnen n (-s;) gymnastics
Tur'ner –in §6 mf gymnast
turnerisch ['turnərɪʃ] adj gymnastic
Turn'gerät n gymnastic apparatus
Turn'halle f gymnasium, gym
Turn'hemd n gym shirt
Turn'hose f trunks
Turnier [tur'nir] n (-s;-e) tournament
Turn'schuhe pl sneakers
Tür'pfosten m doorpost
Tür'rahmen m doorframe
Tür'schild n doorplate
Tür'schwelle f threshold
Tusche ['tuʃə] f (-;-n) (paint) wash;
chinesische T. India ink
tuscheln ['tuʃəln] intr whisper
Tute ['tutə] f (-;-n) (aut) horn
Tüte ['tytə] f (-;-n) paper bag; paper
cone; ice cream cone
tuten ['tutən] intr blow the horn; (coll)
blare away
Twen [tvɛn] m (-s;-s) young man (in
his twenties)
Typ [typ] m (-s;-en) type; (Bauart)
model
Type ['typə] f (-;-n) type; (coll)
strange character
Ty'pennummer f model number

Typhus ['tyfʊs] *m* (–;) typhoid
typisch ['typɪʃ] *adj* (**für**) typical (of)
Tyrann [tY'ran] *m* (–en;–en) tyrant
Tyrannei [tYra'naɪ] *f* (–;–en) tyranny

tyrannisch [tY'ranɪʃ] *adj* tyrannical
tyrannisieren [tYranɪ'zirən] *tr* tyrannize, oppress
Tz ['tetset] *n*—**bis ins Tz** thoroughly

U

U, u [u] *invar n* U, u
u.A.w.g. *abbr* (**um Antwort wird gebeten**) R.S.V.P.
U-Bahn ['uban] *f* (**Untergrundbahn**) subway
übel ['ybəl] *adj* evil; (*schlecht*) bad; (*unwohl*) queasy, sick; (*Geruch, usw.*) nasty, foul; **er ist ein übler Geselle** he's a bad egg; **mir ist ü.** I feel sick; **ü. daran sein** have it rough ‖ *adv* badly; **est steht ü. mit** things don't look good for; **ü. auslegen** misconstrue; **ü. deuten** misinterpret; **ü. ergehen** fare badly; **ü. gelaunt** in bad humor ‖ **Übel** *n* (–s;–) evil; ailment
ü'belgelaunt *adj* ill-humored
ü'belgesinnt *adj* evil-minded
Ü'belkeit *f* (–;) nausea
ü'belnehmen §116 *tr* take amiss; take offense at, resent
ü'belnehmend *adj* resentful
ü'belriechend *adj* foul-smelling
Ü'belstand *m* evil; bad state of affairs
Ü'beltat *f* misdeed, crime, offense
Ü'beltäter **–in** §6 *mf* wrongdoer; criminal
ü'belwollen §162 *intr* (*dat*) be ill-disposed towards ‖ **Übelwollen** *n* (–s;) ill will, malevolence
ü'belwollend *adj* malevolent
üben ['ybən] *tr* practice, exercise; (*e–e Kunst*) cultivate; (*Handwerk*) pursue; (*Gewalt*) use; (*Verrat*) commit; (*mil*) drill; (*sport*) train; **Barmherzigkeit ü. an** (*dat*) have mercy on; **Gerechtigkeit ü. gegen** be fair to; **Nachsicht ü. gegen** be lenient towards; **Rache ü. an** (*dat*) take revenge on ‖ *ref*—**sich im Schifahren ü.** practice skiing
über ['ybər] *adv*—**j–m ü. sein in** (*dat*) be superior to s.o. in; **ü. und ü.** over and over ‖ *prep* (*dat*) over; above, on top of ‖ *prep* (*acc*) by way of, via; (*bei, während*) during; (*nach*) past; over; across; (*betreffend*) about, concerning; **Briefe ü. Briefe** letter after letter; **ein Scheck ü. 10 DM** a check for 10 marks; **es geht nichts ü.** there is nothing better than; **heute übers Jahr** a year from today; **ü. Gebühr** more than was due; **ü. kurz oder lang** sooner or later; **ü. Land** crosscountry
überall' *adv* everywhere, all over
überallher' *adv* from all sides
überallhin' *adv* in every direction
Ü'berangebot *n* over-supply
überan'strengen *tr* overexert, strain ‖ *ref* overexert oneself, strain oneself

überar'beiten *tr* revise, touch up ‖ *ref* —**sich ü.** overwork oneself
Überar'beitung *f* (–;–en) revision, touching up; revised text
ü'beraus *adv* extremely, very
überbacken (überbak'ken) §50 *tr* bake lightly
Ü'berbau *m* (–[e]s; –e & –ten [tən]) superstructure
ü'berbeanspruchen *tr* overwork
ü'berbelasten *tr* overload
ü'berbelegt *adj* overcrowded
ü'berbelichten *tr* (phot) overexpose
ü'berbetonen *tr* overemphasize
überbie'ten §58 *tr* outbid; (fig) outdo
Überbleibsel ['ybərblaɪpsəl] *n* (–s;–) remains; leftovers
Überblen'dung *f* (cin) dissolve
Ü'berblick *m* survey; (fig) synopsis
überblicken (überblik'ken) *tr* survey
überbrin'gen §65 *tr* deliver; convey
Überbrin'ger **–in** §6 *mf* bearer
überbrücken (überbrük'ken) *tr* (& fig) bridge
Überbrückung (Überbrük'kung) *f* (–; –en) bridging; (rr) overpass
Überbrückungs– *comb.fm.* emergency, stop-gap
überdachen [ybər'daxən] *tr* roof over
überdau'ern *tr* outlast
überdecken (überdek'ken) *tr* cover
überden'ken §66 *tr* think over
überdies' *adv* moreover, besides
überdre'hen *tr* (*Uhr*) overwind
Ü'berdruck *m* excess pressure
Ü'berdruckanzug *m* space suit
Ü'berdruckkabine *f* pressurized cabin
Über·druß ['ybərdrʊs] *m* (–drusses;) boredom; (*Übersättigung*) satiety; (*Ekel*) disgust; **bis zum Ü.** ad nauseam
überdrüssig ['ybərdrYsɪç] *adj* (*genit*) sick of, disgusted with
ü'berdurchschnittlich *adj* above the average
Ü'bereifer *m* excessive zeal
ü'bereifrig *adj* overzealous
überei'len *tr* precipitate; rush ‖ *ref* be in too big a hurry; act rashly
übereilt [ybər'aɪlt] *adj* hasty, rash
übereinan'der *adv* one on top of the other
übereinan'derschlagen §132 *tr* cross
überein'kommen §99 *intr* (SEIN) come to an agreement ‖ **Übereinkommen** *n* (–s;–) agreement
Überein'kunft *f* agreement
überein'stimmen *intr* be in agreement; concur; (*Farben, usw.*) harmonize
Überein'stimmung *f* agreement; accord; (*Gleichförmigkeit*) conformity;

(*Einklang*) harmony; **in Ü. mit** in line with

ü′berempfindlich *adj* oversensitive

überfah′ren §71 *tr* run over, run down; (*Fluß, usw.*) cross; **ein Signal ü.** go through a traffic light; **ü. werden** (coll) be taken in || **ü′berfahren** §71 *tr* (*über e–n Fluß, usw.*) take across || *intr* (SEIN) drive over, cross

Ü′berfahrt *f* crossing

Ü′berfall *m* surprise attack, assault; (*Raubüberfall*) holdup; (*Einfall*) raid

überfal′len §72 *tr* (*räuberisch*) hold up; assault; (mil) surprise; (mil) invade, raid; **ü. werden** be overcome (*by sleep*); be seized (*with fear*)

ü′berfällig *adj* overdue

Ü′berfallkommando *n* riot squad

überflie′gen §57 *tr* fly over; (*Buch*) skim through

ü′berfließen §76 *intr* (SEIN) overflow

überflügeln [ybər′flygəln] *tr* outflank; (fig) outstrip

Ü′berfluß *m* abundance; excess; **im Ü. vorhanden sein** be plentiful

ü′berflüssig *adj* superfluous

überflu′ten *tr* overflow, flood, swamp || **ü′berfluten** *intr* (SEIN) overflow

überfor′dern *tr* demand too much of; overwork

Ü′berfracht *f* excess luggage

ü′berführen *tr* carry across; (*Leiche*) transport in state || **überfüh′ren** *tr* (*genit*) convince of; (*genit*) convict of

Überfüh′rung *f* (–;–en) overpass; (*e–s Verbrechers*) conviction

Ü′berfülle *f* superabundance

überfül′len *tr* stuff, jam, pack

Ü′bergabe *f* delivery; (& mil) surrender

Ü′bergang *m* passage; crossing; transition; (jur) transfer; (mil) desertion; (paint) blending; (rr) crossing

Ü′bergangsbeihilfe *f* severance pay

Ü′bergangsstadium *n* transition stage

Ü′bergangszeit *f* transitional period

überge′ben §80 *tr* hand over; give up; (*einreichen*) submit; (& mil) surrender; **dem Verkehr ü.** open to traffic || *ref* vomit, throw up

überge′hen §82 *tr* omit; overlook; **mit Stillschweigen ü.** pass over in silence || **ü′bergehen** §82 *intr* (SEIN) go over, cross; (*sich verändern*) (**in** *acc*) change (into); **auf j–n ü.** devolve upon s.o.; **in andere Hände ü.** change hands; **in Fäulnis ü.** become rotten

Ü′bergewicht *n* overweight; (fig) preponderance; **das Ü. bekommen** become top-heavy; (fig) get the upper hand

ü′bergießen §76 *tr* spill || **übergie′ßen** §76 *tr* pour over, pour on; (*Braten*) baste; **mit Zuckerguß ü.** (culin) ice

ü′bergreifen §88 *intr* (**auf** *acc*) spread (to); (**auf** *acc*) encroach (on)

Ü′bergriff *m* encroachment

ü′bergroß *adj* huge, colossal; oversize

ü′berhaben §89 *tr* have left; (*Kleider*) have on; (fig) be fed up with

überhand′nehmen §116 *intr* get the upper hand; run riot

ü′berhängen §92 *tr* (*Mantel*) put on;

(*Gewehr*) sling over the shoulders || *intr* overhang, project

überhäu′fen *tr* overwhelm, swamp

überhaupt′ *adv* really; anyhow; (*besonders*) especially; (*überdies*) besides; at all; **ü. kein** no...whatever; **ü. nicht** not at all; **wenn ü.** if...at all; if...really

überheblich [ybər′heplıç] *adj* arrogant

überhei′zen, übzerhit′zen *tr* overheat

überhöhen [ybər′hø·ən] *tr* (*Kurve*) bank; (*Preise*) raise too high

ü′berholen *tr* take across; **die Segel ü.** shift sails || *intr* (naut) heel || **überho′len** *tr* outdistance, outrun; (*ausbessern*) overhaul; (*Fahrzeug*) pass; (fig) outstrip

überholt [ybər′hɔlt] *adj* obsolete, out of date; (*repariert*) reconditioned

überhö′ren *tr* not hear, miss; ignore; misunderstand

ü′berirdisch *adj* supernatural

überkandidelt [′ybərkandidəlt] *adj* (coll) nutty, wacky

ü′berkippen *intr* (SEIN) tilt over

überkle′ben *tr* paper over; **ü. mit** cover with

Ü′berkleid *n* outer garment; overalls

ü′berklug *adj* (pej) wise, smart

ü′berkochen *intr* (SEIN) boil over

überkom′men *adj* traditional || §99 *tr* overcome || *intr* (SEIN) be handed down to

überla′den *adj* overdone || §103 *tr* overload

Ü′berlandbahn *f* interurban trolley line

Ü′berlandleitung *f* (elec) high-tension line; (telp) long-distance line

überlas′sen §104 *tr* yield, leave, relinquish; entrust; (com) sell; **das bleibt ihm ü.** he is free to do as he pleases || *ref* (*dat*) give way to

Ü′berlast *f* overload; overweight

überla′sten *tr* overload

überlau′fen *adj* overcrowded; (fig) swamped || §105 *tr* overrun; (*belästigen*) pester; **Angst überlief ihn** fear came over him || **ü′berlaufen** §105 *intr* (SEIN) run over, overflow; boil over; (fig & mil) desert; **die Galle läuft mir über** (fig) my blood boils || *impers*—**mich überläuft es kalt** I shudder

Ü′berläufer –in §6 *mf* (mil) deserter; (pol) turncoat

ü′berlaut *adj* too noisy

überle′ben *tr* outlive, survive || *ref* go out of style

überle′bend *adj* surviving || **Überlebende** §5 *mf* survivor

ü′berlebensgroß *adj* bigger than life

überlebt [ybər′lept] *adj* antiquated

überle′gen *adj* (*dat*) superior (to); (**an** *dat*) superior (in) || *tr* consider, think over || *ref*—**sich** [*dat*] **anders ü.** change one's mind; **sich** [*dat*] **ü.** consider, think over || *intr* think it over || **ü′berlegen** *tr* lay across; (*Mantel*) put on

Überle′genheit *f* (–;) superiority

überlegt′ *adj* well considered; (jur) willful

Überle′gung *f* (–;–en) consideration
überle′sen §107 *tr* read over, peruse
überlie′fern *tr* deliver; hand down, transmit; (mil) surrender
Überlie′ferung *f* (–;–en) delivery; (fig) tradition; (mil) surrender
überli′sten *tr* outwit, outsmart
überma′chen *tr* bequeath
Ü′bermacht *f* superiority; (fig) predominance
ü′bermächtig *adj* overwhelming; predominant
überma′len *tr* paint over
übermannen [ybər′manən] *tr* overpower
Ü′bermaß *n* excess; **bis zum Ü.** to excess
ü′bermäßig *adj* excessive ‖ *adv* excessively; overly
Ü′bermensch *m* superman
ü′bermenschlich *adj* superhuman
übermitteln [ybər′mıtəln] *tr* transmit, convey, forward
Übermitt′lung *f* (–;–en) transmission, conveyance, forwarding
ü′bermorgen *adv* the day after tomorrow
übermüdet [ybər′mydət] *adj* overtired
Ü′bermut *m* exuberance, mischievousness
ü′bermütig *adj* exuberant; haughty
ü′bernächste §9 *adj* next but one; **am übernächsten Tag** the day after tomorrow; **ü. Woche** week after next
übernach′ten *intr* spend the night
Übernach′tung *f* (–;–en) accommodations for the night; spending the night
Ü′bernahme *f* taking over, takeover
ü′bernatürlich *adj* supernatural
überneh′men §116 *tr* take over; assume; undertake; take upon oneself; accept, receive ‖ **ü′bernehmen** §116 *tr* (*Mantel, Schal*) put on; (*Gewehr*) shoulder ‖ **überneh′men** §116 *ref* overreach oneself; **sich beim Essen ü.** overeat
ü′berordnen *tr* place over, set over
ü′berparteilich *adj* nonpartisan
Ü′berproduktion *f* overproduction
überprü′fen *tr* examine again, check; verify; (*Personen*) screen
Überprü′fung *f* (–;–en) checking; checkup
ü′berquellen §119 *intr* (SEIN) (*Teig*) run over; **überquellende Freude** irrepressible joy
überqueren [ybər′kverən] *tr* cross
überra′gen *tr* tower over; (fig) surpass
überraschen [ybər′raʃən] *tr* surprise
Überra′schung *f* (–;–en) surprise
überrech′nen *tr* count over
überre′den *tr* persuade; **j–n zu etw ü.** talk a person into s.th.
Überre′dung *f* (–;) persuasion
ü′berreich *adj* (**an** *dat*) abounding (in) ‖ *adv*—**ü. ausgestattet** well equipped
überrei′chen *tr* hand over, present
ü′berreichlich *adj* superabundant
ü′berreif *adj* overripe
überrei′zen *tr* overexcite; (*Augen, Nerven*) strain
überreizt′ *adj* overwrought

überren′nen §97 *tr* overrun; (fig) overwhelm
Ü′berrest *m* rest, remainder; **irdische Überreste** mortal remains
Ü′berrock *m* topcoat, overcoat
überrum′peln *tr* take by surprise
Überrum′pelung *f* (–;–en) surprise
überrun′den *tr* (sport) lap
übersät [ybər′zet] *adj* (fig) strewn, dotted
übersät′tigen *tr* stuff; cloy; (chem) saturate, supersaturate
Übersät′tigung *f* (chem) supersaturation
Überschall– *comb.fm.* supersonic
überschat′ten *tr* overshadow
überschät′zen *tr* overestimate
Ü′berschau *f* survey
überschau′en *tr* look over, survey; overlook (*a scene*)
überschla′fen §131 *tr* (fig) sleep on
Ü′berschlag *m* rough estimate; (aer) loop; (gym) somersault
überschla′gen *adj* lukewarm ‖ §132 *tr* skip, omit; estimate roughly; consider ‖ *ref* go head over heels; do a somersault; (*Auto*) overturn; (*Boot*) capsize; (*Flugzeug*) do a loop; (beim Landen) nose over; (*Stimme*) break; (fig) (**vor** *dat*) outdo oneself (in) ‖ **ü′berschlagen** §132 *tr* (*Beine*) cross; flip over; **ü. in** (*acc*) (fig) change suddenly to
ü′berschnappen *intr* (SEIN) (*Stimme*) squeak; (coll) flip one's lid
überschnei′den §106 *ref* (*Linien*) intersect; (& fig) overlap
überschrei′ben §62 *tr* sign over
überschrei′en §135 *tr* shout down ‖ *ref* strain one's voice
überschrei′ten §86 *tr* cross, step over; (*Kredit*) overdraw; (*Gesetz*) violate, transgress; (fig) exceed, overstep
Ü′berschrift *f* heading, title
Ü′berschuh *m* overshoe
Ü′berschuß *m* surplus, excess; profit
ü′berschüssig *adj* surplus, excess
überschüt′ten *tr* shower; (& fig) overwhelm, flood
Ü′berschwang *m* (–[e]s;) rapture
überschwem′men *tr* flood, inundate
Überschwem′mung *f* (–;–en) flood, inundation
überschwenglich [′ybərʃveŋlıç] *adj* effusive, gushing
Ü′bersee *f* (–;) overseas
Ü′berseedampfer *m* ocean liner
Ü′berseehandel *m* overseas trade
übersehbar [ybər′zebar] *adj* visible at a glance
überse′hen §138 *tr* survey, look over; (*nicht bemerken*) overlook; (*absichtlich*) ignore; (*erkennen*) realize
übersen′den §140 *tr* send, forward; transmit; (*Geld*) remit
Übersen′dung *f* (–;–en) forwarding; transmission; consignment
ü′bersetzen *tr* ferry across ‖ **überset′zen** *tr* translate
Überset′zung *f* (–;–en) translation; (mach) gear, transmission
Ü′bersicht *f* survey, review; (*Abriß*) abstract; (*Zusammenfassung*) sum-

mary; (*Umriß*) outline; (*Ausblick*) perspective; **jede Ü. verlieren** lose all perspective
ü'bersichtlich *adj* clear; (*Gelände*) open
Ü'bersichtsplan *m* general plan
ü'bersiedeln *intr* (SEIN) move; emigrate
ü'bersinnlich *adj* transcendental
überspan'nen *tr* span; cover; overstrain; (fig) exaggerate
überspannt [ybər'/pant] *adj* eccentric; extravagant
Überspannt'heit *f* (–;–en) eccentricity
Überspan'nung *f* (–;–en) overstraining; (fig) exaggeration; (elec) excess voltage
überspie'len *tr* outplay; outwit; (*Tonbandaufnahme*) transcribe; (*Schüchternheit*) hide
überspitzt [ybər'/pɪtst] *adj* oversubtle
übersprin'gen §142 *tr* jump; (*auslassen*) omit, skip || **ü'berspringen** §142 *intr* (SEIN) jump
ü'bersprudeln *intr* (SEIN) bubble over
ü'berständig *adj* leftover; (*Bier*) flat; (*Obst*) overripe
überste'hen §146 *tr* stand, endure; (*Krankheit, usw.*) get over; (*Operation*) pull through; (*überleben*) survive || **ü'berstehen** §146 *intr* jut out
überstei'gen §148 *tr* climb over; (*Hindernisse*) overcome; (*Erwartungen*) exceed || **ü'bersteigen** §148 *intr* (SEIN) step over
überstim'men *tr* vote down, defeat
überstrah'len *tr* shine upon; (*verdunkeln*) outshine, eclipse
überstrei'chen §85 *tr* paint over
ü'berstreifen *tr* slip on
überströ'men *tr* flood, inundate || **ü'berströmen** *intr* (SEIN) overflow
Ü'berstunde *f* hour of overtime; **Überstunden machen** work overtime
überstür'zen *tr* rush, hurry || *ref* be in too big a hurry; act rashly; (*Ereignisse*) follow one another rapidly
überstürzt [ybər'/tʏrtst] *adj* hasty
überteuern [ybər'tɔɪ⸳ərn] *tr* overcharge
übertölpeln [ybər'tœpəln] *tr* dupe
übertö'nen *tr* drown out
Übertrag ['ybərtrak] *m* (–[e]s;⸚e) (acct) carryover, balance
übertragbar [ybər'trakbar] *adj* transferable; (pathol) contagious
übertra'gen *adj* figurative, metaphorical || §132 *tr* carry over, transfer; (*Amt, Titel*) confer; (*Aufgabe*) assign; (*Vollmacht*) delegate; (*Kurzschrift*) transcribe; (**in** *acc*) translate (into); (acct) transfer; (pathol) spread, communicate; (rad) broadcast, transmit; (**mit** *Relais*) relay; (telv) televise
Übertra'gung *f* (–;–en) carrying over; transfer; assignment; delegation; conferring; transcription; translation; copy; (pathol) spread; (rad) broadcast; relay; (telv) televising
übertref'fen §151 *tr* surpass, outdo
übertrei'ben §62 *tr* overdo; exaggerate; (theat) overact
Übertrei'bung *f* (–;–en) overdoing; exaggeration; (theat) overacting

übertre'ten §152 *tr* (*Gesetz*) transgress, break || *ref*—**sich** [*dat*] **den Fuß ü.** sprain one's ankle || **ü'bertreten** §152 *intr* (SEIN) (sport) go off sides; **ü. zu** (fig) go over to; (relig) be converted to
Übertre'tung *f* (–;–en) violation
Ü'bertritt *m* change, going over; (relig) conversion
übervölkern [ybər'fœlkərn] *tr* overpopulate
Übervöl'kerung *f* (–;) overpopulation
ü'bervoll *adj* brimful; crowded
übervorteilen [ybər'fortaɪlən] *tr* take advantage of, get the better of
überwa'chen *tr* watch over; supervise; (*kontrollieren*) inspect, check; (*polizeilich*) shadow; (rad, telv) monitor
Überwa'chung *f* (–;–en) supervision; inspection; control; surveillance
Überwa'chungsausschuß *m* watchdog committee
überwältigen [ybər'vɛltɪgən] *tr* overpower (fig) overwhelm
überwei'sen §118 *tr* (*Geld*) send; (*zu e-m Spezialisten*) refer
Überwei'sung *f* (–;–en) sending, remittance; referral
ü'berweltlich *adj* otherworldly
ü'berwerfen §160 *tr* throw over || **überwer'fen** §160 *ref* (**mit**) have a run-in (with)
überwie'gen §57 *tr* outweigh || *intr* prevail, preponderate || **Überwiegen** *n* (–s;) prevalence, preponderance
überwie'gend *adj* prevailing; (*Mehrheit*) vast || *adv* predominantly
überwin'den §59 *tr* conquer, overcome || *ref*—**sich ü. zu** (*inf*) bring oneself to (*inf*)
überwintern [ybər'vɪntərn] *intr* pass the winter; (bot) survive the winter
überwu'chern *tr* overrun; (fig) stifle
Ü'berwurf *m* wrap; shawl
Ü'berzahl *f* numerical superiority; majority
überzah'len *tr* & *intr* overpay
überzäh'len *tr* count over, recount
überzählig ['ybərtselɪç] *adj* surplus
überzeu'gen *tr* convince || *ref*—**ü. Sie sich selbst davon!** go and see for yourself!
Überzeu'gung *f* (–;–en) conviction
überzie'hen §163 *tr* cover; (*mit Farbe*) coat; (*Bett*) put fresh linen on; (*Konto*) overdraw; **ein Land mit Krieg ü.** invade a country || **ü'berziehen** §163 *tr* (*Mantel, usw.*) slip on; **j–m eins ü.** (coll) give s.o. a whack
Ü'berzieher *m* (–s;–) overcoat
überzuckern (überzuk'kern) *tr* (& fig) sugarcoat
Ü'berzug *m* coat, film; (*Decke*) cover; (*Hülle*) case; pillow case; (*Kruste*) crust; (*Schale, Rinde*) skin
üblich ['yplɪç] *adj* usual, customary
U'-Boot *n* (**Unterseeboot**) submarine
U'-Bootbunker *m* submarine pen
U'-Bootjäger *m* (aer) antisubmarine aircraft; (nav) subchaser
U'-Bootortungsgerät *n* sonar
U'-Bootrudel *n* (nav) wolf pack
übrig ['ybrɪç] *adj* left (over), remain-

ing, rest (of); **die übrigen** the others, the rest; **ein übriges tun** do more than is necessary; **etw ü. haben für** have a soft spot for; **im übrigen** for the rest, otherwise

ü′brigbehalten §90 *tr* keep, spare

ü′brigbleiben §62 *intr* (SEIN) be left (over) ‖ *impers*—**es blieb mir nichts anderes ü. als zu** (*inf*) I had no choice but to (*inf*)

übrigens [′ybrɪgəns] *adv* moreover; after all; by the way

ü′briglassen §104 *tr* leave, spare

Übung [′ybʊŋ] *f* (−;−en) exercise; practice; (*Gewohnheit*) use; (*Ausbildung*) training; (mil) drill

Ü′bungsbeispiel *n* practical example

Ü′bungsbuch *n* composition book; workbook

Ü′bungsgelände *n* training ground; (*für Bomben*) target area

Ü′bungshang *m* (sport) training slope

Ü′bungsheft *n* composition book; workbook

Ufer [′ufər] *n* (−s;−) (*e–s Flusses*) bank; (*e–s Meers*) shore

U′ferdamm *m* embankment, levee

u′ferlos *adj* fruitless

Uhr [ur] *f* (−;−en) clock; watch; o'clock; **um wieviel Uhr?** at what time; **um zwölf Uhr** at twelve o'clock; **wieviel Uhr ist es?** what time is it?

Uhr′armband *n* (−[e]s;−er) watchband

Uhr′feder *f* watch spring

Uhr′glas *n* watch crystal

Uhr′macher *m* watchmaker

Uhr′werk *n* works, clockwork

Uhr′zeiger *m* hand

Uhr′zeigerrichtung *f*—**entgegen der U.** counterclockwise; **in der U.** clockwise

Uhr′zeigersinn *m*—**im U.** clockwise

Uhu [′uhu] *m* (−s;−s) owl

Ukraine [ʊ′kraɪnə] *f* (−;)—**die U.** the Ukraine

ukrainisch [ʊ′kraɪnɪʃ] *adj* Ukrainian

UK-Stellung [ʊ′kaʃtelʊŋ] *f* (−;−en) military deferment

Ulk [ʊlk] *m* (−[e]s;−e) joke, fun

ulken [′ʊlkən] *intr* (coll) make fun

ulkig [′ʊlkɪç] *adj* funny

Ulme [′ʊlmə] *f* (−;−n) elm

Ultima·tum [ʊltɪ′matum] *n* (−s;−ten [tən] & −ta [ta]) ultimatum

Ultra-, ultra– [ultra] *comb.fm.* ultra–

Ul′trakurzfrequenz *f* ultrashort frequency

ultramontan [ultramɔn′tan] *adj* strict Catholic

ul′trarot *adj* infrared

Ultraschall– *comb.fm.* supersonic

ul′traviolett *adj* ultraviolet

um [ʊm] *adv*—**deine Zeit ist um** your time is up; **je…um so** the…the; **um so besser** all the better; **um so weniger** all the less; **um und um** round and round ‖ *prep* (*acc*) around, about; for; at; **um die Hälfte mehr** half as much again; **um die Wette laufen** race; **um ein Jahr älter** one year older; **um etw eintauschen** exchange for s.th.; **um jeden Preis** at

any price; **um…Uhr** at…o'clock; **um…zu** (*inf*) in order to (*inf*)

um′ackern *tr* plow up, turn over

um′adressieren *tr* readdress

um′ändern *tr* change (around)

Um′änderung *f* (−;−en) change, alteration

um′arbeiten *tr* rework; (*Metall*) recast; (*Buch*) revise; (*Haus*) remodel; (*berichtigen*) emend, correct; (*verbessern*) improve

umar′men *tr* embrace, hug

Umar′mung *f* (−;−en) embrace, hug

Um′bau *m* (−[e]s;−e & −ten) rebuilding; alterations, remodeling; reorganization

um′bauen *tr* remodel; reorganize ‖ **umbau′en** *tr* build around; **umbauter Raum** floor space

um′besetzen *tr* (*Stellungen*) switch around; (pol) reshuffle; (theat) recast

um′biegen §47 *tr* bend (over); bend up, bend down

um′bilden *tr* remodel; reconstruct; (adm) reorganize, (pol) reshuffle

Um′bildung *f* (−;−en) remodeling; reconstruction; reorganization; reshuffling

um′binden §59 *tr* (*Schürze, usw.*) put on ‖ **umbin′den** §59 *tr* (*verletztes Glied, usw.*) bandage

um′blättern *tr* turn ‖ *intr* turn the page(s)

um′brechen §64 *tr* (*Bäume, usw.*) knock down; (*Acker*) plow up ‖ **umbre′chen** *tr* make into page proof

um′bringen §65 *tr* kill

Um′bruch *m* upheaval; (typ) page proof

um′buchen *tr* transfer to another account; book for another date

um′denken §66 *tr* rethink

um′dirigieren *tr* redirect

um′disponieren *tr* rearrange

umdrän′gen *tr* crowd around

um′drehen *tr* turn around; (*Hals*) wring; (*j–s Worte*) twist ‖ *ref* turn around ‖ *intr* turn around

Umdre′hung *f* (−;−en) turn; revolution

Um′druck *m* reprint; (typ) transfer

umeinan′der *adv* around each other

um′erziehen §163 *tr* reeducate

um′fahren §71 *tr* run down ‖ **umfah′ren** §71 *tr* drive around; sail around

um′fallen §72 *intr* (SEIN) fall over, fall down; collapse; give in

Um′fang *m* circumference; perimeter; (*Bereich*) range; (*Ausdehnung*) extent; (*des Leibes*) girth; (fig) scope; (mus) range; **im großen U.** on a large scale

umfan′gen §73 *tr* surround; embrace

um′fangreich *adj* extensive; (*körperlich*) bulky; (*geräumig*) spacious

umfas′sen *tr* embrace; clasp; comprise, cover; include; contain; (mil) envelop

umfas′send *adj* comprehensive; extensive

Umfas′sung *f* (−;−en) embrace; clasp; enclosure, fence; (mil) envelopment

Umfas′sungsmauer ƒ enclosure
umflat′tern *tr* flutter around
umflech′ten §74 *tr* braid
umflie′gen §57 *tr* fly around ‖ **um′flie-gen** §57 *intr* (SEIN) (coll) fall down
umflie′ßen §76 *tr* flow around
um′formen *tr* reshape; (elec) convert
Um′former *m* (–s;–) (elec) converter
Um′frage ƒ inquiry, poll; **öffentliche U.** public opinion poll
umfrieden [ʊm′fridən] *tr* enclose
Um′gang *m* round, circuit; revolution, rotation; (*Zug*) procession; associa-tion, company; (archit) gallery; **ge-schlechtlicher U.** sexual intercourse; **schlechter U.** bad company; **U. mit j–m haben** (or **pflegen**) associate with s.o.
umgänglich [′ʊmgɛŋlɪç] *adj* sociable
Um′gangsformen *pl* social manners
Um′gangssprache ƒ colloquial speech
um′gangssprachlich *adj* colloquial
umgar′nen *tr* (fig) trap
umge′ben §80 *tr* surround
Umgebung [ʊm′gebʊŋ] ƒ (–;–en) sur-roundings, environs, neighborhood; company, associates; background, environment
Umgegend [′ʊmgegənt] ƒ (–;) (coll) neighborhood
umgehen §82 *tr* go around; evade; by-pass; (mil) outflank ‖ **um′gehen** §82 *intr* (SEIN) go around; (*Gerücht*) cir-culate; **an** (or **in**) **e–m Ort u.** haunt a place; **mit dem Gedanken** (or **Plan**) **u. zu** (*inf*) be thinking of (*ger*); **u. mit** deal with, handle; manage; be occupied with; hang around with
um′gehend *adj* immediate; **mit umge-hender Post** by return mail; **umge-hende Antwort erbeten!** please an-swer at your earliest convenience ‖ *adv* immediately
Umge′hung ƒ (–;–en) going around; bypassing; (fig) evasion; (mil) flank-ing movement
Umge′hungsstraße ƒ bypass
umgekehrt [′ʊmgəkert] *adj* reverse; contrary ‖ *adv* on the contrary; vice versa; upside down; inside out
um′gestalten *tr* alter; remodel
um′graben §87 *tr* dig up
umgren′zen *tr* fence in; (fig) limit
Umgren′zung ƒ (–;–en) enclosure; (fig) limit, boundary
um′gruppieren *tr* regroup; (pol) re-shuffle
um′gucken *ref* look around
um′haben §89 *tr* have on, be wearing
Um′hang *m* wrap; cape; shawl
um′hängen *tr* put on; (*Gewehr*) sling; (*Bild*) hang elsewhere
Um′hängetasche ƒ shoulder bag
um′hauen §93 *tr* cut down; (coll) bowl over
umher′ *adv* around, about
umher′blicken *tr* look around
umher′fuchteln *intr* gesticulate
umher′schweifen, umher′streifen *intr* (SEIN) rove, roam about
umhin′ *adv*—**ich kann nicht u.** I can't do otherwise; **ich kann nicht u. zu** (*inf*) I can't help (*ger*)

umhül′len *tr* wrap up, cover; envelop
Umhül′lung ƒ (–;–en) wrapping
Umkehr [′ʊmker] ƒ (–;) return; change; conversion; (elec) reversal
um′kehren *tr* turn around; overturn; (*Tasche*) turn out; (elec) reverse; (gram, math, mus) invert ‖ *intr* (SEIN) turn back, return
Um′kehrung ƒ (–;–en) overturning; re-versal; conversion; inversion
um′kippen *tr* upset ‖ *intr* (SEIN) tilt over
umklam′mern *tr* clasp; cling to; (mil) envelop; **einander u.** (box) clinch
Umklam′merung ƒ (–;–en) embrace; (box) clinch; (mil) envelopment
umklei′den *tr* clothe ‖ *ref* change around ‖ **um′kleiden** *tr* change the clothes of
Um′kleideraum *m* dressing room
um′kommen §99 *intr* (SEIN) perish; (*Essen*) spoil
Um′kreis *m* circuit; vicinity; (geom) circumference; **5 km im U.** within a radius of 5 km
umkrei′sen *tr* circle, revolve around
um′krempeln *tr* (*Ärmel*) roll up; **völ-lig u.** (coll) change completely
um′laden §103 *tr* reload; transship
Um′lauf *m* circulation; (*Umdrehung*) revolution, rotation; (*Flugblatt*) cir-cular; (*Rundschreiben*) circular let-ter; **in U. setzen** circulate
Um′laufbahn ƒ orbit
um′laufen §105 *tr* run down ‖ *intr* (SEIN) circulate ‖ **umlau′fen** §105 *tr* walk around
Um′laut *m* (–es;–e) umlaut, vowel mu-tation; mutated vowel
umlegbar [′ʊmlekbɑr] *adj* reversible
um′legen *tr* lay down; turn down; (*an-ders legen*) shift; (*Kragen*) put on; (*gleichmäßig verteilen*) apportion; (coll) knock down; (vulg) lay
um′leiten *tr* detour, divert
Um′leitung ƒ (–;–en) detour
um′lenken *tr* turn back
um′lernen *tr* relearn, learn anew
um′liegend *adj* surrounding
ummau′ern *tr* wall in
um′modeln *tr* remodel
umnachtet [ʊm′naxtət] *adj* deranged
Umnach′tung ƒ (–;)—**geistige U.** men-tal derangement
um′nähen *tr* hem
umne′beln *tr* fog; (fig) dull; **umnebelter Blick** glassy eyes
um′nehmen §116 *tr* put on
um′packen *tr* repack
um′pflanzen *tr* transplant ‖ **umpflan′-zen** *tr*—**etw mit Blumen u.** plant flowers around s.th.
um′pflügen *tr* plow up, turn over
umrah′men *tr* frame
umranden [ʊm′randən] *tr* edge, border
Umran′dung ƒ (–;–en) edging, edge
umran′ken *tr* twine around; **mit Efeu umrankt** ivy-clad
um′rechnen *tr* convert; **umgerechnet auf** (*acc*) expressed in
Um′rechnungskurs *m* rate of exchange
Um′rechnungstabelle ƒ conversion table
Um′rechnungswert *m* exchange value

um'reißen §53 *tr* pull down; knock down || **umrei'ßen** §53 *tr* outline

umrin'gen *tr* surround

Um'riß *m* outline

Um'rißzeichnung *f* sketch

um'rühren *tr* stir, stir up

um'satteln *tr* resaddle || *intr* change jobs; (educ) change one's course or major; (pol) switch parties

Um'satz *m* turnover, sales

Um'satzsteuer *f* sales tax

umsäu'men *tr* enclose, hem in

um'schalten *tr* switch; (*Strom*) convert || *intr* (**auf** *acc*) switch back (to)

Um'schalter *m* (elec) switch; (typ) shift key

Um'schaltung *f* (–;–en) switching; shifting

Um'schau *f* look around; **U. halten** have a look around

um'schauen *ref* look around

um'schichten *tr* regroup, reshuffle

umschichtig ['ʊmʃɪçtɪç] *adv* alternately

umschif'fen *tr* circumnavigate; (*ein Kap*) double

Um'schlag *m* (sudden) change, shift; envelope; (*e–s Buches*) cover, jacket; cuff; hem; transshipment; (med) compress

um'schlagen §132 *tr* knock down; (*Ärmel*) roll up; (*Bäume*) fell; (*Saum*) turn up; (*Seite*) turn; (*umladen*) transship || *intr* (SEIN) (*Laune, Wetter*) change; (*Wind*) shift; (*kentern*) capsize

Um'schlagpapier *n* wrapping paper

umschlie'ßen §76 *tr* surround, enclose

umschlin'gen §142 *tr* clasp; embrace; wind around

um'schmeißen §53 *tr* (coll) throw over

um'schnallen *tr* buckle on

um'schreiben §62 *tr* rewrite; (*abschreiben*) transcribe; (*Wechsel*) re-endorse; **u. auf** (*acc*) transfer to || **umschrei'ben** §62 *tr* circumscribe; paraphrase

Um'schreibung *f* (–;–en) transcription; transfer || **Umschrei'bung** *f* (–;–en) paraphrase

Um'schrift *f* transcription; (*e–r Münze*) legend

um'schulen *tr* retrain

um'schütteln *tr* shake (up)

um'schütten *tr* spill; pour into another container

umschwär'men *tr* swarm around; (fig) idolize

Um'schweif *m* digression; **ohne Umschweife** point-blank; **Umschweife machen** beat around the bush

umschweifig [ʊm'ʃvaɪfɪç] *adj* round-about

um'schwenken *intr* wheel around; (fig) change one's mind

Um'schwung *m* change; (*Drehung*) revolution; (*Umkehrung*) reversal; (*der Gesinnung*) revulsion

umse'geln *tr* sail around; (*Kap*) double

Umse'gelung *f* (–;–en) circumnavigation

um'sehen §138 *ref* (**nach**) look around (for); (fig) (**nach**) look out (for)

um'sein §139 *intr* (SEIN) (*Zeit*) be up; (*Ferien*) be over

um'setzen *tr* shift; transplant; (*Nährstoffe*) assimilate; (*Schüler*) switch around; (*Ware*) sell; (*verwandeln*) convert; (mus) transpose; **Geld u. in** (*acc*) spend money on; **in die Tat u.** translate into action || *ref*—**sich u. in** (*acc*) (biochem) be converted into

Um'sicht *f* (–;) circumspection

umsichtig ['ʊmzɪçtɪç] *adj* circumspect

um'siedeln *tr* & *intr* (SEIN) resettle

Um'siedlung *f* (–;–en) resettlement

umsonst' *adv* for nothing, gratis; (*vergebens*) in vain

um'spannen *tr* (*Wagenpferde*) change; (elec) transform || **umspan'nen** *tr* span; encompass; include

Um'spanner *m* (–s;–) (elec) transformer

um'springen §142 *intr* (SEIN) (*Wind*) shift; **mit j–m rücksichtslos u.** (coll) treat s.o. thoughtlessly

Um'stand *m* circumstance; factor; fact; (*Einzelheit*) detail; (*Aufheben*) fuss; **in anderen Umständen** (coll) pregnant; **sich** [*dat*] **Umstände machen** go to the trouble; **Umstände machen** be formal; **unter Umständen** under certain conditions

umständehalber ['ʊmʃtɛndəhalbər] *adv* owing to circumstances

umständlich ['ʊmʃtɛntlɪç] *adj* detailed; (*förmlich*) formal; (*zu genau*) fussy; (*verwickelt*) complicated; (*Erzählung*) long-winded, round-about

Um'standskleid *n* maternity dress

Um'standskrämer *m* fusspot

Um'standswort *n* (–[e]s;ℒer) adverb

um'stehend *adj* (*Seite*) next || **Umstehende** §5 *mf* bystander

Um'steige(fahr)karte *f* transfer

um'steigen §148 *intr* (SEIN) transfer

um'stellen *tr* put into a different place, shift; (*Möbel*) rearrange; (**auf** *acc*) convert (to) || *ref* (**auf** *acc*) adjust (to) || **umstel'len** *tr* surround

Um'stellung *f* (–;–en) change of position, shift; conversion; readjustment

um'stimmen *tr* tune to another pitch; make (*s.o.*) change his mind

um'stoßen §150 *tr* knock down; (*Pläne*) upset; (*Vertrag*) annul; (*Urteil*) reverse

umstricken (**umstrik'ken**) *tr* ensnare

umstritten [ʊm'ʃtrɪtən] *adj* contested; controversial

Um'sturz *m* overthrow

um'stürzen *tr* overturn; overthrow; (*Mauer*) tear down; (*Plan*) change, throw out || *intr* (SEIN) fall down

Umstürzler –**in** ['ʊmʃtʏrtslər(ɪn)] §6 *mf* revolutionary, subversive

umstürzlerisch ['ʊmʃtʏrtslərɪʃ] *adj* revolutionary; subversive

Um'tausch *m* exchange

um'tauschen *tr* (**gegen**) exchange (for)

um'tun §154 *tr* (*Kleider*) put on || *ref* —**sich u. nach** look around for

um'wälzen *tr* roll around; (fig) revolutionize || *ref* roll around

umwäl'zend *adj* revolutionary

Umwäl'zung *f* (–;–en) revolution

umwandelbar ['umvandəlbɑr] *adj* (com) convertible

um'wandeln *tr* change; (elec, fin) convert; (jur) commute

Um'wandlung *f* (–;–en) change; (elec, fin) conversion; (jur) commutation

um'wechseln *tr* exchange; (fin) convert

Um'weg *m* detour; **auf Umwegen** indirectly

um'wehen *tr* knock down || **umwe'hen** *tr* blow around

Um'welt *f* environment

Um'weltverschmutzung *f* ecological pollution

um'wenden §140 *tr* turn over || *ref & intr* turn around

umwer'ben §149 *tr* court, go with

um'werfen §160 *tr* throw down; upset; (*Plan*) ruin; (*Kleider*) throw about one's shoulders

umwickeln (umwik'keln) *tr* (*mit Band*) tape

umwin'den *tr* wreathe

umwölken [um'vœlkən] *ref & intr* cloud over

umzäunen [um'tsɔɪnən] *tr* fence in

um'ziehen §163 *ref* change one's clothes || *intr* (SEIN) move || **umzie'hen** §163 *ref*—**der Himmel hat sich umzogen** the sky has become overcast

umzingeln [um'tsɪŋəln] *tr* encircle

Um'zug *m* procession, parade; (*Wohnungswechsel*) moving; (pol) march

un– [un] *comb.fm.* un–, in–, ir–, non–

unabän'derlich *adj* unalterable

un'abhängig *adj* (von) independent (of) || **Unabhängige** §5 *mf* (pol) independent

Un'abhängigkeit *f* independence

unabkömm'lich *adj* unavailable; indispensable; (mil) essential (*on the homefront*); **ich bin augenblicklich u.** I can't get away at the moment

unablässig ['unaplɛsɪç] *adj* incessant

unablösbar [unap'lØsbɑr], **unablöslich** [unap'lØslɪç] *adj* unpayable

unabseh'bar *adj* unforeseeable; immense

unabsetz'bar *adj* irremovable

unabsicht'lich *adj* unintentional

unabwendbar [unap'vɛntbɑr] *adj* inevitable

un'achtsam *adj* careless, inattentive

um'ähnlich *adj* dissimilar, unlike

unanfecht'bar *adj* indisputable

un'angebracht *adj* out of place

un'angefochten *adj* undisputed

un'angemessen *adj* improper; inadequate; unsuitable

un'angenehm *adj* unpleasant, disagreeable; awkward

un'annehmbar *adj* unacceptable

Un'annehmlichkeit *f* unpleasantness; annoyance, inconvenience; **Unannehmlichkeiten** trouble

un'ansehnlich *adj* unsightly; (*unscheinbar*) plain, inconspicuous

un'anständig *adj* indecent; obscene

un'antastbar *adj* unassailable

un'appetitlich *adj* unappetizing; (*ekelhaft*) unsavory

Un'art *f* bad habit; (*Ungezogenheit*)

naughtiness; (*schlechte Manieren*) bad manners

un'artig *adj* ill-behaved, naughty

un'aufdringlich *adj* unostentatious; unobtrusive

un'auffällig *adj* inconspicuous

unauffindbar ['unauffɪntbɑr] *adj* not to be found

unaufgefordert ['unaufgəfordərt] *adj* unasked, uncalled for || *adv* spontaneously

unaufhaltbar ['unaufhaltbɑr], **unaufhaltsam** ['unaufhaltzɑm] *adj* irresistible; relentless

unaufhörlich ['unaufhØrlɪç] *adj* incessant

un'aufmerksam *adj* inattentive

un'aufrichtig *adj* insincere

unaufschiebbar ['unaufʃipbɑr] *adj* not to be postponed, urgent

unausbleiblich ['unausblaɪplɪç] *adj* inevitable

unausführbar ['unausfyrbɑr] *adj* unfeasible, impracticable

unausgeglichen ['unausgəglɪçən] *adj* uneven; (fig) unbalanced

unauslöschbar ['unauslœʃbɑr], **unauslöschlich** ['unauslœʃlɪç] *adj* inextinguishable; (*Tinte*) indelible

unaussprechlich ['unausʃpreçlɪç] *adj* unspeakable, ineffable

unausstehlich ['unausʃtelɪç] *adj* intolerable, insufferable

unbändig ['unbɛndɪç] *adj* wild

un'barmherzig *adj* unmerciful

un'beabsichtigt *adj* unintentional

un'beachtet *adj* unobserved, unnoticed

unbeanstandet ['unbə·anʃtandət] *adj* unopposed, unhampered

unbearbeitet ['unbə·arbaɪtət] *adj* unworked; (*roh*) raw; (*Land*) untilled; (mach) unfinished

unbebaut ['unbəbaut] *adj* uncultivated; (*Gelände*) undeveloped

unbedacht ['unbədaxt] *adj* thoughtless

un'bedenklich *adj* unhesitating; unswerving; unobjectionable, harmless || *adv* without hesitation

un'bedeutend *adj* unimportant; slight

un'bedingt *adj* unconditional, unqualified; implicit

un'befahrbar *adj* impassable

un'befangen *adj* unembarrassed; (*unparteiisch*) impartial; natural, unaffected

unbefleckt ['unbəflɛkt] *adj* immaculate

un'befriedigend *adj* unsatisfactory

un'befriedigt *adj* unsatisfied

un'befugt *adj* unauthorized; (jur) incompetent || **Unbefugte** §5 *mf* unauthorized person

un'begabt *adj* untalented

unbegreif'lich *adj* incomprehensible

un'begrenzt *adj* unlimited

un'begründet *adj* unfounded

Un'behagen *n* discomfort, uneasiness

un'behaglich *adj* uncomfortable

unbehelligt ['unbəhɛlɪçt] *adj* undisturbed, unmolested

unbehindert ['unbəhɪndərt] *adj* unhindered; unrestrained

unbeholfen ['unbəhɔlfən] *adj* clumsy

unbeirrbar ['ʊnbə·ɪrbɑr] *adj* unwavering

unbeirrt ['ʊnbə·ɪrt] *adj* unswerving

un'bekannt *adj* unknown; unfamiliar; unacquainted; (*Ursache*) unexplained || **Unbekannte** §5 *mf* stranger || *f* (math) unknown quantity

unbekümmert ['ʊnbəkʏmərt] *adj* (**um**) unconcerned (about)

un'beladen *adj* unloaded

unbelastet ['ʊnbəlastət] *adj* unencumbered; (*Wagen*) unloaded; carefree

un'belebt *adj* inanimate; (*Straße*) quiet; (com) slack

unbelichtet ['ʊnbəlɪçtət] *adj* (*Film*) unexposed

un'beliebt *adj* unpopular, disliked

unbemannt ['ʊnbəmant] *adj* unmanned

un'bemerkbar *adj* imperceptible

un'bemittelt *adj* poor

un'benommen *adj*—**es bleibt Ihnen u. zu** (*inf*) you are free to (*inf*); **es ist mir u., ob** it's up to me whether

unbenutzbar ['ʊnbənʊtsbɑr] *adj* unusable

unbenutzt ['ʊnbənʊtst] *adj* unused

un'bequem *adj* inconvenient; uncomfortable

unberechenbar ['ʊnbəreçənbɑr] *adj* incalculable; unpredictable

un'berechtigt *adj* unauthorized; unjustified

unbeschadet ['ʊnbəʃadət] *prep* (*genit*) without prejudice to

unbeschädigt ['ʊnbəʃedɪçt] *adj* unhurt; undamaged

un'bescheiden *adj* pushy

unbescholten ['ʊnbəʃɔltən] *adj* of good reputation

un'beschränkt *adj* unlimited; absolute

unbeschreiblich ['ʊnbəʃraɪplɪç] *adj* indescribable

unbesehen ['ʊnbəze·ən] *adv* sight unseen

un'besetzt *adj* unoccupied, vacant

unbesiegbar ['ʊnbəzikbɑr] *adj* invincible

unbesoldet ['ʊnbəzɔldət] *adj* unsalaried

un'besonnen *adj* thoughtless; careless; rash

un'besorgt *adj* unconcerned; carefree

un'beständig *adj* unsteady, inconstant; (*Preise*) fluctuating; (*Wetter*) changeable; (*Person*) fickle, unstable

unbestätigt ['ʊnbəʃtetɪçt] *adj* unconfirmed

un'bestechlich *adj* incorruptible

un'bestimmt *adj* indeterminate; vague; (*unsicher*) uncertain; (*unentschieden*) undecided; (gram) indefinite

unbestraft ['ʊnbəʃtraft] *adj* unpunished

unbestreit'bar *adj* indisputable

unbestritten ['ʊnbəʃtrɪtən] *adj* undisputed, uncontested

unbeteiligt ['ʊnbətaɪlɪçt] *adj* uninterested; indifferent; impartial

un'beträchtlich *adj* trifling, slight

unbeugsam ['ʊnbɔɪkzɑm] *adj* inflexible

unbewacht ['ʊnbəvaxt] *adj* unguarded

unbewaffnet ['ʊnbəvafnət] *adj* unarmed; (*Auge*) naked

un'beweglich *adj* immovable; motionless

unbewiesen ['ʊnbəvizən] *adj* unproved

unbewohnt ['ʊnbəvont] *adj* uninhabited

un'bewußt *adj* unconscious; involuntary

unbezähmbar [ʊnbə'tsembar] *adj* untamable; (fig) uncontrollable

Un'bilden *pl*—**U. der Witterung** inclement weather

Un'bildung *f* lack of education

un'billig *adj* unfair

unbotmäßig ['ʊnbotmesɪç] *adj* unruly; insubordinate

unbrauch'bar *adj* useless, of no use

un'bußfertig *adj* unrepentant

un'christlich *adj* unchristian

und [ʊnt] *conj* and; **und?** so what? **und wenn** even if

Un'dank *m* ingratitude

un'dankbar *adj* ungrateful; thankless

Un'dankbarkeit *f* ingratitude

undatiert ['ʊndatirt] *adj* undated

undenk'bar *adj* unthinkable

undenklich [ʊn'deŋklɪç] *adj*—**seit undenklichen Zeiten** from time immemorial

un'deutlich *adj* unclear, indistinct

un'deutsch *adj* un-German

un'dicht *adj* not tight; leaky

Un'ding *n* nonsense, absurdity

un'duldsam *adj* intolerant

undurchdring'lich *adj* (**für**) impervious (to); **undurchdringliche Miene** poker face

undurchführ'bar *adj* not feasible

un'durchlässig *adj* (**für**) impervious (to)

un'durchsichtig *adj* opaque; (*Beweggründe*) hidden; (*Machenschaften*) shady

un'eben *adj* uneven; bumpy; **nicht u.!** (coll) not bad!

un'echt *adj* false, spurious; artificial, imitation; (*Farbe*) fading

un'edel *adj* ignoble; (*Metall*) base

un'ehelich *adj* illegitimate

Un'ehre *f* dishonor

un'ehrenhaft *adj* dishonorable

un'ehrerbietig *adj* disrespectful

un'ehrlich *adj* dishonest; underhand

un'eigennützig *adj* unselfish

un'einig *adj* disunited; at odds

Un'einigkeit *f* disagreement

uneinnehm'bar *adj* impregnable

un'eins *adj* at odds, at variance

un'empfänglich *adj* (**für**) insusceptible (to)

un'empfindlich *adj* (**gegen**) insensitive (to); (**gegen**) insensible (to)

unend'lich *adj* endless; infinite; **auf u. einstellen** (phot) set at infinity || *adv* endlessly; infinitely; **u. viele** an endless number of

unentbehr'lich *adj* indispensible

unentrinnbar [ʊnɛnt'rɪnbar] *adj* inescapable

un'entschieden *adj* undecided; (*schwankend*) indecisive; (sport) tie || **Unentschieden** *n* (**-s;-**) (sport) tie

Un'entschiedenheit *f* indecision

un'entschlossen *adj* irresolute

Un'entschlossenheit f indecision
unentschuld'bar adj inexcusable
unentwegt ['unɛntvekt] adj staunch; unswerving || adv continuously; untiringly || **Unentwegte** §5 mf die-hard
unentwirrbar ['unɛntvɪrbɑr] adj inextricable
unerbittlich [unɛr'bɪtlɪç] adj inexorable; (Tatsache) hard
un'erfahren adj inexperienced
unerfindlich [unɛr'fɪntlɪç] adj incomprehensible, mysterious
unerforschlich [unɛr'fɔrʃlɪç] adj inscrutable
unerfreulich ['unɛrfrɔɪlɪç] adj unpleasant
unerfüllbar [unɛr'fYlbɑr] adj unattainable
un'ergiebig adj unproductive
un'ergründlich adj unfathomable
un'erheblich adj insignificant; (für) irrelevant (to)
unerhört [unɛr'hørt] adj unheard-of, unprecedented; outrageous || **un'erhört** adj (Bitte) unanswered
un'erkannt adj unrecognized || adv incognito
unerklär'lich adj inexplicable
unerläßlich [unɛr'lɛslɪç] adj indispensable
un'erlaubt adj illicit, unauthorized
un'erledigt adj unsettled, unfinished
unermeßlich [unɛr'mɛslɪç] adj immense
unermüdlich [unɛr'mydlɪç] adj untiring; (Person) indefatigable
unerquicklich [unɛr'kvɪklɪç] adj unpleasant
unerreich'bar adj unattainable, out of reach
unerreicht ['unɛrraɪçt] adj unrivaled
unersättlich [unɛr'zɛtlɪç] adj insatiable
unerschlossen ['unɛrʃlɔsən] adj undeveloped; (Boden) unexploited
unerschöpflich [unɛr'ʃøpflɪç] adj inhaustible
unerschrocken ['unɛrʃrɔkən] adj intrepid, fearless
unerschütterlich [unɛr'ʃYtərlɪç] adj unshakable; imperturbable
unerschwing'lich adj unattainable; beyond one's means; exorbitant
unersetz'bar, unersetz'lich adj irreplaceable; (Schaden) irreparable
unerträg'lich adj intolerable
unerwähnt ['unɛrvɛnt] adj unmentioned; **u. lassen** pass over in silence
unerwartet ['unɛrvartət] adj unexpected, sudden
unerweis'lich adj unprovable
un'erwünscht adj undesired; unwelcome
unerzogen ['unɛrtsogən] adj ill-bred
un'fähig adj incapable, unable; unqualified, inefficient
Un'fähigkeit f inability; inefficiency
Un'fall m accident, mishap
Un'fallflucht f hit-and-run offense
Un'fallstation f first-aid station
Un'falltod m accidental death
Un'fallversicherung f accident insurance
Un'fallziffer m accident rate

unfaß'bar, unfaß'lich adj incomprehensible; inconceivable
unfehl'bar adj infallible; unfailing
Unfehl'barkeit f infallibility
un'fein adj coarse; indelicate
un'fern adj near; **u. von** not far from || prep (genit) not far from
un'fertig adj not ready; not finished; immature
Unflat ['unflɑt] m (-s;) dirt, filth
unflätig ['unflɛtɪç] adj dirty, filthy
un'folgsam adj disobedient
Un'folgsamkeit f disobedience
unförmig ['unfœrmɪç] adj shapeless
un'förmlich adj informal
unfrankiert ['unfraŋkirt] adj unfranked, unstamped
un'frei adj not free; unstamped || adv —**u. schicken** send c.o.d.
un'freiwillig adj involuntary
un'freundlich adj unfriendly, unkind
Un'friede m dissension, discord
un'fruchtbar adj unfruitful, sterile; (fig) fruitless
Unfug ['unfuk] m (-[e]s;) nuisance, disturbance; mischief; misdemeanor; **U. treiben** cause mischief
ungang'bar adj impassable; unsalable
Ungar ['uŋgar] m (-;-n), **Ungarin** ['uŋgarɪn] f (-;-nen) Hungarian
ungarisch ['uŋgarɪʃ] adj Hungarian
Ungarn ['uŋgarn] n (-s;) Hungary
un'gastlich adj inhospitable
ungeachtet ['ungə·axtət] adj not esteemed || prep (genit) regardless of
ungeahnt ['ungə·ant] adj unexpected
ungebärdig ['ungəberdɪç] adj unruly
ungebeten ['ungəbetən] adj unbidden
ungebeugt ['ungəbɔɪkt] adj unbowed; (gram) uninflected
un'gebildet adj uneducated
un'gebräuchlich adj unusual; (veraltet) obsolete
un'gebraucht adj unused
Un'gebühr f indecency, impropriety
un'gebührlich adj indecent, improper
ungebunden ['ungəbundən] adj unbound; (ausschweifend) loose, dissolute; (frei) unrestrained; **ungebundene Rede** prose
ungedeckt ['ungədɛkt] adj uncovered; (Tisch) unset; (Haus) roofless; (Kosten) unpaid; (Scheck) overdrawn
Un'geduld f impatience
un'geduldig adj impatient
un'geeignet adj unfit, unsuitable; unqualified
ungefähr ['ungəfer] adj approximate || adv approximately, about; **nicht von u.** on purpose
ungefährdet ['ungəferdət] adj safe, unendangered
un'gefährlich adj not dangerous
un'gefällig adj discourteous
un'gefüge adj monstrous; clumsy
un'gefügig adj unyielding, inflexible
ungefüttert ['ungəfYtərt] adj unlined
un'gehalten adj (Versprechen) unkept, broken; (über acc) indignant (at)
ungeheißen ['ungəhaɪsən] adv of one's own accord
ungehemmt ['ungəhɛmt] adj unchecked

ungeheuer ['ʊngəhɔɪ·ər] *adj* huge; monstrous ‖ *adv* tremendously ‖ **Ungeheuer** *n* (–s;–) monster
un'geheuerlich *adj* monstrous ‖ *adv* (coll) tremendously
ungehobelt ['ʊngəhobəlt] *adj* unplaned; (fig) uncouth
un'gehörig *adj* improper; (*Stunde*) ungodly
Un'gehörigkeit *f* (–;–en) impropriety
un'gehorsam *adj* disobedient ‖ **Ungehorsam** *m* (–s;) disobedience
un'gekünstelt *adj* unaffected, natural
un'gekürzt *adj* unabridged
un'gelegen *adj* inconvenient
Un'gelegenheiten *pl* inconvenience
un'gelehrig *adj* unteachable
un'gelenk *adj* clumsy; stiff
un'gelernt *adj* (coll) unskilled
Un'gemach *n* discomfort; trouble
un'gemein *adj* uncommon
un'gemütlich *adj* uncomfortable; (*Zimmer*) dreary; (*Person*) disagreeable
un'genannt *adj* anonymous
un'genau *adj* inaccurate, inexact
ungeniert ['ʊnʒenirt] *adj* informal ‖ *adv* freely
ungenieß'bar *adj* inedible; undrinkable; (& fig) unpalatable
un'genügend *adj* insufficient; **u. bekommen** get a failing grade
ungepflastert ['ʊngəpflastərt] *adj* unpaved, dirt
un'gerade *adj* uneven; crooked; (*Zahl*) odd
un'geraten *adj* spoiled
un'gerecht *adj* unjust, unfair
Un'gerechtigkeit *f* injustice
ungereimt ['ʊngəraɪmt] *adj* unrhymed; (*unvernünft*) absurd; **ungereimtes Zeug reden** talk nonsense
un'gern *adv* unwillingly, reluctantly
ungerührt ['ʊngəryrt] *adj* (fig) unmoved
un'geschehen *adj* undone; **u. machen** undo
ungescheut ['ʊngəʃɔɪt] *adv* without fear
Un'geschick *n*, **Un'geschicklichkkeit** *f* awkwardness
un'geschickt *adj* awkward, clumsy
ungeschlacht ['ʊngəʃlaxt] *adj* uncouth
ungeschliffen ['ʊngəʃlɪfən] *adj* unpolished; (*Messer*) blunt; (*Edelstein*) uncut; (fig) rude
ungeschminkt ['ʊngəʃmɪŋkt] *adj* without makeup; (*Wahrheit*) unvarnished
un'gesellig *adj* unsociable
un'gesetzlich *adj* illegal
ungesittet ['ʊngəzɪtət] *adj* unmannerly; uncivilized
ungestört ['ʊngəʃtørt] *adj* undisturbed
ungestraft ['ʊngəʃtraft] *adj* unpunished ‖ *adv* scot-free
ungestüm ['ʊngəʃtym] *adj* impetuous, violent ‖ **Ungestüm** *n* (–[e]s;) impetuosity, violence
un'gesund *adj* unhealthy; unwholesome
ungeteilt ['ʊngətaɪlt] *adj* undivided
un'getreu *adj* disloyal, untrue
ungetrübt ['ʊngətrypt] *adj* cloudless, clear; (fig) untroubled

Ungetüm ['ʊngətym] *n* (–[e]s;–e) monster
ungeübt ['ʊngə·ypt] *adj* untrained; (*Arbeiter*) inexperienced
un'gewandt *adj* unskillful; clumsy
un'gewiß *adj* uncertain; **j–n im ungewissen lassen** keep s.o. in suspense
Un'gewißheit *f* uncertainty
Un'gewitter *n* storm
un'gewöhnlich *adj* unusual
un'gewohnt *adj* unusual; (*genit*) unaccustomed (to)
ungezählt ['ʊngətselt] *adj* countless
Ungeziefer ['ʊngətsifər] *n* (–s;) vermin, bugs
ungeziemend ['ʊngətsimənt] *adj* improper; (*frech*) impudent
un'gezogen *adj* rude; naughty
ungezügelt ['ʊngətsygəlt] *adj* unbridled
un'gezwungen *adj* unforced; natural, easy-going
Un'glaube *m* disbelief, unbelief
un'gläubig *adj* incredulous; (*heidnisch*) infidel ‖ **Ungläubige** §5 *mf* infidel
unglaub'lich *adj* incredible
un'glaubwürdig *adj* untrustworthy; incredible
un'gleich *adj* uneven, unequal; (*unähnlich*) unlike, dissimilar; (*Zahl*) odd ‖ *adv* much, far, by far
un'gleichartig *adj* heterogeneous
un'gleichförmig *adj* unequal; irregular
Un'gleichheit *f* inequality; difference, dissimilarity; unevenness
un'gleichmäßig *adj* disproportionate
Unglimpf ['ʊnglɪmpf] *m* (–[e]s;–e) harshness; wrong, insult
un'glimpflich *adj* harsh
Un'glück *n* (–s;) bad luck; (*Unfall*) accident; disaster, calamity
un'glücklich *adj* unlucky; unfortunate; unhappy
un'glücklicherweise *adv* unfortunately
Un'glücksbote *m* bearer of bad news
Un'glücksbringer *m* (–s;–) jinx
un'glückselig *adj* miserable; disastrous
Un'glücksfall *m* accident, misfortune
Un'glücksmensch *m* unlucky person
Un'glücksrabe *m*, **Un'glücksvogel** *m* unlucky fellow
Un'gnade *f* (–;) disfavor, displeasure
un'gnädig *adj* ungracious; **etw u. aufnehmen** take s.th. amiss
un'gültig *adj* null and void, invalid; **für u. erklären** nullify, void
Un'gültigkeit *f* invalidity
Un'gültigkeitserklärung *f* annulment
Un'gunst *f* disfavor; **zu meinen Ungunsten** to my disadvantage
un'günstig *adj* unfavorable, bad, adverse
un'gut *adj* unkind; **nichts für u.!** no offense!; **ungutes Gefühl** misgivings
un'haltbar *adj* not durable; untenable
un'handlich *adj* unwieldy, unhandy
Un'heil *n* disaster; mischief; **U. anrichten** cause mischief; **U. heraufbeschwören** ask for trouble
unheil'bar *adj* incurable; irreparable
un'heilvoll *adj* ominous; disastrous
un'heimlich *adj* uncanny; sinister
un'höflich *adj* impolite, uncivil

Un'höflichkeit *f* impoliteness
un'hold *adj* unkind || **Unhold** *m* (-[e]s; -e) fiend
un'hörbar *adj* inaudible
un'hygienisch *adj* unsanitary
Uni ['uni] *f* (-;-s) (**Universität**) (coll) university
uniform [uni'form] *adj* uniform || **Uniform** *f* (-;-en) uniform
Uni·kum ['unɪkum] *n* (-s;-s & -ka [ka]) unique example; (coll) queer duck
un'interessant *adj* uninteresting
un'interessiert *adj* (**an** *dat*) uninterested (in)
Union [un'jon] *f* (-;-en) union
universal [unɪver'zal] *adj* universal
Universal'mittel *n* panacea, cure-all
Universal'schlüssel *m* monkey wrench
Universität [unɪverzɪ'tet] *f* (-;-en) university
Universitäts'auswahlmannschaft *f* varsity (team)
Universum [unɪ'verzum] *n* (-s;) universe
Unke ['uŋkə] *f* (-;-n) toad
unken ['uŋkən] *intr* (coll) be a prophet of doom
un'kenntlich *adj* unrecognizable; **u. machen** disguise
Un'kenntnis *f* (-;) ignorance
Un'kenruf *m* croak
un'keusch *adj* unchaste
un'kindlich *adj* precocious; (*Verhalten*) disrespectful
un'kirchlich *adj* secular, worldly
un'klar *adj* unclear; muddy; misty; **im unklaren sein über** (*acc*) be in the dark about
Un'klarheit *f* obscurity
un'kleidsam *adj* unbecoming
un'klug *adj* unwise, imprudent
Un'klugheit *f* imprudence; foolish act
un'kontrollierbar *adj* unverifiable
un'körperlich *adj* incorporeal
Un'kosten *pl* expenses, costs; overhead; **sich in U. stürzen** go to great expense
Un'kraut *n* weed, weeds; **U. jäten** pull weeds
Un'krautvertilgungsmittel *n* weed killer
un'kündbar *adj* binding; (*Darlehen*) irredeemable; (*Stellung*) permanent
un'kundig *adj* (*genit*) ignorant (of), unacquainted (with)
unlängst ['unleŋst] *adv* recently, the other day
un'lauter *adj* unfair
un'leidlich *adj* intolerable
un'lenksam *adj* unruly
unles'bar, unle'serlich *adj* illegible
unleugbar ['unlɔɪkbar] *adj* indisputable, undeniable
un'lieb *adj* disagreeable; **es ist mir u.** I am sorry
un'logisch *adj* illogical
unlös'bar *adj* (*Problem*) unsolvable; (*untrennbar*) inseparable; (chem) insoluble
unlös'lich *adj* (chem) insoluble
Un'lust *f* reluctance; listlessness
un'lustig *adj* reluctant; listless

un'manierlich *adj* impolite
un'männlich *adj* unmanly
Un'maß *n* excess; **im U.** to excess
Un'masse *f* (coll) vast amount, lots
un'maßgeblich *adj* unauthoritative; irrelevant; **nach meiner unmaßgeblichen Meinung** in my humble opinion
un'mäßig *adj* immoderate; excessive
Un'menge *f* (coll)—**e-e U. von** lots of
Un'mensch *m* brute, monster
un'menschlich *adj* inhuman, brutal
Un'menschlichkeit *f* brutality
un'marklich *adj* imperceptible
un'methodisch *adj* unmethodical
un'mißverständlich *adj* unmistakable
un'mittelbar *adj* direct, immediate
un'möbliert *adj* unfurnished
un'modern *adj* outmoded
un'möglich, unmög'lich *adj* impossible
Un'möglichkeit *f* impossibility
Un'moral *f* immorality
un'moralisch *adj* immoral
un'mündig *adj* underage
un'musikalisch *adj* unmusical
Un'mut *m* (**über** *acc*) displeasure (at)
un'mutig *adj* displeased, annoyed
unnachahmlich ['unnaxamlɪç] *adj* inimitable
un'nachgiebig *adj* unyielding
un'nachsichtig *adj* unrelenting, inexorable; strict
unnahbar [un'nabar] *adj* inaccessible
un'natürlich *adj* unnatural
unnenn'bar *adj* inexpressible
un'nötig *adj* unnecessary
unnütz ['unnʏts] *adj* useless; vain
un'ordentlich *adj* disorderly; untidy
Un'ordnung *f* disorder; mess; **in U. bringen** throw into disorder
un'organisch *adj* inorganic
un'paar, un'paarig *adj* unpaired, odd
un'parteiisch, un'parteilich *adj* impartial, disinterested
Un'parteilichkeit *f* impartiality
un'passend *adj* unsuitable; (*unschicklich*) improper; (*unzeitgemäß*) untimely
un'passierbar *adj* impassable
unpäßlich ['unpɛslɪç] *adj* indisposed, ill
un'patriotisch *adj* unpatriotic
un'persönlich *adj* impersonal
un'politisch *adj* nonpolitical
un'populär *adj* unpopular
un'praktisch *adj* impractical; (*unerfahren*) unskillful
Un'rast *f* restlessness
Un'rat *m* (-[e]s;) garbage; dirt; **U. wittern** (coll) smell a rat
un'rätlich, un'ratsam *adj* inadvisable
um'recht *adj* wrong || **Unrecht** *n* (-[e]s;) —**im U. sein** be in the wrong; **j-m U. geben** decide against s.o.; **mit (or zu) U.** wrongly; unjustly; illegally
un'redlich *adj* dishonest
Un'redlichkeit *f* dishonesty
un'reell *adj* unfair
un'regelmäßig *adj* irregular
Un'regelmäßigkeit *f* irregularity
un'reif *adj* unripe, green; (fig) immature
Un'reife *f* unripeness; immaturity
un'rein *adj* unclean; (& fig) impure

ins u. schreiben make a rough copy of

Un'reinheit *f* uncleanness; (& fig) impurity

un'reinlich *adj* dirty

un'rentabel *adj* unprofitable

un'rettbar *adj* irrecoverable

un'richtig *adj* incorrect, wrong

un'ritterlich *adj* unchivalrous

Un'ruh *f* (-;-en) (horol) balance wheel

Un'ruhe *f* restlessness; uneasiness; (*Aufruhr*) commotion, riot; (*Störung*) disturbance; (*Besorgnis*) anxiety

un'ruhig *adj* restless; uneasy; (*laut*) noisy; (*Pferd*) restive; (*Meer*) choppy; (*nervös*) jumpy

un'rühmlich *adj* inglorious

Un'ruhstifter -in §6 *mf* agitator, troublemaker; (*Wirrkopf*) screwball

uns [ʊns] *pers pron* us; to us ‖ *reflex pron* ourselves; **wir sind doch unter uns** we are by ourselves ‖ *recip pron* each other, one another; **wir sehen uns später** we'll meet later

un'sachgemäß *adj* inexpert

un'sachlich *adj* subjective; personal

unsagbar [ʊn'zakbar], **unsäglich** [ʊn'zeklɪç] *adj* unspeakable; (fig) immense

un'sauber *adj* unclean; (*unlauter*) unfair, dirty

un'schädlich *adj* harmless

un'scharf *adj* (*Apparat*) out of focus; (*Bild*) blurred; (*Begriff*) poorly defined

un'schätzbar *adj* inestimable, invaluable

un'scheinbar *adj* inconspicuous, insignificant

un'schicklich *adj* unbecoming; indecent

Un'schicklichkeit *f* impropriety

un'schlüssig *adj* indecisive

Un'schlüssigkeit *f* indecision, hesitation

un'schmackhaft *adj* insipid, unpalatable

un'schön *adj* unlovely; plain, homely; (*Angelegenheit*) unpleasant

Un'schuld *f* innocence; **ich wasche meine Hände in U.** I wash my hands of it

un'schuldig *adj* innocent; (*keusch*) chaste; harmless; **sich für u. erklären** (jur) plead not guilty

un'schwer *adj* not difficult

Un'segen *m* adversity; (*Fluch*) curse

un'selbständig *adj* dependent, helpless

un'selig *adj* unfortunate; (*Ereignis*) fatal

unser ['ʊnzər] §2,3 *poss adj* our ‖ §2,4 *poss pron* ours ‖ *pers pron* us; of us; **erinnerst du dich unser noch?** do you still remember us?; **es waren unser vier** there were four of us

unseresgleichen ['ʊnzərəs'glaɪçən] *pron* people like us; the likes of us

unserige ['ʊnzərɪgə] §2,5 *pron* ours

unserthalben ['ʊnzərt'halbən], **unsertwegen** ['ʊnzərt'vegən] *adv* for our sake, on our behalf, on our account

un'sicher *adj* unsafe; shaky; precarious

Un'sicherheit *f* unsafeness; shakiness; insecurity; precariousness

un'sichtbar *adj* invisible

Un'sinn *m* (-[e]s;) nonsense, rubbish; **U. machen** fool around

un'sinnig *adj* nonsensical

Un'sitte *f* bad habit

un'sittlich *adj* immoral, indecent

Un'sittlichkeit *f* immorality

un'solid(e) *adj* unsolid; (*Person*) loose; (*Firma*) unreliable, shaky

unsortiert ['ʊnzɔrtirt] *adj* unsorted

un'sozial *adj* antisocial

un'sportlich *adj* unsportsmanlike

unsrerseits ['ʊnzrər'zaɪts] *adv* as for us, for our part

unsrige ['ʊnzrɪgə] §2,5 *poss pron* ours

un'ständig *adj* impermanent, temporary

un'statthaft *adj* inadmissible; forbidden

unsterb'lich *adj* immortal

Unsterb'lichkeit *f* immortality

Un'stern *m* unlucky star; (fig) disaster

un'stet *adj* unsteady; restless; changeable

un'stillbar *adj* unappeasable; (*Durst*) unquenchable; (*Hunger*) unsatiable

unstimmig ['ʊn/tɪmɪç] *adj* discrepant; inconsistent

Un'stimmigkeit *f* (-;-en) discrepancy; inconsistency; (*Widerspruch*) disagreement

un'sträflich *adj* blameless; guileless

un'streitig *adj* indisputable

Un'summe *f* enormous sum

un'symmetrisch *adj* asymmetrical

un'sympathisch *adj* unpleasant; **er ist mir u.** I don't like him

un'tadelhaft *adj* blameless; flawless

Un'tat *f* crime

un'tätig *adj* inactive

un'tauglich *adj* unfit, unsuitable; useless; (*Person*) incompetent; **u. machen** disqualify

un'teilbar *adj* indivisible

unten ['ʊntən] *adv* below, beneath; downstairs; **da u.** down there; **er ist bei ihnen u. durch** they are through with him; **nach u.** downstairs; downwards; **tief u.** far below; **u. am Berge** at the foot of the mountain; **u. an der Seite** at the bottom of the page; **von u. her** from underneath

unter ['ʊntər] *prep* (*dat*) under, below; beneath, underneath; (*zwischen*) among; (*während*) during; **ganz u. uns gesagt** just between you and me; **u. aller Kritik** beneath contempt; **u. anderem** among other things; **u. diesem Gesichtspunkt** from this point of view; **u. Null** below zero; **was versteht man unter...?** what is meant by...? ‖ *prep* (*acc*) under, below; beneath, underneath; among ‖ **Unter** *m* (-s;-) (cards) jack

Unter-, unter- *comb.fm.* under-, sub-; lower

Un'terabteilung *f* subdivision

Un'terarm *m* forearm

Un'terart *f* subspecies

Un'terausschuß *m* subcommittee

Un'terbau *m* (-[e]s;-ten) foundation

un′terbelichten *tr* underexpose
un′terbewußt *adj* subconscious
Un′terbewußtsein *n* subconscious
unterbie′ten §58 *tr* undercut, undersell; underbid
un′terbinden §59 *tr* tie underneath ‖ unterbin′den §59 *tr* (*Verkehr*) tie up; (*Blutgefäß*) tie off; (*verhindern*) prevent; (*Angriff*) neutralize
Unterbin′dung *f* stoppage; (surg) ligature
unterblei′ben §62 *intr* (SEIN) remain undone; not take place; be discontinued; **das muß u.** that must be stopped
unterbre′chen §64 *tr* interrupt; (*einstellen*) suspend; (*Schweigen, Stille, Kontakt*) break; (*Verkehr*) hold up; (telp) disconnect; **die Reise in München u.** have a stopover in Munich ‖ *ref* stop short
Unterbre′cher *m* (elec) circuit breaker
Unterbre′chung *f* interruption; disconnection; (*e-r Fahrt*) stopover
unterbrei′ten *tr* submit
un′terbringen §65 *tr* provide a place for; find room for; (*Gäste*) accommodate, put up; (*Stapeln*) store; (*Anleihe*) place; (*Geld*) invest; (*Pferde*) stable; (*Wagen*) park; (*Truppe*) billet; **e-n Artikel bei e-r Zeitung u.** have an article published in a newspaper; **j-n auf e-m Posten** (or **in e-r Stellung**) **u.** find s.o. a job, place s.o.
Un′terbringung *f* (-;-en) accommodations, housing; billet; storage; investment; placement
Un′terbringungsmöglichkeiten *pl* accommodations
unterdes [ʊntər'dɛs], unterdessen [ʊntər'dɛsən] *adv* meanwhile
Un′terdruck *m* low pressure
unterdrücken (unterdrük′ken) *tr* suppress; (*Aufstand*) quell; (*bedrücken*) oppress; (*ersticken*) stifle; (*Seufzer*) repress
Un′terdruckgebiet *n* low-pressure area
Unterdrückung (Unterdrük′kung) *f* (-;) oppression; suppression
untere ['ʊntərə] §9 *adj* lower, inferior
untereinan′der *adv* among one another; mutually; reciprocally
unterentwickelt ['ʊntərɛntvɪkəlt] *adj* underdeveloped
unterernährt ['ʊntərɛrnɛrt] *adj* undernourished
Un′terernährung *f* (-;) undernourishment
Un′terfamilie *f* subfamily
unterfer′tigen *tr* sign
Unterfüh′rung *f* (-;-en) underpass
unterfüt′tern *tr* line
Un′tergang *m* setting; (fig) decline, fall; (naut) sinking
unterge′ben *adj* (*dat*) subject (to), inferior (to) ‖ **Untergebene** §5 *mf* subordinate
un′tergehen §82 *intr* (SEIN) go down, sink; (fig) perish; (astr) set
untergeordnet ['ʊntərgə.ɔrdnət] *adj* subordinate ‖ **Untergeordnete** §5 *mf* subordinate

Un′tergeschoß *n* ground floor; (*Kellergeschoß*) basement
Un′tergestell *n* undercarriage
Un′tergewand *n* underwear
un′tergliedern *tr* subdivide
untergra′ben §87 *tr* undermine
Un′tergrund *m* subsoil
Un′tergrundbahn *f* subway
Un′tergrundbewegung *f* underground movement
un′terhalb *prep* (*genit*) below
Un′terhalt *m* (-[e]s;) support; maintenance, upkeep; livelihood
un′terhalten §90 *tr* hold under ‖ unterhal′ten §90 *tr* maintain; support; (*Briefwechsel*) keep up; (*Feuer*) feed; entertain, amuse ‖ *ref* enjoy oneself, have a good time; amuse oneself; **sich u. mit** talk with
unterhaltsam [ʊntər'haltzam] *adj* entertaining, amusing, enjoyable
Un′terhaltsbeitrag *m* alimony; (*für Kinder*) support
Unterhaltsberechtigte ['ʊntərhaltsbərɛçtɪgtə] §5 *mf* dependent
Un′terhaltskosten *pl* living expenses
Unterhal′tung *f* (-;-en) entertainment, amusement; (*Gespräch*) conversation; (*Aufrechterhaltung*) upkeep; (*Unterstützung*) support
Unterhal′tungskosten *pl* maintenance cost, maintenance
Unterhal′tungslektüre *f* light reading
unterhan′deln *intr* negotiate
Un′terhändler -in §6 *mf* negotiator; (*Vermittler*) mediator
Unterhand′lung *f* (-;-en) negotiation
Un′terhaus *n* (parl) lower house
Un′terhemd *n* undershirt
unterhöh′len *tr* undermine
Un′terholz *n* undergrowth, underbrush
Un′terhose *f* shorts; panties; **in Unterhosen zeigen** (coll) debunk
un′terirdisch *adj* underground, subterranean; (myth) of the underworld
Un′terjacke *f* vest
unterjo′chen *tr* subjugate
Unterjo′chung *f* (-;) subjugation
Un′terkiefer *m* lower jaw
Un′terkinn *n* double chin
Un′terkleid *n* slip
Un′terkleidung *f* (-;) underwear
un′terkommen §99 *intr* (SEIN) find accommodations; find employment ‖ **Unterkommen** *n* (-s;) accommodations; (*Stellung*) job
Un′terkörper *m* lower part of the body
un′terkriegen *tr* (coll) get the better of; **er läßt sich nicht u.** he won't knuckle under
Unterkunft ['ʊntərkunft] *f* (-;⸗e) accommodations; apartment; (*Obdach*) shelter, place to stay; (mil) quarters; **U. und Verpflegung** room and board
Un′terlage *f* foundation; base; pad; desk pad; rubber pad (*for a bed*); (*Teppich*) underpad; (*Beleg*) voucher; (*Urkunde*) document; (archit) support; (geol) substratum; **keine Unterlagen haben** have nothing to go on; **Unterlagen** documentation; data
Un′terland *n* lowland

Unterlaß ['ʊntərlas] *m*—**ohne U.** without letup

unterlas'sen §104 *tr* omit; neglect; skip; stop, cut out

Unterlas'sung *f* (–;–en) omission; neglect; failure

Unterlas'sungssünde *f* sin of omission

unterlau'fen *adj*—**blau u.** black-and-blue; **mit Blut u.** bloodshot || **un'terlaufen** §105 *intr* (SEIN) (*Fehler*) slip in

un'terlegen *tr* lay under, put under; (*Bedeutung, Sinn*) attach; **der Musik Worte u.** set words to music || **unterle'gen** *adj* defeated; (*dat*) inferior (to) || **Unterlegene** §5 *mf* loser

Unterle'genheit *f* (–;) inferiority

Unterlegring ['ʊntərlekrɪŋ] *m*, **Unterlegscheibe** ['ʊntərlekʃaɪbə] *f* washer

Un'terleib *m* abdomen

Unterleibs– *comb.fm.* abdominal

unterlie'gen §108 *intr* (SEIN) (*dat*) be beaten (by), lose (to); **e-m Rabatt u.** be subject to discount || *impers* (SEIN)—**es unterliegt keinem Zweifel, daß** there is no doubt that

Un'terlippe *f* lower lip

unterma'len *tr* put the primer on; **mit Musik u.** accompany with music

untermau'ern *tr* support

Un'termiete *f* (–;) subletting; **in U. abgeben** sublet; **in U. wohnen bei** sublet from

Un'termieter –in §6 *mf* subtenant

unterminie'ren *tr* (fig) undermine

unterneh'men §116 *tr* undertake; (*versuchen*) attempt; **Schritte u.** (fig) take steps || **Unternehmen** *n* (–s;–) undertaking; venture; enterprise; (mil) operation

unterneh'mend *adj* enterprising

Unterneh'mensberater *m* management consultant

Unterneh'mer –in §6 *mf* entrepreneur; (*Arbeitgeber*) employer; (*Bau–*) contractor

Unterneh'mung *f* (–;–en) undertaking; enterprise, business; (mil) operation

Unterneh'mungsgeist *m* initiative

unterneh'mungslustig *adj* enterprising

Un'teroffizier *m* noncommissioned officer, N.C.O.

un'terordnen *tr* (*dat*) subordinate (to) || *ref* (*dat*) submit (to)

unterre'den *ref* (mit) confer (with)

Unterre'dung *f* (–;–en) conference

Unterricht ['ʊntərrɪçt] *m* (–[e]s;–e) instruction, lessons

unterrich'ten *tr* instruct; **u. von** (or **über** *acc*) inform (of, about)

Un'terrichtsfach *n* subject, course

Un'terrichtsfilm *m* educational film; (mil) training film

Un'terrichtsministerium *n* department of public instruction

Un'terrichtsstunde *f* (educ) period

Un'terrichtswesen *n* education; teaching

Un'terrock *m* slip

untersa'gen *tr* forbid, prohibit

Un'tersatz *m* saucer; support; (*Gestell*) stand; (archit) socle; (log) minor premise

unterschät'zen *tr* underrate, underestimate; undervalue

unterschei'den §112 *tr* distinguish || *ref* (von) differ (from)

Unterschei'dung *f* (–;–en) difference, distinction

Un'terschenkel *m* shank

un'terschieben §130 *tr* shove under; (statt *genit*) substitute (for); (*dat*) impute (to), foist (on)

Unterschied ['ʊntərʃit] *m* (–[e]s;–e) difference, distinction; **zum U. von** as distinct from, unlike

un'terschiedlich *adj* different; varying

un'terschiedslos *adj* indiscriminate

unterschla'gen §132 *tr* embezzle; (*Nachricht*) suppress; (*Brief*) intercept

Unterschla'gung *f* (–;–en) embezzlement; suppression; interception

Unterschlupf ['ʊntərʃlupf] *m* (–[e]s;) shelter; hide-out

unterschrei'ben §62 *tr* sign; (fig) subscribe to, agree to

Un'terschrift *f* signature

Un'terseeboot *n* submarine

unterseeisch ['ʊntərze·ɪʃ] *adj* submarine

Un'terseekabel *n* transoceanic cable

Un'terseite *f* underside

untersetzt [ʊntər'zetst] *adj* stocky

Un'tersetzung *f* (–;–en) (mech) reduction

un'tersinken §143 *intr* (SEIN) go down

Un'terstand *m* (mil) dugout

unterste ['ʊntərstə] §9 *adj* lowest, bottom

unterste'hen §146 *ref* dare; **untersteh dich!** don't you dare! || *intr* (*dat*) be under (*s.o.*) || **un'terstehen** §146 *intr* take shelter

un'terstellen *tr* place under; (*Auto*) put into the garage || *ref* take cover || **unterstel'len** *tr* assume, suppose; (*dat*) impute (to); (mil) (*dat*) put under the command (of)

Unterstel'lung *f* (–;–en) assumption; imputation

unterstrei'chen §85 *tr* underline

unterstüt'zen *tr* support, back; help

Unterstüt'zung *f* (–;–en) support, backing; assistance; (*Beihilfe durch Geld*) relief; (ins) benefit

untersu'chen *tr* examine, inspect; investigate; study, do research on; (chem) analyze

Untersu'chung *f* (–;–en) examination; inspection; investigation; study, research; (chem) analysis

Untersu'chungsausschuß *m* fact-finding committee

Untersu'chungsgericht *n* court of inquiry

Untersu'chungshaft *f* (jur) detention

Untersu'chungsrichter *m* examining judge

Untertagebau [ʊntər'tagəbau] *m* (–[e]s;) mine

Untertan ['ʊntərtan] *m* (–s & –en;–en) subject

untertänig [ʊntər'tenɪç] *adj* submissive

Un'tertasse *f* saucer; **fliegende U.** flying saucer

un'tertauchen *tr* submerge; duck ‖ *intr* (SEIN) dive; (fig) disappear ‖ **Unter-tauchen** *n* (-s;) dive; disappearance
Un'terteil *m* & *n* lower part, bottom
untertei'len *tr* subdivide
Untertei'lung *f* (-;-en) subdivision
Un'tertitel *m* subtitle; caption
Un'terton *m* undertone
un'tertreten §152 *intr* (SEIN) take cover
un'tervermieten *tr* sublet
Un'tervertrag *m* subcontract
unterwan'dern *tr* infiltrate
Un'terwäsche *f* underwear
Unterwasser– *comb.fm.* underwater, submarine
Un'terwasserbombe *f* depth charge
Un'terwasserhorchgerät *n* hydrophone
Un'terwasserortungsgerät *n* sonar
unterwegs [ʊntər'veks] *adv* on the way; (com) in transit
unterwei'sen §118 *tr* instruct
Unterwei'sung *f* (-;-en) instruction
Un'terwelt *f* underworld; (myth) lower world
unterwer'fen §160 *tr* subjugate; (*dat*) subject (to) ‖ *ref* (*dat*) submit to, subject oneself to; **sich** [*dat*] **ein Volk u.** subjugate a people
Unterwer'fung *f* (-;) subjugation; submission
unterworfen [ʊntər'vɔrfən] *adj* subject
unterwürfig ['ʊntərvʏrfɪç] *adj* submissive, subservient
unterzeich'nen *tr* sign
Unterzeich'ner –in §6 *mf* signer; signatory
Unterzeichnete [ʊntər'tsaɪçnətə] §5 *mf* undersigned
Unterzeich'nung *f* (-;-en) signing; signature
un'terziehen §163 *tr* put on underneath ‖ **unterzie'hen** §163 *tr* (*dat*) subject (to) ‖ *ref*—**sich der Mühe u. zu** (*inf*) take the trouble to (*inf*); **sich e–r Operation u.** have an operation; **sich e–r Prüfung u.** take an examination
un'tief *adj* shallow ‖ **Untiefe** *f* (-;-n) shoal
Un'tier *n* (& fig) monster
untilg'bar *adj* inextinguishable; (*Tinte*) indelible; (*Anleihe*) irredeemable
untrag'bar *adj* unbearable; (*Kleidung*) unwearable; (*Kosten*) prohibitive
untrenn'bar *adj* inseparable
un'treu *adj* unfaithful ‖ **Untreue** *f* unfaithfulness; infidelity
untröst'lich *adj* inconsolable
untrüg'lich *adj* unerring, infallible
un'tüchtig *adj* incapable; inefficient
Un'tugend *f* bad habit, vice
un'überlegt *adj* thoughtless; rash
unüberseh'bar *adj* vast, huge; incalculable ‖ *adv* very
unübersetz'bar *adj* untranslatable
un'übersichtlich *adj* unclear; (*Kurve*) blind
unübersteig'bar, unübersteig'lich *adj* insurmountable
unübertreff'lich *adj* unsurpassable
unübertroffen [ʊnybər'trɔfən] *adj* unsurpassed
unüberwind'lich *adj* invincible; (*Schwierigkeiten*) insurmountable

unumgäng'lich *adj* indispensable
unumschränkt ['ʊnʊm/rɛŋkt] *adj* unlimited; (pol) absolute
unumstößlich ['ʊnʊm/tøslɪç] *adj* irrefutable; (*unwiderruflich*) irrevocable
unumwunden ['ʊnʊmvʊndən] *adj* blunt
un'unterbrochen *adj* continuous
unverän'derlich *adj* unchangeable, invariable
unverant'wortlich *adj* irresponsible
unveräu'ßerlich *adj* inalienable
unverbesserlich [ʊnfer'bɛsərlɪç] *adj* incorrigible
unverbind'lich *adj* without obligation; (*Verhalten*) proper, formal; (*Antwort*) noncommittal
un'verblümt *adj* blunt, plain
unverbürgt [ʊnfer'bʏrkt] *adj* unwarranted; (*Nachricht*) unconfirmed
un'verdächtig *adj* unsuspected
un'verdaulich *adj* indigestible
unverderbt ['ʊnferderpt], **unverdorben** ['ʊnferdɔrbən] *adj* unspoiled
unverdient ['ʊnferdint] *adj* undeserved
un'verdrossen *adj* indefatigable
unverdünnt ['ʊnferdʏnt] *adj* undiluted
unverehelicht ['ʊnfere·əlɪçt] *adj* unmarried, single
un'vereinbar *adj* incompatible; contradictory
unverfälscht ['ʊnferfɛl/t] *adj* genuine; (*Wein*) undiluted
un'verfänglich *adj* innocent
un'verfroren *adj* brash
un'vergänglich *adj* imperishable
un'vergeßlich *adj* unforgettable
un'vergleich'bar *adj* incomparable
unvergleichlich ['ʊnferglaɪçlɪç] *adj* incomparable
un'verhältnismäßig *adj* disproportionate
un'verheiratet *adj* unmarried
unvergolten ['ʊnfergɔltən] *adj* unrewarded
unverhofft ['ʊnferhɔft] *adj* unhoped-for
unverhohlen ['ʊnferholən] *adj* unconcealed; (fig) open
un'verkäuflich *adj* unsalable
unverkennbar ['ʊnferkenbar] *adj* unmistakable
unverkürzt ['ʊnferkʏrtst] *adj* unabridged
unverlangt ['ʊnferlaŋt] *adj* unsolicited
un'verletzbar, un'verletzlich *adj* undamageable; (fig) inviolable
unverletzt ['ʊnferletst] *adj* safe and sound, unharmed; (*Sache*) undamaged
unvermeid'lich *adj* inevitable
unvermindert ['ʊnfermɪndərt] *adj* undiminished
unvermittelt ['ʊnfermɪtəlt] *adj* sudden
Un'vermögen *n* inability; impotence
un'vermögend *adj* poor; impotent
unvermutet ['ʊnfermutət] *adj* unexpected
un'vernehmlich *adj* imperceptible
Un'vernunft *f* unreasonableness; folly
un'vernünftig *adj* unreasonable; foolish
un'verschämt *adj* brazen, shameless

unverschuldet ['ʊnfɛrʃʊldət] *adj* unencumbered; (*unverdient*) undeserved
un'versehens *adv* unawares, suddenly
unversehrt ['ʊnfɛrzert] *adj* undamaged (*Person*) unharmed
unversichert ['ʊnfɛrzɪçərt] *adj* uninsured
unversiegbar [ʊnfɛr'zikbɑr] **unversieglich** [ʊnfɛr'ziklɪç] *adj* inexhaustible
unversiegelt ['ʊnfɛrzigəlt] *adj* unsealed
un'versöhnlich *adj* irreconcilable
unversorgt ['ʊnfɛrzɔrkt] *adj* unprovided for
Un'verstand *m* lack of judgment
un'verständig *adj* foolish
un'verständlich *adj* incomprehensible
unversucht ['ʊnfɛrzuxt] *adj* untried
un'verträglich *adj* unsociable; quarrelsome; incompatible, contradictory
un'verwandt *adj* steady, unflinching
unverwelklich [ʊnfɛr'vɛlklɪç] *adj* unfading
un'verwendbar *adj* unusable
unverweslich ['ʊnfɛrvezlɪç] *adj* incorruptible
unverwindbar [ʊnfɛr'vɪntbɑr] *adj* irreparable; (*Entäuschung*) lasting
un'verwundbar *adj* invulnerable
unverwüstlich ['ʊnfɛrvystlɪç] *adj* indestructible; (*Stoff*) durable; (fig) irrepressible
unverzagt ['ʊnfɛrtsɑkt] *adj* undaunted
un'verzeihlich *adj* unpardonable
unverzerrt ['ʊnfɛrtsɛrt] *adj* undistorted
unverzinslich ['ʊnfɛrtsɪnslɪç] *adj* (fin) without interest
unverzüglich ['ʊnfɛrtsyklɪç] *adj* prompt, immediate || *adv* without delay
unvollendet ['ʊnfɔlɛndət] *adj* unfinished
un'vollkommen *adj* imperfect
Un'vollkommenheit *f* imperfection
un'vollständig *adj* incomplete; (gram) defective
un'vorbereitet *adj* unprepared; (*Rede*) extemporaneous || *adv* extempore
un'voreingenommen *adj* unbiased
un'vorhergesehen *adj* unforeseen
un'vorsätzlich *adj* unintentional
un'vorsichtig *adj* incautious; careless
un'vorteilhaft *adj* disadvantageous; unprofitable; (*Kleid*) unflattering
un'wahr *adj* untrue
un'wahrhaftig *adj* untruthful
Un'wahrheit *f* untruth, falsehood
un'wahrnehmbar *adj* imperceptible
un'wahrscheinlich *adj* unlikely, improbable
unwan'delbar *adj* unchangeable
unwegsam ['ʊnvekzɑm] *adj* impassable
unweigerlich [ʊn'vaɪgərlɪç] *adj* unhesitating; (*Folge*) necessary || *adv* without fail
un'weit *adj*—**u. von** not far from || *prep* (*genit*) not far from
Un'wesen *n* mischief; **sein U. treiben** be up to one's old tricks
un'wesentlich *adj* unessential; unimportant; (**für**) immaterial (to)
Un'wetter *n* storm

un'wichtig *adj* unimportant
unwiederbringlich [ʊnvidər'brɪŋlɪç] *adj* irretrievable, irreparable
unwiderleg'bar *adj* irrefutable
unwiderruf'lich *adj* irrevocable
unwidersteh'lich *adj* irresistible
Un'wille *m*, **Un'willen** *m* indignation, displeasure; reluctance
un'willig *adj* (**über** *acc*) indignant (at), displeased (at); **u. zu** (*inf*) reluctant to (*inf*)
un'willkommen *adj* unwelcome
un'willkürlich *adj* involuntary
un'wirklich *adj* unreal
un'wirksam *adj* ineffective; inefficient; (chem) inactive; (jur) null and void
Un'wirksamkeit *f* ineffectiveness, inefficiency; (chem) inactivity
unwirsch ['ʊnvɪrʃ] *adj* surly
un'wirtlich *adj* inhospitable
un'wirtschaftlich *adj* uneconomical
unwissend ['ʊnvɪsənt] *adj* ignorant
Unwissenheit ['ʊnvɪsənhaɪt] *f* (–;) ignorance
un'wissenschaftlich *adj* unscientific
un'wissentlich *adv* unwittingly
un'wohl *adj* sickish; **ich fühle mich u.** I don't feel well
un'wohnlich *adj* uninhabitable; (*unbehaglich*) uncomfortable
un'würdig *adj* unworthy
Un'zahl *f* (**von**) huge number (of)
unzähl'bar, **unzählig** [ʊn'tselɪç] *adj* countless, innumerable
un'zart *adj* indelicate
Unze ['ʊntsə] *f* (–;–n) ounce
Un'zeit *f* wrong time
un'zeitgemäß *adj* out-of-date
un'zeitig *adj* untimely; (*Obst*) unripe
unzerbrech'lich *adj* unbreakable
unzerstör'bar *adj* indestructible
unzertrennlich [ʊntser'trɛnlɪç] *adj* inseparable
unziemend ['ʊntsimənt], **un'ziemlich** *adj* unbecoming, unseemly
Un'zucht *f* unchastity; lewdness
un'züchtig *adj* unchaste; lewd
un'zufrieden *adj* dissatisfied
un'zugänglich *adj* inaccessible; aloof
un'zulänglich *adj* inadequate
un'zulässig *adj* inadmissible; (*Beeinflussung, Einmischung*) undue
un'zurechnungsfähig *adj* unaccountable
un'zureichend *adj* inadequate
un'zusammenhängend *adj* incoherent
un'zuträglich *adj* (*dat*) bad (for)
un'zutreffend *adj* not applicable
un'zuverlässig *adj* unreliable
un'zweckmäßig *adj* inappropriate; unsuitable; impractical
un'zweideutig *adj* unambiguous
un'zweifelhaft *adj* undoubted
üppig ['ʏpɪç] *adj* luxurious, plush; (*Mahl*) sumptuous; (*Pflanzenwuchs*) luxuriant; (*sinnlich*) voluptuous
Ur-, ur- [ʊr] *comb.fm.* original; very
ur'alt *adj* very old, ancient
Uran [ʊ'rɑn] *n* (–s;) uranium
Ur'aufführung *f* world première
urbar ['ʊrbɑr] *adj* arable; **u. machen** reclaim
Urbarmachung ['ʊrbɑrmɑxʊŋ] *f* (–;) reclamation

Ur'bewohner *pl* aborigines
Ur'bild *n* prototype; original
ur'deutsch *adj* hundred-percent German
ur'eigen *adj* one's very own; original
Ur'einwohner *pl* aborigines
Ur'eltern *pl* ancestors
Ur'enkel *m* great-grandson
Ur'geschichte *f* prehistory
Ur'großmutter *f* great-grandmother
Ur'großvater *m* great-grandfather
Urheber –in ['urhebər(ɪn)] §6 *mf* originator, author
Ur'heberrecht *n* copyright
Ur'heberschaft *f* (–;–e) authorship
Urin [u'rin] *m* (–s;) urine
urinieren [urɪ'nirən] *intr* urinate
ur'ko'misch *adj* very funny
Urkunde ['urkundə] *f* (–;–n) document; deed; (*Vertrag*) instrument
Ur'kundenmaterial *n* documentation
urkundlich ['urkuntlɪç] *adj* documentary; (*verbürgt*) authentic
Urlaub ['urlaup] *m* (–[e]s;–e) vacation; (mil) furlough
Ur'lauber –in §6 *mf* vacationer
Ur'laubsschein *m* (mil) pass
Ur'laubstag *m* day off
Urne ['urnə] *f* (–;–n) urn; ballot box; zur U. gehen go to the polls
Ur'nengang *m* balloting

ur'plötz'lich *adj* sudden || *adv* all of a sudden
Ur'sache *f* cause, reason; keine U.! don't mention it!
ur'sächlich *adj* causal
Ur'schleim *m* (–es;) protoplasm
Ur'schrift *f* original text, original
Ur'sprung *m* origin, source; beginning; (*Ursache*) cause
ursprünglich ['urʃpryŋlɪç] *adj* original
Ur'stoff *m* primary matter; (chem) element
Ur'teil *n* judgment; (*Ansicht*) view, opinion; (jur) verdict; (*Strafmaß*) (jur) sentence
urteilen ['urtaɪlən] *intr* judge; u. nach judge by
Ur'teilskraft *f* discernment
Ur'teilsspruch *m* verdict; sentence
Ur'text *m* original text
Ur'tier *n* protozoon
Ur'volk *n* aborigines
Ur'wald *m* virgin forest; jungle
ur'weltlich *adj* primeval
urwüchsig ['urvyksɪç] *adj* original; (fig) rough
Ur'zeit *f* remote antiquity
Utensilien [uten'ziljən] *pl* utensils
Uto·pie [uto'pi] *f* (–;–pien ['pi·ən]) utopia; pipe dream
uzen ['utsən] *tr* tease, kid

V

V, v [fau] *invar n* V, v
vag [vak] *adj* vague
Vagabund [vaga'bunt] *m* (–en;–en) vagabond, tramp, bum
vagabundieren [vagabun'dirən] *intr* (HABEN & SEIN) bum around
vage ['vagə] *adj* vague
vakant [va'kant] *adj* vacant
Vakanz [va'kants] *f* (–;–en) vacancy
Vaku·um ['vaku·um] *n* (–s;–ua [u·a]) vacuum
Vakzine [vak'tsinə] *f* (–;–n) vaccine
vakzinieren [vaktsɪ'nirən] *tr* vaccinate
Valet [va'let] *n* (–s;–s) farewell
Valu·ta [va'luta] *f* (–;–ten [tən]) value; (foreign) currency
Vampir ['vampir] *m* (–s;–e) vampire
Vandale [van'dalə] *m* (–n;–n) Vandal; (fig) vandal
Vanille [va'nɪljə] *f* (–;) vanilla
Variante [varɪ'antə] *f* (–;–n) variant
Varietät [varɪ·ɛ'tet] *f* (–;–en) variety
Varieté [varɪ·ɛ'te] *n* (–s;–s) vaudeville; vaudeville stage
variieren [varɪ'irən] *tr* & *intr* vary
Vase ['vazə] *f* (–;–n) vase
Vaselin [vaze'lin] *n* (–s;–e), Vaseline [vaze'linə] *f* (–;–n) vaseline
Vater ['fatər] *m* (–s;–̈) father
Va'terland *n* (native) country
vaterländisch ['fatərlendɪʃ] *adj* national || *adv*—v. gesinnt patriotic
Va'terlandsliebe *f* patriotism
väterlich ['fetərlɪç] *adj* fatherly

väterlicherseits ['fetərlɪçər'zaɪts] *adv* on the father's side
Va'terliebe *f* paternal love
Va'terschaft *f* (–;) fatherhood
Va'terschaftsklage *f* paternity suit
Va'tersname *m* family name, last name
Va'terstadt *f* home town
Va'terstelle *f*—bei j–m V. vertreten be a father to s.o.
Vaterun'ser *n* (–s;–) Lord's Prayer
Vati ['fati] *m* (–s;–s) dad, daddy
Vatikan [vatɪ'kan] *m* (–s;) Vatican
v. Chr. *abbr* (vor Christus) B.C.
Vegetarier –in [vege'tarjər(ɪn)] §6 *mf* vegetarian
Vegetation [vegeta'tsjon] *f* (–;) vegetation
vegetieren [vege'tirən] *intr* vegetate
Veilchen ['faɪlçən] *n* (–s;–) (bot) violet
Vene ['venə] *f* (–;–n) (anat) vein
Venedig [ve'nedɪç] *n* (–s;) Venice
venerisch [ve'nerɪʃ] *adj* venereal; venerisches Leiden venereal disease
Ventil [ven'til] *n* (–s;–e) valve; (bei der Orgel) stop; (fig) outlet
Ventilation [ventɪla'tsjon] *f* (–;) ventilation
Venti·lator [ventɪ'lator] *m* (–s;–latoren [la'torən]) ventilator; fan
ver– [fer] *pref* up, e.g., verbrauchen use up; away, e.g., verjagen chase away; mis–, wrongly, e.g., verstellen misplace, verdrehen turn the wrong

way; (to form verbs from other parts of speech) **verwirklichen** realize, **vergöttern** deify; (to express a sense opposite that of the simple verb) **verlernen** forget, **verkaufen** sell; (to indicate consumption or waste through the action of the verb) **verschreiben** use up in writing; (to indicate intensification or completion) **verhungern** die of hunger; (to indicate cessation of action) **vergären** cease to ferment; (to indicate conversion to another state) **verflüssigen** liquify

verabfolgen [fɛr'apfɔlgən] *tr* hand over; deliver; (*Arznei*) give, administer

verabreden [fɛr'apredən] *tr* agree upon; **schon anderweitig verabredet sein** have a prior engagement || *ref* make an appointment

Verab'redung *f* (-;-en) agreement; appointment

verabreichen [fɛr'apraɪçən] *tr* give

verabsäumen [fɛr'apzɔɪmən] *tr* var of **versäumen**

verabscheuen [fɛr'apʃɔɪ•ən] *tr* detest, loath, abhor

verab'scheuenswert, verab'scheuenswürdig detestable

verabschieden [fɛr'apʃidən] *tr* dismiss; (*Beamte*) put on pension; (*Gesetz*) pass; (mil) disband || *ref* (**von**) take leave (of), say goodbye (to)

Verab'schiedung *f* (-;-en) dismissal; pensioning; (mil) disbanding; (parl) passing, enactment

verach'ten *tr* despise; **nicht zu v.** not to be sneezed at

verächtlich [fɛr'ɛçtlɪç] *adj* contemptuous; (*verachtungswert*) contemptible

Verach'tung *f* (-;) contempt

veralbern [fɛr'albərn] *tr* tease

verallgemeinern [fɛralgə'maɪnərn] *tr & intr* generalize

Verallgemei'nerung *f* (-;-en) generalization

veralten [fɛr'altən] *intr* become obsolete; (*Kleider*) go out of style

veraltet [fɛr'altət] *adj* obsolete; out of date, old-fashioned

Veran•da [ve'randa] *f* (-;-den [dən]) veranda, porch

veränderlich [fɛr'ɛndərlɪç] *adj* changeable; (math) variable

Verän'derlichkeit *f* (-;-en) changeableness; fluctuation; instability

verän'dern [fɛr'ɛndərn] *tr* change; vary || *ref* change; look for a new job

Verän'derung *f* (-;-en) change

verängstigt [fɛr'ɛŋstɪçt] *adj* intimidated

verankern [fɛr'aŋkərn] *tr* anchor, moor

Veran'kerung *f* (-;-en) anchorage, mooring

veranlagen [fɛr'anlɑgən] *tr* (*zu e–r Steuer*) assess; **gut veranlagt** highly talented; **künstlerisch veranlagt** artificially inclined; **schlecht veranlagt** poorly endowed

Veran'lagung *f* (-;-en) talents; disposition; (fin) assessment

veran'lassen *tr* cause, occasion, make; (*bereden*) induce

Veran'lassung *f* (-;-en) cause, occasion; **auf V. von** at the suggestion of; **ohne jede V.** without provocation; **V. geben zu** give rise to

veranschaulichen [fɛr'anʃaulıçən] *tr* make clear, illustrate

veran'schlagen §132 *tr* rate, value; (*im voraus berechnen*) estimate; **zu hoch v.** overrate

Veran'schlagung *f* (-;) estimate

veranstalten [fɛr'anʃtaltən] *tr* organize, arrange; (*Empfang*) give; (*Sammlung*) take up; (*Versammlung*) hold

Veran'stalter -in §6 *mf* organizer

Veran'staltung *f* (-;-en) organization, arrangement; affair; performance, show; meeting; (sport) event, meet

veran'tworten *tr* answer for, account for; (*verteidigen*) defend || *ref* defend oneself, justify oneself

verantwortlich [fɛr'antvɔrtlɪç] *adj* responsible, answerable; **für etw v. zeichnen** sign for s.th.

Verant'wortlichkeit *f* (-;) responsibility; (jur) liability

Verant'wortung *f* (-;-en) responsibility; (*Rechtfertigung*) justification; **auf eigene V.** at one's own risk; **die V. abwälzen auf** (*acc*) pass the buck to; **zur V. ziehen** call to account

Verant'wortungsbewußtsein *n* sense of responsibility

verant'wortungsfreudig *adj* willing to assume responsibility

verant'wortungsvoll *adj* responsible

veräppeln [fɛr'ɛpəln] *tr* (coll) tease

verar'beiten *tr* manufacture, process; (**zu**) make (into); (*verdauen*) digest; (fig) assimilate

verar'beitend *adj* manufacturing

Verar'beitung *f* (-;-en) manufacturing; digestion; (fig) assimilation

verargen [fɛr'argən] *tr—j-m etw v.* blame s.o. for s.th.

verär'gern *tr* annoy

verarmen [fɛr'armən] *intr* (SEIN) grow poor

verästeln [fɛr'ɛstəln] *ref* branch out

verausgaben [fɛr'ausgabən] *tr* pay out || *ref* run short of money

veräußern [fɛr'ɔɪsərn] *tr* sell

Verb [vɛrp] *n* (-s;-en) verb

verbal [vɛr'bal] *adj* verbal

Verband [fɛr'bant] *m* (-[e]s;-̈e) association, union, federation; (aer, nav) formation; (mil) unit; (surg) bandage, dressing; **sich aus dem V. lösen** (aer) peel off

Verband'kasten *m* first-aid kit

Verband'päckchen *n* first-aid pack

Verband'platz *m* first-aid station

Verband'stoff *m* bandage, dressing

verbannen [fɛr'banən] *tr* banish, exile

Verbannte [fɛr'bantə] §5 *mf* exile

Verban'nung *f* (-;-en) banishment; place of exile

verbarrikadie'ren *tr* barricade

verbau'en *tr* (*Gelände*) build up; use up (*in building*); (*Geld*) spend (*in building*); build poorly; **j-m den Weg v. zu** bar s.o.'s way to

verbei'ßen §53 *tr* swallow, suppress ‖ *ref* (in *acc*) stick (to)

verber'gen §54 *tr* & *ref* hide

verbes'sern *tr* improve; correct; (*Aufsatz*) grade; (*Gesetz*) amend; (*Tatsache*) rectify ‖ *ref* improve; better oneself

Verbes'serung *f* (-;-en) improvement; correction; amendment

verbeu'gen *ref* bow

Verbeu'gung *f* (-;-en) bow; curtsy

verbeulen [fɛr'bɔɪlən] *tr* dent; batter

verbie'gen §57 *tr* bend ‖ *ref* warp

verbie'ten §58 *tr* forbid

verbil'den *tr* spoil; educate badly

verbil'ligen *tr* reduce the price of

Verbil'ligung *f* (-;-en) reduction

verbin'den §59 *tr* tie, tie up; join, unite; (*verketten*) link; (*zu Dank verpflichten*) obligate; (*chem*) combine; (*med*) bandage; (*telp*) (**mit**) connect (with), put through (to); **j-m die Augen v.** blindfold s.o. ‖ *ref* unite

verbindlich [fɛr'bɪntlɪç] *adj* obliging; binding; **verbindlichsten Dank!** thank you ever so much!

Verbind'lichkeit *f* (-;-en) obligation; commitment; polite way; (*e-s Vertrags*) binding force

Verbin'dung *f* (-;-en) union; association; alliance; combination; contact; touch; (*Fuge, Gelenk*) joint; (*chem*) compound; (*educ*) fraternity; (*mach, rr, telp*) connection; (*mil*) liaison; **die V. verlieren mit** lose touch with; **e-e V. eingehen** (*chem*) form a compound; **er hat gute Verbindungen** he has good connections; **in V. mit** in conjunction with; **sich in V. setzen mit** get in touch with; **unmittelbare V.** (*telp*) direct call

Verbin'dungsbahn *f* connecting train

Verbin'dungsleitung *f* (*telp*) trunk line

Verbin'dungslinie *f* line of communication

Verbin'dungsoffizier *m* liaison officer

Verbin'dungspunkt *m*, **Verbin'dungsstelle** *f* joint, juncture

Verbin'dungsstück *n* joint, coupling

verbissen [fɛr'bɪsən] *adj* dogged, grim; (*Zorn*) suppressed; **v. sein in** (*dat*) stick doggedly to

Verbis'senheit *f* (-;) doggedness, grimness

verbitten [fɛr'bɪtən] §60 *ref*—**sich** [*dat*] **etw v.** not stand for s.th.

verbittern [fɛr'bɪtərn] *tr* embitter

Verbit'terung *f* (-;) bitterness

verblassen [fɛr'blasən] *intr* (SEIN) grow pale; (*fig*) fade

verblättern [fɛr'blɛtərn] *tr*—**die Seite v.** lose the page

Verbleib [fɛr'blaɪp] *m* (-[e]s;) whereabouts

verblei'ben §62 *intr* (SEIN) remain, be left; (**bei**) persist (in); **wir sind so verblieben, daß** we finally agreed that

verblei'chen §85 *intr* (SEIN) fade

verblen'den *tr* blind; dazzle; (*Mauer*) face; (*Fenster*) wall up

Verblen'dung *f* (-;-en) blindness, infatuation; (*archit*) facing

verblichen [fɛr'blɪçən] *adj* faded

verblödet [fɛr'blødət] *adj* idiotic

verblüffen [fɛr'blʏfən] *tr* dumbfound, flabbergast; bewilder, perplex

Verblüf'fung *f* (-;) bewilderment

verblü'hen *intr* (SEIN) wither; fade

verblümt [fɛr'blymt] *adj* euphemistic

verblu'ten *ref* & *intr* (SEIN) bleed to death

verbocken [fɛr'bɔkən] *tr* bungle

verboh'ren *ref*—**sich v. in** (*acc*) stick stubbornly to

verbohrt [fɛr'bort] *adj* stubborn; odd

verbolzen [fɛr'bɔltsən] *tr* bolt

verbor'gen *adj* secret; latent; hidden ‖ *tr* lend out ‖ **Verborgene** §5 *n*—**im Verborgenen** in secret, on the sly

Verbor'genheit *f* (-;) secrecy; concealment; seclusion

Verbot [fɛr'bot] *n* (-[e]s;-e) prohibition; (*jur*) injunction

verboten [fɛr'botən] *adj* forbidden; **Eintritt v.!** no admittance; **Plakatankleben v.!** post no bills!; **Stehenbleiben v.!** no loitering

verbrämen [fɛr'bremən] *tr* trim, edge; (*fig*) sugar-coat

verbrannt [fɛr'brant] *adj* burnt; torrid; **Politik der verbrannten Erde** scorched-earth policy

Verbrauch' *m* (-[e]s;) use, consumption

verbrau'chen *tr* use up, consume; waste; (*abnutzen*) wear out

Verbrau'cher *m* (-s;-) consumer; (*Benützer*) user; (*Kunde*) customer

Verbrau'chergenossenschaft *f* co-op

Verbrauchs'güter *pl* consumer goods

verbraucht' *adj* used up, consumed; worn out; (*Geld*) spent; (*Luft*) stale

verbre'chen §64 *tr* commit, do ‖ **Verbrechen** *n* (-s;-) crime

Verbre'cher *m* (-s;-) criminal

Verbre'cheralbum *n* rogues' gallery

Verbre'cherin *f* (-;-nen) criminal

verbrecherisch [fɛr'brɛçərɪʃ] *adj* criminal

Verbre'cherkolonie *f* penal colony

verbreiten [fɛr'braɪtən] *tr* spread; (*Frieden, Licht*) shed ‖ *ref* spread; **sich v. über** (*acc*) expatiate on

verbreitern [fɛr'braɪtərn] *tr* & *ref* widen, broaden

Verbrei'terung *f* (-;) widening, broadening

Verbrei'tung *f* (-;) spreading; dissemination; diffusion

verbren'nen §97 *tr* burn; scorch; (*bräunen*) tan; (*Leichen*) cremate ‖ *ref* burn oneself; **sich** [*dat*] **die Finger v.** (& *fig*) burn one's fingers

Verbren'nung *f* (-;-en) burning, combustion; cremation; (*Brandwunde*) burn

Verbren'nungskraftmaschine *f*, **Verbren'nungsmotor** *m* internal combustion engine

Verbren'nungsraum *m* combustion chamber

verbrin'gen §65 *tr* spend, pass; (*wegbringen*) take away

verbrüdern [fɛr'brydərn] *ref* (**mit**) fraternize (with)

Verbrü'derung *f* (-;) fraternizing

verbrü'hen *tr* scald

verbu'chen *tr* book; **etw als Erfolg v.** chalk s.th. up as a success

Ver·bum ['vɛrbʊm] *n* (-s;-ba [ba]) verb

verbunden [fɛr'bʊndən] *adj* connected; **falsch v.!** sorry, wrong number!; **untereinander v.** interconnected; **zu Dank v.** obligated

verbünden [fɛr'bʏndən] *ref*—**sich mit j-m v.** ally oneself with s.o.

Verbun'denheit *f* (-;) connection, ties; solidarity, union

Verbündete [fɛr'bʏndətə] §5 *mf* ally

verbür'gen *tr* guarantee, vouch for ‖ *ref*—**sich v. für** vouch for

verbürgt [fɛr'bʏrkt] *adj* authenticated

verbüßen [fɛr'bysən] *tr* atone for, pay for; **seine Strafe v.** serve one's time

verchromen [fɛr'kroːmən] *tr* chromeplate

Verchro'mung *f* (-;-en) chromeplating

Verdacht [fɛr'daxt] *m* (-[e]s;) suspicion; **in V. kommen** come under suspicion; **V. hegen gegen** have suspicions about; **V. schöpfen** get suspicious

verdächtig [fɛr'dɛçtɪç] *adj* suspicious; (*genit*) suspected (of)

verdächtigen [fɛr'dɛçtɪgən] *tr* cast suspicion on; (*genit*) suspect (of)

Verdäch'tigung *f* (-;-en) insinuation

verdammen [fɛr'damən] *tr* condemn; damn

Verdammnis [fɛr'damnɪs] *f* (-;) damnation, perdition

verdammt' *adj* (sl) damn ‖ *interj* (sl) damn it!

verdamp'fen *tr & intr* (SEIN) evaporate

Verdamp'fung *f* (-;) evaporation

verdan'ken *tr*—**j-m etw v.** be indebted to s.o. for s.th.

verdarb [fɛr'darp] *pret* of **verderben**

verdattert [fɛr'datərt] *adj* (coll) shook up

verdauen [fɛr'dau·ən] *tr* digest

verdaulich [fɛr'daulɪç] *adj* digestible

Verdau'ung *f* (-;) digestion

Verdau'ungsbeschwerden *pl* **Verdau'-ungsstörung** *f* indigestion

Verdau'ungswerkzeug *n* digestive track

Verdeck [fɛr'dɛk] *n* (-[e]s;-e) hood (*of baby carriage*); (aut) convertible top; (naut) deck

verdecken (**verdek'ken**) *tr* cover; hide

verden'ken §66 *tr*—**j-m etw v.** blame s.o. for s.th.

Verderb [fɛr'dɛrp] *m* (-[e]s;) ruin; decay

verderben [fɛr'dɛrbən] §149 *tr* spoil; ruin; (*Magen*) upset; (*verführen*) corrupt ‖ *intr* (SEIN) spoil, go bad; (fig) go to pot ‖ **Verderben** (-s;) ruin; **j-n ins V. stürzen** ruin s.o.

verderblich [fɛr'dɛrplɪç] *adj* ruinous; (*Lebensmittel*) perishable

Verderbnis [fɛr'dɛrpnɪs] *f* (-;) depravity

verderbt [fɛr'dɛrpt] *adj* depraved

Verderbt'heit *f* (-;) depravity

verdeutlichen [fɛr'dɔɪtlɪçən] *tr* make plain, explain

verdeutschen [fɛr'dɔɪtʃən] *tr* translate into (or express in) German

verdich'ten *tr* condense, thicken ‖ *ref* condense; solidify; thicken; (*Nebel, Rauch*) grow thicker; (*Verdacht*) become stronger, grow

verdicken [fɛr'dɪkən] *tr & ref* thicken

verdie'nen *tr* deserve; (*Geld*) earn

Verdienst [fɛr'dinst] *m* (-es;-e) earnings; gain, profit ‖ *n* (-es;-e) merit; deserts; **es ist dein V., daß** it is owing to you that; **nach V.** deservedly; **nach V. behandelt werden** get one's due; **sich** [*dat*] **als** (or **zum**) **V. anrechnen** take credit for it; **V. um** services to

Verdienst'ausfall *m* loss of wages

verdienst'lich *adj* meritorious

Verdienst'spanne *f* margin of profit

verdienst'voll *adj* meritorious

verdient [fɛr'dint] *adj*—**sich um j-n v. machen** serve s.o. well

verdol'metschen *tr* translate orally; interpret

Verdol'metschung *f* (-;) oral translation; interpretation

verdonnern [fɛr'dɔnərn] *tr* (coll) condemn

verdop'peln *tr & ref* double

verdorben [fɛr'dɔrbən] *adj* spoiled; (*Luft*) foul; (*Magen*) upset; (*moralisch*) depraved

verdorren [fɛr'dɔrən] *intr* (SEIN) dry up, wither

verdrän'gen *tr* push aside, crowd out; dislodge; (phys) displace; (psychol) repress, inhibit

Verdrän'gung *f* (-;-en) (phys) displacement; (psychol) repression, inhibition

verdre'hen *tr* twist; (*Augen*) roll; (*Glied*) sprain; (fig) distort; **j-m den Kopf v.** make s.o. fall in love with one

verdreht' *adj* twisted; (fig) distorted; (fig) (*verrückt*) cracked

verdreifachen [fɛr'draɪfaxən] *tr* triple

verdre'schen §67 *tr* (coll) spank

verdrießen [fɛr'drisən] §76 *tr* bother, annoy, get down; **laß es dich nicht v.!** don't let it get you down; **sich keine Mühe v. lassen** spare no pains ‖ *impers*—**es verdrießt mich, daß** it bothers me that

verdrießlich [fɛr'drislɪç] *adj* glum; tiresome, depressing; annoyed

verdroß [fɛr'drɔs] *pret* of **verdrießen**

verdro'ßen *adj* cross; (*mürrisch*) surly; (*lustlos*) listless

verdrucken (**verdruk'ken**) *tr* misprint

verdrücken (**verdrük'ken**) *tr* wrinkle; (coll) eat up, polish off ‖ *ref* (coll) sneak away

Ver·druß [fɛr'drus] *m* (-drusses; -drusse) annoyance, vexation; **j-m etw zum V. tun** do s.th. to spite s.o.

verduften [fɛr'dʊftən] *intr* (SEIN) lose its aroma; (coll) take off, scram

verdummen [fɛr'dʊmən] *tr* make stupid ‖ *intr* (SEIN) become stupid

verdunkeln [fɛr'dʊŋkəln] *tr* darken; obscure; (*Glanz*) dull; (fig) cloud; (astr) eclipse; (mil) black out ‖ *ref* darken; (*Himmel*) cloud over

Verdun'kelung f (-;-en) darkening; (astr) eclipse; (mil) blackout

verdünnen [fɛr'dʏnən] tr thin; dilute; (Gase) rarefy

verdun'sten intr (SEIN) evaporate

Verdun'stung f (-;) evaporation

verdur'sten intr (SEIN) die of thirst

verdutzen [fɛr'dutsən] tr bewilder

veredeln [fɛr'edəln] tr ennoble; (verfeinen) refine; (Rohstoff) process; (Boden) enrich; (Pflanze, Tier) improve

Vere'delung f (-;) refinement; processing; enrichment; improvement

verehelichen [fɛr'e·əlɪçən] ref get married

verehren [fɛr'erən] tr revere; worship; (fig) adore; **j-m etw v.** present s.o. with s.th.

Vereh'rer –in §6 mf worshiper; (Liebhaber) admirer

verehrt [fɛr'ert] adj—**Sehr verehrte gnädige Frau! Dear Madam; Sehr verehrter Herr! Dear Sir; Verehrte Anwesende (or Gäste)! Ladies and Gentlemen!**

Vereh'rung f (-;) reverence, veneration; worship, adoration

vereiden [fɛr'aɪdən], **vereidigen** [fɛr'aɪdɪɡən] tr swear in

Verein [fɛr'aɪn] m (-[e]s;-e) society

vereinbar [fɛr'aɪnbar] adj compatible

vereinbaren [fɛr'aɪnbarən] tr agree to, agree upon || ref—**das läßt sich mit meinen Grundsätzen nicht v.** that is inconsistent with my principles

Verein'barkeit f (-;) compatibility

Verein'barung f (-;) agreement, arrangement; terms; **nur nach V.** by appointment only

vereinen [fɛr'aɪnən] tr unite, join

vereinfachen [fɛr'aɪnfaxən] tr simplify

Verein'fachung f (-;-en) simplification

vereinheitlichen [fɛr'aɪnhaɪtlɪçən] tr standardize

vereinigen [fɛr'aɪnɪɡən] tr unite, join; (verbinden) combine; (verschmelzen) merge; (versammeln) assemble || ref unite, join; (Flüsse) meet; **sich v. mit** team up with; **sich v. lassen mit** be compatible with, square with

Verei'nigten Staa'ten pl United States

Verein'igung f (-;-en) union; combination; society, association

vereinnahmen [fɛr'aɪnnamən] tr take in

vereinsamen [fɛr'aɪnzamən] intr (SEIN) become lonely; become isolated

Verein'samung f (-;) loneliness; isolation

Vereins'meier –in §6 mf (coll) joiner

vereinzeln [fɛr'aɪntsəln] tr isolate

verein'zelt adj isolated; sporadic

vereisen [fɛr'aɪzən] tr (surg) freeze || intr (SEIN) become covered with ice; (aer) ice up

vereiteln [fɛr'aɪtəln] tr frustrate; baffle

verekeln [fɛr'ɛkəln] tr—**j-m etw v.** spoil s.th. for s.o.

veren'den intr (SEIN) die

verengen [fɛr'ɛŋən] tr & ref narrow

verer'ben tr bequeath, leave; (über-**mitteln**) hand down; (Krankheit) transmit || ref run in the family

Verer'bung f (-;-en) inheritance; transmission; heredity

Verer'bungslehre f genetics

verewigen [fɛr'evɪɡən] tr perpetuate

verewigt [fɛr'evɪçt] adj late, deceased

verfah'ren adj bungled, messed up || §71 tr bungle; (Geld, Zeit) spend (on travel) || ref lose one's way, take a track || intr (SEIN) proceed; act || wrong turn; (fig) be on the wrong

Verfahren n (-s;-) procedure, method; system; (chem) process; (jur) proceedings, case

Verfall m (-[e]s;) deterioration, decay; decline, downfall; (Fristablauf) expiration; (von Wechseln) maturity; **in V. geraten** become delapidated

verfal'len adj delapidated; **e-m Rauschgift v. sein** be addicted to a drug || §72 intr (SEIN) decay, go to ruin, decline; (ablaufen) expire; (Kranker) waste away; (Recht) lapse; (Pfand) be forfeited; (Wechsel) mature

Verfall'tag m due date; date of maturity

verfäl'schen tr falsify; (Geld) counterfeit; (Wein) adulterate; (Urkunde) forge

Verfäl'schung f (-;-en) falsification; forging; adulteration

verfan'gen §73 ref become entangled || intr (bei) have an effect (on)

verfänglich [fɛr'fɛŋlɪç] adj (Frage) loaded; (Situation) awkward

verfär'ben ref change color

verfas'sen tr compose, write

Verfas'ser –in §6 mf author

Verfas'sung f (-;-en) constitution; (Zustand) condition; frame of mind, mood

verfas'sungsgemäß, verfas'sungsmäßig adj constitutional

verfas'sungswidrig adj unconstitutional

verfau'len intr (SEIN) rot

verfech'ten §74 tr defend, stand up for

Verfech'ter m (-s;-) champion

verfeh'len tr (Abzweigung, Ziel, Zug) miss; (Wirkung) fail to achieve, not have; **ich werde nicht v. zu** (inf) I will not fail to (inf) || recip—**wir haben uns verfehlt** we missed each other

verfehlt [fɛr'felt] adj wrong

Verfeh'lung f (-;-en) offense; mistake

verfeinden [fɛr'faɪndən] recip become enemies

verfeinern [fɛr'faɪnərn] tr refine, improve || ref become refined, improve

verfertigen [fɛr'fɛrtɪɡən] tr manufacture, make

Verfer'tigung f (-;) manufacture

verfilmen [fɛr'fɪlmən] tr adapt to the screen, make into a movie

Verfil'mung f (-;-en) film version

verfilzen [fɛr'fɪltsən] ref get tangled

verfinstern [fɛr'fɪnstərn] ref get dark

verflachen [fɛr'flaxən] tr flatten || ref & intr (SEIN) flatten out

verflech'ten §74 tr interweave; (fig) implicate, involve

verflie'gen §57 ref (aer) lose one's

bearings || *intr* (SEIN) fly away;
(*Zeit*) fly; evaporate; (fig) vanish
verflie′ßen §76 *intr* (SEIN) flow off;
(*Frist*) run out, expire; (*Farben*)
blend; (*Begriffe, Grenzen*) overlap
verflixt [fer′flıkst] *adj* (sl) darn
verflossen [fer′flɔsən] *adj* past; former
verflu′chen *tr* curse, damn
verflucht′ *adj* (sl) damn || *interj* (sl)
damn it!
verflüchtigen [fer′flʏçtıgən] *tr* vola-
tilize || *ref* evaporate; (fig) disappear
verflüssigen [fer′flʏsıgən] *tr & ref*
liquefy
Verfolg [fer′fɔlk] *m* (–s;) course; **im
V.** (*genit*) in pursuance of
verfol′gen *tr* pursue; follow up; persecute; haunt; (hunt) track; (jur)
prosecute; **j–n steckbrieflich v.** send
out a warrant for the arrest of s.o.
Verfol′ger –in §6 *mf* pursuer; persecutor
Verfol′gung *f* (–;–en) pursuit; persecution; (jur) prosecution
Verfol′gungswahn *m*, **Verfol′gungs-
wahnsinn** *m* persecution complex
verfrachten [fer′fraxtən] *tr* ship; (coll)
bundle off
Verfrach′ter –in §6 *mf* shipper
verfrühen [fer′fry·ən] *ref* be too early
verfügbar [fer′fykbar] *adj* available,
at one's disposal
verfü′gen *tr* decree, order || *ref*—**sich
v. nach** betake oneself to || *intr*—**v.
über** (*acc*) have at one's disposal,
have control over
Verfü′gung *f* (–;–en) decree, order;
disposal; **einstweilige V.** (jur) injunction; **j–m zur V. stehen** be at
s.o.'s disposal; **j–m zur V. stellen** put
at s.o.'s disposal; **letztwillige V.** last
will and testament
verfüh′ren *tr* mislead; (*zum Irrtum*)
lead; (*verlocken*) seduce
Verführ′er –in §6 *mf* seducer
verführerisch [fer′fyrərıʃ] *adj* seductive, tempting
Verführ′rung *f* (–;–en) seduction
vergaffen [fer′gafən] *ref* (coll) (**in**
acc) fall in love (with)
vergammeln [fer′gaməln] *intr* (SEIN)
(coll) go to the dogs
vergangen [fer′gaŋən] *adj* past;
(*Schönheit*) faded
Vergan′genheit *f* (–;) past; background;
(gram) past tense
vergänglich [fer′gɛŋlıç] *adj* transitory
vergasen [fer′gazən] *tr* gas
Verga′ser *m* (–s;–) carburetor
vergaß [fer′gas] *pret* of **vergessen**
verge′ben §80 *tr* forgive (*s.th.*); give
away; (*Chance*) miss, pass up; (*Amt,
freie Stelle*) fill; (*Auftrag*) place;
(*Karten*) misdeal; (*verleihen*) confer; **v. sein** have a previous engage-
ment; be engaged (*to a man*) || *ref*—
sich [*dat*] **etw v.** compromise on s.th.
|| *intr* (*dat*) forgive (*s.o.*).
verge′bens [fer′gebəns] *adv* in vain
vergeb′lich [fer′geplıç] *adj* vain, futile
Verge′bung *f* (–;) forgiveness; bestowal
vergegenwärtigen [fer′gegənvertıgən]
ref—**sich** [*dat*] **etw. v.** visualize s.th.

verge′hen §82 *ref*—**sich an j–m v.** of-
fend s.o.; (*sexuell*) violate s.o. || *intr*
(SEIN) pass, go away; fade || **Verge-
hen** *n* (–s;–) offense, misdemeanor
vergel′ten §83 *tr* requite; **vergelt's
Gott!** (coll) thank you!
Vergel′tung *f* (–;) repayment; retaliation, reprisal
Vergel′tungswaffe *f* V-1 or V-2
vergesellschaften [fergə′zelʃaftən] *tr*
socialize; nationalize
vergessen [fer′gesən] §70 *tr* forget
Verges′senheit *f* (–;)—**in V. geraten**
fall (or sink) into oblivion
vergeßlich [fer′geslıç] *adj* forceful
Vergeß′lichkeit *f* (–;) forgetfulness
vergeuden [fer′gɔıdən] *tr* waste
Vergeu′dung *f* (–;) waste, squandering
vergewaltigen [fergə′valtıgən] *tr* do
violence to; (*Mädchen*) rape
Vergewal′tigung *f* (–;–en) rape
vergewerkschaften [fergə′verkʃaftən]
tr unionize
vergewissern [fergə′vısərn] *ref* (*genit*)
make sure of, ascertain
vergie′ßen §76 *tr* spill; (*Tränen*) shed
vergiften [fer′gıftən] *tr* (& fig) poison;
(*verseuchen*) contaminate || *ref* take
poison
Vergif′tung *f* (–;–en) poisoning; contamination
vergipsen [fer′gıpsən] *tr* plaster
Vergißmeinnicht [fer′gısmaınnıçt] *n*
(–[e]s;–e) forget-me-not
vergittern [fer′gıtərn] *tr* bar up
Vergleich [fer′glaıç] *m* (–[e]s;–e)
comparison; (*Verständigung*) agreement; (*Ausgleich*) settlement; **e–n V.
anstellen zwischen** make a comparison between; **e–n V. treffen** reach a
settlement, come to an agreement
vergleichbar [fer′glaıçbar] *adj* comparable
verglei′chen [fer′glaıçən] §85 *tr* (**mit**)
compare (with, to) || *ref* (**mit**) come
to an agreement (with)
Vergleichs′grundlage *f* basis for comparison
vergleichs′weise *adv* by way of comparison
Verglei′chung *f* (–;–en) comparison;
matching; contrasting
verglü′hen *intr* (SEIN) cease to glow
vergnügen [fer′gnygən] *tr* amuse, de-
light || *ref* enjoy oneself, amuse one-
self || **Vergnügen** *n* (–s;–) delight,
pleasure; **mit V.** with pleasure; **V.
finden an** (*dat*) take delight in; **viel
V.!** (coll) have fun!; **zum V.** for fun
vergnügt [fer′gnykt] *adj* cheerful, gay;
(**über** *acc*) delighted (with)
Vergnü′gung *f* (–;–en) pleasure, amusement
Vergnü′gungspark *m* amusement park
Vergnü′gungsreise *f* pleasure trip
Vergnü′gungssteuer *f* entertainment tax
vergnü′gungssüchtig *adj* pleasure-loving
vergolden [fer′gɔldən] *tr* gild
Vergol′dung *f* (–;–en) gilding
vergönnen [fer′gœnən] *tr* not begrudge
vergöttern [fer′gœtərn] *tr* deify; (fig)
idolize
vergra′ben §87 *tr* (& fig) bury

vergrämen [fɛr'grɛmən] *tr* annoy, anger

vergrämt [fɛr'grɛmt] *adj* haggard

vergrei/fen §88 *ref* (mus) hit the wrong note; **sich v. an** (*dat*) lay violent hands on; (*fremdem Gut*) encroach on; (*Geld*) misappropriate; (*Mädchen*) assault; **sich im Ausdruck v.** express oneself poorly

vergreisen [fɛr'graızən] *intr* (SEIN) age; become senile

vergriffen [fɛr'grıfən] *adj* sold out; (*Buch*) out of print

vergröbern [fɛr'grøbərn] *tr* roughen || *ref* become coarser

vergrößern [fɛr'grøsərn] *tr* enlarge; increase; (*ausdehnen*) expand; (opt) magnify || *ref* become larger

Vergrö/ßerung *f* (–;–en) enlargement; increase; expansion; (opt) magnification

Vergrö/ßerungsapparat *m* (phot) enlarger

Vergrö/ßerungsglas *m* magnifying glass

Vergünstigung [fɛr'gynstıguŋ] *f* (–; –en) privilege; (*bevorzugte Behandlung*) preferential treatment

vergüten [fɛr'gytən] *tr* make good; (*Stahl*) temper; **j–m etw v.** reimburse (or compensate) s.o. for s.th.

Vergü/tung *f* (–;–en) reimbursement, compensation; tempering

verhaften [fɛr'haftən] *tr* apprehend

Verhaf/tung *f* (–;–en) apprehension

verhal/ten *adj* (*Atem*) bated; (*Stimme*) low || §90 *tr* hold back; (*Atem*) hold; (*Lachen*) suppress; (*Stimme*) keep down; **den Schritt v.** slow down; (*stehenbleiben*) stop || *ref* behave, act; be; **A verhält sich zu B wie X zu Y** A is to B as X is to Y; **sich anders v.** be different; **sich ruhig v.** keep quiet || *impers ref*—**wenn es sich so verhält** if that's the case || **Verhalten** *n* (–s;) conduct, behavior; attitude

Verhältnis [fɛr'hɛltnıs] *n* (–ses;–se) proportion, ratio; (*Beziehung*) relation; (*Liebes–*) love affair; **aus kleinen Verhältnissen** of humble birth; **bei sonst gleichen Verhältnissen** other things being equal; **das steht in keinem V. zu** that is all out of proportion to; **Verhältnisse** circumstances, conditions; matters; means

verhält/nismäßig *adj* proportionate || *adv* relatively, comparatively

Verhält/nismaßregeln *pl* instructions

Verhält/niswahl *f* proportional representation

verhält/niswidrig *adj* disproportionate

Verhält/niswort *n* (–[e]s;–̈er) preposition

verhan/deln *tr* discuss; (*Waren*) sell || *intr* negotiate; argue; (*beraten*) confer; (jur) plead a case; **gegen j–n wegen etw v.** (jur) try s.o. for s.th.

Verhand/lung *f* (–;–en) negotiation; discussion; proceedings, trial

verhangen [fɛr'haŋən] *adj* overcast

verhän/gen *tr* (*Fenster*) put curtains on; (*Strafe*) impose; (*Untersuchung*) order; (*Belagerungszustand*) pro-

claim; **mit verhängtem Zügel** at full speed

Verhängnis [fɛr'hɛŋnıs] *n* (–ses;–se) destiny, fate; (*Unglück*) disaster

verhäng/nisvoll *adj* fateful; disastrous

verhärmt [fɛr'hɛrmt] *adj* haggard

verharren [fɛr'harən] *intr* (HABEN & SEIN) remain; (**auf** *dat*, **in** *dat*, **bei**) stick (to)

verhärten [fɛr'hɛrtən] *tr & ref* harden

verhaßt [fɛr'hast] *adj* hated, hateful

verhätscheln [fɛr'hɛtʃəln] *tr* pamper

Verhau [fɛr'hau] *m* (–[e]s;–e) barbwire entanglement

verhau/en §93 *tr* lick, beat up; (*Kind*) spank; (*Auftrag, Ball, usw.*) muff || *ref* make a blunder

verheddern [fɛr'hɛdərn] *ref* get tangled up

verheeren [fɛr'herən] *tr* devastate

verhee/rend *adj* terrible; (coll) awful

Verhee/rung *f* (–;) devastation

verhehlen [fɛr'helən] *tr* conceal

verhei/len *intr* (SEIN) heal up

verheimlichen [fɛr'haımlıçən] *tr* keep secret, conceal

Verheim/lichung *f* (–;) concealment

verhei/raten *tr* marry; (*Tocher*) give away || *ref* (**mit**) get married (to)

Verhei/ratung *f* (–;) marriage

verhei/ßen §95 *tr* promise

Verhei/ßung *f* (–;–en) promise

verhei/ßungsvoll *adj* promising

verhel/fen §96 *intr*—**j–m zu etw v.** help s.o. to acquire s.th.

verherrlichen [fɛr'hɛrlıçən] *tr* glorify

Verherr/lichung *f* (–;) glorification

verhet/zen *tr* instigate

verhexen [fɛr'hɛksən] *tr* bewitch, hex

verhimmeln [fɛr'hıməln] *tr* praise to the skies; (*Schauspieler*) idolize

verhin/dern *tr* prevent

Verhin/derung *f* (–;) prevention; **im Falle seiner V.** in case he's unavailable

verhohlen [fɛr'holən] *adj* hidden

verhöh/nen *tr* jeer at; make fun of

Verhöh/nung *f* (–;) jeering; ridicule

Verhör [fɛr'hør] *n* (–s;–e) interrogation, questioning, hearing

verhö/ren *tr* interrogate, question || *ref* hear wrong

verhudeln [fɛr'hudəln] *tr* (coll) bungle

verhüllen [fɛr'hylən] *tr* cover, veil; wrap up; disguise

Verhül/lung *f* (–;–en) cover; disguise

verhun/gern *intr* (SEIN) starve to death

verhunzen [fɛr'huntsən] *tr* (coll) botch

verhü/ten *tr* prevent, avert

verinnerlicht [fɛr'ınərlıçt] *adj* introspective

verir/ren *ref* lose one's way; (*Augen, Blick*) wander; (*fig*) make a mistake

verirrt [fɛr'ırt] *adj* stray

verja/gen *tr* chase away

verjähren [fɛr'jerən] *intr* (SEIN) fall under the statute of limitations

verjubeln [fɛr'jubəln] *tr* squander

verjüngen [fɛr'jyŋən] *tr* rejuvenate; reduce in scale; taper || *ref* be rejuvenated; taper, narrow

Verjün/gung *f* (–;) rejuvenation; tapering; scaling down

verkatert [fɛr'katərt] *adj* suffering from a hangover
Verkauf' *m* (-[e]s;-e) sale
verkau'fen *tr* sell
Verkäu'fer -in §6 *mf* seller; salesclerk; vendor || *m* salesman || *f* salesgirl, saleswoman
verkäuf'lich *adj* salable
Verkaufs'anzeige *f* for-sale ad
Verkaufs'automat *m* vending machine
Verkaufs'leiter -in §6 *mf* sales manager
Verkaufs'schlager *m* good seller
Verkaufs'steigerung *f* sales promotion
Verkaufs'vertrag *m* agreement of sale
Verkehr [fɛr'ker] *m* (-s;) traffic; commerce; company, association; (*sexuell*) intercourse; (aer, rr) service; (fin) circulation
verkeh'ren *tr* reverse, invert; turn upside down; convert, change; (*Sinn, Worte*) twist || *intr* (*Fahrzeug*) run, run regularly; **mit j-m geschlechtlich v.** have intercourse with s.o.; **mit j-m v.** associate with s.o.
Verkehrs'ader *f* main artery
Verkehrs'ampel *f* traffic light
Verkehrs'andrang *m* heavy traffic
Verkehrs'betrieb *m* public transportation company
Verkehrs'delikt *n* traffic violation
Verkehrs'flugzeug *n* airliner
Verkehrs'insel *f* traffic island
Verkehrs'mittel *n* means of transportation
Verkehrs'ordnungen *pl* traffic regulations
Verkehrs'polizist -in §7 *mf* traffic cop
verkehrs'reich *adj* crowded, congested
verkehrs'stark *adj* busy
Verkehrs'stockung *f*, **Verkehrs'störung** *f* traffic jam
Verkehrs'unfall *m* traffic accident
Verkehrs'unternehmen *n* transportation company
Verkehrs'vorschrift *f* traffic regulation
Verkehrs'wesen *n* traffic, transportation
Verkehrs'zeichen *n* traffic sign
verkehrt [fɛr'kert] *adj* reversed; upside down; inside out; wrong
verken'nen §97 *tr* misunderstand; (*Person*) misjudge, mistake
verketten [fɛr'kɛtən] *tr* chain together; (fig) link
Verket'tung *f* (-;) chaining; (fig) concatenation; (fig) coincidence
verkit'ten *tr* cement; putty; seal, bond
verkla'gen *tr* accuse; (jur) sue
Verklagte [fɛr'klaktə] §5 *mf* defendant
verklat'schen *tr* (coll) slander; (educ) squeal on
verkle'ben *tr* glue, cement; **v. mit** cover with
verklei'den *tr* disguise, dress up; (*täfeln*) panel; line, face; (mil) camouflage
Verklei'dung *f* (-;-en) disguise; paneling; lining, facing; (mil) camouflage
verkleinern [fɛr'klaınərn] *tr* lessen, diminish; (fig) disparage; (math) reduce; **maßstäblich v.** scale down

Verklei'nerung *f* (-;-en) diminution, reduction; (fig) detraction
Verklei'nerungsform *f* diminutive
verklin'gen §142 *intr* (SEIN) die away
verkloppen [fɛr'klɔpən] *tr* (coll) beat up
verknacken [fɛr'knakən] *tr* (coll) sentence
verknallt [fɛr'knalt] *adj*—**in j-n v. sein** (coll) have a crush on s.o.
verknappen [fɛr'knapən] *intr* (SEIN) run short, run low
Verknap'pung *f* (-;) shortage
verknei'fen §88 *ref*—**sich** [*dat*] **etw v.** deny oneself s.th.
verkniffen [fɛr'knıfən] *adj* wry
verknip'sen *tr* (*Film*) waste
verknöchern [fɛr'knœçərn] *intr* (SEIN) ossify; (*Glieder*) become stiff
verknöchert [fɛr'knœçərt] *adj* pedantic; (*Junggeselle*) inveterate
verknoten [fɛr'knotən] *tr* snarl, tie up
verknüp'fen *tr* tie together; (fig) connect, combine, relate
verknusen [fɛr'knuzən] *tr* (coll) stand
verkohlen [fɛr'kolən] *tr* carbonize; char; **j-n v.** (coll) pull s.o.'s leg
verkom'men *adj* decayed; degenerate; (*Gebäude*) squalid || §99 *intr* (SEIN) decay, spoil; (fig) go to the dogs; **v. zu** degenerate into
Verkom'menheit *f* (-;) depravity
verkop'peln *tr* couple; (*Interessen*) (com) consolidate
verkorken [fɛr'kɔrkən] *tr* cork up
verkorksen [fɛr'kɔrksən] *tr* (coll) bungle || *ref*—**sich** [*dat*] **den Magen v.** (coll) upset one's stomach
verkörpern [fɛr'kœrpərn] *tr* embody, personify; (*Rolle*) play
Verkör'perung *f* (-;-en) embodiment, incarnation
verkra'chen *ref*—**sich mit j-m v.** have an argument with s.o. || *intr* (SEIN) (coll) go bankrupt
verkrampft [fɛr'krampft] *adj* cramped
verkrie'chen §102 *ref* hide; (& fig) crawl into a hole; **neben ihm kannst du dich v.!** you're no match for him!
verkrümeln [fɛr'kryməln] *tr* crumble || *ref* (fig) disappear
verkrüm'men *tr* & *ref* bend
Verkrüm'mung *f* (-;) bend, crookedness; curvature
verkrüppeln [fɛr'krypəln] *tr* cripple || *intr* (SEIN) become crippled; (*verkümmern*) become stunted
verkrustet [fɛr'krustət] *adj* caked
verküh'len *ref* catch a cold
verküm'mern *intr* (SEIN) become stunted; (pathol) atrophy
Verküm'merung *f* (-;) atrophy
verkünden [fɛr'kʏndən], **verkündigen** [fɛr'kʏndıgən] *tr* announce, proclaim; (*Urteil*) pronounce
Verkün'digung *f* (-;-en), **Verkün'dung** *f* (-;-en) announcement, proclamation; pronouncement; **Mariä Verkündigung** (feast of the) Annunciation
verkup'peln *tr* couple; (*Mädchen, Mann*) procure; (*Tochter*) sell into prostitution

verkür'zen *tr* shorten; abridge; (*be-schränken*) curtail; (*Zeit*) pass

Verkür'zung *f* (-;-en) shortening; abridgement; curtailment

verla'chen *tr* laugh at

verla'den §103 *tr* load, ship

Verlag [fɛr'lɑk] *m* (-[e]s;-e) publisher; **im V. von** published by

verla'gern *tr* shift; (*aus Sicherheits-gründen*) evacuate ‖ *ref* shift

Verla'gerung *f* (-;-en) shift, shifting; evacuation

Verlags'anstalt *f* publisher

Verlags'buchhandlung *f* publisher and dealer

Verlags'recht *n* copyright

verlangen [fɛr'laŋən] *tr* demand, require; want, ask ‖ *intr*—**v. nach** ask for; long for ‖ **Verlangen** *n* (-s;) demand; request; wish; claim; (*Sehnsucht*) longing, yearning; **auf V.** upon demand, upon request

verlängern [fɛr'lɛŋərn] *tr* lengthen; prolong, extend; **seinen Paß v. lassen** have one's passport renewed

Verlän'gerung *f* (-;-en) lengthening; prolongation, extension; (sport) overtime

Verlän'gerungsschnur *f* extension cord

verlangsamen [fɛr'laŋzɑmən] *tr* slow down

verläppern [fɛr'lɛpərn] *tr* (coll) fritter away

Ver·laß [fɛr'las] *m* (-lasses;) reliance; **es ist kein V. auf ihn** you can't rely on him

verlas'sen *adj* abandoned, deserted; lonesome ‖ §104 *tr* leave; forsake, desert ‖ *ref*—**sich v. auf** (*acc*) rely on

Verlas'senheit *f* (-;) loneliness

verläßlich [fɛr'lɛslɪç] *adj* reliable

verlästern [fɛr'lɛstərn] *tr* slander

Verlä'sterung *f* (-;-en) slander

Verlaub [fɛr'laup] *m*—**mit V.** with your permission; **mit V. zu sagen** if I may say so

Verlauf' *m* (-[e]s;) course; **e-n guten V. haben** turn out well; **nach V. von** after a lapse of

verlau'fen §105 *intr* (SEIN) (*Zeit*) pass, lapse; (*ablaufen*) turn out, come off; (*vorgehen*) proceed, run ‖ *ref* lose one's way; (*Wasser*) run off; (*Menschenmenge*) disperse

verlau'ten *intr* (SEIN) become known, be reported; **kein Wort davon v. lassen** not breathe a word about it; **wie verlautet** as reported ‖ *impers*—**es verlautet** it is reported

verle'ben *tr* spend, pass

verlebt [fɛr'lept] *adj* haggard

verle'gen *adj* embarrassed; confused; **v. um** (*e-e Antwort*) at a loss for; (*Geld*) short of ‖ *tr* move, shift; transfer; misplace; (*Buch*) publish; (*Geleise, Kabel, Rohre*) lay; (*sperren*) block; (*vertagen*) postpone ‖ *ref*—**sich v. auf** (*acc*) apply onself to; devote oneself to; resort to

Verle'genheit *f* (-;) embarrassment; difficulties; predicament; **in V. bringen** embarrass

Verle'ger *m* (-s;-) publisher

Verle'gung *f* (-;-en) move, shift; transfer; postponement; (*von Kabeln, usw.*) laying

verlei'den *tr* spoil, take the joy out of

Verleih [fɛr'laɪ] *m* (-s;-e) rental service

verlei'hen §81 *tr* lend out, loan; rent out; (*Gunst*) grant; (*Titel*) confer; (*Auszeichnung*) award

Verlei'her -in §6 *mf* lender; grantor; (*von Filmen*) distributor

Verlei'hung *f* (-;-en) lending out; rental; grant; bestowal

verlei'ten *tr* mislead; (*zur Sünde, zum Trunk*) lead; (jur) suborn

verler'nen *tr* unlearn, forget

verle'sen §107 *tr* read out; (*Namen*) read off; (*Salat*) clean; (*Gemüse*) sort out ‖ *ref* misread

verletzen [fɛr'letsən] *tr* (& fig) injure, hurt; (*kränken*) offend; (*Gesetz*) break; (*Recht*) violate

verlet'zend *adj* offensive

Verletzte [fɛr'letstə] §5 *mf* injured party

Verlet'zung *f* (-;-en) injury; offense; (*e-s Gesetzes*) breaking; (*e-s Rechtes*) violation

verleug'nen *tr* deny; (*Kind*) disown; (*Glauben*) renounce ‖ *ref*—**sich selbst v.** act contrary to one's nature; **sich vor Besuchern v. lassen** refuse to see visitors

Verleug'nung *f* (-;-en) denial; renunciation; disavowal

verleumden [fɛr'lɔɪmdən] *tr* slander

verleumderisch [fɛr'lɔɪmdərɪʃ] *adj* slanderous, libelous

Verleum'dung *f* (-;-en) slander

verlie'ben *ref*—**sich in j-n v.** fall in love with s.o.

verliebt [fɛr'lipt] *adj* in love

verlieren [fɛr'lirən] §77 *tr* lose ‖ *ref* lose one's way; disappear; disperse

Verlies [fɛr'lis] *n* (-es;-e) dungeon

verlo'ben *ref* (mit) become engaged (to)

Verlöbnis [fɛr'løpnɪs] *n* (-ses;-se) engagement

Verlobte [fɛr'loptə] §5 *m* fiancé; **die Verlobten** the engaged couple ‖ *f* fiancée

Verlo'bung *f* (-;-en) engagement

verlocken (verlok'ken) *tr* lure, tempt; (*verführen*) seduce

verlockend (verlok'kend) *adj* tempting

Verlockung (Verlok'kung) *f* (-;-en) allurement, temptation

verlogen [fɛr'logən] *adj* dishonest

verloh'nen *impers ref*—**es verlohnt sich nicht** it doesn't pay ‖ *impers*—**es verlohnt der Mühe nicht** it is not worth the trouble

verlor [fɛr'lor] *pret* of **verlieren**

verloren [fɛr'lorən] *pp* of **verlieren** ‖ *adj* lost; (*hilflos*) forlorn; (*Ei*) poached; **der verlorene Sohn** the prodigal son

verlo'rengeben §80 *tr* give up for lost

verlo'rengehen §82 *intr* (SEIN) be lost

verlö'schen §110 *tr* extinguish; (*Schrift*) erase ‖ *intr* (SEIN) (*Licht, Kerze*) go out; (*Zorn*) cease

verlo′sen *tr* raffle off, draw lots for

verlö′ten *tr* solder; **e–n v.** (coll) belt one down

verlottern [fɛr′lɔtərn] *intr* (coll) go to the dogs

verlumpen [fɛr′lʊmpən] *tr* (coll) blow, squander || *intr* (coll) go to the dogs

Verlust [fɛr′lʊst] *m* (–[e]s;–e) loss; **in V. geraten** get lost; **Verluste** (mil) casualties

Verlust′liste *f* (mil) casualty list

verma′chen *tr* bequeath, leave

Vermächtnis [fɛr′mɛçtnɪs] *n* (–ses;–se) bequest, legacy

vermählen [fɛr′mɛlən] *tr* marry || *ref* (mit) get married (to)

Vermäh′lung *f* (–;–en) marriage, wedding

vermah′nen *tr* admonish, warn

Vermah′nung *f* (–;–en) admonition

vermaledeien [fɛrmalɛ′daɪ·ən] *tr* curse

vermanschen [fɛr′manʃən] *tr* (coll) make a mess of

vermasseln [fɛr′masəln] *tr* (coll) bungle, muff

vermassen [fɛr′masən] *intr* (SEIN) lose one's individuality

vermauern [fɛr′maʊ·ərn] *tr* wall up

vermehren [fɛr′merən] *tr* & *ref* increase; (*an Zahl*) multiply; **vermehrte Auflage** enlarged edition

vermei′den *tr* avoid

vermeidlich [fɛr′maɪtlɪç] *adj* avoidable

Vermei′dung *f* (–;) avoidance

vermei′nen *tr* suppose; presume, allege

vermeintlich [fɛr′maɪntlɪç] *adj* supposed, alleged; (*erdacht*) imaginary

vermel′den *tr* (poet) announce

vermen′gen *tr* mix, mingle; confound || *ref* (mit) meddle (with)

Vermerk [fɛr′mɛrk] *m* (–[e]s;–e) note

vermer′ken *tr* note, record

vermes′sen *adj* daring, bold || §70 *tr* measure; (*Land*) survey || *ref* measure wrong; **sich v. zu** (*inf*) have the nerve to (*inf*)

Vermes′sung *f* (–;–en) surveying

vermie′ten *tr* rent out; lease out

Vermie′ter –in §6 *mf* (jur) lessor || *m* landlord || *f* landlady

vermindern [fɛr′mɪndərn] *tr* diminish, lessen; (*beschränken*) reduce, cut || *ref* diminish, decrease

Vermin′derung *f* (–;–en) diminution, decrease; reduction, cut

verminen [fɛr′minən] *tr* (mil) mine

vermi′schen *tr* & *ref* mix

Vermi′schung *f* (–;–en) mixture

vermissen [fɛr′mɪsən] *tr* miss

vermißt [fɛr′mɪst] *adj* (mil) missing in action || **Vermißte** §5 *mf* missing person

vermitteln [fɛr′mɪtəln] *tr* negotiate; arrange, bring about; (*beschaffen*) get, procure || *intr* mediate; intercede

vermittels [fɛr′mɪtəls] *prep* (genit) by means of, through

Vermitt′ler –in §6 *mf* mediator, go-between; (com) agent

Vermitt′lung *f* (–;–en) negotiation; mediation; intercession; (*Mittel*) means; agency;

brokerage; (telp) exchange; **durch gütige V.** (genit) through the good offices of

Vermitt′lungsamt *n* (telp) exchange

Vermitt′lungsgebühr *f*, **Vermitt′lungsprovision** *f* commission; brokerage

vermo′dern *intr* (SEIN) rot, decay

vermöge [fɛr′møgə] *prep* (genit) by virtue of

vermö′gen §114 *tr* be able to do; **j–n v. zu** (*inf*) induce s.o. to (*inf*); **sie vermag bei ihm viel** (or **wenig**) she has great (or little) influence with him; **v. zu** (*inf*) have the power to (*inf*) || **Vermögen** *n* (–s;–) ability; capacity, power; fortune, means; property; (fin) capital, assets; **nach bestem V.** to the best of one's ability

vermö′gend *adj* well-to-do, well-off

Vermö′genslage *f* financial situation

Vermö′genssteuer *f* property tax

vermorscht [fɛr′mɔrʃt] *adj* rotten

vermottet [fɛr′mɔtət] *adj* moth-eaten

vermummen [fɛr′mʊmən] *tr* disguise || *ref* disguise oneself

vermuten [fɛr′mutən] *tr* suppose, presume

vermutlich [fɛr′mutlɪç] *adj* presumable || *adv* presumably, I suppose

Vermu′tung *f* (–;–en) guess, conjecture

vernachlässigen [fɛr′naxlɛsɪgən] *tr* neglect

Vernach′lässigung *f* (–;) neglect

verna′geln *tr* nail up; board up

vernä′hen *tr* sew up

vernarben [fɛr′narbən] *intr* (SEIN) heal up

vernarren [fɛr′narən] *ref*—**sich v. in** (*acc*) be crazy about, be stuck on

verna′schen *tr* spend on sweets; (*Mädchen*) make love to

vernebeln [fɛr′nebəln] *tr* (mil) screen with smoke; (fig) hide, cover over

vernehmbar [fɛr′nembɑr] *adj* perceptible

verneh′men §116 *tr* perceive; (*erfahren*) hear, learn; (jur) question; **sich v. lassen** be heard, express an opinion || **Vernehmen** *n* (–s;–)—**dem V. nach** reportedly, according to the report

vernehmlich [fɛr′nemlɪç] *adj* perceptible, audible; distinct

Verneh′mung *f* (–;–en) interrogation

vernei′gen *ref* bow; curtsy

Vernei′gung *f* (–;–en) bow; curtsy

verneinen [fɛr′naɪnən] *tr* say no to; reject, refuse; disavow

vernei′nend *adj* negative

Vernei′nung *f* (–;–en) negation; denial

vernichten [fɛr′nɪçtən] *tr* destroy, annihilate; (*Hoffnung*) dash

vernich′tend *adj* (*Kritik*) scathing; (*Niederlage*) crushing

Vernich′tung *f* (–;) destruction

vernickeln [fɛr′nɪkəln] *tr* nickel-plate

vernie′ten *tr* rivet

Vernunft [fɛr′nʊnft] *f* (–;) reason; good sense; senses; **die gesunde V.** common sense; **V. annehmen** listen to reason; **zur V. bringen** bring to one's senses

Vernunft′ehe *f* marriage of convenience

vernunft′gemäß *adj* reasonable

vernünftig [fɛr′nʏnftɪç] *adj* rational; reasonable; sensible, level-headed

vernunft′los *adj* senseless

vernunft′mäßig *adj* rational; reasonable

veröden [fɛr′ødən] *intr* (SEIN) become desolate

veröffentlichen [fɛr′œfəntlɪçən] *tr* publish; announce

Veröf′fentlichung *f* (–;–en) publication; announcement

verord′nen *tr* decree; (med) prescribe

Verord′nung *f* (–;–en) decree, order; (med) prescription

verpach′ten *tr* farm out; lease, rent out

Verpäch′ter –in §6 *mf* lessor

verpacken (verpak′ken) *tr* pack up

Verpackung (Verpak′kung) *f* (–;–en) packing (material); wrapping

verpas′sen *tr* (*Gelegenheit, Anschluß, usw.*) miss; **j–m e–n Anzug v.** fit s.o. with a suit; **j–m e–e v.** (coll) give s.o. a smack

verpatzen [fɛr′patsən] *tr* (coll) make a mess of

verpesten [fɛr′pɛstən] *tr* infect, contaminate

verpet′zen *tr* (coll) squeal on

verpfän′den *tr* pawn; mortgage; **sein Wort v.** give one's word of honor

verpflan′zen *tr* (bot, surg) transplant

Verpflan′zung *f* (–;–en) (bot, surg) transplant

verpfle′gen *tr* feed; (mil) supply

Verpfle′gung *f* (–;) feeding; board; (mil) rations, supplies

verpflichten [fɛr′pflɪçtən] *tr* obligate, bind; **zu Dank v.** put under obligation

Verpflich′tung *f* (–;–en) obligation; commitment; (jur) liability

verpfuschen [fɛr′pfuʃən] *tr* (coll) botch, bungle, muff

verplap′pern *ref* blab out a secret

verplau′dern *tr* waste in chatting

verpönt [fɛr′pønt] *adj* taboo

verprü′geln *tr* (coll) wallop, thrash

verpuf′fen *intr* (SEIN) fizzle; (fig) fizzle out

verpulvern [fɛr′pulfərn] *tr* (coll) waste, fritter away

verpum′pen *tr* (coll) loan

verpusten [fɛr′pustən] *ref* (coll) catch one's breath

Verputz [fɛr′puts] *m* (–es;–e) finishing coat (of plaster)

verput′zen *tr* plaster; (*aufessen*) polish off; (coll) stand

verquicken [fɛr′kvɪkən] *tr* interrelate

verquollen [fɛr′kvɔlən] *adj* (*Augen*) swollen; (*Gesicht*) puffy; (*Holz*) warped

verrammeln [fɛr′raməln] *tr* barricade

verramschen [fɛr′ramʃən] *tr* (coll) sell dirt-cheap

verrannt [fɛr′rant] *adj*—**v. sein in** (*acc*) be stuck on

Verrat′ *m* (–[e]s;) betrayal; treason

verra′ten §63 *tr* betray

Verräter –in [fɛr′retər(ɪn)] §6 *mf* traitor; betrayer

verräterisch [fɛr′retərɪʃ] *adj* treacherous; (*Spur, usw.*) telltale

verrau′chen *tr* spend on smokes

verräu′chern *tr* fill with smoke

verrech′nen *tr* (*ausgleichen*) balance; (*Scheck*) deposit; (fin) clear ‖ *ref* miscalculate; (fig) be mistaken

Verrech′nung *f* (–;–en) miscalculation; (fin) clearing; **nur zur V.** for deposit only

Verrech′nungsbank *f*, **Verrech′nungskasse** *f* clearing house

verrecken [fɛr′rɛkən] *intr* (SEIN) die; (sl) croak; **verrecke!** drop dead!

verreg′nen *tr* spoil with too much rain

verrei′sen *intr* (SEIN) go on a trip; **v. nach** depart for

verreist [fɛr′raɪst] *adj* out of town

verren′ken *tr* wrench, dislocate ‖ *ref*— **sich** [*dat*] **den Arm v.** wrench one's arm; **sich** [*dat*] **den Hals v.** (coll) crane one's neck

Verren′kung *f* (–;–en) dislocation

verrich′ten *tr* do; (*Gebet*) say; **seine Notdurft v.** ease oneself

Verrich′tung *f* (–;–en) performance; task, duty

verrie′geln *tr* bolt, bar

verringern [fɛr′rɪŋərn] *tr* diminish, reduce ‖ *ref* diminish; be reduced

Verrin′gerung *f* (–;–en) diminution; reduction

verrin′nen §121 *intr* (SEIN) run off; (*Zeit*) pass

verro′sten *intr* (SEIN) rust

verrotten [fɛr′rɔtən] *intr* (SEIN) rot

verrucht [fɛr′ruxt] *adj* wicked

verrücken (verrük′ken) *tr* move, shift

verrückt [fɛr′rʏkt] *adj* crazy; **v. auf etw** crazy about s.th.; **v. nach j–m** crazy about s.o. ‖ **Verrückte** §5 *mf* lunatic

Verrückt′heit *f* (–;–en) craziness, madness; crazy action or act

Verruf′ *m* (–[e]s;) discredit, disrepute

verru′fen *adj* disreputable

verrüh′ren *tr* stir thoroughly

verrut′schen *intr* (SEIN) slip

Vers [fɛrs] *m* (–es;–e) verse

versa′gen *tr* refuse; **versagt sein** have a previous engagement ‖ *ref*—**sich** [*dat*] **etw v.** deny oneself s.th.; **ich kann es mir nicht v. zu** (*inf*) I can't refrain from (*ger*) ‖ *intr* fail; (*Beine, Stimme, usw.*) give out; (*Gewehr*) misfire; (*Motor*) fail to start; **bei e–r Prüfung v.** flunk a test ‖ **Versagen** *n* (–s;–) failure, flop; misfire

Versa′ger *m* (–s;–) failure, flop; (*Patrone*) dud

versal′zen *tr* oversalt; (fig) spoil

versam′meln *tr* gather together, assemble; convoke ‖ *ref* gather, assemble

Versamm′lung *f* (–;–en) assembly, meeting

Versand [fɛr′zant] *m* (–[e]s;) shipment; mailing

Versand′abteilung *f* shipping department

versanden [fɛr′zandən] *intr* (SEIN) silt up; (fig) bog down

Versand′geschäft *n,* **Versand′haus** *n* mail-order house

versäu′men *tr* (*Gelegenheit, Schule, Zug*) miss; (*Geschäft, Pflicht*) neglect; **v. zu** (*inf*) fail to (*inf*)

Versäumnis [fɛr'zɔɪmnɪs] *f* (–;–se), *n* (–ses;–se) omission, neglect; (*educ*) absence; (*jur*) default

verschaf′fen *tr* get, obtain ‖ *ref*—**sich** [*dat*] **etw v.** get; **sich** [*dat*] **Geld v.** raise money; **sich** [*dat*] **Respekt v.** gain respect

verschämt [fɛr'ʃɛmt] *adj* bashful, coy

Verschämt′heit *f* (–;) bashfulness

verschandeln [fɛr'ʃandəln] *tr* deface

verschan′zen *tr* fortify ‖ *ref* entrench oneself; **sich v. hinter** (*dat*) (*fig*) hide behind

Verschan′zung *f* (–;–en) entrenchment

verschär′fen *tr* intensify; aggravate; **verschärfter Arrest** detention on a bread-and-water diet ‖ *ref* get worse

verschei′den §112 *intr* (SEIN) pass away

verschen′ken *tr* give away

verscher′zen *ref*—**sich** [*dat*] **etw v.** throw away, lose (*frivolously*)

verscheu′chen *tr* scare away

verschicken (**verschik′ken**) *tr* send away; (*deportieren*) deport

Verschie′bebahnhof *m* marshaling yard

verschie′ben §130 *tr* postpone; shift; displace; black-market; (rr) shunt, switch ‖ *ref* shift

Verschie′bung *f* (–;–en) postponement; shift, shifting

verschieden [fɛr'ʃidən] *adj* different, various; distinct

verschie′denartig *adj* of a different kind

verschiedenerlei [fɛr'ʃidənərlaɪ] *invar adj* different kinds of

Verschie′denheit *f* (–;–en) difference; variety, diversity

verschiedentlich [fɛr'ʃidəntlɪç] *adv* repeatedly; at times, occasionally

verschie′ßen §76 *tr* (*Schießvorrat*) use up, expend ‖ *intr* (SEIN) (*Farbe*) fade

verschif′fen *tr* ship

Verschif′fung *f* (–;) shipment

verschim′meln *intr* (SEIN) get moldy

verschla′fen *adj* sleepy, drowsy ‖ §131 *tr* miss by sleeping; (*Zeit*) sleep away ‖ *intr* oversleep

Verschla′fenheit *f* (–;) sleepiness

Verschlag′ *m* partition; crate

verschla′gen *adj* sly; (*lau*) lukewarm ‖ §132 *tr* partition off; board up; (*Kisten*) nail shut; (*Seite im Buch*) lose; (naut) drive off course; (tennis) misserve; **j–m den Atem v.** take s.o.'s breath away; **j–m die Sprache** (or **Rede, Stimme**) **v.** make s.o. speechless; **v. werden auf** (*acc*) (or **in** *acc*) be driven to ‖ *impers*— **es verschlägt nichts** it doesn't matter

verschlammen [fɛr'ʃlamən] *intr* (SEIN) silt up

verschlampen [fɛr'ʃlampən] *tr* ruin (*through neglect*); (*verlegen*) misplace ‖ *intr* get slovenly

verschlechtern [fɛr'ʃlɛçtərn] *tr* make worse ‖ *ref* get worse, deteriorate

Verschlech′terung *f* (–;) deterioration

verschleiern [fɛr'ʃlaɪ-ərn] *tr* veil; (*Tatsachen*) cover up; (*Stimme*) disguise; (mil) screen; **die Bilanz v.** juggle the books ‖ *ref* cloud up

verschleiert [fɛr'ʃlaɪ-ərt] *adj* hazy; (*Stimme*) husky; (*Augen*) misty

Verschlei′erung *f* (–;) coverup; camouflaging; (jur) suppression of evidence

verschlei′fen §88 *tr* slur, slur over

Verschleiß [fɛr'ʃlaɪs] *m* (–es;) wear and tear; (Aust) retail trade

verschlei′ßen §53 *tr* wear out; (Aust) retail ‖ *ref* wear out

verschleiß′fest *adj* durable

verschlep′pen *tr* drag off; abduct; (*im Krieg*) displace; (*Verhandlungen*) drag out; (*Seuche*) spread; (*verzögern*) delay

verschleu′dern *tr* waste, squander; (*Waren*) sell dirt-cheap

verschlie′ßen §76 *tr* shut; lock; put under lock and key ‖ *ref* (*dat*) close one's mind to

verschlimmern [fɛr'ʃlɪmərn] *tr* make worse; (*fig*) aggravate ‖ *ref* get worse

verschlin′gen §142 *tr* devour, wolf down; (*verflechten*) intertwine

verschlissen [fɛr'ʃlɪsən] *adj* frayed

verschlossen [fɛr'ʃlɔsən] *adj* shut; (*fig*) reserved, tight-lipped

verschlucken (**verschluk′ken**) *tr* swallow ‖ *ref* swallow the wrong way

verschlungen [fɛr'ʃluŋən] *adj* (*Weg*) winding; (*fig*) intricate

Ver·schluß′ *m* (–schlusses;–schlüsse) fastener; (*Schnapp–*) catch; (*Schloß*) lock; (*e–r Flasche*) stopper; (*Stöpsel*) plug; (*Plombe*) seal; (*e–s Gewehrs*) breechlock; (*phot*) shutter; **unter V.** under lock and key

verschlüsseln [fɛr'ʃlysəln] *tr* code

Verschluß′laut *m* (ling) stop, plosive

verschmach′ten *intr* (SEIN) pine away; **vor Durst v.** be dying of thirst

verschmä′hen *tr* disdain

verschmel′zen §133 *tr & intr* (SEIN) fuse, merge; blend

Verschmel′zung *f* (–;–en) fusion; (com) merger

verschmer′zen *tr* get over

verschmie′ren *tr* smear; soil, dirty; (*verwischen*) blur

verschmitzt [fɛr'ʃmɪtst] *adj* crafty

verschmut′zen *tr* dirty ‖ *intr* (SEIN) get dirty

verschnap′pen *ref* give oneself away

verschnau′fen *ref & intr* stop for breath

verschnei′den §106 *tr* clip, trim; cut wrong; castrate; (*Branntwein, Wein*) blend

verschneit [fɛr'ʃnaɪt] *adj* snow-covered

Verschnitt′ *m* (–[e]s;) blend

verschnup′fen *tr* annoy; **verschnupft sein** have a cold; (coll) be annoyed

verschnü′ren *tr* tie up

verschollen [fɛr'ʃɔlən] *adj* missing, never heard of again; (jur) presumed dead

verscho′nen *tr* spare; **j–n mit etw v.** spare s.o. s.th.

verschönern [fɛr'ʃønərn] *tr* beautify

verschossen [fɛr'ʃɔsən] *adj* faded, discolored; (**in** *acc*) (coll) be madly in love (with)

verschränken [fɛr'ʃrɛŋkən] *tr* fold (*one's arms*)

verschrau'ben *tr* screw tight

verschrei'ben §62 *tr* use up (*in writing*); (jur) make over; (med) prescribe || *ref* make a mistake (*in writing*)

Verschrei'bung *f* (–;–en) prescription

verschrei'en §135 *tr* decry

verschrien [fɛr'ʃri·ən] *adj*—**v. sein als** have the reputation of being

verschroben [fɛr'ʃrobən] *adj* eccentric

Verschro'benheit *f* (–;–en) eccentricity

verschrotten [fɛr'ʃrɔtən] *tr* scrap

verschüch'tern *tr* intimidate

verschul'den *tr* encumber with debts; **etw v.** be guilty of s.th.; be the cause of s.th. || **Verschulden** *n* (–s;) fault

verschuldet [fɛr'ʃuldət] *adj* in debt

Verschul'dung *f* (–;–en) indebtedness; encumbrance

verschüt'ten *tr* spill; (*ausfüllen*) fill up; (*Person*) bury alive

verschwägert [fɛr'ʃvɛgərt] *adj* related by marriage

verschwei'gen §148 *tr* keep secret; **j–m etw v.** keep s.th. from s.o.

Verschwei'gung *f* (–;) concealment

verschwei'ßen *tr* weld (together)

verschwenden [fɛr'ʃvɛndən] *tr* (**an** *acc*) waste (on), squander (on)

Verschwen'der –**in** §6 *mf* spendthrift

verschwenderisch [fɛr'ʃvɛndərɪʃ] *adj* wasteful; lavish, extravagant

Verschwen'dung *f* (–;) waste; extravagance

verschwiegen [fɛr'ʃvigən] *adj* discreet; reserved, reticent

Verschwie'genheit *f* (–;) discretion; reticence; secrecy

verschwim'men §136 *intr* (SEIN) become blurred; (fig) fade

verschwin'den §59 *intr* (SEIN) disappear; **ich muß mal v.** (coll) I have to go (to the toilet); **v. lassen** put out of the way; spirit off || **Verschwinden** *n* (–s;) disappearance

verschwistert [fɛr'ʃvɪstərt] *adj* closely related

verschwit'zen *tr* sweat up; (coll) forget

verschwollen [fɛr'ʃvɔlən] *adj* swollen

verschwommen [fɛr'ʃvɔmən] *adj* hazy, indistinct; (*Bild*) blurred

Verschwom'menheit *f* (–;) haziness

verschwö'ren §137 *tr* forswear || *ref* (**gegen**) plot (against); **sich zu etw v.** plot s.th.

Verschwö'rer –**in** §6 *mf* conspirator

Verschwö'rung *f* (–;–en) conspiracy

verse'hen §138 *tr* (*Amt, Stellung*) hold; (*Dienst, Pflicht*) perform; (*Haushalt, usw.*) look after; (**mit**) provide (with); (eccl) administer the last rites to; **j–s Dienst v.** fill in for s.o.; **mit e–m Saum v.** hem; **mit Giro v.** endorse; **mit Unterschrift v.** sign || *ref* make a mistake; **ehe man es sich versieht** before you know it; **sich v.** (*genit*) expect || **Versehen** *n* (–s;–) mistake, slip; oversight; **aus V.** by mistake

versehentlich [fɛr'ze·əntlɪç] *adv* by mistake, erroneously, inadvertently

versehren [fɛr'zerən] *tr* injure

Versehrte [fɛr'zertə] §5 *mf* disabled person

versen'den §140 *tr* send, ship; **ins Ausland v.** export

versen'gen *tr* scorch; (*Haar*) singe

versen'ken *tr* sink; submerge; lower; (*Kabel*) lay; (*Schraube*) countersink; (naut) scuttle || *ref*—**sich v. in** (*acc*) become engrossed in

Versen'kung *f* (–;–en) sinking; (theat) trapdoor; **in der V. verschwinden** (fig) vanish into thin air

versessen [fɛr'zesən] *adj*—**v. auf** (*acc*) crazy about, obsessed with

verset'zen *tr* move, shift; (*Pflanze*) transplant; (*Schulkind*) promote; (*Beamte*) transfer; (*Schlag*) deal, give; (*verpfänden*) pawn; (*vermischen*) mix; (*Metall*) alloy; (*erwidern*) reply; (*vergeblich warten lassen*) (coll) stand up; (mus) transpose; **in Angst v.** terrify; **in Erstaunen v.** amaze; **in den Ruhestand v.** retire; **in Zorn v.** anger || *ref*—**v. Sie sich in meine Lage** put yourself in my place

Verset'zung *f* (–;–en) moving, shifting; transplanting; transfer; mixing; alloying; (educ) promotion

Verset'zungszeichen *n* (mus) accidental

verseuchen [fɛr'zɔɪçən] *tr* infect, contaminate

Verseu'chung *f* (–;) infection; contamination

Vers'fuß *m* (pros) foot

versicherbar [fɛr'zɪçərbɑr] *adj* insurable

versichern [fɛr'zɪçərn] *tr* assure; assert, affirm; insure || *ref* (*genit*) assure oneself of

Versicherte [fɛr'zɪçərtə] §5 *mf* insured

Versi'cherung *f* (–;–en) assurance; affirmation; insurance

Versi'cherungsanstalt *f* insurance company

Versi'cherungsbeitrag *m* premium

Versi'cherungsfähig *adj* insurable

Versi'cherungsgesellschaft *f* insurance company

Versi'cherungsleistung *f* insurance benefit

Versi'cherungsmathematiker –**in** §6 *mf* actuary

Versi'cherungsnehmer –**in** §6 *mf* insured

versi'cherungspflichtig *adj* subject to mandatory insurance

Versi'cherungspolice *f*, **Versi'cherungsschein** *m* insurance policy

Versi'cherungsträger *m* underwriter

Versi'cherungszwang *m* compulsory insurance

versickern (**versik'kern**) *intr* (SEIN) seep out, trickle away

versie'geln *tr* seal (up); (jur) seal off

Versie'gelung *f* (–;) sealing (off)

versie'gen *intr* (SEIN) dry up

versil'bern *tr* silver-plate; (coll) sell

Versil'berung *f* (–;) silver-plating

versin'ken §143 *intr* (SEIN) (**in** *acc*) sink (into); (fig) (**in** *acc*) lapse (into)
versinnbildlichen [fɛr'zɪnbɪltlɪçən] *tr* symbolize
Version [vɛr'zjon] *f* (–;–en) version
versippt [fɛr'zɪpt] *adj* (**mit**) related (to)
versklaven [fɛr'sklɑvən] *tr* enslave
Vers'kunst *f* versification
Vers'macher –**in** §6 *mf* versifier
Vers'maß *n* meter
versoffen [fɛr'zɔfən] *adj* (coll) drunk
versohlen [fɛr'zolən] *tr* (coll) give (*s.o.*) a good licking
versöhnen [fɛr'zønən] *tr* (**mit**) reconcile (with) ‖ *ref* become reconciled
versöhnlich [fɛr'zønlɪç] *adj* conciliatory
Versöh'nung *f* (–;) reconciliation
Versöh'nungstag *m* Day of Atonement
versonnen [fɛr'zɔnən] *adj* wistful
versor'gen *tr* look after; provide for; (**mit**) supply (with), provide (with)
Versor'ger –**in** §6 *mf* provider, breadwinner
Versor'gung *f* (–;) providing, supplying; (*Unterhalt*) maintenance; (*Alters– und Validen–*) social security
Versor'gungsbetrieb *m* public utility
Versor'gungstruppen *pl* service troops
Versor'gungswege *pl* supply lines
verspan'nen *tr* guy, brace
verspäten [fɛr'ʃpetən] *ref* come late; (rr) be behind schedule
verspätet [fɛr'ʃpetət] *adj* belated, late
Verspä'tung *f* (–;–en) lateness, delay; **mit e–r Stunde V.** one hour behind schedule; **V. haben** be late
verspei'sen *tr* eat up
verspekulie'ren *tr* lose on a gamble ‖ *ref* lose all through speculation
versper'ren *tr* bar, block, obstruct; (*Tür*) lock
verspie'len *tr* lose, gamble away ‖ *intr* —**bei j–m v.** lose favor with s.o.
verspielt [fɛr'ʃpilt] *adj* playful; frivolous
versponnen [fɛr'ʃpɔnən] *adj*—**in Gedanken versponnen** lost in thought
verspot'ten *tr* mock, deride
Verspot'tung *f* (–;) mockery, derision
verspre'chen §64 *tr* promise ‖ *ref* make a mistake in speaking; **ich verspreche mir viel davon** I expect a lot from that ‖ **Versprechen** *n* (–s;–) promise; slip of the tongue
Verspre'chung *f* (–;–en) promise
verspren'gen *tr* scatter, disperse
Versprengte [fɛr'ʃprɛŋtə] §5 *mf* (mil) straggler
versprit'zen *tr* squirt, spatter
versprü'hen *tr* spray
verspü'ren *tr* feel, sense
verstaatlichen [fɛr'ʃtɑtlɪçən] *tr* nationalize
Verstaat'lichung *f* (–;) nationalization
verstädtern [fɛr'ʃtetərn] *tr* urbanize
Verstäd'terung *f* (–;) urbanization
Verstand' *m* (–[e]s;) understanding; intellect; intelligence, brains; (*Vernunft*) reason; (*Geist*) mind; senses; sense; **den V. verlieren** lose one's

mind; **gesunder V.** common sense; **klarer V.** clear head; **nicht bei V. sein** be out of one's mind
Verstan'deskraft *f* intellectual power
verstan'desmäßig *adj* rational
Verstan'desmensch *m* matter-of-fact person
verstän'dig *adj* intelligent; sensible, reasonable; wise
verständigen [fɛr'ʃtɛndɪgən] *tr* (**von**) inform (about), notify (of) ‖ *ref*— **sich v. mit** make oneself understood to; come to an understanding with
Verstän'digung *f* (–;) understanding; information; communication; (telp) quality of reception
verständlich [fɛr'ʃtɛntlɪç] *adj* understandable, intelligible; **sich v. machen** make oneself understood
Verständnis [fɛr'ʃtɛntnɪs] *n* (–ses;–se) (**für**) understanding (of), appreciation (for)
verständ'nislos *adj* uncomprehending
verständ'nisinnig *adj* with deep mutual understanding; (*Blick*) knowing
verständ'nisvoll *adj* understanding; appreciative; (*Blick*) knowing
verstär'ken *tr* strengthen; (*steigern*) intensify; (elec) boost; (mil) reinforce; (rad) amplify
Verstär'ker *m* (–s;–) (rad) amplifier
Verstär'kung *f* (–;–en) strengthening; intensification; (mil) reinforcement; (rad) amplification
verstatten [fɛr'ʃtatən] *tr* permit
verstau'ben *intr* (SEIN) get dusty
verstäu'ben *intr* atomize
verstaubt [fɛr'ʃtaupt] *adj* dusty; (fig) antiquated
verstau'chen *tr* sprain
Verstau'chung *f* (–;–en) sprain
verstau'en *tr* stow away
Versteck [fɛr'ʃtɛk] *m* (–[e]s;–e) hiding place; hideout; **V. spielen** play hide-and-seek
verstecken (**verstek'ken**) *tr* & *ref* hide
versteckt [fɛr'ʃtɛkt] *adj* hidden, veiled; (*Absicht*) ulterior
verste'hen §146 *tr* understand, see; make out; realize; (*Sprache*) know; **e–n Spaß v.** take a joke; **ich verstehe es zu** (*inf*) I know how to (*inf*); **falsch v.** misunderstand; **verstanden?** get it?; **v. Sie mich recht!** don't get me wrong!; **was v. Sie unter** (*dat*)? what do you mean by? ‖ *ref*—(**das**) **versteht sich!** that's understood!; **das versteht sich von selbst!** that goes without saying; **sich gut v. mit** get along well with; **sich v. auf** (*acc*) be skilled in; **sich zu etw v.** (*sich zu etw entschließen*) bring oneself to do s.th.; (*in etw einwilligen*) agree to s.th. ‖ *recip* understand each other
verstei'fen *tr* stiffen; strut, brace, reinforce ‖ *ref* stiffen; **sich v. auf** (*acc*) insist on
verstei'gen §148 *ref* lose one's way in the mountain; **sich dazu v., daß** go so far as to (*inf*)
Verstei'gerer *m* (–s;–) auctioneer
verstei'gern *tr* auction off

Verstei'gerung *f* (-;-en) auction
verstei'nern *intr* (SEIN) become petrified; (fig) be petrified
verstell'bar *adj* adjustable
verstel'len *tr* (*regulieren*) adjust; (*versperren*) block; (*Stimme, usw.*) disguise; (*Weiche*) throw; (*Verkehrsampel*) switch; (*Zeiger e-r Uhr*) move; misplace; **j-m den Weg v.** block s.o.'s way || *ref* put on an act
Verstel'lung *f* (-;-en) adjusting; disguise
versteu'ern *tr* pay taxes on
Versteu'erung *f* (-;) paying of taxes
verstiegen [fɛr'ʃtigən] *adj* (*Idee, Plan*) extravagant, fantastic
verstim'men *tr* put out of tune; (fig) put out of humor
verstimmt [fɛr'ʃtɪmt] *adj* out of tune; (*Magen*) upset; **v. über** (*acc*) upset over
Verstim'mung *f* (-;) bad humor; (*zwischen zweien*) bad feeling, bad blood
verstockt [fɛr'ʃtɔkt] *adj* stubborn; (*Verbrecher*) hardened; (eccl) impenitent
Verstockt'heit *f* (-;) stubbornness; (eccl) impenitence
verstohlen [fɛr'ʃtolən] *adj* furtive
verstop'fen *tr* stop up, clog; (*Straße*) block, jam; (*Leib*) constipate
Verstop'fung *f* (-;) stopping up, clogging; congestion; (pathol) constipation
verstorben [fɛr'ʃtɔrbən] *adj* late, deceased || **Verstorbene** §5 *mf* deceased
verstört [fɛr'ʃtørt] *adj* shaken, bewildered, distracted
Verstört'heit *f* (-;) bewilderment
Verstoß' *m* (**gegen**) violation (of), offense (against)
versto'ßen §150 *tr* disown || *intr*—**v. gegen** violate, break
verstre'ben *tr* prop, brace
verstrei'chen §85 *tr* (*Butter*) spread; (*Risse*) plaster up || *intr* (SEIN) pass, elapse; (*Gelegenheit*) slip by; (*Frist*) expire
verstreu'en *tr* scatter, disperse, strew
verstricken (**verstrik'ken**) *tr* use up in knitting; (fig) involve, **entangle** || *ref* get entangled
verstümmeln [fɛr'ʃtʏməln] *tr* mutilate; (*Funkspruch*) garble
Verstüm'melung *f* (-;-en) mutilation; (rad) garbling
verstummen [fɛr'ʃtumən] *intr* (SEIN) become silent; (*vor Erstaunen*) be dumbstruck; (*Geräusch*) cease
Versuch [fɛr'zux] *m* (-[e]s;-e) try, attempt; (*Probe*) test, trial; (*wissenschaftlich*) experiment; **e-n V. machen mit** have a try at
versu'chen *tr* try; tempt; (*kosten*) taste
Versuchs'anstalt *f* research institute
Versuchs'ballon *m* (& fig) trial balloon
Versuchs'flieger *m* test pilot
Versuchs'flug *m* test flight
Versuchs'kaninchen *n* (fig) guinea pig
Versuchs'reihe *f* series of tests
versuchs'weise *adv* by way of a test; on approval
Versu'chung *f* (-;-en) temptation

versumpfen [fɛr'zumpfən] *intr* (SEIN) become marshy; (coll) go to the dogs
versün'digen *ref* (**an** *dat*) sin (against)
versunken [fɛr'zuŋkən] *adj* sunk; **v. in** (*acc*) (fig) lost in
versü'ßen *tr* sweeten
verta'gen *tr* & *ref* (**auf** *acc*) adjourn (till), recess (till)
Verta'gung *f* (-;-en) adjournment
vertändeln [fɛr'tɛndəln] *tr* trifle away
vertäuen [fɛr'tɔɪ-ən] *tr* (naut) moor
vertau'schen *tr* (**gegen**) exchange (for)
Vertau'schung *f* (-;-en) exchange
verteidigen [fɛr'taɪdɪgən] *tr* defend
Vertei'diger **-in** §6 *mf* defender; (*Befürworter*) advocate; (jur) counsel for the defense || *m* (fb) back
Vertei'digung *f* (-;-en) defense
Vertei'digungsbündnis *n* defensive alliance
Vertei'digungsminister *m* secretary of defense
Vertei'digungsministerium *n* department of defense
Vertei'digungsschrift *f* written defense
Vertei'digungsstellung *f* defensive position
vertei'len *tr* distribute; (*zuteilen*) allot; (*über e-e große Fläche*) scatter; (*steuerlich*) spread out; (*Rollen*) (theat) cast || *ref* spread out
Vertei'ler *m* (-s;-) distributer; (*Anschriftenliste*) mailing list; (*von Durchschlägen*) distribution; (aut) distributor
Vertei'lung *f* (-;-en) distribution; allotment; (theat) casting
verteuern [fɛr'tɔɪ-ərn] *tr* raise the price of
verteufelt [fɛr'tɔɪfəlt] *adj* devilish; a devil of a
vertiefen [fɛr'tifən] *tr* make deeper; (fig) deepen || *ref*—**sich v. in** (*acc*) become absorbed in
Vertie'fung *f* (-;-en) deepening; (*Höhlung*) hollow, depression; (*Nische*) niche; (*Loch*) hole; (fig) absorption
vertiert [fɛr'tirt] *adj* bestial
vertikal [vɛrtɪ'kal] *adj* vertical || **Vertikale** *f* (-;-n) vertical
vertil'gen *tr* exterminate, eradicate; (*aufessen*) (coll) eat, polish off
Vertil'gung *f* (-;) extermination
vertip'pen *tr* type incorrectly || *ref* make a typing error
verto'nen *tr* set to music
Verto'nung *f* (-;-en) musical arrangement
vertrackt [fɛr'trakt] *adj* (coll) odd, strange; (coll) blooming
Vertrag [fɛr'trak] *m* (-[e]s;̈-e) contract, agreement; (dipl) treaty
vertra'gen §132 *tr* stand, take; tolerate || *recip* agree, be compatible; (*Farben*) harmonize; (*Personen*) get along
vertrag'lich *adj* contractual || *adv* by contract, as stipulated; **sich v. verpflichten zu** (*inf*) contract to (*inf*)
verträglich [fɛr'trɛklɪç] *adj* sociable, personable; (*Speise*) digestible
Vertrags'bruch *m* breach of contract
vertragsbrüchig [fɛr'traksbrʏçɪç] *adj* **—v. werden** break a contract

vertrags'gemäß *adj* contractual

vertrags'widrig *adj* contrary to the terms of a contract or treaty

vertrau'en *intr* (*dat*) trust; **v. auf** (*acc*) trust in, have confidence in ‖ **Vertrauen** *n* (**-s;**) trust, confidence; **ganz im V.** just between you and me; **im V.** confidentially

vertrau'enerweckend *adj* inspiring confidence

Vertrau'ensbruch *m* breach of trust

Vertrau'ens·mann *m* (**-[e]s;-er** & **-leute**) confidential agent; (*Vertrauter*) confidant; (*Sprecher*) spokesman; (*Gewährsmann*) informant

Vertrau'ensposten *m*, **Vertrau'ensstellung** *f* position of trust

vertrau'ensvoll *adj* confident; trusting

Vertrau'ensvotum *n* vote of confidence

vertrau'enswürdig *adj* trustworthy

vertrauern [fɛr'trau·ərn] *tr* spend in mourning

vertraulich [fɛr'traulıç] *adj* confidential; intimate

Vertrau'lichkeit *f* (**-;-en**) intimacy, familiarity; **sich** [*dat*] **Vertraulichkeiten herausnehmen** take liberties

verträu'men *tr* dream away

verträumt [fɛr'trɔımt] *adj* dreamy

vertraut [fɛr'traut]*adj* familiar; friendly, intimate ‖ **Vertraute** §5 *mf* intimate friend ‖ *m* confidant ‖ *f* confidante

Vertraut'heit *f* (**-;**) familiarity

vertrei'ben §62 *tr* drive away, expel; (*aus dem Hause*) chase out; (*aus dem Lande*) banish; (*Ware*) sell, market; (*Zeit*) pass, kill

Vertrei'bung *f* (**-;**) expulsion

vertre'ten §152 *tr* represent; substitute for; (*Ansicht, usw.*) advocate ‖ *ref* —**sich** [*dat*] **den Fuß v.** sprain one's ankle; **sich** [*dat*] **die Beine v.** (coll) stretch one's legs

Vertre'ter **-in** §6 *mf* representative; substitute; (*Bevollmächtigte*) proxy; (*im Amt*) deputy; (*Fürsprecher*) advocate; (com) agent

Vertre'tung *f* (**-;-en**) representation; substitution; (com) agency; (pol) mission; **in V.** by proxy; **in V.** (*genit*) signed for

Vertrieb' *m* (**-[e]s;-e**) sale, turnover; retail trade; sales department

Vertriebs'abkommen *n* franchise agreement

Vertriebs'abteilung *f* sales department

Vertriebs'kosten *pl* distribution costs

Vertriebs'leiter **-in** §6 *mf* sales manager

Vertriebs'recht *n* franchise

vertrin'ken §143 *tr* drink up

vertrock'nen *intr* (SEIN) dry up

vertrödeln [fɛr'trødəln] *tr* fritter away

vertrö'sten *tr* string along; **auf später v.** put off till later

vertun' §154 *tr* waste ‖ *ref* (coll) make a mistake

vertu'schen *tr* hush up

verübeln [fɛr'ybəln] *tr* take (*s.th.*) the wrong way; **j-m etw v.** blame s.o. for s.th.

verü'ben *tr* commit, perpetrate

verul'ken *tr* (coll) kid

verunehren [fɛr'unerən] *tr* dishonor

veruneinigen [fɛr'unainıgən] *tr* disunite ‖ *recip* fall out, quarrel

verunglimpfen [fɛr'unglımpfən] *tr* slander, defame

verunglücken [fɛr'unglykən] *intr* (SEIN) have an accident; (coll) fail

Verunglückte [fɛr'unglyktə] §5 *mf* victim, casualty

verunreinigen [fɛr'unrainıgən] *tr* soil, dirty; (*Luft, Wasser*) pollute

Verun'reinigung *f* (**-;**) pollution

verunstalten [fɛr'un/taltən] *tr* disfigure, deface

veruntreuen [fɛr'untrɔı·ən] *tr* embezzle

Verun'treuung *f* (**-;**) embezzlement

verunzieren [fɛr'untsirən] *tr* mar

verursachen [fɛr'urzaxən] *tr* cause

verur'teilen *tr* condemn; sentence

Verur'teilung *f* (**-;-en**) condemnation; sentence

vervielfachen [fɛr'filfaxən] *tr* multiply ‖ *ref* increase considerably

vervielfältigen [fɛr'filfɛltıgən] *tr* multiply; duplicate; mimeograph; (*nachbilden*) reproduce

Verviel'fältigung *f* (**-;-en**) duplication; mimeographing; reproduction; (phot) printing

Verviel'fältigungsapparat *m* duplicator

vervollkommnen [fɛr'fɔlkɔmnən] *tr* improve on, perfect

Vervoll'kommnung *f* (**-;**) improvement, perfection

vervollständigen [fɛr'fɔl/tɛndıgən] *tr* complete

Vervoll'ständigung *f* (**-;**) completion

verwach'sen *adj* overgrown; deformed; hunchbacked; **mit etw v. sein** (fig) be attached to s.th. ‖ *intr* (SEIN) grow together; become deformed; (*Wunde*) heal up; **zu e-r Einheit v.** form a whole

Verwach'sung *f* (**-;-en**) deformity

verwackelt [fɛr'vakəlt] *adj* (phot) blurred

verwah'ren *tr* keep; **v. vor** (*dat*) protect against ‖ *ref*—**sich v. gegen** protest against

verwahrlosen [fɛr'varlozən] *tr* neglect ‖ *intr* (SEIN) (*Gebäude*) deteriorate; (*Kinder*) run wild; (*Personen*) go to the dogs

verwahrlost [fɛr'varlost] *adj* uncared-for; (*Person*) unkempt; (*sittlich*) degenerate; (*Garten*) overgrown with weeds

Verwahr'losung *f* (**-;**) neglect

Verwah'rung *f* (**-;**) care, safekeeping, custody; (fig) protest; **etw in V. nehmen** take care of s.th.; **j-m in V. geben** entrust to s.o.'s care

verwaisen [fɛr'vaizən] *intr* (SEIN) become an orphan, be orphaned

verwaist [fɛr'vaist] *adj* orphaned; (fig) deserted

verwalten [fɛr'valtən] *tr* administer, manage

Verwal'ter **-in** §6 *mf* administrator, manager

Verwal'tung *f* (**-;-en**) administration, management

Verwal'tungsapparat *m* administrative machinery
Verwal'tungsbeamte *m* civil service worker; administrative official
Verwal'tungsdienst *m* civil service
Verwal'tungsrat *m* advisory board; (*e-r Aktiengesellschaft*) board of directors; (*e-s Instituts*) board of trustees
verwan'deln *tr* change, turn, convert; (*Strafe*) commute || *ref* change, turn
Verwand'lung *f* (-;-en) change, transformation; (jur) commutation
verwandt [fer'vant] *adj* (mit) related (to); (*Wissenschaften*) allied; (*Wörter*) cognate; (*Seelen*) kindred || Verwandte §5 *mf* relative, relation
Verwandt'schaft *f* (-;-en) relationship; relatives; (chem) affinity
verwandt'schaftlich *adj* kindred
Verwand'schaftsgrad *m* degree of relationship
verwanzt [fer'vantst] *adj* (coll) full of bugs, lousy
verwar'nen *tr* warn, caution
Verwar'nung *f* (-;-en) warning, caution
verwa'schen *adj* washed-out, faded; (*verschwommen*) vague, fuzzy
verwäs'sern *tr* dilute; (fig) water down
verwe'ben §94 *tr* interweave
verwe'chseln *tr* confuse, get (*various items*) mixed up; (*Hüte, Mäntel*) take by mistake || Verwechseln *n* (-s;)—sie sehen sich zum V. ähnlich they are as alike as two peas
Verwechs'lung *f* (-;-en) mix-up
verwegen [fer'vegən] *adj* bold, daring
verwe'hen *tr* (*Blätter*) blow away; (*Spur*) cover up (with snow) || *intr* (SEIN) be blown in all directions; (*Spur*) be covered up; (*Worte*) drift away
verweh'ren *tr*—j-m etw v. refuse s.o. s.th.; prevent s.o. from getting s.th.
Verwe'hung *f* (-;-en) (snow)drift
verweichlichen [fer'vaiçliçən] *tr* make effeminate; (*Kind*) coddle || *ref* & *intr* become effeminate; grow soft
verweichlicht [fer'vaiçliçt] *adj* effeminate; soft, flabby
Verweich'lichung *f* (-;) effeminacy
verwei'gern *tr* refuse, deny, turn down
Verwei'gerung *f* (-;-en) refusal
verweilen [fer'vailən] *intr* linger, tarry; (fig) dwell
verweint [fer'vaint] *adj* red with tears
Verweis [fer'vais] *m* (-es;-e) reprimand, rebuke; (*Hinweis*) reference
verwei'sen §118 *tr* banish; (*Schüler*) expel; j-m etw v. reprimand s.o. for s.th.; j-n an j-n v. refer s.o. to s.o.; j-n auf etw v. refer s.o. to s.th.
Verwei'sung *f* (-;-en) banishment; expulsion; (an *acc*) referral (to); (auf *acc*) reference (to)
verwel'ken *intr* (SEIN) wither, wilt
verweltlichen [fer'veltliçən] *tr* secularize
verwendbar [fer'ventbar] *adj* applicable; available; usable
Verwend'barkeit *f* (-;) availability; usefulness

verwen'den §140 *tr* use, employ; (auf *acc*, für) apply (to); Zeit und Mühe v. auf (*acc*) spend time and effort on || *ref*—sich bei j-m v. für intercede with s.o. for
Verwen'dung *f* (-;-en) use, employment; application; keine V. haben für have no use for; vielseitige V. versatility
verwen'dungsfähig *adj* usable
verwer'fen §160 *tr* reject; (*Plan*) discard; (*Berufung*) turn down; (*Klage*) dismiss; (*Urteil*) overrule || *ref* (*Holz*) warp; (geol) fault
verwerf'lich *adj* objectionable
Verwer'fung *f* (-;-en) rejection; warping; (geol) fault
verwer'ten *tr* utilize
Verwer'tung *f* (-;-en) utilization
verwesen [fer'vezən] *intr* (SEIN) rot
verweslich [fer'vezliç] *adj* perishable
Verwe'sung *f* (-;) decay
verwet'ten *tr* lose (*in betting*)
verwich'sen *tr* (coll) clobber
verwickeln (verwik'keln) *tr* snarl, entangle; complicate; (fig) involve || *ref*—sich v. in (*acc*) get entangled in; (fig) get involved in
Verwick'lung *f* (-;-en) snarl, tangle; involvement; complexity; complication
verwil'dern *intr* become overgrown; (*Person*) become depraved; (*Kind*) run wild, go wild
verwildert [fer'vildərt] *adj* wild, savage; weed-grown
verwin'den §59 *tr* get over; (*Verlust*) recover from
verwir'ken *tr* forfeit; (*Strafe*) incur || *ref*—sich [*dat*] j-s Gunst v. lose favor with s.o.
verwirklichen [fer'virkliçən] *tr* realize, make come true || *ref* come true
Verwirk'lichung *f* (-;) realization
Verwir'kung *f* (-;-en) forfeiture
verwirren [fer'virən] *tr* throw into disorder; (*Haar*) muss up; confuse
verwirrt [fer'virt] *adj* confused
Verwir'rung *f* (-;-en) confusion; in V. geraten become confused
verwirt'schaften *tr* squander
verwi'schen *tr* wipe out; (*teilweise*) blur; (*verschmieren*) smear; (*Spuren*) cover || *ref* become blurred
verwit'tern *intr* (SEIN) become weather-beaten; (*zerfallen*) crumble away
verwittert [fer'vitərt] *adj* weather-beaten
verwitwet [fer'vitvət] *adj* widowed
verwöhnen [fer'vønən] *tr* pamper, spoil
verworfen [fer'vorfən] *adj* depraved
Verwor'fenheit *f* (-;) depravity
verworren [fer'vorən] *adj* confused
verwundbar [fer'vuntbar] *adj* vulnerable
verwun'den *tr* wound
verwunderlich [fer'vundərliç] *adj* remarkable, astonishing
verwun'dern *tr* astonish || *ref* (über *acc*) be astonished (at), wonder (at)
Verwun'derung *f* (-;) astonishment; j-n in V. setzen astonish s.o.
verwundet [fer'vundət] *adj* wounded

|| **Verwundete** §5 *mf* wounded person
verwunschen [fɛr'vʊnʃən] *adj* enchanted
verwün'schen *tr* damn, curse; (*in Märchen*) bewitch, put a curse on
verwünscht [fɛr'vʏnʃt] *adj* confounded, darn || *interj* darn it!
Verwün'schung *f* (-;-en) curse
verwurzelt [fɛr'vʊrtsəlt] *adj* deeply rooted
verwüsten [fɛr'vystən] *tr* devastate
Verwü'stung *f* (-;-en) devastation
verzagen [fɛr'tsagən] *intr* (SEIN) lose heart, despair; **v. an** (*dat*) give up on
verzagt [fɛr'tsakt] *adj* despondent
Verzagt'heit *f* (-;) despondency
verzäh'len *ref* miscount
verzärteln [fɛr'tsɛrtəln] *tr* pamper
verzau'bern *tr* bewitch, charm; **v. in** (*acc*) change into
Verzehr [fɛr'tser] *m* (-[e]s;) consumption
verzeh'ren *tr* consume; (*Geld*) spend; (*Mahlzeit*) eat || *ref* (**in** *dat*, **vor** *dat*) pine away (with); (**nach**) yearn (for)
verzeh'rend *adj* (*Blick*) longing; (*Fieber*) wasting; (*Leidenschaft*) burning
Verzeh'rung *f* (-;) consumption
verzeich'nen *tr* draw wrong; make a list of; register; catalogue; (opt) distort
Verzeichnis [fɛr'tsaiçnɪs] *n* (-ses;-se) list; catalogue; (*im Buch*) index; (*Inventar*) inventory; (*Tabelle*) table; (telp) directory
verzeihen [fɛr'tsai·ən] §81 *tr* forgive, pardon (*s.th.*); condone || *intr* (*dat*) forgive, pardon (*s.o.*)
verzeihlich [fɛr'tsailiç] *adj* pardonable
Verzei'hung *f* (-;) pardon
verzer'ren *tr* distort; contort
Verzer'rung *f* (-;-en) distortion; contortion; grimace
verzetteln [fɛr'tsetəln] *tr* fritter away; catalogue || *ref* spread oneself too thin
Verzicht [fɛr'tsɪçt] *m* (-[e]s;) renunciation; **V. leisten auf** (*acc*) waive
verzichten [fɛr'tsɪçtən] *intr*—**v. auf** (*acc*) do without; (*verabsäumen*) pass up; (*aufgeben*) give up, renounce; (*Rechte*) waive
verzieh [fɛr'tsi] *pret* of **verzeihen**
verzie'hen §163 *tr* distort; (*Kind*) spoil; **den Mund v.** make a face; **ohne e–e Miene zu v.** without batting an eye || *ref* disappear; (*Schmerz*) go away; (*Menge, Wolken*) disperse; (*Holz*) warp; (*durch Druck*) buckle; (coll) sneak off
verzie'ren *tr* decorate
Verzie'rung *f* (-;-en) decoration; (*Schmuck*) ornament
verzinsen [fɛr'tsɪnzən] *tr* pay interest on; **e–e Summe zu 6% v.** pay 6% interest on a sum || *ref* yield interest; **sich mit 6% v.** yield 6% interest
verzinslich [fɛr'tsɪnsliç] *adj* bearing interest || *adv*—**v. anlegen** put out at interest
Verzin'sung *f* (-;) interest
verzog [fɛr'tsok] *pret* of **verziehen**

verzogen [fɛr'tsogən] *adj* distorted; (*Kind*) spoiled; (*Holz*) warped
verzö'gern *tr* delay; put off, postpone || *ref* be late
Verzö'gerung *f* (-;-en) delay; postponement
verzollen [fɛr'tsɔlən] *tr* pay duty on; (naut) clear; **haben Sie etw zu v.?** do you have anything to declare?
verzückt [fɛr'tsʏkt] *adj* ecstatic
Verzückung [fɛr'tsʏkuŋ] *f* (-;) ecstasy
Verzug' *m* (-[e]s;) delay; (*in der Leistung*) default; **in V. geraten mit** fall behind in; **ohne V.** without delay
verzwei'feln *intr* (HABEN & SEIN) (**an** *dat*) despair (of) || **Verzweifeln** *n*—**es ist zum V.** it's enough to drive one to despair
verzweifelt [fɛr'tsvaifəlt] *adj* desperate
Verzweif'lung *f* (-;) despair
verzweigen [fɛr'tsvaigən] *ref* branch out
verzweigt [fɛr'tsvaikt] *adj* having many branches; (fig) complex
verzwickt [fɛr'tsvɪkt] *adj* (coll) tricky, ticklish
Vestibül [vɛstɪ'byl] *n* (-s;-e) vestibule; (theat) lobby
Veteran [vete'ran] *m* (-en;-en) veteran, ex-serviceman
Veterinär –**in** [veterɪ'ner(ɪn)] §8 *mf* veterinarian
Veto ['veto] *n* (-s;-s) veto
Vetter ['fɛtər] *m* (-s;-) cousin
Vet'ternwirtschaft *f* nepotism
Vexierbild [vɛ'ksirbɪlt] *n* picture puzzle
vexieren [vɛ'ksirən] *tr* tease; pester
V-förmig ['fauførmɪç] *adj* V-shaped
vibrieren [vɪ'brirən] *intr* vibrate
Vieh [fi] (-[e]s;) livestock; cattle; animal, beast
Vieh'bestand *m* livestock
Vieh'bremse *f* horsefly
viehisch ['fi·iʃ] *adj* brutal
Vieh'tränke *f* water hole
Vieh'wagen *m* (rr) cattle car
Vieh'weide *f* cow pasture
Vieh'zucht *f* cattle breeding
Vieh'züchter –**in** §6 *mf* rancher
viel [fil] *adj* much; many; a lot of || *adv* much; a lot || *pron* much; many
viel'beschäftigt *adj* very busy
viel'deutig *adj* ambiguous
Viel'eck *n* polygon
vielerlei ['filər'lai] *invar adj* many kinds of
viel'fach *adj* multiple; manifold || *adv* (coll) often
Vielfach– *comb.fm.* multiple
viel'fältig *adj* manifold, various
Viel'fältigkeit *f* (-;) multiplicity; variety
vielleicht' *adv* maybe, perhaps
vielmalig ['filmaliç] *adj* oft repeated
vielmals ['filmals] *adv* frequently; **danke v.!** many thanks!
vielmehr' *adv* rather, on the contrary
viel'sagend *adj* suggestive
viel'seitig *adj* many-sided, versatile
vielstufig ['filʃtufiç] *adj* multistage
viel'teilig *adj* of many parts
viel'versprechend *adj* very promising

vier [fir] *adj* four; **unter vier Augen** confidentially || *pron* four; **auf allen vieren** on all fours || **Vier** *f* (-;-en) four

vier'beinig *adj* four-legged

Vier'eck *n* quadrangle

vier'eckig *adj* quadrangular

viererlei ['firər'laɪ] *invar adj* four different kinds of

vier'fach, vier'fältig *adv* fourfold, quadruple

Vierfüßer ['firfysər] *m* (-s;-) quadruped

vierhändig ['firhɛndɪç] *adv*—v. spielen (mus) play a duet

Vierlinge ['firlɪŋə] *pl* quadruplets

vier'mal *adv* four times

vierschrötig ['firʃrøtɪç] *adj* stocky

vierstrahlig ['firʃtrɑlɪç] *adj* four-engine (jet)

viert [firt] *pron*—zu v. in fours; wir gehen zu v. the four of us are going

Viertakter ['firtaktər] *m* (-s;-), **Viertaktmotor** ['firtaktmotər] *m* four-cycle engine

Vierte ['firtə] §9 *adj* & *pron* fourth

vier'teilen *tr* quarter

Viertel ['fɪrtəl] *n* (-s;-) quarter; fourth (*part*); (*Stadtteil*) quarter, section

Vierteljahr' *n* quarter (*of a year*)

vierteljäh'rig, vierteljähr'lich *adj* quarterly

vierteln ['fɪrtəln] *tr* quarter

Vier'telnote *f* (*mus*) quarter note

Viertelpfund' *n* quarter of a pound

Viertelstun'de *f* quarter of an hour

viertens ['fɪrtəns] *adv* fourthly

vier'zehn *invar adj* & *pron* fourteen || **Vierzehn** *f* (-;-en) fourteen

vier'zehnte §9 *adj* & *pron* fourteenth

Vier'zehntel *n* (-s;-) fourteenth (*part*)

vierzig ['fɪrtsɪç] *invar adj* & *pron* forty || **Vierzig** *f* (-;-en) forty

vierziger ['fɪrtsɪgər] *invar adj* of the forties; **die v. Jahre** the forties

vierzigste ['fɪrtsɪçstə] §9 *adj* & *pron* fortieth

Vikar [vɪ'kɑr] *m* (-s;-e) vicar

Vil·la ['vɪla] *f* (-;-len [lən]) villa

violett [vɪ·ɔ'let] *adj* violet

Violine [vɪ·ɔ'linə] *f* (-;-n) violin

Violin'schlüssel *m* treble clef

Viper ['vipər] *f* (-;-n) viper

viril [vɪ'ril] *adj* virile

virtuos [vɪrtu'os] *adj* masterly || **Virtuose** [vɪrtu'ozə] *m* (-n;-n), **Virtuosin** [vɪrtu'ozɪn] *f* (-;-nen) virtuoso

Vi·rus ['virʊs] *n* (-;-ren [rən]) virus

Visage [vɪ'zaʒə] *f* (-;-n) (coll) mug

Visier [vɪ'zir] *n* (-s;-e) visor; (*am Gewehr*) sight

visieren [vɪ'zirən] *tr* (*eichen*) gauge; (*Paß*) visa

Vision [vɪ'zjon] *f* (-;-en) vision

visionär [vɪzjɔ'ner] *adj* visionary || **Visionär** *m* (-s;-e) visionary

Visitation [vɪzita'tsjon] *f* (-;-en) inspection; search

Visite [vɪ'zitə] *f* (-;-n) formal call; **Visiten machen** (med) make the rounds

Visi'tenkarte *f* calling card

visuell [vɪzu'el] *adj* visual

Vi·sum ['vizum] *n* (-s;-sa [za]) visa

vital [vɪ'tal] *adj* energetic

Vitalität [vɪtalɪ'tet] *f* (-;) vitality

Vitamin [vɪta'min] *n* (-s;-e) vitamin

Vitamin'mangel *m* vitamin deficiency

Vitrine [vɪ'trinə] *f* (-;-n) showcase

Vize- [fitsə], [vitsə] *comb.fm.* vice-

Vi'zekönig *m* viceroy

Vlies [flis] *n* (-es;-e) fleece

Vogel ['fogəl] *m* (-s;⁻) bird; (coll) chap, bird; **den V. abschießen** (coll) bring down the house; **du hast e-n V.!** (coll) you're cuckoo!

Vo'gelbauer *n* birdcage

Vogelbeerbaum ['fogəlberbaum] *m* mountain ash

vo'gelfrei *adj* outlawed

Vo'gelfutter *n* birdseed

Vo'gelkunde *f* ornithology

Vo'gelmist *m* bird droppings

vögeln ['føgəln] *tr* & *intr* (vulg) screw

Vo'gelperspektive *f*, **Vo'gelschau** *f* bird's-eye view

Vo'gelpfeife *f* bird call

Vo'gelscheuche *f* scarecrow

Vo'gelstange *f* perch

Vogel-Strauß'-Politik *f* burying one's head in the sand; **V. betreiben** bury one's head in the sand

Vo'gelstrich *m*, **Vo'gelzug** *m* migration of birds

Vöglein ['føglaɪn] *n* (-s;-) little bird

Vogt [fokt] *m* (-[e]s;⁻e) (obs) steward; (obs) governor, prefect, magistrate

Vokabel [vɔ'kabəl] *f* (-;-n) vocabulary word

Vokal [vɔ'kal] *m* (-s;-e) vowel

Volk [fɔlk] *n* (-[e]s;⁻er) people, nation; lower classes; (*von Bienen*) swarm; (*von Rebhühnern*) covey

Völker- [fœlkər] *comb.fm.* international

Völ'kerbund *m* League of Nations

Völ'kerfriede *m* international peace

Völ'kerkunde *f* ethnology

Völ'kermord *m* genocide

Völ'kerrecht *n* international law

Völ'kerschaft *f* (-;-en) tribe

Völ'kerwanderung *f* barbarian invasions

volk'reich *adj* populous

Volks'abstimmung *f* plebiscite

Volks'aufwiegler *m* rabble rouser

Volks'ausdruck *m* household expression

Volks'befragung *f* public opinion poll

Volks'begehren *n* national referendum

Volks'bibliotek *f* free library

Volks'charakter *m* national character

Volks'deutsche §5 *mf* German national

Volks'dichter *m* popular poet

volks'eigen *adj* state-owned

Volks'entscheid *m* referendum

Volks'feind *m* public enemy

Volks'gunst *f* popularity

Volks'haufen *m* crowd, mob

Volks'herrschaft *f* democracy

Volks'hochschule *f* adult evening school

Volks'justiz *f* lynch law

Volks′küche f soup kitchen
Volks′kunde f folklore
Volks′lied n folksong
volks′mäßig adj popular
Volks′meinung f popular opinion
Volks′menge f populace, crowd of people
Volks′musik f popular music
Volks′partei f people's party
Volks′republik f people's republic
Volks′schule f grade school
Volks′sitte f national custom
Volks′sprache f vernacular
Volks′stamm m tribe; race
Volks′stimme f popular opinion
Volks′stimmung f mood of the people
Volks′tracht f national costume
Volkstum ['fɔlkstum] n (-s;) nationality
volkstümlich ['fɔlkstymlɪç] adj national; popular
Volks′verführer –in §6 mf demagogue
Volks′versammlung f public meeting
Volks′vertreter –in §6 mf representative
Volks′wirt m political economist
Volks′wirtschaft f national economy
Volks′wirtschaftslehre f (educ) political economy
Volks′wohl n public good
Volks′wohlfahrt f public welfare
Volks′zählung f census
voll [fɔl] adj full, filled; whole, entire; (Tageslicht) broad; (coll) drunk; aus dem vollen schöpfen have unlimited resources; j–n für v. ansehen (or nehmen) take s.o. seriously || adv fully, in full; v. und ganz fully
vollauf′ adv—das genügt v. that's quite enough; v. beschäftigt plenty busy; v. zu tun haben have plenty to do
Voll′beschäftigung f full employment
Voll′besitz m full possession
Voll′blut n, Voll′blutpferd n thoroughbred
vollblütig ['fɔlblytɪç] adj full-blooded
vollbrin′gen §65 tr achieve
vollbusig ['vɔlbuzɪç] adj big-breasted
Voll′dampf m full steam; mit V. (fig) at full blast, full speed
vollenden [fɔl'ɛndən] tr bring to a close, finish, complete; (vervollkommnen) perfect; er hat sein Leben vollendet (poet) he died
vollendet [fɔl'ɛndət] adj perfect
vollends ['fɔlents] adv completely
Vollen′dung f (-;) finishing, completing; (Vollkommenheit) perfection
Völlerei [fœlə'raɪ] f (-;) gluttony
voll′führen tr carry out, execute
voll′füllen tr fill up
Voll′gas n full throttle
Voll′gefühl n—im V. (genit) fully conscious of
Voll′genuß m full enjoyment
vollgepfropft ['fɔlgəpfrɔpft] adj jammed, packed
voll′gießen §76 tr fill up
völlig ['fœlɪç] adj full, complete
voll′jährig adj of age
Voll′jährigkeit f legal age, majority
vollkom′men, voll′kommen adj perfect || adv (coll) absolutely

Vollkom′menheit f (-;) perfection
Voll′kornbrot n whole-grain bread
Voll′kraft f full vigor, prime
voll′machen tr fill up; (coll) dirty
Voll′macht f full authority; (jur) power of attorney; in V. for ... (prefixed to the signature of another at end of letter)
Voll′matrose m able-bodied seaman
Voll′milch f whole milk
Voll′mond m full moon
Voll′pension f full board and lodging
voll′saftig adj juicy, succulent
voll′schenken tr fill up
voll′schlagen §132 ref—sich [dat] den Bauch v. (coll) stuff oneself
voll′schlank adj well filled out
Voll′sitzung f plenary session
Voll′spur f (rr) standard-gauge track
voll′ständig adj full; complete, entire || adv completely, quite
Voll′ständigkeit f (-;) completeness
voll′stopfen tr stuff, cram
vollstrecken (vollstrek′ken) tr (Urteil) carry out; (Testament) execute; ein Todesurteil an j–m v. execute s.o.
Vollstreckung (Vollstrek′kung) f. (-;) execution
voll′tanken tr (aut) fill up || intr (aut) fill it up
volltönend ['fɔltønənt] adj (Stimme) rich; (Satz) well-rounded
Voll′treffer m direct hit
Voll′versammlung f plenary session
Voll′waise f (full) orphan
voll′wertig adj of full value; complete, perfect
vollzählig ['fɔltselɪç] adj complete; sind wir v.? are we all here? || adv in full force
vollzie′hen §163 tr execute, carry out, effect; (Vertrag) ratify; (Ehe) consummate || ref take place
vollzie′hend adj executive
Vollzie′hung f, Vollzug′ m execution, carrying out
Vollzugs′ausschuß m executive committee
Volontär –in [vɔlɔn'ter(ɪn)] §8 mf volunteer; trainee
volontieren [vɔlɔn'tirən] intr work as a trainee
Volt [vɔlt] n (-[e]s;–) (elec) volt
Volu•men [vɔ'lumən] n (-s;– & –mina [mɪna]) (Band; Rauminhalt) volume
vom [fɔm] abbr von dem
von [fɔn] prep (dat) (beim Passiv) by; für den Genitiv) of; (räumlich, zeitlich) from; (über) about, of; von ... an from ... on; von Holz (made) of wood; von Kindheit auf from earliest childhood; von mir aus as far as I am concerned; von selbst automatically
voneinan′der adv from each other; of each other; apart
vonnöten [fɔn'nøtən] invar adj—v. sein be necessary
vonstatten [fɔn'ʃtatən] adv—gut v. gehen go well; v. gehen take place
vor [for] prep (dat) (örtlich) in front of, before; (zeitlich) before, prior to; (Abwehr) against, from; (wegen) of,

with, for; **etw vor sich haben** face s.th.; **heute vor acht Tagen** today a week ago; **vor sich gehen** take place, occur; **vor sich hin** to oneself || *prep* (*acc*) in front of

vorab' *adv* in advance

Vor'abend *m*—**am V.** (*genit*) on the eve of

Vor'ahnung *f* (coll) hunch, idea

voran' *adv* in front, out ahead || *interj* go ahead!, go on!

voran'gehen §82 *intr* (SEIN) go on ahead, take the lead; (fig) set an example; **die Arbeit geht gut voran** the work is coming along well

voran'kommen §99 *intr* (SEIN) make progress; **gut v.** come along well

Vor'anschlag *m* rough estimate

Vor'anzeige *f* preliminary announcement; (cin) preview of coming attractions

Vor'arbeit *f* preliminary work

vor'arbeiten *intr* do the work in advance; do the preliminary work

vorauf' *adv* ahead, in front

voraus' *adv* in front; (*dat*) ahead (of) || **vor'aus** *adv*—**im v.** in advance

Voraus'abteilung *f* (mil) vanguard

voraus'bedingen §142 *tr* stipulate beforehand

voraus'bestellen *tr* reserve

voraus'bestimmen *tr* predetermine

voraus'bezahlen *tr* pay in advance

voraus'eilen *intr* (SEIN) rush ahead

vorausgesetzt [fɔ'rausgəzetst] *adj*—**v., daß** provided that

Voraus'sage *f* prediction; prophecy; (*des Wetters*) forecast; (*Wink*) tip

voraus'sagen *tr* predict; prophesy; (*Wetter*) forecast

Voraus'sagung *f* var of **Voraussage**

voraus'schauen *intr* look ahead

voraus'schicken *tr* send ahead; (fig) mention beforehand

voraus'sehen §138 *tr* foresee

voraus'setzen *tr* presume, presuppose

Voraus'setzung *f* assumption; prerequisite; premise

Voraus'sicht *f* foresight

voraus'sichtlich *adj* probable, presumable || *adv* probably, presumably, the way it looks

Voraus'zahlung *f* advance payment

Vor'bau *m* (-[e]s;-ten) projection; balcony, porch

vor'bauen *tr* build out || *intr* (*dat*) take precautions against

vor'bedacht *adj* premeditated || **Vorbedacht** *m* (-[e]s;)—**mit V.** on purpose; **ohne V.** unintentionally

vor'bedeuten *tr* forebode

Vor'bedeutung *f* (-;-en) foreboding; omen, portent

Vor'bedingung *f* (-;-en) precondition

Vorbehalt ['forbəhalt] *m* (-[e]s;-e) reservation; proviso; **mit allem V. hinnehmen!** take it for what it's worth!; **mit** (*or* **unter**) **dem V., daß** with the proviso that; **stiller** (*or* **innerer**) **V.** mental reservation; **unter V. aller Rechte** all rights reserved

vor'behalten §90 *tr* reserve; **Änderungen v.!** subject to change without

notice || *ref*—**sich** [*dat*] **etw v.** reserve s.th. for oneself

vor'behaltlich *prep* (*genit*) subject to

vor'behaltlos *adj* unreserved, unconditional

vorbei' *adv* over, past, gone; **es ist drei Uhr v.** it's past three o'clock; **v. an** (*dat*) past, by; **v. ist v.** done is done; **v. können** be able to pass

vorbei'eilen *intr* (SEIN)—**an j-m v.** rush past s.o.

vorbei'fahren §71 *intr* (SEIN) drive by

vorbei'fliegen §57 *intr* (SEIN) fly past

vorbei'fließen §76 *intr* (SEIN) flow by

vorbei'gehen §82 *intr* (SEIN) pass; **an j-m v.** pass by s.o. || **Vorbeigehen** *n* —**im V.** in passing

vorbei'gelingen §142 *intr* (SEIN) fail

vorbei'kommen §99 *intr* (SEIN) pass by; (coll) stop in

vorbei'lassen §104 *tr* let pass

Vorbei'marsch *m* parade

vorbei'marschieren *intr* (SEIN) march by

Vor'bemerkung *f* (-;-en) preliminary remark; (parl) preamble

vorbenannt ['forbənant] *adj* aforementioned

vor'bereiten *tr* prepare || *ref* (**auf** *acc*, **für**) get ready (for)

vor'bereitend *adj* preparatory

Vor'bereitung *f* (-;-en) preparation

Vor'bericht *m* preliminary report

Vor'besprechung *f* (-;-en) preliminary discussion

vor'bestellen *tr* order in advance; (*Zimmer, usw.*) reserve

Vor'bestellung *f* (-;-en) advance order; reservation

vor'bestraft *adj* previously convicted

vor'beten *tr* keep repeating || *intr* lead in prayer

vor'beugen *ref* bend forward || *intr* (*dat*) prevent

vor'beugend *adj* preventive

Vor'beugung *f* (-;-en) prevention

Vor'beugungsmittel *n* preventive

Vor'bild *n* model; (*Beispiel*) example

vor'bildlich *adj* exemplary, model

Vor'bildung *f* (-;-en) educational background

Vor'bote *m* forerunner; (fig) harbinger

vor'bringen §65 *tr* bring forward, produce; (*Gründe*) give; (*Plan*) propose; (*Klagen*) prefer; (*Wunsch*) express

vor'buchstabieren *tr* spell out

Vor'bühne *f* apron, proscenium

vor'datieren *tr* antedate

vordem [for'dem] *adv* formerly

Vorder- [fordər] *comb.fm.* front, fore-

Vor'derachse *f* front axle

Vor'derarm *m* forearm

Vor'derbein *n* foreleg

vordere ['fordərə] §9 *adj* front

Vor'derfront *f* front; (fig) forefront

Vor'derfuß *m* front foot

Vor'dergrund *m* foreground

vor'derhand *adv* for the time being

vor'derlastig *adj* (aer) nose-heavy

Vor'derlauf *m* (hunt) foreleg

Vor'dermann *m* (-[e]s;-er) man in front; **j-n auf V. bringen** (coll) put s.o. straight; **V. halten** keep in line

Vor′derpfote *f* front paw
Vor′derrad *n* front wheel
Vor′derradantrieb *m* front-wheel drive
Vor′derreihe *f* front row; front rank
Vor′dersicht *f* front view
Vor′derseite *f* front side, front; *(e-r Münze)* obverse, heads
Vor′dersitz *m* front seat
vorderste [′fɔrdərstə] §9 *adj* farthest front
Vor′dersteven *m* (naut) stem
Vor′derteil *m & n* front section; (naut) prow
Vor′dertür *f* front door
Vor′derzahn *m* front tooth
Vor′derzimmer *n* front room
vor′drängen *tr & ref* press forward
vor′dringen §142 *intr* (SEIN) forge ahead, advance
vor′dringlich *adj* urgent
Vor′druck *m* printed form, blank
vor′ehelich *adj* premarital
vor′eilig *adj* hasty, rash
Vor′eiligkeit *f* (–;) haste, rashness
vor′eingenommen *adj* biased, prejudiced
Vor′eingenommenheit *f* (–;-en) bias, prejudice
Vor′eltern *pl* ancestors, forefathers
vor′enthalten §90 *tr*—**j-m etw v.** withhold s.th. from s.o.
Vor′entscheidung *f* (–;-en) preliminary decision
vor′erst *adv* first of all; for the time being, for the present
vorerwähnt [′forɛrvɛnt] *adj* aforesaid
Vorfahr [′forfar] *m* (-en;-en) forebear
vor′fahren §71 *intr* (SEIN) **(bei)** drive up (to)
Vor′fahrt *f*, **Vor′fahrt(s)recht** *n* right of way
Vor′fall *m* incident; event
vor′fallen §72 *intr* (SEIN) happen
Vor′feld *n* (aer) apron *(of airport)*; (mil) approaches
vor′finden §59 *tr* find there
Vor′freude *f* anticipation
Vor′frühling *m* early spring
vor′fühlen *intr*—**bei j-m v.** feel s.o. out, put out feelers to s.o.
Vorführdame [′forfyrdamə] *f* mannequin
vor′führen *tr* bring forward, produce; display, demonstrate; *(Kleider)* model; *(Film)* show; *(Stück)* (theat) present
Vor′führer –in §6 *mf* projectionist
Vor′führung *f* (–;-en) production; demonstration; showing; show, performance
Vor′gabe *f* points, handicap
Vor′gaberennen *n* handicap (race)
Vor′gabespiel *n* handicap
Vor′gang *m* event, incident, phenomenon; *(Verfahren)* process, procedure; *(Präzedenzfall)* precedent; *(in den Akten)* previous correspondence
Vor′gänger –in §6 *mf* predecessor
Vor′garten *m* front yard
vor′geben §80 *tr* pretend; give as an excuse; **j-m zehn Punkte v.** give s.o. ten points odds ‖ *intr*—**j-m v.** give

s.o. odds ‖ **Vorgeben** *n* (-s;–) pretext
Vor′gebirge *n* foothills; *(Kap)* cape
vorgeblich [′forgɛplɪç] *adj* ostensible
vorgefaßt [′forgəfast] *adj* preconceived
Vor′gefühl *n* inkling; **banges V.** misgivings; **im V. von** or *genit* in anticipation of
vor′gehen §82 *intr* (SEIN) advance; go first; act; take action, proceed; *(sich ereignen)* go on, happen; *(Uhr)* be fast; *(dat)* take precedence (over); **die Arbeit geht vor** work comes first; **was geht hier vor?** what's going on here? ‖ **Vorgehen** *n* (-s;) advance; action, proceeding; **gemeinschaftliches V.** concerted action
vorgelagert [′forgəlagərt] *adj* offshore
Vor′gelände *n* foreground
vorgenannt [′forgənant] *adj* aforementioned
Vor′gericht *n* appetizer
Vor′geschichte *f* previous history; *(Urgeschichte)* prehistory
vor′geschichtlich *adj* prehistoric
Vor′geschmack *m* foretaste
Vorgesetzte [′forgəzɛtstə] §5 *mf* superior; boss; (mil) senior officer
vor′gestern *adv* day before yesterday
vor′gestrig *adj* of the day before yesterday
vorgetäuscht [′forgətɔɪʃt] *adj* make-believe
vor′greifen §88 *intr* (dat) anticipate
Vor′griff *m* anticipation
vor′gucken *intr* (*Unterkleid*) show
vor′haben §89 *tr* have in mind, plan; intend to do; *(ausfragen)* question; *(schelten)* scold; *(Schürze)* (coll) have on ‖ **Vorhaben** *n* (-s;–) intention, plan; project
Vor′halle *f* entrance hall; lobby
vor′halten §90 *tr*—**j-m etw v.** hold s.th. in front of s.o.; (fig) reproach s.o. with s.th. ‖ *intr* last
Vor′haltung *f* (–;-en) reproach; **j-m Vorhaltungen machen über** (acc) reproach s.o. for
Vor′hand *f* (cards) forehand; (tennis) forehand stroke; **die V. haben** (cards) lead off
vorhanden [for′handən] *adj* present, at hand, available; (com) in stock; **v. sein** exist
Vorhan′densein *n* existence; presence
Vor′hang *m* (-[e]s;-̈e) curtain; (theat) (coll) curtain call; **Eiserner V.** iron curtain
Vorhängeschloß [′forhɛŋəʃlɔs] *n* padlock
Vor′hangstange *f* curtain rod
Vor′hangstoff *m* drapery material
Vor′haut *f* foreskin
Vor′hemd *n* dicky, shirt front
vor′her *adv* before, previously; *(im voraus)* in advance
vorher′bestellen *tr* reserve
vorher′bestimmen *tr* predetermine; (eccl) predestine
Vorher′bestimmung *f* predestination
vorher′gehend, vorherig [for′herɪç] *adj* preceding, previous; prior
Vor′herrschaft *f* predominance

vor'herrschen *intr* predominate, prevail

vor'herrschend *adj* predominant, prevailing

Vorher'sage *f* prediction; forecast

vorher'sagen *tr* predict, foretell; (*Wetter*) forecast

vorhin' *adv* a little while ago

vor'historisch *adj* prehistoric

Vor'hof *m* front yard; (anat) auricle

Vor'hut *f* (mil) vanguard

vorige ['fɔrɪgə] §9 *adj* previous, former; **voriges Jahr** last year

Vor'jahr *n* preceding year

vor'jährig *adj* last year's

Vor'kammer *f* (anat) auricle; (aut) precombustion chamber

Vor'kampf *m* (box) preliminary bout; (sport) heat

Vor'kämpfer –in §6 *mf* pioneer

Vorkehrung ['fɔrkeruŋ] *f* (–;–en) precaution; **Vorkehrungen treffen** take precautions

Vor'kenntnis *f* (von) basic knowledge (of); **Vorkenntnisse** rudiments, basics; **Vorkenntnisse nicht erforderlich** no previous experience necessary

vor'knöpfen *ref*—**sich** [*dat*] **j–n** v. (coll) chew s.o. out

Vor'kommando *n* (mil) advance party

vor'kommen §99 *intr* (SEIN) happen; (*Fall*) come up; (*als Besucher*) be admitted; (*scheinen*) seem, look; (*sich finden*) be found; (*zu Besuch*) call on || *ref*—**er kam sich** [*dat*] **dumm vor** he felt silly || *impers*—**es kommt dir nur so vor** you are just imagining it; **es kommt mir vor** it seems to me || **Vorkommen** *n* (–s;–) occurrence; (min) deposit

Vorkommnis ['fɔrkɔmnɪs] *n* (–ses;–se) event, occurrence

Vorkriegs– *comb.fm.* prewar

vor'laden §103 *tr* (jur) summon; (*unter Strafandrohung*) (jur) subpoena

Vor'ladung *f* (–;–en) (jur) summons; (*unter Strafandrohung*) (jur) subpoena

Vor'lage *f* submission, presentation; proposal; (*Muster*) pattern; bedside carpet; (fb) forward pass; (parl) bill

vor'lassen §104 *tr* let go ahead; (*Auto*) let pass; (*zulassen*) admit

Vor'lauf *m* (sport) qualifying heat

Vor'läufer –in §6 *mf* forerunner

vor'läufig *adj* preliminary; temporary || *adv* provisionally; temporarily, for the time being

vor'laut *adj* forward, fresh

Vor'leben *n* past life, former life

Vorlegebesteck ['fɔrlegəbəʃtek] *n* carving set

Vorlegegabel ['fɔrlegəgabəl] *f* carving fork

Vorlegelöffel ['fɔrlegəlœfəl] *m* serving spoon

Vorlegemesser ['fɔrlegəmesər] *n* carving knife

vor'legen *tr* put forward; propose; (*Ausweis, Paß*) show; (*Essen*) serve; (*zur Prüfung, usw.*) submit, present; **den Ball v.** (fb) pass the ball; **ein scharfes Tempo v.** (coll) speed it up;

j–m e–e Frage v. ask s.o. a question || *ref* lean forward

Ver'leger *m* (–s;–) throw rug

Vorlegeschloß ['fɔrlegəʃlɔs] *n* padlock

vor'lesen §107 *tr*—**j–m etw v.** read s.th. to s.o.

Vor'lesung *f* (–;–en) reading; lecture; **e–e V. halten über** (*acc*) give a lecture on

Vor'lesungsverzeichnis *n* university catalogue

vor'letzte §9 *adj* second last; (gram) penultimate

Vor'liebe *f* preference

vorliebnehmen [for'lipnemən] §116 *intr* take pot luck; **v. mit** put up with

vor'liegen §108 *intr* be present; exist; be under consideration; **dem Richter v.** be up before the judge; **heute liegt nichts vor** there's nothing doing today; **mir liegt e–e Beschwerde vor** I have a complaint here; **was liegt gegen ihn vor?** what is the charge against him?

vor'liegend *adj* present, at hand

vor'lügen §111 *tr*—**j–m etw v. über** (*acc*) tell s.o. lies about

vor'machen *tr*—**du kannst mir doch nichts v.** you can't put anything over on me; **j–m etw v.** show s.o. how to do s.th. || *ref*—**er läßt sich** [*dat*] **nichts v.** he's nobody's fool; **sich** [*dat*] **selbst etw v.** fool oneself

Vor'macht *f* leading power; supremacy

Vor'machtstellung *f* (position of) supremacy

vormalig ['fɔrmalɪç] *adj* former

vormals ['fɔrmals] *adv* formerly

Vor'marsch *m* advance

vor'merken *tr* note down; reserve; **sich v. lassen für** put in for

Vor'mittag *m* forenoon, morning

vor'mittags *adv* in the forenoon

Vor'mund *m* guardian

Vor'mundschaft *f* (–;–en) guardianship

vor'mundschaftlich *adj* guardian's

Vor'mundschaftsgericht *n* orphans' court

vorn [fɔrn] *adv* in front; ahead; **ganz v.** all the way up front; **nach v.** forward; **nach v. heraus wohnen** live in the front part of the house; **nach v. liegen** face the front; **von v.** from the front; **von v. anfangen** begin at the beginning

Vor'nahme *f* undertaking

Vor'name *m* first name

vorne ['fɔrnə] *adv* (coll) var of **vorn**

vornehm ['fɔrnem] *adj* distinguished, high-class; **vornehme Welt** high society; **vornehmste Aufgabe** principal task || *adv*—**v. tun** put on airs

vor'nehmen §116 *tr* (*umbinden*) put on; undertake, take up; (*Änderungen*) make; **wieder v.** resume || *ref*—**sich** [*dat*] **ein Buch v.** take up a book; **sich** [*dat*] **etw v.** decide upon s.th.; **sich** [*dat*] **j–n v.** take s.o. to task; **sich** [*dat*] **v. zu** (*inf*) make up one's mind to (*inf*); **sich** [*dat*] **zuviel v.** bite off more than one can chew

Vor'nehmheit *f* (–;) distinction, high rank; distinguished bearing

vor'nehmlich *adv* especially
vor'neigen *ref* bend forward
vorn'herein *adv*—**von v.** from the first
vornweg ['fɔrnvɛk], (fɔrn'vɛk] *adv*— **er ist weit v.** he is way out in front; **mit dem Kopf v.** head first; **mit dem Mund v. sein** be fresh
Vor'ort *m* suburb
Vorort– *comb.fm.* suburban
Vor'ortbahn *f* (rr) suburban line
Vor'ortzug *m* commuter train
Vor'platz *m* front yard; (*Diele*) entrance hall; (*Vorfeld*) (aer) apron
Vor'posten *m* (mil) outpost
Vor'rang *m* precedence; priority; preeminence; **den V. vor j–m haben** have precedence over s.o.
Vor'rat *m* (–[e]s;⁀e) (**an** *dat*) stock (of), supply (of); **auf V. kaufen** buy in quantity; **e–n V. anlegen an** (*dat*) stock
vorrätig ['fɔrrɛtɪç] *adj* in stock
Vor'ratskammer *f* pantry, storeroom
Vor'ratsraum *m* storeroom
Vor'ratsschrank *m* pantry
Vor'raum *m* anteroom
vor'rechnen *tr*—**j–m etw v.** figure out s.th. for s.o.; **j–m seine Fehler v.** enumerate s.o.'s mistakes to s.o.
Vor'recht *n* privilege, prerogative
Vor'rede *f* preface, introduction
vor'reden *tr*—**j–m etw v.** try to make s.o. believe s.th.
Vor'redner –in §6 *mf* previous speaker
Vor'richtung *f* (–;–en) preparation; (*Gerät*) device, appliance, mechanism; (mach) fixture
vor'rücken *tr* move forward ‖ *intr* (SEIN) (*Truppen*) advance; (*Polizei*) move in; (*im Dienst*) be promoted
Vor'runde *f* (sport) play-offs
vors [fors] *abbr* **vor das**
vor'sagen *tr*—**j–m etw v.** recite s.th. to s.o. ‖ *intr* (*dat*) prompt
Vor'sager –in §6 *mf* prompter
Vor'satz *m* purpose, intention; (jur) premeditation; **den V. fassen zu** (*inf*) make up one's mind to (*inf*); **mit V.** on purpose; **seinen V. ausführen** gain one's ends
Vor'satzblatt *n* (bb) end paper
Vor'satzgerät *n* adapter
vorsätzlich ['forzɛtslɪç] *adj* deliberate; (*Mord*) premeditated
Vor'schau *f* (cin) preview
vor'schieben §130 *tr* push forward; offer as an excuse; (fig) plead; **den Riegel v.** (*dat*) (fig) prevent; **Truppen v.** move troops forward
vor'schießen §76 *tr* (*Geld*) (coll) advance ‖ *intr* (SEIN) dart ahead
Vor'schiff *n* (naut) forecastle
Vor'schlag *m* proposal; (*Angebot*) offer; (*Anregung*) suggestion; (*Empfehlung*) recommendation; (mus) grace note; (parl) motion; **in V. bringen** (parl) move
vor'schlagen §132 *tr* propose; suggest; recommend; **zur Wahl v.** nominate
Vor'schlagsliste *f* slate of candidates
Vor'schlußrunde *f* (sport) semifinal
vor'schnell *adj* rash, hasty
vor'schreiben §62 *tr* prescribe, order;

specify; write out; **ich lasse mir nichts v.** I take orders from no one
vor'schreiten §86 *intr* (SEIN) step forward; advance
Vor'schrift *f* order, direction; regulation; (med) prescription
vor'schriftsmäßig *adj* & *adv* according to regulations
vor'schriftswidrig *adj* & *adv* against regulations
Vor'schub *m* assistance; (mach) feed; **V. leisten** (*dat*) encourage; (jur) aid and abet
Vor'schule *f* prep school; (*Elementarschule*) elementary school
Vor'schuß *m* (*Geld–*) advance; (jur) retainer
vor'schützen *tr* pretend, plead
Vor'schützung *f* (–;) pretense
vor'schweben *intr*—**mir schwebte etw anderes vor** I had s.th. else in mind; **das schwebt mir dunkel vor** I have a dim recollection of it
vor'schwindeln *tr*—**j–m etw v.** fool s.o. about s.th.
vor'sehen §138 *tr* schedule, plan; provide; (fin) earmark; **das Gesetz sieht vor, daß** the law provides that ‖ *ref* be careful, take care; **sich mit etw v.** provide oneself with s.th.; **sich v. vor** (*dat*) be on one's guard against
Vor'sehung *f* (–;) Providence
vor'setzen *tr* put forward; (*Silbe*) prefix; **j–m etw v.** set s.th. before s.o. (*to eat*); **j–m j–n v.** set s.o. over s.o.
Vor'sicht *f* caution, care; (*Umsicht*) prudence; **V.!** watch out! (*auf Kisten*) handle with care!; **V., Stufe!** watch your step!
vor'sichtig *adj* cautious, careful
Vor'sichtigkeit *f* (–;) caution
vorsichtshalber ['forzɪçtshalbər] *adv* to be on the safe side, as a precaution
Vor'sichtsmaßnahme *f*, **Vor'sichtsmaßregel** *f* precaution
Vor'silbe *f* prefix
vor'singen §142 *tr*—**j–m etw v.** sing s.th. to s.o. ‖ *intr* lead the choir
Vor'sitz *m* chairmanship, chair; presidency; **den V. haben** (or **führen) bei** preside over; **unter V. von** presided over by
Vorsitzende ['forzɪtsəndə] §5 *mf* chairperson; president
Vor'sorge *f* provision; **V. tragen** (or **treffen) für** make provision for, provide for
vor'sorgen *intr* (**für**) provide (for)
vorsorglich ['forzɔrklɪç] *adv* as a precaution, just in case
Vor'spann *m* (cin) credits; (*Kurzfilm*) (cin) short
Vor'speise *f* appetizer
vor'spiegeln *tr*—**j–m etw v.** delude s.o. with s.th.; **j–m falsche Tatsachen v.** misrepresent facts to s.o.
Vor'spiegelung *f* (–;) sham; pretense; **V. falscher Tatsachen** misrepresentation of facts
Vor'spiel *n* prelude; (*beim Geschlechtsverkehr*) foreplay; (mus) overture; (theat) curtain raiser; **das**

war nur das V.! (fig) that was only the beginning!

vor′spielen *tr*—j–m etw v. play s.th. for s.o.

vor′sprechen §64 *tr*—j–m etw v. pronounce s.th. for s.o.; teach s.o. how to pronounce s.th. || *intr*—bei j–m v. drop in on s.o.; j–m v. audition before s.o.

vor′springen §142 *intr* (SEIN) leap forward; (*aus dem Versteck*) jump out; (*vorstehen*) stick out, protrude

Vor′sprung *m* projection; (*Sims*) ledge; (*Vorteil*) advantage; (sport) head start; (sport) lead

Vor′stadt *f* suburb

vor′städtisch *adj* suburban

Vor′stand *m* board of directors; executive committee, executive board; (*Person*) chairman of the board

vor′stehen §146 *intr* protrude; (*dat*) be at the head of, direct, manage

Vor′steher *m* (–s;–) head, director, manager; (educ) principal

Vor′steherdrüse *f* prostate gland

Vor′steherin *f* (–;–nen) head, director, manager; (educ) principal

vor′stellen *tr* place in front, put ahead; (*Uhr*) set ahead; (*einführen*) introduce, present; (*darstellen*) represent; (*bedeuten*) mean; (*hinweisen auf*) point out || *ref*—sich [*dat*] etw v. imagine s.th., picture s.th.

Vor′stellung *f* (–;–en) introduction, presentation; (*Begriff*) idea; (*Einspruch*) remonstrance, protest; (cin) show; (theat) performance

Vor′stellungsvermögen *n* imagination

Vor′stoß *m* (fig & mil) thrust, drive

vor′stoßen §150 *tr* push forward || *intr* (SEIN) push forward, advance

Vor′strafe *f* previous conviction

Vor′strafenregister *n* previous record

vor′strecken *tr* stretch out; (*Geld*) advance

Vor′stufe *f* preliminary stage

Vor′tag *m* previous day

vor′täuschen *tr* pretend, put on

Vor′teil *m* advantage; profit; (tennis) advantage

vor′teilhaft *adj* advantageous; profitable

Vortrag [′fortrɑk] *m* (–[e]s;–̈e) performance; (*Bericht*) report; (*e–s Gedichtes*) recitation; (*e–r Rede*) delivery; (*Vorlesung*) lecture; (acct) balance (carried over); (mus) recital; **e–n V. halten über** (*acc*) give a lecture on

vor′tragen §132 *tr* perform; present

Vortragende [′fortrɑgəndə] §5 *mf* performer; speaker; lecturer

Vor′tragsfolge *f* program

vortrefflich [′fortrɛflɪç] *adj* excellent

vor′treten §152 *intr* (SEIN) step forward; (fig) stick out, protrude

Vor′tritt *m* (–[e]s;) precedence

vorü′ber *adv* past, by, along; (*zeitlich*) over, gone by

vorü′bergehen §82 *intr* (SEIN) pass; (*an dat*) pass by; (fig) disregard

vorü′bergehend *adj* passing, transitory || **Vorübergehende** §5 *mf* passer-by

vorü′berziehen §163 *intr* (SEIN) march by; (*Gewitter*) blow over

Vor′übung *f* warmup

Vor′untersuchung *f* preliminary investigation

Vor′urteil *n* prejudice

vor′urteilsfrei, vor′urteilslos *adj* unprejudiced

Vor′vergangenheit *f* (gram) past perfect

Vor′verkauf *m* advance sale; (theat) advance reservation

vor′verlegen *tr* advance, move up

Vor′wahl *f* (pol) primary

vor′wählen *intr* dial the area code

Vor′wählnummer *f* (telp) area code

Vor′wand *m* (–[e]s;–̈e) pretext; excuse

vorwärts [′forvɛrts] *adv* forward, on, ahead || *interj* go on!

vor′wärtsbringen §65 *tr* bring forward; (fig) advance

vor′wärtsgehen §82 *intr* (SEIN) progress

vor′wärtskommen §99 *intr* (SEIN) go ahead; progress, make headway

vorweg [for′vɛk] *adv* beforehand; out in front

Vorweg′nahme *f* anticipation

vorweg′nehmen §116 *tr* anticipate; presuppose, assume

vor′weisen §118 *tr* produce, show

Vor′welt *f* prehistoric world

vor′weltlich *adj* primeval

vor′werfen §160 *tr*—j–m etw v. throw s.th. to s.o.; (fig) throw s.th. up to s.o.

vorwiegend [′forvigənt] *adj* predominant || *adv* predominantly, chiefly

Vor′wissen *n* foreknowledge

vor′witzig *adj* inquisitive; brash

Vor′wort *n* (–[e]s;–e) foreword

Vor′wurf *m* reproach, blame; (*e–s Dramas*) subject; **j–m Vorwürfe machen** blame s.o.

vor′wurfslos *adj* irreproachable

vor′wurfsvoll *adj* reproachful

vor′zählen *tr* enumerate

Vor′zeichen *n* omen; (math) sign; (mus) accidental; **negatives V.** minus sign

vor′zeichnen *tr*—j–m etw v. draw or sketch s.th. for s.o.

Vor′zeichnung *f* (–;–en) drawing; (mus) signature

vor′zeigen *tr* produce, show; (*Wechsel*) present

Vor′zeiger –in §6 *mf* bearer

Vor′zeigung *f* (–;–en) producing, showing; presentation

Vor′zeit *f* remote antiquity

vor′zeiten *adv* in days of old

vor′zeitig *adj* premature

vor′ziehen §163 *tr* draw forth; pull out; prefer; (mil) move up

Vor′zimmer *n* anteroom; entrance hall

Vor′zug *m* preference; (*Vorteil*) advantage; (*Überlegenheit*) superiority; (*Vorrang*) priority; (*Vorrecht*) privilege; (*Vorzüglichkeit*) excellence; **e–r Sache den V. geben** prefer s.th.

vorzüglich [′fortsyklɪç] *adj* excellent, first-rate || *adv* especially

Vor′züglichkeit *f* (–;) excellence

Vor′zugsaktie *f* preferred stock

Vor′zugsbehandlung *f* preferential treatment
Vor′zugspreis *m* special price
Vor′zugsrecht *n* priority; privilege
vor′zugsweise *adv* preferably
votieren [vɔ'tirən] *intr* vote
Votiv– [vɔtif] *comb.fm.* votive
Vo•tum ['votum] *n* (–s;–ten [tən] & –ta [ta]) vote

vulgär [vul'gɛr] *adj* vulgar
Vulkan [vul'kan] *m* (–s;–e) volcano
Vulkan′ausbruch *m* eruption
vulkanisch [vul'kanɪʃ] *adj* volcanic
vulkanisieren [vulkanɪ'zirən] *tr* vulcanize
Vulkan′schlot *m* volcanic vent
VW *abbr* (Volkswagen) VW
V-Waffe *f* (Vergeltungswaffe) V-1, V-2

W

W, w [ve] *invar n* W, w
Waage ['vagə] *f* (–;–n) (pair of) scales; (astr) Libra; (gym) horizontal position; **die beiden Dinge halten sich** [dat] **die W.** the two things balance each other; **die W. halten** (*dat*) counterbalance; **j–m die W. halten** be a match for s.o.
waa′gerecht, waagrecht ['vakrɛçt] *adj* horizontal, level
Waagschale ['vakʃalə] *f* scale(s); **in die W. fallen** carry weight; **in die W. werfen** bring to bear
wabbelig ['vabəlɪç] *adj* (coll) flabby
Wabe ['vabə] *f* (–;–n) honeycomb
wach [vax] *adj* awake; (*lebhaft*) lively; (*Geist*) alert; **ganz w.** wide awake
Wach′ablösung *f* changing of the guard
Wach′dienst *m* guard duty
Wache ['vaxə] *f* (–;–n) guard, watch; (*Wachstube*) guardroom; (*Wachlokal*) guardhouse; (*Polizei–*) police station; (*Wachdienst*) guard duty; (*Posten*) guard, sentinel; **auf W.** on guard; **auf W. ziehen** mount guard; **W. schieben** (coll) pull guard duty
wachen ['vaxən] *intr* be awake; **bei j–m w.** sit up with s.o.; **w. über** (*acc*) watch over, guard
wach′habend *adj* on guard duty
wach′halten §90 *tr* keep awake; (fig) keep alive
Wach′hund *m* watchdog
Wach′lokal *n* guardroom; police station
Wach′mann *m* (–[e]s;–leute) (Aust) policeman
Wach′mannschaft *f* (mil) guard detail
Wacholder [va'xɔldər] *m* (–s;–) juniper
Wachol′derbranntwein *m* gin
Wach′posten *m* sentry
wach′rufen §122 *tr* wake up; (*Erinnerung*) bring back
Wachs [vaks] *n* (–es;–e) wax
wachsam ['vaxzam] *adj* vigilant
Wach′samkeit *f* (–;) vigilance
Wachs′bohne *f* wax bean
wachsen ['vaksən] *tr* wax || §155 *intr* (SEIN) grow; (**an** *dat*) increase (in)
wächsern ['vɛksərn] *adj* wax; (fig) waxy
Wachs′figurenkabinett *n* wax museum
Wachs′kerze *f*, **Wachs′licht** *n* wax candle
Wachs′leinwand *f* oilcloth

Wach′stube *f* guardroom
Wachs′tuch *n* oilcloth
Wachstum ['vaxstum] *n* (–s;) growth; increase
Wacht [vaxt] *f* (–;–en) guard, watch
Wächte ['vɛçtə] *f* (–;–n) snow cornice
Wachtel ['vaxtəl] *f* (–;–n) quail
Wach′telhund *m* spaniel
Wächter ['vɛçtər] *m* (–s;–) guard
Wacht′meister *m* police sergeant
Wacht′traum *m* daydream
Wacht′turm *m* watchtower
wackelig ['vakəlɪç] *adj* wobbly; (*Zahn*) loose; (fig) shaky
Wackelkontakt ['vakəlkɔntakt] *m* (elec) loose connection, poor contact
wackeln ['vakəln] *intr* wobble; shake; (*locker sein*) be loose
wacker ['vakər] *adj* decent, honest; (*tapfer*) brave || *adv* heartily
wacklig ['vaklɪç] *adj* var of **wackelig**
Wade ['vadə] *f* (–;–n) (anat) calf
Wa′denbein *n* (anat) fibula
Wa′denkrampf *m* leg cramp
Wa′denstrumpf *m* calf-length stocking
Waffe ['vafə] *f* (–;–n) weapon; branch of service; **die Waffen strecken** surrender; (fig) give up; **zu den Waffen greifen** take up arms
Waffel ['vafəl] *f* (–;–n) waffle
Waf′fenbruder *m* comrade in arms
waf′fenfähig *adj* capable of bearing arms
Waf′fengang *m* armed conflict
Waf′fengattung *f* branch of service
Waf′fengewalt *f* force of arms
Waf′fenkammer *f* armory
Waf′fenlager *n* ordnance depot; **heimliches W.** cache of arms
waf′fenlos *adj* unarmed
Waf′fenruhe *f* truce
Waf′fenschein *m* gun permit
Waf′fenschmied *m* gunsmith
Waf′fenschmuggel *m* gunrunning
Waf′fen-SS *f* (–;) SS combat unit
Waf′fenstillstand *m* armistice
Wagehals ['vagəhals] *m* daredevil
Wagemut ['vagəmut] *m* daring
wagen ['vagən] *tr* dare; risk || *ref* venture, dare || **Wagen** *m* (–s;–) wagon; (*Fahrzeug; Teil e–r Schreibmaschine*) carriage; (aut, rr) car; **der Große Wagen** the Big Dipper; **j–m an den W. fahren** (fig) step on s.o.'s toes
wägen ['vegən] *tr* (& fig) weigh
Wa′genabteil *n* (rr) compartment

Wa′genburg f barricade of wagons
Wa′genheber m (aut) jack
Wa′genpark m fleet of cars
Wa′genpflege f (aut) maintenance
Wa′genschlag m car door, carriage door
Wa′genschmiere f (aut) grease
Wa′genspur f wheel track, rut
Wa′genwäsche f car wash
Wagestück [′vagəʃtʏk] n hazardous venture, daring deed
Waggon [va′gõ] m (-s;-s) railroad car
waghalsig [′vakhalzɪç] adj foolhardy
Wagnis [′vaknɪs] n (-ses;-se) risk
Wahl [val] f (-;-en) choice, option; (Auswahl) selection; (Alternative) alternative; (pol) election; **e-e W. treffen** make a choice; **vor der W. stehen** have the choice
wählbar [′velbar] adj eligible
Wähl′barkeit f (-;) eligibility
Wahl′beeinflussung f interference with the election process
wahl′berechtigt adj eligible to vote
Wahl′beteiligung f election turnout
Wahl′bezirk m ward
wählen [′velən] tr choose; select; (pol) elect; (telp) dial || intr vote
Wäh′ler m (-s;-) voter
Wahl′ergebnis n election returns
Wäh′lerin f (-;-nen) voter
wählerisch [′velərɪʃ] adj choosy, particular
Wäh′lerschaft f (-;-en) constituency
Wäh′lerscheibe f (telp) dial
Wahl′fach n (educ) elective
wahl′fähig adj eligible for election; having a vote
wahl′frei adj (educ) elective
Wahl′gang m ballot
Wahl′kampf m election campaign
Wahl′kreis m constituency; district
Wahl′leiter m campaign manager
Wahl′list f (pol) slate, ticket
Wahl′lokal n polling place
Wahl′lokomotive f (coll) vote getter
wahl′los adj indiscriminate
Wahl′parole f campaign slogan
Wahl′programm n (pol) platform
Wahl′recht n right to vote, suffrage
Wahl′rede f campaign speech
Wahl′spruch m motto; (com, pol) slogan
Wahl′urne f ballot box
Wahl′versammlung f campaign rally
wahl′verwandt adj congenial
Wahl′zelle f voting booth
Wahl′zettel m ballot
Wahn [van] m (-[e]s;) delusion; error; folly; madness
Wahn′bild n phantom, delusion
wähnen [′venən] tr fancy, imagine
Wahn′idee f delusion; (coll) crazy idea
Wahn′sinn m (& fig) madness
wahn′sinnig adj (vor dat) mad (with); (coll) terrible || adv madly; (coll) awfully || **Wahnsinnige** §5 mf lunatic
Wahn′vorstellung f hallucination
Wahn′witz m (& fig) madness
wahn′witzig adj mad; (unverantwortlich) irresponsible
wahr [var] adj true; (wirklich) real; (echt) genuine; **nicht w.?** right?

wahren [′varən] tr keep; (Anschein) keep up; (vor dat) protect (against)
währen [′verən] intr last
während [′verənt] prep (genit) during; (jur) pending || conj while; whereas
wahr′haben §89 tr admit
wahr′haft, wahr′haftig adj true, truthful; (wirklich) real || adv actually
Wahr′haftigkeit f (-;) truthfulness
Wahr′heit f (-;-en) truth; **j-m die W. sagen** give s.o. a piece of one's mind
wahr′heitsgemäß, wahr′heitsgetreu adj true, faithful; truthful
Wahr′heitsliebe f truthfulness
wahr′heitsliebend adj truthful
wahr′lich adv truly; (Bib) verily
wahrnehmbar [′varnembar] adj noticeable
wahr′nehmen §116 tr notice; (benutzen) make use of; (Interesse) protect; (Recht) assert
Wahr′nehmung f (-;-en) observation, perception; (der Interessen) safeguarding
wahr′sagen ref—**sich** [dat] **w. lassen** have one's fortune told || intr prophesy; tell fortunes
Wahr′sagerin f (-;-nen) fortuneteller
wahrscheinlich [var′ʃaɪnlɪç] adj probable, likely || adv probably
Wahrschein′lichkeit f (-;) probability
Wahr′spruch m verdict
Wah′rung f (-;) safeguarding
Wäh′rung f (-;-en) currency; standard
Wäh′rungsabwertung f devaluation
Wäh′rungseinheit f monetary unit
Wahr′zeichen n landmark
Waise [′vaɪzə] f (-;-n) orphan
Wai′senhaus n orphanage
Wal [val] m (-[e]s;-e) whale
Wald [valt] m (-[e]s;⁻er) forest, woods
Wald– comb.fm. forest; sylvan; wild
Wald′aufseher m forest ranger
Wald′brand m forest fire
waldig [′valdɪç] adj wooded
Waldung [′valduŋ] f (-;-en) forest
Wald′wirtschaft f forestry
Wal′fang m whaling
Wal′fänger m (-s;-) whaler
walken [′valkən] tr full
Wal′ker m (-s;-) fuller
Wall [val] m (-[e]s;⁻e) mound; embankment; (mil) rampart
Wallach [′valax] m (-[e]s;-e) gelding
wallen [′valən] intr (sieden) boil; (sprudeln) bubble; (Gewand, Haar) flow, fall in waves || intr (SEIN) go on a pilgrimage; travel, wander
wall′fahren insep intr (SEIN) go on a pilgrimage
Wall′fahrer –in §6 mf pilgrim
Wall′fahrt f pilgrimage
Wall′graben m moat
Wal′lung f (-;) simmering, boiling; bubbling; flow; flutter; (Blutandrang) congestion; **in W. bringen** enrage; **in W. geraten** fly into a rage; **Wallungen** hot flashes
Walnuß [′valnʊs] f walnut
Walroß [′valrɔs] n walrus
Wal′speck m blubber
walten [′valtən] intr rule; hold sway;

Gnade w. lassen show mercy; **seines Amtes w.** attend to one's duties
Wal'tran m whale oil
Walze ['valtsə] f (-;-n) cylinder, drum; roll, roller; (*der Schreibmaschine*) platen
walzen ['valtsən] tr roll
wälzen ['vɛltsən] tr roll; (*Bücher*) pore over; (*Gedanken*) turn over in one's mind; **die Schuld auf j-n w.** shift the blame to s.o. else || ref roll, toss; (*im Kot*) wallow; (*im Blut*) welter
Wal'zer m (-s;-) waltz
Wäl'zer m (-s;-) (coll) thick tome
Walz'werk n rolling mill
Wamme ['vamə] f (-;-n) dewlap; (coll) potbelly
Wampe ['vampə] f (-;-n) (coll) potbelly
wand [vant] pret of **winden** || **Wand** f (-;ːe) wall; partition; (*Fels-*) cliff; **spanische W.** folding screen
Wand'apparat m (telp) wall phone
Wand'bekleidung f wainscot
Wandel ['vandəl] m (-s;) change
wandelbar ['vandəlbar] adj changeable
Wan'delgang m, **Wan'delhalle** f lobby
wandeln ['vandəln] tr change || ref (in acc) change (into) || intr (SEIN) (poet) wander; (poet) walk
Wan'derer –in §6 mf wanderer; hiker
Wan'derlust f wanderlust, itch to travel
wandern ['vandərn] intr (SEIN) wander; hike; (*Vögel*) migrate
Wan'derniere f floating kidney
Wan'derpreis m challenge trophy
Wan'derschaft f (-;) travels, wanderings
Wan'derstab m walking stick
Wan'derung f (-;-en) hike; migration
Wan'dervogel m migratory bird; (coll) rover
Wand'gemälde n mural
Wand'karte f wall map
Wand'leuchter m sconce
Wand'lung f (-;-en) change, transformation; (eccl) consecration
Wand'malerei f wall painting
Wand'pfeiler m pilaster
Wand'schirm m folding screen
Wand'schrank m wall shelves
Wand'spiegel m wall mirror
Wand'steckdose f, **Wand'stecker** m (elec) wall outlet
Wand'tafel f blackboard
wandte ['vantə] pret of **wenden**
Wand'teppich m tapestry
Wange ['vaŋə] f (-;-n) cheek
-wangig [vaŋɪç] comb.fm. –cheeked
Wan'kelmut m fickleness
wan'kelmütig adj fickle
wanken ['vaŋkən] intr stagger; sway, rock; (fig) waver
wann [van] adv & conj when; **w. immer** anytime, whenever
Wanne ['vanə] f (-;-n) tub
Wanst [vanst] m (-es;ːe) belly, paunch
-wanstig [vanstɪç] comb.fm. –bellied
Wanze ['vantsə] f (-;-n) bedbug
Wappen ['vapən] n (-s;-) coat of arms
Wap'penkunde f heraldry

Wap'penschild m escutcheon
wappnen ['vapnən] ref arm oneself; **sich mit Geduld w.** have patience
war [var] pret of **sein**
warb [varp] pret of **werben**
ward [vart] pret of **werden**
Ware ['varə] f (-;-n) ware; article; commodity; **Waren** goods, merchandise
-waren [varən] pl comb.fm. –ware
Wa'renaufzug m freight elevator
Wa'renausgabe f wrapping department
Wa'renbestand m stock
Wa'renbörse f commodity market
Wa'renhaus n department store
Wa'renlager n warehouse; stockroom
Wa'renmarkt m commodity market
Wa'renmuster n, **Wa'renprobe** f sample
Wa'renrechnung f invoice
Wa'renzeichen n trademark
warf [varf] pret of **werfen**
warm [varm] adj (**wärmer** ['vɛrmər]; **wärmste** ['vɛrmstə] §9) warm
Warmblüter ['varmblytər] m (-s;-) warm-blooded animal
warmblütig ['varmblytɪç] adj warm-blooded
Wärme ['vɛrmə] f (-;) warmth, heat
wär'mebeständig adj heatproof
Wär'meeinheit f thermal unit; calory
Wär'megrad m degree of heat, temperature
wärmen ['vɛrmən] tr warm, heat
Wär'meplatte f—**elektrische W.** hotplate
Wärm'flasche f hot-water bottle
warm'halten §90 tr keep warm
warm'herzig adj warm-hearted
warm'laufen §105 intr—**den Motor w. lassen** let the motor warm up
Warmluft'heizung f hot-air heating
Warmwas'serbehälter m hot-water tank
Warmwas'serheizung f hot-water heating
Warmwas'serspeicher m hot-water tank
Warn– [varn] comb.fm. warning
Warn'anlage f warning system
warnen ['varnən] tr (**vor** dat) warn (of), caution (against)
Warn'gebiet n danger zone
Warn'schuß m warning shot
Warn'signal n warning signal
War'nung f (-;-en) warning, caution; **zur W.** as a warning
War'nungsschild n, **Warn'zeichen** n danger sign
Warschau ['varʃau] n (-s;) Warsaw
Warte ['vartə] f (-;-n) watchtower, lookout
War'tefrau f attendant; nurse
War'tefrist f waiting period
warten ['vartən] tr tend, attend to; (*pflegen*) nurse || intr (**auf** acc) wait (for)
Wärter ['vɛrtər] m (-s;-) attendant; (*Pfleger*) male nurse; (*Aufseher*) caretaker; (*Gefängnis–*) guard; (rr) signalman
War'teraum m waiting room
Wärterin ['vɛrtərɪn] f (-;-nen) attendant; nurse

War′tesaal *m,* **War′tezimmer** *n* waiting room
War′tung *f* (–;) maintenance
warum [va′rum] *adv* why
Warze [′vartsə] *f* (–;–n) wart; (*Brust–*) nipple
was [vas] *indef pron* something; **na, so was! well, I never!** ‖ *interr pron* what; **ach was!** go on! **was für ein what kind of,** what sort of; **was haben wir gelacht!** how we laughed! ‖ *rel pron* what; which, that; **was auch immer** no matter what; **was immer** whatever
Wasch– [vaʃ] *comb.fm.* wash, washing
waschbar [′vaʃbɑr] *adj* washable
Wasch′bär *m* racoon
Wasch′becken *n* sink
Wasch′benzin *n* cleaning fluid
Wasch′blau *n* bluing
Wasch′bütte *f* washtub
Wäsche [′vɛʃə] *f* (–;–n) wash, laundry; linen; underwear
Wä′schebeutel *m* laundry bag
wasch′echt *adj* washable; (fig) genuine
Wä′scheklammer *f* clothespin
Wä′schekorb *m* clothesbasket
Wä′scheleine *f* clothesline
waschen [′vaʃən] §158 *tr* wash; launder; (*Gold*) pan; (*Haar*) shampoo; (*reinigen*) purify ‖ *ref* wash; **sich** [*dat*] **die Hände w.** wash one's hands ‖ *intr* wash
Wä′scher [′vɛʃər] *m* (–s;–) washer; laundryman
Wäscherei [vɛʃə′raɪ] *f* (–;–en) laundry
Wäscherin [′vɛʃərɪn] *f* (–;–nen) washerwoman, laundress
Wä′scherolle *f* mangle
Wä′scheschleuder *f* spin-drier
Wä′scheschrank *m* linen closet
Wä′schezeichen *n* laundry mark
Wasch′frau *f* laundress
Wasch′haus *n* laundry
Wasch′korb *m* clothesbasket
Wasch′küche *f* laundry
Wasch′lappen *m* washcloth; (fig) wishy-washy person
Wasch′maschine *f* washmachine, washer
Wasch′mittel *n* detergent
Wasch′raum *m* washroom, lavatory
Wasch′schüssel *f* wash basin
Wasch′tisch *m* washstand
Wasch′trog *m* washtub
Wa′schung *f* (–;–en) washing; ablution
Wasch′weib *n* (coll) gossip (*woman*)
Wasch′zettel *m* laundry list; (*am Schutzumschlag*) blurb
Wasser [′vasər] *n* (–s;–) water; **das W. läuft mir im Mund zusammen** my mouth is. watering; **j–m das W. abgraben** pull the rug out from under s.o.; **mit allen Wassern gewaschen** sharp as a needle
was′serabstoßend *adj* water-repellent
was′serarm *adj* arid
Was′serball *m* water polo
Was′serbau *m* (–[e]s;) harbor and canal construction
Was′serbehälter *m* water tank; reservoir; cistern

Was′serblase *f* bubble; (*auf der Haut*) blister
Was′serbombe *f* depth charge
Was′serbüffel *m* water buffalo
Was′serdampf *m* steam
was′serdicht *adj* watertight, waterproof
Was′sereimer *m* bucket
Was′serfall *m* waterfall, cascade
Was′serfarbe *f* watercolor
Was′serflasche *f* water bottle
Was′serflugzeug *n* seaplane
Was′sergeflügel *n* waterfowl
Was′sergraben *m* drain; moat
Was′serhahn *m* faucet, spigot
Was′serhose *f* waterspout
wässerig [′vesərɪç] *adj* watery
Was′serjungfer *f* dragonfly
Was′serkessel *m* cauldron
Was′serklosett *n* toilet
Was′serkraftwerk *n* hydroelectric plant
Was′serkrug *m* water jug, water pitcher
Was′serkur *f* spa
Was′serland′flugzeug *n* amphibian plane
Was′serland′panzerwagen *m* amphibian tank
Was′serlauf *m* watercourse
Was′serleitung *f* water main; aqueduct
Was′sermangel *m* water shortage
Was′sermann *m* (–[e]s;) (astr) Aquarius
Was′sermelone *f* watermelon
wassern [′vasərn] *intr* land on water; (rok) splash down
wässern [′vesərn] *tr* water; irrigate; (phot) wash ‖ *intr* (*Augen, Mund*) water
Was′serratte *f* water rat; (fig) old salt
Was′serrinne *f* gutter
Was′serrohr *n* water pipe
Was′serscheide *f* watershed, divide
was′serscheu *adj* afraid of water
Was′serschi *m* water ski
Was′serschlauch *m* hose
Wasserspeier [′vasərʃpaɪ·ər] *m* (–s;–) gargoyle
Was′serspiegel *m* surface; water level
Was′sersport *m* aquatics
Was′serstand *m* water level
Was′serstiefel *m* rubber boots
Was′serstoff *m* hydrogen
was′serstoffblond *adj* peroxide-blond
Was′serstoffbombe *f* hydrogen bomb
Was′serstrahl *m* jet of water
Was′serstraße *f* waterway
Was′sersucht *f* dropsy
Was′serung *f* (–;–en) (aer) landing on water; (rok) splashdown
Wäs′serung *f* (–;) watering; irrigation
Was′serverdrängung *f* displacement
Was′serversorgung *f* water supply
Was′servogel *m* waterfowl
Was′serwaage *f* (carp) level
Was′serweg *m* waterway; **auf dem W.** by water
Was′serwerk *n* waterworks
Was′serzähler *m* water meter
Was′serzeichen *n* watermark
wässrig [′vesrɪç] *adj* watery
waten [′vatən] *intr* (SEIN) wade
Watsche [′vatʃə] *f* (–;–n) slap
watscheln [′vatʃəln] *intr* (SEIN) waddle
watschen [′vatʃən] *tr* slap

Watt [vat] *n* (–s;–) (elec) watt
Watte ['vatə] *f* (–;–en) absorbent cotton; wadding
Wat'tebausch *m* swab
Wat'tekugel *f* cotton ball
Wat'tenmeer *n* shallow coastal waters
Wat'testäbchen *n* Q-tip, cotton swab
wattieren [va'tirən] *tr* pad, wad
Wattie'rung *f* (–;–en) padding, wadding
wauwau ['vau'vau] *interj* bow-wow! || **Wauwau** *m* (–s;–s) bow-wow, doggy
weben ['vebən] §109 & §94 *tr* & *intr* weave
We'ber *m* (–s;–) weaver
Weberei [vebə'raɪ] *f* (–;–en) weaving
We'berin *f* (–;–nen) weaver
We'berknecht *m* daddy-long-legs
Webstuhl ['vepʃtul] *m* loom
Webwaren ['vepvɑrən] *pl* textiles
Wechsel ['vɛksəl] *m* (–s;–) change, shift; (*für Studenten*) allowance; (agr) rotation (*of crops*); (fin) bill of exchange; (hunt) run, beaten track; **gezogener W.** draft; **offener W.** letter of credit; **trockener** (or **eigener**) **W.** promissory note
Wech'selbeziehung *f* correlation
Wechselfälle ['vɛksəlfɛlə] *pl* ups and downs, vicissitudes
Wech'selfieber *n* intermittent fever; malaria
Wech'selfrist *f* period of grace (*before bill of exchange falls due*)
Wech'selgeld *n* change, small change
Wech'selgesang *m* antiphony
Wech'selgespräch *n* dialogue
wech'selhaft *adj* changeable
Wech'selkurs *m* rate of exchange
Wech'selmakler –**in** §6 *mf* bill-broker
wechseln ['vɛksəln] *tr* change; vary; (*austauschen*) exchange; **den Besitzer w.** change hands; **die Zähne w.** get one's second set of teeth; **seinen Wohnsitz w.** move || *intr* change; vary
Wech'selnehmer *m* (fin) payee
Wech'selnotierung *f* foreign exchange rate
Wech'selrichter *m* (elec) vibrator (*producing a.c.*)
wech'selseitig *adj* mutual, reciprocal
Wech'selseitigkeit *f* (–;) reciprocity
Wech'selspiel *n* interplay
Wech'selsprechanlage *f* intercom
Wech'selstrom *m* alternating current
Wech'selstube *f* money-exchange office
Wech'seltierchen *n* amoeba
wech'selvoll *adj* (*Landschaft*) changing; (*Leben*) checkered; (*Wetter*) changeable
wech'selweise *adv* mutually; alternately
Wech'selwirkung *f* interaction
Wech'selwirtschaft *f* crop rotation
wecken ['vɛkən] *tr* wake, awaken, rouse
Wecker (**Wek'ker**) *m* (–s;–) alarm clock
Weck'ruf *m* (mil) reveille
Wedel ['vedəl] *m* (–s;–) brush, whisk; (*Schwanz*) tail; (eccl) sprinkler
wedeln ['vedəln] *tr* brush away || *intr*

—**mit dem Fächer w.** fan oneself; **mit dem Schwanz w.** wag its tail
weder ['vedər] *conj*—**weder...noch** neither...nor
weg [vɛk] *adv* away, off; gone; lost || **Weg** [vek] *m* (–[e]s;–e) way, path; road; route, course; (*Art und Weise*) way; (*Mittel*) means; **am Wege** by the roadside; **auf dem besten Wege sein** be well on the way; **auf gütlichem Wege** amicably; **auf halbem Wege** halfway; **aus dem Weg räumen** remove; (fig) bump off; **etw in die Wege leiten** prepare the way for s.th.; introduce s.th.; **j–m aus dem Wege gehen** make way for s.o.; steer clear of s.o.; **Weg und Steg kennen** know every turn in the road
weg'bekommen §99 *tr* (*Fleck*) get out; (*Krankheit*) catch; (*verstehen*) get the hang of; **e–e w.** (coll) get a crack
weg'bleiben §62 *intr* (SEIN) stay away; be omitted
weg'blicken *intr* glance away
weg'bringen §65 *tr* take away; (*Fleck*) get out
Wegebau ['vegəbau] *m* (–[e]s;) road building
Wegegeld ['vegəgɛlt] *n* mileage allowance; turnpike toll
wegen ['vegən] *prep* (*genit*) because of, on account of; for the sake of; (*mit Rücksicht auf*) in consideration of; (*infolge*) in consequence of; (jur) on (the charge of); **von Amts w.** officially; **von Rechts w.** by right
Wegerecht ['vegərɛçt] *n* right of way
weg'essen §70 *tr* eat up
weg'fahren §71 *tr* remove || *intr* (SEIN) drive away, leave
weg'fallen §72 *intr* (SEIN) fall away, fall off; (*ausgelassen werden*) be omitted; (*aufhören*) cease; (*abgeschafft werden*) be abolished
weg'fangen §73 *tr* snap away, snatch
weg'fliegen §57 *intr* (SEIN) fly away
weg'fressen §70 *tr* devour
weg'führen *tr* lead away
Weggang ['vɛkgaŋ] *m* departure
weg'geben §80 *tr* give away
weg'gehen §82 *intr* (SEIN) go away; **w. über** (*acc*) pass over; **wie warme Semmeln w.** go like hotcakes
weg'haben §89 *tr* get rid of; (*Schläge, usw.*) have gotten one's share of; (*verstehen*) catch on to; **der hat eins weg** (sl) he has a screw loose; (sl) he's loaded
weg'jagen *tr* chase away
weg'kehren *tr* sweep away; (*Gesicht*) avert || *ref* turn away
weg'kommen §99 *intr* (SEIN) come away; get away (*verlorengehen*) get lost; **nicht w. über** (*acc*) not get over
weg'können §100 *intr*—**nicht w.** not be able to get away
Wegkreuzung ['vɛkkrɔɪtsuŋ] *f* (–;–en) crossing, intersection
weg'kriegen *tr* get; (*Fleck*) get out
weg'lassen §104 *tr* leave out; let go; cross out; (gram) elide; (math) cancel
weg'legen *tr* put aside

weg'machen *tr* take away; (*Fleck*) take out

wegmüde ['vekmydə] *adj* travel-weary

weg'müssen §115 *intr* have to go

Wegnahme ['vɛknɑmə] *f* (-;-n) taking away; confiscation; (mil) capture

weg'nehmen §116 *tr* take away; (*Raum, Zeit*) take up; (*beschlagnahmen*) confiscate; (mil) capture

weg'packen *tr* pack away || *ref* pack off

weg'raffen *tr* snatch away

Wegrand ['vekrant] *m* wayside

weg'räumen *tr* clear away

weg'reißen §53 *tr* tear off, tear away

weg'rücken *tr* move away

weg'schaffen *tr* remove; get rid of

weg'scheren §129 *tr* clip || *ref* scram

weg'scheuchen *tr* scare away

weg'schicken *tr* send away

weg'schleichen §85 *ref* & *intr* (SEIN) sneak away, steal away

weg'schmeißen §53 *tr* (coll) throw away

weg'schneiden §106 *tr* cut away

weg'sehen §138 *intr* look away; **w. über** (*acc*) shut one's eyes to

weg'setzen *tr* put away || *ref*—**sich w. über** (*acc*) not mind; feel superior to || *intr* (SEIN)—**w. über** (*acc*) jump over

weg'spülen *tr* wash away; (geol) erode

weg'stehlen §147 *ref* slip away

weg'stellen *tr* put aside

weg'stoßen §150 *tr* shove aside

weg'streichen §85 *tr* cross out

weg'treten §152 *intr* (SEIN) step aside; (mil) break ranks; **weggetreten!** (mil) dismissed!; **w. lassen** (mil) dismiss

weg'tun §154 *tr* put away

Wegweiser ['vekvaɪzər] *m* (-s;-) road-sign; (*Buch, Reiseführer*) guide

weg'wenden §120 & §140 *tr* & *ref* turn away

weg'werfen §160 *tr* throw away || *ref* degrade oneself

weg'werfend *adj* disparaging

weg'wischen *tr* wipe away

weg'zaubern *tr* spirit away

weg'ziehen §163 *tr* pull away || *intr* (SEIN) move; (mil) pull out

weh [ve] *adj* painful, sore; **mir ist weh ums Herz** I am sick at heart || *adv*—**sich** [*dat*] **weh tun** hurt oneself; **weh tun** ache || *interj* woe! **weh mir!** woe is me! || **Weh** *n* (-[e]s;-e) pain, ache

wehe ['ve·ə] *adj, adv,* & *interj* var of **weh** || **Wehe** *f* (-;-n) drift

wehen ['ve·ən] *tr* blow; (*Schnee*) drift || *intr* (*Wind*) blow; (*Fahne, Kerzenflamme*) flutter || **Wehen** *pl* labor, labor pains; (fig) travail

Weh'geschrei *n* wails, wailing

Weh'klage *f* wail

weh'klagen *intr* (über *acc*) wail (over); **w. um** lament for

weh'leidig *adj* complaining, whining; **W. tun** whine

Weh'mut *f* (-;) melancholy; nostalgia

weh'mütig *adj* melancholy; nostalgic

Wehr [ver] *f* (-;-en) weapon; (*Abwehr*) defense, resistance; (*Brüstung*)

parapet; **sich zur W. setzen** offer resistance || **Wehr** *n* (-[e]s;-e) dam

Wehr'dienst *m* military service

wehr'dienstpflichtig *adj* subject to military service

Wehr'dienstverweigerer *m* (-s;-) conscientious objector

wehren ['verən] *tr*—**j-m etw w.** keep s.o. (away) from s.th. || *ref* defend oneself; resist, put up a fight; **sich seiner Haut w.** save one's skin || *intr* (*dat*) resist; (*dat*) check

wehr'fähig *adj* fit for military service

wehr'haft *adj* (*Person*) full of fight; (*Burg*) strong

wehr'los *adj* defenseless

Wehr'macht *f* (hist) German armed forces

Wehr'meldeamt *n* draft board

Wehr'paß *m* service record

Wehr'pflicht *f* compulsory military service; **allgemeine W.** universal military training

wehr'pflichtig *adj* subject to military service

Weib [vaɪp] *n* (-[e]s;-er) woman; wife; **ein tolles W.** a luscious doll

Weibchen ['vaɪpçən] *n* (-s;-) (*Tier*) female; (*Ehefrau*) little woman

Weiberfeind ['vaɪbərfaɪnt] *m* woman-hater

Weiberheld ['vaɪbərhɛlt] *m* ladies' man

Weibervolk ['vaɪbərfɔlk] *n* womenfolk

weibisch ['vaɪbɪʃ] *adj* womanish, effeminate

weib'lich *adj* female; womanly; (& gram) feminine

Weib'lichkeit *f* (-;) womanhood; feminine nature; **die holde W.** (hum) the fair sex

Weibs'bild *n* female; (pej) wench

Weibs'stück *n* (sl) woman

weich [vaɪç] *adj* soft; (*Ei*) soft-boiled; (*zart*) tender; (*schwach*) weak; **w. machen** soften up; **w. werden** (& fig) soften; relent

Weich'bild *n* urban area, outskirts

Weiche ['vaɪçə] *f* (-;-n) (anat) side, flank; (rr) switch; **Weichen stellen** throw the switch

weichen ['vaɪçən] *tr* & *intr* soften; soak || §85 *intr* (SEIN) yield; give ground; (*Boden*) give way; (*dat*) give in to; **j-m nicht von der Seite w.** not leave s.o.'s side; **nicht von der Stelle w.** not budge from the spot; **von j-m w.** leave s.o.

Weichensteller ['vaɪçənstɛlər] *m* (-s; -) (rr) switchman

Weich'heit *f* (-;) softness; tenderness

weich'herzig *adj* soft-hearted

Weich'käse *m* soft cheese

weich'lich *adj* soft; tender; flabby; insipid; (*weibisch*) effeminate; (*lässig*) indolent

Weichling ['vaɪçlɪŋ] *m* (-s;-e) weakling

Weich'tier *n* mollusk

Weide ['vaɪdə] *f* (-;-n) pasture; (bot) willow

Wei'deland *n* pasture land

weiden ['vaɪdən] *tr* graze; (*Augen*)

feast ‖ *ref*—**sich w. an** (*dat*) feast
one's eyes on ‖ *intr* graze
Wei′denkorb *m* wicker basket
weidlich ['vaɪtlɪç] *adv* heartily
weidmännisch ['vaɪtmɛnɪʃ] *adj* (hunt)
sportsmanlike
weigern ['vaɪgərn] *ref*—**sich w. zu** (*inf*)
refuse to (*inf*)
Wei′gerung *f* (-;-en) refusal
Weihe ['vaɪ·ə] *f* (-;-n) consecration;
(*e–s Priesters*) ordination
weihen ['vaɪ·ən] *tr* consecrate; (*zum
Priester*) ordain; (*widmen*) dedicate;
dem Tode geweiht doomed to death
‖ *ref* devote oneself
Wei′her *m* (-s;-) pond
wei′hevoll *adj* solemn
Weihnachten ['vaɪnaxtən] *n* (-s;) & *pl*
Christmas; **zu W.** for or at Christmas
Weih′nachtsabend *m* Christmas Eve
Weih′nachtsbaum *m* Christmas tree;
(coll) bombing markers
Weih′nachtsbescherung *f* exchange of
Christmas presents
Weih′nachtsfeier *f* Christmas celebra-
tion; (*in Betrieben*) Christmas party
Weih′nachtsfest *n* feast of Christmas
Weih′nachtsgeschenk *n* Christmas pres-
ent
Weih′nachtsgratifikation *f* Christmas
bonus
Weih′nachtslied *n* Christmas carol
Weih′nachtsmann *m* (-[e]s;) Santa
Claus
Weih′nachtsmarkt *m* Christmas fair
(*at which Christmas decorations are
sold*)
Weih′nachstag *m* Christmas day
Weih′rauch *m* incense
Weih′rauchfaß *n* censer
Weih′wasser *n* holy water
Weih′wedel *m* (eccl) sprinkler
weil [vaɪl] *conj* because, since
weiland ['vaɪlant] *adv* formerly
Weilchen ['vaɪlçən] *n* (-s;) little while
Weile ['vaɪlə] *f* (-;) while
weilen ['vaɪlən] *intr* stay, linger
Wein [vaɪn] *m* (-[e]s;-e) wine;
(*Pflanze*) vine
Wein′bau *m* (-[e]s;) winegrowing
Wein′bauer *m* §6 *mf* winegrower
Wein′beere *f* grape
Wein′berg *m* vineyard
Wein′blatt *n* vine leaf
Wein′brand *m* brandy
weinen ['vaɪnən] *tr* (*Tränen*) shed ‖
intr cry, weep; **vor Freude w.** weep
for joy; **w. um** cry over
weinerlich ['vaɪnərlɪç] *adj* tearful;
(*Stimme*)) whining
Wein′ernte *f* vintage
Wein′essig *m* wine vinegar
Wein′faß *n* wine barrel
Wein′händler *m* wine merchant
Wein′jahr *n* vintage year
Wein′karte *f* wine list
Wein′keller *m* wine cellar
Wein′kelter *f* wine press
Wein′kenner *m* connoisseur of wine
Wein′krampf *m* crying fit
Wein′laub *n* vine leaves
Wein′lese *f* grape picking
Wein′presse *f* wine press

Wein′ranke *f* vine tendril
Wein′rebe *f* grapevine
wein′selig *adj* tipsy, tight
Wein′stock *m* vine
Wein′traube *f* grape; bunch of grapes
weise ['vaɪzə] *adj* wise ‖ **Weise** §5 *m*
wise man, sage ‖ *f* (-;-n) way;
(*Melodie*) tune; **auf diese W.** in this
way
-weise *comb.fm.* –wise; by, e.g., **dut-
zendweise** by the dozen; –ly, e.g.,
glücklicherweise luckily
weisen ['vaɪzən] §118 *tr* point out,
show; (*aus dem Lande*) banish; (*aus
der Schule*) expel; **j–n w. an** (*acc*)
refer s.o. to; **j–n w. nach** direct s.o.
to; **j–n w. von** order s.o. off (*premises, etc.*); **von der Hand w.** refuse;
weit von der Hand w. have nothing
to do with ‖ *ref*—**von sich w.** refuse
‖ *intr*—**w. auf** (*acc*) point to
Weis′heit *f* (-;-en) wisdom; wise saying; **Weisheiten** words of wisdom
Weis′heitszahn *m* wisdom tooth
weis′lich *adv* wisely, prudently
weismachen ['vaɪsmaxən] *tr*—**j–m etw
w.** put s.th. over on s.o.; **mach das
anderen weis!** tell it to the marines!
weiß [vaɪs] *adj* white
weissagen ['vaɪsza:gən] *tr* foretell
Weiß′blech *n* tin plate, tin
Weiß′blechdose *f* tincan
weiß′bluten *tr* bleed white
Weiß′brot *n* white bread
Weiß′dorn *m* (bot) hawthorn
Weiße ['vaɪsə] *f* (-;-n) whiteness;
(Berlin) ale ‖ §5 *m* white man ‖ *f*
white woman ‖ *n* (*im Auge, im Ei*)
white
weißen ['vaɪsən] *tr* whiten; (*tünchen*)
whitewash
weiß′glühend *adj* white-hot
Weiß′glut *f* white heat, incandescence
Weiß′kohl *m*, **Weiß′kraut** *n* cabbage
weiß′lich *adj* whitish
Weiß′metall *n* pewter; Babbitt metal
Weiß′waren *pl* linens
Weiß′wein *m* white wine
Wei′sung *f* (-;-en) directions, instructions; directive
weit [vaɪt] *adj* far, distant; (*ausgedehnt*) extensive; (*breit*) wide, broad;
(*geräumig*) large; (*Gewissen*) elastic;
(*Herz*) big; (*Kleid*) full, big; (*Meer*)
broad; (*Reise, Weg*) long; (*Welt*)
wide; **bei weitem besser** better by
far; **von weitem** from afar ‖ *adv* far,
way; widely; greatly; **w. besser** far
better
weit′ab′ *adv* (**von**) far away (from)
weit′aus′ *adv* by far
Weit′blick *m* farsightedness
weit′blickend *adj* farsighted
Weite ['vaɪtə] *f* (-;-n) width, breadth;
(*Ferne*) distance; (*Umfang*) size;
(*Ausdehnung*) extent; (*Durchmesser*)
diameter; (fig) range; **in die W.
ziehen** go out into the world
weiten ['vaɪtən] *tr* widen; (*Loch*) en-
large; (*Schuh*) stretch ‖ *ref* widen
weiter ['vaɪtər] *adj* farther; further;
wider; **bis auf weiteres** until further
notice; **des weiteren** furthermore;

ohne weiteres without further ado ‖ *adv* farther; further; furthermore; (*voran*) on; **er kann nicht w.** he can't go on; **nur s. w.!** keep it up!; **und so w.** and so forth, and so on
weiter– *comb.fm.* on; keep on, continue to
wei′terbefördern *tr* forward
Wei′terbestand *m* continued existence
wei′terbestehen §146 *intr* survive
wei′terbilden *tr* develop ‖ *ref* continue one's studies
wei′tererzählen *tr* spread (*rumors*)
wei′terfahren §71 *intr* (SEIN) drive on
wei′tergeben §80 *tr* pass on, relay
wei′tergehen §82 *intr* (SEIN) go on
wei′terhin′ *adv* furthermore; again
wei′terkommen §99 *intr* (SEIN) get ahead, make progress
wei′terkönnen §100 *intr* be able to go on; **ich kann nicht weiter** I'm stuck
wei′terleben *intr* live on, survive
wei′termachen *tr & intr* continue ‖ *interj* (mil) as you were!, carry on!
weit′gehend *adj* far-reaching
weit′gereist *adj* widely traveled
weit′greifend *adj* far-reaching
weit′her′ *adv*—**von w.** from afar
weit′her′geholt *adj* far-fetched
weit′herzig *adj* broad-minded
weit′hin′ *adv* far off
weitläufig [′vaɪtlɔɪfɪç] *adj* lengthy, detailed; complicated; (*Verwandte*) distant; (*geräumig*) roomy ‖ *adv* at length, in detail
weit′reichend *adj* far-reaching
weitschweifig [′vaɪtʃvaɪfɪç] *adj* detailed, lengthy; long-winded
weit′sichtig *adj* (& fig) far-sighted
Weit′sprung *m* (sport) long jump
Weit′streckenflug *m* long-distance flight
weit′tragend *adj* long-range; (fig) far-reaching
Weit′winkelobjektiv *n* wide-angle lens
Weizen [′vaɪtsən] *m* (–s;–) wheat
Wei′zenmehl *n* wheat flour
welch [vɛlç] *interr adj* which ‖ *interr pron* which one; (*in Ausrufen*) what …!; **mit welcher** (or **mit welch einer**) **Begeisterung arbeitet er!** with what enthusiasm he works! ‖ *indef pron* any; some ‖ *rel pron* who, which, that
welcherlei [′vɛlçər′laɪ] *invar adj* what kind of; whatever
welk [vɛlk] *adj* withered; (*Haut, Lippen*) wrinkled; (fig) faded
welken [′vɛlkən] *intr* (SEIN) wither; (fig) fade
Wellblech [′vɛlblɛç] *n* corrugated iron
Well′blechhütte *f* Quonset hut
Welle [′vɛlə] *f* (–;–n) wave; (*Wellbaum*) shaft; (gym) circle (*around horizontal bar*); (mach) shaft
wellen [′vɛlən] *tr & ref* wave
Wel′lenbereich *m* wave band
Wel′lenberg *m* crest (*of wave*)
Wel′lenbewegung *f* undulation
Wel′lenbrecher *m* breakwater
wel′lenförmig *adj* wavy
Wel′lenlänge *f* wavelength
Wel′lenlinie *f* wavy line

wel′lenreiten §86 *intr* surf; waterski ‖ **Wellenreiten** *n* (–s;) surfing, surfboard riding; waterskiing
Wel′lenreiter –**in** §6 *mf* surfer; waterskier
Wel′lenreiterbrett *n* surfboard; water ski
Wel′lental *n* trough (*of wave*)
wellig [′vɛlɪç] *adj* wavy
Well′pappe *f* corrugated cardboard
Welt [vɛlt] *f* (–;–en) world
Welt′all *n* universe; outer space
Welt′anschauung *f* outlook on life; ideology
Welt′ausmaß *m*—**im W.** on a global scale
Welt′ausstellung *f* world's fair
welt′bekannt, welt′berühmt *adj* world-renowned
Wel′tenbummler *m* globetrotter
welt′erfahren *adj* sophisticated
Weltergewicht [′vɛltərgəvɪçt] *n* welterweight class
Weltergewichtler [′vɛltərgəvɪçtlər] *m* (–s;–) welterweight boxer
welt′erschütternd *adj* earth-shaking
welt′fremd *adj* secluded; innocent
Welt′friede *m* world peace
Welt′geistlicher *m* secular priest
welt′gewandt *adj* worldly-wise
Welt′karte *f* map of the world
welt′klug *adj* worldly-wise
Welt′körper *m* heavenly body
Welt′krieg *m* world war
Welt′kugel *f* globe
Welt′lage *f* international situation
welt′lich *adj* worldly; secular
Welt′macht *f* world power
Welt′mann *m* (–[e]s;⸚er) man of the world
welt′männisch *adj* sophisticated
Welt′meer *n* ocean
Welt′meinung *f* world opinion
Welt′meister –**in** §6 *mf* world champion
Welt′meisterschaft *f* world championship
Welt′ordnung *f* cosmic order
Welt′postverein *m* postal union
Welt′priester *m* secular priest
Welt′raum *m* (–[e]s;) outer space
Welt′raumfahrer *m* spaceman
Welt′raumfahrt *f* space travel
Welt′raumfahrzeug *n* spacecraft
Welt′raumforschung *f* exploration of outer space
Welt′raumgeschoß *n* space shot
Welt′raumkapsel *f* space capsule
Welt′raumstation *f* space station
Welt′raumstrahlen *pl* cosmic rays
Welt′reich *n* world empire
Welt′reise *f* trip around the world
Welt′rekord *m* world record
Welt′ruf *m* world-wide renown
Welt′ruhm *m* world-wide fame
Welt′schmerz *m* world-weariness
Welt′sicherheitsrat *m* U.N. Security Council
Welt′stadt *f* metropolis (*city with more than one million inhabitants*)
Welt′teil *m* continent
welt′umfassend *adj* world-wide
Welt′weisheit *f* philosophy

wem [vem] *interr & rel pron* to whom
Wem'fall *m* dative case
wen [ven] *interr & rel pron* whom
Wende ['vɛndə] *f* (-;-n) turn; turning point; (gym) face vault, front vault
Wen'dekreis *m* (geog) tropic
Wendeltreppe ['vɛndəltrɛpə] *f* spiral staircase
Wen'demarke *f* (aer) pylon; (sport) turn post
wenden ['vɛndən] §140 *tr* turn; turn around; turn over; (*Geld, Mühe*) spend ‖ *ref* turn; (*Wind, Wetter*) change ‖ *intr* turn, turn around
Wen'depunkt *m* turning point
wendig ['vɛndɪç] *adj* maneuverable; (*Person*) versatile, resourceful
Wen'dung *f* (-;-en) turn; change; (*Redensart*) idiomatic expression
Wen'fall *m* accusative case
wenig ['venɪç] *adj* little; **ein w.** a little, a bit of; **wenige** few, a few, some ‖ *adv* little; not very; seldom ‖ *indef pron* little; **wenige** few, a few
weniger ['venɪgər] *adj* fewer; less; (arith) minus
We'nigkeit *f* (-;) fewness; smallness; pittance; trifle; **meine W.** (coll) poor little me
wenigste ['venɪçstə] §9 *adj* least; very few, fewest; **am wenigsten** least of all
wenigstens ['venɪçstəns] *adv* at least
wenn [ven] *conj* if, in case; (*zeitlich*) when, whenever; **auch w.** even if; **außer w.** except when, except if, unless; **w. anders** provided that; **w. auch** although, even if; **w. schon, denn schon** go all the way ‖ **Wenn** *n* (-;-) if
wenngleich', wennschon' *conj* although
Wenzel ['vɛntsəl] *m* (-s;-) (cards) jack
wer [ver] *interr pron* who, which one; **wer auch immer** whoever; **wer da?** who goes there? ‖ *rel pron* he who, whoever ‖ *indef pron* somebody, anybody
Werbe– [vɛrbə] *comb.fm.* advertising; publicity; commercial
Wer'befernsehen *n* commercial television
Wer'befilm *m* commercial
Wer'befläche *f* advertising space
Wer'begraphik *f* commercial art
Wer'begraphiker –in §6 *mf* commercial artist
werben ['vɛrbən] §149 *tr* (*neue Kunden*) try to get; (mil) recruit ‖ *intr* advertise; **für e–n neuen Handelsartikel w.** advertise a new product; **um ein Mädchen w.** court a girl
Wer'beschrift *f* folder
Wer'bestelle *f* advertising agency
Wer'bung *f* (-;-en) advertising; publicity; courting; recruiting
Werdegang ['vɛrdəgaŋ] *m* career, background; (*Entwicklung*) development; (*Wachstum*) growth; (*Ablauf der Herstellung*) process of production
werden ['vɛrdən] §159 *intr* (SEIN) become, grow, get, turn; **w. zu** change into; **zu nichts w.** come to nought ‖

aux (SEIN) (to form the future) **er wird gehen** he will go; (to form the passive) **er wird geehrt** he is being honored ‖ **Werden** *n* (-s;) becoming, growing; (*Entstehung*) evolution; (*Wachstum*) growth; **im W. sein** be in the process of development; be in the making
wer'dend *adj* nascent; (*Mutter*) expectant; (*Arzt*) future
Werder ['verdər] *m* (-s;-) islet
Wer'fall *m* subjective case
werfen ['vɛrfən] §160 *tr* throw, cast; (*Junge*) produce; (*Blasen*) form, blow; **Falten w.** wrinkle ‖ *ref* (*Holz*) warp; **sich hin und her w.** toss; **sich in die Brust w.** throw out one's chest ‖ *intr* throw; (*Tieren*) produce young
Werft [vɛrft] *f* (-;-e) shipyard
Werft'halle *f* (aer) repair hangar
Werg [vɛrk] *n* (-[e]s;) oakum, tow
Werk [vɛrk] *n* (-[e]s;-e) work; (*Tat*) deed; (*Erzeugnis*) production; (*Leistung*) performance; (*Unternehmen*) undertaking; (*Fabrik*) works, plant, mill; (horol) clockwork; **das ist dein W.** that's your doing; **gutes W.** good deed; **im Werke sein** be in the works; **zu Werke gehen** go to it
Werk'anlage *f* plant, works
Werk'bank *f* (-;⸗e) workbench
werk'fremd *adj* (*Personen*) unauthorized
Werk'meister *m* foreman
Werk'nummer *f* factory serial number
Werks'angehörige §5 *mf* employee
Werk'schutz *m* security force
Werks'kantine *f* factory cafeteria
Werk'statt *f*, **Werk'stätte** *f* workshop
Werk'stattwagen *m* maintenance truck
Werk'stoff *m* manufacturing material
Werk'stück *n* (indust) piece
Werk'tag *m* weekday; working day
werk'tägig *adj* workaday, ordinary
werk'tags *adv* (on) weekdays
werk'tätig *adj* working; practical
Werk'zeug *n* tool
Werk'zeugmaschine *f* machine tool
Wermut ['vermut] *m* (-[e]s;) vermouth; (bot) wormwood
wert [vert] *adj* worth; worthy; esteemed; **etw** [*genit* or *acc*] **w. sein** be worth s.th.; **nicht der Rede w. sein** not worth mentioning; **nichts w.** good for nothing; **Werter Herr X** Dear Mr. X ‖ **Wert** *m* (-[e]s;-e) worth, value; price, rate; (*Wichtigkeit*) importance; (chem) valence; **äußerer W.** face value; **im W. von** valued at; **innerer W.** intrinsic value; **Werte** (com) assets; (phys) data
Wert'angabe *f* valuation
wert'beständig *adj* of lasting value; (*Währung*) stable
Wert'bestimmung *f* appraisal
Wert'brief *m* insured letter
werten ['vertən] *tr* (*bewerten*) value; (*nach Leistung*) rate; (*auswerten*) evaluate
Wert'gegenstand *m* valuable article; **Wertgegenstände** valuables
–wertig [vertɪç] *comb.fm.* –value, –quality, e.g., **geringwertig** low-qual-

ity; (chem) –valent, e.g., **zweiwertig** bivalent

Wer'tigkeit *f* (-;-en) (chem) valence

wert'los *adj* worthless

Wert'papiere *pl* securities

Wert'sachen *pl* valuables

wert'voll *adj* valuable

Wert'zeichen *n* stamp; (*Briefmarke*) postage stamp; (*Banknote*) bill

Wesen ['vezən] *n* (-s;-) being, creature; entity; (*inneres Sein, Kern*) essence; (*Betragen*) conduct, way; (*Getue*) fuss; (*Natur*) nature, character; **einnehmendes W.** pleasing personality; **höchtes W.** Supreme Being

–wesen *n comb.fm.* system

we'senhaft *adj* real; characteristic

we'senlos *adj* unreal; incorporeal

wesentlich ['vezəntlıç] *adj* essential; (*beträchtlich*) substantial

Weser ['vezər] *f* (-;) Weser (River)

Wes'fall *m* genitive case

weshalb [vɛsˈhalp] *adv* why; wherefore

Wespe ['vɛspə] *f* (-;-n) wasp

wessen ['vesən] *interr pron* whose

West [vɛst] *m* (-s;) west; (poet) west wind

Weste ['vɛstə] *f* (-;-n) vest; **e–e reine W.** a clean slate

Westen ['vɛstən] *m* (-s;) west; **im W. von** west of; **nach W.** westward

Westfalen [vɛstˈfɑlən] *n* (-s;) Westphalia

westfälisch [vɛstˈfelɪʃ] *adj* Westphalian

West'gote *m* (-n;-n) Visigoth

Westindien [vɛstˈɪndjən] *n* (-s;) the West Indies

west'lich *adj* west, western; westerly

Westmächte ['vɛstmɛçtə] *pl* Western Powers

westwärts ['vɛstvɛrts] *adv* westward

weswegen [vɛsˈvegən] *adv* why; wherefore

wett [vɛt] *adj* even, quits

Wett– *comb.fm.* competitive

Wett'bewerb *m* (-s;-e) competition, contest; (*Treffen*) meet

Wett'bewerber –**in** §6 *mf* competitor

Wette ['vɛtə] *f* (-;-n) bet, wager; **e–e W. abschließen** (or **eingehen**) make a bet; **mit j–m um die W. laufen** race s.o.; **was gilt die W.?** what do you bet?

Wett'eifer *m* competitiveness, rivalry

wetteifern ['vɛtaɪfərn] *insep intr* compete; **w. um** compete for

Wetter ['vɛtər] *n* (-s;) weather; (min) ventilation; **alle W.!** holy smokes!

wet'terbeständig, wet'terfest *adj* weatherproof

Wet'terglas *n* barometer

wet'terhart *adj* hardy

Wet'terkunde *f* meteorology

Wet'terlage *f* weather conditions

wet'terleuchten *insep impers*—**es wetterleuchtet** there is summer lightning || **Wetterleuchten** *n* (-;) summer lightning, heat lightning

Wet'terverhältnisse *pl* weather conditions

Wet'tervorhersage *f* weather forecast

Wet'terwarte *f* meteorological station

Wet'terwechsel *m* change in the weather

wetterwendisch ['vɛtərvɛndɪʃ] *adj* moody

Wett'fahrer –**in** §6 *mf* racer

Wett'fahrt *f* race

Wett'kampf *m* competition, contest

Wett'kämpfer –**in** §6 *mf* competitor, contestant

Wett'lauf *m* race, foot race

Wett'läufer –**in** §6 *mf* runner

wett'machen *tr* make up for

Wett'rennen *n* race

Wett'rudern *n* boat race

Wett'rüsten *n* armaments race

Wett'schwimmen *n* swimming meet

Wett'segeln *n* regatta

Wett'spiel *n* game, match

Wett'streit *m* contest, match, game

Wett'zettel *m* betting ticket

wetzen ['vetsən] *tr* whet, sharpen

Wetzstein ['vetsʃtaɪn] *m* whetstone

Whisky ['vɪski] *m* (-s;-s) whiskey

wich [vɪç] *pret* of **weichen**

Wichs [vɪks] *m* (es-;-e) gala; **in vollem W.** in full dress; **sich in W. werfen** dress up

Wichse ['vɪksə] *f* (-;-n) shoepolish || *f* (-;) (coll) spanking

wichsen ['vɪksən] *tr* polish; (coll) spank, beat up

Wicht [vɪçt] *m* (-[e]s;-e) elf; dwarf

Wichtel ['vɪçtəl] *m* (-s;-) dwarf

wichtig ['vɪçtɪç] *adj* important || *adv* —**w. tun** act important

Wich'tigkeit *f* (-;) importance

Wichtigtuer ['vɪçtɪçtu·ər] *m* (-s;-) busybody

wichtigtuerisch ['vɪçtɪçtu·ərɪʃ] *adj* officious

Wicke ['vɪkə] *f* (-;-n) (bot) vetch

Wickel ['vɪkəl] *m* (-s;-) wrapper; curler, roller; (*von Garn*) ball; (med) compress

wickeln ['vɪkəln] *tr* wrap; wind (*Haar*) curl; (*Kind*) diaper; (*Zigaretten*) roll

Widder ['vɪdər] *m* (-s;-) ram; (astr) Ram

wider ['vidər] *prep* (*acc*) against, contrary to

wider– *comb.fm.* re–, con–, un–, counter–, contra–, anti–, with–

wi'derborstig *adj* stubborn, contrary

widerfah'ren §71 *intr* (SEIN) (*dat*) befall, happen to

Wi'derhaken *m* barb

Wi'derhall *m* echo, reverberation; (fig) response, reaction

wi'derhallen *intr* echo, resound

Wi'derlager *n* abutment

widerle'gen *tr* refute

wi'derlich *adj* repulsive

wi'dernatürlich *adj* unnatural

widerra'ten §63 *tr*—**j–m etw w.** dissuade s.o. from s.th.

wi'derrechtlich *adj* illegal

Wi'derrede *f* contradiction

Wi'derruf *m* recall; cancellation; retraction; denial; **bis auf W.** until further notice

widerru'fen §122 *tr* revoke; (*Auftrag*)

cancel; (*Befehl*) countermand; (*Behauptung*) retract
Widersacher –in ['vidərzaxər(ın)] §6 *mf* adversary
Wi′derschein *m* reflection
widerset′zen *ref* (*dat*) oppose, resist
widersetz′lich *adj* insubordinate
wi′dersinning *adj* absurd, nonsensical
widerspenstig ['vidərʃpɛnstıç] *adj* refractory, contrary; (*Haar*) stubborn
wi′derspiegeln *tr* reflect ‖ *ref* (**in** *dat*) be reflected (in)
Wi′derspiel *n* contrary, reverse
widerspre′chen §64 *intr* (*dat*) contradict; (*dat*) oppose
widerspre′chend *adj* contradictory
Wi′derspruch *m* contradiction; opposition; **auf heftigen W. stoßen bei** meet with strong opposition from
widersprüchlich ['vidərʃpryçlıç] *adj* contradictory
wi′derspruchsvoll *adj* full of contradictions
Wi′derstand *m* resistance; opposition; (elec) resistance; (elec) resistor
Wi′derstandsnest *n* pocket of resistance
widerste′hen §146 *intr* (*dat*) withstand, resist; (*dat*) be repugnant to
widerstre′ben *intr* (*dat*) oppose, resist; (*dat*) be repugnant to ‖ *impers*—**es widerstrebt mir zu** (*inf*) I hate to (*inf*)
widerstre′bend *adj* reluctant
Wi′derstreit *m* opposition, antagonism; (fig) conflict, clash
widerstrei′ten §86 *intr* (*dat*) clash with
widerwärtig ['vidərvɛrtıç] *adj* nasty
Wi′derwille *m* (**gegen**) dislike (of, for), aversion (to); (*Widerstreben*) reluctance; **mit W.** reluctantly
wi′derwillig *adj* reluctant, unwilling
widmen ['vıtmən] *tr* dedicate, devote ‖ *ref* (*dat*) devote oneself to
Wid′mung *f* (–;–en) dedication
widrig ['vidrıç] *adj* contrary; (*ungünstig*) unfavorable, adverse
wid′rigenfalls *adv* otherwise, or else
wie [vi] *adv* how; (*vergleichend*) as, such as, like; **so…wie** as…as; **und wie!** and how!; **wie, bitte?** what did you say?; **wie dem auch sei** be that as it may; **wie wäre es mit…?** how about…?
wieder ['vidər] *adv* again; anew; (*zurück*) back; (*als Vergeltung*) in return
wieder– *comb.fm.* re-
Wie′derabdruck *m* reprint
wiederan′knüpfen *tr* resume
Wiederauf′bau *m* (–[e]s;) rebuilding
wiederauf′bauen *tr* rebuild, reconstruct
wiederauf′erstehen §146 *intr* (SEIN) rise from the dead
Wiederauf′erstehung *f* resurrection
Wiederauf′führung *f* (theat) revival
wiederauf′kommen §99 *intr* (SEIN) (*Kranker*) recover; (*Mode*) come in again
Wiederauf′nahme *f* resumption; (jur) reopening
Wiederauf′nahmeverfahren *n* retrial
Wiederauf′rüstung *f* rearmament

Wie′derbeginn *m* reopening
wie′derbekommen §99 *tr* recover
wie′derbeleben *tr* revive, resuscitate
wie′derbeschaffen *tr* replace
wie′derbringen §65 *tr* bring back; restore, give back
wiederein′bringen §65 *tr* make up for
wiederein′setzen *tr* (**in** *acc*) reinstate (in); **in Rechte w.** restore to former rights
wiederein′stellen *tr* rehire; (mil) reenlist
Wie′dereintritt *m* (rok) reentry
wie′derergreifen §88 *tr* recapture
wie′dererhalten §90 *tr* get back
wie′dererkennen §97 *tr* recognize
wie′dererlangen *tr* recover, retrieve
wie′dererstatten *tr* restore; (*Geld*) refund
Wie′dergabe *f* return; reproduction; rendering
wie′dergeben §80 *tr* give back; (*Ton*) reproduce; (*spielen, übersetzen*) render; (*Ehre, Gesundheit*) restore
Wie′dergeburt *f* rebirth
wie′dergenesen §84 *intr* (SEIN) recover
wie′dergewinnen §52 *tr* regain
wiedergut′machen *tr* make good
Wiedergut′machung *f* (–;–en) reparation
wiederher′stellen *tr* restore
wie′derholen *tr* bring back; take back ‖ **wiederho′len** *tr* repeat
wiederholt [vidər'hɔlt] *adv* repeatedly
Wiederho′lung *f* (–;–en) repetition
Wiederho′lungszeichen *n* dittomarks; (mus) repeat
Wie′derhören *n*—**auf W.!** (telp) goodbye!
wie′derimpfen *tr* give (*s.o.*) a booster shot
wiederinstand′setzen *tr* repair
wiederkäuen ['vidərkɔı-ən] *tr* ruminate; (fig) repeat over and over ‖ *intr* chew the cud
Wiederkehr ['vidərker] *f* (–;) return; recurrence; anniversary
wie′derkehren *intr* (SEIN) return; recur
wie′derkommen §99 *intr* (SEIN) come back
Wiederkunft ['vidərkʊnft] *f* (–;) return
wie′dersehen §138 *tr* see again ‖ *recip* meet again ‖ **Wiedersehen** *n* (–s;–) meeting again; **auf W.!** see you!
Wie′dertäufer *m* Baptist
wie′dertun §154 *tr* do again, repeat
wie′derum *adv* again; on the other hand
wie′dervereinigen *tr* reunite; reunify
Wie′dervereinigung *f* reunion; (pol) reunification
wie′derverheiraten *tr & recip* remarry
Wie′derverkäufer –in §6 *mf* retailer
Wie′derwahl *f* reelection
wie′derwählen *tr* reelect
wiederzu′lassen §104 *tr* readmit
Wiege ['vigə] *f* (–;–n) cradle
wiegen ['vigən] *tr* (*schaukeln*) rock ‖ *ref*—**sich in den Hüften w.** sway one's hips; **sich w. in** (*acc*) lull oneself into ‖ §57 *tr & intr* weigh
Wie′gendruck *m* incunabulum
Wie′genlied *n* lullaby

wiehern ['vi·ərn] *intr* neigh; **wiehern-des Gelächter** horselaugh
Wien [vin] *n* (-s;) Vienna
Wiener –in ['vinər(ın)] §6 *mf* Viennese
wienerisch ['vinərıʃ] *adj* Viennese
wies [vis] *pret* of **weisen**
Wiese ['vizə] *f* (-;-n) meadow
Wiesel ['vizəl] *n* (-s;-) weasel
Wie'senland *n* meadowland
wieso' *adv* why, how come
wieviel' *adj* how much; **w. Uhr ist es?** what time is it? || *adv & pron* how much || **vieviele** *adj & pron* how many
wievielte [vi'filtə] §9 *adj* which, what; **den wievielten haben wir?** (or **der w. ist heute?**) what day of the month is it?
wiewohl' *conj* although
wild [vılt] *adj* wild; savage; (*grausam*) ferocious; (*Flucht*) headlong; (**auf** *acc*) wild (about); **wilde Ehe** concubinage; **wilder Streik** wildcat strike || **Wild** *n* (-es;) game
Wild'bach *m* torrent
Wild'braten *m* roast venison
Wildbret ['vıltbret] *n* (-s;) game; venison
Wild'dieb *m* poacher
Wilde ['vıldə] §5 *mf* savage; **wie ein Wilder** like a madman
Wild'ente *f* wild duck
Wilderer ['vıldərər] *m* (-s;-) poacher
wildern ['vıldərn] *intr* poach
Wild'fleisch *n* game; venison
wild'fremd' *adj* completely strange
Wild'hüter *m* game warden
Wild'leder *n* doeskin, buckskin; chamois; suede
Wildnis ['vıltnıs] *f* (-;) wilderness
Wild'schwein *n* wild boar
Wild'wasser *n* rapids
Wildwest'film *m* western
wildwüchsig ['vıltvyksıç] *adj* wild
Wille ['vılə] *m* (-ns;-n), **Willen** ['vılən] *m* (-s;-) will; (*Absicht*) intention; **mit W.** on purpose; **um j-s willen** for s.o.'s sake; **wider Willen** unwillingly; unintentionally; **willens sein zu** (*inf*) be willing to (*inf*)
wil'lenlos *adj* irresolute; unstable
Wil'lensfreiheit *f* free will
Wil'lenskraft *f* will power
wil'lensschwach *adj* weak-willed
wil'lensstark *adj* strong-willed
willfah'ren *intr* (*dat*) comply with
willig ['vılıç] *adj* willing, ready
Wil'ligkeit *f* (-;) willingness
willkom'men *adj* welcome; **j-n w. heißen** welcome s.o. || **Willkommen** *m & n* (-s;) welcome
Willkür ['vılkyr] *f* (-;) arbitrariness
will'kürlich *adj* arbitrary·
wimmeln ['vıməln] *intr* (**von**) team (with)
wimmern ['vımərn] *intr* whimper
Wimpel ['vımpəl] *m* (-s;-) streamer; pennant
Wimper ['vımpər] *f* (-;-n) eyelash; **ohne mit der W. zu zucken** without batting an eye
Wim'perntusche *f* mascara

Wind [vınt] *m* (-[e]s;-e) wind; flatulence; (hunt) scent
Wind'beutel *m* (fig) windbag; (aer) windsock; (culin) cream puff
Winde ['vındə] *f* (-;-n) winch, windlass; reel; (naut) capstan
Windel ['vındəl] *f* (-;-n) diaper
win'delweich *adj*—**w. schlagen** (coll) beat to a pulp
winden ['vındən] §59 *tr* wind; twist, coil; (*Kranz*) weave, make || *ref* wriggle; (*Fluß*) wind; (*vor Schmerzen*) writhe
Wind'fang *m* storm porch
Wind'hose *f* tornado
Wind'hund *m* greyhound; (coll) windbag
windig ['vındıç] *adj* windy; (fig) flighty
Wind'kanal *m* wind tunnel
Wind'licht *n* hurricane lamp
Wind'mühle *f* windmill
Wind'pocken *pl* chicken pox
Wind'sack *m* windsock
Wind'schatten *m* lee
Wind'schutzscheibe *f* windshield
Wind'stärke *f* wind velocity
wind'still *adj* calm || **Windstille** *f* calm
Wind'stoß *m* gust
Wind'strömung *f* air current
Win'dung *f* (-;-en) winding, twisting; (*Kurve*) bend; (*e-r Schlange*) coil; (*e-r Schraube*) thread, worm; (*e-r Muschel*) whorl
Wind'zug *m* air current, draft
Wink [vıŋk] *m* (-[e]s;-e) sign; (*Zwinkern*) wink; (*mit der Hand*) wave; (*mit dem Kopfe*) nod; (*Hinweis*) hint, tip; **W. mit dem Zaunpfahl** broad hint
Winkel ['vıŋkəl] *m* (-s;-) corner; (carp) square; (geom) angle; (mil) chevron
winkelig ['vıŋkəlıç] *adj* angular; (*Straße*) crooked
Win'kellinie *f* diagonal
Win'kelmaß *n* (carp) square
Win'kelzug *m* subterfuge; evasion
winken ['vıŋkən] *intr* signal; **mit der Hand** wave; (*mit dem Kopfe*) nod; (*mit dem Auge*) wink; **mit dem Taschentuch w.** wave the handkerchief
Win'ker *m* (-s;-) signalman; (aut) direction signal
winseln ['vınzəln] *intr* whimper, whine
Winter ['vıntər] *m* (-s;-) winter
win'terfest *adj* winterized; (*Pflanzen*) hardy
win'terlich *adj* wintry
Win'terschlaf *m* hibernation; **W. halten** hibernate
Win'tersonnenwende *f* winter solstice
Winzer ['vıntsər] *m* (-s;-) vinedresser; (*Traubenleser*) grape picker
winzig ['vıntsıç] *adj* tiny
Wipfel ['vıpfəl] *m* (-s;-) treetop
Wippe ['vıpə] *f* (-;-n) seesaw
wippen ['vıpən] *intr* seesaw; rock; balance oneself
wir [vir] §11 *pers pron* we
Wirbel ['vırbəl] *m* (-s;-) whirl; eddy; whirlpool; (*Trommel-*) roll; (*Violin-*)

peg; (anat) vertebra; **e–n W. machen** (coll) raise Cain
wirbelig ['vɪrbəlɪç] adj whirling; giddy
Wir'belknochen m (anat) vertebra
wir'bellos adj spineless, invertebrate
wirbeln ['vɪrbəln] tr warble || intr whirl; (Wasser) eddy; (Trommel) roll; (Lerche) warble; **mir wirbelt der Kopf** my head is spinning
Wir'belsäule f spinal column, spine
Wir'belsturm m hurricane, typhoon
Wir'beltier n vertebrate
Wir'belwind m whirlwind
wirken ['vɪrkən] tr work, bring about, effect; (Teig) knead; (Teppich) weave; (Pullover) knit; **Gutes w.** do good; **Wunder w.** work wonders || intr work; be active; function; look, appear; (Worte) tell, hit home; **als Arzt w.** be a doctor; **an e–r Schule (als Lehrer) w.** teach school; **anregend w.** act as a stimulant; **berauschend w. auf** (acc) intoxicate; **beruhigend w. auf** (acc) have a soothing effect on; **gut w.** work well; **lächerlich w.** look ridiculous; **stark w. auf** (acc) touch deeply; **w. auf** (acc) affect, have an effect on; **w. bei** have an effect on; **w. für** work for; **w. gegen** work against, counteract || **Wirken** n (–s;) action, performance; operation
wirk'lich adj real, actual; true || adv really, actually; truly
Wirk'lichkeit f (–;–en) reality; actual fact
Wirk'lichkeitsform f indicative mood
wirksam ['vɪrkzam] adj active; effective; (Hieb) telling; **w. für** good for
Wirk'samkeit f (–;) effectiveness
Wirk'stoff m metabolic substance (vitamin, hormone, or enzyme)
Wir'kung f (–;–en) effect; result; operation, action; influence, impression
Wir'kungsbereich m scope; effective range; (mil) zone of fire
wir'kungsfähig adj active; effective; efficient
Wir'kungskreis m domain, province
wir'kungslos adj ineffective; inefficient
wir'kungsvoll adj effective; efficacious
Wirk'waren pl knitwear
wirr [vɪr] adj confused; (verworren) chaotic; (Haar) disheveled
Wirren ['vɪrən] pl disorders, troubles
Wirr'kopf m scatterbrain
Wirrwarr ['vɪrvar] m (–s;) mix-up, mess
Wirt [vɪrt] m (–[e]s;–e) host; innkeeper; landlord; (biol) host
Wirtin ['vɪrtɪn] f (–;–nen) hostess; innkeeper, innkeeper's wife; landlady
wirt'lich adj hospitable
Wirt'schaft f (–;–en) economy; business; industry and trade; (Haushaltung) housekeeping; (Hauswesen) household; (Gasthaus) inn; (Treiben) goings-on; (Durcheinander) mess; (Umstände) fuss, trouble; **die W. besorgen** (or **führen**) keep house; **gelenkte W.** planned economy
wirtschaften ['vɪrtʃaftən] intr keep

house; economize; (herumhantieren) bustle about; **gut w.** manage well
Wirt'schafter –in §6 mf manager || f housekeeper
Wirt'schaftler –in §6 mf economist; economics teacher
wirt'schaftlich adj economical, thrifty; economic; industrial; (vorteilhaft) profitable
Wirt'schaftsgeld n housekeeping money
Wirt'schaftshilfe f economic aid
Wirt'schaftsjahr n fiscal year
Wirt'schaftslehre f economics
Wirt'schaftspolitik f economic policy
Wirt'schaftsprüfer –in §6 mf certified public accountant, CPA
Wirts'haus n inn, restaurant; bar
wischen ['vɪʃən] tr wipe
Wisch'lappen m dustcloth
Wisch'tuch n dishtowel
wispern ['vɪspərn] tr & intr whisper
Wißbegierde ['vɪsbəgirdə] f (–;) craving for knowledge; curiosity
wissen ['vɪsən] §161 tr & intr know || **Wissen** n (–s;) knowledge; learning; know-how; **meines Wissens** as far as I know
Wis'senschaft f (–;–en) knowledge; science
Wis'senschaftler –in §6 mf scientist
wis'senschaftlich adj scientific; scholarly; learned
Wis'sensdrang m, **Wis'sensdurst** m thirst for knowledge
Wis'sensgebiet n field of knowledge
wis'senswert adj worth knowing
wis'sentlich adj conscious; willful || adv knowingly; on purpose
wittern ['vɪtərn] tr scent, smell
Wit'terung f (–;–en) weather; (hunt) scent; **bei günstiger W.** weather permitting; **e–e feine W. haben** have a good nose
Wit'terungsverhältnisse pl weather conditions
Witwe ['vɪtvə] f (–;–n) widow
Witwer ['vɪtvər] m (–s;–) widower
Witz [vɪts] m (–es;–e) joke; wisecrack; wit; wittiness; **das ist der ganze W.** that's all; **Witze machen** (or **reißen**) crack jokes
Witz'blatt n comics
Witzbold ['vɪtsbɔlt] m (–[e]s;–e) joker
witzig ['vɪtsɪç] adj witty; funny
wo [vo] adv where; **wo auch** (or **wo immer**) wherever; **wo nicht** if not; **wo nur** wherever
woan'ders adv somewhere else
wob [vop] pret of **weben**
wobei' adv whereby; whereat; whereto; at which; in the course of which
Woche ['vɔxə] f (–;–n) week; **heute in e–r W.** a week from today; **in den Wochen sein** be in labor; **in die Wochen kommen** go into labor; **unter der W.** (coll) during the week
Wo'chenbeihilfe f maternity benefits
Wo'chenbett n post-natal period
Wo'chenblatt n weekly (newspaper)
Wo'chenende n weekend
Wo'chengeld n weekly allowance; (für Mütter) maternity benefits

wo'chenlang adj lasting many weeks || adv for weeks
Wo'chenlohn m weekly wages
Wo'chenschau f (cin) newsreel
wöchentlich ['vœçəntlɪç] adj weekly || adv every week; **einmal w.** once a week
-wöchig [vœçɪç] comb.fm. -week
Wöchnerin ['vœçnərɪn] f (-;-nen) recent mother
Wodka ['vɔtka] m (-s;) vodka
wodurch' adv whereby, by which; how
wofern' conj provided that; **w. nicht** unless
wofür' adv wherefore, for which; what for; **w. halten Sie mich?** what do you take me for?
wog [vok] pret of **wägen** & **wiegen**
Woge ['vogə] f (-;-n) billow; **Wogen der Erregung** waves of excitement
woge'gen adv against what; against which; in exchange for what
wogen ['vogən] intr billow, surge, heave; (Getreide) wave; **hin und her w.** fluctuate
woher' adv from where; **w. wissen Sie das?** how do you know this?
wohin' adv whereto, where
wohinge'gen conj whereas
wohl [vol] adj well || adv well; (freilich) to be sure, all right; I guess; possibly, probably; perhaps; **es sich** [dat] **w. sein lassen** have a good time; **nun w.!** well!; **w. daran tun zu** (inf) do well to (inf); **w. dem, der** happy he who; **w. kaum** hardly; **w. oder übel** willy-nilly || **Wohl** n (-[e]s;) good health, well-being; (Wohlfahrt) welfare; (Gedeihen) prosperity; **auf Ihr W.!** to your health! **gemeines W.** common good
wohlan' interj all right then!
wohlauf' adj in good health, well || interj all right then!
wohlbedacht ['volbədaxt] adj well-thought-out
Wohl'befinden n (-;) well-being
Wohl'behagen n comfort, contentment
wohl'behalten adj safe and sound
wohl'bekannt adj well-known
wohl'beschaffen adj in good condition
Wohl'ergehen n well-being
wohl'erzogen adj well-bred
Wohl'fahrt f (-;) welfare
Wohl'fahrtsarbeit f social work
wohl'feil adj cheap
Wohl'gefallen n (-s;) pleasure, satisfaction
wohl'gefällig adj pleasant, agreeable
wohl'gemeint adj well-meant
wohlgemut ['volgəmut] adj cheerful
wohl'genährt adj well-fed
wohl'geneigt adj affectionate
Wohl'geruch m fragrance, perfume
wohl'gesinnt adj well-disposed
wohl'habend adj well-to-do
wohlig ['volɪç] adj comfortable
Wohl'klang m melodious sound
wohl'klingend adj melodious
Wohl'leben n good living, luxury
wohl'riechend adj fragrant
wohl'schmeckend adj tasty
Wohl'sein n good health, well-being

Wohl'stand m prosperity, wealth
Wohl'tat f benefit; (Gunst) kindness, good deed; **e-e W. sein** hit the spot
Wohl'täter -in §6 mf benefactor
wohl'tätig adj charitable; beneficent
Wohl'tätigkeit f charity
wohltuend ['voltu-ənt] adj pleasant
wohl'tun §154 intr do good; (dat) be pleasant (to)
wohl'unterrichtet adj well-informed
wohl'verdient adj well-deserved
wohl'verstanden interj mark my words!
wohl'weislich adv very wisely
wohl'wollen §162 intr (dat) be well-disposed towards || **Wohlwollen** n (-s;) good will; (Gunst) favor
Wohn- [von] comb.fm. residential; dwelling, living
Wohn'anhänger m house trailer
Wohn'block m block of apartments
wohnen ['vonən] intr live, reside; (als Mieter) room
wohn'haft adj residing, living
Wohn'haus n dwelling; apartment house
Wohn'küche f efficiency apartment
Wohn'laube f garden house
wohn'lich adj livable; cozy
Wohn'möglichkeit f living accommodations
Wohn'ort m place of residence; (jur) domicile; **ständiger W.** permanent address
Wohn'raum m living space; room (of a house)
Wohn'sitz m place of residence
Woh'nung f (-;-en) dwelling, home; apartment; room; accommodations
Woh'nungsamt n housing authority
Woh'nungsbau m (-[e]s;) housing construction
Woh'nungsfrage f housing problem
Woh'nungsinhaber -in §6 mf occupant
Woh'nungsmangel m, **Woh'nungsnot** f housing shortage
Wohn'viertel n residential district
Wohn'wagen m mobile home
Wohn'wagenparkplatz m trailer camp
Wohn'zimmer n living room
wölben ['vœlbən] tr vault, arch || ref (über dat or acc) arch (over)
Wöl'bung f (-;-en) curvature; vault
Wolf [vɔlf] m (-[e]s;⸚e) wolf; (Fleisch-) meat grinder; (astr) Lupus; (pathol) lupus
Wolfram ['vɔlfram] n (-s;) tungsten
Wolke ['vɔlkə] f (-;-n) cloud
Wol'kenbildung f cloud formation
Wol'kenbruch m cloudburst
Wol'kendecke f cloudcover
Wol'kenfetzen m wispy cloud
Wol'kenhöhe f (meteor) ceiling
Wol'kenkratzer m (-s;-) skyscraper
Wol'kenwand f cloud bank
wolkig ['vɔlkɪç] adj cloudy, clouded
Wolldecke ['vɔldɛkə] f woolen blanket
Wolle ['vɔlə] f (-;-n) wool
wollen ['vɔlən] adj woolen, wool || §162 tr want, wish; mean, intend; (gern haben) like || intr wish, like; **dem sei, wie ihm wolle** be that as it may; **wie Sie w.** as you please || mod aux want (to), wish (to), intend (to);

be going (to) || **Wollen** *n* (-s;) will; volition

Wollfett ['vɔlfɛt] *n* lanolin

Wollgarn ['vɔlgarn] *n* worsted

wollig ['vɔlıç] *adj* woolly

Wolljacke ['vɔljakə] *f* cardigan

Wollsachen ['vɔlzaxən] *pl* woolens

Wollstoff ['vɔlʃtɔf] *m* woolen fabric

Wollust ['vɔllust] *f* (-;̈e) lust

wollüstig ['vɔllʏstıç] *adj* voluptuous; *(geil)* lewd, lecherous

Wollüstling ['vɔllʏstlıŋ] *m* (-s;-e) voluptuary

Wollwaren ['vɔlvarən] *pl* woolens

womit' *adv* with which; with what; wherewith; **w. kann ich dienen?** (com) can I help you?

womög'lich *adv* possibly, if possible

wonach' *adv* after which, whereupon; according to which

Wonne ['vɔnə] *f* (-;-n) delight; bliss

Won'negefühl *n* blissful feeling

Won'neschauer *m* thrill of delight

won'netrunken *adj* enraptured

won'nevoll, wonnig ['vɔnıç] *adj* blissful

woran' *adv* at which; at what; **ich weiß nicht, w. ich bin** I don't know where I stand

worauf' *adv* on which; on what; whereupon; **w. warten Sie?** what are you waiting for?

woraus' *adv* out of what, from what; out of which, from which; **w. ist das gemacht?** what is this made of?

worden ['vɔrdən] *pp* of **werden**

worin' *adv* in what; in which

Wort [vɔrt] *n* (-[e]s;̈er) word *(individual; literal)* || *n* (-[e]s;-e) word *(expression; figurative)*; *(Ausspruch)* saying; *(Ehrenwort)* word *(of honor)*; **auf ein W.!** may I have a word with you!; **auf mein W.!** word of honor!; **aufs W.** implicitly, to the letter; **das W. ergreifen** begin to speak; (parl) take the floor; **das W. erhalten** (or **haben**) be allowed to speak; (parl) have the floor; **das W. führen** be the spokesman; **hast du Worte!** (coll) can you beat that!; **in Worten** in writing; **j-m das W. erteilen** allow s.o. to speak; **j-m ins W. fallen** cut s.o. short

Wort'art *f* (gram) part of speech

Wort'bedeutungslehre *f* semantics

Wort'beugung *f* declension

Wort'bildung *f* word formation

wort'brüchig *adj*—**w. werden** break one's word

Wörterbuch ['vœrtərbux] *n* dictionary

Wörterverzeichnis ['vœrtərfɛrtsaıçnıs] *n* word index; vocabulary; glossary

Wort'folge *f* word order

Wort'führer –in §6 *mf* spokesman

Wort'gefecht *n* dispute

wort'getreu *adj* literal; verbatim

wort'karg *adj* taciturn

Wortklauber –in ['vɔrtklaubər(ın)] §6 *mf* quibbler, hairsplitter

Wort'laut *m* wording, (fig) letter

wörtlich ['vœrtlıç] *adj* word-for-word; literal; *(Rede)* direct

wort'los *adv* without saying a word

Wort'register *n* word index

Wort'schatz *m* vocabulary

Wort'schwall *m* flood of words, verbiage

Wort'spiel *n* pun

Wort'stamm *m* stem

Wort'stellung *f* word order

Wort'streit *m*, **Wort'wechsel** *m* argument

worüber [vo'rybər] *adv* over what, over which

worum [vo'rum] *adv* about what, about which

worunter [vo'runtər] *adv* under what, under which; among which

wovon' *adv* from what, of what, from which, of which; **w. ist die Rede?** what are they talking about?

wovor' *adv* of what; before which

wozu' *adv* for what; why; to which

Wrack [vrak] *n* (-[e]s;-e & -s) (& fig) wreck

Wrack'gut *n* wreckage

wrang [vraŋ] *pret* of **wringen**

wringen ['vrıŋən] §142 *tr* wring

Wringmaschine ['vrıŋmaʃinə] *f* wringer

Wucher ['vuxər] *m* (-s;) profiteering; **das ist ja W.!** (coll) that's highway robbery!; **W. treiben** profiteer

Wu'cherer –in §6 *mf* profiteer; loan shark

Wu'chergewinn *m* excess profit

wu'cherhaft, wucherisch ['vuxərıʃ] *adj* profiteering, exorbitant

Wu'chermiete *f* excessive rent

wuchern ['vuxərn] *intr* grow luxuriantly; *(Wucher treiben)* profiteer

Wu'cherung *f* (-;-en) (bot) rank growth; (pathol) growth

Wu'cherzinsen *pl* excessive interest

wuchs [vuks] *pret* of **wachsen** || **Wuchs** *m* (-es;) growth; **groß von W.** tall

–wüchsig [vʏksıç] *comb.fm.* -growing, -grown

Wucht [vuxt] *f* (-;-en) weight, force

wuchten ['vuxtən] *tr* lift with effort

wuchtig ['vuxtıç] *adj* heavy; massive

Wühlarbeit ['vylarbaıt] *f* subversive activity

wühlen ['vylən] *intr* dig, burrow; *(Schwein)* root about; *(suchend)* rummage about; (pol) engage in subversive activities; **im Geld w.** be rolling in money; **in Schmutz w.** wallow in filth

Wüh'ler –in §6 *mf* subversive, agitator

Wulst [vulst] *m* (-es;̈e) & *f* (-;̈e) bulge; (aut) rim *(of tire)*

wulstig ['vulstıç] *adj* bulging; *(Lippen)* thick

wund [vunt] *adj* sore; (poet) wounded

Wunde ['vundə] *f* (-;-n) wound; sore

Wunder ['vundər] *n* (-s;-) wonder; miracle; **W. wirken** work wonders

wunderbar ['vundərbar] *adj* wonderful; (& fig) miraculous

Wun'derding *n* marvel

Wun'derdoktor *m* faith healer

Wun'derkind *n* child prodigy

Wun'derkraft *f* miraculous power

wun'derlich *adj* queer, odd

wundern ['vundərn] *tr* amaze || *ref*

(**über** *acc*) be amazed (at) || *impers*
—es sollte mich w., wenn I'd be surprised if; **es wundert mich, daß** I am
surprised that
wun′derschön′ *adv* lovely, gorgeous
Wun′dertat *f* miracle
Wun′dertäter –in §6 *mf* wonder worker
wundertätig *adj* miraculous
wun′dervoll *adj* wonderful, marvelous
Wun′derwerk *n* (& fig) miracle
Wun′derzeichen *n* omen, prodigy
Wund′klammer *f* (surg) clamp
wund′liegen §108 *ref* get bedsores
Wund′mal *n* scar, sore; (relig) wound
wund′reiten §86 *ref* become saddlesore
Wunsch [vunʃ] *m* (**–es;⸚e**) wish;
(**nach**) desire (for); **auf W.** upon request; **ein frommer W.** wishful thinking; **nach W.** as desired
Wünschelrute [ˈvʏnʃəlrutə] *f* divining
rod
Wün′schelrutengänger *m* dowser
wünschen [ˈvʏnʃən] *tr* wish; wish for,
desire; **was w. Sie?** (com) may I help
you? || *intr* wish, please
wün′schenswert *adj* desirable
Wunsch′form *f* (gram) optative
Wunsch′konzert *n* (rad) request program
wunsch′los *adj* contented || *adv*—**w.
glücklich** perfectly happy
wuppdich [ˈvupdɪç] *interj* zip!, in a
flash!; all of a sudden!
wurde [ˈvurdə] *pret* of **werden**
Würde [ˈvʏrdə] *f* (**–;–n**) honor; title;
dignity; post, office; **akademische
W.** academic degree; **unter aller W.**
beneath contempt
wür′delos *adj* undignified
Wür′denträger –in §6 *mf* dignitary
wür′devoll *adj* dignified
würdig [ˈvʏrdɪç] *adj* dignified; (genit)
worthy (of), deserving (of)
würdigen [ˈvʏrdɪgən] *tr* appreciate,
value; (genit) deem worthy (of)
Wurf [vurf] *m* (**–[e]s;⸚e**) throw, cast,
pitch; (fig) hit, success; (zool) litter,
brood
Wurf′anker *m* grapnel
Würfel [ˈvʏrfəl] *m* (**–s;–**) die; cube,

square; (geom) cube; **W. spielen**
play dice
Wür′felbecher *m* dice box
würfelig [ˈvʏrfəlɪç] *adj* cube-shaped;
(*Muster*) checkered
würfeln [ˈvʏrfəln] *intr* play dice
Wür′felzucker *m* cube sugar
Wurf′geschoß *n* projectile, missile
Wurf′pfeil *m* dart
würgen [ˈvʏrgən] *tr* choke; strangle ||
intr choke; **am Essen w.** gag on food
Wurm [vurm] *m* (**–s;⸚er**) (& mach)
worm
wurmen [ˈvurmən] *tr* (coll) bug
wurmig [ˈvurmɪç] *adj* wormy; worm-
eaten
wurmstichig [ˈvurmʃtɪçɪç] *adj* worm-
eaten
Wurst [vurst] *f* (**–;⸚e**) sausage; **es geht
um die W.** now or never; **es ist mir
W.** I couldn't care less
Würstchen [ˈvʏrstçən] *n* (**–s;–**), **Würstel** [ˈvʏrstəl] *n* (**–s;–n**) hotdog
wursteln [ˈvurstəln] *intr* muddle along
Würze [ˈvʏrtsə] *f* (**–;–n**) spice, seasoning; (fig) zest
Wurzel [ˈvurtsəl] *f* (**–;–n**) root; **W.
fassen** (or **schlagen**) take root
wurzeln [ˈvurtsəln] *intr* (HABEN & SEIN)
take root; **w. in** (*dat*) be rooted in
würzen [ˈvʏrtsən] *tr* spice, season
würzig [ˈvʏrtsɪç] *adj* spicy; aromatic
Würz′stoff *m* seasoning
wusch [vuʃ] *pret* of **waschen**
wußte [ˈvustə] *pret* of **wissen**
Wust [vust] *m* (**–es;**) jumble, mess
wüst [vyst] *adj* desert, waste; (*roh*)
coarse; (*wirr*) confused
Wüste [ˈvystə] *f* (**–;–en**) desert
Wüstling [ˈvystlɪŋ] *m* (**–s;–e**) debauchee
Wut [vut] *f* (**–;**) rage, fury; madness
Wut′anfall *m* fit of rage
wüten [ˈvytən] *intr* rage
wü′tend *adj* (auf *acc*) furious (at)
Wüterich [ˈvytərɪç] *m* (**–s;–e**) madman; bloodthirsty villain
wut′schäumend *adj* foaming with rage
wut′schnaubend *adj* in a towering rage
Wut′schrei *m* shout of anger

X

X, x [ɪks] *invar n* X, x
X′-Beine *pl* knock-knees
x′-beinig *adj* knock-kneed
x′-beliebig *adj* any, whatever || **X-
beliebige** §5 *m*—**jeder X.** every Tom,
Dick, and Harry
x′-fach *adj* (coll) hundredfold

x′-mal *adv* umpteen times
X′-Strahlen *pl* x-rays
X′-Tag *m* D-day
x-te [ˈɪkstə] §9 *adj* umpteenth; **die
x-te Potenz** (math) the nth power
Xylophon [ksʏloˈfon] *n* (**–s;–e**) xylophone

Y

Y, y [ˈʏpsɪlɔn] *invar n* Y, y
Yacht [jaxt] *f* (**–;–en**) yacht
Yamswurzel [ˈjamsvurtsəl] *f* (**–;–n**)
(bot) yam

Yankee [ˈjɛŋki] *m* (**–s;–s**) Yankee
Yoghurt [ˈjogurt] *m* & *n* (**–s;**) yogurt
Yo-Yo [ˈjoˈjo] *n* (**–s;–s**) yo-yo
Ypsilon [ˈʏpsɪlɔn] *n* (**–[s];–s**) y

Z

Z, z [tset] *invar n* Z, z
Zacke ['tsakə] *f* (-;-n) sharp point; (*Zinke*) prong; (*Fels–*) crag; (*e–s Kamms, e–r Säge*) tooth; (*am Kleid*) scallop
zacken ['tsakən] *tr* notch; scallop ‖ **Zacken** *m* (-s;-) var of **Zacke**
zackig ['tsakɪç] *adj* toothed; notched; (*Felsen*) jagged; (*spitz*) pointed; (*Kleid*) scalloped; (fig) sharp
zagen ['tsagən] *intr* be faint-hearted
zaghaft ['tsakhaft] *adj* timid
zäh [tse] *adj* tough; (*klebig*) viscous; (*beharrlich*) persistent; (*Gedächtnis*) tenacious; (*halsstarrig*) dogged
zäh′flüssig *adj* viscous
Zäh′flüssigkeit *f* (-;) viscosity
Zä′higkeit *f* (-;) toughness; tenacity; viscosity; doggedness
Zahl [tsal] *f* (-;-en) number; (*Betrag, Ziffer*) figure; **an Z. übertreffen** out-number; **arabische Z.** Arabic numeral; **der Z. nach** in number; **ganze Z.** integer; **gebrochene Z.** fraction; **gerade Z.** even number; **in roten Zahlen stecken** be in the red; **ungerade Z. ödd** number; **wenig an der Z.** few in number
zahlbar ['tsalbar] *adj* payable; **z. bei Lieferung** cash on delivery
zählebig ['tselebɪç] *adj* hardy
zahlen ['tsalən] *tr* pay; (*Schuld*) pay off ‖ *intr* pay
zählen ['tselən] *tr* count; number, amount to ‖ *intr* count; be of importance, count; **nach Tausenden z.** number in the thousands; **z. auf** (*dat*) count on; **z. zu** be numbered among, belong to
Zah′lenangaben *pl* figures
Zah′lenfolge *f* numerical order
zah′lenmäßig *adj* numerical
Zah′ler –in §6 *mf* payer
Zäh′ler (-s;-) counter; recorder; (*für Gas, Elektrizität*) meter; (math) numerator; (parl) teller; (sport) scorekeeper
Zählerableser ['tseləraplezər] *m* (-s;-) meter man
Zahl′karte *f* money-order form
zahl′los *adj* countless, innumerable
Zahl′meister *m* paymaster; (mil) pay officer; (nav) purser
zahl′reich *adj* numerous
Zähl′rohr *n* Geiger counter
Zahl′stelle *f* cashier's window; (*e–r Bank*) branch office
Zahl′tag *m* payday
Zah′lung *f* (-;-en) payment; (*e–r Schuld*) settlement
Zäh′lung *f* (-;-en) counting; computation
Zah′lungsanweisung *f* draft; check; postal money order
Zah′lungsausgleich *m* balance of payments
Zah′lungsbedingungen *pl* (fin) terms
Zah′lungsbestätigung *f* receipt

Zah′lungsbilanz *f* balance of payments; **aktive** (or **passive**) **Z.** favorable (or unfavorable) balance of payments
zah′lungsfähig *adj* solvent
Zah′lungsfähigkeit *f* (-;) solvency
Zah′lungsfrist *f* due date
Zah′lungsmittel *n* medium of exchange; **gesetzliches Z.** legal tender; **bargeldloses Z.** instrument of credit
Zah′lungsschwierigkeiten *pl* financial embarrassment
Zah′lungssperre *f* stoppage of payments
Zah′lungstermin *m* date of payment; (fin) date of maturity
Zah′lungsverzug *m* (fin) default
Zähl′werk *n* meter
Zahl′wort *n* (-[e]s;–er) numeral
Zahl′zeichen *n* figure, cipher
zahm [tsam] *adj* tame; domesticated
zähmen ['tsemən] *tr* tame; domesticate; (fig) control ‖ *ref* control oneself
Zäh′mung *f* (-;) taming; domestication
Zahn [tsan] *m* (-[e]s;–e) tooth; (mach) tooth, cog; **j–m auf den Z. fühlen** sound s.o. out; **mit den Zähnen knirschen** grind one's teeth
Zahn′arzt *m*, **Zahn′ärztin** *f* dentist
Zahn′bürste *f* toothbrush
Zahn′creme *f* toothpaste
zahnen ['tsanən] *intr* cut one's teeth
Zahn′ersatz *m* denture
Zahn′fäule *f* tooth decay, caries
Zahn′fleisch *n* gum
Zahn′füllung *f* (dent) filling
Zahn′heilkunde *f* dentistry
Zahn′klammer *f* (-;-n) (dent) brace
Zahn′krem *f* toothpaste
Zahn′krone *f* (dent) crown
Zahn′laut *m* (phonet) dental
Zahn′lücke *f* gap between the teeth
Zahn′paste *f* toothpaste
Zahn′pflege *f* dental hygiene
Zahn′pulver *n* tooth powder
Zahn′rad *n* cog wheel; (*Kettenrad*) sprocket
Zahn′radbahn *f* cog railway
Zahn′schmerz *m* toothache
Zahn′spange *f* (-;-n) (dent) brace
Zahn′stein *m* (dent) tartar
Zahnstocher ['tsanʃtoxər] *m* (-s;-) toothpick
Zahn′techniker –in §6 *mf* dental technician
Zahn′weh *n* toothache
Zange ['tsaŋə] *f* (-;-en) (pair of) pliers; (pair of) tongs; (*Pinzette*) (pair of) tweezers; (dent, surg, zool) forceps; **j–n in die Z. nehmen** corner s.o. (*with tough questioning*)
Zank ['tsaŋk] *m* (-[e]s;) quarrel, fight
Zank′apfel *m* apple of discord
zanken ['tsaŋkən] *tr* scold ‖ *recip & intr* quarrel, fight
zank′haft, zänkisch ['tsɛŋkɪʃ], **zank′-süchtig** *adj* quarrelsome

Zäpfchen ['tsɛpfçən] n (-s;-) little peg; (anat) uvula; (med) suppository
zapfen ['tsapfən] tr (Bier, Wein) tap || **Zapfen** m (-s;-) plug, bung; (Stift) stud; (Drehpunkt) pivot; (Eis-) icicle; (Tannen-) cone; (carp) tenon; (mach) pin; (mach) journal
Zap′fenstreich m (mil) taps
Zapfhahn ['tsapfhan] m tap, spigot
Zapfsäule ['tsapfzɔɪlə] f (-;-n) (aut) gasoline pump
Zapfstelle ['tsapfʃtɛlə] f (-;-n) (aut) service station, gas station
Zapfwart ['tsapfvart] m (-[e]s;-e) (aut) service station attendant
zappelig ['tsapəlɪç] adj fidgety
zappeln ['tsapəln] intr fidget; squirm; (im Wasser) founder
Zar [tsar] m (-en;-en) czar
Zarge ['tsargə] f (-;-n) border; frame
zart [tsart] adj tender; (Farbe, Haut) soft; (Gesundheit) delicate
zart′fühlend adj tender; sensitive
Zart′gefühl n sensitivity; tact
Zart′heit f (-;) tenderness
zärtlich ['tsɛrtlɪç] adj tender, affectionate
Zärt′lichkeit f (-;-en) tenderness; (Liebkosung) caress
Zaster ['tsastər] m (-s;) (coll) dough
Zauber ['tsaubər] m (-s;-) spell; magic; (fig) charm, glamor
Zauber- comb.fm. magic
Zauberei [tsaubə'raɪ] f (-;-en) magic; witchcraft, sorcery
Zau′berer m (-s;-) magician; sorcerer
Zau′berformel f incantation, spell
zau′berhaft adj magic; enchanting
Zau′berin f (-;-nen) sorceress, witch; enchantress
zauberisch ['tsaubərɪʃ] adj magic
Zau′berkraft f magic power
Zau′berkunst f magic
Zau′berkünstler -in §6 mf magician
Zau′berkunststück n magic trick
Zau′berland n fairyland
zaubern ['tsaubərn] tr produce by magic || intr practice magic; do magic tricks
Zau′berspruch m incantation, spell
Zau′berstab m magic wand
Zau′bertrank m magic potion
Zau′berwerk n witchcraft
Zau′berwort n (-[e]s;-e) magic word
zaudern ['tsaudərn] intr procrastinate; hesitate; linger
Zaum [tsaum] m (-[e]s;̈e) bridle; im Z. halten keep in check
zäumen ['tsɔɪmən] tr bridle
Zaun [tsaun] m (-[e]s;̈e) fence; e-n Streit vom Z. brechen pick a quarrel
Zaun′gast m non-paying spectator
Zaun′könig m (orn) wren
Zaun′pfahl m fence post
zausen ['tsauzən] tr tug at; tousle; ruffle || recip tug at each other
Zebra ['tsebra] n (-s;-s) zebra
Ze′brastreifen m zebra stripe; (auf der Fahrbahn) passenger crossing
Zech- [tsɛç] comb.fm. drinking
Zech′bruder m boozehound
Zeche ['tsɛçə] f (-;-n) (Wirtshausrechnung) check; (min) mine die Z.

prellen (coll) sneak out without paying the bill
zechen ['tsɛçən] intr booze
Ze′cher -in §6 mf heavy drinker
Zech′gelage n drinking party
Zechpreller ['tsɛçprɛlər] m (-s;-) cheat, bilker
Zech′tour f binge; e-e Z. machen go on a binge
Zecke ['tsɛkə] f (-;-n) (ent) tick
Zeder ['tsedər] f (-;-n) cedar
Zehe ['tse·ə] f (-;-n) toe; (Knoblauch-) clove
Ze′hennagel m toenail
Ze′henspitze f tip of the toe; auf den Zehenspitzen (on) tiptoe
zehn [tsen] invar adj & pron ten || **Zehn** f (-;-en) ten
Zehner ['tsenər] m (-s;-) ten; ten-mark bill
zehn′fach, zehn′fältig adj tenfold
Zehnfin′gersystem n touch-type system
Zehn′kampf m decathlon
zehn′mal adv ten times
zehnte ['tsentə] §9 adj & pron tenth || **Zehnte** §5 mfn tenth
Zehntel ['tsentəl] n (-s;-) tenth (part)
zehren ['tserən] intr be debilitating; an den Kräften z. drain one's strength; an der Gesundheit z. undermine one's health; z. an (dat) (fig) gnaw at; z. von live on, live off
Zeh′rung f (-;) provisions; expenses
Zeichen ['tsaɪçən] n (-s;-) sign; signal; token; (Merkmal) distinguishing mark; (Beweis) proof; symbol; (astr) sign; (com) brand; (med) symptom; (rad) call sign; er ist seines Zeichens Anwalt he is a lawyer by profession; zum Z., daß as proof that
Zei′chenbrett n drawing board
Zei′chenbuch n sketchbook
Zei′chengerät n drafting equipment
Zei′chenheft n sketchbook
Zei′chenlehrer -in §6 mf art teacher
Zei′chenpapier n drawing paper
Zei′chensetzung f punctuation
Zei′chensprache f sign language
Zei′chentisch m drawing board
Zei′chentrickfilm m animated cartoon
Zei′chenunterricht m drawing lesson
zeichnen ['tsaɪçnən] tr draw; sketch; (entwerfen) design; (brandmarken) brand; (Anleihe) take out; (Aktien) buy; (Geld) pledge; (Wäsche) mark; (Brief) sign || intr draw; sketch; (hunt) leave a trail of blood; z. für sign for
Zeich′ner -in §6 mf draftsman; (Mode-) designer; (e-r Anleihe) subscriber
zeichnerisch ['tsaɪçnərɪʃ] adj (Begabung) for drawing; (Darstellung) graphic
Zeich′nung f (-;-en) drawing; sketch; design; picture, illustration; diagram; signature; (e-r Anleihe) subscription; (des Holzes) grain
zeich′nungsberechtigt adj authorized to sign
Zeigefinger ['tsaɪgəfɪŋər] m index finger
zeigen ['tsaɪgən] tr show, indicate;

(*in e-r Rede*) point out; (*zur Schau stellen*) display; (*beweisen*) prove; (*dartun*) demonstrate || *ref* appear, show up; prove to be || *intr* point; **z. auf** (*acc*) point to; **z. nach** point toward || *impers ref*—**es zeigt sich, daß** it turns out that; **es wird sich ja z., ob** we shall see whether

Zei'ger *m* (-s;-) pointer; indicator; (*e-r Uhr*) hand

Zeigestock ['tsaɪgəʃtɔk] *m* pointer

Zeile ['tsaɪlə] *f* (-;-n) line; (*Reihe*) row

Zeit [tsaɪt] *f* (-;-en) time; **auf Z.** (com) on credit, on time; **in der letzten Z.** lately; **in jüngster Z.** quite recently; **mit der Z.** in time, in the course of time; **vor Zeiten** in former times; **zu meiner Z.** in my time; **zu rechter Z.** in the nick of time; on time; **zur Z.** at present; **zur Z.** (*genit*) at the time of

Zeit'abschnitt *m* period, epoch

Zeit'abstand *m* interval of time

Zeit'alter *n* age

Zeit'angabe *f* time; date; exact date and hour; **ohne Z.** undated

Zeit'ansage *f* (rad) (giving of) time

Zeit'aufnahme *f* (phot) time exposure

Zeit'aufwand *m* loss of time; (**für**) time spent (on)

Zeit'dauer *f* term, period of time

Zeit'einteilung *f* timetable; timing

Zei'tenfolge *f* sequence of tenses

Zei'tenwende *f* beginning of the Christian era

Zeit'folge *f* chronological order

Zeit'form *f* tense

Zeit'geist *m* spirit of the times

zeit'gemäß *adj* timely; up-to-date

Zeit'genosse *m*, **Zeit'genossin** *f* contemporary

zeitgenössich ['tsaɪtgənœsɪʃ] *adj* contemporary

Zeit'geschichte *f* contemporary history

zeitig ['tsaɪtɪç] *adj* early; (*reif*) mature, ripe

zeitigen ['tsaɪtɪgən] *tr* ripen

Zeit'karte *f* commuter ticket

Zeit'lage *f* state of affairs

Zeit'lang *f*—**e-e Z.** for some time

Zeit'lauf *m* course of time

zeit'lebens *adv* during my (his, your, etc.) life

zeit'lich *adj* temporal; chronological || *adv* in time || **Zeitliche** §5 *n*—**das Z. segnen** depart this world

zeit'los *adj* timeless

Zeit'lupe *f* (cin) slow motion

Zeit'mangel *m* lack of time

Zeit'maß *n* (mus) tempo; (pros) quantity

Zeit'nehmer -**in** §6 *mf* timekeeper

Zeit'ordnung *f* chronological order

Zeit'punkt *m* point of time, moment

Zeitraffer ['tsaɪtrafər] *m* (-s;) time-lapse photography

zeit'raubend *adj* time-consuming

Zeit'raum *m* space of time, period

Zeit'rechnung *f* era

Zeit'schaltgerät *n* timer

Zeit'schrift *f* periodical, magazine

Zeit'spanne *f* span (of time)

Zeit'tafel *f* chronological table

Zei'tung *f* (-;-en) newspaper; journal

Zei'tungsarchiv *n* (journ) morgue

Zei'tungsartikel *m* newspaper article

Zei'tungsausschnitt *m* newspaper clipping

Zei'tungsbeilage *f* supplement

Zei'tungsdeutsch *n* journalese

Zei'tungsente *f* (journ) hoax, spoof

Zei'tungskiosk *m* newsstand

Zei'tungsmeldung *f*, **Zei'tungsnotiz** *f* newspaper item

Zei'tungspapier *n* newsprint

Zei'tungsverkäufer -**in** §6 *mf* newsvendor

Zei'tungswesen *n*—**das Z.** the press

Zeit'vergeudung *f* waste of time

zeit'verkürzend *adj* entertaining

Zeit'verlust *m* loss of time

Zeit'vermerk *m* date

Zeit'verschwendung *f* waste of time

Zeit'vertreib *m* pastime

zeitweilig ['tsaɪtvaɪlɪç] *adj* temporary; periodic || *adv* temporarily; at times, from time to time

Zeit'wende *f* beginning of a new era

Zeit'wert *m* current value

Zeit'wort *n* (-[e]s;ᵉer) verb

Zeit'zeichen *n* time signal

Zeit'zünder *m* time fuse

Zelle ['tsɛlə] *f* (-;-n) cell; (aer) fuselage; (telp) booth

Zel'lenlehre *f* cytology

Zellophan [tsɛlo'fan] *n* (-s;) cellophane

Zellstoff ['tsɛlʃtɔf] *m* cellulose

Zelluloid [tsɛlu'lɔɪt] *n* (-s;) celluloid

Zellulose [tsɛlu'lozə] *f* (-;) cellulose

Zelt ['tsɛlt] *n* (-[e]s;-e) tent

zelten ['tsɛltən] *intr* camp out

Zelt'leinwand *f* canvas

Zelt'pfahl *m* tent pole

Zelt'pflock *m* tent peg, tent stake

Zelt'stange *f*, **Zelt'stock** *m* tent pole

Zement [tse'mɛnt] *m* (-[e]s;) cement

zementieren [tsemɛn'tirən] *tr* cement

Zenit [tse'nit] *m* (-[e]s;) zenith

zensieren [tsɛn'zirən] *tr* censor; (educ) mark, grade

Zen·sor ['tsɛnzɔr] *m* (-s;-soren ['zorən]) censor

Zensur [tsɛn'zur] *f* (-;-en) censorship; (educ) grade, mark

Zentimeter [tsɛnti'metər] *m & n* centimeter

Zentner ['tsɛntnər] *m* (-s;-) hundredweight

Zent'nerlast *f* (fig) heavy load

zentral [tsɛn'tral] *adj* central

Zentral'behörde *f* central authority

Zentrale [tsɛn'tralə] *f* (-;-n) central office; telephone exchange, switchboard; (elec) power station

Zentral'heizung *f* central heating

Zen·trum ['tsɛntrum] *m* (-s;-tren [trən]) center

Zephir ['tsefɪr] *m* (-s;-e) zephyr

Zepter ['tsɛptər] *n* (-s;-) scepter

zer- [tsɛr] *pref* up, to pieces, apart

zerbei'ßen §53 *tr* bite to pieces

zerber'sten §55 *intr* (SEIN) split apart

zerbre'chen §64 *tr* break to pieces, shatter, smash || *ref*—**sich** [*dat*] **den**

Kopf z. über (*acc*) rack one's brains over || *intr* (SEIN) shatter
zerbrech′lich *adj* fragile, brittle
zerbröckeln (**zerbrök′keln**) *tr & intr* (SEIN) crumble
zerdrücken (**zerdrük′ken**) *tr* crush; (*Kleid*) wrinkle; (*Kartoffeln*) mash
Zeremonie [tsɛremə′ni] *f* (-;-nien [′ni·ən]) ceremony
zeremoniell [tsɛremə′njel] *adj* ceremonial || **Zeremoniell** *n* (-s;-e) ceremonial
Zeremo′nienmeister *m* master of ceremonies
zerfah′ren *adj* (*Weg*) rutted; (*zerstreut*) absent-minded; (*konfus*) scatterbrained
Zerfall′ *m* (-s;) decay, ruin; disintegration; (*geistig*) decadence
zerfal′len *adj*—z. sein mit be at variance with || §72 *intr* (SEIN) fall into ruin; decay; disintegrate; z. in (*acc*) divide into; z. mit fall out with
zerfa′sern *tr* unravel || *intr* fray
zerfet′zen *tr* tear to shreds
zerflei′schen *tr* mangle; lacerate
zerflie′ßen §76 *intr* (SEIN) melt; (*Farben*) run
zerfres′sen §70 *tr* eat away, chew up; erode, eat a hole in; corrode
zerge′hen §82 *intr* (SEIN) melt
zerglie′dern *tr* dissect; analyze
zerhacken (**zerhak′ken**) *tr* chop up
zerkau′en *tr* chew well
zerkleinern [tser′klaɪnərn] *tr* cut into small pieces; chop up
zerklop′fen *tr* pound
zerklüftet [tser′klyftət] *adj* jagged
zerknirscht [tser′knɪrʃt] *adj* contrite
Zerknir′schung *f* (-;) contrition
zerknit′tern *tr* (*Papier*) crumple; (*Kleider*) rumple
zerknül′len *tr* crumple up
zerko′chen *tr* overcook
zerkrat′zen *tr* scratch up
zerkrü′meln *tr & intr* (SEIN) crumble
zerlas′sen §104 *tr* melt, dissolve
zerlegbar [tser′lekbɑr] *adj* collapsible; (chem) decomposable; (math) divisible
zerle′gen *tr* take apart; (*zerstückeln*) cut up; (*Braten*) carve; (*Licht*) disperse; (anat) dissect; (chem) break down; (geom, mus) resolve; (gram & fig) analyze; (mach) tear down
zerle′sen *adj* well-thumbed
zerlö′chern *tr* riddle with holes
zerlumpt [tser′lumpt] *adj* tattered
zermah′len *tr* grind
zermal′men *tr* crush
zermür′ben *tr* wear down
Zermür′bung *f* (-;) attrition, wear
zerna′gen *tr* gnaw, chew up; (chem) corrode
zerplat′zen *intr* (SEIN) burst; explode
zerquet′schen *tr* crush; (culin) mash
Zerrbild [′tserbɪlt] *n* distorted picture; caricature
zerrei′ben §62 *tr* grind, pulverize
zerrei′ßen §95 *tr* tear; tear up; (*zerfleischen*) mangle; (fig) split; (pathol) rupture; j-m das Herz z. break s.o.'s heart || *ref*—sich z. für

(fig) knock oneself out for || *intr* (SEIN) tear
zerren [′tserən] *tr* drag; (*Sehne*) pull || *intr* (an *dat*) tug (at)
zerrin′nen §121 *intr* (SEIN) melt away
zerrissen [tser′rɪsən] *adj* torn
Zer′rung *f* (-;-en) strain, muscle pull
zerrütten [tser′rytən] *tr* disorganize; (*Geist*) unhinge; (*Gesundheit*) undermine; (*Nerven*) shatter; (*Ehe*) wreck
zersä′gen *tr* saw up
zerschel′len *intr* (SEIN) be wrecked; (*Schiff*) break up
zerschie′ßen §76 *tr* shoot up
zerschla′gen *adj* battered, broken; exhausted, beat || §132 *tr* beat up; break to pieces; smash; batter
zerschmel′zen *tr & intr* (SEIN) melt
zerschmet′tern *tr* smash, crush
zerschnei′den §106 *tr* cut up; mince
zerset′zen *tr* decompose; electrolyze; (fig) undermine || *ref* decompose, disintegrate
zerspal′ten *tr* split
zersplit′tern *tr* split up; splinter; (*Menge*) disperse; (*Kraft, Zeit*) fritter away || *ref* spread oneself thin
zerspren′gen *tr* blow up; (*Kette*) break; (mil) rout
zersprin′gen §142 *intr* (SEIN) break, burst; (*Glas*) crack; (*Saite*) snap; (*Kopf*) split; (*vor Wut*) explode; (*vor Freude*) burst
zerstamp′fen *tr* crush, pound; trample
zerstäu′ben *tr* pulverize, spray
Zerstäu′ber *m* (-s;-) sprayer; (*für Parfüm*) atomizer
zerste′chen §64 *tr* sting; bite
zerstie′ben *intr* §130 *intr* (SEIN) scatter
zerstö′ren *tr* destroy; (*Fernsprechleitung*) disrupt; (*Leben, Ehe, usw.*) ruin; (*Illusionen*) shatter
Zerstö′rer *m* (-s;-) (& nav) destroyer
Zerstö′rung *f* (-;-en) destruction; ruin; disruption
Zerstö′rungswerk *n* work of destruction
Zerstö′rungswut *f* vandalism
zersto′ßen §150 *tr* pound, crush
zerstreu′en *tr* scatter, disperse; (*Bedenken, Zweifel*) dispel; (*ablenken*) distract; (*Licht*) diffuse || *ref* scatter; amuse oneself
zerstreut′ *adj* dispersed; (*Licht*) diffused; (fig) absent-minded
Zerstreut′heit *f* (-;) absent-mindedness
Zerstreu′ung *f* (-;) scattering; diffusion; diversion; absent-mindedness
zerstückeln [tser′ʃtykəln] *tr* chop up; (*Körper*) dismember; (*Land*) parcel out
zertei′len *tr* divide; (*zerstreuen*) disperse; (*Braten, usw.*) cut up || *ref* divide, separate
Zertifikat [tsertɪfɪ′kɑt] *n* (-[e]s;-e) certificate
zertren′nen *tr* sever
zertre′ten §152 *tr* trample, squash; (*Feuer*) stamp out
zertrümmern [tser′trymərn] *tr* smash, demolish; (*Atome*) split
zerwüh′len *tr* root up; (*Haar*) dishevel; (*Bett, Kissen*) rumple

Zerwürfnis [tsɛr'vʏrfnɪs] *n* (−ses;−se) disagreement, quarrel

zerzau'sen *tr* (*Haar*) muss; (*Federn*) ruffle

Zeter ['tsetər] *n* (−s;)—Z. **und Mordio schreien** (coll) cry bloody murder

zetern ['tsętərn] *intr* cry out, raise an outcry

Zettel ['tsetəl] *m* (−s;−) slip of paper; note; (*Anschlag*) poster; (*zum Ankleben*) sticker; (*zum Anhängen*) tag

Zet'telkartei *f*, **Zet'telkasten** *m*, **Zet'telkatalog** *m* card file

Zeug [tsɔɪk] *n* (−[e]s;−e) stuff, material; (*Stoff*) cloth, fabric; (*Sachen*) things; (*Waren*) goods; (*Geräte*) tools; (*Plunder*) junk; **dummes Z.** silly nonsense; **er hat das Z.** he has what it takes

−zeug *n comb.fm.* stuff; tools; equipment; tackle; instrument; things; **−wear**

Zeuge ['tsɔɪgə] *m* (−n;−n) witness; **als Z. aussagen** testify

zeugen ['tsɔɪgən] *tr* beget; (fig) produce, generate ‖ *intr* produce offspring; testify; **z. für** testify in favor of; **z. von** bear witness to

Zeu'genaussage *f* deposition

Zeu'genbank *f* witness stand

Zeu'genbeeinflussung *f* suborning of witnesses

Zeu'genstand *m* witness stand

Zeugin ['tsɔɪgɪn] *f* (−;−nen) witness

Zeugnis ['tsɔɪknɪs] *n* (−ses;−se) evidence, testimony; proof; (*Schein*) certificate; (educ) report card; **j-m ein Z. ausstellen** (or **schreiben**) write s.o. a letter of recommendation; **Z. ablegen** testify; **zum Z. dessen** in witness whereof

Zeu'gung *f* (−;) procreation; breeding

Zeu'gungstrieb *m* sexual drive

zeu'gungsunfähig *adj* impotent

Zicke ['tsɪkə] *f* (−;−n) (pej) old nanny goat; **Zicken machen** (coll) play tricks

Zicklein ['tsɪklaɪn] *n* (−s;−) kid

Zickzack ['tsɪktsak] *m* (−[e]s;−e) zigzag; **im Z. laufen** run zigzag

Zick'zackkurs *m*—**im Z. fahren** zigzag

Ziege ['tsigə] *f* (−;−n) she-goat

Ziegel ['tsigəl] *m* (−s;−) brick; (*Dach*−) tile

Zie'gelbrenner *m* brickmaker; tilemaker

Zie'gelbrennerei *f* brickyard; tileworks

Zie'geldach *n* tiled roof

Zie'gelstein *m* brick

Zie'genbart *m* goatee

Zie'genbock *m* billy goat

Zie'genhirt *m* goatherd

Zie'genpeter *m* (pathol) mumps

Zieh− [tsi] *comb.fm.* draw; tow−; foster

Zieh'brunnen *m* well

ziehen ['tsi·ən] §163 *tr* pull; (*Folgerung, Kreis, Linie, Los, Schwert, Seitengewehr, Vorhang, Wechsel*) draw; (*Glocke*) ring; **aus der Tasche** pull out; (*Zahn*) extract, pull; (*züchten*) grow, breed; (*Kinder*) raise; (*beim Schach*) move; (*den*

Hut) tip; (*Graben*) dig; (*Mauer*) build; (*Schiff*) tow; (*Blasen*) raise; (*Vergleich*) make; (*Gewehrlauf*) rifle; (math) extract; **auf Fäden z.** string (*pearls*); **auf Flaschen z.** bottle; **auf seine Seite z.** win over to one's side; **den kürzeren z.** get the short end of it; **die Bilanz z.** balance accounts; **die Stirn kraus z.** knit the brows; **Grimassen z.** make faces; **ins Vertrauen z.** take into confidence; **j-n auf die Seite z.** take s.o. aside; **Nutzen z.** derive benefit; **Wasser z.** leak ‖ *ref* (*Holz*) warp; (*Stoff*) stretch; (geog) extend, run; **an sich** (or **auf sich**) **z.** attract; **sich in die Länge z.** drag on ‖ *intr* ache; (**an** *dat*) pull (on); (theat) (coll) pull them in; **an e-r Zigarette z.** puff on a cigarette ‖ *intr* (SEIN) go; march; (*Vögel*) migrate; (*Wohnung wechseln*) move ‖ *impers*—**es zieht** there is a draft; **es zieht mich nach I** feel drawn to ‖ **Ziehen** *n* (−s;) drawing; cultivation; growing; raising; breeding; migration

Zieh'harmonika *f* accordion

Zieh'kind *n* foster child

Zie'hung *f* (−;−en) drawing (*of lots*)

Ziel [tsil] *n* (−[e]s;−e) aim; mark; goal; (*beim Rennsport*) finish line; (*e-r Reise*) destination; (*beim Schießen*) target; (*Grenze*) limit, boundary; (*Zweck*) end, object; (*des Spottes*) butt; (*Frist*) term; (mil) objective; **auf Z.** (com) on credit; **durchs Z. gehen** pass the finish line; **gegen zwei Jahre Z.** (or **mit zwei Jahren Z.**) with two years to pay; **j-m zwei Jahre Z. gewähren** give s.o. two years to pay; **seinem Ehrgeiz ein Z. setzen** set a limit to one's ambition

Ziel'anflug *m* (aer) bomb run

Ziel'band *n* (−[e]s;−er) (sport) tape

ziel'bewußt *adj* purposeful; single-minded

zielen ['tsilən] *intr* take aim; **z. auf** (*acc*) or **nach** aim at

Ziel'fernrohr *n* telescopic sight

Ziel'gerade *f* homestretch

Ziel'gerät *n* gunsight; (aer) bombsight

Ziel'landung *f* pinpoint landing

Ziel'linie *f* (sport) finish line

ziel'los *adj* aimless

Ziel'photographie *f* photo finish

Ziel'punkt *m* objective; bull's-eye

Ziel'scheibe *f* target; (fig) butt

Ziel'setzung *f* objective, target

ziel'sicher *adj* steady, unerring

Ziel'sprache *f* target language

zielstrebig ['tsil/trebɪç] *adj* single-minded, determined

Ziel'sucher *m* (rok) homing device

Ziel'vorrichtung *f* gunsight; bombsight

ziemen ['tsimən] *ref* be proper; **sich für j-n z.** become s.o. ‖ *intr* (*dat*) be becoming to

ziemlich ['tsimlɪç] *adj* fit, suitable; (*leidlich*) middling; (*mäßig*) fair; (*beträchtlich*) considerable ‖ *adv* pretty, rather, fairly; (*fast*) almost, practically

Zier [tsir] *f* (-;), **Zierat** ['tsirɑt] *m* (-s;) ornament, decoration

Zierde ['tsirdə] *f* (-;-n) ornament decoration; (fig) credit, honor

zieren ['tsirən] *tr* decorate, adorn || *ref* be affected, be coy; (*beim Essen*) need to be coaxed; **zier dich doch nicht so!** don't be coy!

Zier'leiste *f* trim(ming)

zier'lich *adj* delicate; (*nett*) nice

Zier'pflanze *f* ornamental plant

Zier'puppe *f* glamour girl

Ziffer ['tsıfər] *f* (-;-n) digit, figure

Zif'ferblatt *n* face (*of a clock*)

zig [tsıç] *invar adj* (coll) umpteen

Zigarette [tsıga'retə] *f* (-;-n) cigarette

Zigaret'tenautomat *m* cigarette machine

Zigaret'tenetui *n* cigarette case

Zigaret'tenspitze *f* cigarette holder

Zigaret'tenstummel *m* cigarette butt

Zigarre [tsı'garə] *f* (-;-n) cigar

Zigeuner –**in** [tsı'gɔɪnər(ın)] §6 *mf* gipsy

Zimbel ['tsımbəl] *f* (-;-n) cymbal

Zimmer ['tsımər] *n* (-s;-) room

Zim'merantenne *f* indoor antenna

Zim'merarbeit *f* carpentry

Zim'merdienst *m* room service

Zim'mereinrichtung *f* furniture

Zim'merer *m* (-s;-) carpenter

Zim'merflucht *f* suite

Zim'mermädchen *n* chambermaid

Zim'mer·mann *m* (-[e]s;-leute) carpenter

zimmern ['tsımərn] *tr* carpenter, build || *intr* carpenter

Zim'mervermieter *m* landlord

–**zimmrig** [tsımrıç] *comb.fm.* –room

zimperlich ['tsımpərlıç] *adj* prudish; fastidious; (*gegen Kälte*) oversensitive

Zimt [tsımt] *m* (-[e]s;) cinnamon

Zink [tsıŋk] *m & n* (-[e]s;) zinc

Zinke ['tsıŋkə] *f* (-;-n) prong; (*e-s Kammes*) tooth; (carp) dovetail

zinken ['tsıŋkən] *tr* dovetail; (*Karten*) mark || **Zinken** *m* (-s;-) (sl) schnozzle

–**zinkig** [tsıŋkıç] *comb.fm.* –pronged

Zinn [tsın] *n* (-[e]s;) tin

Zinne ['tsınə] *f* (-;-n) pinnacle; battlement

zinnoberrot [tsı'nobərrot] *adj* vermilion

Zins [tsıns] *m* (-es;-en) interest; (*Miete*) rent; **auf Zinsen anlegen** put out at interest; **j–m mit Zinsen (und Zinseszinsen) heimzahlen** (coll) pay s.o. back in full; **Zinsen berechnen** charge interest

zins'bringend *adj* interest-bearing

Zin'senbelastung *f* interest charge

Zinseszinsen ['tsınzəstsınzən] *pl* compound interest

zins'frei *adj* rent-free; interest-free

Zins'fuß *m*, **Zins'satz** *m* rate of interest

Zins'schein *m* (interest) coupon; dividend warrant

Zionismus [tsı·ɔ'nısmʊs] *m* (-;) Zionism

Zipfel ['tsıpfəl] *m* (-s;-) tip, point;

edge; (*Ecke*) corner; (*e–r Wurst*) end piece

Zip'felmütze *f* nightcap, tasseled cap

zirka ['tsırka] *adv* approximately

Zirkel ['tsırkəl] *m* (-s;-) circle; (*Reißzeug*) compass; (fig) circle

Zir'kelschluß *m* vicious circle

Zirkon [tsır'kon] *m* (-s;-e) zircon

zirkulieren [tsırku'lirən] *intr* (SEIN) circulate; **z. lassen** circulate

Zirkus ['tsırkʊs] *m* (-;-se) circus

zirpen ['tsırpən] *intr* chirp

zischeln ['tsıʃəln] *tr & intr* whisper

zischen ['tsıʃən] *intr* hiss; sizzle; (*schwirren*) whiz || **Zischen** *n* (-s;) hissing; sizzle; whiz

Zisch'laut *m* hissing sound; (phonet) sibilant

ziselieren [tsızɛ'lirən] *tr* chase

Zisterne [tsıs'tɛrnə] *f* (-;-n) cistern

Zitadelle [tsıta'delə] *f* (-;-n) citadel

Zitat [tsı'tat] *n* (-[e]s;-e) quotation

Zither ['tsıtər] *f* (-;-n) zither

zitieren [tsı'tirən] *tr* quote; **j–n vor Gericht z.** issue s.o. a summons

Zitronat [tsıtrɔ'nat] *n* (-[e]s;-e) candied lemon peel

Zitrone [tsı'tronə] *f* (-;-n) lemon

Zitro'nenlimonade *f* lemonade; (*mit Sodawasser*) lemon soda

Zitro'nenpresse *f* lemon squeezer

Zitro'nensaft *m* lemon juice

Zitro'nensäure *f* citric acid

zitterig ['tsıtərıç] *adj* shaky

zittern ['tsıtərn] *intr* quake, tremble; quiver; (*flimmern*) dance; (*vor dat*) shake (with), shiver (with); **beim dem Gedanken an etw** [*acc*] **z.** shudder at the thought of s.th.

Zit'terpappel ['tsıtərpapəl] *f* aspen

Zitze ['tsıtsə] *f* (-;-n) teat

zivil [tsı'vil] *adj* civil; civilian; (*Preise*) reasonable || **Zivil** *n* (-s;) civilians; **in Z.** in plain clothes

Zivil'courage *f* courage of one's convictions, moral courage

Zivil'ehe *f* civil marriage

Zivilisation [tsıvılıza'tsjon] *f* (-;-en) civilization

zivilisieren [tsıvılı'zirən] *tr* civilize

Zivilist –**in** [tsıvı'lıst(ın)] §7 *mf* civilian

Zivil'klage *f* (jur) civil suit

Zivil'kleidung *f* civilian clothes

Zivil'person *f* civilian

Zobel ['tsobəl] *m* (-s;-) (zool) sable

Zofe ['tsofə] *f* (-;-n) lady-in-waiting

zog [tsok] *pret* of **ziehen**

zögern ['tsøgərn] *intr* hesitate; delay || **Zögern** *n* (-s;) hesitation; delay

Zögling ['tsøklıŋ] *m* (-s;-e) pupil

Zölibat [tsølı'bat] *m & n* (-[e]s;) celibacy

Zoll [tsɔl] *m* (-[e]s;-e) duty, customs; (*Brückenzoll*) toll; (*Maß*) inch

Zoll'abfertigung *f* customs clearance

Zoll'amt *n* customs office

Zoll'beamte §5 *m* customs official

zollen ['tsɔlən] *tr* give, pay; **j–m Achtung z.** show s.o. respect; **j–m Beifall z.** applaud s.o.; **j–m Dank z.** thank s.o.; **j–m Lob z.** praise s.o.

Zoll'erklärung *f* customs declaration

zoll'frei *adj* duty-free
Zoll'grenze *f* customs frontier
–zöllig [ˈtsœlɪç] *comb.fm.* –inch
Zoll'kontrolle *f* customs inspection
zoll'pflichtig *adj* dutiable
Zoll'schein *m* customs clearance
Zoll'schranke *f* customs barrier
Zoll'stab *m*, **Zoll'stock** *m* foot rule
Zoll'tarif *m* tariff
Zone [ˈtsonə] *f* (–;–n) zone; **blaue Z.** limited-parking area; **Z. der Windstille** doldrums
Zoo [tso] *m* (– & –s;–s) zoo
Zoologe [tso·oˈlogə] *m* (–n;–n) zoologist
Zoologie [tso·oloˈgi] *f* (–;) zoology
Zoologin [tso·oˈlogɪn] *f* (–;–nen) zoologist
zoologisch [tso·oˈlogɪʃ] *adj* zoological
Zopf [tsɔpf] *m* (–[e]s;–̈e) plait of hair; pigtail; twisted (bread) roll; **alter Z.** outdated custom
zopfig [ˈtsɔpfɪç] *adj* pedantic; old-fashioned
Zorn [tsɔrn] *m* (–[e]s;) anger, rage
Zorn'anfall *m* fit of anger
Zorn'ausbruch *m* outburst of anger
zornig [ˈtsɔrnɪç] *adj* (**auf** *acc*) angry (at)
zorn'mütig *adj* hotheaded
Zote [ˈtsotə] *f* (–;–n) obscenity; dirty joke; **Zoten reißen** crack dirty jokes; talk dirty
zo'tenhaft, zotig [ˈtsotɪç] *adj* obscene, dirty
Zotte [ˈtsotə] *f* (–;–n) tuft of hair; strand of hair
Zottel [ˈtsotəl] *f* (–;–n) strand of hair
Zot'telhaar *n* stringy hair
zottelig [ˈtsotəlɪç] *adj* stringy (*hair*)
zotteln [ˈtsotəln] *intr* (SEIN) (coll) saunter
zottig [ˈtsotɪç] *adj* shaggy; matted
zu [tsu] *adj* closed, shut || *adv* too; **immer zu!** (or **nur zu!**) go on! || *prep* (*dat*) at, in, on; to; along with; in addition to; beside, near; **zu Anfang** at the beginning; **zu dritt** in threes; **zu Wasser und zu Lande** by land and by sea
zuallererst [tsu·alərˈɛrst] *adv* first of all
zuallerletzt [tsu·alərˈlɛtst] *adv* last of all
zuballern [ˈtsubalərn] *tr* (coll) slam
zu'bauen *tr* wall up, wall in
Zubehör [ˈtsubəhør] *m* & *n* (–s;) accessories; fittings; trimmings; **Wohnung mit allem Z.** apartment with all utilities
Zu'behörteil *m* accessory, attachment, component
zu'beißen §53 *intr* bite; snap at people
zu'bekommen §99 *tr* get in addition; (*Tür, usw.*) manage to close
zu'bereiten *tr* prepare; (*Speise*) cook; (*Getränk*) mix
Zu'bereitung *f* (–;–en) preparation
zu'billigen *tr* grant, allow, concede
zu'binden §59 *tr* tie up; **j–m die Augen z.** blindfold s.o.
zu'bleiben §62 *intr* (SEIN) remain closed

zu'blinzeln *intr* (*dat*) wink at
zu'bringen §65 *tr* (*Zeit*) spend; (coll) manage to shut; (tech) feed
Zu'bringer *m* (–s;–) (tech) feeder
Zu'bringerdienst *m* shuttle service
Zu'bringerstraße *f* access road
Zucht [tsuxt] *f* (–;) breeding; rearing; (*Rasse*) race, stock; (*Pflanzen–*) cultivation; (*Schul–*) education; discipline; training, drill; **Z. halten** maintain discipline
züchten [ˈtsʏçtən] *tr* breed; rear, raise; (bot) grow, cultivate
Züch'ter –in §6 *mf* breeder; grower
Zucht'haus *n* penitentiary, hard labor; **lebenslängliches Z.** life imprisonment
Zuchthäusler –in [ˈtsuxthɔɪzlər(ɪn)] §6 *mf* convict, prisoner at hard labor
Zucht'hengst *m* studhorse
züchtig [ˈtsʏçtɪç] *adj* modest, chaste
züchtigen [ˈtsʏçtɪgən] *tr* chastise
zucht'los *adj* undisciplined
Zucht'losigkeit *f* (–;) lack of discipline
Zucht'meister *m* disciplinarian
Zucht'perle *f* cultured pearl
Züch'tung *f* (–;) breeding; rearing; growing, cultivation
zucken [ˈtsukən] *tr* (*Aschseln*) shrug || *intr* twitch, jerk; (*Blitz*) flash; (*vor Schmerzen*) wince; **mit keiner Wimper z.** not bat an eye; **ohne zu z.** without wincing || *impers*—**es zuckte mir in den Fingern zu** (*inf*) my fingers were itching to (*inf*) || **Zucken** *n* (–s;) twitch
zücken [ˈtsʏkən] *tr* (*Schwert*) draw
Zucker [ˈtsukər] *m* (–s;) sugar
Zuckerdose (**Zuk'kerdose**) *f* sugar bowl
Zuckererbse (**Zuk'kererbse**) *f* sweet pea
Zuckerguß (**Zuk'kerguß**) *m* frosting
Zuckerharnruhr (**Zuk'kerharnruhr**) *f* diabetes
Zuckerhut (**Zuk'kerhut**) *m* sugar loaf
zuckerig [ˈtsukərɪç] *adj* sugary
zuckerkrank (**zuk'kerkrank**) *adj* diabetic || **Zuckerkranke** §5 *mf* diabetic
Zuckerkrankheit (**Zuk'kerkrankheit**) *f* diabetes
Zuckerlecken (**Zuk'kerlecken**) *n* (–s;) (fig) pushover, picnic
Zuckerrohr (**Zuk'kerrohr**) *n* sugar cane
Zuckerrübe (**Zuk'kerrübe**) *f* sugar beet
zuckersüß (**zuk'kersüß'**) *adj* sweet as sugar
Zuckerwerk (**Zuk'kerwerk**) *n*, **Zuckerzeug** (**Zuk'kerzeug**) *n* candy
Zuckung (**Zuk'kung**) *f* (–;–en) twitch, spasm, convulsion
Zu'decke *f* (coll) bed covering
zu'decken *tr* cover up
zudem [tsuˈdem] *adv* moreover, besides
zu'denken §66 *tr*—**j–m etw z.** intend s.th. as a present for s.o.
Zu'drang *m* crowding, rush
zu'drehen *tr* turn off; **j–m den Rücken z.** turn one's back on s.o.
zu'dringlich *adj* obtrusive; **z. werden** make a pass
zu'drücken *tr* close, shut
zu'eignen *tr* dedicate
Zu'eignung *f* (–;–en) dedication

zu'erkennen §97 *tr* confer, award; (jur) adjudge, award

zuerst' *adv* first; at first

zu'erteilen *tr* award; confer, bestow

zu'fahren §71 *intr* (SEIN) drive on; **z. auf** (*acc*) drive in the direction of (*s.th.*); rush at (*s.o.*)

Zu'fahrt *f* access

Zu'fahrtsrampe *f* on-ramp

Zu'fahrtsstraße *f* access road

Zu'fall *m* chance; coincidence; accident; **durch Z.** by chance

zu'fallen §72 *intr* (SEIN) close, shut; **j-m z.** fall to s.o.'s share

zufällig ['tsufɛlɪç] *adj* chance, fortuitous; accidental; casual || *adv* by chance; accidentally

zu'fälligerweise *adv* by chance

Zufalls– *comb.fm.* chance

zu'fassen *intr* set to work; lend a hand; (*e-e Gelegenheit wahrnehmen*) seize the opportunity

Zu'flucht *f* refuge; (fig) recourse; **seine Z. nehmen zu** take refuge in; have recourse to

Zu'fluß *m* influx; (*Nebenfluß*) tributary; (mach) feed

zu'flüstern *intr* (*dat*) whisper to

zufolge [tsu'fɔlgə] *prep* (*genit & dat*) in consequence of; according to

zufrieden [tsu'fridən] *adj* satisfied; **j-n z. lassen** leave s.o. alone

zufrie'dengeben §80 *ref* (**mit**) be satisfied (with), acquiesce (in)

Zufrie'denheit *f* (–;) satisfaction

zufrie'denstellen *tr* satisfy

zufrie'denstellend *adj* satisfactory

Zufrie'denstellung *f* satisfaction

zu'frieren §77 *intr* (SEIN) freeze up

zu'fügen *tr* add; (*Niederlage*) inflict; (*Kummer, Schaden, Schmerz*) cause

Zufuhr ['tsufur] *f* (–;) supply; importation; supplies; (mach) feed

zu'führen *tr* convey, bring; (*Waren*) supply; (mach) feed

Zu'führung *f* (–;–en) conveyance; supply; importation; (elec) lead; (mach) feed

Zug [tsuk] *m* (–[e]s;̈-e) train; pull, tug; drawing, pulling; (*Spannung*) tension; strain; (*beim Rauchen*) puff; (*beim Atmen*) breath, gasp; (*Schluck*) drink, gulp, swig; (*Luft–*) draft; (*Reihe*) row, line; (*Um–*) procession; parade; (*Kriegs–*) campaign; (*Geleit*) escort; (*von Vögeln*) flock; flight, migration; (*von Fischen*) school; (*Rudel*) pack; (*Trupp*) platoon; (*Gespann*) team, yoke; (*Gesichts–*) feature; (*Charakter–*) trait; characteristic; (*Neigung*) trend, tendency; (*im Gewehrlauf*) groove, rifling; (*Strich*) stroke; (*Schnörkel*) flourish; (*Umriß*) outline; (*beim Brettspiel*) move; **auf dem Zuge** on the march; **auf e-n Zug** in one gulp; at one stroke; at a stretch; **du bist am Zug** (& fig) it's your move; **e-n guten Zug haben** drink like a fish; **e-n Zug tun** take a puff; make a move; take a drink; **gut im Zuge sein** (or **im besten Zuge sein**) be going strong; **in e-m Zuge** in one gulp; in one breath; at one stroke; at a stretch; **in großen Zügen** in broad outlines; **in vollen Zügen** thoroughly; **in Zug bringen** start; **nicht zum Zug kommen** not get a chance; **ohne rechten Zug** half-heartedly; **Zug um Zug** in rapid succession

Zu'gabe *f* addition; (theat) encore

Zu'gang *m* access; approach; entrance; (*Zunahme*) increase; (libr) accession

zugänglich ['tsugɛŋlɪç] *adj* accessible; (*Person*) affable; (*benutzbar*) available; (*dat*, **für**) open (to); **nicht z. für** proof against

Zug'artikel *m* (com) popular article

Zug'brücke *f* drawbridge

zu'geben §80 *tr* add; (*erlauben*) allow; (*anerkennen*) admit, concede; (*eingestehen*) confess; (com) throw into the bargain

zugegen [tsu'gegən] *adj* (**bei**) present (at)

zu'gehen §82 *intr* (SEIN) go on; walk faster; (*sich schließen*) shut; **auf j-n z.** go up to s.o.; **j-m etw z. lassen** send s.th. to s.o.

zu'gehören *intr* (*dat*) belong to

zu'gehörig *adj* (*dat*) belonging to

Zu'gehörigkeit *f* (–;) (**zu**) membership (in)

Zügel ['tsygəl] *m* (–s;–) rein; bridle; (fig) curb

zü'gellos *adj* (& fig) unbridled; (*ausschweifig*) dissolute

Zü'gellosigkeit *f* (–;) licentiousness

zügeln ['tsygəln] *tr* bridle; (fig) curb

Zu'geständnis *n* admission, concession

zu'gestehen §146 *tr* admit, concede

zu'getan *adj* (*dat*) fond of

Zug'feder *f* tension spring

Zug'führer *m* (mil) platoon leader; (rr) chief conductor

zu'gießen §76 *tr* add

zugig ['tsugɪç] *adj* drafty

zügig ['tsygɪç] *adj* speedy, fast

Zug'klappe *f* damper

Zug'kraft *f* tensile force; (fig) drawing power

zug'kräftig *adj* attractive, popular

zugleich' *adv* at the same time; **z. mit** together with

Zug'luft *f* draft

Zug'maschine *f* tractor

Zug'mittel *n* (fig) attraction, draw

zu'graben §87 *tr* cover up

zu'greifen §88 *intr* grab hold; lend a hand; (fig) go into action; **greifen Sie zu!** (*bei Tisch*) help yourself!; (*bei Reklamen*) don't miss this opportunity!

Zu'griff *m* grip; (fig) clutches

zugrunde [tsu'grundə] *adv*—**z. gehen** go to ruin; **z. legen** (*dat*) take as a basis (for); **z. liegen** (*dat*) underlie

Zug'tier *n* draft animal

zu'gucken *intr* (coll) look on

zugunsten [tsu'gunstən] *prep* (*genit*) in favor of; for the benefit of

zugute [tsu'gutə] *adv*—**j-m etw z. halten** make allowance to s.o. for s.th.; **j-m z. kommen** stand s.o. in good stead

Zug'verkehr *m* train service

Zug'vogel m migratory bird
zu'haben §89 tr (*Augen*) have closed; (*Mantel*) have buttoned up ‖ intr (*Geschäft*) be closed
zu'halten §90 tr keep closed; (*Ohren*) shut ‖ intr—z. auf (*acc*) head for
Zuhälter ['tsuhɛltər] m (-s;-) pimp
Zuhälterei [tsuhɛltə'raɪ] f (-;) pimping
zuhanden [tsu'handən] prep (*genit*) (*auf Briefumschlägen*) Attn:
Zuhause [tsu'hauzə] n (-s;) home
zu'heilen intr (SEIN) heal up
zu'hören intr (*dat*) listen (to)
Zu'hörer –in §6 mf hearer, listener; die Z. the audience
Zu'hörerschaft f (-;) audience
zu'jauchzen, zu'jubeln intr cheer
zu'klappen tr shut, slam shut
zu'kleben tr glue up, paste up
zu'knallen tr bang, slam shut
zu'kneifen §88 tr—**die Augen z.** blink; **ein Auge z.** wink
zu'knöpfen tr button up
zu'kommen §99 intr (SEIN) (*dat*) reach; (*dat*) be due to; **auf j-n z.** come up to s.o.; **das kommt dir nicht zu** you're not entitled to it; **j-m etw z. lassen** let s.o. have s.th.; send s.th. to s.o. ‖ impers—**mir kommt es nicht zu zu** (*inf*) it's not up to me to (*inf*)
zu'korken tr put the cork on
Zu'kost f vegetables; trimmings
Zukunft ['tsukʊnft] f (-;) future; (gram) future (tense)
zukünftig ['tsukʏnftɪç] adj future ‖ adv in the future ‖ **Zukünftige** §5 m (coll) fiancé ‖ f (coll) fiancée
Zu'kunftsmusik f wishful thinking
Zu'kunftsroman m science fiction
zu'lächeln intr (*dat*) smile at; (*dat*) smile on
Zu'lage f extra pay; pay raise
zulande [tsu'landə] adv—**bei uns z.** in my (or our) country
zu'langen intr suffice, do; (*bei Tisch*) help oneself
zu'länglich adj adequate, sufficient
zu'lassen §104 tr admit; (*erlauben*) allow; (*Tür*) leave shut; (*Fahrzeug*) license; (*Zweifel*) admit of
zulässig ['tsulɛsɪç] adj permissible; **zulässige Abweichung** allowance, tolerance
Zu'lassung f (-;-en) admission; permission; approval; license
Zu'lassungsprüfung f college entrance examination
Zu'lassungsschein m registration card
Zu'lauf m crowd, rush; **Z. haben** be popular; (theat) have a long run
zu'laufen §105 intr (SEIN) run on; run faster; (*dat*) flock to; **auf j-n z.** run up to s.o.; **spitz z.** end in a point
zu'legen tr add; **etw z.** up one's offer ‖ ref—**sich** [dat] **etw. z.** (coll) get oneself s.th.
zuleide [tsu'laɪdə] adv—**j-m etw z. tun** hurt s.o., do s.o. wrong
zu'leiten tr (*Wasser*) (*dat*) let in (to); (*dat*) direct (s.o.) (to); (*Schreiben*) (*dat*) pass on (to); *auf dem Amtsweg*) channel (to); (tech) feed

Zu'leitung f (-;-en) feed pipe; (elec) lead-in wire; (elec) conductor
zuletzt [tsu'lɛtst] adv last; at last; finally; after all
zuliebe [tsu'libə] prep (*dat*) for (s.o.'s) sake
zum [tsum] abbr **zu dem; es ist zum** ...it's enough to make one...
zu'machen tr shut; (*Loch*) close up; (*zuknöpfen*) button up
zumal [tsu'mal] adv especially; **z. da** all the more because
zu'mauern tr wall up
zumindest [tsu'mɪndəst] adv at least
zumute [tsu'mutə] adv—**mir ist gut** (or **wohl**) **z.** I feel good; **mir ist nicht zum Lachen z.** I don't feel like laughing
zumuten ['tsumutən] tr—**j-m etw z.** expect s.th. of s.o. ‖ ref—**sich** [dat] **zuviel z.** attempt too much
Zu'mutung f (-;-en) imposition
zunächst [tsu'nɛçst] adv first, at first, first of all; (*erstens*) to begin with; (*vorläufig*) for the time being ‖ prep (*dat*) next to
zu'nageln tr nail up, nail shut
zu'nähen tr sew up
Zu'nahme f (-;-n) increase; growth; rise
Zu'name m last name, family name
Zünd– (tsʏnt] comb.fm. ignition
zünden ['tsʏndən] tr ignite; kindle; (*Sprengstoff*) detonate ‖ intr ignite, catch fire; (fig) catch on
Zün'der m (-s;-) fuse; detonator
Zünd'flamme f pilot light
Zünd'holz n match
Zünd'kerze f (aut) spark plug
Zünd'nadel f firing pin
Zünd'satz m primer
Zünd'schlüssel m ignition key
Zünd'schnur f fuse
Zünd'stein m flint
Zünd'stoff m fuel
Zün'dung f (-;-en) (aut) ignition
zu'nehmen §116 intr (an *dat*) increase (in); (*steigen*) rise; grow longer
zu'neigen tr (*dat*) tilt toward ‖ ref & intr (*dat*) incline toward(s); **sich dem Ende z.** draw to a close
Zu'neigung f (-;) (für, zu) liking (for)
Zunft [tsʊnft] f (-;-en) guild
Zunge ['tsʊŋə] f (-;-n) tongue
züngeln ['tsʏŋəln] intr dart out the tongue; (*Flamme*) dart, leap up
Zun'genbrecher m tongue twister
zun'genfertig adj glib
Zun'genspitze f tip of the tongue
zunichte [tsu'nɪçtə] adv—**z. machen** destroy; (*Plan*) spoil; (*Theorie*) explode; **z. werden** come to nothing
zu'nicken intr (*dat*) nod to
zunutze [tsu'nutsə] adv—**sich etw z. machen** utilize s.th.
zuoberst [tsu'obərst] adv at the top
zupfen ['tsupfən] tr pull; pluck ‖ intr (an *dat*) tug (at)
zu'prosten intr (*dat*) toast
zur [tsur] abbr **zu der**
zu'rechnen tr add; (*dat*) number among, classify with; (*dat*) attribute to

zu'rechnungsfähig *adj* accountable; responsible; of sound mind
Zu'rechnungsfähigkeit *f* responsibility; sound mind
zurecht– [tsu'reçt] *comb.fm.* right, in order; at the right time
zurecht'biegen §57 *tr* straighten out
zurecht'bringen §65 *tr* set right
zurecht'finden §59 *ref* find one's way; (fig) see one's way
zurecht'kommen §99 *intr* (SEIN) come on time; get on, manage; turn out all right; **mit etw nicht z.** make a mess of s.th.; **mit j–m z.** get along with s.o.
zurecht'legen *tr* lay out in order ‖ *ref*—**sich** [*dat*] **z.** figure out
zurecht'machen *tr* & *ref* get ready
zurecht'schneiden §106 *tr* cut to size
zurecht'setzen *tr* set right, fix, adjust
zurecht'weisen §118 *tr* reprimand
zu'reden *intr* (*dat*) try to persuade; (*dat*) encourage
zu'reichen *tr* reach, pass ‖ *intr* do
zu'reichend *adj* sufficient
zu'reiten §86 *tr* break in
zu'richten *tr* prepare; cook
zu'riegeln *tr* bolt
zürnen ['tsʏrnən] *intr* (*dat*) be angry (with)
zurren ['tsurən] *tr* (naut) lash down
Zurschau'stellung *f* display
zurück [tsu'rʏk] *adv* back; backward; behind; **ein paar Jahre z.** a few years ago ‖ *interj* back up!
zurück– *comb.fm.* back; behind; re–
zurück'behalten §90 *tr* keep back
zurück'bekommen §99 *tr* get back
zurück'bleiben §62 *intr* (SEIN) stay behind; fall behind; (*Uhr*) lose time; (**hinter** *dat*) fall short (of)
Zurück'blenden *n* (cin) flashback
zurück'blicken *intr* look back
zurück'bringen §65 *tr* bring back; **z. auf** (*acc*) (math) reduce to
zurück'datieren *tr* antedate
zurück'drängen *tr* force back; repress
zurück'dürfen §69 *intr* be allowed to return
zurück'erobern *tr* reconquer, win back
zurück'erstatten *tr* return; (*Ausgaben*) refund; (*Kosten*) reimburse
zurück'fahren §71 *tr* drive back ‖ *intr* (SEIN) drive back, ride back; (*vor Schreck*) recoil, start
zurück'finden §59 *ref* find one's way back
zurück'fordern *tr* reclaim, demand back
zurück'führen *tr* lead back; trace back; **z. auf** (*acc*) refer to; attribute to
zurück'geben §80 *tr* give back, return
zurück'gehen §82 *intr* (SEIN) go back; (*Fieber, Preise*) drop; (*Geschwulst*) go down; (mil) fall back
zurück'gezogen *adj* secluded
zurück'greifen §88 *intr*—**z. auf** (*acc*) (fig) fall back on
zurück'halten §90 *tr* hold back; **j–n davon z. zu** (*inf*) keep s.o. from (*ger*) ‖ *intr* **mit etw z.** conceal s.th.
zurück'haltend *adj* reserved; shy
Zurück'haltung *f* (–;–en) reserve

zurück'kehren *intr* (SEIN) return
zurück'kommen §99 *intr* (SEIN) return; **z. auf** (*acc*) come back to, revert to; (*hinweisen*) refer to
zurück'können §100 *intr* be able to return
zurück'lassen §104 *tr* leave behind; outstrip, outrun
zurück'legen *tr* (*Kopf*) lean back; (*Geld*) put aside; (*Jahre*) complete; *Strecke*) cover; (*Ware*) lay away ‖ *ref* lean back
zurück'lehnen *ref* lean back
zurück'liegen §108 *intr* belong to the past ‖ *impers*—**es liegt jetzt zehn Jahre zurück, daß** it's ten years now that
zurück'müssen §115 *intr* have to return
zurück'nehmen §116 *tr* take back; (*widerrufen*) revoke; (*Auftrag*) cancel; (*Vorwurf*) retract; (*Klage*) withdraw; (*Versprechen*) go back on; (*Truppen*) pull back; **das Gas z.** slow down
zurück'prallen *intr* (SEIN) rebound; (*vor Schreck*) start, be startled
zurück'rufen §122 *tr* call back, recall
zurück'schauen *intr* look back
zurück'schicken *tr* send back
zurück'schlagen §132 *tr* beat back, throw back ‖ *intr* strike back
zurück'schrecken *tr* frighten away; (**von**) deter (from) ‖ §109 & §134 *intr* (SEIN) (**von, vor** *dat*) shrink back (from)
zurück'sehnen *ref* yearn to return
zurück'sein §139 *intr* (SEIN) be back; (**in** *dat*) be behind (in)
zurück'setzen *tr* put back; (*im Preis*) reduce; (fig) snub ‖ *ref* sit back
zurück'stecken *tr* put back
zurück'stellen *tr* (*Uhr*) set back; (*Plan*) shelve; (mil) defer
zurück'stoßen §150 *tr* push back; repel
zurück'strahlen *tr* reflect
zurück'streifen *tr* (*Ärmel*) roll up
zurück'treten §152 *intr* (SEIN) step back; (*vom Amt*) resign; (*Wasser, Berge*) recede
zurück'tun §154 *tr* put back
zurück'verfolgen *tr* (*Schritte*) retrace; (fig) trace back
zurück'verweisen §118 *tr* (**an** *acc*) refer back (to); (parl) remand (to)
zurück'weichen §85 *intr* (SEIN) fall back, make way; (*Hochwasser*) recede; (*vor dem Feind*) give ground; **z. vor** (*dat*) shrink from
zurück'weisen §118 *tr* turn back; (*ablehnen*) turn down; (*Angriff*) repel ‖ *intr*—**z. auf** (*acc*) refer to
Zurück'weisung *f* (–;–en) rejection
zurück'wenden §140 *tr* & *ref* turn back
zurück'werfen §160 *tr* throw back; (*e–n Patienten*) set back; (*Strahlen*) reflect; (*Feind*) hurl back
zurück'wirken *intr* (**auf** *acc*) react (on); (*Gesetz*) be retroactive
zurück'zahlen *tr* pay back; (fin) refund
zurück'ziehen §163 *tr* draw back; (*Antrag*) withdraw; (*Geld*) call in; (*Truppen*) pull back; (sport) scratch ‖ *ref* withdraw; (*schlafengehen*) re-

tire; (mil) pull back ‖ *intr* (SEIN) move back; (mil) fall back, retreat

Zu′ruf *m* call; cheer; (parl) acclamation

zu′rufen §122 *tr*—j-m etw z. shout s.th. to s.o.

Zu′sage *f* (-;-n) assent; promise

zu′sagen *tr* promise ‖ *intr* accept an invitation; (*dat*) please; (*dat*) agree (with)

zusammen [tsu′zamən] *adv* together; in common; at the same time

Zusam′menarbeit *f* cooperation

zusam′menarbeiten *intr* cooperate

zusam′menballen *tr* (*Faust*) clench

zusam′menbeißen §53 *tr*—die Zähne z. grit one's teeth

zusam′menbinden §59 *tr* tie together

zusam′menbrauen *tr* concoct ‖ *ref* (*Sturm*) brew

zusam′menbrechen §64 *intr* (SEIN) break down; collapse

Zusam′menbruch *m* collapse; breakdown

zusam′mendrängen *tr* crowd together

zusam′mendrücken *tr* compress

zusam′menfahren §71 *intr* (SEIN) be startled; (mit) collide (with)

zusam′menfallen §72 *intr* (SEIN) fall in, collapse; (*Teig*) fall; (*Person*) lose weight; (mit) coincide (with)

Zusam′menfall *m* coincidence

zusam′menfalten *tr* fold

zusam′menfassen *tr* (*in sich fassen*) comprise; (*verbinden*) combine; (*Macht, Funktionen*) concentrate; (*Bericht*) summarize

zusam′menfassend *adj* comprehensive; summary

Zusam′menfassung *f* (-;-en) summary, résumé

zusam′menfinden §59 *ref* meet

zusam′menfügen *tr* join together; (*Scherben, Teile*) piece together

zusam′mengehen §82 *intr* (SEIN) go together; match; close; shrink

zusam′mengehören *intr* belong together

zusam′mengeraten §63 *intr* (SEIN) collide

zusammengewürfelt [tsu′zaməngevʏrfəlt] *adj* mixed, motely

Zusam′menhalt *m* cohesion; consistency

zusam′menhalten §90 *tr* hold together; compare ‖ *intr* stick together

Zusam′menhang *m* connection, relation; context; coherence

zusam′menhängend *adj* coherent; allied

zusam′menklappen *tr* fold up; die Hacken z. click one's heels ‖ *intr* (SEIN) collapse

zusam′menkommen §99 *intr* (SEIN) come together

Zusammenkunft [tsu′zamənkunft] *f* (-;-̈e) meeting

zusam′menlaufen §105 *intr* (SEIN) run together; come together; flock; (*Milch*) curdle; (*Farben*) run; (*einschrumpfen*) shrink up; (geom) converge

zusammenlegbar [tsu′zamənlekbɑr] *adj* collapsible

zusam′menlegen *tr* put together; (*fal-*

ten) fold; (*Geld*) pool; (*vereinigen*) combine, consolidate ‖ *intr* pool money

zusam′mennehmen §116 *tr* gather up; (*Gedanken*) collect; (*Kräfte, Mut*) muster; alles zusammengenommen considering everything ‖ *ref* pull oneself together

zusam′menpacken *tr* pack up

zusam′menpassen *tr* & *intr* match

zusam′menpferchen *tr* crowd together

Zusam′menprall *m* collision; (fig) (mit) impact (on)

zusam′menprallen *intr* collide

zusam′menraffen *tr* collect in haste; (*ein Vermögen*) amass; (*Kräfte*) summon up, marshal ‖ *ref* pull oneself together

zusam′menreißen §53 *ref* (coll) pull oneself together

zusam′menrollen *tr* roll up

zusam′menrotten *ref* band together, form a gang; (*Aufrührer*) riot

zusam′menrücken *tr* push together ‖ *intr* (SEIN) move closer together

zusam′menschießen *tr* (*Stadt*) shoot up; (*Menschen*) shoot down; (*Geld*) pool

zusam′menschlagen §132 *tr* smash up; (*Absätze*) click; (*Beine, Zeitung*) fold; (*Hände*) clap; (*zerschlagen*) beat up; die Hände über den Kopf z. (fig) throw up one's hands ‖ *intr* (SEIN)—aneinander z. clash

zusam′menschließen §76 *tr* join; link together ‖ *ref* join together, unite

Zusam′menschluß *m* union; alliance

zusam′menschmelzen *intr* (SEIN) fuse; melt away; (fig) dwindle

zusam′menschnüren *tr* tie up

zusam′menschrumpfen *intr* (SEIN) shrivel; (*Geld*) (coll) dwindle away

zusam′mensetzen *tr* put together; (mach) assemble ‖ *ref* sit down together; sich z. aus consist of

Zusam′mensetzung *f* (-;-en) composition; (*Bestandteile*) ingredients; (*Struktur*) structure; (chem, gram) compound

Zusam′menspiel *n* teamwork

zusam′menstauchen *tr* browbeat, chew out

zusam′menstellen *tr* put together; (*Liste*) compile; (*Farben*) match; organize

Zusam′menstoß *m* collision; (*der Meinungen*) clash; (*Treffen*) encounter; (mil) engagement

zusam′menstoßen §150 *tr* knock together; (*Gläser*) touch ‖ *intr* adjoin; mit den Gläsern z. clink glasses ‖ *intr* (SEIN) collide; (*Gegner*) clash

zusam′menstückeln *tr* piece together

zusam′menstürzen *intr* (SEIN) collapse

zusam′mentragen §132 *tr* collect

zusam′mentreffen §151 *intr* (SEIN) meet; coincide ‖ Zusammentreffen *n* (-s;) encounter, meeting; coincidence

zusam′mentreiben §62 *tr* round up; (*Geld*) scrape up

zusam′mentreten §152 *intr* (SEIN) meet

zusam′menwirken *intr* cooperate; collaborate; interact ‖ **Zusammen-wirken** n (–s;) cooperation; inter-action

zusam'menzählen tr count up, add up

zusam'menziehen §163 tr draw to-gether, contract; (*Lippen*) pucker; (*Brauen*) knit; (*Summe*) add up; (*kürzen*) shorten; (*Truppen*) concen-trate ‖ ref contract; (*Gewitter*) brew ‖ intr (SEIN)—**mit j–m z.** move in with s.o.

Zu'satz m addition; (*Ergänzung*) sup-plement; (*Anhang*) appendix; (*Nach-schrift*) postscript; (*Beimischung*) admixture; (*zu e–m Testament*) codi-cil; (parl) rider; **unter Z. von** with the addition of

Zu'satzgerät n attachment

zusätzlich ['tsuzetslɪç] adj additional, extra ‖ adv in addition

zuschanden [tsu'ʃandən] adv—**z. ma-chen** ruin; **z. werden** go to ruin

zu'schauen intr look on; (*dat*) watch

Zu'schauer –in §6 mf spectator

Zu'schauerraum m auditorium

zu'schicken tr (*dat*) send (to)

zu'schieben §130 tr close, shut; (*Rie-gel*) push forward; **j–m die Schuld z.** push the blame on s.o.

Zu'schlag m extra charge; **den Z. er-halten** get the contract (*on a bid*)

zu'schlagen §132 tr (*Tür*) slam; (*Buch*) shut; (*auf Auktionen*) knock down; (*hinzurechnen*) add ‖ intr hit hard

zu'schließen §76 tr shut, lock

zu'schnallen tr buckle (up)

zu'schnappen intr snap shut; **z. lassen** snap shut

zu'schneiden §106 tr cut out; (*Anzug*) cut to size

Zu'schnitt m cut; (fig) style

zu'schnüren tr lace up

zu'schrauben tr screw tight

zu'schreiben §62 tr ascribe; (*Bedeu-tung*) attach; (*Grundstück, usw.*) transfer, sign over ‖ ref—**er hat es sich** [*dat*] **selbst zuzuschreiben** he has himself to thank for it

Zu'schrift f letter, communication

zuschulden [tsu'ʃuldən] adv—**sich** [*dat*] **etw. z. kommen lassen** take the blame for s.th.

Zu'schuß m subsidy; grant; allowance

zu'schütten tr add; (*Graben*) fill up

zu'sehen §138 intr look on; (*dat*) watch; **z., daß** see to it that

zusehends ['tsuze-ənts] adv visibly

zu'senden §120 & §140 tr (*dat*) send to

zu'setzen tr add; (*Geld*) lose ‖ intr (*dat*) pester; (*dat*) be hard on; (mil) (*dat*) put pressure on

zu'sichern tr—**j–m etw z.** assure s.o. of s.th.

Zu'sicherung f (–;–en) assurance

zu'siegeln tr seal up

Zu'speise f side dish

zu'sperren tr lock

zu'spielen tr—**j–m den Ball z.** pass the ball to s.o.; **j–m etw z.** slip s.th. to s.o.

zu'spitzen tr sharpen, make pointy ‖ ref (*Lage*) come to a head

zu'sprechen §64 tr (& jur) award

Zu'spruch m consolation, encourage-ment; (com) customers, clientele

zu'springen §142 intr (SEIN) snap shut

Zu'stand m state, condition; **gegen-wärtiger Z.** status quo; **in gutem Z.** in good condition; **Zustände** state of affairs

zustande [tsu'ʃtandə] adv—**z. bringen** bring about; put across; get away with; **z. kommen** come about, come off; happen; be realized; (*Gesetz*) pass; (*Vertrag*) be reached

zu'ständig adj competent; (*Behörde*) proper; (*verantwortlich*) responsible

Zu'ständigkeit f (–;) jurisdiction

zustatten [tsu'ʃtatən] adv—**z. kommen** come in handy

zu'stehen §146 intr (*dat*) be due to

zu'stellen tr deliver; (jur) serve

Zu'stellung f (–;–en) delivery; (jur) serving

zu'steuern tr (*Geld*) contribute, kick in ‖ intr (*dat*, **auf** *acc*) head for

zu'stimmen intr (*dat*) agree to, approve of (*s.th.*); (*dat*) agree with (*s.o.*)

Zu'stimmung f (–;) consent, approval

zu'stopfen tr plug up

zu'stoßen §150 tr slam ‖ intr (SEIN) lunge; (*dat*) happen to

zu'streben intr (*dat*) strive for

zutage [tsu'tagə] adv to light; **z. liegen** be evident

Zutaten ['tsutatən] pl ingredients

zuteil [tsu'taɪl] adv—**j–m z. werden** fall to s.o.'s share

zu'teilen tr allot; ration; award; (*ge-währen*) grant; confer; (mil) assign

Zu'teilung f (–;–en) allotment, alloca-tion; rationing; (mil) assignment

zu'tragen §132 tr carry; (*Neuigkeiten*) report ‖ ref happen

zuträglich ['tsutreklɪç] adj advanta-geous; (*Klima*) healthful; (*Nahrung*) wholesome; **j–m z. sein** agree with s.o.

zu'trauen tr—**j–m etw z.** give s.o. credit for s.th.; imagine s.o. capable of s.th. ‖ **Zutrauen** n (–s;) (zu) con-fidence (in)

zu'traulich adj trustful; (*zahm*) tame

zu'treffen §151 intr (SEIN) prove right; come true; hold true, be conclusive; **z. auf** (*acc*) apply to

zu'treffend adj correct; to the point; (*anwendbar*) applicable

zu'trinken §143 intr (*dat*) drink to

Zu'tritt m access; admission, entrance; **kein Z.!** no admittance!

zu'tun §154 tr close; (*hinzufügen*) add

zu'verlässig adj reliable; **von zuverläs-siger Seite** on good authority

Zu'verlässigkeit f (–;) reliability

Zuversicht ['tsuferzɪçt] f (–;) confi-dence

zu'versichtlich adj confident

zuviel [tsu'fil] adv & indef pron too much; **einer z.** one too many

zuvor [tsu'for] adv before, previously; first (of all); **kurz z.** shortly before

zuvor- comb.fm. beforehand

zuvor'kommen §99 intr (SEIN) (*dat*) anticipate; **j–m z.** get the jump on s.o.

zuvor'kommend *adj* obliging; polite
zuvor'tun §154 *tr*—es **j—m z.** outdo s.o.
Zu'wachs *m* increase; growth; **auf Z.** (big enough) to allow for growth
zu'wachsen §155 *intr* (SEIN) grow together; (*Wunde*) heal up; (*dat*) accrue (to)
Zu'wachsrate *f* rate of increase
zuwege [tsu'vegə] *adv*—**z. bringen** bring about; achieve; finish; **gut z. sein** be fit as a fiddle
zuweilen [tsu'vaɪlən] *adv* sometimes
zu'weisen §118 *tr* assign, allot
zu'wenden §120 & §140 *tr* (*dat*) turn (*s.th.*) towards; (*dat*) give (*s.th.*) to, devote (*s.th.*) to || *ref* (*dat*) devote oneself to, concentrate on
Zu'wendung *f* (—;—en) gift, donation
zuwenig [tsu'veniç] *adv & pron* too little
zu'werfen §160 *tr* (*Tür*) slam; (*Blick*) cast; (*Grube*) fill up; **j—m etw z.** throw s.o. s.th.
zuwider [tsu'vidər] *adj* (*dat*) distasteful (to) || *prep* (*dat*) contrary to
zuwi'derhandeln *intr* (*dat*) go against
Zuwi'derhandlung *f* (—;—en) violation
zu'winken *intr* (*dat*) wave to; beckon to
zu'zahlen *tr* pay extra
zu'zählen *tr* add
zuzeiten [tsu'tsaɪtən] *adv* at times
zu'ziehen §163 *tr* (*Vorhang*) draw; (*Knoten*) tighten; (*Arzt, Experten*) call in || *ref*—**sich** [*dat*] **etw z.** incur s.th.; contract s.th. || *intr* (SEIN) move in; move (*to a city*)
Zu'ziehung *f*—**unter Z.** (*genit or von*) in consultation with
zuzüglich ['tsutsykliç] *prep* (*genit*) plus; including
zwang [tsvaŋ] *pret of* **zwingen** || **Zwang** *m* (—[e]s;) coercion, force; restraint; obligation; (*Druck*) pressure; (*jur*) duress; **auf j—n Z. ausüben** put pressure on s.o. || *ref*—**sich** [*dat*] **keinen Z. antun** (or **auferlegen**) relax
zwängen ['tsvɛŋən] *tr* force, squeeze || *ref* (**durch**) squeeze (through)
zwang'los *adj* free and easy; informal
Zwang'losigkeit *f* (—;) ease; informality
Zwangs— [tsvaŋs] *comb.fm.* force, compulsory
Zwangs'arbeit *f* hard labor
Zwangs'arbeitslager *n* labor camp
Zwangs'jacke *f* strait jacket
Zwangs'lage *f* tight spot
zwangs'läufig *adj* inevitable
zwangs'mäßig *adj* forced; coercive
Zwangs'maßnahme *f*—**zu Zwangsmaßnahmen greifen** resort to force
Zwangs'verschleppte §5 *mf* displaced person
Zwangs'verwaltung *f* receivership
Zwangs'vorstellung *f* hallucination
zwangs'weise *adv* by force
Zwangs'wirtschaft *f* (econ) government control, controlled economy
zwanzig ['tsvantsiç] *invar adj & pron* twenty || **Zwanzig** *f* (—;—en) twenty
zwanziger ['tsvansigər] *invar adj* of the twenties; **die z. Jahre** the twenties

zwanzigste ['tsvantsiçstə] §9 *adj & pron* twentieth
Zwanzigstel ['tsvantsiçstəl] *n* (—s;—) twentieth (*part*)
zwar [tsvar] *adv* indeed, no doubt, it is true; **und z.** namely, that is
Zweck [tsvek] *m* (—[e]s;—e) purpose, aim, object, point; **es hat keinen Z.** there's no point to it
zweck'dienlich *adj* serviceable, useful
Zwecke ['tsvekə] *f* (—;—n) tack; thumbtack
zweck'entfremden *tr* misuse
zweck'entsprechend *adj* appropriate
zweck'los *adj* pointless
zweck'mäßig *adj* serving its purpose; (*Möbel*) functional
zwecks [tsveks] *prep* (*genit*) for the purpose of
zwei [tsvaɪ] *adj & pron* two; **alle z.** (coll) both; **zu zweien** in twos, two by two, in pairs; **zu zweien hintereinander** in double file || **Zwei** *f* (—;—en) two
zwei'beinig *adj* two-legged
Zwei'bettzimmer *n* double room
Zweidecker ['tsvaɪdekər] *m* (—s;—) biplane
zweideutig ['tsvaɪdɔɪtiç] *adj* ambiguous; (*Witz*) off-color; (*schlüpfrig*) suggestive
zweierlei ['tsvaɪ·ər'laɪ] *invar adj* two kinds of; **das ist z.** (coll) that's different
zwei'fach, zwei'fältig *adj* twofold, double; **in zweifacher Ausfertigung** in duplicate
Zweifami'lienhaus *n* duplex
zwei'farbig *adj* two-tone
Zweifel ['tsvaɪfəl] *m* (—s;—) doubt; **in Z. stellen** (or **ziehen**) call into question; **über allen Zweifeln erhaben** beyond reproach
zwei'felhaft *adj* doubtful; questionable; (*Persönlichkeit*) suspicious
zwei'fellos *adj* doubtless
zweifeln ['tsvaɪfəln] *intr* be in doubt; waver, hesitate; **z. an** (*dat*) doubt
Zwei'felsfall *m*—**im Z.** in case of doubt
Zweif'ler **—in** §6 *mf* skeptic
Zweig [tsvaɪk] *m* (—[e]s;—e) branch
Zweig'anstalt *f*, **Zweig'geschäft** *n* (com) branch
Zweig'gesellschaft *f* (com) affiliate
Zweig'niederlassung *f*, **Zweig'stelle** *f* (com) branch
Zwei'kampf *m* duel, single combat
zwei'mal *adv* twice
zweimalig ['tsvaɪmaliç] *adj* repeated
zweimotorig ['tsvaɪmɔtoriç] *adj* two-engine, twin-engine
zweireihig ['tsvaɪraɪ·iç] *adj* (*Sakko*) double-breasted
zwei'schneidig *adj* double-edged
zwei'seitig *adj* bilateral; reversible
zweisprachig ['tsvaɪʃpraxiç] *adj* bilingual
Zweistär'kenglas *n* bifocal lens; (*Brille*) bifocals
zwei'stimmig *adj* for two voices
zweistufig ['tsvaɪʃtufiç] *adj* (rok) two-stage
zwei'stündig *adj* two-hour

zwei'stündlich *adj* & *adv* every two hours

zweit [tsvaɪt] *adv*—**zu z.** by twos; **wir sind zu z.** there are two of us

Zwei'taktmotor *m* two-cycle engine

Zweit'ausfertigung *f* duplicate

zweit'beste §9 *adj* second-best

zweite ['tsvaɪtə] §9 *adj* & *pron* second; another; **aus zweiter Hand** second-hand; at second hand; **zum zweiten** secondly || **Zweite** §5 *mf* (sport) runner-up

zwei'teilig *adj* two-piece; two-part

zweitens ['tsvaɪtəns] *adv* secondly

zweit'klassig *adj* second-class

Zwerchfell ['tsvɛrçfɛl] *n* diaphragm

Zwerg [tsvɛrk] *m* (-[e]s;-e) dwarf

zwer'genhaft *adj* dwarfish

Zwetsche ['tsvɛtʃə] *f* (-;-n), **Zwetschge** ['tsvɛtʃgə] *f* (-;-n) plum

Zwetsch'genwasser *n* plum brandy

zwicken ['tsvɪkən] *tr* pinch

Zwicker (**Zwik'ker**) *m* (-s;-) pince-nez

Zwickmühle ['tsvɪkmylə] *f* (fig) fix

zwie– [tsvi] *comb.fm.* dis-, two-, double

Zwieback ['tsvibak] *m* (-s;ᵉe & -e) zwieback

Zwiebel ['tsvibəl] *f* (-;-n) onion; (*Blumen–*) bulb

Zwie'gespräch *n* dialogue

Zwie'licht *n* twilight

Zwiesel ['tsvizəl] *f* (-;-n) fork (*of tree*)

Zwie'spalt *m* dissension; schism; discrepancy; **im Z. sein mit** be at variance with

zwiespältig ['tsviʃpɛltɪç] *adj* disunited, divided; divergent

Zwie'tracht *f* (-;) discord

Zwilling ['tsvɪlɪŋ] *m* (-s;-e) twin; **einæige Zwillinge** identical twins

Zwil'lingsbruder *m* twin brother

Zwil'lingsschwester *f* twin sister

Zwinge ['tsvɪŋə] *f* (-;-n) ferrule; clamp; (*Schraubstock*) vise

zwingen ['tsvɪŋən] §142 *tr* force, compel; (*schaffen*) accomplish, swing

zwin'gend *adj* forceful, cogent

Zwin'ger *m* (-s;-) dungeon; cage; dog kennel; bear pit; lists

zwinkern ['tsvɪŋkərn] *intr* blink

Zwirn [tsvɪrn] *m* (-[e]s;-e) thread

Zwirns'faden *m* thread

zwischen ['tsvɪʃən] *prep* (*dat* & *acc*) between, among

Zwi'schenbemerkung *f* interruption

Zwi'schendeck *n* steerage

Zwi'schending *n* cross, mixture

zwischendurch' *adv* in between; at times

Zwi'schenergebnis *n* incomplete result

Zwi'schenfall *m* (unexpected) incident

Zwi'schenhändler –**in** §6 *mf* middleman

Zwi'schenlandung *f* stopover

Zwi'schenlauf *m* (sport) quarterfinal; (sport) semifinal

Zwi'schenpause *f* break, intermission

Zwi'schenraum *m* space, interval

Zwi'schenruf *m* boo; interruption

Zwi'schenrunde *f* (sport) quarterfinal; (sport) semifinal

Zwi'schenspiel *n* interlude

zwi'schenstaatlich *adj* international; interstate

Zwi'schenstation *f* (rr) way station

Zwi'schenstecker *m* (elec) adapter

Zwi'schenstellung *f* (-;-en) intermediate position

Zwi'schenstück *n* insert; (*Verbindung*) connection; (elec) adapter

Zwi'schenstufe *f* intermediate stage

Zwi'schenträger –**in** §6 *mf* gossip

Zwi'schenwand *f* partition wall

Zwi'schenzeit *f* interval, meanwhile

Zwist [tsvɪst] *m* (-es;-e) discord; quarrel; (*Feindschaft*) enmity

Zwi'stigkeit *f* (-;-en) hostility

zwitschern ['tsvɪtʃərn] *tr*—**e–n z.** (coll) have a shot of liquor || *intr* chirp

Zwitter ['tsvɪtər] *m* (-s;-) hermaphrodite

Zwit'terfahrzeug *n* (mil) half-track

zwo [tsvo] *adj* & *pron* (coll) two

zwölf ['tsvœlf] *invar adj* & *pron* twelve || **Zwölf** *f* (-;-en) twelve

Zwölffin'gerdarm *m* duodenum

zwölfte ['tsvœlftə] §9 *adj* & *pron* twelfth

Zwölftel ['tsvœftəl] *n* (-s;-) twelfth (part)

Zyklon [tsʏ'klon] *m* (-s;-e), **Zyklone** [tsʏ'klonə] *f* (-;-n) cyclone

Zyk·lus ['tsʏklʊs] *m* (-;-len [lən]) cycle; (*Reihe*) series, course

Zylinder [tsʏ'lɪndər] *m* (-s;-) cylinder (*e–r Lampe*) chimney; (*Hut*) top hat

zylindrisch [tsʏ'lɪndrɪʃ] *adj* cylindrical

Zyniker ['tsʏnɪkər] *m* (-s;-) cynic; (philos) Cynic

zynisch ['tsʏnɪʃ] *adj* cynical

Zypern ['tsʏpərn] *n* (-s;) Cyprus

Zypresse [tsʏ'prɛsə] *f* (-;-n) cypress

Zyste ['tsʏstə] *f* (-;-n) cyst

GRAMMATICAL EXPLANATIONS

German Pronunciation

All the German letters and their variant spellings are listed below (in column 1) with their IPA symbols (in column 2), a description of their sounds (in column 3), and German examples with phonetic transcription (in column 4).

VOWELS

SPELLING	SYMBOL	APPROXIMATE SOUND	EXAMPLES
a	[a]	Like *a* in English *swat*	Apfel ['apfəl], **lassen** ['lasən], **Stadt** [ʃtat]
a	[ɑ]	Like *a* in English *father*	Vater ['fatər], **laden** ['ladən]
aa	[ɑ]	" "	Paar [pɑr], **Staat** [ʃtat]
ah	[ɑ]	" "	Hahn [hɑn], **Zahl** [tsɑl]
ä	[ɛ]	Like *e* in English *met*	Äpfel ['ɛpfəl], **lässig** ['lɛsɪç], **Städte** ['ʃtɛtə]
ä	[e]	Like *e* in English *they* (without the following sound of *y*)	mäßig ['mesɪç], **Väter** ['fetər]
äh	[e]	" "	ähnlich ['enlɪç], **Zähne** ['tsenə]
e	[ə]	Like *e* in English *system*	Bitte ['bɪtə], **rufen** ['rufən]
e	[ɛ]	Like *e* in English *met*	Kette ['kɛtə], **messen** ['mɛsən]
e	[e]	Like *e* in English *they* (without the following sound of *y*)	Feder ['fedər], **regnen** ['regnən]
ee	[e]	" "	Meer [mer], **Seele** ['zelə]
eh	[e]	" "	Ehre ['erə], **zehn** [tsen]
i	[ɪ]	Like *i* in English *sin*	bin [bɪn], **Fisch** [fɪʃ]
i	[i]	Like *i* in English *machine*	Maschine [ma'ʃinə], **Lid** [lit]
ih	[i]	" "	ihm [im], **ihr** [ir]
ie	[i]	" "	dieser ['dizər], **tief** [tif]
o	[ɔ]	Like *o* in English *often*	Gott [gɔt], **offen** ['ɔfən]
o	[o]	Like *o* in English *note*, but without the diphthongal glide	holen ['holən], **Rose** ['rozə]
oo	[o]	" "	Boot [bot], **Moos** [mos]
oh	[o]	" "	Bohne ['bonə], **Kohle** ['kolə]
ö	[œ]	The lips are rounded for [ɔ] and held without moving while the sound [ɛ] is pronounced.	Götter ['gœtər], **öffnen** ['œfnən]

3a

SPELLING	SYMBOL	APPROXIMATE SOUND	EXAMPLES
ö	[ø]	The lips are rounded for [o] and held without moving while the sound [e] is pronounced.	böse ['bøzə], Löwe ['løvə]
öh	[ø]	" "	Röhre ['rørə], Söhne ['zønə]
u	[ʊ]	Like u in English bush	Busch [bʊʃ], muß [mʊs], Hund [hʊnt]
u	[u]	Like u in English rule	Schule ['ʃulə], Gruß [grus]
uh	[u]	" "	Uhr [ur], Ruhm [rum]
ü	[ʏ]	The lips are rounded for [ʊ] and held without moving while the sound [ɪ] is pronounced.	Hütte ['hʏtə], müssen ['mʏsən]
ü	[y]	The lips are rounded for [u] and held without moving while the sound [i] is pronounced.	Schüler ['ʃylər], Grüße ['grysə]
üh	[y]	" "	Mühle ['mylə], kühn [kyn]
y	[ʏ]	Like ü [ʏ] above	Mystik ['mʏstɪk]
y	[y]	Like ü [y] above	Mythe ['mytə]

DIPHTHONGS

SPELLING	SYMBOL	APPROXIMATE SOUND	EXAMPLES
ai	[aɪ]	Like i in English night	Saite ['zaɪtə], Mais [maɪs]
au	[aʊ]	Like ou in English ouch	kaufen ['kaʊfən], Haus [haʊs]
äu	[ɔɪ]	Like oy in English toy	träumen ['trɔɪmən], Gebäude [gə'bɔɪdə]
ei	[aɪ]	Like i in English night	Zeit [tsaɪt], nein [naɪn]
eu	[ɔɪ]	Like oy in English toy	heute ['hɔɪtə], Eule ['ɔɪlə]

CONSONANTS

SPELLING	SYMBOL	APPROXIMATE SOUND	EXAMPLES
b	[b]	Like b in English boy	Buch [bux], haben ['habən]
b	[p]	Like p in English lap	gelb [gɛlp], lieblich ['liplɪç]
c	[k]	Like c in English car	Clown [klaʊn], Café [ka'fe]
c	[ts]	Like ts in English its	Cäsar ['tsezar], Centrale [tsen'tralə]
ch	[x]	This sound is made by breathing through a space between the back of the tongue and the soft palate.	auch [aʊx], Buche ['buxə]
ch	[ç]	This sound is made by breathing through a space left when the front of the tongue is pressed close to the hard palate with the tip of the tongue behind the lower teeth.	ich [ɪç], Bücher ['byçər], Chemie [çe'mi], durch [dʊrç]

SPELLING	SYMBOL	APPROXIMATE SOUND	EXAMPLES
ch	[k]	Like *k* in English *key*	**Charakter** [ka'raktər], **Chor** [kor]
ch	[ʃ]	Like *sh* in English *shall*	**Chef** [ʃɛf], **Chassis** [ʃa'si]
chs	[ks]	Like *x* in English *box*	**sechs** [zɛks], **Wachs** [vaks]
ck	[k]	Like *k* in English *key* When *ck* in a vocabulary entry in this Dictionary has to be divided by an accent mark, the word is first spelled with *ck* and is then repeated in parentheses with the *ck* changed to *kk* in accordance with the principle which requires this change when the division comes at the end of the line, e.g., **Deckenlicht (Dek'ken-licht).**	**wecken** ['vɛkən], **Ruck** [rʊk]
d	[d]	Like *d* in English *door*	**laden** ['lɑdən], **deutsch** [dɔɪtʃ]
d	[t]	Like *t* in English *time*	**Freund** [frɔɪnt], **Hund** [hʊnt]
dt	[t]	" "	**verwandt** [fɛr'vant], **Stadt** [ʃtat]
f	[f]	Like *f* in English *five*	**Fall** [fal], **auf** [aʊf]
g	[g]	Like *g* in English *go*	**geben** ['gebən], **Regen** ['regən]
g	[k]	Like *k* in English *key*	**Krieg** [krik], **Weg** [vek]
g	[ç]	See **ch** [ç] above	**wenig** ['veniç], **häufig** ['hɔɪfɪç]
h	[h]	Like *h* in English *hat*	**Haus** [haʊs], **Freiheit** ['fraɪhaɪt]
j	[j]	Like *y* in English *yet*	**Jahr** [jɑr], **jener** ['jenər]
k	[k]	Like *k* in English *key*	**Kaffee** [ka'fe], **kein** [kaɪn]
l	[l]	This sound is made with the tip of the tongue against the back of the upper teeth and the side edges of the tongue against the side teeth.	**laden** ['lɑdən], **fahl** [fal]
m	[m]	Like *m* in English *man*	**mehr** [mer], **Amt** [amt]
n	[n]	Like *n* in English *neck*	**Nase** ['nɑzə], **kaufen** ['kaʊfən]
n	[ŋ]	Like *n* in English *sink*	**sinken** ['zɪŋkən], **Funke** ['fʊŋkə]
ng	[ŋ]	" "	**Finger** ['fɪŋər], **Rang** [raŋ]
p	[p]	Like *p* in English *pond*	**Perle** ['pɛrlə], **Opfer** ['ɔpfər]
ph	[f]	Like *f* in English *five*	**Phase** ['fɑzə], **Graphik** ['grɑfɪk]
qu	[kv]	Does not occur in English.	**Quelle** ['kvɛlə], **bequem** [bə'kvem]
r	[r]	This sound is a trilled sound made by vibrating the tip of the tongue against the upper gums or by vibrating the uvula.	**rufen** ['rufən], **Rede** ['redə]

SPELLING	SYMBOL	APPROXIMATE SOUND	EXAMPLES
s	[s]	Like s in English sock	Glas [glɑs], erst [erst]
s	[z]	Like z in English zest	sind [zınt], Eisen ['aızən]
sch	[ʃ]	Like sh in English shall	Schuh [ʃu], Schnee [ʃne]
sp	[ʃp]	Does not occur in English in the initial position.	sparen ['ʃparən], Spott [ʃpɔt]
ss	[s]	This spelling is used only in the intervocalic position and when the preceding vowel sound is one of the following: [a], [ε], [ı], [ɔ], [œ], [u], [Y]	Klasse ['klasə], essen ['ɛsən], wissen ['vısən], Gosse ['gɔsə], Rössel ['rœsəl], Russe ['rusə], müssen ['mYsən]
ß	[s]	This spelling is used instead of ss (a) when in the final position in a word or component, (b) when followed by a consonant, or (c) when intervocalic and preceded by a diphthong or one of the following vowel sounds: [ɑ], [e], [i], [o], [ø], [u], [y]	(a) Fluß [flus], Flußufer ['flusufər], (b) läßt [lest], (c) dreißig ['draısıç], Straße ['ʃtrasə], mäßig ['mesıç], schießen ['ʃisən], stoßen ['ʃtosən], Stößel ['ʃtøsəl], Muße ['musə], müßig ['mysıç]
st	[ʃt]	Does not occur in English in the initial position.	Staub [ʃtaup], stehen ['ʃte·ən]
t	[t]	Like t in English time	Teller ['telər], Tau [tau]
th	[t]	" "	Theater [tɛ'atər], Thema ['tema]
ti+ vowel	[tsj]	Does not occur in English.	Station [sta'tsjon], Patient [pa'tsjent]
tz	[ts]	Like ts in English its	schätzen ['ʃɛtsən], jetzt [jetst]
v	[f]	Like f in English five	Vater ['fatər], brav [braf]
v	[v]	Like v in English vat	November [nɔ'vɛmbər], Verb [vɛrp]
w	[v]	" "	Wasser ['vasər], wissen ['vısən]
x	[ks]	Like x in English box	Export [eks'pɔrt], Taxe ['taksə]
z	[ts]	Like ts in English its	Zahn [tsɑn], reizen ['raıtsən]

German Grammar References

§1. Declension of the Definite Article

	SINGULAR			PLURAL
	MASC	FEM	NEUT	MASC, FEM, NEUT
NOM	der	die	das	die
ACC	den	die	das	die
DAT	dem	der	dem	den
GENIT	des	der	des	der

§2. Declension of the Indefinite Article and the Numeral Adjective

	SINGULAR			PLURAL
1.	MASC	FEM	NEUT	MASC, FEM, NEUT
NOM	ein	eine	ein	
ACC	einen	eine	ein	
DAT	einem	einer	einem	
GENIT	eines	einer	eines	

2. Other words that are declined like **ein** are: **kein** *no, not any* and the possessive adjectives **mein** *my;* **dein** *thy, your;* **sein** *his; her; its;* **ihr** *her; their;* **Ihr** *your;* **unser** *our;* **euer** *your.* Unlike **ein,** they have plural forms, as shown in the following paradigm.

	SINGULAR			PLURAL
	MASC	FEM	NEUT	MASC, FEM, NEUT
NOM	kein	keine	kein	keine
ACC	keinen	keine	kein	keine
DAT	keinem	keiner	keinem	keinen
GENIT	keines	keiner	keines	keiner

3. The **e** of **er** of **unser** and **euer** is generally dropped when followed by an ending, as shown in the following paradigm. And instead of the e of er dropping, the e of final **em** and **en** in these words may drop.

	SINGULAR			PLURAL
	MASC	FEM	NEUT	MASC, FEM, NEUT
NOM	unser	uns(e)re	unser	uns(e)re
ACC	uns(e)ren or unsern	uns(e)re	unser	uns(e)re
DAT	uns(e)rem or unserm	uns(e)rer	uns(e)rem or unserm	uns(e)ren or unsern
GENIT	uns(e)res	uns(e)rer	uns(e)res	uns(e)rer

All adjectives that follow these words are declined in the mixed declension.

4. The pronouns **einer** and **keiner**, as well as all the possessive pronouns, are declined according to the strong declension of adjectives. The neuter forms **eines** and **keines** have the variants **eins** and **keins**.

5. When the possessive adjectives are used as possessive pronouns, they are declined according to the strong declension of adjectives. When preceded by the definite article, they are declined according to the weak declension of adjectives. There are also possessive pronouns with the infix **ig** which are always preceded by the definite article and capitalized and are declined according to the declension of adjectives, e.g., **der, die, das Meinige** *mine*.

§3. Declension of the Demonstrative Pronoun

	SINGULAR			PLURAL
	MASC	FEM	NEUT	MASC, FEM, NEUT
NOM	dieser	diese	dieses or dies	diese
ACC	diesen	diese	dieses or dies	diese
DAT	diesem	dieser	diesem	diesen
GENIT	dieses	dieser	dieses	dieser

Other words that are declined like **dieser** are **jeder** *each;* **jener** *that;* **mancher** *many a;* **welcher** *which.* All adjectives that come after these words are declined in the weak declension.

§4. Declension of Adjectives.
Adjectives have three declensions: 1) the strong declension, 2) the weak declension, and 3) the mixed declension. On both sides of this Dictionary, adjectives occurring in the expressions consisting solely of an adjective and a noun are entered in their weak forms.

1. The strong declension of adjectives, whose endings are shown in the following table, is used when the adjective is not preceded by **der** or by **dieser** or any of the other words listed in §3 or by **ein** or any of the other words listed in §2.

	SINGULAR			PLURAL
	MASC	FEM	NEUT	MASC, FEM, NEUT
NOM	—er	—e	—es	—e
ACC	—en	—e	—es	—e
DAT	—em	—er	—em	—en
GENIT	—en	—er	—en	—er

2. The weak declension of adjectives, whose endings are shown in the following table, is used when the adjective is preceded by **der** or **dieser** or any of the other words listed in §3.

	SINGULAR			PLURAL
	MASC	FEM	NEUT	MASC, FEM, NEUT
NOM	—e	—e	—e	—en
ACC	—en	—e	—e	—en
DAT	—en	—en	—en	—en
GENIT	—en	—en	—en	—en

3. The **der** component of **derselbe** and **derjenige** is the article **der** and is declined like it, while the **—selbe** and **—jenige** components are declined according to the weak declension of adjectives.

4. The mixed declension of adjectives, whose endings are shown in the following table, is used when the adjective is preceded by **ein** or **kein** or any of the other words listed in §2.

8a

	SINGULAR			PLURAL
	MASC	FEM	NEUT	MASC, FEM, NEUT
NOM	–er	–e	–es	–en
ACC	–en	–e	–es	–en
DAT	–en	–en	–en	–en
GENIT	–en	–en	–en	–en

§5. Adjectives Used as Nouns. When an adjective is used as a masculine, feminine, or neuter noun, it is spelled with an initial capital letter and is declined as an adjective in accordance with the principles set forth in §4. We have, for example, **der** or **die Fremde** the foreigner; **der** or **die Angestellte** *the employee*; **ein Angestellter** *a (male) employee*, **eine Angestellte** *a (female) employee*; **das Deutsche** *German* (i.e., *language*). These nouns are entered on both sides of this Dictionary in the weak form of the adjective and their genitives and plurals are not shown.

§6. Many masculine nouns ending in **–er** and **–ier** have feminine forms made by adding **–in**. The masculine forms have genitives made by adding **s** and remain unchanged in the plural, while the feminine forms remain unchanged in the singular and have plurals made by adding **–nen**. For example:

	MASC	FEM
NOM SG	**Verkäufer** *salesperson (salesman)*	**Verkäuferin** *salesperson (saleslady)*
GENIT SG	**Verkäufers**	**Verkäuferin**
NOM PL	**Verkäufer**	**Verkäuferinnen**

§7. Many masculine nouns ending in **–at** (e.g., **Advokat**), or in **–ant** (e.g., **Musikant**), or in **–ist** (*e.g.*, **Artist**), or in **–ent** (e.g., **Student**), or in **–graph** (e.g., **Choreograph**), or in **–ot** (e.g., **Pilot**), or in **–et** (e.g., **Analphabet**), or in **–it** (e.g., **Israelit**), or in **–ast** (e.g., **Phantast**), etc., have feminine forms made by adding **–in**. The masculine forms have genitives and plurals made by adding **–en**, while the femine forms remain unchanged in the singular and have plurals made by adding **–nen**. For example:

	MASC	FEM
NOM SG	**Advokat** *attorney*	**Advokatin** *attorney*
GENIT SG	**Advokaten**	**Advokatin**
NOM PL	**Advokaten**	**Advokatinnen**

§8. Many masculine nouns ending in **–ar** (e.g., **Antiquar**) or in **–är** (e.g., **Milliardär**) have feminine forms made by adding **–in**. The masculine forms have genitives made by adding **–(e)s** and plurals made by adding **–e**, while the feminine forms remain unchanged in the singular and have plurals made by adding **–nen**. For example:

	MASC	FEM
NOM SG	**Antiquar** *antique dealer*	**Antiquarin** *antique dealer*
GENIT SG	**Antiquar(e)s**	**Antiquarin**
NOM PL	**Antiquare**	**Antiquarinnen**

§9. Adjectives are generally given in their uninflected form, the form in which they appear in the predicate, e.g., **billig, reich, alt.** However, those adjectives which do not occur in an uninflected form are given with the weak ending **–e**, which in the nominative is the same for all genders, e.g., **andere, besondere, beste, hohe.**

9a

§10. Adjectives which denote languages may be used as adverbs. When so used with **sprechen, schreiben, können,** and a few others, they are translated in English by the corresponding noun, and actual and immediate action is implied, e.g., **deutsch sprechen** *to speak German* (i.e., to be speaking German right now). Adjectives which denote languages may be capitalized and used as invariable nouns, and when so used with **sprechen, schreiben, können,** and a few other verbs, general action is implied, e.g., **Deutsch sprechen** *to speak German* (i.e., to know how to speak German, to be a speaker of German).

With other verbs, these adjectives used as adverbs are translated by the corresponding noun preceded by "auf" or "in", e.g., **sich auf** (or **in**) **deutsch unterhalten** *to converse in German.*

§11. Personal and Reflexive Pronouns

PERSONS	SUBJECT	PERSONAL DIRECT OBJECT	PERSONAL INDIRECT OBJECT	REFLEXIVE DIRECT OBJECT	REFLEXIVE INDIRECT OBJECT
SG					
1	**ich** *I*	**mich** *me*	**mir** *(to) me*	**mich** *myself*	**mir** *(to) myself*
2	**du** *you*	**dich** *you*	**dir** *(to) you*	**dich** *yourself*	**dir** *(to) yourself*
3 MASC	**er** *he; it*	**ihn** *him; it*	**ihm** *(to) him; (to) it*	**sich** *himself; itself*	**sich** *(to) himself; (to) itself*
3 FEM	**sie** *she; it*	**sie** *her; it*	**ihr** *(to) her; (to) it*	**sich** *herself; itself*	**sich** *(to) herself; (to) itself*
3 NEUT	**es** *it; she; he*	**es** *it; her; him*	**ihm** *(to) it; (to) her; (to) him*	**sich** *itself; herself; himself*	**sich** *(to) itself; (to) herself; (to) himself*
PL					
1	**wir** *we*	**uns** *us*	**uns** *(to) us*	**uns** *ourselves*	**uns** *(to) ourselves*
2	**ihr** *you*	**euch** *you*	**euch** *(to) you*	**euch** *yourselves*	**euch** *(to) yourselves*
3	**sie** *they*	**sie** *them*	**ihnen** *(to) them*	**sich** *themselves*	**sich** *(to) themselves*
2 FORMAL SG & PL	**Sie** *you*	**Sie** *you*	**Ihnen** *(to) you*	**sich** *yourself; yourselves*	**sich** *(to) yourself; (to) yourselves*

er means *it* when it stands for a masculine noun that is the name of an animal or a thing, as **Hund, Tisch.** **sie** means *it* when it stands for a feminine noun that is the name of an animal or a thing, as **Hündin, Feder.** **es** means *she* when it stands for a neuter noun that is the name of a female person, as **Fräulein, Mädchen, Weib**; it means *he* when it stands for a neuter noun that is the name of a male person, as **Söhnchen, Söhnlein.**

The dative means also *from me, from you,* etc., with certain verbs expressing separation such as **entnehmen.**

11a

§12. Separable and Inseparable Prefixes. Many verbs can be compounded either with a prefix, which is always inseparable and unstressed, or with a combining form (conventionally called also a prefix), which can be separable and stressed or inseparable and unstressed. Exceptions are indicated by the abbreviations *sep* and *insep*.

1. The inseparable prefixes are **be–, emp–, ent–, er–, ge–, ver–,** and **zer–,** e.g., **beglei′ten, erler′nen, verste′hen.** They are never stressed.

2. The separable prefixes (i.e., combining forms) are prepositions, e.g., **auf–** as in **auf′tragen,** adverbs, e.g., **vorwärts–** as in **vor′wärtsbringen,** adjectives, e.g., **tot–** as in **tot′schlagen,** nouns, e.g., **maschine–** as in **maschi′neschreiben,** or other verbs, e.g., **stehen–** as in **ste′henbleiben.** They are always stressed except as provided for those listed in the following section.

3. The prefixes (combining forms) **durch, hinter, über, um, unter, wider,** and **wieder,** when their meaning is literal, are separable and stressed, e.g. **durch′schneiden** *cut through, cut in two,* and, when their meaning is figurative or derived, are inseparable and unstressed, e.g., **durchschnei′den** *cut across, traverse.*

4. A compound prefix is (a) inseparable if it consists of an inseparable prefix plus a separable prefix, e.g., **beauf′tragen,** (b) separable if it consists of a separable prefix plus an inseparable prefix, e.g.,**vor′bereiten—er bereitet etwas vor,** and (c) separable if it consists of two separable prefixes, e.g., **vorbei′laufen—sie lief vorbei.** Although verbs falling under (b) are separable, they do not take –ge– in the past participle, e.g., **vor′bereitet** (past participle of **vorbereiten**). But they do take the infix –zu– in the infinitive, e.g., **vor′zubereiten.** Note that compound prefixes falling under (c) are stressed on the second of the two separable components.

§13. German verbs are regarded as reflexive regardless of whether the reflexive pronoun is the direct or indirect object of the verb.

§14. The declension of German nouns is shown by giving the genitive singular followed by the nominative plural, in parentheses after the abbreviation indicating gender. This is done by presenting the whole noun by a hyphen with which the ending and/or the umlaut may or may not be shown according to the inflection; e.g., **Stadt** [ʃtat] *f* (–;⁼e) means **der Stadt** and **die Städte.** If the noun has no plural, the closing parenthesis comes immediately after the semicolon following the genitive singular, e.g., **Kleidung** [ˈklaɪdʊŋ] *f* (–;). In loan words in which the ending changes in the plural, the centered period is used to mark off the portion of the word that has to be detached before the portion showing the plural form is added, e.g., **Da·tum** [ˈdɑtʊm] *n* (–s;–ten [tən]).

When a vowel is added to a word ending in ß, the ß remains if it is preceded by a diphthong or one of the following vowel sounds: [ɑ], [e], [i], [o], [ø], [y], e.g., **Stoß** [ʃtos], plural: **Stöße; Strauß,** plural: **Sträuße,** but changes to ss if it is preceded by one of the following vowel sounds: [a], [ɛ], [ɪ], [ɔ], [œ], [ʊ], [ʏ], e.g., **Roß** [rɔs], plural **Rosses.** In this Dictionary the inflection of words in which ß does not change is shown in the usual way, e.g., **Stoß** [ʃtos] *m* (–es;⁼e); **Strauß** [ʃtraʊs] *m* (–es;⁼e), while the inflection of words in which ß changes to ss is shown in monosyllables by repeating the full word in its inflected forms, e.g., **Roß** [rɔs] *n* (**Rosses; Rosse**) and in polysyllables by marking off with a centered dot the final syllable and then repeating it in its inflected forms, e.g., **Ver·laß** [fɛrˈlas] *m* (–lasses;).

§15. When a word ending in a double consonant is combined with a following word beginning with the same single consonant followed by a vowel, the resultant group of three identical consonants is shortened to two, e.g., **Schiff** combined with **Fahrt** makes **Schiffahrt** and **Schall** combined with **Lehre** makes

12a

Schallehre.[1] However, when such a compound as a vocabulary entry has to be divided by an accent mark, the word is first spelled with two identical consonants and is then repeated in parentheses with three identical consonants, e.g., **Schiffahrt (Schiff′fahrt).** Furthermore, when such a compound has to be divided because the first component comes at the end of a line and is followed by a hyphen and the second component begins the following line, the three consonants are used, e.g., **Schiff–fahrt** and **Schall–lehre.**

When the medial group **ck** in a vocabulary entry has to be divided by an accent mark, the word is first spelled with **ck** and is then repeated in parentheses with the **ck** changed to **kk** in accordance with the orthographic principle which requires this change when the division comes at the end of the line, e.g., **Deckenlicht (Dek′kenlicht).**

---

[1] If the intial consonant of the following word is followed by a consonant instead of a vowel, the group of three identical consonants remains, e.g., **Fetttropfen, Rohstofffrage.**

German Model Verbs

These verbs are models for all the verbs that appear as vocabulary entries in the German-English part of this Dictionary. If a section number referring to this table is not given with an entry, it is understood that the verb is a weak verb conjugated like **loben, reden, handeln,** or **warten.** If a section number is given, it is understood that the verb is a strong, mixed, or irregular verb and that it is identical in all forms with the model referred to in its radical vowel or diphthong and the consonants that follow the radical. Thus **schneiden** is numbered §106 to refer to the model **leiden.** Such words include the model itself, e.g., **denken,** numbered §66 to refer to the model **denken,** compounds of the model, e.g., **bekommen,** numbered §99 to refer to the model **kommen,** and verbs that have the same radical component, e.g., **empfehlen,** numbered §51 to refer to the model **befehlen.**

If a strong or mixed verb in a given function (transitive or intransitive) and/or meaning may be conjugated also as a weak verb, this is indicated by the insertion of the section number of the appropriate weak verb (**loben, handeln, reden,** or **warten**) after the section number of the model strong verb, e.g., **dingen** §142 & §109.

If a strong or mixed verb in a different function is conjugated as a weak verb, this is indicated by dividing the two functions by parallels and showing the conjungation of each by the insertion of the appropriate section numbers, e.g., **hängen** §92 *tr* . . . ‖ §109 *intr*.

If a strong or mixed verb in a different meaning is conjugated as a weak verb, this is indicated by dividing the two meanings by parallels and showing the conjungation of each by the insertion of the appropriate section numbers, e.g., **bewegen** *tr* move, set in motion . . . ‖ §56 *tr* move, induce.

It is understood that verbs with inseparable prefixes, verbs with compound separable prefixes of which the first component is separable and the second inseparable, and verbs ending in –**ieren** do not take **ge** in the past participle.

No account is taken here of the auxiliary used in forming compound tenses. The use of SEIN is indicated in the body of the Dictionary.

Alternate forms are listed in parentheses immediately below the corresponding principal part of the model verb.

	INFINITIVE	3D SG PRESENT INDICATIVE	IMPERFECT INDICATIVE	IMPERFECT SUBJUNCTIVE	PAST PARTICIPLE
§50	backen	bäckt	buk	büke	gebacken
§51	befehlen	befiehlt	befahl	beföhle	befohlen
§52	beginnen	beginnt	begann	begönne (begänne)	begonnen
§53	beißen	beißt	biß	bisse	gebissen
§54	bergen	birgt	barg	bärge (bürge)	geborgen
§55	bersten	birst (berstet)	barst	bärste (börste)	geborsten
§56	bewegen	bewegt	bewog	bewöge	bewogen
§57	biegen	biegt	bog	böge	gebogen
§58	bieten	bietet	bot	böte	geboten
§59	binden	bindet	band	bände	gebunden
§60	bitten	bittet	bat	bäte	gebeten
§61	blasen	bläst	blies	bliese	geblasen
§62	bleiben	bleibt	blieb	bliebe	geblieben
§63	braten	brät	briet	briete	gebraten
§64	brechen	bricht	brach	bräche	gebrochen
§65	bringen	bringt	brachte	brächte	gebracht
§66	denken	denkt	dachte	dächte	gedacht
§67	dreschen	drischt	drosch (drasch)	drösche (dräsche)	gedroschen
§68	dünken	dünkt (deucht)	dünkte (deucht)	dünkte (deuchte)	gedünkt (gedeucht)

15a

	INFINITIVE	3D SG PRESENT INDICATIVE	IMPERFECT INDICATIVE	IMPERFECT SUBJUNCTIVE	PAST PARTICIPLE
§69	dürfen	darf	durfte	dürfte	gedurft (dürfen)
§70	essen	ißt	aß	äße	gegessen
§71	fahren	fährt	fuhr	führe	gefahren
§72	fallen	fällt	fiel	fiele	gefallen
§73	fangen	fängt	fing	finge	gefangen
§74	fechten	ficht	focht	föchte	gefochten
§75	fliehen	flieht	floh	flöhe	geflohen
§76	fließen	fließt	floß	flösse	geflossen
§77	frieren	friert	fror	fröre	gefroren
§78	gären	gärt	gor	göre	gegoren
§79	gebären	gebiert	gebar	gebäre	geboren
§80	geben	gibt	gab	gäbe	gegeben
§81	gedeihen	gedeiht	gedieh	gediehe	gediehen
§82	gehen	geht	ging	ginge	gegangen
§83	gelten	gilt	galt	gälte (gölte)	gegolten
§84	genesen	genest	genas	genäse	genesen
§85	gleichen	gleicht	glich	gliche	geglichen
§86	gleiten	gleitet	glitt	glitte	geglitten
§87	graben	gräbt	grub	grübe	gegraben
§88	greifen	greift	griff	griffe	gegriffen
§89	haben	hat	hatte	hätte	gehabt
§90	halten	hält	hielt	hielte	gehalten

16a

	INFINITIVE	3D SG PRESENT INDICATIVE	IMPERFECT INDICATIVE	IMPERFECT SUBJUNCTIVE	PAST PARTICIPLE
§91	handeln	handelt	handelte	handelte	gehandelt
§92	hängen	hängt	hing	hinge	gehangen
§93	hauen	haut	hieb	hiebe	gehauen
§94	heben	hebt	hob	höbe	gehoben
§95	heißen	heißt	hieß	hieße	geheißen
§96	helfen	hilft	half	hälfe (hülfe)	geholfen
§97	kennen	kennt	kannte	kennte	gekannt
§98	kiesen	kiest	kor	köre	gekoren
§99	kommen	kommt	kam	käme	gekommen
§100	können	kann	konnte	könnte	gekonnt (können)
§101	kreischen	kreischt	kreischte (krisch)	kreischte (krische)	gekreischt (gekrischen)
§102	kriechen	kriecht	kroch	kröche	gekrochen
§103	laden	lädt	lud	lüde	geladen
§104	lassen	läßt	ließ	ließe	gelassen
§105	laufen	läuft	lief	liefe	gelaufen
§106	leiden	leidet	litt	litte	gelitten
§107	lesen	liest	las	läse	gelesen
§108	liegen	liegt	lag	läge	gelegen
§109	loben	lobt	lobte	lobte	gelobt
§110	löschen	lischt	losch	lösche	geloschen
§111	lügen	lügt	log	löge	gelogen

	INFINITIVE	3D SG PRESENT INDICATIVE	IMPERFECT INDICATIVE	IMPERFECT SUBJUNCTIVE	PAST PARTICIPLE
§112	meiden	meidet	mied	miede	gemieden
§113	melken	melkt	molk	mölke	gemolken
§114	mögen	mag	mochte	möchte	gemocht (mögen)
§115	müssen	muß	mußte	müßte	gemußt (müssen)
§116	nehmen	nimmt	nahm	nähme	genommen
§117	pflegen	pflegt	pflog	pflöge	gepflogen
§118	preisen	preist	pries	priese	gepriesen
§119	quellen	quillt	quoll	quölle	gequollen
§120	reden	redet	redete	redete	geredet
§121	rinnen	rinnt	rann	ränne (rönne)	geronnen
§122	rufen	ruft	rief	riefe	gerufen
§123	salzen	salzt	salzte	salzte	gesalzen
§124	saufen	säuft	soff	söffe	gesoffen
§125	saugen	saugt	sog	söge	gesogen
§126	schaffen	schafft	schuf	schüfe	geschaffen
§127	schallen	schallt	scholl	schölle	geschollen
§128	scheinen	scheint	schien	schiene	geschienen
§129	scheren	schert (schiert)	schor	schöre	geschoren
§130	schieben	schiebt	schob	schöbe	geschoben
§131	schlafen	schläft	schlief	schliefe	geschlafen

18a

	INFINITIVE	3D SG PRESENT INDICATIVE	IMPERFECT INDICATIVE	IMPERFECT SUBJUNCTIVE	PAST PARTICIPLE
§132	schlagen	schlägt	schlug	schlüge	geschlagen
§133	schmelzen	schmilzt	schmolz	schmölze	geschmolzen
§134	schrecken	schrickt	schrak	schräke	geschrocken
§135	schreien	schreit	schrie	schriee	geschrie(e)n
§136	schwimmen	schwimmt	schwamm	schwämme (schwömme)	geschwommen
§137	schwören	schwört	schwur (schwor)	schwüre	geschworen
§138	sehen	sieht	sah	sähe	gesehen
§139	sein	ist	war	wäre	gewesen
§140	senden	sendet	sandte	sendete	gesandt
§141	sieden	siedet	sott	sötte	gesotten
§142	singen	singt	sang	sänge	gesungen
§143	sinken	sinkt	sank	sänke	gesunken
§144	sitzen	sitzt	saß	säße	gesessen
§145	sollen	soll	sollte	sollte	gesollt (sollen)
§146	stehen	steht	stand	stände (stünde)	gestanden
§147	stehlen	stiehlt	stahl	stähle (stöhle)	gestohlen
§148	steigen	steigt	stieg	stiege	gestiegen
§149	sterben	stirbt	starb	stürbe	gestorben
§150	stoßen	stößt	stieß	stieße	gestoßen

	INFINITIVE	3D SG PRESENT INDICATIVE	IMPERFECT INDICATIVE	IMPERFECT SUBJUNCTIVE	PAST PARTICIPLE
§151	treffen	trifft	traf	träfe	getroffen
§152	treten	tritt	trat	träte	getreten
§153	triefen	trieft	troff	tröffe	getroffen
§154	tun	tut	tat	täte	getan
§155	wachsen	wächst	wuchs	wüchse	gewachsen
§156	wägen	wiegt	wog	wöge	gewogen
§157	warten	wartet	wartete	wartete	gewartet
§158	waschen	wäscht	wusch	wüsche	gewaschen
§159	werden	wird	wurde	würde	geworden
			(ward)		(worden)
§160	werfen	wirft	warf	würfe	geworfen
§161	wissen	weiß	wußte	wüßte	gewußt
§162	wollen	will	wollte	wollte	gewollt
					(wollen)
§163	ziehen	zieht	zog	zöge	gezogen
§164	klimmen	klimmt	klomm	klömme	geklommen
§165	küren	kürt	kor	köre	gekoren
§166	schinden	schindet	schund	schünde	geschunden

Die Aussprache des Englischen

Die nachstehenden Lautzeichen bezeichnen fast alle Laute der englischen Sprache:

VOKALE

LAUTZEICHEN	UNGEFÄHRER LAUT	BEISPIEL
[æ]	Offener als *ä* in *hätte*	**hat** [hæt]
[ɑ]	Wie *a* in *Vater* Wie *a* in *Mann*	**father** ['fɑðər] **proper** ['prɑpər]
[ɛ]	Wie *e* in *Fett*	**met** [mɛt]
[e]	Offener als *eej* in *Seejungfrau*	**fate** [fet] **they** [ðe]
[ə]	Wie *e* in *finden*	**haven** ['hɛvən] **pardon** ['pɑrdən]
[i]	Wie *ie* in *sie*	**she** [ʃi] **machine** [mə'ʃin]
[ɪ]	Offener als *i* in *bitte*	**fit** [fɪt] **beer** [bɪr]
[o]	Offenes *o* mit anschließendem kurzem (halbvokalischem) *u*	**nose** [noz] **road** [rod] **row** [ro]
[ɔ]	Wie *o* in *oft*	**bought** [bɔt] **law** [lɔ]
[ʌ]	Wie *er* in *jeder* (umgangssprachlich)	**cup** [kʌp] **come** [kʌm] **mother** ['mʌðər]
[ʊ]	Wie *u* in *Fluß*	**pull** [pʊl] **book** [bʊk] **wolf** [wʊlf]
[u]	Wie *u* in *Fluß*	**move** [muv] **tomb** [tum]

DIPHTHONGE

LAUTZEICHEN	UNGEFÄHRER LAUT	BEISPIEL
[aɪ]	Wie *ei* in *nein*	**night** [naɪt] **eye** [aɪ]
[aʊ]	Wie *au* in *Haus*	**found** [faʊnd] **cow** [kaʊ]
[ɔɪ]	Wie *eu* in *heute*	**voice** [vɔɪs] **oil** [ɔɪl]

KONSONANTEN

LAUTZEICHEN	UNGEFÄHRER LAUT	BEISPIEL
[b]	Wie *b* in *bin*	**bed** [bɛd] **robber** ['rɑbər]

21a

LAUTZEICHEN	UNGEFÄHRER LAUT	BEISPIEL
[d]	Wie *d* in *du*	dead [dɛd] add [æd]
[dʒ]	Wie *dsch* in *Dschungel*	gem [dʒɛm] jail [dʒel]
[ð]	*d* als Reibelaut ausgesprochen	this [ðɪs] Father ['faðər]
[f]	Wie *f* in *fett*	face [fes] phone [fon]
[g]	Wie *g* in *gehen*	go [go] get [gɛt]
[h]	Wie *h* in *Haus*	hot [hɑt] alcohol ['ælkə͵hɔl]
[j]	Wie *j* in *ja*	yes [jɛs] unit ['junɪt]
[k]	Wie *k* in *kann*	cat [kæt] chord [kɔrd] kill [kɪl]
[l]	Wie *l* in *lang*, aber mit angehobenem Zungenrücken	late [let] allow [ə'laʊ]
[m]	Wie *m* in *mehr*	more [mor] command [kə'mænd]
[n]	Wie *n* in *Nest*	nest [nɛst] manner ['mænər]
[ŋ]	Wie *ng* in *singen*	king [kɪŋ] conquer ['kaŋkər]
[p]	Wie *p* in *Pech*	pen [pɛn] cap [kæp]
[r]	Im Gegensatz zum deutschen gerollten Zungenspitzen– oder Zäpfchen–r, ist das englische *r* mit retroflexer Zungenstellung und gerundeten Lippen zu artikulieren.	run [rʌn] far [fɑr] art [ɑrt] carry ['kæri]
[s]	Wie *s* in *es*	send [sɛnd] cellar ['sɛlər]
[ʃ]	Wie *sch* in *Schule*	shall [ʃæl] machine [mə'ʃin] nation ['neʃən]
[t]	Wie *t* in *Tee*	ten [tɛn] dropped [drɑpt]
[tʃ]	Wie *tsch* in *deutsch*	child [tʃaɪld] much [mʌtʃ] nature ['netʃər]
[θ]	Ist als stimmloser linguadentaler Lispellaut zu artikulieren	think [θɪŋk] truth [truθ]
[v]	Wie *w* in *was*	vest [vɛst] over ['ovər] of [ɑv]
[w]	Ist als Halbvokal zu artikulieren	work [wʌrk] tweed [twid] queen [kwin]
[z]	Ist stimmhaft zu artikulieren wie *s* in *so*	zeal [zil] busy ['bɪzi] his [hɪz] winds [wɪndz]
[ʒ]	Wie *j* in *Jalousie*	azure ['eʒər] measure ['mɛʒər]

Aussprache der zusammengesetzten Wörter

Im englisch-deutschen Teil dieses Wörterbuches ist die Aussprache aller einfachen englischen Wörter in einer Neufassung der Lautzeichen des Internationalen Phonetischen Alphabets in eckigen Klammern angegeben.

22a

Außer den mit Präfixen, Suffixen und Wortbildungselementen gebildeten Zusammensetzungen gibt es im Englischen drei Arten von zusammengesetzten Wörtern: (1) zusammengeschriebene, z.B. **bookcase** Bücherregal, (**2**) mit Bindestrich geschriebene, z.B. **short-circuit** kurzschließen, und (3) getrennt geschriebene, z.B. **post card** Postkarte. Die Aussprache der englischen zusammengesetzten Wörter ist nicht angegeben, sofern die Aussprache der Bestandteile an der Stelle angegeben ist, wo sie als selbständige Stichwörter erscheinen; angegeben ist jedoch die Betonung durch Haupt– und Nebentonakzent und zwar jeweils am Ende der betonten Silben, z.B. **book′case′, short′-cir′cuit, post′ card′**.

In Hauptwörtern, in denen der Nebenton auf den Bestandteilen **–man** und **–men** liegt, wird der Vokal dieser Bestandteile wie in den Wörtern **man** und **men** ausgesprochen, z.B. **mailman** [′meɪˌmæn] und **mailmen** [′meɪˌmɛn]. In Hauptwörtern, in denen diese Bestandteile unbetont bleiben, wird der Vokal beider Bestandteile als schwa ausgesprochen, z.B. **policeman** [pə′lismən] und **policemen** [pə′lismən]. Es gibt Hauptwörter, in denen diese Bestandteile entweder mit dem Nebenton oder unbetont ausgesprochen werden, z.B. **doorman** [′dorˌmæn] oder [′dormən] und **doormen** [′dorˌmen] oder [′dormən]. In diesem Wörterbuch ist die Lautschrift für diese Wörter nicht angegeben, sofern sie für den ersten Bestandteil dort angeführt ist, wo er als Stichwort erscheint; angegeben sind jedoch Haupt- und Nebenton:

> **mail′man** *s* (**–men′**)
> **police′man** *s* (**–men**)
> **door′man′** & **door′man** *s* (**–men′** & **–men**)

Aussprache des Partizip Perfekt

Bei Wörtern, die auf **–ed** (oder **–d** nach stummem **e**) enden und nach den nachstehenden Regeln ausgesprochen werden, ist die Aussprache in diesem Wörterbuch nicht angegeben, sofern sie für die endungslose Form dort angegeben ist, wo diese als Stichwort erscheint. Die Doppelschreibung des Schlußkonsonanten nach einfachem betontem Vokal hat keinen Einfluß auf die Aussprache der Endung **–ed**.

Die Endung **–ed** (oder **–d** nach stummen **e**) der Vergangenheit, des Partizip Perfekt und gewisser Adjektive hat drei verschiedene Aussprachen je nach dem Klang des Konsonanten am Stammende.

1) Wenn der Stamm auf einen stimmhaften Konsonanten mit Ausnahme von [d] ausgeht, nämlich [b], [g], [l], [m], [n], [ŋ], [r], [v], [z], [ʒ], oder auf einen Vokal, wird **–ed** als [d] ausgesprochen.

KLANG DES STAMMENDES	INFINITIV	VERGANGENHEIT UND PARTIZIP PERFEKT
[b]	**ebb** [ɛb]	**ebbed** [ɛbd]
	rob [rɑb]	**robbed** [rɑbd]
	robe [rob]	**robed** [robd]
[g]	**egg** [ɛg]	**egged** [ɛgd]
	sag [sæg]	**sagged** [sægd]
[l]	**mail** [mel]	**mailed** [meld]
	scale [skel]	**scaled** [skeld]
[m]	**storm** [stɔrm]	**stormed** [stɔrmd]
	bomb [bɑm]	**bombed** [bɑmd]
	name [nem]	**named** [nemd]
[n]	**tan** [tæn]	**tanned** [tænd]
	sign [saɪn]	**signed** [saɪnd]
	mine [maɪn]	**mined** [maɪnd]
[ŋ]	**hang** [hæŋ]	**hanged** [hæŋd]
[r]	**fear** [fɪr]	**feared** [fɪrd]
	care [kɛr]	**cared** [kɛrd]
[v]	**rev** [rɛv]	**revved** [rɛvd]
	save [sev]	**saved** [sevd]
[z]	**buzz** [bʌz]	**buzzed** [bʌzd]
[ð]	**smooth** [smuð]	**smoothed** [smuðd]
	bathe [beð]	**bathed** [beðd]
[ʒ]	**massage** [mə′saʒ]	**massaged** [mə′saʒd]
[dʒ]	**page** [pedʒ]	**paged** [pedʒd]
Klang des Vokals	**key** [ki]	**keyed** [kid]
	sigh [saɪ]	**sighed** [saɪd]
	paw [pɔ]	**pawed** [pɔd]

2) Wenn der Stamm auf einen stimmlosen Konsonanten mit Ausnahme von [t] ausgeht, nämlich: [f], [k], [p], [s], [θ], [ʃ] oder [tʃ], wird –ed als [t] ausgesprochen.

KLANG DES STAMMENDES	INFINITIV	VERGANGENHEIT UND PARTIZIP PERFEKT
[f]	**loaf** [lof] **knife** [naɪf]	**loafed** [loft] **knifed** [naɪft]
[k]	**back** [bæk] **bake** [bek]	**backed** [bækt] **baked** [bekt]
[p]	**cap** [kæp] **wipe** [waɪp]	**capped** [kæpt] **wiped** [waɪpt]
[s]	**hiss** [hɪs] **mix** [mɪks]	**hissed** [hɪst] **mixed** [mɪkst]
[θ]	**lath** [læθ]	**lathed** [læθt]
[ʃ]	**mash** [mæʃ]	**mashed** [mæʃt]
[tʃ]	**match** [mætʃ]	**matched** [mætʃt]

3) Wenn der Stamm auf einen Dentallaut ausgeht, nämlich: [t] oder [d], wird –ed als [ɪd] oder [əd] ausgesprochen.

KLANG DES STAMMENDES	INFINITIV	VERGANGENHEIT UND PARTIZIP PERFEKT
[t]	**wait** [wet] **mate** [met]	**waited** ['wetɪd] **mated** ['metɪd]
[d]	**mend** [mɛnd] **wade** [wed]	**mended** ['mɛndɪd] **waded** ['wedɪd]

Es ist zu beachten, daß die Doppelschreibung des Schlußkonsonanten nach einem einfachen betonten Vokal die Aussprache der Endung –ed nicht beeinflußt: **batted** ['bætɪd], **dropped** [drɑpt], **robbed** [rɑbd].

Diese Regeln gelten auch für zusammengesetzte Adjektive, die auf –ed enden. Für diese Adjektive ist nur die Betonung angegeben, sofern die Aussprache der beiden Bestandteile ohne die Endung –ed dort angegeben ist, wo sie als Stichwörter erscheinen, z.B. **o'pen-mind'ed.**

Es ist jedoch zu beachten, daß bei manchen Adjektiven, deren Stamm auf einen anderen Konsonanten als [d] oder [t] ausgeht, das –ed als [ɪd] ausgesprochen wird; in diesem Fall ist die volle Aussprache in phonetischer Umschrift angegeben, z.B. **blessed** ['blɛsɪd], **crabbed** ['kræbɪd].

PART TWO

English-German

A

A, a [e] *s* erster Buchstabe des englischen Alphabets; (mus) **A** *n;* **A flat** As *n;* **A sharp** Ais *n*

a [e], [ə] *indef art* ein || *prep* pro; **once a year** einmal im Jahr

abandon [ə'bændən] *s*—**with a.** rückhaltlos || *tr* (*forsake*) verlassen; (*give up*) aufgeben; (*a child*) aussetzen; (*a position*) (mil) überlassen; **a. oneself to** sich ergeben (*dat*)

abase [ə'bes] *tr* demütigen

abasement [ə'besmənt] *s* Demütigung *f*

abashed [ə'bæʃt] *adj* fassungslos

abate [ə'bet] *tr* mäßigen || *intr* nachlassen

abbess ['æbɪs] *s* Äbtissin *f*

abbey ['æbi] *s* Abtei *f*

abbot ['æbət] *s* Abt *m*

abbreviate [ə'brivɪ͵et] *tr* abkürzen

abbreviation [ə͵brivɪ'eʃən] *s* Abkürzung *f*

ABC's [͵e͵bi'siz] *spl* Abc *n*

abdicate ['æbdɪ͵ket] *tr* niederlegen; (*a right, claim*) verzichten auf (*acc*) || *intr* abdanken

abdomen ['æbdəmən] *s* Unterleib *m*

abdominal [æb'damɪnəl] *adj* Unterleibs-

abduct [æb'dʌkt] *tr* entführen

abet [ə'bet] *v* (*pret & pp* **abetted;** *ger* **abetting**) *tr* (*a person*) aufhetzen; (*a crime*) Vorschub leisten (*dat*)

abeyance [ə'be·əns] *s*—**in a.** in der Schwebe

ab·hor [æb'hɔr] *v* (*pret & pp* **–horred;** *ger* **-horring**) *tr* verabscheuen

abhorrent [æb'hɔrənt] *adj* verhaßt

abide [ə'baɪd] *v* (*pret & pp* **abode** [ə'bod] *& abided*) *intr*—**a. by** (*an agreement*) sich halten an (*acc*); (*a promise*) halten

ability [ə'bɪlɪti] *s* Fähigkeit *f;* **to the best of one's a.** nach bestem Vermögen

abject [æb'dʒekt] *adj* (*servile*) unterwürfig; (*poverty*) äußerst

ablative ['æblətɪv] *s* Ablativ *m*

ablaze [ə'blez] *adj* in Flammen; (**with**) glänzend (vor *dat*); (*excited*) (**with**) erregt (vor *dat*)

able ['ebəl] *adj* fähig, tüchtig; **be a. to** (*inf*) können (*inf*)

able-bodied ['ebəl'badid] *adj* kräftig; (mil) wehrfähig; **a. seaman** Vollmatrose *m*

ably ['ebli] *adv* mit Geschick

abnormal [æb'nɔrməl] *adj* abnorm

abnormality [͵æbnɔr'mælɪti] *s* Ungewöhnlichkeit *f;* (pathol) Mißbildung *f*

abnor'mal psychol'ogy *s* Psychopathologie *f*

aboard [ə'bord] *adv* an Bord; **all a.!** (*a ship*) alles an Bord! (*a bus, plane, train*) alles einsteigen! || *prep* (*a ship*) an Bord (*genit*); (*a bus, train*) in (*dat*)

abode [ə'bod] *s* Wohnsitz *m*

abolish [ə'balɪʃ] *tr* aufheben, abschaffen

abominable [ə'bamɪnəbəl] *adj* abscheulich

aborigines [͵æbə'rɪdʒɪ͵niz] *spl* Ureinwohner *pl,* Urvolk *n*

abort [ə'bɔrt] *tr* (rok) vorzeitig zur Explosion bringen || *intr* fehlgebären; (fig) fehlschlagen

abortion [ə'bɔrʃən] *s* Abtreibung *f*

abortive [ə'bɔrtɪv] *adj* (fig) mißlungen; **prove a.** fehlschlagen

abound [ə'baʊnd] *intr* reichlich vorhanden sein; **a. in** reich sein an (*dat*)

about [ə'baʊt] *adv* umher, herum; (*approximately*) ungefähr, etwa; **be a. to** (*inf*) im Begriff sein zu (*inf*) || *prep* (*around*) um (*acc*); (*concerning*) über (*acc*); (*approximately at*) gegen (*acc*)

about′ face′ *interj* kehrt!

about′-face′ *s*—**do an a.** (fig) umschwenken; **complete a.** (fig) völliger Umschwung *m*

above [ə'bʌv] *adj* obig || *adv* oben, droben || *prep* (*position*) über (*dat*); (*direction*) über (*acc*); (*physically*) oberhalb (*genit*); **a. all** vor allem

above′board′ *adj & adv* ehrlich, redlich

above′-men′tioned *adj* obenerwähnt, obig

abrasion [ə'breʒən] *s* Abschleifen *n;* (*of the skin*) Abschürfung *f*

abrasive [ə'bresɪv] *adj* abschleifend; (*character*) auf die Nerven gehend || *s* Schleifmittel *n*

abreast [ə'brest] *adj & adv* nebeneinander; **keep a. of** Schritt halten mit

abridge [ə'brɪdʒ] *tr* verkürzen

abridgement [ə'brɪdʒmənt] *s* Verkürzung *f*

abroad [ə'brɔd] *adv* im Ausland; (*direction*) ins Ausland; (*out of doors*) draußen

abrogate ['æbrə͵get] *tr* abschaffen

abrupt [ə'brʌpt] *adj* (*sudden*) jäh; (*curt*) schroff; (*change*) unvermittelt; (*style*) abgerissen

abscess ['æbses] *s* Geschwür *n,* Abszeß *m*

abscond [æb'skand] *intr* (**with**) durchgehen (mit)

absence ['æbsəns] *s* Abwesenheit *f;* (*lack*) Mangel *m;* **in the a. of** in Ermangelung von (or *genit*)

ab'sence without' leave' s unerlaubte Entfernung f von der Truppe
absent ['æbsənt] adj abwesend; **be a. fehlen** || [æb'sent] tr—a. **oneself** (stay away) fernbleiben; (go away) sich entfernen
absentee [,æbsən'ti] s Abwesende mf
ab'sent-mind'ed adj geistesabwesend
absolute ['æbsə,lut] adj absolut
absolutely ['æbsə,lutli] adv absolut, völlig || [,æbsə'lutli] adv (coll) ganz bestimmt, jawohl; **a. not!** keine Rede!
absolve [æb'salv] tr (from sin, an obligation) lossprechen; (sins) vergeben
absorb [æb'sorb] tr aufsaugen; (a shock) dämpfen; (engross) ganz in Anspruch nehmen; **be absorbed in** vertieft sein in (acc)
absorbent [æb'sorbənt] adj aufsaugend
absor'bent cot'ton s Verbandswatte f
absorb'ing adj (fig) packend
abstain [æb'sten] intr (from) sich enthalten (genit); (parl) sich der Stimme enthalten
abstention [æb'stenʃən] s (from) Enthaltung f (von); (parl) Stimmenthaltung f
abstinence ['æbstɪnəns] s Enthaltsamkeit f; (from) Enthaltung f (von)
abstinent ['æbstɪnənt] adj enthaltsam
abstract ['æbstrækt] adj abstrakt || s (summary) Abriß m; **in the a.** an und für sich (betrachtet) || [æb'strækt] tr (the general from the specific) abstrahieren; (summarize) kurz zusammenfassen; (purloin) entwenden
abstruse [æb'strus] adj dunkel
absurd [æb'sʌrd] adj unsinnig
absurdity [æb'sʌrdɪti] s Unsinn m
abundance [ə'bʌndəns] s (of) Fülle f (von), Überfluß m (an dat, von)
abundant [ə'bʌndənt] adj reichlich; **a. in** reich an (dat)
abuse [ə'bjus] s (misuse) Mißbrauch m; (insult) Beschimpfung f; (physical ill-treatment) Mißhandlung f || [ə'bjuz] tr mißbrauchen; (insult) beschimpfen; (ill-treat) mißhandeln; (a girl) schänden
abusive [ə'bjusɪv] adj mißbräuchlich; (treatment) beleidigend; **a. language** Schimpfworte pl; **become a.** ausfällig werden
abut [ə'bʌt] v (pret & pp **abutted;** ger **abutting**) intr—a. **on** grenzen an (acc)
abutment [ə'bʌtmənt] s (of arch) Strebepfeiler m; (of bridge) Widerlager n
abyss [ə'bɪs] s Abgrund m
academic [,ækə'demɪk] adj akademisch
academ'ic gown' s Talar m
academy [ə'kædəmi] s Akademie f
accede [æk'sid] intr beistimmen; **a. to** (s.o.'s wishes) gewähren; (an agreement) beitreten (dat); **a. to the throne** den Thron besteigen
accelerate [æk'selə,ret] tr & intr beschleunigen

accelerator [æk'selə,retər] s Gashebel m
accent ['æksent] s (stress) Betonung f; (peculiar pronunciation) Akzent m || [æk'sent] tr betonen
ac'cent mark' s Tonzeichen n, Akzent m
accentuate [æk'sentʃu,et] tr betonen
accept [æk'sept] tr annehmen; (one's fate, blame) auf sich [acc] nehmen; (put up with) hinnehmen; (recognize) anerkennen
acceptable [æk'septəbəl] adj annehmbar; (pleasing) angenehm; (welcome) willkommen
acceptance [æk'septəns] s Annahme f; (recognition) Anerkennung f
access ['ækses] s Zugang m; (to a person) Zutritt m; (data proc) Zugriff m
accessible [æk'sesɪbəl] adj (to) zugänglich (für)
accession [æk'seʃən] s (to an office) Antritt m; **a. to the throne** Thronbesteigung f
accessory [æk'sesəri] adj (subordinate) untergeordnet; (additional) zusätzlich || s Zubehörteil n; (to a crime) Teilnehmer –in mf; (after the fact) Begünstiger –in mf; (before the fact) Anstifter –in mf
ac'cess road' s Zufahrtsstraße f; (on a turnpike) Zubringerstraße f
accident ['æksɪdənt] s (mishap) Unfall m; (chance) Zufall m; **by a.** zufälligerweise; **have an a.** verunglücken
accidental [,æksɪ'dentəl] adj zufällig; **a. death** Unfalltot m || s (mus) Versetzungszeichen n
acclaim [ə'klem] s Beifall m || tr (e.g., as king) begrüßen, akklamieren
acclamation [,æklə'meʃən] s Beifall m
acclimate [ə'klaɪmət] tr akklimatisieren || intr (to) sich gewöhnen (an acc)
accommodate [ə'kamə,det] tr (oblige) aushelfen (dat); (have room for) Platz haben für
accom'modating adj gefällig
accommodation [ə,kamə'deʃən] s (convenience) Annehmlichkeit f; (adaptation, adjustment) Anpassung f; (willingness to please) Gefälligkeit f; (compromise) Übereinkommen n; **accommodations** (lodgings) Unterkunft f
accompaniment [ə'kʌmpənɪmənt] s Begleitung f
accompanist [ə'kʌmpənɪst] s Begleiter –in mf
accompa·ny [ə'kʌmpəni] v (pret & pp **-nied**) tr begleiten
accomplice [ə'kamplɪs] m Mitschuldige mf
accomplish [ə'kamplɪʃ] tr (a task) vollenden; (a goal) erreichen
accom'plished adj (skilled) ausgezeichnet
accomplishment [ə'kamplɪʃmənt] s (completion) Vollendung f; (achievement) Leistung f
accord [ə'kord] s Übereinstimmung f; **in a. with** übereinstimmend mit; **of**

one's own a. aus eigenem Antriebe || *tr* gewähren || *intr* übereinstimmen

accordingly [ə'kɔrdɪŋli] *adv* demgemäß

accord'ing to' *prep* gemäß (*dat*), laut (*genit* or *dat*), nach (*dat*)

accordion [ə'kɔrdɪ·ən] *s* Akkordeon *n*

accost [ə'kɔst] *tr* ansprechen

account [ə'kaʊnt] *s* Rechnung *f*; (*narrative*) Erzählung *f*; (*report*) Bericht *m*; (*importance*) Bedeutung *f*; (*com*) Konto *n*; **by all accounts** nach allem, was man hört; **call to a.** zur Rechenschaft ziehen; **on a. of** wegen; **on no a.** auf keinen Fall; **render an a. of s.th. to s.o.** j-m Rechenschaft von etw ablegen; **settle accounts with** (coll) abrechnen mit; **take into a.** in Betracht ziehen

accountable [ə'kaʊntəbəl] *adj* (*explicable*) erklärlich; (*responsible*) **(for)** verantwortlich (für)

accountant [ə'kaʊntənt] *s* Rechnungsführer –in *mf*, Buchhalter –in *mf*

account'ing *s* Rechnungswesen *n*

accouterments [ə'kutərmənts] *spl* Ausrüstung *f*

accredit [ə'krɛdɪt] *tr* (*e.g., an ambassador*) beglaubigen; (*a school*) bestätigen; (*a story*) als wahr anerkennen; (*give credit for*) gutschreiben

accrue [ə'kru] *intr* anwachsen; (*said of interest*) auflaufen || *intr* sich anhäufen

accumulation [ə,kjumjə'leʃən] *s* Anhäufung *f*

accuracy ['ækjərəsi] *s* Genauigkeit *f*

accurate ['ækjərɪt] *adj* genau

accursed [ə'kʌrsɪd], [ə'kʌrst] *adj* verwünscht

accusation [,ækjə'zeʃən] *s* Anschuldigung *f*; (jur) Anklage *f*

accusative [ə'kjuzətɪv] *s* Akkusativ *m*

accuse [ə'kjuz] *tr* **(of)** beschuldigen (*genit*); (jur) **(of)** anklagen (wegen)

accustom [ə'kʌstəm] *tr* **(to)** gewöhnen (an *acc*); **become accustomed to** sich gewöhnen an (*acc*)

ace [es] *s* (aer, cards) As *n*

acetate ['æsɪ,tet] *s* Azetat *n*; (tex) Azetatseide *f*

ace'tic ac'id [ə'sitɪk] *s* Essigsäure *f*

acetone ['æsɪ,ton] *s* Azeton *n*

acet'ylene torch' [ə'sɛtɪ,lin] *s* Schweißbrenner *m*

ache [ek] *s* Schmerz *m* || *intr* schmerzen; **a. for** (coll) sich sehnen nach

achieve [ə'tʃiv] *tr* erlangen; (*success*) erzielen; (*a goal*) erreichen

achievement [ə'tʃivmənt] *s* (*something accomplished*) Leistung *f*; (*great deed*) Großtat *f*; (*heroic deed*) Heldentat *f*; (*of one's object*) Erreichung *f*

achieve'ment test' *s* Leistungsprüfung *f*

Achil'les' ten'don [ə'kɪlis] *s* Achillessehne *f*

acid ['æsɪd] *adj* sauer || *s* Säure *f*

acidity [ə'sɪdɪti] *s* Säure *f*, Schärfe *f*; (*of the stomach*) Magensäure *f*

ac'id test' *s* (fig) Feuerprobe *f*

acidy ['æsɪdi] *adj* säuerlich, säurig

acknowledge [æk'nɑlɪdʒ] *tr* anerken-

nen; (*admit*) zugeben; (*receipt*) bestätigen

acknowledgment [æk'nɑlɪdʒmənt] *s* Anerkennung *f*; (*e.g., of a letter*) Bestätigung *f*

acme ['ækmi] *s* Höhepunkt *m*

acne ['ækni] *s* (pathol) Akne *f*

acolyte ['ækə,laɪt] *s* Ministrant *m*

acorn ['ekɔrn] *s* Eichel *f*

acoustic(al) [ə'kustɪk(əl)] *adj* akustisch, Gehör–, Hör–

acous'tical tile' *s* Dämmplatte *f*

acoustics [ə'kustɪks] *s & spl* Akustik *f*

acquaint [ə'kwent] *tr*—**a. s.o. with s.th.** j-n mit etw bekanntmachen, j-m etw mitteilen; **be acquainted with** kennen; **get acquainted with** kennenlernen

acquaintance [ə'kwentəns] *s* Bekanntschaft *f*; (*person*) Bekannte *mf*

acquiesce [,ækwɪ'ɛs] *intr* **(in)** einwilligen (in *acc*)

acquiescence [,ækwɪ'ɛsəns] *s* **(in)** Einwilligung *f* (in *acc*)

acquire [ə'kwaɪr] *tr* erwerben, sich [*dat*] anschaffen; **a. a taste for** Geschmack gewinnen an (*dat*)

acquisition [,ækwɪ'zɪʃən] *s* Anschaffung *f*

acquisitive [ə'kwɪzɪtɪv] *adj* gewinnsüchtig

acquit [ə'kwɪt] *v* (*pret & pp* **acquitted**; *ger* **acquitting**) *tr* freisprechen

acquittal [ə'kwɪtəl] *s* Freispruch *m*

acre ['ekər] *s* Acre *m*

acreage ['ekərɪdʒ] *s* Fläche *f*

acrid ['ækrɪd] *adj* beißend, scharf

acrobat ['ækrə,bæt] *s* Akrobat –in *mf*

acrobatic [,ækrə'bætɪk] *adj* akrobatisch || **acrobatics** *spl* Akrobatik *f*; (aer) Kunstflug *m*

acronym ['ækrənɪm] *s* Akronym *n*

across [ə'krɔs] *adv* herüber, hinüber; **a. from** gegenüber (*dat*); **ten feet a.** zehn Fuß im Durchmesser || *prep* (quer) über (*acc*); (*on the other side of*) jenseits (*genit*); **come a.** (*a person*) treffen; (*a thing*) stoßen auf (*acc*); **come a. with it!** (*say it!*) heraus damit!; (*give it!*) her damit!

across'-the-board' *adj* allgemein

acrostic [ə'krɔstɪk] *s* Akrostichon *n*

act [ækt] *s* Tat *f*, Handlung *f*; (coll) Theater *n*; (jur) Gesetz *n*; (telv) Nummer *f*; (theat) Akt *m*, Aufzug *m*; **catch in the act** auf frischer Tat ertappen || *tr* spielen; || *intr* (*take action*) handeln; (*function*) wirken; (*behave*) **(like)** sich benehmen (wie); (theat & fig) Theater spielen; **act as** dienen als; **act as if** so tun, als ob; **act on** (*follow*) befolgen; (*affect*) (ein)wirken auf (*acc*)

act'ing *adj* stellvertretend; (theat) Bühnen– || *s* (*as an art*) Schauspielkunst *f*

action ['ækʃən] *s* Tätigkeit *f*, Tat *f*; (*effect*) Wirkung *f*; (jur) Klage *f*; (mil) Gefecht *n*; (tech) Wirkungsweise *f*; **go into a.** eingreifen; **put out of a.** (mil) außer Gefecht setzen; (tech) außer Betrieb setzen; **see a.** (mil) an der Front kämpfen

activate ['æktɪ͵vet] *tr* aktivieren; (mil) aufstellen
active ['æktɪv] *adj* tätig; (*member*) ordentlich; (gram, mil) aktiv
ac'tive voice' *s* Tätigkeitsform *f*
activist ['æktɪvɪst] *s* Aktivist –in *mf*
activity [æk'tɪvɪti] *s* Tätigkeit *f*
act' of God' *s* höhere Gewalt *f*
act' of war' *s* Angriffshandlung *f*
actor ['æktər] *s* Schauspieler *m*
actress ['æktrɪs] *s* Schauspielerin *f*
actual ['æktʃʊ·əl] *adj* wirklich
actually ['æktʃʊ·əli] *adv* (*really*) wirklich; (*as a matter of fact*) eigentlich
actuary ['æktʃʊ͵eri] *s* Aktuar –in *mf*
actuate ['æktʃʊ͵et] *tr* in Bewegung setzen; (*incite*) antreiben
acumen [ə'kjumən] *s* Scharfsinn *m*
acupuncture ['ækjə͵pʌŋktʃər] *s* Akupunktur *f*
acute [ə'kjut] *adj* (*stage, appendicitis pain*) akut; (*pain*) scharf; (*need*) vordringlich; (*vision*) scharf; (*hearing*) fein; (*problem*) brennend; (*shortage*) bedenklich; (*angle*) spitz
A.D. *abbr* n. Chr. (*nach Christus*)
ad [æd] *s* (coll) Anzeige *f;* **put an ad in the papers** inserieren
adage ['ædɪdʒ] *s* Sprichwort *n*
adamant ['ædəmənt] *adj* unnachgiebig
Ad'am's ap'ple ['ædəmz] *s* Adamsapfel *m*
adapt [ə'dæpt] *tr* (to) anpassen (*dat* or an *acc*); **a. to the stage** für die Bühne bearbeiten; **a. to the screen** verfilmen ‖ *intr* sich anpassen
adaptation [͵ædæp'teʃən] *s* (*adjustment*) (to) Anpassung *f* (an *acc*); (*reworking, rewriting*) (for) Bearbeitung *f* (für)
adapter [ə'dæptər] *s* Zwischenstück *n;* (elec) Zwischenstecker *m*
add [æd] *tr* hinzufügen; (math) addieren; **add** (*e.g., 10%*) **to the price** auf den Preis aufschlagen; **add up** zusammenrechnen ‖ *intr* (math) addieren; **add to** (*in number*) vermehren; (*in size*) vergrößern; **add up** (coll) stimmen; **add up to** betragen
adder ['ædər] *s* Natter *f*, Otter *f*
addict ['ædɪkt] *s* Süchtige *mf* ‖ [ə'dɪkt] *tr*—**a. oneself to** sich ergeben (*dat*)
addict'ed *adj* ergeben; **a. to drugs** rauschgiftsüchtig
addiction [ə'dɪkʃən] *s* (to) Sucht *f* (nach)
add'ing machine' *s* Addiermaschine *f*
addition [ə'dɪʃən] *s* Hinzufügung *f*, Zusatz *m;* (*to a family, possessions*) Zuwachs *m;* (*to a building*) Anbau *m;* (math) Addition *f;* **in a.** außerdem; **in a. to** außer
additional [æ'dɪʃənəl] *adj* zusätzlich
additive ['ædɪtɪv] *s* Zusatz *m*
address [ə'dres], ['ædres] *s* Adresse *f*, Anschrift *f* ‖ [ə'dres] *s* Rede *f;* **deliver an a.** e–e Rede halten ‖ *tr* (*a letter*) (to) adressieren (an *acc*); (*words, a question*) (to) richten (an *acc*); (*an audience*) e–e Ansprache halten an (*acc*)
adduce [ə'd(j)us] *tr* anführen

adenoids ['ædə͵nɔɪdz] *spl* Polypen *pl*
adept [ə'dept] *adj* (in) geschickt (in *dat*)
adequate ['ædɪkwɪt] *adj* angemessen; (to) ausreichend (für)
adhere [æd'hɪr] *intr* (to) haften (an *dat*); (fig) (to) festhalten (an *dat*)
adherence [æd'hɪrəns] *s* (to) Festhalten *n* (an *dat*); (fig) (to) Festhalten *n* (an *dat*), Beharren *n* (bei)
adherent [æd'hɪrənt] *s* Anhänger –in *mf*
adhesion [æd'hiʒən] *s* (*sticking*) Ankleben *n;* (*loyalty*) Anhänglichkeit *f;* (pathol, phys) Adhäsion *f*
adhesive [æd'hisɪv] *adj* anklebend ‖ *s* Klebemittel *n*, Klebstoff *m*
adhe'sive tape' *s* Heftpflaster *m*
adieu [ə'd(j)u] *s* (adieus & adieux) Lebewohl *n* ‖ *interj* lebe wohl!
adjacent [ə'dʒesənt] *adj* (to) angrenzend (an *acc*); (*angles*) Neben–
adjective ['ædʒɪktɪv] *s* Eigenschaftswort *n*, Adjektiv *n*
adjoin [ə'dʒɔɪn] *tr* angrenzen an (*acc*) ‖ *intr* angrenzen, naheliegen
adjoin'ing *adj* angrenzend; **a. rooms** Nebenzimmer *pl*
adjourn [ə'dʒʌrn] *tr* vertagen ‖ *intr* sich vertagen
adjournment [ə'dʒʌrnmənt] *s* Vertagung *f*
adjudge [ə'dʒʌdʒ] *tr* (*a prize*) zusprechen; **a. s.o. guilty** j–n für schuldig erklären
adjudicate [ə'dʒudɪ͵ket] *tr* gerichtlich entscheiden
adjunct ['ædʒʌŋkt] *s* (to) Zusatz *m* (zu)
adjust [ə'dʒʌst] *tr* (*to the right position*) einstellen; (*to an alternate position*) verstellen; (*fit*) (to) anpassen (*dat* or an *acc*); (*differences*) ausgleichen; (*an account*) bereinigen; (ins) berechnen ‖ *intr* (to) sich anpassen (*dat* or an *acc*)
adjustable [ə'dʒʌstəbəl] *adj* verstellbar
adjuster [ə'dʒʌstər] *s* (ins) Schadenssachverständiger –in *mf*
adjustment [ə'dʒʌstmənt] *s* (to) Anpassung *f* (*dat* or an *acc*); (*of an account*) Bereinigung *f;* (ins) Berechnung *f;* (mach) Einstellung *f*
adjutant ['ædʒətənt] *s* Adjutant *m*
ad-lib [͵æd'lɪb] *v* (*pret & pp*) **–libbed;** *ger* **–libbing**) *tr & intr* improvisieren
ad·man ['ædmən] *s* (**–men**) Werbefachmann *m;* (*writer*) Werbetexter *m*
administer [æd'mɪnɪstər] *tr* verwalten; (*help*) leisten; (*medicine*) eingeben; (*an oath*) abnehmen; (*punishment*) verhängen; (*a sacrament*) spenden; **a. justice** Recht sprechen ‖ *intr*— **a. to** dienen (*dat*)
administration [æd͵mɪnɪs'treʃən] *s* (*of an institution*) Verwaltung *f;* (*of an official*) Amtsführung *f;* (*government*) Regierung *f;* (*period of government*) Regierungszeit *f;* (*of a president*) Amtszeit *f;* (*of tests*) Durchführung *f;* (*of an oath*) Abnahme *f;* (*of a sacrament*) Spendung *f;* **a. of justice** Rechtspflege *f*

administrator [æd'mɪnɪs ˌtretər] s Verwalter –in *mf*
admiral ['ædmɪrəl] s Admiral *m*
admiration [ˌædmɪ're ʃən] s Bewunderung *f*
admire [æd'maɪr] *tr* (**for**) bewundern (wegen)
admirer [æd'maɪrər] s Bewunderer –in *mf;* (*of a woman*) Verehrer *m*
admissible [æd'mɪsɪbəl] *adj* (& jur) zulässig
admission [æd'mɪ ʃən] s (*entry*) Eintritt *m;* (*permission to enter*) Eintrittserlaubnis *f;* (*entry fee*) Eintrittsgebühr *f;* (*of facts*) Anerkennung *f;* (*of guilt*) Eingeständis *n;* (*enrollment*) (**to**, **into**) Aufnahme *f* (in *acc*); (**to**) (*a profession*) Zulassung *f* (zu)
ad·mit [æd'mɪt] *v* (*pret & pp* **–mitted**; *ger* **–mitting**) *tr* (hin)einlassen; (**to**) (*a hospital, a society*) aufnehmen (in *acc*); (**to**) (*a profession*) zulassen (zu); (*accept*) anerkennen; (*concede*) zugeben; (*a crime, guilt*) eingestehen || *intr*—**a. of** zulassen
admittance [æd'mɪtəns] s Eintritt *m;* **no a.** Eintritt verboten
admittedly [æd'mɪtɪdli] *adv* anerkanntermaßen
admixture [æd'mɪkst ʃər] s Beimischung *f*
admonish [æd'manɪ ʃ] *tr* ermahnen
admonition [ˌædmə'nɪ ʃən] s Ermahnung *f*
ado [ə'du] s Getue *n;* **much ado about nothing** viel Lärm um nichts; **without further ado** ohne weiteres
adobe [ə'dobi] s Lehmstein *m*
adolescence [ˌædə'lɛsəns] s Jugendalter *n*
adolescent [ˌædə'lɛsənt] *adj* jugendlich || *s* Jugendliche *mf*
adopt [ə'dapt] *tr* (*a child*) adoptieren; (*an idea*) annehmen
adopt'ed child' s Adoptivkind *n*
adoption [ə'dap ʃən] s (*of a child*) Adoption *f;* (*of an idea*) Annahme *f*
adorable [ə'dorəbəl] *adj* anbetungswürdig; (coll) entzückend
adore [ə'dor] *tr* anbeten; (coll) entzückend finden
adorn [ə'dorn] *tr* schmücken
adornment [ə'dornmənt] s Schmuck *m*
adrenaline [ə'drenəlɪn] s Adrenalin *n*
adrift [ə'drɪft] *adj*—**be a.** treiben; (fig) weder aus noch ein wissen
adroit [ə'drɔɪt] *adj* geschickt, gewandt
adulation [ˌædjə'le ʃən] s Schmeichelei *f*
adult [ə'dʌlt], ['ædʌlt] *adj* erwachsen || *s* Erwachsene *mf*
adult' educa'tion s Erwachsenenbildung *f*
adulterate [ə'dʌltə ˌret] *tr* verfälschen; (*e.g., wine*) panschen
adulterer [ə'dʌltərər] s Ehebrecher *m*
adulteress [ə'dʌltərɪs] s Ehebrecherin *f*
adulterous [ə'dʌltərəs] *adj* ehebrecherisch
adultery [ə'dʌltəri] s Ehebruch *m*
advance [æd'væns] s Fortschritt *m;* (*money*) Vorschuß *m;* **in a.** im vor-

aus; **make advances to** (*e.g., a girl*) Annäherungsversuche machen bei || *tr* vorrücken; (*a clock*) vorstellen; (*money*) vorschießen; (*a date*) aufschieben; (*an opinion*) vorbringen; (*s.o.'s interests*) fördern; (*in rank*) befördern || *intr* vorrücken
advancement [æd'vænsmənt] s Fortschritt *m;* (*promotion*) Beförderung *f;* (*of a cause*) Förderung *f*
advance' pay'ment s Voraus(be)zahlung *f*
advantage [æd'væntɪdʒ] s Vorteil *m;* **be of a.** nützlich sein; **take a. of** ausnutzen; **to a.** vorteilhaft
advantageous [ˌædvən'tedʒəs] *adj* vorteilhaft
advent ['ædvɛnt] s Ankunft *f;* **Advent** Advent *m*, Adventszeit *f*
adventure [æd'vɛnt ʃər] s Abenteuer *n*
adventurer [æd'vɛnt ʃərər] s Abenteurer *m*
adventuress [æd'vɛnt ʃərɪs] s Abenteurerin *f*
adventurous [æd'vɛnt ʃərəs] *adj* (*person*) abenteuerlustig; (*undertaking*) abenteuerlich
adverb ['ædvʌrb] s Umstandswort *n*
adverbial [æd'vʌrbɪ·əl] *adj* adverbial
adversary ['ædvər ˌsɛri] s Gegner –in *mf*
adverse [æd'vʌrs], ['ædvʌrs] *adj* ungünstig, nachteilig
adversity [æd'vɛrsiti] s Unglück *n,* Not *f*
advertise ['ædvər ˌtaɪz] *tr* Reklame machen für || *intr* Reklame machen; **a. for** durch Inserat suchen
advertisement [ˌædvər'taɪzmənt], [æd'vertɪsmənt] s Anzeige *f,* Reklame *f*
ad'vertising a'gency s Reklamebüro *n*
ad'vertising campaign' s Werbefeldzug *m*
ad'vertising man' s (*solicitor*) Anzeigenvermittler *m;* (*writer*) Werbetexter *m*
advice [æd'vaɪs] s Rat *m,* Ratschlag *m;* **a piece of a.** ein Rat *m;* **get a. from** sich [*dat*] Rat holen bei; **give a. to** raten (*dat*)
advisable [æd'vaɪzəbəl] *adj* ratsam
advise [æd'vaɪz] *tr* raten (*dat*); (**of**) benachrichtigen (von); (**on**) beraten (über *acc*); **a. s.o. against s.th.** j–m von etw abraten
advisement [æd'vaɪzmənt] s—**take under a.** in Betracht ziehen
adviser [æd'vaɪzər] s Berater –in *mf*
advisory [æd'vaɪzəri] *adj* Beratungs–
advi'sory board' s Beirat *m*
advocate ['ædvə ˌket] s Fürsprecher –in *mf;* (jur) Advokat –in *mf* || *tr* befürworten
aeon ['i·ən], ['i·an] s Äon *m*
aerial ['ɛrɪ·əl] *adj* Luft– || s Antenne *f*
aerodynamic [ˌɛrodaɪ'næmɪk] *adj* aerodynamisch || **aerodynamics** s Aerodynamik *f*
aeronautic(al) [ˌɛrə'nɔtɪk(əl)] *adj* aeronautisch || **aeronautics** s Aeronautik *f,* Luftfahrt *f*
aerosol ['ɛrə ˌsol] s Sprühdose *f*

aerospace ['ɛrəspes] *adj* Raum—
aesthetic [ɛs'θɛtɪk] *adj* ästhetisch ||
aesthetics *s* Ästhetik *f*
afar [ə'fɑr] *adv*—**a. off** weit weg; **from
a.** von weit her
affable ['æfəbəl] *adj* leutselig
affair [ə'fɛr] *s* Angelegenheit *f;* (*event,
performance*) Veranstaltung *f;* (*romantic involvement*) Verhältnis *n*
affect [ə'fɛkt] *tr* (*influence*) berühren;
(*injuriously*) angreifen; (*pretend*)
vortäuschen
affectation [,æfɛk'teʃən] *s* Geziertheit
f
affect'ed *adj* affektiert
affection [ə'fɛkʃən] *s* (**for**) Zuneigung
f (zu); (pathol) Erkrankung *f*
affectionate [ə'fɛkʃənɪt] *adj* liebevoll
affidavit [,æfɪ'devɪt] *s* (schriftliche)
eidesstattliche Erklärung *f*
affiliate [ə'fɪlɪ,et] *s* Zweiggesellschaft
f || *tr* angliedern || *intr* sich anglie-
dern
affinity [ə'fɪnɪti] *s* Verwandschaft *f*
affirm [ə'fʌrm] *tr* & *intr* behaupten
affirmation [,æfər'meʃən] *s* Behauptung *f*
affirmative [ə'fʌrmətɪv] *adj* bejahend
|| *s* Bejahung *f;* **in the a.** bejahend,
positiv
affix [ə'fɪks] *tr* (*a seal*) aufdrücken;
(**to**) befestigen (an *dat*), anheften (an
acc)
afflict [ə'flɪkt] *tr* plagen; **afflicted with**
erkrankt an (*dat*)
affliction [ə'flɪkʃən] *s* Elend *n,* Leiden
n; (*grief*) Betrübnis *f*
affluence ['æflu·əns] *s* Wohlstand *m*
affluent ['æflu·ənt] *adj* wohlhabend
af'fluent socie'ty *s* Wohlstandsgesell-
schaft *f*
afford [ə'ford] *tr* (*confer*) gewähren;
(*time*) erübrigen; (*be able to meet
the expense of*) sich [*dat*] leisten
affront [ə'frʌnt] *s* Beleidigung *f* || *tr*
beleidigen
afire [ə'faɪr] *adj* & *adv* in Flammen
aflame [ə'flem] *adj* & *adv* in Flammen
afloat [ə'flot] *adj* flott, schwimmend;
(*awash*) überschwemmt; (*at sea*) auf
dem Meer; (*in circulation*) im Umlauf; **keep a.** (& fig) über Wasser
halten; **stay a.** (& fig) sich über
Wasser halten
afoot [ə'fut] *adj* & *adv* (*on foot*) zu
Fuß; (*in progress*) im Gange
aforesaid [ə'for,sed] *adj* vorerwähnt
afoul [ə'faul] *adj* (*entangled*) ver-
wickelt || *adv*—**run a. of the law** mit
dem Gesetz in Konflikt geraten
afraid [ə'fred] *adj* ängstlich; **be a. (of)**
(*inf*) sich scheuen zu (*inf*)
afresh [ə'frɛʃ] *adv* aufs neue
Africa ['æfrɪkə] *s* Afrika *n*
African ['æfrɪkən] *adj* afrikanisch ||
s Afrikaner –in *mf*
aft [æft] *adv* (nach) achtern
after ['æftər] *adj* später; (naut) achter
|| *adv* nachher, darauf || *prep* nach
(*dat*); **a. all** immerhin; **a. that** da-
rauf; **be a. s.o.** hinter j–m her sein ||
conj nachdem
af'ter-din'ner speech' *s* Tischrede *f*

af'tereffect' *s* Nachwirkung *f;* **have an
a.** nachwirken
af'terlife' *s* (*later life*) zukünftiges
Leben *n;* (*life after death*) Leben *n*
nach dem Tode
aftermath ['æftər,mæθ] *s* Nach-
wirkungen *pl;* (agr) Grummet *n*
af'ternoon' *s* Nachmittag *m;* **in the a.**
am Nachmittag, nachmittags; **this a.**
heute nachmittag
af'ter-shave' lo'tion *s* Rasierwasser *n*
af'tertaste' *s* Nachgeschmack *m*
af'terthought' *s* nachträglicher Einfall
m
afterward(s) ['æftərwərd(z)] *adv* später
af'terworld' *s* Jenseits *n*
again [ə'gen] *adv* wieder, noch einmal;
half as much a. anderthalbmal so
viel; **what's his name a.?** wie heißt
er doch schnell?
against [ə'genst] *prep* gegen (*acc*); **a.
it** dagegen; **a. the rules** regelwidrig;
be up a. it (coll) in der Klemme sein
age [edʒ] *s* Alter *n,* Lebensalter *n;*
(*period of history*) Zeitalter *n;* **at the
age of** mit, im Alter von; **come of
age** mündig werden; **for ages** e–e
Ewigkeit; **of age** volljährig; **of the
same age** gleichaltrig; **twenty years
of age** zwanzig Jahre alt || *tr* alt
machen; (*wine*) ablagern || *intr*
altern; (*said of wine*) lagern
aged [edʒd] *adj* alt, e.g., **a. three** drei
Jahre alt || ['edʒɪd] *adj* bejahrt
age' lim'it *s* Altersgrenze *f*
agency ['edʒənsi] *s* (*instrumentality*)
Vermittlung *f;* (*activity*) Tätigkeit
f; (adm) Behörde *f;* (com) Agentur *f*
agenda [ə'dʒɛndə] *s* Tagesordnung *f*
agent ['edʒənt] *s* Handelnde *mf;* (biol,
chem) Agens *n;* (com) Agent –in *mf*
agglomeration [ə,glɑmə'reʃən] *s* Anhäufung *f*
aggravate ['ægrə,vet] *tr* erschweren,
verschärfen; (coll) ärgern
aggravation [,ægrə'veʃən] *s* Erschwe-
rung *f,* Verschärfung *f;* (coll) Ärger
m
aggregate ['ægrɪ,get] *adj* gesamt || *s*
Aggregat *n;* **in the a.** im ganzen || *tr*
anhäufen
aggression [ə'grɛʃən] *s* Agression *f*
aggressive [ə'grɛsɪv] *adj* aggressiv
aggressor [ə'grɛsər] *s* Aggressor *m*
aggrieved [ə'grivd] *adj* (*saddened*) betrübt; (jur) geschädigt
aghast [ə'gæst] *adj* entsetzt
agile ['ædʒɪl] *adj* flink; (*mind*) rege
agility [ə'dʒɪlɪti] *s* Flinkheit *f;* (*of the
mind*) Regsamkeit *f*
agitate ['ædʒɪ,tet] *tr* hin und her be-
wegen; (fig) beunruhigen || *intr* agi-
tieren
agitator ['ædʒɪ,tetər] *s* Unruhestifter
–in *mf;* (*in a washer*) Rührapparat *m*
aglow [ə'glo] *adj* & *adv* (er)glühend
agnostic [æg'nɑstɪk] *adj* agnostisch ||
s Agnostiker –in *mf*
ago [ə'go] *adv* vor (*dat*), e.g., **a year
ago** vor e–m Jahr; **long ago** vor langer Zeit
agog [ə'gɑg] *adv* gespannt, erpicht
agonize ['ægə,naɪz] *intr* sich quälen

ag'onizing *adj* qualvoll

agony ['ægəni] *s* Qual *f;* (*death struggle*) Todeskampf *m*

agrarian [ə'grɛrɪ-ən] *adj* landwirtschaftlich, agrarisch

agree [ə'gri] *intr* übereinstimmen; **a. on** (or **upon**) sich einigen über (*acc*); **a. to** zustimmen (*dat*); **a. to** (*inf*) übereinkommen zu (*inf*); **a. with** (& gram) übereinstimmen mit; (*affect one's health*) bekommen (*dat*)

agreeable [ə'gri-əbəl] *adj* angenehm

agreed' *interj* abgemacht!, einverstanden!

agreement [ə'grimənt] *s* Abkommen *n,* Vereinbarung *f;* (*contract*) Vertrag *m;* (& gram) Übereinstimmung *f*

agriculture ['ægrɪ‚kʌltʃər] *s* Landwirtschaft *f,* Ackerbau *m*

aground [ə'graund] *adv* gestrandet; **run a.** stranden, auf Grund laufen

ahead [ə'hɛd] *adj* & *adv* (*in the front*) vorn; (*to the front*) nach vorn; (*in advance*) voraus; (*forward*) vorwärts; **a. of** vor (*dat*); **get a.** vorwärtskommen; **go a.** vorangehen; **go a.!** los!; **go a. with** fortfahren mit; **look a.** an die Zukunft denken

ahoy [ə'hɔɪ] *interj* ahoi!

aid [ed] *s* Hilfe *f,* Beihilfe *f* ‖ *tr* helfen (*dat*); **aid and abet** Vorschub leisten (*dat*)

aide [ed] *s* Gehilfe *m*

aide-de-camp ['eddə'kæmp] *s* (**aides-de-camp**) Adjutant *m*

ail [el] *tr* schmerzen; **what ails you?** was fehlt Ihnen? ‖ *intr* (*have pain*) Schmerzen haben; (*be ill*) erkrankt sein

ail'ing *adj* leidend, kränklich

ailment ['elmənt] *s* Leiden *n*

aim [em] *s* Ziel *n;* (fig) Ziel *n,* Zweck *m;* **is your aim good?** zielen Sie gut?; **take aim** zielen ‖ *tr* (*a gun, words*) (**at**) richten auf (*acc*); **aim to** (*inf*) beabsichtigen zu (*inf*) ‖ *intr* zielen; **aim at** (& fig) zielen auf (*acc*); **aim for** streben nach

aimless ['emlɪs] *adj* ziellos, planlos

air [ɛr] *s* Luft *f;* (mus) Melodie *f;* **be on the air** (*an announcer*) senden; (*a program*) gesendet werden; **be up in the air** (fig) in der Luft hängen; **by air** per Flugzeug; **go off the air** die Sendung beenden; **go on the air** die Sendung beginnen; **in the open air** im Freien; **put on airs** groß tun; **walk on air** sich wie im Himmel fühlen ‖ *tr* lüften

air'base' *s* Flugstützpunkt *m*

airborne ['ɛr‚bɔrn] *adj* aufgestiegen; **a. troops** Luftlandetruppen *pl*

air'brake' *s* Druckluftbremse *f*

air'-condi'tion *tr* klimatisieren

air' condi'tioner *s* Klimaanlage *f*

air' cov'er *s* Luftsicherung *f*

air'craft' *s* (*pl* **aircraft**) Flugzeug *n*

air'craft car'rier *s* Flugzeugträger *m*

air' cur'rent *s* Luftströmung *f*

air' fare' *s* Flugpreis *m*

air'field' *s* Flugplatz *m*

air'force' *s* Luftstreitkräfte *pl*

air'ing *s* Lüftung *f*

air' lane' *s* Flugschneise *f*

air'lift' *s* Luftbrücke *f* ‖ *tr* auf dem Luftwege transportieren

air'line(s)' *s* Luftverkehrsgesellschaft *f*

air'line pi'lot *s* Flugkapitän *m*

air'lin'er *s* Verkehrsflugzeug *n*

air'mail' *s* Luftpost *f*

air'-mail let'ter *s* Luftpostbrief *m*

air'-mail stamp' *s* Luftpostbriefmarke *f*

air'plane' *s* Flugzeug *n*

air' pock'et *s* Luftloch *n*

air' pollu'tion *s* Luftverunreinigung *f*

air'port' *s* Flughafen *m,* Flugplatz *m*

air' raid' *s* Fliegerangriff *m*

air'-raid drill' *s* Luftschutzübung *f*

air'-raid shel'ter *s* Luftschutzraum *m*

air'-raid war'den *s* Luftschutzwart *m*

air'-raid warn'ing *s* Fliegeralarm *m*

air' recon'naissance *s* Luftaufklärung *f*

air'show' *s* Flugvorführung *f*

air'sick' *adj* luftkrank

air'sleeve', air'sock' *s* Windsack *m*

air'strip' *s* Start– und Landestreifen *m*

air' suprem'acy *s* Luftherrschaft *f*

air'tight' *adj* luftdicht

air' time' *s* (rad, telv) Sendezeit *f*

air'-traffic control' *s* Flugsicherung *f*

air'waves' *spl* Rundfunk *m;* **on the a.** im Rundfunk

air'way' *s* Luft(verkehrs)linie *f*

air'wor'thy *adj* lufttüchtig

airy ['ɛri] *adj* (*room*) luftig; (*lively*) lebhaft; (*flippant*) leichtsinnig

aisle [aɪl] *s* Gang *m;* (archit) Seitenschiff *n*

ajar [ə'dʒɑr] *adj* angelehnt

akimbo [ə'kɪmbo] *adj*—**with arms a.** die Arme in die Hüften gestemmt

akin [ə'kɪn] *adj* verwandt; **a. to** ähnlich (*dat*)

alabaster ['ælə‚bæstər] *s* Alabaster *m*

alacrity [ə'lækrɪti] *s* Bereitwilligkeit *f*

alarm [ə'lɑrm] *s* Alarm *m;* (*sudden fear*) Bestürzung *f;* (*apprehension*) Unruhe *f* ‖ *tr* alarmieren

alarm' clock' *s* Wecker *m*

alas [ə'læs] *interj* o weh!

Albania [æl'benɪ-ə] *s* Albanien *n*

Albanian [æl'benɪ-ən] *adj* albanisch ‖ *s* Alban(i)er –in *mf*

albatross ['ælbə‚trɔs] *s* Albatros *m*

album ['ælbəm] *s* Album *n*

albumen [æl'bjumən] *s* Eiweiß *n*

alchemy ['ælkɪmi] *s* Alchimie *f*

alcohol ['ælkə‚hɔl] *s* Alkohol *m*

alcoholic [‚ælkə'hɔlɪk] *adj* alkoholisch ‖ *s* Alkoholiker –in *mf*

alcove ['ælkov] *s* Alkoven *m*

alder ['ɔldər] *s* (bot) Erle *f*

al'der-man *s* (*–men*) Stadtrat *m*

ale [el] *s* Ale *n,* englisches Bier *n*

alert [ə'lʌrt] *adj* wachsam ‖ *s* (*state of readiness*) Alarmbereitschaft *f;* **on the a.** alarmbereit; (fig) auf der Hut ‖ *tr* alarmieren

alfalfa [æl'fælfə] *s* Luzerne *f*

algae ['ældʒi] *spl* Algen *pl*

algebra ['ældʒɪbrə] *s* Algebra *f*

Algeria [æl'dʒɪrɪ-ə] *s* Algerien *n*

Algerian [æl'dʒɪrɪ-ən] *adj* algerisch ‖ *s* Algerier –in *mf*

Algiers [æl'dʒɪrz] *s* Algier *n*

alias ['elɪ·əs] *adv* alias, sonst...genannt ‖ *s* Deckname *m*
ali·bi ['ælɪ,baɪ] *s* (**–bis**) Alibi *n;* (*excuse*) Ausrede *f*
alien ['eljən], ['elɪ·ən] *adj* fremd ‖ *s* Fremde *mf*, Ausländer –in *mf*
alienate ['eljə,net], ['elɪ·ə,net] *tr* entfremden; (*jur*) übertragen
alight [ə'laɪt] *v* (*pret & pp* **alighted** & **alit** [ə'lɪt]) *intr* aussteigen; (*said of a bird*) (**on**) sich niederlassen (auf *dat* or *acc*); (aer) landen
align [ə'laɪn] *tr* (**with**) ausrichten (nach); (aut) einstellen; **a. oneself with** sich anschließen an (*acc*) ‖ *intr* —**a. with** sich ausrichten nach
alignment [ə'laɪnmənt] *s* Ausrichten *n;* (pol) Ausrichtung *f;* **bring into a.** gleichschalten; **out of a.** schlecht ausgerichtet
alike [ə'laɪk] *adj* gleich, ähnlich; **look a.** sich [*dat*] ähnlich sehen; (*resemble completely*) gleich aussehen
alimony ['ælɪ,moni] *s* Unterhaltskosten *pl*
alive [ə'laɪv] *adj* lebendig; (*vivacious*) lebhaft; **keep a.** am Leben bleiben; **keep s.o. a.** j–n am Leben erhalten
alka·li ['ælkə,laɪ] *s* (**–lis** & **–lies**) Laugensalz *n*, Alkali *n*
alkaline ['ælkə,laɪn] *adj* alkalisch
all [ɔl] *adj* all, ganz; **all day long** den ganzen Tag; **all kinds of** allerlei; **all the time** fortwährend; **for all that** trotzdem ‖ *adv* ganz, völlig; **all along** schon immer; **all at once** auf einmal; **all gone** alle; **all in** (coll) völlig erschöpft; **all over** (*everywhere*) überall; (*ended*) ganz vorbei; **all right** gut, schön; **all the better** um so besser; **all the same** dennoch; **not be all there** (coll) nicht ganz richtig im Kopf sein ‖ *s*—**after all** schließlich; **all in all** im großen und ganzen; **and all** gesamt, e.g., **he went, family and all** er ging mit gesamter Familie; **in all** insgesamt; **not at all** überhaupt nicht, gar nicht ‖ *indef pron* alle; (*everything*) alles
all'-around' *adj* vielseitig
allay [ə'le] *tr* beschwichtigen; (*hunger, thirst*) stillen
all'-clear' *s* Entwarnung *f*
allege [ə'ledʒ] *tr* behaupten; (*advance as an excuse*) vorgeben
alleged' *adj* angeblich, mutmaßlich
allegiance [ə'lidʒəns] *s* Treue *f*
allegoric(al) [,ælɪ'gɔrɪk(əl)] *adj* allegorisch
allegory ['ælɪ,gori] *s* Allegorie *f*
allergic [ə'lʌrdʒɪk] *adj* allergisch
allergy ['ælərdʒi] *s* Allergie *f*
alleviate [ə'livɪ,et] *tr* lindern
alley ['æli] *s* Gasse *f;* (*for bowling*) Kegelbahn *f*
alliance [ə'laɪ·əns] *s* Bündnis *n*
allied' *adj* (*field*) benachbart; (*science*) verwandt; (mil, pol) alliiert
alligator ['ælɪ,getər] *s* Alligator *m*
all'-inclu'sive *adj* Pauschal–
alliteration [ə,lɪtə're/ən] *s* Stabreim *m*, Alliteration *f*
all'-know'ing *adj* allwissend

allocate ['ælə,ket] *tr* zuteilen
al·lot [ə'lat] (*pret & pp* **–lotted; ger –lotting**) *tr* zuteilen, austeilen
all'-out' *adj* vollkommen, total
allow [ə'lau] *tr* erlauben, gestatten; (*admit*) zugeben; (*e.g., a discount*) gewähren; **be allowed to** (*inf*) dürfen (*inf*) ‖ *intr*—**a. for** bedenken
allowable [ə'lau·əbəl] *adj* zulässig
allowance [ə'lau·əns] *s* (*tolerance*) Duldung *f;* (*permission*) Erlaubnis *f;* (*ration*) Zuteilung *f*, Ration *f;* (*pocket money*) Taschengeld *n;* (*discount*) Abzug *m;* (*salary for a particular expense*) Zuschuß *m*, Zulage *f;* (*for groceries*) Wirtschaftsgeld *n;* (*mach*) Toleranz *f;* **make a. for** berücksichtigen
alloy ['ælɔɪ] *s* Legierung *f* ‖ [ə'lɔɪ] *tr* legieren
all'-pow'erful *adj* allmächtig
all' right' *adj*—**be a.** in Ordnung sein ‖ *interj* schon gut!
All' Saints'' Day' *s* Allerheiligen *n*
All' Souls'' Day' *s* Allerseelen *n*
all'spice' *s* Nelkenpfeffer *m*
all'-star' *adj* (*sport*) aus den besten Spielern bestehend
allude [ə'lud] *intr*—**a. to** anspielen auf (*acc*)
allure [ə'lur] *s* Charme *m* ‖ *tr* anlocken
allurement [ə'lurmənt] *s* Verlockung *f*
allur'ing *adj* verlockend
allusion [ə'luʒən] *s* (**to**) Anspielung *f* (auf *acc*)
al·ly ['ælaɪ], [ə'laɪ] *s* Alliierte *mf*, Verbündete *mf* ‖ [ə'laɪ] *v* (*pret & pp* **–lied**) *tr*—**a. oneself with** sich verbünden mit
almanac ['ɔlmə,næk] *s* Almanach *m*
almighty [ɔl'maɪti] *adj* allmächtig
almond ['amənd] *s* Mandel *f*
almost ['ɔlmost], [ɔl'most] *adv* fast
alms [amz] *s & spl* Almosen *n*
aloft [ə'lɔft] *adv* (*position*) oben; (*direction*) nach oben; **raise a.** emporheben
alone [ə'lon] *adj* allein; **let a.** (*not to mention*) geschweige denn; (*not bother*) in Ruhe lassen ‖ *adv* allein
along [ə'lɔŋ] *adv* vorwärts, weiter; **all a.** schon immer; **a. with** zusammen mit; **get a. with** sich gut vertragen mit; **go a. with** mitgehen mit; (*agree with*) sich einverstanden erklären mit ‖ *prep* (*direction*) entlang (*acc*); (*position*) an (*dat*), längs (*genit*)
along'side' *adv* (naut) längsseits; **a. of** im Vergleich zu ‖ *prep* neben (*dat*); (naut) längsseits (*genit*)
aloof [ə'luf] *adj* zurückhaltend ‖ *adv*— **keep a.** (**from**) sich fernhalten (von); **stand a.** für sich bleiben
aloud [ə'laud] *adv* laut
alphabet ['ælfə,bɛt] *s* Alphabet *n*
alphabetic(al) [,ælfə'bɛtɪk(əl)] *adj* alphabetisch
alpine ['ælpaɪn] *adj* alpin, Alpen–
Alps [ælps] *spl* Alpen *pl*
already [ɔl'redi] *adv* schon, bereits
Alsace [æl'ses], ['ælsæs] *s* Elsaß *n*
Alsatian [æl'se/ən] *adj* elsässisch ‖ *s*

Elsässer –in *mf;* (*dog*) deutscher Schäferhund *m*

also ['ɔlso] *adv* auch

altar ['ɔltər] *s* Altar *m*

al'tar boy' *s* Ministrant *m*

alter ['ɔltər] *tr* ändern; (*castrate*) kastrieren || *intr* sich ändern

alteration [ˌɔltə'reʃən] *s* Änderung *f;* **alterations** (*in construction*) Umbau *m*

alternate ['ɔltərnɪt] *adj* abwechselnd || *s* Ersatzmann *m* || ['ɔltərˌnet] *tr* (ab)wechseln; (*e.g., hot and cold compresses*) zwischen (*dat*) und (*dat*) abwechseln || *intr* miteinander abwechseln

al'ternating cur'rent *s* Wechselstrom *m*

alternative [ɔl'tʌrnətɪv] *adj* Ausweich-, Alternativ- || *s* Alternative *f*

although [ɔl'ðo] *conj* obgleich, obwohl

altimeter [æl'tɪmɪtər] *s* Höhenmesser *m*

altitude ['æltɪˌt(j)ud] *s* Höhe *f*

al·to ['ælto] *s* (**–tos**) Alt *m*, Altstimme *f;* (*singer*) Altist *m*

altogether [ˌɔltə'gɛðər] *adv* durchaus; (*in all*) insgesamt

altruist ['æltru·ɪst] *s* Altruist –in *mf*

alum ['æləm] *s* Alaun *m*

aluminum [ə'lumɪnəm] *s* Aluminium *n*

alu'minum foil' *s* Aluminiumfolie *f*

alum·na [ə'lʌmnə] *s* (**–nae** [ni]) ehemalige Studentin *f*

alum·nus [ə'lʌmnəs] *s* (**–ni** [naɪ]) ehemaliger Student *m*

always ['ɔlwɪz], ['ɔlwez] *adv* immer

A.M. *abbr* (**ante meridiem**) vormittags; (**amplitude modulation**) Amplitudenmodulation *f*

amalgam [ə'mælgəm] *s* Amalgam *n;* (fig) Mischung *f*, Gemenge *n*

amalgamate [ə'mælgəˌmet] *tr* amalgamieren || *intr* sich amalgamieren

amass [ə'mæs] *tr* aufhäufen, ansammeln

amateur ['æmətər] *adj* Amateur– || *s* Amateur *m*, Liebhaber *m*

amaze [ə'mez] *tr* erstaunen

amaz'ing *adj* erstaunlich

Amazon ['æməˌzɑn] *s* (*river*) Amazonas *m;* (fig) Mannweib *n;* (myth) Amazone *f*

ambassador [æm'bæsədər] *s* Botschafter –in §6 *mf;* (fig) Bote *m*

ambassadorial [æmˌbæsə'dɔrɪ·əl] *adj* Botschafts–

amber ['æmbər] *adj* Bernstein–; (*in color*) bernsteinfarben || *s* Bernstein *m*

ambiguity [ˌæmbɪ'gju·ɪti] *s* Doppelsinn *m*, Zweideutigkeit *f*

ambiguous [æm'bɪgjʊ·əs] *adj* doppelsinnig, zweideutig

ambit ['æmbɪt] *s* Bereich *m*

ambition [æm'bɪʃən] *s* Ehrgeiz *m;* (*aim, object*) Ambition *f*

ambitious [æm'bɪʃəs] *adj* ehrgeizig

ambivalent [æm'bɪvələnt] *adj* (chem) ambivalent; (psychol) zwiespältig

amble ['æmbəl] *s* (*of a person*) gemächlicher Gang *m;* (*of a horse*) Paßgang *m* || *intr* schlendern; (*said of a horse*) im Paßgang gehen

ambulance ['æmbjələns] *s* Krankenwagen *m*

ambulatory ['æmbjələˌtori] *adj* gehfähig

ambuscade [ˌæmbəs'ked] *s* Hinterhalt *m*

ambush ['æmbuʃ] *s* Hinterhalt *m* || *tr* aus dem Hinterhalt überfallen

ameliorate [ə'miljəˌret] *tr* verbessern || *intr* besser werden

amen ['e'mɛn], ['ɑ'mɛn] *s* Amen *n* || *interj* amen!

amenable [ə'mɛnəbəl] *adj* (*docile*) fügsam; **a. to** (*e.g., flattery*) zugänglich (*dat*); (*e.g., laws*) unterworfen (*dat*)

amend [ə'mɛnd] *tr* (*a law*) (ver)bessern; (*one's ways*) (ab)ändern || *intr* sich bessern

amendment [ə'mɛndmənt] *s* Änderungsantrag *m;* (*by addition*) Zusatzantrag *m;* (*to the constitution*) Zusatzartikel *m*

amends [ə'mɛndz] *s & spl* Genugtuung *f;* **make a. for** wiedergutmachen

amenity [ə'mɛnɪti] *s* (*pleasantness*) Annehmlichkeit *f;* **amenities** (*of life*) Annehmlichkeiten *pl*

America [ə'mɛrɪkə] *s* Amerika *n*

American [ə'mɛrɪkən] *adj* amerikanisch || *s* Amerikaner –in *mf*

Americanize [ə'mɛrɪkəˌnaɪz] *tr* amerikanisieren

amethyst ['æmɪθɪst] *s* Amethyst *m*

amiable ['emɪ·əbəl] *adj* liebenswürdig

amicable ['æmɪkəbəl] *adj* freundschaftlich, gütlich

amid [ə'mɪd] *prep* inmitten (*genit*)

amidships [ə'mɪdʃɪps] *adv* mittschiffs

amiss [ə'mɪs] *adj* (*improper*) unpassend; (*wrong*) verkehrt; **there is s.th. a.** etwas stimmt nicht || *adv* verkehrt; **go a.** danebengehen; **take a.** übelnehmen

amity ['æmɪti] *s* Freundschaft *f*

ammo ['æmo] *s* (sl) Muni *m*

ammonia [ə'monɪ·ə] *s* (*gas*) Ammoniak *n;* (*solution*) Salmiakgeist *m*

ammunition [ˌæmjə'nɪʃən] *s* Munition *f*

amnesia [æm'niʒɪ·ə] *s* Amnesie *f*

amnes·ty ['æmnɪsti] *s* Amnestie *f* || *v* (*pret & pp.* **–tied**) *tr* begnadigen

amoeba [ə'mibə] *s* Amöbe *f*

among [ə'mʌŋ] *prep* (*position*) unter (*dat*); (*direction*) unter (*acc*); **a. other things** unter anderem

amorous ['æmərəs] *adj* amourös

amortize ['æmərˌtaɪz] *tr* tilgen

amount [ə'maunt] *s* (*sum*) Betrag *m;* (*quantity*) Menge *f* || *intr*—**a. to** betragen

ampere ['æmpɪr] *s* Ampere *n*

amphibian [æm'fɪbɪ·ən] *s* Amphibie *f*

amphibious [æm'fɪbɪ·əs] *adj* amphibisch

amphitheater ['æmfɪˌθi·ətər] *s* Amphitheater *n*

ample ['æmpəl] *adj* (*sufficient*) genügend; (*spacious*) geräumig

amplifier ['æmplɪˌfaɪ·ər] *s* Verstärker *m*

ampli·fy ['æmplɪˌfaɪ] *v* (*pret & pp* **–fied**) *tr* (*a statement*) erweitern; (electron, rad, phys) verstärken

amplitude ['æmplɪ‚t(j)ud] *s* Weite *f;* (electron, rad, phys) Amplitude *f*

am'plitude modula'tion *s* Amplitudenmodulation *f*

amputate ['æmpjə‚tet] *tr* amputieren

amputee [‚æmpje'ti] *s* Amputierte *mf*

amuck [ə'mʌk] *adv*—**run a.** Amok laufen

amulet ['æmjəlɪt] *s* Amulett *n*

amuse [ə'mjuz] *tr* amüsieren, belustigen

amusement [ə'mjuzmənt] *s* Vergnügen *n*

amuse'ment park' *s* Vergnügungspark *m*

amus'ing *adj* amüsant

an [æn], [ən] *indef art* ein

anachronism [ə'nækrə‚nɪzəm] *s* Anachronismus *m*

analogous [ə'næləgəs] *adj* (**to**) analog (*dat*), ähnlich (*dat*)

analogy [ə'nælədʒi] *s* Analogie *f*

analy·sis [ə'nælɪsɪs] *s* (**-ses** [‚siz]) Analyse *f;* (*of a literary work*) Zergliederung *f*

analyst ['ænəlɪst] *s* Analytiker –in *mf*

analytic(al) [‚ænə'lɪtɪk(əl)] *adj* analytisch

analyze ['ænə‚laɪz] *tr* analysieren

anarchist ['ænərkɪst] *s* Anarchist –in *mf*

anarchy ['ænərki] *s* Anarchie *f*

anatomic(al) [‚ænə'tamɪk(əl)] *adj* anatomisch

anatomy [ə'nætəmi] *s* Anatomie *f*

ancestor ['ænsɛstər] *s* Vorfahr *m,* Ahne *m*

ancestral [æn'sɛstrəl] *adj* angestammt, Ahnen–; (*inherited*) Erb–, ererbt

ancestry ['ænsɛstri] *s* Abstammung *f*

anchor ['æŋkər] *s* Anker *m;* **cast a.** vor Anker gehen; **weigh a.** den Anker lichten ‖ *tr* verankern ‖ *intr* ankern

anchorage ['æŋkərɪdʒ] *s* Ankerplatz *m*

anchovy ['æntʃovi] *s* Anschovis *f*

ancient ['entʃənt] *adj* (*very old*) uralt; (*civilization*) antik ‖ **the ancients** *spl* die alten Griechen und Römer

an'cient his'tory *s* alte Geschichte *f*

and [ænd], [ənd] *conj* und; **and how!** und ob! **and so forth** und so weiter

andiron ['ænd‚aɪ·ərn] *s* Kaminbock *m*

anecdote ['ænɪk‚dot] *s* Anekdote *f*

anemia [ə'nimɪ·ə] *s* Anämie *f*

anemic [ə'nimɪk] *adj* anämisch, blutarm

anesthesia [‚ænɪs'θiʒə] *s* Anästhesie *f;* **general a.** Vollnarkose *f;* **local a.** Lokalanästhesie *f*

anesthetic [‚ænɪs'θɛtɪk] *adj* betäubend ‖ *s* Betäubungsmittel *n;* **local a.** örtliches Betäubungsmittel *n*

anesthetize [æ'nɛsθɪ‚taɪz] *tr* betäuben

anew [ə'n(j)u] *adv* von neuem, aufs neue

angel ['endʒəl] *s* Engel *m;* (*financial backer*) Hintermann *m*

angelic(al) [æn'dʒɛlɪk(əl)] *adj* engelgleich, engelhaft

anger ['æŋgər] *s* Zorn *m* ‖ *tr* erzürnen

angina pectoris [æn'dʒaɪnə'pɛktərɪs] *s* Brustbeklemmung *f,* Herzbräune *f*

angle ['æŋgəl] *s* Winkel *m;* (*point of view*) Gesichtswinkel *m;* (*ulterior motive*) Hintergedanken *m;* (*side*) Seite *f*

angler ['æŋglər] *s* Angler –in *mf*

angry ['æŋgri] *adj* zornig, böse; (*wound*) entzündet; **a. at** (*s.th.*) zornig über (*acc*); **a. with** (*s.o.*) zornig auf (*acc*)

anguish ['æŋgwɪʃ] *s* Qual *f,* Pein *f*

angular ['æŋgjələr] *adj* kantig

animal ['ænɪməl] *adj* tierisch, Tier— ‖ *s* Tier *n*

animate ['ænɪmɪt] *adj* belebt; (*lively*) lebhaft ‖ ['ænɪ‚met] *tr* beleben, beseelen; (*make lively*) aufmuntern

an'imated cartoon' *s* Zeichentrickfilm *m*

animation [‚ænɪ'meʃən] *s* Lebhaftigkeit *f;* (cin) Herstellung *f* von Zeichentrickfilm

animosity [‚ænɪ'masɪti] *s* Feindseligkeit *f*

anion ['æn‚aɪ·ən] *s* Anion *n*

anise ['ænɪs] *s* Anis *m*

anisette [‚ænɪ'sɛt] *s* Anisett *m*

ankle ['æŋkəl] *s* Fußknöchel *m*

an'kle support' *s* Knöchelstütze *f*

anklet ['æŋklɪt] *s* (*ornament*) Fußring *m;* (*sock*) Söckchen *n*

annals ['ænəlz] *spl* Annalen *pl*

anneal [ə'nil] *tr* ausglühen; (*the mind*) stählen

annex ['ænɛks] *s* (*building*) Anbau *m,* Nebengebäude *n;* (*supplement*) Zusatz *m* ‖ [ə'nɛks] *tr* annektieren

annexation [‚ænɛks'eʃən] *s* Einverleibung *f;* (pol) Annexion *f*

annihilate [ə'naɪ·ɪ‚let] *tr* vernichten; (fig) zunichte machen

annihilation [ə‚naɪ·ɪ'leʃən] *s* Vernichtung *f*

anniversary [‚ænɪ'vʌrsəri] *s* Jahrestag *m*

annotate ['ænə‚tet] *tr* mit Anmerkungen versehen

annotation [‚ænə'teʃən] *s* Anmerkung *f*

announce [ə'naʊns] *tr* ankündigen, anmelden; (rad) ansagen, melden

announcement [ə'naʊnsmənt] *s* Ankündigung *f;* (rad) Durchsage *f*

announcer [ə'naʊnsər] *s* Ansager –in *mf*

annoy [ə'nɔɪ] *tr* ärgern; **be annoyed at** sich ärgern über (*acc*)

annoyance [ə'nɔɪ·əns] *s* Ärger *m*

annoy'ing *adj* ärgerlich

annual ['ænju·əl] *adj* jährlich, Jahres–; (*plant*) einjährig ‖ *s* (*book*) Jahrbuch *n;* (bot) einjährige Pflanze *f*

annuity [ə'n(j)u·ɪti] *s* Jahresrente *f*

an·nul [ə'nʌl] *v* (*pret & pp* **-nulled;** *ger* **-nulling**) *tr* annullieren

annulment [ə'nʌlmənt] *s* Annullierung *f;* (*of marriage*) Nichtigkeitserklärung *f*

anode ['ænod] *s* Anode *f*

anoint [ə'nɔɪnt] *tr* salben

anomaly [ə'naməli] *s* Anomalie *f*

anonymous [ə'nanɪməs] *adj* anonym

another [ə'nʌðər] *adj* (*a different*) ein anderer; (*an additional*) noch ein; **a. Caesar** ein zweiter Cäsar ‖ *pron* (*a different one*) ein anderer; (*an additional one*) noch einer

answer ['ænsər] *s* Antwort *f*; (*to a problem*) Lösung *f* || *tr* (*a person*) antworten (*dat*); (*a question, letter*) beantworten; (*need, description*) entsprechen (*dat*); (*enemy fire*) antworten auf (*acc*); **a. an ad** sich auf e–e Anzeige melden; **a. the door** die Tür öffnen; **a. the telephone** ans Telefon gehen || *intr* antworten; (telp) sich melden; **a. back** e–n losen Mund haben; **a. for** verantworten; **a. to** (*a description*) entsprechen (*dat*)

an'swering serv'ice *s* Fernsprechauftragsdienst *m*

ant [ænt] *s* Ameise *f*

antagonism [æn'tægə,nɪzəm] *s* Feindseligkeit *f*

antagonize [æn'tægə,naɪz] *tr* sich [*dat*] zum Gegner machen

antarctic [ænt'ɑrktɪk] *adj* antarktisch || **the Antarctic** *s* die Antarktis

Antarc'tic Cir'cle *s* südlicher Polarkreis *m*

Antarc'tic O'cean *s* südliches Eismeer *n*

ante ['ænti] *s* (cards) Einsatz *m*; (com) Scherflein *n* || *tr* (cards) einsetzen || *intr* (*in a joint venture*) sein Scherflein beitragen; (*pay up*) (coll) blechen; (cards) einsetzen

antecedent [,ænti'sidənt] *adj* vorhergehend || *s* (gram) Beziehungswort *n*; **antecedents** Antezedenzien *pl*

antechamber ['ænti,tʃembər] *s* Vorzimmer *n*

antelope ['ænti,lop] *s* Antilope *f*

anten·na [æn'tɛnə] *s* (**-nae** [ni]) (ent) Fühler *m* || *s* (**-nas**) (rad) Antenne *f*

antepenult [,ænti'pinʌlt] *s* drittletzte Silbe *f*

anthem ['ænθəm] *s* Hymne *f*

ant'hill' *s* Ameisenhaufen *m*

anthology [æn'θɑlədʒi] *s* Anthologie *f*

anthropology [,ænθrə'pɑlədʒi] *s* Anthropologie *f*, Lehre *f* vom Menschen

antiaircraft [,ænti'ɛr,kræft] *adj* Flak–, Flugabwehr– || *s* Flak *f*

antiair'craft gun' *s* Flak *f*

antibiotic [,æntɪbaɪ'ɑtɪk] *s* Antibiotikum *n*

antibody ['ænti,bɑdi] *s* Antikörper *m*

anticipate [æn'tɪsɪ,pet] *tr* (*expect*) erwarten; (*remarks, criticism, etc.*) vorwegnehmen; (*trouble*) vorausahnen; (*pleasure*) vorausempfinden; (*s.o.'s wish or desire*) zuvorkommen (*dat*)

anticipation [æn,tɪsɪ'peʃən] *s* Erwartung *f*, Vorfreude *f*

antics ['æntɪks] *spl* Possen *pl*

antidote ['ænti,dot] *s* Gegengift *n*

antifreeze ['ænti,friz] *s* Gefrierschutzmittel *n*

antiknock [,ænti'nak] *adj* klopffest || *s* Antiklopfmittel *n*

antipathy [æn'tɪpəθi] *s* Abneigung *f*, Antipathie *f*

antiquarian [,ænti'kwɛri·ən] *adj* altertümlich || *s* Altertumsforscher –in *mf*

antiquated ['ænti,kwetɪd] *adj* veraltet

antique [æn'tik] *adj* (ur)alt, antik || *s* Antiquität *f*

antique' deal'er *s* Antiquitätenhändler –in *mf*

antique' shop' *s* Antiquitätenladen *m*

antiquity [æn'tɪkwɪti] *s* Altertum *n*, Vorzeit *f*; **antiquities** Antiquitäten *pl*, Altertümer *pl*

antirust [,ænti'rʌst] *adj* Rostschutz–

anti-Semitic [,æntɪsɪ'mɪtɪk] *adj* antisemitisch, judenfeindlich

antiseptic [,ænti'sɛptɪk] *adj* antiseptisch || *s* Antiseptikum *n*

antitank [,ænti'tæŋk] *adj* Panzer–: (*unit*) Panzerjäger–

antitank' mine' *s* Tellermine *f*

antithe·sis [æn'tɪθɪsɪs] *s* (**-ses** [,siz]) Gegensatz *m*, Antithese *f*

antitoxin [,ænti'taksɪn] *s* Gegengift *n*

antitrust [,ænti'trʌst] *adj* Antitrust–

antiwar [,ænti'wɔr] *adj* antimilitaristisch

antler ['æntlər] *s* Geweihsprosse *f*; (**pair of**) **antlers** Geweih *n*

antonym ['æntənɪm] *s* Antonym *n*

anus ['enəs] *s* After *m*

anvil ['ænvɪl] *s* Amboß *m*

anxiety [æŋ'zaɪ·əti] *s* (**over**) Besorgnis *f* (um); (psychol) Beklemmung *f*

anxious ['æŋkʃəs] *adj* (**about**) besorgt (um or wegen); (**for**) gespannt (auf *acc*), begierig (auf *acc*); **I am a. to** (*inf*) es liegt mir daran zu (*inf*)

any ['ɛni] *indef adj* irgendein, irgendwelch; (*a little*) etwas; **any (possible)** etwaig; **any (you wish)** jeder beliebige; **do you have any money on you?** haben Sie Geld bei sich?; **I do not have any money** ich habe kein Geld || *adv*—**any more** (*e.g., coffee*) noch etwas; (*e.g., apples*) noch ein paar; **not any better** keinwegs besser; **not ...any longer** nicht mehr; **not ...any more** mehr nicht mehr

an'ybod'y *indef pron* var of **anyone**

an'yhow' *adv* sowieso, trotzdem; (*in any event*) jedenfalls

an'yone' *indef pron* (irgend)jemand, irgendeiner; **a. but you** jeder andere als du; **a. else** sonstnochwer; **ask a.** frag wen du willst; **I don't see a.** ich sehe niemand

an'yplace' *adv* (coll) var of **anywhere**

an'ything' *indef pron* (irgend)etwas, (irgend)was; **a. but** alles andere als; **a. else?** noch etwas?, sonst etwas?; **a. you want** was du willst; **not ...a.** nichts; **not for a. in the world** um keinen Preis

an'ytime' *adv* zu jeder (beliebigen) Zeit; (*at some unspecified time*) irgendwann

an'yway' *adv* sowieso, trotzdem

an'ywhere' *adv* (*position*) irgendwo; (*everywhere*) an jedem beliebigen Ort; (*direction*) irgendwohin; (*everywhere*) an jeden beliebigen Ort; (*to any extent*) einigermaßen, e.g., **a. near correct** einigermaßen richtig; **get a.** (*achieve success*) es zu etwas bringen

apace [ə'pes] *adv* schnell, rasch

apart [ə'pɑrt] *adv* (*to pieces*) auseinander; (*separately*) einzeln, für sich; a. **from** abgesehen von

apartment [ə'pɑrtmənt] s Wohnung *f*

apart'ment house' s Apartmenthaus *n*

apathetic [ˌæpə'θɛtɪk] *adj* apathisch, teilnahmslos

apathy ['æpəθi] s Apathie *f*

ape [ep] s Affe *m* || *tr* nachäffen

aperture ['æpərtʃər] s Öffnung *f;* (phot) Blende *f*

apex ['epɛks] s (**apexes** & **apices** ['æpɪˌsiz]) Spitze *f;* (fig) Gipfel *m*

aphid ['æfɪd] s Blattlaus *f*

aphorism ['æfəˌrɪzəm] s Aphorismus *m*

apiary ['epɪˌɛri] s Bienenhaus *n*

apiece [ə'pis] *adv* pro Stück; (*per person*) pro Person

aplomb [ə'plɔm] s sicheres Auftreten *n*

apogee ['æpəˌdʒi] s Erdferne *f*

apologetic [əˌpɑlə'dʒɛtɪk] *adj* (*remark*) entschuldigend; (*letter, speech*) Entschuldigungs–; **be a.** (**about**) Entschuldigungen vorbringen (für)

apologize [ə'pɑləˌdʒaɪz] *intr* sich entschuldigen; **a. to s.o. for s.th.** sich bei j–m wegen etw entschuldigen

apology [ə'pɑlədʒi] s (*excuse*) Entschuldigung *f;* (*apologia*) Verteidigung *f*

apoplec'tic stroke' [ˌæpə'plɛktɪk] s Schlaganfall *m*

apoplexy ['æpəˌplɛksi] s Schlaganfall *m*

apostle [ə'pɑsəl] s Apostel *m*

apostolic [ˌæpəs'tɑlɪk] *adj* apostolisch

apostrophe [ə'pɑstrəfi] s (gram) Apostroph *m;* (rhet) Anrede *f*

apothecary [ə'pɑθɪˌkɛri] s (*druggist*) Apotheker *m;* (*drugstore*) Apotheke *f*

appall [ə'pɔl] *tr* entsetzen

appall'ing *adj* entsetzlich

appara·tus [ˌæpə'retəs], [ˌæpə'rætəs] s (**–tus** & **–tuses**) Apparat *m*

apparel [ə'pærəl] s Kleidung *f*, Tracht *f*

apparent [ə'pærənt] *adj* (*visible*) sichtbar; (*obvious*) offenbar; (*seeming*) scheinbar

apparition [ˌæpə'rɪʃən] s Erscheinung *f;* (*ghost*) Gespenst *n*

appeal [ə'pil] s (*request*) Appell *m*, dringende Bitte *f;* (*to reason, etc.*) Appell *m;* (*charm*) Anziehungskraft *f;* (jur) (**to**) Berufung *f* (an *acc*) || *tr*—**a. a case** Berufung einlegen in e–r Rechtssache || *intr*—**a. to** (*entreat*) dringend bitten; (*be attractive to*) reizen; (jur) appellieren an (*acc*)

appear [ə'pir] *intr* erscheinen; (*seem*) scheinen; (*come before the public*) sich zeigen; (jur) sich stellen; (theat) auftreten; **a. as a guest** (telv) gastieren

appearance [ə'pɪrəns] s Erscheinen *n;* (*outward look*) Aussehen *n;* (*semblance*) Anschein *m;* (*on the stage*) Auftreten *n;* (jur) Erscheinen *n;* **for the sake of appearances** anstandshalber; **to all appearances** allem Anschein nach

appease [ə'piz] *tr* beruhigen; (*hunger*)

stillen; (*pain*) mildern; (dipl) beschwichtigen

appeasement [ə'pizmənt] s Beruhigung *f;* (*of hunger*) Stillung *f;* (dipl) Beschwichtigung *f*

appel'late court' [ə'pɛlɪt] s Berufungsgericht *n*

append [ə'pɛnd] *tr* anhängen; (*a signature*) hinzufügen

appendage [ə'pɛndɪdʒ] s Anhang *m*

appendectomy [ˌæpən'dɛktəmi] s Blinddarmoperation *f*

appendicitis [əˌpɛndɪ'saɪtɪs] s Blinddarmentzündung *f*, Appendizitis *f*

appen·dix [ə'pɛndɪks] s (**–dixes** & **—dices** [dɪˌsiz]) Anhang *m;* (anat) Appendix *m*

appertain [ˌæpər'ten] *intr* (**to**) gehören (zu), gebühren (*dat*)

appetite ['æpɪˌtaɪt] s (**for**) Appetit *m* (auf *acc*)

appetizer ['æpɪˌtaɪzər] s Vorspeise *f*

ap'petizing *adj* appetitlich

applaud [ə'plɔd] *tr* Beifall klatschen (*dat*); (*praise*) billigen || *intr* Beifall klatschen

applause [ə'plɔz] s Beifall *m*, Applaus *m*

apple ['æpəl] s Apfel *m*

ap'plecart' s—**upset the a.** die Pläne über den Haufen werfen

ap'ple of one's eye' s Augapfel *m*

ap'ple pie' s gedeckte Apfeltorte *f*

ap'ple-pol'isher s (coll) Speichellecker *m*

ap'plesauce' s Apfelmus *n*

ap'ple tree' s Apfelbaum *m*

appliance [ə'plaɪ·əns] s Gerät *n*, Vorrichtung *f*

applicable ['æplɪkəbəl] *adj* (**to**) anwendbar (auf *acc*); **not a.** nicht zutreffend

applicant ['æplɪkənt] s Bewerber –in *mf*

application [ˌæplɪ'keʃən] s (*use*) Anwendung *f;* (*for a job*) Bewerbung *f;* (*for a grant*) Antrag *m;* (*zeal*) Fleiß *m;* (med) Anlegen *n*

applica'tion blank' s (*for a job*) Bewerbungsformular *n;* (*for a grant*) Antragsformular *n*

applied' *adj* angewandt

apply [ə'plaɪ] *v* (*pret & pp* **–plied**) *tr* anwenden; (med) anlegen; **a. oneself to** sich befleißigen (*genit*); **a. the brakes** bremsen || *intr* gelten; **a. for** (*a job*) sich bewerben um; (*a grant*) beantragen

appoint [ə'pɔɪnt] *tr* (*a person*) ernennen; (*a time, etc.*) festsetzen

appointment [ə'pɔɪntmənt] s Ernennung *f;* (*post*) Stelle *f;* (*engagement*) Verabredung *f;* **by a. only** nur nach Vereinbarung; **have an a. with** (*e.g., a dentist*) bestellt sein zu

appoint'ment book' s Terminkalender *m*

apportion [ə'pɔrʃən] *tr* zumessen

appraisal [ə'prezəl] s Abschätzung *f*

appraise [ə'prez] *tr* (ab)schätzen

appraiser [ə'prezər] s Schätzer –in *mf*

appreciable [ə'priʃɪ·əbəl] *adj* (*notice-*

able) merklich; (*considerable*) erheblich

appreciate [ə'priʃɪ ˌet] *tr* dankbar sein für; (*danger*) erkennen; (*regard highly*) hochschätzen || *intr* (im Werte) steigen

appreciation [ə ˌpriʃɪ'eʃən] *s* (*gratitude*) Dank *m*. Anerkennung *f;* (*for art*) Verständnis *n;* (*high regard*) Schätzung *f;* (*increase in value*) Wertzuwachs *m*

appreciative [ə'priʃɪ-ətɪv] *adj* (*of*) dankbar (für)

apprehend [ˌæprɪ'hɛnd] *tr* verhaften, ergreifen; (*understand*) begreifen

apprehension [ˌæprɪ'hɛnʃən] *s* (*arrest*) Verhaftung *f;* (*fear*) Befürchtung *f;* (*comprehending*) Begreifen *n*

apprehensive [ˌæprɪ'hɛnsɪv] *adj* (*of*) besorgt (um)

apprentice [ə'prɛntɪs] *s* Lehrling *m*

appren'ticeship' *s* Lehre *f;* **serve an a.** in der Lehre sein

apprise, apprize [ə'praɪz] *tr* (**of**) benachrichtigen (von)

approach [ə'protʃ] *s* Annäherung *f;* (*e.g., a road*) Zugang *m*, Zufahrt *f;* *e.g., to a problem*) Behandlung *f;* (*tentative sexual approach*) Annäherungsversuch *m;* (aer) Anflug *m* || *tr* sich nähern (*dat*); (*e.g., a problem*) behandeln; (*perfection*) nahekommen (*dat*); (aer) anfliegen || *intr* sich nähern

approachable [ə'protʃəbəl] *adj* zugänglich

approbation [ˌæprə'beʃən] *s* (*approval*) Beifall *m;* (*sanction*) Billigung *f*

appropriate [ə'proprɪ-ɪt] *adj* (**to**) angemessen (*dat*) || [ə'proprɪ ˌet] *tr* (*take possession of*) sich [*dat*] aneignen; (*authorize*) bewilligen

approval [ə'pruvəl] *s* (*approbation*) Beifall *m;* (*sanction*) Billigung *f;* **meet with s.o.'s a.** j-s Beifall finden; **on a.** auf Probe

approve [ə'pruv] *tr* (*sanction*) genehmigen; (*judge favorably*) billigen; (*a bill*) (parl) annehmen || *intr*—**a. of** billigen

approvingly [ə'pruvɪŋli] *adv* beifällig

approximate [ə'praksɪmɪt] *adj* annähernd || [ə'praksɪ ˌmet] *tr* (*come close to*) nahekommen (*dat*); (*estimate*) schätzen; (*simulate closely*) täuschend nachahmen

approximately [ə'praksɪmɪtli] *adv* ungefähr, etwa

apricot ['eprɪ ˌkat] *s* Aprikose *f*

ap'ricot tree' *s* Aprikosenbaum *m*

April ['eprɪl] *s* April *m*

A'pril fool' *interj* April, April!

A'pril Fools'' Day' *s* der erste April *m*

apron ['eprən] *s* Schürze *f;* (aer) Vorfeld *n;* (theat) Vorbühne *f*

apropos [ˌæprə'po] *adj* passend || *adv* —**a. of** in Bezug auf (*acc*)

apse [æps] *s* Apsis *f*

apt [æpt] *adj* (*suited to the occasion*) passend; (*suited to the purpose*) geeignet; (*metaphor*) zutreffend; **be apt to** (*inf*) (*be prone to*) dazu neigen zu

(*inf*); **he is apt to believe it** er wird es wahrscheinlich glauben

aptitude ['æptɪ ˌt(j)ud] *s* Eignung *f*

ap'titude test' *s* Eignungsprüfung *f*

aqualung ['ækwə ˌlʌŋ] *s* Tauchergerät *n*

aquamarine [ˌækwəmə'rin] *adj* blaugrün || *s* Aquamarin *m*

aquari·um [ə'kwɛrɪ-əm] *s* (**–ums & –a** [ə]) Aquarium *n*

aquatic [ə'kwætɪk] *adj* Wasser– || **aquatics** *spl* Wassersport *m*

aqueduct ['ækwə ˌdʌkt] *s* Aquädukt *n*

aq'uiline nose' ['ækwɪ ˌlaɪn] *s* Adlernase *f*

Arab ['ærəb] *adj* arabisch || *s* Araber –in *mf*

Arabia [ə'rebɪ-ə] *s* Arabien *n*

Arabic ['ærəbɪk] *adj* arabisch || *s* Arabisch *n*

arable ['ærəbəl] *adj* urbar, Acker–

arbiter ['arbɪtər] *s* Schiedsrichter *m*

arbitrary ['arbɪ ˌtrɛri] *adj* (*act*) willkürlich; (*number*) beliebig; (*person, government*) tyrannisch

arbitrate ['arbɪ ˌtret] *tr* schlichten || *intr* als Schiedsrichter fungieren

arbitration [ˌarbɪ'treʃən] *s* Schlichtung *f*

arbitrator ['arbɪ ˌtretər] *s* Schiedsrichter *m*

arbor ['arbər] *s* Laube *f;* (mach) Achse *f*

arbore·tum [ˌarbə'ritəm] *s* (**–tums & –ta** [tə]) Baumgarten *m*

arc [ark] *s* (astr, geom, mach) Bogen *m;* (elec) Lichtbogen *m*

arcade [ar'ked] *s* Bogengang *m*, Arkade *f*

arcane [ar'ken] *adj* geheimnisvoll

arch [artʃ] *adj* (*liar, etc.*) abgefeimt || *s* Bogen *m* || *tr* wölben; (*span*) überwölben || *intr* sich wölben

archaeologist [ˌarkɪ'alədʒɪst] *s* Archäolog(e) *m*, Archäologin *f*

archaeology [ˌarkɪ'alədʒɪ] *s* Archäologie *f*

archaic [ar'ke-ɪk] *adj* (*word*) veraltet; (*manner, notion*) antiquiert

archangel ['ark ˌendʒəl] *s* Erzengel *m*

archbishop ['artʃ'bɪʃəp] *s* Erzbischof *m*

archduke ['artʃ'd(j)uk] *s* Erzherzog *m*

archenemy ['artʃ ˌɛnimi] *s* Erzfeind *m*

archer ['artʃər] *s* Bogenschütze *m*

archery ['artʃəri] *s* Bogenschießen *n*

archipela·go [ˌarkɪ'peləgo] *s* (**–gos & –goes**) Inselmeer *n;* (*group of islands*) Inselgruppe *f*, Archipel *m*

architect ['arkɪ ˌtɛkt] *s* Architekt –in *mf*

architecture ['arkɪ ˌtɛktʃər] *s* Architektur *f*, Baukunst *f*

archives ['arkaɪvz] *spl* Archiv *n*

arch'way' *s* Bogengang *m*, Torbogen *m*

arctic ['arktɪk] *adj* arktisch, nördlich || **the Arctic** *s* die Arktis

Arc'tic Cir'cle *s* nördlicher Polarkreis *m*

arc' weld'ing *s* Lichtbogenschweißung *f*

ardent ['ardənt] *adj* feurig, eifrig

ardor ['ardər] *s* Eifer *m*, Inbrust *f*

arduous ['ɑrdʒʊ·əs] *adj* mühsam
area ['ɛrɪ·ə] *s* (*surface*) Fläche *f*; (*district*) Gegend *f*; (*field of enterprise*) Bereich *m*, Gebiet *n*; (*of danger*) Zone *f*
arena [ə'rinə] *s* Arena *f*, Kampfbahn *f*
Argentina [ˌɑrdʒən'tinə] *s* Argentinien *n*
argue ['ɑrgju] *tr* erörtern; (*maintain*) behaupten; **a. into** (*ger*) dazu überreden zu (*inf*) || *intr* (**with**) streiten (mit); **a. for** (or **against**) **s.th.** für (or gegen) etw eintreten; **don't a.!** keine Widerrede!
argument ['ɑrgjəmənt] *s* (*discussion*) Erörterung *f*; (*point*) Beweisgrund *m*; (*disagreement*) Auseinandersetzung *f*; (*theme*) Thema *n*
argumentative [ˌɑrgjə'mɛntətɪv] *adj* streitsüchtig
aria ['ɑrɪ·ə], ['ɛrɪ·ə] *s* Arie *f*
arid ['ærɪd] *adj* trocken, dürr
aridity [ə'rɪdɪti] *s* Trockenheit *f*
arise [ə'raɪz] *v* (*pret* **arose** [ə'roz]; *pp* **arisen** [ə'rɪzən]) *intr* (*come into being*) (**from**) entstehen (aus); (*get out of bed*) aufstehen; (*from a seat*) sich erheben; (*occur*) aufkommen, auftauchen; (*said of an opportunity*) sich bieten; (*stem*) (**from**) stammen (von)
aristocracy [ˌærɪs'tɑkrəsi] *s* Aristokratie *f*
aristocrat [ə'rɪstəˌkræt] *s* Aristokrat –in *mf*
aristocratic [əˌrɪstə'krætɪk] *adj* aristokratisch
arithmetic [ə'rɪθmətɪk] *s* Arithmetik *f*
arithmetical [ˌærɪθ'mɛtɪkəl] *adj* arithmetisch, rechnerisch
ark [ɑrk] *s* Arche *f*
ark' of the cov'enant *s* Bundeslade *f*
arm [ɑrm] *s* Arm *m*; (*of a chair*) Seitenlehne *f*; (*weapon*) Waffe *f*; **keep s.o. at arm's length** sich j–m vom Leibe halten; **take up arms** zu den Waffen greifen; **up in arms** in Aufruhr || *tr* bewaffnen; || *intr* sich bewaffen
armament ['ɑrməmənt] *s* Kriegsausrüstung *f*, Bewaffnung *f*
ar'maments race' *s* Rüstungswettlauf *m*
armature ['ɑrməˌtʃər] *s* (*of doorbell or magnet*) Anker *m*; (*of a motor or dynamo*) Läufer *m*; (biol) Panzer *m*
arm'chair' *s* Lehnsessel *m*; (*unpadded*) Lehnstuhl *m*
armed' for'ces *spl* Streitkräfte *pl*
armed' rob'bery *s* bewaffneter Raubüberfall *m*
Armenia [ɑr'minɪ·ə] *s* Armenien *n*
armful ['ɑrmˌfʊl] *s* Armvoll *m*
armistice ['ɑrmɪstɪs] *s* Waffenstillstand *m*
armor ['ɑrmər] *s* Panzer *m* || *tr* panzern
ar'mored car' *s* Panzerwagen *m*
armor-piercing ['ɑrmərˌpɪrsɪŋ] *adj* panzerbrechend
ar'mor plat'ing ['pletɪŋ] *s* Panzerung *f*
armory ['ɑrməri] *s* (*large arms storage*) Arsenal *n*; (*arms repair and storage room of a unit*) Waffenkam-

mer *f*; (*arms factory*) Waffenfabrik *f*; (*drill hall*) Exerzierhalle *f*
arm'pit' *s* Achselhöhle *f*
arm'rest' *s* Armlehne *f*
army ['ɑrmi] *adj* Armes–, Heeres– || *s* Armee *f*, Heer *n*; **join the a.** zum Militär gehen
aroma [ə'romə] *s* Aroma *n*, Duft *m*
aromatic [ˌærə'mætɪk] *adj* aromatisch
around [ə'raʊnd] *adv* ringsherum; **be a. in der Nähe sein; get a. viel herumkommen; get a. to** (*inf*) dazukommen zu (*inf*) || *prep* um (*acc*) herum; (*approximately*) etwa; (*near*) bei (*dat*); **a. town** in der Stadt
arouse [ə'raʊz] *tr* aufwecken; (fig) erwecken
arraign [ə'ren] *tr* (*accuse*) anklagen; (jur) vor Gericht stellen
arrange [ə'rendʒ] *tr* arrangieren; (*in a certain order*) (an)ordnen; (*a time*) festsetzen; (mus) bearbeiten || *intr*— **a. for** Vorkehrungen treffen für
arrangement [ə'rendʒmənt] *s* Anordnung *f*; (*agreement*) Vereinbarung *f*; (mus) Bearbeitung *f*; **make arrangements to** (*inf*) Vorbereitungen treffen, um zu (*inf*)
array [ə're] *s* (*of troops, facts*) Ordnung *f*; (*large number or quantity*) Menge *f*; (*apparel*) Staat *m* || *tr* ordnen; (*dress up*) putzen
arrears [ə'rɪrz] *spl* Rückstand *m*; **in a.** rückständig
arrest [ə'rɛst] *s* Verhaftung *f*; **make an a. e–e** Verhaftung vornehmen; **place under a.** in Haft nehmen; **under a.** verhaftet || *tr* verhaften; (*attention*) fesseln; (*a disease, progress*) hemmen
arrival [ə'raɪvəl] *s* Ankunft *f*; (*of merchandise*) Eingang *m*; (*a person*) Ankömmling *m*
arrive [ə'raɪv] *intr* ankommen; (*said of time, an event*) kommen; **a. at** (*a conclusion, decision*) erlangen
arrogance ['ærəgəns] *s* Anmaßung *f*
arrogant ['ærəgənt] *adj* anmaßend
arrogate ['ærəˌget] *tr* sich [*dat*] anmaßen
arrow ['æro] *s* Pfeil *m*
ar'rowhead' *s* Pfeilspitze *f*
arsenal ['ɑrsənəl] *s* Arsenal *n*
arsenic ['ɑrsɪnɪk] *s* Arsen *n*
arson ['ɑrsən] *s* Brandstiftung *f*
arsonist ['ɑrsənɪst] *s* Brandstifter –in *mf*
art [ɑrt] *s* Kunst *f*
artery ['ɑrtəri] *s* Pulsader *f*; (*highway*) Verkehrsader *f*
artful ['ɑrtfəl] *adj* (*cunning*) schlau, listig; (*skillful*) kunstvoll
arthritic [ɑr'θrɪtɪk] *adj* arthritisch, gichtisch || *s* Arthritiker –in *mf*
arthritis [ɑr'θraɪtɪs] *s* Arthritis *f*
artichoke ['ɑrtɪˌtʃok] *s* Artischocke *f*
article ['ɑrtɪkəl] *s* (*object*) Gegenstand *m*; (com, gram, journ, jur) Artikel *m*
articulate [ɑr'tɪkjəlɪt] *adj* deutlich || [ɑr'tɪkjəˌlet] *tr & intr* deutlich aussprechen
artifact ['ɑrtɪˌfækt] *s* Artefakt *n*
artifice ['ɑrtɪfɪs] *s* Kunstgriff *m*
artificial [ˌɑrtɪ'fɪʃəl] *adj* Kunst–,

künstlich; (*emotion, smile*) gekünstelt
artillery [ɑr'tɪləri] *s* Artillerie *f*
artil'lery·man *s* (**-men**) Artillerist *m*
artisan ['ɑrtɪzən] *s* Handwerker –in
mf
artist ['ɑrtɪst] *s* Künstler –in *mf*
artistic [ɑr'tɪstɪk] *adj* künstlerisch
artistry ['ɑrtɪstri] *s* Kunstfertigkeit *f*
artless ['ɑrtlɪs] *adj* (*lacking art*) unkünstlerisch; (*made without skill*)
stümperhaft; (*ingenuous*) unbefangen
arts' and crafts' *spl* Kunstgewerbe *n*
arts' and sci'ences *spl* Geistes– und
Naturwissenschaften *pl*
arty ['ɑrti] *adj* (coll) gekünstelt
Aryan ['ɛrɪ·ən], ['ɑrjən] *adj* arisch ||
s Arier –in *mf;* (*language*) Arisch *n*
as [æz], [əz] *adv* wie; as...as (eben)so
...wie; **as far as Berlin** bis nach
Berlin; **as far as I know** soviel ich
weiß; **as far back as 1900** schon im
Jahre 1900; **as for me** was mich betrifft; **as if** als ob; **as long as** so-
lange; (*with the proviso that*) vorausgesetzt, daß; **as soon as** sobald wie;
as though als ob; **as well** ebensogut,
auch; **as yet** bis jetzt || *rel pron* wie,
was || *prep* als; **as a rule** in der
Regel || *conj* wie; (*while*) als,
während; (*because*) da, weil, indem;
as it were sozusagen
asbestos [æs'bɛstəs] *adj* Asbest– || *s*
Asbest *m*
ascend [ə'sɛnd] *tr* (*stairs*) hinaufstei-
gen; (*a throne, mountain*) besteigen
|| *intr* emporsteigen; (*said of a bal-
loon, plane*) aufsteigen
ascendancy [ə'sɛndənsi] *s* Überlegenheit *f*
ascension [ə'sɛnʃən] *s* Aufsteigen *n*
Ascen'sion Day' *s* Himmelfahrtstag *m*
ascent [ə'sɛnt] *s* (*on foot*) Besteigung
f; (*by vehicle*) Auffahrt *f;* (*upward
slope*) Steigung *f;* (& fig) Aufstieg *m*
ascertain [,æsər'ten] *tr* feststellen
ascetic [ə'sɛtɪk] *adj* asketisch || *s*
Asket –in *mf*
ascribe [ə'skraɪb] *tr*—**a. to** zuschreiben (*dat*)
aseptic [ə'sɛptɪk] *adj* aseptisch
ash [æʃ] *s* Asche *f;* (*tree*) Esche *f;*
ashes Asche *f;* (*mortal remains*)
sterbliche Überreste *pl*
ashamed [ə'ʃemd] *adj*—**be** (or **feel**)
a. (**of**) sich schämen (*genit*)
ash'can' *s* Ascheneimer *m*
ashen ['æʃən] *adj* aschgrau
ashore [ə'ʃor] *adv* (*position*) am Land;
(*direction*) ans Land
ash'tray' *s* Aschenbecher *m*
Ash' Wednes'day *s* Aschermittwoch *m*
Asia ['eʒə], ['eʃə] *s* Asien *n*
A'sia Mi'nor *s* Kleinasien *n*
aside [ə'saɪd] *adv* zur Seite; **a. from**
außer || *s* (theat) Seitenbemerkung *f*
asinine ['æsɪ,naɪn] *adj* eselhaft
ask [æsk] *tr* (*request*) bitten; (*demand*)
auffordern; (*a high price*) fordern;
(*inquire of*) fragen; **ask a question
(of s.o.)** (j–m) e-e Frage stellen; **ask
in** hereinbitten; **that is asking too
much** das ist zuviel verlangt || *intr*

fragen; **ask for** bitten um; **ask for
trouble** sich [*dat*] selbst Schwierigkeiten machen
askance [əs'kæns] *adv*—**look a. at**
schief ansehen
askew [ə'skju] *adv* schräg
ask'ing *s*—**for the a.** umsonst
asleep [ə'slip] *adj* schlafend; (*numb*)
eingeschlafen; **be a.** schlafen; **fall a.**
einschlafen
asp [æsp] *s* Natter *f*
asparagus [ə'spærəgəs] *s* Spargel *m*
aspect ['æspɛkt] *s* Gesichtspunkt *m*
aspen ['æspən] *s* Espe *f*
aspersion [ə'spʌrʒən] *s* (eccl) Bespren-
gung *f;* **cast aspersions on** verleumden
asphalt ['æsfɔlt], ['æsfælt] *s* Asphalt
m || *tr* asphaltieren
asphyxiate [æs'fɪksɪ,et] *tr* & *intr* ersticken
aspirant [ə'spaɪrənt] *s* Bewerber –in
mf
aspirate ['æspɪrɪt] *s* Hauchlaut *m* ||
['æspɪ,ret] *tr* behauchen
aspire [ə'spaɪr] *intr* (**after, to**) streben
(nach); **a. to** (*inf*) danach streben zu
(*inf*)
aspirin ['æspɪrɪn] *s* Aspirin *n*
ass [æs] *s* Esel *m;* (*vulg*) Arsch *m;*
make an ass of oneself (sl) sich
lächerlich machen
assail [ə'sel] *tr* angreifen, anfallen;
(*with questions*) bestürmen
assassin [ə'sæsɪn] *s* Meuchelmörder
–in *mf*
assassinate [ə'sæsɪ,net] *tr* ermorden
assassination [ə,sæsɪ'neʃən] *s* Meuchelmord *m*, Ermordung *f*
assault [ə'sɔlt] *s* Überfall *m;* (*rape*)
Vergewaltigung *f;* (*physical violence*)
(jur) tätlicher Angriff *m;* (*threat of
violence*) (jur) unmittelbare Bedro-
hung *f;* (mil) Sturm *m* || *tr* (er-)
stürmen, anfallen; (jur) tätlich beleidigen
assault' and bat'tery *s* schwere tätliche
Beleidigung *f*
assay [ə'se], ['æse] *s* Prüfung *f* ||
[ə'se] *tr* prüfen
assemble [ə'sɛmbəl] *tr* versammeln;
(mach) montieren || *intr* sich ver-
sammeln
assembly [ə'sɛmbli] *s* Versammlung *f;*
(mach) Montage *f;* (pol) Unterhaus
n
assem'bly line' *s* Fließband *n*
assent [ə'sɛnt] *s* Zustimmung *f* || *intr*
(**to**) zustimmen (*dat*)
assert [ə'sʌrt] *tr* behaupten; **a. oneself**
sich behaupten
assertion [ə'sʌrʃən] *s* Behauptung *f;*
(*of rights*) Geltendmachung *f*
assess [ə'sɛs] *tr* (*damage*) festsetzen;
(*property*) (**at**) (ab)schätzen (auf
acc); **assessed value** Schätzungswert
m
assessment [ə'sɛsmənt] *s* (*of damage*)
Festsetzung *f;* (*valuation*) Einschät-
zung *f;* (*of real estate*) Veranlagung
f
assessor [ə'sɛsər] *s* Steuereinschätzer
m

asset ['æset] *s* Vorzug *m;* (com) Aktivposten *m;* **assets** Vermögenswerte *pl;* **assets and liabilities** Aktiva und Passiva *pl*

assiduous [ə'sɪdʒu·əs] *adj* emsig

assign [ə'saɪn] *tr* zuweisen; (*homework*) aufgeben; (*transfer*) (jur) abtreten; (mil) zuteilen

assignment [ə'saɪnmənt] *s* Zuweisung *f;* (*homework*) Aufgabe *f;* (*task*) Auftrag *m,* Aufgabe *f;* (*transference*) (jur) Abtretung *f;* (*to a unit*) (mil) Zuteilung *f*

assimilate [ə'sɪmɪ‚let] *tr* angleichen ‖ *intr* sich angleichen

assimilation [ə‚sɪmɪ'leʃən] *s* Assimilierung *f,* Angleichung *f*

assist [ə'sɪst] *s* (sport) Zuspiel *n* ‖ *tr* beistehen (*dat*) ‖ *intr*—**a. in** beistehen bei, behilflich sein bei

assistance [ə'sɪstəns] *s* Hilfe *f*

assistant [ə'sɪstənt] *adj* Hilfs-, Unter- ‖ *s* (*helper*) Gehilfe *m,* Gehilfin *f*

associate [ə'soʃɪ·ɪt] *adj* Mit-, beigeordnet; (*member*) außerordentlich ‖ *s* (*companion*) Gefährte *m,* Gefährtin *f;* (*colleague*) Kollege *m,* Kollegin *f;* (com) Partner –in *mf* ‖ [ə'soʃɪ‚et] *tr* verbinden ‖ *intr* (**with**) verkehren (mit)

asso'ciate profes'sor *s* außerordentlicher Professor *m*

association [ə‚soʃɪ'eʃən] *s* (*connection*) Verbindung *f;* (*social intercourse*) Verkehr *m;* (*society*) Verband *m;* (*suggested ideas, feelings*) Assoziation *f*

assonance ['æsənəns] *s* Assonanz *f*

assorted [ə'sɔrtɪd] *adj* verschieden

assortment [ə'sɔrtmənt] *s* Sortiment *n*

assuage [ə'swedʒ] *tr* (*pain*) lindern; (*hunger*) befriedigen; (*thirst*) stillen

assume [ə's(j)um] *tr* (*a fact as true; a certain shape, property, habit*) annehmen; (*a duty*) auf sich nehmen; (*office*) antreten; (*power*) ergreifen; **assuming that** vorausgesetzt, daß

assumed' *adj* (*feigned*) erheuchelt; **a. name** Deckname *m*

assumption [ə'sʌmpʃən] *s* (*supposition*) Annahme *f;* (*e.g., of power*) Übernahme *f*

assurance [ə'ʃurəns] *s* Versicherung *f*

assure [ə'ʃur] *tr* versichern

aster ['æstər] *s* Aster *f*

asterisk ['æstə‚rɪsk] *s* Sternchen *n*

astern [ə'stʌrn] *adv* achtern, achteraus

asthma ['æzmə] *s* Asthma *n*

astonish [ə'stɑnɪʃ] *tr* in Erstaunen setzen; **be astonished at** staunen über (*acc*), sich wundern über (*acc*)

aston'ishing *adj* erstaunlich

astonishment [ə'stɑnɪʃmənt] *s* Erstaunen *n,* Verwunderung *f*

astound [ə'staund] *tr* überraschen

astound'ing *adj* erstaunlich

astray [ə'stre] *adv*—**go a.** irregehen; **lead a.** irreführen

astride [ə'straɪd] *adv* rittlings ‖ *prep* (*a road*) an beiden Seiten (*genit*); (*a horse*) rittlings auf (*dat*)

astringent [əs'trɪndʒənt] *adj* stopfend ‖ *s* Stopfmittel *n*

astrology [ə'strɑlədʒi] *s* Astrologie *f*

astronaut ['æstrə‚nɔt] *s* Astronaut *m*

astronautics [‚æstrə'nɔtɪks] *s* Raumfahrtwissenschaft *f,* Astronautik *f*

astronomer [ə'strɑnəmər] *s* Astronom –in *mf*

astronomic(al) [‚æstrə'nɑmɪk(əl)] *adj* astronomisch

astronomy [ə'strɑnəmi] *s* Astronomie *f*

astute [ə'st(j)ut] *adj* scharfsinnig; (*cunning*) schlau

asunder [ə'sʌndər] *adv* auseinander

asylum [ə'saɪləm] *s* (*refuge*) Asyl *n;* (*for the insane*) Irrenhaus *n*

at [æt], [ət] *prep* (*position*) an (*dat*), auf (*dat*), in (*dat*), bei (*dat*), zu (*dat*); (*direction*) auf (*acc*), gegen (*acc*), nach (*dat*), zu (*dat*); (*manner, circumstance*) auf (*acc*), in (*dat*), unter (*dat*), bei (*dat*), zu (*dat*); (*time*) um (*acc*), bei (*dat*), auf (*dat*) zu (*dat*); **at all** (*in questions*) überhaupt; **at high prices** zu hohen Preisen; **even at that** sogar so

atheism ['eθi‚ɪzəm] *s* Atheismus *m*

atheist ['eθi·ɪst] *s* Atheist –in *mf*

Athens ['æθɪns] *s* Athen *n*

athlete ['æθlit] *s* Sportler –in *mf*

ath'lete's foot' *s* Fußflechte *f*

athletic [æθ'letɪk] *adj* athletisch, Sport-, Turn- ‖ **athletics** *s* Athletik *f*

Atlantic [æt'læntɪk] *adj* atlantisch ‖ *s* Atlantik *m*

atlas ['ætləs] *s* Atlas *m*

atmosphere ['ætməs‚fɪr] *s* (& fig) Atmosphäre *f*

atmospheric [‚ætməs'ferɪk] *adj* atmosphärisch

atom ['ætəm] *s* Atom *n*

atomic [ə'tɑmɪk] *adj* atomisch, atomar, Atom-

atom'ic age' *s* Atomzeitalter *n*

atom'ic bomb' *s* Atombombe *f*

atom'ic pow'er *s* Atomkraft *f;* **atomic powers** (pol) Atommächte *pl*

atomizer ['ætə‚maɪzər] *s* Zerstäuber *m*

atone [ə'ton] *intr*—**a. for** büßen

atonement [ə'tonmənt] *s* Buße *f*

atrocious [ə'troʃəs] *adj* gräßlich

atrocity [ə'trɑsɪti] *s* Greueltat *f*

atro·phy ['ætrəfi] *s* Verkümmerung *f,* Atrophie *f* ‖ *v* (*pret & pp* –phied) *tr* auszehren ‖ *intr* verkümmern

attach [ə'tætʃ] *tr* (*with glue, stitches, tacks*) (**to**) anheften (an *acc*); (*connect*) (**to**) befestigen (an *acc*); (*importance*) (**to**) beimessen (*dat*); (*a person*) (jur) verhaften; (*a thing*) (jur) beschlagnahmen; (mil) (**to**) zuteilen (*dat*); **a. oneself to** sich anschließen an (*acc*); **be attached to** festhalten an (*dat*); (fig) verwachsen sein mit

attaché [‚ætə'ʃe] *s* Attaché *m*

attaché' case' *s* Aktenköfferchen *n*

attachment [ə'tætʃmənt] *s* Befestigung *f;* (*regard*) (**to**) Zuneigung *f* (*zu*); (*device*) Zusatzgerät *n;* (*of a person*) (jur) Verhaftung *f;* (*of a thing*) (jur) Beschlagnahme *f*

attack [ə'tæk] *s* Angriff *m;* (pathol)

Anfall *m* ‖ *tr* & *intr* angreifen;
(pathol) überfallen
attain [ə'ten] *tr* erreichen, erzielen ‖
intr—**a. to** erreichen
attainment [ə'tenmənt] *s* Erreichen *n;*
attainments Fertigkeiten *pl*
attempt [ə'tempt] *s* Versuch *m; (as-sault)* Attentat *n* ‖ *tr* versuchen
attend [ə'tend] *tr* beiwohnen *(dat);*
(school, church) besuchen; *(accom-pany)* begleiten; *(a patient)* behan-deln ‖ *intr*—**a. to** nachgehen *(dat),*
erledigen
attendance [ə'tendəns] *s* Besuch *m;*
(number in attendance) Besucherzahl
f; (med) Behandlung *f*
attendant [ə'tendənt] *s* *(servant, waiter)* Diener –in *mf; (keeper)*
Wärter –in *mf; (at a gas station)*
Tankwart *m; (escort)* Begleiter –in
mf
attention [ə'tenʃən] *s* Aufmerksamkeit
f; Acht *f;* **a. Mr. X.** zu Händen von
Herrn X; **call a. to** hinweisen auf
(acc); **call s.o.'s a. to** j–n aufmerk-sam machen auf *(acc);* **pay a.** acht-geben; **pay a. to** achten auf *(acc);*
stand at a. stillstehen ‖ *interj* (mil)
Achtung!
attentive [ə'tentɪv] *adj* aufmerksam
attenuate [ə'tɛnju ‚et] *tr (dilute, thin)*
verdünnen; *(weaken)* abschwächen
attest [ə'tɛst] *tr* bezeugen ‖ *intr*—**a. to**
bezeugen
attic ['ætɪk] *s* Dachboden *m; (as liv-ing quarters)* Mansarde *f*
attire [ə'taɪr] *s* Putz *m* ‖ *tr* kleiden
attitude ['ætɪ ‚t(j)ud] *s* Haltung *f;* (aer,
rok) Lage *f*
attorney [ə'tʌrni] *s* Rechtsanwalt *m*
attor'ney gen'eral *s* **(attorneys general)**
Justizminister *m*
attract [ə'trækt] *tr* anziehen, reizen;
(attention) erregen
attraction [ə'trækʃən] *s* Anziehungs-kraft *f; (that which attracts)* Anzie-hungspunkt *m; (in a circus, variety show)* Attraktion *f;* (theat) Zugstück
n
attractive [ə'træktɪv] *adj* reizvoll;
(price, offer) günstig
attribute ['ætrɪ ‚bjut] *s* Attribut *n* ‖
[ə'trɪbjut] *tr* **(to)** zuschreiben *(dat)*
attrition [ə'trɪʃən] *s* Abnutzung *f,* Ver-schleiß *m*
attune [ə't(j)un] *tr* **(to)** abstimmen
(auf *acc)*
auburn ['ɔbərn] *adj* kastanienbraun
auction ['ɔkʃən] *s* Auktion *f* ‖ *tr*—**a.
off** versteigern; **be auctioned off**
unter den Hammer kommen
auctioneer [‚ɔkʃən'ɪr] *s* Versteigerer
–in *mf*
audacious [ɔ'deʃəs] *adj (daring)* kühn;
(brazen) keck
audacity [ɔ'dæsɪti] *s (daring)* Kühn-heit *f; (insolence)* Unverschämtheit *f*
audience ['ɔdɪ·əns] *s (spectators)* Pu-blikum *n; (formal hearing)* Audienz
f; (rad) Zuhörerschaft *f;* (telv) Fern-sehpublikum *n*
au'dio fre'quency ['ɔdɪ ‚o] *s* Tonfre-quenz *f,* Hörfrequenz *f*

au'dio-vis'ual *adj* audiovisuell; **a. aids**
Lehrmittel *pl*
audit ['ɔdɪt] *s* Rechnungsprüfung *f* ‖
tr prüfen, revidieren; *(a lecture)* als
Gasthörer belegen
audition [ɔ'dɪʃən] *s* Hörprobe *f* ‖ *tr*
vorspielen (or vorsingen) lassen ‖
intr vorspielen, vorsingen
auditor ['ɔdɪtər] *s* (com) Rechnungs-prüfer –in *mf;* (educ) Gasthörer –in
mf
auditorium [‚ɔdɪ'tɔrɪ·əm] *s* Hörsaal *m*
auger ['ɔgər] *s* Bohrer *m*
augment [ɔg'ment] *tr (in size)* ver-größern; *(in number)* vermehren ‖
intr sich vergrößern; sich vermehren
augur ['ɔgər] *s* Augur *m* ‖ *intr* weis-sagen; **a. well for** Gutes versprechen
für
augury ['ɔgəri] *s* Weissagung *f*
august [ɔ'gʌst] *adj* erhaben ‖ **August**
['ɔgəst] *s* August *m*
aunt [ænt], [ɑnt] *s* Tante *f*
auricle ['ɔrɪkəl] *s* äußeres Ohr *n; (of
the heart)* Herzohr *n*
auspices ['ɔspɪsɪz] *spl* Auspizien *pl*
auspicious [ɔs'pɪʃəs] *adj* glückverhei-ßend
austere [ɔs'tɪr] *adj (stern)* streng; *(sim-ple)* einfach; *(frugal)* genügsam;
(style) schmucklos
Australia [ɔ'streljə] *s* Australien *n*
Australian [ɔ'streljən] *adj* australisch
‖ *s* Australier –in *mf*
Austria ['ɔstrɪ·ə] *s* Österreich *n*
Austrian ['ɔstrɪ·ən] *adj* österreichisch
‖ *s* Österreicher –in *mf; (dialect)*
Österreichisch *n*
authentic [ɔ'θentɪk] *adj* authentisch
authenticate [ɔ'θentɪ ‚ket] *tr (establish
as genuine)* als echt erweisen; *(a
document)* beglaubigen
author ['ɔθər] *s (of a book)* Autor –in
mf; (creator) Urheber –in *mf*
authoritative [ɔ'θɔrɪ ‚tetɪv] *adj* maß-gebend
authority [ɔ'θɔrɪti] *s (power; expert)*
Autorität *f; (right)* Recht *n; (ap-proval)* Genehmigung *f; (source)*
Quelle *f; (commanding influence)*
Ansehen *n; (authoritative body)* Be-hörde *f;* **on one's own a.** auf eigene
Verantwortung; **the authorities** die
Behörden
authorize ['ɔθə ‚raɪz] *tr* autorisieren
au'thorship' *s* Autorschaft *f*
au·to ['ɔto] *s* **(–tos)** Auto *n*
autobiography [‚ɔtobaɪ'ɑgrəfi] *s*
Selbstbiographie *f*
autocratic [‚ɔtə'krætɪk] *adj* autokra-tisch
autograph ['ɔtə ‚græf] *s* Autogramm *n*
‖ *tr* autographieren
automat ['ɔtə ‚mæt] *s* Automaten-restaurant *n*
automatic [‚ɔtə'mætɪk] *adj* automa-tisch ‖ *s* Selbstladepistole *f*
automat'ic transmis'sion *s* Automatik
f
automation [‚ɔtə'meʃən] *s* Automa-tion *f*
automa·ton [ɔ'tɑmə ‚tɑn] *s* **(–tons** &
–ta [tə]) Automat *m*

automobile [‚ɔtəmoˈbil] s Automobil n

automotive [‚ɔtəˈmotɪv] adj Auto-

autonomous [ɔˈtʌnəməs] adj autonom

autonomy [ɔˈtɑnəmi] s Autonomie f

autopsy [ˈɔtɑpsi] s Obduktion f

autumn [ˈɔtəm] adj Herbst– ‖ s Herbst m

autumnal [ɔˈtʌmnəl] adj herbstlich

auxiliary [ɔgˈzɪljəri] adj Hilfs– ‖ s (helper) Helfer –in mf; (gram) Hilfszeitwort n; **auxiliaries** (mil) Hilfstruppen pl

avail [əˈvel] s—**to no a.** nutzlos; **without a.** vergeblich ‖ tr nützen (dat); **a. oneself of** sich bedienen (genit) ‖ intr nützen

available [əˈveləbəl] adj vorhanden; (articles, products) erhältlich; (e.g., documents) zugänglich; **be a.** (for consultation, etc.) zu sprechen sein; **make a. (to)** zur Verfügung stellen (dat)

avalanche [ˈævə‚læntʃ] s Lawine f

avarice [ˈævərɪs] s Habsucht f, Geiz m

avaricious [‚ævəˈrɪʃəs] adj geizig

avenge [əˈvendʒ] tr (a person) rächen; (a crime) ahnden; **a. oneself on** sich rächen an (dat)

avenger [əˈvendʒər] s Rächer –in mf

avenue [ˈævə‚n(j)u] s (wide street) Straße f; (fig) Weg m

average [ˈævərɪdʒ] adj Durchschnitts– ‖ s Durchschnitt m; (naut) Havarie f; **on the a.** im Durchschnitt ‖ tr (amount to, as a mean quantity) durchschnittlich betragen; (find the average of) den Durchschnitt berechnen von; (earn on the average) durchschnittlich verdienen; (travel on the average) durchschnittlich zurücklegen

averse [əˈvʌrs] adj **(to)** abgeneigt (dat)

aversion [əˈvʌrʒən] s **(to)** Abneigung f (gegen)

avert [əˈvʌrt] tr abwenden

aviary [ˈevɪ‚ɛri] s Vogelhaus n

aviation [‚evɪˈeʃən] s Flugwesen n

aviator [ˈevɪ‚etər] s Flieger –in mf

avid [ˈævɪd] adj gierig

avocation [‚ævəˈkeʃən] s Nebenbeschäftigung f

avoid [əˈvɔɪd] tr (a person) meiden; (a thing) vermeiden

avoidable [əˈvɔɪdəbəl] adj vermeidbar

avoidance [əˈvɔɪdəns] s (of a person) Meidung f; (of a thing) Vermeidung f

avow [əˈvaʊ] tr bekennen, gestehen

avowal [əˈvaʊ·əl] s Bekenntnis n

avowed′ adj (declared) erklärt; (acknowledged) offen anerkannt

await [əˈwet] tr erwarten

awake [əˈwek] adj wach, munter ‖ v (pret & pp **awoke** [əˈwok] & **awaked**) tr wecken; (fig) erwecken ‖ intr erwachen

awaken [əˈweken] tr wecken; (fig) erwecken ‖ intr erwachen

awak′ening s Erwachen n; **a rude a.** ein unsanftes Erwachen

award [əˈwɔrd] s Preis m, Prämie f ‖ tr (to) zuerkennen (dat)

aware [əˈwer] adj—**be a. of** sich [dat] bewußt sein (genit)

awareness [əˈwernɪs] s Bewußtsein n

awash [əˈwɑʃ] adj überschwemmt

away [əˈwe] adj abwesend; (on a trip) verreist; (sport) Auswärts– ‖ adv fort, (hin)weg; **do a. with** abschaffen; **make a. with** (kill) umbringen

awe [ɔ] s (of) Ehrfurcht f (vor dat); **stand in awe of s.o.** vor j–m Ehrfurcht haben

awesome [ˈɔsəm] adj ehrfurchtgebietend

awful [ˈɔfəl] adj ehrfurchtgebietend; (coll) furchtbar

awfully [ˈɔfəli] adv (coll) furchtbar

awhile [əˈhwaɪl] adv eine Zeitlang

awkward [ˈɔkwərd] adj ungeschickt; (situation) peinlich

awl [ɔl] s Ahle f, Pfriem m

awning [ˈɔnɪŋ] s Markise f

awry [əˈraɪ] adv—**go a.** schiefgehen

ax [æks] s Axt f, Beil n

axiom [ˈæksɪ·əm] s Axiom n

axiomatic [‚æksɪ·əˈmætɪk] adj axiomatisch

axis [ˈæksɪs] s (axes [ˈæksiz]) Achse f

axle [ˈæksəl] s Achse f

ay(e) [aɪ] adv (yes) ja; **aye, aye, sir!** zu Befehl, Herr (Leutnant, etc.) ‖ s Ja n, Jastimme f; **the ayes have it** die Mehrheit ist dafür

azalea [əˈzeljə] s Azalee f

azure [ˈæʒər] adj azurblau ‖ s Azur m

B

B, b [bi] zweiter Buchstabe des englischen Alphabets; (mus) H n; **B flat** B n; **B sharp** His n

babble [ˈbæbəl] s Geschwätz n; (of brook) Geplätscher n ‖ tr schwätzen ‖ intr schwätzen; (said of a brook) plätschern

babe [beb] s Kind n; (naive person) Kindskopf m; (pretty girl) Puppe f

baboon [bæˈbun] s (zool) Pavian m

ba·by [ˈbebi] s Baby n; (youngest child) Nesthäkchen n ‖ v (pret & pp –bied) tr verzärteln

ba′by bot′tle s Saugflasche f

ba′by car′riage s Kinderwagen m

ba′by grand′ s Stutzflügel m

ba′by pow′der s Kinderpuder m

ba′by-sit′ v (pret & pp –sat; ger –sitting) intr Kinder hüten

ba′by-sit′ter s Babysitter m

ba′by talk′ s Babysprache f
ba′by teeth′ spl Milchzähne pl
baccalaureate [‚bækə'lɔrɪ·ɪt] s (bachelor's degree) Bakkalaureat n; (service) Gottesdienst m bei der akademischen Promotion
bacchanal ['bækənəl] s (devotee) Bacchantin f; (orgy) Bacchanal n
bachelor ['bætʃələr] s Junggeselle m
bach′elorhood′ s Junggesellenstand m
Bach′elor of Arts′ s Bakkalaureus m der Geisteswissenschaften
Bach′elor of Sci′ence s Bakkalaureus m der Naturwissenschaften
bacil·lus [bə'sɪləs] s (–li [laɪ]) Bazillus m, Stäbchenbakterie f
back [bæk] adj Hinter–, Rück– ‖ s (of a man, animal) Rücken m, Kreuz n; (of a hand, book, knife, mountain) Rücken m; (of a head, house, door, picture, sheet) Rückseite f; (of a fabric) linke Seite f; (of a seat) Rückenlehne f; (of a coin) Kehrseite f; (of clothing) Rückenteil m; (sport) Verteidiger m; at the b. of (e.g., a room) hinten in (dat); b. to b. (coll) nacheinander; behind s.o.'s b. hinter j–s Rücken; have one's b. to the wall an die Wand gedrückt sein; turn one's b. on s.o. (& fig) j–m den Rücken kehren ‖ adv zurück; b. and forth hin und her; b. home bei uns (zulande); ‖ tr (a person) den Rücken decken (dat); (a candidate, product) befürworten; (a horse) setzen auf (acc); b. up (a car) rückwärts laufen lassen; b. water rückwärts rudern; das Schiff rückwärts fahren lassen; (fig) sich zurückziehen ‖ intr —b. down klein beigeben; b. down from abstehen von; b. out of zurücktreten von; b. up zurückfahren; zurückgehen; (said of a sewer) zurückfließen
back′ache′ s Rückenschmerzen pl
back′bit′ing s Anschwärzerei f
back′bone′ s Rückgrat n; (fig) Willenskraft f
back′break′ing adj mühsam
back′ door′ s Hintertür f
back′drop′ s (fig & theat) Hintergrund m
backer ['bækər] s Förderer m, Unterstützer m; (com) Hintermann m
back′fire′ s Fehlzündung f ‖ intr fehlzünden; (fig) nach hinten losgehen
back′ground′ adj Hintergrund– ‖ s (& fig) Hintergrund m; (e.g., of an applicant) Vorbildung f, Erfahrung f
back′hand′ s (tennis) Rückhandschlag m
back′hand′ed adj Rückhand–; (compliment) zweideutig
back′ing s Unterstützung f; (material) versteifende Ausfütterung f
back′lash′ s (& fig) Rückschlag m; (mach) toter Gang m
back′log′ s Rückstand m
back′ or′der s rückständiger Auftrag m
back′ pay′ s rückständiger Lohn m
back′ seat′ s Rücksitz m
back′side′ s Rückseite f; (coll) Gesäß n

back′space′ intr den Wagen zurückschieben
back′space key′ s Rücktaste f
back′spin′ s Rückeffet n
back′stage′ adv hinten auf der Bühne
back′ stairs′ spl Hintertreppe f
back′stop′ s (baseball) Ballfang m
back′ stretch′ s Gegengerade f
back′stroke′ s Rückenschwimmen n
back′swept′ adj pfeilförmig
back′ talk′ s freche Antworten pl
back′track′ intr denselben Weg zurückgehen; (fig) e–n Rückzieher machen
back′up′ s (stand-by) Beistand m; (in traffic) Verkehrsstauung f
back′up light′ s (aut) Rückfahrscheinwerfer m
backward ['bækwərd] adj rückwärts gerichtet, Rück–; (country) zurückständig; (in development) zurückgeblieben; (shy) zurückhaltend ‖ adv rückwärts, zurück; (fig) verkehrt; b. and forward vor und zurück
backwardness ['bækwərdnɪs] s Rückständigkeit f; (shyness) Zurückhaltung f
back′wash′ s zurücklaufende Strömung f
back′wa′ter s Rückstau m; (fig) Öde f
back′woods′ spl Hinterwälder pl
back′yard′ s Hinterhof m
bacon ['bekən] s Speck m; bring home the b. (sl) es schaffen
bacteria [bæk'tɪrɪ·ə] spl Bakterien pl
bacteriological [bæk‚tɪrɪ·ə'lɑdʒɪkəl] adj bakteriologisch
bacteriology [bæk‚tɪrɪ'ɑlədʒi] s Bakteriologie f, Bakterienkunde f
bacteri·um [bæk'tɪrɪ·əm] s (–a [ə]) Bakterie f
bad [bæd] adj schlecht, schlimm; (unfavorable) ungünstig; (risk) zweifelhaft; (debt) uneinbringlich; (check) ungedeckt; (blood) böse; (breath) übelriechend; (language) anstößig; (pain) stark; bad for schädlich (dat); from bad to worse immer schlimmer; I feel bad about it es tut mir leid; too bad! schade!
bad′ egg′ s (sl) übler Kunde m
badge [bædʒ] s Abzeichen n
badger ['bædʒər] s Dachs m ‖ tr quälen
bad′ luck′ s Ünglück n, Pech n
badly ['bædli] adv schlecht, übel; (coll) dringend; b. wounded schwerverwundet; be b. off übel dran sein
badminton ['bædmɪntən] s Federballspiel n
bad′-tem′pered adj schlecht gelaunt
baffle ['bæfəl] s Sperre f; (on loudspeaker) Schallwand f ‖ tr verwirren; (gas) drosseln
baf′fling adj verwirrend
bag [bæg] s Sack m; (for small items) Tüte f; (for travel) Reisetasche f; (sl) Frauenzimmer n; (hunt) Strecke f; bag and baggage mit Sack und Pack; it's in the bag wir haben wir in der Tasche ‖ v (pret & pp bagged; ger bagging) tr einsacken; (hunt) zur Strecke bringen ‖ intr sich bauschen
baggage ['bægɪdʒ] s Gepäck n

bag'gage car' s Gepäckwagen m
bag'gage check' s Gepäckschein m
bag'gage count'er s Gepäckabfertigung f
bag'gage room' s Gepäckaufbewahrung f
baggy ['bægɪ] adj bauschig
bag'pipe' s Dudelsack m; **play the b.** dudeln
bail [bel] s Kaution f; **be out on b.** gegen Kaution auf freiem Fuß sein; **put up b. for** bürgen für || tr—**b. out** (water) ausschöpfen; (fig) retten; (jur) durch Kaution aus der Haft befreien || intr Wasser schöpfen; **b. out** (aer) abspringen
bailiff ['belɪf] s (agr) Gutsverwalter m; (jur) Gerichtsvollzieher m
bailiwick ['belɪwɪk] s (fig) Spezialgebiet n; (jur) Amtsbezirk m
bait [bet] s (& fig) Köder m || tr (traps) mit Köder versehen; (lure) ködern; (harass) quälen
bake [bek] tr (bread) backen; (meat) braten; (in a kiln) brennen || intr backen; (meat) braten
baked' goods' spl Gebäck n, Backwaren pl
baked' pota'to s gebackene Pellkartoffel f
baker ['bekər] s Bäcker –in mf
bak'er's doz'en s dreizehn Stück pl
bakery ['bekəri] s Bäckerei f
bak'ing pow'der s Backpulver n
bak'ing so'da s Backpulver n
balance ['bæləns] s (equilibrium) Gleichgewicht n; (remainder) Rest m; (scales) Waage f; (in a bank account) Bankguthaben n; (fig) Fassung f; (com) Bilanz f; || tr balancieren; (offset) abgleichen; (make come out even) ausgleichen || intr balancieren
bal'ance of pay'ments s Devisenbilanz f
bal'ance of pow'er s Gleichgewicht n der Kräfte
bal'ance sheet' s Bilanz f
bal'ance wheel' s (horol) Unruh f
balcony ['bælkəni] s Balkon m; (theat) Rang m
bald [bɔld] adj kahl; (eagle) weißköpfig; (fig) unverblümt
bald'head'ed adj kahlköpfig
baldness ['bɔldnɪs] s Kahlheit f
bald' spot' s Kahlstelle f
bale [bel] s Ballen m || tr in Ballen verpacken
baleful ['belfəl] adj unheilvoll
balk [bɔk] intr (at) scheuen (vor dat)
Balkan ['bɔlkən] adj Balkan– || s— **the Balkans** der Balkan
balky ['bɔki] adj störrisch
ball [bɔl] s Ball m; (dance) Ball m; (of yarn) Knäuel m & n; (of the foot) Ballen m; **be on the b.** (coll) bei der Sache sein; **have a lot on the b.** (coll) viel auf dem Kasten haben
ballad ['bæləd] s Ballade f
ball'-and-sock'et joint' s Kugelgelenk n
ballast ['bæləst] s (aer, naut) Ballast m; (rr) Schotter m || tr (aer, naut) mit Ballast beladen; (rr) beschottern

ball' bear'ing s Kugellager n
ballerina [,bælə'rinə] s Ballerina f
ballet [bæ'le] s Ballett n
ball' han'dling s (sport) Balltechnik f
ballistic [bə'lɪstɪk] adj ballistisch || **ballistics** s Ballistik f
balloon [bə'lun] s Ballon m
ballot ['bælət] s Stimmzettel m || intr abstimmen
bal'lot box' s Wahlurne f
ball'-point pen' s Kugelschreiber m
ball'room' s Ballsaal m, Tanzsaal m
ballyhoo ['bælɪ,hu] s Tamtam n || tr Tamtam machen um
balm [bam] s (& fig) Balsam m
balmy ['bami] adj mild, lind; **be b.** (coll) e–n Tick haben
baloney [bə'loni] s (sausage) (coll) Bolognawurst f; (sl) Quatsch m
balsam ['bɔlsəm] s Balsam m
Baltic ['bɔltɪk] adj baltisch || s Ostsee f
baluster ['bæləstər] s Geländersäule f
balustrade ['bæləs,tred] s Brüstung f
bamboo [bæm'bu] s Bambus m, Bambusrohr n
bamboozle [bæm'buzəl] tr (cheat) anschmieren; (mislead) irreführen; (perplex) verwirren
ban [bæn] s Verbot n; (eccl) Bann m; || v (pret & pp **banned**; ger **banning**) tr verbieten
banal ['benəl] adj banal
banana [bə'nænə] s Banane f; (tree) Bananenbaum m
band [bænd] s (e.g., of a hat) Band n; (stripe) Steifen m; (gang) Bande f; (mus) Musikkapelle f; (rad) Band n || intr—**b. together** sich zusammenrotten
bandage ['bændɪdʒ] s Verband m || tr verbinden
Band'-Aid' s (trademark) Schnellverband m
bandit ['bændɪt] s Bandit m
band'lead'er s Kapellmeister m
band' saw' s Bandsäge f
band'stand' s Musikpavillon m
band'wag'on s—**climb the b.** mitlaufen
bane [ben] s Ruin m
baneful ['benfəl] adj verderblich
bang [bæŋ] s Knall m; **bangs** Ponyfrisur f; **with a b.** mit Krach || tr knallen lassen; (a door) zuschlagen; || intr knallen; (said of a door) zuschlagen; || interj bums! paff!
bang'-up' adj (sl) tipptopp, prima
banish ['bænɪʃ] tr verbannen
banishment ['bænɪʃmənt] s Verbannung f
banister ['bænɪstər] s Geländer n
bank [bæŋk] s Bank f; (of a river) Ufer n; (in a road) Überhöhung f; (aer) Schräglage f; (rr) Böschung f; || tr (money) in e–r Bank deponieren; (a road) überhöhen; (aer) in Schräglage bringen || intr (at) ein Bankkonto haben (bei); (aer) in die Kurve gehen; **b. on** bauen auf (acc)
bank' account' s Bankkonto n
bank' bal'ance s Bankguthaben n
bank'book' s Sparbuch n, Bankbuch n
banker ['bæŋkər] s Bankier –in mf

bank'ing s Bankwesen n
bank' note' s Geldschein m
bank'roll' s Rolle f von Geldscheinen
|| tr (sl) finanzieren
bankrupt ['bæŋkrʌpt] adj bankrott; **go
b.** Pleite machen || tr bankrott
machen
bankruptcy ['bæŋkrʌptsi] s Bankrott m
bank' state'ment s Bankausweis m
bank' tell'er s Kassierer –in mf
banner ['bænər] s Fahne f, Banner n
banquet ['baŋkwɪt] s Bankett n || intr
tafeln
banter ['bæntər] s Neckerei f || intr
necken
baptism ['bæptɪzəm] s Taufe f
baptismal [bæp'tɪzməl] adj Tauf–
baptis'mal certi'ficate s Taufschein m
bap'tism of fire' s Feuertaufe f
Baptist ['bæptɪst] s Baptist –in mf,
Wiedertäufer m
baptistery ['bæptɪstəri] s Taufkapelle
f
baptize [bæp'taɪz] tr taufen
bar [bɑr] s Stange f; (of a door, window) Riegel m; (of gold, etc.) Barren
m; (of chocolate, soap) Riegel m;
(barroom) Bar f; (counter) Schanktisch m; (obstacle) (to) Schranke f
(gegen); (jur) Gerichtshof m, An-
waltschaft f; (bar line) (mus) Takt-
strich m; (measure) Takt m; (naut)
Barre f; **be admitted to the bar** zur
Advokatur zugelassen werden; **be-
hind bars** hinter Gittern; || prep—
bar none ohne Ausnahme || v (pret
& pp barred; ger barring) tr (a door)
verriegeln; (a window) vergittern;
(the way) versperren; **bar s.o. from**
j–n hindern an (dat)
barb [bɑrb] s Widerhaken m; (fig)
Stachelrede f; (bot) Bart m
barbarian [bɑr'berɪ-ən] s Barbar m
barbaric [bɑr'bærɪk] adj barbarisch
barbarism ['bɑrbə,rɪzəm] s Barbarei
f; (gram) Barbarismus m
barbarity [bɑr'berɪti] s Barbarei f
barbarous ['bɑrbərəs] adj barbarisch
barbecue ['bɑrbɪ,kju] s am Spieß (or
am Rost) gebratenes Fleisch n; (grill)
Bratrost m; (outdoor meal) Garten-
grillfest n || tr am Spieß (or am Rost)
braten
barbed' wire' s Stacheldraht m
barbed'-wire entan'glement s Drahtverhau m
barber ['bɑrbər] s Friseur m
bar'ber chair' s Friseursessel m
bar'bershop' s Friseurladen m
bard [bɑrd] s Barde m
bare [ber] adj nackt, bloß; (tree, wall)
kahl; (facts) nackt; (majority) knapp
|| tr entblößen; (heart, thoughts)
offenbaren; (teeth) fletschen
bare'back' adj & adv sattellos
bare'faced' adj unverschämt
bare'foot' adj & adv barfuß
bare'head'ed adj & adv barhäuptig
barely ['berli] adv kaum, bloß
bar'fly' s Kneipenhocker m
bargain ['bɑrgɪn] s (deal) Geschäft n;
(cheap purchase) Sonderangebot n;
into the b. obendrein; **it's a b.!** abge-

macht! || tr—**b. away** mit Verlust
verkaufen || intr handeln; **b. for** ver-
handeln über (acc)
bar'gain price' s Preisschlager m
bar'gain sale' s Sonderverkauf m
barge [bɑrdʒ] s Lastkahn m; || intr—
b. in hereinstürzen; **b. into** stürzen
in (acc)
baritone ['bærɪ,ton] s Bariton m
barium ['berɪ-əm] s Barium n
bark [bɑrk] s (of a tree) Rinde f; (of a
dog) Bellen n, Gebell n; (boat) Barke
f; || tr—**b. out** bellend hervorstoßen
|| intr bellen; **b. at** anbellen
barker ['bɑrkər] s Anreißer m
barley ['bɑrli] s Gerste f; **grain of b.**
Graupe f
bar'maid' s Schankmädchen n, Bar-
dame f
barn [bɑrn] s Scheune f; (for animals)
Stall m
barnacle ['bɑrnəkəl] s Entenmuschel f
barn'storm' intr auf dem Lande
Theateraufführungen versanstalten;
(pol) auf dem Lande Wahlreden halten
barn'yard' s Scheunenhof m
barometer [bə'rɑmɪtər] s Barometer n
barometric [,bærə'metrɪk] adj baro-
metrisch
baron ['bærən] s Baron m
baroness ['bærənɪs] s Baronin f
baroque [bə'rok] adj barock || s
(style, period) Barock m & n
barracks ['bærəks] s (temporary wood-
en structure) Baracke f; (mil) Kaserne f
barrage [bə'rɑʒ] s Sperrfeuer n; **moving b.** Sperrfeuerwalze f
barrel ['bærəl] s Faß n, Tonne f; (of a
gun) Lauf m; (of money, fun) große
Menge f; **have over the b.** (sl) in der
Gewalt haben || intr (coll) rasen,
sausen
barren ['bærən] adj dürr, unfruchtbar;
(landscape) kahl
barricade ['bærɪ,ked] s Barrikade f
|| tr verbarrikadieren
barrier ['bærɪ-ər] s Schranke f, Schlag-
baum m; (e.g., on a street) Sperre f
bar'room' s Schenkstube f, Bar f
bartend ['bɑr,tend] intr Getränke aus-
schenken
bar'tend'er s Schankwirt m, Barmixer
m
barter ['bɑrtər] s Tauschhandel m || tr
tauschen || intr Tauschhandel treiben
basalt [bə'sɔlt], ['bæsɔlt] s Basalt m
base [bes] adj gemein, niedrig; (metal)
unedel || s (cosmetic) Schminkunter-
lage f; (fig) Grundlage f; (archit)
Basis f, Fundament n; (baseball)
Mal n; (chem) Base f; (geom) Grund-
linie f, Grundfläche f; (math) Basis
f; (mil) Stützpunkt m || tr (mil) sta-
tionieren; **b. on** stützen auf (acc),
gründen auf (acc)
base'ball' s Baseball m
base'board' s Wandleiste f
basement ['besmənt] s Kellergeschoß
n
bash [bæʃ] s heftiger Schlag m
bashful ['bæʃfəl] adj schüchtern

basic [ˈbesɪk] *adj* grundsätzlich; *(e.g., salary)* Grund–; (chem) basisch
basically [ˈbesɪkəli] *adv* grundsätzlich
ba′sic train′ing *s* Grundausbildung *f*
basilica [bəˈsɪlɪkə] *s* Basilika *f*
basin [ˈbesɪn] *s* Becken *n;* (geol) Mulde *f;* (naut) Bassin *n*
ba·sis [ˈbesɪs] *s* (–ses [siz]) Basis *f*, Grundlage *f;* **b. of comparison** Vergleichsgrundlage *f;* **put on a firm b.** (fin) sanieren
bask [bæsk] *intr* (& fig) sich sonnen
basket [ˈbæskɪt] *s* (& sport) Korb *m*
bas′ketball′ *s* Basketball *m*, Korbball *m*
bas-relief [ˌbɑrɪˈlif] *s* Flachrelief *n*
bass ⌊bes] *adj* Baß– ‖ *s* (mus) Baß *m* ‖ [bæs] *s* (ichth) Flußbarsch *m*, Seebarsch *m*
bass′ clef′ *s* Baßschlüssel *m*
bass′ drum′ *s* große Trommel *f*
bass′ fid′dle *s* Baßgeige *f*
bassoon [bəˈsun] *s* Fagott *n*
bass viol [ˈbesˈvaɪ·əl] *s* Gambe *f*
bastard [ˈbæstərd] *adj* Bastard–; *(illegitimate in birth)* unehelich ‖ *s* Bastard *m;* (vulg) Schweinehund *m*
baste [best] *tr (thrash)* verprügeln; *(scold)* schelten; *(culin)* begießen; *(sew)* lose (an)heften
bastion [ˈbæstʃən] *s* Bastion *f*
bat [bæt] *s* (sport) Schläger *m;* (zool) Fledermaus *f;* **go to bat for s.o.** (fig) für j–n eintreten ‖ *v (pret & pp* **batted;** *ger* **batting)** *tr* schlagen; **without batting an eye** ohne mit der Wimper zu zucken
batch [bætʃ] *s* Satz *m*, Haufen *m;* *(of bread)* Schub *m;* *(of letters)* Stoß *m*
bated [ˈbetɪd] *adj*—**with b. breath** mit verhaltenem Atem
bath [bæθ] *s* Bad *n;* **take a b.** ein Bad nehmen
bathe [beʃ] *tr & intr* baden
bather [ˈbeðər] *s* Badende *mf*
bath′house′ *s* Umkleideräume *pl*
bath′ing *s* Baden *n*, Bad *n*
bath′ing cap′ *s* Badehaube *f*
bath′ing suit′ *s* Badeanzug *m*
bath′ing trunks′ *spl* Badehose *f*
bath′robe′ *s* Bademantel *m*
bath′room′ *s* Badezimmer *n*
bath′room fix′tures *spl* Armaturen *pl*
bath′room scales *spl* Personenwaage *f*
bath′ tow′el *s* Badetuch *n*
bath′tub′ *s* Badewanne *f*
baton [bæˈtɑn] *s* (mil) Kommandostab *m;* (mus) Taktstock *m*
battalion [bəˈtæljən] *s* Bataillon *n*
batter [ˈbætər] *s* Teig *m;* (baseball) Schläger –in *mf* ‖ *tr* zerschlagen; (aer) bombardieren; **b. down** niederschlagen; **b. in** einschlagen
bat′tering ram′ *s* Sturmbock *m*
battery [ˈbætəri] *s* Batterie *f;* *(secondary cell)* Akkumulator *m;* (arti) Batterie *f;* (nav) Geschützgruppe *f*
battle [ˈbætəl] *s* Schlacht *f;* (& fig) Kampf *m;* **do b.** kämpfen; **in b.** im Felde ‖ *tr* bekämpfen ‖ *intr* kämpfen
bat′tle array′ *s* Schlachtordnung *f*
bat′tleax′ *s* Streitaxt *f;* (fig) Drachen *m*
bat′tle cruis′er *s* Schlachtkreuzer *m*

bat′tle cry′ *s* Schlachtruf *m;* (fig) Schlagwort *n*
bat′tle fatigue′ *s* Kriegsneurose *f*
bat′tlefield′ *s* Schlachtfeld *n*
bat′tlefront′ *s* Front *f*, Hauptkampflinie *f*
bat′tleground′ *s* Kampfplatz *m*
battlement [ˈbætəlmənt] *s* Zinne *f*
bat′tle scar′ *s* Kampfmal *n*
bat′tleship′ *s* Schlachtschiff *n*
bat′tle wag′on *s* (coll) Schlachtschiff *n*
batty [ˈbæti] *adj* (sl) doof
bauble [ˈbɔbəl] *s* Tand *m;* *(jester's staff)* Narrenstab *m*
Bavaria [bəˈverɪ·ə] *s* Bayern *n*
Bavarian [bəˈverɪ·ən] *adj* bayerisch ‖ *s* Bayer –in *mf*
bawd [bɔd] *s* Dirne *f*
bawdy [ˈbɔdi] *adj* unzüchtig
bawl [bɔl] *s* Geplärr *n* ‖ *tr*—**b. out** *(names, etc.)* ausschreien; *(scold)* anschnauzen ‖ *intr* (coll) plärren
bay [be] *adj* kastanienbraun ‖ *s* Bucht *f;* *(horse)* Rotfuchs *m;* (bot) Lorbeer *m;* **keep at bay** in Schach halten ‖ *intr* laut bellen; **bay at** anbellen
bayo·net [ˈbe·ənɪt] *s* Bajonett *n*, Seitengewehr *n;* **with fixed bayonets** mit aufgepflanztem Bajonett ‖ *v (pret & pp* **–net(t)ed;** *ger* **–net(t)ing)** *tr* mit dem Bajonett erstechen
bay′ win′dow *s* Erkerfenster *n*
bazaar [bəˈzɑr] *s* Basar *m*, Markt *m*
bazooka [bəˈzukə] *s* Panzerfaust *f*
be [bi] *v (pres* **am** [æm], **is** [ɪz], **are** [ɑr]; *pret* **was** [wɑz], [wʌz], **were** [wʌr]; *pp* **been** [bɪn]) *intr* sein; **be about** in der Nähe sein; **be about to** *(inf)* im Begriff sein zu *(inf)*; **be after s.o.** hinter j–m her sein; **be along** hier sein; **be behind in** im Rückstand sein mit; **be behind s.o.** j–m den Rücken decken; **be from** *(a country)* stammen aus, sein aus; **be in** zu Hause sein; **be in for** zu erwarten haben; **be in for it** in der Patsche sitzen; **be in on** dabei sein bei; **be off** weggehen; **be on to s.o.** j–m auf die Schliche kommen; **be out** nicht zu Hause sein, aus sein; **be out for s.th.** auf der Suche nach etw sein; **be up** auf sein; **be up to s.th.** etw im Sinn haben; **how are you?** wie geht es Ihnen?, wie befinden Sie sich?; **how much is that?** wieviel kostet das?; **there are, there is** es gibt *(acc)* ‖ *aux*—**he is studying** er studiert; **he is to go** er soll gehen; **he was hit** er ist getroffen worden ‖ *impers*—**how is it that...?** wie kommt es, daß...?; **it is cold** es ist kalt; **it is to be seen that** es ist darauf zu sehen, daß
beach [bitʃ] *s* Strand *m;* **on the b.** am Strand, an der See ‖ *tr* auf den Strand ziehen; **be beached** stranden
beach′comb′er *s* Strandgutjäger *m;* *(wave)* Strandwelle *f*
beach′head′ *s* Landekopf *m*
beach′ tow′el *s* Badetuch *m*
beach′ umbrel′la *s* Strandschirm *m*
beacon [ˈbikən] *s* Leuchtfeuer *n*, Bake *f;* *(lighthouse)* Leuchtturm *m;* (aer)

Scheinwerfer *m* ‖ *tr* lenken ‖ *intr* leuchten

bead [bid] (*of glass, wood, sweat*) Perle *f;* (*of a gun*) Korn *n;* **beads** (eccl) Rosenkranz *m;* **draw a b. on** zielen auf (*acc*)

beagle ['bigel] *s* Spürhund *m*

beak [bik] *s* Schnabel *m;* (*nose*) (sl) Rübe *f*

beam [bim] *s* (*of wood*) Balken *m;* (*of light, heat, etc.*) Strahl *m;* (*fig*) Glanz *m;* (aer) Leitstrahl *m;* (*width of a vessel*) (naut) größte Schiffsbreite *f;* (*horizontal structural member*) (naut) Deckbalken *m;* **b. of light** Lichtkegel *m;* **off the b.** (sl) auf dem Holzweg; **on the b.** (sl) auf Draht ‖ *intr* strahlen; **b. at** anstrahlen

bean [bin] *s* Bohne *f;* (*head*) (sl) Birne *f;* **spill the beans** (sl) alles ausquatschen

bean'pole' *s* (& coll) Bohnenstange *f*

bear [bɛr] *adj* (*market*) flau, Baisse– ‖ *s* Bär *m;* (st. exch.) Baissier *m* ‖ *v* (*pret* **bore** [bor]; *pp* **borne** [born]) *tr* (*carry*) tragen; (*endure*) dulden, ertragen; (*children*) gebären; (*date*) tragen; (*a name, sword*) führen; (*a grudge, love*) hegen; (*a message*) überbringen; (*the consequences*) auf sich [*acc*] nehmen; **bear in mind** bedenken, beachten; **bear fruit** Früchte tragen; (fig) Frucht tragen; **bear out** bestätigen ‖ *intr*—**bear down on** losgehen auf (*acc*); (naut) zufahren auf (*acc*); **bear left** sich links halten; **bear on** sich beziehen auf (*acc*); **bear up (well) against** gut ertragen; **bear with** Geduld haben mit

bearable ['bɛrəbəl] *adj* erträglich

beard [bɪrd] *s* Bart *m*

beard'ed *adj* bärtig

beardless ['bɪrdlɪs] *adj* bartlos

bearer ['bɛrər] *s* Träger –in *mf;* (*of a message*) Überbringer –in *mf;* (com) Inhaber –in *mf*

bear' hug' *s* (coll) Knutsch *m*

bear'ing *s* Körperhaltung *f;* (mach) Lager *n;* (**on**) Beziehung *f* (auf *acc*); **bearings** (aer, naut) Lage *f*, Richtung *f*, Peilung *f;* **lose one's bearings** die Richtung verlieren

bear'skin' *s* Bärenfell *n*

beast [bist] *s* Tier *n;* (fig) Bestie *f*

beastly ['bistli] *adj* bestialisch; **b. weather** Hundewetter *n*

beast' of bur'den *s* Lasttier *n*

beat [bit] *adj* (sl) erschöpft ‖ *s* (*of the heart*) Schlag *m;* (*of a policeman*) Runde *f*, Revier *n;* (mus) Takt *m* ‖ *v* (*pret* **beat;** *pp* **beat & beaten**) *tr* (*eggs, a child, record, team, etc.*) schlagen; (*a carpet*) ausklopfen; (*metal*) hämmern; (*a path*) treten; **b. it!** hau ab!; **b. one's brains out** sich [*dat*] den Kopf zerbrechen; **b. s.o. to it** j–m zuvorkommen; **b. up** verprügeln ‖ *intr* schlagen, klopfen; **b. against** peitschen gegen; **b. down** niederprallen

beati·fy [bɪ'ætɪ,faɪ] *v* (*pret* & *pp* **–fied**) *tr* seligsprechen

beat'ing *s* Prügel *pl*

beatitude [bɪ'ætɪ,t(j)ud] *s* Seligpreisung *f*

beau [bo] *s* (**beaus & beaux** [boz]) Liebhaber *m*

beautician [bju'tɪʃən] *s* Kosmetiker –in *mf;* (*hairdresser*) Friseuse *f*

beautiful ['bjutɪfəl] *adj* schön

beauti·fy ['bjutɪ,faɪ] *v* (*pret* & *pp* **–fied**) *tr* verschönern

beauty ['bjuti] *s* (*quality; woman*) Schönheit *f;* (coll) Prachtexemplar *n*

beau'ty queen' *s* Schönheitskönigin *f*

beau'ty shop' *s* Frisiersalon *m*

beau'ty sleep' *s* Schönheitsschlaf *m*

beau'ty spot' *s* Schönheitsmal *n*

beaver ['bivər] *s* Biber *m*

because [bɪ'kɔz] *conj* weil, da ‖ *interj* darum!

because' of' *prep* wegen (*genit*)

beck [bɛk] *s* Wink *m;* **be at s.o.'s b. and call** j–m ganz zu Diensten sein

beckon ['bɛkən] *tr* zuwinken (*dat*); (*summon*) heranwinken ‖ *intr* winken; **b. to s.o.** j–m zuwinken

become [bɪ'kʌm] *v* (*pret* **–came;** *pp* **–come**) *tr* (*said of clothes*) gut anstehen (*dat*); (*said of conduct*) sich schicken für ‖ *intr* werden; **what has b. of him?** was ist aus ihm geworden?

becom'ing *adj* (*said of clothes*) kleidsam; (*said of conduct*) schicklich

bed [bɛd] *s* (*for sleeping; of a river*) Bett *n;* (*of flowers*) Beet *n;* (*of straw*) Lager *n;* (geol) Lager *n;* (rr) Unterbau *m;* **put to bed** zu Bett bringen

bed'bug' *s* Wanze *f*

bed'clothes' *spl* Bettwäsche *f*

bed'ding *s* Bettzeug *n;* (*for animals*) Streu *f*

bed'fel'low *s*—**strange bedfellows** ein seltsames Paar *n*

bedlam ['bɛdləm] *s* (fig) Tollhaus *n;* **there was b.** es ging zu wie im Tollhaus

bed' lin'en *s* Bettwäsche *f*

bed'pan' *s* Bettschüssel *f*

bed'post' *s* Bettpfosten *m*

bedraggled [bɪ'drægəld] *adj* beschmutzt

bedridden ['bɛd,rɪdən] *adj* bettlägerig

bed'rock' *s* Grundgestein *n;* (fig) Grundlage *f*

bed'room' *s* Schlafzimmer *n*

bed'side' *s*—**at s.o.'s b.** an j–s Bett

bed'sore' *s* wundgelegene Stelle *f;* **get bedsores** sich wundliegen

bed'spread' *s* Bettdecke *f*, Tagesdecke *f*

bed'spring' *s* (*one coil*) Sprungfeder *f;* (*framework of springs*) Sprungfedermatratze *f*

bed'stead' *s* Bettgestell *n*

bed'time' *s* Schlafenszeit *f;* **it's past b.** es ist höchste Zeit, zu Bett zu gehen

bee [bi] *s* Biene *f*

beech [bitʃ] *s* Buche *f*

beech'nut' *s* Buchecker *f*

beef [bif] *s* Rindfleisch *n;* (*brawn*) (coll) Muskelkraft *f;* (*human flesh*) (coll) Fleisch *n;* (*complaint*) (sl) Gemecker *n* ‖ *tr*—**b. up** (coll) ver-

stärken || *intr* (*complain*) (sl)
meckern
beef' broth' *s* Kraftbrühe *f*
beef'steak' *s* Beefsteak *n*
beefy ['bifi] *adj* muskulös
bee'hive' *s* Bienenstock *m*, Bienenkorb *m*
bee'line' *s*—**make a b. for** schnurstracks losgehen auf (*acc*)
beer [bɪr] *s* Bier *n*
bee' sting' *s* Bienenstich *m*
beeswax ['biz ˌwæks] *s* Bienenwachs *n*
beet [bit] *s* Rübe *f*
beetle ['bitəl] *s* Käfer *m*
be·fall [bɪ'fɔl] *v* (*pret* **–fell** ['fɛl]; *pp* **–fallen** ['fɔlən] *tr* betreffen, zustoßen || *intr* sich ereignen
befit'ting *adj* passend
before [bɪ'for] *adv* vorher, früher || *prep* (*position or time*) vor (*dat*); (*direction*) vor (*acc*); **b. long** binnen kurzem; **b. now** schon früher || *conj* bevor, ehe
before'hand' *adv* zuvor, vorher
befriend [bɪ'frɛnd] *tr* sich [*dat*] (*j–n*) zum Freund machen, sich anfreunden mit
befuddle [bɪ'fʌdəl] *tr* verwirren
beg [bɛg] *v* (*pret* & *pp* begged; *ger* begging) *tr* bitten um; (*a meal*) betteln um; **beg s.o. to** (*inf*) j–n bitten zu (*inf*); **I beg your pardon** (ich bitte um) Verzeihung! || *intr* betteln; (*said of a dog*) Männchen machen; **beg for** bitten um, flehen um; **beg off** absagen
be·get [bɪ'gɛt] *v* (*pret* **–got** ['gɑt]; *pp* **–gotten** & **–got**; *ger* **–getting**) *tr* erzeugen
beggar ['bɛgər] *s* Bettler **–in** *mf*
be·gin [bɪ'gɪn] *v* (*pret* **–gan** ['gæn]; *pp* **–gun** ['gʌn]; *ger* **–ginning** ['gɪnɪŋ]) *tr* beginnen, anfangen || *intr* beginnen, anfangen; **to b. with** zunächst
beginner [bɪ'gɪnər] *s* Anfänger **–in** *mf*
begin'ning *s* Beginn *m*, Anfang *m*
begrudge [bɪ'grʌdʒ] *tr*—**b. s.o. s.th.** j–m etw mißgönnen
beguile [bɪ'gaɪl] *tr* (*mislead*) verleiten; (*charm*) betören
behalf [bɪ'hæf] *s*—**on b. of** zugunsten (*genit*), für; (*as a representative of*) im Namen (*genit*), im Auftrag von
behave [bɪ'hev] *intr* sich benehmen
behavior [bɪ'hevjər] *s* Benehmen *n*
behead [bɪ'hɛd] *tr* enthaupten
behind [bɪ'haɪnd] *adj* (*in arrears*) (**in**) im Rückstand (mit); **the clock is ten minutes b.** die Uhr geht zehn Minuten nach || *adv* (*in the rear*) hinten, hinterher; (*to the rear*) nach hinten, zurück; **from b.** von hinten || *s* (sl) Hintern *m*, Popo *m* || *prep* (*position*) hinter (*dat*); (*direction*) hinter (*acc*); **be b. schedule** sich verspäten; **b. time** zu spät sein; **b. the times** hinter dem Mond
be·hold [bɪ'hold] *v* (*pret* & *pp* **–held** ['hɛld]) *tr* betrachten || *interj* schau!
behoove [bɪ'huv] *impers*—**it behooves me** es geziemt mir
beige [beʒ] *adj* beige || *s* Beige *n*
be'ing *adj*—**for the time b.** einstweilen

|| *s* Dasein *n*; (*creature*) Wesen *n*; **come into b.** entstehen
belabor [bɪ'lebər] *tr* herumreiten auf (*dat*)
belated [bɪ'letɪd] *adj* verspätet
belch [bɛltʃ] *s* Rülpser *m* || *tr* (*fire*) ausspeien || *intr* rülpsen
beleaguer [bɪ'ligər] *tr* belagern
belfry ['bɛlfri] *s* Glockenturm *m*
Belgian ['bɛlʒən] *adj* belgisch || *s* Belgier **–in** *mf*
Belgium ['bɛldʒəm] *s* Belgien *n*
belief [bɪ'lif] *s* (**in**) Glaube(n) *m* (an *acc*)
believable [bɪ'livəbəl] *adj* glaublich
believe [bɪ'liv] *tr* (*a thing*) glauben; (*a person*) glauben (*dat*) || *intr* glauben; **b. in** glauben an (*acc*); **I don't b. in war** ich halte nicht viel vom Kriege
believer [bɪ'livər] *s* Gläubige *mf*
belittle [bɪ'lɪtəl] *tr* herabsetzen
bell [bɛl] *s* Glocke *f*; (*small bell*) Klingel *f*; (*of a wind instrument*) Schalltrichter *m*; (*box*) Gong *m*
bell'boy' *s* Hotelboy *m*
bell'hop' *s* (sl) Hotelpage *m*
belligerent [bə'lɪdʒərənt] *adj* streitlustig || *s* kriegführender Staat *m*
bell' jar' *s* Glasglocke *f*
bellow ['bɛlo] *s* Gebrüll *n*; **bellows** Blasebalg *m*; (phot) Balgen *m* || *tr* & *intr* brüllen
bell' tow'er *s* Glockenturm *m*
bel·ly ['bɛli] *s* Bauch *m*; (*of a sail*) Bausch *m* || *v* (*pret* & *pp* **–lied**) *intr* bauschen
bel'lyache' *s* (coll) Bauchweh *n* || *intr* (sl) jammern
bel'ly but'ton *s* Nabel *m*
bel'ly danc'er *s* Bauchtänzerin *f*
bel'ly flop' *s* Bauchklatscher *m*
bellyful ['bɛli ˌful] *s*—**have a b. of** die Nase voll haben von
bel'ly-land'ing *s* Bauchlandung *f*
belong [bɪ'lɔŋ] *intr* **b. to** (*designating ownership*) gehören (*dat*); (*designating membership*) gehören zu; **where does this table b.?** wohin gehört dieser Tisch?
belongings [bɪ'lɔŋɪŋz] *spl* Sachen *pl*
beloved [bɪ'lʌvɪd], [bɪ'lʌvd] *adj* geliebt || *s* Geliebte *mf*
below [bɪ'lo] *adv* (*position*) unten; (*direction*) nach unten, hinunter || *prep* (*position*) unter (*dat*), unterhalb (*genit*); (*direction*) unter (*acc*)
belt [bɛlt] *s* Riemen *m*, Gurt *m*, Gürtel *m*; (geol) Gebiet *n*; (mach) Treibriemen *m*; **tighten one's b.** den Riemen enger schnallen || *tr* (sl) e–n heftigen Schlag versetzen (*dat*)
belt' buck'le *s* Gürtelschnalle *f*
belt'way' *s* Verkehrsgürtel *m*
bemoan [bɪ'mon] *tr* betrauern, beklagen
bench [bɛntʃ] *s* Bank *f*; (jur) Gerichtshof *m*; (sport) Reservebank *f*, Bank *f*
bend [bɛnd] *s* Biegung *f*; (*in a road*) Kurve *f*; **bends** (pathol) Tauchkrankheit *f* || *v* (*pret* & *pp* bent [bɛnt]) *tr* biegen, beugen; (*a bow*) spannen ||

intr sich biegen, sich beugen; **b. down** sich bücken; **b. over backwards** (fig) sich [*dat*] übergroße Mühe geben

beneath [bɪ'niθ] *adv* unten ‖ *prep* (*position*) unter (*dat*), unterhalb (*genit*); (*direction*) unter (*acc*); **b. me** unter meiner Würde

benediction [‚benɪ'dɪkʃən] *s* Segen *m*

benefactor ['benɪ‚fæktər] *s* Wohltäter –in *mf*

beneficence [bɪ'nefɪsəns] *s* Wohltätigkeit *f*

beneficent [bɪ'nefɪsənt] *adj* wohltätig

beneficial [‚benɪ'fɪʃəl] *adj* heilbringend, gesund; (**to**) nützlich (*dat*)

beneficiary [‚benɪ'fɪʃɪ‚ɛri] *s* Begünstigte *mf*; (ins) Bezugsberechtigte *mf*

benefit ['benɪfɪt] *s* Nutzen *m*; (*fundraising performance*) Benefiz *n*; (ins) Versicherungsleistung *f*

benevolence [bɪ'nevələns] *s* Wohlwollen *n*

benevolent [bɪ'nevələnt] *adj* wohlwollend

benign [bɪ'naɪn] *adj* gütig; (pathol) gutartig

bent [bent] *adj* krumm, verbogen; **b. on** versessen auf (*acc*) ‖ *s* Hang *m*

benzene [ben'zin] *s* Benzol *n*

bequeath [bɪ'kwið] *tr* vermachen

bequest [bɪ'kwest] *s* Vermächtnis *n*

berate [bɪ'ret] *tr* ausschelten, rügen

be·reave [bɪ'riv] *v* (*pret & pp* **–reaved & –reft** ['reft]) *tr* (**of**) berauben (*genit*)

bereavement [bɪ'rivmənt] *s* Trauerfall *m*

beret [bə're] *s* Baskenmütze *f*

Berlin [bər'lɪn] *adj* Berliner, berlinerisch ‖ *s* Berlin *n*

Berliner [bər'lɪnər] *s* Berliner –in *mf*

berry ['beri] *s* Beere *f*

berserk [bər'sʌrk] *adj* wütend ‖ *adv*— **go b.** wütend werden

berth [bʌrθ] *s* Schlafkoje *f*; (naut) Liegeplatz *m*; (rr) Bett *n*; **give s.o. wide b.** um j–n e–n weiten Bogen machen ‖ *tr* am Kai festmachen

be·seech [bɪ'sitʃ] *v* (*pret & pp* **–sought** ['sɔt] & **–seeched**) *tr* anflehen

be·set [bɪ'set] *v* (*pret & pp* **–set**; *ger* **–setting**) *tr* bedrängen, umringen

beside [bɪ'saɪd] *prep* (*position*) neben (*dat*), bei (*dat*); (*direction*) neben (*acc*); **be b. oneself with** außer sich [*dat*] sein vor (*dat*)

besides [bɪ'saɪdz] *adv* überdies, außerdem ‖ *prep* außer (*dat*)

besiege [bɪ'sidʒ] *tr* belagern

besmirch [bɪ'smʌrtʃ] *tr* beschmutzen

be·speak [bɪ'spik] *v* (*pret* **–spoke** ['spok]; *pp* **–spoken** ['spokən]) *tr* bezeigen

best [best] *adj* beste; **b. of all, very b.** allerbeste ‖ *adv* am besten; **had b.** es wäre am besten, wenn ‖ *s*—**at b.** bestenfalls; **be at one's b.** in bester Form sein; **for the b.** zum Besten; **make the b. of** sich abfinden mit; **to the b. of one's ability** nach bestem Vermögen

bestial ['bestʃəl] *adj* bestialisch

best' man' *s* Brautführer *m*

bestow [bɪ'sto] *tr* verleihen

bestowal [bɪ'sto·əl] *s* Verleihung *f*

best' sel'ler *s* (*book*) Bestseller *m*

bet [bet] *s* Wette *f*; **make a bet** e–e Wette abschließen (or eingehen) ‖ *v* (*pret & pp* **bet & betted**; *ger* **betting**) *tr* (**on**) wetten (auf *acc*) ‖ *intr* wetten; **you bet!** aber sicher!

betray [bɪ'tre] *tr* verraten; (*a secret*) preisgeben; (*ignorance*) offenbaren; (*a trust*) mißbrauchen

betrayal [bɪ'tre·əl] *s* Verrat *m*

betrayer [bɪ'tre·ər] *s* Verräter –in *mf*

better ['betər] *adj* besser; **the b. part of** der größere Teil (*genit*) ‖ *s*— **change for the b.** sich zum Besseren wenden; **get the b. of** übervorteilen; **one's betters** die Höherstehenden *pl*; ‖ *adv* besser; **all the b.** um so besser; **b. off** besser daran; (*financially*) wohlhabender; **so much the b.** desto besser; **you had b. do it at once** am besten tust du es sofort; **you had b. not** das will ich dir nicht geraten haben ‖ *tr* verbessern; **b. oneself** sich verbessern

bet'ter half' *s* (coll) bessere Hälfte *f*

betterment ['betərmənt] *s* Besserung *f*

bettor ['betər] *s* Wettende *mf*

between [bɪ'twin] *adv*—**in b.** dazwischen ‖ *prep* (*position*) zwischen (*dat*); (*direction*) zwischen (*acc*); **just b. you and me** ganz unter uns gesagt

bev·el ['bevəl] *adj* schräg ‖ *s* schräge Kante *f* ‖ *v* (*pret & pp* **–el(l)ed**; *ger* **–el(l)ing**) *tr* abschrägen

beverage ['bevərɪdʒ] *s* Getränk *n*

bevy ['bevi] *s* Schar *f*

bewail [bɪ'wel] *tr* beklagen

beware [bɪ'wer] *intr* sich hüten; **b.!** gib acht!; **b. of** sich hüten vor (*dat*); **b. of imitations** vor Nachahmungen wird gewarnt

bewilder [bɪ'wɪldər] *tr* verblüffen

bewilderment [bɪ'wɪldərmənt] *s* Verblüffung *f*

bewitch [bɪ'wɪtʃ] *tr* (fig) bezaubern

beyond [bɪ'jand] *adv* jenseits ‖ *s*— **the b.** das Jenseits ‖ *prep* jenseits (*genit*), über (*acc*) hinaus; (fig) über (*acc*), außer (*dat*); **he is b. help** ihm ist nicht mehr zu helfen; **that's b. me** das geht über meinen Verstand

B'-girl' *s* (coll) Animiermädchen *n*

bias ['baɪ·əs] *s* Voreingenommenheit *f* ‖ *tr* (**against**) einnehmen (gegen)

bi'ased *adj* voreingenommen

bib [bɪb] *s* Latz *m*, Lätzchen *n*

Bible ['baɪbəl] *s* Bibel *f*

Biblical ['bɪblɪkəl] *adj* biblisch

bibliographer [‚bɪblɪ'agrəfər] *s* Bibliograph –in *mf*

bibliography [‚bɪblɪ'agrəfi] *s* Bücherverzeichnis *n*; (*science*) Bücherkunde *f*

bi·ceps ['baɪseps] *s* (**–cepses** [sepsɪz] & **–ceps**) Bizeps *m*

bicker ['bɪkər] *intr* (sich) zanken

bick'ering *s* Gezänk *n*

bicuspid [baɪ'kʌspɪd] *s* kleiner Backenzahn *m*

bicycle ['baɪsɪkəl] s Fahrrad n
bid [bɪd] s Angebot n; (cards) Meldung f; (com) Kostenvoranschlag m || v (pret **bade** [bæd] & **bid**; pp **bidden** ['bɪdən]) tr (ask) heißen; (at auction) bieten; (cards) melden, reizen || intr (cards) reizen; (com) ein Preisangebot machen; **bid for** sich bewerben um
bidder ['bɪdər] s (at an auction) Bieter –in mf; **highest b.** Meistbietende mf
bid'ding s (at an auction) Bieten n; (request) Geheiß n; (cards) Reizen n
bide [baɪd] tr—**b. one's time** seine Gelegenheit abwarten
biennial [baɪ'ɛnɪ·əl] adj zweijährig
bier [bɪr] s Totenbahre f
bifocals [baɪ'fokəlz] spl Zweistärkenbrille f
big [bɪg] adj (bigger; biggest) groß
bigamist ['bɪgəmɪst] s Bigamist m
bigamous ['bɪgəməs] adj bigamisch
bigamy ['bɪgəmi] s Bigamie f
big'-boned' adj starkknochig
big' busi'ness s das große Geschäft; (collectively) Großunternehmertum n
Big' Dip'per s Großer Bär m
big' game' s Hochwild n
big'-heart'ed adj großherzig
big'mouth' s (sl) Großmaul n
bigot ['bɪgət] s Fanatiker –in mf
bigoted ['bɪgətɪd] adj bigott, fanatisch
bigotry ['bɪgətri] s Bigotterie f
big' shot' s (coll) hohes Tier n, Bonze m
big'-time' adj groß, erstklassig; **b. operator** Großschieber –in mf
big' toe' s große Zehe f
big' top' s (coll) großes Zirkuszelt n
big' wheel' s (coll) hohes Tier n
big'wig' s (coll) Bonze m
bike [baɪk] s (coll) Rad n
bikini [bɪ'kini] s Bikini m
bilateral [baɪ'lætərəl] adj beiderseitig, verbindlich
bile [baɪl] s Galle f
bilge [bɪldʒ] s Bilge f, Kielraum m
bilge' wat'er s Bilgenwasser n
bilingual [baɪ'lɪŋgwəl] adj zweisprachig
bilk [bɪlk] tr (out of) prellen (um)
bill [bɪl] s Rechnung f; (paper money) Geldschein m, Schein m; (of a bird) Schnabel m; (parl) Gesetzvorlage f; **pass a b.** ein Gesetz verabschieden || tr in Rechnung stellen
bill'board' s Anschlagtafel f
bill' collec'tor s Einkassierer –in mf
billet ['bɪlət] s (mil) Quartier n || tr (mil) einquartieren, unterbringen
bill'fold' s Brieftasche f
bil'liard ball' s Billardkugel f
billiards ['bɪljərdz] s Billard n
bil'liard ta'ble s Billardtisch m
billion ['bɪljən] s Milliarde f; (Brit) Billion f (million million)
bill' of exchange' s Tratte f, Wechsel m
bill' of fare' s Speisekarte f
bill' of health' s Gesundheitszeugnis n; **he gave me a clean b.** (fig) er hat mich für einwandfrei befunden
bill' of lad'ing ['ledɪŋ] s Frachtbrief m

bill' of rights' s erste zehn Zusatzartikel pl zur Verfassung (der U.S.A.)
bill' of sale' s Kaufurkunde f
billow ['bɪlo] s Woge f || intr wogen
bil'ly club' ['bɪli] s Polizeiknüppel m
bil'ly goat' s (coll) Ziegenbock m
bind [baɪnd] s—**in a b.** in der Klemme || v (pret & pp **bound** [baʊnd]) tr binden; (obligate) verpflichten; (bb) einbinden
binder ['baɪndər] s Binder –in mf; (e.g., cement) Bindemittel n; (for loose papers) Aktendeckel m; (mach) Garbenbinder m
bindery ['baɪndəri] s Buchbinderei f
bind'ing adj (on) verbindlich (für) || s Binden n; (for skis) Bindung f; (bb) Einband n
binge [bɪndʒ] s (sl) Zechtour f; **go on a b.** (sl) e–e Zechtour machen
binoculars [baɪ'nɑkjələrz] spl Fernglas n
biochemistry [ˌbaɪ·ə'kɛmɪstri] s Biochemie f
biographer [baɪ'ɑgrəfər] s Biograph –in mf
biographic(al) [ˌbaɪ·ə'græfɪk(əl)] adj biographisch
biography [baɪ'ɑgrəfi] s Biographie f
biologic(al) [ˌbaɪ·ə'lɑdʒɪk(əl)] adj biologisch
biologist [baɪ'ɑlədʒɪst] s Biologe m, Biologin f
biology [baɪ'ɑlədʒi] s Biologie f
biophysics [ˌbaɪ·ə'fɪzɪks] s Biophysik f
biopsy ['baɪ·ɑpsi] s Biopsie f
bipartisan [baɪ'pɑrtɪzən] adj Zweiparteien–
biped ['baɪpɛd] s Zweifüßer m
bird [bɪrd] s Vogel m; **for the birds** für die Katz; **kill two birds with one stone** zwei Fliegen mit e–r Klappe schlagen
bird'cage' s Bauer n, Vogelkäfig m
bird' call' s Vogelruf m, Lockpfeife f
bird' dog' s Hühnerhund m
bird' of prey' s Raubvogel m
bird'seed' s Vogelfutter n
bird's'-eye view' s Vogelperspektive f
birth [bʌrθ] s Geburt f; (origin) Herkunft f; **give b. to** gebären
birth' certi'ficate s Geburtsurkunde f
birth' control' s Geburtenbeschränkung f
birth'day' s Geburtstag m
birth'day cake' s Geburtstagskuchen m
birth'day par'ty s Geburtstagsfeier f
birth'day pres'ent s Geburtstagsgeschenk n
birth'day suit' s (hum) Adamskostüm n
birth'mark' s Muttermal n
birth'place' s Geburtsort m
birth' rate' s Geburtenziffer f
birth'right' s Geburtsrecht n
biscuit ['bɪskɪt] s Keks m
bisect [baɪ'sɛkt] tr halbieren || intr sich teilen
bishop ['bɪʃəp] s Bischof m; (chess) Läufer m
bison ['baɪsən] s Bison m
bit [bɪt] s Bißchen n; (of food) Stück-

chen *n; (of time)* Augenblick *m;* (*part of a bridle*) Gebiß *n; (drill)* Bohrer *m;* **a bit** (*somewhat*) ein wenig; **a little bit** ein klein wenig; **bit by bit** brockenweise; **bits and pieces** Brocken *pl;* **every bit as** ganz genauso

bitch [bɪtʃ] *s* Hündin *f;* (*vulg*) Weibsbild *n*

bite [baɪt] *s* Biß *m;* (*wound*) Bißwunde *f;* (*of an insect*) Stich *m;* (*of a snake*) Biß *m;* (*snack*) Imbiß *m;* (*fig*) Bissigkeit *f;* **I have a b.** (*in fishing*) es beißt e–r an ‖ *v* (*pret* **bit** [bɪt]; *pp* **bit** & **bitten** ['bɪtən]) *tr* beißen; (*said of insects*) stechen; (*said of snakes*) beißen; **b. one's nails** an den Nägeln kauen ‖ *intr* beißen; (*said of fish*) anbeißen; (*said of the wind*) schneiden; **b. into** anbeißen

bit'ing *adj* (*remark*) bissig; (*cold, wind*) schneidend

bit' part' *s* kleine Rolle *f*

bitter ['bɪtər] *adj* (& *fig*) bitter; (*Person, Blick*) bitterböse

bitterly ['bɪtərli] *adv* bitterlich

bitterness ['bɪtərnɪs] *s* Bitterkeit *f*

bitters ['bɪtərz] *spl* Magenbitter *m*

bitu'minous coal' [bɪ't(j)umɪnəs] *s* Fettkohle *f*

bivouac ['bɪvwæk] *s* Biwak *n* ‖ *intr* biwakieren

bizarre [bɪ'zɑr] *adj* bizarr

blab [blæb] *v* (*pret* & *pp* **blabbed;** *ger* **blabbing**) *tr* ausplaudern ‖ *intr* plaudern

blabber ['blæbər] *intr* schwatzen

blab'bermouth' *s* Schwatzmaul *n*

black [blæk] *adj* schwarz ‖ *s* Schwarz *n;* (*black person*) Neger –in *mf,* Schwarze *mf* ‖ *tr* schwärzen; **b. out** (*mil*) verdunkeln ‖ *intr*—**b. out** die Besinnung verlieren

black'-and-blue' *adj* blau unterlaufen; **beat s.o. b.** j–n grün und blau schlagen

black' and white' *s*—**in b.** schwarz auf weiß, schriftlich

black'-and-white' *adj* schwarzweiß

black'ball' *tr* (*ostracize*) ausschließen; (*vote against*) stimmen gegen

black'ber'ry *s* Brombeere *f*

black'berry bush' *s* Brombeerstrauch *m*

black'bird' *s* Amsel *f*

black'board' *s* Tafel *f,* Wandtafel *f*

blacken ['blækən] *tr* schwärzen; (*a name*) anschwärzen

black' eye' *s* blaues Auge *n;* **give s.o. a b.** (*fig*) j–m Schaden zufügen

black'head' *s* Mitesser *m*

blackish ['blækɪʃ] *adj* schwärzlich

black'jack' *s* (*club*) Totschläger *m;* (*cards*) Siebzehnundvier *n* ‖ *tr* niederknüppeln

black'list' *s* schwarze Liste *f* ‖ *tr* auf die schwarze Liste setzen

black' mag'ic *s* schwarze Kunst *f*

black'mail' *s* Erpressung *f* ‖ *tr* erpressen

blackmailer ['blæk,melər] *s* Erpresser –in *mf*

black' mar'ket *s* Schwarzmarkt *m*

black' marketeer' *s* Schwarzhändler –in *mf*

black'out' *s* (*fainting*) Bewußtlosigkeit *f;* (*of memory*) kurze Gedächtnisstörung *f;* (*of news*) Nachrichtensperre *f;* (*mil*) Verdunkelung *f;* (*telv*) Sperre *f;* (*theat*) Auslöschen *n* aller Rampenlichter

black' sheep' *s* (*fig*) schwarzes Schaf *n*

black'smith' *s* Grobschmied *m;* (*person who shoes horses*) Hufschmied *m*

bladder ['blædər] *s* Blase *f*

blade [bled] *s* (*of a sword, knife*) Klinge *f;* (*of grass*) Halm *m;* (*of a saw, ax, shovel, oar*) Blatt *n;* (*of a propeller*) Flügel *m*

blame [blem] *s* Schuld *f* ‖ *tr* die Schuld geben (*dat*); **b. s.o. for** j–m Vorwürfe machen wegen; **I don't b. you for laughing** ich nehme es Ihnen nicht übel, daß Sie lachen

blameless ['blemlɪs] *adj* schuldlos

blame'wor'thy *adj* tadelnswert, schuldig

blanch [blæntʃ] *tr* erbleichen lassen; (*celery*) bleichen; (*almonds*) blanchieren ‖ *intr* erbleichen

bland [blænd] *adj* sanft, mild

blandish ['blændɪʃ] *tr* schmeicheln (*dat*)

blank [blæŋk] *adj* (*cartridge*) blind; (*piece of paper, space, expression*) leer; (*form*) unausgefüllt; (*tape*) unbespielt; (*nonplussed*) verblüfft; **my mind went b.** ich konnte mich an nichts erinnern ‖ *s* (*cartridge*) Platzpatrone *f;* (*unwritten space*) leere Stelle *f;* (*form*) Formular *n;* (*unfinished piece of metal*) Rohling *m* ‖ *tr* (*sport*) auf Null halten

blank' check' *s* Blankoscheck *m*

blanket ['blæŋkɪt] *adj* generell, umfassend ‖ *s* Decke *f*

blank' verse' *s* Blankvers *m*

blare [bler] *s* Lärm *m;* (*of trumpets*) Geschmetter *n* ‖ *intr* schmettern; (*aut*) laut hupen

blasé [blɑ'ze] *adj* blasiert; **b. attitude** Blasiertheit *f*

blaspheme [blæs'fim] *tr* & *intr* lästern

blasphemous ['blæsfɪməs] *adj* lästerlich

blasphemy ['blæsfɪmi] *s* Lästerung *f*

blast [blæst] *s* (*of an explosion*) Luftdruck *m;* (*of a horn, trumpet, air*) Stoß *m;* (*of air*) Luftzug *m;* **at full b.** (*fig*) auf höchsten Touren ‖ *tr* (*e.g., a tunnel*) sprengen; (*ruin*) (fig) verderben; (*criticize*) wettern gegen; (*blight*) versengen; **b. it!** verdammt! ‖ *intr*—**b. off** (*rok*) starten

blast' fur'nace *s* Hochofen *m*

blast'-off' *s* (*rok*) Start *m*

blatant ['bletənt] *adj* (*lie, infraction*) eklatant; (*nonsense*) schreiend

blaze [blez] *s* Brand *m;* **b. of color** Farbenpracht *f;* **b. of glory** Ruhmesglanz *m;* **b. of light** Lichterglanz *m;* **go to blazes!** (sl) geh zum Teufel!; **like blazes** wie verrückt ‖ *tr*—**b. a trail** e–n Weg markiern; (*fig*) e–n Weg bahnen ‖ *intr* lodern; **b. away at** drauflosschießen auf (*acc*)

blazer ['blezər] *s* Sportjacke *f*
blaz'ing *adj* (*sun*) prall
bleach [blitʃ] *s* Bleichmittel *n* ‖ *tr* bleichen; (*hair*) blondieren ‖ *intr* bleichen
bleachers ['blitʃərs] *spl* Zuschauersitze *pl* im Freien
bleak [blik] *adj* öde, trostlos
bleary-eyed ['blıri ˌaıd] *adj* triefäugig
bleat [blit] *s* Blöken *n* ‖ *intr* blöken; (*said of a goat*) meckern
bleed [blid] *v* (*pret & pp* **bled** [blɛd]) *tr* (*brakes*) entlüften; (*med*) zur Ader lassen; **b. white** (fig) zum Weißbluten bringen ‖ *intr* bluten; **b. to death** verbluten
blemish ['blɛmıʃ] *s* Fleck *m*, Makel *m*; (fig) Schandfleck *m*
blend [blɛnd] *s* Mischung *f*; (*liquor*) Verschnitt *m* ‖ *v* (*pret & pp* **blended** & **blent** [blɛnt]) *tr* mischen; (*wine, liquor*) verschneiden ‖ *intr* sich vermischen; (*said of colors*) zueinander passen, zusammenpassen
bless [blɛs] *tr* segnen; **God b. you!** (*after a sneeze*) Gesundheit!
blessed ['blɛsıd] *adj* selig
bless'ing *s* Segen *m*, Gnade *f*; **b. in disguise** Glück *n* im Unglück
blight [blaıt] *s* (fig) Gifthauch *m*; (agr) Brand *m*, Mehltau *m* ‖ *tr* (fig) verderben; (agr) schädigen
blight'ed *adj* brandig
blimp [blımp] *s* unstarres Luftschiff *n*
blind [blaınd] *adj* blind; (*curve*) unübersichtlich; **go b.** erblinden ‖ *s* Jalousie *f*; (hunt) Attrappe *f* ‖ *tr* blenden; (fig) verblenden
blind' al'ley *s* (& fig) Sackgasse *f*
blind' date' *s* Verabredung *f* mit e–r (or e–m) Unbekannten
blinder ['blaındər] *s* Scheuklappe *f*
blind' fly'ing *s* Blindflug *m*
blind'fold' *adj* mit verbundenen Augen ‖ *adv* blindlings ‖ *tr* die Augen verbinden (*dat*)
blind' man' *s* Blinder *m*
blind'man's' bluff' *s* Blindekuhspiel *n*
blindness ['blaındnıs] *s* Blindheit *f*
blink [blıŋk] *s* Blinken *n*; (*with the eyes*) Blinzeln *n*; **on the b.** (sl) kaputt ‖ *tr*—**b. one's eyes** mit den Augen zwinkern ‖ *intr* (*said of a light*) blinken; (*said of the eyes*) blinzeln
blinker ['blıŋkər] *s* (*for horses*) Scheuklappe *f*; (aut) Blinker *m*
blip [blıp] *s* (radar) Leuchtfleck *m*
bliss [blıs] *s* Wonne *f*
blissful ['blısfəl] *adj* glückselig
blister ['blıstər] *s* Blase *f*; (*from a burn*) Brandblase *f* ‖ *intr* (*said of the skin*) Blasen ziehen; (*said of paint*) Blasen werfen
blithe [blaıð] *adj* fröhlich
blitzkrieg ['blıts ˌkrig] *s* Blitzkrieg *m*
blizzard ['blızərd] *s* Blizzard *m*
bloat [blot] *tr* aufblähen ‖ *intr* anschwellen
bloc [blɑk] *s* (parl) Stimmblock *m*; (pol) Block *m*
block [blɑk] *s* (*of wood*) Klotz *m*; (*toy*) Bauklotz *m*; (*for chopping*) Hackklotz *m*; (*of houses*) Häuser-

block *m*; (*of seats*) Reihe *f*; (mach) Rolle *f*; (sport) Block *m*; **five blocks from here** fünf Straßen weiter ‖ *tr* versperren; (*traffic, a street, a player*) blockieren; (*a ball*) abfangen; (*a hat*) aufdämpfen; **be blocked** sich stauen; **b. off** (*a street*) absperren; **b. up** verstopfen, versperren
blockade [blɑ'ked] *s* Blockade *f*, Sperre *f* ‖ *tr* blockieren, sperren
blockade' run'ner *s* Blockadebrecher *m*
blockage ['blɑkıdʒ] *s* Stockung *f*
block' and tac'kle *s* Flaschenzug *m*
block'head' *s* Klotz *m*, Dummkopf *m*
blond [blɑnd] *adj* blond ‖ *s* Blonde *m*
blonde [blɑnd] *s* Blondine *f*
blood [blʌd] *s* Blut *n*; (*lineage*) Geblüt *n*; **in cold b.** kaltblütig
blood' circula'tion *s* Blutkreislauf *m*
blood' clot' *s* Blutgerinnsel *n*
bloodcurdling ['blʌd ˌkʌrdlıŋ] *adj* haarsträubend
blood' do'nor *s* Blutspender –in *mf*
blood'hound' *s* (& fig) Bluthund *m*
bloodless ['blʌdlıs] *adj* blutlos; (*revolution*) unblutig
blood' poi'soning *s* Blutvergiftung *f*
blood' pres'sure *s* Blutdruck *m*
blood' rela'tion *s* Blutsverwandte *mf*
blood'shed' *s* Blutvergießen *n*
blood'shot' *adj* blutunterlaufen
blood'stain' *s* Blutfleck *m*, Blutspur *f*
blood'stained' *adj* blutbefleckt
blood'stream' *s* Blutstrom *m*
blood'suck'er *s* (& fig) Blutsauger *m*
blood' test' *s* Blutprobe *f*
blood'thirst'y *adj* blutdürstig
blood' transfu'sion *s* Blutübertragung *f*
blood' type' *s* Blutgruppe *f*
blood' ves'sel *s* Blutgefäß *n*
blood·y ['blʌdi] *adj* blutig; (*bloodstained*) blutbefleckt ‖ *v* (*pret & pp* –**ied**) *tr* mit Blut beflecken
bloom [blum] *s* Blüte *f* ‖ *intr* blühen
blossom ['blɑsəm] *s* Blüte *f* ‖ *intr* blühen
blot [blɑt] *s* Fleck *m*; (fig) Schandfleck *m* ‖ *v* (*pret & pp* **blotted**; *ger* **blotting**) *tr* (*smear*) beschmieren; (*with a blotter*) (ab)löschen; **b. out** ausstreichen; (fig) auslöschen ‖ *intr* (*said of ink*) klecksen
blotch [blɑtʃ] *s* Klecks *m*; (*on the skin*) Ausschlag *m*
blotter ['blɑtər] *s* Löscher *m*
blot'ting pa'per *s* Löschpapier *n*
blouse [blaus] *s* Bluse *f*
blow [blo] *s* Schlag *m*, Hieb *m*; (fig) Schlag *m*; **come to blows** handgemein werden ‖ *v* (*pret* **blew** [blu]; *pp* **blown**) *tr* blasen; (*money*) (sl) verschwenden; (*a fuse*) durchbrennen; **b. a whistle** pfeifen; **b. off steam** sich austoben; **b. one's top** (coll) hochgehen; **b. out** (*a candle*) ausblasen; **b. up** (*inflate*) aufblasen; (*with explosives*) sprengen; (phot) vergrößern ‖ *intr* blasen; **b. out** (*said of a candle*) auslöschen; (*said of a tire*) platzen; **blow over** vorüberziehen; **b. up** (& fig) in die Luft gehen
blower ['blo·ər] *s* Gebläse *n*, Bläser *m*

blow'out' s (sl) Gelage n; (aut) Reifenpanne f
blow'pipe' s Blasrohr n
blow'torch' s Lötlampe f
blubber ['blʌbər] s Tran m || intr (cry
noisily) jaulen
bludgeon ['blʌdʒən] s Knüppel m || tr
mit dem Knüppel bearbeiten
blue [blu] adj blau; (fig) bedrückt || s
Blau n; **blues** (mus) Blues m; **have
the blues** trüb gestimmt sein; **out of
the b.** aus heiterem Himmel
blue'ber'ry s Heidelbeere f
blue'bird' s Blaukehlchen n
blue' chip' s (cards) blaue Spielmarke
f; (fin) sicheres Wertpapier n
blue'-col'lar work'er s Arbeiter m
blue' jeans' spl Jeans pl
blue' moon' s—once in a b. alle Jubel-
jahre einmal
blue'print' s Blaupause f
blue' streak' s—talk a b. (coll) in e–r
Tour reden
bluff [blʌf] adj schroff; (person) derb
|| s (coll) Bluff m; (geol) Steilküste
f; **call s.o.'s b.** j–m beim Wort neh-
men || tr & intr bluffen
bluffer ['blʌfər] s Bluffer m
blu'ing s Waschblau n
bluish ['blu·ɪʃ] adj bläulich
blunder ['blʌndər] s Schnitzer m; ||
intr e–n Schnitzer machen; **b. into**
stolpern in (acc); **b. upon** zufällig
geraten auf (acc)
blunt [blʌnt] adj stumpf; (fig) plump,
unverblümt || tr abstumpfen
bluntly ['blʌntli] adv unverblümt
blur [blʌr] s Verschwommenheit f || v
(pret & pp blurred; ger blurring) tr
verwischen || intr verschwommen
werden
blurb [blʌrb] s Reklametext m
blurred adj verschwommen; (vision)
unscharf
blurt [blʌrt] tr—b. out herausplatzen
blush [blʌʃ] s Röte f, Schamröte f ||
intr (at) erröten (über acc)
bluster ['blʌstər] s Prahlerei f || intr
(said of a person) prahlen, poltern;
(said of wind) toben
blustery ['blʌstəri] adj stürmisch
boa constrictor ['bo·ə kən'strɪktər] s
Abgottschlange f, Königsschlange f
boar [bor] s Eber m; (wild boar) Wildschwein n
board [bord] s Brett n; (of administra-
tors) Ausschuß m, Behörde f, Rat m;
(meals) Kost f; (educ) Schultafel f;
above b. offen; **on b.** an Bord || tr
(a ship) besteigen; (a plane, train)
einsteigen in (acc); (paying guests)
beköstigen; **b. up** mit Brettern ver-
nageln || intr (with) in Kost sein
(bei)
boarder ['bordər] s Kostgänger –in mf
board'inghouse' s Pension f
board'ing pass' s Bordkarte f
board'ing school' s Internat n
board'ing stu'dent s Interne mf
board' of direc'tors s Verwaltungsrat
m, Aufsichtsrat m
board' of educa'tion s Unterrichtsmi-
nisterium n

board' of health' s Gesundheitsbehörde
f
board' of trade' s Handelskammer f
board' of trustees' s Verwaltungsrat m
board'walk' s Strandpromenade f
boast [bost] s Prahlerei f; (cause of
pride) Stolz m || tr sich rühmen
(genit) || intr (about) prahlen (mit)
boastful ['bostfəl] adj prahlerisch
boat [bot] s Boot n; **in the same b.**
(fig) in der gleichen Lage
boat'house' s Bootshaus n
boat'ing s Bootsfahrt f; **go b.** e–e Boot-
fahrt machen
boat'race' s Bootrennen n
boat' ride' s Bootsfahrt f
boatswain ['bosən] s Hochbootsmann
m
bob [bab] s (jerky motion) Ruck m;
(hairdo) Bubikopf m; (of a fishing
line) Schwimmer m; (of a plumb
line) Senkblei n || v (pret & pp
bobbed; ger bobbing) tr (hair) kurz
schneiden || intr sich hin und her be-
wegen; **bob up and down** sich auf
und ab bewegen
bobbin ['babɪn] s Klöppel m
bobble ['babəl] tr (coll) ungeschickt
handhaben
bob'by pin' ['babi] s Haarklammer f
bob'sled' s Bob m, Rennschlitten m
bode [bod] tr bedeuten
bodily ['badɪli] adj leiblich; **b. injury**
Körperverletzung f || adv leibhaftig
body ['badi] s Körper m; (of a person
or animal) Körper m; (corpse) Leiche
f; (collective group) Körperschaft f;
(of a plane, ship) Rumpf m; (of a
vehicle) Karosserie f; (of beer, wine)
Schwere f; (of a letter) Text m; **b. of
water** Gewässer n; **in a b.** geschlossen
bod'yguard' s Leibgarde f
bod'y o'dor s Körpergeruch m
bog [bag] s Sumpf m || v (pret & pp
bogged; ger bogging) intr—bog down
steckenbleiben
bogey·man ['bogi ˌmæn] s (–men) Kin-
derschreck m
bogus ['bogəs] adj schwindelhaft
Bohemia [bo'himɪ·ə] s Böhmen n
Bohemian [bo'himɪ·ən] adj böhmisch
|| s (person) Böhme m, Böhmin f;
(fig) Bohemien m; (language) Böhmisch n
boil [bɔɪl] s (pathol) Geschwür n;
bring to a b. zum Sieden bringen ||
tr kochen, sieden || intr kóchen, sie-
den; **b. away** verkochen; **b. over**
überkochen
boiled' ham' s gekochter Schinken m
boiled' pota'toes spl Salzkartoffeln pl
boiler ['bɔɪlər] s (electrical water
tank) Boiler m; (kettle) Kessel m
boil'ermak'er s Kesselschmied m
boil'er room' s Heizraum m
boil'ing adj siedend || adv—be b. mad
vor Zorn kochen; **b. hot** siedeheiß
boil'ing point' s Siedepunkt m
boisterous ['bɔɪstərəs] adj ausgelassen
bold [bold] adj kühn, gewagt; (outlines) deutlich
bold'face' s Fettdruck m

boldness ['boldnɪs] s Kühnheit f
Bolshevik ['bolʃəvɪk] adj bolsche-
wistisch || s Bolschewik –in mf
bolster ['bolstər] s Nackenrolle f || tr
unterstützen
bolt [bolt] s Bolzen m; (door lock)
Riegel m; (of cloth) Stoffballen m;
(of lightning) Blitzstrahl m; **b. out of
the blue** Blitz m aus heiterem Him-
mel || tr (a door) verriegeln; (a po-
litical party) im Stich lassen; (food)
hinunterschlingen || intr davonstür-
zen; (said of a horse) durchgehen
bomb [bam] s (dropped from the air)
Bombe f; (planted) Sprengladung f;
(fiasco) (sl) Versager m || tr (from
the air) bombardieren; (blow up)
sprengen || intr (sl) versagen
bombard [bam'bard] tr bombardieren,
beschießen; (fig) bombardieren
bombardier [,bambər'dɪr] s Bomben-
schütze m
bombardment [bam'bardmənt] s Bombardement n, Beschießung f
bombast ['bambæst] s Schwulst m
bombastic [bam'bæstɪk] adj schwülstig
bomb' bay' s Bombenschacht m
bomb' cra'ter s Bombentrichter m
bomber ['bamər] s Bomber m
bomb'ing s Bombenabwurf m
bomb'ing run' s Bomben(ziel)anflug m
bomb'proof' adj bombenfest, bomben-
sicher
bomb'shell' s (& fig) Bombe f
bomb' shel'ter s Bombenkeller m
bomb'sight' s Bombenzielgerät n
bomb' squad' s Entschärfungskom-
mando n
bona fide ['bonə,faɪd] adj ehrlich,
echt; (offer) solide
bonanza [bo'nænzə] s Goldgrube f
bond [band] s Fessel f; (fin) Obligation f
bondage ['bandɪdʒ] s Knechtschaft f
bond'hold'er s Inhaber –in mf e-r Obligation
bonds·man ['bandzmən] s (–men)
Bürge m
bone [bon] s Knochen m, Bein n; (of
fish) Gräte f; **bones** Gebein n; (mortal remains) Gebeine pl; **have a b. to
pick with** ein Hühnchen zu rupfen
haben mit; **make no bones about it**
nicht viel Federlesens machen mit;
to the b. bis ins Mark || tr (meat)
ausbeinen; (fish) ausgräten || intr—
b. up for (sl) büffeln für
bone'-dry' adj knochentrocken
bone'head' s Dummkopf m
boneless ['bonlɪs] adj ohne Knochen;
(fish) ohne Gräten
boner ['bonər] s (coll) Schnitzer m;
pull a b. (coll) e–n Schnitzer machen
bonfire ['ban,faɪr] s Freudenfeuer n
bonnet ['banɪt] s Haube f
bonus ['bonəs] s Gratifikation f
bony ['boni] adj knochig; (fish) grätig
boo [bu] s Pfuiruf m || tr niederbrüllen
|| intr pfui rufen || interj (to jeer)
pfui!; (to scare someone) huh!
boob [bub] s (sl) Blödkopf m
booby ['bubi] s (sl) Blödkopf m
boo'by hatch' s (sl) Affenkasten m

boo'by prize' s Trostpreis m
boo'by trap' s Minenfalle f
boogey·man ['bugi,mæn], ['bogi-
,mæn] s (–men') Schreckgespenst n
book [buk] s Buch n; (of stamps, tickets, matches) Heftchen n; **keep books**
Bücher führen || tr buchen; (e.g.,
seats) vorbestellen
book'bind'er s Buchbinder –in mf
book'bind'ery s Buchbinderei f
book'bind'ing s Buchbinderei f
book'case' s Bücherschrank m
book' end' s Bücherstütze f
bookie ['buki] s (coll) Buchmacher –in
mf
book'ing s Buchung f
bookish ['bukɪʃ] adj lesefreudig
book'keep'er s Buchhalter –in mf
book'keep'ing s Buchhaltung f
book' learn'ing s Schulweisheit f
booklet ['buklɪt] s Büchlein n
book'mak'er s Buchmacher –in mf
book'mark' s Lesezeichen n
book'rack' s Büchergestell n
book' review' s Buchbesprechung f
book'sel'ler s Buchhändler –in mf
book'shelf' s (–shelves) Bücherregal n
book'stand' s Bücher(verkaufs)stand m
book'store' s Buchhandlung f
book'worm' s (& fig) Bücherwurm m
boom [bum] s (noise) dumpfes Dröhnen n; (of a crane) Ausleger m; (cin,
telv) Galgen m; (econ) Boom m,
Hochkonjunktur f; (naut) Baum m,
Spiere f; (st.exch.) Hausse f || intr
dröhnen; (said of an organ) brummen
boomerang ['bumə,ræŋ] s Bumerang
m
boon [bun] s Wohltat f, Segen m
boon' compan'ion s Zechkumpan m
boor [bur] s Rüpel m, Flegel m
boorish ['burɪʃ] adj flegelhaft
boost [bust] s (push) Auftrieb m; (in
pay) Gehaltserhöhung f || tr fördern;
(prices) in die Höhe treiben; (elec)
verstärken; **b. business** die Wirtschaft ankurbeln
booster ['bustər] s (backer) Förderer
m, Förderin f
boost'er rock'et s Hilfsrakete f
boost'er shot' s (med) Nachimpfung f
boot [but] s Stiefel m; (kick) Fußtritt
m; **to b.** noch dazu; **you can bet your
boots on that** (sl) darauf kannst du
Gift nehmen || tr (sl) stoßen; (fb)
kicken; **b. out** (sl) 'rausschmeißen
booth [buθ] s (at a fair) Marktbude f;
(for telephone, voting) Zelle f
boot'leg' adj geschmuggelt || v (pret &
pp –legged; ger –legging) tr (make
illegally) illegal brennen; (smuggle)
schmuggeln
bootlegger ['but,lɛgər] s Alkohol-
schmuggler m, Bootlegger m
bootlicker ['but,lɪkər] s (sl) Kriecher
m
booty ['buti] s Beute f
booze [buz] s (coll) Schnaps m || intr
(coll) saufen
booze' hound' s Saufbold m, Saufaus m
border ['bordər] s Rand m; (of a country) Grenze f; (of a dress, etc.) Saum

m, Borte *f* ‖ *tr* umranden, begrenzen; **be bordered by** grenzen an (*acc*) ‖ *intr*—**b. on** (& fig) grenzen an (*acc*)

bor'derline' *s* Grenzlinie *f*

bor'derline case' *s* Grenzfall *m*

bore [bor] *s* (*drill hole*) Bohrloch *n*; (*of a gun*) Bohrung *f*; (*of a cylinder*) innerer Zylinderdurchmesser *m*; (fig) langweiliger Mensch *m* ‖ *tr* bohren; (fig) langweilen

boredom ['bordəm] *s* Langeweile *f*

bor'ing *adj* langweilig ‖ *s* Bohren *n*

born [bɔrn] *adj* geboren; **he was b.** (*said of a living person*) er ist geboren; (*said of a deceased person*) er war geboren

borough ['bʌro] *s* Städtchen *n*

borrow ['bɔro] *tr* leihen

borrower ['bɔro·ər] *s* Entleiher –in *mf*; (fin) Kreditnehmer –in *mf*

bor'rowing *s* Borgen *n*; (fin) Kreditaufnahme *f*; (ling) Lehnwort *n*

bosom ['buzəm] *s* Busen *m*; (fig) Schoß *m*

bos'om friend' *s* Busenfreund *m*

boss [bɔs] *s* (coll) Chef *m*, Boß *m*; (*of a shield*) Buckel *m*; (pol) Bonze *m* ‖ *tr* (**around**) herumkommandieren

bossy ['bɔsi] *adj* herrschsüchtig

botanical [bə'tænɪkəl] *adj* botanisch

botanist ['batənɪst] *s* Botaniker –in *mf*

botany ['batəni] *s* Botanik *f*

botch [batʃ] *tr* (coll) verpfuschen

both [boθ] *adj & pron* beide ‖ *conj*— **both... and** sowohl... als auch

bother ['baðər] *s* Belästigung *f*, Mühe *f* ‖ *tr* (*annoy*) belästigen, stören; (*worry*) bedrücken; (*said of a conscience*) quälen ‖ *intr* sich bemühen; **b. about** sich bekümmern um; **b. with** (*a thing*) sich befassen mit; (*a person*) verkehren mit

bothersome ['baðərsəm] *adj* lästig

bottle ['batəl] *s* Flasche *f* ‖ *tr* in Flaschen abfüllen; **bottled up** aufgestaut

bot'tleneck' *s* Flaschenhals *m*; (fig) Engpaß *m*, Stauung *f*

bot'tle o'pener *s* Flaschenöffner *m*

bottom ['batəm] *adj* niedrigste, unterste ‖ *s* Boden *m*; (*of a well, shaft, river, valley*) Sohle *f*; (*of a mountain*) Fuß *m*; (*of an affair*) Grund *m*; (*buttocks*) Hintern *m*; **at the b. of the page** unten auf der Seite; **bottoms up!** prosit, ex!; **get to the b. of a problem** e–r Frage auf den Grund gehen; **reach b.** (fig) den Nullpunkt erreichen

bottomless ['batəmlɪs] *adj* bodenlos

bough [bau] *s* Ast *m*

bouillon ['buljan] *s* Kraftbrühe *f*

bouil'lon cube' *s* Bouillonwürfel *m*

boulder ['boldər] *s* Felsblock *m*

bounce [bauns] *s* Aufprall *m*; (fig) Schwung *m* ‖ *tr* (*a ball*) aufprallen lassen; (*throw out*) (sl) 'rausschmeißen ‖ *intr* aufprallen, aufspringen; (*said of a check*) (coll) platzen

bouncer ['baunsər] *s* (sl) Rausschmeißer *m*

bounc'ing *adj* (*baby*) stramm

bound [baund] *adj* gebunden, gefesselt; (*book*) gebunden; (*in duty*) verpflichtet; **be b. for** unterwegs sein nach; **be b. up with** eng verbunden sein mit; **I am b. to** (*inf*) ich muß (*inf*) ‖ *s* Sprung *m*, Satz *m*; **bounds** Grenzen *pl*, Schranken *pl*; **in bounds** (sport) in; **keep within bounds** in Schranken halten; **know no bounds** weder Maß noch Ziel kennen; **out of bounds** (sport) aus; **within the bounds of** im Bereich (*genit*) ‖ *tr* begrenzen ‖ *intr* aufprallen, aufspringen

boundary ['baundəri] *s* Grenze *f*; (fig) Umgrenzung *f*

boun'dary line' *s* Grenzlinie *f*

boun'dary stone' *s* Grenzstein *m*

boundless ['baundlɪs] *adj* grenzenlos

bountiful ['bauntɪfəl] *adj* (*generous*) freigebig; (*ample*) reichlich

bounty ['baunti] *s* (*generosity*) Freigebigkeit *f*; (*gift*) Geschenk *n*; (*reward*) Prämie *f*

bouquet [bu'ke] *s* Strauß *m*; (*aroma*) Blume *f*

bout [baut] *s* (*box*) Kampf *m*; (fencing) Gang *m*; (pathol) Anfall *m*

bow [bau] *s* Verbeugung *f*; (naut) Bug *m* ‖ *intr* sich verbeugen; **bow and scrape before** sich schmiegen und biegen vor (*dat*); **bow down** sich bücken; **bow out** sich geschickt zurückziehen; **bow to** sich (ver)neigen vor (*dat*) ‖ [bo] *s* (*weapon*) Bogen *m*; (*of a violin*) Geigenbogen *m*; (*bowknot*) Schleife *f*; **bow and arrow** Pfeil *m* und Bogen *m* ‖ *intr* (mus) geigen

bowel ['bau·əl] *s* Darm *m*; **bowels** Eingeweide *pl*; **bowels of the earth** Erdinnere *n*

bow'el move'ment *s* Stuhlgang *m*

bowl [bol] *s* Napf *m*, Schüssel *f*; (*of a pipe*) Kopf *m*; (*washbowl, toilet bowl*) Becken *n*; (*of a spoon*) Höhlung *f*; (sport) Stadion *n* ‖ *tr* umhauen; (fig) umwerfen ‖ *intr* kegeln

bowlegged ['bo‿leg(ɪ)d] *adj* O-beinig

bowler ['bolər] *s* Kegler –in *mf*

bowl'ing *s* Kegeln *n*

bowl'ing al'ley *s* Kegelbahn *f*

bowl'ing ball' *s* Kegelkugel *f*

bowl'ing pin' *s* Kegel *m*

bowstring ['bo‿strɪŋ] *s* Bogensehne *f*

bow' tie' [bo] *s* Schleife *f*, Fliege *f*

bow' win'dow [bo] *s* Bogenfenster *n*

bowwow ['bau'wau] *interj* wauwau!

box [baks] *s* (*small and generally of cardboard*) Schachtel *f*; (*larger and generally of cardboard*) Karton *m*; (*generally of wood*) Kasten *m*; (*larger and generally of wood*) Kiste *f*; (*of strips of wood*) Spanschachtel *f*; (theat) Loge *f*; (typ) Kasten *m*; **box of candy** Bonbonniere *f*; **box on the ear** Ohrfeige *f* ‖ *tr* (sport) boxen; **box in** einschließen; **box s.o.'s ears** j–n ohrfeigen ‖ *intr* (sport) boxen

box'car' *s* geschlossener Güterwagen *m*

boxer ['baksər] *s* (sport, zool) Boxer *m*

box'ing *s* Boxen *n*, Boxsport *m*

box'ing glove' *s* Boxhandschuh *m*

box'ing match' s Boxkampf m
box' kite' s Kastendrachen m
box' of'fice s (cin, theat) Kasse f
box' seat' s Logenplatz m
box'wood' s Buchsbaum m
boy [bɔɪ] s Junge m; (servant) Boy m
boycott ['bɔɪkɑt] s Boykott m ‖ tr boykottieren
boy'friend' s Freund m
boy'hood' s Knabenalter n
boyish ['bɔɪ·ɪʃ] adj jungenhaft
boy' scout' s Pfadfinder m
bra [brɑ] s (coll) BH m
brace [bres] s (carp) Strebe f, Stütze f; (dent) Zahnklammer f, Zahnspange f; (hunt) Paar n; (med) Schiene f; (typ) geschweifte Klammer f ‖ tr verstreben; (fig) stärken; **b. oneself** sich zusammenreißen; **b. oneself against** sich stemmen gegen; **b. oneself for** seinen Mut zusammennehmen für; **b. up** (fig) aufpulvern
brace' and bit' s Bohrwinde f
bracelet ['breslɪt] s Armband n
brac'ing adj (invigorating) erfrischend
bracket ['brækɪt] s Winkelstütze f, Konsole f; (wall bracket) Wandarm m; (mounting clip) Befestigungsschelle f; (typ) eckige Klammer f ‖ tr einklammern; (arti) eingabeln
brackish ['brækɪʃ] adj brackig
brag [bræg] v (pret & pp bragged; ger bragging) intr (about) prahlen (mit)
braggart ['brægərt] s Prahler –in mf
brag'ging adj prahlerisch ‖ s Prahlerei f
braid [bred] s (of hair) Flechte f; (flat trimming) Tresse f, Litze f; (round trimming) Kordel f ‖ tr (hair, rope) flechten; (trim with braid) mit Tresse (or Borten) besetzen
braille [brel] s Blindenschrift f
brain [bren] s Hirn n; **brains** Hirn n; (fig) Grütze f ‖ tr (coll) den Schädel einschlagen (dat)
brain'child' s Geistesfrucht f
brainless ['brenlɪs] adj hirnlos
brain'storm' s (coll) Geistesblitz m
brain'wash' tr Gehirnwäsche vornehmen bei
brain'wash'ing s Gehirnwäsche f
brain' wave' s Hirnwelle f; (fig) Geistesblitz m
brain'work' s Gehirnarbeit f
brainy ['breni] adj geistreich
braise [brez] tr schmoren, dünsten
brake [brek] s Bremse f; **put on the brakes** bremsen ‖ intr bremsen
brake' drum' s Bremstrommel f
brake' light' s Bremslicht n
brake' lin'ing s Bremsbelag m
brake'man s (–men) Bremser m
brake'ped'al s Bremspedal n
brake' shoe' s (aut) Bremsbacke f
bramble ['bræmbəl] s Dornbusch m
bran [bræn] s Kleie f
branch [bræntʃ] s (of a tree) Ast m; (smaller branch; of lineage) Zweig m; (of river) Arm m; (of a road, railroad) Abzweigung f; (of science, work, a shop) Branche f, Unterabteilung f; (com) Filiale f, Nebenstelle

f ‖ intr—**b. off** abzweigen; **b. out** sich verzweigen
branch' line' s Seitenlinie f
branch' of'fice s Zweigstelle f
branch' of serv'ice s Truppengattung f
brand [brænd] s (kind) Marke f; (trademark) Handelsmarke f; (on cattle) Brandmal n; (branding iron) Brandeisen n; (dishonor) Schandfleck m ‖ tr (& fig) brandmarken
brand'ing i'ron s Brandeisen n
brandish ['brændɪʃ] tr schwingen; (threateningly) schwenken
brand'-new' adj nagelneu
brandy ['brændi] s Branntwein m
brash [bræʃ] adj schnodd(e)rig, frech
brass [bræs] adj Messing– ‖ s Messing n; (mil) hohe Offiziere pl; (mus) Blechinstrumente pl
brass' band' s Blechblaskapelle f
brassiere [brə'zɪr] s Büstenhalter m
brass' knuck'les spl Schlagring m
brass' tacks' spl—**get down to b.** (coll) zur Sache kommen
brat [bræt] s (coll) Balg m
bravado [brə'vɑdo] s Bravour f, Angabe f
brave [brev] adj tapfer, mutig ‖ s indianischer Krieger m ‖ tr trotzen (dat)
bravery ['brevəri] s Tapferkeit f
bra·vo ['brɑvo] s (–vos) Bravo n ‖ interj bravo!
brawl [brɔl] s Rauferei f ‖ intr raufen
brawler ['brɔlər] s Raufbold m
brawn [brɔn] s Muskelkraft f
brawny ['brɔni] adj muskulös, kräftig
bray [bre] s Eselsschrei m ‖ intr schreien, iahen
braze [brez] tr (brassplate) mit Messing überziehen; (solder) hartlöten
brazen ['brezən] adj Messing–, ehern; (fig) unverschämt ‖ tr—**b. it out** unverschämt durchsetzen
Brazil [brə'zɪl] s Brasilien n
Brazilian [brə'zɪljən] adj brasilianisch, brasilisch ‖ s Brasilier –in mf
Brazil' nut' s Paranuß f
breach [britʃ] s Bruch m; (mil) Bresche f ‖ tr (mil) durchbrechen
breach' of con'tract s Vertragsbruch m
breach' of prom'ise s Verlöbnisbruch m
breach' of the peace' s Friedensbruch m
breach' of trust' s Vertrauensbruch m
bread [bred] s Brot n; (money) (sl) Pinke f ‖ tr (culin) panieren
bread' and but'ter s Butterbrot n; (livelihood) Lebensunterhalt m
bread' box' s Brotkasten m
bread' crumb' s Brotkrume f
bread'ed adj paniert
bread'ed veal' cut'let s Wiener Schnitzel n
bread' knife' s Brotmesser n
breadth [bredθ] s Breite f
bread'win'ner s Brotverdiener –in mf
break [brek] s Bruch m; (split, tear) Riß m; (crack) Sprung m; (in relations) Bruch m; (in a forest) Lichtung f; (in the clouds) Lücke f; (recess) Pause f; (rest from work)

Arbeitspause *f;* (*luck*) Glück *n;* (*chance*) Chance *f;* (box) Lösen *n;* **bad b.** Pech *n;* **b. in the weather** Wetterumschlag *m;* **give s.o. a b.** j-m e-e Chance geben; **make a b. for** losstürzen auf (*acc*); **take a b.** e-e Pause machen; **tough b.** Pech *n;* **without a b.** ohne Unterbrechung ‖ *v* (*pret* **broke** [brok]; *pp* **broken** ['brokən]) *tr* (& fig) brechen; (*snap*) zerreißen; (*a string*) durchreißen; (*a dish*) zerbrechen; (*an appointment*) nicht einhalten; (*contact*) unterbrechen; (*an engagement*) auflösen; (*a law, limb*) verletzen; (*monotony*) auflockern; (*a record*) brechen; (*a seal*) erbrechen; (*a window*) einschlagen; (*one's word, promise*) nicht halten; **b. down** (*into constituents*) zerlegen; (*s.o.'s resistance*) überwinden; (mach) abmontieren; **b. in** (*a horse*) zureiten; (*a car*) einfahren; (*a person*) anlernen; **b. loose** losreißen; **b. off** abbrechen, losbrechen; (*an engagement*) auflösen; **b. open** aufbrechen; **b. s.o. from s.th.** j-m etw abgewöhnen; **b. the news (to)** die Nachricht eröffnen (*dat*), die Nachricht beibringen (*dat*); **b. to pieces** zerbrechen; (*a meeting*) auflösen; (*forcibly*) sprengen; **break wind** e-n Darmwind abgehen lassen ‖ *intr* brechen; (*snap*) reißen; (*said of the voice*) mutieren; (*said of waves*) sich brechen; (*said of large waves*) sich überschlagen; (*said of the weather*) umschlagen; **b. down** zusammenbrechen; (mach) versagen; **b. even** gerade die Unkosten decken; **b. loose** losbrechen, sich losreißen; **b. out** (*said of fire, an epidemic, prisoner*) ausbrechen; **b. up** (*said of a meeting*) sich auflösen

breakable ['brekəbəl] *adj* zerbrechlich
breakage ['brekɪdʒ] *s* Bruch *m;* (*cost of broken articles*) Bruchschaden *m*
break'down' *s* (*of health, discipline, morals*) Zusammenbruch *m;* (*disintegration*) Zersetzung *f;* (*of costs, etc.*) Aufgliederung *f;* (aut) Panne *f;* (chem) Analyse *f;* (elec) Durchschlag *m;* (*of a piece of equipment*) (mach) Versagen *n;* (*e.g., of power supply, factory equipment*) Betriebsstörung *f*
breaker ['brekər] *s* Sturzwelle *f;* **breakers** Brandung *f*
breakfast ['brɛkfəst] *s* Frühstück *n* ‖ *intr* frühstücken
break'neck' *adj* halsbrecherisch
break' of day' *s* Tagesanbruch *m*
break'through' *s* Durchbruch *m*
break'up' *s* Aufbrechen *n;* (*of a meeting*) Auflösung *f*
break'wa'ter *s* Wellenbrecher *m*
breast [brɛst] *s* Brust *f;* (*of a woman*) Brust *f,* Busen *m;* **beat one's b.** sich an die Brust schlagen; **make a clean b. of** sich [*dat*] vom Herzen reden
breast'bone' *s* Brustbein *n*
breast' feed'ing *s* Stillen *n*
breast'plate' *s* Brustharnisch *m*
breast'stroke' *s* Brustschwimmen *n*

breath [brɛθ] *s* Atem *m;* (*single inhalation*) Atemzug *m;* (fig) Hauch *m;* **b. of air** Lüftchen *n;* **gasp for b.** nach Luft schnappen; **have bad b.** aus dem Mund riechen; **in the same b.** im gleichen Atemzug; **save one's b.** sich [*dat*] seine Worte ersparen; **take a deep b.** tief Luft holen; **take one's b. away** j-m den Atem verschlagen; **waste one's b.** in den Wind reden
breathe [bri ð] *tr* atmen, schöpfen; **b. a sigh of relief** aufatmen; **b. life into** beseelen; **b. one's last** die Seele aushauchen; **b. out** ausatmen; **not b. a word about it** kein Wort davon verlauten lassen ‖ *intr* atmen, hauchen; **b. again** aufatmen; **b. on** anhauchen
breath'ing space' *s* Atempause *f*
breathless ['brɛθlɪs] *adj* atemlos
breath'-tak'ing *adj* atemberaubend
breech [brit ʃ] *s* Verschlußstück *n*
breed [brid] *s* Zucht *f,* Stamm *m;* (*sort, group*) Schlag *m;* (*of animals*) Rasse *f* ‖ *v* (*pret & pp* **bred** [brɛd]) *tr* (*beget*) erzeugen; (*raise*) züchten; (fig) hervorrufen ‖ *intr* sich vermehren
breeder ['bridər] *s* Züchter –in *mf*
breed'ing *s* (*of animals*) Züchtung *f,* Aufzucht *f;* (fig) Erziehung *f*
breeze [briz] *s* Lüftchen *n,* Brise *f* ‖ *intr*—**b. by** vorbeiflitzen; **b. in** frisch und vergnügt hereinkommen
breezy ['brizi] *adj* luftig; (fig) keß
brevity ['brɛvɪti] *s* Kürze *f*
brew [bru] *s* Brühe *f;* (*of beer*) Bräu *m* ‖ *tr* (*tea, coffee*) aufbrühen; (*beer*) brauen ‖ *intr* ziehen; (*said of a storm*) sich zusammenbrauen; **something is brewing** etwas ist im Anzuge
brewer ['bru·ər] *s* Brauer –in *mf*
brewery ['bru·əri] *s* Brauerei *f*
bribe [braɪb] *s* Bestechungsgeld *n* ‖ *tr* bestechen
bribery ['braɪbəri] *s* Bestechung *f*
brick [brɪk] *s* Ziegelstein *m*
bricklayer ['brɪk ˌle·ər] *s* Maurer *m*
brick'work' *s* Mauerwerk *n*
brick'yard' *s* Ziegelei *f*
bridal ['braɪdəl] *adj* Braut–, Hochzeits–
brid'al gown' *s* Brautkleid *n*
brid'al veil' *s* Brautschleier *m*
bride [braɪd] *s* Braut *f*
bride'groom' *s* Bräutigam *m*
brides'maid' *s* Brautjungfer *f*
bridge [brɪdʒ] *s* (*over a river*) Brücke *f;* (*of eyeglasses*) Steg *m;* (*of a nose*) Nasenrücken *m;* (cards) Bridge *n;* (dent) Zahnbrücke *f;* (naut) Kommandobrücke *f* ‖ *tr* (& fig) überbrücken
bridge'head' *s* Brückenkopf *m*
bridge'work' *s* (dent) Brückenarbeit *f*
bridle ['braɪdəl] *s* Zaum *m,* Zügel *m* ‖ *tr* aufzäumen, zügeln
bri'dle path' *s* Reitweg *m*
brief [brif] *adj* kurz; **be b.** sich kurz fassen ‖ *s* (jur) Schriftsatz *m* ‖ *tr* einweisen, orientieren
brief' case' *s* Aktentasche *f*

brief'ing s Einsatzbesprechung f
brier ['braɪ-ər] s Dornbusch m
brig [brɪg] s (naut) Brigg f; (nav) Knast m
brigade [brɪ'ged] s Brigade f
brigadier' **gen'eral** [‚brɪgə'dɪr] s Brigadegeneral m
brigand ['brɪgənd] s Brigant m
bright [braɪt] adj hell; (color) lebhaft; (face) strahlend; (weather) heiter; (smart) gescheit, aufgeweckt || adv —b. and early in aller Frühe
brighten ['braɪtən] tr aufhellen || intr sich aufhellen
bright'-eyed' adj helläugig
brightness ['braɪtnɪs] s Helle f
bright' side' s (fig) Lichtseite f
bright' spot' s (fig) Lichtblick m
brilliance ['brɪljəns], **brilliancy** ['brɪljənsi] s Glanz m
brilliant ['brɪljənt] adj (& fig) glänzend
brim [brɪm] s Rand m; (of a hat) Krempe f; **to the b.** bis zum Rande || v (pret & pp **brimmed;** ger **brimming**) intr—b. **over (with)** (fig) überschäumen (vor dat)
brimful ['brɪm‚fʊl] adj übervoll
brim'stone' s Schwefel m
brine [braɪn] s Salzwasser n, Sole f; (for pickling) Salzlake f
bring [brɪŋ] v (pret & pp **brought** [brɔt]) tr bringen; **b. about** zustande bringen; **b. back** zurückbringen; (memories) zurückrufen; **b. down** herunterbringen; (shoot down) abschießen; **b. down the house** (fig) Lachstürme entfesseln; **b. forth** (e.g., complaints) hervorbringen; **b. forward** vorbringen; **b. it about that** es durchsetzen, daß; **b. on** herbeiführen; **b. oneself to** (inf) sich überwinden zu (inf); **b. to** wieder zu sich bringen; **b. together** zusammenbringen; **b. up** (children) erziehen; (a topic) zur Sprache bringen
bring'ing-up' s Erziehung f
brink [brɪŋk] s (& fig) Rand m
brisk [brɪsk] adj (pace, business) flott; (air) frisch, scharf
bristle ['brɪsəl] s Borste f || intr sich sträuben
bristly ['brɪsli] adj borstig
Britain ['brɪtən] s Britannien n
British ['brɪtɪʃ] adj britisch || **the B.** spl die Briten pl
Britisher ['brɪtɪʃər] s Brite m, Britin f
Briton ['brɪtən] s Brite m, Britin f
Brittany ['brɪtəni] s die Bretagne f
brittle ['brɪtəl] adj brüchig, spröde
broach [brotʃ] tr zur Sprache bringen
broad [brɔd] adj breit; (daylight) hellicht; (outline) grob; (sense) weit; (view) allgemein, umfassend
broad'cast' s Sendung f, Übertragung f || v (pret & pp —cast) tr (rumors, etc.) ausposaunen || (pret & pp —cast & —casted) tr & intr senden, übertragen
broadcaster ['brɔd‚kæstər] s Rundfunksprecher –in mf
broad'casting sta'tion s Sender m
broad'casting stu'dio s Senderaum m

broad'cloth' s feiner Wäschestoff m
broaden ['brɔdən] tr verbreitern || intr sich verbreitern
broad'-gauge' adj (rr) breitspurig
broad'-mind'ed adj großzügig
broad'-shoul'dered adj breitschultrig
broad'side' s (guns on one side of ship) Breitseite f; (fig) Schimpfkanonade f
brocade [bro'ked] s Brokat m
broccoli ['brɑkəli] s Spargelkohl m
brochure [bro'ʃʊr] s Broschüre f
broil [brɔɪl] tr am Rost braten, grillen
broiler ['brɔɪlər] s Bratrost m
broke [brok] adj (coll) abgebrannt, pleite; **go b.** (coll) pleite gehen
broken ['brokən] adj zerbrochen; (limb, spirit, English) gebrochen; (home) zerrüttet; (line) gestrichelt
bro'ken-down' adj erschöpft; (horse) abgearbeitet
bro'ken-heart'ed adj mit gebrochenem Herzen
broker ['brokər] s Makler –in mf
brokerage ['brokərɪdʒ] s Maklergeschäft n; (fee) Maklergebühr f
bromide ['bromaɪd] s Bromid n; (coll) Binsenweisheit f
bromine ['bromin] s Brom n
bronchial ['brɑŋkɪ-əl] adj bronchial
bron'chial tube' s Luftröhre f, Bronchie f
bronchitis [brɑŋ'kaɪtɪs] s Bronchitis f
bron·co ['brɑŋko] s (–cos) kleines halbwildes Pferd n
bronze [brɑnz] adj Bronze– || s Bronze f || tr bronzieren || intr sich bräunen
brooch [brotʃ], [brutʃ] s Brosche f
brood [brud] s Brut f, Junge pl || tr ausbrüten || intr brüten; (coll) sinnieren; **b. over** grübeln über (acc)
brook [brʊk] s Bach m || tr dulden
broom [brum] s Besen m
broom'stick' s Besenstiel m
broth [brɔθ] s Brühe f
brothel ['brɑθəl] s Bordell n
brother ['brʌðər] s Bruder m; **brother(s) and sister(s)** Geschwister pl
broth'erhood' s (& relig) Brüderschaft f
broth'er-in-law' s (brothers-in-law) Schwager m
brotherly ['brʌðərli] adj brüderlich
brow [brau] s Stirn f
brow'beat' v (pret —beat; pp —beaten) tr einschüchtern
brown [braun] adj braun || s Bräune f || tr & intr bräunen
brownish ['braunɪʃ] adj bräunlich
brown'-nose' tr (sl) kriechen (dat)
brown' sug'ar s brauner Zucker m
browse [brauz] intr grasen, weiden; (through books) schmökern, stöbern; (through a store) herumsuchen
bruise [bruz] s Quetschung f || tr quetschen
brunette [bru'nɛt] adj brünett || s Brünette f
brunt [brʌnt] s Anprall m; **bear the b.** die Hauptlast tragen
brush [brʌʃ] s Bürste f; (of an artist; for shaving) Pinsel m; (brief encoun-

ter) kurzer Zusammenstoß *m;* (*light touch*) leichte Berührung *f;* (bot) Gebüsch *n;* (elec) Bürste *f;* || *tr* bürsten; **b. aside** beiseite schieben; **b. off** abbürsten; (*devour*) verschlingen; (*make light of*) abwimmeln || *intr*—**b. against** streifen; **b. up on** auffrischen

brush'-off' *s* (coll) Laufpaß *m*

brush'wood' *s* Unterholz *n*, Niederwald *m*

brusque [brʌsk] *adj* brüsk

Brussels ['brʌsəlz] *s* Brüssel *n*

Brus'sels sprouts' *spl* Rosenkohl *m*

brutal ['brutəl] *adj* brutal

brutality [bru'tælɪti] *s* Brutalität *f*

brute [brut] *adj* viehisch; (*strength*) roh || *s* Tier *n;* (fig) Unmensch *m*

brutish ['brutɪʃ] *adj* tierisch, roh

bubble ['bʌbəl] *s* Blase *f*, Bläschen *n* || *intr* sprudeln; **b. over** (**with**) übersprudeln (vor *dat*)

bub'ble bath' *s* Schaumbad *n*

bub'ble gum' *s* Knallkaugummi *m*

bubbly ['bʌbli] *adj* sprudelnd; (*Person*) lebhaft

buck [bʌk] *s* Bock *m;* (sl) Dollar *m;* **pass the b.** (coll) die Verantwortung abschieben || *tr* (fig) kämpfen gegen; **b. off** abwerfen || *intr* bocken; **b. for** (*a promotion*) sich bemühen um

bucket ['bʌkɪt] *s* Eimer *m*

buck'et seat' *s* Schalensitz *m*

buckle ['bʌkəl] *s* Schnalle *f;* (*bend*) Ausbauchung *f* || *tr* zuschnallen || *intr* (*from heat, etc.*) zusammensacken; **b. down** sich auf die Hosen setzen

buck' pri'vate *s* gemeiner Soldat *m*

buckram ['bʌkrəm] *s* Buckram *n*

buck'shot' *s* Rehposten *m*

buck'tooth' *s* (**–teeth**) vorstehender Zahn *m*

buck'wheat' *s* Buchweizen *m*

bud [bʌd] *s* Knospe *f*, Keim *m;* **nip in the bud** (fig) im Keime ersticken || *v* (*pret & pp* **budded;** *ger* **budding**) *intr* knospen, keimen, ausschlagen

buddy ['bʌdi] *s* (coll) Kumpel *m*

budge [bʌdʒ] *tr* (von der Stelle) bewegen || *intr* sich (von der Stelle) bewegen

budget ['bʌdʒɪt] *s* Budget *n*, Haushaltsplan *m;* (*of a state*) Staatshaushalt *m* || *tr* einteilen, vorausplanen

budgetary ['bʌdʒɪ ,teri] *adj* Budget–

buff [bʌf] *adj* lederfarben || *s* Lederfarbe *f;* (coll) Schwärmer –in *mf* || *tr* polieren

buffa·lo ['bʌfə ,lo] *s* (**–loes & –los**) Büffel *m*

buffer ['bʌfər] *s* Puffer *m;* (*polisher*) Polierer *m;* (rr) Prellbock *m*

buff'er state' *s* Pufferstaat *m*

buffet [bu'fe] *s* (*meal*) Büfett *n;* (*furniture*) Kredenz *f* || ['bʌfɪt] *tr* herumstoßen

buffoon [bə'fun] *s* Hanswurst *m*

bug [bʌg] *s* Insekt *n*, Käfer *m;* (*defect*) (coll) Defekt *m;* (electron) Abhörgerät *n*, Wanze *f;* **bugs** Ungeziefer *n* || *v* (*pret & pp* **bugged;** *ger* **bugging**) *tr* (*annoy*) (sl) ärgern;

(electron) (sl) Abhörgeräte einbauen in (*dat*)

bug'-eyed' *adj* (sl) mit großen Augen

buggy ['bʌgi] *adj* verwanzt; (*crazy*) (sl) verrückt || *s* Wagen *m*

bugle ['bjugal] *s* Signalhorn *n*

bu'gle call' *s* Signal *n*

bugler ['bjuglər] *s* Hornist –in *mf*

build [bɪld] *s* Bauart *f*, Gestalt *f;* (*of a person*) Körperbau *m* || *v* (*pret & pp* **built** [bɪlt]) *tr* bauen; (*a bridge*) schlagen; (*with stone or brick*) mauern; (*a fire*) anmachen; **b. up** aufbauen; (*an area*) ausbauen; (*hopes*) erwecken

builder ['bɪldər] *s* Baumeister *m*

build'ing *s* Gebäude *n*

build'ing and loan' associa'tion *s* Bausparkasse *f*

build'ing block' *s* Zementblock *m;* (*for children*) Bauklötzchen *n*

build'ing con'tractor *s* Bauunternehmer *m*

build'ing in'dustry *s* Bauindustrie *f*

build'ing lot' *s* Bauplatz *m*, Grundstück *n*

build'ing mate'rial *s* Baustoff *m*

build'-up' *s* (coll) Propaganda *f*

built'-in' *adj* Einbau–

built'-up' *adj* bebaut

bulb [bʌlb] *s* (bot) Knolle *f*, Zwiebel *f;* (elec) Glühbirne *f;* (phot) Blitzlampe *f*

Bulgaria [bʌl'gɑrɪ·ə] *s* Bulgarien *n*

Bulgarian [bʌl'gɑrɪ·ən] *adj* bulgarisch || *s* Bulgare *m*, Bulgarin *f;* (*language*) Bulgarisch *n*

bulge [bʌldʒ] *s* Ausbauchung *f*, Beule *f;* (*of a sail*) Bausch *m;* (mil) Frontvorsprung *m* || *intr* sich bauschen; (*said of eyes*) hervortreten

bulg'ing *adj* (*belly, muscles*) hervorspringend; (*eyes*) hervorquellend; (*sails*) gebläht; **b. with** bis zum Platzen gefüllt mit

bulk [bʌlk] *adj* Massen–, unverpackt || *s* Masse *f;* (*main part*) Hauptteil *m;* **in b.** unverpackt || *intr*—**b. large** e–e große Rolle spielen

bulk'head' *s* (aer) Spant *m;* (naut) Schott *n*

bulky ['bʌlki] *adj* sperrig

bull [bul] *s* Bulle *m*, Stier *m;* (sl) Quatsch *m;* (eccl) Bulle *f;* (st. exch.) Haussier *m;* **like a b. in a china shop** wie ein Elefant im Porzellanladen; **shoot the b.** (sl) quatschen; **take the b. by the horns** den Stier an den Hörnern packen; **throw the b.** (sl) aufschneiden

bull'dog' *s* Bulldogge *f*

bull'doze' *tr* planieren; (fig) überfahren

bulldozer ['bʌl ,dozər] *s* Planierraupe *f*

bullet ['bulɪt] *s* Kugel *f*

bul'let hole' *s* Schußöffnung *f*

bulletin ['bulətɪn] *s* (*report*) Bulletin *n;* (*flyer*) Flugschrift *f*

bul'letin board' *s* Anschlagbrett *n*

bul'letproof' *adj* kugelsicher

bull'fight' *s* Stierkampf *m*

bull'fight'er *s* Stierkämpfer –in *mf*

bull'frog' *s* Ochsenfrosch *m*

bull'-head'ed *adj* dickköpfig
bull' horn' *s* Richtungslautsprecher *m*
bullion ['buljən] *s* Barren *m;* (mil, nav) Kordel *f*
bull' mar'ket *s* Spekulationsmarkt *m*
bullock ['bulək] *s* Ochse *m*
bull'pen' *s* Stierpferch *m;* (baseball) Übungsplatz *m* für Reservewerfer
bull'ring' *s* Stierkampfarena *f*
bull' ses'sion *s* (sl) zwanglose Diskussion *f*
bull's'-eye' *s* (*of a target*) Schwarze *n;* (*round window*) Bullauge *n;* hit the b. ins Schwarze treffen
bul·ly ['buli] *adj—*b. for you! großartig! || *s* Raufbold *m* || *v* (*pret & pp* –lied) *tr* tyrannisieren
bulrush ['bul‚rʌʃ] *s* Binse *f*
bulwark ['bulwərk] *s* Bollwerk *n*
bum [bʌm] (sl) Strolch *m;* give s.o. the bum's rush j–n auf den Schub bringen || *v* (*pret & pp* bummed; *ger* bumming) *tr* (sl) schinden, schnorren || *intr—*bum around bummeln
bumblebee ['bʌmbəl‚bi] *s* Hummel *f*
bump [bʌmp] *s* Stoß *m*, Bums *m;* (*swelling*) Beule *f;* (*in the road*) holp(e)rige Stelle *f* || *tr* (an)stoßen; b. off (sl) abknallen; b. one's head against s.th. mit dem Kopf gegen etw stoßen || *intr* zusammenstoßen; b. against stoßen an (*acc*); b. into stoßen gegen; (*meet unexpectedly*) in die Arme laufen (*dat*)
bumper ['bʌmpər] *s* Stoßstange *f*
bumpkin ['bʌmpkɪn] *s* Tölpel *m*
bumpy ['bʌmpi] *adj* holperig; (aer) böig
bum' steer' *s—*give s.o. a b. (coll) nasführen
bun [bʌn] *s* Kuchenbrötchen *n;* (*of hair*) Haarknoten *m*
bunch [bʌntʃ] *s* Bündel *n;* (*of grapes*) Traube *f;* (*group*) Schar *f*, Bande *f;* b. of flowers Blumenstrauß *m;* b. of grapes Weintraube *f* || *tr—*b. together zusammenfassen || *intr—*b. together sich zusammendrängen
bundle ['bʌndəl] *s* Bündel *n;* (*heap*) Stoß *m;* (*of straw*) Schütte *f;* b. of nerves Nervenbündel *n* || *tr* bündeln; b. off (coll) verfrachten; b. up sich warm anziehen
bung [bʌŋ] *s* Spund *m* || *tr* verspunden
bungalow ['bʌŋgə‚lo] *s* Bungalow *m*
bung'hole' *s* Spundloch *n*
bungle ['bʌŋgəl] *s* Pfuscherei *f* || *tr* verpfuschen || *intr* pfuschen
bungler ['bʌŋglər] *s* Pfuscher –in *mf*
bun'gling *adj* stümperhaft || *s* Stümperei *f*
bunk [bʌŋk] *s* Schlafkoje *f;* (sl) Unsinn *m* || *intr* (with) schlafen (mit)
bunk' bed' *s* Etagenbett *n*
bunker ['bʌŋkər] *s* Bunker *m*
bunny ['bʌni] *s* Kaninchen *n*
bunt'ing *s* (*cloth*) Fahnentuch *n;* (*decoration*) Fahnenschmuck *m;* (orn) Ammer *f*
buoy [bɔɪ], ['bu·i] *s* Boje *f* || *tr—*b. up flott erhalten; (fig) Auftrieb geben (*dat*)

buoyancy ['bɔɪ·ənsi] *s* Auftrieb *m;* (fig) Spannkraft *f*
buoyant ['bɔɪ·ənt] *adj* schwimmend; (fig) lebhaft
burden ['bʌrdən] *s* Bürde *f*, Last *f;* (fig) Belastung *f* || *tr* belasten
bur'den of proof' *s* Beweislast *f*
burdensome ['bʌrdənsəm] *adj* lästig
bureau ['bjuro] *s* Kommode *f;* (*office*) Büro *n;* (*department*) Amt *n*
bureaucracy [bju'rɑkrəsi] *s* Bürokratie *f*, Beamtenschaft *f*
bureaucrat ['bjurə‚kræt] *s* Bürokrat –in *mf*
bureaucratic [‚bjurə'krætɪk] *adj* bürokratisch
burglar ['bʌrglər] *s* Einbrecher –in *mf*
bur'glar alarm' *s* Einbruchssicherung *f*
burglarize ['bʌrglə‚raɪz] *tr* einbrechen in (*acc*)
bur'glarproof' *adj* einbruchssicher
burglary ['bʌrgləri] *s* Einbruchdiebstahl *m*
Burgundy ['bʌrgəndi] *s* Burgund *n;* (*wine*) Burgunder *m*
burial ['berɪ·əl] *s* Beerdigung *f*
bur'ial ground' *s* Begräbnisplatz *m*
burlap ['bʌrlæp] *s* Sackleinwand *f*
burlesque [bər'lɛsk] *adj* burlesk || *s* Burleske *f* || *tr* burlesk behandeln
burlesque' show' *s* Variété *n*
burly ['bʌrli] *adj* stämmig, beleibt
Burma ['bʌrmə] *s* Birma *n*
Bur·mese [bər'miz] *adj* birmanisch || *s* (–mese) (*person*) Birmane *m*, Birmanin *f;* (*language*) Birmanisch *n*
burn [bʌrn] *s* Brandwunde *f;* || *v* (*pret & pp* burned & burnt [bʌrnt]) *tr* (ver)brennen; be burned up (coll) fauchen; b. down niederbrennen; b. up (coll) wütend machen || *intr* (ver)brennen; (*said of food*) anbrennen; b. out ausbrennen; (elec) durchbrennen; b. up ganz verbrennen; (*during reentry*) verglühen
burner ['bʌrnər] *s* Brenner *m*
burn'ing *adj* (& fig) brennend
burnish ['bʌrnɪʃ] *tr* polieren
burn'out' *s* (rok) Brennschluß *m*
burnt *adj* verbrannt; (*smell*) brenzlig
burp [bʌrp] *s* Rülpser *m* || *tr* rülpsen lassen || *intr* rülpsen
burr [bʌr] *s* (*growth on a tree*) Auswuchs *m;* (*in metal*) Grat *m;* (bot) Klette *f*
burrow ['bʌro] *s* Bau *m* || *tr* graben || *intr* sich eingraben, wühlen
bursar ['bʌrsər] *s* Schatzmeister *m*
burst [bʌrst] *s* Bersten *n;* (*split*) Riß *m;* Bruch *m;* b. of gunfire Feuerstoß *m* || *v* (*pret & pp* burst) *tr* (auf)sprengen, zum Platzen bringen || *intr* bersten, platzen; (*split*) reißen; (*said of a boil*) aufgehen; b. into (e.g., a room) hereinstürzen in (*acc*); b. into tears in Tränen ausbrechen; b. open aufplatzen; b. out laughing loslachen
bur·y ['bɛri] *v* (*pret & pp* –ied) *tr* beerdigen, begraben; be buried in thought in Gedanken versunken sein; b. alive verschütten
bus [bʌs] *s* (busses & buses) Autobus *m*, Bus *m* || *v* (*pret & pp*) bussed &

bused; *ger* bussing & busing) *tr* &
intr mit dem Bus fahren
bus′ boy′ *s* Pikkolo *m*
bus′ driv′er *s* Autobusfahrer –in *mf*
bush [buʃ] *s* Busch *m;* **beat around
the b.** um die Sache herumreden
bushed *adj* (coll) abgeklappert
bushel [′buʃəl] *s* Scheffel *m;* **by the b.**
scheffelweise
bush′ing *s* Buchse *f*
bushy [′buʃi] *adj* strauchbewachsen;
(*brows*) buschig
business [′bɪznɪs] *adj* Geschäfts– ‖ *s*
Geschäft *n;* (*company*) Firma *f,* Betrieb *m;* (*employment*) Beruf *m,* Gewerbe *n;* (*duty*) Pflicht *f;* (*right*)
Recht *n;* (coll) Sache *f;* **be in b.** ge-
schäftlich tätig sein; **do b. with** Geschäfte machen mit; **get down to b.**
(coll) zur Sache kommen; **go about
one's b.** seiner Arbeit nachgehen; **he
means b.** (coll) er meint es ernst;
know one's b. seine Sache verstehen;
make s.th. one's b. sich [*dat*] etw
angelegen sein lassen; **mind your
own b.** kümmere dich um deine
eigenen Sachen; **that's none of your
b.** das geht dich gar nichts an; **the
whole b.** die ganze Geschichte; **you
have no b. here** du hast hier nichts
zu suchen
busi′ness call′ *s* Dienstgespräch *n*
busi′ness card′ *s* Geschäftskarte *f*
busi′ness cen′ter *s* Geschäftszentrum *n*
busi′ness col′lege *s* Handelsschule *f*
busi′ness dis′trict *s* Geschäftsviertel *n*
busi′ness expens′es *spl* Geschäftsspesen
pl
busi′ness hours′ *s* Geschäftszeit *f*
busi′ness let′ter *s* Geschäftsbrief *m*
busi′nesslike′ *adj* sachlich; (pej) ge-
schäftsmäßig
busi′ness·man′ *s* (**–men′**) Geschäfts-
mann *m*
busi′ness reply′ card′ *s* Rückantwort-
karte *f*
busi′ness suit′ *s* Straßenanzug *m*
busi′ness·wom′an *s* (**–wom′en**) Ge-
schäftsfrau *f*
bus′ line′ *s* Autobuslinie *f*
bus′ stop′ *s* Autobushaltestelle *f*
bust [bʌst] *s* (*chest*) Busen *m;* (*measurement*) Oberweite *f;* (*statue*) Brustbild *n;* (*blow*) Faustschlag *m;*
(*failure*) (sl) Platzen *n;* (*binge*) (sl)
Sauftour *f* ‖ *tr* (sl) kaputtmachen;
(mil) degradieren ‖ *intr* (*break*) (sl)
kaputtgehen
bustle [′bʌsəl] *s* (*activity*) Hochbe-
trieb *m,* Trubel *m* ‖ *intr* umher-
hasten; **b. about** herumsausen
bus′tling *adj* geschäftig
bus·y [′bɪzi] *adj* tätig, beschäftigt;
(*day, life*) arbeitsreich; (*street*) lebhaft, verkehrsstark; (telp) belegt, besetzt; **be b.** (*be occupied*) zu tun
haben; (*be unavailable*) nicht zu
sprechen sein ‖ *v* (*pret & pp* **–ied**)
tr beschäftigen
bus′ybod′y *s* Wichtigtuer –in *mf*
bus′y sig′nal *s* (telp) Besetztzeichen *n*
but [bʌt] *adv* nur, lediglich, bloß;
(*just, only*) erst; **all but** beinahe ‖

prep außer (*dat*); (*after negatives*)
als; **all but one** alle bis auf einen ‖
conj aber; (*after negatives*) sondern
butcher [′butʃər] *s* Fleischer –in *mf,*
Metzger –in *mf;* (fig) Schlächter –in
mf ‖ *tr* schlachten; (fig) abschlachten
butch′er knife′ *s* Fleischermesser *n*
butch′er shop′ *s* Metzgerei *f*
butchery [′butʃəri] *s* (*slaughterhouse*)
Schlachthaus *n;* (fig) Gemetzel *n*
butler [′bʌtlər] *s* Haushofmeister *m*
butt [bʌt] *s* (*of a gun*) Kolben *m;* (*of
a cigarette*) Stummel *m;* (*with the
horns, head*) Stoß *m;* (*of ridicule*)
Zielscheibe *f* ‖ *tr* stoßen ‖ *intr*
stoßen; **b. in** (sl) sich einmischen,
dazwischenfahren
butter [′bʌtər] *s* Butter *f* ‖ *tr* mit Butter bestreichen; (*bread*) schmieren;
b. s.o. up (coll) j–m Honig um den
Mund schmieren
but′terball′ *s* Butterkugel *f;* (*chubby
child*) Pummelchen *n*
but′tercup′ *s* Butterblume *f,* Hahnenfuß *m*
but′ter dish′ *s* Butterdose *f*
but′terfly′ *s* Schmetterling *m;* (sport)
Schmetterlingsstil *m*
but′ter knife′ *s* Buttermesser *n*
but′termilk′ *s* Buttermilch *f*
buttocks [′bʌtəks] *spl* Hinterbacken *pl*
button [′bʌtən] *s* Knopf *m* ‖ *tr* knöpfen; **button up** zuknöpfen
but′tonhole′ *s* Knopfloch *n* ‖ *tr* im
Gespräch festhalten
buttress [′bʌtrɪs] *s* Strebepfeiler *m;*
(fig) Stütze *f* ‖ *tr* (durch Strebepfeiler) stützen; (fig) (unter)stützen
butt′-weld′ *tr* stumpfschweißen
buxom [′bʌksəm] *adj* beleibt
buy [baɪ] *s* Kauf *m* ‖ *v* (*pret & pp*
bought [bɔt]) *tr* kaufen; (*bus ticket,
train ticket*) lösen; (*accept, believe*)
glauben; **buy off** (*bribe*) bestechen;
buy out auskaufen; **buy up** aufkaufen
buyer [′baɪ·ər] *s* Käufer –in *mf*
buzz [bʌz] *s* Summen *n,* Surren *n;*
(telp) (coll) Anruf *m* ‖ *tr* (coll) (aer)
dicht vorbeisausen an (*dat*); (telp)
(coll) anrufen ‖ *intr* summen, surren; **b. around** herumsausen
buzzard [′bʌzərd] *s* Bussard *m*
buzz′ bomb′ *s* Roboterbombe *f,* V-
Waffe *f*
buzzer [′bʌzər] *s* Summer *m;* **did the
b. sound?** ist der Summer ertönt
buzz′ saw′ *s* Kreissäge *f,* Rundsäge *f*
by [baɪ] *adv* vorüber, vorbei; **by and
by** nach und nach; **by and large** im
großen und ganzen ‖ *prep* (*agency*)
von (*dat*), durch (*acc*); (*position*)
bei (*dat*), an (*dat*), neben (*dat*); (*no
later than*) bis spätestens; (*in division*) durch (*acc*); (*indicating mode
of transportation*) mit (*dat*); (*indicating authorship*) von (*dat*); (*according to*) nach (*dat*); (*past*) an
(*dat*) vorbei; (*by means of*) mit
(*dat*); **by** (*ger*) indem (*ind*); **by an
inch** um e–n Zoll; **by day** bei Tag;
by far bei weitem; **by heart** auswendig; **by itself** (*automatically*) von
selbst; **by land** zu Lande; **by mail**

per Post; **by myself** ganz allein; **by nature** von Natur aus; **by now** schon; **by the pound** per Pfund; **two by four** zwei mal vier

bye [baɪ] *s* (sport) Freilos *n*

bye′bye′ *interj* Wiedersehen!

bygone ['baɪ ˌgɔn] *adj* vergangen ‖ *s*— **let bygones be bygones** laß(t) das Vergangene ruhen

by′law′ *s* Satzung *f;* **bylaws** (*of an organization*) Statuten *pl*, Satzungen *pl*

by′-line′ *s* (journ) Verfasserangabe *f*

by′pass′ *s* Umgehungsstraße *f*, Umleitung *f;* (elec) Nebenschluß *m* ‖ *tr* umgehen

by′prod′uct *s* Nebenprodukt *n*

bystander ['baɪ ˌstændər] *s* Umstehende *mf*

by′way′ *s* Seitenweg *m*

by′word′ *s* Sprichwort *n*

Byzantine ['bɪzən ˌtin], [bɪ'zæntin] *adj* byzantinisch ‖ *s* Byzantiner –in *mf*

Byzantium [bɪ'zænʃɪˌəm], [bɪ'zæntɪˌəm] *s* Byzanz *n*

C

C, c [si] *s* dritter Buchstabe des englischen Alphabets; (mus) **C** *n;* **C flat** Ces *n;* **C sharp** Cis *n*

cab [kæb] *s* Taxi *n;* (*of a truck*) Fahrerkabine *f*

cabaret [ˌkæbə're] *s* Kabarett *n*

cabbage ['kæbɪdʒ] *s* Kohl *m*, Kraut *n*

cab′driv′er *s* Taxifahrer –in *mf*

cabin ['kæbɪn] *s* Hütte *f;* (aer) Kabine *f;* (naut) Kajüte *f*, Kabine *f*

cab′in boy′ *s* Schiffsjunge *m*

cabinet ['kæbɪnɪt] *adj* Kabinetts– ‖ *s* (*in a kitchen*) Küchenschrank *m;* (*for a radio*) Gehäuse *n;* (pol) Kabinett *n*, Ministerrat *m*

cab′inetmak′er *s* Tischler *m*

cable ['kebəl] *s* Kabel *n*, Seil *n;* (naut) Tau *m;* (telg) Kabelnachricht *f* ‖ *tr & intr* kabeln

ca′ble car′ *s* Seilbahn *f*, Schwebebahn *f*

ca′blegram′ *s* Kabelnachricht *f*

caboose [kə'bus] *s* (rr) Dienstwagen *m*

cab′stand′ *s* Taxistand *m*

cache [kæʃ] *s* Geheimlager *n*, Versteck *n;* **c. of arms** Waffenlager *n*

cachet [kæ'ʃe] *s* Siegel *n;* (fig) Stempel *m;* (pharm) Kapsel *f*

cackle ['kækəl] *s* (*of chickens*) Gegacker *n;* (*of geese*) Geschnatter *n* ‖ *intr* gackern, gackeln; schnattern

cac·tus ['kæktəs] *s* (–tuses *&* –ti [taɪ]) Kaktus *m*

cad [kæd] *s* (sl) Saukerl *m*, Schuft *m*

cadaver [kə'dævər] *s* Kadaver *m*, Leiche *f*

caddie ['kædi] *s* Golfjunge *m* ‖ *intr* die Schläger tragen

cadence ['kedəns] *s* (*rhythm*) Rhythmus *m;* (*flow of language*) Sprechrhythmus *m;* (mus) Kadenz *f*

cadet [kə'det] *s* Offizier(s)anwärter –in *mf*

cadre ['kædri] *s* Kader *m*

Caesar′ean opera′tion [sɪ'zɛrɪˌən] *s* Kaiserschnitt *m*

café [kæ'fe] *s* Cafe *n*

cafeteria [ˌkæfə'tɪrɪˌə] *s* Selbstbedienungsrestaurant *n*

caffeine ['kæ'fin] *s* Koffein *n*

cage [kedʒ] *s* Käfig *m* ‖ *tr* in e–n Käfig sperren

cagey ['kedʒi] *adj* (coll) schlau

cahoots [kə'huts] *s*—**be in c.** (sl) unter e–r Decke stecken

Cain [ken] *s*—**raise C.** Krach schlagen

caisson ['kesən] *s* Senkkasten *m*

cajole [kə'dʒol] *tr* beschwatzen

cake [kek] *s* Kuchen *m;* (*round cake*) Torte *f;* (*of soap*) Riegel *m;* **he takes the c.** (coll) er schießt den Vogel ab; **that takes the c.** (coll) das ist die Höhe ‖ *intr* zusammenbacken; **c. on** anbacken

calamitous [kə'læmɪtəs] *adj* unheilvoll

calamity [kə'læmɪti] *s* Unheil *n*

calci·fy ['kælsɪ ˌfaɪ] *v* (*pret & pp* –fied) *tr & intr* verkalken

calcium ['kælsɪˌəm] *s* Kalzium *n*

calculate ['kælkjə ˌlet] *tr* berechnen ‖ *intr* rechnen

cal′culated risk′ *s*—**take a c.** ein bewußtes Risiko eingehen

cal′culating *adj* berechnend

calculation [ˌkælkjə'leʃən] *s* Berechnung *f;* **rough c.** Überschlagsrechnung *f*

calculator ['kælkjə ˌletər] *s* Rechenmaschine *f;* (data proc) Rechner *m*

calcu·lus ['kælkjələs] *s* (–luses *&* –li [ˌlaɪ]) (math) Differenzial– und Integralrechnung *f;* (pathol) Stein *m*

caldron ['kɔldrən] *s* Kessel *m*

calendar ['kæləndər] *s* Kalender *m*

calf [kæf] *s* (**calves** [kævz] (*of a cow*) Kalb *n;* (*of certain other mammals*) Junge *n;* (anat) Wade *f*

calf′skin′ *s* Kalbleder *n*

caliber ['kælɪbər] *s* (*&* fig) Kaliber *n*

calibrate ['kælɪ ˌbret] *tr* kalibrieren

cali·co ['kælɪ ˌko] *s* (–coes *&* –cos) Kaliko *m*

calisthenics [ˌkælɪs'θenɪks] *spl* Leibesübungen *pl*

calk [kɔk] *tr* abdichten, kalfatern

calk′ing *s* Kalfaterung *f*

call [kɔl] *s* Ruf *m;* (*visit*) Besuch *m;* (*reason*) Grund *m;* (com) (**for**) Nachfrage *f* (nach); (naut) Anlaufen *n;* (telp) Anruf *m;* **on c.** auf Abruf ‖ *tr* rufen; (*name*) nennen; (*wake*) wecken; (*a meeting*) einberufen; (*a game*) absagen; (*a strike*) ausrufen; (*by phone*) anrufen; (*a witness*) vorladen; (*a doctor; taxi*) kommen las-

sen; **be called** heißen; **c. down** (coll)
herunterputzen; **c. in** (a doctor, specialist) hinzuziehen; (for advice) zu
Rate ziehen; (currency) einziehen;
(capital) kündigen; **c. it a day** (coll)
Schluß machen; **c. off** absagen; **c.
out** ausrufen; (the police) einsetzen;
c. s.o. names j–n beschimpfen; **c. up**
(mil) einberufen; (telp) anrufen ‖
intr rufen; (cards) ansagen; **c. for**
(require) erfordern; (fetch) abholen;
(help) rufen um; (a person) rufen
nach; **c. on** (a pupil) aufrufen; (visit)
e–n Besuch machen bei; **c. to s.o.**
j–m zurufen; **c. upon** auffordern
call' bell' s Rufglocke f
call' boy' s Hotelpage m; (theat) In-
spezientengehilfe m
caller ['kɔlər] s Besucher –in mf
call' girl' s Callgirl n
call'ing s Beruf m; (relig) Berufung f
call'ing card' s Visitenkarte f
call'ing-down' s (coll) Standpauke f
call' num'ber s (libr) Standortnummer
f
callous ['kæləs] adj schwielig; (fig)
gefühllos, abgestumpft
call'up' s (mil) Einberufung f
callus ['kæləs] s Schwiele f
calm [kɑm] adj ruhig ‖ s Ruhe f;
(naut) Flaute f ‖ tr beruhigen; **c.
down** beruhigen ‖ intr—**c. down** sich
beruhigen
calorie ['kæləri] s Kalorie f
calumny ['kæləmni] s Verleumdung f
Calvary ['kælvəri] s Golgatha n
calve [kæv] intr kalben
cam [kæm] s Nocken m
camel ['kæməl] s Kamel n
camellia [kə'miljə] s Kamelie f
came•o ['kæmɪ‚o] s (–os) Kamee f
camera ['kæmərə] s Kamera f
cam'era•man' s (–men') Kameramann
m
camouflage ['kæmə‚flaʒ] s Tarnung f
‖ tr tarnen
camp [kæmp] s (& fig) Lager n ‖ intr
kampieren, lagern, campen
campaign [kæm'pen] s (& fig) Feldzug
m; (pol) Wahlfeldzug m ‖ intr an
e–m Feldzug teilnehmen; **c. for** (pol)
Wahlpropaganda machen für
campaigner [kæm'penər] s (for a specific cause) Befürworter –in mf;
(pol) Wahlredner –in mf
campaign' slo'gan s Wahlparole f
campaign' speech' s Wahlrede f
camper ['kæmpər] s Camper m
camp'fire' s Lagerfeuer n
camp'ground s Campingplatz m
camphor ['kæmfər] s Kampfer m
camp'ing s Camping n
campus ['kæmpəs] s Universitätsge-
lände n
cam'shaft' s Nockenwelle f
can [kæn] s Dose f, Büchse f; (for
gasoline, water) Kanister m ‖ v
(pret & pp **canned;** ger **canning**) tr
einmachen; (sl) 'rausschmeißen ‖ v
(pret & cond) (could) aux—**I can
come** ich kann kommen; **I cannot
come** ich kann nicht kommen
Canada ['kænədə] s Kanada n

Canadian [kə'nedɪ•ən] adj kanadisch
‖ s Kanadier –in mf
canal [kə'næl] s Kanal m; (anat)
Gang m
canary [kə'nɛri] s Kanarienvogel m ‖
the Canaries spl die Kanarischen
Inseln pl
can•cel ['kænsəl] v (pret & pp –el(l)ed;
ger –el(l)ing) tr (an event) absagen;
(an order) rückgängig machen;
(something written) (aus)streichen,
annulieren; (stamps) entwerten; (a
debt) tilgen; (a newspaper) abbestellen; (math) streichen; **c. out** ausgleichen
cancellation [‚kænsə'leʃən] s (of an
event) Absage f; (of an order) Annullierung f; (of something written)
Streichung f; (of a debt) Tilgung f;
(of a stamp) Entwertung f; (of a
newspaper) Abbestellung f
cancer ['kænsər] s Krebs m
cancerous ['kænsərəs] adj krebsartig
candela•brum [‚kændə'labrəm] s
(–bra [brə] & –brums) Armleuchter
m
candid ['kændɪd] adj offen
candidacy ['kændɪdəsi] s Kandidatur
f
candidate ['kændɪ‚det] s (for) Kandidat –in mf (für)
candied ['kændid] adj kandiert
candle ['kændəl] s Kerze f
can'dlelight' s Kerzenlicht n
can'dlepow'er s Kerzenstärke f
can'dlestick' s Kerzenhalter m
candor ['kændər] s Offenheit f
can•dy ['kændi] s Süßwaren pl; **piece
of c.** Bonbon m & n ‖ v (pret & pp
–died) tr glacieren, kandieren
can'dy store' s Süßwarengeschäft n
cane [ken] s (plant; stem) Rohr n;
(walking stick) Stock m ‖ tr mit e–m
Stock züchtigen
cane' sug'ar s Rohrzucker m
canine ['kenaɪn] adj Hunde– ‖ s
(tooth) Eckzahn m, Reißzahn m
canister ['kænɪstər] s Dose f
canker ['kæŋkər] s (bot) Brand m;
(pathol) Mundgeschwür n
canned' goods' spl Dosenkonserven pl
canned' mu'sic s Konservenmusik f
canned' veg'etables spl Gemüsekon-
serven pl
cannery ['kænəri] s Konservenfabrik f
cannibal ['kænɪbəl] s Kannibale m
can'ning adj Konserven– ‖ s Konser-
venfabrikation f
cannon ['kænən] s Kanone f
cannonade [‚kænə'ned] s Kanonade f,
Beschießung f ‖ tr beschießen
can'nonball' s Kanonenkugel f
can'non fod'der s Kanonenfutter n
canny ['kæni] adj (shrewd) schlau;
(sagacious) klug
canoe [kə'nu] s Kanu n
canoe'ing s Kanufahren n
canoeist [kə'nu•ɪst] s Kanufahrer m
canon ['kænən] s Kanon m; (of a
cathedral) Domherr m
canonical [kə'nɑnɪkəl] adj kanonisch
‖ **canonicals** spl kirchliche Amts-
tracht f

canonize ['kænə,naɪz] *tr* heiligsprechen

can'on law' *s* kanonisches Recht *n*

can' o'pener *s* Dosenöffner *m*

canopy ['kænəpi] *s* Baldachin *m;* (*above a king or pope*) Thronhimmel *m;* (*of a bed*) Betthimmel *m*

cant [kænt] *s* (*insincere statements*) unaufrichtiges Gerede *n;* (*jargon of thieves*) Gaunersprache *f;* (*technical phraseology*) Jargon *m*

cantaloupe ['kæntə,lop] *s* Kantalupe *f*

cantankerous [kæn'tæŋkərəs] *adj* mürrisch, zänkisch

cantata [kən'tɑtə] *s* Kantate *f*

canteen [kæn'tin] *s* (*service club, service store*) Kantine *f;* (*flask*) Feldflasche *f*

canter ['kæntər] *s* kurzer Galopp *m* || *intr* im kurzen Galopp reiten

canticle ['kæntɪkəl] *s* Lobgesang *m*

canton ['kæntən] *s* Kanton *m*

canvas ['kænvəs] *s* Leinwand *f;* (naut) Segeltuch *n;* (*a painting*) Gemälde *n*

canvass ['kænvəs] *s* (econ) Werbefeldzug *m;* (pol) Wahlfeldzug *m* || *tr* (*a district*) (pol) bearbeiten; (*votes*) (pol) werben

canyon ['kænjən] *s* Schlucht *f*

cap [kæp] *s* Kappe *f*, Mütze *f;* (*of a jar*) Deckel *m;* (*twist-off type*) Kapsel *f;* (*for a toy pistol*) Knallblättchen *n;* (typ) großer Buchstabe *m;* **use caps** (typ) großschreiben || *v* (*pret & pp* **capped; ger capping**) *tr* (*a bottle*) mit e-r Kapsel versehen; (*e.g., with snow*) bedecken; (*outdo*) übertreffen; (*success*) krönen

capability [,kepə'bɪlɪti] *s* Fähigkeit *f*

capable ['kepəbəl] *adj* tüchtig; **c. of** fähig (*genit*); (*ger*) fähig zu (*inf*)

capacious [kə'peʃəs] *adj* geräumig

capacity [kə'pæsɪti] *adj* maximal, Kapazitäts– || *s* (*ability*) Fähigkeit *f;* (*content*) Fassungsvermögen *n;* (*of a truck, bridge*) Tragfähigkeit *f;* (tech) Kapazität *f;* **in my c. as** in meiner Eigenschaft als

cap' and gown' *s* Barett *n* und Talar *m*

cape [kep] *s* Umhang *m;* (geog) Kap *n*

Cape' of Good' Hope' *s* Kap *n* der Guten Hoffnung

caper ['kepər] *s* Luftsprung *m;* (*prank*) Schabernack *m;* (culin) Kaper *f* || *intr* hüpfen

capita ['kæpɪtə] *spl*—**per c.** pro Kopf, pro Person

capital ['kæpɪtəl] *adj* (*importance*) äußerste, höchste; (*city*) Haupt–; (*crime*) Kapital– || *s* (*city*) Hauptstadt *f;* (archit) Kapitell *n;* (fin) Kapital *n;* (typ) Großbuchstabe *m*

cap'ital gains' *spl* Kapitalzuwachs *m*

capitalism ['kæpɪtə,lɪzəm] *s* Kapitalismus *m*

capitalist ['kæpɪtəlɪst] *s* Kapitalist –in *mf*

capitalistic [,kæpɪtə'lɪstɪk] *adj* kapitalistisch

capitalize ['kæpɪtə,laɪz] *tr* (fin) kapitalisieren; (typ) groß schreiben (or drucken) || *intr*—**c. on** Nutzen ziehen aus

cap'ital let'ter *s* Großbuchstabe *m*

cap'ital pun'ishment *s* Todesstrafe *f*

capitol ['kæpɪtəl] *s* Kapitol *n*

capitulate [kə'pɪtʃə,let] *intr* kapitulieren

capon ['kepɑn] *s* Kapaun *m*

caprice [kə'pris] *s* Grille *f*, Kaprice *f*

capricious [kə'prɪʃəs] *adj* kapriziös

capsize ['kæpsaɪz] *tr* zum Kentern bringen || *intr* kentern

capsule ['kæpsəl] *s* Kapsel *f*

captain ['kæptən] *s* (*of police, of firemen, in the army*) Hauptmann *m;* (naut, sport) Kapitän *m;* (nav) Kapitän *m* zur See; (sport) Mannschaftsführer *m*

caption ['kæpʃən] *s* (*heading of an article*) Überschrift *f;* (*wording under a picture*) Bildunterschrift *f;* (cin) Untertitel *m*

captivate ['kæptɪ,vet] *tr* fesseln

captive ['kæptɪv] *adj* gefangen || *s* Gefangene *mf*

cap'tive au'dience *s* unfreiwillige Zuhörerschaft *f*

captivity [kæp'tɪvɪti] *s* Gefangenschaft *f*

captor ['kæptər] *s* Fänger –in *mf*

capture ['kæptʃər] *s* Fangen *n*, Gefangennahme *f;* (naut) Kaperung *f* || *tr* (*animals*) fangen; (*soldiers*) gefangennehmen; (*a ship*) kapern; (*a town*) erobern; (*a prize*) gewinnen

car [kɑr] *s* (aut, rr) Wagen *m*

carafe [kə'ræf] *s* Karaffe *f*

caramel ['kærəməl] *s* Karamelle *f*

carat ['kærət] *s* Karat *n*

caravan ['kærə,væn] *s* Karawane *f*

car'away seed' ['kærə,we] *s* Kümmelkorn *n*

carbide ['kɑrbaɪd] *s* Karbid *n*

carbine ['kɑrbaɪn] *s* Karabiner *m*

carbohydrate [,kɑrbo'haɪdret] *s* Kohlenhydrat *n*

carbol'ic ac'id [kɑr'bɑlɪk] *s* Karbolsäure *f*

carbon ['kɑrbən] *s* (chem) Kohlenstoff *m;* (elec) Kohlenstift *m*

carbonated ['kɑrbə,netɪd] *adj* kohlensäurehaltig, Brause–

car'bon cop'y *s* Durchschlag *m;* **make a c. of** durchschlagen

car'bon diox'ide *s* Kohlendioxyd *n*

car'bon monox'ide *s* Kohlenoxyd *n*

car'bon pa'per *s* Kohlepapier *n*

carbuncle ['kɑrbʌŋkəl] *s* (*stone*) Karfunkel *m;* (pathol) Karbunkel *m*

carburetor ['kɑrb(j)ə,retər] *s* Vergaser *m*

carcass ['kɑrkəs] *s* Kadaver *m*, Aas *n;* (*without offal*) Rumpf *m*

car' coat' *s* Stutzer *m*

card [kɑrd] *s* Karte *f;* (*person*) (coll) Kerl *m;* (text) Krempel *f* || *tr* (text) kardätschen

card'board' *s* Kartonpapier *n;* (*thick pasteboard*) Pappe *f;* **piece of c.** Papp(en)deckel *m*

card'board box' *s* Pappkarton *m*, Pappschachtel *f*

card' cat'alogue *s* Kartothek *f*

card' file' s Kartei f
cardiac ['kardı,æk] adj Herz– ‖ s
(remedy) Herzmittel n; (patient)
Herzkranke mf
cardinal ['kardınəl] adj Kardinal– ‖ s
(eccl, orn) Kardinal m
card' in'dex s Karthotek f, Kartei f
card'sharp' s Falschspieler –in mf
card' trick' s Kartenkunststück n
care [kɛr] s (accuracy) Sorgfalt f;
(worry) Sorge f, Kummer m; (prudence) Vorsicht f; (upkeep) Pflege
f; **be under a doctor's c.** unter der
Aufsicht e–s Arztes stehen; **c. of** (on
letters) bei; **take c.** aufpassen; **take
c. not to** (inf) sich hüten zu (inf);
take c. of s.o. (provide for s.o.) für
j–n sorgen; (attend to) sich um j–n
kümmern; **take c. of s.th.** etw besorgen; (e.g., one's clothes) schonen
‖ intr—**c. about** sich kümmern um;
c. for (like) mögen, gern haben;
(have concern for) sorgen für; (attend to) pflegen; **c. to** (inf) Lust
haben zu (inf); **for all I c.** von mir
aus
careen [kə'rin] tr auf die Seite legen
‖ intr (aut) sich in die Kurve neigen
career [kə'rɪr] adj Berufs– ‖ s Karriere f
career' wo'man s berufstätige Frau f
care'free' adj unbelastet, sorgenfrei
careful ['kɛrfəl] adj (cautious) vorsichtig; (accurate) sorgfältig; **b. c.!**
gib acht!
careless ['kɛrlɪs] adj (incautious) unvorsichtig; (remark) unbedacht; (inaccurate) nachlässig
carelessness ['kɛrlɪsnɪs] s Unvorsich-
tigkeit f; Nachlässigkeit f
caress [kə'rɛs] s Liebkosung f ‖ tr
liebkosen
caret ['kærət] s Auslassungszeichen n
caretaker ['kɛr,tekər] s Verwalter m
care'worn' adj abgehärmt, vergrämt
car'fare' s Fahrgeld n
car·go ['kargo] s (–goes & –gos)
Fracht f
car'go compart'ment s Frachtraum m
car'go plane' s Frachtflugzeug n
Caribbean [,kærı'bi·ən], [kə'rıbı·ən]
adj karibisch ‖ s Karibisches Meer n
caricature ['kærıkət∫ər] s Karikatur f
‖ tr karikieren
caries ['kɛriz] s (dent) Karies f
carillon ['kærı,lan] s Glockenspiel n
car' lift' s (aut) Hebebühne f
car'load' s Wagenladung f
carnage ['karnıdʒ] s Blutbad n
carnal ['karnəl] adj fleischlich
car'nal know'ledge s Geschlechtsverkehr m
carnation [kar'ne∫ən] s Nelke f
carnival ['karnıvəl] s Karneval m
carnivorous [kar'nıvərəs] adj fleisch-
fressend
car·ol ['kærəl] s Weihnachtslied n ‖
v (pret & pp –ol(l)ed; ger –l(l)ing)
intr Weihnachtslieder singen
carom ['kærəm] s (billiards) Karambolage f ‖ intr (fig) zusammenstoßen; (billiards) karambolieren
carouse [kə'rauz] intr zechen

carp [karp] s Karpfen m ‖ intr nörgeln
carpenter ['karpəntər] s Zimmermann
m
carpentry ['karpəntri] s Zimmerei f
carpet ['karpıt] s Teppich m ‖ tr mit
Teppichen belegen
car'pet sweep'er s Teppichkehrmaschine f
car'port' s Autoschuppen m
car'-ren'tal serv'ice s Autovermietung
f
carriage ['kærıdʒ] s Kutsche f; (of a
typewriter) Wagen m; (bearing)
Körperhaltung f; (econ) Transportkosten pl
car' ride' s Autofahrt f
carrier ['kærı·ər] s Träger m; (company) Transportunternehmen n
car'rier pig'eon s Brieftaube f
carrion ['kærı·ən] s Aas n
carrot ['kærət] s Karotte f, Mohrrübe
f
carrousel [,kærə'zɛl] s Karussell n
car·ry ['kæri] v (pret & pp –ried) tr
tragen; (wares) führen; (a message)
überbringen; (a tune) halten; (said
of transportation) befördern; (insurance) haben; (math) übertragen;
(parl) durchbringen; **be carried**
(said of a motion, bill) angenommen
werden; **be carried away by** (& fig)
mitgerissen werden von; **c. away** (an
audience) mitreißen; **c. off** (a prize)
davontragen; **c. on** weiterführen; (a
business) betreiben, führen; **c. out**
hinaustragen; (a duty) erfüllen;
(measures) durchführen; (a sentence) vollstrecken; (an order) ausführen; **c. over** (acct) übertragen;
c. s.th. too far etw übertreiben; **c.
through** durchsetzen; ‖ intr (said of
sounds) tragen; (parl) durchgehen;
c. on (continue) weitermachen; (act
up) (coll) toben; **c. on with** ein Verhältnis haben mit
car'rying char'ges spl Kreditgebühren
pl
car'ry-o'ver s Überbleibsel n; (acct)
Übertrag m
cart [kart] s Karren m ‖ tr mit dem
Handwagen befördern; **c. away** (or
c. off) abfahren
cartel [kar'tɛl] s Kartell n
cartilage ['kartılıdʒ] s Knorpel m
carton ['kartən] s Karton m; **a c. of
cigarettes** e–e Stange Zigaretten
cartoon [kar'tun] s Karikatur f;
(comic strip) Karikaturenreihe f;
(cin) Zeichentrickfilm m; (paint)
Entwurf m natürlicher Größe ‖ tr
karikieren
cartoonist [kar'tunıst] s Karikaturen-
zeichner –in mf
cartridge ['kartrıdʒ] s Patrone f;
(phot) Filmpatrone f
car'tridge belt' s Patronengurt m
cart'wheel' s Wagenrad n; **turn a c.**
ein Rad schlagen
carve [karv] tr (wood) schnitzen;
(meat) tranchieren, vorschneiden;
(stone) meißeln; **c. out** (e.g., a career) aufbauen

carver ['kɑrvər] s (at table) Vor-
schneider –in mf
carv'ing knife' s Tranchiermesser n
car' wash' s Wagenwäsche f
cascade [kæs'ked] s Kaskade f || intr
kaskadenartig herabstürzen
case [kes] s (instance) Fall m; (situation) Sache f; (box) Kiste f; (for
a knife, etc.) Hülle f; (for cigarettes)
Etui n; (for eyeglasses) Futteral n;
(for shipping) Schutzkarton m; (of
a watch) Gehäuse n; (of sickness)
Krankheitsfall m; (sick person) Patient –in mf; (gram) Fall m; (jur)
Fall m, Sache f, Prozeß m; (typ)
Setzkasten m; **as the c. may be** je
nachdem; **have a strong c.** schlüssige
Beweise haben; **if that's the c.** wenn
es sich so verhält; **in any c.** auf jeden
Fall, jedenfalls; **in c.** falls; **in c. of**
im Falle (genit); **in c. of emergency**
im Notfall; **in no c.** keinesfalls || tr
(sl) genau ansehen; **the c. at issue**
der vorliegende Fall
case' his'tory s Vorgeschichte f; (med)
Krankengeschichte f
casement ['kesmənt] s Fensterflügel m
case'ment win'dow s Flügelfenster n
cash [kæʃ] adj Bar– || s Bargeld n;
(cash payment) Barzahlung f; **c. and
carry** nur gegen Barzahlung und
eigenen Transport; **in c.** per Kasse;
out of c. nicht bei Kasse; **pay c. for**
bar bezahlen || tr einlösen || intr—
c. in on (coll) Nutzen ziehen aus
cash'box' s Schatulle f, Kasse f
cash' dis'count s Kassaskonto n
cashew' nut' [kə'ʃu], ['kæʃu] s Ka-
schunuß f
cashier [kæ'ʃɪr] s Kassierer –in mf
cashmere ['kæʃmɪr] s Kaschmir m
cash' on deliv'ery adv per Nachnahme
cash' reg'ister m Registrierkasse f
cas'ing s (wrapping) Verpackung f;
(housing) Gehäuse n; (of a window
or door) Futter n; (of a tire) Mantel
m; (of a sausage) Wurstdarm m
casi·no [kə'sino] s (–nos) Kasino n
cask [kæsk] s Faß n, Tonne f
casket ['kæskɪt] s Sarg m
casserole ['kæsə‚rol] s Kasserolle f
cassette [kæ'sɛt] s Kassette f
cassock ['kæsək] s (eccl) Soutane f
cast [kæst] s (throw) Wurf m; (act of
molding) Guß m; (mold) Gußform
f; (object molded) Abguß m; (hue)
Abtönung f; (surg) Gipsverband m;
(theat) (Rollenbesetzung f || v (pret
& pp cast) tr werfen; (a net, anchor)
auswerfen; (a ballot) abgeben; (lots)
ziehen; (skin, horns) abwerfen; (a
shadow, glance) werfen; (metal)
gießen; (a play or motion picture)
die Rollen besetzen in (dat); **be c.
down** niedergeschlagen sein; **c. aside**
(reject) verwerfen; || intr (angl) die
Angel auswerfen; **c. off** (naut) los-
werfen
castanet [‚kæstə'nɛt] s Kastagnette f
cast'away' adj verworfen; (naut)
schiffbrüchig || s (naut) Schiff-
brüchige mf
caste [kæst] s Kaste f

caster ['kæstər] s (under furniture)
Rolle f; (shaker) Streuer m
castigate ['kæstɪ‚get] tr züchtigen;
(fig) geißeln
cast'ing s Wurf m; (act of casting)
(metal) Guß m; (the object cast)
(metal) Gußstück n; (theat) Rollen-
verteilung f
cast'ing rod' s Wurfangel f
cast' i'ron s Gußeisen n
cast'-i'ron adj gußeisern; (fig) eisern
castle ['kæsəl] s Schloß n, Burg, f;
(chess) Turm m || intr (chess) ro-
chieren
cast'off' adj abgelegt || s (e.g., dress)
abgelegtes Kleidungsstück n; (person) Verstoßene mf
cas'tor oil' ['kæstər] s Rizinusöl n
castrate ['kæstret] tr kastrieren
casual ['kæʒu·əl] adj (cursory) beiläufig; (occasional) gelegentlich; (incidental) zufällig; (informal) zwanglos; (unconcerned) gleichgültig
casualty ['kæʒu·əltɪ] s (victim) Opfer
n; (accident) Unfall m; (person injured) Verunglückte mf; (person
killed) (mil) Gefallene mf; (person
wounded) (mil) Verwundete mf;
casualties (in an accident) Verunglückte pl; (in war) Verluste pl
cas'ualty list' s Verlustliste f
cat [kæt] s Katze f; (guy) (sl) Typ m;
(malicious woman) (sl) falsche Katze
f
catacomb ['kætə‚kom] s Katakombe f
catalog(ue) ['kætə‚lɔg] s Katalog m;
(list) Verzeichnis n; (of a university)
Vorlesungsverzeichnis n || tr kata-
logisieren
catalyst ['kætəlɪst] s Katalysator m
catapult ['kætə‚pʌlt] s Katapult m &
n || tr katapultieren, abschleudern
cataract ['kætə‚rækt] s Katarakt m;
(pathol) grauer Star m; **remove
s.o.'s c.** j–m den Star stechen
catastrophe [kə'tæstrəfi] s Katastrophe f
cat'call' s Auspfeifen n || tr auspfeifen
catch [kætʃ] s Fang m; (of fish) Fisch-
fang m; (device) Haken m, Klinke
f; (desirable partner) Partie f; (fig)
Haken m; || v (pret & pp caught
[kɔt]) tr fangen; (s.o. or s.th. falling) auffangen; (by pursuing) abfangen; (s.o. or s.th. that has es-
caped) einfangen; (by surprise)
ertappen, erwischen; (in midair)
aufschnappen; (take hold of) fassen;
(said of a storm) überraschen; (e.g.,
a train) erreichen; **c. a cold** sich erkälten; **c. fire** in Brand geraten; **c.
hold of** ergreifen; **c. it** (coll) sein
Fett kriegen; **c. one's breath** wieder
Atem schöpfen; **c. one's eye** j–m ins
Auge fallen; **get caught on** hängen-
bleiben an (dat) || intr (said of a
bolt, etc.) einschnappen; **c. on** (said
of an idea) Anklang finden; **catch up** aufholen;
c. up on nachholen; **c. up with** einholen
catch'ing adj (disease) ansteckend;
(attractive) anziehend

catch'word' s (slogan) Schlagwort n;
(actor's cue) Stichwort n; (pol)
Parteiparole f
catchy ['kætʃi] adj einschmeichelnd
catechism ['kætɪ,kɪzəm] s Katechis-
mus m
category ['kætɪ,gori] s Kategorie f
cater ['ketər] tr Lebensmittel liefern
für || intr—c. to schmeicheln (dat);
(deliver food to) Lebensmittel liefern für
cater-corner ['kætər,kɔrnər] adj &
adv diagonal
caterer ['ketərər] s Lebensmittelliefe-
rant –in mf
caterpillar ['kætər,pɪlər] s (ent,
mach) Raupe f
cat'fish' s Katzenwels m, Katzenfisch
m
cat'gut' s (mus) Darmseite f; (surg)
Katgut n
cathedral [kə'θidrəl] s Dom m
catheter ['kæθɪtər] s Katheter n
cathode ['kæθod] s Kathode f
catholic ['kæθəlɪk] adj universal;
Catholic katholisch || Catholic s
Katholik –in mf
cat'nap' s Nickerchen n
catnip ['kætnɪp] s Baldrian m
catsup ['kætsəp], ['ketʃəp] s Ketschup
m
cattle ['kætəl] spl Vieh n
cat'tle car' s (rr) Viehwagen m
cat'tle-man s (–men) Viehzüchter m
cat'tle ranch' s Viehfarm f
catty ['kæti] adj boshaft
cat'walk' s Steg m, Laufplanke f
Caucasian [kɔ'keʒən] adj kaukasisch
|| s Kaukasier –in mf
caucus ['kɔkəs] s Parteiführerver-
sammlung f
cauliflower ['kɔlɪ,flau·ər] s Blumen-
kohl m
cause [kɔz] s (origin) Ursache f; (reason) Grund m; (person) Urheber –in
mf; (occasion) Anlaß m; for a good
c. für e–e gute Sache || tr verursa-
chen; c. s.o. to (inf) j–n veranlassen
zu (inf)
cause'way' s Dammweg m
caustic ['kɔstɪk] adj (& fig) ätzend
cauterize ['kɔtə,raɪz] tr verätzen
caution ['kɔʃən] s (carefulness) Vor-
sicht f; (warning) Warnung f || tr
(against) warnen (vor dat)
cautious ['kɔʃəs] adj vorsichtig
cavalcade ['kævəl,ked] s Kavalkade f
cavalier [,kævə'lɪr] adj hochmütig ||
s Kavalier m
cavalry ['kævəlri] s Kavallerie f
cav'alry-man s (–men) Kavallerist m
cave [kev] s Höhle f || intr—c. in
(collapse) einstürzen
cave'-in' s Einsturz m
cave' man' s Höhlenmensch m
cavern ['kævərn] s (große) Höhle f
caviar ['kævɪ,ar] s Kaviar m
cav·il ['kævɪl] v (pret & pp –l(l)ed;
ger –l(l)ing) intr (at, about) herum-
nörgeln (an dat)
cavity ['kævɪti] s Hohlraum m; (anat)
Höhle f; (dent) Loch n
cavort [kə'vɔrt] intr (coll) herumtollen

caw [kɔ] s Krächzen n || intr krächzen
cease [sis] s—without c. unaufhörlich
|| tr einstellen; (ger) aufhören (zu
inf); c. fire das Feuer einstellen ||
intr aufhören
cease'fire' s Feuereinstellung f
ceaseless ['sislɪs] adj unaufhörlich
cedar ['sidər] s Zeder f
cede [sɪd] tr abtreten, überlassen
cedilla [sɪ'dɪlə] s Cedille f
ceiling ['silɪŋ] s Decke f; (fin) oberste
Grenze f; hit the c. (coll) platzen
ceil'ing light' s Deckenlicht n
ceil'ing price' s Höchstpreis m
celebrant ['selɪbrənt] s Zelebrant m
celebrate ['selɪ,bret] tr (a feast) fei-
ern; (mass) zelebrieren || intr feiern;
(eccl) zelebrieren
cel'ebrat'ed adj (for) berühmt (wegen)
celebration [,selɪ'breʃən] s Feier f;
(eccl) Zelebrieren n; in c. of zur
Feier (genit)
celebrity [sɪ'lebrɪti] s Berühmtheit f;
(person) Prominente mf
celery ['seləri] s Selleriestengel m
celestial [sɪ'lestʃəl] adj himmlisch;
(astr) Himmels–
celibacy ['selɪbəsi] s Zölibat m & n
celibate ['selɪbɪt] adj ehelos
cell [sel] s Zelle f
cellar ['selər] s Keller m
cellist ['tʃelɪst] s Cellist –in mf
cel·lo ['tʃelo] s (–los) Cello n
cellophane ['selə,fen] s Zellophan n
celluloid ['seljə,lɔɪd] s Zelluloid n
Celt [selt], [kelt] s Kelte m, Keltin f
Celtic ['seltɪk], ['keltɪk] adj keltisch
cement [sɪ'ment] s (glue) Bindemittel
n; (used in building) Zement m || tr
zementieren; (glue) kitten; (fig) (be)-
festigen
cement' mix'er s Betonmischmaschine
f
cemetery ['semɪ,teri] s Friedhof m
censer ['sensər] s Räucherfaß n
censor ['sensər] s (of printed matter,
films) Zensor m; (of morals) Sitten-
richter m || tr zensieren
cen'sorship' s Zensur f
censure ['senʃər] s Tadel m || tr tadeln
census ['sensəs] s Volkszählung f
cent [sent] s Cent m
centaur ['sentɔr] s Zentaur m
centennial [sen'tenɪ·əl] adj hundert-
jährig || s Hundertjahrfeier f
center ['sentər] s Zentrum n, Mittel-
punkt m; (pol) Mitte f || tr in den
Mittelpunkt stellen; (tech) (zentrie-
ren || intr—c. on sich konzentrieren
auf (acc)
cen'ter aisle' s Mittelgang m
cen'ter cit'y s Stadtmitte f
cen'terpiece' s Tischaufsatz m
centigrade ['sentɪ,gred] s Celsius, e.g.,
one degree c. ein Grad Celsius
centimeter ['sentɪ,mitər] s Zentimeter
m
centipede ['sentɪ,pid] s Hundertfüßler
m
central ['sentrəl] adj zentral
Cen'tral Amer'ica s Mittelamerika n
centralize ['sentrə,laɪz] tr zentrali-
sieren

centri′fugal force′ [sɛn′trɪfjəgəl] s Fliehkraft f
centrifuge [′sɛntrɪ‚fjudʒ] s Zentrifuge f
century [′sɛntʃəri] s Jahrhundert n
ceramic [sɪ′ræmɪk] adj keramisch ‖ **ceramics** s (art) Keramik f; spl Töpferwaren pl
cereal [′sɪrɪ‚əl] adj Getreide– ‖ s (grain) Getreide n; (dish) Getreide- flockengericht n
cerebral [′sɛrɪbrəl] adj Gehirn–
ceremonial [‚sɛrɪ′monɪ‚əl] adj zere- moniell, feierlich
ceremonious [‚sɛrɪ′monɪ‚əs] adj zere- moniös, umständlich
ceremony [′sɛrɪ‚moni] s Zeremonie f
certain [′sʌrtən] adj (sure) sicher, be- stimmt; (particular but unnamed) gewiß; **be c.** feststehen; **for c.** gewiß; **make c. of** sich vergewissern (genit); **make c. that** sich vergewissern, daß
certainly [′sʌrtənlɪ] adv sicher(lich); (as a strong affirmative) allerdings
certainty [′sʌrtənti] s Sicherheit f
certificate [sər′tɪfɪkɪt] s Schein m; (educ) Abgangszeugnis n
certification [‚sʌrtɪfɪ′keʃən] s Be- scheinigung f, Beglaubigung f
cer′tified adj beglaubigt
cer′tified check′ s durch Bank be- stätigter Scheck m
cer′tified pub′lic account′ant s amt- lich zugelassener Wirtschaftsprüfer m
certi•fy [′sʌrtɪ‚faɪ] v (pret & pp –fied) bescheinigen, beglaubigen
cervix [′sʌrvɪks] s (cervices [sər- ′vaɪsiz]) Genick n
cessation [sɛ′seʃən] s (of territory) Abtretung f; (of activities) Einstel- lung f
cesspool [′sɛs‚pul] s Senkgrube f
chafe [tʃef] tr (the skin) wund- scheuern ‖ intr (rub) scheuern; (be- come sore) sich wundreiben; (be irritated) (at) sich ärgern über (acc)
chaff [tʃæf] s Spreu f
chaf′ing dish′ s Speisenwärmer m
chagrin [ʃə′grɪn] s Verdruß m ‖ tr verdrießen
chain [tʃen] s Kette f ‖ tr (to) an- ketten (an acc)
chain′ gang′ s Kettensträflinge pl
chain′ reac′tion s Kettenreaktion f
chain′ smok′er s Kettenraucher –in mf
chain′ store′ s Kettenladen m
chair [tʃɛr] s Stuhl m; (upholstered) Sessel m; (of the presiding officer) Vorsitz m; (presiding officer) Vor- sitzende mf; (educ) Lehrstuhl m ‖ tr den Vorsitz führen von
chair′la′dy s Vorsitzende f
chair′ lift′ s Sessellift m
chair′man s (–men) Vorsitzende m
chair′manship′ s Vorsitz m
chalice [′tʃælɪs] s Kelch m
chalk [tʃɔk] s Kreide f ‖ tr—**c. up** ankreiden; (coll) verbuchen
challenge [′tʃælɪndʒ] s Aufforderung f; (to a duel) Herausforderung f; (jur) Ablehnung f; (mil) Anruf m ‖ tr auffordern; (to a duel) herausfor-

dern; (a statement, right) bestreiten; (jur) ablehnen; (mil) anrufen
chamber [′tʃembər] s Kammer f; (parl) Sitzungssaal m
chamberlain [′tʃembərlɪn] s Kammer- herr m
cham′bermaid′ s Stubenmädchen n
cham′ber of com′merce s Handels- kammer f
chameleon [kə′milɪ‚ən] s Chamäleon n
chamfer [′tʃæmfər] s Schrägkante f ‖ tr abschrägen; (furrow) auskehlen
cham•ois [′ʃæmi] s (–ois) Sämischle- der n; (zool) Gemse f
champ [tʃæmp] s (coll) Meister m ‖ tr kauen; **champ the bit** am Gebiß kauen
champagne [ʃæm′pen] s Champagner m, Sekt m
champion [′tʃæmpɪ‚ən] s (of a cause) Verfechter –in mf; (sport) Meister –in mf ‖ tr eintreten für
cham′pionship′ s Meisterschaft f
chance [tʃæns] adj zufällig ‖ s (acci- dent) Zufall m; (opportunity) Chance f, Gelegenheit f; (risk) Risiko n; (possibility) Möglichkeit f; (lottery ticket) Los n; **by c.** zufällig; **c. of a lifetime** einmalige Gelegenheit f; **chances are (that)** aller Wahrschein- lichkeit nach; **on the c. that** für den Fall, daß; **take a c.** ein Risiko ein- gehen; **take no chances** nichts riskie- ren; ‖ tr riskieren ‖ intr geschehen; **c. upon** stoßen auf (acc)
chancel [′tʃænsəl] s Altarraum m
chancellery [′tʃænsələri] s Kanzlei f
chancellor [′tʃænsələr] s Kanzler m; (hist) Reichskanzler m
chandelier [‚ʃændə′lɪr] s Kronleuch- ter m
change [tʃendʒ] s Veränderung f; (in times, styles, etc.) Wechsel m; (in attitude, relations, etc.) Wandel m; (small coins) Kleingeld n; (of weath- er) Umschlag m; **c. for the better** Verbesserung f; **c. for the worse** Verschlechterung f; **for a c.** zur Ab- wechslung; **give c. for a dollar** auf e–n Dollar herausgeben; **need a c.** Luftveränderung brauchen ‖ tr ver- ändern; (plans) ändern; (money, subject, oil) wechseln; (a baby) trockenlegen; (stations, channels) umschalten; **c. around** umändern; **c. hands** den Besitzer wechseln; **c. one's mind** sich anders besinnen; **c. trains** (or **buses, streetcars**) umstei- gen ‖ intr sich verändern; (said of a mood, wind, weather) umschlagen; (said of a voice) mutieren; (change clothes) sich umziehen **change into** sich wandeln in (acc)
changeable [′tʃendʒəbəl] adj veränder- lich
changeless [′tʃendʒlɪs] adj unveränder- lich
change′ of heart′ s Sinnesänderung f
change′ of life′ s Wechseljahre pl
change′ of scen′ery s Ortsveränderung f
change′-o′ver s Umstellung f

chan·nel ['tʃænəl] s (strait) Kanal m; (of a river) Fahrrinne f; (groove) Rinne f; (furrow) Furche f; (fig) Weg m; (telv) Kanal m; **through official channels** auf dem Amtswege || v (pret & pp **–nel(l)ed; ger –nel(l)ing**) tr lenken; (furrow) kanalisieren

chant [tʃænt] s Gesang m; (singsong) Singsang m; (eccl) Kirchengesang m || tr singen

chanter ['tʃæntər] s Kantor m

chaos ['ke·as] s Chaos n

chaotic [ke'atɪk] adj chaotisch

chap [tʃæp] s (in the skin) Riß m; (coll) Kerl m || v (pret & pp **chapped; ger chapping**) tr (the skin) rissig machen || intr rissig werden, aufspringen

chapel ['tʃæpəl] s Kapelle f

chaperon ['ʃæpə‚ron] s Begleiter –in mf; (of a young couple) Anstandsdame f || tr als Anstandsdame begleiten

chaplain ['tʃæplɪn] s Kaplan m

chapter ['tʃæptər] s Kapitel n; (of an organization) Ortsgruppe f

char [tʃar] v (pret & pp **charred; ger charring**) tr verkohlen

character ['kærɪktər] s Charakter m; (letter) Schriftzeichen n; (typewriter space) Anschlag m; (coll) Kauz m; (theat) handelnde Person f; **be out of c.** nicht passen

characteristic [‚kærɪktə'rɪstɪk] adj (of) charakteristisch (für) || s Charakterzug m, Kennzeichen n

characterize ['kærɪktə‚raɪz] tr charakterisieren, kennzeichnen

charade [ʃə'red] s Scharade f

charcoal ['tʃar‚kol] s Holzkohle f; (for sketching) Zeichenkohle f

charge [tʃardʒ] s (accusation) Anklage f; (fee) Gebühr f; (custody) Obhut f; (responsibility) Pflicht f; (ward) Pflegebefohlene mf; (of an explosive or electricity) Ladung f; (assault) Ansturm m; (of a judge to the jury) Rechtsbelehrung f; **be in c. of** verantwortlich sein für; **charges** Spesen pl; **take c. of** die Verantwortung übernehmen für; **there is no c.** es kostet nichts; **under s.o.'s c.** unter j–s Aufsicht || tr (a battery) (auf)-laden; (with) anklagen (wegen); (a jury) belehren; (mil) stürmen; **c. s.o. ten marks for** j–m zehn Mark berechnen für; **c. s.o.'s account** auf j–s Rechnung setzen || intr (mil) anrechnen für; **c. to s.o.'s account** auf j–s Rechnung setzen || intr (mil) anstürmen

charge' account' s laufendes Konto n

charger ['tʃardʒər] s (elec) Ladevorrichtung f; (hist) Schlachtroß n

chariot ['tʃærɪ·ət] s Kampfwagen m

charitable ['tʃærɪtəbəl] adj (generous) freigebig; (lenient) nachsichtig; **c. institution** wohltätige Stiftung f

charity ['tʃærɪti] s (giving of alms) Wohltätigkeit f; (alms) Almosen n; (institution) Wohlfahrtsinstitut n; (love of neighbor) Nächstenliebe f

charlatan ['ʃarlətən] s Scharlatan m

Charles [tʃarlz] s Karl m

char'ley horse' ['tʃarli] s (coll) Muskelkater m

charm [tʃarm] s Charme m; (trinket) Amulett n || tr verzaubern; (fig) entzücken

charm'ing adj scharmant, reizend

chart [tʃart] s Karte f; (table) Tabelle f; (naut) Seekarte f || tr entwerfen, auf e–r Karte graphisch darstellen

charter ['tʃartər] adj (plane, etc.) Charter– || s Freibrief m, Charter m; (of an organization) Gründungsurkunde f und Satzungen pl || tr chartern

char'ter mem'ber s gründendes Mitglied n

char·woman ['tʃar‚wumən] s (–women [‚wɪmɪn] Putzfrau f

chase [tʃes] s (pursuit) Verfolgung f; (hunt) Jagd f || tr jagen; (girls) nachsteigen (dat); **c. away** verjagen; **c. out** vertreiben || intr—**c. after** nachlaufen (dat)

chasm ['kæzəm] s (& fig) Abgrund m

chas·sis ['tʃæsi] s (–sis [siz]) Chassis n; (aut) Fahrgestell n

chaste [tʃest] adj keusch

chasten ['tʃesən] tr züchtigen

chastise [tʃæs'taɪz] tr züchtigen

chastity ['tʃæstɪti] s Keuschheit f

chat [tʃæt] s Plauderei f || v (pret & pp **chatted; ger chatting**) intr plaudern

chattel ['tʃætəl] s Sklave m; **chattels** Hab und Gut n

chatter ['tʃætər] s (talk) Geplapper n; (of teeth) Klappern n || intr (talk) plappern; (said of teeth) klappern

chat'terbox' s (coll) Plappermaul n

chauffeur ['ʃofər], [ʃo'fʌr] s Chauffeur m || tr fahren

cheap [tʃip] adj (inexpensive) billig; (shoddy) minderwertig; (base) gemein; (stingy) geizig; **feel c.** sich verlegen fühlen || adv billig; **get off c.** mit e–m blauen Auge davonkommen

cheapen ['tʃipən] tr herabsetzen

cheat [tʃit] s Betrüger –in mf || tr (out of) betrügen (um) || intr schwindeln; (at cards) mogeln; **c. on** (e.g., a wife) betrügen

cheat'ing s Betrügerei f; (at cards) Mogelei f

check [tʃek] s (of a bank) Scheck m; (for luggage) Schein m; (in a restaurant) Rechnung f; (inspection) Kontrolle f; (test) Nachprüfung f; (repulse) Rückschlag m; (restraint) (on) Hemmnis n (für); (square) Karo n; (chess) Schach n; **hold in c.** in Schach halten || tr (restrain) hindern; (inspect) kontrollieren; (test) nachprüfen, überprüfen; (a hat, coat) abgeben, (luggage) aufgeben; (figures) nachrechnen; (chess) Schach bieten (dat); **c. off** abhaken || intr (agree) übereinstimmen; **c. out** (of a hotel) sich abmelden; **c. up on** überprüfen; (a person) sich erkundigen über (*acc*); **c. with** (*corre-spond to*) übereinstimmen mit; (*con-sult*) sich besprechen mit || *interj* Schach!

check'book' *s* Scheckbuch *n*, Scheck-heft *n*

checker ['tʃɛkər] *s* Kontrolleur *m;* (*in checkers*) Damestein *m;* **checkers** Damespiel *n*

check'erboard' *s* Damebrett *n*

check'ered *adj* kariert; (*life, career*) wechselvoll

check'ing account' *s* Scheckkonto *n*

check' list' *s* Kontrolliste *f*

check'mate' *s* Schachmatt *n;* (fig) Niederlage *f* || *tr* (& fig) matt setzen || *interj* schachmatt!

check'-out count'er *s* Kasse *f*

check'point' *s* Kontrollstelle *f*

check'room' *s* Garderobe *f*

check'up' *s* Überprüfung *f;* (med) ärzt-liche Untersuchung *f*

cheek [tʃik] *s* Backe *f*, Wange *f;* (coll) Frechheit *f*

cheek'bone' *s* Backenknochen *m*

cheek' by jowl' *adv* Seite an Seite

cheeky ['tʃiki] *adj* (coll) frech

cheer [tʃɪr] *s* (*applause*) Beifallsruf *m;* (*encouragement*) Ermunterung *f;* (sport) Ermunterungsruf *m;* **three cheers for** ein dreifaches Hoch auf (*acc*) || *tr* zujubeln (*dat*); **c. on** an-feuern; **c. up** aufmuntern; **c. up!** nur Mut!

cheerful ['tʃɪrfəl] *adj* heiter; (*room, surroundings*) freundlich

cheer'lead'er *s* Anführer –in *mf* beim Beifallsrufen

cheerless ['tʃɪrlɪs] *adj* freudlos

cheese [tʃiz] *s* Käse *m*

cheeseburger ['tʃiz‚bʌrgər] *s* belegtes Brot *n* mit Frikadelle und über-backenem Käse

cheese' cake' *s* Käsekuchen *m*

cheese' cloth' *s* grobe Baumwollgaze *f*

cheesy ['tʃizi] *adj* (sl) minderwertig

chef [ʃɛf] *s* Küchenchef *m*

chemical ['kɛmɪkəl] *adj* chemisch; (*fertilizer*) Kunst– || *s* Chemikalie *f*

chemist ['kɛmɪst] *s* Chemiker –in *mf*

chemistry ['kɛmɪstri] *s* Chemie *f*

cherish ['tʃɛrɪʃ] *tr* (*hold dear*) schät-zen; (*hopes, thoughts*) hegen

cherry ['tʃɛri] *s* Kirsche *f*

cher'ry tree' *s* Kirschbaum *m*

cher·ub ['tʃɛrəb] *s* (**–ubim** [əbɪm]) Cherub *m* || *s* (**–ubs**) Engelskopf *m*

chess [tʃɛs] *s* Schach *n*

chess'board' *s* Schachbrett *n*

chess'man' *s* (**–men'**) Schachfigur *f*

chest [tʃɛst] *s* Truhe *f;* (anat) Brust *f*

chestnut ['tʃɛsnət] *adj* kastanienbraun || *s* Kastanie *f;* (*tree*) Kastanien-baum *m;* (*horse*) Rotfuchs *m*

chest' of drawers' *s* Kommode *f*

chevron ['ʃɛvrən] *s* (mil) Winkel *m*

chew [tʃu] *s* Kauen *n;* (*stick of to-bacco*) Priem *m* || *tr* kauen; **c. the cud** wiederkauen; **c. the rag** (sl) schwatzen

chew'ing gum' *s* Kaugummi *m*

chew'ing tobac'co *s* Kautabak *m*

chic [ʃik] *adj* schick || *s* Schick *m*

chicanery [ʃɪ'kenəri] *s* Schikane *f*

chick [tʃɪk] *s* Küken *n;* (*girl*) (sl) kesse Biene *f*

chicken ['tʃɪkən] *adj* Hühner–; (sl) feig(e) || *s* Huhn *n*, Hühnchen *n*

chick'en coop' *s* Hühnerstall *m*

chick'en-heart'ed *adj* feig(e)

chick'en pox' *s* Windpocken *pl*

chick'en wire' *s* Maschendraht *m*

chick'pea' *s* Kichererbse *f*

chicory ['tʃɪkəri] *s* Zichorie *f*

chide [tʃaɪd] *v* (*pret & pp* **chided** & **chid** [tʃɪd];* pp* **chided**) *tr* tadeln

chief [tʃif] *adj* Haupt–, Ober–, oberste; (*leading*) leitend || *s* Chef *m*, Ober-haupt *n;* (*of an Indian tribe*) Häupt-ling *m*

chief' exec'utive *s* Regierungsober-haupt *n*

chief' jus'tice *s* Vorsitzender *m* des obersten Gerichtshofes

chiefly ['tʃifli] *adv* vorwiegend

chief' of police' *s* Polizeipräsident *m*

chief' of staff' *s* Generalstabschef *m*

chief' of state' *s* Staatschef *m*

chieftain ['tʃiftən] *s* Häuptling *m*

chiffon [ʃɪ'fan] *s* Chiffon *m*

child [tʃaɪld] *s* (**children** ['tʃɪldrən]) Kind *n;* **with c.** schwanger

child' abuse' *s* Kindermißhandlung *f*

child'birth' *s* Niederkunft *f*

child'hood' *s* Kindheit *f*

childish ['tʃaɪldɪʃ] *adj* kindisch

childless ['tʃaɪldlɪs] *adj* kinderlos

child'like' *adj* kindlich

child' prod'igy *s* Wunderkind *n*

child's' play' *s* (*fig*) Kinderspiel *n*

child' support' *s* Alimente *pl*

child' wel'fare *s* Jugendfürsorge *f*

Chile ['tʃɪli] *s* Chile *n*

chili ['tʃɪli] *s* Cayennepfeffer *m*

chil'i sauce' *s* Chillisoße *f*

chill [tʃɪl] *s* (*coldness*) Kälte *f;* (*sen-sation of cold or fear*) Schau(d)er *m;* **chills** Fieberschau(d)er *m* || *tr* kühlen; (*hopes, etc.*) dämpfen; (*met-als*) abschrecken; **be chilled to the bone** durchfrieren || *intr* abkühlen

chilly ['tʃɪli] *adj* (& fig) frostig; **feel chilly** frösteln

chime [tʃaɪm] *s* Geläut *n;* **chimes** Glockenspiel *n* || *intr* (*said of bells*) läuten; (*said of a doorbell*) ertönen; (*said of a clock*) schlagen; **c. in** (coll) beipflichten

chimera [kaɪ'mɪrə] *s* Hirngespinst *n*

chimney ['tʃɪmni] *s* Schornstein *m;* (*of a lamp*) Zylinder *m*

chimpanzee [tʃɪm'pænzi] *s* Schim-panse *m*

chin [tʃɪn] *s* Kinn *n;* **keep one's c. up** die Ohren steifhalten; **up to the c.** bis über die Ohren

china ['tʃaɪnə] *s* Porzellan *n* || **China** *s* China *n*

chi'na clos'et *s* Porzellanschrank *m*

chi'na·man *s* (**–men**) (pej) Chinese *m*

chin'aware' *s* Porzellanwaren *pl*

Chi·nese [tʃaɪ'niz] *adj* chinesisch || *s* (**–nese**) Chinese *m*, Chinesin *f;* (*lan-guage*) Chinesisch *n*

Chi'nese lan'tern *s* Lampion *m*

chink [tʃɪŋk] *s* Ritze *f;* (*of coins or*

glasses) Klang *m* || *tr* (*glasses*) anstoßen

chin'-up' *s* Klimmzug *m*

chip [tʃɪp] *s* Span *m*, Splitter *m;* (*in china*) angestoßene Stelle *f;* (*in poker*) Spielmarke *f;* **a c. off the old block** (coll) ganz der Vater; **have a c. on one's shoulder** (coll) vor Zorn geladen sein || *v* (*pret & pp* **chipped;** *ger* **chipping**) *tr* (e.g., *a cup*) anschlagen; **c. in** (coll) beitragen; **c. off** abbrechen || *intr* (leicht) abbrechen; **c. in** (**with**) einspringen (mit); **c. off** (*said of paint*) abblättern

chipmunk ['tʃɪp͵mʌŋk] *s* Streifenhörnchen *n*

chipper ['tʃɪpər] *adj* (coll) munter

chiropodist [kaɪ'rɑpədɪst], [kɪ'rɑpədɪst] *s* Fußpfleger –*in mf*

chiropractor ['kaɪrə͵præktər] *s* Chiropraktiker –*in mf*

chirp [tʃʌrp] *s* Gezwitscher *n* || *intr* zwitschern

chis·el ['tʃɪzəl] *s* Meißel *m* || *v* (*pret & pp* –**el[l]ed;** *ger* –**il[l]ing**) *tr* meißeln; (sl) bemogeln || meißeln; (sl) mogeln

chiseler ['tʃɪzələr] *s* (sl) Mogler *m*

chitchat ['tʃɪt͵tʃæt] *s* Schnickschnack *m*

chivalrous ['ʃɪvəlrəs] *adj* ritterlich

chivalry ['ʃɪvəlri] *s* Rittertum *n;* (*politeness*) Ritterlichkeit *f*

chive [tʃaɪv] *s* Schnittlauch *m*

chloride ['klɔraɪd] *s* Chlorid *n*

chlorine ['klɔrin] *s* Chlor *n*

chloroform ['klɔrə͵fɔrm] *s* Chloroform *n* || *tr* chloroformieren

chlorophyll ['klɔrəfɪl] *s* Chlorophyll *n*

chock-full ['tsɑk'fʊl] *adj* zum Bersten voll

chocolate ['tʃəkəlɪt] *adj* Schokoladen–; (*in color*) schokoladenfarben || *s* Schokolade *f;* (*chocolate-covered candy*) Praline *f*

choc'olate bar' *s* Schokoladentafel *f*

choice [tʃɔɪs] *adj* (aus)erlesen || *s* Wahl *f;* (*selection*) Auswahl *f*

choir [kwaɪr] *s* Chor *m;* (archit) Chor *m*

choir'boy' *s* Chorknabe *m*

choir' loft' *s* Chorgalerie *f*

choir'mas'ter *s* Chordirigent *m*

choke [tʃok] *s* (aut) Starterklappe *f* || *tr* erwürgen, ersticken; **c. back** (*tears*) herunterschlucken; **c. down** herunterwürgen; **c. up** verstopfen || *intr* ersticken; **c. on** ersticken an (*dat*)

choker ['tʃokər] *s* enges Halsband *n*

cholera ['kɑlərə] *s* Cholera *f*

cholesterol [kə'lestə͵rol] *s* Blutfett *n*

choose [tʃuz] *v* (*pret* **chose** [tʃoz]; *pp* **chosen** ['tʃozən]) *tr & intr* wählen

choosy ['tʃuzi] *adj* (coll) wählerisch

chop [tʃɑp] *s* Hieb *m;* (culin) Kotelett *n*, Schnitzel *n;* **chops** (sl) Maul *n* || *v* (*pret & pp* **chopped;** *ger* **chopping**) *tr* hacken; **c. down** niederhauen; **c. off** abhacken; **c. up** zerhacken

chopper ['tʃɑpər] *s* (ax) Hackbeil *n;* (coll) Hubschrauber *m*

chop'ping block' *s* Hackklotz *m*

choppy ['tʃɑpi] *adj* (sea) bewegt

chop'stick' *s* Eßstäbchen *n*

choral ['korəl] *adj* Chor-, Sänger–

chorale [ko'rɑl] *s* Choral *m*

chord [kɔrd] *s* (anat) Band *n;* (geom) Sehne *f;* (*combination of notes*) (mus) Akkord *m;* (mus & fig) Saite *f*

chore [tʃor] *s* Hausarbeit *f*

choreography [͵korɪ'ɑgrəfi] *s* Choreographie *f*

chorus ['korəs] *s* Chor *m;* (*refrain*) Kehrreim *m*

cho'rus girl' *s* Revuetänzerin *f*

chowder ['tʃaʊdər] *s* Fischsuppe *f*

Christ [kraɪst] *s* Christus *m*

Christ' child' *s* Christkind *n*

christen ['krɪsən] *tr* taufen

Christendom ['krɪsəndəm] *s* Christenheit *f*

chris'tening *s* Taufe *f;* **c. of a ship** Schiffstaufe *f*

Christian ['krɪstʃən] *adj* christlich || Christ –*in mf*

Chris'tian E'ra *s* christliche Zeitrechnung *f*

Christianity [͵krɪstɪ'ænɪti] *s* (*faith*) Christentum *n;* (*all Christians*) Christenheit *f*

Chris'tian name' *s* Taufname *m*

Christmas ['krɪsməs] *adj* Weihnachts– || *s* Weihnachten *pl*, Weihnachtsfest *n*

Christ'mas card' *s* Weihnachtskarte *f*

Christ'mas car'ol *s* Weihnachtslied *n*

Christ'mas Eve' *s* Heiliger Abend *m*

Christ'mas gift' *s* Weihnachtsgeschenk *n*

Christ'mas tree' *s* Christbaum *m*

Christ'mas tree' lights' *spl* Weihnachtskerzen *pl*

Christopher ['krɪstəfər] *s* Christoph *m*

chromatic [kro'mætɪk] *adj* chromatisch

chrome [krom] *adj* Chrom– || *s* Chrom *n* || *tr* verchromen

chrome'plate' *tr* verchromen

chromium ['kromɪ·əm] *s* Chrom *n*

chromosome ['kromə͵som] *s* Chromosom *n*

chronic ['krɑnɪk] *adj* chronisch

chronicle ['krɑnɪkəl] *s* Chronik *f* || *tr* aufzeichnen

chronicler ['krɑnɪklər] *s* Chronist –*in mf*

chronological [͵krɑnə'lɑdʒɪkəl] *adj* chronologisch

chronology [krə'nɑlədʒi] *s* Chronologie *f*

chronometer [krə'nɑmɪtər] *s* Chronometer *n*

chrysanthemum [krɪ'sænθɪməm] *s* Chrysantheme *f*

chubby ['tʃʌbi] *adj* pummelig

chuck [tʃʌk] *s* (culin) Schulterstück *n;* (mach) Klemmfutter *n* || *tr* schmeißen

chuckle ['tʃʌkəl] *s* Glucksen *n* || *intr* glucksen

chug [tʃʌg] *s* Tuckern *n* || *v* (*pret & pp* **chugged;** *ger* **chugging**) *intr* tuckern; **c. along** tuckernd fahren

chum [tʃʌm] s (coll) Kumpel m ‖ v (pret & pp **chummed;** ger **chumming**) intr—c. **around with** sich eng anschließen an (acc)

chummy ['tʃʌmi] adj eng befreundet

chump [tʃʌmp] s (coll) Trottel m

chunk [tʃʌŋk] s Klotz m, Stück n

church [tʃʌrtʃ] adj Kirchen–, kirchlich ‖ s Kirche f

churchgoer ['tʃʌrtʃ,go·ər] s Kirchgänger –in mf

church' pic'nic s Kirchweih f

church'yard' s Kirchhof m

churl [tʃʌrl] s Flegel m

churlish ['tʃʌrlɪʃ] adj flegelhaft

churn [tʃʌrn] s Butterfaß n ‖ tr (cream) buttern; **c. up** aufwühlen ‖ intr sich heftig bewegen

chute [ʃut] s (for coal, etc.) Rutsche f; (for laundry, etc.) Abwurfschacht m; (sliding board) Rutschbahn f; (in a river) Stromschnelle f; (aer) Fallschirm m

cider ['saɪdər] s Apfelwein m

cigar [sɪ'gɑr] s Zigarre f

cigarette [,sɪgə'rɛt] s Zigarette f

cigarette' cough' s Raucherhusten m

cigarette' light'er s Feuerzeug n

cigar' store' s Rauchwarenladen m

cinch [sɪntʃ] s Sattelgurt m; (sure thing) totsichere Sache f; (snap) (sl) Kinderspiel n; (likely candidate) totsicherer Kandidat m ‖ tr (sl) sich [dat] sichern

cinder ['sɪndər] s (ember) glühende Kohle f; (slag) Schlacke f; **cinders** Asche f

Cinderella [,sɪndə'rɛlə] s Aschenbrödel n

cin'der track' s (sport) Aschenbahn f

cinema ['sɪnəmə] s Kino n

cinematography [,sɪnəmə'tɑgrəfi] s Kinematographie f

cinnamon ['sɪnəmən] s Zimt m

cipher ['saɪfər] s Ziffer f; (zero) Null f; (code) Chiffre f ‖ tr chiffrieren

circle ['sʌrkəl] s Kreis m; **circles under the eyes** Ränder pl unter den Augen ‖ tr einkreisen; (go around) umkreisen ‖ intr kreisen

circuit ['sʌrkɪt] s (course) Kreislauf m; (elec) Stromkreis m; (jur) Bezirk m

cir'cuit break'er s Ausschalter m

cir'cuit court' s Bezirksgericht n

circuitous [sər'kju·ɪtəs] adj weitschweifig

circular ['sʌrkjələr] adj kreisförmig; (saw) Kreis– ‖ s Rundschreiben n

circulate ['sʌrkjə,let] tr in Umlauf setzen; (a rumor) verbreiten; (fin) girieren ‖ intr umlaufen; (said of blood) kreisen; (said of a rumor) umgehen

circulation [,sʌrkjə'leʃən] s (of blood) Kreislauf m; (of a newspaper) Auflage f; (of money) Umlauf m

circumcize ['sʌrkəm,saɪz] tr beschneiden

circumference [sər'kʌmfərəns] s Umfang m

circumflex ['sʌrkəm,flɛks] s Zirkumflex m

circumlocution [,sʌrkəmlo'kjuʃən] s Umschreibung f

circumscribe ['sʌrkəm,skraɪb] tr (geom) umschreiben; (fig) umgrenzen

circumspect ['sʌrkəm,spɛkt] adj umsichtig

circumstance ['sʌrkəm,stæns] s Umstand m; **circumstances** (financial situation) Verhältnisse pl

cir'cumstan'tial ev'idence [,sʌrkəm-'stænʃəl] s Indizienbeweis m

circumvent [,sʌrkəm'vɛnt] tr umgehen

circus ['sʌrkəs] s Zirkus m

cistern ['sɪstərn] s Zisterne f

citadel ['sɪtədəl] s Burg f

citation [saɪ'teʃən] s Zitat n; (jur) Vorladung f; (mil) Belobung f

cite [saɪt] tr (quote) anführen; (jur) vorladen; (mil) belobigen

citizen ['sɪtɪzən] s Bürger –in mf

cit'izenship' s Staatsangehörigkeit f

cit'rus fruit' ['sɪtrəs] s Zitrusfrucht f

city ['sɪti] s Stadt f

cit'y coun'cil s Stadtrat m

cit'y fa'ther s Stadtrat m

cit'y hall' s Rathaus n

city' plan'ning s Stadtplanung f

civic ['sɪvɪk] adj bürgerlich, Bürger– ‖ **civics** s Staatsbürgerkunde f

civil ['sɪvɪl] adj (life, duty) bürgerlich; (service) öffentlich; (polite) höflich; (jur) privatrechtlich

civ'il cer'emony s standesamtliche Trauung f

civ'il defense' s zivile Verteidigung f

civ'il engineer'ing s Hoch– und Tiefbau m

civilian [sɪ'vɪljən] adj bürgerlich, Zivil– ‖ s Zivilist –in mf

civilization [,sɪvɪlɪ'zeʃən] s Zivilisation f, Kultur f

civilize ['sɪvɪ,laɪz] tr zivilisieren

civ'il rights' spl Bürgerrechte pl

civ'il serv'ant s Staatsbeamte m, Staatsbeamtin f

civ'il serv'ice s Staatsdienst m

civ'il war' s Bürgerkrieg m

claim [klem] s Anspruch m; (assertion) Behauptung f; (for public land) beanspruchtes Land n ‖ tr beanspruchen; (assert) behaupten; (attention) erfordern; **c. to be** sich ausgeben für

claim' check' s Aufgabeschein m

clairvoyance [klɛr'vɔɪ·əns] s Hellsehen n

clairvoyant [klɛr'vɔɪ·ənt] adj hellseherisch; **be c.** hellsehen ‖ s Hellseher –in mf

clam [klæm] s eßbare Meermuschel f

clamber ['klæmər] intr klettern

clammy ['klæmi] adj feuchtkalt

clamor ['klæmər] s Geschrei n ‖ intr (for) schreien (nach)

clamorous ['klæmərəs] adj schreiend

clamp [klæmp] s Klammer f; (surg) Klemme f ‖ tr (ver)klammern ‖ intr —c. **down** on einschreiten gegen

clan [klæn] s Stamm m; (pej) Sippschaft f

clandestine [klæn'dɛstɪn] adj heimlich

clang [klæŋ] s Geklirr n ‖ intr klirren

clank [klæŋk] s Geklirr n, Gerassel n || intr klirren, rasseln

clannish ['klænɪʃ] adj stammesbewußt

clap [klæp] s (of the hands) Klatschen n; (of thunder) Schlag m || v (pret & pp **clapped**; ger **clapping**) tr (a tax, fine, duty) (**on**) auferlegen (dat); **clap hands** in die Hände klatschen || intr Beifall klatschen

clapper ['klæpər] s Klöppel m

clap'trap' s Phrasendrescherei f

claque [klæk] s Claque f

clari·fy ['klærɪ‚faɪ] v (pret & pp –**fied**) tr erklären

clarinet [‚klærɪ'nɛt] s Klarinette f

clarity ['klærɪti] s Klarheit f

clash [klæʃ] s (sound) Geklirr n; (of interests, etc.) Widerstreit m || intr (conflict) kollidieren; (said of persons) aufeinanderstoßen; (said of ideas) im Widerspruch stehen; (said of colors) nicht zusammenpassen

clasp [klæsp] s (fastener) Schließe f, Spange f; (on a necktie) Klammer f; (embrace) Umarmung f; (of hands) Händedruck m || tr umklammern; **c. s.o.'s hand** j–m die Hand drücken

class [klæs] s (group) Klasse f; (period of instruction) Stunde f; (year) Jahrgang m; **have c.** (sl) Niveau haben || tr einstufen

classic ['klæsɪk] adj klassisch || s Klassiker m

classical ['klæsɪkəl] adj klassisch; **c. antiquity** Klassik f; **c. author** Klassiker m

classicist ['klæsɪsɪst] s Kenner –in mf der Klassik

classification [‚klæsɪfɪ'keʃən] s Klassifikation f, Anordnung f

clas'sified adj geheimzuhaltend

clas'sified ad' s kleine Anzeige f

classi·fy ['klæsɪ‚faɪ] v (pret & pp –**fied**) tr klassifizieren

class'mate' s Klassenkamerad m

class' reun'ion s Klassentreffen n

class'room' s Klassenzimmer n

classy ['klæsi] adj (sl) pfundig

clatter ['klætər] s Geklapper n || intr klappern

clause [klɔz] s Satzteil m; (jur) Klausel f

clavicle ['klævɪkəl] s Schlüsselbein n

claw [klɔ] s Klaue f, Kralle f; (of a crab) Schere f || tr zerkratzen; (a hole) scharren || intr kratzen

clay [kle] adj tönern || s Ton m, Lehm m

clay' pig'eon s Tontaube f

clean [klin] adj sauber, rein; (cut) glatt; (features) klar || adv (coll) völlig || tr reinigen, putzen; **c. out** (clear out by force) räumen; (empty) ausleeren; (sl) ausbeuten; **c. up** (a room) aufräumen || intr putzen; **c. up** sich zurechtmachen; (in gambling) (sl) schwer einheimsen

clean'-cut' adj (of a person) ordentlich; (clearly outlined) klar umrissen

cleaner ['klinər] s (person, device) Reiniger m; **cleaners** (establishment) Reinigungsanstalt f

clean'ing flu'id s flüssiges Reinigungsmittel n

clean'ing wo'man s Reinemachefrau f

cleanliness ['klɛnlɪnɪs] s Sauberkeit f

cleanse [klɛnz] tr reinigen

cleanser ['klɛnzər] s Reinigungsmittel n

clean'-shav'en adj glattrasiert

clean'up' s Reinemachen n; (e.g., of vice, graft) Säuberungsaktion f

clear [klɪr] adj klar; (sky, weather) heiter; (light) hell; (profit) netto; (conscience) rein; (proof) offenkundig || adv (coll) völlig; (fin) netto || tr klären; (streets) freimachen; (the table) abräumen; (a room) räumen; (a forest) roden; (the air) reinigen; (an obstacle without touching it) setzen über (acc); (a path) bahnen; (as profit) rein gewinnen; (at customs) zollamtlich abfertigen; (one's name) reinwaschen; **c. away** wegräumen; (doubts) beseitigen; **c. up** klarlegen || intr sich klären; **c. out** (coll) sich davonmachen; **c. up** sich aufklären

clearance ['klɪrəns] s (approval) Genehmigung f; (at customs) Zollabfertigung f; (of a bridge) lichte Höhe f; (aer) Starterlaubnis f; (mach) Spielraum m

clear'ance sale' s Räumungsverkauf m

clear'-cut' adj klar, eindeutig

clear'-head'ed adj verständig

clear'ing s (in a woods) Lichtung f

clear'ing house' s Abstimmungszentrale f; (fin) Verrechnungsstelle f

clear'-sight'ed adj scharfsichtig

cleat [klit] s Stollen m

cleavage ['klivɪdʒ] s Spaltung f

cleave [kliv] v (pret & pp **cleft** [klɛft] & **cleaved**) tr zerspalten || intr (split) sich spalten; (**to**) kleben (an dat)

cleaver ['klivər] s Hackbeil n

clef [klɛf] s Notenschlüssel m

cleft [klɛft] s Riß m, Spalt m

clemency ['klɛmənsi] s Milde f; (jur) Begnadigung f

clement ['klɛmənt] adj mild

clench [klɛntʃ] tr (a fist) ballen; (the teeth) zusammenbeißen

clerestory ['klɪr‚stori] s Lichtgaden m

clergy ['klɛrdʒi] s Geistlichkeit f

cler'gy·man s (–men) Geistliche m

cleric ['klɛrɪk] s Kleriker m

clerical ['klɛrɪkəl] adj Schreib–, Büro–; (eccl) geistlich

cler'ical er'ror s Schreibfehler m

cler'ical staff' s Schreibkräfte pl

cler'ical work' s Büroarbeit f

clerk [klʌrk] s (in a store) Verkäufer –in mf; (in an office) Büroangestellte mf; (in a post office) Schalterbeamte m; (jur) Gerichtsschreiber –in mf

clever ['klɛvər] adj (intelligent) klug; (adroit) geschickt; (witty) geistreich; (ingenious) findig

cleverness ['klɛvərnɪs] s (intelligence) Klugheit f; (adroitness) Geschicklichkeit f; (ingeniousness) Findigkeit f

cliché [kli'ʃe] s Klischee n

click [klɪk] *s* Klicken *n; (of the tongue)* Schnalzen *n; (of a lock)* Einschnappen *n* || *tr* klicken lassen; **c. one's heels** die Hacken zusammenschlagen || *intr* klicken; *(said of heels)* knallen; *(said of a lock)* einschnappen || *impers*—**it clicks** (coll) es klappt

client [ˈklaɪ·ənt] *s (customer)* Kunde *m,* Kundin *f; (of a company)* Auftraggeber –in *mf; (jur)* Klient –in *mf*

clientele [ˌklaɪ·ənˈtel] *s* Kundschaft *f;* (com, jur) Klientel *f*

cliff [klɪf] *s* Klippe *f,* Felsen *m*

climate [ˈklaɪmɪt] *s* Klima *n*

climax [ˈklaɪmæks] *s* Höhepunkt *m*

climb [klaɪm] *s* Aufstieg *m,* Besteigung *f;* (aer) Steigungsflug *m* || *tr* ersteigen, besteigen; *(stairs)* hinaufsteigen; **climb a tree** auf e–n Baum klettern; || *intr* steigen, klettern; *(said of a street)* ansteigen

climber [ˈklaɪmər] *s* Kletterer –in *mf; (of a mountain)* Bergsteiger –in *mf;* (bot) Kletterpflanze *f*

clinch [klɪntʃ] *s* (box) Clinch *m* || *tr (settle)* entscheiden || *intr* clinchen

clincher [ˈklɪntʃər] *s* (coll) Trumpf *m*

cling [klɪŋ] *v (pret & pp* **clung** [klʌŋ]) *intr* haften; **c. to** sich anklammern an *(acc); (said of a dress)* sich anschmiegen an *(acc);* (fig) festhalten an *(dat)*

clinic [ˈklɪnɪk] *s* Klinik *f*

clinical [ˈklɪnɪkəl] *adj* klinisch

clink [klɪŋk] *s* Klirren *n; (prison)* (sl) Kittchen *n* || *tr*—**c. glasses** mit den Gläsern anstoßen || *intr* klirren

clip [klɪp] *s* Klammer *f;* **go at a good c.** ein scharfes Tempo gehen || *v (pret & pp* **clipped;** *ger* **clipping)** *tr (a hedge)* beschneiden; *(hair)* schneiden; *(wings)* stutzen; *(sheep)* scheren; *(from newspapers, etc.)* ausschneiden; *(syllables)* verschlucken; (sl) schröpfen; **c. together** zusammenklammern

clip′board′ *s* Manuskripthalter *m*

clip′ joint′ *s* (sl) Nepplokal *n*

clipper [ˈklɪpər] *s* (aer) Klipperflugzeug *m;* (naut) Klipper *m;* **clippers** Haarschneidemaschine *f*

clip′ping *s (act)* Stutzen *n; (from newspapers)* Ausschnitt *m;* **clippings** *(of paper)* Schnitzel *pl; (scraps)* Abfälle *pl*

clique [klik] *s* Sippschaft *f*

cliquish [ˈklikɪʃ] *adj* cliquenhaft

cloak [klok] *s* Umhang *m;* (fig) Deckmantel *m;* **under the c. of darkness** im Schutz der Dunkelheit || *tr* (fig) bemänteln

cloak′-and-dag′ger *adj* Spionage–

cloak′room′ *s* Garderobe *f*

clobber [ˈklabər] *tr* (coll) verwichsen

clock [klak] *s* Uhr *f* || *tr (a runner)* abstoppen

clock′mak′er *s* Uhrmacher –in *mf*

clock′ tow′er *s* Uhrturm *m*

clock′wise′ *adv* im Uhrzeigersinn

clock′work′ *s* Uhrwerk *n;* **like c.** wie am Schnürchen

clod [klad] *s* Klumpen *m,* Scholle *f*

clodhopper [ˈklad ˌhapər] *s* Bauerntölpel *m*

clog [klag] *s* Verstopfung *f; (shoe)* Holzschuh *m* || *v (pret & pp* **clogged;** *ger* **clogging)** *tr* verstopfen || *intr* sich verstopfen

cloister [ˈklɔɪstər] *s* Kloster *n; (covered walk)* Kreuzgang *m*

close [klos] *adj (near)* nahe; *(tight)* knapp; *(air)* schwül; *(ties; friend)* eng; *(attention)* gespannt; *(game)* beinahe gleich; *(observer)* scharf; *(surveillance)* streng; *(supervision)* genau; *(inspection)* eingehend; *(resemblance; competition)* stark; *(shave)* glatt; *(translation)* wortgetreu; *(stingy)* geizig; *(order)* (mil) geschlossen; **c. to** *(position)* nahe an *(dat),* neben *(dat); (direction)* nahe an *(acc),* neben *(acc)* || *adv* dicht, eng; **from c. up** in der Nähe || [kloz] *s* Schluß *m,* Ende *n;* **bring to a c.** zu Ende bringen; **draw to a c.** zu Ende gehen || *tr* schließen; *(an account, deal)* abschließen; **c. down** stillegen; **c. off** abschließen; *(a road)* sperren; **c. out** (com) ausverkaufen; **c. up** zumachen || *intr* sich schließen; **c. in** immer näher kommen; **c. in on** umschließen

close-by [ˈklosˈbaɪ] *adj* nebenan

close-cropped [ˈklosˈkrapt] *adj* kurz geschoren

closed [klozd] *adj* geschlossen; **c. today** (public sign) heute Betriebsruhe

closed′ shop′ *s* Unternehmen *n* mit Gewerkschaftszwang

closefisted [ˈklosˈfɪstəd] *adj* geizig

close-fitting [ˈklosˈfɪtɪŋ] *adj* eng anliegend

close-mouthed [ˈklosˈmauðd] *adj* verschwiegen

close′ or′der drill′ [klos] *s* (mil) geschlosssenes Exerzieren *n*

closeout [ˈkloz ˌaut] *s* Räumungsausverkauf *m*

close′ shave′ [klos] *s* glatte Rasure *f;* (fig) knappes Entkommen *n;* **have a c.** mit knapper Not davonkommen

closet [ˈklazɪt] *s* Schrank *m*

close-up [ˈklos ˌap] *s* Nahaufnahme *f*

clos′ing *adj* Schluß–; *(day)* scheidend || *s* Schließung *f; (of an account)* Abschluß *m; (of a factory)* Stillegung *f; (of a road)* Sperrung *f*

clos′ing price′ *s* Schlußkurs *m*

clos′ing time′ *s (of a shop)* Geschäftsschluß *m; (of bars)* Polizeistunde *f*

clot [klat] *s* Klumpen *m; (of blood)* Gerinnsel *n* || *v (pret & pp* **clotted;** *ger* **clotting)** *intr* gerinnen

cloth [klɔθ] *s* Stoff *m,* Tuch *n; (for cleaning, etc.)* Lappen *m;* **the c.** die Geistlichkeit

clothe [kloð] *v (pret & pp* **clothed &** **clad** [klæd]) *tr* ankleiden, (be)kleiden; (fig) **(in)** einhüllen (in *acc)*

clothes [kloz], [kloθz] *spl* Kleider *pl;* **change one's clothes** sich umziehen; **put on one's clothes** sich anziehen

clothes′bas′ket *s* Wäschekorb *m*

clothes′brush′ *s* Kleiderbürste *f*

clothes′ clos′et *s* Kleiderschrank *m*

clothes' dri'er s Wäschetrockner m
clothes' hang'er s Kleiderbügel m
clothes'line' s Wäscheleine f
clothes'pin' s Wäscheklammer f
clothier ['kloðjǝr] s Kleiderhändler m; (cloth maker) Tuchmacher m; (cloth dealer) Tuchhändler m
clothing ['kloðɪŋ] s Kleidung f
cloud [klaʊd] s Wolke f; **be up in the clouds** (fig) in höheren Regionen schweben || tr bewölken; (a liquid) trüben; (fig) verdunkeln || intr— **c. over** (or up) sich bewölken
cloud'burst' s Wolkenbruch m
cloud'-capped' adj von Wolken bedeckt
cloudiness ['klaʊdɪnɪs] s Bewölktheit f
cloudless ['klaʊdlɪs] adj unbewölkt
cloudy ['klaʊdi] adj bewölkt; (liquid) trüb(e)
clout [klaʊt] s (blow) (coll) Hieb m; (influence) (coll) Einfluß m || tr— **c. s.o.** (coll) j–m eins herunterhauen
clove [klov] s Gewürznelke f; **c. of garlic** Knoblauchzehe f
clo'ven hoof' ['klovǝn] s (as a sign of the devil) Pferdefuß m
clover ['klovǝr] s Klee m
clo'ver·leaf' s (–leaves) Kleeblatt n
clown [klaʊn] s Clown m, Hanswurst m
clownish ['klaʊnɪʃ] adj närrisch
cloy [klɔɪ] tr übersättigen
club [klʌb] s (weapon) Keule f; (organization) Klub m; (cards) Kreuz n; (golf) Schläger m || (pret & pp **clubbed; ger clubbing**) tr verprügeln
club' car' s (rr) Salonwagen m
club'house' s Klubhaus n
cluck [klʌk] s Glucken n || intr glucken
clue [klu] s Schlüssel m, Anhaltspunkt m
clump [klʌmp] s (of earth) Klumpen m; (of hair, grass) Büschel n; (of trees) Gruppe f; (heavy tramping sound) schwerer Tritt m; **c. of bushes** Gebüsch n || intr—**c. along** trapsen
clumsy ['klʌmzi] adj ungeschickt, plump; **c. ox** Tölpel m
cluster ['klʌstǝr] s (bunch growing together) Büschel n; (of grapes) Traube f; (group) Gruppe f || intr— **c. around** sich zusammendrängen um
clutch [klʌtʃ] s Griff m; (aut) Kupplung f; **fall into s.o.'s clutches** j–m in die Klauen geraten; **let out the c.** einkuppeln; **step on the c.** auskuppeln || tr packen
clutter ['klʌtǝr] s Durcheinander n || tr—**c. up** vollstopfen
Co. abbr (**Company**) Gesellschaft f
c/o abbr (**care of**) per Adresse, bei
coach [kotʃ] s Kutsche f; (rr) Personenwagen m; (sport) Trainer m || tr Nachhilfeunterricht geben (dat); (sport) trainieren || intr (sport) trainieren
coach'ing s Nachhilfeunterricht m; (sport) Training n
coach'man s (–men) Kutscher m

coagulate [ko'ægjǝ,let] tr gerinnen lassen || intr gerinnen
coal [kol] s Kohle f
coal'bin' s Kohlenkasten m
coal'-black' adj kohlrabenschwarz
coal' car' s (rr) Kohlenwagen m
coal'deal'er s Kohlenhändler m
coalesce [,ko·ǝ'lɛs] intr zusammenwachsen, sich vereinigen
coalition [,ko·ǝ'lɪʃǝn] s Koalition f
coal' mine' s Kohlenbergwerk n
coal' min'ing s Kohlenbergbau m
coal' oil' s Petroleum n
coal'yard' s Kohlenlager n
coarse [kors] adj (& fig) grob
coast [kost] s Küste f; **the c. is clear** (coll) die Luft ist rein || intr im Leerlauf fahren; **c. along** (fig) sich mühelos fortbewegen
coastal ['kostǝl] adj küstennah, Küsten–
coaster ['kostǝr] s (for a glass) Untersatz m; (naut) Küstenfahrer m
coast'guard' s Küstenwachdienst m
coast'line' s Küstenlinie f
coat [kot] s (of a suit) Jacke f, Rock m; (topcoat) Mantel m; (of fur) Fell n; (of enamel, etc.) Belag m; (of paint) Anstrich m || tr (e.g., with teflon) beschichten; (e.g., with chocolate) überziehen; (e.g., with oil) beschmieren
coat'ed adj überzogen; (tongue) belegt
coat' hang'er s Kleiderbügel m
coat'ing s Belag m, Überzug m
coat' of arms' s Wappen n
coat'rack' s Kleiderständer m
coat'room' s Garderobe f
coat'tail' s Rockschoß m; (of formal wear) Frackschoß m
coauthor ['ko,ɔθǝr] s Mitautor m
coax [koks] tr schmeicheln (dat); **c. s.o. to** (inf) j–n überreden zu (inf)
cob [kɑb] s Kolben m
cobalt ['kobɔlt] s Kobalt m
cobbler ['kɑblǝr] s Flickschuster m
cobblestone ['kɑbǝl,ston] s Pflasterstein m, Kopfstein m
cobra ['kobrǝ] s Kobra f
cob'web' s Spinn(en)gewebe n
cocaine [ko'ken] s Kokain n
cock [kɑk] s Hahn m; (faucet) Wasserhahn m; (of a gun) Gewehrhahn m || tr (one's ears) spitzen; (one's hat) schief aufsetzen; (the firing mechanism) spannen
cock-a-doodle-doo ['kɑkǝ,dudǝl'du] s Kikeriki n
cock'-and-bull' sto'ry s Lügengeschichte f
cockeyed ['kɑk,aɪd] adj (cross-eyed) nach innen schielend; (slanted to one side) (sl) schief; (drunk) (sl) blau; (absurd) (sl) verrückt
cock'fight' s Hahnenkampf m
cock'pit' s Hahnenkampfplatz m; (aer) Kabine f, Kanzel f
cock'roach' s Schabe f
cock'sure' adj todsicher
cock'tail' s Cocktail m
cock'tail dress' s Cocktailkleid n
cock'tail par'ty s Cocktailparty f

cock'tail shak'er s Cocktailmischgefäß n
cocky ['kɑki] adj (coll) frech
cocoa ['koko] s Kakao m
coconut ['kokə‚nʌt] s Kokosnuß f
co'conut palm', **co'conut tree'** s Kokospalme f
cacoon [kə'kun] s Kokon m
C.O.D., **c.o.d.** abbr (**cash on delivery**) per Nachnahme
cod [kɑd] s Kabeljau m
coddle ['kɑdəl] tr hätscheln
code [kod] s Geheimschrift f; (jur) Kodex m || tr verschlüsseln, chiffrieren
codefendant [‚kodɪ'fendənt] s Mitangeklagte mf
code' name' s Deckname m
code' of hon'or s Ehrenkodex m
code' of laws' s Gesetzsammlung f
code' word' s Kennwort n
codex ['kodɛks] s (**codices** ['kodɪ‚siz]) Kodex m
cod'fish' s Kabeljau m
codicil ['kɑdɪsɪl] s Kodizill n
codi·fy ['kodɪ‚faɪ] v (pret & pp **–fied**) tr kodifizieren
cod'-liver oil' s Lebertran m
coed, co-ed ['ko‚ed] s Studentin f
coeducation [‚ko‚edʒə'keʃən] s Koedukation f
coeducational [‚ko‚edʒə'keʃənəl] adj Koedukations–
coefficient [‚ko·ɪ'fɪʃənt] s Koeffizient m
coerce [ko'ʌrs] tr zwingen
coercion [ko'ʌrʃən] s Zwang m
coexist [‚ko·ɪg'zɪst] intr koexistieren
coexistence [‚ko·ɪg'zɪstəns] s Koexistenz f
coffee ['kɔfi] s Kaffee m
cof'fee bean' s Kaffeebohne f
cof'fee break' s Kaffeepause f
cof'fee fiend' s Kaffeetante f
cof'fee grounds' spl Kaffeesatz m
cof'fee pot' s Kaffeekanne f
cof'fee shop' s Kaffeestube f
coffer ['kɔfər] s Truhe f; (archit) Deckenfeld n; **coffers** Schatzkammer f
cof'ferdam' s (caisson) Kastendamm m; (naut) Kofferdamm m
coffin ['kɔfɪn] s Sarg m
cog [kɑg] s Zahn m; (cogwheel) Zahnrad n
cogency ['kodʒənsi] s Beweiskraft f
cogent ['kodʒənt] adj triftig
cognac ['konjæk], ['kɑnjæk] s Kognak m
cognizance ['kɑgnɪzəns] s Kenntnis f; **take c. of s.th.** etw zur Kenntnis nehmen
cognizant ['kɑgnɪzənt] adj—**be c. of** Kenntnis haben von
cog'wheel' s Zahnrad n
cohabit [ko'hæbɪt] intr in wilder Ehe leben
coheir [ko'er] s Miterbe m, Miterbin f
cohere [ko'hɪr] intr zusammenhängen
cohesion [ko'hiʒən] s Kohäsion f
coiffeur [kwɑ'fʌr] s Friseur m
coiffure [kwɑ'fjur] s Frisur f
coil [kɔɪl] s (something wound in a spiral) Spirale f, Rolle f; (of tubing) Schlange f; (single wind) Windung f; (elec) Spule f || tr aufrollen; (naut) aufschießen || intr—**c. up** sich zusammenrollen
coil' spring' s Spiralfeder f
coin [kɔɪn] s Münze f, Geldstück n || tr münzen, (& fig) prägen
coinage ['kɔɪnɪdʒ] s (minting) Prägen n; (coins collectively) Münzen pl; (fig) Prägung f
coincide [‚ko·ɪn'saɪd] intr (**with**) zusammentreffen (mit); (in time) (**with**) gleichzeitig geschehen (mit)
coincidence [ko'ɪnsɪdəns] s Zufall m; **by mere c.** rein zufällig
coin' machine' s Münzautomat m
coin' slot' s Münzeinwurf m
coition [ko'ɪʃən], **coitus** ['ko·ɪtəs] s Koitus m, Beischlaf m
coke [kok] s Koks m; (coll) Coca-Cola n
colander ['kʌləndər] s Sieb n
cold [kold] adj kalt || s Kälte f; (indisposition) Erkältung f
cold' blood' s—**in c.** kaltblütig
cold'-blood'ed adj kaltblütig
cold' chis'el s Kaltmeißel m
cold' com'fort s (fig) geringer Trost m
cold' cream' s Cold Cream n
cold' cuts' spl kalter Aufschnitt m
cold' feet' spl—**have c.** (fig) Angst haben
cold' front' s Kaltfront f
cold'-heart'ed adj kaltherzig
coldness ['koldnɪs] s Kälte f
cold' should'er s—**give s.o. the c.** j-m die kalte Schulter zeigen
cold' snap' s plötzlicher Kälteeinbruch m
cold' stor'age s Lagerung f im Kühlraum
cold' war' s kalter Krieg m
cold' wave' s (meteor) Kältewelle f
coleslaw ['kol‚slɔ] s Krautsalat m
colic ['kɑlɪk] s Kolik f
coliseum [‚kɑlɪ'si·əm] s Kolosseum n
collaborate [kə'læbə‚ret] intr mitarbeiten; (pol) kollaborieren
collaboration [kə‚læbə're/ən] s Mitarbeit f; (pol) Kollaboration f
collaborator [kə'læbə‚retər] s Mitarbeiter –in mf; (pol) Kollaborateur m
collapse [kə'læps] s (of a bridge, etc.) Einsturz m; (com) Krach m; (pathol) Zusammenbruch m, Kollaps m || intr einstürzen; (fig) zusammenbrechen
collapsible [kə'læpsɪbəl] adj zusammenklappbar
collaps'ible boat' s Faltboot n
collar ['kɑlər] s Kragen m; (of a dog) Halsband n; (of a horse) Kummet n; (mach) Ring m, Kragen m
collate [kə'let] tr kollationieren
collateral [kə'lætərəl] adj kollateral, Seiten– || s (fin) Deckung f
collation [kə'le/ən] s Kollation f
colleague ['kɑlig] s Kollege m, Kollegin f
collect ['kɑlɛkt] s (eccl) Kollekte f || [kə'lɛkt] adj—**make a c. call** ein R-

Gespräch führen ‖ *adv*—**call c.** ein
R-Gespräch führen; **send c.** gegen
Nachnahme schicken ‖ *tr* (*money*)
(ein)kassieren; (*stamps, coins*) sammeln; (*e.g., examination papers*) ein-
sammeln; (*taxes*) abheben; (*one's
thoughts*) zusammennehmen; **c. oneself** sich fassen ‖ *intr* sich (ver)-
sammeln; (*pile up*) sich anhäufen
collect'ed *adj* (*works*) gesammelt;
(*self-possessed*) gefaßt
collection [kə'lɛkʃən] *s* (*of stamps,
etc.*) Sammlung *f;* (*accumulation*)
Ansammlung *f;* (*of money*) Einzie-
hung *f;* (*in a church*) Kollekte *f;* (*of
mail*) Leerung *f* des Briefkastens;
(com) Kollektion *f*
collec'tion a'gency *s* Inkassobüro *n*
collec'tion bas'ket *s* Klingelbeutel *m*
collective [kə'lɛktɪv] *adj* kollektiv,
Sammel-, Gesamt- ‖ *s* (pol) Kollektiv *n*
collec'tive bar'gaining *s* Tarifverhand-
lungen *pl*
collec'tive farm' *s* Kolchose *f*
collector [kə'lɛktər] *s* (*e.g., of stamps*)
Sammler –in *mf;* (*bill collector*) Einkassierer –in *mf;* (*of taxes*) Einneh-
mer –in *mf;* (*of tickets*) Fahrkarten-
abnehmer –in *mf*
college ['kɑlɪdʒ] *s* College *n;* (*e.g., of
cardinals*) Kollegium *n*
collide [kə'laɪd] *intr* zusammenstoßen
collie ['kɑli] *s* Collie *m*
collision [kə'lɪʒən] *s* Zusammenstoß *m*
colloquial [kə'lokwɪ·əl] *adj* umgangssprachlich, Umgangs–
colloquialism [kə'lokwɪ·ə ˌlɪzəm] *s*
Ausdruck *m* der Umgangssprache
colloquy ['kɑləkwi] *s* Gespräch *n*
collusion [kə'luʒən] *s* Kollusion *f;* **be
in c.** kolludieren
colon ['kolən] *s* (anat) Dickdarm *m;*
(gram) Doppelpunkt *m*
colonel ['kʌrnəl] *s* Oberst *m*
colonial [kə'lonɪ·əl] *adj* Kolonial– ‖ *s*
Einwohner –in *mf* e–r Kolonie
colonialism [kə'lonɪ·ə ˌlɪzəm] *s* Kolo-
nialismus *m*
colonize ['kɑlə ˌnaɪz] *tr* besiedeln
colonnade [ˌkɑlə'ned] *s* Säulengang *m*
colony ['kɑləni] *s* Kolonie *f*
color ['kʌlər] *adj* (film, photo, photography, slide, television) Farb– ‖
s Farbe *f;* **lend c. to** beleben; **show
one's colors** sein wahres Gesicht zeigen; **the colors** die Flagge; **with flying colors** glänzend ‖ *tr* färben;
(fig) (schön)färben ‖ *intr* sich verfärben; (*become red*) erröten
col'or-blind' *adj* farbenblind
col'ored *adj* farbig
col'or-fast' *adj* farbecht
colorful ['kʌlərfəl] *adj* bunt, farben-
reich; (fig) farbig
col'oring *s* Kolorit *n*, Färbung *f*
col'oring book' *s* Malbuch *n*
colorless ['kʌlərlɪs] *adj* farblos
col'or ser'geant *s* Fahnenträger *m*
colossal [kə'lɑsəl] *adj* kolossal
colossus [kə'lɑsəs] *s* Koloß *m*
colt [kolt] *s* Füllen *n*
Columbus [kə'lʌmbəs] *s* Kolumbus *m*

column ['kɑləm] *s* Säule *f;* (*syndi-
cated article*) Kolumne *f;* (mil) Kolonne *f;* (typ) Spalte *f*, Rubrik *f;* **c.
of smoke** Rauchsäule *f*
columnist ['kɑləmɪst] *s* Kolumnist –in
mf
coma ['komə] *s* Koma *n*
comb [kom] *s* Kamm *m;* (*honeycomb*)
Wabe *f;* (*of a rooster*) Kamm *m* ‖
tr kämmen; (*an area*) absuchen
com·bat ['kɑmbæt] (*e.g., pilot,
strength, unit, zone*) Kampf– ‖ *s*
Kampf *m*, Streit *m* ‖ ['kɑmbæt],
[kɑm'bæt] *v* (*pret & pp* –**bat**[t]**ed;**
ger –**bat**[t]**ing**) *tr* bekämpfen ‖ *intr*
kämpfen
combatant ['kɑmbətənt] *s* Kämpfer
–in *mf*
com'bat fatigue' *s* Kriegsneurose *f*
combative ['kɑmbətɪv] *adj* streitsüchtig
comber ['komər] *s* Sturzwelle *f*
combination [ˌkɑmbɪ'neʃən] *s* Verbindung *f;* (com) Konzern *m*
combine ['kɑmbaɪn] *s* (agr) Mähdrescher *m;* (com) Interessengemein-
schaft *f* ‖ [kəm'baɪn] *tr* kombinie-
ren, verbinden
combustible [kəm'bʌstɪbəl] *adj* (ver)-
brennbar ‖ *s* Brennstoff *m*
combustion [kəm'bʌstʃən] *s* Verbrennung *f*
combus'tion cham'ber *s* Brennkammer
f
combus'tion en'gine *s* Verbrennungs-
maschine *f*
come [kʌm] *v* (*pret* **came** [kem]; *pp*
come) *intr* kommen; **c. about** geschehen, sich ereignen; **c. across**
(*discover*) stoßen auf (*acc*); (*said of
a speech, etc.*) ankommen; **c. across
with** (coll) blechen; **c. after** folgen
(*dat*); (*fetch*) holen kommen; **c.
along** mitkommen; (coll) vorwärtskommen; **c. apart** auseinanderfallen;
c. around herumkommen; (*said of a
special day*) wiederkehren; (*improve*) wieder zu sich kommen;
(*change one's view*) von e–r Ansicht
abgehen; **c. back** zurückkehren; (*recur to the mind*) wieder einfallen;
c. between treten zwischen (*acc*); **c.
by** vorbeikommen; (*acquire*) geraten
an (*acc*); **c. clean** (sl) mit der Wahrheit herausrücken; **c. down** (*said of
prices*) sinken; (& fig) herunterkom-
men; **c. down with** erkranken an
(*dat*); **c. first** (*have priority*) zuerst
an die Reihe kommen; **c. for** abholen; **c. forward** vortreten; **c. from**
herkommen; (*e.g., a rich family*)
stammen aus; (*e.g., school*) kommen
aus; **c. in** hereinkommen; **c. in for**
(coll) erhalten; **c. in second** den
zweiten Platz belegen; **c. off** (*said
of a button*) abgehen; (*come loose*)
losgehen; (*said of an event*) verlaufen; **c. on!** los!; **c. out** herauskommen; (*said of a spot*) herausgehen;
(*said of a publication*) erscheinen;
c. out against (or **for**) sich erklären
gegen (or für); **c. over** (*said of fear,
etc.*) überlaufen; **c. to** (*amount to*)

betragen; (*after fainting*) wieder zu
sich kommen; **c. together** zusammenkommen; **c. true** in Erfüllung gehen;
c. up (*occur*) vorkommen; (*said of
a number*) herauskommen; (*said of
plants*) aufgehen; (*in conversation*)
zur Sprache kommen; (*said of a
storm*) heranziehen; **c. upon** kommen auf (*acc*); **c. up to** entsprechen
(*dat*); **for years to c.** auf Jahre hinaus; **how c.?** (coll) wieso?; **it comes
easy to me** es fällt mir leicht
come'back' *s* Comeback *n*
comedian [kə'mɪdɪ·ən] *s* Komiker *m*;
(pej) Komödiant –in *mf*
comedienne [kə͵mɪdɪ'en] *s* Komikerin
f
come'down' *s* (coll) Abstieg *m*
comedy ['kamədi] *s* Komödie *f*
comely ['kʌmli] *adj* anmutig
come'-on' *s* (sl) Lockmittel *n*
comet ['kamɪt] *s* Komet *m*
comfort ['kʌmfərt] *s* (*solace*) Trost *m*;
(*of a room, etc.*) Behaglichkeit *f*;
(*person or thing that comforts*) Tröster *m*; (*bed cover*) Steppdecke *f* ‖
tr trösten
comfortable ['kʌmfərtəbəl] *adj* behaglich, bequem; (*income*) ausreichend;
be (or **feel**) **c.** sich wohl fühlen
comforter ['kʌmfərtər] *s* Tröster *m*;
(*bed cover*) Steppdecke *f*
com'forting *adj* tröstlich
com'fort sta'tion *s* Bedürfnisanstalt *f*
comic ['kamɪk] *adj* komisch ‖ *s* Komiker *m*; **comics** Comics *pl*, Witzblatt *n*
comical ['kamɪkəl] *adj* komisch
com'ic op'era *s* Operette *f*
com'ic strip' *s* Bildstreifen *m*
com'ing *adj* künftig, kommend; **c.
soon** (*notice at theater*) demnächst
‖ *s* Kommen *n*, Ankunft *f*; **c. of age**
Mündigwerden *n*
comma ['kamə] *s* Komma *n*, Beistrich
m
command [kə'mænd] *s* (*order*) Befehl
m; (*of language*) Beherrschung *f*;
(mil) Kommando *n*; (*jurisdiction*)
(mil) Kommandobereich *m*; **at s.o.'s
c.** auf j–s Befehl; **be in c. of** (mil)
das Kommando führen über (*acc*);
have a good c. of gut beherrschen;
take c. of (mil) das Kommando
übernehmen über (*acc*) ‖ *tr* (*a person*) befehlen (*dat*); (*respect, silence*) gebieten; (*troops*) führen; (*a
high price*) erzielen ‖ *intr* (mil) kommandieren
commandant [͵kamən'dænt] *s* Kommandant *m*
commandeer [͵kamən'dɪr] *tr* (coll)
organisieren; (mil) requirieren
commander [kə'mændər] *s* Truppen-
führer *m*; (*of a company*) Chef *m*;
(*of a military unit from battalion to
corps*) Kommandeur *m*; (*of an
army*) Befehlshaber *m*; (nav) Fre-
gattenkapitän *m*
comman'der in chief' *s* Oberbefehls-
haber *m*
command'ing *adj* (*appearance*) eindrucksvoll; (*view*) weit; (*position*)

beherrschend; (*general*) kommandie-
rend
command'ing of'ficer *s* Einheitsführer
m
commandment [kə'mændmənt] *s* Gebot *n*
command' post' *s* Befehlsstand *m*
commemorate [kə'mɛmə͵ret] *tr* gedenken (*genit*), feiern
commemoration [kə͵mɛmə're∫ən] *s*
Gedenkfeier *f*; **in c. of** zum Gedächtnis von
commence [kə'mɛns] *tr & intr* anfangen
commencement [kə'mɛnsmənt] *s* Anfang *m*; (educ) Schulentlassungsfeier
f
commend [kə'mɛnd] *tr* (*praise*) (&
mil) belob(ig)en; (*entrust*) empfehlen
commendable [kə'mɛndəbəl] *adj* lobenswert
commendation [͵kamən'de∫ən] *s* Be-
lobigung *f*
comment ['kamənt] *s* Bemerkung *f*,
Stellungnahme *f*; **no c.!** kein Kommentar! ‖ *intr* Bemerkungen machen; **c. on** kommentieren
commentary ['kamən͵tɛri] *s* Kommentar *m*
commentator ['kamən͵tetər] *s* Kom-
mentator –in *mf*; (*of a text*) Erklärer
–in *mf*
commerce ['kamərs] *s* Handel *m*
commercial [kə'mʌr∫əl] *adj* Handels-,
Geschäfts-, kommerziell ‖ *s* (rad,
telv) Werbesendung *f*
commer'cial art' *s* Gebrauchsgraphik *f*
commercialism [kə'mʌr∫ə͵lɪzəm] *s*
Handelsgeist *m*
commercialize [kə'mʌr∫ə͵laɪz] *tr*
kommerzialisieren
commiserate [kə'mɪzə͵ret] *intr*—**c.
with** bemitleiden
commissar ['kamɪ͵sar] *s* (pol) Kommissar *m*
commissary ['kamɪ͵sɛri] *s* (*deputy*)
Kommissar *m*; (*store*) Militärversor-
gungsstelle *f*
commission [kə'mɪ∫ən] *s* (*order*) Auftrag *m*; (*of a crime*) Begehung *f*;
(*committee*) Kommission *f*; (*percentage*) Provision *f*; (mil) Offizierspatent *n*; **out of c.** außer Betrieb;
‖ *tr* beauftragen; (*a work*) bestellen;
(*a ship*) in Dienst stellen; (mil) ein
Offizierspatent verleihen (*dat*)
commis'sioned of'ficer *s* Offizier –in
mf
commissioner [kə'mɪ∫ənər] *s* Kommissar –in *mf*
com·mit [kə'mɪt] *v* (*pret & pp*
–**mitted**; *ger* –**mitting**) *tr* (*a crime*)
begehen; (*entrust*) anvertrauen; (*give
over*) übergeben; (*to an institution*)
einweisen; **c. oneself to** sich festlegen auf (*acc*); **c. to memory** auswendig lernen; **c. to writing** zu Papier bringen
commitment [kə'mɪtmənt] *s* (**to**) Festlegung *f* (auf *acc*); (*to an asylum*)
Anstaltsüberweisung *f*
committee [kə'mɪti] *s* Ausschuß *m*
commode [kə'mod] *s* Kommode *f*

commodious [kə'modɪ·əs] *adj* geräumig
commodity [kə'madɪtɪ] *s* Ware *f*
common ['kamən] *adj* (*language, property, interest*) gemeinsam; (*general*) allgemein; (*people*) einfach; (*soldier*) gemein; (*coarse, vulgar*) gemein; (*frequent*) häufig ‖ *s*—**in c.** gemeinsam
com'mon denom'inator *s* gemeinsamer Nenner *m;* **reduce to a c.** auf e-n gemeinsamen Nenner bringen
commoner ['kamənər] *s* Bürger –in *mf*
com'mon-law mar'riage *s* wilde Ehe *f*
Com'mon Mar'ket *s* Gemeinsamer Markt *m*
com'mon noun' *s* Gattungsname *m*
com'monplace' *adj* alltäglich ‖ *s* Gemeinplatz *m*
com'mon sense' *s* gesunder Menschenverstand *m*
com'mon stock' *s* Stammaktien *pl*
commonweal ['kamən‚wil] *s* Gemeinwohl *n*
com'monwealth' *s* (*republic*) Republik *f;* (*state in U.S.A.*) Bundesstaat *m*
commotion [kə'moʃən] *s* Aufruhr *m*
commune ['kamjun] *s* Kommune *f* ‖ [kə'mjun] *intr* sich vertraulich besprechen
communicable [kə'mjunɪkəbəl] *adj* übertragbar
communicant [kə'mjunɪkənt] *s* Kommunikant –in *mf*
communicate [kə'mjunɪ‚ket] *tr* mitteilen; (*a disease*) (**to**) übertragen (auf *acc*) ‖ *intr* sich besprechen
communication [kə‚mjunɪ'keʃən] *s* Mitteilung *f;* (*message*) Nachricht *f;* **communications** Nachrichtenwesen *n;* (mil) Fernmeldewesen *n*
communicative [kə'mjunɪ‚ketɪv] *adj* mitteilsam
communion [kə'mjunjən] *s* Gemeinschaft *f;* (Prot) Abendmahl *n;* (R. C.) Kommunion *f*
commun'ion rail' *s* Altargitter *n*
communiqué [kə‚mjunɪ'ke] *s* Kommuniqué *n*
communism ['kamjə‚nɪzəm] *s* Kommunismus *m*
communist ['kamjənɪst] *s* kommunistisch ‖ *s* Kommunist –in *mf*
community [kə'mjunɪtɪ] *s* Gemeinschaft *f;* (*people living together*) Gemeinde *f*
communize ['kamjə‚naɪz] *tr* kommunistisch machen
commutation [‚kamjə'teʃən] *s* (jur) Umwandlung *f*
commuta'tion tick'et *s* Zeitkarte *f*
commutator ['kamjə‚tetər] *s* (elec) Kommutator *m*, Kollektor *m*
commute [kə'mjut] *tr* (jur) umwandeln ‖ *intr* pendeln
commuter [kə'mjutər] *s* Pendler –in *mf*
commut'er train' *s* Pendelzug *m*
compact [kəm'pækt] *adj* kompakt, dicht ‖ ['kampækt] *s* (*for cosmetics*) Kompaktdose *f;* (*agreement*) Vertrag *m;* (aut) Kompaktwagen *m*

companion [kəm'pænjən] *s* Kumpan –in *mf;* (*one who accompanies*) Begleiter –in *mf*
companionable [kə'pænjənəbəl] *adj* gesellig
compan'ionship' *s* Gesellschaft *f*
compan'ionway' *s* Kajütstreppe *f*
company ['kʌmpəni] *s* (*companions*) Umgang *m;* (& com) Gesellschaft *f;* (mil) Kompanie *f;* (theat) Truppe *f;* **keep c. with** verkehren mit; **keep s.o. c.** j–m Gesellschaft leisten
com'pany command'er *s* Kompaniechef *m*
comparable ['kampərəbəl] *adj* vergleichbar
comparative [kəm'pærətɪv] *adv* vergleichend; (gram) komparativ ‖ *s* (gram) Komparativ *m*
comparatively [kəm'pærətɪvli] *adv* verhältnismäßig
compare [kəm'pɛr] *s*—**beyond c.** unvergleichlich ‖ *tr* (**with, to**) vergleichen (mit); (gram) steigern; **as compared with** im Vergleich zu
comparison [kəm'pærɪsən] *s* Vergleich *m;* (gram) Steigerung *f*
compartment [kəm'partmənt] *s* Fach *n;* (rr) Abteil *n*
compass ['kʌmpəs] *s* Kompaß *m;* (geom) Zirkel *m;* **within the c. of** innerhalb (*genit*)
com'pass card' *s* Kompaßrose *f*
compassion [kəm'pæʃən] *s* Mitleid *n*
compassionate [kəm'pæʃənɪt] *adj* mitleidig
compatible [kəm'pætɪbəl] *adj* vereinbar
com·pel [kəm'pɛl] *v* (*pret & pp* –**pelled;** *ger* –**pelling**) *tr* zwingen, nötigen
compendious [kəm'pɛndɪ·əs] *adj* gedrängt
compendi·um [kəm'pɛndɪ·əm] *s* (–**ums** & –**a** [ə]) Abriß *m*, Kompendium *n*
compensate ['kampən‚set] *tr* entschädigen ‖ *intr*—**c. for** Ersatz leisten (or bieten) für
compensation [‚kampən'seʃən] *s* (*for damages*) Entschädigung *f;* (*remuneration*) Entgeld *n*
compete [kəm'pit] *intr* (**with**) konkurrieren (mit); (**for**) sich mitbewerben (um); (sport) am Wettkampf teilnehmen
competence ['kampɪtəns] *s* (*mental state*) Zurechnungsfähigkeit *f;* (*ability*) (**in**) Fähigkeit *f* (zu)
competent ['kampɪtənt] *adj* (*able*) fähig, tüchtig; (*witness*) zulässig
competition [‚kampɪ'trʃən] *s* Wettbewerb *m;* (com) Konkurrenz *f;* (sport) Wettkampf *m*
competitive [kəm'pɛtɪtɪv] *adj* (*bidding*) Konkurrenz–; (*prices*) konkurrenzfähig; (*person*) ehrgeizig; (*exam*) Auslese–
competitor [kəm'pɛtɪtər] *s* Mitbewerber –in *mf;* (com) Konkurrent –in *mf;* (sport) Wettkämpfer –in *mf*
compilation [‚kampɪ'leʃən] *s* Zusammenstellung *f;* (*book*) Sammelwerk *n*

compile [kəm'paɪl] *tr* zusammenstellen, kompilieren; (*Material*) zusammentragen

complacence [kəm'plesəns], **complacency** [kəm'plesənsi] *s* Selbstgefälligkeit *f*

complacent [kəm'plesənt] *adj* selbstgefällig

complain [kəm'plen] *intr* klagen; **c. to s.o. about** sich bei j—m beklagen über (*acc*)

complaint [kəm'plent] *s* Klage *f*; (*ailment*) Beschwerde *f*

complement ['kamplɪmənt] *s* (& gram) Ergänzung *f*; (geom) Komplement *n*; (nav) Bemannung *f* || ['kamplɪ‚ment] *tr* ergänzen

complete [kəm'plit] *adj* ganz, vollkommen, vollständig; (*works*) sämtlich || *tr* (*make whole*) vervollständigen; (*make perfect*) vollenden; (*finish*) beenden; (*a job*) erledigen

completely [kəm'plitli] *adv* völlig

completion [kəm'pliʃən] *s* Vollendung *f*

complex [kəm'plɛks], ['kamplɛks] *adj* verwickelt || ['kamplɛks] *s* Komplex *m*

complexion [kəm'plɛkʃən] *s* Gesichtsfarbe *f*; (*appearance*) Aussehen *n*

complexity [kəm'plɛksɪti] *s* Kompliziertheit *f*

compliance [kəm'plaɪ·əns] *s* Einwilligung *f*; **in c. with your wishes** Ihren Wünschen gemäß

complicate ['kamplɪ‚ket] *tr* komplizieren

com'plicat'ed *adj* kompliziert

complication [‚kamplɪ'keʃən] *s* Verwicklung *f*; (& pathol) Komplikation *f*

complicity [kəm'plɪsɪti] *s* (**in**) Mitschuld *f* (an *dat*)

compliment ['kamplɪmənt] *s* Kompliment *n*; (*praise*) Lob *n*; **compliments** Empfehlungen *pl*; **pay s.o. a (high) c.** j—m ein (großes) Lob spenden || *tr* (**on**) beglückwünschen (zu)

complimentary [‚kamplɪ'mɛntəri] *adj* (*remark*) schmeichelhaft; (*free*) Frei—

com·ply ['kəm'plaɪ] *v* (*pret & pp* –**plied**) *intr* sich fügen; **c. with** einwilligen in (*acc*); **c. with the rules** sich an die Vorschriften halten

component [kəm'ponənt] *adj* Teil— || *s* Bestandteil *m*; (math, phys) Komponente *f*

compose [kəm'poz] *tr* (*writings*) verfassen; (*a sentence*) bilden; (mus) komponieren; (typ) setzen; **be composed of** bestehen aus; **c. oneself** sich fassen

composed' *adj* ruhig, gefaßt

composer [kəm'pozər] *s* Verfasser –in *mf*; (mus) Komponist –in *mf*

composite [kəm'pazɪt] *adj* zusammengesetzt || *s* Zusammensetzung *f*

composition [‚kampə'zɪʃən] *s* (chem) Zusammensetzung *f*; (*educ*) Aufsatz *m*; (mus, paint) Komposition *f*; (typ) Schriftsatz *m*

composi'tion book' *s* Übungsheft *n*

compositor [kəm'pazɪtər] *s* Setzer –in *mf*

composure [kəm'poʒər] *s* Fassung *f*

compote ['kampot] *s* (*stewed fruit*) Kompott *n*; (*dish*) Kompottschale *f*

compound ['kampaund] *adj* zusammengesetzt; (*fracture*) kompliziert || *s* Zusammensetzung *f*; (*enclosure*) umzäumtes Gelände *n*; (chem) Verbindung *f*; (gram) Kompositum *n*; (mil) Truppenlager *n* || [kam'paund] *tr* zusammensetzen

com'pound in'terest *s* Zinseszinsen *pl*

comprehend [‚kamprɪ'hɛnd] *tr* auffassen

comprehensible [‚kamprɪ'hɛnsɪbəl] *adj* faßlich, begreiflich

comprehension [‚kamprɪ'hɛnʃən] *s* Auffassung *f*; (*ability to understand*) Fassungskraft *f*

comprehensive [‚kamprɪ'hɛnsɪv] *adj* umfassend

compress ['kamprɛs] *s* (med) Kompresse *f* || [kəm'prɛs] *tr* komprimieren

compressed' *adj* komprimiert; (*air*) Druck—; (fig) gedrängt

compression [kəm'prɛʃən] *s* Kompression *f*, Druck *m*

comprise [kəm'praɪz] *tr* umfassen; **be comprised of** bestehen aus

compromise ['kamprə‚maɪz] *s* Kompromiß *m* || *tr* kompromittieren; (*principles*) preisgeben || *intr* (**on**) e—n Kompromiß schließen (über *acc*)

comptroller [kəm'trolər] *s* Rechnungsprüfer *m*

compulsion [kəm'pʌlʃən] *s* Zwang *m*

compulsive [kəm'pʌlsɪv] *adj* triebhaft

compulsory [kəm'pʌlsəri] *adj* obligatorisch, Zwangs—; **c. military service** allgemeine Wehrpflicht *f*

compute [kəm'pjut] *tr* berechnen || *intr* rechnen

computer [kəm'pjutər] *s* Computer *m*

comput'er lan'guage *s* Maschinensprache *f*

comrade ['kamræd] *s* Kamerad *m*

con [kan] *v* (*pret & pp* **conned**; *ger* **conning**) *tr* beschwindeln

concave [kan'kev] *adj* konkav

conceal [kən'sil] *tr* verheimlichen

concealment [kən'silmənt] *s* Verheimlichung *f*; (*place*) Versteck *n*

concede [kən'sid] *tr* zugestehen, zubilligen; **c. victory** (pol) den Wahlsieg überlassen || *intr* nachgeben

conceit [kən'sit] *s* (*vanity*) Einbildung *f*, Dünkel *m*; (*witty expression*) Witz *m*

conceit'ed *adj* eingebildet

conceivable [kən'sivəbəl] *adj* denkbar

conceive [kən'siv] *tr* begreifen; (*a desire*) hegen; (*a child*) empfangen

concentrate ['kansən‚tret] *tr* konzentrieren; (*troops*) zusammenziehen || *intr* (**on**) sich konzentrieren (auf *acc*); (*gather*) sich sammeln

concentration [‚kansən'treʃən] *s* Konzentration *f*

concentric [kən'sɛntrɪk] *adj* konzentrisch

concept ['kansɛpt] *s* Begriff *m*

conception [kən'sɛpʃən] s (idea) Vorstellung f; (design) Entwurf m; (biol) Empfängnis f
concern [kən'sʌrn] s (worry) Besorgnis f; (matter) Angelegenheit f; (com) Firma f; **that is no c. of mine** das geht mich nichts an || tr betreffen, angehen; **as far as I am concerned** von mir aus; **c. oneself about** sich bekümmern um; **c. oneself with** sich befassen mit; **to whom it may c.** Bescheinigung
concern'ing prep betreffend (acc), betreffs (genit), über (acc)
concert ['kɑnsərt] s (mus) Konzert n; **in c. (with)** im Einvernehmen (mit) || [kən'sʌrt] tr zusammenfassen
concession [kən'sɛʃən] s Konzession f
conciliate [kən'sɪlɪ‚et] tr versöhnen
conciliatory [kən'sɪlɪ‚ə‚tori] adj versöhnlich
concise [kən'saɪs] adj kurz, bündig
conclude [kən'klud] tr schließen; **c. from s.th. that** aus etw schließen, daß; **to be concluded** Schluß folgt || intr (**with**) schließen (mit)
conclusion [kən'kluʒən] s Schluß m; **draw conclusions from** Schlüsse ziehen aus; **in c.** zum Schluß; **jump at conclusions** voreilige Schlüsse ziehen
conclusive [kən'klusɪv] adj (decisive) entscheidend; (proof) schlagkräftig
concoct [kən'kɑkt] tr (brew) zusammenbrauen; (plans) schmieden
concoction [kən'kɑkʃən] s Gebräu n
concomitant [kən'kɑmɪtənt] adj begleitend || s Begleitumstand m
concord ['kɑŋkɔrd] s Eintracht f
concordance [kən'kɔrdəns] s Übereinstimmung f; (book) Konkordanz f
concourse ['kɑŋkors] s (of people) Zusammenlaufen n, Anlauf m; (of rivers) Zusammenfluß m; (rr) Bahnhofshalle f
concrete ['kɑnkrit], [kən'krit] adj (not abstract) konkret; (solid) fest; (evidence) schlüssig; (of concrete) Beton–; (math) benannt || s Beton m || tr betonieren
con'crete block' s Betonblock m
con'crete noun' s Konkretum n
concubine ['kɑŋkjə‚baɪn] s Nebenfrau f; (mistress) Konkubine f
con·cur [kən'kʌr] v (pret & pp -curred; ger -curring) intr (agree) übereinstimmen; (coincide) (**with**) zusammenfallen (mit); **c. in** (an opinion) beistimmen (dat)
concurrence [kən'kʌrəns] s (agreement) Einverständis n; (coincidence) Zusammentreffen n; (geom) Schnittpunkt m
condemn [kən'dɛm] tr verdammen; (& jur) verurteilen; (a building) für unbewohnlich erklären
condemnation [‚kɑndɛm'neʃən] s Verurteilung f; (of a building, ship, plane) Untauglichkeitserklärung f
condense [kən'dɛns] tr (make thicker) verdichten; (writing) zusammendrängen; || intr kondensieren
condenser [kən'dɛnsər] s Kondensator m

condescend [‚kɑndɪ'sɛnd] intr sich herablassen
condescend'ing adj herablassend
condescension [‚kɑndɪ'sɛnʃən] s Herablassung f
condiment ['kɑndɪmənt] s Würze f
condition [kən'dɪʃən] s (state) Zustand m; (state of health) Verfassung f; (stipulation) Bedingung f; **conditions** (e.g. for working; of the weather) Verhältnisse pl; **on c. that** unter der Bedingung, daß || tr (impose stipulations on) bedingen; (accustom) (**to**) gewöhnen (an acc); (sport) in Form bringen
conditional [kən'dɪʃənəl] adj bedingt
condi'tional clause' s Bedingungssatz m
conditionally [kən'dɪʃənəli] adv bedingungsweise
condole [kən'dol] intr (**with**) kondolieren (dat)
condolence [kən'doləns] s Beileid n
condom ['kɑndəm] s Präservativ n
condominium [‚kɑndə'mɪnɪ·əm] s Eigentumswohnung f
condone [kən'don] tr verzeihen
conducive [kən'd(j)usɪv] adj—**c. to** förderlich (dat)
conduct ['kɑndʌkt] s (behavior) Betragen n; (guidance) Führung f || [kən'dʌkt] tr (business, a campaign, a tour) führen; (elec, phys) leiten; (mus) dirigieren; **c. oneself** sich betragen || intr (mus) dirigieren
conductor [kən'dʌktər] s (elec, phys) Leiter m; (mus) Dirigent m; (rr) Schaffner m
conduit ['kɑnd(ʊ)ɪt] s Röhre f; (elec) Isolierrohr n
cone [kon] s (ice cream cone; paper cone) Tüte f; (bot) Zapfen m; (geom) Kegel m, Konus m
confection [kən'fɛkʃən] s Konfekt n
confectioner [kən'fɛkʃənər] s Zuckerbäcker –in mf
confec'tioner's sug'ar s Puderzucker m
confectionery [kən'fɛkʃə‚nɛri] s (shop) Konditorei f; (sweets) Zuckerwerk n
confederacy [kən'fɛdərəsi] s Bündnis n; (conspiracy) Verschwörung f
confederate [kən'fɛdərɪt] adj verbündet || s Bundesgenosse m, Bundesgenossin f; (accomplice) Helfershelfer –in mf || [kən'fɛdə‚ret] tr verbünden || intr sich verbünden
confederation [kən‚fɛdə'reʃən] s Bund m
con·fer [kən'fʌr] v (pret & pp -ferred; ger -ferring) tr (on, upon) verleihen (dat) || intr sich besprechen, konferieren
conference ['kɑnfərəns] s Konferenz f; (sport) Verband m
con'ference call' s Sammelverbindung f
confess [kən'fɛs] tr (ein)gestehen, bekennen; (sins) beichten || intr gestehen
confession [kən'fɛʃən] s Geständnis n, Bekenntnis n; (of sins) Beichte f; **go to c.** beichten

confessional [kən'fɛʃənəl] *s* Beicht-
stuhl *m*
confes'sion of faith' *s* Glaubensbekenntnis *n*
confessor [kən'fɛsər] *s* Beichtvater *m*
confidant [,kɑnfɪ'dænt] *s* Vertraute
mf
confide [kən'faɪd] *tr* (to) anvertrauen
(*dat*) ‖ *intr*—**c. in** vertrauen (*dat*)
confidence ['kɑnfɪdəns] *s* (*trust*) (in)
Vertrauen *n* (auf *acc*, zu); (*assurance*) Zuversicht *f;* **in c.** im Vertrauen
con'fidence man' *s* Bauernfänger *m*
confident ['kɑnfɪdənt] *adj* zuversichtlich; **be c. of** sich [*dat*] sicher sein
(*genit*)
confidential [,kɑnfɪ'dɛnʃəl] *adj* vertraulich
confine ['kɑnfaɪn] *s*—**the confines** die
Grenzen *pl* ‖ *tr* [kən'faɪn] *tr* (*limit*)
(to) beschränken (auf *acc*); (*shut in*)
einsperren; **be confined** (*in pregnancy*) niederkommen; **be confined
to bed** bettlägerig sein
confinement [kən'faɪnmənt] *s* Beschränkung *f;* (*arrest*) Haft *f;* (*childbirth*) Niederkunft *f*
confirm [kən'fʌrm] *tr* bestätigen;
(Prot) konfirmieren; (R.C.) firmen;
confirm in writing verbriefen
confirmation [,kɑnfər'meʃən] *s* Bestätigung *f;* (Prot) Konfirmation *f;*
(R.C.) Firmung *f*
confirmed' *adj* (*e.g., report*) bestätigt;
(*inveterate*) unverbesserlich; **c. bachelor** Hagestolz *m*
confiscate ['kɑnfɪs,ket] *tr* beschlagnahmen, konfiszieren
confiscation [,kɑnfɪs'keʃən] *s* Beschlagnahme *f*
conflagration [,kɑnflə'greʃən] *s* Brand
m, Feuerbrunst *f*
conflict ['kɑnflɪkt] *s* (*of interests, of
evidence*) Konflikt *m;* (*fight*) Zusammenstoß *m* ‖ [kən'flɪkt] *intr*
(with) im Widerspruch stehen (zu)
conflict'ing *adj* einander widerspre-
chend
con'flict of in'terest *s* Interessenkon-
flikt *m*, Interessenkollision *f*
confluence ['kɑnfluəns] *s* Zusammenfluß *m*
conform [kən'fɔrm] *tr* anpassen ‖ *intr*
übereinstimmen; (to) sich anpassen
(*dat*)
conformity [kən'fɔrmɪti] *s* (*adaptation*) (to) Anpassung *f* (an *acc*);
(*agreement*) (with) Übereinstimmung
f (mit)
confound [kɑn'faʊnd] *tr* (*perplex*) verblüffen; (*throw into confusion*) verwirren; (*erroneously identify*) (with)
verwechseln (mit) ‖ ['kɑn'faʊnd]
tr—**c. it!** zum Donnerwetter!
confound'ed *adj* (coll) verwünscht
confrere ['kɑnfrɛr] *s* Kollege *m*
confront [kən'frʌnt] *tr* (*face*) gegenüberstehen (*dat*); (*a problem, an
enemy*) entgegentreten (*dat*); **be
confronted with** gegenüberstehen
(*dat*); **c. s.o. with** j-n konfrontieren
mit

confrontation [,kɑnfrən'teʃən] *s* Konfrontation *f;* (*of witnesses*) Gegenüberstellung *f*
confuse [kən'fjuz] *tr* (*e.g., names*)
verwechseln; (*persons*) verwirren
confused' *adj* konfus, verwirrt, wirr
confusion [kən'fjuʒən] *s* Verwechslung *f;* (*disorder, chaos*) Verwirrung
f
confute [kən'fjut] *tr* widerlegen
congeal [kən'dʒil] *tr* erstarren lassen
‖ *intr* erstarren
congenial [kən'dʒinjəl] *adj* (*person*)
sympathisch; (*surroundings*) angenehm
congenital [kən'dʒɛnɪtəl] *adj* angeboren
congen'ital de'fect *s* Geburtsfehler *m*
congest [kən'dʒɛst] *tr* überfüllen
congest'ed *adj* überfüllt; (*area*) übervölkert; (*with traffic*) verkehrsreich
congestion [kən'dʒɛstʃən] *s* Über-
füllung *f;* (*of traffic*) Verkehrsstockung *f;* (*of population*) Übervölkerung *f;* (*pathol*) Blutandrang *m*
congratulate [kən'grætʃə,let] *tr* gratulieren (*dat*); **c. s.o. on** j-m gratulieren zu
congratulations [kən,grætʃə'leʃənz]
spl Glückwunsch *m;* **c.!** ich gratuliere!
congregate ['kɑŋgrɪ,get] *intr* sich
(ver)sammeln, zusammenkommen
congregation [,kɑŋgrɪ'geʃən] *s* Versammlung *f;* (eccl) Gemeinde *f*
congress ['kɑŋgrɛs] *s* Kongreß *m*
congressional [kən'grɛʃənəl] *adj* Kongreß–
congress·man ['kɑŋgrɪsmən] *s* (–men)
Abgeordnete *m*
con'gress·wom'an *s* (–wom'en) Abgeordnete *f*
congruent ['kɑŋgruənt] *adj* kongruent
conical ['kɑnɪkəl] *adj* kegelförmig
conjecture [kən'dʒɛkʃər] *s* Vermutung
f, Mutmaßung *f* ‖ *tr & intr* vermuten
conjugal ['kɑndʒəgəl] *adj* ehelich
conjugate ['kɑndʒə,get] *tr* abwandeln
conjugation [,kɑndʒə'geʃən] *s* Ab-
wandlung *f*
conjunction [kən'dʒʌŋkʃən] *s* Binde-
wort *n;* **in c. with** in Verbindung mit
conjure [kən'dʒur] *tr* (*appeal solemnly to*) beschwören ‖ ['kʌndʒər] *tr*—
c. away wegzaubern; **c. up** heraufbeschwören
conk [kɑŋk] *tr* (sl) hauen ‖ *intr*—**c.
out** (sl) versagen
connect [kə'nɛkt] *tr* verbinden; (&
fig) verknüpfen; (elec) (to) anschließen (an *acc*); (telp) (with) verbinden
(mit) ‖ *intr* verbunden sein; (*said of
trains, etc.*) (with) Anschluß haben
(an *acc*); (box) treffen
connect'ing *adj* Verbindungs–, Binde–;
(*trains, buses*) Anschluß–; (*rooms*)
mit Zwischentür
connect'ing rod' *s* Schubstange *f*
connection [kə'nɛkʃən] *s* (*e.g., of a
pipe*) Verbindung *f;* (*of ideas*) Ver-
knüpfung *f;* (*context*) Zusammenhang *m;* (*part that connects*) Ver-
bindungsteil *m;* (*elec*) Schaltung *f;*

(mach, rr, telp) Verbindung *f;* **con-nections** Beziehungen *pl;* **in c. with** in Zusammenhang mit

con'ning tow'er ['kɑnɪŋ] *s* Kommandoturm *m*

connive [kə'naɪv] *intr*—**c. at** ein Auge zudrücken bei; **c. with** im geheimen Einverständnis stehen mit

connotation [,kɑno'teʃən] *s* Nebenbedeutung *f*

connote [kə'not] *tr* mitbezeichnen

conquer ['kɑŋkər] *tr* (*win in war*) erobern; (*overcome*) überwinden

conquerer ['kɑŋkərər] *s* Eroberer *m*

conquest ['kɑŋkwɛst] *s* Eroberung *f*

conscience ['kɑnʃəns] *s* Gewissen *n*

conscientious [,kɑnʃɪ'ɛnʃəs] *adj* gewissenhaft, pflichtbewußt

conscien'tious objec'tor [əb'dʒɛktər] *s* Wehrdienstverweigerer *m*

conscious ['kɑnʃəs] *adj* bei Bewußtsein; **c. of** bewußt (*genit*)

consciousness ['kɑnʃəsnɪs] *s* Bewußtsein *n;* (*awareness*) (**of**) Kenntnis *f* (*genit* or *von*); **regain c.** wieder zu sich kommen

conscript ['kɑnskrɪpt] *s* Dienstpflichtige *m;* (mil) Wehrdienstpflichtige *m* ‖ [kən'skrɪpt] *tr* ausheben

conscription [kən'skrɪpʃən] *s* Dienstpflicht *f;* (*draft*) Aushebung *f*

consecrate ['kɑnsɪ,kret] *tr* weihen

consecration [,kɑnsɪ'kreʃən] *s* Einweihung *f;* (*at Mass*) Wandlung *f*

consecutive [kən'sɛkjətɪv] *adj* aufeinanderfolgend

consensus [kən'sɛnsəs] *s* allgemeine Übereinstimmung *f;* **the c. of opinion** die übereinstimmende Meinung

consent [kən'sɛnt] *s* Zustimmung *f;* **by common c.** mit allgemeiner Zustimmung ‖ *intr* zustimmen; **c. to** (*inf*) sich bereit erklären zu (*inf*)

consequence ['kɑnsɪ,kwɛns] *s* Folge *f;* (*influence*) Einfluß *m;* **in c. of** infolge (*genit*); **it is of no c.** es hat nichts auf sich; **suffer the consequences** die Folgen tragen

consequently ['kɑnsɪ,kwɛntli] *adv* folglich, infolgedessen, mithin

conservation [,kɑnsər've ʃən] *s* Bewahrung *f;* (*of energy, etc.*) Erhaltung *f;* (*supervision of natural resources*) Naturschutz *m;* (*ecology*) Umweltschutz *m*

conservatism [kən'sʌrvə,tɪzəm] *s* Konservatismus *m*

conservative [kən'sʌrvətɪv] *adj* konservativ; (*estimate*) vorsichtig ‖ *s* Konservative *mf*

conservatory [kən'sʌrvə,tori] *s* Treibhaus *n;* (mus) Konservatorium *n*

conserve [kən'sʌrv] *tr* sparsam umgehen mit

consider [kən'sɪdər] *tr* (*take into account*) berücksichtigen; (*show consideration for*) Rücksicht nehmen auf (*acc*); (*reflect on*) sich [*dat*] überlegen; (*regard as*) halten für, betrachten als; **all things considered** alles in allem

considerable [kən'sɪdərəbəl] *adj* beträchtlich, erheblich

considerate [kən'sɪdərɪt] *adj* (**towards**) rücksichtsvoll (gegen)

consideration [kən,sɪdə'reʃən] *s* (*taking into account*) Berücksichtigung *f;* (*regard*) (**for**) Rücksicht *f* (auf *acc*); **be an important c.** e–e wichtige Rolle spielen; **be under c.** in Betracht gezogen werden; **for a c.** entgeltlich; **in c. of** in Anbetracht (*genit*); **take into c.** in Betracht ziehen; **with c.** rücksichtsvoll

consid'ering *adv* (coll) den Umständen nach ‖ *prep* in Anbetracht (*genit*)

consign [kən'saɪn] *tr* (*ship*) versenden; (*address*) adressieren

consignee [,kɑnsaɪ'ni] *s* Adressat –in *mf*

consignment [kən'saɪnmənt] *s* (*act of sending*) Versand *m;* (*merchandise sent*) Sendung *f;* **on c.** in Kommission

consist [kən'sɪst] *intr*—**c. in** bestehen in (*dat*); **c. of** bestehen aus

consistency [kən'sɪstənsi] *s* Konsequenz *f;* (*firmness*) Festigkeit *f;* (*viscosity*) Dickflüssigkeit *f;* (*agreement*) Übereinstimmung *f;* (*steadfastness*) (**in**) Beständigkeit *f* (in *dat*)

consistent [kən'sɪstənt] *adj* (*performer*) stetig; (*performance*) gleichmäßig; (*free from contradiction*) konsequent; **c. with** in Übereinstimmung mit

consistory [kən'sɪstəri] *s* Konsistorium *n*

consolation [,kɑnsə'leʃən] *s* Trost *m*

console ['kɑnsol] *s* (*for radio or record player*) Musiktruhe *f;* (*of an organ*) Spieltisch *m;* (*television*) Fernsehtruhe *f* ‖ [kən'sol] *tr* trösten

consolidate [kən'sɑlɪ,det] *tr* (*a position*) festigen; (*debts*) konsolidieren; (*combine*) zusammenlegen

consonant ['kɑnsənənt] *adj* (**with**) im Einklang (mit) ‖ *s* Mitlaut *m*

consort ['kɑnsɔrt] *s* (*male*) Gemahl *m;* (*female*) Gemahlin *f* ‖ [kən'sɔrt] *intr* (**with**) Umgang haben (mit)

consorti·um [kən'sɔrtɪ·əm] *s* (–**a** [ə]) Konsortium *n*

conspicuous [kən'spɪkju·əs] *adj* auffallend, auffällig; **c. for** bemerkenswert wegen

conspiracy [kən'spɪrəsi] *s* Verschwörung *f*

conspirator [kən'spɪrətər] *s* Verschwörer –in *mf*

conspire [kən'spaɪr] *intr* sich verschwören

constable ['kɑnstəbəl] *s* Gendarm *m*

constancy ['kɑnstənsi] *s* Beständigkeit *f*

constant ['kɑnstənt] *adj* (*continuous*) dauernd, ständig; (*faithful*) treu; (*resolute*) standhaft; (*element, time element*) fest; (fig & tech) konstant ‖ *s* (math, phys) Konstante *f*

constantly ['kɑnstəntli] *adv* immerfort

constellation [,kɑnstə'leʃən] *s* Sternbild *n*

consternation [,kɑnstər'neʃən] *s* Bestürzung *f*

constipate ['kɑnstɪ ,pet] *tr* verstopfen
constipation [,kɑnstɪ 'peʃən] *s* Verstopfung *f*
constituency [kən'stɪtʃʊ·ənsi] *s* Wählerschaft *f*
constituent [kən'stɪtʃʊ·ənt] *adj* wesentlich; **c. part** Bestandteil *m* ‖ *s* Komponente *f;* (pol) Wähler –in *mf*
constitute ['kɑnstɪ ,t(j)ut] *tr* (*make up*) ausmachen, bilden; (*found*) gründen
constitution [,kɑnstɪ 't(j)uʃən] *s* (*of a country or organization*) Verfassung *f;* (*bodily condition*) Konstitution *f;* (*composition*) Zusammensetzung *f*
constitutional [,kɑnstɪ 't(j)uʃənəl] *adj* (*according to a constitution*) konstitutionell; (*crisis, amendment, etc.*) Verfassungs–
constrain [kən'stren] *tr* zwingen
constraint [kən'strent] *s* Zwang *m;* (jur) Nötigung *f*
constrict [kən'strɪkt] *tr* zusammenziehen
construct [kən'strʌkt] *tr* errichten; (eng, geom, gram) konstruieren
construction [kən'strʌkʃən] *s* (*act of building*) Errichtung *f;* (*manner of building*) Bauweise *f;* (*interpreta.tion*) Auslegung *f;* (eng, geom, gram) Konstruktion *f;* **under c.** im Bau
constructive [kən'strʌktɪv] *adj* konstruktiv
construe [kən'stru] *tr* (*interpret*) auslegen; (gram) konstruieren
consul ['kɑnsəl] *s* Konsul *m*
consular ['kɑns(j)ələr] *adj* konsularisch
consulate ['kɑns(j)əlɪt] *s* Konsulat *n*
con'sul gen'eral *s* Generalkonsul *m*
consult [kən'sʌlt] *tr* konsultieren, um Rat fragen; (*a book*) nachschlagen ‖ *intr*—**c. with** sich beraten mit
consultant [kən'sʌltənt] *s* Berater –in *mf*
consultation [,kɑnsəl'teʃən] *s* Beratung *f;* (& med) Konsultation *f*
consume [kən's(j)um] *tr* verzehren; (*use up*) verbrauchen; (*time*) beanspruchen
consumer [kən's(j)umər] *s* Konsument –in *mf,* Verbraucher –in *mf*
consum'er goods' *spl* Konsumgüter *pl*
consummate [kən'sʌmɪt] *adj* vollendet; (pej) abgefeimt ‖ ['kɑnsə ,met] *tr* vollziehen
consumption [kən'sʌmpʃən] *s* (*of food*) Verzehr *m;* (econ) (**of**) Verbrauch *m* (an *dat*); (pathol) Schwindsucht *f*
consumptive [kə'sʌmptɪv] *adj* schwindsüchtig ‖ *s* Schwindsüchtige *mf*
contact ['kɑntækt] *s* Kontakt *m,* Berührung *f;* (fig) (**with**) Verbindung *f* (mit); (elec) Kontakt *m* ‖ *tr* (coll) sich in Verbindung setzen mit
con'tact lens' *s* Haftschale *f*
contagion [kən'tedʒən] *s* Ansteckung *f*
contagious [kən'tedʒəs] *adj* ansteckend
contain [kən'ten] *tr* enthalten; (*an*

enemy) aufhalten; (*one's feelings*) verhalten; **c. oneself** sich beherrschen
container [kən'tenər] *s* Behälter *m*
containment [kən'tenmənt] *s* (mil, pol) Eindämmung *f*
contaminate [kən'tæmɪ ,net] *tr* verunreinigen; (fig) vergiften
contamination [kən ,tæmɪ'neʃən] *s* Verunreinigung *f;* (fig) Vergiftung *f*
contemplate ['kɑntəm ,plet] *tr* betrachten; (*intend*) beabsichtigen ‖ *intr* nachdenken
contemplation [,kɑntəm'pleʃən] *s* Betrachtung *f;* (*consideration*) Erwägung *f*
contemporaneous [kən ,tempə'renɪ·əs] *adj* (**with**) gleichzeitig (mit)
contemporary [kən'tempə ,reri] *adj* zeitgenössisch; (*modern*) modern ‖ *s* Zeitgenosse *m,* Zeitgenossin *f*
contempt [kən'tempt] *s* Verachtung *f;* **beneath c.** unter aller Kritik
contemptible [kən'temptɪbəl] *adj* verachtungswürdig
contempt' of court' *s* Mißachtung *f* des Gerichtes
contemptuous [kən'temptʃʊ·əs] *adj* verachtungsvoll, verächtlich
contend [kən'tend] *tr* behaupten ‖ *intr* (**for**) sich bewerben (um); (**with**) kämfen (mit)
contender [kən'tendər] *s* (**for**) Bewerber –in *mf* (um)
content [kən'tent] *adj* (**with**) zufrieden (mit); **c. to** (*inf*) bereit zu (*inf*) ‖ *s* Zufriedenheit *f;* **to one's heart's c.** nach Herzenslust ‖ ['kɑntənt] *s* Inhalt *m;* (chem) Gehalt *m;* **contents** Inhalt *m* ‖ [kən'tent] *tr* zufriedenstellen; **c. oneself with** sich begnügen mit
content'ed *adj* zufrieden
contention [kən'tenʃən] *s* (*strife*) Streit *m;* (*assertion*) Behauptung *f*
contest ['kɑntest] *s* (**for**) Wettkampf *m* (um); (*written competition*) Preisausschreiben *n* ‖ [kən'test] *tr* (*argue against*) bestreiten; (*a will*) anfechten; (mil) kämpfen um; **contested** umstritten
contestant [kən'testənt] *s* Bewerber –in *mf;* (sport) Wettkämpfer –in *mf*
context ['kɑntekst] *s* Zusammenhang *m*
contiguous [kən'tɪgjʊ·əs] *adj* einander berührend; (**to**) angrenzend (an *acc*)
continence ['kɑntɪnəns] *s* Enthaltsamkeit *f*
continent ['kɑntɪnənt] *adj* enthaltsam ‖ *s* Kontinent *m*
continental [,kɑntɪ'nentəl] *adj* kontinental, Kontinental–
contingency [kən'tɪndʒənsi] *s* Zufall *m*
contingent [kən'tɪndʒənt] *adj* (**upon**) abhängig (von) ‖ *s* (mil) Kontingent *n*
continual [kən'tɪnjʊ·əl] *adj* immer wiederkehrend
continuation [kən ,tɪnjʊ'eʃən] *s* Fortsetzung *f;* (*continued existence*) Fortdauer *f*
continue [kən'tɪnju] *tr* fortsetzen; **c.**

to (*inf*) fortfahren zu (*inf*); weiter–, e.g., **c. to read** weiterlesen; **to be continued** Fortsetzung folgt || *intr* fortfahren; (*said of things*) anhalten

continuity [,kɑntɪ'n(j)u·ɪti] *s* Stetigkeit *f*

continuous [kən'tɪnju·əs] *adj* ununterbrochen, anhaltend

contortion [kən'tɔrʃən] *s* Verzerrung *f*

contour ['kɑntʊr] *s* Kontur *f*

con'tour line' *s* Schichtlinie *f*

con'tour map' *s* Landkarte *f* mit Schichtlinien

contraband ['kɑntrə,bænd] *adj* Schmuggel– || *s* Konterbande *f*, Schmuggelware *f*

contraceptive [,kɑntrə'sɛptɪv] *adj* empfängnisverhütend || *s* Empfängnisverhütungsmittel *n*

contract ['kɑntrækt] *s* Vertrag *m*, Kontrakt *m*; (*order*) Auftrag *m* || [kən'trækt] *tr* (*marriage*) (ab)schließen; (*a disease*) sich [*dat*] zuziehen; (*e.g., a muscle*) zusammenziehen; (*debts*) geraten in (*acc*); (ling) kontrahieren || *intr* (*shrink*) sich zusammenziehen; **c. to** (*inf*) sich vertraglich verpflichten zu (*inf*)

contract'ing *adj* vertragsschließend

contraction [kən'trækʃən] *s* (& ling) Zusammenziehung *f*, Kontraktion *f*; (*contracted word*) Verkürzung *f*

contractor ['kɑntræktər] *s* (*supplier*) Lieferant *m*; (*builder*) Bauunternehmer *m*

contradict [,kɑntrə'dɪkt] *tr* widersprechen (*dat*)

contradiction [,kɑntrə'dɪkʃən] *s* Widerspruch *m*

contradictory [,kɑntrə'dɪktəri] *adj* widerspruchsvoll

contrail ['kɑn,trel] *s* Kondensstreifen *m*

contral·to [kən'trælto] *s* (**–tos**) (*person*) Altistin *f*; (*voice*) Alt *m*

contraption [kən'træpʃən] *s* (coll) Vorrichtung *f*; (*car*) (coll) Kiste *f*

contrary ['kɑntreri] *adj* konträr, gegensätzlich; (*person*) querköpfig; **c. to nature** naturwidrig || *s* Gegenteil *n*; **on the c.** im Gegenteil

contrast ['kɑntræst] *s* Gegensatz *m* || [kən'træst] *tr* (**with**) gegenüberstellen (*dat*) || *intr* (**with**) im Gegensatz stehen (zu)

contravene [,kɑntrə'vin] *tr* zuwiderhandeln (*dat*)

contribute [kən'trɪbjut] *tr* beitragen, spenden || *intr*—**c. to** beitragen zu; (*with help*) mitwirken an (*dat*)

contribution [,kɑntrɪ'bjuʃən] *s* Beitrag *m*; (*of money*) Spende *f*

contributor [kən'trɪbjutər] *s* Spender –in *mf*; (*to a periodical*) Mitarbeiter –in *mf*

contrite [kən'traɪt] *adj* reuig

contrition [kən'trɪʃən] *s* Reue *f*

contrivance [kən'traɪvəns] *s* (*device*) Vorrichtung *f*; (*expedient*) Kunstgriff *m*; (*act of contriving*) Aushecken *n*

contrive [kən'traɪv] *tr* (*invent*) erfin-

den; (*devise*) ersinnen; **c. to** (*inf*) es fertig bringen zu (*inf*) || *intr* Anschläge aushecken

con·trol [kən'trol] *s* Kontrolle *f*, Gewalt *f*; (mach) Steuerung *f*; (mach) (*devise*) Regler *m*; **be out of c.** nicht zu halten sein; **be under c.** in bester Ordnung sein; **controls** (aer) Steuerwerk *n*; **gain c. over** die Herrschaft gewinnen über (*acc*); **have c. over s.o.** über j–n Gewalt haben; **keep under c.** im Zaume halten || *v* (*pret* & *pp* **–trolled**; *ger* **–trolling**) *tr* (*dominate*) beherrschen; (*verify*) kontrollieren; (*contain*) eindämmen; (*steer*) steuern; (*regulate*) regeln; **c. oneself** sich beherrschen

control' pan'el *s* Schaltbrett *n*

control' room' *s* Kommandoraum *m*; (rad) Regieraum *m*

control' stick' *s* (aer) Steuerknüppel *m*

control' tow'er *s* (*at an airport*) Kontrollturm *m*; (*on an aircraft carrier*) Kommandoturm *m*

controversial [,kɑntrə'vʌrʃəl] *adj* umstritten, strittig; **c. subject** Streitfrage *f*

controversy ['kɑntrə,vʌrsi] *s* Kontroverse *f*, Auseinandersetzung *f*

controvert [,kɑntrə'vʌrt] *tr* (*argue against*) bestreiten; (*argue about*) streiten über (*acc*)

contusion [kən't(j)uʒən] *s* Quetschung *f*

convalesce [,kɑnvə'lɛs] *intr* genesen

convalescence [,kɑnvə'lɛsəns] *s* Genesung *f*

convalescent [,kɑnvə'lɛsənt] *s* Genesende *mf*

convales'cent home' *s* Genesungsheim *n*

convene [kən'vin] *tr* versammeln || *intr* sich versammeln

convenience [kən'vinjəns] *s* Bequemlichkeit *f*; **at one's c.** nach Belieben; **at your earliest c.** möglichst bald; **modern conveniences** moderner Komfort *m*

convenient [kən'vinjənt] *adj* gelegen

convent ['kɑnvent] *s* Nonnenkloster *n*

convention [kən'vɛnʃən] *s* (*professional meeting*) Tagung *f*; (*political meeting*) Konvent *m*; (*accepted usage*) Konvention *f*

conventional [kən'vɛnʃənəl] *adj* konventionell, herkömmlich

converge [kən'vʌrdʒ] *intr* zusammenlaufen; **c. on** sich stürzen auf (*acc*)

conversation [,kɑnvər'seʃən] *s* Gespräch *n*

conversational [,kɑnvər'seʃənəl] *adj* Gesprächs–

converse ['kɑnvʌrs] *adj* gegenteilig || *s* (**of**) Gegenteil *n* (von) || [kən'vʌrs] *intr* sich unterhalten

conversion [kən'vʌrʒən] *s* (**into**) Umwandlung *f* (in *acc*); (*of a factory*) (**to**) Umstellung *f* (auf *acc*); (*of a building*) (**into**) Umbau *m* (zu); (*of currency*) (**into**) Umwechslung *f* (in *acc*); (elec) (**to**) Umformung *f* (in *acc*); (math) Umrechnung *f*; (phys) Umsetzung *f*; (relig) Bekehrung *f*

convert [ˈkɑnvʌrt] s (**to**) Bekehrte mf (zu) ‖ [kənˈvʌrt] tr (**into**) umwandeln (in acc); (a factory) (**to**) umstellen (auf acc); (a building) (**into**) umbauen (zu); (currency) (**into**) umwechseln (in acc); (biochem) (**into**) umsetzen (in acc); (chem) (**into**) umwandeln (in acc), verwandeln (in acc); (elec) (**to**) umformen (in acc); (math) (**to**) umrechnen (in acc); (phys) (**to**) umsetzen (in acc); (relig) (**to**) bekehren (zu) ‖ intr (**to**) sich bekehren (zu)

converter [kənˈvʌrtər] s (elec) Umformer m, Stromrichter m

convertible [kənˈvʌrtɪbəl] adj umwandelbar; (fin) konvertierbar ‖ s (aut) Kabriolett n

convex [ˈkɑnvɛks], [kɑnˈvɛks] adj konvex

convey [kənˈve] tr (transport) befördern; (greetings, message) übermitteln; (sound) fortpflanzen; (meaning) ausdrücken; (a property) abtreten

conveyance [kənˈve·əns] s (act) Beförderung f; (means) Transportmittel n; (jur) Abtretung f

conveyor [kənˈve·ər] s Beförderer –in mf

convey'or belt' s Förderband n

convict [ˈkɑnvɪkt] s Sträfling m ‖ [kənˈvɪkt] tr (of) überführen (genit)

conviction [kənˈvɪkʃən] s (of a crime) Verurteilung f; (certainty) Überzeugung f; **convictions** Gesinnung f

convince [kənˈvɪns] tr (of) überzeugen (von)

convivial [kənˈvɪvɪ·əl] adj gesellig

convocation [ˌkɑnvəˈkeʃən] s Zusammenberufung f; (educ) Eröffnungsfeier f

convoke [kənˈvok] tr zusammenberufen

convoy [ˈkɑnvɔɪ] s (of vehicles) Kolonne f, Konvoi m; (nav) Geleitzug m

convulse [kənˈvʌls] tr erschüttern

convulsion [kənˈvʌlʃən] s Krampf m; **go into convulsions** Krämpfe bekommen

coo [ku] intr girren

cook [kʊk] s Koch m, Köchin f ‖ tr braten, backen; (boil) kochen; **c. up** (fig) zusammenbrauen ‖ intr braten, backen; (boil) kochen

cook'book' s Kochbuch n

cookie [ˈkʊki] s Plätzchen n, Keks m & n; **cookies** pl Gebäck n

cook'ing s Kochen n; **do one's own c.** sich selbst beköstigen

cool [kul] adj (& fig) kühl; **keep c.!** ruhig Blut!; **keep one's c.** (coll) ruhig Blut bewahren ‖ s Kühle f ‖ tr kühlen; **c. down** (fig) beruhigen; **c. off** abkühlen ‖ intr (& fig) sich abkühlen

cooler [ˈkulər] s Kühler m; (sl) Kittchen n

cool'-head'ed adj besonnen

coolie [ˈkuli] s Kuli m

coolness [ˈkulnɪs] s (& fig) Kühle f

coon [kun] s (zool) Waschbär m

coop [kup] s (building) Hühnerstall m; (enclosure) Hühnerhof m; (jail) (sl) Kittchen n; **fly the c.** (sl) auskneifen ‖ tr—**c. up** einsperren

co-op [ˈko·ɑp] s Konsumverein m

cooper [ˈkupər] s Küfer m, Böttcher m

cooperate [koˈɑpəˌret] intr (**in**) mitwirken (an dat, bei); (**with**) mitarbeiten (mit)

cooperation [koˌɑpəˈreʃən] s Mitwirkung f, Mitarbeit f

cooperative [koˈɑpəˌretɪv] adj hilfsbereit

coordinate [koˈɔrdɪnɪt] adj gleichrangig; (gram) beigeordnet ‖ s (math) Koordinate f ‖ [koˈɔrdɪˌnet] tr koordinieren

coordination [koˌɔrdɪˈneʃən] s Koordination f; (gram) Beiordnung f

cootie [ˈkuti] s (sl) Laus f

co-owner [ˈkoˌonər] s Miteigentümer –in mf

cop [kɑp] s (sl) Bulle m ‖ v (pret & pp copped; ger copped) tr (catch) (sl) erwischen; (steal) (sl) klauen ‖ intr—**cop out** (coll) auskneifen

copartner [koˈpɑrtnər] s Mitinhaber –in mf

cope [kop] intr—**c. with** sich messen mit, aufkommen gegen

cope'stone' s Schlußstein m

copier [ˈkɑpɪ·ər] s Kopiermaschine f

copilot [ˈkoˌpaɪlət] s Kopilot m

coping [ˈkopɪŋ] s Mauerkappe f

copious [ˈkopɪ·əs] adj reichlich

cop'-out' s (act) Kneifen n; (person) Drückeberger m

copper [ˈkɑpər] adj kupfern, Kupfer–; (color) kupferrot ‖ s Kupfer n; (coin) Kupfermünze f; (sl) Schupo m

cop'persmith' s Kupferschmied m

copter [ˈkɑptər] s (coll) Hubschrauber m

copulate [ˈkɑpjəˌlet] intr sich paaren

cop·y [ˈkɑpi] s Kopie f; (of a book) Exemplar n; (typ) druckfertiges Manuskript n ‖ v (pret & pp –ied) tr kopieren; (in school) abschreiben

cop'ybook' s Schreibheft n, Heft n

cop'ycat' s (imitator) Nachäffer –in mf

cop'yright' s Urheberrecht n, Verlagsrecht n ‖ tr urheberrechtlich schützen, verlagsrechtlich schützen

cop'ywrit'er s Texter –in mf

coquette [koˈket] s Kokette f

coquettish [koˈketɪʃ] adj kokett

coral [ˈkɔrəl] adj Korallen– ‖ s Koralle f

cor'al reef' s Korallenriff n

cord [kɔrd] s Schnur f, Strick m; (of wood) Klafter n; (elec) Leitungsschnur f

cordial [ˈkɔrdʒəl] adj herzlich ‖ s Likör m; (med) Herzstärkung f

cordiality [kərˈdʒælɪti] s Herzlichkeit f

cordon [ˈkɔrdən] s Kordon m, Absperrkette f ‖ tr—**c. off** absperren

corduroy [ˈkɔrdəˌrɔɪ] s Kordsamt m; **corduroys** Kordsamthose f

core [kor] s (of fruit) Kern m; (of a

cable) Seele *f;* (fig) Kern *m,* Mark *n;* (elec) Spulenkern *m*

cork [kɔrk] *s* Kork *m; (stopper)* Pfropfen *m,* Korken *m ‖ tr* verkorken

corker ['kɔrkər] *s* (sl) Schlager *m*

cork'ing *adj* (sl) fabelhaft

cork'oak', cork' tree' *s* Korkeiche *f*

cork'screw' *s* Korkenzieher *m*

corn [kɔrn] *s (Indian corn)* Mais *m; (on a foot)* Hühnerauge *n; (joke)* (sl) Kalauer *m*

corn'bread' *s* Maisbrot *n*

corn'cob' *s* Maiskolben *m*

corn'cob pipe' *s* Maiskolbenpfeife *f*

corn'crib' *s* Maisspeicher *m*

cornea ['kɔrnɪ·ə] *s* Hornhaut *f*

corned' beef' ['kɔrnd] *s* Pökelfleisch *n*

corner ['kɔrnər] *adj* Eck– ‖ *s* Ecke *f; (secluded spot)* Winkel *m; (curve)* Kurve *f;* **c. of the eye** Augenwinkel *m;* **from all corners of the world** von allen Ecken und Enden; **turn the c.** um die Ecke biegen ‖ *tr (a person)* in die Zange nehmen; *(the market)* aufkaufen

cor'nerstone' *s* Eckstein *m; (of a new building)* Grundstein *m*

cornet [kɔr'nɛt] *s* (mus) Kornett *n*

corn' exchange' *s* Getreidebörse *f*

corn'field' *s* Maisfeld *n; (grain field)* (Brit) Kornfeld *n*

corn'flakes' *spl* Maisflocken *pl*

corn' flour' *s* Maismehl *n*

corn'flow'er *s* Kornblume *f*

corn' frit'ter *s* Maispfannkuchen *m*

corn'husk' *s* Maishülse *f*

cornice ['kɔrnɪs] *s* Gesims *n*

corn' liq'uor *s* Maisschnaps *m*

corn' meal' *s* Maismehl *n*

corn' on the cob' *s* Mais *m* am Kolben

corn' silk' *s* Maisfasern *pl*

corn'stalk' *s* Maisstengel *m*

corn'starch' *s* Maisstärke *f*

cornucopia [ˌkɔrnə'kopɪ·ə] *s* Füllhorn *n*

corny ['kɔrni] *adj (sentimental)* rührselig; *(joke)* blöd

corollary ['kɔrəˌlɛri] *s* **(to)** Folge *f* (von)

coron·a [kə'ronə] *s* **(–nas & –nae** [ni]) (astr) Hof *m,* Korona *f;* (archit) Kranzleiste *f*

coronary ['kɔrəˌnɛri] *adj* koronar

coronation [ˌkɔrə'neʃən] *s* Krönung *f*

coroner ['kɔrənər] *s* Gerichtsmediziner *m*

cor'oner's in'quest *s* Totenschau *f*

coronet ['kɔrəˌnɛt] *s* Krönchen *n; (worn by the nobility)* Adelskrone *f; (worn by women)* Diadem *n*

corporal ['kɔrpərəl] *adj* körperlich ‖ *s* (mil) Obergefreite *m*

corporate ['kɔrpərɪt] *adj* korporativ

corporation [ˌkɔrpə'reʃən] *s* (fin) Aktiengesellschaft *f;* (jur) Körperschaft *f*

corpora'tion law'yer *s* Syndikus *m*

corporeal [kɔr'porɪ·əl] *adj* körperlich

corps [kor] *s* **(corps** [korz]) Korps *n*

corpse [kɔrps] *s* Leiche *f,* Leichnam *m*

corps'man *s* **(–men)** Sanitäter *m*

corpulent ['kɔrpjələnt] *adj* beleibt

corpuscle ['kɔrpəsəl] *s* Blutkörperchen *n*

cor·ral [ke'ræl] *s* Pferch *m ‖ v (pret & pp –ralled; ger –ralling) tr* zusammenpferchen

correct [kə'rɛkt] *adj* richtig; *(manners)* korrekt; *(time)* genau; **be c.** *(said of a thing)* stimmen; *(said of a person)* recht haben ‖ *tr* korrigieren; *(examination papers)* verbessern; *(beat)* züchtigen; *(scold)* zurechtweisen; *(an unjust situation)* ausgleichen

correction [kə'rɛkʃən] *s* Berichtigung *f; (of examination papers)* Verbesserung *f,* Korrektur *f; (punishment)* Bestrafung *f*

corrective [kə'rɛktɪv] *adj (measures)* Gegen–; *(lenses, shoes)* Ausgleichs–

correctness [kə'rɛktnɪs] *s* Richtigkeit *f; (in manners)* Korrektheit *f*

correlate ['kɔrəˌlet] *tr* in Wechselbeziehung bringen ‖ *intr* in Wechselbeziehung stehen

correlation [ˌkɔrə'leʃən] *s* Wechselbeziehung *f,* Korrelation *f*

correlative [kə'rɛlətɪv] *adj* korrelativ ‖ *s* Korrelat *n*

correspond [ˌkɔrɪ'spɑnd] *intr* einander übereinstimmen; **(to, with)** entsprechen *(dat); (exchange letters)* **(with)** im Briefwechsel stehen (mit)

correspondence [ˌkɔrɪ'spɑndəns] *s (act of corresponding)* Übereinstimmung *f; (instance of correspondence)* Entsprechung *f; (exchange of letters; letters)* Korrespondenz *f*

correspon'dence course' *s* Fernkursus *m*

correspondent [ˌkɔrɪ'spɑndənt] *s* Briefpartner –in *mf;* (journ) Korrespondent –in *mf*

correspond'ing *adj* entsprechend

corridor ['kɔrɪdər] *s* Korridor *m*

corroborate [kə'rɑbəˌret] *tr* bestätigen

corrode [kə'rod] *tr & intr* korrodieren

corrosion [kə'roʒən] *s* Korrosion *f*

corrosive [kə'rosɪv] *adj* ätzend; *(influence)* schädigend ‖ *s* Ätzmittel *n*

cor'rugated card'board ['kɔrəˌgetɪd] *s* Wellpappe *f*

cor'rugated i'ron *s* Wellblech *n*

corrupt [kə'rʌpt] *adj (text)* verderbt; *(morally)* verdorben; *(open to bribes)* bestechlich ‖ *tr* verderben; *(bribe)* bestechen

corruption [kə'rʌpʃən] *s* Verderbtheit *f; (bribery)* Korruption *f*

corsage [kɔr'saʒ] *s* Blumensträußchen *n* zum Anstecken

corsair ['kɔrsɛr] *s* Korsar *m*

corset ['kɔrsɪt] *s* Korsett *n*

Corsica ['kɔrsɪkə] *s* Korsika *n*

Corsican ['kɔrsɪkən] *adj* korsisch

cortege [kɔr'teʒ] *s* Gefolge *n; (at a funeral)* Leichenzug *m*

cor·tex ['kɔrˌtɛks] *s* **(–tices** [tɪˌsiz]) Rinde *f,* Kortex *m*

cortisone ['kɔrtɪˌson] *s* Cortison *n*

corvette [kɔr'vɛt] *s* (naut) Korvette *f*

cosmetic [kaz'metɪk] *adj* kosmetisch ‖ *s* Kosmetikum *n;* **cosmetics** Kosmetikartikel *pl*

cosmic ['kazmɪk] *adj* kosmisch
cosmonaut ['kazmə,nɔt] *s* Kosmonaut –in *mf*
cosmopolitan [,kazə'pɑlɪtən] *adj* kosmopolitisch ‖ *s* Kosmopolit –in *mf*
cosmos ['kazməs] *s* Kosmos *m*
cost [kɔst] *s* Preis *m;* **at all costs** (fig) um jeden Preis; **at c.** zum Selbstkostenpreis; **at the c. of** auf Kosten (*genit*); **costs** Kosten *pl;* (jur) Gerichtskosten *pl* ‖ *v* (*pret & pp* **cost**) *intr* kosten
cost' account'ing *s* Kostenrechnung *f*
costly ['kɔstlɪ] *adj* kostspielig; (*of great value*) kostbar
cost' of liv'ing *s* Lebenshaltungskosten *pl*
costume ['kast(j)um] *s* Kostüm *n;* (*national dress*) Tracht *f*
cos'tume ball' *s* Kostümball *m*
cos'tume jew'elry *s* Modeschmuck *m*
cot [kat] *s* Feldbett *n*
coterie ['kotəri] *s* Klüngel *m*, Koterie *f*
cottage ['katɪdʒ] *s* Hütte *f;* (*country house*) Landhaus *n*
cot'tage cheese' *s* Quark *m*, Quarkkäse *m*
cot'ter pin' ['katər] *s* Schließbolzen *m*
cotton ['katən] *s* (*fiber, yarn*) Baumwolle *f;* (*unspun cotton*) Watte *f;* (*sterilized cotton*) Verbandswatte *f*
cot'ton field' *s* Baumwollfeld *n*
cot'ton gin' *s* Entkörnungsmaschine *f*
cot'ton mill' *s* Baumwollspinnerei *f*
cot'ton pick'er ['pɪkər] *s* Baumwollpflücker –in *mf;* (*machine*) Baumwollpflückmaschine *f*
cot'tonseed oil' *s* Baumwollsamenöl *n*
cot'ton waste' *s* Putzwolle *f*
couch [kautʃ] *s* Couch *f*, Liege *f* ‖ *tr* (*words*) fassen; (*thoughts*) ausdrücken
cougar ['kugər] *s* Puma *m*
cough [kɔf] *s* Husten *m* ‖ *tr—***c. up** aushusten; (*money*) (sl) blechen ‖ *intr* husten; (*in order to attract attention*) sich räuspern
cough' drop' *s* Hustenbonbon *m & n*
cough' syr'up *s* Hustentropfen *pl*
could [kud] *aux*—**he c.** (*was able*) er konnte; **if he c.** (*were able*) wenn er könnte
council ['kaunsəl] *s* Rat *m;* (eccl) Konzil *n*
coun'cil·man *s* (**–men**) Stadtratsmitglied *n*
councilor ['kaunsələr] *s* Rat *m*
coun·sel ['kaunsəl] *s* Rat *m;* (*for the defense*) Verteidiger –in *mf;* (*for the prosecution*) Anklagevertreter –in *mf* ‖ *v* (*pret & pp* **-sel[l]ed;** *ger* **-sel[l]ing**) *tr* raten (*dat*) ‖ *intr* Rat geben
counselor ['kaunsələr] *s* Berater –in *mf*
count [kaunt] *s* Zahl *f;* (*nobleman*) Graf *m;* (jur) Anklagepunkt *m;* **lose c.** sich verzählen ‖ *tr* zählen; (*the costs*) berechnen; **c. in** einschließen; **c. off** abzählen; **c. out** (*money, a boxer*) auszählen ‖ *intr* zählen; **c. for little** (or **much**) wenig (or viel)

gelten; **c. off** (mil) abzählen; **c. on** zählen auf (*acc*)
count'down' *s* Countdown *m & n*
countenance ['kauntɪnəns] *s* Antlitz *n* ‖ *tr* (*tolerate*) zulassen; (*approve*) billigen
counter ['kauntər] *adj* Gegen– ‖ *adv* —**c. to** wider; **run c. to** zuwiderlaufen (*dat*) ‖ *s* Zähler *m;* (*in games*) Spielmarke *f;* (*in a store*) Ladentisch *m*, Theke *f;* (*in a restaurant*) Büffet *n;* (*in a bank*) Schalter *m;* **under the c.** (fig) heimlich ‖ *tr* widerstreben (*dat*); (*in speech*) widersprechen (*dat*) ‖ *intr* Gegenmaßnahmen treffen; (box) kontern, nachschlagen
coun'teract' *tr* entgegenwirken (*dat*)
coun'terattack' *s* Gegenangriff *m* ‖ **coun'terattack'** *tr* e–n Gegenangriff machen auf (*acc*) ‖ *intr* e–n Gegenangriff machen
coun'terbal'ance *s* Gegengewicht *n* ‖ **coun'terbal'ance** *tr* das Gegengewicht halten (*dat*)
coun'terclock'wise *adj* linksläufig ‖ *adv* entgegen der Uhrzeigerrichtung
coun'teres'pionage *s* Gegenspionage *f*
counterfeit ['kauntərfɪt] *adj* gefälscht ‖ *s* Fälschung *f;* (*money*) Falschgeld *n* ‖ *tr* fälschen
counterfeiter ['kauntər,fɪtər] *s* Falschmünzer –in *mf*
coun'terfeit mon'ey *s* Falschgeld *n*
coun'terintel'ligence *s* Spionageabwehr *f*
countermand ['kauntər,mænd] *s* Gegenbefehl *m* ‖ *tr* widerrufen
coun'termeas'ure *s* Gegenmaßnahme *f*
coun'teroffen'sive *s* Gegenoffensive *f*
coun'terpart' *s* Gegenstück *n;* (*person*) Ebenbild *n*
coun'terpoint' *s* (mus) Kontrapunkt *m*
coun'terrevolu'tion *s* Konterrevolution *f*
coun'tersign' *s* Gegenzeichen *n* ‖ *tr & intr* mitunterzeichnen
coun'tersink' *v* (*pret & pp* **-sunk**) *tr* (*a screw*) versenken; (*a hole*) ausfräsen
coun'terspy' *s* Gegenspion –in *mf*
coun'terstroke' *s* Gegenstoß *m*
coun'terweight' *s* Gegengewicht *n*
countess ['kauntɪs] *s* Gräfin *f*
countless ['kauntlɪs] *adj* zahllos
countrified ['kantrɪ,faɪd] *adj* ländlich; (*boorish*) bäu(e)risch
country ['kantri] *adj* (*air, house, life, road*) Land– ‖ *s* (*state; rural area*) Land *n;* (*land of birth*) Heimatland *n;* **in the c.** auf dem Lande; **to the c.** aufs Land
coun'try club' *s* exklusiver Klub *m* auf dem Lande
coun'tryfolk' *spl* Landvolk *n*
coun'try gen'tleman *s* Landedelmann *m*
coun'try·man *s* (**–men**) Landsmann *m*
coun'tryside' *s* Landschaft *f*, Land *n*
coun'try-wide' *adj* über das ganze Land verbreitet (or ausgedehnt)
county ['kaunti] *s* Kreis *m*
coun'ty seat' *s* Kreisstadt *f*

coup [ku] *s* Coup *m*

coup d'état [ku de 'ta] *s* Staatsstreich *m*

coupe [ku'pe], [kup] *s* Coupé *n*

couple ['kʌpəl] *s* Paar *n*; (*of lovers*) Liebespaar *n*; (*man and wife*) Ehepaar *n*; (phys) Kräftepaar *n*; **a c. of** ein paar, e.g., **a c. of days ago** vor ein paar Tagen ‖ *tr* koppeln ‖ *intr* sich paaren

couplet ['kʌplɪt] *s* Verspaar *n*

coupling ['kʌplɪŋ] *s* Verbindungsstück *n*; (rad) Kopplung *f*; (rr) Kupplung *f*

coupon ['k(j)upɑn] *s* Gutschein *m*

courage ['kʌrɪdʒ] *s* Mut *m*, Courage *f*; **get up the c. to** (*inf*) sich [*dat*] ein Herz fassen zu (*inf*)

courageous [kə'redʒəs] *adj* mutig

courier ['kʌrɪ·ər] *s* Eilbote *m*; (*tour guide*) Reiseleiter –in *mf*

course [kors] *s* (*direction*) Richtung *f*, Kurs *m*; (*of a river, of time*) Lauf *m*; (*method of procedure*) Weg *m*, Weise *f*, Kurs *m*; (*in racing*) Bahn *f*; (archit) Schicht *f*; (culin) Gang *m*; (educ) Kurs *m*; **c. of action** Handlungsweise *f*; **go off c.** (aer) sich verfliegen; **in due c.** zur rechten Zeit; **in the c. of** im Verlaufe von (or *genit*); (*with expressions of time*) im Laufe (*genit*); **of c.** natürlich; **run its c.** seinen Verlauf nehmen

court [kort] *s* (*of a king*) Hof *m*; (*of justice*) Gericht *n*; (*yard*) Hof *m*; (tennis) Platz *m*; **in c.** (or **into c.** or **to c.**) vor Gericht; **out of c.** außergerichtlich ‖ *tr* (*a girl*) werben um; (*danger*) suchen; (*disaster*) heraufbeschwören

courteous ['kʌrtɪ·əs] *adj* höflich

courtesan ['kortɪʒən] *s* Kurtisane *f*

courtesy ['kʌrtɪsi] *s* Höflichkeit *f*; **by c. of** freundlicherweise zur Verfügung gestellt von

court'house' *s* Gerichtsgebäude *n*

courtier ['kortɪ·ər] *s* Höfling *m*

court' jest'er *s* Hofnarr *m*

courtly ['kortli] *adj* höfisch

court'-mar'tial *s* (**courts-martial**) Kriegsgericht *n* ‖ *v* (*pret & pp* –tial[l]ed; *ger* –tial[l]ing) *tr* vor ein Kriegsgericht stellen

court'room' *s* Gerichtssaal *m*

court'ship' *s* Werbung *f*

court'yard' *s* Hof *m*

cousin ['kʌzɪn] *s* Vetter *m*; (*female*) Kusine *f*

cove [kov] *s* Bucht *f*

covenant ['kʌvənənt] *s* Vertrag *m*; (Bib) Bund *m*

cover ['kʌvər] *s* Decke *f*; (*lid*) Deckel *m*; (*wrapping*) Hülle *f*; (e.g., *of a bed*) Bezug *m*; (*of a book*) Einband *m*; (*protection*) Schutz *m*; (mil) Deckung *f*; **from c. to c.** von vorn bis hinten; **take c.** sich unterstellen; **under c.** im Geheimen; **under c. of night** im Schutz der Dunkelheit ‖ *tr* bedecken, decken; (*conceal*) verdecken; (*distances*) zurücklegen; (*a sales territory*) bearbeiten; (*a bet*) die gleiche Summe setzen gegen; (*ex-*

penses, losses) decken; (*upholstered furniture*) beziehen; (*deal with*) behandeln; (*include*) umfassen; (*material in class*) durchnehmen; (*said of a reporter*) berichten über (*acc*); (*said of plants*) bewachsen; (*with insurance*) versichern, decken; (*protect with a gun*) sichern; (*threaten with a gun*) in Schach halten; (*have within range*) beherrschen; **c. up** zudecken; (*conceal*) verheimlichen ‖ *intr*—**c. for** einspringen für

coverage ['kʌvərɪdʒ] *s* (*area covered*) Verbreitungsgebiet *n*; (*of news*) Berichterstattung *f*; (ins) Versicherungsschutz *m*; (rad, telv) Sendebereich *m*

coveralls ['kʌvər‚ɔlz] *spl* Monteuranzug *m*

cov'ered wag'on *s* Planwagen *m*

cov'er girl' *s* Covergirl *n*

cov'ering *s* Decke *f*, Bedeckung *f*

covert ['kovərt] *adj* verborgen

cov'erup' *s* Beschönigung *f*, Bemäntelung *f*

covet ['kʌvɪt] *tr* begehren

covetous ['kʌvɪtəs] *adj* begehrlich

covetousness ['kʌvɪtəsnɪs] *s* Begehrlichkeit *f*

covey ['kʌvi] *s* (*brood*) Brut *f*; (*small flock*) Schwarm *m*; (*bevy*) Schar *f*

cow [kau] *s* Kuh *f* ‖ *tr* einschüchtern

coward ['kau·ərd] *s* Feigling *m*, Memme *f*

cowardice ['kau·ərdɪs] *s* Feigheit *f*

cowardly ['kau·ərdli] *adj* feig(e)

cow'bell' *s* Kuhglocke *f*

cow'boy' *s* Cowboy *m*

cower ['kau·ər] *intr* kauern

cow'herd' *s* Kuhhirt *m*

cow'hide' *s* Rindsleder *n*

cowl [kaul] *s* (*on a chimney*) Schornsteinkappe *f*; (aer) Motorhaube *f*; (eccl) Kapuze *f*

cowling ['kaulɪŋ] *s* (aer) Motorhaube *f*

co-worker ['ko ‚wʌrkər] *s* Mitarbeiter –in *mf*

cowpox ['kau ‚pɑks] *s* Kuhpocken *pl*

coxswain ['kɑksən] *s* Steuermann *m*

coy [kɔɪ] *adj* spröde

coyote [kaɪ'oti], ['kaɪ·ot] *s* Kojote *m*, Präriewolf *m*, Steppenwolf *m*

cozy ['kozi] *adj* gemütlich

C.P.A. ['si'pi'e] *s* (**certified public accountant**) amtlich zugelassener Wirtschaftsprüfer *m*

crab [kræb] *s* Krabbe *f*; (*grouch*) Sauertopf *m*

crab' ap'ple *s* Holzapfel *m*

crabbed ['kræbɪd] *adj* mürrisch; (*handwriting*) unleserlich; (*style*) schwer verständlich, verworren

crabby ['kræbi] *adj* mürrisch, grämlich

crack [kræk] *adj* erstklassig; (*troops*) Elite- ‖ *s* Riß *m*, Sprung *m*; (*of a whip or rifle*) Knall *m*; (*blow*) (sl) Klaps *m*; (*opportunity*) (sl) Gelegenheit *f*; (*try*) (sl) Versuch *m*; (*cutting remark*) (sl) Seitenhieb *m*; **at the c. of dawn** bei Tagesanbruch; **take a c. at** (sl) versuchen ‖ *tr* spalten; (*a nut, safe*) knacken; (*an egg*) aufschlagen;

(*a code*) entziffern; (*hit*) (sl) e–n Klaps geben (*dat*); (chem) spalten; **c. a joke** e–n Witz reißen; **c. a smile** lächeln ‖ *intr* (*make a cracking sound*) knacken, krachen; (*develop a crack*) rissig werden; (*said of a whip or rifle*) knallen; (*said of a voice*) umschlagen; (*said of ice*) (zer) springen; **c. down on** scharf vorgehen gegen; **c. up** (coll) überschnappen; (aut) aufknallen

cracked *adj* (*split*) rissig; (*crazy*) (sl) übergeschnappt

cracker ['krækər] *s* Keks *m* & *n*

crack'erjack' *adj* (coll) erstklassig ‖ *s* (coll) Kanone *f*

crackle ['krækəl] *s* Krakelierung *f* ‖ *tr* krakelieren ‖ *intr* prasseln

crack'pot' *adj* (sl) verrückt ‖ *s* (sl) Verrückte *mf*

crack' shot' *s* Meisterschütze *m*

crack'-up' *s* (aut) Zusammenstoß *m*

cradle ['kredəl] *s* Wiege *f;* (telp) Gabel *f* ‖ *tr* in den Armen wiegen

craft [kræft] *s* Handwerk *n*, Gewerbe *n;* (naut) Fahrzeug *n;* **by c.** durch List ‖ *spl* Fahrzeuge *pl*, Schiffe *pl;* **small c.** kleine Schiffe *pl*

craftiness ['kræftɪnɪs] *s* List *f*

crafts·man ['kræftsmən] *s* (–men) Handwerker *m*

crafts'manship' *s* Kunstfertigkeit *f*

crafty ['kræfti] *adj* arglistig

crag [kræg] *s* Felszacke *f*

cram [kræm] *v* (*pret & pp* **crammed;** *ger* **cramming**) *tr* vollstopfen; **c. into** hineinstopfen in (*acc*) ‖ *intr* (educ) büffeln, ochsen; **c. into** sich hineinzwängen in (*acc*)

cram' course' *s* Presse *f*

cramp [kræmp] *s* Krampf *m;* (*clamp*) Klammer *f* ‖ *tr* einschränken, beengen

cramped *adj* eng

cranberry ['kræn ‚beri] *s* Preiselbeere *f*

crane [kren] *s* (mach) Kran *m;* (orn) Kranich *m* ‖—**c. one's neck** den Hals recken

crani·um ['krenɪ·əm] *s* (–a [ə]) *s* Hirnschale *f*, Schädel *m*

crank [kræŋk] *s* Kurbel *f;* (*grouch*) (coll) Griesgram *m;* (*eccentric*) (coll) Sonderling *m* ‖ *tr* kurbeln; **c. up** ankurbeln

crank'case' *s* Kurbelgehäuse *n*

crank'shaft' *s* Kurbelwelle *f*

cranky ['kræŋki] *adj* launisch

cranny ['kræni] *s* Ritze *f*

crap [kræp] *s* (*nonsense*) (sl) Unsinn *m;* **craps** Würfel *pl;* **shoot craps** Würfel spielen

crash [kræʃ] *s* Krach *m;* (aer) Absturz *m;* (aut) Zusammenstoß *m;* (econ) Zusammenbruch *m* ‖ *tr* zerschmettern; (*a party*) hineinplatzen in (*acc*); (aer) zum Absturz bringen ‖ *intr* (*produce a crashing sound*) krachen; (*shatter*) zerbrechen; (*collapse*) zusammenstürzen; (aer) abstürzen; (aut) zusammenstoßen; **c. into** fahren gegen

crash' dive' *s* Schnelltauchen *n*

crash'-dive' *intr* schnelltauchen

crash' hel'met *s* Sturzhelm *m*

crash' land'ing *s* Bruchlandung *f*

crash' pro'gram *s* Gewaltkur *f*

crass [kræs] *adj* kraß

crate [kret] *s* Lattenkiste *f;* (*old car, old plane*) (coll) Kiste *f* ‖ *tr* in e–r Lattenkiste verpacken

crater ['kretər] *s* Krater *m;* (*of a bomb*) Trichter *m*

crave [krev] *tr* ersehnen ‖ *intr*—**c. for** verlangen nach

craven ['krevən] *adj* feige ‖ *s* Feigling *m*

crav'ing *s* (**for**) Verlangen *n* (nach)

craw [krɔ] *s* Kropf *m*

crawl [krɔl] *s* Kriechen *n* ‖ *intr* kriechen; (*said of the skin*) kribbeln; (*said of a swimmer*) kraulen; (*said of cars*) schleichen; **c. along** im Schneckentempo gehen (or fahren); **c. into a hole** (& fig) sich verkriechen; **c. with** wimmeln von

crayon ['kre·ən] *s* (*wax crayon*) Wachsmalkreide *f;* (*colored pencil*) Farbstift *m;* (*artist's crayon*) Zeichenkreide *f*

craze [krez] *s* Mode *f*, Verrücktheit *f* ‖ *tr* verrückt machen

crazy ['krezi] *adj* verrückt; (*senseless*) sinnlos; **c. about** verrückt nach; **c. idea** Wahnidee *f;* **drive c.** verrückt machen

cra'zy bone' *s* Musikantenknochen *m*

creak [krik] *s* (*high-pitched sound*) Quietschen *n;* (*low-pitched sound*) Knarren *n* ‖ *intr* quietschen; knarren

creaky ['kriki] *adj* quietschend; knarrend

cream [krim] *adj* Sahne–, Rahm–; (*color*) creme, cremefarben ‖ *s* Sahne *f*, Rahm *m;* (*cosmetic*) Creme *f;* (*color*) Cremefarbe *f;* (fig) Creme *f* ‖ *tr* (*milk*) abrahmen; (*trounce*) (sl) schlagen

cream' cheese' *s* Rahmkäse *m*, Sahnekäse *m*

creamery ['kriməri] *s* Molkerei *f*

cream' pit'cher *s* Sahnekännchen *n*

cream' puff' *s* Windbeutel *m*

cream' sep'arator ['sepə ‚retər] *s* Milchschleuder *f*, Milchzentrifuge *f*

creamy ['krimi] *adj* sahnig

crease [kris] *s* Falte *f;* (*in trousers*) Bügelfalte *f* ‖ *tr* falten; (*trousers*) bügeln ‖ *intr* knittern

create [kri'et] *tr* (er)schaffen; (*excitement, an impression*) hervorrufen; (*noise*) verursachen; (*appoint*) ernennen, machen zu; (*a role, fashions*) kreieren

creation [kri'eʃən] *s* Schaffung *f;* (*of the world*) Schöpfung *f;* (*in fashions*) Modeschöpfung *f*

creative [kri'etɪv] *adj* schöpferisch

creator [kri'etər] *s* Schöpfer *m*

creature ['kritʃər] *s* Kreatur *f*, Geschöpf *n;* **every living c.** jedes Lebewesen *n*

credence ['kridəns] *s* Glaube *m*

credentials [krɪ'denʃəlz] *spl* Beglaubigungsschreiben *n*, Akkreditiv *n*

credenza [krɪ'denzə] *s* Kredenz *f*

credibility [ˌkrɛdɪ'bɪlɪti] *s* Glaubwürdigkeit *f*
credibil'ity gap' *s* Vertrauenslücke *f*
credible ['krɛdɪbəl] *adj* glaubwürdig
credit ['krɛdɪt] *s* (*credence*) Glaube *m*; (*honor*) Ehre *f*; (*recognition*) Anerkennung *f*;·(educ) Anrechnungspunkt *m*; (fin) Kredit *m*; (*credit balance*) (fin) Guthaben *n*; **be a c. to** Ehre machen (*dat*); **credits** (cin) Vorspann *m*; **give s.o. c. for s.th.** j-m etw hoch anrechnen; **on c.** auf Kredit; **on thirty days' c.** auf dreißig Tage Ziel; **take c. for** sich [*dat*] als Verdienst anrechnen; **to s.o.'s c.** zu j-s Ehre ‖ *tr* (*believe*) glauben (*dat*); (*an account*) gutschreiben (*dat*); **c. s.o. with s.th.** j-m etw hoch anrechnen
creditable ['krɛdɪtəbəl] *adj* ehrenwert
cre'dit card' *s* Kreditkarte *f*
cre'dit hour' *s* (educ) Anrechnungspunkt *m*
creditor ['krɛdɪtər] *s* Gläubiger –in *mf*
cre'dit rat'ing *s* Bonität *f*
credulous ['krɛdʒələs] *adj* leichtgläubig
creed [krid] *s* (& fig) Glaubensbekenntnis *n*
creek [krik] *s* Bach *m*
creep [krip] *s* Kriechen *n*; (sl) Spinner *m*; **it gives me the creeps** mir gruselt ‖ *v* (*pret & pp* **crept** [krɛpt]) *intr* kriechen, schleichen; (*said of plants*) kriechen; **c. along** dahinschleichen; **c. up on** heranschleichen an (*acc*); **it makes my flesh c.** es macht mich schaudern
creeper ['kripər] *s* Kletterpflanze *f*
creepy ['kripi] *adj* schaudererregend; (*sensation*) gruselig; **have a c. feeling** gruseln
cremate ['krimet] *tr* einäschern
cremation [krɪ'meʃən] *s* Einäscherung *f*
crematory ['krimə,tori] *s* Krematorium *n*
crepe [krep] *s* Krepp *m*; (*mourning band*) Trauerflor *m*
crepe' pa'per *s* Kreppapier *n*
crescent ['krɛsənt] *s* Mondsichel *f*
cres'cent roll' *s* Hörnchen *n*
cress [krɛs] *s* (bot) Kresse *f*
crest [krɛst] *s* (*of a hill, wave, or rooster*) Kamm *m*; (*of a helmet*) Helmbusch *m*; (*of a bird*) Federbüschel *n*
crestfallen ['krɛst,fɔlən] *adj* niedergeschlagen
Crete [krit] *s* Kreta *n*
crevice ['krɛvɪs] *s* Riß *m*
crew [kru] *s* Gruppe *f*; (aer, nav) Besatzung *f*; (*of a boat*) (sport) Mannschaft *f*; (*rowing*) (sport) Rudersport *m*
crew' cut' *s* Bürstenschnitt *m*
crib [krɪb] *s* (*manger*) Krippe *f*; (*for children*) Kinderbettstelle *f*; (*bin*) Speicher *m*; (*student's pony*) Eselsbrücke *f* ‖ *v* (*pret & pp* **cribbed;** *ger* **cribbing**) *tr & intr* abbohren
cricket ['krɪkɪt] *s* (*ent*) Grille *f*;

(sport) Kricketspiel *n*; **not c.** (coll) nicht fair
crime [kraɪm] *s* Verbrechen *n*
criminal ['krɪmɪnəl] *adj* verbrecherisch; (*act, case, code, court, law*) Straf-; (*investigation, trial, police*) Kriminal– ‖ *s* Verbrecher –in *mf*
crim'inal charge' *s* Strafanzeige *f*
crim'inal neg'ligence *s* grobe Fahrlässigkeit *f*
crim'inal offense' *s* strafbare Handlung *f*
crim'inal rec'ord *s* Strafregister *n*
crimp [krɪmp] *s* Welle *f*; **put a c. in** (coll) e-n Dämpfer aufsetzen (*dat*) ‖ *tr* wellen, riffeln
crimson ['krɪmzən] *adj* karmesinrot ‖ *s* Karmesin *n*
cringe [krɪndʒ] *intr* sich krümmen; (*fawn*) kriechen
crinkle ['krɪŋkəl] *s* Runzel *f* ‖ *tr* runzeln; (*one's nose*) rümpfen
cripple ['krɪpəl] *s* Krüppel *m* ‖ *tr* verkrüppeln; (fig) lähmen, lahmlegen
cri·sis ['kraɪsɪs] *s* (–ses [siz]) Krise *f*
crisp [krɪsp] *adj* (*brittle*) knusprig; (*firm and fresh*) mürb; (*air, clothes*) frisch; (*manner*) forsch
crisscross ['krɪs,krɔs] *adj & adv* kreuz und quer ‖ *tr* kreuz und quer markieren ‖ *intr* sich kreuzen
criteri·on [kraɪ'tɪrɪ·ən] *s* (–a [ə] & –ons) Kennzeichen *n*, Kriterium *n*
critic ['krɪtɪk] *s* Kritiker –in *mf*
critical ['krɪtɪkəl] *adj* kritisch
criticism ['krɪtɪ,sɪzəm] *s* Kritik *f*
criticize ['krɪtɪ,saɪz] *tr* kritisieren
critique [krɪ'tik] *s* (*review*) Rezension *f*; (*critical discussion*) Kritik *f*
croak [krok] *s* (*of a frog*) Quaken *n*; (*of a raven*) Krächzen *n* ‖ *intr* quaken; krächzen; (*die*) (sl) verrecken
cro·chet [kro'ʃə] *s* Häkelarbeit *f* ‖ *v* (*pret & pp* –**cheted** ['ʃed]; *ger* –**cheting** ['ʃe·ɪŋ]) *tr & intr* häkeln
crochet' nee'dle *s* Häkelnadel *f*
crock [krak] *s* irdener Topf *m*, Krug *m*
crockery ['krakəri] *s* irdenes Geschirr *n*
crocodile ['krakə,daɪl] *s* Krokodil *n*
croc'odile tears' *spl* Krokodilstränen *pl*
crocus ['krokəs] *s* (bot) Krokus *m*
crone [kron] *s* altes Weib *n*
crony ['kroni] *s* alter Kamerad *m*
crook [kruk] *s* (*of a shepherd*) Hirtenstab *m*; (sl) Gauner *m* ‖ *tr* krümmen
crooked ['krukɪd] *adj* krumm; (*dishonest*) unehrlich
croon [krun] *tr & intr* schmalzig singen
crooner ['krunər] *s* Schnulzensänger *m*
crop [krap] *s* Ernte *f*; (*whip*) Peitsche *f*; (*of a bird*) Kropf *m*; (*large number*) Menge *f*; **the crops** die ganze Ernte ‖ *v* (*pret & pp* **cropped;** *ger* **cropping**) *tr* stutzen; (*said of an animal*) abfressen ‖ *intr*—**c. up** auftauchen
crop' fail'ure *s* Mißerte *f*
croquet [kro'ke] *s* Krocket *n*

croquette [kro'kɛt] *s* (culin) Krokette *f*

crosier ['kroʒər] *s* Bischofsstab *m*

cross [krɔs] *adj* Quer-, Kreuz-; (biol) Kreuzungs-; (*angry*) (**with**) ärgerlich (auf *acc*, über *acc*) || *s* (& fig) Kreuz *n*; (biol) Kreuzung *f* || *tr* (*arms, legs, streets, plans, breeds*) kreuzen; (*a mountain*) übersteigen; (*oppose*) in die Quere kommen (*dat*); **c. my heart!** Hand aufs Herz!; **c. oneself** sich bekreuzigen; **c. s.o.'s mind** j-m durch den Kopf gehen; **c. out** ausstreichen || *intr* sich kreuzen; **c. over to** hinübergehen zu

cross'bones' *spl* gekreuzte Skelettknochen *pl*

cross'bow' *s* (hist) Armbrust *f*

cross'breed' *v* (*pret & pp* **-bred**) *tr* kreuzen

cross'-coun'try *adj* (*vehicle*) geländegängig || **cross'-coun'try** *s* (sport) Langlauf *m*

cross'cur'rent *s* Gegenströmung *f*

cross'-exam'ine *tr* ins Kreuzverhör nehmen

cross'-examina'tion *s* Kreuzverhör *n*

cross'-eyed' *adj* schieläugig

cross'fire' *s* Kreuzfeuer *n*

cross'ing *s* (*of streets*) Kreuzung *f*; (*of the ocean*) Überfahrt *f*, Überquerung *f*; (rr) Übergang *m*

cross'piece' *s* Querstück *n*

cross'-pur'pose *s*—**be at cross-purposes** einander entgegenarbeiten

cross' ref'erence *s* Querverweis *m*

cross'road' *s* Querweg *m*; **crossroads** Straßenkreuzung *f*; (fig) Scheideweg *m*

cross' sec'tion *s* Querschnitt *m*

cross'wind' *s* Seitenwind *m*

cross'wise' *adj* & *adv* quer, in die Quere

cross'word puz'zle *s* Kreuzworträtsel *n*

crotch [krɑtʃ] *s* (*of a tree*) Gabelung *f*; (*of a body or trousers*) Schritt *m*

crotchety ['krɑtʃɪti] *adj* verschroben

crouch [krautʃ] *s* Hocke *f* || *intr* hocken

croup [krup] *s* (*of a horse*) Kruppe *f*; (pathol) Halsbräune *f*

croupier ['krupɪ·ər] *s* Croupier -in *mf*

crouton ['krutɑn] *s* gerösteter Brotwürfel *m*

crow [kro] *s* (*cry*) Krähen *n*; (*bird*) Krähe *f*; **as the c. flies** schnurgrade; **eat c.** klein beigeben || *intr* krähen

crow'bar' *s* Stemmeisen *n*

crowd [kraud] *s* Menge *f*; (*mob*) Masse *f*; (*set*) Gesellschaft *f* || *tr* vollstopfen; (*push*) stoßen; **c. out** verdrängen || *intr* (*around*) sich drängen (um); **c. into** sich hineindrängen in (*acc*)

crowd'ed *adj* überfüllt; (*street*) belebt

crown [kraun] *s* Krone *f*; (dent) Zahnkrone *f* || *tr* krönen, bekränzen; (checkers) zur Dame machen; (sl) eins aufs Dach geben (*dat*); (dent) überkronen

crown' jew'els *spl* Kronjuwelen *pl*

crown' prince' *s* Kronprinz *m*

crown' prin'cess *s* Kronprinzessin *f*

crow's'-feet' *spl* (*wrinkles*) Krähenfüße *pl*

crow's'-nest' *s* (naut) Krähennest *n*

crucial ['kruʃəl] *adj* entscheidend; (*point*) springend; **c. question** Gretchenfrage *f*; **c. test** Feuerprobe *f*

crucible ['krusɪbəl] *s* Schmelztiegel *m*

crucifix ['krusɪfɪks] *s* Kruzifix *n*

crucifixion [,krusɪ'fɪkʃən] *s* Kreuzigung *f*

cruci·fy ['krusɪ,faɪ] *v* (*pret & pp* **-fied**) *tr* kreuzigen

crude [krud] *adj* (*raw, unrefined*) roh; (*person*) grob, ungeschliffen; **c. joke** plumper Scherz *m*

crudity ['krudɪti] *s* Roheit *f*

cruel ['kru·əl] *adj* (**to**) grausam (gegen)

cruelty ['kru·əlti] *s* Grausamkeit *f*; **c. to animals** Tierquälerei *f*

cruet ['kru·ɪt] *s* Fläschchen *n*; (relig) Meßkännchen *n*

cruise [kruz] *s* Kreuzfahrt *f* || *intr* (aer) mit Reisegeschwindigkeit fliegen; (aut) herumfahren; (naut) kreuzen

cruiser ['kruzər] *s* (nav) Kreuzer *m*

cruise' ship' *s* Vergnügungsdampfer *m*

cruller ['krʌlər] *s* Krapfen *m*

crumb [krʌm] *s* Krümel *m*; (& fig) Bröckchen *n*; (sl) Schweinehund *m*

crumble ['krʌmbəl] *tr* & *intr* zerbröckeln

crumbly ['krʌmbli] *adj* bröcklig

crummy ['krʌmi] *adj* (sl) schäbig

crumple ['krʌmpəl] *tr* zerknittern || *intr* (*said of clothes*) faltig werden; (*collapse*) zusammenbrechen

crunch [krʌntʃ] *s* Knacken *n*; (*of snow*) Knirschen *n*; (*tight situation*) Druck *m* || *tr* knirschend kauen || *intr* (*said of snow*) knirschen; **c. on** knirschend kauen

crusade [kru'sed] *s* Kreuzzug *m*

crusader [kru'sedər] *s* Kreuzfahrer *m*

crush [krʌʃ] *s* Gedränge *n*; **have a c. on s.o.** (coll) in j-n vernarrt sein || *tr* (zer)quetschen, zerdrücken; (*grain*) schroten; (*stone*) zerkleinern; (*suppress*) unterdrücken; (*oppress*) bedrücken; (*hopes*) knicken; (*overwhelm*) zerschmettern; (min) pochen; **c. out** (*a cigarette*) ausdrücken || *intr* zerdrückt werden

crush'ing *adj* (*victory*) entscheidend; (*defeat*) vernichtend; (*experience*) überwältigend

crust [krʌst] *s* Kruste *f*; (sl) Frechheit *f*

crustacean [krʌs'teʃən] *s* Krebstier *n*

crustaceous [krʌs'teʃəs] *adj* Krebs-

crusty ['krʌsti] *adj* krustig, rösch; (*surly*) mürrisch

crutch [krʌtʃ] *s* (& fig) Krücke *f*

crux [krʌks] *s* Kern *m*, Kernpunkt *m*

cry [kraɪ] *s* (*cries*) (*shout*) Schrei *m*, Ruf *m*; (*weeping*) Weinen *n*; **a far cry from** etw ganz anderes als; **cry for help** Hilferuf *m*; **have a good cry** sich ordentlich ausweinen || *v* (*pret & pp* **cried**) *tr* schreien, rufen; **cry one's eyes out** sich [*dat*] die Augen aus dem Kopf weinen || *intr* (*weep*) weinen; (*shout*) schreien; **cry for help** um Hilfe rufen; **cry on s.o.'s shoulder** j–m seine Not klagen; **cry out against** scharf verurteilen; **cry out in** (*pain*) schreien vor (*dat*); **cry over** nachweinen (*dat*)

cry'ba'by s (**–bies**) Schreihals *m*

cry'ing *adj*—**c. jag** Schreikrampf *m*; **c. shame** schreiende Ungerechtigkeit *f* || *s* Weinen *n*; **for c. out loud!** um Himmels willen!

crypt [krɪpt] s Totengruft *f*, Krypta *f*

cryptic(al) ['krɪptɪk(əl)] *adj* (*secret*) geheim; (*puzzling*) rätselhaft; (*coded*) verschlüsselt

crystal ['krɪstəl] *adj* Kristall– || s Kristall *m*; (*cut glass*) Kristallglas *n*; (*of a watch*) Uhrglas *n*

crys'tal ball' s Kristall *m*

crystalline ['krɪstəlɪn], ['krɪstə͵laɪn] *adj* kristallinisch, kristallen

crystallize ['krɪstə͵laɪz] *tr* kristallisieren || *intr* kristallisieren; (fig) feste Form annehmen

cub [kʌb] s Junge *n*

Cuba ['kjubə] s Kuba *n*

Cuban ['kjubən] *adj* kubanisch || s Kubaner –in *mf*

cubbyhole ['kʌbɪ͵hol] s gemütliches Zimmerchen *n*

cube [kjub] s Würfel *m*; (math) dritte Potenz *f* || *tr* in Würfel schneiden; (math) kubieren

cubic ['kjubɪk] *adj* Raum–; (math) kubisch; **c. foot** Kubikfuß *m*

cub' report'er s unerfahrener Reporter *m*

cub' scout' s Wölfling *m*

cuckold ['kʌkəld] s Hahnrei *m* || *tr* zum Hahnrei machen

cuckoo ['kuku] *adj* (sl) verrückt || s Kuckuck *m*

cuck'oo clock' s Kuckucksuhr *f*

cucumber ['kjukʌmbər] s Gurke *f*

cud [kʌd] s—**chew the cud** wiederkäuen

cuddle ['kʌdəl] *tr* herzen || *intr* sich kuscheln; **c. up** sich behaglich zusammenkuscheln

cudg·el ['kʌdʒəl] s Prügel *m* || *v* (pret & pp **–el[l]ed**; ger **–el[l]ing**) *tr* verprügeln

cue [kju] s Hinweis *m*; (billiards) Billardstock *m*; (theat) Stichwort *n*; **take the cue from s.o.** sich nach j–m richten || *tr* das Stichwort geben (*dat*)

cuff [kʌf] s (*of a shirt*) Manschette *f*; (*of trousers*) Aufschlag *m*; (*blow*) Ohrfeige *f*; **off the c.** aus dem Handgelenk

cuff' link' s Manschettenknopf *m*

cuisine [kwɪ'zin] s Küche *f*

culinary ['kjulɪ͵neri] *adj* kulinarisch, Koch–; **c. art** Kochkunst *f*

cull [kʌl] *tr* (*choose*) auslesen; (*pluck*) pflücken

culminate ['kʌlmɪ͵net] *intr* (**in**) kulminieren (in *dat*), gipfeln (in *dat*)

culmination [͵kʌlmɪ'neʃən] s Gipfel *m*

culpable ['kʌlpəbəl] *adj* schuldhaft

culprit ['kʌlprɪt] s Schuldige *mf*

cult [kʌlt] s Kult *m*, Kultus *m*

cultivate ['kʌltɪ͵vet] *tr* (*soil*) bearbeiten; (*plants*) ziehen; (*activities*) betreiben; (*an art*) pflegen; (*friendship*) hegen

cul'tivat'ed *adj* kultiviert

cultivation [͵kʌltɪ'veʃən] s (*of the soil*) Bearbeitung *f*; (*of the arts*) Pflege *f*; (*of friendship*) Hegen *n*; **under c.** bebaut

cultivator ['kʌltɪ͵vetər] s (mach) Kultivator *m*

cultural ['kʌltʃərəl] *adj* kulturell, Kultur–

culture ['kʌltʃər] s Kultur *f*

cul'tured *adj* kultiviert

cul'ture me'dium s Nährboden *m*

culvert ['kʌlvərt] s Rinnstein *m*

cumbersome ['kʌmbərsəm] *adj* (*unwieldy*) unhandlich; (*slow-moving*) schwerfällig; (*burdensome*) lästig

cunning ['kʌnɪŋ] *adj* (arg)listig || s List *f*, Arglist *f*, Schlauheit *f*

cup [kʌp] s Tasse *f*; (*of a bra*) Körbchen *n*; (fig, bot, relig) Kelch *m*; (sport) Pokal *m* || *v* (pret & pp **cupped**; ger **cupping**) *tr* (*the hands*) wölben; (med) schröpfen

cupboard ['kʌbərd] s Schrank *m*

cupidity [kju'pɪdɪti] s Habgier *f*

cupola ['kjupələ] s Kuppel *f*

cur [kʌr] s Köter *m*; (pej) Halunke *m*

curable ['kjurəbəl] *adj* heilbar

curate ['kjurɪt] s Kaplan *m*

curative ['kjurətɪv] *adj* heilend, Heil–

curator ['kju͵retər] s Kustos *m*

curb [kʌrb] s (*of a street*) Randstein *m*; (*of a horse*) Kandare *f* || *tr* (& fig) zügeln; (*a person*) an die Kandare nehmen

curb'stone' s Bordstein *m*

curd [kʌrd] s Quark *m*; **curds** Quark *m*

curdle ['kʌrdəl] *tr* gerinnen lassen; (fig) erstarren lassen || *intr* gerinnen, stocken; (fig) erstarren

cure [kjur] s (*restoration to health*) Heilung *f*; (*remedy*) Heilmittel *n*; (*treatment*) Kur *f* || *tr* (*a disease, evil*) heilen; (*by smoking*) räuchern; (*by drying*) trocknen; (*by salting*) einsalzen || *intr* heilen

cure'–all' s Allheilmittel *n*

curfew ['kʌrfju] s Ausgehverbot *n*; (*enforced closing time*) Polizeistunde *f*

curi·o ['kjurɪ͵o] s (**–os**) Kuriosität *f*

curiosity [͵kjurɪ'asɪti] s Neugier *f*; (*strange article*) Kuriosität *f*

curious ['kjurɪ·əs] *adj* neugierig; (*odd*) kurios, merkwürdig

curl [kʌrl] s (*of hair*) Locke *f*; (*of smoke*) Rauchkringel *m* || *tr* locken; (*lips*) verächtlich schürzen || *intr* sich kräuseln; **c. up** sich zusammenrollen; (*said of an edge*) sich umbiegen

curler ['kʌrlər] s Haarwickler *m*

curlicue ['kʌrlɪ͵kju] s Schnörkel *m*

curly ['kʌrli] *adj* lockig; (*leaves, etc.*) gekräuselt

currant ['kʌrənt] s (*raisin*) Korinthe *f*; (genus *Ribes*) Johannisbeere *f*

currency ['kʌrənsi] s (money) Währung f; (circulation) Umlauf m; foreign c. Devisen pl; gain c. in Gebrauch kommen
current ['kʌrənt] adj (year, prices, account) laufend; (events) aktuell,
Tages–; be c. Gültigkeit haben; (said
of money) gelten || s (& elec) Strom
m
currently ['kʌrəntli] adv gegenwärtig
curricu·lum [kə'rɪkjələm] s (–lums &
–la [lə]) Lehrplan m
cur·ry ['kʌri] s Curry m || v (pret &
pp –ried) tr (a horse) striegeln; c.
favor with s.o. sich bei j–m ein-
zuschmeicheln suchen
cur'rycomb' s Striegel m
cur'ry pow'der s Currypulver n
curse [kʌrs] s Fluch m; put a c. on
verwünschen || tr verfluchen || intr
(at) fluchen (auf acc)
cursed ['kʌrsɪd], [kʌrst] adj verflucht
curse' word' s Fluchwort n, Schimpf-
wort n
cursive ['kʌrsɪv] adj Kurrent–
cursory ['kʌrsəri] adj flüchtig
curt [kʌrt] adj barsch, schroff
curtail [kər'tel] tr einschränken
curtain ['kʌrtɪn] s Gardine f; (drape)
Vorhang m; (theat) Vorhang m ||
tr—c. off mit Vorhängen abteilen
cur'tain call' s Vorhang m, Hervorruf
m
cur'tain rod' s Gardinenstange f
curt·sy ['kʌrtsi] s Knicks m || v (pret
& pp –sied) intr (to) knicksen (vor
dat)
curvaceous [kʌr've∫əs] adj kurvenreich
curvature ['kʌrvət∫ər] s (of the spine)
Verkrümmung f; (of the earth)
Krümmung f
curved adj krumm
cushion ['ku∫ən] s Kissen n, Polster
m & n; (billiards) Bande f || tr pol-
stern; (a shock) abfedern
cuss [kʌs] s (sl) Kerl m; (curse) (sl)
Fluch m || tr (sl) verfluchen || intr
(sl) fluchen
cussed ['kʌsɪd] adj (sl) verflucht
cussedness ['kʌsɪdnɪs] s (sl) Bosheit f
custard ['kʌstərd] s Eierkrem f
custodian [kəs'todɪ·ən] s (e.g., of records) Verwalter m; (of inmates)
Wärter m; (caretaker) Hausmeister
m
custody ['kʌstədi] s Verwahrung f,
Obhut f; (jur) Gewahrsam m; c. of
(children) Sorgerecht für; in the c.
of in der Obhut (genit); take into c.
in Gewahrsam nehmen
custom ['kʌstəm] s Brauch m, Sitte f;
(habit) Gewohnheit f; customs Zollkontrolle f; pay customs on s.th. für
etw Zoll bezahlen
customary ['kʌstə‚mɛri] adj gebräuchlich
cus'tom-built' adj nach Wunsch ge-
baut
customer ['kʌstəmər] s Kunde m,
Kundin f; (in a restaurant) Gast m;
(telp) Teilnehmer –in mf
cus'tom-made' adj nach Maß angefertigt

cus'toms clear'ance s Zollabertigung f
cus'toms declara'tion s Zollerklärung
f; (form) Abfertigungsschein m
cus'toms inspec'tion s Zollkontrolle f
cus'toms of'fice s Zollamt n
customs of'ficer s Zollbeamte m, Zoll-
beamtin f
cus'tom tai'lor s Maßschneider m
cut [kʌt] adj (glass) geschliffen; cut
flowers Schnittblumen pl; cut out
for wie geschaffen für (or zu) || s
Schnitt m; (piece cut off) Abschnitt
m; (slice) Schnitte f; (wound)
Schnittwunde f; (of a garment)
Schnitt m, Fasson f; (of the profits)
Anteil m; (in prices, pay) Kürzung
f, Senkung f; (absence from school)
Schwänzen n; (of meat) Stück n;
(cards) Abheben n; (tennis) Dreh-
schlag m; a cut above e–e Stufe
besser als || v (pret & pp cut; ger
cutting) tr schneiden; (glass, precious stones) schleifen; (grass)
mähen; (hedges) stutzen; (hay) machen; (a tunnel) bohren; (a motor)
abstellen; (production) drosseln;
(pay) kürzen, vermindern; (class)
(coll) schwänzen; (prices) herabsetzen, kürzen; (whiskey) (coll) panschen; (cards) abheben; (tennis)
schneiden; cut back (plants) stutzen;
(fig) abbauen; cut down fällen; cut
it out! Schluß damit!; cut off abschneiden; (a tail) kupieren; (gas,
telephone, electricity) absperren;
(troops) absprengen; cut one's finger
sich in den Finger schneiden; cut
out the nonsense! laß den Quatsch!;
cut short (e.g., a vacation) abkürzen;
(a person) das Wort abschneiden
(dat); cut up zerstückeln || intr
schneiden; cut down on einschränken, verringern; cut in sich einmischen; (at a dance) ablösen; cut
in ahead of s.o. vor j–m einbiegen;
cut up (sl) wild darauf losschießen
cut-and-dried ['kʌtən'draɪd] adj fix
und fertig
cut'away' s Cut m
cut'back' s Einschränkung f
cute [kjut] adj (pretty) niedlich;
(shrewd) (coll) klug
cut' glass' s geschliffenes Glas n
cuticle ['kjutɪkəl] s Nagelhaut f
cutie ['kjuti] s (sl) flotte Biene f
cutlass ['kʌtləs] s Entermesser n
cutlery ['kʌtləri] s Schneidwerkzeuge
pl
cutlet ['kʌtlɪt] s Schnitzel n
cut'-off' s (turn-off) Abzweigung f;
(cut-off point) (acct) gemeinsamer
Endpunkt m; (elec) Ausschaltvor-
richtung f; (mach) Absperrvorrich-
tung f
cut'-off date' s Abschlußtag m
cut'-out' s Ausschnitt m; (design to be
cut out) Ausschneidemuster n; (aut)
Auspuffklappe f
cut'-rate' adj (price) Schleuder–
cutter ['kʌtər] s (naut) Kutter m
cut'throat' adj halsabschneiderisch ||
s Halsabschneider –in mf
cut'ting adj schneidend; (tools)

Schneide–; (*remark*) scharf || *s* Abschnitt *m;* (*of prices*) Herabsetzung *f;* (hort) Steckling *m;* **cuttings** Abfälle *pl*

cut'ting board' *s* Schneidebrett *n*

cut'ting edge' *s* Schnittkante *f*

cut'ting room' *s* (cin) Schneideraum *m*

cuttlefish ['kʌtəl‚fɪʃ] *s* Tintenfisch *m*

cyanamide [saɪ'ænə‚maɪd] *s* (chem) Zyanamid *n;* (com) Kalkstickstoff *m*

cycle ['saɪkəl] *s* Kreis *m;* (*of an internal combustion engine*) Takt *m;* (phys) Periode *f* || *intr* radeln

cyclic(al) ['sɪklɪk(əl)] *adj* zyklisch, kreisförmig

cyclist ['saɪklɪst] *s* Radfahrer –in *mf*

cyclone ['saɪklon] *s* Zyklon *m*

cyclotron ['saɪklə‚tran] *s* Zyklotron *n,* Beschleuniger *m*

cylinder ['sɪlɪndər] *s* Zylinder *m*

cyl'inder block' *s* Zylinderblock *m*

cyl'inder bore' *s* Zylinderbohrung *f*

cyl'inder head' *s* Zylinderkopf *m*

cylindric(al) [sɪ'lɪndrɪk(əl)] *adj* zylindrisch

cymbal ['sɪmbəl] *s* Becken *n*

cynic ['sɪnɪk] *adj* (philos) zynisch || *s* Menschenverächter –in *mf;* (philos) Zyniker *m*

cynical ['sɪnɪkəl] *adj* zynisch

cynicism ['sɪnɪ‚sɪzəm] *s* Zynismus *m;* (*cynical remark*) zynische Bemerkung *f*

cypress ['saɪprəs] *s* Zypresse *f*

Cyprus ['saɪprəs] *s* Zypern *n*

Cyrillic [sɪ'rɪlɪk] *adj* kyrillisch

cyst [sɪst] *s* Zyste *f*

czar [zar] *s* Zar *m*

czarina [za'rinə] *s* Zarin *f*

Czech [tʃɛk] *adj* tschechisch || *s* Tscheche *m,* Tschechin *f;* (*language*) Tschechisch *n*

Czechoslovakia [‚tʃɛkəslo'vækɪ·ə] *s* die Tschechoslowakei *f*

D

D, d [di] *s* vierter Buchstabe des englischen Alphabets; (mus) D; **D flat** Des *n;* **D sharp** Dis *n*

D.A. *abb* (**District Attorney**) Staatsanwalt *m*

dab [dæb] *s* (*of color*) Klecks *m;* (*e.g., of butter*) Stückchen *n* || *v* (*pret & pp* **dabbed;** *ger* **dabbing**) *tr* betupfen || *intr*—**dab at** betupfen

dabble ['dæbəl] *tr* bespritzen || *intr* (*splash about*) plantschen; **d. in** herumstümpern in (*dat*)

dachshund ['daks‚hʊnd] *s* Dachshund *m*

dad [dæd] *s* (coll) Vati *m*

daddy ['dædi] *s* (coll) Vati *m*

dad'dy-long'legs' *s* (**–legs**) Weberknecht *m*

daffodil ['dæfədɪl] *s* gelbe Narzisse *f*

daffy ['dæfi] *adj* (coll) doof

dagger ['dægər] *s* Dolch *m;* (typ) Kreuzzeichen *n;* **look daggers at s.o.** j–n mit Blicken durchbohren

dahlia ['dæljə] *s* Georgine *f,* Dahlie *f*

daily ['deli] *adj* täglich, Tages– || *adv* täglich || *s* Tageszeitung *f*

dainty ['denti] *adj* zart; (*food*) lecker; (*finiky*) wählerisch

dairy ['deri] *s* Molkerei *f*

dair'y farm' *s* Meierei *f*

dair'y farm'er *s* Meier –in *mf*

dais ['de·ɪs] *s* Tribüne *f*

daisy ['dezi] *s* Gänseblümchen *n*

dal·ly ['dæli] *v* (*pret & pp* **–lied**) *intr* (*delay*) herumtrödeln; (*play amorously*) liebäugeln

dam [dæm] *s* Damm *m;* (*female quadruped*) Muttertier *n* || *v* (*pret & pp* **dammed;** *ger* **damming**) *tr* eindämmen; **dam up** anstauen

damage ['dæmɪdʒ] *s* Schaden *m;* **damages** (jur) Schadenersatz *m;* **do d.** Schaden anrichten; **sue for damages**

auf Schadenersatz klagen || *tr* beschädigen; (*a reputation*) beeinträchtigen

dam'aging *adj* (*influence*) schädlich; (*evidence*) belastend

dame [dem] *s* Dame *f;* (sl) Weibsbild *n*

damn [dæm] *adj* (sl) verflucht || *s*— **I don't give a d. about it** (sl) ich mache mir e–n Dreck daraus; **not be worth a d.** (sl) keinen Pfifferling wert sein || *tr* verdammen; (*curse*) verfluchen; **d. it!** (sl) verflucht!

damnation [dæm'neʃən] *s* Verdammnis *f*

damned *adj* verdammt; (sl) verflucht || *adv* (sl) verdammt || **the d.** *spl* die Verdammten *pl*

damp [dæmp] *adj* feucht || *s* Feuchtigkeit *f* || *tr* (be)feuchten; (*a fire; enthusiasm*) dämpfen; (elec, mus, phys) dämpfen

dampen ['dæmpən] *tr* befeuchten; (fig) dämpfen

damper ['dæmpər] *s* (*of a fireplace*) Schieber *m;* (*of a stove*) Ofenklappe *f;* (mus) Dämpfer *m;* **put a d. on** e–n Dämpfer aufsetzen (*dat*)

dampness ['dæmpnɪs] *s* Feuchtigkeit *f*

damsel ['dæmzəl] *s* Jungfrau *f*

dance [dæns] *s* Tanz *m* || *tr & intr* tanzen

dance' band' *s* Tanzkapelle *f*

dance' floor' *s* Tanzfläche *f*

dance' hall' *s* Tanzsaal *m,* Tanzlokal *n*

dancer ['dænsər] *s* Tänzer –in *mf*

dance' step' *s* Tanzschritt *m*

danc'ing part'ner *s* Tanzpartner –in *mf*

dandelion ['dændɪ‚laɪ·ən] *s* Löwenzahn *m*

dandruff ['dændrəf] *s* Schuppen *pl*

dandy ['dændi] *adj* (coll) pfundig, nett ‖ *s* Stutzer *m*

Dane [den] *s* Däne *m*, Dänin *f*

danger ['dendʒər] *s* (**to**) Gefahr *f* (für)

dan'ger list' *s*—**be on the d.** in Lebensgefahr sein

dangerous ['dendʒərəs] *adj* gefährlich

dangle ['dæŋgəl] *tr* schlenkern, baumeln lassen ‖ *intr* baumeln

Danish ['deniʃ] *adj* dänisch ‖ *s* (*language*) Dänisch *n*

Dan'ish pas'try *s* feines Hefegebäck *n*

dank [dæŋk] *adj* feucht

Danube ['dænjub] *s* Donau *f*

dapper ['dæpər] *adj* schmuck

dappled ['dæpəld] *adj* scheckig, bunt

dare [dɛr] *s* Herausforderung *f* ‖ *tr* wagen; (*a person*) herausfordern; **d. to** (*inf*) es wagen zu (*inf*); **don't you d. go** unterstehen Sie sich, wegzugehen!; **I d. say** ich darf wohl behaupten ‖ *intr*—**don't you d.!** unterstehen Sie sich!

dare'dev'il *s* Waghals *m*, Draufgänger *m*

dar'ing *adj* (*deed*) verwegen; (*person*) wagemutig ‖ *s* Wagemut *m*

dark [dɑrk] *adj* finster; (*color, beer, complexion*) dunkel; (fig) düster ‖ *s* Finsternis *n*, Dunkel *n*; **be in the d. about** im unklaren sein über (*acc*)

Dark' A'ges *spl* frühes Mittelalter *n*

dark-complexioned ['dɑrkkəm'plɛkʃənd] *adj* dunkelhäutig

darken ['dɑrkən] *tr* (*a room*) verfinstern ‖ *intr* sich verfinstern; (fig) sich verdüstern

dark'-eyed' *adj* schwarzäugig

dark' horse' *s* Außenseiter *m*

darkly ['dɑrkli] *adv* geheimnisvoll

darkness ['dɑrknɪs] *s* Finsternis *f*

dark'room' *s* (phot) Dunkelkammer *f*

darling ['dɑrlɪŋ] *adj* lieb ‖ *s* Liebchen *n*

darn [dɑrn] *adj* (coll) verwünscht ‖ *adv* (coll) verdammt ‖ *s*—**I don't give a d. about it** ich pfeif drauf! ‖ *tr* (*stockings*) stopfen; **d. it!** (coll) verflixt!; **I'll be darned if** der Kuckuck soll mich holen, wenn

darn'ing nee'dle *s* Stopfnadel *f*

dart [dɑrt] *s* Wurfspieß *m*, Pfeil *m*; (sew) Abnäher *m*; **darts** (*game*) Pfeilwerfen *n*; **play darts** Pfeile werfen ‖ *intr* huschen; **d. ahead** vorschießen; **d. off** davonstürzen

dash [dæʃ] *s* (*rush*) Ansturm *m*; (*smartness*) Schneidigkeit *f*; (*spirit*) Schwung *m*; (*of solids*) Prise *f*; (*of liquids*) Schuß *m*; (sport) Kurzstreckenlauf *m*; (typ) Gedankenstrich *m*; **make a d. for** losstürzen auf (*acc*) ‖ *tr* (*throw*) schleudern; (*hopes*) niederschlagen, knicken; **d. off** (*a letter*) hinwerfen ‖ *intr* stürmen, stürzen

dash'board' *s* (aut) Armaturenbrett *n*

dash'ing *adj* schneidig, forsch

dastardly ['dæstərdli] *adj* feige

data ['detə] *s* or *spl* Daten *pl*, Angaben *pl*

da'ta proc'essing *s* Datenverarbeitung *f*

date [det] *s* Datum *n*; (*fixed time*) Termin *m*; (*period*) Zeitraum *m*; (*appointment*) (coll) Verabredung *f*; (*person on a date*) Freund –in *mf*; (bot) Dattel *f*; (jur) Termin *m*; **have a d. with** verabredet sein mit; **make a d. with** sich verabreden mit; **out of d.** veraltet; **to d.** bis heute; **what is the d. today?** der wievielte ist heute? ‖ *tr* datieren; (coll) ausgehen mit ‖ *intr*—**d. back to** zurückgehen auf (*acc*); **d. from** stammen aus

dat'ed *adj* (*provided with a date*) datiert; (*out-of-date*) zeitgebunden

date' line' *s* Datumsgrenze *f*

date'line' *s* (journ) Datumszeile *f*

date' palm' *s* Dattelpalme *f*

dative ['detɪv] *s* Dativ *m*, Wemfall *m*

daub [dɔb] *s* Bewurf *m* ‖ *tr* (*a canvas*) beschmieren; (*a wall*) bewerfen; (*e.g. mud, plaster*) (**on**) schmieren (auf *acc*) ‖ *intr* (paint) klecksen

daughter ['dɔtər] *s* Tochter *f*

daugh'ter-in-law' *s* (**daughters-in-law**) Schwiegertocher *f*

daunt [dɔnt] *tr* einschüchtern

dauntless ['dɔntlɪs] *adj* furchtlos

davenport ['dævən‚port] *s* Diwan *m*

davit ['dævɪt] *s* (naut) Bootskran *m*

daw [dɔ] *s* (orn) Dohle *f*

dawdle ['dɔdəl] *intr* trödeln, bummeln

dawn [dɔn] *s* Morgendämmerung *f*; (fig) Anbeginn *m* ‖ *intr* dämmern; **d. on s.o.** j–m zum Bewußtsein kommen

day [de] *adj* Tage-, Tages– ‖ *s* Tag *m*; (*specific date*) Termin *m*; **all day long** den ganzen Tag; **by day** am Tage, bei Tage; **by the day** tageweise; **call it a day** (coll) Feierabend machen; **day after day** Tag für Tag; **day by day** Tag für Tag; **day in, day out** tagaus, tagein; **day off** Urlaubstag *m*, Ruhetag *m*; **every other day** jeden zweiten Tag; **in days of old** in alten Zeiten; **in his day** zu seiner Zeit; **in those days** damals; **one day** e–s Tages; **one of these days** demnächst; **the day after** am folgenden Tag; **the day after tomorrow** übermorgen; **the day before** am Vortag; **the day before yesterday** vorgestern; **the other day** neulich, unlängst; **these days** heutzutage; **to this very day** bis auf den heutigen Tag; **what day of the week is it?** welchen Wochentag haben wir?

day' bed' *s* Ruhebett *n*, Liege *f*

day'break' *s* Tagesanbruch *m*

day'-by-day' *adj* tagtäglich, Tag für Tag

day'-care cen'ter *s* Kindertagesstätte *f*, Kindergarten *m*

day' coach' *s* (rr) Personenwagen *m*

day'dream' *s* Träumerei *f*, Wachtraum *m*; (*wild ideas*) Phantasterei *f* ‖ *intr* mit offenen Augen träumen

day'dream'er *s* Träumer –in *mf*

day' la'borer *s* Tagelöhner –in *mf*

day'light' *adj* Tageslicht– ‖ *s* Tageslicht *n*; **in broad d.** am hellichten Tag; **knock the daylights out of** (sl) zur Sau machen

day'light-sav'ing time' s Sommerzeit f
day' nurs'ery s Kleinkinderbewahranstalt f
day' of reck'oning s Jüngster Tag m
day' shift' s Tagschicht f
day'time' s Tageszeit f; **in the d.** bei Tage, am Tage
daze [dez] s Benommenheit f; **be in a d.** benommen sein || tr betäuben
dazzle ['dæzəl] s Blenden n || tr (& fig) blenden
dazz'ling adj blendend
D-day ['di ,de] s X-Tag m; (hist) Invasionstag m
deacon ['dikən] s Diakon m
deaconess ['dikənɪs] s Diakonisse f
dead [dɛd] adj tot; (plant) abgestorben, dürr; (faint, sleep) tief; (numb) gefühllos; (volcano, fire) erloschen; (elec) stromlos; (sport) tot, nicht im Spiel; **d. as a doornail** mausetot; **d. shot** unfehlbarer Schütze m; **d. stop** völliger Stillstand m; **d. silence** Totenstille f || adv völlig, tod— || s— **in the d. of night** mitten in der Nacht; **in the d. of winter** im tiefsten Winter
dead' beat' s (sl) Nichtstuer –in mf
dead' bolt' s Absteller m
dead' calm' s Windstille f
dead' cen'ter s genaue Mitte f; (dead point) (mach) toter Punkt m
deaden ['dɛdən] tr (pain) betäuben; (a nerve) abtöten; (sound) dämpfen
dead' end' s (& fig) Sackgasse f
dead'head' s Dummkopf m
dead' heat' s totes Rennen n
dead'-let'ter of'fice s Abteilung f für unbestellbare Briefe
dead'line' s (letzter) Termin m; (journ) Redaktionsschluß m; **meet the d.** den Termin einhalten; **set a d. for** terminieren
dead'lock' s Stillstand m; **break the d.** den toten Punkt überwinden; **reach a d.** steckenbleiben || tr zum völligen Stillstand bringen; **become deadlocked** stocken
deadly ['dɛdli] adj (fatal) tödlich; **d. enemy** Todfeind –in mf; **d. fear** Todesangst f || adv—**d. dull** sterbenlangweilig; **d. pale** leichenblaß
dead'ly sins' spl Todsünden pl
dead'pan' adj (look) ausdrucklos; (person) schafsgesichtig
dead' pan' s (coll) Schafsgesicht n
dead' reck'oning s (naut) Koppelkurs m
dead' ring'er ['rɪŋər] s (coll) Doppelgänger m
dead'wood' s (& fig) totes Holz n
deaf [dɛf] adj taub; **d. and dumb** taubstumm; **d. to** (fig) taub gegen; **turn a d. ear to** taube Ohren haben für
deafen ['dɛfən] tr betäuben
deaf'ening adj ohrenbetäubend
deaf'-mute' adj taubstumm || s Taubstumme mf
deafness ['dɛfnɪs] s Taubheit f
deal [dil] s (business transaction) Geschäft n; (underhanded agreement) Schiebung f; (cards) Austeilen n, Geben n; **a good d. of** (coll) ziemlich viel; **a good d. worse** (coll) viel (or weit) schlechter; **a great d. of** (coll) sehr viel; **give s.o. a good d.** (be fair to s.o.) j–n fair behandeln; (make s.o. a good offer) j–m ein gutes Angebot machen; **give s.o. a raw d.** j–m übel mitspielen; **it is my d.** (cards) ich muß geben; **it's a d.!** abgemacht!; **make a d.** (coll) ein Abkommen treffen || v (pret & pp dealt [dɛlt]) tr (a blow) versetzen; (cards) austeilen, geben || intr (cards) geben; **d. at** (a store) kaufen bei; **d. in** handeln mit; **d. with** (settle) erledigen; (occupy oneself or itself with) sich befassen mit; (treat, e.g., fairly) behandeln; (patronize) kaufen bei; (do business with) in Geschäftsbeziehungen stehen mit; **I'll d. with you later** mit Ihnen werde ich später abrechnen!
dealer ['dilər] s Geber –in mf; (com) Händler –in mf
deal'ings spl (business dealings) Handel m; (relations) Umgang m; **I'll have no d. with** ich will nichts zu tun haben mit
dean [din] s (eccl, educ) Dekan m
dean'ship' s (eccl, educ) Dekanat n
dear [dɪr] adj lieb, traut; (expensive) teuer; **Dear Madam** Sehr verehrte gnädige Frau!; **Dear Mrs. X** Sehr geehrte Frau X; **Dear Mr. X** Sehr geehrter Herr X!; **Dear Sir** Sehr geehrter Herr! || s Liebling m, Schatz m || interj—**oh d.!** ach herrje!
dearie ['dɪri] s (coll) Liebchen n
dearth [dʌrθ] s (of) Mangel m (an dat)
death [dɛθ] s Tod m; (in the family) Todesfall m; **at death's door** sterbenskrank; **catch a d. of a cold** sich [dat] den Tod holen; **he'll be the d. of me yet** er bringt mich noch ins Grab; **put to d.** hinrichten; **to the d.** bis aufs Messer; **work to d.** totarbeiten
death'bed' s Totenbett n, Sterbebett n
death'blow' s Gnadenstoß m; (fig) Todesstoß m
death' certif'icate s Totenschein m
death' house' s Todeshaus n
death' knell' s Grabgeläute n
deathless ['dɛθlɪs] adj unsterblich
deathly ['dɛθli] adj tödlich, Todes–, Toten– || adv toten–
death' mask' s Totenmaske f
death' pen'alty s Todesstrafe f
death' rate' s Sterblichkeitsziffer f
death' rat'tle s Todesröcheln n
death' sen'tence s Todesurteil n
death' strug'gle s Todeskampf m
death' trap' s (fig) Mausefalle f
death' war'rant s Hinrichtungsbefehl m
debacle [de'bakəl] s Zusammenbruch m
de·bar [dɪ'bar] v (pret & pp –barred; ger –barring) tr (from) ausschließen (aus)
debark [dɪ'bark] tr ausschiffen || intr sich ausschiffen, an Land gehen
debarkation [,dibar'keʃən] s Ausschiffung f

debase [dɪ'bes] *tr* entwürdigen; (*currency*) entwerten

debatable [dɪ'betəbəl] *adj* strittig

debate [dɪ'bet] *s* Debatte *f* ‖ *tr & intr* debattieren

debauch [dɪ'bɔtʃ] *s* Schwelgerei *f* ‖ *tr* verderben; (*seduce*) verführen; **d. oneself** verkommen

debauched' *adj* ausschweifend

debauchee [,debə'tʃi] *s* Wüstling *m*

debauchery [dɪ'bɔtʃəri] *s* Schwelgerei *f*

debenture [dɪ'bentʃər] *s* (*bond*) Obligation *f*; (*voucher*) Schuldschein *m*

debilitate [dɪ'bɪlɪ,tet] *tr* entkräften

debility [dɪ'bɪlɪti] *s* Schwäche *f*

debit ['debɪt] *s* Debet *n*, Soll *n*; (*as entry*) Belastung *f*

de'bit bal'ance *s* Sollsaldo *n*

de'bit side' *s* Soll *n*, Sollseite *f*

debonair [,debə'nɛr] *adj* (*courteous*) höflich; (*carefree*) heiter und sorglos

debris [de'bri] *s* Trümmer *pl*

debt [det] *s* Schuld *f*; **be in s.o.'s d.** j–m verpflichtet sein; **run into d.** in Schulden geraten

debtor ['detər] *s* Schuldner –in *mf*

de·bug [dɪ'bʌg] *v pret & pp* **–bugged;** *ger* **–bugging**) *tr* (*remove defects from*) bereinigen; (*electron*) Abhörgeräte entfernen aus

debut [de'bju], ['debju] *s* Debüt *n*; **make one's d.** debütieren

debutante ['debju,tɑnt] *s* Debütantin *f*

decade ['deked] *s* Jahrzehnt *n*, Dekade *f*

decadence ['dekədəns] *s* Dekadenz *f*

decadent ['dekədənt] *adj* dekadent; (*art*) entartet

decal ['dikæl] *s* Abziehbild *n*

decanter [dɪ'kæntər] *s* Karaffe *f*

decapitate [dɪ'kæpɪ,tet] *tr* enthaupten

decathlon [dɪ'kæθlɑn] *s* Zehnkampf *m*

decay [dɪ'ke] *s* (*rotting*) Verwesung *f*; (fig) Verfall *m*; (dent) Karies *f*; **fall into d.** (& fig) in Verfall geraten ‖ *intr* verfaulen; (fig) verfallen

decease [dɪ'sis] *s* Ableben *n*

deceased' *adj* verstorben ‖ *s* Verstorbene *mf*

deceit [dɪ'sit] *s* Betrügerei *f*

deceitful [dɪ'sitfəl] *adj* betrügerisch

deceive [dɪ'siv] *tr* betrügen ‖ *intr* trügen

decelerate [dɪ'selə,ret] *tr* verlangsamen ‖ *intr* seine Geschwindigkeit verringern

December [dɪ'sembər] *s* Dezember *m*

decency ['disənsi] *s* Anstand *m*; **decencies** Anstandsformen *pl*

decent ['disənt] *adj* anständig

decentralize [dɪ'sentrə,laɪz] *tr* dezentralisieren

deception [dɪ'sepʃən] *s* (*act of deceiving*) Betrug *m*; (*state of being deceived*) Täuschung *f*

deceptive [dɪ'septɪv] *adj* trügerisch; (*misleading*) irreführend; (*similarity*) täuschend

decide [dɪ'saɪd] *tr* entscheiden ‖ *intr* **(on)** sich entscheiden, sich entschließen (über *acc*, für)

deciduous [dɪ'sɪdʒu·əs] *adj* blattabwerfend; **d. tree** Laubbaum *m*

decimal ['desɪməl] *adj* dezimal ‖ *s* Dezimalzahl *f*

dec'imal place' *s* Dezimalstelle *f*

dec'imal point' *s* (*in German the comma is used to separate the decimal fraction from the integer*) Komma *n*

decimate ['desɪ,met] *tr* dezimieren

decipher [dɪ'saɪfər] *tr* entziffern

decision [dɪ'sɪʒən] *s* Entscheidung *f*, Entschluß *m*; (jur) Urteil *n*

decisive [dɪ'saɪsɪv] *adj* entscheidend

deck [dek] *s* (*of cards*) Spiel *n*; (data proc) Kartensatz *m*; (naut) Deck *n*, Verdeck *n* ‖ *tr* (coll) zu Boden schlagen; **d. out** ausschmücken

deck' chair' *s* Liegestuhl *m*

deck' hand' *s* gemeiner Matrose *m*

deck' land'ing *s* (aer) Trägerlandung *f*

declaim [dɪ'klem] *tr & intr* deklamieren

declaration [,deklə'reʃən] *s* Erklärung *f*; (*at customs*) Zollerklärung *f*

declarative [dɪ'klærətɪv] *adj*—**d. sentence** Aussagesatz *m*

declare [dɪ'klɛr] *tr* erklären; (*tourist's belongings*) verzollen; (*commercial products*) deklarieren; **d. oneself against** sich aussprechen gegen

declension [dɪ'klɛnʃən] *s* Deklination *f*

declinable [dɪ'klaɪnəbəl] *adj* deklinierbar

decline [dɪ'klaɪn] *s* (*decrease*) Abnahme *f*; (*in prices*) Rückgang *m*; (*deterioration*) Verschlechterung *f*; (*slope*) Abhang *m*; (fig) Niedergang *m*; **be on the d.** in Abnahme begriffen sein ‖ *tr* (*refuse*) ablehnen; (gram) deklinieren ‖ *intr* (*refuse*) ablehnen; (*descend*) sich senken; (*sink*) sinken; (*draw to a close*) zu Ende gehen

declivity [dɪ'klɪvɪti] *s* Abhang *m*

decode [di'kod] *tr* entschlüsseln

decompose [,dikəm'poz] *tr* zerlegen ‖ *intr* sich zersetzen, verwesen

decomposition [,dikɑmpə'zɪʃən] *s* Zersetzung *f*, Verwesung *f*

decompression [,dikəm'preʃən] *s* Dekompression *f*

decontaminaiton [,dikən,tæmɪ'neʃən] *s* Entseuchung *f*

décor [de'kɔr] *s* Dekor *m*

decorate ['dekə,ret] *tr* dekorieren, (aus)schmücken; (*a new room*) einrichten; (*e.g., with a badge*) auszeichnen

decoration [,dekə'reʃən] *s* Schmuck *m*; (*medal*) Orden *m*, Ehrenzeichen *n*, Dekoration *f*

decorative ['dekərətɪv] *adj* dekorativ

decorator ['dekə,retər] *s* Dekorateur –in *mf*

decorous ['dekərəs] *adj* schicklich

decorum [dɪ'korəm] *s* Schicklichkeit *f*

decoy ['dikɔɪ] *s* (*bird or person*) Lockvogel *m*; (*anything used as a lure*) Lockmittel *n* ‖ [dɪ'kɔɪ] *tr* locken

decrease ['dikris] *s* Abnahme *f* ‖

[dɪ'kris] *tr* verringern || *intr* abnehmen

decree [dɪ'kri] *s* Dekret *n*, Verordnung *f* || *tr* dekretieren, verordnen

decrepit [dɪ'krɛpɪt] *adj* (age-worn) altersschwach; (frail) gebrechlich

de·cry [dɪ'kraɪ] *v* (pret & pp **–cried**) *tr* (disparage) herabsetzen; (censure openly) kritisieren

dedicate ['dɛdɪ,ket] *tr* (a book, one's life) (to) widmen (dat); (a building) einweihen

dedication [,dɛdɪ'keʃən] *s* Widmung *f*; (of a building, etc.) Einweihung *f*; (to) Hingabe *f* (an acc)

deduce [dɪ'd(j)us] *tr* (from) schließen (aus)

deduct [dɪ'dʌkt] *tr* abziehen, abrechnen

deduction [dɪ'dʌkʃən] *s* Abzug *m*; (conclusion) Schluß *m*, Folgerung *f*

deed [did] *s* (act) Tat *f*; (jur) Besitzurkunde *f*

deem [dim] *tr* halten für; **d. s.o. worthy of my confidence** j–n meines Vertrauens für würdig halten

deep [dip] *adj* tief; (recondite) dunkel; (impression) tiefgehend; (color, sound) tief, dunkel; **be d. in debt** tief in Schulden stecken; **four (ranks) d.** in Viererreihen; **in d. water** (fig) in Schwierigkeiten; **that's too d. for me** das ist mir zu hoch || *adv* tief; **d. down** in tief innen in (dat) || *s* Tiefe *f*, Meer *n*

deepen ['dipən] *tr* (& fig) vertiefen || *intr* sich vertiefen

deep'-freeze' *v* (pret **–freezed** & **–froze**; pp **–freezed** & **–frozen**) *tr* tiefkühlen

deep'-fry' *v* (pret & pp **–fried**) *tr* fritieren

deep'-laid' *adj* schlau angelegt

deep' mourn'ing *s* tiefe Trauer *f*

deep'-root'ed *adj* tiefsitzend

deep'-set' *adj* (eyes) tiefliegend

deer [dɪr] *s* Hirsch *m*, Reh *n*, Rotwild *n*

deer'skin' *s* Hirschleder *n*, Wildleder *n*

deface [dɪ'fes] *tr* (disfigure) verunstalten; (make illegible) unleserlich machen

defacement [di'fesmənt] *s* Verunstaltung *f*

de facto [di'fækto] *adj* & *adv* tatsächlich, de facto

defamation [,dɛfə'meʃən] *s* Verleumdung *f*

defame [dɪ'fem] *tr* verleumden

default [dɪ'fɔlt] *s* (in duties) Unterlassung *f*; (fin) Verzug *m*; **by d.** (jur) durch Nichterscheinen; (sport) durch Nichtantreten; **in d. of** in Ermangelung (genit) || *tr* nicht erfüllen; (fin) nicht zahlen || *intr* seinen Verpflichtungen nicht nachkommen; (fin) in Verzug sein

defeat [dɪ'fit] *s* Niederlage *f*; (parl) Niederstimmen *n*; **admit d.** sich geschlagen geben || *tr* besiegen, schlagen; (frustrate) hilflos machen; (plans) zunichte machen; (a bill) niederstimmen; **d. the purpose** den Zweck verfehlen

defeatism [dɪ'fitɪzəm] *s* Defätismus *m*

defeatist [dɪ'fitɪst] *s* Defätist –in *mf*

defecate ['dɛfɪ,ket] *intr* Stuhl haben

defect ['difɛkt] *s* Defekt *m*; (physical or mental defect) Gebrechen *n*; (imperfection) Mangel *m*; (in manufacture) Fabrikationsfehler *m* || [dɪ'fɛkt] *intr* (from) (a religion) abfallen (von); (a party) abtrünnig werden (von); (to) überlaufen (zu)

defection [dɪ'fɛkʃən] *s* Abfall *m*; (to) Übertritt *m* (zu)

defective [dɪ'fɛktɪv] *adj* fehlerhaft; (gram) unvollständig; (tech) defekt

defector [dɪ'fɛktər] *s* (pol) Abtrünnige *mf*, Überläufer –in *mf*

defend [dɪ'fɛnd] *tr* verteidigen

defendant [dɪ'fɛndənt] *s* (in civil suit) Beklagte *mf*; (in criminal suit) Angeklagte *mf*

defender [dɪ'fɛndər] *s* Verteidiger –in *mf*; (sport) Titelverteidiger –in *mf*

defense [dɪ'fɛns] *s* (& jur, sport) Verteidigung *f*; (tactical) (mil) Abwehr *f*; **d. against** (e.g., disease) Schutz *m* vor (dat)

defenseless [dɪ'fɛnslɪs] *adj* schutzlos

defensible [dɪ'fɛnsɪbəl] *adj* verteidigungsfähig; (argument, claim) verfechtbar

defensive [dɪ'fɛnsɪv] *adj* defensiv; (mil) Verteidigungs-, Abwehr- || *s* Defensive *f*; (tactical) Abwehr *f*; **be on the d.**—sich in der Defensive befinden

de·fer [dɪ'fʌr] *v* (pret & pp **–ferred**; ger **–ferring**) *tr* verschieben; (mil) zurückschieben || *intr*—**d. to** nachgeben (dat)

deference ['dɛfərəns] *s* (courteous regard) Ehrerbietung *f*; (yielding) Nachgiebigkeit *f*; **in d. to** aus Rücksicht gegen; **with all due d. to** bei aller Achtung vor (dat)

deferential [,dɛfə'rɛnʃəl] *adj* ehrerbietig, rücksichtsvoll

deferment [dɪ'fʌrmənt] *s* Aufschub *m*; (mil) Zurückstellung *f*

defiance [dɪ'faɪəns] *s* Trotz *m*; **in d. of s.o.** j–m zum Trotz

defiant [dɪ'faɪənt] *adj* trotzig

deficiency [dɪ'fɪʃənsi] *s* (of) Mangel *m* (an dat); (shortcoming) Defekt *m*; (deficit) Defizit *n*

deficient [dɪ'fɪʃənt] *adj* mangelhaft; **be d. in** Mangel haben an (dat); **mentally d.** schwachsinnig

deficit ['dɛfɪsɪt] *s* Defizit *n*

defilade [,dɛfi'led] *s* Deckung *f* || *tr* gegen Feuer sichern

defile [dɪ'faɪl], ['difaɪl] *s* Hohlweg *m* || [dɪ'faɪl] *tr* beflecken

defilement [dɪ'faɪlmənt] *s* Befleckung *f*

define [dɪ'faɪn] *tr* definieren, bestimmen; (e.g., boundaries) festlegen

definite ['dɛfɪnɪt] *adj* bestimmt

definition [,dɛfɪ'nɪʃən] *s* Definition *f*, Bestimmung *f*; (opt) Bildschärfe *f*

definitive [dɪ'fɪnɪtɪv] *adj* endgültig

deflate [dɪ'flet] *tr* Luft ablassen aus; (prices) herabsetzen; (s.o.'s ego, hopes) e–n Stoß versetzen (dat)

deflation [dɪ'fleʃən] s (fin) Deflation f

deflect [dɪ'flɛkt] tr ablenken || intr (from) abweichen (von)

deflection [dɪ'flɛkʃən] s Ablenkung f; Abweichung f; (of an indicator) Ausschlag m; (of light rays) Beugung f; (radar, telv) Ablenkung f

deflower [dɪ'flaʊ·ər] tr entjungfern

defoliate [di'folɪ‚et] tr entblättern

deforest [di'fɔrɛst] tr abholzen

deform [dɪ'fɔrm] tr entstellen

deformed' adj verwachsen, mißförmig

deformity [dɪ'fɔrmɪti] s (state of being deformed) Mißgestalt f; (deformed part) Verwachsung f; (ugliness) Häßlichkeit f

defraud [dɪ'frɔd] tr (of) betrügen (um)

defray [dɪ'fre] tr tragen, bestreiten

defrock [di'frak] tr das Priesteramt entziehen (dat)

defrost [dɪ'frɔst] tr entfrosten

defroster [dɪ'frɔstər] s Entfroster m

deft [dɛft] adj flink, fingerfertig

defunct [dɪ'fʌŋkt] adj (person) verstorben; (no longer in operation) stillgelegt; (no longer in effect) außer Kraft (befindlich); (newspaper) eingegangen

de·fy [dɪ'faɪ] v (pret & pp –fied) tr trotzen (dat); (challenge) herausfordern; **d. description** sich nicht beschreiben lassen

degeneracy [dɪ'dʒɛnərəsi] s Entartung f

degenerate [dɪ'dʒɛnərɪt] adj entartet, verkommen || [dɪ'dʒɛnə‚ret] intr entarten; (into) ausarten (in acc)

degrade [dɪ'gred] tr degradieren; (bring into low esteem) entwürdigen

degrad'ing adj entwürdigend

degree [dɪ'gri] s Grad m; (gram) Steigerungsstufe f; **by degrees** gradweise; **d. of latitude** Breitengrad m; **d. of longitude** Längengrad m; **take one's d.** promovieren; **to a d.** einigermaßen; **to a high d.** in hohem Maße

dehumanize [dɪ'hjumə‚naɪz] tr entmenschlichen

dehumidifier [‚dihju'mɪdɪ‚faɪ·ər] s Luftentfeuchter m

dehumidi·fy [‚dihju'mɪdɪ‚faɪ] v (pret & pp –fied) entfeuchten

dehydrate [di'haɪdret] tr (vegetables) dörren, das Wasser entziehen (dat); (chem) dehydrieren || intr das Wasser verlieren

dehy'drated adj (vegetables) Trocken–; (body) dehydriert

deice [di'aɪs] tr enteisen

dei·fy ['di·ɪ‚faɪ] v (pret & pp –fied) tr (a man) zum Gott erheben; (a woman) zur Göttin erheben

deject'ed adj niedergeschlagen

dejection [dɪ'dʒɛkʃən] s Niederge-schlagenheit f, Mutlosigkeit f

delay [dɪ'le] s Aufschub m, Verzögerung f; **without d.** unverzüglich || tr (postpone) aufschieben; (detain) aufhalten || intr zögern

delectable [dɪ'lɛktəbəl] adj ergötzlich

delegate ['dɛlɪ‚get], ['dɛlɪgɪt] s De-

legierte mf || ['dɛlɪ‚get] tr delegieren; (authority) übertragen

delegation [‚dɛlɪ'geʃən] s (persons delegated) Delegation f; (e.g., of authority) Übertragung f

delete [dɪ'lit] tr tilgen

deletion [dɪ'liʃən] s Tilgung f

deliberate [dɪ'lɪbərɪt] adj (intentional) vorsätzlich, bewußt; (slow) gemessen, bedächtig || [dɪ'lɪbə‚ret] intr überlegen; (said of several persons) beratschlagen; **d. on** sich beraten über (acc)

deliberately [dɪ'lɪbərɪtli] adv mit Absicht

deliberation [dɪ‚lɪbə'reʃən] s Überlegung f; (by several persons) Beratung f; (slowness) Bedächtigkeit f

delicacy ['dɛlɪkəsi] s Zartheit f; (fine food) Delikatesse f

delicate ['dɛlɪkɪt] adj fein, delikat; (situation) heikel; (health) zart

delicatessen [‚dɛlɪkə'tɛsən] s (food) Delikatessen pl; (store) Delikatessengeschäft n

delicious [dɪ'lɪʃəs] adj köstlich

delight [dɪ'laɪt] s Freude f; (high degree of pleasure) Entzücken n; **take d. in** Freude finden an (dat) || tr entzücken, erfreuen; **be delighted by** sich freuen an (dat); **I'll be delighted to come** ich komme mit dem größten Vergnügen || intr—**d. in** sich ergötzen an (dat)

delightful [dɪ'laɪtfəl] adj entzückend

delimit [dɪ'lɪmɪt] tr abgrenzen

delineate [dɪ'lɪnɪ‚et] tr zeichnen

delinquency [dɪ'lɪŋkwənsi] s Pflicht-vergessenheit f; (misdeed) Vergehen n

delinquent [dɪ'lɪŋkwənt] adj pflicht-vergessen; (guilty) straffällig; (overdue) rückständig; (in default) säumig || s Straffällige mf

delirious [dɪ'lɪrɪ·əs] adj irre; (with) rasend (vor dat)

delirium [dɪ'lɪrɪ·əm] s Fieberwahn m

deliver [dɪ'lɪvər] tr liefern; (a message) überreichen; (free) befreien; (mail) zustellen; (a speech) halten; (a blow) versetzen; (a verdict) aussprechen; (a child) zur Welt bringen; (votes) bringen; (a ball) werfen; (relig) erlösen

deliverance [dɪ'lɪvərəns] s Erlösung f

delivery [dɪ'lɪvəri] s Lieferung f; (freeing) Befreiung f; (of mail) Zustellung f; (of a speaker, actor, singer) Vortragsweise f; (of a pitcher) Wurf m; (childbirth) Entbindung f

deliv'ery·man' s (–men') Austräger m

deliv'ery room' s Kreißsaal m

deliv'ery truck' s Lieferwagen m

dell [dɛl] s enges Tal n

delouse [di'laʊs] tr entlausen

delta ['dɛltə] s Delta n

delude [dɪ'lud] tr täuschen

deluge ['dɛljudʒ] s Überschwemmung f; (fig) Hochflut f; **Deluge** (Bib) Sintflut f || tr überschwemmen; (with letters, etc.) überschütten

delusion [dɪ'luʒən] s (state of being deluded) Täuschung f; (misconcep-

tion) Wahnvorstellung *f;* (psychiatry) Wahn *m;* **delusions of grandeur** Größenwahn *m*

deluxe [dɪ'lʊks], [dɪ'lʌks] *adj* Luxus-

delve [dɛlv] *intr*—**d. into** sich vertiefen in (*acc*)

demagogue ['dɛmə‚gɑg] *s* Volksverführer –in *mf*

demand [dɪ'mænd] *s* Verlangen *n;* (com) (**for**) Nachfrage *f* (nach); **in** (**great**) **d.** (sehr) gefragt; **make demands on** Ansprüche erheben auf (*acc*); **on d.** auf Verlangen ‖ *tr* (**from** or **of**) verlangen (von), fordern (von)

demand'ing *adj* anspruchsvoll; (*strict*) streng

demarca'tion line' [‚dimɑr'keʃən] *s* Demarkationslinie *f*

demean [dɪ'min] *tr* erniedrigen

demeanor [dɪ'minər] *s* Benehmen *n*

demented [dɪ'mɛntɪd] *adj* wahnsinnig

demerit [dɪ'mɛrɪt] *s* (*fault*) Fehler *m;* (*deficiency mark*) Minuspunkt *m*

demigod ['dɛmɪ‚gɑd] *s* Halbgott *m*

demijohn ['dɛmɪ‚dʒɑn] *s* Korbflasche *f*

demilitarize [di'mɪlɪtə‚raɪz] *tr* entmilitarisieren

demise [dɪ'maɪz] *s* Ableben *n*

demitasse ['dɛmɪ‚tæs], ['dɛmɪ‚tɑs] *s* Mokkatasse *f*

demobilize [di'mobɪ‚laɪz] *tr & intr* demobilisieren

democracy [dɪ'mɑkrəsi] *s* Demokratie *f*

democrat ['dɛmə‚kræt] *s* Demokrat –in *mf*

democratic [‚dɛmə'krætɪk] *adj* demokratisch

demolish [dɪ'mɑlɪʃ] *tr* (*raze*) niederreißen; (*destroy*) zertrümmern; (*an argument*) vernichten; (*devour*) (coll) verschlingen

demolition [‚dɛmə'lɪʃən], [‚dimə'lɪʃən] *s* (*act of razing*) Abbruch *m;* (*by explosives*) Sprengung *f;* **demolitions** Sprengstoff *m*

demoli'tion squad' *s* Sprengkommando *n*

demoli'tion work' *s* Sprengarbeiten *pl*

demon ['dimən] *s* Dämon *m,* böser Geist *m*

demonstrable [dɪ'mɑnstrəbəl] *adj* beweisbar

demonstrate ['dɛmən‚stret] *tr* (*prove*) beweisen; (*explain*) dartun; (*display*) zeigen; (*a product, process*) vorführen ‖ *intr* (pol) demonstrieren

demonstration [‚dɛmən'streʃən] *s* (com) Vorführung *f;* (pol) Demonstration *f*

demonstrative [dɪ'mɑnstrətɪv] *adj* (*showing emotions*) gefühlvoll; (*illustrative*) anschaulich; (gram) hinweisend

demonstrator ['dɛmən‚stretər] *s* (*of products*) Vorführer –in *mf;* (*model used in demonstration*) Vorführmodell *n;* (pol) Demonstrant –in *mf*

demoralize [dɪ'mɔrə‚laɪz] *tr* demoralisieren

demote [dɪ'mot] *tr* (*an employee*) her-

abstufen; (*a student*) zurückversetzen; (mil) degradieren

demotion [dɪ'moʃən] *s* (*of an employee*) Herabstufung *f;* (*of a student*) Zurückversetzung *f;* (mil) Degradierung *f*

de·mur [dɪ'mʌr] *v* (*pret & pp* –**murred;** *ger* –**murring**) *intr* Einwände erheben

demure [dɪ'mjʊr] *adj* zimperlich

den [dɛn] *s* (*of animals; of thieves*) Höhle *f;* (*comfortable room*) Freizeitraum *m*

denaturalize [di'nætʃərə‚laɪz] *tr* ausbürgern

denial [dɪ'naɪ·əl] *s* (*of an assertion*) Leugnung *f;* (*of guilt*) Leugnen *n;* (*of a request*) Ablehnung *f;* (*of faith*) Ableugnung *f;* (*of rights*) Verweigerung *f;* (*of a report*) Dementi *n*

denigrate ['dɛnɪ‚gret] *tr* anschwärzen

denim ['dɛnɪm] *s* Drillich *m*

denizen ['dɛnɪzən] *s* Bewohner –in *mf*

Denmark ['dɛnmɑrk] *s* Dänemark *n*

denomination [dɪ‚nɑmɪ'neʃən] *s* Bezeichnung *f;* (*class, kind*) Klasse *f;* (*of money*) Nennwert *m;* (*of shares*) Stückelung *f;* (relig) Konfession *f,* Bekenntnis *n;* **in denominations of five and ten dollars** in Fünf– und Zehndollarnoten

denotation [‚dino'teʃən] *s* Bedeutung *f*

denote [dɪ'not] *tr* (*mean*) bedeuten; (*indicate*) anzeigen

dénouement [‚denu'mã] *s* Auflösung *f*

denounce [dɪ'naʊns] *tr* (*inform against*) denunzieren; (*condemn openly*) brandmarken, anprangern; (*a treaty*) kündigen

dense [dɛns] *adj* dicht; (coll) beschränkt

density ['dɛnsɪti] *s* Dichte *f*

dent [dɛnt] *s* Beule *f* ‖ *tr* einbeulen

dental ['dɛntəl] *adj* Zahn–; (ling) dental ‖ *s* (ling) Zahnlaut *m*

den'tal hygiene' *s* Zahnpflege *f*

den'tal sur'geon *s* Zahnarzt *m,* Zahnärztin *f*

dentifrice ['dɛntɪfrɪs] *s* Zahnputzmittel *n*

dentist ['dɛntɪst] *s* Zahnarzt *m,* Zahnärztin *f*

dentistry ['dɛntɪstri] *s* Zahnheilkunde *f*

denture ['dɛntʃər] *s* künstliches Gebiß *n*

denunciation [dɪ‚nʌnsɪ'eʃən] *s* (*informing against*) Denunzierung *f;* (*public condemnation*) Brandmarkung *f*

de·ny [dɪ'naɪ] *v* (*pret & pp* –**nied**) *tr* (*a statement*) leugnen; (*officially*) dementieren; (*a request*) ablehnen; (*one's faith*) ableugnen; (*rights*) verweigern; **d. oneself s.th.** sich [*dat*] etw versagen; **d. s.o. s.th.** j–m etw aberkennen

deodorant [di'odərənt] *s* Deodorant *n*

deodorize [di'odə‚raɪz] *tr* desodorieren

deoxidize [di'ɑksɪ‚daɪz] *tr* desoxydieren

depart [dɪ'pɑrt] *intr* (*on foot*) fortgehen; (*in a vehicle or boat*) abfahren; (*by plane*) abfliegen; (*on horseback*) abreiten; (*on a trip*) abreisen; (*deviate*) abweichen

department [dɪ'pɑrtmənt] *s* (*subdivision*) Abteilung *f;* (*field*) Fach *n;* (*principal branch of government*) Ministerium *n;* (*government office*) Amt *n;* (*educ*) Abteilung *f*

depart′ment head′ *s* Abteilungsleiter –in *mf*

depart′ment store′ *s* Kaufhaus *n,* Warenhaus *n*

departure [dɪ'pɑrtʃər] *s* (*on foot*) Weggehen *n;* (*by car, boat, train*) Abfahrt *f,* Abreise *f;* (*by plane*) Abflug *m;* (*deviation*) Abweichung *f*

depend [dɪ'pɛnd] *intr* (**on**) abhängen (**von**); (*rely on*) sich verlassen (**auf** *acc*); **depending on** je nach; **depending on how** je nachdem; **it all depends** (coll) es kommt darauf an

dependable [dɪ'pɛndəbəl] *adj* zuverlässig

dependence [dɪ'pɛndəns] *s* Abhängigkeit *f*

dependency [dɪ'pɛndənsi] *s* Schutzgebiet *n*

dependent [dɪ'pɛndənt] *adj* (**on**) abhängig (**von**) ‖ *s* Abhängige *mf;* (*for tax purposes*) Unterhaltsberechtigte *mf*

depict [dɪ'pɪkt] *tr* schildern

deplete [dɪ'plit] *tr* entleeren; (fig) erschöpfen

deplorable [dɪ'plorəbəl] *adj* (*situation*) beklagenswert; (*regrettable*) bedauerlich; (*bad*) schlecht

deplore [dɪ'plor] *tr* bedauern

deploy [dɪ'plɔɪ] *tr* entfalten ‖ *intr* sich entfalten

deployment [dɪ'plɔɪmənt] *s* Entfaltung *f*

depolarize [di'polə‚raɪz] *tr* depolarisieren

deponent [dɪ'ponənt] *s* (gram) Deponens *n;* (jur) Deponent –in *mf*

depopulate [di'pɑpjə‚let] *tr* entvölkern

deport [dɪ'port] *tr* deportieren; **d. oneself** sich benehmen

deportation [‚dipor'teʃən] *s* Deportation *f*

deportment [dɪ'portmənt] *s* Benehmen *n*

depose [dɪ'poz] *tr* (*from office*) absetzen; (jur) bezeugen ‖ *intr* (jur) unter Eid aussagen; (*in writing*) (jur) eidesstattlich versichern

deposit [dɪ'pɑzɪt] *s* (*partial payment*) Anzahlung *f;* (*at a bank*) Einlage *f;* (*for safekeeping*) Hinterlegung *f;* (geol) Ablagerung *f;* (min) Vorkommen *n;* **for d. only** nur zur Verrechnung ‖ *tr* (*set down*) niederlegen; (*money at a bank*) einlegen; (*a check*) verrechnen; (*as part payment*) anzahlen; (*for safekeeping*) deponieren; (geol) ablagern; (*a coin*) (telp) einwerfen

depositor [dɪ'pɑzɪtər] *s* Einzahler –in *mf;* (*of valuables*) Hinterleger –in *mf*

depos′it slip′ *s* Einzahlungsbeleg *m*

depot ['dipo], ['dɛpo] *s* (*bus station; storage place*) Depot *n;* (*train station*) Bahnhof *m*

depraved [dɪ'prevd] *adj* verworfen

depravity [dɪ'præviti] *s* Verworfenheit *f*

deprecate ['dɛprɪ‚ket] *tr* mißbilligen

depreciate [dɪ'priʃɪ‚et] *tr* (*money, stocks*) abwerten; (*for tax purposes*) abschreiben; (*value or price*) herabsetzen; (*disparage*) geringschätzen ‖ *intr* im Wert sinken

depreciation [dɪ‚priʃɪ'eʃən] *s* (*decrease in value*) Wertminderung *f;* (*of currency or stocks*) Abwertung *f;* (*for tax purposes*) Abschreibung *f*

depress [dɪ'prɛs] *tr* niederdrücken; (*sadden*) deprimieren; (*cause to sink*) herunterdrücken

depressed′ *adj* (*saddened*) niedergeschlagen; (*market*) flau

depressed′ ar′ea *s* Notstandsgebiet *n*

depress′ing *adj* deprimierend

depression [dɪ'prɛʃən] *s* (*mental state; economic crisis*) Depression *f;* (geol) Vertiefung *f*

deprive [dɪ'praɪv] *tr*—**d. s.o. of s.th.** j-m etw entziehen; (*withhold*) j-m etw vorenthalten

depth [dɛpθ] *s* Tiefe *f;* **go beyond one's d.** den Boden unter den Füßen verlieren; **in d.** gründlich

depth′ charge′ *s* Wasserbombe *f*

depth′ of field′ *s* (phot) Tiefenschärfe *f*

deputation [‚dɛpjə'teʃən] *s* Abordnung *f*

deputize ['dɛpjə‚taɪz] *tr* abordnen

deputy ['dɛpjəti] *s* Vertreter –in *mf;* (pol) Abgeordnete *mf*

derail [dɪ'rel] *tr* zum Entgleisen bringen ‖ *intr* entgleisen

derailment [dɪ'relmənt] *s* Entgleisung *f*

deranged [dɪ'rendʒd] *adj* geistesgestört

derangement [dɪ'rendʒmənt] *s* Geistesgestörtheit *f*

derby ['dɑrbi] *s* (*hat*) Melone *f;* (*race*) Derbyrennen *n*

derelict ['dɛrɪlɪkt] *adj* (*negligent*) (**in**) nachlässig (**in** *dat*); (*abandoned*) herrenlos ‖ *s* (*ship; bum*) Wrack *n*

dereliction [‚dɛrɪ'lɪkʃən] *s* (*neglect*) Vernachlässigung *f*

deride [dɪ'raɪd] *tr* verspotten

derision [dɪ'rɪʒən] *s* Spott *m*

derivation [‚dɛrɪ'veʃən] *s* (gram, math) Ableitung *f*

derivative [dɪ'rɪvətɪv] *adj* abgeleitet ‖ *s* (chem) Derivat *n;* (gram, math) Ableitung *f*

derive [dɪ'raɪv] *tr* (*obtain*) gewinnen; (gram, math) ableiten; **d. pleasure from s.th.** Freude an etw finden ‖ *intr* (**from**) herstammen (**von**)

dermatologist [‚dʌrmə'tɑlədʒɪst] *s* Hautarzt *m,* Hautärztin *f*

derogatory [dɪ'rɑgə‚tori] *adj* abfällig

derrick ['dɛrɪk] *s* (*over an oil well*) Bohrturm *m;* (naut) Ladebaum *m*

dervish ['dʌrvɪʃ] *s* Derwisch *m*

desalinization [di‚sɛlɪnɪ'zeʃən] *s* Entsalzung *f*

desalt [di'sɔlt] *tr* entsalzen
descend [dɪ'sɛnd] *tr* hinuntergehen ‖ *intr* (*dismount, alight*) absteigen; (*said of a plane*) niedergehen; (*from a tree, from heaven*) herabsteigen; (*said of a road*) sich senken; (*pass by inheritance*) (**to**) übergehen (auf *acc*); **be descended from** abstammen von; **d. upon** hereinbrechen über (*acc*)
descendant [dɪ'sɛndənt] *s* Abkömmling *m*, Nachkomme *m*; **descendants** Nachkommenschaft *f*
descendent [dɪ'sɛndənt] *adj* absteigend
descent [dɪ'sɛnt] *s* Abstieg *m*; (*lineage*) Herkunft *f*; (*of a plane or parachute*) Niedergehen *n*; (*slope*) Abhang *m*; (*hostile raid*) (**on**) Überfall *m* (auf *acc*)
describe [dɪ'skraɪb] *tr* beschreiben
description [dɪ'skrɪpʃən] *s* Beschreibung *f*; (*type*) Art *f*; **beyond d.** unbeschreiblich
descriptive [dɪ'skrɪptɪv] *adj* beschreibend
de·scry [dɪ'skraɪ] *v* (*pret & pp* –scried*) *tr* erspähen, erblicken
desecrate ['dɛsɪ͵kret] *tr* entweihen
desecration [͵dɛsɪ'kreʃən] *s* Entweihung *f*
desegregate [di'sɛgrɪ͵get] *tr* die Rassentrennung aufheben in (*dat*)
desegregation [di͵sɛgrɪ'geʃən] *s* Aufhebung *f* der Rassentrennung
desert ['dɛzərt] *adj* öde, wüst; (*sand, warfare, etc.*) Wüsten– ‖ *s* Wüste *f*; (fig) Öde *f* ‖ [dɪ'zʌrt] *s* Verdienst *m*; **get one's just deserts** seinen wohlverdienten Lohn empfangen ‖ *tr* verlassen ‖ *intr* (mil) desertieren; (**to**) überlaufen (zu)
deserter [dɪ'zʌrtər] *s* Deserteur *m*
desertion [dɪ'zʌrʃən] *s* Verlassen *n*; (*of a party*) Abfall *m*; (mil) Fahnenflucht *f*
deserve [dɪ'zʌrv] *tr* verdienen
deservedly [dɪ'zʌrvɪdli] *adv* mit Recht
deserv'ing *adj* (**of**) würdig (*genit*)
design [dɪ'zaɪn] *s* (*outline*) Entwurf *m*; (*pattern*) Muster *n*; (*plan*) Plan *m*; (*plot*) Anschlag *m*; (*of a building, etc.*) Bauart *f*; (*aim*) Absicht *f*; **designs on** böse Absichten auf (*acc*) ‖ *tr* (*make a preliminary sketch of*) entwerfen; (*draw up detailed plans for*) konstruieren; **designed for** gedacht für
designate ['dɛzɪg͵net] *tr* (**as**) bezeichnen (als); (**to**) ernennen (zu)
designation [͵dɛzɪg'neʃən] *s* (*act of designating*) Kennzeichnung *f*; (*title*) Bezeichnung *f*; (*appointment*) Ernennung *f*
designer [dɪ'zaɪnər] *s* (*of patterns*) Musterzeichner –in *mf*; (*of fashions*) Modeschöpfer –in *mf*; (theat) Dekorateur –in *mf*
design'ing *adj* intrigant; (*calculating*) berechnend
desirable [dɪ'zaɪrəbəl] *adj* wünschenswert, begehrenswert
desire [dɪ'zaɪr] *s* (*wish*) Wunsch *m*; (*interest*) Lust *f*; (*craving*) Begierde

f; (*thing desired*) Gewünschte *n* ‖ *tr* wünschen
desirous [dɪ'zaɪrəs] *adj* (**of**) begierig (nach)
desist [dɪ'zɪst] *intr* (**from**) ablassen (von)
desk [dɛsk] *s* Schreibtisch *m*; (*of a teacher*) Pult *n*; (*of a pupil*) Schulbank *f*; (*in a hotel*) Kasse *f*
desk' cop'y *s* Freiexemplar *n*
desk' lamp' *s* Tischlampe *f*
desk' pad' *s* Schreibunterlage *f*
desolate ['dɛsəlɪt] *adj* (*barren*) öde; (*joyless*) trostlos; (*deserted*) verlassen; (*delapidated*) verfallen ‖ ['dɛsə͵let] *tr* verwüsten
desolation [͵dɛsə'leʃən] *s* (*devastation*) Verwüstung *f*; (*dreariness*) Trostlosigkeit *f*
despair [dɪs'pɛr] *s* Verzweiflung *f* ‖ *intr* (**of**) verzweifeln (an *dat*)
despair'ing *adj* verweifelt
despera·do [͵dɛspə'rado], [͵dɛspə'redo] *s* (–does & –dos) Desperado *m*
desperate ['dɛspərɪt] *adj* verzweifelt
desperation [͵dɛspə'reʃən] *s* Verzweiflung *f*
despicable ['dɛspɪkəbəl] *adj* verächtlich, verachtungswürdig
despise [dɪ'spaɪz] *tr* verachten
despite [dɪ'spaɪt] *prep* trotz (*genit*)
despondency [dɪ'spɑndənsi] *s* Kleinmut *m*
despondent [dɪ'spɑndənt] *adj* kleinmütig
despot ['dɛspɑt] *s* Despot –in *mf*
despotic [dɛs'pɑtɪk] *adj* despotisch
despotism ['dɛspə͵tɪzəm] *s* Despotie *f*; (*as a system*) Despotismus *m*
dessert [dɪ'zʌrt] *s* Nachtisch *m*
destination [͵dɛstɪ'neʃən] *s* (*of a trip*) Bestimmungsort *m*, Reiseziel *n*; (*purpose*) Bestimmung *f*
destine ['dɛstɪn] *tr* (**for**) bestimmen (zu or für)
destiny ['dɛstɪni] *s* Schicksal *n*; (*doom*) Verhängnis *n*
destitute ['dɛstɪ͵t(j)ut] *adj* mittellos; **d. of** ohne
destitution [͵dɛstɪ't(j)uʃən] *s* äußerste Armut *f*
destroy [dɪ'strɔɪ] *tr* vernichten, zerstören; (*animals, bacteria*) töten
destroyer [dɪ'strɔɪ·ər] *s* (nav) Zerstörer *m*
destroy'er es'cort *s* Zerstörergeleitschutz *m*
destruction [dɪ'strʌkʃən] *s* Zerstörung *f*; (*of species*) Ausrottung *f*
destructive [dɪ'strʌktɪv] *adj* zerstörend; (*criticism*) vernichtend; (*tendency*) destruktiv
desultory ['dɛsəl͵tori] *adj* (*without plan*) planlos; (*fitful*) sprunghaft; (*remark*) deplaciert
detach [dɪ'tætʃ] *tr* ablösen; (*along a perforation*) abtrennen; (mil) abkommandieren
detachable [dɪ'tætʃəbəl] *tr* abnehmbar, ablösbar
detached' *adj* (*building*) alleinstehend; (*objective*) objektiv; (*aloof*) distanziert

detachment [dɪ'tæt∫mənt] *s* Objektivität *f;* (*aloofness*) Abstand *m;* (mil) Trupp *m*, Kommando *n*

detail [dɪ'tel], ['ditel] *s* Enzelheit *f*, Detail *n;* (mil) Kommando *n*, Trupp *m;* **details** (pej) Kleinkram *m;* **in d.** ausführlich ‖ [dɪ'tel] (*relate in detail*) ausführlich berichten; (*list*) einzeln aufzählen; (mil) abkommandieren

de'tail draw'ing *s* Detailzeichnung *f*

detailed' *adj* ausführlich; **d. work** Kleinarbeit *f*

detain [dɪ'ten] *tr* zurückhalten; (jur) in Haft behalten

detect [dɪ'tɛkt] *tr* (*discover*) entdecken; (*catch*) ertappen

detection [dɪ'tɛk∫ən] *s* Entdeckung *f*

detective [dɪ'tɛktɪv] *s* Detektiv *m*

detec'tive sto'ry *s* Kriminalroman *m*

detector [dɪ'tɛktər] *s* (*e.g., of smoke*) Spürgerät *n;* (*of objects*) Suchgerät *n;* (rad) Detektor *m*

détente [de'tɑnt] *s* Entspannung *f*, Détente *f*

detention [dɪ'tɛn∫ən] *s* (jur) Haft *f*

deten'tion camp' *s* Internierungslager *n*

deten'tion home' *s* Haftanstalt *f*

de•ter [dɪ'tʌr] *v* (*pret & pp* **–terred;** *ger*–**terring**) *tr* (**from**) abschrecken (von), abhalten (von)

detergent [dɪ'tʌrdʒənt] *s* Reinigungsmittel *n;* (*in a washer*) Waschmittel *n*

deteriorate [dɪ'tɪrɪ-ə‚ret] *tr* verschlechtern ‖ *intr* sich verschlechtern

deterioration [dɪ‚tɪrɪ-ə're∫ən] *s* Verschlechterung *f*, Verfall *m*

determination [dɪ‚tʌrmɪ'ne∫ən] *s* Bestimmung *f;* (*resoluteness*) Entschlossenheit *f;* (*of boundaries*) Festlegung *f*

determine [dɪ'tʌrmɪn] *tr* (*fix conclusively*) bestimmen; (*boundaries*) festlegen; (*decide*) entscheiden

deter'mined *adj* entschlossen

deterrent [dɪ'tʌrənt] *adj* abschreckend ‖ *s* Abschreckungsmittel *n*

detest [dɪ'tɛst] *tr* verabscheuen

detestable [dɪ'tɛstəbəl] *adj* abscheulich

dethrone [dɪ'θron] *tr* entthronen

detonate ['dɛtə‚net] *tr* explodieren lassen ‖ *intr* explodieren

detour ['ditur] *s* (*for cars*) Umleitung *f;* (*for pedestrians*) Umweg *m* ‖ *tr* umleiten ‖ *intr* e–n Umweg machen

detract [dɪ'trækt] *tr* ablenken ‖ *intr*—**d. from** beeinträchtigen

detraction [dɪ'træk∫ən] *s* Beeinträchtigung *f*

detractor [dɪ'træktər] *s* Verleumder –in *mf*

detrain [dɪ'tren] *tr* ausladen ‖ *intr* aussteigen

detriment ['dɛtrɪmənt] *s* Nachteil *m*

detrimental [‚detrɪ'mɛntəl] *adj* (**to**) nachteilig (für), schädlich (für)

deuce [d(j)us] *s* (*in cards or dice*) Zwei *f;* (*in tennis*) Einstand *m;* **what the d.?** was zum Teufel?

devaluate [dɪ'vælju‚et] *tr* abwerten

devaluation [di‚vælju'e∫ən] *s* Abwertung *f*

devastate ['dɛvəs‚tet] *tr* verheeren

develop [dɪ'vɛləp] *tr* entwickeln; (*one's mind*) (aus)bilden; (*a habit*) annehmen; (*a disease*) sich [*dat*] zuziehen; (*cracks*) bekommen; (*land*) nutzbar machen; (*a mine*) ausbauen; (phot) entwickeln ‖ *intr* sich entwickeln; (*said of habits*) sich herausbilden; **d. into** sich entwickeln zu

developer [dɪ'vɛləpər] *s* (*of land*) Spekulant –in *mf;* (phot) Entwickler *m*

development [dɪ'vɛləpmənt] *s* Entwicklung *f;* (*of relations, of a city*) Ausbau *m;* (*of land*) Nutzbarmachung *f;* (*of housing*) Siedlung *f;* (*an event*) Ereignis *n;* (educ) Ausbildung *f;* (phot) Entwicklung *f*

deviate ['divɪ‚et] *intr* abweichen

deviation [‚divɪ'e∫ən] *s* Abweichung *f*

device [dɪ'vaɪs] *s* Vorrichtung *f*, Gerät *n;* (*means*) Mittel *n;* (*crafty scheme*) Kniff *m;* (*literary device*) Kunstgriff *m;* (heral) Sinnbild *n;* **leave s.o. to his own devices** j–n sich [*dat*] selbst überlassen

dev•il ['dɛvəl] *s* Teufel *m;* **a d. of a** (coll) verteufelt; **between the d. and the deep blue sea** zwischen zwei Feuern; **poor d.** armer Teufel; **the d. with you!** (coll) scher dich zum Teufel!; **what** (**who,** *etc.*) **the d.?** was (wer, *etc.*) zum Teufel? ‖ *v* (*pret & pp* –**il[l]ed;** *ger* –**il[l]ing**) *tr* (culin) mit viel Gewürz zubereiten

devilish ['dɛv(ə)lɪ∫] *adj* teuflisch

dev'il-may-care' *adj* (*informal*) wurstig; (*reckless*) verwegen

devilment ['dɛvɪlmənt] *s* Unfug *m*

deviltry ['dɛvɪltri] *s* Unfug *m*

devious ['divɪ-əs] *adj* abweichend; (*tricky*) unredlich; (*reasoning*) abwegig

devise [dɪ'vaɪz] *tr* ersinnen; (jur) vermachen

devoid [dɪ'vɔɪd] *adj*—**d. of** ohne

devolve [dɪ'valv] *intr*—**d. on** zufallen (*dat*)

devote [dɪ'vot] *tr* widmen

devot'ed *adj* (*dedicated*) ergeben; (*affectionate*) liebevoll

devotee [‚dɛvə'ti] *s* Anhänger –in *mf*

devotion [dɪ'vo∫ən] *s* Ergebenheit *f;* (*devoutness*) Frömmigkeit *f;* (*special prayer*) (**to**) Gebet *n* (zu); **devotions** Andacht *f*

devour [dɪ'vaur] *tr* verschlingen; (*said of fire*) verzehren

devout [dɪ'vaut] *adj* fromm; (*e.g., hope*) innig

dew [d(j)u] *s* Tau *m;* **dew is falling** es taut

dew'drop' *s* Tautropfen *m*

dew'lap' *s* Wamme *f*

dewy ['d(j)u-i] *adj* tauig

dexterity [dɛks'tɛrɪti] *s* Geschicklichkeit *f*, Handfertigkeit *f*

dexterous ['dɛkstərəs] *adj* handfertig

dextrose ['dɛkstroz] *s* Traubenzucker *m*

diabetes [‚daɪ-ə'bitɪs] *s* Zuckerkrankheit *f*

diabetic [‚daɪ·ə'bɛtɪk] *adj* zuckerkrank *mf*
diabolic(al) [‚daɪ·ə'bɑlɪk(ə)l] *adj* teuflisch
diacritical [‚daɪ·ə'krɪtɪkəl] *adj* diakritisch
diadem ['daɪ·ə‚dɛm] *s* Diadem *n*
diaere·sis [daɪ'ɛrɪsɪs] *s* (**-ses** [‚siz] Diäresis *f*; (*mark*) Trema *n*
diagnose [‚daɪ·əg'nos], [‚daɪ·əg'noz] *tr* diagnostizieren
diagno·sis [‚daɪ·əg'nosɪs] *s* (**-ses** [siz]) Diagnose *f*
diagonal [daɪ'ægənəl] *adj* diagonal ‖ *s* Diagonale *f*
diagonally [daɪ'ægənəli] *adv*—**d. across from** schräg gegenüber von
diagram ['daɪ·ə‚græm] *s* Diagramm *n*
di·al ['daɪ·əl] *s* Zifferblatt *n;* (tech) Skalenscheibe *f;* (telp) Wählscheibe *f* ‖ *v* (*pret* & *pp* **-al[l]ed;** *ger* **-al[l]ing**) *tr* & *intr* (telp) wählen
di'aling *s* (telp) Wählen *n* der Nummer
dialogue ['daɪ·ə‚lɔg] *s* Dialog *m*
di'al tel'ephone *s* Selbstanschlußtelefon *n*
di'al tone' *s* Summton *m*, Amtszeichen *n*
diameter [daɪ'æmɪtər] *s* Durchmesser *m*
diamond ['daɪmənd] *adj* diamanten; (*in shape*) rautenförmig ‖ *s* Diamant *m; (cut diamond)* Brillant *m; (rhombus)* Raute *f;* (baseball) Spielfeld *n;* (cards) Karo *n*
dia'mond ring' *s* Brillantring *m*
diaper ['daɪpər] *s* Windel *f;* **change the diapers of** trockenlegen, wickeln
diaphanous [daɪ'æfənəs] *adj* durchsichtig, durchscheinend
diaphragm ['daɪ·ə‚fræm] *s* (*for birth control*) Gebärmutterkappe *f;* (anat) Zwerchfell *n;* (phot) Blende *f;* (tech, telp) Membran *f*
diarrhea [‚daɪ·ə'ri·ə] *s* Durchfall *m*
diary ['daɪ·əri] *s* Tagebuch *n*
diastole [daɪ'æstəli] *s* Diastole *f*
diatribe ['daɪ·ə‚traɪb] *s* Schmährede *f*
dice [daɪs] *spl* Würfel *pl* ‖ *tr* in Würfel schneiden
dice'box' *s* Würfelbecher *m*
dichotomy [daɪ'kɑtəmi] *s* Zweiteilung *f;* (bot) Gabelung *f*
dicker ['dɪkər] *intr* (**about**) feilschen (um)
dickey ['dɪki] *s* Hemdbrust *f*
dictaphone ['dɪktə‚fon] *s* Diktaphon *n*
dictate ['dɪktet] *s* Diktat *n;* **the dictates of conscience** das Gebot des Gewissens ‖ *tr* & *intr* diktieren
dictation [dɪk'teʃən] *s* Diktat *n*
dictator ['dɪktetər] *s* Diktator *m*
dictatorial [‚dɪktə'torɪ·əl] *adj* diktatorisch; (*power*) unumschränkt
dic'tatorship' *s* Diktatur *f*
diction ['dɪkʃən] *s* Ausdrucksweise *f*
dictionary ['dɪkʃə‚neri] *s* Wörterbuch *n*
dic·tum ['dɪktəm] *s* (**-ta** [tə]) (*saying*) Spruch *m;* (*pronouncement*) Ausspruch *m*
didactic [daɪ'dæktɪk] *adj* lehrhaft

die [daɪ] *s* (**dice** [daɪs]) Würfel *m;* **the die is cast** die Würfel sind gefallen ‖ *s* (**dies**) (*coining die*) Prägestempel *m; (casting die)* Form *f; (forging die)* Gesenk *n; (threader)* Schneidkopf *m* ‖ *v* (*pret* & *pp* **died;** *ger* **dying**) *tr*—**die a natural death** e–s natürlichen Todes sterben ‖ *intr* sterben; (*said of plants and animals*) eingehen; **be dying for** (coll) sich sehnen nach; **die down** (*said of the wind*) sich legen; (*said of noise*) ersterben; **die from** sterben an (*dat*); **die laughing** sich totlachen; **die of hunger** verhungern; **die of thirst** verdursten; **die out** aussterben; (*said of fire*) erlöschen; **I am dying to** (*inf*) (coll) ich würde schrecklich gern (*inf*)
die'-hard' *s* Unentwegte *mf*
die'sel en'gine ['dizəl] *s* Dieselmotor *m*
die'sel oil' *s* Dieselöl *n*
die'stock' *s* Gewindeschneidkluppe *f*
diet ['daɪ·ət] *s* Kost *f;* (*special menu*) Diät *f;* (parl) Reichstag *m;* **be on a d.** diät leben; **put on a d.** auf Diät setzen ‖ *intr* diät leben
dietary ['daɪ·ə‚teri] *adj* Diät–; **d. laws** rituelle Diätvorschriften *pl*
dietetic [‚daɪ·ə'tetɪk] *adj* diätetisch ‖ **dietetics** *spl* Diätetik *f*
dietitian [‚daɪ·ə'tɪʃən] *s* Diätspezialist –in *mf*
differ ['dɪfər] *intr* sich unterscheiden; (*said of opinions*) auseinandergehen; **d. from** abweichen von; **d. in** verschieden sein in (*dat*); **d. with** anderer Meinung sein als
difference ['dɪfərəns] *s* Unterschied *m;* (*argument*) Streit *m;* (math) Differenz *f;* **d. of opinion** Meinungsverschiedenheit *f;* **it makes no d. to me** es ist mir gleich; **split the d.** den Rest teilen
different ['dɪfərənt] *adj* verschieden; **a d. kind of** e–e andere Art von; **d. from** anders als, verschieden von; **d. kinds of** verschiedene
differential [‚dɪfə'renʃəl] *adj* (econ, elec, mach, math, phys) Differential– ‖ *s* (*difference*) Unterschied *m;* (mach) Differentialgetriebe *n;* (math) Differential *n*
dif'feren'tial cal'culus *s* Differentialrechnung *f*
differentiate [‚dɪfə'renʃɪ‚et] *tr* unterscheiden; (math) differenzieren ‖ *intr* —**d. between** unterscheiden zwischen (*dat*)
difficult ['dɪfɪ‚kʌlt] *adj* schwierig, schwer
difficulty ['dɪfɪ‚kʌlti] *s* Schwierigkeit *f;* **I have d. in** (*ger*) es fällt mir schwer zu (*inf*); **with d.** mit Mühe
diffuse [dɪ'fjus] *adj* (weit) zerstreut; (*style*) diffus ‖ [di'fjuz] *tr* (*spread*) verbreiten; (*pour out*) ausgießen; (phys) diffundieren ‖ *intr* sich zerstreuen
diffusion [dɪ'fjuʃən] *s* (*spread*) Verbreitung *f;* (phys) Diffusion *f*
dig [dɪg] *s* (*jab*) Stoß *m; (sarcasm)*

Seitenhieb *m;* (archeol) Ausgrabung
f || *v* (*pret & pp* dug [dʌg] & digged;
ger digging) *tr* graben; (*a ditch*)
auswerfen; (*potatoes*) ausgraben;
(*understand*) (sl) kapieren; (*look at*)
(sl) anschauen; (*appreciate*) (sl)
schwärmen für; dig up ausgraben;
(*find*) auftreiben; (*information*) ausfindig machen; (*money*) aufbringen;
|| *intr* graben, wühlen; dig in (*with
the hands*) hineinfassen; (*work hard*)
(coll) schuften; (mil) sich eingraben;
dig for (*e.g., gold*) schürfen nach
digest ['daɪdʒɛst] *s* Zusammenfassung
f; (jur) Gesetzessammlung *f* || [daɪ-
'dʒɛst] *tr* verdauen; (*in the mind*)
verarbeiten || *intr* verdauen
digestible [daɪ'dʒɛstɪbəl] *adj* verdaulich, verträglich
digestion [daɪ'dʒɛstʃən] *s* Verdauung
f
digestive [daɪ'dʒɛstɪv] *adj* Ver-
dauungs–; d. tract Verdauungsappa-
rat *m*
digit ['dɪdʒɪt] *s* (math) Ziffer *f* (unter
zehn); (math) Stelle *f*
digital ['dɪdʒɪtəl] *adj* digital, Digital–
dig'ital comput'er *s* digitale Rechen-
anlage *f*
digitalis [dɪdʒɪ'tælɪs] *s* Digitalis *n*
dignified ['dɪgnɪˌfaɪd] *adj* würdig
digni-fy ['dɪgnɪˌfaɪ] *v* (*pret & pp*
–fied) *tr* ehren
dignitary ['dɪgnɪˌtɛri] *s* Würdenträger
–in *mf*
dignity ['dɪgnɪti] *s* Würde *f;* d. of man
Menschenwürde *f;* stand on one's d.
sich [*dat*] nichts vergeben
digress [daɪ'grɛs] *intr* (from) abschweifen (von)
digression [daɪ'grɛʃən] *s* Abschwei-
fung *f*
dike [daɪk] *s* Deich *m*
dilapidated [dɪ'læpɪˌdetɪd] *adj* baufällig
dilate [daɪ'let] *tr* ausdehnen || *intr*
sich ausdehnen
dilation [daɪ'leʃən] *s* Ausdehnung *f*
dilatory ['dɪləˌtori] *adj* saumselig;
(*tending to cause delay*) hinhaltend
dilemma [dɪ'lɛmə] *s* Dilemma *n*
dilettan-te [ˌdɪlə'tænti], ['dɪləˌtɑnt]
s (–tes & –ti [ti]) Dilettant –in *mf*
diligence ['dɪlɪdʒəns] *s* Fleiß *m*
diligent ['dɪlɪdʒənt] *adj* fleißig
dill [dɪl] *s* Dill *m*
dillydal-ly ['dɪlɪˌdæli] *v* (*pret & pp*
–lied) *intr* herumtrödeln
dilute [dɪ'lut], [daɪ'lut] *adj* verdünnt
|| [dɪ'lut] *tr* verdünnen; (*with water*)
verwässern || *intr* sich verdünnen
dilution [dɪ'luʃən] *s* Verdünnung *f;*
(*with water*) Verwässerung *f*
dim [dɪm] *adj* (dimmer; dimmest) *adj*
(*light, eyesight*) schwach; (*poorly
lighted*) schwach beleuchtet; (*dull*)
matt; (*chances, outlook*) schlecht;
(*indistinct*) undeutlich; take a dim
view of (*disapprove of*) mißbilligen;
(*be pessimistic about*) sich [*dat*]
etw schwarz ausmalen || *v* (*pret &
pp* dimmed; *ger* dimming) *tr* trüben;
(*lights*) abblenden || *intr* sich ver-

dunkeln; (*said of lights, hopes*) verblassen
dime [daɪm] *s* Zehncentstück *n*
dime' nov'el *s* Groschenroman *m*
dimension [dɪ'mɛnʃən] *s* Maß *n*, Ausdehnung *f;* dimensions Ausmaß *n*
diminish [dɪ'mɪnɪʃ] *tr* (ver)mindern,
verringern || *intr* sich vermindern
diminutive [dɪ'mɪnjətɪv] *adj* winzig;
(gram) Verkleinerungs– || *s* Ver-
kleinerungsform *f*
dimmer ['dɪmər] *s* (aut) Abblendvor-
richtung *f*
dimple ['dɪmpəl] *s* Grübchen *n*
dim'wit' *s* Schwachsinnige *mf*
din [dɪn] *s* Getöse *n* || *v* (*pret & pp*
dinned; *ger* dinning) *tr* betäuben;
din s.th. into s.o. j–m etw einhäm-
mern
dine [daɪn] *intr* speisen; d. out auswärts speisen
diner ['daɪnər] *s* Tischgast *m;* (*small
restaurant*) speisewagenähnliches
Speiselokal *n;* (rr) Speisewagen *m*
dinette [daɪ'nɛt] *s* Speisenische *f*
dingbat ['dɪŋˌbæt] *s* (sl) (*person*)
Dingsda *m;* (*thing*) Dingsda *n*
ding-dong ['dɪŋˌdɔŋ] *interj* bimbam!,
klingklang!
dinghy ['dɪŋgi] *s* Beiboot *n;* rubber d.
Schlauchboot *n*
dingy ['dɪndʒi] *adj* (*gloomy*) düster;
(*shabby*) schäbig
din'ing car' *s* (rr) Speisewagen *m*
din'ing hall' *s* Speisesaal *m*
din'ing room' *s* Eßzimmer *n*
dinner ['dɪnər] *s* (*supper*) Abendessen
n; (*main meal*) Hauptmahlzeit *f;*
(*formal meal*) Diner *n;* after d. nach
Tisch; at d. bei Tisch; before d. vor
Tisch
din'ner guest' *s* Tischgast *m*
din'ner jac'ket *s* Smoking *m*
din'ner mu'sic *s* Tafelmusik *f*
din'ner par'ty *s* Tischgesellschaft *f*
din'ner time' *s* Tischzeit *f*
dinosaur ['daɪnəˌsɔr] *s* Dinosaurier *m*
dint [dɪnt] *s*—by d. of kraft (*genit*)
diocesan [daɪ'ɑsɪsən] *adj* Diözesan–
diocese ['daɪ-əˌsis] *s* Diözese *f*
diode ['daɪ-od] *s* (electron) Diode *f*
dioxide [daɪ'ɑksaɪd] *s* Dioxyd *n*
dip [dɪp] *s* (*in the road*) Neigung *f;*
(*short swim*) kurzes Bad *n;* (*dunk*)
Eintauchen *n;* (*sauce*) Tunke *f;* (*of
ice cream*) Portion *f* || *v* (*pret & pp*
dipped; *ger* dipping) *tr* eintauchen;
(*e.g., doughnuts*) eintunken; (*a flag*)
senken || *intr* sich senken; dip into
(*e.g., reserves*) angreifen; dip into
one's pockets (fig) in die Tasche
greifen
diphtheria [dɪf'θɪrɪ-ə] *s* Diphtherie *f*
diphthong ['dɪfθɔŋ] *s* Doppelvokal *m*
diploma [dɪ'plomə] *s* Diplom *n*
diplomacy [dɪ'ploməsi] *s* Diplomatie *f*
diplomat ['dɪpləˌmæt] *s* Diplomat –in
mf
diplomatic [ˌdɪplə'mætɪk] *adj* (& *fig*)
diplomatisch
dipper ['dɪpər] *s* Schöpflöffel *m*
dipsomania [ˌdɪpsə'mɛnɪ-ə] *s* Trunk-
sucht *f*

dip' stick' s (aut) Ölstandmesser m
dire [daɪr] adj (terrible) gräßlich;
(need) äußerste
direct [dɪ'rɛkt] adj direkt, unmittelbar; (frank) unverblümt; (quotation)
wörtlich || tr (order) beauftragen;
(a company) leiten; (traffic) regeln;
(a movie, play) Regie führen bei;
(an orchestra) dirigieren; (attention,
glance) (to) richten (auf acc); (a
person) (to) verweisen (an acc);
(words, letter) (to) richten (an acc)
direct' call' s Selbstwählverbindung f
direct' cur'rent s Gleichstrom m
direct' dis'course s direkte Rede f
direct' hit' s Volltreffer m
direction [dɪ'rɛkʃən] s Richtung f;
(order) Anweisung f; (leadership)
Leitung f, Führung f; (cin, theat)
Regie f; (mus) Stabführung f; **directions** Weisungen pl; (for use) Gebrauchsanweisung f; **in all directions**
nach allen Richtungen
directional [dɪ'rɛkʃənəl] adj Richt–
direc'tion find'er s Peilgerät n
direc'tion sig'nal s (aut) Richtungs-
anzeiger m
directive [dɪ'rɛktɪv] s Anweisung f
direct' ob'ject s direktes Objekt n
direct' op'posite s genaues Gegenteil n
director [dɪ'rɛktər] s Leiter –in mf,
Direktor –in mf; (cin, theat) Regisseur –in mf; (mus) Dirigent –in mf;
(rad, telv) Sendeleiter –in mf
direc'torship' s Direktorat n
directory [dɪ'rɛktəri] s Verzeichnis n
dirge [dʌrdʒ] s Trauergesang m
dirigible ['dɪrɪdʒɪbəl] s lenkbares
Luftschiff n
dirt [dʌrt] s Schmutz m, Dreck m;
(moral filth) Schmutz m; (soil) Erde
f
dirt'-cheap' adj spottbillig
dirt' farm'er s kleiner Farmer m
dirt' road' s unbefestigte Straße f
dirt•y ['dʌrti] adj schmutzig, dreckig;
(morally) schmutzig; **d. business**
Schweinerei f; **d. dog** Sauhund m;
d. joke Zote f; **d. lie** gemeine Lüge
f; **d. linen** schmutzige Wäsche f; **d.
look** böser Blick m; **d. trick** übler
Streich m; **that's a d. shame** das ist
e–e Gemeinheit! || v (pret & pp
–ied) tr beschmutzen
disability [,dɪsə'bɪlɪti] s Invalidität f
disable [dɪs'ebəl] tr (e.g., a worker)
arbeitsunfähig machen; (make un-
suited for combat) kampfunfähig
machen; (jur) rechtsunfähig machen
disa'bled adj invalide; (mil) kampfunfähig; **d. veteran** Kriegsversehrte
mf; **d. person** Invalide mf
disabuse [,dɪsə'bjuz] tr—**d. of** befreien von
disadvantage [,dɪsəd'væntɪdʒ] s Nachteil m; **place at a d.** benachteiligen
disadvantageous [dɪs,ædvən'tedʒəs]
adj nachteilig
disagree [,dɪsə'gri] intr nicht übereinstimmen; (be contradictory) einander widersprechen; (quarrel) (sich)
streiten; **d. with** (said of food) nicht
bekommen (dat); **d. with s.o. on**

anderer Meinung über (acc) als j–d
sein
disagreeable [,dɪsə'grɪ·əbəl] adj unangenehm
disagreement [,dɪsə'grimənt] s (un-
likeness) Verschiedenheit f; (dissention) Uneinigkeit f; (quarrel) Meinungsverschiedenheit f
disappear [,dɪsə'pɪr] intr verschwinden
disappearance [,dɪsə'pɪrəns] s Verschwinden n
disappoint [,dɪsə'pɔɪnt] tr enttäuschen; **be disappointed at (or with)**
enttäuscht sein über (acc)
disappointment [,dɪsə'pɔɪntmənt] s
Enttäuschung f
disapproval [,dɪsə'pruvəl] s Mißbilli-
gung f
disapprove [,dɪsə'pruv] tr mißbilligen; (e.g., an application) nicht ge-
nehmigen || intr—**d. of** mißbilligen
disarm [dɪs'ɑrm] tr (& fig) entwaffen;
(a bomb) entschärfen || intr ab-
rüsten
disarmament [dɪs'ɑrməmənt] s Ab-
rüstung f
disarm'ing adj (fig) entwaffend
disarray [,dɪsə're] s Unordnung f ||
tr in Unordnung bringen, verwirren
disassemble [,dɪsə'sɛmbəl] tr zerlegen
disaster [dɪ'zæstər] s Unheil n
disas'ter ar'ea s Katastrophengebiet n
disastrous [dɪ'zæstrəs] adj unheilvoll
disavow [,dɪsə'vau] tr ableugnen
disavowal [,dɪsə'vau·əl] s Ableugnung
f
disband [dɪs'bænd] tr auflösen || intr
sich auflösen
dis•bar [dɪs'bɑr] v (pret & pp –barred;
ger –barring) tr aus dem Anwalts-
stand ausschließen
disbelief [,dɪsbɪ'lif] s Unglaube m
disbelieve [,dɪsbɪ'liv] tr & intr nicht
glauben
disburse [dɪs'bʌrs] tr auszahlen
disbursement [dɪs'bʌrsmənt] s Aus-
zahlung f
disc [dɪsk] s var of **disk**
discard [dɪs'kɑrd] s Ablegen n || tr
(clothes, cards, habits) ablegen; (a
plan) verwerfen
discern [dɪ'sʌrn] tr (perceive) wahrnehmen; **be able to d. right from
wrong** zwischen Gut und Böse unterscheiden können
discern'ing adj scharfsinnig
discernment [dɪ'sʌrnmənt] s Scharfsinn m
discharge [dɪs'tʃɑrdʒ] s (of a gun)
Abfeuern n; (of a battery) Ent-
ladung f; (of water) Abfluß m; (of
smoke) Ausströmen n; (of duties)
Erfüllung f; (of debts) Tilgung f;
(of employees, patients, soldiers)
Entlassung f; (of a prisoner) Freilas-
sung f; (pathol) Ausfluß m || tr (a
gun) abfeuern; (e.g., water) ergießen; (smoke) ausstoßen; (debts) tilgen; (duties) erfüllen; (an office)
verwalten; (an employee, patient,
soldier) entlassen || intr (said of a
gun) losgehen; (said of a battery)

sich entladen; (*pour out*) abfließen; (pathol) eitern

disciple [dɪ'saɪpəl] *s* Jünger *m*

disciplinarian [,dɪsɪplɪ'nɛrɪ·ən] *s* Zuchtmeister *m*

disciplinary ['dɪsɪplɪ,nɛri] *adj* Disziplinar–

discipline ['dɪsɪplɪn] *s* Disziplin *f;* (*punishment*) Züchtigung *f* ‖ *tr* disziplinieren; (*punish*) züchtigen

disclaim [dɪs'klem] *tr* leugnen; (jur) verzichten auf (*acc*)

disclose [dɪs'kloz] *tr* enthüllen

disclosure [dɪs'kloʒər] *s* Enthüllung *f*

discolor [dɪs'kʌlər] *tr* verfärben ‖ *intr* sich verfärben

discoloration [dɪs,kʌlə'reʃən] *s* Verfärbung *f*

discomfiture [dɪs'kʌmfɪtʃər] *s* (*defeat*) Niederlage *f;* (*frustration*) Enttäuschung *f;* (*confusion*) Verwirrung *f*

discomfort [dɪs'kʌmfərt] *s* Unbehagen *n* ‖ *tr* Unbehagen verursachen (*dat*)

disconcert [,dɪskən'sʌrt] *tr* aus der Fassung bringen

dis'concert'ed *adj* fassungslos

disconnect [,dɪskə'nɛkt] *tr* trennen; (elec) ausschalten; (mach) auskuppeln; (telp) unterbrechen

disconsolate [dɪs'kansəlɪt] *adj* trostlos

discontent [,dɪskən'tɛnt] *s* Unzufriedenheit *f* ‖ *tr* unzufrieden machen

dis'content'ed *adj* (**with**) mißvergnügt (über *acc*)

discontinue [,dɪskən'tɪnju] *tr* (*permanently*) einstellen; (*temporarily*) aussetzen; (*a newspaper*) abbestellen; **d.** (ger) aufhören zu (*inf*)

discord ['dɪskɔrd] *s* Mißklang *m;* (*dissention*) Zwietracht *f*

discordance [dɪs'kɔrdəns] *s* Uneinigkeit *f*

discotheque [,dɪsko'tɛk] *s* Diskothek *f*

discount ['dɪskaʊnt] *s* (*in price*) Rabatt *m;* (*cash discount*) Kassaskonto *n;* (*deduction from nominal value*) Diskont *m;* **at a d.** mit Rabatt; (st. exch.) unter pari ‖ *tr* (*disregard*) außer acht lassen; (*minimize*) geringen Wert beimessen (*dat*); (*for cash payment*) e–n Abzug gewähren auf (*acc*); (*e.g., a promissory note*) diskontieren

dis'count store' *s* Rabattladen *m*

discourage [dɪs'kʌrɪdʒ] *tr* (*dishearten*) entmutigen; **d. s.o. from** (ger) (*deter*) j–n davon abschrecken zu (*inf*); (*dissuade*) j–m davon abraten zu (*inf*)

discour'aged *adj* mutlos

discouragement [dɪs'kʌrɪdʒmənt] *s* (*act*) Entmutigung *f;* (*state*) Mutlosigkeit *f;* (*deterrent*) Abschreckung *f*

discourse ['dɪskors] *s* (*conversation*) Gespräch *n;* (*formal treatment*) Abhandlung *f;* (*lecture*) Vortrag *m* ‖ [dɪs'kors] *intr* (**on**) sich unterhalten (über *acc*)

discourteous [dɪs'kʌrtɪ·əs] *adj* unhöflich

discourtesy [dɪs'kʌrtəsi] *s* Unhöflichkeit *f*

discover [dɪs'kʌvər] *tr* entdecken

discovery [dɪs'kʌvəri] *s* Entdeckung *f*

discredit [dɪs'krɛdɪt] *s* (*disrepute*) Mißkredit *m;* (*disbelief*) Zweifel *m* ‖ *tr* (*destroy confidence in*) in Mißkredit bringen; (*disbelieve*) anzweifeln; (*disgrace*) in Verruf bringen

discreditable [dɪs'krɛdɪtəbəl] *adj* schändlich

discreet [dɪs'krit] *adj* diskret

discrepancy [dɪs'krɛpənsi] *s* Unstimmigkeit *f*

discretion [dɪs'krɛʃən] *s* Diskretion *f,* Besonnenheit *f;* **at one's d.** nach Belieben; **leave to s.o.'s d.** in j–s Belieben stellen

discriminate [dɪs'krɪmɪ,net] *tr* voneinander unterscheiden ‖ *intr*—**d. against** diskriminieren

discrimination [dɪs,krɪmɪ'neʃən] *s* (*distinction*) Unterscheidung *f;* (*prejudicial treatment*) Diskriminierung *f*

discriminatory [dɪs'krɪmɪnə,tori] *adj* diskriminierend

discus ['dɪskʌs] *s* Diskus *m*

discuss [dɪs'kʌs] *tr* besprechen, diskutieren; (*formally*) erörtern

discussion [dɪs'kʌʃən] *s* Diskussion *f;* (*formal consideration*) Erörterung *f*

disdain [dɪs'den] *s* Geringschätzung *f* ‖ *tr* geringschätzen

disdainful [dɪs'denfəl] *adj* geringschätzig; **be d. of** geringschätzen

disease [dɪ'ziz] *s* Krankheit *f*

diseased' *adj* krank, erkrankt

disembark [,dɪsɛm'bark] *tr* ausschiffen, landen ‖ *intr* an Land gehen, landen

disembarkation [dɪs,ɛmbar'keʃən] *s* Ausschiffung *f*

disembow·el [,dɪsɛm'baʊ·əl] *v* (*pret* & *pp* –el[l]ed; *ger* –el[l]ing) *tr* ausweiden

disenchant [,dɪsɛn'tʃænt] *tr* ernüchtern

disenchantment [,dɪsɛn'tʃæntmənt] *s* Ernüchterung *f*

disengage [,dɪsɛn'gedʒ] *tr* (*a clutch*) ausrücken; (*the enemy*) sich absetzen von; (*troops*) entflechten; **d. the clutch** auskuppeln ‖ *intr* loskommen; (mil) sich absetzen

disengagement [,dɪsɛn'gedʒmənt] *s* Lösung *f;* (mil) Truppenentflechtung *f*

disentangle [,dɪsɛn'tæŋgəl] *tr* entwirren

disentanglement [,dɪsɛn'tæŋgəlmənt] *s* Entwirrung *f*

disfavor [dɪs'fevər] *s* Ungunst *f*

disfigure [dɪs'fɪgjər] *tr* entstellen

disfigurement [dɪs'fɪgjərmənt] *s* Entstellung *f*

disfranchise [dɪs'fræntʃaɪz] *tr* die Bürgerrechte entziehen (*dat*)

disgorge [dɪs'gɔrdʒ] *tr* ausspeien ‖ *intr* sich ergießen

disgrace [dɪs'gres] *s* Schande *f;* (*of a family*) Schandfleck *m* ‖ *tr* in Schande bringen; (*a girl*) schänden; **be disgraced** in Schande kommen

disgraceful [dɪs'gresfəl] *adj* schändlich, schimpflich
disgruntled [dɪs'grʌntəld] *adj* mürrisch
disguise [dɪs'gaɪz] *s* (*clothing*) Verkleidung *f*; (*insincere manner*) Verstellung *f* ‖ *tr* (*by dress*) verkleiden; (*e.g., the voice*) verstellen
disgust [dɪs'gʌst] *s* (**at**) Ekel *m* (vor *dat*) ‖ *tr* anekeln
disgust'ing *adj* ekelhaft
dish [dɪʃ] *s* Schüssel *f*, Platte *f*; (*food*) Gericht *n*; **do the dishes** das Geschirr spülen ‖ *tr*—**d. out** (*coll*) austeilen
dish'cloth' *s* Geschirrlappen *m*
dishearten [dɪs'hɑrtən] *tr* entmutigen
disheveled [dɪ'ʃɛvəld] *adj* unordentlich
dishonest [dɪs'ɑnɪst] *adj* unehrlich
dishonesty [dɪs'ɑnɪsti] *s* Unehrlichkeit *f*
dishonor [dɪs'ɑnər] *s* Unehre *f* ‖ *tr* verunehren
dishonorable [dɪs'ɑnərəbəl] *adj* (*person*) ehrlos; (*action*) unehrenhaft
dishon'orable dis'charge *s* Entlassung *f* wegen Wehrunwürdigkeit
dish'pan' *s* Aufwaschschüssel *f*
dish'rack' *s* Abtropfkörbchen *n*
dish'rag' *s* Spüllappen *m*
dish'tow'el *s* Geschirrtuch *n*
dish'wash'er *s* (*person*) Aufwäscher –in *mf*; (*appliance*) Geschirrspülmaschine *f*
dish'wa'ter *s* Spülwasser *n*
disillusion [,dɪsɪ'luʒən] *s* Ernüchterung *f* ‖ *tr* ernüchtern
disillusionment [,dɪsɪ'luʒənmənt] *s* Ernüchterung *f*
disinclination [dɪs,ɪnklɪ'neʃən] *s* Abneigung *f*, Abgeneigtheit *f*
disinclined [,dɪsɪn'klaɪnd] *adj* abgeneight
disinfect [,dɪsɪn'fɛkt] *tr* desinfizieren
disinfectant [,dɪsɪn'fɛktənt] *adj* desinfizierend ‖ *s* Desinfektionsmittel *n*
disinherit [,dɪsɪn'hɛrɪt] *tr* enterben
disintegrate [dɪs'ɪntɪ,gret] *tr* (& fig) zersetzen ‖ *intr* zerfallen
disintegration [dɪs,ɪntɪ'greʃən] *s* (& fig) Zerfall *m*
disin·ter [,dɪsɪn'tʌr] *v* (*pret & pp* –terred; *ger* –terring) *tr* ausgraben
disinterested [dɪs'ɪntə,rɛstɪd] *adj* (*unbiased*) unparteiisch; (*uninterested*) desinteressiert
disjunctive [dɪs'dʒʌŋktɪv] *adj* disjunktiv
disk [dɪsk] *s* Scheibe *f*
disk' brake' *s* Scheibenbremse *f*
disk' jock'ey *s* Schallplattenjockei *m*
dislike [dɪs'laɪk] *s* (**of**) Abneigung *f* (gegen) ‖ *tr* nicht mögen
dislocate ['dɪslo,ket] *tr* verschieben; (*a shoulder*) verrenken; (fig) stören
dislocation [,dɪslo'keʃən] *s* Verschiebung *f*; (*of a shoulder*) Verrenkung *f*; (fig) Störung *f*
dislodge [dɪs'lɑdʒ] *tr* losreißen; (mil) aus der Stellung werfen
disloyal [dɪs'lɔɪ·əl] *adj* untreu
disloyalty [dɪs'lɔɪ·əlti] *s* Untreue *f*
dismal ['dɪzməl] *adj* trübselig, düster
dismantle [dɪs'mæntəl] *tr* demontieren

dismay [dɪs'me] *s* Bestürzung *f* ‖ *tr* bestürzen
dismember [dɪs'mɛmbər] *tr* zerstückeln
dismiss [dɪs'mɪs] *tr* verabschieden; (*an employee*) (**from**) entlassen (aus); (*a case*) (jur) abweisen; (mil) wegtreten lassen; **d. as** abtun als; **dismissed!** (mil) wegtreten!
dismissal [dɪs'mɪsəl] *s* Entlassung *f*; (jur) Abweisung *f*
dismount [dɪs'maʊnt] *tr* (*throw down*) abwerfen; (mach) abmontieren ‖ *intr* (*from a carriage*) herabsteigen; (*from a horse*) absitzen
disobedience [,dɪsə'bidɪ·əns] *s* Ungehorsam *m*, Unfolgsamkeit *f*
disobedient [,dɪsə'bidɪ·ənt] *adj* ungehorsam, unfolgsam
disobey [,dɪsə'be] *tr* nicht gehorchen (*dat*) ‖ *intr* nicht gehorchen
disorder [dɪs'ɔrdər] *s* Unordnung *f*; (*public disturbance*) Unruhe *f*; (*pathol*) Erkrankung *f*; **throw into d.** in Unordnung bringen
disorderly [dɪs'ɔrdərli] *adj* unordentlich, liederlich
disor'derly con'duct *s* ungebührliches Benehmen *n*
disor'derly house' *s* Bordell *n*; (*gambling house*) Spielhölle *f*
disorganize [dɪs'ɔrgə,naɪz] *tr* zerrütten, desorganisieren
disown [dɪs'on] *tr* verleugnen
disparage [dɪ'spærɪdʒ] *tr* herabsetzen, geringschätzen
disparate ['dɪspərɪt] *adj* ungleichartig
disparity [dɪ'spærɪti] *s* (*inequality*) Ungleichheit *f*; (*difference*) Unterschied *m*
dispassionate [dɪs'pæʃənɪt] *adj* leidenschaftslos
dispatch [dɪ'spætʃ] *s* Abfertigung *f*; (*message*) Depesche *f*; **with d.** in Eile ‖ *tr* (*send off*) absenden; (*e.g., a truck*) abfertigen; (*e.g., a task*) schnell erledigen; (*kill*) töten; (*eat fast*) (coll) verputzen
dispatcher [dɪ'spætʃər] *s* (*of vehicles*) Fahrbereitschaftsleiter –in *mf*
dis·pel [dɪ'spɛl] *v* (*pret & pp* –pelled; *ger* –pelling) *tr* vertreiben; (*thoughts, doubts*) zerstreuen
dispensary [dɪ'spɛnsəri] *s* Arzneiausgabestelle *f*; (mil) Krankenrevier *n*
dispensation [,dɪspɛn'seʃən] *s* (eccl) (**from**) Dispens *m* (von); **by divine d.** durch göttliche Fügung
dispense [dɪ'spɛns] *tr* (*exempt*) (**from**) entbinden (von); (pharm) zubereiten und ausgeben; **d. justice** Recht sprechen ‖ *intr*—**d. with** verzichten auf (*acc*)
dispersal [dɪ'spʌrsəl] *s* Auflockerung *f*
disperse [dɪ'spʌrs] *tr* zerstreuen; (*a crowd*) zersprengen; (*one's troops*) auflockern; (*the enemy*) auseinandersprengen ‖ *intr* (*said of clouds, etc.*) sich verziehen; (*said of crowds*) auseinandergehen
dispirited [dɪ'spɪrɪtɪd] *adj* niedergeschlagen

displace [dɪs'ples] *tr* (*people in war*) verschleppen; (phys) verdrängen

displacement [dɪs'plesmənt] *s* Vertreibung *f*; (phys) Verdrängung *f*

display [dɪ'sple] *s* (*of energy, wealth*) Entfaltung *f*; (*of goods*) Ausstellung *f*; (*pomp*) Aufwand *m*; **on d.** zur Schau || *tr* (*wares*) ausstellen; (*reveal*) entfalten; (*flaunt*) protzen mit

display' case' *s* Vitrine *f*

display' room' *s* Ausstellungsraum *m*

display' win'dow *s* Schaufenster *n*

displease [dɪs'pliz] *tr* mißfallen (*dat*); **be displeased with** Mißfallen finden an (*dat*) || *intr* mißfallen

displeas'ing *adj* mißfällig

displeasure [dɪs'plɛʒər] *s* Mißfallen *n*

disposable [dɪ'spozəbəl] *adj* Einweg–

disposal [dɪ'spozəl] *s* (*riddance*) Beseitigung *f*; (*of a matter*) Erledigung *f*; (*distribution*) Anordnung *f*; **be at s.o.'s d.** j–m zur Verfügung stehen; **have at one's d.** verfügen über (*acc*); **put at s.o.'s d.** j–m zur Verfügung stellen

dispose [dɪ'spoz] *tr* (*incline*) **(to)** geneigt machen (zu); (*arrange*) anordnen || *intr*—**d. of** (*a matter*) erledigen; (*get rid of*) loswerden

disposed' *adj* gesinnt; **d. to** (*ger*) geneigt zu (*inf*)

disposition [ˌdɪspə'zɪʃən] *s* (*settlement*) Erledigung *f*; (*nature*) Gemütsart *f*; (*inclination*) Neigung *f*

dispossess [ˌdɪspə'zɛs] *tr*—**d. s.o. of s.th.** j–m etw enteignen

disproof [dɪs'pruf] *s* Widerlegung *f*

disproportionate [ˌdɪsprə'porʃənɪt] *adj* unverhältnismäßig **be d. to** im Mißverhältnis stehen zu

disprove [dɪs'pruv] *tr* widerlegen

dispute [dɪs'pjut] *s* (*quarrel*) Streit *m*; (*debate*) Wortgefecht *n*; **beyond d.** unstreitig; **in d.** umstritten || *tr* bestreiten || *intr* disputieren

disqualification [dɪsˌkwɑlɪfɪ'keʃən] *s* Disqualifizierung *f*

disqualify [dɪs'kwɑlɪˌfaɪ] *v* (*pret & pp* –**fied**) *tr* (*make unfit*) **(for)** untauglich machen (für); (*declare ineligible*) disqualifizieren

disquiet [dɪs'kwaɪ·ət] *tr* beunruhigen

disqui'eting *adj* beunruhigend

disregard [ˌdɪsrɪ'gɑrd] *s* (*lack of attention*) Nichtbeachtung *f*; (*disrespect*) Mißachtung *f* || *tr* (*not pay attention to*) nicht beachten; (*treat without due respect*) mißachten

disrepair [ˌdɪsrɪ'per] *s* Verfall *m*; **fall into d.** verfallen

disreputable [dɪs'rɛpjətəbəl] *adj* verrufen

disrepute [ˌdɪsrɪ'pjut] *s* Verruf *m*

disrespect [ˌdɪsrɪ'spɛkt] *s* Nichtachtung *f*, Mißachtung *f* || *tr* nicht achten

disrespectful [ˌdɪsrɪ'spɛktfəl] *adj* respektlos, unehrerbietig

disrobe [dɪs'rob] *tr* entkleiden || *intr* sich entkleiden

disrupt [dɪs'rʌpt] *tr* (*throw into confusion*) in Verwirrung bringen; (*interrupt*) unterbrechen; (*cause to*

break down) zum Zusammenbruch bringen

dissatisfaction [ˌdɪssætɪs'fækʃən] *s* Unzufriedenheit *f*

dissat'isfied' *adj* unzufrieden

dissatis·fy [dɪs'sætɪsˌfaɪ] *v* (*pret & pp* –**fied**) *tr* nicht befriedigen

dissect [dɪ'sɛkt] *tr* (fig) zergliedern; (anat) sezieren

dissection [dɪ'sɛkʃən] *s* (fig) Zergliederung *f*; (anat) Sektion *f*

dissemble [dɪ'sɛmbəl] *tr* verbergen || *intr* heucheln

disseminate [dɪ'sɛmɪˌnet] *tr* verbreiten

dissension [dɪ'sɛnʃən] *s* Uneinigkeit *f*

dissent [dɪ'sɛnt] *s* abweichende Meinung *f* || *intr* **(from)** anderer Meinung sein (als)

dissenter [dɪ'sɛntər] *s* Andersdenkende *mf*; (relig) Dissident –in *mf*

dissertation [ˌdɪsər'teʃən] *s* Dissertation *f*

disservice [dɪ'sʌrvɪs] *s* schlechter Dienst *m*; **do s.o. a d.** j–m e–n schlechten Dienst erweisen

dissidence [ˈdɪsɪdəns] *s* Meinungsverschiedenheit *f*

dissident [ˈdɪsɪdənt] *adj* andersdenkend || *s* Dissident –in *mf*

dissimilar [dɪ'sɪmɪlər] *adj* unähnlich

dissimilate [dɪ'sɪmɪˌlet] *tr* (phonet) dissimilieren

dissimulate [dɪ'sɪmjəˌlet] *tr* verheimlichen || *intr* heucheln

dissipate [ˈdɪsɪˌpet] *tr* (*squander*) vergeuden; (*scatter*) zerstreuen; (*dissolve*) auflösen || *intr* (*scatter*) sich zerstreuen; (*dissolve*) sich auflösen

dis'sipat'ed *adj* ausschweifend

dissipation [ˌdɪsɪ'peʃən] *s* (*squandering*) Vergeudung *f*; (*dissolute mode of life*) Ausschweifung *f*; (phys) Dissipation *f*

dissociate [dɪ'soʃɪˌet] *tr* trennen; **d. oneself from** abrücken von

dissolute [ˈdɪsəˌlut] *adj* ausschweifend

dissolution [ˌdɪsə'luʃən] *s* Auflösung *f*

dissolve [dɪ'zɑlv] *s* (cin) Überblendung *f* || *tr* auflösen; (cin) überblenden || *intr* sich auflösen; (cin) überblenden

dissonance [ˈdɪsənəns] *s* Mißklang *m*

dissuade [dɪ'swed] *tr* **(from)** abbringen (von); **d. s.o. from** (*ger*) j–n davon abbringen zu (*inf*)

dissyllabic [ˌdɪsɪ'læbɪk] *adj* zweisilbig

distaff [ˈdɪstæf] *s* Spinnrocken *m*; (fig) Frauen *pl*

dis'taff side' *s* weibliche Linie *f*

distance [ˈdɪstəns] *s* Entfernung *f*; (*between two points*) Abstand *m*; (*stretch*) Strecke *f*; (*of a race*) Rennstrecke *f*; **from a d.** aus einiger Entfernung; **go the d.** bis zum Ende aushalten; **in the d.** in der Ferne; **keep one's d.** zurückhaltend sein; **keep your d.** bleib mir vom Leib!; **within easy d. of** nicht weit weg von; **within walking d. of** zu Fuß erreichbar von

distant [ˈdɪstənt] *adj* entfernt; (*reserved*) zurückhaltend

distaste [dɪs'test] *s* **(for)** Abneigung *f* (gegen), Ekel *m* (vor *dat*)

distasteful [dɪs'testfəl] *adj* (*unpleasant*) **(to)** unangenehm (*dat*); (*offensive*) **(to)** ekelhaft (*dat*)

distemper [dɪs'tɛmpər] *s* (*of dogs*) Staupe *f;* (*paint*) Temperafarbe *f*

distend [dɪs'tɛnd] *tr* (*swell*) aufblähen; (*extend*) ausdehnen ‖ *intr* (*swell*) anschwellen; (*extend*) (aus)-dehnen

distension [dɪs'tɛnʃən] *s* Aufblähung *f;* Ausdehnung *f*

distill [dɪ'stɪl] *tr* destillieren; (*e.g., whiskey*) brennen

distillation [,dɪstɪ'leʃən] *s* Destillation *f;* (*of whiskey*) Brennen *n*

distiller [dɪs'tɪlər] *s* Brenner *m*

distillery [dɪs'tɪləri] *s* Brennerei *f*

distinct [dɪ'stɪŋkt] *adj* (*clear*) deutlich; (*different*) verschieden; **as d. from** zum Unterschied von; **keep d.** auseinanderhalten

distinction [dɪs'tɪŋkʃən] *s* (*difference*) Unterschied *m;* (*differentiation*) Unterscheidung *f;* (*honor*) Auszeichnung *f;* (*eminence*) Vornehmheit *f;* **have the d. of** (*ger*) den Vorzug haben zu (*inf*)

distinctive [dɪs'tɪŋktɪv] *adj* (*distinguishing*) unterscheidend; (*characteristic*) kennzeichnend

distinguish [dɪs'tɪŋgwɪʃ] *tr* (*differentiate*) unterscheiden; (*classify*) einteilen; (*honor*) auszeichnen; (*characterize*) kennzeichnen; (*discern*) erkennen ‖ *intr* **(between)** unterscheiden (zwischen *dat*)

distin'guished *adj* (*eminent*) prominent; **(for)** berühmt (wegen)

distort [dɪs'tɔrt] *tr* verzerren; (*the truth*) entstellen; **distorted picture** Zerrbild *n*

distortion [dɪs'tɔrʃən] *s* Verzerrung *f;* (*of the truth*) Entstellung *f*

distract [dɪ'strækt] *tr* ablenken

distraction [dɪ'strækʃən] *s* (*diversion of attention*) Ablenkung *f;* (*entertainment*) Zerstreuung *f;* **drive s.o. to d.** j–n zum Wahnsinn treiben

distraught [dɪ'strɔt] *adj* (*bewildered*) verwirrt; (*deeply agitated*) **(with)** aufgewühlt (von); (*crazed*) **(with)** rasend (vor *dat*)

distress [dɪ'strɛs] *s* (*anxiety*) Kummer *m;* (*mental pain*) Betrübnis *f;* (*danger*) Notstand *m,* Bedrängnis *f;* (*naut*) Seenot *f* ‖ *tr* betrüben

distress'ing *adj* betrüblich

distress' sig'nal *s* Notzeichen *n*

distribute [dɪ'strɪbjut] *tr* verteilen; (*divide*) einteilen; (*apportion*) (jur) aufteilen

distribution [,dɪstrɪ'bjuʃən] *s* Verteilung *f;* (*geographic range*) Verbreitung *f;* (*of films*) Verleih *m;* (*marketing*) Vertrieb *m;* (*of dividends*) Ausschüttung *f;* (jur) Aufteilung *f*

distributor [dɪ'strɪbjətər] *s* Verteiler –in *mf;* (*of films*) Verleiher –in *mf;* (*dealer*) Lieferant –in *mf;* (aut) Verteiler *m*

distri'butorship' *s* Vertrieb *m*

district ['dɪstrɪkt] *s* Bezirk *m*

dis'trict attor'ney *s* Staatsanwalt *m*

distrust [dɪs'trʌst] *s* Mißtrauen *n* ‖ *tr* mißtrauen (*dat*)

distrustful [dɪs'trʌstfəl] *adj* **(of)** mißtrauisch (gegen)

disturb [dɪs'tʌrb] *tr* stören; (*disquiet*) beunruhigen; **d. the peace** die öffentliche Ruhe stören

disturbance [dɪs'tʌrbəns] *s* (*interruption*) Störung *f;* (*breach of peace*) Unruhe *f*

disunited [,dɪsju'naɪtɪd] *adj* uneinig

disunity [dɪs'junɪti] *s* Uneinigkeit *f*

disuse [dɪs'jus] *s* Nichtverwendung *f;* **fall into d.** außer Gebrauch kommen

ditch [dɪtʃ] *s* Graben *m* ‖ *tr* (*discard*) (sl) wegschmeißen; (aer) (coll) auf dem Wasser notlanden mit ‖ *intr* (aer) (coll) notwassern

dither ['dɪðər] *s*—**be in a d.** verdattert sein

dit·to ['dɪto] *adj* (coll) dito ‖ *s* (**–tos**) Kopie *f* ‖ *tr* vervielfältigen

dit'to mark' *s* Wiederholungszeichen *n*

ditty ['dɪti] *s* Liedchen *n*

diva ['divɑ] *s* (mus) Diva *f*

divan ['daɪvæn], [dɪ'væn] *s* Diwan *m*

dive [daɪv] *s* Kopfsprung *m;* (coll) Spelunke *f;* (aer) Sturzflug *m;* (nav) Tauchen *n;* (sport) Kunstsprung *m;* **make a d. for** (fig) sich stürzen auf (*acc*) ‖ *v* (*pret & pp* **dived & dove** [dov]) *intr* (*submerge*) tauchen; (*plunge head first*) e–n Kopfsprung machen; (aer) e–n Sturzflug machen; (nav) (unter)tauchen; (sport) e–n Kunstsprung machen

dive'-bomb' *tr & intr* im Sturzflug mit Bomben angreifen

dive' bomb'er *s* Sturzkampfbomber *m*

diver ['daɪvər] *s* Taucher –in *mf;* (orn) Taucher *m;* (sport) Kunstspringer –in *mf*

diverge [daɪ'vʌrdʒ] *intr* (*said of roads, views*) sich teilen; (*from the norm*) abweichen; (geom, phys) divergieren

diverse [daɪ'vʌrs] *adj* (*different*) verschieden; (*of various kinds*) vielförmig

diversi·fy [daɪ'vʌrsɪ,faɪ] *v* (*pret & pp* **–fied**) *tr* abwechslungsreich gestalten

diversion [daɪ'vʌrʒən] *s* Ablenkung *f;* (*recreation*) Zeitvertreib *m;* (mil) Ablenkungsmanöver *n*

diversity [daɪ'vʌrsɪti] *s* Mannigfaltigkeit *f*

divert [daɪ'vʌrt] *tr* (*attention*) ablenken; (*traffic*) umleiten; (*a river*) ableiten; (*money*) abzweigen; (*entertain*) zerstreuen

divest [daɪ'vɛst] *tr*—**d. oneself of** sich entäußern (*genit*); **d. s.o. of** (*e.g., office, power*) j–n entkleiden (*genit*); (*e.g., rights, property*) j–m (*seine Rechte, etc.*) entziehen

divide [dɪ'vaɪd] *s* (geol) Wasserscheide *f* ‖ *tr* teilen; (*cause to disagree*) entzweien; (math) **(by)** teilen (durch); **d. into** einteilen in (*acc*); **d. off** (*a room*) abteilen; **d. up** (**among**) aufteilen (unter *acc*) ‖ *intr* (*said of a road*) sich teilen; **d. into** sich teilen in (*acc*)

dividend ['dɪvɪ,dɛnd] *s* Dividende *f;* (math) Dividend *m;* **pay dividends** Dividenden ausschütten; (fig) sich lohnen

divid'ing line' *s* Trennungsstrich *m*

divination [,dɪvɪ'neʃən] *s* Weissagung *f*

divine [dɪ'vaɪn] *adj* göttlich ‖ *s* Geistlicher *m* ‖ *tr* (er)ahnen

divine' prov'idence *s* göttliche Vorsehung *f*

divine' right' of kings' *s* Königtum *n* von Gottes Gnaden

div'ing *s* Tauchen *n* (sport) Kunstspringen *n*

div'ing bell' *s* Taucherglocke *f*

div'ing board' *s* Sprungbrett *n*

div'ing suit' *s* Taucheranzug *m*

divin'ing rod' *s* Wünschelrute *f*

divinity [dɪ'vɪnɪti] *s* (*divine nature*) Göttlichkeit *f;* (*deity*) Gottheit *f*

divisible [dɪ'vɪzɪbəl] *adj* teilbar

division [dɪ'vɪʒən] *s* Teilung *f;* (*dissention*) Uneinigkeit *f;* (adm) Abteilung *f;* (math, mil) Division *f;* (sport) Sportklasse *f*

divisor [dɪ'vaɪzər] *s* (math) Teiler *m;* Divisor *m*

divorce [dɪ'vors] *s* Scheidung *f;* **apply for a d.** die Scheidungsklage einreichen; **get a d.** sich scheiden lassen ‖ *tr* (*said of a spouse*) sich scheiden lassen von; (*said of a judge*) scheiden; (*separate*) trennen

divorcee [dɪvor'si] *s* Geschiedene *f*

divulge [dɪ'vʌldʒ] *tr* ausplaudern

dizziness ['dɪzɪnɪs] *s* Schwindel *m*

dizzy ['dɪzi] *adj* schwindlig; (*causing dizziness*) schwindelerregend; (*mentally confused*) benommen; (*foolish*) damisch; (*feeling, spell*) Schwindel–

do [du] *v* (*3d pers* **does** [dʌz]; *pret* **did** [dɪd]; *pp* **done** [dʌn]; *ger* **doing** ['du·ɪŋ] *tr* tun, machen; (*damage*) anrichten; (*one's hair*) frisieren; (*an injustice*) antun; (*a favor, disservice*) erweisen; (*time in jail*) absitzen; (*miles per hour*) fahren; (*tour*) (coll) besichtigen; (*Shakespeare, etc., in class*) durchnehmen; **do duty as** dienen als; **do in** (sl) umbringen; **do over** (*with paint*) neu anstreichen; (*with covering*) neu überziehen; **what can I do for you?** womit kann ich dienen? ‖ *intr* tun, machen; (*suffice*) genügen; **do away with** abschaffen; (*persons*) aus dem Wege räumen; **do away with oneself** sich [*dat*] das Leben nehmen; **do without** auskommen ohne; **I am doing well** es geht mir gut; (*financially*) ich verdiene gut; (*e.g., in history*) ich komme gut voran; **I'll make it do** ich werde schon damit auskommen; **nothing doing!** ausgeschlossen! **that will do!** genug· davon!; **that won't do!** das geht nicht! ‖ *aux* used in English but not specifically expressed in German: 1) in questions, e.g., **do you speak German?** sprechen Sie deutsch?; 2) in negative sentences,

e.g., **I do not live here** ich wohne hier nicht; 3) for emphasis, e.g., **I do feel better** ich fühle mich wirklich besser; 4) in imperative entreaties, e.g., **do come again** besuchen Sie mich doch wieder!; 5) in elliptical sentences, e.g., **I like Berlin. So do I** Mir gefällt Berlin. Mir auch.; **he drinks, doesn't he?** er trinkt, nicht wahr?; 6) in inversions after adverbs such as hardly, rarely, scarcely, little, e.g., **little did she realize that**...sie hatte keine Ahnung, daß... ‖ *impers*—**it doesn't do to** (*inf*) es ist unklug zu (*inf*); **it won't do you any good to stay here** es wird Ihnen nicht viel nützen, hier zu bleiben

docile ['dɑsɪl] *adj* gelehrig; (*easy to handle*) fügsam, lenksam

dock [dɑk] *s* Anlegeplatz *m;* (jur) Anklagebank *f;* **docks** Hafenanlagen *pl;* **in the d.** (jur) auf der Anklagebank ‖ *tr* (*a ship, space vehicle*) docken; (*a tail*) stutzen; (*pay*) kürzen; **d. an employee** (**for**) e–m Arbeitnehmer den Lohn kürzen (um) ‖ *intr* (naut) (am Kai) anlegen; (rok) docken, koppeln

docket ['dɑkɪt] *s* (*agenda*) Tagesordnung *f;* (jur) Prozeßliste *f*

dock' hand' *s* Hafenarbeiter *m*

dock'ing *s* (naut) Anlegen *n;* (rok) Andocken *n*

dock' work'er *s* Dockarbeiter *m*

dock'yard' *s* Werft *f*

doctor ['dɑktər] *s* Doktor *m;* (*physician*) Arzt *m*, Ärztin *f* ‖ *tr* (*records*) frisieren; (*adapt, e.g., a play*) zurechtmachen ‖ *intr* (coll) in ärztlicher Behandlung stehen

doctorate ['dɑktərɪt] *s* Doktorwürde *f*

doctrine ['dɑktrɪn] *s* Doktrin *f*, Lehre *f*

document ['dɑkjəmənt] *s* Urkunde *f* ‖ ['dɑkjə,mɛnt] *tr* dokumentieren

documentary [,dɑkjə'mɛntəri] *adj* dokumentarisch ‖ *s* Dokumentarfilm *m*

documentation [,dɑkjəmən'teʃən] *s* Dokumentation *f*

doddering ['dɑdərɪŋ] *adj* zittrig

dodge [dɑdʒ] *s* Winkelzug *m* ‖ *tr* (*e.g., a blow*) ausweichen (*dat*); (*e.g., a responsibility*) sich drücken vor (*dat*) ‖ *intr* ausweichen

do·do ['dodo] *s* (**–does** & **–dos**) (coll) Depp *m*

doe [do] *s* Rehgeiß *f*, Damhirschkuh *f*

doer ['du·ər] *s* Täter –in *mf*

doe'skin' *s* Rehleder *n*

doff [dɔf] *tr* (*a hat*) abnehmen; (*clothes*) ausziehen; (*habits*) ablegen

dog [dɔg] *s* Hund *m;* **dog eats dog** jeder für sich; **go to the dogs** (coll) vor die Hunde gehen; **lucky dog!** (coll) Glückspitz!; **put on the dog** (coll) großtun ‖ *v* (*pret* & *pp* **dogged**; *ger* **dogging**) *tr* nachspüren (*dat*)

dog' bis'cuit *s* Hundekuchen *m*

dog' days' *spl* Hundstage *pl*

dog'-eared' *adj* mit Eselsohren

dog'face' *s* (mil) Landser *m*

dog'fight' s (aer) Kurbelei f
dogged ['dɔgɪd] adj verbissen
doggerel ['dɔgərəl] s Knittelvers m
doggone ['dɔg'gɔn] adj (sl) verflixt
dog'house' s Hundehütte f; **in the d.** (fig) in Ungnade
dog' ken'nel s Hundezwinger m
dogma ['dɔgmə] s Dogma n
dogmatic [dɔg'mætɪk] adj dogmatisch
do-gooder ['du'gʊdər] s Humanitätsapostel m
dog' show' s Hundeschau f
dog's' life' s Hundeleben n
Dog' Star' s Hundestern m
dog' tag' s Hundemarke f; (mil) Erkennungsmarke f
dog'-tired' adj hundemüde
dog'wood' s Hartriegel m
doily ['dɔɪli] s Zierdeckchen n
do'ing s Werk n; **doings** Tun und Treiben n; (events) Ereignisse pl
doldrums ['dɔldrəmz] spl Kalmengürtel m; **in the d.** (fig) deprimiert
dole [dol] s Spende f; **be on the d.** stempeln gehen || tr—**d. out** verteilen
doleful ['dolfəl] adj trübselig
doll [dal] s Puppe f || tr—**d. up** (coll) aufdonnern || intr (coll) sich aufdonnern
dollar ['dalər] s Dollar m
doll' car'riage s Puppenwagen m
dolly ['dali] s Püppchen n; (cart) Schiebkarren m
dolphin ['dalfɪn] s Delphin m
dolt [dolt] s Tölpel m
domain [do'men] s (& fig) Domäne f
dome [dom] s Kuppel f
dome' light' s (aut) Deckenlicht n
domestic [də'mɛstɪk] adj (of the home) Haus–, häuslich, Haushalts–; (produced at home) einheimisch, inländisch, Landes–; (tame) Haus–; (e.g., policy) Innen–, innere || s Hausangestellte mf
domesticate [də'mɛstɪ‚ket] tr zähmen
domicile ['damɪ‚saɪl] s Wohnsitz m
dominance ['damɪnəns] s Vorherrschaft f
dominant ['damɪnənt] adj vorherrschend; (factor) entscheidend
dominate ['damɪ‚net] tr beherrschen || intr (**over**) herrschen (über acc)
domination [‚damɪ'neʃən] s Beherrschung f, Herrschaft f
domineer [‚damɪ'nɪr] tr & intr tyrannisieren
domineer'ing adj tyrannisch
dominion [də'mɪnjən] s (sovereignty) (**over**) Gewalt f (über acc); (domain) Domäne f; (of British Empire) Dominion n
domi•no ['damɪ‚no] s (**-noes** & **nos**) Dominostein m; **dominoes** ssg Dominospiel n
don [dan] s Universitätsprofessor m || v (pret & pp **donned**; ger **donning**) tr anlegen; (a hat) sich [dat] aufsetzen
donate ['donet] tr schenken, spenden
donation [do'neʃən] s Schenkung f; (small contribution) Spende f
done [dʌn] adj erledigt; (culin) gar, fertig; **d. for** kaputt; **d. with** (com-

pleted) fertig; **get** (s.th.) **d.** fertigbekommen; **well d.** (culin) durchgebraten
donkey ['dʌŋki] s Esel m
donor ['donər] s Spender –in mf
doodad ['dudæd] s (gadget) Dings n; (decoration) Tand m
doodle ['dudəl] s Gekritzel n || tr bekritzeln || intr kritzeln
doom [dum] s Verhängnis n || tr verdammen, verurteilen
doomed adj todgeweiht
doomsday ['dumz‚de] s der Jüngste Tag
door [dor] s Tür f; **from d. to d.** von Haus zu Haus; **out of doors** draußen, im Freien; **show s.o. the d.** j–m die Tür weisen; **two doors away** zwei Häuser weiter
door'bell' s Türklingel f; **the d. is ringing** es klingelt
door'bell but'ton s Klingelknopf m
door'frame' s Türrahmen m
door'han'dle s Türgriff m, Türklinke f
door'jamb' s Türpfosten m
door'knob' s Türknopf m
door'man' s (**-men'**) Portier m
door'mat' s Abtreter m, Türmatte f
door'nail' s—**dead as a d.** mausetot
door'post' s Türpfosten m
door'sill' s Türschwelle f
door'step' s Türstufe f
door'stop' s Türanschlag m
door'-to-door' sales'man s Hausierer m
door'-to-door sel'ling s Hausieren n
door'way' s Türöffnung f; (fig) Weg m
dope [dop] s (drug) (sl) Rauschgift n; (information) (sl) vertraulicher Tip m; (fool) (sl) Trottel m; (aer) Lack m || tr (a racehorse) (sl) dopen; (a person) (sl) betäuben, verdrogen; (aer) lackieren; **d. out** (sl) herausfinden, ausarbeiten;. **d. up** (sl) verdrogen
dope' ad'dict s (sl) Rauschgiftsüchtige mf
dope' push'er s (sl) Rauschgiftschieber –in mf
dope'sheet' s (sl) vertraulicher Bericht m
dope' traf'fic s (sl) Rauschgifthandel m
dopey ['dopi] adj (**dopier; dopiest**) (sl) dämlich; (from sleep) (coll) schlaftrunken
dormant ['dɔrmənt] adj ruhend, untätig; (bot) in der Winterruhe
dormer ['dɔrmər] s Bodenfenster n; (the whole structure) Mansarde f
dor'mer win'dow s Bodenfenster n
dormitory ['dɔrmɪ‚tori] s (building) Studentenheim n; (room) Schlafsaal m
dormouse ['dɔr‚maʊs] s (**mice** [‚maɪs]) Haselmaus f
dor'sal fin' ['dɔrsəl] s Rückenflosse f
dosage ['dosɪdʒ] s Dosierung f
dose [dos] s (& fig) Dosis f
dossier ['dasɪ‚e] s Dossier m
dot [dat] s Punkt m, Tupfen m; **on the dot** auf die Sekunde; **three o'clock on the dot** Punkt drei Uhr || v (pret

& *pp* dotted; *ger* dotting) *tr* punktieren; tüpfeln; **dot one's i's** den
Punkt aufs i setzen; (fig) übergenau
sein
dotage ['dotɪdʒ] *s*—be in one's d.
senil sein
dotard ['dotərd] *s* kindischer Greis *m*
dote [dot] *intr*—d. on vernarrt sein in
(*acc*)
dot'ing *adj* (on) vernarrt (in *acc*)
dots' and dash'es *spl* (telg) Punkte
und Striche *pl*
dot'ted *adj* (*pattern*) getüpfelt; (*with
flowers, etc.*) übersät; (*line*) punk-
tiert
double ['dʌbəl] *adj* doppelt ‖ *s* Doppelte *n;* (*person*) Doppelgänger *m*
(cin, theat) Double *n;* **doubles** (tennis) Doppel *n;* **on the d.** im Ge-
schwindschritt ‖ *tr* (ver)doppeln;
(*the fist*) ballen; (*cards*) doppeln;
(naut) umsegeln ‖ *intr* sich verdop-
peln; (cards) doppeln; **d. back** umkehren; **d. up with** sich biegen vor
(*dat*)
dou'ble-bar'reled *adj* (*gun*) doppelläu-
fig; (fig) mit zweifacher Wirkung
dou'ble bass' [bes] *s* Kontrabaß *m*
dou'ble bed' *s* Doppelbett *n*
dou'ble-breast'ed *adj* doppelreihig
dou'ble' chin' *s* Doppelkinn *n*
dou'ble cross' *s* Schwindel *m*
dou'ble-cross' *tr* beschwindeln
dou'ble-cross'er *s* Schwindler –in *mf*
dou'ble date' *s* Doppelrendezvous *n*
dou'ble-deal'er *s* Betrüger –in *mf*
dou'ble-deal'ing *s* Doppelzüngigkeit *f*
dou'ble-deck'er *s* (*ship, bus*) Doppel-
decker *m;* (*sandwich*) Doppelsand-
wich *n;* (*bed*) Etagenbett *n*
dou'ble-edged' *adj* (& fig) zweischneidig
double entendre ['dʌbəlɑn'tɑndrə] *s*
(*ambiguity*) Doppelsinn *m;* (*ambiguous term*) doppelsinniger Ausdruck
m
dou'ble en'try *s* (com) doppelte Buch-
führung *f*
dou'ble expo'sure *s* Doppelbelichtung
f
dou'ble fea'ture *s* Doppelprogramm *n*
dou'blehead'er *s* Doppelspiel *n*
dou'ble-joint'ed *adj* mit Gummigelen-
ken
dou'blepark' *tr* & *intr* falsch parken
dou'ble-spaced' *adj* mit doppeltem Zei-
lenabstand
dou'ble stand'ard *s* zweierlei Maß *n*
doublet ['dʌblɪt] *s* (*duplicate; counterfeit stone*) Dublette *f;* (hist) Wams
m; (ling) Doppelform *f*
dou'ble take' *s* (fig) Spätzündung *f*
dou'ble-talk' *s* zweideutige Rede *f*
dou'ble time' *s* (*wage rate*) doppelter
Lohn *m;* (mil) Eilschritt *m*
dou'ble track' *s* (rr) doppelgleisige
Bahnlinie *f*
doubly ['dʌbli] *adv* doppelt
doubt [daut] *s* Zweifel *m;* **be still in
d.** (*said of things*) noch zweifelhaft
sein; **beyond d.** ohne (jeden) Zweifel;
in case of d. im Zweifelsfalle; **no d.**
zweifellos; **raise doubts** Bedenken

erregen; **there is no d. that** es unter-
liegt keinem Zweifel, daß ‖ *tr* bezweifeln ‖ *intr* zweifeln
doubter ['dautər] *s* Zweifler –in *mf*
doubtful ['dautfəl] *adj* zweifelhaft
doubtless ['dautlɪs] *adj* & *adv* zweifellos
douche [duʃ] *s* (*device*) Irrigator *m;*
(*act of cleansing*) Spülung *f* ‖ *tr* &
intr spülen
dough [do] *s* Teig *m;* (sl) Pinke *f*
dough'boy' *s* (sl) Landser *m*
dough'nut' *s* Krapfen *m*
doughty ['dauti] *adj* wacker
doughy ['do·i] *adj* teigig
dour [daur], [dur] *adj* mürrisch
douse [daus] *tr* eintauchen; (**with**)
übergießen (mit); (*a fire*) auslöschen
dove [dʌv] *s* (& pol) Taube *f*
dovecote ['dʌv‚kot] *s* Taubenschlag *m*
dove'tail' *s* (carp) Schwalbenschwanz
m ‖ *tr* verzinken; (fig) ineinander-
fügen ‖ *intr* ineinanderpassen
dowager ['dau·ədʒər] *s* Witwe *f* (von
Stand); (coll) Matrone *f*
dowdy ['daudi] *adj* schlampig
dow·el ['dau·əl] *s* Dübel *m* ‖ *v* (*pret
& pp* –el[l]ed; *ger* –el[l]ing) *tr*
(ein)dübeln
down [daun] *adj* (*prices*) gesunken;
(*sun*) untergegangen; **be d. for** vor-
gemerkt sein für; **be d. on s.o.** auf
j–m herumtrampeln; **be d. three
points** (sport) drei Punkte zurück
sein; **be d. with a cold** mit e–r Erkältung im Bett liegen; **d. and out**
völlig erledigt; **d. in the mouth** nie-
dergedrückt ‖ *adv* herunter, hinunter; **d. from** von...herab; **d. there**
da unten; **d. to** bis hinunter zu; **d.
to the last man** bis zum letzten
Mann; **d. with...!** nieder mit...! ‖
s (*of fowl*) Daune *f;* (*fine hair*)
Flaum *m;* **downs** grasbedecktes
Hügelland *n* ‖ *prep* (postpositive)
(*acc*) herunter, hinunter; **a little way
d. the road** etwas weiter auf der
Straße; **d. the river** flußabwärts ‖ *tr*
niederschlagen; (*a glass of beer*)
(coll) hinunterstürzen; (aer) abschießen
down'cast' *adj* niedergeschlagen
down'draft' *s* Abwind *m*, Fallwind *m*
down'fall' *s* Untergang *m*
down'grade' *s* Gefälle *n;* **on the d.** (fig)
im Niedergang ‖ *tr* herabsetzen;
niedriger einstufen
down'heart'ed *adj* niedergeschlagen
down'hill' *adj* bergabgehend; (*in skiing*) Abfahrts– ‖ *adv* bergab; **he's
going d.** (coll) mit ihm geht es abwärts
down' pay'ment *s* Anzahlung *f*
down'pour' *s* Regenguß *m*, Sturzregen
m
down'right' *adj* ausgesprochen; (*lie*)
glatt; (*contradiction*) schroff ‖ *adv*
ausgesprochen
down'spout' *s* Fallrohr *n*
down'stairs' *adj* unten befindlich ‖ *adv*
(*position*) unten; (*direction*) nach
unten
down'stream' *adv* stromabwärts

down'stroke' s (in writing) Grund-
strich m; (of a piston) Abwärtshub
m
down'-the-line' adj vorbehaltlos
down-to-earth' adj nüchtern
down'town' adj im Geschäftsviertel
gelegen || adv (position) im Ge-
schäftsviertel; (direction) ins Ge-
schäftsviertel, in die Stadt || s
Geschäftsviertel n
down'trend' s Baissestimmung f
downtrodden ['daυn‚trɑdən] adj un-
terdrückt
downward ['daυnwərd] adj Abwärts–
|| adv abwärts
downwards ['daυnwərdz] adv abwärts
downy ['daυni] adj flaumig; (soft)
weich wie Flaum
dowry ['daυri] s Mitgift f
dowser ['daυzər] s (rod) Wünschelrute f; (person) Wünschelrutengän-
ger m
doze [doz] s Schläfchen n || intr dösen
dozen ['dʌzən] s Dutzend n; **a d. times**
dutzendmal
Dr. abbr (Doctor) Dr.; (in addresses:
Drive) Str.
drab [dræb] adj (drabber; drabbest)
graubraun; (fig) trüb
drach·ma ['drækmə] s (–mas & –mae
[mi]) Drachme f
draft [dræft] s (of air; drink) Zug m;
(sketch) Entwurf m; (fin) Tratte f;
(mil) Einberufung f; **on d.** vom Faß
|| tr (sketch) entwerfen, abfassen;
(mil) einberufen
draft' age' s wehrpflichtiges Alter n
draft' beer' s Schankbier n
draft' board' s Wehrmeldeamt n
draft' dodg'er ['dɑdʒər] s Drückeberger m
draftee [‚dræf'ti] s Dienstpflichtige
mf
draft'ing s (of a document) Abfassung
f; (mechanical drawing) Zeichnen n;
(mil) Aushebung f
draft'ing board' s Zeichenbrett n
draft'ing room' s Zeichenbüro n
drafts·man ['dræftsmən] s (–men)
Zeichner m
drafty ['dræfti] adj zugig
drag [dræg] s (sledge) Lastschlitten
m; (in smoking) (coll) Zug m; (boring person) langweiliger Mensch m;
(s.th. tedious) etwas langweiliges;
(encumbrance) (on) Hemmschuh m
(für); (aer) Luftwiderstand m; (for
recovering objects) (naut) Schleppnetz n; (for retarding motion) (naut)
Schleppanker m || v (pret & pp
dragged; ger dragging) tr schleppen,
schleifen; **d. one's feet** schlurfen;
(fig) sich [dat] Zeit lassen; **d. out**
dahinschleppen; (protract) verschleppen; **d. through the mud** (fig) in den
Schmutz zerren; **d. up** (fig) aufwär-
men || intr (said of a long dress,
etc.) schleifen; (said of time) dahinschleichen; **d. on** (be prolonged) sich
hinziehen
drag'net' s Schleppnetz n
dragon ['drægən] s Drache m
drag'onfly' s Libelle f

dragoon [drə'gun] s Dragoner m || tr
(coerce) zwingen
drag' race' s Straßenrennen n; (sport)
Kurzstreckenrennen n
drain [dren] s (sewer) Kanal m; (under a sink) Abfluß m; (fig) (on)
Belastung f (genit); (surg) Drain m;
down the d. (fig) zum Fenster hin-
aus || tr (land) entwässern; (water)
ableiten; (a cup, glass) austrinken;
(fig) verzehren || intr ablaufen;
(culin) abtropfen
drainage ['drenɪdʒ] s Ableitung f;
(e.g., of land) Entwässerung f; (surg)
Drainage f
drain'age ditch' s Abflußgraben m
drain' cock' s Entleerungshahn m
drain'pipe' s Abflußrohr n
drain' plug' s Abflußstöpsel m
drake [drek] s Enterich m
dram [dræm] s Dram n
drama ['drɑmə] s Drama n; (art and
genre) Dramatik f
dra'ma crit'ic s Theaterkritiker –in mf
dramatic [drə'mætɪk] adj dramatisch
|| **dramatics** s Dramatik f; spl (pej)
Schauspielerei f
dramatist ['dræmətɪst] s Dramatiker
–in mf
dramatize ['dræmə‚taɪz] tr dramati-
sieren
drape [drep] s Vorhang m; (hang of a
drape or skirt) Faltenwurf m || tr
drapieren
drapery ['drepəri] s Vorhänge pl
dra'pery mate'rial s Vorhangstoff m
drastic ['dræstɪk] adj drastisch
draught [dræft] s & tr var of **draft**
draw [drɔ] s (in a lottery) Ziehen n;
(that which attracts) Schlager m;
(power of attraction) Anziehungs-
kraft f; **end in a d.** unentschieden
ausgehen || v (pret **drew** [dru]; pp
drawn [drɔn]) tr (pictures) zeichnen;
(a line, comparison, parallel, conclusion, lots, winner, sword, wagon)
ziehen; (a crowd) anlocken; (a distinction) machen; (blood) vergießen; (curtains) zuziehen; (a check)
ausstellen; (water) schöpfen; (cards)
nehmen; (rations) (mil) in Empfang
nehmen; **d. a blank** (coll) –e Niete
ziehen; **d. aside** beiseiteziehen; **d. attention to** die Aufmerksamkeit lenken auf (acc); **d. into** (e.g., an argument) hineinziehen in (acc); **d. lots
for** losen um; **d. out** (protract) in
die Länge ziehen; (money from a
bank) abheben; **d. s.o. out** j–n aus-
holen; **d. the line** (fig) e–e Grenze
ziehen; **d. up** (a document) verfas-
sen; (plans) entwerfen || intr zeich-
nen; **d. away** sich entfernen; **d. back**
sich zurückziehen; **d. near** heran-
nahen; **d. on** zurückgreifen auf (acc);
d. to a close sich dem Ende zuneigen
draw'back' s Nachteil m
draw'bridge' s Zugbrücke f
drawee [‚drɔ'i] s Trassat –in mf
drawer ['drɔ·ər] s Zeichner –in mf;
(com) Trassant –in mf || [drɔr] s
Schublade f; **drawers** Unterhose f
draw'ing s (of pictures) Zeichnen n;

(picture) Zeichnung *f; (in a lottery)* Ziehung *f*, Verlosung *f*
draw'ing board' *s* Reißbrett *n*
draw'ing card' *s* Zugnummer *f*
draw'ing room' *s* Empfangszimmer *n*
drawl [drɔl] *s* gedehntes Sprechen *n* ‖ *intr* gedehnt sprechen
drawn [drɔn] *adj (face)* **(with)** verzerrt *(vor dat); (sword)* blank
dray [dre] *s* niedriger Rollwagen *m; (sledge)* Schleife *f*
dread ⌊dred⌋ *adj* furchtbar ‖ *s* Furcht *f* ‖ *tr* fürchten
dreadful ['dredfəl] *adj* furchtbar
dream [drim] *s* Traum *m; (aspiration, ambition)* Wunschtraum *m; (ideal)* (coll) Gedicht *n* ‖ *v (pret & pp* **dreamed & dreamt** [dremt] *tr* träumen; **d. away** verträumen; **d. up** zusammenträumen ‖ *intr* träumen; **d. of** *(long for)* sich *[dat]* enträumen; **I dreamt of her** mir träumte von ihr
dreamer ['drimər] *s* Träumer –in *mf*
dream'land' *s* Traumland *n*
dream'-like' *adj* traumhaft
dream'world' *s* Traumwelt *f*
dreamy ['drimi] *adj (place)* verträumt; *(eyes)* träumerisch
dreary ['drɪri] *adj* trüb, trist
dredge [dredʒ] *s* Bagger *m* ‖ *tr* (aus)-baggern ‖ *intr* baggern
dredger ['dredʒər] *s* Bagger *m*
dredg'ing *s* Baggern *n*
dregs [dregz] *spl* Bodensatz *m; (of society)* Abschaum *m*, Auswurf *m*
drench [drentʃ] *tr* durchnässen
Dres'den chi'na ['drezdən] *s* Meißner Porzellan *n*
dress [dres] *s* Kleidung *f; (woman's dress)* Kleid *n* ‖ *tr* anziehen; *(a store window)* dekorieren; *(skins)* gerben; *(a salad, goose, chicken)* zubereiten; *(vines)* beschneiden; *(stones)* behauen; *(ore)* aufbereiten; *(wounds)* verbinden; *(hair)* frisieren; (tex) appretieren; **d. down** (coll) ausschimpfen; **d. ranks** die Glieder ausrichten; **get dressed** sich anziehen ‖ *intr* sich anziehen; **d. up** sich fein machen
dress' affair' *s* Galaveranstaltung *f*
dresser ['dresər] *s* Frisierkommode *f*; **be a good d.** sich gut kleiden
dress'ing *s (stuffing for fowl)* Füllung *f; (for salad)* Soße *f;* (surg) Verband *m*
dress'ing down' *s* Gardinenpredigt *f*
dress'ing room' *s* Umkleideraum *m;* (theat) Garderobe *f*
dress'ing sta'tion *s* Verbandsplatz *m*
dress'ing ta'ble *s* Frisierkommode *f*
dress'mak'er *s* Schneiderin *f*
dress'mak'ing *s* Modenschneiderei *f*
dress' rehear'sal *s* Kostümprobe *f*
dress' shirt' *s* Frackhemd *n*
dress' shop' *s* Modenhaus *n*, Modengeschäft *n*
dress' suit' *s* Frackanzug *m*, Frack *m*
dress' un'iform *s* Paradeuniform *f*
dressy ['dresi] *adj (showy)* geschniegelt; *(stylish)* modisch; *(for formal affairs)* elegant
dribble ['drɪbəl] *s (trickle)* Getröpfel

n; (sport) Dribbeln *n* ‖ *tr & intr* tröpfeln; (sport) dribbeln
driblet ['drɪblɪt] *s* Bißchen *n*
dried [draɪd] *adj* Trocken–, Dörr–
dried' beef' *s* Dörrfleisch *n*
dried' fruit' *s* Dörrobst *n*
dried'-up' *adj* ausgetrocknet, verdorrt
drier ['draɪ·ər] *s* Trockner *m; (for the hair)* Haartrockenhaube *f; (hand model)* Fön *m*
drift [drɪft] *s (of sand, snow)* Wehe *f; (tendency)* Richtung *f*, Neigung *f; (intent)* Absicht *f; (meaning)* Sinn *m;* (aer, naut, rad) Abtrift *f; (flow of the ocean current)* (naut) Drift *f* ‖ *intr (said of sand, snow)* sich anhäufen; *(said of a boat)* treiben; **d. away** *(said of sounds)* verwehen; *(said of a crowd)* sich verlaufen; **d. shut** verweht werden
drifter ['drɪftər] *s* zielloser Mensch *m*
drift' ice' *s* Treibeis *n*
drift'wood' *s* Treibholz *n*
drill [drɪl] *s (tool)* Bohrer *m; (exercise)* Drill *m;* (tex) Drillich *m* ‖ *tr* bohren; *(exercise)* drillen; **d. s.th. into s.o.** j–m etw einpauken ‖ *intr* bohren; *(exercise)* drillen
drill'mas'ter *s* (mil) Ausbilder *m*
drill' press' *s* Bohrpresse *f*
drink [drɪŋk] *s* Trunk *m* ‖ *v (pret* **drank** [dræŋk]; *pp* **drunk** [drʌŋk] *tr* trinken; *(said of animals)* saufen; (pej) saufen; **d. away** *(money)* versaufen; **d. down** hinunterkippen; **d. in** *(air)* einschlürfen; *(s.o.'s words)* verschlingen ‖ *intr* trinken; *(excessively)* saufen; **d. to** trinken auf *(acc);* **d. up** austrinken
drinkable ['drɪŋkəbəl] *adj* trinkbar
drinker ['drɪŋkər] *s* Trinker –in *mf;* **heavy drinker** Zecher –in *mf*
drink'ing foun'tain *s* Trinkbrunnen *m*
drink'ing par'ty *s* Zechgelage *n*
drink'ing song' *s* Trinklied *n*
drink'ing straw' *s* Strohhalm *m*
drink'ing trough' *s* Viehtränke *f*
drink'ing wa'ter *s* Trinkwasser *n*
drip [drɪp] *s* Tröpfeln *n* ‖ *v (pret & pp* **dripped**; *ger* **dripping**) *tr & intr* tröpfeln
drip' cof'fee *s* Filterkaffee *m*
drip'-dry' *adj* bügelfrei
drip' pan' *s* Bratpfanne *f*
drip'pings *spl* Bratenfett *n*
drive [draɪv] *s (in a car)* Fahrt *f; (road)* Fahrweg *m; (energy)* Schwungkraft *f; (inner urge)* Antrieb *m; (campaign)* Aktion *f; (for raising money)* Spendeaktion *f;* (golf) Treibschlag *m;* (mach) Antrieb *m;* (mil) Vorstoß *m;* (tennis) Treibschlag *m;* **go for a d.** spazierenfahren ‖ *v (pret* **drove** [drov]; *pp* **driven** ['drɪvən] *tr (a car, etc.)* fahren; *(e.g., cattle)* treiben; *(a tunnel)* vortreiben; **d. a hard bargain** zäh um den Preis feilschen; **d. away** abtreiben; **d.** *(oneself, a horse)* **hard** abjagen; **d. home** nahebringen; **d. in** *(a nail)* einschlagen; **d. off course** (naut) verschlagen; **d. on** antreiben; **d. out** austreiben; **d. s.o. to** *(inf)* j–n

dazu bringen zu (*inf*); **d. to despair** zur Verzweiflung treiben ‖ *intr* fahren; **d. along** mitfahren; **d. at** abzielen auf (*acc*); **d. away** wegfahren; **d. by** vorbeifahren an (*dat*); **d. in** einfahren; **d. on** weiterfahren; **d. out** herausfahren; **d. up** anfahren
drive′ belt′ *s* Treibriemen *m*
drive′-in′ *s* Autorestaurant *n;* (cin) Autokino *n*
driv·el [′drɪvəl] *s* (*slobber*) Geifer *m;* (*nonsense*) Faselei *f* ‖ *v* (*pret & pp* –el[l]ed; *ger* –el[l]ing) *intr* sabbern; (fig) faseln
driver [′draɪvər] *s* (*of a car*) Fahrer –in *mf;* (*of a locomotive, streetcar*) Führer *m;* (golf) Treibschläger *m;* (mach) Treibhammer *m*
driv′er's li′cense *s* Führerschein *m*
drive′ shaft′ *s* Antriebswelle *f*
drive′way′ *s* Einfahrt *f*
drive′-yourself′ serv′ice *s* Autovermietung *f* an Selbstfahrer
driv′ing *adj* (*rain*) stürmisch ‖ *s* (aut) Steuerung *f*
driv′ing instruc′tor *s* Fahrlehrer –in *mf*
driv′ing les′son *s* Fahrstunde *f*
driv′ing school′ *s* Autofahrschule *f*
drizzle [′drɪzəl] *s* Nieselregen *m* ‖ *impers*—**it is drizzling** es nieselt
droll [drol] *adj* drollig
dromedary [′dramə‚deri] *s* Dromedar *n*
drone [dron] *s* (*bee; loafer*) Drohne *f;* (*buzz*) Gesumme *n;* (*monotonous speech*) Geleier *n* ‖ *tr* (e.g., *prayers*) leiern ‖ *intr* summen; (fig) leiern
drool [drul] *intr* sabbern
droop [drup] *s* Herabhängen *n;* (*stoop*) gebeugte Haltung *f* ‖ *intr* herabhängen; (*said of flowers*) zu welken beginnen; (fig) den Kopf hängen lassen
droopy [′drupi] *adj* (*saggy*) schlaff herabhängend; (*dejected*) mutlos; (*shoulders*) abfallend; (*flowers*) welkend
drop [drap] *s* (*of liquid*) Tropfen *m;* (*candy*) Fruchtbonbon *m & n;* (*fall*) Fall *m;* (*height differential*) Gefälle *n;* (*reduction*) Abnahme *f;* (*in prices*) Rückgang *m;* (*in temperature*) Sturz *m;* (*of bombs or supplies*) Abwurf *m;* (*of paratroopers*) Absprung *m;* **a fifty-meter d.** ein Fall *m* aus e-r Höhe von fünfzig Metern; **d. by d.** tropfenweise; **d. in the bucket** Tropfen *m* auf e-n heißen Stein ‖ *v* (*pret & pp* **dropped;** *ger* **dropping**) *tr* (*let fall*) fallenlassen; (*bombs, supplies*) abwerfen; (*a subject, remarks, hints*) fallenlassen; (*the eyes, voice*) senken; (*anchor; young of animals*) werfen; (*money in gambling*) (sl) verlieren; (*terminate*) einstellen; (*from membership roll*) ausschließen; (*paratroopers*) absetzen; **d. it!** laß das!; **d. s.o. a line** j-m ein paar Zeilen schreiben ‖ *intr* fallen; (*drip*) tropfen; (*said of prices, temperature*) sinken, fallen; (*keel over*) umfallen; (*said of a curtain*) niedergehen; **d. behind** zurück-

fallen; **d. dead!** (sl) laß dich begraben!; **d. in on s.o.** auf e-n Sprung bei j-m vorbeikommen; **d. off to sleep** einschlafen; **d. out** sich zurückziehen; (sport) ausscheiden; **d. out of school** von der Schule abgehen
drop′ ar′ea *s* (aer) Abwurfraum *m*
drop′ cur′tain *s* (bemalter) Vorhang *m*
drop′ ham′mer *s* Fallhammer *m*
drop′-leaf ta′ble *s* Tisch *m* mit herunterklappbaren Flügeln
drop′light′ *s* Hängelampe *f*
drop′out′ *s* Gescheiterte *mf;* (educ) Abgänger –in *mf*
dropper [′drapər] *s* (med) Tropfer *m*
drop′ping *adj* (*prices*) rückgängig ‖ *s* (*of bombs, supplies*) Abwurf *m;* **droppings** tierischer Kot *m*
dropsy [′drapsi] *s* Wassersucht *f*
drop′ ta′ble *s* Klapptisch *m*
dross [dros] *s* (*slag*) Schlacke *f;* (*waste*) Abfall *m*
drought [draut] *s* Dürre *f*
drove [drov] *s* Herde *f*
drown [draun] *tr* (& fig) ertränken; **d. out** übertönen ‖ *intr* ertrinken
drowse [drauz] *intr* dösen
drowsiness [′drauzɪnɪs] *s* Schläfrigkeit *f*
drowsy [′drauzi] *adj* schläfrig, dösig
drub [drʌb] *v* (*pret & pp* **drubbed;** *ger* **drubbing**) *tr* (*flog*) verprügeln; (sport) entscheidend schlagen
drudge [drʌdʒ] *s* Packesel *m* ‖ *intr* sich placken, schuften
drudgery [′drʌdʒəri] *s* Plackerei *f*
drug [drʌg] *s* Droge *f*, Arznei *f;* (*narcotic*) Betäubungsmittel *n;* (*addictive narcotic*) Rauschgift *n* ‖ *v* (*pret & pp* **drugged;** *ger* **drugging**) *tr* betäuben
drug′ ad′dict *s* Rauschgiftsüchtige *mf*
drug′ addic′tion *s* Rauschgiftsucht *f*
druggist [′drʌgɪst] *s* Apotheker –in *mf*
drug′store′ *s* Apotheke *f*, Drogerie *f*
drug′ traf′fic *s* Rauschgifthandel *m*
druid [′dru·ɪd] *s* Druide *m*
drum [drʌm] *s* (*musical instrument; container*) Trommel *f* ‖ *v* (*pret & pp* **drummed;** *ger* **drumming**) *tr* trommeln; **d. s.th. into s.o.** j-m etw einpauken; **d. the table** auf den Tisch trommeln; **d. up** zusammentrommeln ‖ *intr* trommeln
drum′ and bu′gle corps′ *s* Musikzug *m*
drum′beat′ *s* Trommelschlag *m*
drum′fire′ *s* (mil) Trommelfeuer *n*
drum′head′ *s* Trommelfell *n*
drum′ ma′jor *s* Tambourmajor *m*
drum′ majorette′ *s* Tambourmajorin *f*
drummer [′drʌmər] *s* Trommler –in *mf*
drum′stick′ *s* Trommelschlegel *m;* (culin) Unterschenkel *m*
drunk [drʌŋk] *adj* betrunken ‖ *s* Säufer –in *mf*
drunkard [′drʌŋkərd] *s* Trunkenbold *m*
drunken [′drʌŋkən] *adj* betrunken
dry [draɪ] *adj* trocken; (*boring*) trokken; (*wine*) herb; (*thirsty*) durstig; (*rainless*) regenarm; (*wood*) dürr ‖ *v* (*pret & pp* –dried) *tr* (ab)trocknen;

(*e.g.*, *fruit*) dörren; **dry off** abtrocknen; **dry out** austrocknen; **dry up** austrocknen; (fig) erschöpfen || *intr* trocknen; **dry out** austrocknen; **dry up** vertrocknen; (*said of grass, flowers*) verdorren; (fig) versiegen; (*keep quiet*) (sl) die Klappe halten

dry′ bat′tery *s* Trockenbatterie *f*
dry′ cell′ *s* Tockenelement *n*
dry′-clean′ *tr* (*chemically*) reinigen
dry′ clean′er's *s* Reinigungsanstalt *f*
dry′ clean′ing *s* chemische Reinigung *f*
dry′ dock′ *s* Trockendock *n*
dry′-eyed′ *adj* ungerührt
dry′ goods′ *spl* Schnittwaren *pl*
dry′ ice′ *s* Trockeneis *n*
dry′ land′ *s* fester Boden *m*
dry′ meas′ure *s* Trockenmaß *n*
dryness ['draɪnɪs] *s* Trockenheit *f*, Dürre *f*; (fig) Nüchternheit *f*
dry′ nurse′ *s* Säuglingsschwester *f*
dry′ rot′ *s* Trockenfäule *f*
dry′ run′ *s* Vorübung *f*; (*test run*) Probelauf *m*; (*with blank ammunition*) Zielübung *f*
dry′ sea′son *s* Trockenzeit *f*
dual ['d(j)u·əl] *adj* Zwei–, doppelt; (tech) Doppel–
dualism ['d(j)u·ə‚lɪzəm] *s* Dualismus *m*
du′al-pur′pose *adj* e–m doppelten Zweck dienend
dub [dʌb] *v* (*pret & pp* **dubbed**; *ger* **dubbing**) *tr* (*nickname*) betiteln; (cin) synchronisieren; (golf) schlecht treffen; (hist) zum Ritter schlagen
dub′bing *s* (cin) Synchronisierung *f*
dubious ['d(j)ubɪ·əs] *adj* zweifelhaft
ducal ['d(j)ukəl] *adj* herzoglich
duchess ['dʌtʃɪs] *s* Herzogin *f*
duchy ['dʌtʃi] *s* Herzogtum *n*
duck [dʌk] *s* Ente *f* || *tr* (*the head*) ducken; (*in water*) (unter)tauchen; (*evade*) sich drücken vor (*dat*) || *intr* ducken; (*go under the surface*) untertauchen
duck′ing *s*—**give s.o. a d.** j–n untertauchen
duck′ pond′ *s* Ententeich *m*
duck′ soup′ *s* (sl) Kinderspiel *n*
ducky ['dʌki] *adj* (coll) nett, lieb
duct [dʌkt] *s* Rohr *n*, Kanal *m*, Leitung *f*; (anat, elec) Kanal *m*
duct′less gland′ ['dʌktlɪs] *s* endokrine Drüse *f*
duct′work′ *s* Rohrleitungen *pl*
dud [dʌd] *s* (sl & mil) Versager *m*, Blindgänger *m*; **duds** (coll) Klamotten *pl*
dude [d(j)ud] *s* (*dandy*) Geck *m*
dude′ ranch′ *s* Vergnügungsfarm *f*
due [d(j)u] *adj* (*payment*; *bus*, *train*) fällig; (*proper*) gehörig; (*consideration*) reiflich; **be due to** (*as a cause*) beruhen auf (*dat*); (*said of an honor*) gebühren (*dat*); (*said of money*) zustehen (*dat*); **be due to** (*inf*) sollen, müssen; **in due course** im gegebenen Moment; **in due time** zur rechten Zeit || *adv* (naut) genau || *s*—**dues** Beitrag *m*; **get one's due** nach Verdienst behandelt werden; **give every-**

one his due jedem geben, was ihm gebührt
due′ date′ *s* (*of a payment*) Termin *m*
duel ['d(j)u·əl] *s* Duell *n*; **fight a d.** sich duellieren || *v* (*pret & pp* **duel[l]ed**; *ger* **duel[l]ing**) *intr* sich duellieren
dues-paying ['d(j)uz‚pe·ɪŋ] *adj* beitragzahlend
duet [d(j)u'ɛt] *s* Duett *n*
due′ to′ *prep* wegen (*genit*)
duf′fle bag′ ['dʌfəl] *s* (mil) Kleidersack *m*
dug′out′ *s* (*boat*) Einbaum *m*; (baseball, mil) Unterstand *m*
duke [d(j)uk] *s* Herzog *m*
dukedom ['d(j)ukdəm] *s* Herzogtum *n*
dull [dʌl] *adj* (*not sharp*) stumpf; (*pain*) dumpf; (*not shining*) glanzlos, matt; (*uninteresting*) nüchtern, geistlos; (*stupid*) stumpfsinnig; (com) flau || *tr* stumpf machen; (fig) abstumpfen || *intr* stumpf werden; (fig) abstumpfen
dullard ['dʌlərd] *s* Dummkopf *m*
dullness ['dʌlnɪs] *s* (*of a blade*) Stumpfheit *f*; (*of color*) Mattheit *f*; (*of a speech, etc.*) Stumpfsinn *m*
duly ['d(j)uli] *adv* ordnungsgemäß
dumb [dʌmb] *adj* stumm; (*stupid*) dumm || *adv*—**play d.** sich unwissend stellen
dumb′bell′ *s* Hantel *f*; (sl) Dummkopf *m*
dumbstruck ['dʌm‚strʌk] *adj* wie auf den Mund geschlagen
dumb′ wait′er *s* (*elevator*) Speiseaufzug *m*; (*serving table*) Serviertisch *m*
dumdum ['dʌm‚dʌm] *s* Dumdumgeschoß *n*
dumfound ['dʌm‚faund] *tr* verblüffen
dummy ['dʌmi] *adj* (*not real*) Schein–; (mil) blind, Übungs– || *s* (*representation for display*) Attrappe *f*; (*clothes form*) Schneiderpuppe *f*; (*doll*) Ölgötze *m*; (cards) Strohmann *m*; (mil) Übungspatrone *f*; (typ) Blindband *m*
dump [dʌmp] *s* (*trash heap*) Schuttabladeplatz *m*; (sl) Bude *f*; (mil) Lager *n*; **be down in the dumps** (coll) Trübsal blasen || *tr* (aus)kippen; (*fling down*) hinplumpsen; (*garbage*) abladen; (com) verschleudern; **be dumped** (*be fired*) entlassen werden; **no dumping** (public sign) Schuttabladen verboten
dumpling ['dʌmplɪŋ] *s* Kloß *m*, Knödel *m*
dump′ truck′ *s* Kipper *m*
dumpy ['dʌmpi] *adj* rundlich
dun [dʌn] *adj* schwarzbraun || *v* (*pret & pp* **dunned**; *ger* **dunning**) *tr* drängen
dunce [dʌns] *s* Schwachkopf *m*
dunce′ cap′ *s* Narrenkappe *f*
dune [d(j)un] *s* Düne *f*
dung [dʌŋ] *s* Dung *m*, Mist *m* || *tr* düngen
dungarees [‚dʌŋgə'riz] *spl* Drillichhose *f*, Drillichanzug *m*
dungeon ['dʌndʒən] *s* Verlies *n*; (hist) Bergfried *m*

dung'hill' s Düngerhaufen m
dunk [dʌŋk] tr eintunken
duo ['d(j)u·o] s (duet) Duett n; (a pair) Duo n
duode·num [͵d(j)u·ə'dinəm] s (–na [nə]) Zwölffingerdarm m
dupe [d(j)up] s Düpierte mf ‖ tr düpieren, übertölpeln
duplex ['d(j)uplɛks] s Doppelhaus n
duplicate ['d(j)uplɪkɪt] adj Duplikat–; (parts) Ersatz–; **d. key** Nachschlüssel m ‖ s Duplikat n, Abschrift f; **in d.** abschriftlich ‖ ['d(j)uplɪ͵ket] tr (make a copy of) kopieren; (make many copies of) vervielfältigen; (reproduce by writing) abschreiben; (repeat) wiederholen; (perform again) nachmachen
duplication [͵d(j)uplɪ'keʃən] s Vervielfältigung f
duplicator ['d(j)uplɪ͵ketər] s Vervielfältigungsapparat m
duplicity [d(j)u'plɪsɪti] s Duplizität f
durable ['d(j)urəbəl] adj dauerhaft
duration [d(j)u're/ən] s Dauer f
duress ['d(j)urɛs] s (jur) Nötigung f
during ['d(j)urɪŋ] prep während (genit), bei (dat); **d. the meal** bei Tisch; **d. the day** tagsüber
dusk [dʌsk] s Abenddämmerung f
dust [dʌst] s Staub m; **cover with d.** bestauben; **make d.** stauben ‖ tr (free of dust) abstauben; (sprinkle, spray with insecticides) bestäuben
dust' bowl' s Staubsturmgebiet n
dust' cloth' s Staubtuch n
dust' collec'tor s Staubfänger m
duster ['dʌstər] s (feather duster) Staubwedel m; (for insecticides) Zerstäuber m
dust'ing pow'der s Streupulver n
dust' jac'ket s Schutzumschlag m
dust' mop' s Mop m
dust'pan' s Kehrichtschaufel f
dust'proof' adj staubdicht
dust' rag' s Staublappen m
dusty ['dʌsti] adj staubig
Dutch [dʌtʃ] adj niederländisch; **go D.** (coll) getrennt bezahlen ‖ s (language) Niederländisch n; **in D.** (coll)

in der Patsche; **the D.** die Niederländer
Dutch'man s (–men) Niederländer m
Dutch' treat' s (coll) Beisammensein n bei getrennter Kasse
dutiable ['d(j)utɪ·əbəl] adj steuerpflichtig
dutiful ['d(j)utɪfəl] adj pflichtgetreu
duty ['d(j)uti] s (to) Pflicht f (gegenüber dat); (service) Dienst m; (task) Aufgabe f; (tax) Zoll m, Abgabe f; **be in d. bound to** (inf) pflichtgemäß müssen (inf); **do d. as** (said of a thing) dienen als; (said of a person) Dienst tun als; **off d.** außer Dienst, dienstfrei; **on. d.** im Dienst; **pay d. on** verzollen
du'ty-free' adj zollfrei
du'ty ros'ter s (mil) Diensteinteilung f
dwarf [dwɔrf] adj zwergenhaft, Zwerg– ‖ s Zwerg m ‖ tr (stunt) in der Entwicklung behindern; (fig) in den Schatten stellen
dwell [dwɛl] v (pret & pp **dwelled** & **dwelt** [dwɛlt]) intr wohnen; **d. on** verweilen bei
dwell'ing s Wohnung f
dwell'ing house' s Wohnhaus n
dwindle ['dwɪndəl] intr schwinden, abnehmen; **d. away** dahinschwinden
dye [daɪ] s Farbe f ‖ v (pret & pp **dyed**; ger **dyeing**) tr färben
dyed'-in-the-wool' adj (fig) in der Wolle gefärbt
dye'ing s Färben n
dyer ['daɪ·ər] s Färber –in mf
dy'ing adj (person) sterbend; (words) letzte ‖ s Sterben n
dynamic [daɪ'næmɪk] adj dynamisch ‖ **dynamics** s Dynamik f; **dynamics** spl (fig) Triebkraft f
dynamite ['daɪnə͵maɪt] s Dynamit n ‖ tr sprengen
dyna·mo ['daɪnə͵mo] s (–mos) Dynamo m
dynastic [daɪ'næstɪk] adj dynastisch
dynasty ['daɪnəsti] s Dynastie f
dysentery ['dɪsən͵teri] s Ruhr f
dyspepsia [dɪs'pɛpsɪ·ə] s Verdauungsstörung f

E

E, e [i] s fünfter Buchstabe des englischen Alphabets; (mus) E n; **E flat** Es n; **E sharp** Eis n
each [itʃ] indef adj jeder; **e. and every** jeder einzelne ‖ adv je, pro Person, pro Stück ‖ indef pron jeder; **e. other** einander, sich
eager ['igər] adj eifrig; **e. for** begierig nach; **e. to** (inf) begierig zu (inf)
ea'ger bea'ver s (coll) Streber –in mf
eagerness ['igərnɪs] s Eifer m
eagle ['igəl] s Adler m
ea'gle-eyed' adj adleräugig
ear [ɪr] s Ohr n; (of corn, wheat) Ähre f; (fig) Gehör n; **be all ears**

ganz Ohr sein; **bend s.o.'s ears** (sl) j–m die Ohren vollreden; **be up to one's ears in** bis über die Ohren stecken in (dat); **by ear** nach Gehör; **ear for music** musikalisches Gehör n; **fall on deaf ears** kein Gehör finden; **in one ear and out the other** zu e–m Ohr hinein und zum anderen hinaus; **turn a deaf ear to** taub sein gegen
ear'ache' s Ohrenschmerzen pl
ear'drops' spl (med) Ohrentropfen pl
ear'drum' s Trommelfell n
earl [ʌrl] s Graf m
ear'lobe' s Ohrläppchen n

early ['ʌrli] *adj* früh; (*reply*) baldig; (*far back in time*) Früh–; **at the earliest possible moment** baldigst; **at your earliest convenience** bei erster Gelegenheit; **be too e.** sich verfrühen || *adv* früh, frühzeitig; (*too soon*) zu früh; **as e. as** schon

ear'ly bird' *s* Frühaufsteher –in *mf*

ear'ly ris'er *s* Frühaufsteher –in *mf*

ear'ly warn'ing sys'tem *s* Vorwarnungssystem *n*

ear'mark' *s* (fig) Kennzeichen *n* || *tr* (*mark out*) kennzeichnen; (*e.g., funds*) (**for**) bestimmen (für)

ear'muffs' *spl* Ohrenschützer *m*

earn [ʌrn] *tr* (*money*) verdienen; (*a reputation*) sich [*dat*] erwerben; (*interest*) einbringen

earnest ['ʌrnɪst] *adj* ernst, ernsthaft || *s*—**are you in e.?** ist das Ihr Ernst?; **be in e. about** es ernst meinen mit; **in e.** im Ernst

ear'phone' *s* Kopfhörer *m*

ear'piece' *s* (*earphone*) Hörer *m;* (*of eyeglasses*) Bügel *m*

ear'ring' *s* Ohrring *m*

ear'shot' *s*—**within e.** in Hörweite

ear'split'ting *adj* ohrenbetäubend

earth [ʌrθ] *s* Erde *f;* **come down to e.** auf den Boden der Wirklichkeit zurückkehren; **on e.** (coll) in aller Welt

earthen ['ʌrθən] *adj* irden

earth'enware' *s* Tonwaren *pl*

earthly ['ʌrθli] *adj* irdisch; **be of no e. use** völlig unnütz sein; **e. possessions** Glücksgüter *pl*

earth'quake' *s* Erdbeben *n*

earth'shak'ing *adj* welterschütternd

earth'work' *s* Schanze *f*

earth'worm' *s* Regenwurm *m*

earthy ['ʌrθi] *adj* erdig; (fig) deftig

ear'wax' *s* Ohrenschmalz *n*

ease [iz] *s* (*facility*) Leichtigkeit *f;* (*comfort*) Bequemlichkeit *f;* (*informality*) Zwanglosigkeit *f;* **at e.!** (mil) rührt euch!; **feel at e. with s.o.** sich in j–s Gegenwart wohl fühlen; **put at e.** beruhigen; **with e.** mühelos || *tr* (*work*) erleichtern; (*pain*) lindern; (*move carefully*) lavieren; **e. out** (*of a job*) hinausmanövrieren || *intr*—**e. up** nachlassen; **e. up on** (*work*) es sich ⌈*dat*⌉ leichter machen mit

easel ['izəl] *s* Staffelei *f*

easement ['izmənt] *s* (jur) Dienstbarkeit *f*

easily ['izəli] *adv* leicht, mühelos; **e. satisfied** genügsam

easiness ['izɪnɪs] *s* Leichtigkeit *f*

east [ist] *adj* Ost–, östlich || *adv* ostwärts, nach Osten; **e. of** östlich von || *s* Osten *m;* **the East** der Osten

east'bound' *adj* nach Osten fahrend

Easter ['istər] *adj* Oster– || *s* Ostern *n & pl*

easterly ['istərli] *adj* österlich

eastern ['istərn] *adj* Ost–

East'ertide' *s* Osterzeit *f*

East'-Ger'man mark' *s* Ostmark *f*

eastward ['istwərd] *adv* ostwärts

easy ['izi] *adj* leicht; (*terms*) günstig; (*virtue*) locker; (*pace*) gemächlich; **e. on the eye** knusprig; **e. to digest**

leichtverdaulich; **have an e. time of it** leichtes Spiel haben; **it's e. for you to talk** du hast gut reden!; **make e.** erleichtern || *adv*—**e. come, e. go** wie gewonnen, so zerronnen; **get off e.** gnädig davonkommen; **take it e.** (*relax*) es sich [*dat*] leicht machen; **take on'e time**) sich [*dat*] Zeit lassen; (*in parting*) mach's gut! (*remain calm*) reg dich nicht auf!; **take it e. on** (*a person*) schonend umgehen mit; (*a thing*) sparsam umgehen mit

eas'y chair' *s* Lehnsessel *m*

eas'ygo'ing *adj* ungeniert, ungezwungen

eas'y mark' *s* (coll) leichte Beute *f*

eat [it] *s*—**eats** *pl* (coll) Essen *n* || *v* (*pret* **ate** [et]; *pp* **eaten** ['itən]) *tr* essen; (*said of animals*) fressen; **eat away** zerfressen; **eat one's fill** sich satt essen; **eat one's heart out** sich in Kummer verzehren; **eat one's words** das Gesagte zurücknehmen; **eat up** aufessen; **what's eating him?** was hat er denn? || *intr* essen; **eat out** auswärts essen

eatable ['itəbəl] *adj* eßbar

eaves [ivz] *spl* Dachrinne *f,* Traufe *f*

eaves'drop' *v* (*pret & pp* –**dropped;** *ger* –**dropping**) *intr* horchen; **e. on** belauschen

eaves'drop'per *s* Horcher –in *mf*

ebb [eb] *s* Ebbe *f;* **at a low ebb** sehr heruntergekommen || *intr* ebben; (fig) nachlassen

ebb' and flow' *s* Ebbe und Flut *f*

ebb' tide' *s* Ebbe *f*

ebony ['ɛbəni] *s* Ebenholz *n*

ebullient [ɪ'bʌljənt] *adj* überschwenglich, hochbegeistert

eccentric [ɛk'sɛntrɪk] *adj* (& fig) exzentrisch || *s* Sonderling *m,* Kauz *m;* (mach) Exzenter *m*

eccentricity [ˌɛksɛn'trɪsɪti] *s* Verschrobenheit *f,* Tick *m*

ecclesiastic [ɪˌklizɪ'æstɪk] *adj* kirchlich; (*law*) Kirchen– || *s* Geistlicher *m*

echelon ['ɛʃəˌlɑn] *s* (*level*) Befehlsebene *f;* (*group occupying a particular level*) Stabsführung *f;* (*flight formation*) Staffel *f;* **in echelons** staffelförmig || *tr* staffeln

ech·o ['ɛko] *s* (–**oes**) Echo *n* || *tr* (*sounds*) zurückwerfen; (fig) nachsprechen || *intr* widerhallen, echoen

éclair [e'klɛr] *s* Eclair *n*

eclectic [ɛk'lɛktɪk] *adj* eklektisch || *s* Eklektiker –in *mf*

eclipse [ɪ'klɪps] *s* Verfinsterung *f;* **go into e.** sich verfinstern; **in e.** im Schwinden || *tr* verfinstern; (fig) in den Schatten stellen

eclogue ['ɛklɔg] *s* Ekloge *f*

ecological [ˌɛkə'lɑdʒɪkəl] *adj* ökologisch

ecology [ɪ'kɑlədʒi] *s* Ökologie *f*

economic [ˌikə'nɑmɪk], [ˌɛkə'nɑmɪk] *adj* wirtschaftlich, Wirtschafts–

economical [ˌikə'nɑmɪkəl], [ˌɛkə'nɑmɪkəl] *adj* sparsam

economics [ˌikə'nɑmɪks], [ˌɛkə'nɑmɪks] *s* Wirtschaftswissenschaften *pl*

economist [ɪˈkɑnəmɪst] *s* Volkswirt-schaftler –in *mf*
economize [ɪˈkɑnəˌmaɪz] *intr* sparen
economy [ɪˈkɑnəmi] *s* Wirtschaft *f;* *(thriftiness)* Sparsamkeit *f; (a sav-ing)* Ersparnis *f*
ecstasy [ˈɛkstəsi] *s* Verzückung *f;* **go into e.** in Verzückung geraten
ecstatic [ɛkˈstætɪk] *adj* verzückt
ecumenic(al) [ˌɛkjəˈmɛnɪk(əl)] *adj* ökumenisch
eczema [ɛgˈzimə] *s* Ausschlag *m*
ed·dy [ˈɛdi] *s* Strudel *m* ‖ *v (pret & pp –died) intr* strudeln
edelweiss [ˈedəlˌvaɪs] *s* Edelweiß *n*
edge [ɛdʒ] *s (of a knife)* Schneide *f; (of a forest, town, water, road)* Rand *m; (e.g., of a table)* Kante *f; (keen-ness)* Schärfe *f;* (bb) Schnitt *m;* **have an e. on s.o.** den Vorteil gegenüber j–m haben; **on e.** *(said of a person or teeth)* kribbelig; *(said of nerves)* aufs äußerste gespannt; **take the e. off** abstumpfen; (fig) die Schärfe nehmen *(dat)* ‖ *tr (a lawn)* beschnei-den; *(put a border on)* einfassen; **e. out** (sport) knapp schlagen ‖ *intr* —**e. forward** langsam vorrücken
edge'wise' *adv*—**not get a word in e.** nicht zu Worte kommen können
edg'ing *s* Umrandung *f,* Besatz *m*
edgy [ˈɛdʒi] *adj* kribbelig
edible [ˈɛdɪbəl] *adj* eßbar, genießbar
edict [ˈidɪkt] *s* Edikt *n,* Erlaß *m*
edification [ˌɛdɪfɪˈkeʃən] *s* Erbauung *f*
edifice [ˈɛdɪfɪs] *s* Bauwerk *n,* Ge-bäude *n*
edi·fy [ˈɛdɪˌfaɪ] *v (pret & pp –fied) tr* erbauen; **be edified by** sich er-bauen an *(dat)*
ed'ifying *adj* erbaulich
edit [ˈɛdɪt] *tr (a book)* herausgeben; *(a newspaper)* redigieren; (cin) schneiden
edition [ɛˈdɪʃən] *s* Ausgabe *f*
editor [ˈɛdɪtər] *s (of a newspaper or magazine)* Redakteur –in *mf; (of a book)* Herausgeber –in *mf; (of edi-torials)* Leitartikler –in *mf;* (cin) Schnittmeister –in *mf*
editorial [ˌɛdɪˈtori·əl] *adj* redaktio-nell, Redaktions– ‖ *s* Leitartikel *m*
editorialize [ˌɛdɪˈtori·əˌlaɪz] *intr* (on) seine Meinung zum Ausdruck bringen (über *acc); (report with a slant)* ten-denziös berichten
edito'rial of'fice *s* Redaktion *f*
edito'rial staff' *s* Redaktion *f*
ed'itor in chief' *s* Chefredakteur –in *mf*
educate [ˈɛdʒʊˌket] *tr* bilden, erziehen
education [ˌɛdʒʊˈkeʃən] *s* Bildung *f,* Erziehung *f;* (educ) Pädagogik *f*
educational [ˌɛdʒʊˈkeʃənəl] *adj* Bil-dungs–; **e. background** Vorbildung *f;* **e. film** Lehrfilm *m;* **e. institution** Lehranstalt *f*
educator [ˈɛdʒʊˌketər] *s* Erzieher –in *mf*
educe [ɪˈd(j)us] *tr* hervorholen
eel [il] *s* Aal *m*
eerie, eery [ˈɪri] *adj* unheimlich

efface [ɪˈfes] *tr* austilgen; **e. oneself** sich zurückhalten
effect [ɪˈfɛkt] *s* (on) Wirkung *f* (auf *acc); (consequence)* (on) Auswirkung *f* (auf *acc); (impression)* Eindruck *m;* **effects** *(movable property)* Habe *f;* **for e.** zum Effekt; **go into e.** in Kraft treten; **have an e. on** wirken auf *(acc);* **in e.** praktisch; **put into e.** in Kraft setzen; **take e.** zur Geltung kommen; **to the e. that** des Inhalts, daß ‖ *tr* bewirken
effective [ɪˈfɛktɪv] *adj* wirkungsvoll; *(actual)* effektiv; **e. against** wirksam gegen; **e. date** Tag *m* des Inkraft-tretens; **e. from** mit Wirkung von; **e. immediately** mit sofortiger Wir-kung; **e. strength** (mil) Iststärke *f*
effectual [ɪˈfɛktʃʊ·əl] *adj* wirksam
effectuate [ɪˈfɛktʃʊˌet] *tr* bewirken
effeminacy [ɪˈfɛmɪnəsi] *s* Verweichli-chung *f*
effeminate [ɪˈfɛmɪnɪt] *adj* verweich-licht
effervesce [ˌɛfərˈvɛs] *intr* aufbrausen
effervescence [ˌɛfərˈvɛsəns] *s* Aufbrau-sen *n,* Moussieren *n*
effervescent [ˌɛfərˈvɛsənt] *adj (liquid; personality)* aufbrausend
effete [ɪˈfit] *adj* entkräftet
efficacious [ˌɛfɪˈkeʃəs] *adj* wirksam
efficacy [ˈɛfɪkəsi] *s* Wirksamkeit *f,* Wirkungskraft *f*
efficiency [ɪˈfɪʃənsi] *s* Tüchtigkeit *f;* (phys) Nutzeffekt *m;* (tech) Lei-stungsfähigkeit *f*
efficient [ɪˈfɪʃənt] *adj* tüchtig; (tech) leistungsfähig
effigy [ˈɛfɪdʒi] *s* Abbild *n;* **hang in e.** symbolisch hängen
effort [ˈɛfərt] *s (exertion)* Mühe *f;* *(attempt)* Bestreben *n;* **efforts** Be-mühungen *pl;* **make an honest e. to** *(inf)* sich redlich bemühen zu *(inf)*
effortless [ˈɛfərtlɪs] *adj* mühelos
effrontery [ɪˈfrʌntəri] *s* Frechheit *f,* Unverschämtheit *f*
effusion [ɪˈfjuʒən] *s* Erguß *m*
effusive [ɪˈfjusɪv] *adj* überschweng-lich
egg [ɛg] *s* Ei *n;* **bad egg** (sl) übler Geselle *m;* **good egg** (sl) feiner Kerl *m;* **lay an egg** ein Ei legen; (fig) e–e völlige Niete sein ‖ *tr*—**egg on** an-stacheln
egg'beat'er *s* Schneeschläger *m*
egg'cup' *s* Eierbecher *m*
egg'head' *s* (coll) Intelligenzler –in *mf*
eggnog [ˈɛgˌnɑg] *s* Eierlikör *m,* Egg-Nog *m*
egg'plant' *s* Eierfrucht *f*
egg'shell' *s* Eierschale *f*
egg' white' *s* Eiweiß *n*
egg' yolk' *s* Eigelb *n,* Eidotter *m*
ego [ˈigo] *s* Ego *n,* Ich *n;* (coll) Ich-sucht *f*
egocentric [ˌigoˈsɛntrɪk] *adj* egozen-trisch
egoism [ˈigoˌɪzəm] *s* Selbstsucht *f*
egoist [ˈigo·ɪst] *s* Egoist *m*
egotism [ˈigoˌtɪzəm] *s* Ichsucht *f*
egotistic(al) [ˌigoˈtɪstɪk(əl)] *adj* ego-tistisch, geltungsbedürtig

egregious [ɪ'gridʒəs] *adj* unerhört
egress ['igres] *s* Ausgang *m*
Egypt ['idʒɪpt] *s* Ägypten *n*
Egyptian [ɪ'dʒɪp/ən] *adj* ägyptisch ||
s Ägypter –in *mf;* (*language*) Ägyptisch *n*
eiderdown ['aɪdər͵daʊn] *s* Eiderdaunen *pl;* (*cover*) Daunenbett *n*
eight [et] *adj & pron* acht || *s* Acht *f*
eight'ball' *s*—**be behind the e.** (sl) in der Klemme sitzen
eighteen ['et'tin] *adj & pron* achtzehn || *s* Achtzehn *f*
eighteenth ['et'tinθ] *adj* achtzehnte ||
s (*fraction*) Achtzehntel *n;* **the e.**
(*in dates or in a series*) der Achzehnte
eighth [etθ] *adj* achte || *s* (*fraction*) Achtel *n;* **the e.** (*in dates or in a series*) der Achte
eighth' note' *s* (mus) Achtelnote *f*
eightieth ['etɪ·ɪθ] *adj* achtzigste || *s* (*fraction*) Achtzigstel *n;* **the e.** der Achtzigste
eighty ['eti] *adj & pron* achtzig || *s* Achtzig *f;* **the eighties** die achtziger Jahre *pl*
eigh'ty-one' *adj & pron* einundachtzig
either ['iðər], ['aɪðər] *adj*—**e. one is correct** beides ist richtig; **e. way** auf die e-e oder andere Art; **in e. case** in jedem der beiden Fälle; **on e. side** auf beiden Seiten || *adv*—**not...e.** auch nicht || *pron* einer von beiden; **e. of you** einer von euch beiden; **I didn't see e.** ich habe beide nicht gesehen || *conj*—**e....or** entweder... oder
ejaculate [ɪ'dʒækjə͵let] *tr* ausstoßen; (physiol) ejakulieren
eject [ɪ'dʒɛkt] *tr* ausstoßen; (*from a property*) (**from**) hinauswerfen (aus)
ejection [ɪ'dʒɛk/ən] *s* Ausstoßung *f*
ejec'tion seat' *s* Schleudersitz *m*
eke [ik] *tr*—**eke out a living** das Leben fristen
el [ɛl] *s* (coll) Hochbahn *f*
elaborate [ɪ'læbərɪt] *adj* (*detailed*) weitläufig; (*ornate*) kunstvoll; (*idea*) compliziert || [ɪ'læbə͵ret] *tr* ausarbeiten || *intr*—**e. on** sich verbreiten über (*acc*)
elaboration [ɪ͵læbə'reʃən] *s* Ausarbeitung *f*
elapse [ɪ'læps] *intr* verrinnen
elastic [ɪ'læstɪk] *adj* elastisch; (*conscience*) weit || *s* Gummiband *n*
elasticity [͵ɪlæs'tɪsɪti] *s* Elastizität *f*
elated [ɪ'letɪd] *adj* freudig erregt
elation [ɪ'leʃən] *s* Hochgefühl *n*
elbow ['ɛlbo] *s* Ellbogen *m;* (*of a pipe*) Rohrknie *n;* **at one's e.** bei der Hand; **rub elbows with s.o.** mit j-m in nähere Berührung kommen || *tr*—**e. one's way** sich [*dat*] seinen Weg bahnen
el'bow grease' *s* (coll) Knochenschmalz *n*
el'bowroom' *s* Spielraum *m*
elder ['ɛldər] *adj* älter || *s* Ältere *mf;* (bot) Holunder *m;* (eccl) Kirchenälteste *mf*
el'derber'ry *s* Holunderbeere *f*

elderly ['ɛldərli] *adj* ältlich
el'der states'man *s* profilierter Staatsmann *m*
eldest ['ɛldɪst] *adj* älteste
elect [ɪ'lɛkt] *adj* erlesen; (*elected but not yet installed*) zukünftig; (relig) auserwählt || **the e.** *spl* die Auserwählten *pl* || *tr* wählen; **e. s.o. president** j-n zum Präsidenten wählen
election [ɪ'lɛk/ən] *adj* Wahl– || *s* Wahl *f*
elec'tion campaign' *s* Wahlkampf *m*
elec'tion day' *s* Wahltag *m*
electioneer [ɪ͵lɛk/ə'nɪr] *intr* Stimmen werben
elective [ɪ'lɛktɪv] *adj* (educ) wahlfrei; (pol) Wahl– || *s* (educ) Wahlfach *n*
electoral [ɪ'lɛktərəl] *adj* Wahl–
elec'toral col'lege *s* Wahlmänner *pl*
electorate [ɪ'lɛktərɪt] *s* Wählerschaft *f*
electric(al) [ɪ'lɛktrɪk(əl)] *adj* elektrisch, Elektro–
elec'trical appli'ance *s* Elektrogerät *n*
elec'trical engineer' *s* Elektroingenieur *m*
elec'trical engineer'ing *s* Elektrotechnik *f*
elec'tric blan'ket *s* Heizdecke *f*
elec'tric bulb' *s* Glühbirne *f*
elec'tric chair' *s* elektrischer Stuhl *m;* (*penalty*) Hinrichtung *f* auf dem elektrischen Stuhl
elec'tric cir'cuit *s* Stromkreis *m*
elec'tric eel' *s* Zitteraal *m*
elec'tric eye' *s* Photozelle *f*
elec'tric fan' *s* Ventilator *m*
elec'tric fence' *s* elektrisch geladener Drahtzaun *m*
electrician [ɪ͵lɛk'trɪ/ən] *s* Elektriker –in *mf*
electricity [͵ɪlɛk'trɪsɪti] *s* Elektrizität *f;* (*current*) Strom *m*
elec'tric light' *s* elektrisches Licht *n*
elec'tric me'ter *s* Stromzähler *m*
elec'tric saw' *s* Motorsäge *f*
elec'tric shav'er *s* elektrischer Rasierapparat *m*
elec'tric storm' *s* Gewittersturm *m*
elec'tric stove' *s* Elektroherd *m*
electri•fy [ɪ'lɛktrɪ͵faɪ] *v* (*pret & pp* –fied*) *tr* (& fig) elektrisieren; (*a streetcar, railroad*) elektrifizieren
electrocute [ɪ'lɛktrə͵kjut] *tr* durch elektrischen Strom töten; (jur) auf dem elektrischen Stuhl hinrichten
electrode [ɪ'lɛktrod] *s* Elektrode *f*
electrolysis [ɪ͵lɛk'tralɪsɪs] *s* Elektrolyse *f*
electrolyte [ɪ'lɛktrə͵laɪt] *s* Elektrolyt *m*
electromagnet [ɪ͵lɛktrə'mægnət] *s* Elektromagnet *m*
electromagnetic [ɪ͵lɛktrəmæg'nɛtɪk] *adj* elektromagnetisch
electron [ɪ'lɛktran] *s* Elektron *n*
electronic [ɪ͵lɛk'tranɪk] *adj* elektronisch, Elektronen– || **electronics** *s* Elektronik *f*
electron'ic flash' *s* Röhrenblitz *m;* (*device*) Blitzgerät *n*
electronic [ɪ͵lɛk'tranɪk] *adj* elektroplattieren, galvanisieren

electrostatic [ɪ ˌlɛktrə'stætɪk] *adj* elektrostatisch
electrotype [ɪ'lɛktrə ˌtaɪp] *s* Galvano *n* ‖ *tr* galvanoplastisch vervielfältigen
elegance ['ɛlɪgəns] *s* Eleganz *f*
elegant ['ɛlə ˌgənt] *adj* elegant
elegiac [ˌɛlə'dʒaɪ·æk] *adj* elegisch
elegy ['ɛlɪdʒi] *s* Elegie *f*
element ['ɛlɪmənt] *s* (& fig) Element *n; (e.g., of truth)* Körnchen *n*
elementary [ˌɛlɪ'mɛntəri] *adj* elementar, grundlegend
elemen'tary school' *s* Grundschule *f*
elephant ['ɛlɪfənt] *s* Elefant *m*
elevate ['ɛlɪ ˌvet] *tr* erheben, erhöhen
el'evated *adj (eyes)* erhoben; *(style)* erhaben ‖ *s* (coll) Hochbahn *f*
elevation [ˌɛlɪ'veʃən] *s (height)* Höhe *f; (hill)* Anhöhe *f; (above sealevel)* Seehöhe *f; (to the throne)* Erhebung *f;* (archit) Aufriß *m;* (arti) Richthöhe *f;* (astr, relig) Elevation *f*
elevator ['ɛlɪ ˌvetər] *s* Aufzug *m,* Fahrstuhl *m;* (aer) Höhenruder *n;* (agr) Getreidespeicher *m*
el'evator op'erator *s* Fahrstuhlführer –in *mf*
el'evator shaft' *s* Fahrstuhlschacht *m*
eleven [ɪ'lɛvən] *adj & pron* elf ‖ *s* Elf *f*
eleventh [ɪ'lɛvənθ] *adj* elfte ‖ *s (fraction)* Elftel *n; the e.* (in dates and in a series) der Elfte
elev'enth hour' *s*—at the e. (fig) kurz vor Torschluß
elf [ɛlf] *s* (**elves** [ɛlvz]) Elf *m,* Elfe *f*
elicit [ɪ'lɪsɪt] *tr* hervorlocken; *(an answer)* entlocken
elide [ɪ'laɪd] *tr* elidieren
eligible ['ɛlɪdʒɪbəl] *adj* qualifiziert; *(entitled)* berechtigt; *(for office)* wählbar; *(for marriage)* heiratsfähig
el'igible bach'elor *s* Heiratskandidat *m*
eliminate [ɪ'lɪmɪ ˌnet] *tr* ausscheiden; (alg) eliminieren
elimination [ɪ ˌlɪmɪ'neʃən] *s* Ausscheidung *f*
elimina'tion bout' *s* Ausscheidungskampf *m*
elision [ɪ'lɪʒən] *s* Auslassung *f*
elite [e'lit] *adj* Elite– ‖ *s* Elite *f*
elixir [ɪ'lɪksər] *s* Elixier *n*
elk [ɛlk] *s* Elch *m*
ellipse [ɪ'lɪps] *s* (geom) Ellipse *f*
ellip·sis [ɪ'lɪpsɪs] *s* (**–ses** [siz]) (gram) Ellipse *f*
elliptic(al) [ɪ'lɪptɪk(əl)] *adj* elliptisch
elm [ɛlm] *s* Ulme *f*
elocution [ˌɛlə'kjuʃən] *s* (art) Vortragskunst *f; (style)* Vortragsweise *f*
elope [ɪ'lop] *intr* ausreißen
elopement [ɪ'lopmənt] *s* Ausreißen *n*
eloquence ['ɛləkwəns] *s* Beredsamkeit *f*
eloquent ['ɛləkwənt] *adj* beredt
else [ɛls] *adj* sonst; **someone else's house** das Haus e–s anderen; **what e.?** was sonst?; *(in addition)* was noch? ‖ *adv* sonst, anders; **nowhere e.** sonst nirgends; **or e.** sonst, andernfalls; **where e.?** wo sonst?
else'where' *adv (position)* woanders;

(direction) sonstwohin; **from e.** anderswoher
elucidate [ɪ'lusɪ ˌdet] *tr* erläutern
elucidation [ɪ ˌlusɪ'deʃən] *s* Erläuterung *f*
elude [ɪ'lud] *tr* entgehen *(dat)*
elusive [ɪ'lusɪv] *adj* schwer zu fassen; *(memory)* unzuverlässig
emaciated [ɪ'meʃɪ ˌetɪd] *adj* abgezehrt
emanate ['ɛmə ˌnet] *intr*—e. from *(said of gases)* ausströmen aus; *(said of rays)* ausstrahlen aus; (fig) ausgehen von
emancipate [ɪ'mænsɪ ˌpet] *tr* emanzipieren
emasculate [ɪ'mæskjə ˌlet] *tr* (& fig) entmannen
embalm [ɛm'bam] *tr* einbalsamieren
embankment [ɛm'bæŋkmənt] *s* Damm *m*
embar·go [ɛm'bargo] *s* (**–goes**) Sperre *f,* Embargo *n* ‖ *tr* sperren
embark [ɛm'bark] *intr* **(for)** sich einschiffen (nach); **e. upon** sich einlassen auf *(acc)*
embarkation [ˌɛmbar'keʃən] *s* Einschiffung *f*
embarrass [ɛm'bærəs] *tr* in Verlegenheit bringen
embar'rassed *adj* verlegen; **feel e.** sich genieren
embar'rassing *adj* peinlich
embarrassment [ɛm'bærəsmənt] *s* Verlegenheit *f*
embassy ['ɛmbəsi] *s* Botschaft *f*
em·bed [ɛm'bed] *v* *(pret & pp* **–bedded;** *ger* **–bedding)** *tr* einbetten; **e. in concrete** einbetonieren
embellish [ɛm'belɪʃ] *tr* verschönern
embellishment [ɛm'belɪʃmənt] *s* Verschönerung *f*
ember ['ɛmbər] *s* glühende Kohle *f;* **embers** Glut *f*
Em'ber day' *s* Quatember *m*
embezzle [ɛm'bezəl] *tr* unterschlagen
embezzlement [ɛm'bezəlmənt] *s* Unterschlagung *f,* Veruntreuung *f*
embezzler [ɛm'bezlər] *s* Veruntreuer –in *mf*
embitter [ɛm'bɪtər] *tr* verbittern
emblazon [ɛm'blezən] *tr (decorate)* verzieren; *(extol)* verherrlichen; (heral) heraldisch darstellen
emblem ['ɛmbləm] *s* Sinnbild *n*
emblematic(al) [ˌɛmblə'mætɪk(əl)] *adj* sinnbildlich
embodiment [ɛm'badɪmənt] *s* Verkörperung *f*
embod·y [ɛm'badi] *v* *(pret & pp* **–ied)** *tr* verkörpern
embolden [ɛm'boldən] *tr* ermutigen
embolism ['ɛmbə ˌlɪzəm] *s* Embolie *f*
emboss [ɛm'bɔs] *tr* bossieren
embossed' *adj* getrieben
embrace [ɛm'bres] *s* Umarmung *f* ‖ *tr* umarmen; *(include)* umfassen; *(a religion, idea)* annehmen ‖ *intr* sich umarmen
embrasure [ɛm'breʒər] *s* Schießscharte *f*
embroider [ɛm'brɔɪdər] *tr* sticken
embroidery [ɛm'brɔɪdəri] *s* Stickerei *f*
embroi'dery nee'dle *s* Sticknadel *f*

embroil [ɛm'brɔɪl] *tr* verwickeln

embroilment [ɛm'brɔɪlmənt] *s* Verwicklung *f*

embry·o ['ɛmbrɪ,o] *s* (**-os**) Embryo *m*

embryology [,ɛmbrɪ'alədʒi] *s* Embryologie *f*

embryonic [,ɛmbrɪ'anɪk] *adj* embryonal

emend [ɪ'mɛnd] *tr* berichtigen

emendation [,imɛn'deʃən] *s* Berichtigung *f*

emerald ['ɛmərəld] *adj* smaragdgrün ‖ *s* Smaragd *m*

emerge [ɪ'mʌrdʒ] *intr* (*come forth*) hervortreten; (*surface*) auftauchen; (*result*) (**from**) herauskommen (bei)

emergence [ɪ'mʌrdʒəns] *s* Hervortreten *n*; (*surfacing*) Auftauchen *n*

emergency [ɪ'mʌrdʒənsi] *adj* Not- ‖ *s* Notlage *f*; **in case of e.** im Notfall

emeritus [ɪ'mɛrɪtəs] *adj* emeritiert

emersion [ɪ'mʌrʒən] *s* Auftauchen *n*

emery ['ɛməri] *s* Schmirgel *m*

em'ery cloth' *s* Schmirgelleinwand *f*

em'ery wheel' *s* Schmirgelrad *n*

emetic [ɪ'mɛtɪk] *adj* Brech- ‖ *s* Brechmittel *n*

emigrant ['ɛmɪgrənt] *s* Auswanderer –in *mf*

emigrate ['ɛmɪ,gret] *intr* auswandern

emigration [,ɛmɪ'greʃən] *s* Auswanderung *f*

eminence ['ɛmɪnəns] *s* (*height*) Anhöhe *f*; (*fame*) Berühmtheit *f*; **Eminence** (*title of a cardinal*) Eminenz *f*; **rise to e.** zu Ruhm und Würde gelangen

eminent ['ɛmɪnənt] *adj* hervorragend

emissary ['ɛmɪ,sɛri] *s* Abgesandte *mf*

emission [ɪ'mɪʃən] *s* (biol) Erguß *m*; (phys) Ausstrahlung *f*

emis'sion control' *s* Abgasentgiftung *f*

emit [ɪ'mɪt] *v* (*pret & pp* **emitted**; *ger* **emitting**) *tr* von sich geben; (*rays*) ausstrahlen; (*gases*) ausströmen; (*sparks*) sprühen

emolument [ɛ'maljəmənt] *s* Vergütung *f*

emotion [ɪ'moʃən] *s* Gemütsbewegung *f*

emotional [ɪ'moʃənəl] *adj* (*e.g., disorder*) Gemüts-; (*person*) gefühlvoll; (*e.g., sermon*) ergreifend; (*mawkish*) rührselig

emperor ['ɛmpərər] *s* Kaiser *m*

empha·sis ['ɛmfəsɪs] *s* (**-ses** [,siz]) Betonung *f*

emphasize ['ɛmfə,saɪz] *tr* betonen

emphatic [ɛm'fætɪk] *adj* nachdrücklich

emphysema [,ɛmfɪ'simə] *s* Emphysem *n*

empire ['ɛmpaɪr] *s* Reich *n*; (*Roman period*) Kaiserzeit *f*

Em'pire fur'niture *s* Empiremöbel *n*

empiric(al) [ɛm'pɪrɪk(əl)] *adj* erfahrungsmäßig, empirisch

empiricist [ɛm'pɪrɪsɪst] *s* Empiriker –in *mf*

emplacement [ɛm'plesmənt] *s* Stellung *f*

employ [ɛm'plɔɪ] *s* Dienst *m* ‖ *tr* (*hire*) anstellen; (*keep in employ-* *ment*) beschäftigen; (*use*) verwenden; (*troops, police*) einsetzen

employee [ɛm'plɔɪ·i], [,ɛmplɔɪ'i] *s* Arbeitnehmer –in *mf*

employer [ɛm'plɔɪ·ər] *s* Arbeitgeber –in *mf*

employment [ɛm'plɔɪmənt] *s* (*work*) Beschäftigung *f*, Arbeit *f*; (*use*) Verwendung *f*; (*e.g., of troops*) Einsatz *m*; **out of e.** arbeitslos

employ'ment a'gency *s* Arbeitsvermittlung *f*

empower [ɛm'pau·ər] *tr* ermächtigen

empress ['ɛmprɪs] *s* Kaiserin *f*

emptiness ['ɛmptɪnɪs] *s* Leere *f*; (fig) Nichtigkeit *f*

emp·ty ['ɛmpti] *adj* leer; **e. talk** leere Worte *pl*; **on an e. stomach** auf nüchternen Magen ‖ **empties** *spl* Leergut *n* ‖ *v* (*pret & pp* **-tied**) *tr* (aus)leeren ‖ *intr*—**e. into** münden in (*acc*)

emp'ty-hand'ed *adj* mit leeren Händen

emp'ty-head'ed *adj* hohlköpfig

emulate ['ɛmjə,let] *s* nacheifern (*dat*)

emulation [,ɛmjə'leʃən] *s* Nacheiferung *f*

emulator [,ɛmjə'letər] *s* Nacheiferer –in *mf*

emulsi·fy [ɪ'mʌlsɪ,faɪ] *v* (*pret & pp* **-fied**) *tr* emulgieren

emulsion [ɪ'mʌlʃən] *s* Emulsion *f*; (phot) Schicht *f*

enable [ɛn'ebəl] *tr* befähigen

enact [ɛn'ækt] *tr* erlassen

enactment [ɛn'æktmənt] *s* Erlassen *n*

enam·el [ɪ'næməl] *s* Email *n*; (dent) Zahnschmelz *m* ‖ *v* (*pret & pp* **-el[l]ed**; *ger* **-el[l]ing**) *tr* emaillieren

enam'el paint' *s* Emaillack *m*

enam'elware' *s* Emailwaren *pl*

enamored [ɛ'næmərd] *adj*—**be e. of** verliebt sein in (*acc*)

encamp [ɛn'kæmp] *tr* in e–m Lager unterbringen ‖ *intr* lagern, sich lagern

encampment [ɛn'kæmpmənt] *s* (*camping*) Lagern *n*; (*campsite*) Lager *n*

encase [ɛn'kes] *tr* einschließen

enchant [ɛn't ʃænt] *tr* verzaubern; (fig) bezaubern

enchanter [ɛn't ʃæntər] *s* Zauberer –in *mf*

enchant'ing *adj* bezaubernd

enchantment [ɛn't ʃæntmənt] *s* (*state*) Verzauberung *f*; (*cause of enchantment*) Zauber *m*

enchantress [ɛn't ʃæntrɪs] *s* Zauberin *f*

encircle [ɛn'sʌrkəl] *tr* umgeben; (mil) einschließen

encirclement [ɛn'sʌrkəlmənt] *s* (mil) Einschließung *f*

enclave ['ɛnklev] *s* Enklave *f*

enclitic [ɛn'klɪtɪk] *adj* enklitisch ‖ *s* Enklitikon *n*

enclose [ɛn'kloz] *tr* einschließen; (*land*) umzäunen; (*in a letter*) beilegen; **e. in parentheses** einklammern; **please find enclosed** in der Anlage erhalten Sie

enclosure [ɛn'kloʒər] *s* Umzäunung *f*; (*in a letter*) Anlage *f*

encomi·um [ɛn'komɪ·əm] s (–ums & –a [ə]) Lobpreisung f, Enkomion n

encompass [ɛn'kʌmpəs] tr umfassen

encore ['ɑnkor] s (performance) Zugabe f; (recall) Dakaporuf m || interj da capo!; noch einmal!

encounter [ɛn'kaʊntər] s Begegnung f; (hostile meeting) Zusammenstoß m; (mil) Gefecht n || tr begegnen (dat)

encourage [ɛn'kʌrɪdʒ] tr ermutigen

encouragement [ɛn'kʌrɪdʒmənt] s Ermutigung f

encroach [ɛn'krotʃ] intr—e. on übergreifen auf (acc); (rights) beeinträchtigen

encroachment [ɛn'krotʃmənt] s Übergriff m

encrust [ɛn'krʌst] tr überkrusten

encumber [ɛn'kʌmbər] tr belasten; (with debts) verschulden

encumbrance [ɛn'krʌmbrəns] s Belastung f

encyclical [ɛn'sɪklɪkəl] s Enzyklika f

encyclopedia [ɛn,saɪklə'pidɪ·ə] s Enzyklopädie f

encyclopedic [ɛn,saɪklə'pidɪk] adj enzyklopädisch

end [ɛnd] s Ende n; (purpose) Zweck m; (goal) Ziel n; (closing) Schluß m; (outcome) Ausgang m, Ergebnis n; **at the end of one's strength** am Rande seiner Kraft; **come to a bad end** ein schlimmes Ende finden; **come to an end** zu Ende gehen; **end in itself** Selbstzweck m; **gain one's ends** seinen Vorsatz ausführen; **go off the deep end** sich unnötig aufregen; **in the end** schließlich; **make both ends meet** gerade auskommen; **no end of** unendlich viel(e); **on end** hochkant; (without letup) ununterbrochen; **put an end to** ein Ende machen (dat); **that will be the end of me** das überlebe ich nicht; **to no end** vergebens || tr beenden || intr enden; (gram) auslauten; **end in a point** spitz zulaufen; **end up (in)** (coll) landen (in dat); **end up with** beenden mit

end'-all' s Schluß m vom Ganzen

endanger [ɛn'dendʒər] tr gefährden

endear [ɛn'dɪr] tr—e. s.o. to j–n einschmeicheln bei

endear'ing adj gewinnend

endearment [ɛn'dɪrmənt] s Beliebtheit f

endeavor [ɛn'dɛvər] s Bestreben n || intr—e. to (inf) sich bestreben zu (inf), versuchen zu (inf)

endemic [ɛn'dɛmɪk] adj endemisch || s Endemie f, endemische Krankheit f

end'ing s Beendigung f, Abschluß m; (gram) Endung f

endive ['ɛndaɪv] s Endivie f

endless ['ɛndlɪs] adj endlos; **an e. number of** unendlich viele

end'most' adj entfernteste

endocrine ['ɛndo,kraɪn] adj endokrin

endorse [ɛn'dɔrs] tr (confirm) bestätigen; (a check) indossieren

endorsee [,ɛndɔr'si] s Indossat –in mf

endorsement [ɛn'dɔrsmənt] s Indossament n; (approval) Bestätigung f

endorser [ɛn'dɔrsər] s Indossant –in mf; (backer) Hintermann m

endow [ɛn'daʊ] tr (provide with income) dotieren; (with talent) begaben

endowment [ɛn'daʊmənt] s Dotierung f; (talent) Begabung f

endow'ment fund' s Stiftungsvermögen n

endurance [ɛn'd(j)ʊrəns] s Dauer f; (ability to hold out) Ausdauer f

endur'ance test' s Dauerprobe f

endure [ɛn'd(j)ʊr] tr aushalten || intr fortdauern

endur'ing adj dauerhaft

enema ['ɛnəmə] s Einlauf m

enemy ['ɛnəmi] adj feindlich, Feind– || s Feind m; **become enemies** sich verfeinden

energetic [,ɛnər'dʒɛtɪk] adj energisch

energy ['ɛnərdʒi] s Energie f

enervate ['ɛnər,vet] tr entkräften

enfeeble [ɛn'fibəl] tr entkräften

enfilade ['ɛnfɪ,led] s (mil) Flankenfeuer n || tr mit Flankenfeuer bestreichen

enfold [ɛn'fold] tr einhüllen

enforce [ɛn'fɔrs] tr durchsetzen; (obedience) erzwingen

enforcement [ɛn'fɔrsmənt] s Durchsetzung f

enfranchise [ɛn'fræntʃaɪz] tr (admit to citizenship) einbürgern; (give the right to vote to) das Wahlrecht verleihen (dat)

engage [ɛn'gedʒ] tr (hire) anstellen; (reserve) vorbestellen; (attention) fesseln; (gears) einrücken; (one's own troops) einsetzen; (the enemy) angreifen; **be engaged in** beschäftigt sein mit; **e. in** verwickeln in (acc) || intr (mach) (ein)greifen; **e. in** sich einlassen in (acc)

engaged' adj verlobt; **get e. (to)** sich verloben (mit)

engaged' cou'ple s Brautleute pl

engagement [ɛn'gedʒmənt] s (betrothal) Verlobung f; (appointment) Verabredung f; (obligation) Verpflichtung f; (mil) Gefecht n; **have a previous e.** verabredet sein

engage'ment ring' s Verlobungsring m

engag'ing adj gewinnend

engender [ɛn'dʒɛndər] tr hervorbringen

engine ['ɛndʒɪn] s Maschine f; (aer, aut) Motor m; (rr) Lokomotive f

engineer [,ɛndʒə'nɪr] s Ingenieur m, Techniker m; (mil) Pionier m; (rr) Lokomotivführer m; **engineers** (mil) Pioniertruppe f || tr errichten; (fig) bewerkstelligen

engineer'ing s Ingenieurwesen n

engineer'ing school' s Technikum n

en'gine house' s Spritzenhaus n

en'gine room' s Maschinenraum m

England ['ɪŋglənd] s England n

English ['ɪŋglɪʃ] adj englisch || s (spin) Effet n; (language) Englisch n; **in plain E.** unverblümt; **the E.** die Engländer

Eng'lish Chan'nel s Ärmelkanal m

Eng'lish horn' s Englischhorn n

Eng'lish·man s (**-men**) Engländer m

Eng'lish-speak'ing adj englischsprechend

Eng'lish·wom'an s (**-wom'en**) Engländerin f

engraft [ɛn'græft] tr aufpropfen; (fig) einprägen

engrave [ɛn'grev] tr gravieren

engraver [ɛn'grevər] s Graveur m

engrav'ing s Kupferstich m

engross [ɛn'gros] tr in Anspruch nehmen; (a document) mit großen Buchstaben schreiben; **become engrossed in** sich versenken in (acc)

engross'ing adj fesselnd

engulf [ɛn'gʌlf] tr (fig) verschlingen

enhance [ɛn'hæns] tr erhöhen; **be enhanced** sich erhöhen

enhancement [ɛn'hænsmənt] s Erhöhung f

enigma [ɪ'nɪgmə] s Rätsel n

enigmatic(al) [ˌɪnɪg'mætɪk(əl)] adj rätselhaft

enjoin [ɛn'dʒɔɪn] tr (forbid) (**from** ger) verbieten (dat) (zu inf); **e. s.o. to** (inf) j–m auferlegen zu (inf)

enjoy [ɛn'dʒɔɪ] tr (take pleasure in) Gefallen finden an (dat); (have the advantage of) genießen, sich erfreuen (genit); **e. doing s.th.** gern etw tun; **e. oneself** sich gut unterhalten; **e. to the full** auskosten; **I e. the wine** mir schmeckt der Wein

enjoyable [ɛn'dʒɔɪ·əbəl] adj erfreulich; **thoroughly e.** genußreich

enjoyment [ɛn'dʒɔɪmənt] s Genuß m

enkindle [ɛn'kɪndəl] tr entzünden

enlarge [ɛn'lardʒ] tr vergrößern || intr sich vergrößern; **e. upon** näher eingehen auf (acc)

enlargement [ɛn'lardʒmənt] s Vergrößerung f

enlarger [ɛn'lardʒər] s (phot) Vergrößerungsapparat m

enlighten [ɛn'laɪtən] tr aufklären

enlightenment [ɛn'laɪtənmənt] s (act) Aufklärung f; (state) Aufgeklärtheit f

enlist [ɛn'lɪst] tr (services) in Anspruch nehmen; (mil) anwerben; **e. s.o. in a cause** j–n für e–e Sache gewinnen || intr (**in**) sich freiwillig melden (zu)

enlist'ed man' s Soldat m; **enlisted men** Mannschaften pl

enlistment [ɛn'lɪstmənt] s Anwerbung f; (period of service) Militärdienstzeit f

enliven [ɛn'laɪvən] tr beleben

enmesh [ɛn'mɛʃ] tr verstricken

enmity ['ɛnmɪti] s Feindschaft f

ennoble [ɛn'nobəl] tr veredeln, adeln

ennui ['anwi] s Langeweile f

enormity [ɪ'nɔrmɪti] s Ungeheuerlichkeit f

enormous [ɪ'nɔrməs] adj enorm, ungeheuer

enough [ɪ'nʌf] adj & adv genug, genügend; **be e.** genügen; **I have e. of it** ich bin es satt; **it's e. to drive one crazy** es ist zum Verrücktwerden

enounce [ɪ'nauns] tr (declare) verkünden; (pronounce) aussprechen

enrage [ɛn'redʒ] tr wütend machen

enraged' adj (**at**) wütend (über acc)

enrapture [ɛn'ræptʃər] tr hinreißen

enrich [ɛn'rɪtʃ] tr (a person with money; the mind, a program) bereichern; (soil) fruchtbarer machen; (food, metals, gases) anreichern

enrichment [ɛn'rɪtʃmənt] s Bereicherung f; (of food, metals, gases) Anreicherung f

enroll [ɛn'rol] tr als Mitglied aufnehmen || intr (educ) sich immatrikulieren lassen

enrollment [ɛn'rolmənt] s (in a course or school) Schülerzahl f; (of a society) Mitgliederzahl f

en route [an 'rut] adv unterwegs

ensconce [ɛn'skans] tr verbergen

ensemble [an'sambəl] s Ensemble n

ensign ['ɛnsɪn] s (flag) (mil) Fahne f; (flag) (nav) Flagge f; (emblem) Abzeichen n; (nav) Leutnant m zur See

enslave [ɛn'slev] tr versklaven

enslavement [ɛn'slevmənt] s Versklavung f

ensnare [ɛn'snɛr] tr (fig) umgarnen

ensue [ɛn's(j)u] intr (**from**) (er)folgen (aus)

ensu'ing adj darauffolgend

ensure [ɛn'ʃur] tr gewährleisten

entail [ɛn'tel] tr mit sich bringen

entangle [ɛn'tæŋgəl] tr verwickeln; **get entangled** sich verwickeln

entanglement [ɛn'tæŋgəlmənt] s Verwicklung f; (mil) Drahtverhau m

enter ['ɛntər] tr (a room) betreten, treten in (acc); (political office) antreten; (a university) beziehen; (a protest) erheben; (a career) einschlagen; (in the records) eintragen; **e. the army** Soldat werden || intr eintreten, hereinkommen; (by car) einfahren; (sport) melden; (theat) auftreten; **e. into** (an agreement) treffen; (a contract) abschließen; **e. upon** anfangen; (a career) einschlagen; (an office, inheritance) antreten; (year of life) eintreten in (acc)

enterprise ['ɛntər ˌpraɪz] s Unternehmen n; (spirit) Unternehmungsgeist m

en'terprising adj unternehmungslustig

entertain [ˌɛntər'ten] tr unterhalten; (guests) bewirten; (doubts, hopes, suspicions) hegen || intr Gäste haben

entertainer [ˌɛntər'tenər] s Unterhaltungskünstler –in mf

entertain'ing adj unterhaltsam || s—**do a lot of e.** ein großes Haus führen

entertainment [ˌɛntər'tenmənt] s Unterhaltung f

entertain'ment tax' s Vergnügungssteuer f

enthrall [ɛn'θrəl] tr bezaubern, fesseln

enthrone [ɛn'θron] tr auf den Thron setzen; **be enthroned** thronen

enthuse [ɛn'θ(j)uz] tr (coll) begeistern

enthusiasm [ɛn'θ(j)uzi ˌæzəm] s Begeisterung f, Schwärmerei f

enthusiast [ɛn'θ(j)uzɪ‚æst] *s* Schwär-mer –in *mf*
enthusiastic [ɛn‚θ(j)uzɪ'æstɪk] *adj* (**about**) begeistert (über *acc* or von)
entice [ɛn'taɪs] *tr* (ver)locken
enticement [ɛn'taɪsmənt] *s* Verlockung *f*
entic'ing *adj* verlockend
entire [ɛn'taɪr] *adj* ganz, gesamt; (*trust*) voll
entirely [ɛn'taɪrli] *adv* ganz, gänzlich
entirety [ɛn'taɪrti] *s*—**in its e.** in seiner Gesamtheit
entitle [ɛn'taɪtəl] *tr* (*call*) betiteln; (**to**) berechtigen (zu); **be entitled to** Anspruch haben auf (*acc*); **be en-titled to** (*inf*) berechtigt sein zu (*inf*)
entity ['ɛntɪti] *s* Wesen *n*
entomb [ɛn'tum] *tr* bestatten
entombment [ɛn'tummənt] *s* Bestat-tung *f*
entomology [‚ɛntə'malədʒi] *s* Ento-mologie *f*
entourage [‚antu'raʒ] *s* Begleitung *f*
entrails ['ɛntrelz] *spl* Eingeweide *pl*
entrain [ɛn'tren] *tr* verladen ‖ *intr* einsteigen
entrance ['ɛntrəns] *s* Eingang *m*; (*drive*) Einfahrt *f*; (*of a home*) Flur *m*; (*upon office*) Antritt *m*; (theat) Auftritt *m*; **make one's e.** eintreten ‖ [ɛn'træns] *tr* mitreißen
en'trance examina'tion *s* Aufnahme-prüfung *f*
en'trance fee' *s* Eintrittspreis *m*
entrant ['ɛntrənt] *s* (**in**) Teilnehmer –in *mf* (an *dat*)
en·trap [ɛn'træp] *v* (*pret & pp* –trapped; *ger* –trapping) *tr* verleiten
entreat [ɛn'trit] *tr* anflehen
entreaty [ɛn'triti] *s* dringende Bitte *f*; **at his e.** auf seine Bitte
entrée ['ɑntre] *s* (*access*) Zutritt *m*; (*before main course*) Vorspeise *f*; (*between courses*) Zwischengericht *n*; (*main course*) Hauptgericht *n*
entrench [ɛn'trɛntʃ] *tr* verschanzen; **be entrenched in** (fig) eingewurzelt sein in (*dat*)
entrenchment [ɛn'trɛntʃmənt] *s* (*activ-ity*) Schanzbau *m*; (*the result*) Ver-schanzung *f*
entrepreneur [ɑntrəprə'nʌr] *s* Unter-nehmer –in *mf*
entrust [ɛn'trʌst] *tr* (**to**) anvertrauen (*dat*)
entry ['ɛntri] *s* Eintritt *m*; (*by car*) Einfahrt *f*; (*door*) Eingang *m*, Ein-gangstür *f*; (*into a country*) Einreise *f*; (*into office*) Antritt *m*; (*in a dic-tionary*) Stichwort *n*; (*into a race*) Nennung *f*; (*contestant*) Bewerber –in *mf*; (com) Buchung *f*; (theat) Auftritt *m*; **unlawful e.** Hausfriedens-bruch *m*
entwine [ɛn'twaɪn] *tr* umwinden
enumerate [ɪ'n(j)umə‚ret] *tr* aufzählen
enunciate [ɪ'nʌnsɪ‚et] *tr* aussprechen ‖ *intr* deutlich aussprechen
envelop [ɛn'vɛləp] *tr* (*said of crowds, waves*) verschlingen; (*said of mist, clouds, darkness*) umhüllen; (mil) umfassen

envelope ['ɛnvə‚lop] *s* Umschlag *m*
envelopment [ɛn'vɛləpmənt] *s* Um-hüllung *f*; (mil) Umfassung *f*
envenom [ɛn'vɛnəm] *tr* vergiften
enviable ['ɛnvɪ·əbəl] *adj* beneidens-wert
envious ['ɛnvɪ·əs] *adj* (**of**) neidisch (auf *acc*)
environment [ɛn'vaɪrənmənt] *s* (*eco-logical condition*) Umwelt *f*; (*sur-roundings*) Umgebung *f*
environmental [ɛn‚vaɪrən'mɛntəl] *adj* Umwelt–; umgebend, Umgebungs–
environmentalist [ɛn‚vaɪrən'mɛntəlɪst] Umweltschützer –in *mf*
environs [ɛn'vaɪrənz] *spl* Umgebung *f*
envisage [ɛn'vɪzɪdʒ] *tr* ins Auge fassen
envoy ['ɛnvɔɪ] *s* Gesandte *mf*
en·vy ['ɛnvi] *s* Neid *m* ‖ *v* (*pret & pp* –vied) *tr* (**for**) beneiden (um)
enzyme ['ɛnzaɪm] *s* Enzym *n*
epaulet, epaulette ['ɛpə‚lɛt] *s* Epau-lette *f*, Schulterstück *n*
ephemeral [ɛ'fɛmərəl] *adj* flüchtig
epic ['ɛpɪk] *adj* episch; **e. poetry** Epik *f* ‖ *s* Epos *n*, Heldengedicht *n*
epicure ['ɛpɪ‚kjʊr] *s* Feinschmecker –in *mf*
epicurean [‚ɛpɪkju'ri·ən] *adj* genuß-süchtig; (philos) epikureisch ‖ *s* Ge-nußmensch *m*; (philos) Epikureer *m*
epidemic [‚ɛpɪ'dɛmɪk] *adj* epidemisch ‖ *s* Epidemie *f*, Seuche *f*
epidermis [‚ɛpɪ'dʌrmɪs] *s* Oberhaut *f*
epigram ['ɛpɪ‚græm] *s* Epigramm *n*
epigraph ['ɛpɪ‚græf] *s* Inschrift *f*
epigraphy [ɛ'pɪgrəfi] *s* Inschriften-kunde *f*
epilepsy ['ɛpɪ‚lɛpsi] *s* Epilepsie *f*
epileptic [‚ɛpɪ'lɛptɪk] *adj* epileptisch ‖ *s* Epileptiker –in *mf*
epilogue ['ɛpɪ‚lɔg] *s* Nachwort *n*
Epiphany [ɪ'pɪfəni] *s* Dreikönigsfest *n*
episcopal [ɪ'pɪskəpəl] *adj* bischöflich
Episcopalian [ɪ‚pɪskə'pɛli·ən] *adj* Episkopal– ‖ *s* Episkopale *m*, Epis-kopalin *f*
epis'copal see' *s* Bischofssitz *m*
episcopate [ɪ'pɪskə‚pet] *s* Bischofs-amt *n*
episode ['ɛpɪ‚sod] *s* Episode *f*
epistemology [ɪ‚pɪstə'malədʒi] *s* Epi-stemologie *f*, Erkenntnistheorie *f*
epistle [ɪ'pɪsəl] *s* Epistel *f*
epitaph ['ɛpɪtæf] *s* Grabinschrift *f*
epithet ['ɛpɪ‚θɛt] *s* Beiwort *n*
epitome [ɪ'pɪtəmi] *s* Auszug *m*; (fig) Verkörperung *f*
epitomize [ɪ'pɪtə‚maɪz] *tr*—**e–n Aus-zug machen von** or **aus**; (fig) ver-körpern
epoch ['ɛpək], ['ipak] *s* Epoche *f*
epochal ['ɛpəkəl] *adj* epochal
e'poch-mak'ing *adj* bahnbrechend
Ep'som salts' ['ɛpsəm] *spl* Bittersalz *n*
equable ['ɛkwəbəl] *adj* gleichmäßig; (*disposition*) gleichmütig
equal ['ikwəl] *adj* gleich; (*in birth or status*) ebenbürtig; (*in worth*) gleich-wertig; (*in kind*) gleichartig; **be e. to** (*e.g., a task*) gewachsen sein (*dat*); **be on e. terms** (*be on the same level*) auf gleichem Fuß stehen; **other**

things being e. bei sonst gleichen Verhältnissen ‖ s Gleiche *mfn;* **her** or **their e.(s)** ihresgleichen; **my (your,** *etc.*) **e.(s)** meines– (deines–, *etc.*) gleichen ‖ v (*pret & pp* **equal[l]ed;** *ger* **equal[l]ing** *tr* gleichkommen (*dat*); (*a record*) erreichen; (math) ergeben

equality [ɪ'kwɑlɪti] s Gleichheit *f;* (*in standing*) Gleichberechtigung *f*

equalize ['ikwə,laiz] *tr* gleichmachen

equally ['ikwəli] *adv* gleich, ebenso

equanimity [,ikwə'nimiti] s Gleichmut *m*

equate [i'kwet] *tr* (**to** or **with**) gleichsetzen (*dat* or mit)

equation [i'kweʒən] s Gleichung *f*

equator [i'kwetər] s Äquator *m*

equatorial [,ikwə'tori·əl] *adj* äquatorial

equestrian [ɪ'kwɛstrɪ·ən] *adj* Reiter–; **e. statue** Reiterstandbild *n* ‖ s Kunstreiter –in *mf*

equilateral [,ikwɪ'lætərəl] *adj* gleichseitig

equilibrium [,ikwɪ'lɪbrɪ·əm] s Gleichgewicht *n;* (fig) Gleichmaß *n*

equinox ['ikwɪ,nɑks] s Tagundnachtgleiche *f*

equip [ɪ'kwɪp] v (*pret & pp* **equipped;** *ger* **equipping**) *tr* ausrüsten, ausstatten

equipment [ɪ'kwɪpmənt] s Ausrüstung *f,* Ausstattung *f*

equipoise ['ikwɪ,pɔiz] s Gleichgewicht *n*

equitable ['ɛkwɪtəbəl] *adj* gerecht

equity ['ɛkwɪti] s (*fairness*) Unparteilichkeit *f;* (fin) Nettowert *m*

equivalent [ɪ'kwɪvələnt] *adj* gleichwertig; (**to**) gleichbedeutend (mit) ‖ s Gegenwert *m;* (**of**) Äquivalent *n* (für)

equivocal [ɪ'kwɪvəkəl] *adj* zweideutig

equivocate [ɪ'kwɪvə,ket] *intr* zweideutig reden

equivocation [ɪ'kwɪvə,keʃən] s Zweideutigkeit *f*

era ['irə], ['irə] s Zeitalter *n*

eradicate [ɪ'rædɪ,ket] *tr* ausrotten

erase [ɪ'res] *tr* ausradieren; (*a tape recording*) löschen; (*a blackboard*) abwischen; (fig) auslöschen

eraser [ɪ'resər] s Radiergummi *m;* (*for a blackboard*) Tafelwischer *m*

erasure [ɪ'reʃər], [ɪ'reʒər] s (*action*) Ausradieren *n;* (*erased spot*) Rasur *f*

ere [ɛr] *prep* (poet) vor (*dat*) ‖ *conj* (poet) ehe, bevor

erect [ɪ'rɛkt] *adj* aufrecht, straff; (*hair*) gesträubt; **with head e.** erhobenen Hauptes ‖ *tr* errichten

erection [ɪ'rɛkʃən] s Errichtung *f;* (*of sexual organs*) Erektion *f*

erg [ʌrg] s Erg *n*

ermine ['ʌrmɪn] s Hermelinpelz *m*

erode [ɪ'rod] *tr* (*corrode*) zerfressen; (fig) unterhöhlen; (geol) erodieren ‖ *intr* zerfressen werden

erosion [ɪ'roʒən] s (*corrosion*) Zerfressen *n;* (fig) Unterhöhlung *f;* (geol) Erosion *f*

erotic [ɪ'rɑtɪk] *adj* erotisch

err [ʌr] *intr* irren, sich irren

errand ['ɛrənd] s Bersorgung *f;* **run an e.** e–e Besorgung machen

er'rand boy' s Laufbursche *m*

erratic [ɪ'rætɪk] *adj* regellos, ziellos; (geol) erratisch

erroneous [ɪ'roni·əs] *adj* irrtümlich

erroneously [ɪ'roni·əsli] *adv* irrtümlicherweise, versehentlich

error ['ɛrər] s Fehler *m,* Irrtum *m*

erudite ['ɛr(j)υ,daɪt] *adj* gelehrt

erudition [,ɛr(j)υ'dɪʃən] s Gelehrsamkeit *f*

erupt [ɪ'rʌpt] *intr* ausbrechen

eruption [ɪ'rʌpʃən] s Ausbruch *m;* (pathol) Ausschlag *m*

escalate ['ɛskə,let] *tr & intr* eskalieren

escalation [,ɛskə'leʃən] s Eskalierung *f*

escalator ['ɛskə,letər] s Rolltreppe *f*

es'calator clause' s Indexklausel *f*

escapade ['ɛskə,ped] s Eskapade *f*

escape [ɛs'kep] s Flucht *f;* (*of gas or liquid*) Ausströmen *n;* **have a narrow e.** mit knapper Not davonkommen ‖ *intr* (*said of gas or liquid*) ausströmen; (**from**) flüchten (aus)

escape' clause' s Ausweichklausel *f*

escapee [,ɛskə'pi] s Flüchtling *m*

escape' hatch' s Notausstieg *m*

escapement [ɛs'kepmənt] s (horol) Hemmung *f*

escape' wheel' s (horol) Hemmungsrad *n*

escapism [ɛs'kepɪzəm] s Wirklichkeitsflucht *f*

escarpment [ɛs'kɑrpmənt] s (geol) Steilabhang *m;* (mil) Abdachung *f*

eschew [ɛs'tʃu] *tr* (ver)meiden

escort ['ɛskɔrt] s Geleit *n,* Schutzgeleit *n;* (*person*) Begleiter *m;* (mil) Begleitmannschaft *f,* Bedeckung *f;* (nav) Geleitschutz *m* ‖ [ɛs'kɔrt] *tr* begleiten; (mil, nav) geleiten

es'cort ves'sel s Geleitschiff *n*

escutcheon [ɛs'kʌtʃən] s Wappenschild *m;* (*doorplate*) Schlüssellochschild *n*

Eskimo ['ɛskɪ,mo] *adj* Eskimo– ‖ s (**-mos & -mo**) Eskimo *m*

esopha·gus [i'sɑfəgəs] s (**-gi** [,dʒaɪ]) Speiseröhre *f*

esoteric [,ɛso'tɛrɪk] *adj* esoterisch

especial [ɛs'pɛʃəl] *adj* besondere

especially [ɛs'pɛʃəli] *adv* besonders

espionage [,ɛspɪ·ə'nɑʒ] s Spionage *f*

espousal [ɛs'pauzəl] s (**of**) Annahme *f* (von)

espouse [ɛs'pauz] *tr* annehmen

esprit de corps [ɛs'pri də 'kɔr] s Korpsgeist *m,* Gemeinschaftsgeist *m*

espy [ɛs'paɪ] v (*pret & pp* **espied**) *tr* erspähen

essay ['ɛse] s Aufsatz *m,* Essay *n* ‖ [ɛ'se] *tr* probieren

essayist ['ɛse·ɪst] s Essayist –in *mf*

essence ['ɛsəns] s Wesenheit *f;* (*scent*) Duft *m;* (*extract*) Essenz *f;* (philos) inneres Wesen *n;* **in e.** im wesentlichen

essential [ɛ'sɛnʃəl] *adj* (**to**) wesentlich (für) ‖ s Hauptsache *f;* **the essentials** die Grundzüge *pl*

establish [ɛs'tæblɪʃ] *tr* (*found*) gründen; (*a business, an account*) eröffnen; (*relations, connections*) herstellen; (*order*) schaffen; (*a record*) aufstellen; (*a fact*) feststellen

establishment [ɛs'tæblɪʃmənt] *s* (*act*) Gründung *f*; (*institution*) Anstalt *f*; (*business*) Unternehmen *n*; **the Establishment** das Establishment

estate [ɛs'tet] *s* (*landed property*) Landgut *n*; (*possessions*) Vermögen *n*; (*property of deceased person*) Nachlaß *m*; (*social station*) Stand *m*

esteem [ɛs'tim] *s* Hochachtung *f*; **hold in e.** achten ‖ *tr* achten

esthete ['ɛsθit] *s* Ästhetiker –in *mf*

esthetic [ɛs'θɛtɪk] *adj* ästhetisch ‖ **esthetics** *s* Ästhetik *f*

estimable ['ɛstɪməbəl] *adj* schätzenswert

estimate ['ɛstɪ͵met], ['ɛstɪmɪt] *s* Kostenanschlag *m*; (*judgment of value*) Schätzung *f*; **rough e.** Überschlag *m* ‖ ['ɛstɪ͵met] *tr* (*costs*) veranschlagen; (*the value*) abschätzen; (*homes, damages*) schätzen; (**at**) beziffern (auf *acc*); **e. roughly** überschlagen

estimation [͵ɛstɪ'meʃən] *s* Schätzung *f*; **in my e.** nach meiner Schätzung

Estonia [ɛs'tonɪ·ə] *s* Estland *n*

estrangement [ɛs'trendʒmənt] *s* Entfremdung *f*

estuary ['ɛstʃu͵ɛri] *s* (*of a river*) Mündung *f*; (*inlet*) Meeresarm *m*

etch [ɛtʃ] *tr* radieren, ätzen

etcher ['ɛtʃər] *s* Radierer –in *mf*

etch'ing *s* Radierung *f*; (*as an art*) Radierkunst *f*

eternal [ɪ'tʌrnəl] *adj* ewig

eternity [ɪ'tʌrnɪti] *s* Ewigkeit *f*

ether ['iθər] *s* Äther *m*

ethereal [ɪ'θɪrɪ·əl] *adj* ätherisch

ethical ['ɛθɪkəl] *adj* ethisch, sittlich

ethics ['ɛθɪks] *s* Ethik *f*, Sittenlehre *f*

Ethiopia [͵iθɪ'opɪ·ə] *s* Äthiopien *n*

Ethiopian [͵iθɪ'opɪ·ən] *adj* äthiopisch ‖ *s* Äthiopier –in *mf*; (*language*) Äthiopisch *n*

ethnic(al) ['ɛθnɪk(əl)] *adj* völkisch; **e. group** Volksgruppe *f*

ethnography [ɛθ'nɑɡrəfi] *s* Ethnographie *f*

ethnology [ɛθ'nɑlədʒi] *s* Völkerkunde *f*

ethyl ['ɛθɪl] *s* Äthyl *m*

ethylene ['ɛθɪ͵lin] *s* Äthylen *n*

etiquette ['ɛtɪ͵kɛt] *s* Etikette *f*

etymology [͵ɛtɪ'mɑlədʒi] *s* Etymologie *f*

ety·mon ['ɛtɪ͵mɑn] *s* (**–mons** & **–ma** [mə]) Etymon *n*

eucalyp·tus [͵jukə'lɪptəs] *s* (**–tuses** & **–ti** [taɪ]) Eukalyptus *m*

Eucharist ['jukərɪst] *s*—**the E.** das heilige Abendmal, die Eucharistie *f*

eugenics [ju'dʒɛnɪks] *s* Rassenhygiene *f*

eulogize ['julə͵dʒaɪz] *tr* lobpreisen

eulogy ['julədʒi] *s* Lobrede *f*

eunuch ['junək] *s* Eunuch *m*

euphemism ['jufɪ͵mɪzəm] *s* Euphemismus *m*

euphemistic [͵jufə'mɪstɪk] *adj* euphemistisch, verblümt

euphonic [ju'fɑnɪk] *adj* wohlklingend

euphony ['jufəni] *s* Wohlklang *m*

euphoria [ju'forɪ·ə] *s* Euphorie *f*

euphoric [ju'forɪk] *adj* euphorisch

euphuism ['jufju͵ɪzəm] *s* gezierte Ausdrucksweise *f*

Europe ['jurəp] *s* Europa *n*

European [͵jurə'pi·ən] *adj* europäisch ‖ *s* Europäer –in *mf*

Europe'an plan' *s* Hotelpreis *m* ohne Mahlzeiten

euthanasia [͵juθə'neʒə] *s* Euthanasie *f*

evacuate [ɪ'vækju͵et] *tr* evakuieren; (*med*) entleeren; (*an area*) räumen ‖ *intr* sich zurückziehen

evacuation [ɪ͵vækju'eʃən] *s* Evakuierung *f*; (*med*) Entleerung *f*

evade [ɪ'ved] *tr* ausweichen (*dat*); (*duties*) vernachlässigen; (*laws*) umgehen; (*prosecution, responsibility*) sich entziehen (*dat*); (*taxes*) hinterziehen

evaluate [ɪ'vælju͵et] *tr* (*e.g., jewels*) (ab)schätzen; (*e.g., a performance*) beurteilen

evaluation [ɪ͵vælju'eʃən] *s* Abschätzung *f*; (*judgment*) Beurteilung *f*

evangelic(al) [͵ivæn'dʒɛlɪk(əl)], [͵ɛvən'dʒɛlɪk(əl)] *adj* evangelisch

Evangelist [ɪ'vændʒəlɪst] *s* Evangelist *m*

evaporate [ɪ'væpə͵ret] *tr* eindampfen ‖ *intr* (*above boiling point*) verdampfen; (*below boiling point*) verdunsten; (fig) sich verflüchtigen

eva'porated milk' *s* Kondensmilch *f*

evasion [ɪ'veʒən] *s* (*dodge*) Ausweichen *n*; (*of the law*) Umgehung *f*; (*of responsibility*) Vernachlässigung *f*; (*in speech*) Ausflucht *f*

evasive [ɪ'vesɪv] *adj* ausweichend

eve [iv] *s* Vorabend *m*

even ['ivən] *adj* (*smooth*) eben, gerade; (*number*) gerade; (*uniform*) gleichmäßig; (*chance*) gleich; (*temperament*) ruhig, ausgeglichen; **an e. break** gleiche Aussichten *pl*; **an e. dozen** genau ein Dutzend; **be e.** (coll) quitt sein; **e. with** auf gleicher Höhe mit; **get e. with** mit j–m abrechnen ‖ *adv* selbst, sogar; (*before comparatives*) noch; (*as intensifier before nouns and pronouns*) selbst; **break e.** gerade auf seine Kosten kommen; **e. if** selbst wenn, wenn auch; **e. so** trotzdem; **e. though** obgleich; **e. today** noch heute; **e. when** selbst wenn ‖ *tr* ebnen; **e. up** ausgleichen

e'ven-hand'ed *adj* unparteiisch

evening ['ivnɪŋ] *adj* Abend– ‖ *s* Abend *m*; **in the e.** am Abend; **this e.** heute abend

eve'ning gown' *s* Abendkleid *n*

eve'ning pa'per *s* Abendblatt *n*

eve'ning school' *s* Abendschule *f*

evenly ['ivənli] *adv* gleichmäßig; **e. matched** (sport) gleichwertig

ev'en-mind'ed *adj* gleichmütig

evenness ['ivənnɪs] *s* (*smoothness*)

Ebenheit f; (uniformity) Gleich-
mäßigkeit f
event [ɪ'vɛnt] s Ereignis n; (sport)
Veranstaltung f; **at all events, in any
e.** auf jeden Fall; **in the e. of** im
Falle (genit)
eventful [ɪ'vɛntfəl] adj ereignisvoll
eventual [ɪ'vɛntʃʊ·əl] adj schließlich
eventuality [ɪ‚vɛntʃʊ'ælɪti] s Möglichkeit f
eventually [ɪ'vɛntʃʊ‚əli] adj schließlich
ever ['ɛvər] adv je, jemals; (before
comparatives) immer; **did you e.!** hat
man schon sowas gehört!; **e. after**
die ganze Zeit danach; **e. so** noch
so; **e. so much** (coll) sehr; **hardly e.**
fast nie
ev'ergreen' adj immergrün ‖ s Immergrün n
ev'erlast'ing adj ewig; (continual)
fortwährend; (iron) ewig
ev'ermore' adv immer; **for e.** in Ewigkeit
every ['ɛvri] adj jeder; (confidence)
voll; **e. bit** (coll) völlig; **e. now and
then** ab und zu; **e. once in a while**
dann und wann; **e. other day** alle
zwei Tage; **e. time (that)** jedesmal
(wenn)
ev'erybod'y indef pron jeder, jeder-
mann
ev'eryday' adj alltäglich, Alltags–
ev'eryone', ev'ery one' indef pron (of)
jeder (von); **e. else** alle anderen
ev'erything' indef pron alles
ev'erywhere' adv (position) überall;
(direction) überallhin
evict [ɪ'vɪkt] tr delogieren
eviction [ɪ'vɪkʃən] s Delogierung f
evidence ['ɛvɪdəns] s Beweismaterial
n, Beweise pl; (piece of evidence)
Beweis m; **as e. of** zum Beweis
(genit); **for lack of e.** wegen Mangels
an Beweisen; **give e.** aussagen; **in e.**
sichtbar
evident ['ɛvɪdənt] adj (obvious) offen-
sichtlich; (visible) ersichtlich; **be e.**
zutage liegen
evidently ['ɛvɪdəntli] adv offenbar
evil ['ivəl] adj übel, böse ‖ s Übel n
e'vildo'er s Übeltäter –in mf
e'vildo'ing s Missetat f
e'vil eye' s böser Blick m
e'vil-mind'ed adj übelgesinnt
E'vil One' s Böse m
evince [ɪ'vɪns] tr bekunden
evoke [ɪ'vok] tr hervorrufen
evolution [‚ɛvə'luʃən] s Evolution f
evolve [ɪ'vɑlv] tr entwickeln, entfalten
‖ intr sich entwickeln, sich entfalten
ewe [ju] s Mutterschaf n
ewer ['ju·ər] s Wasserkanne f
exact [ɛg'zækt] adj genau ‖ tr (e.g.,
money) beitreiben; (obedience) erzwingen
exact'ing adj (strict) streng; (task)
aufreibend; (picky) anspruchsvoll
exactly [ɛg'zæktli] adv genau
exactness [ɛg'zæktnɪs] s Genauigkeit f
exact' sci'ences spl Realien pl
exaggerate [ɛg'zædʒə‚ret] tr übertreiben

exaggeration [ɛg‚zædʒə'reʃən] s Über-
treibung f
exalt [ɛg'zɔlt] tr erheben
exam [ɛg'zæm] s (coll) Prüfung f
examination [ɛg‚zæmɪ'neʃən] s Prüfung f, Examen n; (jur) Verhör n,
Vernehmung f; (med) Untersuchung
f; **direct e.** (jur) direkte Befragung
f; **fail an e.** bei e-r Prüfung durchfallen; **on closer e.** bei näherer Prüfung; **pass an e.** e-e Prüfung bestehen; **take an e.** e-e Prüfung ablegen
examine [ɛg'zæmɪn] tr prüfen; (jur)
verhören, vernehmen; (med) untersuchen
examinee [ɛg‚zæmɪ'ni] s Prüfling m
examiner [ɛg'zæmɪnər] s (educ) Prüfer –in mf; (med) Untersucher –in
mf
example [ɛg'zæmpəl] s Beispiel n; **for
e.** zum Beispiel; **make an e. of** ein
Exempel statuieren an (dat); **set a
good e.** mit gutem Beispiel vorangehen
exasperate [ɛg'zæspə‚ret] tr reizen
excavate ['ɛkskə‚vet] tr ausgraben
excavation [‚ɛkskə've ʃən] s Ausgrabung f
excavator ['ɛkskə‚vetər] s (archeol)
Ausgräber –in mf; (mach) Trockenbagger m
exceed [ɛk'sid] tr überschreiten
exceedingly [ɛk'sidɪŋli] adv außerordentlich
ex·cel [ɛk'sɛl] v (pret & pp –celled;
ger –celling) tr übertreffen ‖ intr
(in) sich auszeichnen (in dat)
excellence ['ɛksələns] s Vorzüglichkeit
f
excellency ['ɛksələnsi] s Vorzüglichkeit f; **Your Excellency** Eure Exzellenz
excellent ['ɛksələnt] adj ausgezeichnet
excelsior ['ɛk'sɛlsɪ·ər] s Holzwolle f
except [ɛk'sɛpt] adv—**e. for** abgesehen
von; **e. if** außer wenn; **e. that** außer
daß; **e. when** außer wenn ‖ prep
außer (dat), ausgenommen (acc) ‖
tr ausnehmen, ausschließen
exception [ɛk'sɛpʃən] s Ausnahme f;
by way of e. ausnahmsweise; **take e.
to** Anstoß nehmen an (dat); **without
e.** ausnahmslos; **with the e. of** mit
Ausnahme von
exceptional [ɛk'sɛpʃənəl] adj außergewöhnlich. Sonder–
excerpt ['ɛksʌrpt] s Auszug m ‖ [ɛk-
'sʌrpt] tr exzerpieren
excess ['ɛksɛs], [ɛk'sɛs] adj überschüssig ‖ [ɛk'sɛs] s (surplus)
Überschuß m; (immoderate amount)
(of) Übermaß n (von or an dat);
carry to e. übertreiben; **excesses**
Ausschreitungen pl; **in e. of** mehr
als; **to e.** übermäßig
ex'cess bag'gage s Überfracht f
excessive [ɛk'sɛsɪv] adj übermäßig
ex'cess-prof'its tax' s Mehrgewinnsteu-
er f
exchange [ɛks'tʃɛndʒ] s Austausch m;
(e.g., of purchases) Umtausch m;
(of words) Wechselgespräch n; (of

money) Geldwechsel *m;* (fin) Börse *f;* (mil) Kantine *f;* (telp) Vermittlung *f;* **e. of letters** Briefwechsel *m;* **in e.** dafür; **in e. for** für || *tr* (*trade*) tauschen; (*replace*) auswechseln; **e. for** umtauschen gegen; **e. places with s.o.** mit j–m tauscnen

exchequer [ɛks'tʃɛkər] *s* Staatskasse *f;* (*department*) Schatzamt *n*

ex'cise tax' ['ɛksaɪz] *s* Verbrauchssteuer *f*

excitable [ɛk'saɪtəbəl] *adj* erregbar

excite [ɛk'saɪt] *tr* erregen, aufregen

excitement [ɛk'saɪtmənt] *s* Erregung *f*, Aufregung *f*

excit'ing *adj* erregend, aufregend

exclaim [ɛks'klem] *tr & intr* ausrufen

exclamation [,ɛksklə'meʃən] *s* Ausruf *m*

exclama'tion point' *s* Ausrufungszeichen *n*

exclude [ɛks'klud] *tr* ausschließen

exclusion [ɛks'kluʒən] *s* Ausschließung *f,* Ausschluß *m;* **to the e. of** unter Ausschluß (*genit*)

exclusive [ɛks'klusɪv] *adj* (*rights, etc.*) alleinig, ausschließlich; (*club*) exklusiv; (*shop*) teuer; **e. of** ausschließlich (*genit*)

excommunicate [,ɛkskə'mjunɪ,ket] *tr* exkommunizieren

excommunication [,ɛkskə,mjunɪ'keʃən] *s* Exkommunikation *f*, Kirchenbann *m*

excoriate [ɛks'korɪ,et] *tr* (fig) heruntermachen

excrement ['ɛkskrəmənt] *s* Exkremente *pl*

excrescence [ɛks'krɛsəns] *s* Auswuchs *m*

excruciating [ɛks'kruʃɪ,etɪŋ] *adj* qualvoll

exculpate ['ɛkskʌl,pet] *tr* entschuldigen

excursion [ɛks'kʌrʒən] *s* (*side trip*) Abstecher *m;* (*short trip*) Ausflug *m*

excusable [ɛks'kjuzəbəl] *adj* entschuldbar, verzeihlich

excuse [ɛks'kjus] *s* Ausrede *f;* **give as an e.** vorgeben; **make excuses** sich ausreden || [ɛks'kjuz] *tr* entschuldigen; **e. me!** entschuldigen Sie!; **you may be excused now** Sie können jetzt gehen

execute ['ɛksɪ,kjut] *tr* (*a condemned man*) hinrichten; (*by firing squad*) erschießen; (*perform*) durchführen, vollziehen; (*a will, a sentence*) vollstrecken; (mus) vortragen

execution [,ɛksɪ'kjuʃən] *s* Hinrichtung *f;* (*by firing squad*) Erschießung *f;* (*performance*) Durchführung *f*, Vollziehung *f;* (mus) Vortrag *m*

executioner [,ɛksɪ'kjuʃənər] *s* Scharfrichter *m*

executive [ɛg'zɛkjətɪv] *adj* vollziehend, exekutiv || *s* (com) Manager *m,* leitender Angestellte *mf;* **the Executive** (*pol*) die Exekutive *f*

exec'utive commit'tee *s* Vollzugsausschuß *m,* Vorstand *m*

exec'utive or'der *s* Durchführungsverordnung *f*

executor [ɛg'zɛkjətər] *s* Vollstrecker *m*

executrix [ɛg'zɛkjətrɪks] *s* Vollstreckerin *f*

exemplary [ɛg'zɛmpləri] *adj* vorbildlich, mustergültig

exempli·fy [ɛg'zɛmplɪ,faɪ] *v* (*pret & pp* –fied) *tr* (*demonstrate*) an Beispielen erläutern; (*embody*) als Beispiel dienen für

exempt [ɛg'zɛmpt] *adj* (**from**) befreit (von) || *tr* befreien; (mil) freistellen

exemption [ɛg'zɛmpʃən] *s* Befreiung *f;* (mil) Freistellung *f*

exercise ['ɛksər,saɪz] *s* Übung *f;* (*of the body*) Bewegung *f;* (*of power*) Ausübung *f;* (mil) Exerzieren *n;* **take e.** sich [*dat*] Bewegung machen || *tr* üben; (*the body, a horse*) bewegen; (*power, influence*) ausüben; (mil) exerzieren || *intr* üben; (mil) exerzieren

exert [ɛg'zʌrt] *tr* ausüben; **e. every effort** alle Kräfte rühren; **e. oneself** sich anstrengen

exertion [ɛg'zʌrʃən] *s* Anstrengung *f;* (*e.g., of power*) Ausübung *f*

exhalation [,ɛks·hə'leʃən] *s* Ausatmung *f;* (*of gases*) Gasabgabe *f*

exhale [ɛks'hel] *tr & intr* ausatmen

exhaust [ɛg'zɔst] *s* (aut) Auspuff *m* || *tr* erschöpfen

exhaust'ed *adj* erschöpft

exhaust' fan' *s* Absaugventilator *m*

exhaust' gas' *s* Abgas *n*

exhaust'ing *adj* anstrengend, mühselig

exhaustion [ɛg'zɔstʃən] *s* Erschöpfung *f*

exhaustive [ɛg'zɔstɪv] *adj* erschöpfend

exhaust' pipe' *s* Auspuffrohr *n*

exhaust' valve' *s* Auspuffventil *n*

exhibit [ɛg'zɪbɪt] *s* (*exhibition*) Ausstellung *f;* (*object exhibited*) Ausstellungsstück *n;* (jur) Beleg *m* || *tr* zur Schau stellen; (*wares*) ausstellen; (*e.g., courage*) zeigen

exhibition [,ɛksɪ'bɪʃən] *s* Ausstellung *f*

exhilarating [ɛg'zɪlə,retɪŋ] *adj* erheiternd

exhort [ɛg'zɔrt] *tr* ermahnen

exhume [ɛks'hjum] *tr* exhumieren

exigency ['ɛksɪdʒənsi] *s* (*demand, need*) Erfordnis *n;* (*state of urgency*) Dringlichkeit *f*

exigent ['ɛksɪdʒənt] *adj* dringlich

exile ['ɛgzaɪl] *s* Exil *n;* (*person*) Verbannte *mf* || *tr* verbannen

exist [ɛg'zɪst] *intr* existieren; (*continue to be*) bestehen; **e. from day to day** dahinleben

existence [ɛg'zɪstəns] *s* Existenz *f,* Dasein *n;* **be in e.** bestehen; **come into e.** entstehen

existential [,ɛgzɪs'tɛnʃəl] *adj* existentiell

existentialism [,ɛgzɪs'tɛnʃə,lɪzəm] *s* Existentialismus *m*

exit ['ɛgzɪt] *s* Ausgang *m;* (*by car*) Ausfahrt *f;* (theat) Abgang *m* || *intr* (theat) abtreten

exodus ['ɛksədəs] *s* Abwanderung *f*

exonerate [ɛg'zɑnə,ret] *tr* entlasten

exorbitant [ɛg'zɔrbɪtənt] *adj* schwindelhaft; **e. price** Wucherpreis *m*
exorcise ['ɛksɔr‚saɪz] *tr* exorzieren
exotic [ɛg'zɑtɪk] *adj* exotisch
expand [ɛks'pænd] *tr* (aus)dehnen; (*enlarge*) erweitern; (*math*) entwikkeln || *intr* sich ausdehnen
expanse [ɛks'pæns] *s* Weite *f*, Fläche *f*
expansion [ɛks'pænʃən] *s* Ausdehnung *f*; (*expanded part*) Erweiterung *f*
expansive [ɛks'pænsɪv] *adj* expansiv; (fig) mitteilsam
expatiate [ɛks'peʃɪ‚et] *intr* (**on**) sich verbreiten (über *acc*)
expatriate [ɛks'petrɪ‚ɪt] *adj* ausgebürgert || *s* Ausgebürgerte *mf* || [ɛks'petrɪ‚et] *tr* ausbürgern
expect [ɛks'pɛkt] *tr* erwarten || *intr*—**she's expecting** (coll) sie ist in anderen Umständen
expectancy [ɛks'pɛktənsi] *s* Ewartung *f*
expectant [ɛks'pɛktənt] *adj* erwartungsvoll; (*mother*) werdende
expectation [‚ɛkspɛk'teʃən] *s* Erwartung *f*
expectorate [ɛks'pɛktə‚ret] *tr & intr* spucken
expediency [ɛks'pidɪ·ənsi] *s* Zweckmäßigkeit *f*
expedient [ɛks'pidɪ·ənt] *adj* zweckmäßig || *s* Mittel *n*, Hilfsmittel *f*
expedite ['ɛkspɪ‚daɪt] *tr* beschleunigen; (*a document*) ausstellen
expedition [‚ɛkspɪ'dɪʃən] *s* Expedition *f*
expedi'tionary force' [‚ɛkspɪ'dɪʃə‚nɛri] *s* (mil) Expeditionsstreitkräfte *pl*
expeditious [‚ɛkspɪ'dɪʃəs] *adj* schleunig
ex·pel [ɛks'pɛl] *v* (*pret & pp* **–pelled; ger –pelling**) *tr* (aus)treiben; (*a student*) (**from**) verweisen (von)
expend [ɛks'pɛnd] *tr* (*time, effort, etc.*) aufwenden; (*money*) ausgeben
expendable [ɛks'pɛndəbəl] *adj* entbehrlich
expenditure [ɛks'pɛndɪtʃər] *s* Aufwand *m*; (*of money*) Ausgabe *f*
expense [ɛks'pɛns] *s* Ausgabe *f*; **at s.o.'s e.** (& fig) auf j-s Kosten; **expenses** Unkosten *pl*; **go to great e.** sich in Unkosten stürzen
expense' account' *s* Spesenkonto *n*
expensive [ɛks'pɛnsɪv] *adj* kostspielig
experience [ɛks'pɪrɪ·əns] *s* Erfahrung *f*; (*an event*) Erlebnis *n*; **no previous e. necessary** Vorkenntnisse nicht erforderlich || *tr* erfahren; (*pain*) erdulden; (*loss*) erleiden
expe'rienced *adj* erfahren
experiment [ɛks'pɛrɪmənt] *s* Experiment *n*, Versuch *m* || [ɛks'pɛrɪ‚mɛnt] *intr* experimentieren, Versuche anstellen
experimental [ɛks‚pɛrɪ'mɛntəl] *adj* experimentell, Versuchs–
expert ['ɛkspərt] *adj* fachmännisch, erfahren; **e. advice** Gutachten *n* || *s* Fachmann *m*; (jur) Sachverständige *mf*

expertise [‚ɛkspɛr'tiz] *s* (*opinion*) Gutachten *n*; (*skill*) Sachkenntnis *f*
expiate ['ɛkspɪ‚et] *tr* sühnen, büßen
expiation [‚ɛkspɪ'eʃən] *s* Sühnung *f*
expiration [‚ɛkspɪ'reʃən] *s* Verfall *m*
expira'tion date' *s* Verfalltag *m*
expire [ɛks'paɪr] *tr* ausatmen || *intr* verfallen; (*die*) verscheiden
explain [ɛks'plen] *tr* erklären, erläutern; (*justify*) rechtfertigen
explanation [‚ɛksplə'neʃən] *s* Erklärung *f*, Erläuterung *f*
explanatory [ɛks'plænə‚tori] *adj* erklärend, erläuternd
expletive ['ɛksplɪtɪv] *s* Füllwort *n*
explicit [ɛks'plɪsɪt] *adj* ausdrücklich
explode [ɛks'plod] *tr* explodieren lassen; (*a theory*) verwerfen || *intr* explodieren; (*said of a grenade*) krepieren; (**with**) platzen (vor *dat*)
exploit ['ɛksplɔɪt] *s* Heldentat *f*, Großtat *f* || [ɛks'plɔɪt] *tr* ausnutzen; (pej) ausbeuten; (min) abbauen
exploitation [‚ɛksplɔɪ'teʃən] *s* Ausnutzung *f*; (pej) Ausbeutung *f*; (min) Abbau *m*
exploration [‚ɛksplə'reʃən] *s* Erforschung *f*
explore [ɛks'plor] *tr* erforschen
explorer [ɛks'plorər] *s* Forscher –in *mf*
explosion [ɛks'ploʒən] *s* Explosion *f*
explosive [ɛks'plosɪv] *adj* explosiv, Spreng– || *s* (*explosive substance*) Sprengstoff *m*; (*device*) Sprengkörper *m*
explo'sive charge' *s* Sprengladung *f*
exponent [ɛks'ponənt] *s* Exponent *m*
export ['ɛksport] *adj* Ausfuhr– || *s* Ausfuhr *m*, Export *m*; **exports** Ausfuhrgüter *pl* || [ɛks'port] *tr* ausführen
exportation [‚ɛkspor'teʃən] *s* Ausfuhr *m*
exporter ['ɛksportər], [ɛks'portər] *s* Ausfuhrhändler –in *mf*, Exporteur –in *mf*
expose [ɛks'poz] *tr* (*to danger, ridicule, sun*) aussetzen; (*bare*) entblößen; (*a person*) (**as**) bloßstellen (als), entlarven (als); (phot) belichten
exposé [‚ɛkspo'ze] *s* Enthüllung *f*
exposition [‚ɛkspə'zɪʃən] *s* Ausstellung *f*; (rhet) Exposition *f*
expostulate [ɛks'pɑstʃə‚let] *intr* protestieren; **e. with s.o. about** j–m ernste Vorhaltungen machen über (*acc*)
exposure [ɛks'poʒər] *s* (*of a child*) Aussetzung *f*; (*laying bare*) Entblößung *f*; (*unmasking*) Entlarvung *f*; (*of a building*) Lage *f*; (phot) Belichtung *f*
expo'sure me'ter *s* Belichtungsmesser *m*
expound [ɛks'paund] *tr* erklären
express [ɛks'prɛs] *adj* ausdrücklich || *s* (rr) Expreß *m*; **by e.** als Eilgut || *tr* ausdrücken; (*feelings*) zeigen; **e. oneself** sich äußern
express' com'pany *s* Paketpostgesellschaft *f*
expression [ɛks'prɛʃən] *s* Ausdruck *m*

expressive [εks'prεsɪv] *adj* ausdrucks-voll

express' train' *s* Expreßzug *m*

express'way' *s* Schnellverkehrsstraße *f*

expropriate [εks'proprɪ ‚et] *tr* enteignen

expulsion [εks'pʌlʃən] *s* Austreibung *f; (from school or a game)* Verweisung *f*

expunge [εks'pʌndʒ] *tr* ausstreichen

expurgate ['εkspər ‚get] *tr* säubern

exquisite ['εkskwɪzɪt], [εks'kwɪzɪt] *adj* exquisit, vorzüglich

ex-service-man [‚εks'sɑrvɪs ‚mæn] *s* (**-men'**) ehemaliger Soldat *m*

extant ['εkstənt] *adj* noch bestehend

extemporaneous [εks ‚tεmpə'renɪ·əs] *adj* aus dem Stegreif, unvorbereitet

extempore [εks'tεmpəri] *adj* unvorbereitet ‖ *adv* aus dem Stegreif

extemporize [εks'tεmpə ‚raɪz] *tr & intr* extemporieren

extend [εks'tεnd] *tr (expand)* ausdehnen; *(a line)* fortführen; *(time)* verlängern; *(congratulations, invitation)* aussprechen; *(one's hand)* ausstrecken; *(a building)* ausbauen ‖ *intr* (**to**) sich erstrecken (bis); **e. beyond** hinausgehen über *(acc)*

extension [εks'tεnʃən] *s* Ausdehnung *f; (of time, credit)* Verlängerung *f;* (archit) Anbau *m;* (telp) Nebenanschluß *m*

exten'sion cord' *s* Verlängerungsschnur *f*

exten'sion lad'der *s* Ausziehleiter *f*

exten'sion ta'ble *s* Ausziehtisch *m*

extensive [εks'tεnsɪv] *adj* umfassend

extent [εks'tεnt] *s* Umfang *m*, Ausmaß *n;* **to some e.** eingermaßen; **to the full e.** in vollem Umfang; **to what e.** inwiefern

extenuating [εks'tεnju ‚etɪŋ] *adj* mildernd

exterior [εks'tɪrɪ·ər] *adj* Außen-, äußere ‖ *s* Äußere *n*

exterminate [εks'tɑrmɪ ‚net] *tr* vertilgen, ausrotten

extermination [εks ‚tɑrmɪ'neʃən] *s* Vertilgung *f; (of vermin)* Raumentwesung *f*

exterminator [εks'tɑrmɪ ‚netər] *s* Raumentweser *m*

external [εks'tɑrnəl] *adj* Außen-, äußerlich ‖ **externals** *spl* Äußerlichkeiten *pl*

extinct [εks'tɪŋkt] *adj (volcano)* erloschen; *(animal)* ausgestorben; **become e.** aussterben

extinguish [εks'tɪŋgwɪʃ] *tr* auslöschen; **be extinguished** erlöschen

extinguisher [εks'tɪŋgwɪʃər] *s* Löschgerät *n*

extirpate ['εkstər ‚pet] *tr* ausrotten

ex-tol [εks'tol] *v (pret & pp* **-tolled;** *ger* **-tolling)** *tr* erheben, lobpreisen

extort [εks'tɔrt] *tr* erpressen

extortion [εks'tɔrʃən] *s* Erpressung *f*

extortionate [εks'tɔrʃənɪt] *adj* überhöht

extra ['εkstrə] *adj* übrig; *(special)* Sonder-, Extra-; **meals are e.** Mahlzeiten werden zusätzlich berechnet ‖ *adv* extra, besonders ‖ *s* (cin) Statist –in *mf;* (journ) Sonderausgabe *f;* (theat) Komparse *m;* **extras** *(expenses)* Nebenausgaben *pl; (accessories)* Zubehör *n*

extract ['εkstrækt] *s* Extrakt *m*, Auszug *m; (excerpt)* Ausschnitt *m* ‖ [εks'trækt] *tr* extrahieren, ausziehen; (dent, math) ziehen

extraction [εks'trækʃən] *s (lineage)* Abstammung *f;* (dent) Zahnziehen *n;* (min) Gewinnung *f*

extracurricular [‚εkstrəkə'rɪkjələr] *adj* außerplanmäßig

extradite ['εkstrə ‚daɪt] *tr* ausliefern

extradition [‚εkstrə'dɪʃən] *s* Auslieferung *f*

ex'tra in'come *s* Nebeneinkünfte *pl*

ex'tramar'ital *adj* außerehelich

extramural [‚εkstrə'mjʊrəl] *adj* außerhalb der Schule stattfindend

extraneous [εks'trenɪ·əs] *adj* unwesentlich

extraordinary [‚εks'trɔrdɪ ‚nεri] *adj* außerordentlich

ex'tra pay' *s* Zulage *f*

extrapolate [εks'træpə ‚let] *tr & intr* extrapolieren

extrasensory [‚εkstrə'sεnsəri] *adj* übersinnlich

extravagance [εks'trævəgəns] *s* Verschwendung *f*

extravagant [εks'trævəgənt] *adj* verschwenderisch, extravagant; *(idea, plan)* überspannt

extreme [εks'trim] *adj* äußerst; *(radical)* extrem; *(old age)* höchst; *(necessity)* dringend ‖ *s* Äußerste *n;* **at the other e.** am entgegengesetzten Ende; **carry to extremes** auf die Spitze treiben; **in the e.** äußerst

extremely [εks'trimli] *adj* äußerst

extreme' unc'tion *s* die Letzte Ölung

extremist [εks'trimɪst] *s* Extremist –in *mf*

extremity [εks'trεmɪti] *s* Äußerste *n*, äußerstes Ende *n;* **be reduced to extremities** aus dem letzten Loch pfeifen; **extremities** *(hands and feet)* Extremitäten *pl*

extricate ['εkstrɪ ‚ket] *tr* befreien

extrinsic [εks'trɪnsɪk] *adj* äußerlich

extrovert ['εkstrə ‚vʌrt] *s* Extravertierte *mf*

extrude [εks'trud] *tr* ausstoßen

exuberant [εg'z(j)ubərənt] *adj (luxuriant)* üppig; *(lavish)* überschwenglich

exude [εg'zud] *tr* ausschwitzen; (fig) ausstrahlen

exult [εg'zʌlt] *intr* jauchzen

exultant [εg'zʌltənt] *adj* jauchzend

eye [aɪ] *s* Auge *n; (of a needle)* Öhr *n;* **an eye for an eye** Auge um Auge; **be all eyes** große Augen machen; **by eye** nach dem Augenmaß; **close one's eyes** to die Augen schließen vor *(dat);* **have an eye for** Sinn haben für; **have good eyes** gut sehen; **in my eyes** nach meiner Ansicht; **in the eyes of the law** vom Standpunkt des Gesetzes aus; **keep a close eye on** s.o. j–m auf die Finger sehen; **keep an eye on s.th.** ein wachsames Auge auf etw [*acc*] haben; **keep one's eyes peeled** scharf aufpassen; **lay eyes on** zu Gesicht bekommen; **makes eyes at** verliebte Blicke zuwerfen (*dat*); **see eye to eye with** völlig übereinstimmen mit; **with an eye to** mit Rücksicht auf (*acc*) ‖ *v* (*pret & pp* **eyed;** *ger* **eying & eyeing**) *tr* mustern, schielen nach

eye'ball' *s* Augapfel *m*

eye'brow' *s* Augenbraue *f*

eye'brow pen'cil *s* Augenbrauenstift *m*

eye' cat'cher *s* Blickfang *m*

eye'cup' *s* Augenspülglas *n*

eye' drops' *spl* Augentropfen *pl*

eyeful ['aɪfʊl] *s*—**get an e.** etw Hübsches sehen

eye'glass' *s* Augenglas *n;* **eyeglasses** Brille *f*

eye'lash' *s* Wimper *f*

eyelet ['aɪlɪt] *s* Öse *f*

eye'lid' *s* Lid *n,* Augenlid *n*

eye'o'pener *s* (*surprise*) Überraschung *f;* (*liquor*) Schnäpschen *n*

eye'piece' *s* Okular *n*

eye'shade' *s* Augenschirm *m*

eye' shad'ow *s* Lidschatten *m*

eye'shot' *s*—**within e.** in Sehweite

eye'sight' *s* Augenlicht *n,* Sehkraft *f;* (*range*) Sehweite *f;* **have bad** (or **good**) **e.** schlechte (or gute) Augen haben

eye' sock'et *s* Augenhöhle *f*

eye'sore' *s* (fig) Dorn *m* im Auge

eye'strain' *s* Überanstrengung *f* der Augen

eye'tooth' *s* (-**teeth**) Augenzahn *m;* **cut one's eyeteeth** (fig) erfahrener werden

eye'wash' *s* Augenwasser *n;* (sl) Schwindel *m*

eye'wit'ness *s* Augenzeuge *m,* Augenzeugin *f*

F

F, f [ɛf] *s* sechster Buchstabe des englischen Alphabets; (mus) F *n;* **F flat** Fes *n;* **F sharp** Fis *n*

fable ['febəl] *s* Fabel *f,* Märchen *n*

fabric ['fæbrɪk] *s* Gewebe *n;* (*cloth*) Stoff *m;* (fig) Gefüge *n*

fabricate ['fæbrɪ,ket] *tr* herstellen; (*lies*) erfinden

fabrication [,fæbrɪ'keʃən] *s* Herstellung *f;* (fig) Erfindung *f*

fabulous ['fæbjələs] *adj* fabelhaft

façade [fə'sad] *s* Fassade *f*

face [fes] *s* Gesicht *n;* (*dial*) Zifferblatt *n;* (tex) rechte Seite *f;* (typ) Satzspiegel *m;* **f. to f. with** Auge in Auge mit; **in the f. of** angesichts (*genit*); **lose f.** sich blamieren; **make faces at s.o.** j-m Gesichter schneiden; **on the f. of it** augenscheinlich; **save f.** das Gesicht wahren; **show one's f.** sich blicken lassen ‖ *tr* (& fig) ins Auge sehen (*dat*); (*said of a building*) liegen nach; (*e.g., with brick*) verkleiden; **be faced with** stehen vor (*dat*); **facing** gegenüber (*dat*); **have to f. the music** die Suppe löffeln müssen ‖ *intr* (*in some direction*) liegen; **about f.!** (mil) kehrt!; **he faced up to it like a man** er stellte seinen Mann

face' card' *s* Bildkarte *f,* Figur *f*

face' cream' *s* Gesichtskrem *f*

face' lift'ing *s* Gesichtsstraffung *f;* (*of a building*) Schönheitsreparatur *f*

face' pow'der *s* Gesichtspuder *m*

facet ['fæsɪt] *s* Facette *f;* (fig) Aspekt *m*

facetious [fə'siʃəs] *adj* scherzhaft

face' val'ue *s* Nennwert *m;* **take at f.** (fig) für bare Münze nehmen

facial ['feʃəl] *adj* Gesichts-; **f. expression** Miene *f* ‖ *s* Gesichtspflege *f*

facilitate [fə'sɪlɪ,tet] *tr* erleichtern

facility [fə'sɪlɪti] *s* (*ease*) Leichtigkeit *f;* (*skill*) Geschicklichkeit *f;* **facilities** Einrichtungen *pl*

fac'ing *s* (archit) Verkleidung *f;* (sew) Besatz *m*

facsimile [fæk'sɪmɪli] *s* Faksimile *n*

fact [fækt] *s* Tatsache *f;* **apart from the f. that** abgesehen davon, daß; **facts of the case** Tatbestand *m;* **in f.** tatsächlich; **it is a f. that** es steht fest, daß

fact'-find'ing *adj* Untersuchungs–

faction ['fækʃən] *s* Clique *f*

factional ['fækʃənəl] *adj* klüngelhaft

factor ['fæktər] *s* (& math) Faktor *m*

factory ['fæktəri] *s* Fabrik *f*

factual ['fæktʃʊ-əl] *adj* sachlich

faculty ['fækəlti] *s* Vermögen *n;* (educ) Lehrkörper *m*

fad [fæd] *s* Mode *f;* **latest fad** letzter Schrei *m*

fade [fed] *tr* verblassen lassen; **f. in** einblenden; **f. out** ausblenden ‖ *intr* (*said of colors, memories*) verblassen; (*said of cloth, wallpaper, etc.*) verschießen; (*said of flowers*) verwelken; **f. away** (*said of sounds*) abklingen; **f. in** (cin, rad, telv) einblenden; **f. out** (cin, rad, telv) ausblenden

fade'-in' *s* (cin, rad, telv) Einblenden *n*

fade'-out' *s* (cin, rad, telv) Ausblenden *n*

fag [fæg] *s* (*cigarette*) (sl) Glimmstengel *m;* (*homosexual*) (sl) Schwuler *m* ‖ *v* (*pret & pp* **fagged;** *ger* **fagging**) *tr*—**fag out** (sl) auspumpen

fagged *adj* (sl) erschöpft

fagot ['fægət] *s* Reisigbündel *n*

fail [fel] *s*—**without f.** ganz bestimmt ‖ *tr* (*an examination*) durchfallen bei; (*a student*) durchfallen lassen; (*friends*) im Stich lassen; (*a father*) enttäuschen; **failing this** widrigenfalls; **I f. to see** ich kann nicht einsehen; **words f. me** mir fehlen die

Worte ‖ *intr* (*said of a person or device*) versagen; (*said of a project, attempt*) fehlschlagen; (*said of crops*) schlecht ausfallen; (*said of strength*) abnehmen; (*said of health*) sich verschlechtern; (com) in Konkurs geraten

failure ['feljər] *s* Versagen *n;* (*person*) Versager –in *mf;* (*lack of success, unsuccessful venture*) Mißerfolg *m;* (*omission*) Versäumnis *n;* (*deterioration*) Schwäche *f;* (*educ*) ungenügende Zensur *f;* (com) Konkurs *m*

faint [fent] *adj* schwach; (*slight*) leise; **feel f.** sich schwach fühlen ‖ *s* Ohnmacht *f* ‖ *intr* ohnmächtig werden

faint'-heart'ed *adj* kleinmütig

faint'ing spell' *s* Ohnmachtsanfall *m*

fair [fer] *adj* (*just*) gerecht, fair; (*blond*) blond; (*complexion*) hell; (*weather*) heiter; (*chance, knowledge*) mittelmäßig; (*warning*) rechtzeitig; **f. to middling** gut bis mäßig ‖ *s* Jahrmarkt *m*, Messe *f*

fair' game' *s* (& fig) Freiwild *n*

fair'ground' *s* Jahrmarktplatz *m*

fairly ['ferli] *adv* ziemlich

fair'-mind'ed *adj* unparteiisch

fairness ['fernıs] *s* Gerechtigkeit *f;* **in f. to s.o.** um j–m Gerechtigkeit widerfahren zu lassen

fair' play' *s* fair Play *n*

fair' sex', the *s* das schöne Geschlecht

fair'way' *s* (golf) Spielbahn *f;* (naut) Fahrwasser *n*

fair'-weath'er *adj* (*friend*) unzuverlässig

fairy ['feri] *adj* Feen– ‖ *s* Fee *f;* (sl) Schwule *mf*

fair'y god'mother *s* gute Fee *f*

fair'yland' *s* Märchenland *n*

fair'ytale' *s* (& fig) Märchen *n*

faith [feθ] *s* Glaube(n) *m;* (in) Vertrauen *n* (auf *acc* or zu); **on the f. of** im Vertrauen auf (*acc*); **put one's f. in** Glauben schenken (*dat*)

faithful ['feθfəl] *adj* (to) (ge)treu (*dat*); (*exact*) genau, wahrheitsgemäß ‖ **the f.** *spl* die Gläubigen

faith' heal'er *s* Gesundbeter –in *mf*

faithless ['feθlıs] *adj* treulos

fake [fek] *adj* verfälscht ‖ *s* Fälschung *f;* (*person*) Simulant –in *mf* ‖ *tr* vortäuschen, simulieren; (*forge*) fälschen

faker ['fekər] *s* Simulant –in *mf*

falcon ['fɔ(l)kən] *s* Falke *m*

falconer ['fɔ(l)kənər] *s* Falkner *m*

fall [fɔl] *adj* Herbst– ‖ *s* Fall *m;* (*of prices, of a government*) Sturz *m;* (*moral*) Verfall *m;* (*of water*) Fall *m;* (*autumn*) Herbst *m;* (Bib) Sündenfall *m;* ‖ *v* (*pret* **fell** [fel]; *pp* **fallen** ['fɔlən] *intr* (*said of a person, object, rain, snow, holiday, prices, temperature*) fallen; (*said of a town*) gestürzt werden; **f. apart** auseinanderfallen; **f. away** wegfallen; **f. back** zurückfallen; (mil) sich zurückziehen; **f. back on** zurückgreifen auf (*acc*); **f. behind** (in) zurückbleiben (mit); **f. below** unterschreiten; **f. down** umfallen; (*said only of per-*

sons) hinfallen; **f. down on the job** versagen; **f. due** fällig werden; **f. flat** (coll) flachfallen; **f. for** reinfallen auf (*acc*); **f. from** abfallen von; **f.. from grace** in Ungnade fallen; **f. in** (*said of a roof*) einstürzen; (mil) antreten; **f. in love with** sich verlieben in (*acc*); **f. in step** Tritt fassen; **f. into** (e.g., *a hole*) hereinfallen in (*acc*); (e.g., *trouble*) geraten in (*acc*); **f. into ruin** zerfallen; **f. in with s.o.** j–n zufällig treffen; **f. off** abfallen; (com) zurückgehen; **f. out** (*said of hair*) ausfallen; **f. out with** sich verfeinden mit; **f. over** umfallen; **f. short** knapp werden; (arti) kurz gehen; **f. short of** zurückbleiben hinter (*dat*); **f. through** durchfallen; **f. to s.o.'s share** j–m zufallen; **f. under s.o.'s influence** unter j–s Einfluß geraten; **f. upon** herfallen über (*acc*)

fallacious [fə'leʃəs] *adj* trügerisch

fallacy ['fæləsi] *s* Trugschluß *m*, Fehlschluß *m*

fall' guy' *s* (sl) Sündenbock *m*

fallible ['fælıbəl] *adj* fehlbar

fall'ing off' *s* Rückschritt *m*

fall'ing rocks' *spl* (public sign) Steinschlag *m*

fall'ing star' *s* Sternschnuppe *f*

fall'out' *s* radioaktiver Niederschlag *m*

fallow ['fælo] *adj* (agr) brach; **lie f.** (& fig) brachliegen

false [fɔls] *adj* falsch, Miß–; (*start, step*) Fehl–; (*bottom*) doppelt; (*ceiling*) Zwischen–

false' alarm' *s* blinder Alarm *m;* (fig) Schreckschuß *m*

false' face' *s* Maske *f*

false' front' *s* (fig) (coll) Mache *f*

false'-heart'ed *adj* treulos

false'hood' *s* Unwahrheit *f*

false' pretens'es *spl* Hochstapelei *f*

false' teeth' *spl* (künstliches) Gebiß *n*

falset·to [fɔl'seto] *s* (**–tos**) Falset *n*

falsi·fy ['fɔlsı‚faı] *v* (*pret* & *pp* **–fied**) *tr* (ver)fälschen

falsity ['fɔlsıti] *s* Falschheit *f*

falter ['fɔltər] *intr* schwanken; (*in speech*) stocken

fame [fem] *s* Ruf, *m*, Ruhm *m*

famed *adj* (for) berühmt (wegen, durch)

familiar [fə'mıljər] *adj* bekannt; (*expression*) geläufig; (e.g., *sight*) gewohnt; (*close*) vertraut; **become f. with** sich bekannt machen mit

familiarity [fə‚mılı'ærıti] *s* Vertrautheit *f;* (*closeness*) Vertraulichkeit *f*

familiarize [fə'mıljə‚raız] *tr* bekannt machen

family ['fæm(ı)li] *adj* Familien–; **in a f. way** in anderen Umständen ‖ *s* Familie *f*

fam'ily doc'tor *s* Hausarzt *m*

fam'ily man' *s* häuslicher Mann *m*

fam'ily name' *s* Familienname *m*

fam'ily tree' *s* Stammbaum *m*

famine ['fæmın] *s* Hungersnot *f*

famish ['fæmıʃ] *tr* (ver)hungern lassen ‖ *intr* verhungern

fam'ished *adj* ausgehungert

famous ['feməs] *adj* (**for**) berühmt (wegen, durch)

fan [fæn] *s* Fächer *m*, Wedel *m*; (*electric*) Ventilator *m*; (sl) Fan *m* ‖ *v* (*pret & pp* **fanned**; *ger* **fanning**) *tr* fächeln; (*a fire*) anfachen; (*passions*) entfachen ‖ *intr*—**fan out** (*said of roads*) fächerförmig auseinandergehen; (mil) ausschwärmen

fanatic [fə'nætɪk] *adj* fanatisch ‖ *s* Fanatiker –in *mf*

fanatical [fə'nætɪkəl] *adj* fanatisch

fanaticism [fə'nætɪ‚sɪzəm] *s* Fanatismus *m*

fan' belt' *s* (aut) Keilriemen *m*

fan'cied *adj* eingebildet

fancier ['fænsɪ·ər] *s* Liebhaber –in *mf*

fanciful ['fænsɪfəl] *adj* phantastisch

fan-cy ['fænsi] *adj* (extra)fein; (*e.g., dress*) Luxus–; (sport) Kunst–; **f. price** Phantasiepreis *m* ‖ *s* Phantasie *f*; **passing f.** vorübergehender Spleen *m*; **take a f. to** Gefallen finden an (*dat*) ‖ *v* (*pret & pp* **–cied**) *tr* sich [*dat*] vorstellen

fan'cy foods' *spl* Feinkost *f*

fan'cy-free' *adj* ungebunden

fan'fare' *s* Fanfare *f*; (*fuss*) Tamtam *n*

fang [fæŋ] *s* Fangzahn *m*; (*of a snake*) Giftzahn *m*

fan' mail' *s* Verehrerbriefe *pl*

fantastic(al) [fæn'tæstɪk(əl)] *adj* phantastisch, toll

fantasy ['fæntəsi] *s* Phantasie *f*

far [far] *adj* (*& fig*) weit; **at the far end** am anderen Ende; **far cry from** etw ganz anderes als; **far side** *f*, dere Seite *f*; **in the far future** in der fernen Zukunft ‖ *adv* weit; **as far as** soweit; (*up to*) bis zu, bis an (*acc*); **as far as I am concerned** was mich anbelangt; **as far as I know** soviel ich weiß; **as far as that goes** was das betrifft; **by far** weitaus, bei weitem; **far and away** weitaus, **far away** weit entfernt; **far below** tief unten; **far better** weit besser; **far from it!** weit gefehlt!; **far from ready** noch lange nicht fertig; **far into the night** tief in die Nacht hinein; **far out** (sl) ausgefallen; **from far** von weitem; (*from a distant place*) von weit her; **go far** es weit bringen; **go far towards** (*ger*) viel beitragen zu (*inf*); **go too far** das Maß überschreiten; **not far from** unweit von; **so far** soweit, bisher

far'away' *adj* weit entfernt; (fig) träumerisch

farce [fars] *s* Possenspiel *n*, Farce *f*; (fig) Posse *f*, Schwank *m*

farcical ['farsɪkəl] *adj* possenhaft

fare [fer] *s* (*travel price*) Fahrpreis *m*; (*money for travel*) Fahrgeld *n*; (*passenger*) Fahrgast *m*; (*food*) Kost *f* ‖ *intr* (er)gehen; **how did you f., well or ill?** wie ist es Ihnen ergangen, gut oder schlecht?

Far' East', the *s* der Ferne Osten

Far' East'ern *adj* fernöstlich

fare'well' *s* Valet *n*, Lebewohl *n*; **bid s.o. f.** j-m Lebewohl sagen ‖ *interj* lebe wohl!; lebt wohl!

farewell' din'ner *s* Abschiedsschmaus *m*

farewell' par'ty *s* Abschiedsfeier *f*

far-fetched ['far‚fɛt∫t] *adj* gesucht

far-flung ['far'flʌŋ] *adj* weit ausgedehnt

farina [fə'rinə] *s* Grießmehl *n*

farm [farm] *adj* landwirtschaftlich ‖ *s* Farm *f*, Bauernhof *m* ‖ *tr* bebauen, bewirtschaften ‖ *intr* Landwirtschaft betreiben, Bauer sein

farm' hand' *s* Landarbeiter *m*

farm'house' *s* Bauernhaus *n*

farm'ing *adj* landwirtschaftlich ‖ *s* Landwirtschaft *f*

farm'land' *s* Ackerland *n*

farm' machin'ery *s* Landmaschinen *pl*

farm'yard' *s* Bauernhof *m*

far'-off' *adj* fernliegend

far'-reach'ing *adj* weitreichend; (*decision*) folgenschwer

far'-sight'ed *adj* weitsichtig; (fig) weitblickend

farther ['farðər] *adj & adv* weiter

farthest ['farðɪst] *adj* weiteste ‖ *adv* am weitesten

farthing ['farðɪŋ] *s*—**not worth a f.** keinen Pfifferling wert

fascinate ['fæsɪ‚net] *tr* faszinieren

fas'cinating *adj* faszinierend

fascination [‚fæsɪ'ne∫ən] *s* Faszination *f*

fascism ['fæʃɪzəm] *s* Faschismus *m*

fascist ['fæʃɪst] *s* Faschist –in *mf*

fashion ['fæʃən] *s* Mode *f*; (*manner*) Art *f*, Weise *f*; **after a f.** in gewisser Weise; **in f.** in Mode; **out of f.** aus der Mode ‖ *tr* gestalten, bilden

fashionable ['fæʃənəbəl] *adj* (*modern*) modisch; (*elegant*) elegant

fash'ion magazine' *s* Modenzeitschrift *f*

fash'ion plate' *s* Modedame *f*

fash'ion show' *s* Mode(n)schau *f*

fast [fæst] *adj* schnell; (*dye*) dauerhaft; (*company*) flott; (*life*) locker; (phot) lichtstark; **be f.** (*said of a clock*) vorgehen; **f. train** Schnellzug *m*; **pull a f. one on s.o.** (coll) j–m ein Schnippchen schlagen ‖ *adv* schnell; (*firmly*) fest; **as f. as possible** schnellstens; **be f. asleep** im tiefen Schlaf liegen; **hold f.** festhalten; **not so f.!** nicht so stürmisch! ‖ *s* Fasten *n* ‖ *intr* fasten

fast' day' *s* Fasttag *m*

fasten ['fæsən] *tr* festmachen, sichern; (*a buckle*) schnallen; (**to**) befestigen (an *dat*); **f. one's seat belt** sich anschnallen; **f. the blame on** die Schuld zuschieben (*dat*) ‖ *intr*—**f. upon** sich heften an (*acc*)

fastener ['fæsənər] *s* Verschluß *m*

fastidious [fæs'tɪdɪ·əs] *adj* wählerisch

fast'ing *s* Fasten *n*

fat [fæt] *adj* (*fatter; fattest*) fett; (*plump*) dick, fett; (*profits*) reich ‖ *s* Fett *n*; **chew the fat** (sl) schwatzen

fatal ['fetəl] *adj* tödlich; (*mistake*) verhängnisvoll; **f. to** verhängnisvoll für

fatalism ['fetə‚lɪzəm] *s* Fatalismus *m*

fatalist ['fetəlɪst] *s* Fatalist –in *mf*

fatality [fə'tælɪti] s Todesfall m; (accident victim) Todesopfer n; (disaster) Unglück n

fat' cat' s (sl) Geldgeber –in mf

fate [fet] s Schicksal n, Verhängnis n; the Fates die Parzen pl

fated ['fetɪd] adj vom Schicksal bestimmt

fateful ['fetfəl] adj verhängnisvoll

fat'head' s (coll) dummes Luder n

father ['faðər] s Vater m; (eccl) Pater m || tr (beget) erzeugen; (originate) hervorbringen

fa'therhood' s Vaterschaft f

fa'ther-in-law' s (fathers-in-law) Schwiegervater m

fa'therland' s Vaterland n

fatherless ['faðərlɪs] adj vaterlos

fatherly ['faðərli] adj väterlich

Fa'ther's Day' s Vatertag m

fathom ['fæðəm] s Klafter f || tr sondieren; (fig) ergründen

fathomless ['fæðəmlɪs] adj unergründlich

fatigue [fə'tig] s Ermattung f; (mil) Arbeitsdienst m; fatigues (mil) Arbeitsanzug m || tr abmatten

fat·so ['fætso] s (–sos & –soes) (coll) Fettkloß m

fatten ['fætən] tr mästen || intr—f. up (coll) sich mästen

fatty ['fæti] adj fettig, fett; f. tissue Fettgewebe n || s (coll) Dicke mf

fatuous ['fætʃu·əs] adj albern

faucet ['fɔsɪt] s Wasserhahn m

fault [fɔlt] s (blame) Schuld f; (misdeed) Vergehen n, Fehler m; (defect) Defekt m; (geol) Verwerfung f; (tennis) Fehlball m; at f. schuld; find f. with etw zu tadeln finden an (dat); to a f. allzusehr || intr (geol) sich verwerfen

fault'find'er s Krittler –in mf

fault'find'ing adj tadelsüchtig || s Krittelei f

faultless ['fɔltlɪs] adj fehlerfrei

faulty ['fɔlti] adj fehlerhaft

faun [fɔn] s (myth) Faun m

fauna ['fɔnə] s Fauna f

favor ['fevər] s (kind act) Gefallen m; (good will) Gunst f; in f. of zugunsten (genit), für; in s.o.'s f. zu j–s Gunsten; lose f. with s.o. sich [dat] j–s Gunst verwirken; speak in f. of s.th. für etw aussprechen || tr begünstigen; (prefer) bevorzugen; (a sore limb) schonen

favorable ['fevərəbəl] adj günstig; (criticism) positiv; (report) beifällig

favorite ['fevərɪt] adj Lieblings– || s Liebling m; (sport) Favorit –in mf

favoritism ['fevərɪ,tɪzəm] s Günstlingswirtschaft f

fawn [fɔn] s Rehkalb n || intr—f. on schmeicheln (dat)

fawn'ing adj schmeichlerisch

faze [fez] tr (coll) auf die Palme bringen

FBI [,ɛf,bi'aɪ] s (Federal Bureau of Investigation) Bundessicherheitspolizei f

fear [fɪr] s (of) Furcht f (vor dat), Angst f (vor dat); for f. of aus Angst vor (dat); for f. of (ger) um nicht zu (inf); stand in f. of sich fürchten vor (dat) || tr fürchten, sich fürchten vor (dat); f. the worst das Schlimmste befürchten || intr sich fürchten; f. for besorgt sein um

fearful ['fɪrfəl] adj (afraid) furchtsam; (terrible) furchtbar

fearless ['fɪrlɪs] adj furchtlos

feasible ['fɪzɪbəl] adj durchführbar

feast [fist] s Fest n; (sumptuous meal) Schmaus m || tr—f. one's eyes on seine Augen weiden an (dat) || intr schwelgen; f. on sich gütlich tun an (dat)

feast'day' s Festtag m

feast'ing s Schmauserei f

feat [fit] s Kunststück n; f. of arms Waffentat f

feather ['fɛðər] s Feder f; a f. in his cap ein Triumph für ihn || tr mit Federn versehen; (aer) auf Segelstellung fahren; (crew) flach drehen; f. one's nest sich warm betten

feath'er bed' s Federbett n

feath'erbed'ding s Anstellung f unnötiger Arbeitskräfte

feath'erbrain' s Schwachkopf m

feath'er dust'er s Staubwedel m

feath'eredge' s feine Kante f

feath'erweight' adj Federgewichts– || s (boxer) Federgewichtler m

feathery ['fɛðəri] adj federartig; (light as feathers) federleicht

feature ['fitʃər] s (of the face) Gesichtszug m; (characteristic) Merkmal n; f. film Spielfilm m; main f. Grundzug m; (cin) Hauptfilm m || tr als Hauptschlager herausbringen; (cin) in der Hauptrolle zeigen

fea'ture writ'er s Sonderberichterstatter –in mf

February ['fɛbru,ɛri] s Februar m

feces ['fisiz] spl Kot m, Stuhl m

feckless ['fɛklɪs] adj (incompetent) unfähig; (ineffective) unwirksam; (without spirit) geistlos

fecund ['fikənd] adj fruchtbar

federal ['fɛdərəl] adj Bundes–, bundesstaatlich; f. government Bundesregierung f

federate ['fɛdə,ret] adj verbündet || tr zu e–m Bund vereinigen || intr sich verbünden

federation [,fɛdə'reʃən] s Staatenbund m

fed' up' [fɛd] adj—be f. die Nase voll haben; be f. with s.th. etw satt haben

fee [fi] s Gebühr f; (of a doctor) Honorar n

feeble ['fibəl] adj schwächlich

fee'ble-mind'ed adj schwachsinnig

feed [fid] s Futter n; (mach) Zuführung f || v (pret & pp fed [fɛd]) tr (animals) füttern; (persons) zu Essen geben; (in a restaurant) verpflegen; (e.g., a nation) nähren; (a fire) unterhalten; (mach) zuführen || intr fressen; f. on sich ernähren von

feed'back' s Rückwirkung f; (electron) Rückkoppelung f

feed' bag' s Futtersack m; put on the f. (sl) futtern

feeder ['fidər] *s* (elec) Speiseleitung *f;* (mach) Zubringer *m*
feed′er line′ *s* (aer, rr) Zubringerlinie *f*
feed′ing *s* (*of animals*) Fütterung *f;* (& mach) Speisung *f*
feed′ trough′ *s* Futtertrog *m*
feed′ wire′ *s* (elec) Zuleitungsdraht *m*
feel [fil] *s* Gefühl *n; get the f. of* sich gewöhnen an (*acc*) || *v* (*pret & pp* **felt** [fɛlt]) *tr* fühlen; (*a pain*) spüren; **f. one's way** sich vortasten; (fig) sondieren; **f. s.o. out** bei j–m vorfühlen || *intr* (*sick, tired, well*) sich fühlen; **f. about for** herumtasten nach; **f. for s.o.** mit j–m fühlen; **f. like** (*ger*) Lust haben zu (*inf*); **f. up to** sich gewachsen fühlen (*dat*); **his head feels hot** sein Kopf fühlt sich heiß an; **how do you f. about it?** was halten Sie davon?; **I don't quite f. myself** ich fühle mich nicht ganz wohl; **I f. as if** es ist mir, als wenn; **make itself felt** sich fühlbar machen
feeler ['filər] *s* (ent) Fühler *m; put out feelers to* vorfühlen bei
feel′ing *s* Gefühl *n; bad f.* Verstimmung *f;* **good f.** Wohlwollen *n;* **have a f. for** Sinn haben für; **have a f. that** das Gefühl haben, daß; **with f.** gefühlsvoll
feign [fen] *tr* vortäuschen; **f. death** sich totstellen
feint [fent] *s* Finte *f*, Scheinangriff *m*
feldspar ['fɛld‚spar] *s* Feldspat *m*
feline ['filaɪn] *adj* katzenartig
fell [fɛl] *adj* grausam || *tr* fällen
fellow ['fɛlo] *s* (coll) Kerl *m;* (*of a society*) Mitglied *n*
fel′low be′ing *s* Mitmensch *m*
fel′low citizen *s* Mitbürger –in *mf*
fel′low coun′tryman *s* Landsmann *m*
fel′low crea′ture *s* Mitgeschöpf *n*
fel′lowman′ *s* (**–men′**) Mitmensch *m*
fel′low mem′ber *s* Mitglied *n*
fel′lowship′ *s* Kameradschaft *f;* (educ) Stipendium *n*
fel′low stu′dent *s* Kommilitone *m*
fel′low trav′eler *s* Mitreisende *mf;* (pol) Mitläufer –in *mf*
felon ['fɛlən] *s* Schwerverbrecher –in *mf*
felony ['fɛləni] *s* Schwerverbrechen *n*
felt [fɛlt] *adi* Filz– || *s* Filz *m*
felt′ pen′ *s* Filzschreiber *m*, Faserstift *m*
female ['fimel] *adj* weiblich || *s* (*of animals*) Weibchen *n;* (pej) Weibsbild *n*
feminine ['fɛmɪnɪn] *adj* weiblich
feminism ['fɛmɪ‚nɪzəm] *s* Feminismus *m*
fen [fɛn] *s* Bruch *m* & *n*
fence [fɛns] *s* Zaun *m;* (*of stolen goods*) Hehler *m;* **on the f.** (fig) unentschlossen || *tr*—**f. in** einzäunen; **f. off** abzäunen || *intr* (sport) fechten
fence′ post′ *s* Zaunpfahl *m*
fenc′ing *s* Fechten *n*
fend [fend] *tr*—**f. off** abwehren || *intr* —**f. for oneself** für sich selbst sorgen
fender ['fendər] *s* (aut) Kotflügel *m*
fennel ['fɛnəl] *s* Fenchel *m*
ferment ['fʌrment] *s* Gärmittel *n;* (fig)

Unruhe *f* || [fər'ment] *tr* in Gärung bringen || *intr* gären
fermentation [‚fʌrmən'teʃən] *s* Gärung *f*
fern [fʌrn] *s* Farn *m*
ferocious [fə'roʃəs] *adj* wild
ferocity [fə'rasɪti] *s* Wildheit *f*
ferret ['fɛrɪt] *s* Frettchen *n* || *tr*—**f. out** aufspüren
Fer′ris wheel′ ['fɛrɪs] *s* Riesenrad *n*
ferrule ['fɛrul], ['fɛrəl] *s* Stockzwinge *f*, Zwinge *f*
fer·ry ['fɛri] *s* Fähre *f* || *v* (*pret & pp* **–ried**) *tr* übersetzen
fer′ryboat′ *s* Fährboot *n*
fer′ry·man′ *s* (**–men′**) Fährmann *m*
fertile ['fʌrtɪl] *adj* fruchtbar
fertility [fər'tɪlɪti] *s* Fruchtbarkeit *f*
fertilization [‚fʌrtɪlɪ'zeʃən] *s* Befruchtung *f;* (*of soil*) Düngung *f*
fertilize ['fʌrtɪ‚laɪz] *tr* (*a field*) düngen; (*an egg*) befruchten
fertilizer ['fʌrtɪ‚laɪzər] *s* Kunstdünger *m*
fervent ['fʌrvənt] *adj* inbrünstig
fervid ['fʌrvid] *adj* brennend
fervor ['fʌrvər] *s* Inbrunst *f*
fester ['fɛstər] *intr* schwären, eitern; (fig) nagen
festival ['fɛstɪvəl] *adj* festlich, Fest– || *s* Fest *n;* (mus, theat) Festspiele *pl*
festive ['fɛstɪv] *adj* festlich
festivity [fɛs'tɪvɪti] *s* Feierlichkeit *f*
festoon [fɛs'tun] *s* Girlande *f* || *tr* mit Girlanden schmücken
fetch [fɛtʃ] *tr* holen, abholen
fetch′ing *adj* entzückend
fete [fet] *s* Fest *n*
fetid ['fɛtɪd], ['fitɪd] *adj* stinkend
fetish ['fɛtɪʃ], ['fitɪʃ] *s* Fetisch *m*
fetlock ['fɛtlak] *s* Köte *f;* (*tuft of hair*) Kötenzopf *m*
fetter ['fɛtər] *s* Fessel *f* || *tr* fesseln
fettle ['fɛtəl] *s*—**in fine f.** in Form
fetus ['fitəs] *s* Leibesfrucht *f*
feud [fjud] *s* Fehde *f*
feudal ['fjudəl] *adj* feudal
feudalism ['fjudə‚lɪzəm] *s* Feudalismus *m*
fever ['fivər] *s* Fieber *n*
feverish ['fivərɪʃ] *adj* fieberig; **be f.** fiebern
few [fju] *adj & pron* wenige; **a few** ein paar
fiancé [‚fi·an'se] *s* Verlobte *m*
fiancée [‚fi·an'se] *s* Verlobte *f*
fias·co [fɪ'æsko] *s* (**–cos** & **–coes**) Fiasko *n*
fib [fɪb] *s* Flunkerei *f* || *v* (*pret & pp* **fibbed;** *ger* **fibbing**) *intr* flunkern
fibber ['fɪbər] *s* Flunkerer –in *mf*
fiber ['faɪbər] *s* Faser *f*
fibrous ['faɪbrəs] *adj* faserig
fickle ['fɪkəl] *adj* wankelmütig
fickleness ['fɪkəlnɪs] *s* Wankelmut *m*
fiction ['fɪkʃən] *s* Dichtung *f*, Romanliteratur *f*
fictional ['fɪkʃənəl] *adj* romanhaft
fic′tion writ′er *s* Romanschriftsteller –in *mf*
fictitious [fɪk'tɪʃəs] *adj* fingiert
fiddle ['fɪdəl] *s* Fiedel *f*, Geige *f* || *tr* fiedeln; **f. away** (*time*) vergeuden ||

intr fiedeln; **f. with** herumfingern an (*dat*)
fiddler ['fɪdlər] *s* Fiedler –in *mf*
fid/dlestick/ *s* Fiedelbogen *m* ‖ **fiddlesticks** *interj* Quatsch!
fidelity [fɪ'delɪti] *s* Treue *f*
fidget ['fɪdʒɪt] *intr* zappeln; **f. with** nervös spielen mit
fidgety ['fɪdʒɪti] *adj* zappelig
fiduciary [fɪ'd(j)uʃɪ‚ɛri] *adj* treuhänderisch; (*note*) ungedeckt ‖ *s* Treuhänder –in *mf*
fief [fif] *s* (hist) Lehen *n*
field [fild] *adj* (*artillery, jacket, hospital, kitchen*) Feld– ‖ . *s* Feld *n*; (*under cultivation*) Acker *m*; (*contestants collectively*) Wettbewerbsteilnehmer *pl*; (*specialty*) Gebiet *n*; (aer) Flugplatz *m*; (elec) Feld *n*; (*of a motor*) (elec) Magnetfeld *n*; (sport) Spielfeld *n*
field/ am/bulance *s* Sanitätskraftwagen *m*
field/ day/ *s* (fig) großer Tag *m*
fielder ['fildər] *s* Feldspieler *m*
field/ ex/ercise *s* Truppenübung *f*
field/ glass/es *spl* Feldstecher *m*
field/ hock/ey *s* Rasenhockey *n*
field/mar/shal *s* Feldmarschall *m*
field/ mouse/ *s* Feldmaus *f*
field/ of vi/sion *s* Blickfeld *n*
field/ pack/ *s* (mil) Tornister *m*
field/ piece/ *s* Feldgeschütz *n*
field/ trip/ *s* Studienfahrt *f*
field/ work/ *s* praktische Arbeit *f*
fiend [find] *s* (*devil*) Teufel *m*; (*wicked person*) Unhold *m*; (*addict*) Süchtige *mf*
fiendish ['findɪʃ] *adj* teuflisch
fierce [fɪrs] *adj* wild, wütend; (*vehement*) heftig; (*menacing*) drohend; (*heat*) glühend
fiery ['faɪri], ['faɪ‚əri] *adj* feurig
fife [faɪf] *s* Querpfeife *f*
fifteen ['fɪf'tin] *adj & pron* fünfzehn ‖ *s* Fünfzehn *f*
fifteenth ['fɪf'tinθ] *adj & pron* fünfzehnte ‖ *s* (*fraction*) Fünfzehntel *n*; **the f.** (*in dates or a series*) der Fünfzehnte
fifth [fɪfθ] *adj & pron* fünfte ‖ *s* (*fraction*) Fünftel *n*; **the f.** (*in dates or a series*) der Fünfte
fifth/ col/umn *s* (pol) Fünfte Kolonne *f*
fiftieth ['fɪftɪ‚ɪθ] *adj & pron* fünfzigste ‖ *s* (*fraction*) Fünfzigstel *n*
fifty ['fɪfti] *adj & pron* fünfzig ‖ *s* Fünfzig *f*; **the fifties** die fünfziger Jahre
fif/ty-fif/ty *adv* halbpart; **go f. with s.o.** mit j–m halbpart machen
fig [frg] *s* Feige *f*; (fig) Pfifferling *m*
fight [faɪt] *s* Kampf *m*, Gefecht *n*; (*quarrel*) Streit *m*; (*brawl*) Rauferei *f*; (box) Boxkampf *m*; **pick a f.** Zank suchen ‖ *tr* bekämpfen; (*a case*) durchkämpfen; **f. back** (*tears*) niederkämpfen; **f. it out** ausfechten; **f. one's way out** sich durchkämpfen ‖ *intr* kämpfen; (*quarrel*) streiten; (*brawl*) raufen
fighter ['faɪtər] *adj* (aer) Jagd– ‖ *s*

Kämpfer –in *mf*; (aer) Jäger *m*; (box) Boxkämpfer *m*
fight/er pi/lot *s* Jagdflieger *m*
fight/ing *s* Schlägerei *f*; (*quarreling*) Streiten *n*; (mil) Kampfhandlungen *pl*
fig/ leaf/ *s* Feigenblatt *n*
figment ['fɪgmənt] *s*—**f. of the imagination** Hirngespinst *n*
fig/ tree/ *s* Feigenbaum *m*
figurative ['fɪgjərətɪv] *adj* bildlich; (*meaning*) übertragen
figure ['fɪgjər] *s* Figur *f*; (*personage*) Persönlichkeit *f*; (*number*) Zahl *f*; **be good at figures** ein guter Rechner sein; **cut a fine** (or **poor**) **f.** e–e gute (or schlechte) Figur abgeben; **run into three figures** in die Hunderte gehen ‖ *tr* (coll) glauben, meinen; **f. out** ausknobeln ‖ *intr*—**f. large** e–e große Rolle spielen; **f. on** rechnen mit
fig/urehead/ *s* Strohmann *m*; (naut) Bugfigur *f*; **a mere f.** e–e bloße Nummer
fig/ure of speech/ *s* Redewendung *f*
fig/ure skat/ing *s* Kunstlauf *m*
figurine [‚fɪgjə'rin] *s* Figurine *f*
filament ['fɪləmənt] *s* Faser *f*, Faden *m*; (elec) Glühfaden *m*
filbert ['fɪlbərt] *s* Haselnuß *f*
filch [fɪltʃ] *tr* mausen
file [faɪl] *s* (*tool*) Feile *f*; (*record*) Akte *f*; (*cards*) Kartei *f*; (*row*) Reihe *f*; **put on f.** zu den Akten legen ‖ *tr* (*with a tool*) feilen; (*letters, etc.*) ablegen, abheften; (*a complaint*) erheben; (*a report*) erstatten; (*a claim*) anmelden; (*a petition*) einreichen; **f. suit** e–n Prozeß anstrengen ‖ *intr*—**f. for** sich bewerben um; **f. out** im Gänsemarsch herausmarschieren; **f. past** vorbeidefilieren (an *dat*)
file/ cab/inet *s* Aktenschrank *m*
file/ card/ *s* Karteikarte *f*
filial ['fɪlɪ‚əl] *adj* kindlich
filibuster ['fɪlɪ‚bʌstər] *s* Obstruktion *f* ‖ *intr* Obstruktion treiben
filigree ['fɪlɪ‚gri] *s* Filigran *n*
fil/ing *s* Feilen *n*; (*of records*) Ablegen *n* von Akten; (*of a claim*) Anmeldung *f*; (*of a complaint*) Erhebung *f*; (*of a petition*) Einreichung *f*; **filings** Feilspäne *pl*
Filipi-no [‚fɪlɪ'pino] *adj* filipinisch ‖ *s* (**-nos**) Filipino *m*
fill [fɪl] *s* (*fullness*) Fülle *f*; (*land fill*) Aufschüttung *f*; **eat one's f.** sich satt essen; **I have had my f. of it** ich habe es satt ‖ *tr* füllen; (*an order*) ausführen; (*a pipe*) stopfen; (*a position*) besetzen; (*dent*) plombieren, füllen; **f. full** vollfüllen; **f. in** (*empty space*) ausfüllen; (*one's name*) einsetzen; (*a hole, grave*) zuwerfen; **f. it up** (aut) volltanken; **f. up** auffüllen; (*a tank*) nachfüllen; (*a bag*) anfüllen; (*a glass*) vollschenken; **f. with smoke** verräuchern ‖ *intr* sich füllen; (*said of sails*) sich blähen; **f. in for** einspringen für; **f. out** rund werden; **f. up** sich füllen
filler ['fɪlər] *s* Füller *m*; (*of a cigar*)

Einlage *f;* (journ) Lückenbüßer *m;* (paint) Grundierfirnis *m*

fillet ['fɪlət] *s* (*headband*) Kopfbinde *f;* (archit) Leiste *f* || [fɪ'le] *s* (culin) Filet *n* || *tr* filetieren

fillet' of beef' *s* Rinderfilet *n*

fillet' of sole' *s* Seezungenfilet *n*

fill'ing *s* (culin, dent) Füllung *f*

fill'ing sta'tion *s* Tankstelle *f*

fillip ['fɪlɪp] *s* Schnippchen *n;* (*on the nose*) Nasenstüber *m*

filly ['fɪli] *s* Stutenfüllen *n*

film [fɪlm] *s* (*thin layer*) Schicht *f;* (cin, phot) Film *m;* **f. of grease** Fettschicht *f*

film' fes'tival *s* Filmfestspiele *pl*

film' li'brary *s* Filmarchiv *n*

film' speed' *s* Filmempfindlichkeit *f*

film' star' *s* Filmstar *m*

film'strip' *s* Bildstreifen *m*

filmy ['fɪlmi] *adj* trüb

filter ['fɪltər] *s* Filter *m;* (rad) Sieb *n* || *tr* filtern; (rad) sieben

fil'tering *s* Filtrierung *f*

fil'ter pa'per *s* Filterpapier *n*

fil'ter tip' *s* Filtermundstück *n;* (coll) Filterzigarette *f*

filth [fɪlθ] *s* Schmutz *m;* (fig) Unflätigkeit *f,* Zote *f*

filthy ['fɪlθi] *adj* schmutzig (*talk*) unflätig; (*lucre*) schnöd(e) || *adv*—**f. rich** (sl) klotzig reich

filtrate ['fɪltret] *s* Filtrat *n* || *tr & intr* filtrieren

filtration [fɪl'treʃən] *s* Filtrierung *f*

fin [fɪn] *s* Flosse *f;* (*of a shark or whale*) Finne *f;* (*of a bomb*) Steuerschwanz *m;* (aer) Flosse *f*

final ['faɪnəl] *adj* End-, Schluß–; (*definitive*) endgültig || *s* (educ) Abschlußprüfung *f;* **finals** (sport) Endrunde *f,* Endspiel *n*

finale [fɪ'nɑli] *s* Finale *n*

finalist ['faɪnəlɪst] *s* Finalist –in *mf*

finality [faɪ'nælɪti] *s* Endgültigkeit *f*

finally ['faɪnəli] *adv* schließlich

finance ['faɪnæns], [fɪ'næns] *s* Finanz *f;* **finances** Finanzwesen *n* || *tr* finanzieren

financial [fɪ'nænʃəl], [faɪ'nænʃəl] *adj* (*e.g., policy, situation, crisis, aid*) Finanz–; (*e.g., affairs, resources, embarrassment*) Geld–

financier [ˌfɪnən'sɪr], [ˌfaɪnən'sɪr] *s* Finanzmann *m*

financ'ing, fi'nancing *s* Finanzierung *f*

finch [fɪntʃ] *s* Fink *m*

find [faɪnd] *s* Fund *m;* (archeol) Bodenfund *m* || *v* (*pret & pp* **found** [faʊnd]) *tr* finden; (math) bestimmen; **f. one's way** sich zurechtfinden; **f. one's way back** zurückfinden; **f. out** herausfinden; **f. s.o. guilty** j–n für schuldig erklären || *intr*—**f. out about s.th.** hinter etw [*acc*] kommen

finder ['faɪndər] *s* Finder –in *mf*

find'ing *s* Finden *n;* **findings** Tatbestand *m*

fine [faɪn] *adj* fein; (*excellent*) hervorragend; (*weather*) schön; **f.!** gut! || *s* Geldstrafe *f* || *tr* mit e–r Geldstrafe belegen

fine' arts' *spl* schöne Künste *pl*

fineness ['faɪnnɪs] *s* Feinheit *f;* (*of a coin or metal*) Feingehalt *m*

fine' point' *s* Feinheit *f*

fine' print' *s* Kleindruck *m*

finery ['faɪnəri] *s* Putz *m,* Staat *m*

fine-spun ['faɪnˌspʌn] *adj* feingesponnen

finesse [fɪ'nɛs] *s* Finesse *f;* (cards) Impaß *m* || *tr & intr* impassieren

fine-toothed ['faɪnˌtuθt] *adj* feingezahnt; **go over with a f. comb** unter die Lupe nehmen

fine' tooth' *s* Feinheit *f*

fine' tun'ing *s* Feineinstellung *f*

finger ['fɪŋgər] *s* Finger *m;* **have a f. in the pie** die Hand im Spiel haben; **keep your fingers crossed** halten Sie mir den Daumen; **not lift a f.** keinen Finger rühren; **put the f. on s.o.** (sl) j–n verpetzen; **snap one's fingers** mit den Fingern schnellen; **twist around one's little f.** um den kleinen Finger wickeln || *tr* befingern

fin'ger bowl' *s* Fingerschale *f*

fin'gering *s* (mus) Fingersatz *m*

fin'gernail' *s* Fingernagel *m*

fin'gernail pol'ish *s* Nagellack *m*

fin'gerprint' *s* Fingerabdruck *m* || *tr*— **f. s.o.** j–m die Fingerabdrücke abnehmen

fin'gertip' *s* Fingerspitze *f;* **have at one's fingertips** parat haben

finicky ['fɪnɪki] *adj* wählerisch

finish ['fɪnɪʃ] *s* Ende *n,* Abschluß *m;* (*polish*) Lack *m,* Politur *f;* **put a f. on** fertig bearbeiten || *tr* beenden; (*complete*) vollenden; (*put a finish on*) fertig bearbeiten; (*smooth*) glätten; (*polish*) polieren; (*ruin*) kaputt machen; **f. drinking** austrinken; **f. eating** aufessen; **f. off** (*supplies*) aufbrauchen; (*food*) aufessen; (*a drink*) austrinken; (*kill*) (sl) erledigen; **f. reading** (*a book*) auslesen

fin'ished *adj* beendet, fertig; **be all f.** fix und fertig sein

fin'ished pro'duct *s* Fertigprodukt *n*

fin'ishing coat' *s* Deckanstrich *m*

fin'ishing mill' *s* Nachwalzwerk *n*

fin'ishing school' *s* Mädchenpensionat *n*

fin'ishing touch'es *spl*—**put the f. to** die letzte Hand legen an (*acc*)

fin'ish line' *s* Ziel *n,* Ziellinie *f*

finite ['faɪnaɪt] *adj* endlich

fi'nite verb' *s* Verbum *n* finitum

fink [fɪŋk] *s* (*informer*) (sl) Verräter –in *mf;* (*strikebreaker*) (sl) Streikbrecher –in *mf*

Finland ['fɪnlənd] *s* Finnland *n*

Finn [fɪn] *s* Finne *m,* Finnin *f*

Finnish ['fɪnɪʃ] *adj* finnisch || *s* (*language*) Finnisch *n*

fir [fʌr] *s* Tanne *f*

fir' cone' *s* Tannenzapfen *m*

fire [faɪr] *s* Feuer *n;* (*conflagration*) Brand *m;* (mil) Feuer *n;* **come under f.** unter Beschuß geraten; **on f. in** Brand; **open f.** Feuer eröffnen; **set on f.** in Brand stecken || *tr* (*a gun, pistol, shot*) abfeuern; (*bricks, ceramics*) brennen; (*an oven*) befeuern; (*an employee*) entlassen; (*throw* *hard*) feuern; **f. questions at s.o.** j–n mit Fragen bombardieren; **f. up** (& fig) anfeuern ‖ *intr* feuern, schießen; **f. away!** schieß los!; **f. on** (mil) beschießen

fire′ alarm′ *s* Feuermeldung *f;* (*box*) Feuermelder *m*

fire′arm′ *s* Schußwaffe *f*

fire′ball′ *s* Feuerball *m;* (*hustler*) Draufgänger *m*

fire′bomb′ *s* Brandbombe *f* ‖ *tr* mit Brandbomben belegen

fire′brand′ *s* (fig) Aufwiegler –in *mf*

fire′break′ *s* Feuerschneise *f*

fire′ brigade′ *s* Feuerwehr *f*

fire′bug′ *m* (coll) Brandstifter –in *mf*

fire′ chief′ *s* Branddirektor *m*

fire′ com′pany *s* Feuerwehr *f*

fire′crack′er *s* Knallfrosch *m*

fire′damp′ *s* Schlagwetter *pl*

fire′ depart′ment *s* Feuerwehr *f*

fire′ drill′ *s* Feueralarmübung *f;* (*by a fire company*) Feuerwehrübung *f*

fire′ en′gine *s* Spritze *f*

fire′ escape′ *s* Feuerleiter *f*

fire′ extin′guisher *s* Feuerlöscher *m*

fire′fly′ *s* Glühwurm *m*

fire′ hose′ *s* Spritzenschlauch *m*

fire′house′ *s* Feuerwache *f*

fire′ hy′drant *s* Hydrant *m*

fire′ insur′ance *s* Brandversicherung *f*

fire′ i′rons *spl* Kamingeräte *pl*

fire′lane′ *s* Feuer(schutz)schneise *f*

fire′man *s* (**–men**) Feuerwehrmann *m;* (*stoker*) Heizer *m*

fire′place′ *s* Kamin *m*, Herd *m*

fire′plug′ *s* Hydrant *m*

fire′ pow′er *s* (mil) Feuerkraft *f*

fire′proof′ *adj* feuerfest ‖ *tr* feuerfest machen

fire′ sale′ *s* Ausverkauf *m* von feuerbeschädigten Waren

fire′ screen′ *s* Feuervorhang *m*

fire′side′ *s* Kamin *m*, Herd *m*

fire′trap′ *s* feuergefährdetes Gebäude *n*

fire′ wall′ *s* Brandmauer *f*

fire′wa′ter *s* (coll) Feuerwasser *n*

fire′wood′ *s* Brennholz *n*

fire′works′ *spl* Feuerwerk *n*

fir′ing *s* (*of a weapon*) Abfeuern *n;* (*of an employee*) Entlassung *f*

fir′ing line′ *s* Feuerlinie *f*

fir′ing range′ *s* Schießstand *m*

fir′ing squad′ *s* Erschießungskommando *n;* (*for ceremonies*) Ehrensalutkommando *n;* **put to the f.** an die Wand stellen

firm [fʌrm] *adj* fest ‖ *s* (com) Firma *f*

firmament [′fʌrməmənt] *s* Firmament *n*

firmness [′fʌrmnɪs] *s* Festigkeit *f*

first [fʌrst] *adj* erste; **very f.** allererste ‖ *adv* erst, erstens; **f. of all** zunächst ‖ *s* (aut) erster Gang *m;* **at f.** zuerst; **f. come, f. served** wer zuerst kommt, mahlt zuerst; **from the f.** von vornherein; **the f.** (*in dates or in a series*) der Erste

first′ aid′ *s* Erste Hilfe *f*

first′-aid′ kit′ *s* Verbandpäckchen *n*

first′-aid′ sta′tion *s* Unfallstation *f;* (mil) Verbandsplatz *m*

first′-born′ *adj* erstgeboren

first′-class′ *adj* erstklassig ‖ *adv* erster Klasse

first′-class′ mail′ *s* Briefpost *f*

first′-class′ tic′ket *s* Fahrkarte *f* (or Flugkarte *f*) erster Klasse

first′ cous′in *s* leiblicher Vetter *m*, leibliche Cousine *f*

first′-degree′ *adj* ersten Grades

first′ draft′ *s* Konzept *n*

first′ fin′ger *s* Zeigefinger *m*

first′ floor′ *s* Parterre *n*, Erdgeschoß *n*

first′ fruits′ *spl* Erstlinge *pl*

first′ lieuten′ant *s* Oberleutnant *m*

firstly [′fʌrstli] *adv* erstens

first′ mate′ *s* Obersteuermann *m*

first′ name′ *s* Vorname *m*

first′ night′ *s* (theat) Erstaufführung *f*

first-nighter [′fɪrst′naɪtər] *s* (theat) Premierenbesucher –in *mf*

first′ offend′er *s* noch nicht Vorbestrafte *mf*

first′ of′ficer *s* erster Offizier *m*

first′ prize′ *s* Hauptgewinn *m*, Haupttreffer *m*

first′-rate′ *adj* erstklassig

first′ ser′geant *s* Hauptfeldwebel *m*

fir′ tree′ *s* Tannenbaum *m*

fiscal [′fɪskəl] *adj* (*period, year*) Rechnungs–; (*policy*) Finanz–

fish [fɪʃ] *s* Fisch *m;* **drink like a f.** wie ein Bürstenbinder saufen; **like a f. out of water** nicht in seinem Element ‖ *tr* fischen ‖ *intr* fischen; **f. for** angeln nach

fish′bone′ *s* Gräte *f*, Fischgräte *f*

fish′ bowl′ *s* Fischglas *n*

fisher [′fɪʃər] *s* Fischer –in *mf*

fish′er·man *s* (**–men**) Angler *m*

fishery [′fɪʃəri] *s* Fischerei *f*

fish′hook′ *s* Angelhaken *m*

fish′ing *adj* Fisch–, Angel– ‖ *s* Fischen *n*

fish′ing line′ *s* Angelschnur *f*

fish′ing reel′ *s* Angelschnurrolle *f*

fish′ing rod′ *s* Angelrute *f*

fish′ing tack′le *s* Fischgerät *n*

fish′ mar′ket *s* Fischmarkt *m*

fishmonger [′fɪʃ‚mʌŋgər] *s* Fischhändler –in *mf*

fish′pond′ *s* Fischteich *m*

fish′ sto′ry *s* Jägerlatein *n*

fish′tail′ *s* (aer) Abbremsen *n* ‖ *intr* (aer) abbremsen

fishy [′fɪʃi] *adj* fischig; (*eyes, look*) ausdruckslos; (*suspicious*) anrüchig; **there's s.th. f. about it** das geht nicht mit rechten Dingen zu

fission [′fɪʃən] *s* (phys) Spaltung *f*

fissionable [′fɪʃənəbəl] *adj* spaltbar

fissure [′fɪʃər] *s* Riß *m*, Spalt *m*

fist [fɪst] *s* Faust *f;* **make a f.** die Faust ballen; **shake one's f. at s.o.** j–m mit der Faust drohen

fist′ fight′ *s* Handgemenge *n*

fisticuffs [′fɪstɪ‚kʌfs] *spl* Faustschläge *pl*

fit [fɪt] *adj* (**fitter; fittest**) gesund; (*for*) tauglich (für, zu); (sport) gut in Form; **be fit as a fiddle** kerngesund sein; **be fit to be tied** Gift und Galle spucken; **feel fit** auf der Höhe sein; **fit for military service**

diensttauglich; **fit to eat** genießbar; **fit to drink** trinkbar; **keep fit** in Form bleiben; **see fit to** (*inf*) es für richtig halten zu (*inf*) || *s* (*of clothes*) Sitz *m*; **by fits and starts** ruckweise; **fit of anger** Wutanfall *m*; **fit of laughter** Lachkrampf *m*; **give s.o. fits** j–n auf die Palme bringen; **it is a good** (or **a bad**) **fit** es sitzt gut (or schlecht); **throw a fit** e–n Wutanfall kriegen || *v* (*pret & pp* **fitted;** *ger* **fitting**) *tr* passen (*dat*); **fit in** (*for an appointment*) einschieben; **fit out** ausrüsten, ausstatten || *intr* passen; **fit into** sich einfügen in (*acc*); **fit in with** passen zu; **fit together** zusammenpassen

fitful ['fɪtfəl] *adj* unregelmäßig

fitness ['fɪtnɪs] *s* Tauglichkeit *f*; **physical f.** gute körperliche Verfassung *f*

fit'ting *adj* passend, angemessen || *s* (*of a garment*) Anprobe *f*; (*mach*) Montage *f*; **fittings** Armaturen *pl*

five [faɪv] *adj & pron* fünf || *s* Fünf *f*

five'-year plan' *s* Fünfjahresplan *m*

fix [fɪks] *s* (*determination of a position*) Standortbestimmung *f*; (*position*) Standort *m*; (*injection of heroin*) (sl) Schuß *m*; **be in a fix** (coll) in der Klemme sein || *tr* befestigen; (*a price, time*) festsetzen; (*repair*) reparieren, wieder in Ordnung bringen; (*get even with*) (sl) erledigen, das Handwerk legen (*dat*); (*one's glance*) (**on**) heften (auf *acc*); (*the blame*) (**on**) zuschreiben (*dat*); (*a game*) (sl) auf unehrliche Weise beeinflussen; (*bayonets*) aufpflanzen; (phot) fixieren

fixed *adj* (*unmovable*) unbeweglich; (*stare*) starr; (*income*) fest; (*idea, cost*) fix; **f. date** Termin *m*

fixer ['fɪksər] *s* (phot) Fixiermittel *n*

fix'ing *s* (*making fast*) Befestigung *f*; (*of a date, etc.*) Festsetzung *f*; **fixings** (culin) Zutaten *pl*

fix'ing bath' *s* (phot) Fixierbad *n*

fixture ['fɪkstʃər] *s* Installationsteil *m*; **he is a permanent f.** er gehört zum Inventar

fizz [fɪz] *s* Zischen *n* || *intr* zischen

fizzle ['fɪzəl] *s* (coll) Pleite *f* || *intr* aufzischen; **f. out** verpuffen

flabbergast ['flæbər‚gæst] *tr* verblüffen

flabby ['flæbi] *adj* schlaff, schlapp

flag [flæg] *s* Fahne *f*, Flagge *f* || *v* (*pret & pp* **flagged;** *ger* **flagging**) *tr* signalisieren || *intr* nachlassen

flag'pole' *s* Fahnenmast *m*

flagrant ['flegrənt] *adj* schreiend

flag'ship' *s* Flaggschiff *n*

flag'staff' *s* Flaggenmast *m*

flag'stone' *s* Steinfliese *f*

flag' stop' *s* (rr) Bedarfshaltestelle *f*

flail [flel] *s* Dreschflegel *m* || *tr* dreschen || *intr*—**f. about** um sich schlagen

flair [fler] *s* Spürsinn *m*, feine Nase *f*

flak [flæk] *s* Flak *f*, Flakfeuer *n*

flake [flek] *s* (*thin piece*) Schuppe *f*; (*of snow, soap*) Flocke *f* || *intr* Schuppen bilden; **f. off** abblättern

flaky ['fleki] *adj* (*skin*) schuppig; (*pastry*) blätterig; (sl) überspannt

flamboyant [flæm'bɔɪ‚ənt] *adj* (*person*) angeberisch; (*style*) überladen

flame [flem] *s* Flamme *f*; **be in flames** in Flammen stehen; **burst into flames** in Flammen aufgehen || *intr* flammen

flamethrower ['flem‚θro‚ər] *s* Flammenwerfer *m*

flam'ing *adj* flammend

flamin·go [flə'mɪŋgo] *s* (**–gos** & **–goes**) (orn) Flamingo *m*

flammable ['flæməbəl] *adj* brennbar

Flanders ['flændərz] *s* Flandern *n*

flange [flændʒ] *s* (*of a pipe*) Flansch *m*; (*of a wheel*) (rr) Spurkranz *m*

flank [flæŋk] *s* (anat, mil, zool) Flanke *f* || *tr* flankieren

flank'ing move'ment *s* (mil) Umgehung *f*

flannel ['flænəl] *adj* flanellen || *s* Flanell *m*

flap [flæp] *s* Klappe *f*; **f. of the wing** Flügelschlag *m* || *v* (*pret & pp* **flapped;** *ger* **flapping**) *tr*—**f. the wings** mit den Flügeln schlagen || *intr* flattern

flare [fler] *s* Leuchtsignal *n*; (*of anger, excitement*) Aufbrausen *n*; (*of a skirt*) Glocke *f*; (mil) Leuchtrakete *f*, Leuchtbombe *f* || *intr* flackern; (*said of a skirt*) glockenförmig abstehen; **f. up** auflodern; (fig) aufbrausen

flare'-up' *s* Auflodern *n*; (*of anger*) Aufbrausen *n*

flash [flæʃ] *s* Blitz *m*; (*of a gun*) Mündungsfeuer *n*; (phot) Blitzlicht *n*; **f. of genious** Geistesblitz *m*; **f. of light** Lichtstrahl *m*; **f. of lightning** Blitzstrahl *m*; **in a f.** im Nu || *tr* (*a glance*) zuwerfen; (*a message*) funkeln; **f. a light in s.o.'s face** j–m ins Gesicht leuchten || *intr* blitzen; (*said of eyes*) funkeln; **f. by** vorbeisausen; **f. on** aufleuchten; **f. through one's mind** j–m durch den Kopf schießen

flash'back' *s* (cin) Rückblende *f*

flash' bulb' *s* Blitzlichtbirne *f*

flash' cube' *s* Blitzlichtwürfel *m*

flash' flood' *s* plötzliche Überschwemmung *f*

flash' gun' *s* Blitzlichtgerät *n*

flash'light' *s* Taschenlampe *f*

flash' pic'ture, flash' shot' *s* Blitzlichtaufnahme *f*

flashy ['flæʃi] *adj* auffällig; (*clothes*) protzig; (*colors*) grell

flask [flæsk] *s* Taschenflasche *f*; (*for laboratory use*) Glaskolben *m*

flat [flæt] *adj* (**flatter; flattest**) platt, flach; (*food*) fad(e); (*rate*) Pauschal–; (*tire*) platt; (*color*) matt; (*beer, soda*) schal; (*lie*) glatt; (*denial*) entschieden; (mus) erniedrigt; **be f.** (mus) zu tief singen || *adv* (*e.g., in exactly ten minutes*) genau; **fall f.** (fig) flachfallen; **go f.** schal werden; **lie f.** flach liegen || *s* (*apartment*) Wohnung *f*; (*tire*) Reifenpanne *f*

flat'boat' *s* Flachboot *n*

flat-broke ['flæt'brok] *adj* (coll) völlig pleite
flat'car' *s* Plattformwagen *m*
flat' feet' *spl* Plattfüße *pl*
flat'-foot'ed *adj* plattfüßig; **catch f.** auf frischer Tat ertappen
flat'i'ron *s* Bügeleisen *n*
flatly ['flætli] *adv* rundweg, reinweg
flatten ['flætən] *tr* (*paper, cloth*) glattstreichen; (*raze*) einebnen; **f. out** abplatten; (aer) abfangen || *intr* sich verflachen; (aer) ausschweben
flatter ['flætər] *tr* schmeicheln (*dat*); **be flattered** sich geschmeichelt fühlen; **f. oneself** sich [*dat*] einbilden
flatterer ['flætərər] *s* Schmeichler –in *mf*
flat'tering *adj* schmeichelhaft
flattery ['flætəri] *s* Schmeichelei *f*
flat' tire' *s* Reifenpanne *f*
flat'top' *s* (coll) Flugzeugträger *m*
flat' trajec'tory *s* Rasanz *f*
flatulence ['flætʃələns] *s* Blähung *f*
flat'ware' *s* (*silverware*) Eßbestecke *pl*
flaunt [flɔnt] *tr* prunken mit
flavor ['flevər] *s* Aroma *n* || *tr* würzen
fla'voring *s* Würze *f*
flavorless ['flevərlɪs] *adj* fad(e)
flaw [flɔ] *s* Fehler *m;* (*crack*) Riß *m;* (*in glass, precious stone*) Blase *f*
flawless ['flɔlɪs] *adj* tadellos
flax [flæks] *s* Flachs *m,* Lein *m*
flaxen ['flæksən] *adj* flachsen
flax'seed' *s* Leinsamen *m*
flay [fle] *tr* ausbalgen
flea [fli] *s* Floh *m*
flea'bag' *s* (*sleeping bag*) (coll) Flohkiste *f;* (*hotel*) (coll) Penne *f*
flea'bite' *s* Flohbiß *m*
flea'mar'ket *s,* Flohmarkt *m*
fleck [flɛk] *s* Fleck *m*
fledgling ['flɛdʒlɪŋ] *s* eben flügge gewordener Vogel *m;* (fig) Grünschnabel *m*
flee [fli] *v* (*pret & pp* fled [flɛd]) *intr* fliehen
fleece [flis] *s* Vlies *n* || *tr* (coll) rupfen
fleecy ['flisi] *adj* wollig; **f. clouds** Schäfchenwolken *pl*
fleet [flit] *adj* flink || *s* Flotte *f;* (aer) Geschwader *n;* (nav) Kriegsflotte *f;* **f. of cars** Wagenpark *m*
fleet'ing *adj* flüchtig
Flemish ['flemɪʃ] *adj* flämisch || *s* Flämisch *n*
flesh [flɛʃ] *s* Fleisch *n;* **in the f.** leibhaftig
flesh'-col'ored *adj* fleischfarben
fleshiness ['flɛʃɪnɪs] *s* Fleischigkeit *f*
flesh' wound' *s* Fleischwunde *f*
fleshy ['flɛʃi] *adj* fleischig
flex [flɛks] *tr* biegen; (*muscles*) anspannen
flexible ['flɛksɪbəl] *adj* biegsam
flex(i)time ['flɛks(ɪ) ,taɪm] *s* Gleitzeit *f*
flick [flɪk] *s* Schnippen *n* || *tr* (**away**) wegschnippen
flicker ['flɪkər] *s* (*of a flame*) Flakkern *n;* (*of eyelids*) Zucken *n* || *intr* flackern
flier ['flaɪ-ər] *s* Flieger –in *mf;* (*handbill*) Flugblatt *n*

flight [flaɪt] *s* Flug *m;* (*fleeing*) Flucht *f;* (*of birds, geese*) Schar *f;* (*of stairs*) Treppe *f;* **f. of stairs** Treppenflucht *f;* **f. of the imagination** Geistesschwung *m;* **live two flights up** zwei Treppen hoch wohnen; **put to f.** in die Flucht schlagen; **take to f.** sich davonmachen
flight' bag' *s* (aer) Reisetasche *f*
flight' deck' *s* (nav) Landedeck *n*
flight' engineer' *s* Bordmechaniker *m*
flight' instruc'tor *s* Fluglehrer –in *mf*
flight' path' *s* Flugstrecke *f*
flighty ['flaɪti] *adj* leichtsinnig
flim·flam ['flɪm ,flæm] *s* (*nonsense*) Unsinn *m;* (*deception*) Betrügerei *f* || *v* (*pret & pp* **–flammed;** *ger* **–flamming**) *tr* (coll) betrügen
flimsy ['flɪmzi] *adj* (*material*) hauchdünn; (*excuse, construction*) schwach
flinch [flɪntʃ] *intr* (**at**) zurückweichen (vor *dat*), zusammenfahren (vor *dat*)
flinch'ing *s*—**without f.** ohne mit der Wimper zu zucken
fling [flɪŋ] *s* Wurf *m;* **go on** (or **have**) **a f.** sich austoben; **have a f. at** versuchen || *v* (*pret & pp* flung [flʌŋ]) *tr* schleudern; **f. off** abschleudern; **f. open** aufreißen
flint [flɪnt] *s* Feuerstein *m*
flinty ['flɪnti] *adj* steinhart; (fig) hart
flip [flɪp] *adj* leichtfertig || *s* (*of a coin*) Hochwerfen *n;* (*somersault*) Purzelbaum *m* || *v* (*pret & pp* **flipped;** *ger* **flipping**) *tr* schnellen; (*a coin*) hochwerfen; **f. one's lid** (sl) rasend werden; **f. over** umdrehen
flippancy ['flɪpənsi] *s* Leichtfertigkeit *f*
flippant ['flɪpənt] *adj* leichtfertig
flipper ['flɪpər] *s* Flosse *f*
flirt [flʌrt] *s* Flirt *m* || *intr* kokettieren, flirten; (*with an idea*) liebäugeln
flirtation [flʌr'teʃən] *s* Liebelei *f*
flit [flɪt] *v* (*pret & pp* **flitted;** *ger* **flitting**) *intr* flitzen; **f. by** vorbeiflitzen; (*said of time*) verfliegen
float [flot] *s* Schwimmkörper *m;* (*of a fishing line*) Schwimmer *m;* (*raft*) Floß *n;* (*in parades*) Festwagen *m* || *tr* (*logs*) flößen; (*a loan*) auflegen || *intr* schwimmen; (*in the air*) schweben; **f. about** herumtreiben
float'ing kid'ney *s* Wanderniere *f*
float'ing mine' *s* Treibmine *f*
flock [flɑk] *s* (*of sheep*) Herde *f;* (*of birds*) Schar *f,* Schwarm *m;* (*of people*) Menge *f* || *intr* herbeiströmen; **come flocking** herbeigeströmt kommen; **f. around** sich scharen um; **f. into** strömen in (*acc*); **f. to** zulaufen (*dat*); **f. together** sich zusammenscharen
floe [flo] *s* Eisscholle *f*
flog [flɑg] *v* (*pret & pp* **flogged;** *ger* **flogging**) *tr* prügeln
flood [flʌd] *s* Flut *f;* (*caused by heavy rains*) Überschwemmung *f;* (*sudden rise of a river*) Hochwasser *n;* (fig) Schwall *m;* (Bib) Sintflut *f* || *tr* (& fig) überschwemmen; (*e.g., with mail*) überschütten

flood'gate' s (& fig) Schleusentor n
flood'light' s Flutlicht n ‖ tr anstrahlen
flood' tide' s Flut f; **at f.** zur Zeit der Flut
flood' wa'ters spl Flutwasser n
floor [flor] s Fußboden m; (story) Stock m; (parl) Sitzungssaal m; **have the f.** das Wort haben; **may I have the f.?** ich bitte ums Wort; **on the third f.** im zweiten Stock ‖ tr zu Boden strecken; (coll) verblüffen
floor'board' s Diele f
floor'ing s Fußbodenbelag m
floor' lamp' s Stehlampe f
floor' plan' s Grundriß m
floor' pol'ish s Bohnermasse f
floor' sam'ple s Vorführungsmuster n
floor' show' s Kabarett n
floor' tile' s Bodenfliese f
floor'walk'er s Abteilungsaufseher –in mf
floor' wax' s Bohnerwachs n
flop [flɑp] s (coll) Mißerfolg m; (person) Niete f; (fall) (coll) Plumps m; **take a f.** (coll) plumpsen ‖ v (pret & pp **flopped;** ger **flopping**) intr (fall) (coll) plumpsen; (fail) (coll) versagen; (theat) (coll) durchfallen; **f. down** in (coll) sich plumpsen lassen in (acc)
flora ['florə] s Pflanzenwelt f
floral ['florəl] adj Blumen-
Florence ['florəns] s Florenz n
florescence [flo'rɛsəns] s Blüte f
florid ['florɪd] adj (ornate) überladen; (complexion) blühend
florist ['florɪst] s Blumenhändler –in mf
floss [flɔs] s Rohseide f; (of corn) Narbenfäden pl
floss' silk' s Florettseide f
flossy ['flɔsi] adj seidenweich
flotilla [flo'tɪlə] s Flotille f
flotsam ['flɑtsəm] s Wrackgut n
flot'sam and jet'sam s Treibgut n; (trifles) Kleinigkeiten pl
flounce [flaʊns] s Volant m ‖ tr mit Volants besetzen ‖ intr erregt stürmen
flounder ['flaʊndər] s Flunder f ‖ intr taumeln; (fig) ins Schwimmen kommen
flour [flaʊr] s Mehl n
flourish ['flʌrɪʃ] s (in writing) Schnörkel m; (in a speech) Floskel f; (gesture) große Geste f; (mus) Tusch m; **f. of trumpets** Trompetengeschmetter n ‖ tr (banners) schwenken; (swords) schwingen ‖ intr blühen, gedeihen
flour'ishing adj blühend; (business) schwunghaft
flour' mill' s Mühle f
floury ['flaʊri] adj mehlig
flout [flaʊt] tr verspotten ‖ intr—**f. at** spotten über (acc)
flow [flo] s Fluß m ‖ intr fließen, rinnen; (said of hair, clothes) wallen; **f. by** vorbeifließen; **f. into** zuströmen (dat)
flower ['flaʊ-ər] s Blume f; **cut flowers** Schnittblumen pl ‖ intr blühen

flow'er bed' s Blumenbeet n
flow'er gar'den s Blumengarten m
flow'er girl' s Blumenmädchen n
flow'erpot' s Blumentopf m
flow'er shop' s Blumenladen m
flow'er show' s Blumenausstellung f
flow'er stand' s Blumenstand m
flowery ['flaʊ·əri] adj blumig; (fig) geziert; **f. phrase** Floskel f
flu [flu] s (coll) Grippe f
flub [flʌb] v (pret & pp **flubbed;** ger **flubbing**) tr (coll) verkorksen
fluctuate ['flʌktʃu ,et] intr schwanken
fluctuation [,flʌktʃu'eʃən] s Schwankung f
flue [flu] s Rauchrohr n
fluency ['flu·ənsi] s Geläufigkeit f
fluent ['flu·ənt] adj (speaker) redegewandt; (speech) fließend
fluently ['flu·əntli] adv fließend
fluff [flʌf] s Staubflocke f; (blunder) Schnitzer m ‖ tr verpfuschen; **f. up** (a pillow) schütteln; (a rug) aufrauhen
fluffy ['flʌfi] adj flaumig
fluid ['flu·ɪd] adj flüssig ‖ s Flüssigkeit f
fluke [fluk] s Ankerflügel m; (coll) Dusel m
flunk [flʌŋk] s Durchfallen n ‖ tr (a test) (coll) durchfallen in (dat); (a student) (coll) durchfallen lassen ‖ intr (coll) durchfallen
flunky ['flʌŋki] s Schranze mf
fluorescent [flo'rɛsənt] adj fluoreszierend
fluores'cent light' s Leuchtstofflampe f
fluores'cent tube' s Leuchtröhre f
fluoridate ['florɪ ,det] tr mit e–m Fluorid versetzen
fluoride ['florɑɪd] s Fluorid n
fluorine ['florin] s Fluor n
fluorite ['florɑɪt] s Fluorkalzium n
fluoroscope ['florə ,skop] s Fluoroskop n
flurry ['flʌri] s (of snow) Schneegestöber m; (st. exch.) kurzes Aufflakkern n; **f. of activity** fieberhafte Tätigkeit f
flush [flʌʃ] adj (even) eben, glatt; (well-supplied) gut bei Kasse; (full to overflowing) übervoll ‖ adv direkt ‖ s (on the cheeks) Erröten n; (of youth) Blüte f; (of a toilet) Spülung f; (cards) Flöte f; **f. of victory** Siegesrausch m ‖ tr (a toilet) spülen; (hunt) auftreiben; **f. down** hinunterspülen; **f. out** (animals) auftreiben ‖ intr erröten
flush' switch' s Unterputzschalter m
flush' tank' s Spülkasten m
flush' toi'let s Spülklosett n
fluster ['flʌstər] s Verwirrung f ‖ tr verwirren
flute [flut] s (archit) Kannelüre f; (mus) Flöte f ‖ tr riffeln
flut'ing s (archit) Kannelierung f
flutist ['flutɪst] s Flötist –in mf
flutter ['flʌtər] s Flattern n; (excitement) Aufregung f ‖ tr—**f. one's eyelashes** mit den Wimpern klimpern ‖ intr flattern

flux [flʌks] *s* (*flow*) Fließen *n*, Fluß *m; (for fusing metals)* Schmelzmittel *n;* **in f.** im Fluß

fly [flai] *s* Fliege *f; (of trousers)* Schlitz *m;* (angl) künstliche Fliege *f;* **flies** (theat) Soffitten *pl;* **fly in the ointment** Haar *n* in der Suppe ‖ *v* (*pret* **flew** [flu]; *pp* **flown** [flon]) *tr* fliegen ‖ *intr* fliegen; (*rush*) stürzen; (*said of rumors*) schwirren; (*said of time*) verfliegen; **fly around** umherfliegen; (*e.g., the globe*) umfliegen; **fly at s.o.** auf j-n losgehen; **fly away** abfliegen; **fly in all directions** nach allen Seiten zerstieben; **fly low** tief fliegen; **fly off the handle** (fig) aus der Haut fahren; **fly open** aufspringen; **fly over** überfliegen; **fly past** vorbeifliegen (an *dat*); **let fly** (*e.g., an arrow*) schnellen

fly' ball' *s* (baseball) Flugball *m*
fly'-by-night' *adj* unverläßlich ‖ *s* (coll) Schwindelunternehmen *n*
fly' cast'ing *s* Fischen *n* mit der Wurfangel
flyer ['flaɪ·ər] *s* var of **flier**
fly'-fish' *intr* mit künstlichen Fliegen angeln
fly'ing *adj* fliegend; (*boat, field, time*) Flug-; (*suit, club, school*) Flieger- ‖ *s* Fliegen *n*
fly'ing but'tress *s* Strebebogen *m*
fly'ing col'ors *spl*—**come through with f.** e-n glänzenden Sieg erringen
fly'ing sau'cer *s* fliegende Untertasse *f*
fly'leaf' *s* (**-leaves'**) Vorsatzblatt *n*
fly'pa'per *s* Fliegenfänger *m*
fly' rod' *s* Angelrute *f*
fly'speck' *s* Fliegendreck *m*
fly' swat'ter [ˌswatər] *s* Fliegenklappe *f*
fly'trap' *s* Fliegenfalle *f*
fly'wheel' *s* Schwungrad *n*
foal [fol] *s* Fohlen *n* ‖ *intr* fohlen
foam [fom] *s* Schaum *m; (of waves)* Gischt *m; (from the mouth)* Geifer *m* ‖ *intr* schäumen; (*said of waves*) branden
foam' rub'ber *s* Schaumgummi *m*
foamy ['fomi] *adj* (*full of foam*) schaumig; (*beer*) schäumend; (*foamlike*) schaumartig
F.O.B., f.o.b. [ˌɛf ˌoˈbi] *adv* (**free on board)** frei an Bord
focal ['fokəl] *adj* fokal; **be the f. point** im Brennpunkt stehen; **f. point** (fig & opt) Brennpunkt *m*
fo·cus ['fokəs] *s* (**-cuses & -ci** [saɪ]) (math, opt) Brennpunkt *m;* (pathol) Herd *m;* **bring into f.** richtig (or scharf) einstellen; **in f.** scharf eingestellt; **out of f.** unscharf ‖ *v* (*pret & pp* **-cus[s]ed;** *ger* **-cus[s]ing**) *tr* (*a camera*) einstellen; (*attention, etc.*) (**on**) richten (auf *acc*) ‖ *intr* sich scharf einstellen
fo'cusing *s* Scharfeinstellung *f*
fodder ['fadər] *s* Futter *n*
foe [fo] *s* Feind -in *mf*
fog [fɔg] *s* Nebel *m;* (fig) Verwirrung *f;* (phot) Grauschleier *m* ‖ *v* (*pret & pp* **fogged;** *ger* **fogging**) *tr* ver-

nebeln; (fig) umnebeln ‖ *intr* (phot) verschleiern; **fog up** beschlagen
fog' bank' *s* Nebelbank *f*
fog' bell' *s* Nebelglocke *f*
fog'-bound' *adj* durch Nebel festgehalten
fogey ['fogi] *s* Kauz *m*
foggy ['fɔgi] *adj* neblig, nebelhaft; (phot) verschleiert; **he hasn't the foggiest idea** er hat nicht die leiseste Ahnung
fog'horn' *s* Nebelhorn *n*
fog' light' *s* (aut) Nebelscheinwerfer *m*
foible ['fɔɪbəl] *s* Schwäche *f*
foil [fɔɪl] *s* (*of metal*) Folie *f; (of a mirror)* Spiegelbelag *m;* (fig) (**to**) Hintergrund *m* (für); (fencing) Florett *n* ‖ *tr* (*a plan*) durchkreuzen; (*an attempt*) vereiteln
foist [fɔɪst] *tr*—**f. s.th. on s.o.** j-m etw anhängen
fold [fold] *s* Falte *f; (in stiff material)* Falz *m; (for sheep)* Pferch *m; (flock of sheep)* Schafherde *f;* (relig) Herde *f* ‖ *tr* falten; (*stiff material*) falzen; (*e.g., a chair*) zusammenklappen; (*the arms*) kreuzen; (*the wash*) zusammenlegen ‖ *intr* sich (zusammen) falten; (com) zusammenbrechen
folder ['folder] *s* (*loose-leaf binder*) Schnellhefter *m; (manila folder)* Mappe *f; (brochure)* Prospekt *m*
fold'ing *adj* (*bed, chair, camera, wing*) Klapp-
fold'ing door' *s* Falttür *f*
fold'ing screen' *s* spanische Wand *f*
foliage ['folɪ·ɪdʒ] *s* Laubwerk *n*, Laub *n*
foli·o ['folɪ ˌo] *adj* Folio-, in Folio ‖ *s* (**-os**) (*page*) Folioblatt *n; (book)* Foliant *m* ‖ *tr* paginieren
folk [fok] *adj* Volks- ‖ **folks** *spl* (*people*) Leute *pl; (family)* Angehörige *pl*
folk' dance' *s* Volkstanz *m*
folk'lore' *s* Volkskunde *f*
folk' mu'sic *s* Volksmusik *f*
folk' song' *s* Volkslied *n*
folksy ['foksi] *adj* (*person*) leutselig; (*speech, expression*) volkstümlich
folk' tale' *s* Volkssage *f*
folk'ways' *spl* volkstümliche Lebensweise *f*
follicle ['falɪkəl] *s* Follikel *n*
follow ['falo] *tr* folgen (*dat*); (*instructions*) befolgen; (*a goal, events, news*) verfolgen; (*in office*) folgen auf (*acc*); (*a profession*) ausüben; (*understand*) folgen können (*dat*); **f. one another** aufeinanderfolgen; (*said of events*) sich überstürzen; **f. up** nachgehen (*dat*); **f. your nose!** immer der Nase nach! ‖ *intr* (nach)folgen; **as follows** folgendermaßen; **f. after** nachfolgen (*dat*); **f. through** (sport) ganz durchziehen; **f. upon** folgen auf (*acc*); **it follows that** daraus folgt, daß
follower ['falo·ər] *s* Anhänger -in *mf*
fol'lowing *adj* nachstehend, folgend ‖ *s* Gefolgschaft *f*
fol'low-up' *adj* Nach- ‖ *s* weitere Verfolgung *f*

folly ['fɑli] *s* Torheit *f;* **follies** (theat) Revue *f*
foment [fo'ment] *tr* schüren, anstiften
fond [fɑnd] *adj* (*hope, wish*) sehnlich; **become f. of** lieb gewinnen; **be f. of** gern haben; **be f. of reading** gern lesen
fondle ['fɑndəl] *tr* liebkosen
fondness ['fɑndnɪs] *s* Verliebtheit *f;* (**for**) Hang *m* (zu), Vorliebe *f* (für)
font [fɑnt] *s* (*for holy water*) Weih-wasserbecken *n;* (*for baptism*) Tauf-becken *n;* (typ) Schriftart *f*
food [fud] *adj* Nähr-, Speise– || *s* (*on the table*) Essen *n;* (*in a store*) Le-bensmittel *pl;* (*requirement for life*) Nahrung *f;* (*for animals*) Futter *n;* (*for plants*) Nährstoff *m;* **f. and drink** Speis' und Trank; **f. for thought** Stoff *m* zum Nachdenken
food' poi'soning *s* Nahrungsmittelver-giftung *f*
food'stuffs' *spl* Nahrungsmittel *pl*
food' val'ue *s* Nährwert *m*
fool [ful] *s* Narr *m;* **born f.** Mondkalb *n;* **make a f. of oneself** sich blamie-ren || *tr* täuschen, anführen || *intr—* **f. around** herumtrödeln; **f. around with** herumspielen mit; (*romanti-cally*) sich herumtreiben mit
fool'har'dy *adj* tollkühn
fool'ing *s* Späße *pl;* **f. around** Firlefanz *m;* **no f.!** na, so was!
foolish ['fulɪʃ] *adj* töricht, albern
foolishness ['fulɪnɪs] *s* Torheit *f*
fool'-proof' *adj* narrensicher
fools'cap' *s* Narrenkappe *f;* (*paper size*) Kanzleipapier *n*
foot [fut] *s* (**feet** [fit]) Fuß *m;* **be** (**back**) **on one's feet** (wieder) auf den Beinen sein; **f. of the bed** Fußende *n* des Bettes; **on f.** zu Fuß; **put one's best f. forward** sich ins rechte Licht setzen; **put one's f. down** (fig) ein Machtwort sprechen; **put one's f. in it** (coll) ins Fettnäpfchen treten; **stand on one's own two feet** auf eigenen Füßen stehen || *tr—***f. the bill** blechen
footage ['futɪdʒ] *s* Ausmaß *n* in Fuß
foot'-and-mouth' disease' *s* Maul- und-Klauenseuche *f*
foot'ball' *s* Fußball *m*
foot'board' *s* (*in a car*) Trittbrett *n;* (*of a bed*) Fußbrett *n*
foot'bridge' *s* Steg *m*
foot'fall' *s* Schritt *m*
foot'hills' *spl* Vorgebirge *n*
foot'hold' *s* (& fig) Halt *m;* **gain a f.** festen Fuß fassen
foot'ing *s* Halt *m;* **lose one's f.** aus-gleiten; **on an equal f. with** auf gleichem Fuße mit
foot'lights' *spl* Rampenlicht *n*
foot'man *s* (**-men**) Lakai *m*
foot'note' *s* Fußnote *f*
foot'path' *s* Fußpfad *m*, Fußsteig *m*
foot'print' *s* Fußstapfe *f*
foot' race' *s* Wettlauf *m*
foot'rest' *s* Fußraste *f*
foot' rule' *s* Zollstock *m*
foot' sol'dier *s* Infanterist *m*
foot'sore' *adj* fußkrank

foot'step' *s* Tritt *m;* **follow in s.o.'s footsteps** in j-s Fußstapfen treten
foot'stool' *s* Schemel *m*
foot'wear' *s* Schuhwerk *n*
foot'work' *s* (sl) Lauferei *f;* (sport) Beinarbeit *f*
foot'worn' *adj* abgetreten
fop [fɑp] *s* Geck *m*
for [fɔr] *prep* für; (*a destination*) nach (*dat*); (with an English present per-fect tense) schon (*acc*), e.g., **I have been living here for a month** ich wohne hier schone e–n Monat (or seit e–m Monat; (with an English future tense) für or auf (*acc*); **for good** für immer; **for joy** vor Freude; **for years** jahrelang || *conj* denn
forage ['fɔrɪdʒ] *s* Furage *f* || *intr* fu-ragieren
foray ['fɔre] *s* (*raid*) Raubzug *m;* (*e.g., into politics*) Streifzug *m* || *intr* plündern
for·bear [fɔr'bɛr] *v* (*pret* **–bore** ['bor];* *pp* **–borne** ['born]) *tr* unter-lassen || *intr* ablassen
forbearance [fɔr'bɛrəns] *s* (*patience*) Geduld *f;* (*leniency*) Nachsicht *f*
for·bid [fɔr'bɪd] *v* (*pret* **-bade** ['bæd] & **–bad** ['bæd];* *pp* **–bidden** ['bɪdən]) *tr* verbieten
forbid'ding *adj* abschreckend; (*dan-gerous*) gefährlich
force [fors] *s* (*strength*) Kraft *f;* (*com-pulsion*) Gewalt *f;* (phys) Kraft *f;* **be in f.** in Kraft sein; **by f.** gewalt-sam; **come into f.** in Kraft treten; **forces** (mil) Streitkräfte *pl;* **have the f. of** gelten als; **resort to f.** zu Zwangsmaßnahmen greifen; **with full f.** mit voller Wucht || *tr* zwingen; (*plants*) treiben; (*a door*) aufspren-gen; (*e.g., an issue*) forcieren; (**into**) zwängen (in *acc*); **f. down** hinunter-drücken; (aer) zur Landung zwingen; **f. one's way** sich drängen; **f. s.th. on s.o.** j–m etw aufdrängen
forced' land'ing *s* Notlandung *f*
forced' march' *s* Gewaltmarsch *m*
forceful ['forsfəl] *adj* eindrucksvoll
for·ceps ['fɔrsɛps] *s* (**–ceps** & **–cipes** [sɪ ‚piz]) (dent, surg, zool) Zange *f*
forcible ['fɔrsɪbəl] *adj* (*strong*) kräf-tig; (*violent*) gewaltsam
ford [fɔrd] *s* Furt *f* || *tr* durchwaten
fore [for] *adj* Vorder– || *adv* (naut) vorn || *s*—**come to the f.** hervortre-ten || *interj* (golf) Achtung!
fore' and aft' *adv* längsschiffs
fore'arm' *s* Vorderarm *m*, Unterarm *m*
fore'bears' *spl* Vorfahren *pl*
forebode [for'bod] *tr* vorbedeuten
forebod'ing *s* (*omen*) Vorzeichen *n;* (*presentiment*) Vorahnung *f*
fore'cast' *s* Voraussage *f* || *v* (*pret* & *pp* **-cast** & **–casted**) *tr* voraussagen
forecastle ['foksəl] *s* Back *f*
foreclose' *tr* (*a mortgage*) für verfallen erklären; (*shut out*) ausschließen
foredoom' *tr* im voraus verurteilen
fore'fa'thers *spl* Vorfahren *pl*
fore'fin'ger *s* Zeigefinger *m*
fore'front' *s* Spitze *f*
fore'go'ing *adj* vorhergehend

fore'gone' conclu'sion s ausgemachte Sache f
fore'ground' s Vordergrund m
forehead ['fɔrɪd] s Stirn(e) f
foreign ['fɔrɪn] adj (e.g., aid, product) Auslands–; (e.g., body, language, word, worker) Fremd–; (e.g., minister, office, policy, trade) Außen–; (e.g., affairs, service) auswärtig
foreigner ['fɔrɪnər] s Ausländer –in mf
for'eign exchange' s Devisen pl
fore'leg' s Vorderbein n
fore'lock' s Stirnlocke f
fore'man s (–men) Vorarbeiter m; (jur) Obmann m; (min) Steiger m
foremast ['fɔr ,mæst] s Fockmast m
fore'most' adj vorderste || adv zuerst
fore'noon' s Vormittag m
fore'part' s vorderster Teil m
fore'paw' s Vorderpfote f
fore'quart'er s Vorderviertel n
fore'run'ner s Vorbote m
fore'sail' s Focksegel n
fore-see' v (pret –saw'; pp –seen') tr voraussehen
foreseeable [for'si·əbəl] adj absehbar
foreshad'ow tr ahnen lassen
foreshort'en tr verkürzen
fore'sight' s Voraussicht f
fore'sight'ed adj umsichtig
fore'skin' s Vorhaut f
forest ['fɔrɪst] s Wald m, Forst m
forestall' tr zuvorkommen (dat)
for'est fire' s Waldbrand m
for'est rang'er s Forstbeamte m
forestry ['fɔrɪstri] s Forstwirtschaft f
fore'taste' s Vorgeschmack m
fore-tell' v (pret & pp –told') tr vorhersagen, weissagen
fore'thought' s Vorsorge f, Vorbedacht m
forev'er adv ewig, für immer; **f. and ever** auf immer und ewig
forewarn' tr (of) vorher warnen (vor dat)
fore'word' s Vorwort n
forfeit ['fɔrfɪt] s Einbuße f || tr einbüßen, verwirken
forfeiture ['fɔrfɪtʃər] s Verwirkung f
forgather [fɔr'gæðər] intr sich treffen
forge [fɔrdʒ] s Schmiede f || tr schmieden; (documents) fälschen || intr— **forge ahead** vordringen
forger ['fɔrdʒər] s Fälscher –in mf
forgery ['fɔrdʒəri] s Fälschung f; (coin) Falschgeld n
for·get [fɔr'get] v (pret –got; pp –got & –gotten, ger –getting) tr vergessen; **f. it!** spielt keine Rolle!; **f. oneself** sich vergessen
forgetful fɔr'getfəl] adj vergeßlich
forgetfulness [fɔr'getfəlnɪs] s Vergeßlichkeit f
forget'-me-not' s Vergißmeinnicht n
forgivable [fɔr'gɪvəbəl] adj verzeihlich
for-give [fɔr'gɪv] v (pret –gave; pp –given) tr (a person) vergeben (dat); (a thing) vergeben
forgiveness [fɔr'gɪvnɪs] s Vergebung f
forgiv'ing adj versöhnlich
for·go [fɔr'go] v (pret –went; pp –gone) tr verzichten auf (acc)

fork [fɔrk] s Gabel f; (in the road) Gabelung f; (of a tree) Astgabelung f || tr gabeln; **f. over** (coll) übergeben
forked adj gabelförmig; (tongue) gespalten
fork'lift truck' s Gabelstapler m
forlorn [fɔr'lɔrn] adj (forsaken) verlassen; (wretched) elend; (attempt) verzweifelt
forlorn' hope' s aussichtsloses Unternehmen n
form [fɔrm] s Form f, Gestalt f; (paper to be filled out) Formular n || tr formen, bilden; (a plan) fassen; (a circle, alliance) schließen; (suspicions) schöpfen; (a habit) annehmen; (blisters) werfen || intr sich bilden
formal ['fɔrməl] adj formell, förmlich
for'mal call' s Höflichkeitsbesuch m
for'mal educa'tion s Schulbildung f
formality [fɔr'mælɪti] s Formalität f; **without f.** ohne Umstände
format ['fɔrmæt] s Format n
formation [fɔr'meʃən] s Bildung f; (aer) Verband m; (geol, mil) Formation f
former ['fɔrmər] adj ehemalig, früher; **the f.** jener
formerly ['fɔrmərli] adv ehemals, früher
form'-fit'ting adj—**be f.** e–e gute Paßform haben
formidable ['fɔrmɪdəbəl] adj (huge) gewaltig; (dreadful) schrecklich
formless ['fɔrmlɪs] adj formlos
form' let'ter s Rundbrief m
formu·la ['fɔrmjələ] s (–las & –lae [,li]) Formel f; (baby food) Kindermilch f
formulate ['fɔrmjə ,let] tr formulieren
formulation [,fɔrmjə'leʃən] s Formulierung f
fornicate ['fɔrnɪ ,ket] intr Unzucht treiben
fornication [,fɔrnɪ'keʃən] s Unzucht f
for·sake [fɔr'sek] v (pret –sook ['sʊk]; pp –saken ['sekən]) tr verlassen
fort [fɔrt] s Burg f; (mil) Fort n
forte [fɔrt] s Stärke f
forth [fɔrθ] adv hervor; **and so f.** und so fort; **from that day f.** von dem Tag an
forth'com'ing adj bevorstehend
forth'right' adj ehrlich, offen
forth'with' adv sofort
fortieth ['fɔrtɪ·ɪθ] adj & pron vierzigste || s (fraction) Vierzigstel n; (in a series) Vierzigste mfn
fortification [,fɔrtɪfɪ'keʃən] s Befestigung f
forti·fy ['fɔrtɪ ,faɪ] v (pret & pp –fied) tr (a place) befestigen; (e.g., with liquor) kräftigen; (encourage) ermutigen
fortitude ['fɔrtɪ ,t(j)ud] s Seelenstärke f
fortnight ['fɔrtnaɪt] s vierzehn Tage pl
fortress ['fɔrtrɪs] s Festung f
fortuitous [fɔr't(j)u·ɪtəs] adj zufällig
fortunate ['fɔrtʃənɪt] adj glücklich
fortunately ['fɔrtʃənɪtli] adv glücklicherweise

fortune ['fɔrtʃən] s Glück n; (money) Vermögen n; **make a f.** sich [dat] ein Vermögen erwerben; **have one's f. told** sich [dat] wahrsagen lassen; **tell fortunes** wahrsagen

for'tune hunt'er s Mitgiftjäger –in mf

for'tunetell'er s Wahrsagerin f

forty ['fɔrti] adj & pron vierzig ‖ s Vierzig f; **the forties** die vierziger Jahre

fo·rum ['forəm] s (–rums & –ra [rə]) (& fig) Forum n

forward ['fɔrwərd] adj vordere, Vorwärts–; (person) keck; (mil) vorgeschoben ‖ adv vorwärts, nach vorn; **bring f.** (an idea) vorschlagen; (a proposal) vorbringen; **come f.** sich melden; **look f. to** sich freuen auf (acc); **put f.** vorlegen ‖ s (fb) Stürmer m ‖ tr befördern; **please f.** bitte nachsenden ‖ interj—**f., march!** im Gleichschritt, marsch!

fossil ['fɑsɪl] adj versteinert ‖ s Fossil n

foster ['fɔstər] adj (child, father, mother, home) Pflege–; (brother, sister) Milch– ‖ tr pflegen

foul [faul] adj übel; (in smell) übelriechend; (air, weather) schlecht; (language) unflätig; (means) unfair ‖ s (sport) Foul n ‖ tr (make dirty) besudeln; (the lines) verwickeln; (sport) foulen; **f. up** durcheinanderbringen ‖ intr (sport) foulen

foul' line' s (baseball) Grenzlinie f; (basketball) Freiwurflinie f

foul-mouthed ['faul‚mauðd], ['faul‚mauθt] adj zotige Reden führend

foul' play' s unfaires Spiel n; (crime) Verbrechen n, Mord m

found [faund] tr gründen; (cast) gießen

foundation [faun'deʃən] s (act) Gründung f; (of a structure) Fundament n; (fund) Stiftung f; (fig) Grundlage f; **lay the foundation of** (& fig) den Grund legen zu

founda'tion gar'ments spl Miederwaren pl

founda'tion wall' s Grundmauer f

founder ['faundər] s Gründer –in mf; (metal) Gießer –in mf ‖ intr (said of a ship) sinken; (fail) scheitern

foundling ['faundlɪŋ] s Findling m

foundry ['faundri] s Gießerei f

found'ry·man s (–men) Gießer m

fount [faunt] s Quelle f

fountain ['fauntən] s Springbrunnen m

foun'tainhead' s Urquell m

foun'tain pen' s Füller m

four [for] adj & pron vier ‖ s Vier f; **on all fours** auf allen vieren

four'-cy'cle adj (mach) Viertakt–

four'-en'gine adj viermotorig

fourflusher ['for‚flʌʃər] s Angeber m

four'foot'ed adj vierfüßig

four' hun'dred adj & pron vierhundert ‖ spl—**the Four Hundred** die oberen Zehntausend

four'lane' adj Vierbahn–

four'-leaf' adj vierblätterig

four'-leg'ged adj vierbeinig

four'-letter word' s unanständiges Wort n

foursome ['forsəm] s Viererspiel n; (group of four) Quartet n

fourteenth [for'tinθ] adj & pron vierzehnte ‖ s (fraction) Vierzehntel n; **the f.** (in dates and in a series) der Vierzehnte

fourth [forθ] adj & pron vierte ‖ s (fraction) Viertel n; **the f.** (in dates and in a series) der Vierte

fourth' estate' s Presse f

fowl [faul] s Huhn n, Geflügel n

fox [fɑks] s (& fig) Fuchs m

fox'glove' s (bot) Fingerhut m

fox'hole' s (mil) Schützenloch n

fox' hound' s Hetzhund m

fox' hunt' s Fuchsjagd f

fox' ter'rier s Foxterrier m

fox' trot' s Foxtrott m

foyer ['fɔɪ·ər] s (of a theater) Foyer n; (of a house) Diele f

fracas ['frekəs] s Aufruhr m

fraction ['frækʃən] s Bruchteil m; **fractions** Bruchrechnung f

fractional ['frækʃənəl] adj Bruch–

fracture ['fræktʃər] s Bruch m ‖ tr sich [dat] brechen

fragile ['frædʒɪl] adj zerbrechlich

fragment ['frægmənt] s Bruchstück n; (of writing) Fragment n

fragmentary ['frægmən‚teri] adj bruchstückhaft; (writing) fragmentarisch

fragmenta'tion bomb' [‚frægmən'teʃən] s Splitterbombe f

fragrance ['fregrəns] s Duft m

fragrant ['fregrənt] adj duftend; **be f.** duften

frail [frel] adj schwach, hinfällig; (fragile) zerbrechlich

frailty ['frelti] s Schwachheit f

frame [frem] s (e.g., of a picture, door) Rahmen m; (of glasses) Fassung f; (of a house) Balkenwerk n; (structure) Gestell n; (anat) Körperbau m; (cin, telv) Bild n; (naut) Spant n ‖ tr (a picture) einrahmen; (a plan) ersinnen; (sl) reinhängen

frame' house' s Holzhaus n

frame' of mind' s Gemütsverfassung f

frame' of ref'erence s Bezugspunkte pl

frame'-up' s abgekartete Sache f

frame'work' s Gebälk n, Fachwerk n; (fig) Rahmen m; (aer) Aufbau m

franc [fræŋk] s Franc m; (Swiss) Franken m

France [fræns] s Frankreich n

Frances ['frænsɪs] s Franziska f

franchise ['frænt‚aɪz] s Konzession f; (right to vote) Wahlrecht n

Francis ['frænsɪs] s Franz m

Franciscan [fræn'sɪskən] adj Franziskaner– ‖ s Franziskaner m

frank [fræŋk] adj offen ‖ s Freivermerk m; **Frank** (masculine name) Franz m; (medieval German person) Franke m, Frankin f ‖ tr franieren

frankfurter ['fræŋkfərtər] s Würstel n

frankincense ['fræŋkɪn‚sens] s Weihrauch m

Frankish ['fræŋkɪʃ] adj fränkisch

frankness ['fræŋknɪs] s Offenheit f; (bluntness) Freimut m

frantic ['fræntɪk] adj (with) außer sich (vor dat); (efforts) krampfhaft

fraternal [frə'tʌrnəl] *adj* brüderlich; (*twins*) zweieiig

fraternity [frə'tʌrnɪti] *s* Bruderschaft *f;* (educ) Studentenverbindung *f*

fraternize ['frætər ‚naɪz] *intr* (**with**) sich anfreunden (mit)

fraud [frɔd] *s* Betrug *m;* (*person*) (coll) Betrüger –in *mf*

fraudulent ['frɔdjələnt] *adj* betrügerisch

fraught [frɔt] *adj*—**f. with** voll mit; **f. with danger** gefahrvoll

fray [fre] *s* Schlägerei *f;* (*battle*) Kampf *m* ‖ *tr* ausfranzen; (*the nerves*) aufreiben ‖ *intr* (*said of edges*) sich ausfranzen; (*become threadbare*) sich durchscheuern

freak [frik] *s* Mißbildung *f;* (*whimsy*) Laune *f;* (*enthusiast*) Enthusiast –in *mf;* (*abnormal person*) verrückter Kerl *m;* **f. of nature** Monstrum *n*

freakish ['frikɪʃ] *adj* grotesk; (*capricious*) launisch

freckle ['frɛkəl] *s* Sommersprosse *f*

freckled ['frɛkəld], **freckly** ['frɛkli] *adj* sommersprossig

Frederick ['frɛdərɪk] *s* Friedrich *m*

free [fri] *adj* (**freer** ['fri·ər]; **freest** ['fri·ɪst]) frei; (*off duty*) dienstfrei; **for f.** (coll) gratis; **f. with** (*e.g., money, praise*) freigebig mit; **go f.** frei ausgehen; **he is f. to** (*inf*) es steht ihm frei zu (*inf*); **set f.** freilassen ‖ *adv* umsonst, kostenlos ‖ *v* (*pret & pp* **freed** [frid]; *ger* **freeing** ['fri·ɪŋ] *tr* (*liberate*) befreien; (*untie*) losmachen

free' and ea'sy *adj* zwanglos

freebooter ['fri ‚butər] *s* Freibeuter *m*

free'born' *adj* freigeboren

freedom ['fridəm] *s* Freiheit *f*

free'dom of assem'bly *s* Versammlungsfreiheit *f*

free'dom of speech' *s* Redefreiheit *f*

free'dom of the press' *s* Pressefreiheit *f*

free'dom of wor'ship *s* Glaubensfreiheit *f*

free' en'terprise *s* freie Wirtschaft *f*

free'-for-all' *s* allgemeine Prügelei *f*

free' hand' *s* freie Hand *f*

free'-hand draw'ing *s* (*activity*) Freihandzeichnen *n;* (*product*) Freihandzeichnung *f*

free'hand'ed *adj* freigebig

free'hold' *s* (jur) Freigut *n*

free' kick' *s* (fb) Freistoß *m*

free'-lance' *adj* freiberuflich ‖ *intr* freiberuflich tätig sein

free-lancer ['fri ‚lænsər] *s* Freiberufliche *mf*

free' li'brary *s* Volksbibliothek *f*

free'man *s* (**-men**) Ehrenbürger *m*

Free'ma'son *s* Freimaurer *m*

Free'ma'sonry *s* Freimaurerei *f*

free' of charge' *adj & adv* kostenlos

free' on board' *adv* frei an Bord

free' play' *s* (fig & mach) Spielraum *m*

free' port' *s* Freihafen *m*

free' sam'ple *s* (*of food*) Gratiskostprobe *f;* (*of products*) Gratismuster *n*

free' speech' *s* Redefreiheit *f*

free'-spo'ken *adj* freimütig

free'stone' *adj* mit leicht auslösbarem Kern

free'think'er *s* Freigeist *m*

free' thought' *s* Freigeisterei *f*

free' trade' *s* Freihandel *m*

free'way' *s* Autobahn *f*

free' will' *s* Willensfreiheit *f;* **of one's own f.** aus freien Stücken

freeze [friz] *s* Frieren *n* ‖ *v* (*pret* **froze** [froz]; *pp* **frozen** ['frozən]) *tr* frieren; (*assets*) einfrieren; (*prices*) stoppen; (*food*) tiefkühlen; (surg) vereisen ‖ *intr* (ge)frieren; (*e.g., with fear*) erstarren; **f. over** zufrieren; **f. to death** erfrieren; **f. up** vereisen

freeze'-dry' *v* (*pret & pp* **-dried**) *tr* gefriertrocknen

freezer ['frizər] *s* (*chest*) Tiefkühltruhe *f;* (*cabinet*) Tiefkühlschrank *m*

freez'er compart'ment *s* Gefrierfach *n*

freez'ing *s* Einfrieren *n;* **below f.** unter dem Gefrierpunkt

freight [fret] *s* (*load*) Fracht *f;* (*cargo*) Frachtgut *n;* (*fee*) Frachtgebühr *f;* **by f.** als Frachtgut ‖ *tr* beladen

freight' car' *s* Güterwagen *m*

freight' el'vator *s* Warenaufzug *m*

freighter ['fretər] *s* Frachter *m*

freight' of'fice *s* Güterabfertigung *f*

freight' train' *s* Güterzug *m*

freight' yard' *s* Güterbahnhof *m*

French [frɛntʃ] *adj* französisch ‖ *s* (*language*) Französisch *n;* **the F.** die Franzosen

French' doors' *spl* Glastüre *pl*

French' fries' *spl* Pommes frites *pl*

French' horn' *s* (mus) Waldhorn *n*

French' leave' *s*—**take F.** sich französisch empfehlen

French'man *s* (**-men**) Franzose *m*

French' roll' *s* Schrippe *f*

French' toast' *s* arme Ritter *pl*

French' win'dow *s* Flügelfenster *n*

French' wom'an *s* (**-wom'en**) Französin *f*

frenzied ['frɛnzid] *adj* rasend

frenzy ['frɛnzi] *s* Raserei *f*

frequency ['frikwənsi] *s* Häufigkeit *f;* (phys) Frequenz *f*

fre'quency modula'tion *s* Frequenzmodulation *f*

frequent ['frikwənt] *adj* häufig ‖ [fri-'kwənt] *tr* besuchen, frequentieren

frequently ['frikwəntli] *adv* häufig

fres·co ['frɛsko] *s* (**-coes & -cos**) Fresko *n,* Freskogemälde *n*

fresh [frɛʃ] *adj* frisch; (coll) frech ‖ *adv* neu, kürzlich

fresh'-baked' *adj* neugebacken

freshen ['frɛʃən] *tr* erfrischen; **f. up** auffrischen ‖ *intr*—**f. up** sich auffrischen

freshet ['frɛʃɪt] *s* Hochwasser *n;* (*fresh-water stream*) Fluß *m*

fresh'man *s* (**-men**) Fuchs *m*

freshness ['frɛʃnɪs] *s* Frische *f;* (coll) Naseweisheit *f*

fresh' wa'ter *s* Süßwasser *n*

fresh'-wa'ter *adj* Süßwasser–

fret [frɛt] *s* Verdruß *m;* (carp) Laubsägewerk *n;* (mus) Bund *m* ‖ *v* (*pret*

& *pp* **fretted;** *ger* **fretting**) *tr* gitter-
förmig verzieren || *intr* sich ärgern
fretful ['fretfəl] *adj* verdrießlich
fret'work' *s* Laubsägewerk *n*
Freudian ['frɔɪdɪ·ən] *adj* Freudsch ||
s Freudianer –in *mf*
friar ['fraɪ·ər] *s* Klosterbruder *m*
fricassee [ˌfrɪkə'si] *s* Frikassee *n*
friction ['frɪkʃən] *s* Reibung *f;* (fig)
Reiberei *f*, Mißhelligkeit *f*
fric'tion tape' *s* Isolierband *n*
Friday ['fraɪdɪ] *s* Freitag *m*
fried [fraɪd] *adj* gebraten, Brat–,
Back–
fried' chick'en *s* Backhuhn *n*
fried' egg' *s* Spiegelei *n*
fried' pota'toes *spl* Bratkartoffeln *pl*
friend [frend] *s* Freund –in *mf;* **be
(close) friends** (eng) befreundet sein;
make friends (with) sich anfreunden
(mit)
friendliness ['frendlɪnɪs] *s* Freundlichkeit *f*
friendly ['frendli] *adj* freundlich; **on f.
terms with** in freundschaftlichem
Verhältnis mit
friend'ship' *s* Freundschaft *f*
frieze [friz] *s* Fries *m*
frigate ['frɪgɪt] *s* Fregatte *f*
fright [fraɪt] *s* Schrecken *m*
frighten ['fraɪtən] *tr* schrecken; **be
frightened** erschrecken; **f. away** verscheuchen, vertreiben
frightful ['fraɪtfəl] *adj* schrecklich
frigid ['frɪdʒɪd] *adj* eiskalt; (pathol)
Frigid
frigidity [frɪ'dʒɪdɪti] *s* Kälte *f;* (pathol)
Frigidität *f*
Frig'id Zone' *s* kalte Zone *f*
frill [frɪl] *s* (*ruffle*) Volant *m*, Krause
f; (*frippery*) Schnörkel *m;* **put on
frills** sich aufgeblasen benehmen;
with all the frills mit allen Schikanen
fringe [frɪndʒ] *s* Franse *f* || *tr* mit
Fransen besetzen; (fig) einsäumen
fringe' ar'ea *s* Randgebiet *n*
fringe' ben'efit *s* zusätzliche Sozial-
leistung *f*
frippery ['frɪpəri] *s* (*cheap finery, trifles*) Flitterkram *m*
frisk [frɪsk] *tr* (sl) durchsuchen || *intr*
—**f. about** herumtollen
frisky ['frɪski] *adj* ausgelassen
fritter ['frɪtər] *s* Beignet *m* || *tr*—**f.
away** vertrödeln, verzetteln
fritz [frɪts] *s*—**on the f.** kaputt
frivolous ['frɪvələs] *adj* leichtfertig;
(*object*) geringfügig
friz [frɪz] *s* (**frizzes**) Kraushaar *n* ||
v (*pret* & *pp* **frizzed;** *ger* **frizzing**) *tr*
kräuseln || *intr* sich kräuseln
frizzle ['frɪzəl] *s* Kraushaar *n* || *tr*
(*hair*) kräuseln; (*food*) knusprig bra-
ten || *intr* sich kräuseln; (*sizzle*)
zischen
frizzy ['frɪzi] *adj* kraus
fro [fro] *adv*—**to and fro** hin und her
frock [frak] *s* Kleid *n;* (eccl) Mönchs-
kutte *f*
frog [frag] *s* (*animal; slight hoarseness*) Frosch *m*
frog'man' *s* (**–men'**) Froschmann *m*
frol·ic ['fralɪk] *s* Spaß *m* || *v* (*pret* &

pp **–icked;** *ger* **–icking**) *intr* Spaß
machen; (*frisk about*) herumtollen
frolicsome ['fralɪksəm] *adj* ausgelassen
from [frʌm] *prep* von (dat), aus (*dat*),
von (*dat*) aus; **f. afar** von weitem;
f. now on künftig; **f. ... on** von ...
an
front [frʌnt] *adj* Vorder–, vordere ||
s (*façade*) Vorderseite *f;* (*of a shirt,
dress*) Einsatz *m;* (*cover-up*) Aushängeschild *n;* (meteor, mil) Front
f; **from the f.** von vorn; **in f.** vorn;
in f. of vor (*dat or acc*); **in the f.
of the book** vorn im Buch; **put on
a bold f.** Mut zeigen; **they put on a
big f.** alles Fassade! || *tr* gegenüber-
liegen (*dat*) || *intr*—**f. for s.o.** j–m
als Strohmann dienen; **f. on** mit der
Front liegen nach
frontage ['frʌntɪdʒ] *s* Straßenfront *f*
frontal ['frʌntəl] *adj* Frontal–; (anat)
Stirn–
fron'tal view' *s* Vorderansicht *f*
front' door' *s* Haustür *f*
front' foot' *s* Vorderfuß *m*
frontier [frʌn'tɪr] *s* (*border*) Grenze
f; (*area*) Grenzland *n;* (fig) Grenz-
bereich *m*
frontiers'man *s* (**–men**) Pionier *m*
frontispiece ['frʌntɪsˌpis] *s* Titelbild
n
front' line' *s* Front *f*, Frontlinie *f*
front'-line' *adj* Front–, Gefechts–
front' page' *s* Titelseite *f*
front' porch' *s* Veranda *f*
front' rank' *s* (mil) vorderes Glied *n;*
be in the f. (fig) im Vordergrund
stehen
front' row' *s* erste Reihe *f*
front' run'ner *s* (pol) Spitzenkandidat
–in *mf*
front' seat' *s* Vordersitz *m*
front' steps' *spl* Vordertreppe *f*
front' yard' *s* Vorgarten *m*, Vorplatz *m*
frost [frɔst] *s* (*freezing*) Frost *m;*
(*frozen dew*) Reif *m* || *tr* mit Reif
überziehen; (culin) glasieren
frost'bite' *s* Erfrierung *f*
frost'bit'ten *adj* erfroren
frost'ed glass' *s* Mattglas *n*
frost'ing *s* Glasur *f*
frost' line' *s* Frostgrenze *f*
frosty ['frɔsti] *adj* (& fig) frostig
froth [frɔθ] *s* (*foam*) Schaum *m;*
(*slaver*) Geifer *m* || *intr* schäumen;
geifern
frothy ['frɔθi] *adj* schäumend
froward ['frowərd] *adj* eigensinnig
frown [fraun] *s* Stirnrunzeln *n* || *intr*
die Stirn runzeln; **f. at** böse anschauen; **f. on** mißbilligen
frowsy, frowzy ['frauzi] *adj* (*slovenly*)
schlampig; (*ill-smelling*) muffig
froz'en as'sets ['frozən] *spl* eingefro-
rene Guthaben *pl*
froz'en foods' *spl* tiefgekühlte Lebensmittel *pl*
frugal ['frugəl] *adj* frugal
fruit [frut] *adj* (*tree*) Obst–, Süd-
frucht– || *s* Frucht *f*, Obst *n*, Süd-
früchte *pl;* (fig) Frucht *f*
fruit' cake' *s* Stolle *f*, Stollen *m*

fruit′ cup′ s gemischte Früchte pl
fruit′ fly′ s Obstfliege f
fruitful ['frutfəl] adj fruchtbar
fruition [fru'ɪ/ən] s Reife f; **come to f.** zur Reife gelangen
fruit′ jar′ s Konservenglas n
fruit′ juice′ s Fruchtsaft m, Obstsaft m
fruitless ['frutlɪs] adj (& fig) fruchtlos
fruit′ sal′ad s Obstsalat m
fruit′ stand′ s Obststand m
frump [frʌmp] s Scharteke f
frumpish ['frʌmpɪ/] adj schlampig
frustrate ['frʌstret] tr (discourage) frustrieren; (an endeavor) vereiteln
frustration [frʌs'tre/ən] s Frustration f; (of an endeavor) Vereitelung f
fry [fraɪ] s Gebratenes n || v (pret & pp **fried**) tr & intr braten
fry′ing pan′ s Bratpfanne f; **jump out of the f. into the fire** vom Regen unter die Traufe kommen
fuchsia ['fju/ə] s (bot) Fuchsie f
fudge [fʌdʒ] s weiches, milchhaltiges, mit Kakao versetztes Zuckerwerk n
fuel ['fju·əl] s Brennstoff m; (for engines) Treibstoff m; (fig) Nahrung f; **add f. to the flames** Öl ins Feuer gießen || v (pret & pp **fuel[l]ed**; ger **fuel[l]ing**) tr mit Brennstoff versorgen || intr tanken
fu′el dump′ s Treibstofflager n
fu′el gauge′ s Benzinuhr f
fu′el tank′ s Treibstoffbehälter m
fugitive ['fjudʒɪtɪv] adj flüchtig || s Flüchtling m
fugue [fjug] s (mus) Fuge f
ful·crum ['fʌlkrəm] s (–crums & –cra [krə]) Stützpunkt m, Drehpunkt m
fulfill [ful'fɪl] tr erfüllen
fulfillment [ful'fɪlmənt] s Erfüllung f
full [ful] adj voll; (with food) satt; (clothes) weit; (hour) ganz; (life) inhaltsreich; (voice) wohlklingend; (professor) ordentlich; **f. of** voller, voll von; **too f.** übervoll; **work f. time** ganztägig arbeiten || adv—**f. well** sehr gut || s—**in f.** voll, ganz || tr (tex) walken
full′back′ s (fb) Außenverteidiger m
full′-blood′ed adj vollblütig
full-blown ['ful'blon] adj (flower) voll aufgeblüht; (fig) voll erblüht
full′-bod′ied adj (wine) stark, schwer
full′ dress′ s Gesellschaftsanzug m; (mil) Paradeanzug m
full′-dress′ adj Gala–, formell
full′-faced′ adj pausbackig; (portrait) mit voll zugewandtem Gesicht
full-fledged ['ful'flɛdʒd] adj richtiggehend
full-grown ['ful'gron] adj voll ausgewachsen
full′ house′ s (cards) Full house n; (theat) volles Haus n
full′-length′ adj (dress) in voller Größe; (portrait) lebensgroß; (movie) abendfüllend
full′ moon′ s Vollmond m
full′-page′ adj ganzseitig
full′ pay′ s volles Gehalt n
full′ profes′sor s Ordinarius m
full′-scale′ adj in voller Größe
full′-sized′ adj in natürlicher Größe

full′ speed′ adv auf höchsten Touren
full′ stop′ s (gram) Punkt m; **come to a f.** völlig stillstehen
full′ swing′ s—**in f.** in vollem Gange
full′ throt′tle s Vollgas n
full′ tilt′ adv auf höchsten Touren
full′-time′ adj ganztägig
full′ view′ s—**in f.** direkt vor den Augen
fully ['ful(l)i] adj völlig; **be f. booked** ausverkauft sein
fulsome ['fulsəm] adj (excessive) übermäßig; (offensive) widerlich
fumble ['fʌmbəl] tr (a ball) fallen lassen || intr fummeln; **f. for** umherfühlen nach
fume [fjum] s Gas n, Dampf m || intr dampfen; (smoke) rauchen; **f. with rage** vor Wut schnauben
fumigate ['fjumɪ‚get] tr ausräuchern
fun [fʌn] s Spaß m; **be (great) fun** (viel) Spaß machen; **for fun** zum Spaß; **for the fun of it** spaßeshalber; **have fun!** viel Spaß!; **make fun of** sich lustig machen über (acc); **poke fun at** witzeln über (acc)
function ['fʌnk/ən] s Funktion f; (office) Amt n; (formal occasion) Feier f || intr funktionieren; (officiate) fungieren
functional ['fʌnk/ənəl] adj (practical) Zweck–, zweckmäßig; (disorder) funktionell, Funktions–
functionary ['fʌnk/ə‚neri] s Funktionär –in mf
fund [fʌnd] s Fonds m; (fig) Vorrat m **funds** Geldmittel pl || tr fundieren
fundamental [‚fʌndə'mentəl] adj grundlegend, Grund– || s Grundbegriff m
fundamentalist [‚fʌndə'mentəlɪst] s Fundamentalist –in mf
fundamentally [‚fʌndə'mentəli] adv im Grunde, prinzipiell
funeral ['fjunərəl] adj Leichen–, Trauer–, Begräbnis– || s Begräbnis n
fu′neral direc′tor s Bestattungsunternehmer –in mf
fu′neral home′ s Aufbahrungshalle f
fu′neral proces′sion s Trauergefolge n
fu′neral serv′ice s Trauergottesdienst m
fu′neral wreath′ s Totenkranz m
funereal [fju'nɪrɪ·əl] adj düster
fungus ['fʌngəs] s (funguses & fungi ['fʌndʒaɪ]) Pilz m, Schwamm m
funicular [fju'nɪkjələr] s Drahtseilbahn f
funk [fʌnk] s (fear) Mordsangst f; **be in a f.** niedergeschlagen sein
fun·nel ['fʌnəl] s Trichter m; (naut) Schornstein m || v (pret & pp **–nel[l]ed**; ger **–nel[l]ing**) tr durch e–n Trichter gießen; (fig) (into) konzentrieren (auf acc)
funnies ['fʌniz] spl Witzseite f
funny ['fʌni] adj komisch; (strange, suspicious) sonderbar; **don't try anything f.** mach mir keine Dummheiten!
fun′ny bone′ s Musikantenknochen m
fun′ny bus′iness s dunkle Geschäfte pl
fun′ny ide′as spl Flausen pl

fun′ny pa′per s Witzblatt n
fur [fʌr] adj (coat, collar) Pelz– ‖ s
Pelz m; (on the tongue) Belag m
furbish [′fʌrbɪʃ] tr aufputzen
furious [′fjurɪ‑əs] adj (at) wütend
(auf acc); **be f.** wüten
furl [fʌrl] tr zusammenrollen
fur′-lined′ adj pelzgefüttert
furlong [′fʌrlɒŋ] s Achtelmeile f
furlough [′fʌrlo] s (mil) Urlaub m; **go
on f.** auf Urlaub kommen ‖ tr beurlauben
furnace [′fʌrnɪs] s Ofen m
furnish [′fʌrnɪʃ] tr (a room) möblieren; (e.g., an office) ausstatten;
(proof) liefern; (supply) (with) versehen (mit)
fur′nished room′ s möbliertes Zimmer
n
furnishings [′fʌrnɪʃɪŋz] spl Ausstattung f
furniture [′fʌrnɪtʃər] s Möbel pl; **piece
of f.** Möbelstück n
fur′niture store′ s Möbelhandlung f
furor [′fjurɒr] s (rage) Wut f; (uproar) Furore f; (vogue) Mode f;
cause a f. Furore machen
furrier [′fʌrɪ‑ər] s Pelzhändler –in mf
furrow [′fʌro] s Furche f ‖ tr furchen
furry [′fʌri] adj pelzig
further [′fʌrðər] adj weiter; (particulars) näher ‖ adv weiter ‖ tr fördern
furtherance [′fʌrðərəns] s Förderung f
fur′thermore′ adv überdies, außerdem
furthest [′fʌrðɪst] adj weiteste ‖ adv
am weitesten
furtive [′fʌrtɪv] adj verstohlen

fury [′fjuri] s Wut f; **Fury** (myth)
Furie f
fuse [fjuz] s (of an explosive) Zünder
m; (elec) Sicherung f; **blown f.**
durchgebrannte Sicherung f ‖ tr verschmelzen ‖ intr verschmelzen; (fig)
sich vereinigen
fuse′ box′ s Sicherungskasten m
fuselage [′fjuzəlɪdʒ] s (aer) Rumpf m
fusible [′fjuzɪbəl] adj schmelzbar
fusillade [′fjusə‚led] s Feuersalve f;
(fig) Hagel m
fusion [′fjuʒən] s Verschmelzung f;
(pol, phys) Fusion f
fuss [fʌs] s Getue n; **make a f. over**
viel Aufhebens machen von ‖ intr
sich aufregen; **f. around** herumwirt-
schaften; **f. over** viel Aufhebens machen von; **f. with** herumspielen mit
fuss′ bud′get, fuss′pot′ s Umstandskrä-
mer m
fussy [′fʌsi] adj (given to detail) umständlich; (fastidious) heikel; (irritable) reizbar; **be f.** Umstände machen
fustian [′fʌstʃən] s (bombast) Schwulst
m; (tex) Barchent m
fusty [′fʌsti] adj (musty) muffig; (old-
fashioned) veraltet
futile [′fjutəl] adj vergeblich, nutzlos
futility [fju′tɪlɪti] s Nutzlosigkeit f
future [′fjutʃər] adj (zu)künftig ‖ s
Zukunft f; **futures** (econ) Terminge-
schäfte pl; **in the f.** künftig
fuzz [fʌz] s (from cloth) Fussel f; (on
peaches) Flaum m
fuzzy [′fʌzi] adj flaumig; (unclear) unklar; (hair) kraus

G

G, g [dʒi] s siebenter Buchstabe des
englischen Alphabets
gab [gæb] s (coll) Geschwätz n ‖ v
(pret & pp **gabbed;** ger **gabbing**)
intr schwatzen
gabardine [′gæbər‚din] s Gabardine m
gabble [′gæbəl] s Geschnatter n ‖ intr
schnattern
gable [′gebəl] s Giebel m
ga′ble end′ s Giebelwand f
ga′ble roof′ s Giebeldach n
gad [gæd] v (pret & pp **gadded;** ger
gadding) intr—**gad about** umher-
streifen
gad′about′ s Bummler –in mf
gad′fly′ s Viehbremse f; (fig) Störenfried m
gadget [′gædʒɪt] s (coll) Gerät n
Gaelic [′gelɪk] adj gälisch ‖ s (language) Gälisch n
gaff [gæf] s Fischhaken m
gag [gæg] s (something put into the
mouth) Knebel m; (joke) Witz m;
(hoax, trick) amüsanter Trick m ‖
v (pret & pp **gagged;** ger **gagging**) tr
knebeln; (said of a tight collar) würgen; (fig) mundtot machen ‖ intr
(on food) würgen

gage [gedʒ] s (challenge) Fehdehandschuh m; (pawn) Pfand m
gaiety [′ge‑ɪti] s Fröhlichkeit f
gaily [′geli] adv fröhlich
gain [gen] s Gewinn m; (advantage)
Vorteil m; **g. in weight** Gewichtszunahme f ‖ tr gewinnen; (pounds)
zunehmen; (a living) verdienen; (a
victory) erringen; **g. a footing** festen
Fuß fassen; **g. ground** (mil & fig)
Terrain gewinnen; **g. speed** schneller
werden; **g. weight** an Gewicht zunehmen ‖ intr (said of a car) aufholen;
(said of a clock) vorgehen; **g. from**
Gewinn haben von; **g. in** gewinnen
an (dat); **g. on s.o.** j-m den Vorteil
abgewinnen
gainful [′genfəl] adj einträglich
gainfully [′genfəli] adv—**g. employed**
erwerbstätig
gain′say′ v (pret & pp **–said** [‚sed],
[‚sed]) tr (a thing) verneinen; (a
person) widersprechen (dat)
gait [get] s Gang m, Gangart f
gala [′gælə] [′gelə] adj festlich ‖ s
(celebration) Feier f; (dress) Gala f
galaxy [′gæləksi] s Galaxis f; (fig)
glänzende Versammlung f

gale [gel] s Sturm m, Sturmwind m;
   gales of laughter Lachensalven pl
gale' warn'ing s Sturmwarnung f
gall [gɔl] s Galle f; (audacity) Unver-
   schämtheit f || tr (rub) wundreiben;
   (vex) ärgern, belästigen
gallant ['gælənt] adj (tapfer); (stately)
   stattlich || [gə'lænt] adj galant || s
   Galan m
gallantry ['gæləntri] s (bravery) Tapferkeit f; (courteous behavior) Ritterlichkeit f
gall' blad'der s Gallenblase f
galleon ['gælɪ·ən] s Galeone f
gallery ['gæləri] s (arcade) Säulen-
   halle f; (art, theat) Galerie f; (min)
   Stollen m; play to the g. (coll) Effekthascherei treiben
galley ['gæli] s (a ship) Galeere f; (a
   kitchen) Kombüse f; (typ) Setzschiff
   n
gal'ley proof' s (typ) Fahne f
gal'ley slave' s Galeerensklave m
Gallic ['gælɪk] adj gallisch
gall'ing adj verdrießlich
gallivant ['gælɪ‚vænt] intr bummeln
gallon ['gælən] s Gallone f
galloon [gə'lun] s Tresse f
gallop ['gæləp] s Galopp m; at full g.
   in gestrecktem Galopp || tr in Ga-
   lopp setzen || intr galoppieren
gal·lows ['gæloz] s (-lows & -lowses)
   Galgen m
gal'lows bird' s (coll) Galgenvogel m
gall'stone' s Gallenstein m
galore [gə'lor] adv im Überfluß
galosh [gə'laʃ] s Galosche f
galvanize ['gælvə‚naɪz] tr galvanisieren
gambit ['gæmbɪt] s (fig) Schachzug
   m; (chess) Gambit n
gamble ['gæmbəl] s Hasardspiel n;
   (risk) Risiko n; (com) Spekulations-
   geschäft n || tr—g. away verspielen
   || intr spielen, hasardieren
gambler ['gæmblər] s Spieler -in mf;
   (fig) Hasardeur m, Hasardeuse f
gam'bling s Spielen n, Spiel n
gam'bling house' s Spielhölle f
gam'bling ta'ble s Spieltisch m
gam·bol ['gæmbəl] s Luftsprung m || v
   (pret & pp -bol[l]ed; ger -bol[l]ing)
   intr umhertollen
gambrel ['gæmbrəl] s (hock) Hachse
   f; (in a butcher shop) Spriegel m
gam'brel roof' s Mansardendach n
game [gem] adj bereit; (fight) tapfer;
   (leg) lahm; (hunt) Wild–, Jagd– || s
   Spiel n; (e.g., of chess) Partie f; (fig)
   Absicht f; (culin) Wildbret n; (hunt)
   Wild n, Jagdwild n; have the g. in
   the bag den Sieg in der Tasche haben; play a losing g. auf verlorenem
   Posten kämpfen; the g. is up das
   Spiel ist aus
game' bird' s Jagdvogel m
game' board' s Spielbrett n
game'cock' s Kampfhahn m
gameness ['gemnɪs] f Tapferkeit f
game' of chance' s Glücksspiel n
game' preserve' s Wildpark m
game' war'den s Jagdaufseher m
gamut ['gæmət] s Skala f

gamy ['gemi] adj nach Wild riechend;
   g. flavor Wildgeschmack m
gander ['gændər] s Gänserich m; take
   a g. at (coll) e–n Blick werfen auf
   (acc)
gang [gæŋ] s (group of friends) Gesellschaft f; (antisocial group) Bande
   f; (of workers) Kolonne f || intr—
   g. up (on) sich zusammenrotten
   (gegen)
gangling ['gæŋglɪŋ] adj schlaksig
gangli·on ['gæŋglɪ·ən] s (-ons & -a
   [ə]) (cystic tumor) Überbein n; (of
   nerves) Nervenknoten m
gangly ['gæŋgli] adj schlaksig
gang'plank' s Laufplanke f, Steg m
gangrene ['gæŋgrin] s Gangrän n,
   Brand m || intr brandig werden
gangrenous ['gæŋgrɪnəs] adj brandig
gangster ['gæŋstər] s Gangster m
gang'way' s (passageway) Durchgang
   m; (naut) Laufplanke f || interj aus
   dem Weg!
gantlet ['gɔntlət] s (rr) Gleisverschlin-
   gung f
gantry ['gæntri] s (rok) Portalkran m;
   (rr) Signalbrücke f
gan'try crane' s Portalkran m
gap [gæp] s Lücke f; (in the mountains) Schlucht f; (mil) Bresche f
gape [gep] s Riß m, Sprung m; (gap-
   ing) Gaffen n || intr gaffen; (said of
   wounds, etc.) klaffen; g. at angaffen
garage [gə'raʒ] s Garage f; (repair
   shop) Reparaturwerkstatt f; put into
   the g. unterstellen
garb [garb] s Tracht f
garbage ['garbɪdʒ] s Müll m; (nonsense) Unsinn m
gar'bage can' s Mülltonne f
gar'bage dispos'al s Müllabfuhr f
gar'bage dump' s Müllplatz m
gar'bage man' s Müllfahrer m
gar'bage truck' s Müllabfuhrwagen m
garble ['garbəl] tr verstümmeln
garden ['gardən] s Garten m; gardens
   Gartenanlage f
gardener ['gardənər] s Gärtner -in mf
gar'den hose' s Gartenschlauch m
gardenia [gar'dini·ə] s Gardenie f
gar'dening s Gartenarbeit f
gar'den par'ty s Gartengesellschaft f
gargle ['gargəl] s Mundwasser n || tr
   & intr gurgeln
gargoyle ['gargɔɪl] s Wasserspeier m
garish ['gerɪʃ], ['gærɪʃ] adj grell
garland ['garlənd] s Girlande f
garlic ['garlɪk] s Knoblauch m
garment ['garmənt] s Kleidungsstück n
garner ['garnər] tr (grain) aufspeichern; (gather) ansammeln
garnet ['garnɪt] s Granat m
garnish ['garnɪʃ] s Verzierung f;
   (culin) Garnierung f || tr verzieren;
   (culin) garnieren
garret ['gærɪt] s Dachstube f
garrison ['gærɪsən] s (troops) Garnison f, Besatzung f; (fort) Festung f
   || tr mit e–r Garnison versehen;
   (troops) in Garnison stationieren
gar'rison cap' s Schiffchen n
garrote [gə'rat], [gə'rot] s Garrotte f
   || tr garrottieren

garrulous ['gær(j)ələs] *adj* schwatzhaft
garter ['gɑrtər] *s* Strumpfband *n*
gar'ter belt' *s* Strumpfhaltergürtel *m*
gas [gæs] *adj* (e.g., *generator, light, main, meter*) Gas– ‖ *s* Gas *n;* (coll) Benzin *n*, Sprit *m;* (*empty talk*) (sl) leeres Geschwätz *n;* **get gas** (coll) tanken; **step on the gas** (coll) Gas geben ‖ *v* (*pret & pp* **gassed; ger gassing**) *tr* vergasen ‖ *intr* (sl) schwatzen; **gas up** (coll) volltanken
gas' attack' *s* Gasangriff *m*
gas' burn'er *s* Gasbrenner *m*
gas' en'gine *s* Gasmotor *m*
gaseous ['gæsɪ·əs], ['gæʃəs] *adj* gasförmig
gas' fit'ter *s* Gasinstallateur *m*
gash [gæʃ] *s* tiefe Schnittwunde *f* ‖ e–e tiefe Schnittwunde beibringen (*dat*)
gas' heat' *s* Gasheizung *f*
gas'hold'er *s* Gasbehälter *m*
gasi·fy ['gæsɪ ˌfaɪ] *v* (*pret & pp* **–fied**) *tr* in Gas verwandeln ‖ *intr* zu Gas werden
gas' jet' *s* Gasflamme *f*
gasket ['gæskɪt] *s* Dichtung *f*
gas' mask' *s* Gasmaske *f*
gasoline [ˌgæsə'lin] *s* Benzin *n*
gasoline' pump' *s* Benzinzapfsäule *f*
gasp [gæsp] *s* Keuchen *n* ‖ *tr* (**out**) hervorstoßen ‖ *intr* keuchen; **g. for air** nach Luft schnappen; **g. for breath** nach Atem ringen
gas' range' *s* Gasherd *m*
gas' sta'tion *s* Tankstelle *f*
gas' sta'tion attend'ant *s* Tankwart *m*
gas' stove' *s* Gasherd *m*
gas' tank' *s* Benzinbehälter *m*
gastric ['gæstrɪk] *adj* gastrisch
gas'tric juice' *s* Magensaft *m*
gastronomy [gæs'trɑnəmi] *s* Gastronomie *f*
gas'works' *spl* Gasanstalt *f*
gate [get] *s* Tor *n*, Pforte *f;* (rr) Sperre *f;* (sport) eingenommenes Eintrittsgeld *n;* **crash the g.** ohne Eintrittskarte durchschlupfen
gate' crash'er [ˌkræʃər] *s* unberechtigter Zuschauer *m*
gate'keep'er *s* Pförtner –in *mf*
gate'post' *s* Torpfosten *m*
gate'way' *s* Tor *n*, Torweg *m*
gather ['gæðər] *tr* (*things*) sammeln; (*people*) versammeln; (*flowers, fruit, peas*) pflücken; (*courage*) aufbringen; (*the impression*) gewinnen; (*information*) einziehen; (*strength, speed*) zunehmen an (*dat*); (*conclude*) (**from**) schließen (aus); **g. together** versammeln; **g. up** aufheben; (*curtains, dress*) raffen ‖ *intr* sich (an)sammeln; (*said of clouds*) sich zusammenziehen; **g. around** sich scharen um
gath'ered *adj* (*skirt*) gerafft
gath'ering *s* Versammlung *f;* (sew) Kräuselfalten *pl*
gaudy ['gɔdi] *adj* (*overdone*) überladen; (*color*) grell
gauge [gedʒ] *s* (*instrument*) Messer *m*, Anzeiger *m;* (*measurement*) Eichmaß *n;* (*of wire*) Stärke *f;* (*of a shot-*

gun) Kaliber *n;* (fig) Maß *n;* (mach) Lehre *f;* (rr) Spurweite *f* ‖ *tr* messen; (*check for accuracy*) eichen; (fig) abschätzen
Gaul [gɔl] *s* Gallien *n;* (*native*) Gallier –in *mf*
Gaulish ['gɔlɪʃ] *adj* gallisch
gaunt [gɔnt] *adj* hager
gauntlet ['gɔntlɪt] *s* Panzerhandschuh *m;* (fig) Fehdehandschuh *m;* **run the g.** Spießruten laufen
gauze [gɔz] *s* Gaze *f*
gavel ['gævəl] *s* Hammer *m*
gawk [gɔk] *s* (coll) Depp *m* ‖ *intr*—**g. at** (coll) blöde anstarren
gawky ['gɔki] *adj* schlaksig
gay [ge] *adj* lustig; (*homosexual*) schwul
gay' blade' *s* lebenslustiger Kerl *m*
gaze [gez] *intr* starren; **g. at** anstarren; (*in astonishment*) anstaunen
gazelle [gə'zel] *s* Gazelle *f*
gazetteer [ˌgæzə'tɪr] *s* Ortslexikon *n*
gear [gɪr] *s* (*equipment*) Ausrüstung *f;* (aut) Schaltgetriebe *n*, Gang *m;* (mach) Zahnrad *n;* **gears** Räderwerk *n;* **in g.** eingeschaltet; **in high g.** im höchsten Gang; (fig) auf Touren; **shift gears** umschalten; **throw into g.** einschalten; **throw out of g.** (fig) aus dem Gleichgewicht bringen ‖ *tr*—**g. to** anpassen (*dat*)
gear'box' *s* Schaltgetriebe *n*
gear'shift' *s* Gangschaltung *f;* (*lever*) Schalthebel *m*
gear'wheel' *s* Zahnrad *n*
gee [dʒi] *interj* nanu!
Geiger counter ['gaɪgər ˌkaʊntər] *s* Geigerzähler *m*
gel [dʒel] *s* Gel *n* ‖ *v* (*pret & pp* **gelled; ger gelling**) *intr* gelieren; (coll) klappen
gelatin ['dʒelətɪn] *s* Gelatine *f*
geld [geld] *v* (*pret & pp* **gelded & gelt** [gelt]) *tr* kastrieren
geld'ing *s* Wallach *m*
gem [dʒem] *s* Edelstein *m;* (fig) Perle *f*
Gemini ['dʒemɪ ˌnaɪ] *s* (astr) Zwillinge *pl*
gender ['dʒendər] *s* Geschlecht *n*
gene [dʒin] *s* Gen *n*, Erbanlage *f*
genealogical [ˌdʒini·ə'lɑdʒɪkəl] *adj* genealogisch, Stamm–
genealog'ical ta'ble *s* Stammtafel *f*
genealog'ical tree' *s* Stammbaum *m*
genealogy [ˌdʒinɪ'ælədʒi] *s* Genealogie *f*
general ['dʒenərəl] *adj* allgemein, Gesamt– ‖ *s* General *m;* **in g.** im allgemeinen
Gen'eral Assem'bly *s* Vollversammlung *f*
gen'eral deliv'ery *adv* postlagernd
gen'eral head'quarters *spl* Oberkommando *n*
generalissi·mo [ˌdʒenərə'lɪsɪmo] *s* (**–mos**) Generalissimus *m*
generality [ˌdʒenə'rælɪti] *s* Allgemeingültigkeit *f;* **generalities** Gemeinplätze *pl*
generalization [ˌdʒenərəlɪ'zeʃən] *s* Verallgemeinerung *f*

generalize ['dʒenərə,laɪz] *tr* & *intr* verallgemeinern

generally ['dʒenərəli] *adv* im allgemeinen; *(usually)* gewöhnlich; *(mostly)* meistens

gen'eral man'ager *s* Generaldirektor –in *mf*

gen'eral plan' *s* Übersichtsplan *m*

gen'eral post' of'fice *s* Oberpostamt *n*

gen'eral practi'tioner *s* praktischer Arzt *m*

gen'eralship' *s* Führereingenschaften *pl*

gen'eral staff' *s* Generalstab *m*

gen'eral store' *s* Gemischtwarenhandlung *f*

gen'eral strike' *s* Generalstreik *m*

generate ['dʒenə,ret] *tr (procreate)* zeugen; (fig) verursachen; (elec) erzeugen; (geom) bilden

gen'erating sta'tion *s* Kraftwerk *n*

generation [,dʒenə're/ən] *s* Generation *f*; **present g.** Mitwelt *f*; **younger g.** junge Generation *f*

genera'tion gap' *s* Generationsproblem *n*

generator ['dʒenə,retər] *s* Erzeuger *m*; (chem, elec) Generator *m*; (elec) Stromerzeuger *m*

generic [dʒɪ'nerɪk] *adj* generisch, Gattungs–; **g. name** Gattungsname *m*

generosity [,dʒenə'rɑsɪti] *s* Freigebigkeit *f*

generous ['dʒenərəs] *adj* freigebig

gene·sis ['dʒenɪsɪs] *s* (**–ses** [,siz]) Genese *f*, Entstehung *f*; **Genesis** (Bib) Genesis *f*

genetic [dʒɪ'netɪk] *adj* genetisch

genet'ic engineer' *s* Gen-Ingenieur *m*

genet'ic engineer'ing *s* Gen-Manipulation *f*

genetics [dʒɪ'netɪks] *s* Genetik *f*, Vererbungslehre *f*

Geneva [dʒɪ'nivə] *adj* Genfer ‖ *s* Genf *n*

Genevieve ['dʒenə,viv] *s* Genoveva *f*

genial ['dʒinɪ·əl] *adj* freundlich

genie ['dʒini] *s* Kobold *m*

genital ['dʒenɪtəl] *adj* Genital– ‖ **genitals** *spl* Genitalien *pl*

genitive ['dʒenɪtɪv] *s* Genitiv *m*, Wesfall *m*

genius ['dʒinɪ·əs] *s* (**geniuses**) Genie *n* ‖ *s* (**genii** ['dʒini,aɪ]) Genius *m*

Genoa ['dʒeno·ə] *s* Genua *n*

genocidal [,dʒenə'saɪdəl] *adj* rassenmörderisch

genocide ['dʒenə,saɪd] *s* Rassenmord *m*

genre ['ʒɑnrə] *s* Genre *n*

genteel [dʒen'til] *adj* vornehm

gentile ['dʒentaɪl] *adj* nichtjüdisch; *(pagan)* heidnisch ‖ *s* Nichtjude *m*, Nichtjüdin *f*; *(pagan)* Heide *m*, Heidin *f*

gentility [dʒen'tɪlɪti] *s* Vornehmheit *f*

gentle ['dʒentəl] *adj* sanft, mild; *(tame)* zahm

gen'tle·man *s* (**–men**) Herr *m*, Gentleman *m*

gentlemanly ['dʒentəlmənli] *adj* weltmännisch

gen'tleman's agree'ment *s* Kavaliersab-

kommen *n*, Gentleman's Agreement *n*

gentleness ['dʒentəlnɪs] *s* Sanftmut *f*

gen'tle sex' *s* zartes Geschlecht *n*

gentry ['dʒentri] *s* feine Leute *pl*

genuflection [,dʒenju'flek/ən] *s* Kniebeugung *f*

genuine ['dʒenju·ɪn] *adj* echt

genus ['dʒinəs] *s* (**genera** ['dʒenərə] & **genuses**) (biol, log) Gattung *f*

geographer [dʒɪ'ɑgrəfər] *s* Geograph –in *mf*

geographic(al) [,dʒɪ·ə'græfɪk(əl)] *adj* geographisch

geography [dʒɪ'ɑgrəfi] *s* Geographie *f*

geologic(al) [,dʒɪ·ə'lɑdʒɪk(əl)] *adj* geologisch

geolog'ical e'ra *s* Erdalter *n*

geologist [dʒɪ'ɑlədʒɪst] *s* Geologe *m*, Geologin *f*

geology [dʒɪ'ɑlədʒi] *s* Geologie *f*

geometric(al) [,dʒi·ə'metrɪk(əl)] *adj* geometrisch

geometrician [dʒɪ,ɑmɪ'trɪ/ən] *s* Geometer –in *mf*

geometry [dʒɪ'ɑmɪtri] *s* Geometrie *f*

geophysics [,dʒi·ə'fɪzɪks] *s* Geophysik *f*

geopolitics [,dʒi·ə'pɑlɪtɪks] *s* Geopolitik *f*

George [dʒɔrdʒ] *s* Georg *m*

geranium [dʒɪ'renɪ·əm] *s* Geranie *f*

geriatrics [,dʒerɪ'ætrɪks] *s* Geriatrie *f*

germ [dʒʌrm] *s* Keim *m*

German ['dʒʌrmən] *adj* & *adv* deutsch ‖ *s* Deutsche *mf*; *(language)* Deutsch *n*; **in G.** auf deutsch

germane [dʒer'men] *adj* **(to)** passend **(zu)**

Germanize ['dʒʌrmə,naɪz] *tr* eindeutschen

Ger'man mea'sles *s* & *spl* Röteln *pl*

Ger'man shep'herd *s* deutscher Schäferhund *m*

Ger'man sil'ver *s* Alpaka *n*, Neusilber *n*

Germany ['dʒʌrməni] *s* Deutschland *n*

germ' cell' *s* Keimzelle *f*

germicidal [,dʒʌrmɪ'saɪdəl] *adj* keimtötend

germicide ['dʒʌrmɪ,saɪd] *s* Keimtöter *m*

germinate ['dʒʌrmɪ,net] *intr* keimen

germ' war'fare *s* bakteriologische Kriegsführung *f*

gerontology [,dʒerɑn'tɑlədʒi] *s* Gerontologie *f*

gerund ['dʒerənd] *s* Gerundium *n*

gerundive [dʒɪ'rʌndɪv] *s* Gerundiv *n*

gestation [dʒes'te/ən] *s* Schwangerschaft *f*; *(in animals)* Trächtigkeit *f*

gesticulate [dʒes'tɪkjə,let] *intr* gestikulieren, sich gebärden

gesticulation [dʒes,tɪkjə'le/ən] *s* Gebärdenspiel *n*, Gestikulation *f*

gesture ['dʒest/ər] *s* Geste *f* ‖ *intr* Gesten machen

get [get] *v* (*pret* **got** [gɑt]; *pp* **got** & **gotten** ['gɑtən]; *ger* **getting**) *tr (acquire)* bekommen; *(receive)* erhalten; *(procure)* beschaffen, besorgen; *(fetch)* holen; *(understand)* (coll) kapieren; *(s.o. to do s.th.)* dazu

bringen; (*reach by telephone*) erreichen; (*make, e.g., dirty*) machen;
(*convey, e.g., a message*) übermitteln; **get across** klarmachen; **get back**
zurückbekommen; **get down** (*depress*) verdrießen; (*swallow*) hin-
unterwürgen; **get going** in Gang setzen; **get hold of** (*a person*) erwischen; (*a thing*) erlangen; (*grip*)
ergreifen; **get off** (*e.g., a lid*) ab-
bekommen; **get one's way** sich durchsetzen; **get out** (*e.g., a spot*) heraus-
bekommen; **get s.o.** used to j-n gewöhnen an (*acc*); **get s.th. into one's
head** sich [*dat*] etw in den Kopf setzen; **get the hang of** (coll) wegbe-
kommen; **get the jump on s.o.** j-m
zuvorkommen; **get the worst of it**
am schlechtesten dabei wegkommen;
get (*s.th.*) **wrong** falsch verstehen;
you're going to get it! (coll) du wirst
es kriegen! ‖ *intr* (*become*) werden;
get about sich fortbewegen; **get
ahead in the world** in der Welt fortkommen; **get along** auskommen; **get
along with** zurechtkommen mit; **get
around** herumkommen; **get around
to it** dazu kommen; **get at** herankom-
men an (*acc*); (*e.g., the real reason*)
herausfinden; **get away** (*run away*)
entlaufen; (*escape*) entkommen; **get
away from me!** geh weg von mir!;
get away with davonkommen mit;
get back at s.o. es j-m heimzahlen;
get by (*e.g., the guards*) vorbeikommen an (*dat*); (*on little money*)
durchkommen; **get down** (*step
down*) absteigen; **get down to brass
tacks** (*or business*) zur Sache kommen; **get going** sich auf den Weg
machen; **get going!** mach, daß du
weiter kommst!; **get into** (*a vehicle*)
einsteigen in (*acc*); (*trouble, etc.*)
geraten in (*acc*); **get loose** sich losmachen; **get lost** verloren gehen, abhanden kommen; (*lose one's way*)
sich verirren; **get lost!** (sl) hau ab!;
get off aussteigen; **get off with** (*a
light sentence*) davonkommen mit;
get on (*e.g., a train*) einsteigen (in
acc); **get on one's feet again** sich
hochrappeln; **get on with** (*s.o.*) zurechtkommen mit; **get out** aussteigen;
get out of a tight spot sich aus der
Schlinge ziehen; **get over** (*a hurdle*)
nehmen; (*a misfortune*) überwinden;
(*a sickness*) überstehen; **get ready**
sich fertig machen; **get through**
durchkommen; **get through to s.o.**
sich verständlich machen (*dat*); (telp)
erreichen; **get to be** werden; **get together** (*meet*) sich treffen; (*agree*)
(on) sich einig werden (über *acc*);
get to the bottom of ergründen; **get
up** aufstehen; **get used to** sich gewöhnen an (*acc*); **get well** gesund
werden; **get with it!** (coll) zur
Sache!
get'away' *s* Entkommen *n;* (sport)
Start *m;* **make one's g.** entkommen
get'away car' *s* Fluchtwagen *m*
get'-togeth'er *s* zwangloses Treffen *n*
get'up' *s* (coll) Aufzug *m*

get' up' and go' *s* Unternehmungsgeist
m
gewgaw ['g(j)ugɔ] *s* Plunder *m*
geyser ['gaɪzər] *s* Geiser *m*
ghastly ['gæstli] *adj* (*ghostly*) gespenstisch; (*e.g., crime*) grausig; (*in-
tensely unpleasant*) schrecklich
gherkin ['gʌrkɪn] *s* Essiggurke *f*
ghet·to ['geto] *s* (**–tos**) Getto *n*
ghost [gost] *s* Gespenst *n*, Geist *m;*
(telv) Doppelbild *n;* **give up the g.**
den Geist aufgeben; **not a g. of a
chance** nicht die geringsten Aussichten
ghostly ['gostli] *adj* gespenstisch
ghost' sto'ry *s* Spukgeschichte *f*
ghost' town' *s* Geisterstadt *f*
ghost' writ'er *s* Ghostwriter *m*
ghoul [gul] *s* (& fig) Unhold *m*
ghoulish ['gulɪʃ] *adj* teuflisch
GHQ ['dʒi'et'kju] *s* (**General Headquarters**) Oberkommando *n*
GI ['dʒi'aɪ] *s* (**GI's**) (coll) Landser *m*
giant ['dʒaɪ·ənt] *adj* riesig, Riesen– ‖
s Riese *m,* Riesin *f*
giantess ['dʒaɪ·əntɪs] *s* Riesin *f*
gibberish ['dʒɪbərɪʃ], ['gɪbərɪʃ] *s*
Klauderwelsch *n*
gibbet ['dʒɪbɪt] *s* Galgen *m* ‖ *tr* hängen
gibe [dʒaɪb] *s* Spott *m* ‖ *intr* spotten;
g. at verspotten
giblets ['dʒɪblɪts] *spl* Gänseklein *n*
giddiness ['gɪdɪnɪs] *s* Schwindelgefühl
n; (*frivolity*) Leichtsinn *m*
giddy ['gɪdi] *adj* (*dizzy*) schwindlig;
(*height*) schwindelerregend; (*frivolous*) leichtsinnig
gift [gɪft] *s* Geschenk *n;* (*natural ability*) Begabung *f*
gift'ed *adj* begabt
gift'horse' *s*—**never look a g. in the
mouth** e–m geschenkten Gaul schaut
man nicht ins Maul
gift' of gab' *s* (coll) gutes Mundwerk *n*
gift' shop' *s* Geschenkartikelladen *m*
gift'-wrap' *v* (*pret & pp* **–wrapped;** *ger*
–wrapping) *tr* als Geschenk verpacken
gift'wrap'ping *s* Geschenkverpackung
f
gigantic [dʒaɪ'gæntɪk] *adj* riesig
giggle ['gɪgəl] *s* Gekicher *n* ‖ *intr*
kichern
gigly ['gɪgli] *adj* allezeit kichernd
gigo·lo ['dʒɪgə‚lo] *s* (**–los**) Gigolo *m*
gild [gɪld] *v* (*pret & pp* **gilded & gilt**
[gɪlt]) *tr* vergolden
gild'ing *s* Vergoldung *f*
gill [gɪl] *s* (*of a fish*) Kieme *f;* (*of a
cock*) Kehllappen *m*
gilt [gɪlt] *adj* vergoldet ‖ *s* Vergoldung *f*
gilt' edge' *s* Goldschnitt *m*
gilt'-edged' *adj* mit Goldschnitt versehen; (*first-class*) (coll) erstklassig
gimlet ['gɪmlɪt] *s* Handbohrer *m*
gimmick ['gɪmɪk] *s* (sl) Trick *m*
gin [dʒɪn] *s* Wacholderbranntwein *m,*
Gin *m;* (*snare*) Schlinge *f* ‖ *v* (*pret
& pp* **ginned;** *ger* **ginning**) *tr* ent-
körnen
ginger ['dʒɪndʒər] *s* Ingwer *m*

gin'ger ale' *s* Ingwerlimonade *f*
gin'gerbread' *s* Pfefferkuchen *m*
gingerly ['dʒɪndʒərlɪ] *adv* sacht(e)
gin'gersnap' *s* Ingwerplätzchen *n*
gingham ['gɪnəm] *s* Gingham *m*
giraffe [dʒɪ'ræf] *s* Giraffe *f*
gird [gʌrd] *v* (*pret & pp* **girt** [gʌrt]
& **girded**) *tr* gürten; **g. oneself with
a sword** sich [*dat*] ein Schwert um-
gürten
girder ['gʌrdər] *s* Tragbalken *m*
girdle ['gʌrdəl] *s* Gürtel *m*
girl [gʌrl] *s* Mädchen *n*, Mädel *n*
girl' friend' *s* Freundin *f*, Geliebte *f*
girl'hood' *s* Mädchenzeit *f*
girlish ['gʌrlɪʃ] *adj* mädchenhaft
girl' scout' *s* Pfadfinderin *f*
girth [gʌrθ] *s* Umfang *m;* (*for a horse*)
Sattelgurt *m*
gist [dʒɪst] *s* Kernpunkt *m;* **g. of the
matter** des Pudels Kern
give [gɪv] *s* Elastizität *f;* (*yielding*)
Nachgeben *n* ‖ *v* (*pret* **gave** [gev];
pp **given** ['gɪvən]) *tr* geben; (*a gift,
credence*) schenken; (*free of charge*)
verschenken; (*contribute*) spenden;
(*hand over*) übergeben; (*a report*)
erstatten; (*a reason, the time*) angeben; (*attention, recognition*) zollen; (*a lecture*) halten; (*an award*)
zusprechen; (*homework*) aufgeben;
(*a headache, etc.*) verursachen; (*joy*)
machen; (*a reception*) veranstalten;
(*a blow*) versetzen; **g. away** weg-
geben; (*divulge*) verraten; **g. away
the bride** Brautvater sein; **g. back**
zurückgeben; **g. ground** zurückweichen; **g. it to 'em!** (coll) hau zu!;
g. off von sich geben; (*steam*) ausströmen lassen; **g. oneself away** sich
verplappern; **g. oneself up** sich stellen; **g. or take** mehr oder weniger;
g. out ausgeben; **g. rise to** Anlaß
geben zu; **g. up** aufgeben; (*a business*) schließen; **g. up for lost** ver-
lorengeben; **g. way** weichen; **g. way
to** sich überlassen (*dat*) ‖ *intr* (*yield*)
nachgeben; (*collapse*) einstürzen; **g.
in to** nachgeben (*dat*), weichen (*dat*);
g. out (*said of the voice, legs*) versagen; (*said of strength*) nachlassen;
g. up aufgeben; (mil) die Waffen
strecken; **g. up on** verzagen an (*dat*)
give'-and-take' *s* Kompromiß *m* & *n;*
(*exchange of opinion*) Meinungs-
austausch *m*
give'away' *s* (*betrayal of a secret*) unbeabsichtigte Preisgabe *f;* (*promo-
tional article*) Gratisprobe *f*
give'away show' *s* Preisrätselsendung *f*
given ['gɪvən] *adj* gegeben; (*time*)
festgesetzt; (math, philos) gegeben;
g. to drinking dem Trunk ergeben
giv'en name' *s* Vorname *m*
giver ['gɪvər] *s* Geber –in *mf;* (*of a
contribution*) Spender –in *mf*
gizzard ['gɪzərd] *s* Geflügelmagen *m*
gla'cial per'iod ['gleʃəl] *s* Eiszeit *f*
glacier ['gleʃər] *s* Gletscher *m*
glad [glæd] *adj* (**gladder; gladdest**)
froh; **be g.** (**about**) sich freuen (über
acc); **g. to** (*inf*) erfreut zu (*inf*); **g. to
meet you** sehr erfreut!, sehr ange-

nehm!; **I'll be g. to do it for you**
ich werde das gern für Sie tun
gladden ['glædən] *tr* erfreuen
glade [gled] *s* Waldwiese *f*, Waldlich-
tung *f*
gladiator ['glædɪˌetər] *s* Gladiator *m*
gladiola [ˌglædɪ'olə] *s* Gladiole *f*
gladly ['glædlɪ] *adv* gern(e)
gladness ['glædnɪs] *s* Freude *f*
glad' rags' *spl* (sl) Sonntagsstaat *m*
glad' tid'ings *spl* Freundenbotschaft *f*
glamorous ['glæmərəs] *adj* bezaubernd
glamour ['glæmər] *s* (*of a girl*) Zauber
m; (*of an event*) Glanz *m*
glam'our girl' *s* gefeierte Schönheit *f;*
(pej) Zierpuppe *f*
glance [glæns] *s* Blick *m;* **at a g., at
first g.** auf den ersten Blick; ‖ *intr*
(**at**) blicken (auf *acc* or nach); **g.
around** umherblicken; **g. off** abglei-
ten an (*dat*); **g. through** (or **over**)
flüchtig durchsehen; **g. up** auf-
blicken
gland [glænd] *s* Drüse *f*
glanders ['glændərz] *spl* Rotskrank-
heit *f*
glare [gler] *s* grelles Licht *n;* (*look*)
böser Blick *m* ‖ *intr* blenden; (*look*)
böse starren; **g. at** böse anstarren
glar'ing *adj* (*light*) grell; (fig) schreiend, aufdringlich
glass [glæs] *adj* gläsern, Glas– ‖ *s*
Glas *n;* **glasses** Brille *f*
glass' bead' *s* Glasperle *f*
glass' blow'er ['bloˌər] *s* Glasbläser
–in *mf*
glass' blow'ing *s* Glasbläserei *f*
glass' case' *s* Schaukasten *m*
glass' cut'ter *s* Glasschleifer –in *mf;*
(*tool*) Glasschneider *m*
glassful ['glæsful] *s* Glas *n*
glass'ware' *s* Glaswaren *pl*
glass' wool' *s* Glaswolle *f*
glass'works' *s* Glasfabrik *f*, Glashütte
f
glassy ['glæsɪ] *adj* (*surface*) spiegel-
glatt; (*eyes*) glasig
glaucoma [glau'komə] *s* Glaukom *n*,
grüner Star *m*
glaze [glez] *s* (*on ceramics*) Glasur *f;*
(*on paintings*) Lasur *f;* (*of ice*)
Glatteis *n* ‖ *tr* (*ceramics, baked
goods*) glasieren; (*a window*) ver-
glasen; (*a painting*) lasieren
glazed *adj* (*ceramics, baked goods*) gla-
siert; (*eyes*) glasig; **g. tile** Kachel *f*
glazier ['glezər] *s* Glaser –in *mf*
gleam [glim] *s* Lichtstrahl *m;* **g. of
hope** Hoffnungsschimmer *m* ‖ *intr*
strahlen
glean [glin] *tr* & *intr* auflesen; (fig)
zusammentragen
gleanings ['glinɪŋz] *spl* Nachlese *f*
glee [gli] *s* Frohsinn *m*
glee' club' *s* Gesangverein *m*
glen [glen] *s* Bergschlucht *f*
glib [glɪb] *adj* (**glibber; glibbest**)
(*tongue*) beweglich; (*person*) zungen-
fertig
glide [glaɪd] *s* Gleiten *n;* (aer) Gleit-
flug *m;* (*with a glider*) (aer) Segel-
flug *m;* (ling) Gleitlaut *m;* (mus)
Glissando *n* ‖ *intr* gleiten

glider ['glaɪdər] s (porch swing) Schaukelbett n; (aer) Segelflugzeug n

glid'er pi'lot s Segelflieger –in mf

glid'ing s Segelfliegen n

glimmer ['glɪmər] s Schimmer m; g. of hope Hoffnungsschimmer m ‖ intr schimmern

glim'mering adj flimmernd ‖ s Flimmern n

glimpse [glɪmps] s flüchtiger Blick m; catch a g. of flüchtig zu sehen bekommen ‖ tr flüchtig erblicken ‖ intr—g. at e-n flüchtigen Blick werfen auf (acc)

glint [glɪnt] s Lichtschimmer m ‖ intr schimmern

glisten ['glɪsən] s Glanz m ‖ intr glänzen

glitter ['glɪtər] s Glitzern n, Glanz m ‖ intr glitzern, glänzen

gloat [glot] intr schadenfroh sein; g. over sich weiden an (dat)

gloat'ing s Schadenfreude f

global ['globəl] adj global, Welt-

globe [glob] s Erdkugel f, Globus m

globe'-trot'ter s Weltenbummler –in mf

globule ['glabjul] s Kügelchen n

glockenspiel ['glakən ,spil] s Glockenspiel n

gloom [glum] s Düsternis f; (fig) Trübsinn m

gloominess ['glumɪnɪs] s Düsterkeit f; (fig) Trübsinn m

gloomy ['glumi] adj düster; (depressing) bedrückend; (depressed) trübsinning

glorification ['glorɪfɪ ,keʃən] s Verherrlichung f

glori·fy ['glorɪ ,faɪ] v (pret & pp –fied) tr verherrlichen

glorious ['glorɪ·əs] adj (full of glory) glorreich; (magnificent) herrlich

glo·ry ['glori] s Ruhm m; (magnificence) Herrlichkeit f; be in one's g. im siebenten Himmel sein ‖ v (pret & pp –ried) intr—g. in frohlocken über (acc)

gloss [glɔs] s (shine) Glanz m; (notation) Glosse f ‖ tr glossieren; g. over verschleiern

glossary ['glɔsəri] s Glossar n

glossy ['glɔsi] adj glänzend

glottis ['glatɪs] s Stimmritze f

glove [glʌv] s Handschuh m; fit like a g. wie angegossen passen

glove' compart'ment s Handschuhfach n

glow [glo] s Glühen n ‖ intr glühen; g. with (fig) (er)glühen vor (dat)

glower ['glau·ər] s finsterer Blick m ‖ intr finster blicken; g. at finster anblicken

glow'ing adj glühend; (account) begeistert

glow'worm' s Glühwurm m

glucose ['glukos] s Glukose f

glue [glu] s Leim m, Klebemittel n ‖ tr (wood) leimen; (paper) kleben

gluey ['glu·i] adj leimig

glum [glʌm] adj (glummer; glummest) verdrießlich

glut [glʌt] s Übersättigung f; a g. on the market e-e Überschwemmung des Marktes ‖ v (pret & pp glutted; ger glutting) tr übersättigen; (com) überschwemmen

glutton ['glʌtən] s Vielfraß m

gluttonous ['glʌtənəs] adj gefräßig

gluttony ['glʌtəni] s Gefräßigkeit f

glycerine ['glɪsərɪn] s Glyzerin n

gnarled [nɑrld] adj knorrig

gnash [næʃ] tr—g. one's teeth mit den Zähnen knirschen

gnat [næt] s Mücke f

gnaw [nɔ] tr zernagen; g. off abnagen ‖ intr (on) nagen (an dat)

gnome [nom] s Gnom m, Berggeist m

go [go] s—be on the go auf den Beinen sein; have a lot of go viel Mumm in den Knochen haben; it's no go es geht nicht; let's have a go at it probieren wir's mal; make a go of it es zu e-m Erfolg machen ‖ v (pret went [wɛnt]; pp gone [gɔn]) tr—g. it alone es ganz allein(e) machen ‖ intr gehen; (depart) weggehen; (travel) fahren, reisen; (operate) arbeiten; (belong) gehören; (turn out) verlaufen; (collapse) zusammenbrechen; (fail, go out of order) kaputtgehen; (said of words) lauten; (said of bells) läuten; (said of a buzzer) ertönen; (said of awards) zugeteilt werden; (said of a road) führen; be going to, e.g., I am going to study ich werde studieren; go about umhergehen; (a task) in Angriff nehmen; go about it darangehen; go after (run after) nachlaufen; (strive for) streben nach; go against the grain gegen den Strich gehen; go ahead vorausgehen; go ahead! voran!; go along with (accompany) mitgehen mit; (agree with) zustimmen mit; go and see for yourself überzeugen Sie sich selbst davon!; go around herumgehen; (suffice) (aus)reichen; (an obstacle) umgehen; go at (a person) losgehen auf (acc); (a thing) herangehen an (acc); go away weggehen; go bad schlecht werden; go back zurückkehren; (ride back) zurückfahren; go back on (one's word) brechen; go beyond überschreiten; go by (pass by) vorbeigehen (an dat); (said of time) vergehen; (act according to) sich richten nach; go down niedergehen; (said of the sun or a ship) untergehen; (said of a swelling) zurückgehen; (said of a fever or a price) sinken; go down in history in die Geschichte eingehen; go for (fetch) holen; (apply to) gelten für; (be enthusiastic about) schwärmen für; (have a crush on) verknallt sein in (acc); (be sold for) verkauft werden für; (attack) losgehen auf (acc); go in hineingehen; (said of the sun) verschwinden; go in for schwärmen für; (sport) treiben; go into eintreten in (acc); (arith) enthalten sein in (dat); go into detail ins Detail gehen; **go in with** s.o. on sich beteiligen mit j–m an (dat); **go off** (depart) weggehen; (said of a gun) losgehen; (said of a bomb) explodieren; **go on** (happen) vorgehen; (continue) weitergehen; (**with**) fortfahren (mit); (theat) auftreten; **go on!** (expressing encouragement) nur zu!; (expressing disbelief) ach was!; **go on reading** weiterlesen; **go on to** (another theme) übergehen auf (acc); **go over** (check) überprüfen; (review) noch einmal durchgehen; (figures) nachrechnen; (be a success) einschlagen; **go over to** hinübergehen zu; (the enemy) übergehen zu; **go out** (e.g., of the house) hinausgehen; (on an errand or socially; said of a light) ausgehen; **go out of one's way** sich besonders anstrengen; **go out to dinner** auswärts essen; **go through** (penetrate) durchdringen; (a traffic signal) überfahren; (endure) durchmachen; **go through with** zu Ende führen; **go to** (said of a prize) zugeteilt werden (dat); **go together** zueinanderpassen; **go to it!** los!; **go to show** ein Beweis sein für; **go with** (fit, match) passen zu; (associate with) verkehren mit; **go without** entbehren; **go under an assumed name** e–n angenommenen Namen führen; **go up to s.o.** auf j–n zugehen

goad [god] s Stachel m || tr antreiben; **g. on** (fig) anstacheln

go'-ahead' sig'nal n freie Bahn f

goal [gol] s Ziel n; (sport) Tor n; **make a goal** (sport) ein Tor schießen

goalie ['goli] s Torwart m

goal'keep'er s Torwart m

goal' line' s Torlinie f

goal' post' s Torpfosten m

goat [got] s Ziege f, Geiß f; (male goat) Ziegenbock m; **get s.o.'s g.** (sl) j–n auf die Palme bringen

goatee [go'ti] s Ziegenbart m, Spitzbart m

goat' herd' s Ziegenhirt m

goat'skin' s Ziegenfell n

gob [gab] s (coll) Klumpen m; (sailor) (coll) Blaujacke f; **gobs of money** (coll) ein Haufen m Geld

gobble ['gabəl] s Kollern n || tr verschlingen; **g. up** (food) herunterschlingen; (e.g., land) zusammenraffen || intr (said of a turkey) kollern

gobbledegook ['gabəldɪ‚guk] s (coll) Amtssprache f

gobbler ['gablər] s (coll) Fresser –in mf; (orn) (coll) Puter m, Truthahn m

go'-between' s Vermittler –in mf, Unterhändler –in mf

goblet ['gablɪt] s Kelchglas n

goblin ['gablɪn] s Kobold m

go'cart' s (walker) Laufstuhl m; (stroller) Sportwagen m; (small racer) Go-Kart m; (handcart) Handwagen m

god [gad] s Gott m; **God forbid!** Gott bewahre!; **God knows** weiß Gott; **my God!** du lieber Gott!; **so help**

me **God!** so wahr mir Gott helfe!; ye **gods!** heiliger Strohsack!

god'child' s (–chil'dren) Patenkind n

goddess ['gadɪs] s Göttin f

god'fa'ther s Pate m; **be a g.** Pate stehen

God'-fear'ing adj gottesfürchtig

god'forsak'en adj gottverlassen

god'head' s Göttlichkeit f; **Godhead** Gott m

godless ['gadlɪs] adj gottlos

god'like' adj göttlich

godly ['gadli] adj gottselig

god'moth'er s Patin f; **be a g.** Patin stehen

god'send' s Segen m

God'speed' s—**wish s.o. G.** j–m Lebewohl sagen

go-getter ['go‚getər] s Draufgänger m

goggle ['gagəl] intr glotzen

gog'gle-eyed' adj glotzäugig

goggles ['gagəlz] spl Schutzbrille f

go'ing adj (rate) gültig, üblich; **g. on** (e.g., six o'clock) gegen; **I'm g. to do it** ich werde es tun

go'ing concern' s schwunghaftes Geschäft n

go'ing-o'ver s Überprüfung f; (beating) Prügel pl

go'ings on' spl Treiben n, Wirtschaft f

goiter ['gɔɪtər] s Kropf m

gold [gold] adj Gold– || s Gold n

gold' bar' s Goldbarren m

gold'brick' s (mil) Drückeberger m

gold'-brick' intr faulenzen

gold'-brick'ing s (mil) Drückebergerei f

gold'crest' s Goldhähnchen n

gold' dig'ger ['dɪgər] s Goldgräber m; (sl) Vamp m

golden ['goldən] adj golden; (opportunity) günstig

gold'en age' s Glanzzeit f, Goldenes Zeitalter n

gold'en calf', **the** s das Goldene Kalb

gold'en ea'gle s Goldadler m

Gold'en Fleece', **the** (myth) das Goldene Vlies

gold'en mean' s goldene Mitte f

gold'en rule' s goldene Regel f

gold'en wed'ding s goldene Hochzeit f

gold'-filled' adj vergoldet

gold' fill'ing s (dent) Goldplombe f

gold'finch' s Goldfink m, Stieglitz m

gold'fish' s Goldfisch m

goldilocks ['goldɪ‚laks] s (bot) Hahnenfuß m

gold' leaf' s Blattgold n

gold'mine' s Goldbergwerk n

gold' nug'get s Goldklumpen m

gold' plate' s Goldgeschirr n

gold'-plate' tr vergolden

gold'smith' s Goldschmied –in mf

gold' stand'ard s Goldwährung f

golf [galf] s Golf n || intr Golf spielen

golf' bag' s Köcher m

golf' club' s Golfschläger m; (organization) Golfklub m

golf' course' s Golfplatz m

golfer ['galfər] s Golfspieler –in mf

golf' links' spl Golfplatz m

gondola ['gandələ] s Gondel f

gon'dola car' s offener Güterwagen m
gondolier [ˌgʌndə'lɪr] s Gondelführer m
gone [gɔn] adj hin, weg; (ruined) futsch; **all g.** ganz weg; (sold out) ausverkauft; **he is g.** er ist fort
goner ['gɔnər] s (coll) verlorener Mensch m
gong [gɔŋ] s Gong m, Tamtam n
gonorrhea [ˌgɑnə'riːə] s Tripper m
goo [gu] s (sl) klebrige Masse f
good [gʊd] adj (**better; best**) gut; (well behaved) brav, artig; (in health) gesund; (valid) gültig; **as g.** as so gut wie; **be g. enough to** (inf) so gut sein und; **g. and** recht, e.g., **g. and cheap** recht billig; **g. at** gut in (dat); **g. for** (suited to) geeignet zu; (effective against) wirksam für; (valid for) gültig für; **g. for you!** (serves you right!) das geschieht dir recht!; (expressing congratulations) ich gratuliere!, bravo!; **make g.** wiedergutmachen; (losses) vergüten; (a promise) erfüllen; ‖ s Gut n; (welfare) Wohl n; (advantage) Nutzen m; (philos) Gut n, das Gute; **be up to no g.** nichts Gutes im Schilde führen; **catch with the goods** auf frischer Tat ertappen; **do g.** wohltun; **for g.** für immer; **goods** Waren pl; **to the g.** als Nettogewinn; **what g. is it?**, **what's the g. of it?** was nutzt es?
good'-by', **good'-bye'** s Lebewohl n; **say g. (to)** sich verabschieden (von) ‖ interj auf Wiedersehen!; (on the telephone) auf Wiederhören!
good' day' interj guten Tag!
good' deed' s Wohltat f
good' egg' s (sl) feiner Kerl m
good' eve'ning interj guten Abend!
good' fel'low s netter Kerl m
good'-fel'lowship s gute Kameradschaft f
good'-for-noth'ing adj nichtsnutzig ‖ s Taugenichts m, Nichtsnutz m
Good' Fri'day s Karfreitag m
good' grac'es spl—**be in s.o.'s g. in** j–s Gunst stehen
good'-heart'ed adj gutherzig
good'-hu'mored adj gutgelaunt, gutmütig
good'-look'ing adj gutaussehend, hübsch
goodly ['gʊdli] adj beträchtlich; **a g. number of** viele
good' morn'ing interj guten Morgen!
good'-na'tured adj gutmütig
goodness ['gʊdnɪs] s Güte f; **for g. sake!** um Himmels willen!; **g. knows** weiß Gott; **thank g.** Gott sei Dank!
good' night' interj gute Nacht!
good' sense' s Sinn m; (common sense) gesunder Menschenverstand m; **make g. Sinn** haben
good'-sized' adj ziemlich groß
good'-tem'pered adj ausgeglichen
good' time' s—**have a g.** sich gut unterhalten; **keep g.** taktfest sein
good' turn' s Gefallen m; **one g. deserves another** e–e Hand wäscht die andere

good' will' s Wohlwollen n; (com) Geschäftswert m
goody ['gʊdi] s Näscherei f ‖ interj pfundig!
gooey ['gu·i] adj klebrig
goof [guf] s (person) (sl) Depp m; (mistake) (sl) Schnitzer m ‖ tr (sl) verpfuschen ‖ intr (sl) e–n Schnitzer machen; **g. off** (sl) faulenzen
goof'ball' s (pill) (sl) Beruhigungspille f; (eccentric person) (sl) Sonderling m
goofy ['gufi] adj (sl) dämlich; **g. about** (sl) vernarrt in (acc)
goon [gun] s (sl) Dummkopf m; (in strikes) bestellter Schläger m
goose [gus] s (**geese** [gis]) Gans f; (culin) Gänsebraten m; **cook s.o.'s g.** j–n erledigen
goose'ber'ry s Stachelbeere f
goose' egg' s Gänseei n; (sl) Null f
goose' flesh' s Gänsehaut f
goose'neck' s Schwanenhals m
goose' pim'ples spl Gänsehaut f
goose' step' s Stechschritt m
goose'-step' v (pret & pp —**stepped**; ger —**stepping**) intr im Stechschritt marschieren
gopher ['gofər] s Taschenratte f
gore [gor] s geronnenes Blut n ‖ tr aufspießen
gorge [gɔrdʒ] s Schlucht f ‖ tr vollstopfen ‖ intr schlingen
gorgeous ['gɔrdʒəs] adj prachtvoll
gorilla [gə'rɪlə] s Gorilla m
gorse [gɔrs] s Stechginster m
gory ['gori] adj blutig
gosh [gɑʃ] interj herrjeh!
Gospel ['gɑspəl] s Evangelium n
gos'pel truth' s reine Wahrheit f
gossamer ['gɑsəmər] s Sommerfäden pl
gossip ['gɑsɪp] s Klatsch m; (woman) Klatschweib n; (man) Schwätzer m ‖ intr klatschen, tratschen
gos'sip col'umn s Klatschspalte f
gossipmonger ['gɑsɪpˌmʌŋgər] s Klatschbase f
gossipy ['gɑsɪpi] adj tratschsüchtig
Goth [gɑθ] s Gote m, Gotin f
Gothic ['gɑθɪk] adj gotisch ‖ s (language) Gotisch n
Goth'ic arch' s Spitzbogen m
gouge [gaudʒ] s (tool) Hohlmeißel m; (hole made by a gouge) ausgemeißelte Vertiefung f ‖ tr aushöhlen; (overcharge) übervorteilen; **g. out** (eyes) herausdrücken
gouger ['gaudʒər] s Wucherer –in mf
goulash ['gulɑʃ] s Gulasch n
gourd [gord], [gʊrd] s Kürbis m
gourmand ['gʊrmənd] s (glutton) Schlemmer –in mf; (gourmet) Feinschmecker m
gourmet ['gʊrme] s Feinschmecker m
gout [gaut] s Gicht f
govern ['gʌvərn] tr regieren; (fig) beherrschen; (gram) regieren ‖ intr regieren
governess ['gʌvərnɪs] s Gouvernante f
government ['gʌvərnmənt] adj Regierungs-, Staats- ‖ s Regierung f

gov'ernment con'tract s Staatsauftrag m

gov'ernment control' s Zwangsbewirtschaftung f

gov'ernment employ'ee s Staatsbeamte m, Staatsbeamtin f

gov'ernment grant' s Staatszuschuß m

gov'ernment-in-ex'ile s Exilregierung f

governor ['gʌvərnər] s Statthalter m, Gouverneur m; (mach) Regler m

gov'ernorship' s Statthalterschaft f

gown [gaun] s Damenkleid n; (of a judge, professor) Robe f, Talar m

grab [græb] s—make a g. for grapschen nach || v (pret & pp grabbed; ger grabbing) tr schnappen; g. hold of anpacken || intr—g. for greifen nach

grab' bag' s Glückstopf m

grace [gres] s (mercy, divine favor) Gnade f; (charm) Grazie f; (table prayer) Tischgebet n; (charm) Grazie f; Graces (myth) Grazien pl

graceful ['gresfəl] adj graziös, anmutig

gracious ['greʃəs] adj gnädig; (living) angenehm || interj lieber Himmel!

gradation [gre'deʃən] s Stufenfolge f

grade [gred] s (level) Stufe f, Grad m; (quality) Qualität f; (class year) Schulklasse f; (mark in a course, test) Zensur f; (slope) Steigung f; (mil) Dienstgrad m || tr (sort) einstufen; (evaluate) bewerten; (make level) planieren; (educ) zensieren

grade' cross'ing s (rr) Schienenübergang m

grade' school' s Grundschule f

gradient ['gredɪ-ənt] s Neigung f

gradual ['grædʒʊ-əl] adj allmählich

graduate ['grædʒʊ-ɪt] adj (student) graduiert; (course) Graduierten– || s Promovierte mf; (from a junior college) Abiturient –in mf; (from a university) Absolvent –in mf || ['grædʒʊ‚et] tr & intr graduieren, promovieren; g. from absolvieren

grad'uated adj (tax) abgestuft; (marked by divisions of measurement) graduiert; g. scale Gradmesser m

graduation [‚grædʒʊ'eʃən] s Graduierung f, Promotion f; (marking on a vessel or instrument) Gradeinteilung f

gradua'tion ex'ercises spl Schlußfeier f

graft [græft] s (illegal gain) Schiebung f; (money involved in graft) Schmiergeld n; (twig) (hort) Pfropfreis n; (place where scion is inserted) (hort) Propfstelle f; (organ transplanted) (surg) verpflanztes Gewebe n; (transplanting) (surg) Gewebeverpflanzung f || tr (hort) pfropfen; (surg) verpflanzen

gra'ham bread' ['gre-əm] s Grahambrot n

gra'ham crack'er s Grahamplätzchen n

gra'ham flour' s Grahammehl n

grain [gren] s Korn n; (of leather) Narbe f; (in wood, marble) Maserung f; (unit of weight) Gran n; (cereals) Getreide n; (phot) Korn n; against the g. (& fig) gegen den Strich; g. of truth Körnchen n Wahrheit

grain' el'evator s Getreidesilo m

grain'field' s Saatfeld n, Kornfeld n

gram [græm] s Gramm n

grammar ['græmər] s Grammatik f

gram'mar school' s Grundschule f

grammatical [grə'mætɪkəl] adj grammatisch, grammatikalisch

gramophone ['græmə‚fon] s Grammophon n

granary ['grenəri] s Getreidespeicher m

grand [grænd] adj großartig; (large and striking) grandios; (lofty) erhaben; (wonderful) (coll) herrlich

grand'aunt' s Großtante f

grand'child' s (–chil'dren) Enkelkind n

grand'daugh'ter s Enkelin f

grand' duch'ess s Großfürstin f, Großherzogin f

grand' duch'y s Großfürstentum n, Großherzogtum n

grand' duke' s Großfürst m, Großherzog m

grandee [græn'di] s Grande m

grandeur ['grændʒər], ['grændʒʊr] s Großartigkeit f, Erhabenheit f

grand'fath'er s Großvater m

grand'father's clock' s Standuhr f

grandiose ['grændɪ‚os] adj grandios

grand' ju'ry s Anklagekammer f

grand' lar'ceny s schwerer Diebstahl m

grand' lodge' s Großloge f

grandma ['græn(d)‚ma], ['græm‚ma] s (coll) Oma f

grand'moth'er s Großmutter f

grand'neph'ew s Großneffe m

grand'niece' s Großnichte f

grandpa ['græn(d)‚pa], ['græm‚pa] s (coll) Opa m

grand'par'ents spl Großeltern pl

grand' pian'o s Konzertflügel m

grand' slam' s Schlemm m

grand'son' s Enkel m

grand'stand' s Tribüne f

grand' to'tal s Gesamtsumme f

grand'un'cle s Großonkel m

grand' vizier' s Großwesir m

grange [grendʒ] s Farm f; (organization) Farmervereinigung f

granite ['grænɪt] adj Granit– || s Granit m

granny ['græni] s (coll) Oma f

grant [grænt] s (of money) Beihilfe f; (of a pardon) Gewährung f; (of an award) Verleihung f || tr (permission) geben; (credit) bewilligen; (a favor) gewähren; (a request) erfüllen; (a privilege, award) verleihen; (admit) zugeben; granted that angenommen, daß; take for granted als selbstverständlich hinnehmen

grantee [græn'ti] s Empfänger –in mf

grant'-in-aid' s (grants-in-aid) (by the government) Subvention f; (educ) Stipendium n

grantor ['græntər] s Verleiher –in mf

granular ['grænjələr] adj körnig

granulate ['grænjə‚let] tr körnen

gran'ulated sug'ar s Streuzucker m
granule ['grænjul] s Körnchen n
grape [grep] s Weintraube f
grape' ar'bor s Weinlaube f
grape'fruit' s Pampelmuse f
grape' juice' s Most m, Traubensaft m
grape' pick'er s Weinleser –in mf
grape'vine' s Weinstock m; through the
  g. gerüchtweise
graph [græf] s Diagramm n
graphic(al) ['græfik(əl)] adj graphisch;
  (description) anschaulich, bildhaft
graph'ic arts' spl Graphik f
graphite ['græfait] s Graphit m
graph' pa'per s Millimeterpapier n
grapnel ['græpnəl] s Wurfanker m
grapple ['græpəl] s Enterhaken m;
  (fight) Handgemenge n || tr packen
  || intr (use a grapple) (naut) e–n
  Enterhaken gebrauchen; g. with (&
  fig) ringen mit
grap'pling hook', grap'pling i'ron s
  Wurfanker m; (naut) Enterhaken m
grasp [græsp] s Griff m; (control) Gewalt f; (comprehension) Verständnis
  n; (reach) Reichweite f; have a good
  g. of gut beherrschen || tr (& fig)
  fassen || intr—g. at schnappen nach
grasp'ing adj habgierig, geldgierig
grass [græs] s Gras n; (lawn) Rasen
  m; (pasture land) Weide f
grass' court' s Rasenspielplatz m
grass'hop'per s Grashüpfer m
grass' land' s Weideland n, Grasland
  n
grass'-roots' adj (coll) volkstümlich
grass' seed' s Grassamen m
grass' wid'ow s Strohwitwe f
grassy ['græsi] adj grasig
grate [gret] s (on a window) Gitter n;
  (of a furnace) Rost m || tr (e.g.,
  cheese) reiben; g. the teeth mit den
  Zähnen knirschen || intr knirschen;
  g. on one's nerves an den Nerven
  reißen
grateful ['gretfəl] adj dankbar
grater ['gretər] s (culin) Reibeisen n
grati-fy ['græti ,fai] v (pret & pp
  –fied) tr befriedigen; be gratified by
  sich freuen über (acc)
grat'ifying adj erfreulich
grat'ing adj knirschend || s Gitter n
gratis ['grætis], ['gretis] adj & adv
  unentgeltlich
gratitude ['græti ,t(j)ud] s Dankbarkeit f
gratuitious [grə't(j)u·itəs] adj unentgeltlich; (undeserving) unverdient
gratuity [grə't(j)u·iti] s Trinkgeld n
grave [grev] adj (face) ernst; (condition) besorgniserregend; (mistake)
  folgenschwer; (sound) tief || s Grab
  n; (accent) Gravis m
gravedigger ['grev ,digər] s Toten-
  gräber m
gravel ['grævəl] s (rounded stones)
  Kies m; (crushed stones) Schotter
  m; (pathol) Harngrieß m || tr mit
  Kies (or Schotter) bestreuen
gravelly ['grævəli] adj heiser
grav'el pit' s Kiesgrube f
grav'el road' s Schotterstraße f

grave'stone' s Grabstein m
grave'yard' s Friedhof m
gravitate ['grævi ,tet] intr gravitieren;
  g. towards (fig) neigen zu
gravitation [,grævi 'te/ən] s Gravitation f, Massenanziehung f
gravitational [,grævi 'te/ənəl] adj Gra-
  vitations–, Schwer–
gravita'tional force' s Schwerkraft f
gravita'tional pull' s Anziehungskraft
  f
gravity ['græviti] s (seriousness) Ernst
  m; (of a situation) Schwere f; (phys)
  Schwerkraft f
gravy ['grevi] s Soße f; (coll) leichter
  Gewinn m
gra'vy boat' s Soßenschüssel f
gra'vy train' s (sl) Futterkrippe f
gray [gre] adj grau || s Grau n || intr
  ergrauen
gray'beard' s Graubart m
gray'-haired' adj grauhaarig
grayish ['gre·i/] adj gräulich
gray' mat'ter s graue Substanz f
graze [grez] tr (said of a bullet) strei-
  fen; (cattle) weiden lassen || intr
  weiden
graz'ing land' s Weide f
grease [gris] s Fett n, Schmiere f ||
  [gris], [griz] tr (aut) schmieren
grease' gun' [gris] s Schmierpresse f
grease' paint' s Schminke f
grease' pit' s (aut) Schmiergrube f
grease' spot' s Fettfleck m
greasy ['grisi], ['grizi] adj fett(ig)
great [gret] adj groß; (wonderful)
  (coll) großartig; a g. many (of) e–e
  große Anzahl von; g. fun Heidenspaß
  m; g. guy Prachtkerl m
great'-aunt' s Großtante f
Great' Bear' s Großer Bär m
Great' Brit'ain s Großbritannien n
Great' Dane' s deutsche Dogge f
great'-grand'child' s (–chil'dren) Urenkel m
great'-grand'daugh'ter s Urenkelin f
great'-grand'fa'ther s Urgroßvater m
great'-grand'moth'er s Urgroßmutter f
great'-grand'par'ents spl Urgroßeltern
  pl
great'-grand'son's Urenkel m
greatly ['gretli] adv sehr, stark
great'-neph'ew s Großneffe m
greatness ['gretnis] s Größe f
great'-niece' s Großnichte f
great'-un'cle s Großonkel m
Grecian ['gri/ən] adj griechisch
Greece [gris] s Griechenland n
greed [grid] s Habgier f, Gier f
greediness ['gridinis] s Gierigkeit f
greedy ['gridi] adj (for) gierig (nach)
Greek [grik] adj griechisch || s (per-
  son) Grieche m, Griechin f; (language) Griechisch n; that's G. to me
  das kommt mir spanisch vor
green [grin] adj grün; (unripe) unreif;
  (inexperienced) unerfahren, neu; become g. grünen; turn g. with envy
  grün vor Neid werden || s (& golf)
  Grün n; greens Blattgemüse n
green'back' s (coll) Geldschein m
greenery ['grinəri] s Grün n

green'-eyed' *adj* grünäugig; (fig) neidisch
green'gro'cer *s* Obst– und Gemüsehändler –in *mf*
green'horn' *s* Ausländer –in *mf*
green'house' *s* Gewächshaus *n*
greenish ['grinɪʃ] *adj* grünlich
Green'land *s* Grönland *n*
green' light' *s* (fig) freie Fahrt *f*
greenness ['grinnɪs] *s* Grün *n;* (*inexperience*) Unerfahrenheit *f*
green' pep'per *s* Paprikaschote *f*
green'room' *s* (theat) Aufenthaltsraum *m*
greensward ['grin‚swɔrd] *s* Rasen *m*
green' thumb' *s*—**have a g.** gärtnerisches Geschick besitzen
greet [grit] *tr* grüßen; (*welcome*) begrüßen
greet'ing *s* Gruß *m;* (*welcoming*) Begrüßung *f;* **greetings** Grüße *pl*
greet'ing card' *s* Glückwunschkarte *f*
gregarious [grɪ'gɛrɪ·əs] *adj* gesellig
Gregor'ian cal'endar [grɪ'gɔrɪ·ən] *s* Gregorianischer Kalender *m*
Gregor'ian chant' *s* Gregorianischer Gesang *m*
grenade [grɪ'ned] *s* Granate *f*
grenade' launch'er *s* Gewehrgranatgerät *n*
grey [gre] *adj, s,* & *intr* var of **gray**
grey'hound' *s* Windhund *m*
grid [grɪd] *s* (*on a map*) Gitternetz *n;* (culin) Bratrost *m;* (electron) Gitter *n*
griddle ['grɪdəl] *s* Bratpfanne *f;* (*cookie sheet*) Backblech *n*
grid'dlecake' *s* Pfannkuchen *m*
grid'i'ron *s* Bratrost *m;* (sport) Spielfeld *n;* (theat) Schnürboden *m*
grid' leak' *s* (electron) Gitterwiderstand *m*
grief [grif] *s* Kummer *m;* **come to g.** zu Fall (or Schaden) kommen, scheitern
grief'-strick'en *adj* gramgebeugt
grievance ['grivəns] *s* Beschwerde *f*
grieve [griv] *tr* bekümmern ‖ *intr* (*over*) sich grämen (über *acc*)
grievous ['grivəs] *adj* (*causing grief*) schmerzlich; (*serious*) schwerwiegend
griffin ['grɪfɪn] *s* Greif *m*
grill [grɪl] *s* Grill *m* ‖ *tr* grillen; (*an accused person*) scharf verhören
grille [grɪl] *s* Gitter *n*
grim [grɪm] *adj* (**grimmer; grimmest**) grimmig; **g. humor** Galgenhumor *m*
grimace ['grɪməs], [grɪ'mes] *s* Grimasse *f* ‖ *intr* Grimassen schneiden
grime [graɪm] *s* Schmutz *m,* Ruß *m*
grimness ['grɪmnɪs] *s* Grimmigkeit *f*
grimy ['graɪmi] *adj* schmutzig, rußig
grin [grɪn] *s* Grinsen *n,* Schmunzeln *n* ‖ *v* (*pret & pp* **grinned;** *ger* **grinning**) *intr* grinsen, schmunzeln; **I had to g. and bear it** ich mußte gute Miene zum bösen Spiel machen
grind [graɪnd] *s* (*of coffee, grain*) Mahlen *n;* (*hard work*) Schinderei *f;* (*a student*) (coll) Streber –in *mf;* **the daily g.** der graue Alltag ‖ *v* (*pret & pp* **ground** [graʊnd]) *tr* (*coffee,*

grain) mahlen; (*glass, tools*) schleifen; (*meat*) zermahlen; (*in a mortar*) stampfen; **g. down** zerreiben; **g. one's teeth** mit den Zähnen knirschen; **g. out** (*e.g., articles*) ausstoßen; (*tunes*) leiern
grinder ['graɪndər] *s* (*molar*) (dent) Backenzahn *m;* (*mach*) Schleifmaschine *f*
grind'stone' *s* Schleifstein *m*
grip [grɪp] *s* Griff *m;* (*handle*) Handgriff *m;* (*handbag*) Reisetasche *f;* (*power*) Gewalt *f;* **come to grips with** in Angriff nehmen; **have a good g. on** (fig) sicher beherrschen; **lose one's g.** (fig) den Halt verlieren ‖ *v* (*pret & pp* **gripped;** *ger* **gripping**) *tr* (& fig) packen
gripe [graɪp] *s* Meckerei *f* ‖ *intr* (**about**) meckern (über *acc*)
grippe [grɪp] *s* (pathol) Grippe *f*
grip'ping *adj* fesselnd, packend
grisly ['grɪzli] *adj* gräßlich
grist [grɪst] *s* Mahlkorn *n;* **that's g. for his mill** das ist Wasser auf seine Mühle
gristle ['grɪsəl] *s* Knorpel *m*
gristly ['grɪsli] *adj* knorpelig
grist'mill' *s* Getreidemühle *f*
grit [grɪt] *s* (*abrasive particles*) Grieß *m;* (*pluck*) (coll) Mumm *m;* **grits** Schrotmehl *n* ‖ *v* (*pret & pp* **gritted;** *ger* **gritting**) *tr* (*one's teeth*) zusammenbeißen
gritty ['grɪti] *adj* grießig
grizzly ['grɪzli] *adj* gräulich
griz'zly bear' *s* Graubär *m*
groan [gron] *s* Stöhnen *n;* **groans** Geächze *n* ‖ *intr* stöhnen; (*grumble*) (coll) brumen
grocer ['grosər] *s* Lebensmittelhändler –in *mf*
grocery ['grosəri] *s* (*store*) Lebensmittelgeschäft *n;* **groceries** Lebensmittel *pl*
gro'cery store' *s* Lebensmittelgeschäft *n*
grog [grɑg] *s* Grog *m*
groggy ['grɑgi] *adj* benommen
groin [grɔɪn] *s* (anat) Leiste *f,* Leistengegend *f;* (archit) Rippe *f*
groom [grum] *s* Bräutigam *m;* (*stableboy*) Reitknecht *m* ‖ *tr* (*a person, animal*) pflegen; (*for a position*) heranziehen
groove [gruv] *s* Kerbe *f;* (*for letting off water*) Rinne *f;* (*of a record*) Rille *f;* (*in a barrel*) Zug *m;* **in the g.** (fig) im richtigen Fahrwasser
grope [grop] *tr*—**g. one's way** sich vorwärtstasten ‖ *intr* tappen; **g. about** herumtappen; **g. for** tappen nach, tasten nach
gropingly ['gropɪŋli] *adv* tastend
gross [gros] *adj* (*coarse, vulgar*) roh, derb; (*mistake*) grob; (*crass, extreme*) kraß; (*without deductions*) Brutto– ‖ *s* Gros *n* ‖ *tr* e–n Bruttogewinn haben von
grossly ['grosli] *adv* sehr, stark
gross' na'tional prod'uct *s* Bruttosozialprodukt *n*

gross′ receipts′ *spl* Bruttoeinnahmen *pl*

grotesque [gro′tɛsk] *adj* grotesk

grot·to [′grɑto] *s* (**–toes** & **–tos**) Grotte *f*, Höhle *f*

grouch [grɑʊtʃ] *s* (coll) Brummbär *m*, Griesgram *m* ‖ *intr* brummen

grouchy [′grɑʊtʃi] *adj* (coll) brummig

ground [grɑʊnd] *s* Grund *m*, Boden *m*; (*reason*) Grund *m*; (elec) Erde f; **every inch of g.** jeder Fußbreit Boden; **grounds** (*e.g., of an estate*) Anlagen *pl*; (*reasons*) Gründe *pl*; (*of coffee*) Satz *m*; **break g.** mit dem Bau beginnen; **gain g.** (an) Boden gewinnen; **hold one's g.** seinen Standpunkt behaupten; **level to the g.** dem Erdboden gleichmachen; **lose g.** (an) Boden verlieren; **low g.** Niederung f; **new g.** (fig) Neuland *n*; **on the grounds that** mit der Begründung, daß; **run into the g.** (fig) bis zum Überdruß wiederholen; **stand one's g.** standhalten; **yield g.** (fig) nachgeben ‖ *tr* (*a pilot*) Startverbot erteilen (*dat*); (*a ship*) auflaufen lassen; (elec) erden; **be grounded by bad weather** wegen schlechten Wetters am Starten gehindert werden

ground′ connec′tion *s* (elec) Erdung f

ground′ crew′ *s* (aer) Bodenmannschaft f

ground′ floor′ *s* Parterre *n*, Erdgeschoß *n*

ground′ glass′ *s* Mattglas *n*

ground′ hog′ *s* Murmeltier *n*

groundless [′grɑʊndlɪs] *adj* grundlos

ground′ meat′ *s* Hackfleisch *n*

ground′ plan′ *s* Grundriß *m*; (fig) Entwurf *m*

ground′ speed′ *s* Geschwindigkeit f über Grund

ground′ swell′ *s* Dünung f; (fig) wogende Erregung f

ground′-to-air′ *adj* Boden-Bord-

ground′ wa′ter *s* Grundwasser *n*

ground′ wire′ *s* (elec) Erdleitung f

ground′work′ *s* Grundlage f

group [grup] *adj* Gruppen– ‖ *s* Gruppe f; (*consisting of 18 aircraft*) Geschwader *n* ‖ *tr* gruppieren ‖ *intr* sich gruppieren

group′ing *s* Gruppierung f

group′ insur′ance *s* Gruppenversicherung f

group′ ther′apy *s* Gruppentherapie f

grouse [grɑʊs] *s* Waldhuhn *n* ‖ *intr* (sl) meckern

grout [grɑʊt] *s* dünner Mörtel *m* ‖ *tr* verstreichen

grove [grov] *s* Gehölz *n*, Hain *m*

grov·el [′grʌvəl], [′grɑvəl] *v* (*pret* & *pp* **–el[l]ed**; *ger* **–el[l]ing**) *intr* (& fig) kriechen; **g. in filth** in Schmutz wühlen

grow [gro] *v* (*pret* **grew** [gru]; *pp* **grown** [gron]) *tr* (*plants*) pflanzen, züchten; (*grain*) anbauen; (*a beard*) sich [*dat*] wachsen lassen; **the ram grows horns** dem Widder wachsen Hörner ‖ *intr* wachsen; (*become*) werden; (*become bigger*) größer werden;

den; **g. fond of** liebgewinnen; **g. luxuriantly** wuchern; **g. older** an Jahren zunehmen; **g. on s.o.** j–m ans Herz wachsen; **g. out of** (*clothes*) herauswachsen aus; (fig) entstehen aus; **g. pale** erblassen; **g. together** zusammenwachsen; (*close*) zuwachsen; **g. up** aufwachsen; **g. wild** (*luxuriantly*) wuchern; (*in the wild*) wild wachsen

grower [′gro·ər] *s* Züchter –in *mf*

growl [grɑʊl] *s* (*of a dog, stomach*) Knurren *n*; (*of a bear*) Brummen *n* ‖ *tr* (*words*) brummen ‖ *intr* knurren; (*said of a bear*) brummen; **g. at** anknurren

grown [gron] *adj* erwachsen

grown′-up′ *adj* erwachsen ‖ *s* (**grownups**) Erwachsene *mf*

growth [groθ] *s* Wachstum *n*; (*increase*) Zuwachs *m*; (pathol) Gewächs *n*; **full g.** volle Größe f

grub [grʌb] *s* Larve f, Made f; (sl) Fraß *m* ‖ *v* (*pret* & *pp* **grubbed**; *ger* **grubbing**) *tr* ausjäten ‖ *intr* wühlen; **g. for** graben nach

grubby [′grʌbi] *adj* (*dirty*) schmutzig

grudge [grʌdʒ] *s* Mißgunst f, Groll *m*; **bear** (or **have**) **a g. against s.o.** j–m grollen ‖ *tr* mißgönnen

grudg′ing *adj* mißgünstig

grudg′ingly *adv* (nur) ungern

gruel [′gru·əl] *s* Haferschleim *m*

gruel′ing *adj* strapaziös

gruesome [′grusəm] *adj* grausig

gruff [grʌf] *adj* barsch

grumble [′grʌmbəl] *s* Murren *n* ‖ *intr* (*over*) murren (über *acc*)

grumbler [′grʌmblər] *s* Brummbär *m*

grumpy [′grʌmpi] *adj* übellaunig

grunt [grʌnt] *s* Grunzen *n* ‖ *tr* & *intr* grunzen

G′-string′ *s* (*of a dancer*) letzte Hülle f; (*of a native*) Lendenschurz *m*

guarantee [,gærən′ti] *s* Garantie f ‖ *tr* garantieren für

guarantor [′gærən ,tɔr] *s* Garant –in *mf*

guaranty [′gærənti] *s* Garantie f ‖ *v* (*pret* & *pp* **–tied**) *tr* garantieren

guard [gɑrd] *s* (*watch*; *watchman*) Wache f; (*person*) Wächter –in *mf*; (fb) Verteidiger *m*; (mach) Schutzvorrichtung f; (*soldier*) (mil) Posten *m*; (*soldiers*) (mil) Wachmannschaft f, Wache f; **be on g. against** sich hüten vor (*dat*); **be on one's g.** auf der Hut sein; **keep under close g.** scharf bewachen; **mount g.** Wache beziehen; **relieve the g.** die Wache ablösen; **stand g.** Posten (or Wache) stehen; (*during a robbery*) Schmiere stehen ‖ *tr* bewachen; (fig) hüten; **g. one's tongue** seine Zunge im Zaum halten ‖ *intr—***g. against** sich vorsehen gegen ‖ **g. over** wachen über (*acc*)

guard′ de′tail *s* Wachmannschaft f

guard′ du′ty *s* Wachdienst *m*; **pull g.** Wache schieben

guard′house′ *s* (*building used by guards*) Wache f; (*military jail*) Arrestlokal *n*

guardian ['gɑrdɪ·ən] *s* (*custodian*) Wächter –in *mf;* (jur) Vormund *m*
guard′ian an′gel *s* Schutzengel *m*
guard′ianship′ *s* Obhut *f;* (jur) Vormundschaft *f*
guard′rail′ *s* Geländer *n*
guard′room′ *s* Wachstube *f*, Wachlokal *n*
guerrilla [gə'rɪlə] *s* Guerillakämpfer –in *mf*
gueril′la war′fare *s* Guerillakrieg *m*
guess [gɛs] *s* Vermutung *f;* anybody's g. reine Vermutung *f;* **take a good g.** gut raten || *tr* vermuten; **you guessed it!** geraten! || *intr* raten; **g. at** schätzen
guesser ['gɛsər] *s* Rater –in *mf*
guess′work′ *s* Raten *n*, Mutmaßung *f*
guest [gɛst] *adj* Gast–, Gäste– || *s* Gast *m;* **be a g. of** zu Gaste sein bei
guest′ book′ *s* Gästebuch *n*
guest′ perform′ance *s* Gastspiel *n;* **give a g.** (theat) gastieren
guest′ perform′er *s* Gast *m*
guest′ room′ *s* Gästezimmer *n*
guest′ speak′er *s* Gastredner –in *mf*
guffaw [gə'fɔ] *s* Gewieher *n* || *intr* wiehern
guidance ['gaɪdəns] *s* Leitung *f*, Führung *f;* (educ) Studienberatung *f;* **for your g.** zu Ihrer Orientierung
guid′ance coun′selor *s* Studienberater –in *mf*
guide [gaɪd] *s* Führer –in *mf;* (*book*) Reiseführer *m;* (*tourist escort*) Reiseführer –in *mf;* (*for gardening, etc.*) Leitfaden *m* || *tr* führen; (rok) lenken
guide′book′ *s* Reiseführer *m*, Führer *m*
guid′ed mis′sile *s* Fernlenkkörper *m*
guid′ed tour′ *s* Führung *f*
guide′line′ *s* Richtlinie *f*
guide′post′ *s* Wegweiser *m*
guide′ word′ *s* Stichwort *n*
guild [gɪld] *s* Zunft *f*, Gilde *f*
guile [gaɪl] *s* Arglist *f*
guileful ['gaɪlfəl] *adj* arglistig
guileless ['gaɪllɪs] *adj* arglos
guillotine ['gɪlə‚tin] *s* Fallbeil *n*, Guillotine *f* || *tr* mit dem Fallbeil (or mit der Guillotine) hinrichten
guilt [gɪlt] *s* Schuld *f*
guilt′-rid′den *adj* schuldbeladen
guilty ['gɪlti] *adj* (of) schuldig (*genit*); (*conscience*) schlecht; **plead g.** sich schuldig bekennen; **plead not g.** sich für nicht schuldig erklären
guil′ty par′ty *s* Schuldige *mf*
guil′ty ver′dict *s* Schuldspruch *m*
guin′ea fowl′ ['gɪni], **guin′ea hen′** *s* Perlhuhn *n*
guin′ea pig′ *s* Meerschweinchen *n;* (fig) Versuchskaninchen *n*
guise [gaɪz] *s* Verkleidung *f;* **under the g. of** unter dem Schein (*genit*)
guitar [gɪ'tɑr] *s* Gitarre *f*
guitarist [gɪ'tɑrɪst] *s* Gitarrenspieler –in *mf*
gulch [gʌltʃ] *s* Bergschlucht *f*
gulf [gʌlf] *s* Golf *m;* (fig) Kluft *f*
Gulf′ Stream′ *s* Golfstrom *m*
gull [gʌl] *s* Möwe *f;* (coll) Tölpel *m* || *tr* übertölpeln

gullet ['gʌlɪt] *s* Gurgel *f*, Schlund *m*
gullible ['gʌlɪbəl] *adj* leichtgläubig
gully ['gʌli] *s* Wasserrinne *f*
gulp [gʌlp] *s* Schluck *m*, Zug *m;* **at one g.** in e–m Zuge || *tr* schlucken; **g. down** schlingen || *intr* schlucken
gum [gʌm] *s* Gummi *m & n;* (*chewing gum*) Kaugummi *m & n;* (anat) Zahnfleisch *n* || *v* (*pret & pp* **gummed;** *ger* **gumming**) *tr* (*e.g., labels*) gummieren; **gum up the works** (coll) die Arbeit (or das Spiel) vermasseln
gum′ ar′abic *s* Gummiarabikum *n*
gum′boil′ *s* (pathol) Zahngeschwür *n*
gum′drop′ *s* Gummibonbon *m & n*
gummy ['gʌmi] *adj* klebrig
gumption ['gʌmpʃən] *s* Unternehmungsgeist *m*, Mumm *m*
gun [gʌn] *s* Gewehr *n;* (*handgun*) Handfeuerwaffe *f;* (arti) Geschütz *n;* **stick to one's guns** bei der Stange bleiben || *v* (*pret & pp* **gunned;** *ger* **gunning**) *tr*—**gun down** niederschießen; **gun the engine** Gas geben || *intr* auf die Jagd gehen; **be out gunning for** auf dem Korn haben; **gun for game** auf die Jagd gehen
gun′ bar′rel *s* Gewehrlauf *m;* (arti) Geschützrohr *n*
gun′ bat′tle *s* Feuerkampf *m*
gun′ belt′ *s* Wehrgehänge *n*
gun′boat′ *s* Kanonenboot *n*
gun′ car′riage *s* Lafette *f*
gun′cot′ton *s* Schießbaumwolle *f*
gun′ crew′ *s* Bedienungsmannschaft *f*
gun′ emplace′ment *s* Geschützstand *m*
gun′ fight′ *s* Schießerei *f*
gun′fire′ *s* Geschützfeuer *n*
gun′man *s* (**–men**) bewaffneter Bandit *m*
gun′ met′al *s* Geschützlegierung *f*
gun′ mount′ *s* Lafette *f;* (*of swivel type*) Schwenklafette *f*
gunner ['gʌnər] *s* Kanonier *m;* (aer) Bordschütze *m*
gunnery ['gʌnəri] *s* Geschützwesen *n*
gun′nery prac′tice *s* Übungsschießen *n*
gunnysack ['gʌni‚sæk] *s* Jutesack *m*
gun′ per′mit *s* Waffenschein *m*
gun′point′ *s*—**at g.** mit vorgehaltenem Gewehr
gun′pow′der *s* Schießpulver *n*
gun′run′ning *s* Waffenschmuggel *m*
gun′shot′ *s* Schuß *m;* (*range*) Schußweite *f*
gun′shot wound′ *s* Schußwunde *f*
gun′-shy′ *adj* schußscheu
gun′sight′ *s* Visier *n*
gun′smith′ *s* Büchsenmacher *m*
gun′stock′ *s* Gewehrschaft *m*
gun′ tur′ret *s* Geschützturm *m;* (aer) Schwalbennest *n*
gunwale ['gʌnəl] *s* Schandeckel *m*
guppy ['gʌpi] *s* Millionenfisch *m*
gurgle ['gʌrgəl] *s* Glucksen *n*, Gurgeln *n* || *intr* glucksen, gurgeln
gush [gʌʃ] *s* Guß *m;* (fig) Erguß *m* || *intr* sich ergießen; **g. out** hervorströmen; **g. over** (fig) viel Aufhebens machen von
gusher ['gʌʃər] *s* Schwärmer –in *mf;* (*oil well*) sprudelnde Ölquelle *f*

gush'ing adj (fig) überschwenglich
gushy ['gʌ/i] adj schwärmerisch
gusset ['gʌsɪt] s Zwickel m
gust [gʌst] s Stoß m; (of wind) Windstoß m, Bö f
gusto ['gʌsto] s Gusto m
gusty ['gʌsti] adj böig
gut [gʌt] s Darm m; **guts** Eingeweide pl; (coll) Schneid m || v (pret & pp **gutted**; ger **gutting**) tr ausbrennen; **be gutted** ausbrennen
gutter ['gʌtər] s Gosse f; (of a roof) Dachrinne f
gut'tersnipe' s (coll) Straßenjunge m
guttural ['gʌtərəl] adj kehlig; (ling) Kehl- || s (ling) Kehllaut m
guy [gaɪ] s Halteseil n; (of a tent) Spannschnur f; (coll) Kerl m; **dirty guy** (coll) Sauigel m; **great guy** Prachtkerl m || tr verspannen
guy' wire' s Spanndraht m
guzzle ['gʌzəl] tr & intr saufen
guzzler ['gʌzlər] s Säufer –in mf
gym [dʒɪm] adj (coll) Turn- || s (coll) Turnhalle f
gym' class' s (coll) Turnstunde f

gymnasi·um [dʒɪm'nezɪ·əm] s (–ums & –a [ə]) Turnhalle f
gymnast ['dʒɪmnæst] s Turner –in mf
gymnastic [dʒɪm'næstɪk] adj Turn-, gymnastisch; **g. exercise** Turnübung f || **gymnastics** spl Gymnastik f, Turnen n
gynecologist [ˌgaɪnə'kɑlədʒɪst] s Gynäkologe m, Gynäkologin f
gynecology [ˌgaɪnə'kɑlədʒi] s Gynäkologie f
gyp [dʒɪp] s (sl) Nepp m; (person) Nepper m; **that's a gyp** das ist Nepp! || v (pret & pp **gypped**; ger **gypping**) tr neppen
gyp' joint' s Nepplokal n
gypper ['dʒɪpər] s Nepper m
gypsy ['dʒɪpsi] adj Zigeuner- || s Zigeuner –in mf
gyp'sy moth' s Großer Schwammspinner m
gyrate ['dʒaɪret] intr sich drehen; kreiseln
gyration [dʒaɪ'reʃən] s Kreiselbewegung f
gyroscope ['dʒaɪrə ˌskop] s Kreisel m

H

H, h [etʃ] s achter Buchstabe des englischen Alphabets
haberdasher ['hæbər ˌdæʃər] s Inhaber –in mf e-s Herrenmodengeschäfts
haberdashery ['hæbər ˌdæʃəri] s Herrenmodengeschäft n
habit ['hæbɪt] s Gewohnheit f; (eccl) Ordenskleid n; **be in the h. of** (ger) pflegen zu (inf); **break s.o. of that h. of smoking** j-m das Rauchen abgewöhnen; **from h.** aus Gewohnheit; **get into the h. of smoking** sich [dat] das Rauchen angewöhnen; **make a h. of it** es zur Gewohnheit werden lassen
habitat ['hæbɪ ˌtæt] s Wohngebiet n
habitation [ˌhæbɪ'teʃən] s Wohnort m
habitual [hə'bɪtʃu·əl] adj gewohnheitsmäßig, Gewohnheits-
hack [hæk] s (blow) Hieb m; (notch) Kerbe f; (rasping cough) trockener Husten m; (worn-out horse) Schindmähre f; (hackney) Droschke f; (taxi) (coll) Taxi n; (writer) (coll) Schreiberling m || tr hacken, hauen; (basketball) auf den Arm schlagen || intr Taxi fahren
hackney ['hækni] s (carriage) Droschke f; (horse) gewöhnliches Gebrauchspferd n
hackneyed ['hæknid] adj abgedroschen
hack'saw' s Metallsäge f, Bügelsäge f
haddock ['hædək] s Schellfisch m
haft [hæft] s Griff m
hag [hæg] s Vettel f; (witch) Hexe f
haggard ['hægərd] adj hager
haggle ['hægəl] intr (over) feilschen (um)

hag'gling s Feilschen n
Hague, the [heg] s den Haag m
hail [hel] s Hagel m; **h. of bullets** Kugelhagel m || tr (a taxi, ship) anrufen; (acclaim) preisen; (as) begrüßen (als) || intr hageln; **h. from** stammen aus (or von) || interj Heil!
Hail' Mar'y s Ave Maria n
hail'stone' s Hagelkorn n, Schloße f
hail'storm' s Hagelschauer m
hair [her] s (single hair) Haar n; (collectively) Haare pl; **by a h.** um ein Haar; **do s.o.'s h.** j-n frisieren; **get in s.o.'s h.** j-m auf die Nerven gehen lassen; **split hairs** Haarspalterei treiben
hair'breadth' s—**by a h.** um Haaresbreite
hair'brush' s Haarbürste f
hair' clip' s Spange f, Klammer f
hair'cloth' s Haartuch n
hair'curl'er s Lockenwickler m
hair'cut' s Haarschnitt m; **get a h.** sich [dat] die Haare schneiden lassen
hair'do' s (–dos) Frisur f
hair'dress'er s Friseur m, Friseuse f
hair'dri'er s Haartrockner m
hair' dye' s Haarfärbemittel n
hariness ['herɪnɪs] s Behaartheit f
hairless ['herlɪs] adj haarlos
hair'line' s Haaransatz m
hair' net' s Haarnetz n
hair' oil' s Haaröl n
hair'piece' s Haarteil m
hair'pin' s Haarnadel f
hair'-pin curve' s Haarnadelkurve f
hair'-rais'ing adj haarsträubend
hair' rinse' s Spülmittel n

hair'roll'er *s* Haarwickler *m*
hair' set' *s* Wasserwelle *f*
hair' shirt' *s* Büßerhemd *n*
hair'split'ting *s* Haarspalterei *f*
hair' spray' *s* Haarspray *m*
hair'spring' *s* Haarfeder *f*, Spirale *f*
hair'style' *s* Frisur *f*
hair' ton'ic *s* Haarwasser *n*
hairy ['heri] *adj* haarig, behaart
Haiti ['heti] *s* Haiti *n*
halberd ['hælbərd] *s* Hellebarde *f*
hal'cyon days' ['hælsı-ən] *spl* (fig)
glückliche Zeit *f*
hale [hel] *adj* gesund; **h. and hearty**
gesund und munter
half [hæf] *adj* halb; **at h. price** zum
halben Preis; **have h. a mind to** (*inf*)
halb und halb entschlossen sein zu
(*inf*); **one and a h.** eineinhalb || *adv*
halb; **h. as much** als nur halb so wie;
h. as much again um die Hälfte mehr;
h. past three halb vier; **not h.** durch-
aus nicht || *s* (**halves** [hævz]) Hälfte
f; **cut in h.** in die Hälfte schneiden;
go halves with halbpart machen mit
half'-and-half' *adj & adv* halb und
halb || *s* Halb-und-halb-Mischung *f*
half'back' *s* (fb) Läufer *m*
half'-baked' *adj* halb gebacken; (*plans,*
etc.) halbfertig; (*person*) unerfahren
half'-blood' *s* Halbblut *n*
half'-breed' *s* Halbblut *n*, Mischling *m*
half' broth'er *s* Halbbruder *m*
half'-cocked' *adv* (coll) nicht ganz
vorbereitet
half'-day' *adv* halbtags
half'-full' *adj* halbvoll
half'-heart'ed *adj* zaghaft
half'-hour' *adj* halbstündig || *s* halbe
Stunde *f*; **every h.** halbstündlich
half' leath'er *s* (bb) Halbleder *n*
half'-length' *adj* halblang; (*portrait*) in
Halbfigur
half'-length por'trait *s* Brustbild *n*
half'-light' *s* Halbdunkel *n*
half-mast' *s*—**at h.** auf halbmast
half'-meas'ure *s* Halbheit *f*
half'-moon' *s* Halbmond *m*
half' note' *s* (mus) halbe Note *f*
half' pay' *s* Wartegeld *n*; **be on h.**
Wartegeld beziehen
half' pint' *s* (sl) Zwerg *m*
half' sis'ter *s* Halbschwester *f*
half' sleeves' *spl* halblange Ärmel *pl*
half' sole' *s* Halbsohle *f*
half'-staff' *s*—**at h.** auf halbmast
half'-tim'bered *adj* Fachwerk—
half' time' *s* (sport) Halbzeit *f*
half'-time' *adj* Halbzeit—
half' ti'tle *s* Schmutztitel *m*
half'tone' *s* (mus, paint, typ) Halbton
m
half'-track' *s* Halbkettenfahrzeug *n*
half'-truth' *s* halbe Wahrheit *f*
half'way' *adj* auf halbem Wege liegend
|| *adv* halbwegs, auf halbem Wege;
meet s.o. h. j-m auf dem halbem
Wege entgegenkommen
half'way meas'ure *s* Halbheit *f*
half'-wit' *s* Schwachkopf *m*
half'-wit'ted *adj* blöd
halibut ['hælıbət] *s* Heilbutt *m*

halitosis [,hælı'tosıs] *s* Mundgeruch *m*
hall [hɔl] *s* (*entranceway*) Diele *f*, Flur
m; (*passageway*) Gang *m*; (*large*
meeting room) Saal *m*; (*building*)
Gebäude *n*
hall'mark' *s* Kennzeichen *n*
hal·lo [hə'lo] *s* (**-los**) Hallo *n* || *interj*
hallo!
hall' of fame' *s* Ruhmeshalle *f*
hallow ['hælo] *tr* heiligen
hallucination [hə,lusı'neʃən] *s* Sinnes-
täuschung *f*, Halluzination *f*
hall'way' *s* Flur *m*, Diele *f*; (*passage-*
way) Gang *m*
ha·lo ['helo] *s* (**-los**) Glorienschein *m*;
(astr) Ring *m*, Hof *m*
halogen ['hælədʒən] *s* Halogen *n*
halt [hɔlt] *s* Halt *m*, Stillstand *m*; (*rest*)
Rast *f*; **bring to a h.** zum Stillstand
bringen; **call a h. to** halten lassen;
come to a h. stehenbleiben || *tr* an-
halten || *intr* halten; (*rest*) rasten ||
interj halt!
halter ['hɔltər] *s* (*for a horse*) Halfter
m; (*noose*) Strick *m*
halt'ing *adj* (*gait*) hinkend; (*voice*)
stockend
halve [hæv] *tr* halbieren
halyard ['hæljərd] *s* Fall *n*
ham [hæm] *s* (*pork*) Schinken *m*; (*back*
of the knee) Kniekehle *f*; (*actor*)
(sl) Schmierenschauspieler –in *mf*;
(rad) (sl) Funkamateur *m*
hamburger ['hæm,bʌrgər] *s* Hackfleisch *n*, deutsches Beefsteak *n*
hamlet ['hæmlıt] *s* Dörfchen *n*
hammer ['hæmər] *s* Hammer *m*; (*of a*
bell) Klöppel *m*; (sport) Wurfham-
mer *m* || *tr* hämmern; **h. in** (*a nail*)
einschlagen; (*e.g., rules*) einhäm-
mern; **h. out** aushämmern || *intr*
hämmern; **h. away at** (fig) herum-
arbeiten an (*dat*)
hammock ['hæmək] *s* Hängematte *f*
hamper ['hæmpər] *s* Wäschebehälter
m || *tr* behindern
hamster ['hæmstər] *s* Hamster *m*
ham'string' *s* Kniesehne *f* || *v* (*pret &*
pp **-strung**) *tr* (fig) lähmen
hand [hænd] *s* Hand *f*; (*applause*) Beifall *m*; (*handwriting*) Handschrift *f*;
(*of a clock*) Zeiger *m*; (*help*) Hilfe
f; **all hands on deck!** (naut) alle
Mann an Deck!; **at first h.** aus erster
Hand; **at h.** vorhanden, zur Hand;
at the hands of von seiten (*genit*);
be on h. zur Stelle sein; **by h.** mit
der Hand; **change hands** in andere
Hände übergehen; **fall into s.o.'s**
hands in j-s Hände fallen; **from h.**
to mouth von der Hand in den Mund;
get one's hands on in die Hände
bekommen; **get the upper h.** die
Oberhand gewinnen; **give s.o. a free**
h. j-m freies Spiel lassen; **give s.o. a**
h. (*help s.o.*) j-m helfen; (*applaud*
s.o.) j-m Beifall spenden; **go h. in h.**
with (fig) Hand in Hand gehen mit;
h. and foot eifrig; **h. in h.** Hand in
Hand; **hands off!** Hände weg!; **hands**
up! Hände hoch!; **have a good h.**
(cards) gute Karten haben; **have a h.**

in die Hand im Spiel haben bei;
have one's hands full alle Hände voll
zu tun haben; **have well in h.** gut in
der Hand haben; **hold hands** sich bei
den Händen halten; **in one's own h.**
eigenhändig; **I wash my hands of it**
ich wasche meine Hände in Unschuld; **join hands** (fig) sich zusam-
menschließen; **new h.** Neuling m; **on
all hands** auf allen Seiten; **on h.**
(com) vorrätig; **on one h. ... on the
other** einerseits ... anderseits; **out of
h.** außer Rand und Band; **play into
s.o.'s hands** j–m in die Hände spielen; **put one's h. on** (fig) finden;
show one's h. (fig) seine Karten aufdecken; **take a h. in** mitarbeiten an
(dat); **throw up one's hands** verzweifelt die Hände hochwerfen; **try
one's h. at** versuchen; **win hands
down** spielend gewinnen; **with a
heavy h.** streng || tr (zu)reichen; **h.
down** (to s.o. below) herunter-
reichen; (e.g., traditions) überliefern; **h. in** (e.g., homework) abgeben; (an application) einreichen; **h.
out** austeilen; **h. over** übergeben;
(relinquish) aushändigen, hergeben;
I have to h. it to you (coll) ich muß
dir recht geben
hand'bag' s Handtasche f, Tasche f
hand'ball' s Handball m
hand'bill' s Handzettel m
hand'book' s Handbuch n
hand' brake' s (aut) Handbremse f
hand'breadth' s Handbreit f
hand' cart' s Handkarren m
hand'clasp' s Händedruck m
hand'cuff' s Handschelle f || tr Hand-
schellen anlegen (dat)
–handed [ˌhændɪd] suf –händig
handful ['hænd ˌfʊl] s Handvoll f; (a
few) ein paar; (fig) Nervensäge f
hand'glass' s Leselupe f
hand' grenade' s Handgranate f
handi·cap ['hændɪ ˌkæp] s Handikap
n, Benachteiligung f || v (pret & pp
–capped; ger –capping) tr handika-
pen, benachteiligen
hand'icap race' s Vorgaberennen n
handicraft ['hændɪ ˌkræft] s Handwerk
n
handily ['hændɪli] adv (dexterously)
geschickt; (easily) mit Leichtigkeit
handiwork ['hændɪ ˌwʌrk] s Handarbeit f; (fig) Werk n, Schöpfung f
handkerchief ['hæŋkərtʃɪf] s Taschentuch n
handle ['hændəl] s Griff m; (of a pot)
Henkel m; (of a frying pan, broom,
etc.) Stiel m; (of a crank) Hand-
kurbel f; (of a pump) Schwengel m;
(of a door) Drücker m; (name) (coll)
Name m; (title) (coll) Titelkram m;
fly off the h. vor Wut platzen || tr
(touch) berühren; (tools, etc.) handhaben; (operate) bedienen; (fig) erledigen; (com) handeln mit; **h. with
care!** Vorsicht!; **know how to h.
customers** es verstehen, mit Kunden
umzugehen || intr—**h. well** sich leicht
lenken lassen

han'dlebars' spl Lenkstange f, (mustache) (coll) Schnauzbart m
handler ['hændlər] s (sport) Trainer m
han'dling s (e.g., of a car) Lenkbarkeit
f; (of merchandise, theme, ball) Behandlung f; (of a tool) Handhabung
f
han'dling charg'es spl Umschlagspesen
pl
hand' lug'gage s Handgepäck n
hand'made' adj handgemacht
hand'-me-downs' spl getragene Kleider
pl
hand' mir'ror s Handspiegel m
hand'-op'erated adj mit Handbetrieb
hand' or'gan s Drehorgel f
hand'out' s milde Gabe f; (sheet)
Handzettel m
hand'-picked' adj handgepflückt; (fig)
ausgesucht
hand'rail' s Geländer n
hand'saw' s Handsäge f
hand'shake' s Handschlag m, Händedruck m
handsome ['hænsəm] adj schön
hand'-to-hand' fight'ing s Nahkampf
m
hand'-to-mouth' adj von der Hand in
den Mund
hand'work' s Handarbeit f
hand'writ'ing s Handschrift f
handwritten ['hænd ˌrɪtən] adj hand-
schriftlich; **h. letter** Handschreiben
n
handy ['hændi] adj handlich; (practical) praktisch; (person) geschickt;
come in h. gelegen kommen; **have h.**
zur Hand haben
hand'y·man' s (–men') Handlanger m
hang [hæŋ] s (of curtains, clothes)
Fall m; **get the h. of** (coll) sich
einarbeiten in (acc); **I don't give a
h. about it** (coll) es ist mir Wurst ||
v (pret & pp hung [hʌŋ]) tr hängen;
(a door) einhängen; (wallpaper) ankleben; **h. one's head** den Kopf hängen lassen; **h. out** heraushängen; **h.
up** aufhängen; (the receiver) (telp)
auflegen; **I'll be hanged if** ich will
mich hängen lassen, wenn || intr
hängen; (float) schweben; **h. around**
herumlungern; **h. around the bar**
sich in der Bar herumtreiben; **h.
around with** umgehen mit; **h. back**
sich zurückhalten; **h. by** (a thread,
rope) hängen an (dat); **h. down**
niederhängen; **h. in the balance** in
der Schwebe sein; **h. on** durchhalten;
h. on s.o.'s words an j–s Worten
hängen; **h. on to** festhalten; (retain)
behalten; **h. together** zusammen-
halten; **h. up** (telp) einhängen || v
(pret & pp hanged & hung) tr hängen
hangar ['hæŋər] s Hangar m
hang'-dog look' s Armesündergesicht n
hanger ['hæŋər] s Kleiderbügel m
hang'er-on' s (hangers-on) Mitläufer
–in mf
hang'ing adj (herab)hängend || s Hän-
gen n
hang'man s (–men) Henker m
hang'nail' s Niednagel m

hang'out' s Treffpunkt m
hang'o'ver s (coll) Kater m
hank [hæŋk] s Strähne f
hanker ['hæŋkər] intr (for) sich sehnen (nach)
hanky-panky ['hæŋki'pæŋki] s (coll)
Schwindel m
haphazard [,hæp'hæzərd] adj wahllos
haphazardly [,hæp'hæzərdli] adv aufs
Geratewohl
hapless ['hæplɪs] adj unglücklich
happen ['hæpən] intr geschehen; h. to
see zufällig sehen; h. upon zufällig
stoßen auf (acc); what happens now?
was soll nun werden?
hap'pening s Ereignis n
happily ['hæpɪli] adv glücklich
happiness ['hæpɪnɪs] s Glück n
happy ['hæpi] adj glücklich; be h.
about s.th. über etw erfreut sein;
be h. to (inf) sich freuen zu (inf);
h. as a lark quietschvergnügt
Hap'py Birth'day interj Herzlichen
Glückwunsch zum Geburtstag!
hap'py-go-luck'y adj unbekümmert
hap'py me'dium s—strike a h. e-n
glücklichen Ausgleich treffen
Hap'py New' Year' interj Glückliches
Neujahr!
harangue [hə'ræŋ] s leidenschaftliche
Rede f || tr e-e leidenschaftliche
Rede halten an (acc)
harass [hə'ræs], ['hærəs] tr schikanieren; (mil) stören
harass'ing fire' s (mil) Störungsfeuer n
harassment [hə'ræsmənt], ['hærəs-
mənt] s Schikane f; (mil) Störung f
harbinger ['harbɪndʒər] s Vorbote m
|| tr anmelden
harbor ['harbər] adj Hafen– || s Hafen
m || tr (give refuge to) beherbergen;
(hide) verbergen; (thoughts) hegen
har'bor mas'ter s Hafenmeister m
hard [hard] adj (substance, water,
words) hart; (problem) schwierig;
(worker) fleißig; (blow, times, work)
schwer; (life) mühsam; (fact) nackt;
(rain) heftig; (winter) streng; (drinks)
alkoholisch; be h. on s.o. j–m schwer
zusetzen; have a h. time Schwierigkeiten haben; h. to believe kaum zu
glauben; h. to please anspruchsvoll;
h. to understand schwer zu verstehen
|| adv hart; (energetically) fleißig; he
was h. put to (inf) es fiel ihm schwer
zu (inf); rain h. stark regnen; take h.
schwer nehmen; try h. mit aller Kraft
versuchen
hard'-and-fast' adj fest
hard-bitten ['hard,bɪtən] adj verbissen
hard'-boiled' adj (egg) hartgekocht;
(coll) hartgesotten
hard' can'dy s Bonbons pl
hard' cash' s bare Münze f
hard' ci'der s Apfelwein m
hard' coal' s Steinkohle f
hard'-earned' adj schwer verdient
harden ['hardən] tr & intr (er)härten
hard'ened adj (criminal) hartgesotten
hard'ening s Verhärtung f
hard'-head'ed adj nüchtern
hard'-heart'ed adj hartherzig

hardihood ['hardɪ,hud] s Kühnheit f;
(insolence) Frechheit f
hardiness ['hardɪnɪs] s Ausdauer f,
Widerstandsfähigkeit f
hard' la'bor s Zwangsarbeit f
hard' luck' s Pech n
hardly ['hardli] adv kaum, schwerlich;
h. ever fast gar nicht
hardness ['hardnɪs] s Härte f
hard'-of-hear'ing adj schwerhörig
hard'-pressed' adj schwer bedrängt
hard'-shell' adj hartschalig; (coll) unnachgiebig
hard'ship' s Mühsal f
hard'top' s (aut) Hardtop n
hard' up' adj (for money) schlecht bei
Kasse; h. for in Verlegenheit um
hard'ware' s Eisenwaren pl; (e.g., on
doors, windows) Beschläge pl; military h. militärische Ausrüstung f
hard'ware store' s Eisenwarenhandlung
f
hard'wood' s Hartholz n
hard'wood floor' s Hartholzboden m
hard'-work'ing adj fleißig
hardy ['hardi] adj (plants) winterfest;
(person) widerstandsfähig
hare [her] s Hase m
hare'brained' adj unbesonnen
hare'lip' s Hasenscharte f
harem ['herəm] s Harem m
hark [hark] intr horchen; h. back to
zurückgehen auf (acc)
harlequin ['harləkwɪn] s Harlekin m
harlot ['harlət] s Hure f
harm [harm] s Schaden m; do h. Schaden anrichten; I meant no h. by it
ich meinte es nicht böse; out of
harm's way in Sicherheit; there's no
h. in trying ein Versuch kann nicht
schaden || tr beschädigen; (e.g., a
reputation, chances) schaden (dat);
h. s.o. (physically) j–m etw zuleide
tun; (fig) schaden (dat)
harmful ['harmfəl] adj schädlich
harmless ['harmlɪs] adj unschädlich
harmonic [har'manɪk] adj harmonisch
|| s (mus) Oberton m
harmonica [har'manɪkə] s Harmonika
f
harmonious [har'monɪ·əs] adj harmonisch
harmonize ['harmə,naɪz] intr harmonieren
harmony ['harməni] s Harmonie f; be
in h. with im Einklang stehen mit
harness ['harnɪs] s Geschirr n; die in
the h. in den Sielen sterben || tr an-
schirren; (e.g., a river, power) nutzbar machen
har'ness mak'er s Sattler m
har'ness rac'ing s Trabrennen n
harp [harp] s Harfe f || intr—h. on
herumreiten auf (dat)
harpist ['harpɪst] s Harfner –in mf
harpoon [har'pun] s Harpune f || tr
harpunieren
harpsichord ['harpsɪ,kɔrd] s Cembalo
n
harpy ['harpi] s (myth) Harpyie f
harrow ['hæro] s Egge f || tr eggen
har'rowing adj schrecklich

har·ry ['hæri] v (pret & pp **-ried**) tr
martern

Harry ['hæri] s Heinz m

harsh [hɑrʃ] adj (conditions) hart;
(tone) schroff; (light) grell; (treatment) rauh

harshness ['hɑrʃnɪs] s Härte f; Schroff-
heit f; Grelle f; Rauheit f

hart [hɑrt] s Hirsch m

harum-scarum ['herəm'skɛrəm] adj
wild || adv wie ein Wilder

harvest ['hɑrvɪst] s Ernte f; **bad h.**
Mißernte f || tr & intr ernten

harvester ['hɑrvɪstər] s Schnitter –in
mf; (mach) Mähmaschine f

har'vest moon' s Erntemond m

has-been ['hæz͵bɪn] s (coll) Gestrige
mf

hash [hæʃ] s Gehacktes n; **make h. of**
(coll) verwursteln || tr zerhacken

hashish ['hæʃiʃ] s Haschisch n

hasp [hæsp] s Haspe f

hassle ['hæsəl] s (coll) Streit m

hassock ['hæsək] s Hocker m

haste [hest] s Hast f, Eile f; **in (all) h.**
in (aller) Eile; **make h.** sich beeilen

hasten ['hesən] tr beschleunigen || intr
hasten, eilen

hasty ['hesti] adj eilig; (rash) hastig

hat [hæt] s Hut m; **keep under one's h.**
für sich behalten

hat'band' s Hutband n

hat'block' s Hutform f

hat'box' s Hutschachtel f

hatch [hætʃ] s (opening) (aer, naut)
Luke f; (cover) (naut) Lukendeckel
m || tr (eggs) ausbrüten; (a scheme)
aushecken; (mark with strokes)
schraffieren || intr Junge ausbrüten;
(said of chicks) aus dem Ei kriechen

hat'check girl' s Garderobe(n)fräulein
n

hatchet ['hætʃɪt] s Beil n; **bury the h.**
die Streitaxt begraben

hatch'ing s Schraffierung f

hatch'way' s (naut) Luke f

hate [het] s Haß m || tr hassen; **I h. to**
(inf) es widerstrebt mir zu (inf)

hateful ['hetfəl] adj verhaßt

hatless ['hætlɪs] adj hutlos

hat'pin' s Hutnadel f

hat'rack' s Hutständer m

hatred ['hetrɪd] s Haß m

haughtiness ['hɔtɪnɪs] s Hochmut m

haughty ['hɔti] adj hochmütig

haul [hɔl] s Schleppen n; (hauling distance) Transportstrecke f; (amount
caught) Fang m; **make a big h.** (fig)
reiche Beute machen; **over the long
h.** auf die Dauer || tr (tug) schlep-
pen; (transport) transportieren; **h.
ashore** ans Land ziehen; **h. down** (a
flag) einholen; **h. into court** vor
Gericht schleppen; **h. out of bed** aus
dem Bett herausholen || intr—**h. off**
(naut) abdrehen; **h. off and hit** aus-
holen um zu schlagen

haulage ['hɔlɪdʒ] s Transport m;
(costs) Transportkosten pl

haunch [hɔntʃ] s (hip) Hüfte f; (hind
quarter of an animal) Keule f

haunt [hɔnt] s Aufenthaltsort m || tr
verfolgen; **h. a place** an e–m Ort
umgehen; **this place is haunted** es
spukt hier

haunt'ed house' s Haus n in dem es
spukt

have [hæv] s—**the haves and the have-
nots** die Besitzenden und die Besitz-
losen || v (pret & pp **had** [hæd]) tr
haben; (a baby) bekommen; (a drink)
trinken; (food) essen; **h. back** (coll)
zurückhaben; **h. in mind** vorhaben;
h. it in for s.o. j–n auf dem Strich
haben; **h. it out with s.o.** sich mit
j–m aussprechen; **h. it your way**
meinetwegen machen Sie es, wie Sie
wollen; **h. left** übrig haben; **h. on**
(clothes) anhaben; (a hat) aufhaben;
(e.g., a program) vorhaben; **h. on
one's person** bei sich tragen; **h. to
do with s.o.** mit j–m zu tun haben;
h. what it takes das Zeug dazu haben; **I've had it!** jetzt langt's mir
aber!; **I will not h. it!** ich werde es
nicht dulden!; **you had better** es
wäre besser, wenn Sie; **what would
you h. me do?** was soll ich machen?
|| intr—**h. done with it** fertig sein
damit; **h. off** frei haben || aux (to
form compound past tenses) haben,
e.g., **he has paid the bill** er hat die
Rechnung bezahlt; (to form compound past tenses of certain intransitive verbs of motion and change of
condition, of the verb **bleiben,** and
of the transitive verb **eingehen**) sein,
e.g., **she has gone to the theater** sie
ist ins Theater gegangen; **they h.
become rich** sie sind reich geworden;
you h. stayed too long Sie sind zu
lange geblieben; **I h. assumed an
obligation** ich bin e–e Verpflichtung
eingegangen; (to express causation)
lassen, e.g., **I am having a new suit
made** ich lasse mir e–n neuen Anzug
machen; (to express necessity) müssen, e.g., **I h. to study now** jetzt muß
ich studieren; **that will h. to do** das
wird genügen müssen

haven ['hevən] s Hafen m

haversack ['hævər͵sæk] s Brotbeutel m

havoc ['hævək] s Verwüstung f; **wreak
h. on** verwüsten

haw [hɔ] s (bot) Mehlbeere f; (in
speech) Äh n || tr nach links lenken
|| intr nach links gehen || interj (to
a horse) hü!

Hawaii [hə'waɪ·i] s Hawaii n

Hawaiian [hə'waɪjən] adj hawaiisch

Hawai'ian Is'lands spl Hawaii-Inseln
pl

hawk [hɔk] s Habicht m || tr (wares)
verhökern; **h. up** aushusten || intr
sich räuspern

hawker ['hɔkər] s Straßenhändler –in
mf

hawse [hɔz] s (hole) (naut) Klüse f;
(prow) (naut) Klüsenwand f

hawse'hole' s (naut) Klüse f

hawser ['hɔzər] s (naut) Trosse f, Tau
n

hawthorn ['hɔθɔrn] s Weißdorn m

hay [he] s Heu n; **hit the hay** (sl) sich

in die Falle hauen; **make hay** Heu machen
hay′ fe′ver s Heufieber n
hay′field′ s Kleefeld n
hay′fork′ s Heugabel f
hay′loft′ s Heuboden m
hay′mak′er s (box) Schwinger m
hay′rack′ s Heuraufe f
hayrick [′he ‚rɪk] s Heuschober m
hay′ride′ s Ausflug m in e–m teilweise mit Heu gefüllten Wagen
hay′seed′ s (coll) Bauerntölpel m
hay′stack′ s Heuschober m
hay′wire′ adj (sl) übergeschnappt; **go h.** (go wrong) schiefgehen; (go insane) überschnappen
hazard [′hæzərd] s (danger) Gefahr f; (risk) Risiko n || tr riskieren
hazardous [′hæzərdəs] adj gefährlich
haze [hez] s Dunst m; (fig) Unklarheit f || tr (students) piesacken
hazel [′hezəl] adj (eyes) nußbraun || s (bush) Hasel f
ha′zelnut′ s Haselnuß f
haziness [′hezɪnɪs] s Dunstigkeit f; (fig) Verschwommenheit f
haz′ing s (of students) Piesacken n
hazy [′hezi] adj dunstig; (recollection) verschwommen
H-bomb [′etʃ ‚bɑm] s Wasserstoffbombe f
he [hi] pers pron er; **he who** wer || s Männchen n
head [hɛd] adj Kopf–; (chief) Haupt–, Ober–, Chef– || s (of a body, cabbage, nail, lettuce, pin) Kopf m; (of a gang, family) Haupt m; (of a firm) Chef m; (of a school) Direktor –in mf; (of a department) Leiter –in mf; (of a bed) Kopfende n; (of a coin) Bildseite f; (of a glass of beer) Blume f; (of cattle) Stück n; (of stairs) oberer Absatz m; (of a river) Quelle f; (of a parade, army) Spitze f; (toilet) Klo n; **a h.** pro Person, pro Kopf; **at the h. of** an der Spitze (genit); **be at the h. of** vorstehen (dat); **be h. and shoulders above s.o.** haushoch über j–m stehen; (be far superior to s.o.) j–m haushoch überlegen sein; **be over one's h.** über j–s Verstand gehen; **bring to a h.** zur Entscheidung bringen; **by a h.** um e–e Kopflänge; **from h. to foot** von Kopf bis Fuß; **go over s.o.'s h.** über j–s Verstand gehen; (adm) über j–s Kopf hinweg handeln; **go to s.o.'s h.** j–m zu Kopfe steigen; **have a good h. for** begabt sein für; **h. over heels** kopfüber; (in love) bis über die Ohren; (in debt) bis über den Hals; **heads or tails?** Kopf oder Wappen?; **heads up!** aufpassen!; **keep one's h. above water** sich über Wasser halten; **lose one's h.** den Kopf verlieren; **my h. is spinning** es schwindelt mir; **not be able to make h. or tail of** nicht klug werden aus; **out of one's h.** nicht ganz richtig im Kopf; **per h.** pro Kopf; **put heads together** die Köpfe zusammenstecken; **talk over**

s.o.'s h. über j–s Kopf hinwegreden; **talk s.o.'s h. off** j–n dumm und dämlich reden; **take it into one's h.** es sich [dat] in den Kopf setzen || tr (be in charge of) leiten; (a parade, army, expedition) anführen; (steer, guide) lenken; **h. a list** als erster auf e–r Liste stehen; **h. off** abwehren; **h. up** (a committee) vorsitzen (dat) || intr—**h. back** zurückkehren; **h. for** auf dem Wege sein nach; (aer) anfliegen; (naut) ansteuern; **h. home** sich heimbegeben; **where are you heading?** wo wollen Sie hin?
head′ache′ s Kopfweh n, Kopfschmerzen pl
head′band′ s Kopfband n
head′board′ s Kopfbrett n
head′cold′ s Schnupfen m
head′ doc′tor s Chefarzt m, Chefärztin f
head′dress′ s Kopfputz m
–headed [‚hɛdɪd] suf –köpfig
head first adv kopfüber; (fig) Hals über Kopf
head′gear′ s Kopfbedeckung f
head′hunt′er s Kopfjäger m
head′ing s Überschrift f; (aer) Steuerkurs m
headland [′hɛdlənd] s Landspitze f
headless [′hɛdlɪs] adj kopflos; (without a leader) führerlos
head′light′ s (aut) Scheinwerfer m
head′line′ s (in a newspaper) Schlagzeile f; (at the top of a page) Überschrift f; **hit the headlines** (coll) Schlagzeilen liefern
head′lin′er s Hauptdarsteller –in mf
head′long′ adj stürmisch || adv kopfüber
head′man s (–men) Häuptling m, Chef m
head′mas′ter s Direktor m
head′mis′tress s Direktorin f
head′ nurse′ s Oberschwester f
head′ of′fice s Hauptgeschäftsstelle f
head′ of gov′ernment s Regierungschef m
head′ of hair′ s—beautiful h. schönes volles Haar n
head′ of the fam′ily s Familienoberhaupt n
head′-on′ adj Frontal– || adv frontal
head′phones spl Kopfhörer pl
head′piece′ s Kopfbedeckung f; (brains) (coll) Kopf m; (typ) Zierleiste f
head′quar′ters s Hauptquartier n; (of police) Polizeidirektion f; (mil) Hauptquartier n, Stabsquartier n
head′quarters com′pany s Stabskompanie f
head′rest′ s Kopflehne f; (aut) Kopfstütze f
head′ restrain′er s (aut) Kopfstütze f
head′set′ s Kopfhörer m
head′ shrink′er s (coll) Psychiater –in mf
head′stand′ s Kopfstand m
head′ start′ s Vorsprung m
head′stone′ s Grabstein m
head′strong′ adj starrköpfig

head′ wait′er s Oberkellner m
head′wa′ters spl Quellflüsse pl
head′way′ s Vorwärtsbewegung f; (fig) Fortschritte pl
head′wear′ s Kopfbedeckung f
head′wind′ s Gegenwind m
head′work′ s Kopfarbeit f
heady [ˈhɛdi] adj (wine) berauschend; (news) spannend; (impetuous) unbesonnen
heal [hil] tr & intr heilen; **h. up** zuheilen
healer [ˈhilər] s Heilkundige mf
heal′ing s Heilung f
health [hɛlθ] s Gesundheit f; **drink to s.o.'s h.** auf j–s Wohl trinken; **in good h.** gesund; **in poor h.** kränklich; **to your h.!** auf Ihr Wohl!
health′ certi′ficate s Gesundheitspaß m
healthful [ˈhɛlθfəl] adj heilsam; (climate) bekömmlich
health′ insur′ance s Krankenversicherung f
health′ resort′ s Kurort m
healthy [ˈhɛlθi] adj gesund; (respect) gehörig; **keep h.** sich gesund halten
heap [hip] s Haufen m; **in heaps** haufenweise ‖ tr beladen; **h.** (e.g., praise) **on s.o.** j–n überhäufen mit; **h. up** anhäufen
hear [hɪr] v (pret & pp **heard** [hʌrd]) tr hören; (find out) erfahren; (get word) Bescheid bekommen; **h. s.o.'s lessons** j–n überhören; **h. s.o. out** j–n ganz ausreden lassen ‖ intr hören; **h. about** hören über (acc) or von; **h. from** Nachricht bekommen von; **h. of** hören von; **h. wrong** sich verhören; **he wouldn't h. of it** er wollte nichts davon hören
hearer [ˈhɪrər] s Hörer –in mf; **hearers** Zuhörer pl
hear′ing s Hören n, Gehör n; (jur) Verhör n; **within h.** in Hörweite
hear′ing aid′ s Hörgerät n, Hörapparat m
hear′say′ s Hörensagen n; **know s.th. by h.** etw nur vom Hörensagen kennen; **that's mere h.** das ist bloßes Gerede
hearse [hʌrs] s Leichenwagen m
heart [hɑrt] s Herz n; **after my own h.** nach meinem Herzen; **at h.** im Grunde genommen; **be the h. and soul of** die Seele sein (genit); **by h.** auswendig; **cross my h.!** Hand aufs Herz!; **cry one's h. out** sich ausweinen; **eat one's h. out** sich vor Kummer verzehren; **get to the h. of** auf den Grund kommen (dat); **have a h.** (coll) ein Herz haben; **have one's h. in s.th.** mit dem Herzen bei etw sein; **have the h. to** (inf) es übers Herz bringen zu (inf); **h. and soul** mit Leib und Seele; **hearts** (cards) Herz n; **lose h.** den Mut verlieren; **lose one's h. to** sein Herz verlieren an (acc); **set one's h. on** sein Herz hängen an (acc); **take h.** Mut fassen; **take to h.** beherzigen; **to one's heart's content** nach Herzenslust; **wear one's h. on one's sleeve** das Herz auf der

Zunge tragen; **with all one's h.** mit ganzem Herzen
heart′ache′ s Herzweh n
heart′ attack′ s Herzanfall m
heart′beat′ s Herzschlag m
heart′break′ s Herzeleid n
heart′break′er s Herzensbrecher –in mf
heartbroken [ˈhɑrt‚brokən] adj trostlos
heart′burn′ s Sodbrennen n
heart′ disease′ s Herzleiden n
–hearted [‚hɑrtɪd] suf –herzig
hearten [ˈhɑrtən] tr ermutigen
heart′ fail′ure s Herzschlag m
heartfelt [ˈhɑrt‚fɛlt] adj herzinnig, tiefempfunden; (wishes) herzlich
hearth [hɑrθ] s Herd m
hearth′stone′ s Kaminplatte f
heartily [ˈhɑrtɪli] adv (with zest) herzhaft; (sincerely) von Herzen
heartless [ˈhɑrtlɪs] adj herzlos
heart′ mur′mur s Herzgeräusch n
heart′-rend′ing adj herzzerreißend
heart′sick′ adj tief betrübt
heart′ strings′ spl—**pull at s.o.'s h.** j–m ans Herz greifen
heart′ throb′ s Schwarm m
heart′ trans′plant s Herzverpflanzung f
heart′ trou′ble s Herzbeschwerden pl
heart′wood′ s Kernholz n
hearty [ˈhɑrti] adj herzhaft; (meal) reichlich; (eater) stark; (appetite) gut
heat [hit] s Hitze f, Wärme f; (heating) Heizung f; (sexual) Brunst f; (in the case of dogs) Läufigkeit f; (of battle) Eifer m; (sport) Rennen n, Einzelrennen n; **be in h.** brunsten; (said of dogs) läufig sein; **final h.** Schlußrennen n; **put the h. on** (sl) unter Druck setzen; **qualifying h.** Vorlauf m ‖ tr (e.g., food) wärmen; (fluids) erhitzen; (a house) heizen; **h. up** aufwärmen ‖ intr—**h. (up)** warm (or heiß) werden
heat′ed adj erhitzt; (fig) erregt
heater [ˈhitər] s Heizkörper m; (oven) Heizofen m
heath [hiθ] s Heide f
hea·then [ˈhiðən] adj heidnisch ‖ s (–then & –thens) Heide m, Heidin f
heathendom [ˈhiðəndəm] s Heidentum n
heather [ˈhɛðər] s Heiderkraut n
heat′ing s Heizung f
heat′ing pad′ s Heizkissen n
heat′ing sys′tem s Heizanlage f
heat′ light′ning s Wetterleuchten n
heat′ prostra′tion s Hitzekollaps m
heat′-resis′tant adj hitzebeständig
heat′ shield′ s (rok) Hitzeschild m
heat′stroke′ s Hitzschlag m
heat′ treat′ment s Wärmebehandlung f
heat′ wave′ s Hitzewelle f
heave [hiv] s Hub m; (throw) Wurf m; **heaves** (vet) schweres Atmen n ‖ v (pret & pp **heaved** & **hove** [hov]) tr heben; (throw) werfen; (a sigh) ausstoßen; (the anchor) lichten ‖ intr (said of the breast or sea) wogen; (retch) sich übergeben; **h. in sight** auftauchen; **h. to** (naut) stoppen

heaven ['hɛvən] s Himmel m; **for heaven's sake** um Himmels willen; **good heavens!** ach du lieber Himmel!; **the heavens** der Himmel
heavenly ['hɛvənli] adj himmlisch
hea'venly bod'y s Himmelskörper m
heavenwards ['hɛvənwərdz] adv himmelwärts
heavily ['hɛvɪli] adv schwer; **h. in debt** überschuldet
heavy ['hɛvi] adj schwer; (food) schwer verdaulich; (fine, price) hoch; (walk) schwerfällig; (heart) bedrückt, schwer; (traffic, frost, rain) stark; (fog) dicht; (role) (theat) ernst, düster; **h. drinker** Gewohnheitstrinker –in mf; **h. seas** Sturzsee f; **h. with sleep** schlaftrunken
heavy'-armed' adj schwerbewaffnet
heav'y-du'ty adj Hochleistungs–, Schwerlast–
heav'y-du'ty truck' s Schwerlastwagen m
heav'y-heart'ed adj bedrückt
heav'y in'dustry s Schwerindustrie f
heav'yset' adj untersetzt
heav'y weight' adj Schwergewicht– ‖ s Schwergewichtler m
Hebrew ['hibru] adj hebräisch ‖ s Hebräer –in mf; (language) Hebräisch n
hecatomb ['hɛkə,tom] s Hekatombe f
heck [hɛk] s—**give s.o. h.** (sl) j–m tüchtig einheizen; **what the h. are you doing?** (sl) was zum Teufel tust du? ‖ interj (sl) verflixt!
heckle ['hɛkəl] tr durch Zwischenrufe belästigen
heckler ['hɛklər] s Zwischenrufer –in mf
hectic ['hɛktɪk] adj hektisch
hectograph ['hɛktə,græf] s Hektograph m ‖ tr hektographieren
hedge [hɛdʒ] s Hecke f ‖ tr—**h. in** (or **h. off**) einhegen ‖ intr sich den Rücken decken
hedge'hog' s Igel m
hedge'hop' v (pret & pp –hopped; ger hopping) intr (aer) heckenspringen
hedge'hop'ping s (aer) Heckenhüpfen n
hedge'row' s Hecke f
hedonism ['hidə,nɪzəm] s Hedonismus m
hedonist ['hidənɪst] s Hedonist –in mf
heed [hid] s Acht f; **pay h. to** achtgeben auf (acc); **take h.** achtgeben ‖ tr beachten ‖ intr achtgeben
heedful ['hidfəl] adj (of) achtsam (auf acc)
heedless ['hidlɪs] adj achtlos; **h. of** ungeachtet (genit)
heehaw ['hi,hɔ] s Iah n ‖ interj iah!
heel [hil] s (of the foot) Ferse f; (of a shoe) Absatz m; (of bread) Brotende n; (sl) Schurke m; **down at the h.** abgerissen; **cool one's heels** [dat] die Beine in den Bauch stehen; **take to one's heels** Fersengeld geben ‖ intr (said of a dog) auf den Fersen folgen
hefty ['hɛfti] adj (heavy) schwer; (muscular) stämmig; (blow) zünftig

heifer ['hɛfər] s Färse f
height [haɪt] s Höhe f; (e.g., of power) Gipfel m; **h. of the season** Hochsaison f
heighten ['haɪtən] tr erhöhen; (fig) verschärfen
heinous ['henəs] adj abscheulich
heir [ɛr] s Erbe; m; **become h. to** erben; **become s.o.'s h.** j–n beerben
heir' appar'ent s (heirs apparent) Thronerbe m
heiress ['ɛrɪs] s Erbin f
heir'loom' s Erbstück n
heir' presump'tive s (heirs presumptive) mutmaßlicher Erbe m
Helen ['hɛlən] s Helene f
helicopter ['hɛlɪ,kɑptər] s Hubschrauber m
heliport ['hɛlɪ,pɔrt] s Hubschrauberlandeplatz m
helium ['hilɪ·əm] s Helium n
helix ['hilɪks] s (helixes & helices ['hɛlɪ,siz]) Spirale f; (archit) Schnecke f
hell [hɛl] s Hölle f
hell'bent' adj—**h. on** (sl) erpicht auf (acc)
hell'cat' s (shrew) Hexe f
Hellene ['hɛlin] s Hellene m, Hellenin f
Hellenic [hɛ'lɛnɪk] adj hellenisch
hell'fire' s Höllenfeuer n
hellish ['hɛlɪʃ] adj höllisch
hel·lo [hɛ'lo] s (–los) Hallo n ‖ interj guten Tag!; (in southern Germany and Austria) Grüß Gott!; (to get s.o.'s attention and in answering the telephone) hallo!
helm [hɛlm] s (& fig) Steuerruder n
helmet ['hɛlmɪt] s Helm m
helms'man s (–men) Steuermann m
help [hɛlp] s Hilfe f; (domestic) Hilfe f, Hilfskraft f; (temporary) Aushilfe f; **h. wanted** (in newspapers) Stellenangebot n; **there's no h. for it** da ist nicht zu helfen; **with the h. of** mit Hilfe (genit) ‖ tr helfen (dat); **can I h. you?** womit kann ich (Ihnen) dienen?; **h. along** nachhelfen (dat); **h. down from** herunterhelfen (dat) von (dat); **h. oneself** sich bedienen; (at table) zugreifen; **h. oneself to** sich [dat] nehmen; **h. out** aushelfen (dat); **h. s.o. on** (or **off**) **with the coat** j–m in den (or aus dem) Mantel helfen; **I cannot h.** (ger), **I cannot h. but** (inf) ich kann nicht umhin zu (inf); **sorry, that can't be helped** es tut mir leid, aber es geht nicht anders ‖ intr helfen ‖ interj Hilfe!
helper ['hɛlpər] s Gehilfe m, Gehilfin f
helpful ['hɛlpfəl] adj (person) hilfsbereit; (e.g., suggestion) nützlich
help'ing s Portion f
help'ing hand' s hilfreiche Hand f
helpless ['hɛlplɪs] adj hilflos, ratlos
helter-skelter ['hɛltər'skɛltər] adj wirr ‖ adv holterdiepolter
hem [hɛm] s Saum m ‖ v (pret & pp hemmed; ger hemming) tr säumen; **hem in** umringen ‖ intr stocken; **hem**

and haw nicht mit der Sprache herauswollen || *interj* hm!

hemisphere ['hɛmɪ,sfɪr] *s* Halbkugel *f*

hemistich ['hɛmɪ,stɪk] *s* Halbvers *m*

hem'line' *s* Rocklänge *f*

hem'lock' *s* (*conium*) Schierling *m;* (*poison*) Schierlingsgift *n;* (*Tsuga canadensis*) Kanadische Hemmlocktanne *f*

hemoglobin [,hɪmə'globɪn] *s* Blutfarbstoff *m*, Hämoglobin *n*

hemophilia [,hɪmə'fɪlɪ·ə] *s* Bluterkrankheit *f*, Hämophilie *f*

hemorrhage ['hɛmərɪdʒ] *s* Blutung *f*

hemorrhoids ['hɛmə,rɔɪdz] *spl* Hämorrhoiden *pl*

hemostat ['hɪmə,stæt] *s* Unterbindungsklemme *f*

hemp [hɛmp] *s* Hanf *m*

hem'stitch' *s* Hohlsaum *m* || *tr* mit e-m Hohlsaum versehen

hen [hɛn] *s* Henne *f*, Huhn *n*

hence [hɛns] *adv* von hier; (*therefore*) daher, daraus; **a year h.** in e-m Jahr

hence'forth' *adv* hinfort, von nun an

hench·man ['hɛntʃmən] *s* (**-men**) Anhänger *m;* (*gang member*) Helfershelfer *m*

hen'house' *s* Hühnerstall *m*

henna ['hɛnə] *s* Henna *f*

hen' par'ty *s* (coll) Damengesellschaft *f*

hen'peck' *tr* unter dem Pantoffel haben; **be henpecked** unter dem Pantoffel stehen; **henpecked husband** Pantoffelheld *m*

Henry ['hɛnri] *s* Heinrich *m*

hep [hɛp] *adj* (**to**) eingeweiht (in *acc*)

her [hʌr] *poss adj* ihr; (if the antecedent is neuter, e.g., Fräulein) sein || *pers pron* sie; (if the antecedent is neuter) es; (indirect object) ihr; (if the antecedent is neuter) ihm

herald ['hɛrəld] *s* Herold *m;* (fig) Vorbote *m* || *tr* ankündigen; **h. in** einführen

heraldic [hɛ'rældɪk] *adj* heraldisch; **h. figure** Wappenbild *n;* **h. motto** Wappenspruch *m*

heraldry ['hɛrəldri] *s* Wappenkunde *f*

herb [(h)ʌrb] *s* Kraut *n*, Gewürz *n;* (pharm) Arzneikraut *n*

herculean [hʌrkju'li·ən] *adj* herkulisch

herd [hʌrd] *s* Herde *f;* (of game) Rudel *n;* **the common h.** der Pöbel || *tr* hüten; **h. together** zusammenpferchen || *intr* in e-r Herde gehen (or leben)

herds'man *s* (**-men**) Hirt *m*

here [hɪr] *adv* (*position*) hier; (*direction*) hierher, her; **h. and there** hie(r) und da; **h. below** in diesem Leben; **h. goes!** jetzt gilt's!; **here's to you!** auf Ihr Wohl!; **neither h. nor there** belanglos || *interj* hier!

hereabouts ['hɪrə,bauts] *adv* hier in der Nähe

hereaf'ter *adv* hiernach || *s* Jenseits *n*

hereby' *adv* hierdurch

hereditary [hɪ'rɛdɪ,tɛri] *adj* erblich, Erb–; **be h.** sich vererben

heredity [hɪ'rɛdɪti] *s* Vererbung *f*

herein' *adv* hierin

hereof' *adv* hiervon

hereon' *adv* hierauf

heresy ['hɛrəsi] *s* Ketzerei *f*

heretic ['hɛrətɪk] *s* Ketzer –in *mf*

heretical [hɪ'rɛtɪkəl] *adj* ketzerisch

heretofore [,hɪrtu'for] *adv* zuvor

here'upon' *adv* daraufhin

herewith' *adv* hiermit; (*in a letter*) anbei, in der Anlage

heritage ['hɛrɪtɪdʒ] *s* Erbe *n*

hermet'ically sealed' [hʌr'mɛtɪkəli] *adj* hermetisch verschlossen

hermit ['hʌrmɪt] *s* Einsiedler –in *mf;* (eccl) Eremit *m*

hermitage ['hʌrmɪtɪdʒ] *s* Eremitage *f*

herni·a ['hʌrnɪ·ə] *s* (**–as** & **–ae** [,i]) Bruch *m*

he·ro ['hɪro] *s* (**–roes**) Held *n*

heroic [hɪ'ro·ɪk] *adj* heldenhaft, Helden–; (pros) heroisch || **heroics** *spl* Heldentaten *pl*

hero'ic age' *s* Helden(zeit)alter *n*

hero'ic coup'let *s* heroisches Reimpaar *n*

hero'ic verse' *s* heroisches Vermaß *n*

heroin ['hɛro·ɪn] *s* Heroin *n*

heroine ['hɛro·ɪn] *s* Heldin *f*

heroism ['hɛro,ɪzəm] *s* Heldenmut *m*

heron ['hɛrən] *s* (orn) Fischreiher *m*

he'ro wor'ship *s* Heldenverehrung *f*

herring ['hɛrɪŋ] *s* Hering *m*

her'ringbone' *s* (*pattern*) Grätenmuster *n;* (*parquetry*) Riemenparkett *n*

hers [hʌrz] *poss pron* der ihre (or ihrige), ihrer

herself' *reflex pron* sich; **she's not h. today** sie ist heute gar nicht wie sonst || *intens pron* selbst, selber

hesitancy ['hɛzɪtənsi] *s* Zaudern *n*

hesitant ['hɛzɪtənt] *adj* zögernd

hesitate ['hɛzɪ,tet] *intr* zögern

hesitation [,hɛzɪ'teʃən] *s* Zögern *n*

heterodox ['hɛtərə,daks] *adj* andersgläubig, heterodox

heterodyne ['hɛtərə,daɪn] *adj* Überlagerungs– || *tr* & *intr* überlagern

heterogeneous [,hɛtərə'dʒɪnɪ·əs] *adj* heterogen

hew [hju] *v* (*pret* **hewed;** *pp* **hewed** & **hewn**) *tr* (stone) hauen; (trees) fällen; **hew down** umhauen

hex [hɛks] *s* (spell) Zauber *m;* (witch) Hexe *f;* **put a hex on** (coll) behexen || *tr* (coll) behexen

hexagon ['hɛksəgan] *s* Hexagon *n*

hey [he] *interj* hei!; **hey there!** heda!

hey'day' *s* Hochblüte *f*, Glanzzeit *f*

H'-hour' *s* (mil) X-Zeit *f*

hi [haɪ] *interj* he!; **hi there!** heda!

hia·tus [haɪ'etəs] *s* (**–tuses** & **–tus**) Lücke *f;* (ling) Hiatus *m*

hibernate ['haɪbər,net] *intr* (& fig) Winterschlaf halten

hibernation [,haɪbər'neʃən] *s* Winterschlaf *m*

hibiscus [haɪ'bɪskəs] *s* Hibiskus *m*

hiccough, hiccup ['hɪkəp] *s* Schluckauf *m*

hick [hɪk] *s* Tölpel *m*

hickory ['hɪkəri] *s* Hickorybaum *m*

hick' town' *s* Kuhdorf *n*

hidden ['hɪdən] *adj* verborgen, versteckt; (*secret*) geheim
hide [haɪd] *s* Haut *f*, Fell *n* || *v* (*pret* **hid** [hɪd]; *pp* **hid** & **hidden** ['hɪdən] *tr* verstecken; (*a view*) verdecken; (*fig*) verbergen; **h. from** verheimlichen vor (*dat*) || *intr* (**out**) sich verstecken
hide'-and-seek' *s* Versteckspiel *n*; **play h.** Versteck spielen
hide'away' *s* Schlupfwinkel *m*
hide'bound' *adj* engherzig
hideous ['hɪdɪ·əs] *adj* gräßlich
hide'out' *s* (coll) Versteck *n*
hid'ing *s* Verstecken *n*; **be in h.** sich versteckt halten; **get a h.** (coll) Prügel bekommen
hid'ing place' *s* Versteck *n*
hierarchy ['haɪ·ə‚rɑrki] *s* Hierarchie *f*
hieroglyphic [‚haɪ·ərə'glɪfɪk] *adj* Hieroglphen– || *s* Hieroglyphe *f*
hi-fi ['haɪ'faɪ] *adj* Hif-fi– || *s* Hi-Fi *n*
high [haɪ] *adj* hoch; (*wind*) stark; (*hopes*) hochgespannt; (*fever*) heftig (*spirits*) gehoben; **h. and dry** auf dem Trockenen; **h. and mighty** hochfahrend; **it is h. time** es ist höchste Zeit || *adv* hoch; **h. and low** weit und breit || *s* (*e.g., in prices*) Hochstand *m*; (aut) höchster Gang *m*; (meteor) Hoch *n*; **on h.** oben; **shift into h.** den höchsten Gang einschalten
high' al'tar *s* Hochaltar *m*
high'ball' *s* Highball *m*
high'born' *adj* hochgeboren
high'boy' *s* hochbeinige Kommode *f*
high'brow' *adj* intellektuell || *s* Intellektuelle *mf*
high' chair' *s* Kinderstuhl *m*
High' Church' *s* Hochkirche *f*
high'-class' *adj* vornehm, herrschaftlich
high' command' *s* Oberkommando *n*
high' cost' of liv'ing *s* hohe Lebenshaltungskosten *pl*
high'er educa'tion *s* Hochschulbildung *f*
high'er-up' *s* (coll) hohes Tier *n*
high'est bid' ['haɪ·ɪst] *s* Meistgebot *n*
high'est bid'der *s* Meistbietende *mf*
high' explo'sive *s* hochexplosiver Sprengstoff *m*
highfalutin [‚haɪfə'lutən] *adj* hochtönend
high' fidel'ity *s* äußerst getreue Tonwiedergabe *f*, High Fidelity *f*
high'-fidel'ity *adj* klanggetreu
high' fre'quency *s* Hochfrequenz *f*
high'-fre'quency *adj* hochfrequent
high' gear' *s* höchster Gang *m*; **shift into h.** den höchsten Gang einschalten; (fig) auf Hochtouren gehen
High' Ger'man *s* Hochdeutsch *n*
high'-grade' *adj* hochfein, Qualitäts–
high'-grade steel' *s* Edelstahl *m*
high'-hand'ed *adj* anmaßend
high' heel' *s* Stöckel *m*
high'-heeled shoe' *s* Stöckelschuh *m*
high' horse' *s*—**come off one's h.** klein beigeben; **get up on one's h.** sich aufs hohe Roß setzen

high' jinks' [‚dʒɪŋks] *spl* Ausgelassenheit *f*
high' jump' *s* (sport) Hochsprung *m*
highland ['haɪlənd] *s* Hochland *n*; **highlands** Hochland *n*
highlander ['haɪləndər] *s* Hochländer –in *mf*
high' life' *s* Prasserei *f*, Highlife *n*
high'light' *s* (*big moment*) Höhepunkt *m*; (*in a picture*) Glanzlicht *n* || *tr* hervorheben; (*in a picture*) Glanzlichter aufsetzen (*dat*)
highly ['haɪli] *adv* hoch, hoch–, höchst; **h. sensitive** hochempfindlich; **speak h. of** in den höchsten Tönen sprechen von; **think h. of** große Stücke halten auf (*acc*)
High' Mass' *s* Hochamt *n*
high'-mind'ed *adj* hochgesinnt
high'-necked' *adj* hochgeschlossen
highness ['haɪnɪs] *s* Höhe *f*; **Highness** (*title*) Hoheit *f*
high' noon' *s*—**at h.** am hellen Mittag
high'-oc'tane *adj* mit hoher Oktanzahl
high'-pitched' *adj* (*voice*) hoch; (*roof*) steil
high'-pow'ered *adj* starkmotorig; **h. engine** Hochleistungsmotor *m*
high' pres'sure *s* Hochdruck *m*
high'-pres'sure *adj* Hochdruck–; **h. area** Hochdruckgebiet *n* || *tr* (com) bearbeiten
high'-priced' *adj* kostspielig
high' priest' *s* Hohe(r)priester *m*
high'-qual'ity *adj* Qualitäts–, hochwertig
high'-rank'ing *adj* hochgestellt
high' rise' *s* Hochbau *m*, Hochhaus *n*
high'road' *s* (fig) sicherer Weg *m*
high' school' *s* Oberschule *f*
high' sea' *s*—**on the high seas** auf offenem Meer
high' soci'ety *s* vornehme Welt *f*, High Society *f*
high'-sound'ing *adj* hochtönend
high'-speed' *adj* Schnell–; (phot) lichtstark
high'-speed steel' *s* Schnelldrehstahl *m*
high'-spir'ited *adj* hochgemut; (*horse*) feurig
high' spir'its *spl* gehobene Stimmung *f*
high-strung ['haɪ'strʌŋ] *adj* überempfindlich
high' ten'sion *s* Hochspannung *f*
high'-ten'sion *adj* Hochspannungs–
high'-test' gas'oline *s* Superbenzin *n*
high' tide' *s* Flut *f*
high' time' *s* höchste Zeit *f*; (sl) Heidenspaß *m*
high' trea'son *s* Hochverrat *m*
high' volt'age *s* Hochspannung *f*
high'-volt'age *adj* Hochspannungs–
high'-wa'ter mark' *s* Hochwassermarke *f*; (fig) Höhepunkt *m*
high'way' *s* Landstraße *f*, Chaussee *f*
high'way'man *s* (**-men**) Straßenräuber *m*
high'way patrol' *s* Straßenstreife *f*
high'way rob'bery *s* Straßenraub *m*
hijack ['haɪ‚dʒæk] *tr* (*a truck*) überfallen und rauben; (*a plane*) entführen

hijacker [ˈhaɪ͵dʒækər] s (of a truck) Straßenräuber –in mf; (of a plane) Entführer –in mf

hiˈjackˈing s Entführung f

hike [haɪk] s Wanderung f; (in prices) Erhöhung f ‖ tr (prices) erhöhen ‖ intr wandern

hiker [ˈhaɪkər] s Wanderer –in mf

hikˈing s Wandern n

hilarious [hɪˈlɛrɪ·əs] adj heiter

hill [hɪl] s Hügel m; **go over the h.** (mil) ausbüxen; **over the h.** (coll) auf dem absteigenden Ast ‖ tr häufeln

hillˈbilˈly adj hinterwäldlerisch ‖ s Hinterwäldler –in mf

hillˈ counˈtry s Hügelland n

hillock [ˈhɪlək] s Hügelchen n

hillˈside s Hang m

hilly [ˈhɪli] adj hügelig

hilt [hɪlt] s Griff m; **armed to the h.** bis an die Zähne bewaffnet; **to the h.** (fig) gründlich

him [hɪm] pers pron (dative) ihm; (accusative) ihn

himselfˈ reflex pron sich; **he is not h. today** er ist heute gar nicht wie sonst ‖ intens pron selbst, selber

hind [haɪnd] adj Hinter– ‖ s Hirschkuh f

hinder [ˈhɪndər] tr (ver)hindern

hindˈmostˈ adj hinterste

hindˈquarˈter s Hinterviertel n; (of a horse) Hinterhand f; (of venison) Ziemer m

hindrance [ˈhɪndrəns] s (to) Hindernis n (für)

hindˈsightˈ s späte Einsicht f

Hindu [ˈhɪndu] adj Hindu– ‖ s Hindu m

hinge [hɪndʒ] s Scharnier n; (of a door) Angel f ‖ intr—**h. on** abhängen von

hint [hɪnt] s Wink m, Andeutung f; **give a broad h.** e–n Wink mit dem Zaunpfahl geben; **take the h.** den Wink verstehen ‖ intr—**h. at** andeuten

hinterland [ˈhɪntər͵lænd] s Hinterland n

hip [hɪp] adj (sl) im Bild ‖ s Hüfte f; (of a roof) Walm m

hipˈbone s Hüftbein n

hipˈjoint s Hüftgelenk n

hipped adj—**h. on** (coll) erpicht auf (acc)

hippopota·mus [͵hɪpə ˈpatəməs] s (-muses & –mi [͵maɪ]) Nilpferd n

hipˈ roofˈ s Walmdach n

hire [haɪr] s Miete f; (salary) Lohn m; **for h.** zu vermieten ‖ tr (workers) anstellen; (rent) mieten; **h. oneself out to** sich verdingen bei; **h. out** vermieten

hiredˈ handˈ s Lohnarbeiter –in mf

hireling [ˈhaɪrlɪŋ] s Mietling m

his [hɪz] poss adj sein ‖ poss pron seiner, der seine (or seinige)

Hispanic [hɪsˈpænɪk] adj hispanisch

hiss [hɪs] s Zischen n ‖ tr auszischen ‖ intr zischen

hissˈing s Zischen n, Gezisch n

hissˈing soundˈ s Zischlaut m

hist [hɪst] interj st!

historian [hɪsˈtorɪ·ən] s Historiker –in mf

historic [hɪsˈtɔrɪk] adj historisch bedeutsam

historical [hɪsˈtɔrɪkəl] adj historisch, geschichtlich

history [ˈhɪstəri] s Geschichte f

historionic [͵hɪstrɪ ˈanɪk] adj schauspielerisch; (fig) übertrieben ‖ **histrionics** spl theatralisches Benehmen n

hit [hɪt] s Schlag m, Stoß m; (a success) Schlager m; (sport) Treffer m; (theat) Zugstück n ‖ v (pret & pp **hit**; ger **hitting**) tr (e.g., with the fist) schlagen; (a note, target) treffen; **hit bottom** (fig) auf dem Nullpunkt angekommen sein; **hit it off** gut miteinander auskommen; **hit one's head against** mit dem Kopf stoßen gegen; **hit s.o. hard** (said of misfortunes, etc.) schwer treffen; **hit the road** sich auf den Weg machen; **hit the sack** sich hinhauen ‖ intr schlagen; **hit on** (or **upon**) kommen auf (acc)

hitˈ-and-runˈ adj (driver) flüchtig; **h. accident** Unfall m mit Fahrerflucht; **h. attack** Zerstörangriff m

hitch [hɪtʃ] s (difficulty) Haken m; (knot) Stich m; (term of service) Dienstzeit f; **that's the h.** das ist ja gerade der Haken; **without a h.** reibungslos ‖ tr spannen; **h. a ride** (to) per Anhalter fahren (nach); **h. to the wagon** vor (or an) den Wagen spannen; **h. up** (horses) anspannen; (trousers) hochziehen

hitchˈhikeˈ intr per Anhalter fahren

hitchˈing postˈ s Pfosten m (zum Anbinden von Pferden)

hither [ˈhɪðər] adv her, hierher; **h. and thither** hierhin und dorthin

hithertoˈ adv bisher

hitˈ or missˈ adv aufs Geratewohl

hitˈ-or-missˈ adj planlos

hitter [ˈhɪtər] s Schläger m

hive [haɪv] s Bienenstock m; **hives** (pathol) Nesselausschlag m

hoard [hord] s Hort m ‖ tr & intr horten; (food) hamstern

hoarder [ˈhordər] s Hamsterer –in mf

hoardˈing s Horten n; (of food) Hamstern n

hoarfrost [ˈhor͵frɔst] s Rauhreif m

hoarse [hors] adj heiser

hoarseness [ˈhorsnɪs] s Heiserkeit f

hoary [ˈhori] adj ergraut; (fig) altersgrau

hoax [hoks] s Schnabernack m ‖ tr anführen

hob [hab] s Kamineinsatz m

hobble [ˈhabəl] s Humpeln n ‖ intr humpeln

hobby [ˈhabi] s Hobby n

hobˈbyhorseˈ s (stick with horse's head) Steckenpferd n; (rocking horse) Schaukelpferd n

hobˈgobˈlin s Kobold m; (bogy) Schreckgespenst n

hobˈnailˈ s grober Schuhnagel m

hob·nob [ˈhɑbˌnɑb] v (pret & pp
–nobbed; ger –nobbing) intr—**h. with**
freundschaftlich verkehren mit
ho·bo [ˈhobo] s (–bos & –boes) Landstreicher m
hock [hɑk] s (of a horse) Sprunggelenk
n; **in h.** verpfändet ‖ tr (hamstring)
lähmen; (pawn) (coll) verpfänden
hockey [ˈhɑki] s Hockey n
hoc′key stick′ s Hockeystock m
hock′shop′ s (coll) Leihhaus n
hocus-pocus [ˈhokəsˈpokəs] s Hokuspokus m
hod [hɑd] s Mörteltrog m
hodgepodge [ˈhɑdʒˌpɑdʒ] s Mischmasch m
hoe [ho] s Hacke f, Haue f ‖ tr hacken
hog [hɔg] s Schwein n ‖ v (pret & pp
hogged; ger hogging) tr (sl) gierig
an sich reißen; **hog the road** rücksichtslos fahren
hog′back′ s scharfer Gebirgskamm m
hog′ bris′tle s Schweinsborste f
hoggish [ˈhɔgɪʃ] adj schweinisch, gefräßig
hog′wash′ s (nonsense) Quatsch m
hoist [hɔɪst] s (apparatus for lifting)
Hebezeug n; (act of lifting) Hochwinden n ‖ tr hochwinden; (a flag,
sail) hissen
hokum [ˈhokəm] s (nonsense) (coll)
Quatsch m; (flimflam) (coll) Effekthascherei f
hold [hold] s Halt m, Griff m; (naut)
Raum m; (sport) Griff m; **get h. of**
(catch) erwischen; (acquire) erwerben; **get h. of oneself** sich fassen;
take h. of anfassen ‖ v (pret & pp
held [hɛld] tr halten; (contain) enthalten; (regard as) halten für; (one's
breath) anhalten; (an audience) fesseln; (a meeting, election, court) abhalten; (an office, position) beklei-
den, innehaben; (talks) führen; (a
viewpoint) vertreten; (a meet) (sport)
veranstalten; **able to h. one's liquor**
trinkfest; **h. back** zurückhalten;
(news) geheimhalten; **h. dear** wert-
halten; **h. down** niederhalten; **h. in
contempt** verachten; **h. it!** halt!; **h.
off** abhalten; **h. office** amtieren; **h.
one's ground** die Stellung halten;
h. one's own seinen Mann stehen;
h. one's own against sich behaupten
gegen; **h. one's tongue** den Mund
halten; **h. open** (a door) aufhalten;
h. out (a hand) hinhalten; (proffer)
vorhalten; **h. over** (e.g., a play) verlängern; **h. s.th. against s.o.** j–m
etw nachtragen; **h. sway** walten; **h.
under** niederhalten; **h. up** (raise)
hochhalten; (detain) aufhalten; (traffic) behindern; (rob) (räuberisch)
überfallen; **h. up to ridicule** dem
Spott preisgeben; **h. the line** (telp) am
Apparat bleiben; **h. the road well**
e–e gute Straßenlage haben; **h. together** zusammenhalten; **h. water**
(fig) stichhaltig sein ‖ intr (said of
a knot) halten; **h. back** sich zurückhalten; **h. forth** (coll) dozieren; **h. on**
warten; **h. on to** festhalten, sich

festhalten an (dat); **h. out** aushalten;
h. out for abwarten; **h. true** gelten;
h. true for zutreffen auf (acc); **h. up**
(wear well) halten
holder [ˈholdər] s (device) Halter m;
(e.g., of a title) Inhaber –in mf
hold′ing s (of a meeting) Abhaltung f;
(of an office) Bekleidung f; **holdings**
Besitz m, Bestand m
hold′ing com′pany s Holdinggesell-
schaft f
hold′ing pat′tern s (aer) Platzrunde f
hold′-o′ver s Überbleibsel n
hold′up′ s (delay) Aufenthalt m; (robbery) Raubüberfall m; (in traffic)
Verkehrsstauung f
hold′up man′ s Räuber m
hole [hol] s Loch n; (of animals) Bau
m; **h. in the wall** Loch n; **in a h.** in
der Patsche; **in the h.** hängengeblie-
ben, e.g., **I am ten dollars in the h.**
ich bin mit zehn Dollar hängenge-
blieben; **pick holes in** (fig) herum-
kritisieren an (dat); **wear holes in**
völlig abtragen ‖ intr—**h. out** (golf)
ins Loch spielen; **h. up** sich vergra-
ben; (fig) sich verstecken
holiday [ˈhɑlɪˌde] s Feiertag m; (vacation) Ferien pl; **take a h.** e–n
freien Tag machen, Urlaub nehmen
hol′iday mood′ s Ferienstimmung f
holiness [ˈholɪnɪs] s Heiligkeit f; **His
Holiness** Seine Heiligkeit
Holland [ˈhɑlənd] s Holland n
Hollander [ˈhɑləndər] s Holländer –in
mf
hollow [ˈhɑlo] adj hohl ‖ s Höhle f,
Höhlung f; (geol) Talmulde f ‖ tr—
h. out aushöhlen
hol′low-cheeked′ adj hohlwangig
hol′low-eyed′ adj hohläugig
holly [ˈhɑli] s Stechpalme f
holm′ oak′ [hom] s Steineiche f
holocaust [ˈhɑləˌkɔst] s Brandopfer n;
(disaster) Brandkatastrophe f
holster [ˈholstər] s Pistolentasche f
holy [ˈholi] adj heilig; **h. smokes!**
(coll) heiliger Strohsack!
Ho′ly Commun′ion s Kommunion f,
das Heilige Abendmahl
ho′ly day′ s Feiertag m
Ho′ly Ghost′ s Heiliger Geist m
Ho′ly of Ho′lies s Allerheiligste n
ho′ly or′ders spl Priesterweihe f
Ho′ly Scrip′ture s die Heilige Schrift
Ho′ly See′ s Heiliger Stuhl m
Ho′ly Sep′ulcher s Heiliges Grab n
Ho′ly Spir′it s Heiliger Geist m
ho′ly wa′ter s Weihwasser n
Ho′ly Week′ s Karwoche f
Ho′ly Writ′ s die Heilige Schrift
homage [ˈ(h)ɑmɪdʒ] s Huldigung f;
pay h. to huldigen (dat)
home [hom] adj inländisch, Innen– ‖
adv nach Hause, heim; **bring h. to
s.o.** j–m beibringen ‖ s Heim n;
(house) Haus n, Wohnung f; (place
of residence) Wohnort m; (institution) Heim n; **at h.** zu Hause, daheim; **at h. and abroad** im In– und
Ausland; **feel at h.** sich zu Hause
fühlen; **for the h.** für den Hausbe-

darf; **from h.** von zu Hause; **h. for
the aged** Altersheim *n;* **h. for the
blind** Blindenheim *n;* **h. of one's own**
Zuhause *n*
home' address' *s* Privatadresse *f*
home'-baked' *adj* hausbacken
home' base' *s* (aer) Heimatflughafen *m*
home'bod'y *s* Stubenhocker –in *mf*
homebred ['hom,brɛd] *adj* einheimisch
home'-brew' *s* selbstgebrautes Getränk
n
home'-brewed' *adj* selbstgebraut
home'com'ing *s* Heimkehr *f*
home' comput'er *s* Heimcomputer *m*
home' coun'try *s* Heimatstaat *m*
home' econom'ics *s* Hauswirtschafts-
lehre *f*
home'-fried pota'toes *spl,* **home' fries'**
[,fraɪz] *spl* Bratkartoffeln *pl*
home' front' *s* Heimatfront *f*
home'-grown' *adj* selbstgezogen
home' guard' *s* Landsturm *m*
home'land' *s* Heimatland *n*
homeless ['homlɪs] *adj* obdachlos || *s*
Obdachlose *mf*
home'like' *adj* anheimelnd
homely ['homli] *adj* unschön
home'made' *adj* selbstgemacht; (culin)
selbstgebacken
home'mak'er *s* Hausfrau *f*
home' of'fice *s* Hauptbüro *n*
home' own'er *s* Hausbesitzer –in *mf*
home' plate' *s* Schlagmal *n*
home' rem'edy *s* Hausmittel *n*
home' rule' *s* Selbstverwaltung *f*
home' run' *s* (baseball) Vier-Mal-Lauf
m
home'sick' *adj*—**be h.** Heimweh haben
home'sick'ness *s* Heimweh *n*
homespun ['hom,spʌn] *adj* selbstgemacht; (fig) einfach
home'stead' *s* Siedlerstelle *f*
home'stretch' *s* Zielgerade *f*
home' team' *s* Ortsmannschaft *f*
home'town' *adj* Heimat– || *s* Heimat-
stadt *f*
homeward ['homwərd] *adv* heimwärts
home'ward jour'ney *s* Heimreise *f*
home'work' *s* Hausaufgabe *f*
homey ['homi] *adj* anheimelnd
homicidal [,hamɪ'saɪdəl] *adj* mörderisch
homicide ['hamɪ,saɪd] *s* (act) Totschlag *m;* (person) Totschläger –in
mf
hom'icide squad' *s* Mordkommission *f*
homily ['hamɪli] *s* Homilie *f*
hom'ing device' ['homɪŋ] *s* Zielsucher
m
hom'ing pi'geon *s* Brieftaube *f*
homogeneous [,homə'dʒɪnɪ·əs] *adj* homogen
homogenize [ha'madʒə,naɪz] *tr* homo-
genisieren
homonym ['hamənɪm] *s* Homonym *n*
homosexual [,homə'sɛkʃʊ·əl] *adj* ho-
mosexuell || *s* Homosexuelle *mf*
hone [hon] *s* Wetzstein *m* || *tr* honen
honest ['anɪst] *adj* ehrlich, aufrecht
honestly ['anɪstli] *adv* ehrlich; **to tell
you h.** offengestanden || *interj* auf
mein Wort!

honesty ['anɪsti] *s* Ehrlichkeit *f*
hon·ey ['hʌni] *s* Honig *m;* (as a term
of endearment) Schatz *m,* Liebling
m || *v* (pret & pp –**eyed** & –**ied**) *tr*
versüßen; (speak sweetly to)
schmeicheln (dat)
hon'eybee' *s* Honigbiene *f*
hon'eycomb' *s* Honigwabe *f* || *tr* (e.g.,
a hill) wabenartig durchlöchern
hon'eyed *adj* mit Honig gesüßt; (fig)
honigsüß
hon'ey lo'cust *s* Honigdorn *m*
hon'eymoon' *s* Flitterwochen *pl* || *intr*
die Flitterwochen verbringen
hon'eysuck'le *s* Geißblatt *n*
honk [hɔŋk] *s* (aut) Hupensignal *n* ||
tr—**h. the horn** hupen || *intr* hupen
honkytonk ['hɔŋkɪ,tɔŋk] *s* (sl) Tingeltangel *m* & *n*
honor ['anər] *s* Ehre *f;* (award) Auszeichnung *f;* (chastity) Ehre *f;* **be
held in h.** in Ehren gehalten werden;
consider it an h. es sich [dat] zur
Ehre anrechnen; **do the honors** die
Honneurs machen; **have the h. of**
(ger) sich beehren zu (inf); **in s.o.'s
h.** j–m zu Ehren; **your Honor** Euer
Gnaden || *tr* ehren; (favor) beehren;
(a check) honorieren; **feel honored**
sich geehrt fühlen
honorable ['anərəbəl] *adj* (person) ehrbar; (intentions) ehrlich; (peace
treaty) ehrenvoll
honorari·um [,anə'rɛrɪ·əm] *s* (–**ums** &
–**a** [ə]) Honorar *n;* **give an h. to**
honorieren
hon'orary degree' *s* Ehrendoktorat *n*
honorific [,anə'rɪfɪk] *adj* ehrend,
Ehren– || *s* Ehrentitel *m*
hooch [hutʃ] *s* (sl) Fusel *m,* Schnaps
m
hood [hʊd] *s* Haube *f;* (of a monk)
Kapuze *f;* (of a baby carriage) Verdeck *n;* (sl) Gangster *m;* (aut)
Motorhaube *f;* (culin) Rauchabzug
m; (educ) Talarüberwurf *m* || *tr* mit
e–r Haube versehen; (fig) verhüllen
hoodlum ['hʊdləm] *s* Ganove *m*
hoodoo ['hudu] *s* Unglücksbringer *m*
|| *tr* Unglück bringen (dat)
hood'wink' *tr* täuschen
hooey ['hu·i] *s* (sl) Quatsch *m*
hoof [huf], [hʊf] *s* Huf *m* || *tr*—**h. it**
auf Schusters Rappen reiten
hoof'beat' *s* Hufschlag *m*
hook [hʊk] *s* Haken *m;* (angl) Angelhaken *m;* (baseball) Kurvball *m;*
(box) Haken *m;* (golf) Hook *m;* **by
h. or by crook** so oder so; **h., line,
and sinker** mit allem Drum und
Dran; **off the h.** (coll) aus der
Schlinge; **on one's own h.** (coll) auf
eigene Faust || *tr* festhaken, ein-
haken; (e.g., a boyfriend) angeln;
(steal) schnappen; (box) e–n Haken
versetzen (dat); (golf) nach links
verziehen; **h. up** zuhaken; (elec) an-
schließen || *intr* sich krümmen; **h. up
with s.o.** sich j–m anschließen
hook' and eye' *s* Haken *m* und Öse *f*
hook'-and-lad'der truck' *s* Feuerwehr-
fahrzeug *n* mit Drehleiter

hooked *adj* hakenförmig; **h. on drugs** rauschgiftsüchtig
hooker ['hʊkər] *s* (sl) Nutte *f*
hook'nose' *s* Hakennase *f*
hook'up' *s* (elec, electron) Schaltung *f*; (electron) Schaltbild *n*; (rad, telv) Gemeinschaftsschaltung *f*
hook'worm' *s* Hakenwurm *m*
hooky ['hʊki] *s*—**play h.** schwänzen
hooligan ['hulɪɡən] *s* Straßenlümmel *m*
hoop [hup] *s* Reifen *m* ‖ *tr* binden
hoop' skirt' *s* Reifrock *m*
hoot [hut] *s* Geschrei *n*; **not give a h. about** keinen Pfifferling geben für ‖ *intr* schreien; **h. at** anschreien
hoot' owl' *s* Waldkauz *m*
hop [hap] *s* Hopser *m*; (*dance*) Tanz *m*; hops (bot) Hopfen *m* ‖ *v* (*pret & pp* hopped; *ger* hopping) *tr* (*e.g., a train*) aufspringen auf (*acc*); **hop a ride** (coll) mitfahren ‖ *intr* hüpfen; **hop around** herumhüpfen
hope [hop] *s* (**of**) Hoffnung *f* (auf *acc*); **beyond h.** hoffnungslos; **not get up one's hopes** sich [*dat*] keine Hoffnungen machen ‖ *tr* hoffen ‖ *intr* hoffen; **h. for** hoffen auf (*acc*); **h. for the best** das Beste hoffen; **I h.** (*parenthetical*) hoffentlich
hope' chest' *s* Aussteuertruhe *f*
hopeful ['hopfəl] *adj* hoffnungsvoll ‖ *s* (pol) Kandidat –in *mf*
hopefully ['hopfəli] *adv* hoffentlich
hopeless ['hoplɪs] *adj* hoffnungslos
hopper ['hapər] *s* Fülltrichter *m*; (*in a toilet*) Spülkasten *m*; (*storage container*) Vorratsbehälter *m*; (data proc) Kartenmagazin *n*
hop'per car' *s* (rr) Selbstentladewagen *m*
hop'ping mad' *adj* fuchsteufelswild
hop'scotch' *s* Himmel und Hölle
horde [hord] *s* Horde *f*
horehound ['hor ˌhaʊnd] *s* (*lozenge*) Hustenbonbon *m*; (bot) Andorn *m*
horizon [hə'raɪzən] *s* Horizont *m*
horizontal [ˌharɪ'zɑntəl] *adj* horizontal, waagrecht ‖ *s* Horizontale *f*
horizon'tal bar' *s* (gym) Reck *n*
horizon'tal controls' *spl* (aer) Seitenleitwerk *n*
horizon'tal sta'bilizer *s* (aer) Höhenflosse *f*
hormone ['hɔrmon] *s* Hormon *n*
horn [hɔrn] *s* (*of an animal; wind instrument*) Horn *n*; (aut) Hupe *f*; **blow one's own h.** (coll) ins eigene Horn stoßen; **blow the h.** (aut) hupen; **horns** (*of an animal*) Geweih *n* ‖ *intr*—**h. in** (**on**) (coll) sich eindrängen (in *acc*)
hornet ['hɔrnɪt] *s* Hornisse *f*
hor'net's nest' *s*—**stir up a h.** in ein Wespennest stechen
horn' of plen'ty *s* Füllhorn *n*
horn'-rimmed glass'es *spl* Hornbrille *f*
horny ['hɔrni] *adj* (*callous*) schwielig; (*having horn-like projections*) verhornt; (sl) geil
horoscope ['hɔrə ˌskop] *s* Horoskop *n*; **cast s.o.'s h.** j–m das Horoskop stellen

horrible ['hɔrɪbəl] *adj* (& *coll*) schrecklich
horrid ['hɔrɪd] *adj* abscheulich
horri-fy ['hɔrɪ ˌfaɪ] *v* (*pret & pp* –fied) *tr* erschrecken, entsetzen
horror ['hɔrər] *s* Schrecken *m*, Entsetzen *n*
hor'ror sto'ry *s* Schauergeschichte *f*
hors d'oeuvre [ɔr'dʌrv] *s* (**hors d'oeuvres** [ɔr'dʌrvz]) Vorspeise *f*
horse [hɔrs] *s* Pferd *n*; (carp) Sägebock *m*; **back the wrong h.** (fig) auf's falsche Pferd setzen; **bet on a h.** auf ein Pferd setzen; **hold your horses** immer mit der Ruhe!; **h. of another color** e–e andere Sache; **mount a h.** zu Pferd steigen; **straight from the horse's mouth** direkt von der Quelle ‖ *intr*—**h. around** (sl) herumalbern; **stop horsing around** laß den Unsinn!
horse'back' *s*—**on h.** zu Pferd ‖ *adv*—**ride h.** reiten
horse'back rid'ing *s* Reiten *n*
horse' blan'ket *s* Pferdedecke *f*
horse' chest'nut *s* Roßkastanie *f*
horse' col'lar *s* Kummet *n*
horse' doc'tor *s* (coll) Roßarzt *m*
horse'fly' *s* Pferdebremse *f*
horse'hair' *s* Roßhaar *n*, Pferdehaar *n*
horse'laugh' *s* wieherndes Gelächter *n*
horse'man *s* (**–men**) Reiter *m*
horse'manship' *s* Reitkunst *f*
horse' meat' *s* Pferdefleisch *n*
horse' op'era *s* (coll) Wildwestfilm *m*
horse'play' *s* grober Unfug *m*
horse'pow'er *s* Pferdestärke *f*
horse' race' *s* Pferderennen *n*
horse'rad'ish *s* Meerrettich *m*, Kren *m*
horse' sense' *s* gesunder Menschenverstand *m*
horse' shoe' *s* Hufeisen *n* ‖ *tr* beschlagen
horse'shoe mag'net *s* Hufeisenmagnet *m*
horse' show' *s* Pferdeschau *f*
horse' tail' *s* Pferdeschwanz *m*
horse' trad'er *s* Pferdehändler *m*; (fig) Kuhhändler *m*
horse' trad'ing *s* Pferdehandel *m*; (fig) Kuhhandel *m*
horse'whip' *s* Reitpeitsche *f* ‖ *v* (*pret & pp* –whipped; *ger* –whipping) *tr* mit der Reitpeitsche schlagen
horse'wom'an *s* (**–wom'en**) Reiterin *f*
horsy ['hɔrsi] *adj* pferdeartig; (*horse-loving*) pferdeliebend
horticultural [ˌhɔrtɪ'kʌltʃərəl] *adj* Gartenbau-
horticulture ['hɔrtɪ ˌkʌltʃər] *s* Gartenbau *m*, Gärtnerei *f*
hose [hoz] *s* Schlauch *m* ‖ *s* (**hose**) Strumpf *m*; (*collectively*) Strümpfe *pl*
hosiery ['hoʒəri] *s* Strumpfwaren *pl*; (*mill*) Strumpffabrik *f*
hospice ['haspɪs] *s* Hospiz *n*
hospitable ['haspɪtəbəl], [has'pɪtəbəl] *adj* gastlich, gastfreundlich
hospital ['haspɪtəl] *s* Hospital *n*, Krankenhaus *n*; (mil) Lazarett *n*
hospitality [ˌhaspɪ'tælɪti] *s* Gast-

freundschaft *f;* **show s.o. h.** j–m
Gastfreundschaft gewähren
hospitalize [ˈhɑspɪtəˌlaɪz] *tr* ins
Krankenhaus einweisen
hos′pital ship′ *s* Lazarettschiff *f*
hos′pital train′ *s* Sanitätszug *m*
hos′pital ward′ *s* Kranken(haus)station
f
host [host] *s* Gastgeber *m;* (*at an inn*)
Wirt *m;* (*in a television show*) Leiter
m; (*multitude*) Heerschar *f;* (*army*)
Heer *n;* **Host** (relig) Hostie *f*
hostage [ˈhɑstɪdʒ] *s* Geisel *mf*
hostel [ˈhɑstəl] *s* Herberge *f*
hostelry [ˈhɑstəlri] *s* Gasthaus *n*
hostess [ˈhostɪs] *s* Gastgeberin *f;* (*at
an inn*) Wirtin *f;* (*on an airplane*)
Stewardeß *f;* (*in a restaurant*) Emp-
fangsdame *f;* (*on a television show*)
Leiterin *f*
hostile [ˈhɑstɪl] *adj* feindlich; **(to)**
feindselig (gegen)
hostility [hasˈtɪlɪti] *s* Feindseligkeit *f;*
hostilities Feindseligkeiten *pl*
hot [hɑt] *adj* heiß; (*spicy*) scharf;
(*meal*) warm; (*stolen, sought by the
police, radioactive; jazz, tip*) heiß;
(*trail, scent*) frisch; (*in heat*) geil;
be hot (*said of the sun*) stechen; **get
into hot water** in die Patsche geraten;
hot and bothered aufgeregt; **hot from
the press** frisch von der Presse; **hot
on s.o.'s trail** j–m dicht auf der Spur;
hot stuff (sl) toller Kerl *m;* **I am hot**
mir ist heiß; **I don't feel so hot** (coll)
ich fühle mich nicht besonders; **she's
not so hot** (coll) sie is nicht so toll
hot′ air′ *s* Heißluft *f;* (sl) blauer Dunst
m
hot′-air heat′ *s* Heißlufteizung *f*
hot′bed′ *s* Frühbeet *n;* (fig) Brutstätte
f
hot′-blood′ed *adj* heißblütig
hot′ cake′ *s* Pfannkuchen *m;* **sell like
hot cakes** wie warme Semmeln weggehen
hotchpotch [ˈhɑtʃˌpɑtʃ] *s* (coll) Mischmasch *m*
hot′ dog′ *s* warmes Würstel *n*
hotel [hoˈtɛl] *adj* Hotel– ‖ *s* Hotel *n;*
(*small hotel*) Gasthof *m*
hotel′ busi′ness *s* Hotelgewerbe *n*
hotel′man *s* (–men) Hotelbesitzer *m*
hot′foot′ *adv* in aller Eile ‖ *tr*—**h. it**
schleunigst eilen; **h. it after s.o.** j–m
nacheilen
hot′head′ *s* Hitzkopf *m*
hot′-head′ed *adj* hitzköpfig
hot′house′ *s* Treibhaus *n,* Gewächshaus
n
hot′ line′ *s* (telp) heißer Draht *m*
hot′ mon′ey *s* (sl) Fluchtkapital *n*
hot′ pep′per *s* scharfe Paprikaschote *f*
hot′ plate′ *s* Heizplatte *f*
hot′ pota′to *s* (coll) schwieriges Problem *n*
hot′ rod′ *s* (sl) frisiertes altes Auto *n*
hot′ rod′der [ˌrɑdər] *s* (sl) Fahrer *m*
e–s frisierten Autos
hot′ seat′ *s* (sl) elektrischer Stuhl *m*
hot′ springs′ *spl* Thermalquellen *pl*
hot′ tem′per *s* hitziges Temperament *n*

hot′-tem′pered *adj* hitzig, hitzköpfig
hot′ war′ *s* Schießkrieg *m*
hot′ wa′ter *s* Heißwasser *n;* **be in h.**
(fig) in der Tinte sitzen; **get into h.**
(fig) in die Patsche geraten
hot′-wa′ter bot′tle *s* Gummiwärm-
flasche *f*
hot′-wa′ter heat′er *s* Heißwasserberei-
ter *m*
hot′-wa′ter heat′ing *s* Heißwasserhei-
zung *f*
hot′-wa′ter tank′ *s* Heißwasserspeicher
m
hound [haund] *s* Jagdhund *m* ‖ *tr*
hetzen
hour [aur] *s* Stunde *f;* **after hours**
nach Arbeitsschluß; **at any h.** zu
jeder Tageszeit; **by the h.** stunden-
weise; **every h.** stündlich; **for an h.**
e–e Stunde lang; **for a solid h.** e–e
geschlagene Stunde lang; **for hours**
stundenlang; **h. of death** Todes-
stunde *f;* **h. overtime** Überstunde *f;*
in the small hours in den frühen
Morgenstunden; **keep late hours** spät
zu Bett gehen; **keep regular hours**
zur Zeit aufstehen und schlafengehen; **on the h.** zur vollen Stunde
–hour *suf* –stündig
hour′glass′ *s* Stundenglas *n*
hour′ hand′ *s* Stundenzeiger *m*
hourly [ˈaurli] *adj* stündlich; **h. rate**
Stundensatz *m;* **h. wages** Stunden-
lohn *m* ‖ *adv* stündlich
house [haus] *adj* (*boat, dress*) Haus–
‖ *s* (**houses** [ˈhauzɪz]) Haus *n;* **h.
and home** Haus und Hof; **h. for rent**
Haus *n* zu vermieten; **keep h. (for
s.o.)** (j–m) den Haushalt führen; **on
the h.** auf Kosten des Wirts; **put
one's h. in order** (fig) seine Angelegenheiten in Ordnung bringen ‖
[hauz] *tr* unterbringen
house′ arrest′ *s* Hausarrest *m*
house′boat′ *s* Hausboot *n*
house′break′ing *s* Einbruchsdiebstahl
m
housebroken [ˈhausˌbrokən] *adj* stu-
benrein
house′ clean′ing *s* Hausputz *m;* (fig)
Säuberungsaktion *f*
house′fly′ *s* Stubenfliege *f*
houseful [ˈhausˌful] *s* Hausvoll *n*
house′guest′ *s* Logierbesuch *m*
house′hold′ *adj* Haushalts– ‖ *s* Haushalt *m*
house′hold′er *s* Haushaltsvorstand *m*
house′hold fur′nishings *spl* Hausrat *m*
house′hold needs′ *spl* Hausbedarf *m*
house′hold word′ *s* Alltagswort *n*
house′ hunt′ing *s* Wohungssuche *f*
house′keep′er *s* Haushälterin *f*
house′keep′ing *s* Hauswirtschaft *f*
house′maid′ *s* Dienstmädchen *n*
house′moth′er *s* Hausmutter *f*
house′ of cards′ *s* Kartenhaus *n*
House′ of Com′mons *s* Unterhaus *n*
house′ of corec′tion *s* Zuchthaus *n,*
Besserungsanstalt *f*
house′ of ill′ repute′ *s* öffentliches
Haus *n*
House′ of Lords′ *s* Oberhaus *n*

house' physi'cian s Krankenhausarzt m; (in a hotel) Hausarzt m
house'-to-house' adv von Haus zu Haus; **sell h.** hausieren
house'warm'ing s Einzugsfest n
house'wife' s (wives') Hausfrau f
house'work' s Hausarbeit f
hous'ing s Unterbringung f, Wohnung f; (mach) Gehäuse n
hous'ing devel'opment s Siedlung f
hous'ing pro'ject s Sozialsiedlung f
hous'ing short'age s Wohnungsnot f
hous'ing un'it s Wohneinheit f
hovel ['hʌvəl], ['hɑvəl] s Hütte f
hover ['hʌvər] intr schweben; (fig) pendeln; **h. about** sich herumtreiben in der Nähe von
Hov'ercraft' s (trademark) Schwebefahrzeug n
how [haʊ] adv wie; **and how!** und wie!; **how about** ...? (would you care for ...?) wie wäre es mit ...?; (what's the progress of ...?) wie steht es mit ...?; (what do you think of ...?) was halten Sie von ...?; **how are you?** wie befinden Sie sich?; **how beautiful!** wie schön!; **how come?** wieso?, wie kommt es?; **how do you do?** (as a greeting) guten Tag!; (at an introduction) freut mich sehr!; **how many** wie viele; **how much** wieviel; **how on earth** wie in aller Welt; **how the devil** wie zum Teufel || s Wie n
how-do-you-do ['haʊdəjə'du] s—**that's a fine h.!** (coll) das ist e-e schöne Geschichte!
howev'er adv jedoch, aber; (with adjectives and adverbs) wie ... auch immer; **h. it may be** wie es auch sein mag
howitzer ['haʊ·ɪtsər] s Haubitze f
howl [haʊl] s Geheul n, Gebrüll n || tr heulen, brüllen; **h. down** (a speaker) niederschreien; **h. out** hinausbrüllen || intr (said of a dog, wolf, wind, etc.) heulen; (in pain, anger) brüllen; **h. with laughter** vor Lachen brüllen
howler ['haʊlər] s (coll) Schnitzer m
hub [hʌb] s Nabe, f, Radnabe f
hubbub ['hʌbʌb] s Rummel m
hubby ['hʌbi] s (coll) Mann m
hub'cap' s Radkappe f
huckleberry ['hʌkəl‚beri] s Heidelbeere f
huckster ['hʌkstər] s (hawker) Straßenhändler m; (peddler) Hausierer m; (adman) Reklamefachmann m || tr verhökern
huddle ['hʌdəl] s (fb) Zusammendrängen n; **go into a h.** die Köpfe zusammenstecken || intr sich zusammendrängen; (fb) sich um den Mannschaftsführer drängen
hue [hju] s Farbton m
hue' and cry' s Zetergeschrei n
huff [hʌf] s Aufbrausen n; **in a h.** beleidigt
huffy ['hʌfi] adj übelnehmerisch
hug [hʌg] s Umarmung f; **give s.o. a hug** j-n an sich drücken || v (pret & pp **hugged**; ger **hugging**) tr umar-

men; **hug the road** gut auf der Straße liegen; **hug the shore** sich dicht an der Küste halten || intr einander herzen
huge [hjudʒ] adj riesig, ungeheuer; **h. success** (theat) Bombenerfolg m
hulk [hʌlk] s (body of an old ship) Schiffsrumpf m; (old ship used as a warehouse, etc.) Hulk m & f; **h. of a man** Koloß m
hulk'ing adj ungeschlacht
hull [hʌl] s (of seed) Schale f; (naut) Schiffsrumpf m || tr schälen
hullabaloo [‚hʌləbə'lu] s Heidenlärm m
hum [hʌm] s Summen n || v (pret & pp **hummed**; ger **humming**) tr summen; **hum** (e.g., a tune) **to oneself** vor sich hin summen || intr summen; (fig) in lebhafter Bewegung sein
human ['hjumən] adj menschlich, Menschen–
hu'man be'ing s Mensch m, menschliches Wesen n
humane [hju'men] adj human
humaneness [hju'mennɪs] s Humanität f
humanistic [hjumə'nɪstɪk] adj humanistisch
humanitarian [hju‚mænɪ'terɪ·ən] adj menschenfreundlich || s Menschenfreund –in mf
humanity [hju'mænɪti] s (mankind) Menschheit f; (humaneness) Humanität f, Menschlichkeit f; **humanities** Geisteswissenschaften pl; (Greek and Latin studies) klassische Philologie f
humanize ['hjumə‚naɪz] tr zivilisieren
hu'mankind' s Menschengeschlecht n
humanly ['hjumənli] adv menschlich; **h. possible** menschenmöglich; **h. speaking** nach menschlichen Begriffen
hu'man na'ture s menschliche Natur f
hu'man race' s Menschengeschlecht n
humble ['(h)ʌmbəl] adv demütig; (origens) niedrig; **in my h. opinion** nach meiner unmaßgeblichen Meinung || tr demütigen
hum'ble pie' s—eat h. sich demütigen
hum'bug' s Humbug m
hum'drum' adj eintönig
humer·us ['hjumərəs] s (-i [‚aɪ]) Oberarmknochen m
humid ['hjumɪd] adj feucht
humidifier [hju'mɪdɪ‚faɪ·ər] s Verdunster m
humidity [hju'mɪdɪti s Feuchtigkeit f
humiliate [hju'mɪlɪ‚et] tr erniedrigen
humil'iating adj schmachvoll
humiliation [hju‚mɪlɪ'eʃən] s Erniedrigung f
hum'mingbird' s Kolibri m
humor ['(h)jumər] s (comic quality) Komik f; (frame of mind) Laune f; **in bad** (or **good**) **h.** bei schlechter (or guter) Laune || tr bei guter Laune halten
humorist ['(h)jumərɪst] s Humorist –in mf
humorous ['(h)jumərəs] adj humorvoll
hump [hʌmp] s Buckel m; (of a camel)

Höcker *m;* *(slight elevation)* kleiner Hügel *m;* **over the h.** (fig) über den Berg ‖ *tr*—**h.** its back *(said of an animal)* e-n Buckel machen
hump'back' *s* Buckel *m;* *(person)* Bucklige *mf*
Hun [hʌn] *s* (hist) Hunne *m,* Hunnin *f*
hunch [hʌntʃ] *s* *(hump)* Buckel *m;* (coll) Ahnung *f* ‖ *intr*—**h.** over sich bücken über *(acc)*
hunch'back' *s* Bucklige *mf*
hunch'backed' *adj* bucklig
hunched *adj*—**h. up** zusammengekauert
hundred ['hʌndrəd] *adj & pron* hundert ‖ *s* Hundert *n;* **by the h.**(s) hundertweise; **hundreds (and hundreds) of** Hunderte (und aber Hunderte) von
hun'dredfold' *adj & adv* hundertfach
hundredth ['hʌndrədθ] *adj & pron* hundertste; **for the h. time** (fig) zum X-ten Male; **h. anniversary** Hundertjahrfeier *f* ‖ *s* *(fraction)* Hundertstel *n*
hun'dredweight' *s* Zentner *n*
Hungarian [hʌŋ'gerɪ·ən] *adj* ungarisch ‖ *s* *(person)* Ungar -in *mf;* *(language)* Ungarisch *n*
Hungary ['hʌŋgəri] *s* Ungarn *n*
hunger ['hʌŋgər] *s* Hunger *m* ‖ *intr* hungern; **h. for** hungern nach
hun'ger strike' *s* Hungerstreik *m*
hungry ['hʌŋgri] *adj* hungrig; **be h.** Hunger haben; **be h. for** (fig) begierig sein nach; **go h.** am Hungertuch nagen; **I feel h.** es hungert mich
hunk [hʌŋk] *s* großes Stück *n*
hunt [hʌnt] *s* Jagd *f;* *(search)* **(for)** Suche *f* (nach); **on the h. for** auf der Suche nach ‖ *tr* jagen; *(a horse)* jagen mit; *(look for)* suchen; **h. down** erjagen ‖ *intr* jagen; **h. for** suchen; *(game)* jagen; *(a criminal)* fahnden nach; **go hunting** auf die Jagd gehen
hunter ['hʌntər] *s* Jäger -in *mf;* *(horse)* Jagdpferd *n*
hunt'ing *adj* *(e.g., dog, knife, season)* Jagd– ‖ *s* Jägerei *f;* *(on horseback)* Parforcejagd *f*
hunt'ing ground' *s* Jagdrevier *n*
hunt'ing li'cense *s* Jagdschein *m*
hunt'ing lodge' *s* Jagdhütte *f*
huntress ['hʌntrɪs] *s* Jägerin *f*
hunts'man *s* (–men) Weidmann *m*
hurdle ['hʌrdəl] *s* Hürde *f;* (fig) Hindernis *n;* **hurdles** (sport) Hürdenlauf *m* ‖ *tr* überspringen; (fig) überwinden
hurdygurdy ['hʌrdi'gʌrdi] *s* Drehorgel *f*
hurl [hʌrl] *s* Wurf *m* ‖ *tr* scheudern; **h. abuse at s.o.** j–m Beleidigungen ins Gesicht schleudern; **h. down** zu Boden werfen
hurrah [hə'ra], **hurray** [hə're] *s* Hurra *n* ‖ *interj* hurra!
hurricane ['hʌrɪ‚ken] *s* Orkan *m*
hur'ricane lamp' *s* Sturmlaterne *f*
hurried ['hʌrid] *adj* eilig, flüchtig
hurriedly ['hʌrɪdli] *adv* eilig, eilends
hur·ry ['hʌri] *s* Eile *f;* **be in too much of a h.** sich übereilen; **in a h.** in Eile; **there's no h.** es hat keine Eile ‖ *v*

(pret & pp –**ried**) *tr* *(prod)* antreiben; *(expedite)* beschleunigen; *(an activity)* zu schnell tun; *(to overhasty action)* drängen ‖ *intr* eilen; **h. away** wegeilen; **h. over s.th.** etw flüchtig erledigen; **h. up** sich beeilen
hurt [hʌrt] *adj* *(injured, offended)* verletzt; **feel h.** (about) sich verletzt (or gekränkt) fühlen (durch) ‖ *s* Verletzung *f* ‖ *v* *(pret & pp* hurt) *tr* *(a person, animal, feelings)* verletzen; *(e.g., a business)* schaden *(dat);* **it hurts him to think of it** es schmerzt ihn, daran zu denken ‖ *intr* (& fig) weh tun, schmerzen; **my arm hurts** mir tut der Arm weh; **that won't h.** das schadet nichts; **will it h. if I'm late?** macht es etw aus, wenn ich zu spät komme?
hurtle ['hʌrtəl] *tr* schleudern ‖ *intr* stürzen
husband ['hʌzbənd] *s* Ehemann *m;* **my h.** mein Mann *m* ‖ *tr* haushalten mit
hus'bandman *s* (–men) Landwirt *m*
husbandry ['hʌzbəndri] *s* Landwirtschaft *f*
hush [hʌʃ] *s* Stille *f* ‖ *tr* zur Ruhe bringen; **h. up** *(suppress)* vertuschen ‖ *intr* schweigen ‖ *interj* still!
hush'-hush' *adj* streng vertraulich und geheim
hush' mon'ey *s* Schweigegeld *n*
husk [hʌsk] *s* Hülse *f;* *(of corn)* Maishülse *f* ‖ *tr* enthülsen
husky ['hʌski] *adj* stämmig; *(voice)* belegt ‖ *s* Eskimohund *m*
hussy ['hʌsi] *s* *(prostitute)* Dirne *f;* *(saucy girl)* Fratz *m*
hustle ['hʌsəl] *s* (coll) Betriebsamkeit *f;* **h. and bustle** Getriebe *n* ‖ *tr* *(jostle, rush)* drängen; *(wares, girls)* an den Mann bringen; *(customers)* bearbeiten; *(money)* betteln ‖ *intr* rührig sein; *(shove)* sich drängen; *(hasten)* hasten; *(make money by fraud)* Betrügereien verüben; *(engage in prostitution)* Prostitution betreiben
hustler ['hʌslər] *s* rühriger Mensch *m*
hut [hʌt] *s* Hütte *f;* (mil) Baracke *f*
hutch [hʌtʃ] *s* Stall *m*
hyacinth ['haɪ·əsɪnθ] *s* Hyazinthe *f*
hybrid ['haɪbrɪd] *adj* hybrid ‖ *s* Kreuzung *f*
hydrant ['haɪdrənt] *s* Hydrant *m*
hydrate ['haɪdret] *s* Hydrat *n* ‖ *tr* hydratisieren, hydrieren
hydraulic [haɪ'drɔlɪk] *adj* hydraulisch ‖ **hydraulics** *s* Hydraulik *f*
hydrau'lic brakes' *spl* Öldruckbremsen *pl*
hydrocarbon [‚haɪdrə'karbən] *s* Kohlenwasserstoff *m*
hydrochlor'ic ac'id [‚haɪdrə'klorɪk] *s* Salzsäure *f*
hydroelectric [‚haɪdro·ɪ'lektrɪk] *adj* hydroelektrisch
hydroelec'tric plant' *s* Wasserkraftwerk *n*
hydrofluo'ric ac'id [‚haɪdrəflu'orɪk] *s* Flußsäure *f*
hydrofoil ['haɪdrə‚fɔɪl] *s* Tragflügelboot *n*

hydrogen ['haɪdrədʒən] *s* Wasserstoff *m*
hy'drogen bomb' *s* Wasserstoffbombe *f*
hy'drogen perox'ide *s* Wasserstoff-superoxyd *n*
hydrometer [haɪ'drɑmɪtər] *s* Hydrometer *m*
hydrophobia [,haɪdrə'fobɪ·ə] *s* Wasserscheu *f;* (*rabies*) Tollwut *f*
hydrophone ['haɪdrə,fon] *s* Unterwasserhorchgerät *n*, Hydrophon *n*
hydroplane ['haɪdrə,plen] *s* (aer) Wasserflugzeug *n;* (aer) Gleitfläche *f;* (naut) Gleitboot *n;* (*in a submarine*) (nav) Tiefenruder *n*
hydroxide [haɪ'drɑksaɪd] *s* Hydroxyd *n*
hyena [haɪ'inə] *s* Hyäne *f*
hygiene ['haɪdʒin] *s* Hygiene *f;* (educ) Gesundheitslehre *f*
hygienic [haɪ'dʒinɪk] *adj* hygienisch
hymn [hɪm] *s* Hymne *f;* (eccl) Kirchenlied *n*
hymnal ['hɪmnəl] *s* Gesangbuch *n*
hymn'book' *s* Gesangbuch *n*
hyperacidity [,haɪpərə'sɪdɪti] *s* Übersäuerung *f*
hyperbola [haɪ'pʌrbələ] *s* Hyperbel *f*
hyperbole [haɪ'pʌrbəli] *s* Hyperbel *f*
hypersensitive [,haɪpər'sɛnsɪtɪv] *adj* (to) überempfindlich (gegen)
hypertension [,haɪpər'tɛnʃən] *s* Hypertonie *f*
hyphen ['haɪfən] *s* Bindestrich *m*

hyphenate ['haɪfə,net] *tr* mit Bindestrich schreiben
hypnosis [hɪp'nosɪs] *s* Hypnose *f*
hypnotic [hɪp'nɑtɪk] *adj* hypnotisch
hypnotism ['hɪpnə,tɪzəm] *s* Hypnotismus *m*
hypnotist ['hɪpnətɪst] *s* Hypnotiseur *m*
hypnotize ['hɪpnə,taɪz] *tr* hypnotisieren
hypochondriac [,haɪpə'kɑndrɪ,æk] *s* Hypochonder *m*
hypocrisy [hɪ'pɑkrəsi] *s* Heuchelei *f*
hypocrite ['hɪpəkrɪt] *s* Heuchler –in *mf;* **be a h.** heucheln
hypocritical [,hɪpə'krɪtɪkəl] *adj* heuchlerisch
hypodermic [,haɪpə'dʌrmɪk] *adj* subkutan ‖ *s* (*injection*) subkutane Spritze *f*
hypoderm'ic nee'dle *s* Injektionsnadel *f*
hypotenuse [haɪ'pɑtɪ,n(j)us] *s* Hypotenuse *f*
hypothe·sis [haɪ'pɑθɪsɪs] *s* (–ses [,siz]) Hypothese *f*
hypothetic(al) [,haɪpə'θɛtɪk(əl)] *adj* hypothetisch
hysterectomy [,hɪstə'rɛktəmi] *s* Hysterektomie *f*
hysteria [hɪs'tɪrɪ·ə] *s* Hysterie *f*
hysteric [hɪs'tɛrɪk] *adj* hysterisch ‖ **hysterics** *spl* Hysterie *f;* **go into hysterics** e–n hysterischen Anfall bekommen
hysterical [hɪs'tɛrɪkəl] *adj* hysterisch

I

I, i [aɪ] *s* elfter Buchstabe des englischen Alphabets
I *pers pron* ich
iambic [aɪ'æmbɪk] *adj* jambisch
Iberian [aɪ'bɪrɪ·ən] *adj* iberisch
ibex ['aɪbeks] *s* (**ibexes** & **ibices** ['ɪbɪ,siz]) Steinbock *m*
ice [aɪs] *s* Eis *n;* **break the ice** (coll) das Eis brechen; **cut no ice** (coll) nicht ziehen ‖ *tr* (*a cake*) glasieren ‖ *intr*—**ice up** vereisen
ice' age' *s* Eiszeit *f*
iceberg ['aɪs,bʌrg] *s* Eisberg *m*
ice'boat' *s* (sport) Segelschlitten *m*
ice'bound' *adj* (*boat*) eingefroren; (*port, river*) zugefroren
ice'box' *s* Eisschrank *m;* (*refrigerator*) Kühlschrank *m*
ice'break'er *s* Eisbrecher *m*
ice' buck'et *s* Sektkübel *m*
ice'cap' *s* Eiskappe *f*
ice' cream' *s* Eis *n*, Eiskrem *f*
ice'-cream cone' *s* Tüte *f* Eis
ice' cube' *s* Eiswürfel *m*
ice'-cube tray' *s* Eiswürfelschale *f*
iced' tea' *s* Eistee *m*
ice' floe' *s* Eisscholle *f*
ice' hock'ey *s* Eishockey *n*
Iceland ['aɪslənd] *s* Island *n*

Icelander ['aɪs,lændər] *s* Isländer –in *mf*
Icelandic [aɪs'lændɪk] *adj* isländisch ‖ *s* (*language*) Isländisch *n*
ice'man' *s* (**–men'**) Eismann *m*
ice' pack' *s* (geol) Packeis *n;* (med) Eisbeutel *m*
ice' pick' *s* Eispfriem *m;* (mount) Eispickel *m*
ice' skate' *s* Schlittschuh *m*
ice'-skate' *intr* eislaufen
ichthyology [,ɪkθɪ'ɑlədʒi] *s* Ichthyologie *f*, Fischkunde *f*
icicle ['aɪsɪkəl] *s* Eiszapfen *m*
icing ['aɪsɪŋ] *s* Glasur *f*, Zuckerguß *m;* (aer) Vereisung *f*
icon ['aɪkɑn] *s* Ikone *f*
iconoclast [aɪ'kɑnə,klæst] *s* Bilderstürmer –in *mf*
icy ['aɪsi] *adj* (& fig) eisig
id [ɪd] *s* (psychol) Es *n*
I.D. card ['aɪ'di'kɑrd] *s* Ausweis *m*
idea [aɪ'di·ə] *s* Idee *f*, Vorstellung *f;* (*intimation*) Ahnung *f;* **crazy i.** Schnapsidee *f;* **have big ideas** große Rosinen im Kopf haben; **that's the i.!** so ist's richtig!; **the i.!** na so was!; **what's the i.?** wie kommen Sie darauf?

ideal [aɪ'di·əl] *adj* ideal ‖ *s* Ideal *n*
idealism [aɪ'di·ə,lɪzəm] *s* Idealismus *m*
idealist [aɪ'di·əlɪst] *s* Idealist –in *mf*
idealistic [aɪ,di·əl'ɪstɪk] *adj* idealistisch
idealize [aɪ'di·ə,laɪz] *tr* idealisieren
identical [aɪ'dɛntɪkəl] *adj* identisch
identification [aɪ'dɛntɪfɪ'keʃən] *s* Identifizierung *f*
identifica'tion tag' *s* Erkennungsmarke *f*
identi·fy [aɪ'dɛntɪ,faɪ] *v* (*pret* & *pp* –fied) *tr* identifizieren; **i. oneself** sich ausweisen ‖ *intr*—**i. with** sich einfühlen in (*acc*)
identity [aɪ'dɛntɪti] *s* Identität *f;* **prove one's i.** sich ausweisen
iden'tity card' *s* Ausweis *m*
ideological [,aɪdɪ·ə'ladʒɪkəl] *adj* ideologisch
ideology [,aɪdɪ'alədʒi] *s* Ideologie *f*
idiocy ['ɪdɪ·əsi] *s* Idiotie *f*
idiom ['ɪdɪ·əm] *s* (*phrase*) Redewendung *f;* (*language, style*) Idiom *n*
idiomatic [,ɪdɪ·ə'mætɪk] *adj* idiomatisch; **i. expression** (idiomatische) Redewendung *f*
idiosyncrasy [,ɪdɪ·ə'sɪnkrəsi] *s* Idiosynkrasie *f*
idiot ['ɪdɪ·ət] *s* Idiot *m*, Trottel *m*
idiotic [,ɪdɪ'atɪk] *adj* idiotisch
idle ['aɪdəl] *adj* (*person, question, hours*) müßig; (*machine, factory*) stillstehend; (*capital*) tot; (*fears*) grundlos; (*talk, threats*) leer; **lie i.** stilliegen; **stand i.** stillstehen ‖ *s* (aut) Leerlauf *m* ‖ *tr* arbeitslos machen; **i. away** vertrödeln ‖ *intr* (aut) leerlaufen
idleness ['aɪdəlnɪs] *s* Müßiggang *m*
idler ['aɪdlər] *s* Müßiggänger *m*
i'dling *s* (aut) Leerlauf *m*
idol ['aɪdəl] *s* Abgott *m;* (fig) Idol *n*
idolatry [aɪ'dalətri] *s* Abgötterei *f*
idolize ['aɪdə,laɪz] *tr* vergöttern
idyll ['aɪdəl] *s* Idyll *n*, Idylle *f*
idyllic [aɪ'dɪlɪk] *adj* idyllisch
if [ɪf] *s* Wenn *n* ‖ *conj* wenn; (*whether*) ob
igloo ['ɪglu] *s* Schneehütte *f*, Iglu *m* & *n*
ignite [ɪg'naɪt] *tr* & *intr* zünden
ignition [ɪg'nɪʃən] *adj* Zünd– ‖ *s* Entzünden *n;* (aut) Zündung *f*
igni'tion key' *s* Zündschlüssel *m*
igni'tion switch' *s* Zündschloß *n*
ignoble [ɪg'nobəl] *adj* unedel
ignominious [,ɪgnə'mɪnɪ·əs] *adj* schmachvoll, schändlich
ignoramus [,ɪgnə'reməs] *s* Ignorant –in *mf*
ignorance ['ɪgnərəns] *s* Unwissenheit *f;* (**of**) Unkenntnis *f* (*genit*)
ignorant ['ɪgnərənt] *adj* unwissend; **be i. of** nicht wissen
ignore [ɪg'nor] *tr* ignorieren; (*words*) überhören; (*rules*) nicht beachten
ilk [ɪlk] *s*—**of that ilk** derselben Art
ill [ɪl] *adj* (**worse** [wʌrs]; **worst** [wʌrst]) krank; (*repute*) schlecht; (*feelings*) feindselig; **fall** (*or* **take**)

ill krank werden ‖ *adv* schlecht; **he can ill afford to** (*inf*) er kann es sich [*dat*] kaum leisten zu (*inf*); **take s.th. ill** etw übelnehmen
ill'-advised' *adj* (*person*) schlecht beraten; (*action*) unbesonnen
ill'-at-ease' *adj* unbehaglich
ill'-bred' *adj* ungezogen
ill'-consid'ered *adj* unbesonnen
ill'-disposed' *adj*—**be i. towards** übelgesinnt sein (*dat*)
illegal [ɪ'ligəl] *adj* illegal
illegible [ɪ'lɛdʒɪbəl] *adj* unlesbar
illegitimate [,ɪlɪ'dʒɪtɪmɪt] *adj* unrechtmäßig; (*child*) illegitim
ill'-fat'ed *adj* unglücklich
illgotten ['ɪl,gɑtən] *adj* unrechtmäßig erworben
ill' health' *s* Kränklichkeit *f*
ill'-hu'mored *adj* übelgelaunt
illicit [ɪ'lɪsɪt] *adj* unerlaubt
illiteracy [ɪ'lɪtərəsi] *s* Analphabetentum *n*
illiterate [ɪ'lɪtərɪt] *adj* analphabetisch ‖ *s* Analphabet –in *mf*
ill'-man'nered *adj* ungehobelt
ill'-na'tured *adj* bösartig
illness ['ɪlnɪs] *s* (& fig) Krankheit *f*
illogical [ɪ'ladʒɪkəl] *adj* unlogisch
ill'-spent' *adj* verschwendet
ill'-starred' *adj* unglücklich
ill'-suit'ed (**to**) *adj* unpassend (*dat*)
ill'-tem'pered *adj* schlechtgelaunt
ill'-timed' *adj* unpassend
ill'-treat' *tr* mißhandeln
illuminate [ɪ'lumɪ,net] *tr* beleuchten; (*public buildings, manuscripts*) illuminieren; (*enlighten*) erleuchten; (*explain*) erklären
illumination [ɪ,lumɪ'neʃən] *s* Beleuchten *n;* Erleuchtung *f;* Illuminierung *f*
illusion [ɪ'luʒən] *s* Illusion *f*
illusive [ɪ'lusɪv] *adj* trügerisch
illusory [ɪ'lusəri] *adj* illusorisch
illustrate ['ɪləs,tret] *tr* (*exemplify*) erläutern; (*a book*) illustrieren; **illustrated lecture** Lichtbildervortrag *m;* **richly illustrated** bilderreich
illustration [,ɪləs'treʃən] *s* Erläuterung *f;* (*in a book*) Abbildung *f*
illustrative [ɪ'lʌstrətɪv] *adj* erläuternd; **i. material** Anschauungsmaterial *n*
illustrator ['ɪləs,tretər] *s* Illustrator *m*
illustrious [ɪ'lʌstrɪ·əs] *adj* berühmt
ill' will' *s* Feindschaft *f*
image ['ɪmɪdʒ] *s* Bild *n;* (*reflection*) Spiegelbild *n;* (*statue*) Standbild *n;* (*before the public*) Image *n;* (opt, phot, telv) Bild *n;* **the spitting i. of his father** ganz der Vater
imagery ['ɪmɪdʒ(ə)ri] *s* Bildersprache *f*
imaginable [ɪ'mædʒɪnəbəl] *adj* erdenklich
imaginary [ɪ'mædʒɪ,nɛri] *adj* imaginär
imagination [ɪ,mædʒɪ'neʃən] *s* Phantasie *f*, Einbildungskraft *f;* **that's pure i.** das ist pure Einbildung
imaginative [ɪ'mædʒɪnətɪv] *adj* phantasievoll
imagine [ɪ'mædʒɪn] *tr* sich [*dat*] vorstellen, sich [*dat*] denken; **i. oneself**

in sich hineindenken in (acc); **you're
only imagining things** das bilden Sie
sich [*dat*] nur ein || *intr*—**I can i.**
das läßt sich denken; **I i. so ich**
glaube schon; **just i.** denken Sie nur
mal!

imbecile ['ɪmbɪsɪl] *adj* geistesschwach
|| *s* Geistesschwache *mf*

imbecility [ˌɪmbɪ'sɪlɪti] *s* Geistes-
schwäche *f*, Blödheit *f*

imbibe [ɪm'baɪb] *tr* aufsaugen; (coll)
trinken; (fig) (geistig) aufnehmen

imbue [ɪm'bju] *tr* durchfeuchten; (fig)
(with) durchdringen (mit)

imitate ['ɪmɪˌtet] *tr* nachahmen, nachmachen; **i. s.o. in everything** j–m
alles nachmachen

imitation [ˌɪmɪ'teʃən] *adj* unecht,
nachgemacht || *s* Nachahmung *f*; **in
i. of** nach dem Muster (*genit*)

imita′tion leath′er *s* Kunstleder *n*

imitator ['ɪmɪˌtetər] *s* Nachahmer –in
mf

immaculate [ɪ'mækjəlɪt] *adj* makellos;
(*sinless*) unbefleckt

immaterial [ˌɪmə'tɪrɪ·əl] *adj* immateriell, unkörperlich; (*unimportant*)
unwesentlich; **it's i. to me** es is mir
gleichgültig

immature [ˌɪmə'tjʊr] *adj* unreif

immaturity [ˌɪmə'tjʊrɪti] *s* Unreife *f*

immeasurable [ɪ'mɛʒərəbəl] *adj* unermeßlich

immediacy [ɪ'midɪ·əsi] *s* Unmittelbar-
keit *f*

immediate [ɪ'midɪ·ɪt] *adj* sofortig;
(*direct*) unmittelbar

immediately [ɪ'midɪ·ɪtli] *adv* sofort;
i. afterwards gleich darauf

immemorial [ˌɪmɪ'morɪ·əl] *adj* uralt;
since time i. seit Menschengedenken

immense [ɪ'mɛns] *adj* unermeßlich

immensity [ɪ'mɛnsɪti] *s* Unermeßlichkeit *f*

immerse [ɪ'mʌrs] *tr* (unter)tauchen;
immersed in (*books, thought, work*)
vertieft in (*acc*); **i. oneself in** sich
vertiefen in (*acc*)

immersion [ɪ'mʌrʒən] *s* Untertauchen
n; (fig) Versunkenheit *f*

immigrant ['ɪmɪgrənt] *adj* einwandernd
|| *s* Einwanderer –in *mf*

immigrate ['ɪmɪˌgret] *intr* einwandern

immigration [ˌɪmɪ'greʃən] *s* Einwan-
derung *f*

imminent ['ɪmɪnənt] *adj* drohend

immobile [ɪ'mobɪl] *adj* unbeweglich

immobilize [ɪ'mobɪˌlaɪz] *tr* unbeweglich machen; (*tanks*) bewegungsun-
fähig machen; (*troops*) fesseln;
(med) ruhigstellen

immoderate [ɪ'madərɪt] *adj* unmäßig

immodest [ɪ'madɪst] *adj* unbescheiden

immolate ['ɪməˌlet] *tr* opfern

immoral [ɪ'mɔrəl] *adj* unsittlich

immorality [ˌɪmə'rælɪti] *s* Unsittlichkeit *f*

immortal [ɪ'mɔrtəl] *adj* unsterblich

immortality [ˌɪmɔr'tælɪti] *s* Unsterb-
lichkeit *f*

immortalize [ɪ'mɔrtəˌlaɪz] *tr* unsterblich machen

immovable [ɪ'muvəbəl] *adj* unbeweglich

immune [ɪ'mjun] *adj* (*free, exempt*)
(**from**) immun (gegen); (*not responsive*) **(to)** gefeit (gegen); (med) **(to)**
immun (gegen)

immunity [ɪ'mjunɪti] *s* Immunität *f*

immunization [ˌɪmjunɪ'zeʃən] *s*
Schutzimpfung *f*, Immunisierung *f*

immunize ['ɪmjəˌnaɪz] *tr* (**against**) immunisieren (gegen)

immutable [ɪ'mjutəbəl] *adj* unwandel-
bar

imp [ɪmp] *s* Schlingel *m*

impact ['ɪmpækt] *s* Anprall *m;* (*of a
shell*) Aufschlag *m;* (fig) Einwirkung
f

impair [ɪm'pɛr] *tr* beeinträchtigen

impale [ɪm'pel] *tr* pfählen

impan·el [ɪm'pænəl] *v* (*pret & pp
-el[l]ed; ger -el[l]ing*) *tr* in die Ge-
schworenenliste eintragen

impart [ɪm'part] *tr* mitteilen

impartial [ɪm'parʃəl] *adj* unparteiisch

impassable [ɪm'pæsɪbəl] *adj* (*on foot*)
ungangbar; (*by car*) unbefahrbar

impasse ['ɪmpæs] *s* Sackgasse *f;* reach
an i. in e–e Sackgasse geraten

impassible [ɪm'pæsɪbəl] *adj* (**to**) unempfindlich (für)

impassioned [ɪm'pæʃənd] *adj* leiden-
schaftlich

impassive [ɪm'pæsɪv] *adj* (*person*) teilnahmslos; (*expression*) ausdruckslos

impatience [ɪm'peʃəns] *s* Ungeduld *f*

impatient [ɪm'peʃənt] *adj* ungeduldig

impeach [ɪm'pitʃ] *tr* (*an official*) wegen Amtsmißbrauchs unter Anklage
stellen; (*a witness, motives*) in Zweifel ziehen

impeachment [ɪm'pitʃmənt] *s* (*of an
official*) öffentliche Anklage *f;* (*of a
witness, motives*) Anzweiflung *f*

impeccable [ɪm'pɛkəbəl] *adj* makellos

impecunious [ˌɪmpɪ'kjunɪ·əs] *adj* mittellos

impede [ɪm'pid] *tr* behindern, erschweren

impediment [ɪm'pɛdɪmənt] *s* Behinderung *f;* (*of speech*) Sprachfehler *m*

im·pel [ɪm'pɛl] *v* (*pret & pp -pelled;
ger -pelling*) *tr* antreiben

impending [ɪm'pɛndɪŋ] *adj* nahe bevorstehen; (*threatening*) drohend

impenetrable [ɪm'pɛnətrəbəl] *adj* un-
durchdringlich; (fig) unergründlich

impenitent [ɪm'pɛnɪtənt] *adj* unbußfertig

imperative [ɪm'pɛrətɪv] *adj* dringend
nötig || *s* Imperativ *m*

imper′ative mood′ *s* Befehlsform *f*

imperceptible [ˌɪmpər'sɛptɪbəl] *adj*
nicht wahrnehmbar, unmerklich

imperfect [ɪm'pʌrfɪkt] *adj* unvollkom-
men || *s* (gram) Imperfekt(um) *n*

imperfection [ˌɪmpər'fɛkʃən] *s* Unvoll-
kommenheit *f;* (*flaw*) Fehler *m*

imperial [ɪm'pɪrɪ·əl] *adj* kaiserlich

imperialism [ɪm'pɪrɪ·əˌlɪzəm] *s* Imperialismus *m*

imperialist [ɪm'pɪrɪ·əlɪst] *adj* imperia-
listisch || *s* Imperialist –in *mf*

imper·il [ɪm'pɛrɪl] v (pret & pp
–il[l]ed; ger –il[l]ing) tr gefährden
imperious [ɪm'pɛrɪ·əs] adj herrisch, anmaßend
imperishable [ɪm'pɛrɪʃəbəl] adj unver-
gänglich
impersonal [ɪm'pʌrsənəl] adj unpersönlich
impersonate [ɪm'pʌrsə,net] tr (imitate) nachahmen; (e.g., an officer)
sich ausgeben als; (theat) darstellen
impersonator [ɪm'pʌrsə,netər] s Imitator –in mf
impertinence [ɪm'pʌrtɪnəns] s Ungezogenheit f
impertinent [ɪm'pʌrtɪnənt] adj ungezogen
imperturbable [,ɪmpʌr'tʌrbəbəl] adj
unerschütterlich
impetuous [ɪm'pɛtʃʊ·əs] adj ungestüm
impetus ['ɪmpɪtəs] s (& fig) Antrieb
m
impiety [ɪm'paɪ·əti] s Gottlosigkeit f
impinge [ɪm'pɪndʒ] intr—i. on (an)
stoßen an (acc); (said of rays) fallen
auf (acc); (fig) eingreifen in (acc)
impious ['ɪmpɪ·əs] adj gottlos
impish ['ɪmpɪʃ] adj spitzbübisch
implant [ɪm'plænt] tr einpflanzen
implement ['ɪmplɪmənt] s Werkzeug
n, Gerät n || ['ɪmplɪ,mɛnt] tr durch-
führen
implicate ['ɪmplɪ,ket] tr (in) verwickeln (in acc)
implication [,ɪmplɪ'keʃən] s (involvement) Verwicklung f; (implying) Andeutung f; **implications** Folgerungen
pl
implicit [ɪm'plɪsɪt] adj (approval) stillschweigend; (trust) unbedingt
implied [ɪm'plaɪd] adj stillschweigend
implore [ɪm'plor] tr anflehen
im·ply [ɪm'plaɪ] v (pret & pp –plied)
tr (express indirectly) andeuten; (involve) in sich schließen; (said of
words) besagen
impolite [,ɪmpə'laɪt] adj unhöflich
import ['ɪmport] s Import m, Einfuhr
f; (meaning) Bedeutung f; **imports**
Einfuhrwaren pl || [ɪm'port], ['ɪm-
port] tr importieren, einführen
importance [ɪm'portəns] s Wichtigkeit
f; **a man of i.** ein Mann m von Bedeutung; **of no i.** unwichtig
important [ɪm'portənt] adj wichtig
im'port du'ty s Einfuhrzoll m
importer [ɪm'portər] s Importeur m
importune [,ɪmpor't(j)un] adj auf-
dringlich || tr bestürmen
impose [ɪm'poz] tr (on, upon) auf-
erlegen (dat) || intr—i. on über Ge-
bühr beanspruchen
impos'ing adj imposant
imposition [,ɪmpə'zɪʃən] s (of hands,
of an obligation) Auferlegung f; (taking unfair advantage) Zumutung f
impossible [ɪm'pasɪbəl] adj unmöglich
impostor [ɪm'pastər] s Hochstapler m
imposture [ɪm'pastjər] s Hochstapelei
f
impotence ['ɪmpətəns] s Machtlosig-
keit f; (pathol) Impotenz f

impotent ['ɪmpətənt] adj machtlos;
(pathol) impotent
impound [ɪm'paund] tr beschlagnahmen
impoverish [ɪm'pavərɪʃ] tr arm machen; **become impoverished** verarmen
impracticable [ɪm'præktɪkəbəl] adj unausführbar
impractical [ɪm'præktɪkəl] adj un-
praktisch
impregnable [ɪm'prɛgnəbəl] adj unein-
nehmbar
impregnate [ɪm'prɛgnet] tr (saturate)
imprägnieren; (& fig) schwängern
impresari·o [,ɪmprɪ'sarɪ,o] s (–os)
Impresario m
impress [ɪm'prɛs] tr (affect) imponieren (dat), beeindrucken; (imprint,
emphasize) einprägen; **i. s.th. on s.o.**
j–m etw einprägen
impression [ɪm'prɛʃən] s Eindruck m;
(stamp) Gepräge n; **try to make an i.**
Eindruck schinden
impressive [ɪm'prɛsɪv] adj eindrucksvoll
imprint ['ɪmprɪnt] s Aufdruck m; (fig)
Eindruck m || [ɪm'prɪnt] tr (on) auf-
drucken (auf acc); **i. on s.o.'s memory** j–m ins Gedächtnis einprägen
imprison [ɪm'prɪzən] tr einsperren
imprisonment [ɪm'prɪzənmənt] s Haft
f; (penalty) Freiheitsstrafe f; (captivity) Gefangenschaft f
improbable [ɪm'prabəbəl] adj unwahrscheinlich
impromptu [ɪm'prampt(j)u] adj & adv
aus dem Stegreif || s Stegreifstück n
improper [ɪm'prapər] adj ungehörig,
unschicklich; (use) unzulässig
improve [ɪm'pruv] tr verbessern; (relations) ausbauen; (land) kultivieren;
(a salary) aufbessern; **i. oneself** sich
bessern; (financially) sich verbessern
|| intr bessern; (com) sich erholen;
i. on Verbesserungen vornehmen an
(dat)
improvement [ɪm'pruvmənt] s Verbesserung f; (reworking) Umarbeitung
f; (of money value) Erholung f; (of
a salary) Aufbesserung f; (in health)
Besserung f; **be an i. on** ein Fortschritt sein gegenüber
improvident [ɪm'pravɪdənt] adj unbedacht
improvise ['ɪmprə,vaɪz] tr improvisie-
ren || intr improvisieren; (mus) phan-
tasieren
imprudence [ɪm'prudəns] s Unklugheit
f
imprudent [ɪm'prudənt] adj unklug
impudence ['ɪmpjədəns] s Unverschämtheit f
impudent ['ɪmpjədənt] adj unverschämt
impugn [ɪm'pjun] tr bestreiten
impulse ['ɪmpʌls] s Impuls m; **act on i.**
impulsiv handeln
impulsive [ɪm'pʌlsɪv] adj impulsiv
impunity [ɪm'pjunɪti] s Straffreiheit
f; **with i.** ungestraft
impure [ɪm'pjʊr] adj (& fig) unrein

impurity [ɪm'pjʊrɪti] s (& fig) Unreinheit f
impute [ɪm'pjut] tr (**to**) unterstellen (dat)
in [ɪn] adv (position) drin, drinnen; (direction away from the speaker) hinein; (direction toward the speaker) herein; **be all in** ganz erschöpft sein; **be in** da sein; (said of a political party) an der Macht sein; (be in style) in Mode sein; **be in for** zu erwarten haben; **have it in for** auf dem Strich haben || s—**the ins and outs of** die Einzelheiten (genit) || prep (position) in (dat); (direction) in (acc); (e.g., the morning, afternoon, evening) am; (a field, the country; one eye) auf (dat); (one's opinion; all probability) nach (dat); (circumstances; a reign) unter (dat); (ink; one stroke) mit (dat); (because of pain, joy, etc.) vor (dat); **he doesn't have it in him to** (inf) er hat nicht das Zeug dazu zu (inf); **in German** auf deutsch
inability [ˌɪnə'bɪlɪti] s Unfähigkeit f; **i. to pay** Zahlungsunfähigkeit f
inaccessible [ˌɪnæk'sɛsɪbəl] adj unzugänglich
inaccuracy [ɪn'ækjərəsi] s Ungenauigkeit f
inaccurate [ɪn'ækjərɪt] adj ungenau
inaction [ɪn'ækʃən] s Untätigkeit f
inactive [ɪn'æktɪv] adj untätig; (chem) unwirksam; (st. exch.) lustlos
inactivity [ˌɪnæk'tɪvɪti] s Untätigkeit f
inadequate [ɪn'ædɪkwɪt] adj unangemessen
inadmissible [ˌɪnəd'mɪsɪbəl] adj unstatthaft, unzulässig
inadvertent [ˌɪnəd'vʌrtənt] adj versehentlich
inadvisable [ˌɪnəd'vaɪzəbəl] adj nicht ratsam
inalienable [ɪn'eljənəbəl] adj unveräußerlich
inane [ɪn'en] adj leer, unsinnig
inanimate [ɪn'ænɪmɪt] adj unbeseelt
inappropriate [ˌɪnə'proprɪ·ɪt] adj unangemessen
inarticulate [ˌɪnɑr'tɪkjəlɪt] adj unartikuliert, undeutlich
inartistic [ˌɪnɑr'tɪstɪk] adj unkünstlerisch, kunstlos
inasmuch as [ˌɪnəz'mʌtʃ ˌæz] conj da
inattentive [ˌɪnə'tɛntɪv] adv (**to**) unaufmerksam (or unachtsam) (gegenüber)
inaudible [ɪn'ɔdɪbəl] adj unhörbar
inaugural [ɪn'ɔg(j)ərəl] adj Antritts–
inaugurate [ɪn'ɔg(j)ə·ˌret] tr feierlich eröffnen; (a new policy) einleiten
inauguration [ɪnˌɔg(j)ə'reʃən] s Eröffnung f; (of an official) Amtsantritt m
inauspicious [ˌɪnɔ'spɪʃəs] adj ungünstig
inborn ['ɪn‚bɔrn] adj angeboren
inbred ['ɪn‚brɛd] adj angeboren, ererbt
in'breed'ing s Inzucht f

incalculable [ɪn'kælkjələbəl] adj unberechenbar
incandescent [ˌɪnkən'dɛsənt] adj Glüh–
incantation [ˌɪnkæn'teʃən] s Beschwörung f
incapable [ɪn'kepəbəl] adj untüchtig; **i. of** (ger) nicht fähig zu (inf)
incapacitate [ˌɪnkə'pæsɪ‚tet] tr unfähig machen; (jur) für geschäftsunfähig erklären
incarcerate [ɪn'kɑrsə‚ret] tr einkerkern
incarnate [ɪn'kɑrnet] adj—**God i.** Gottmensch m; **the devil i.** der Teufel in Menschengestalt
incarnation [ˌɪnkɑr'neʃən] s (fig) Verkörperung f; (eccl) Fleischwerdung f
incendiary [ɪn'sɛndɪ‚ɛri] adj Brand–; (fig) aufhetzend || s Brandstifter –in mf
incense ['ɪnsəns] s Weihrauch m || tr (eccl) beräuchern || [ɪn'sɛns] tr erzürnen
in'cense burn'er s Räuchergefäß n
incentive [ɪn'sɛntɪv] s Anreiz m
inception [ɪn'sɛpʃən] s Anfang m
incessant [ɪn'sɛsənt] adj unaufhörlich
incest ['ɪnsɛst] s Blutschande f
incestuous [ɪn'sɛstʃʊ·əs] adj blutschänderisch
inch [ɪntʃ] s Zoll m; **beat within an i. of one's life** fast zu Tode prügeln; **by inches** nach und nach; **not yield an i.** keinen Fußbreit nachgeben || intr—**i. along** dahinschleichen; **i. forward** langsam vorrücken
incidence ['ɪnsɪdəns] s Vorkommen n
incident ['ɪnsɪdənt] s Vorfall m; (adverse event) Zwischenfall m
incidental [ˌɪnsɪ'dɛntəl] adj zufällig; **i. to** gehörig zu || **incidentals** spl Nebenausgaben pl
incidentally [ˌɪnsɪ'dɛntəli] adv übrigens
incinerate [ɪn'sɪnə‚ret] tr einäschern
incinerator [ɪn'sɪnə‚retər] s Verbrennungsofen m
incipient [ɪn'sɪpɪ·ənt] adv beginnend
incision [ɪn'sɪʒən] s Schnitt m
incisive [ɪn'saɪsɪv] adj (biting) beißend; (penetrating) durchdringend; (sharp) scharf
incisor [ɪn'saɪzər] s Schneidezahn m
incite [ɪn'saɪt] tr aufreizen, aufhetzen
inclement [ɪn'klɛmənt] adj ungünstig
inclination [ˌɪnklɪ'neʃən] s (& fig) Neigung f
incline ['ɪnklaɪn] s Abhang m || [ɪn'klaɪn] tr neigen || intr (towards) sich neigen (nach or zu); (fig) (towards) neigen (zu); **the roof inclines sharply** das Dach fällt steil ab
include [ɪn'klud] tr einschließen; **i. among** rechnen unter (acc); **i. in** einrechnen in (acc)
includ'ed adj (mit) inbegriffen
includ'ing prep einschließlich (genit)
inclusive [ɪn'klusɪv] adj umfassend, gesamt; **all i.** alles inbegriffen; **from ... to ... i.** von ... zu ... einschließlich (or inklusive); **i. of** einschließlich (genit)

incognito [ɪn'kagnɪ ˌto] *adv* inkognito

incoherent [ˌɪnko'hɪrənt] *adj* unzusammenhängend; **be i.** (*said of a person*) nicht ganz bei sich sein

incombustible [ˌɪnkəm'bʌstɪbəl] *adj* unverbrennbar

income ['ɪnkʌm] *s* (**from**) Einkommen *n* (aus)

in'come tax' *s* Einkommensteuer *f*

in'come-tax return' *s* Einkommensteuererklärung *f*

in'com'ing *adj* (e.g., *tide*) hereinkommend; (*bus, train*) ankommend; (*official*) neu eintretend; **i. goods, i. mail** Eingänge *pl*

incomparable [ɪn'kampərəbəl] *adj* unvergleichlich

incompatible [ˌɪnkəm'pætɪbəl] *adj* (**with**) unvereinbar (mit); (*persons*) unverträglich

incompetent [ɪn'kampɪtənt] *adj* untauglich; (*not legally qualified*) nicht zuständig; (*not legally capable*) geschäftsunfähig; (*inadmissible*) unzulässig ‖ *s* Nichtkönner –in *mf*

incomplete [ˌɪnkəm'plit] *adj* unvollständig

incomprehensible [ˌɪnkamprɪ'hɛnsɪbəl] *adj* unbegreiflich

inconceivable [ˌɪnkən'sivəbəl] *adj* undenkbar

inconclusive [ˌɪnkən'klusɪv] *adj* (*not convincing*) nicht überzeugend; (*leading to no result*) ergebnislos

incongruous [ɪn'kaŋgru·əs] *adj* nicht übereinstimmend

inconsequential [ɪn ˌkansɪ'kwenʃəl] *adj* belanglos

inconsiderate [ˌɪnkən'sɪdərɪt] *adj* unüberlegt; (**towards**) rücksichtslos (gegen)

inconsistency [ˌɪnkən'sɪstənsi] *s* (*lack of logical connection*) Inkonsequenz *f*; (*contradiction*) Unstimmigkeit *f*; (*instability*) Unbeständigkeit *f*

inconsistent [ˌɪnkən'sɪstənt] *adj* inkonsequent; (*uneven*) unbeständig

inconspicuous [ˌɪnkən'spɪkju·əs] *adj* unauffällig

inconstant [ɪn'kanstənt] *adj* unbeständig

incontinent [ɪn'kantɪnənt] *adj* zügellos

incontrovertible [ˌɪnkantrə'vʌrtɪbəl] *adj* unwiderlegbar

inconvenience [ˌɪnkən'vini·əns] *s* Ungelegenheit *f* ‖ *tr* bemühen, belästigen

inconvenient [ˌɪnkən'vini·ənt] *adj* ungelegen

incorporate [ɪn'kɔrpə ˌret] *tr* einverleiben; (*an organization*) zu e-r Körperschaft machen ‖ *intr* e-e Körperschaft werden

incorporation [ɪn ˌkɔrpə're∫ən] *s* Einverleibung *f*; (*jur*) Körperschaftsbildung *f*

incorrect [ˌɪnkə'rɛkt] *adj* unrichtig, falsch; (*conduct*) unschicklich

incorrigible [ɪn'kɔrɪdʒɪbəl] *adj* unverbesserlich

increase ['ɪnkris] *s* Zunahme *f*; **be on the i.** steigen; **i. in costs** Kostensteigerung *f*; **i. in pay** Gehaltserhöhung *f*; (mil) Solderhöhung *f*; **i. in population** Bevölkerungszunahme *f*; **i. in prices** Preiserhöhung *f*; **i. in rent** Mieterhöhung *f*; **i. in taxes** Steuererhöhung *f*; **i. in value** Wertsteigerung *f*; **i. in weight** Gewichtszunahme *f* ‖ [ɪn'kris] *tr* (*in size*) vergrößern; (*in height*) erhöhen; (*in quantity*) vermehren; (*in intensity*) verstärken; (*prices*) heraufsetzen ‖ *intr* zunehmen, sich vergrößern; (*rise*) sich erhöhen; (*in quantity*) sich vermehren; (*in intensity*) sich verstärken; **i. in** zunehmen an (*dat*)

increasingly [ɪn'krisɪŋli] *adv* immer mehr; **i. more difficult** immer schwieriger

incredible [ɪn'krɛdɪbəl] *adj* unglaublich

incredulous [ɪn'krɛdʒələs] *adj* ungläubig

increment ['ɪnkrɪmənt] *s* Zunahme *f*, Zuwachs *m*; (*in pay*) Gehaltszulage *f*

incriminate [ɪn'krɪmɪ ˌnet] *tr* belasten

incrust [ɪn'krʌst] *tr* überkrusten

incubate ['ɪnkjə ˌbet] *tr & intr* brüten

incubator ['ɪnkjə ˌbetər] *s* Brutapparat *m*

inculcate [ɪn'kʌlket], ['ɪnkʌl ˌket] *tr* (**in**) einprägen (*dat*)

incumbency [ɪn'kʌmbənsi] *s* (*obligation*) Obliegenheit *f*; (*term of office*) Amtszeit *f*

incumbent [ɪn'kʌmbənt] *adj*—**be i. on** obliegen (*dat*) ‖ *s* Amtsinhaber –in *mf*

incunabula [ˌɪnkju'næbjələ] *spl* (typ) Wiegendrucke *pl*

in·cur [ɪn'kʌr] *v* (*pret & pp* –**curred;** *ger* –**curring**) *tr* sich [*dat*] zuziehen; (*debts*) machen; (*a loss*) erleiden; (*a risk*) eingehen

incurable [ɪn'kjurəbəl] *adj* unheilbar ‖ *s* unheilbarer Kranke *m*

incursion [ɪn'kʌrʒən] *s* Einfall *m*

indebted [ɪn'dɛtɪd] *adj* (**to**) verschuldet (bei); **be i. to s.o. for s.th.** j–m etw zu verdanken haben

indecency [ɪn'disənsi] *s* Unsittlichkeit *f*

indecent [ɪn'disənt] *adj* unsittlich; **i. assault** Sittlichkeitsvergehen *n*

indecision [ˌɪndɪ'sɪʒən] *s* Unentschlossenheit *f*

indecisive [ˌɪndɪ'saɪsɪv] *adj* (*person*) unentschlossen; (*battle*) nicht entscheidend

indeclinable [ˌɪndɪ'klaɪnəbəl] *adj* undeklinierbar

indeed [ɪn'did] *adv* ja, zwar ‖ *interj* jawohl!

indefatigable [ˌɪndɪ'fætɪgəbəl] *adj* unermüdlich

indefensible [ˌɪndɪ'fɛnsɪbəl] *adj* nicht zu verteidigen(d); (*argument*) unhaltbar; (*behavior*) unentschuldbar

indefinable [ˌɪndɪ'faɪnəbəl] *adj* undefinierbar

indefinite [ɪn'dɛfɪnɪt] *adj* (*unlimited*) unbegrenzt; (*not exact*) unbestimmt; (*answer*) ausweichend; (*vague*) undeutlich; (gram) unbestimmt indelible [ɪn'dɛlɪbəl] adj (ink, pencil) wasserfest; (fig) unauslöschlich

indelicate [ɪn'dɛlɪkɪt] adj unzart

indemnification [ɪn,dɛmnɪfɪ'keʃən] s Schadenersatzleistung f

indemni·fy [ɪn'dɛmnɪ,faɪ] v (pret & pp –fied) tr entschädigen

indemnity [ɪn'dɛmnɪti] s Schadenersatz m

indent [ɪn'dɛnt] tr (notch) einkerben; (the coast) tiefe Einschnitte bilden in (dat); (typ) einrücken || intr (typ) einrücken

indentation [,ɪndɛn'teʃən] s Kerbe f; (typ) Absatz m

indenture [ɪn'dɛntʃər] s (service contract) Arbeitsvertrag m; (apprentice contract) Lehrvertrag m || tr vertraglich binden

independence [,ɪndɪ'pɛndəns] s Unabhängigkeit f

independent [,ɪndɪ'pɛndənt] adj (of) unabhängig (von) || s Unabhängige mf

indescribable [,ɪndɪ'skraɪbəbəl] adj unbeschreiblich

indestructible [,ɪndɪ'strʌktɪbəl] adj unzerstörbar

index ['ɪndɛks] s (indexes & indices ['ɪndɪ,siz]) (in a book) Register n; (fig) (to) Hisweis m (auf acc); Index Index m || tr registrieren; (a book) mit e–m Register versehen

in'dex card' s Karteikarte f

in'dex fin'ger s Zeigefinger m

India ['ɪndɪ·ə] s Indien n

In'dia ink' s chinesische Tusche f

Indian ['ɪndɪ·ən] adj indisch; (e.g., chief, tribe) Indianer– || s (of India) Inder –in mf; (of North America) Indianer –in mf; (of Central or South America) Indio m

In'dian corn' s Mais m

In'dian file' adv in Gänsemarsch

In'dian O'cean s Indischer Ozean m

In'dian sum'mer s Altweibersommer m

indicate ['ɪndɪ,ket] tr angeben, anzeigen

indication [,ɪndɪ'keʃən] s Angabe f; (of s.th. imminent) (of) Anzeichen n (für); give i. of anzeigen

indicative [ɪn'dɪkətɪv] adj (gram) indikativ; be i. of hindeuten auf (acc) || s (gram) Wirklichkeitsform f, Indikativ m

indicator ['ɪndɪ,ketər] s Zeiger m

indict [ɪn'daɪt] tr (for) anklagen (wegen)

indictment [ɪn'daɪtmənt] s Anklage f

indifference [ɪn'dɪfərəns] s (to) Gleichgültigkeit f (gegen or gegenüber)

indifferent [ɪn'dɪfərənt] adj (mediocre) mittelmäßig; (to) gleichgültig (gegen)

indigenous [ɪn'dɪdʒɪnəs] adj (to) einheimisch (in dat)

indigent ['ɪndɪdʒənt] adj bedürftig

indigestible [,ɪndɪ'dʒɛstɪbəl] adj unverdaulich

indigestion [,ɪndɪ'dʒɛstʃən] s Verdauungsstörung f, Magenverstimmung f

indignant [ɪn'dɪgnənt] adj (at) empört (über acc)

indignation [,ɪndɪg'neʃən] s (at) Empörung f (über acc)

indignity [ɪn'dɪgnɪti] s Beleidigung f

indigo ['ɪndɪ,go] adj Indigo– || s Indigo m & n

indirect [,ɪndɪ'rɛkt] adj indirekt

in'direct dis'course s indirekte Rede f

in'direct ques'tion s indirekter Fragesatz m

indiscreet [,ɪndɪs'krit] adj indiskret

indiscretion [,ɪndɪs'krɛʃən] s Indiskretion f

indiscriminate [,ɪndɪs'krɪmɪnɪt] adj unterschiedslos

indispensable [,ɪndɪs'pɛnsəbəl] adj unentbehrlich

indisposed adj (ill) unpäßlich; i. to abgeneigt (dat)

indissoluble [,ɪndɪ'saljəbəl] adj unauflösbar

indistinct [,ɪndɪ'stɪŋkt] adj undeutlich

individual [,ɪndɪ'vɪdʒu·əl] adj individuell, Einzel–, einzeln || s Individuum n

individ'ual case' s Einzelfall m

individuality [,ɪndɪ,vɪdʒu'ælɪti] s Individualität f

individually [,ɪndɪ'vɪdʒu·əli] adv einzeln

indivisible [,ɪndɪ'vɪzɪbəl] adj unteilbar

Indochina ['ɪndo't ʃaɪnə] s Indochina n

indoctrinate [ɪn'daktrɪ,net] tr (in) schulen (in dat), unterweisen (in dat)

indoctrination [,ɪndaktrɪ'neʃən] s Schulung f, Unterweisung f

Indo-European ['ɪndo,jurə'pi·ən] adj indogermanisch || s (language) Indogermanisch n

indolence ['ɪndələns] s Trägheit f

indolent ['ɪndələnt] adj träge

Indonesia [,ɪndo'niʒə] s Indonesien n

Indonesian [,ɪndo'niʒən] adj indonesisch || s Indonesier –in mf

indoor ['ɪn,dor] adj Haus–, Zimmer–, Innen–; (sport) Hallen–

indoors [ɪn'dorz] adv innen, drin(nen)

in'door shot' s (phot) Innenaufnahme f

induce [ɪn'd(j)us] tr veranlassen, bewegen; (bring about) verursachen; (elec, phys) induzieren

inducement [ɪn'd(j)usmənt] s Anreiz m

induct [ɪn'dʌkt] tr (into) einführen (in acc); (mil) (into) einberufen (zu)

inductee [,ɪn'dʌkti] s Einberufene mf

induction [ɪn'dʌkʃən] s Einführung f; (elec, log) Induktion f; (mil) Einberufung f

induc'tion coil' s Induktionsspule f

indulge [ɪn'dʌldʒ] tr (a desire) frönen (dat); (a person) befriedigen; (children) verwöhnen; i. oneself in schwelgen in (dat) || intr (coll) trinken; i. in s.th. sich [dat] etw gestatten

indulgence [ɪn'dʌldʒəns] s (of a desire) Frönen n; (tolerance) Duldung f; (relig) Ablaß m; ask s.o.'s i. j–n um Nachsicht bitten

indulgent [ɪn'dʌldʒənt] adj schonend; (toward) nachsichtig (gegen)

industrial [ɪn'dʌstri·əl] adj (e.g., bank,

center, alcohol, product, worker) Industrie–; *(e.g., accident, medicine)* Betriebs–; *(e.g., revolution)* industri- ell; *(e.g., school, engineering)* Gewerbe–

industrialist [ɪn'dʌstrɪ·əlɪst] *s* Industrielle *mf*

industrialize [ɪn'dʌstrɪ·ə‚laɪz] *tr* industrialisieren

indus'trial man'agement *s* Betriebswirtschaft *f*

industrious [ɪn'dʌstrɪ·əs] *adj* fleißig

industry ['ɪndəstri] *s* Industrie *f; (energy)* Fleiß *m*

inebriated [ɪn'ibrɪ‚etɪd] *adj* betrunken

inedible [ɪn'ɛdɪbəl] *adj* ungenießbar

ineffable [ɪn'ɛfəbəl] *adj* unaussprechlich

ineffective [‚ɪnɪ'fɛktɪv] *adj* unwirksam; *(person)* untüchtig

ineffectual [‚ɪnɪ'fɛktʃʊ·əl] *adj* unwirksam

inefficient [‚ɪnɪ'fɪʃənt] *adj* untüchtig; *(process, procedure)* unrationell; *(mach)* nicht leistungsfähig

ineligible [ɪn'ɛlɪdʒɪbəl] *adj* nicht wählbar; *(not suitable)* ungeeignet

inept [ɪn'ɛpt] *adj* ungeschickt

inequality [‚ɪnɪ'kwɑlɪti] *s* Ungleichheit *f*

inequity [ɪn'ɛkwɪti] *s* Ungerechtigkeit *f*

inertia [ɪn'ʌrʃə] *s* Trägheit *f*

inescapable [‚ɪnɛs'kepəbəl] *adj* unentrinnbar, unabwendbar

inevitable [ɪn'ɛvɪtəbəl] *adj* unvermeidlich, unausweichlich

inexact [‚ɪnɛg'zækt] *adj* ungenau

inexcusable [‚ɪnɛks'kjuzəbəl] *adj* unentschuldbar

inexhaustible [‚ɪnɛg'zɔstɪbəl] *adj* unerschöpflich

inexorable [ɪn'ɛksərəbəl] *adj* unerbittlich

inexpensive [‚ɪnɛk'spɛnsɪv] *adj* billig

inexperience [‚ɪnɛk'spɪrɪ·əns] *s* Unerfahrenheit *f*

inexpe'rienced *adj* unerfahren

inexplicable [ɪn'ɛksplɪkəbəl] *adj* unerklärlich

inexpressible [‚ɪnɛk'sprɛsɪbəl] *adj* unaussprechlich

infallibility [‚ɪnfælɪ'bɪlɪti] *s* Unfehlbarkeit *f*

infallible [ɪn'fælɪbəl] *adj* unfehlbar

infamous ['ɪnfəməs] *adj* schändlich

infamy ['ɪnfəmi] *s* Schändlichkeit *f*

infancy ['ɪnfənsi] *s* Kindheit *f;* **be still in its i.** (fig) noch in den Kinderschuhen stecken

infant ['ɪnfənt] *adj* Säuglings– ‖ *s* Kleinkind *n*, Säugling *m*

infantile ['ɪnfən‚taɪl] *adj* infantil

in'fantile paral'ysis *s* Kinderlähmung *f*

infantry ['ɪnfəntri] *s* Infanterie *f*

in'fantry·man *s* (–men) Infanterist *m*

infatuated [ɪn'fætʃʊ‚etɪd] *adj* betört

infatuation [ɪn‚fætʃʊ'eʃən] *s* Betörung *f*

infect [ɪn'fɛkt] *tr* anstecken, infizieren; **become infected** sich anstecken

infection [ɪn'fɛkʃən] *s* Ansteckung *f*

infectious [ɪn'fɛkʃəs] *adj* (& *fig*) ansteckend

in·fer [ɪn'fʌr] *v* (*pret* & *pp* **–ferred; ger –ferring**) *tr* folgern

inference ['ɪnfərəns] *s* Folgerung *f*

inferior [ɪn'fɪrɪ·ər] *adj* (*in rank*) niedriger; (*in worth*) minderwertig; **(to)** unterlegen (*dat*)

inferiority [ɪn‚fɪrɪ'ɑrɪti] *s* Unterlegenheit *f;* (*in worth*) Minderwertigkeit *f*

inferior'ity com'plex *s* Minderwertigkeitskomplex *m*

infernal [ɪn'fʌrnəl] *adj* höllisch

infest [ɪn'fɛst] *tr* in Schwärmen überfallen; **be infested with** wimmeln von

infidel ['ɪnfɪdəl] *adj* ungläubig ‖ *s* Ungläubige *mf*

infidelity [‚ɪnfɪ'dɛlɪti] *s* Untreue *f*

in'field' *s* (baseball) Innenfeld *n*

infiltrate [ɪn'fɪltret], ['ɪnfɪl‚tret] *tr* (*filter through*) infiltrieren; (mil) durchsickern durch; (pol) unterwandern ‖ *intr* infiltrieren

infinite ['ɪnfɪnɪt] *adj* unendlich

infinitive [ɪn'fɪnɪtɪv] *s* (gram) Nennform *f*, Infinitiv *m*

infinity [ɪn'fɪnɪti] *s* Unendlichkeit *f;* **to i.** endlos

infirm [ɪn'fʌrm] *adj* schwach; (*from age*) altersschwach

infirmary [ɪn'fʌrməri] *s* Krankenstube *f;* (mil) Revier *n*

infirmity [ɪn'fʌrmɪti] *s* Schwachheit *f*

inflame [ɪn'flem] *tr* (fig & pathol) entzünden; **become inflamed** sich entzünden

inflammable [ɪn'flæməbəl] *adj* entzündbar, feuergefährlich

inflammation [‚ɪnflə'meʃən] *s* Entzündung *f*

inflammatory [ɪn'flæmə‚tori] *adj* aufrührerisch; (pathol) Entzündungs–

inflate [ɪn'flet] *tr* aufblasen; (*tires*) aufpumpen

inflation [ɪn'fleʃən] *s* (econ) Inflation *f*

inflationary [ɪn'fleʃə‚neri] *adj* inflationistisch

inflect [ɪn'flɛkt] *tr* (*the voice*) modulieren; (gram) flektieren

inflection [ɪn'flɛkʃən] *s* (*of the voice*) Tonfall *m;* (gram) Flexion *f*

inflexible [ɪn'flɛksɪbəl] *adj* unbiegsam; (*person*) unbeugsam; (*law*) unabänderlich

inflict [ɪn'flɪkt] *tr* (*punishment*) (**on**) auferlegen (*dat*); (*a defeat*) (**on**) zufügen (*dat*); (*a wound*) (**on**) beibringen (*dat*)

influence ['ɪnflu·əns] *s* (**on**) Einfluß *m* (auf *acc*) ‖ *tr* beeinflussen

influential [‚ɪnflu'ɛnʃəl] *adj* einflußreich, maßgebend

influenza [‚ɪnflu'ɛnzə] *s* Grippe *f*

influx ['ɪnflʌks] *s* Zufluß *m*

inform [ɪn'fɔrm] *tr* (**of**) benachrichtigen (von) ‖ *intr*—**i. against** anzeigen

informal [ɪn'fɔrməl] *adj* zwanglos

informant [ɪn'fɔrmənt] *s* Gewährsmann *m*

information [‚ɪnfər'meʃən] *s* Nachricht *f*, Auskunft *f;* (*items of information*)

Informationen *pl;* **a piece of** i. e–e Auskunft *f;* **for your i.** zu Ihrer Information
informa'tion desk' *s* Auskunftsstelle *f*
informative [ɪn'fɔrmətɪv] *adj* belehrend
informed' *adj* unterrichtet
informer [ɪn'fɔrmər] *s* Denunziant –in *mf*
infraction [ɪn'frækʃən] *s* **(of)** Verstoß *m* (gegen)
infrared [,ɪnfrə'rɛd] *adj* infrarot
infrequent [ɪn'frikwənt] *adj* selten
infringe [ɪn'frɪndʒ] *tr* verletzen ‖ *intr* **—i. on** eingreifen in (acc)
infringement [ɪn'frɪndʒmənt] *s* (of a law) Verletzung *f;* (of a right) Eingriff *m* (in acc)
infuriate [ɪn'fjʊrɪ ,et] *tr* wütend machen
infuse [ɪn'fjuz] *tr* (& fig) **(into)** einflößen (dat)
infusion [ɪn'fjuʒən] *s* (& fig) Einflößung *f;* (med) Infusion *f*
ingenious [ɪn'dʒinɪ·əs] *adj* erfinderisch
ingenuity [,ɪndʒɪ'n(j)u·ɪti] *s* Erfindungsgabe *f,* Scharfsinn *m*
ingenuous [ɪn'dʒɛnju·əs] *adj* aufrichtig; (naive) naiv
ingest [ɪn'dʒɛst] *tr* zu sich nehmen
inglorious [ɪn'glɔrɪ·əs] *adj* (shameful) unrühmlich; (without honor) ruhmlos
ingot ['ɪŋɡət] *s* Block *m;* (of gold or silver) Barren *m*
ingrained', **in'grained** *adj* eingewurzelt
ingrate ['ɪngret] *s* Undankbare *mf*
ingratiate [ɪn'greʃɪ ,et] *tr*—**i. oneself with** sich einschmeicheln bei
ingra'tiating *adj* einschmeichelnd
ingratitude [ɪn'grætɪ ,t(j)ud] *s* Undankbarkeit *f,* Undank *m*
ingredient [ɪn'gridɪ·ənt] *s* Bestandteil *m;* (culin) Zutat *f*
in'grown' *adj* eingewachsen
inhabit [ɪn'hæbɪt] *tr* bewohnen
inhabitant [ɪn'hæbɪtənt] *s* Bewohner –in *mf,* Einwohner –in *mf*
inhale [ɪn'hel] *tr & intr* einatmen; inhalieren
inherent [ɪn'hɪrənt] *adj* innewohnend; (right) angeboren
inherit [ɪn'herɪt] *tr* (biol, jur) erben
inheritance [ɪn'herɪtəns] *s* Erbschaft *f*
inher'itance tax' *s* Erbschaftssteuer *f*
inheritor [ɪn'herɪtər] *s* Erbe *m,* Erbin *f*
inhibit [ɪn'hɪbɪt] *tr* hemmen, inhibieren
inhibition [,ɪnɪ'bɪʃən] *s* Hemmung *f*
inhospitable [ɪn'hɑspɪtəbəl] *adj* ungastlich; (place) unwirtlich
inhuman [ɪn'hjumən] *adj* unmenschlich
inhumane [,ɪnju'men] *adj* inhuman
inhumanity [,ɪnhju'mænɪti] *s* Unmenschlichkeit *f*
inimical [ɪ'nɪmɪkəl] *adj* **(to)** abträglich (dat)
iniquity [ɪ'nɪkwɪti] *s* Niederträchtigkeit *f,* Ungerechtigkeit *f*
ini·tial [ɪn'ɪʃəl] *adj* anfänglich ‖ *s* Anfangsbuchstabe *m,* Initiale *f* ‖ *v*

(pret & pp **–tial[l]ed;** ger **–tial[l]ing**) *tr* mit den Initialen unterzeichnen
initially [ɪ'nɪʃəli] *adv* anfangs
initiate [ɪ'nɪʃɪ ,et] *tr* einführen; (reforms) einleiten; **(into)** aufnehmen in (acc)
initiation [ɪ ,nɪʃɪ'eʃən] *s* Einführung *f;* **(into)** Aufnahme *f* (in acc)
initiative [ɪ'nɪʃ(ɪ)ətɪv] *s* Unternehmungsgeist *m;* **take the i.** die Initiative ergreifen
inject [ɪn'dʒɛkt] *tr* (a needle) einführen; (a word) dazwischenwerfen; (e.g., bigotry into a campaign) einfließen lassen; (a liquid) (med) injizieren
injection [ɪn'dʒɛkʃən] *s* (mach) Einspritzung *f;* (med) Injektion *f*
injudicious [,ɪndʒu'dɪʃəs] *adj* unverständig
injunction [ɪn'dʒʌŋkʃən] *s* Gebot *n;* (jur) gerichtliche Verfügung *f*
injure ['ɪndʒər] *tr* verletzen; (fig) schädigen
injurious [ɪn'dʒʊrɪ·əs] *adj* schädlich
injury ['ɪndʒəri] *s* Verletzung *f;* **(to)** Schädigung *f* (genit)
injustice [ɪn'dʒʌstɪs] *s* Ungerechtigkeit *f*
ink [ɪŋk] *s* Tinte *f* ‖ *tr* schwärzen
inkling ['ɪŋklɪŋ] *s* leise Ahnung *f*
ink' pad' *s* Stempelkissen *n*
ink' spot' *s* Tintenklecks *m*
inky ['ɪŋki] *adj* tiefschwarz
inlaid ['ɪn ,led] *adj* eingelegt
in'laid floor' *s* Parkettfußboden *m*
inland ['ɪnlənd] *adj* Binnen– ‖ *adv* landeinwärts ‖ *s* Binnenland *n*
in'-laws' *spl* angeheiratete Verwandte *pl*
inlay ['ɪn ,le] *s* Einlegearbeit *f;* (dent) gegossene Plombe *f*
in'let *s* Meeresarm *m;* (opening) Öffnung *f*
in'mate *s* Insasse *m,* Insassin *f*
inn [ɪn] *s* Gasthaus *n,* Wirtshaus *n*
innards ['ɪnərdʒ] *spl* (coll) Innere *n*
innate [ɪ'net] *adj* angeboren
inner ['ɪnər] *adj* innere, inwendig, Innen–
in'nermost' *adj* innerste
in'nerspring mat'tress *s* Federkernmatratze *f*
in'ner tube' *s* Schlauch *m*
inning ['ɪnɪŋ] *s* Runde *f*
inn'keep'er *s* Wirt *m,* Wirtin *f*
innocence ['ɪnəsəns] *s* Unschuld *f;* (of a crime) Schuldlosigkeit *f*
innocent ['ɪnəsənt] *adj* (of) unschuldig (an dat); (harmless) harmlos; (guileless) arglos ‖ *s* Unschuldige *mf*
innocuous [ɪ'nɑkju·əs] *adj* harmlos
innovation [,ɪnə've ʃən] *s* Neuerung *f*
innovative ['ɪnə ,vetɪv] *adj* (person) neuerungssüchtig; (thing) Neuerungs–
innuen·do [,ɪnju'endo] *s* **(–does)** Unterstellung *f*
innumerable [ɪ'n(j)umərəbəl] *adj* unzählbar, unzählig
inoculate [ɪn'ɑkjə ,let] *tr* impfen
inoculation [ɪn ,ɑkjə'leʃən] *s* Impfung *f*

inoffensive [ˌɪnə'fɛnsɪv] *adj* unschädlich

inopportune [ɪnˌɑpər't(j)un] *adj* ungelegen

inordinate [ɪn'ɔrdɪnɪt] *adj* übermäßig

inorganic [ˌɪnɔr'gænɪk] *adj* unorganisch; (chem) anorganisch

in'put' *adj* (data proc) Eingabe– ‖ *s* (*in production*) Aufwand *m;* (data proc) Eingabe *f,* Eingangsinformation *f;* (elec) Stromzufuhr *f*

inquest ['ɪnkwɛst] *s* Untersuchung *f*

inquire [ɪn'kwaɪr] *intr* anfragen; **i. about** sich erkundigen nach; **i. into** untersuchen; **i. of** sich erkundigen bei

inquiry [ɪn'kwaɪri], ['ɪnkwɪri] *s* Anfrage *f;* (*investigation*) Untersuchung *f;* **make inquiries (about)** Erkundigungen einziehen (über *acc*)

inquisition [ˌɪnkwɪ'zɪʃən] *s* Inquisition *f*

inquisitive [ɪn'kwɪzɪtɪv] *adj* wißbegierig

in'road *s* (*raid*) Einfall *m;* (fig) Eingriff *m*

ins' and outs' *spl* alle Kniffe *pl*

insane [ɪn'sen] *adj* wahnsinnig; (*absurd*) unsinnig

insane' asy'lum *s* Irrenanstalt *f*

insanity [ɪn'sænɪti] *s* Wahnsinn *m*

insatiable [ɪn'seʃəbəl] *adj* unersättlich

inscribe [ɪn'skraɪb] *tr* (*a name*) einschreiben; (*a book*) widmen; (*a monument*) mit e-r Inschrift versehen

inscription [ɪn'skrɪpʃən] *s* Inschrift *f;* (*of a book*) Widmung *f*

inscrutable [ɪn'skrutəbəl] *adj* unerforschlich

insect ['ɪnsɛkt] *s* Insekt *n,* Kerbtier *n*

insecticide [ɪn'sɛktɪˌsaɪd] *s* Insektenvertilgungsmittel *n,* Insektizid *n*

insecure [ˌɪnsɪ'kjur] *adj* unsicher

insecurity [ˌɪnsɪ'kjurɪti] *s* Unsicherheit *f*

insensitive [ɪn'sɛnsɪtɪv] *adj* (**to**) unempfindlich (gegen)

inseparable [ɪn'sɛpərəbəl] *adj* untrennbar; (*friends*) unzertrennlich

insert ['ɪnsʌrt] *s* Einsatzstück *n* ‖ [ɪn'sʌrt] *tr* einfügen; (*a coin*) einwerfen

insertion [ɪn'sʌrʃən] *s* Einfügung *f;* (*of a coin*) Einwurf *m*

in'set' (*of a map*) Nebenkarte *f;* (*inserted piece*) Einsatz *m*

in'shore' *adj* Küsten– ‖ *adv* auf die Küste zu

in'side' *adj* innere, Innen–; (*information*) vertraulich ‖ *adv* innen, drinnen; **come i.** hereinkommen; **i. of** innerhalb von; **i. out** verkehrt; **know i. out** in– und auswendig kennen; **turn i. out** umdrehen ‖ *s* Innenseite *f,* Innere *n;* **on the i.** innen ‖ *prep* innerhalb (*genit*)

insider [ɪn'saɪdər] *s* Eingeweihte *mf*

in'side track' *s* (sport) Innenbahn *f;* **have the i.** (fig) im Vorteil sein

insidious [ɪn'sɪdɪ-əs] *adj* hinterlistig

in'sight' *s* Einsicht *f*

insigni·a [ɪn'sɪgnɪ-ə] *s* (**–a & –as**) Ab-

zeichen *n;* **i. of office** Amtsabzeichen *pl;* **i. of rank** Rangabzeichen *pl*

insignificant [ˌɪnsɪg'nɪfɪkənt] *adj* bedeutungslos, geringfügig

insincere [ˌɪnsɪn'sɪr] *adj* unaufrichtig

insincerity [ˌɪnsɪn'sɛrɪti] *s* Unaufrichtigkeit *f*

insinuate [ɪn'sɪnjuˌet] *tr* andeuten

insipid [ɪn'sɪpɪd] *adj* (& fig) fad(e)

insist [ɪn'sɪst] *intr*—**i. on** bestehen auf (*dat*); **i. on** (*ger*) darauf bestehen zu (*inf*)

insistent [ɪn'sɪstənt] *adj* beharrlich

insofar as [ˌɪnso'fɑr ˌæz] *conj* insoweit als

insolence ['ɪnsələns] *s* Unverschämtheit *f*

insolent ['ɪnsələnt] *adj* unverschämt

insoluble [ɪn'saljəbəl] *adj* unlösbar

insolvency [ɪn'salvənsi] *s* Zahlungsunfähigkeit *f,* Insolvenz *f*

insolvent [ɪn'salvənt] *adj* zahlungsunfähig

insomnia [ɪn'samnɪ-ə] *s* Schlaflosigkeit *f*

insomuch as [ˌɪnso'mʌtʃəz] *conj* insofern als

inspect [ɪn'spɛkt] *tr* (*view closely*) besichtigen; (*check*) kontrollieren; (aut) untersuchen; (mil) besichtigen

inspection [ɪn'spɛkʃən] *s* Besichtigung *f;* Kontrolle *f;* (aut) Untersuchung *f;* (mil) Truppenbesichtigung *f*

inspector [ɪn'spɛktər] *s* Kontrolleur *m;* (*of police*) Inspektor *m*

inspiration [ˌɪnspɪ'reʃən] *s* Begeisterung *f*

inspire [ɪn'spaɪr] *tr* begeistern; (*feelings*) erwecken

inspir'ing *adj* begeisternd

instability [ˌɪnstə'bɪlɪti] *s* Unbeständigkeit *f*

install [ɪn'stɔl] *tr* (*appliances*) installieren; (*in office*) einführen

installation [ˌɪnstə'leʃən] *s* (*of appliances*) Installation *f;* (mil) Anlage *f*

installment [ɪn'stɔlmənt] *s* Installation *f;* (*in a serialized story*) Fortsetzung *f;* (*partial payment*) Rate *f;* **in installments** ratenweise

install'ment plan' *s* Teilzahlungsplan *m*

instance ['ɪnstəns] *s* (*case*) Fall *m;* (*example*) Beispiel *n;* (jur) Instanz *f;* **for i.** zum Beispiel

instant ['ɪnstənt] *adj* augenblicklich; (*foods*) gebrauchsfertig ‖ *s* Augenblick *m;* **this i.** sofort

instantaneous [ˌɪnstən'tenɪ-əs] *adj* augenblicklich, sofortig

instead [ɪn'stɛd] *adv* statt dessen

instead' of *prep* (an)statt (*genit*); (*ger*) anstatt zu (*inf*)

in'step' *s* Rist *m*

instigate ['ɪnstɪˌget] *tr* anstiften

instigation [ˌɪnstɪ'geʃən] *s* Anstiftung *f*

instigator ['ɪnstɪˌgetər] *s* Anstifter –in *mf*

instill [ɪn'stɪl] *tr* einflößen

instinct ['ɪnstɪŋkt] *s* Trieb *m,* Instinkt *m;* **by i.** instinktiv

instinctive [ɪn'stɪŋktɪv] *adj* instinktiv

institute ['ɪnstɪ ˌt(j)ut] s Institut n ‖ tr einleiten

institution [ˌɪnstɪ't(j)uʃən] s Anstalt f

instruct [ɪn'strʌkt] tr anweisen, beauftragen; (teach) unterrichten

instruction [ɪn'strʌkʃən] s (teaching) Unterricht m; **instructions** Anweisungen pl; **instructions for use** Gebrauchsanweisung f

instructive [ɪn'strʌktɪv] adj lehrreich

instructor [ɪn'strʌktər] s Lehrer –in mf; (at a university) Dozent –in mf

instrument ['ɪnstrəmənt] s Instrument n; (tool) Werkzeug n; (jur) Dokument n

instrumental [ˌɪnstrə'mentəl] adj (mus) instrumental; **he was i. in my getting an award** er war mir behilflich, e–n Preis zu erhalten

instrumentality [ˌɪnstrəmən'tælɪti] s Vermittlung f

in'strument land'ing s Instrumentenlandung f

in'strument pan'el s Armaturenbrett n

insubordinate [ˌɪnsə'bɔrdɪnɪt] adj widersetzlich

insubordination [ˌɪnsəbɔrdɪ'neʃən] s Widersetzlichkeit f

insufferable [ɪn'sʌfərəbəl] adj unausstehlich

insufficient [ˌɪnsə'fɪʃənt] adj ungenügend, unzureichend

insular ['ɪns(j)ələr] adj insular

insulate ['ɪnsə ˌlet] tr isolieren

insulation [ˌɪnsə'leʃən] s Isolierung f; (insulating material) Isolierstoff m

insulator ['ɪnsə ˌletər] s Isolator m

insulin ['ɪnsəlɪn] s Insulin n

insult ['ɪnsʌlt] s Beleidigung f ‖ [ɪn-'sʌlt] tr beleidigen, beschimpfen

insurance [ɪn'ʃurəns] adj Versicherungs– ‖ s Versicherung f

insure [ɪn'ʃur] tr versichern

insured' adj (letter, package) Wert– ‖ s Versicherungsnehmer –in mf

insurer [ɪn'ʃurər] s Versicherer –in mf

insurgent [ɪn'sʌrdʒənt] adj aufständisch ‖ s Aufständische mf

insurmountable [ˌɪnsər'mauntəbəl] adj unübersteigbar; (fig) unüberwindlich

insurrection [ˌɪnsə'rekʃən] s Aufstand m

intact [ɪn'tækt] adj unversehrt

in'take' s (aut) Einlaß m; **i. of food** Nahrungsaufnahme f

in'take valve' s Einlaßventil n

intangible [ɪn'tændʒɪbəl] adj immateriell

integer ['ɪntɪdʒər] s ganze Zahl f

integral ['ɪntɪgrəl] adj wesentlich; (math) Integral– ‖ s Integral n

integrate ['ɪntɪ ˌgret] tr eingliedern; (a school) die Rassentrennung aufheben in (dat); (& math) integrieren

integration [ˌɪntɪ'greʃən] s Integration f; (of schools) Aufhebung f der Rassentrennung

integrity [ɪn'tegrɪti] s Redlichkeit f

intellect ['ɪntə ˌlekt] s Intellekt m

intellectual [ˌɪntə'lekt/ʊ–əl] adj intellektuell; (freedom, history) Geistes– ‖ s Intellektuelle mf

intelligence [ɪn'telɪdʒəns] s Intelligenz f, Klugheit f; (information) Nachricht f; (department) Nachrichtendienst m; **gather i.** Nachrichten einziehen

intel'ligence quo'tient s Intelligenz-Quotient m

intel'ligence test' s Begabungsprüfung f

intelligent [ɪn'telɪdʒənt] adj intelligent, klug

intelligentsia [ɪn ˌtelɪ'dʒentsɪ-ə] s Intelligenz f, geistige Oberschicht f

intelligible [ɪn'telɪdʒɪbəl] adj (to) verständlich (dat)

intemperate [ɪn'tempərɪt] adj unmäßig; (in drink) trunksüchtig

intend [ɪn'tend] tr beabsichtigen; **be intended for** bestimmt sein für, gemünzt sein auf (acc) **i. by** bezwecken mit; **i. for s.o.** j–m zudenken

intend'ed s (coll) Verlobte mf

intense [ɪn'tens] adj intensiv, stark

intensi-fy [ɪn'tensɪ ˌfaɪ] v (pret & pp –fied) tr steigern, verstärken ‖ intr sich steigern, stärker werden

intensity [ɪn'tensɪti] s Stärke f

intensive [ɪn'tensɪv] adj intensiv; (gram) verstärkend

inten'sive care' s Intensivstation f

intent [ɪn'tent] adj (on) erpicht (auf acc) ‖ s Absicht f; **to all intents and purposes** praktisch genommen

intention [ɪn'tenʃən] s Absicht f; **good i.** guter Wille m; **have honorable intentions** es ehrlich meinen; **with the i. of** (ger) in der Absicht zu (inf)

intentional [ɪn'tenʃənəl] adj absichtlich

intently [ɪn'tentli] adv gespannt

in-ter [ɪn'tʌr] v (pret & pp –terred; ger –terring) tr beerdigen

interact [ˌɪntər'ækt] intr zusammenwirken, aufeinander wirken

interaction [ˌɪntər'ækʃən] s Wechselwirkung f

inter·breed [ˌɪntər'brid] v (pret & pp –bred) tr kreuzen ‖ intr sich kreuzen

intercede [ˌɪntər'sid] intr Fürsprache einlegen; **i. for s.o. with** Fürsprache einlegen für j–n bei

intercept [ˌɪntər'sept] tr (a letter, aircraft) abfangen; (a radio message) abhören; (cut off, check) den Weg abschneiden (dat)

interceptor [ˌɪntər'septər] s (aer) Abfangjäger m

intercession [ˌɪntər'seʃən] s Fürsprache f; (relig) Fürbitte f

interchange ['ɪntər ˌtʃendʒ] s Wechsel m; (on a highway) Anschlußstelle f ‖ [ˌɪntər'tʃendʒ] tr auswechseln ‖ intr (with) abwechseln (mit)

interchangeable [ˌɪntər'tʃendʒəbəl] adj auswechselbar, austauschbar

intercom ['ɪntər ˌkɑm] s Wechselsprachanlage f

intercourse ['ɪntər ˌkors] s Verkehr m; (sexual) Geschlechtsverkehr m

interdependent [ˌɪntərdɪ'pendənt] adj voneinander abhängig

interdict ['ɪntər ˌdɪkt] s Verbot n; (eccl) Interdikt n ‖ [ˌɪntər'dɪkt] tr

verbieten; **i. s.o. from** (*ger*) j-m verbieten zu (*inf*)
interest ['ɪnt(ə)rɪst] *s* (**in**) Interesse *n*
(an *dat*, für); (fin) Zinsen *pl;* **at i.**
gegen Zinsen; **be in s.o.'s i.** in j-s
Interesse liegen; **have an i. in** be-
teiligt sein an (*dat*) or bei; **interests**
Belange *pl;* **pay i.** (*bring in interest*)
Zinsen abwerfen; (*pay out interest*)
Zinsen zahlen; **take an i. in** sich
interessieren für; **with i.** (& fig) mit
Zinsen ‖ *tr* (**in**) interessieren (für)
in'terested *adj*—**i. in** interessiert an
(*dat*); **the i. parties** die Beteiligten *pl*
in'teresting *adj* interessant
in'terest rate' *s* Zinsfuß *m*, Zinssatz *m*
interfere [,ɪntər'fɪr] *intr* (*said of a
thing*) dazwischenkommen; (*said of
a person*) eingreifen; (**in** or **with**) sich
(ein)mengen (in *acc*); **i. with** (rad,
telv) stören; **i. with s.o.'s work** j-n
bei seiner Arbeit stören
interference [,ɪntər'fɪrəns] *s* Einmischung *f;* (phys) Interferenz *f;*
(rad, telv) Störung *f*
interim ['ɪntərɪm] *adj* Zwischen– ‖ *s*
Zwischenzeit *f*
interior [ɪn'tɪrɪ·ər] *adj* innere, Innen–
‖ *s* Innere *n;* (*of a building*) Innen-
raum *m;* (*of a country*) Inland *n*
inte'rior dec'orator *s* Innenarchitekt
–in *mf*
interject [,ɪntər'dʒɛkt] *tr* dazwischenwerfen
interjection [,ɪntər'dʒɛkʃən] *s* Zwi-
schenwurf *m;* (gram) Interjektion *f*
interlard [,ɪntər'lard] *tr* (& fig) spicken
interlinear [,ɪntər'lɪnɪ·ər] *adj* Interlinear–
interlock [,ɪntər'lak] *tr* miteinander
verbinden ‖ *intr* sich ineinander-
schließen
interloper [,ɪntər'lopər] *s* Eindringling
m
interlude ['ɪntər,lud] *s* (*interval*)
Pause *f;* (fig, mus, theat) Zwischen-
spiel *n*
intermediary [,ɪntər'midɪ ,ɛri] *adj* ver-
mittelnd ‖ *s* Vermittler –in *mf*
intermediate [,ɪntər'midɪ·ɪt] *adj* zwi-
schenliegend, Zwischen–
interment [ɪn'tʌrmənt] *s* Beerdigung *f*
intermez·zo [,ɪntər'metso] *s* (–**zos** &
zi [tsi]) Intermezzo *n*
intermingle [,ɪntər'mɪŋgəl] *tr* vermischen ‖ *intr* sich vermischen
intermission [,ɪntər'mɪʃən] *s* Unterbrechung *f;* (theat) Pause *f*
intermittent [,ɪntər'mɪtənt] *adj* inter-
mittierend
intermix [,ɪntər'mɪks] *tr* vermischen ‖
intr sich vermischen
intern ['ɪntʌrn] *s* Assistenzarzt *m*, Assistenzärztin *f*
internal [ɪn'tʌrnəl] *adj* innere, intern;
(*domestic*) einheimisch; (*trade,
rhyme*) Binnen–
inter'nal-combus'tion en'gine *s* Ver-
brennungsmotor *m*
inter'nal med'icine *s* innere Medizin *f*
inter'nal rev'enue *s* Steueraufkommen
n

international [,ɪntər'næʃənəl] *adj* international
interna'tional date' line' *s* internationale Datumsgrenze *f*
interna'tional law' *s* Völkerrecht *n*
interne'cine war' [,ɪntər'nisɪn] *s* ge-
genseitiger Vernichtungskrieg *m*
internee [,ɪntər'ni] *s* Internierte *mf*
internment [ɪn'tʌrnmənt] *s* Internie-
rung *f*
in'ternship' *s* Pflichtzeit *f* als Assistenzarzt (or Assistenzärztin)
interoffice [,ɪntər'afɪs] *adj* Haus–
interplanetary [,ɪntər'plænɪ ,tɛri] *adj*
interplanetarisch
interplay ['ɪntər ,ple] *s* Wechselspiel *n*
interpolate [ɪn'tʌrpə ,let] *tr* interpolie-
ren
interpose [,ɪntər'poz] *tr* (*an obstacle*)
dazwischensetzen; (*a remark*) einwerfen
interpret [ɪn'tʌrprɪt] *tr* (& mus) inter-
pretieren; (*translate*) verdolmetschen
‖ *intr* dolmetschen
interpretation [ɪn,tʌrprɪ'teʃən] *s* (&
mus) Interpretation *f*
interpreter [ɪn'tʌrprɪtər] *s* Dolmet-
scher –in *mf;* **act as i.** dolmetschen
interrogate [ɪn'tɛrə ,get] *tr* ausfragen;
(jur) verhören, vernehmen
interrogation [ɪn ,tɛrə'geʃən] *s* Verhör
n
interrogative [,ɪntər'ragətɪv] *adj*
Frage–
interrupt [,ɪntə'rʌpt] *tr* unterbrechen
interruption [,ɪntə'rʌpʃən] *s* Unterbrechung *f;* (*in industry*) Betriebsstörung *f*
intersect [,ɪntər'sɛkt] *tr* durchschnei-
den ‖ *ref* sich kreuzen
intersection [,ɪntər'sɛkʃən] *s* Straßenkreuzung *f;* (math) Schnittpunkt *m*
intersperse [,ɪntər'spʌrs] *tr* durchsetzen
interstate ['ɪntər ,stet] *adj* zwischen-
staatlich
interstellar [,ɪntər'stɛlər] *adj* interstellar
interstice [ɪn'tʌrstɪs] *s* Zwischenraum
m
intertwine [,ɪntər'twaɪn] *tr* verflechten
‖ *intr* sich verflechten
interval ['ɪntərvəl] *s* Abstand *m;* (mus)
Stufe *f*, Intervall *n*
intervene [,ɪntər'vin] *intr* dazwischenkommen; (*interfere*) eingreifen; (*intercede*) intervenieren
intervention [,ɪntər'vɛnʃən] *s* Dazwischenkommen *n;* Eingreifen *n;* Intervention *f*
interview ['ɪntər ,vju] *s* Interview *n* ‖
tr interviewen
inter·weave [,ɪntər'wiv] *v* (*pret* –**wove**
& –**weaved;** *pp* –**wove**, –**woven** &
–**weaved**) *tr* durchweben, durchflech-
ten
intestate [ɪn'tɛstet] *adj* ohne Testament
intestine [ɪn'tɛstɪn] *s* Darm *m;* **intestines** Gedärme *pl*
intimacy ['ɪntɪməsi] *s* Vertraulichkeit
f; **intimacies** Intimitäten *pl*
intimate ['ɪntɪmɪt] *adj* intim, vertraut

‖ *s* Vertraute *mf* ‖ [ˈɪntɪ ˌmet] *tr* andeuten

intimation [ˌɪntɪˈmeʃən] *s* Andeutung *f*

intimidate [ɪnˈtɪmɪ ˌdet] *tr* einschüchtern

intimidation [ˌɪntɪmɪˈdeʃən] *s* Einschüchterung *f*

into [ˈɪntu], [ˈɪntʊ] *prep* in (*acc*)

intolerable [ɪnˈtɑlərəbəl] *adj* unerträglich

intolerance [ɪnˈtɑlərəns] *s* (**of**) Intoleranz *f* (**gegen**)

intolerant [ɪnˈtɑlərənt] *adj* (**of**) intolerant (**gegen**)

intonation [ˌɪntoˈneʃən] *s* Tonfall *m*

intone [ɪnˈton] *tr* intonieren

intoxicate [ɪnˈtɑksɪ ˌket] *tr* berauschen; (*poison*) vergiften

intoxication [ɪn ˌtɑksɪˈkeʃən] *s* (& *fig*) Rausch *m;* (*poisoning*) Vergiftung *f*

intractable [ɪnˈtræktəbəl] *adj* (*person*) störrisch; (*thing*) schwer zu bearbeiten(d)

intransigent [ɪnˈtrænsɪdʒənt] *adj* unversöhnlich

intransitive [ɪnˈtrænsɪtɪv] *adj* intransitiv

intravenous [ˌɪntrəˈvinəs] *adj* intravenös

intrepid [ɪnˈtrɛpɪd] *adj* unerschrocken

intricate [ˈɪntrɪkɪt] *adj* verwickelt

intrigue [ɪnˈtrig], [ˈɪntrig] *s* Intrige *f* ‖ [ɪnˈtrig] *tr* fesseln ‖ *intr* intrigieren

intrigu'ing *adj* fesselnd

intrinsic(al) [ɪnˈtrɪnsɪk(əl)] *adj* innere, innerlich; (*value*) wirklich

introduce [ˌɪntrəˈd(j)us] *tr* einführen; (*strangers*) vorstellen

introduction [ˌɪntrəˈdʌkʃən] *s* Einführung *f;* (*of strangers*) Vorstellung *f;* (*in a book*) Einleitung *f*

introductory [ˌɪntrəˈdʌktəri] *adj* (*offer, price*) Einführungs–; (*remarks*) einleitend

introspection [ˌɪntrəˈspɛkʃən] *s* Selbstbeobachtung *f*

introspective [ˌɪntrəˈspɛktɪv] *adj* introspektiv

introvert [ˈɪntrə ˌvʌrt] *s* Introvertierte *f*

intrude [ɪnˈtrud] *intr* (**on**) sich aufdrängen (dat); **am I intruding?** störe ich?

intruder [ɪnˈtrudər] *s* Eindringling *m*

intrusion [ɪnˈtruʒən] *s* Eindrängen *n,* Stören *n*

intrusive [ɪnˈtrusɪv] *adj* störend, lästig

intuition [ˌɪnt(j)uˈɪʃən] *s* Intuition *f*

inundate [ˈɪnən ˌdet] *tr* überschwemmen

inundation [ˌɪnənˈdeʃən] *s* Überschwemmung *f*

inure [ɪnˈjʊr] *tr* (**to**) abhärten (**gegen**)

invade [ɪnˈved] *tr* (*a country*) eindringen in (*acc*); (*rights*) verletzen; (*privacy*) stören

invader [ɪnˈvedər] *s* Eindringling *m;* (mil) Angreifer *m*

invalid [ɪnˈvælɪd] *adj* ungültig ‖ [ˈɪnvəlɪd] *adj* kränklich ‖ *s* Invalide *m*

invalidate [ɪnˈvælɪ ˌdet] *tr* ungültig machen; (*a law*) außer Kraft setzen

invalidity [ˌɪnvəˈlɪdɪti] *s* Ungültigkeit *f*

invaluable [ɪnˈvæljʊ·əbəl] *adj* unschätzbar

invariable [ɪnˈvɛrɪ·əbəl] *adj* unveränderlich

invasion [ɪnˈveʃən] *s* Invasion *f*

invective [ɪnˈvɛktɪv] *s* Schmähung *f*

inveigh [ɪnˈve] *intr*—**i. against** schimpfen über (*acc*) or auf (*acc*)

inveigle [ɪnˈvigel] *tr* verleiten; **i. s.o. into** (*ger*) j–n verleiten zu (*inf*)

invent [ɪnˈvent] *tr* erfinden; (*a story*) sich [*dat*] ausdenken

invention [ɪnˈvenʃən] *s* Erfindung *f*

inventive [ɪnˈventɪv] *adj* erfinderisch

inventiveness [ɪnˈventɪvnɪs] *s* Erfindungsgabe *f*

inventor [ɪnˈventər] *s* Erfinder –in *mf*

invento·ry [ˈɪnvən ˌtɔri] *s* (*stock*) Inventar *n;* (*act*) Inventur *f;* (*list*) Bestandsverzeichnis *n;* **take i.** Inventur machen ‖ *v* (*pret* & *pp* –**ried**) *tr* inventarisieren

inverse [ɪnˈvʌrs] *adj* umgekehrt

inversion [ɪnˈvʌrʒən] *s* Umkehrung *f;* (gram) Umstellung *f*

invert [ɪnˈvʌrt] *tr* umkehren; (gram) umstellen

invertebrate [ɪnˈvʌrtɪ ˌbret] *adj* wirbellos ‖ *s* wirbelloses Tier *n*

invest [ɪnˈvest] *tr* (**in**) investieren (in *acc*); (mil) belagern; **i. with** ausstatten mit

investigate [ɪnˈvestɪ ˌget] *tr* untersuchen

investigation [ɪn ˌvestɪˈgeʃən] *s* Untersuchung *f*

investigator [ɪnˈvestɪ ˌgetər] *s* Untersucher –in *mf*

investment [ɪnˈvestmənt] *s* Anlage *f,* Investition *f;* (*with an office*) Amtseinführung *f;* (mil) Belagerung *f*

investor [ɪnˈvestər] *s* Investor –in *mf*

inveterate [ɪnˈvetərɪt] *adj* (*habitual*) eingefleischt; (*firmly established*) eingewurzelt

invidious [ɪnˈvɪdɪ·əs] *adj* haßerregend

invigorate [ɪnˈvɪgə ˌret] *tr* beleben

invig'orating *adj* belebend

invincible [ɪnˈvɪnsɪbəl] *adj* unbesiegbar

invisible [ɪnˈvɪzɪbəl] *adj* unsichtbar

invis'ible ink' *s* Geheimtinte *f*

invitation [ˌɪnvɪˈteʃən] *s* Einladung *f*

invite [ɪnˈvaɪt] *tr* einladen; **i. in** hereinbitten

invit'ing *adj* lockend

invocation [ˌɪnvəˈkeʃən] *s* Anrufung *f;* (relig) Bittgebet *n*

invoice [ˈɪnvɔɪs] *s* Faktura *f,* Warenrechnung *f;* **as per i.** laut Rechnung ‖ *tr* fakturieren

invoke [ɪnˈvok] *tr* anrufen; (*cite*) zitieren

involuntary [ɪnˈvɑlən ˌteri] *adj* (*against one's will*) unfreiwillig; (*without one's will*) unwillkürlich

invol'untary man'slaughter *s* unbeabsichtigte Tötung *f*

involve [ɪn'vɑlv] *tr* verwickeln; (*include*) einschließen; (*affect*) betreffen; (*entail*) zur Folge haben
involved' *adj* verwickelt, kompliziert; **be i. in** (*e.g., construction*) beschäftigt sein bei; (*e.g., a crime*) verwickelt sein in (*acc*); **be i. with** (*e.g., a married person*) e–e Affäre haben mit
involvement [ɪn'vɑlʌmənt] *s* Verwicklung *f*
invulnerable [ɪn'vʌlnərəbəl] *adj* unverwundbar
inward ['ɪnwərd] *adj* inner(lich) ‖ *adv* nach innen
inwardly ['ɪnwərdli] *adv* innerlich
iodine ['aɪ·ə ˌdin] *s* (chem) Jod *n* ‖ ['aɪ·ə ˌdaɪn] *s* (pharm) Jodtinktur *f*
ion ['aɪ·ən], ['aɪ·ɑn] *s* Ion *n*
ionize ['aɪ·ə ˌnaɪz] *tr* ionisieren
IOU ['aɪ ˌo'ju] *s* (**I owe you**) Schuldschein *m*
I.Q. ['aɪ'kju] *s* (**intelligence quotient**) Intelligenz-Quotient *m*
Iran [ɪ'rɑn], [aɪ'ræn] *s* Iran *m*
Iranian [aɪ'reni·ən] *adj* iranisch ‖ *s* Iran(i)er –in *mf*
Iraq [ɪ'rɑk] *s* Irak *m*
Ira·qi [ɪ'rɑki] *adj* irakisch ‖ *s* (**–qis**) Iraker –in *mf*
irascible [ɪ'ræsɪbəl] *adj* jähzornig
irate ['aɪret], [aɪ'ret] *adj* zornig
ire [aɪr] *s* Zorn *m*
Ireland ['aɪrlənd] *s* Irland *n*
iris ['aɪrɪs] *s* (anat, bot) Iris *f*
Irish ['aɪrɪʃ] *adj* irisch ‖ *s* (*language*) Irisch *n;* **the I.** die Iren *pl*
I'rish·man *s* (**–men**) Ire *m*
I'rishwom'an *s* (**–wom'en**) Irin *f*
irk [ʌrk] *tr* ärgern
irksome ['ʌrksəm] *adj* ärgerlich
iron ['aɪ·ərn] *adj* (& fig) eisern ‖ *s* Eisen *n;* (*for pressing clothes*) Bügeleisen *n* ‖ *tr* bügeln; **i. out** ausbügeln; (fig) ins Reine bringen
ironclad ['aɪ·ərn ˌklæd] *adj* (fig) unumstößlich
i'ron cur'tain *s* eiserner Vorhang *m*
ironic(al) [aɪ'rɑnɪk(əl)] *adj* ironisch
i'roning *s* (*act*) Bügeln *n;* (*clothes*) Bügelwäsche *f*
i'roning board' *s* Bügelbrett *n*
i'ron lung' *s* eiserne Lunge *f*
i'ron ore' *s* Eisenerz *n*
irony ['aɪrəni] *s* Ironie *f*
irradiate [ɪ'redi ˌet] *tr* bestrahlen; (*light*) ausstrahlen; (*a face*) aufheitern
irrational [ɪ'ræʃənəl] *adj* irrational
irreconcilable [ˌɪrɛkən'saɪləbəl] *adj* unversöhnlich
irredeemable [ˌɪrɪ'diməbəl] *adj* (*loan, bond*) nicht einlösbar; (*hopeless*) hoffnungslos
irrefutable [ˌɪrɪ'fjutəbəl] *adj* unwiderlegbar
irregular [ɪ'regjələr] *adj* unregelmäßig
irregularity [ɪ ˌregjə'lærɪti] *s* Unregelmäßigkeit *f*
irrelevant [ɪ'rɛləvənt] *adj* (**to**) nicht anwendbar (auf *acc*)
irreligious [ˌɪrɪ'lɪdʒəs] *adj* irreligiös

irreparable [ɪ'rɛpərəbəl] *adj* unersetzlich
irreplaceable [ˌɪrɪ'plesɪbəl] *adj* unersetzlich
irrepressible [ˌɪrɪ'prɛsɪbəl] *adj* unbezähmbar
irreproachable [ˌɪrɪ'protʃəbəl] *adj* untadelig
irresistible [ˌɪrɪ'zɪstɪbəl] *adj* unwiderstehlich
irresolute [ɪ'rɛzəlut] *adj* unentschlossen, unschlüßig
irrespective [ˌɪrɪ'spɛktɪv] *adj*—**i. of** ohne Rücksicht auf (*acc*)
irresponsible [ˌɪrɪ'spɑnsɪbəl] *adj* unverantwortlich
irretrievable [ˌɪrɪ'trivəbəl] *adj* unwiederbringlich, unrettbar
irreverent [ɪ'rɛvərənt] *adj* unehrerbietig
irrevocable [ɪ'rɛvəkəbəl] *adj* unwiderruflich
irrigate ['ɪrɪ ˌget] *tr* verwässern; (med) irrigieren
irrigation [ˌɪrɪ'geʃən] *s* Bewässerung *f*
irritable ['ɪrɪtəbəl] *adj* reizbar
irritant ['ɪrɪtənt] *s* Reizstoff *m*
irritate ['ɪrɪ ˌtet] *tr* reizen, irritieren
ir'ritating *adj* ärgerlich
irritation [ˌɪrɪ'teʃən] *s* Reizung *f*
irruption ['ɪrʌpʃən] *s* Einbruch *m*
isinglass ['aɪzɪŋ ˌglæs] *s* Fischleim *m;* (*mica*) Glimmer *m*
Islam ['ɪsləm] *s* Islam *m*
island ['aɪlənd] *s* Insel *f*
islander ['aɪləndər] *s* Insulaner –in *mf*
isle [aɪl] *s* kleine Insel *f*
isolate ['aɪsə ˌlet] *tr* isolieren
isolation [ˌaɪsə'leʃən] *s* Isolierung *f*
isolationist [ˌaɪsə'leʃənɪst] *s* Isolationist –in *mf*
isola'tion ward' *s* Isolierstation *f*
isometric [ˌaɪsə'mɛtrɪk] *adj* isometrisch
isosceles [aɪ'sɑsə ˌliz] *adj* gleichschenklig
isotope ['aɪsə ˌtop] *s* Isotop *n*
Israel ['ɪzrɪ·əl] *s* Israel *n*
Israe·li [ɪz'reli] *adj* israelisch ‖ *s* (**–li**) Israeli *m*
Israelite ['ɪzrɪ·ə ˌlaɪt] *adj* israelitisch ‖ *s* Israelit –in *mf*
issuance ['ɪʃʊ·əns] *s* Ausgabe *f*
issue ['ɪʃʊ] *s* (*of a magazine*) Nummer *f;* (*result*) Ausgang *m;* (*e.g., of securities*) Ausgabe *f,* Emission *f;* (*under discussion*) Streitpunkt *m;* (*offspring*) Nachkommenschaft *f;* **avoid the i.** der Frage ausweichen; **be at i.** zur Debatte stehen; **make an i. of it** e–e Streitfrage daraus machen; **take i. with** anderer Meinung sein als ‖ *tr* (*orders, supplies, stamps, stocks*) ausgeben; (*a pass*) ausstellen ‖ *intr* (**from**) herauskommen (aus)
isthmus ['ɪsməs] *s* Landenge *f*
it [ɪt] *pron* es; **about it** darüber, davon; **it is I** ich bin es
Italian [ɪ'tælɪ·ən] *adj* italienisch ‖ *s* (*person*) Italiener –in *mf;* (*language*) Italienisch *n*
italicize [ɪ'tælɪ ˌsaɪz] *tr* kursiv drucken

italics [ɪˈtælɪks] *spl* Kursivschrift *f*

Italy [ˈɪtəli] *s* Italien *n*

itch [ɪtʃ] *s* Jucken *n;* (pathol) Krätze *f* ‖ *intr* jucken; **I am itching to** (*inf*) es reizt mich zu (*inf*); **my nose itches me** es juckt mich in der Nase

itchy [ˈɪtʃi] *adj* juckend; (pathol) krätzig

item [ˈaɪtəm] *s* Artikel *m;* (*in a list*) Punkt *m;* (com) Posten *m;* (journ) Nachricht *f;* **hot i.** (coll) Schlager *m*

itemize [ˈaɪtəˌmaɪz] *tr* einzeln aufführen

itinerant [aɪˈtɪnərənt], [ɪˈtɪnərənt] *adj* Wander–, reisend ‖ *s* Reisende *mf*

itinerary [aɪˈtɪnəˌrɛri] *s* Reiseplan *m*

its [ɪts] *poss adj* sein

itself *reflex pron* sich; **in i.** an und für sich ‖ *intens pron* selbst, selber

ivied [ˈaɪvid] *adj* efeubewachsen

ivory [ˈaɪvəri] *adj* elfenbeinern, Elfenbein–; (*color*) kremfarben ‖ *s* Elfenbein *n;* **tickle the ivories** in die Tasten greifen

i'vory tow'er *s* (fig) Elfenbeinturm *m*

ivy [ˈaɪvi] *s* Efeu *m*

J

J, j [dʒe] *s* zehnter Buchstabe des englischen Alphabets

jab [dʒæb] *s* Stoß *m;* (box) Gerade *f* ‖ *v* (*pret & pp* **jabbed;** *ger* **jabbing**) *tr* stoßen; (box) mit der Gerade stoßen

jabber [ˈdʒæbər] *tr & intr* plappern

jack [dʒæk] *s* (*money*) (sl) Pinke *f;* (aut) Wagenheber *m;* (cards) Bube *m;* (telp) Klinke *f;* **Jack** Hans *m* ‖ *tr*—**j. up** (aut) heben; (*prices*) hinaufschrauben

jackal [ˈdʒækəl] *s* Schakal *m*

jack'ass' *s* Esel *m*

jacket [ˈdʒækɪt] *s* Jacke *f;* (*of a book*) Umschlag *m;* (*of a potato*) Schale *f*

Jack' Frost' *s* Herr Winter *m*

jack'ham'mer *s* Preßlufthammer *m*

jack'-in-the-box' *s* Kastenteufel *m*

jack'knife' *s* (–knives) Klappmesser *n;* (*dive*) Hechtbeuge *f* ‖ *intr* zusammenklappen

jack'-of-all'-trades' *s* Hansdampf *m* in allen Gassen

jack'pot' *s* Jackpot *m;* **hit the j.** das Große Los gewinnen

jack' rab'bit *s* Hase *m*

Jacob [ˈdʒekəb] *s* Jakob *m*

jade [dʒed] *adj* jadegrün ‖ *s* (*stone*) Jade *m;* (*color*) Jadegrün *n;* (*horse*) Schindmähre *f*

jad'ed *adj* ermattet

jag [dʒæg] *s* Zacke *f;* **have a jag on** (sl) e–n Schwips haben

jagged [ˈdʒægɪd] *adj* zackig, schartig

jaguar [ˈdʒægwɑr] *s* Jaguar *m*

jail [dʒel] *s* Gefängnis *n,* Untersuchungsgefängnis *n;* **be in j.** sizten ‖ *tr* einsperren

jail'bird' *s* Knastbruder *m*

jailer [ˈdʒelər] *s* Gefängniswärter *m*

jalopy [dʒəˈlɑpi] *s* Rumpelkasten *m*

jal'ousie win'dow [ˈdʒæləsi] *s* Glasjalousie *f*

jam [dʒæm] *s* Marmelade *f;* **be in a jam** (coll) in der Patsche sitzen ‖ *v* (*pret & pp* **jammed;** *ger* **jamming**) *tr* (*a room*) überfüllen; (*a street*) verstopfen; (*a finger*) quetschen; (rad) stören; **be jammed in** eingezwängt sein; **jam on the brakes** auf die Bremsen drücken; **jam s.th. into**

etw stopfen in (*acc*) ‖ *intr* (*said of a window*) klemmen; (*said of gears*) sich verklemmen; (*said of a gun*) Ladehemmung haben; **jam into** sich hineinquetschen in (*acc*)

jamb [dʒæm] *s* Pfosten *m*

jamboree [ˌdʒæmbəˈri] *s* Trubel *m;* (*of scouts*) Pfadfindertreffen *n*

James [dʒemz] *s* Jakob *m*

jam'ming *s* (rad) Störung *f*

Jane [dʒen] *s* Johanna *f*

Janet [ˈdʒænɪt] *s* Hanna *f*

jangle [ˈdʒæŋgəl] *s* Rasseln *n* ‖ *tr* rasseln lassen; **j. s.o.'s nerves** j–m auf die Nerven gehen ‖ *intr* rasseln

janitor [ˈdʒænɪtər] *s* Hausmeister *m*

January [ˈdʒænjuˌɛri] *s* Januar *m*

Japan [dʒəˈpæn] *s* Japan *n*

Japanese [ˌdʒæpəˈniz] *adj* japanisch ‖ *s* Japaner –in *mf;* (*language*) Japanisch *n*

Jap'anese bee'tle *s* Japankäfer *m*

jar [dʒɑr] *s* Krug *m;* (*e.g., of jam*) Glas *n;* (*jolt*) Stoß *m* ‖ *v* (*pret & pp* **jarred;** *ger* **jarring**) *tr* (*jolt*) anstoßen; (fig) erschüttern ‖ *intr* nicht harmonieren; **jar on the nerves** auf die Nerven gehen

jargon [ˈdʒɑrgən] *s* Jargon *m*

jasmine [ˈdʒæzmɪn] *s* Jasmin *m*

jaundice [ˈdʒɔndɪs] *s* Gelbsucht *f*

jaun'diced *adj* gelbsüchtig

jaunt [dʒɔnt] *s* Ausflug *m*

jaunty [ˈdʒɔnti] *adj* (*sprightly*) lebhaft; (*clothes*) fesch

javelin [ˈdʒæv(ə)lɪn] *s* Speer *m*

jaw [dʒɔ] *s* Kiefer *m;* **the jaws of death** die Klauen des Todes

jaw'bone' *s* Kiefer *m* ‖ *intr* (sl) sich stark machen

jay [dʒe] *s* (orn) Häher *m*

jay'walk' *intr* verkehrswidrig die Straße überqueren

jazz [dʒæz] *s* Jazz *m* ‖ *tr*—**j. up** (coll) aufmöbeln

jazz' band' *s* Jazzband *f*

jazzy [ˈdʒæzi] *adj* bunt, grell

jealous [ˈdʒɛləs] *adj* (**of**) eifersüchtig (auf *acc*)

jealousy [ˈdʒɛləsi] *s* Eifersucht *f*

jeans [dʒinz] *spl* Jeans *pl*

jeep [dʒip] s Jeep m
jeer [dʒɪr] s Hohn m || tr verhöhnen || intr höhnen; **j. at** verhöhnen
Jeffrey ['dʒefri] s Gottfried m
Jehovah [dʒɪ'hovə] s Jehova m
jell [dʒɛl] s Gelee n || intr gelieren; (fig) zum Klappen kommen
jellied ['dʒɛlid] adj geliert
jelly ['dʒɛli] s Gallerte f
jel′lyfish′ s Qualle f; (pej) Waschlappen m
jeopardize ['dʒepər‚daɪz] tr gefährden
jeopardy ['dʒepərdi] s Gefahr f
jerk [dʒʌrk] s Ruck m; (sl) Knülch m || tr ruckweise ziehen || intr zucken
jerky ['dʒʌrki] adj ruckartig
jersey ['dʒʌrzi] s (material) Jersey m; (shirt) Jersey n; (sport) Trikot n
jest [dʒest] s Scherz m; **in j.** scherzweise || intr scherzen
jester ['dʒestər] s Hofnarr m; (joker) Spaßvogel m
Jesuit ['dʒeʒʊ·ɪt] adj Jesuiten– || s Jesuit m
Jesus ['dʒizəs] s Jesus m
jet [dʒet] adj Düsen– || s (stream) Strahl m; (nozzle) Düse f; (plane) Jet m, Düsenflugzeug n || v (pret & pp jetted; ger jetting) herausströmen; (aer) jetten
jet′-black′ adj rabenschwarz
jet′ propul′sion s Düsenantrieb m
jetsam ['dʒetsəm] s Seewurfgut n
jet′ stream′ s Strahlströmung f
jettison ['dʒetɪsən] s Seewurf m || tr (aer) abwerfen; (naut) über Bord werfen
jetty ['dʒeti] s (warf) Landungsbrücke f; (breakwater) Hafendamm m
Jew [dʒu] s Jude m, Jüdin f
jewel ['dʒu·əl] s (& fig) Juwel n; (in a watch) Stein m
jew′el box′ s Schmuckkästchen n
jewel(l)er ['dʒu·ələr] s Juwelier –in mf
jewelry ['dʒu·əlri] s Jewelen pl; **piece of j.** Schmuckstück n
jew′elry store′ s Juweliergeschäft n
Jewish ['dʒu·ɪʃ] adj jüdisch
Jew′s′ harp′ s Maultrommel f
jib [dʒɪb] s Ausleger m; (naut) Klüver m
jibe [dʒaɪb] intr (coll) übereinstimmen
jiffy ['dʒɪfi] s—**in a j.** im Nu
jig [dʒɪg] s (dance) Gigue f; (tool) Spannvorrichtung f; **the jig is up** (sl) das Spiel ist aus
jigger ['dʒɪgər] s Schnapsglas n; (gadget) Dingsbums n; (naut) Besan m
jiggle ['dʒɪgəl] tr & intr rütteln
jig′saw′ s Laubsäge f
jig′saw puz′zle s Puzzelspiel n
jilt [dʒɪlt] tr (a girl) sitzenlassen; (a boy) den Laufpaß geben (dat)
jim·my ['dʒɪmi] s Brecheisen n || v (pret & pp –mied) tr mit dem Brecheisen aufbrechen
jingle ['dʒɪŋgəl] s (of coins) Klimpern n; (bell) Schelle f; (verse) Verseklingel n || tr klimpern mit || intr klimpern; (said of verses) klingeln
jin·go ['dʒɪŋgo] s (–goes) Chauvinist –in mf; **by j.!** alle Wetter!

jinx [dʒɪŋks] s Unglücksrabe m || tr Pech bringen (dat); **be jinxed** vom Pech verfolgt sein
jitters ['dʒɪtərz] spl—**have the j.** wahnsinnig nervös sein; **give s.o. the j.** j-n wahnsinnig nervös machen
jittery ['dʒɪtəri] adj durchgedreht
Joan [dʒon] s Johanna f
job [dʒab] s (employment) Job m; (task, responsibility) Aufgabe f; **bad job** Machwerk n; **do a good job** gute Arbeit leisten; **fall down on the job** seine Pflicht nicht erfüllen; **know one's job** seine Sache verstehen; **on the job** bei der Arbeit; (fig) auf Draht; **out of a job** arbeitslos
jobber ['dʒabər] s (middleman) Zwischenhändler –in mf; (pieceworker) Akkordarbeiter –in mf
job′hold′er s Stelleninhaber –in mf
jobless ['dʒablɪs] adj stellungslos
jockey ['dʒaki] s Jockei m || tr manövrieren
jog [dʒag] s Dauerlauf m; (of a horse) Trott m || v (pret & pp jogged; ger jogging) tr (shake) rütteln; (the memory) auffrischen || intr trotten; (for exercise) langsam rennen, Dauerlauf machen
John [dʒan] s Johann m; **john** (sl) Klo n
Johnny ['dʒani] s Hans m
John′ny-come′-late′ly s Neuling m, Nachzügler m
join [dʒɔɪn] tr verbinden; (a club) beitreten (dat); (a person) sich anschließen (dat); (two parts) zusammenfügen; **j. the army** zum Militär gehen || intr sich verbinden; **j. in** sich beteiligen an (dat); **j. up** (mil) einrücken
joiner ['dʒɔɪnər] s (coll) Vereinsmeier m; (carp) Tischler m
joint [dʒɔɪnt] adj (account, venture) gemeinschaftlich; (return) gemeinsam; (committee) gemischt; (heir, owner) Mit– || s Verbindungspunkt m; (in plumbing) Naht f; (sl) Bumslokal n; (anat, bot, mach) Gelenk n; (carp) Fuge f; (culin) Bratenstück n; **throw out of j.** auskugeln
jointly ['dʒɔɪntli] adv gemeinsam
joint′-stock′ com′pany s Aktiengesellschaft f
joist [dʒɔɪst] s Tragbalken m
joke [dʒok] s Witz m; **he can't take a j.** er versteht keinen Spaß; **make a j. of** ins Lächerliche ziehen; **play a j. on** e-n Streich spielen (dat) || intr Spaß machen; **j. about** witzeln über (acc); **j. around** schäkern; **joking aside** Spaß beiseite
joker ['dʒokər] s Spaßvogel m; (pej) Knülch m; (cards) Joker m
jolly ['dʒali] adj lustig
jolt [dʒolt] s Stoß m || tr stoßen || intr holpern; **j. along** dahinholpern
Jordan ['dʒɔrdən] s (country) Jordanien n; (river) Jordan m
josh [dʒaʃ] tr & intr hänseln
jostle ['dʒasəl] tr & intr drängeln
jot [dʒat] s—**not a jot** kein Jota || v

(*pret & pp* **jotted;** *ger* **jotting**) *tr*—
jot down notieren
journal ['dʒʌrnəl] *s* (*daily record*) Tagebuch *n;* (*magazine*) Zeitschrift *f*
journalism ['dʒʌrnə‚lɪzəm] *s* Journa-
lismus *m,* Zeitungswesen *n*
journalist ['dʒʌrnəlɪst] *s* Journalist –in
mf
journey ['dʒʌrni] *s* Reise *f;* **go on a j.**
verreisen ‖ *intr* reisen
jour′ney·man *adj* tüchtig ‖ *s* (**–men**)
Geselle *m*
joust [dʒaʊst] *s* Tjost *f* ‖ *intr* turnieren
jovial ['dʒovɪ·əl] *adj* jovial
jowls [dʒaʊlz] *spl* Hängebacken *pl*
joy [dʒɔɪ] *s* Freude *f*
joyful ['dʒɔɪfəl] *adj* froh, freudig
joyless ['dʒɔɪlɪs] *adj* freudlos
joy′ ride′ *s* (coll) Schwarzfahrt *f*
joy′ stick′ *s* (aer) Steuerknüppel *m*
Jr. *abbr* (**Junior**) jr., jun.
jubilant ['dʒubɪlənt] *adj* frohlockend
jubilation [‚dʒubɪ'leʃən] *s* Jubel *m*
jubilee ['dʒubɪ‚li] *s* Jubiläum *n*
Judaea [dʒu'di·ə] *s* Judäa *n*
Judaic [dʒu'de·ɪk] *adj* jüdisch
Judaism ['dʒudə‚ɪzəm] *s* Judaismus *m*
judge [dʒʌdʒ] *s* (*in a competition*)
Preisrichter –in *mf;* (box) Punkt-
richter *m;* (jur) Richter –in *mf* ‖ *tr*
(**by**) beurteilen (**nach**); (*distances*)
abschätzen; (jur) richten ‖ *intr* urteilen; (jur) richten; **judging by his
words** seinen Worten nach zu urteilen
judge′ ad′vocate *s* Kriegsgerichtsrat *m*
judgment ['dʒʌdʒmənt] *s* (& jur) Urteil
n; **in my j.** meines Erachtens; **show
good j.** ein gutes Urteilsvermögen
haben; **sit in j. over** zu Gericht sitzen
über (*acc*)
Judg′ment Day′ *s* Tag *m* des Gerichts
judicial [dʒu'dɪʃəl] *adj* Rechts–
judiciary [dʒu'dɪ/ɪ‚ɛri] *adj* richterlich
‖ *s* (*branch*) richterliche Gewalt *f;*
(*judges*) Richterstand *m*
judicious [dʒu'dɪʃəs] *adj* klug
judo ['dʒudo] *s* Judo *n*
jug [dʒʌg] *s* Krug *m;* (*jail*) Kittchen *n*
juggle ['dʒʌgəl] *tr* jonglieren; (*accounts*) frisieren ‖ *intr* jonglieren
juggler ['dʒʌglər] *s* Gaukler –in *mf*
Jugoslav ['jugo‚slav] *adj* jugoslawisch
‖ *s* Jugoslawe *m,* Jugoslawin *f*
Jugoslavia [‚jugo'slavi·ə] *s* Jugoslawien *n*
jug′ular vein′ ['dʒʌgjələr] *s* Halsader
f
juice [dʒus] *s* Saft *m*
juicy ['dʒusi] *adj* saftig
jukebox ['dʒuk‚bɑks] *s* Musikautomat
m
July [dʒu'laɪ] *s* Juli *m*
jumble ['dʒʌmbəl] *s* Wust *m* ‖ *tr*
durcheinanderwerfen
jumbo ['dʒʌmbo] *adj* Riesen–
jump [dʒʌmp] *s* Sprung *m;* (aer) Absprung *m;* **get the j. on** zuvorkommen
(*dat*) ‖ *tr* überspringen; (*attack*)
überfallen; (*a hurdle*) nehmen; (*in*

checkers) schlagen; **j. bail** die Kaution verfallen lassen; **j. channels** den
amtlichen Weg nicht einhalten; **j.
rope** seilspringen; **j. ship** vom Schiff
weglaufen; **j. the gun** übereilt handeln; (sport) zu früh starten; **j. the
track** entgleisen ‖ *intr* springen; (*be
startled*) auffahren; **j. at** (*a chance*)
stürzen auf (*acc*); **j. down s.o.'s
throat** j–n anfahren
jump′ ball′ *s* (basketball) Sprungball *m*
jumper ['dʒʌmpər] *s* (*dress*) Jumper *m;*
(elec) Kurzschlußbrücke *f*
jump′-off′ *s* Beginn *m;* (sport) Start *m*
jump′ rope′ *s* Springseil *n*
jumpy ['dʒʌmpi] *adj* unruhig, nervös
junction ['dʒʌŋkʃən] *s* Verbindung *f;*
(*of roads, rail lines*) Knotenpunkt *m*
juncture ['dʒʌŋktʃər] *s* Verbindungs-
stelle *f;* **at this j.** in diesem Augenblick
June [dʒun] *s* Juni *m*
June′ bug′ *s* Maikäfer *m*
jungle ['dʒʌŋgəl] *s* Dschungel *m, n & f*
junior ['dʒunjər] *adj* jünger ‖ *s* Student –in *mf* im dritten Studienjahr
juniper ['dʒunɪpər] *s* Wacholder *m*
junk [dʒʌŋk] *s* Altwaren *pl;* (*scrap
iron*) Schrott *m;* (*useless stuff*)
Plunder *m;* (naut) Dschunke *f*
junket ['dʒʌŋkɪt] *s* Vergnügungsreise
f auf öffentliche Kosten
junk′ mail′ *s* Wurfsendung *f*
junk′yard′ *s* Schrottplatz *m*
junta ['hʌntə], ['dʒʌntə] *s* Junta *f*
jurisdiction [‚dʒurɪs'dɪkʃən] *s* Zu-
ständigkeit *f;* **have j. over** zuständig
sein für
jurisprudence [‚dʒurɪs'prudəns] *s*
Rechtswissenschaft *f*
jurist ['dʒurɪst] *s* Jurist –in *mf*
juror ['dʒurər] *s* Geschworene *mf*
jury ['dʒuri] *s* Geschworene *pl*
ju′ry box′ *s* Geschworenenbank *f*
ju′ry tri′al *s* Schwurgerichtsverfahren *n*
just [dʒʌst] *adj* gerecht ‖ *adv* gerade;
(*only*) nur; (*simply*) einfach
justice ['dʒʌstɪs] *s* Gerechtigkeit *f;* (*of
a claim*) Berechtigung *f;* (*judge*)
Richter *m;* **bring to j.** vor Gericht
bringen; **do j. to** (*a meal*) wacker
zusprechen (*dat*); (*said of a picture*)
gerecht werden (*dat*)
jus′tice of the peace′ *s* Friedensrichter
m
justification [‚dʒʌstɪfɪ'keʃən] *s* Rechtfertigung *f*
justi·fy ['dʒʌstɪ‚faɪ] *v* (*pret & pp*
–fied) *tr* rechtfertigen
justly ['dʒʌstli] *adv* mit Recht
jut [dʒʌt] *v* (*pret & pp* **jutted;** *ger*
jutting) *intr*—**jut out** hervorragen
juvenile ['dʒuvə‚naɪl] *adj* (*books,
court*) Jugend–; (*childish*) unreif
ju′venile delin′quency *s* Jugendkrimi-
nalität *f*
ju′venile delin′quent *s* jugendlicher
Verbrecher *m*
juxtapose [‚dʒʌkstə'poz] *tr* nebenein-
anderstellen

K

K, k [ke] *s* elfter Buchstabe des englischen Alphabets
kale [kel] *s* Grünkohl *m*
kaleidoscopic [kə‚laɪdə'skɑpɪk] *adj* (& *fig*) kaleidoskopisch
kangaroo [‚kæŋgə'ru] *s* Känguruh *n*
kangaroo court' *s* Scheingericht *n*
kashmir ['kaeʃmɪr] *s* (tex) Kaschmir *m*
kayo ['ke'o] *s* K.o. *m* ‖ *tr* k.o. schlagen
keel [kil] *s* Kiel *m;* **on an even k.** (fig) gleichmäßig ‖ *intr*—**k. over** umkippen; (naut) kentern
keen [kin] *adj* (*sharp*) scharf; (*interest*) lebhaft; **k. on** scharf auf (*acc*)
keenness ['kinnɪs] *s* Schärfe *f*
keep [kip] *s* Unterhalt *m;* (*of a castle*) Bergfried *m;* **for keeps** (*forever*) für immer; (*seriously*) im Ernst ‖ *v* (*pret & pp* **kept** [kɛpt]) *tr* (*retain*) behalten; (*detain*) aufhalten; (*save for s.o.*) aufbewahren; (*a secret*) bewahren; (*a promise*) (ein)halten; (*animals*) halten; (*books*) (acct) führen; **be kept in school** nachsitzen müssen; **k. at arm's length** vom Leibe halten; **k. at bay** sich erwehren (*genit*); **k. away** fernhalten; **k. back** zurückhalten; (*retain*) zurückbehalten; **k.** (*s.o.*) **company** Gesellschaft leisten (*dat*); **k. down** (*one's head*) niederhalten; (*one's voice*) verhalten; (*prices*) niedrig halten; **k. from** abhalten von; **k. from** (*ger*) daran hindern zu (*inf*); **k. going** im Gange halten; **k. good time** gut gehen; **k. guard** Wache halten; **k. house** den Haushalt führen; **k. in good condition** instand halten; **k. in mind** sich [*dat*] merken; **k. it up!** nur so weiter; **k. on** (*a garment*) anbehalten; (*a hat*) aufbehalten; **k. oneself from** (*ger*) es fertigbringen nicht zu (*inf*); **k. one's temper** sich beherrschen; **k. out** ausschließen; (*light*) nicht durchlassen; (*rain*) abhalten; **k. posted** auf dem laufenden halten; **k. score** die Punktliste führen; **k. secret** geheimhalten; **k. step** Tritt halten; **k. s.th. from s.o.** j-m etw verschweigen; **k. track of** sich [*dat*] merken; **k. under wraps** (coll) totschweigen; **k. up** instand halten; (*appearances*) wahren; (*correspondence*) unterhalten; **k. up the good work!** arbeiten Sie weiter so gut!; **k. waiting** warten lassen; **k. warm** warm halten; **k. your shirt on!** (coll) daß du die Nase im Gesicht behältst! ‖ *intr* (*said of food*) sich halten; **k. at** beharren bei; **k. at it!** bleib dabei!; **k. away** sich fernhalten; **k. cool** (fig) die Nerven behalten; **k. cool!** ruhig Blut!; **k. from** sich enthalten (*genit*); **k. from** (*ger*) es unterlassen zu (*inf*); **k. from laughing** sich das Lachen verkneifen;

k. going weitermachen; **k. moving** weitergehen; **k. on** (*ger*) weiter (*inf*), e.g., **k. on driving** weiterfahren; **k. out!** Eintritt verboten! **k. out of** sich fernhalten von; **k. quiet** sich ruhig verhalten; **k. quiet!** sei still!; **k. to the right** sich rechts halten; **k. up with** (*work*) nachkommen mit; **k. up with the Joneses** mit den Nachbarn Schritt halten; **k. within** bleiben innerhalb (*genit*)
keeper ['kipər] *s* (*of animals*) Halter –in *mf;* (*at a zoo*) Tierwärter –in *mf;* (*watchman*) Wächter *m*
keep'ing *s* Verwahrung *f;* **in k. with** in Einklang mit
keep'sake' *s* Andenken *n*
keg [kɛg] *s* Faß *n*
ken [kɛn] *s* Gesichtskreis *m*
kennel ['kɛnəl] *s* Hundezwinger *m*
kep·i ['kepi], ['kɛpi] *s* (**-is**) Kappi *n*
kerchief ['kʌrtʃɪf] *s* (*for the head*) Kopftuch *n;* (*for the neck*) Halstuch *n*
kernel ['kʌrnəl] *s* (*of fruit*) Kern *m;* (*of grain*) Korn *n;* (fig) Kern *m*
kerosene [‚kerə'sin] *s* Petroleum *n*
kerplunk [kər'plʌŋk] *interj* bums!
ketchup ['ketʃəp] *s* Ketchup *m* & *n*
kettle ['kɛtəl] *s* Kessel *m*
ket'tledrum' *s* Kesselpauke *f*
key [ki] *adj* (*ring, hole, industry, position*) Schlüssel– ‖ *s* (& *fig*) Schlüssel *m;* (*of a map*) Zeichenerklärung *f;* (*of a typewriter, piano, organ*) Taste *f;* (*of windinstrument*) Klappe *f;* (*reef*) Riff *n;* (*low island*) Insel *f;* (mus) Tonart *f;* **key of C major** C-dur; **off key** falsch ‖ *tr* (mach) festkeilen
key'board' *s* Tastatur *f*
keyed *adj*—**k. to** gestimmt auf (*acc*); **k. up** in Hochspannung
key' man' *s* Schlüsselfigur *f*
key'note *s* Grundgedanke *m;* (mus) Tonika *f*
key'note address' *s* programmatische Rede *f*
keynoter ['kɪ ‚notər] *s* Programmatiker –in *mf*
keypuncher ['ki ‚pʌntʃər] *s* Locher –in *mf*
key'stone' *s* Schlußstein *m;* (fig) Grundlage *f*
key' word' *s* Stichwort *n*
kha·ki ['kæki] *adj* Khaki– ‖ *s* (**-kis**) Khaki *m;* **khakis** Khakiuniform *f*
kibitz ['kɪbɪts] *intr* (coll) kiebitzen
kibitzer ['kɪbɪtsər] *s* (coll) Kiebitz *m*
kick [kɪk] *s* Fußtritt *m;* (*of a rifle*) Rückstoß *m;* (*of a horse*) Schlag *m;* (*final spurt*) (sport) Endspurt *m;* **give s.o. a k.** j-m e-n Fußtritt versetzen; **I get a (great) k. out of him** er macht mir (riesigen) Spaß ‖ *tr* treten, stoßen; (fb) kicken; **be kicked upstairs** (coll) die Treppe hinauffallen;

I could k. myself ich könnte mich
ohrfeigen; k. a goal (fb) ein Tor
schießen; k. (s.o.) around schlecht
behandeln; (e.g., an idea) beschwatzen; k. in (money) beisteuern; k.
open (a door) aufstoßen; k. out (coll)
rausschmeißen; k. s.o. in the shins
j–n gegen das Schienbein treten; k.
the bucket (sl) krepieren; k. up a
storm Krach schlagen ‖ intr (said
of a gun) stoßen; (said of a horse)
ausschlagen; (complain) (about)
meckern (über acc); k. around Europe in Europa herumbummeln; k.
off (fb) anspielen
kick'back' s Schmiergeld n
kick'off' s (commencement) Beginn m;
(fb) Anstoß m
kid [kɪd] s Zicklein n; (coll) Kind n
‖ v (pret & pp kidded; ger kidding)
tr necken ‖ intr scherzen; no kidding! mach keine Witze!
kid' gloves' spl Glacéhandschuhe pl;
handle with k. (fig) mit Glacéhand-
schuhen anfassen
kid'nap' v (pret & pp –nap(p)ed; ger
–nap(p)ing) tr kidnappen, entführen
kidnap(p)er ['kɪd,næpər] s Kidnapper
m
kid'nap(p)ing s Kidnapping s
kidney ['kɪdni] s Niere f
kid'ney bean' s rote Bohne f
kid'ney-shaped' adj nierenförmig
kid'ney stone' s Nierenstein m
kid'ney trans'plant s Nierenverpflan-
zung f; (transplanted kidney) ver-
pflanzte Niere f
kid'ney trou'ble s Nierenleiden n
kid' stuff' s (coll) Kinderei f
kill [kɪl] s (aer) Abschuß m; (hunt)
Jagdbeute f; (nav) Versenkung f ‖
tr töten; (murder) ermorden, killen;
(plants) zum Absterben bringen;
(time) totschlagen; (a proposal,
plans, competition) zu Fall bringen;
(the motor) abwürgen; (the ball)
stark schlagen; (a bottle) austrinken;
be killed in action (im Felde) fallen;
it won't k. you (coll) es wird dich
nicht umbringen; k. off abschlachten;
k. oneself sich umbringen; k. two
birds with one stone zwei Fliegen
mit e–r Klappe schlagen; she is
dressed to k. sie ist totschick angezogen
killer ['kɪlər] s Totschläger –in mf,
Killer m
kill'er whale' s Schwertwal m
kill'ing s Tötung f; make a k. e–n un-
erhofften Gewinn erzielen
kill'joy' s Spaßverderber m
kiln ['kɪl(n)] s Brennofen m
kil·o ['kɪlo], ['kilo] s (–os) Kilo n
kilocycle ['kɪlə,saɪkəl] s Kilohertz n
kilogram ['kɪlə,græm] s Kilogramm n
kilohertz ['kɪlə,hɑrts] s Kilohertz n
kilometer [kɪ'lɑmɪtər] s Kilometer m;
kilometers per hour Stundenkilo-
meter pl
kilowatt ['kɪlə,wɑt] s Kilowatt n
kil'owatt'-hour' s Kilowattstunde f
kilt [kɪlt] s Kilt m

kilter ['kɪltər] s—out of k. nicht in
Ordnung
kimo·no [kɪ'mono] s (–nos) Kimono m
kin [kɪn] s Sippe f; the next of kin
die nächsten Angehörigen
kind [kaɪnd] adj liebenswürdig; (to)
gütig (zu), freundlich (zu); would
you be so k. as to (inf)? würden
Sie so gefällig sein zu (inf)?; with
k. regards mit freundlichen Grüßen
‖ s Art f, Sorte f; all kinds of
allerlei; another k. of ein anderer;
any k. of irgendwelcher; every k. of
jede Art von; in. k. (fig) auf gleiche
Weise; k. of (coll) etwas; nothing of
the k. nichts dergleichen; that k. of
derartig; two (three) kinds of zweierlei (dreierlei); what k. of was für ein
kindergarten ['kɪndər,gɑrtən] s Vor-
schule f, Vorschuljahr n
kind'-heart'ed adj gutmütig
kindle ['kɪndəl] tr anzünden; (fig) erwecken ‖ intr sich entzünden
kindling ['kɪndlɪŋ] s Entzündung f;
(wood) Kleinholz n
kindly ['kaɪndli] adj gütig, freundlich
‖ adv freundlich; (please) bitte
kindness ['kaɪndnɪs] s Freundlichkeit
f; (deed) Gefälligkeit f
kindred ['kɪndrɪd] adj verwandtschaft-
lich; (fig) verwandt ‖ s Verwandtschaft f
kinescope ['kɪnɪ,skop] s (trademark)
Fernsehempfangsröhre f
kinetic [kɪ'netɪk] adj kinetisch ‖
kinetics s Kinetik f
king [kɪŋ] s König m; (cards, chess)
König m; (checkers) Dame f
kingdom ['kɪŋdəm] s Königreich n;
(of animals, etc.) Reich n; k. of
heaven Himmelreich n
king'fish'er s Königsfischer m
kingly ['kɪŋli] adj königlich
king'pin' s (coll) Boß m; (bowling)
König m
king'ship' s Königtum n
king'-size' adj übergroß
kink [kɪŋk] s (in a wire) Knick m; (in
the hair) Kräuselung f; (in a muscle)
Muskelkrampf m; (flaw) Fehler m
kinky ['kɪŋki] adj gekräuselt
kin'ship' s Verwandtschaft f
kins'man s (–men) Blutsverwandte m
kins'wom'an s (–wom'en) Blutsverwandte f
kipper ['kɪpər] s Räucherhering m ‖
tr einsalzen und räuchern
kiss [kɪs] s Kuß m ‖ tr & intr küssen
kisser ['kɪsər] s (sl) Fresse f
kit [kɪt] s (equipment) Ausrüstung f;
(tool kit) Werkzeugkasten m; (for
models) Modellsatz m; (e.g., for a
convention) Mappe f; the whole kit
and caboodle (things) der ganze
Kram; (persons) die ganze Sippschaft
kitchen ['kɪtʃən] s Küche f
kitchenette [,kɪtʃə'net] s Kochnische
f
kit'chen knife' s Küchenmesser n
kit'chen police' s (mil) Küchendienst
m
kit'chen range' s Herd m, Kochherd m

kit′chen sink′ s Ausguß m
kit′chenware′ s Küchengeschirr n
kite [kaɪt] s Drachen m; (orn) Weih m; **fly a k.** e-n Drachen steigen lassen; **go fly a k.!** (coll) scher dich zum Kuckuck!
kith′ and kin′ [kɪθ] spl Freunde and Verwandte pl
kitten [′kɪtən] s Kätzchen n
kitty [′kɪti] s Kätzchen n; (cards) gemeinsame Kasse f; **Kitty** Käthchen n
kleptomaniac [‚kleptə′menɪ ‚æk] s Kleptomane m, Kleptomanin f
knack [næk] s—**have a k. for** Talent haben für; **have the k. of it** den Griff heraus haben
knapsack [′næp ‚sæk] s Rucksack m
knave [nev] s Schelm m; (cards) Bube m
knavery [′nevəri] s Schelmenstreich m
knead [nid] tr kneten
knead′ing trough′ s Teigmulde f
knee [ni] s Knie n; **bring s.o. to his knees** j-n auf die Knie zwingen; **go down on one's knees** niederknien; **on bended knees** kniefällig
knee′ bend′ s Kniebeuge f
knee′ breech′es spl Kniehose f
knee′cap′ s Kniescheibe f
knee′-deep′ adj knietief
knee′-high′ adj kniehoch
knee′ jerk′ s Patellarreflex m
kneel [nil] v (pret & pp **knelt** [nɛlt] & **kneeled**) intr knien
knee′-length′ adj kniefrei
knee′pad′ s (sport) Knieschützer m
knee′pan′ s Kniescheibe f
knee′ swell′ s (of organ) Knieschweller m
knell [nɛl] s Totengeläute n
knickers [′nɪkərz] spl Knickerbockerhosen pl
knicknack [′nɪk ‚næk] s Nippsache f
knife [naɪf] s (**knives** [naɪvz]) Messer n ‖ tr erstechen
knife′ sharp′ener s Messerschleifer m
knife′ switch′ s (elec) Messerschalter m
knight [naɪt] s Ritter m; (chess) Springer m ‖ tr zum Ritter schlagen
knight′hood′ s Ritterschaft f
knightly [′naɪtli] adj ritterlich
knit [nɪt] v (pret & pp **knitted** & **knit**; ger **knitting**) tr stricken; **k. one's brows** die Brauen runzeln ‖ intr stricken; (said of bones) zusammenheilen
knit′ goods′ spl Trikotwaren pl
knit′ted dress′ s Strickkleid n
knit′ting s (act) Strickerei f; (materials) Strickzeug n
knit′ting machine′ s Strickmaschine f
knit′ting nee′dle s Stricknadel f
knit′ting yarn′ s Strickgarn n
knit′wear′ s Strickwaren pl
knob [nab] s (of a door) Drücker m; (lump) Auswuchs m; (in wood) Knorren m; (of a radio) Knopf m
knock [nak] s (& aut) Klopfen n ‖ tr (criticize) tadeln; **k. a hole through** durchbrechen; **k. around** herumstoßen; (mistreat) unsanft behandeln;

k. down niederschlagen; (with a car) umfahren; (trees) umbrechen; (at auctions) zuschlagen; **k. it off!** (sl) hör mal auf!; **k. oneself out over** sich [dat] die Zähne ausbeißen an (dat); **k. one's head against the wall** mit dem Kopf gegen die Wand rennen; **k. out** ausschlagen; (exhaust) (coll) strapazieren; (a tank) abschießen; (box) k.o. schlagen; **k. over** umwerfen; **k. together** (build hurriedly) schnell zusammenhauen; **k. to the ground** zu Boden schlagen; **k. up a girl** (sl) e-m Mädchen ein Kind anhängen ‖ intr (an)klopfen; (aut) klopfen; **k. about** herumbummeln; **k. against** stoßen an (acc); **k. off (from)** (coll) aufhören (mit)
knock′down′ s (box) Niederschlag m
knocker [′nakər] s Türklopfer m; **knockers** (sl) Brüste pl
knock-kneed [′nak ‚nid] adj x-beinig
knock′-knees′ spl X-beine pl
knock′out′ s (woman) (coll) Blitzmädel n; (box) Knockout m
knock′out drops′ spl Betäubungsmittel n
knock′-out punch′ s K.o.-Schlag m
knoll [nol] s Hügel m
knot [nat] s Knoten m; (in wood) Knorren m; (of people) Gruppe f; (naut) Knoten m; **tie a k.** e-n Knoten machen; **tie the k.** (coll) sich verheiraten ‖ tr e-n Knoten machen in (acc); (two ends) zusammenknoten
knot′hole′ s Astloch n
knotty [′nati] adj knorrig; (problem) knifflig
know [no] s—**be in the k.** Bescheid wissen ‖ v (pret **knew** [n(j)u]; pp **known**) tr (facts) wissen; (be familiar with) kennen; (a language) können; **come to k.** erfahren; **get to k.** kennenlernen; **known** bekannt; **k. one's way around** sich auskennen; **k. the ropes** (coll) Bescheid wissen; **what's what** (coll) den Rummel kennen ‖ intr wissen; **he ought to k. better** er sollte mehr Verstand haben; **k. about** wissen über (acc); **k. of** wissen von; **not that I k. of** (coll) nicht, daß ich wüßte; **you k.** (coll) wissen Sie
knowable [′no‑əbəl] adj kenntlich
know′-how′ s Sachkenntnis f
know′ing adj (glance) vielsagend
knowingly [′no‑ɪŋli] adv wissentlich; (intentionally) absichtlich
know′-it-all′ s Naseweis m
knowledge [′nalɪdʒ] s Wissen n, Kenntnisse pl; (information) (of) Kenntnis f (von); **basic k. of** Grundkenntnisse pl in (dat); **come to s.o.'s k.** j-m zur Kenntnis kommen; **to my k.** soweit (or soviel) ich weiß; **to the best of my k.** nach bestem Wissen; **without my k.** ohne mein Mitwissen; **working k. of** praktisch verwertbare Kenntnisse pl (genit)
knowledgeable [′nalɪdʒəbəl] adj kenntnisreich
known [non] adj bekannt; **become k.**

kundwerden; **k. all over town** stadt-
bekannt; **make k.** bekanntgeben
know'-noth'ing *s* Nichtswisser *m*
knuckle ['nʌkəl] *s* Knöchel *m*, Finger-
knöchel *m;* (mach) Gelenkstück *n;*
k. of ham Eisbein *n* ‖ *intr*—**k. down
to work** sich ernsthaft an die Arbeit
machen; **k. under** klein beigeben
k.o. ['ke'o] *s* K.o. *m* ‖ *tr* k.o.-schlagen
Koran [ko'ræn] *s* Koran *m*
Korea [ko'ri·ə] *s* Korea *n*

Korean [ko'ri·ən] *adj* koreanisch ‖ *s*
Koreaner –in *mf;* (*language*) Koreanisch *n*
kosher ['koʃər] *adj* (& coll) koscher
kowtow ['kau'tau] *intr* e–n Kotau
machen; **k. to** kriechen vor (*dat*)
K.P. ['ke'pi] *s* (**kitchen police**) (mil)
Küchendienst *m*
Kremlin ['krɛmlɪn] *s* Kreml *m*
kudos ['k(i)udɑs] *s* (coll) Ruhm *m*,
Renommee *n*

L

L, l [ɛl] *s* zwölfter Buchstabe des englischen Alphabets
lab [læb] *s* (coll) Labor *n*
la·bel ['lebəl] *s* Etikett *n;* (*brand*)
Marke *f;* (fig) Bezeichnung *f* ‖ *v*
(*pret & pp* **–bel[l]ed;** *ger* **—bel[l]ing**)
tr etikettieren; (fig) bezeichnen
labial ['lebɪ·əl] *adj* Lippen– ‖ *s* Lip-
penlaut *m*, Labial *m*
labor ['lebər] *adj* Arbeits–, Arbeiter–
‖ *s* Arbeit *f;* (*toil*) Mühe *f;* **be in
l.** in den Wehen liegen ‖ *tr* (*a point*)
ausführlich eingehen auf (*acc*) ‖ *intr*
sich abmühen; (*at*) arbeiten (an *dat*);
(*exert oneself*) sich anstrengen; (*said
of a ship*) stampfen; **l. under** zu leiden haben unter (*dat*)
la'bor and man'agement *spl* Arbeitnehmer und Arbeitgeber *pl*
laboratory ['læbərə,tori] *s* Laborato-
rium *n*
lab'oratory techni'cian *s* Laborant –in
mf
la'bor camp' *s* Zwangsarbeitslager *n*
la'bor con'tract *s* Tarifvertrag *m*
la'bor dis'pute *s* Arbeitsstreitigkeit *f*
la'bored *adj* (e.g., *breathing*) mühsam;
(*style*) gezwungen
laborer ['lebərər] *s* Arbeiter –in *mf;*
(*unskilled*) Hilfsarbeiter –in *mf*
la'bor force' *s* Arbeitskräfte *pl*
laborious [lə'borɪ·əs] *adj* mühsam,
schwierig
la'bor law' *s* Arbeitsrecht *n*
la'bor lead'er *s* Arbeiterführer –in *mf*
la'bor mar'ket *s* Arbeitsmarkt *m*
la'bor move'ment *s* Arbeiterbewegung
f
la'bor pains' *spl* Geburtswehen *pl*
la'bor-sav'ing *adj* arbeitssparend; **l.
device** Hilfsgerät *n*
la'bor short'age *s* Mangel *m* an Arbeits-
kräften
la'bor supply' *s* Arbeitsangebot *n*
la'bor un'ion *s* Gewerkschaft *f*
laburnum [lə'bʌrnəm] *s* Goldregen *m*
labyrinth ['læbɪrɪnθ] *s* Labyrinth *n*
lace [les] *adj* (*collar, dress*) Spitzen–
‖ *s* Spitze *f;* (*shoestring*) Schnürsenkel *m* ‖ *tr* (e.g., *shoes*) schnüren;
(*braid*) flechten; (*drinks*) (coll) mit
e–m Schuß Branntwein versetzen;
(*beat*) (coll) prügeln; **l. up** zuschnü-
ren

lacerate ['læsə,ret] *tr* zerfleischen
laceration [,læsə'reʃən] *s* Fleischwunde *f*
lace' trim'ming *s* Spitzenbesatz *m*
lace'work' *s* Spitzenarbeit *f*
lachrymose ['lækrɪ,mos] *adj* tränen-
reich
lac'ing *s* Schnürung *f;* (coll) Prügel *pl*
lack [læk] *s* (*of*) Mangel *m* (an *dat*);
for l. of aus Mangel an (*dat*); **l. of
space** Raummangel *m;* **l. of time**
Zeitmangel *m* ‖ *tr*—**I l.** es mangelt
mir an (*dat*) ‖ *intr*—**be lacking** fehlen; **he is lacking in courage** ihm
fehlt der Mut
lackadaisical [,lækə'dezɪkəl] *adj* teilnahmslos, gleichgültig
lackey ['læki] *s* Lakai *m*
lack'ing *prep* mangels (*genit*)
lack'lus'ter *adj* glanzlos
laconic [lə'kɑnɪk] *adj* lakonisch
lacquer ['lækər] *s* Lack *m* ‖ *tr* lackieren
lac'quer ware' *s* Lackwaren *pl*
lacrosse [lə'krɔs] *s* Lacrosse *n*
lacu·na [lə'kjunə] *s* (**–nas** & **–nae** [ni])
Lücke *f*, Lakune *f*
lacy ['lesi] *adj* spitzenartig
lad [læd] *s* Bube *m*
la'dies' man' *s* Weiberheld *m*, Salonlöwe *m*
la'dies' room' *s* Damentoilette *f*
ladle ['ledəl] *s* Schöpflöffel *m* ‖ *tr*
ausschöpfen
lady ['ledi] *s* Dame *f;* **ladies and gentlemen** meine Damen und Herren!
la'dybird', la'dybug' *s* Marienkäfer *m*
la'dy compan'ion *s* Gesellschaftsdame
f
la'dyfin'ger *s* Löffelbiskuit *m* & *n*
la'dy-in-wait'ing *s* (**ladies-in-waiting**)
Hofdame *f*
la'dy-kil'ler *s* Schwerenöter *m*
la'dylike' *adj* damenhaft
la'dylove' *s* Geliebte *f*
la'dy of the house' *s* Hausherrin *f*
la'dy's maid' *s* Zofe *f*
la'dy's man' *s* var of **ladies' man**
lag [læg] *s* Zurückbleiben *n;* (aer)
Rücktrift *f;* (phys) Verzögerung *f* ‖
v (*pret & pp* **lagged;** *ger* **lagging**) *intr*
(**behind**) zurückbleiben (hinter *dat*)
la'ger beer' ['lɑgər] *s* Lagerbier *n*
laggard ['lægərd] *s* Nachzügler *m*

lagoon [lə'gun] *s* Lagune *f*
laid' up' *adj* (with) bettlägerig (infolge von); **be l. in bed** auf der Nase liegen
lair [ler] *s* Höhle *f*, Lager *n*
laity ['le·ɪti] *s* Laien *pl*
lake [lek] *s* See *m*
Lake' Con'stance ['kɑnstəns] *s* der Bodensee
lamb [læm] *s* Lamm *n*; (culin) Lammfleisch *n*
lambaste [læm'best] *tr* (*berate*) (coll) herunterputzen; (*beat*) (coll) verdreschen
lamb' chop' *s* Hammelrippchen *n*
lambkin ['læmkɪn] *s* Lammfell *n*
lame [lem] *adj* (*person, leg; excuse*) lahm; **be l. in one leg** auf e–m Bein lahm sein ‖ *tr* lähmen
lament [lə'ment] *s* Jammer *m*; (*dirge*) Klagelied *n* ‖ *tr* beklagen ‖ *intr* wehklagen
lamentable ['læməntəbəl] *adj* beklagenswert; (pej) jämmerlich
lamentation [ˌlæmə'teʃən] *s* Wehklage *f*
laminate ['læmɪˌnet] *tr* schichten
lamp [læmp] *s* Lampe *f*
lamp' chim'ney *s* Lampenzylinder *m*
lamp'light' *s* Lampenlicht *n*
lamp'light'er *s* Laternenanzünder *m*
lampoon [læm'pun] *s* Schmähschrift *f* ‖ *tr* mit e–r Schmähschrift verspotten
lamp'post' *s* Laternenpfahl *m*
lamp'shade' *s* Lampenschirm *m*
lance [læns] *s* Lanze *f*; (surg) Lanzette *f* ‖ *tr* (surg) aufstechen
lance' cor'poral *s* (Brit) Hauptgefreite *m*
lancet ['lænsɪt] *s* Lanzette *f*
land [lænd] *s* (*dry land; country*) Land *n*; (*ground*) Boden *m*; **by l.** zu Lande ‖ *tr* (*a plane, troops, punch*) landen; (*a ship, fish*) an Land bringen; (*a job*) (coll) kriegen; **l. s.o. in trouble** j–n in Schwierigkeiten bringen ‖ *intr* (aer, naut, & fig) landen; (*said of a blow*) treffen; **l. on s.o.'s head** j–m auf den Kopf fallen; **l. on water** auf dem Wasser aufsetzen
land' breeze' *s* Landwind *m*
land'ed prop'erty *s* Landbesitz *m*
land'fall' *s* (*sighting of land*) Sichten *n* von Land; **make l.** landen
land' forc'es *spl* Landstreitkräfte *pl*
land'ing *s* Landung *f*; (*of a staircase*) Absatz *m*; **l. on the moon** Mondlandung *f*
land'ing craft' *s* Landungsboot *n*
land'ing field' *s* Landeplatz *m*
land'ing force' *s* Landekorps *n*
land'ing gear' *s* Fahrgestell *n*
land'ing par'ty *s* Landeabteilung *f*
land'ing stage' *s* Landungssteg *m*
land'ing strip' *s* Start- und Landestreifen *m*
land'la'dy *s* (*of an apartment*) Hauswirtin *f*; (*of an inn*) Gastwirtin *f*
land'locked' *adj* landumschlossen
land'lord' *s* (*of an apartment*) Hauswirt *m*; (*of an inn*) Gastwirt *m*
landlubber ['lændˌlʌbər] *s* Landratte *f*

land'mark' *s* Landmarke *f*; (*cardinal event*) Markstein *m*
land' of'fice *s* Grundbuchamt *n*
land'-office bus'iness *s* (fig) Bombengeschäft *n*
land'own'er *s* Grundbesitzer –in *mf*
landscape ['lændˌskep] *s* Landschaft *f*; (paint) Landschaftsbild *n* ‖ *tr* landschaftlich gestalten
land'scape ar'chitect *s* Landschaftsarchitekt –in *mf*
land'scape paint'er *s* Landschaftsmaler –in *mf*
land'slide' *s* Bergrutsch *m*; (pol) Stimmenrutsch *m*
landward ['lændwərd] *adv* landwärts
land' wind' [wɪnd] *s* Landwind *m*
lane [len] *s* Bahn *f*; (*country road*) Feldweg *m*; (aer) Flugschneise *f*; (aut) Fahrbahn *f*; (naut) Fahrtroute *f*; (sport) Laufbahn *f*; (sport) Schwimmbahn *f*
language ['læŋgwɪdʒ] *s* Sprache *f*
lan'guage instruc'tion *s* Sprachunterricht *m*
lan'guage teach'er *s* Sprachlehrer –in *mf*
languid ['læŋgwɪd] *adj* schlaff
languish ['læŋgwɪʃ] *intr* schmachten
languor ['læŋgər] *s* Mattigkeit *f*
languorous ['læŋgərəs] *adj* matt
lank [læŋk] *adj* schlank; (*hair*) glatt
lanky ['læŋki] *adj* schlaksig
lanolin ['lænəlɪn] *s* Lanolin *n*
lantern ['læntərn] *s* Laterne *f*
lan'tern slide' *s* Diapositiv *n*
lanyard ['lænjərd] *s* (*around the neck*) Halsschnur *f*; (naut) Taljereep *n*
Laos ['le·ɑs] *s* Laos *n*
Laotian [le'oʃən] *adj* laotisch ‖ *s* Laote *m*, Laotin *f*; (*language*) Laotisch *n*
lap [læp] *s* (*of the body or clothing*) Schoß *m*; (*of the waves*) Plätschern *n*; (sport) Runde *f* ‖ *v* (*pret & pp* **lapped;** *ger* **lapping**) *tr* schlappen; (sport) überrunden; **lap up** auf(sch)lecken ‖ *intr*—**lap against** (*e.g., a boat, shore*) plätschern gegen; **lap over** hinausragen über (*acc*)
lap' dog' *s* Schoßhund *m*
lapel [lə'pɛl] *s* Aufschlag *m*
Lap'land' *s* Lappland *n*
Laplander ['læpˌlændər] *s* Lappländer –in *mf*
Lapp [læp] *s* Lappe *m*, Lappin *f*; (*language*) Lappisch *n*
lapse [læps] *s* (*error*) Versehen *n*; (*of time*) Ablauf *m*; **after a l. of** nach Ablauf von; **l. of duty** Pflichtversäumnis *f*; **l. of memory** Gedächtnislücke *f* ‖ *intr* (*said of a right, an insurance policy*) verfallen; (*said of time*) ablaufen; **l. into** verfallen in (*acc*); **l. into unconsciousness** das Bewußtsein verlieren
lap'wing' *s* Kiebitz *m*
larceny ['lɑrsəni] *s* Diebstahl *m*
larch [lɑrtʃ] *s* (bot) Lärche *f*
lard [lɑrd] *s* Schmalz *n* ‖ *tr* spicken
larder ['lɑrdər] *s* Speisekammer *f*
large [lɑrdʒ] *adj* groß; **at l.** (*as a whole*) gesamt; (*at liberty*) auf freiem

Fuß; (said of an official) zur beson-
deren Verfügung; **become larger** sich
vergrößern; **on a l. scale** in großem
Umfang
large′ intes′tine s Dickdarm m
largely [′lɑrdʒli] adv größtenteils
largeness [′lɑrdʒnĭs] s Größe f
large′-scale′ adj Groß–; (map) in großem Maßstab; (production) Serien–
largesse [′lɑrdʒĕs] s (generosity) Freigebigkeit f; (handout) Geldverteilung
f
lariat [′læri·ət] s Lasso m & n; (for
grazing animals) Halteseil n
lark [lɑrk] s (orn) Lerche f; **for a l.**
zum Spaß
lark′spur′ s (bot) Rittersporn m
lar·va [′lɑrvə] s (-vae [vi]) Larve f
laryngitis [ˌlærɪn′dʒaɪtɪs] s Kehlkopf-
entzündung f, Laryngitis f
larynx [′lærɪŋks] s (larynxes & laryn-
ges [lə′rɪndʒiz]) Kehlkopf m
lascivious [lə′sɪvi·əs] adj wollüstig
lasciviousness [lə′sɪvi·əsnɪs] s Wol-
lüstigkeit f
laser [′lezər] s Laser m
lash [læʃ] s Peitsche f; (as a punishment) Peitschenhieb m; (of the eye)
Wimper f ‖ tr (whip) peitschen;
(bind) (to) anbinden (an acc); (said
of rain, storms) peitschen ‖ intr—
l. out (at) ausschlagen (nach)
lass [læs] s Mädel n
lassitude [′læsɪˌt(j)ud] s Mattigkeit f
last [læst] adj letzte; **very l.** allerletzte
‖ adv zuletzt; **l. of all** zuallerletzt ‖
s Letzte mfn; (of a cobbler) Schuh-
leisten m; **at l.** schließlich; **at long l.**
zu guter Letzt; **look one′s l. on** zum
letzten Mal blicken auf (acc); **see the**
l. of s.o. j–n nicht mehr wiedersehen;
to the l. bis zum Letzten ‖ intr (remain unchanged) anhalten; (for a
specific time) dauern; (said of money,
supplies) reichen; (said of a person)
aushalten
last′ing adj dauerhaft, andauernd; **l.**
effect Dauerwirkung f; **l. for months**
monatelang
Last′ Judg′ment s Jüngstes Gericht n
lastly [′læstli] adv zuletzt
last′-min′ute adj in letzter Minute
last′-minute news′ s neueste Nachrichten pl
last′ night′ adv gestern abend
last′ quar′ter s (astr) abnehmendes
Mondviertel n; (com) letztes Quartal
n
last′ resort′ s letztes Mittel n
last′ sleep′ s Todesschlaf m
last′ straw′ s—**that′s the l.** das schlägt
dem Faß den Boden aus
Last′ Sup′per, the s das Letzte Abendmahl
last′ week′ adv vorige Woche
last′ will′ and test′ament s letztwillige
Verfügung f
last′ word′ s letztes Wort n; **the l.**
(fig) der letzte Schrei
latch [lætʃ] s Klinke f ‖ tr zuklinken
‖ intr einschnappen; **l. on to** (coll)
spitzkriegen

latch′key′ s Hausschlüssel m
late [let] adj (after the usual time)
spät; (at a late hour) zu später Stunde; (deceased) verstorben; **be l.** sich
verspäten; (said of a train) Verspätung haben; **keep l. hours** spät
aufbleiben ‖ adv spät; **come l.** zu
spät kommen; **of l.** kürzlich; **see you**
later (coll) bis später!
latecomer [′letˌkʌmər] s Nachzügler m
lateen′ sail′ [læ′tin] s Lateinsegel n
lateen′ yard′ s Lateinrah f
lately [′letli] adv neulich, unlängst
lateness [′letnɪs] s Verspätung f
latent [′letənt] adj latent, verborgen
later [′letər] adj später ‖ adv später,
nachher; **l. on** späterhin
lateral [′lætərəl] adj seitlich, Seiten–
lath [læθ] s Latte f ‖ tr belatten
lathe [leð] s Drehbank f; **turn on a l.**
drechseln
lather [′læðər] s Seifenschaum m; (of
a horse) schäumender Schweiß m ‖
tr einseifen ‖ intr schäumen
lathing [′læθɪŋ] s Lattenwerk n
Latin [′lætɪn] adj lateinisch ‖ s
(Romance-speaking person) Romane
m, Romanin f; (language) Lateinisch
n
La′tin Amer′ica s Lateinamerika n
La′tin-Amer′ican adj lateinamerika-
nisch ‖ s Lateinamerikaner –in mf
latitude [′lætɪˌt(j)ud] s Breite f; (fig)
Spielraum m
latrine [lə′trin] s Latrine f
latter [′lætər] adj (later) später; (final)
End–; (recent) letzte; **in the l. part**
of (e.g., the year) in der zweiten
Hälfte (genit); **the l.** dieser
lat′ter-day′ adj (later) später; (recent)
letzte
Lat′ter-day Saint′ s Heilige mf der
Jüngsten Tage
lattice [′lætɪs] s Gitter n ‖ tr vergittern
lat′ticework′ s Gitterwerk n
Latvia [′lætvɪ·ə] s Lettland n
Latvian [′lætvɪ·ən] adj lettisch ‖ s
Lette m, Lettin f; (language) Lettisch
n
laud [lɔd] tr loben, preisen
laudable [′lɔdəbəl] adj löblich
laudanum [′lɔd(ə)nəm] s Opiumtink-
tur f
laudatory [′lɔdəˌtɔri] adj Lob–
laugh [læf] s Lachen n, Gelächter n;
for laughs zum Spaß; **have a good l.**
sich auslachen ‖ tr—**l. off** sich lachend hinwegsetzen über (acc) ‖ intr
lachen; **it′s easy for you to l.** Sie
haben leicht lachen!; **l. about** lachen
über (acc); **l. at** (deride) auslachen;
(find amusement in) lachen über
(acc)
laughable [′læfəbəl] adj lächerlich
laugh′ing adj lachend; **it′s no l. matter**
es ist nichts zum Lachen
laugh′ing gas′ s Lachgas n
laugh′ingstock′ s Gespött n
laughter [′læftər] s Gelächter n, Lachen n; **roar with l.** vor Lachen
brüllen
launch [lɔntʃ] s (open boat) Barkasse

f || *tr* (*a boat*) aussetzen; (*a ship*) vom Stapel laufen lassen; (*a plane*) katapultieren; (*a rocket*) starten; (*a torpedo*) abschießen; (*an offensive*) beginnen; **be launched** (naut) vom Stapel laufen; (rok) starten || *intr*—**l. into** sich stürzen in (*acc*)

launch'ing *s* (*of a ship*) Stapellauf *m*; (*of a torpedo*) Ausstoß *m*; (*of a rocket*) Abschuß *m*, Start *m*

launch' pad' *s* (rok) Startrampe *f*

launder ['lɔndər] *tr* waschen

laundress ['lɔndrɪs] *s* Wäscherin *f*

laundry ['lɔndrɪ] *s* (*clothes*) Wäsche *f*; (*room*) Waschküche *f*; (*business*) Wäscherei *f*

laun'drybag' *s* Wäschebeutel *m*

laun'drybas'ket *s* Wäschekorb *m*

laun'dry list' *s* Waschzettel *m*

laun'dry·man' *s* (–men') Wäscher *m*

laun'dry·wom'an *s* (–wom'en) Wäscherin *f*

laurel ['lɔrəl] *s* Lorbeer *m*

lau'rel tree' *s* Lorbeerbaum *m*

lava ['lɑvə] *s* Lava *f*

lavatory ['lævə‚tori] *s* Waschraum *m*; (*toilet*) Toilette *f*

lavender ['lævəndər] *adj* lavendelfarben || *s* (bot) Lavendel *m*

lavish ['lævɪʃ] *adj* (*person*) verschwenderisch; (*dinner*) üppig || *tr*—**l. care on** hegen und pflegen; **l. s.th. on s.o.** j–n mit etw überhäufen

lavishness ['lævɪʃnɪs] *s* Üppigkeit *f*

law [lɔ] *s* Gesetz *n*; (*system*) Recht *n*; (*as a science*) Rechtswissenschaft *f*; (relig) Gebot *n*; **according to law** dem Recht entsprechend; **act within the law** sich ans Gesetz halten; **against the law** gesetzwidrig; **become law** Gesetzkraft erlangen; **by law** gesetzlich; **go against the law** gegen das Gesetz handeln; **lay down the law** gebieterisch auftreten; **practice law** den Anwaltsberuf ausüben; **study law** Jura studieren; **take the law into one's own hands** sich [*dat*] selbst sein Recht verschaffen; **under the law** nach dem Gesetz

law'-abid'ing *adj* friedlich

law' and or'der *s* Ruhe und Ordnung *pl*

law'-and-or'der *adj* für Ruhe und Ordnung

law'break'er *s* Rechtsbrecher –in *mf*

law'break'ing *s* Rechtsbruch *m*

law'court' *s* Gerichtshof *m*, Gericht *n*

lawful ['lɔfəl] *adj* gesetzmäßig

lawless ['lɔlɪs] *adj* gesetzlos

lawlessness ['lɔlɪsnɪs] *s* Gesetzlosigkeit *f*

law'mak'er *s* Gesetzgeber *m*

lawn [lɔn] *s* Rasen *m*; (tex) Batist *m*

lawn' mow'er *s* Rasenmäher *m*

lawn' par'ty *s* Gartenfest *m*

lawn' sprin'kler *s* Rasensprenger *m*

law' of dimin'ishing returns' *s* Gesetz *n* der abnehmenden Erträge

law' of'fice *s* Anwaltsbüro *n*

law' of na'tions *s* Völkerrecht *n*

law' of na'ture *s* Naturgesetz *n*

law' of probabil'ity *s* Wahrscheinlichkeitsgesetz *n*

law' of supply' and demand' *s* Gesetz *n* von Angebot und Nachfrage

law' of the land' *s* Landesgesetz *n*

law' school' *s* juristiche Fakultät *f*

law' stu'dent *s* Student –in *mf* der Rechtswissenschaft

law'suit' *s* Klage *f*, Prozeß *m*

lawyer ['lɔjər] *s* Advokat –in *m*, Anwalt –in *mf*

lax [læks] *adj* lax, nachlässig

laxative ['læksətɪv] *s* Abführmittel *n*

laxity ['læksɪti] *s* Laxheit *f*

lay [le] *adj* (*not of the clergy*) Laien-, weltlich; (*non-expert*) laienhaft || *s* (*poem*) Lied *n* || *v* (*pret & pp* **laid** [led]) *tr* legen; (*eggs; foundation, bricks, lineoleum*) legen; (*cables, pipes, tracks*) verlegen; (*vulg*) umlegen; **be laid up with** das Bett hüten müssen wegen (*genit*); **I'll lay you two to one** ich wette mit dir zwei zu eins; **lay aside** beiseite legen; (*save*) sparen; **lay bare** bloßlegen; **lay down** niederlegen; (*principles*) aufstellen; **lay claim to** Anspruch erheben auf (*acc*); **lay it on thick** dick auftragen; **lay low** (*said of an illness*) bettlägerig machen; **lay off** (*workers*) vorübergehend entlassen; **lay open** freilegen; **lay out** auslegen; (*a garden*) anlegen; (*money*) aufwenden; (*a corpse*) aufbahren; (surv) abstecken; **lay siege to** belagern; **lay waste** verwüsten || *intr* (*said of hens*) legen; **lay for** auflauern (*dat*); **lay into** (*beat*) (coll) verdreschen; (*scold*) (coll) heruntermachen; **lay off** (*abstain from*) sich enthalten (*genit*); (*let alone*) in Ruhe lassen; **lay over** (*on a trip*) sich aufhalten; **lay to** (naut) stilliegen

lay' broth'er *s* Laienbruder *m*

layer ['le·ər] *s* Schicht *f*; (bot) Ableger *m*; **in layers** schichtenweise; **l. of fat** Fettschicht *f*; **thin l.** Hauch *m*

lay'er cake' *s* Schichttorte *f*

layette [le'εt] *s* Babyausstattung *f*

lay' fig'ure *s* Gliederpuppe *f*

lay'man *s* (–men) Laie *m*; **layman's** laienhaft

lay'off' *s* vorübergehende Entlassung *f*

lay' of the land' *s* Gestaltung *f* des Terrains; (fig) Gesichtspunkt *m* der Angelegenheit

lay'out' *s* Anlage *f*, Anordnung *f*; (typ) Layout *n*; **l. of rooms** Raumverteilung *f*

laziness ['lezɪnɪs] *s* Faulheit *f*

lazy ['lezi] *adj* faul

la'zybones' *s* (coll) Faulpelz *m*

la'zy Su'san *s* drehbares Tablett *n*

lea [li] *s* (poet) Aue *f*

lead [led] *adj* Blei– || *s* Blei *n*; (*in a pencil*) Mine *f*; (*plumb line*) Bleilot *n* || *v* (*pret & pp* **leaded**; *ger* **leading**) *tr* verbleien; (typ) durchschießen || [lid] *s* Führung *f*; (cards) Vorhand *f*; (elec) Zuführung *f*; (sport) Vorsprung *m*; (theat) Hauptrolle *f*; **be in the l.** an der Spitze stehen; **have the l.** die Führung haben; **take the l.** die Führung übernehmen || *v* (*pret & pp*

led [lɛd]) *tr* führen, leiten; (*to error, drinking, etc.*) verleiten; (*a parade*) anführen; (*a life*) führen; **l. astray** verführen; **l. away** wegführen; (*e.g., a criminal*) abführen; **l. back** zurückführen; **l. by the nose** an der Nase herumführen; **l. on** weiterführen; (*deceive*) täuschen; **l. the way** vorangehen || *intr* führen; (cards) anspielen; **l. nowhere** zu nichts führen; **l. off** den Anfang machen; **l. to** hinausgehen auf (*acc*); **l. up to** hinauswollen auf (*acc*) **where will all this l. to?** wo soll das alles hinführen?

leaden ['lɛdən] *adj* bleiern; (*in color*) bleifarbig; (*sluggish*) schwerfällig; **l. sky** bleierner Himmel *m*

leader ['lidər] *s* Führer –in *mf*; (*of a band*) Dirigent –in *mf*; (*of a film*) Vorspann *m*; (*lead article*) Leitartikel *m*

lead'ership' *s* Führung *f*

leading ['lidɪŋ] *adj* (*person, position, power*) führend

lead'ing ide'a *s* Leitgedanke *m*

lead'ing la'dy *s* Hauptdarstellerin *f*

lead'ing man' *s* Hauptdarsteller *m*

leading' ques'tion *s* Suggestivfrage *f*

lead'ing role' *s* Hauptrolle *f*

lead'-in wire' *s* Zuleitungsdraht *m*

lead' pen'cil [lɛd] *s* Bleistift *m*

lead' pipe' [lɛd] *s* Bleirohr *n*

lead' poi'soning [lɛd] *s* Bleivergiftung *f*

leaf [lif] *s* (**leaves** [livz]) Blatt *n*; (*of a folding door*) Flügel *m*; (*of a folding table*) Tischklappe *f*; (*insertable table board*) Einlegebrett *n*; **turn over a new l.** ein neues Leben anfangen || *intr*—**l. through** durchblättern

leafage ['lifɪdʒ] *s* Laubwerk *n*

leafless ['liflɪs] *adj* blattlos

leaflet ['liflɪt] *s* Werbeprospekt *m*, Flugblatt *n*; (bot) Blättchen *n*

leafy ['lifi] *adj* (*abounding in leaves*) belaubt; (*e.g., vegetables*) Blatt–

league [lig] *s* Bund *m*; (*unit of distance*) Meile *f*; (sport) Liga *f*; **in l. with** verbündet mit || *tr* verbünden || *intr* sich verbünden

League' of Na'tions *s* Völkerbund *m*

leak [lik] *s* Leck *n*; **spring a l.** ein Leck bekommen; **take a l.** (vulg) schiffen || *tr* (*e.g., a story to the press*) durchsickern lassen || *intr* (*said of a container*) leck sein; (*said of a boat*) lecken; (*said of a fluid*) auslaufen; (*said of a spigot*) tropfen; **l. out** (& fig) durchsickern

leakage ['likɪdʒ] *s* Lecken *n*; (& fig) Durchsickern *n*; (com) Schwund *m*; (elec) Streuung *f*

leaky ['liki] *adj* leck

lean [lin] *adj* mager || *v* (*pret & pp* **leaned** & **leant** [lɛnt]) *tr* (**against**) lehnen (an *acc* or gegen) || *intr* lehnen; **l. against** sich anlehnen an (*acc*); **l. back** sich zurücklehnen; **l. forward** sich vorbeugen; **l. on** sich stützen auf (*acc*); **l. over** (*e.g., a railing*) sich neigen über (*acc*); **l. toward** (fig) neigen zu

lean'ing *adj* sich neigend; (*tower*) schief || *s* (**toward**) Neigung *f* (zu)

leanness ['linnɪs] *s* Magerkeit *f*

lean'-to' *s* (**–tos**) Anbau *m* mit Pultdach

lean' years' *spl* magere Jahre *pl*

leap [lip] *s* Sprung *m*, Satz *m*; **by leaps and bounds** sprungweise; **l. in the dark** (fig) Sprung *m* ins Ungewisse || *v* (*pret & pp* **leaped** & **leapt** [lɛpt]) *tr* überspringen || *intr* springen; **l. at** anspringen; **l. at an opportunity** e–e Gelegenheit beim Schopf ergreifen; **l. forward** vorspringen; **l. up** emporschnellen

leap'frog' *s* Bocksprung *m*; **play l.** Bocksprünge machen

leap' year' *s* Schaltjahr *n*

learn [lʌrn] *v* (*pret & pp* **learned** & **learnt** [lʌrnt]) *tr* lernen; (*find out*) erfahren; **l. s.th. from s.o.**

learned ['lʌrnɪd] *adj* (*person, word*) gelehrt; (*for or of scholars*) Gelehrten–

learn'ed jour'nal *s* Gelehrtenzeitschrift *f*

learn'ed soci'ety *s* Gelehrtenvereinigung *f*

learn'ed world' *s* Gelehrtenwelt *f*

learn'ing *s* (*act*) Lernen *n*; (*erudition*) Gelehrsamkeit *f*

lease [lis] *s* Mietvertrag *m*; (*of land*) Pachtvertrag *m* || *tr* (*in the role of landlord*) vermieten; (*land*) verpachten; (*in the role of tenant*) mieten; (*land*) pachten

lease'hold' *adj* Pacht– || *s* Pachtbesitz *m*

leash [liʃ] *s* Leine *f*, Hundeleine *f*; **keep on the l.** an der Leine führen; **strain at the l.** (fig) an der Leine zerren || *tr* an die Leine nehmen

leas'ing *s* Miete *f*; (*of land*) Pachtung *f*; **l. out** Vermietung *f*; (*of land*) Verpachtung *f*

least [list] *adj* mindeste, wenigste || *adv* am wenigsten; **l. of all** am wenigsten von allen || *s* Geringste *mfn*; **at l.** mindestens, wenigstens; **at the very l.** zum mindesten; **not in the l.** nicht im mindesten

leather ['lɛðər] *adj* ledern || *s* Leder *n*

leath'er bind'ing *s* Ledereinband *m*

leath'erbound' *adj* ledergebunden

leath'erneck' *s* (sl) Marineinfanterist *m*

leathery ['lɛðəri] *adj* (*e.g., steak*) (coll) lederartig

leave [liv] *s* (*permission*) Erlaubnis *f*; (mil) Urlaub *m*; **on l.** auf Urlaub; **take l.** (**from**) Abschied nehmen (von); **take l. of one's senses** (coll) den Verstand verlieren || *v* (*pret & pp* **left** [lɛft]) *tr* (*go away from*) verlassen; (*undone, open, etc.*) lassen; (*a message, bequest*) hinterlassen; (*a job*) aufgeben; (*a scar*) zurücklassen; (*forget*) liegenlassen, stehenlassen; (*e.g., some food for s.o.*) übriglassen; **be left** übrig sein; **l. alone** (*a thing*) bleibenlassen; (*a person*) in Frieden lassen; **l. behind** (*said of a deceased person*) hinterlassen; (*forget*) liegenlassen; **l. home** von zu Hause fortgehen; **l. it at that!** überlaß es mir!; **l. lying about** herumliegen lassen; **l. nothing to chance** nichts dem Zufall überlassen; **l. nothing undone** nichts unversucht lassen; **l. open** offen lassen; **l. out** auslassen; **l. standing** stehenlassen; **l.** (*e.g., work*) **undone** liegenlassen || *intr* fortgehen; (*on travels*) abreisen; (*said of vehicles*) abfahren; (aer) abfliegen; **l. off** (*e.g., from reading*) aufhören

leaven ['lɛvən] *s* Treibmittel *n* || *tr* säuern

leav'ening *s* Treibstoff *m*

leave' of ab'sence *s* Urlaub *m*

leave'-tak'ing *s* Abschiednehmen *n*

leavings ['livɪŋz] *spl* Überbleibsel *pl*

Leba·nese [ˌlɛbə'niz] *adj* libanesisch || *s* (**–nese**) Libanese *m*, Libanesin *f*

Lebanon ['lɛbənən] *s* Libanon *n*

lecher ['lɛtʃər] *s* Lüstling *m*

lecherous ['lɛtʃərəs] *adj* wollüstig

lechery ['lɛtʃəri] *s* Wollust *f*

lectern ['lɛktərn] *s* Lesepult *n*

lector ['lɛktər] *s* (eccl) Lektor *m*

lecture ['lɛktʃər] *s* Vorlesung *f*, Vortrag *m;* (coll) Standpauke *f;* **give a l. on** e–n Vortrag halten über (*acc*)**; give s.o. a l.** j–m den Text lesen || *tr* (coll) abkanzeln || *intr* lesen

lecturer ['lɛktʃərər] *s* Vortragende *mf;* (*at a university*) Dozent –in *mf*

lec'ture room' *s* Hörsaal *m*

ledge [lɛdʒ] *s* Sims *m* & *n;* (*of a cliff*) Felsenriff *n*

ledger ['lɛdʒər] *s* (acct) Hauptbuch *n*

lee [li] *s* Lee *f*

leech [litʃ] *s* Blutegel *m;* (fig) Blutsauger –in *mf*

leek [lik] *s* (bot) Porree *m*, Lauch *m*

leer [lɪr] *s* lüsterner Seitenblick *m* || *intr* (at) lüstern schielen (nach)

leery ['lɪri] *adj* mißtrauisch; **be l. of** mißtrauen (*dat*)

lees [liz] *spl* Hefe *f*

lee' side' *s* Leeseite *f*

leeward ['liwərd] *adv* leewärts || *s* Leeseite *f*

Lee'ward Is'lands *spl* Inseln *pl* unter dem Winde

lee'way' *s* (coll) Spielraum *m;* (aer, naut) Abtrift *f*

left [lɛft] *adj* linke; (*left over*) übrig || *adv* links; **l. face!** (mil) links um! || *s* (*left hand*) Linke *f;* **on our l.** zu unserer Linken; **the l.** (pol) die Linke; **the third street to the l.** die dritte Querstraße links; **to the l.** nach links; **to the l. of** links von

left' field' *s* (baseball) linkes Außenfeld *n*

left' field'er ['fildər] *s* Spieler *m* im linken Außenfeld

left'-hand drive' *s* Linkssteuerung *f*

left'-hand'ed *adj* linkshändig; (*compliment*) fragwürdig; (*counterclockwise*) linksgängig; (*clumsy*) linkisch

left-hander ['lɛft'hændər] *s* Linkshänder –in *mf*

leftish ['lɛftɪʃ] *adj* linksgerichtet

leftist ['lɛftɪst] *s* Linksradikaler *m;* (pol) Linkspolitiker –in *mf*

left'o'ver *adj* übriggeblieben || **leftovers** *spl* Überbleibsel *pl*

left'-wing' *adj* Links–

left' wing' *s* (pol) linker Flügel *m;* (sport) Linksaußen *m*

left-winger ['lɛft'wɪŋər] *s* (coll) Linkspolitiker –in *mf*

lefty ['lɛfti] *adj* (coll) linkshändig || *s* (coll) Linkshänder –in *mf*

leg [lɛg] *s* (*of a body, of furniture, of trousers*) Bein *n;* (*stretch*) Etappe *f;* (*of a compass*) Schenkel *m;* (*of a boot*) Schaft *m;* **be on one's last legs** auf dem letzten Loche pfeifen; **pull s.o.'s leg** (coll) j–n auf die Schippe nehmen; **run one's legs off** sich abrennen; **you don't have a leg to stand on** Sie haben keinerlei Beweise

legacy ['lɛgəsi] *s* Vermächtnis *n*

legal ['ligəl] *adj* (*according to the law*) gesetzlich, legal; (*pertaining to or approved by law*) Rechts–, juristisch; **take l. action** den Rechtweg beschreiten; **take l. steps against s.o.** gerichtlich gegen j–n vorgehen

le'gal advice' *s* Rechtsberatung *f*

le'gal advis'er *s* Rechtsberater –in *mf*

le'gal age' *s* Volljährigkeit *f;* **of l.** großjährig

le'gal aid' *s* Rechtshilfe *f*

le'gal ba'sis *s* Rechtsgrundlage *f*

le'gal case' *s* Rechtsfall *m*

le'gal claim' *s* Rechtsanspruch *m*

le'gal en'tity *s* juristische Person *f*

le'gal force' *s* Rechtskraft *f*

le'gal grounds' *spl* Rechtsgrund *m*

le'gal hol'iday *s* gesetzlicher Feiertag *m*

legality [lɪ'gæliti] *s* Gesetzlichkeit *f*, Rechtlichkeit *f*

legalize ['ligə,laɪz] *tr* legalisieren

le'gal jar'gon *s* Kanzleisprache *f*

le'gal profes'sion *s* Rechtsanwaltsberuf *m*

le'gal rem'edy *s* Rechtsmittel *n*

le'gal ten'der *s* gesetzliches Zahlungsmittel *n;* **be l.** gelten

le'gal ti'tle *s* Rechtsanspruch *m*

legate ['lɛgɪt] *s* Legat –in *mf*

legatee [ˌlɛgə'ti] *s* Legatar –in *mf*

legation [lɪ'geʃən] *s* Gesandtschaft *f*

legend ['lɛdʒənd] *s* Legende *f*

legendary ['lɛdʒən,dɛri] *adj* legendär

legerdemain [ˌlɛdʒərdɪ'men] *s* Taschenspielerei *f*

leggings ['lɛgɪŋz] *spl* hohe Gamaschen *pl*

leggy ['lɛgi] *adj* langbeinig

Leg'horn' *s* (*chicken*) Leghorn *n;* (*town in Italy*) Livorno *n*

legibility [ˌlɛdʒɪ'bɪliti] *s* Lesbarkeit *f*

legible ['lɛdʒɪbəl] *adj* lesbar

legion ['lidʒən] *s* Legion *f;* (fig) Heerschar *f*

legionnaire [ˌlidʒə'nɛr] *s* Legionär *m*

legislate ['lɛdʒɪs,let] *tr* durch Gesetzgebung bewirken || *intr* Gesetze geben

legislation [ˌlɛdʒɪs'leʃən] *s* Gesetzgebung *f*

legislative [ˈlɛdʒɪs‚letɪv] *adj* gesetzgebend
legislator [ˈlɛdʒɪs‚letər] *s* Gesetzgeber –in *mf*
legislature [ˈlɛdʒɪs‚letʃər] *s* Legislatur *f*
legitimacy [lɪˈdʒɪtɪməsi] *s* Rechtmäßigkeit *f*
legitimate [lɪˈdʒɪtɪmɪt] *adj* gesetzmäßig, legitim; (*child*) ehelich ‖ [lɪˈdʒɪtɪ‚met] *tr* legitimieren
legit′imate the′ater *s* literarisch wertvolles Theater *n*
legitimize [lɪˈdʒɪtɪ‚maɪz] *tr* legitimieren
leg′ of lamb′ *s* Lammkeule *f*
leg′ of mut′ton *s* Hammelkeule *f*
leg′ room′ *s* Beinfreiheit *f*
leg′work′ *s* Vorarbeiten *pl*
leisure [ˈliʒər] *s* Muße *f;* at l. mit Muße; at s.o.'s l. wenn es j–m paßt
lei′sure class′ *s* wohlhabende Klasse *f*
lei′sure hours′ *spl* Mußestunden *pl*
leisurely [ˈliʒərli] *adj & adv* gemächlich
lei′sure time′ *s* Freizeit *f*
lemon [ˈlɛmən] *adj* Zitronen– ‖ *s* Zitrone *f;* (sl) Niete *f*
lemonade [‚lɛmɪˈned] *s* Zitronenlimonade *f*
lem′on squeez′er *s* Zitronenpresse *f*
lend [lɛnd] *v* (*pret & pp* lent [lɛnt]) *tr* leihen, borgen; l. at five percent interest zu fünf Prozent Zinsen anlegen; l. itself to sich eignen zu or für; l. oneself to sich hergeben zu; l. out ausleihen, verborgen; l. s.o. a hand j–m zur Hand gehen
lender [ˈlɛndər] *s* Verleiher –in *mf*
lend′ing li′brary *s* Leihbücherei *f*
length [lɛŋθ] *s* Länge *f;* (*of time*) Dauer *f;* (*in horse racing*) Pferdelänge *f;* at great l. sehr ausführlich; at l. ausführlich; (*finally*) schließlich; at some l. ziemlich ausführlich; go to any l. alles Erdenkliche tun; go to great lengths sich sehr bemühen; keep s.o. at arm's l. zu j–m Abstand wahren; stretch out full l. sich der Länge nach ausstrecken
lengthen [ˈlɛŋθən] *tr* verlängern; (*a vowel*) dehnen
length′ening *s* Verlängerung *f;* (ling) Dehnung *f*
length′wise′ *adj & adv* der Länge nach
lengthy [ˈlɛŋθi] *adj* langwierig
leniency [ˈlini‚ənsi] *s* Milde *f*
lens [lɛnz] *s* Linse *f;* (*combination of lenses*) Objektiv *n*
Lent [lɛnt] *s* Fastenzeit *f*
Lenten [ˈlɛntən] *adj* Fasten–
lentil [ˈlɛntɪl] *s* (bot) Linse *f*
leopard [ˈlɛpərd] *s* Leopard *m*
leper [ˈlɛpər] *s* Aussätzige *mf*
leprosy [ˈlɛprəsi] *s* Aussatz *m*, Lepra *f*
lesbian [ˈlɛzbɪ‚ən] *adj* lesbisch ‖ *s* Lesbierin *f*
lesbianism [ˈlɛzbɪ‚ə‚nɪzəm] *s* lesbische Liebe *f*
lesion [ˈliʒən] *s* Wunde *f*
less [lɛs] *comp adj* weniger, geringer;

l. and l. immer weniger ‖ *adv* weniger, minder; l. than weniger als ‖ *s*—do with l. mit weniger auskommen; for l. billiger; in l. than no time in Null Komma nichts ‖ *prep* abzüglich (*genit* or *acc*); (arith) weniger (*acc*), minus (*acc*)
lessee [lɛˈsi] *s* Mieter –in *mf;* (*of land*) Pächter –in *mf*
lessen [ˈlɛsən] *tr* vermindern ‖ *intr* sich vermindern, abnehmen
lesser [ˈlɛsər] *comp adj* minder, geringer
lesson [ˈlɛsən] *s* Unterrichtsstunde *f*, Stunde *f;* (*in a textbook*) Lektion *f;* (*warning*) Lehre *f;* learn a l. from e–e Lehre ziehen aus; let that be l. to you! lassen Sie sich das e–e Lehre sein
lessor [ˈlɛsər] *s* Vermieter –in *mf;* (*of land*) Verpächter –in *mf*
lest [lɛst] *conj* damit nicht; (after expressions of fear) daß
let [lɛt] *v* (*pret & pp* let; *ger* letting) *tr* lassen; I really let him have it! (coll) ich hab's ihm ordentlich gegeben!; let alone in Ruhe lassen; (*not to mention*) geschweige denn; let down herunterlassen; (*disappoint*) enttäuschen; let drop fallen lassen; let fly fliegen lassen; (coll) loslassen; let go fortlassen, loslassen; let go ahead vorlassen; let in hereinlassen; (*water*) zuleiten; let in on (*e.g., a secret*) einweihen in (*acc*); let it go, e.g., I'll let it go this time diesmal werde ich es noch hingehen lassen; let lie liegenlassen; let know wissen lassen, Bescheid geben (*dat*); let off (*e.g., at the next corner*) absetzen; let off easy noch so davonkommen lassen; let off scot-free straflos laufen lassen; let one's hair down (fig) sich gehenlassen; let out (*seams, air, water*) auslassen; (*e.g., a yell*) von sich geben; let pass durchlassen; let s.o. have s.th. j–m etw zukommen lassen; let stand (fig) gelten lassen; let through durchlassen; let things slide die Dinge laufen lassen; let things take their course den Dingen ihren Lauf lassen; let's go! los!; let us (or let's) (*inf*), e.g., let's (or let us) sing singen wir ‖ *intr* (*be rented out*) (for) vermietet werden (für); let fly with (coll) loslegen mit; let go of loslassen; let on that sich [*dat*] anmerken lassen, daß; let up nachlassen; let up on (coll) ablassen von
let′down′ *s* Hereinfall *m*
lethal [ˈliθəl] *adj* tödlich
lethargic [lɪˈθɑrdʒɪk] *adj* lethargisch
lethargy [ˈlɛθərdʒi] *s* Lethargie *f*
letter [ˈlɛtər] *s* Brief *m*, Schreiben *n;* (*of the alphabet*) Buchstabe *m;* by l. brieflich, schriftlich; to the l. aufs Wort ‖ *tr* beschriften
let′ter box′ *s* Briefkasten *m*
let′ter car′rier *s* Briefträger –in *mf*
let′ter drop′ *s* Briefeinwurf *m*
let′tered *adj* gelehrt
let′ter file′ *s* Briefordner *m*

let'terhead' s Briefkopf m

let'tering s (act) Beschriften n; (inscription) Beschriftung f

let'ter of condol'ence s Beileidsbrief m

let'ter of cred'it s Kreditbrief m

let'ter of recommenda'tion s Empfehlungsbrief m

letter o'pener s Brieföffner m

let'terper'fect adj buchstabengetreu

let'terpress' s (typ) Hochdruck m

let'ter scales' spl Briefwaage f

let'ter to the ed'itor s Leserbrief m

lettuce ['letɪs] s Salat m

let'up' s Nachlassen n; without l. ohne Unterlaß

leukemia [lu'kimɪ·ə] s Leukämie f

Levant [lɪ'vænt] s Levante f

Levantine [lɪ'væntin] adj levantinisch || s Levantiner –in mf

levee ['levi] s Uferdamm m

lev·el ['levəl] adj eben, gerade; (flat) flach; (spoonful) gestrichen; be l. with so hoch sein wie; do one's l. best sein Möglichstes tun; have a l. head ausgeglichen sein; keep a l. head e–n klaren Kopf behalten || s (& fig) Niveau n; (tool) Wasserwaage f; at higher levels höheren Ortes; be up to the usual l. (fig) auf der gewöhnlichen Höhe sein; on a l. with (& fig) auf gleicher Höhe mit; on the l. (fig) ehrlich || v (pret & pp –el[l]ed; ger –el[l]ing tr (a street, ground) planieren; l. (e.g., a rifle) at richten auf (acc); (e.g., complaints) richten gegen; l. off nivellieren; (aer) abfangen; l. to the ground dem Erdboden gleichmachen || intr— l. off sich verflachen; (said of prices) sich stabilisieren; (aer) in Horizontalflug übergehen; l. with s.o. mit j–m offen sein

lev'elhead'ed adj besonnen, vernünftig

lever ['livər] s Hebel m, Brechstange f || tr mit e–r Brechstange fortbewegen

leverage ['livərɪdʒ] s Hebelkraft f; (fig) Einfluß m

leviathan [lɪ'vaɪ·əθən] s Leviathan m

levitate ['levɪ,tet] tr schweben lassen || intr frei schweben

levitation [,levɪ'teʃən] s Schweben n

levity ['levɪti] s Leichtsinn m

lev·y ['levi] s Truppenaushebung f; (of taxes) Erhebung f; (tax) Steuer f || v (pret & pp –vied) tr (troops) ausheben; (taxes) erheben; l. war on Krieg führen gegen

lewd [lud] adj unzüchtig

lewdness ['ludnɪs] s Unzucht f

lexical ['leksɪkəl] adj lexikalisch

lexicographer [,leksɪ'kagrəfər] s Lexikograph –in mf

lexicographic(al) [,leksɪkə'græfɪk(əl)] adj lexikographisch

lexicography [,leksɪ'kagrəfi] s Lexikographie f

lexicology [,leksɪ'kalədʒi] s Wortforschung f, Lexikologie f

lexicon ['leksɪkən] s Wörterbuch n

liability [,laɪ·ə'bɪlɪti] s (ins) Haftpflicht f; (jur) Haftung f; liabilities Schulden pl; (acct) Passiva pl

liabil'ity insur'ance s Haftpflichtversicherung f

liable ['laɪ·əbəl] adj (jur) (for) haftbar (für); be l. to (inf) (coll) leicht können (inf); l. for damages schadenersatzpflichtig

liaison [li'ezən] s Verbindung f; (illicit affair) Liaison f; (ling) Bindung f

liai'son of'ficer s Verbindungsoffizier m

liar ['laɪ·ər] s Lügner –in mf

libation [laɪ'beʃən] s Opfertrank m

li·bel ['laɪbəl] s Verleumdung f; (in writing) Schmähschrift f || v (pret & pp –bel[l]ed; ger –bel[l]ing) tr verleumden

libelous ['laɪbələs] adj verleumderisch

li'bel suit' s Verleumdungsklage f

liberal ['lɪbərəl] adj (views) liberal, freisinnig; (with money) freigebig; (gift) großzügig; (interpretation) weitherzig; (education) allgemeinbildend; (pol) liberal || s Liberale mf

lib'eral arts' spl Geisteswissenschaften pl

liberalism ['lɪbərə,lɪzəm] s Liberalismus m

liberality [,lɪbə'rælɪti] s Freigebigkeit f, Großzügigkeit f

liberate ['lɪbə,ret] tr befreien; (chem) freimachen

liberation [,lɪbə'reʃən] s Befreiung f; (chem) Freimachen n

liberator ['lɪbə,retər] s Befreier –in mf

libertine ['lɪbər,tin] s Wüstling m

liberty ['lɪbərti] s Freiheit f; take liberties sich [dat] Freiheiten herausnehmen; you are at l. to (inf) es steht Ihnen frei zu (inf)

libidinous [lɪ'bɪdɪnəs] adj wollüstig

libido [lɪ'bido] s Libido f

librarian [laɪ'brerɪ·ən] s Bibliothekar –in mf

library ['laɪ,breri] s Bibliothek f

li'brary card' s Benutzerkarte f

libret·to [lɪ'breto] s (–tos) Operntext m, Libretto n

Libya ['lɪbɪ·ə] s Libyen n

Libyan ['lɪbɪ·ən] adj libysch || s Libyer –in mf

license ['laɪsəns] s Lizenz f, Genehmigung f; (document) Zulassungsschein m; (for a business, restaurant) Konzession f; (to drive) Führerschein m; (excessive liberty) Zügellosigkeit f || tr konzessionieren; (aut) zulassen

li'cense num'ber s (aut) Kennzeichen n

li'cense plate' or tag' s Nummernschild n

licentious [laɪ'senʃəs] adj unzüchtig

lichen ['laɪkən] s (bot) Flechte f

lick [lɪk] s Lecken n || tr lecken; (thrash) (coll) wichsen; (defeat) (coll) schlagen; (said of a flame) züngeln an (dat); l. clean auslecken; l. into shape auf Hochglanz bringen; l. off ablecken; l. one's chops sich [dat] die Lippen lecken; l. s.o.'s boots vor j–m kriechen; l. up auflecken

lick'ing s Prügel pl; give s.o. a good l. j–n versohlen

licorice ['lɪkərɪs] *s* Lakritze *f*

lid [lɪd] *s* Deckel *m*

lie [laɪ] *s* Lüge *f;* **give the lie to s.o.**
(or **s.th.**) j–n (or etw) Lügen strafen;
tell a lie lügen ‖ *v* (*pret* & *pp* **lied;**
ger **lying**) *tr*—**lie one's way out of**
sich herauslügen aus ‖ *intr* lügen;
lie like mad das Blaue vom Himmel
herunter lügen; **lie to** belügen ‖ *v*
(*pret* **lay** [le]; *pp* **lain** [len]; *ger*
lying) *intr* liegen; **lie down** sich hin-
legen; **lie down!** (*to a dog*) leg dich!;
lie in wait auf der Lauer liegen; **lie
in wait for** auflauern (*dat*); **lie low**
sich versteckt halten; (*bide one's
time*) abwarten; **take s.th. lying down**
etw widerspruchslos hinnehmen

lie' detec'tor *s* Lügendetektor *m*

lien [lin] *s* Pfandrecht *n*

lieu [lu] *s*—**in l. of** statt (*genit*)

lieutenant [lu'tɛnənt] *s* Leutnant *m;*
(nav) Kapitänleutnant *m*

lieuten'ant colo'nel *s* Oberstleutnant *m*

lieuten'ant comman'der *s* Korvetten-
kapitän *m*

lieuten'ant gen'eral *s* Generalleutnant
m

lieuten'ant gov'ernor *s* Vizegouverneur
m

lieuten'ant jun'ior grade' *s* (nav) Oberleutnant *m* zur See

lieuten'ant sen'ior grade' *s* (nav) Kapitänleutnant *m*

life [laɪf] *adj* (*imprisonment*) lebenslänglich ‖ *s* (**lives** [laɪvz]) Leben *n;*
(*e.g., of a car*) Lebensdauer *f;* **all
my l.** mein ganzes Leben lang; **as big
as l.** in voller Lebensgröße; **bring
back to l.** wieder zum Bewußtsein
bringen; **bring to l.** ins Leben bringen; **for dear l.** ums liebe Leben;
for l. auf Lebenszeit; **full of l.** voller
Leben; **I can't for the l. of me** ich
kann beim besten Willen nicht; **lives
lost** Menschenleben *pl;* **not on your
l.** auf keinen Fall; **put l. into** beleben; **such is l.!** so ist nun mal das
Leben; **take one's l.** sich [*dat*] das
Leben nehmen; **upon my l!** so wahr
ich lebe!; **you can bet your l. on
that!** darauf kannst du Gift nehmen!

life'-and-death' *adj* auf Leben und Tod

life' annu'ity *s* Lebensrente *f*

life' belt' *s* Schwimmgürtel *m*

life'blood' *s* Lebensblut *n*

life'boat' *s* Rettungsboot *n*

life' buoy' *s* Rettungsboje *f*

life' expect'ancy *s* Lebenserwartung *f*

life' guard' *s* (*at a pool*) Bademeister
–in *mf;* (*at the shore*) Strandwärter
–in *mf*

life' impris'onment *s* lebenslängliche
Haft *f*

life' insur'ance *s* Lebensversicherung *f*

life' jack'et *s* Schwimmweste *f*

lifeless ['laɪflɪs] *adj* leblos; (fig)
schwunglos

life'-like' *adj* naturgetreu, lebensecht

life' line' *s* Rettungsleine *f;* (*for a
diver*) Signalleine *f;* (*supply line*)
Lebensader *f*

life'long' *adj* lebenslänglich

life' mem'ber *s* Mitglied *n* auf Lebenszeit

life' of lei'sure *s* Wohlleben *n*

life' of plea'sure *s* Wohlleben *n*

life' of Ri'ley ['raɪli] *s* Herrenleben *n*

life' of the par'ty *s*—**be the l.** die ganze
Gesellschaft unterhalten

life' preserv'er [prɪ ˌzʌrvər] *s* Rettungs-
ring *m*

lifer ['laɪfər] *s* (sl) Lebenslängliche *mf*

life' raft' *s* Rettungsfloß *n*

lifesaver ['laɪf ˌsevər] *s* Rettungs-
schwimmer –in *mf;* (fig) rettender
Engel *m*

life' sen'tence *s* Verurteilung *f* zu le-
benslänglicher Haft

life'-size(d)' *adj* lebensgroß

life' span' *s* Lebensdauer *f*

life' style' *s* Lebensweise *f*

life'time' *adj* lebenslänglich ‖ *s* Leben
n; **for a l.** auf Lebenszeit; **once in a
l.** einmal im Leben

life' vest' *s* Schwimmweste *f*

life'work' *s* Lebenswerk *n*

lift [lɪft] *s* (*elevator*) Aufzug *m;* (aer
& fig) Auftrieb *m;* **give s.o. a l.** j–n
im Wagen mitnehmen ‖ *tr* heben;
(*gently*) lüpfen; (*with effort*) wuchten; (*weights*) stemmen; (*the receiver*) abnehmen; (*an embargo*) aufheben; (*steal*) (sl) klauen; **l. up** aufheben; (*the eyes*) erheben; **not l. a
finger** keinen Finger rühren ‖ *intr*
(*said of a mist*) steigen; **l. off** (rok)
starten

lift'-off' *s* (rok) Start *m*

lift' truck' *s* Lastkraftwagen *m* mit
Hebevorrichtung

ligament ['lɪgəmənt] *s* Band *n*

ligature ['lɪgətʃər] *s* (mus) Bindung *f;*
(*act*) (surg) Abbinden *n;* (*filament*)
(surg) Abbindungsschnur *f;* (typ)
Ligatur *f*

light [laɪt] *adj* (*clothing, meal, music,
heart, wine, sleep, punishment,
weight*) leicht; (*day, beer, color,
complexion, hair*) hell; **as l. as day**
tageshell; **l. as a feather** federleicht;
make l. of auf die leichte Schulter
nehmen; (*belittle*) als bedeutungslos
hinstellen ‖ *s* Licht *n;* **according to
his lights** nach dem Maß seiner Einsicht; **bring to l.** ans Licht bringen;
come to l. ans Licht kommen; **do
you have a l.?** haben Sie Feuer?;
in the l. of im Lichte (*genit*), angesichts (*genit*); **put in a false l.** in ein
falsches Licht stellen; **see the l. of
day** (*be born*) das Licht der Welt
erblicken; **shed l. on** Licht werfen
auf (*acc*); **throw quite a different l.
on** ein ganz anderes Licht werfen
auf (*acc*) ‖ *v* (*pret* & *pp* **lighted** &
lit [lɪt]) *tr* (*a fire, cigarette*) anzünden; (*an oven*) anheizen; (*a
street*) beleuchten; (*a hall*) erleuchten; (*a face*) aufleuchten lassen ‖
intr sich entzünden; **l. up** (*said of a
face*) aufleuchten; (*light a cigarette*)
sich [*dat*] e–e Zigarette anstecken

light'-blue' *adj* lichtblau, hellblau

light' bulb' *s* Glühbirne *f*

light-complexioned ['laɪtkəm'plɛkʃənd] *adj* von heller Hautfarbe

lighten ['laɪtən] *tr* (*in weight*) leichter machen; (*brighten*) erhellen; (fig) erleichtern || *intr* (*become brighter*) sich aufhellen; (*during a storm*) blitzen

lighter ['laɪtər] *s* Feuerzeug *n;* (naut) Leichter *m*

ligh'ter flu'id *s* Feuerzeugbenzin *n*

light'-fin'gered *adj* geschickt; (*thievish*) langfingerig

light'-foot'ed *adj* leichtfüßig

light'-head'ed *adj* leichtsinnig; (*dizzy*) schwindlig

light'-heart'ed *adj* leichtherzig

light'-heavy'weight' *adj* (box) Halbschwergewichts– || *s* Halbschwergewichtler *m*

light'house' *s* Leuchtturm *m*

light'ing *s* Beleuchtung *f*

light'ing effects' *spl* Lichteffekte *pl*

light'ing fix'ture *s* Beleuchtungskörper *m*

lightly ['laɪtli] *adv* leicht; (*without due consideration*) leichthin; (*disparagingly*) geringschätzig

light' me'ter *s* Lichtmesser *m*

lightness ['laɪtnɪs] *s* (*in weight*) Leichtigkeit *f;* (*in shade*) Helligkeit *f*

lightning ['laɪtnɪŋ] *s* Blitz *m* || *impers* —**it is l.** es blitzt

light'ning arrest'er [ə‚rɛstər] *s* Blitzableiter *m*

light'ning bug' *s* Leuchtkäfer *m*

light'ning rod' *s* Blitzableiter *m*

light'ning speed' *s* Windeseile *f*

light' op'era *s* Operette *f*

light' read'ing *s* Unterhaltungslektüre *f*

light'ship' *s* Leuchtschiff *n*

light' sleep' *s* Dämmerschlaf *m*

light' switch' *s* Lichtschalter *m*

light' wave' *s* Lichtwelle *f*

light'weight' *adj* (box) Leichtgewichts– || *s* (*coll*) geistig Minderbemittelter *m;* (box) Leichtgewichtler *m*

light'-year' *s* Lichtjahr *n*

likable ['laɪkəbəl] *adj* sympathisch, lieb

like [laɪk] *adj* gleich, ähnlich; **be l.** gleichen (*dat*) || *adv*—**l. crazy** (coll) wie verrückt || *s*—**and the l.** und dergleichen; **likes and dislikes** Neigungen und Abneigungen *pl* || *tr* gern haben, mögen; **I l. him** er ist mir sympathisch; **I l. the picture** das Bild gefällt mir; **I l. the food** das Essen schmeckt mir; **l. to** (*inf*), e.g., **I l. to read** ich lese gern || *intr*— **as you l.** wie Sie wollen; **if you l.** wenn Sie wollen || *prep* wie; **feel l.** (*ger*) Lust haben zu (*inf*); **feel l. hell** (sl) sich elend fühlen; **it looks l.** es sieht nach ... aus; **l. greased lightning** wie geschmiert; **that's just l. him** das sieht ihm ähnlich; **there's nothing l. traveling** es geht nichts übers Reisen

likelihood ['laɪklɪ‚hʊd] *s* Wahrscheinlichkeit *f*

likely ['laɪkli] *adj* wahrscheinlich; **a l. story!** (iron) e–e glaubhafte Geschichte!; **it's l. to rain** es wird wahrscheinlich regen

like'-mind'ed *adj* gleichgesinnt

liken ['laɪkən] *tr* (**to**) vergleichen (mit)

likeness ['laɪknɪs] *s* Ähnlichkeit *f;* **a good l. of** ein gutes Portrait (*genit*)

like'wise' *adv* gleichfalls, ebenso

lik'ing *s* (**for**) Zuneigung *f* (*zu*); **not to my l.** nicht nach meinem Geschmack; **take a l. to** Zuneigung fassen zu

lilac ['laɪlək] *adj* lila || *s* Flieder *m*

lilt [lɪlt] *s* rhythmischer Schwung *m;* (*lilting song*) lustiges Lied *n*

lily ['lɪli] *s* Lilie *f*

lil'y of the val'ley *s* Maiglöckchen *n*

lil'y pad' *s* schwimmendes Seerosenblatt *n*

lil'y-white' *adj* lilienweiß

li'ma bean' ['laɪmə] *s* Limabohne *f*

limb [lɪm] *s* Glied *n;* (*of a tree*) Ast *m;* **go out on a l.** (fig) sich exponieren; **limbs** Gliedmaßen *pl*

limber ['lɪmbər] *adj* geschmeidig || *tr* —**l. up** geschmeidig machen || *intr*— sich geschmeidig machen

lim·bo ['lɪmbo] *s* (**–bos**) Vorhölle *f;* (fig) Vergessenheit *f*

lime [laɪm] *s* Kalk *m;* (bot) Limonelle *f*

lime'kiln' *s* Kalkofen *m*

lime'light' *s* (& fig) Rampenlicht *n*

limerick ['lɪmərɪk] *s* Limerick *m*

lime'stone' *adj* Kalkstein– || *s* Kalkstein *m*

limit ['lɪmɪt] *s* Grenze *f;* **go the l.** zum Äußersten gehen; **off limits** Zutritt verboten; **set a l. to** e–e Grenze ziehen (*dat*); **that's the l.!** das ist denn doch die Höhe!; **there's a l. to everything** alles hat seine Grenzen; **within limits** in Grenzen; **without l.** schrankenlos || *tr* begrenzen; (**to**) beschränken (auf *acc*)

limitation [‚lɪmɪ'teʃən] *s* Begrenzung *f*, Beschränkung *f*

lim'ited *adj* (**to**) beschränkt (*auf* acc)

lim'ited-ac'cess high'way *s* Autobahn *f*

lim'ited mon'archy *s* konstitutionelle Monarchie *f*

limitless ['lɪmɪtlɪs] *adj* grenzenlos

limousine ['lɪmə‚zin], [‚lɪmə'zin] *s* Limousine *f*

limp [lɪmp] *adj* (& fig) schlaff || *s* Hinken *n;* **walk with a l.** hinken || *intr* (& fig) hinken

limpid ['lɪmpɪd] *adj* durchsichtig

linchpin ['lɪntʃ‚pɪn] *s* Achsnagel *m*

linden ['lɪndən] *s* Linde *f*, Lindenbaum *m*

line [laɪn] *s* Linie *f*, Strich *m;* (*boundary*) Grenze *f;* (*of a page*) Zeile *f;* (*of verse*) Verszeile *f;* (*of a family*) Zweig *m;* (*sphere of activity*) Fach *n;* (e.g., *of a streetcar*) Linie *f*, Strecke *f;* (*wrinkle*) Furche *f;* (*of articles for sale*) Sortiment *n;* (*for wash*) Leine *f;* (*queue*) Schlange *f;* (sl) zungenfertiges Gerede *n;* (angl) Schnur *f;* (mil) Linie *f*, Front *f;* (telp) Leitung *f;* **all along the l.** (fig) auf der ganzen Linie; **along the lines**

of nach dem Muster von; **draw the l. (at)** (fig) e–e Grenze ziehen (bei); **fall into l.** sich einfügen; **forget one's lines** (theat) steckenbleiben; **form a l.** sich in e–r Reihe aufstellen; **get a l. on** (coll) herausklamüsern; **give s.o. a l.** (sl) j–m schöne Worte machen; **hold the l.** die Stellung halten; (telp) am Apparat bleiben; **in l. of duty** im Dienst; **in l. with** in Übereinstimmung mit; **keep in l.** in der Reihe bleiben; **keep s.o. in l.** j–n im Zaum halten; **stand in l.** Schlange stehen; **the l. is busy** (telp) Leitung besetzt! || *tr* linieren; (e.g., *a coat*) füttern; (*a face*) furchen; (*a drawer*) ausschlagen; (*a wall*) verkleiden; **l. one's purse** sich [*dat*] den Beutel spicken; **l. the streets** in den Straßen Spalier bilden; **l. up** ausrichten; (mil) aufstellen || *intr*—**l. up** Schlange stehen; (mil) antreten; **l. up for** sich anstellen nach
lineage ['lɪnɪ·ɪdʒ] *s* Abkunft *f*, Abstammung *f*
lineal ['lɪnɪ·əl] *adj* (*descent*) direkt; (*linear*) geradlinig
lineaments ['lɪnɪ·əmənts] *spl* Gesichtszüge *pl*
linear ['lɪnɪ·ər] *adj* (*arranged in a line*) geradlinig; (*involving a single dimension*) Längen–; (*using lines*) Linien–; (math) linear
lined' pa'per *s* Linienpapier *n*
line'man *s* (**–men**) (rr) Streckenwärter *m;* (telp) Telephonarbeiter *m*
linen ['lɪnən] *adj* Leinen– || *s* Leinen *n;* (*in the household*) Wäsche *f;* (*of the bed*) Bettwäsche *f;* **linens** Weißzeug *n;* **put fresh l. on the bed** das Bett überziehen
lin'en clos'et *s* Wäscheschrank *m*
lin'en cloth' *s* Leinwand *f*
lin'en goods' *spl* Weißwaren *pl*
line' of approach' *s* (aer) Anflugschneise *f*
line' of bus'iness *s* Geschäftszweig *m*
line' of communica'tion *s* Verbindungslinie *f*
line' of fire' *s* Schußlinie *f*
line' of sight' *s* (*of a gun*) Visierlinie *f;* (astr) Sichtlinie *f*
liner ['laɪnər] *s* Einsatz *m;* (naut) Linienschiff *n*
lines'man *s* (**–men**) (sport) Linienrichter *m*
line'up' *s* (*at a police station*) Gegenüberstellung *f;* (sport) Aufstellung *f*
linger ['lɪŋgər] *intr* (*tarry*) verweilen; (*said of memories*) nachwirken; (*said of a melody*) nachtönen; **l. over** verweilen bei
lingerie [,læn3ə'ri] *s* Damenunterwäsche *f*
lin'gering *adj* (*disease*) schleichend; (*tune*) nachklingend; (*memory, taste, feeling*) nachwirkend
lingo ['lɪŋgo] *s* Kauderwelsch *n*
linguist ['lɪŋgwɪst] *s* Sprachwissenschaftler –in *mf*
linguistic [lɪŋ'gwɪstɪk] *adj* (e.g., *skill*) sprachlich; (*of linguistics*) sprach-

wissenschaftlich || **linguistics** *s* Sprachwissenschaft *f*
liniment ['lɪnɪmənt] *s* Einreibemittel *n*
lin'ing *s* (*of a coat*) Futter *n;* (*of a brake*) Bremsbelag *m;* (e.g., *of a wall*) Verkleidung *f*
link [lɪŋk] *s* Glied *n;* (fig) Bindeglied *n* || *tr* verbinden; (fig) verketten; **l. to** verbinden mit; (fig) in Verbindung bringen mit || *intr*—**l. up** (rok) dokken; **l. up with** sich anschließen an (*acc*)
linnet ['lɪnɪt] *s* (orn) Hänfling *m*
linoleum [lɪ'nolɪ·əm] *s* Linoleum *n*
linotype ['laɪnə,taɪp] *s* (trademark) Linotype *f*
lin'seed oil' ['lɪn ,sid] *s* Leinöl *n*
lint [lɪnt] *s* Fussel *f*
lintel ['lɪntəl] *s* Sturz *m*
lion ['laɪ·ən] *s* Löwe *m*
li'on cage' *s* Löwenzwinger *m*
lioness ['laɪ·ənɪs] *s* Löwin *f*
lionize ['laɪ·ə ,naɪz] *tr* zum Helden des Tages machen
li'ons' den' *s* Löwengrube *f*
li'on's share' *s* Löwenanteil *m*
li'on tam'er *s* Löwenbändiger –in *mf*
lip [lɪp] *s* Lippe *f;* (*edge*) Rand *m;* **bite one's lips** sich auf die Lippen beißen; **smack one's lips** sich [*dat*] die Lippen lecken
lip' read'ing *s* Lippenlesen *n*
lip' serv'ice *s* Lippenbekenntnis *n;* **pay l. to** ein Lippenbekenntnis ablegen zu
lip'stick' *s* Lippenstift *m*
lique·fy ['lɪkwɪ ,faɪ] *v* (*pret & pp* **–fied**) *tr* verflüssigen || *intr* sich verflüssigen
liqueur [lɪ'kʌr] *s* Likör *m*
liquid ['lɪkwɪd] *adj* flüssig; (*clear*) klar || *s* Flüssigkeit *f*
liq'uid as'sets *spl* flüssige Mittel *pl*
liquidate ['lɪkwɪ ,det] *tr* (*a debt*) tilgen; (*an account*) abrechnen; (*a company*) liquidieren
liquidation [,lɪkwɪ 'deʃən] *s* (*of a debt*) Tilgung *f;* (*of an account*) Abrechnung *f;* (*of a company*) Liquidation *f*
liquidity [lɪ'kwɪdɪti] *s* flüssiger Zustand *m;* (fin) Liquidität *f*
liq'uid meas'ure *s* Hohlmaß *m*
liquor ['lɪkər] *s* Spirituosen *pl*, Schnaps *m;* **have a shot of l.** einen zwitschern
liquorice ['lɪkərɪs] *s* Lakritze *f*
li'quor li'cense *s* Schankerlaubnis *f*
Lisbon ['lɪzbən] *s* Lissabon *n*
lisp [lɪsp] *s* Lispeln *n* || *tr & intr* lispeln
lissome ['lɪsəm] *adj* biegsam, gelenkig
list [lɪst] *s* Liste *f*, Verzeichnis *n;* (naut) Schlagseite *f* **enter the lists** (& fig) in die Schranken treten; **make a l. of** verzeichnen || *tr* verzeichnen || *intr* (naut) Schlagseite haben
listen ['lɪsən] *intr* horchen, zuhören; **l. closely** die Ohren aufsperren; **l. for** achten auf (*acc*); **l. in** mithören; **l. to** zuhören (*dat*); (*a thing*) horchen auf (*acc*); (*obey*) gehorchen (*dat*); (*take advice from*) hören auf (*acc*); **l. to reason** auf e–n Rat hören; **l. to the radio** Radio hören

listener ['lɪsənər] *s* Zuhörer –in *mf;* (rad) Rundfunkhörer –in *mf*

lis'tening *adj* Abhör–, Horch–

lis'tening post' *s* Horchposten *m*

listless ['lɪstlɪs] *adj* lustlos

list' price' *s* Listenpreis *m*

litany ['lɪtəni] *s* (& fig) Litanei *f*

liter ['litər] *s* Liter *m* & *n*

literacy ['lɪtərəsi] *s* Kenntnis *f* des Lesens und Schreibens

literal ['lɪtərəl] *adj* buchstäblich; (*person*) pedantisch; **l. sense** wörtlicher Sinn *m*

literally ['lɪtərəli] *adv* buchstäblich

literary ['lɪtə‚reri] *adj* literarisch; **l. language** Literatursprache *f;* **l. reference** Schrifttumsangabe *f*

literate ['lɪtərɪt] *adj* des Lesens und des Schreibens kundig; (*educated*) gebildet || *s* Gebildete *mf*

literati [‚lɪtə'rati] *spl* Literaten *pl*

literature ['lɪtərətʃər] *s* Literatur *f;* (com) Drucksachen *pl*

lithe [laɪð] *adj* gelenkig

lithia ['lɪθɪ·ə] *s* (chem) Lithiumoxyd *n*

lithium ['lɪθɪ·əm] *s* Lithium *n*

lithograph ['lɪθə‚græf] *s* Steindruck *m* || *tr* lithographieren

lithographer [lɪ'θɑgrəfər] *s* Lithograph –in *mf*

lithography [lɪ'θɑgrəfi] *s* Steindruck *m*, Lithographie *f*

Lithuania [‚lɪθu'enɪ·ə] *s* Litauen *n*

Lithuanian [‚lɪθu'enɪ·ən] *adj* litauisch || *s* Litauer –in *mf;* (*language*) Litauisch *n*

litigant ['lɪtɪgənt] *adj* prozessierend; **the l. parties** die streitenden Parteien || *s* Prozeßführer –in *mf*

litigate ['lɪtɪ‚get] *tr* prozessieren gegen || *intr* prozessieren

litigation [‚lɪtɪ'geʃən] *s* Rechsstreit *m*

lit'mus pa'per ['lɪtməs] *s* Lackmuspapier *n*

litter ['lɪtər] *s* (*stretcher*) Tragbahre *f;* (*bedding for animals*) Streu *f;* (*of pigs, dogs*) Wurf *m;* (*trash*) herumliegender Abfall *m;* (hist) Sänfte *f* || *tr* verunreinigen || *intr* (*bear young*) werfen; (*strew litter*) Abfälle wegwerfen; **no littering!** das Wegwerfen von Abfällen ist verboten!

lit'terbug' *s*—**don't be a l.** wirf keine Abfälle weg

little ['lɪtəl] *adj* (*in size*) klein; (*in amount*) wenig || *adv* wenig; **l. by l.** nach und nach || *s*—**after a l.** nach kurzer Zeit; **a l.** ein wenig, ein bißchen; **make l. of** wenig halten von

Lit'tle Bear' *s* Kleiner Bär *m*

Lit'tle Dip'per *s* Kleiner Wagen *m*, Kleiner Bär *m*

lit'tle fin'ger *s* kleiner Finger *m*

lit'tle peo'ple *s* kleine Leute *pl;* (myth) Heinzelmännchen *pl*

Lit'tle Red Rid'inghood' *s* Rotkäppchen *n*

lit'tle slam' *s* (cards) Klein-Schlemm *m*

liturgic(al) [lɪ'tʌrdʒɪk(əl)] *adj* liturgisch

liturgy ['lɪtərdʒi] *s* Liturgie *f*

livable ['lɪvəbəl] *adj* (*place*) wohnlich; (*life*) erträglich

live [laɪv] *adj* lebendig; (*coals*) glühend; (*ammunition*) scharf; (elec) stromführend; (rad, telv) live; **l. program** Originalsendung *f* || *adv* (rad, telv) live || [lɪv] *tr* leben; (*a life*) führen; **l. down** durch einwandfreien Lebenswandel vergessen machen; **l. it up** (coll) das Leben genießen; **l. out** (*survive*) überleben || *intr* leben; (*reside*) wohnen; (*reside temporarily*) sich aufhalten; **l. and learn!** man lernt nie aus!; **l. for the moment** in den Tag hineinleben; **l. high off the hog** in Saus und Braus leben; **l. off s.o.** j–m auf der Tasche liegen; **l. on** (*subsist on*) sich nähren von; (*continue to live*) fortleben; **l. through** durchmachen; **l. to see** erleben; **l. up to** gerecht werden (*dat*)

livelihood ['laɪvlɪ‚hud] *s* Lebensunterhalt *m*

liveliness ['laɪvlɪnɪs] *s* Lebhaftigkeit *f*

livelong ['lɪv‚lɔŋ] *adj*—**all the l. day** den lieben langen Tag

lively ['laɪvli] *adj* lebhaft; (*street*) belebt

liven ['laɪvən] *tr* aufmuntern || *intr* munter werden

liver ['lɪvər] *s* (anat) Leber *f*

liverwurst ['lɪvər‚wurst] *s* Leberwurst *f*

livery ['lɪvəri] *s* Livree *f*

liv'ery sta'ble *s* Mietstallung *f*

live' show' [laɪv] *s* Originalsendung *f*, Livesendung *f*

livestock ['laɪv‚stɑk] *s* Viehstand *m*

live' wire' [laɪv] *s* geladener Draht *m;* (coll) energiegeladener Mensch *m*

livid ['lɪvɪd] *adj* bleifarben; (*enraged*) wütend

liv'ing *adj* (*alive*) lebend, lebendig; (*for living*) Wohn–; **not a l. soul** keine Mutterseele *f* || *s* Unterhalt *n;* **good l.** Wohlleben *n;* **make a l. (as)** sein Auskommen haben (als); **what do you do for a l.?** wie verdienen Sie Ihren Lebensunterhalt?

liv'ing accommoda'tions *spl* Unterkunft *f*

liv'ing be'ing *s* Lebewesen *n*

liv'ing condi'tions *spl* Lebensbedingungen *pl*

liv'ing expens'es *spl* Unterhaltskosten *pl*

liv'ing quar'ters *spl* Unterkunft *f*

liv'ing room' *s* Wohnzimmer *n*

liv'ing-room set' (or **suite'**) *s* Polstergarnitur *f*

liv'ing space' *s* Lebensraum *m*

liv'ing wage' *s* Existenzminimum *n*

lizard ['lɪzərd] *s* Eidechse *f*

load [lod] *s* Last *f*, Belastung *f;* (*in a truck*) Fuhre *f;* **get a l. of that!** schau dir das mal an!; **have a l. on** (sl) einen sitzen haben; **loads of** (coll) Mengen von; **that's a l. off my mind** mir ist dabei ein Stein vom Herzen gefallen || *tr* (*a truck, gun*) laden; (*cargo on a ship*) einladen; (*with work*) überladen; (*with worries*) belasten; **l. down** belasten; **l. the cam-**

era den Film einlegen; **l. up** aufladen || *intr* das Gewehr laden

load′ed *adj* (*rifle*) scharf geladen; (*dice*) falsch; (*question*) verfänglich; (*very rich*) (sl) steinreich; (*drunk*) (sl) sternhagelvoll; **fully l.** (aut) mit allen Schikanen

loader [′lodər] *s* (*worker*) Ladearbeiter –in *mf;* (*device*) Verladevorrichtung *f*

load′ing *s* Ladung *f*, Verladung *f*

load′ing plat′form *s* Ladebühne *f*

load′ing ramp′ *s* Laderampe *f*

load′ lim′it *s* Tragfähigkeit *f;* (elec) Belastungsgrenze *f*

load′stone′ *s* Magneteisenstein *m*

loaf [lof] *s* (**loaves** [lovz]) Laib *m* || *intr* faulenzen; **l. around** herumlungern

loafer [′lofər] *s* Faulenzer *m*

loaf′ing *s* Faulenzen *n*

loam [lom] *s* Lehm *m*

loamy [′lomi] *adj* lehmig

loan [lon] *s* Anleihe *f*, Darlehe(n) *n* || *tr* (ver)leihen, borgen; **l. out** leihen

loan′ com′pany *s* Leihanstalt *f*

loan′ shark′ *s* (coll) Wucherer *m*

loan′ word′ *s* Lehnwort *n*

loath [loθ] *adj*—**be l. to** (*inf*) abgeneigt sein zu (*inf*)

loathe [loð] *tr* verabscheuen

loathing [′loðıŋ] *s* (**for**) Abscheu *m* (vor *dat*)

loathsome [′loðsəm] *adj* abscheulich

lob [lab] *s* (tennis) Lobball *m* || *v* (*pret & pp* **lobbed;** *ger* **lobbing**) *tr* lobben, hochschlagen

lob·by [′labi] *s* (*of a hotel or theater*) Vorhalle *f*, Foyer *n;* (pol) Interessengruppe *f* || *v* (*pret & pp* **–bied**) *intr* antichambrieren

lob′bying *s* Beeinflussung *f* von Abgeordneten, Lobbying *n*

lobbyist [′labı·ıst] *s* Lobbyist –in *mf*

lobe [lob] *s* (anat) Lappen *m*

lobster [′labstər] *s* Hummer *m; ***red as a l.** (fig) krebsrot

local [′lokəl] *adj* örtlich, Orts–; (*produce*) heimisch || *s* (*group*) Ortsgruppe *f;* (rr) Personenzug *m*

lo′cal anesthe′sia *s* Lokalanästhese *f*

lo′cal call′ *s* (telp) Ortsgespräch *n*

lo′cal col′or *s* Lokalkolorit *n*

lo′cal deliv′ery *s* Ortszustellung *f*

locale [lo′kæl] *s* Ort *m*

lo′cal gov′ernment *s* Gemeindeverwaltung *f*

locality [lo′kælıti] *s* Örtlichkeit *f*

localize [′lokə‚laız] *tr* lokalisieren

lo′cal news′ *s* Lokalnachrichten *pl*

lo′cal pol′itics *s* Kommunalpolitik *f*

lo′cal show′er *s* Strichregen *m*

lo′cal tax′ *s* Gemeindesteuer *f*

lo′cal time′ *s* Ortszeit *f*

lo′cal traf′fic *s* Nahverkehr *m*, Ortsverkehr *m*

locate [lo′ket], [′loket] *tr* (*find*) ausfindig machen; (*a ship, aircraft*) orten; (*the trouble*) finden, feststellen; (*set up, e.g., an office*) errichten; **be located** liegen, gelegen sein || *intr* sich niederlassen

location [lo′keʃən] *s* Lage *f; ***on l.** (cin) auf Außenaufnahme

lock [lak] *s* Schloß *n;* (*of hair*) Locke *f;* (*of a canal*) Schleuse *f;* **l., stock, and barrel** mit allem Drum und Dran; **under l. and key** unter Verschluß || *tr* zusperren; (*arms*) verschränken; **l. in** einsperren; **l. out** aussperren; **l. up** (*a house*) zusperren; (*imprison*) einsperren || *intr* (*said of a lock*) zuschnappen; (*said of brakes*) sperren; **l. together** (*said of bumpers*) sich ineinander verhaken

locker [′lakər] *s* (*as in a gym or barracks*) Spind *m & n;* (*for luggage*) Schließfach *n*

lock′er room′ *s* Umkleideraum *m*

locket [′lakıt] *s* Medaillon *n*

lock′jaw′ *s* Maulsperre *f*

lock′ nut′ *s* Gegenmutter *f*

lock′out′ *s* Aussperrung *f*

lock′smith′ *s* Schlosser –in *mf*

lock′smith shop′ *s* Schlosserei *f*

lock′ step′ *s* Marschieren *n* in dicht geschlossenen Gliedern

lock′ stitch′ *s* Kettenstich *m*

lock′up′ *s* (coll) Gefängnis *n*

lock′ wash′er *s* Sicherungsring *m*

locomotion [‚lokə′moʃən] *s* (*act*) Fortbewegung *f;* (*power*) Fortbewegungsfähigkeit *f*

locomotive [‚lokə′motıv] *s* Lokomotive *f*

lo·cus [′lokəs] *s* (**–ci** [saı]) Ort *m;* (geom) geometrischer Ort *m*

locust [′lokəst] *s* (*black locust*) (bot) Robinie *f;* (*carob*) (bot) Johannisbrotbaum *m;* (Cicada) (ent) Zikade *f*

lode [lod] *s* (min) Gang *m*

lode′star′ *s* Leitstern *m*

lodge [ladʒ] *s* (*of Masons*) Loge *f;* (*for hunting*) Jagdhütte *f;* (*for weekending*) Wochenendhäuschen *n;* (*summer house*) Sommerhäuschen *n* || *tr* unterbringen; **l. a complaint** e–e Beschwerde einreichen || *intr* wohnen; (*said of an arrow, etc.*) steckenbleiben

lodger [′ladʒər] *s* Untermieter –in *mf*

lodg′ing *s* Unterkunft *f;* **lodgings** Logis *n*

loft [lɔft] *s* Speicher *m;* (*for hay*) Heuboden *m;* (*of a church*) Chor *m;* (*of a golf club*) Hochschlaghaltung *f* || *tr* (*a golf club*) in Hochschlaghaltung bringen; (*a golf ball*) hochschlagen

loftiness [′lɔftınıs] *s* Erhabenheit *f*

lofty [′lɔfti] *adj* (*style*) erhaben; (*high*) hochragend; (*elevated in rank*) gehoben; (*haughty*) anmaßend

log [lɔg] *s* (*trunk*) Baumstamm *m;* (*for the fireplace*) Holzklotz *m;* (*record book*) Tagebuch *n;* (aer, naut) Log *n;* **sleep like a log** wie ein Klotz schlafen || *v* (*pret & pp* **logged**) *ger* **logging**) *tr* (*trees*) fällen und abästen; (*cut into logs*) in Klötze schneiden; (*an area*) abholzen; (*enter into a logbook*) in das Logbuch eintragen; (*traverse*) zurücklegen

logarithm [′lɔgə‚rıðəm] *s* Logarithmus *m*

log'book' s (aer, naut) Logbuch n
log' cab'in s Blockhaus n, Blockhütte f
logger ['lɔgər] s Holzfäller m
log'gerhead' s—at **loggerheads** auf Kriegsfuß
log'ging s Holzarbeit f
logic ['lɑdʒɪk] s Logik f
logical ['lɑdʒɪkəl] adj logisch
logician [loˈdʒɪʃən] s Logiker –in mf
logistic(al) [loˈdʒɪstɪk(əl)] adj logistisch
logistics [loˈdʒɪstɪks] s Logistik f
log'jam' s aufgestaute Baumstämme pl; (fig) völlige Stockung f
log'wood' s Kampescheholz n
loin [lɔɪn] s (of beef) Lendenstück n; (anat) Lende f; **gird up one's loins** (fig) sich rüsten
loin'cloth' s Lendentuch n
loin' end' s (of pork) Rippenstück n
loiter ['lɔɪtər] tr—l. **away** vertrödeln || intr trödeln; (hang around) herumlungern
loiterer ['lɔɪtərər] s Bummler –in mf
loi'tering s Trödelei f; **no l.** Herumlungern verboten!
loll [lɑl] intr sich bequem ausstrecken
lollipop ['lɑlɪ ˌpɑp] s Lutschbonbon m & n
Lombardy ['lʌmbərdi] s die Lombardei
London ['lʌndən] adj Londoner || s London n
Londoner ['lʌndənər] s Londoner –in mf
lone [lon] adj (sole) alleinig; (solitary) einzelstehend
loneliness ['lonlɪnɪs] s Einsamkeit f
lonely ['lonli] adj einsam; **become l.** vereinsamen
loner ['lonər] s Einzelgänger m
lonesome ['lonsəm] adj einsam; **be l. for** sich sehnen nach
lone' wolf' s (fig) Einzelgänger m
long [lɔŋ] adj (longer ['lɔŋgər]; longest ['lɔŋgɪst]) lang; (way, trip) weit; (detour) groß; **a l. time** lange; **a l. time since** schon lange her, daß; **in the l. run** auf die Dauer || adv lange; **as l. as** so lange wie; **but not for l.** aber nicht lange; **l. after** lange nach; **l. ago** vor langer Zeit; **l. live ...!** es lebe ...!; **l. since** längst; **so l.!** bis dann! || intr—**l. for** sich sehnen nach; **l. to** (inf) sich danach sehnen zu (inf)
long'boat' s Pinasse f
long' dis'tance s (telp) Ferngespräch n; **call l.** ein Ferngespräch anmelden
long'-dis'tance adj (sport) Langstrecken–
long'-dis'tance call' s Ferngespräch n
long'-dis'tance flight' s Langstreckenflug m
long'-drawn'-out' adj ausgedehnt; (story) langatmig
longevity [lanˈdʒɛvɪti] s Langlebigkeit f
long' face' s langes Gesicht n
long'hair' adj (fig) intellektuell || s (fig) Intellektueller m; (mus) (coll) konservativer Musiker m
long'hand' s Langschrift f; **in l.** mit der Hand geschrieben

long'ing adj sehnsüchtig || s (for) Sehnsucht f (nach)
longitude ['lɑndʒɪ ˌt(j)ud] s Länge f
longitudinal [ˌlɑndʒɪˈt(j)udɪnəl] adj Longitudinal–
long' jump' s Weitsprung m
long-lived ['lɔŋ'laɪvd] adj langlebig
long'-play'ing rec'ord s Langspielplatte f
long'-range' adj (plan) auf lange Sicht; (aer) Langstrecken–
long'shore'man s (–men) Hafenarbeiter m
long' shot' s (coll) riskante Wette f; **by a l.** bei weitem
long'stand'ing adj althergebracht, alt
long'-suf'fering adj langmütig
long' suit' s (fig) Stärke f; (cards) lange Farbe f
long'-term' adj langfristig
long-winded ['lɔŋ'wɪndɪd] adj langatmig
look [luk] s (glance) Blick m; (appearance) Aussehen n; (expression) Ausdruck m; **from the looks of things** wie die Sache aussieht; **give a second l.** sich [dat] genauer ansehen; **have a l. around** Umschau halten; **have a l. at s.th.** sich [dat] etw ansehen; **I don't like the looks of it** die Sache gefällt mir nicht; **looks** Ansehen n; **new l.** verändertes Aussehen n; (latest style) neueste Mode f; **take a l. at s.th.** sich [dat] etw ansehen || tr—he **looks his age** man sieht ihm sein Alter an; **l. one's best** sich in bester Verfassung zeigen; **l. one's last at** zum letzten Mal ansehen; **l. s.o. in the eye** j–m in die Augen sehen; **l. s.o. over** j–n mustern; **l. s.th. over** etw (über)prüfen (or durchsehen); **l. up** (e.g., a word) nachschlagen; (e.g., a friend) aufsuchen; **l. up and down** von oben bis unten mustern || intr schauen; (appear, seem) aussehen; **l. after** (e.g., children) betreuen; (a household, business) besorgen; (a departing person) nachblicken (dat); **l. ahead** vorausschauen; **l. around (for)** sich [dat] umsehen (nach); **l. at** anschauen; **l. back (on)** zurücksehen (auf acc); **l. down** herabsehen; (cast the eyes down) die Augen niederschlagen; **l. down on** herabsehen auf (acc); (in contempt) über die Achseln ansehen; **l. for** suchen; (e.g., a criminal) fahnden nach; **l. forward to** sich freuen auf (acc); **l. hard at** scharf ansehen; **l. into** (a mirror, the future) blicken in (acc); (a matter) nachgehen (dat); **l. like** gleichen (dat); (e.g., rain) aussehen nach; **l. on** zuschauen; **l. on s.o. as** j–n betrachten als; **l. out** aufpassen; **l. out for** aussehen nach; **l. out on** (a view) hinausgehen auf (acc); **l. over** hinwegsehen über (acc); **l. sharp!** jetzt aber hoppla!; **l. through** (e.g., a window) blicken durch; (s.o. or s.o.'s motives) durchschauen; **l. up** (raise one's gaze) aufschauen; **l. up to s.o.** zu j–m hinaufsehen; **things**

are beginning to l. up es wird langsam besser; **things don't l. so good for** est steht übel mit; **what does he l. like?** wie sieht er aus?

look'ing glass' s Spiegel m

look'out' s (watchman) Wachposten m; (observation point) Ausguck m; (matter of concern) Sache f; **be a l.** Schmiere stehen; **be on the l.** (for) Auschau halten (nach)

look'out man' s—**be the l.** Schmiere stehen

look'out tow'er s Aussichtsturm m

loom [lum] s Webstuhl m || intr undeutlich und groß auftauchen; **l. large** von großer Bedeutung scheinen

loon [lun] s (orn) Taucher m

loony ['luni] adj verrückt; **be l.** spinnen

loop [lup] s Schleife f, Schlinge f; (e.g., on a dress for a hook) Öse f; (aer) Looping m; **do a l.** (aer) e-n Looping drehen || tr schlingen || intr Schlingen (or Schleifen) bilden

loop'hole' s Guckloch n; (in a fortification) Schießscharte f; (in a law) Lücke f

loose [lus] adj locker, los; (wobbly) wackelig; (morally) locker, unsolid; (unpacked) unverpackt; (translation) frei; (interpretation) dehnbar; (dress, tongue) lose; (skin) schlaff; **l. connection** (elec)' Wackelkontakt m || adv—**break l.** (from an enclosure) ausbrechen; (e.g., from a hitching) sich losmachen; (said of a storm, hell) losbrechen; **come l.** losgehen; **cut l.** (act up) (coll) außer Rand und Band geraten; **turn l.** befreien; **work l.** sich lockern; (said of a button) abgehen; (said of a brick, stone, shoestring) sich lösen || s—**on the l.** ungehemmt, frei || tr (a boat) losmachen; (a knot) lösen

loose' change' s Kleingeld n

loose' end' s (fig) unerledigte Kleinigkeit f; **at loose ends** im ungewissen

loose'-leaf note'book s Loseblattbuch n

loosen ['lusən] tr lockern, locker machen || intr locker werden

looseness ['lusnɪs] s Lockerheit f

loot [lut] s Beute f || tr erbeuten; (plunder) plündern; (e.g., art treasures) verschleppen

lop [lɑp] v (pret & pp lopped; ger lopping) tr—**lop off** abhacken

lope [lop] s Trab m || intr—**l. along** in großen Schritten laufen

lop'sid'ed adj schief; (score) einseitig

loquacious [lo'kweʃəs] adj geschwätzig

lord [lɔrd] s Herr m; (Brit) Lord m; **Lord** Herrgott m || tr—**l. it over** sich als Herr aufspielen über (acc)

lordly ['lɔrdli] adj würdig; (haughty) hochmütig

Lord's' Day' s Tag m des Herrn

lord'ship' s Herrschaft f

Lord's' Prayer' s Vaterunser n

Lord's' Sup'per s heiliges Abendmahl n

lore [lor] s Kunde f; (traditional wisdom) überlieferte Kunde f

lorry ['lɔri] s (Brit) Lastkraftwagen m

lose [luz] v (pret & pp lost [lɔst]) tr verlieren; (several minutes, as a clock does) zurückbleiben; (in betting) verwetten; (in gambling) verspielen; (the page in a book) verblättern; **l. one's way** sich verirren; (on foot) sich verlaufen; (by car) sich verfahren || intr verlieren; (sport) geschlagen werden; **l. to** (sport) unterliegen (dat)

loser ['luzər] s Unterlegene mf; **be the l.** mit langer Nase abziehen

los'ing adj verlierend; (com) verlustbringend || **losings** spl Verluste pl

los'ing game' s aussichtsloses Spiel n

loss [lɔs] s (in) Verlust m (an dat); **at a l.** in Verlegenheit; (com) mit Verlust; **be at a l. for words** nach Worten suchen; **inflict l. on s.o.** j-m Schaden zufügen; **l. of appetite** Appetitlosigkeit f; **l. of blood** Blutverlust m; **l. of face** Blamage f; **l. of life** Verluste pl an Menschenleben; **l. of memory** Gedächtnisverlust m; **l. of sight** Erblindung f; **l. of time** Zeitverlust m; **straight l.** Barverlust m

lost [lɔst] adj verloren; **be l.** (said of a thing) verlorengehen; (not know one's way) sich verirrt haben; **be l. on s.o.** auf j-n keinen Eindruck machen; **get l.** in Verlust geraten; **get l.!** hau ab!; **l. in thought** in Gedanken versunken

lost'-and-found' depart'ment s Fundbüro n

lost' cause' s aussichtslose Sache f

lot [lɑt] s (fate) Los n, Schicksal n; (in a drawing) Los n; (portion of land) Grundstück n; (cin) Filmgelände n; (com) Posten m, Partie f; **a lot** viel, sehr; **a lot of** (or **lots of**) viel(e); **the lot** das Ganze

lotion ['loʃən] s Wasser n

lottery ['lɑtəri] s Lotterie f

lot'tery tick'et s Lotterielos n

lotto ['lɑto] s Lotto n

lotus ['lotəs] s Lotos m

loud [laud] adj laut; (colors) schreiend

loud-mouthed ['laud,mauðd] adj laut

loud'speak'er s Lautsprecher m

lounge [laundʒ] s Aufenthaltsraum m || intr sich recken; **l. around** herumlungern

lounge' chair' s Klubsessel m

lounge' liz'ard s (sl) Salonlöwe m

louse [laus] s (lice [laɪs]) Laus f; (sl) Sauhund m || tr—**l. up** (sl) versauen

lousy ['lauzi] adj verlaust; (sl) lausig; **l. with** (people) wimmelnd von; **l. with money** stinkreich

lout [laut] s Lümmel m

louver ['luvər] s Jalousie f

lovable ['lʌvəbəl] adj liebenswürdig

love [lʌv] adj Liebes- || s (for, of) Liebe f (zu); **be in l. with** verliebt sein in (acc); **for the l. of God** um Gottes willen; **fall (madly) in l. with** sich (heftig) verlieben in (acc); **Love** (at the end of a letter) herzliche Grüße; **l. at first sight** Liebe f auf den ersten Blick; **make l. to** herzen;

(sl) geschlechtlich verkehren mit; **not for l. or money** nicht für Gold und gute Worte; **there's no l. lost between them** sie schätzen sich nicht || *tr* lieben; (*like*) gern haben; **l. to dance** sehr gern tanzen

love' affair' *s* Liebeshandel *m*, Liebesverhältnis *n*

love'birds' *spl* (coll) Unzertrennlichen *pl*

love' child' *s* Kind *n* der Liebe

love' feast' *s* (eccl) Liebesmahl *n*

love' game' *s* (tennis) Nullpartie *f*

love' knot' *s* Liebesschleife *f*

loveless ['lʌvlɪs] *adj* lieblos

love' let'ter *s* Liebesbrief *m*

lovelorn ['lʌv ,lɔrn] *adj* vor Liebe vergehend

lovely ['lʌvli] *adj* lieblich

love'-mak'ing *s* Geschlechtsverkehr *m*

love' match' *s* Liebesheirat *f*

love' po'em *s* Liebesgedicht *n*

love' po'tion *s* Liebestrank *m*

lover ['lʌvər] *s* Liebhaber *m*; **lovers** Liebespaar *n*

love' scene' *s* Liebesszene *f*

love' seat' *s* Sofasessel *n*

love'sick' *adj* liebeskrank

love' song' *s* Liebeslied *n*

love' to'ken *s* Liebespfand *n*

lov'ing *adj* liebevoll; **Your l.** ... Dich liebender ...

lov'ing-kind'ness *s* Herzensgüte *f*

low [lo] *adj* (*building, mountain, forehead, birth, wages, estimate, prices, rent*) niedrig; (*number*) nieder; (*altitude, speed*) gering; (*not loud*) leise; (*vulgar*) gemein; (*grades, company*) schlecht; (*fever*) leicht; (*pulse, pressure*) schwach; (*ground*) tiefgelegen; (*bow, voice*) tief; (*almost empty*) fast leer; (*supplies, funds*) knapp; **be low** (*said of the sun, water*) niedrigstehen; **be low in funds** knapp bei Kasse sein; **feel low** niedergeschlagen sein; **have a low opinion of** e-e geringe Meinung haben von || *adv* niedrig; **lay low** über den Haufen werfen; **lie low** sich versteckt halten; (*bide one's time*) abwarten; **run low** knapp werden; **sing low** tief singen; **sink low** tief sinken || *s* (*low point*) (fig) Tiefstand *m*; (meteor) Tief *n* || *intr* muhen, brüllen

low' blow' *s* (box) Tiefschlag *m*

low'born' *adj* von niederer Herkunft

low'brow' *s* Spießbürger *m*

low'-cost hous'ing *s* sozial geförderter Wohnungsbau *m*

Low' Coun'tries, the *spl* die Niederlande

low'-cut' *adj* tiefausgeschnitten

low'-down' *adj* schurkisch || *s* (*unadorned facts*) unverblümte Wahrheit *f*; (*inside information*) Geheimnachrichten *pl*

lower ['lo·ər] *comp adj* untere; (*e.g., deck, house, jaw, lip*) Unter– || *tr* herunterlassen; (*the eyes, voice, water level, temperature*) senken; (*prices*) herabsetzen; (*a flag, sail*) streichen; (*lifeboats*) aussetzen; **l.**

oneself sich herablassen || ['lau·ər] *intr* finster blicken; **l. at** finster anblicken

low'er ab'domen ['lo·ər] *s* Unterbauch *m*

low'er berth' ['lo·ər] *s* untere Koje *f*

low'er case' ['lo·ər] *s* Kleinbuchstaben *pl*

lower-case ['lo·ər'kes] *adj* klein

low'er course' ['lo·ər] *s* (*of a river*) Unterlauf *m*

low'er mid'dle class' ['lo·ər] *s* Kleinbürgertum *n*

lowermost ['lo·ər ,most] *adj* niedrigste

low'er world' ['lo·ər] *s* Unterwelt *f*

low'-fly'ing *adj* tieffliegend

low' fre'quency *s* Niederfrequenz *f*

low'-fre'quency *adj* Niederfrequenz–

low' gear' *s* erster Gang *m*

low'-grade' *adj* minderwertig

low'ing *s* Gebrüll *n*

lowland ['loland] *s* Flachland *n*; **Lowlands** (*in Scotland*) Unterland *n*

low' lev'el *s* Tiefstand *m*

low'-lev'el attack' *s* Tiefangriff *m*

low'-lev'el flight' *s* Tiefflug *m*

lowly ['loli] *adj* bescheiden; (*humble in spirit*) niederträchtig

low'-ly'ing *adj* tiefliegend

Low' Mass' *s* stille Messe *f*

low'-mind'ed *adj* niedrig gesinnt

low' neck' *s* (*of a dress*) Ausschnitt *m*

low'-necked' *adj* tief ausgeschnitten

low'-pitched' *adj* (*sound*) tief; (*roof*) mit geringer Neigung

low'-pres'sure *adj* Tiefdruck–, Unterdruck–

low'-priced' *adj* billig

low' shoe' *s* Halbschuh *m*

low'-speed' *adj* mit geringer Geschwindigkeit; (*film*) unempfindlich

low'-spir'ited *adj* niedergeschlagen

low' spir'its *spl* Niedergeschlagenheit *f*; **be in l.** niedergeschlagen sein

low' tide' *s* Ebbe *f*; (fig) Tiefstand *m*

low' wa'ter *s* Niedrigwasser *n*

low'-wa'ter mark' *s* (fig) Tiefpunkt *m*

loyal ['lɔɪ·əl] *adj* treu, loyal

loyalist ['lɔɪ·əlɪst] *s* Regierungstreue *mf*

loyalty ['lɔɪ·əlti] *s* Treue *f*

lozenge ['lazɪndʒ] *s* Pastille *f*

LP ['ɛl'pi] *s* (trademark) (**long-playing record**) Langspielplatte *f*

Ltd. *abbr* (Brit) (**Limited**) Gesellschaft *f* mit beschränkter Haftung

lubricant ['lubrɪkənt] *s* Schmiermittel *n*

lubricate ['lubrɪ ,ket] *tr* (ab)schmieren

lubrication [,lubrɪ'keʃən] *s* Schmierung *f*

lucerne [lu'sʌrn] *s* (bot) Luzerne *f*; **Lucerne** Luzern *n*

lucid ['lusɪd] *adj* (*clear*) klar, deutlich; (*bright*) hell

luck [lʌk] *s* Glück *n*; (*chance*) Zufall *m*; **as l. would have it** wie es der Zufall wollte; **be down on one's l.** an seinem Glück verzagen; **be in l.** Glück haben; **be out of l.** Unglück haben; **dumb l.** (coll) Sauglück *n*; **have tough l.** (coll) Pech haben;

rotten l. (coll) Saupech *n;* **try one's l.**
sein Glück versuchen; **with l. you
should win** wenn Sie Glück haben,
werden Sie gewinnen
luckily ['lʌkɪli] *adv* zum Glück
luckless ['lʌklɪs] *adj* glücklos
lucky ['lʌki] *adj* glücklich; **be l.** Glück
haben; **l. dog** (coll) Glückspilz *m;*
l. penny Glückspfennig *m*
luck'y shot' *s* Glückstreffer *m*
lucrative ['lukrətɪv] *adj* gewinnbrin-
gend
ludicrous ['ludɪkrəs] *adj* lächerlich
lug [lʌg] *s* (*pull, tug*) Ruck *m;* (*lout*)
(sl) Lümmel *m;* (elec) Öse *f* ‖ *v* (*pret
& pp* **lugged;** *ger* **lugging**) *tr* schleppen
luggage ['lʌgɪdʒ] *s* Gepäck *n;* **excess l.**
Mehrgepäck *n;* **piece of l.** Gepäckstück *n*
lug'gage car'rier *s* Gepäckträger *m*
lug'gage compart'ment *s* (aer) Frachtraum *m*
lug'gage rack' *s* Gepäckablage *f;* (*on
the roof of a car*) Dachgepäckträger
m
lug'gage receipt' *s* Aufgabeschein *m*
lugubrious [lʊ'g(j)ubrɪ·əs] *adj* tieftrau-
rig
lukewarm ['luk ˌwɔrm] *adj* lau, lauwarm
lull [lʌl] *s* Windstille *f;* (com) Flaute
f ‖ *tr* einlullen; (*e.g., fears*) beschwichtigen; **l. to sleep** einschläfern
‖ *intr* nachlassen
lullaby ['lʌlə ˌbaɪ] *s* Wiegenlied *n*
lumbago [lʌm'bego] *s* Hexenschluß
m
lumber ['lʌmbər] *s* Bauholz *n* ‖ *intr*
sich schwerfällig fortbewegen
lum'berjack' *s* Holzfäller *m*
lum'ber·man' *s* (**–men'**) (*dealer*) Holz-
händler *m;* (*lumberjack*) Holzfäller
m
lum'beryard' *s* Holzplatz *m*
luminary ['lumɪ ˌneri] *s* Leuchtkörper
m; (fig) Leuchte *f*
luminescent [ˌlumɪ'nɛsənt] *adj* lumi-
neszierend
luminous ['lumɪnəs] *adj* leuchtend,
Leucht–
lu'minous di'al *s* Leuchtzifferblatt *n*
lu'minous paint' *s* Leuchtfarbe *f*
lummox ['lʌməks] *s* Lümmel *m*
lump [lʌmp] *s* (*e.g., of clay*) Klumpen
m; (*on the body*) Beule *f;* **have a l.
in one's throat** e–n Kloß (or Knödel)
im Hals haben; **l. of sugar** Würfel *m*
Zucker ‖ *tr*—**l. together** (fig) zusammenwerfen
lumpish ['lʌmpɪʃ] *adj* klumpig
lump' sug'ar *s* Würfelzucker *m*
lump' sum' *s* Pauschalbetrag *m*
lumpy ['lʌmpi] *adj* klumpig; (*sea*) bewegt
lunacy ['lunəsi] *s* Irrsinn *m*
lu'nar eclipse' ['lunər] *s* Mondfinster-
nis *f*
lu'nar land'ing *s* Mondlandung *f*
lu'nar mod'ule *s* (rok) Mondfähre *f*
lu'nar year' *s* Mondjahr *n*
lunatic ['lunətɪk] *s* Irre *mf*

lu'natic asy'lum *s* Irrenhaus *n*
lu'natic fringe' *s* Extremisten *pl*
lunch [lʌntʃ] *s* (*at noon*) Mittagessen
n, Lunch *m;* (*light meal*) Zwischen-
mahlzeit *f;* **eat l.** zu Mittag essen;
have (*s.th.*) **for l.** zum Mittagessen
haben ‖ *intr* zu Mittag essen, lun-
chen
lunch' coun'ter *s* Theke *f*
luncheon ['lʌntʃən] *s* gemeinsames
Mittagessen *n*
luncheonette [ˌlʌntʃə'nɛt] *s* Imbißstube *f*
lunch' hour' *s* Mittagsstunde *f*
lunch'room' *s* Imbißhalle *f*
lunch'time' *s* Mittagszeit *f*
lung [lʌŋ] *s* Lunge *f;* **at the top of
one's lungs** aus voller Kehle
lunge ['lʌndʒ] *s* Sprung *m* vorwärts;
(fencing) Ausfall *m* ‖ *tr* (*a horse*)
an der Longe laufen lassen ‖ *intr*—
e–n Sprung vorwärts machen; (*with
a sword*) (*at*) e–n Ausfall machen
(gegen); **l. at** losstürzen auf (*acc*)
lurch [lʌrtʃ] *s* Torkeln *n,* Taumeln *n;*
leave in a l. im Stich lassen ‖ *intr*
torkeln; (*said of a ship*) zur Seite
rollen
lure [lʊr] *s* Köder *m* ‖ *tr* ködern; (fig)
verlocken; **l. away** weglocken
lurid ['lʊrɪd] *adj* (*light*) gespenstisch;
(*sunset*) düsterrot; (*gruesome*) grausig; (*pallid*) fahl
lurk [lʌrk] *intr* lauern
luscious ['lʌʃəs] *adj* köstlich; **a l. doll**
(coll) ein tolles Weib
lush [lʌʃ] *adj* üppig
lust [lʌst] *s* Wollust *f;* (*for*) Begierde
f (nach) ‖ *intr* (**after, for**) gieren
(nach)
luster ['lʌstər] *s* Glanz *m;* (*e.g., chandelier*) Lüster *m*
lusterless ['lʌstərlɪs] *adj* matt
lus'terware' *s* Tongeschirr *n* mit Lüster
lustful ['lʌstfəl] *adj* lüstern, geil
lustrous ['lʌstrəs] *adj* glänzend
lusty ['lʌsti] *adj* kräftig
lute [lut] *s* Laute *f*
Lutheran ['luθərən] *adj* lutherisch ‖ *s*
Lutheraner –in *mf*
luxuriance [lʌg'ʒʊrɪ·əns] *s* Üppigkeit *f*
luxuriant [lʌg'ʒʊrɪ·ənt] *adj* üppig
luxuriate [lʌg'ʒʊrɪ ˌet] *intr* (*thrive*)
gedeihen; (*delight*) (**in**) schwelgen
(in *dat*)
luxurious [lʌg'ʒʊrɪ·əs] *adj* luxuriös; **l.
living** Prasserei *f*
luxury ['lʌgʒəri] *s* Extravaganz *f,*
Luxus *m;* (*object of luxury*) Luxusar-
tikel *m;* **live a life of l.** im vollen
leben
lye [laɪ] *s* Lauge *f*
ly'ing *adj* lügenhaft ‖ *s* Lügen *n*
ly'ing-in' **hos'pital** *s* Entbindungsan-
stalt *f*
lymph [lɪmf] *s* Lymphe *f*
lymphatic [lɪm'fætɪk] *adj* lymphatisch
lynch [lɪntʃ] *tr* lynchen
lynch'ing *s* Lynchen *n*
lynch' law' *s* Lynchjustiz *f*
lynx [lɪŋks] *s* Luchs *m*
lynx'-eyed' *adj* luchsäugig

lyre [laɪr] s (mus) Leier *f*
lyric [ˈlɪrɪk] *adj* lyrisch; **l. poetry**
Lyrik *f* ‖ s lyrisches Gedicht *n;* (*of
a song*) Text *m*

lyrical [ˈlɪrɪkəl] *adj* lyrisch
lyricism [ˈlɪrɪˌsɪzəm] *s* Lyrik *f*
lyricist [ˈlɪrɪsɪst] *s* (*of a song*) Texter
–in *mf;* (*poet*) lyrischer Dichter *m*

M

M, m [ɛm] *s* dreizehnter Buchstabe des
englischen Alphabets
ma [mɑ] *s* (coll) Mama *f*
ma'am [mæm] *s* (coll) gnädige Frau *f*
macadam [məˈkædəm] *s* Makadam-
decke *f*
macadamize [məˈkædəˌmaɪz] *tr* ma-
kadamisieren
maca'dam road' *s* Straße *f* mit Maka-
damdecke
macaroni [ˌmækəˈroni] *spl* Makkaroni
pl
macaroon [ˌmækəˈrun] *s* Makrone *f*
macaw [məˈkɔ] *s* (orn) Ara *m*
mace [mes] *s* Stab *m*, Amtsstab *m*
mace'bear'er *s* Träger *m* des Amts-
stabes
machination [ˌmækɪˈneʃən] *s* Intrige
f; **machinations** Machenschaften *pl*
machine [məˈʃin] *s* Maschine *f;* (pol)
Apparat *m;* **by m.** maschinell ‖ *tr*
spannabhebend formen
machine'-driv'en *adj* mit Maschinenan-
trieb
machine' gun' *s* Maschinengewehr *n*
machine'-gun' *v* (*pret & pp* –gunned;
ger –gunning) *tr* unter Maschinenge-
wehrfeuer nehmen
machine' gun'ner *s* Maschinengewehr-
schütze *m*
machine'-made' *adj* maschinell herge-
stellt
machinery [məˈʃinəri] *s* (& fig) Maschinerie *f*
machine' screw' *s* Maschinenschraube
f
machine' shop' *s* Maschinenhalle *f*
machine' tool' *s* Werkzeugmaschine *f*
machinist [məˈʃinɪst] *s* (*maker and
repairer of machines*) Maschinen-
bauer *m;* (*machine operator*) Ma-
schinenschlosser –in *mf*
mackerel [ˈmækərəl] *s* Makrele *f*
mad [mæd] *adj* (**madder; maddest**) verrückt; (*angry*) böse; **be mad about**
vernarrt sein in (*acc*); **be mad at**
böse sein auf (*acc*); **drive mad** verrückt machen; **go mad** verrückt
werden
madam [ˈmædəm] *s* gnädige Frau *f;*
(*of a brothel*) (sl) Bordellmutter *f*
mad'cap' *adj* ausgelassen ‖ *s* Wildfang
m
madden [ˈmædən] *tr* verrückt machen;
(*make angry*) zornig machen
made'-to-or'der *adj* nach Maß angefertigt
made'-up' *adj* (*story*) erfunden; (*artificial*) künstlich; (*with cosmetics*) ge-
schminkt

mad'house' *s* Irrenhaus *n*, Narrenhaus
n
madly [ˈmædli] *adv* (coll) wahnsinnig
mad'man' *s* (–men') Verrückter *m*
madness [ˈmædnɪs] *s* Wahnsinn *m*
Madonna [məˈdɑnə] *s* Madonna *f*
maelstrom [ˈmelstrəm] *s* (& fig) Strudel *m*
magazine [ˌmægəˈzin] *s* (*periodical*)
Zeitschrift *f;* (*illustrated*) Illustrierte
f; (*warehouse for munitions; cartridge container*) Magazin *n;* (*for a
camera*) Kassette *f*
magazine' rack' *s* Zeitschriftenständer
m
Maggie [ˈmægi] *s* Gretchen *n*
maggot [ˈmægət] *s* Made *f*
Magi [ˈmedʒaɪ] *spl*—**the three M.**
(Bib) die drei Weisen *pl* aus dem
Morgenland
magic [ˈmædʒɪk] *adj* (*enchanting*) zau-
berhaft; (*trick, word, wand*) Zauber–
‖ *s* Zauberkunst *f*
magician [məˈdʒɪʃən] *s* Zauberer –in
mf
ma'gic lan'tern *s* Laterna magica *f*
magisterial [ˌmædʒɪsˈtɪrɪ·əl] *adj* (*of
a magistrate*) obrigkeitlich; (*authoritative*) autoritativ; (*pompous*) anmaßend
magistrate [ˈmædʒɪsˌtret] *s* Polizei-
richter *m*
magnanimous [mægˈnænɪməs] *adj* groß-
mütig
magnate [ˈmægnet] *s* Magnat *m*
magnesium [mægˈnizɪ·əm] *s* Magnesium *n*
magnet [ˈmægnɪt] *s* Magnet *m*
magnetic [mægˈnɛtɪk] *adj* magnetisch;
(*personality*) fesselnd
magnetism [ˈmægnɪˌtɪzəm] *s* Magnetismus *m;* (fig) Anziehungskraft *f*
magnetize [ˈmægnɪˌtaɪz] *tr* magnetisieren
magnificence [mægˈnɪfɪsəns] *s* Pracht
f
magnificent [mægˈnɪfɪsənt] *adj* prächtig
magnifier [ˈmægnɪˌfaɪ·ər] *s* (electron)
Verstärker *m*
magni·fy [ˈmægnɪˌfaɪ] *v* (*pret & pp*
–fied) *tr* vergrößern; (fig) übertreiben
mag'nifying glass' *s* Lupe *f*
magnitude [ˈmægnɪˌt(j)ud] *s* (& astr)
Größe *f*
magno'lia tree' [mægˈnolɪ·ə] *s* Magno-
lia *f*
magpie [ˈmægˌpaɪ] *s* (& fig) Elster *f*
mahlstick [ˈmɑlˌstɪk] *s* Malerstock *m*

mahogany [mə'hɑgəni] s Mahagoni n
mahout [mə'haut] s Elefantentreiber m
maid [med] s Dienstmädchen n
maiden ['medən] s Jungfer f; (poet) Maid f
maid'enhair' s (bot) Jungfernhaar n
maid'enhead' s Jungfernhäutchen n
maid'enhood' s Jungfräulichkeit f
maidenly ['medənli] adj jungfräulich
maid'en name' s Mädchenname m
maid'en voy'age s Jungfernfahrt f
maid'-in-wait'ing s (maids-in-waiting) Hofdame f
maid' of hon'or s erste Brautjungfer f
maid'serv'ant s Dienstmädchen n
mail [mel] adj Post– || s Post f; (armor) Kettenpanzer m; by m. brief-lich; by return m. postwendend || tr (put into the mail) aufgeben; (send) abschicken; m. to zuschicken (dat)
mail'bag' s Postsack m
mail'boat' s Postschiff n
mail'box' s Briefkasten m
mail' car'rier s Briefträger –in mf
mail' deliv'ery s Postzustellung f
mail' drop' s Briefeinwurf m
mailer ['melər] s (phot) Versandbeutel m
mail'ing s Absendung f
mail'ing list' s Postversandliste f
mail'ing per'mit s Zulassung f zum portofreien Versand
mail'man' s (–men') Briefträger m
mail' or'der s Bestellung f durch die Post
mail'-order house' s Versandhaus n
mail' plane' s Postflugzeug n
mail' train' s Postzug m
mail' truck' s Postauto n
maim [mem] tr verstümmeln
main [men] adj Haupt– || s Hauptlei-tung f; in the main hauptsächlich
main' clause' s (gram) Hauptsatz m
main' course' s Hauptgericht n
main' deck' s Hauptdeck n
main' floor' s Erdgeschoß n
mainland ['men ˌlænd] s Festland n
main' line' s (rr) Hauptstrecke f
mainly ['menli] adv größtenteils
mainmast ['men ˌmæst] s Großmast m
main' of'fice s Hauptbüro n, Zentrale f
main' point' s springender Punkt m
mainsail ['men ˌsel] s Großsegel n
main'spring' s (horol & fig) Triebfeder f
main'stay' s (fig) Hauptstütze f; (naut) Großstag n
main' street' s Hauptstraße f
maintain [men'ten] tr aufrechterhalten; (e.g., a family) unterhalten; (assert) behaupten; (one's reputation) wah-ren; (e.g., in good condition) bewah-ren; (order, silence) halten; (a road) instand halten
maintenance ['mentɪnəns] s (upkeep) Instandhaltung f; (support) Unter-halt m; (e.g., of an automobile) War-direktor m
maître d'hôtel [ˌmetərdo'tɛl] s (head waiter) Oberkellner m; (owner)

Hotelbesitzer m; (manager) Hotel-tung f
majestic [mə'dʒɛstɪk] adj majestätisch
majesty ['mædʒɪsti] s Majestät f
major ['medʒər] adj Haupt–; (mus) –Dur || s (educ) Hauptfach n; (mil) Major m || intr—m. in als Haupt-fach studieren
majordomo ['medʒər'domo] s Haus-hofmeister m
ma'jor gen'eral s Generalmajor m
majority [mə'dʒɔrɪti] adj Mehrheits– || s Mehrheit f; (full age) Mündig-keit f; (mil) Majorsrang m; (parl) Stimmenmehrheit f; be in the m. in der Mehrheit sein; in the m. of cases in der Mehrzahl der Fälle; the m. of people die meisten Menschen
major'ity vote' s Mehrheitsbeschluß m
ma'jor league' s Oberliga f
make [mek] s Fabrikat n, Marke f || tr machen; (in a factory) herstellen; (cause) lassen; (force) zwingen; (clothes) anfertigen; (money) verdie-nen; (a reputation, name) erwerben; (a choice) treffen; (a confession) ablegen; (a report) erstatten; (plans) schmieden; (changes) vornehmen; (a movie) drehen; (contact) herstellen; (a meal) (zu)bereiten; (conditions) stellen; (rules, assertions) aufstellen; (a bet, compromise, peace) schließen; (excuses, requests, objections) vor-bringen; (a protest) erheben; (a goal) schießen (or erzielen); (a compari-son) ziehen; (a speech) halten; (e.g., a good father) abgeben; (be able to fit through, e.g., a window) gehen durch; (e.g., a train, bus, destina-tion) erreichen; (e.g., ten miles) zurücklegen; (a girl) (sl) verführen; (arith) machen; m. (s.o.) believe weismachen (dat); m. into verarbei-ten zu; m. of halten von; m. out (e.g., writing) entziffern; (e.g., a per-son at a distance) erkennen; (under-stand) kapieren; (a blank or form) ausfüllen; (a check, receipt) ausstel-len; m. over to (jur) überschreiben auf (acc); m. s.o. out to be a liar j–n als Lügner hinstellen; m. s.th. of oneself es weit bringen; m. the most of ausnutzen; m. time Zeit gewinnen; m. time with (a woman) (coll) flirten mit; m. up (e.g., a list) zusammenstellen; (a bill) ausstellen; (a sentence) bilden; (a story) sich [dat] ausdenken; m. up one's mind (about) sich [dat] schlüssig werden (über acc); m. way! Platz da!; m. way for ausweichen vor (dat) || intr—m. believe schauspielern; m. believe that nur so tun, als ob; m. do with sich behelfen mit; m. for los-steuern auf (acc); m. off with durch-brennen mit; m. out well gut aus-kommen; m. sure of sich vergewis-sern (genit); m. sure that vergewis-sern, daß; m. up (after a quarrel) sich versöhnen; m. up for (past mis-takes) wieder gutmachen; (lost time) wieder einbringen

make′-believe′ *adj* Schein-, vorgetäuscht ‖ *s* Schein *m*, Mache *f*
maker [ˈmekər] *s* Hersteller –in *mf;*
Maker Schöpfer *m*
make′shift′ *adj* behelfsmäßig, Behelfs–
‖ *s* Notbehelf *m*
make′-up′ *s* Aufmachung *f; (cosmetic)*
Make-up *n*, Schminke *f; (of a team)*
Aufstellung *f;* (theat) Maske *f;* (typ)
Umbruch *m;* **apply m.** sich schmin-
ken
make′weight′ *s* Gewichtszugabe *f*
mak′ing *s* Herstellung *f;* **be in the m.**
im Werden sein; **have the makings
of** das Zeug haben zu; **this is of his
own m.** dies ist sein eigenes Werk
maladjusted [ˌmælə'dʒʌstɪd] *adj* unausgeglichen
maladroit [ˌmælə'drɔɪt] *adj* ungeschickt
malady [ˈmælədi] *s* (& fig) Krankheit
f
malaise [mæ'lez] *s (physical)* Unwohl-
sein *n; (mental)* Unbehagen *n*
malaria [mə'lerɪ·ə] *s* Malaria *f*
Malaya [mə'le·ə] *s* Malaya *n*
Malaysia [mə'leʒɪ·ə] *s* Malaysia *n*
malcontent [ˈmælkən ˌtent] *adj* unzufrieden ‖ *s* Unzufriedene *mf*
male [mel] *adj* männlich ‖ *s* Mann *m;*
(bot) männliche Pflanze *f;* (zool)
Männchen *n*
malediction [ˌmælɪ'dɪkʃən] *s* Ver-
wünschung *f*
malefactor [ˈmælɪˌfæktər] *s* Übeltäter
–in *mf*
male′ nurse′ *s* Pfleger *m*
malevolence [mæ'levələns] *s* Böswillig-
keit *f*
malevolent [mə'levələnt] *adj* böswillig
malfeasance [ˌmæl'fizəns] *s* strafbare
Handlung *f;* **m. in office** Amtsvergehen *n*
malfunction [mæl'fʌŋkʃən] *s* technische Störung *f*
malice [ˈmælɪs] *s* Bosheit *f*
malicious [mə'lɪʃəs] *adj* boshaft
malign [mə'laɪn] *adj* böswillig ‖ *tr*
verleumden
malignancy [mə'lɪgnənsi] *s* (pathol)
Bösartigkeit *f*
malignant [mə'lɪgnənt] *adj* böswillig;
(pathol) bösartig
malinger [mə'lɪŋgər] *intr* simulieren
malingerer [mə'lɪŋgərər] *s* Simulant
–in *mf*
mall [mɔl] *s (promenade)* Lauben-
promenade *f; (shopping center)* über-
dachtes Einkaufszentrum *n*, Mall *f*
mallard [ˈmælərd] *s* Stockente *f*
malleable [ˈmælɪ·əbəl] *adj* schmiedbar
mallet [ˈmælɪt] *s* Schlegel *m*
mallow [ˈmælo] *s* Malve *f*
malnutrition [ˌmæln(j)u'trɪʃən] *s* Unterernährung *f*
malodorous [mæl'odərəs] *adj* übelriechend
malpractice [mæl'præktɪs] *s* ärztlicher
Kunstfehler *m*
malt [mɔlt] *s* Malz *n*
maltreat [mæl'trit] *tr* mißhandeln
mamma [ˈmɑmə] *s* Mama *f*, Mutti *f*

mammal [ˈmæməl] *s* Säugetier *n*
mammalian [mæ'melɪ·ən] *adj* Säugetier– ‖ *s* Säugetier *n*
mam′mary gland′ [ˈmæməri] *s* Milch-
drüse *f*
mam′ma's boy′ *s* Muttersöhnchen *n*
mammoth [ˈmæməθ] *adj* ungeheuer
(groß) ‖ *s* (zool) Mammut *n*
man [mæn] *s* (men [menɪ]) *(adult male)*
Mann *m; (human being)* Mensch *m;
(servant)* Diener *m; (worker)* Arbeiter *m; (mankind)* die Menschheit
f; (checkers) Stein *m;* **man alive!**
Menschenskind! ‖ *v* (pret & pp
manned; ger **manning**) *tr* besetzen;
(nav, rok) bemannen
man′ about town′ *s* weltgewandter
Mann *m*
manacle [ˈmænəkəl] *s* Handschelle *f* ‖
tr fesseln
manage [ˈmænɪdʒ] *tr (a business,
household)* leiten; *(an estate)* verwalten; *(tools, weapons)* handhaben;
(e.g., a boat, car) völlig in der Gewalt haben; *(children)* fertig werden
mit; **I'll m. it** ich werde es schon
schaffen; **m. the situation** die Sache
deichseln ‖ *intr* zurechtkommen;
(with, on) auskommen (mit); **m. to**
(inf) es fertigbringen zu *(inf)*
manageable [ˈmænɪdʒəbəl] *adj* handlich; *(hair)* fügsam
management [ˈmænɪdʒmənt] *s* Unter-
nehmensführung *f; (group which
manages)* Direktion *f; (as opposed
to labor)* Management *n*
man′agement consult′ant *s* Unterneh-
mungsberater –in *mf*
manager [ˈmænədʒər] *s* Manager *m,*
Geschäftsführer –in *mf; (of a bank
or hotel)* Direktor –in *mf; (of an
estate)* Verwalter –in *mf; (of a department)* Abteilungsleiter –in *mf;
(of a star, theater, athlete)* Manager
m
managerial [ˌmænə'dʒɪrɪ·əl] *adj* Lei-
tungs–, Führungs–
man′aging *adj* geschäftsführend
man′aging direc′tor *s* Geschäftsführer
–in *mf*
Manchuria [mæn't∫urɪ·ə] *s* Mandschurei *f*
man′darin or′ange [ˈmændərɪn] *s*
Mandarine *f*
mandate [ˈmændet] *s* Mandat *n* ‖ *tr*
(to) zuweisen *(dat)*
mandatory [ˈmændə ˌtori] *adj* verbindlich
mandolin [ˈmændəlɪn] *s* Mandoline *f*
mandrake [ˈmændrek] *s* (bot) Alraune *f*
mane [men] *s* Mähne *f*
maneuver [mə'nuvər] *s* Manöver *n;* **go
on maneuvers** (mil) ins Manöver ziehen ‖ *tr* manövrieren; **m. s.o. into**
(ger) j–n dazubringen zu *(inf)*
maneuverability [məˌnuvərə'bɪlɪti] *s*
Manövrierbarkeit *f*
maneuverable [mə'nuvərəbəl] *adj* ma-
növrierfähig
manful [ˈmænfəl] *adj* mannhaft
manganese [ˈmæŋgə ˌniz] *s* Mangan *n*

mange [mendʒ] s Räude f
manger ['mendʒər] s Krippe f
mangle ['mæŋɡəl] s Mangel f || tr
(tear apart) zerfleischen; (wash)
mangeln
mangy ['mendʒi] adj räudig; (fig)
schäbig
man'han'dle tr grob behandeln
man'hole' s Kanalschacht m, Mann-
loch n
man'hole cov'er s Schachtdeckel m
man'hood' s (virility) Männlichkeit f;
(age) Mannesalter n
man'-hour' s Arbeitsstunde f pro Mann
man'hunt' s Fahndung f
mania ['meni·ə] s Manie f
maniac ['meni,æk] s Geisteskranke
mf
maniacal [mə'nai·əkəl] adj manisch
manicure ['mæni,kjur] s Maniküre f,
Handpflege f || tr maniküren
manicurist ['mæni,kjurist] s Maniküre f
manifest ['mæni,fest] adj offenkundig,
offenbar || s (aer, naut) Manifest n
|| tr bekunden, bezeigen
manifestation [,mænifes'teʃən] s
(manifesting) Offenbarung f; (indication) Anzeichen n
manifes·to [,mæni'festo] s (-toes)
Manifest n
manifold ['mæni,fold] adj mannigfal-
tig || s (aut) Rohrverzweigung f
manikin ['mænikin] s Männchen n;
(for teaching anatomy) anatomisches
Modell n; (mannequin) Mannequin n
man' in the moon' s Mann m im Mond
man' in the streets' s Durchschnitts-
mensch m
manipulate [mə'nipjə,let] tr manipulieren
man'kind' s Menschheit f
manliness ['mænlinis] s Männlichkeit
f
manly ['mænli] adj mannhaft, männlich
man'-made' adj künstlich
manna ['mænə] s Manna n, Himmels-
brot n
manned' space'craft s bemanntes
Raumfahrzeug n
mannequin ['mænikin] s (clothes
model) Mannequin n; (in a display
window) Schaufensterpuppe f
manner ['mænər] s Art f, Weise f;
(custom) Sitte f; after the m. of
nach der Art von; by all m. of means
auf jeden Fall; by no m. of means
auf keinen Fall; in a m. gewissermaßen; in a m. of speaking sozusagen; in like m. gleicherweise; in
the following m. folgendermaßen; in
this m. auf diese Weise; it's bad
manners to (inf) es schickt sich nicht
zu (inf); m. of death Todesart f;
manners Manieren pl
mannerism ['mænə,rizəm] s Manie-
riertheit f
mannerly ['mænərli] adj manierlich
mannish ['mæniʃ] adj männisch;
(woman) unweiblich
man' of let'ters s Literat m

man' of the world' s Weltmann m
man' of war' s Kriegsschiff n
manor ['mænər] s Herrengut n
man'or house' s Herrenhaus n
man'pow'er s Arbeitskräfte pl; (mil)
Kriegsstärke f
man'serv'ant s (menservants) Diener m
mansion ['mænʃən] s Herrenhaus n
man'slaugh'ter s Totschlag m
mantel ['mæntəl] s Kaminsims m & n
man'telpiece' s Kaminsims m & n
mantilla [mæn'tilə] s Mantille f
mantle ['mæntəl] s (& fig) Mantel m;
(of a gaslight) Glühstrumpf m; (geol)
Mantel m || tr verhüllen
manual ['mænju·əl] adj manuell, Hand–
|| s (book) Handbuch n, Leitfaden
m; (mus) Manual n
man'ual control' s Handbedienung f
man'ual dexter'ity s Handfertigkeit f
man'ual la'bor s Handarbeit f
man'ual of arms' s (mil) Dienstvor-
schrift f
man'ual train'ing s Werkunterricht m
manufacture [,mænjə'fæktʃər] s Herstellung f; (production) Erzeugnis n
|| tr herstellen; (clothes) konfektio-
nieren
manufac'tured goods' spl Fertigwaren
pl
manufacturer [,mænjə'fæktʃərər] s
Hersteller –in mf
manure [mə'n(j)ur] s Mist m || tr
misten
manuscript ['mænjə,skript] adj hand-
schriftlich || s Manuskript n
many ['meni] adj viele; a good (or
great) m. sehr viele; how m. wieviele; in so m. words ausdrücklich;
m. a mancher, manch ein; m. a person manch einer; m. a time manchmal; twice as m. noch einmal so
viele || pron viele; as m. as ten nicht
weniger als zehn; how m. wieviele
man'y-sid'ed adj vielseitig
map [mæp] s Karte f, Landkarte f; (of
a city) Plan m; (of a local area)
Spezialkarte f; map of the world
Weltkarte f; put on the map (coll)
ausposaunen || v (pret & pp mapped;
ger mapping) tr kartographisch aufnehmen; map out planen
maple ['mepəl] s Ahorn m
ma'ple sug'ar s Ahornzucker m
ma'ple syr'up s Ahornsirup m
mar [mar] v (pret & pp marred; ger
marring) tr (detract from the beauty
of) verunzieren; (e.g., a reputation)
beeinträchtigen
marathon ['mærə,θan] s Dauerwett-
bewerb m
mar'athon race' s Marathonlauf m
maraud [mə'rɔd] tr & intr plündern
marauder [mə'rɔdər] s Plünderer m
marble ['marbəl] adj marmorn || s
Marmor m; (little glass ball) Murmel
f; (marbles (game) Murmelspiel n ||
tr marmorieren
mar'ble quar'ry s Marmorbruch m
march [martʃ] s Marsch m; (festive
parade) Umzug m; March März m;
on the m. auf dem Marsch; steal a

m. on s.o. j-m den Rang ablaufen;
the m. of time der Lauf der Zeit || *tr*
marschieren || *intr* marschieren; **m.
by** vorbeimarschieren (an *dat*); **m.
off** abmarschieren || *interj* marsch!
marchioness ['mɑrʃənɪs] *s* Marquise *f*
mare [mer] *s* Stute *f*
Margaret ['mɑrgərɪt] *s* Margarete *f*
margarine ['mɑrdʒərɪn] *s* Margarine *f*
margin ['mɑrdʒɪn] *s* (*of a page*) Rand
m; (*leeway*) Spielraum *m;* (fin)
Spanne *f;* **by a narrow m.** mit knap-
pem Abstand; **leave a m.** am Rande
Raum lassen; **m. of profit** Gewinn-
spanne *f;* **m. of safety** Sicherheits-
faktor *m;* **win by a ten-second m.**
mit zehn Sekunden Abstand gewinnen; **write in the m.** an dem Rand
schreiben
marginal ['mɑrdʒɪnəl] *adj* (*costs, profits, case*) Grenz–; (*in the margin*)
Rand–
mar'ginal note' *s* Randbemerkung *f*
mar'gin release' *s* Randauslöser *m*
mar'gin set'ter *s* Randsteller *m*
marigold ['mærɪ,gold] *s* Ringelblume
f
marijuana [,mɑrɪ'hwɑnə] *s* Marihuana
n
marinate ['mærɪ,net] *tr* marinieren
marine [mə'rin] *adj* See–, Meer(es)– ||
s (*fleet*) Marine *f;* (*fighter*) Marineinfanterist *m;* **marines** Marinetruppen
pl
Marine' Corps' *s* Marineinfanterie-
korps *n*
mariner ['mærɪnər] *s* Seemann *m*
marionette [,mærɪ-ə'net] *s* Marionette
f
marital ['mærɪtəl] *adj* ehelich, Gatten–
mar'ital sta'tus *s* Familienstand *m*
maritime ['mærɪ,taɪm] *adj* See–
marjoram ['mɑrdʒərəm] *s* Majoran *m*
mark [mɑrk] *s* (& fig) Zeichen *n;*
(*stain, bruise*) Fleck *m,* Mal *n;* (*German unit of currency*) Mark *f;* (educ)
Zensur *f;* **be an easy m.** (coll) leicht
reinzulegen sein; **hit the m.** ins
Schwarze treffen; **make one's m.** sich
durchsetzen; **m. of confidence** Ver-
trauensbeweis *m;* **m. of favor** Gunst-
bezeichnung *f;* **m. of respect** Zeichen
n der Hochachtung; **on your marks!**
auf die Plätze; **wide of the m.** am
Ziel vorbei || *tr* (aus)zeichnen, be-
zeichnen; (*student papers*) zensieren;
(*cards*) zinken; (*labels*) beschriften;
(*laundry*) zeichnen; (*the score*) anschreiben; **m. down** aufschreiben,
niederschreiben; (com) im Preis herabsetzen; **m. my words!** merken Sie
sich, was ich sage!; **m. off** abgrenzen;
(surv) abstecken; **m. time** (mil & fig)
auf der Stelle treten; (mus) den Takt
schlagen; **m. up** (*e.g., a wall*) beschmieren; (com) im Preis heraufsetzen
mark'down' *s* Preisnachlaß *m*
marked *adj* (*difference*) merklich; **a m.
man** ein Gezeichneter *m*
marker ['mɑrkər] *s* (*of scores*) Anschreiber –in *mf;* (*commemorative*

marker) Gedenktafel *f;* (*on a firing
range*) Anzeiger *m;* (*bombing marker*) Leuchtbombe *f;* (*felt pen*) Filzschreiber *m*
market ['mɑrkɪt] *s* Markt *m;* (*grocery
store*) Lebensmittelgeschäft *n;* (*stock
exchange*) Börse *f;* (*ready sale*) Absatz *m;* **be in the m. for** Bedarf haben
an (*dat*); **be on the m.** zum Verkauf
stehen; **put on the m.** auf den Markt
bringen || *tr* verkaufen
marketable ['mɑrkɪtəbəl] *adj* markt-
fähig
mar'ket anal'ysis *s* Marktanalyse *f*
mar'keting *s* (econ) Marketing *n;* **do
the m.** Einkäufe machen
mar'keting research' *s* Absatzforschung *f*
mar'ketplace' *s* Marktplatz *m*
mar'ket price' *s* Marktpreis *m*
mar'ket town' *s* Marktflecken *m*
mar'ket val'ue *s* Marktwert *m;* (st.
exch.) Kurswert *m*
mark'ing *s* Kennzeichen *n*
marks·man ['mɑrksmən] *s* (**–men**)
Schütze *m*
marks'manship' *s* Schießkunst *f*
mark'up' *s* (com) Gewinnaufschlag *m*
marl [mɑrl] *s* Mergel *m* || *tr* mergeln
marmalade ['mɑrmə,led] *s* Marmelade
f
maroon [mə'run] *adj* rotbraun, kasta-
nienbraun || *s* Kastanienbraun *n* || *tr*
aussetzen; **be marooned** von der Au-
ßenwelt abgeschnitten sein
marquee [mɑr'ki] *s* Schutzdach *n*
marquess ['mɑrkwɪs] *s* Marquis *m*
marquis ['mɑrkwɪs] *s* Marquis *m*
marquise [mɑr'kiz] *s* Marquise *f*
marriage ['mærɪdʒ] *s* Heirat *f;* (*state*)
Ehe *f,* Ehestand *m;* **by m.** angeheiratet, schwägerlich; **give in m.** verheiraten
marriageable ['mærɪdʒəbəl] *adj* heiratsfähig; **m. age** (*of a girl*) Mannbarkeit
f
mar'riage brok'er *s* Heiratsvermittler
–in *mf*
mar'riage cer'emony *s* Trauung *f*
mar'riage li'cense *s* Heiratsurkunde *f*
mar'riage of conven'ience *s* Vernunft-
ehe *f*
mar'riage por'tion *s* Mitgift *f*
mar'riage propos'al *s* Heiratsantrag *m*
mar'riage vow' *s* Ehegelöbnis *n*
mar'ried cou'ple *s* Ehepaar *n*
mar'ried state' *s* Ehestand *m*
marrow ['mæro] *s* Knochenmark *n;*
(fig) Mark *n*
mar·ry ['mæri] *v* (*pret & pp* **–ried**) *tr*
heiraten; (*said of a priest or minister*)
trauen; **m. off (to)** verheiraten (mit)
|| *intr* heiraten; **m. rich** e–e gute
Partie machen
Mars [mɑrz] *s* Mars *m*
marsh [mɑrʃ] *s* Sumpf *m*
mar·shal ['mɑrʃəl] *s* Zeremonienmeister *m;* (*police officer*) Bezirkspoli-
zeichef *m;* (mil) Marschall *m* || *v*
(*pret & pp* **–shal[l]ed;** ger **–shal[l]ing**)
tr (*troops*) ordnungsgemäß aufstellen; (*strength*) zusammenraffen

marsh'land' s Sumpfland n
marsh' mal'low s (bot) Eibisch m
marsh'mal'low s (candy) Konfekt n aus Stärkesirup, Zucker, Stärke, Gelatine, und geschlagenem Eiweiß
marshy ['marʃi] adj sumpfig
mart [mart] s Markt m
marten ['martən] s (zool) Marder m
Martha ['marθə] s Martha f
martial ['marʃəl] adj Kriegs–
mar'tial law' s Standrecht n; **declare m.** das Standrecht verhängen; **under m.** standrechtlich
martin ['martɪn] s Mauerschwalbe f; Martin Martin m
martinet [,martɪ'nɛt] s Pauker –in mf; (mil) Schleifer m
martyr ['martər] s Märtyrer –in mf || tr martern
martyrdom ['martərdəm] s Märtyrertum n
mar·vel ['marvəl] s Wunder n || v (pret & pp –vel[l]ed; ger –vel[l]ing) intr (at) sich wundern (über acc)
marvelous ['marvələs] adj wundervoll; (coll) pfundig
Marxist ['marksɪst] adj marxistisch || Marxist –in mf
marzipan ['marzɪ,pæn] s Marzipan n
mascara [mæs'kærə] s Lidtusche f
mascot ['mæskət] s Maskotte f
masculine ['mæskjəlɪn] adj männlich
mash [mæʃ] s Brei m; (in brewing) Maische f || tr zerquetschen; (potatoes) zerdrücken
mashed' pota'toes spl Kartoffelbrei m
mask [mæsk] s Maske f || tr maskieren
masked' ball' s Maskenball m
mason ['mesən] s Maurer m; Mason Freimaurer m
Masonic [mə'sanɪk] adj Freimaurer–
masonite ['mesə,naɪt] s Holzfaserplatte f
masonry ['mesənri] s Mauerwerk n; Masonry Freimaurerei f
masquerade [,mæskə'red] s (& fig) Maskerade f || intr (& fig) sich maskieren; **m. as** sich ausgeben als
mass [mæs] adj Massen– || s Masse f; (eccl) Messe; **the masses** die breite Masse f || tr massieren || intr sich ansammeln
massacre ['mæsəkər] s Massaker n || tr massakrieren, niedermetzeln
massage [mə'saʒ] s Massage f || tr massieren
masseur [mə'sʌr] s Masseur m
masseuse [mə'suz] s Masseuse f
massif ['mæsɪf] s Gebirgsstock m
massive ['mæsɪv] adj massiv
mass' me'dia ['midɪ·ə] spl Massenmedien pl
mass' meet'ing s Massenversammlung f
mass' mur'der s Massenmord m
mass'-produce' tr serienmäßig herstellen
mass' produc'tion s Serienherstellung f
mast [mæst] s Mast m; (food for swine) Mast f
master ['mæstər] adj (bedroom, key, switch, cylinder) Haupt– || s Herr m,

Meister m; (male head of a household) Hausherr m; (of a ship) Kapitän m || tr beherrschen
mas'ter build'er s Baumeister m
mas'ter car'penter s Zimmermeister m
mas'ter cop'y s Originalkopie f
masterful ['mæstərfəl] adj herrisch; (masterly) meisterhaft
masterly ['mæstərli] adj meisterhaft
mas'ter mechan'ic s Schlossermeister m
mas'termind' s führender Geist m || tr planen und überwachen
Mas'ter of Arts' s Magister m der freien Künste
mas'ter of cer'emonies s Zeremonienmeister m
mas'ter of the house' s Hausherr m
mas'terpiece' s Meisterstück n
mas'ter ser'geant s Oberfeldwebel m
mas'ter stroke' s Meisterstreich m
mas'terwork' s Meisterwerk n
mastery ['mæstəri] s (of) Beherrschung f (genit); **gain m. over** die Oberhand gewinnen über (acc)
mast'head' s (naut) Topp m; (typ) Impressum n
masticate ['mæstɪ,ket] tr zerkauen || intr kauen
mastiff ['mæstɪf] s Mastiff m
masturbate ['mæstər,bet] intr onanieren
masturbation [,mæstər'beʃən] s Onanie f
mat [mæt] s (for a floor) Matte f; (before the door) Türvorleger m; (under cups, vases, etc.) Zierdeckchen n || v (pret & pp matted; ger matting) tr (cover with matting) mit Matten belegen; (the hair) verfilzen || intr sich verfilzen
match [mætʃ] s Streichholz n; (for marriage) Partie f; (sport) Match n; **be a good m.** zueinanderpassen; **a m. for** gewachsen sein (dat); **be no m. for** sich nicht messen können mit; **meet one's m.** seinen Mann finden || tr (fit together) zusammenstellen; (harmonize with) passen zu; (equal) (in) gleichkommen (in dat); (funds) in gleicher Höhe aufbringen; (adapt) in Übereinstimmung bringen mit; **be well matched** auf gleicher Höhe sein; **m. up** zusammenpassen; **m. wits with** sich geistig messen mit || intr zueinanderpassen
match'book' s Streichholzbrief m
match' box' s Streichholzschachtel f
match'ing adj (clothes) passend; (funds) in gleicher Höhe || s Paarung f
match'mak'er s Heiratsvermittler –in mf; (sport) Veranstalter m
mate [met] s Genosse m, Kamerad m; (in marriage) Ehepartner m; (one of a pair, e.g., of gloves) Gegenstück n; (especially of birds) Männchen n, Weibchen n; (naut) Maat m || tr paaren || intr sich paaren
material [mə'tɪrɪ,əl] adj materiell; (important) wesentlich || s Material n, Stoff m; (tex) Stoff m

materialist [mə'tɪrɪ·əlɪst] *s* Materialist –in *mf*

materialistic [mə,tɪrɪ·ə'lɪstɪk] *adj* materialistisch

materialize [mə'tɪrɪ·ə,laɪz] *intr* sich verwirklichen

materiel [mə,tɪrɪ'el] *s* Material *n;* (mil) Kriegsmaterial *n*

maternal [mə'tʌrnəl] *adj* mütterlich; (*relatives*) mütterlicherseits

maternity [mə'tʌrnɪti] *s* Mutterschaft *f*

mater'nity dress' *s* Umstandskleid *n*

mater'nity hos'pital *s* Wöchnerinnenheim *n*

mater'nity ward' *s* Wöchnerinnenstation *f*

math [mæθ] *s* (coll) Mathe *f*

mathematical [,mæθɪ'mætɪkəl] *adj* mathematisch

mathematician [,mæθɪmə'tɪʃən] *s* Mathematiker –in *mf*

mathematics [,mæθɪ'mætɪks] *s* Mathematik *f*

matinée [,mætɪ'ne] *s* Nachmittagsvorstellung *f*

mat'ing sea'son *s* Paarungszeit *f*

matins ['mætɪnz] *spl* Frühmette *f*

matriarch ['metrɪ,ɑrk] *s* Stammesmutter *f*

matriarchal [,metrɪ'ɑrkəl] *adj* matriarchalisch

matriarchy ['metrɪ,ɑrki] *s* Matriarchat *n*

matricide ['mætrɪ,saɪd] *s* (*act*) Muttermord *m;* (*person*) Muttermörder –in *mf*

matriculate [mə'trɪkjə,let] *tr* immatrikulieren ǁ *intr* sich immatrikulieren

matriculation [mə,trɪkjə'leʃən] *s* Immatrikulation *f*

matrimonial [,mætrɪ'monɪ·əl] *adj* Ehe–

matrimony ['mætrɪ,moni] *s* Ehestand *m*

ma·trix ['metrɪks] *s* (–trices [trɪ,siz] & –trixes) (*mold*) Gießform *f;* (math) Matrix *f;* (typ) Matrize *f*

matron ['metrən] *s* Matrone *f*

matronly ['metrənli] *adj* matronenhaft, gesetzt

matt [mæt] *adj* (phot) matt

matter ['mætər] *s* Stoff *m;* (*affair*) Sache *f*, Angelegenheit *f;* (*pus*) Eiter *m;* (phys) Materie *f;* **as a m. of course** routinemäßig; **as matters now stand** wie die Sache jetzt liegt; **for that m.** was das betrifft; **it's a m. of** es handelt sich um; **it's a m. of life and death** es geht um Leben und Tod; **m. of opinion** Ansichtssache *f;* **m. of taste** Geschmackssache *f;* **something is the m. with his heart** er hat was am Herz; **no laughing m.** nichts zum Lachen; **no m.** ganz gleich; **what's the m. (with)?** was ist los (mit)? ǁ *intr* von Bedeutung sein; **it doesn't m.** es macht nichts (aus); **it doesn't m. to me** es liegt mir nichts daran; **it matters a great deal to me** es liegt mir sehr viel daran

mat'ter of fact' *s* Tatsache *f;* **as a m.** tatsächlich

mat'ter-of-fact' *adj* sachlich, nüchtern

Matthew ['mæθju] *s* Matthäus *m*

mattock ['mætək] *s* Breithacke *f*

mattress ['mætrɪs] *s* Matratze *f*

mature [mə'tʃʊr] *adj* (& fig) reif ǁ *tr* reifen lassen ǁ *intr* reifen; (fin) fällig werden

maturity [mə'tʃʊrɪti] *s* Reife *f;* (fin) Verfall *m*

maudlin ['mɔdlɪn] *adj* rührselig

maul [mɔl] *tr* schlimm zurichten

maulstick ['mɔl,stɪk] *s* Mahlstock *m*

mausole·um [,mɔsə'li·əm] *s* (–ums & –a [ə]) Mausoleum *n*

maw [mɔ] *s* (*mouth of an animal*) Rachen *m;* (*stomach of an animal*) Tiermagen *m;* (*of birds*) Kropf *m*

mawkish ['mɔkɪʃ] *adj* rührselig

maxim ['mæksɪm] *s* Maxime *f*, Lehrspruch *m*

maximum ['mæksɪməm] *adj* Höchst–; **m. load** Höchstbelastung *f* ǁ *s* Maximum *n*

May [me] *s* Mai *m* ǁ **may** *v* (*pret* **might** [maɪt] *aux* (expressing possibility) mögen, können; (expressing permission) dürfen; (expressing a wish) mögen; **be that as it may** wie dem auch sei; **come what may** komme, was da wolle; **it may be too late** es ist vielleicht zu spät; **that may be** das kann (or mag) sein

maybe ['mebi] *adv* vielleicht

May' Day' *s* der erste Mai

mayhem ['mehəm] *s* Körperverletzung *f*

mayonnaise [,me·ə'nez] *s* Mayonnaise *f*

mayor [mɛr] *s* Bürgermeister *m;* (*of a large city*) Oberbürgermeister *m*

May'pole' *s* Maibaum *m*

May' queen' *s* Maikönigin *f*

maze [mez] *s* Irrgarten *m;* (fig) Gewirr *n*

me [mi] *pers pron* (*direct object*) mich; (*indirect object*) mir; **this one is on me** das geht auf meine Rechnung

mead [mid] *s* (hist) Met *m;* (poet) Aue *f*

meadow ['mɛdo] *s* Wiese *f*

mead'owland' *s* Wiesenland *n*

meager ['migər] *adj* karg, kärglich

meal [mil] *s* Mahl *n*, Mahlzeit *f;* (*grain*) grobes Mehl *n*

meal' tick'et *s* Gutschein *m* für e–e Mahlzeit

meal'time' *s* Essenszeit *f*

mealy ['mili] *adj* mehlig

mealy-mouthed ['mili,maʊðd] *adj* zurückhaltend

mean [min] *adj* (*nasty*) bösartig; (*lowly*) gemein, niedrig; (*shabby*) schäbig; (*in statistics*) mittlere; no **m.** kein schlechter ǁ *s* (log) Mittelbegriff *m;* (math) Mittel *n;* **by all means** unbedingt; **by every means** mit allen Mitteln; **by fair means or foul** ganz gleich wie; **by lawful means** auf dem Rechtswege; **by means of**

meander   205   medium size

mittels (*genit*); **by no means** keineswegs; **live beyond one's means** über seine Verhältnisse leben; **live within one's means** seinen Verhältnissen entsprechend leben; **means** (*way*) Mittel *n;* (*resources*) Mittel *pl,* Vermögen *n;* **means of transportation** Verkehrsmittel *n;* **means to an end** Mittel *pl* zum Zweck; **of means** bemittelt ‖ *v* (*pret & pp* **meant** [mɛnt]) *tr* (*intend, intend to say*) meinen; (*signify*) bedeuten; **be meant for** (*said, e.g., of a remark*) gelten (*dat*); (*said, e.g., of a gift*) bestimmt sein für; **it means a lot to me to** (*inf*) mir liegt viel daran zu (*inf*); **m. business** es ernst meinen; **m. little** (or **much**) wenig (or viel) gelten; **m. no harm** es nicht böse meinen; **m. s.o. no harm** j–n nicht verletzen wollen; **m. the world to s.o.** j–m alles bedeuten; **what is meant by ...?** was versteht man unter ...? ‖ *intr*—**m. well** es gut meinen

meander [mɪˈændər] *intr* sich winden

mean'ing *s* Bedeutung *f;* **take on m.** e–n Sinn bekommen; **what's the m. of this?** was soll das heißen?

meaningful [ˈminɪŋfəl] *adj* sinnvoll

meaningless [ˈminɪŋlɪs] *adj* sinnlos

mean'-look'ing *adj* bösartig aussehend

meanness [ˈminnɪs] *s* Gemeinheit *f;* (*nastiness*) Bösartigkeit *f*

mean'time', mean'while' *adv* mittlerweile ‖ *s*—**in the m.** mittlerweile, in der Zwischenzeit

measles [ˈmizəlz] *s* Masern *pl;* (*German measles*) Röteln *pl*

measly [ˈmizli] *adj* kümmerlich, lumpig

measurable [ˈmɛʒərəbəl] *adj* meßbar

measure [ˈmɛʒər] *s* Maß *n;* (*step*) Maßnahme *f;* (*law*) Gesetz *n;* (*mus*) Takt *m;* **beyond m.** übermäßig; **for good m.** obendrein; **in a great m.** in großem Maß; **to some m.** gewissermaßen; **take drastic measures** durchgreifen; **take measures to** (*inf*) Maßnahmen ergreifen um zu (*inf*); **take s.o.'s m.** (fig) j–n einschätzen ‖ *tr* messen; **m. off** abmessen; **m. out** ausmessen ‖ *intr* messen; **m. up to** gewachsen sein (*dat*)

measurement [ˈmɛʒərmənt] *s* (*measured dimension*) Maß *n;* (*measuring*) Messung *f;* **measurements** Maße *pl;* **take s.o.'s measurements for** j–m Maß nehmen zu

meas'uring cup' *s* Meßbecher *m*

meas'uring tape' *s* Meßband *n*

meat [mit] *s* Fleisch *n;* (*of a nut, of the matter*) Kern *m*

meat'ball' *m* Fleischklößchen *n*

meat' grind'er *s* Fleischwolf *m*

meat'hook' *s* Fleischhaken *m*

meat'mar'ket *s* Fleischmarkt *m*

meat' pie' *s* Fleischpastete *f*

meaty [ˈmiti] *adj* fleischig; (fig) kernig

Mecca [ˈmɛkə] *s* Mekka *n*

mechanic [məˈkænɪk] *s* Mechaniker *m,* Schlosser *m;* (aut) Autoschlosser *m;* **mechanics** Mechanik *f*

mechanical [məˈkænɪkəl] *adj* mechanisch

mechan'ical engineer' *s* Maschinenbauingenieur *m*

mechan'ical engineer'ing *s* Maschinenbau *m*

mechanism [ˈmɛkəˌnɪzəm] *s* Mechanismus *m*

mechanize [ˈmɛkəˌnaɪz] *tr* mechanisieren

medal [ˈmɛdəl] *s* Medaille *f,* Orden *m*

medallion [mɪˈdæljən] *s* Medaillon *n*

meddle [ˈmɛdəl] *intr* sich einmischen; **m. with** sich abgeben mit

meddler [ˈmɛdlər] *s* zudringliche Person *f*

meddlesome [ˈmɛdəlsəm] *adj* zudringlich

media [ˈmidɪə] *spl* Medien *pl*

median [ˈmidɪ.ən] *adj* mittlere, Mittel- ‖ *s* (arith) Mittelwert *m;* (geom) Mittellinie *f*

me'dian strip' *s* Mittelstreifen *m*

mediate [ˈmidɪˌet] *tr & intr* vermitteln

mediation [ˌmidɪˈeʃən] *s* Vermittlung *f*

mediator [ˈmidɪˌetər] *s* Vermittler –in *mf*

medic [ˈmɛdɪk] *s* (mil) Sanitäter *m*

medical [ˈmɛdɪkəl] *adj* (*of a doctor*) ärztlich; (*of medicine*) medizinisch; (*of the sick*) Kranken–

med'ical bul'letin *s* Krankheitsbericht *m*

med'ical corps' *s* Sanitätstruppe *f*

med'ical profes'sion *s* Arztberuf *m*

med'ical school' *s* medizinische Fakultät *f*

med'ical sci'ence *s* Heilkunde *f*

med'ical stu'dent *s* Medizinstudent –in *mf*

medication [ˌmɛdɪˈkeʃən] *s* Medikament *n*

medicinal [məˈdɪsɪnəl] *adj* medizinisch

medicine [ˈmɛdɪsən] *s* Medizin *f,* Arznei *f;* (*profession*) Medizin *f;* **practice m.** den Arztberuf ausüben

med'icine cab'inet *s* Hausapotheke *f*

med'icine kit' *s* Reiseapotheke *f*

med'icine man' *s* Medizinmann *m*

medic·o [ˈmɛdɪˌko] *s* (–cos) (coll) Mediziner –in *mf*

medieval [ˌmidɪˈivəl], [ˌmɛdɪˈivəl] *adv* mittelalterlich

mediocre [ˌmidɪˈokər] *adj* mittelmäßig

mediocrity [ˌmidɪˈakrɪti] *s* Mittelmäßigkeit *f*

meditate [ˈmɛdɪˌtet] *tr* vorhaben ‖ *intr* (on) meditieren (über *acc*)

meditation [ˌmɛdɪˈteʃən] *s* Meditation *f*

Mediterranean [ˌmɛdɪtəˈrenɪ.ən] *adj* Mittelmeer– ‖ *s* Mittelmeer *n*

medi·um [ˈmidɪ.əm] *adj* Mittel–, mittlere ‖ *s* (–ums & –a [ə]) Mittel *n;* (*culture*) Nährboden *m;* (*in spiritualism, communications*) Medium *n;* **through the m. of** vermittels (*genit*)

me'dium of exchange' *s* Tauschmittel *n*

me'dium-rare' *adj* halb durchgebraten

me'dium size' *s* Mittelgröße *f*

med'ium-sized' *adj* mittelgroß
medley ['mɛdli] *s* Mischmasch *m;* (mus) Potpourri *n*
medul·la [mɪ'dʌlə] *s* (–las & –lae [li]) Knochenmark *n,* Mark *n*
meek [mik] *adj* sanftmütig; **m. as a lamb** lammfromm
meekness ['miknɪs] *s* Sanftmut *m*
meerschaum ['mɪrʃəm] *s* Meerschaum *m*
meet [mit] *adj* passend || *s* (sport) Treffen *n,* Veranstaltung *f.* || *v* (*pret* & *pp* met [mɛt]) *tr* begegnen (*dat*), treffen; (*make the acquaintance of*) kennenlernen; (*demands*) befriedigen; (*obligations*) nachkommen (*dat*); (*wishes*) erfüllen; (*a deadline*) einhalten; **m. s.o. at the train** j–n von der Bahn abholen; **m. s.o. halfway** j–m auf halbem Wege entgegenkommen; **m. the train** zum Zug gehen; **pleased to m. you** freut mich sehr, sehr angenehm || *intr* (*said of persons, of two ends*) zusammenkommen; (*said of persons*) sich treffen; (*in conference*) tagen; (*said of roads, rivers*) sich vereinigen; **make both ends m.** gerade mit dem Geld auskommen; **m. again** sich wiedersehen; **m. up with s.o.** j–n einholen; **m. with** zusammentreffen mit; **m. with an accident** verunglücken; **m. with a refusal** e–e Fehlbitte tun; **m. with approval** Beifall finden; **m. with success** Erfolg haben
meet'ing *s* (*of an organization*) Versammlung *f;* (*e.g., of a committee*) Sitzung *f;* (*of individuals*) Zusammenkunft *f*
meet'ing place' *s* Treffpunkt *m*
megacycle ['mɛgə,saɪkəl], **megahertz** ['mɛgə,hʌrts] *s* (elec) Megahertz *n*
megalomania [,mɛgəlo'mɛnɪ-ə] *s* Größenwahn *m*
megaphone ['mɛgə,fon] *s* Sprachrohr *n*
megohm ['mɛg,om] *s* Megohm *n*
melancholy ['mɛlən,kɑli] *adj* schwermütig || *s* Schwermut *f*
melee ['mele], ['mele] *s* Gemenge *n*
mellow ['mɛlo] *adj* (*very ripe*) mürb(e); (*wine*) abgelagert; (*voice*) schmelzend; (*person*) gereift || *tr* zur Reife bringen; (fig) mildern || *intr* mürb(e) werden; (fig) mild werden
melodic [mɪ'lɑdɪk] *adj* melodisch
melodious [mɪ'lodɪ-əs] *adj* melodisch
melodrama ['mɛlo,drɑmə] *s* (& fig) Melodrama *n*
melody ['mɛlədi] *s* Melodie *f*
melon ['mɛlən] *s* Melone *f*
melt [mɛlt] *tr* & *intr* schmelzen
melt'ing point' *s* Schmelzpunkt *m*
melt'ing pot' *s* (& fig) Schmelztiegel *m*
member ['mɛmbər] *s* Glied *n;* (*person*) Mitglied *n,* Angehörige *mf;* **m. of the family** Familienangehörige *mf*
mem'bership *s* Mitgliedschaft *f;* (*collectively*) Mitglieder *pl;* (*number of members*) Mitgliederzahl *f*
mem'bership card' *s* Mitgliedskarte *f*

membrane ['mɛmbren] *s* Häutchen *n,* Membran(e) *f*
memen·to [mɪ'mɛnto] *s* (–tos & –toes) Erinnerung *f,* Memento *n*
mem·o ['mɛmo] *s* (–os) (coll) Notiz *f*
mem'o book' *s* Notizbuch *n,* Agenda *f*
memoirs ['mɛmwarz] *spl* Memoiren *pl*
mem'o pad' *s* Notizblock *m,* Agenda *f*
memorable ['mɛmərəbəl] *adj* denkwürdig
memoran·dum [,mɛmə'rændəm] *s* (–dums & –da [də]) Notiz *f,* Vermerk *m;* (dipl) Memorandum *n*
memorial [mɪ'morɪ-əl] *adj* Gedächtnis–. Erinnerungs– || *s* Denkmal *n*
Memor'ial Day' *s* Gefallenengedenktag *m*
memorialize [mɪ'morɪ-ə,laɪz] *tr* gedenken (*genit*)
memorize ['mɛmə,raɪz] *tr* auswendig lernen
memory ['mɛməri] *s* (*faculty*) Gedächtnis *n;* (of) Gedenken *n* (an *acc*), Erinnerung *f* (an *acc*); **commit to m.** auswendig lernen; **escape one's m.** seinem Gedächtnis entfallen; **from m.** aus dem Gedächtnis; **in m. of** zur Erinnerung an (*acc*); **of blessed m.** seligen Angedenkens; **within the m. of men** seit Menschengedenken
menace ['mɛnɪs] *s* (to) Drohung *f* (*genit*) || *tr* bedrohen
menagerie [mə'nædʒəri] *s* Menagerie *f*
mend [mɛnd] *s* Besserung *f;* **on the m.** auf dem Wege der Besserung || *tr* (*clothes*) ausbessern; (*socks*) stopfen; (*repair*) reparieren
mendacious [mɛn'deʃəs] *adj* lügnerisch
mendicant ['mɛndɪkənt] *adj* Bettel– || *s* Bettelmönch *m*
menfolk ['mɛn,fok] *spl* Mannsleute *pl*
menial ['minɪ-əl] *adj* niedrig || *s* Diener –in *mf*
menopause ['mɛnə,pɔz] *s* Wechseljahre *pl*
menses ['mɛnsiz] *spl* Monatsfluß *m*
men's' room' *s* Herrentoilette *f*
men's' size' *s* Herrengröße *f*
men's' store' *s* Herrenbekleidungsgeschäft *n*
menstruate ['mɛnstru,et] *intr* menstruieren
menstruation [,mɛnstru'eʃən] *s* Menstruation *f*
men's' wear' *s* Herrenbekleidung *f*
mental ['mɛntəl] *adj* geistig, Geistes–
men'tal an'guish *s* Seelenpein *f*
men'tal arith'metic *s* Kopfrechnen *n*
men'tal capac'ity *s* Fassungskraft *f*
men'tal disor'der *s* Geistesstörung *f*
men'tal institu'tion *s* Nervenheilanstalt *f*
mentality [mɛn'tælɪti] *s* Mentalität *f*
mentally ['mɛntəli] *adv* geistig, Geistes–; **m. alert** geistesgegenwärtig; **m. disturbed** geistesgestört; **m. lazy** denkfaul
men'tal reserva'tion *s* geistiger Vorbehalt *m*
men'tal telep'athy *s* Gedankenübertragung *f*
mention ['mɛnʃən] *s* Erwähnung *f;*

make m. of erwähnen ‖ *tr* erwähnen, nennen; **be mentioned** zur Sprache kommen; **don't m. it!** keine Ursache!; **not worth mentioning** nicht der Rede wert

menu ['mɛnju] *s* Speisekarte *f*

meow [mi'aʊ] *s* Miauen *n* ‖ *intr* miauen

mercantile ['mʌrkən‚til], ['mʌrkən‚taɪl] *adj* Handels-, kaufmännisch

mercenary ['mʌrsə‚nɛri] *adj* gewinnsüchtig ‖ *s* Söldner *m*

merchandise ['mʌrtʃən‚daɪz] *s* Ware *f* ‖ *tr* handeln

mer'chandising *s* Verkaufspolitik *f*

merchant ['mʌrtʃənt] *s* Händler, Kaufmann *m*

mer'chant·man *s* (**–men**) Handelsschiff *n*

mer'chant marine' *s* Handelsmarine *f*

mer'chant ves'sel *s* Handelsschiff *n*

merciful ['mʌrsɪfəl] *adj* barmherzig

merciless ['mʌrsɪlɪs] *adj* erbarmungslos

mercurial [mɛr'kjʊrɪ·əl] *adj* quecksilbrig

mercury ['mʌrkjəri] *s* Quecksilber *n*

mercy ['mʌrsi] *s* Barmherzigkeit *f;* **be at s.o.'s m.** in j–s Gewalt sein; **be at the m. of** (*e.g., the wind, waves*) preisgegeben sein (*dat*); **beg for m.** um Gnade flehen; **show no m.** keine Gnade walten lassen; **show s.o. m.** sich j–s erbarmen; **throw oneself on the m. of** sich auf Gnade und Ungnade ergeben (*dat*); **without m.** ohne Gnade

mere [mɪr] *adj* bloß, rein

merely ['mɪrli] *adv* nur, lediglich

meretricious [‚mɛrɪ'trɪʃəs] *adj* (*tawdry*) flitterhaft; (*characteristic of a prostitute*) dirnenhaft

merge [mʌrdʒ] *tr* verschmelzen ‖ *intr* sich verschmelzen

merger ['mʌrdʒər] *s* (com) Fusion *f;* (jur) Verschmelzung *f*

meridian [mə'rɪdɪ·ən] *s* (astr) Meridian *m;* (geog) Meridian *m*, Längenkreis *m*

meringue [mə'ræŋ] *s* (*topping*) Eierschnee *m;* (*pastry*) Schaumgebäck *n*

merit ['mɛrɪt] *s* Verdienst *n;* **of great m.** hochverdient ‖ *tr* verdienen

meritorious [‚mɛrə'torɪ·əs] *adj* verdienstvoll

merlin ['mʌrlɪn] *s* (orn) Merlinfalke *m*

mermaid ['mʌr‚med] *s* Seejungfer *f*

merriment ['mɛrɪmənt] *s* Fröhlichkeit *f*

merry ['mɛri] *adj* fröhlich, heiter

Mer'ry Christ'mas *s* fröhliche Weihnachten *pl*

mer'ry-go-round' *s* Karussell *n*

mer'rymak'er *s* Zecher –in *mf*

mesh [mɛʃ] *s* Masche *f;* (*network*) Netzwerk *n;* (mach) Ineinandergreifen *n;* **meshes** (fig) Schlingen *pl* ‖ *intr* ineinandergreifen

mesmerize ['mɛsmə‚raɪz] *tr* hypnotisieren

mess [mɛs] *s* (*disorder*) Durcheinander *n;* (*dirty condition*) Schweinerei *f;* (*for officers*) Messe *f;* **a nice m.!** e–e schöne Wirtschaft!; **get into a m.** in die Klemme geraten; **make a m.** Schmutz machen; **make a m. of** verpfuschen; **what a m.!** nette Zustände! ‖ *tr*—**m. up** (*dirty*) beschmutzen; (*put into disarray*) in Unordnung bringen ‖ *intr*—**m. around** herumtrödeln; **m. around with** herummurksen an (*dat*)

message ['mɛsɪdʒ] *s* Botschaft *f*

messenger ['mɛsəndʒər] *s* Bote *m*, Botin *f*

mess' hall' *s* Messe *f*

Messiah [mə'saɪ·ə] *s* Messias *m*

mess' kit' *s* Eßgeschirr *n*

messy ['mɛsi] *adj* (*disorderly*) unordentlich; (*dirty*) dreckig

metabolism [mə'tæbə‚lɪzəm] *s* Stoffwechsel *m*

metal ['mɛtəl] *s* Metall *n*

metallic [mɪ'tælɪk] *adj* metallisch

metallurgy ['mɛtə‚lʌrdʒi] *s* Hüttenwesen *n*, Metallurgie *f*

met'alwork' *s* Metallarbeit *f*

metamorpho·sis [‚mɛtə'mɔrfəsɪs] *s* (**–ses** [‚siz]) Verwandlung *f*

metaphor ['mɛtə‚fɔr] *s* Metapher *f*

metaphorical [‚mɛtə'fɔrɪkəl] *adj* bildlich

metaphysical [‚mɛtə'fɪzɪkəl] *adj* metaphysisch

metaphysics [‚mɛtə'fɪzɪks] *s* Metaphysik *f*

metathe·sis [mɪ'tæθɪsɪs] *s* (**–ses** [‚siz]) Metathese *f*, Lautversetzung *f*

mete [mit] *tr*—**m. out** austeilen

meteor ['mitɪ·ər] *s* Meteor *m*

meteoric [‚mitɪ'ɔrɪk] *adj* meteorisch; (fig) kometenhaft

meteorite ['mitɪ·ə‚raɪt] *s* Meteorit *m*

meteorologist [‚mitɪ·ə'ralədʒɪst] *s* Meteorologe *m*, Meteorologin *f*

meteorology [‚mitɪ·ə'ralədʒi] *s* Meteorologie *f*, Wetterkunde *f*

meter ['mitər] *s* Meter *m* & *n;* (*instrument*) Messer *m*, Zähler *m;* (pros) Versmaß *n*

me'ter read'er *s* Zählerableser –in *mf*

methane ['mɛθen] *s* Methan *n*, Sumpfgas *n*

method ['mɛθəd] *s* Methode *f*

methodic(al) [mɪ'θɑdɪk(əl)] *adj* methodisch

Methodist ['mɛθədɪst] *s* Methodist –in *mf*

methodology [‚mɛθə'dalədʒi] *s* Methodenlehre *f*

Methuselah [mɪ'θuzələ] *s* Methusalem *m*

meticulous [mɪ'tɪkjələs] *adj* übergenau

metric(al) ['mɛtrɪk(əl)] *adj* metrisch

metrics ['mɛtrɪks] *s* Metrik *f*

metronome ['mɛtrə‚nom] *s* Metronom *n*

metropolis [mɪ'trapəlɪs] *s* Metropole *f*

metropolitan [‚mɛtrə'palɪtən] *adj* großstädtisch ‖ *s* (eccl) Metropolit *m*

mettle ['mɛtəl] *s* (*temperament*) Veranlagung *f;* (*courage*) Mut *m*

mettlesome ['mɛtəlsəm] *adj* mutig

mew [mju] s Miau n || intr miauen

Mexican ['mɛksɪkən] adj mexikanisch || s Mexikaner –in mf

Mexico ['mɛksɪ ‚ko] s Mexiko n

mezzanine ['mɛzə ‚nin] s Zwischenge-schoß n

mica ['maɪkə] s Glimmer m, Marien-glas n

Michael ['maɪkəl] s Michel m

microbe ['maɪkrob] s Mikrobe f

microbiology [‚maɪkrəbaɪ'alədʒi] s Mikrobiologie f

microcosm ['maɪkrə ‚kazəm] s Mikro-kosmos m

microfilm ['maɪkrə ‚fɪlm] s Mikrofilm m || tr mikrofilmen

microgroove ['maɪkrə ‚gruv] s Mikro-rille f

mic'rogroove rec'ord s Schallplatte f mit Mikrorillen

microphone ['maɪkrə ‚fon] s Mikro-phon n

microscope ['maɪkrə ‚skop] s Mikro-skop n

microscopic [‚maɪkrə'skɑpɪk] adj mi-kroskopisch

microwave ['maɪkrə ‚wev] s Mikro-welle f

mid [mɪd] adj mittlere

midair' s—in m. mitten in der Luft

mid'day' adj mittäglich, Mittags– || s Mittag m

middle ['mɪdəl] adj mittlere || s Mitte f, Mittel n; in the m. of inmitten (genit), mitten in (dat)

mid'dle age' s mittleres Lebensalter n; Middle Ages Mittelalter n

middle-aged ['mɪdəl ‚edʒd] adj mitt-leren Alters

mid'dle class' s Mittelstand m

mid'dle-class' adj bürgerlich

mid'dle dis'tance s Mittelgrund m

mid'dle ear' s Mittelohr n

Mid'dle East', the s der Mittlere Osten

mid'dle fin'ger s Mittelfinger m

Mid'dle High' Ger'man s Mittelhoch-deutsch n

Mid'dle Low' Ger'man s Mittelnieder-deutsch n

mid'dle·man' s (–men') Mittelsmann m, Zwischenhändler m

mid'dleweight box'er s Mittelgewichtler m

mid'dleweight divi'sion s Mittelgewicht n

middling ['mɪdlɪŋ] adj mittelmäßig || adv leidlich, ziemlich

middy ['mɪdi] s (nav) Fähnrich m zur See

midget ['mɪdʒɪt] s Zwerg m

mid'get rail'road s Liliputbahn f

mid'get submarine' s Kleinst-U-Boot n

midland ['mɪdlənd] adj binnenländisch

mid'night adj mitternächtlich; burn the m. oil bis in die tiefe Nacht arbeiten || s Mitternacht f; at m. um Mitter-nacht

midriff ['mɪdrɪf] s (of a dress) Mittel-teil m; (diaphragm) Zwerchfell n; (middle part of the body) Magen-grube f; have a bare m. die Taille frei lassen

mid'shipman' s (–men') Fähnrich m zur See

midst [mɪdst] s Mitte f; from our m. aus unserer Mitte; in the m. of mit-ten in (dat)

mid'stream' s—in m. in der Mitte des Stromes

mid'sum'mer s Mittsommer m

mid'-term' adj mitten im Semester || midterms spl Prüfungen pl mitten im Semester

mid'way' adj in der Mitte befindlich || adv auf halbem Weg || s Mitte f des Weges; (at a fair) Mittelstraße f

mid'week' s Wochenmitte f

mid'wife' s (–wives') Hebamme f

mid'win'ter s Mittwinter m

mid'year' adj in der Mitte des Studien-jahres || midyears spl Prüfungen pl in der Mitte des Studienjahres

mien [min] s Miene f

miff [mɪf] s kleine Auseinandersetzung f || tr ärgern

might [maɪt] s Macht f, Kraft f; with m. and main mit aller Kraft || aux used to form the potential mood, e.g., she m. lose her way sie könnte sich verirren; we m. as well go es ist wohl besser, wenn wir gehen

mightily ['maɪtəli] adv gewaltig; (coll) enorm

mighty ['maɪti] adj mächtig || adv (coll) furchtbar

migraine ['maɪgren] s Migräne f

mi'grant work'er ['maɪgrənt] s Wan-derarbeiter –in mf

migrate ['maɪgret] intr wandern, zie-hen

migration [maɪ'greʃən] s Wanderung f; (e.g., of birds) Zug m

migratory ['maɪgrə ‚tori] adj Wander–

mi'gratory bird' s Zugvogel m

Milan [mɪ'læn] s Mailand n

mild [maɪld] adj mild, lind

mildew ['mɪl ‚d(j)u] s Mehltau m

mildly ['maɪldli] adv leicht, schwach; to put it m. gelinde gesagt

mildness ['maɪldnɪs] s Milde f

mile [maɪl] s Meile f; for miles meilen-weit; miles apart meilenweit ausein-ander; miles per hour Stundenge-schwindigkeit

mileage ['maɪlɪdʒ] s Meilenzahl f; (charge) Meilengeld n

mile'post' s Wegweiser m mit Entfer-nungsangabe

mile'stone' s (& fig) Meilenstein m

militancy ['mɪlɪtənsi] s Kampfgeist m

militant ['mɪlɪtənt] adj militant || s Kämpfer –in mf

militarism ['mɪlɪtə ‚rɪzəm] s Militaris-mus m

militarize ['mɪlɪtə ‚raɪz] tr auf den Krieg vorbereiten

military ['mɪlə ‚teri] adj militärisch; (academy, band, government) Mili-tär– || s Militär n

mil'itary campaign' s Feldzug m

mil'itary cem'etery s Soldatenfriedhof m

mil'itary obliga'tions spl Wehrpflicht f

mil'itary police' s Militärpolizei f

mil′itary police′man s (**–men**) Militär-
polizist m
mil′itary sci′ence s Kriegswissenschaft
f
militate [′mɪlɪ ‚tet] intr (**against**) entgegenwirken (dat)
militia [mɪ′lɪʃə] s Miliz f
mili′tia·man s (**–men**) Milizsoldat m
milk [mɪlk] s Milch f ‖ tr (& fig)
melken
milk′ bar′ s Milchbar f
milk′ car′ton s Milchtüte f
milk′maid′ s Milchmädchen n
milk′man′ s (**–men′**) Milchmann m
milk′ pail′ s Melkeimer m
milk′shake′ s Milchmischgetränk n
milk′sop′ s Milchbart m
milk′ tooth′ s Milchzahn m
milk′weed′ s Wolfsmilch f, Seiden-
pflanze f
milky [′mɪlki] adj milchig
Milk′y Way′ s Milchstraße f
mill [mɪl] s Mühle f; (factory) Fabrik
f, Werk n; **put through the m.** (coll)
durch e–e harte Schule schicken ‖ tr
(grain) mahlen; (coins) rändeln;
(with a milling machine) fräsern;
(chocolate) quirlen ‖ intr—**m. around**
durcheinanderlaufen
millenial [mɪ′lenɪ·əl] adj tausendjährig
millenni·um [mɪ′lenɪ·əm] s (**–ums** &
–a [ə]) Jahrtausend n
miller [′mɪlər] s Müller m
millet [′mɪlɪt] s Hirse f
milligram [′mɪlɪ ‚græm] s Milligramm
n
millimeter [′mɪlɪ ‚mitər] s Millimeter
n
milliner [′mɪlɪnər] s Putzmacher –in
mf
mil′linery shop′ [′mɪlɪ ‚neri] s Damen-
hutgeschäft n
mill′ing s (of grain) Mahlen n; (of
wood or metal) Fräsen n
mill′ing machine′ s Fräsmaschine f
million [′mɪljən] adj—**one m. people**
e–e Million Menschen; **two m. people**
zwei Millionen Menschen ‖ s Million
f
millionaire [‚mɪljən′er] s Millionär –in
mf
millionth [′mɪljənθ] adj & pron millionste ‖ s (fraction) Millionstel n
mill′pond′ s Mühlteich m
mill′stone′ s Mühlstein m
mill′ wheel′ s Mühlrad n
mime [maɪm] s Mime m, Mimin f ‖ tr
mimen
mimeograph [′mɪmɪ·ə ‚græf] s Vervielfältigungsapparat m ‖ tr vervielfältigen
mim·ic [′mɪmɪk] s Mimiker –in mf ‖
v (pret & pp **–icked**; ger **–icking**) tr
nachäffen
mimicry [′mɪmɪkri] s Nachäffen n;
(zool) Mimikry f
mimosa [mɪ′mosə] s Mimose f
minaret [‚mɪnə′ret] s Minarett n
mince [mɪns] tr (meat) zerhacken; **not
m. words** kein Blatt vor den Mund
nehmen
mince′meat′ s Pastetenfüllung f;

(chopped meat) Hackfleisch n; **make
m. of** (fig) in die Pfanne hauen
mind [maɪnd] s Geist m; **bear in m.**
denken an (acc); **be of one m.** ein
Herz und e–e Seele sein; **be of two
minds** geteilter Meinung sein; **be out
of one's m.** nicht bei Trost sein;
call to m. erinnern; (remember) sich
erinnern; **change one's m.** sich anders besinnen; **give s.o. a piece of
one's m.** j-m gründlich die Meinung
sagen; **have a good m. to** (inf) große
Lust haben zu (inf); **have in m.** im
Sinn haben zu (inf); **have one's m.
on s.th.** ständig an etw denken
müssen; **I can't get her out of my m.**
sie will mir nicht aus dem Sinn;
know one's own m. wissen, was man
will; **of sound m.** zurechnungsfähig;
put s.th. out of one's m. sich [dat]
etw aus dem Sinn schlagen; **set one's
m. on** sein Sinnen und Trachten
richten auf (acc); **slip s.o.'s m.** j-m
entfallen; **to my m.** meines Erachtens ‖ tr (watch over) aufpassen auf
(acc); (obey) gehorchen (dat); (be
troubled by; take care of) sich kümmern um; **do you m. if I smoke?**
macht es Ihnen etw aus, wenn ich
rauche?; **do you m. the smoke?** macht
Ihnen der Rauch etw aus?; **I don't
m. your smoking** ich habe nichts dagegen, daß (or wenn) Sie rauchen;
m. your own business! kümmere dich
um deine Angelegenheit!; **m. you!**
wohlgemerkt! ‖ intr—**I don't m.** es
macht mir nichts aus; **I don't m. if
I do** (coll) ja, recht gern; **never m.!**
schon gut!
–minded [‚maɪndɪd] suf –mütig. -ge-
sinnt, –sinnig
mindful [′maɪndfəl] adj (of) eingedenk
(genit); **be m. of** achten auf (acc)
mind′ read′er s Gedankenleser –in mf
mind′ read′ing s Gedankenlesen n
mine [maɪn] s Bergwerk n, Mine f;
(fig) Fundgrube f; (mil) Mine f ‖
poss pron meiner ‖ tr (e.g., coal)
abbauen; (mil) verminen ‖ intr—**m.
for** graben nach
mine′ detec′tor s Minensuchgerät n
mine′field′ s Minenfeld n
minelayer [′maɪn ‚le·ər] s Minenleger
m
miner [′maɪnər] s Bergarbeiter m
mineral [′mɪnərəl] adj mineralisch,
Mineral– ‖ s Mineral n
mineralogy [‚mɪnə′rɑlədʒi] s Mineralogie f
min′eral resourc′es spl Bodenschätze
pl
min′eral wa′ter s Mineralwasser n
mine′sweep′er s Minenräumboot n
mingle [′mɪŋgəl] tr vermengen ‖ intr
(with) sich mischen (unter acc)
miniature [′mɪnɪ·ətʃər], [′mɪnɪtʃər]
adj Miniatur–, Klein– ‖ s Miniatur f
minimal [′mɪnɪməl] adj minimal, Mindest–
minimize [′mɪnɪ ‚maɪz] tr auf das
Minimum herabsetzen; (fig) bagatellisieren

minimum ['mınıməm] *adj* minimal, Mindest– ‖ *s* Minimum *n; (lowest price)* untere Preisgrenze *f*
min'imum wage' *s* Mindestlohn *m*
min'ing *adj* Bergbau– ‖ *s* Bergbau *m,* Bergwesen *n;* (mil) Minenlegen *n*
minion ['mınjən] *s* Günstling *m*
miniskirt ['mını,skʌrt] *s* Minirock *m*
minister ['mınıstər] *s* (eccl) Geistlicher *m;* (pol) Minister *m* ‖ *intr*—**m. to** dienen *(dat)*; *(aid)* Hilfe leisten *(dat)*
ministerial [,mınıs'tırı·əl] *adj* (eccl) geistlich; (pol) ministeriell
ministry ['mınıstri] *s* *(office)* (eccl) geistliches Amt *n; (the clergy)* (eccl) geistlicher Stand *m;* (pol) Ministerium *n*
mink [mıŋk] *s* (zool) Nerz *m; (fur)* Nerzfell *n*
mink' coat' *s* Nerzmantel *m*
minnow ['mıno] *s* Pfrille *f,* Elritze *f*
minor ['maınər] *adj* minder, geringer, Neben– ‖ *s* *(person)* Minderjährige *mf;* (educ) Nebenfach *n;* (log) Untersatz *m;* (mus) Moll *n* ‖ *intr*—**m. in** als Nebenfach studieren
minority [mı'nɔrıti] *adj* Minderheits– ‖ *s* Minderheit *f; (of votes)* Stimmenminderheit *f; (ethnic group)* Minorität *f*
mi'nor key' *s* Molltonart *f;* **in a m.** in Moll
minstrel ['mınstrəl] *s* (hist) Spielmann *m*
mint [mınt] *s* Münzanstalt *f;* (bot) Minze *f* ‖ *tr* münzen
mintage ['mıntıdʒ] *s* Prägung *f*
minuet [,mınju'et] *s* Menuett *n*
minus ['maınəs] *adj* negativ ‖ *prep* minus, weniger; *(without)* (coll) ohne *(acc)*
mi'nus sign' *s* Minuszeichen *n*
minute [maı'n(j)ut] *adj* winzig ‖ ['mınıt] *s* Minute *f;* **minutes** Protokoll *n;* **take the minutes** das Protokoll führen
–minute [mınıt] *suf* –minutig
min'ute hand' *s* Minutenzeiger *m*
minutiae [mı'n(j)uʃı·i] *spl* Einzelheiten *pl*
minx [mıŋks] *s* Range *f*
miracle ['mırəkəl] *s* Wunder *n*
mir'acle play' *s* Mirakelspiel *n*
miraculous [mı'rækjələs] *adj* wunderbar; *(e.g., power)* Wunder–
mirage [mı'rɑʒ] *s* Luftspiegelung *f;* (fig) Luftbild *n,* Täuschung *f*
mire [maır] *s* Morast *m,* Schlamm *m*
mirror ['mırər] *s* Spiegel *m* ‖ *tr* spiegeln
mirth [mʌrθ] *s* Fröhlichkeit *f*
miry ['maıri] *adj* sumpfig, schlammig
misadventure [,mısəd'ventʃər] *s* Mißgeschick *n*
misanthrope ['mısən,θrop] *s* Menschenfeind *m*
misapprehension [,mısæprı'henʃən] *s* Mißverständnis *n*
misappropriate [,mısə'proprı,et] *tr* sich *[dat]* widerrechtlich aneignen
misbehave [,mısbı'hev] *intr* sich schlecht benehmen

misbehavior [,mısbı'hevı·ər] *s* schlechtes Benehmen *n*
miscalculate [mıs'kælkjə,let] *tr* falsch berechnen ‖ *intr* sich verrechnen
miscalculation [,mıskælkjə'leʃən] *s* Rechenfehler *m*
miscarriage [mıs'kærıdʒ] *s* Fehlgeburt *f;* (fig) Fehlschlag *m*
miscar'riage of jus'tice *s* Justizirrtum *m*
miscar·ry [mıs'kæri] *v* *(pret & pp* –ried) *intr* e-e Fehlgeburt haben; *(said of a plan)* scheitern, fehlschlagen
miscellaneous [,mısə'lenı·əs] *adj* vermischt
miscellany ['mısə,leni] *s* Gemisch *n; (of literary works)* Sammelband *m*
mischief ['mıstʃıf] *s* Unfug *m;* **be up to m.** e-n Unfug im Kopf haben; **cause m.** Unfug treiben; **get into m.** etw anstellen
mis'chief-mak'er *s* Störenfried *m*
mischievous ['mıstʃıvəs] *adj* mutwillig
misconception [,mıskən'sepʃən] *s* falsche Auffassung *f*
misconduct [mıs'kɑndʌkt] *s* schlechtes Benehmen *n;* **m. in office** Amtsvergehen *n* ‖ [,mıskən'dʌkt] *tr* schlecht verwalten; **m. oneself** sich schlecht benehmen
misconstrue [,mıskən'stru] *tr* falsch auffassen
miscount [mıs'kaunt] *s* Rechenfehler *m* ‖ *tr* falsch zählen ‖ *intr* sich verzählen
miscreant ['mıskrı·ənt] *s* Schurke *m*
miscue [mıs'kju] *s* (fig) Fehler *m;* (billiards) Kicks *m* ‖ *intr* (billiards) kicksen; (theat) den Auftritt verpassen
mis·deal ['mıs,dil] *s* falsches Geben *n* ‖ [mıs'dil] *v* *(pret & pp* –**delt** [delt]) *tr* falsch geben ‖ *intr* sich vergeben
misdeed [mıs'did] *s* Missetat *f*
misdemeanor [,mısdı'minər] *s* Vergehen *n*
misdirect [,mısdı'rekt], [,mısdaı'rekt] *tr* (& fig) fehlleiten
misdoing [mıs'du·ıŋ] *s* Missetat *f*
miser ['maızər] *s* Geizhals *m*
miserable ['mızərəbəl] *adj* elend; **feel m.** sich elend fühlen; **make life m. for s.o.** j–m das Leben sauer machen
miserly ['maızərli] *adj* geizig
misery ['mızəri] *s* Elend *n*
misfeasance [mıs'fizəns] *s* (jur) Amtsmißbrauch *m*
misfire [mıs'faır] *s* Versagen *n* ‖ *intr* versagen
misfit ['mısfıt] *s* *(clothing)* schlecht sitzendes Kleidungsstück *n; (person)* Gammler *m*
misfortune [mıs'fɔrtʃən] *s* Unglück *n*
misgiving [mıs'gıvıŋ] *s* böse Ahnung *f;* **full of misgivings** ahnungsvoll
misgovern [mıs'gʌvərn] *tr* schlecht verwalten
misguidance [mıs'gaıdəns] *s* Irreführung *f*
misguide [mıs'gaıd] *tr* irreleiten
misguid'ed *adj* irregeleitet

mishap ['mɪʃæp] s Unfall m
mishmash ['mɪʃ‚mæʃ] s Mischmasch m
misinform [‚mɪsɪn'fɔrm] tr falsch informieren, falsch unterrichten
misinterpret [‚mɪsɪn'tʌrprɪt] tr mißdeuten, falsch auffassen
misjudge [mɪs'dʒʌdʒ] tr (e.g., a person, situation) falsch beurteilen; (distance) falsch schätzen
mis·lay [mɪs'le] v (pret & pp –laid) tr verlegen, verkramen
mis·lead [mɪs'lid] v (pret & pp –led) tr irreführen
mislead'ing adj irreführend
mismanage [mɪs'mænɪdʒ] tr schlecht verwalten; (funds) verwirtschaften
mismanagement [mɪs'mænɪdʒmənt] s Mißwirtschaft f, schlechte Verwaltung f
mismarriage [mɪs'mærɪdʒ] s Mißheirat f
misnomer [mɪs'nomər] s Felhbezeichnung f
misplace [mɪs'ples] tr verlegen
misprint ['mɪs‚prɪnt] s Druckfehler m || [mɪs'prɪnt] tr verdrucken
mispronounce [‚mɪsprə'nauns] tr falsch aussprechen
mispronunciation [‚mɪsprənʌnsɪ'eʃən] s falsche Aussprache f
misquote [mɪs'kwot] tr falsch zitieren
misread [mɪs'rid] v (pret & pp –read ['rɛd]) tr falsch lesen || intr sich verlesen
misrepresent [‚mɪsrɛprɪ'zɛnt] tr falsch darstellen; m. the facts to s.o. j–m falsche Tatsachen vorspiegeln
miss [mɪs] s Fehlschlag m, Versager m; **Miss** Fräulein n; **Miss America** die Schönheitskönigin von Amerika || tr (a target; one's calling; a person, e.g., at the station; a town along the road; one's way) verfehlen; (feel the lack of) verpassen; (school, a train, an opportunity) versäumen; **m. one's step** fehltreten; **m. the mark** vorbeischießen; (fig) sein Ziel verfehlen; **m. the point** die Pointe nicht verstanden haben || intr fehlen; (in shooting) vorbeischießen
missal ['mɪsəl] s Meßbuch n
misshapen [mɪs'ʃepən] adj mißgestaltet
missile ['mɪsɪl] s Geschoß n; (rok) Rakete f
missing ['mɪsɪŋ] adj—**be m.** fehlen; (said, e.g., of a child) vermißt werden; **m. in action** vermißt
miss'ing per'son s Vermißte mf
miss'ing-per'sons bu'reau s Suchdienst m
mission ['mɪʃən] s Mission f; **m. in life** Lebensaufgabe f
missionary ['mɪʃən‚ɛri] adj Missions– || s Missionar –in mf
missis ['mɪsɪz] s—**the m.** (the wife) die Frau; (of the house) (coll) die Frau des Hauses
missive ['mɪsɪv] s Sendschreiben n
mis·spell [mɪs'spɛl] v (pret & pp –spelled & –spelt) tr & intr falsch schreiben

misspell'ing s Schreibfehler m
misspent [mɪs'spɛnt] adj vergeudet
misstate [mɪs'stet] tr falsch angeben
misstatement [mɪs'stetmənt] s falsche Angabe f
misstep [mɪs'stɛp] s (& fig)Fehltritt m
mist [mɪst] s feiner Nebel m || tr umnebeln || intr (said of the eyes) sich trüben; **mist over** nebeln
mis·take [mɪs'tek] s Fehler m; **by m.** aus Versehen || v (pret –took ['tuk]; pp –taken) tr verkennen; **m. s.o. for s.o. else** j–n mit e–m anderen verwechseln
mistaken [mɪs'tekən] adj falsch, irrig; **be m. (about)** sich irren (in dat); **unless I'm m.** wenn ich mich nicht irre
mistak'en iden'tity s Personenverwechslung f
mistakenly [mɪs'tekənli] adv versehentlich
mister ['mɪstər] s Herr m || interj (pej) Herr!
mistletoe ['mɪsəl‚to] s Mistel f
mistreat [mɪs'trit] tr mißhandeln
mistreatment [mɪs'tritmənt] s Mißhandlung f
mistress ['mɪstrɪs] s Herrin f; (lover) Mätresse f, Geliebte f
mistrial [mɪs'traɪ·əl] s fehlerhaft geführter Prozeß m
mistrust [mɪs'trʌst] s Mißtrauen n || tr mißtrauen (dat)
misty ['mɪsti] adj neblig; (eyes) umflort; (fig) unklar
misunder·stand [‚mɪsʌndər'stænd] v (pret & pp –stood) tr & intr mißverstehen
misunderstanding [‚mɪsʌndər'stændɪŋ] s Mißverständnis n
misuse [mɪs'jus] s Mißbrauch m || [mɪs'juz] tr mißbrauchen; (mistreat) mißhandeln
misword [mɪs'wʌrd] tr in falsche Worte fassen
mite [maɪt] s (ent) Milbe f
miter ['maɪtər] s Bischofsmütze f || tr auf Gehrung verbinden
mi'ter box' s Gehrlade f
mitigate ['mɪtɪ‚get] tr lindern
mitigation [‚mɪtɪ'geʃən] s Linderung f
mitt [mɪt] s Fausthandschuh m; (sl) Flosse f; (baseball) Fängerhandschuh m
mitten ['mɪtən] s Fausthandschuh m
mix [mɪks] s Mischung f, Gemisch n || tr (ver)mischen; (a drink) mixen; (a cake) anrühren; **mix in** beimischen; **mix up** vermischen; (confuse) verwirren || intr sich (ver)mischen; **mix with** vekehren mit
mixed adj vermischt; (feelings, company, doubles) gemischt
mixed' drink' s Mixgetränk n
mixed' mar'riage s Mischehe f
mixer ['mɪksər] s Mischer –in mf; (of cocktails) Mixer –in mf; (mach) Mischmaschine f; **a good m.** ein guter Gesellschafter
mixture ['mɪkstʃər] s (e.g., of gases)

Gemisch *n; (e.g., of tobacco, coffee)* Mischung *f;* (pharm) Mixtur *f*
mix'-up' *s* Wirrwar *m,* Verwechslung *f*
mizzen ['mɪzən] *s* Besan *m*
mnemonic [nə'manɪk] *s* Gedächtnishilfe *f*
moan [mon] *s* Stöhnen *n* ‖ *intr* stöhnen; **m. about** jammern über *(acc)* or um
moat [mot] *s* Schloßgraben *m*
mob [mab] *s* *(populace)* Pöbel *m;* *(crush of people)* Andrang *m; (gang of criminals)* Verbrecherbande *f* ‖ *v* *(pret & pp* **mobbed;** *ger* **mobbing)** *tr* *(crowd into)* lärmend eindringen in *(acc); (e.g., a consulate)* angreifen; *(a celebrity)* umringen
mobile ['mobɪl] *adj* fahrbar; (mil) motorisiert
mo'bile home' *s* Wohnwagen *m*
mobility [mo'bɪlɪti] *s* (& mil) Bewegglichkeit *f*
mobilization [,mobɪlɪ'zeʃən] *s* Mobilisierung *f*
mobilize ['mobɪ,laɪz] *tr* mobilisieren; *(strength)* aufbieten
mob' rule' *s* Pöbelherrschaft *f*
mobster ['mabstər] *s* Gangster *m*
moccasin ['makəsɪn] *s* Mokassin *m; (snake)* Mokassinschlange *f*
Mo'cha cof'fee ['mokə] *s* Mokka *m*
mock [mak] *adj* Schein– ‖ *tr* verspotten; *(imitate)* nachäffen ‖ *intr* spotten; **m.** at sich lustig machen über *(acc);* **m. up** improvisieren
mocker ['makər] *s* Spötter –in *mf*
mockery ['makəri] *s* Spott *m,* Spöttelei *f;* **make a m. of** hohnsprechen *(dat)*
mock'ing *adj* spöttisch
mock'ingbird' *s* Spottdrossel *f*
mock' tri'al *s* Schauprozeß *m*
mock' tur'tle soup' *s* falsche Schildkrötensuppe *f*
mock'-up' *s* Schaumodell *n*
modal ['modəl] *adj* modal, Modal–
mode [mod] *s* Modus *m;* (mus) Tonart *f*
mod·el ['madəl] *adj* vorbildlich; *(student, husband)* Muster– ‖ *s (e.g., of a building)* Modell *n; (at a fashion show)* Vorführdame *f; (for art or photography)* Modell *n; (example for imitation)* Vorbild *n,* Muster *n; (make)* Typ *m,* Bauart *f* ‖ *v (pret & pp* –el[l]ed; *ger* –el[l]ing) *tr (clothes)* vorführen; **m. oneself on** sich *[dat]* ein Muster nehmen an *(dat);* **m. s.th. on** etw formen nach; (fig) etw gestalten nach ‖ *intr* (for) Modell stehen *(zu dat)*
mod'el air'plane *s* Flugzeugmodell *n*
mod'el num'ber *s* (aut) Typennummer *f*
moderate ['madərɪt] *adj (climate)* gemäßigt; *(demand)* maßvoll; *(price)* angemessen; *(e.g., in drinking)* mäßig; **of m. means** minderbemittelt ‖ ['madə,ret] *tr* mäßigen; *(a meeting)* den Vorsitz führen über *(acc)* or bei; *(a television show)* moderieren ‖ *intr* sich mäßigen
moderation [,madə'reʃən] *s* Mäßigung

f, Maß *n;* **in m.** mit Maß; **observe m.** Maß halten
moderator ['madə,retər] *s* Moderator *m*
modern ['madərn] *adj* modern, zeitgemäß
mod'ern Eng'lish *s* Neuenglisch *n*
mod'ern his'tory *s* Neuere Geschichte *f*
modernize ['madər,naɪz] *tr* modernisieren
mod'ern lan'guages *spl* neuere Sprachen *pl*
mod'ern times' *spl* die Neuzeit *f*
modest ['madɪst] *adj* bescheiden
modesty ['madɪsti] *s* Bescheidenheit *f*
modicum ['madɪkəm] *s* bißchen; **a m. of truth** ein Körnchen Wahrheit
modification [,madɪfɪ'keʃən] *s* Abänderung *f*
modifier ['madɪ,faɪ·ər] *s* (gram) nähere Bestimmung *f*
modi·fy ['madɪ,faɪ] *v (pret & pp* –fied) *tr* abändern; (gram) näher bestimmen
modish ['modɪʃ] *adj* modisch
modulate ['madʒə,let] *tr & intr* modulieren
modulation [,madʒə'leʃən] *s* Modulation *f*
mohair ['mo,hɛr] *s* Mohair *m*
Mohammedan [mo'hæmɪdən] *adj* mohammedanisch ‖ *s* Mohammedaner –in *mf*
Mohammedanism [mo'hæmɪdə,nɪzəm] *s* Mohammedanismus *m*
moist [mɔɪst] *adj* feucht; *(eyes)* tränenfeucht
moisten ['mɔɪsən] *tr* anfeuchten; *(lips)* befeuchten ‖ *intr* feucht werden
moisture ['mɔɪstʃər] *s* Feuchtigkeit *f*
molar ['molər] *s* Backenzahn *m*
molasses [mə'læsɪz] *s* Melasse *f*
mold [mold] *s* Form *f; (mildew)* Schimmel *m;* (typ) Matrize *f* ‖ *tr* formen ‖ *intr* (ver)schimmeln
molder ['moldər] *s* Former –in *mf;* (fig) Bildner –in *mf* ‖ *intr* modern
mold'ing *s* Formen *n;* (carp) Gesims *n*
moldy ['moldi] *adj* mod(e)rig, schimmlig
mole [mol] *s (breakwater)* Hafendamm *m; (blemish)* Muttermal *n;* (zool) Maulwurf *m*
molecular [mə'lɛkjələr] *adj* molekular
molecule ['malɪ,kjul] *s* Molekül *n*
mole'skin' *s (fur)* Maulwurfsfell *n;* (tex) Englischleder *n*
molest [mə'lest] *tr* belästigen
molli·fy ['malɪ,faɪ] *v (pret & pp* –fied) *tr* besänftigen
mollusk ['maləsk] *s* Weichtier *n*
mollycoddle ['malɪ,kadəl] *s* Weichling *m* ‖ *tr* verweichlichen
Mol'otov cock'tail ['malətəf] *s* Flaschengranate *f*
molt [molt] *s intr* sich mausern
molten ['moltən] *adj* schmelzflüssig
molybdenum [mə'lɪbdɪnəm] *s* Molybdän *n*
mom [mam] *s* (coll) Mama *f,* Mutti *f*
moment ['momənt] *s* Moment *m,* Au-

genblick *m*; **a m. ago** nur eben; **at a moment's notice** jeden Augenblick; **at any m.** jederzeit; **at the m.** im Augenblick, zur Zeit; **of great m.** von großer Tragweite; **the very m. I spotted her** sobald ich sie erblickte

momentarily ['momən ˌterɪli] *adv* momentan; (*in a moment*) gleich

momentary ['momən ˌtɛri] *adj* vorübergehend

momentous [mo'mɛntəs] *adj* folgenschwer

momen·tum [mo'mɛntəm] *s* (**–tums & –ta** [tə]) (*phys*) Moment *n*; (*fig*) Schwung *m*; **gather m.** Schwung bekommen

monarch ['monərk] *s* Monarch *m*

monarchical [mə'narkɪkəl] *adj* monarchisch

monarchy ['monərki] *s* Monarchie *f*

monastery ['monəs ˌteri] *s* Kloster *n*

monastic [mə'næstɪk] *adj* Kloster–, Mönchs–

monasticism [mə'næstɪ ˌsɪzəm] *s* Mönchswesen *n*

Monday ['mʌndi], ['mʌnde] *s* Montag *m*; **on M.** am Montag

monetary ['monɪ ˌteri] *adj* (*e.g., crisis, unit*) Währungs–; (*e.g., system, value*) Geld–

mon'etary stand'ard *s* Münzfuß *m*

money ['mʌni] *adj* Geld– || *s* Geld *n*; **big m.** schweres Geld; **get one's money's worth** reell bedient werden; **make m. (on)** Geld verdienen (an *dat*); **put m. on** Geld setzen auf (*acc*)

mon'eybag' *s* Geldbeutel *m*; **moneybags** (coll) Geldsack *m*

mon'ey belt' *s* Geldgürtel *m*

moneychanger ['mʌni ˌtʃendʒər] *s* Wechsler –in *mf*

moneyed ['mʌnid] *adj* vermögend

mon'ey exchange' *s* Geldwechsel *m*

mon'eylend'er *s* Geldverleiher –in *mf*

mon'eymak'er *s* (*fig*) Goldgrube *f*

mon'ey or'der *s* Postanweisung *f*

Mongol ['moŋgəl] *adj* mongolid || *s* Mongole *m*, Mongolin *f*

Mongolian [moŋ'golɪ·ən] *adj* mongolisch || *s* (*language*) Mongolisch *n*

mon·goose ['moŋgus] *s* (**–gooses**) Mungo *m*

mongrel ['mʌŋgrəl] *s* Bastard *m*

monitor ['monɪtər] *s* (*at school*) Klassenordner *m*; (*rad, telv*) Überwachungsgerät *n*, Monitor *m* || *tr* überwachen

monk [mʌŋk] *s* Mönch *m*

monkey ['mʌŋki] *s* Affe *m*; (*female*) Äffin *f*; **make a m. of** zum Narren halten || *intr*—**m. around** (*trifle idly*) herumalbern; **m. around with s.o.** es mit j–m treiben; **m. around with s.th.** an etw [*dat*] herummurksen

mon'keybusi'ness *s* (*underhanded conduct*) Gaunerei *f*; (*frivolous behavior*) (sl) Unfug *m*

mon'keyshine' *s* (sl) Possen *m*

mon'key wrench' *s* Engländer *m*

monocle ['monəkəl] *s* Monokel *n*

monogamous [mə'nagəməs] *adj* monogam

monogamy [mə'nagəmi] *s* Einehe *f*

monogram ['monə ˌgræm] *s* Monogramm *n*

monograph ['monə ˌgræf] *s* Monographie *f*

monolithic [ˌmonə'lɪθɪk] *adj* (& fig) monolithisch

monologue ['monə ˌlog] *s* Monolog *m*

monomania [ˌmonə'menɪ·ə] *s* Monomanie *f*

monoplane ['monə ˌplen] *s* Eindecker *m*

monopolize [mə'napə ˌlaɪz] *tr* monopolisieren

monorail ['monə ˌrel] *s* Einschienenbahn *f*

monosyllable ['monə ˌsɪləbəl] *s* einsilbiges Wort *n*

monotheism [ˌmonə'θi·ɪzəm] *s* Monotheismus *m*

monotonous [mə'natənəs] *adj* eintönig

monotony [mə'natəni] *s* Eintönigkeit *f*

monotype ['monə ˌtaɪp] *s* Monotype *f*

monoxide [mə'naksaɪd] *s* Monoxyd *n*

monsignor [man'sinjər] *s* (**monsignors & monsignori** [ˌmonsi'njori]) (eccl) Monsignore *m*

monsoon [man'sun] *s* Monsun *m*

monster ['manstər] *s* (& fig) Ungeheuer *n*

monstrance ['manstrəns] *s* Monstranz *f*

monstrosity [mans'trasɪti] *s* Monstrosität *f*, Ungeheuerlichkeit *f*

monstrous ['manstrəs] *adj* ungeheuer(lich)

month [mʌnθ] *s* Monat *m*

monthly ['mʌnθli] *adj* & *adv* monatlich || *s* Monatszeitschrift *f*

monument ['manjəmənt] *s* Denkmal *n*

monumental [ˌmanjə'mentəl] *adj* monumental

moo [mu] *s* Muhen *n* || *intr* muhen

mood [mud] *s* Laune *f*, Stimmung *f*; (gram) Aussageweise *f*, Modus *m*; **be in a bad m.** schlechtgelaunt sein; **be in the m. for s.th.** zu etw gelaunt sein

moody ['mudi] *adj* launisch

moon [mun] *s* Mond *m* || *intr*—**m. about** herumlungern

moon'beam' *s* Mondstrahl *m*

moon'light' *s* Mondschein *m* || *intr* schwarzarbeiten

moon'light'er *s* Doppelverdiener –in *mf*

moon'light'ing *s* Schwarzarbeit *f*

moon'lit' *adj* mondhell

moon'shine' *s* Mondschein *m*; (sl) schwarz gebrannter Whisky *m*

moonshiner ['mun ˌʃaɪnər] *s* Schwarzbrenner –in *mf*

moon'shot' *s* Mondgeschoß *n*

moor [mur] *s* Moor *n*, Heidemoor *n*; **Moor** Mohr *m* || *tr* (naut) vertäuen || *intr* (naut) festmachen

moor'ing *s* (*act*) Festmachen *n*; **moorings** (*cables*) Vertäuung *f*; (*place*) Liegeplatz *m*

Moorish ['murɪʃ] *adj* maurisch

moose [mus] *s* (**moose**) amerikanischer Elch *m*

moot [mut] *adj* umstritten

mop [mɑp] *s* Mop *m;* (*of hair*) Wust *m* ‖ *v* (*pret & pp* **mopped;** *ger* **mopping**) *tr* mit dem Mop wischen; **mop up** mit dem Mop aufwischen; (mil) säubern

mope [mop] *intr* Trübsal blasen

moped ['mopəd] *s* Moped *n*

mop'ping-up' opera'tion *s* (mil) Säuberungsaktion *f*

moral ['mɔrəl] *adj* moralisch ‖ *s* Moral *f;* **morals** Sitten *pl*

morale [mə'ræl] *s* Moral *f*

morality [mə'rælɪti] *s* Sittlichkeit *f*

moralize ['mɔrə‚laɪz] *intr* moralisieren

morass [mə'ræs] *s* Morast *m*

moratori·um [‚mɔrə'tori·əm] *s* (–ums & a– [ə]) Moratorium *n*

Moravia [mə'revɪ·ə] *s* Mähren *n*

morbid ['mɔrbɪd] *adj* krankhaft, morbid

mordacious [mɔr'deʃəs] *adj* bissig

mordant ['mɔrdənt] *adj* beißend

more [mor] *comp adj* mehr; **one m. minute** noch e–e Minute ‖ *comp adv* mehr; **all the m.** erst recht; **all the m. because** zumal, da; **m. and m.** immer mehr; **m. and m. expensive** immer teurer; **m. or less** gewissermaßen; **m. than anything** über alles; **no m.** nicht mehr; **not any m.** nicht mehr; **once m.** noch einmal; **the more ... the** (expressing quantity) je mehr ... desto; (expressing frequency) je öfter ... desto ‖ *s* mehr; **see m. of s.o.** j–n noch öfter sehen; **what's m.** außerdem ‖ *pron* mehr

more'o'ver *adv* außerdem, übrigens

morgue [mɔrg] *s* Leichenschauhaus *n;* (journ) Archiv *n,* Zeitungsarchiv *n*

morning ['mɔrnɪŋ] *adj* Morgen– ‖ *s* Morgen *m;* **from m. till night** von früh bis spät; **in the early m.** in früher Morgenstunde; **in the m.** am Morgen; **this m.** heute morgen; **tomorrow m.** morgen früh

morn'ing-af'ter pill' *s* Pille *f* danach

morn'ing-glo'ry *s* Trichterwinde *f*

morn'ing sick'ness *s* morgendliches Erbrechen *n*

morn'ing star' *s* Morgenstern *m*

Moroccan [mə'rakən] *adj* marokkanisch ‖ *s* Marokkaner –in *mf*

morocco [mə'rako] *s* (*leather*) Saffian *m;* **Morocco** Marokko *n*

moron ['mɔran] *s* Schwachsinnige *mf*

morose [mə'ros] *adj* mürrisch

morphine ['mɔrfin] *s* Morphium *n*

morphology [mɔr'falədʒi] *s* Morphologie *f*

morrow ['mɔro] *s*—**on the m.** am folgenden Tag

Morse' code' [mɔrs] *s* Morsealphabet *n*

morsel ['mɔrsəl] *s* Bröckchen *n*

mortal ['mɔrtəl] *adj* sterblich ‖ *s* Sterbliche *mf*

mor'tal dan'ger *s* Lebensgefahr *f*

mor'tal en'emy *s* Todfeind *m*

mor'tal fear' *s* Heidenangst *f*

mortality [mɔr'tælɪti] *s* Sterblichkeit *f*

mortally ['mɔrtəli] *adv* tödlich

mor'tal remains' *spl* irdische Überreste *pl*

mor'tal sin' *s* Todsünde *f*

mor'tal wound' *s* Todeswunde *f*

mortar ['mɔrtər] *s* (*vessel*) Mörser *m;* (archit) Mörtel *m;* (mil) Granatwerfer *m*

mor'tarboard' *s* Mörtelbrett *n*

mor'tar fire' *s* Granatwerferfeuer *n*

mor'tar shell' *s* Granate *f*

mortgage ['mɔrgɪdʒ] *s* Hypothek *f* ‖ *tr* mit e–r Hypothek belasten

mortgagee [‚mɔrgɪ'dʒi] *s* Hypothengläubiger –in *mf*

mortgagor ['mɔrgɪdʒər] *s* Hypothekenschuldner –in *mf*

mortician [mɔr'tɪʃən] *s* Leichenbestatter –in *mf*

morti·fy ['mɔrtɪ‚faɪ] *v* (*pret & pp* **–fied**) *tr* (*the flesh*) abtöten; (*humiliate*) demütigen; **m. oneself** sich kasteien

mortise ['mɔrtɪs] *s* (carp) Zapfenloch *n* ‖ *tr* (carp) verzapfen

mortuary ['mɔrtʃu‚ɛri] *s* Leichenhalle *f*

mosaic [mo'ze·ɪk] *adj* mosaisch ‖ *s* Mosaik *n*

Moscow ['masko], ['maskau] *s* Moskau *n*

Moses ['mozɪz], ['mozɪs] *s* Moses *m*

mosey ['mozi] *intr* (coll) dahinschlürfen

Mos·lem ['mazləm] *adj* muselmanisch ‖ *s* (–**lems** & –**lem**) Moslem –in *mf*

mosque [mask] *s* Moschee *f*

mosqui·to [məs'kito] *s* (–**toes** & –**tos**) Moskito *m,* Mücke *f*

mosqui'to net' *s* Moskitonetz *n*

moss [mɔs] *s* Moos *n*

mossy ['mɔsi] *adj* bemoost

most [most] *super adj* meist ‖ *super adv* am meisten; (*very*) höchst; **m. of all** am allermeisten ‖ *s*—**at (the) m.** höchstens; **make the m. of** möglichst gut ausnützen; **m. of** die meisten; **m. of the day** der größte Teil des Tages; **the m.** das meiste, das Höchste ‖ *pron* die meisten

mostly ['mostli] *adv* meistens

motel [mo'tɛl] *s* Motel *n*

moth [mɔθ] *s* Nachtfalter *m;* (*clothes moth*) Motte *f*

moth'ball' *s* Mottenkugel *f;* **put into mothballs** (nav) stillegen, einmotten ‖ *tr* (& fig) einmotten

moth-eaten ['mɔθ‚itən] *adj* mottenzerfressen

mother ['mʌðər] *s* Mutter *f* ‖ *tr* (*produce*) gebären; (*take care of as a mother*) bemuttern

moth'er coun'try *s* Mutterland *n*

moth'erhood' *s* Mutterschaft *f*

moth'er-in-law' *s* (**mothers-in-law**) Schwiegermutter *f*

motherless ['mʌðərlɪs] *adj* mutterlos

motherly ['mʌðərli] *adj* mütterlich

mother-of-pearl ['mʌðərəv'pʌrl] *adj* perlmuttern ‖ *s* Perlmutter *f*

Moth'er's Day' *s* Muttertag *m*

moth'er's help'er *s* Stütze *f* der Hausfrau

moth'er supe'rior s (Schwester) Oberin f

moth'er tongue' s Muttersprache f

moth' hole' s Mottenfraß m

mothy ['mɔθi] adj mottenzerfressen

motif [moʹtif] s (mus, paint) Motiv n

motion ['moʃən] s Bewegung f; (parl) Antrag m; **make a m.** e–n Antrag stellen; **set in m.** in Bewegung setzen ‖ tr zuwinken (dat); **m. s.o. to** (inf) j–n durch e–n Wink auffordern zu (inf)

motionless ['moʃənlɪs] adj bewegungslos

mo'tion pic'ture s Film m; **be in motion pictures** beim Film sein

mo'tion-pic'ture adj Film–

mo'tion-pic'ture the'ater s Kino n

motivate ['motɪ‚vet] tr begründen, motivieren

motive ['motɪv] s Anlaß m, Beweggrund m

mo'tive pow'er s Triebkraft f

motley ['matli] adj bunt zusammengewürfelt

motor ['motər] adj Motor– ‖ s Motor m

motorcade ['motər‚ked] s Wagenkolonne f

mo'torcy'cle s Motorrad n

mo'torcyc'list s Motorradfahrer –in mf

mo'toring s Autofahren n

motorist ['motərɪst] s Autofahrer –in mf

motorize ['motə‚raɪz] tr motorisieren

mo'tor launch' s Motorbarkasse f

mo'tor·man s (–men) Straßenbahnführer m

mo'tor pool' s Fahrbereitschaft f

mo'tor scoot'er s Motorroller m

mo'tor ve'hicle s Kraftfahrzeug n

mottle ['matəl] tr sprenkeln

mot·to ['mato] s (–toes & –tos) Motto n

mound [maʊnd] s Wall m, Erdhügel m

mount [maʊnt] s (mountain) Berg m; (riding horse) Reittier n ‖ tr (a horse, mountain) besteigen; (stairs) hinaufgehen; (e.g., a machinegun) in Position bringen; (a precious stone) fassen; (photographs in an album) einkleben; (photographs on a backing) aufkleben; **m.** (e.g., a gun) **on** montieren auf (acc)

mountain ['maʊntən] s Berg m; **down the m.** bergab; **up the m.** bergauf

moun'tain climb'er s Bergsteiger –in mf

moun'tain climb'ing s Bergsteigen n

mountaineer [‚maʊntə'nɪr] s Bergbewohner –in mf

mountainous ['maʊntənəs] adj gebirgig

moun'tain pass' s Gebirgspaß m, Paß m

moun'tain rail'road s Bergbahn f

moun'tain range' s Gebirge n

moun'tain scen'ery s Berglandschaft f

mountebank ['maʊntə‚bæŋk] s Quacksalber m; (charlatan) Scharlatan m

mount'ing s Montage f; (of a precious stone) Fassung f

mourn [morn] tr betrauren ‖ intr

trauern; **mourn for** betrauern, trauern um

mourner ['mornər] s Leidtragende mf

mournful ['mornfəl] adj traurig

mourn'ing s Trauer f; **be in m.** Trauer tragen

mourn'ing band' s Trauerflor m

mourn'ing clothes' spl Trauerkleidung f; **wear m.** Trauer tragen

mouse [maʊs] s (mice [maɪs]) Maus f

mouse'hole' s Mauseloch n

mouse'trap' s Mausefalle f

moustache [məs'tæʃ] s Schnurbart m

mouth [maʊθ] s (mouths [maʊðz]) Mund m; (of an animal) Maul n; (of a gun, bottle, river) Mündung f; (sl) Maul n; **keep one's m. shut** den Mund halten; **make s.o.'s m. water** j–m das Wasser im Munde zusammenlaufen lassen

mouthful ['maʊθ‚fʊl] s Mundvoll m; (sl) großes Wort n

mouth' or'gan s Mundharmonika f

mouth'piece' s (of an instrument) Ansatz m; (box) Mundstück n; (fig) Sprachrohr n

mouth'wash' s Mundwasser n

movable ['muvəbəl] adj beweglich, mobil ‖ **movables** spl Mobilien pl

move [muv] s (movement) Bewegung f; (step, measure) Maßnahme f; (resettlement) Umzug m; (checkers) Zug m; (parl) Vorschlag m; **be on the m.** unterwegs sein; **don't make a m.!** keinen Schritt!; **get a m. on** (coll) sich rühren; **it's your m.** (& fig) du bist am Zug; **she won't make a m. without him** sie macht keinen Schritt ohne ihn ‖ tr bewegen; (emotionally) rühren; (shove) rücken; (checkers) e–n Zug machen mit; (parl) beantragen; **m. the bowels** abführen; **m. up** (mil) vorschieben ‖ intr (stir) sich bewegen; (change residence) umziehen; (in society) verkehren; (checkers) ziehen; (com) Absatz haben; **m. away** wegziehen; **m. back** zurückziehen; **m. for** (e.g., a new trial) beantragen; **m. in** zuziehen; **m. into** (a home) beziehen; **m. on** fortziehen; **m. out** (of) ausziehen (aus); **m. over** (make room) zur Seite rücken; **m. up** (to a higher position) vorrücken; (into a vacated position) nachrücken; (said of a team) aufsteigen

movement ['muvmənt] s (& fig) Bewegung f; (mus) Satz m

mover ['muvər] s Möbeltransporteur m; (parl) Antragsteller –in mf

movie ['muvi] adj (actor, actress, camera, projector) Film– ‖ s (coll) Film m; **movies** Kino n; **go to the movies** ins Kino gehen

mov'ie cam'era s Filmkamera f

moviegoer ['muvi‚go·ər] s Kinobesucher –in mf

mov'ie house' s Kino n

mov'ie screen' s Filmleinwand f

mov'ie set' s Filmkulisse f

mov'ie the'ater s Kino n

mov'ing adj beweglich; (force) treibend; (fig) herzergreifend ‖ s (*change of residence*) Umzug m

mov'ing pic'ture s Lichtspiel n, Film m

mov'ing spir'it s führender Kopf m

mow [mo] v (pret **mowed;** pp **mowed & mown**) tr mähen; **mow down** (*enemies*) niedermähen

mower ['mo·ər] s Mäher m

m.p.h. ['ɛm'pi'etʃ] spl (**miles per hour**) Stundenmeilen; **drive sixty m.p.h.** mit sechzig Stundenmeilen fahren

Mr. [mɪstər] s Herr m

Mrs. ['mɪsɪz] s Frau f

Ms. [mɪz] s Fräulein n

much [mʌtʃ] adj, adv & pron viel; **as m. again** noch einmal soviel; **how m.** wieviel; **m. less** (*not to mention*) geschweige denn; **not so m.** as nicht einmal; **so m. so** so sehr; **so m. the better** um so besser; **very m.** sehr

mucilage ['mjusɪlɪdʒ] s Klebstoff m

muck [mʌk] s (& fig) Schmutz m

muck'rake' intr (coll) Korruptionsfälle enthüllen

muckraker ['mʌk‚rekər] s (coll) Korruptionsschnüffler –in mf

mucky ['mʌki] adj schmutzig

mucous ['mjukəs] adj schleimig

muc'ous mem'brane s Schleimhaut f

mucus ['mjukəs] s Schleim m

mud [mʌd] s Schlamm m; **drag through the mud** (fig) in den Schmutz ziehen

mud' bath' s Schlammbad n, Moorbad n

muddle ['mʌdəl] s Durcheinander n ‖ tr durcheinanderbringen ‖ intr—**m. through** sich durchwursteln

mud'dlehead' s Wirrkopf m

mud·dy ['mʌdi] adj schlammig; (fig) trüb ‖ v (pret & pp **–died**) trüben

mud'hole' s Schlammloch n

mudslinging ['mʌd‚slɪŋɪŋ] s (fig) Verleumdung f

muff [mʌf] s Muff m ‖ tr (coll) verpfuschen

muffin ['mʌfɪn] s Teekuchen m aus Backpulverteig

muffle ['mʌfəl] tr (*sounds*) dämpfen; **m. up** (*wrap up*) einhüllen

muf'fled adj dumpf

muffler ['mʌflər] s (*scarf*) Halstuch n; (aut) Auspufftopf m

mufti ['mʌfti] s Zivil n

mug [mʌg] s Krug m; (*for beer*) Seidel n; (*thug*) (sl) Rocker m; (*face*) (sl) Fratze f ‖ v (pret & pp **mugged;** ger **mugging**) tr (sl) photographieren; (*assault*) (sl) überfallen ‖ intr (sl) Gesichter schneiden

muggy ['mʌgi] adj schwül

mug' shot' s (sl) Polizeiphoto n

mulat·to [mə'læto] s (**–toes**) Mulatte m, Mulattin f

mulberry ['mʌl‚bɛri] s Maulbeere f

mul'berry tree' s Maulbeerbaum m

mulch [mʌltʃ] s Streu n

mulct [mʌlkt] tr (of) betrügen (um)

mule [mjul] s Maulesel m, Maultier n

mulish ['mjulɪʃ] adj störrisch

mull [mʌl] intr—**m. over** nachgrübeln über (*acc*)

mullion ['mʌljən] s Mittelpfosten m

multicolored ['mʌltɪ‚kələrd] adj bunt

multigraph ['mʌltɪ‚græf] s (trademark) Vervielfältigungsmaschine f ‖ tr vervielfältigen

multilateral [‚mʌltɪ'lætərəl] adj mehrseitig

multimillionaire ['mʌltɪ‚mɪljə'nɛr] s vielfacher Millionär m

multiple ['mʌltɪpəl] adj mehrfach, Vielfach– ‖ s (math) Vielfaches n

multiplication [‚mʌltɪplɪ'keʃən] s Vermehrung f; (arith) Multiplikation f

multiplica'tion ta'ble s Einmaleins n

multiplicity [‚mʌltɪ'plɪsɪti] s Vielfältigkeit f

multi·ply ['mʌltɪ‚plaɪ] v (pret & pp **–plied**) tr vervielfältigen; (biol) vermehren; (math) multiplizieren ‖ intr sich vervielfachen; (biol) sich vermehren

multistage ['mʌltɪ‚stedʒ] adj mehrstufig

multistory ['mʌltɪ‚stori] adj mehrstöckig

multitude ['mʌltɪ‚t(j)ud] s (*large number*) Vielheit f; (*of people*) Masse f

mum [mʌm] adj still; **keep mum about** Stillschweigen beobachten über (*acc*); **mum's the word!** Mund halten!

mumble ['mʌmbəl] tr & intr murmeln

mummery ['mʌməri] s Hokuspokus m

mummy ['mʌmi] s Mumie f

mumps [mʌmps] s Ziegenpeter m, Mumps m

munch [mʌntʃ] tr & intr geräuschvoll kauen

mundane [mʌn'den] adj irdisch

municipal [mju'nɪsɪpəl] adj städtisch

muni'cipal bond' s Kommunalobligation f

municipality [mju‚nɪsɪ'pælɪti] s Stadt f, Gemeinde f; (*governing body*) Stadtverwaltung f

munificent [mju'nɪfɪsənt] adj freigebig

munificence [mju'nɪfɪsəns] s Freigebigkeit f

munitions [mju'nɪʃəns] s Kriegsmaterial n, Munition f

muni'tions dump' s Munitionsdepot n

muni'tions fac'tory s Rüstungsfabrik f

mural ['mjurəl] s Wandgemälde n

murder ['mʌrdər] s Mord m ‖ tr (er)morden; (*a language*) radebrechen

murderer ['mʌrdərər] s Mörder m

murderess ['mʌrdərɪs] s Mörderin f

mur'der mys'tery s Krimi m

murderous ['mʌrdərəs] adj mörderisch

mur'der plot' s Mordanschlag m

murky ['mʌrki] adj düster

murmur ['mʌrmər] s Gemurmel n ‖ tr & intr murmeln

muscle ['mʌsəl] s Muskel m; **muscles** Muskulatur f

muscular ['mʌskjələr] adj muskulös

Muse [mjuz] s Muse f ‖ **muse** intr (over) nachsinnen (über acc)

museum [mju'zi·əm] s Museum n

mush [mʌʃ] s (*corn meal*) Maismehlbrei m; (*soft mass*) Matsch m; (*sentimental talk*) Süßholzraspeln n

mush'room' s Pilz m, Champignon m

|| *intr* wie Pilze aus dem Boden schießen

mushy ['mʌʃi] *adj* matschig; *(sentimental)* rührselig

music ['mjusɪk] *s* Musik *f;* *(score)* Noten *pl;* **face the m.** die Sache ausbaden; **set to m.** vertonen

musical ['mjuzɪkəl] *adj* musikalisch || *s* (cin) Singspielfilm *m;* (theat) Musical *n,* Singspiel *n*

mu'sical in'strument *s* Musikinstrument *n*

musicale [ˌmjusɪ'kæl] *s* Musikabend *m*

mu'sic box' *s* Spieldose *f*

musician [mju'zɪʃən] *s* Musikant –in *mf;* *(accomplished artist)* Musiker –in *mf*

musicology [ˌmjuzɪ'kalədʒi] *s* Musikwissenschaft *f*

mu'sic stand' *s* Notenständer *m*

mus'ing *s* Grübelei *f*

musk [mʌsk] *s* Moschus *m*

musket ['mʌskɪt] *s* Muskete *f*

musk'rat' *s* Bisamratte *f*

muslin ['mʌzlɪn] *s* Musselin *m*

muss [mʌs] *tr* (hair) zerzausen; (dirty) schmutzig machen; (rumple) zerknittern

mussel ['mʌsəl] *s* Muschel *f*

mussy ['mʌsi] *adj* (hair) zerzaust; (clothes) zerknittert

must [mʌst] *s* (a necessity) Muß *n;* (new wine) Most *m;* (mold) Moder *m* || *mod*—**I m.** (inf) ich muß (inf)

mustache [məs'tæʃ] *s* Schnurrbart *m*

mustard ['mʌstərd] *s* Senf *m*

mus'tard plas'ter *s* Senfpflaster *n*

muster ['mʌstər] *s* Appell *m;* **pass m.** die Prüfung bestehen || *tr* (troops) antreten lassen; (courage, strength) aufbringen; **m. out** ausmustern

musty ['mʌsti] *adj* mod(e)rig

mutation [mju'teʃən] *s* (biol) Mutation *f*

mute [mjut] *adj* (& ling) stumm || *s* (ling) stummer Buchstabe *m;* (mus) Dämpfer || *tr* (mus) dämpfen

mutilate ['mjutɪ ˌlet] *tr* verstümmeln

mutineer [ˌmjutɪ'nɪr] *s* Meuterer *m*

mutinous ['mjutɪnəs] *adj* meuterisch

muti·ny ['mjutɪni] *s* Meuterei *f* || *v* (pret & pp –nied) *intr* meutern

mutt [mʌt] *s* (coll) Köter *m*

mutter ['mʌtər] *s* Gemurmel *n* || *tr* & *intr* murmeln

mutton ['mʌtən] *s* (culin) Hammel *m*

mut'ton-head' *s* (sl) Hammel *m*

mutual ['mjutʃu·əl] *adj* gegenseitig; (friends) gemeinsam

mu'tual fund' *s* Investmentfond *m*

mu'tual insur'ance com'pany *s* Versicherungsgesellschaft *f* auf Gegenseitigkeit

mutually ['mjutʃu·əli] *adv* gegenseitig

muzzle ['mʌzəl] *s* Maulkorb *m;* (of a gun) Rohrmündung *f;* (snout) Schnauze *f* || *tr* (an animal) e–n Maulkorb anlegen (dat); (e.g., the press) mundtot machen

muz'zle flash' *s* Mündungsfeuer *n*

my [maɪ] *poss adj* mein

myopic [maɪ'apɪk] *adj* kurzsichtig

myriad ['mɪrɪ·əd] *adj* Myriade *f*

myrrh [mʌr] *s* Myrrhe *f*

myrtle ['mʌrtəl] *s* Myrte *f*

myself ['maɪ'sɛlf] *reflex pron* mich; (indirect object) mir || *intens pron* selbst, selber

mysterious [mɪs'tɪrɪ·əs] *adj* mysteriös

mystery ['mɪstəri] *s* Geheimnis *n;* (fi) Rätsel *n;* (relig) Mysterium *n*

mys'tery nov'el *s* Kriminalroman *m*

mys'tery play' *s* Mysterienspiel *n*

mystic ['mɪstɪk] *adj* mystisch || *s* Mystiker –in *mf*

mystical ['mɪstɪkəl] *adj* mystisch

mysticism ['mɪstɪ ˌsɪzəm] *s* Mystik *f*

mystification [ˌmɪstɪfɪ'keʃən] *s* Verwirrung *f*

mysti·fy ['mɪstɪ ˌfaɪ] *v* (pret & pp –fied) *tr* verwirren

myth [mɪθ] *s* Mythe *f,* Mythos *m;* (ill-founded belief) Märchen *n*

mythical ['mɪθɪkəl] *adj* mythisch

mythological [ˌmɪθə'ladʒɪkəl] *adj* mythologisch

mythology [mɪ'θalədʒi] *s* Mythologie *f*

N

N, n [ɛn] *s* vierzehnter Buchstabe des englischen Alphabets

nab [næb] *v* (pret & pp nabbed; ger –nabbing) *tr* (coll) schnappen

nadir ['nedɪr] *s* (fig) Tiefpunkt *m;* (astr) Nadir *m*

nag [næg] *s* Gaul *m;* **old nag** Schindmähre *f* || *v* (pret & pp nagged; ger nagging) *tr* zusetzen (dat) || *intr* nörgeln; **nag at** herumnörgeln an (dat)

nag'ging *adj* nörgelnd || *s* Nörgelei *f*

naiad ['naɪ·æd] *s* Najade *f*

nail [nel] *s* Nagel *m;* **hit the n. on the head** den Nagel auf den Kopf treffen || *tr* (to) annageln (an acc); (catch)

(coll) erwischen; (box) (coll) treffen; **n. down** (fig) festnageln; **n. shut** zunageln

nail' clip'pers *spl* Nagelzange *f*

nail' file' *s* Nagelfeile *f*

nail' pol'ish *s* Nagellack *m*

nail' scis'sors *s* & *spl* Nagelschere *f*

naïve [na'iv] *adj* naiv

naked ['nekɪd] *adj* nackt; (eye) bloß

nakedness ['nekɪdnɪs] *s* Nacktheit *f*

name [nem] *s* Name *m;* (reputation) Name *m,* Ruf *m;* **by n.** dem Namen nach; **by the n. of** namens; **in n. only** nur dem Namen nach; **of the same n.** gleichnamig; **spell one's n.** sich

schreiben; **what is your n.?** wie hei-
ßen Sie? || *tr* nennen; (*nominate*)
ernennen; **be named after** heißen
nach; **n. after** nennen nach; **named**
namens
name'-call'ng *s* Beschimpfung *f*
name' day' *s* Namenstag *m*
nameless ['nemlɪs] *adj* namenlos
namely ['nemli] *adv* nämlich, und
zwar
name'plate' *s* Namensschild *n*
name'sake' *s* Namensvetter *m*
nanny ['næni] *s* Kindermädchen *n*
nan'ny goat' *s* (coll) Ziege *f*
nap [næp] *s* Schläfchen *n;* (tex) Noppe
f; **take a nap** ein Schläfchen machen
|| *v* (*pret & pp* **napped;** *ger* **napping)**
intr schlummern; **catch s.o. napping**
(fig) j-n überrumpeln
napalm ['nepɑm] *s* Napalm *n*
nape [nep] *s*—**n. of the neck** Nacken
m
naphtha ['næfθə] *s* Naphtha *f & n*
napkin ['næpkɪn] *s* Serviette *f*
nap'kin ring' *s* Serviettenring *m*
narcissism ['nɑrsɪ‚sɪzəm] *s* Narzißmus
m
narcissus [nɑr'sɪsəs] *s* (bot) Narzisse *f*
narcotic [nɑr'kɑtɪk] *adj* narkotisch ||
s (med) Betäubungsmittel *n,* Narko-
tikum *n;* (*addictive drug*) Rauschgift
n; (*addict*) Rauschgiftsüchtige *mf*
narrate [næ'ret] *tr* erzählen
narration [næ're‚ən] *s* Erzählung *f*
narrative ['nærətɪv] *adj* erzählend || *s*
Erzählung *f*
narrator [næ'retər] *s* Erzähler *m;* (telv)
Moderator *m*
narrow ['næro] *adj* eng, schmal; (*e.g.,*
margin) knapp || **narrows** *spl*
Meerenge *f* || *tr* verengen || *intr* sich
verengen
nar'row escape' *s*—**have a n.** mit
knapper Not entkommen
nar'row-gauge rail'road *s* Schmalspur-
bahn *f*
narrowly ['næroli] *adv* mit knapper
Not
nar'row-mind'ed *adj* engstirnig
nasal ['nezəl] *adj* (*of the nose*) Nasen-;
(*sound*) näselnd || *s* (phonet) Nasen-
laut *m*
nasalize ['nezə‚laɪz] *tr* nasalieren ||
intr näseln
na'sal twang' *s* Näseln *n*
nascent ['nesənt] *adj* werdend
nastiness ['næstɪnɪs] *s* Ekligkeit *f*
nasturtium [nə'stʌrʃəm] *s* Kapuziner-
kresse *f*
nasty ['næsti] *adj* (*person, smell, taste*)
ekelhaft; (*weather*) scheußlich; (*dog,
accident, tongue*) böse; **n. to** garstig
zu or gegen
nation ['neʃən] *s* Nation *f,* Volk *n*
national ['næʃənəl] *adj* national, Lan-
des- || *s* Staatsangehörige *mf*
na'tional an'them *s* Nationalhymne *f*
na'tional defense' *s* Landesverteidigung
f
nationalism ['næʃənə‚lɪzəm] *s* Nationalismus *m*
nationality [‚næʃə'nælɪti] *s* (*citizen-*

ship) Staatsangehörigkeit *f;* (*ethnic
identity*) Nationalität *f*
nationalization [‚næʃənəlɪ'zeʃən] *s*
Verstaatlichung *f*
nationalize ['næʃənə‚laɪz] *tr* verstaatlichen
na'tional park' *s* Naturschutzpark *m*
na'tional so'cialism *s* Nationalsozialis-
mus *m*
na'tionwide' *adj* im ganzen Land
native ['netɪv] *adj* eingeboren; (*prod-
ucts*) heimisch, Landes- || *s* Eingebo-
rene *mf;* **be a n. of** beheimatet sein
in (*dat*)
na'tive coun'try *s* Vaterland *n*
na'tive land' *s* Heimatland *n*
na'tive tongue' *s* Muttersprache *f*
nativity [nə'tɪvɪti] *s* Geburt *f;* (astrol)
Nativität *f;* **the Nativity** die Geburt
Christi
NATO ['neto] *s* (**North Atlantic Treaty
Organization**) NATO *f*
natty ['næti] *adj* elegant
natural ['nætʃərəl] *adj* natürlich; (*be-
havior*) ungezwungen || *s* (mus)
weiße Taste *f;* (*symbol*) (mus) Auf-
lösungszeichen *n;* **a n.** (*person*) (coll)
ein Naturtalent *n;* (*thing*) (coll) e-e
totsichere Sache *f*
na'tural his'tory *s* Naturgeschichte *f*
naturalism ['nætʃərə‚lɪzəm] *s* Natura-
lismus *m*
naturalist ['nætʃərəlɪst] *s* (*student of
natural history*) Naturforscher –in
mf; (paint, philos) Naturalist –in *mf*
naturalization [‚nætʃərəlɪ'zeʃən] *s* Ein-
bürgerung *f*
naturalize ['nætʃərə‚laɪz] *tr* einbürgern
na'tural law' *s* Naturgesetz *n*
na'tural phenom'enon *s* (*occurring in
nature*) Naturereignis *n;* (*not supernatural*) natürliche Erscheinung *f*
na'tural re'sources *spl* Bodenschätze *pl*
na'tural sci'ence *s* Naturwissenschaft *f*
na'tural state' *s* Naturzustand *m*
nature ['netʃər] *s* die Natur; (*quali-
ties*) Natur *f,* Beschaffenheit *f;* **by n.**
von Natur aus
naught [nɔt] *s* Null *f;* **all for n.** ganz
umsonst; **bring to n.** zuschanden machen; **come to n.** zunichte werden
naughty ['nɔti] *adj* unartig, ungezogen
nausea ['nɔʃɪ‚ə], ['nɔsɪ‚ə] *s* Übelkeit *f*
nauseate ['nɔʃɪ‚et], ['nɔsɪ‚et] *tr* Übelkeit erregen (*dat*)
naus'eating *adj* Übelkeit erregend
nauseous ['nɔʃɪ‚əs], ['nɔsɪ‚əs] *adj*
(*causing nausea*) Übelkeit erregend;
I feel n. mir ist übel
nautical ['nɔtɪkəl] *adj* See-, nautisch
nau'tical mile' ['nɔtɪkəl] *s* Seemeile *f*
nau'tical term' *s* Ausdruck *m* der See-
mannssprache *f*
naval ['nevəl] *adj* (*e.g., battle, blockade, cadet, victory*) See-; (*unit*)
Flotten-; (*academy, officer*) Marine-
na'val base' *s* Flottenstützpunkt *m*
na'val cap'tain *s* Kapitän *m* zur See
na'val engage'ment *s* Seegefecht *n*
na'val forc'es *s* Seestreitkräfte *pl*
na'val suprem'acy *s* Seeherrschaft *f*

nave [nev] s (of a church) Schiff n; (of a wheel) Nabe f
navel ['nevəl] s Nabel m
na'vel or'ange s Navelorange f
navigable ['nævɪgəbəl] adj schiffbar
navigate ['nævɪ‚get] tr (traverse) befahren; (steer) steuern || intr (aer, naut) navigieren
navigation [‚nævɪ'geʃən] s (plotting courses) Navigation f; (sailing) Schiffahrt f
naviga'tion chart' s Navigationskarte f
naviga'tion light' s (aer, naut) Positionslicht n
navigator ['nævɪ‚getər] s Seefahrer m; (aer) Navigator m
navy ['nevi] adj Marine– || s Kriegsmarine f
na'vy bean' s Weiße Bohne f
na'vy blue' adj marineblau || s Marineblau n
na'vy yard' s Marinewerft f
nay [ne] adv nein || s Nein n; (parl) Neinstimme f; **the nays have it** die Mehrheit stimmt dagegen
Nazarene [‚næzə'rin] adj aus Nazareth || s Nazarener m
Nazi ['nɑtsi] adj Nazi– || s Nazi m
Nazism ['nɑtsɪzəm] s Nazismus m
N.C.O. ['en'si'o] s (**noncommissioned officer**) Unteroffizier m
neap' tide' [nip] s Nippflut f
near [nɪr] adj nahe(liegend); (escape) knapp; **n. at hand** zur Hand || adv nahe; **draw n. (to)** sich nähern (dat); **live n.** (e.g., a church) in der Nähe wohnen, (genit) || prep nahe (dat), nahe an (dat), bei (dat); **n. here** hier in der Nähe
near'by' adj nahe(gelegen) || adv in der Nähe
Near' East', the s der Nahe Osten
nearly ['nɪrli] adv beinahe, fast
nearness ['nɪrnɪs] s Nähe f
near'-sight'ed adj kurzsichtig
near'-sight'edness s Kurzsichtigkeit f
neat [nit] adj sauber, ordentlich; (simple but tasteful) nett f; (cute) niedlich; (tremendous) (coll) prima
neatness ['nitnɪs] s Sauberkeit f
nebu·la ['nɛbjələ] s (**-lae** [‚li] & **-las**) (astr) Nebelfleck m
nebulous ['nɛbjələs] adj nebelhaft; (astr) Nebel–
necessarily [‚nesɪ'serɪli] adv notwendigerweise, unbedingt
necessary ['nesɪ‚seri] adj notwendig, nötig; (consequence) zwangsläufig; **if n.** notfalls
necessitate [nɪ'sesɪ‚tet] tr notwendig machen, enfordern
necessity [nɪ'sesɪti] s (state of being necessary) Notwendigkeit f; (something necessary) Bedürfnis n; (poverty) Not f; **in case of n.** im Notfall; **necessities of life** Lebensbedürfnisse pl; **of n.** notwendigerweise
neck [nɛk] s Hals m; (of a dress) Halsausschnitt m; **break one's n. (& fig)** sich [dat] den Hals brechen; **get it in the n.** (sl) eins aufs Dach kriegen; **get s.o. off one's n.** sich [dat] j–n

vom Halse schaffen; **n. and n.** Seite an Seite || intr (coll) sich knutschen
–necked [‚nɛkt] suf –halsig, –nackig
neckerchief ['nɛkərtʃɪf] s Halstuch n
neck'ing s Abknutscherei f
necklace ['nɛklɪs] s Halsband n; (metal chain) Halskette f
neck'line' s Halsausschnitt m; **with a low n.** tief ausgeschnitten
neck'tie' s Krawatte f, Schlips m
necrology [nɛ'krɑlədʒi] s (list of the dead) Totenliste f; (obituary) Nekrolog m
necromancer ['nɛkrə‚mænsər] s Geistesbeschwörer –in mf
necromancy ['nɛkrə‚mænsi] s Geistesbeschwörung f
necropolis [nɛ'krɑpəlɪs] s Nekropolis f
nectar ['nɛktər] s (bot, myth) Nektar m
nectarine [‚nɛktə'rin] s Nektarine f
nee [ne] adj geborene, e.g., **Mrs. Mary Schmidt, nee Müller** Frau Maria Schmidt, geborene Müller
need [nid] s Bedarf m, Bedürfnis n; **be in n. in Not sein**; **be in n. of repair** reparaturbedürftig sein; **be in n. of s.th.** etw nötig haben; **if n. be** erforderlichenfalls; **meet s.o.'s needs** j–s Bedarf decken; **needs** Bedarfsartikel pl || tr benötigen, brauchen; **as needed** nach Bedarf
needful ['nidfəl] adj nötig
needle ['nidəl] s Nadel f || tr (prod) anstacheln; **n. s.o. about** gegen j–n sticheln wegen
nee'dlepoint', nee'dlepoint lace' s Nadelspitze f
needless ['nidlɪs] adj unnötig; **n. to say** es erübrigt sich zu sagen
nee'dlework' s Näharbeit f
needy ['nidi] adj bedürftig
ne'er [nɛr] adv nie
ne'er'-do-well' s Tunichtgut m
nefarious [nɪ'feri·əs] adj ruchlos
negate [nɪ'get] tr verneinen
negation [nɪ'geʃən] s Verneinung f
negative ['nɛgətɪv] adj negativ || s Verneinung f; (elec) negativer Pol m; (gram) Verneinungswort n; (phot) Negativ n
neglect [nɪ'glɛkt] s Vernachlässigung f || tr vernachlässigen; **n. to (inf)** unterlassen zu (inf)
négligée, negligee [‚nɛglɪ'ʒe] s Negligé n
negligence ['nɛglɪdʒəns] s Fahrlässigkeit f
negligent ['nɛglɪdʒənt] adj fahrlässig
negligible ['nɛglɪdʒɪbəl] adj geringfügig
negotiable [nɪ'goʃɪ·əbəl] adj diskutierbar; (fin) übertragbar, bankfähig
negotiate [nɪ'goʃɪ‚et] tr (a contract) abschließen; (a curve) nehmen || intr verhandeln
negotiation [nɪ‚goʃɪ'eʃən] s Verhandlung f; **carry on negotiations with** in Verhandlungen stehen mit; **enter negotiations with** in Verhandlungen treten mit

negotiator [nɪ'goʃɪ͵etər] s Unterhändler –in mf
Ne·gro ['nigro] s (–groes) Neger –in mf
neigh [ne] s Wiehern n ‖ intr wiehern
neighbor ['nebər] s Nachbar –in mf; (fellow man) Nächste m ‖ tr angrenzen an (acc) ‖ intr—**n. on** angrenzen an (acc)
neigh'borhood' s Nachbarschaft f; (vicinity) Umgebung f; **in the n. of** (coll) etwa
neigh'boring adj benachbart, Nachbar–, angrenzend
neighborliness ['nebərlɪnɪs] s gutnachbarliche Beziehungen pl
neighborly ['nebərli] adj (gut)nachbarlich
neither [niðər] indef adj keiner ‖ indef pron (of) keiner (von); **n. of them** keiner von beiden ‖ conj noch, ebensowenig; auch nicht, e.g., **n. do I** ich auch nicht; **neither ... nor** weder ... noch; **that's n. here nor there** das hat nichts zu sagen
neme·sis ['nɛməsɪs] s (–ses [͵siz]) Nemesis f
Neolith'ic Age' [͵ni·ə'lɪθɪk] s Neusteinzeit f
neologism [ni'alə͵dʒɪzəm] s Neubildung f, Neologismus m
neon ['ni·an] s Neon n
ne'on light' s Neonröhre f
ne'on sign' s Neonreklame f
neophyte ['ni·ə͵faɪt] s Neuling m; (relig) Neubekehrte mf
nephew ['nɛfju] s Neffe m
nepotism ['nɛpə͵tɪzəm] s Nepotismus m
Neptune ['nɛpt(j)un] s Neptun m
neptunium [nɛp't(j)unɪ·əm] s Neptunium n
nerve [nʌrv] adj Nerven– ‖ s Nerv m; (courage) Wagemut m; (gall) (coll) Unverfrorenheit f; **get on s.o.'s nerves** j–m auf die Nerven gehen; **lose one's n.** die Nerven verlieren; **nerves of steel** Nerven pl wie Drahtseile
nerve' cen'ter s Nervenzentrum n
nerve'-rack'ing adj nervenaufreibend
nervous ['nʌrvəs] adj nervös; (system) Nerven–; (horse) kopfscheu; **be a n. wreck** mit den Nerven herunter sein
ner'vous break'down s Nervenzusammenbruch m
nervousness ['nʌrvəsnɪs] s Nervosität f
nervy ['nʌrvi] adj (brash) unverschämt; (courageous) mutig
nest [nɛst] s Nest n ‖ intr nisten
nest' egg' s (fig) Sparpfennig m
nestle ['nɛsəl] intr (**up to**) sich anschmiegen (an acc)
net [nɛt] adj Rein– ‖ adv netto, rein ‖ s Netz n; (for fire victims) Sprungtuch n ‖ v (pret & pp **netted**); ger **netting**) tr (e.g., fish, butterflies) mit dem Netz fangen; (said of an enterprise) netto einbringen; (said of a person) rein verdienen
net'ball' s (tennis) Netzball m

Netherlander ['nɛðər͵lændər] s Niederländer –in mf
Netherlands, the ['nɛðərləndz] s & spl die Niederlande
net'ting s Netzwerk n
nettle ['nɛtəl] s Nessel f ‖ tr reizen
net'work' s Netzwerk n; (rad, telv) Sendergruppe f
neuralgia [n(j)υ'ræ1dʒə] s Neurologie f
neuritis [n(j)υ'raɪtɪs] s Nervenentzündung f
neurologist [n(j)υ'ralədʒɪst] s Nervenarzt m, Nervenärztin f
neurology [n(j)υ'ralədʒi] s Nervenheilkunde f, Neurologie f
neuron ['n(j)υran] s Neuron n
neuro·sis [n(j)υ'rosɪs] s (–ses [siz]) Neurose f
neurotic [n(j)υ'ratɪk] adj neurotisch ‖ s Neurotiker –in mf
neuter ['n(j)utər] adj (gram) sächlich ‖ s (gram) Neutrum n
neutral ['n(j)utrəl] adj neutral ‖ s Neutrale mf; (aut) Leerlauf m
neutrality [n(j)u'trælɪti] s Neutralität f
neutralize ['n(j)utrə͵laɪz] tr (a bomb) entschärfen; (& chem) neutralisieren; (troops) lahmlegen; (an attack) unterbinden
neutron ['n(j)utran] s Neutron n
never ['nɛvər] adv nie(mals); **n. again** nie wieder; **n. before** noch nie; **n. mind!** spielt keine Rolle!
ne'vermore' adv nimmermehr
ne'vertheless' adv nichtsdestoweniger
new [n(j)u] adj neu; (wine) jung; (inexperienced) unerfahren; **what's new?** was gibt's Neues?
new' arriv'al s Neuankömmling m
new'born' adj neugeboren
New'cas'tle s—**carry coals to N.** Eulen nach Athen tragen
newcomer ['n(j)u͵kʌmər] s Neuankömmling m
newel ['n(j)u·əl] s Treppenspindel f
new'el post' s Geländerpfosten m
newfangled ['n(j)u͵fæŋgəld] adj neumodisch
Newfoundland ['n(j)ufənd͵lænd] s Neufundland n ‖ [n(j)u'faundlənd] s (dog) Neufundländer m
newly ['n(j)uli] adv neu, Neu–
new'lyweds' spl Neuvermählten pl
new' moon' s Neumond m
new-mown ['n(j)u͵mon] adj frischgemäht
newness ['n(j)unɪs] s Neuheit f
news [n(j)uz] s Nachricht f; (rad, telv) Nachrichten pl; **that's not n. to me** das ist mir nicht neu; **piece of n.** Neuigkeit f
news' a'gency s Nachrichtenagentur f
news'boy' s Zeitungsjunge m
news' bul'letin s Kurznachricht f
news'cast' s Nachrichtensendung f
news'cast'er s Nachrichtensprecher –in mf
news'deal'er s Zeitungshändler –in mf
news' ed'itor s Nachrichtenredakteur –in mf

news'let'ter s Rundschreiben n
news'man' s (−**men'**) Journalist m;
(dealer) Zeitungshändler m
news'pa'per adj Zeitungs– || s Zeitung
f
news'paper clip'ping s Zeitungsaus-
schnitt m
news'paper·man' s (−**men'**) Journalist
m; (dealer) Zeitungshändler m
news'paper se'rial s Zeitungsroman m
news'print' s Zeitungspapier n
news'reel' s Wochenschau f
news' report' s Nachrichtensendung f
news' report'er s Zeitungsreporter −in
mf
news' room' s Nachrichtenbüro n
news'stand' s Zeitungskiosk m
news'wor'thy adj berichtenswert
New' Tes'tament s Neues Testament n
New' World' s Neue Welt f
New' Year' s Neujahr n; **happy N.!**
glückliches Neues Jahr!
New' Year's' Eve' s Silvesterabend m
New' Zea'land ['zilənd] s Neuseeland
n
next [nɛkst] adj nächste; **be n.** an der
Reihe sein; **come n.** folgen; **in the n.
place** darauf; **n. best** nächstbeste; **n.
time** das nächste Mal; **n. to** (locally)
gleich neben (dat); (almost) sogut
wie; **the n. day** am nächsten Tag ||
adv dann, danach; **what should I do
n.?** was soll ich als Nächstes tun?
next'-door' adj—**n. neighbor** unmittel-
barer Nachbar m || **next'-door'** adv
nebenan; **n. to** direkt neben (dat)
next' of kin' s (pl: **next of kin**) nächster Angehöriger m
niacin ['naɪ·əsɪn] s Niacin n
Niag'ara Falls' [naɪ'ægrə] s Niagara-
fall m
nib [nɪb] s Spitze f; (of a pen) Feder-
spitze f
nibble ['nɪbəl] tr knabbern || intr (on)
knabbern (an dat)
Nibelung ['nibəluŋ] s (myth) Nibelung
m
nice [naɪs] adj nett; (pretty) hübsch;
(food) lecker; (well-behaved) artig;
(distinction) fein; **have a n. time** sich
gut unterhalten; **n. and warm** schön
warm
nicely ['naɪsli] adv nett; **he's doing n.**
es geht ihm recht gut; **that will do n.**
das paßt gut
nicety ['naɪsəti] s Feinheit f; **niceties
of life** Annehmlichkeiten pl des
Lebens
niche [nɪtʃ] s Nische f; (fig) rechter
Platz m
nick [nɪk] s Kerbe f, Scharte f; **in the
n. of time** gerade im rechten Augen-
blick || tr kerben
nickel ['nɪkəl] s Nickel n; (coin) Fünf-
centstück n || tr vernickeln
nick'el-plate' tr vernickeln
nick'name' s Spitzname m || tr e−n
Spitznamen geben (dat)
nicotine ['nɪkə,tin] s Nikotin n; **low
in n.** nikotinarm
niece [nis] s Nichte f
nifty ['nɪfti] adj (coll) fesch, prima

niggard ['nɪgərd] s Knauser −in mf
niggardly ['nɪgərdli] adj knauserig
night [naɪt] adj (light, shift, train,
watch) Nacht– || s Nacht f; **all n.**
(long) die ganze Nacht (über); **at n.**
nachts; **last n.** gestern abend; **n.
after n.** Nacht für Nacht; **n. before
last** vorgestern abend
night' cap' s Nachtmütze f; (drink)
Schlummertrunk m
night' club' s Nachtklub m
night'fall' s Anbruch m der Nacht; **at
n.** bei Anbruch der Nacht
night'gown' s Damennachthemd n
nightingale ['naɪtən,gel] s Nachtigall
f
night'light' s Nachtlicht n
night'long' adj & adv die ganze Nacht
dauernd
nightly ['naɪtli] adj & adv allnächtlich
night'mare' s Alptraum m
nightmarish ['naɪt,merɪʃ] adj alpartig
night' owl' s (coll) Nachteule f
night' school' s Abendschule f
night'time' s Nachtzeit f; **at n.** zur
Nachtzeit
night' watch'man s Nachtwächter m
nihilism ['naɪ·ɪ,lɪzəm] s Nihilismus m
nil [nɪl] s Nichts n, Null f
Nile [naɪl] s Nil m
nimble ['nɪmbəl] adj flink
nincompoop ['nɪnkəm,pup] s Trottel
m
nine [naɪn] adj & pron neun || s Neun
f
nineteen ['naɪn'tin] adj & pron neun-
zehn || s Neunzehn f
nineteenth ['naɪn'tinθ] adj & pron
neunzehnte || s (fraction) Neunzehn-
tel n; **the nineteenth** (in dates or in
a series) der Neunzehnte
ninetieth ['naɪntɪ·ɪθ] adj & pron neun-
zigste || s (fraction) Neunzigstel n
ninety ['naɪnti] adj & pron neunzig ||
s Neunzig f; **the nineties** die neunziger Jahre
nine'ty-first' adj & pron einundneun-
zigste
nine'ty-one' adj & pron einundneunzig
ninny ['nɪni] s (coll) Trottel m
ninth [naɪnθ] adj & pron neunte || s
(fraction) Neuntel n; **the n.** (in dates
or in a series) der Neunte
nip [nɪp] s (pinch) Kneifen n; (of cold
weather) Schneiden n; (of liquor)
Schluck m || v (pret & pp **nipped;**
ger **nipping**) tr (pinch) kneifen; (alcohol) nippen; **nip in the bud** im
Keime ersticken
nippers ['nɪpərz] spl Zwickzange f
nipple ['nɪpəl] s (of a nursing bottle)
Lutscher m; (anat) Brustwarze f;
(mach) Schmiernippel m
nippy ['nɪpi] adj schneidend
nirvana [nɪr'vɑnə] s Nirwana n
nit [nɪt] s (ent) Nisse f
niter ['naɪtər] s Salpeter m
nit'pick'er s (coll) Pedant −in mf
nitrate ['naɪtret] s Nitrat n || tr ni-
trieren
ni'tric ac'id ['naɪtrɪk] s Salpetersäure
f

nitride ['naɪtraɪd] s Nitrid n
nitrogen ['naɪtrədʒən] s Stickstoff m
nitroglycerin [ˌnaɪtrə'glɪsərɪn] s Nitroglyzerin n
ni'trous ac'id ['naɪtrəs] s salpetrige Säure f
ni'trous ox'ide s Stickstoffoxydul n
nit'wit' s Trottel m
no [no] adj kein; **no admittance** Zutritt verboten; **no ... of any kind** keinerlei; **no offense!** nichts für ungut!; **no parking** Parkverbot; **no smoking** Rauchen verboten; **no thoroughfare** Durchgang verboten; **no ... whatever** überhaupt kein || adv nein; **no?** nicht wahr?; **no longer** (or **no more**) nicht mehr || s Nein n; **give no for an answer** mit (e–m) Nein antworten
No'ah's Ark' ['no-əz] s Arche f Noah(s)
nobility [no'bɪlɪti] s (nobleness; aristocracy) Adel m; (noble rank) Adelsstand m; **n. of mind** Seelenadel m
noble ['nobəl] adj (rank) ad(e)lig; (character, person) edel || s Adliger m; **nobles** Edelleute pl
no'ble·man s (–men) Edelmann m
no'blemind'ed adj edelgesinnt
nobleness ['nobəlnɪs] s Vornehmheit f
no'ble·wom'an s (–wom'en) Edelfrau f
nobody ['no ˌbɑdi] s indef pron niemand, keiner; **n. else** sonst keiner || s (coll) Null f
nocturnal [nɑk'tʌrnəl] adj nächtlich
nod [nɑd] s Kopfnicken n || v (pret & pp **nodded;** ger **nodding**) tr—**nod one's head** mit dem Kopf nicken || intr nicken; **nod to** zunicken (dat)
node [nod] s (anat, astr, math, phys) Knoten m
nodule ['nɑdʒul] s Knötchen n; (bot) Knollen m
noise [nɔɪz] s Geräusch n; (disturbingly loud) Lärm m || tr—**n. abroad** ausposaunen
noiseless ['nɔɪzlɪs] adj geräuschlos
noisy ['nɔɪzi] adj lärmend, geräuschvoll
nomad ['nomæd] s Nomade m, Nomadin f
no' man's' land' s Niemandsland n
nomenclature ['nomən ˌkletʃər] s Nomenklatur f
nominal ['nɑmɪnəl] adj nominell
nominate ['nɑmɪ ˌnet] tr ernennen; **n. as candidate** als Kandidaten aufstellen
nomination [ˌnɑmɪ'neʃən] s Ernennung f; (of a candidate) Aufstellung f
nominative ['nɑmɪnətɪv] s Nominativ m
nominee [ˌnɑmɪ'ni] s Designierte mf
non– [nɑn] pref Nicht–, nicht–
non'accept'ance s Nichtannahme f
non'belli'gerent adj nicht am Krieg teilnehmend
non'break'able adj unzerbrechlich
non'-Cath'olic adj nichtkatholisch || s Nichtkatholik –in mf
nonchalant [ˌnɑnʃə'lɑnt] adj zwanglos

noncom ['nɑn ˌkɑm] s (coll) Kapo m
non'com'batant s Nichtkämpfer m
non'commis'sioned of'ficer s Unteroffizier m
noncommittal [ˌnɑnkə'mɪtəl] adj nichtssagend; (person) zurückhaltend
nondescript ['nɑndɪ ˌskrɪpt] adj unbestimmbar
none [nʌn] adv—**n. too** keineswegs zu || indef pron keiner; **that's n. of your business** das geht dich nichts an
nonen'tity s Nichts n; (fig) Null f
non'exis'tent adj nichtexistent
nonfic'tion s Sachbücher pl
nonfulfill'ment s Nichterfüllung f
non'interven'tion s Nichteinmischung f
non'met'al s Nichtmetall n, Metalloid n
non'nego'tiable adj unübertragbar; (demands) unabdingbar
nonpar'tisan adj überparteilich
nonpay'ment s Nichtbezahlung f
non'polit'ical adj unpolitisch
non·plus [nɑn'plʌs] s Verlegenheit f || v (pret & pp –**plus[s]ed;** ger –**plus[s]ing**) tr verblüffen
nonprof'it adj gemeinnützig
nonres'ident adj nich ansässig || s Nichtansässige mf
non'return'able adj (bottles, etc.) Einweg–; (merchandise) nicht rücknehmbar
non'scienti'fic adj nichtwissenschaftlich
non'sectar'ian adj keiner Sekte angehörend
nonsense ['nɑnsəns] s Unsinn m
nonsen'sical adj unsinnig, widersinnig
non'skid' adj rutschsicher
nonsmok'er s Nichtraucher –in mf
non'stop' adj & adv ohne Zwischenlandung
nonvi'olence s Gewaltlosigkeit f
nonvi'olent adj gewaltlos
noodle ['nudəl] s Nudel f; (head) (coll) Birne f
noo'dle soup' s Nudelsuppe f
nook [nuk] s Ecke f; (fig) Winkel m
noon [nun] s Mittag m; **at n.** zu Mittag
no' one', no'-one' indef pron niemand, keiner; **n. else** kein anderer
noon' hour' s Mittagsstunde f
noon'time' adj mittäglich || s Mittagszeit f
noose [nus] s Schlinge f
nor [nɔr] conj (after **neither**) noch; auch nicht, e.g., **nor do I** ich auch nicht
Nordic ['nɔrdɪk] adj nordisch
norm [nɔrm] s Norm f
normal ['nɔrməl] adj normal
normalcy ['nɔrməlsi] s Normalzustand m
normalize ['nɔrmə ˌlaɪz] tr normalisieren
Norman ['nɔrmən] adj normannisch || s Normanne m, Normannin f
Normandy ['nɔrməndi] s die Normandie
Norse [nɔrs] adj altnordisch || s (language) Altnordisch n; **the N.** die Skandinavier pl
Norse'man s (–men) Nordländer m

north [nɔrθ] *adj* nördlich, Nord– || *adv* nach Norden || *s* Norden *m;* **to the n. of** im Norden von

North′ Amer′ica *s* Nordamerika *n*

North′ Amer′ican *adj* nordamerikanisch || *s* Nordamerikaner –in *mf*

north′east′ *adj & adv* nordöstlich || *s* Nordosten *m*

north′east′er *s* Nordostwind *m*

northerly [′nɔrðərli] *adj* nördlich

northern [′nɔrðərn] *adj* (*direction*) nördlich; (*race*) nordisch

north′ern expo′sure *s* Nordseite *f*

North′ern Hem′isphere *s* nördliche Halbkugel *f*

north′ern lights′ *spl* Nordlicht *n*

nor′thernmost′ *adj* nördlichst

North′ Pole′ *s* Nordpol *m*

North′ Sea′ *s* Nordsee *f*

northward [′nɔrθwərd] *adv* nach Norden

north′west′ *adj & adv* nordwestlich || *s* Nordwesten *m*

north′ wind′ *s* Nordwind *m*

Norway [′nɔrwe] *s* Norwegen *n*

Norwegian [nɔr′widʒən] *adj* norwegisch || *s* Norweger –in *mf;* (*language*) Norwegisch *n*

nose [noz] *s* Nase *f;* (aer) Nase *f,* Bug *m;* **by a n.** (sport) um e-e Nasenlänge; **blow one′s n.** sich schneuzen; **lead around by the n.** an der Nase herumführen; **pay through the n.** e-n zu hohen Preis bezahlen; **turn one′s n. up** at die Nase rümpfen über (*acc*) || *tr*—**n. out** (fig) mit knappem Vorsprung besiegen; (sport) um e-e Nasenlänge schlagen || *intr*—**n. about** herumschnüffeln; **n. over** (aer) sich überschlagen

nose′bleed′ *s* Nasenbluten *n*

nose′ cone′ *s* (rok) Raketenspitze *f*

nose′ dive′ *s* (aer) Sturzflug *m*

nose′-dive′ *intr* e-n Sturzflug machen

nose′ drops′ *spl* Nasentropfen *pl*

nose′gay′ *s* Blumenstrauß *m*

nose′-heav′y *adj* (aer) vorderlastig

nostalgia [na′stældʒə] *s* Heimweh *n*

nostalgic [na′stældʒɪk] *adj* wehmütig

nostril [′nastrɪl] *s* (anat) Nasenloch *n;* (zool) Nüster *f*

nostrum [′nastrəm] *s* Allheilmittel *n*

nosy [′nozi] *adj* neugierig

not [nat] *adv* nicht; **not at all** überhaupt nicht; **not even** nicht einmal; **not one** keiner; **not only ... but also** nicht nur ... sondern auch

notable [′notəbəl] *adj* bemerkenswert || *s* Standesperson *f*

notarial [no′terɪ·əl] *adj* notariell

notarize [′notə‚raɪz] *tr* notariell beglaubigen

no′tary pub′lic [′notəri] *s* (**notaries public**) Notar *m,* Notarin *f*

notation [no′teʃən] *s* (*note*) Aufzeichnung *f;* (*system of symbols*) Bezeichnung *f;* (*method of noting*) Schreibweise *f*

notch [natʃ] *s* Kerbe *f;* (*in a belt*) Loch *n;* (*degree, step*) Grad *m;* (*of a wheel*) Zahn *m* || *tr* einkerben

note [not] *s* Notiz *f;* (*to a text*) An-

merkung *f;* (*slip*) Zettel *m;* (*e.g., of doubt*) Ton *m;* (mus) Note *f;* **jot down notes** sich [*dat*] Notizen machen; **make a n. of** sich [*dat*] notieren; **take n. of** zur Kenntnis nehmen; **take notes** sich [*dat*] Notizen machen || *tr* beachten; **n. down** notieren; **n. in passing** am Rande bemerken

note′book′ *s* Heft *n,* Notizbuch *n*

note′ pad′ *s* Schreibblock *m*

note′wor′thy *adj* beachtenswert

nothing [′nʌθɪŋ] *indef pron* nichts; **be for n.** vergebens sein; **come to n.** platzen; **for n.** (*gratis*) umsonst; **have n. to go on** keine Unterlagen haben; **next to n.** soviel wie nichts; **n. at all** gar nichts; **n. but** lauter; **n. doing!** kommt nicht in Frage!; **n. else** sonst nichts; **n. new** nichts Neues; **there is n. like** es geht nichts über (*acc*)

nothingness [′nʌθɪŋnɪs] *s* (*nonexistence*) Nichts *n;* (*utter insignificance*) Nichtigkeit *f*

notice [′notɪs] *s* (*placard*) Anschlag *m;* (*in the newspaper*) Anzeige *f;* (*attention*) Beachtung *f;* (*announcement*) Ankündigung; (*notice of termination*) Kündigung *f;* **at a moment′s n.** jeden Moment; **escape s.o.′s n.** j-m entgehen; **give s.o. a week′s n.** j-m acht Tage vorher kündigen; **take n. of** Notiz nehmen von; **until further n.** bis auf weiteres || *tr* (be)merken, wahrnehmen; **be noticed by s.o.** j-m auffallen; **n. s.th. about s.o.** j-m etw anmerken

noticeable [′notɪsəbəl] *adj* wahrnehmbar

notification [‚notɪfɪ′keʃən] *s* Benachrichtigung *f*

noti·fy [′notɪ‚faɪ] *v* (*pret & pp* **–fied**) *tr* (*about*) benachrichtigen (von)

notion [′noʃən] *s* (*idea*) Vorstellung *f;* **I have a good n. to** (*inf*) ich habe gute Lust zu (*inf*); **notions** Kurzwaren *pl*

notoriety [‚notə′raɪ·ɪti] *s* Verruf *m*

notorious [no′tori·əs] *adj* (*for*) notorisch (*wegen*)

no′-trump′ *adj* ohne Trumpf || *s* Ohne-Trumpf-Ansage *f*

notwithstanding [‚natwɪθ′stændɪŋ] *adv* trotzdem || *prep* trotz (*genit*)

noun [naun] *s* Hauptwort *n*

nourish [′nʌrɪʃ] *tr* (er)nähren

nour′ishing *adj* nahrhaft, Nähr–

nourishment [′nʌrɪʃmənt] *s* (*feeding*) Ernährung *f;* (*food*) Nahrung *f*

Nova Scotia [′novə′skoʃə] *s* Neuschottland *n*

novel [′navəl] *adj* neuartig || *s* Roman *m*

novelist [′navəlɪst] *s* Romanschriftsteller –in *mf*

novelty [′navəlti] *s* Neuheit *f*

November [no′vembər] *s* November *m*

novena [no′vinə] *s* Novene *f*

novice [′navɪs] *s* Neuling *m;* (eccl) Novize *m,* Novizin *f*

novitiate [no′vɪʃɪ·ɪt] *s* Noviziat *n*

novocaine [′novə‚ken] *s* Novokain *n*

now [nau] *adv* jetzt; (*without tem-*

poral force) nun; **before now** schon früher; **by now** nachgerade; **from now on** von nun ab, fortan; **now and then** dann und wann; **now ... now** bald ... bald; **now or never** jetzt oder nie

nowadays ['naʊ·ə ‚dez] *adv* heutzutage

no'way', **no'ways'** *adv* keineswegs

no'where' *adv* nirgends

noxious ['nɑkʃəs] *adj* schädlich

nozzle ['nɑzəl] *s* Düse *f;* (*on a can*) Schnabel *m*

nth [ɛnθ] *adj*—**nth times** zig mal; **to the nth degree** (fig) im höchsten Maße

nuance ['n(j)u·ɑns] *s* Nuance *f*

nub [nʌb] *s* Knoten *m;* (*gist*) Kernpunkt *m*

nuclear ['n(j)uklɪ·ər] *adj* nuklear; (*energy, fission, fusion, physics, reactor, weapon*) Kern-

nu'clear pow'er *s* Atomkraft *f*

nu'clear pow'er plant' *s* Atomkraftwerk *n*

nucleolus [n(j)u'kli·ələs] *s* Nukleolus *m*

nucleon ['n(j)ukli·ɑn] *s* Nukleon *n*

nucle·us ['n(j)ukli·əs] *s* (**–uses** & **i-** [‚aɪ]) Kern *m*

nude [n(j)ud] *adj* nackt ‖ *s* (*nude figure*) Akt *m;* **in the n.** nackt

nudge [nʌdʒ] *s* Stups *m* ‖ *tr* stupsen

nudist ['n(j)udɪst] *s* Nudist –in *mf*

nudity ['n(j)udɪti] *s* Nacktheit *f*

nugget ['nʌgɪt] *s* Klumpen *m*

nuisance ['n(j)usəns] *s* Ärgernis *n;* **be a n.** lästig sein

nui'sance raid' *s* Störungsangriff *m*

null' and void' [nʌl] *adj* null und nichtig

nulli·fy ['nʌlɪ ‚faɪ] *v* (*pret* & *pp* **–fied**) *tr* (*e.g., a law*) für ungültig erklären; (*e.g., the effects*) aufheben

numb [nʌm] *adj* taub; (**with**) starr (vor *dat*); (fig) betäubt; **grow n.** erstarren ‖ *tr* (& fig) betäuben; (*said of cold*) starr machen

number ['nʌmbər] *s* Nummer *f;* (*count*) Zahl *f,* Anzahl *f;* (*article*) (com) Artikel *m;* (gram) Zahl *f;* (mus) Stück *n;* **in n.** der Zahl nach; **get s.o.'s n.** (coll) j–m auf die Schliche kommen ‖ *tr* (*e.g., pages*) numerieren; (*amount to*) zählen; **be numbered among** zählen zu; **n. among** zählen zu

numberless ['nʌmbərlɪs] *adj* zahllos

num'bers game' *s* Zahlenlotto *n*

numbness ['nʌmnɪs] *s* Taubheit *f;* (*from cold*) Starrheit *f*

numeral ['n(j)umərəl] *adj* Zahl- ‖ *s* Zahl *f,* Ziffer *f;* (gram) Zahlwort *n*

numerator ['n(j)umə ‚retər] *s* Zähler *m*

numerical [n(j)u'mɛrɪkəl] *adj* numerisch; **n. order** Zahlenfolge *f;* **n. superiority** Überzahl *f;* **n. value** Zahlenwert *m*

numerous ['n(j)umərəs] *adj* zahlreich

numismatic [‚n(j)umɪz'mætɪk] *adj* numismatisch ‖ **numismatics** *s* Münzkunde *f*

numskull ['nʌm ‚skʌl] *s* Dummkopf *m*

nun [nʌn] *s* Nonne *f*

nunci·o ['nʌnʃɪ·o] *s* (**–os**) Nuntius *m*

nuptial ['nʌpʃəl] *adj* Braut-, Hochzeits- ‖ **nuptials** *spl* Trauung *f*

Nuremberg ['n(j)ʊrəm ‚bʌrg] *s* Nürnberg *n*

nurse [nʌrs] *s* Krankenschwester *f;* (*male*) Krankenpfleger *m;* (*wet nurse*) Amme *f* ‖ *tr* (*the sick*) pflegen; (*a child*) stillen; (*hopes*) hegen; **n. a cold** e–e Erkältung kurieren

nurse'maid' *s* Kindermädschen *n*

nursery ['nʌrsəri] *s* Kinderstube *f;* (*for day care*) Kindertagesstätte *f;* (hort) Baumschule *f,* Pflanzschule *f*

nurs'ery·man *s* (**–men**) Kunstgärtner *m*

nurs'ery rhyme' *s* Kinderlied *n*

nurs'ery school' *s* Kindergarten *m*

nurse'·s aide' *s* Schwesterhelferin *f*

nurs'ing *s* (*as a profession*) Krankenpflege *f;* (*of a person*) Pflege *f;* (*of a baby*) Stillen *n*

nurs'ing home' *s* Pflegeheim *n*

nurture ['nʌrtʃər] *s* Nahrung *f* ‖ *tr* (er)nähren

nut [nʌt] *s* Nuß *f;* (sl) verrückter Kerl *m;* (mach) Mutter *f,* Schraubenmutter *f;* **be nuts** (sl) verrückt sein; **be nuts about** (sl) vernarrt sein in (*acc*); **go nuts** (sl) e–n Klaps kriegen

nut'crack'er *s* Nußknacker *m*

nutmeg ['nʌt ‚mɛg] *s* (*spice*) Muskatnuß *f;* (*tree*) Muskat *m*

nutrient ['nutrɪ·ənt] *s* Nährstoff *m*

nutriment ['n(j)utrɪmənt] *s* Nährstoff *m*

nutrition [n(j)u'trɪʃən] *s* Ernährung *f*

nutritious [n(j)u'trɪʃəs] *adj* nahrhaft

nutritive ['n(j)utrɪtɪv] *adj* nahrhaft, Nähr-

nut'shell' *s* Nußschale *f;* **in a n.** mit wenigen Worten

nutty ['nʌti] *adj* nußartig; (sl) spleenig, verrückt

nuzzle ['nʌzəl] *tr* sich mit der Schnauze (or Nase) reiben an (*dat*) ‖ *intr* (*burrow*) mit der Schnauze wühlen; **n. up to** sich anschmiegen an (*acc*)

nylon ['naɪlɑn] *s* Nylon *n*

nymph [nɪmf] *s* Nymphe *f*

nymphomaniac [‚nɪmfə'menɪ·æk] *s* Nymphomanin *f*

O

O, o [o] *s* fünfzehnter Buchstabe des englischen Alphabets

oaf [of] *s* Tölpel *m*

oak [ok] *adj* eichen ‖ *s* Eiche *f*

oak' leaf' clus'ter *s* Eichenlaub *n*

oak' tree' *s* Eichbaum *m*

oakum ['okəm] *s* Werg *n*

oar [or], [ɔr] *s* Ruder *n,* Riemen *m*

oar'lock' s Ruderdolle f
oars'man' s (**–men'**) Ruderer m
oa·sis [o'esɪs] s (**–ses** [siz]) Oase f
oath [oθ] s (**oaths** [oðz]) Eid m; **o. of allegiance** Treueid m; **o. of office** Amtseid m; **under o.** eidlich
oat'meal' s Hafergrütze f, Hafermehl n
oats [ots] spl Hafer m; **he's feeling his o.** (coll) ihn sticht der Hafer; **sow one's wild o.** (coll) sich [dat] die Hörner ablaufen
obbligato [,ɑblɪ'gato] adj hauptstimmig || s Obligato m
obdurate ['ɑbdjərɪt] adj verstockt
obedience [o'bidɪ·əns] s (**to**) Gehorsam m (gegenüber dat, gegen); **blind o.** Kadavergehorsam m
obedient [o'bidɪ·ənt] adj (**to**) gehorsam (dat)
obeisance [o'bisəns] s Ehrerbietung f
obelisk ['ɑbəlɪsk] s Obelisk m
obese [o'bis] adj fettleibig
obesity [o'bisɪti] s Fettleibigkeit f
obey [o'be] tr gehorchen (dat); (a law, order) befolgen || intr gehorchen
obfuscate [ɑb'fʌsket] tr verdunkeln
obituary [o'bɪtʃu,eri] adj Todes– || s Todesanzeige f, Nachruf m
object ['ɑbdʒɪkt] s Gegenstand m; (aim) Ziel n, Zweck m; (gram) Ergänzung f, Objekt n; **money is no o.** Geld spielt keine Rolle || [ɑb'dʒɛkt] intr (**to**) Einwände erheben (gegen)
objection [ɑb'dʒɛk/ən] s Einwand m; **I have no o. to his staying** ich habe nichts dagegen (einzuwenden), daß er bleibe
objectionable [ɑb'dʒɛk/ənəbəl] adj nicht einwandfrei
objective [ɑb'dʒɛktɪv] adj sachlich, objektiv || s Ziel n
objec'tive case' s Objektsfall m
ob'ject les'son s Lehre f
obligate ['ɑblɪ,get] tr verpflichten; **be obligated to s.o.** j–m zu Dank verbunden sein
obligation [,ɑblɪ'ge/ən] s Verpflichtung f
obligatory ['ɑblɪgə,tori], [ə'blɪgə,tori] adj verpflichtend, obligatorisch
oblige [ə'blaɪdʒ] tr (bind) verpflichten; (do a favor to) gefällig sein (dat); **be obliged to** (inf) müssen (inf); **feel obliged to** (inf) sich bemüßigt fühlen zu (inf); **I'm much obliged to you** ich bin Ihnen sehr verbunden
oblig'ing adj gefällig
oblique [ə'blik] adj schief
obliterate [ə'blɪtə,ret] tr auslöschen; (traces) verwischen; (writing) unleserlich machen
oblivion [ə'blɪvɪ·ən] s Vergessenheit f
oblivious [ə'blɪvɪ·əs] adj—**be o. of** sich [dat] nicht bewußt sein (genit)
oblong ['ɑblɔŋ] adj länglich || s Rechteck n
obnoxious [əb'nɑk/əs] adj widerlich
oboe ['obo] s Oboe f
oboist ['obo·ɪst] s Oboist –in mf
obscene [ɑb'sin] adj obszön

obscenity [ɑb'sɛnɪti] s Obszönität f
obscure [əb'skjʊr] adj dunkel, obskur || tr verdunkeln
obscurity [əb'skjʊrɪti] s Dunkelheit f
obsequies ['ɑbsɪkwiz] spl Totenfeier f
obsequious [əb'sikwɪ·əs] adj unterwürfig
observance [əb'zʌrvəns] s Beachtung f, Befolgung f; (celebration) Feier f
observant [əb'zʌrvənt] adj beobachtend
observation [,ɑbzər've/ən] s Beobachtung f; **keep under o.** beobachten
observa'tion tow'er s Aussichtsturm m
observatory [əb'zʌrvə,tori] s Sternwarte f, Observatorium n
observe [əb'zʌrv] tr (a person, rules) beobachten; (a holiday) feiern; **o. silence** Stillschweigen bewahren
obsess [əb'sɛs] tr verfolgen; **obsessed** (by) besessen (von)
obsession [əb'sɛ/ən] s Besessenheit f
obsolescent [,ɑbsə'lɛsənt] adj veraltend
obsolete ['ɑbsə,lit] adj veraltet; **become o.** veralten
obstacle ['ɑbstəkəl] s Hindernis n
ob'stacle course' s Hindernisbahn f
obstetrical [ɑb'stɛtrɪkəl] adj Geburtshilfe–, Entbindungs–
obstetrician [,ɑbstə'trɪ/ən] s Geburtshelfer –in mf
obstetrics [ɑb'stɛtrɪks] s Geburtshilfe f
obstinacy ['ɑbstɪnəsi] s Starrheit f
obstinate ['ɑbstɪnɪt] adj starr
obstreperous [əb'strɛpərəs] adj (clamorous) lärmend; (unruly) widerspenstig
obstruct [əb'strʌkt] tr (e.g., a pipe) verstopfen; (a view, way) versperren; (traffic) behindern; **o. justice** die Rechtspflege behindern
obstruction [əb'strʌk/ən] s (of a view, way) Versperrung f; (of traffic) Behinderung f; (obstacle) Hindernis n; (parl, pol) Obstruktion f
obtain [əb'ten] tr erhalten, erlangen || intr bestehen
obtrusive [əb'trusɪv] adj aufdringlich
obtuse [əb't(j)us] adj (& fig) stumpf
obviate ['ɑbvɪ,et] tr erübrigen
obvious ['ɑbvɪ·əs] adj naheliegend; **it is o.** es liegt auf der Hand
occasion [ə'keʒən] s Gelegenheit f; (reason) Anlaß m; **on o.** gelegentlich; **on the o. of** anläßlich (genit) || tr veranlassen
occasional [ə'keʒənəl] adj gelegentlich
occasionally [ə'keʒənəli] adv gelegentlich, zuweilen
occident ['ɑksɪdənt] s Abendland n
occidental [,ɑksɪ'dɛntəl] adj abendländisch || s Abendländer –in mf
occlusion [ə'kluʒən] s Okklusion f
occult [ə'kʌlt] adj geheim, okkult
occupancy ['ɑkjəpənsi] s Besitz m, Besitzergreifung f; (of a home) Einzug m
occupant ['ɑkjəpənt] s Besitzer –in mf; (of a home) Inhaber –in mf; (of a car) Insasse m, Insassin f
occupation [,ɑkjə'pe/ən] s (employ-

ment) Beruf *m*, Beschäftigung *f*;
(mil) Besetzung *f*, Besatzung *f*
occup'ational disease' [͵akjə'peʃənəl]
s Berufskrankheit *f*
occupa'tional ther'apy *s* Beschäfti-
gungstherapie *f*
occupa'tion troops' *spl* Besatzungstrup-
pen *pl*
occu·py ['ɑkjə ͵paɪ] *v* (*pret & pp* –**pied**)
tr in Besitz nehmen; (*a house*) bewohnen; (*time*) in Anspruch nehmen;
(*keep busy*) beschäftigen; (mil) besetzen; **occupied** (*said of a seat or
toilet*) besetzt; (*said of a person*)
beschäftigt; **o. oneself with** sich befassen mit
oc·cur [ə'kʌr] *v* (*pret & pp* –**curred**;
ger –**curring**) *intr* sich ereignen;
(*come to mind*) (**to**) einfallen (*dat*)
occurrence [ə'kʌrəns] *s* Ereignis *n*;
(*e.g., of a word*) Vorkommen *n*
ocean ['oʃən] *s* Ozean *m*
oceanic [͵oʃɪ'ænɪk] *adj* Ozean–, ozea-
nisch
o'cean lin'er *s* Ozeandampfer *m*
oceanography [͵oʃən'ɑgrəfi] *s* Ozeanographie *f*
ocher ['okər] *s* Ocker *m & n*
o'clock [ə'klɑk] *adv* Uhr; **at . . . o'clock**
, **um . . . Uhr**
octane ['ɑkten] *s* Oktan *n*
oc'tane num'ber *s* Oktanzahl *f*
octave ['ɑktɪv], ['ɑktev] *s* Oktave *f*
October [ɑk'tobər] *s* Oktober *m*
octogenarian [͵ɑktədʒɪ'nerɪ·ən] *s*
Achtzige *mf*
octo·pus ['ɑktəpəs] *s* (–**puses** & –**pi**
[͵paɪ]) Seepolyp *m*
ocular ['ɑkjələr] *adj* Augen–
oculist ['ɑkjəlɪst] *s* Augenarzt *m*, Augenärztin *f*
odd [ɑd] *adj* (*strange*) seltsam, eigenartig; (*number*) ungerade; (*e.g.,
glove*) einzeln; **two hundred odd
pages** etwas über zweihundert Seiten
‖ **odds** *spl* (*probability*) Wahrscheinlichkeit *f*; (*advantage*) Vorteil *m*;
(*in gambling*) Vorgabe *f*; **at odds**
uneinig; **lay** (*or* **give**) **odds** vorgeben;
the odds are two to one die Chancen
stehen zwei zu eins
odd' ball' *s* (sl) Sonderling *m*
oddity ['ɑdɪti] *s* Seltsamkeit *f*
odd' jobs' *spl* Gelegenheitsarbeit *f*;
(*chores*) kleine Aufgaben *pl*
odds' and ends' *spl* Kleinkram *m*
ode [od] *s* Ode *f*
odious ['odɪ·əs] *adj* verhaßt
odor ['odər] *s* Duft *m*, Geruch *m*; **be
in bad o.** in schlechtem Ruf stehen
odorless ['odərlɪs] *adj* geruchlos
odyssey ['ɑdɪsi] *s* Irrfahrt *f*; **Odyssey**
Odyssee *f*
of [ɑv], [əv] *prep* von (*dat*); *genit*,
e.g., **the name of the dog** der Name
des Hundes
off [ɔf] *adj* (*free from work*) dienstfrei; (*poor, bad*) schlecht; (*electric
current*) ausgeschaltet, abgeschaltet;
be badly off in schlechten Verhältnissen sein; **be off** (*said of a clock*)
nachgehen; (*said of a measurement*)

falsch sein; (*said of a person*) im
Irrtum sein; (*be crazy*) nicht ganz
richtig im Kopf sein; **be well off** in
guten Verhältnissen sein; **the deal**
(*or* **party**) **is off** es ist aus mit dem
Geschäft (or mit der Party) ‖ *adv*
(*distant*) weg; **he was off in a flash**
er war im Nu weg; **I must be off**
ich muß fort ‖ *prep* von (*dat*); **off
duty** außer Dienst; **off limits** Zutritt
verboten
offal ['ɔfəl] *s* (*refuse*) Abfall *m*; (*of
butchered meat*) Innereien *pl*
off' and on' *adv* ab und zu
off'beat' *adj* (sl) ungewöhnlich
off' chance' *s* geringe Chance *f*
off'-col'or *adj* schlüpfrig
off'-du'ty *adj* außerdienstlich
offend [ə'fend] *tr* beleidigen ‖ *intr*—
o. against verstoßen gegen
offender [ə'fendər] *s* Missetäter –in
mf; **first o.** nicht Vorbestrafte *mf*;
second o. Vorbestrafte *mf*
offense [ə'fens] *s* (**against**) Vergehen
n (gegen); **give o.** Anstoß geben;
no o.! nichts für ungut!; **take o. (at)**
Anstoß nehmen (an *dat*)
offensive [ə'fensɪv] *adj* anstößig; (*odor*)
ekelhaft; (*action*) offensiv ‖ *s* Offensive *f*; **take the o.** die Offensive ergreifen
offer ['ɔfər] *s* Angebot *n* ‖ *tr* anbieten; (*a price*) bieten; (*help, resistance*) leisten; (*friendship*) schenken;
o. an excuse e–e Entschuldigung vorbringen; **o. as an excuse** als Entschuldigung vorbringen; **o. for sale** feil-
bieten; **o. one's services** sich anbieten; **o. up** aufopfern ‖ *intr*—**o. to**
(*inf*) sich erbieten zu (*inf*)
of'fering *s* (*act*) Opferung *f*; (*gift*)
Opfergabe *f*
offertory ['ɔfər ͵tori] *s* Offertorium *n*
off'hand' *adj* (*excuse*) unvorbereitet;
(*manner*) lässig ‖ *adv* kurzerhand
office ['ɔfɪs] *s* (*room*) Büro *n*, Amt *n*;
(*position*) Amt *n*; (*of a doctor*)
Sprechzimmer *n*; **be in o.** amtieren;
through the good offices of durch die
freundliche Vermittlung (*genit*); **run
for o.** für ein Amt kandidieren
of'fice boy' *s* Bürojunge *m*
of'fice build'ing *s* Bürogebäude *n*
of'ficehold'er *s* Amtsträger –in *mf*
of'fice hours' *spl* Dienststunden *pl*; (*of
a doctor, lawyer*) Sprechstunde *f*
officer ['ɔfɪsər] *s* (adm) Beamte *m*,
Beamtin *f*; (com) Direktor –in *mf*;
(mil) Offizier –in *mf*
of'ficer can'didate *s* Offiziersanwärter
–in *mf*
of'ficers' mess' *s* Offizierskasino *n*;
(nav) Offiziersmesse *f*
of'fice seek'er *s* Amtsbewerber –in *mf*
of'fice supplies' *spl* Bürobedarf *m*
of'fice work' *s* Büroarbeit *f*
official [ə'fɪʃəl] *adj* amtlich; (*in line
of duty*) Dienst–; (*visit*) offiziell;
(*document*) öffentlich; **on o. business**
dienstlich ‖ *s* Beamte *m*, Beamtin *f*;
top officials Spitzenkräfte *pl*
offi'cial busi'ness *s* Dienstsache *f*

offi'cial call' s (telp) Dienstgespräch n
officialdom [ə'fɪʃəldəm] s Beamtentum n
officialese [ə,fɪʃə'liz] s Amtssprache f
officially [ə'fɪʃəli] adv offiziell
offi'cial use' s Dienstgebrauch m
officiate [ə'fɪʃɪ,et] intr amtieren; **o. at a marriage** e–n Traugottesdienst halten
officious [ə'fɪʃəs] adj dienstbeflissen
offing ['ɔfɪŋ] s—**in the o.** in Aussicht
off'-lim'its adj gesperrt
off'print' s Abdruck m, Sonderdruck m
off'-seas'on adj—**o. prices** Preise pl während der Vor– und Nachsaison ‖ s Vor– und Nachsaison f
off'set' s (compensation) Ausgleich m; (typ) Offsetdruck m ‖ **off'set'** v (pret –set; ger –setting) tr ausgleichen
off'set press' s Offsetdruck m
off'shoot' s Ableger m
off'shore' adj küstennah
off'side' adv (sport) abseits
off'spring' s Sprößling m
off'stage' adj hinter der Bühne befindlich ‖ adv hinter der Bühne
off'-the-cuff' adj aus dem Stegreif
off'-the-rec'ord adj im Vertrauen
often ['ɔfən] adv oft, häufig; **every so o.** von Zeit zu Zeit; **quite o.** öfters
of'tentimes' adv oftmals
ogive ['odʒaɪv] s (diagonal vaulting rib) Gratrippe f; (pointed arch) Spitzbogen m
ogle ['ogəl] tr liebäugeln mit ‖ intr liebäugeln
ogre ['ogər] s Scheusal n; (myth) Menschenfresser m
oh [o] interj oh!; **oh, dear!** o weh!
ohm [om] s Ohm n
oil [ɔɪl] s Öl n; **strike oil** auf Öl stoßen ‖ tr ölen
oil' burn'er s Ölbrenner m
oil'can' s Ölkanne f
oil'cloth' s Wachsleinwand f
oil' col'or s Ölfarbe f
oil' drum' s Ölfaß n
oil' field' s Ölfeld n
oil' gauge' s Ölstandsanzeiger m
oil' heat' s Ölheizung f
oil' lev'el s Ölstand m
oil'man' s (–men') Ölhändler m
oil' paint'ing s Ölgemälde n
oil' pres'sure s Öldruck m
oil' rig' s Ölbohrinsel f
oil' shale' s Ölschiefer m
oil' slick' s Öllache f
oil' tank' s Ölbehälter m
oil' tank'er s Öltanker m
oil' well' s Ölquelle f
oily ['ɔɪli] adj ölig; (unctious) salbungsvoll
ointment ['ɔɪntmənt] s Salbe f
O.K. ['o'ke] adj in Ordnung, okay ‖ s Billigung f ‖ v (pret & pp **O.K.'d**; ger **O.K.'ing**) tr billigen ‖ intr okay!
old [old] adj alt; **as old as the hills** uralt; (said of a person) steinalt
old' age' s Alter n, Greisenalter n
old'-age' home' s Altersheim n
old' coun'try s Heimatland n
olden ['oldən] adj alt

old'-fash'ioned adj altmodisch
old' fog'(e)y ['fogi] s alter Kauz m
Old' Glo'ry s Sternenbanner n
old' hand' s alter Hase m
old' hat' adj bärtig
old' la'dy s Greisin f; (wife) (pej) Alte f
old' maid' s alte Jungfer f
old' man' s Greis m; (mil) Alter m
old' mas'ter s (paint) alter Meister m
old' moon' s letztes Viertel n
old' salt' s alter Seebär m
oldster ['oldstər] s alter Knabe m
Old' Tes'tament s Altes Testament n
old'-time' adj altväterisch
old'-tim'er s (coll) alter Hase m
old' wives'' tale' s Altweibergeschichte f
Old' World' s alte Welt f
oleander [,oli'ændər] s Oleander m
olfactory [ɑl'fæktəri] adj Geruchs–
oligarchy ['ɑlɪ,gɑrki] s Oligarchie f
olive ['ɑlɪv] s Olive f
ol'ive branch' s Ölzweig m
ol'ive grove' s Olivenhain m
ol'ive oil' s Olivenöl n
ol'ive tree' s Ölbaum m, Olivenbaum m
olympiad [o'lɪmpɪ,æd] s Olympiade f
Olympian [o'lɪmpɪ-ən] adj olympisch
Olympic [o'lɪmpɪk] adj olympisch ‖ **the Olympics** spl die Olympischen Spiele
omelet, omelette ['ɑmə,lɛt] s Eierkuchen m, Omelett n
omen ['omən] s Omen n, Vorzeichen n
ominous ['ɑmɪnəs] adj ominös, unheilvoll
omission [o'mɪʃən] s Auslassung f; (of a deed) Unterlassung f
omit [o'mɪt] v (pret & pp **omitted**; ger **omitting**) tr (a word) auslassen; (a deed) unterlassen; **be omitted** ausfallen; **o.** (ger) es unterlassen zu (inf)
omnibus ['ɑmnɪ,bʌs] adj Sammel–, Mantel– ‖ s Omnibus m, Autobus m
omnipotent [ɑm'nɪpətənt] adj allmächtig
omnipresent [,ɑmnɪ'prɛzənt] adj allgegenwärtig
omniscient [ɑm'nɪʃənt] adj allwissend
on [ɔn] adj (in progress) im Gange; (light, gas, water) an; (radio, television) angestellt; (switch) eingeschaltet; (brakes) angezogen; **be on to s.o.** j–n durchsehen; **be on to s.th.** über etw [acc] im Bilde sein ‖ adv weiter; **on and off** dann und wann; **on and on** in e–m fort ‖ prep auf (dat or acc), an (dat or acc); (concerning) über (acc)
once [wʌns] adv einmal; (formerly) einst; **at o.** auf einmal; (immediately) sofort; **not o.** nicht ein einziges Mal; **o. and for all** ein für allemal; **o. before** früher einmal; **o. in a while** ab und zu; **o. more** noch einmal; **o. upon a time there was** es war einmal ‖ s—**this o.** dieses (eine) Mal ‖ conj sobald
once'-o'ver s—**give** (s.o. or s.th.) **the o.** rasch mustern
one [wʌn] adj ein; (one certain, e.g.,

Mr. Smith) ein gewisser; **for one thing** zunächst; **her one care** ihre einzige Sorge; **it's all one to me** es ist mir ganz gleich; **one and a half hours** anderthalb Stunden; **one day** e–s Tages; **one more** noch ein; **one more thing** noch etwas; **one o'clock** ein Uhr, eins; **on the one hand ... on the other** einerseits ... andererseits ‖ *s* Eins *f* ‖ *pron* einer; **I for one** was mich betrifft, ich jedenfalls; **one after another** einer nach dem anderen; **one after the other** nacheinander; **one another** einander, sich; **one at a time, please!** einer nach dem anderen, bitte!; **one behind the other** hintereinander; **one by one** einer nach dem anderen; **one of these days** früher oder später; **one on top of the other** übereinander, aufeinander; **one to nothing** eins zu Null; **this one** dieser da, der da; **with one another** miteinander ‖ *indef pron* man; **one's** sein

one'-armed' *adj* einarmig
one'-eyed' *adj* einäugig
one'-horse town' *s* Kuhdorf *n*
one'-leg'ged *adj* einbeinig
onerous ['ɑnərəs] *adj* lästig
oneself' *reflex pron* sich; **be o.** sein, wie man immer ist; **by o.** allein; **to o.** vor sich [*acc*] hin
one'-sid'ed *adj* (& *fig*) einseitig
one'-track' *adj* eingleisig; (*fig*) einseitig
one'-way street' *s* Einbahnstraße *f*
one'-way tick'et *s* einfache Fahrkarte *f*
one'-week' *adj* achttägig
onion ['ʌnjən] *s* Zwiebel *f;* **know 'one's onions** (coll) Bescheid wissen
on'ionskin' *s* Durchschlagpapier *n*
on'look'er *s* Zuschauer –in *mf*
only ['onli] *adj* (*son, hope*) einzig ‖ *adv* nur; **not only ... but also** nicht nur ... sondern auch; **o. too** nur (all)zu; **o. too well** zur Genüge; **o. yesterday** erst gestern ‖ *conj* aber; **o. that** nur daß
on'ly-begot'ten *adj* eingeboren
onomatopoeia [ˌɑnəˌmætə'pi·ə] *s* Lautmalerei *f*
on'-ramp' *s* Zufahrtsrampe *f*
on'rush' *s* Ansturm *m*
on'set' *s* Anfang *m;* (*attack*) Angriff *m*
onslaught ['ɑnˌslɔt] *s* Angriff *m*
on'to *prep* auf (*acc*) hinauf; **be o. s.o.** hinter j–s Schliche kommen; **be o. s.th.** über etw [*acc*] im Bilde sein
onus ['onəs] *s* Last *f;* **o. of proof** Beweislast *f*
onward(s) ['ɑnwərd(z)] *adv* vorwärts
onyx ['ɑnɪks] *s* Onyx *m*
oodles ['udəlz] *spl* (coll) (**of**) Unmengen *pl* (von)
ooze [uz] *s* Sickern *n;* (*mud*) Schlamm *m* ‖ *tr* ausschwitzen ‖ *intr* sickern; **o. out** durchsickern
opal ['opəl] *s* Opal *m*
opaque [o'pek] *adj* undurchsichtig; (*stupid*) stumpf
open ['opən] *adj* (*window, position, sea, question, vowel*) offen; (*air, field, seat*) frei; (*business, office*)

geöffnet; (*seam*) geplatzt; (*account*) laufend; (*meeting*) öffentlich; **be o.** offenstehen; **get o.** aufbekommen; **have an o. mind about s.th.** sich noch nicht auf etw [*acc*] festgelegt haben; **keep o.** offenhalten; **lay oneself o. to** sich aussetzen (*dat*); **o. to** (*the public*) zugänglich (*dat*); (*criticism*) ausgesetzt (*dat*); (*doubt*) unterworfen (*dat*); **o. to bribery** bestechlich; **o. to question** strittig ‖ *s*—**come out into the o.** (fig) mit seinen Gedanken herauskommen; **in the o.** im Freien ‖ *tr* öffnen, aufmachen; (*a business, account, meeting, hostilities, fire*) eröffnen; (*a book*) aufschlagen; (*eyes in surprise*) aufreißen; (*a box, bottle*) anbrechen; (*an umbrella*) aufspannen; **o. the attack** losschlagen; **o. to traffic** dem Verkehr übergeben; **o. wide** weit aufreißen ‖ *intr* sich öffnen, aufgehen; (*said of a school, speech, play*) beginnen; **o. onto** hinausgehen auf (*acc*); **o. up** sich auftun; **o. with hearts** (cards) Herz ausspielen
o'pen-air' *adj* Freiluft–; (theat) Freilicht–; **o. concert** Konzert *n* im Freien
opener ['opənər] *s* Öffner *m*, **for openers** (coll) für den Anfang
o'pen-eyed' *adj* mit offenen Augen
o'pen-hand'ed *adj* freigebig
o'pen-heart'ed *adj* offenherzig
o'pen house' *s* allgemeiner Besuchstag *m*
o'pening *adj* (*scene*) erste; (*remarks*) Eröffnungs– ‖ *s* Öffnung *f;* (*of a speech, play*) Anfang *m;* (*of a store, etc.*) Eröffnung *f;* (*vacant job*) freie (or offene) Stelle *f;* (*in the woods*) Lichtung *f;* (*good opportunity*) günstige Gelegenheit *f;* (theat) Erstaufführung *f*
o'pening night' *s* Eröffnungsvorstellung *f,* Premiere *f*
o'pening num'ber *s* erstes Stück *n*
o'pen-mind'ed *adj* aufgeschlossen
openness ['opənnɪs] *s* Offenheit *f*
o'pen sea'son *s* Jagdzeit *f*
o'pen se'cret *s* offenes Geheimnis *n*
o'pen shop' *s* offener Betrieb *m* (für den kein Gewerkschaftszwang besteht)
opera ['ɑpərə] *s* Oper *f*
op'era glass'es *spl* Opernglas *n*
op'era house' *s* Opernhaus *n*
operate ['ɑpəˌret] *tr* (*a machine, gun*) bedienen; (*a tool*) handhaben; (*a business*) betreiben; **be operated by electricity** elektrisch betrieben werden ‖ *intr* (*said of a device, machine*) funktionieren, laufen; (surg) operieren; **o. on** (surg) operieren
operatic [ˌɑpə'rætɪk] *adj* opernhaft
op'erating costs' *spl* Betriebskosten *pl*
op'erating instruc'tions *spl* Bedienungsanweisung *f*
op'erating room' *s* Operationssaal *m*
op'erating ta'ble *s* Operationstisch *m*
operation [ˌɑpə'reʃən] *s* (*process*) Verfahren *n;* (*of a machine*) Bedie-

nung *f;* (*of a business*) Leitung *f;* (mil) Operation *f,* Aktion *f;* (surg) Operation *f;* **be in o.** (*said of a machine*) in Betrieb sein; (*said of a law*) in Kraft sein; **have** (or **undergo**) **an o.** sich e–r Operation unterziehen; **in a single o.** in e–m einzigen Arbeitsgang; **put into o.** in Betrieb setzen

operational [ˌɑpəˈreʃənəl] *adj* (*ready to be used*) betriebsbereit; (*pertaining to operations*) Betriebs– Arbeits–; (mil) Einsatz–, Operations–

opera'tions room' *s* (aer) Bereitschaftsraum *m*

operative [ˈɑpərətɪv] *adj* funktionsfähig, wirkend; **become o.** in Kraft treten ‖ *s* Agent –in *mf*

operator [ˈɑpəˌretər] *s* (*of a machine*) Bedienende *mf;* (*of an automobile*) Fahrer –in *mf;* (sl) Schieber –in *mf;* (telp) Telephonist –in *mf;* **o.!** (telp) Zentrale!

op'erator's li'cense *s* Führerschein *m*

operetta [ˌɑpəˈrɛtə] *s* Operette *f*

ophthalmologist [ˌɑfθəlˈmɑlədʒɪst] *s* Augenarzt *m,* Augenärztin *f*

ophthalmology [ˌɑfθəlˈmɑlədʒi] *s* Augenheilkunde *f,* Ophthalmologie *f*

opiate [ˈopiˌet] *s* Opiat *n;* (fig) Betäubungsmittel *n*

opinion [əˈpɪnjən] *s* Meinung *f;* **be of the o.** der Meinung sein; **give an o. on** begutachten; **have a high o. of** große Stücke halten auf (*acc*); **in my o.** meiner Meinung nach, meines Erachtens

opinionated [əˈpɪnjəˌnetɪd] *adj* von sich eingenommen

opin'ion poll' *s* Meinungsumfrage *f*

opium [ˈopiˌəm] *s* Opium *n*

o'pium den' *s* Opiumhöhle *f*

o'pium pop'py *s* Schlafmohn *m*

opossum [əˈpɑsəm] *s* Opossum *n*

opponent [əˈponənt] *s* Gegner –in *mf*

opportune [ˌɑpərˈt(j)un] *adj* gelegen

opportunist [ˌɑpərˈt(j)unɪst] *s* Opportunist –in *mf*

opportunity [ˌɑpərˈt(j)unɪti] *s* Gelegenheit *f*

oppose [əˈpoz] *tr* sich widersetzen (*dat*); (*for comparison*) gegenüberstellen; **be opposed to s.th.** gegen etw sein

oppos'ing *adj* (*team, forces*) gegnerisch; (*views*) entgegengesetzt

opposite [ˈɑpəsɪt] *adj* (*side, corner*) gegenüberliegend; (*meaning*) entgegengesetzt; (*view*) gegenteilig; **o. angle** (geom) Gegenwinkel *m;* **o. to** gegenüber (*dat*) ‖ *s* Gegensatz *m,* Gegenteil *n* ‖ *prep* gegenüber (*dat*)

op'posite num'ber *s* Gegenstück *n,* Gegenspieler –in *mf*

opposition [ˌɑpəˈzɪʃən] *s* Widerstand *m;* (pol) Opposition *f;* **meet with stiff o.** auf heftigen Widerstand stoßen; **offer o.** Widerstand leisten

oppress [əˈpres] *tr* unterdrücken

oppression [əˈprɛʃən] *s* Unterdrückung *f*

oppressive [əˈprɛsɪv] *adj* bedrückend

oppressor [əˈprɛsər] *s* Unterdrücker –in *mf*

opprobrious [əˈprobri·əs] *adj* schändlich

opprobrium [əˈprobri·əm] *s* Schande *f*

opt [ɑpt] *intr*—**opt for** optieren für

optic [ˈɑptɪk] *adj* Augen– ‖ **optics** *s* Optik *f*

optical [ˈɑptɪkəl] *adj* optisch

op'tical illus'ion *s* optische Täuschung *f*

optician [ɑpˈtɪʃən] *s* Optiker –in *mf*

op'tic nerve' *s* Augennerv *m*

optimism [ˈɑptɪˌmɪzəm] *s* Optimismus *m*

optimist [ˈɑptɪmɪst] *s* Optimist –in *mf*

optimistic [ˌɑptɪˈmɪstɪk] *adj* optimistisch

option [ˈɑpʃən] *s* (*choice*) Wahl *f;* (*alternative*) Alternative *f;* (ins) Option *f*

optional [ˈɑpʃənəl] *adj* wahlfrei; **be o.** freistehen

optometrist [ɑpˈtɑmɪtrɪst] *s* Augenoptiker –in *mf*

optometry [ɑpˈtɑmɪtri] *s* Optometrie *f*

opulent [ˈɑpjələnt] *adj* (*wealthy*) reich; (*luxurious*) üppig

or [ɔr] *conj* oder

oracle [ˈɔrəkəl] *s* Orakel *n*

oracular [oˈrækjələr] *adj* orakelhaft

oral [ˈorəl] *adj* mündlich

o'ral hygiene' *s* Mundpflege *f*

orange [ˈɔrɪndʒ] *adj* orange ‖ *s* Orange *f,* Apfelsine *f*

orangeade [ˌɔrɪndʒˈed] *s* Orangeade *f*

or'ange blos'som *s* Orangenblüte *f*

or'ange grove' *s* Orangenhain *m*

or'ange tree' *s* Orangenbaum *m*

orang-outang [oˈræŋuˌtæŋ] *s* Orang-Utan *m*

oration [oˈreʃən] *s* Rede *f*

orator [ˈɔrətər] *s* Redner –in *mf*

oratorical [ˌɔrəˈtɔrɪkəl] *adj* rednerisch

oratori·o [ɔrəˈtɔriˌo] *s* (**-os**) Oratorium *n*

oratory [ˈɔrəˌtori] *s* Redekunst *f*

orb [ɔrb] *s* Kugel *f;* (*of the moon or sun*) Scheibe *f*

orbit [ˈɔrbɪt] *s* Umlaufbahn *f;* **send into o.** in die Umlaufbahn schicken ‖ *tr* umkreisen

orbital [ˈɔrbɪtəl] *adj* Kreisbahn–

orchard [ˈɔrtʃərd] *s* Obstgarten *m*

orchestra [ˈɔrkɪstrə] *s* Orchester *n*

or'chestra pit' *s* Orchesterraum *m*

orchestrate [ˈɔrkɪˌstret] *tr* orchestrieren

orchid [ˈɔrkɪd] *s* Orchidee *f*

ordain [ɔrˈden] *tr* verordnen; (eccl) ordinieren, zum Priester weihen

ordeal [ɔrˈdil] *s* Qual *f;* (hist) Gottesurteil *n;* **o. by fire** Feuerprobe *f*

order [ˈɔrdər] *s* (*command*) Befehl *m;* (*decree*) Verordnung *f;* (*order, arrangement*) Ordnung *f;* (*medal*) Orden *m;* (*sequence*) Reihenfolge *f;* (architt, bot, zool) Ordnung *f;* (com) (**for**) Auftrag *m* (auf *acc*), Bestellung *f* (auf *acc*); (eccl) Orden *m;* (jur) Beschluß *m;* **according to orders** befehlsgemäß; **be in good o.** in gutem

Zustand sein; **be the o. of the day** (coll) an der Tagesordnung sein; **be under orders to** (inf) Befehl haben zu (inf); **by o. of** auf Befehl von (or genit); **call to o.** (a meeting) für eröffnet erklären; (reestablish order) zur Ordnung rufen; **in o.** (functioning) in Ordnung; (proper, in place) angebracht; **in o. of** geordnet nach; **in o. that** damit; **in o. to** (inf) um ... zu (inf); **make to o.** nach Maß machen; **of a high o.** von ausgezeichneter Art; **on o.** (com) in Auftrag; **o.!, o.!** zur Ordnung! **out of o.** (defective) außer Betrieb; (not functioning at all) nicht in Ordnung; (disarranged) in Unordnung; (parl) im Widerspruch zur Geschäftsordnung, unzulässig; **put in o.** in Ordnung bringen; **restore to o.** die Ordnung wiederherstellen; **you are out of o.** Sie haben nicht das Wort || tr (command) befehlen, anordnen; (decree) verordnen; (com) bestellen; **as ordered** auftragsgemäß; **o. around** herumkommandieren; **o. in advance** vor(her)bestellen; **o. more of** nachbestellen; **o. s.o. off** (e.g., the premises) j-n weisen von

or′der blank′ s Auftragsformular n
orderliness [′ɔrdərlɪnɪs] s (of a person) Ordnungsliebe f; (of a room, etc.) Ordnung f
orderly [′ɔrdərli] adj ordentlich || s (med) Krankenwärter m; (mil) Bursche m
or′derly room′ s (mil) Schreibstube f
or′der slip′ s Bestellzettel m
ordinal [′ɔrdɪnəl] adj Ordnungs– || s Ordnungszahl f
ordinance [′ɔrdɪnəns] s Verfügung f; (of a city) Verordnung f
ordinary [′ɔrdɪ‚neri] adj gewöhnlich; (member) ordentlich; **o. person** Alltagsmensch m || s Gewöhnliche n; (eccl) Ordinarius m; **nothing out of the o.** nichts Ungewöhnliches; **out of the o.** außerordentlich
ordination [‚ɔrdɪ′neʃən] s Priesterweihe f
ordnance [′ɔrdnəns] s Waffen und Munition pl; (arti) Geschützwesen n
ore [or] s Erz n
organ [′ɔrgən] s (means) Werkzeug n; (publication) Organ n; (adm, biol) Organ n; (mus) Orgel f
organdy [′ɔrgəndi] s Organdy m
or′gan grind′er s Drehorgelspieler m
organic [ɔr′gænɪk] adj organisch
organism [′ɔrgə‚nɪzəm] s Organismus m
organist [′ɔrgənɪst] s Organist –in mf
organization [‚ɔrgənɪ′zeʃən] s Organisation f
organizational [‚ɔrgənɪ′zeʃənəl] adj organisatorisch
organize [′ɔrgə‚naɪz] tr organisieren
organizer [′ɔrgə‚naɪzər] s Organisator –in mf
or′gan loft′ s Orgelbühne f
orgasm [′ɔrgæzəm] s Orgasmus m
orgy [′ɔrdʒi] s Orgie f

Orient [′ɔrɪ‚ənt] s Orient m || **orient** [′ɔrɪ‚ɛnt] tr orientieren
oriental [‚ɔrɪ′ɛntəl] adj orientalisch || **Oriental** s Orientale m, Orientalin f
orientation [‚ɔrɪ‚ən′teʃən] s Orientierung f; (of new staff members) Einführung f
orifice [′ɔrɪfɪs] s Öffnung f
origin [′ɔrɪdʒɪn] s Ursprung m; (of a person or word) Herkunft f
original [ə′rɪdʒɪnəl] adj ursprünglich; (first) Ur–; (novel, play) originell; (person) erfinderisch || s Original n
originality [ə‚rɪdʒɪ′nælɪti] s Originalität f
ori′ginal research′ s Quellenstudium n
ori′ginal sin s Erbsünde f, Sündenfall m
originate [ə′rɪdʒɪ‚net] tr hervorbringen || intr (from) entstehen (aus); **o. in** seinen Ursprung haben in (dat)
originator [ə′rɪdʒɪ‚netər] s Urheber –in mf
oriole [′ɔrɪ‚ol] s Goldamsel f, Pirol m
ormolu [′ɔrmə‚lu] s Malergold n
ornament [′ɔrnəmənt] s Verzierung f, Schmuck m || [′ɔrnə‚mɛnt] tr verzieren
ornamental [‚ɔrnə′mɛntəl] adj Zier–
ornamentation [‚ɔrnəmən′teʃən] s Verzierung f
ornate [ɔr′net] adj überladen; (speech) bilderreich
ornery [′ɔrnəri] adj (cantankerous) mürrisch; (vile) gemein
ornithology [‚ɔrnɪ′θalədʒi] s Vogelkunde f, Ornithologie f
orphan [′ɔrfən] s Waise f; **become an o.** verwaisen
orphanage [′ɔrfənɪdʒ] s Waisenhaus n
or′phaned adj verwaist; **be o.** verwaisen
or′phans′ court′ s Vormundschaftsgericht n
orthodox [′ɔrθə‚daks] adj orthodox
orthography [ɔr′θagrəfi] s Orthographie f, Rechtschreibung f
orthopedist [‚ɔrθə′pidɪst] s Orthopäde m, Orthopädin f
oscillate [′asɪ‚let] intr schwingen
oscillation [‚asɪ′leʃən] s Schwingung f
oscillator [′asɪ‚letər] s Oszillator m
osier [′oʒər] s Korbweide f
osmosis [as′mosɪs] s Osmose f
osprey [′aspri] s Fischadler m
ossi•fy [′asɪ‚faɪ] v (pret & pp –fied) tr verknöchern lassen || intr verknöchern
ostensible [as′tɛnsɪbəl] adj vorgeblich
ostentation [‚astən′teʃən] s Zurschaustellung f, Prahlerei f
ostentatious [‚astən′teʃəs] adj prahlerisch, prunksüchtig
osteopath [′astɪ‚ə‚pæθ] s Osteopath –in mf
osteopathy [‚astɪ′apəθi] s Osteopathie f
ostracism [′astrə‚sɪzəm] s Ächtung f; (hist) Scherbengericht n
ostracize [′astrə‚saɪz] tr verfemen
ostrich [′astrɪtʃ] s Strauß m
Ostrogoth [′astrə‚gaθ] s Ostgote m

other ['ʌðər] *adj* andere, sonstig; **among o. things** unter anderem; **every o. day** jeden zweiten Tag; **none o. than** he kein anderer als er; **on the o. hand** andererseits; **o. things being equal** unter gleichen Voraussetzungen; **someone or o.** irgend jemand; **some ... or o.** irgendein; **the o. day** unlängst ‖ *adv*—**o. than** anders als ‖ *indef pron* andere; **the others** die anderen

otherwise ['ʌðər ˌwaɪz] *adj* sonstig ‖ *adv* sonst; **I can't do o.** ich kann nicht umhin; **o. engaged** anderweitig beschäftigt; **think o.** anders denken

otter ['atər] *s* Otter *m;* (*snake*) Otter *f*

Ottoman ['atəmən] *adj* osmanisch ‖ **ottoman** *s* (*couch*) Ottomane *m;* (*cushioned stool*) Polsterschemel *m;* **O.** Osmane *m*

ouch [autʃ] *interj* au!

ought [ɔt] *aux* used to express obligation, e.g., **you o. to tell her** Sie sollten es ihr sagen; **they o. to have been here** sie hätten hier sein sollen

ounce [auns] *s* Unze *f*

our [aur] *poss adj* unser

ours [aurz] *poss pron* der uns(e)rige, der uns(e)re, uns(e)rer; **a friend of o.** ein Freund von uns; **this is o.** das gehört uns

ourselves [aur'sɛlvz] *reflex pron* uns; **we are by o.** wir sind doch unter uns ‖ *intens pron* selbst, selber

oust [aust] *tr* (**from**) verdrängen (aus); **o. from office** seines Amtes entheben

ouster ['austər] *s* Amtsenthebung *f*

out [aut] *adj*—**an evening out** ein Ausgehabend *m;* **be out** (*of the house*) ausgegangen sein; (*said of a light, fire*) aus sein; (*said of a new book*) erschienen sein; (*said of a secret*) enthüllt sein; (*said of flowers*) aufgeblüht sein; (*said of a dislocated limb*) verrenkt sein; (*be out of style*) aus der Mode sein; (*be at an end*) aus sein; (*be absent from work*) der Arbeit fernbleiben; (*be on strike*) streiken; **be out after s.o.** hinter j—m her sein; **be out for a good time** dem Vergnügen nachgehen; **be out on one's feet** (coll) erledigt sein; **be out ten marks** zehn Mark eingebüßt haben; **be out to** (*inf*) darauf ausgehen (or aus sein) zu (*inf*); **that's out** das kommt nicht in Frage; **the best thing out** das Beste, was es gibt ‖ *adv* (*gone forth; ended, terminated*) aus; **out of** (*curiosity, pity, etc.*) aus (*dat*); (*fear*) vor (*dat*); (*a certain number*) von (*dat*); (*deprived of*) beraubt (*genit*); **out of breath** außer Atem; **out of money** ohne Geld; **out of place** verlegt; (*not appropriate or proper*) unpassend; **out of the window** zum Fenster hinaus ‖ *s* (*pretext*) Ausweg *m;* **be on the outs with s.o.** mit j—m auf gespanntem Fuße sein ‖ *prep* aus (*dat*) ‖ *interj* (sport) aus!; **out with it!** heraus damit!

out' and away' *adv* bei weitem

out'-and-out' *adj* abgefeimt

out'-ar'gue *tr* in Grund und Boden argumentieren

out'bid' *v* (*pret* —**bid**; *pp* —**bid** & —**bidden**) *ger* —**bidding**) *tr* überbieten

out'board mo'tor *s* Außenbordmotor *m*

out'bound' *adj* nach auswärts bestimmt; (*traffic*) aus der Stadt fließend

out'break' *s* Ausbruch *m*

out'build'ing *s* Nebengebäude *n*

out'burst' *s* Ausbruch *m;* **o. of anger** Zornausbruch *m*

out'cast' *adj* ausgestoßen ‖ *s* Ausgestoßene *mf*

out'come' *s* Ergebnis *n*

out'cry' *s* Ausruf *m;* **raise an o.** ein Zetergeschrei erheben

out'-dat'ed *adj* zeitlich überholt

out'dis'tance *tr* hinter sich [*dat*] lassen

out'do' *v* (*pret* —**did**; *pp* —**done**) *tr* überbieten, übertreffen; **not to be outdone by s.o. in zeal** j—m nichts an Eifer nachgeben; **o. oneself in** sich überbieten in (*dat*)

out'door' *adj* Außen-

out'doors' *adv* draußen, im Freien ‖ *s*—**in the outdoors** im Freien

out'door shot' *s* (*phot*) Außenaufnahme *f*

out'door swim'ming pool' *s* Freibad *n*

out'door the'ater *s* Naturtheater *n*

out'door toil'et *s* Abtritt *m*

outer ['autər] *adj* äußere, Außen-

out'er ear' *s* Ohrmuschel *f*

out'er gar'ment *s* Überkleid *n*

out'ermost' *adj* äußerste

out'er space' *s* Weltall *n*, Weltraum *m*

out'field' *s* (baseball) Außenfeld *n*

out'fit' *s* (*equipment*) Ausrüstung *f;* (*set of clothes*) Ausstattung *f;* (*uniform*) Kluft *f;* (*business firm*) Gesellschaft *f;* (mil) Einheit *f* ‖ *v* (*pret* —**fitted**; *ger* —**fitting**) *tr* (*with equipment*) ausrüsten; (*with clothes*) neu ausstaffieren

out'flank' *tr* überflügeln, umfassen

out'flow' *s* Ausfluß *m*

out'go'ing *adj* (*sociable*) gesellig; (*officer*) bisherig; (*tide*) zurückgehend; (*train, plane*) abgehend

out'grow' *v* (*pret* —**grew**; *pp* —**grown**) *tr* herauswachsen aus; (fig) entwachsen (*dat*)

out'growth' *s* Auswuchs *m;* (fig) Folge *f*

out'ing *s* Ausflug *m*

outlandish [aut'lændɪʃ] *adj* fremdartig; (*prices*) überhöht

out'last' *tr* überdauern

out'law' *s* Geächtete *mf* ‖ *tr* ächten

out'lay' *s* Auslage *f*, Kostenaufwand *m* ‖ **out'lay'** *v* (*pret* & *pp* —**laid**) *tr* auslegen

out'let' *s* (*for water*) Abfluß *m*, Ausfluß *m;* (fig) (**for**) Ventil *n* (für); (com) Absatzmarkt *m;* (elec) Steckdose *f;* **find an o. for** (fig) Luft machen (*dat*); **no o.** Sackgasse *f*

out'line' *s* (*profile*) Umriß *m;* (*sketch*) Umrißzeichnung *f;* (*summary*) Grundriß *m;* **rough o.** knapper Umriß *m* ‖ *tr* umreißen out'live' *tr* überleben

out'look' *s* (*place giving a view*) Ausguck *m;* (*view from a place*) Ausblick *m;* (*point of view*) Anschauung *f;* (*prospects*) Aussichten *pl*

out'ly'ing *adj* Außen–

out'maneu'ver *tr* ausmanövrieren; (fig) überlisten

outmoded [‚aʊt'moʊdɪd] *adj* unmodern

out'num'ber *tr* an Zahl übertreffen

out'-of-bounds' *adj* (fig) nicht in den Schranken; (sport) im Aus

out'-of-court' set'tlement *s* außergerichtlicher Vergleich *m*

out'-of-date' *adj* veraltet

out'-of-door' *adj* Außen–

out'-of-doors' *adj* Außen– || *adv* im Freien, draußen || *s*—in the o. im Freien

out'-of-pock'et *adj*—o. expenses Barauslagen *pl*

out' of print' *adj* vergriffen

out'-of-the-way' *adj* abgelegen

out' of tune' *adj* verstimmt

out' of work' *adj* arbeitslos, erwerbslos

out'pace' *tr* überholen

out'pa'tient *s* ambulant Behandelte *mf*

out'patient clin'ic *s* Ambulanz *f*

out'play' *tr* überspielen

out'point' *tr* (sport) nach Punkten schlagen

out'post' *s* (mil) Vorposten *m*

out'pour'ing *s* (& fig) Erguß *m*

out'put' *s* (*of a machine or factory*) Arbeitsleistung *f;* (*of a factory*) Produktion *f;* (mech) Nutzleistung *f;* (min) Förderung *f*

out'rage' *s* Unverschämtheit *f;* (**against**) Verletzung *f* (*genit*) || *tr* gröblich beleidigen

outrageous [aʊt'redʒəs] *adj* unverschämt

out'rank' *tr* im Rang übertreffen

out'rid'er *s* Vorreiter *m*

outrigger [‚aʊt‚rɪɡər] *s* Ausleger *m;* (*of a racing boat*) Outrigger *m*

out'right' *adj* (*lie, refusal*) glatt; (*loss*) total; (*frank*) offen || *adv* (*completely*) völlig; (*without reserve*) ohne Vorbehalt; (*at once*) auf der Stelle; **buy o.** per Kasse kaufen; **refuse o.** glatt ablehnen

out'run' *v* (*pret* –ran; *pp* –run; *ger* –running) *tr* hinter sich [*dat*] lassen

out'sell' *v* (*pret & pp* –sold) *tr* e–n größeren Umsatz haben als

out'set' *s* Anfang *m*

out'shine' *v* (*pret & pp* –shone) *tr* überstrahlen

out'side' *adj* (*help, interference*) von außen; (*world, influence, impressions*) äußere; (*lane, work*) Außen– || *adv* draußen || *s* Außenseite *f,* Äußere *n;* **at the (very) o.** (aller–) höchstens; **from the o.** von außen || *prep* außerhalb (*genit*)

outsider [‚aʊt'saɪdər] *s* Außenstehende *mf;* (sport) Außenseiter *m*

out'size' *adj* übergroß || *s* Übergröße *f*

out'skirts' *spl* Randgebiet *n,* Stadtrand *m*

out'smart' *tr* überlisten

out'spo'ken *adj* freimütig

out'spread' *adj* (*legs*) gespreizt; (*arms, wings*) ausgebreitet

out'stand'ing *adj* hervorragend, profiliert; (*money, debts*) ausstehend

out'strip' *v* (*pret & pp* –stripped; *ger* –stripping) *tr* (& fig) hinter sich [*dat*] lassen

out'vote' *tr* überstimmen

outward ['aʊtwərd] *adj* äußerlich, äußere || *adv* auswärts, nach außen

outwardly ['aʊtwərdli] *adv* äußerlich

outwards ['aʊtwərdz] *adv* auswärts

out'weigh' *tr* an Gewicht übertreffen; (fig) überwiegen

out'wit' *v* (*pret & pp* –witted; *ger* –witting) *tr* überlisten

oval ['oʊvəl] *adj* oval || *s* Oval *n*

ovary ['oʊvəri] *s* Eierstock *m*

ovation [o'veʃən] *s* Huldigung *f,* Ovation *f*

oven ['ʌvən] *s* Ofen *m;* (*for baking*) Backofen *m*

over ['oʊvər] *adj* (*ended*) vorbei, aus; **it's o. with him** es ist vorbei mit ihm; **o. and done with** total erledigt || *adv*—**all o.** (*everywhere*) überall; (*on the body*) über und über; **children of twelve and o.** Kinder von zwölf Jahren und darüber; **come o.!** komm herüber!; **o.!** (*turn the page*) bitte wenden!; **o. again** noch einmal; **o. against** gegenüber (*dat*); **o. and above** obendrein; **o. and out!** (rad) Ende!; **o. and o. again** immer wieder; **o. in Europe** drüben in Europa; **o. there** dort, da drüben || *prep* (*position*) über (*dat*); (*motion*) über (*acc*); (*because of*) wegen (*genit*); (*in the course of, e.g., a cup of tea*) bei (*dat*); (*during; more than*) über (*acc*); **all o. town** (*position*) in der ganzen Stadt; (*direction*) durch die ganze Stadt; **be o. s.o.** über j–m stehen; **b. o. s.o.'s head** j–m zu hoch sein; **from all o. Germany** aus ganz Deutschland; **o. and above** außer (*genit*); **o. the radio** im Radio

o'veract' *tr & intr* (theat) übertreiben

o'verac'tive *adj* übermäßig tätig

overage ['oʊvər'edʒ] *adj* über das vorgeschriebene Alter hinaus

o'verall' *adj* Gesamt– || o'veralls' *spl* Monteuranzug *m;* (*trousers*) Überziehhose *f*

o'verambi'tious *adj* allzu ehrgeizig

o'veranx'ious *adj* überängstlich; (*overeager*) übereifrig

o'verawe' *tr* einschüchtern

o'verbear'ing *adj* überheblich

o'verboard' *adv* über Bord; **go o. about** sich übermäßig begeistern für

o'vercast' *adj* bewölkt, bedeckt; **become o.** sich bewölken || *s* Bewölkung *f*

o'vercharge' *s* Überteuerung *f;* (elec) Überladung *f* || o'vercharge' *tr* e–n Überpreis abverlangen (*dat*); (elec) überladen

o'vercoat' *s* Mantel *m,* Überrock *m*

o'ver·come' *v* (*pret* –came; *pp* –come)

tr überwältigen; **be o. with joy** vor Freude hingerissen sein

o'vercon'fidence *s* zu großes Selbstvertrauen *n*

o'vercon'fident *adj* zu vertrauensvoll

o'vercook' *tr* (*overboil*) zerkochen; (*overbake*) zu lange backen, zu lange braten

o'vercrowd' *tr* überfüllen; (*a room, hotel, hospital*) überbelegen

o'ver·do' *v* (*pret* –**did;** *pp* –**done**) *tr* übertreiben; **o. it** sich überanstrengen

o'verdone' *adj* (culin) übergar

o'verdose' *s* Überdosis *f*

o'verdraft' *s* Überziehung *f*

o'ver·draw' *v* (*pret* –**drew;** *pp* –**drawn**) *tr* überziehen

o'verdress' *intr* sich übertrieben kleiden

o'verdrive' *s* (aut) Schongang *m*

o'verdue' *adj* überfällig

o'ver·eat' *v* (*pret* –**ate;** *pp* –**eaten**) *intr* sich überessen

o'verem'phasis *s* Überbetonung *f*

o'verem'phasize *tr* überbetonen

o'veres'timate *tr* überschätzen

o'verexcite' *tr* überreizen

o'verexert' *tr* überanstrengen

o'verexer'tion *s* Überanstrengung *f*

o'verexpose' *tr* (phot) überbelichten

o'verexpo'sure *s* Überbelichtung *f*

o'verextend' *tr* übermäßig ausweiten

o'verflow' *s* (*inundation*) Überschwemmung *f;* (*surplus*) Überschuß *m;* (*outlet for surplus liquid*) Überlauf *m;* **filled to o.** bis zum Überfließen gefüllt || **o'verflow'** *tr* überfluten; **o. the banks** über die Ufer treten || *intr* überfließen

o'ver·fly' *v* (*pret* –**flew;** *pp* –**flown**) *tr* überfliegen

o'verfriend'ly *adj* katzenfreundlich

o'vergrown' *adj* überwachsen; (*child*) lang aufgeschossen; **become o.** (*said of a garden*) verwildern; **become o. with** überwuchert werden von

o'verhang' *s* Überhang *m* || **o'ver·hang'** *v* (*pret & pp* –**hung**) *tr* hervorragen über (*acc*); (*threaten*) bedrohen || *intr* überhängen

o'verhaul' *s* Überholung *f* || **o'verhaul'** *tr* (*repair; overtake*) überholen

o'verhead' *adj* (*line*) oberirdisch; (*valve*) obengesteuert || *adv* droben || *s* (econ) Gemeinkosten *pl,* laufende Unkosten *pl*

o'verhead door' *s* Federhubtor *n*

o'verhead line' *s* (*of a trolley*) Oberleitung *f*

o'ver·hear' *v* (*pret & pp* –**heard**) *tr* mitanhören; **be o.** belauscht werden

o'verheat' *tr* überhitzen; (*a room*) überheizen || *intr* heißlaufen

o'verindulge' *tr* verwöhnen || *intr* (**in**) sich allzusehr ergehen (in *dat*)

o'verkill' *s* Overkill *m*

overjoyed [ˌovər'dʒɔɪd] *adj* überglücklich

overland ['ovərˌlænd] *adj* Überland–; **o. route** Landweg *m* || *adv* über Land

o'verlap' *s* Überschneiden *n* || **o'verlap'** *v* (*pret & pp* –**lapped;** *ger* –**lapping**)

tr sich überschneiden mit || *intr* (& fig) sich überschneiden

o'verlap'ping *s* (& fig) Überschneidung *f*

o'verlay' *s* Auflage *f;* (*for a map*) Planpause *f;* **o. of gold** Goldauflage *f*

o'verload' *s* Überbelastung *f;* (elec) Überlast *f* || **o'verload'** *tr* überlasten; (*a truck*) überladen; (*in radio communications*) übersteuern; (elec) überlasten

o'verlook' *tr* (*by mistake*) übersehen; (*a mistake*) hinwegsehen über (*acc*); (*a view*) überblicken

overly ['ovərli] *adv* übermäßig

o'vernight' *adj*—**o. stop** Aufenthalt *m* von e–r Nacht; **o. things** Nachtzeug *n* || *adv* über Nacht; **stay o.** übernachten

o'vernight' bag' *s* Nachtzeugtasche *f*

o'verpass' *s* Überführung *f*

o'ver·pay' *v* (*pret & pp* –**paid**) *tr & intr* überbezahlen

o'verpay'ment *s* Überbezahlung *f*

o'verpop'ulat'ed *adj* übervölkert

o'verpop'ula'tion *s* Übervölkerung *f*

o'verpow'er *tr* (& fig) überwältigen

o'verproduc'tion *s* Überproduktion *f*

o'verrate' *tr* zu hoch schätzen

o'verreach' *tr* (*extend beyond*) hinausragen über (*acc*); (*an arm*) zu weit ausstrecken; **o. oneself** sich übernehmen

o'verrefined' *adj* überspitzt

o'verripe' *adj* überreif

o'verrule' *tr* (*an objection*) zurückweisen; (*a proposal*) verwerfen; (*a person*) überstimmen

o'verrun' *s* Überproduktion *f* || **o'ver·run'** *v* (*pret* –**ran;** *pp* –**run;** *ger* –**running**) *tr* überrennen; (*said of a flood*) überschwemmen; **o. with** (*weeds*) überwuchert von; (*tourists*) überlaufen von; (*vermin*) wimmeln von

o'versalt' *tr* versalzen

o'versea(s)' *adj* Übersee– || *adv* nach Übersee

o'ver·see' *v* (*pret & pp* –**saw;** *pp* –**seen**) *tr* beaufsichtigen

o'verse'er *s* Aufseher –in *mf*

o'versen'sitive *adj* überempfindlich

o'vershad'ow *tr* überschatten; (fig) in den Schatten stellen

o'vershoe' *s* Überschuh *m*

o'ver·shoot' *v* (*pret & pp* –**shot**) *tr* (& fig) hinausschießen über (*acc*)

o'versight' *s* Versehen *n;* **through an o.** aus Versehen

o'versimplifica'tion *s* allzu große Vereinfachung *f*

o'versize' *adj* übergroß || *s* Übergröße *f*

o'ver·sleep' *v* (*pret & pp* –**slept**) *tr & intr* verschlafen

o'verspe'cialized *adj* überspezialisiert

o'verstaffed' *adj* (mit Personal) übersetzt

o'verstay' *tr* überschreiten

o'ver·step' *v* (*pret & pp* –**stepped;** *ger* –**stepping**) *tr* überschreiten

o'verstock' tr überbevorraten
o'verstrain' tr überanstrengen
o'verstuffed' adj überfüllt; (furniture) überpolstert
o'versupply' s zu großer Vorrat m; (com) Überangebot n || o'versup·ply' v (pret & pp –plied) tr überreichlich versehen; (com) überreichlich anbieten
overt ['ovərt], [o'vʌrt] adj offenkundig
o'ver·take' v (pret –took; pp –taken) tr (catch up to) einholen; (pass) überholen; (suddenly befall) überfallen
o'vertax' tr überbesteuern; (fig) überfordern, übermäßig in Anspruch nehmen
o'ver-the-coun'ter adj (pharm) rezeptfrei; (st. exch.) freihändig
o'verthrow' s Sturz m || o'ver·throw' (pret –threw; pp –thrown) tr stürzen
o'vertime' adj Überstunden– || adv—work o. Überstunden arbeiten; work five hours o. fünf Überstunden machen || s Überstunden pl; (sport) Spielverlängerung f
o'vertired' adj übermüdet
o'vertone' s (fig) Nebenbedeutung f; (mus) Oberton m
o'vertrump' tr überstechen
overture ['ovərtʃər] s Antrag m; (mus) Ouvertüre f
o'verturn' tr umstürzen || intr umkippen; (aut) sich überschlagen
overweening [,ovər'winiŋ] adj hochmütig
o'verweight' adj zu schwer || s Übergewicht n; (of freight) Überfracht f
overwhelm [,ovər'whɛlm] tr (with some feeling) überwältigen; (e.g., with questions, gifts) überschütten; (with work) überbürden
o'verwhelm'ing adj überwältigend
overwind [,ovər'waɪnd] v (pret & pp –wound) tr überdrehen
o'verwork' s Überarbeitung f, Überanstrengung f || o'verwork' tr überfordern || intr sich überarbeiten
o'verwrought' adj überreizt

o'verzeal'ous adj übereifrig
ow [aʊ] interj au!
owe [o] tr schulden (dat), schuldig sein (dat); he owes her everything er verdankt ihr alles
ow'ing adj—it is o. to you that es ist dein Verdienst, daß; o. to infolge (genit)
owl [aʊl] s Eule f; (barn owl, screech owl) Schleiereule f
own [on] adj eigen || s—be left on one's own sich [dat] selbst überlassen sein; be on one's own auf eigenen Füßen stehen; come into one's own zu seinem Recht kommen; hold one's own sich behaupten; of one's own für sich allein; on one's own (initiative) aus eigener Initiative; (responsibility) auf eigene Faust || tr besitzen; (acknowledge) anerkennen; who owns this house? wem gehört dieses Haus? || intr—own to sich bekennen zu; own up to zugeben (dat)
owner ['onər] s Eigentümer –in mf
own'ership' s Eigentum n; (legal right of possession) Eigentumsrecht n; under new o. unter neuer Leitung
ox [ɑks] s (oxen ['ɑksən]) Ochse m
ox'cart' s Ochsenkarren m
oxfords ['ɑksfərdz] spl Halbschuhe pl
oxide ['ɑksaɪd] s Oxyd n
oxidize ['ɑksɪ ,daɪz] tr & intr oxydieren
oxydation [,ɑksɪ'deʃən] s Oxydation f
oxygen ['ɑksɪdʒən] s Sauerstoff m
oxygenate ['ɑksɪdʒə ,net] tr mit Sauerstoff anreichern
ox'ygen mask' s Sauerstoffmaske f
ox'ygen tank' s Sauerstofflasche f
ox'ygen tent' s Sauerstoffzelt n
oxytone ['ɑksɪ ,ton] adj oxytoniert || s Oxytonon n
oyster ['ɔɪstər] s Auster f
oys'ter bed' s Austernbank f
oys'ter farm' s Austernpark m
oys'ter·man s (–men) Austernfischer m
oys'tershell' s Austernschale f
oys'ter stew' s Austernragout n
ozone ['ozon] s Ozon n
O'zone layer' s Ozonschicht f

P

P, p [pi] s sechzehnter Buchstabe des englischen Alphabets
pace [pes] s Schritt m; (speed) Tempo n; at a fast p. in schnellem Tempo; keep p. with Schritt halten mit; put s.o. through his paces j–n auf Herz und Nieren prüfen; set the p. das Tempo angeben; (sport) Schrittmacher sein || tr (the room, floor) abschreiten; p. off abschreiten || intr—p. up and down (in) auf und ab schreiten (in dat)
pace'mak'er s Schrittmacher m
pacific [pə'sɪfɪk] adj pazifisch; the

Pacific Ocean der Pazifische (or Stille) Ozean || s—the Pacific der Pazifik
pacifier ['pæsɪ ,faɪ·ər] s Friedensvermittler –in mf; (for a baby) Schnuller m
pacifism ['pæsɪ ,fɪzəm] s Pazifismus m
pacifist ['pæsɪfɪst] s Pazifist –in mf
paci·fy ['pæsɪ ,faɪ] v (pret & pp –fied) tr (a country) befrieden; (a person) beruhigen
pack [pæk] s Pack m, Packen m; (of a soldier) Gepäck n; (of wolves, submarines) Rudel n; (of hounds) Meute

f; (*of cigarettes*) Päckchen *n,* Schachtel *f;* (*on pack animals*) Last *f;* (med) Packung *f;* **p. of cards** Spiel *n* Karten; **p. of lies** Lug und Trug || *tr* (*a trunk*) packen; (*clothes*) einpacken; (*seal*) abdichten; **p. in** (*above normal capacity*) einpferchen; **p. up** zusammenpacken || *intr* packen; **send s.o. packing** j-m Beine machen

package ['pækɪdʒ] *adj* (*price, tour, agreement*) Pauschal– || *s* Paket *n* || *tr* (ver)packen

pack'age deal' *s* Koppelgeschäft *n*

pack' an'imal *s* Packtier *n*

packet ['pækɪt] *s* Paket *n,* Päckchen *n;* (naut) Postschiff *n*

pack'ing *s* (*act*) Packen *n;* (*seal*) Dichtung *f;* (*wrapper*) Verpackung *f*

pack'ing case' *s* Packkiste *f*

pack'ing house' *s* Konservenfabrik *f*

pack'sad'dle *s* Packsattel *m*

pact [pækt] *s* Pakt *m;* **make a p.** paktieren

pad [pæd] *s* (*of writing paper*) Block *m;* (*ink pad*) Stempelkissen *n;* (*cushion*) Kissen *n;* (*of butter*) Stück *n;* (*under a rug*) Unterlage *f;* (*living quarters*) Bude *f;* (rok) Abschußrampe *f;* (sport) Schützer *m;* (surg) Bausch *m* || *v* (*pret & pp* **padded;** *ger* **padding**) *tr* (*e.g., the shoulders*) wattieren; (*writing*) ausbauschen

pad'ded cell' *s* Gummizelle *f*

pad'ding *s* Wattierung *f;* (coll) Ballast *m*

paddle ['pædəl] *s* (*of a canoe*) Paddel *n;* (*for table tennis*) Schläger *m* || *tr* paddeln; (*spank*) prügeln || *intr* paddeln

pad'dle wheel' *s* Schaufelrad *n*

paddock ['pædək] *s* Pferdekoppel *f;* (*at the races*) Sattelplatz *m*

pad'dy wag'on ['pædi] *s* (sl) Grüne Minna *f*

pad'lock' *s* Vorhängeschloß *n* || *tr* mit e-m Vorhängeschloß verschließen

paean ['pi·ən] *s* Siegeslied *n*

pagan ['pegən] *adj* heidnisch || *s* Heide *m,* Heidin *f*

paganism ['pegə‚nɪzəm] *s* Heidentum *n*

page [pedʒ] *s* Seite *f;* (*in a hotel or club; at court*) Page *m* || *tr* (*summon*) über den Lautsprecher (or durch Pagen) holen lassen || *intr*— **p. through** durchblättern

pageant ['pædʒənt] *s* Festspiel *n;* (*procession*) Festzug *m*

pageantry ['pædʒəntri] *s* Schaugepränge *n*

page'boy' *s* Pagenfrisur *f*

page' proof' *s* Umbruchabzug *m*

pagoda [pə'godə] *s* Pagode *f*

paid' in full' [ped] *adj* voll bezahlt

paid'-up' *adj*(*debts*) abgezahlt; (*policy, capital*) voll eingezahlt

pail [pel] *s* Eimer *m*

pain [pen] *s* Schmerz *m;* **on p. of death** bei Todesstrafe; **take pains** sich bemühen || *tr & intr* schmerzen || *impers*—**it pains me to** (*inf*) es fällt mir schwer zu (*inf*)

painful ['penfəl] *adj* schmerzhaft; (fig) peinlich

pain' in the neck' *s* (coll) Nervensäge *f*

pain'kill'er *s* schmerzstillendes Mittel *n*

painless ['penlɪs] *adj* schmerzlos

pains'tak'ing *adj* (*work*) mühsam; (*person*) sorgfältig

paint [pent] *s* Farbe *f;* (*for a car*) Lack *m* || *tr* (be)malen; (*e.g., a house*) (an) streichen; (*a car*) lackieren; (*with watercolors*) aquarellieren; (fig) schildern; **p. the town red** tüchtig auf die Pauke hauen || *intr* malen; (*with house paint*) überstreichen

paint'box' *s* Malkasten *m*

paint'brush' *s* Pinsel *m*

paint' can' *s* Farbendose *f*

painter ['pentər] *s* Maler –in *mf;* (*of houses, etc.*) Anstreicher –in *mf*

paint'ing *s* Malerei *f;* (*picture*) Gemälde *n*

paint' remov'er *s* Farbenabbeizmittel *n*

paint' spray'er *s* Farbspritzpistole *f*

pair [per] *s* Paar *n;* **p. of glasses** e–e Brille *f;* **a p. of gloves** ein Paar *n* Handschule; **a p. of pants** e–e Hose *f;* **a p. of scissors** e–e Schere *f;* **a p. of twins** ein Zwillingspaar *n;* **in pairs** paarweise || *tr* paaren; **p. off** paarweise ordnen; (coll) verheiraten || *intr*—**p. off** sich paarweise absondern

pajamas [pə'dʒɑməz] *s* Pyjama *m*

Pakistan ['pækɪ‚stæn] *s* Pakistan *n*

Pakista·ni [‚pækɪ'stæni] *adj* pakistanisch || *s* (**–nis**) Pakistaner –in *mf*

pal [pæl] *s* Kamerad *m* || *v* (*pret & pp* **palled;** *ger* **palling**) *intr*—**pal around with** dick befreundet sein mit

palace ['pælɪs] *s* Palast *m*

palatable ['pælətəbəl] *adj* (& fig) mundgerecht

palatal ['pælətəl] *adj* Gaumen– || *s* (phonet) Gaumenlaut *m*

palate ['pælɪt] *s* Gaumen *m*

palatial [pə'leʃəl] *adj* palastartig

Palatinate [pə'lætɪ‚net] *s* Rheinpfalz *f*

pale [pel] *adj* (*face, colors, recollection*) blaß; **turn pale** erblassen, erbleichen || *s* Pfahl *m* || *intr* erblassen; **pale beside** (fig) verblassen neben (*dat*)

pale'face' *s* Bleichgesicht *n*

Palestine ['pælɪs‚taɪn] *s* Palästina *n*

palette ['pælɪt] *s* Palette *f*

palisade [‚pælɪ'sed] *s* Palisade *f;* (*line of cliffs*) Flußklippen *pl*

pall [pɔl] *s* Bahrtuch *n;* (*of smoke, gloom*) Hülle *f* || *intr* (on) zuviel werden (*dat*)

pall'bear'er *s* Sargträger *m*

pallet ['pælɪt] *s* Lager *n*

palliate ['pælɪ‚et] *tr* lindern; (fig) bemänteln

pallid ['pælɪd] *adj* blaß, bleich

pallor ['pælər] *s* Blässe *f*

palm [pɑm] *s* (*of the hand*) Handfläche *f;* (*tree*) Palme *f;* **grease s.o.'s palm** j-n schmieren; **palm of victory** Siegespalme *f* || *tr* (*a card*) in der Hand verbergen; **palm s.th. off on s.o.** j-m etw andrehen

palmette [pæl'mɛt] *s* Palmette *f*
palmet·to [pæl'mɛto] *s* (**-tos** & **-toes**) Fächerpalme *f*
palmist ['pɑmɪst] *s* Wahrsager –in *mf*
palmistry ['pɑmɪstri] *s* Handlesekunst *f*
palm' leaf' *s* Palmblatt *n*
Palm' Sun'day *s* Palmsonntag *m*
palm' tree' *s* Palme *f*
palpable ['pælpəbəl] *adj* greifbar
palpitate ['pælpɪˌtet] *intr* klopfen
palsied ['pɔlzid] *adj* lahm, gelähmt
palsy ['pɔlzi] *s* Lähmung *f*
paltry ['pɔltri] *adj* armselig
pamper ['pæmpər] *tr* verwöhnen
pamphlet ['pæmflɪt] *s* Flugschrift *f*
pan [pæn] *s* Pfanne *f*; (sl) Visage *f* || *tr* (gold) waschen; (a camera) schwenken; (criticize sharply) (coll) verreißen || *intr* (cin) panoramieren; **pan out** glücken, klappen
panacea [ˌpænə'si·ə] *s* Allheilmittel *n*
Panama ['pænəmɑ] *s* Panama *n*
Pan'ama Canal' *s* Panamakanal *m*
Pan-American [ˌpænə'mɛrɪkən] *adj* panamerikanisch
pan'cake' *s* (flacher) Pfannkuchen *m* || *intr* (aer) absacken, bumslanden
pan'cake land'ing *s* Bumslandung *f*
panchromatic [ˌpænkro'mætɪk] *adj* panchɪomatisch
pancreas ['pænkrɪ·əs] *s* Bauchspeicheldrüse *f*
pandemic [pæn'dɛmɪk] *adj* pandemisch
pandemonium [ˌpændə'moni·əm] *s* Höllenlärm *m*
pander ['pændər] *s* Kuppler *m* || *intr* kuppeln; **p. to** Vorschub leisten (dat)
pane [pen] *s* Scheibe *f*
panegyric [ˌpænɪ'dʒɪrɪk] *s* Lobrede *f*
pan·el ['pænəl] *s* Tafel *f*, Feld *n*; (in a door) Füllung *f*; (for instruments) Schlattafel *f*; (of experts) Diskussionsgruppe *f*; (archit) Paneel *n*; (jur) Geschworenenliste *f* || *v* (pret & pp **-el[l]ed**; ger **-el[l]ing**) *tr* täfeln
pan'el discus'sion *s* Podiumsdiskussion *f*
pan'eling *s* Täfelung *f*
panelist ['pænəlɪst] *s* Diskussionsteilnehmer –in *mf*
pang [pæŋ] *s* stechender Schmerz *m*; (fig) Angst *f*; **pangs of conscience** Gewissensbisse *pl*; **pangs of hunger** nagender Hunger *m*
pan'han'dle *s* Pfannenstiel *m*; (geog) Landzunge *f* || *intr* (sl) betteln
pan'han'dler *s* (sl) Bettler –in *mf*
pan·ic ['pænɪk] *s* Panik *f* || *v* (pret & pp **-icked**; ger **-icking**) *tr* in Panik versetzen || *intr* von panischer Angst erfüllt werden
pan'ic-strick'en *adj* von panischem Schrecken erfaßt
panicky ['pænɪki] *adj* übernervös
panoply ['pænəpli] *s* Pracht *f*; (full suit of armor) vollständige Rüstung *f*
panorama [ˌpænə'ræmə] *s* Panorama *n*
pansy ['pænzi] *s* Stiefmütterchen *n*
pant [pænt] *s* Keuchen *n*; **pants** Hose

f, Hosen *pl* || *intr* keuchen; **p. for** or **after** gieren nach
pantheism ['pænθɪˌɪzəm] *s* Pantheismus *m*
pantheon ['pænθɪˌɑn] *s* Pantheon *n*
panther ['pænθər] *s* Panther *m*
panties ['pæntiz] *spl* Schlüpfer *m*
pantomime ['pæntəˌmaɪm] *s* Pantomime *f*
pantry ['pæntri] *s* Speisekammer *f*
pap [pæp] *s* Brei *m*, Kleister *m*
papa ['pɑpə] *s* Papa *m*, Vati *m*
papacy ['pepəsi] *s* Papsttum *n*
papal ['pepəl] *adj* päpstlich
Pa'pal State' *s* Kirchenstaat *m*
paper ['pepər] *adj* (money, plate, towel) Papier– || *s* Papier *n*; (before a learned society) Referat *n*; (newspaper) Zeitung *f*; **papers** (documents) Papiere *pl* || *tr* tapezieren
pa'perback' *s* Taschenbuch *n*, Pappband *m*
pa'per bag' *s* Papiertüte *f*, Tüte *f*
pa'perboy' *s* Zeitungsjunge *m*
pa'per clip' *s* Büroklammer *f*
pa'per cone' *s* Tüte *f*
pa'per cup' *s* Papierbecher *m*
pa'per cut'ter *s* Papierschneidemaschine *f*
pa'perhang'er *s* Tapezierer –in *mf*
pa'perhang'ing *s* Tapezierarbeit *f*
pa'pering *s* Tapezieren *n*
pa'per mill' *s* Papierfabrik *f*
pa'per nap'kin *s* Papierserviette *f*
pa'perweight' *s* Briefbeschwerer *m*
pa'perwork' *s* Schreibarbeit *f*
papier-mâché [ˌpepərme'ʃe] *s* Papiermaché *n*, Pappmaché *n*
paprika [pæ'prikə] *s* Paprika *m*
papy·rus [pə'paɪrəs] *s* (**-ri** [raɪ]) Papyrus *m*
par [pɑr] *s* (fin) Pari *n*; (golf) festgesetzte Schlagzahl *f*; **at par** pari, auf Pari; **on a par with** auf gleicher Stufe mit; **up to par** (coll) auf der Höhe
parable ['pærəbəl] *s* Gleichnis *n*
parabola [pə'ræbələ] *s* Parabel *f*
parachute ['pærəˌʃut] *s* Fallschirm *m* || *tr* mit dem Fallschirm abwerfen || *intr* abspringen
par'achute jump' *s* Fallschirmabsprung *m*
parachutist ['pærəˌʃutɪst] *s* Fallschirmspringer –in *mf*
parade [pə'red] *s* Parade *f* || *tr* zur Schau stellen || *intr* paradieren; (mil) aufmarschieren
paradigm ['pærədɪm], ['pærəˌdaɪm] *s* Musterbeispiel *n*, Paradigma *n*
paradise ['pærəˌdaɪs] *s* Paradies *n*
paradox ['pærəˌdɑks] *s* Paradox *n*
paradoxical [ˌpærə'dɑksɪkəl] *adj* paradox
paraffin ['pærəfɪn] *s* Paraffin *n*
paragon ['pærəˌgɑn] *s* Musterbild *n*
paragraph ['pærəˌgræf] *s* Absatz *m*, Paragraph *m*
parakeet ['pærəˌkit] *s* Sittich *m*
paral·lel ['pærəˌlɛl] *adj* parallel; **be (or run) p. to** parallel verlaufen zu || *s* Parallele *f*; (of latitude) Breiten-

kreis *m;* (fig) Gegenstück *n;* **without p.** ohnegleichen ‖ *v* (*pret & pp* **-lel[l]ed; ger -lel[l]ing**) *tr* parallel verlaufen zu; (*match*) gleichkommen (*dat*); (*correspond to*) entsprechen (*dat*)

par'allel bars' *spl* Barren *m*

paraly·sis [pə'rælɪsɪs] *s* (**-ses** [,siz]) Lähmung *f,* Paralyse *f*

paralytic [,pærə'lɪtɪk] *adj* paralytisch ‖ *s* Paralytiker –in *mf*

paralyze ['pærə,laɪz] *tr* lähmen, paralysieren; (*traffic*) lahmlegen

parameter [pə'ræmɪtər] *s* Parameter *m*

paramilitary [,pærə'mɪlɪ,teri] *adj* halbmilitärisch

paramount ['pærə,maunt] *adj* oberste; **be p. an erster Stelle stehen; of p. importance** von äußerster Wichtigkeit

paranoia [,pærə'nɔɪ·ə] *s* Paranoia *f*

paranoiac [,pærə'nɔɪ·æk] *adj* paranoisch ‖ *s* Paranoiker –in *mf*

paranoid ['pærə,nɔɪd] *adj* paranoid

parapet ['pærə,pet] *s* (*of a wall*) Brustwehr *f;* (*of a balcony*) Geländer *n*

paraphernalia [,pærəfər'nelɪ·ə] *s* Zubehör *n,* Ausrüstung *f*

paraphrase ['pærə,frez] *s* Umschreibung *f* ‖ *tr* umschreiben

parasite ['pærə,saɪt] *s* (& fig) Parasit *m*

parasitic(al) [,pærə'sɪtɪk(əl)] *adj* parasitisch

parasol ['pærə,sɔl] *s* Sonnenschirm *m*

paratrooper ['pærə,trupər] *s* Fallschirmjäger *m*

par·cel ['parsəl] *s* Paket *n;* (com) Posten *m* ‖ *v* (*pret & pp* **-cel[l]ed; ger -cel[l]ing**) *tr*—**p.** out aufteilen

par'cel post' *s* Paketpost *f*

parch [partʃ] *tr* ausdörren; **my throat is parched** mir klebt die Zunge am Gaumen

parchment ['partʃmənt] *s* Pergament *n*

pardon ['pardən] *s* Verzeihung *f;* (jur) Begnadigung *f;* **I beg your p.** ich bitte um Entschuldigung; **p.?** wie, bitte? ‖ *tr* (*a person*) verzeihen (*dat*); (*an act*) verzeihen; (*officially*) begnadigen

pardonable ['pardənəbəl] *adj* verzeihlich

pare [per] *tr* (*nails*) schneiden; (*e.g., potatoes*) (ab)schälen; (*costs*) beschneiden

parent ['perənt] *s* Elternteil *m;* **parents** Eltern *pl*

parentage ['perəntɪdʒ] *s* Abstammung *f*

parental [pə'rentəl] *adj* elterlich

parenthe·sis [pə'renθɪsɪs] *s* (**-ses** [,siz]) Klammer *f;* (*expression in parentheses*) Parenthese *f*

parenthetic(al) [,perən'θetɪk(əl)] *adj* parenthetisch

parenthood ['perənt,hud] *s* Elternschaft *f*

pariah [pə'raɪ·ə] *s* Paria *m*

par'ing knife' *s* Schälmesser *n*

Paris ['pærɪs] *s* Paris *n*

parish ['pærɪʃ] *adv* Pfarr– ‖ *s* Pfarrgemeinde *f*

parishioner [pə'rɪʃənər] *s* Gemeindemitglied *n,* Pfarrkind *n*

Parisian [pə'rɪʒən] *adj* Pariser ‖ *s* Pariser –in *mf*

parity ['pærɪti] *s* Parität *f*

park [park] *s* Park *m* ‖ *tr* abstellen, parken ‖ *intr* parken

park'ing *s* Parken *n;* **no p.** (public sign) Parken verboten

park'ing light' *s* Parklicht *n*

park'ing lot' *s* Parkplatz *m*

park'ing lot' atten'dant' *s* Parkplatzwärter –in *mf*

park'ing me'ter *s* Parkuhr *f*

park'ing place', park'ing space *s* Parkplatz *m,* Parkstelle *f*

park'ing tick'et *s* gebührenpflichtige Verwarnung *f* (wegen falschen Parkens)

park'way' *s* Aussichtsautobahn *f*

parley ['parli] *s* Unterhandlung *f* ‖ *intr* unterhandeln

parliament ['parləmənt] *s* Parlament *n*

parliamentary [,parlə'mentəri] *adj* parlamentarisch

parlor ['parlər] *s* Salon *m;* (*living room*) Wohnzimmer *n*

par'lor game' *s* Gesellschaftsspiel *n*

parochial [pə'roki·əl] *adj* Pfarr–; (fig) beschränkt

paro'chial school' *s* Pfarrschule *f*

paro·dy ['pærədi] *s* Parodie *f* ‖ *v* (*pret & pp* **-died**) *tr* parodieren

parole [pə'rol] *s* bedingte Strafaussetzung *f;* **be out on p.** bedingt entlassen sein ‖ *tr* bedingt entlassen

par·quet [par'ke], [par'ket] *v* (*pret & pp* **-queted** ['ked]; *ger* **-queting** ['ke·ɪŋ]) *tr* parkettieren

parquetry ['parkɪtri] *s* Parkettfußboden *m*

parrot ['pærət] *s* Papagei *m* ‖ *tr* nachplappern

par·ry ['pæri] *s* Parade *f* ‖ *v* (*pret & pp* **-ried**) *tr* parieren

parse [pars] *tr* zergliedern

parsimonious [,parsɪ'moni·əs] *adj* sparsam

parsley ['parsli] *s* Petersilie *f*

parsnip ['parsnɪp] *s* Pastinak *m*

parson ['parsən] *s* Pfarrer *m*

parsonage ['parsənɪdʒ] *s* Pfarrhaus *n*

part [part] *adv*—**p. ... p.** zum Teil ... zum Teil ‖ *s* Teil *m & n;* (*section*) Abschnitt *m;* (*spare part*) Ersatzteil *m;* (*of a machine, etc.*) Bestandteil *m;* (*share*) Anteil *m;* (*of the hair*) Scheitel *m;* (mus) Partie *f;* (theat) Rolle *f;* **do one's p.** das Seinige tun; **for his p.** seinerseits; **for the most p.** größtenteils; **have a p. in** Anteil haben an (*dat*); **in p.** zum Teil, teilweise; **make a p.** (*in the hair*) e-n Scheitel ziehen; **on his p.** seinerseits; **p. and parcel** ein wesentlicher Bestandteil *m;* **take p.** (in) teilnehmen (an *dat*); **take s.o.'s p.** j-s Partei ergreifen ‖ *tr* (ab)scheiden; (*the hair*) scheiteln; **p. company** von

einander scheiden || *intr* sich tren-
nen; **p. with** hergeben
par·take [pɑr'tek] *v* (*pret* **-took;** *pp*
taken) *intr*—**p. in** teilnehmen an
(*dat*); **p. of** zu sich nehmen
partial ['pɑrʃəl] *adj* Teil-, partiell;
(*prejudiced*) parteiisch; **be p. to** bevorzugen
partiality [‚pɑrʃɪ'ælɪti] *s* Parteilichkeit *f*, Befangenheit *f*
partially ['pɑrʃəli] *adv* teilweise
participant [pɑr'tɪsɪpənt] *s* Teilnehmer –in *mf*
participate [pɑr'tɪsɪ‚pet] *intr* (**in**) teilnehmen (an *dat*)
participation [pɑɪ‚tɪsɪ'peʃən] *s* (**in**)
Teilnahme *f* (*an* dat)
participle ['pɑrtɪ‚sɪpəl] *s* Mittelwort
n, Partizip *n*
particle ['pɑrtɪkəl] *s* Teilchen *n;* (gram,
phys) Partikel *f*
particular [pɑr'tɪkjələr] *adj* (*specific*)
bestimmt; (*individual*) einzeln; (*meticulous*) peinlich genau; (*especial*)
peinlich genau; (*choosy*) heikel || *s*
Einzelheit *f;* **in p.** insbesondere
partisan ['pɑrtɪzən] *adj* parteiisch || *s*
(mil) Partisan –in *mf;* (pol) Partei-
gänger –in *mf*
partition [pɑr'tɪʃən] *s* Teilung *f;* (*wall*)
Scheidewand *f* || *tr* (auf)teilen; **p. off**
abteilen
partly ['pɑrtli] *adv* teils, teilweise
partner ['pɑrtnər] *s* Partner –in *mf*
part'nership' *s* Partnerschaft *f*
part' of speech' *s* Wortart *f*
partridge ['pɑrtrɪdʒ] *s* Rebhuhn *n*
part'-time' *adj* & *adv* nicht vollzeitlich
part'-time work' *s* Teilzeitarbeit *f*
party ['pɑrti] *s* Gesellschaft *f*, Party *f;*
(jur) Partei *f;* (mil) Kommando *n;*
(pol) Partei *f;* (telp) Teilnehmer –in
mf; **be a p. to** sich hergeben zu
par'ty affilia'tion *s* Parteizugehörigkeit
f
par'ty line' *s* (pol) Parteilinie *f;* (telp)
Gemeinschaftsanschluß *m*
par'ty mem'ber *s* Parteigenosse *m*, Par-
teigenossin *f*
par'ty pol'itics *s* Parteipolitik *f*
paschal ['pæskəl] *adj* Oster–
pass [pæs] *s* (*over a mountain; permit*) Paß *m;* (*erotic advance*) An-
näherungsversuch *m;* (fencing) Stoß
m; (fb) Paßball *m;* (mil) Urlaubs-
schein *m;* (theat) Freikarte *f;* **make
a p. at** (*flirt with*) e–n Annäherungs-
versuch machen bei; (aer) vorbeiflie-
gen an (*dat*) || *tr* (*go by*) vorbeigehen
an (*dat*), passieren; (*a test*) bestehen;
(*a student in a test*) durchlassen; (*a
bill*) verabschieden; (*hand over*)
reichen; (*judgment*) abgeben; (*sentence*) sprechen; (*time*) verbringen;
(*counterfeit money*) in Umlauf bringen; (*a car*) überholen; (*e.g., a kidney stone*) ausscheiden; (*a ball*)
weitergeben; (**to**) zuspielen (*dat*); **p.
around** herumgehen lassen; **p. away**
(*time*) vertreiben; **p. in** einhändigen;
p. off as ausgeben als; **p. on** weiter-
leiten; (*e.g., news*) weitersagen; **p.**

out ausgeben; **p. over in silence** unerwähnt lassen; **p. up** verzichten auf
(*acc*) || *intr* (**by**) vorbeikommen (an
dat), vorbeigehen (an *dat*); (*in a car*)
(**by**) vorbeifahren (an *dat*); (*in a
test*) durchkommen; (*e.g., from father
to son*) übergehen; (cards) passen;
(parl) zustandekommen; **bring to p.**
herbeiführen; **come to p.** geschehen;
p.! (cards) passe!; **p. away** verschei-
den; **p. for** gelten als; **p. on** ab-
scheiden; **p. out** ohnmächtig werden;
p. over (*disregard*) hinweggehen über
(*acc*); **p. through** durchgehen (*durch*);
(*said of an army*) durchziehen
(durch); (*said of a train*) berühren
passable ['pæsəbəl] *adj* (*road*) gangbar; (*by car*) befahrbar; (*halfway
good*) leidlich, passabel
passage ['pæsɪdʒ] *s* Korridor *m*, Gang
m; (*crossing*) Überfahrt *f;* (*in a
book*) Stelle *f;* (*of a law*) Annahme
f; (*of time*) Ablauf *m;* **book p. for**
e–e Schiffskarte bestellen nach
pas'sageway' *s* Durchgang *m*, Passage *f*
pass'book' *s* Sparbuch *n*
passenger ['pæsəndʒər] *s* Passagier –in
mf; (*in public transportation*) Fahrgast *m;* (*in a car*) Insasse *m*, Insassin *f*
pas'senger car' *s* Personenkraftwagen
m
pas'senger plane' *s* Passagierflugzeug *n*
pas'senger train' *s* Personenzug *m*
passer-by ['pæsər'baɪ] *s* (**passers-by**)
Passant –in *mf*
pass'ing *adj* vorübergehend; **a p. grade**
die Note „befriedigend" || *s* (*act of
passing*) Vorbeigehen *n;* (*of a law*)
Verabschiedung *f;* (*of time*) Verstreichen *n;* (*dying*) Hinscheiden *n;*
in p. im Vorbeigehen; (*as under-
statement*) beiläufig; **no p.** (public
sign) Überholen verboten
passion ['pæʃən] *s* Leidenschaft *f;* (*of
Christ*) Passion *f;* **fly into a p.** in
Zorn geraten; **have a p. for** e–e
Vorliebe haben für
passionate ['pæʃənɪt] *adj* leidenschaft-
lich
pas'sion play' *s* Passionsspiel *n*
passive ['pæsɪv] *adj* (& gram) passiv
|| *s* Passiv(um) *n*
pass'key' *s* (*master key*) Hauptschlüssel
m; (*skeleton key*) Nachschlüssel *m*
Pass'o'ver *s* Passah *n*
pass'port *s* Paß *m*, Reisepaß *m*
pass'port of'fice *s* Paßamt *n*
pass'word' *s* (mil) Kennwort *n*
past [pæst] *adj* (*e.g., week*) vergangen;
(*e.g., president*) ehemalig, früher;
(*gone*) vorbei; **for some time p.** seit
einiger Zeit || *s* Vergangenheit *f* ||
prep (*e.g., one o'clock*) nach; (*beyond*) über (*acc*) hinaus; **get p.** (*an
opponent*) (sport) umspielen; **go p.**
vorbeigehen an (*dat*); **it's way p.
bedtime** es ist schon längst Zeit zum
Schlafengehen
paste [pest] *s* (*glue*) Kleister *m;* (culin)
Brei *m*, Paste *f* || *tr* (*e.g., a wall*)
(**with**) bekleben (mit); **p. on** aufkle-

ben auf (*acc*); **p. together** zusammenkleben

paste'board' *s* Pappe *f*

pastel [pæs'tɛl] *adj* pastellfarben ‖ *s* Pastell *n*

pastel' col'or *s* Pastellfarbe *f*

pasteurize ['pæstə‚raɪz] *tr* pasteurisieren

pastime ['pæs‚taɪm] *s* Zeitvertreib *m*

past' mas'ter *s* Experte *m*

pastor ['pæstər] *s* Pastor *m*

pastoral ['pæstərəl] *adj* Schäfer-, Hirten-; (eccl) Hirten-, pastoral ‖ *s* Schäfergedicht *n*

pas'toral let'ter *s* Hirtenbrief *m*

pastorate ['pæstərɪt] *s* Pastorat *n*

pastry ['pestri] *s* Gebäck *n;* **pastries** Backwaren *pl*

pas'try shop' *s* Konditorei *f*

past' tense' *s* Vergangenheit *f*

pasture ['pæstʃər] *s* Weide *f* ‖ *tr* & *intr* weiden

pas'ture land' *s* Weideland *n*

pasty ['pesti] *adj* (*sticky*) klebrig; (*complexion*) bläßlich

pat [pæt] *adj* (*answer*) treffend; **have s.th. down pat** etw in- und auswendig wissen ‖ *adv*—**stand pat** bei der Stange bleiben ‖ *s* Klaps *m;* (*of butter*) Klümpchen *n* ‖ *tr* tätscheln; **pat s.o. on the back** j-m auf die Schulter klopfen; (fig) j-n beglückwünschen

patch [pætʃ] *s* (*of clothing, land, color*) Fleck *m;* (*garden bed*) Beet *n;* (*for clothing, inner tube*) Flicken *m;* (*over the eye*) Binde *f;* (*for a wound*) Pflaster *n* ‖ *tr* flicken; **p. together** (& fig) zusammenflicken; **p. up** (*a friendship*) kitten; (*differences*) beilegen

patch'work' *s* Flickwerk *n;* (fig) Stückwerk *n*

patch'work quilt' *s* Flickendecke *f*

pate [pet] *s* (coll) Schädel *m*

patent ['petənt] *adj* öffentlich ‖ ['pætənt] *adj* Patent-, e.g., **p. lawyer** Patentanwalt *m* ‖ *s* Patent *n;* **p. pending** Patent angemeldet ‖ *tr* patentieren

pa'tent leath'er ['pætənt] *s* Lackleder *n*

pa'tent-leath'er shoe' *s* Lackschuh *m*

pat'ent med'icine ['pætənt] *s* rezeptfreies Medikament *n*

pat'ent rights' ['pætənt] *spl* Schutzrechte *pl*

paternal [pə'tʌrnəl] *adj* väterlich

paternity [pə'tʌrnɪti] *s* Vaterschaft *f*

path [pæθ] *s* Pfad *m;* (astr) Lauf *m;* **clear a p.** e-n Weg bahnen; **cross s.o.'s p.** j-s Weg kreuzen

pathetic [pə'θɛtɪk] *adj* (*moving*) rührend; (*evoking contemptuous pity*) kläglich

path'find'er *s* Pfadfinder *m;* (aer) Beleuchter *m*

pathologist [pə'θɑlədʒɪst] *s* Pathologe *m,* Pathologin *f*

pathology [pə'θɑlədʒi] *s* Pathologie *f*

pathos ['peθɑs] *s* Pathos *n*

path'way' *s* Weg *m,* Pfad *m*

patience ['peʃəns] *s* Geduld *f*

patient ['peʃənt] *adj* geduldig ‖ *s* Patient –in *mf*

pati·o ['pæti·o] *s* (**-os**) Terasse *f*

patriarch ['petri‚ɑrk] *s* Patriarch *m*

patrician [pə'trɪʃən] *adj* patrizisch ‖ *s* Patrizier –in *mf*

patricide ['pætrɪ‚saɪd] *s* (*act*) Vatermord *m;* (*person*) Vatermörder –in *mf*

patrimony ['pætrɪ‚moni] *s* väterliches Erbe *n*

patriot ['petri·ət] *s* Patriot –in *mf*

patriotic [‚petri'ɑtɪk] *adj* patriotisch

patriotism ['petri·ə‚tɪzəm] *s* Patriotismus *m*

pa·trol [pə'trol] *s* Patrouille *f,* Streife *f* ‖ *v* (*pret* & *pp* **-trolled;** *ger* **-trolling**) *tr* & *intr* patrouillieren

patrol' car' *s* Streifenwagen *m*

patrol'man *s* (**-men**) Polizeistreife *f*

patrol' wag'on *s* Gefangenenwagen *m*

patron ['petrən] *s* Schutzherr *m;* (com) Kunde *m,* Kundin *f;* (eccl) Schutzpatron *m*

patronage ['petrənɪdʒ] *s* Patronat *n*

patroness ['petrənɪs] *s* Schutzherrin *f;* (eccl) Schutzpatronin *f*

patronize ['petrə‚naɪz] *tr* beschützen, protegieren; (com) als Kunde besuchen; (theat) regelmäßig besuchen

pa'tronizing *adj* gönnerhaft

pa'tron saint' *s* Schutzheilige *mf*

patter ['pætər] *s* (*of rain*) Prasseln *n;* (*of feet*) Getrappel *n* ‖ *intr* (*said of rain*) prasseln; (*said of feet*) trappeln

pattern ['petərn] *s* Muster *n;* (sew) Schnittmuster *n*

patty ['pæti] *s* Pastetchen *n*

paucity ['pɔsɪti] *s* Knappheit *f*

paunch [pɔntʃ] *s* Wanst *m*

paunchy ['pɔnʃi] *adj* dickbäuchig

pauper ['pɔpər] *s* Arme *mf;* (*person on welfare*) Unterstützte *mf*

pause [pɔz] *s* Pause *f;* (mus) Fermate *f* ‖ *intr* pausieren

pave [pev] *tr* pflastern; **p. the way for** (fig) anbahnen

pavement ['pevmənt] *s* Pflaster *n;* (*sidewalk*) Bürgersteig *m,* Trottoir *n*

pavilion [pə'vɪljən] *s* Pavillon *m*

pav'ing *s* Pflasterung *f*

pav'ing stone' *s* Pflasterstein *m*

paw [pɔ] *s* Pfote *f* ‖ *tr* (*scratch*) kratzen; (coll) befummeln; **paw the ground** auf dem Boden scharren ‖ *intr* (*said of a horse*) mit dem Huf scharren

pawl [pɔl] *s* Sperrklinke *f*

pawn [pɔn] *s* Pfand *f;* (fig) Schachfigur *f;* (chess) Bauer *m* ‖ *tr* verpfänden

pawn'brok'er *s* Pfandleiher –in *mf*

pawn'shop' *s* Pfandhaus *n*

pawn' tick'et *s* Pfandschein *m*

pay [pe] *s* Lohn *m;* (mil) Sold *m* ‖ *v* (*pret* & *pp* **paid** [ped]) *tr* bezahlen; (*a visit*) abstatten; (*a dividend*) ausschütten; (*a compliment*) machen; **pay back** zurückzahlen; **pay damages** Schadenersatz leisten; **pay down** anzahlen; **pay extra** nachzahlen; **pay in advance** vorausbezahlen; **pay in full**

begleichen; **pay interest on** verzinsen;
pay off (*a debt*) abbezahlen; (*a per-son*) entlohnen; **pay one's way** ohne
Verlust arbeiten; **pay out** auszahlen;
pay s.o. back for s.th. j-m etw heim-zahlen; **pay taxes on** versteuern; **pay up** (*a debt*) abbezahlen; (ins) voll
einzahlen ‖ *intr* zahlen; (*be worth-while*) sich lohnen; **pay extra** zu-zahlen; **pay for** (*a purchase*) (be)-zahlen für; (*suffer for*) büßen
payable ['pe‧əbəl] *adj* fällig, zahlbar
pay' check' *s* Lohnscheck *m*
pay'day' *s* Zahltag *m*
pay' dirt' *s*—**hit p.** sein Glück machen
payee [pe'i] *s* (*of a draft*) Zahlungs-empfänger –in *mf;* (*of a check*)
Wechselnehmer –in *mf*
pay' en'velope *s* Lohntüte *f*
payer ['pe‧ər] *s* Zahler –in *mf*
pay'load' *s* Nutzlast *f;* (*explosive en-ergy*) Sprengladung *f*
pay'mas'ter *s* Zahlmeister *m*
payment ['pemənt] *s* Zahlung *f;* **in p. of** zur Bezahlung (*genit*)
pay' phone' *s* Münzfernsprecher *m*
pay' raise' *s* Gehaltserhöhung *f*
pay' rate' *s* Lohnsatz *m*
pay'roll' *s* Lohnliste *f;* (*money paid*)
gesamte Lohnsumme *f*
pay' sta'tion *s* Telephonautomat *m*
pea [pi] *s* Erbse *f*
peace [pis] *s* Friede(n) *m;* (*quiet*)
Ruhe *f;* **be at p. with** in Frieden
leben mit; **keep the p.** die öffent-liche Ruhe bewahren
peaceable ['pisəbəl] *adj* friedfertig
Peace' Corps' *s* Friedenskorps *n*
peace'-lov'ing *adj* friedliebend
peace'mak'er *s* Friedenstifter –in *mf*
peace' negotia'tions *spl* Friedensver-handlungen *pl*
peace' of mind' *s* Seelenruhe *f*
peace'pipe' *s* Friedenspfeife *f*
peace'time' *adj* Friedens– ‖ *s*—**in p. in** Friedenszeiten
peace' trea'ty *s* Friedensvertrag *m*
peach [pitʃ] *s* Pfirsich *m*
peach' tree' *s* Pfirsichbaum *m*
peachy ['pitʃi] *adj* (coll) pfundig
pea'cock' *s* Pfau *m*
pea'hen' *s* Pfauenhenne *f*
pea' jack'et *s* (nav) Matrosenjacke *f*
peak [pik] *adj* Spitzen– ‖ *s* (& fig)
Gipfel *m;* (*of a cap*) Mützenschirm
m; (elec) Leistungsspitze *f;* (phys)
Scheitelwert *m*
peak' hours' *spl* (*of traffic*) Hauptver-kehrszeit *f;* (elec) Stoßzeit *f*
peak' load' *s* (elec) Spitzenlast *f*
peak' vol'tage *s* Spitzenspannung *f*
peal [pil] *s* Geläute *n* ‖ *intr* erschallen
peal' of laugh'ter *s* Lachsalve *f*
peal' of thun'der *s* Donnergetöse *n*
pea'nut' *s* Erdnuß *f;* **peanuts** (coll)
kleine Fische *pl*
pea'nut but'ter *s* Erdnußbutter *f*
pear [per] *s* Birne *f*
pearl [pʌrl] *adj* Perlen– ‖ *s* Perle *f*
pearl' neck'lace *s* Perlenkette *f*
pearl' oys'ter *s* Perlenauster *f*
pear' tree' *s* Birnbaum *m*

peasant ['pεzənt] *adj* Bauern–, bäuer-lich ‖ *s* Bauer *m*, Bäuerin *f*
peasantry ['pεzəntri] *s* Bauernstand *m*
pea'shoot'er *s* Blasrohr *n*
pea' soup' *s* Erbsensuppe *f;* (fig)
Waschküche *f*
peat [pit] *s* Torf *m*
peat' moss' *s* Torfmull *m*
pebble ['pεbəl] *s* Kiesel *m;* **pebbles**
Geröll *n*
peck [pεk] *s* (*measure*) Viertelscheffel
m; (*e.g., of a bird*) Schnabelhieb *n;*
(*kiss*) (coll) flüchtiger Kuß *m;* (*of trouble*) (coll) Menge *f* ‖ *tr* hacken;
(*food*) aufpicken ‖ *intr* hacken,
picken; (*eat food*) picken; **p. at**
hacken nach; (*food*) (coll) herum-stochern in (*dat*)
peculation [ˌpεkjə'leʃən] *s* Geldunter-schlagung *f*
peculiar [pɪ'kjuljər] *adj* eigenartig,
absonderlich; **p. to** eigen (*dat*)
peculiarity [ˌpɪkjulɪ'ærɪti] *s* Eigenheit
f, Absonderlichkeit *f*
pedagogic(al) [ˌpεdə'gadʒɪk(əl)] *adj*
pädagogisch, erzieherisch
pedagogue ['pεdəˌgag] *s* Pädagoge *m*,
Erzieher *m*
pedagogy ['pεdəˌgadʒi] *s* Pädagogik *f*,
Erziehungskunde *f*
ped‧al ['pεdəl] *s* Pedal *n* ‖ *v* (*pret &
pp* –al[l]ed; *ger* –al[l]ing) *tr* fahren
‖ *intr* die Pedale treten
pedant ['pεdənt] *s* Pedant –in *mf*
pedantic [pɪ'dæntɪk] *adj* pedantisch
pedantry ['pεdəntri] *s* Pedanterie *f*
peddle ['pεdəl] *tr* hausieren mit ‖ *intr*
hausieren
peddler ['pεdlər] *s* Hausierer –in *mf*
pedestal ['pεdɪstəl] *s* Sockel *m*, Posta-ment *n;* **put s.o. on a p.** (fig) j–n
aufs Podest erheben
pedestrian [pɪ'dεstrɪ‧ən] *adj* Fuß-gänger–; (fig) schwunglos ‖ *s* Fuß-gänger –in *mf*
pediatrician [ˌpidɪ‧ə'trɪʃən] *s* Kinder-arzt *m*, Kinderärztin *f*
pediatrics [ˌpidɪ'ætrɪks] *s* Kinderheil-kunde *f*
pediment ['pεdɪmənt] *s* Giebelfeld *n*
peek [pik] *s* schneller Blick *m* ‖ *intr*
gucken; **p. at** angucken
peekaboo ['pikəˌbu] *adj* durchsichtig
‖ *interj* guck, guck!
peel [pil] *s* Schale *f* ‖ *tr* schälen; **p.
off** abschälen ‖ *intr* sich schälen;
(*said of paint*) abbröckeln; **p. off**
(aer) sich aus dem Verband lösen
peep [pip] *s* schneller Blick *m;* heim-licher Blick *m;* **not another p. out
of you!** kein Laut mehr aus dir! ‖
intr gucken; (*look carefully*) lugen;
p. out hervorlugen
peep'hole' *s* Guckloch *n*
peep' show' *s* Fleischbeschau *f*
peer [pɪr] *s* Gleichgestellte *mf* ‖ *intr*
blicken; **p. at** mustern
peerless ['pɪrlɪs] *adj* unvergleichlich
peeve [piv] *s* (coll) Beschwerde *f* ‖ *tr*
(coll) ärgern
peeved *adj* verärgert
peevish ['pivɪʃ] *adj* sauertöpfisch

peg [pɛg] *s* Pflock *m; (for clothes)* Haken *m; (e.g., of a violin)* Wirbel *m;* **take down a peg or two** ducken || *v (pret & pp* **pegged;** *ger* **pegging)** *tr* festpflocken; *(prices)* festlegen; *(throw)* (sl) schmeißen; *(identify)* (sl) erkennen
peg'board' *s* Klammerplatte *f*
Peggy ['pɛgi] *s* Gretchen *n,* Gretl *f & n*
peg' leg' *s* Stelzbein *n*
Pekin·ese [,pikɪ'niz] *s* **(–ese)** Pekinese *m*
pelf [pɛlf] *s* (pej) Mammon *m*
pelican ['pɛlɪkən] *s* Pelikan *m*
pellet ['pɛlɪt] *s* Kügelchen *n; (bullet)* Schrotkugel *f,* Schrotkorn *n*
pell-mell ['pɛl'mɛl] *adj* verworren || *adv* durcheinander
pelt [pɛlt] *s* Fell *n,* Pelz *m; (whack)* Schlag *m* || *tr* **(with)** bewerfen (mit); *(with questions)* bombardieren
pelvis ['pɛlvɪs] *s* Becken *n*
pen [pɛn] *s* Feder *f; (fountain pen)* Füllfederhalter *m; (enclosure)* Pferch *m; (prison)* (sl) Kittchen *n* || *v (pret & pp* **penned;** *ger* **penning)** *tr (a letter)* verfassen || *(pret & pp* **penned & pent;** *ger* **penning)** *tr*—**pen in** pferchen
penal ['pinəl] *adj* strafrechtlich, Straf–
pe'nal code' *s* Strafgesetzbuch *n*
penalize ['pinə,laɪz] *tr* bestrafen; (box) mit Strafpunkten belegen
penalty ['pɛnəlti] *s* Strafe *f; (point deducted)* (sport) Strafpunkt *m;* **under p. of death** bei Todesstrafe
pen'alty ar'ea *s* (sport) Strafraum *m*
pen'alty box' *s* Strafbank *f*
pen'alty kick' *s* Strafstoß *m*
penance ['pɛnəns] *s* Buße *f*
penchant ['pɛnʃənt] *s* **(for)** Hang *m* (zu)
pen·cil ['pɛnsəl] *s* Bleistift *m* || *v (pret & pp* **–cil[l]ed;** *ger* **–cil[l]ing)** *tr* mit Bleistift anzeichnen
pen'cil push'er *s* (coll) Schreiberling *m*
pen'cil sharp'ener *s* Bleistiftspitzer *m*
pendant ['pɛndənt] *s* Anhänger *m; (electrical fixture)* Hängeleuchter *m*
pendent ['pɛndənt] *adj* (herab)hängend
pend'ing *adj* schwebend; **be p.** in (der) Schwebe sein || *prep (during)* während *(genit); (until)* bis zu *(dat)*
pendulum ['pɛndʒələm] *s* Pendel *n*
pen'dulum bob' *s* Pendelgewicht *n*
penetrate ['pɛnɪ,tret] *tr* eindringen in *(acc)* || *intr* eindringen
penetration [,pɛnɪ'treʃən] *s* Durchdringen *n; (of, e.g., a country)* Eindringen *n* (in *acc*); *(in ballistics)* Durchschlagskraft *f*
penguin ['pɛŋgwɪn] *s* Pinguin *m*
penicillin [,pɛnɪ'sɪlɪn] *s* Penizillin *n*
peninsula [pə'nɪnsələ] *s* Halbinsel *f*
pe·nis ['pinɪs] *s* **(–nes** [niz] **& –nises)** Penis *m*
penitence ['pɛnɪtəns] *s* Bußfertigkeit *f*
penitent ['pɛnɪtənt] *adj* bußfertig || *s* Büßer –in *mf;* (eccl) Beichtkind *n*
penitentiary [,pɛnɪ'tɛnʃəri] *s* Zuchthaus *n*
pen'knife' *s* **(–knives')** Federmesser *n*

penmanship ['pɛnmən,ʃɪp] *s* Schreibkunst *f*
pen' name' *s* Schriftstellername *m*
pennant ['pɛnənt] *s* Wimpel *m;* (nav) Stander *m*
penniless ['pɛnɪlɪs] *adj* mittellos
penny ['pɛni] *s* Pfennig *m; (U.S.A.)* Cent *m*
pen'ny pinch'er [,pɪntʃər] *s* Pfennigfuchser *m*
pen' pal' *s* Schreibfreund –in *mf*
pension ['pɛnʃən] *s* Pension *f,* Rente *f;* **put on p.** pensionieren || *tr* pensionieren
pensioner ['pɛnʃənər] *s* Pensionär –in *mf;* (ins) Rentenempfänger –in *mf*
pen'sion fund' *s* Pensionskasse *f*
pensive ['pɛnsɪv] *adj* sinnend
pentagon ['pɛntə,gan] *s* Fünfeck *n;* **the Pentagon** das Pentagon
Pentecost ['pɛntɪ,kɔst] *s* Pfingsten *n*
penthouse ['pɛnt,haʊs] *s* Wetterdach *n; (exclusive apartment)* Penthouse *n*
pent-up ['pɛnt'ʌp] *adj* verhalten
penult ['pinʌlt] *s* vorletzte Silbe *f*
penurious [pɪ'nʊrɪ·əs] *adj* karg
penury ['pɛnjəri] *s* Kargheit *f*
peony ['pi·əni] *s* Pfingstrose *f*
people ['pipəl] *spl* Leute *pl,* Menschen *pl;* **his p.** die Seinen; **p. like him** seinesgleichen; **p. say** man sagt, die Leute sagen || *s* **(peoples)** Volk *n* || *tr* bevölkern
pep [pɛp] *s* (coll) Schwungkraft *f* || *v (pret & pp* **pepped;** *ger* **pepping)** *tr*— **pep up** aufpulvern
pepper ['pɛpər] *s (spice)* Pfeffer *m; (plant)* Paprika *f; (vegetable)* Paprikaschote *f* || *tr* pfeffern
pep'per mill' *s* Pfeffermühle *f*
pep'permint' *adj* Pfefferminz– || *s* Pfefferminze *f*
pep'per shak'er *s* Pfefferstreuer *m*
peppery ['pɛpəri] *adj* pfefferig
per [pʌr] *prep* pro *(acc);* **as per** laut *(genit & dat)*
perambulator [pər'æmbjə,letər] *s* Kinderwagen *m*
per capita [pər'kæpɪtə] pro Kopf
perceivable [pər'sivəbəl] *adj* wahrnehmbar
perceive [pər'siv] *tr* wahrnehmen
percent [pər'sɛnt] *s* Prozent *n*
percentage [pər'sɛntɪdʒ] *s* Prozentsatz *m;* **p. of** *(e.g., the profit)* Anteil *m* an *(dat); (e.g., of a group)* Teil *m (genit)*
perceptible [pər'sɛptəbəl] *adj* wahrnehmbar
perception [pər'sɛpʃən] *s* Wahrnehmung *f*
perch [pʌrtʃ] *s* Stange *f;* (ichth) Barsch *m* || *tr* setzen || *intr* sitzen
percolate ['pʌrkə,let] *tr* durchseihen; *(coffee)* perkolieren || *intr* durchsickern
percolator ['pʌrkə,letər] *s* Perkolator *m*
percussion [pər'kʌʃən] *s* Schlag *m;* (med) Perkussion *f*
percus'sion in'strument *s* Schlaginstrument *n*

per di'em allow'ance [pər'daɪ·əm] s Tagegeld n
perdition [pər'dɪʃən] s Verdammnis f
perennial [pə'renɪ·əl] adj immerwährend; (bot) ausdauernd ‖ s ausdauernde Pflanze f
perfect ['pʌrfɪkt] adj perfekt, vollkommen; **he is a p. stranger to me** er ist mir völlig fremd ‖ s (gram) Perfekt(um) n ‖ [pər'fɛkt] tr vervollkommen
perfection [pər'fɛkʃən] s Vollkommenheit f; **to p.** vollkommen
perfectionist [pər'fɛkʃənɪst] s Perfektionist –in mf
perfectly ['pʌrfɪktli] adv völlig, durchaus; **p. well** ganz genau
perfidious [pər'fɪdɪ·əs] adj treulos
perfidy ['pʌrfɪdi] s Treubruch m
perforate ['pʌrfə‚ret] tr durchlöchern
per'forated line' s durchlochte Linie f
perforation [‚pʌrfə'reʃən] s gelochte Linie f
perforce [pər'fors] adv notgedrungen
perform [pər'fɔrm] tr ausführen; (an operation) vornehmen; (theat) aufführen ‖ intr (öffentlich) auftreten; (mach) funktionieren
performance [pər'fɔrməns] s Ausführung f; (mach) Leistung f; (theat) Aufführung f
performer [pər'fɔrmər] s Künstler –in mf
perform'ing arts' spl darstellende Künste pl
perfume [pər'fjum] s Parfüm n ‖ tr parfümieren
perfunctorily [pər'fʌŋktərɪli] adv oberflächlich
perfunctory [pər'fʌŋktəri] adj oberflächlich
perhaps [pər'hæps] adv vielleicht
per hour' pro Stunde, in der Stunde
peril ['pɛrɪl] s Gefahr f; **at one's own p.** auf eigene Gefahr
perilous ['pɛrɪləs] adj gefährlich
perimeter [pə'rɪmɪtər] s (math) Umfang m; (mil) Rand m
period ['pɪrɪ·əd] s Periode f, Zeitabschnitt m; (menstrual period) Periode f; (educ) Stunde f; (gram) Punkt m; (sport) Viertel n; **extra p.** (sport) Verlängerung f; **for a p. of** für die Dauer von; **p.!** und damit punktum!; **p. of grace** Frist f; **p. of life** Lebensalter n; **p. of time** Zeitdauer pl
pe'riod fur'niture s Stilmöbel pl
periodic [‚pɪrɪ'adɪk] adj zeitweilig
periodical [‚pɪrɪ'adɪkəl] s Zeitschrift f
peripheral [pə'rɪfərəl] adj peripher
periphery [pə'rɪfəri] s Peripherie f
periscope ['pɛrɪ‚skop] s Periskop n
perish ['pɛrɪʃ] intr umkommen; (said of wares) verderben
perishable ['pɛrɪʃəbəl] adj vergänglich; (food) leicht verderblich
perjure ['pʌrdʒər] tr—**p. oneself** Meineid begehen
perjury ['pʌrdʒəri] s Meineid m; **commit p.** e–n Meineid leisten
perk [pʌrk] tr—**p. up** (the head) aufwerfen; (the ears) spitzen ‖ intr

(percolate) (coll) perkolieren; **p. up** lebhaft werden
permanence ['pʌrmənəns] s Dauer f
permanent ['pʌrmənənt] adj (fort)dauernd, bleibend ‖ s Dauerwelle f
per'manent address' s ständiger Wohnort m
per'manent job' s Dauerstellung f
per'manent wave' s Dauerwelle f
permeable ['pʌrmɪ·əbəl] adj durchlässig
permeate ['pʌrmɪ‚et] tr durchdringen ‖ intr durchsickern
permissible [pər'mɪsɪbəl] adj zulässig
permission [pər'mɪʃən] s Erlaubnis f; **with your p.** mit Verlaub
permissive [pər'mɪsɪv] adj nachsichtig
per·mit ['pʌrmɪt] s Erlaubnis f; (document) Erlaubnisschein m ‖ [pər'mɪt] v (pret & pp –mitted; ger –mitting) tr erlauben, gestatten; **be permitted to** (inf) dürfen (inf)
permute [pər'mjut] tr umsetzen; (math) permutieren
pernicious [pər'nɪʃəs] adj (to) schädlich (für)
perox'ide blonde' [pə'raksaɪd] s Wasserstoffblondine f
perpendicular [‚pʌrpən'dɪkjələr] adj senkrecht ‖ s Senkrechte f
perpetrate ['pʌrpɪ‚tret] tr verüben
perpetual [pər'pɛtʃʊ·əl] adj (everlasting) ewig; (continual) unaufhörlich
perpetuate [pər'pɛtʃʊ‚et] tr verewigen
perplex [pər'plɛks] tr verblüffen
perplexed' adj verblüfft
perplexity [pər'plɛksɪti] s Verblüffung f
persecute ['pʌrsɪ‚kjut] tr verfolgen
persecution [‚pʌrsɪ'kjuʃən] s Verfolgung f
persecutor ['pʌrsɪ‚kjutər] s Verfolger –in mf
perseverance [‚pʌrsɪ'vɪrəns] s Ausdauer f, Beharrlichkeit f
persevere [‚pʌrsɪ'vɪr] intr ausdauern; **p. in** (cling to) beharren auf (acc); (e.g., efforts, studies) fortfahren mit
Persia ['pʌrʒə] s Persien n
Persian ['pʌrʒən] adj persisch ‖ s Perser –in mf; (language) Persisch n
Per'sian rug' s Perserteppich m
persimmon [pər'sɪmən] s Persimone f
persist [pər'sɪst] intr andauern; **p. in** verbleiben bei
persistent [pər'sɪstənt] adj andauernd
person ['pʌrsən] s Person f; **in p.** persönlich; **per p.** pro Person
personable ['pʌrsənəbəl] adj (attractive) ansehnlich; (good-natured) verträglich
personage ['pʌrsənɪdʒ] s Persönlichkeit f
personal ['pʌrsənəl] adj persönlich; (private) Privat–; **become p.** anzüglich werden
per'sonal da'ta spl Personalien pl
per'sonal hygiene' s Körperpflege f
per'sonal in'jury s Personenschaden m
personality [‚pʌrsə'nælɪti] s Persönlichkeit f
personally ['pʌrsənəli] adv persönlich

per'sonal pro'noun *s* Personalprono-
men *n*
personi•fy [pər'sɑnɪ ˌfɑɪ] *v* (*pret & pp*
–fied) *tr* personifizieren, verkörpern
personnel [ˌpʌrsə'nɛl] *s* Personal *n*
per'son-to-per'son call' *s* Gespräch *n*
mit Voranmeldung
perspective [pər'spɛktɪv] *s* Perspektive
f
perspicacious [ˌpʌrspɪ'keʃəs] *adj*
scharfsinnig
perspiration [ˌpʌrspɪ'reʃən] *s* Schweiß
m; (*perspiring*) Schwitzen *n*
perspire [pər'spɑɪr] *intr* schwitzen
persuade [pər'swed] *tr* überreden
persuasion [pər'weʒən] *s* Überredung
f
persuasive [pər'swesɪv] *adj* redegewandt
pert [pʌrt] *adj* keck; (*sprightly*) lebhaft
pertain [pər'ten] *intr*—p. to betreffen,
sich beziehen auf (*acc*)
pertinacious [ˌpʌrtɪ'neʃəs] *adj* beharrlich
pertinent ['pʌrtɪnənt] *adj* einschlägig;
be p. to sich beziehen auf (*acc*)
perturb [pər'tʌrb] *tr* beunruhigen
peruse [pə'ruz] *tr* sorgfältig durchlesen
pervade [pər'ved] *tr* durchdringen
perverse [pər'vʌrs] *adj* (*abnormal*)
pervers; (*obstinate*) verstockt
perversion [pər'vʌrʒən] *s* Perversion *f*;
(*of truth*) Verdrehung *f*
perversity [pər'vʌrsɪti] *s* Perversität *f*
pervert ['pʌrvərt] *s* perverser Mensch
m || [pər'vʌrt] *tr* (*corrupt*) verder-
ben; (*twist*) verdrehen; (*misapply*)
mißbrauchen
pesky ['pɛski] *adj* (coll) lästig
pessimism ['pɛsɪ ˌmɪzəm] *s* Pessimis-
mus *m*
pessimist ['pɛsɪmɪst] *s* Pessimist –in
mf
pessimistic [ˌpɛsɪ'mɪstɪk] *adj* pessimistisch
pest [pɛst] *s* (*insect*) Schädling *m*; (*annoying person*) Plagegeist *m*; (*pestilence*) Pest *f*
pest' control' *s* Schädlingsbekämpfung
f
pester ['pɛstər] *tr* piesacken; (*with
questions*) belästigen
pesticide ['pɛstɪ ˌsɑɪd] *s* Pestizid *n*
pestilence ['pɛstɪləns] *s* Pestilenz *f*
pestle ['pɛsəl] *s* Stößel *m*
pet [pɛt] *adj* Lieblings– || *s* (*animal*)
Haustier *n*; (*person*) Liebling *m*;
(*favorite child*) Schoßkind *n* || *v*
(*pret & pp* **petted; *ger* petting**) *tr*
streicheln || *intr* sich abknutschen
petal ['pɛtəl] *s* Blumenblatt *n*
Peter ['pitər] *s* Peter *m* || *intr*—peter
out im Sande verlaufen
pet' ide'a *s* Lieblingsgedanke *m*
petition [pɪ'tɪʃən] *s* Eingabe *f*; (jur)
Gesuch *n* || *tr* (*s.o.*) ersuchen
pet' name' *s* Kosename *m*
petri•fy ['pɛtrɪ ˌfɑɪ] *v* (*pret & pp* –fied)
tr (& fig) versteinern; **be petrified**
versteinern; (fig) zu Stein werden

petroleum [pə'trolɪ-əm] *s* Petroleum *n*
pet' shop' *s* Tierhandlung *f*
petticoat ['pɛtɪ ˌkot] *s* Unterrock *m*
pet'ting *s* Petting *n*
petty ['pɛti] *adj* klein, geringfügig;
(*narrow*) engstirnig
pet'ty cash' *s* Handkasse *f*
pet'ty lar'ceny *s* geringer Diebstahl *m*
pet'ty of'ficer *s* (nav) Bootsmann *m*
petulant ['pɛtjələnt] *adj* verdrießlich
petunia [pə't(j)unɪ-ə] *s* Petunie *f*
pew [pju] *s* Bank *f*, Kirchenstuhl *m*
pewter ['pjutər] *s* Weißmetall *n*
Pfc. ['pi'ɛf'si] *s* (**private first class**)
Gefreiter *m*
phalanx ['fælæŋks] *s* Phalanx *f*
phantasm ['fæntæzəm] *s* Trugbild *n*
phantom ['fæntəm] *s* Phantom *n*
Pharaoh ['fero] *s* Pharao *m*
Pharisee ['færi ˌsi] *s* Pharisäer *m*
pharmaceutical [ˌfɑrmə'sutɪkəl] *adj*
pharmazeutisch
pharmacist ['fɑrməsɪst] *s* Apotheker
–in *mf*
pharmacy ['fɑrməsi] *s* Apotheke *f*;
(*science*) Pharmazie *f*
pharynx ['færɪŋks] *s* Rachenhöhle *f*
phase [fez] *s* Phase *f* || *tr* in Phasen
einteilen; **p. out** abwickeln
pheasant ['fɛzənt] *s* Fasan *m*
phenobarbital [ˌfino'bɑrbɪ ˌtæl] *s*
Phenobarbital *n*
phenomenal [fɪ'nɑmɪnəl] *adj* phänomenal
phenome•non [fɪ'nɑmɪ ˌnɑn] *s* (**–na**
[nə]) (& fig) Phänomen *n*, Erscheinung *f*
phial ['fɑɪ-əl] *s* Phiole *f*
philanderer [fɪ'lændərər] *s* Schürzenjäger *m*
philanthropist [fɪ'lænθrəpɪst] *s* Men-
schenfreund –in *mf*, Philanthrop –in
mf
philanthropy [fɪ'lænθrəpi] *s* Menschen-
liebe *f*, Philanthropie *f*
philately [fɪ'lætəli] *s* Briefmarken-
kunde *f*
Philippine ['fɪlɪ ˌpin] *adj* philippinisch
|| **the Philippines** *spl* die Philippinen
Philistine ['fɪlɪstin] *adj* (& fig) phi-
listerhaft || *s* (& fig) Philister *m*
philologist [fɪ'lɑlədʒɪst] *s* Philologe *m*,
Philologin *f*
philology [fɪ'lɑlədʒi] *s* Philologie *f*
philosopher [fɪ'lɑsəfər] *s* Philosoph *m*
philosophic(al) [ˌfɪlə'sɑfɪk(əl)] *adj*
philosophisch
philosophy [fɪ'lɑsəfi] *s* Philosophie *f*
phlebitis [flɪ'bɑɪtɪs] *s* Venenentzün-
dung *f*
phlegm [flɛm] *s* Schleim *m*
phlegmatic(al) [flɛg'mætɪk(əl)] *adj*
phlegmatisch
phobia ['fobɪ-ə] *s* Phobie *f*
Phoenicia [fɪ'nɪʃə] *s* Phönizien *n*
Phoenician [fɪ'nɪʃən] *adj* phönizisch ||
s Phönizier *m*
phoenix ['finɪks] *s* Phönix *m*
phone [fon] *s* (coll) Telephon *n*; **on the
p.** am Apparat || *tr* (coll) anrufen ||
intr telephonieren
phone' call' *s* (coll) Anruf *m*

phonetic [fo'nɛtɪk] *adj* phonetisch, Laut– ‖ **phonetics** *s* Lautlehre *f*, Phonetik *f*

phonograph ['fonə‚græf] *s* Grammophon *n*

pho'nograph rec'ord *s* Schallplatte *f*

phonology [fə'nalədʒi] *s* Lautlehre *f*

phony ['foni] *adj* falsch, Schein– ‖ *s* Schwindler –in *mf*

phosphate ['fasfet] *s* Phosphat *n*

phosphorescent [‚fasfə'rɛsənt] *adj* phosphoreszierend

phospho·rus ['fasfərəs] *s* (–ri [‚raɪ]) Phosphor *m*

pho·to ['foto] *s* (–tos) (coll) Photo *n*

pho'tocop'y *s* Photokopie *f* ‖ *v* (pret & pp –ied) *tr* photokopieren

pho'toengrav'ing *s* Lichtdruckverfahren *n*

pho'to fin'ish *s* Zielphotographie *f*

photogenic [‚foto'dʒɛnɪk] *adj* photogen

photograph ['fotə‚græf] *s* Photographie *f* ‖ *tr & intr* photographieren

photographer [fə'tagrəfər] *s* Photograph –in *mf*

photography [fə'tagrəfi] *s* Photographie *f*

photostat ['fotə‚stæt] *s* (trademark) Photokopie *f* ‖ *tr* photokopieren

phrase [frez] *s* Sinngruppe *f* ‖ *tr* formulieren; (mus) phrasieren

phrenology [frə'nalədʒi] *s* Schädellehre *f*

physic ['fɪzɪk] *s* Abführmittel *n;* **physics** *s* Physik *f*

physical ['fɪzɪkəl] *adj* körperlich, physisch ‖ *s* (*examination*) ärztliche Untersuchung *f*

phys'ical condi'tion *s* Gesundheitszustand *m*

phys'ical de'fect *s* körperliches Gebrechen *n*

phys'ical educa'tion *s* Leibeserziehung *f*

phys'ical ex'ercise *s* Leibesübungen *pl;* (*calisthenics*) Bewegung *f*

phys'ical hand'icap *s* Körperbehinderung *f*

physician [fɪ'zɪʃən] *s* Arzt *m*, Ärztin *f*

physicist ['fɪzɪsɪst] *s* Physiker –in *mf*

physics ['fɪzɪks] *s* Physik *f*

physiognomy [‚fɪzɪ'agnəmi] *s* Gesichtsbildung *f*, Physiognomie *f*

physiological [‚fɪzɪ·ə'ladʒɪkəl] *adj* physiologisch

physiology [‚fɪzɪ'alədʒi] *s* Physiologie *f*

physique [fɪ'zik] *s* Körperbau *m*

pi [paɪ] *s* (math) Pi *n* ‖ *tr* (typ) zusammenwerfen

pianist ['pi·ənɪst] *s* Pianist –in *mf*

pian·o [pɪ'æno] *s* (–os) Klavier *n*

pian'o stool' *s* Klavierschemel *m*

picayune [‚pɪkə'jun] *adj* (*paltry*) geringfügig; (*person*) kleinlich

picco·lo ['pɪkəlo] *s* (–los) Pikkoloflöte *f*

pick [pɪk] *s* (*tool*) Spitzhacke *f;* (*choice*) Auslese *f;* **the p. of the crop** das Beste von allem ‖ *tr* (*choose*) sich [*dat*] aussuchen; (*e.g., fruit*) pflücken; (*one's teeth*) stochern in (*dat*); (*one's nose*) bohren in (*dat*); (*a lock*) mit e–m Dietrich öffnen; (*a quarrel*) suchen; (*a bone*) abnagen; **p. off** abpflücken; (*shoot*) (coll) abknallen; **p. out** auswählen; **p. s.o.'s brains** j–s Ideen klauen; **p. s.o.'s pocket** j–m die Tasche ausräumen; **p. up** (*lift up*) aufheben; (*a girl*) (coll) aufgabeln; (*a suspect*) aufgreifen; (*with a car*) abholen; (*passengers; the scent*) aufnehmen; (*a language; news*) aufschnappen; (*a habit*) annehmen; (*a visual object*) erkennen; (*strength*) wieder erlangen; (*weight*) zunehmen an (*dat*); **p. up speed** in Fahrt kommen ‖ *intr*—**p. and choose** wählerisch suchen; **p. at** herumstochern in (*dat*); **p. on her-** umreiten auf (*dat*); **p. up** (*improve in health or business*) sich (wieder) erholen

pick'ax' *s* Picke *f*, Pickel *m*

picket ['pɪkɪt] *s* Holzpfahl *m;* (*of strikers*) Streikposten *m* ‖ *tr* durch Streikposten absperren, Streikposten stehen vor (*dat*) ‖ *intr* Streikposten stehen

pick'et fence' *s* Lattenzaun *m*

pick'et line' *s* Streikkette *f*

pickle ['pɪkəl] *s* Essiggurke *f;* **be in a p.** (*coll*) im Schlamassel sitzen ‖ *tr* (ein)pökeln

pick'led *adj* (sl) blau

pick'led her'ring *s* Rollmops *m*

pick'pock'et *s* Taschendieb *m*

pick'up' *s* (*of a car*) Beschleunigungsvermögen *n;* (*girl*) Straßenbekanntschaft *f;* (*restorative*) Stärkungsmittel *n*, Erfrischung *f;* (*a stop to pick up*) Abholung *f;* (*of a phonograph*) Schalldose *f*

pick'up truck' *s* offener Lieferwagen *m*

picky ['pɪki] *adj* wählerisch

pic·nic ['pɪknɪk] *s* Picknick *n* ‖ *v* (pret & pp –nicked; ger –nicking) *intr* picknicken

pictorial [pɪk'torɪ·əl] *adj* illustriert ‖ *s* Illustrierte *f*

picture ['pɪktʃər] *s* Bild *n;* (fig) Vorstellung *f;* **look the p. of health** kerngesund aussehen ‖ *tr* sich [*dat*] vorstellen

pic'ture gal'lery *s* Gemäldegalerie *f*

pic'ture post'card *s* Ansichtspostkarte *f*

picturesque [‚pɪktʃə'rɛsk] *adj* malerisch, pittoresk; (*language*) bilderreich

pic'ture tube' *s* Bildröhre *f*

pic'ture win'dow *s* Panoramafenster *n*

piddling ['pɪdlɪŋ] *adj* lumpig

pie [paɪ] *s* Torte *f;* (*meat-filled*) Pastete *f;* **pie in the sky** Luftschloß *n*

piece [pis] *s* Stück *n;* (checkers) Stein *m;* (chess) Figur *f;* (mil) Geschütz *n;* (mus, theat) Stück *n;* **a p. of advice** ein Rat *m;* **a p. of bad luck** ein unglücklicher Zufall *m;* **a p. of furniture** ein Möbelstück *n;* **a p. of luggage** ein Gepäckstück *n;* **a p. of**

news e–e Neuigkeit *f;* **a p. of paper**
ein Blatt Papier; **a p. of toast** e–e
geröstete Brotscheibe *f;* **say one's p.**
seine Meinung sagen
piece'meal' *adv* stückweise
piece'work' *s* Akkordarbeit *f;* **do p.**
in Akkord arbeiten
piece'work'er *s* Akkordarbeiter –in *mf*
pier [pɪr] *s* Landungsbrücke *f,* Pier *m*
& *f; (of a bridge)* Pfeiler *m*
pierce [pɪrs] *tr* durchstechen, durchbohren
pierc'ing *adj (look, pain)* scharf, ste-
chend; *(cry)* gellend; *(cold)* schneidend
piety ['paɪ·əti] *s* Frömmigkeit *f*
pig [pɪg] *s* Schwein *n*
pigeon ['pɪdʒən] *s* Taube *f*
pi'geonhole' *s* Fach *n* ‖ *tr* auf die lange
Bank schieben
pi'geon loft' *s* Taubenschlag *m*
pi'geon-toed' *adj & adv* mit einwärts
gerichteten Zehen
piggish ['pɪgɪʃ] *adj* säuisch
piggyback ['pɪgi ‚bæk] *adv* huckepack
pig'gy bank' *s* Sparschweinchen *n*
pig'head'ed *adj* dickköpfig
pig' i'ron *s* Roheisen *n*
pigment ['pɪgmənt] *s* Pigment *n*
pig'pen' *s* Schweinekoben *m*
pig'skin' *s* Schweinsleder *n;* (sport)
(coll) Fußball *m*
pig'sty' *s* Schweinestall *m*
pig'tail' *s (hair style)* Rattenschwanz *m*
pike [paɪk] *s* Pike *f,* Spieß *m; (high-*
way) Landstraße *f;* (ichth) Hecht *m*
piker ['paɪkər] *s* (coll) Knicker *m*
pilaster [pɪ'læstər] *s* Wandpfeiler *m*
pile [paɪl] *s (heap)* Haufen *m; (e.g.,*
of papers) Stoß *m; (stake)* Pfahl *m;*
(fortune) (coll) Menge *f;* (atom.
phys) Meiler *m,* Reaktor *m;* (elec,
phys) Säule *f;* (tex) Flor *m;* **piles**
(pathol) Hämorrhoiden *pl;* **piles of**
money (coll) Heidengeld *n* ‖ *tr* anhäufen, aufhäufen; **p. it on** (coll)
dick auftragen ‖ *intr—***p. into** sich
drängen in *(acc);* **p. on** sich übereinander stürzen; **p. out** of sich hinaus-
drängen aus; **p. up** sich (an)häufen
pile' driv'er *s* Pfahlramme *f,* Rammbär *m*
pilfer ['pɪlfər] *tr* mausen, stibitzen
pilgrim ['pɪlgrɪm] *s* Pilger –in *mf*
pilgrimage ['pɪlgrɪmɪdʒ] *s* Pilgerfahrt
f; **go on a p.** pilgern
pill [pɪl] *s* (& fig) Pille *f*
pillar ['pɪlər] *s* Pfeiler *m,* Säule *f*
pill'box' *s* Pillenschachtel *f;* (mil) Bunker *m*
pillo·ry ['pɪləri] *s* Pranger *m* ‖ *v (pret*
& pp **–ried)** *tr* an den Pranger stellen; (fig) anprangern
pillow ['pɪlo] *s* Kopfkissen *n*
pil'lowcase' *s* Kopfkissenbezug *m*
pilot ['paɪlət] *adj (experimental)* Versuchs– ‖ *s* (aer) Pilot *m,* Flugzeug-
führer –in *mf;* (naut) Lotse *m* ‖ *tr*
(aer) steuern, führen; (naut) steuern,
lotsen
pi'lothouse' *s* (naut) Ruderhaus *n*
pi'lot light' *s* Sparflamme *f*

pi'lot's li'cense *s* Flugzeugführerschein
m
pimp [pɪmp] *s* Zuhälter *m* ‖ *intr* kuppeln
pimp'ing *s* Zuhälterei *f*
pimple ['pɪmpəl] *s* Pickel *m*
pimply ['pɪmpli] *adj* pickelig
pin [pɪn] *s* Stecknadel *f; (ornament)*
Anstecknadel *f;* (bowling) Kegel *m;*
(mach) Pinne *f,* Zapfen *m;* **be on**
pins and needles wie auf Nadeln sitzen ‖ *v (pret & pp* **pinned)** *ger* **pin-**
ning) *tr (fasten with a pin)* mit e–r
Nadel befestigen; *(e.g., a dress)* abstecken; *(e.g., under a car)* einklem-
men; *(e.g., against the wall)* drücken;
(in wrestling) auf die Schultern legen; **pin down** *(a person)* festlegen;
(troops) niederhalten; **pin one's**
hopes on seine Hofnungen setzen auf
(acc); **pin s.th. on s.o.** (fig) j–m etw
anhängen; **pin up** *(a sign)* anschlagen; *(the hair, a dress)* aufstecken
pinafore ['pɪnə ‚for] *s* Latz *m*
pin'ball machine' *s* Spielautomat *m*
pin' boy' *s* Kegeljunge *m*
pincers ['pɪnsərz] *s & spl* Kneifzange *f*
pinch [pɪntʃ] *s* Kneifen *n; (of salt)*
Prise *f;* **give s.o. a p.** j–n kneifen;
in a p. zur Not, in der Not ‖ *tr*
kneifen, zwicken; *(steal)* (sl) klauen;
(arrest) (coll) schnappen; **I got my**
finger pinched in the door ich habe
mir den Finger in der Tür geklemmt;
p. and scrape every penny sich *[dat]*
jeden Groschen vom Munde abspa-
ren; **p. off** abzwicken ‖ *intr (said of*
shoe) (& fig) drücken
pinchers ['pɪntʃərz] *s & spl* Kneifzange *f*
pinch'-hit' *v (pret & pp* **–hit;** *ger* **–hit-**
ting) *intr* einspringen
pinch' hit'ter *s* Ersatzmann *m*
pin'cush'ion *s* Nadelkissen *n*
pine [paɪn] *adj* Kiefern– ‖ *s* Kiefer *f*
‖ *intr—***p. away** sich abzehren; **p. for**
sich sehnen nach
pine'ap'ple *s* Ananas *f*
pine' cone' *s* Kiefernzapfen *m*
pine' nee'dle *s* Kiefernnadel *f*
ping [pɪŋ] *s* Päng *n; (of a motor)*
Klopfen *n* ‖ *intr* (aut) klopfen
ping-pong ['pɪŋ ‚paŋ] *s* Ping-pong *n*
pin'head' *s* (& fig) Stechnadelkopf *m*
pink [pɪŋk] *adj* rosa ‖ *s* Rosa *n*
pin' mon'ey *s* Nadelgeld *n*
pinnacle ['pɪnəkəl] *s* Zinne *f*
pin'point' *adj* haarscharf; **p. landing**
Ziellandung *f* ‖ *tr* markieren
pin'prick' *s* Nadelstich *m*
pint [paɪnt] *s* Schoppen *m,* Pinte *f*
pin'up girl' *s* Pin-up-Girl *n*
pin'wheel' *s (toy)* Windmühle *f; (fire-*
works) Feuerrad *n*
pioneer [‚paɪ·ə'nɪr] *s* Bahnbrecher –in
mf; (fig & mil) Pionier *m* ‖ *tr* (fig)
den Weg freimachen für ‖ *intr* (fig)
Pionierarbeit leisten
pious ['paɪ·əs] *adj* fromm
pip [pɪp] *s (in fruit)* Kern *m; (on dice)*
Punkt *m; (on a radarscope)* Leucht-
punkt *m; (of chickens)* Pips *m*

pipe [paɪp] *s* Rohr *n; (for smoking; of
an organ)* Pfeife *f* ‖ *tr* durch ein
Rohr (weiter)leiten ‖ *intr* pfeifen;
p. down (sl) das Maul halten; **p. up**
(coll) anfangen zu sprechen, loslegen
pipe' clean'er *s* Pfeifenreiniger *m*
pipe' dream' *s* Wunschtraum *m*
pipe' joint' *s* Rohranschluß *m*
pipe' line' *s* Rohrleitung *f*, Pipeline *f;
(of information)* Informationsquelle
f
pipe' or'gan *s* Orgel *f*
piper ['paɪpər] *s* Pfeifer –in *mf*
pipe' wrench' *s* Rohrzange *f*
piping ['paɪpɪŋ] *adv*—**p. hot** siedend
heiß ‖ *s* Rohrleitung *f; (on uniforms)*
Biese *f;* (sew) Paspel *f*
piquancy ['pikənsi] *s* Pikanterie *f*
piquant ['pikənt] *adj* pikant
pique [pik] *s* Pik *m* ‖ *tr* verärgern; **be
piqued at** pikiert sein über *(acc)*
piracy ['paɪrəsi] *s* Seeräuberei *f*
pirate ['paɪrɪt] *s* Seeräuber *m* ‖ *tr (a
book)* (ungesetzlich) nachdrucken
pirouette [ˌpɪru'ɛt] *s* Pirouette *f*
pista'chio nut' [pɪs'tæʃɪ·o] *s* Pistazien-
nuß *f*
pistol ['pɪstəl] *s* Pistole *f*
pis'tol point' *s*—**at p.** mit vorgehaltener
Pistole
piston ['pɪstən] *s* Kolben *m*
pis'ton ring' *s* Kolbenring *m*
pis'ton rod' *s* Kolbenstange *f*
pis'ton stroke' *s* Kolbenhub *m*
pit [pɪt] *s* Grube *f; (in fruit)* Kern *m;
(trap)* Fallgrube *f; (in the skin)*
Narbe *f; (from corrosion)* Rostgrüb-
chen *n; (in auto racing)* Box *f; (for
cockfights)* Kampfplatz *m;* (min)
Schacht *m;* (theat) Parkett *n;* (mus)
Orchester *n;* **pit of the stomach** Ma-
gengrube *f* ‖ *v (pret & pp pitted; ger
pitting) tr (a face)* mit Narben bedecken; *(fruit)* entkernen; *(through
corrosion)* anfressen; **pit A against
B** A gegen B ausspielen; **pit one's
strength against s.th.** seine Kraft mit
etw messen
pitch [pɪtʃ] *s* Pech *n; (of a roof)* Dach-
schräge *f; (downward slope)* Gefälle
n; (of a ship) Stampfen *n; (of a
screw, thread)* Teilung *f; (of a propeller)* Steigung *f;* (throw) Wurf *m;
(sales talk)* Verkaufsgespräch *n;*
(mus) Tonhöhe *f* ‖ *tr (seal with
pitch)* verpichen; *(a tent)* aufschlagen; *(a ball)* dem Schläger zuwerfen;
(hay) mit der Heugabel werfen ‖
intr (naut) stampfen; **p. and toss**
schlingern; **p. in** mithelfen
pitch' ac'cent *s* musikalischer Tonak-
zent *m*
pitch'-black' *adj* pechrabenschwarz
pitcher ['pɪtʃər] *s (jug)* Krug *m*
pitch'fork' *s* Heugabel *f*
pitch'ing *s* (naut) Stampfen *n*
pit'fall' *s* Fallgrube *f;* (fig) Falle *f*
pith [pɪθ] *s (& fig)* Mark *n*
pithy ['pɪθi] *adj (& fig)* markig
pitiable ['pɪtɪ·əbəl] *adj* erbarmenswert
pitiful ['pɪtɪfəl] *adj* erbärmlich
pitiless ['pɪtɪlɪs] *adj* erbarmungslos

pit'ted *adj (by corrosion)* angefressen;
(fruit) entkernt
pit·y ['pɪti] *s* Erbarmen *n*, Mitleid *n;*
have p. on Mitleid haben mit; **it's a
p. that** (es ist) schade, daß; **move to
p.** jammern; **what a p.!** wie schade!
‖ *v (pret & pp –ied) tr* sich erbarmen *(genit)*, bemitleiden
pivot ['pɪvət] *s* Drehpunkt *m* ‖ *intr*
(on) sich drehen (um); (mil) schwenken
placard ['plækɑrd] *s* Plakat *n*
placate ['pleket] *tr* begütigen
place [ples] *s (seat; room)* Platz *m;
(area, town, etc.)* Ort *m*, Ortschaft
f; (in a book; in a room) Stelle *f;
(situation)* Lage *f; (spot to eat in,
dance in, etc.)* Lokal *n;* **all over the
p.** überall; **at your p.** (coll) bei Ihnen;
in my p. an meiner Stelle; **in p. of**
anstelle von (or *genit)*; **in the first p.**
erstens; **know one's p.** wissen, wohin
man gehört; **out of p.** (& fig) nicht
am Platz; **p. to stay** Unterkunft *f;*
put s.o. in his p. j–n in seine Schranken verweisen; **take one's p.** antreten; **take p.** stattfinden; **take s.o.'s p.**
an j–s Stelle treten ‖ *tr* setzen, stellen; *(an advertisement)* aufgeben;
(an order) erteilen; *(find a job for)*
unterbringen; **I can't p. him** ich weiß
nicht, wo ich ihn hintun soll; **p. a
call** (telp) ein Gespräch anmelden ‖
intr (in horseracing) sich als Zweiter
placieren; (sport) sich placieren
place·bo [plə'sibo] *s* (–bos & –boes)
Placebo *n*
place' card' *s* Tischkarte *f*
place' mat' *s* Tischmatte *f*
placement ['plesmənt] *s* Unterbringung
f
place'-name' *s* Ortsname *m*
place' of birth' *s* Geburtsort *m*
place' of employ'ment *s* Arbeitsstätte
f
place' of res'idence *s* Wohnsitz *m*
placid ['plæsɪd] *adj* ruhig, sanftmütig
plagiarism ['pledʒə ˌrɪzəm] *s* Plagiat *n*
plagiarist ['pledʒərɪst] *s* Plagiator –in
mf
plagiarize ['pledʒə ˌraɪz] *intr* ein Plagiat begehen
plague [pleg] *s* Seuche *f* ‖ *tr* heim-
suchen
plaid [plæd] *adj* buntkariert ‖ *s* Schot-
tenkaro *n*
plain [plen] *adj (simple)* einfach;
(clear) klar; *(fabric)* einfarbig;
(homely) unschön; *(truth)* rein;
(food) bürgerlich; *(paper)* unlin(i)-
iert; *(speech)* unverblümt; *(alcohol)*
unverdünnt ‖ *s* Ebene *f*
plain' clothes' *spl*—**in p.** in Zivil
plain'-clothes' man' *s* Geheimpolizist
m
plaintiff ['plentɪf] *s* Kläger –in *mf*
plaintive ['plentɪv] *adj* Klage-, kla-
gend
plait [plet], [plæt] *s* Flechte *f;* **p. of
hair** Zopf *m* ‖ *tr* flechten
plan [plæn] *s* Plan *m; (intention)* Vorhaben *n;* **according to p.** planmäßig;

what are your plans for this evening? was haben Sie für heute abend vor? || v (pret & pp **planned;** ger **planning**) tr planen; (one's time) einteilen; **p. to** (inf) vorhaben zu (inf) || intr—p. for Pläne machen für; **p. on** rechnen mit

plane [plen] s (airplane) Flugzeug n, Maschine f; (airfoil) Tragfläche f; (carp) Hobel m; (geom) Ebene f; **on a high p.** (fig) auf e-m hohen Niveau || tr hobeln; **p. down** abhobeln

plane' connec'tion s Fluganschluß m

plane' geom'etry s Planimetrie f

planet ['plænɪt] s Planet m

planetari·um [ˌplænɪ'tɛrɪ·əm] s (–a [ə] & –ums) Planetarium n

planetary ['plænəˌtɛri] adj Planeten–

plane' tick'et s Flugkarte f

plane' tree' s Platane f

plank [plæŋk] s Brett n, Planke f; (pol) Programmpunkt m

planned' par'enthood s Familienplanung f

plant [plænt] s (factory) Anlage f; (spy) Spion –in mf; (bot) Pflanze f || tr (an)pflanzen; (a field) bepflanzen; (a colony) gründen; (as a spy) als Falle aufstellen; (a bomb) verstecken; **p. oneself** sich hinstellen

plantation [plæn'teʃən] s Plantage f

planter ['plæntər] s (person who plants; plantation owner) Pflanzer –in mf; (decorative container) Blumentrog m; (mach) Pflanzmaschine f

plasma ['plæzmə] s Plasma n

plaster ['plæstər] s Verputz m; (med) Pflaster n || tr verputzen; (e.g., with posters) bepflastern; **be plastered** (sl) besoffen sein

plas'terboard' s Gipsdiele f

plas'ter cast' s (med) Gipsverband m; (sculp) Gipsabguß m

plasterer ['plæstərər] s Stukkateur m

plas'tering s Verputz m

plas'ter of Par'is s Gips m

plastic ['plæstɪk] adj Plastik– || s Plastik n

plas'tic sur'gery s Plastik f

plas'tic wood' s Holzpaste f

plate [plet] s (dish) Teller m; (of metal) Platte f; (in a book) Tafel f; (elec, phot, typ) Platte f; (electron) Plattenelektrode f || tr plattieren

plateau [plæ'to] s Plateau n

plate' glass' s Tafelglas n

platen ['plætən] s Schreibmaschinenwalze f

platform ['plætˌfɔrm] s Plattform f; (for a speaker) Bühne f; (for loading) Rampe f; (pol) Programm n; (rr) Bahnsteig m

plat'form shoes' spl Plateauschuhe pl

plat'ing s (e.g., of gold) Plattierung f; (armor) Panzerung f

platinum ['plætɪnəm] s Platin n

plat'inum blonde' s Platinblondine f

platitude ['plætɪˌt(j)ud] s Gemeinplatz m

Plato ['pleto] s Plato m

Platonic [plə'tɑnɪk] adj platonisch

platoon [plə'tun] s Zug m

platter ['plætər] s Platte f

plausible ['plɔzɪbəl] adj plausibel

play [ple] s Spiel n; (mach) Spielraum m; (sport) Spielzug m; (theat) Stück n; **in p.** im Spiel; **out of p.** aus dem Spiel || tr spielen; (a card) ausspielen; (an opponent) spielen gegen; **p. back** (a tape, record) abspielen; **p. down** bagatellisieren; **p. the horses** bei Pferderennen wetten || intr spielen; (records, tapes) abspielen; **p. about** (the lips) umspielen; **p. along** mitspielen; **p. around with** herumspielen mit; **p. for** (stakes) spielen um; (a team) spielen für; **p. into s.o.'s hands** j–m in die Hände spielen; **p. safe** auf Nummer Sicher gehen; **p. up to** schmeicheln (dat)

play'back' s (reproduction) Wiedergabe f; (device) Abspielgerät n

play'boy' s Playboy m

player ['ple·ər] s Spieler –in mf; (sport) Sportler –in mf; (theat) Schauspieler –in mf

playful ['plefəl] adj spielerisch

play'ground' s Spielplatz m

play'house' s Theater n; (for children) Spielhaus n

play'ing card' s Spielkarte f

play'ing field' s Spielfeld n

play'mate' s Spielkamerad –in mf

play'-offs' spl Vorrunde f

play' on words' s Wortspiel n

play'pen' s Laufgitter n

play'room' s Spielzimmer n

play'-school' s Kindergarten m

play'thing' s (& fig) Spielzeug n

playwright ['pleˌraɪt] s Schauspieldichter –in mf

plea [pli] s Bitte f; (jur) Plädoyer n

plead [plid] v (pret & pp **pleaded &** **pled** [plɛd]) tr (ignorance) vorschützen || intr plädieren; **p. guilty** sich schuldig bekennen; **p. not guilty** sich als nichtschuldig erklären; **p. with s.o.** j–n anflehen

pleasant ['plɛzənt] adj angenehm

pleasantry ['plɛzəntri] s Heiterkeit f; (remark) Witz m

please [pliz] tr gefallen (dat); **be pleased to** (inf) sich freuen zu (inf); **be pleased with** sich freuen über (acc); **pleased to meet you!** sehr angenehm || intr gefallen; **as one pleases** nach Gefallen; **do as you p.** tun Sie, wie Sie wollen; **if you p.** wenn ich bitten darf; (iron) gefälligst; **p.!** bitte!

pleas'ing adj angenehm, gefällig

pleasure ['plɛʒər] s Vergnügen n

pleas'ure trip' s Vergnügungsreise f

pleat [plit] s Plissee n || tr plissieren

pleat'ed skirt' s Plisseerock m

plebeian [plɪ'bi·ən] adj plebejisch || s Plebejer –in mf

plect·rum ['plɛktrəm] s (–rums & –ra [rə]) Plektron n; (for zither) Schlagring m

pledge [plɛdʒ] s (solemn promise) Gelübde n; (security for a payment)

Pfand *n;* (fig) Unterpfand *n* ‖ *tr* geloben; (*money*) zeichnen

plenary ['plinəri] *adj* Plenar-, Voll—

ple′nary indul′gence *s* vollkommener Ablaß *m*

ple′nary ses′sion *s* Plenum *n*

plenipotentiary [ˌplenɪpə'tenʃɪ ˌɛri] *adj* bevollmächtigt ‖ *s* Bevollmächtigte *mf*

plentiful ['plentɪfəl] *adj* reichlich

plenty ['plenti] *s* Fülle *f;* **have p. of** Überfluß haben an (*dat*); **have p. to do** vollauf zu tun haben ‖ *adv* (coll) reichlich

pleurisy ['plʊrɪsi] *s* Brustfellentzündung *f*

plexiglass ['plɛksɪ ˌglæs] *s* Plexiglas *n*

pliant ['plaɪ-ənt] *adj* biegsam; (fig) gefügig

pliers ['plaɪ-ərz] *s & spl* Zange *f*

plight [plaɪt] *s* Notlage *f*

plod [plɑd] *v* (*pret & pp* **plodded;** *ger* **plodding**) *intr* stapfen; **p. along** mühsam weitermachen

plop [plɑp] *v* (*pret & pp* **plopped;** *ger* **plopping**) *tr* plumpsen lassen ‖ *intr* plumpsen ‖ *interj* plumps!

plot [plɑt] *s* (*conspiracy*) Komplott *n;* (*of a story*) Handlung *f;* (*of ground*) Grundstück *n* ‖ *v* (*pret & pp* **plotted;** *ger* **plotting**) *tr* (*a course*) abstecken; (*intrigues*) schmieden; (*e.g., murder*) planen ‖ *intr* sich verschwören

plough [plaʊ] *s, tr & intr* var of **plow**

plow [plaʊ] *s* Pflug *m* ‖ *tr* pflügen; **p. up** umpflügen; **p. under** unterpflügen ‖ *intr* pflügen; **p. through the waves** durch die Wellen streichen

plow′man *s* (**–men**) Pflüger *m*

plow′share *s* Pflugschar *f*

pluck [plʌk] *s* (*tug*) Ruck *m;* (fig) Schneid *m* ‖ *tr* (*e.g., a chicken*) rupfen; (*flowers, fruit*) pflücken; (*eyebrows*) auszupfen; (mus) zupfen ‖ *intr*—**p. up** Mut fassen

plug [plʌg] *s* (*for a sink*) Pfropfen *m;* (*of tobacco*) Priem *m;* (*old horse*) alter Klepper *m;* (*advertising*) Befürwortung *f;* (aut) Zündkerze *f;* (elec) Stecker *m* ‖ *v* (*pret & pp* **plugged;** *ger* **plugging**) *tr* (*a hole*) zustopfen; **p. in** an die Steckdose anschließen ‖ *intr*—**p. away** (*work hard*) schuften; (*study hard*) pauken

plum [plʌm] *s* Pflaume *f*

plumage ['plumɪdʒ] *s* Gefieder *n*

plumb [plʌm] *adj* lotrecht ‖ *adv* (coll) völlig ‖ *s* Lot *n;* **out of p.** aus dem Lot ‖ *tr* loten, sondieren

plumb′ bob′ *s* Lot *n*

plumber ['plʌmər] *s* Installateur *m*

plumb′ing *s* (*plumbing work*) Installateurarbeit *f;* (*pipes*) Rohrleitung *f*

plumb′ line′ *s* Lotschnur *f*

plume [plum] *s* Feder *f;* (*on a helmet*) Helmbusch *m;* **p. of smoke** Rauchfahne *f* ‖ *tr* (*adorn with plumes*) mit Federn schmücken; **p. itself** sich putzen

plummet ['plʌmɪt] *s* Lot *n* ‖ *intr* stürzen

plump [plʌmp] *adj* rundlich ‖ *tr* plumpsen; **p. oneself down** sich schwerfällig hinwerfen

plum′ tree′ *s* Pflaumenbaum *m*

plunder ['plʌndər] *s* (*act*) Plünderung *f;* (*booty*) Beute *f* ‖ *tr & intr* plündern

plunderer ['plʌndərər] *s* Plünderer *m*

plunge [plʌndʒ] *s* Sturz *m* ‖ *tr* stürzen ‖ *intr* (*fall*) stürzen; (*throw oneself*) sich stürzen

plunger ['plʌndʒər] *s* Saugglocke *f*

plunk [plʌŋk] *adv* (*squarely*) (coll) genau ‖ *tr* (*e.g., a guitar*) zupfen; **p. down** klirrend auf den Tisch legen

pluperfect [ˌplu'pʌrfɛkt] *s* Vorvergangenheit *f,* Plusquamperfekt(um) *n*

plural ['plʊrəl] *adj* Plural— ‖ *s* Mehrzahl *f,* Plural *m*

plurality [plʊ'rælɪti] *s* Mehrheit *f;* (pol) Stimmenmehrheit *f*

plus [plʌs] *adj* Plus—; (elec) positiv ‖ *s* Plus *n* ‖ *prep* plus (*acc*)

plush [plʌʃ] *adj* (coll) luxuriös

plus′ sign′ *s* Pluszeichen *n*

plutonium [plu'tonɪ-əm] *s* Plutonium *n*

ply [plaɪ] *s* (*of wood, etc.*) Schicht *f;* (*of yarn*) Strähne *f* ‖ *v* (*pret & pp* **plied**) *tr* (*e.g., a needle*) (eifrig) handhaben; (*a trade*) betreiben; (*with questions*) bestürmen; (*a waterway*) regelmäßig befahren ‖ *intr* (**between**) verkehren (zwischen *dat*)

ply′wood′ *s* Sperrholz *n*

pneumatic [n(j)u'mætɪk] *adj* pneumatisch

pneumat′ic drill′ *s* Preßluftbohrer *m*

pneumonia [n(j)u'monɪ-ə] *s* Lungenentzündung *f*

poach [potʃ] *tr* (*eggs*) pochieren ‖ *intr* wildern

poached′ egg′ *s* verlorenes Ei *n*

poacher ['potʃər] *s* Wilderer *m*

pock [pɑk] *s* Pocke *f,* Pustel *f*

pocket ['pɑkɪt] *adj* (*comb, flap, knife, money, watch*) Taschen— ‖ *s* Tasche *f;* (billiards) Loch *n;* (mil) Kessel *m* ‖ *tr* in die Tasche stecken; (billiards) ins Loch spielen

pock′etbook′ *s* Handtasche *f;* (*book*) Taschenbuch *n*

pock′et cal′culator *s* Taschenrechner *m*

pock′mark′ *s* Pockennarbe *f*

pock′marked′ *adj* pockennarbig

pod [pɑd] *s* Hülse *f*

podi·um ['podɪ-əm] *s* (**–ums & –a** [ə]) Podium *n*

poem ['po·ɪm] *s* Gedicht *n*

poet ['po·ɪt] *s* Dichter *m,* Poet *m*

poetaster ['po·ɪt ˌæstər] *s* Dichterling *m*

poetess ['po·ɪtɪs] *s* Dichterin *f*

poetic [po'ɛtɪk] *adj* dichterisch, poetisch ‖ **poetics** *s* Poetik *f*

poetry ['po·ɪtri] *s* Dichtung *f;* **write p.** dichten, Gedichte schreiben

poignant ['pɔɪn(j)ənt] *adj* (*touching*) ergreifend; (*pungent*) scharf; (*cutting*) beißend

point [pɔɪnt] *s* (*dot, score*) Punkt *m;*

(*tip*) Spitze *f;* (*of a joke*) Pointe *f;* (*of a statement*) Hauptpunkt *m;* (*side of a character*) Seite *f;* (*purpose*) Sinn *m;* (*matter, subject*) Sache *f;* (*of a compass*) Kompaßstrich *m;* (*to show decimals*) Komma *n;* (aut) Zündkontakt *m;* (geog) Landspitze *f;* (typ) Punkt *m;* **at this p.** in diesem Augenblick; **be on the p. of** (*ger*) gerade im Begriff sein zu (*inf*); **come to the p.!** zur Sache!; **get the p.** verstehen; **in p. of fact** tatsächlich; **make a p. of** bestehen auf (*dat*); **make it a p. to** (*inf*) es sich [*dat*] zur Pflicht machen zu (*inf*); **not to the p.** nicht zur Sache gehörig; **off the p.** unzutreffend; **on points** (sport) nach Punkten; **p. at issue** strittiger Punkt *m;* **p. of order!** zur Tagesordnung!; **p. of time** Zeitpunkt *m;* **score a p.** (fig) e-n Punkt für sich buchen; **that's beside the p.** darum handelt es sich nicht; **there's no p. to it** es hat keinen Zweck; **to the p.** zutreffend; **up to a certain p.** bis zu e-m gewissen Grade ‖ *tr* (*e.g., a gun*) (**at**) richten (auf *acc*); **p. out** (auf)zeigen; **p. s.th. out to s.o.** j-n auf etw [*acc*] hinweisen; **p. the finger at** mit dem Finger zeigen auf (*acc*) ‖ *intr* mit dem Finger zeigen; **p. to** deuten auf (*acc*); (fig) hinweisen auf (*acc*)

point'-blank' *adj* (*refusal*) glatt; (*shot*) rasant, Kernschuß–; **at p. range** auf Kernschußweite ‖ *adv* (*at close range*) aus nächster Nähe; (fig) glatt; (arti) auf Kernschußweite

point'ed *adj* spitzig; (*remark*) anzüglich; (*gun*) gerichtet; (*arch, nose*) Spitz–

pointer ['pɔɪntər] *s* (*of a meter*) Zeiger *m;* (*stick*) Zeigestock *m;* (*advice*) Tip *m;* (*hunting dog*) Vorstehhund *m*

pointless ['pɔɪntlɪs] *adj* zwecklos

point' of hon'or *s* Ehrensache *f*

point' of law' *s* Rechtsfrage *f*

point' of view' *s* Gesichtspunkt *m*

poise [pɔɪz] *s* sicheres Auftreten *n* ‖ *tr* im Gleichgewicht halten ‖ *intr* schweben

poison ['pɔɪzən] *s* Gift *n* ‖ *tr* (& fig) vergiften

poi'son gas' *s* Giftgas *n*

poi'son i'vy *s* Giftsumach *m*

poisonous ['pɔɪzənəs] *adj* giftig

poke [pok] *s* Stoß *m,* Knuff *m* ‖ *tr* anstoßen, knuffen; (*the fire*) schüren; (*head, nose*) stecken; **p. fun at** sich lustig machen über (*acc*); **p. out** (*an eye*) ausstechen; **p. s.o. in the ribs** j-m e-n Rippenstoß geben ‖ *intr* bummeln; **p. around** herumstochern; (*be slow*) herumbummeln; (*in another's business*) herumstöbern

poker ['pokər] *s* Schürhaken *m;* (cards) Poker *n*

pok'er face' *s* Pokergesicht *n*

poky ['poki] *adj* bummelig

Poland ['polənd] *s* Polen *n*

polar ['polər] *adj* Polar–

po'lar bear' *s* Eisbär *m*

polarity [po'lærɪti] *s* Polarität *f*

polarize ['polə͵raɪz] *tr* polarisieren

pole [pol] *s* (*rod*) Stange *f;* (*for telephone lines, flags, etc.*) Mast *m;* (astr, geog, phys) Pol *m;* **Pole** Pole *m,* Polin *f* ‖ *tr* (*a raft, boat*) staken

pole'cat' *s* Iltis *m*

polemic(al) [pə'lɛmɪk(əl)] *adj* polemisch

polemics [pə'lɛmɪks] *s* Polemik *f*

pole'star' *s* Polarstern *m*

pole'-vault' *intr* stabhochspringen

pole' vault'ing *s* Stabhochsprung *m*

police [pə'lis] *adj* polizeilich ‖ *s* Polizei *f* ‖ *tr* polizeilich überwachen; (*clean up*) (mil) säubern

police' es'cort *s* Polozeibedeckung *f*

police'man *s* (**–men**) Polizist *m*

police' of'ficer *s* Polizeibeamte *m,* Polizeibeamtin *f*

police' pre'cinct *s* Polizeirevier *n*

police' state' *s* Polizeistaat *m*

police' sta'tion *s* Polizeiwache *f*

police'wom'an *s* (**–wom'en**) Polizistin *f*

policy ['palɪsi] *s* Politik *f;* (ins) Police *f*

polio ['poli͵o] *s* Polio *f*

polish ['palɪʃ] *s* (*material; shine*) Politur *f;* (*for shoes*) Schuhcreme *f;* (fig) Schliff *m* ‖ *tr* polieren; (*fingernails*) lackieren; (*shoes, silver, etc.*) putzen; (*floors*) bohnern; (fig) abschleifen; **p. off** (*eat*) (sl) verdrücken; (*an opponent*) (sl) erledigen; (*work*) (sl) hinhauen ‖ *intr*—**p. up on** aufpolieren ‖ **Polish** ['polɪʃ] *adj* polnisch ‖ *s* Polnisch *n*

polite [pə'laɪt] *adj* höflich

politeness [pə'laɪtnɪs] *s* Höflichkeit *f*

politic ['palɪtɪk] *adj* diplomatisch

political [pə'lɪtɪkəl] *adj* politisch

poli'tical econ'omy *s* Volkswirtschaft *f*

poli'tical sci'ence *s* Staatswissenschaften *pl*

politician [͵palɪ'tɪʃən] *s* Politiker –in *mf*

politics ['palɪtɪks] *s* Politik *f;* **be in p.** sich politisch betätigen; **talk p.** politisieren

polka ['po(l)kə] *s* Polka *f*

pol'ka-dot' *adj* getupft

poll [pol] *s* (*voting*) Abstimmung *f;* (*of public opinion*) Umfrage *f;* **be defeated at the polls** e-e Wahlniederlage erleiden; **go to the polls** zur Wahl gehen; **polls** (*voting place*) Wahllokal *n;* **take a p.** e-e Umfrage halten ‖ *tr* befragen

pollen ['palən] *s* Pollen *m*

poll'ing booth' *s* Wahlzelle *f*

pollster ['polstər] *s* Meinungsforscher –in *mf*

poll' tax' *s* Kopfsteuer *f*

pollute [pə'lut] *tr* verunreinigen

pollution [pə'luʃən] *s* Verunreinigung *f*

polo ['polo] *s* (sport) Polo *n*

po'lo shirt' *s* Polohemd *n*

polygamist [pə'lɪgəmɪst] *s* Polygamist *m*

polygamy [pə'lɪgəmi] *s* Polygamie *f*

polyglot ['palɪ͵glat] *s* Polyglott *m*

polygon ['pɑlɪ ,gɑn] s Vieleck n
polyp ['pɑlɪp] s Polyp m
polytheism [,pɑlɪ'θi ,ɪzəm] s Vielgötterei f, Polytheismus m
polytheistic [,pɑlɪθi'ɪstɪk] adj polytheistisch
pomade [pə'med] s Pomade f
pomegranate ['pɑm ,grænɪt] s Granatapfel m; (tree) Granatapfelbaum m
Pomerania [,pɑmə'renɪ-ə] s Pommern n
pom·mel ['pʌməl] s (of a sword) Degenkopf m; (of a saddle) Sattelknopf m || v (pret & pp –mel[l]ed; ger –el[l]ing) tr mit der Faust schlagen
pomp [pɑmp] s Pomp m, Prunk m
pompous ['pɑmpəs] adj hochtrabend
pon·cho ['pɑntʃo] s (–chos) Poncho m
pond [pɑnd] s Teich m
ponder ['pɑndər] tr erwägen; (words) abwägen || intr (over) nachsinnen (über acc)
ponderous ['pɑndərəs] adj schwerfällig
pontiff ['pɑntɪf] s (eccl) Papst m; (hist) Pontifex m
pontifical [pɑn'tɪfɪkəl] adj pontifikal
pontoon [pɑn'tun] s Ponton m; (aer) Schwimmer m
pony ['poni] s (small horse; hair style) Pony n; (crib) Eselsbrücke f
poodle ['pudəl] s Pudel m
pool [pul] s (small pond) Tümpel m; (of blood) Lache f; (swimming pool) Schwimmbecken n; (in betting) Pool m; (game) Billiard n; (fin) Pool m || tr zusammenlegen
pool'room' s Billardsalon m
pool' ta'ble s Billardtisch m
poop [pup] s Heck n || tr (sl) erschöpfen; **be pooped (out)** erschöpft sein
poor [pur] adj arm; (e.g., in spelling) schwach; (soil, harvest) schlecht; (miserable) armselig; **p. in** arm an (dat)
poor' box' s Opferstock m
poor'house' s Armenhaus n
poorly ['purli] adv schlecht
pop [pɑp] adj (concert, singer, music) Pop– || s Puff m, Knall m; (dad) Vati m; (soda) Brauselimonade f; (mus) Popmusik f || v (pret & pp popped; ger popping) tr (corn) rösten; (cause to pop) knallen lassen; **pop the question** (coll) e–n Heiratsantrag machen || intr (make a popping noise) knallen; (said of popcorn) aufplatzen; **pop in** (visit unexpectedly) (coll) hereinplatzen; **pop off** (sl) das Maul aufreißen; **pop up** (appear) (coll) auftauchen; (jump up) hochfahren
pop'corn' s Puffmais m
pope [pop] s Papst m
pop'eyed' adj glotzäugig
pop'gun' s Knallbüchse f
poplar ['pɑplər] s Pappel f
poppy ['pɑpi] s Mohnblume f, Mohn m
pop'pycock' s (coll) Quatsch m
pop'pyseed' s Mohn m
popsicle ['pɑp ,sɪkəl] s Eis n am Stiel
populace ['pɑpjələs] s Pöbel m

popular ['pɑpjələr] adj populär; (e.g., music, expression) volkstümlich; **p. with** beliebt bei
popularity [,pɑpjə'lærɪti] s Popularität f, Beliebtheit f
popularize ['pɑpjələ ,rɑɪz] tr popularisieren
populate ['pɑpjə ,let] tr bevölkern
population [,pɑpjə'leʃən] s Bevölkerung f
popula'tion explo'sion s Bevölkerungsexplosion f
populous ['pɑpjələs] adj volkreich
porcelain ['pɔrs(ə)lɪn] s Porzellan n
porch [portʃ] s Vorbau m, Veranda f
porcupine ['pɔrkjə ,pɑɪn] s Stachelschwein n
pore [por] s Pore f || intr—**p. over** eifrig studieren
pork [pork] adj Schweine– || s Schweinefleisch n
pork'chop' s Schweinekotelett n
pornography [pɔr'nɑgrəfi] s Pornographie f
porous ['porəs] adj porös
porphyry ['pɔrfɪri] s Porphyr m
porpoise ['pɔrpəs] s Tümmler m
porridge ['pɔrɪdʒ] s Brei m
port [port] s Hafen m; (wine) Portwein m; (slit for shooting) Schießscharte f; (naut) Backbord m & n; **to p.** (naut) backbord
portable ['portəbəl] adj tragbar; (radio, television, typewriter) Koffer–
portal ['portəl] s Portal m
portend [pɔr'tend] tr vorbedeuten
portent ['pɔrtənt] s schlimmes Vorzeichen n, böses Omen n
portentous [pɔr'tentəs] adj unheildrohend
porter ['portər] s (in a hotel) Hausdiener m; (at a station) Gepäckträger m; (doorman) Portier m
portfoli·o [port'folɪ ,o] s (–os) Aktenmappe f; (fin) Portefeuille n; **without p.** ohne Geschäftsbereich
port'hole' s (for shooting) Schießscharte f; (naut) Bullauge n
porti·co ['portɪ ,ko] s (–coes & –cos) Säulenvorbau m, Portikus m
portion ['pɔrʃən] s Anteil m; (serving) Portion f; (dowry) Heiratsgut n || tr —**p. out** austeilen, einteilen
portly ['portli] adj wohlbeleibt
port' of call' s Anlaufhafen m
port' of en'try s Einfuhrhafen m
portrait ['portret] s Porträt n
portray [por'tre] tr porträtieren; (fig) beschreiben; (theat) darstellen
portrayal [por'tre-əl] s Porträtieren n; (fig) Beschreibung f; (theat) Darstellung f
port'side' s Backbord m & n
Portugal ['portʃəgəl] s Portugal n
Portuguese ['portʃə ,giz] adj portugiesisch || s Portugiese m, Portugiesin f; (language) Portugiesisch n
port' wine' s Portwein m
pose [poz] s Haltung f, Pose f || tr (a question, problem) stellen || intr posieren; **p. as** sich ausgeben als; **p. for an artist** e–m Künstler Modell ste-

hen; **p. for a picture** sich e–m Photographen stellen

posh [pɑʃ] *adj* (sl) großartig

position [pəˈzɪʃən] *s* Stellung *f;* (*situation, condition*) Lage *f;* (*job; place of defense*) Stellung *f;* (*point of view*) Standpunkt *m;* (aer, naut) Standort *m;* (astr, mil, naut) Position *f;* **be in a p. to** (*inf*) in der Lage sein zu (*inf*); **in p.** am rechten Platz; **p. wanted** (*as in an ad*) Stelle gesucht; **take a p. on** Stellung nehmen zu; **take one's p.** sich aufstellen

positive [ˈpɑzɪtɪv] *adj* (*reply, result, attitude*) positiv; (*answer*) zustimmend; (*sure*) sicher; (*offer*) fest; (elec, math, med, phot, phys) positiv ‖ *s* (gram) Positiv *m;* (phot) Positiv *n*

posse [ˈpɑsi] *s* Polizeiaufgebot *n*

possess [pəˈzɛs] *tr* besitzen; **be possessed by the devil** von dem Teufel besessen sein

possession [pəˈzɛʃən] *s* Besitz *m;* (*property*) Eigentum *n;* **be in p. of s.th.** etw besitzen; **take p. of s.th.** etw in Besitz nehmen

possessive [pəˈzɛsɪv] *adj* eifersüchtig; (gram) besitzanzeigend, Besitz–

possibility [ˌpɑsɪˈbɪlɪti] *s* Möglichkeit *f*

possible [ˈpɑsɪbəl] *adj* möglich; **make p.** ermöglichen

possibly [ˈpɑsɪbli] *adv* möglicherweise

possum [ˈpɑsəm] *s* Opossum *n;* **play p.** sich verstellen; (*play dead*) sich tot stellen

post [post] *s* (*pole*) Pfahl *m;* (*job; of a sentry*) Posten *m;* (*military camp*) Standort *m* ‖ *tr* (*a notice*) anschlagen; (*a guard*) aufstellen; **p. bond** Kaution stellen; **p. no bills** Plakatankleben verboten

postage [ˈpostɪdʒ] *s* Porto *n*

post′age due′ *s* Nachporto *n*

post′age stamp′ *s* Briefmarke *f*

postal [ˈpostəl] *adj* Post–

post′al mon′ey or′der *s* Postanweisung *f*

post′card′ *s* Ansichtskarte *f*

post′date′ *tr* nachdatieren

post′ed *adj*—**keep s.o. p.** j–n auf dem laufenden halten

poster [ˈpostər] *s* Plakat *n*

posterity [pɑsˈtɛrɪti] *s* Nachkommenschaft *f*, Nachwelt *f*

postern [ˈpostərn] *s* Hintertür *f*

post′ exchange′ *s* Marketenderei *f*

post′haste′ *adv* schnellstens

posthumous [ˈpɑstʃʊməs] *adj* posthum

post′man *s* (–men) Briefträger *m*

post′mark′ *s* Poststempel *m* ‖ *tr* abstempeln

post′mas′ter *s* Postmeister *m*

post′master gen′eral *s* Postminister *m*

post-mortem [ˌpostˈmɔrtəm] *s* Obduktion *f*

post′ of′fice *s* Post *f*, Postamt *n*

post′-office box′ *s* Postschließfach *n*

post′paid′ *adv* frankiert

postpone [postˈpon] *tr* (**till, to**) aufschieben (auf *acc*)

postponement [postˈponmənt] *s* Aufschub *m*

post′script′ *s* Nachschrift *f*

posture [ˈpɑstʃər] *s* Haltung *f*

post′war′ *adj* Nachkriegs–

posy [ˈpozi] *s* Sträußchen *n*

pot [pɑt] *s* Topf *m;* (*for coffee, tea*) Kanne *f;* (*in gambling*) Einsatz *m;* **go to pot** (sl) hops gehen; **pots and pans** Kochgeschirr *n*

potash [ˈpɑtˌæʃ] *s* Pottasche *f*, Kali *n*

potassium [pəˈtæsɪ·əm] *s* Kalium *n*

pota·to [pəˈteto] *s* (**–toes**) Kartoffel *f*

pota′to chips′ *spl* Kartoffelchips *pl*

potbellied [ˈpɑtˌbelɪd] *adj* dickbäuchig

pot′bel′ly *s* Spitzbauch *m*

potency [ˈpotənsi] *s* Stärke *f;* (physiol) Potenz *f*

potent [ˈpotənt] *adj* (*powerful*) mächtig; (*persuasive*) überzeugend; (*e.g., drugs*) wirksam; (physiol) potent

potentate [ˈpotənˌtet] *s* Potentat *m*

potential [pəˈtenʃəl] *adj* möglich; (phys) potentiell ‖ *s* (& elec, math, phys) Potential *n*

pot′hold′er *s* Topflappen *m*

pot′hole′ *s* Schlagloch *n*

potion [ˈpoʃən] *s* Trank *m*

pot′luck′ *s*—**take p.** mit dem vorliebnehmen, was es gerade gibt

pot′ roast′ *s* Schmorbraten *m*

pot′sherd′ *s* Topfscherbe *f*

pot′ shot′ *s* müheloser Schuß *m;* **take a p. at** unfair bekritteln

pot′ted *adj* Topf–

potter [ˈpɑtər] *s* Töpfer *m*

pot′ter′s clay′ *s* Töpferton *m*

pot′ter′s wheel′ *s* Töpferscheibe *f*

pottery [ˈpɑtəri] *s* Tonwaren *pl*

potty [ˈpɑti] *s* (coll) Töpfchen *n*

pouch [pautʃ] *s* Beutel *m*

poultice [ˈpoltɪs] *s* Breiumschlag *m*

poultry [ˈpoltri] *s* Geflügel *n*

poul′try·man *s* (**–men**) Geflügelzüchter *m;* (*dealer*) Geflügelhändler *m*

pounce [pauns] *intr*—**p. on** sich stürzen auf (*acc*)

pound [paund] *s* Pfund *n;* (*for animals*) Pferch *m* ‖ *tr* (zer)stampfen; (*meat*) klopfen; **p. the sidewalks** Pflaster treten ‖ *intr* (*said of the heart*) klopfen; **p. on** (*e.g., a door*) hämmern an (*acc*)

–pound *suf* –pfündig

pound′ ster′ling *s* Pfund *n* Sterling

pour [por] *tr* gießen; (*e.g., coffee*) einschenken; **p. away** wegschütten ‖ *intr* (meteor) gießen; **p. out of** (*e.g., a theater*) strömen aus ‖ *impers*—**it's pouring** es gießt

pout [paut] *s* Schmollen *n* ‖ *intr* schmollen

pout′ing *adj* (*lips*) aufgeworfen ‖ *s* Schmollen *n*

poverty [ˈpɑvərti] *s* Armut *f*

pov′erty-strick′en *adj* verarmt

POW [ˈpiˈoˈdʌblˌju] *s* (**prisoner of war**) Kriegsgefangener *m*

powder [ˈpaudər] *s* Pulver *n;* (*cosmetic*) Puder *m* ‖ *tr* (*e.g., the face*) pudern; (*plants*) stäuben; (*a cake*) bestreuen ‖ *intr* zu Pulver werden

pow'der box' s Puderdose f
pow'dered milk' s Milchpulver n
pow'dered sug'ar s Staubzucker m
pow'der keg' s Pulverfaß n
pow'der puff' s Puderquaste f
pow'der room' s Damentoilette f
powdery ['paʊdəri] adj pulverig
power ['paʊ·ər] s Macht f; (personal control) Gewalt f; (electricity) Strom m; (math) Potenz f; (opt) Vergrößerungskraft f; (phys) Leistung f; (pol) Macht f; **be in p.** an der Macht sein; **be in s.o.'s p.** in j–s Gewalt sein; **be within s.o.'s p.** in j–s Macht liegen; **come to p.** an die Macht gelangen; **have the p. to** (inf) vermögen zu (inf); **more p. to you!** viel Erfolg!; **the powers that be** die Obrigkeit f || tr antreiben
pow'er brake' s (aut) Servobremse f
pow'er dive' s (aer) Vollgassturzflug m
pow'er drill' s Elektrobohrer m
pow'er-driv'en adj mit Motorantrieb
pow'er fail'ure s Stromausfall m
powerful ['paʊ·ərfəl] adj mächtig; (opt) stark
pow'erhouse' s Kraftwerk n; (coll) Kraftprotz m
pow'erhun'gry adj herrschsüchtig
powerless ['paʊ·ərlɪs] adj machtlos
pow'er line' s Starkstromleitung f
pow'er mow'er s Motorrasenmäher m
pow'er of attorn'ey s Vollmacht f
pow'er plant' s (powerhouse) Kraftwerk n; (aer, aut) Triebwerk n
pow'er shov'el s Löffelbagger m
pow'er sta'tion s Kraftwerk n
pow'er steer'ing s Servolenkung f
pow'er supply' s Stromversorgung f
practicable ['præktɪkəbəl] adj praktikabel, durchführbar
practical ['præktɪkəl] adj praktisch
prac'tical joke' s Streich m
practically ['præktɪkəli] adv praktisch; (almost) fast, so gut wie
prac'tical nurse' s praktisch ausgebildete Krankenschwester f
practice ['præktɪs] s (exercise) Übung f; (habit) Gewohnheit f; (of medicine, law) Praxis f; **in p.** (in training) in der Übung; (in reality) in der Praxis; **make it a p. to** (inf) es sich [dat] zur Gewohnheit machen zu (inf); **out of p.** aus der Übung || tr (a profession) tätig sein als; (patience, reading, dancing, etc.) sich üben in (dat); (music, gymnastics) treiben; (piano, etc.) üben || intr üben; (said of a doctor) praktizieren; **p. on** (e.g., the violin, piano, parallel bars) üben auf (dat)
prac'tice game' s Übungsspiel n
prac'tice teach'er s Studienreferendar –in mf
practitioner [præk'tɪʃənər] s Praktiker –in mf
pragmatic [præg'mætɪk] adj pragmatisch
pragmatism ['prægmə,tɪzəm] s Sachlichkeit f; (philos) Pragmatismus m
Prague [prɑg] s Prag n
prairie ['prɛri] s Steppe f, Prärie f

praise [prez] s Lob n || tr (for) loben (wegen); **p. to the skies** verhimmeln
praise'wor'thy adj lobenswert
prance [præns] intr tänzeln
prank [præŋk] s Schelmenstreich m
prate [pret] intr schwätzen
prattle ['prætəl] s Geplapper n || intr plappern, schwätzen
prawn [prɔn] s Garnele f
pray [pre] tr & intr beten
prayer [prɛr] s Gebet n; **say a p.** ein Gebet sprechen
prayer' book' s Gebetbuch n
preach [pritʃ] tr & intr predigen
preacher ['pritʃər] s Prediger m
preamble ['pri,æmbəl] s Präambel f
precarious [prɪ'kɛrɪ·əs] adj prekär
precaution [prɪ'kɔʃən] s Vorsichtsmaßnahme f; **as a p.** vorsichtshalber; **take precautions** Vorkehrungen treffen
precede [prɪ'sid] tr vorausgehen (dat) || intr vorangehen
precedence ['prɛsɪdəns] s Vorrang m; **take p. over** den Vorrang haben vor (dat)
precedent ['prɛsɪdənt] s Präzedenzfall m; **set a p.** e–n Präzedenzfall schaffen
preced'ing adj vorhergehend
precept ['prisɛpt] s Vorschrift f
precinct ['prisɪŋkt] s Bezirk m
precious ['prɛʃəs] adj (expensive) kostbar; (valuable) wertvoll; (excessively refined) geziert; (child) lieb || adv **p. few** (coll) herzlich wenige
pre'cious stone' s Edelstein m
precipice ['prɛsɪpɪs] s Abgrund m
precipitate [prɪ'sɪpɪ,tet] adj steil abfallend || s (chem) Niederschlag m || tr (hurl) (into) stürzen (in acc); (bring about) heraufbeschwören; (vapor) (chem) niederschlagen; (from a solution) (chem) ausfällen || intr (chem, meteor) sich niederschlagen
precipitation [prɪ,sɪpɪ'teʃən] s (meteor) Niederschlag m
precipitous [prɪ'sɪpɪtəs] adj jäh
precise [prɪ'saɪs] adj präzis, genau
precision [prɪ'sɪʒən] s Präzision f
preclude [prɪ'klud] tr ausschließen
precocious [prɪ'koʃəs] adj frühreif
preconceived [,prikən'sivd] adj vorgefaßt
predatory ['prɛdə,tori] adj Raub-
predecessor ['prɛdɪ,sɛsər] s Vorgänger –in mf
predestination [,pridɛstɪ'neʃən] s Prädestination f
predicament [prɪ'dɪkəmənt] s Mißliche Lage f
predicate ['prɛdɪkɪt] s (gram) Aussage f, Prädikat n || ['prɛdɪ,ket] tr (of) aussagen (über acc); (base) (on) gründen (auf acc)
predict [prɪ'dɪkt] tr voraussagen
prediction [prɪ'dɪkʃən] s Voraussage f
predispose [,pridɪs'poz] tr (to) im voraus geneigt machen (zu); (pathol) empfänglich machen (für)
predominant [prɪ'dɑmɪnənt] adj vorwiegend

preeminent [prɪ'emɪnənt] *adj* hervorragend

preempt [prɪ'empt] *tr* (*a program*) ersetzen; (*land*) durch Vorkaufsrecht erwerben

preen [prin] *tr* putzen

prefabricated [pri'fæbrɪ‚ketɪd] *adj* Fertig–

preface ['prefɪs] *s* Vorwort *n*, Vorrede *f* || *tr* einleiten

prefer [prɪ'fʌr] *v* (*pret & pp* –ferred; *ger* –ferring) *tr* bevorzugen; (*charges*) vorbringen; **I p. to wait** ich warte lieber

preferable ['prefərəbəl] *adj* (**to**) vorzuziehen(d) (*dat*)

preferably ['prefərəbli] *adv* vorzugsweise

preferred' stock' *s* Vorzugsaktie *f*

prefix ['prifɪks] *s* Vorsilbe *f*, Präfix *n* || *tr* vorsetzen

pregnancy ['pregnənsi] *s* Schwangerschaft *f*; (*of animals*) Trächtigkeit *f*

pregnant ['pregnənt] *adj* schwanger; (*animals*) trächtig; (*fig*) inhaltsschwer

prehistoric [‚prihɪs'tɔrɪk] *adj* vorgeschichtlich, prähistorisch

prejudice ['predʒədɪs] *s* Voreingenommenheit *f*; (*detriment*) Schaden *m* || *tr* beeinträchtigen; **p. s.o. against** j–n einnehmen gegen

pre'judiced *adj* voreingenommen

prejudicial [‚predʒə'dɪʃəl] *adj* (**to**) schädlich (für)

prelate ['prelɪt] *s* Prälat *m*

preliminary [prɪ'lɪmɪ‚neri] *adj* einleitend, Vor– || *s* Vorbereitung *f*

prelude ['prel(j)ud] *s* (fig, mus, theat) Vorspiel *n*

premarital [pri'mærɪtəl] *adj* vorehelich

premature [‚primə't(j)ʊr] *adj* verfrüht; **p. birth** Frühgeburt *f*

premeditated [pri'medɪ‚tetɪd] *adj* vorbedacht; (*murder*) vorsätzlich

premier [prɪ'mɪr] *s* Premier *m*

premiere [prɪ'mɪr] *s* Erstaufführung *f*

premise ['premɪs] *s* Voraussetzung *f*; **on the premises** an Ort und Stelle; **the premises** das Lokal

premium ['primɪ‚əm] *s* Prämie *f*; **at a p.** (*in demand*) sehr gesucht; (*at a high price*) über pari

premonition [‚primə'nɪʃən] *s* Vorahnung *f*

preoccupation [pri‚akjə'peʃən] *s* (**with**) Beschäftigtsein *n* (mit)

preoccupied [pri'akjə‚paɪd] *adj* ausschließlich beschäftigt

preparation [‚prepə'reʃən] *s* Vorbereitung *f*; (med) Präparat *n*

preparatory [prɪ'pærə‚tori] *adj* vorbereitend; **p. to** vor (*dat*)

prepare [prɪ'per] *tr* vorbereiten; (*a meal*) zubereiten; (*a prescription*) anfertigen; (*a document*) abfassen

preparedness [prɪ'perɪdnɪs] *s* Bereitschaft *f*; (mil) Einsatzbereitschaft *f*

pre-pay [pri'pe] *v* (*pret & pp* –paid) *tr* im voraus bezahlen

preponderant [prɪ'pandərənt] *adj* überwiegend

preposition [‚prepə'zɪʃən] *s* Präposition *f*, Verhältniswort *n*

prepossessing [‚pripə'zesɪŋ] *adj* einnehmend

preposterous [prɪ'pastərəs] *adj* lächerlich

prep' school' [prep] *s* Vorbereitungsschule *f*

prerecorded [‚priri'kɔrdɪd] *adj* vorher aufgenommen

prerequisite [pri'rekwɪzɪt] *s* Voraussetzung *f*, Vorbedingung *f*

prerogative [prɪ'ragətɪv] *s* Vorrecht *n*

presage ['presɪdʒ] *s* Vorzeichen *n* || [prɪ'sedʒ] *tr* ein Vorzeichen sein für

Presbyterian [‚prezbɪ'tɪri‚ən] *adj* presbyterianisch || *s* Presbyterianer –in *mf*

prescribe [prɪ'skraɪb] *tr* vorschreiben; (med) verordnen

prescription [prɪ'skrɪpʃən] *s* Vorschrift *f*; (med) Rezept *n*, Verordnung *f*

presence ['prezəns] *s* Anwesenheit *f*

pres'ence of mind' *s* Geistesgegenwart *f*

present ['prezənt] *adj* (*at this place*) anwesend; (*of the moment*) gegenwärtig || *s* (*gift*) Geschenk *n*; (*present time or tense*) Gegenwart *f*; **at p.** zur Zeit; **for the p.** vorläufig || [prɪ'zent] *tr* bieten; (*facts*) darstellen; (*introduce*) vorstellen; (theat) vorführen; **p. s.o. with s.th.** j–m etw verehren

presentable [prɪ'zentəbəl] *adj* presentabel

presentation [‚prezən'teʃən] *s* Vorstellung *f*; (theat) Aufführung *f*

pres'ent-day' *adj* heutig, aktuell

presentiment [prɪ'zentɪmənt] *s* Ahnung *f*

presently ['prezəntli] *adv* gegenwärtig; (*soon*) alsbald

preservation [‚prezər've ʃən] *s* Erhaltung *f*; (**from**) Bewahrung *f* (vor *dat*)

preservative [prɪ'zʌrvətɪv] *s* Konservierungsmittel *n*

preserve [prɪ'zʌrv] *s* Revier *n*; **preserves** Konserven *pl* || *tr* konservieren; **p. from** schützen vor (*dat*)

preside [prɪ'zaɪd] *intr* (**over**) den Vorsitz führen (über *acc* or bei)

presidency ['prezɪdənsi] *s* Präsidentschaft *f*

president ['prezɪdənt] *s* Präsident –in *mf*; (*of a university*) Rektor –in *mf*; (*of a board*) Vorsitzende *mf*

presidential [‚prezɪ'dentʃəl] *adj* Präsidenten–

press [pres] *adj* (*agency, agent, conference, gallery, report, secretary*) Presse– || *s* (*wine press; printing press; newspapers*) Presse *f*; **go to p.** in Druck gehen || *tr* drucken; (*a suit*) (auf)bügeln; (*a person*) bedrängen; (*fruit*) ausdrücken; **be pressed for** knapp sein an (*dat*); **p. s.o. to** (*inf*) j–n dringend bitten zu (*inf*); **p. the button** auf den Knopf drücken || *intr* (*said of time*) drängen; **p. for** drängen auf (*acc*); **p. forward** sich vorwärtsdrängen

press' box' s Pressekabine f
press' card' s Presseausweis m
press'ing adj dringend, dringlich
press' release' s Pressemitteilung f
pressure ['prɛʃər] s Druck m; (of work) Andrang m; (aut) Reifendruck m; **put p. on** unter Druck setzen || tr drängen
pres'sure cook'er s Schnellkochtopf m
pres'sure group' s Interessengruppe f
pressurize ['prɛʃə‚raɪz] tr druckfest machen
prestige [prɛs'tiʒ] s Prestige n
presumably [prɪ'z(j)uməbli] adv vermutlich
presume [prɪ'z(j)um] tr vermuten || intr vermuten; **p. on** pochen auf (acc)
presumption [prɪ'zʌmpʃən] s Vermutung f; (presumptuousness) Anmaßung f
presumptuous [prɪ'zʌmptʃu‧əs] adj anmaßend
presuppose [‚prisə'poz] tr voraussetzen
pretend [prɪ'tɛnd] tr vorgeben; **he pretended that he was a captain** er gab sich für e-n Hauptmann aus || intr so tun, als ob
pretender [prɪ'tɛndər] s Quaksalber m; **p. to the throne** Thronbewerber m
pretense [prɪ'tɛns], ['pritəns] s Schein m; **under false pretenses** unter Vorspiegelung falscher Tatsachen; **under the p. of** unter dem Vorwand (genit)
pretentious [prɪ'tɛnʃəs] adj (person) anmaßend; (home) protzig
pretext ['pritɛkst] s Vorwand m
pretty ['prɪti] adj hübsch || adv (coll) ziemlich
pretzel ['prɛtsəl] s Brezel f
prevail [prɪ'vel] intr (predominate) (vor)herrschen; (triumph) (against) sich behaupten (gegen); **p. on** überreden
prevail'ing adj (fashion, view) (vor)herrschend; (situation) obwaltend
prevalence ['prɛvələns] s Vorherrschen n
prevalent ['prɛvələnt] adj vorherrschend; **be p.** herrschen
prevaricate [prɪ'værɪ‚ket] intr Ausflüchte machen
prevent [prɪ'vɛnt] tr verhindern; (war, danger) abwenden; **p. s.o. from** j-n hindern an (dat); **p. s.o. from** (ger) j-n daran hindern zu (inf)
prevention [prɪ'vɛnʃən] s Verhütung f
preventive [prɪ'vɛntɪv] adj vorbeugend || s Schutzmittel n
preview ['pri‚vju] s Vorschau f
previous ['privɪ‧əs] adj vorhergehend, vorig; Vor-, e.g., **p. conviction** Vorstrafe f; **p. day** Vortag m; **p. record** Vorstrafenregister n
previously ['privɪ‧əsli] adv vorher
prewar ['pri‚wɔr] adj Vorkriegs–
prey [pre] s Beute f, Raub m; (fig) Opfer n; **fall p. to** (& fig) zum Opfer fallen (dat) || intr—**p. on** erbeuten; (exploit) ausbeuten; **p. on s.o.'s mind** an j-s Gewissen nagen

price [praɪs] s Preis m; (st. exch.) Kurs m; **at any p.** um jeden Preis; **at the p. of** im Wert von || tr mit Preisen versehen; (inquire about the price of) nach dem Preis fragen (genit)
price' control' s Preiskontrolle f
price' fix'ing s Preisbindung f
price' freeze' s Preisstopp m
priceless ['praɪslɪs] adj unbezahlbar; (coll) sehr komisch
price' range' s Preislage f
price' rig'ging s Preistreiberei f
price' tag' s Preiszettel m, Preisschild n
price'-wage' spi'ral s Preis-Lohn-Spirale f
price' war' s Preiskrieg m
prick [prɪk] s (& fig) Stich m || tr stechen; **p. up** (ears) spitzen
prickly ['prɪkli] adj stachelig, Stech–
prick'ly heat' s Hitzepickel pl
pride [praɪd] s Stolz m; (pej) Hochmut m; **swallow one's p.** seinen Stolz in die Tasche stecken; **take p. in** stolz sein auf (acc) || tr—**p. oneself on** sich viel einbilden auf (acc)
priest [prist] s Priester m
priestess ['prɪstɪs] s Priesterin f
priest'hood' s Priestertum n
priestly ['pristli] adj priesterlich
prig [prɪg] s Tugendbold m
prim [prɪm] adj (primmer; primmest) spröde
primacy ['praɪməsi] s Primat m & n
primarily [praɪ'mɛrɪli] adv vor allem
primary ['praɪ‚mɛri] adj primär, Haupt–; (e.g., color, school) Grund– || s (pol) Vorwahl f
primate ['praɪmet] s (zool) Primat m
prime [praɪm] adj (chief) Haupt–; (best) erstklassig || s Blüte f; (math) Primzahl f; **p. of life** Lenz m des Lebens || tr (a pump) ansaugen lassen; (ammunition) scharfmachen; (a surface for painting) grundieren; (with information) vorher informieren
prime' min'ister s Ministerpräsident m; (in England) Premierminister m
primer ['prɪmər] s Fibel f || ['praɪmər] s (for painting) Grundierfarbe f; (of an explosive) Zündsatz m; (aut) Einspritzpumpe f
prime' time' s schönste Zeit f
primeval [praɪ'mivəl] adj urweltlich, Ur–; **p. world** Urwelt f
primitive ['prɪmɪtɪv] adj primitiv || s Primitive mf, Urmensch m
primp [prɪmp] tr aufputzen || intr sich aufputzen, sich zieren
prim'rose' s Himmelschlüssel m
prince [prɪns] s Prinz m, Fürst m
Prince' Al'bert s Gehrock m
princely ['prɪnsli] adj prinzlich
princess ['prɪnsɪs] s Prinzessin f, Fürstin f
principal ['prɪnsɪpəl] adj Haupt– || s (educ) Schuldirektor –in mf; (fin) Kapitalbetrag m, Kapital n
principality [‚prɪnsɪ'pælɪti] s Fürstentum n

principally ['prɪnsɪpəli] *adv* größtenteils

principle ['prɪnsɪpəl] *s* Grundsatz *m*, Prinzip *n*; **in p.** im Prinzip

print [prɪnt] *s* (*lettering*; *design on cloth*) Druck *m*; (*printed dress*) bedrucktes Kleid *n*; (phot) Abzug *m*; **in cold p.** schwarz auf weiß; **out of p.** vergriffen ‖ *tr* drucken; (*e.g., one's name*) in Druckschrift schreiben; (phot) kopieren; (tex) bedrucken

print′ed mat′ter *s* Drucksache *f*

printer ['prɪntər] *s* Drucker *m*; (phot) Kopiermaschine *f*

prin′ter's ink′ *s* Druckerschwärze *f*

print′ing *s* Drucken *n*; (*of a book*) Buchdruck *m*; (*subsequent printing*) Abdruck *m*; (phot) Kopieren *n*, Abziehen *n*

print′ing press′ *s* Druckerpresse *f*

print′ shop′ *s* Druckerei *f*

prior ['praɪ·ər] *adj* vorherig; **p. to** vor (*dat*) ‖ *s* (eccl) Prior *m*

priority [praɪ'ɔrɪti] *s* Priorität *f*

prism ['prɪzəm] *s* Prisma *n*

prison ['prɪzən] *s* Gefängnis *n*

pris′on camp′ *s* Gefangenenlager *n*

prisoner ['prɪz(ə)nər] *s* Gefangene *mf*; (*in a concentration camp*) Häftling *m*; **be taken p.** in Gefangenschaft geraten; **take p.** gefangennehmen

pris′oner of war′ *s* Kriegsgefangene *mf*

prissy ['prɪsi] *adj* zimperlich

privacy ['praɪvəsi] *s* Zurückgezogenheit *f*; **disturb s.o.'s p.** j–s Ruhe stören

private ['praɪvɪt] *adj* privat; (*personal*) persönlich; **keep p.** geheimhalten ‖ *s* (mil) Gemeine *mf*; **in p.** privat(im); **privates Geschlechtsteile** *pl*

pri′vate cit′izen *s* Privatperson *f*

pri′vate eye′ *s* (coll) Privatdetektiv *m*

pri′vate first′ class′ *s* Gefreite *mf*

privately ['praɪvɪtli] *adv* privat(im)

privet ['prɪvɪt] *s* Liguster *m*

privilege ['prɪvɪlɪdʒ] *s* Privileg *n*

privy ['prɪvi] *adj*—**p. to** eingeweiht in (*acc*) ‖ *s* Abtritt *m*

prize [praɪz] *s* Preis *m*, Prämie *f*; (nav) Prise *f* ‖ *tr* schätzen

prize′ fight′ *s* Preisboxkampf *m*

prize′ fight′er *s* Berufsboxer *m*

prize′ ring′ *s* Boxring *m*

pro [pro] *s* (**pros**) (coll) Profi *m*; **the pros and the cons** das Für und Wider ‖ *prep* für (*acc*)

probability [,prabə'bɪlɪti] *s* Wahrscheinlichkeit *f*; **in all p.** aller Wahrscheinlichkeit nach

probable ['prabəbəl] *adj* wahrscheinlich

probate ['probet] *s* Testamentsbestätigung *f* ‖ *tr* bestätigen

pro′bate court′ *s* Nachlaßgericht *n*

probation [pro'beʃən] *s* Probe *f*; (jur) Bewährungsfrist *f*; **on p.** auf Probe; (jur) mit Bewährung

proba′tion of′ficer *s* Bewährungshelfer –in *mf*

probe [prob] *s* (jur) Untersuchung *f*;

(mil) Sondierungsangriff *m*; (rok) Versuchsrakete *f*; (surg) Sonde *f* ‖ *tr* (*with the hands*) abtasten; (fig & surg) sondieren

problem ['prabləm] *s* Problem *n*; (math) Aufgabe *f*

prob′lem child′ *s* Sorgenkind *n*

procedure [pro'sidʒər] *s* Verfahren *n*

proceed [pro'sid] *intr* (*go on*) fortfahren; (*act*) verfahren; **p. against** (jur) vorgehen gegen; **p. from** kommen von; **p. to** (*inf*) darangehen zu (*inf*)

proceed′ing *s* Vorgehen *n*; **proceedings** (*of a society*) Sitzungsberichte *pl*; (jur) Verfahren *n*

proceeds ['prosidz] *spl* Erlös *n*

process ['prases] *s* Verfahren *n*, Prozeß *m*; **be in p.** im Gang sein; **in the p.** dabei ‖ *tr* (*raw materials*) verarbeiten; (*applications*) bearbeiten; (*persons*) abfertigen; (phot) entwickeln und vervielfältigen

procession [pro'sɛʃən] *s* Prozession *f*

proclaim [pro'klem] *tr* ankündigen; (*law*) bekanntmachen; **p. (as) a holiday** zum Feiertag erklären

proclamation [,praklə'meʃən] *s* Aufruf *m*, Proklamation *f*

procrastinate [pro'kræstɪ,net] *intr* zaudern

proctor ['præktər] *s* Aufsichtsführende *mf* ‖ *tr* beaufsichtigen

procure [pro'kjur] *tr* besorgen, verschaffen; (*said of a pimp*) verkuppeln

procurement [pro'kjurmənt] *s* Besorgung *f*

procurer [pro'kjurər] *s* Kuppler *m*

prod [prad] *s* Stoß *m*; (*stick*) Stachelstock *m* ‖ *v* (*pret & pp* **prodded**; *ger* **prodding**) *tr* stoßen; **prod s.o. into** (*ger*) j–n dazu anstacheln zu (*inf*)

prodigal ['pradɪgəl] *adj* verschwenderisch

prod′igal son′ *s* verlorener Sohn *m*

prodigious [pro'dɪdʒəs] *adj* großartig

prodigy ['pradɪdʒi] *s* Wunderzeichen *n*; (*talented child*) Wunderkind *n*

produce ['prod(j)us] *s* (*product*) Erzeugnis *n*; (*amount produced*) Ertrag *m*; (*fruits and vegetables*) Bodenprodukte *pl* ‖ [pro'd(j)us] *tr* produzieren; (*manufacture*) herstellen; (*said of plants, trees*) hervorbringen; (*interest, profit*) abwerfen; (*proof*) beibringen; (*papers*) vorlegen; (cin) produzieren; (theat) inszenieren ‖ *intr* (bot) tragen; (econ) Gewinne abwerfen

pro′duce depart′ment *s* Obst– und Gemüseabteilung *f*

producer [pro'd(j)usər] *s* Hersteller *m*; (cin, theat) Produzent –in *mf*

product ['pradʌkt] *s* Erzeugnis *n*, Produkt *n*

production [pro'dʌkʃən] *s* Erzeugung *f*, Produktion *f*; (fa, lit) Werk *n*

productive [pro'dʌktɪv] *adj* produktiv

profane [pro'fen] *adj* profan; **p. language** Fluchen *n* ‖ *tr* profanieren

profanity [pro'fænɪti] *s* Fluchen *n*; **profanities** Flüche *pl*

profess [pro'fɛs] *tr* gestehen
profession [pro'fɛʃən] *s* Beruf *m;* (*of faith*) Bekenntnis *n;* **by p.** von Beruf
professional [pro'fɛʃənəl] *adj* berufs-mäßig, professionell ‖ *s* (*expert*) Fachmann *m;* (sport) Profi *m*
profes'sional jea'lousy *s* Brotneid *m*
professor [pro'fɛsər] *s* Professor –in *mf*
profes'sorship' *s* Professur *f*
proffer ['prafər] *s* Angebot *n* ‖ *tr* an-bieten
proficient [pro'fɪʃənt] *adj* tüchtig
profile ['profaɪl] *s* Profil *n;* (*bio-graphical sketch*) Kurzbiographie *f*
profit ['prafɪt] *s* Gewinn *m;* **show a p.** e–n Gewinn abwerfen ‖ *tr* nutzen ‖ *intr* (**by**) Nutzen ziehen aus
profitable ['prafɪtəbəl] *adj* einträglich
profiteer [‚prafɪ'tɪr] *s* Wucherer *m,* Schieber *m* ‖ *intr* wuchern, schieben
prof'it shar'ing *s* Gewinnbeteiligung *f*
profligate ['praflɪgɪt] *adj* verkommen; (*extravagant*) verschwenderisch ‖ *s* verkommener Mensch *m;* (*spend-thrift*) Verschwender –in *mf*
profound [pro'faund] *adj* (*knowledge*) gründlich; (*change*) tiefgreifend
profuse [prə'fjus] *adj* überreichlich
progeny ['pradʒəni] *s* (& bot) Nach-kommenschaft *f;* (*of animals*) Junge *pl*
progno·sis [prag'nosɪs] *s* (**–ses** [siz]) Prognose *f*
prognosticate [prag'nastɪ‚ket] *tr* vor-aussagen
pro·gram ['progræm] *s* Programm *n;* (*radio or television show*) Sendung *f* ‖ *v* (*pret & pp* **–grammed;** *ger* **–gramming**) *tr* programmieren
progress ['pragres] *s* Fortschritt *m;* **be in progress** im Gang sein ‖ [prə-'gres] *intr* (*make progress*) fortschrei-ten; (*develop*) sich fortentwickeln
progressive [prə'gresɪv] *adj* fortschritt-lich; (*party*) Fortschritts– ‖ *s* Fort-schrittler –in *mf*
prog'ress report' *s* Tätigkeitsbericht *m*
prohibit [pro'hɪbɪt] *tr* verbieten
prohibition [‚pro·ə'bɪʃən] *s* Verbot *n;* (hist) Prohibition *f*
prohibitive [pro'hɪbɪtɪv] *adj* (*costs*) unertragbar; (*prices*) unerschwinglich
project ['pradʒɛkt] *s* Project *n,* Vor-haben *n* ‖ [prə'dʒɛkt] *tr* (*light, film*) projizieren; (*plan*) vorhaben ‖ *intr* vorspringen, vorragen
projectile [prə'dʒɛktɪl] *s* (*fired from a gun*) Projektil *n;* (*thrown object*) Wurfgeschoß *n*
projection [prə'dʒɛkʃən] *s* (*jutting out*) Vorsprung *m,* Vorbau *m;* (cin) Pro-jektion *f*
projector [prə'dʒɛktər] *s* Projektor *m*
proletarian [‚proli'tɛrɪ·ən] *adj* prole-tarisch ‖ *s* Proletarier –in *mf*
proletariat [‚proli'tɛrɪ·ət] *s* Proletariat *n*
proliferate [prə'lɪfə‚ret] *intr* sich stark vermehren
prolific [prə'lɪfɪk] *adj* fruchtbar
prolix [pro'lɪks] *adj* weitschweifig

prologue ['prolog] *s* Prolog *m*
prolong [pro'loŋ] *tr* verlängern
promenade [‚pramɪ'ned] *s* Promenade *f* ‖ *intr* promenieren
promenade' deck' *s* Promenadendeck *n*
prominent ['pramɪnənt] *adj* hervorra-gend, prominent; (*chin*) vorstehend
promiscuity [‚pramɪs'kju·ɪti] *s* Pro-miskuität *f*
promiscuous [pro'mɪskju·əs] *adj* unter-schiedslos; (*sexually*) locker
promise ['pramɪs] *s* Versprechen *n* ‖ *tr* versprechen
prom'ising *adj* (*thing*) aussichtsreich; (*person*) vielversprechend
prom'issory note' ['pramɪ‚sori] *s* Eigenwechsel *m*
promontory ['pramən‚tori] *s* Land-spitze *f*
promote [prə'mot] *tr* (*in rank*) beför-dern; (*a cause*) fördern; (*a pupil*) versetzen; (*wares*) werben für
promoter [prə'motər] *s* Förderer –in *mf;* (sport) Veranstalter –in *mf*
promotion [prə'moʃən] *s* (*in rank*) Be-förderung *f;* (*of a cause*) Förderung *f;* (*of a pupil*) Versetzung *f*
prompt [prampt] *adj* prompt ‖ *tr* ver-anlassen; (theat) soufflieren (*dat*)
prompter ['pramptər] *s* Souffleur *m,* Souffleuse *f*
promp'ter's box' *s* Souffleurkasten *m*
promptness ['pramptnɪs] *s* Pünktlich-keit *f*
promulgate [pro'mʌlget] *tr* bekannt-machen
prone [pron] *adj*—**be p. to** neigen zu; **in the p. position** auf Anschlag liegend
prong [proŋ] *s* (*of a fork*) Zinke *f;* (*of a deer*) Sprosse *f*
pronoun ['pronaun] *s* Fürwort *n*
pronounce [prə'nauns] *tr* (*enunciate*) aussprechen; **p. sentence** das Straf-ausmaß festsetzen; **p. s.o.** (*e.g., guilty, insane, man and wife*) er-klären für
pronouncement [prə'naunsmənt] *s* (*an-nouncement*) Erklärung *f;* (*of a sen-tence*) (jur) Verkündung *f*
pronunciation [prə‚nʌnsɪ'eʃən] *s* Aus-sprache *f*
proof [pruf] *adj*—**p. against** (fig) ge-feit gegen; **90 p. 45** prozentig ‖ *s* Beweis *m;* (phot) Probebild *n;* (typ) Korrekturbogen *m*
proof'read'er *s* Korrektor –in *mf*
prop [prap] *s* Stütze *f;* **props** (coll) Beine *pl;* (theat) Requisiten *pl* ‖ *v* (*pret & pp* **propped;** *ger* **propping**) *tr* stützen; **p. oneself up** sich auf-stemmen; **p. up** abstützen
propaganda [‚prapə'gændə] *s* Propa-ganda *f*
propagate ['prapə‚get] *tr* fortpflanzen; (fig) propagieren ‖ *intr* sich fort-pflanzen
pro·pel [prə'pɛl] *v* (*pret & pp* **–pelled;** *ger* **–pelling**) *tr* antreiben
propeller [prə'pɛlər] *s* (aer) Propeller *m;* (naut) Schraube *f*
propensity [prə'pensɪti] *s* Neigung *f*

proper ['prɑpər] *adj* passend; (*way, time*) richtig; (*authority*) zuständig; (*strictly so-called*) selbst, e.g., Germany p. Deutschland selbst
properly ['prɑpərli] *adj* gehörig
prop'er name' *s* Eigenname *m*
property ['prɑpərti] *s* Eigentum *n;* (*land*) Grundstück *n;* (*quality*) Eigenschaft *f*
prop'erty dam'age *s* Sachschaden *m*
prop'erty tax' *s* Grundsteuer *f*
prophecy ['prɑfɪsi] *s* Prophezeiung *f*
prophe∙sy ['prɑfɪ ˌsaɪ] *v* (*pret & pp* –sied) *tr* prophezeien
prophet ['prɑfɪt] *s* Prophet *m*
prophetess ['prɑfɪtɪs] *s* Prophetin *f*
prophylactic [ˌprofɪ'læktɪk] *adj* prophylaktisch ‖ *s* Prophylaktikum *n;* (*condom*) Präservativ *n*
propitiate [prə'pɪʃɪ ˌet] *tr* versöhnen
propitious [prə'pɪʃəs] *adj* günstig
prop'jet' *s* Flugzeug *n* mit Turboprop
proportion [prə'pɔrʃən] *s* Verhältnis *n;* **in p.** to im Verhältnis zu; **out of p.** to in keinem Verhältnis zu; **proportions** Proportionen *pl* ‖ *tr* bemessen; **well proportioned** gut proportioniert
proposal [prə'pozəl] *s* Vorschlag *m;* (*of marriage*) Heiratsantrag *m*
propose [prə'poz] *tr* vorschlagen; (*intend*) beabsichtigen; **p. a toast to** e-n Toast ausbringen auf (*acc*) ‖ *intr* (**to**) e-n Heiratsantrag machen (*dat*)
proposition [ˌprɑpə'zɪʃən] *s* Vorschlag *m;* (log, math) Lehrsatz *m* ‖ *tr* ansprechen
propound [prə'paund] *tr* vortragen
proprietor [prə'praɪ∙ətər] *s* Inhaber *m*
proprietress [prə'praɪ∙ətrɪs] *s* Inhaberin *f*
propriety [prə'praɪ∙əti] *s* Anstand *m;* **proprieties** Anstandsformen *pl*
propulsion [prə'pʌlʃən] *s* Antrieb *m*
prorate [pro'ret] *tr* anteilmäßig verteilen
prosaic [pro'ze∙ɪk] *adj* prosaisch
proscribe [pro'skraɪb] *tr* proskribieren
prose [proz] *adj* Prosa– ‖ *s* Prosa *f*
prosecute ['prɑsɪ ˌkjut] *tr* verfolgen
prosecutor ['prɑsɪ ˌkjutər] *s* Ankläger –in *mf*
proselytize ['prɑsɪlə ˌtaɪz] *intr* Anhänger gewinnen
prose' writ'er *s* Prosaiker –in *mf*
prosody ['prɑsədi] *s* Silbenmessung *f*
prospect ['prɑspɛkt] *s* Aussicht *f;* (*person*) Interessent –in *mf;* **hold out the p. of s.th.** etw in Aussicht stellen ‖ *intr* (**for**) schürfen (nach)
prospector ['prɑspɛktər] *s* Schürfer *m*
prospectus [prə'spɛktəs] *s* Prospekt *m*
prosper ['prɑspər] *intr* gedeihen
prosperity [prɑs'pɛrɪti] *s* Wohlstand *m*
prosperous ['prɑspərəs] *adj* wohlhabend
prostitute ['prɑstɪ ˌt(j)ut] *s* Prostituierte *f* ‖ *tr* prostituieren
prostrate ['prɑstret] *adj* hingestreckt; (*exhausted*) erschöpft ‖ *tr* niederwerfen; (fig) niederzwingen

prostration [prɑs'treʃən] *s* Niederwerfen *n;* (*abasement*) Demütigung *f*
protagonist [pro'tægənɪst] *s* Protagonist *m,* Hauptfigur *f*
protect [prə'tɛkt] *tr* (be)schützen; (*interests*) wahrnehmen; **p. from** schützen vor (*dat*)
protection [prə'tɛkʃən] *s* (**from**) Schutz *m* (vor *dat*)
protector [prə'tɛktər] *s* Beschützer *m*
protein ['protin] *s* Protein *n*
protest ['protɛst] *s* Protest *m* ‖ [pro'tɛst] *tr & intr* protestieren
Protestant ['prɑtɪstənt] *adj* protestantisch ‖ *s* Protestant –in *mf*
protocol ['protə ˌkɑl] *s* Protokoll *n*
proton ['protɑn] *s* Proton *n*
protoplasm ['protə ˌplæzəm] *s* Protoplasma *n*
prototype ['protə ˌtaɪp] *s* Prototyp *m*
protozo∙an [ˌprotə'zo∙ən] *s* (–a [ə]) Einzeller *m*
protract [pro'trækt] *tr* hinziehen
protrude [pro'trud] *intr* hervorstehen
proud [praud] *adj* (**of**) stolz (auf *acc*)
prove [pruv] *v* (*pret* **proved;** *pp* **proved & proven** ['pruvən]) *tr* beweisen; **p. a failure** sich nicht bewähren; **p. one's worth** sich bewähren ‖ *intr*— **p. right** zutreffen; **p. to be** sich erweisen als
proverb ['prɑvərb] *s* Sprichwort *n*
proverbial [prə'vʌrbɪ∙əl] *adj* sprichwörtlich
provide [prə'vaɪd] *tr* (*s.th.*) besorgen; **p. s.o. with s.th.** j–n mit etw versorgen ‖ *intr*—**p. for** (*e.g., a family*) sorgen für; (*e.g., a special case*) vorsehen; (*the future*) voraussehen
provid'ed *adj* (**with**) versehen (mit) ‖ *conj* vorausgesetzt, daß
Providence ['prɑvɪdəns] *s* Vorsehung *f*
providential [ˌprɑvɪ'dɛntʃəl] *adj* von der Vorsehung beschlossen
provid'ing *conj* vorausgesetzt, daß
province ['prɑvɪns] *s* (*district*) Provinz *f;* (*special field*) Ressort *n*
provision [prə'vɪʒən] *s* (*providing*) Versorgung *f;* (*stipulation*) Bestimmung *f;* **make p. for** Vorsorge treffen für; **provisions** Lebensmittelvorräte *pl* ‖ *tr* (mil) verpflegen
provisional [prə'vɪʒənəl] *adj* vorläufig
provi∙so [prə'vaɪzo] *s* (–sos & –soes) Vorbehalt *m*
provocation [ˌprɑvə'keʃən] *s* Provokation *f*
provocative [prə'vakətɪv] *adj* aufreizend
provoke [prə'vok] *tr* (*a person*) provozieren; (*e.g., laughter*) erregen
provok'ing *adj* ärgerlich
prow [prau] *s* Bug *m*
prowess ['prau∙ɪs] *s* Tapferkeit *f*
prowl [praul] *intr* herumschleichen
prowl' car' *s* Streifenwagen *m*
prowler ['praulər] *s* mutmaßlicher Einbrecher *m*
proximity [prɑk'sɪmɪti] *s* Nähe *f*
proxy ['prɑksi] *s* Stellvertreter –in *mf;* **by p.** in Vertretung

prude [prud] *s* prüde Person *f*
prudence ['prudəns] *s* Klugheit *f; (caution)* Vorsicht *f*
prudent ['prudənt] *adj* klug; *(cautious)* umsichtig
prudish ['prudıʃ] *adj* prüde
prune [prun] *s* Zwetschge *f* || *tr* stuzen
Prussia ['prʌʃɪ·ə] *s* Preußen *n*
Prussian ['prʌʃən] *adj* preußisch || *s* Preuße *m*, Preußin *f*
pry [praɪ] *v (pret & pp* **pried)** *tr*—**pry open** aufbrechen; **pry s.th. out of s.o.** etw aus j–m herauspressen || *intr* herumschnüffeln; **pry into** seine Nase stecken in *(acc)*
P.S. ['pi'es] *s* **(postscript)** NS
psalm [sam] *s* Psalm *m*
pseudo– ['sudo] *adj* Pseudo–, falsch
pseudonym ['sudənɪm] *s* Deckname *m*
psyche ['saɪki] *s* Psyche *f*
psychiatrist [saɪ'kaɪ·ətrɪst] *s* Psychiater –in *mf*
psychiatry [saɪ'kaɪ·ətri] *s* Psychiatrie *f*
psychic ['saɪkɪk] *adj* psychisch || *s* Medium *n*
psychoanalysis [ˌsaɪko·ə'nælɪsɪs] *s* Psychoanalyse *f*
psychoanalyze [ˌsaɪko'ænəˌlaɪz] *tr* psychoanalytisch behandeln
psychologic(al) [ˌsaɪko'ladʒɪk(əl)] *adj* psychologisch
psychologist [saɪ'kalədʒɪst] *s* Psychologe *m*, Psychologin *f*
psychology [saɪ'kalədʒi] *s* Psychologie *f*
psychopath ['saɪkəˌpæθ] *s* Psychopath –in *mf*
psycho·sis [saɪ'kosɪs] *s* **(–ses** [siz]) Psychose *f*
psychotic [saɪ'katɪk] *adj* psychotisch || *s* Psychosekranke *mf*
pto'main poi'soning ['tomen] *s* Fleischvergiftung *f*
pub [pʌb] *s* Kneipe *f*
puberty ['pjubərti] *s* Pubertät *f*
public ['pʌblɪk] *adj* öffentlich || *s* Öffentlichkeit *f*, Publikum *n*
pub'lic address' sys'tem *s* Lautsprecheranlage *f*
publication [ˌpʌblɪ'keʃən] *s* Veröffentlichung *f*
pub'lic domain' *n*—**in the p. d.** gemeinfrei
publicity [pʌb'lɪsɪti] *s* Publizität *f*
publicize ['pʌblɪˌsaɪz] *tr* bekanntmachen
pub'lic opin'ion *s* öffentliche Meinung *f*
pub'lic-opin'ion poll' *s* öffentliche Meinungsumfrage *f*
pub'lic pros'ecutor *s* Staatsanwalt *m*
pub'lic rela'tions *spl* Kontaktpflege *f*
pub'lic serv'ant *s* Staatsangestellte *mf*
pub'lic util'ity *s* öffentlicher Versorgungsbetrieb *m*
publish ['pʌblɪʃ] *tr* veröffentlichen
publisher ['pʌblɪʃər] *s* Verleger –in *mf*
pub'lishing house' *s* Verlag *m*
puck [pʌk] *s* Puck *m*
pucker ['pʌkər] *tr (the lips)* spitzen || *intr*—**p. up** den Mund spitzen
pudding ['pudɪŋ] *s* Pudding *m*

puddle ['pʌdəl] *s* Pfütze *f*, Lache *f*
pudgy ['pʌdʒi] *adj* dicklich
puerile ['pju·ərɪl] *adj* knabenhaft
puff [pʌf] *s (on a cigarette)* Zug *m; (of smoke)* Rauchwölkchen *n; (on sleeves)* Puff *m* || *tr (e.g., a cigar)* paffen; **p. oneself up** sich aufblähen; **p. out** ausblasen || *intr* keuchen; **p. on** *(a pipe, cigar)* paffen an *(dat)*
pugilist ['pjudʒɪlɪst] *s* Faustkämpfer *m*
pugnacious [pʌg'neʃəs] *adj* kampflustig
pug-nosed ['pʌgˌnozd] *adj* stupsnasig
puke [pjuk] *s* (sl) Kotze *f* || *intr* (sl) kotzen
pull [pul] *s* Ruck *m; (influence)* Beziehungen *pl; (of gravity)* Anziehungskraft *f* || *tr* ziehen; *(a muscle)* zerren; *(proof)* (typ) abziehen; **p. down** *(e.g., a shade)* herunterziehen; *(a building)* niederreißen; **p. off** (coll) zuwegebringen; **p. oneself together** sich zusammennehmen; **p. out** *(weeds)* herausreißen; **p. up** *(e.g., a chair)* heranrücken || *intr* **(on)** ziehen (an *dat);* **p. back** sich zurückziehen; **p. in** *(arrive)* ankommen; **p. out** *(depart)* abfahren; **p. over to the side** an den Straßenrand heranfahren; **p. through** durchkommen; **p. up** *(e.g., in a car)* vorfahren
pullet ['pulɪt] *s* Hühnchen *n*
pulley ['puli] *s* Rolle *f; (pulley block)* Flaschenzug *m*
pull'o'ver *s* Pullover *m*
pulmonary ['pʌlməˌneri] *adj* Lungen–
pulp [pʌlp] *s* Brei *m; (to make paper)* Papierbrei *m;* **beat to a p.** windelweich schlagen
pulpit ['pulpɪt] *s* Kanzel *f*
pulsate ['pʌlset] *intr* pulsieren
pulsation [pʌl'seʃən] *s* Pulsieren *n*
pulse [pʌls] *s* Puls *m;* **take s.o.'s p.** j–m den Puls fühlen
pulverize ['pʌlvəˌraɪz] *tr* pulverisieren
pum'ice stone' ['pʌmɪs] *s* Bimsstein *m*
pum·mel ['pʌməl] *v (pret & pp* **–mel[l]**ed; *ger* **–mel[l]ing)** *tr* mit der Faust schlagen
pump [pʌmp] *s* Pumpe *f; (shoe)* Pump *m* || *tr* pumpen; *(for information)* ausfragen; **p. up** *(a tire)* aufpumpen
pump'han'dle *s* Pumpenschwengel *m*
pumpkin ['pʌmpkɪn] *s* Kürbis *m*
pun [pʌn] *s* Wortspiel *n* || *v (pret & pp* **punned;** *ger* **punning)** *intr* ein Wortspiel machen
punch [pʌntʃ] *s* Faustschlag *m; (to make holes)* Locher *m; (drink)* Punsch *m* || *tr* mit der Faust schlagen; *(a card)* lochen; *(a punch clock)* stechen
punch' bowl' *s* Punschschüssel *f*
punch' card' *s* Lochkarte *f*
punch' clock' *s* Kontrolluhr *f*
punch'-drunk' *adj* von Faustschlägen betäubt
punch'ing bag' *s* Punchingball *m*
punch' line' *s* Pointe *f*
punctilious [pʌŋk'tɪlɪ·əs] *adj* förmlich
punctual ['pʌŋktʃu·əl] *adj* pünktlich
punctuate ['pʌŋktʃuˌet] *tr* interpunktieren

punctuation [ˌpʌŋktʃu'eʃən] s Interpunktion f
punctua'tion mark' s Satzzeichen n
puncture ['pʌŋktʃər] s Loch n ‖ tr durchstechen; **p. a tire** e–e Reifenpanne haben
punc'ture-proof' adj pannensicher
pundit ['pʌndɪt] s Pandit m
pungent ['pʌndʒənt] adj beißend, scharf
punish ['pʌnɪʃ] tr (be)strafen
punishment ['pʌnɪʃmənt] s Strafe f, Bestrafung f; (educ) Strafarbeit f
punk [pʌŋk] adj (sl) mies; **I feel p.** mir ist mies ‖ s (sl) Rocker m
punster ['pʌnstər] s Wortspielmacher m
puny ['pjuni] adj kümmerlich, winzig
pup [pʌp] s junger Hund m
pupil ['pjupəl] s Schüler –in mf; (of the eye) Pupille f
puppet ['pʌpɪt] s Marionette f
pup'pet gov'ernment s Marionettenregierung f
pup'pet show' s Marionettentheater n
puppy ['pʌpi] s Hündchen n
pup'py love' s Jugendliebe f
purchase ['pʌrtʃəs] s Kauf m; (leverage) Hebelwirkung f ‖ tr kaufen
pur'chasing pow'er s Kaufkraft f
pure [pjur] adj (& fig) rein
purgative ['pʌrgətɪv] s Abführmittel n
purgatory ['pʌrgə,tori] s Fegefeuer n
purge [pʌrdʒ] s (pol) Säuberungsaktion f ‖ tr reinigen; (pol) säubern
puri·fy ['pjurɪ,faɪ] v (pret & pp –fied) tr reinigen, läutern
puritan ['pjurɪtən] adj puritanisch ‖ **Puritan** s Puritaner –in mf
purity ['pjuriti] s Reinheit f
purloin [pər'lɔɪn] tr entwenden
purple ['pʌrpəl] adj purpurn ‖ s Purpur m
purport ['pʌrport] s Sinn m ‖ [pər'port] tr vorgeben; (imply) besagen
purpose ['pʌrpəs] s Absicht f; (goal) Zweck m; **on p.** absichtlich; **to no p.** ohne Erfolg
purposely ['pʌrpəsli] adv absichtlich
purr [pʌr] s Schnurren n ‖ intr schnurren
purse [pʌrs] s Beutel m; (handbag) Handtasche f ‖ tr—**p. one's lips** den Mund spitzen
purse' strings' spl—**hold the p.** über das Geld verfügen
pursue [pər's(j)u] tr (a person; a plan, goal) verfolgen; (studies, profession) betreiben; (pleasures) suchen
pursuit [pər's(j)ut] s Verfolgung f; **in hot p.** hart auf den Fersen
pursuit' plane' s Jäger m
purvey [pər've] tr liefern, versorgen
pus [pʌs] s Eiter m
push [puʃ] s Schub m; (mil) Offensive f ‖ tr (e.g., a cart) schieben; (jostle) stoßen; (a button) drücken auf (acc); **p. around** (coll) schlecht behandeln; **p. aside** beiseite schieben; (curtains) zurückschlagen; **p. one's way through** sich durchdrängen; **p. through** durchsetzen ‖ intr drängen

push' but'ton s Druckknopf m
push' cart' s Verkaufskarren m
push'o'ver s (snap) (coll) Kinderspiel n; (sucker) Gimpel m; (easy opponent) leicht zu besiegender Gegner m
push'-up' s (gym) Liegestütz m
pushy ['puʃi] adj zudringlich
puss [pus] s (cat) Mieze f; (face) (sl) Fresse f
pussy ['pʌsi] adj eit(e)rig ‖ ['pusi] s Mieze f
puss'y wil'low s Salweide f
put [put] v (pret & pp put; ger putting) tr (stand) stellen; (lay) legen; (set) setzen; **feel put out** ungehalten sein; **put across to** beibringen (dat); **put aside** beiseite legen; **put down** (a load) abstellen; (a rebellion) niederschlagen; (in writing) aufschreiben; **put in** (e.g., a windowpane) einsetzen; (e.g., a good word) einlegen; (time) (on) verwenden (auf acc); **put off** (a person) hinhalten; (postpone) aufschieben; **put on** (clothing) anziehen; (a hat) aufsetzen; (a ring) anstecken; (an apron) umbinden; (the brakes) betätigen; (to cook) ansetzen; (a play) aufführen; **put on an act** sich in Szene setzen; **put oneself into** sich hineindenken in (acc); **put oneself out** sich [dat] Umstände machen; **put on its feet again** (com) auf die Beine stellen; **put s.o. on to s.th.** j–n auf etw [acc] bringen; **put out** (a fire) löschen; (lights) auslöschen; (throw out) herauswerfen; (a new book) herausbringen; **put out of action** kampfunfähig machen; **put over on s.o.** j–n übers Ohr hauen; **put through** durchsetzen; (a call) (telp) herstellen; **put (s.o.) through to** (telp) j–n verbinden mit; **put to good use** gut verwenden; **put up** (erect) errichten; (bail) stellen; (for the night) unterbringen; **put up a fight** sich zur Wehr setzen; **put up to** anstiften zu; **to put it mildly** gelinde gesagt ‖ intr —**put on** sich verstellen; **put out to sea** (said of a ship) in See gehen; **put up with** sich abfinden mit
put'-on' adj vorgetäuscht ‖ s (affectation) Affektiertheit f; (parody) Jux m
put-put ['pʌt'pʌt] s Tacktack n ‖ intr —**p. along** knattern
putrid ['pjutrɪd] adj faul(ig)
putt [pʌt] tr & intr (golf) putten
putter ['pʌtər] s (golf) Putter m ‖ intr —**p. around** herumwursteln
put·ty ['pʌti] s Kitt m ‖ v (pret & pp –tied) tr (ver)kitten
put'ty knife' s Spachtel m & f
put'-up job' s abgekartete Sache f
puzzle ['pʌzəl] s Rätsel n; (game) Geduldspiel n ‖ tr verwirren; **be puzzled** verwirrt sein; **p. out** enträtseln ‖ intr —**p. over** tüfteln an (dat)
puzzler ['pʌzlər] s Rätsel n
puz'zling adj rätselhaft
PW ['pi'dʌbəl,ju] s (prisoner of war) Kriegsgefangene mf

pygmy ['pɪgmi] s Pygmäe m, Pygmäin
f
pylon ['paɪlɑn] s (entrance to Egyptian temple) Pylon m; (aer) Wendemarke f; (elec) Leitungsmast m
pyramid ['pɪrəmɪd] s Pyramide f

pyre [paɪr] s Scheiterhaufen m
Pyrenees ['pɪrɪ ˌniz] spl Pyrenäen pl
pyrotechnics [ˌpaɪrə'teknɪks] spl
Feuerwerkskunst f, Pyrotechnik f
python ['paɪθɑn] s Pythonschlange f
pyx [pɪks] s (eccl) Pyxis f

Q

Q, q [kju] s siebzehnter Buchstabe des
englischen Alphabets
quack [kwæk] s Quacksalver m, Kurpfuscher m ‖ intr schnattern
quadrangle ['kwɑd ˌræŋgəl] s Viereck
n; (inner yard) Innenhof m, Lichthof
m
quadrant ['kwɑdrənt] s Quadrant m
quadratic [kwɑd'rætɪk] adj quadratisch
quadruped ['kwɑdru ˌpɛd] s Vierfüßer
m
quadruple [kwɑd'rupəl] adj vierfach ‖
s Vierfache n ‖ tr vervierfachen ‖
intr sich vervierfachen
quadruplets [kwɑd'ruplɛts] spl Vierlinge pl
quaff [kwɑf] tr in langen Zügen trinken
quagmire ['kwæg ˌmaɪr] s Morast m
quail [kwel] s Wachtel f ‖ intr verzagen
quaint [kwent] adj seltsam
quake [kwek] s Zittern n; (geol) Beben n ‖ intr zittern; (geol) beben
Quaker ['kwekər] s Quäker –in mf
qualification [ˌkwɑlɪfɪ'keʃən] s (for)
Qualifikation f (für)
quali·fy ['kwɑlɪ ˌfai] v (pret & pp
–fied) tr qualifizieren; (modify) einschränken ‖ intr sich qualifizieren
quality ['kwɑlɪti] s (characteristic)
Eigenschaft f; (grade) Qualität f
qualm [kwɑm] s Bedenken n
quandary ['kwɑndəri] s Dilemma n
quantity ['kwɑntɪti] s Menge f, Quantität f; (math) Größe f; (pros) Silbenmaß n; **buy in q.** auf Vorrat kaufen
quan'tum the'ory ['kwɑntəm] s Quantentheorie f
quarantine ['kwɔrən ˌtin] s Quarantäne f ‖ tr unter Quarantäne stellen
quar·rel ['kwɔrəl] s Streit m; **pick a
q.** Händel suchen ‖ v (pret & pp
–rel[l]ed; ger –el[l]ing) intr (over)
streiten (über acc or um)
quarrelsome ['kwɔrəlsəm] adj streitsüchtig, händelsüchtig
quar·ry ['kwɔri] s Steinbruch m; (hunt)
Jagdbeute f ‖ v (pret & pp –ried) tr
brechen
quart [kwɔrt] s Quart n
quarter ['kwɔrtər] s Viertel n; (of a
city) Stadtviertel n; (of the moon)
Mondviertel n; (of the sky) Himmelsrichtung f; (coin) Vierteldollar m;
(econ) Quartal n; (sport) Viertelzeit
f; **a q. after one** (ein) Viertel nach

eins; **a q. of an hour** e–e Viertelstunde f; **a q. to eight** dreiviertel
acht, (ein) viertel vor acht; **at close
quarters** im Nahkampf; **from all
quarters** von überall; **give no q.**
keinen Pardon geben; **quarters** (&
mil) Unterkunft f, Quartier n ‖ tr
(lodge) einquartieren; (divide into
four, tear into quarters) vierteilen ‖
intr im Quartier liegen
quar'ter-deck' s Quarterdeck n
quar'terfi'nal s Zwischenrunde f
quar'ter-hour' s Viertelstunde f
quarterly ['kwɔrtərli] adj vierteljährig;
(econ) Quartals– ‖ s Vierteljahresschrift f
quar'termas'ter s Quartiermeister m
Quar'termaster Corps' s Versorgungstruppen pl
quar'ter note' s (mus) Viertelnote f
quar'ter rest' s (mus) Viertelpause f
quartet [kwɔr'tet] s Quartett n
quartz [kwɔrts] s Quarz m
quash [kwɑʃ] tr niederschlagen
quatrain ['kwɑtren] s Vierzeiler m
quaver ['kwevər] s Zittern n; (mus)
Triller m ‖ intr zittern; (mus) trillern, tremolieren
queasy ['kwizi] adj übel
queen [kwin] s Königin f; (cards)
Dame f
queen' bee' s Bienenkönigin f
queen' dow'ager s Königinwitwe f
queenly ['kwinli] adj königlich
queen' moth'er s Königinmutter f
queer [kwɪr] adj sonderbar; (homosexual) schwul ‖ s (homosexual)
Schwule mf
queer' duck' s (coll) Unikum n
quell [kwɛl] tr unterdrücken
quench [kwɛntʃ] tr (thirst) löschen;
(a fire) (aus)löschen
que·ry ['kwɪri] s Frage f ‖ v (pret &
pp –ried) tr befragen; (cast doubt
on) bezweifeln
quest [kwɛst] s Suche f; **in q. of** auf
der Suche nach
question ['kwɛstʃən] s Frage f; **ask
(s.o.) a q.** (j–m) e–e Frage stellen;
be out of the q. außer Frage stehen;
beyond q. außer Frage; **call into q.**
in Frage stellen; **call the q.** (parl) um
Abstimmung bitten; **in q.** betreffend;
it is a q. of (ger) es handelt sich
darum zu (inf); **q. of time** Zeitfrage
f; **that's an open q.** darüber läßt sich
streiten; **there's no q. about it** darüber besteht kein Zweifel ‖ tr be-

fragen; (*said of the police*) verhören; (*cast doubt on*) bezweifeln
questionable ['kwestʃənəbəl] *adj* fraglich, fragwürdig; (*doubtful*) zweifelhaft; (*character*) bedenklich
ques'tioning *s* Verhör *n*, Vernehmung *f*
ques'tion mark' *s* Fragezeichen *n*
questionnaire [‚kwestʃə'ner] *s* Frage-
bogen *m*
queue [kju] *s* Schlange *f* ‖ *intr*—**q. up**
sich anstellen
quibble ['kwɪbəl] *s* Deutelei *f* ‖ *intr*
(*about*) deuteln (an *dat*)
quibbler ['kwɪblər] *s* Wortklauber *m*
quick [kwɪk] *adj* schnell, fix ‖ *s*—**cut
to the q.** bis ins Mark treffen
quicken ['kwɪkən] *tr* beschleunigen ‖
intr sich beschleunigen
quick'lime' *s* gebrannter ungelöschter
Kalk *m*
quick' lunch' *s* Schnellimbiß *m*
quick'sand' *s* Treibsand *m*
quick'sil'ver *s* Quecksilber *n*
quick'-tem'pered *adj* jähzornig
quick'-wit'ted *adj* scharfsinnig
quiet ['kwaɪ‧ət] *adj* ruhig; (*person*)
schweigsam; (*still*) still; (*street*) un-
belebt; **be q.!** sei still!; **keep q.**
schweigen ‖ *s* Stille *f* ‖ *tr* beruhigen
‖ *intr*—**q. down** sich beruhigen; (*said
of excitement, etc.*) sich legen
quill [kwɪl] *s* Feder *f*, Federkiel *m*;
(*of a porcupine*) Stachel *m*
quilt [kwɪlt] *s* Steppdecke *f* ‖ *tr* steppen
quince [kwɪns] *s* Quitte *f*
quince' tree' *s* Quittenbaum *m*
quinine ['kwaɪnaɪn] *s* Chinin *n*
quintessence [kwɪn'tesəns] *s* Inbegriff
m
quintet [kwɪn'tet] *s* Quintett *n*
quintuplets [kwɪn'tʌplets] *spl* Fünf-
linge *pl*
quip [kwɪp] *s* witziger Seitenhieb *m* ‖
v (*pret & pp* **quipped;** *ger* **quipping**)
tr witzig sagen ‖ *intr* witzeln

quire [kwaɪr] *s* (bb) Lage *f*
quirk [kwʌrk] *s* Eigenart *f*; (*subterfuge*) Ausflucht *f*; (*sudden change*)
plötzliche Wendung *f*
quit [kwɪt] *adj* quitt; **let's call it quits!**
(coll) Strich drunter! ‖ *v* (*pret & pp*
quit & quitted; *ger* **quitting**) *tr* aufgeben; (*e.g., a gang*) abspringen von;
q. it! hören Sie damit auf! ‖ *intr*
aufhören; (*at work*) seine Stellung
aufgeben
quite [kwaɪt] *adv* recht, ganz; **q. a disappointment** e–e ausgesprochene Enttäuschung *f*; **q. recently** in jüngster
Zeit; **q. the reverse** genau das Gegenteil
quitter ['kwɪtər] *s* Schlappmacher *m*
quiver ['kwɪvər] *s* Zittern *n*; (*to hold
arrows*) Köcher *m* ‖ *intr* zittern
quixotic [kwɪks'ɑtɪk] *adj* überspannt
quiz [kwɪz] *s* Prüfung *f*; (*game*) Quiz
n ‖ *v* (*pret & pp* **quizzed;** *ger* **quiz-
zing**) *tr* ausfragen; **q. s.o. on s.th.**
j–n etw abfragen
quiz'mas'ter *s* Quizonkel *m*
quiz' show' *s* Quizshow *f*
quizzical ['kwɪzɪkəl] *adj* (*puzzled*)
verwirrt; (*strange*) seltsam; (*mocking*) spöttisch
quoit [kwɔɪt] *s* Wurfring *m*
quondam ['kwɑndæm] *adj* ehemalig
Quon'set hut' ['kwɑnsət] *s* Nissen-
hütte *f*
quorum ['kwɔrəm] *s* beschlußfähige
Anzahl *f*
quota ['kwotə] *s* Quote *f*, Anteil *m*;
(*work*) Arbeitsleistung *f*
quotation [kwo'teʃən] *s* Zitat *n*; (*price*)
Notierung *f*
quota'tion marks' *spl* Anführungszei-
chen *pl*
quote [kwot] *s* Zitat *n*; (*of prices*)
Notierung *f* ‖ *tr* zitieren; (*prices*)
notieren ‖ *interj*—**q. . . . unquote** Beginn des Zitats! . . . Ende des Zitats!
quotient ['kwoʃənt] *s* Quotient *m*

R

R, r [ɑr] *s* achtzehnter Buchstabe des
englischen Alphabets
rabbet ['ræbɪt] *s* Falz *m* ‖ *tr* falzen
rabbi ['ræbaɪ] *s* Rabbiner *m*
rabbit ['ræbɪt] *s* Kaninchen *n*
rabble ['ræbəl] *s* Pöbel *m*
rab'ble-rous'er *s* Volksaufwiegler –in
mf
rabid ['ræbɪd] *adj* rabiat; (*dog*) toll-
wütig
rabies ['rebiz] *s* Tollwut *f*
raccoon [ræ'kun] *s* Waschbär *m*
race [res] *s* Rasse *f*; (*contest*) Wettren-
nen *n*; (fig) Wettlauf *m* ‖ *tr* um die
Wette laufen mit; (*in a car*) um die
Wette fahren mit; (*a horse*) rennen
lassen; (*an engine*) hochjagen ‖ *intr*

rennen; (*on foot*) um die Wette laufen; (*in a car*) um die Wette fahren
race' driv'er *s* Rennfahrer –in *mf*
race' horse' *s* Rennpferd *n*
racer ['resər] *s* (*person*) Wettfahrer
–in *mf*; (*car*) Rennwagen *m*; (*in
speed skating*) Schnelläufer –in *mf*
race' ri'ot *s* Rassenaufruhr *m*
race' track' *s* Rennbahn *f*
racial ['reʃəl] *adj* rassisch, Rassen-
rac'ing *s* Rennsport *m*
racism ['resɪzəm] *s* Rassenhaß *m*
rack [ræk] *s* (*shelf*) Regal *n*, Ablage *f*;
(*for clothes, bicycles, hats*) Ständer
m; (*for luggage*) Gepäcknetz *n*; (*for
fodder*) Futterraufe *f*; (*for torture*)
Folter *f*; (*toothed bar*) Zahnstange *f*;

go to r. and ruin völlig zugrunde gehen; put to the r. auf die Folter spannen || *tr* (*with pain*) quälen; r. one's brains (*over*) sich [*dat*] den Kopf zerbrechen (über *acc*)

racket ['rækɪt] *s* (*noise*) Krach *m;* (*illegal business*) Schiebergeschäft *n;* (*tennis*) Rakett *n*

racketeer [ˌrækɪ'tɪr] *s* Schieber –in *mf*

racketeer'ing *s* Schiebertum *n*

rack' rail'way *s* Zahnradbahn *f*

racy ['resi] *adj* (*off-color*) schlüpfrig; (*vivacious, pungent*) rassig

radar ['redɑr] *s* Radar *n*

ra'darscope' *s* Radarschirm *m*

radial ['redɪ·əl] *adj* radial

radiance ['redɪ·əns] *s* Strahlung *f*

radiant ['redɪ·ənt] *adj* (with) strahlend (vor *dat*); (*phys*) Strahlungs–

radiate ['redɪ‚et] *tr* & *intr* ausstrahlen

radiation [ˌredɪ'eʃən] *s* Strahlung *f*

radia'tion belt' *s* Strahlungsgürtel *m*

radia'tion treat'ment *s* Bestrahlung *f;* give r. treatment to bestrahlen

radiator ['redɪ‚etər] *s* Heizkörper *m;* (aut) Kühler *m*

ra'diator cap' *s* Kühlerverschluß *m*

radical ['rædɪkəl] *adj* radikal || *s* Radikale *mf*

radically ['rædɪkəli] *adv* von Grund auf

radi·o ['redɪ‚o] *s* (–os) Radio *n*, Rundfunk *m;* go on the r. im Rundfunk sprechen || *tr* funken

ra'dioac'tive *adj* radioaktiv

ra'dio announc'er *s* Rundfunkansager –in *mf*

ra'dio bea'con *s* (aer) Funkfeuer *n*

ra'dio beam' *s* Funkleitstrahl *m*

ra'dio broad'cast *s* Rundfunksendung *f*

radiocar'bon dat'ing *s* Radiokarbonmethode *f*

ra'diofre'quency *s* Hochfrequenz *f*

radiogram ['redɪ‚o‚græm] *s* Radiogramm *n*

radiologist [ˌredɪ'ɑldʒɪst] *s* Röntgenologe *m*, Röntgenologin *f*

radiology [redɪ'ɑldʒi] *s* Röntgenologie *f*

ra'dio net'work *s* Rundfunknetz *n*

ra'dio op'erator *s* Funker –in *mf*

radioscopy [ˌredɪ'ɑskəpi] *s* Durchleuchtung *f*

ra'dio set' *s* Radioapparat *m*

ra'dio sta'tion *s* Rundfunkstation *f*

radish ['rædɪʃ] *s* Radieschen *n*

radium ['redɪ·əm] *s* Radium *n*

radi·us ['redɪ·əs] *s* (–i [ˌaɪ] & –uses) Halbmesser *m;* (anat) Speiche *f;* within a r. of in e–m Umkreis von

raffish ['ræfɪʃ] *adj* gemein, niedrig

raffle ['ræfəl] *s* Tombola *f* || *tr*—r. off in e–r Tombola verlosen

raft [ræft] *s* Floß *n;* a r. of (coll) ein Haufen *m*

rafter ['ræftər] *s* Dachsparren *m;* rafters Sparrenwerk *n*

rag [ræg] *s* Lumpen *m;* chew the rag (sl) quasseln

ragamuffin ['rægə‚mʌfɪn] *s* Lump *m*

rag' doll' *s* Stoffpuppe *f*

rage [redʒ] *s* Wut *f;* all the r. letzter Schrei *m;* be the r. die große Mode sein; fly into a r. in Wut geraten || *intr* wüten, toben

ragged ['rægɪd] *adj* zerlumpt, lumpig

rag'man *s* (–men) Lumpenhändler *m*

ragout [ræ'gu] *s* Ragout *n*

rag'weed' *s* Ambrosiapflanze *f*

raid [red] *s* Beutezug *m;* (*by police*) Razzia *f;* (mil) Überfall *m* || *tr* überfallen; e–e Razzia machen auf (*acc*)

raider ['redər] *s* (naut) Kaperkreuzer *m;* raiders (mil) Kommandotruppe *f*

rail [rel] *s* Geländerstange *f;* (naut) Reling *f;* (rr) Schiene *f;* by r. per Bahn ||—r. at beschimpfen

rail'head' *s* Schienenkopf *m*

rail'ing *s* Geländer *n;* (naut) Reling *f*

rail'road' *s* Eisenbahn *f* || *tr* (*a bill*) durchpeitschen

rail'road cross'ing *s* Bahnübergang *m*

rail'road embank'ment *s* Bahndamm *m*

rail'road sta'tion *s* Bahnhof *m*

rail'road tie' *s* Schwelle *f*

rail'way' *adj* Eisenbahn– || *s* Eisenbahn *f*

raiment ['remənt] *s* Kleidung *f*

rain [ren] *s* Regen *m;* it looks like r. es sieht nach Regen aus; r. or shine bei jedem Wetter || *tr*—r. cats and dogs Bindfäden regnen; r. out verregnen || *intr* regnen

rainbow ['ren‚bo] *s* Regenbogen *m*

rain'coat' *s* Regenmantel *m*

rain'drop' *s* Regentropfen *m*

rain'fall' *s* Regenfall *m;* (*amount of rain*) Regenmenge *f*

rain' gut'ter *s* Dachrinne *f*

rain' pipe' *s* Fallrohr *n*

rain'proof' *adj* regenfest, regendicht

rainy ['reni] *adj* regnerisch; (*e.g., day, weather*) Regen–; save money for a r. day sich [*dat*] e–n Notpfennig aufsparen

rain'y sea'son *s* Regenzeit *f*

raise [rez] *s* Lohnerhöhung *f;* (in *poker*) Steigerung *f* || *tr* (*lift*) heben, erheben; (*increase*) erhöhen, steigern; (*erect*) aufstellen; (*children*) großziehen; (*a family*) ernähren; (*grain, vegetables*) anbauen; (*animals*) züchten; (*dust*) aufwirbeln; (*money, troops*) aufbringen; (*blisters*) ziehen; (*a question*) aufwerfen; (*hopes*) erwecken; (*a laugh, smile*) hervorrufen; (*the ante*) steigern; (*a siege*) aufheben; (*from the dead*) auferwecken; r. Cain (or hell) Krach schlagen; r. the arm (*before striking*) mit dem Arm ausholen; r. the price of verteuern; r. to a higher power potenzieren || *intr* (*in poker*)

raisin ['rezən] *s* Rosine *f*

rake [rek] *s* Rechen *m;* (*person*) Wüstling *m* || *tr* rechen; (*with gunfire*) bestreichen; r. in (*money*) kassieren; r. together (or up) zusammenrechen

rake'-off' *s* (coll) Gewinnanteil *m*

rakish ['rekɪʃ] *adj* (*dissolute*) liederlich; (*jaunty*) schmissig

ral·ly ['ræli] *s* (*meeting*) Massenversammlung *f;* (*recovery*) Erholung *f;*

(mil) Umgruppierung *f* || *v* (*pret &
pp* -lied) *tr* (wieder) sammeln || *intr*
sich (wieder) sammeln; (*recover*) sich
erholen

ram [ræm] *s* Schafbock *m* || *v* (*pret &
pp* rammed; *ger* ramming) *tr* rammen; **ram s.th. down s.o.'s throat**
j-m etw aufdrängen

ramble ['ræmbəl] *intr*—**r. about** her-
umwandern; **r. on** daherreden

ramification [ˌræmɪfɪ'keʃən] *s* Ver-
zweigung *f*

ramp [ræmp] *s* Rampe *f*

rampage ['ræmpedʒ] *s* Toben *n*, Wüten
n; **go on a r.** toben, wüten

rampant ['ræmpənt] *adj*—**be r.** grassieren

rampart ['ræmpɑrt] *s* Wall *m*, Ring-
wall *m*

ram'rod' *s* Ladestock *m*; (*cleaning rod*)
Reinigungsstock *m*

ram'shack'le *adj* baufällig

ranch [ræntʃ] *s* Ranch *f*

rancid ['rænsɪd] *adj* ranzig

random ['rændəm] *adj* zufällig, Zufalls–; **at r.** aufs Geratewohl

range [rendʒ] *s* (row) Reihe *f*; (*mountains*) Bergkette *f*; (*stove*) Herd *m*;
(*for firing practice*) Schießplatz *m*;
(*of a gun*) Schießweite *f*; (*distance*)
Reichweite *f*; (mus) Umfang *m*; **at
a r. of** in e–r Entfernung von; **at
close r.** auf kurze Entfernung; **come
within s.o.'s r.** j–m vor den Schuß
kommen; **out of r.** außer Reichweite;
(*in shooting*) außer Schußweite;
within r. in Reichweite; (*in shooting*)
in Schußweite || *tr* reihen || *intr*—
r. from ... to sich bewegen zwischen
(*dat*) ... und

range' find'er *s* Entfernungsmesser *m*

ranger ['rendʒər] *s* Förster *m*; **rangers**
Stoßtruppen *pl*

rank [ræŋk] *adj* (*rancid*) ranzig;
(*smelly*) stinkend; (*absolute*) kraß;
(*excessive*) übermäßig; (*growth*)
üppig || *s* Rang *m*; **according to r.**
standesgemäß; **person of r.** Standes-
person *f* || *tr* einreihen, rangieren;
be ranked as gelten als || *intr* ran-
gieren; **r. above** stehen über (*dat*);
r. among zählen zu; **r. below** stehen
unter (*dat*); **r. with** mitzählen zu

rank' and file' *s* die breite Masse

rank'ing of'ficer *s* Rangälteste *mf*

rankle ['ræŋkəl] *tr* nagen an (*dat*) ||
intr nagen

ransack ['rænsæk] *tr* durchstöbern

ransom ['rænsəm] *s* Lösegeld *n* || *tr*
auslösen

rant [rænt] *intr* schwadronieren

rap [ræp] *s* (*on the door*) Klopfen *n*;
(*blow*) Klaps *m*; **not give a rap for**
husten auf (*acc*); **take the rap** den
Kopf hinhalten; **there was a rap on
the door** es klopfte an der Tür || *v*
(*pret & pp* rapped; *ger* rapping) *tr*
(*strike*) schlagen; (*criticize*) tadeln ||
intr (*talk freely*) offen reden; **(on)**
klopfen (an *dat*)

rapacious [rə'peʃəs] *adj* raffgierig;
(*animal*) raubgierig

rape [rep] *s* Vergewaltigung *f* || *tr*
vergewaltigen

rapid ['ræpɪd] *adj* rapid(e); (*river*)
reißend || **rapids** *spl* Stromschnelle *f*

rap'id-fire' *adj* Schnell–; (mil) Schnell-
feuer–

rap'id trans'it *s* Nahschnellverkehr *m*

rapier ['repɪ·ər] *s* Rapier *n*

rapist ['repɪst] *s* sexueller Gewaltver-
brecher *m*

rap' ses'sion *s* zwanglose Diskussion *f*

rapt [ræpt] *adj* (*attention*) gespannt;
(*in thought*) vertieft

rapture ['ræptʃər] *s* Entzückung *f*; **go
into raptures** in Entzücken geraten

rare [rɛr] *adj* selten; (culin) halbgar

rare' bird' *s* (fig) weißer Rabe *m*

rare·fy ['rɛrɪˌfaɪ] *v* (*pret & pp* -fied)
tr verdünnen

rarely ['rɛrli] *adv* selten

rarity ['rɛrɪti] *s* Rarität *f*

rascal ['ræskəl] *s* Bengel *m*

rash [ræʃ] *adj* vorschnell, unbesonnen
|| *s* Ausschlag *m*

rasp [ræsp] *s* (*sound*) Kratzlaut *m*;
(*tool*) Raspel *f* || *tr* raspeln

raspberry ['ræzˌbɛri] *s* Himbeere *f*

rat [ræt] *s* Ratte *f*; (*deserter*) (sl)
Überläufer –in *mf*; (*informer*) (sl)
Spitzel *m*; (*scoundrel*) (sl) Gauner
m; **smell a rat** (coll) den Braten
riechen || *intr*—**rat on** (sl) verpetzen

ratchet ['rætʃɪt] *s* (*wheel*) Sperrad *n*;
(*pawl*) Sperrklinke *f*

rate [ret] *s* Satz *m*; (*for mail, freight*)
Tarif *m*; **at any r.** auf jeden Fall;
at the r. of (*a certain speed*) mit der
Geschwindigkeit von; (*a certain
price*) zum Preis von; **at the r. of a
dozen per week** ein Duzend pro
Woche; **at this** (or **that**) **r.** bei diesem
Tempo || *tr* bewerten || *intr* (coll)
hochgeschätzt sein

rate' of exchange' *s* Kurs *m*

rate' of in'terest *s* Zinssatz *m*

rather ['ræðər] *adv* ziemlich; **I would
r. wait** ich würde lieber warten; **r.
... than** lieber ... als || *interj* na ob!

rati·fy ['rætɪˌfaɪ] *v* (*pret & pp* -fied)
tr ratifizieren, bestätigen

rat'ing *s* Beurteilung *f*; (mach) Leistung *f*; (mil) Dienstgrad *m*; (sport)
Bewertung *f*

ra·tio ['reʃ(ɪ)ˌo] *s* (-tios) Verhältnis
n

ration ['ræʃən], ['reʃən] *s* Ration *f*;
rations (mil) Verpflegung *f* || *tr*
rationieren

ra'tion card' *s* Bezugsschein *m*

ra'tioning *s* Rationierung *f*

rational ['ræʃənəl] *adj* vernünftig

rationalize ['ræʃənəˌlaɪz] *tr & intr*
rationalisieren

rat' poi'son *s* Rattengift *n*

rat' race' *s* (fig) Hetzjagd *f*

rattle ['rætəl] *s* Geklapper *n*; (*toy*)
Klapper *f*, Schnarre *f* || *tr* (*confuse*)
verwirren; **get s.o. rattled** j–n aus
dem Konzept bringen; **r. off** herun-
terschnarren; **r. the dishes** mit dem
Geschirr klappern || *intr* klappern;
(*said of a machine gun*) knattern;

(*said of windows*) klirren; **r. on** daherplappern
rat'tlebrain' *s* Hohlkopf *m*
rat'tlesnake' *s* Klapperschlange *f*
rat'tletrap' *s* (coll) Kiste *f*, Karre *f*
rat'trap' *s* Rattenfalle *f*
raucous ['rɔkəs] *adj* heiser
ravage ['rævɪdʒ] *s* Verwüstung *f*, Verheerung *f* ‖ *tr* verwüsten, verheeren
rave [rev] *s* (*coll*) Modeschrei *m* ‖ *intr* irrereden; **r. about** schwärmen von
raven ['revən] *adj* (*black*) rabenschwarz ‖ *s* Kolkrabe *m*, Rabe *m*
ravenous ['rævənəs] *adj* rasend
ravine [rə'vin] *s* Bergschlucht *f*
rav'ing *adj* (coll) toll ‖ *adv*—**r. mad** tobsüchtig
ravish ['rævɪʃ] *tr* vergewaltigen
rav'ishing *adv* entzückend
raw [rɔ] *adj* roh; (*weather*) naßkalt; (*throat*) rauh; (*recruit*) unausgebildet; (*skin*) wundgerieben; (*leather*) ungegerbt; (*wool*) ungesponnen
raw'-boned' *adj* hager
raw' deal' *s* (sl) unfaire Behandlung *f*
raw'hide' *s* Rohhaut *f*
raw' mate'rial *s* Rohstoff *m*
ray [re] *s* Strahl *m*; (ichth) Rochen *m*; **ray of hope** Hoffnungsstrahl *m*
rayon ['re·ɑn] *adj* kunstseiden ‖ *s* Kunstseide *f*, Rayon *m*
raze [rez] *tr* abtragen; **r. to the ground** dem Erdboden gleichmachen
razor ['rezər] *s* Rasiermesser *n*; (*safety razor*) Rasierapparat *m*
ra'zor blade' *s* Rasierklinge *f*
razz [ræz] *tr* (sl) aufziehen
re [ri] *prep* betreffs (*genit*)
reach [ritʃ] *s* Reichweite *f*; **beyond the r. of s.o.** für j–n unerreichbar; **out of r.** unerreichbar; **within easy r.** leicht zu erreichen; **within r.** in Reichweite ‖ *tr* (*a goal, person, city, advanced age, an understanding*) erreichen; (*a certain amount*) sich belaufen auf (*acc*); (*a compromise*) schließen; (*an agreement*) treffen; (*e.g., the ceiling*) heranreichen an (*acc*); **r. out** ausstrecken ‖ *intr* (*extend*) reichen, sich erstrecken; **r. for** greifen nach; **r. into one's pocket** in die Tasche greifen
react [rɪ'ækt] *intr* (**to**) reagieren (auf *acc*); **r. upon** zurückwirken auf (*acc*)
reaction [rɪ'ækʃən] *s* Reaktion *f*
reactionary [rɪ'ækʃən͵eri] *adj* reaktionär ‖ *s* Reaktionär –in *mf*
reac'tion time' *s* Reaktionszeit *f*
reactor [rɪ'æktər] *s* Reaktor *m*
read [rid] *v* (*pret & pp* **read** [red]) *tr* lesen; **r. a paper on** referieren über (*acc*); **r. off** verlesen; **r. over** durchlesen; **r. to** vorlesen (*dat*) ‖ *intr* lesen; (*said of a passage*) lauten; (*said of a thermometer*) zeigen; **r. up on** studieren
readable ['ridəbəl] *adj* lesbar
reader ['ridər] *s* (*person*) Leser –in *mf*; (*book*) Lesebuch *n*
readily ['rɛdɪli] *adv* gern(e)
readiness ['rɛdɪnɪs] *s* Bereitwilligkeit *f*; (*preparedness*) Bereitschaft *f*

read'ing *s* (*act*) Lesen *n*; (*material*) Lektüre *f*; (*version*) Lesart *f*; (eccl, parl) Lesung *f*
read'ing glass'es *spl* Lesebrille *f*
read'ing lamp' *s* Leselampe *f*
read'ing room' *s* Lesesaal *m*
readjustment [͵ri·ə'dʒʌstmənt] *s* Umstellung *f*
read·y ['redi] *adj* (*done*) fertig; **be r.** (*stand in readiness*) in Bereitschaft stehen; **get r.** sich fertig (or bereit) machen; **get s.th. r.** etw fertigstellen; **r. for** bereit zu; **r. for take-off** startbereit; **r. for use** gebrauchsfertig; **r. to** (*inf*) bereit zu (*inf*) ‖ *v* (*pret & pp* **–ied**) *tr* fertigmachen
read'y cash' *s* flüssiges Geld *n*
read'y-made' *adj* von der Stange
read'y-made' clothes' *spl* Konfektion *f*
reaffirm [͵ri·ə'fʌrm] *tr* nochmals beteuern
real ['ri·əl] *adj* wirklich; (*genuine*) echt; (*friend*) wahr
re'al estate' *s* Immobilien *pl*
re'al-estate' a'gent *s* Immobilienmakler –in *mf*
re'al-estate tax' *s* Grundsteuer *f*
realist ['ri·əlɪst] *s* Realist –in *mf*
realistic [ri·ə'lɪstɪk] *adj* wirklichkeitsnah, realistisch
reality [rɪ'ælɪti] *s* Wirklichkeit *f*; **in r.** wirklich; **realities** (*facts*) Tatsachen *pl*
realize ['ri·ə͵laɪz] *tr* einsehen; (*a profit*) erzielen; (*a goal*) verwirklichen; (*a good*) realisieren
really ['ri·əli] *adv* wirklich; **not r.** eigentlich nicht
realm [rɛlm] *s* Königreich *n*; (fig) Reich *n*, Gebiet *n*; **within the r. of possibility** im Rahmen des Möglichen
realtor ['ri·əltər] *s* Immobilienmakler –in *mf*
ream [rim] *s* Ries *n* ‖ *tr* ausbohren
reamer ['rimər] *s* Reibahle *f*
reap [rip] *tr* (*cut*) mähen; (& fig) ernten
reaper ['ripər] *s* Mäher –in *mf*; (mach) Mähmaschine *f*
reappear [͵ri·ə'pɪr] *intr* wiederauftauchen, wiedererscheinen
rearmament [ri'ɑrməmənt] *s* Wiedererscheinen *n*
reappoint [͵ri·ə'pɔɪnt] *tr* wieder anstellen
rear [rɪr] *adj* hintere, rückwärtig ‖ *s* Hinterseite *f*; (*of an army*) Nachhut *f*; (sl) Hintern *m*; **bring up the r.** den Schluß bilden; (mil) den Zug beschließen; **from the r.** von hinten; **to the r.** nach hinten; **to the r., march!** kehrt, marsch! ‖ *tr* (*children*) aufziehen; (*animals*) züchten; (*a structure, one's head*) aufrichten ‖ *intr* sich bäumen
rear' ad'miral *s* Konteradmiral *m*
rear' ax'le *s* Hinterachse *f*
rear' end' *s* (sl) Hintern *m*
rear' guard' *s* (mil) Nachhut *f*
rear' gun'ner *s* Heckschütze *m*

rearm [ri'ɑrm] *tr* wieder aufrüsten
rearmament [ri'ɑrməmənt] *s* Wieder-
aufrüstung *f*
rearrange [ˌri·ə'rendʒ] *tr* umstellen
rear' seat' *s* Hintersitz *m*
rear'-view mir'ror *s* Rückspiegel *m*
rear'-wheel drive' *s* Hinterradantrieb
m
rear' win'dow *s* (aut) Heckfenster *n*
reason ['rizən] *s* Vernunft *f;* (*cause*)
Grund *m;* **by r.** of auf Grund (*genit*);
for this r. aus diesem Grund; **listen
to r.** sich belehren lassen; **not listen
to r.** sich [*dat*] nichts sagen lassen;
not without good r. nicht umsonst ||
*tr—***r. out** durchdenken || *intr—***r.**
with vernünftig reden mit
reasonable ['rizənəbəl] *adj* (*person*)
vernünftig; (*price*) solid; (*wares*)
preiswert
reassemble [ˌri·ə'sembəl] *tr* (*people*)
wieder versammeln; (mach) wieder
zusammenbauen || *intr* sich wieder
sammeln
reassert [ˌri·ə'sɛrt] *tr* wieder behaupten
reassurance [ˌri·ə'ʃurəns] *s* Beruhigung
f
reassure [ri·ə'ʃur] *tr* beruhigen
reawaken [ˌri·ə'wekən] *tr* wieder er-
wecken || *intr* wieder erwachen
rebate ['ribet] *s* Rabatt *m*
re·bel ['rɛbəl] *adj* Rebellen- || *s* Rebell
–in *mf* || [ri'bɛl] *v* (*pret & pp*
–belled; *ger* **–belling**) *intr* rebellieren
rebellion [ri'bɛljən] *s* Aufstand *m,*
Rebellion *f*
rebellious [ri'bɛljəs] *adj* aufständisch
rebirth ['ribʌrθ] *s* Wiedergeburt *f*
rebore [ri'bor] *tr* nachbohren
rebound ['ri‚baʊnd] *s* Rückprall *m* ||
[ri'baʊnd] *intr* zurückprallen
rebroad·cast [ri'brɔd‚kæst] *s* Wieder-
holungssendung *f* || *v* (*pret & pp*
–cast & **–casted**) *tr* nochmals übertragen
rebuff [ri'bʌf] *s* Zurückweisung *f* || *tr*
schroff abweisen
re·build [ri'bɪld] *v* (*pret & pp* **–built**)
tr wiederaufbauen; (mach) über-
holen; (*confidence*) wiederherstellen
rebuke [ri'bjuk] *s* Verweis *m* || *tr* ver-
weisen
re·but [ri'bʌt] *v* (*pret & pp* **–butted;**
ger **–butting**) *tr* widerlegen
rebuttal [ri'bʌtəl] *s* Widerlegung *f*
recall [ri'kɔl], ['rikɔl] *s* (*recollection*)
Erinnerungsvermögen *n;* (com) Zurücknahme *f;* (dipl, pol) Abberufung
f; **beyond r.** unwiderruflich || [ri'kɔl]
tr (*remember*) sich erinnern an (*dat*);
(*an ambassador*) abberufen; (*workers*) zurückrufen; (mil) wiederein-
berufen
recant [ri'kænt] *tr* & *intr* (öffentlich)
widerrufen
re·cap ['ri‚kæp] *s* Zusammenfassung
f || *v* (*pret & pp* **–capped;** *ger* **–cap-
ping**) *tr* zusammenfassen; (*a tire*)
runderneuern
recapitulate [ˌrikə'pɪtʃə‚let] *tr* zusammenfassen

recapitulation [ˌrikə‚pɪtʃə'leʃən] *s*
Rekapitulation *f,* Zusammenfassung
f
re·cast ['ri‚kæst] *s* Umguß *m* ||
[ri'kæst] *v* (*pret & pp* **–cast**) *tr* um-
gießen; (*a sentence*) umarbeiten;
(theat) neubesetzen
recede [ri'sid] *intr* zurückgehen; (*become more distant*) zurückweichen
reced'ing *adj* (*forehead, chin*) fliehend
receipt [ri'sit] *s* Quittung *f;* **acknowledge r. of** den Empfang bestätigen
(*genit*); **receipts** Eingänge *pl* || *tr*
quittieren
receive [ri'siv] *tr* bekommen, erhalten;
(*a guest*) empfangen; (*pay*) beziehen;
(rad) empfangen
receiver [ri'sivər] *s* Empfänger –in *mf;*
(jur) Zwangsverwalter –in *mf;* (telp)
Hörer *m*
receiv'ership' *s* Zwangsverwaltung *f*
recent ['risənt] *adj* neu, jung; **in r.
years** in den letzten Jahren; **of r. date**
neueren Datums
recently ['risəntli] *adv* kürzlich
receptacle [ri'sɛptəkəl] *s* Behälter *m;*
(elec) Steckdose *f*
reception [ri'sɛpʃən] *s* (& rad) Empfang *m*
recep'tion desk' *s* Empfang *m*
receptionist [ri'sɛpənɪst] *s* Empfangs-
dame *f;* (med) Sprechstundenhilfe *f*
receptive [ri'sɛptɪv] *adj* (**to**) aufgeschlossen (für)
recess [ri'sɛs], ['risɛs] *s* (*alcove*)
Nische *f;* (*cleft*) Einschnitt *m;* (*at
school*) Pause *f;* (jur) Unterbrechung
f; (parl) Ferien *pl* || [ri'sɛs] *tr*
(*place in a recess*) versenken || *intr*
(*until*) sich vertagen (auf *acc*)
recession [ri'sɛʃən] *s* Rezession *f,*
Rückgang *m*
recharge [ri'tʃɑrdʒ] *tr* wieder aufladen
recipe ['rɛsɪ‚pi] *s* Rezept *n*
recipient [ri'sɪpi·ənt] *s* Empfänger –in
mf
reciprocal [ri'sɪprəkəl] *adj* gegenseitig
reciprocate [ri'sɪprə‚ket] *tr* sich er-
kenntlich zeigen für || *intr* sich er-
kenntlich zeigen
reciprocity [ˌrɛsɪ'prɑsɪti] *s* Gegenseitigkeit *f*
recital [ri'saɪtəl] *s* Vortrag *m*
recite [ri'saɪt] *tr* vortragen
reckless ['rɛklɪs] *adj* (*careless of consequences*) unbekümmert; (*lacking
caution*) leichtsinnig; (*negligent*)
fahrlässig
reck'less driv'ing *s* rücksichtsloses Fahren *n*
reckon ['rɛkən] *tr* (*count*) rechnen;
(*compute*) (coll) schätzen || *intr*
rechnen; (coll) schätzen; **r. on** rechnen auf (*acc*); **r. with** (*deal with*)
abrechnen mit; (*take into consideration*) rechnen mit
reck'oning *s* (*accounting*) Abrechnung
f; (*computation*) Berechnung *f;* (aer,
naut) Besteck *n*
reclaim [ri'klem] *tr* (*demand back*)
zurückfordern; (*from wastes*) rück-
gewinnen; (*land*) urbar machen

reclamation [,reklə'meʃən] s (*of land*) Urbarmachung *f*

recline [rɪ'klaɪn] *intr* ruhen; **r. against** sich lehnen an (*acc*); **r. in** (*a chair*) sich zurücklehnen in (*dat*)

recluse ['reklus] s Einsiedler –in *mf*

recognition [,rekəg'nɪʃən] s Wiedererkennung *f*; (*acknowledgement*) Anerkennung *f*; **gain r.** zur Geltung kommen

recognizable [,rekəg'naɪzəbəl] *adj* erkennbar

recognize ['rekəg,naɪz] *tr* (**by**) erkennen (an *dat*); **r. as** anerkennen als

recoil ['rikɔɪl] s (*of a rifle*) Rückstoß *m*; (arti) Rücklauf *m* ‖ [rɪ'kɔɪl] *intr* (*in fear*) zurückfahren; (**from**, *e.g.*, *a challenge*) zurückschrecken vor (*dat*); (*said of a rifle*) zurückstoßen; (arti) zurücklaufen

recoilless [rɪ'kɔɪlɪs] *adj* rückstoßfrei

recollect [,rekə'lekt] *tr* sich erinnern an (*acc*)

recollection [,rekə'lekʃən] s Erinnerung *f*

recommend [,rekə'mend] *tr* empfehlen

recommendation [,rekəmən'deʃən] s Empfehlung *f*

recompense ['rekəm,pens] s (**for**) Vergütung *f* (für) ‖ *tr* vergüten

reconcile ['rekən,saɪl] *tr* (**with**) versöhnen (mit); **become reconciled** sich versöhnen; **r. oneself to** sich abfinden mit

reconciliation [,rekən,sɪlɪ'eʃən] s Versöhnung *f*, Aussöhnung *f*

recondite ['rekən,daɪt] *adj* (*deep*) tiefgründig; (*obscure*) dunkel

recondition [,rikən'dɪʃən] *tr* wiederinstandsetzen

reconnaissance [rɪ'kanɪsəns] s Aufklärung *f*

reconnoiter [,rekə'nɔɪtər] *tr* erkunden ‖ *intr* aufklären

reconquer [ri'kaŋkər] *tr* zurückerobern

reconquest [ri'kaŋkwest] s Zurückeroberung *f*

reconsider [,rikən'sɪdər] *tr* noch einmal erwägen

reconstruct [,rikən'strʌkt] *tr* (*rebuild*) wiederaufbauen; (*make over*) umbauen; (*e.g.*, *events of a case*) rekonstruieren

record ['rekərd] *adj* Rekord– ‖ s (*highest achievement*) Rekord *m*; (*document*) Akte *f*, Protokoll *n*; (*documentary evidence*) Aufzeichnung *f*; (mus) Schallplatte *f*; **have a criminal r.** vorbestraft sein; **keep a r. of** Buch führen über (*acc*); **make a r. of** zu Protokoll nehmen; **off the r.** inoffiziell; **on r.** bisher registriert; **set a r.** e–n Rekord aufstellen ‖ [rɪ'kɔrd] *tr* (*in writing*) aufzeichnen; (*officially*) protokollieren; (*on tape or disk*) aufnehmen ‖ *intr* Schallplatten aufnehmen

rec'ord chang'er s Plattenwechsler *m*

recorder [rɪ'kɔrdər] s Protokollführer –in *mf*; (*device*) Zähler *m*; (*on tape*

or disk) Aufnahmegerät; (mus) Blockflöte *f*

rec'ord hold'er s Rekordler –in *mf*

record'ing *adj* aufzeichnend; (*on tape or disk*) Aufnahme– ‖ s Aufzeichnung *f*; (*on tape or disk*) Tonaufnahme *f*

record'ing sec'retary s Protokollführer –in *mf*

rec'ord play'er s Plattenspieler *m*

recount ['ri ,kaunt] s Nachzählung *f* ‖ [ri'kaunt] *tr* (*count again*) nachzählen ‖ [rɪ'kaunt] *tr* (*relate*) im einzelnen erzählen

recoup [rɪ'kup] *tr* (*losses*) wieder einbringen; (*a fortune*) wiedererlangen; (*reimburse*) entschädigen

recourse [rɪ'kors], ['rikors] s (**to**) Zuflucht *f* (zu); (jur) Regreß *m*; **have r. to** seine Zuflucht nehmen zu

recover [rɪ'kʌvər] *tr* (*get back*) wiedererlangen; (*losses*) wiedereinbringen; (*e.g.*, *a spent rocket*) bergen; (*one's balance*) wiederfinden; (*e.g.*, *a chair*) neu beziehen ‖ *intr* (**from**) sich erholen (von)

recovery [rɪ'kʌvəri] s Wiedererlangung *f*, Rückgewinnung *f*; (*of health*) Genesung *f*; (*of a rocket*) Bergung *f*

recreation [,rekrɪ'eʃən] s Erholung *f*

recrea'tion room' s Unterhaltungsraum *m*

recruit [rɪ'krut] s Rekrut *m* ‖ (& mil) rekrutieren; **be recruited from** sich rekrutieren aus

recruit'ing of'ficer s Werbeoffizier *m*

recruitment [rɪ'krutmənt] s Rekrutierung *f*; (mil) Rekrutenaushebung *f*

rectangle ['rek ,tæŋgəl] s Rechteck *n*

rectangular [rek'tæŋgjələr] *adj* rechteckig

rectifier ['rektə ,faɪ·ər] s Berichtiger *m*; (elec) Gleichrichter *m*

recti•fy ['rektɪ ,faɪ] *v* (*pret & pp* –**fied**) *tr* berichtigen; (elec) gleichrichten

rector ['rektər] s Rektor *m*

rectory ['rektəri] s Pfarrhaus *n*

rec•tum ['rektəm] s (–**ta** [tə]) Mastdarm *m*

recumbent [rɪ'kʌmbənt] *adj* liegend

recuperate [rɪ'k(j)upə ,ret] *intr* sich (wieder) erholen

re•cur [rɪ'kʌr] *v* (*pret & pp* –**curred**; *ger* –**curring**) *intr* wiederkehren

recurrence [rɪ'kʌrəns] s Wiederkehr *f*

red [red] *adj* (**redder**; **reddest**) rot ‖ s Rot *n*, Röte *f*; **be in the red** in den Roten Zahlen stecken; **Red** (pol) Rote *mf*; **see red** wild werden

red' ant' s rote Waldameise *f*

red'bird' s Kardinal *m*

red'blood'ed *adj* lebensprühend

red'breast' s Rotkehlchen *n*

red' cab'bage s Rotkohl *m*

red' car'pet s (fig) roter Teppich *m*

red' cent' s—**not give a r. for** keinen roten Heller geben für

red'-cheeked' *adj* rotbäckig

Red' Cross', **the** s das Rote Kreuz

redden ['redən] *tr* röten, rot machen ‖ *intr* erröten, rot werden

reddish ['redɪʃ] *adj* rötlich

redecorate [rɪ'dɛkə͵ret] *tr* neu dekorieren

redeem [rɪ'dim] *tr* zurückkaufen; (*a pawned article, promise*) einlösen; **r. oneself** seine Ehre wiederherstellen

redeemable [rɪ'diməbəl] *adj* (fin) ablösbar, kündbar

Redeemer [rɪ'dimər] *s* Erlöser *m*

redemption [rɪ'dempʃən] *s* Rückkauf *m*, Wiedereinlösung *f*; (relig) Erlösung *f*

red'-haired' *adj* rothaarig

red'-hand'ed *adj*—**catch s.o. r.** j–n auf frischer Tat ertappen

red'head' *s* Rotkopf *m*

red' her'ring *s* Bückling *m*; (fig) Ablenkungsmanöver *n*

red'-hot' *adj* glühend heiß, rotglühend

redirect [͵ridɪ'rɛkt] *tr* umdirigieren

rediscover [͵ridɪs'kʌvər] *tr* wiederentdecken

red'-let'ter day' *s* Glückstag *m*

red' light' *s* rotes Licht *n*

red'-light' dis'trict *s* Bordellviertel *n*

red' man' *s* Rothaut *f*

redness ['rɛdnɪs] *s* Röte *f*

re·do ['ri'du] *v* (*pret* **–did**; *pp* **–done**) *tr* neu machen; (*redecorate*) renovieren

redolent ['rɛdələnt] *adj* (**with**) duftend (nach)

redoubt [rɪ'daʊt] *s* Redoute *f*

redound [rɪ'daʊnd] *intr*—**r. to** gereichen zu

red' pep'per *s* spanischer Pfeffer *m*

redress [rɪ'drɛs] *s* Wiedergutmachung *f* ‖ *tr* wiedergutmachen

Red' Rid'inghood' *s* Rotkäppchen *n*

red'skin' *s* Rothaut *f*

red' tape' *s* Amtsschimmel *m*

reduce [rɪ'd(j)us] *tr* reduzieren, verringern; (*prices*) herabsetzen; (math) (ab)kürzen

reduction [rɪ'dʌkʃən] *s* Verminderung *f*; (*gradual reduction*) Abbau *m*; (*in prices*) Absetzung *f*; (*in weight*) Abnahme *f*

redundant [rɪ'dʌndənt] *adj* überflüssig

red' wine' *s* Rotwein *m*

red'wing' *s* Rotdrossel *f*

red'wood' *s* Rotholz *n*

reecho [ri'ɛko] *tr* wiederhallen lassen ‖ *intr* wiederhallen

reed [rid] *s* Schilf *n*; (*in mouthpiece*) Rohrblatt *n*; (*of metal*) Zunge *f*; (*pastoral pipe*) Hirtenflöte *f*

reedit [rɪ'ɛdɪt] *tr* neu herausgeben

reeducate [ri'ɛdʒʊ͵ket] *tr* umerziehen

reef [rif] *s* Riff *n*; (naut) Reff *n* ‖ *tr* (naut) reffen

reek [rik] *intr* (**of**) riechen (nach)

reel [ril] *s* (*sway*) Taumeln *n*; (*for cables*) Trommel *f*; (angl, cin) Spule *f*; (min, naut) Haspel *f* ‖ *tr* (angl, cin) spulen; (min, naut) haspeln; **r. in** (*a fish*) einholen; **r. off** abhaspeln; (fig) herunterrasseln ‖ *intr* taumeln

reelect [͵ri·ɪ'lɛkt] *tr* wiederwählen

reelection [͵ri·ɪ'lɛkʃən] *s* Wiederwahl *f*

reenlist [͵ri·ɛn'lɪst] *tr* wieder anwerben ‖ *intr* sich weiterverpflichten

reenlistment [͵ri·ɛn'lɪstmənt] *s* Weiterverpflichtung *f*

reentry [rɪ'ɛntri] *s* Wiedereintritt *m*

reexamination [͵ri·ɛg͵zæmɪ'neʃən] *s* Nachprüfung *f*

re·fer [rɪ'fʌr] *v* (*pret* & *pp* **–ferred**; *ger* **–ferring**) *tr*—**r. s.o. to** j–n verweisen an (*acc*) ‖ *intr*—**r. to** hinweisen auf (*acc*); (*e.g., to an earlier correspondence*) sich beziehen auf (*acc*)

referee [͵rɛfə'ri] *s* (box) Ringrichter *m*; (sport) Schiedsrichter *m* ‖ *tr* als Schiedsrichter fungieren bei ‖ *intr* als Schiedsrichter fungieren

reference ['rɛfərəns] *s* (**to**) Hinweis *m* (auf *acc*); (*person or document*) Referenz *f*; **in r. to** in Bezug auf (*acc*); **make r. to** hinweisen auf (*acc*)

ref'erence lib'rary *s* Handbibliothek *f*

ref'erence work' *s* Nachschlagewerk *n*

referen·dum [͵rɛfə'rɛndəm] *s* (**–da** [də]) Volksentscheid *m*

referral [rɪ'fʌrəl] *s* (**to**) Zuweisung *f* (an *acc*, auf *acc*); **by r.** auf Empfehlung

refill ['rifɪl] *s* Nachfüllung *f*; (*for a pencil, ball-point pen*) Ersatzmine *f* ‖ [ri'fɪl] *tr* nachfüllen

refine [rɪ'faɪn] *tr* (*metal*) läutern; (*oil, sugar*) raffinieren; (fig) verfeinern

refinement [rɪ'faɪnmənt] *s* Läuterung *f*; (*of oil, sugar*) Raffination *f*; (fig) Verfeinerung *f*

refinery [rɪ'faɪnəri] *s* Raffinerie *f*

reflect [rɪ'flɛkt] *tr* (& fig) widerspiegeln ‖ *intr* (*throw back rays*) reflektieren; (**on**) nachdenken (über *acc*); **r. on** (*comment on*) sich äußern über (*acc*); (*bring reproach on*) ein schlechtes Licht werfen auf (*acc*)

reflection [rɪ'flɛkʃən] *s* (*e.g., of light*) Reflexion *f*; (*reflected image*) Spiegelbild *n*; (*thought*) Überlegung *f*; **that's no r. on you** das färbt nicht auf Sie ab

reflector [rɪ'flɛktər] *s* Reflektor *m*

reflex ['riflɛks] *s* Reflex *m*

reflexive [rɪ'flɛksɪv] *adj* (gram) reflexiv ‖ *s* Reflexivform *f*

reforestation [͵rifɔrɪs'teʃən] *s* Aufforstung *f*

reform [rɪ'fɔrm] *s* Reform *f* ‖ *tr* reformieren, verbessern ‖ *intr* sich bessern

reformation [͵rɛfər'meʃən] *s* Besserung *f*; **Reformation** Reformation *f*

reformatory [rɪ'fɔrmə͵tori] *s* Besserungsanstalt *f*

reformer [rɪ'fɔrmər] *s* Reformator –in *mf*

reform' school' *s* Besserungsanstalt *f*

refraction [rɪ'frækʃən] *s* Ablenkung *f*

refrain [rɪ'fren] *s* Kehrreim *m* ‖ *intr*—**r. from** sich enthalten (*genit*); **r. from** (*ger*) es unterlassen zu (*inf*)

refresh [rɪ'frɛʃ] *tr* erfrischen; (*the memory*) auffrischen

refresh'er course' [rɪ'frɛʃər] *s* Auffrischungskurs *m*

refresh'ing *adj* erfrischend

refreshment [rɪ'frɛʃmənt] s Erfrischung f

refresh'ment stand' s Erfrischungsstand m

refrigerant [rɪ'frɪdʒərənt] s Kühlmittel n

refrigerate [rɪ'frɪdʒə,ret] tr kühlen

refrigerator [rɪ'frɪdʒə,retər] s Kühlschrank m; (walk-in type) Kühlraum m

refrig'erator car' s (rr) Kühlwagen m

re•fuel [ri'fjul] v (pret & pp –fuel[l]ed; ger –fuel[l]ing) tr auftanken || intr tanken

refuge ['rɛfjudʒ] s Zuflucht f; take r. in (sich) flüchten in (acc)

refugee [,rɛfju'dʒi] s Flüchtling m

refugee' camp' s Flüchtlingslager n

refund ['rifʌnd] s Zurückzahlung f || [rɪ'fʌnd] tr (pay back) zurückzahlen || [ri'fʌnd] tr (fund again) neu fundieren

refurnish [ri'fʌrnɪʃ] tr neu möblieren

refusal [rɪ'fjuzəl] s Ablehnung f

refuse ['rɛfjus] s Abfall m || [rɪ'fjuz] tr ablehnen; r. to (inf) sich weigern zu (inf)

refutation [,rɛfju'teʃən] s Widerlegung f

refute [rɪ'fjut] tr widerlegen

regain [rɪ'gen] tr zurückgewinnen

regal ['rigəl] adj königlich

regale [rɪ'gel] tr (delight) ergötzen; (entertain) reichlich bewirten

regalia [rɪ'gelɪ•ə] spl Insignien pl

regard [rɪ'gard] s (for) Rücksicht f (auf acc); best regards to herzlichster Gruß an (acc); have little r. for wenig achten; in every r. in jeder Hinsicht; in (or with) r. to in Hinsicht auf (acc); in this r. in dieser Hinsicht; without r. for ohne Rücksicht auf (acc) || tr betrachten; as regards in Bezug auf (acc)

regard'ing prep hinsichtlich (genit)

regardless [rɪ'gardlɪs] adv (coll) ungeniert; r. of ungeachtet (genit)

regatta [rɪ'gætə] s Regatta f

regency ['ridʒənsi] s Regentschaft f

regenerate [rɪ'dʒɛnə,ret] tr regenerieren

regent ['ridʒənt] s Regent –in mf

regicide ['rɛdʒɪ,saɪd] s (act) Königsmord m; (person) Königsmörder –in mf

regime [re'ʒim] s Regime n

regiment ['rɛdʒɪmənt] s (mil) Regiment n || ['rɛdʒɪ,mənt] tr reglementieren

regimental [,rɛdʒɪ'mɛntəl] adj Regiments–

region ['ridʒən] s Gegend f, Region f

regional ['ridʒənəl] adj regional

register ['rɛdʒɪstər] s Register n, Verzeichnis n || tr registrieren; (students) immatrikulieren; (feelings) erkennen lassen || intr sich einschreiben lassen; (at a hotel) sich eintragen lassen

reg'istered let'ter s eingeschriebener Brief m

reg'istered nurse' s (staatlich) geprüfte Krankenschwester f

registrar ['rɛdʒɪstrar] s Registrator –in mf

registration [,rɛdʒɪs'treʃən] s (e.g., of firearms) Registrierung f; (for a course; at a hotel) Anmeldung f; (of a trademark) Eintragung f; (aut) Zulassung f; (educ) Einschreibung f

registra'tion blank' s Meldeformular n

registra'tion fee' s Anmeldegebühr f

registra'tion num'ber s Registriernummer f

regression [rɪ'grɛʃən] s Rückgang m

regret [rɪ'grɛt] s (over) Bedauern n (über acc) || v (pret & pp –regretted; ger regretting) tr bedauern; I r. to say es tut mir leid, sagen zu müssen

regrettable [rɪ'grɛtəbəl] adj bedauerlich

regroup [rɪ'grup] tr umgruppieren

regular ['rɛgjələr] adj (usual) gewöhnlich; (pulse, breathing, features, intervals) regelmäßig; r. army stehendes Heer n; r. guy (coll) Pfundskerl m; r. officer Berufsoffizier –in mf

regularity [,rɛgjə'lærɪti] s Regelmäßigkeit f

regulate ['rɛgjə,let] tr regeln

regulation [,rɛgjə'leʃən] s Regelung f; (rule) Vorschrift f, Bestimmung f; against regulations vorschriftswidrig

regulator ['rɛgjə,letər] s Regler m

rehabilitate [,rihə'bɪlɪ,tet] tr rehabilitieren

rehash [ri'hæʃ] tr (coll) aufwärmen

rehearsal [rɪ'harsəl] s Probe f

rehearse [rɪ'hars] tr & intr proben

rehire [ri'haɪr] tr wiedereinstellen

reign [ren] s Regierung f; (period of rule) Regierungszeit f || intr regieren; r. over herrschen über (acc)

reimburse [ri•ɪm'bʌrs] tr (costs) rückerstatten; r. s.o. for s.th. j–m etw vergüten

rein [ren] s Zügel m; give free r. to die Zügel schießen lassen (dat) || tr —r. in (a horse) parieren

reincarnation [,ri•ɪnkar'neʃən] s Reinkarnation f, Wiedergeburt f

rein'deer' s Rentier n

reinforce [,ri•ɪn'fors] tr verstärken

reinforced' concrete' s Stahlbeton m

reinforcement [,ri•ɪn'forsmənt] s Verstärkung f; reinforcements (mil) Verstärkungen pl

reinstate [,ri•ɪn'stet] tr (in) wiedereinsetzen in (acc)

reiterate [ri'ɪtə,ret] tr wiederholen

reject ['ridʒɛkt] s Ausschußware f || [rɪ'dʒɛkt] tr ablehnen, zurückweisen; (a request, appeal) abweisen

rejection [rɪ'dʒɛkʃən] s Ablehnung f; (of a request, appeal) Abweisung f

rejoice [rɪ'dʒɔɪs] intr frohlocken

rejoin [rɪ'dʒɔɪn] tr (answer) erwidern; (a group) sich wieder anschließen (dat)

rejoinder [rɪ'dʒɔɪndər] s Erwiderung f; (jur) Duplik f

rejuvenate [rɪ'dʒuvɪ,net] tr verjüngen

rekindle [ri'kɪndəl] tr wieder anzünden; (fig) wieder entzünden

relapse [rɪ'læps] s (& pathol) Rückfall

m || *intr* (**into**) wieder verfallen (in *acc*)

relate [rɪˈlet] *tr* (*a story*) erzählen; (*connect*) verknüpfen; **r. s.th. to s.th.** etw auf etw [*acc*] beziehen || *intr*—**r. to** in Beziehung stehen mit

relat′ed *adj* (*by blood*) verwandt; (*by marriage*) verschwägert; (*subjects*) benachbart

relation [rɪˈleʃən] *s* Beziehung *f,* Verhältnis *n;* (*relative*) Verwandte *mf;* **in r. to** in Bezug auf (*acc*); **relations** (*sex*) Verkehr *m*

rela′tionship′ *s* (*connection*) Beziehung *f;* (*kinship*) Verwandschaft *f*

relative [ˈrɛlətɪv] *adj* relativ, verhältnismäßig; **r. to** bezüglich (*genit*) || *s* Verwandte *mf*

rel′ative clause′ *s* Relativsatz *m*

rel′ative pro′noun *s* Relativpronomen *n*

relativity [ˌrɛləˈtɪvɪti] *s* Relativität *f*

relax [rɪˈlæks] *tr* auflockern; (*muscles*) entspannen || *intr* sich entspannen

relaxation [ˌrɪlækˈseʃən] *s* Entspannung *f;* **r. of tension** Entspannung *f*

relay [ˈrile] *s* Relais *n;* (sport) Staffel *f* || [riˈle] *v* (*pret & pp* –**layed**) *tr* übermitteln; (*through relay stations*) übertragen

re′lay race′ *s* Staffellauf *m*

re′lay team′ *s* Staffel *f*

release [rɪˈlis] *s* (**from**) Entlassung *f* (aus); (*of bombs*) Abwurf *m;* (*of news*) Mitteilung *f* || *tr* entlassen; (*a film, book*) freigeben; (*bombs*) abwerfen; (*energy*) freisetzen; (*brakes*) lösen; **r. the clutch** auskuppeln

relegate [ˈrɛlɪˌget] *tr* verweisen (an *acc*); **r. to second position** auf den zweiten Platz verweisen

relent [rɪˈlent] *intr* (*let up*) nachlassen; (*yield*) sich erweichen lassen

relentless [rɪˈlentlɪs] *adj* (*tireless*) unermüdlich; (*unappeasable*) unerbittlich; (*never-ending*) unaufhörlich

relevant [ˈrɛlɪvənt] *adj* sachdienlich

reliable [rɪˈlaɪ·əbəl] *adj* zuverlässig

reliance [rɪˈlaɪ·əns] *s* Vertrauen *n*

relic [ˈrɛlɪk] *s* Reliquie *f;* **r. of the past** Zeuge *m* der Vergangenheit

relief [rɪˈlif] *s* Erleichterung *f;* (*for the poor*) Armenunterstützung *f;* (*replacement*) Ablösung *f;* (*sculpture*) Relief *n;* **on r.** von Sozialhilfe lebend; **bring r.** Linderung schaffen; **go on r.** stempeln gehen

relief′ map′ *s* Reliefkarte *f*

relieve [rɪˈliv] *tr* erleichtern; (*from guard duty*) ablösen; **r. oneself** seine Notdurft verrichten

religion [rɪˈlɪdʒən] *s* Religion *f*

religious [rɪˈlɪdʒəs] *adj* religiös; (*order*) geistlich

relinquish [rɪˈlɪŋkwɪʃ] *tr* aufgeben; **r. the right to s.th. to s.o.** j–m das Recht auf etw [*acc*] überlassen

relish [ˈrɛlɪʃ] *s* (**for**) Genuß *m* (an *acc*); (*condiment*) Würze *f* || *tr* genießen

reluctance [rɪˈlʌktəns] *s* Widerstreben *n*

reluctant [rɪˈlʌktənt] *adj* widerstrebend; **be r. to do s.th.** etw ungern tun

reluctantly [rɪˈlʌktəntli] *adv* ungern

re·ly [rɪˈlaɪ] *v* (*pret & pp* –**lied**) *intr*— **r. on** sich verlassen auf (*acc*)

remain [rɪˈmen] *s*—**remains** Überreste *pl;* (*corpse*) sterbliche Reste *pl* || *intr* bleiben; (*at end of letter*) verbleiben; **r. behind** zurückbleiben; **r. seated** sitzenbleiben; **r. steady** (*said of prices*) sich behaupten

remainder [rɪˈmendər] *s* Restbestand *m,* Rest *m* || *tr* verramschen

remark [rɪˈmɑrk] *s* Bemerkung *f* || *tr* bemerken

remarkable [rɪˈmɑrkəbəl] *adj* markant, bemerkenswert

remar·ry [rɪˈmæri] *v* (*pret & pp* –**ried**) *tr* sich wiederverheiraten mit || *intr* sich wiederverheiraten

reme·dy [ˈrɛmɪdi] *s* (**for**) Heilmittel *n* (für); (fig) (**for**) Gegenmittel *n* (gegen) || *v* (*pret & pp* –**died**) *tr* abhelfen (*dat*); (*damage, shortage*) abheben

remember [rɪˈmembər] *tr* sich erinnern an (*acc*); **r. me to** empfehlen Sie mich (*dat*) || *intr* sich erinnern

remembrance [rɪˈmembrəns] *s* Erinnerung *f;* **in r. of** zum Andenken an (*acc*)

remind [rɪˈmaɪnd] *tr* (**of**) erinnern (an *acc*); **r. s.o. to** (*inf*) j–n mahnen zu (*inf*)

reminder [rɪˈmaɪndər] *s* (*note*) Zettel *m;* (*from a creditor*) Mahnung *f*

reminisce [ˌrɛmɪˈnɪs] *intr* in Erinnerungen schwelgen

remiss [rɪˈmɪs] *adj* nachlässig

remission [rɪˈmɪʃən] *s* Nachlaß *m*

re·mit [rɪˈmɪt] *v* (*pret & pp* –**mitted;** *ger* –**mitting**) *tr* (*in cash*) übersenden; (*by check*) überweisen; (*forgive*) vergeben

remittance [rɪˈmɪtəns] *s* (*in cash*) Übersendung *f;* (*by check*) Überweisung *f*

remnant [ˈrɛmnənt] *s* Rest *m;* (*of cloth*) Stoffrest *m*

remod·el [rɪˈmɑdəl] *v* (*pret & pp* –**el[l]ed;** *ger* –**el[l]ing**) *tr* umgestalten; (*a house*) umbauen

remonstrate [rɪˈmɑnstret] *intr* protestieren; **r. with s.o.** j–m Vorwürfe machen

remorse [rɪˈmɔrs] *s* Gewissensbisse *pl*

remorseful [rɪˈmɔrsfəl] *adj* reumütig

remote [rɪˈmot] *adj* fern; (*possibility*) vage; (*idea*) blaß; (*resemblance*) entfernt; (*secluded*) abgelegen

remote′ control′ *s* Fernsteuerung *f;* (telv) Fernbedienung *f;* **guide by r.** fernlenken

removable [rɪˈmuvəbəl] *adj* entfernbar

removal [rɪˈmuvəl] *s* Entfernung *f;* (*by truck*) Abfuhr *f;* (*from office*) Absetzung *f*

remove [rɪˈmuv] *tr* entfernen; (*clothes*) ablegen; (*one's hat*) abnehmen; (*e.g., dishes from the table*) abräumen; (*a stain*) entfernen; (*from office*) absetzen; (*furniture*) ausräumen

remuneration [rɪ͵mjunə'reʃən] s Vergütung f
renaissance [͵rɛnə'sɑns] s Renaissance f
rend [rɛnd] v (pret & pp **rent** [rɛnt]) tr (& fig) zerreißen
render ['rɛndər] tr (give) geben; (a service) leisten; (honor) erweisen; (thanks) abstatten; (a verdict) fällen; (translate; play, e.g., on the piano) wiedergeben; **r. harmless** unschädlich machen
rendez·vous ['rɑndə͵vu] s (-vous [͵vuz]) Rendezvous n, Treffpunkt m; (mil) Sammelplatz m || v (pret & pp -voused [͵vud]; ger -vousing [͵vu·ɪŋ]) intr sich treffen; (mil) sich versammeln
rendition [rɛn'dɪʃən] s Wiedergabe f
renegade ['rɛnɪ͵ged] s Renegat –in mf
renege [rɪ'nɪg] s Renonce f || intr (cards) nicht bedienen; **r. on** nicht einhalten
renew [rɪ'n(j)u] tr erneuern; (e.g., a passport) verlängern lassen
renewable [rɪ'n(j)u·əbəl] adj erneuerbar
renewal [rɪ'n(j)u·əl] s Erneuerung f; (e.g., of a passport) Verlängerung f
renounce [rɪ'nauns] tr verzichten auf (acc)
renovate ['rɛnə͵vet] tr renovieren; (fig) erneuern
renovation [͵rɛnə'veʃən] s Renovierung f
renown [rɪ'naun] s Ruhm m
renowned [rɪ'naund] adj (for) berühmt (wegen)
rent [rɛnt] adj zerrissen || s Miete f; (tear) Riß m || tr mieten; **r. out** vermieten
rental ['rɛntəl] s Miete f
rent'al serv'ice s Verleih m
rent'ed car' s Mietwagen m, Mietauto n
renter ['rɛntər] s Mieter –in mf
renunciation [rɪ͵nʌnsɪ'eʃən] s (of) Verzicht m (auf acc)
reopen [ri'opən] tr wieder öffnen; (a business) wieder eröffnen; (an argument; school year) wieder beginnen || intr (said of a shop or business) wieder geöffnet werden; (said of a school year) wieder beginnen
reopening [ri'opənɪŋ] s (of a business) Wiedereröffnung f; (of school) Wiederbeginn m; (jur) Wiederaufnahme f
reorder [ri'ɔrdər] tr nachbestellen
reorganization [͵ri·ɔrgənɪ'zeʃən] s Reorganisation f, Neuordnung f
reorganize [ri'ɔrgə͵naɪz] tr reorganisieren; (an administration) umbilden
repack [ri'pæk] tr umpacken
repair [rɪ'pɛr] s Ausbesserung f, Reparatur f; **in bad r.** in schlechtem Zustand; **keep in good r.** im Stande halten || tr ausbessern, reparieren || intr (to) sich begeben (nach, zu)
repair' gang' s Störungstrupp m
repair' shop' s Reparaturwerkstatt f
repaper [ri'pepər] tr neu tapezieren

reparation [͵rɛpə'reʃən] s Wiedergutmachung f; **reparations** Reparationen pl, Kriegsentschädigung f
repartee [͵rɛpɑr'ti] s schlagfertige Antwort f
repast [rɪ'pæst] s Mahl n
repatriate [ri'petrɪ͵et] tr repatriieren
re·pay [rɪ'pe] v (pret & pp –paid) tr (e.g., a loan) zurückzahlen; (a person) entschädigen; **r. a favor** e–n Gefallen erwidern
repayment [rɪ'pemənt] s Rückzahlung f; (reprisal) Vergeltung f
repeal [rɪ'pil] s Aufhebung f || tr aufheben, außer Kraft setzen
repeat [rɪ'pit] tr wiederholen; (a story, gossip) weitererzählen; **r. s.th. after s.o.** j–m etw nachsagen
repeat'ed adj abermalig, mehrmalig
repeatedly [rɪ'pitɪdli] adv wiederholt
re·pel [rɪ'pɛl] v (pret & pp –pelled; ger –pelling) tr (an enemy, an attack) zurückschlagen; (e.g., water) abstoßen
repellent [rɪ'pɛlənt] s Bekämpfungsmittel n
repent [rɪ'pɛnt] tr bereuen || intr Reue empfinden; **r. of** bereuen
repentance [rɪ'pɛntəns] s Reue f
repentant [rɪ'pɛntənt] adj reuig
repercussion [͵ripər'kʌʃən] s Rückwirkung f
repertory ['rɛpər͵tori] s Repertoire n
repetition [͵rɛpɪ'tɪʃən] s Wiederholung f
replace [rɪ'ples] tr (with) ersetzen (durch)
replaceable [rɪ'plesəbəl] adj ersetzbar
replacement [rɪ'plesmənt] s (act) Ersetzen n; (substitute part) Ersatz m; (person) Ersatzmann m
replay ['ripli] s (sport) Wiederholungsspiel n || [ri'ple] tr nochmals spielen
replenish [rɪ'plɛnɪʃ] tr wieder auffüllen
replete [rɪ'plit] adj angefüllt
replica ['rɛplɪkə] s Replik f
re·ply [rɪ'plaɪ] s Erwiderung f; (letter) Antwortschreiben n; **in r. to your letter** in Beantwortung Ihres Schreibens || v (pret & pp –plied) tr & intr erwidern
report [rɪ'port] s Bericht m; (rumor) Gerücht n; (e.g., of a gun) Knall m || tr (give an account of) berichten; (give notice of) melden; **r. s.o. to the police** j–n bei der Polizei anzeigen || intr (to) sich melden (bei); **r. in** sich anmelden
report' card' s Zeugnis n
reportedly [rɪ'portɪdli] adv angeblich
reporter [rɪ'portər] s Reporter –in mf
repose [rɪ'poz] s Ruhe f || intr ruhen
repository [rɪ'pɑzɪ͵tori] s Verwahrungsort m; (of information) Fundgrube f
represent [͵rɛprɪ'zɛnt] tr vertreten; (depict) darstellen
representation [͵rɛprɪzɛn'teʃən] s Vertretung f; (depiction) Darstellung f
representative [͵rɛprɪ'zɛntətɪv] adj (function) stellvertretend; (government) parlamentarisch; (typical) (of)

typisch **(für)** ‖ *s* Vertreter –in *mf;*
(pol) Abgeordnete *mf*
repress [rɪ'prɛs] *tr* unterdrücken;
(psychoanal) verdrängen
repression [rɪ'prɛʃən] *s* Unterdrückung
f; (psychoanal) Verdrängung *f*
reprieve [rɪ'priv] *s* Strafaufschub *m;*
(fig) Gnadenfrist *f,* Atempause *f*
reprimand ['rɛprɪ,mænd] *s* Verweis
m; **give s.o. a r.** j–m e–n Verweis
erteilen ‖ *tr* **(for)** zurechtweisen
(wegen, für), rügen (wegen, für)
reprint ['rɪprɪnt] *s* Nachdruck *m* ‖
[rɪ'prɪnt] *tr* nachdrucken
reprisal [rɪ'praɪzəl] *s* Vergeltung *f;*
take reprisals against or **on** Repres-
salien ergreifen gegen
reproach [rɪ'protʃ] *s* Vorwurf *m* ‖ *tr*
(for) tadeln (wegen); **r. s.o. with**
s.th. j–m etw vorwerfen
reproduce [,riprə'd(j)us] *tr* reproduzieren; *(copies)* vervielfältigen; *(an*
experiment) wiederholen; *(a play)*
neuaufführen; *(a sound)* wiedergeben; *(a lost limb)* regenerieren ‖ *intr*
sich fortpflanzen
reproduction [,riprə'dʌkʃən] *s* Repro-
duktion *f;* *(making copies)* Vervielfältigung *f;* *(of sound)* Wiedergabe *f;*
(biol) Fortpflanzung *f*
reproductive [,riprə'dʌktɪv] *adj* Fort-
pflanzungs–
reproof [rɪ'pruf] *s* Rüge *f*
reprove [rɪ'pruv] *tr* rügen
reptile ['rɛptaɪl] *s* Kriechtier *n*
republic [rɪ'pʌblɪk] *s* Republik *f*
republican [rɪ'pʌblɪkən] *adj* republikanisch ‖ *s* Republikaner –in *mf*
repudiate [rɪ'pjudɪ,et] *tr* *(disown)* verleugnen; *(a charge)* zurückweisen; *(a*
debt) nicht anerkennen; *(a treaty)*
für unverbindlich erklären; *(a*
woman) verstoßen
repugnant [rɪ'pʌgnənt] *adj* widerwärtig
repulse [rɪ'pʌls] *s* *(refusal)* Zurück-
weisung *f;* *(setback)* Rückschlag *m* ‖
tr zurückweisen; (mil) zurückschlagen
repulsive [rɪ'pʌlsɪv] *adj* abstoßend
reputable ['rɛpjətəbəl] *adj* anständig
reputation [,rɛpjə'teʃən] *s* Ruf *m,* Ansehen *n;* **have the r. of being** im Rufe
stehen zu sein
repute [rɪ'pjut] *s*—**be held in high r.**
hohes Ansehen genießen; **bring into**
bad r. in üble Nachrede bringen;
of r. von Ruf ‖ *tr*—**she is reputed to**
be a beauty sie soll e–e Schönheit
sein
reputedly [rɪ'pjutɪdli] *adv* angeblich
request [rɪ'kwɛst] *s* Bitte *f,* Gesuch *n;*
at his r. auf seine Bitte; **on r.** auf
Wunsch ‖ *tr* *(a person)* bitten; *(a*
thing) bitten um, ersuchen
Requiem ['rɛkwɪ,ɛm] *s* *(Mass)* Seelen-
messe *f;* *(chant, composition)*
Requiem *n*
require [rɪ'kwaɪr] *tr* erfordern; **if re-**
quired erforderlichenfalls
requirement [rɪ'kwaɪrmənt] *s* Anfor-
derung *f*
requisite ['rɛkwɪzɪt] *adj* erforderlich ‖

s Erfordernis *n;* *(required article)*
Requisit *n*
requisition [,rɛkwɪ'zɪʃən] *s* Anforde-
rung *f;* (mil) Requisition *f* ‖ *tr* anfordern; (mil) beschlagnahmen
requital [rɪ'kwaɪtəl] *s* *(retaliation)*
Vergeltung *f;* *(for a kindness)* Beloh-
nung *f*
requite [rɪ'kwaɪt] *tr* vergelten; **r. s.o.**
for a favor sich j–m für e–n Gefallen
erkenntlich zeigen
re-read [ri'rid] *v* *(pret & pp* –**read**
[rɛd]) *tr* nachlesen
rerun ['rirʌn] *s* (cin) Reprise *f*
resale ['ri,sel] *s* Wiederverkauf *m*
rescind [rɪ'sɪnd] *tr* *(an order)* rückgängig machen; *(a law)* aufheben
rescue ['rɛskju] *s* Rettung *f,* Bergung
f ‖ *tr* retten, bergen
rescuer ['rɛskju·ər] *s* Retter –in *mf*
research [rɪ'sʌrtʃ], ['risʌrtʃ] *s* Forschung *f;* **do r. on** Forschungen betreiben über *(acc)* ‖ *intr* forschen
researcher ['risʌrtʃər] *s* Forscher –in
mf
re-sell [ri'sɛl] *v* *(pret & pp* –**sold**) *tr*
wiederverkaufen, weiterverkaufen
resemblance [rɪ'zɛmbləns] *s* **(to)** Ähnlichkeit *f* (mit); **bear a close r. to s.o.**
große Ähnlichkeit mit j–m haben
resemble [rɪ'zɛmbəl] *tr* ähneln *(dat)*
resent [rɪ'zɛnt] *tr*—**I r. your remark**
Ihre Bemerkung paßt mir nicht
resentful [rɪ'zɛntfəl] *adj* grollend
resentment [rɪ'zɛntmənt] *s* Groll *m;*
feel r. toward Groll hegen gegen
reservation [,rɛzər've/ən] *s* Vorbestel-
lung *f;* *(Indian land)* Reservation *f;*
do you have a r.? haben Sie vorbe-
stellt?; **make reservations** vorbestellen
reserve [rɪ'zʌrv] *s* *(discretion)* Zurückhaltung *f;* (econ, mil) Reserve *f;*
without r. rückhaltlos ‖ *tr* *(e.g.,*
seats) reservieren, belegen; **r. judg-**
ment mit seinem Urteil zurückhalten
reserved' *adj* *(place)* belegt; *(person)*
zurückhaltend
reserve' of'ficer *s* Reserveoffizier *m*
reservist [rɪ'zʌrvɪst] *s* Reservist –in *mf*
reservoir ['rɛzər,vwɑr] *s* Staubecken
m
re-set [ri'sɛt] *v* *(pret & pp* –**set;** *ger*
–**setting)** *tr* *(a gem)* neu fassen;
(mach) nachstellen; (typ) neu setzen
resettle [ri'sɛtəl] *tr & intr* umsiedeln
reshape [ri'ʃep] *tr* umformen
reshuffle [ri'ʃʌfəl] *tr* *(cards)* neu
mischen; (pol) umgruppieren
reside [rɪ'zaɪd] *intr* wohnen
residence ['rɛzɪdəns] *s* Wohnsitz *m;*
(for students) Studentenheim *n*
resident ['rɛzɪdənt] *adj* wohnhaft ‖ *s*
Einwohner –in *mf*
residential [,rɛzɪ'dɛntʃəl] *adj* Wohn–
residue ['rɛzɪ,d(j)u] *s* Rest *m;* (chem)
Rückstand *m*
resign [rɪ'zaɪn] *tr* *(an office)* niederlegen; **r. oneself to** sich ergeben in
(acc) ‖ *intr* zurücktreten
resignation [,rɛzɪg'neʃən] *s* *(from an*
office) Rücktritt *m;* *(submissive*

state) Ergebung *f;* **hand in one's r.**
sein Entlassungsgesuch einreichen

resilience [rɪ'zɪlɪ-əns] *s* Elastizität *f;*
(fig) Spannkraft *f*

resilient [rɪ'zɪlɪ-ənt] *adj* elastisch;
(fig) unverwüstlich

resin ['rɛzɪn] *s* Harz *m*

resist [rɪ'zɪst] *tr* widerstehen (*dat*) ||
intr Widerstand leisten

resistance [rɪ'zɪstəns] *s* (& elec) Widerstand *m*

resole [ri'sol] *tr* neu besohlen

resolute ['rɛzə‚lut] *adj* entschlossen

resolution [rɛzə'luʃən] *s* (*resoluteness*)
Entschlossenheit *f;* (parl) Beschluß
m; **make good resolutions** gute Vor-
sätze fassen

resolve [rɪ'zɔlv] *s* Vorsatz *m* || *tr* auf-
lösen; (*a question, problem*) lösen;
r. to (*inf*) beschließen zu (*inf*) || *intr*
—**r. into** sich auflösen in (*acc*); **r.
upon s.th.** sich [*dat*] etw vornehmen

resonance ['rɛzənəns] *s* Resonanz *f*

resort [rɪ'zɔrt] *s* (*refuge*) Zuflucht *f;*
(*for health*) Kurort *m;* (*for vacation*)
Ferienort *m,* Sommerfrische *f;* **as a
last r.** als letztes Mittel || *intr*—**r. to**
greifen zu

resound [rɪ'zaʊnd] *intr* widerhallen

resource ['risɔrs] *s* Mittel *n;* **resources**
(fin) Geldmittel *pl*

resourceful [rɪ'sɔrsfəl] *adj* findig

respect [rɪ'spɛkt] *s* (*esteem*) Achtung
f, Respekt *m;* (*reference*) Hinsicht *f;*
in every r. in jeder Hinsicht; **pay
one's respects to s.o.** j–m seine Auf-
wartung machen; **with r. to** mit Be-
zug auf (*acc*) || *tr* achten

respectable [rɪ'spɛktəbəl] *adj* achtbar;
(*e.g., firm*) angesehen

respect'ed *adj* angesehen

respectful [rɪ'spɛktfəl] *adj* ehrerbietig

respectfully [rɪ'spɛktfəli] *adv*—**r. yours**
hochachtungsvoll, Ihr … or Ihre …

respective [rɪ'spɛktɪv] *adj* jeweilig

respectively [rɪ'spɛktɪvli] *adv* beziehungsweise

respiration [‚rɛspɪ'reʃən] *s* Atmung *f*

respirator ['rɛspɪ‚retər] *s* Atemgerät *n*

respiratory ['rɛspɪrə‚tori] *adj* At-
mungs–

respite ['rɛspɪt] *s* (*pause*) Atempause
f; (*reprieve*) Aufschub *m;* **without r.**
ohne Unterlaß

resplendent [rɪ'splɛndənt] *adj* glänzend

respond [rɪ'spɑnd] *tr* antworten || *intr*
(*reply*) (**to**) antworten (auf *acc*); (*react*) (**to**) ansprechen (auf *acc*)

response [rɪ'spɑns] *s* Antwort *f;* (*reaction*) Reaktion *f;* (fig) Widerhall
m; **in r. to** als Antwort auf (*acc*)

responsibility [rɪ‚spɑnsɪ'bɪlɪti] *s* Verantwortung *f*

responsible [rɪ'spɑnsɪbəl] *adj* (*position*) verantwortlich; (*person*) verant-
wortungsbewußt; **be held r. for** verantwortlich gemacht werden für; **be
r. for** (*be answerable for*) verantwortlich sein für; (*be to blame for*) schuld
sein an (*dat*); (*be the cause of*) die
Ursache sein (*genit*); (*be liable for*)
haften für

responsive [rɪ'spɑnsɪv] *adj*—**be r. to**
ansprechen auf (*acc*)

rest [rɛst] *s* (*repose*) Ruhe *f;* (*from
work*) Ruhepause *f;* (*e.g., from walking*) Rast *f;* (*remainder*) Rest *m;*
(*support*) Stütze *f;* (mus) Pause *f;*
all the r. (*in number*) alle andern;
(*in quantity*) alles übrige; **be at r.**
(*be calm*) beruhigt sein; (*be dead*)
ruhen; (*not be in motion*) sich in
Ruhelage befinden; **come to r.** stehenbleiben; **put one's mind to r.** sich
beruhigen; **take a r.** sich ausruhen;
the r. of the boys die übrigen (or
andern) Jungen || *tr* ruhen lassen,
ausruhen; (*support, e.g., one's elbow*)
stützen || *intr* sich ausruhen; **r. on**
lasten auf (*dat*); (*be based on*) be-
ruhen auf (*dat*); **r. with** liegen bei

restaurant ['rɛstərənt] *s* Restaurant *n*

restful ['rɛstfəl] *adj* ruhig

rest' home' *s* Erholungsheim *n*

rest'ing place' *s* Ruheplatz *m;* **final r.**
letzte Ruhestätte *f*

restitution [‚rɛstɪ't(j)uʃən] *s* Wiedergutmachung *f;* **make r.** Genugtuung
leisten

restive ['rɛstɪv] *adj* (*restless*) unruhig;
(*balky*) störrisch

restless ['rɛstlɪs] *adj* ruhelos

restock [ri'stɑk] *tr* wieder auffüllen;
(*waters*) wieder mit Fischen besetzen

restoration [‚rɛstə'reʃən] *s* (*of a work
of art or building*) Restaurierung *f*

restore [rɪ'stor] *tr* (*order*) wiederherstellen; (*a painting, building*) restau-
rieren; (*stolen goods*) zurückerstat-
ten; **r. to health** wiederherstellen

restrain [rɪ'stren] *tr* zurückhalten;
(*feelings; a horse*) zügeln; (*e.g.,
trade*) einschränken; **r. s.o. from**
(*ger*) j–n davon abhalten zu (*inf*)

restrain'ing or'der *s* Unterlassungsur-
teil *n*

restraint [rɪ'strent] *s* Zurückhaltung *f;*
(*force*) Zwang *m*

restrict [rɪ'strɪkt] *tr* begrenzen; **r. to**
beschränken auf (*acc*)

restrict'ed ar'ea *s* Sperrgebiet *n*

rest' room' *s* Abort *m,* Toilette *f*

result [rɪ'zʌlt] *s* Ergebnis *n,* Resultat
n; (*consequence*) Folge *f;* **as a r. of**
als Folge (*genit*); **without r.** ergeb-
nislos || *intr*—**r. from** sich ergeben
aus; **r. in** führen zu

result' clause' *s* Folgesatz *m*

resume [rɪ'zum] *tr* wieder aufnehmen;
(*a journey*) fortsetzen

résumé ['rɛzʊ‚me] *s* Zusammenfassung
f

resumption [rɪ'zʌmpʃən] *s* Wiederaufnahme *f*

resurface [ri'sʌrfɪs] *tr*—**r. the road
with** die Straßendecke erneuern von
|| *intr* (naut & fig) wiederauftauchen

resurrect [‚rɛzə'rɛkt] *tr* (*the dead*)
wieder zum Leben erwecken; (fig)
wieder aufleben lassen

resurrection [‚rɛzə'rɛkʃən] *s* Auferste-
hung *f*

resuscitate [rɪ'sʌsɪ‚tet] *tr* wiederbe-
leben

retail ['ritel] *adj* Kleinhandels– || *adv* im Kleinhandel || *tr* im Kleinhandel verkaufen || *intr*—**r. at two dollars** im Kleinverkauf zwei Dollar kosten

re'tail busi'ness *s* Kleinhandel *m*

retailer ['ritelər] *s* Kleinhändler –in *mf*

retain [rɪ'ten] *tr* (zurück)behalten; (*a lawyer*) sich [*dat*] nehmen

retainer [rɪ'tenər] *s* (hist) Gefolgsmann *m*; (jur) Honorarvorschuß *m*

retain'ing wall' *s* Stützmauer *f*

retake ['ritek] *s* (cin) Neuaufnahme *f* || [ri'tek] *tr* (*a town*) zurückerobern; (cin) nochmals aufnehmen

retaliate [rɪ'tælɪ,et] *intr* (**against**) Vergeltung üben (an *dat*)

retaliation [rɪ,tælɪ'eʃən] *s* Vergeltung *f*

retaliatory [rɪ'tælɪ-ə,tori] *adj* Vergeltungs–

retard [rɪ'tard] *tr* verzögern

retard'ed *adj* zurückgeblieben

retch [retʃ] *intr* würgen

retch'ing *s* Würgen *n*

retell [ri'tel] *tr* wiedererzählen

retention [rɪ'tenʃən] *s* Beibehaltung *f*

re•think [rɪ'θɪŋk] *v* (*pret & pp* –**thought**) *tr* umdenken

reticence ['retɪsəns] *s* Verschwiegenheit *f*

reticent ['retɪsənt] *adj* verschwiegen

retina ['retɪnə] *s* Netzhaut *f*, Retina *f*

retinue ['retɪ,n(j)u] *s* Gefolge *n*

retire [rɪ'taɪr] *tr* pensionieren || *intr* (*from employment*) in den Ruhestand treten; (*withdraw*) sich zurückziehen; (*go to bed*) sich zur Ruhe begeben

retired' *adj* pensioniert

retirement [rɪ'taɪrmənt] *s* Ruhestand *m*; **go into r.** in den Ruhestand treten, sich pensionieren lassen

retire'ment pay' *s* Pension *f*

retire'ment plan' *s* Pensionsplan *m*

retir'ing *adj* zurückhaltend

retort [rɪ'tɔrt] *s* schlagfertige Erwiderung *f*; (chem) Retorte *f* || *tr & intr* erwidern

retouch [ri'tʌtʃ] *tr* retuschieren

retrace [ri'tres] *tr* zurückverfolgen

retract [rɪ'trækt] *tr* (*a statement*) widerrufen; (*claws; landing gear*) einziehen

retract'able land'ing gear' [rɪ'træktəbəl] *s* Verschwindfahrgestell *n*

retrain [ri'tren] *tr* umschulen

retread ['ri,tred] *s* (aut) runderneuerter Reifen *m* || *tr* runderneuern

retreat [rɪ'trit] *s* (*quiet place*) Ruhesitz *m*; (mil) Rückzug *m*; (rel) Exerzitien *pl*; **beat a hasty r.** eilig den Rückzug antreten || *intr* sich zurückziehen

retrench [rɪ'trentʃ] *tr* einschränken || *intr* sich einschränken

retribution [,retrɪ'bjuʃən] *s* Vergeltung *f*

retrieval [rɪ'trivəl] *s* Wiedererlangung *f*

retrieve [rɪ'triv] *tr* wiedererlangen; (*a loss*) wettmachen; (hunt) apportieren

retriever [rɪ'trivər] *s* Apportierhund *m*

retroactive [,retro'æktɪv] *adj* (**from**) rückwirkend von ... an

retrogressive [,retrə'gresɪv] *adj* rückläufig

retrorocket ['retro,rakɪt] *s* Bremsrakete *f*

retrospect ['retrə,spekt] *s*—**in r.** rückblickend

re•try [ri'traɪ] *v* (*pret & pp* –**tried**) *tr* (jur) nochmals verhandeln

return [rɪ'tʌrn] *s* Rückkehr *f*; (*giving back*) Rückgabe *f*; (*the way back*) Rückweg *m*; (*tax form*) Steuererklärung *f*; (*profit*) Umsatz *m*; (tennis) Rückschlag *m*; **in r.** dafür; **in r. for** als Entgelt für; **returns** (*profits*) Ertrag *m*; (*of an election*) Ergebnisse *pl* || *tr* zurückgeben; (*send back*) zurücksenden; (*put back*) zurückstellen; (*thanks*) abstatten; (*a verdict*) fällen; (*a favor, love, gun fire*) erwidern; (tennis) zurückschlagen || *intr* zurückkehren; **r. to** (e.g., *a topic*) zurückkommen auf (*acc*)

return' address' *s* Rückadresse *f*

return' flight' *s* Rückflug *m*

return' match' *s* Revanchepartie *f*

return' tick'et *s* Rückfahrkarte *f*; (aer) Rückflugkarte *f*

reunification [ri,junɪfɪ'keʃən] *s* (pol) Wiedervereinigung *f*

reunion [ri'junjən] *s* Treffen *n*

rev [rev] *v* (*pret & pp* **revved**; *ger* **revving**) *tr* (**up**) auf Touren bringen || *intr* auf Touren kommen

revamp [ri'væmp] *tr* umgestalten

reveal [rɪ'vil] *tr* offenbaren

reveille ['revəli] *s* Wecken *n*

rev•el ['revəl] *s* Gelage *n* || *v* (*pret & pp* –**el[l]ed**; *ger* –**el[l]ing**) *intr* ein Gelage halten; **r. in** (fig) schwelgen in (*dat*)

revelation [,revə'ləʃən] *s* Offenbarung *f*; **Revelations** (Bib) Offenbarung *f*

reveler ['revələr] *s* Zecher –in *mf*

revelry ['revəlri] *s* Zechgelage *n*

revenge [rɪ'vendʒ] *s* Rache *f*; **take r. on s.o. for s.th.** sich an j–m für etw rächen || *tr* rächen

revengeful [rɪ'vendʒfəl] *adj* rachsüchtig

revenue ['revə,n(j)u] *s* (*yield*) Ertrag *m*; (*internal revenue*) Steueraufkommen *n*

rev'enue stamp' *s* Banderole *f*

reverberate [rɪ'vʌrbə,ret] *intr* widerhallen

revere [rɪ'vɪr] *tr* verehren

reverence ['revərəns] *s* (*respect given or received*) Ehrerbietung *f*; (*respect felt*) Ehrfurcht *f*

reverend ['revərənd] *adj* ehrwürdig; **the Reverend ...** Hochwürden ...

reverie ['revəri] *s* Träumerei *f*; **be lost in r.** in Träumen versunken sein

reversal [rɪ'vʌrsəl] *s* Umkehrung *f*; (*of opinion*) Umschwung *m*

reverse [rɪ'vʌrs] *adj* umgekehrt; (*side*) linke || *s* (*back side*) Rückseite *f*; (*opposite*) Gegenteil *n*; (*setback*) Rückschlag *m*; (*of a coin*) Revers *m*;

(aut) Rückwärtsgang *m* || *tr* umkehren, umdrehen; (*a decision*) umstoßen || *intr* sich rückwärts bewegen

reverse' side' *s* Rückseite *f*, Kehrseite *f*

reversible [rɪ'vʌrsɪbəl] *adj* (*decision*) umstoßbar; (*material*) zweiseitig; (chem, phys) umkehrbar; (mach) umsteuerbar

revert [rɪ'vʌrt] *intr*—**r. to** zurückkommen auf (*acc*); (jur) zurückfallen an (*acc*)

review [rɪ'vju] *s* (**of**) Überblick *m* (über *acc*); (*of a lesson*) Wiederholung *f*; (*of a book*) Besprechung *f*; (*periodical*) Rundschau *m*; (mil) Besichtigung *f*; **pass in r.** mustern || *tr* (*a lesson*) wiederholen; (*a book*) besprechen; (*e.g., the events of the day*) überblicken; (mil) besichtigen

reviewer [rɪ'vju·ər] *s* Besprecher –in *mf*

revile [rɪ'vaɪl] *tr* schmähen

revise [rɪ'vaɪz] *tr* (*a book*) umarbeiten; (*one's opinion*) revidieren

revised' edi'tion *s* verbesserte Auflage *f*

revision [rɪ'vɪʒən] *s* Neubearbeitung *f*

revival [rɪ'vaɪvəl] *s* Wiederbelebung *f*; (rel) Erweckung *f*; (theat) Reprise *f*

reviv'al meet'ing *s* Erweckungsversammlung *f*

revive [rɪ'vaɪv] *tr* wieder aufleben lassen; (*memories*) aufrühren; (*a victim*) wieder zu Bewußtsein bringen || *intr* wieder aufleben

revoke [rɪ'vok] *tr* widerrufen

revolt [rɪ'volt] *s* Aufstand *m* || *tr* abstoßen || *intr* revoltieren

revolt'ing *adj* abstoßend

revolution [ˌrevə'luʃən] *s* Revolution *f*; (*turn*) Umdrehung *f*; **revolutions per minute** Drehzahl *f*

revolutionary [ˌrevə'luʃə‚neri] *adj* revolutionär || *s* Revolutionär –in *mf*

revolve [rɪ'volv] *intr* (**around**) sich drehen (um)

revolver [rɪ'volvər] *s* Revolver *m*

revolv'ing *adj* Dreh–

revue [rɪ'vju] *s* (theat) Revue *f*

revulsion [rɪ'vʌlʃən] *s* Abscheu *m*

reward [rɪ'wɔrd] *s* Belohnung *f* || *tr* belohnen

reward'ing *adj* lohnend

re·wind [rɪ'waɪnd] *v* (*pret* & *pp* **-wound**) *tr* (*a tape, film*) umspulen; (*a clock*) wieder aufziehen

rewire [rɪ'waɪr] *tr* Leitungen neu legen in (*dat*)

rework [rɪ'wʌrk] *tr* umarbeiten

re·write [rɪ'raɪt] *v* (*pret* **-wrote**; *pp* **-written**) *tr* umschreiben

rhapsody ['ræpsədi] *s* Rhapsodie *f*

rheostat ['ri·ə‚stæt] *s* Rheostat *m*

rhetoric ['retərɪk] *s* Redekunst *f*

rhetorical [rɪ'tɔrɪkəl] *adj* rhetorisch

rheumatic [ru'mætɪk] *adj* rheumatisch

rheumatism ['rumə‚tɪzəm] *s* Rheumatismus *m*

Rhine [raɪn] *s* Rhein *m*

Rhineland ['raɪn‚lænd] *s* Rheinland *n*

rhine'stone' *s* Rheinkiesel *m*

rhinoceros [raɪ'nɑsərəs] *s* Nashorn *n*

rhubarb ['rubɑrb] *s* Rhabarber *m*; (sl) Krach *m*

rhyme [raɪm] *s* Reim *m* || *tr* & *intr* reimen

rhythm ['rɪðəm] *s* Rhythmus *m*

rhythmic(al) ['rɪðmɪk(əl)] *adj* rhythmisch

rib [rɪb] *s* Rippe *f* || *v* (*pret* & *pp* **ribbed**; *ger* **ribbing**) *tr* (coll) sich lustig machen über (*acc*)

ribald ['rɪbəld] *adj* zotig

ribbon ['rɪbən] *s* Band *n*; (*decoration*) Ordensband *n*; (*for a typewriter*) Farbband *n*

rice [raɪs] *s* Reis *m*

rich [rɪtʃ] *adj* reich; (*voice*) volltönend; (*soil*) fruchtbar; (*funny*) (coll) köstlich; **r. in** reich an (*dat*) || **riches** *spl* Reichtum *n*

rickets ['rɪkɪts] *s* Rachitis *f*

rickety ['rɪkɪti] *adj* (*building*) baufällig; (*furniture*) wackelig

rid [rɪd] *v* (*pret* & *pp* **rid**; *ger* **ridding**) *tr* (**of**) befreien (von); **get rid of** loswerden

riddance ['rɪdəns] *s* Befreiung *f*; **good r.!** den (or die or das) wäre ich glücklich los!

riddle ['rɪdəl] *s* Rätsel *n*

ride [raɪd] *s* Fahrt *f*; **give s.o. a r.** j-n im Auto mitnehmen; **take for a r.** (*murder*) entführen und umbringen; (*dupe*) hochnehmen || *v* (*pret* **rode** [rod]; *pp* **ridden** ['rɪdən]) *tr* (*a bicycle*) fahren; (*a horse*) reiten; (*a train, bus*) fahren mit; (*harass*) hetzen; **r. out** (*a storm*) gut überstehen || *intr* (*e.g., in a car*) fahren; (*on a horse*) reiten; **let s.th. r.** sich mit etw abfinden

rider ['raɪdər] *s* (*on horseback*) Reiter –in *mf*; (*on a bicycle*) Radfahrer –in *mf*; (*in a vehicle*) Fahrer –in *mf*; (*to a document*) Zusatzklausel *f*

ridge [rɪdʒ] *s* (*of a hill*; *of the nose*) Rücken *m*; (*of a roof*) Dachfirst *m*

ridge'pole' *s* Firstbalken *m*

ridicule ['rɪdɪ‚kjul] *s* Spott *m* || *tr* verspotten

ridiculous [rɪ'dɪkjələs] *adj* lächerlich; **look r.** lächerlich wirken

rid'ing acad'emy *s* Reitschule *f*

rid'ing boot' *s* Reitstiefel *m*

rid'ing breech'es *spl* Reithose *f*

rid'ing hab'it *s* Reitkostüm *n*

rife [raɪf] *adj* häufig; **r. with** voll von

riffraff ['rɪf‚ræf] *s* Gesindel *n*

rifle ['raɪfəl] *s* Gewehr *n* || *tr* ausplündern

rift [rɪft] *s* (& fig) Riß *m*

rig [rɪg] *s* (*gear*) Ausrüstung *f*; (*horse and carriage*) Gespann *n*; (*truck*) Laster *m*; (*oil drill*) Bohrturm *m*; (*getup*) (coll) Aufmachung *f*; (naut) Takelung *f* || *v* (*pret* & *pp* **rigged**; *ger* **rigging**) *tr* (auf)takeln; (*prices, elections, accounts*) manipulieren

rig'ging *s* Takelung *f*

right [raɪt] *adj* (*side, glove, angle*) recht; (*just*) gerecht; (*correct*) richtig; (*moment*) richtig; **do you have the r. time?** können Sie mir die ge-

naue Uhrzeit sagen?; **be in one's r.
mind** bei klarem Verstand sein; **it is
all r.** es ist schon gut; **r.? nicht
wahr?; that's r.!** eben!; **the r. thing**
das Richtige; **you are r.** Sie haben
recht || *adv* direkt; (*to the right*)
rechts; **r. along** durchaus; **r. away**
sofort, gleich; **r. behind the door**
gleich hinter der Tür; **r. glad** (coll)
recht froh; **r. here** gleich hier; **r.
now** (*at the moment*) momentan;
(*immediately*) sofort; **r. through**
durch und durch || *s* Recht *n;* (box)
Rechte *f;* **all rights reserved** alle
Rechte vorbehalten; **by rights** von
Rechts wegen; **in the r.** im Recht;
on the r. rechts, zur Rechten || *tr*
aufrichten; (*an error*) berichtigen;
(*a wrong*) wiedergutmachen || *interj*
stimmt!
righteous ['raɪtʃəs] *adj* gerecht, recht-
schaffen; (*smug*) selbstgerecht
rightful ['raɪtfəl] *adj* (*owner*) rechtmäßig; (*claim, place*) berechtigt
right'-hand' *adj* zur Rechten; (*glove*)
recht
right'-hand'ed *adj* rechtshändig
right-hander ['raɪt'hændər] *s* Rechts-
händer –in *mf*
right'-hand man' *s* rechte Hand *f*
rightist ['raɪtɪst] *adj* rechtsstehend || *s*
Rechtspolitiker –in *mf*
rightly ['raɪtli] *adv* richtig; (*rightfully*)
rechtmäßig
right' of way' *s* (*in traffic*) Vorfahrts-
recht *n;* (*across another's land*)
Grunddienstbarkeit *f*
right' wing' *s* rechter Flügel *m*
rigid ['rɪdʒɪd] *adj* steif, starr
rigmarole ['rɪgmə‚rol] *s* (*meaningless
talk*) Geschwafel *n;* (*fuss*) Getue *n*
rigorous ['rɪgərəs] *adj* hart, streng
rile [raɪl] *tr* aufbringen
rill [rɪl] *s* Bächlein *n*
rim [rɪm] *s* Rand *m;* (*of eyeglasses*)
Fassung *f;* (*of a wheel*) Felge *f*
rind [raɪnd] *s* Rinde *f*
ring [rɪŋ] *s* (*for the fingers; for boxing; of criminals or spies; of a circus;
circle under the eyes*) Ring *m;* (*of a
bell, voice, laughter*) Klang *m;* **give
s.o. a r.** (telp) j–n anrufen; **run rings
around s.o.** j–n in die Tasche stecken
|| *v* (*pret & pp* **ringed**) *tr* umringen;
r. in einschließen || *v* (*pret* **rang**
[ræŋ]; *pp* **rung** [rʌŋ]) *tr* läuten; **r.
the bell** läuten, klingeln; **r. out** aus-
läuten; **r. up** anrufen || *intr* läuten,
klingeln; **my ears are ringing** mir
klingen die Ohren; **r. for s.o.** nach
j–m klingeln; **r. out** laut schallen;
the bell is ringing es läutet
ring'ing *adj* schallend || *s* Läuten *n;*
(*in the ears*) Klingen *n*
ring'lead'er *s* Rädelsführer *m*
ring'mas'ter *s* Zirkusdirektor *m*
ring'side' *s* Ringplatz *m*
ring'worm' *s* Scherpilzflechte *f*
rink [rɪŋk] *s* Eisbahn *f;* (*for roller-
skating*) Rollschuhbahn *f*
rinse [rɪns] *s* Spülen *n* || *tr* ausspülen
riot ['raɪ‚ət] *s* Aufruhr *m;* **r. of colors**

Farbengemisch *n;* **run r.** sich austo-
ben; (*said of plants*) wuchern || *intr*
sich zusammenrotten
ri'ot act' *s*—**read the r. to s.o.** j–m die
Leviten lesen
rioter ['raɪ‚ətər] *s* Aufrührer –in *mf*
rip [rɪp] *s* Riß *m* || *v* (*pret & pp*
ripped; *ger* **ripping**) *tr* (zer)reißen;
rip off abreißen; (*the skin*) abziehen;
(*cheat*) betrügen || *intr* reißen
rip' cord' *s* Reißlinie *f*
ripe [raɪp] *adj* reif
ripen ['raɪpən] *tr* (& fig) reifen lassen
|| *intr* (& fig) reifen
rip' off' *s* (sl) Wucher *m*
ripple ['rɪpəl] *s* leichte Welle *f* || *intr*
leichte Wellen schlagen
rise [raɪz] *s* Aufsteigen *n;* (*in prices*)
Steigerung *f;* (*of heavenly bodies*)
Aufgang *m;* (*increase, e.g., in population*) Zunahme *f;* (*in the ground*)
Erhebung *f;* **get a r. out of s.o.** j–n
zu e–r Reaktion veranlassen; **give
r. to** veranlassen || *v* (*pret* **rose**
[roz]; *pp* **risen** ['rɪzən]) *intr* (*said
of the sun, of a cake*) aufgehen; (*said
of a river, prices, temperature, barometer*) steigen; (*said of a road*)
ansteigen; (*get out of bed*) aufstehen;
(*stand up*) sich erheben; (*from the
dead*) auferstehen; (*said of anger*)
hochsteigen; **r. to the occasion** sich
der Lage gewachsen zeigen; **r. up
from the ranks** von der Pike auf
dienen
riser ['raɪzər] *s* (*of a staircase*) Fut-
terbrett *n;* **early r.** Frühaufsteher
–in *mf;* **late r.** Langschläfer –in *mf*
risk [rɪsk] *s* Risiko *n;* **run the r. of**
(*ger*) Gefahr laufen zu (*inf*) || *tr*
wagen, aufs Spiel setzen
risky ['rɪski] *adj* riskant, gewagt
risque [rɪs'ke] *adj* schlüpfrig
rite [raɪt] *s* Ritus *m;* **last rites** Ster-
besakramente *pl*
ritual ['rɪtʃu·əl] *adj* rituell || *s* Ritual
n
ri·val ['raɪvəl] *adj* rivalisierend || *s*
Rivale *m*, Rivalin *f* || *v* (*pret & pp*
–val[l]ed; *ger* **–val[l]ing**) *tr* rivalisieren, wetteifern mit
rivalry ['raɪvəlri] *s* Rivalität *f*
river ['rɪvər] *adj* Fluß– || *s* Fluß *m*
riv'er ba'sin *s* Flußgebiet *n*
riv'erfront' *s* Flußufer *n*
riv'erside' *adj* am Flußufer gelegen ||
s Flußufer *n*
rivet ['rɪvɪt] *s* Niet *m* || *tr* nieten
riv'et gun' *s* Nietmaschine *f*
riv'eting *s* (*act*) Vernieten *n;* (*connection*) Nietnaht *f*
rivulet ['rɪvjəlɪt] *s* Flüßchen *n*
R.N. ['ɑr'en] *s* (**registered nurse**) staatlich geprüfte Krankenschwester *f*
roach [rotʃ] *s* (ent) Schabe *f;* (ichth)
Plötze *f*
road [rod] *s* (& fig) Weg *m;* **be (much)
on the r.** (viel) auf Reisen sein; **go
on the r.** auf Tour gehen; (theat) auf
Tournee gehen
road'bed' *s* Bahnkörper *m*
road'block' *s* Straßensperre *f*

road′ hog′ s rücksichtsloser Autofahrer m

road′ house′ s Wirtshaus n, Rasthaus n

road′ map′ s Straßenkarte f, Autokarte f

road′side′ adj Straßen– || s Straßenrand m

road′side inn′ s Rasthaus n

road′sign′ s Wegweiser m

road′stead s Reede f

road′ test′ s (aut) Probefahrt f

road′way′ s Fahrweg m

roam [rom] tr durchstreifen || intr herumstreifen

roar [ror] s Gebrüll n; (of a waterfall, sea, wind) Brausen n; (of an engine) Dröhnen n; (laughter) schallendes Gelächter n || intr brüllen; (said of a waterfall, sea, wind) brausen; r. at anbrüllen; (e.g., a joke) schallend lachen über (acc); r. by vorbeibrausen; r. with brüllen vor (dat)

roast [rost] adj gebraten || s Braten m || tr (meat, fish) braten, rösten; (coffee, chestnuts) rösten; (a person) (coll) durch den Kakao ziehen || intr braten

roast′ beef′ s Roastbeef n

roaster ['rostər] s (appliance) Röster m, Röstapparat m; (fowl) Brathuhn n

roast′ pork′ s Schweinsbraten m

rob [rab] v (pret & pp robbed; ger robbing) tr (a thing) rauben; (a person) (of) berauben (genit)

robber ['rabər] s Räuber –in mf

robbery ['rabəri] s Raubüberfall m

robe [rob] s Robe f; (house robe) Hausrock m || tr feierlich ankleiden || intr sich feierlich ankleiden

robin ['rabın] s Rotkehlchen n

robot ['robat] s Roboter m

robust [ro'bʌst] adj robust

rock [rak] adj (mus) Rock– || s Fels m; (one that is thrown) Stein m; (mus) Rockmusik f; on the rocks mit Eiswürfeln; (ruined) kaputt || tr schaukeln, wiegen; r. the boat (fig) die Sache ins Wanken bringen; r. to sleep in den Schlaf wiegen || intr schwanken, wanken; (said of a boat) schaukeln

rock′-bot′tom adj äußerst niedrig || s Tiefpunkt m

rock′ can′dy s Kandiszucker m

rock′ crys′tal s Bergkristall m

rocker ['rakər] s Schaukelstuhl m; go off one's r. (coll) den Verstand verlieren

rocket ['rakıt] s Rakete f

rock′et launch′er s Raketenwerfer m

rocketry ['rakətri] s Raketentechnik f

rock′et ship′ s Rakentenflugkörper m

rock′ gar′den s Steingarten m

rock′ing chair′ s Schaukelstuhl m

rock′ing horse′ s Schaukelpferd n

rock-'n'-roll ['rakən'rol] s Rock 'n Roll m

rock′ salt′ s Steinsalz n

rocky ['raki] adj felsig; (shaky) wacklig

rod [rad] s Stab m, Stange f; (whip)

Zuchtrute f; (of the retina; of a microorganism) Stäbchen n; (revolver) (sl) Schießeisen n; (angl) Angelrute f; (Bib) Reis n; (mach) Pleuelstange f; (surg) Absteckpfahl m

rodent ['rodənt] s Nagetier n

roe [ro] s (deer) Reh n; (ichth) Rogen m

rogue [rog] s Schuft m, Schurke m

rogues′′ gal′lery s Verbrecheralbum n

roguish ['rogıʃ] adj schurkisch

role, rôle [rol] s Rolle f

roll [rol] s Rolle f; (bread) Brötchen n; (of thunder, of a ship) Rollen n; (of drums) Wirbel m; (of fat) Wulst m; call the r. die Namen verlesen; (mil) Appell halten || tr rollen; (cigarettes) drehen; (metals, roads) walzen; r. over überrollen; r. up zusammenrollen; (sleeves) zurückstreifen || intr sich wälzen; be rolling in money im Geld wühlen

roll′back′ s (com) Senkung f

roll′call′ s Namensverlesung f; (mil) Appell m

roll′er bear′ing s Rollenlager n

roll′er coast′er s Berg-und-Tal-Bahn f

roll′er skate′ s Rollschuh m

roll′er-skate′ intr rollschuhlaufen

roll′er tow′el s Rollhandtuch n

roll′ing mill′ s Walzwerk n

roll′ing pin′ s Nudelholz n, Teigrolle f

roll′ing stock′ s (rr) rollendes Material n

roly-poly ['roli'poli] adj dick und rund

roman ['romən] adj (typ) Antiqua–; **Roman** römisch || s (typ) Antiqua f; **Roman** Römer –in mf

Ro′man can′dle s Leuchtkugel f

Ro′man Cath′olic adj römisch-katholisch || s Katholik –in mf

romance [ro'mæns] adj (ling) romanisch || s Romanze f

Romanesque [,romə'nesk] adj romanisch || s das Romanische

Ro′man nose′ s Römernase f

Ro′man nu′meral s römische Ziffer f

romantic [ro'mæntık] adj romantisch

romanticism [ro'mæntı,sızəm] s Romantik f

romp [ramp] intr umhertollen

rompers ['rampərz] spl Spielanzug m

roof [ruf] s Dach n; (aut) Verdeck n; **raise the r.** (coll) Krach machen; r. of the mouth Gaumendach n

roofer ['rufər] s Dachdecker m

roof′ gar′den s Dachgarten m

roof′ tile′ s Dachziegel m

rook [ruk] s (chess) Turm m; (orn) Saatkrähe f || tr (coll) (out of) beschwindeln (um)

rookie ['ruki] s (coll) Neuling m

room [rum] s Zimmer n; (space) Raum m, Platz m; **make r.** Platz machen; r. for complaint Anlaß m zur Klage; **take up too much r.** zu viel Platz in Anspruch nehmen || intr wohnen

room′ and board′ s Kost und Quartier f

room′ clerk′ s Empfangschef m

roomer ['rumər] s Mieter –in mf

room'ing house' s Pension f
room'mate' s Zimmergenosse m
room' serv'ice s Bedienung f aufs Zimmer
roomy ['rumi] adj geräumig
roost [rust] s Hühnerstange f; **rule the r.** Hahn im Korb sein || intr auf der Stange sitzen
rooster ['rustər] s Hahn m
root [rut] s Wurzel f; **get to the r. of s.th.** etw [dat] auf den Grund gehen; **take r.** Wurzel schlagen; (fig) sich einbürgern || tr—**be rooted in** wurzeln in (dat); **rooted to the spot** festgewurzelt; **r. out** ausrotten || intr —**r. about** wühlen; **r. for** zujubeln (dat)
rope [rop] s Strick m, Seil n; **know the ropes** alle Kniffe kennen || tr mit e–m Seil festbinden; (a steer) mit e–m Lasso einfangen; **r. in** (coll) einwickeln; **r. off** absperren
rosary ['rozəri] s Rosenkranz m
rose [roz] adj rosenrot || s Rose f
rose'bud' s Rosenknospe f
rose'bush' s Rosenstock m
rose'-col'ored adj rosenfarbig; (fig) rosa(rot)
rosemary ['roz‚meri] s Rosmarin m
rosin ['razın] s Harz n; (for violin bow) Kolophonium n
roster ['rustər] s Namenliste f; (educ) Stundenplan m; (mil, naut) Dienstplan m
rostrum ['rustrəm] s Rednerbühne f
rosy ['rozi] adj (& fig) rosig
rot [rut] s Fäulnis f; (sl) Quatsch m || v (pret & pp **rotted**; ger **rotting**) tr faulen lassen || intr verfaulen
rotate ['rotet] tr rotieren lassen; (tires) auswechseln; (agr) wechseln || intr rotieren; (take turns) sich abwechseln
rotation [ro'te/ən] s Rotation f; **in r.** wechselweise; **r. of crops** Wechselwirtschaft f
rote [rot] s—**by r.** mechanisch
rotisserie [ro'tısəri] s Fleischbraterei f
rotten ['rutən] adj faul; (trick) niederträchtig; **feel r.** (sl) sich elend fühlen
rotund [ro'tʌnd] adj rundlich
rotunda [ro'tʌndə] s Rotunde f
rouge [ruʒ] s Rouge n || tr schminken
rough [rʌf] adj (hands, voice, person) rauh; (piece of wood) roh; (work, guess, treatment) grob; (water, weather) stürmisch; (road) uneben; **have it r.** viel durchmachen || tr— **r. in** roh entwerfen; (carp) grob bearbeiten; **r. it** primitiv leben; **r. up** grob behandeln
rough' draft' s Konzept n
roughen ['rʌfən] tr aufrauhen
rough'house' s Radau m || intr Radau machen
roughly ['rʌfli] adv grob; (about) etwa
rough'neck' s (coll) Rauhbein n
roulette [ru'lɛt] s Roulett n
round [raund] adj rund || s Runde f; (of applause) Salve f; (shot) Schuß m; (of drinks) Lage f; (of a sentinel,

policeman, inspector, mailman) Rundgang m; **daily r.** Alltag m || prep um (acc) herum || tr (make round) runden; (a corner) herumgehen (or herumfahren) um (acc); **r. off** abrunden; (finish) vollenden; **r. up** (animals) zusammentreiben; (persons) zusammenbringen; (criminals) ausheben
round'house' s (rr) Lokomotivschuppen m
round'-shoul'dered adj mit runden Schultern
round' steak' s Kugel f
round'-ta'ble adj am runden Tisch
round' trip' s Hin-und Rückfahrt f; (aer) Hin- und Rückflug m
round'-trip' tick'et s Rückfahrkarte f
round'up' s (of cattle) Zusammentreiben n; (of criminals) Aushebung f
rouse [rauz] tr (from) aufwecken (aus)
rout [raut] s völlige Niederlage f; (mil) wilde Flucht f; **put to r.** in die Flucht schlagen || tr (mil) zersprengen
route [rut], [raut] s Route f, Weg m || tr leiten
routine [ru'tin] adj routinemäßig || s Routine f; **be r.** die Regel sein
rove [rov] intr umherwandern
row [rau] s Krach m; **raise a row** (coll) Krach machen || [ro] Reihe f; **in a row** hintereinander || tr rudern
rowboat ['ro‚bot] s Ruderboot n
rowdy ['raudi] adj flegelhaft || s Flegel m
rower ['ro·ər] s Ruderer –in mf
rowing ['ro·ıŋ] s Rudersport m
royal ['rɔɪ·əl] adj königlich
royalist ['rɔɪ·əlıst] adj königstreu || s Königstreue mf
royalty ['rɔɪ·əlti] s (royal status) Königswürde f; (personage) fürstliche Persönlichkeit f; (collectively) fürstliche Persönlichkeiten pl; (author's compensation) Tantieme f; (inventor's compensation) Lizenzgebühr f
r.p.m. ['ur'pi'em] spl (revolutions per minute) Drehzahl f
R.S.V.P. abbr u.A.w.g. (um Antwort wird gebeten)
rub [rʌb] s Reiben n; **there's the rub** (coll) da sitzt der Haken || v (pret & pp **rubbed**; ger **rubbing**) tr reiben; **rub down** abreiben; **rub elbows with** verkehren mit; **rub in** einreiben; **rub it in** (sl) es (j–m) unter die Nase reiben; **rub out** ausradieren; (sl) umbringen; **rub s.o. the wrong way** j–m auf die Nerven gehen || intr reiben; **rub against** sich reiben an (dat); **rub off on** (fig) abfärben auf (acc)
rubber ['rʌbər] adj Gummi– || s Gummi m & n; (cards) Robber m; **rubbers** Gummischuhe pl
ru'ber band' s Gummiband n
rubberize ['rʌbə‚raız] tr gummieren
rub'ber plant' s Kautschukpflanze f
rub'ber stamp' s Gummistempel m
rub'ber-stamp' tr abstempeln; (coll) automatisch genehmigen
rubbery ['rʌbəri] adj gummiartig
rub'bing al'cohol s Franzbranntwein m

rubbish ['rʌbɪʃ] s (trash) Abfall m; (nonsense) dummes Zeug n
rubble ['rʌbəl] s Schutt m; (used in masonry) Bruchstein m
rub'down' s Abreibung f
rubric ['rubrɪk] s Rubrik f
ruby ['rubi] adj rubinrot || s Rubin m
ruckus ['rʌkəs] s (coll) Krawall m
rudder ['rʌdər] s (aer) Seitenruder n; (naut) Steuerruder n
ruddy ['rʌdi] adj rosig
rude [rud] adj grob
rudeness ['rudnɪs] s Grobheit f
rudiments ['rudɪmənts] spl Grundlagen pl
rue [ru] tr bereuen
rueful ['rufəl] adj reuig; (pitiable) kläglich; (mournful) wehmütig
ruffian ['rʌfɪ‧ən] s Raufbold m
ruffle ['rʌfəl] s Rüsche f; (in water) Kräuseln n; (of a drum) gedämpfter Trommelwirbel m || tr kräuseln; (feathers, hair) sträuben
rug [rʌg] s Teppich m
rugged ['rʌgɪd] adj (country) wild; (robust) kräftig; (life) hart
ruin ['ru‧ɪn] s Ruine f; (undoing) Ruin m; **go to r.** zugrunde gehen; **lie in ruins** in Trümmern liegen; **ruins** (debris) Trümmer pl || tr ruinieren
rule [rul] s (reign) Herrschaft f; (regulation) Regel f; **as a r.** in der Regel; **become the r.** zur Regel werden || tr beherrschen; (paper) linieren; **r. out** ausschließen || intr (**over**) herrschen (über acc)
rule' of law' s Rechtsstaatlichkeit f
rule' of thumb' s Faustregel f; **by r.** über den Daumen gepeilt
ruler ['rulər] s Herrscher –in mf; (for measuring) Lineal n
rul'ing adj herrschend || s Regelung f
rum [rʌm] s Rum m
Rumania [ru'menɪ‧ə] s Rumänien n
Rumanian [ru'menɪ‧ən] adj rumänisch || s Rumäne m, Rumänin f; (language) Rumänisch n
rumble ['rʌmbəl] s (of thunder) Rollen n; (of a truck) Rumpeln n || intr rollen; rumpeln
ruminate ['rumɪ‚net] tr & intr wiederkäuen
rummage ['rʌmɪdʒ] intr—r. **through** durchsuchen
rum'mage sale' s Ramschverkauf m
rumor ['rumər] s Gerücht n || tr—**it is rumored that** es geht das Gerücht, daß
rump [rʌmp] s (of an animal) Hinterteil m & n; (buttocks) Gesäß n
rumple ['rʌmpəl] tr (clothes) zerknittern; (hair) zerzausen
rump' steak' s Rumpsteak n
rumpus ['rʌmpəs] s (coll) Krach m; **raise a r.** (coll) Krach machen
rum'pus room' s Spielzimmer n
run [rʌn] s Lauf m; (in stockings) Laufmasche f; (fin) Run m; (theat) Laufzeit f; **be on the run** auf der Flucht sein; **in the long run** auf die Dauer; **run of bad luck** Pechsträhne f; **run of good luck** Glückssträhne f ||

v (pret ran [ræn]; pp run; ger running) tr (a machine) bedienen; (a business, household) führen; (a distance) laufen; (a blockade) brechen; (a cable) verlegen; **run a race** um die Wette laufen; **run down** (with a car) niederfahren; (clues) nachgehen (dat); (a citation) aufspüren; (through gossip) schlechtmachen; **run off** (typ) Abzüge machen von; **run over** (with a vehicle) überfahren; (rehearse) nochmal durchgehen; **run through** (with a sword) erstechen; **run up** (bills) auflaufen lassen; (prices) in die Höhe treiben; (a flag) hissen || intr laufen, rennen; (flow) fließen; (said of buses, etc.) verkehren; (said of the nose) laufen, e.g., **ihm läuft die Nase** his nose is running; (said of colors) auslaufen; (said of a meeting) dauern; (said of a lease) (for) gelten (auf acc); **run across** zufällig treffen; **run after** nachlaufen (dat); **run around** herumlaufen; **run around** with sich herumtreiben mit; **run away** weglaufen; (said of a spouse) durchgehen; **run down** (said of a clock) ablaufen; **run dry** austrocknen; **run for** kandidieren für; **run high**, e.g., **feelings ran high** die Gemüter waren erhitzt; **run in the family** in der Familie liegen; **run into** (e.g., a tree) fahren gegen; (e.g., trouble, debt) geraten in (acc); (e.g., a friend) unerwartet treffen; **run into the thousands** in die Tausende gehen; **run low** knapp werden; **run out** (said of liquids) ausgehen; (said of supplies, time) zu Ende gehen; **run out of** ausgehen, e.g., **they ran out of supplies** die Vorräte gingen ihnen aus; **run over** (said of a pot) überlaufen; **run up against** stoßen auf (acc); **run up to s.o.** j-m entgegenlaufen; **run wild** verwildern
run'-around' s—**give s.o. the r.** j-n von Pontius zu Pilatus schicken
run'away' adj flüchtig; (horse) durchgegangen || s Ausreißer m; (horse) Durchgänger m
run'down' s kurze Zusammenfassung f
run'-down' adj (condition) heruntergekommen; (clock) abgelaufen; (battery) entladen
rung [rʌŋ] s (of a ladder) Sprosse f; (of a chair) Querleiste f
run-in' s (coll) Zusammenstoß m
runner ['rʌnər] s Läufer –in mf; (of a sled or skate) Kufe f; (of a sliding door) Laufschiene f; (rug) Läufer m; (bot) Ausläufer m; (mil) Meldegänger m
run'ner-up' s (runners-up) Zweitbeste mf; (sport) Zweite mf
run'ning adj (water) fließend; (debts, expenses, sore) laufend || s Laufen n, Lauf m; **be in the r.** gut im Rennen liegen; **be out of the r.** (out of the race) aus dem Rennen ausgeschieden sein; (not among the front runners) keine Aussichten haben

run′ning board′ s Trittbrett n
run′ning start′ s fliegender Start m
run′off′ s (sport) Entscheidungslauf m
run′off elec′tion s entscheidende Vor-
 wahl f
run′-of-the-mill′ adj Durchschnitts–
runt [rʌnt] s Dreikäsehoch m
run′way′ s Startbahn f
rupture [′rʌptʃər] s Bruch m ‖ tr (relations) abbrechen; be ruptured e–n
 Bruch (or Riß) bekommen; r. oneself sich [dat] e–n Bruch zuziehen ‖
 intr platzen
rural [′rurəl] adj ländlich
ruse [ruz] s List f
rush [rʌʃ] adj dringend ‖ s Eile f; (for)
 Ansturm m (auf acc); (bot) Binse f;
 be in a r. es eilig haben; what′s your
 r.? wozu die Eile? ‖ tr (a person)
 hetzen; (a defensive position) im
 Sturm nehmen; (work) schnell erledigen; (goods) schleunigst schicken;
 (e.g., to a hospital) schleunigst schaffen; be rushed for time sehr wenig
 Zeit haben; r. through (a bill) durch-
 peitschen; r. up (reinforcements)
 schnell herbeischaffen ‖ intr eilen,
 sich stürzen; r. at zustürzen auf

(acc); r. forward vorstürmen; r. into
 stürzen in (acc); r. up to zuschießen
 auf (acc); the blood rushed to his
 head ihm stieg das Blut in den Kopf
rush′ hours′ spl Hauptverkehrszeit f
rush′ or′der s Eilauftrag m
russet [′rʌsɪt] adj rotbraun
Russia [′rʌʃə] s Russland n
Russian [′rʌʃən] adj russisch ‖ s Russe
 m, Russin f; (language) Russisch n
rust [rʌst] s Rost m ‖ tr rostig machen
 ‖ intr (ver)rosten
rustic [′rʌstɪk] adj (rural) ländlich;
 (countryish) bäuerlich ‖ s Bauer m
rustle [′rʌsəl] s Rauschen n; (of silk)
 Knistern n ‖ tr rascheln mit; (cattle)
 stehlen ‖ intr rauschen; (said of silk)
 knistern
rust′proof′ adj rostfrei
rusty [′rʌsti] adj rostig; (fig) einge-
 rostet
rut [rʌt] s Geleise n, Spur f; (fig) alter
 Trott m
ruthless [′ruθlɪs] adj erbarmungslos
rye [raɪ] s (grain) Roggen m; (whiskey)
 Roggenwhisky m
rye′ bread′ s Roggenbrot n
rye′ grass′ s Raigras n

S

S, s [ɛs] s neunzehnter Buchstabe des
 englischen Alphabets
Sabbath [′sæbəθ] s Sabbat m
sabbat′ical year′ [sə′bætɪkəl] s ein-
 jähriger Urlaub m (e–s Professors)
saber [′sebər] s Säbel m
sable [′sebəl] adj schwarz ‖ s (fur)
 Zobelpelz m; (zool) Zobel m
sabotage [′sæbə‚taʒ] s Sabotage f ‖ tr
 sabotieren
saboteur [‚sæbə′tʌr] s Saboteur –in
 mf
saccharin [′sækərɪn] s Saccharin n
sachet [sæ′ʃe] s Duftkissen n
sack [sæk] s Sack m; (bed) (coll) Falle
 f; hit the s. (coll) in die Falle gehen
 ‖ tr einsacken; (dismiss) (coll) an
 die Luft setzen; (mil) ausplündern
sack′cloth′ s Sacktuch n; in s. and ashes
 in Sack und Asche
sacrament [′sækrəmənt] s Sakrament n
sacramental [‚sækrə′mentəl] adj sakra-
 mental
sacred [′sekrəd] adj heilig; s. to geweiht (dat)
sacrifice [′sækrɪ‚faɪs] s Opfer n; at a
 s. mit Verlust ‖ tr opfern
sacrilege [′sækrɪlɪdʒ] s Sakrileg n
sacrilegious [‚sækrɪ′lɪdʒəs] adj frevel-
 haft, gotteslästerlich
sacristan [′sækrɪstən] s Sakristan m
sacristy [′sækrɪsti] s Sakristei f
sad [sæd] adj traurig; (plight) schlimm
sadden [′sædən] tr traurig machen
saddle [′sædəl] s Sattel m ‖ tr satteln;
 be saddled with auf dem Halse haben

sad′dlebag′ s Satteltasche f
sadism [′sedɪzəm] s Sadismus m
sadistic [se′dɪstɪk] adj sadistisch
sadness [′sædnɪs] s Traurigkeit f
sad′ sack′ s (sl) Trauerkloß m
safe [sef] adj (from) sicher (vor dat);
 (arrival) glücklich; s. and sound heil
 und gesund; (said of a thing) unversehrt; to be on the s. side vorsichtshalber ‖ s Geldschrank m
safe′-con′duct s sicheres Geleit n
safe′-depos′it box′ s Schließfach n
safe′ dis′tance s Sicherheitsabstand m
safe′guard′ s Schutz m ‖ tr schützen
safe′keep′ing s sicherer Gewahrsam m
safety [′sefti] adj Sicherheits– ‖ s
 Sicherheit f
safe′ty belt′ s Sicherheitsgurt m
safe′ty pin′ s Sicherheitsnadel f
safe′ty ra′zor s Rasierapparat m
safe′ty valve′ s Sicherheitsventil n
saffron [′sæfrən] adj safrangelb ‖ s
 Safran m
sag [sæg] s Senkung f ‖ v (pret & pp
 sagged; ger sagging) intr sich senken;
 (said of a cable) durchhängen; (fig)
 sinken
sagacious [sə′geʃəs] adj scharfsinnig
sage [sedʒ] adj weise, klug ‖ s Weise
 m; (plant) Salbei f
sage′brush′ s Beifuß m
sail [sel] s Segel n; set s. for in See
 stechen nach ‖ tr (a boat) fahren;
 (the sea) segeln über (acc) ‖ intr
 segeln; (depart) abfahren; s. across
 übersegeln; s. along the coast an der

Küste entlangsegeln; **s. into** (coll) herunterputzen

sail'boat' s Segelboot n

sail'cloth' s Segeltuch n

sail'ing s Segelfahrt f; (sport) Segelsport m; **it will be smooth s.** (fig) es wird alles glattgehen

sail'ing ves'sel s Segelschiff n

sailor ['selər] s Matrose m

Saint [sent] s Heilige mf; **S. George** der heilige Georg, Sankt Georg

Saint' Bernard' s (dog) Bernhardiner m

sake [sek] s—**for her s.** ihretwegen; **for his s.** seinetwegen; **for my s.** meinetwegen; **for our s.** unsertwegen; **for their s.** ihretwegen; **for the s. of** um (genit) willen; **for your s.** deinetwegen, Ihretwegen

salable ['seləbəl] adj verkäuflich

salacious [sə'leʃəs] adj (person) geil; (writing, pictures) obszön

salad ['sæləd] s Salat m

sal'ad bowl' s Salatschüssel f

sal'ad dress'ing s Salatsoße f

sal'ad oil' s Salatöl n

salami [sə'lɑmi] s Salami f

salary ['sæləri] s Gehalt n

sale [sel] s Verkauf m; (special sale) Ausverkauf m; **be up for s.** zum Kauf stehen; **for s.** zu verkaufen; **sales** (com) Absatz m, Umsatz m; **put up for s.** zum Verkauf anbieten

sales'' clerk' s Verkäufer –in mf

sales'girl' s Ladenmädchen n

sales'la'dy s Verkäuferin f

sales'man s (–men) Verkäufer m

sales'manship' s Verkaufstüchtigkeit f

sales' promo'tion s Verkaufsförderung f

sales' slip' s Kassenzettel m, Bon m

sales' tax' s Umsatzsteuer f

saliva [sə'laɪvə] s Speichel m

sallow ['sælo] adj bläßlich

sal·ly ['sæli] s (side trip) Abstecher m; (mil) Ausfall m || v (pret & pp –lied) intr (mil) ausfallen; **s. forth** sich aufmachen

salmon ['sæmən] adj lachsfarben || s Lachs m

saloon [sə'lun] s Kneipe f; (naut) Salon m

salt [sɔlt] s Salz n || tr salzen; **s. away** (coll) auf die hohe Kante legen

salt'cel'lar s Salzfaß n

salt'ed meat' s Salzfleisch n

salt' mine' s Salzbergwerk n; **back to the salt mines** zurück zur Tretmühle

salt'pe'ter s Salpeter m

salt' shak'er s Salzfaß n

salty ['sɔlti] adj salzig

salutary ['sæljə,teri] adj heilsam

salute [sə'lut] s Salut m || tr & intr salutieren

salvage ['sælvɪdʒ] s (saving by ship) Bergung f; (property saved by ship) Bergungsgut n; (discarded material) Altmaterial n || tr bergen; (discarded material) verwerten

salvation [sæl've∫ən] s Heil n

Salva'tion Ar'my s Heilsarmee f

salve [sæv] s Salbe f || tr (one's conscience) beschwichtigen

sal·vo ['sælvo] s (–vos & –voes) Salve f

Samaritan [sə'mærɪtən] s Samariter –in mf; **good S.** barmherziger Samariter m

same [sem] adj—**at the s. time** gleichzeitig; **it's all the s. to me** es ist mir ganz gleich; **just the s.** trotzdem; **thanks, s. to you!** danke, gleichfalls!; **the s.** derselbe

sameness ['semnɪs] s Eintönigkeit f

sample ['sæmpəl] s Muster n, Probe f || tr (aus)probieren

sancti·fy ['sæŋktɪ,faɪ] v (pret & pp –fied) tr heiligen

sanctimonious [,sæŋktɪ'monɪ·əs] adj scheinheilig

sanction ['sæŋkʃən] s Sanktion f || tr sanktionieren

sanctity ['sæŋktɪti] s Heiligkeit f

sanctuary ['sæŋktʃʊ,eri] s (shrine) Heiligtum n; (of a church) Altarraum m; (asylum) Asyl n

sand [sænd] s Sand m || tr mit Sandpapier abschleifen; (a road, sidewalk) mit Sand bestreuen

sandal ['sændəl] s Sandale f

san'dalwood' s Sandelholz n

sand'bag' s Sandsack m

sand'bank' s Sandbank f

sand' bar' s Sandbank f

sand'blast' tr sandstrahlen

sand'box' s Sandkasten m

sand' cas'tle s Strandburg f

sand' dune' s Sanddüne f

sand'glass' s Sanduhr f

sand'man s (–men) (fig) Sandmann m

sand'pa'per s Sandpapier n || tr mit Sandpapier abschleifen

sand'stone' s Sandstein m

sand'storm' s Sandsturm m

sandwich ['sændwɪtʃ] s belegtes Brot n, Sandwich n || tr (in between) einzwängen (zwischen dat)

sandy ['sændi] adj sandig; (color) sandfarben

sane [sen] adj geistig gesund; (e.g., advice) vernünftig

sanguine ['sæŋgwɪn] adj (about) zuversichtlich (in Bezug auf acc)

sanitarium [,sænɪ'terɪ·əm] s Heilanstalt f, Sanatorium n

sanitary ['sænɪ,teri] adj sanitär

san'itary nap'kin s Damenbinde f

sanitation [,sænɪ'teʃən] s Gesundheitswesen n; (in a building) sanitäre Einrichtungen pl

sanity ['sænɪti] s geistige Gesundheit f

Santa Claus ['sæntə,klɔz] s der Weihnachtsmann m, der Nikolaus

sap [sæp] s Saft m; (coll) Schwachkopf m || v (pret & pp sapped; ger sapping) tr (strength) erschöpfen

sapling ['sæplɪŋ] s junger Baum m

sapphire ['sæfaɪr] s Saphir m

Saracen ['særəsən] adj sarazenisch || s Sarazene m, Sarazenin f

sarcasm ['sɑrkæzəm] s Sarkasmus m

sarcastic [sɑr'kæstɪk] adj sarkastisch

sarcophagus [sɑr'kɑfəgəs] s Sarkophag m

sardine [sɑr'din] s Sardine f; **packed**

in like sardines zusammengedrängt
wie die Heringe
Sardinia [sɑr'dɪnɪ·ə] s Sardinien n
Sardinian [sɑr'dɪnɪ·ən] adj sardinisch
|| s Sardinier –in mf; (language)
Sardinisch n
sash [sæʃ] s Schärpe f; (of a window)
Fensterrahmen m
sass [sæs] s (coll) Revolverschnauze f
|| tr (coll) (off) patzig antworten
(dat)
sassy ['sæsi] adj (coll) patzig
Satan ['setən] s Satan m
satanic(al) [sə'tænɪk(əl)] adj satanisch
satchel ['sætʃəl] s Handtasche f
sate [set] tr übersättigen
satellite ['sætə‚laɪt] s Satellit m
sat'ellite coun'try s Satellitenstaat m
satiate ['seʃɪ‚et] tr sättigen
satin ['sætɪn] s Seidenatlas m
satire ['sætaɪr] s Satire f
satiric(al) [sə'tɪrɪk(əl)] adj satirisch
satirize ['sætɪ‚raɪz] tr verspotten
satisfaction [‚sætɪs'fækʃən] s Befrie-
digung f, Genugtuung f
satisfactory [‚sætɪs'fæktəri] adj frie-
denstellend, genügend
satis·fy ['sætɪs‚faɪ] v (pret & pp –fied)
tr (desires, needs) befriedigen; (re-
quirements) genügen (dat); (a person) zufriedenstellen; **be satisfied
with** zufrieden sein mit || intr be-
friedigen
saturate ['sætʃə‚ret] tr (& chem) sättigen, saturieren
satura'tion bomb'ing s Bombenteppich
m
satura'tion point' s Sättigungspunkt m
Saturday ['sætər‚de] s Samstag m; **on
S.** am Samstag
sauce [sɔs] s Soße f; (coll) Frechheit f
|| tr mit Soße zubereiten; (season)
würzen
sauce'pan' s Stielkasserolle f
saucer ['sɔsər] s Untertasse f
saucy ['sɔsi] adj (impertinent) frech;
(amusingly flippant) keß; (trim) flott
sauerkraut ['saur‚kraut] s Sauerkraut
n
saunter ['sɔntər] s Schlendern n || intr
schlendern
sausage ['sɔsɪdʒ] s Wurst f
saute [so'te] v (pret & pp **sauteed**) tr
sautieren
savage ['sævɪdʒ] adj wild || s Wilde mf
savant ['sævənt] s Gelehrte m
save [sev] tr (rescue) retten; (money,
fuel) sparen; (keep, preserve) aufheben; (trouble) ersparen; (time) gewinnen; (stamps) sammeln; **s. face**
das Gesicht wahren; **s. from** bewah-
ren vor (dat) || prep außer (dat)
sav'ing adj (grace) seligmachend; (qual-
ity) ausgleichend || s (of souls) Ret-
tung f; (in) Ersparnis f (an dat);
savings Ersparnisse pl
sav'ings account' s Sparkonto n
sav'ings bank' s Sparkasse f
sav'ings certi'ficate s Sparbon m
sav'ings depos'it s Spareinlage f
savior ['sevjər] s Retter –in mf;
Saviour Heiland m

savor ['sevər] s Wohlgeschmack m ||
tr auskosten || intr—s. of (smell of)
riechen nach; (taste of) schmecken
nach
savory ['sevəri] adj wohschmeckend
saw [sɔ] s Säge f; (saying) Sprichwort
n || tr sägen; **saw up** zersägen
saw'dust' s Sägespäne pl
saw'horse' s Sägebock m
saw'mill' s Sägemühle f
Saxon ['sæksən] adj sächsisch || s
Sachse m, Sachsin f
Saxony ['sæksəni] s Sachsen n
saxophone ['sæksə‚fon] s Saxophon n
say [se] s—**have a** (or **no**) **say in** etw
(or nichts) zu sagen haben bei; **have
one's say** (**about**) seine Meinung
äußern (über acc) || v (pret & pp
said [sed]) tr sagen; (Mass) lesen;
(a prayer) sprechen; (one's prayers)
verrichten; (said of a newspaper
article, etc.) besagen; **it says in the
papers** in der Zeitung steht; (let's)
say sagen wir; **no sooner said than
done** gesagt, getan; **say!** (to draw
attention) sag mal!; (to elicit agreement) gelt!; **say s.th. behind s.o.'s
back** j–m etw nachsagen; **she is said
to be clever** sie soll klug sein; **that
is not to say** das will nicht sagen;
that is to say das heißt; **they say**
man sagt; **to say nothing of** ganz zu
schweigen von; **you don't say so!**
tatsächlich!
say'ing s Sprichwort n; **as the s. goes**
wie man zu sagen pflegt; **it goes without s.** das versteht sich von selbst
say'-so' s (assertion) Behauptung f;
(order) Anweisung f; (final authority)
letztes Wort n
scab [skæb] s Schorf m; (sl) Streikbrecher –in mf
scabbard ['skæbərd] s Schwertscheide
f
scabby ['skæbi] adj schorfig
scads [skædz] spl (sl) e–e Menge f
scaffold ['skæfəld] s Gerüst n; (for
executions) Schafott n
scaf'folding s Baugerüst n
scald [skɔld] tr verbrühen; (milk) auf-
kochen
scale [skel] s (on fish, reptiles) Schuppe f; (pan of a balance) Waagschale
f; (of a thermometer, wages) Skala f;
(mus) Tonleiter f; **on a grand s.** im
großen Stil; **on a large** (or **small**) **s.**
in großem (or kleinem) Maßstab;
s. 1:1000 Maßstab 1:1000; **scales**
Waage f; **to s.** maßstabgerecht || tr
erklettern; **s. down** maßstäblich verkleinern; (prices) herabsetzen
scallop ['skæləp] s Kammuschel f;
(sew) Zacke f || tr auszacken; (culin)
überbacken
scalp [skælp] s Kopfhaut f; (Indian
trophy) Skalp m || tr skalpieren
scalpel ['skælpəl] s Skalpell n
scaly ['skeli] adj schuppig
scamp [skæmp] s Fratz m, Wildfang m
scamper ['skæmpər] intr herumtollen;
s. away davonlaufen
scan [skæn] v (pret & pp **scanned; ger**

scanning) *tr* (*a page*) überfliegen;
(*a verse*) skandieren; (*examine*) genau prüfen; (radar, telv) abtasten

scandal ['skændəl] *s* Skandal *m*

scandalize ['skændə‚laız] *tr* schockieren

scandalmonger ['skændəl‚mʌŋgər] *s*
Lästermaul *n*

scandalous ['skændələs] *adj* skandalös

scan'dal sheet' *s* Sensationsblatt *n*

Scandinavia [‚skændı'nevı‑ə] *s* Skandinavien *n*

Scandinavian [‚skændı'nevı‑ən] *adj*
skandinavisch ‖ *s* Skandinavier –in
mf; (*language*) Skandinavisch *n*

scansion ['skænʃən] *s* Skandieren *n*

scant [skænt] *adj* gering; **a s. two
hours** knapp zwei Stunden

scantily ['skæntıli] *adv*—**s. clad** leicht
bekleidet

scanty ['skænti] *adj* kärglich, knapp

scapegoat ['skep‚got] *s* Sündenbock *m*

scar [skɑr] *s* Narbe *f;* (fig) Makel *m* ‖
v (*pret & pp* **scarred;** *ger* **scarring**)
tr (*e.g., a face*) entstellen; (*e.g., a
tabletop*) verschrammen; (fig) bein-
trächtigen

scarce [skɛrs] *adj* knapp, rar; **make
oneself s.** (coll) das Weite suchen

scarcely ['skɛrsli] *adv* kaum; **be s.
able to** (*inf*) Not haben zu (*inf*)

scarcity ['skɛrsıti] *s* (**of**) Knappheit *f*
(an *dat*), Mangel *m* (an *dat*)

scare [skɛr] *s* Schrecken *m;* **be scared**
erschrecken; **be scared stiff** e–e
Hundeangst haben; **give s.o. a s.** j–m
e–n Schrecken einjagen ‖ *tr* erschrecken; **s. away** verscheuchen; **s.
up** (*money*) auftreiben ‖ *intr* erschrecken

scare'crow' *s* Vogelscheuche *f*

scarf [skɑrf] *s* (**scarfs & scarves**
[skɑrvz]) Schal *m*

scarlet ['skɑrlıt] *adj* scharlachrot ‖ *s*
Scharlachrot *n*

scar'let fe'ver *s* Scharlach *m*

scarred *adj* narbig, schrammig

scary ['skɛri] *adj* schreckerregend

scat [skæt] *interj* weg!

scathing ['skeðıŋ] *adj* vernichtend

scatter ['skætər] *tr* zerstreuen ‖ *intr*
sich zerstreuen

scat'terbrain' *s* Wirrkopf *m*

scat'tered show'ers *spl* einzelne Schauer *pl*

scenari‑o [sı'nɛrı‑o] *s* (**–os**) Drehbuch
n

scene [sin] *s* Szene *f;* **be on the s.** zur
Stelle sein; **behind the scenes** hinter
den Kulissen; **make a s.** e–e Szene
machen; **s. of the crime** Tatort *m*

scenery ['sinəri] *s* Landschaft *f;* (theat)
Bühnenausstattung *f*

scenic ['sinık] *adj* landschaftlich;
(theat) szenisch

scent [sent] *s* Duft *m;* (*of a dog*) Witterung *f;* (hunt) Spur *f;* **have a s.**
duften ‖ *tr* wittern

scepter ['septər] *s* Zepter *n*

sceptic ['skeptık] *s* Skeptiker –in *mf*

scepticism ['skeptı‚sızəm] *s* (*doubt*)
Skepsis *f;* (*doctrine*) Skeptizismus *m*

schedule ['skedjʊl] *s* Plan *m;* (*for
work*) Arbeitsplan *m;* (*in travel*)
Fahrplan *m;* (*at school*) Stundenplan
m; (*appendix to a tax return*) Ein-
kommensteuerformular *n;* (*table*)
Einkommensteuertabelle *f;* **on s.**
fahrplanmäßig ‖ *tr* ansetzen; **the
plane is scheduled to arrive at six**
nach dem Flugplan soll die Maschine
um sechs Uhr ankommen

scheme [skim] *s* (*schematic*) Schema
n; (*plan, program*) Plan *m;* (*intrigue*)
Intrige *f* ‖ *tr* planen ‖ *intr* Ränke
schmieden

schemer ['skimər] *s* Ränkeschmied *m*

schilling ['ʃılıŋ] *s* (Aust) Schilling *m*

schism ['sızəm] *s* (fig) Spaltung *f;*
(eccl) Schisma *n*

schizophrenia [‚skıtso'frinı‑ə] *s* Schizophrenie *f*, Bewußtseinsspaltung *f*

schizophrenic [‚skıtso'frenık] *adj* schizophren

schmaltzy ['ʃmɔltsi] *adj* schmalzig

scholar ['skɑlər] *s* Gelehrte *mf*

scholarly ['skɑlərli] *adj* gelehrt

schol'arship' *s* Gelehrsamkeit *f;*
(*award*)) Stipendium *n*

scholastic [skə'læstık] *adj* Schul–,
Bildungs–; (hist) scholastisch

school [skul] *adj* (*book, house, master,
room, teacher, yard, year*) Schul– ‖
s Schule *f;* (*of a university*) Fakultät
f; (*of fish*) Schwarm *m;* **s. is over**
die Schule ist aus ‖ *tr* schulen

school' age' *s* schulpflichtiges Alter *n;*
of s. schulpflichtig

school'bag' *s* Schulranzen *m*

school' board' *s* Schulausschuß *m*

school'boy' *s* Schüler *m*

school'girl' *s* Schülerin *f*

school'ing *s* (*formal education*) Schulbildung *f;* (*training*) Schulung *f*

school'mate' *s* Mitschüler –in *mf*

schooner ['skunər] *s* Schoner *m*

sciatica [saı'ætıkə] *s* Hüftschmerz *m*

science ['saı‑əns] *s* Wissenschaft *f;* **the
sciences** die Naturwissenschaften *pl*

sci'ence fic'tion *s* Science-fiction *f*

scientific [‚saı‑ən'tıfık] *adj* wissenschaftlich

scientist ['saı‑əntıst] *s* Wissenschaftler
–in *mf*

scimitar ['sımıtər] *s* Türkensäbel *m*

scintillate ['sıntı‚let] *intr* funkeln

scion ['saı‑ən] *s* Sprößling *m;* (bot)
Pfropfreis *n*

scissors ['sızərz] *s & spl* Schere *f;*
(*in wrestling*) Zangengriff *m*

scoff [skɔf] *s* Spott *m* ‖ *intr* (**at**) spotten (über *acc*)

scold [skold] *tr & intr* schelten

scold'ing *s* Schelte *f;* **get a s.** Schelte
bekommen

sconce [skɑns] *s* Wandleuchter *m*

scoop [skup] *s* (*ladle*) Schöpfkelle *f;*
(*for sugar, flour*) Schaufel *f;* (*amount
scooped*) Schlag *m;* (journ) Knüller
m ‖ *tr* schöpfen; **s. out** ausschaufeln;
s. up scheffeln

scoot [skut] *intr* (coll) flitzen

scooter ['skutər] *s* Roller *m*

scope [skop] *s* (*extent*) Umfang *m;*

(*range*) Reichweite *f*; **give free s. to the imagination** der Phatasie freien Lauf lassen; **give s.o. free s.** j–m freie Hand geben; **within the s. of** im Rahmen (*genit*) or von

scorch [skɔrtʃ] *tr* versengen

scorched'-earth' pol'icy *s* Politik *f* der verbrannten Erde

scorch'ing *adj & adv* sengend

score [skor] *s* (*of a game*) Punktzahl *f*; (*final score*) Ergebnis *n*; (*notch*) Kerbe *f*; (*mus*) Partitur *f*; **a s. of** zwanzig; **have an old s. to settle with s.o.** mit j–m e–e alte Rechnung zu begleichen haben; **keep s.** die Punktzahl anschreiben; **know the s.** (*coll*) auf Draht sein; **on that s.** diesbezüglich; **what's the s.?** wie steht das Spiel? ‖ *tr* (*points*) erzielen; (*goals*) schießen; (*notch*) einkerben; (*mus*) in Partitur setzen ‖ *intr* e–n Punkt erzielen

score'board' *s* Anzeigetafel *f*

score'card' *s* Punktzettel *m*

score'keep'er *s* Anschreiber –in *mf*

score'sheet' *s* Spielberichtsbogen *m*

scorn [skɔrn] *s* Verachtung *f*; **laugh to s.** auslachen ‖ *tr* verachten

scornful [ˈskɔrnfəl] *adj* verächtlich

scorpion [ˈskɔrpɪ-ən] *s* Skorpion *m*

Scot [skɑt] *s* Schotte *m*, Schottin *f*

Scotch [skɑtʃ] *adj* schottisch; (sl) geizig ‖ *s* schottischer Whisky *m*; (*dialect*) Schottisch *n* ‖ *tr* (*a rumor*) ausrotten; (*with a chock*) blockieren; (*render harmless*) unschädlich machen

Scotch'man *s* (**–men**) Schotte *m*

Scotch' pine' *s* gemeine Kiefer *f*

Scotch' tape' *s* (trademark) durchsichtiger Klebstreifen *m*

scot'-free' *adj* ungestraft

Scotland [ˈskɑtlənd] *s* Schottland *n*

Scottish [ˈskɑtɪʃ] *adj* schottisch ‖ *s* (*dialect*) Schottisch *n*; **the S.** die Schotten *pl*

scoundrel [ˈskaʊndrəl] *s* Lump *m*

scour [skaʊr] *tr* scheuern; (*the city*) absuchen

scourge [skʌrdʒ] *s* Geißel *f* ‖ *tr* geißeln

scout [skaʊt] *s* Pfadfinder *m*; (mil, sport) Kundschafter *m* ‖ *tr* aufklären ‖ *intr* kundschaften

scout'mas'ter *s* Pfadfinderführer *m*

scowl [skaʊl] *s* finsterer Blick *m* ‖ *intr* finster blicken; **s. at** grollend ansehen

scram [skræm] *v* (*pret & pp* **scrammed;** *ger* **scramming**) *intr* (coll) abhauen

scramble [ˈskræmbəl] *s* (for) Balgerei *f* (um) ‖ *tr* (*mix up*) durcheinandermischen; (*a message*) unverständlich machen; **s. eggs** Rührei machen ‖ *intr* (*e.g., over rocks*) klettern; **s. for s.th.** sich um etw reißen; **s. to one's feet** sich aufrappeln

scram'bled eggs' *spl* Rührei *n*;

scrap [skræp] *s* (*of metal*) Schrott *m*; (*of paper*) Fetzen *m*; (*of food*) Rest *m*; (*refuse*) Abfall *m*; (*quarrel*) (coll) Zank *m*; (*fight*) (coll) Rauferei *f* ‖ *v* (*pret & pp* **scrapped;** *ger*

scrapping) *tr* ausrangieren ‖ *intr* (*quarrel*) (coll) zanken; (*fight*) (coll) raufen

scrap'book' *s* Einklebebuch *n*

scrape [skrep] *s* Kratzer *m*; (coll) Patsche *f* ‖ *tr* schaben; (*the skin*) abscheuern; **s. off** abschaben; **s. together** (or up) zusammenkratzen

scrap' heap' *s* Schrotthaufen *m*; (*refuse heap*) Abfallhaufen *m*

scrap' i'ron *s* Schrott *m*, Alteisen *n*

scrapper [ˈskræpər] *s* Zänker –in *mf*

scrappy [ˈskræpi] *adj* (*made of scraps*) zusammengestoppelt; (coll) rauflustig

scratch [skrætʃ] *s* Kratzer *m*, Schramme *f*; **start from s.** wieder ganz von vorne anfangen ‖ *tr* kratzen; (sport) streichen; **s. open** aufkratzen; **s. out** (*a line*) ausstreichen; (*eyes*) aushacken; **s. the surface of** nur streifen ‖ *intr* kratzen; (*scratch oneself*) sich kratzen

scratch' pad' *s* Notizblock *m*

scratch' pa'per *s* Schmierpapier *n*

scrawl [skrɔl] *s* Gekritzel *n* ‖ *tr & intr* kritzeln

scrawny [ˈskrɔni] *adj* spindeldürr

scream [skrim] *s* Aufschrei *m*; **he's a s.!** er ist zum Schreien! ‖ *tr & intr* schreien

screech [skritʃ] *s* Kreischen *n* ‖ *intr* (*said of tires, brakes*) kreischen; (*said of an owl*) schreien

screech' owl' *s* Kauz *m*

screen [skrin] *s* Wandschirm *m*; (*for a window*) Fliegengitter *n*; (*camouflage*) Tarnung *f*; (aer) (**of**) Abschirmung *f* (durch); (cin) Leinwand *f*; (nav) Geleitschutz *m*; (radar, telv) Leinwand *f* ‖ *tr* (*sand, gravel, coal; applications*) durchsieben; (*applicants*) überprüfen; (*a porch, windows*) mit Fliegengittern versehen; (mil) verschleiern; **s. off** abschirmen

screen'play' *s* Filmdrama *n*; (*scenario*) Drehbuch *n*

screen' test' *s* Probeaufnahme *f*

screw [skru] *s* Schraube *f*; **he has a s. loose** (coll) bei ihm ist e–e Schraube locker ‖ *tr* schrauben; (*cheat*) (sl) hereinlegen; (vulg) vögeln; **s. tight** festschrauben; **s. up** (*courage*) aufbringen; (*bungle*) (coll) verpfuschen

screw'ball' *adj* (coll) verrückt ‖ *s* (coll) Wirrkopf *m*

screw'driv'er *s* Schraubenzieher *m*

screw'-on cap' *s* Schraubendeckel *m*

screwy [ˈskru-i] *adj* (sl) verrückt

scribble [ˈskrɪbəl] *s* Gekritzel *n* ‖ *tr & intr* kritzeln

scribe [skraɪb] *s* Schreiber *m*; (Bib) Schriftgelehrte *m*

scrimmage [ˈskrɪmɪdʒ] *s* (fb) Übungsspiel *n*

scrimp [skrɪmp] *tr* knausern mit ‖ *intr* (**on**) knausern (mit)

scrimpy [ˈskrɪmpi] *adj* knapp

script [skrɪpt] *s* (*handwriting*) Handschrift *f*; (cin) Drehbuch *n*; (rad) Textbuch *n*; (typ) Schreibschrift *f*

scriptural [ˈskrɪptʃərəl] *adj* biblisch; **s. passage** Bibelstelle *f*

Scripture ['skrɪptʃər] s die Heilige Schrift; *(Bible passage)* Bibelzitat n
script'writ'er s (cin) Drehbuchautor m
scrofula ['skrɑfjələ] s Skrofeln pl
scroll [skrol] s Schriftrolle f; (archit) Schnörkel m
scroll'work' s Schnörkelverzierung f
scro·tum ['skrotəm] s (-ta [tə] or -tums) Hodensack m
scrounge [skraʊndʒ] tr stibitzen ‖ intr —s. around for herumstöbern nach
scrub [skrʌb] s Schrubben n; *(shrubs)* Buschwerk n; (sport) Ersatzmann m ‖ v (pret & pp scrubbed; ger scrubbing) tr schrubben
scrub'bing brush' s Scheuerbürste f
scrub'wom'an s (-wom'en) Scheuerfrau f
scruff [skrʌf] s—s. of the neck Genick n
scruple ['skrupəl] s Skrupel m
scrupulous ['skrupjələs] adj skrupulös
scrutinize ['skrutɪ ˌnaɪz] tr genau prüfen; *(a person)* mustern
scrutiny ['skrutɪni] s genaue Prüfung f
scud [skʌd] s Wolkenfetzen m
scuff [skʌf] tr *(a shoe, waxed floor)* abschürfen ‖ intr *(shuffle)* schlurfen
scuffle ['skʌfəl] s Rauferei f ‖ intr raufen
scuff' mark' s Schmutzfleck m
scull [skʌl] s (sport) Skull m ‖ intr (sport) skullen
scullery ['skʌləri] s Spülküche f
scul'lery maid' s Spülerin f
sculptor ['skʌlptər] s Bildhauer m
sculptress ['skʌlptrɪs] s Bildhauerin f
sculptural ['skʌlptʃərəl] adj bildhauerisch
sculpture ['skʌlptʃər] s *(art)* Bildhauerei f; *(work of art)* Skulptur f ‖ tr meißeln ‖ intr bildhauern
scum [skʌm] s (& fig) Abschaum m
scummy ['skʌmi] adj schaumig; (fig) niederträchtig
scurrilous ['skʌrɪləs] adj skurril
scur·ry ['skʌri] v (pret & pp -ried) intr huschen
scurvy ['skʌrvi] adj gemein ‖ s Skorbut m
scuttle ['skʌtəl] s (naut) Springluke f ‖ tr *(hopes, plans)* vernichten; (naut) selbst versenken
scut'tlebutt' s (coll) Latrinenparole f
scut'tling s Selbstversenkung f
scythe [saɪð] s Sense f
sea [si] s See f, Meer n; at sea auf See; go to sea zur See gehen; heavy seas hoher (or schwerer) Seegang m
sea'board' s Küstenstrich m
sea' breeze' s Seebrise f
sea'coast' s Seeküste f, Meeresküste f
seafarer ['si ˌferər] s Seefahrer m
seafaring ['si ˌferɪŋ] s Seefahrt f
sea'food' s Fischgerichte pl
sea'go'ing adj seetüchtig
sea' gull' s Seemöwe f, Möwe f
seal [sil] s Siegel n; (zool) Seehund m ‖ tr *(a document)* siegeln; *(a deal, s.o.'s fate)* besiegeln; *(against leakage)* verschließen, abdichten; s. off (mil) abriegeln; s. up abdichten

sea' legs' spl—get one's s. seefest werden
sea'lev'el s Meereshöhe f
seal'ing wax' s Siegellack m
seal'skin' s Seehundsfell n
seam [sim] s *(groove)* Fuge f; (geol) Lager n; (min) Flöz n; (sew) Naht f
sea'man s (-men) Seemann m; (nav) Matrose m
sea' mile' s Seemeile f
seamless ['simlɪs] adj nahtlos
sea' mon'ster s Meeresungeheuer n
seamstress ['simstrɪs] s Näherin f
seamy ['simi] adj verrufen; s. side (fig) Schattenseite f
séance ['se·ɑns] s Séance f
sea'plane' s Seeflugzeug n
sea'port' s Seehafen m
sea'port town' s Hafenstadt f
sea' pow'er s Seemacht f
sear [sɪr] tr versengen
search [sʌrtʃ] s Durchsuchung f; *(for a person)* (for) Fahndung f *(nach)*; in s. of auf der Suche nach ‖ tr durchsuchen ‖ intr suchen; s. for suchen, fahnden nach
search'ing adj gründlich; *(glance)* forschend
search'light' s Scheinwerfer m
search' war'rant s Haussuchungsbefehl m
seascape ['si ˌskep] s Seegemälde n
sea' shell' s Muschel f
sea'shore' s Strand m
sea'shore resort' s Seebad n
sea'sick' adj seekrank
sea'sick'ness s Seekrankheit f
sea'side' adj Meeres-, See-
season ['sizən] s Jahreszeit f; *(appropriate period)* Saison f; **closed s.** (hunt) Schonzeit f; **dry s.** Trockenzeit f; **in and out of s.** jederzeit; **in s.** zur rechten Zeit; **out of s.** *(game)* außerhalb der Saison; *(fruits, vegetables)* nicht auf dem Markt; **peak s.** Hochsaison f ‖ tr *(food)* würzen; *(wine)* lagern; *(wood)* austrocknen lassen; *(tobacco)* reifen lassen; *(soldiers)* abhärten ‖ intr (e.g., said of wine) (ab)lagern
seasonal ['sizənəl] adj jahreszeitlich; *(caused by seasons)* saisonbedingt
sea'sonal work' s Saisonarbeit f
sea'soned adj erfahren; *(troops)* kampfgewohnt, fronterfahren
sea'soning s Würze f
sea'son's greet'ings spl Festgrüße pl
sea'son tick'et s Dauerkarte f
seat [sit] s Sitz m, Platz m; *(of trousers)* Gesäß n; **have a s.** Platz nehmen; **keep one's s.** sitzenbleiben ‖ tr *(a person)* e-n Platz anweisen *(dat)*; *(said of a room)* Sitzplätze bieten für; **be seated** sich hinsetzen
seat' belt' s (aer, aut) Sicherheitsgurt m; **fasten seat belts!** bitte anschnallen!
seat' cov'er s (aut) Auto-Schonbezug m
seat'ing capac'ity s (for) Sitzgelegenheit f (für); **have a s. of** fassen
seat' of gov'ernment s Regierungssitz m
sea'wall' s Strandmauer f

sea'way' s Seeweg m; (heavy sea) schwerer Seegang m
sea'weed' s Alge f, Seetang m
sea'wor'thy adj seetüchtig
secede [sɪ'sid] intr sich trennen
secession [sɪ'sɛʃən] s Sezession f
seclude [sɪ'klud] tr abschließen
seclud'ed adj abgeschieden; (life) zurückgezogen; (place) abgelegen
seclusion [sɪ'kluʒən] s Zurückgezogenheit f, Abgeschiedenheit f
second ['sɛkənd] adj zweite; **be s. to none** niemandem nachstehen; **in the s. place** zweitens; **s. in command** stellvertretender Kommandeur m ‖ s (unit of time) Sekunde f; (moment) Augenblick m; (in boxing or duelling) Sekundant m; **George the Second** Georg der Zweite; **the s.** (of the month) der zweite ‖ pron zweite ‖ tr unterstützen
secondary ['sɛkən,dɛri] adj sekundär, Neben– ‖ s (elec) Sekundärwicklung f; (fb) Spieler pl in der zweiten Reihe
sec'ondary school' s Oberschule
sec'ondary-school teach'er s Oberlehrer –in mf
sec'ondary sourc'es spl Sekundärliteratur f
sec'ondary tar'get s Ausweichziel n
sec'ond best' s Zweitbeste mfn
sec'ond-best' adj zweitbeste; **come off s.** den kürzeren ziehen
sec'ond-class' adj zweitklassig; **s. ticket** Fahrkarte f zweiter Klasse
sec'ond cous'in s Cousin m (or Kusine f) zweiten Grades
sec'ond fid'dle s—**play s.** die zweite Geige spielen
sec'ond hand' s (horol) Sekundenzeiger m
sec'ondhand' adj (car) gebraucht (information) aus zweiter Hand; (books) antiquarisch
sec'ondhand book'store s Antiquariat n
sec'ondhand deal'er s Altwarenhändler –in mf
sec'ond lieuten'ant s Leutnant m
secondly ['sɛkəndli] adv zweitens
sec'ond mate' s (naut) zweiter Offizier m
sec'ond na'ture s zweite Natur f
sec'ond-rate' adj zweitklassig
sec'ond sight' s zweites Gesicht n
sec'ond thought' s—**have second thoughts** Bedenken hegen; **on s.** bei weiterem Nachdenken
sec'ond wind' s—**get one's s.** wieder zu Kräften kommen
secrecy ['sikrəsi] s Heimlichkeit f
secret ['sikrɪt] adj geheim ‖ s Geheimnis n; **in s.** insgeheim; **keep no secrets from** keine Geheimnisse haben vor (dat); **keep s.** geheimhalten; **make no s. of** kein Hehl machen aus
secretary ['sɛkrə,tɛri] s (man, desk, bird) Sekretär m; (female) Sekretärin f; (in government) Minister m
sec'retary-gen'eral s Generalsekretär m
sec'retary of com'merce s Handelsminister m

sec'retary of defense' s Verteidigungsminister m
sec'retary of la'bor s Arbeitsminister m
sec'retary of state' s Außenminister m
sec'retary of the inter'ior s Innenminister m
sec'retary of the treas'ury s Finanzminister n
se'cret bal'lot s geheime Abstimmung f
secrete [sɪ'krit] tr (hide) verstecken; (physiol) absondern, ausscheiden
secretive ['sikrɪtɪv] adj verschwiegen
se'cret police' s Geheimpolizei f
se'cret serv'ice s Geheimdienst m
sect [sɛkt] s Sekte f
sectarian [sɛk'tɛri·ən] adj sektiererisch; (school) Konfessions–
section ['sɛkʃən] s (segment, part) Teil m; (of a newspaper, chapter) Abschnitt m; (of a city) Viertel n; (group) Abteilung f; (cross section) thin slice, e.g., of tissue) Schnitt m; (jur) Paragraph m; (mil) Halbzug m; (rr) Strecke f; (surg) Sektion f ‖ tr—**s. off** abteilen
sectional ['sɛkʃənəl] adj (view) Teil–; (pride) Lokal–
sec'tional fur'niture s Anbaumöbel n
sec'tion hand' s Schienenleger m
sector ['sɛktər] s Sektor m
secular ['sɛkjələr] adj weltlich ‖ s Weltpriester m, Weltgeistlicher m
secularism ['sɛkjələ,rɪzəm] s Weltlichkeit f, Säkularismus m
secure [sɪ'kjʊr] adj sicher ‖ tr (make fast) sichern; (obtain) sich [dat] beschaffen
security [sɪ'kjʊrɪti] s (& jur) Sicherheit f; **securities** Wertpapiere pl
sedan [sɪ'dæn] s Limousine f
sedan' chair' s Sänfte f
sedate [sɪ'det] adj gesetzt
sedation [sɪ'deʃən] s Beruhigung f
sedative ['sɛdətɪv] s Beruhigungsmittel n
sedentary ['sɛdən,tɛri] adj sitzend
sedge [sɛdʒ] s (bot) Segge f
sediment ['sɛdɪmənt] s Bodensatz m; (geol) Ablagerung f, Sediment n
sedition [sɪ'dɪʃən] s Aufruhr m
seditious [sɪ'dɪʃəs] adj aufrührerisch
seduce [sɪ'd(j)us] tr verführen
seducer [sɪ'd(j)usər] s Verführer –in mf
seduction [sɪ'dʌkʃən] s Verführung f
seductive [sɪ'dʌktɪv] adj verführerisch
sedulous ['sɛdʒələs] adj emsig
see [si] s (eccl) (erz)bischöflicher Stuhl m ‖ v (pret saw [sɔ]; pp seen [sin]) tr sehen; (comprehend) verstehen; (realize) einsehen; (a doctor) gehen zu; **see red** rasend werden; **see s.o. off** j–n an den Zug (ans Flugzeug) bringen; **see s.o. to the door** j–n zur Tür geleiten; **see s.th. through** etw durchstehen; **that remains to be seen** das wird man erst sehen ‖ intr sehen; **see through** (fig) durchschauen; **see to** sich kümmern um; **see to it that** sich darum kümmern,

daß; **you see** (*parenthetical*) wissen Sie

seed [sid] *s* Samen *m;* (*collective* & fig) Saat *f;* (*in fruit*) Kern *m;* (physiol) Samen *m;* **go to s.** in Samen schießen; **seeds** (fig) Keim *m* || *tr* besäen

seed'bed' *s* Samenbeet *n*

seed'ed rye' bread' *s* Kümmelbrot *n*

seedless ['sidlɪs] *adj* kernlos

seedling ['sidlɪŋ] *s* Sämling *m*

seedy ['sidi] *adj* (*person*) heruntergekommen; (*thing*) schäbig

see'ing *s* Sehen *n* || *conj*—**s. that** in Anbetracht dessen, daß

See'ing Eye' dog' *s* Blindenhund *m*

seek [sik] *v* (*pret* & *pp* **sought** [sɔt]) *tr* suchen; **s. s.o.'s advice** j-s Rat erbitten; **s. to** (*inf*) versuchen zu (*inf*) || *intr*—**s. after** suchen nach

seem [sim] *intr* scheinen || *impers*—**it seems to me** es kommt mir vor

seemingly ['simɪŋli] *adv* anscheinend

seemly ['simli] *adj* schicklich

seep [sip] *intr* sickern

seepage ['sipɪdʒ] *s* Durchsickern *n*

seer [sɪr] *s* Seher *m*

seeress ['sɪrɪs] *s* Seherin *f*

see'saw' *s* Schaukelbrett *n,* Wippe *f* || *intr* wippen; (fig) schwanken

seethe [sið] *intr* sieden; **s. with** (fig) sieden vor (*dat*)

segment ['sɛgmənt] *s* Abschnitt *m*

segregate ['sɛgrɪ‚get] *tr* trennen, absondern

segregation [‚sɛgrɪ'geʃən] *s* Absonderung *f;* (*of races*) Rassentrennung *f*

seismograph ['saɪzmə‚græf] *s* Erdbebenmesser *m,* Seismograph *m*

seismology [saɪz'malədʒi] *s* Erdbebenkunde *f,* Seismologie *f*

seize [siz] *tr* anfassen; (*a criminal*) festnehmen; (*a town, fortress*) einnehmen; (*an opportunity*) ergreifen; (*power*) an sich reißen; (*confiscate*) beschlagnahmen

seizure ['siʒər] *s* Besitzergreifung *f;* (*confiscation*) Beschlagnahme *f;* (pathol) plötzlicher Anfall *m*

seldom ['sɛldəm] *adv* selten

select [sɪ'lɛkt] *adj* erlesen || *tr* auslesen, auswählen

select'ed *adj* ausgesucht

selection [sɪ'lɛkʃən] *s* Auswahl *f*

selective [sɪ'lɛktɪv] *adj* Auswahl–; (rad) trennscharf

selec'tive serv'ice *s* allgemeine Wehrpflicht *f*

self [sɛlf] *s* (**selves** [sɛlvz]) Selbst *n,* Ich *n;* **be one's old s. again** wieder der alte sein; **his better s.** sein besseres Ich || *pron*—**payable to s.** auf Selbst ausgestellt

self'-addressed en'velope *s* mit Anschrift versehener Freiumschlag *m*

self'-assur'ance *s* Selbstbewußtsein *n*

self'-cen'tered *adj* ichbezogen

self'-conceit'ed *adj* eingebildet

self'-con'fident *adj* selbstsicher

self'-con'scious *adj* befangen

self'-control' *s* Selbstbeherrschung *f*

self'-decep'tion *s* Selbsttäuschung *f*

self'-defense' *s* Selbstverteidigung *f;* **in s.** aus Notwehr

self'-deni'al *s* Selbstverleugnung *f*

self'-destruc'tion *s* Selbstvernichtung *f*

self'-determina'tion *s* Selbstbestimmung *f*

self'-dis'cipline *s* Selbstzucht *f*

self'-ed'ucated per'son *s* Autodidakt –in *mf*

self'-employed' *adj* selbständig

self'-esteem' *s* Selbsteinschätzung *f*

self'-ev'ident *adj* selbstverständlich

self'-explan'ator'y *adj* keiner Erklärung bedürftig

self'-gov'ernment *s* Selbstverwaltung *f*

self'-impor'tant *adj* eingebildet

self'-indul'gence *s* Genußsucht *f*

self'-in'terest *s* Eigennutz *m*

selfish ['sɛlfɪʃ] *adj* eigennützig

selfishness ['sɛlfɪʃnɪs] *s* Eigennutz *m*

selfless ['sɛlflɪs] *adj* selbstlos

self'-love' *s* Selbstliebe *f*

self'-made man' *s* Selfmademan *m*

self'-por'trait *s* Selbstbildnis *n*

self'-possessed' *adj* selbstbeherrscht

self'-praise' *s* Eigenlob *n*

self'-preserva'tion *s* Selbsterhaltung *f*

self'-reli'ant *adj* selbstsicher

self'-respect' *s* Selbstachtung *f*

self'-right'eous *adj* selbstgerecht

self'-sac'rifice *s* Selbstaufopferung *f*

self'same' *adj* ebenderselbe

self'-sat'isfied *adj* selbstzufrieden

self'-seek'ing *adj* selbstsüchtig

self'-serv'ice *adj* mit Selbstbedienung || *s* Selbstbedienung *f*

self'-styled' *adj* von eigenen Gnaden

self'-suffi'cient *adj* selbstgenügsam

self'-support'ing *adj* finanziell unabhängig

self'-taught' *adj* autodidaktisch

self'-willed' *adj* eigenwillig

self'-wind'ing *adj* automatisch

sell [sɛl] (*pret* & *pp* **sold** [sold]) *tr* verkaufen; (*at auction*) versteigern; (*wares*) führen; **be sold on** (coll) begeistert sein von; **s. dirt cheap** verramschen; **s. s.o. on s.th.** (coll) j-n zu etw überreden; **s. out** ausverkaufen; (*betray*) verraten; **s. short** (st. exch.) in blanko verkaufen || *intr* sich verkaufen; **s. for** verkauft werden für; **s. short** fixen

seller ['sɛlər] *s* Verkäufer –in *mf;* **good s.** (com) Reißer *m*

Seltzer ['sɛltsər] *s* Selterswasser *n*

selvage ['sɛlvɪdʒ] *s* (*of fabric*) Salleiste *f;* (*of a lock*) Eckplatte *f*

semantic [sɪ'mæntɪk] *adj* semantisch || **semantics** *s* Wortbedeutungslehre *f*

semaphore ['sɛmə‚for] *s* Winkzeichen *n;* (rr) Semaphor *m* || *intr* winken

semblance ['sɛmbləns] *s* Anschein *m*

semen ['simən] *s* Samen *m*

semicircle ['sɛmɪ‚sʌrkəl] *s* Halbkreis *m*

semicolon ['sɛmɪ‚kolən] *s* Strichpunkt *m*

semiconductor [‚sɛmɪkən'dʌktər] *s* Halbleiter *m*

semiconscious [‚sɛmɪ'kanʃəs] *adj* halbbewußt

semifinal [,semɪ'faɪnəl] *adj* Halb-
finale– || *s* Halbfinale *n*, Vorschluß-
runde *f*
seminar ['semɪ,nɑr] *s* Seminar *n*
seminarian [,semɪ'nerɪ·ən] *s* Seminarist *m*
seminary ['semɪ,neri] *s* Seminar *n*
semiprecious [,semɪ'preʃəs] *adj* halb-
edel
Semite ['semaɪt] *s* Semit –in *mf*
Semitic [sɪ'mɪtɪk] *adj* semitisch
semitrailer ['semɪ,trelər] *s* Schleppan-
hänger *m*
senate ['senɪt] *s* Senat *m*
senator ['senətər] *s* Senator *m*
senatorial [,senə'torɪ·əl] *adj* (*of one
senator*) senatorisch; (*of the senate*)
Senats–
send [send] *v* (*pret & pp* **sent** [sent])
tr schicken, senden; (rad, telv) senden; **s. back** zurückschicken; **s. back
word** zurücksagen lassen; **s. down**
(box) niederschlagen; **s. forth**
(*leaves*) treiben; **s. off** absenden; **s.
on** (*forward*) weiterbefördern; **s.
word that** benachrichtigen, daß ||
intr—**s. for** (*e.g., free samples*) bestellen; (*e.g., a doctor*) rufen lassen
sender ['sendər] *s* Absender –in *mf;*
(telg) Geber –in *mf*
send'-off' *s* Abschiedsfeier *f*
senile ['sinaɪl] *adj* senil
senility [sɪ'nɪlɪti] *s* Senilität *f*
senior ['sinjər] *adj* (*in age*) älter; (*in
rank*) ranghöher; (*class*) oberste;
Mr. John Smith Senior Herr John
Smith senior || *s* Älteste *mf;* (*stu-
dent*) Student –in *mf* im letzten
Studienjahr
sen'ior cit'izen *s* bejahrter Mitbürger
m
seniority [sin'jɑrɪti] *s* Dienstalter *n*
sen'ior of'ficer *s* Vorgesetzte *mf*
sen'ior part'ner *s* geschäftsführender
Partner *m*
sen'ior year' *s* letztes Studienjahr *n*
sensation [sen'seʃən] *s* (*feeling*) Gefühl *n;* (*cause of interest*) Sensation *f*
sensational [sen'seʃənəl] *adj* sensationell
sensationalism [sen'seʃənə,lɪzəm] *s*
Sensationsgier *f*
sense [sens] *s* (*e.g., of sight; meaning*)
Sinn *m;* (*feeling*) Gefühl *n;* (*common sense*) Verstand *m;* **be out of
one's senses** von Sinnen sein; **bring
s.o. to his senses** j–n zur Vernunft
bringen; **in a s.** in gewissem Sinne;
in the broadest s. im weitesten Sinne;
make s. Sinn haben; **there's no s. to
it** da steckt kein Sinn drin || *tr*
spüren, fühlen
senseless ['senslɪs] *adj* sinnlos; (*from
a blow*) bewußtlos
sense' of direc'tion *s* Ortssinn *m*
sense' of du'ty *s* Pflichtgefühl *n*
sense' of guilt' *s* Schuldgefühl *n*
sense' of hear'ing *s* Gehör *n*
sense' of hon'or *s* Ehrgefühl *n*
sense' of hu'mor *s* Humor *m*
sense' of jus'tice *s* Gerechtigkeits-
gefühl *n*

sense' of responsibil'ity *s* Verantwor-
tungsbewußtsein *n*
sense' of sight' *s* Gesichtssinn *m*
sense' of smell' *s* Geruchssinn *m*
sense' of taste' *s* Geschmackssinn *m*
sense' of touch' *s* Tastsinn *m*
sense' or'gan *s* Sinnesorgan *n*
sensibility [,sensɪ'bɪlɪti] *s* Empfindlichkeit *f*
sensible ['sensɪbəl] *adj* vernünftig
sensitive ['sensɪtɪv] *adj* (**to,** *e.g.,* **cold**)
empfindlich (gegen); (*touchy*) überempfindlich; **s. post** Vertrauensposten
m; **very s.** überempfindlich
sensitize ['sensɪ,taɪz] *tr* (phot) licht-
empfindlich machen
sensory ['sensəri] *adj* Sinnes–
sen'sory depriva'tion *s* Reizentzug *m*
sensual ['senʃu·əl] *adj* sinnlich
sensuality [,senʃu'ælɪti] *s* Sinnlichkeit
f, Sinnenlust *f*
sensuous ['senʃu·əs] *adj* sinnlich
sentence ['sentəns] *s* (gram) Satz *m;*
(jur) Urteil *n;* **pronounce s.** das Ur-
teil verkünden || *tr* verurteilen
sentiment ['sentɪmənt] *s* Empfindung
f
sentimental [,sentɪ'mentəl] *adj* sentimental, rührselig
sentinel ['sentɪnəl] *s* Posten *m;* **stand
s. Wache** stehen
sentry ['sentri] *s* Wachposten *m*
sen'try box' *s* Schilderhaus *n*
separable ['sepərəbəl] *adj* trennbar
separate ['sepərɪt] *adj* getrennt; **under
s. cover** separat || ['sepə,ret] *tr*
trennen; (*segregate*) absondern;
(*scatter*) zerstreuen; (*discharge*) ent-
lassen; **s. into** teilen in (*acc*) || *intr*
sich trennen, sich scheiden
sep'arated *adj* (*couple*) getrennt
separation [,sepə're ʃən] *s* Trennung *f*
September [sep'tembər] *s* September
m
sep'tic tank' ['septɪk] *s* Kläranlage *f*
sepulcher ['sepəlkər] *s* Grabmal *n*
sequel ['sikwəl] *s* Fortsetzung *f;* (fig)
Nachspiel *n*
sequence ['sikwəns] *s* Reihenfolge *f*
se'quence of tens'es *s* Zeitenfolge *f*
sequester [sɪ'kwestər] *tr* (*remove*) entfernen; (*separate*) absondern; (jur)
sequestrieren
sequins ['sikwɪnz] *spl* Flitter *m*
ser·aph ['serəf] *s* (**–aphs &** **–aphim**
[əfɪm]) Seraph *m*
Serb [sʌrb] *adj* serbisch || *s* Serbe *m,*
Serbin *f*
Serbia ['sʌrbɪ·ə] *s* Serbien *n*
serenade [,serə'ned] *s* Ständchen *n* ||
tr ein Ständchen bringen (*dat*)
serene [sɪ'rin] *adj* heiter; (*sea*) ruhig
serenity [sɪ'renɪti] *s* Heiterkeit *f*
serf [sʌrf] *s* Leibeigene *mf*
serfdom ['sʌrfdəm] *s* Leibeigenschaft
f
serge [sʌrdʒ] *s* (tex) Serge *f*
sergeant ['sɑrdʒənt] *s* Feldwebel *m*
ser'geant-at-arms' *s* (**sergeants-at-arms**)
Ordnungsbeamter *m*
ser'geant first' class' *s* Oberfeldwebel
m

ser'geant ma'jor s (sergeant majors) Hauptfeldwebel m

serial ['sɪrɪ·əl] s Fortsetzungsroman m, Romanfolge f

serialize ['sɪrɪ·ə‚laɪz] tr in Fortsetzungen veröffentlichen

se'rial num'ber s laufende Nummer f; (of a product) Fabriknummer f

se·ries ['sɪriz] s (–ries) Serie f, Reihe f; in s. reihenweise; (elec) hintereinandergeschaltet

serious ['sɪrɪ·əs] adj ernst; (mistake) schwerwiegend; (illness) gefährlich

seriously ['sɪrɪ·əsli] adv ernstlich; s. wounded schwerverwundet; take s. ernst nehmen

seriousness ['sɪrɪ·əsnɪs] s Ernst m

sermon ['sʌrmən] s Predigt f

sermonize ['sʌrmə‚naɪz] intr e-e Moralpredigt halten

serpent ['sʌrpənt] s Schlange f

serrated ['sɛretɪd] adj sägeartig

se·rum ['sɪrəm] s (–rums & –ra [rə]) Serum n

servant ['sʌrvənt] s Diener –in mf; (domestic) Hausdiener –in mf

serv'ant girl' s Dienstmädchen n

serve [sʌrv] s (tennis) Aufschlag m || tr (a master, God) dienen (dat); (food) servieren; (a meal) anrichten; (guests) bedienen; (time in jail) verbüßen; (one's term in the service) abdienen; (the purpose) erfüllen; (tennis) aufschlagen; s. mass (eccl) zur Messe dienen; s. notice on s.o. j–n vorladen; s. up (food) auftragen || intr (& mil) dienen; (at table) servieren; s. as dienen als; s. on a committe e–m Ausschuß angehören

server ['sʌrvər] s (eccl) Ministrant m; (tennis) Aufschläger m

service ['sʌrvɪs] s (diplomatic, secret, foreign, public, etc.) Dienst m; (in a restaurant) Bedienung f; (set of table utensils) Besteck n; (set of dishes) Service n; (assistance at a repair shop) Service m; (maintenance) Wartung f; (transportation) Verkehr m; (relig) Gottesdienst m; (tennis) Aufschlag m; at your s. zu Ihren Diensten; be in s. (mach) in Betrieb sein; be in the s. (mil) beim Militär sein; be of s. behilflich sein; do s.o. a s. j–m e–n Dienst erweisen; essential services lebenswichtige Betriebe pl; fit for active s. kriegverwendungsfähig; see s. Kriegsdienst tun; the services die Waffengattungen pl || tr (mach) warten

serviceable ['sʌrvɪsəbəl] adj (usable) verwendungsfähig; (helpful) nützlich; (durable) haltbar

serv'ice club' s (mil) Soldatenklub m

serv'ice en'trance s Dienstboteneingang m

serv'ice·man' s (–men') Monteur m; (at a gas station) Tankwart m; (mil) Soldat m

serv'ice rec'ord s Wehrpaß m

serv'ice sta'tion s Tankstelle f

serv'ice-station atten'dant s Tankwart m

serv'ice troops' spl Versorgungstruppen pl

servile ['sʌrvaɪl] adj kriecherisch

serv'ing s Portion f; (e.g., of a subpoena) Zustellung f

serv'ing cart' s Servierwagen m

servitude ['sʌrvɪ‚t(j)ud] s Knechtschaft f

ses'ame seed' ['sɛsəmi] s Sesamsamen m

session ['sɛʃən] s Sitzung f, Tagung f; (educ) Semester n; be in session tagen

set [sɛt] adj (price, time) festgesetzt; (rule) festgelegt; (speech) wohlüberlegt; be all set fix und fertig sein; be set in one's ways festgefahren sein || s (group of things belonging together) Satz m, Garnitur f; (of chess or checkers) Spiel n; (clique) Sippschaft f; (rad, telv) Apparat m; (tennis) Satz m; (theat) Bühnenbild n; younger set Nachwuchs m || v (pret & pp set; ger setting) tr (put) setzen; (stand) stellen; (lay) legen; (a clock, a trap) stellen; (the hair) legen; (a record) aufstellen; (an example) geben; (a time, price) festsetzen; (the table) decken; (jewels) (ein)fassen; (a camera) einstellen; (surg) einrenken; (typ) setzen; set ahead (a clock) vorstellen; set back (a clock) nachstellen; (a patient) zurückwerfen; set down niedersetzen; set down in writing schriftlich niederlegen; set foot in (or on) betreten; set forth (explain) erklären; set free freilassen; set in order in Ordnung bringen; set limits to Schranken setzen (dat); set off (a bomb) sprengen lassen; set (s.o.) over (j–n) überordnen (dat); set right wieder in Ordnung bringen; set store by Gewicht beimessen (dat); set straight (on) aufklären (über acc); set the meeting for two die Versammlung auf zwei Uhr ansetzen; set up (at the bar) (coll) zu e–m Gläschen einladen; (mach) montieren; (typ) (ab)setzen; set up housekeeping Wirtschaft führen; set up in business etablieren || intr (said of cement) abbinden; (astr) untergehen; set about (ger) darangehen zu (inf); set in einsetzen; set out (for) sich auf den Weg machen (nach); set out on (a trip) antreten; set to work sich an die Arbeit machen

set'back' s Rückschlag m, Schlappe f

set'screw' s Stellschraube f

settee [sɛ'ti] s Polsterbank f

setter ['sɛtər] s Vorstehhund m

set'ting s (of the sun) Niedergang m; (of a story) Ort m der Handlung; (of a gem) Fassung f; (theat) Bühnenbild n

settle ['sɛtəl] tr (conclude) erledigen; (decide) entscheiden; (an argument) schlichten; (a problem) erledigen; (an account) begleichen; (one's affairs) in Ordnung bringen; (a creditor's claim) befriedigen; (a lawsuit) durch Vergleich beilegen; (a region)

besiedeln; (*people*) ansiedeln ‖ *intr*
(*in a region*) sich niederlassen; (*said
of a building*) sich senken; (*said of
a ship*) absacken; (*said of dust*) sich
legen; (*said of a liquid*) sich klären;
(*said of suspended particles*) sich
setzen; (*said of a cold*) (**in**) sich
festsetzen (in *dat*); **s. down** (*in a
chair*) sich niederlassen; (*calm
down*) sich beruhigen; **s. down to**
(*e.g., work*) sich machen an (*acc*);
s. for sich einigen auf (*acc*); **s. on**
sich entscheiden für; **s. up** (fin) die
Verbindlichkeit vergleichen
settlement ['setəlmənt] *s* (*colony*) Siedlung *f*; (*agreement*) Abkommen *n*;
(*of an argument*) Beilegung *f*; (*of
accounts*) Abrechnung *f*; (*of a debt*)
Begleichung *f*; **reach a s.** e–n Vergleich schließen
settler ['setlər] *s* Ansiedler –in *mf*
set'up' *s* Aufbau *m*, Anlage *f*
seven ['sevən] *adj & pron* sieben ‖ *s*
Sieben *f*
seventeen ['sevən'tin] *adj & pron* siebzehn ‖ *s* Siebzehn *f*
seventeenth ['sevən'tinθ] *adj & pron*
siebzehnte ‖ *s* (*fraction*) Siebzehntel
n; **the s.** (*in dates or a series*) der
Siebzehnte
seventh ['sevənθ] *adj & pron* sieb(en)te
‖ *s* (*fraction*) Sieb(en)tel *n*; **the s.**
(*in dates or a series*) der Sieb(en)te
seventieth ['sevəntɪ·ɪθ] *adj & pron*
siebzigste ‖ *s* (*fraction*) Siebzigstel *n*
seventy ['sevəntɪ] *adj & pron* siebzig
‖ *s* Siebzig *f*; **the seventies** die siebziger Jahre
sev'enty-first' *adj & pron* einundsieb-
zigste
sev'enty-one' *adj* einundsiebzig
sever ['sevər] *tr* (ab)trennen; (*relations*) abbrechen
several ['sevərəl] *adj & indef pron*
mehrere; **s. times** mehrmals
severance ['sevərəns] *s* Trennung *f*;
(*of relations*) Abbruch *m*
sev'erance pay' *s* (& mil) Abfindungs-
entschädigung *f*
severe [sɪ'vɪr] *adj* (*judge, winter, cold*)
streng; (*blow, sentence, winter*) hart;
(*illness, test*) schwer; (*criticism*)
scharf
severity [sɪ'verɪtɪ] *s* Strenge *f*; Härte
f; Schärfe *f*
sew [so] *v* (*pret* **sewed;** *pp* **sewed &
sewn**) *tr & intr* nähen
sewage ['su·ɪdʒ] *s* Abwässer *pl*
sew'age-dispos'al plant' *s* Kläranlage
f
sewer ['su·ər] *s* Kanal *m* ‖ ['so·ər] *s*
Näher –in *mf*
sewerage ['su·ərɪdʒ] *s* Kanalisation *f*
sew'er pipe' ['su·ər] *s* Abwasserleitung
f
sew'ing *s* Näharbeit *f*
sew'ing bas'ket *s* Nähkasten *m*
sew'ing kit' *s* Nähzeug *n*
sew'ing machine' *s* Nähmaschine *f*
sex [seks] *adj* (*crime, education, har-
mone*) Sexual– ‖ *s* Geschlecht *n*;
(*intercourse*) Sex *m*

sex appeal' *s* Sex-Appeal *m*
sex' pot' *s* (coll) Sexbombe *f*
sextent ['sekstənt] *s* Sextant *m*
sexton ['sekstən] *s* Küster *m*
sexual ['sekʃu·əl] *adj* geschlechtlich,
Geschlechts–, sexuell
sex'ual in'tercourse *s* Geschlechtsverkehr *m*
sexuality [sekʃu'ælɪtɪ] *s* Sexualität *f*
sexy ['seksi] *adj* sexy
shabbily ['sfæbɪlɪ] *adv* schäbig; (*in
treatment*) stiefmütterlich
shabby ['sfæbi] *adj* schäbig
shack [sfæk] *s* Bretterbude *f*
shackle ['sfækəl] *s* (naut) Schäkel *m;*
shackles Fesseln *pl* ‖ *tr* fesseln
shad [sfæd] *s* Shad *m*, Alse *f*
shade [sfed] *s* Schatten *m;* (*for a window*) Rollo *n;* (*of a lamp*) Schirm *m;*
(*hue*) Schattierung *f;* **throw into the
s.** (fig) in den Schatten stellen ‖ *tr*
beschatten; (paint) schattieren
shad'ing *s* Schattierung *f*
shadow ['sfædo] *s* Schatten *m* ‖ *tr* (*a
person*) beschatten
shad'ow box'ing *s* Schattenboxen *n*
shadowy ['sfædo·ɪ] *adj* (*like a shadow*)
schattenhaft; (*indistinct*) verschwommen; (*shady*) schattig
shady ['sfedi] *adj* schattig; (coll) dunkel; **s. character** Dunkelmann *m;* **s.
deal** Lumperei *f;* **s. side** (& fig)
Schattenseite *f*
shaft [sfæft] *s* Schaft *m;* (*of an elevator*) Schacht *m;* (*handle*) Stiel *m;* (*of
a wagon*) Deichsel *f;* (*of a column*)
Säulenschaft *m;* (*of a transmission*)
Welle *f*
shaggy ['sfægi] *adj* zottig, struppig
shake [sfek] *s* Schütteln *n;* **he's no
great shakes** mit ihm ist nicht viel
los ‖ *v* (*pret* **shook** [sfuk]; *pp*
shaken) *tr* schütteln; **s. a leg!** (coll)
rühr dich ein bißchen; **s. before using** vor Gebrauch schütteln; **s. down**
(sl) erpressen; **s. hands** sich [*dat*]
die Hand geben; **s. hands with s.o.**
j–m die Hand drücken; **s. off** (&
fig) abschütteln; **s. one's head** mit
dem Kopf schütteln; **s. out** (*a rug*)
ausschütteln; **s. up** aufschütteln; (fig)
aufrütteln ‖ *intr* (**with**) zittern (vor
dat), beben (vor *dat*)
shake'down' *s* (sl) Erpressung *f*
shake'down cruise' *s* Probefahrt *f*
shaker ['sfekər] *s* (*for salt*) Streuer *m;*
(*for cocktails*) Shaker *m*
shake'-up' *s* Umgruppierung *f*
shaky ['sfeki] *adj* (& fig) wacklig
shale [sfel] *s* Schiefer *m*
shale' oil' *s* Schieferöl *n*
shall [sfæl] *v* (*pret* **should** [sfud]) *aux*
(*to express future tense*) werden, e.g.,
I **s.** go ich werde gehen; (*to express
obligation*) sollen, e.g., **s. I stay?** soll
ich bleiben?
shallow ['sfælo] *adj* (*river, person*)
seicht; (*water, bowl*) flach ‖ **shallows**
spl Untiefe *f*
sham [sfæm] *adj* Schein– ‖ *s* Schein *m*
‖ *v* (*pret & pp* **shammed;** *ger* **sham-
ming**) *tr* vortäuschen

sham' bat'tle s Scheingefecht n
shambles ['ʃæmbəlz] s Trümmerhaufen m
shame [ʃem] s Schande f; (feeling of shame) Scham f; **put s.o. to s.** (outdo s.o.) j–n in den Schatten stellen; **s. on you!** schäm dich!; **what a s.!** wie schade! || tr beschämen
shame'faced' adj verschämt
shameful ['ʃemfəl] adj schändlich
shameless ['ʃemlɪs] adj unverschämt
shampoo [ʃæm'pu] s Shampoo n || tr shampoonieren
shamrock ['ʃæmrɑk] s Kleeblatt n
Shanghai [ʃæŋ'haɪ] s Schanghai n || **shanghai** ['ʃæŋhaɪ] tr schanghaien
shank [ʃæŋk] s Unterschenkel m; (of an anchor, column, golf club) Schaft m; (cut of meat) Schenkel m
shanty ['ʃænti] s Bude f
shan'tytown' s Bretterbudensiedlung f
shape [ʃep] s Form f, Gestalt f; **in bad s.** (coll) in schlechter Form; **in good s.** in gutem Zustand; **out of s.** aus der Form; **take s.** sich gestalten || tr formen, gestalten || intr—**s. up** (coll) sich zusammenfassen
shapeless ['ʃeplɪs] adj formlos
shapely ['ʃepli] adj wohlgestaltet
share [ʃer] s Anteil m; (st. exch.) Aktie f; **do one's s.** das Seine tun || tr teilen || intr—**s. in** teilhaben an (dat)
share'hold'er s Aktionär –in mf
shark [ʃɑrk] s Hai m, Haifisch m
sharp [ʃɑrp] adj scharf; (pointed) spitzig; (keen) pfiffig || adv pünktlich || s (mus) Kreuz n
sharpen ['ʃɑrpən] tr schärfen; (a pencil) spitzen
sharply ['ʃɑrpli] adv scharf
sharp'shoot'er s Scharfschütze m
shatter ['ʃætər] tr zersplittern; (the nerves) zerrütten; (dreams) zerstören || intr zersplittern
shat'terproof' adj splittersicher
shave [ʃev] s—**get a s.** sich rasieren lassen || tr rasieren || intr sich rasieren
shav'ing brush' s Rasierpinsel m
shav'ing cream' s Rasierkrem m
shav'ing mug' s Rasiernapf m
shawl [ʃɔl] s Schal m
she [ʃi] s Weibchen n || pers pron sie
sheaf [ʃif] s (sheaves [ʃivz]) Garbe f
shear [ʃɪr] s—**shears** Schere f || v (pret sheared; pp sheared & shorn [ʃorn]) tr scheren; **s. off** abschneiden
sheath [ʃiθ] s Scheide f
sheathe [ʃið] tr in die Scheide stecken
shed [ʃɛd] s Schuppen m || v (pret & pp shed; ger shedding) tr (leaves) abwerfen; (tears) vergießen; (hair, leaves) verlieren; (peace) verbreiten; **s. light on** (fig) Licht werfen auf (acc)
sheen [ʃin] s Glanz m
sheep [ʃip] s (sheep) Schaf n
sheep'dog' s Schäferhund m
sheep'fold' s Schafhürde f, Schafpferch
sheepish ['ʃipɪʃ] adj (embarrassed) verlegen; (timid) schüchtern

sheep'skin' s Schaffell n; (coll) Diplom n
sheep'skin coat' s Schafpelz m
sheer [ʃɪr] adj rein; (tex) durchsichtig; **by s. force** durch bloße Gewalt || intr—**s. off** (naut) abscheren
sheet [ʃit] s (for the bed) Leintuch n; (of paper) Blatt n, Bogen m; (of metal) Blech n; (naut) Segelleine f; **come down in sheets** (fig) in Strömen regnen; **s. of ice** Glatteis n; **s. of flame** Feuermeer n
sheet' i'ron s Eisenblech n
sheet' mu'sic s Notenblatt n
she'-goat' s Ziege f
sheik [ʃik] s Scheich m
shelf [ʃɛlf] s (shelves [ʃɛlvz]) Regal n; **put on the s.** (fig) auf die lange Bank schieben
shell [ʃɛl] s Schale f; (conch) Muschel f; (of a snail) Gehäuse n; (of a tortoise) Panzer m; (explosive) Granate f; (bullet) Patrone f || tr (eggs) schälen; (nuts) aufknacken; (mil) beschießen; **s. out money** (coll) mit dem Geld herausrücken || intr—**s. out** (coll) blechen
shel·lac [ʃə'læk] s Schellack m || v (pret & pp –lacked; ger –lacking) tr mit Schellack streichen; (sl) verdreschen
shell'fish' s Schalentier n
shell' hole' s Granattrichter m
shell' shock' s Bombenneurose f
shelter ['ʃɛltər] s Obdach n; (fig) Schutz m || tr schützen
shelve [ʃɛlv] tr auf ein Regal stellen; (fig) auf die lange Bank schieben
shenanigans [ʃɪ'nænɪgənz] spl Possen pl
shepherd ['ʃepərd] s Hirt m; (fig) Seelenhirt m || tr hüten
shep'herd dog' s Schäferhund m
shepherdess ['ʃepərdɪs] s Hirtin f
sherbet ['ʃɑrbət] s Speiseeis n
sheriff ['ʃerɪf] s Sheriff m
sherry ['ʃeri] s Sherry m
shield [ʃild] s Schild m; (fig) Schutz m; (rad) Röhrenabschirmung f || tr (from) schützen (vor dat); (elec, mach) abschirmen
shift [ʃɪft] adj (worker, work) Schicht– || s Schicht f; (change) Verschiebung f; (loose-fitting dress) Kittelkleid n || tr (a meeting) verschieben; (the blame) (on) (ab)schieben (auf acc); **s. gears** umschalten || intr (said of the wind) umspringen; **s. for oneself** sich allein durchschlagen; **s. into second gear** in den zweiten Gang umschalten
shift' key' s Umschalttaste f
shiftless ['ʃɪftlɪs] adj träge
shifty ['ʃɪfti] adj schlau, gerissen
shimmer ['ʃɪmər] s Schimmer m || intr schimmern, flimmern
shin [ʃɪn] s Schienbein n
shin'bone' s Schienbein n
shine [ʃaɪn] s Schein m, Glanz m || v (pret & pp shined) tr polieren; (shoes) wichsen || v (pret & pp shone [ʃon]) intr scheinen; (said of the

eyes) leuchten; (*be outstanding*) (**in**) glänzen (in *dat*)

shiner [ˈʃaɪnər] *s* (sl) blaues Auge *n*

shingle [ˈʃɪŋgəl] *s* (*for a roof*) Schindel *f*; (*e.g., of a doctor*) Aushängeschild *n* ‖ *tr* mit Schindeln decken

shin'ing *adj* (*eyes*) leuchtend, strahlend; (*example*) glänzend

shiny [ˈʃaɪni] *adj* blank, glänzend

ship [ʃɪp] *s* Schiff *n* ‖ *v* (*pret & pp* **shipped**; *ger* **shipping**) *tr* senden; **s. water** e–e Sturzsee bekommen ‖ *intr*—**s. out** absegeln

ship'board' *s* Bord *m*; **on s.** an Bord

ship'build'er *s* Schiffbauer *m*

ship'build'ing *s* Schiffbau *m*

shipment [ˈʃɪpmənt] *s* Lieferung *f*

ship'ping *s* Absendung *f*, Verladung *f*; (*ships*) Schiffe *pl*

ship'ping clerk' *s* Expedient –in *mf*

ship'ping depart'ment *s* Versandabteilung *f*

ship'shape' *adj* ordentlich

ship'wreck' *s* Schiffbruch *m* ‖ *tr* scheitern lassen; **be s.** schiffbrüchig sein ‖ *intr* Schiffbruch erleiden

ship'yard' *s* Werft *f*

shirk [ʃɪrk] *tr* sich drücken vor (*dat*) ‖ *intr* (**from**) sich drücken (vor *dat*)

shirt [ʃʌrt] *s* Hemd *n*; **keep your s. on!** (sl) regen Sie sich nicht auf!

shirt' col'lar *s* Hemdkragen *m*

shirt'sleeve' *s* Hemdsärmel *m*

shirttail' *s* Hemdschoß *m*

shit [ʃɪt] *s* (vulg) Scheiße *f* ‖ *v* (*pret & pp* **shit**) *tr & intr* (vulg) scheißen

shiver [ˈʃɪvər] *s* Schauder *m* ‖ *intr* (**at**) schaudern (vor *dat*); (**with**) zittern (vor *dat*)

shoal [ʃol] *s* Untiefe *f*

shock [ʃɑk] *s* Schock *m*; (*of hair*) Schopf *m*; (agr) Schober *m*; (elec) Schlag *m* ‖ *tr* schockieren; (elec) e–n Schlag versetzen (*dat*)

shock' absorb'er [æbˈsɔrbər] *s* Stoßdämpfer *m*

shock'ing *adj* schockierend

shock' troops' *spl* Stoßtruppen *pl*

shock' wave' *s* Stoßwelle *f*

shoddy [ˈʃɑdi] *adj* schäbig

shoe [ʃu] *s* Schuh *m* ‖ *v* (*pret & pp* **shod** [ʃɑd]) *tr* beschlagen

shoe'horn' *s* Schuhlöffel *m*

shoe'lace' *s* Schuhband *n*, Schnürsenkel *m*

shoe'mak'er *s* Schuster *m*

shoe' pol'ish *s* Schuhwichse *f*

shoe'shine' *s* Schuhputzen *n*

shoe' store' *s* Schuhladen *m*

shoe' string' *s* Schuhband *m*; **on a s.** mit ein paar Groschen

shoe'tree' *s* Schuhspanner *m*

shoo [ʃu] *tr* (**away**) wegscheuchen ‖ *interj* sch!

shook-up [ˈʃukˈʌp] *adj* (coll) verdattert

shoot [ʃut] *s* Schößling *m* ‖ *v* (*pret & pp* **shot** [ʃɑt]) *tr* (an)schießen, (ab)-schießen; (*kill*) erschießen; (*dice*) werfen; (cin) drehen; (phot) aufnehmen; **s. down** (aer) abschießen; **s. the breeze** zwanglos plaudern; **s. up** (*e.g., a town*) zusammenschie-

ßen ‖ *intr* schießen; **s. at** schießen auf (*acc*); **s. by** vorbeisausen an (*dat*); **s. up** (*in growth*) aufschießen; (*said of flames*) emporschlagen; (*said of prices*) emporschnellen

shoot'ing *s* Schießerei *f*; (*execution*) Erschießung *f*; (*of a film*) Drehen *n*

shoot'ing gal'lery *s* Schießbude *f*

shoot'ing match' *s* Preisschießen *n*

shoot'ing star' *s* Sternschnuppe *f*

shoot'ing war' *s* heißer Krieg *m*

shop [ʃɑp] *s* Laden *m*, Geschäft *n*; **talk s.** fachsimpeln ‖ *v* (*pret & pp* **shopped**; *ger* **shopping**) *intr* einkaufen; **go shopping** einkaufen gehen; **s. around for** sich in einigen Läden umsehen nach

shop'girl' *s* Ladenmädchen *n*

shop'keep'er *s* Ladeninhaber –in *mf*

shoplifter [ˈʃɑpˌlɪftər] *s* Ladendieb –in *mf*

shop'lift'ing *s* Ladendiebstahl *m*

shopper [ˈʃɑpər] *s* Einkäufer –in *mf*

shop'ping *s* Einkaufen *n*; (*purchases*) Einkäufe *pl*

shop'ping bag' *s* Einkaufstasche *f*

shop'ping cen'ter *s* Einkaufcenter *n*

shop'ping dis'trict *s* Geschäftsviertel *n*

shop'ping spree' *s* Einkaufsorgie *f*

shop'talk' *s* Fachsimpelei *f*

shop'win'dow *s* Schaufenster *n*

shop'worn' *adj* (fig) abgerissen

shore [ʃor] *s* Küste *f*; (*beach*) Strand *m*; (*of a river*) Ufer *n*; **go to the s.** ans Meer fahren ‖ *tr*—**s. up** abstützen

shore' leave' *s* Landurlaub *m*

shore'line' *s* Küstenlinie *f*; (*of a river*) Uferlinie *f*

shore' patrol' *s* Küstenstreife *f*

short [ʃɔrt] *adj* kurz; (*person*) klein; (*loan*) kurzfristig; **a s. time ago** vor kurzem; **be s. of**, e.g., **I am s. of bread** das Brot geht mir aus; **be s. with s.o.** j–n kurz abfertigen; **cut s.** abbrechen; **fall s. of** zurückbleiben hinter (*dat*); **get the s. end** das Nachsehen haben; **I am three marks s.** es fehlen mir drei Mark; **in s.** kurzum; **s. of breath** außer Atem; **s. of cash** knapp bei Kasse ‖ *s* (cin) Kurzfilm *m*; (elec) Kurzschluß *m* ‖ *tr* (elec) kurzschließen

shortage [ˈʃɔrtɪdʒ] *s* (**of**) Mangel *m* (an *dat*); (com) Minderbetrag *m*

short'cake' *s* Mürbekuchen *m*

short'-change' *tr* zu wenig Wechselgeld herausgeben (*dat*); (fig) betrügen

short' cir'cuit *s* Kurzschluß *m*

short'-cir'cuit *tr* kurzschließen

short'com'ing *s* Fehler *m*, Mangel *m*

short'cut' *s* Abkürzung *f*; **take a s.** den Weg abkürzen

shorten [ˈʃɔrtən] *tr* abkürzen

short'ening *s* Abkürzung *f*; (culin) Backfett *n*

short'hand' *adj* stenographisch ‖ *s* Stenographie *f*; **in s.** stenographisch; **take down in s.** stenographieren

short-lived [ˈʃɔrtˈlaɪvd] *adj* kurzlebig

shortly [ˈʃɔrtli] *adv* in kurzem; **s. after** kurz nach

short'-or'der cook' s Schnellimbißkoch
m, Schnellimbißköchin f
short'-range' adj Nah–, auf kurze Sicht
shorts [ʃɔrts] s (underwear) Unterhose
f; (walking shorts) kurze Hose f;
(sport) Sporthose f
short'-sight'ed adj kurzsichtig
short' sto'ry s Novelle f
short'-tem'pered adj leicht aufbrausend
short'-term' adj kurzfristig
short'wave' adj Kurzwellen– || s Kurz-
welle f
short'wind'ed adj kurzatmig
shot [ʃɑt] adj (sl) kaputt; (drunk) (sl)
besoffen; **my nerves are s.** ich bin
mit meinen Nerven ganz herunter ||
s Schuß m; (shooter) Schütze m;
(pellets) Schrot m; (injection) Spritze
f; (snapshot) Aufnahme f; (of liquor)
Gläschen n; **be a good s.** gut schießen; **s. in the arm** (fig) Belebungs-
spritze f; **s. in the dark** Sprung m
ins Ungewisse; **take a s. at** e–n Schuß
abgeben auf (acc); (fig) versuchen;
wild s. Schuß m ins Blaue
shot'gun' s Schrotflinte f
shot'gun wed'ding s Mußehe f
shot'-put' s (sport) Kugelstoßen n
should [ʃud] aux (to express softened
affirmation) **I s. like to know** ich
möchte wissen; **I s. think so** das will
ich meinen; (to express obligation)
how s. I know? wie sollte ich das
wissen?; **you shouldn't do that** Sie
sollten das nicht tun; (in conditional
clauses) **if it s. rain tomorrow** wenn
es morgen regnen sollte
shoulder [ˈʃoldər] s Schulter f, Achsel
f; (of a road) Bankett n; **have broad
shoulders** e–n breiten Rücken haben
|| tr (a rifle) schultern; (responsibil-
ity) auf sich nehmen
shoul'der bag' s Umhängetasche f
shoul'der blade' s Schulterblatt n
shoul'der strap' s (of underwear) Trä-
gerband n; (mil) Schulterriemen m
shout [ʃaut] s Schrei m, Ruf m || tr
schreien, rufen; **s. down** (coll) nieder-
schreien || intr schreien, rufen
shove [ʃʌv] s Stoß m; **give s.o. a s.**
j–m e–n Stoß versetzen || tr stoßen;
(e.g., furniture) rücken; **s. around**
(coll) herumschubsen; **s. forward**
vorschieben || intr drängeln; **s. off**
(coll) abschieben; (naut) vom Land
abstoßen
shov·el [ˈʃʌvəl] s Schaufel f || v (pret
& pp –el[l]ed; ger –el[l]ing) tr schaufeln
show [ʃo] s (exhibition) Ausstellung f;
(outer appearance) Schau f; (spectacle) Theater n; (cin, theat) Vorstellung f; **by s. of hands** durch
Handzeichen; **make a s. of s.th.** mit
etw Staat machen; **only for s.** nur zur
Schau || v (pret **showed;** pp **shown**
[ʃon] & **showed**) tr zeigen; (prove)
beweisen, nachweisen; (said of evidence, tests) ergeben; (tickets, passport, papers) vorweisen; **s. around**
(a person) herumführen; (a thing)
herumzeigen || intr zu sehen sein;

(said of a slip) vorgucken; **s. off**
(with) großtun (mit); **s. up** erscheinen
show' busi'ness s Unterhaltungsindu-
strie f
show'case' s Schaukasten m, Vitrine f
show'down' s entscheidender Wendepunkt m; (e.g., in a western) Kraft-
probe f; (cards) Aufdecken n der
Karten
shower [ˈʃau·ər] s (rain) Schauer m;
(bath) Dusche f; (shower room)
Duschraum m; (of stones, arrows)
Hagel m; (of bullets, sparks) Regen
m; (for a bride) Party f zur Über-
reichung der Brautgeschenke; **take a
s.** (sich) duschen || intr (with gifts)
überschütten || intr duschen; (me-
teor) schauern
show'er bath' s Dusche f, Brausebad n
show' girl' s Revuegirl n
show'ing s Zeigen n; (cin) Vorführung
f
show'ing off' s Großtuerei f
show'man (–men) s Schauspieler m
show'-off' s Protz m
show'piece' s Schaustück n
show'room' s Ausstellungsraum m
show' win'dow s Schaufenster n
showy [ˈʃo·i] adj prunkhaft
shrapnel [ˈʃræpnəl] s Schrapnell n
shred [ʃred] s Fetzen m; (least bit)
Spur f; **tear to shreds** in Fetzen reißen; (an argument) gründlich wider-
legen || v (pret & pp **shredded** &
shred; ger **shredding**) tr zerfetzen;
(paper) in Streifen schneiden; (culin)
schnitzeln
shredder [ˈʃredər] s (of paper) Reiß-
wolf m; (culin) Schnitzelmaschine f
shrew [ʃru] s böse Sieben f
shrewd [ʃrud] adj schlau
shriek [ʃrik] s Gekreische n, gellender
Schrei m || intr kreischen
shrill [ʃrɪl] adj schrill
shrimp [ʃrɪmp] s Garnele f; (coll)
Knirps m
shrine [ʃraɪn] s Heiligtum n
shrink [ʃrɪŋk] v (pret **shrank** [ʃræŋk]
& **shrunk** [ʃrʌŋk]; pp **shrunk** &
shrunken) tr einlaufen lassen || intr
schrumpfen; **s. back from** zurückschrecken vor (dat); **s. from** sich
scheuen vor (dat); **s. up** einschrumpfen
shrinkage [ˈʃrɪŋkɪdʒ] s Schrumpfung f
shriv·el [ˈʃrɪvəl] s (pret & pp –el[l]ed;
ger –el[l]ing) intr schrumpfen; **s. up**
zusammenschrumpfen
shriv'eled adj schrumpelig
shroud [ʃraud] s Leichentuch n; (fig)
Hülle f; (naut) Want f || tr (in) ein-
hüllen (in acc)
shrub [ʃrʌb] s Strauch m
shrubbery [ˈʃrʌbəri] s Strauchwerk n
shrug [ʃrʌg] s Zucken n || v (pret &
pp **shrugged;** ger **shrugging**) tr zuk-
ken; **s. off** mit e–m Achselzucken
abtun; **s. one's shoulders** mit den
Achseln zucken || intr mit den Ach-
seln zucken
shuck [ʃʌk] tr enthülsen
shudder [ˈʃʌdər] s Schau(d)er m ||

intr (**at**) schau(d)ern (vor *dat*); **s. at the thought of s.th.** bei dem Gedanken an etw [*acc*] zittern

shuffle [ˈʃʌfəl] *s* Schlurfen *n;* (cards) Mischen *n;* **get lost in the s.** (fig) unter den Tisch fallen ‖ *tr* (*cards*) mischen; (*the feet*) schleifen; ‖ *intr* die Karten mischen; (*walk*) schlurfen; **s. along** latschen

shun [ʃʌn] *v* (*pret & pp* **shunned;** *ger* **shunning**) *tr* (*a person*) meiden; (*a thing*) (ver)meiden

shunt [ʃʌnt] *s* (elec) Nebenschluß *m* ‖ *tr* (*shove aside*) beiseite schieben; (**across**) parallelschalten (zu); (rr) rangieren

shut [ʃʌt] *adj* zu ‖ (*pret & pp* **shut;** *ger* **shutting**) *tr* schließen, zumachen; **be s. down** stilliegen; **s. down** stillegen; **s. off** absperren; **s. one's eyes to** hinwegsehen über (*acc*); **s. out** ausperren; **s. s.o. up** j–m den Mund stopfen ‖ *intr* sich schließen; **s. up!** (coll) halt's Maul!

shut'down' *s* Stillegung *f*

shutter [ˈʃʌtər] *s* Laden *m;* (phot) Verschluß *m*

shuttle [ˈʃʌtəl] *s* Schiffchen *n* ‖ *intr* pendeln, hin- und herfahren

shut'tle bus' *s* Pendelbus *m*

shut'tlecock' *s* Federball *m*

shut'tle serv'ice *s* Pendelverkehr *m*

shut'tle train' *s* Pendelzug *m*

shy [ʃaɪ] *adj* (**shyer; shyest**) schüchtern; **be a dollar shy** e–n Dollar los sein ‖ *intr* (*said of a horse*) stutzen; **shy at** zurückscheuen vor (*dat*); **shy away from** sich scheuen vor (*dat*)

shyness [ˈʃaɪnɪs] *s* Scheu *f*

shyster [ˈʃaɪstər] *s* Winkeladvokat *m*

Siamese' twins' [ˌsaɪ·əˈmiz] *spl* Siamesische Zwillinge *pl*

Siberia [saɪˈbɪrɪ·ə] *s* Sibirien *n*

Siberian [saɪˈbɪrɪ·ən] *adj* sibirisch ‖ *s* Sibirier –in *mf*

sibilant [ˈsɪbɪlənt] *s* Zischlaut *m*

siblings [ˈsɪblɪŋs] *spl* Geschwister *pl*

sibyl [ˈsɪbɪl] *s* Sibylle *f*

sic [sɪk] *adv* sic ‖ *v* (*pret & pp* **sicked;** *ger* **sicking**) *tr*—**sic 'em!** (coll) faß!; **sic the dog on s.o.** den Hund auf j–n hetzen

Sicilian [sɪˈsɪljən] *adj* sizilianisch ‖ *s* Sizilianer –in *mf*

Sicily [ˈsɪsɪli] *s* Sizilien *n*

sick [sɪk] *adj* krank; **be s. and tired of s.th.** etw gründlich satt haben; **be s. as a dog** sich hundeelend fühlen; **I am s. to my stomach** mir ist übel; **play s.** krankfeiern

sick' bay' *s* Schiffslazarett *n*

sick'bed' *s* Krankenbett *n*

sicken [ˈsɪkən] *tr* krank machen; (*disgust*) anekeln ‖ *intr* krank werden

sick'ening *adj* (fig) ekelhaft

sick' head'ache *s* Kopfschmerzen *pl* mit Übelkeit

sickle [ˈsɪkəl] *s* Sichel *f*

sick' leave' *s* Krankenurlaub *m*

sickly [ˈsɪkli] *adj* kränklich; (*smile*) erzwungen

sickness [ˈsɪknɪs] *s* Krankheit *f*

sick' room' *s* Krankenzimmer *n*

side [saɪd] *adj* Neben–, Seiten– ‖ *s* Seite *f;* (*of a team, government*) Partei *f;* (*edge*) Rand *m;* **at my s.** mir zur Seite; **dark s.** Schattenseite *f;* **off sides** (sport) abseits; **on the father's s.** väterlicherseits; **on the s.** (coll) nebenbei; **this s. up** Vorsicht, nicht stürzen; **to be on the safe s.** um ganz sicher zu gehen ‖ *intr*— **s. with s.o.** j–s Partei ergreifen

side' aisle' *s* Seitengang *m;* (*of a church*) Seitenschiff *n*

side' al'tar *s* Nebenaltar *m*

side'arm' *s* Seitengewehr *n*

side'board *s* Anrichte *f,* Büffet *n*

side'burns' *spl* Koteletten *pl*

side' dish' *s* Nebengericht *n*

side' door' *s* Seitentür *f*

side' effect' *s* Nebenwirkung *f*

side' en'trance *s* Seiteneingang *m*

side' glance' *s* Seitenblick *m*

side' is'sue *s* Nebenfrage *f*

side' job' *s* Nebenverdienst *m*

side'kick' *s* (coll) Kumpel *m*

side'line' *s* (*occupation*) Nebenbeschäftigung *f;* (fb) Seitenlinie *f* ‖ *tr* (coll) an der aktiven Teilnahme hindern

side' of ba'con *s* Speckseite *f*

side' road' *s* Seitenweg *m*

side'sad'dle *adv*—**ride s.** im Damensattel reiten

side' show' *s* Nebenvorstellung *f;* (fig) Episode *f*

side'split'ting *adj* zwerchfellerschütternd

side'-step' *v* (*pret & pp* **–stepped;** *ger* **–stepping**) *tr* ausweichen (*dat*)

side' street' *s* Seitenstraße *f*

side' stroke' *s* Seitenschwimmen *n*

side'track' *s* Seitengeleise *n* ‖ *tr* (& fig) auf ein Seitengeleise schieben

side' trip' *s* Abstecher *m*

side' view' *s* Seitenansicht *f*

side'walk' *s* Bürgersteig *m,* Gehsteig *m*

sideward [ˈsaɪdwərd] *adj* nach der Seite gerichtet ‖ *adv* seitwärts

side'ways' *adv* seitlich, seitwärts

sid'ing *s* (*of a house*) Verkleidung *f;* (rr) Nebengeleise *n*

sidle [ˈsaɪdəl] *intr*—**s. up to s.o.** sich heimlich an j–n heranmachen

siege [sidʒ] *s* Belagerung *f;* **lay s. to** belagern

siesta [siˈestə] *s* Mittagsruhe *f*

sieve [sɪv] *s* Sieb *n* ‖ *tr* durchsieben

sift [sɪft] *tr* (durch)sieben; (fig) sichten; **s. out** aussieben

sigh [saɪ] *s* Seufzer *m;* **with a s.** seufzend ‖ *intr* seufzen

sight [saɪt] *s* Anblick *m;* (*faculty*) Sehvermögen *n;* (*on a weapon*) Visier *n;* **at first s.** auf den ersten Blick; **at s.** sofort; **be a s.** (coll) unmöglich aussehen; **by s.** vom Sehen; **catch s. of** erblicken; **in s.** in Sicht; **lose s. of** aus den Augen verlieren; **out of s.** außer Sicht; **s. for sore eyes** Augentrost *m;* **sights** Sehenswürdigkeiten *pl;* **s. unseen** unbesehen; **within s.** in Sehweite ‖ *tr* sichten

sight′see′ing s Besichtigung f; **go s.**
sich [dat] die Sehenswürdigkeiten
ansehen
sight′seeing tour′ s Rundfahrt f
sightseer ['saɪt ˌsi·ər] s Tourist –in mf
sign [saɪn] s (signboard) Schild n;
(symbol, omen, signal) Zeichen n;
(symptom, indication) Kennzeichen
n; (trace) Spur f; (math, mus) Vorzeichen n; **s. of life** Lebenszeichen n
‖ tr unterschreiben; **s. away** aufgeben; **s. over (to)** überschreiben (auf
acc) ‖ intr unterschreiben; **s. for**
zeichnen für; **s. in** sich eintragen;
s. off (rad) die Sendung beenden;
s. out sich austragen; **s. up** (mil)
sich anwerben lassen; **s. up for** (e.g.,
courses, work) sich anmelden für
sig·nal ['sɪgnəl] adj auffallend ‖ s (by
gesture) Zeichen n, Wink m; (aut,
rad, rr, telv) Signal n ‖ v (pret &
pp –nal[l]ed; ger –nal[l]ing) tr signalisieren; (a person) ein Zeichen
geben (dat)
sig′nal corps′ s Fernmeldetruppen pl
sig′nal·man s (–men) (nav) Signalgast
m; (rr) Bahnwärter m
signatory ['sɪgnə ˌtori] s Unterzeichner
–in mf
signature ['sɪgnətʃər] s Unterschrift f
sign′board′ s Aushängeschild n
signer ['saɪnər] s Unterzeichner –in mf
sig′net ring′ ['sɪgnɪt] s Siegelring m
significance [sɪg'nɪfɪkəns] s Bedeutung
f
significant [sɪg'nɪfɪkənt] adj bedeutsam
signi·fy ['sɪgnɪ ˌfaɪ] v (pret & pp –fied)
bedeuten, bezeichnen
sign′ lan′guage s Zeichensprache f
sign′ of the cross′ s Kreuzzeichen n;
make the s. sich bekreuzigen
sign′post′ s Wegweiser m
silence ['saɪləns] s Ruhe f, Stille f;
(reticence) Schweigen n; **in s.** schweigend ‖ tr zum Schweigen bringen;
(a conscience) beschwichtigen
silent ['saɪlənt] adj (night, partner)
still; (movies) stumm; (person)
schweigend; **be s.** stillschweigen; **keep
s.** schweigen
silhouette [ˌsɪlu'et] s Schattenbild n,
Silhouette f ‖ tr silhouettieren
silicon ['sɪlɪkən] s Silizium n
silicone ['sɪlɪkon] s Silikon n
silk [sɪlk] adj seiden ‖ s Seide f
silken ['sɪlkən] adj seiden
silk′ hat′ s Zylinder m
silk′ mill′ s Seidenfabrik f
silk′ worm′ s Seidenraupe f
silky ['sɪlki] adj seiden, seidenartig
sill [sɪl] s (of a window) Sims m & n;
(of a door) Schwelle f
silliness ['sɪlɪnɪs] s Albernheit f
silly ['sɪli] adj albern, blöd(e)
si·lo ['saɪlo] s (–los) Getreidesilo m;
(rok) Raketenbunker m, Silo m
silt [sɪlt] s Schlick m ‖ intr—**s. up**
verschlammen
silver ['sɪlvər] adj silbern ‖ s Silber
n; (for the table) Silberzeug n;
(money) Silbergeld n

sil′verfish′ s Silberfischchen n
sil′ver foil′ s Silberfolie f
sil′ver lin′ing s (fig) Silberstreifen m
sil′ver plate′ s Silbergeschirr n
sil′ver-plat′ed adj versilbert
sil′versmith′ s Silberschmied m
sil′ver spoon′ s—**be born with a s. in
one's mouth** ein Sonntagskind sein
sil′verware′ s Silbergeschirr n
silvery ['sɪlvəri] adj silbern
similar ['sɪmɪlər] adj (to) ähnlich (dat)
similarity [ˌsɪmɪ'læriti] s Ähnlichkeit
f
simile ['sɪmɪli] s Gleichnis n
simmer ['sɪmər] tr leicht kochen lassen ‖ intr brodeln; **s. down** (coll)
sich abreagieren
simper ['sɪmpər] s selbstgefälliges
Lächeln n ‖ intr selbstgefällig lächeln
simple ['sɪmpəl] adj einfach; (truth)
rein; (fact) bloß
sim′ple-mind′ed adj einfältig
simpleton ['sɪmpəltən] s Einfaltspinsel
m
simpli·fy ['sɪmplɪ ˌfaɪ] v (pret & pp
–fied) tr vereinfachen
simply ['sɪmpli] adv einfach
simulate ['sɪmjə ˌlet] tr (illness) simulieren; (e.g., a rocket flight) am Modell vorführen
sim′ulated adj unecht
simultaneous [ˌsaɪməl'teni·əs] adj
gleichzeitig, simultan
sin [sɪn] s Sünde f ‖ v (pret & pp
sinned; ger sinning) intr sündigen;
sin against sich versündigen an (dat)
since [sɪns] adv seitdem, seither ‖ prep
seit (dat); **s. then** seither; **s. when**
seit wann ‖ conj (temporal) seit-
(dem); (causal) da
sincere [sɪn'sɪr] adj aufrichtig
sincerely [sɪn'sɪrli] adv aufrichtig, ehrlich; **Sincerely yours** Ihr ergebener,
Ihre ergebene
sincerity [sɪn'seriti] s Aufrichtigkeit f
sinecure ['saɪnɪ ˌkjʊr] s Sinekure f
sinew ['sɪnju] s Sehne f, Flechse f;
(fig) Muskelkraft f
sinewy ['sɪnju·i] adj sehnig; (fig)
kräftig, nervig
sinful ['sɪnfəl] adj sündhaft
sing [sɪŋ] v (pret **sang** [sæŋ] & **sung**
[sʌŋ]; pp **sung**) tr & intr singen
singe [sɪndʒ] v (singeing) tr sengen;
(the hair) versengen
singer ['sɪŋər] s Sänger –in mf
single ['sɪŋgəl] adj einzeln; (unmarried) ledig; **not a s. word** kein einziges Wort ‖ tr—**s. out** herausgreifen
sin′gle bed′ s Einzelbett n
sin′glebreast′ed adj einreihig
sin′gle file′ s Gänsemarsch m
sin′gle-hand′ed adj einhändig
sin′gle-lane′ adj einbahnig
sin′gle life′ s Ledigenstand m
sin′gle-mind′ed adj zielstrebig
sin′gle room′ s Einzelzimmer n
sin′gle-track′ adj (& fig) eingleisig
sing′song′ adj eintönig ‖ s Singsang m
singular ['sɪŋgjələr] adj (outstanding)
ausgezeichnet; (unique) einzig; (odd)
seltsam ‖ s (gram) Einzahl f

sinister ['sinistər] *adj* unheimlich

sink [siŋk] *s* (*in the kitchen*) Ausguß *m*; (*in the bathroom*) Waschbecken *n* ‖ *v* (*pret* sank [sæŋk] & sunk [sʌŋk]; *pp* sunk) *tr* (*a ship; a post*) versenken; (*money*) investieren; (*min*) abteufen; **s. a well** e–n Brunnen bohren ‖ *intr* sinken; (*said of a building*) sich senken; **he is sinking fast** seine Kräfte nehmen rapide ab; **s. in** (coll) einleuchten; **s. into** (*an easychair*) sich fallen lassen in (*acc*); (*poverty*) geraten in (*acc*); (*unconsciousness*) fallen in (*acc*)

sink'ing feel'ing *s* Beklommenheit *f*

sink'ing fund' *s* Schuldentilgungsfonds *m*

sinless ['sinlis] *adj* sünd(en)los

sinner ['sinər] *s* Sünder –in *mf*

sinuous ['sinju·əs] *adj* gewunden

sinus ['sainəs] *s* Stirnhöhle *f*

sip [sip] *s* Schluck *m* ‖ *v* (*pret* & *pp* sipped; *ger* sipping) *tr* schlürfen

siphon ['saifən] *s* Siphon *m*, Saugheber *m* ‖ *tr* entleeren; **s. off** absaugen; (*profits*) abschöpfen

sir [sir] *s* Herr *m*; **yes sir!** jawohl!; **Dear Sir** Sehr geehrter Herr

sire [sair] *s* (& zool) Vater *m* ‖ *tr* zeugen

siren ['sairən] *s* (& myth) Sirene *f*

sirloin ['sʌrlɔin] *s* Lendenbraten *m*

sissy ['sisi] *s* Schlappschwanz *m*

sister ['sistər] *s* Schwester *f*

sis'ter-in-law' *s* (sisters-in-law) Schwägerin *f*

sisterly ['sistərli] *adj* schwesterlich

sit [sit] *v* (*pret* & *pp* sat [sæt]; *ger* sitting) *intr* sitzen; **sit down** sich (hin)setzen; **sit for a painter** e–m Maler Modell stehen; **sit in on** (*a meeting*) dabeisein bei; **sit up and beg** Männchen machen

sit'down strike' *s* Sitzstreik *m*

site [sait] *s* (*position, location*) Lage *f*; (*piece of ground*) Gelände *n*

sit'ting *s*—at one s. auf e–n Sitz

sit'ting duck' *s* wehrloses Ziel *n*

sit'ting room' *s* Gemeinschaftsraum *m*

situated ['sitʃu ‚etid] *adj* gelegen; **be s.** liegen

situation [‚sitʃu'eʃən] *s* Lage *f*; **s. wanted** Stelle gesucht

six [siks] *adj* & *pron* sechs ‖ *s* Sechs *f*

sixteen ['siks'tin] *adj* & *pron* sechzehn ‖ *s* Sechzehn *f*

sixteenth ['siks'tinθ] *adj* & *pron* sechzehnte ‖ *s* (*fraction*) Sechzehntel *n*; **the s.** (*in dates or in series*) der Sechzehnte

sixth [siksθ] *adj* & *pron* sechste ‖ *s* (*fraction*) Sechstel *n*; **the s.** (*in dates or in series*) der Sechste

sixtieth ['siksti·θ] *adj* & *pron* sechzig ‖ *s* (*fraction*) Sechzigstel *n*

sixty ['siksti] *adj* & *pron* sechzig ‖ *s* Sechzig *f*; **the sixties** die sechziger Jahre

six'ty-four dol'lar ques'tion *s* Preisfrage *f*

sizable ['saizəbəl] *adj* beträchtlich

size [saiz] *s* Größe *f*; (*of a book,* *paper*) Format *n* ‖ *tr* grundieren; **s. up** einschätzen

sizzle ['sizəl] *s* Zischen *n* ‖ *intr* zischen

skate [sket] *s* Schlittschuh *m* ‖ *intr* Schlittschuh laufen

skat'ing rink' *s* Eisbahn *f*

skein [sken] *s* Strähne *f*

skeleton ['skelitən] *s* Gerippe *n*

skel'eton crew' *s* Minimalbelegschaft *f*

skel'eton key' *s* Dietrich *m*

skeptic ['skeptik] *s* Zweifler –in *mf*

skeptical ['skeptikəl] *adj* skeptisch

skepticism ['skepti ‚sizəm] *s* (*doubt*) Skepsis *f*; (philos) Skeptizismus *m*

sketch [sketʃ] *s* Skizze *f*; (theat) Sketch *m* ‖ *tr* & *intr* skizzieren

sketch'book' *s* Skizzenbuch *n*

sketchy ['sketʃi] *adj* skizzenhaft

skewer ['skju·ər] *s* Fleischspieß *m*

ski [ski] *s* Schi *m* ‖ *intr* schilaufen

ski' boot' *s* Schistiefel *m*

skid [skid] *s* Rutschen *n*, Schleudern *n*; **go into a s.** ins Schleudern geraten ‖ *v* (*pret* & *pp* skidded; *ger* skidding) *intr* rutschen, schleudern

skid' mark' *s* Bremsspur *f*

skid'proof' *adj* bremssicher

skid' row' [ro] *s* Elendsviertel *n*

skiff [skif] *s* Skiff *n*

ski'ing *s* Schilaufen *n*

ski' jack'et *s* Anorak *m*

ski' jump' *s* Schisprung *m*; (*chute*) Sprungschanze *f*

ski' jump'ing *s* Schispringen *n*

ski' lift' *s* Schilift *m*

skill [skil] *s* Fertigkeit *f*

skilled *adj* gelernt

skillet ['skilit] *s* Bratpfanne *f*

skillful ['skilfəl] *adj* geschickt

skim [skim] *v* (*pret* & *pp* skimmed; *ger* skimming) *tr* (*milk*) abrahmen; (*a book*) überfliegen; **s. off** abschöpfen ‖ *intr*—**s. over the water** über das Wasser streichen; **s. through** (*a book*) flüchtig durchblättern

skim' milk' *s* entrahmte Milch *f*

skimp [skimp] *intr* (on) knausern (mit)

skimpy ['skimpi] *adj* (*person*) knauserig; (*thing*) knapp, dürftig

skin [skin] *s* Haut *f*; (*fur*) Fell *n*; (*of fruit*) Schale *f*; **by the s. of one's teeth** mit knapper Not; **get under s.o.'s s.** j–m auf die Nerven gehen ‖ *v* (*pret* & *pp* skinned; *ger* skinning) *tr* (*an animal*) enthäuten; (*a knee*) aufschürfen; (*fleece*) das Fell über die Ohren ziehen (*dat*); (*defeat*) schlagen; **s. alive** zur Sau machen

skin'-deep' *adj* oberflächlich

skin' div'er *s* Schwimmtaucher –in *mf*

skin'flint' *s* Geizhals *m*

skin' graft' *s* Hautverpflanzung *f*

skinny ['skini] *adj* spindeldürr, mager

skin'tight' *adj* hauteng

skip [skip] *s* Sprung *m* ‖ *v* (*pret* & *pp* skipped; *ger* skipping) *tr* (*omit*) auslassen; (*a page*) überblättern; **s. it!** Schwamm drüber!; **s. rope** Seil springen; **s. school** Schule schwänzen ‖ *intr* springen; **s. out** abhauen

ski' pole' *s* Schistock *m*

skipper ['skɪpər] s Kapitän m
skirmish ['skʌrmɪʃ] s Scharmützel n ‖ intr scharmützeln
skir'mish line' s (mil) Schützenlinie f
skirt [skʌrt] s Rock m ‖ tr (border) umsäumen; (pass along) sich entlangziehen (an dat)
ski' run' s Schipiste f
skit [skɪt] s Sket(s)ch m
skittish ['skɪtɪʃ] adj (lively) lebhaft; (horse) scheu
skull [skʌl] s Schädel m
skull' and cross'bones s Totenkopf m
skull'cap' s Käppchen n
skunk [skʌŋk] s Stinktier n; (sl) Saukerl m
sky [skaɪ] s Himmel m; **out of the clear blue sky** wie aus heiterem Himmel; **praise to the skies** über den grünen Klee loben
sky'-blue' adj himmelblau
sky'div'er s Fallschirmspringer –in mf
sky'div'ing s Fallschirmspringen n
sky'lark' s Feldlerche f
sky'light' s Dachluke f
sky'line' s Horizontlinie f; (of a city) Stadtsilhouette f
sky'rock'et s Rakete f ‖ intr in die Höhe schießen
sky'scrap'er s Wolkenkratzer m
sky'writ'ing s Himmelsschrift f
slab [slæb] s Platte f, Tafel f
slack [slæk] adj schlaff; (period) flau ‖ s Spielraum m; **slacks** Herrenhose f, Damenhose f ‖ intr—**s. off** nachlassen
slacken ['slækən] tr (slow down) verlangsamen; (loosen) lockern ‖ intr nachlassen
slack' per'iod s Flaute f
slack' sea'son s Sauregurkenzeit f
slag [slæg] s Schlacke f
slag' pile' s Schlackenhalde f
slake [slek] tr (thirst, lime) löschen
slalom ['slɑləm] s Slalom m
slam [slæm] s Knall m; (cards) Schlemm m ‖ v (pret & pp **slammed;** ger **slamming**) tr zuknallen; **s. down** hinknallen ‖ intr knallen
slander ['slændər] s Verleumdung f ‖ tr verleumden
slanderous ['slændərəs] adj verleumderisch
slang [slæŋ] s Slang m
slant [slænt] s Schräge f; (view) Einstellung f; (personal point of view) Tendenz f ‖ tr abschrägen; (fig) färben
slap [slæp] s Klaps m; **s. in the face** Ohrfeige f ‖ v (pret & pp **slapped;** ger **slapping**) tr schlagen; (s.o.'s face) ohrfeigen; **s. together** zusammenhauen
slap'stick' adj Radau– ‖ s Radaukomödie f
slash [slæʃ] s Schnittwunde f ‖ tr aufschlitzen; (prices) drastisch herabsetzen
slat [slæt] s Stab m
slate [slet] s Schiefer m; (to write on) Schiefertafel f; (of candidates) Vorschlagsliste f ‖ tr (a roof) mit Schie-

fer decken; (schedule) planen; **he is slated to speak** er soll sprechen
slate' roof' s Schieferdach n
slattern ['slætərn] s (slovenly woman) Schlampe f; (slut) Dirne f
slaughter ['slɔtər] s Schlachten n; (massacre) Metzelei f ‖ tr schlachten; (massacre) niedermetzeln
slaugh'terhouse' s Schlachthaus n
Slav [slɑv], (slæv] adj slawisch ‖ s (person) Slawe m, Slawin f
slave [slev] s Sklave m, Sklavin f ‖ intr (coll) schuften; **s. at a job** sich mit e–r Arbeit abquälen
slave' driv'er s (fig) Leuteschinder m
slaver ['slævər] s Geifer m
slavery ['slevəri] s Sklaverei f
slave' trade' s Sklavenhandel m
Slavic ['slɑvɪk], ['slævɪk] adj slawisch
slavish ['slevɪʃ] adj sklavisch
slay [sle] v (pret **slew** [slu]; pp **slain** [slen]) tr erschlagen
slayer ['sle·ər] s Totschläger –in mf
sled [slɛd] s Schlitten m ‖ v (pret & pp **sledded;** ger **sledding**) intr Schlitten fahren
sledge [slɛdʒ] s Schlitten m
sledge' ham'mer s Vorschlaghammer m
sleek [slik] adj (hair) glatt; (cattle) fett ‖ tr glätten
sleep [slip] s Schlaf m; **get enough s.** sich ausschlafen ‖ v (pret & pp **slept** [slɛpt]) tr (accommodate) Schlafgelegenheiten bieten für; **s. off a hangover** seinen Kater ausschlafen ‖ intr schlafen; **I didn't s. a wink** ich habe kein Auge zugetan; **s. like a log** wie ein Murmeltier schlafen; **s. with** (a woman) schlafen mit
sleeper ['sliper] s Schläfer –in mf; (sleeping car) Schlafwagen m; (fig) überraschender Erfolg m
sleepiness ['slipɪnɪs] s Schläfrigkeit f
sleep'ing bag' s Schlafsack m
Sleep'ing Beau'ty s Dornröschen n
sleep'ing car' s Schlafwagen m
sleep'ing compart'ment s Schlafabteil n
sleep'ing pill' s Schlaftablette f
sleep'ing sick'ness s Schlafkrankheit f
sleepless ['sliplɪs] adj schlaflos
sleep'walk'er s Nachtwandler –in mf
sleepy ['slipi] adj schläfrig
sleep'yhead' s Schlafmütze f
sleet [slit] s Schneeregen m; (on the ground) Glatteis n ‖ impers—**it is sleeting** es gibt Schneeregen, es graupelt
sleeve [sliv] s Ärmel m; (mach) Muffe f; **have s.th. up one's s.** etw im Schilde führen; **roll up one's sleeves** die Ärmel hochkrempeln
sleeveless ['slivlɪs] adj ärmellos
sleigh [sle] s Schlitten m
sleigh' bell' s Schlittenschelle f
sleigh' ride' s Schlittenfahrt f; **go for**
sleight' of hand' [slaɪt] s Taschenspielertrick m
slender ['slɛndər] adj schlank; (means) gering
sleuth [sluθ] s Detektiv m
slice [slaɪs] s Scheibe f, Schnitte f;

(tennis) Schnittball *m* ‖ *tr* aufschneiden

slicer [ˈslaɪsər] *s* Schneidemaschine *f*

slick [slɪk] *adj* glatt; (*talker*) raffiniert

slicker [ˈslɪkər] *s* Regenmantel *m*

slide [slaɪd] *s* (*slip*) Rutsch *m;* (*chute*) Rutschbahn *f;* (*of a microscope*) Objektträger *m;* (phot) Diapositiv *n* ‖ *v* (*pret & pp* **slid** [slɪd]) *tr* schieben ‖ *intr* rutschen; **let things s.** die Dinge laufen lassen

slide′ rule′ *s* Rechenschieber *m*

slide′ valve′ *s* Schieberventil *n*

slide′ view′er *s* Bildbetrachter *m*

slid′ing door′ *s* Schiebetür *f*

slid′ing scale′ *s* gleitende Skala *f*

slight [slaɪt] *adj* gering(fügig); (*illness*) leicht; (*petite*) zart ‖ *tr* mißachten

slim [slɪm] *adj* schlank; (*chance*) gering ‖ *intr*—**s. down** abnehmen

slime [slaɪm] *s* Schlamm *m;* (e.g., *of fish, snakes*) Schleim *m*

slimy [ˈslaɪmi] *adj* schleimig; (*muddy*) schlammig

sling [slɪŋ] *s* (*to hurl stones*) Schleuder *f;* (*for a broken arm*) Schlinge *f* ‖ *v* (*pret & pp* **slung** [slʌŋ]) *tr* schleudern; **s. over the shoulders** umhängen

sling′shot′ *s* Schleuder *f*

slink [slɪŋk] *v* (*pret & pp* **slunk** [slʌŋk]) *intr* schleichen; **s. away** wegschleichen

slip [slɪp] *s* (*slide*) Ausrutschen *n;* (*cutting*) Ableger *m;* (*underwear*) Unterrock *m;* (*paper*) Zettel *m;* (*pillowcase*) Kissenbezug *m;* (*error*) Flüchtigkeitsfehler *m;* (*for ships*) Schlipp *m;* **give s.o. the s.** j—m entwischen; **s. of the pen** Schreibfehler *m;* **s. of the tongue** Sprechfehler *m* ‖ *v* (*pret & pp* **slipped;** *ger* **slipping**) *tr*—**s. in** (*a remark*) einfließen lassen; (*poison*) heimlich schütten; **s. on** (*a glove*) überstreifen; (*a coat*) überziehen; (*a ring*) auf den Finger streifen; **s. s.o. money** j—m etw Geld zustecken; **s. s.o.'s mind** j—m entfallen ‖ *intr* rutschen; (e.g., *out of or into a room*) schlüpfen; (*lose one's balance*) ausgleiten; **let s.** sich [*dat*] entgehen lassen; **s. by** verstreichen; **s. in** (*said of errors*) unterlaufen; **s. through one's fingers** durch die Finger gleiten; **s. out on s.o.** j—m entschlüpfen; **s. up** (on) danebenhauen (bei); **you are slipping** (coll) Sie lassen in der Leistung nach

slip′cov′er *s* Schonbezug *m*

slip′knot′ *s* Schleife *f*

slipper [ˈslɪpər] *s* Pantoffel *m*

slippery [ˈslɪpəri] *adj* glatt

slipshod [ˈslɪp‚ʃɑd] *adj* schlampig; **do s. work** schludern

slip′stream *s* Luftschraubenstrahl *m*

slip′-up′ *s* (coll) Flüchtigkeitsfehler *m*

slit [slɪt] *s* Schlitz *m* ‖ *v* (*pret & pp* **slit;** *ger* **slitting**) *tr* schlitzen; **s. open** aufschlitzen

slit′-eyed′ *adj* schlitzäugig

slither [ˈslɪðər] *intr* gleiten

slit′ trench′ *s* (mil) Splittergraben *m*

sliver [ˈslɪvər] *s* Splitter *m*, Span *m*

slob [slɑb] *s* (sl) Schmutzfink *m*

slobber [ˈslɑbər] *s* Geifer *m* ‖ *intr* geifern

sloe [slo] *s* (bot) Schlehe *f*

sloe′-eyed′ *adj* schlitzäugig

slog [slɑg] *v* (*pret & pp* **slogged;** *ger* **slogging**) *intr* stapfen

slogan [ˈslogən] *s* Schlagwort *n*

sloop [slup] *s* Schaluppe *f*

slop [slɑp] *s* Spülicht *n;* (*bad food*) (sl) Fraß *m* ‖ *v* (*pret & pp* **slopped;** *ger* **slopping**) *tr* (*hogs*) füttern; (*spill*) verschütten

slope [slop] *s* Abhang *m;* (*of a road*) Gefälle *n;* (*of a roof*) Neigung *f* ‖ *tr* abschrägen ‖ *intr* sich neigen; (*said of a road*) abfallen

sloppy [ˈslɑpi] *adj* schlampig; (*weather*) matschig

slosh [slɑʃ] *intr* schwappen

slot [slɑt] *s* Schlitz *m*

sloth [sloθ] *s* Faulheit *f*, Trägheit *f;* (zool) Faultier *n*

slothful [ˈsloθfəl] *adj* faul, träge

slot′ machine′ *s* Spielautomat *m*

slouch [slautʃ] *s* nachlässige Haltung *f;* (*person*) Schlappschwanz *m* ‖ *intr* in schlechter Haltung sitzen; **s. along** latschen

slouch′ hat′ *s* Schlapphut *m*

slough [slau] *s* Sumpf *m* ‖ [slʌf] *s* (*of a snake*) abgestreifte Haut *f;* (pathol) Schorf *m* ‖ *tr* (& fig) abstreifen ‖ *intr* (*said of a snake*) sich häuten

Slovak [ˈslovak], [ˈslovæk] *adj* slowakisch ‖ *s* (*person*) Sklowake *m*, Slowakin *f;* (*language*) Slowakisch *n*

slovenly [ˈslʌvənli] *adj* schlampig

slow [slo] *adj* langsam; (*dawdling*) bummelig; (*mentally*) schwer von Begriff; (com) flau; **be s.** (horol) nachgehen ‖ *adv* langsam ‖ *tr*—**s. down** verlangsamen ‖ *intr*—**s. down** (*in driving*) langsamer fahren; (*in working*) nachlassen; **s. down** (public sign) Schritt fahren

slow′down′ *s* Bummelstreik *m*

slow′ mo′tion *s* (cin) Zeitlupe *f;* **in s.** (cin) im Zeitlupentempo

slow′-mo′tion *adj* Zeitlupen—

slow′poke′ *s* (coll) langsamer Mensch *m*

slow′-wit′ted *adj* schwer von Begriff

slug [slʌg] *s* Rohling *m;* (*drink*) Zug *m* (zool) Wegschnecke *f* ‖ *v* (*pret & pp* **slugged;** *ger* **slugging**) *tr* (coll) hart mit der Faust treffen

sluggard [ˈslʌgərd] *s* Faulpelz *m*

sluggish [ˈslʌgɪʃ] *adj* träge

sluice [slus] *s* Schleuse *f*

sluice′ gate′ *s* Schleusentor *n*

slum [slʌm] *s* Elendsviertel *n*

slumber [ˈslʌmbər] *s* Schlummer *m* ‖ *intr* schlummern

slum′ dwell′ing *s* Elendsquartier *n*

slump [slʌmp] *s* (st. exch.) Baisse *f;* **s. in sales** Absatzstockung *f* ‖ *intr* zusammensacken; (*said of prices*) stürzen

slur [slʌr] *s* (*insult*) Verleumdung *f;* (mus) Bindezeichen *n* ‖ *v* (*pret & pp* **slurred;** *ger* **slurring**) *tr* (*words*)

verschleifen; (mus) binden; **s. over**
hinweggehen über (acc)
slurp [slʌrp] s Schlürfen n || tr & intr
schlürfen
slush [slʌʃ] s Matsch m, Schneematsch
m
slush' fund' s Schmiergeld n
slushy ['slʌʃi] adj matschig
slut [slʌt] s Nutte f
sly [slaɪ] adj (**slyer** & **slier; slyest** &
sliest) schlau || s—**on the sly** im Ver-
borgenen
sly' fox' s Pfiffikus m
smack [smæk] s (blow) Klaps m;
(sound) Klatsch m; (kiss) Schmatz
m; **s. in the face** Backpfeife f || tr
klapsen; **s. one's lips** schmatzen ||
intr—**s. of** riechen nach
small [smɔl] adj klein; (difference) gering; (comfort) schlecht; (petty)
kleinlich
small' arms' spl Handwaffen pl
small' busi'ness s Kleinbetrieb m
small' cap'ital s (typ) Kapitälchen n
small' change' s Kleingeld n
small' fry' s kleine Fische pl
small' intes'tine s Dünndarm m
small'-mind'ed adj engstirnig
small' of the back' s Kreuz n
smallpox ['smɔl‚paks] s Pocken pl
small' print' s Kleindruck m
small' talk' s Geplauder n
small'-time' adj klein
small'-town' adj kleinstädtisch
smart [smart] adj (bright) klug; (neat,
trim) schick; (car) schneidig; (pej)
überklug || s Schmerz m || intr weh
tun; (burn) brennen
smart' al'eck s [‚ælɪk] s Neunmalkluge
mf
smart'-look'ing adj schnittig
smart' set' s elegante Welt f
smash [smæʃ] s (hit) (coll) Bombe f;
(tennis) Schmetterschlag m || tr zer-
schmettern; (e.g., a window) einschlagen; (sport) schmettern; **s. up**
zerknallen || intr zerbrechen; **s. into**
krachen gegen
smash' hit' s (theat) Bombenerfolg m
smash'-up' s (aut) Zusammenstoß m
smattering ['smætərɪŋ] s (of) oberflächliche Kenntnis f (genit)
smear [smɪr] s Schmiere f; (smudge)
Schmutzfleck m; (vilification) Verun-
glimpfung f; (med) Abstrich m || tr
(spread) schmieren; (make dirty) beschmieren; (vilify) verunglimpfen;
(trounce) vollständig fertigmachen
smear' campaign' s Verleumdungsfeld-
zug m
smell [smɛl] s Geruch m; (aroma) Duft
m; (sense) Geruchssinn m || v (pret
& pp **smelled** & **smelt** [smɛlt]) tr
riechen; (danger, trouble) wittern ||
intr (of) riechen (nach)
smell'ing salts' pl Riechsalz n
smelly ['smɛli] adj übelriechend
smelt [smɛlt] s (fish) Stint m || tr
schmelzen, verhütten
smile [smaɪl] s Lächeln n || intr lä-
cheln; **s. at** anlächeln; (clandestinely)
zulächeln (dat); **s. on** lächeln (dat)

smirk [smɪrk] s Grinsen n || intr grin-
sen
smite [smaɪt] v (pret **smote** [smot];
pp **smitten** ['smɪtən] & **smit** [smɪt])
tr schlagen; (said of a plague) befallen; **smitten with** hingerissen von
smith [smɪθ] s Schmied m
smithy ['smɪθi] s Schmiede f
smock [smak] s Kittel m, Bluse f
smog [smag] s Smog m
smoke [smok] s Rauch m; (heavy
smoke) Qualm m; **go up in s.** (fig) in
Dunst und Rauch aufgehen || tr rau-
chen; (meat) räuchern || intr rauchen;
(said of a chimney) qualmen
smoke' bomb' s Rauchbombe f
smoked' ham' s Räucherschinken m
smoker ['smokər] s Raucher –in mf;
(sl) obszöner Film m
smoke' screen' s Rauchvorhang m
smoke'stack' s Schornstein m
smok'ing s Rauchen n; **no s.** (public
sign) Rauchen verboten
smok'ing car' s Raucherwagen m
smok'ing jack'et s Hausjacke f
smoky ['smoki] adj rauchig
smolder ['smoldər] intr (& fig) schwelen
smooch [smutʃ] intr sich abknutschen
smooth [smuð] adj (surface; talker;
landing, operation) glatt; (wine) mild
|| tr glätten; **s. away** (difficulties)
beseitigen; **s. out** glätten; **s. over** beschönigen
smooth'-faced' adj glattwangig
smooth-shaven ['smuð'ʃevən] adj glattrasiert
smooth'-talk'ing adj schönrednerisch
smoothy ['smuði] s Schönredner –in mf
smother ['smʌðər] tr ersticken; **s. with
kisses** abküssen
smudge [smʌdʒ] s Schmutzfleck m || tr
beschmutzen || intr schmutzig werden
smug [smʌg] adj (**smugger; smuggest**)
selbstgefällig
smuggle ['smʌgəl] tr & intr schmuggeln
smuggler ['smʌglər] s Schmuggler –in
mf
smug'gling s Schmuggel m
smut [smʌt] s Schmutz m
smutty ['smʌti] adj schmutzig, obszön
snack [snæk] s Imbiß m
snack' bar' s Imbißstube f, Snack Bar f
snaffle ['snæfəl] s Trense f
snag [snæg] s—**hit a s.** auf Schwierig-
keiten stoßen || v (pret & pp **snagged;**
ger **snagging**) tr hängenbleiben mit
snail [snel] s Schnecke f; **at a snail's
pace** im Schneckentempo
snake [snek] s Schlange f || intr sich
schlängeln
snake'bite' s Schlangenbiß m
snake' in the grass' s heimtückischer
Mensch m
snap [snæp] s (sound) Knacks m; (on
clothes) Druckknopf m; (of a dog)
Biß m; (liveliness) Schwung m; (easy
work) Kinderspiel n || v (pret & pp
snapped; ger **snapping**) tr (break)
zerreißen, entzweibrechen; (a picture) knipsen; **s. a whip** mit der

Peitsche knallen; **s. back** (*words*)
hervorstoßen; (*the head*) zurückwer-
fen; **s. off** abbrechen; **s. one's fingers**
mit den Fingern schnalzen; **s. s.o.'s
head off** j-n zusammenstauchen; **s.
up** gierig an sich reißen; (*buy up*)
aufkaufen ‖ *intr* (*tear*) zerreißen;
(*break*) entzweibrechen; **s. at** schnappen nach; (*fig*) anfahren; **s. out of it!**
komm zu dir!; **s. shut** zuschnappen;
s. to it! mach zu!
snap'drag'on *s* (bot) Löwenmaul *n*
snap' fas'tener *s* Druckknopf *m*
snap' judg'ment *s* vorschnelles Urteil *n*
snap'per soup' ['snæpər] *s* Schildkrötensuppe *f*
snappish ['snæpɪʃ] *adj* bissig
snappy ['snæpi] *adj* (*caustic*) bissig;
(*lively*) energisch; **make it s.!** mach
schnell!
snap'shot' *s* Schnappschuß *m*
snare [sner] *s* Schlinge *f* ‖ *tr* mit e-r
Schlinge fangen; (fig) fangen
snare' drum' *s* Schnarrtrommel *f*
snarl [snɑrl] *s* (*tangle*) Verwicklung *f*;
(*sound*) Knurren *n* ‖ *tr* verwickeln;
s. traffic e-e Verkehrsstockung verursachen ‖ *intr* knurren
snatch [snætʃ] *s*—**in snatches** ruckweise; **snatches** (*of conversation*)
Bruchstücke *pl* ‖ *tr* schnappen; **s.
away from** entreißen (*dat*); **s. up**
schnappen
snazzy ['snæzi] *adj* (sl) schmissig
sneak [snik] *s* Schleicher –in *mf* ‖ *tr*
(*e.g., a drink*) heimlich trinken; **s. in**
einschmuggeln ‖ *intr* schleichen; **s.
away** sich davonschleichen; **s. in** sich
einschleichen; **s. out** sich heraus-
schleichen; **s. up on s.o.** an j-n heranschleichen
sneaker ['snikər] *s* Tennisschuh *m*
sneaky ['sniki] *adj* heimtückisch
sneer [snɪr] *s* Hohnlächeln *n* ‖ *intr*
höhnisch grinsen; **s. at** spötteln über
(*acc*)
sneeze [sniz] *s* Niesen *n* ‖ *tr*—**not to
be sneezed at** nicht zu verachten ‖
intr niesen
snicker ['snɪkər] *s* Kichern *n* ‖ *intr*
kichern
snide' remark' [snaɪd] *s* Anzüglichkeit
f
sniff [snɪf] *s* Schnüffeln *n* ‖ *tr* (be)rie-
chen; **s. out** ausschnüffeln ‖ *intr* (at)
schnüffeln (an *dat*)
sniffle ['snɪfəl] *s* Geschnüffel *n;* **snif-
fles** Schnupfen *m* ‖ *intr* schniefen
snip [snɪp] *s* (*cut*) Einschnitt *m*; (*small
piece snipped off*) Schnippel *m* ‖ *v*
(*pret & pp* **snipped;** *ger* **snipping**) *tr*
& *intr* schnippeln
snipe [snaɪp] *intr*—**s. at** aus dem
Hinterhalt schießen auf (*acc*)
sniper ['snaɪpər] *s* Heckenschütze *m*
snippet ['snɪpɪt] *s* Schnippelchen *n;*
(*small person*) Knirps *m*
snippy ['snɪpi] *adj* schroff, barsch
snitch [snɪtʃ] *tr* (coll) klauen ‖ *intr*
(coll) petzen; **s. on** (coll) verpfeifen
sniv·el ['snɪvəl] *s* (*whining*) Gewimmer *n;* (*mucus*) Nasenschleim *m* ‖ *v*

(*pret & pp* **–el[l]ed;** *ger* **–el[l]ing**)
intr (*whine*) wimmern; (*cry with
sniffling*) schluchzen; (*have a runny
nose*) e-e tropfende Nase haben
snob [snɑb] *s* Snob *m*
snob' appeal' *s* Snobappeal *m*
snobbery ['snɑbəri] *s* Snobismus *m*
snobbish ['snɑbɪʃ] *adj* snobistisch
snoop [snup] *s* (coll) Schnüffler –in *mf*
‖ *intr* (coll) schnüffeln
snoopy ['snupi] *adj* schnüffelnd
snoot [snut] *s* (sl) Rüssel *m;* **make a s.**
e-e Schnute ziehen
snooty ['snuti] *adj* hochnäsig
snooze [snuz] *s* (coll) Nickerchen *n* ‖
intr (coll) ein Nickerchen machen
snore [snor] *s* Schnarchen *n* ‖ *intr*
schnarchen
snort [snɔrt] *s* Schnauben *n* ‖ *tr*
wütend schnauben ‖ *intr* prusten;
(*said of a horse*) schnauben; (*with
laughter*) vor Lachen prusten
snot [snɑt] *s* (sl) Rotz *m*
snotty ['snɑti] *adj* (sl & fig) rotzig
snout [snaʊt] *s* Schnauze *f*, Rüssel *m*
snow [sno] *s* Schnee *m* ‖ *tr* (sl) ein-
wickeln; **s. in** einschneien; **s. under**
mit Schnee bedecken ‖ *impers*—**it is
snowing** es schneit
snow'ball' *s* Schneeball *m* ‖ *intr* (fig)
lawinenartig anwachsen
snow'bank' *s* Schneeverwehung *f*
snow'bird' *s* Schneefink *m*
snow' blind'ness *s* Schneeblindheit *f*
snow' blow'er *s* Schneefräse *f*
snow'bound' *adj* eingeschneit
snow'-capped' *adj* schneebedeckt
snow' chain' *s* (aut) Schneekette *f*
snow'-clad' *adj* verschneit
snow'drift' *s* Schneeverwehung *f*
snow'fall' *s* Schneefall *m*
snow'flake' *s* Schneeflocke *f*
snow' flur'ry *s* Schneegestöber *n*
snow' job' *s*—**give s.o. a s.** (sl) j-n
hereinlegen
snow'man *s* (**–men**) Schneemann *m*
snow'mobile' *s* Motorschlitten *m*
snow'plow' *s* Schneepflug *m*
snow'shoe' *s* Schneeteller *m*
snow' shov'el *s* Schneeschaufel *f*
snow'storm' *s* Schneesturm *m*
snow' tire' *s* Winterreifen *m*
Snow' White' *s* Schneewittchen *n*
snow'-white' *adj* schneeweiß
snowy ['sno·i] *adj* schneeig
snub [snʌb] *s* verächtliche Behandlung
f ‖ *v* (*pret & pp* **snubbed;** *ger* **snub-
bing**) *tr* (*ignore*) schneiden; (*treat
contemptuously*) verächtlich behandeln
snubby ['snʌbi] *adj* (*nose*) etwas abgestumpft; (*person*) abweisend
snub'-nosed' *adj* stupsnasig
snuff [snʌf] *s* Schnupftabak *m;* (*of a
candle*) Schnuppe *f;* **up to s.** (sl)
auf Draht ‖ *tr*—**s. out** (*a candle*)
auslöschen; (*suppress*) unterdrücken
snuff'box' *s* Schnupftabakdose *f*
snug [snʌg] *adj* (**snugger; snuggest**)
behaglich; (*fit*) eng angeschmiegt; **s.
as a bug in a rug** wie die Made im
Speck

snuggle ['snʌgəl] *intr*—**s. up (to)** sich schmiegen (an *acc*)

so [so] *adv* (with adjectives or adverbs) so; *(thus)* so; *(for this reason)* daher; *(then)* also; **and so forth** und so weiter; **or so** etwa, e.g., **ten miles or so** etwa zehn Meilen; **so as to** *(inf)* um zu *(inf)*; **so far** bisher; **so far as** soviel; **so far, so good** soweit ganz gut; **so I see!** das seh' ich!; **so long!** (coll) bis bald!; **so much** soviel; **so much the better** um so besser; **so that** damit; **so what?** na, und?

soak [sok] *s* Einweichen *n* ‖ *tr* einweichen; *(soak through and through)* durchnässen; *(overcharge)* (sl) schröpfen; **soaked to the skin** bis auf die Haut durchnäßt ‖ *intr* weichen

so'-and-so' *s* (–sos) Soundso *mf*

soap [sop] *s* Seife *f* ‖ *tr* einseifen

soap'box der'by *s* Seifenkistenrennen *n*

soap'box or'ator *s* Straßenredner –in *mf*

soap' bub'ble *s* Seifenblase *f*

soap' dish' *s* Seifenschale *f*

soap' flakes' *spl* Seifenflocken *pl*

soap' op'era *s* (rad) rührselige Hörspielreihe *f*; (telv) rührselige Fernsehspielreihe *f*

soap' pow'der *s* Seifenpulver *n*

soap'stone' *s* Seifenstein *m*

soap'suds' *spl* Seifenlauge *f*

soapy ['sopi] *adj* seifig; *(like soap)* seifenartig

soar [sor] *intr* schweben, (auf)steigen; *(prices)* steigen

sob [sab] *s* Schluchzen *n* ‖ *v* (*pret & pp* **sobbed;** *ger* **sobbing**) *intr* schluchzen

sober ['sobər] *adj* nüchtern ‖ *tr* **(up)** ernüchtern ‖ *intr*—**s. up** wieder nüchtern werden

sobriety [so'braɪəti] *s* Nüchternheit *f*

sob' sto'ry *s* Schmachtfetzen *m*

so'-called' *adj* sogenannt

soccer ['sakər] *s* Fußball *m*

soc'cer play'er *s* Fußballer *m*

sociable ['soʃəbəl] *adj* gesellig

social ['soʃəl] *adj* gesellschaftlich ‖ *s* geselliges Beisammensein *n*

so'cial climb'er *s* Streber –in *mf*

socialism ['soʃə,lɪzəm] *s* Sozialismus *m*

socialist ['soʃəlɪst] *s* Sozialist –in *mf*

socialistic [,soʃə'lɪstɪk] *adj* sozialistisch

socialite ['soʃə,laɪt] *s* Prominente *mf*

socialize ['soʃə,laɪz] *intr* **(with)** verkehren (mit)

so'cialized med'icine *s* staatliche Gesundheitspflege *f*

so'cial reg'ister *s* Register *n* der prominenten Mitglieder der oberen Gesellschaftsklasse

so'cial sci'ence *s* Sozialwissenschaft *f*

so'cial secu'rity *s* Sozialversicherung *f*

so'cial wel'fare *s* Sozialfürsorge *f*

so'cial work'er *s* Sozialfürsorger –in *mf*

society [sə'saɪəti] *s* Gesellschaft *f*; *(an organization)* Verein *m*

soci'ety col'umn *s* Gesellschaftsspalte *f*

soci'ety for the preven'tion of cru'elty to an'imals *s* Tierschutzverein *m*

sociological [,sosɪ·ə'ladʒɪkəl] *adj* sozialwissenschaftlich, soziologisch

sociologist [,sosɪ'alədʒɪst] *s* Soziologe *m*, Soziologin *f*

sociology [,sosɪ'alədʒi] *s* Soziologie *f*

sock [sak] *s* Socke *f*; (sl) Faustschlag *m* ‖ *tr*—**s. it to him!** gib's ihm!; **s.o.** j–m eine 'runterhauen

socket ['sakɪt] *s* (anat) Höhle *f*; (elec) Steckdose *f*; (mach) Muffe *f*

sock'et joint' *s* (anat) Kugelgelenk *n*

sock'et wrench' *s* Steckschlüssel *m*

sod [sad] *s* Rasenstück *n* ‖ *v* (*pret & pp* **sodded;** *ger* **sodding**) *tr* mit Rasen bedecken

soda ['sodə] *s* *(refreshment)* Limonade *f*; *(in mixed drinks)* Selterswasser *n*; *(chem)* Soda *f & n*

so'da crack'er *s* Keks *m*

so'da wa'ter *s* Sodawasser *n*

sodium ['sodɪ·əm] *s* Natrium *n*

sofa ['sofə] *s* Sofa *n*

soft [soft] *adj* *(not hard or tough)* weich; *(not loud)* leise; *(light, music)* sanft; *(sleep, breeze)* leicht; *(effeminate)* verweichlicht; *(muscles)* schlaff; **be s. on** weich sein gegenüber *(dat)*

soft'-boiled egg' *s* weichgekochtes Ei *n*

soft' coal' *s* Braunkohle *f*

soft' drink' *s* alkoholfreies Getränk *n*

soften ['sɔfən] *tr* aufweichen; *(palliate)* lindern; *(water)* enthärten; **s. up** (mil) zermürben ‖ *intr* (& fig) weich werden

soft'-heart'ed *adj* weichherzig

soft' job' *s* Druckposten *m*

soft' land'ing *s* (rok) weiche Landung *f*

soft' pal'ate *s* Hintergaumen *m*

soft'-ped'al *v* (*pret & pp* **–al[l]ed;** *ger* **–al[l]ing**) *tr* zurückhaltender vorbringen

soft'-soap' *tr* (coll) schmeicheln *(dat)*

soggy ['sagi] *adj* *(soaked)* durchnäßt; *(ground)* sumpfig

soil [sɔɪl] *s* Boden *m* ‖ *tr* beschmutzen ‖ *intr* schmutzen

soil' pipe' *s* Abflußrohr *n*

sojourn ['sodʒʌrn] *s* Aufenthalt *m* ‖ *intr* sich vorübergehend aufhalten

solace ['salɪs] *s* Trost *m* ‖ *tr* trösten

solar ['solər] *adj* Sonnen–

so'lar plex'us ['plɛksəs] *s* (anat) Sonnengeflecht *n*

solder ['sadər] *s* Lötmetall *n* ‖ *tr* löten

sol'dering i'ron *s* Lötkolben *m*

soldier ['soldʒər] *s* Soldat *m*

sole [sol] *adj* einzig, alleinig ‖ *s* (*of a shoe, foot*) Sohle *f*; *(fish)* Scholle *f* ‖ *tr* (be)sohlen

solely ['soli] *adv* einzig und allein

solemn ['saləm] *adj* feierlich; *(expression)* ernst

solemnity [sə'lɛmnɪti] *s* Feierlichkeit *f*

solicit [sə'lɪsɪt] *tr* *(beg for)* dringend bitten um; *(accost)* ansprechen; *(new members, customers)* werben

solicitor [sə'lɪsɪtər] *s* (com) Agent –in *mf*; (jur) Rechtsanwalt *m*

solicitous [sə'lɪsɪtəs] *adj* fürsorglich
solid ['salɪd] *adj* (*hard, firm, e.g., ice, ground*) fest; (*sturdy, e.g., person, furniture; firm, e.g., foundation, learning; financially sound*) solid(e); (*compact*) kompakt, massiv; (*durable*) dauerhaft; (*gold*) gediegen; (*meal, blow*) kräftig; (*hour*) ganz, geschlagen; (*of one color*) einfarbig; (*color*) getönt; (*of one mind*) einmütig; (*grounds, argument*) stichhaltig; (*row of houses*) geschlossen; (*clouds, fog*) dicht; (geom) Raum– || *s* (geom, phys) Körper *m*
solidarity [,salɪ'dærɪti] *s* Solidarität *f*, Verbundenheit *f*
sol'id food' *s* feste Nahrung *f*
sol'id geo'metry *s* Stereometrie *f*
solidi·fy [sə'lɪdɪ,faɪ] *v* (*pret & pp* –fied*) tr* fest werden lassen; (fig) konsolidieren || *intr* fest werden
solidity [sə'lɪdɪti] *s* (*state*) Festigkeit *f*; (*soundness*) Solidität *f*
solidly ['salɪdli] *adv*—**be s. behind s.o.** sich mit j–m solidarisch erklären
sol'id-state' *adj* Transistor–
soliloquy [sə'lɪləkwi] *s* Selbstgespräch *n*
solitaire ['salɪ,ter] *s* Solitär *m*
solitary ['salɪ,teri] *adj* allein; (*life*) zurückgezogen; (*exception*) einzig; (*lonely*) einsam
sol'itary confine'ment *s* Einzelhaft *f*
solitude ['salɪ,t(j)ud] *s* Einsamkeit *f*; (*lonely spot*) abgelegener Ort *m*
so·lo ['solo] *adj & adv* solo || *s* (–los) Solo *n*
so'lo flight' *s* Soloflug *m*
soloist ['solo·ɪst] *s* Solist –in *mf*
so'lo part' *s* (mus) Solostimme *f*
solstice ['salstɪs] *s* Sonnenwende *f*
soluble ['saljəbəl] *adj* (fig) (auf)lösbar; (chem) löslich
solution [sə'luʃən] *s* Lösung *f*
solvable ['salvəbəl] *adj* (auf)lösbar
solve [salv] *tr* (auf)lösen
solvency ['salvənsi] *s* Zahlungsfähigkeit *f*
solvent ['salvənt] *adj* zahlungsfähig; (chem) (auf)lösend || *s* Lösungsmittel *n*
somber ['sambər] *adj* düster, trüb(e)
some [sʌm] *indef adj* (with singular nouns) etwas; (with plural nouns) manche; (sometimes not translated) e.g., **I am buying s. stockings** ich kaufe Strümpfe; (coll) toll, e.g., **s. girl!** tolles Mädchen!; **at s. time or other** irgendeinmal, irgendwann; **s. ... or other** irgendein; **s. other way** sonstwie || *adv* (with numerals) etwa, ungefähr || *indef pron* manche; (*part of*) ein Teil *m*; **s. of these people** einige Leute; **s. of us** manche von uns
some'bod'y *indef pron* jemand, irgendwer; **s. else** jemand anderer || *s*—**be a s.** etwas Besonderes sein
some'day' *adv* e–s Tages
some'how' *adv* irgendwie; (*for some reason or other*) aus irgendeinem Grunde

some'one' *indef pron* jemand, irgendwer; **s. else** jemand anderer; **s. else's** fremd, e.g., **s. else's property** fremdes Eigentum
some'place' *adv* irgendwo; (*direction*) irgendwohin
somersault ['sʌmər,sɔlt] *s* Purzelbaum *m*; (gym) Überschlag *m*; **do a s.** e–n Purzelbaum schlagen || *intr* sich überschlagen
some'thing *indef pron* etwas; **he is s. of an expert** er ist e–e Art Experte; **s. else** etwas anderes; **s. or other** irgend etwas
some'time' *adv* einmal; **s. today** irgendwann heute
some'times' *adv* manchmal; **sometimes ... sometimes ...** mal ... mal ...
some'way', some'ways' *adv* irgendwie
some'what' *adv* etwas
some'where' *adv* irgendwo; (*direction*) irgendwohin; **from s. else** sonstwoher; **s. else** sonstwo
somnambulist [sam'næmbjəlɪst] *s* Nachtwandler –in *mf*
somnolent ['samnələnt] *adj* schläfrig
son [sʌn] *s* Sohn *m*
sonar ['sonar] *s* Sonar *n*
sonata [sə'natə] *s* Sonate *f*
song [sɔŋ] *s* Lied *n;* (*of birds*) Gesang *m*; **for a s.** (coll) um ein Spottgeld
Song' of Songs' *s* (Bib) Hohelied *n*
sonic ['sanɪk] *adj* Schall–
son'ic boom' *s* Kopfwellenknall *m*
son'-in-law' *s* (sons-in-law) Schwiegersohn *m*
sonnet ['sanɪt] *s* Sonett *n*
sonny ['sʌni] *s* Söhnchen *n*, Kleiner *m*
Son' of Man', the *s* (Bib) der Menschensohn
sonorous [sə'norəs] *adj* sonor
soon [sun] *adv* bald; **as s. as** sobald; **as s. as possible** sobald wie möglich; **just as s.** (*expressing preference*) genauso gern(e); **no sooner said than done** gesagt, getan; **sooner** (expressing time) früher, eher; (*expressing preference*) lieber, eher; **sooner or later** über kurz oder lang; **the sooner the better** je eher, je besser; **too s.** zu früh
soot [sʊt] *s* Ruß *m*
soothe [suð] *tr* beschwichtigen, beruhigen; **have a soothing effect on** beruhigend wirken auf (*acc*)
soothsayer ['suθ,se·ər] *s* Wahrsager *m*
sooty ['suti] *adj* rußig
sop [sap] *s* eingetunktes Stück *n* Brot; (*something given to pacify*) Beschwichtigungsmittel *n;* (*bribe*) Schmiergeld *n;* (*spineless person*) Waschlappen *m* || *v* (*pret & pp* sopped*;* *ger* sopping*) tr* (*dip*) eintunken; **sop up** aufsaugen
sophist ['safɪst] *s* Sophist –in *mf*
sophisticated [sə'fɪstɪ,ketɪd] *adj* (*person*) weltklug; (*way of life*) verfeinert; (*highly developed*) hochentwickelt
sophistication [sə,fɪstɪ'keʃən] *s* Weltklugheit *f*
sophistry ['safɪstri] *s* Sophisterei *f*

sophomore [ˈsɑfəˌmor] s Student –in mf im zweiten Studienjahr

sop'ping adj klatschnaß || adv—s. **wet** klatschnaß

sopran·o [səˈpræno] adj Sopran– || s (–os) (uppermost voice) Sopran m; (soprano part) Sopranpartie f; (singer) Sopranist –in mf

sorcerer [ˈsɔrsərər] s Zauberer m

sorceress [ˈsɔrsərɪs] s Zauberin f

sorcery [ˈsɔrsəri] s Zauberei f

sordid [ˈsɔrdɪd] adj schmutzig; (improper) unlauter

sore [sor] adj wund; (sensitive) empfindlich; (coll) (at) bös (auf acc); be s. weh tun; s. **spot** (& fig) wunder Punkt m || s Wunde f

sore'head' s (coll) Verbitterte mf

sorely [ˈsorli] adv sehr

soreness [ˈsornɪs] s Empfindlichkeit f

sore' throat' s Halsweh n

sorority [səˈrɔrɪti] s Studentinnenvereinigung f

sorrel [ˈsɔrəl] adj fuchsrot || s Fuchs m; (bot) Sauerampfer m

sorrow [ˈsɔro] s Kummer m || intr (for or over) Kummer haben (um)

sorrowful [ˈsɔrəfəl] adj betrübt

sorry [ˈsɔri] adj traurig, betrübt; (appearance) armselig; **I am** s. es tut mir leid; **I am** (or **feel**) s. **for him** er tut mir leid

sort [sɔrt] s Art f, Sorte f; **all sorts of** alle möglichen; **nothing of the** s. nichts dergleichen; **out of sorts** unpäßlich; s. **of** (coll) (with adjectives) etwas; (with verbs) irgendwie; (with nouns) so 'n, e.g., **I had a** s. **of feeling that** ich hatte so 'ne Ahnung, daß; **these sorts of** derartige; **what** s. **of** was für ein || tr sortieren; s. **out** aussortieren; (fig) sichten

sortie [ˈsɔrti] s (from a fortress) Ausfall m; (aer) Einzeleinsatz m || intr e–n Ausfall machen

so'-so' adj & adv soso, leidlich

sot [sɑt] s Trunkenbold m

soul [sol] s (spiritual being; inhabitant) Seele f; **not a** s. (coll) keine Seele f; **upon my** s.! meiner Seele!

sound [saʊnd] adj Schall–, Ton–; (healthy) gesund; (valid) einwandfrei; (basis) tragfähig; (sleep) fest; (beating) (coll) tüchtig; (business) solid; (judgment) treffsicher || s Laut m, Ton m; (noise) Geräusch n; (of one's voice) Klang m; (narrow body of water) Sund m; (phys) Schall m; (surg) Sonde f || adv—be s. **asleep** fest schlafen || tr ertönen lassen; (med) sondieren; (naut) loten; s. **s.o. out** (coll) j–m auf den Zahn fühlen; s. **the alarm** Alarm schlagen; s. **the all-clear** entwarnen || intr (er)klingen, (er)tönen; (seem) klingen; (naut) loten; **it sounds good to me** es kommt mir gut vor; s. **off** (coll) sich laut beschweren

sound' bar'rier s Schallgrenze f, Schallmauer f

sound' effects' spl Klangeffekte pl

sound' film' s Tonfilm m

sound'ing s Lotung f; **take soundings** loten

sound'ing board' s (on an instrument) Resonanzboden m; (over an orchestra or speaker) Schallmuschel f; (board for damping sounds) Schalldämpfungsbrett n

soundly [ˈsaʊndli] adv tüchtig

sound'proof' adj schalldicht || tr schalldicht machen

sound' stu'dio s (cin) Tonatelier n

sound' techni'cian s Tontechniker m

sound' track' s (cin) Tonstreifen m

sound' truck' s Lautsprecherwagen m

sound' wave' s Schallwelle f

soup [sup] s Suppe f; (thick fog) (coll) Waschküche f; **in the** s. (coll) in der Patsche || tr—s. **up** (aut) frisieren

soup' kitch'en s Volksküche f

soup'meat' s Suppenfleisch n

soup' plate' s Suppenteller m

soup'spoon' s Suppenlöffel m

sour [saʊr] adj (& fig) sauer || tr säuern; (fig) verbittern || intr säuern; (fig) versauern

source [sors] s Quelle f

source' lan'guage s Ausgangssprache f

source' mate'rial s Quellenmaterial n

sour' cher'ry s Weichsel f

sour' grapes' spl (fig) saure Trauben pl

sour' note' s (& fig) Mißklang m

sour'puss' s (sl) Sauertopf m

souse [saʊs] s (sl) Säufer –in mf

soused adj (sl) besoffen

south [saʊθ] adj Süd–, südlich || adv (direction) nach Süden; s. **of** südlich von || s Süd(en) m

South' Amer'ica s Südamerika n

south'east' adj Südost– || adv (direction) südöstlich; s. **of** südöstlich von || s Südost(en) m

south'east'ern adj südöstlich

southerly [ˈsʌðərli] adj südlich

southern [ˈsʌðərn] adj südlich

southerner [ˈsʌðərnər] s Südländer –in mf; (in the U.S.A.) Südstaatler –in mf

south'paw' adj (coll) linkshändig || s (coll) Linkshänder –in mf

South' Pole' s Südpol m

South' Seas' spl Südsee f

southward [ˈsaʊθwərd] adv südwärts

south'west' adj Südwest– || adv südwestlich; s. **of** südwestlich von || s Südwest(en) m

south'west'ern adj südwestlich

souvenir [ˌsuvəˈnɪr] s Andenken n

sovereign [ˈsavrɪn] adj souverän || s Souverän m, Landesfürst m

sov'ereign rights' spl Hoheitsrechte pl

sovereignty [ˈsavrɪnti] s Souveränität f

soviet [ˈsovɪˌet] adj sowjetisch || s Sowjet m; **the Soviets** die Sowjets pl

So'viet Rus'sia s Sowjetrußland n

So'viet Un'ion s Sowjetunion f

sow [saʊ] s Sau f || [so] v (pret sowed; pp sowed & sown) tr & intr säen

soybean [ˈsɔɪˌbin] s Sojabohne f

spa [spɑ] s Bad n, Badekurort m

space [spes] s Raum m; (between ob-

jects) Zwischenraum *m;* (typ) Spatium *n;* **take up s.** Platz einnehmen || *tr* in Abständen anordnen; (typ) spationieren

space′ age′ *s* Weltraumzeitalter *n*

space′ bar′ *s* (typ) Leertaste *f*

space′ cap′sule *s* (rok) Raumkapsel *f*

space′craft′ *s* Weltraumfahrzeug *n*

space′ flight′ *s* Raumflug *m*

space′man′ *s* (–men′) Raumfahrer *m*

space′ probe′ *s* Sonde *f*

space′ship′ *s* Raumschiff *n*

space′ shot′ *s* Weltraumabschuß *m*

space′ shut′tle *s* Raumfähre *f*

space′ suit′ *s* Raumanzug *m*

space′ trav′el *s* Raumfahrt *f*

spacious [′speʃəs] *adj* geräumig

spade [sped] *s* Spaten *m;* (cards) Pik *n;* **call a s. a s.** das Kind beim richtigen Namen nennen

spade′work′ *s* (fig) Pionierarbeit *f*

spaghetti [spə′gɛti] *s* Spahetti *pl*

Spain [spen] *s* Spanien *n*

span [spæn] *s* (& fig) Spanne *f;* (*of a bridge*) Joch *n;* **s. of time** Zeitspanne *f* || *v* (*pret & pp* **spanned;** *ger* **spanning**) *tr* (e.g., *the waist*) umspannen; (*a river*) überbrücken; (*said of a bridge*) überspannen

spangle [′spæŋgəl] *s* Flitter *m* || *tr* mit Flitter besetzen

Spaniard [′spænjərd] *s* Spanier –in *mf*

spaniel [′spænjəl] *s* Wachtelhund *m*

Spanish [′spænɪʃ] *adj* spanisch || *s* Spanisch *n;* **the S.** die Spanier

Span′ish-Amer′ican *adj* spanischamerikanisch || *s* Amerikaner –in *mf* mit spanischer Muttersprache

Span′ish moss′ *s* Moosbärte *pl*

spank [spæŋk] *tr* (ver)hauen

spank′ing *adj* (*quick*) flink; (*breeze*) frisch || *adv*—**s. new** funkelnagelneu || *s* Schläge *pl*

spar [spɑr] *s* (aer) Holm *m;* (mineral) Spat *m;* (naut) Spiere *f* || *v* (*pret & pp* **sparred;** *ger* **sparring**) *intr* sparren

spare [sper] *adj* Ersatz–; (*thin*) mager; (*time*) frei; (*leftover*) übrig || *s* (aut) Ersatzreifen *m* || *tr* (*a person*) schonen; (*time, money*) erübrigen; (*expense*) scheuen; (*do without*) entbehren; **have to s.** übrig haben; **s. s.o. s.th.** j–m etw ersparen

spare′ bed′ *s* Gastbett *n*

spare′ part′ *s* Ersatzteil *n*

spare′rib′ *s* Rippenspeer *n*

spare′ time′ *s* Freizeit *f*

spare′-time′ *adj* nebenberuflich

spare′ tire′ *s* Ersatzreifen *m*

spar′ing *adj* sparsam; **be s. with** sparsam umgehen mit

spark [spɑrk] *s* Funke(n) *m* || *tr* (*set off*) auslösen; (*stimulate*) anregen || *intr* Funken sprühen

spark′ gap′ *s* Funkenstrecke *f*

sparkle [′spɑrkəl] *s* Funkeln *n* || *intr* funkeln; (*said of wine*) moussieren

spark′ plug′ *s* Zündkerze *f*

spar′ring part′ner *s* Übungspartner *m*

sparrow [′spæro] *s* Spatz *m,* Sperling *m*

spar′row hawk′ *s* Sperber *m*

sparse [spɑrs] *adj* spärlich

Spartan [′spɑrtən] *adj* spartanisch || *s* Spartaner –in *mf*

spasm [′spæzəm] *s* Krampf *m,* Zukkung *f*

spasmodic [spæz′mɑdɪk] *adj* sprunghaft; (pathol) krampfartig

spastic [′spæstɪk] *adj* spastisch

spat [spæt] *s* (coll) Wortwechsel *m*

spatial [′speʃəl] *adj* räumlich

spatter [′spætər] *s* Spritzen *n;* (*stain*) Spritzfleck *m* || *tr* verspritzen

spatula [′spætʃələ] *s* Spachtel *m & f*

spawn [spɔn] *s* Fischlaich *m* || *tr* hervorbringen || *intr* (*said of fish*) laichen

spay [spe] *tr* die Eierstöcke entfernen aus

speak [spik] *v* (*pret* **spoke** [spok]; *pp* **spoken**) *tr* sprechen; **s. one's mind** sich aussprechen || *intr* (**about**) sprechen (über *acc,* von); **generally speaking** im allgemeinen; **so to s.** sozusagen; **speaking!** (telp) am Apparat!; **s. to** sprechen mit; (*give a speech to*) sprechen zu; **s. up** lauter sprechen; (*say something*) den Mund aufmachen; **s. up!** heraus mit der Sprache!; **s. up for** eintreten für

speak′-eas′y *s* Flüsterkneipe *f*

speaker [′spikər] *s* Sprecher –in *mf;* (*before an audience*) Redner –in *mf;* (parl) Sprecher –in *mf;* (rad) Lautsprecher *m*

spear [spɪr] *s* Speer *m* || *tr* durchbohren; (*a piece of meat*) aufspießen; (*fish*) mit dem Speer fangen

spear′head′ *s* Speerspitze *f;* (mil) Stoßkeil *m* || *tr* an der Spitze stehen von

spear′mint′ *s* Krauseminze *f*

special [′speʃəl] *adj* besonder, Sonder– || *s* (rr) Sonderzug *m;* **today's s.** Stammgericht *n*

spe′cial deliv′ery *s* Eilzustellung *f;* (*tab on envelope*) Eilsendung *f*

spec′ial-deliv′ery let′ter *s* Eilbrief *m*

specialist [′speʃəlɪst] *s* Spezialist –in *mf*

specialization [ˌspeʃəlɪ′zeʃən] *s* Spezialisierung *f*

specialize [′speʃəˌlaɪz] *intr* sich spezialisieren; **specialized knowledge** Fachkenntnisse *pl*

spe′cial of′fer *s* (com) Sonderangebot *n*

specialty [′speʃəlti] *s* Spezialität *f;* (*special field*) Spezialfach *n*

spe′cialty shop′ *s* Spezialgeschäft *n*

specie [′spisi] *s*—**in s.** der Art nach

spe·cies [′spisiz] *s* (–cies) Gattung *f*

specific [spɪ′sɪfɪk] *adj* spezifisch

specification [ˌspesɪfɪ′keʃən] *s* Spezifizierung *f;* **specifications** (tech) technische Beschreibung *f*

specif′ic grav′ity *s* spezifisches Gewicht *n*

speci·fy [′spesɪˌfaɪ] *v* (*pret & pp* **–fied**) *tr* spezifizieren; (*stipulate*) bestimmen

specimen [′spesɪmən] *s* (*example*) Exemplar *n;* (*test sample*) Probe *f*

specious [′spiʃəs] *adj* Schein–

speck [spɛk] s Fleck m; (in the distance) Pünktchen n; **s. of dust** Stäubchen n; **s. of grease** Fettauge n

speckle ['spɛkəl] s Sprenkel m ‖ tr sprenkeln

spectacle ['spɛktəkəl] s Schauspiel n, Anblick m; **spectacles** Brille f

spec'tacle case' s Brillenfutteral n

spectacular [spɛk'tækjələr] adj sensationell ‖ s (cin) Monsterfilm m

spectator ['spɛktetər] s Zuschauer –in mf

specter ['spɛtər] s Gespenst n

spec·trum ['spɛktrəm] s (–tra [trə]) Spektrum n

speculate ['spɛkjə‚let] intr spekulieren; **s. in** spekulieren in (dat); **s. on** Überlegungen anstellen über (acc)

speculation [‚spɛkjə'leʃən] s Spekulation f

speculative ['spɛkjələtɪv] adj (com) Spekulations–; (philos) spekulativ

speculator ['spɛkjə‚letər] s Spekulant –in mf

speech [spitʃ] s Sprache f; (address) Rede f; **give a s.** e–e Rede halten

speech' defect' s Sprachfehler m

speech' imped'iment s Sprachstörung f

speechless ['spitʃlɪs] adj sprachlos

speed [spid] s Geschwindigkeit f; (gear) Gang m; **at top s.** mit Höchstgeschwindigkeit; **pick up s.** auf Touren kommen ‖ v (pret & pp **speeded** & **sped** [spɛd]) tr beschleunigen; **s. up** forcieren; **s. it up** (coll) ein scharfes Tempo vorlegen ‖ intr (aut) rasen; (above the speed limit) (aut) zu schnell fahren

speed'boat' s Schnellboot n

speed'ing s (aut) Schnellfahren n; **be arrested for s.** wegen Überschreitung der Höchstgeschwindigkeit verhaftet werden; **no s.** (public sign) Schnellfahren verboten

speed' lim'it s Geschwindigkeitsgrenze f

speed' of light' s Lichtgeschwindigkeit f

speed' of sound' s Schallgeschwindigkeit f

speedometer [spi'dɑmɪtər] s Tachometer n; (mileage indicator) Meilenzähler m, Kilometerzähler m

speed' rec'ord s Geschwindigkeitsrekord m

speed' trap' s Autofalle f

speed'way' s (aut) Rennstrecke f

speedy ['spidi] adj schnell, schleunig; (reply) baldig

speed' zone' s Geschwindigkeitsbeschränkung f

spell [spɛl] s (short period) Zeitlang f; (attack) Anfall m; (magical influence) Bann m; **be under s.o.'s s.** in j–s Bann stehen; **cast a s.** bannen ‖ v (pret & pp **spelled** & **spelt** [spɛlt]) tr buchstabieren; (in writing) schreiben; **s. out** Buchstaben für Buchstaben lesen; (fig) auseinanderklamüsern; **s. trouble** Schwie-

rigkeiten bedeuten ‖ intr buchstabieren

spell'bind'er s faszinierender Redner m

spell'bound' adj gebannt

spell'ing s Schreibweise f; (orthography) Rechtschreibung f

spell'ing bee' s orthographischer Wettbewerb m

spelt [spɛlt] s Spelz m

spelunker [spɪ'lʌŋkər] s Höhlenforscher –in mf

spend [spɛnd] v (pret & pp **spent** [spɛnt]) tr (money) ausgeben; (time) verbringen; **s. the night** übernachten; **s. time and effort on** Zeit und Mühe verwenden auf (acc)

spend'thrift' s Verschwender –in mf

spent [spɛnt] adj (exhausted) erschöpft; (cartridge) leergeschossen

sperm [spʌrm] s Sperma n

sperm' whale' s Pottwal m

spew [spju] tr erbrechen; (fig) ausspeien ‖ intr sich erbrechen; (fig) herausströmen

sphere [sfɪr] s Kugel f, Sphäre f; (fig) Bereich m; **s. of influence** Einflußsphäre f

spherical ['sfɛrɪkəl] adj sphärisch, kugelförmig

sphinx [sfɪŋks] s (**sphinxes** & **sphinges** ['sfɪndʒiz]) Sphinx f

spice [spaɪs] s Gewürz n, Würze f; (fig) Würze f ‖ tr würzen

spick-and-span ['spɪkənd'spæn] adj blitzblank

spicy ['spaɪsi] adj würzig; (fig) pikant

spider ['spaɪdər] s Spinne f

spi'derweb' s Spinnengewebe n

spiffy ['spɪfi] adj (sl) fesch

spigot ['spɪgət] s Wasserhahn m

spike [spaɪk] s (nail) langer Nagel m; (in volleyball) Schmetterball m; (bot) Ähre f; (rr) Schwellenschraube f; (sport) Dorn m ‖ tr (a drink) e–n Schuß Alkohol tun in (acc); (in volleyball) schmettern

spill [spɪl] s (spilling) Vergießen n; (stain) Fleck m, Klecks m; (fall) Sturz m; **take a s.** stürzen ‖ v (pret & pp **spilled** & **spilt** [spɪlt]) tr verschütten; (a rider) abwerfen; **s. out** ausschütten; **s. the beans** (sl) alles ausplaudern ‖ intr überlaufen; **s. over into** (fig) übergreifen auf (acc)

spill'way' s Überlauf m

spin [spɪn] s (rotation) Umdrehung f; (short ride) kurze Fahrt f; (aer) Trudeln n; **go for a s.** e–e Spritztour machen; **go into a s.** (aer) ins Trudeln kommen ‖ v (pret & pp **spun** [spʌn]; ger **spinning**) tr (rotate) drehen; (tex) spinnen; **s. out** (a story) ausspinnen; **s. s.o. around** j–n im Kreise herumwirbeln ‖ intr kreiseln, sich drehen; (tex) spinnen; **my head is spinning** mir dreht sich alles im Kopf

spinach ['spɪnɪtʃ] s Spinat m

spi'nal col'umn ['spaɪnəl] s Wirbelsäule f

spi'nal cord' s Rückenmark n

spi′nal flu′id s Rückenmarksflüssigkeit f

spindle [ˈspɪndəl] s Spindel f

spin′-dry′ v (pret & pp **-dried**) tr schleudern

spin′-dry′er s Trockenschleuder m

spine [spaɪn] s Rückgrat n, Wirbelsäule f; (bb) Buchrücken m

spineless [ˈspaɪnlɪs] adj (& fig) rückgratlos

spinet [ˈspɪnɪt] s Spinett n

spinner [ˈspɪnər] s Spinner –in mf; (mach) Spinnmaschine f

spin′ning adj (rotating) sich drehend; (tex) Spinn– || s (tex) Spinnen n

spin′ning wheel′ s Spinnrad n

spinster [ˈspɪnstər] s alte Jungfer f

spi·ral [ˈspaɪrəl] adj spiralig || s Spirale f; **s. of rising prices and wages** Lohn-Preis-Spirale f || v (pret & pp **-ral[l]ed**; ger **-ral[l]ing**) intr sich in die Höhe schrauben

spi′ral stair′case s Wendeltreppe f

spire [spaɪr] s Spitze f

spirit [ˈspɪrɪt] s Geist m; (enthusiasm) Schwung m; (ghost) Geist m; **in high spirits** in gehobener Stimmung; **in low spirits** in gedrückter Stimmung; **spirits** Spirituosen pl; **that's the right s.!** das ist die richtige Einstellung! || tr—**s. away** wegzaubern

spir′ited adj lebhaft; (horse) feurig

spiritless [ˈspɪrɪtlɪs] adj schwunglos

spiritual [ˈspɪrɪtʃu·əl] adj (incorporeal) geistig; (of the soul) seelisch; (religious) geistlich || s geistliches Negerlied n

spiritualism [ˈspɪrɪtʃuə ˌlɪzəm] s Spiritismus m

spiritualist [ˈspɪrɪtʃu·əlɪst] s Spiritist –in mf

spir′itual life′ s Seelenleben n

spit [spɪt] s Spucke f; (culin) Spieß m || v (pret & pp **spat** [spæt] & **spit**; ger **spitting**) tr & intr spucken

spite [spaɪt] s Trotz m; **for s.** aus Trotz; **in s. of** trotz (genit) || tr kränken; **he did it to s. me** er hat es mir zum Trotz getan

spiteful [ˈspaɪtfəl] adj gehässig

spit′fire′ s (coll) Sprühteufel m

spit′ting im′age s (coll) Ebenbild n

spittoon [spɪˈtun] s Spucknapf m

splash [splæʃ] s Platschen n; (noise of falling into water) Klatschen n; **make a s.** (coll) Aufsehen erregen || tr (a person, etc.) bespritzen; (e.g., water) spritzen || intr klatschen, patschen; **s. about** planschen; **s. down** (rok) wassern || interj schwaps!, platsch!

splash′down′ s (rok) Wasserung f

splatter [ˈsplætər] tr & intr kleckern

spleen [splin] s Milz f; (fig) schlechte Laune f; **vent one's s. on** seiner schlechten Laune Luft machen gegenüber (dat)

splendid [ˈsplendɪd] adj prächtig, herrlich; (coll) großartig

splendor [ˈsplendər] s Herrlichkeit f

splice [splaɪs] s Spleiß m || tr (a rope) spleißen; (film) zusammenkleben

splint [splɪnt] s Schiene f; **put in splints** schienen

splinter [ˈsplɪntər] s Splitter m || tr (zer)splittern

splin′ter group′ s Splittergruppe f

split [splɪt] adj rissig || s Riß m, Spalt m; (fig) Spaltung f; (gym) Spagat m || v (pret & pp **split**; ger **splitting**) tr spalten; (pants) platzen; (profits, the difference) sich teilen in (acc); **s. hairs** Haarspalterei treiben; **s. one's sides laughing** vor Lachen platzen; **s. open** aufbrechen || intr (into) sich spalten (in acc); **splitting headache** rasende Kopfschmerzen pl; **s. up** (said of a couple) sich trennen

split′ infin′itive s gespaltener Infinitiv m

split′-lev′el adj mit Zwischenstockwerk versehen

split′ personal′ity s gespaltene Persönlichkeit f

split′ sec′ond s Sekundenbruchteil m

splotch [splatʃ] s Klecks m || tr kleckern

splotchy [ˈsplatʃi] adj fleckig

splurge [splʌrdʒ] s—**go on a s.** verschwenderischen Aufwand treiben || tr verschwenden || intr (on) verschwenderische Ausgaben machen (für)

splutter [ˈsplʌtər] s Geplapper n || tr (words) heraussprudeln; (besplatter) bespritzen || intr plappern; (said, e.g., of grease) spritzen

spoil [spɔɪl] s—**spoils** Beute f || v (pret & pp **spoiled** & **spoilt** [spɔɪlt]) tr (perishable goods; fun) verderben; (a child) verziehen, verwöhnen || intr verderben, schlecht werden; **spoiling for a fight** zanksüchtig

spoilage [ˈspɔɪlɪdʒ] s Verderb m

spoil′ sport′ s Spielverderber –in mf

spoils′ sys′tem s Futterkrippensystem n

spoke [spok] s Speiche f

spokes′man s (**-men**) Wortführer –in mf

sponge [spʌndʒ] s Schwamm m || tr schnorren || intr schnorren; **s. on** (coll) schmarotzen bei

sponge′ cake′ s Sandtorte f

sponger [ˈspʌndʒər] s Schmarotzer –in mf

sponge′ rub′ber s Schaumgummi m & n

spongy [ˈspʌndʒi] adj schwammig

sponsor [ˈspansər] s Förderer –in mf; (of a program) Sponsor m; (of an immigrant) Bürge m, Bürgin f; (at baptism or confirmation) Pate m, Patin f || tr fördern; (a program) finanziell fördern

spontaneity [spantəˈni·ɪti] s Spontaneität f

spontaneous [spanˈtenɪ·əs] adj spontan

sponta′neous combus′tion s Selbstverbrennung f

spontaneously [spanˈtenɪ·əsli] adv von selbst, unaufgefordert

spoof [spuf] *s* (*hoax*) Jux *m;* (*parody*) (**on**) Parodie *f* (auf *acc*) ‖ *intr* albern

spook [spuk] *s* (coll) Spuk *m*

spooky ['spuki] *adj* spukhaft

spool [spul] *s* Spule *f*, Rolle *f*

spoon [spun] *s* Löffel *m;* **wooden s.** Kochlöffel *m* ‖ *tr* (**out**) löffeln

spoonerism ['spunə‚rɪzəm] *s* Schüttelreim *m*

spoon'-feed' *v* (*pret & pp* **–fed**) *tr* (fig) es leicht machen (*dat*)

spoonful ['spunful] *s* Löffel *m*

sporadic [spə'rædɪk] *adj* vereinzelt

spore [spor] *s* Spore *f*

sport [sport] *adj* Sport– ‖ *s* Sport *m;* (biol) Spielart *f;* **a good s.** ein Pfundskerl *m;* **go in for sports** sporteln; **in s.** im Spaß; **make s. of** sich lustig machen über (*acc*); **play sports** Sport treiben; **poor s.** Spielverderber –in *mf;* **sports** Sport *m;* (*sportscast*) Sportbericht *m* ‖ *intr* sich belustigen

sport'ing event' *s* Sportveranstaltung *f*

sport'ing goods' *spl* Sportwaren *pl*

sport' jac'ket *s* Sportjacke *f*

sports' car' *s* Sportwagen *m*

sports'cast *s* Sportbericht *m*

sports'cast'er *s* Sportberichterstatter *m*

sports' fan' *s* Sportfreund –in *mf*

sport' shirt' *s* Sporthemd *n*

sports'man *s* (**–men**) Sportsmann *m*

sports'manlike *adj* sportlich

sports'manship' *s* sportliches Verhalten *n*

sports' news' *s* Sportnachrichten *pl*

sports'wear' *s* Sportkleidung *f*

sports' world' *s* Sportwelt *f*

sports' writ'er *s* Sportjournalist –in *mf*

sporty ['sporti] *adj* auffallend

spot [spat] *s* (*stain*) Fleck(en) *m;* (*place*) Platz *m*, Ort *m;* (*as on a leopard*) Tüpfel *m & n;* **be on the s.** (*be present*) zur Stelle sein; (*be in difficulty*) in der Klemme sein; **hit the s.** gerade das Richtige sein; **on the s.** auf der Stelle; **put on the s.** in Verlegenheit bringen ‖ *v* (*pret & pp* **spotted;** *ger* **spotting**) *tr* (*stain*) beflecken; (*espy*) erblicken; (*points in betting*) vorgeben

spot' announce'ment *s* Durchsage *f*

spot' cash' *s* ungebundene Barmittel *pl*

spot' check' *s* Stichprobe *f*

spot'-check' *tr* stichprobenweise prüfen

spotless ['spatlɪs] *adj* makellos

spot'light' *s* Scheinwerfer *m;* **in the s.** (fig) im Rampenlicht der Öffentlichkeit ‖ *tr* (fig) in den Vordergrund stellen

spot' remov'er [rɪ‚muvər] *s* Fleckputzmittel *n*

spotty ['spati] *adj* fleckig; (*uneven*) ungleichmäßig

spot' weld'ing *s* Punktschweißung *f*

spouse [spaus] *s* Gatte *m*, Gattin *f*

spout [spaut] *s* (*of a pot*) Tülle *f;* (*jet of water*) Strahl *m* ‖ *tr* (& fig) hervorsprudeln ‖ *intr* spritzen; (coll) große Reden schwingen

sprain [spren] *s* Verstauchung *f* ‖ *tr* verstauchen; **s. one's ankle** sich [*dat*] den Fuß vertreten

sprat [spræt] *s* (ichth) Sprotte *f*

sprawl ['sprɔl] *intr* (**out**) alle viere von sich ausstrecken; (*said of a city*) sich weit ausbreiten

spray [spre] *s* (*of ocean*) Gischt *m;* (*from a can*) Spray *n;* (*from a fountain*) Sprühwasser *n;* **s. of flowers** Blütenzweig *m* ‖ *tr* spritzen; (*liquids*) zerstäuben; (*plants*) besprühen

sprayer ['spre·ər] *s* Zerstäuber *m;* (*for a garden*) Gartenspritze *f*

spray' gun' *s* Spritzpistole *f*

spray' paint' *s* Spritzfarbe *f*

spread [sprɛd] *s* (*act of spreading*) Ausbreitung *f;* (*extent*) Verbreitung *f;* (*e.g., of a tree*) Umfang *m;* (*on bread*) Aufstrich *m;* (*bedspread*) Bettdecke *f;* (*large piece of land*) weite Fläche *f;* (*of a shot*) Streubereich *m & n;* (*sumptuous meal*) Gelage *n* ‖ *v* (*pret & pp* **spread**) *tr* (*warmth, light, news, rumors*) verbreiten; (*mortar, glue*) auftragen; (*e.g., butter*) aufstreichen; (*the legs*) spreizen; (*manure*) streuen; **s. oneself too thin** sich verzetteln; **s. out over a year** über ein Jahr verteilen ‖ *intr* sich verbreiten; (*said of margarine*) sich aufstreichen lassen

spree [spri] *s* Bummel *m;* (*carousal*) Zechgelage *n;* **go on a buying s.** sich in e–e Kauforgie stürzen

sprig [sprɪg] *s* Zweiglein *n*

sprightly ['spraɪtli] *adj* lebhaft; (*gait*) federnd

spring [sprɪŋ] *adj* Frühlings– ‖ *s* (*of water*) Quelle *f;* (*season*) Frühling *m;* (*resilience*) Sprungkraft *f;* (*of metal*) Feder *f;* (*jump*) Sprung *m;* **springs** (aut) Federung *f* ‖ *v* (*pret* **sprang** [spræŋ] **&** **sprung** [sprʌŋ]; *pp* **sprung** [sprʌŋ]) *tr* (*a trap*) zuschnappen lassen; (*a leak*) bekommen; (*a question*) (**on**) plötzlich stellen (*dat*); (*a surprise*) (**on**) bereiten (*dat*); **s. the news on s.o.** j–n mit der Nachricht überraschen ‖ *intr* springen; **s. back** zurückschnellen; **s. from** entspringen (*dat*); **s. up** aufspringen; (*said of industry, towns*) aus dem Boden schießen

spring'board' *s* (& fig) Sprungbrett *n*

spring' chic'ken *s* Hähnchen *n;* **she's no s.** (sl) sie ist nicht die Jüngste

spring' fe'ver *s* Frühlingsmüdigkeit *f*

spring'time' *s* Frühlingszeit *f*

spring' wa'ter *s* Quellwasser *n*

springy ['sprɪŋi] *adj* federnd

sprinkle ['sprɪŋkəl] *s* Spritzen *n;* (*light rain*) Sprühregen *m* ‖ *tr* (*water, streets, lawns, laundry*) sprengen; (*e.g., sugar*) streuen ‖ *intr* sprühen

sprinkler ['sprɪŋklər] *s* (*truck*) Sprengwagen *m;* (*for the lawn*) Rasensprenger *m;* (eccl) Sprengwedel *m*

sprin'kling *s* Sprengung *f;* **a s. of** (*e.g., sugar*) ein bißchen; (*e.g., of people*) ein paar

sprin'kling can' *s* Gießkanne *f*
sprin'kling sys'tem *s* Feuerlöschanlage *f*
sprint [sprɪnt] *s* Sprint *m* ‖ *intr* sprinten
sprinter ['sprɪntər] *s* Sprinter –in *mf*
sprite [spraɪt] *s* Kobold *m*, Elfe *f*
sprocket ['sprɑkɪt] *s* Zahnrad *n*
sprout [spraʊt] *s* Sproß *m* ‖ *intr* sprießen
spruce [sprus] *adj* schmuck ‖ *s* (bot) Fichte *f* ‖ *intr*—s. up sich schmücken
spry [spraɪ] *adj* (spryer & sprier; spryest & spriest) flink
spud [spʌd] *s* (*for weeding*) Jäthacke *f*; (*potatoe*) (coll) Kartoffel *f*
spume [spjum] *s* Schaum *m*
spun' glass' *s* Glasfaser *f*
spunk [spʌŋk] *s* (coll) Mumm *m*
spunky ['spʌŋki] *adj* (coll) feurig
spur [spʌr] *s* (*on riding boot; on a rooster*) Sporn *m*; (*of a mountain*) Ausläufer *m*; (fig) Ansporn *m*; (archit) Strebe *f*; (bot) Stachel *m*; (rr) Seitengleis *n*; **on the s. of the moment** der Eingebung des Augenblicks folgend ‖ *v* (*pret & pp* **spurred;** *ger* **spurring**) *tr* die Sporen geben (*dat*); **s. on** anspornen
spurious ['spjʊrɪ·əs] *adj* unecht
spurn [spʌrn] *tr* verschmähen
spurt [spʌrt] *s* Ruck *m*; (sport) Spurt *m*; **in spurts** ruckweise ‖ *tr* speien ‖ *intr* herausspritzen; (sport) spurten
sputnick ['spʌtnɪk] *s* Sputnik *m*
sputter ['spʌtər] *s* Stottern *n* ‖ *tr* umherspritzen; (*words*) hervorsprudeln ‖ *intr* (*said of a person, engine*) stottern; (*said of a candle, fire*) flackern
sputum ['spjutəm] *s* Sputum *n*
spy [spaɪ] *s* Spion –in *mf* ‖ *v* (*pret & pp* **spied**) *tr*—**spy out** ausspionieren ‖ *intr* spionieren
spy'glass' *s* Fernglas *n*
spy'ing *s* Spionage *f*
spy' ring' *s* Spionageorganization *f*
squabble ['skwɑbəl] *s* Zank *m* ‖ *intr* zanken
squad [skwɑd] *s* (gym) Riege *f*; (mil) Gruppe *f*; (sport) Mannschaft *f*
squad' car' *s* Funkstreifenwagen *m*
squad' lead'er *s* (mil) Gruppenführer *m*
squadron ['skwɑdrən] *s* (aer) Staffel *f*; (nav) Geschwader *n*
squalid ['skwɑlɪd] *adj* verkommen
squall [skwɔl] *s* Bö *f*
squander ['skwɑndər] *tr* verschwenden
square [skwɛr] *adj* quadratisch; (*mile, meter, foot*) Quadrat–; (*fellow, meal*) anständig; (*even*) quitt; **ten meters s.** zehn Meter im Quadrat; **ten s. meters** zehn Quadratmeter ‖ *s* Quadrat *n*; (*city block*) Häuserblock *m*; (*open area*) Platz *m*; (*of a checkerboard or chessboard*) Feld *n*; (carp) Winkel *m*; (math) zweite Potenz *f* ‖ *tr* quadrieren; (*a number*) ins Quadrat erheben; (*accounts*) abrechnen ‖ *intr*—s. off in Kampfstellung gehen; **s. with** (*agree with*)

übereinstimmen mit; (*be frank with*) aufrichtig sein zu
square' dance' *s* Reigen *m*
square' deal' *s* reelles Geschäft *n*
square' root' *s* Quadratwurzel *f*
squash [skwɑʃ] *s* (bot) Kürbis *m* ‖ *tr* (*a hat*) zerdrücken; (*a finger, grape*) quetschen; (fig) unterdrücken ‖ *intr* zerdrückt (or zerquetscht) werden
squashy ['skwɑʃi] *adj* weich, matschig
squat [skwɑt] *adj* gedrungen, untersetzt ‖ *s* Hocken *n* ‖ *v* (*pret & pp* **squatted;** *ger* **squatting**) *intr* hocken; **s. down** sich (hin)hocken
squatter ['skwɑtər] *s* Ansiedler –in *mf* ohne Rechtstitel
squaw [skwɔ] *s* Indianerin *f*
squawk [skwɔk] *s* Geschrei *n*; (sl) Schimpferei *f* ‖ *intr* schreien; (sl) schimpfen
squeak [skwik] *s* (*of a door*) Quietschen *n*; (*of a mouse*) Pfeifen *n* ‖ *intr* quietschen; (*said of a mouse*) pfeifen
squeal [skwil] *s* Quieken *n* ‖ *intr* (*said of a pig*) quieken; (*said of a mouse*) pfeifen; (sl) petzen; **s. for joy** vor Vergnügen quietschen; **s. on** (sl) (*a pupil*) verpetzen; (*to the police*) verpfeifen
squealer ['skwilər] *s* (sl) Petze *f*
squeamish ['skwimɪʃ] *adj* zimperlich
squeeze [skwiz] *s* Druck *m*; **s. of the hand** Händedruck *m* ‖ *tr* drücken; (*oranges*) auspressen; **s. into** (*e.g., a trunk*) hineinquetschen; **s. out** auspressen; **s. together** zusammenpressen; (*e.g., people*) zusammenpferchen ‖ *intr*—s. **in** sich eindrängen; **s. through** sich durchzwängen (durch)
squelch [skwɛltʃ] *s* schlagfertige Antwort *f* ‖ *tr* niederschmettern
squid [skwɪd] *s* Tintenfisch *m*
squill [skwɪl] *s* (bot) Meerzwiebel *f*; (zool) Heuschreckenkrebs *m*
squint [skwɪnt] *s* Schielen *n* ‖ *intr* (*look with eyes partly closed*) blinzeln; (*be cross-eyed*) schielen; (*look askance*) (**at**) argwöhnisch blicken (auf *acc*)
squint'-eyed' *adj* schielend
squire [skwaɪr] *s* (hist) Knappe *m*; (jur) Friedensrichter *m*
squirm [skwʌrm] *intr* (**through**) sich winden (durch); (*be restless*) zappeln; **s. out of** sich herauswinden aus
squirrel ['skwʌrəl] *s* Eichhörnchen *n*
squirt [skwʌrt] *s* Spritzer *m*; (*boy*) (coll) Stöpsel *m* ‖ *tr* (ver)spritzen ‖ *intr* spritzen; **s. out** herausspritzen
S'S' troops' ['ɛs'ɛs] *spl* Schutzstaffel *f*
stab [stæb] *s* Stich *m*; (*wound*) Stichwunde *f*; **make a s. at** (coll) probieren ‖ *v* (*pret & pp* **stabbed;** *ger* **stabbing**) *tr* stechen; (*kill*) erstechen; (*a pig*) abstechen; **s. s.o. in the back** j–m in den Rücken fallen
stability [stə'bɪlɪti] *s* Stabilität *f*
stabilization [ˌstebɪlɪ'zeʃən] *s* (*e.g., of prices*) Stabilisierung *f*; (aer) Dämpfung *f*

stabilize ['stebɪ‚laɪz] *tr* stabilisieren
stabilizer ['stebɪ‚laɪzər] *s* (aer) Flosse *f*
stab′ in the back′ *s* Stoß *m* aus dem Hinterhalt
stable ['stebəl] *adj* stabil || *s* Stall *m* || *tr* unterbringen
sta′ble boy′ *s* Stalljunge *m*
stack [stæk] *s* (*of papers, books*) Stapel *m;* (*of wheat*) Schober *m;* (*of a ship*) Schornstein *m;* (*of rifles*) Pyramide *f;* **stacks** (libr) Bücherregale *pl* || *tr* (*wood, wheat*) aufstapeln; (*rifles*) zusammensetzen; (*cards*) packen
stadi·um ['stedɪ·əm] *s* (**–ums** & **–a** [ə]) Stadion *n*
staff [stæf] *s* (*rod*) Stab *m;* (*personnel*) Personal *n;* (*of a newspaper*) Redaktion *f;* (mil) Stab *m;* (mus) Notensystem *n* || *tr* mit Personal besetzen
staff′ of′ficer *s* Stabsoffizier *m*
staff′ ser′geant *s* Feldwebel *m*
stag [stæg] *adj* Herren– || *adv*—**go s.** ohne Damenbegleitung sein || *s* Hirsch *m*
stage [stedʒ] *s* (*of a theater*) Bühne *f;* (*phase*) Stadium *n;* (*stretch*) Strecke *f;* (*of life*) Etappe *f;* (*of a rocket*) Stufe *f;* (*scene*) Szene *f;* **at this s.** in diesem Stadium; **by easy stages** etappenweise; **final stages** Endstadien *pl* || *tr* (*a play*) inszenieren; (*a comeback*) veranstalten
stage′coach′ *s* Postkutsche *f*
stage′craft′ *s* Bühnenkunst *f*
stage′ direc′tion *s* Bühnenanweisung *f*
stage′ door′ *s* Bühneneingang *m*
stage′ effect′ *s* Bühnenwirkung *f*
stage′ fright′ *s* Lampenfieber *n*
stage′ hand′ *s* Bühnenarbeiter –in *mf*
stage′ light′ing *s* Bühnenbeleuchtung *f*
stage′ man′ager *s* Bühnenleiter –in *mf*
stage′ play′ *s* Bühnenstück *n*
stage′ prop′erties *spl* Theaterrequisiten *pl*
stagestruck ['stedʒ‚strʌk] *adj* theaterbegeistert
stagger ['stægər] *s* Taumeln *n* || *tr* (*e.g., lunch hours*) staffeln; (& fig) erschüttern || *intr* taumeln
stag′gering *adj* taumelnd; (*blow, loss*) vernichtend; (*news*) erschütternd
stagnant ['stægnənt] *adj* (*water*) stillstehend; (*air*) schlecht; (fig) träge
stagnate ['stægnet] *intr* stagnieren
stag′ par′ty *s* Herrenabend *m*
staid [sted] *adj* gesetzt
stain [sten] *s* Fleck *m;* (*paint*) Beize *f* || *tr* beflecken; (*wood*) beizen
stained′-glass win′dow *s* buntes Glasfenster *n*
stainless ['stenlɪs] *adj* rostfrei
stair [ster] *s* Stufe *f;* **stairs** Treppe *f*
stair′case′ *s* Treppenhaus *n*
stair′way′ *s* Treppenaufgang *m*
stair′well′ *s* Treppenschacht *m*
stake [stek] *s* Pfahl *m;* (*bet*) Einsatz *m;* **be at s.** auf dem Spiel stehen; **die at the s.** auf dem Scheiterhaufen sterben; **play for high stakes** viel riskieren; **pull up stakes** (coll) ab-

hauen || *tr* (*plants*) mit e–m Pfahl stützen; **s. off** abstecken; **s. out a claim** (fig) e–e Forderung umreißen
stake′-out′ *s* polizeiliche Überwachung *f*
stalactite [stə'læktaɪt] *s* Stalaktit *m*
stalagmite [stə'lægmaɪt] *s* Stalagmit *m*
stale [stel] *adj* (*baked goods*) altbacken; (*e.g., beer*) schal; (*air*) verbraucht; (*joke*) abgedroschen; **get s.** abstehen
stale′mate′ *s* (fig) Sackgasse *f;* (chess) Patt *n* || *tr* (fig) in e–e Sackgasse treiben; (chess) patt setzen
stalk [stɔk] *s* (*of grain*) Halm *m;* (*of a plant*) Stiel *m* || *tr* beschleichen; **s. game** pirschen
stall [stɔl] *s* (*for animals*) Stall *m;* (*booth*) Bude *f;* (sl) Vorwand *m* || *tr* (*a motor*) abwürgen; (*a person*) aufhalten || *intr* ausweichen; (aut) absterben; **s. for time** Zeit zu gewinnen suchen
stallion ['stæljən] *s* Hengst *m*
stalwart ['stɔlwərt] *adj* stämmig; (*supporter*) treu
stamen ['stemən] *s* Staubfaden *m*
stamina ['stæmɪnə] *s* Ausdauer *f*
stammer ['stæmər] *s* Stammeln *n* || *tr* & *intr* stammeln
stammerer ['stæmərər] *s* Stammler –in *mf*
stamp [stæmp] *s* (*mark*) Gepräge *n;* (*device for stamping*) Stempel *m;* (*for postage*) Briefmarke *f* || *tr* (*e.g., a document*) stempeln; (*a letter*) freimachen; (*the earth*) stampfen; **s. one's foot** mit dem Fuß aufstampfen; **s. out** (*a fire*) austreten; (*a rebellion*) niederschlagen
stampede [stæm'pid] *s* panische Flucht *f* || *tr* in die Flucht jagen || *intr* in wilder Flucht davonrennen
stamped′ en′velope *s* Freiumschlag *m*
stamp′ing grounds′ *spl* Lieblingsplatz *m*
stamp′ machine′ *s* Briefmarkenautomat *m*
stamp′ pad′ *s* Stempelkissen *n*
stance [stæns] *s* Haltung *f,* Stellung *f*
stanch [stɑntʃ] *tr* stillen
stand [stænd] *s* (*booth*) Stand *m;* (*platform*) Tribüne *f;* (*e.g., for bicycles*) Ständer *m;* (*view, position*) Standpunkt *m;* (*piece of furniture*) Ständer *m;* **take a s.** (on) Stellung nehmen (zu); **take one's s.** (*e.g., near the door*) sich stellen; **s. of timber** Waldbestand *m;* **stands** (sport) Tribüne *f;* **take the s.** (jur) als Zeuge auftreten || *v* (*pret* & *pp* **stood** [stʊd]) *tr* (*put*) stellen; (*the cold, hardships*) aushalten; (*a person*) leiden; **s. a chance** e–e Chance haben; **s. guard** Posten stehen; **s. one's ground** sich behaupten; **s. s.o. up** j–n aufsitzen lassen; **s. the test** sich bewähren || *intr* stehen; (*have validity*) gelten; **she wants to know where she stands** sie will wissen, wie sie daran ist; **s. aside** auf die Seite treten; **s. at attention** stillstehen; **s.**

back zurückstehen; **s. behind s.o.**
(fig) hinter j–m stehen; **s. by** (*in
readiness*) in Bereitschaft stehen; (*a
decision*) bleiben bei; (*e.g., for the
latest news*) am Apparat bleiben; **s.
by s.o.** j–m beistehen; **s. firm** fest
bleiben; **s. for** (*champion*) eintreten
für; (*tolerate*) sich [*dat*] gefallen
lassen; (*mean*) bedeuten; **s. good for**
gutstehen für; **s. idle** stillstehen; **s.
on end** sich sträuben, *e.g.,* **my hair
stood on end** mir sträubten sich die
Haare; **s. on one's head** kopfstehen;
s. out (*project*) abstehen; (*be conspicuous*) hervorstechen; **s. out
against** sich abzeichnen gegen; **s.
s.o. in good stead** j–m zugute kommen; **s. up** aufstehen; **s. up against**
aufkommen gegen; **s. up for** (*a thing*)
verfechten; (*a person*) die Stange
halten (*dat*); **s. up to s.o.** j–m die
Stirn bieten; **s. up under** aushalten
standard ['stændərd] *adj* Standard–,
Normal– || *s* Standard *m;* (*banner*)
Banner *n*
stand'ard-bear'er *s* Bannerträger *m*
stand'ard-gauge track' *s* Normalspur *f*
standardize ['stændər‚daɪz] *tr* normen
stand'ard of liv'ing *s* Lebensstandard
m
stand'ard time' *s* Normalzeit *f*
stand'-by' *adj* Reserve– || *s*—**on s. in
Bereitschaft**
standee [stæn'di] *s* Stehplatzinhaber
–in *mf*
stand'in' *s* (coll) Ersatzmann *m;* (cin,
theat) Double *n*
stand'ing *adj* (*army, water, rule*) stehend; (*committee*) ständig; (*jump*)
aus dem Stand || *s* Stehen *n;* (*social*)
Stellung *f;* (*of a team*) Stand *m;* **in
good s.** treu; **of long s.** langjährig
stand'ing or'der *s* (com) Dauerauftrag
m
stand'ing room' *s* Stehplatz *m;* **s. only**
nur noch Stehplätze
stand'-off' *s* Unentschieden *n*
stand-offish ['stænd'ɔfɪʃ] *adj* zurückhaltend
stand'out' *s* Blickfang *m*
stand'point' *s* Standpunkt *m*
stand'still' *s* Stillstand *m;* **come to a s.**
zum Stillstand kommen
stanza ['stænzə] *s* Strophe *f*
staple ['stepəl] *adj* Haupt–, Stapel– ||
s (*food*) Hauptnahrungsmittel *n;*
(*product*) Hauptprodukt *n;* (*clip*)
Heftklammer *f* || *tr* mit Draht heften
stapler ['steplər] *s* Heftmaschine *f*
star [star] *adj* Spitzen–; (astr) Stern–
|| *s* Stern *m;* (cin, rad, telv, theat)
Star *m;* **I saw stars** (fig) Sterne tanz-
ten mir vor den Augen || *v* (*pret &
pp* **starred**; *ger* **starring**) *tr* (cin, rad,
sport, telv, theat) als Star heraus-
stellen; (typ) mit Sternchen kenn-
zeichnen || *intr* Star sein
starboard ['starbərd] *adj* Steuerbord–
|| *s* Steuerbord *n*
starch [startʃ] *s* Stärke *f* || *tr* stärken
starchy ['startʃi] *adj* stärkenhaltig
stare [ster] *s* starrer Blick *m* || *tr*—

s. down durch Anstarren aus der
Fassung bringen || *intr* starren; **s. at**
anstarren; **s. into space** ins Leere
blicken, ins Blaue starren
star'fish' *s* Seestern *m*
stargazer ['star‚gezər] *s* Sterngucker
–in *mf*
stark [stark] *adj* (*landscape*) kahl;
(*sheer*) völlig || *adv* völlig
stark'-na'ked *adj* splitter(faser)nackt
starlet ['starlət] *s* Sternchen *n*
star'light' *s* Sternenlicht *n*
starling ['starlɪŋ] *s* (orn) Star *m*
star'lit' *adj* sternhell
Star' of Da'vid *s* David(s)stern *m*
starry ['stari] *adj* gestirnt; (*night*)
sternklar; (*sky*) Stern–
star'ry-eyed' *adj* verträumt
Stars' and Stripes' *spl* Sternenbanner *n*
Star'-Spangled Ban'ner *s* Sternenbanner *n*
start [start] *s* Anfang *m;* (*sudden
springing movement*) plötzliches
Hochfahren *n;* (*lead, advantage*) Vorgabe *f,* Vorsprung *m;* (*of a race*)
Start *m;* **give s.o. a s.** j–m auf die
Beine helfen || *tr* anfangen; (*a mo-
tor*) anlassen; (*a rumor*) in die Welt
setzen; (*a conversation*) anknüpfen;
s. a fire ein Feuer anmachen; (*said
of an arsonist*) e–n Brand legen ||
intr anfangen; **s. in to** (*inf*) anfangen
zu (*inf*); **s. out** (*begin*) anfangen;
(*start walking*) losgehen; **s. out on**
(*a trip*) antreten; **to s. with** zunächst
start'ing gate' *s* Startmaschine *f*
start'ing gun' *s* Startpistole *f;* **at the s.**
beim Startschuß
start'ing point' *s* Ausgangspunkt *m*
startle ['startəl] *tr* erschrecken; **be
startled** zusammenfahren
starvation [star'veʃən] *s* Hunger *m;*
die of s. verhungern
starva'tion di'et *s* Hungerkur *f*
starva'tion wag'es *spl* Hungerlohn *m*
starve [starv] *tr* verhungern lassen;
s. out aushungern || *intr* hungern;
(coll) furchtbaren Hunger haben; **s.
to death** verhungern
state [stet] *adj* staatlich, Staats–; (*as
opposed to federal*) bundesstaatlich
|| *s* (*condition*) Zustand *m;* (*govern-
ment*) Staat *m;* (*of the U.S.A.*) Bun-
desstaat *m* || *tr* angeben; (*a rule,
problem*) aufstellen; **as stated above**
wie oben angegeben
State' Depart'ment *s* Außenministerium
n
stateless ['stetlɪs] *adj* staatenlos
stately ['stetli] *adj* stattlich
statement ['stetmənt] *s* Angabe *f;*
(*from a bank*) Abrechnung *f;* (jur)
Aussage *f*
state' of affairs' *s* Lage *f*
state' of emer'gency *s* Notstand *m*
state' of health' *s* Gesundheitszustand
m
state' of mind' *s* Geisteszustand *m*
state' of war' *s* Kriegszustand *m*
state'-owned' *adj* staatseigen; (*in com-
munistic countries*) volkseigen
state' police' *s* Staatspolizei *f*

state'room' s (in a palace) Prunkzimmer n; (on a ship) Passagierkabine f

states'man s (-men) Staatsmann m

states'manlike' adj staatsmännisch

states'manship' s Staatskunst f

static ['stætɪk] adj statisch || s (rad) Nebengeräusche pl

station ['steʃən] s (social) Stellung f; (of a bus, rail line) Bahnhof m; (mil) Standort m || tr aufstellen; (mil) stationieren

stationary ['steʃə,nɛri] adj stationär

sta'tion break' s Werbepause f

stationer ['steʃənər] s Schreibwarenhändler –in mf

stationery ['steʃə,nɛri] s Briefpapier n

sta'tionery store' s Schreibwarenhandlung f

sta'tion house' s Polizeiwache f

sta'tion identifica'tion s (rad) Pausenzeichen n

sta'tionmas'ter s Bahnhofsvorsteher m

sta'tions of the cross' spl Kreuzweg m

sta'tion wag'on s Kombiwagen m

statistic [stə'tɪstɪk] s Angabe f; **statistics** (science) Statistik f || spl (data) Statistik f

statistical [stə'tɪstɪkəl] adj statistisch

statistician [,stætɪs'tɪʃən] s Statistiker –in mf

statue ['stætʃu] s Statue f

statuesque [,stætʃu'ɛsk] adj statuenhaft

stature ['stætʃər] s Gestalt f; (fig) Format n

status ['stetəs] s (in society) Stellung f; (e.g., mental) Stand m

sta'tus quo' [kwo] s Status m quo

sta'tus sym'bol s Statussymbol n

statute ['stætʃut] s Satzung f, Statut n

statutory ['stætʃu,tori] adj statutenmäßig

staunch [stɔntʃ] adj unentwegt

stave [stev] s (of a barrel) Daube f; (of a chair) Steg m; (of a ladder) Sprosse f; (mus) Notensystem n || tr—s. off abwenden

stay [ste] s (visit) Aufenthalt m; (prop) Stütze f; (of execution) Aufschub m || intr bleiben; **have to s. in** (after school) nachsitzen müssen; **s. away** wegbleiben; **s. behind** zurückbleiben; (in school) sitzenbleiben

stay'-at-home' s Stubenhocker –in mf

stead [stɛd] s Statt f; **in s.o.'s s.** an j–s Statt

stead'fast' adj standhaft

stead·y ['stɛdi] adj fest, beständig; (hands) sicher; (ladder) fest; (pace) gleichmäßig; (progress) ständig; (nerves) stark; (prices) stabil; (work) regelmäßig; **s. customer** Stammkunde m, Stammkundin f; **s. now!** immer langsam! || v (pret & pp –ied) tr festigen

steak [stek] s Beefsteak n

steal [stil] s—**it's a s.** (coll) das ist geschenkt || v (pret **stole** [stol]; pp **stolen**) tr stehlen; (a kiss) rauben; **s. s.o.'s thunder** j–m den Wind aus den Segeln nehmen; **s. the show** den Vogel abschießen || intr stehlen; **s.**

away wegstehlen; **s. up on s.o.** sich an j–n heranschleichen

stealth [stɛlθ] s—**by s.** heimlich

stealthy ['stɛlθi] adj verstohlen

steam [stim] s Dampf m; (vapor) Dunst m; (fig) Kraft f; **full s. ahead!** Volldampf voraus!; **let off s.** Dampf ablassen; (fig) sich [dat] Luft machen; **put on s.** (fig) Dampf dahinter machen || tr dämpfen; (culin) dünsten; **s. up** beschlagen || intr dampfen; (culin) dünsten; **s. up** sich beschlagen

steam' bath' s Dampfbad n

steam'boat' s Dampfer m

steam' en'gine s Dampfmaschine f

steamer ['stimər] s Dampfer m

steam' heat' s Dampfheizung f

steam' i'ron s Dampfbügeleisen n

steam' roll'er s (& fig) Dampfwalze f || tr glattwalzen; (fig) niederwalzen

steam'ship' s Dampfschiff n

steam'ship line' s Dampfschiffahrtslinie f

steam' shov'el s Dampflöffelbagger m

steamy ['stimi] adj dampfig, dunstig

steed [stid] s Streitroß n

steel [stil] adj stählern, Stahl– || s Stahl m || tr stählen; **s. oneself against s.th.** sich gegen etw wappnen

steel' wool' s Stahlwolle f

steel'works' spl Stahlwerk n

steely ['stili] adj (fig) stählern

steelyard ['stiljərd] s Schnellwaage f

steep [stip] adj steil; (prices) happig || tr (immerse) eintauchen; (soak) einweichen; **be steeped in** (e.g., prejudice) durchdrungen sein von; (be expert in) ein Kenner sein (genit); **s. oneself in** sich versenken in (acc)

steeple ['stipəl] s Kirchturm m

stee'plechase' s Hindernisrennen n

steer [stɪr] s Stier m || tr lenken, steuern; **s. a middle course** e–n Mittelweg einschlagen || intr lenken, steuern; **s. clear of** vermeiden

steerage ['stɪrɪdʒ] s Zwischendeck n

steer'ing wheel' s Steuerrad n

stellar ['stɛlər] adj (role) Star–; (attraction) Haupt–; (astr) Stern(en)–

stem [stem] s (of a plant) Halm m; (of a word; of a tree) Stamm m; (of a leaf, fruit; of a glass; of a smoke pipe) Stiel m; (of a watch) Aufziehwelle f; (naut) Steven m; **from s. to stern** von vorn bis achtern || v (pret & pp **stemmed**; ger **stemming**) tr (check) hemmen; (fruit) entstielen; (the flow) (an)stauen; (the blood) stillen; (in skiing) stemmen || intr— **s. from** (ab)stammen von

stench [stɛntʃ] s Gestank m

sten·cil ['stɛnsɪl] s (for printing) Schablone f; (for typing) Matrize f || v (pret & pp –cil[l]ed; ger –cil[l]ing) tr mittels Schablone aufmalen

stenographer [stə'nɑgrəfər] s Stenograph –in mf

stenography [stə'nɑgrəfi] s Stenographie f

step [stɛp] s Schritt m; (of a staircase) Stufe f; (footprint) Fußtritt m;

(*measure*) Maßnahme *f;* **be out of s.** nicht Schritt halten; **in. s.** im Takt; **keep in s. with the times** mit der Zeit Schritt halten; **s. by s.** schrittweise; **watch your s.!** Vorsicht! ‖ *v* (*pret & pp* **stepped;** *ger* **stepping**) *tr*—**s. down** (elec) heruntertransformieren; **s. off** abschreiten ‖ *intr* schreiten, treten; **s. aside** beiseitetreten; **s. back** zurücktreten; **s. forward** vortreten; **s. on** betreten; **s. on it** (coll) sich beeilen; **s. on s.o.'s toes** (fig) j–m auf die Zehen treten; **s. out** hinausgehen; **s. out on** (*a marriage partner*) betrügen
step'broth'er *s* Stiefbruder *m*
step'child' *s* (**-chil'dren**) Stiefkind *n*
step'daugh'ter *s* Stieftochter *f*
step'fa'ther *s* Stiefvater *m*
step'lad'der *s* Stehleiter *f*
step'moth'er *s* Stiefmutter *f*
steppe [step] *s* Steppe *f*
step'ping stone' *s* Trittstein *m;* (fig) Sprungbrett *n*
step'sis'ter *s* Stiefschwester *f*
step'son' *s* Stiefsohn *m*
stere·o ['sterɪ‚o] *adj* Stereo– ‖ *s* (**-os**) (*sound*) Stereoton *m*, Raumton *m;* (*reproduction*) Raumtonwiedergabe *f;* (*set*) Stereoapparat *m*
stereotyped ['sterɪ·ə‚taɪpt] *adj* (& fig) stereotyp
sterile ['sterɪl] *adj* keimfrei
sterility [ste'rɪlɪti] *s* Sterilität *f*
sterilize ['sterɪ‚laɪz] *tr* sterilisieren
sterling ['stʌrlɪŋ] *adj* (fig) gediegen ‖ *s* (*currency*) Sterling *m;* (*sterling silver*) Sterlingsilber *n;* (*articles of sterling silver*) Sterlingsilberwaren *pl*
stern [stʌrn] *adj* streng; (*look*) finster ‖ *s* (naut) Heck *n*
stethoscope ['steθə‚skop] *s* Stethoskop *n*
stevedore ['stivə‚dor] *s* Stauer *m*
stew [st(j)u] *s* Ragout *n*, Stew *n* ‖ *tr & intr* dünsten; (& fig) schmoren
steward ['st(j)u·ərd] *s* (aer, naut) Steward *m;* (*of an estate*) Gutsverwalter *m;* (*of a club*) Tafelmeister *m*
stewardess ['st(j)u·ərdɪs] *s* (aer, naut) Stewardeß *f*
stewed' fruit' *s* Kompott *n*
stick [stɪk] *s* Stecken *m*, Stock *m;* (*for punishment*) Prügel *pl;* (*of candy or gum*) Stange *f;* **the sticks** (coll) die Provinz *f* ‖ *tr* (*with a sharp point; into one's pocket*) stecken; (*paste*) (**on**) ankleben (*an acc*); **s. it out** durchhalten; **s. one's finger** sich in den Finger stechen; **s. out** herausstrecken; **s. up** (sl) überfallen und berauben ‖ *intr* (*adhere*) kleben; (*be stuck, be tight*) klemmen; **nothing sticks in his mind** (coll) bei ihm bleibt nichts haften; **s. around** (coll) in der Nähe bleiben; **s. by** (coll) bleiben bei; **s. close to** sich heften an (*acc*); **s. out** (*said of ears*) abstehen; (*be visible*) heraushängen; **s. to** (fig) beharren auf (*dat*); **s. together** zusammenkleben; (fig) zusammenhalten; **s. up for** sich einsetzen für

sticker ['stɪkər] *s* Klebezettel *m*
stick'-in-the-mud' *s* (coll) Schlafmütze *f*
stickler ['stɪklər] *s* (**for**) Pedant *m* (in *dat*)
stick'pin' *s* Krawattennadel *f*
stick'-up' *s* (sl) Raubüberfall *m*
sticky ['stɪki] *adj* klebrig; (*air*) schwül; (*ticklish*) heikel
stiff [stɪf] *adj* steif; (*difficult*) schwer; (*drink*) stark; (*opposition*) hartnäckig; (*sentence*) streng; (*bearing*) steif; (*price*) hoch; **s. as a board** stocksteif ‖ *s* (*corpse*) (sl) Leiche *f;* **big s.** (sl) blöder Kerl *m*
stiffen ['stɪfən] *tr* versteifen ‖ *intr* sich versteifen
stiffly ['stɪfli] *adv* gezwungen
stiff'-necked' *adj* mit steifem Hals; (fig) eigensinnig
stifle ['staɪfəl] *tr* (*a yawn*) unterdrücken; (*a person*) ersticken
stig·ma ['stɪgmə] *s* (**-mas** & **mata** [mətə]) Brandmal *n;* **stigmata** Wundmale *pl* Christi
stigmatize ['stɪgmə‚taɪz] *tr* brandmarken
stile [staɪl] *s* Stiege *f*
stilet·to [stɪ'leto] *s* (**-os**) Stilett *n*
still [stɪl] *adj* still, ruhig ‖ *adv* (*up to this time, as yet, even*) noch; (*yet, nevertheless*) dennoch; **keep s.** stillbleiben ‖ *s* (*stillness*) Stille *f;* (*for whiskey*) Brennapparat *m;* (cin) Einzelphotographie *f;* (phot) Standphoto *n* ‖ *tr* stillen
still'born' *adj* totgeboren
still' life' *s* (**still lifes** & **still lives**) Stilleben *n*
stilt [stɪlt] *s* Stelze *f*
stilt'ed *adj* (*style*) geschraubt; (archit) auf Pfeilern ruhend
stimulant ['stɪmjələnt] *s* Reizmittel *n;* **act as a s.** anregend wirken
stimulate ['stɪmjə‚let] *tr* anregen
stimulation [‚stɪmjə'leʃən] *s* Anregung *f*
stimu·lus ['stɪmjələs] *s* (**-li** [‚laɪ]) (& fig) Reizmittel *n;* (fig) Ansporn *m*
sting [stɪŋ] *s* Biß *m*, Stich *m;* (*stinging organ*) Stachel *m* ‖ *v* (*pret & pp* **stung** [stʌŋ]) *tr & intr* stechen
stingy ['stɪndʒi] *adj* geizig
stink [stɪŋk] *s* Gestank *m;* (sl) Krach *m* ‖ *v* (*pret* **stank** [stæŋk]; **stunk** [stʌŋk]) *tr*—**s. up** verstänkern ‖ *intr* stinken
stinker ['stɪŋkər] *s* (sl) Stinker *m*
stinky ['stɪŋki] *adj* stinkend, stinkig
stint [stɪnt] *s* bestimmte Arbeit *f;* **without s.** freigebig ‖ *tr* einschränken ‖ *intr* (**on**) knausern (mit)
stipend ['staɪpənd] *s* (*salary*) Gehalt *n;* (*of a scholarship*) Zuwendung *f*
stipple ['stɪpəl] *tr* punktieren
stipulate ['stɪpjə‚let] *tr* bedingen; **as stipulated** wie vertraglich festgelegt
stipulation [‚stɪpjə'leʃən] *s* Bedingung *f*
stir [stʌr] *s* (*movement*) Bewegung *f;* (*unrest*) Unruhe *f;* (*commotion, ex-*

citement) Aufsehen *n;* **create quite a s.** großes Aufsehen erregen ‖ *v* (*pret & pp* **stirred; ger stirring**) *tr* e.g., *with a spoon*) (um)rühren; (*said of a breeze*) bewegen; (*the fire*) schüren; **s. up** (*hatred*) entfachen; (*trouble*) stiften; (*people*) aufhetzen ‖ *intr* sich rühren

stir'ring *adj* erregend; (*times*) bewegt; (*speech*) mitreißend; (*song*) schwungvoll

stirrup ['stʌrəp] *s* Steigbügel *m*

stitch [stɪtʃ] *s* Stich *m;* (*in knitting*) Masche *f;* **stitches** (surg) Naht *f;* **s. in the side** Seitenstechen *n* ‖ *tr* heften; (surg) nähen

stock [stɑk] *s* (*supplies*) Lager *n;* (*of a gun*) Schaft *m;* (*lineage*) Zucht *f;* (*of paper*) Papierstoff *m;* (culin) Fond *m;* (st. exch.) Aktie *f;* **in s.** vorrätig, auf Lager; **not put much s. in** nicht viel Wert legen auf (*acc*); **out of s.** nicht (mehr) vorrätig; (*books*) vergriffen; **stocks** (hist) Stock *m;* **take s.** den Bestand aufnehmen; **take s. of** (fig) in Betracht ziehen ‖ *tr* auf Lager halten; (*a stream*) (mit Fischen) besetzen; (*a farm*) ausstatten ‖ *intr*—**s. up (on)** sich eindecken (mit)

stockade [stɑ'ked] *s* Palisade *f;* (mil) Gefängnis *n*

stock'breed'er *s* Viehzüchter –in *mf*

stock'brok'er *s* Börsenmakler –in *mf*

stock' car' *s* (aut) Serienwagen *m;* (sport) als Rennwagen hergerichteter Personenkraftwagen *m*

stock' com'pany *s* (com) Aktiengesellschaft *f;* (theat) Repertoiregruppe *f*

stock' div'idend *s* Aktiendividende *f*

stock' exchange' *s* Börse *f*

stock'hold'er *s* Aktionär –in *mf*

stock'ing *s* Strumpf *m*

stock' in trade' *s* Warenbestand *m;* (fig) Rüstzeug *n*

stock'pile' *s* Vorrat *m* ‖ *tr* aufstapeln

stock'room' *s* Lagerraum *m*

stocky ['stɑki] *adj* untersetzt

stock'yard' *s* Viehhof *m*

stodgy ['stɑdʒi] *adj* gezwungen

stogy ['stogi] *s* (coll) Glimmstengel *m*

stoic ['sto·ɪk] *adj* stoisch ‖ *s* Stoiker *m*

stoke [stok] *tr* (*a fire*) schüren; (*a furnace*) heizen

stoker ['stokər] *s* Heizer *m*

stole [stol] *s* (*woman's fur piece*) Pelzstola *f;* (eccl) Stola *f*

stolid ['stɑlɪd] *adj* unempfindlich

stomach ['stʌmək] *s* Magen *m;* (fig) (for) Lust *f* (zu) ‖ *tr* (*food*) verdauen; (fig) vertragen

stom'ach ache' *s* Magenschmerzen *pl*

stone [ston] *adj* steinern ‖ *s* Stein *m;* (*of fruit*) Kern *m;* (pathol) Stein *m* ‖ *tr* steinigen; (*fruit*) entsteinen

stone' age' *s* Steinzeit *f*

stone'-broke' *adj* (coll) völlig abgebrannt

stone'-deaf' *adj* stocktaub

stone' ma'son *s* Steinmetz *m*

stone' quar'ry *s* Steinbruch *m*

stone's' throw' *s* Katzensprung *m*

stony ['stoni] *adj* steinig

stooge [studʒ] *s* Lakai *m*

stool [stul] *s* Schemel *m;* (e.g., *at a bar*) Hocker *m;* (*bowel movement*) Stuhl *m*

stool' pi'geon *s* Polizeispitzel *m*

stoop [stup] *s* Beugung *f;* (*condition of the body*) gebeugte Körperhaltung *f;* (*porch*) kleine Verande *f* ‖ *intr* sich bücken; (*demean oneself*) sich erniedrigen

stoop'-shoul'dered *adj* gebeugt

stop [stɑp] *s* (*for a bus or streetcar*) Haltestelle *f;* (*layover*) Aufenthalt *m;* (*station*) Station *f;* (*of an organ*) Register *m;* (ling) Verschlußlaut *m;* **bring to a s.** zum Halten bringen; **come to a s.** anhalten; **put a s. to** ein Ende machen (*dat*) ‖ *v* (*pret & pp* **stopped; ger stopping**) *tr* (*an activity*) aufhören mit; (*ger*) aufhören (zu *inf*); (e.g., *a thief, car*) anhalten; (*bring to a stop with difficulty*) zum Halten bringen; (*delay, detain*) aufhalten; (*a leak*) stopfen; (*a check*) sperren; (*payment*) einstellen; (*the blood*) stillen; (*traffic*) lahmlegen; **s. down** (phot) abblenden; **s. s.o. from** (*ger*) j-n davonhalten zu (*inf*) ‖ *intr* (*cease*) aufhören; (*come to a stop; break down*) stehenbleiben; (*said of a person stopping for a short time or of a vehicle at an unscheduled stop*) anhalten; (*said of a vehicle at a scheduled stop*) halten; **s. at nothing** vor nichts zurückschrecken; **s. dead** plötzlich stehenbleiben; **s. in** vorbeikommen; **s. off at** e-n kurzen Halt machen bei

stop'gap' *adj* Not–, Behelfs– ‖ *s* Notbehelf *m*

stop'light' *s* (*on a car*) Bremslicht *n;* (*traffic light*) Verkehrsampel *f*

stop'o'ver *s* Fahrtunterbrechung *f;* (aer) Zwischenlandung *f*

stoppage ['stɑpɪdʒ] *s* (*of a pipe*) Verstopfung *f;* (*of payment, of work*) Einstellung *f;* (pathol) Verstopfung *f*

stopper ['stɑpər] *s* Stöpsel *m;* (*made of cork*) Korken *m*

stop' sign' *s* Haltezeichen *n*

stop'watch' *s* Stoppuhr *f*

storage ['storɪdʒ] *s* Lagerung *f*

stor'age bat'tery *s* Akkumulator *m*

stor'age charge' *s* Lagergebühr *f*

stor'age room' *s* Rumpelkammer *f;* (com) Lagerraum *m*

stor'age tank' *s* Sammelbehälter *m*

store [stor] *s* (*small shop*) Laden *m;* (*large shop*) Geschäft *n;* (*supply*) Vorrat *m;* **be in s. for** bevorstehen (*dat*); **have in s. for** bereithalten für; **set great s. by** viel Wert legen auf (*acc*); **s. of knowledge** Wissenschatz *m* ‖ *tr* einlagern; (*in the attic*) auf den Speicher stellen; **s. up** aufspeichern

store'house' *s* Lagerhaus *n;* (fig) Schatz *m*, Fundgrube *f*

store'keep'er *s* Ladeninhaber –in *mf*

store'room' s Lagerraum m, Vorrats-
raum m
stork [stɔrk] s Storch m
storm [stɔrm] s Sturm m; (thunderstorm) Gewitter n; (fig) Sturm m;
take by s. (& fig) im Sturm nehmen
|| tr (er)stürmen || intr stürmen
storm' cloud' s Gewitterwolke f
storm' door' s Doppeltür f
storm' warn'ing s Sturmwarnung f
storm' win'dow s Doppelfenster n
stormy ['stɔrmi] adj stürmisch
story ['stori] s Geschichte f; (floor)
Stock m, Stockwerk n; **that's another
s.** das ist e-e Sache für sich
sto'rybook' s Geschichtenbuch n
sto'rytell'er s Erzähler –in mf
stout [staut] adj beleibt; (heart) tapfer
|| s Starkbier n
stout'-heart'ed adj beherzt
stove [stov] s Ofen m, Küchenherd m
stove'pipe' s Ofenrohr n; (coll) Angst-
röhre f
stow [sto] tr stauen; **s. away** verstauen
|| intr—**s. away** als blinder Passagier
mitreisen
stowage ['sto·ɪdʒ] s Stauen n; (costs)
Staugebühr f
stow'away' s blinder Passagier m
straddle ['strædəl] tr mit gespreizten
Beinen sitzen auf (dat)
strafe [stref] tr im Tiefflug mit Bord-
waffen angreifen
straggle ['strægəl] intr abschweifen
straggler ['stræglər] s Nachzügler –in
mf; (mil) Versprengte m
straight [stret] adj gerade; (honest)
aufrecht; (candid) offen; (hair) glatt;
(story) wahr; (uninterrupted) ununterbrochen; (whiskey) unverdünnt
|| adv (directly) direkt; (without in-
terruption) ununterbrochen; **give it
to s.o. s.** j-m die ungeschminkte
Wahrheit sagen; **go s.** (fig) seinen
geraden Weg gehen; **is my hat on s.?**
sitzt mein Hut richtig?; **make s. for**
zuhalten auf (acc); **set the record s.**
den Sachverhalt klarstellen; **s. ahead**
(immer) geradeaus; **s. as an arrow**
pfeilgerade; **s. from the horse's
mouth** (coll) aus erster Hand; **s.
home** schnurstracks nach Hause; **s.
off** ohne weiteres || s (cards) Buch n
straight'away' adv geradewegs, sofort
|| s (sport) Gerade f
straighten ['stretən] tr gerade machen;
(e.g., a tablecloth) glattziehen; **s. out**
(fig) wieder in Ordnung bringen; **s.
s.o.'s tie** j-m die Krawatte zurecht-
rücken; **s. up** (a room) aufräumen ||
intr gerade werden; **s. up** sich aufrichten
straight' face' s—**keep a s.** keine
Miene verziehen
straight'for'ward adj aufrichtig
straight' left' s (box) linke Gerade f
straight' man' s Stichwortgeber m
straight' ra'zor s Rasiermesser n
straight' right' s (box) rechte Gerade f
straight'way' adv auf der Stelle
strain [stren] s Belastung f; (of a muscle or tendon) Zerrung f; (task re-

quiring effort) (coll) Strapaze f;
(stock, family) Linie f; (trait) Erbei-
genschaft f; (bot) Art f; **without s.**
mühelos || tr (filter) durchseihen;
(the eyes, nerves) überanstrengen;
s. oneself (make a great effort) sich
überanstrengen; (in lifting) sich
überheben; **s. the truth** übertreiben
|| intr sich anstrengen; **s. after** sich
abmühen um; **s. at** ziehen an (dat),
zerren an (dat)
strained adj (smile) gezwungen; (relations) gespannt
strainer ['strenər] s Seiher m, Filter m
strait [stret] s Straße f; **financial straits**
finanzielle Schwierigkeiten pl; **straits**
Meerenge f
strait' jack'et s Zwangsjacke f
strait'-laced' adj sittenstreng
strand [strænd] s Strähne f; (beach)
Strand m; **s. of pearls** Perlenschnur
f || tr auf den Strand setzen; (fig)
stranden lassen; **be stranded** (fig) in
der Patsche sitzen; **get stranded** auflaufen; **leave s.o. stranded** j-n im
Stich lassen
strange [strendʒ] adj (quaint) sonderbar; (foreign) fremd; **s. character**
Sonderling m || adv—**s. to say** merk-
würdigerweise
stranger ['strendʒər] s Fremde mf
strangle ['stræŋgəl] tr erwürgen || intr
ersticken
stran'glehold' s Würgegriff m
strap [stræp] s Riemen m, Gurt m; (of
metal) Band n || v (pret & pp
strapped; ger **strapping**) tr (to) anschnallen (an acc); (a razor) abziehen
strap'ping adj stramm
stratagem ['strætədʒəm] s Kriegslist f
strategic(al) [strə'tidʒɪk(əl)] adj strategisch
strategist ['strætɪdʒɪst] s Stratege m
strategy ['strætɪdʒi] s Strategie f
stratification [,strætɪfɪ'keʃən] s Schich-
tung f
strati·fy ['strætɪ,faɪ] v (pret & pp
-fied) tr schichten || intr Schichten
bilden
stratosphere ['strætə,sfɪr] s Strato-
sphäre f
stra·tum ['stretem], ['strætəm] s (-ta
[tə] & -tums) Schicht f
straw [strɔ] adj (e.g., hat, man, mat)
Stroh– || s Stroh n; (single stalk; for
drinking) Strohhalm m; **that's the
last s.!** das schlägt dem Faß den
Boden aus!
straw'ber'ry s Erdbeere f
straw'berry blond' adj rotblond
straw' mat'tress s Strohsack m
straw' vote' s Probeabstimmung f
stray [stre] adj (e.g., bullet) verirrt;
(cat, dog) streunend; **s. shell** (mil)
Ausreißer m || s verirrtes Tier n ||
intr herumirren; (fig) abschweifen
streak [strik] s Streifen m; **like a s.**
wie der Blitz; **s. of bad luck** Pech-
strähne f; **s. of luck** Glückssträhne
f; **s. of light** Lichtstreifen m || tr
streifen || intr streifig werden; **s.
along** vorbeisausen

streaky ['striki] *adj* gestreift; (*uneven*) (coll) ungleich(mäßig)

stream [strim] *s* Fluß *m;* (*of people, cars, air, blood, lava*) Strom *m;* (*of words*) Schwall *m;* (*of tears*) Flut *f;* (*of a liquid*) Strahl *m* || *intr* (aus)-strömen

streamer ['strimər] *s* (*pennant*) Wimpel *m;* (*ribbon*) herabhängendes Band *n;* (*rolled crepe paper*) Papierschlange *f*

stream'line' *tr* in Stromlinienform bringen; (fig) reorganizieren

stream'lined' *adj* stromlinienförmig

street [strit] *s* Straße *f*

street'car' *s* Straßenbahn *f*

street' clean'er *s* Straßenkehrer –in *mf;* (*truck*) Straßenkehrmaschine *f*

street' fight' *s* Straßenschlacht *f*

street'light' *s* Straßenlaterne *f*

street' sign' *s* Straßenschild *n*

street' ven'dor *s* Straßenhändler –in *mf*

street'walk'er *s* Straßendirne *f*

strength [strɛŋθ] *s* Kraft *f;* (*strong point; potency of alcohol; moral or mental power*) Stärke *f;* (mil) Kopfstärke *f;* **bodily s.** Körperkraft *f;* **on the s. of** auf Grund (*genit*)

strengthen ['strɛŋθən] *tr* stärken; (fig) bestärken || *intr* stärker werden

strenuous ['strɛnju·əs] *adj* anstrengend; **s. effort** Kraftanstrengung *f*

stress [strɛs] *s* (*emphasis, weight*) Nachdruck *m;* (*mental*) Belastung *f;* (mus, pros) Ton *m,* Betonung *f;* (phys) Beanspruchung *f,* Spannung *f* || *tr* (& mus, pros) betonen

stress' ac'cent *s* Betonungsakzent *m*

stress' mark' *s* Betonungszeichen *n*

stretch [strɛtʃ] *s* (*of road*) Strecke *f;* (*of the limbs*) Strecken *n;* (*of water*) Fläche *f;* (*of a racetrack*) Gerade *f;* (*of years*) Zeitspanne *f;* **do a s.** (sl) brummen; **in one s.** in e–m Zug || *tr* (*a rope*) spannen; (*one's neck*) rekken; (*shoes, gloves*) ausdehnen; (*wire*) ziehen; (*strings of an instrument*) straffziehen; **s. a point** es nicht allzu genau nehmen; **s. oneself** sich strecken; **s. one's legs** sich [*dat*] die Beine vertreten; **s. out** (*e.g., hands*) ausstrecken || *intr* sich (aus)-dehnen; (*said of a person*) sich strecken; **s. out on** sich ausstrecken auf (*dat*)

stretcher ['strɛtʃər] *s* Tragbahre *f*

stretch'erbear'er *s* Krankenträger *m*

strew [stru] *v* (*pret* strewed; *pp* strewed & strewn) *tr* (aus)streuen; **s. with** bestreuen mit

stricken ['strɪkən] *adj* (**with** *e.g., misfortune*) heimgesucht (von); (**with** *e.g., fear, grief*) ergriffen (von); (**with** *a disease*) befallen (von)

strict [strɪkt] *adj* streng; **in s. confidence** streng vertraulich

strictly ['strɪktli] *adv* streng; **s. speaking** genau genommen

stricture ['strɪktʃər] *s* (**on**) kritische Bemerkung *f* (über *acc*)

stride [straɪd] *s* Schritt *m;* **hit one's s.** auf Touren kommen; **make great**

strides große Fortschritte machen; **take in s.** ruhig hinnehmen || *v* (*pret* strode [strod]; *pp* stridden ['strɪdən]) *intr* schreiten; **s. along** tüchtig ausschreiten

strident ['straɪdənt] *adj* schrill

strife [straɪf] *s* Streit *m,* Hader *m*

strike [straɪk] *s* (*work stoppage*) Streik *m;* (*blow*) Schlag *m;* (*discovery, e.g., of oil*) Fund *m;* (baseball) Fehlschlag *m;* **go on s.** in Streik treten || *v* (*pret & pp* struck [strʌk]) *tr* (*a person, the hours, coins, strings of an instrument*) schlagen; (*a match*) anstreichen; (*a bargain*) schließen; (*a note*) greifen; (*go on strike against*) bestreiken; (*a tent*) abbrechen; (*oil*) stoßen auf (*acc*); (*run into*) auffahren auf (*acc*); (*s.o. blind, dumb*) machen; (*s.o. with fear*) erfüllen; (*a blow*) versetzen; (*a pose*) einnehmen; (*seem to s.o.*) erscheinen (*dat*); **s. it rich** auf e–e Goldader stoßen; **s. fear into s.o.** j–m e–n Schrecken einjagen; **s. up** (*a conversation, an acquaintance*) anknüpfen; (*a song*) anstimmen || *intr* (*said of a person or clock*) schlagen; (*said of workers*) streiken; (*said of lightning*) einschlagen; **s. home** Eindruck machen; **s. out** (& fig) fehlschlagen

strike'break'er *s* Streikbrecher –in *mf*

striker ['straɪkər] *s* Streikende *mf*

strik'ing *adj* auffallend; (*example*) treffend; (*workers*) streikend

strik'ing pow'er *s* Schlagkraft *f*

string [strɪŋ] *s* Bindfaden *m;* (*row, series*) Reihe *f;* (*of a bow*) Sehne *f;* (*of a musical instrument*) Saite *f;* **pull strings** (fig) der Drahtzieher sein; **s. of pearls** Perlenkette *f;* **strings** (mus) Streicher *pl;* **with no strings attached** ohne einschränkende Bedingungen || *v* (*pret & pp* strung [strʌŋ]) *tr* (*pearls*) auf e–e Schnur (auf)reihen; (*a bow*) spannen; **s. along** hinhalten; **s. up** (coll) aufknüpfen

string' band' *s* Streichorchester *n*

string' bean' *s* grüne Bohne *f;* (*tall, thin person*) Bohnenstange *f*

stringed' in'strument *s* Saiteninstrument *n*

stringent ['strɪndʒənt] *adj* streng

string' quartet' *s* Streichquartett *n*

stringy ['strɪŋi] *adj* (*vegetables*) holzig; (*meat*) sehnig; (*hair*) zottelig

strip [strɪp] *s* Streifen *m* || *v* (*pret & pp* stripped; *ger* stripping) *tr* (off) abziehen; (*clothes*) (off) abstreifen; (*a thread*) überdrehen; (*gears*) beschädigen; **s. down** abmontieren; **s.o. of office** j–n seines Amtes entkleiden || *intr* sich ausziehen

stripe [straɪp] *s* Streifen *m;* (*elongated welt*) Striemen *m;* (mil) Tresse *f* || *tr* streifen

strip' mine' *s* Tagebau *m*

stripper ['strɪpər] *s* Stripperin *f*

strip'tease' *s* Entkleidungsnummer *f*

stripteaser ['strɪp ,tizər] *s* Stripperin *f*

strive [straɪv] *v* (*pret* strove [strov];

pp **striven** ['strɪvən]) *intr* **(for)** streben (nach); **s. to** (*inf*) sich bemühen
zu (*inf*)
stroke [strok] *s* Schlag *m*; (*caress with
the hand*) Streicheln *n*; (*of a piston*)
Hub *m*; (*of a pen, brush*) Strich *m*;
(*of a sword*) Hieb *m*; (*in swimming*)
Schwimmstoß *m*; (*of the leg*) Bein-
stoß *m*; (*of an oar*) Schlag *m*; (pathol)
Schlaganfall *m*; **at a single** *m*; mit
e-m Schlag; **at the s. of twelve**
Schlag zwölf Uhr; **not do a s. of
work** keinen Strich tun; **she'll have
a s.** (coll) dann trifft sie der Schlag;
s. of genius Genieblitz *m*; **s. of luck**
Glücksfall *m*; **with a s. of the pen**
mit e-m Federstrich ‖ *tr* streicheln
stroll [strol] *s* Spaziergang *m* ‖ *intr*
spazieren
stroller ['strolər] *s* Spaziergänger –in
mf; (*for a baby*) Kindersportwagen
m
strong [strɔŋ] *adj* kräftig; (*firm*) fest;
(*drink, smell, light, wind, feeling*)
stark; (*glasses*) scharf; (*wine*) schwer;
(*suspicion*) dringend; (*memory*) gut;
(*candidate*) aussichtsreich; (*argument*) triftig
strong'-arm' *adj* (e.g., *methods*)
Zwangs–
strong'box' *s* Geldschrank *m*
strong'hold' *s* Feste *f*; (fig) Hochburg
f
strong' lan'guage *s* Kraftausdrücke *pl*
strongly ['strɔŋli] *adv* nachdrücklich;
feel s. about sich sehr einsetzen für
strong'-mind'ed *adj* willensstark
strontium ['strɑn/ɪ·əm] *s* Strontium *n*
strop [strɑp] *s* Streichriemen *m* ‖ *v*
(*pret & pp* **stropped**; *ger* **stropping**)
tr abziehen
strophe ['strofi] *s* Strophe *f*
structural ['strʌkt/ərəl] *adj* strukturell,
Bau–
structure ['strʌkt/ər] *s* Struktur *f*;
(*building*) Bau *m*
struggle ['strʌgəl] *s* Kampf *m* ‖ *intr*
(for) kämpfen (um); **s. against** an-
kämpfen gegen; **s. to one's feet** sich
mit Mühe erheben
strum [strʌm] *v* (*pret & pp* **strummed**;
ger **strumming**) *tr* klimpern auf (*dat*)
strumpet ['strʌmpɪt] *s* Dirne *f*
strut [strʌt] *s* (*brace*) Strebebalken *m*;
(*haughty walk*) stolzer Gang *m* ‖ *v*
(*pret & pp* **strutted**; *ger* **strutting**)
intr stolzieren
strychnine ['strɪknaɪn] *s* Strychnin *n*
stub [stʌb] *s* (*of a checkbook*) Abschnitt *m*; (*of a ticket*) Kontroll-
abschnitt *m*; (*of a candle, pencil,
cigarette*) Stummel *m* ‖ *v* (*pret &
pp* **stubbed**; *ger* **stubbing**) *tr*—**s. one's
toe** sich an der Zehe stoßen
stubble ['stʌbəl] *s* Stoppel *f*; (*facial
hair*) Bartstoppeln *pl*
stubbly ['stʌbli] *adj* stopp(e)lig
stubborn ['stʌbərn] *adj* eigensinnig;
(e.g., *resistance*) hartnäckig; (*hair*)
widerspenstig
stubby ['stʌbi] *adj* kurz und dick;
(*person*) untersetzt

stuc•co ['stʌko] *s* (**-coes** & **-cos**) Verputz *m* ‖ *tr* verputzen
stuc'co work' *s* Verputzarbeit *f*
stuck [stʌk] *adj*—**be s.** feststecken;
(*said, e.g., of a lock*) klemmen; **be
s. on** vernarrt sein in (*acc*); **get s.**
steckenbleiben
stuck'-up' *adj* (coll) hochnäsig
stud [stʌd] *s* (*ornament*) Ziernagel *m*;
(*horse*) Zuchthengst *m*; (archit)
Wandpfosten *m* ‖ *v* (*pret & pp*
studded; *ger* **studding**) *tr* mit Zier-
nägeln verzieren
stud' bolt' *s* Schraubenbolzen *m*
student ['st(j)udənt] *adj* Studenten– ‖
s (*in college*) Student –in *mf*; (*in
grammar or high school*) Schüler
–in *mf*; (*scholar*) Gelehrte *mf*
stu'dent bod'y *s* Studentenschaft *f*
stu'dent nurse' *s* Krankenpflegerin *f* in
Ausbildung
stud' farm' *s* Gestüt *n*
stud'horse' *s* Zuchthengst *m*
stud'ied *adj* gesucht
studi•o ['st(j)udɪ ,o] *s* (**-os**) (fa, phot)
Atelier *n*; (cin, fa, phot, telv) Studio
n
studious ['st(j)udɪ·əs] *adj* fleißig
stud•y ['stʌdi] *s* Studium *n*; (*room*)
Studierzimmer *n*; (paint) Studie *f* ‖
v (*pret & pp* **-ied**) *tr & intr* studieren
stuff [stʌf] *s* Stoff *m*; (coll) Kram *m*;
do your s.! (coll) schieß los!; **know
one's s.** (coll) sich auskennen ‖ *tr*
(*animals*) ausstopfen; (*a cushion*)
polstern; (e.g., *cotton in the ears*)
sich [*dat*] stopfen; (culin) füllen;
s. oneself sich vollstopfen
stuffed' shirt' *s* steifer, eingebildeter
Mensch *m*
stuff'ing *s* Polstermaterial *n*; (culin)
Fülle *f*
stuffy ['stʌfi] *adj* (*room*) stickig; (*nose*)
verstopft; (*person*) steif
stumble ['stʌmbəl] *intr* stolpern; (*in
reading*) holpern; **s. across** stoßen
auf (*acc*)
stum'bling block' *s* Stein *m* des An-
stoßes
stump [stʌmp] *s* (*of an arm, tree, cigarette, pencil*) Stummel *m* ‖ *tr* (*a cigarette*) ausdrücken; (*nonplus*) verblüffen; (*a district, state*) als Wahlredner bereisen
stump' speak'er *s* Wahlredner –in *mf*
stun [stʌn] *v* (*pret & pp* **stunned**; *ger*
stunning) *tr* betäuben
stun'ning *adj* (coll) phantastisch
stunt [stʌnt] *s* Kunststück *n*; **do stunts**
Kunststücke vorführen ‖ *tr* hemmen
stunt'ed *adj* verkümmert
stunt' fly'ing *s* Kunstflug *m*
stunt' man' *s* (**men'**) Sensationsdarstel-
ler *m*
stupe•fy ['st(j)upɪ ,faɪ] *v* (*pret & pp*
-fied) *tr* verblüffen
stupendous [st(j)u'pendəs] *adj* erstaunlich
stupid ['st(j)upɪd] *adj* dumm, blöd
stupidity [st(j)u'pɪdɪti] *s* Dummheit *f*
stupor ['st(j)upər] *s* Stumpfsinn *m*
sturdy ['stʌrdi] *adj* (*person*) kräftig;

(*thing*) stabil; (*resolute*) standhaft; (*plant*) widerstandsfähig

sturgeon ['stʌrdʒən] *s* Stör *m*

stutter ['stʌtər] *s* Stottern *n* || *tr & intr* stottern

sty [staɪ] *s* Schweinestall *m;* (pathol) Gerstenkorn *n*

style [staɪl] *s* Stil *m;* (*manner*) Art *f;* (*fashion*) Mode *f;* (*cut of suit*) Schnitt *m;* **be in s.** in Mode sein; **go out of s.** veralten; **live in s.** auf großem Fuße leben || *tr* (*title*) betiteln; (*e.g., clothes*) gestalten; (*hair*) nach der Mode frisieren

stylish ['staɪlɪʃ] *adj* modisch; (*person*) modisch gekleidet

stylistic [staɪ'lɪstɪk] *adj* stilistisch

stymie ['staɪmi] *tr* vereiteln

styp'tic pen'cil ['stɪptɪk] *s* Alaunstift *m*

suave [swɑv] *adj* verbindlich

sub [sʌb] *s* (naut) U-boot *n;* (sport) Ersatzspieler –in *mf*

sub'chas'er *s* U-bootjäger *m*

sub'commit'tee *s* Unterausschuß *m*

subconscious [sʌb'kɑnʃəs] *adj* unterbewußt || *s* Unterbewußtsein *n*

sub'con'tinent *s* Subkontinent *m*

sub'con'tract *s* Nebenvertrag *m* || *tr* e–n Nebenvertrag abschließen über (*acc*)

sub'con'tractor *s* Unterlieferant –in *mf*

sub'divide', **sub'divide'** *tr* unterteilen || *intr* sich unterteilen

sub'divi'sion *s* (*act*) Unterteilung *f;* (*unit*) Unterabteilung *f*

subdue [səb'd(j)u] *tr* (*an enemy*) unterwerfen; (*one who is struggling*) überwältigen; (*light, sound*) dämpfen; (*feelings, impulses*) bändigen

sub'floor' *s* Blindboden *m*

sub'head' *s* Untertitel *m*

subject ['sʌbdʒɪkt] *adj* (**to**) untertan (*dat*); **be s. to** (*e.g., approval, another country*) abhängig sein von; (*e.g., colds*) neigen zu; (*e.g., laws of nature, change*) unterworfen sein (*dat*); **s. to change without notice** Änderungen vorbehalten || *s* Thema *n;* (*of a kingdom*) Untertan –in *mf;* (educ) Fach *n;* (fa) Vorwurf *m;* (gram) Satzgegenstand *m*, Subjekt *n;* (libr) Stichwort *n;* **change the s.** das Thema wechseln; **get off the s.** vom Thema abkommen || [səb'dʒɛkt] *tr* (& fig) unterwerfen (*dat*)

subjection [səb'dʒɛkʃən] *s* Unterwerfung *f*

subjective [səb'dʒɛktɪv] *adj* subjektiv; **s. case** Werfall *m*

sub'ject mat'ter *s* Inhalt *m*

subjugate ['sʌdʒə͵get] *tr* unterjochen

subjunctive [səb'dʒʌŋktɪv] *adj* konjunktiv(isch) || *s* Konjunktiv *m*

sub'lease' *s* Untermiete *f* || **sub'lease'** *tr & intr* (*to s.o.*) untervermieten; (*from s.o.*) untermieten

sublet [səb'lɛt] *v* (*pret & pp* –**let;** *ger* –**letting**) *tr & intr* (*to s.o.*) untervermieten; (*from s.o.*) untermieten

sublimate ['sʌblɪmət] *s* (chem) Sublimat *n* || ['sʌblɪ͵met] *tr* sublimieren

sublime [sə'blaɪm] *adj* erhaben || *s* Erhabene *n*

submachine' gun' *s* Maschinenpistole *f*

sub'marine' *adj* U-boot– || *s* U-boot *n*

sub'marine' base' *s* U-bootstützpunkt *m*

submerge [səb'mʌrdʒ] *tr & intr* untertauchen; **ready to s.** tauchklar

submersion [səb'mʌrʒən] *s* Untertauchen *n*

submission [səb'mɪʃən] *s* (**to**) Unterwerfung *f* (unter *acc*); (*of a document*) Vorlage *f;* (*of a question*) Unterbreitung *f*

submissive [səb'mɪsɪv] *adj* unterwürfig

sub•mit [səb'mɪt] *v* (*pret & pp* –**mitted;** *ger* –**mitting**) *tr* (*a question*) unterbreiten; (*a document*) vorlegen; (*suggest*) der Ansicht sein || *intr* (**to**) sich unterwerfen (*dat*)

subordinate [səb'ɔrdɪnɪt] *adj* (*lower in rank*) untergeordnet; (*secondary*) Neben– || *s* Untergebene *mf* || [səb'ɔrdɪ͵net] *tr* (**to**) unterordnen (*dat*)

subor'dinate clause' *s* Nebensatz *m*

suborn [sə'bɔrn] *tr* verleiten; (*bribe*) bestechen

sub'plot' *s* Nebenhandlung *f*

subpoena [sʌb'pina] *s* Vorladung *f* || *tr* (unter Strafandrohung) vorladen

subscribe [səb'skraɪb] *tr* unterschreiben; (*money*) zeichnen || *intr*—**s. to** (*a newspaper*) abonnieren; (*to a series of volumes*) subskribieren; (*an idea*) billigen

subscriber [səb'skraɪbər] *s* Abonnent –in *mf*

subscription [səb'skrɪpʃən] *s* (**to**) Abonnement *n* (auf *acc*); (*to a series of volumes*) Subskription *f* (auf *acc*); **take out a s. to** sich abonnieren auf (*acc*)

sub'sec'tion *s* Unterabteilung *f*

subsequent ['sʌbsɪkwənt] *adj* (nach)-folgend; **s. to** anschließend an (*acc*)

subsequently ['sʌbsɪkwəntli] *adv* anschließend

subservient [səb'sʌrvɪ·ənt] *adj* (**to**) unterwürfig (gegenüber *dat*)

subside [səb'saɪd] *intr* nachlassen; (geol) sich senken

subsidiary [səb'sɪdɪ͵ɛri] *adj* Tochter– || *s* Tochtergesellschaft *f*

subsidize ['sʌbsɪ͵daɪz] *tr* subventionieren

subsidy ['sʌbsɪdi] *s* Subvention *f*

subsist [səb'sɪst] *intr* (*exist*) existieren; **s. on** leben von

subsistence [səb'sɪstəns] *s* (*existence*) Dasein *n;* (*livelihood*) Lebensunterhalt *m;* (philos) Subsistenz *f*

subsist'ence allow'ance *s* Unterhaltszuschuß *m*

sub'soil' *s* Untergrund *m*

subsonic [səb'sɑnɪk] *adj* Unterschall–

sub'spe'cies *s* Unterart *f*

substance ['sʌbstəns] *s* Substanz *f*, Stoff *m;* **in s.** im wesentlichen

substand'ard *adj* unter dem Niveau

substantial [səb'stænʃəl] *adj* (*sum, amount*) beträchtlich; (*difference*) wesentlich; (*meal*) kräftig; **be in s. agreement** im wesentlichen übereinstimmen

substantiate [səb'stænʃɪ‚et] *tr* begründen, nachweisen

substantive ['sʌbstəntɪv] *adj* wesentlich ‖ *s* (gram) Substantiv *m*

sub'sta'tion *s* Nebenstelle *f*; (*post-office*) Zweigpostamt *n*; (elec) Umspannwerk *n*

substitute ['sʌbstɪ‚t(j)ut] *s* (*person*) Stellvertreter –in *mf*; (*material*) Austauschstoff *m*; (pej) Ersatz *m*; (sport) Ersatzspieler –in *mf*; **act as a s. for** vertreten; **beware of substitutes** vor Nachamung wird gewarnt ‖ *tr*—**s. A for B** B durch A ersetzen ‖ *intr*—**s. for** einspringen für

sub'stitute teach'er *s* Aushilfslehrer –in *mf*

substitution [‚sʌbstɪ't(j)uʃən] *s* Einsetzung *f*; (chem, math, ling) Substitution *f*; (sport) Auswechseln *n*

sub'stra'tum *s* (**–ta** [tə] **& –tums**) Unterlage *f*; (biol) Nährboden *m*

sub'struc'ture *s* Unterbau *m*

subsume [sʌb'sjum] *tr* unterordnen

subterfuge ['sʌbtər‚fjudʒ] *s* Winkelzug *m*

subterranean [‚sʌbtə'renɪ‚ən] *adj* unterirdisch

sub'ti'tle *s* Untertitel *m*

subtle ['sʌtəl] *adj* fein; (*poison*) schleichend; (*cunning*) raffiniert

subtlety ['sʌtəlti] *s* Feinheit *f*

subtract [səb'trækt] *tr* subtrahieren

subtraction [səb'trækʃən] *s* Subtraktion *f*

suburb ['sʌbʌrb] *s* Vorstadt *f*, Vorort *m*; **the suburbs** der Stadtrand

suburban [sə'bʌrbən] *adj* Vorstadt–

suburbanite [sə'bʌrbə‚naɪt] *s* Vorstadtbewohner –in *mf*

subvention [səb'venʃən] *s* Subvention *f*

subversion [səb'vʌrʒən] *s* Umsturz *m*

subversive [səb'vʌrsɪv] *adj* umstürzlerisch ‖ *s* Umstürzler –in *mf*

subver'sive activ'ity *s* Wühlarbeit *f*

subvert [səb'vʌrt] *tr* (*a government*) stürzen; (*the law*) umstoßen; (*corrupt*) (sittlich) verderben

sub'way' *s* U-Bahn *f*, Untergrundbahn *f*

succeed [sək'sid] *tr* folgen (*dat*) ‖ *intr* (*said of persons*) (**in**) Erfolg haben (**mit**); (*said of things*) gelingen; **I succeeded in** (*ger*) es gelang mir zu (*inf*); **not s.** mißglücken; **s. to the throne** die Thronfolge antreten

success [sək'ses] *s* Erfolg *m*; (*play, song, piece of merchandise*) Knüller *m*; **be a s.** Erfolg haben; **without s.** erfolglos

successful [sək'sesfəl] *adj* erfolgreich

succession [sək'seʃən] *s* Reihenfolge *f*; (*as heir*) Erbfolge *f*; **in s.** nacheinander; **s. to** (e.g., *an office, estate*) Übernahme *f* (*genit*)

successive [sək'sesɪv] *adj* aufeinanderfolgend

successor [sək'sesər] *s* Nachfolger –in

mf; **s. to the throne** Thronfolger –in *mf*

succor ['sʌkər] *s* Beistand *m* ‖ *tr* beistehen (*dat*)

succotash ['sʌkə‚tæʃ] *s* Gericht *n* aus Süßmais und grünen Bohnen

succulent ['sʌkjələnt] *adj* saftig

succumb [sə'kʌm] *intr* (**to**) erliegen (*dat*)

such [sʌtʃ] *adj* solch; **as s. als solcher; no s. thing** nichts dergleichen; **some s. thing** irgend so (et)was; **s. and s.** der und der; **s. as** wie (etwa); **s. a long time** so lange; **s. as it is** wie es nun einmal ist

suck [sʌk] *s* Saugen *n*; (*licking*) Lutschen *n* ‖ *tr* saugen; **s. in** einsaugen; (sl) reinlegen ‖ *intr* saugen; **s. on** (e.g., *candy*) lutschen

sucker ['sʌkər] *s* (coll) Gimpel *m*; (*carp*) Karpfenfisch *m*; (bot) Wurzelschößling *m*; (zool) Saugröhre *f*

suckle ['sʌkəl] *tr* stillen; (*animals*) säugen

suck'ling *s* Säugling *m*

suck'ling pig' *s* Spanferkel *n*

suction ['sʌkʃən] *s* Saugen *n*, Sog *m*

suc'tion cup' *s* Saugnapf *m*

suc'tion pump' *s* Saugpumpe *f*

sudden ['sʌdən] *adj* plötzlich, jäh; **all of a s.** (ganz) plötzlich

suddenly ['sʌdənli] *adv* plötzlich

suds [sʌdz] *spl* Seifenschaum *m*

sudsy ['sʌdzi] *adj* schaumig

sue [s(j)u] *tr* (**for**) verklagen (**auf** *acc*) ‖ *intr* (**for**) klagen (**auf** *acc*)

suede [swed] *adj* Wildleder– ‖ *s* Wildleder *n*

suet ['s(j)u·ɪt] *s* Talg *m*

suffer ['sʌfər] *tr* erleiden; (*damage*) nehmen; (*put up with*) ertragen ‖ *intr* (**from**) leiden (**an** *dat*)

sufferance ['sʌfərəns] *s* stillschweigende Einwilligung *f*

suf'fering *s* Leiden *n*

suffice [sə'faɪs] *intr* ausreichen

sufficient [sə'fɪʃənt] *adj* (**for**) ausreichend (**für**)

suffix ['sʌfɪks] *s* Nachsilbe *f*

suffocate ['sʌfə‚ket] *tr & intr* ersticken

suffrage ['sʌfrɪdʒ] *s* Stimmrecht *n*

suffuse [sə'fjuz] *tr* übergießen

sugar ['ʃugər] *s* Zucker *m* ‖ *tr* zuckern

sug'ar beet' *s* Zuckerrübe *f*

sug'ar bowl' *s* Zuckerdose *f*

sug'ar cane' *s* Zuckerrohr *n*

sug'ar-coat' *tr* (& fig) überzuckern

sug'ar dad'dy *s* Geldonkel *m*

sug'ar ma'ple *s* Zuckerahorn *m*

sug'ar tongs' *spl* Zuckerzange *f*

sugary ['ʃugəri] *adj* zuckerig

suggest [səg'dʒest] *tr* vorschlagen; (*hint*) andeuten

suggestion [səg'dʒestʃən] *s* Vorschlag *m*

suggestive [səg'dʒestɪv] *adj* (*remark*) zweideutig; (*thought-provoking*) anregend; (e.g., *dress*) hauteng; **be s. of** erinnern an (*acc*)

suicidal [‚su·ɪ'saɪdəl] *adj* selbstmörderisch

suicide ['su·ɪ‚saɪd] *s* Selbstmord *m*;

(*person*) Selbstmörder –in *mf;* **commit s.** Selbstmord begehen

suit [sut] *s* (*men's*) Anzug *m;* (*women's*) Kostüm *n;* (cards) Farbe *f;* (jur) Prozeß *m;* **bring s. (against)** e–e Klage einbringen (gegen); **follow s.** Farbe bekennen; (fig) sich nach den anderen richten || *tr* (*please*) passen (*dat*); (*correspond to*) entsprechen (*dat*); (*said, e.g., of colors, style*) gut passen (*dat*); **be suited for** sich eignen für; **s. s.th. to** etw anpassen (*dat*); **s. yourself!** wie Sie wollen!

suitable ['sutəbəl] *adj* (**to**) geeignet (für)

suit'case' *s* Handkoffer *m*

suit' coat' *s* Sakko *m & n*

suite [swit] *s* (*series of rooms*) Zimmerflucht *f;* (*set of furniture*) Zimmergarnitur *f;* (mus) Suite *f*

suitor ['sutər] *s* Freier *m*

sul'fa drug' *s* Sulfonamid *n*

sulfate ['sʌlfet] *s* Sulfat *n*

sulfide ['sʌlfaɪd] *s* Sulfid *n*

sulfur ['sʌlfər] *adj* Schwefel– || *s* Schwefel *m* || *tr* einschwefeln

sulfur'ic ac'id [sʌl'f(j)ʊrɪk] *s* Schwefelsäure *f*

sul'fur mine' *s* Schwefelgrube *f*

sulk [sʌlk] *intr* trotzen

sulky ['sʌlki] *adj* trotzend, mürrisch || *s* (sport) Traberwagen *m*

sulk'y race' *s* Trabrennen *n*

sullen ['sʌlən] *adj* mißmutig

sul·ly ['sʌli] *v* (*pret & pp* **–lied**) *tr* besudeln

sulphur ['sʌlfər] var of **sulfur**

sultan ['sʌltən] *s* Sultan *m*

sultry ['sʌltri] *adj* schwül

sum [sʌm] *s* Summe *f,* Betrag *m;* **in sum** kurz gesagt || *v* (*pret & pp* **summed;** *ger* **summing**)—**sum up** summieren; (*summarize*) zusammenfassen; (*make a quick estimate of*) kurz abschätzen

sumac, sumach ['ʃumæk] *s* Sumach *m*

summarize ['sʌmə͵raɪz] *tr* zusammenfassen

summary ['sʌməri] *adj* summarisch || *s* Zusammenfassung *f*

sum'mary court'martial *s* summarisches Militärgericht *n*

summer ['sʌmər] *s* Sommer *m*

sum'mer cot'tage *s* Sommerwohnung *f*

sum'mer resort' *s* Sommerfrische *f*

sum'mer school' *s* Sommerkurs *m*

sum'mertime' *s* Sommerzeit *f*

summery ['sʌməri] *adj* sommerlich

summit ['sʌmɪt] *s* (& fig) Gipfel *m*

sum'mit con'ference *s* Gipfelkonferenz *f*

sum'mit talks' *spl* Gipfelgespräche *pl*

summon ['sʌmən] *tr* (*e.g., a doctor*) kommen lassen; (*a conference*) einberufen; (jur) vorladen; **s. up** (*courage, strength*) aufbieten

summons ['sʌmənz] *s* (jur) Vorladung *f*

sumptuous ['sʌmptʃʊ-əs] *adj* üppig

sun [sʌn] *s* Sonne *f* || *v* (*pret & pp* **sunned;** *ger* **sunning**) *tr* sonnen; **sun oneself** sich sonnen

sun' bath' *s* Sonnenbad *n*

sun'beam' *s* Sonnenstrahl *m*

sun'burn' *s* Sonnenbrand *m*

sun'burned' *adj* sonnverbrannt

sundae ['sʌnde] *s* Eisbecher *m* mit Sirup, Nüssen, Früchten und Schlagsahne

Sunday ['sʌnde] *adj* sonntäglich; **dressed in one's S. best** sonntäglich gekleidet || *s* Sonntag *m;* **on S.** am Sonntag

Sun'day driv'er *s* Sonntagsfahrer –in *mf*

Sun'day school' *s* Sonntagsschule *f*

sunder ['sʌndər] *tr* trennen

sun'di'al *s* Sonnenuhr *f*

sun'down' *s* Sonnenuntergang *m*

sun'-drenched' *adj* sonnenüberflutet

sundries ['sʌndriz] *pl* Diverses *n*

sundry ['sʌndri] *adj* verschiedene

sun'fish' *s* Sonnenfisch *m*

sun'flow'er *s* Sonnenblume *f*

sun'glass'es *pl* Sonnenbrille *f*

sun' hel'met *s* Tropenhelm *m*

sunken ['sʌŋkən] *adj* (*ship*) gesunken; (*eyes; garden*) tiefliegend; (*treasure*) versunken; (*cheeks*) eingefallen; **s. rocks** blinde Klippe *f*

sun' lamp' *s* Höhensonne *f*

sun'light' *s* Sonnenlicht *n*

sunny ['sʌni] *adj* sonnig

sun'ny side' *s* Sonnenseite *f*

sun' par'lor *s* Glasveranda *f*

sun'rise' *s* Sonnenaufgang *m*

sun' roof' *s* (aut) Schiebedach *n*

sun'set' *s* Sonnenuntergang *m*

sun'shade' *s* Sonnenschirm *m;* (*awning*) Sonnendach *n;* (phot) Gegenlichtblende *f*

sun'shine' *s* Sonnenschein *m*

sun'spot' *s* Sonnenfleck *m*

sun'stroke' *s* Sonnenstich *m*

sun'tan' *s* Sonnenbräune *f*

sun'tanned' *adj* sonnengebräunt

sun' vis'or *s* (aut) Sonnenblende *f*

sup [sʌp] *v* (*pret & pp* **supped;** *ger* **supping**) *intr* zu Abend essen

super ['supər] *adj* (*oversized*) Super–; (sl) prima || *s* (theat) Komparse *m*

su'perabun'dance *s* (of) Überfülle *f* (an *dat*)

su'perabun'dant *adj* überreichlich

superannuated [͵supər'ænju͵etɪd] *adj* (*person*) pensioniert; (*thing*) veraltet

superb [su'perb] *adj* prachtvoll, herrlich

su'perbomb' *s* Superbombe *f*

su'perbomb'er *s* Riesenbomber *m*

supercilious [͵supər'sɪlɪ-əs] *adj* hochnäsig

superficial [͵supər'fɪʃəl] *adj* oberflächlich

superfluous [su'pʌrflu-əs] *adj* überflüssig

su'perhigh'way' *s* Autobahn *f*

su'perhu'man *adj* übermenschlich

su'perimpose' *tr* darüberlegen; (elec, phys) überlagern

su'perintend' *tr* die Aufsicht führen über (*acc*), beaufsichtigen

superintendent [͵supərɪn'tendənt] *s* Oberaufseher –in *mf;* (*in industry*)

Betriebsleiter –in *mf;* (*of a factory*)
Werksleiter –in *mf;* (*of a building*)
Hausverwalter –in *mf;* (educ) Schul-
inspektor –in *mf*
superior [sə'pɪrɪ·ər] *adj* (*physically*)
höher; (*in rank*) übergeordnet; (*quality*) hervorragend; **s. in** überlegen an
(*dat*); **s. to** überlegen (*dat*) || *s* Vor-
gesetzte *mf*
supe'rior court' *s* Obergericht *n*
superiority [sə‚pɪrɪ'arɪti] *s* (**in**) Überlegenheit *f* (in *dat,* an *dat*); (mil)
Übermacht *f*
superlative [su'pʌrlətɪv] *adj* hervorragend; (gram) superlativisch, Super-
lativ– || *s* (gram) Superlativ *m*
su'perman' *s* (**–men'**) Übermensch *m*
su'permar'ket *s* Supermarkt *m*
su'pernat'ural *adj* übernatürlich || *s*
Übernatürliche *n*
supersede [‚supər'sid] *tr* ersetzen
su'persen'sitive *adj* überempfindlich
su'person'ic *adj* Überschall–
superstition [‚supər'stɪʃən] *s* Aberglau-
be *m;* (*superstitious idea*) abergläu-
bische Vorstellung *f*
superstitious [‚supər'stɪʃəs] *adj* abergläubisch
su'perstruc'ture *s* Überbau *m;* (*of a
bridge*) Oberbau *m;* (*of a building or
ship*) Aufbauten *pl*
supervise ['supər‚vaɪz] *tr* beaufsichtigen
supervision [‚supər'vɪʒən] *s* Beaufsichtigung *f*
supervisor ['supər‚vaɪzər] *s* Vorgesetzte *mf*
su'pine posi'tion ['supaɪn] *s* Rücken-
lage *f*
supper ['sʌpər] *s* Abendessen *n;* **eat s.**
zu Abend essen
sup'pertime' *s* Abendbrotzeit *f*
supplant [sə'plænt] *tr* ersetzen
supple ['sʌpəl] *adj* geschmeidig; (*mind*)
beweglich
supplement ['sʌplɪmənt] *s* (*e.g., to a
diet*) (**to**) Ergänzung *f* (*genit*); (*to
a writing*) Anhang *m;* (*to a news-
paper*) Beilage *f* || ['sʌplɪ‚ment] *tr*
ergänzen
supplementary [‚sʌplɪ'mentəri] *adj* er-
gänzend
suppliant ['sʌplɪ·ənt] *adj* flehend || *s*
Bittsteller –in *mf*
supplicant ['sʌplɪkənt] *s* Bittsteller –in
mf
supplicate ['sʌplɪ‚ket] *tr* flehen
supplication [‚sʌplɪ'keʃən] *s* Flehen *n*
supplier [sə'plaɪ·ər] *s* Lieferant –in *mf*
sup·ply [sə'plaɪ] *s* (*supplying*) Versorgung *f;* (*stock*) (**of**) Vorrat *m* (an
dat); (com) Angebot *n;* **supplies** Vorräte *pl;* (*e.g., office supplies, dental
supplies*) Bedarfsartikel *pl;* (mil)
Nachschub *m* || *v* (*pret & pp* **–plied**)
tr (**with**) versorgen (mit); (*deliver*)
liefern; (*procure*) beschaffen; (*with
a truck*) zuführen; (*equip*) (**with**)
versehen (mit); (*a demand*) befriedigen; (*a loss*) ausgleichen; (*missing
words*) ergänzen; (mil) mit Nach-
schub versorgen

supply' and demand' *spl* Angebot *n*
und Nachfrage *f*
supply' base' *s* Nachschubstützpunkt
m
supply' line' *s* Versorgungsweg *m;*
(mil) Nachschubweg *m*
support [sə'port] *adj* Hilfs– || *s* (*prop,
brace, stay; person*) Stütze *f;* (*of a
family*) Unterhalt *m;* **in s. of** zur
Unterstützung (*genit*); **without s.**
(*unsubstantiated*) haltlos; (*unprovided*) unversorgt; **with the s. of**
mit dem Beistand von || *tr* stützen,
tragen; (*back*) unterstützen; (*a family*) erhalten; (*a charge*) erhärten; (*a
claim*) begründen
supporter [sə'portər] *s* (*of a family*)
Ernährer –in *mf;* (*backer*) Förderer
–in *mf;* (*jockstrap*) Suspensorium *n*
support'ing role' *s* Nebenrolle *f*
suppose [sə'poz] *tr* annehmen; **be supposed to** sollen; **I s. so** ich glaube
schon; **s. it rains** gesetzt den Fall (or
angenommen), es regnet; **s. we take
a walk** wie wäre es, wenn wir e–n
Spaziergang machten?; **what is that
supposed to mean?** was soll das be-
deuten? || *intr* vermuten
supposed' *adj* mutmaßlich
supposedly [sə'pozɪdli] *adv* angeblich
supposition [‚sʌpə'zɪʃən] *s* Annahme
f
suppository [sə'pazɪ‚tori] *s* Zäpfchen
n
suppress [sə'pres] *tr* unterdrücken;
(*news, scandal*) verheimlichen
suppression [sə'preʃən] *s* Unterdrük-
kung *f;* (*of news, truth, scandal*) Verheimlichung *f*
suppurate ['sʌpjə‚ret] *intr* eitern
supremacy [sə'preməsi] *s* Oberherr-
schaft *f*
supreme [sə'prim] *adj* Ober–, höchste
supreme' author'ity *s* Obergewalt *f*
Supreme' Be'ing *s* höchstes Wesen *n*
supreme' command' *s* Oberkommando
n; **have s.** den Oberbefehl führen
supreme' command'er *s* oberster Befehlshaber *m*
Supreme' Court' *s* Oberster Gerichtshof *m*
surcharge ['sʌr‚tʃɑrdʒ] *s* (**on**) Zuschlag *m* (zu)
sure [ʃur] *adj* sicher, gewiß; (*shot,
cure*) unfehlbar; (*shot, footing,
ground, way, proof*) sicher; **are you
s. you won't come?** kommen Sie
wirklich nicht?; **be s. of** sicher sein
(*genit*); **be s. to** (*inf*) vergiß nicht zu
(*inf*); **feel s. of oneself** s–r selbst
sicher sein; **for s.** sicherlich; **she is
s. to come** sie wird sicher(lich) kommen; **s. enough** wirklich; **to be s.**
(*parenthetically*) zwar
sure'-foot'ed *adj* trittsicher
surely ['ʃurli] *adv* sicher(lich), gewiß
surety ['ʃur(ɪ)ti] *s* Bürgschaft *f;* **stand
s. (for**) bürgen (für)
surf [sʌrf] *s* Brandung *f* || *intr* wellen-
reiten
surface ['sʌrfɪs] *adj* (*superficial*) oberflächlich; (*apparent rather than real*)

Schein– ‖ *s* Oberfläche *f; (of a road)*
Belag *m; (aer)* Tragfläche *f;* **on the
s.** oberflächlich (betrachtet) ‖ *tr (a
road)* mit e–m Belag versehen ‖ *intr*
auftauchen
sur'face mail' *s* gewöhnliche Post *f*
sur'face-to-air' mis'sile *s* Boden-Luft-
Rakete *f*
sur'face-to-sur'face mis'sile *s* Boden-
Boden-Rakete *f*
surf'board' *s* Wellenreiterbrett *n*
surf'board'ing *s* Wellenreiten *n*
surfeit ['sʌrfɪt] *s* Übersättigung *f* ‖ *tr*
übersättigen
surfer ['sʌrfər] *s* Wellenreiter –in *mf*
surf'ing *s* Wellenreiten *n*
surge [sʌrdʒ] *s (forward rush of a wave
or crowd)* Wogen *n; (swelling wave)*
Woge *f; (swelling sea)* Wogen *n;*
(elec) Stromstoß *m* ‖ *intr (said of
waves or a crowd)* wogen; *(said of
emotions, blood)* **(up)** (auf)wallen
surgeon ['sʌrdʒən] *s* Chirurg –in *mf*
surgery ['sʌrdʒəri] *s* Chirurgie *f;*
(room) Operationssaal *m;* **undergo s.**
sich e–r Operation unterziehen
surgical ['sʌrdʒɪkəl] *adj* chirurgisch;
(resulting from surgery) Operations–
surly ['sʌrli] *adj* bärbeißig
surmise [sər'maɪz] *s* Vermutung *f* ‖ *tr
& intr* vermuten
surmount [sər'maunt] *tr* überwinden
surname ['sʌr ˌnem] *s (family name)*
Zuname *m; (epithet)* Beiname *m* ‖
tr e–n Zunamen (or Beinamen) geben
(dat)
surpass [sər'pæs] *tr* **(in)** übertreffen
(an dat)
surplice ['sʌrplɪs] *s* Chorhemd *n*
surplus ['sʌrplʌs] *adj* überschüssig,
Über– ‖ *s* **(of)** Überschuß *m (an dat)*
surprise [sər'praɪz] *adj* Überraschungs–
‖ *s* Überraschung *f;* **take by s.**
überraschen; **to my (great) s.** zu
meiner (großen) Überraschung ‖ *tr*
überraschen; **be surprised at** sich
wundern über *(acc);* **be surprised to
see how** staunen, wie; **I am surprised
that** es wundert mich, daß
surpris'ing *adj* überraschend
surrealism [sə'ri·ə ˌlɪzəm] *s* Surrealis-
mus *m*
surrender [sə'rɛndər] *s (e.g., of a fortress)* Übergabe *f; (of an army or
unit)* Kapitulation *f; (of rights)* Aufgabe *f; (of a prisoner)* Auslieferung
f ‖ *tr* übergeben; *(rights)* aufgeben;
(a prisoner) ausliefern ‖ *intr* sich
ergeben
surren'der val'ue *s* (ins) Rückkaufs-
wert *m*
surreptitious [ˌsʌrɛp'tɪʃəs] *adj* heimlich; *(glance)* verstohlen
surround [sə'raund] *tr* umgeben; *(said
of a crowd, police)* umringen; (mil)
einschließen
surround'ing *adj* umliegend ‖ **surroundings** *spl* Umgebung *f*
surtax ['sʌr ˌtæks] *s* Steuerzuschlag *m*
surveillance [sər'vel(j)əns] *s* Überwachung *f;* **keep under s.** unter Po-
lizeiaufsicht halten

survey ['sʌrve] *s* **(of)** Überblick *m*
(über *acc); (of opinions)* Umfrage
f; (of land) Vermessung *f; (plan or
description of the survey)* Lageplan
m ‖ [sʌr've] *tr* überblicken; *(a person)* mustern; *(land)* vermessen;
(people for their opinion) befragen
sur'vey course' *s* Einführungskurs *m*
survey'ing *s* Landvermessung *f*
surveyor [sər've·ər] *s* Landmesser *m*
survival [sər'vaɪvəl] *s* Überleben *n;*
(after death) Weiterleben *n*
surviv'al of the fit'test *s* Überleben *n*
des Tüchtigsten
survive [sər'vaɪv] *tr (a person)* überleben; *(a thing)* überstehen; **be sur-
vived by** hinterlassen ‖ *intr* am Leben
bleiben
surviv'ing *adj* überlebend
survivor [sər'vaɪvər] *s* Überlebende *mf*
susceptible [sə'sɛptɪbəl] *adj (impres-
sionable)* eindrucksfähig; **be s. of**
zulassen; **be s. to** *(disease, infection)*
anfällig sein für; *(flattery)* empfänglich sein für
suspect ['sʌspɛkt] *adj* verdächtig ‖ *s*
Verdächtige *mf* ‖ [səs'pɛkt] *tr* in
Verdacht haben; *(surmise)* vermuten;
(have a hint of) ahnen; **s. s.o. of** j–n
verdächtigen *(genit)*
suspend [səs'pɛnd] *tr (from a job, office)* suspendieren; *(payment, hostilities, proceedings, a game)* einstellen;
(a rule) zeitweilig aufheben; *(a sentence)* aussetzen; *(a player)* sperren;
(from a club) zeitweilig ausschließen;
(from) hängen (an *dat)*
suspenders [səs'pɛndərz] *spl* Hosenträ-
ger *pl*
suspense [səs'pɛns] *s* Spannung *f;* **hang
in s.** in der Schwebe sein; **keep in s.**
im ungewissen lassen
suspension [səs'pɛnʃən] *s* Aufhängung
f; (of a sentence) Aussetzung *f; (of
work)* Einstellung *f; (e.g., of telephone service)* Sperrung *f;* (aut) Federung *f;* (chem) Suspension *f;* **s. of
driver's license** Führerscheinentzug
m
suspen'sion bridge' *s* Hängebrücke *f*
suspen'sion points' *spl (indicating unfinished thoughts)* Gedankenpunkte
pl; (indicating omission) Auslassungs-
punkte *pl*
suspicion [səs'pɪʃən] *s* Verdacht *m;*
above s. über jeden Verdacht erhaben; **be under s.** unter Verdacht
stehen; **on s. of murder** unter Mord-
verdacht
suspicious [səs'pɪʃəs] *adj (person)* verdächtig; *(e.g., glance)* argwöhnisch;
(character) zweifelhaft
sustain [səs'ten] *tr* aufrechterhalten;
(a loss, defeat, injury) erleiden; *(a
family)* ernähren; *(an army)* verpflegen; *(a motion, an objection)*
stattgeben *(dat); (a theory, position)*
erhärten; *(a note)* dehnen
sustenance ['sʌstɪnəns] *s (nourishment)*
Nahrung *f; (means of livelihood)*
Unterhalt *m*
swab [swɑb] *s* (med, surg) Tupfer *m;*

(*matter collected on a swab*) Abstrich *m;* (naut) Schwabber *m* ‖ *v* (*pret & pp* **swabbed;** *ger* **swabbing**) *tr* (med, surg) abtupfen; (naut) schrubben

Swabia ['swebɪ·ə] *s* Schwaben *n*

Swabian ['swebɪ·ən] *adj* schwäbisch ‖ *s* Schwabe *m,* Schwäbin *f;* (*dialect*) Schwäbisch *n*

swad′dling clothes′ ['swɑdlɪŋ] *spl* Windeln *pl*

swagger ['swægər] *s* (*strut*) Stolzieren *n;* (*swaggering manner*) Prahlerei *f* ‖ *intr* stolzieren; (*show off*) prahlen

swain [swen] *s* (*lover*) Liebhaber *m;* (*country lad*) Bauernbursche *m*

swallow ['swɑlo] *s* Schluck *m;* (orn) Schwalbe *f* ‖ *tr* schlucken; (fig) hinunterschlucken ‖ *intr* schlucken; **s. the wrong way** sich verschlucken

swamp [swɑmp] *s* Sumpf *m,* Moor *n* ‖ *tr* überfluten; (*with work*) überhäufen

swamp′land′ *s* Moorland *n*

swampy ['swɑmpi] *adj* sumpfig

swan [swɑn] *s* Schwan *m*

swan′ dive′ *s* Schwalbensprung *m*

swank [swæŋk], **swanky** ['swæŋki] *adj* (*luxurious*) schick; (*ostentatious*) protzig

swan′s′-down′ *s* Schwanendaunen *pl*

swan′ song′ *s* Schwanengesang *n*

swap [swɑp] *s* (coll) Tauschgeschäft *n* ‖ *v* (*pret & pp* **swapped;** *ger* **swapping**) *tr & intr* (coll) tauschen

swarm [swɑrm] *s* Schwarm *m;* (*of children*) Schar *f* ‖ *intr* schwärmen; **s. around** umschwärmen; **s. into** sich drängen in (*acc*); **s. with** (fig) wimmeln von

swarthy ['swɔrði] *adj* dunkelhäutig

swashbuckler ['swɑʃ͵bʌklər] *s* Eisenfresser *m*

swastika ['swɑstɪkə] *s* Hakenkreuz *n*

swat [swɑt] *s* Schlag *m* ‖ (*pret & pp* **swatted;** *ger* **swatting**) *tr* schlagen

swath [swɔθ] *s* Schwaden *m*

swathe [sweð] *tr* umwickeln, einwikkeln

sway [swe] *s* Schwanken *n,* Schwingen *n;* (*domination*) Herrschaft *f* ‖ *tr* (*e.g., tree*) hin– und herbewegen; (*influence*) beeinflussen; (*cause to vacillate*) ins Wanken bringen ‖ *intr* schwanken

sway′-back′ *s* Senkrücken *m*

swear [swer] *v* (*pret* **swore** [swor]; *pp* **sworn** [sworn]) *tr* schwören; **s. in** vereidigen; **s. s.o. to secrecy** j–n auf Geheimhaltung vereidigen ‖ *intr* schwören; (coll) fluchen; **s. at** schimpfen über (*acc*) *or* auf (*acc*); **s. by** schwören bei; **s. off** abschwören (*dat*); **s. on a stack of Bibles** Stein und Bein schwören; **s. to** (*a statement*) beschwören; **s. to it** darauf schwören

swear′ing-in′ *s* Vereidigung *f*

swear′word′ *s* Fluchwort *n*

sweat [swɛt] *s* Schweiß *m;* **break out in s.** in Schweiß geraten ‖ *v* (*pret & pp* **sweat** & **sweated**) *tr* (*blood*)

schwitzen; (*metal*) seigern; (*a horse*) in Schweiß bringen; **s. off** abschwitzen; **s. out** (sl) geduldig abwarten; **s. up** durchschwitzen ‖ *intr* schwitzen

sweater ['swɛtər] *s* Sweater *m,* Pullover *m*

sweat′er girl′ *s* vollbusiges Mädchen *n*

sweat′ shirt′ *s* Trainingsbluse *f*

sweat′ shop′ *s* (sl) Knochenmühle *f*

sweaty ['sweti] *adj* verschwitzt; (*hand*) schweißig

Swede [swid] *s* Schwede *m,* Schwedin *f*

Swedish ['swidɪʃ] *adj* schwedisch ‖ *s* Schwedisch *n*

sweep [swip] *s* (*sweeper*) Kehrer –in *mf;* (*of the arm, scythe, weapon*) Schwung *m;* (*of an oar*) Schlag *m;* (*range*) Reichweite *f;* (*continuous stretch*) ausgedehnte Strecke *f;* **in one clean s.** mit e–m Schlag; **make a clean s. of it** reinen Tisch machen ‖ *v* (*pret & pp* **swept** [swept]) *tr* kehren, fegen; (*mines*) räumen; (*with machine-gun fire*) bestreichen; (*with a searchlight*) absuchen; **he swept her off her feet** er hat sie im Sturm erobert; **s. clean** reinemachen ‖ *intr* kehren, fegen

sweeper ['swipər] *s* Kehrer –in *mf;* (*carpet sweeper*) Teppichkehrer *m*

sweep′ing *adj* weitreichend ‖ **sweepings** *spl* Kehricht *m & n*

sweep′-sec′ond *s* Zentralsekundenzeiger *m*

sweep′stakes′ *s & spl* Lotterie *f;* (sport) Toto *m & n*

sweet [swit] *adj* süß; (*person*) lieb; (*butter*) ungesalzen; **be s. on** scharf sein auf (*acc*) ‖ **sweets** *spl* Süßigkeiten *pl*

sweet′bread′ *s* Bries *n*

sweet′bri′er *s* Heckenrose *f*

sweet′ corn′ *s* Zuckermais *m*

sweeten ['switən] *tr* süßen; (fig) versüßen ‖ *intr* süß(er) werden

sweet′heart′ *s* Liebste *mf,* Schatz *m*

sweetish ['switɪʃ] *adj* süßlich

sweet′ mar′joram *s* Gartenmajoran *m*

sweet′meats′ *spl* Zuckerwerk *n*

sweetness ['switnɪs] *s* Süßigkeit *f*

sweet′ pea′ *s* Gartenwicke *f*

sweet′ pep′per *s* grüner Paprika *m*

sweet′ pota′to *s* Süßkartoffel *f*

sweet′-scent′ed *adj* wohlriechend

sweet′ tooth′ *s*—**have a s.** gern naschen

sweet′ wil′liam *s* Fleischnelke *f*

swell [swɛl] *adj* (coll) prima ‖ *s* (*of the sea*) Wellengang *m;* (*of an organ*) Schweller *m* ‖ *v* (*pret* **swelled;** *pp* **swelled** & **swollen** ['swolən]) *tr* zum Schwellen bringen; (*the number*) vermehren; (*a musical tone*) anschwellen lassen ‖ *intr* schwellen

swell′ing *s* Schwellung *f*

swelter ['swɛltər] *intr* unter der Hitze leiden

swept′-back′ *adj* (aer) keilförmig

swerve [swʌrv] *s* Abweichung *f* ‖ *tr* ablenken ‖ *intr* scharf abbiegen

swift [swɪft] *adj* geschwind, rasch

swig [swɪg] *s* (coll) kräftiger Schluck

m || *v* (*pret* & *pp* **swigged; *ger* swig-ging**) *tr* in langen Zügen trinken

swill [swɪl] *s* Spülicht *n;* (*for swine*) Schweinefutter *n;* (*deep drink*) tüchtiger Schluck *m* || *tr* & *intr* gierig trinken

swim [swɪm] *s* Schwimmen *n;* **take a s.** schwimmen || *v* (*pret* **swam** [swæm]; *pp* **swum** [swʌm]; *ger* **swimming**) *tr* (*e.g., a lake*) durchschwimmen; (*cause to swim*) schwimmen lassen; (*challenge in swimming*) um die Wette schwimmen mit || *intr* schwimmen; **my head is swimming** mir schwindelt der Kopf

swimmer ['swɪmər] *s* Schwimmer –in *mf*

swim'ming *adj* Schwimm– || *s* Schwimmen *n;* (*sport*) Schwimmsport *m*

swim'ming pool' *s* Schwimmbecken *n*

swim'ming suit' *s* Badeanzug *m*

swim'ming trunks' *spl* Badehose *f*

swindle ['swɪndəl] *s* Schwindel *m* || *tr* gaunern; **s. s.th. out of** etw erschwindeln von

swindler ['swɪndlər] *s* Schwindler –in *mf*

swind'ling *s* Schwindelei *f*

swine [swaɪn] *s* Schwein *n*

swine'herd' *s* Schweinehirt *m*

swing [swɪŋ] *s* (*for children*) Schaukel *f;* (*swinging movement*) Hin– und Herschwingen *n;* (box) Schwinger *m;* (mus) Swing *m;* **in full s.** in vollem Gang; **take a s. at** s.o. nach j–m schlagen || *v* (*pret* & *pp* **swung** [swʌŋ]) *tr* schwingen; (*children on a swing*) schaukeln; (*an election*) entscheidend beeinflussen; **s.** (*e.g., a car*) **around** herumdrehen; **we'll s. it somhow** (coll) wir werden es schon schaffen || *intr* pendeln; (*on a swing*) schaukeln; **s. around** sich umdrehen; **s. into action** in Schwung kommen; **things are swinging around here** (coll) hier geht es lustig zu

swing'ing door' *s* Pendeltür *f*

swinish ['swaɪnɪʃ] *adj* schweinisch

swipe [swaɪp] *s* (coll) Hieb *m;* **take a s. at** (coll) schlagen nach || *tr* (*hit with full force*) (coll) kräftig schlagen; (*steal*) (sl) mausen

swirl [swʌrl] *s* Wirbel *m* || *tr* (**about**) herumwirbeln; || *intr* wirbeln; (*said of water*) Strudel bilden

swish [swɪʃ] *s* (*e.g., of a whip*) Sausen *n;* (*of a dress*) Rauschen *n* || *tr* (*a whip*) sausen lassen; **s. its tail** mit dem Schwanz wedeln || *intr* (*said of a whip*) sausen; (*said of a dress*) rauschen

Swiss [swɪs] *adj* schweizerisch || *s* Schweizer –in *mf*

Swiss' cheese' *s* Schweizer Käse *m*

Swiss' franc' *s* Schweizerfranken *m*

Swiss' Guard' *s* Schweizergarde *f*

switch [swɪtʃ] *s* (*exchange*) Wechsel *m,* Umschwung *m;* (*stick*) Rute *f;* (elec) Schalter *m;* (rr) Weiche *f* || *tr* wechseln; (*e.g., coats by mistake*) verwechseln; (rr) rangieren; **s. off** (elec, rad, telv) ausschalten; **s. on**

(elec, rad, telv) einschalten || *intr* Plätze wechseln

switch'-blade knife' *s* feststellbares Messer *n*

switch'board' *s* Schaltbrett *n,* Zentrale *f*

switch'board op'erator *s* Telephonist –in *mf*

switch' box' *s* Schaltkasten *m*

switch'man *s* (–men) (rr) Weichensteller *m*

switch' tow'er *s* (rr) Blockstation *f*

switch'yard' *s* Rangierbahnhof *m*

Switzerland ['swɪtsərlənd] *s* die Schweiz

swiv·el ['swɪvəl] *s* Drehlager *n* || *v* (*pret* & *pp* **–el[l]ed; *ger* –el[l]ing**) *tr* herumdrehen || *intr* sich drehen

swiv'el chair' *s* Drehstuhl *m*

swiz'zle stick' ['swɪzəl] *s* Rührstäbchen *n*

swollen ['swolən] *adj* (an)geschwollen; (*eyes*) verquollen

swoon [swun] *s* Ohnmacht *f* || *intr* ohnmächtig werden

swoop [swup] *s* Herabstoßen *n;* **in one fell s.** mit e–m Schlag || *intr*—**s. down** (**on**) herabstoßen (auf *acc*)

sword [sord] *s* Schwert *n;* **put to the s.** mit dem Schwert hinrichten

sword' belt' *s* Schwertgehenk *n*

sword'fish' *s* Schwertfisch *m*

swords'man *s* (–men) Fechter *m*

sworn [sworn] *adj* (*statement*) eidlich; **s. enemy** Todfeind *m*

sycamore ['sɪkəmor] *s* Platane *f*

sycophant ['sɪkəfənt] *s* Sykophant *m*

syllabary ['sɪlə‚beri] *s* Silbenschrift *f*

syllabification [sɪ‚læbɪfɪ'keʃən] *s* Silbentrennung *f*

syllable ['sɪləbəl] *s* Silbe *f*

sylla·bus ['sɪləbəs] *s* (**–bai** [‚baɪ] & **–buses**) Lehrplan *m*

syllogism ['sɪlə‚dʒɪzəm] *s* Syllogismus *m*

sylvan ['sɪlvən] *adj* Wald–

symbol ['sɪmbəl] *s* Sinnbild *n,* Symbol *n*

symbolic(al) [sɪm'balɪk(əl)] *adj* sinnbildlich, symbolisch

symbolism ['sɪmbə‚lɪzəm] *s* Symbolik *f*

symbolize ['sɪmbə‚laɪz] *tr* symbolisieren

symmetric(al) [sɪ'mɛtrɪk(əl)] *adj* symmetrisch

symmetry ['sɪmɪtri] *s* Symmetrie *f*

sympathetic [‚sɪmpə'θɛtɪk] *adj* mitfühlend; (physiol) sympathisch

sympathize ['sɪmpə‚θaɪz] *intr*—**s. with** mitfühlen mit; (*be in accord with*) sympathisieren mit

sympathizer ['sɪmpə‚θaɪzər] *s* Sympathisant –in *mf*

sympathy ['sɪmpəθi] *s* Mitleid *n;* **be in s. with** im Einverständnis sein mit; **offer one's sympathies to s.o.** j–m sein Beileid bezeigen

sym'pathy card' *s* Beileidskarte *f*

sym'pathy strike' *s* Sympathiestreik *m*

symphonic [sɪm'fanɪk] *adj* sinfonisch

symphony ['sɪmfəni] *s* Sinfonie *f*

symposi·um [sım'pozı·əm] s (–a [ə] & –ums) Symposion n
symptom ['sımptəm] s (of) Symptom n (für)
symptomatic [,sımtə'mætık] adj (of) symptomatisch (für)
synagogue ['sınə ,gɔg] s Synagoge f
synchronize ['sıŋkrə ,naız] tr synchronisieren
synchronous ['sıŋkrənəs] adj synchron; (elec) Synchron–
syncopate ['sıŋkə ,pet] tr synkopieren
syncopation [,sıŋkə'peʃən] s Synkope f
syncope ['sıŋkə ,pi] s Synkope f
syndicate ['sındıkıt] s Interessengemeinschaft f, Syndikat n || ['sındı ,ket] tr zu e–m Syndikat zusammenschließen; (a column) in mehreren Zeitungen zugleich veröffentlichen || intr ein Syndikat bilden
synod ['sınəd] s Synode f
synonym ['sınənım] s Synonym n
synonymous [sı'nanəməs] adj sinnverwandt; **s. with** gleichbedeutend mit

synop·sis [sı'napsıs] s (–ses [siz]) Zusammenfassung f
synoptic [sı'naptık] adj synoptisch
syntax ['sıntæks] s Satzlehre f, Syntax f
synthe·sis ['sınθısıs] s (–ses [,siz]) Synthese f
synthesize ['sınθı ,saız] tr (& chem) zusammenfügen
synthetic [sın'θɛtık] adj künstlich, Kunst– || s Kunststoff m
syphilis ['sıfılıs] s Syphilis f
Syria ['sırı·ə] s Syrien n
Syrian ['sırı·ən] adj syrisch || s Syrer –in mf; (language) Syrisch n
syringe [sı'rındʒ] s Spritze f || tr (inject) einspritzen; (wash) ausspritzen
syrup ['sırəp] s Sirup m
system ['sıstəm] s System n; (bodily system) Organismus m
systematic(al) [,sıstə'mætık(əl)] adj systematisch, planmäßig
systematize ['sıstəmə ,taız] tr systematisieren, systematisch ordnen
systole ['sıstəli] s Systole f

T

T, t [ti] s zwanzigster Buchstabe des englischen Alphabets
tab [tæb] s (label) Etikett n; (on file cards) Karteireiter m; **keep tabs on** (coll) genau kontrollieren; **pick up the tab** (coll) die Zeche bezahlen || v (pret & pp tabbed; ger tabbing) tr (designate) ernennen
tabby ['tæbi] s getigerte Katze f
tabernacle ['tæbər ,nækəl] s Tabernakel n
table ['tebəl] s Tisch m; (list, chart) Tafel f, Tabelle f; (geol) Tafel f; **at t.** bei Tisch; **the tables have turned** das Blatt hat sich gewendet || tr (parl) verschieben
tab·leau ['tæblo] s (–leaus & leaux [loz]) Tableau n
ta'blecloth' s Tischtuch n
ta'bleland' s Tafelland n
ta'ble man'ners spl Tischmanieren pl
ta'ble of con'tents s Inhaltsverzeichnis n
ta'ble salt' s Tafelsalz n
ta'ble set'ting s Gedeck n
ta'blespoon' s Eßlöffel m
tablespoonful ['tebəl ,spun ,ful] s Eßlöffel m
tablet ['tæblıt] s (writing pad) Schreibblock m; (med) Tablette f
ta'ble talk' s Tischgespräch n
ta'ble ten'nis s Tischtennis n
ta'bletop' s Tischplatte f
ta'bleware' s Tafelgeschirr n
ta'ble wine' s Tafelwein m
tabloid ['tæblɔıd] adj konzentriert || s Bildzeitung f; (pej) Sensationsblatt n
taboo [tə'bu] adj tabu || s Tabu n || tr für Tabu erklären

tabular ['tæbjələr] adj tabellarisch
tabulate ['tæbjə ,let] tr tabellarisieren
tabulator ['tæbjə ,letər] s Tabelliermaschine f
tacit ['tæsıt] adj stillschweigend
taciturn ['tæsıtərn] adj schweigsam
tack [tæk] s (nail) Zwecke f, Stift m; (stitch) Heftstich m; (stickiness) Klebrigkeit f; (course of action) Kurs m; (gear for a riding horse) Reitgeschirr n; (course run obliquely to the wind) Schlag m; **be on the wrong t.** (fig) auf dem Holzweg sein || tr (down) mit Zwecken befestigen; (sew) heften; **t. on** (to) anfügen (an acc) || intr (fig & naut) lavieren
tackle ['tækəl] s (gear) Ausrüstung f; (for lifting) Flaschenzug m; (fb) Halbstürmer m; (naut) Takelwerk n || tr (a problem) anpacken; (fb) packen
tacky ['tæki] adj klebrig; (gaudy) geschmacklos
tact [tækt] s Takt m, Feingefühl n
tactful ['tæktfəl] adj taktvoll
tactical ['tæktıkəl] adj taktisch
tac'tical u'nit s Kampfeinheit f
tactician [tæk'tıʃən] s Taktiker m
tactics ['tæktıks] spl (& fig) Taktik f
tactless ['tæktlıs] adj taktlos
tadpole ['tæd ,pol] s Kaulquappe f
taffeta ['tæfıtə] s Taft m
taffy ['tæfi] s Sahnebonbon n
tag [tæg] s (label) Etikett n; (loose end) loses Ende n; (on a shoestring) Stift m; (loop for hanging up a coat) Aufhänger m; (on a fish hook) Glitzerschmuck m; (game) Haschen n; **play tag** sich haschen; **tags** (aut)

Nummernschild *n* || *v* (*pret & pp*
tagged; *ger* **tagging**) *tr* (*mark with
a tag*) mit e–m Etikett versehen;
(*touch*) haschen; (*hit solidly*) heftig
schlagen; (*give a traffic ticket to*)
e–n Strafzettel geben (*dat*) || *intr*—
tag after s.o. sich an j–s Sohlen
heften

tag' line' *s* (*e.g., of a play*) Schlußworte
pl; (*favorite phrase*) stehende Redensart *f*

tail [tel] *s* Schwanz *m;* (*of a horse,
comet*) Schweif *m;* (*of a shirt*) Schoß
m; (aer) Heck *n;* **tails** ein Frack *m;*
(*of a coin*) Rückseite *f;* **turn t.** ausreißen; **wag its t.** mit dem Schwanz
wedeln || *tr* (coll) beschatten || *intr*
—**t. after** nachlaufen (*dat*); **t. off**
abflauen

tail' end' *s* (*e.g., of a conversation*)
Schlußteil *n;* **come in at the t. end** als
letzter durchs Ziel gehen

tail'gate' *s* (*of a station wagon*) Heck-
tür *f;* (*of a truck*) Ladeklappe *f* ||
intr dicht hinter e–m anderen fahren

tail' gun'ner *s* (aer) Heckschütze *m*

tail'-heav'y *adj* schwanzlastig

tail'light' *s* (aer) Hecklicht *n;* (aut)
Rücklicht *n*

tailor ['telər] *s* Schneider *m* || *tr &
intr* schneidern

tai'loring *s* Schneiderarbeit *f*

tai'lor-made suit' *s* Maßanzug *m*

tai'lor shop' *s* Schneiderei *f*

tail'piece' *s* (*appendage*) Anhang *m;*
(*of a stringed instrument*) Saiten-
halter *m;* (typ) Zierleiste *f*

tail' pipe' *s* (aut) Auspuffrohr *n*

tail'skid' *s* (aer) Sporn *m*

tail'spin' *s*—**go into a t.** abtrudeln

tail' wheel' *s* (aer) Spornrad *n*

tail'wind' *s* Rückenwind *m*

taint [tent] *s* Fleck *m;* (fig) Schand-
fleck *m* || *tr* beflecken; (*food*) ver-
derben

take [tek] *s* (*income*) (sl) Einnahmen
pl; (*loot*) (sl) Beute *f;* (angl) Fang
m; (cin) Szenenaufnahme *f;* **be on
the t.** (sl) sich bestechen lassen || *v*
(*pret* **took** [tʊk]; *pp* **taken**) *tr* nehmen; (*in a car*) mitnehmen; (*bring,
carry*) bringen; (*subtract*) abziehen;
(*require*) erfordern; (*insults, criticism*) hinnehmen; (*bear, stand*) ertragen; (*with a camera*) aufnehmen;
(*food, pills*) einnehmen; (*s.o.'s temperature*) messen; (*courage*) schöpfen; (*a deep breath*) holen; (*precautions*) treffen; (*responsibility*) übernehmen; (*an oath, test*) ablegen;
(*inventory*) aufnehmen; (*a walk, trip,
examination, turn, notes*) machen;
(*the consequences*) tragen; (*measures*) ergreifen; (*a certain amount
of time to travel*) in Anspruch nehmen; (*a step*) tun; (*advice*) befolgen;
(*a game*) gewinnen; (*e.g., third
place*) belegen; (*a trick*) (cards)
stechen; (gram) regieren; **be able to
t. a lot** e–n breiten Rücken haben;
be taken in by s.o. j–m auf den
Leim gehen; **I'm not going to t. that**

das lasse ich nicht auf mir sitzen;
t. along mitnehmen; **t. aside** bei-
seitenehmen; **t. at one's word** beim
Wort nehmen; **t. away** wegschaffen;
t. away from wegnehmen (*dat*); **t.
back** zurücknehmen; **t.** (*e.g., s.o.'s
hat*) **by mistake** verwechseln; **t. down**
herunternehmen; (*in writing*) aufschreiben; (*dictation*) aufnehmen;
(*minutes*) zu Protokoll nehmen; **t. in**
(*money*) einnehmen; (*washing*) ins
Haus nehmen; (*as guest*) beherbergen; (*deceive*) täuschen; (*encompass*)
umfassen; (*observe*) beobachten;
(*sightsee*) besichtigen; (*sew*) enger
machen; **t. it out on s.o.** seinen Zorn
an j–m auslassen; **t. it that** annehmen, daß; **taken** (*occupied*) besetzt;
t. off (*subtract*) abziehen; (*clothes*)
ausziehen; (*a coat*) ablegen; (*gloves*)
abstreifen; (*a hat*) abnehmen; (*a
tire, wheel*) abmontieren; (*e.g., a
day from work*) sich [*dat*] freineh-
men; **t.** (*e.g., wares*) **off s.o.'s hands**
j–m abnehmen; **t. on** (*hire*) anstellen; (*passengers*) aufnehmen; **t. out**
(*from a container*) herausnehmen; (*a
spot*) entfernen; (*a girl*) ausführen;
(*a mortgage, loan*) (ins)
abschließen; (libr) sich [*dat*] ausleihen; **t. over** übernehmen; **t. s.o.
for** j–n halten für; **t. up** aufnehmen;
(*absorb*) aufsaugen; (*a profession*)
ergreifen; (*room, time*) wegnehmen;
(*a collection*) veranstalten; (*a skirt*)
kürzer machen; **t. upon oneself** auf
sich nehmen; **t. up** (*a matter*) **with**
besprechen mit || *intr* (*said of an
injection*) anschlagen; (*said of seed-
lings, skin transplants*) anwachsen;
how long does it t.? wie lange dauert
es?; **how long does it t. to** (*inf*)?
wie lange braucht man, um zu (*inf*)?;
t. after nachgeraten (*dat*); **t. off**
(*depart*) (coll) abhauen; (*from work*)
wegbleiben; (aer, rok) starten; (aut)
abfahren; **t. over for s.o.** für j–n
einspringen; **t. to** (*a person*) warm
werden mit; (*an idea*) aufgreifen; **t.
up with** sich abgeben mit

take'-home pay' *s* Nettolohn *m*

take'-off' *s* Karikatur *f;* (aer) Start *m*

take'-off ramp' *s* (*in skiing*) Schanzen-
tisch *m*

take'o'ver *s* Übernahme *f*

tal'cum pow'der ['tælkəm] *s* Feder-
weiß *n*

tale [tel] *s* Geschichte *f;* **tell tales out
of school** aus der Schule plaudern

tale'bear'er *s* Zuträger –in *mf*

talent ['tælənt] *s* Talent *n*

tal'ented *adj* talentiert, begabt

talisman ['tælɪsmən] *s* Talisman *m*

talk [tɔk] *s* Gespräch *n;* (*gossip*) Geschwätz *n;* (*lecture*) Vortrag *m;*
(*speech*) Rede *f;* **cause t.** von sich
reden machen; **give a t. on** e–n Vortrag halten über (*acc*); **t. of the town**
Stadtgespräch *n* || *tr* reden; (*busi-
ness, politics, etc.*) sprechen über
(*acc*); **t. down** zum Schweigen bringen; (aer) heruntersprechen; **t. one-**

self hoarse sich heiser reden; **t. one's way out of** sich herausreden aus; **t. over** besprechen; **t. sense** vernünftig reden; **t. s.o. into** (*ger*) j–n überreden zu (*inf*); **t. up** Reklame machen für || *intr* reden; (*chat*) schwätzen; **t. back** scharf erwidern; **t. big** große Töne reden; **t. dirty** Zoten reißen; **t. down to** herablassend reden zu; **talking of food** à propos Essen; **t. on** (*a topic*) e–n Vortrag halten über (*acc*); **t. to the walls** in den Wind reden

talkative ['tɔkətɪv] *adj* redselig

talker ['tɔkər] *s* Plauderer –in *mf;* **big t.** Schaumschläger *m*

talkie ['tɔki] *s* (cin) Sprechfilm *m*

talk′ing-to′ *s* Denkzettel *m*

tall [tɔl] *adj* hoch; (*person*) hochgewachsen; **t. story** Mordsgeschichte *f*

tallow ['tælo] *s* Talg *m*

tal·ly ['tæli] *s* (*reckoning*) Rechnung *f;* (*game score*) Punktzahl *f* || *v* (*pret & pp* –lied) *tr* (up) berechnen || *intr* (with) übereinstimmen (mit)

tallyho [,tælɪ'ho] *interj* hallo!

tal′ly sheet′ *s* Zählbogen *m*

talon ['tælən] *s* Klaue *f*

tambourine [,tæmbə'rin] *s* Tamburin *n*

tame [tem] *adj* zahm; (*docile*) gefügig; (*dull*) langweilig || *tr* zähmen; (*e.g., lions*) bändigen || *intr*—**t. down** (*said of a person*) gesetzter werden

tamp [tæmp] *tr* (*a tobacco pipe*) stopfen; (*earth, cement*) stampfen; (*a drill hole*) zustopfen

tamper ['tæmpər] *s* Stampfer *m* || *intr* —**t. with** sich einmischen in (*acc*); (*machinery*) herumbasteln an (*dat*); (*documents*) frisieren

tampon ['tæmpɑn] *s* Damenbinde *f;* (surg) Tampon *m* || *tr* (surg) tamponieren

tan [tæn] *adj* gelbbraun || *s* Sonnenbräunung *f* || *v* (*pret & pp* **tanned;** *ger* **tanning**) *tr* (*the skin*) bräunen; (*leather*) gerben || *intr* sich bräunen

tandem ['tændəm] *adj & adv* hintereinander (geordnet) || *s* Tandem *n;* **in t.** hintereinander

tang [tæŋ] *s* Herbheit *f;* (*sound*) Geklingel *n*

tangent ['tændʒənt] *adj*—**be t. to** tangieren || *s* Tangente *f;* **fly off on a t.** plötzlich vom Thema abschweifen

tangerine [,tændʒə'rin] *s* Mandarine *f*

tangible ['tændʒɪbəl] *adj* (& fig) greifbar

tangle ['tæŋgəl] *s* Verwicklung *f;* (*twisted strands; confused jumble*) Gewirr *n;* (*conflict*) Auseinandersetzung *f* || *tr* verwirren; **get tangled** sich verfilzen || *intr* sich verwirren; **t. with** sich in e–n Kampf einlassen mit

tango ['tæŋgo] *s* Tango *m* || *intr* Tango tanzen

tangy ['tæŋi] *adj* herb

tank [tæŋk] *s* Behälter *m;* (*of a toilet*) Spülkasten *m;* (mil) Panzer *m*

tank′ attack′ *s* Panzerangriff *m*

tank′ car′ *s* (rr) Kesselwagen *m,* Tankwagen *m*

tanker ['tæŋkər] *s* (*truck*) Tankwagen *m;* (*ship*) Tanker *m;* (*plane*) Tankflugzeug *n*

tank′ trap′ *s* Panzersperre *f*

tank′ truck′ *s* Tankwagen *m*

tanned *adj* gebräunt

tanner ['tænər] *s* Gerber –in *mf*

tannery ['tænəri] *s* Gerberei *f*

tantalize ['tæntə,laɪz] *tr* quälen

tantamount ['tæntə,maunt] *adj*—**be t. to** gleichkommen (*dat*)

tantrum ['tæntrəm] *s* Koller *m;* **throw a t.** e–n Koller kriegen

tap [tæp] *s* (*light blow*) Klaps *m;* (*on a window or door*) Klopfen *n;* (*faucet*) Wasserhahn *m;* (*in a cask*) Faßhahn *m;* (elec) Anzapfung *f;* (mach) Gewindebohrer *m;* (surg) Punktion *f;* **on tap** vom Faß; **play taps** (mil) den Zapfenstreich blasen || *v* (*pret & pp* **tapped;** *ger* **tapping**) *tr* (*a cask, powerline, telephone*) anzapfen; (*fluids*) abzapfen; (*a person on the shoulder*) antippen; (*a hole*) mit e–m Gewinde versehen; **tap one's foot** (*to mark time*) Takt treten; **tap s.o. for** (*money*) (coll) j–n anpumpen um; **tap s.o.'s spine** j–n punktieren; **tap the window** am Fenster klopfen || *intr* tippen

tap′ dance′ *s* Steptanz *m*

tap′-dance′ *intr* steppen

tap′ dan′cer *s* Stepper –in *mf*

tape [tep] *s* Band *n;* (electron) Tonband *n;* (*friction tape*) Isolierband *n;* (*of paper*) Papierstreifen *m;* (med) Klebstreifen *m;* (sport) Zielband *n* || *tr* (mit Band) umwickeln; (electron) auf Tonband aufnehmen

tape′ meas′ure *s* Meßband *n*

taper ['tepər] *s* Wachsfaden *m* || *tr* zuspitzen || *intr* spitz zulaufen; **t. off** langsam abnehmen

tape′ record′er *s* Tonbandgerät *n*

ta′pered *adj* kegelförmig, Keil–

tapestry ['tæpɪstri] *s* Wandteppich *m*

tape′worm′ *s* Bandwurm *m*

tapioca [,tæpɪ'okə] *s* Tapioka *f*

tappet ['tæpɪt] *s* (mach) Stößel *m*

tap′room′ *s* Ausschank *m*

tap′root′ *s* Pfahlwurzel *f*

tap′ wa′ter *s* Leitungswasser *n*

tap′ wrench′ *s* Gewindeschneidkluppe *f*

tar [tɑr] *s* Teer *m* || *v* (*pret & pp* **tarred;** *ger* **tarring**) *tr* teeren

tardy ['tɑrdi] *adj* säumig

target ['tɑrgɪt] *s* Ziel *n;* (*on a firing range; of ridicule*) Zielscheibe *f*

tar′get ar′ea *s* Zielraum *m*

tar′get date′ *s* Zieltag *m*

tar′get lan′guage *s* Zielsprache *f*

tar′get prac′tice *s* Scheibenschießen *n*

tariff ['tærɪf] *s* Tarif *m*

tarnish ['tɑrnɪʃ] *tr* matt (or blind) machen; (fig) beflecken || *intr* matt (or blind) werden

tar′ pa′per *s* Teerpappe *f*

tarpaulin ['tɑrpəlɪn] *s* Plane *f*

tar·ry ['tɑri] *adj* teerig || ['tæri] *v*

(*pret & pp* **-ried**) *intr* verweilen; (*stay*) bleiben

tart [tɑrt] *adj* sauer; (*reply*) scharf ‖ *s* Tortelett *n*

tartar ['tɑrtər] *s* (dent) Zahnstein *m*

tar'tar sauce' *s* pikante Soße *f*

task [tæsk] *s* Aufgabe *f;* **take to t.** zur Rede stellen

task' force' *s* Sonderverband *m*

task'mas'ter *s* Zuchtmeister *m*

tassel ['tæsəl] *s* Quaste *f;* (*on corn*) Narbenfäden *pl*

taste [test] *s* (& *fig*) Geschmack *m;* **develop a t. for** Geschmack gewinnen an (*dat*); **have a bad t.** schlecht ‖ *intr*—**t. like** (or **of**) schmecken; **have bad t.** e–n schlechten Geschmack haben; **in bad t.** geschmacklos; **in good t.** geschmackvoll; **to t.** (culin) nach Gutdünken ‖ *tr* schmecken; (*try out*) kosten; (*e.g., the pepper in soup*) herausschmecken; **t. blood** (fig) Blut lecken nach

taste' bud' *s* Geschmacksknospe *f*

tasteful ['testfəl] *adj* geschmackvoll

tasteless ['testlɪs] *adj* (& fig) geschmacklos

tasty ['testi] *adj* schmackhaft

tatter ['tætər] *s* Lumpen *m* ‖ *tr* zerfetzen

tat'tered *adj* zerlumpt

tattle ['tætəl] *intr* petzen

tattler ['tætlər] *s* Petze *f*

tat'tletale' *s* Petze *f*

tattoo [tæ'tu] *s* Tätowierung *f* ‖ *tr* tätowieren

taunt [tɔnt] *s* Stichelei *f* ‖ *tr* sticheln gegen

taut [tɔt] *adj* straff, prall

tavern ['tævərn] *s* Schenke *f*

tawdry ['tɔdri] *adj* aufgedonnert

tawny ['tɔni] *adj* gelbbraun

tax [tæks] *s* Steuer *f* ‖ *tr* besteuern; (fig) beanspruchen; **tax s.o. with** j–n rügen wegen

taxable ['tæksəbəl] *adj* steuerpflichtig

tax' assess'ment *s* Steuereinschätzung *f*

taxation [tæk'seʃən] *s* Besteuerung *f*

tax' brac'ket *s* Steuerklasse *f*

tax' collec'tor *s* Steuereinnehmer –in *mf*

tax' cut' *s* Steuersenkung *f*

tax' evas'ion *s* Steuerhinterziehung *f*

tax' exemp'tion *s* steuerfreier Betrag *m*

tax•i ['tæksi] *s* Taxi *n;* **go by t.** mit e–m Taxi fahren ‖ *v* (*pret & pp* **-ied;** *ger* **-iing** & **-ying**) *tr* (aer) rollen lassen ‖ *intr* mit e–m Taxi fahren; (aer) rollen

tax'icab' *s* Taxi *n*

tax'i danc'er *s* Taxigirl *n*

taxidermist ['tæksɪ,dʌrmɪst] *s* Tierpräparator –in *mf*

tax'i driv'er *s* Taxifahrer –in *mf*

tax'ime'ter *s* Taxameter *m*

tax'i stand' *s* Taxistand *m*

tax'pay'er *s* Steuerzahler –in *mf*

tax' rate' *s* Steuersatz *m*

tax' return' *s* Steuererklärung *f*

tea [ti] *s* Tee *m*

tea' bag' *s* Teebeutel *m*

tea' cart' *s* Teewagen *m*

teach [titʃ] *v* (*pret & pp* **taught** [tɔt]) *tr* lehren; (*instruct*) unterrichten; **t. school** an e–r Schule unterrichten; **t. s.o. manners** j–m Manieren beibringen; **t. s.o. music** j–n in Musik unterrichten; **t. s.o. (to play) tennis** j–m das Tennisspielen beibringen ‖ *intr* lehren, unterrichten

teacher ['titʃər] *s* Lehrer –in *mf*

teach'er's pet' *s* Liebling *m* des Lehrers (or der Lehrerin)

teach'ing *s* Lehren *n;* (*profession*) Lehrberuf *m*

teach'ing aid' *s* Lehrmittel *n*

teach'ing staff' *s* Lehrkörper *m*

tea'cup' *s* Teetasse *f*

teak [tik] *s* Teakholz *n*

tea'ket'tle *s* Teekessel *m*

tea' leaves' *spl* Teesatz *m*

team [tim] *s* Team *n;* (*of draught animals*) Gespann *n;* (sport) Mannschaft *f* ‖ *tr* (*draft animals*) zusammenspannen ‖ *intr*—**t. up with** sich vereinigen mit

team' cap'tain *s* Spielführer –in *mf*

team'mate' *s* Mannschaftskamerad –in *mf*

teamster ['timstər] *s* Fuhrmann *m;* (*trucker*) Lastwagenfahrer *m*

team'work' *s* Gemeinschaftsarbeit *f;* (sport) Zusammenspiel *n*

tea'pot' *s* Teekanne *f*

tear [tɪr] *s* Träne *f;* **bring tears to the eyes** Tränen in die Augen treiben; **burst into tears** in Tränen ausbrechen ‖ [tɛr] *s* Riß *m* ‖ *v* (*pret tore* [tor]; *pp torn* [torn]) *tr* (zer)reißen; **t. apart** (*meat*) zerreißen; (*a speech*) zerpflücken; **t. away** wegreißen; **t. down** (*a building*) abreißen; (mach) zerlegen; (*a person*) sich [*dat*] das Maul zerreißen über (*acc*); **t. off** abreißen; **t. open** aufreißen; **t. oneself away** sich losreißen; **t. out** ausreißen; **t. up** (*a street*) aufreißen; (*e.g., letter*) zerreißen ‖ *intr* (zer)reißen; **t. along** (*at high speed*) dahinsausen

teardrop ['tɪr,drɑp] *s* Träne *f*

tear' gas' [tɪr] *s* Tränengas *n*

tear-jerker ['tɪr,dʒʌrkər] *s* (sl) Schnulze *f*

tea'room' *s* Teestube *f*

tease [tiz] *tr* necken; (*e.g., a dog*) quälen; (*hair*) auflockern

teas'ing *s* Neckerei *f*

tea'spoon' *s* Teelöffel *m*

teaspoonful ['ti,spun,ful] *s* Teelöffel *m*

teat [tit] *s* Zitze *f*

technical ['tɛknɪkəl] *adj* technisch, Fach–

tech'nical in'stitute *s* technische Hochschule *f*

technicality [,tɛknɪ'kælɪti] *s* technische Einzelheit *f*

tech'nical school' *s* Technikum *n*

tech'nical term' *s* Fachausdruck *m*

technician [tɛk'nɪʃən] *s* Techniker –in *mf*

technique [tɛk'nik] *s* Technik *f*

technocrat ['tɛknə ˌkræt] *s* Technokrat *m*

technological [ˌtɛknə'lɑdʒɪkəl] *adj* technologisch

technology [tɛk'nɑlɪdʒi] *s* Technologie *f*

ted′dy bear′ ['tɛdi] *s* Teddybär *m*

tedious ['tidɪ·əs] *adj* langweilig

tee [ti] *s* (*mound*) Abschlagplatz *m;* (*wooden or plastic peg*) Aufsatz *m;* **to a tee** aufs Haar ‖ *tr*—**tee off** (sl) aufregen; **tee up** (golf) auf den Aufsatz stellen ‖ *intr*—**tee off** (golf) abschlagen

teem [tim] *intr* (**with**) wimmeln (von)

teem′ing *adj* wimmelnd; (*rain*) strömend

teen-age ['tin ˌedʒ] *adj* halbwüchsig

teen-ager ['tin ˌedʒər] *s* Teenager *m*

teens [tinz] *spl* Jugendalter *n* (*vom dreizehnten bis neunzehnten Lebensjahr*); **in one′s t.** in den Jugendjahren

teeny ['tini] *adj* (coll) winzig

tee′ shot′ *s* (golf) Abschlag *m*

teeter ['titər] *s* Schaukeln *n* ‖ *intr* schaukeln

teethe [tið] *intr* zahnen

teeth′ing ring′ *s* Beißring *m*

teetotaler [ti'totələr] *s* Abstinenzler –in *mf*

tele·cast ['tɛlɪ ˌkæst] *s* Fernsehsendung *f* ‖ *v* (*pret & pp* –**cast** & –**casted**) *tr* im Fernsehen übertragen

telecommunications [ˌtɛlɪkə ˌmjunɪ'keʃəns] *spl* Fernmeldewesen *n*

telegram ['tɛlɪ ˌgræm] *s* Telegramm *n*

telegraph ['tɛlɪ ˌgræf] *s* Telegraph *m* ‖ *tr & intr* telegraphieren

telegrapher [tɪ'lɛgrəfər] *s* Telegraphist –in *mf*

tel′egraph pole′ *s* Telegraphenstange *f*

telemeter [tɪ'lɛmɪtər] *s* Telemeter *n*

telepathy [tɪ'lɛpəθi] *s* Telepathie *f*

telephone ['tɛlɪ ˌfon] *s* Telephon *n,* Fernsprecher *m;* **be on the t.** am Apparat sein; **by t.** telephonisch; **speak on the t. with** telephonieren mit ‖ *tr & intr* anrufen

tel′ephone booth′ *s* Telephonzelle *f*

tel′ephone call′ *s* Telephonanruf *m*

tel′ephone direc′tory *s* Teilnehmerverzeichnis *n*

tel′ephone exchange′ *s* Telephonzentrale *f*

tel′ephone num′ber *s* Telephonnummer *f*

tel′ephone op′erator *s* Telephonist –in *mf*

tel′ephone receiv′er *s* Telephonhörer *m*

tel′ephoto lens′ ['tɛlɪ ˌfoto] *s* Teleobjektiv *n*

telescope ['tɛlɪ ˌskop] *s* Fernrohr *n,* Perspektiv *n* ‖ *tr* ineinanderschieben; (fig) verkürzen ‖ *intr* sich ineinanschieben

telescopic [ˌtɛlɪ'skɑpɪk] *adj* teleskopisch

telescop′ic sight′ *s* Zielfernrohr *n*

Teletype ['tɛlɪ ˌtaɪp] *s* (trademark) Fernschreiber *m* ‖ **teletype** *tr* durch Fernschreiber übermitteln ‖ *intr* fernschreiben

tel′etype′writ′er *s* Fernschreiber *m*

televiewer ['tɛlɪ ˌvju·ər] *s* Fernsehteilnehmer –in *mf*

televise ['tɛlɪ ˌvaɪz] *tr* im Fernsehen übertragen (or senden)

television ['tɛlɪ ˌvɪʒən] *adj* Fernseh– ‖ *s* Fernsehen *n;* **watch t.** fernsehen

tel′evision net′work *s* Fernsehnetz *n*

tel′evision screen′ *s* Bildschirm *m*

tel′evision set′ *s* Fernsehapparat *m;* **color t.** Farbfernsehapparat *m*

tel′evision show′ *s* Fernschau *f*

telex ['tɛlɛks] *s* Fernschreiber *m;* (*message*) Telex *n* ‖ *tr* fernschreiben

tell [tɛl] *v* (*pret & pp* **told** [told]) *tr* (*the truth, a lie*) sagen; (*relate*) erzählen; (*a secret*) anvertrauen; (*let know*) Bescheid sagen (*dat*); (*inform*) bestellen; (*express*) ausdrücken; (*the reason*) angeben; (*distinguish*) auseinanderhalten; **be able to t. time** die Uhr lesen können; **t. apart** auseinanderhalten; **t. me another!** (sl) das machst du mir nicht weis!; **t. s.o. off** j–n abkanzeln; **t. s.o. that** (*assure s.o. that*) j–m versichern, daß; **t. s.o. to** (*inf*) j–m sagen, daß er (*inf*) soll; **t. s.o. where to get off** (sl) j–m e–e Zigarre verpassen; **to t. the truth** ehrlich gesagt; **you can t. by looking at her that** man sieht es ihr an, daß ‖ *intr*—**don′t t. me!** na, so was!; **t. on** (*betray*) verraten; (*produce a marked effect on*) sehr mitnehmen; **you′re telling me!** wem sagst du das!

teller ['tɛlər] *s* (*of a bank*) Kassierer –in *mf;* (*of votes*) Zähler –in *mf*

tell′ing *adj* (*blow*) wirksam

tell′-tale′ *adj* verräterisch

temper ['tɛmpər] *s* (*anger*) Zorn *m;* (*of steel*) Härtegrad *m;* **bad t.** großer Zorn *m;* **even t.** Gleichmut *m;* **lose one′s t.** in Wut geraten ‖ *tr* (**with**) mildern (durch); (*steel*) härten; (mus) temperieren

temperament ['tɛmpərəmənt] *s* Temperament *n*

temperamental [ˌtɛmpərə'mɛntəl] *adj* launisch, temperamentvoll

temperance ['tɛmpərəns] *s* Mäßigkeit *f*

temperate ['tɛmpərɪt] *adj* mäßig; (*climate*) gemäßigt

Tem′perate Zone′ *s* gemäßigte Zone *f*

temperature ['tɛmərətʃər] *s* Temperatur *f*

tempest ['tɛmpɪst] *s* Sturm *m;* **a t. in a teapot** ein Sturm im Wasserglas

tempestuous [tɛm'pɛstʃu·əs] *adj* stürmisch

temple ['tɛmpəl] *s* Tempel *m;* (*of glasses*) Bügel *m;* (anat) Schläfe *f*

tem·po ['tɛmpo] *s* (–**pos** & –**pi** [pi]) Tempo *n*

temporal ['tɛmpərəl] *adj* zeitlich

temporary ['tɛmpə ˌrɛri] *adj* zeitweilig; (*credit, solution*) Zwischen–

temporize ['tɛmpə ˌraɪz] *intr* Zeit zu gewinnen suchen

tempt [tɛmpt] *tr* versuchen; (*said of things*) reizen, locken

temptation [tɛmp'teʃən] s Versuchung f

tempter ['tɛmptər] s Versucher m

tempt'ing adj verlockend

temptress ['tɛmptrɪs] s Versucherin f

ten [tɛn] adj & pron zehn ‖ s Zehn f

tenable ['tɛnəbəl] adj haltbar

tenacious [tɪ'neʃəs] adj (obstinate) nartnäckig; (memory) verläßlich

tenacity [tɪ'næsɪti] s Hartnäckigkeit f

tenant ['tɛnənt] s Mieter –in mf

ten'ant farm'er s Pächter –in mf

tend [tɛnd] tr (flocks) hüten; (the sick) pflegen; (a machine) bedienen ‖ intr—t. to (attend to) sich kümmern um; (inf) dazu neigen zu (inf); **t. toward(s)** neigen zu

tendency ['tɛndənsi] s Tendenz f

tender ['tɛndər] adj zart ‖ s Angebot n; (nav, rr) Tender m ‖ tr anbieten

ten'derfoot' s Neuankömmling m; (boy-scout) neu aufgenommener Pfadfinder m

ten'derheart'ed adj zartfühlend

ten'derloin' s Rindslendenstück n

tenderness ['tɛndərnɪs] s Zartheit f

tendon ['tɛndən] s Sehne f

tendril ['tɛndrɪl] s Ranke f

tenement ['tɛnɪmənt] s (dwelling) Wohnung f; (rented dwelling) Mietwohnung f

ten'ement house' s Mietskaserne f

tenet ['tɛnɪt] s Grundsatz m, Lehrsatz m

ten'fold' adj & adv zehnfach

tennis ['tɛnɪs] s Tennis n

ten'nis court' s Tennisplatz m

ten'nis rack'et s Tennisschläger m

tenor ['tɛnər] s (drift, meaning; singer; voice range) Tenor m

ten'pin' s Kegel m

tense [tɛns] adj gespannt, straff; **make t.** spannen ‖ s (gram) Tempus n, Zweitform f

tension ['tɛnʃən] s (& elec) Spannung f; (phys) Spannkraft f

tent [tɛnt] s Zelt n

tentacle ['tɛntəkəl] s Fühler m; (bot) Tentakel m

tentative ['tɛntətɪv] adj vorläufig

tenth [tɛnθ] adj & pron zehnte ‖ s (fraction) Zehntel n; **the t.** (in dates and in series) der Zehnte

tent' pole' s Zeltstange f

tenuous ['tɛnju·əs] adj (thin) dünn; (rarefied) verdünnt; (insignificant) unbedeutend; (weak) schwach

tenure ['tɛnjər] s (possession) Besitz m; (educ) Anstellung f auf Lebenszeit; **t. of office** Amtsdauer f

tepid ['tɛpɪd] adj lauwarm

term [tʌrm] s (expression) Ausdruck m; (time period) Frist f; (of office) Amtszeit f; (jur) Sitzungsperiode f; (math) Glied n; (log) Begriff m; **be on good terms with** in guten Beziehungen stehen mit; **come to terms with** handelseinig werden mit; **in plain terms** unverblümt; **in terms of** im Sinne von; **in terms of praise** mit lobenden Worten; **on easy terms** zu günstigen Bedingungen; **on equal terms** auf gleichem Fuß; **on t.** (com) auf Zeit; **not be on speaking terms with** nicht sprechen mit; **tell s.o. in no uncertain terms** j–m gründlich die Meinung sagen; **terms** (of a contract, treaty, payment) Bedingungen pl ‖ tr bezeichnen

termagant ['tʌrməgənt] s Xanthippe f

terminal ['tʌrmɪnəl] adj End–; (disease) unheilbar ‖ s (aer) Flughafenempfangsgebäude n; (pole) (elec) Pol m; (rr) Kopfbahnhof m

terminate ['tʌrmɪˌnet] tr (end) beenden; (limit) begrenzen ‖ intr enden, endigen; (gram) (in) auslauten (auf acc)

termination [ˌtʌrmɪ'neʃən] s Beendigung f; (gram) Endung f

terminology [ˌtʌrmɪ'nɑlɪdʒi] s Terminologie f

term' insur'ance s Versicherung f auf Zeit

terminus ['tʌrmɪnəs] s (end) Endpunkt m; (boundary) Grenze f; (rr) Endstation f

termite ['tʌrmaɪt] s Termite f

term' pa'per s Referat n

terrace ['tɛrəs] s Terrasse f ‖ tr abstufen, terrassieren

terra cotta ['tɛrə'kɑtə] s Terrakotta f

ter'ra-cot'ta adj Terrakotta–

terrain [tɛ'ren] s Gelände n, Terrain n

terrestrial [tə'rɛstrɪ·əl] adj irdisch

terrible ['tɛrɪbəl] adj furchtbar

terribly ['tɛrɪbli] adv (coll) furchtbar

terrier ['tɛrɪ·ər] s Terrier m

terrific [tə'rɪfɪk] adj (frightful) fürchterlich; (intense) (coll) gewaltig; (splendid) (coll) prima

terri·fy ['tɛrɪˌfaɪ] v (pret & pp –fied) tr Entsetzen einjagen (dat)

ter'rifying adj schrecklich

territorial [ˌtɛrɪ'torɪ·əl] adj territorial; **t. waters** Hoheitsgewässer pl

territory ['tɛrɪˌtori] s Gebiet n, Territorium n; (of a salesman) Absatzgebiet n; (pol) Hoheitsgebiet n; (sport) Spielhälfte f

terror ['tɛrər] s Schrecken m; **in t.** vor Schrecken

terrorism ['tɛrəˌrɪzəm] s Terrorismus m

terrorist ['tɛrərɪst] s Terrorist –in mf

terrorize ['tɛrəˌraɪz] tr terrorisieren

ter'ror-strick'en adj schreckerfüllt

ter'ry cloth' ['tɛri] s Frottee m & n

terse [tʌrs] adj knapp

tertiary ['tʌrʃɪˌɛri] adj Tertiär–

test [tɛst] s Probe f, Prüfung f; (criterion) Prüfstein m; (med) Probe f; **put to the t.** auf die Probe stellen ‖ tr (for) prüfen (auf acc); (chem) (for) analysieren (auf acc); **t. out** (coll) ausprobieren

testament ['tɛstəmənt] s Testament n

testator [tɛs'tetər] s Erblasser –in mf

test' ban' s Atomstopp m

test' case' s Probefall m; (jur) Präzedenzfall m

test'flight' s Probeflug m

testicle ['tɛstɪkəl] s Hoden m

testi·fy ['tɛstɪˌfaɪ] v (pret & pp –fied)

intr (**against**) zeugen (**gegen**), aussagen (**gegen**); **t. to** bezeugen
testimonial [ˌtɛstɪˈmonɪ-əl] *adj* (*dinner*) Ehren– ‖ *s* Anerkennungsschreiben *n*
testimony [ˈtɛstɪ ˌmoni] *s* Zeugnis *n*
test' pa'per *s* Prüfungsarbeit *f*
test' pi'lot *s* Versuchsflieger –in *mf*
test' tube' *s* Reagenzglas *n*
testy [ˈtɛsti] *adj* reizbar
tetanus [ˈtetənəs] *s* Starrkrampf *m*
tether [ˈteðər] *s* Haltestrick *m;* **be at the end of one's t.** nicht mehr weiter wissen ‖ *tr* anbinden
Teuton [ˈt(j)utən] *s* Teutone *m,* Teutonin *f*
Teutonic [t(j)uˈtɑnɪk] *adj* teutonisch
text [tɛkst] *s* Text *m*
text'book' *s* Lehrbuch *n*
textile [ˈtɛkstaɪl] *adj* Textil– ‖ *s* Webstoff *m;* **textiles** Textilien *pl*
textual [ˈtɛkstʃʊ-əl] *adj* textlich
texture [ˈtɛkstʃər] *s* (*structure*) Gefüge *n;* (*of a fabric*) Gewebe *n;* (*of a play*) Aufbau *m*
Thai [taɪ] *adj* Thai– ‖ *s* (*person*) Thai –in *mf;* (*language*) Thai *n*
Thailand [ˈtaɪlənd] *s* Thailand *n*
Thames [tɛmz] *s* Themse *f*
than [ðæn] *conj* als; **t. ever** denn je
thank [θæŋk] *adj* (*offering*) Dank– ‖ **thanks** *spl* Dank *m;* **give thanks to** danken (*dat*); **many thanks!** vielen Dank!; **return thanks** danksagen; **thanks a lot!** danke vielmals!; **thanks to her, I** ich verdanke es ihr, daß ich ‖ *tr* danken (*dat*); **t. God!** Gott sei Dank!; **t. goodness!** gottlob!; **t. you!** danke schön!; **t. you ever so much!** verbindlichsten Dank!; **you have only yourself to t. for** das hast du dir nur selbst zu verdanken
thankful [ˈθæŋkfəl] *adj* dankbar
thankless [ˈθæŋklɪs] *adj* undankbar
Thanksgiv'ing Day' *s* Danksagungstag *m*
that [ðæt] *adj* jener, der; **t. one** der da, jener ‖ *adv* (*coll*) so, derart ‖ *rel pron* der, welcher; (*after indefinite pronouns*) was ‖ *dem pron* das; **about t.** darüber; **after t.** danach; **and that's t.** und damit punktum!; **at t.** so, dabei; **by t.** dadurch; **for all t.** trotz alledem; **for t.** dafür; **from t.** daraus; **in t.** darin, daran; **on t.** darauf, drauf; **t. is** das heißt; **that's out** das kommt nicht in Frage!; **t. will do!** das reicht! ‖ *conj* daß
thatch [θætʃ] *s* Dachstroh *n*
thatched' roof' *s* Strohdach *n*
thaw [θɔ] *s* Tauwetter *n* ‖ *tr & intr* (auf)tauen
the [ðə], [ði] *def art* der, die, das ‖ *adv*—**so much the better** um so besser; **the ... the** je ... desto, je ... um so
theater [ˈθi-ətər] *s* Theater *n*
the'atergo'er *s* Theaterbesucher –in *mf*
the'ater of war' *s* Kriegsschauplatz *m*
theatrical [θɪˈætrɪkəl] *adj* (& *fig*) theatralisch
thee [ði] *pers pron* dich; **to t.** dir

theft [θɛft] *s* Diebstahl *m*
their [ðɛr] *poss adj* ihr
theirs [ðɛrz] *poss pron* ihrer
them [ðɛm] *pron* sie; **to t.** ihnen
theme [θim] *s* Thema *n;* (*essay*) Aufsatz *m;* (*mus*) Thema *n*
theme' song' *s* Kennmelodie *f*
themselves' *intens pron* selbst, selber ‖ *reflex pron* sich
then [ðɛn] *adv* (*next; in that case*) dann; (*at that time*) damals; **by t.** bis dahin; **from t. on** von da an; **t. and there** auf der Stelle; **till t.** bis dahin; **what t.?** was dann?
thence [ðɛns] *adv* von ..., von dort; (*from that fact*) daraus
thence'forth' *adv* von da an
theologian [ˌθi-əˈlodʒən] *s* Theologe *m,* Theologin *f*
theological [ˌθi-əˈlɑdʒɪkəl] *adj* theologisch
theology [θiˈɑlədʒi] *s* Theologie *f*
theorem [ˈθi-ərəm] *s* Lehrsatz *m*
theoretical [ˌθi-əˈrɛtɪkəl] *adj* theoretisch
theorist [ˈθi-ərɪst] *s* Theoretiker –in *mf*
theorize [ˈθi-əˌraɪz] *intr* theoretisieren
theory [ˈθi-əri] *s* Theorie *f,* Lehre *f*
the'ory of relativ'ity *s* Relativitätstheorie *f*
therapeutic [ˌθɛrəˈpjutɪk] *adj* therapeutisch ‖ **therapeutics** *s* Therapeutik *f*
therapy [ˈθɛrəpi] *s* Therapie *f*
there [ðɛr] *adv* (*position*) da; (*direction*) dahin; **down t.** da unten; **not be all t.** (*coll*) nicht ganz richtig sein; **over t.** da drüben; **t. are** es gibt, es sind; **t. is** es gibt, es ist; **t., t.!** sachte, sachte!; **up t.** da (or dort) oben
there'abouts' *adv* daherum; **ten people or t.** so ungefähr zehn Leute
there'af'ter *adv* danach
there'by' *adv* dadurch, damit
therefore [ˈðɛrˌfor] *adv* deshalb, darum
there'in' *adv* darin
there'of' *adv* davon
there'to' *adv* dazu
there'upon' *adv* daraufhin, danach
there'with' *adv* damit
thermal [ˈθʌrməl] *adj* Thermal–, Wärme–
thermodynamic [ˌθʌrmodaɪˈnæmɪk] *adj* thermodynamisch ‖ **thermodynamics** *s* Thermodynamik *f,* Wärmelehre *f*
thermometer [θerˈmɑmɪtər] *s* Thermometer *n*
thermonuclear [ˌθɛrmoˈn(j)uklɪ-ər] *adj* thermonuklear
ther'mos bot'tle [ˈθʌrməs] *s* Thermosflasche *f*
thermostat [ˈθʌrməˌstæt] *s* Thermostat *m*
thesau·rus [θɪˈsɔrəs] *s* (**–ri** [raɪ]) Thesaurus *m*
these [ðiz] *dem adj & pron* diese
the·sis [ˈθisɪs] *s* (**–ses** [siz]) These *f*
they [ðe] *pers pron* sie; **t. say** man sagt
thick [θɪk] *adj* dick; (*dense*) dicht;

(*stupid*) stumpfsinnig; (*lips*) wulstig; (*intimate*) (coll) dick; **t. with dust** dick bedeckt mit Staub || *adv*—**be in t. with** (coll dicke Beziehungen haben mit; **come t. and fast** Schlag auf Schlag gehen; **lay it on t.** (coll) dick auftragen || *s*—**in the t. of** mitten in (*dat*); **through t. and thin** durch dick und dünn

thicken ['θɪkən] *tr* verdicken; (*make denser*) verdichten; (*a sauce*) eindicken || *intr* sich verdicken; (*become denser*) sich verdichten; (*said of liquids*) sich verfestigen; (*said of a sauce*) eindicken; **the plot thickens** der Knoten schürzt sich

thicket ['θɪkɪt] *s* Dickicht *n*

thick'head' *s* (coll) Dickkopf *m*

thick'-head'ed *adj* (coll) dickköpfig

thickness ['θɪknɪs] *s* Dicke *f*

thick'-set' *adj* stämmig

thick'skinned' *adj* (coll) dickfellig

thief [θif] *s* (**thieves** [θivz] Dieb –in *mf*

thieve [θiv] *intr* stehlen

thievery ['θivəri] *s* Dieberei *f*

thievish ['θivɪʃ] *adj* diebisch

thigh [θaɪ] *s* Schenkel *m*, Oberschenkel *m*

thighbone' *s* Oberschenkelknochen *m*

thimble ['θɪmbəl] *s* Fingerhut *m*

thin [θɪn] *adj* (**thinner; thinnest**) dünn; (*hair*) schütter; (*lean*) mager; (*excuse*) schwach; (*soup*) wäßrig || *v* (*pret & pp* **thinned**; *ger* **thinning**) *tr* (*a liquid*) verdünnen; (*a forest*) lichten; **t. out** (*plants*) vereinzeln || *intr* (*said of hair*) sich lichten; **t. out** (*said of a crowd*) sich verlaufen

thing [θɪŋ] *s* Ding *n*, Sache *f*; **among other things** unter anderem; **first t.** zu allerest; **how are things?** wie geht's?; **I'll do no such t.!** ich werde mich schön hüten; **of all things!** na sowas!; **the real t.** das Richtige; **things** (*the situation*) die Lage *f*; (*belongings*) Sachen *pl*

think [θɪŋk] *v* (*pret & pp* **thought** [θɔt]) *tr* denken; (*regard*) halten; (*believe*) glauben, denken; **he thinks he's clever** er hält sich für klug; **that's what you t.!** ja, denkste!; **t. better of it** sich e–s Besseren besinnen; **t. it best to** (*inf*) es für das Beste halten zu (*inf*); **t. little of** nicht viel halten von; **t. nothing of it!** es ist nicht der Rede wert!; **t. over** sich [*dat*] überlegen; **t. up** sich [*dat*] ausdenken; **what do you t. you're doing?** was soll das? || *intr* denken; **be thinking of** (*ger*) beabsichtigen zu (*inf*); **do you t. so?** meinen Sie?; **t. about** (*call to consciousness*) denken an (*acc*); (*reflect on*) nachdenken über (*acc*); (*be concerned about*) bedacht sein auf (*acc*); **t. twice before** es sich [*dat*] zweimal überlegen, bevor

thinker ['θɪŋkər] *s* Denker –in *mf*

thin'-lipped' *adj* dünnlippig

thinner ['θɪnər] *s* Verdünnungsmittel *n*

third [θɪrd] *adj & pron* dritte || *s* (*frac-*

tion) Drittel *n*; (mus) Terz *f*; **the third** (*in dates and in series*) der Dritte

third'-class' *adj & adv* dritter Klasse

third' degree' *s*—**give s.o. the t.** j–n e–m Folterverhör unterwerfen

third' par'ty *s* Dritter *m*, dritte Seite *f*

third'-rate' *adj* drittrangig

thirst [θʌrst] *s* (for) Durst *m* (nach); **t. for knowledge** Wissensdurst *m*; **t. for power** Herrschsucht *f* || *intr* **(for)** dürsten (nach)

thirsty ['θʌrsti] *adj* durstig; **be t.** Durst haben

thirteen ['θʌr'tin] *adj & pron* dreizehn || *s* Dreizehn *f*

thirteenth ['θʌr'tinθ] *adj & pron* dreizehnte || *s* (*fraction*) Dreizehntel *n*; **the t.** (*in dates and in series*) der Dreizehnte

thirtieth ['θʌrtɪ·ɪθ] *adj & pron* dreißigste || *s* (*fraction*) Dreißigstel *n*; **the t.** (*in dates and in series*) der Dreißigste

thirty ['θʌrti] *adj & pron* dreißig || *s* Dreißig *f*; **the thirties** die dreißiger Jahre

thir'ty-one' *adj & pron* einunddreißig

this [ðɪs] *dem adj* dieser; **t. afternoon** heute nachmittag; **t. evening** heute abend; **t. minute** augenblicklich; **t. one** dieser || *adv* (coll) so || *dem pron* dieser, der; **about t.** hierüber; (*concerning this*) davon; **t. and that** dies und jenes

thistle ['θɪsəl] *s* Distel *f*

thither ['θɪðər] *adv* dorthin, hinzu

thong [θɔŋ] *s* Riemen *m*; (*sandal*) Sandale *f*

tho·rax ['θoræks] *s* (**–raxes & –races** [rə,siz]) Brustkorb *m*

thorn [θɔrn] *s* Dorn *m*; **t. in the side** Dorn *m* im Fleisch

thorny ['θɔrni] *adj* dornig; (fig) heikel

thorough ['θʌro] *adj* gründlich; (coll) tüchtig

thor'oughbred' *adj* reinrassig || *s* Vollblut *n*; (*horse*) Vollblutpferd *n*, Rassepferd *n*

thor'oughfare' *s* Durchgang *m*; **no t.** (*public sign*) Durchgang verboten

thor'oughgo'ing *adj* gründlich

thoroughly ['θʌroli] *adv* gründlich

those [ðoz] *dem adj & pron* jene, die da

thou [ðaʊ] *pers pron* du

though [ðo] *adv* immerhin || *conj* obwohl

thought [θɔt] *s* Gedanke(n) *m*; **be lost in t.** in Gedanken versunken sein; **give some t. to** sich [*dat*] Gedanken machen über (*acc*); **have second thoughts** sich [*dat*] eines Besseren besinnen; **on second t.** nach reiflicher Überlegung; **the mere t.** schon der Gedanke

thoughtful ['θɔtfəl] *adj* (*reflective*) nachdenklich; (*e.g., essay*) gedankenvoll; (*considerate*) aufmerksam; (*gift*) sinnig; **t. of** bedacht auf (*acc*)

thoughtless ['θɔtlɪs] *adj* gedankenlos

thought'-provok'ing *adj* anregend

thousand ['θauzənd] *adj & pron* tausend; **a t. times** tausendmal ‖ *s* Tausend *f;* **by the t.** zu Tausenden
thousandth ['θauzəndθ] *adj & pron* tausendste ‖ *s* (*fraction*) Tausendstel *n*
thrash [θræʃ] *tr* (& fig) dreschen; **t. out** (*debate*) gründlich erörten ‖ *intr* dreschen; **t. about** sich hin– und herwerfen
thrash'ing *s* Dreschen *n;* (*beating*) Dresche *f*
thread [θred] *s* Faden *m;* (*of a screw*) Gewinde *n;* (*of a story*) Faden *m;* **hang by a t.** an e–m Faden hängen ‖ *tr* (*a needle*) einfädeln; (*pearls*) aufreihen; (mach) Gewinde schneiden in (*acc*)
thread'bare' *adj* fadenscheinig
threat [θret] *s* Drohung *f*
threaten ['θrɛtən] *tr* drohen (*dat*), bedrohen; **t. so. with s.th.** j–m etw androhen ‖ *intr* drohen
three [θri] *adj & pron* drei ‖ *s* Drei *f;* **in threes** zu dritt
three' cheers' *spl* ein dreimaliges Hoch *n*
three'-dimen'sional *adj* dreidimensional
three'-en'gine *adj* dreimotorig
three'-piece' *adj* (*suit*) dreiteilig
three'-ply' *adj* dreischichtig
three'-point land'ing *s* Dreipunktlandung *f*
threnody ['θrɛnədi] *s* Klagelied *n*
thresh [θrɛʃ] *tr* dreschen; **t. out** (*debate*) gründlich erörten ‖ *intr* dreschen
thresh'ing floor' *s* Dreschtenne *f*
thresh'ing machine' *s* Dreschmaschine *f*
threshold ['θrɛʃold] *s* Türschwelle *f;* (psychol) Schwelle *f*
thrice [θraɪs] *adv* dreimal
thrift [θrɪft] *s* Sparsamkeit *f*
thrifty ['θrɪfti] *adj* sparsam
thrill [θrɪl] *s* Nervenkitzel *m* ‖ *tr* erregen, packen
thriller ['θrɪlər] *s* Thriller *m*
thrill'ing *adj* packend, spannend
thrive [θraɪv] *v* (*pret* **thrived** & **throve** [θrov]; *pp* **thrived** & **thriven** ['θrɪvən]) *intr* gedeihen
throat [θrot] *s* Kehle *f;* **clear one's t.** sich räuspern; **cut one another's t.** (fig) sich gegenseitig kaputt machen; **cut one's own t.** (fig) sich [*dat*] sein eigenes Grab schaufeln; **jump down s.o.'s t.** j–m an die Gurgel fahren; **sore t.** Halsweh *n*
throb [θrɑb] *s* Schlagen *n;* (*of a motor*) Dröhnen *n* ‖ *v* (*pret* & *pp* **throbbed;** *ger* **throbbing**) *intr* schlagen; (*said of a motor or head*) dröhnen
throes [θroz] *spl* Schmerzen *pl;* **be in the t. of death** im Todeskampf liegen
thrombosis [θrɑm'bosɪs] *s* Thrombose *f*
throne [θron] *s* Thron *m*
throng [θrɔŋ] *s* Menschenmenge *f* ‖ *tr* umdrängen; (*the streets*) sich drängen in (*acc*) ‖ *intr* (**around**) sich drängen (um)
throttle ['θrɑtəl] *s* Drossel(klappe) *f*

‖ *tr* drosseln; (*a person*) erwürgen ‖ *intr*—**t. back** (*aut*) das Gas zurücknehmen
through [θru] *adj* (*traffic, train*) Durchgangs–; (*street*) durchgehend; (*finished*) fertig; (coll) quitt ‖ *adv*— **t. and t.** durch und durch ‖ *prep* durch (*acc*)
throughout' *adv* durch und durch ‖ *prep* hindurch (*acc*) (postpositive), e.g., **t. the summer** den ganzen Sommer hindurch; **t. the world** in der ganzen Welt
throw [θro] *s* Wurf *m;* (*scarf*) Überwurf *m* ‖ *v* (*pret* **threw** [θru]; *pp* **thrown** [θron]) *tr* werfen; (*a rider*) abwerfen; (*sparks*) sprühen; (*a party, banquet*) geben; (*a game*) absichtlich verlieren; (*into confusion*) bringen; **t. away** wegwerfen; **t. down** niederwerfen; (*overturn*) umwerfen; **t. in** (*e.g., a few extras*) als Zugabe geben; **t. off** (fig) aus dem Gleichgewicht bringen; **t. out** hinauswerfen; (*a person*) vor die Tür setzen; (*the chest*) herausdrücken; **t. out of the game** vom Platz verweisen; **t. the book at s.o.** (fig) j–n zur Höchststrafe verurteilen; **t. up to s.o.** j–m vorwerfen ‖ *intr* werfen; **t. up** sich erbrechen
throw'away' *adj* Einweg–
throw'back' *s* (**to**) Rückkehr *f* (zu)
throw' rug' *s* Vorleger *m*
thrum [θrʌm] *v* (*pret* & *pp* **thrummed;** *ger* **thrumming**) *intr* (**on**) mit den Fingern trommeln (auf *acc*)
thrush [θrʌʃ] *s* (orn) Drossel *f*
thrust [θrʌst] *s* (*shove*) Stoß *m;* (*stab*) Hieb *m;* (aer, archit, geol, rok) Schub *m;* (mil) Vorstoß *m* ‖ *v* (*pret* & *pp* **thrust**) *tr* stoßen
thud [θʌd] *s* Bums *m* ‖ *v* (*pret* & *pp* **thudded;** *ger* **thudding**) *tr* & *intr* bumsen ‖ *interj* bums!
thug [θʌg] *s* Rocker *m*
thumb [θʌm] *s* Daumen *m;* **be all thumbs** zwei linke Hände haben; **be under s.o.'s t.** unter j–s Fuchtel stehen; **thumbs down!** pfui!; **thumbs up!** Kopf hoch! ‖ *tr* (*a book*) abgreifen; **t. a ride** per Anhalter fahren; **t. one's nose at s.o.** j–m e–e lange Nase machen ‖ *intr*—**t. through** durchblättern
thumb' in'dex *s* Daumenindex *m*
thumb'print' *s* Daumenabdruck *m*
thumb'screw' *s* Flügelschraube *f*
thumb'tack' *s* Reißnagel *m*
thump [θʌmp] *s* Bums *m* ‖ *tr* & *intr* bumsen ‖ *interj* bums!
thump'ing *adj* (coll) enorm
thunder ['θʌndər] *s* Donner *m* ‖ *tr* & *intr* donnern
thun'derbolt' *s* Donnerkeil *m*
thun'derclap' *s* Donnerschlag *m*
thunderous ['θʌndərəs] *adj* donnernd
thun'dershow'er *s* Gewitterregen *m*
thun'derstorm' *s* Gewitter *n*
thunderstruck ['θʌndər ˌstrʌk] *adj* (fig) wie vom Schlag getroffen
Thursday ['θʌrzde] *s* Donnerstag *m;* **on T.** am Donnerstag

thus [ðʌs] *adv* so; (*consequently*) also; **t. far** soweit

thwack [θwæk] *s* heftiger Schlag *m* || *tr* klatschen

thwart [θwɔrt] *adj* Quer– || *s* (naut) Ruderbank *f* || *tr* (*plans*) durchkreuzen; (*a person*) in die Quere kommen (*dat*)

thy [ðaɪ] *poss adj* dein

thyme [taɪm] *s* Thymian *m*

thy'roid gland' ['θaɪrɔɪd] *s* Schilddrüse *f*

thyself [ðaɪ'sɛlf] *intens pron* selbst, selber || *reflex pron* dich

tiara [taɪ'erə] *s* Tiara *f;* (*lady's headdress*) Diadem *n*

tibia ['tɪbɪ·ə] *s* Schienbein *n*

tic [tɪk] *s* (pathol) Tick *m*

tick [tɪk] *s* (*of a clock*) Ticken *n;* (*mattress case*) Überzug *m;* (ent) Zecke *f;* **on t.** (coll) auf Pump || *tr—* **be ticked off** (at) (sl) verärgert sein (über *acc*); **t. off** (*names, items*) abhaken; (*the minutes*) ticken || *intr* ticken; **t. by** vergehen

ticker ['tɪkər] *s* (*watch*) (sl) Uhr *f,* Armbanduhr *f;* (*heart*) (sl) Herz *n;* (st. exch.) Börsentelegraph *m*

tick'er tape' *s* Papierstreifen *m* (des Börsentelegraphen)

tick'er-tape parade' *s* Konfettiregenparade *f*

ticket ['tɪkɪt] *s* Karte *f;* (*for travel*) Fahrkarte *f;* (*by air*) Flugkarte *f;* (*for admission*) Eintrittskarte *f;* (*in a lottery*) Los *n;* (*for a traffic violation*) Strafzettel *m;* (pol) Wahlliste *f* || *tr* etikettieren; (*aut*) mit e–m Strafzettel versehen

tick'et a'gency *s* Vorverkaufsstelle *f*

tick'et a'gent *s* Fahrkartenverkäufer –in *mf*

tick'et of'fice *s* Kartenverkaufsstelle *f*

tick'et win'dow *s* Schalter *m*

tick'ing *s* Ticken *n*

tickle ['tɪkəl] *s* Kitzel *m* || *tr* kitzeln || *intr* jucken

ticklish ['tɪklɪʃ] *adj* kitzlig; (*touchy*) heikel

ticktock ['tɪk ˌtɑk] *adv—***go t.** ticktack machen || *s* Ticken *n*

tid'al wave' ['taɪdəl] *s* Flutwelle *f*

tidbit ['tɪd ˌbɪt] *s* Leckerbissen *m*

tiddlywinks ['tɪdli ˌwɪŋks] *s* Flohhüpfspiel *n*

tide [taɪd] *s* Gezeiten *pl;* **against the t.** (fig) gegen den Strom; **the t. is coming in** die Flut steigt; **the t. is going out** die Flut fällt || *tr—***t. s.o. over** j–n über Wasser halten

tide'land' *s* Watt *n*

tide'wa'ter *s* Flutwasser *n*

tidings ['taɪdɪŋz] *spl* Botschaft *f*

ti·dy ['taɪdi] *adj* ordentlich; (*sum*) hübsch || *v* (*pret & pp* **–died**) *tr* in Ordnung bringen; **t. up** aufräumen || *intr—***t. up** aufräumen

tie [taɪ] *adj* (sport) unentschieden || *s* (*cord*) Schnur *f;* (*ribbon*) Band *n;* (*necktie*) Krawatte *f;* (*knot*) Schleife *f;* (mus) Ligatur *f;* (parl) Stimmengleichheit *f;* (rr) Schwelle *f;* (sport)

Unentschieden *n;* **end in a tie** punktgleich enden; **ties** (*e.g., of friendship*) Bande *pl* || *v* (*pret & pp* **tied;** *ger* **tying**) *tr* binden; **be tied up** (*said of a person or telephone*) besetzt sein; **get tied up** (*in traffic*) steckenbleiben; **my hands are tied** mir sind die Hände gebunden; **tie in with** verknüpfen mit; **tie oneself down** sich festlegen; **tie to** festbinden an (*dat*); **tie up** (*a wound*) verbinden; (*traffic*) lahmlegen; (*money*) fest anlegen; (*production*) stillegen; (*the telephone*) blockieren; (*a boat*) festmachen

tie'back' *s* Gardinenhalter *m*

tie'clasp' *s* Krawattenhalter *m*

tie'pin' *s* Krawattennadel *f*

tier [tɪr] *s* Reihe *f;* (theat) Rang *m*

tie'rod' *s* (aut) Zugstange *f*

tie'-up' *s* (*of traffic*) Stockung *f*

tiger ['taɪgər] *s* Tiger *m*

ti'ger shark' *s* Tigerhai *m*

tight [taɪt] *adj* (*firm*) fest; (*clothes*) eng; (*taut*) straff; (*scarce*) knapp; (*container*) dicht; (*drunk*) beschwipst; (*with money*) knaus(e)rig; **feel t. in the chest** sich beengt fühlen || *adv* fest; **hold t.** festhalten; **sit t.** sich nicht rühren; **pull t.** strammziehen || **tights** *spl* Trikot *m & n*

tighten ['taɪtən] *tr* (*a rope*) straff spannen; (*a belt*) enger schnallen; (*a jar lid*) festziehen; (*a screw*) anziehen; (*a spring*) spannen; (*a knot*) zuziehen

tight'-fist'ed *adj* knaus(e)rig

tight'-fit'ting *adj* eng anliegend

tight'-lipped' *adj* verschlossen

tight'rope' *s* Drahtseil *n;* **walk a t.** auf e–m festgespannten Drahtseil gehen

tight' spot' *s* (coll) Klemme *f*

tight' squeeze' *s* (coll) Zwickmühle *f*

tight'wad' *s* Geizkragen *m*

tigress ['taɪgrɪs] *s* Tigerin *f*

tile [taɪl] *s* (*for the floor or wall*) Fliese *f;* (*for the roof*) Dachziegel *m;* (*glazed tile*) Kachel *f* || *tr* (*a roof*) mit Ziegeln decken; (*a floor*) mit Fliesen auslegen; (*a bathroom*) kacheln

tile' roof' *s* Ziegeldach *n*

till [tɪl] *s* Kasse *f* || *tr* ackern || *prep* bis (*acc*); **t. now** bisher || *conj* bis

tiller ['tɪlər] *s* (naut) Pinne *f*

tilt [tɪlt] *s* Kippen *n;* **full t.** mit voller Wucht || *tr* kippen; (*a bottle, the head*) neigen; **t. back** (*e.g., a chair*) zurücklehnen; **t. over** umkippen || *intr* kippen; **t. over** umkippen

timber ['tɪmbər] *s* Holz *n;* (*for structural use*) Bauholz *n;* (*rafter*) Balken *m*

tim'berland' *s* Waldland *n*

tim'ber line' *s* Baumgrenze *f*

timbre ['tɪmbər] *s* Klangfarbe *f*

time [taɪm] *s* Zeit *f;* (*limited period*) Frist *f;* (*instance*) Mal *n;* (mus) Takt *m;* **all the t.** ständig; **all this t.** die ganze Zeit; **any number of times** x-mal; **at no t.** nie; **at one t.** einst; **at some t.** irgendwann; **at that t.**

damals; **at the present t.** derzeit; **at times** manchmal; **at what t.?** um wieviel Uhr?; **by this t.** nunmehr; **do t.** (sl) sitzen; **do you have the t.?** können Sie mir sagen, wie spät es ist?; **for a t.** e–e Zeitlang; **for the last t.** zum letzten Mal; **for the t. being** vorläufig; **give s.o. a hard t.** j–m das Leben schwer machen; **have a good t.** sich gut unterhalten; **have a hard t.** (ger) es schwer haben zu (inf); **in no t.** im Nu; **in t.** zur rechten Zeit; (in the course of time) mit der Zeit; **make good t.** Fortschritte machen; **on one's own t.** in der Freizeit; **on t.** pünktlich; (on schedule) fahrplanmäßig; (com) auf Raten; **several times** mehrmals; **take one's t.** sich [dat] Zeit lassen; **there's t. for that** das hat Zeit; **this t. tomorrow** morgen um diese Zeit; **t.!** (sport) Zeit!; **t. is up!** die Zeit ist um!; **t. of life** Lebensalter n; **times** Zeiten pl; (math) mal, e.g., **two times two** zwei mal zwei; **t. will tell** die Zeit wird es lehren; **what t. is it?** wieviel Uhr ist es? || tr (mit der Uhr) messen; **t. s.th. right** die richtige Zeit wählen für
time′ bomb′ s Zeitbombe f
time′card′ s Stechkarte f
time′ clock′ s Stechuhr f
time′-consum′ing adj zeitraubend
time′ expo′sure s (phot) Zeitaufnahme f
time′ fuse′ s Zeitzünder m
time′-hon′ored adj altehrwürdig
time′keep′er s Zeitnehmer –in mf
time′-lag′ s Verzögerung f
timeless ['taɪmlɪs] adj zeitlos
time′ lim′it s Frist f; **set a t. on** befristen
timely ['taɪmli] adj zeitgerecht; (topic) aktuell
time′ pay′ment s Ratenzahlung f
time′piece′ s Uhr f
timer ['taɪmər] s (person) Zeitnehmer –in mf; (device) Schaltuhr f; (aut) Zündunterbrecher m; (phot) Zeitauslöser m
time′ sig′nal s Zeitzeichen n
time′ stud′y s Zeitstudien pl
time′ta′ble s Zeittabelle f; (aer) Flugplan m; (rr) Fahrplan m
time′work′ s Zeitlohnarbeit f
time′worn′ adj abgenutzt
time′ zone′ s Zeitzone f
timid ['tɪmɪd] adj ängstlich
tim′ing s genaue zeitliche Berechnung f; (aut) Zündeinstellung f
timorous ['tɪmərəs] adj furchtsam
tin [tɪn] adj Zinn– || s (element) Zinn n; (tin plate) Weißblech n
tin′ can′ s Blechdose f
tincture ['tɪŋktʃər] s Tinktur f
tinder ['tɪndər] s Zunder m
tin′derbox′ s (fig) Pulverfaß n
tin′ foil′ s Zinnfolie f
ting-a-ling ['tɪŋə‚lɪŋ] s Klingeling m
tinge [tɪndʒ] s (of color) Stich m; (fig) Spur f || v (pret tingeing & tinging) tr leicht färben

tingle ['tɪŋgəl] s Kribbeln n, Prickeln n || intr kribbeln, prickeln
tinker ['tɪŋkər] s (bungler) Pfuscher m || intr basteln
tinkle ['tɪŋkəl] s Klingeln n || intr klingeln
tin′ mine′ s Zinnbergwerk n
tinsel ['tɪnsəl] s Lametta f; (fig) Flitterkram m
tin′smith′ s Klempner m
tin′ sol′dier s Zinnsoldat m
tint [tɪnt] s Farbton m || tr tönen, leicht färben
tint′ed glass′ s (aut) blendungsfreies Glas n
tiny ['taɪni] adj winzig
tip [tɪp] s Spitze f; (gratuity) Trinkgeld n; (hint) Tip m; **it's on the tip of my tongue** es schwebt mir auf der Zunge || v (pret & pp tipped; ger tipping) tr schief halten; (a waiter) ein Trinkgeld geben (dat); **tip off** e–n Tip geben (dat); **tip one's hat** auf den Hut tippen || intr—**tip over** umtippen
tip′-off′ s Tip m, rechtzeitiger Wink m
tipple ['tɪpəl] tr & intr süffeln
tippler ['tɪplər] s Säufer –in mf
tipster ['tɪpstər] s Wettberater m
tipsy ['tɪpsi] adj beschwipst
tip′toe′ s—**on t.** auf den Zehenspitzen || v (pret & pp –toed; ger –toeing) intr auf den Zehenspitzen gehen
tip′top′ adj tipptopp
tirade ['taɪred] s Tirade f
tire [taɪr] s Reifen m || tr ermüden; **t. out** strapazieren || intr ermüden
tired adj müde; **be t. of** (ger) es satt haben zu (inf); **be t. of coffee** den Kaffee satt haben; **t. out** abgespannt
tire′ gauge′ s Reifendruckmesser m
tireless ['taɪrlɪs] adj unermüdlich
tire′ pres′sure s Reifendruck m
tiresome ['taɪrsəm] adj (tiring) ermüdend; (boring) langweilig
tissue ['tɪʃju] s Gewebe n; (thin paper) Papiertaschentuch n; **t. of lies** Lügengewebe n
tis′sue pa′per s Seidenpapier n
tit [tɪt] s (sl) Brust f; **tit for tat** wie du mir, so ich dir
Titan ['taɪtən] s Titan(e) m
titanic [taɪ'tænɪk] adj titanisch
titanium [taɪ'tenɪ‐əm] s Titan n
tithe [taɪð] s Kirchenzehnt m || tr (pay one tenth of) den Zehnten bezahlen von; (exact a tenth from) den Zehnten erheben von
Titian ['tiʃən] adj tizianrot
titillate ['tɪtɪ‚let] tr & intr kitzeln, (angenehm) reizen
title ['taɪtəl] s Titel m; (to a property) Eigentumsrecht n; (claim) Rechtstitel m; (of a chapter) Überschrift f; (honor) Würde f; (aut) Kraftfahrzeugbrief m || tr titulieren
ti′tle bout′ s (box) Titelkampf m
ti′tled adj ad(e)lig
ti′tle deed′ s Eigentumsurkunde f
ti′tle hold′er s Titelverteidiger –in mf
ti′tle page′ s Titelblatt n
ti′tle role′ s Titelrolle f

titter ['tɪtər] s Gekicher n ‖ intr kichern
titular ['tɪtələr] adj Titular–
to [tu], [tʊ] adv—**to and fro** hin und her ‖ prep zu (dat); (a city, country, island) nach (dat); (as far as) bis (acc); (in order to) um ... zu (inf); (against, e.g., a wall) an (dat or acc); **a quarter to eight** viertel vor acht; **how far is it to the town?** wie weit ist es bis zur Stadt?; **to a T** haargenau
toad [tod] s Kröte f
toad'stool' s Giftpilz m
toad·y ['todi] s Schranze m & f ‖ v (pret & pp –ied) intr (to) scharwenzeln (um)
to-and-fro ['tu·ənd'fro] adj Hin– und Her– ‖ adv hin und her
toast [tost] s (bread; salutation) Toast m; **drink a t. to** e–n Toast ausbringen auf (acc) ‖ tr (bread) rösten
toaster ['tostər] s Toaster m
toast'mas'ter s Toastmeister m
tobac·co [tə'bæko] s (–cos) Tabak m
tobac'co pouch' s Tabaksbeutel m
toboggan [tə'bagən] s Rodel m & f ‖ intr rodeln
tocsin ['taksɪn] s Alarmglocke f
today [tʊ'de] adv heute ‖ s—**from t. on** von heute an; **today's** heutig
toddle ['tadəl] s Watscheln n ‖ intr watscheln
toddler ['tadlər] s Kleinkind n
toddy ['tadi] s Toddy m
to-do [tə'du] s Getue n
toe [to] s Zehe f; **be on one's toes** auf Draht sein; **step on s.o.'s toes** j–m auf die Zehen treten ‖ v (pret & pp toed; ger toeing) tr—**toe the line** nicht aus der Reihe tanzen
toe' dance' s Spitzentanz m
toe'-in' s (aut) Spur f
toe'nail' s Zehennagel m
together [tʊ'gɛðər] adv zusammen; **t. with** mitsamt (dat), samt (dat)
togetherness [tʊ'gɛðərnɪs] s Zusammengehörigkeit f
tog'gle switch' ['tagəl] s (elec) Kippschalter m
togs [tagz] spl Klamotten pl
toil [tɔɪl] s Mühe f; **toils** Schlingen pl ‖ intr sich mühen
toilet ['tɔɪlɪt] s (room) Toilette f; (bathroom fixture) Klosett n
toi'let ar'ticle s Toilettenartikel m
toi'let bowl' s Klosettschüssel f
toi'let pa'per s Klosettpapier n
toi'let seat' s Toilettenring m
token ['tokən] adj (payment) symbolisch; (strike) Warn– ‖ Zeichen n; (proof) Beweis m; **by the same t.** aus dem gleichen Grund; **as** (or **in**) **t. of** zum Beweis (genit)
tolerable ['talərəbəl] adj erträglich
tolerably ['talərəbli] adv leidlich
tolerance ['talərəns] s Duldsamkeit f; (mach) Toleranz f
tolerant ['talərənt] adj (of) duldsam (gegen), tolerant (gegen)
tolerate ['talə‚ret] tr dulden
toleration [‚talə'reʃən] s Duldung f

toll [tol] adj (road) gebührenpflichtig ‖ s Wegezoll m; (at a bridge) Brückenzoll m; (of bells) Läuten n; (number of victims) Zahl f der Opfer; (fig) Tribut m; (telp) Gebühr f für ein Ferngespräch; **take a heavy t. of** life viele Menschenleben kosten ‖ tr & intr läuten
toll' booth' s Zahlkasse f
toll' bridge' s Zollbrücke f
toll' call' s Ferngespräch n
toll' collec'tor s Zolleinnehmer –in mf
toma·to [tə'meto] s (–toes) Tomate f
toma'to juice' s Tomatensaft f
tomb [tum] s Grab n, Grabmal n
tomboy ['tam‚bɔɪ] s Wildfang m
tomb'stone' s Grabstein m
tomcat ['tam‚kæt] s Kater m
tome [tom] s Band m
tomfoolery [tam'fuləri] s Albernheit f
Tom'my gun' ['tami] s Maschinenpistole f
tom'myrot' s Blödsinn m
tomorrow [tʊ'mɔro] adv morgen; **t. evening** morgen abend; **t. morning** morgen früh; **t. night** morgen abend; **t. noon** morgen mittag ‖ s morgen; **tomorrow's** morgig
tom-tom ['tam‚tam] s Hindutrommel f
ton [tʌn] s Tonne f
tone [ton] s Ton m; (of color) Farbton m; (phot) Tönung f ‖ tr tönen; (phot) tönen; **t. down** dämpfen ‖ intr milder werden
tone'-control knob' s (rad) Klangregler m
tongs [tɔŋz] spl Zange f
tongue [tʌŋ] s Zunge f; (language) Sprache f; (of a shoe) Zunge f; (of a buckle) Dorn m; (of a bell) Klöppel m; (of a wagon) Deichsel f; (carp) Feder f; **hold one's t.** den Mund halten
tongue'-tied' adj zungenlahm; (fig) sprachlos
tongue' twist'er s Zungenbrecher m
tonic ['tanɪk] adj tonisch ‖ s (med) Tonikum n; (mus) Tonika f
tonight [tʊ'naɪt] adv heute nacht; (this evening) heute abend
tonnage ['tʌnɪdʒ] s Tonnage f
tonsil ['tansɪl] s Mandel f
tonsilitis [‚tansɪ'laɪtɪs] s Mandelentzündung f
tonsure ['tanʃər] s Tonsur f
too [tu] adv (also) auch; (excessively) zu; **too bad!** Schade!
tool [tul] s (& fig) Werkzeug n ‖ tr (with tools) bearbeiten
tool'box' s Werkzeugkasten m
tool'mak'er s Werkzeugmacher m
tool' shed' s Geräteschuppen m
toot [tut] s (aut) Hupen n ‖ tr (a trumpet) blasen; **t. the horn** (aut) hupen ‖ intr (aut) hupen
tooth [tuθ] s (teeth [tiθ]) Zahn m; (of a rake) Zinke f; **t. and nail** mit aller Gewalt
tooth'ache' s Zahnschmerz m, Zahnweh n

tooth'brush' s Zahnbürste f
tooth' decay' s Zahnfäule f
toothless ['tuθlɪs] adj zahnlos
tooth'paste' s Zahnpaste f
tooth'pick' s Zahnstocher m
tooth' pow'der s Zahnpulver n
top [tɑp] adj oberste; (speed, price, form) Höchst–; (team) Spitzen–; (first-class) erstklassig || s Spitze f; (of a mountain) Gipfel m; (of a tree) Wipfel m; (of a car) Verdeck n; (of a box) Deckel m; (of a garment) Oberteil m & n; (of a bottle) Verschluß m; (of an object) obere Seite f; (of the water) Oberfläche f; (of a turnip) Kraut n; (toy) Kreisel m; **at the top of one's voice** aus voller Kehle; **at the top of the page** oben auf der Seite; **be tops with s.o.** (coll) bei j–m ganz groß angeschrieben sein; **from top to bottom** von oben bis unten; **on top** (& fig) obenauf; **on top of** (position) auf (dat); (direction) auf (acc); **on top of that** obendrein || v (pret & pp **topped**; ger **topping**) tr (a tree) kappen; (surpass) übertreffen; **that tops everything** das übersteigt alles; **top off** (a meal, an evening) abschließen; **to top it off** zu guter Letzt
topaz ['topæz] s Topas m
top' brass' s (mil) hohe Tiere pl
top'coat' s Überzieher m
top' dog' s (coll) Erste mf
top' ech'elon s Führungsspitze f
top' hat' s Zylinder m
top'-heav'y adj oberlastig
topic ['tɑpɪk] s Gegenstand m, Thema n
topical ['tɑpɪkəl] adj aktuell
top' kick' s (mil) Spieß m
topless ['tɑplɪs] adj Oben-ohne–
topmast ['tɑp ˌmest] s Toppmast m
top'most' adj oberste
top'notch' adj erstklassig
top' of the head' s Scheitel m
topography [tə'pɑgrəfi] s Topographie f
topple ['tɑpəl] tr & intr stürzen
topsail ['tɑpsəl] s Toppsegel n
top'-se'cret adj streng geheim
top' ser'geant s Hauptfeldwebel m
top'side' adv auf Deck || s Oberseite f
top'soil' s Mutterboden m
topsy-turvy ['tɑpsi 'tʌrvi] adj drunter und drüber || adv—**turn t.** durcheinanderbringen
torch [tɔrtʃ] s Fackel f; (Brit) Taschenlampe f; **carry the t. for** (coll) verknallt sein in (acc)
torch'bear'er s (& fig) Fackelträger m
torch'light' s Fackelschein m
torch'light parade' s Fackelzug m
torment ['tɔrment] s Qual f || [tɔr'ment] tr quälen
tormentor [tɔr'mentər] s Quäler –in mf
torn [tɔrn] adj zerrissen, rissig
torna·do [tɔr'nedo] s (–does & –dos) Tornado m, Windhose f
torpe·do [tɔr'pido] s (–does) Torpedo m || tr torpedieren

torpe'do boat' s Torpedoboot n
torpe'do tube' s Ausstoßrohr n
torpid ['tɔrpɪd] adj träge
torque [tɔrk] s Drehmoment n
torrent ['tɔrənt] s Sturzbach m; (of words) Schwall m; **in torrents** stromweise
torrential [tə'rentʃəl] adj—**t. rain** Wolkenbruch m
torrid ['tɔrɪd] adj brennend
Tor'rid Zone' s heiße Zone f
tor·so ['tɔrso] s (–sos) (of a statue) Torso m; (of a human body) Rumpf m
tortoise ['tɔrtəs] s Schildkröte f
tor'toise shell' s Schildpatt n
torture ['tɔrtʃər] s Folter f, Qual f || tr foltern, quälen
toss [tɔs] s Wurf m; (of the head) Zurückwerfen n; (of a ship) Schlingern n; (of a coin) Loswurf m || tr (throw) werfen; (the head) zurückwerfen; (a ship) hin– und herwerfen; (a coin) hochwerfen; **t. off** (work) hinhauen; **t. s.o. for** mit j–m losen um || intr (naut) schlingern; **t. for** e–e Münze hochwerfen um; **t. in bed** sich im Bett hin –und herwerfen
toss'up' s Loswurf m; **it's a t. whether** es hängt ganz vom Zufall ab, ob
tot [tɑt] s Knirps m
to·tal ['totəl] adj Gesamt–, total || s Gesamtsumme f || v (pret & pp –tal[l]ed; ger –tal[l]ling) tr (add up) zusammenrechnen; (amount to) sich belaufen auf (acc); (sl) (Wagen) ganz kaputt machen
totalitarian [to ˌtælɪ'terɪ·ən] adj totalitär
tote [tot] tr schleppen
totem ['totəm] s Totem n
totter ['tatər] intr schwanken
touch [tʌtʃ] s Berührung f; (sense of touch) Tastsinn m; (e.g., of a fever) Anflug m; (trace, small bit) Spur f; (of a pianist) Anschlag m; **get in t. with** in Verbindung treten mit; **keep in t. with** in Verbindung bleiben mit; **put in t. with** in Verbindung setzen mit; **with sure t.** mit sicherer Hand || tr berühren; (fig) rühren; **he's a little touched** (coll) er hat e–n kleinen Klaps; **t. bottom** anstoßen; **t. glasses** mit den Gläsern anstoßen; **t. off** auslösen; **t. s.o. for** (coll) j–n anpumpen um; **t. up** (with cosmetics) auffrischen; (paint, phot) retuschieren || intr sich berühren; **t. down** (aer) aufsetzen; **t. on** (a topic) berühren; (e.g., arrogance) grenzen an (acc)
touch' and go' s—**be t.** auf der Kippe stehen
touch'ing adj rührend, herzergreifend
touch'stone' s (fig) Prüfstein m
touch'-type' intr blindschreiben
touchy ['tʌtʃi] adj (spot, person) empfindlich; (situation) heikel
tough [tʌf] adj (strong) derb; (meat) zäh; (life) mühselig; (difficult) schwierig || s Gassenjunge m
toughen ['tʌfən] tr zäher machen; **t.**

up (*through training*) ertüchtigen ‖
intr (**up**) zäher werden
tough' luck' s Pech n
tour [tʊr] s (*of a country*) Tour f; (*of
a city*) Rundfahrt f; (*of a museum*)
Führung f; (*mus, theat*) Tournee f;
go on t. auf Tournee gehen ‖ tr besichtigen; (*a country*) bereisen ‖ intr
auf der Reise sein; (*theat*) auf Tournee sein
tour' guide' s Reiseführer –in mf
tourism ['tʊrɪzəm] s Touristik f
tournament ['tʊrnəmənt] s Turnier n
tourney ['tʊrni] s Turnier n
tourniquet ['tʊrnɪ,kɛt] s Aderpresse f
tousle ['taʊzəl] tr (zer)zausen
tow [to] s—**have in tow** im Schlepptau
haben; **take in tow** ins Schlepptau
nehmen ‖ tr schleppen; **tow away**
abschleppen
toward(s) [tord(z)] prep (*with respect
to*) gegenüber (*dat*); (*a goal, direction*) auf (*acc*), zu; (*shortly before*)
gegen (*acc*); (*for*) für (*acc*); (*facing*)
zugewandt (*dat*)
tow'boat' s Schleppschiff n
tow·el ['taʊ·əl] s Handtuch n ‖ v (*pret
& pp* –el[l]ed; *ger* –el[l]ing) tr mit
e–m Handtuch abtrocknen
tow'el rack' s Handtuchhalter m
tower ['taʊ·ər] s Turm m; **t. of strength**
starker Hort m ‖ intr ragen; **t. over**
überragen
tow'ering adj hochragend; (*rage*) rasend
tow'ing serv'ice s Schleppdienst m
tow'line' s Schlepptau n
town [taʊn] adj städtisch, Stadt– ‖ s
Stadt f; **in t.** in der Stadt; **out of t.**
verreist; **go to t. on** Feuer und
Flamme sein für
town' coun'cil s Stadtrat m
town' hall' s Rathaus n
town' house' s Stadthaus n
town'ship' s Gemeinde f
tow'rope' s Schlepptau n; (*for a
glider*) Startseil n
tow' truck' s Abschleppwagen m
toxic ['tɑksɪk] adj Gift–, toxisch ‖ s
Giftstoff m
toy [tɔɪ] adj Spielzeug– ‖ s Spielzeug
n; **toys** Spielsachen pl; (*com*) Spiel-
waren pl ‖ intr spielen; **toy with**
(fig) herumspielen mit
toy' dog' s Schoßhund m
toy' shop' s Spielwarengeschäft n
toy' sol'dier s Spielzeugsoldat m
trace [tres] s Spur f; (*of a harness*)
Strang m; **without a t.** spurlos ‖ tr
(*a drawing*) durchpausen; (*lines*)
nachziehen; (*track*) ausfindig machen; **t. (back) to** zurückführen auf
(*acc*)
tracer ['tresər] s Suchzettel m
trac'er bul'let s Leuchtspurgeschoß n
trac'ing pa'per s Pauspapier n
track [træk] s Spur f; (*of a foot*) Fuß-
spur f; (*of a wheel*) Radspur f;
(*chain of a tank*) Raupenkette f;
(*parallel rails*) Geleise n; (*single rail*)
Gleis n, Schiene f; (*station platform*)
Bahnsteig m; (*path*) Pfad m; (*course

for running*) Laufbahn f; (*course for
motor and horse racing*) Rennbahn f;
(*running as a sport*) Laufen n; **be off
the t.** (fig) auf dem Holzweg sein;
go off the t. (*derail*) entgleisen; **in
one's tracks** mitten auf dem Weg;
jump the t. aus den Schienen springen ‖ tr verfolgen; **t. down** (*game,
a criminal*) zur Strecke bringen; (*a
rumor, reference*) nachgehen (*dat*);
t. up (*a rug*) schmutzig treten
track'-and-field' adj Leichtathletik-
trackless ['træklɪs] adj pfadlos; (*vehicle*) schienenlos
track' meet' s Leichtathletikwettkampf
m
tract [trækt] s Strich m; (*treatise*)
Traktat n; **t. of land** Grundstück n
traction ['trækʃən] s (med) Ziehen n;
(*of the road*) Griffigkeit f
tractor ['træktər] s Traktor m; (*of
a tractor-trailer*) Zugmaschine f
trac'tor-trail'er s Sattelschlepper m mit
e–m Anhänger
trade [tred] s Handel m; (*calling, job*)
Gewerbe n; (*exchange*) Tausch m;
by t. von Beruf ‖ tr (aus)tauschen;
t. in (*e.g., a used car*) in Zahlung
geben ‖ intr Handel treiben
trade' agree'ment s Handelsabkommen
n
trade' bar'riers spl Handelsschranken
pl
trade'-in val'ue s Handelswert m
trade'mark' s Warenzeichen n
trade' name' s (*of products*) Handels-
bezeichnung f; (*of a firm*) Firmen-
name m
trader ['tredər] s Händler –in mf
trade' school' s Gewerbeschule f
trade' se'cret s Geschäftsgeheimnis n
trades'man s (–men) Handelsmann m
trade' un'ion s Gewerkschaft f
trade'wind' s Passatwind m
trad'ing post' s Handelsniederlassung f
trad'ing stamp' s Rabattmarke f
tradition [trə'dɪʃən] s Tradition f
traditional [trə'dɪʃənəl] adj herkömmlich, traditionell
traf·fic ['træfɪk] s Verkehr m; (*trade*)
(**in**) Handel m (**in** dat) ‖ v (*pret &
pp* –ficked; *ger* –ficking) intr—**t. in**
handeln in (*dat*)
traf'fic ac'cident s Verkehrsunfall m
traf'fic cir'cle s Kreisverkehr m
traf'fic is'land s Verkehrsinsel f
traf'fic jam' s Verkehrsstockung f
traf'fic lane' s Fahrbahn f
traf'fic light' s Verkehrsampel f; **go
through a t.** bei Rot durchfahren
traf'fic sign' s Verkehrszeichen n
traf'fic tick'et s Strafzettel m
traf'fic viola'tion s Verkehrsdelikt n
tragedian [trə'dʒidɪ·ən] s Tragiker m
tragedy ['trædʒɪdi] s (& *fig*) Tragödie f
tragic ['trædʒɪk] adj tragisch
trail [trel] s (*path*) Fährte f; **be on
s.o.'s t.** j–m auf der Spur sein; **t. of
smoke** Rauchfahne f ‖ tr (*on foot*)
nachgehen (*dat*); (*in a vehicle*) nach-
fahren (*dat*); (*in a race*) nachhinken
(*dat*) ‖ intr (*said of a robe*) schleifen

trailer ['trelər] s Anhänger m; (mobile home) Wohnwagen m
trail'er camp' s Wohnwagenparkplatz m
train [tren] s (of railway cars) Zug m; (of a dress) Schleppe f; (following) Gefolge n; (of events) Folge f; **go by t.** mit dem Zug fahren; **t. of thought** Gedankengang m ‖ tr ausbilden; (for a particular job) anlernen; (the memory) üben; (plants) am Spalier aufziehen; (an animal) dressieren; (a gun) (on) zielen (auf acc); (sport) trainieren ‖ intr üben; (sport) trainieren
trained adj geschult, ausgebildet
trainee [tre'ni] s Anlernling m
trainer ['trenər] s (of domestic animals) Dresseur m, Dresseuse f; (of wild animals) Dompteur m, Dompteuse f; (aer) Schulflugzeug n; (sport) Sportwart –in mf
train'ing s Ausbildung f; (of animals) Dressur f; (sport) Training n
train'ing school' s (vocational school) Berufsschule f; (reformatory) Erziehungsanstalt f
trait [tret] s Charakterzug m
traitor ['tretər] s Verräter –in mf; (of a country) Hochverräter –in mf
trajectory [trə'dʒɛktəri] s Flugbahn f
tramp [træmp] s Landstreicher –in mf; (loose woman) Frauenzimmer n ‖ tr trampeln; (traverse on foot) durchstreifen ‖ intr vagabundieren; **t. on** herumtrampeln auf (dat)
trample ['træmpəl] s Getrampel n ‖ tr trampeln; **t. to death** tottreten; **t. under foot** (fig) mit Füßen treten ‖ intr—**t. on** herumtrampeln auf (dat); (fig) mit Füßen treten
trampoline ['træmpə,lin] s Trampolin n
trance [træns] s Trance f
tranquil ['træŋkwɪl] adj ruhig
tranquilize ['træŋkwɪ,laɪz] tr beruhigen
tranquilizer ['træŋkwɪ,laɪzər] s Beruhigungsmittel n
tranquillity [træn'kwɪlɪti] s Ruhe f
transact [træn'zækt] tr abwickeln
transaction [træn'zækʃən] s Abwicklung f; **transactions** (of a society) Sitzungsbericht m
transatlantic [,trænsət'læntɪk] adj transatlantisch
transcend [træn'sɛnd] tr übersteigen
transcendental [,trænsən'dɛntəl] adj übersinnlich; (philos) transzendental
transcribe [træn'skraɪb] tr (copy) umschreiben; (dictated or recorded material) übertragen; (mus) transkribieren; (phonet) in Lautschrift wiedergeben; (rad) auf Band aufnehmen
transcript ['trænskrɪpt] s Transkript n
transcription [træn'skrɪpʃən] s Umschrift f; (mus) Transkription f
transept ['trænsept] s Querschiff n
trans·fer ['trænsfər] s (of property) Übertragung f (of money) Überweisung f; (of an employee) Versetzung f; (of a passenger) Umsteigen n; (ticket) Umsteigefahrschein

m ‖ [træns'fʌr], ['trænsfər] v (pret & pp –ferred; ger –ferring) tr (property) übertragen; (money) überweisen; (to another account) umbuchen; (an employee) versetzen ‖ intr (to) versetzt werden (nach, zu); (said of a passenger) umsteigen
transfix [træns'fɪks] tr durchbohren
transform [træns'fɔrm] tr (a person) verwandeln; (into) umwandeln (in acc); (elec) umspannen
transformer [træns'fɔrmər] s (elec) Stromwandler m, Transformator m
transfusion [træns'fjuʒən] s (med) Übertragung f, Transfusion f
transgress [træns'grɛs] tr überschreiten
transgression [træs'grɛʃən] s Vergehen n
transient ['trænʃənt] adj vorübergehend; (fleeting) flüchtig ‖ s Durchreisende mf
transistor [træn'sɪstər] adj Transistor– ‖ s Transistor m
transistorize [træn'sɪstə,raɪz] tr transistorisieren
transit ['trænzɪt] s (astr) Durchgang m; (com) Transit m; **in t.** unterwegs
transition [træn'zɪʃən] s Übergang m
transitional [træn'zɪʃənəl] adj Übergangs–
transitive ['trænsɪtɪv] adj transitiv
transitory ['trænsɪ,tori] adj vergänglich
translate [træns'let] tr übersetzen; **t. into action** in die Tat umsetzen
translation [træns'leʃən] s Übersetzung f
translator [træns'letər] s Übersetzer –in mf
transliterate [træns'lɪtə,ret] tr transkribieren
translucent [træns'lusənt] adj durchscheinend, lichtdurchlässig
transmigration [,trænsmaɪ'greʃən] s— **t. of the soul** Seelenwanderung f
transmission [træns'mɪʃən] s (of a text) Textüberlieferung f; (of news, information) Übermittlung f; (aut) Getriebe n; (rad, telv) Sendung f
trans·mit [træns'mɪt] v (pret & pp –mitted; ger –mitting) tr (send forward) übersenden; (disease, power, light, heat) übertragen; (e.g., customs) überliefern; (by inheritance) vererben; (rad, telp, telv) senden
transmitter [træns'mɪtər] s (rad, telg, telv) Sender m
transmutation [,trænsmu'teʃən] s Umwandlung f; (biol) Transmutation f; (chem, phys) Umwandlung f
transmute [træns'mjut] tr umwandeln
transoceanic [,trænzoʃɪ'ænɪk] adj überseeisch, Übersee–
transom ['trænsəm] s (crosspiece) Querbalken m; (window over a door) Oberlicht n mit Kreuzsprosse; (of a boat) Spiegel m
transparency [træns'pɛrənsi] s Durchsichtigkeit f, Transparenz f; (phot) Diapositiv n
transparent [træns'pɛrənt] adj durchsichtig, transparent

transpire [træns'paɪr] *intr* (*happen*) sich ereignen; (*leak out*) (fig) durchsickern

transplant ['træns‚plænt] *s* (bot, surg) Verpflanzung *f* ‖ [træns'plænt] *tr* (bot, surg) verpflanzen

transport ['trænsport] *s* Beförderung *f*. Transport *m;* (nav) Truppentransporter *m* ‖ [træns'port] *tr* befördern

transportation [‚trænspor'teʃən] *s* Beförderung *f;* (*public transportation*) Verkehrsmittel *n;* **do you need t.?** brauchen Sie e-e Fahrgelegenheit?

trans'port plane' *s* Transportflugzeug *n*

transpose [træns'poz] *tr* umstellen; (math, mus) transponieren

trans·ship [træns'ʃɪp] *v* (*pret & pp* **-shipped;** *ger* **-shipping**) *tr* (com, naut) umladen

trap [træp] *s* (& fig) Falle *f;* (*snare*) Schlinge *f;* (*pit*) Fallgrube *f;* (*under a sink*) Geruchsverschluß *m;* (*mouth*) (sl) Klappe *f;* (chem) Abscheider *m;* (golf) Sandbunker *m;* **fall** (or **walk**) **into a t.** in die Falle gehen; **set a trap** e-e Falle stellen ‖ *v* (*pret & pp* **trapped;** *ger* **trapping**) *tr* mit e-r Falle fangen; (fig) erwischen; (mil) einfangen

trap' door' *s* Falltür *f*, Klapptür *f;* (theat) Versenkung *f*

trapeze [trə'piz] *s* Trapez *n;* (gym) Schwebereck *n*

trapezoid ['træpɪ‚zɔɪd] *s* Trapez *n*

trapper ['træpər] *s* Fallensteller *m*

trappings ['træpɪŋz] *spl* Staat *m;* (*caparison*) Staatsgeschirr *n*

trap'shoot'ing *s* Tontaubenschießen *n*

trash [træʃ] *s* Abfälle *pl;* (*junk*) Schund *m;* (*artistically inferior material*) Kitsch *m;* (*worthless people*) Gesindel *n*

trash' can' *s* Mülleimer *m*, Abfalleimer *m*

trashy ['træʃi] *adj* kitschig; (*literature*) Schund–

travail [trə'vel] *s* Plackerei *f;* (*labor of childbirth*) Wehen *pl*

trav·el ['trævəl] *s* Reisen *n;* (*trip*) Reise *f;* (*e.g., of a bullet, rocket*) Bewegung *f;* (*of moving parts*) Lauf *m;* **travels** Reiseerlebnisse *pl* ‖ *v* (*pret & pp* **-el[l]ed;** *ger* **-el[l]ing**) *tr* bereisen ‖ *intr* reisen; (*said of a vehicle or passenger*) fahren; (astr, aut, mach, phys) sich bewegen

trav'el a'gency *s* Reisebüro *n*

traveler ['trævələr] *s* Reisende *mf*

trav'eler's check' *s* Reisescheck *m*

trav'el fold'er *s* Reiseprospekt *m*

trav'eling bag' *s* Reisetasche *f*

trav'eling sales'man *s* (**-men**) Geschäftsreisende *m*

travelogue ['trævə‚lɔg] *s* Reisebericht *m;* (cin) Reisefilm *m*

traverse [trə'vʌrs] *tr* durchqueren ‖ *intr* (*said of a gun*) sich drehen

traves·ty ['trævɪsti] *s* Travestie *f* ‖ *v* (*pret & pp* **-tied**) *tr* travestieren

trawl [trɔl] *s* Schleppnetz *n* ‖ *tr* mit dem Schleppnetz fangen ‖ *intr* mit dem Schleppnetz fischen

trawler ['trɔlər] *s* Schleppnetzboot *n*

tray [tre] *s* Tablett *n;* (phot) Schale *f*

treacherous ['trɛtʃərəs] *adj* verräterisch; (*e.g., ice*) trügerisch

treachery ['trɛtʃəri] *s* Verrat *m*

tread [trɛd] *s* (*step*) Tritt *m;* (*imprint*) Spur *f;* (*on a tire*) Profil *n* ‖ *v* (*pret* **trod** [trɑd]; *pp* **trodden** ['trɑdən] & **trod**) *tr* betreten ‖ *intr* (**on**) treten (auf *acc*)

treadle ['trɛdəl] *s* Trittbrett *n*

tread'mill' *s* (& fig) Tretmühle *f*

treason ['trizən] *s* Verrat *m*

treasonable ['trizənəbəl] *adj* verräterisch

treasure ['trɛʒər] *s* Schatz *m* ‖ *tr* sehr schätzen

treasurer ['trɛʒərər] *s* Schatzmeister –in *mf*

treasury ['trɛʒəri] *s* Schatzkammer *f;* (*chest*) Tresor *m;* (*public treasury*) Staatsschatz *m;* **Treasury** Finanzministerium *n*

treat [trit] *s* Hochgenuß *m* ‖ *tr* behandeln; (*regard*) (**as**) betrachten (als); **t. oneself to s.th.** sich [*dat*] etw genehmigen; **t. s.o. to s.th** j-n bewirten mit

treatise ['tritɪs] *s* Abhandlung *f*

treatment ['tritmənt] *s* Behandlung *f*

treaty ['triti] *s* Vertrag *m*

treble ['trɛbəl] *adj* (*threefold*) dreifach; (mus) Diskant– ‖ *s* Diskant *m;* (*voice*) Diskantstimme *f* ‖ *tr* verdreifachen ‖ *intr* sich verdreifachen

tre'ble clef' *s* Violinschlüssel *m*

tree [tri] *s* Baum *m*

treeless ['trilɪs] *adj* baumlos

tree'top' *s* Baumwipfel *m*

tree' trunk' *s* Baumstamm *m*

trellis ['trɛlɪs] *s* Spalier *n;* (*gazebo*) Gartenhäuschen *n*

tremble ['trɛmbəl] *s* Zittern *n* ‖ *intr* zittern; (geol) beben; **t. all over** am ganzen Körper zittern

tremendous [trɪ'mɛndəs] *adj* ungeheuer

tremor ['trɛmər] *s* Zittern *n;* (geol) Beben *n*

trench [trɛntʃ] *s* Graben *m;* (mil) Schützengraben *m*

trenchant ['trɛntʃənt] *adj* schneidend; (*policy*) durchschlagend

trench' war'fare *s* Stellungskrieg *m*

trend [trɛnd] *s* Richtung *f*, Trend *m*

trespass ['trɛspəs] *s* unbefugtes Betreten *n;* (*sin*) Sünde *f* ‖ *intr* unbefugt fremdes Eigentum betreten; **no trespassing** (public sign) Betreten verboten; **t. on** unbefugt betreten

trespasser ['trɛspəsər] *s* Unbefugte *mf*

tress [trɛs] *s* Flechte *f*

trestle ['trɛsəl] *s* Gestell *n;* (*of a bridge*) Brückenbock *m*

trial ['traɪ·əl] *s* (*attempt*) Versuch *m;* (*hardship*) Beschwernis *f;* (jur) Prozeß *m;* **a week's t.** e-e Woche Probezeit; **be on t. for** vor Gericht stehen wegen; **be brought up** (or **come up**) **for t.** zur Verhandlung kommen; **new t.** Wiederaufnahmeverfahren *n;* **on t.** (com) auf Probe; **put on t.** vor Gericht bringen

tri′al and er′ror s—**by t.** durch Ausprobieren

tri′al balloon′ s Versuchsballon m

tri′al by ju′ry s Verhandlung f vor dem Schwurgericht

tri′al or′der s Probeauftrag m

tri′al run′ s Probelauf m

triangle [′traɪ‚æŋgəl] s Dreieck n

triangular [traɪ′æŋgjələr] adj dreieckig

tribe [traɪb] s Stamm m; (pej) Sippschaft f

tribunal [traɪ′bjunəl] s Tribunal n

tributary [′trɪbjə‚teri] adj zinspflichtig || s Nebenfluß m

tribute [′trɪbjut] s Tribut m, Zins m; **pay t. to** Anerkennung zollen (dat)

trice [traɪs] s—**in a t.** im Nu

trick [trɪk] s Trick m; (prank) Streich m; (technique) Kniff m; (artifice) Schlich m; (cards) Stich m; **be on to s.o.'s tricks** j-s Schliche kennen; **be up to one's old tricks** sein Unwesen treiben; **do the t.** die Sache schaffen; **play a dirty t. on s.o.** j-m e-n gemeinen Streich spielen || tr reinlegen; **t. s.o. into** (ger) j-n durch Kniffe dazu bringen zu (inf)

trickery [′trɪkəri] s Gaunerei f

trickle [′trɪkəl] s Tröpfeln n || intr tröpfeln, rieseln

trickster [′trɪkstər] s Gauner m

tricky [′trɪki] adj (wily) listig; (touchy) heikel; (difficult) verzwickt

trident [′traɪdənt] s Dreizack m

tried [traɪd] adj bewährt, probat

trifle [′traɪfəl] s Kleinigkeit f; **a t.** (e.g., too big) ein bißchen || tr— **t. away** vertändeln || intr tändeln

trif′ling adj geringfügig || s Tändelei f

trigger [′trɪgər] s Abzug m; **pull the t.** abdrücken || tr auslösen

trig′ger-hap′py adj schießwütig

trigonometry [‚trɪgə′namətri] s Trigonometrie f

trill [trɪl] s Triller m || tr & intr trillern

trillion [′trɪljən] s Billion f; (Brit) Trillion f

trilogy [′trɪlədʒi] s Trilogie f

trim [trɪm] adj (trimmer; trimmest) (figure) schick; (well-kept) gepflegt || s (e.g., of a hat) Zierleiste f; (naut) Trimm m; **be in t.** in Form sein || v (pret & pp **trimmed**; ger **trimming**) tr (clip) stutzen; (decorate) dekorieren; (a Christmas tree) schmücken; (beat) (coll) schlagen; (naut) trimmen

trim′ming s (e.g., of a dress) Besatz m; (of hedges) Stutzen n; **take a t.** (coll) e-e Niederlage erleiden; **trimmings** (decorations) Verzierungen pl; (food) Zutaten pl; (scraps) Abfälle pl; **with all the trimmings** (fig) mit allen Schikanen

trinity [′trɪnɪti] s Dreiheit f; **Trinity** Dreifaltigkeit f

trinket [′trɪŋkɪt] s Schmuckgegenstand m

tri·o [′tri·o] s (–os) (& mus) Trio n

trip [trɪp] s Reise f; (on drugs) Trip m; **go on** (or **take**) **a t.** e-e Reise machen || v (pret & pp **tripped**; ger **tripping**) tr ein Bein stellen (dat); **t. up** (fig) zu Fall bringen || intr stolpern

tripartite [traɪ′partaɪt] adj Dreiparteien–; (of three powers) Dreimächte–

tripe [traɪp] s Kutteln pl; (sl) Schund m

trip′ham′mer s Schmiedehammer m

triple [′trɪpəl] adj dreifach || s Dreifache n || tr verdreifachen

triplet [′trɪplɪt] s (offspring) Drilling m; (mus) Triole f

triplicate [′trɪplɪkɪt] adj dreifach || s—**in t.** in dreifacher Ausfertigung

tripod [′traɪpad] s Dreifuß m; (phot) Stativ n

triptych [′trɪptɪk] s Triptychon n

trite [traɪt] adj abgedroschen

triumph [′traɪ·əmf] s Triumph m || intr (**over**) triumphieren (über acc)

triumphal [traɪ′ʌmfəl] adj Sieges–

triumphant [traɪ′ʌmfənt] adj triumphierend

trivia [′trɪvɪ·ə] spl Nichtigkeiten pl

trivial [′trɪvɪ·əl] adj trivial, alltäglich; (person) oberflächlich

triviality [‚trɪvɪ′ælɪti] s Trivialität f, Nebensächlichkeit f

Trojan [′trodʒən] adj trojanisch || s Trojaner –in mf

troll [trol] s (myth) Troll m || tr & intr mit der Schleppangel fischen

trolley [′trali] s Straßenbahn f

trollop [′traləp] s (slovenly woman) Schlampe f; (prostitute) Dirne f

trombone [′trambon] s Posaune f

troop [trup] s Trupp m; (mil) Truppe f

trooper [′truper] s Kavallerist m; **swear like a t.** fluchen wie ein Kutscher

troop′ship′ s Truppentransporter m

trophy [′trofi] s Trophäe f; (sport) Pokal m

tropical [′trapɪkəl] adj Tropen–

tropics [′trapɪks] spl Tropen pl

trot [trat] s Trab m || v (pret & pp **trotted**; ger **trotting**) tr—**t. out** (coll) zur Schau stellen || intr traben

troubadour [′trubə‚dor] s Minnesänger m

trouble [′trʌbəl] s (inconvenience, bother) Mühe f; (difficulty) Schwierigkeit f; (physical distress) Leiden n; (civil disorder) Unruhe f; **ask for t.** das Schicksal herausfordern; **be in t.** in Schwierigkeiten sein; (be pregnant) schwanger sein; **cause s.o. a lot of t.** j-m viel zu schaffen machen; **get into t.** in Schwierigkeiten geraten; **go to a lot of t.** sich [dat] viel Mühe machen; **it was no t. at all!** gern geschehen!; **make t.** Geschichten machen; **take the t. to** (inf) sich der Mühe unterziehen zu (inf); **that's the t.** da liegt die Schwierigkeit; **what's the t.?** was ist los? || tr (worry) beunruhigen; (bother) belästigen; (disturb) stören; (said of ills) plagen

trou′blemak′er s Unruhestifter –in mf

troubleshooter [′trʌbəl‚ʃutər] s Stö-

rungssucher –in *mf;* (*in disputes*) Friedensstifter –in *mf*
troublesome ['trʌbəlsəm] *adj* lästig
trough [trɔf] *s* Trog *m;* (*of a wave*) Wellental *n*
troupe [trup] *s* Truppe *f*
trousers ['trauzərz] *spl* Hose *f*
trous-seau [tru'so] *s* (–seaux & –seaus) Brautausstattung *f*
trout [traut] *s* Forelle *f*
trowel ['trau-əl] *s* Kelle *f*
truant ['tru-ənt] *adj* schwänzend || *s*— **play t.** die Schule schwänzen
truce [trus] *s* Waffenruhe *f*
truck [trʌk] *s* Last(kraft)wagen *m;* (*for luggage*) Gepäckwagen *m* || *tr* mit Lastkraftwagen befördern
truck'driv'er *s* Lastwagenfahrer *m*
trucker ['trʌkər] *s* (*driver*) Lastwagenfahrer *m;* (*owner of a trucking firm*) Fuhrunternehmer –in *mf*
truck' farm'ing *s* Gemüsebau *m*
truculent ['trʌkjələnt] *adj* gehässig
trudge [trʌdʒ] *intr* stapfen
true [tru] *adj* wahr; (*loyal*) (ge)treu; (*genuine*) echt; (*sign*) sicher; **come t.** sich verwirklichen; **prove t.** sich als wahr erweisen; **that's t.** das stimmt
truffle ['trʌfəl] *s* Trüffel *f*
truism ['tru-ɪzəm] *s* Binsenwahrheit *f*
truly ['truli] *adv* wirklich; **Yours t.** Hochachtungsvoll
trump [trʌmp] *s* Trumpf *m* || *tr* trumpfen; **t. up** erdichten || *intr* trumpfen
trumpet ['trʌmpɪt] *s* Trompete *f* || *intr* (*said of an elephant*) trompeten
truncheon ['trʌntʃən] *s* Gummiknüppel *m*
trunk [trʌŋk] *s* (*chest*) Koffer *m;* (*of a tree*) Stamm *m;* (*of a living body*) Rumpf *m;* (*of an elephant*) Rüssel *m;* (aut) Kofferraum *m;* **trunks** (sport) Sporthose *f*
trunk' line' *s* Fernverkehrsweg *m*
truss [trʌs] *s* (archit) Tragwerk *n;* (med) Bruchband *n* || *tr* (archit) stützen; (*bind*) festbinden
trust [trʌst] *s* (in) Vertrauen *n* (auf *acc*); (com) Trust *m;* (jur) Treuhand *f* || *tr* trauen (*dat*); (*hope*) hoffen || *intr*—**t. in** vertrauen auf (*acc*)
trust' com'pany *s* Treuhandgesellschaft *f*
trustee [trʌs'ti] *s* Aufsichtsrat *m;* (jur) Treuhänder –in *mf*
trustee'ship *s* Treuhandverwaltung *f*
trustful ['trʌstfəl] *adj* zutraulich
trust' fund' *s* Treuhandfonds *m*
trust'wor'thy *adj* vertrauenswürdig
trusty ['trʌsti] *adj* treu || *s* Kalfaktor *m*
truth [truθ] *s* Wahrheit *f;* **in t.** wahrlich
truthful ['truθfəl] *adj* (*person*) ehrlich; (*e.g., account*) wahrheitsgemäß
try [traɪ] *s* Versuch *m* || *v* (*pret & pp* **tried**) *tr* versuchen; (*one's patience*) auf e-e harte Probe stellen; (*a case*) verhandeln; **be tried for** vor Gericht kommen wegen; **try on** anprobieren; (*a hat*) aufprobieren; **try out** erproben; (*new food*) kosten; **try s.o. for**

gegen j–n verhandeln wegen || *intr* versuchen
try'ing *adj* anstrengend
try'out' *s* (sport) Ausscheidungskampf *m*
T'-shirt' *s* T-Shirt *n*
tub [tʌb] *s* Wanne *f;* (*boat*) Kasten *m*
tubby ['tʌbi] *adj* (coll) kugelrund
tube [t(j)ub] *s* (*pipe*) Rohr *n*, Röhre *f;* (*e.g., of toothpaste*) Tube *f;* (*of rubber*) Schlauch *m;* (rad) Röhre *f*
tuber [t(j)ubər] *s* (bot) Knolle *f*
tubercle ['t(j)ubərkəl] *s* Tuberkel *m*
tuberculosis [t(j)u,bʌrkjə'losɪs] *s* Lungenschwindsucht *f*
tuck [tʌk] *s* (sew) Abnäher *m* || *tr* (*into one's pocket, under a mattress*) stecken; (*under one's arm*) klemmen; (*into bed*) packen; **t. in** reinstecken; **t. up** (*trousers*) hochkrempeln; (*a skirt, dress*) hochschürzen
Tuesday ['t(j)uzde] *s* Dienstag *m;* **on T.** am Dienstag
tuft [tʌft] *s* Büschel *m & n* || *tr* (*e.g., a mattress*) durchheften
tug [tʌg] *s* (*pull*) Zug *m;* (*boat*) Schlepper *m* || *v* (*pret & pp* **tugged;** *ger* **tugging**) *tr* schleppen || *intr* (at) zerren (an *dat*)
tug'boat' *s* Schleppdampfer *m*
tug' of war' *s* Tauziehen *n*
tuition [t(j)u'ɪʃən] *s* Schulgeld *n*
tulip ['t(j)ulɪp] *s* Tulpe *f*
tumble ['tʌmbəl] *s* (*fall*) Sturz *m;* (gym) Purzelbaum *m* || *intr* (*fall*) stürzen; (gym) Saltos machen; **t. down the stairs** die Treppe herunterpurzeln
tum'ble-down' *adj* baufällig
tumbler ['tʌmblər] *s* (*glass*) Trinkglas *n;* (*of a lock*) Zuhaltung *f;* (*acrobat*) Akrobat –in *mf*
tumor ['t(j)umər] *s* Geschwulst *f*
tumult ['t(j)umʌlt] *s* Getümmel *n*
tuna ['tunə] *s* Thunfisch *m*
tune [t(j)un] *s* Melodie *f;* **be in t.** richtig gestimmt sein; **be out of t.** falsch singen; (*said of a piano*) verstimmt sein; **change one's t.** e–n anderen Ton anschlagen || *tr* stimmen; **t. up** (aut) neu einstellen || *intr*— **t. in on** (rad) einstellen; **t. up** (*said of an orchestra*) stimmen
tungsten ['tʌŋstən] *s* Wolfram *n*
tunic ['t(j)unɪk] *s* Tunika *f*
tun'ing fork' *s* Stimmgabel *f*
tun·nel ['tʌnəl] *s* Tunnel *m;* (min) Stollen *m* || *v* (*pret & pp* **-nel[l]ed;** *ger* **-nel[l]ing**) *intr* e–n Tunnel bohren
turban ['tʌrbən] *s* Turban *m*
turbid ['tʌrbɪd] *adj* trüb(e)
turbine ['tʌrbɪn] *s* Turbine *f*
turboprop ['tʌrbo,prɑp] *s* Turboprop *m*
turbulence ['tʌrbjələns] *s* Turbulenz *f*
tureen [t(j)u'rin] *s* Terrine *f*
turf [tʌrf] *s* Rasendecke *f;* (*of a gang*) (sl) Gebiet *n;* **the t.** der Turf
Turk [tʌrk] *s* Türke *m*, Türkin *f*
turkey ['tʌrki] *s* Truthahn *m;* (*female*) Truthenne *f;* **Turkey** die Türkei

Turkish ['tʌrkıʃ] *adj* türkisch ‖ *s* Türkisch *n*
Tur'kish tow'el *s* Frottiertuch *n*
turmoil ['tʌrmɔıl] *s* Getümmel *n*
turn [tʌrn] *s* (*rotation*) Drehung *f*; (*change of direction or condition*) Wendung *f*; (*curve*) Kurve *f*; (*by a driver*) Abbiegen *n*; (*of a century*) Wende *f*; (*of a spool*) Windung *f*; **at every t.** bei jeder Gelegenheit; **good t.** Gunst *f*; **it's his t.** er ist dran; **out of t.** außer der Reihe; **take turns** sich abwechseln ‖ *tr* drehen; (*the page*) umblättern; (*one's head*) wenden; **t. down** (*refuse*) ablehnen; (*a radio*) leiser stellen; (*a bed*) aufdecken; (*a collar*) umschlagen; (*an appeal*) (jur) verwerfen; **t. in** (*an application, resignation*) einreichen; (*lost articles*) abgeben; (*a person*) anzeigen; **t. into** verwandeln in (*acc*); **t. loose** frei lassen; **t. off** (*light, gas*) abdrehen; (*rad, telv*) abstellen; **t. on** (*gas, light*) andrehen; (*excite*) (coll) in Erregung versetzen; (*rad, telv*) anstellen; **t. out** produzieren; (*pockets*) umkehren; (*eject*) vor die Tür setzen; **t. over** (*property*) abtreten; (*a business*) übertragen; (*e.g., weapons*) abliefern; **t. up** (*a card, sleeve*) aufschlagen ‖ *intr* (*rotate*) sich drehen; (*in some direction*) sich wenden; **it turned out that** es stellte sich heraus, daß; **t. against** (fig) sich wenden gegen; **t. around** sich herumdrehen; **t. back** umdrehen; **t. down** (*a street*) einbiegen in (*acc*); **t. in** (*go to bed*) zu Bett gehen; **t. into** werden zu; **t. out** ausfallen; **t. out for** sich einfinden zu; **t. out for the best** sich zum Guten wenden; **t. out in force** vollzählig erscheinen; **t. out to be** sich erweisen als; **t. over** (*tip over*) umkippen; (aut) anspringen; **t. to s.o. for help** sich an j–n um Hilfe wenden; **t. towards** sich wenden gegen; **t. up** auftauchen
turn'coat' *s* Überläufer –in *mf*
turn'ing point' *s* Wendepunkt *m*
turnip ['tʌrnıp] *s* Steckrübe *f*
turn'out' *s* Beteiligung *f*
turn'o'ver *s* Umsatz *m*
turn'pike' *s* Autobahn *f*
turnstile ['tʌrn͵staıl] *s* Drehkreuz *n*
turn'ta'ble *s* Plattenteller *m*; (rr) Drehscheibe *f*
turpentine ['tʌrpən͵taın] *s* Terpentin *n*
turpitude ['tʌrpı͵t(j)ud] *s* Verworfenheit *f*
turquoise ['tʌrk(w)ɔız] *adj* türkisfarben ‖ *s* Türkis *m*
turret ['tʌrıt] *s* Turm *m*
turtle ['tʌrtəl] *s* Schildkröte *f*
tur'tledove' *s* Turteltaube *f*
tur'tleneck' *s* Rollkragen *m*
tusk [tʌsk] *s* (*of an elephant*) Stoßzahn *m*; (*of a boar*) Hauer *m*
tussle ['tʌsəl] *s* Rauferei *f* ‖ *intr* raufen
tutor ['t(j)utər] *s* Hauslehrer –in *mf*
tuxe·do [tʌk'sido] *s* (**–dos**) Smoking *m*

twang [twæŋ] *s* (*of a musical instrument*) Schwirren *n*; (*of the voice*) Näseln *n* ‖ *intr* schwirren; näseln
tweed [twid] *adj* aus Tweed ‖ *s* Tweed *m*
tweet [twit] *s* Gezwitscher *n* ‖ *intr* zwitschern
tweezers ['twizərz] *spl* Pinzette *f*
twelfth [twɛlfθ] *adj* & *pron* zwölfte ‖ *s* (*fraction*) Zwölftel *n*; **the t.** (*in dates or in series*) der Zwölfte
twelve [twɛlv] *adj* & *pron* zwölf ‖ *s* Zwölf *f*
twentieth ['twentı·ıθ] *adj* & *pron* zwanzigste ‖ *s* (*fraction*) Zwanzigstel *n*; **the t.** (*in dates or in series*) der Zwanzigste
twenty ['twenti] *adj* & *pron* zwanzig ‖ *s* Zwanzig *f*; **the twenties** die zwanziger Jahre
twen'ty-one' *adj* & *pron* einundzwanzig
twice [twaıs] *adv* zweimal
twiddle ['twıdəl] *tr* müßig herumdrehen; **t. one's thumbs** Daumen drehen
twig [twıg] *s* Zweig *m*
twilight ['twaı͵laıt] *adj* dämmerig ‖ *s* Abenddämmerung *f*
twin [twın] *adj* (*brother, sister*) Zwillings–; (*double*) Doppel– ‖ *s* Zwilling *m*
twine [twaın] *s* (*for a package*) Bindfaden *m*; (sew) Zwirn *m* ‖ *tr*—**t. around** winden um
twin'-en'gine *adj* zweimotorig
twinge [twındz] *s* stechender Schmerz *m*
twinkle ['twıŋkəl] *s* Funkeln *n*; **in a t.** im Nu ‖ *intr* funkeln
twirl [twʌrl] *s* Wirbel *m* ‖ *tr* herumwirbeln ‖ *intr* wirbeln
twist [twıst] *s* (*turn*) Drehung *f*; (*distortion*) Verdrehung *f*; (*strand*) Flechte *f*; (*bread roll*) Zopf *m*; (*dance*) Twist *m* ‖ *tr* (*revolve*) drehen; (*wind*) winden; (*an arm, words*) verdrehen; **t. one's ankle** sich [*dat*] den Knöchel vertreten ‖ *intr* sich drehen; (*wind*) sich winden
twister ['twıstər] *s* (coll) Windhose *f*
twit [twıt] *s* (sl) Depp *m* ‖ *v* (*pret* & *pp* **twitted**; *ger* **twitting**) *tr* verspotten; (*upbraid*) rügen
twitch [twıtʃ] *s* Zucken *n* ‖ *intr* zucken
twitter ['twıtər] *s* Zwitschern *n* ‖ *intr* zwitschern
two [tu] *adj* & *pron* zwei ‖ *s* Zwei *f*; **by twos** zu zweit; **in two** entzwei; **put two and two together** Schlußfolgerungen ziehen
two'-edged' *adj* zweischneidig
two'-faced' *adj* doppelzüngig
two' hun'dred *adj* & *pron* zweihundert
two'-piece' *adj* (*suit*) zweiteilig
twosome ['tusəm] *s* (*of lovers*) Liebespaar *n*; (golf) Einzelspiel *n*
two'-time' *tr* untreu sein (*dat*)
two'-tone' *adj* zweifarbig
two'-way traf'fic *s* Gegenverkehr *m*
tycoon [taı'kun] *s* Industriekapitän *m*
type [taıp] *s* (*kind*) Art *f*; (*of person*; *of manufacture*) Typ *m*; (typ) Drucktype *f*, Letter *f* ‖ *tr* & *intr* tippen

type'face' s Schriftbild n
type'script' s Maschinenschrift f
type'set'ter s Schriftsetzer –in mf
type'write' v (pret **–wrote;** pp **–written**) tr & intr mit der Maschine schreiben
type'writ'er s Schreibmaschine f
type'writer rib'bon s Farbband n
ty'phoid fe'ver ['taɪfɔɪd] s Typhus m
typhoon [taɪ'fun] s Taifun m
typical ['tɪpɪkəl] adj (of) typisch (für)
typi·fy ['tɪpɪ,faɪ] v (pret & pp **–fied**) tr (characterize) typisch sein für; (exemplify) ein typisches Beispiel sein für
typ'ing er'ror s Tippfehler m

typist ['taɪpɪst] s Maschinenschreiber –in mf
typographic(al) [,taɪpə'græfɪk(əl)] adj typographisch; (error) Druck–
typography [taɪ'pɑgrəfi] s (the skill) Buchdruckerkunst f; (the work) Buchdruck m
tyrannical [tɪ'rænɪkəl] adj tyrannisch
tyrannize ['tɪrə,naɪz] tr tyrannisieren
tyranny ['tɪrəni] s Tyrannei f
tyrant ['taɪrənt] s Tyrann m
ty·ro ['taɪro] s (**–ros**) Neuling m
Tyrol [tɪ'rol] s Tirol n
Tyrolean [tɪ'rolɪ·ən] adj tirolerisch || s Tiroler –in mf

U

U, u [ju] s einundzwanzigster Buchstabe des englischen Alphabets
ubiquitous [ju'bɪkwɪtəs] adj allgegenwärtig
udder ['ʌdər] s Euter n
ugliness ['ʌglɪnɪs] s Häßlichkeit f
ugly ['ʌgli] adj häßlich
Ukraine [ju'kren] s Ukraine f
Ukrainian [ju'krenɪ·ən] adj ukrainisch || s (person) Ukrainer –in mf; (language) Ukrainisch n
ulcer ['ʌlsər] s Geschwür n
ulcerate ['ʌlsə,ret] intr eitern
ulte'rior mo'tive [ʌl'tɪrɪ·ər] s Hintergedanke m
ultimate ['ʌltɪmɪt] adj äußerste; (goal) höchst; (result) End– || s Letzte n
ultima·tum [,ʌltɪ'metəm] s (**–tums &** **–ta** [tə]) Ultimatum n
ul'trahigh fre'quency ['ʌltrə,haɪ] s Ultrahochfrequenz f
ultramodern [,ʌltrə'mɑdərn] adj ultramodern
ultraviolet [,ʌltrə'vaɪ·əlɪt] adj ultraviolett || s Ultraviolett n
ultravi'olet lamp' s Höhensonne f
umbil'ical cord' [ʌm'bɪlɪkəl] adj Nabelschnur f
umbrage ['ʌmbrɪdʒ] s—**take u. at** Anstoß nehmen an (dat)
umbrella [ʌm'brelə] s Regenschirm m; (aer) Abschirmung f
umlaut ['umlaut] s Umlaut m || tr umlauten
umpire ['ʌmpaɪr] s Schiedsrichter –in mf || tr als Schiedsrichter leiten || intr Schiedsrichter sein
umpteen [ʌmp'tin] adj zig; **u. times** zigmal
UN ['ju'ɛn] s (**United Nations**) UNO f
unable [ʌn'ebəl] adj unfähig
unabridged [ʌnə'brɪdʒd] adj ungekürzt
unaccented [,ʌnæk'sentɪd] adj unbetont
unacceptable [,ʌnæk'septɪbəl] adj unannehmbar
unaccountable [,ʌnə'kauntəbəl] adj

nicht verantwortlich; (strange) seltsam
unaccounted-for [,ʌnə'kauntɪd,fɔr] adj unerklärt; (acct) nicht belegt
unaccustomed [,ʌnə'kʌstəmd] adj (to) nicht gewöhnt (an acc)
unaffected [,ʌnə'fektɪd] adj nicht affektiert; **u. by** unbeeinflusst von
unafraid [,ʌnə'fred] adj—**be u. (of)** sich nicht fürchten (vor dat)
unalterable [ʌn'ɔltərəbəl] adj unabänderlich
unanimity [,junə'nɪmɪti] s Stimmeneinheit f
unanimous [ju'nænɪməs] adj (persons) einmütig; (vote) einstimmig
unannounced [,ʌnə'naunst] adj unangemeldet
unanswered [ʌn'ænsərd] adj (question) unbeantwortet; (claim, statement) unwiderlegt; (request) nicht erhört
unappreciative [,ʌnə'priʃɪ·ətɪv] adj (of) unempfänglich (für)
unapproachable [,ʌnə'protʃəbəl] adj unzugänglich
unarmed [ʌn'ɑrmd] adj unbewaffnet
unasked [ʌn'æskt] adj (advice) unerbeten; (uninvited) ungeladen
unassailable [,ʌnə'seləbəl] adj unangreifbar
unassuming [,ʌnə's(j)umɪŋ] adj nicht anmaßend
unattached [,ʌnə'tætʃt] adj (to) nicht befestigt (an dat); (person) ungebunden; (mil) zur Verfügung stehend
unattainable [,ʌnə'tenəbəl] adj unerreichbar
unattended [,ʌnə'tendɪd] adj unbeaufsichtigt
unattractive [,ʌnə'træktɪv] adj reizlos
unauthorized [ʌn'ɔθəraɪzd] adj unberechtigt
unavailable [,ʌnə'veləbəl] adj (person) unabkömmlich; (thing) nicht verfügbar
unavenged [,ʌnə'vendʒd] adj ungerächt
unavoidable [,ʌnə'vɔɪdəbəl] adj unvermeidlich

unaware [ˌʌnəˈwɛr] *adj* **(of)** nicht bewußt (*genit*)

unawares [ˌʌnəˈwɛrz] *adv* (*unexpectedly*) unversehens; (*unintentionally*) versehentlich; **catch u.** überraschen

unbalanced [ʌnˈbælənst] *adj* nicht im Gleichgewicht; (fig) unausgeglichen

un·bar [ʌnˈbɑr] *v* (*pret & pp* **–barred;** *ger* **–barring**) *tr* aufriegeln

unbearable [ʌnˈbɛrəbəl] *adj* unerträglich

unbeaten [ʌnˈbitən] *adj* (& fig) ungeschlagen

unbecoming [ˌʌnbɪˈkʌmɪŋ] *adj* (*improper*) ungeziemend; (*clothing*) unkleidsam

unbelievable [ˌʌnbɪˈlivəbəl] *adj* unglaublich

unbeliever [ˌʌnbɪˈlivər] *s* Ungläubige *mf*

unbending [ʌnˈbɛndɪŋ] *adj* unbeugsam

unbiased [ʌnˈbaɪ·əst] *adj* unvoreingenommen

unbidden [ʌnˈbɪdən] *adj* ungebeten

un·bind [ʌnˈbaɪnd] *v* (*pret & pp* **–bound**) *tr* losbinden

unbleached [ʌnˈblitʃt] *adj* ungebleicht

unbolt [ʌnˈbolt] *tr* aufriegeln

unborn [ˈʌnbɔrn] *adj* ungeboren

unbosom [ʌnˈbuzəm] *tr*—**u. oneself to** sich offenbaren (*dat*)

unbowed [ʌnˈbaud] *adj* ungebeugt

unbreakable [ʌnˈbrekəbəl] *adj* unzerbrechlich

unbridled [ʌnˈbraɪdəld] *adj* ungezügelt

unbroken [ʌnˈbrokən] *adj* (*intact*) ungebrochen; (*line, series*) ununterbrochen; (*horse*) nicht zugeritten

unbuckle [ʌnˈbʌkəl] *tr* aufschnallen

unburden [ʌnˈbʌrdən] *tr* entlasten; **u. oneself** sein Herz ausschütten

unburied [ʌnˈberid] *adj* unbeerdigt

unbutton [ʌnˈbʌtən] *adj* aufknöpfen

uncalled-for [ʌnˈkɔld ˌfɔr] *adj* unangebracht

uncanny [ʌnˈkæni] *adj* unheimlich

uncared-for [ʌnˈkɛrd ˌfɔr] *adj* verwahrlost

unceasing [ʌnˈsisɪŋ] *adj* unaufhörlich

unceremonious [ˌʌnsɛrɪˈmoni·əs] *adj* (*informal*) ungezwungen; (*rude*) unsanft

uncertain [ʌnˈsɑrtən] *adj* unsicher

uncertainty [ʌnˈsɑrtənti] *s* Unsicherheit *f*

unchain [ʌnˈtʃen] *tr* losketten; (fig) entfesseln

unchangeable [ʌnˈtʃendʒəbəl] *adj* unveränderlich

uncharacteristic [ˌʌnkærɪktəˈrɪstɪk] *adj* wesensfremd

uncharted [ʌnˈtʃɑrtɪd] *adj* auf keiner Karte verzeichnet

unchaste [ʌnˈtʃest] *adj* unkeusch

unchecked [ʌnˈtʃɛkt] *adj* ungehemmt

unchristian [ʌnˈkrɪstʃən] *adj* unchristlich

uncivilized [ʌnˈsɪvɪ ˌlaɪzd] *adj* unzivilisiert

unclad [ʌnˈklæd] *adj* unbekleidet

unclaimed [ʌnˈklemd] *adj* nicht abgeholt

unclasp [ʌnˈklæsp] *tr* loshaken; (*the arms, hands*) öffnen

unclassified [ʌnˈklæsɪ ˌfaɪd] *adj* nicht klassifiziert; (*not secret*) nicht geheim

uncle [ˈʌnkəl] *s* Onkel *m*

unclean [ʌnˈklin] *adj* unsauber; (relig) unrein

unclear [ʌnˈklɪr] *adj* unklar

un·clog [ʌnˈklɑg] *v* (*pret & pp* **–clogged;** *ger* **–clogging**) *tr* von e-m Hindernis befreien

uncombed [ʌnˈkomd] *adj* ungekämmt

uncomfortable [ʌnˈkʌmfərtəbəl] *adj* unbequem; **feel u.** sich nicht recht wohl fühlen

uncommitted [ˌʌnkəˈmɪtɪd] *adj* (*troops*) nicht eingesetzt; (*delegates, nations*) unentschieden

uncommon [ʌnˈkɑmən] *adj* ungewöhnlich; (*outstanding*) außergewöhnlich

uncomplaining [ˌʌnkʌmˈplenɪŋ] *adj* klaglos

uncompromising [ʌnˈkɑmprə ˌmaɪzɪŋ] *adj* unbeugsam

unconcealed [ˌʌnkənˈsild] *adj* unverholen

unconcerned [ˌʌnkənˈsɑrnd] *adj* (*about*) unbesorgt (um)

unconditional [ˌʌnkənˈdɪʃənəl] *adj* bedingungslos

unconfirmed [ˌʌnkənˈfɪrmd] *adj* unbestätigt, unverbürgt

unconquerable [ʌnˈkɑŋkərəbəl] *adj* unüberwindlich

unconquered [ʌnˈkɑŋkərd] *adj* unbezwungen

unconscious [ʌnˈkɑnʃəs] *adj* bewußtlos; (*of*) nicht bewußt (*genit*) ‖ *s—* **the u.** das Unbewußte

unconstitutional [ˌʌnkɑnstɪˈt(j)uʃənəl] *adj* verfassungswidrig

uncontested [ˌʌnkənˈtɛstɪd] *adj* unbestritten

uncontrollable [ˌʌnkənˈtroləbəl] *adj* unkontrollierbar; (fig) unbändig

unconventional [ˌʌnkənˈvɛntʃənəl] *adj* unkonventionell

uncork [ʌnˈkɔrk] *tr* entkorken

uncouple [ʌnˈkʌpəl] *tr* abkoppeln

uncouth [ʌnˈkuθ] *adj* ungehobelt; (*appearance*) ungeschlacht

uncover [ʌnˈkʌvər] *tr* aufdecken

unctuous [ˈʌŋktʃu·əs] *adj* salbungsvoll

uncultivated [ʌnˈkʌltɪ ˌvetɪd] *adj* unbebaut

uncultured [ʌnˈkʌltʃərd] *adj* (fig) unkultiviert

uncut [ʌnˈkʌt] *adj* nicht abgeschnitten; (*gem*) ungeschliffen; (*grain*) ungemäht

undamaged [ʌnˈdæmɪdʒd] *adj* unbeschädigt, unversehrt

undaunted [ʌnˈdɔntɪd] *adj* unverzagt

undecided [ˌʌndɪˈsaɪdɪd] *adj* (*person*) unschlüssig; (*thing*) unentschieden

undefeated [ˌʌndɪˈfitɪd] *adj* unbesiegt

undefended [ˌʌndɪˈfɛndɪd] *adj* unverteidigt

undefiled [ˌʌndɪˈfaɪld] *adj* unbefleckt

undefined [ˌʌndɪˈfaɪnd] *adj* unklar

undeliverable [ˌʌndɪˈlɪvərəbəl] *adj* unbestellbar

undeniable [ˌʌndɪ'naɪ·əbəl] *adj* un-leugbar
under ['ʌndər] *adj* Unter– || *adv* unter–, e.g., **go u.** untergehen || *prep* unter (*position*) (*dat*); (*direction*) unter (*acc*)
un'derage' *adj* unmündig
un'der·bid' *v* (*pret & pp* –**bid;** *ger* –**bidding**) *tr* unterbieten
un'derbrush' *s* Unterholz *n*
un'dercar'riage *s* Fahrgestell *n*
un'derclothes' *spl* Unterwäsche *f*
un'dercov'er *adj* Geheim–; **u. agent** Spitzel *m*
un'dercur'rent *s* (& *fig*) Unterströmung *f*
un'dercut' *v* (*pret & pp* –**cut;** *ger* –**cutting**) *tr* unterbieten
un'derdevel'oped *adj* unterentwickelt
un'derdog' *s* (coll) Unterlegene *mf*
un'derdone' *adj* nicht durchgebraten
un'deres'timate *tr* unterschätzen
un'derexpose' *tr* (phot) unterbelichten
un'dergar'ment *s* Unterkleidung *f*
un'der·go' *v* (*pret* –**went;** *pp* –**gone**) durchmachen; (*an operation*) sich unterziehen (*dat*)
un'dergrad'uate *s* Collegestudent –in *mf*
un'derground' *adj* unterirdisch; (*fig*) Untergrund–; (*water*) Grund–; (*min*) unter Tage || **un'derground'** *s* (*secret movement*) Untergrundbewegung *f*; **go u.** untertauchen
un'dergrowth' *s* Buschholz *n*, Unterholz *n*
un'derhand' *adj* (*throw*) unter Schulterhöhe (ausgeführt)
un'derhand'ed *adj* hinterhältig
un'derline', **un'derline'** *tr* unterstreichen
underling ['ʌndərlɪŋ] *s* Handlanger *m*
un'dermine' *tr* (& *fig*) untergraben
underneath [ˌʌndər'niθ] *adj* Unter– || *adv* unten || *s* Unterseite *f* || *prep* (*position*) unter (*dat*), unterhalb (*genit*); (*direction*) unter (*acc*)
un'dernour'ished *adj* unterernährt
un'dernour'ishment *s* Unterernährung *f*
un'derpad' *s* (*of a rug*) Unterlage *f*
un'derpaid' *adj* unterbezahlt
un'derpass' *s* Straßenunterführung *f*
un'der·pin' *v* (*pret & pp* –**pinned;** *ger* –**pinning**) *tr* untermauern
un'derplay' *tr* unterspielen
un'derpriv'ileged *adj* benachteiligt
un'derrate' *tr* unterschätzen
un'derscore' *tr* (& *fig*) unterstreichen
un'dersea' *adj* Unterwasser–
un'dersec'retar'y *s* Untersekretär –in *mf*
un'der·sell' *v* (*pret & pp* –**sold;** *ger* –**selling**) *tr* (*a person*) unterbieten; (*goods*) verschleudern
un'dershirt' *s* Unterhemd *n*
un'derside' *s* Unterseite *f*
un'dersigned' *adj* unterschrieben || **un'dersigned'** *s* Unterzeichnete *mf*
un'der·stand' *v* (*pret & pp* –**stood**) *tr* verstehen; **it's understood that** es ist selbstverständlich, daß; **make oneself understood** sich verständlich machen

understandable [ˌʌndər'stændəbəl] *adj* verständlich
understandably [ˌʌndər'stændəbli] *adv* begreiflicherweise
un'derstand'ing *adj* verständnisvoll || *s* (**of**) Verständnis *n* (für); (*between persons*) Einvernehmen *n;* (*agreement*) Übereinkommen *n;* **come to an u. with s.o.** sich mit j–m verständigen; **it is my u. that** wie ich verstehe
un'derstud'y *s* Ersatzmann *m;* (cin, theat) Ersatzschauspieler –in *mf*
un'der·take' *v* (*pret* –**took;** *pp* –**taken**) *tr* unternehmen
undertaker ['ʌndər ˌtekər] *s* Leichenbestatter –in *mf*
un'dertak'ing *s* Unternehmen *n*
un'dertone' *s* leise Stimme *f;* (fig) Unterton *m*
un'dertow' *s* Sog *m*
un'derwa'ter *adj* Unterwasser–
un'derwear' *s* Unterwäsche *f*
un'derweight' *adj* untergewichtig
un'derworld' *s* (*of criminals*) Unterwelt *f;* (myth) Totenreich *n*
un'der·write', **un'der·write'** *v* (*pret* –**wrote;** *pp* –**written**) *tr* unterschreiben; (ins) versichern
un'derwrit'er *s* Unterzeichner –in *mf;* (ins) Versicherer –in *mf;* (st. exch.) Wertpapiermakler –in *mf;* **underwriters** Emissionsfirma *f*
undeserved [ˌʌndɪ'zʌrvd] *adj* unverdient
undeservedly [ˌʌndɪ'zʌrvɪdli] *adv* unverdientermaßen
undesirable [ˌʌndɪ'zaɪrəbəl] *adj* unerwünscht || *s* Unerwünschte *mf*
undeveloped [ˌʌndɪ'veləpt] *adj* unentwickelt; (*land*) unerschlossen
undies ['ʌndiz] *spl* (coll) Unterwäsche *f*
undigested [ˌʌndɪ'dʒestɪd] *adj* (& fig) unverdaut
undignified [ʌn'dɪgnɪ ˌfaɪd] *adj* würdelos
undiluted [ˌʌndɪ'lutɪd] *adj* unverdünnt
undiminished [ˌʌndɪ'mɪnɪʃt] *adj* unvermindert
undisciplined [ʌn'dɪsəplɪnd] *adj* undiszipliniert, zuchtlos
undisputed [ˌʌndɪs'pjutɪd] *adj* unbestritten, unangefochten
undisturbed [ˌʌndɪs'tʌrbd] *adj* ungestört
undivided [ˌʌndɪ'vaɪdɪd] *adj* ungeteilt
un·do [ʌn'du] *v* (*pret* –**did;** *pp* –**done**) *tr* (*a knot*) aufschnüren; (*a deed*) ungeschehen machen
undo'ing *s* Ruin *m*
undone [ʌn'dʌn] *adj* (*not done*) ungetan; (*ruined*) ruiniert; **come u.** sich lösen; **leave nothing u.** nichts unversucht lassen
undoubtedly [ʌn'dautɪdli] *adv* zweifellos
undramatic [ˌʌndrə'mætɪk] *adj* undramatisch
undress [ʌn'drɛs] *s*—**in a state of u.** (*nude*) in unbekleidetem Zustand; (*in a negligee*) im Negligé || *tr* ausziehen || *intr* sich ausziehen

undrinkable [ʌn'drɪŋkəbəl] *adj* nicht trinkbar

undue [ʌn'd(j)u] *adj* (*inappropriate*) unangemessen; (*excessive*) übermäßig

undulate ['ʌndjə‚let] *intr* wogen

undulating ['ʌndjə‚letɪŋ] *adj* wellenförmig

unduly [ʌn'd(j)uli] *adv* übermäßig

undying [ʌn'daɪ·ɪŋ] *adj* unsterblich

un'earned in'come ['ʌnʌrnd] *s* Kapitalrente *f*

unearth [ʌn'ʌrθ] *tr* ausgraben; (fig) aufstöbern

unearthly [ʌn'ʌrθli] *adj* unirdisch; (*cry*) schauerlich; **at an u. hour** (*early*) in aller Herrgottsfrühe

uneasy [ʌn'izi] *adj* (*worried*) ängstlich; (*ill at ease*) unbehaglich

uneatable [ʌn'itəbəl] *adj* ungenießbar

uneconomic(al) [‚ʌnɛkə'nɑmɪk(əl)] *adj* unwirtschaftlich

uneducated [ʌn'ɛdjə‚ketɪd] *adj* ungebildet

unemployed [‚ʌnɛm'plɔɪd] *adj* arbeitslos || *s* Arbeitslose *mf*

unemployment [‚ʌnɛm'plɔɪmənt] *s* Arbeitslosigkeit *f*

unemploy'ment compensa'tion *s* Arbeitslosenunterstützung *f;* **collect u.** (sl) Stempeln gehen

unencumbered [‚ʌnən'kʌmbərd] *adj* unbelastet

unending [ʌn'ɛndɪŋ] *adj* endlos

unequal [ʌn'ikwəl] *adj* ungleich; **u. to** nicht gewachsen (*dat*)

unequaled [ʌn'ikwəld] *adj* ohnegleichen

unequivocal [‚ʌnə'kwɪvəkəl] *adj* eindeutig

unerring [ʌn'ɛrɪŋ] *adj* unfehlbar

UNESCO [ju'nesko] *s* (**United Nations Educational, Scientific, and Cultural Organization**) UNESCO *f*

unessential [‚ʌnɛ'sɛnʃəl] *adj* unwesentlich

uneven [ʌn'ivən] *adj* (*not smooth*) uneben; (*unbalanced*) ungleich; (*not uniform*) ungleichmäßig; (*number*) ungerade

uneventful [‚ʌnɪ'vɛntfəl] *adj* ereignislos

unexceptional [‚ʌnɛk'sɛpʃənəl] *adj* nicht außergewöhnlich

unexpected [‚ʌnɛk'spɛktɪd] *adj* unerwartet

unexplained [‚ʌnɛk'splend] *adj* unerklärt

unexplored [‚ʌnɛk'splord] *adj* unerforscht

unexposed [‚ʌnɛk'spozd] *adj* (phot) unbelichtet

unfading [ʌn'fedɪŋ] *adj* unverwelklich

unfailing [ʌn'felɪŋ] *adj* unfehlbar

unfair [ʌn'fer] *adj* unfair; (*competition*) unlauter

unfaithful [ʌn'feθfəl] *adj* treulos

unfamiliar [‚ʌnfə'mɪljər] *adj* unbekannt

unfasten [ʌn'fæsən] *tr* losbinden; (*e.g., a seat belt*) aufschnallen

unfathomable [ʌn'fæðəməbəl] *adj* unergründlich

unfavorable [ʌn'fevərəbəl] *adj* ungünstig

unfeasible [ʌn'fizəbəl] *adj* unausführbar

unfeeling [ʌn'filɪŋ] *adj* unempfindlich

unfilled [ʌn'fɪld] *adj* ungefüllt; (*post*) unbesetzt

unfinished [ʌn'fɪnɪʃt] *adj* unfertig; (*business*) unerledigt

unfit [ʌn'fɪt] *adj* (**for**) ungeeignet (für); (*not qualified*) (**for**) untauglich (für); **u. for military service** wehrdienstuntauglich

unfold [ʌn'fold] *tr* (*a chair*) aufklappen; (*cloth, paper*) entfalten; (*ideas, plans*) offenbaren

unforeseeable [‚ʌnfor'si·əbəl] *adj* unabsehbar

unforeseen [‚ʌnfor'sin] *adj* unvorhergesehen

unforgettable [‚ʌnfor'gɛtəbəl] *adj* unvergeßlich

unfortunate [ʌn'fortʃənɪt] *adj* unglücklich

unfortunately [ʌn'fortʃənɪtli] *adv* leider

unfounded [ʌn'faundɪd] *adj* unbegründet

un·freeze [ʌn'friz] *v* (*pret* **–froze;** *pp* **–frozen**) *tr* auftauen; (*prices*) freigeben

unfriendly [ʌn'frɛndli] *adj* unfreundlich

unfruitful [ʌn'frutfəl] *adj* unfruchtbar

unfulfilled [‚ʌnfəl'fɪld] *adj* unerfüllt

unfurl [ʌn'fʌrl] *tr* (*a flag*) entrollen; (*sails*) losmachen

unfurnished [ʌn'fʌrnɪʃt] *adj* unmöbliert

ungainly [ʌn'genli] *adj* plump

ungentlemanly [ʌn'dʒɛntəlmənli] *adj* unfein, unedel

ungodly [ʌn'gɑdli] *adj* (*hour*) ungehörig

ungracious [ʌn'greʃəs] *adj* ungnädig

ungrammatical [‚ʌngrə'mætɪkəl] *adj* ungrammatisch

ungrateful [ʌn'gretfəl] *adj* undankbar

ungrudgingly [ʌn'grʌdʒɪŋli] *adv* gern

unguarded [ʌn'gɑrdɪd] *adj* unbewacht; (*moment*) unbedacht

unguent ['ʌŋgwɛnt] *s* Salbe *f*

unhandy [ʌn'hændi] *adj* unhandlich; (*person*) unbeholfen

unhappy [ʌn'hæpi] *adj* unglücklich

unharmed [ʌn'hɑrmd] *adj* unversehrt

unharness [ʌn'hɑrnɪs] *tr* abschirren

unhealthful [ʌn'hɛlθfəl] *adj* ungesund

unhealthy [ʌn'hɛlθi] *adj* ungesund

unheard-of [ʌn'hʌrd‚ɑv] *adj* unerhört

unheated [ʌn'hitɪd] *adj* ungeheizt

unhesitating [ʌn'hɛzɪ‚tetɪŋ] *adj* (*immediate*) unverzüglich; (*unswerving*) unbeirrbar; (*support*) bereitwillig

unhinge [ʌn'hɪndʒ] *tr* (fig) aus den Angeln heben

unhitch [ʌn'hɪtʃ] *tr* (*horses*) ausspannen; (*undo*) losmachen

unholy [ʌn'holi] *adj* unheilig

unhook [ʌn'huk] *tr* losmachen; (*a dress*) aufhaken; (*the receiver*) abnehmen

unhoped-for [ʌn'hopt ,fɔr] *adj* unverhofft
unhurt [ʌn'hʌrt] *adj* unbeschädigt; (*person*) unversehrt
unicorn ['junɪ ,kɔrn] *s* Einhorn *n*
unification [,junɪfɪ'keʃən] *s* Vereinigung *f*
uniform ['junɪ ,fɔrm] *adj* gleichförmig || *s* Uniform *f*
uniformity [,junɪ'fɔrmɪti] *s* Gleichförmigkeit *f*
uni‧fy ['junɪ ,faɪ] *v* (*pret & pp* –fied) *tr* vereinigen
unilateral [,junɪ'lætərəl] *adj* einseitig
unimpaired [,ʌnɪm'pɛrd] *adj* ungeschwächt
unimpeachable [,ʌnɪm'pitʃəbəl] *adj* unantastbar
unimportant [,ʌnɪm'pɔrtənt] *adj* unwichtig
uninflected [,ʌnɪn'flɛktɪd] *adj* (gram) unflektiert
uninhabited [,ʌnɪn'hæbɪtɪd] *adj* unbewohnt
uninspired [,ʌnɪn'spaɪrd] *adj* schwunglos
unintelligible [,ʌnɪn'tɛlɪdʒəbəl] *adj* unverständlich
unintentional [,ʌnɪn'tɛnʃənəl] *adj* unabsichtlich
uninterested [ʌn'ɪntə ,rɛstɪd] *adj* (in) uninteressiert (an *dat*)
uninteresting [ʌn'ɪntə ,rɛstɪŋ] *adj* uninteressant
uninterrupted [,ʌnɪntə'rʌptɪd] *adj* ununterbrochen
uninvited [,ʌnɪn'vaɪtɪd] *adj* ungeladen
union ['junjən] *adj* Gewerkschafts– || *s* Vereinigung *f;* (*harmony*) Eintracht *f;* (*of workers*) Gewerkschaft *f;* (pol) Union *f*
unionize ['junjə ,naɪz] *tr* gewerkschaftlich organisieren || *intr* sich gewerkschaftlich organisieren
un'ion shop' *s* Betrieb *m,* der nur Gewerkschaftsmitglieder beschäftigt
unique [ju'nik] *adj* einzigartig
unison ['junɪsən] *s* Einklang *m*
unit ['junɪt] *s* (& mil) Einheit *f*
unite [ju'naɪt] *tr* vereinigen; (chem) verbinden || *intr* sich vereinigen; (chem) sich verbinden
Unit'ed King'dom *s* Vereinigtes Königreich *n*
Unit'ed Na'tions *spl* Vereinte Nationen *pl*
Unit'ed States' *s* Vereinigte Staaten *pl*
unity ['junɪti] *s* (*harmony*) Einigkeit *f;* (*e.g., of a nation*) Einheit *f;* (fa) Einheitlichkeit *f*
universal [,junɪ'vʌrsəl] *adj* universal, allgemein || *s* Allgemeine *n;* (philos) Allgemeinbegriff *m*
u'niver'sal joint' *s* Kardangelenk *n*
u'niver'sal mil'itary train'ing *s* allgemeine Wehrpflicht *f*
universe ['junɪ ,vʌrs] *s* Universum *n*
university [,junɪ'vʌrsɪti] *adj* Universitäts– || *s* Universität *f*
unjust [ʌn'dʒʌst] *adj* ungerecht
unjustified [ʌn'dʒʌstɪ ,faɪd] *adj* ungerechtfertigt

unjustly [ʌn'dʒʌstli] *adv* zu Unrecht
unkempt [ʌn'kɛmpt] *adj* ungekämmt; (fig) verwahrlost
unkind [ʌn'kaɪnd] *adj* unfreundlich
unknown [ʌn'non] *adj* unbekannt
un'known quan'tity *s* Unbekannte *f*
Un'known Sol'dier *s* Unbekannter Soldat *m*
unlatch [ʌn'lætʃ] *tr* aufklinken
unlawful [ʌn'lɔfəl] *adj* gesetzwidrig
unleash [ʌn'liʃ] *tr* losbinden; (fig) entfesseln
unleavened [ʌn'lɛvənd] *adj* ungesäuert
unless [ʌn'lɛs] *conj* wenn ... nicht
unlettered [ʌn'lɛtərd] *adj* ungebildet
unlicensed [ʌn'laɪsənst] *adj* unerlaubt
unlike [ʌn'laɪk] *adj* (*unequal*) ungleich; (*dissimilar*) unähnlich || *prep* im Gegensatz zu (*dat*); **be u. s.o.** anders als jemand sein
unlikely [ʌn'laɪkli] *adj* unwahrscheinlich
unlimited [ʌn'lɪmɪtɪd] *adj* unbeschränkt
unlined [ʌn'laɪnd] *adj* (*clothes*) ungefüttert; (*paper*) unliniert; (*face*) faltenlos
unload [ʌn'lod] *tr & intr* ausladen
unload'ing *s* Ausladen *n;* (naut) Löschen *n*
unlock [ʌn'lak] *tr* aufsperren
unloose [ʌn'lus] *tr* lösen
unloved [ʌn'lʌvd] *adj* ungeliebt
unlucky [ʌn'lʌki] *adj* unglücklich
un‧make [ʌn'mek] *v* (*pret & pp* –made) *tr* rückgängig machen; (*a bed*) abdecken
unmanageable [ʌn'mænɪdʒəbəl] *adj* (*person, animal*) widerspenstig; (*thing*) unhandlich
unmanly [ʌn'mænli] *adj* unmännlich
unmanned [ʌn'mænd] *adj* (rok) unbemannt
unmannerly [ʌn'mænərli] *adj* unmännlich
unmarketable [ʌn'markɪtəbəl] *adj* nicht marktgängig
unmarriageable [ʌn'mærɪdʒəbəl] *adj* nicht heiratsfähig
unmarried [ʌn'mærid] *adj* unverheiratet
unmask [ʌn'mæsk] *tr* (& fig) demaskieren || *intr* sich demaskieren
unmatched [ʌn'mætʃt] *adj* (*not matched*) ungleichartig; (*unmatchable*) unvergleichlich
unmerciful [ʌn'mʌrsɪfəl] *adj* unbarmherzig
unmesh [ʌn'mɛʃ] *tr* (mach) ausrücken
unmindful [ʌn'maɪndfəl] *adj* uneingedenk
unmistakable [,ʌnmɪs'tekəbəl] *adj* unmißverständlich
unmitigated [ʌn'mɪtɪ ,getɪd] *adj* ungemildert; (*liar*) Erz–
unmixed [ʌn'mɪkst] *adj* ungemischt
unmoor [ʌn'mur] *tr* losmachen || *intr* sich losmachen
unmoved [ʌn'muvd] *adj* (fig) ungerührt
unmuzzle [ʌn'mʌzəl] *tr* den Maulkorb abnehmen (*dat*)

unnatural [ʌn'nætʃərəl] *adj* unnatürlich; (*forced*) gezwungen
unnecessary [ʌn'nesə‚seri] *adj* unnötig
unneeded [ʌn'nidɪd] *adj* nutzlos
unnerve [ʌn'nʌrv] *tr* entnerven
unnoticeable [ʌn'notɪsəbəl] *adj* unbemerkbar
unnoticed [ʌn'notɪst] *adj* unbemerkt
unobserved [‚ʌnəb'zʌrvd] *adj* unbeobachtet
unobtainable [‚ʌnəb'tenəbəl] *adj* nicht erhältlich
unobtrusive [‚ʌnəb'trusɪv] *adj* unaufdringlich
unoccupied [ʌn'akjə‚paɪd] *adj* (*room, house*) leerstehend; (*seat*) unbesetzt; (*person*) unbeschäftigt
unofficial [‚ʌnə'fɪʃəl] *adj* inoffiziell
unopened [ʌn'opənd] *adj* ungeöffnet
unopposed [‚ʌnə'pozd] *adj* (*without opposition*) widerspruchslos; (*unresisted*) unbehindert
unorthodox [ʌn'ɔrθə‚daks] *adj* unorthodox; (relig) nicht orthodox
unpack [ʌn'pæk] *tr* auspacken
unpalatable [ʌn'pælətəbəl] *adj* unschmackhaft; (fig) widerlich
unparalleled [ʌn'pærə‚leld] *adj* unvergleichlich
unpardonable [ʌn'pardənəbəl] *adj* unverzeihlich
unpatriotic [‚ʌnpetrɪ'atɪk] *adj* unpatriotisch
unpaved [ʌn'pevd] *adj* ungepflastert
unperceived [‚ʌnpər'sivd] *adj* unbemerkt
unpleasant [ʌn'plɛzənt] *adj* unangenehm; (*person*) unsympathisch
unpopular [ʌn'papjələr] *adj* unbeliebt
unpopularity [ʌn‚papjə'lærɪti] *s* Unbeliebtheit *f*
unprecedented [ʌn'presɪ‚dentɪd] *adj* unerhört; (jur) ohne Präzedenzfall
unpredictable [‚ʌnprɪ'dɪktəbəl] *adj* unberechenbar; (*weather*) wechselhaft
unprejudiced [ʌn'predʒədɪst] *adj* unvoreingenommen
unprepared [‚ʌnprɪ'perd] *adj* unvorbereitet
unpresentable [‚ʌnprɪ'zentəbəl] *adj* nicht präsentabel
unpretentious [‚ʌnprɪ'tenʃəs] *adj* anspruchslos
unprincipled [ʌn'prɪnsɪpəld] *adj* haltlos
unproductive [‚ʌnprə'dʌktɪv] *adj* unproduktiv; (**of**) unergiebig (an *dat*)
unprofessional [‚ʌnprə'feʃənəl] *adj* (*work*) unfachmännisch; (*conduct*) berufswidrig
unprofitable [ʌn'prafɪtəbəl] *adj* (*useless*) nutzlos; (fi) unrentabel
unpronounceable [‚ʌnprə'naunsəbəl] *adj* unaussprechlich
unprotected [‚ʌnprə'tektɪd] *adj* (*place*) ungeschützt; (*person*) unbeschützt
unpropitious [‚ʌnprə'pɪʃəs] *adj* ungünstig
unpublished [ʌn'pʌblɪʃt] *adj* unveröffentlicht
unpunished [ʌn'pʌnɪʃt] *adj* ungestraft
unqualified [ʌn'kwalə‚faɪd] *adj* un-

qualifiziert; (*full, complete*) unbedingt
unquenchable [ʌn'kwɛntʃəbəl] *adj* unstillbar
unquestionably [ʌn'kwɛstʃənəbli] *adv* fraglos, unbezweifelbar
unquestioning [ʌn'kwɛstʃənɪŋ] *adj* (*obedience*) bedingungslos
unquiet [ʌn'kwaɪ‚ət] *adj* unruhig
unrav·el [ʌn'rævəl] *v* (*pret* & *pp* **-el[l]ed;** *ger* **-el[l]ling**) *tr* (a knitted *fabric*) auftrennen; (fig) entwirren ‖ *intr* sich fasern; (fig) sich entwirren
unreachable [ʌn'ritʃəbəl] *adj* unerreichbar
unreal [ʌn'ri‚əl] *adj* unwirklich
unreality [‚ʌnrɪ'ælɪti] *s* Unwirklichkeit *f*
unreasonable [ʌn'rizənəbəl] *adj* unvernünftig
unrecognizable [ʌn'rekəg‚naɪzəbəl] *adj* unerkennbar
unreel [ʌn'ril] *tr* abspulen
unrefined [‚ʌnrɪ'faɪnd] *adj* roh
unrelated [‚ʌnrɪ'letɪd] *adj* (**to**) ohne Beziehung (zu)
unrelenting [‚ʌnrɪ'lentɪŋ] *adj* unerbittlich
unreliable [‚ʌnrɪ'laɪ·əbəl] *adj* unzuverlässig; (fin) unsolid(e)
unremitting [‚ʌnrɪ'mɪtɪŋ] *adj* unablässig
unrepentant [‚ʌnrɪ'pentənt] *adj* unbußfertig
unrequited [‚ʌnrɪ'kwaɪtɪd] *adj* unerwidert
unreserved [‚ʌnrɪ'zʌrvd] *adj* vorbehaltlos
unresponsive [‚ʌnrɪ'spansɪv] *adj* (**to**) unempfänglich (für)
unrest [ʌn'rest] *s* Unruhe *f*
unrestricted [‚ʌnrɪ'strɪktɪd] *adj* uneingeschränkt
unrewarded [‚ʌnrɪ'wɔrdɪd] *adj* unbelohnt
unrhymed [ʌn'raɪmd] *adj* ungereimt
un·rig [ʌn'rɪg] *v* (*pret* & *pp* **-rigged;** *ger* **-rigging**) *tr* abtakeln
unripe [ʌn'raɪp] *adj* unreif
unrivaled [ʌn'raɪvəld] *adj* unübertrefflich
unroll [ʌn'rol] *tr* aufrollen; (*e.g., a cable*) abrollen ‖ *intr* sich aufrollen; sich abrollen
unromantic [‚ʌnro'mæntɪk] *adj* unromantisch
unruffled [ʌn'rʌfəld] *adj* unerschüttert
unruly [ʌn'ruli] *adj* ungebärdig
unsaddle [ʌn'sædəl] *tr* (a *horse*) absatteln; (*a rider*) aus dem Sattel werfen
unsafe [ʌn'sef] *adj* unsicher
unsaid [ʌn'sed] *adj* ungesagt
unsalable [ʌn'seləbəl] *adj* unverkäuflich
unsanitary [ʌn'sænɪ‚teri] *adj* unhygienisch
unsalted [ʌn'sɔltɪd] *adj* ungesalzen
unsatisfactory [ʌn‚sætɪs'fæktəri] *adj* unbefriedigend
unsatisfied [ʌn'sætɪs‚faɪd] *adj* unbefriedigt

unsavory [ʌn'sevəri] *adj* unschmack-haft; (fig) widerlich
unscathed [ʌn'skeðd] *adj* unversehrt
unscientific [ˌʌnsaɪ·ən'tɪfɪk] *adj* un-wissenschaftlich
unscramble [ʌn'skræmbəl] *tr* (*a mes-sage*) entziffern; (fig) entflechten
unscrew [ʌn'skru] *tr* aufschrauben
unscrupulous [ʌn'skrupjələs] *adj* skru-pellos
unseal [ʌn'sil] *tr* entsiegeln; (*eyes, lips*) öffnen
unseasonable [ʌn'sizənəbəl] *adj* unzei-tig; (*weather*) nicht der Jahreszeit entsprechend
unseasoned [ʌn'sizənd] *adj* ungewürzt
unseat [ʌn'sit] *tr* (*a rider*) aus dem Sattel heben; (*an official*) aus dem Posten verdrängen
unseemly [ʌn'simli] *adj* ungehörig
unseen [ʌn'sin] *adj* ungesehen
unselfish [ʌn'selfɪʃ] *adj* selbstlos
unsettle [ʌn'setəl] *tr* beunruhigen
unsettled [ʌn'setəld] *adj* (*matter, bill*) unerledigt; (*without a residence*) ohne festen Wohnsitz; (*restless*) un-ruhig; (*life*) unstet
unshackle [ʌn'ʃækəl] *tr* die Fesseln abnehmen (*dat*)
unshakable [ʌn'ʃekəbəl] *adj* unerschüt-terlich
unshapely [ʌn'ʃepli] *adj* mißgestaltet
unshaven [ʌn'ʃevən] *adj* unrasiert
unsheathe [ʌn'ʃið] *tr* aus der Scheide ziehen
unshod [ʌn'ʃɑd] *adj* unbeschuht
unsightly [ʌn'saɪtli] *adj* unansehnlich
unsinkable [ʌn'sɪŋkəbəl] *adj* nicht ver-senkbar
unskilled [ʌn'skɪld] *adj* ungelernt; **u. laborer** Hilfsarbeiter –in *mf*
unskillful [ʌn'skɪlfəl] *adj* ungewandt
unsnarl [ʌn'snɑrl] *tr* entwirren
unsociable [ʌn'soʃəbəl] *adj* ungesellig
unsolicited [ˌʌnso'lɪsɪtɪd] *adj* unver-langt
unsold [ʌn'sold] *adj* unverkauft
unsophisticated [ˌʌnsə'fɪstɪˌketɪd] *adj* unverfälscht; (*naive*) arglos
unsound [ʌn'saund] *adj* ungesund; (*sleep*) unruhig; **of u. mind** geistes-krank
unspeakable [ʌn'spikəbəl] *adj* unsag-bar
unspoiled [ʌn'spɔɪld] *adj* unverdorben
unsportsmanlike [ʌn'sportsmən ˌlaɪk] *adj* unsportlich
unstable [ʌn'stebəl] *adj* unbeständig; (*e.g., ladder*) wacklig; (*hand*) zittrig; (*market, walk*) schwankend; (*incon-stant*) unbeständig; (chem) unbestän-dig
unstinted [ʌn'stɪntɪd] *adj* uneinge-schränkt
unstinting [ʌn'stɪntɪŋ] *adj* freigebig
unstitch [ʌn'stɪtʃ] *tr* auftrennen
unstressed [ʌn'strest] *adj* unbetont
unsuccessful [ˌʌnsək'sesfəl] *adj* er-folglos
unsuitable [ʌn'sutəbəl] *adj* ungeeignet; (*inappropriate*) unangemessen
unsullied [ʌn'sʌlid] *adj* unbefleckt

unsung [ʌn'sʌŋ] *adj* unbesungen
unsuspected [ˌʌnsəs'pɛktɪd] *adj* unver-dächtig; (*not known to exist*) un-geahnt
unsuspecting [ˌʌnsəs'pɛktɪŋ] *adj* arglos
unswerving [ʌn'swʌrvɪŋ] *adj* unentwegt
unsympathetic [ˌʌnsɪmpə'θɛtɪk] *adj* teilnahmslos
unsystematic(al) [ˌʌnsɪstə'mætɪk(əl)] *adj* unsystematisch
untactful [ʌn'tæktfəl] *adj* taktlos
untalented [ʌn'tæləntɪd] *adj* unbegabt
untamed [ʌn'temd] *adj* ungezähmt
untangle [ʌn'tæŋgəl] *tr* (& fig) ent-wirren
untenable [ʌn'tenəbəl] *adj* unhaltbar
untested [ʌn'testɪd] *adj* ungeprüft
unthankful [ʌn'θæŋkfəl] *adj* undank-bar
unthinking [ʌn'θɪŋkɪŋ] *adj* gedanken-los
untidy [ʌn'taɪdi] *adj* unordentlich
un·tie [ʌn'taɪ] *v* (*pret & pp* –**tied;** *ger* –**tying**) *tr* aufbinden; (*a knot*) lösen; **my shoe is untied** mein Schuh ist auf-gegangen
until [ʌn'tɪl] *prep* bis (*acc*); **u. further notice** bis auf weiteres ‖ *conj* bis
untimely [ʌn'taɪmli] *adj* frühzeitig; (*at the wrong time*) unzeitgemäß
untiring [ʌn'taɪrɪŋ] *adj* unermüdlich
untold [ʌn'told] *adj* (*suffering*) unsäg-lich; (*countless*) zahllos
untouched [ʌn'tʌtʃt] *adj* unangetastet; (fig) ungerührt
untoward [ʌn'tord] *adj* (*unfavorable*) ungünstig; (*unruly*) widerspenstig
untrained [ʌn'trend] *adj* unausgebil-det; (*eye*) ungeschult; (sport) un-trainiert
untried [ʌn'traɪd] *adj* (*unattempted*) unversucht; (*untested*) unerprobt; (*case*) (jur) nicht verhandelt
untroubled [ʌn'trʌbəld] *adj* (*mind, times*) ruhig; (*peace*) ungestört
untrue [ʌn'tru] *adj* unwahr; (*unfaith-ful*) un(ge)treu; (*not exact*) ungenau
untrustworthy [ʌn'trʌst ˌwʌrði] *adj* un-glaubwürdig
untruth [ʌn'truθ] *s* Unwahrheit *f*
untruthful [ʌn'truθfəl] *adj* (*statement*) unwahr; (*person*) unaufrichtig
untwist [ʌn'twɪst] *tr* aufflechten ‖ *intr* aufgehen
unusable [ʌn'juzəbəl] *adj* nicht ver-wendbar; (*unconsumable*) unbenutz-bar
unusual [ʌn'juʒʊ·əl] *adj* ungewöhnlich
unutterable [ʌn'ʌtərəbəl] *adj* unaus-sprechlich
unvarnished [ʌn'vɑrnɪʃt] *adj* nicht ge-firnißt; (*truth*) ungeschminkt
unveil [ʌn'vel] *tr* (*a monument*) ent-hüllen; (*a face*) entschleiern
unventilated [ʌn'venti ˌletɪd] *adj* un-gelüftet
unvoiced [ʌn'vɔɪst] *adj* (ling) stimmlos
unwanted [ʌn'wɑntɪd] *adj* uner-wünscht
unwarranted [ʌn'wɑrəntɪd] *adj* unge-rechtfertigt
unwary [ʌn'weri] *adj* unvorsichtig

unwavering [ʌn'wevərɪŋ] *adj* standhaft
unwelcome [ʌn'wɛlkəm] *adj* unwillkommen
unwell [ʌn'wɛl] *adj* unwohl
unwept [ʌn'wɛpt] *adj* unbeweint
unwholesome [ʌn'holsəm] *adj* schädlich; (& fig) unbekömmlich
unwieldy [ʌn'wildi] *adj* (*person*) schwerfällig; (*thing*) unhandlich
unwilling [ʌn'wɪlɪŋ] *adj* (*involuntary*) unfreiwillig; (*reluctant*) widerwillig; (*obstinate*) eigensinnig; **be u. to** (*inf*) nicht (*inf*) wollen
unwillingly [ʌn'wɪlɪŋli] *adv* ungern
un·wind [ʌn'waɪnd] *v* (*pret & pp* –wound) *tr* abwickeln ‖ *intr* sich abwickeln; (fig) sich entspannen
unwise [ʌn'waɪz] *adj* unklug
unwished-for [ʌn'wɪʃt‚fɔr] *adj* unerwünscht
unwitting [ʌn'wɪtɪŋ] *adj* unwissentlich
unworkable [ʌn'wʌrkəbəl] *adj* (*plan*) unausführbar; (*material*) nicht zu bearbeiten(d)
unworldly [ʌn'wʌrldli] *adj* nicht weltlich; (*naive*) weltfremd
unworthy [ʌn'wʌrði] *adj* unwürdig
un·wrap [ʌn'ræp] *v* (*pret & pp* –wrapped; *ger* –wrapping) *tr* auspacken ‖ *intr* aufgehen
unwrinkled [ʌn'rɪŋkəld] *adj* faltenlos
unwritten [ʌn'rɪtən] *adj* ungeschrieben; (*agreement*) mündlich
unyielding [ʌn'jildɪŋ] *adj* unnachgiebig
up [ʌp] *adj & adv* (*at a height*) oben; (*to a height*) hinauf; **be up** (*be out of bed; said of a shade*) aufsein; (baseball) am Schlag sein; **be up and around again** wieder auf dem Damm sein; **be up to** (*be ready for*) gewachsen sein (*dat*); (*e.g., mischief*) vorhaben; **from ten dollars and up** von zehn Dollar aufwärts; **it's up to you** es hängt von Ihnen ab; **prices are up** die Preise sind gestiegen; **up and down** (*back and forth*) auf und ab; (*from head to toe*) von oben bis unten; **up there** da oben; **up to** (*e.g., one hour*) bis zu; **up to the ears in debt** bis über die Ohren in Schulden ‖ *v* (*pret & pp* **upped;** *ger* **upping**) *tr* erhöhen ‖ *prep* (*acc*) hinauf (postpositive)
up-and-coming ['ʌpən'kʌmɪŋ] *adj* (coll) unternehmungslustig
up-and-up ['ʌpən'ʌp] *s*—**be on the u.** aufrichtig sein
upbraid' *tr* Vorwürfe machen (*dat*)
upbringing ['ʌp‚brɪŋɪŋ] *s* Erziehung *f*
update' *tr* aufs laufende bringen
up'draft' *s* Aufwind *m*
upend' *tr* hochkant stellen
up'grade' *s* Steigung *f*; **on the u.** (fig) im Aufsteigen ‖ **up'grade'** *tr* (*reclassify*) höher einstufen; (*improve*) verbessern
upheaval [ʌp'hivəl] *s* Umbruch *m*
up'hill' *adj* ansteigend; (fig) mühsam; **u. struggle** harter Kampf *m* ‖ *adv* bergauf
uphold' *v* (*pret & pp* –held) *tr* (*the law*) unterstützen; (*a verdict*) bestätigen

upholster [ʌp'holstər] *tr* (auf)polstern
upholsterer [ʌp'holstərər] *s* Polsterer –in *mf*
upholstery [ʌp'holstəri] *s* Polsterung *f*
up'keep' *s* Instandhaltung *f;* (*maintenance costs*) Instandhaltungskosten *pl*
upland ['ʌplənd] *adj* Hochlands–, Berg– ‖ **the uplands** *spl* das Hochland
up'lift' *s* (fig) Aufschwung *m;* **moral u.** moralischer Auftrieb *m* ‖ **up'lift'** *tr* (fig) geistig (or moralisch) erheben
upon [ə'pɑn] *prep* (*position*) an (*dat*), auf (*dat*); (*direction*) an (*acc*), auf (*acc*); **u. my word!** auf mein Wort!
upper ['ʌpər] *adj* obere, Ober– ‖ **uppers** *spl* Oberleder *n*
up'per-case' *adj* in Großbuchstaben gedruckt (or geschrieben)
up'per class'es *spl* Oberschicht *f*
up'percut' *s* (box) Aufwärtshaken *m*
up'per deck' *s* Oberdeck *n*
up'per hand' *s* Oberhand *f*
up'per lip' *s* Oberlippe *f*
up'permost' *adj* oberste
uppish ['ʌpɪʃ] *adj* (coll) hochnäsig
uppity ['ʌpɪti] *adj* (coll) eingebildet
upraise' *tr* erheben
up'right' *adj* aufrecht; (fig) redlich ‖ *s* (fb) Torpfosten *m*
up'ris'ing *s* Aufstand *m*
up'roar' *s* Aufruhr *m*
uproarious [ʌp'rorɪ·əs] *adj* (*noisy*) lärmend; (*laughter*) schallend; (*applause*) tosend; (*very funny*) zwerchfellerschütternd
uproot' *tr* entwurzeln
ups' and downs' *spl* Auf und Ab *n*
upset' *adj* (*over*) verstimmt (über *acc*) ‖ **up'set'** *s* unerwartete Niederlage *f* ‖ **up'set'** *v* (*pret & pp* –set; *ger* –setting*) *tr* (*throw over*) umwerfen; (*tip over*) umkippen; (*plans*) umstoßen; (*a person*) aufregen; (*the stomach*) verderben
up'shot' *s* Ergebnis *n*
up'side down' *adv* verkehrt; **turn u.** auf den Kopf stellen
up'stage' *adv* in den (or im) Hintergrund der Bühne ‖ *tr* (coll) ausstechen
up'stairs' *adj* im oberen Stockwerk ‖ *adv* (*position*) oben; (*direction*) nach oben ‖ *s* oberes Stockwerk *n*
upstand'ing *adj* aufrecht; (*sincere*) aufrichtig
up'start' *s* Emporkömmling *m*
up'stream' *adj* weiter stromaufwärts gelegen ‖ *adv* stromaufwärts
up'stroke' *s* Aufstrich *m;* (mach) Hub *m*
up'surge' *s* Aufwallung *f*
up'sweep' *s* Hochfrisur *f*
up'swing' *s* (fig) Aufschwung *m*
upsy-daisy ['ʌpsɪ'dezi] *interj* hopsasa!
up-to-date' ['ʌptə'det] *adj* (*modern*) zeitgemäß; (*with latest information*) auf dem neuesten Stand
up'-to-the-min'ute news' ['ʌptəðə'mɪnɪt] *s* Zeitfunk *m*
up'trend' *s* steigende Tendenz *f*

up'turn' s Aufschwung m
upturned' adj nach oben gebogen; **u. nose** Stupsnase f
upward ['ʌpwərd] adj nach oben gerichtet; (tendency) steigend || adv aufwärts
U'ral Moun'tains ['jurəl] spl Ural m
uranium [juˈrenɪ·əm] adj Uran– || s Uran n
urban ['ʌrbən] adj städtisch, Stadt–
urbane [ʌrˈben] adj weltgewandt
urbanite ['ʌrbə‚naɪt] s Städter –in mf
urbanize ['ʌrbə‚naɪz] tr verstädtern
ur'ban renew'al s Altstadtsanierung f
urchin ['ʌrtʃɪn] s Bengel m
ure·thra [juˈriθrə] s (–thras & –thrae [θri]) Harnröhre f
urge [ʌrdʒ] s Drang m, Trieb m || tr drängen; **u. on** antreiben
urgency ['ʌrdʒənsi] s Dringlichkeit f
urgent ['ʌrdʒənt] adj dringend
urinal ['jurɪnəl] s (in a toilet) Urinbecken n; (in a sick bed) Urinflasche f
urinary ['jurɪ‚nɛri] adj Harn–, Urin–
urinate ['jurɪ‚net] intr harnen
urine ['jurɪn] s Harn m, Urin m
urn [ʌrn] s Urne f; (for coffee) Kaffeemaschine f
urology [jɪˈralədʒi] s Urologie f
us [ʌs] per pron uns
U.S.A. ['ju'ɛs'e] s (United States of America) USA pl
usable ['juzəbəl] adj (consumable items) verwendbar; (non-consumable items) benutzbar
usage ['jusɪdʒ] s (using) Gebrauch m; (treatment) Behandlung f; (ling) Sprachgebrauch m; **rough u.** starke Beanspruchung f
use [jus] s (of consumable items) Verwendung f, Gebrauch m; (of non-consumable items) Benutzung f; (application) Anwendung f; (advantage) Nutzen m; (purpose) Zweck m; (consumption) Verbrauch m; **I have no use for him** ich habe nichts für ihn übrig; **in use** in Gebrauch; **it's no use** es nützt nichts; **make use of** ausnutzen; **of use** von Nutzen; **there's no use in** (ger) es hat keinen Zweck zu (inf) || [juz] tr (ge)brauchen, verwenden; (non-consumable items) benutzen; (apply) anwenden; (e.g.,

troops) einsetzen; **use up** verbrauchen || intr—**he used to live here** er wohnte früher hier
used [juzd] adj gebraucht; (car) Gebraucht–; **be u. to** gewöhnt sein an (acc); **be u. to** (ger) gewöhnt sein zu (inf); **get s.o. u. to** j–n gewöhnen an (acc); **get u. to** sich gewöhnen an (acc)
useful ['jusfəl] adj nützlich
usefulness ['jusfəlnɪs] s Nützlichkeit f; (usability) Brauchbarkeit f
useless ['juslɪs] adj nutzlos; (not usable) unbrauchbar
user ['juzər] s (of gas, electric) Verbraucher –in mf; (e.g., of a book) Benutzer –in mf
usher ['ʌʃər] s Platzanweiser –in mf || tr—**u. in** hereinführen; (a new era) einleiten
U.S.S.R. ['ju'ɛs'ɛs'ɑr] s (Union of Soviet Socialist Republics) UdSSR f
usual ['juʒʊ·əl] adj gewöhnlich; **as u.** wie gewöhnlich
usually ['juʒʊ·əli] adv gewöhnlich
usurp [juˈzʌrp] tr usurpieren
usurper [juˈzʌrpər] s Usurpator –in mf
usury ['juʒəri] s Wucher m
utensil [juˈtɛnsɪl] s Gerät n; **utensils** Utensilien pl
uter·us ['jutərəs] s (–i [‚aɪ]) Gebärmutter f
utilitarian [‚jutɪlɪˈtɛrɪ·ən] adj utilitaristisch, Nützlichkeits–
utility [juˈtɪlɪti] s (usefulness) Nützlichkeit f; (company) öffentlicher Versorgungsbetrieb m; **apartment with all utilities** Wohnung f mit allem Zubehör; **utilities** Gas, Wasser, Strom pl
utilize ['jutɪ‚laɪz] tr verwerten
utmost ['ʌt‚most] adj äußerste, höchste || s—**do one's u.** sein Äußerstes tun; **to the u.** auf äußerste; **to the u. of one's power** nach besten Kräften
utopia [juˈtopɪ·ə] s Utopie f
utopian [juˈtopɪ·ən] adj utopisch
utter ['ʌtər] adj völlig, Erz– || tr (a sigh) ausstoßen; (a sound) hervorbringen; (feelings) ausdrücken; (words) äußern
utterance ['ʌtərəns] s Äußerung f
utterly ['ʌtərli] adv ganz und gar, völlig

V

V, v [vi] s zweiundzwanzigster Buchstabe des englischen Alphabets
vacancy ['vekənsi] s (emptiness) Leere f; (unfilled job) freie Stelle f; **no v.** (public sign) kein freies Zimmer
vacant ['vekənt] adj frei; (stare) geistesabwesend; (lot) unbebaut
vacate [ve'ket] tr (a home) räumen; (a seat) freimachen || intr ausziehen
vacation [ve'keʃən] s Urlaub m; (educ)

Ferien pl; **on v.** auf Urlaub || intr Urlaub machen
vacationer [ve'keʃənər] s Urlauber –in mf
vaccinate ['væksɪ‚net] tr impfen
vaccination [‚væksɪ'neʃən] s Impfung f
vaccina'tion certi'ficate s Impfschein m
vaccine [væk'sin] s Impfstoff m

vacillate ['væsɪ ˌlet] *intr* schwanken
vacuous ['vækjʊ·əs] *adj* nichtssagend
vacu·um ['vækjʊ·əm] *s* (–ums & –a [ə]) Vakuum *n* ‖ *tr* & *intr* staubsaugen
vac'uum clean'er *s* Staubsauger *m*
vac'uum pump' *s* Absaugepumpe *f*
vac'uum tube' *s* Vakuumröhre *f*
vagabond ['vægə ˌband] *s* Landstreicher –in *mf*
vagary ['vegəri] *s* Laune *f*
vagina [və'dʒaɪnə] *s* Scheide *f*
vagrancy ['vegrənsi] *s* Landstreicherei *f*
vagrant ['vegrənt] *adj* vagabundierend ‖ *s* Landstreicher –in *mf*
vague [veg] *adj* unbestimmt, vage
vain [ven] *adj* (*proud*) eitel; (*pointless*) vergeblich; **in v.** vergebens
vainglo'rious *adj* prahlerisch
valance ['væləns] *s* Quervolant *m*
vale [vel] *s* Tal *n*
valedictory [ˌvælɪ'dɪktəri] *s* Abschiedsrede *f*
valence ['veləns] *s* Wertigkeit *f*
valentine ['vælən ˌtaɪn] *s* Valentinsgruß *m*
vale' of tears' *s* Jammertal *n*
valet ['vælɪt] *s* Kammerdiener *m*
valiant ['væljənt] *adj* tapfer
valid ['vælɪd] *adj* (*law, ticket*) gültig; (*argument, objection*) wohlbegründet; (*e.g., contract*) rechtsgültig; **be v.** gelten
validate ['vælɪ ˌdet] *tr* bestätigen
validation [ˌvælɪ'deʃən] *s* Bestätigung *f*
validity [və'lɪdɪti] *s* Gültigkeit *f*
valise [və'lis] *s* Reisetasche *f*
valley ['væli] *s* Tal *n*
valor ['vælər] *s* Tapferkeit *f*
valorous ['vælərəs] *adj* tapfer
valuable ['væljʊ·əbəl] *adj* wertvoll ‖ **valuables** *spl* Wertsachen *pl*
value ['væljʊ] *s* Wert *m* ‖ *tr* (at) schätzen (auf *acc*)
val'ue judg'ment *s* Werturteil *n*
valueless ['væljʊlɪs] *adj* wertlos
valve [vælv] *s* (anat, mach, zool) Klappe *f*; (mach, mus) Ventil *n*
vamp [væmp] *s* (coll) Vamp *m*
vampire ['væmpaɪr] *s* Vampir *m*
van [væn] *s* Möbelwagen *m*; (*panel truck*) Kastenwagen *m*; (fig) Avantgarde *f*; (mil) Vorhut *f*
vandal ['vændəl] *s* Vandale *m*; **Vandal** Vandale *m*
vandalism ['vændə ˌlɪzəm] *s* Vandalismus *m*
vane [ven] *s* (*of a windmill, fan, propeller*) Flügel *m*; (*in a turbine*) Schaufel *f*
vanguard ['væn ˌgard] *s* (fig) Spitze *f*; (mil) Vorhut *f*
vanilla [və'nɪlə] *s* Vanille *f*
vanish ['vænɪʃ] *intr* (ver)schwinden; **v. into thin air** sich in blauen Dunst auflösen
van'ishing cream' *s* Tagescreme *f*
vanity ['vænɪti] *s* (*arrogance*) Anmaßung *f*; (*emptiness*) Nichtigkeit *f*; (*furniture*) Frisiertisch *m*

van'ity case' *s* Kosmetikköfferchen *n*
vanquish ['væŋkwɪʃ] *tr* besiegen
van'tage point' ['væntɪdʒ] *s* (*advantage*) günstiger Ausgangspunkt *m*; (*view*) Aussichtspunkt *m*
vapid ['væpɪd] *adj* schal, fad(e)
vapor ['vepər] *s* Dampf *m*, Dunst *m*
vaporize ['vepə ˌraɪz] *tr* & *intr* verdampfen
vaporizer ['vepə ˌraɪzər] *s* Inhalationsapparat *m*
va'por trail' *s* Kondensstreifen *m*
variable ['verɪ·əbəl] *adj* veränderlich; (*wind*) aus wechselnden Richtungen ‖ *s* (math) Veränderliche *f*
variance ['verɪ·əns] *s* Veränderung *f*; (*difference*) Abweichung *f*; (*argument*) Streit *m*; **be at v. with** (*a person*) in Zwiespalt sein mit; (*a thing*) in Widerspruch stehen zu
variant ['verɪ·ənt] *adj* abweichend ‖ *s* Variante *f*
variation [ˌverɪ'eʃən] *s* Veränderung *f*; (alg, biol, mus) Variation *f*
var'icose vein' ['værɪ ˌkos] *s* Krampfader *f*
varied ['verid] *adj* abwechslungsreich; (*diverse*) verschieden
variegated ['verɪ·ə ˌgetɪd] *adj* (*diverse*) verschieden; (*in color*) bunt
variety [və'raɪ·əti] *s* (*choice*) Auswahl *f*; (*difference*) Verschiedenheit *f*; (*sort*) Art *f*; (biol) Spielart *f*; **for a v. of reasons** aus verschiedenen Gründen
vari'ety show' *s* Variétévorstellung *f*
various ['verɪ·əs] *adj* verschieden; (*several*) mehrere
varnish ['varnɪʃ] *s* Firnis *m*, Lack *m* ‖ *tr* firnissen
varsity ['varsɪti] *adj* Auswahl– ‖ *s* Auswahlmannschaft *f*
var·y ['veri] *v* (*pret* & *pp* –ied) *tr* & *intr* abwechseln, variieren
vase [ves], [vez] *s* Vase *f*
vaseline ['væsə ˌlin] *s* (trademark) Vaseline *f*
vassal ['væsəl] *s* Lehensmann *m*
vast [væst] *adj* riesig; (*majority*) überwiegend; **v. amount** Unmasse *f*
vastness ['væstnɪs] *s* Unermeßlichkeit *f*
vat [væt] *s* Bottich *m*
Vatican ['vætɪkən] *adj* vatikanisch; (*city*) Vatikan– ‖ *s* Vatikan *m*
Vat'ican Coun'cil *s* Vatikanisches Konzil *n*
vaudeville ['vɔdvɪl] *s* Varieté *n*
vaude'ville show' *s* Variétévorstellung *f*
vault [vɔlt] *s* (*underground chamber*) Gruft *f*; (*of a bank*) Tresor *m*; (*archit*) Gewölbe *n*; **v. of heaven** Himmelsgewölbe *n* ‖ *tr* überspringen
vaunt [vɔnt] *s* Prahlerei *f* ‖ *tr* sich rühmen (*genit*) ‖ *intr* sich rühmen
veal [vil] *s* Kalbfleisch *n*
veal' cut'let *s* Kalbskotelett *n*
veer [vɪr] *intr* drehen, wenden
vegetable ['vedʒɪtəbəl] *adj* pflanzlich; (*garden, soup*) Gemüse–; (*kingdom, life, oil, dye*) Pflanzen– ‖ *s* Gemüse *n*; **vegetables** Gemüse *n*

vegetarian [ˌvedʒɪ'tɛrɪ·ən] *adj* vegetarisch || *s* Vegetarier –in *mf*
vegetate ['vedʒɪ ˌtet] *intr* vegetieren
vegetation [ˌvedʒɪ'teʃən] *s* Vegetation *f*
vehemence ['vi·ɪməns] *s* Heftigkeit *f*
vehement ['vi·ɪmənt] *adj* heftig
vehicle ['vi·ɪkəl] *s* Fahrzeug *n*
veil [vel] *s* Schleier *m* || *tr* (& fig) verschleiern
veiled *adj* verschleiert; (*threat*) verhüllt
vein [ven] *s* Vene *f;* (geol, min) Ader *f*
vellum ['veləm] *s* Velin *n*
velocity [vɪ'lɑsɪti] *s* Geschwindigkeit *f*
velvet ['vɛlvɪt] *adj* Samt– || *s* Samt *m*
velveteen [ˌvɛlvɪ'tin] *s* Baumwollsamt *m*
velvety ['vɛlvɪti] *adj* samtartig
vend [vend] *tr* verkaufen
vend'ing machine' *s* Automat *m*
vendor ['vendər] *s* Verkäufer –in *mf*
veneer [və'nɪr] *s* Furnier *n;* (fig) Tünche *f* || *tr* furnieren
venerable ['venərəbəl] *adj* ehrwürdig
venerate ['venə ˌret] *tr* verehren
veneration [ˌvenə'reʃən] *s* Verehrung *f*
Venetian [vɪ'niʃən] *adj* venezianisch || *s* Venezianer –in *mf*
Vene'tian blind' *s* Fensterjalousie *f*
vengeance ['vendʒəns] *s* Rache *f;* take v. on sich rächen an (*dat*); with a v. mit Gewalt
vengeful ['vendʒfəl] *adj* rachsüchtig
venial ['vinɪ·əl] *adj* (*sin*) läßlich
Venice ['venɪs] *s* Venedig *n*
venison ['venɪsən] *s* Wildbret *n*
venom ['venəm] *s* Gift *n;* (fig) Geifer *m*
venomous ['venəməs] *adj* giftig
vent [vent] *s* Öffnung *f;* give v. to Luft machen (*dat*) || *tr* auslassen
ventilate ['ventɪ ˌlet] *tr* ventilieren
ventilation [ˌventɪ'leʃən] *s* Ventilation *f*
ventilator ['ventɪ ˌletər] *s* Ventilator *m*
ventricle ['ventrɪkəl] *s* Ventrikel *m*
ventriloquist [ven'trɪləkwɪst] *s* Bauchredner –in *mf*
venture ['ventʃər] *s* Unternehmen *n* || *tr* wagen || *intr* (on) sich wagen (an *acc*); v. out sich hinauswagen; v. to (*inf*) sich vermessen zu (*inf*)
venturesome ['ventʃərsəm] *adj* (*person*) wagemutig; (*deed*) gewagt
venue ['venju] *s* zuständiger Gerichtsort *m;* change of v. Änderung *f* des Gerichtsstandes
Venus ['vinəs] *s* Venus *f*
veracity [vɪ'ræsɪti] *s* Wahrhaftigkeit *f*
veranda [və'rændə] *s* Veranda *f*
verb [vɜrb] *s* Verb *n*, Zeitwort *n*
verbal ['vɜrbəl] *adj* (*oral*) mündlich; (*gram*) verbal
verbatim [vər'betɪm] *adj* wortgetreu
verbiage ['vɜrbɪ·ɪdʒ] *s* Wortschwall *m*
verbose [vər'bos] *adj* weitschweifig
verdant ['verdənt] *adj* grün
verdict ['vɜrdɪkt] *s* Urteilsspruch *m* (der Geschworenen); give a v. e–n Spruch fällen

verdigris ['vʌrdɪ ˌgris] *s* Grünspan *m*
verge [vʌrdʒ] *s* (fig) Rand *m;* on the v. of (*ger*) nahe daran zu (*inf*) || *intr*—v. on grenzen an (*acc*)
verifiable [ˌvɛrɪ'faɪ·əbəl] *adj* nachprüfbar
verification [ˌvɛrɪfɪ'keʃən] *s* Nachprüfung *f*
veri·fy ['vɛrɪ ˌfaɪ] *v* (*pret & pp* –fied) *tr* nachprüfen
verily ['vɛrɪli] *adv* (Bib) wahrlich
veritable ['vɛrɪtəbəl] *adj* echt
vermilion [vər'mɪljən] *adj* zinnoberrot
vermin ['vʌrmɪn] *s* (*objectionable person*) Halunke *m;* v. *spl* Schädlinge *pl;* (*objectionable persons*) Gesindel *n*
vermouth [vər'muθ] *s* Wermut *m*
vernacular [vər'nækjələr] *adj* volkssprachlich || *s* Volkssprache *f*
ver'nal e'quinox ['vʌrnəl] *s* Frühlingstagundnachtgleiche *f*
versatile ['vʌrsətɪl] *adj* beweglich
verse [vʌrs] *s* (& Bib) Vers *m;* (*stanza*) Strophe *f*
versed [vʌrst] *adj* (in) bewandert in (*dat*)
versification [ˌvʌrsɪfɪ'keʃən] *s* (*metrical structure*) Versbau *m;* (*versifying*) Verskunst *f;* (*metrical version*) Versfassung *f*
versifier ['vʌrsɪ ˌfaɪ·ər] *s* Verseschmied *m*
version ['vʌrʒən] *s* Version *f*
ver·so ['vʌrso] *s* (–sos) (*of a coin*) Revers *m;* (typ) Verso *n*
versus ['vʌrsəs] *prep* gegen (*acc*)
verte·bra ['vʌrtɪbrə] *s* (–brae [ˌbri] & –bras) Rückenwirbel *m*, Wirbel *m*
vertebrate ['vʌrtɪ ˌbret] *s* Wirbeltier *n*
ver·tex ['vʌrteks] *s* (–texes & –tices [tɪ ˌsiz]) Scheitelpunkt *m*
vertical ['vʌrtɪkəl] *adj* senkrecht || *s* Vertikale *f*
ver'tical hold' *s* (telv) Vertikaleinstellung *f*
ver'tical take'off *s* Senkrechtstart *m*
vertigo ['vʌrtɪ ˌgo] *s* Schwindel *m*, Schwindelgefühl *n*
very ['vɛri] *adj*—that v. day an demselben Tag; the v. thought der bloße Gedanke; the v. truth die reine Wahrheit; the v. man genau der Mann || *adv* sehr; the v. best der allerbeste; the v. same ebenderselbe
vesicle ['vesɪkəl] *s* Bläschen *n*
vespers ['vespərz] *spl* Vesper *f*
vessel ['vesəl] *s* (*ship*) Schiff *n;* (*container*) Gefäß *n*
vest [vest] *s* Weste *f;* (*for women*) Leibchen *n* || *tr* (with) bekleiden (mit); be vested in zustehen (*dat*)
vest'ed in'terest *s* (*for personal benefits*) persönliches Interesse *n;* (jur) rechtmäßiges Interesse *n*
vestibule ['vestɪ ˌbjul] *s* Vestibül *n*
vestige ['vestɪdʒ] *s* Spur *f*
vestment ['vestmənt] *s* Gewand *n*
vest'-pock'et *adj* Westentaschen–
vestry ['vestri] *s* Sakristei *f;* (*committee*) Gemeindevertretung *f*
vetch [vetʃ] *s* Wicke *f*

veteran ['vetərən] *s* Veteran *m;* (sport) Senior *m*

veterinarian [ˌvetərɪ'nerɪ·ən] *s* Tierarzt *m*, Tierärztin *f*

veterinary ['vetərɪ ˌnerɪ] *adj* (college) tierärztlich; **v.. medicine** Tierheilkunde *f*

ve·to ['vito] *s* (**-toes**) Veto *n* ‖ *tr* ein Veto einlegen gegen

vex [veks] *tr* ärgern

vexation [vek'seʃən] *s* Ärger *m*

V'-forma'tion *s* (aer) Staffelkeil *m*

via ['vi·ə] *prep* über (acc)

viable ['vaɪ·əbəl] *adj* lebensfähig

viaduct ['vaɪ·ə ˌdʌkt] *s* Viadukt *m*

vial ['vaɪ·əl] *s* Phiole *f*

viands ['vaɪ·əndz] *spl* Lebensmittel *pl*

vibrate ['vaɪbret] *intr* vibrieren; **cause to v.** in Schwingung versetzen

vibration [vaɪ'breʃən] *s* Schwingung *f*

vicar ['vɪkər] *s* Vikar *m*

vicarage ['vɪkərɪdʒ] *s* Pfarrhaus *n*

vicarious [vaɪ'kerɪ·əs] *adj* (pleasure) nachempfunden; (taking the place of another) stellvertretend; **v. experience** Ersatzbefriedigung *f*

vice [vaɪs] *s* Laster *n*

vice'-ad'miral *s* Vizeadmiral *m*

vice'-con'sul *s* Vizekonsul *m*

vice'-pres'ident *s* Vizepräsident –in *mf*

viceroy ['vaɪsrɔɪ] *s* Vizekönig *m*

vice' squad' *s* Sittenpolizei *f*

vice versa ['vaɪsə'vʌrsə] *adv* umgekehrt

vicinity [vɪ'sɪnɪti] *s* Umgebung *f;* **in the v. of** in der Nähe (genit)

vicious ['vɪʃəs] *adj* (temper) bösartig; (dog) bissig; (person, gossip) heimtückisch

vi'cious cir'cle *s* Zirkelschluß *m*

vicissitudes [vɪ'sɪsɪ ˌtjudz] *spl* Wechselfälle *pl*

victim ['vɪktɪm] *s* Opfer *n;* (animal) Opfertier *n;* **fall v. to** zum Opfer fallen (dat)

victimize ['vɪktɪ ˌmaɪz] *tr* (make a victim of) benachteiligen; (dupe) hereinlegen

victor ['vɪktər] *s* Sieger –in *mf*

victorious [vɪk'torɪ·əs] *adj* siegreich

victory ['vɪktəri] *adj* Sieges– ‖ *s* Sieg *m;* (myth) Siegesgöttin *f;* **flushed with v.** siegestrunken

victuals ['vɪtəlz] *spl* Viktualien *pl*

vid'eo sig'nal ['vɪdɪ ˌo] *s* Bildsignal *n*

vid'eo tape' *s* Bildband *n*

vid'eo tape' record'er *s* Bildbandgerät *n*

vid'eo tape' record'ing *s* Bildbandaufnahme *f*

vie [vaɪ] *v* (pret & pp **vied;** ger **vying**) *intr* (**with**) wetteifern (mit)

Vienna [vɪ'enə] *s* Wien *n*

Vien·nese [ˌvi·ə'niz] *adj* wienerisch ‖ *s* (**-nese**) Wiener –in *mf*

Vietnam [ˌvɪ·et'nam] *s* Vietnam *n*

Vietnam·ese [vɪ ˌetnə'miz] *adj* vietnamesisch ‖ *s* (**-se**) Vietnamese *m*, Vietnamesin *f*

view [vju] *s* Aussicht *f;* (opinion) Ansicht *f;* **come into v.** in Sicht kommen; **in my v.** meiner Ansicht nach;

in v. of angesichts (genit); **with a v. to** (ger) in der Absicht zu (inf) ‖ *tr* betrachten; (sights) besichtigen

viewer ['vju·ər] *s* Zuschauer –in *mf*

view'find'er *s* Bildsucher *m*

view'point' *s* Standpunkt *m*

vigil ['vɪdʒɪl] *s* Nachtwache *f;* **keep v.** wachen

vigilance ['vɪdʒɪləns] *s* Wachsamkeit *f*

vigilant ['vɪdʒɪlənt] *adj* wachsam

vignette [vɪn'jet] *s* Vignette *f*

vigor ['vɪgər] *s* (physical) Kraft *f;* (mental) Energie *f;* (intensity) Wucht *f*

vigorous ['vɪgərəs] *adj* (strong) kräftig; (act) energisch

vile [vaɪl] *adj* gemein; (coll) scheußlich

vileness ['vaɪlnɪs] *s* Gemeinheit *f*

vili·fy ['vɪlɪ ˌfaɪ] *v* (pret & pp **-fied**) *tr* verleumden

villa ['vɪlə] *s* Villa *f*

village ['vɪlɪdʒ] *s* Dorf *n*, Ort *m*

villager ['vɪlɪdʒər] *s* Dorfbewohner –in *mf*

villain ['vɪlən] *s* Bösewicht *m*, Schurke *m*

villainous ['vɪlənəs] *adj* schurkisch

villainy ['vɪləni] *s* Schurkerei *f*

vim [vɪm] *s* Mumm *m*

vindicate ['vɪndɪ ˌket] *tr* rechtfertigen

vindictive [vɪn'dɪktɪv] *adj* rachsüchtig

vine [vaɪn] *s* Rebe *f;* (creeper) Ranke *f*

vinegar ['vɪnɪgər] *s* Essig *m*

vine' grow'er [ˌgro·ər] *s* Winzer *m*

vineyard ['vɪnjərd] *s* Weinberg *m*

vintage ['vɪntɪdʒ] *adj* Qualitäts– ‖ *s* Weinernte *f*

vin'tage year' *s* Weinjahr *n*

vintner ['vɪntnər] *s* Weinbauer –in *mf*

vinyl ['vaɪnɪl] *adj* Vinyl–

viola [vaɪ'olə] *s* Bratsche *f*, Viola *f*

violate ['vaɪ·ə ˌlet] *tr* (a law) verletzen; (a promise) brechen; (the peace) stören; (a custom, shrine) entweihen; (a girl) vergewaltigen

violation [ˌvaɪ·ə'leʃən] *s* (of the law) Verletzung *f;* (of a shrine) Entweihung *f;* (of a girl) Vergewaltigung *f*

violence ['vaɪ·ələns] *s* Gewalt *f*

violent ['vaɪ·ələnt] *adj* (person) gewalttätig; (deed) gewaltsam; (anger, argument) heftig

violet ['vaɪ·əlɪt] *adj* violett ‖ *s* Veilchen *n*

violin [ˌvaɪ·ə'lɪn] *s* Geige *f*

violinist [ˌvaɪ·ə'lɪnɪst] *s* Geiger –in *mf*

violoncel·lo [ˌvaɪ·ələn'tʃelo] *s* (**-los**) Violoncello *n*

viper ['vaɪpər] *s* Natter *f*, Viper *f*

virgin ['vʌrdʒɪn] *adj* Jungfern–; (land) unberührt ‖ *s* Jungfrau *f*

virginity [vər'dʒɪnɪti] *s* Jungfräulichkeit *f*

virility [vɪ'rɪlɪti] *s* Zeugungskraft *f*

virology [vaɪ'rɑlədʒi] *s* Virusforschung *f*

virtual ['vʌrtʃʊ·əl] *adj* faktisch; (opt, tech) virtuell

virtue ['vʌrtʃu] *s* Tugend *f;* **by v. of** kraft (genit), vermöge (genit)

virtuosity [ˌvʌrtʃʊˈɑsɪtɪ] s Virtuosität f

virtuo·so [ˌvʌrtʃʊˈoso] s (-sos & -si [si]) Virtuose m, Virtuosin f

virtuous [ˈvʌrtʃʊ·əs] adj tugendhaft

virulence [ˈvɪrjələns] s Virulenz f

virulent [ˈvɪrjələnt] adj virulent

virus [ˈvaɪrəs] s Virus n

visa [ˈvizə] s Visum n

visage [ˈvɪzɪdʒ] s Antlitz n

viscera [ˈvɪsərə] s Eingeweide pl

viscosity [vɪsˈkɑsɪtɪ] s Viskosität f

viscount [ˈvaɪkaunt] s Vicomte m

viscountess [ˈvaɪkauntɪs] s Vicomtesse f

viscous [ˈvɪskəs] adj zähflüssig

vise [vaɪs] s Schraubstock m

visibility [ˌvɪzɪˈbɪlɪtɪ] s Sichtbarkeit f; (meteor) Sicht f

visible [ˈvɪzɪbəl] adj sichtbar

visibly [ˈvɪzɪblɪ] adv zusehends

vision [ˈvɪʒən] s (faculty) Sehvermögen n; (appearance) Vision f; of great v. von großem Weitblick

visionary [ˈvɪʒəˌnerɪ] adj visionär ‖ s Visionär –in mf

visit [ˈvɪzɪt] s Besuch m; (official) Visite f ‖ tr besuchen; (a museum, town) besichtigen

visitation [ˌvɪzɪˈteʃən] s Visitation f; Visitation of our Lady Heimsuchung f Mariä

vis'iting hours' spl Besuchszeit f

vis'iting nurse' s Fürsorgerin f

visitor [ˈvɪzɪtər] s Besucher –in mf; have visitors Besuch haben

visor [ˈvaɪzər] s Schirm m; (on a helmet) Visier n

vista [ˈvɪstə] s (& fig) Ausblick m

Vistula [ˈvɪstʃʊlə] s Weichsel f

visual [ˈvɪʒʊ·əl] adj visuell

vis'ual aids' spl Anschauungsmaterial n

visualize [ˈvɪʒʊ·əˌlaɪz] tr sich [dat] vorstellen

vital [ˈvaɪtəl] adj (lebens)wichtig; (signs, functions) Lebens– ‖ vitals spl edle Teile pl

vitality [vaɪˈtælɪtɪ] s Lebenskraft f

vitalize [ˈvaɪtəˌlaɪz] tr beleben

vitamin [ˈvaɪtəmɪn] s Vitamin n

vi'tamin defi'ciency s Vitaminmangel m

vitiate [ˈvɪʃɪˌet] tr verderben

vitreous [ˈvɪtrɪ·əs] adj glasartig

vitriolic [ˌvɪtrɪˈɑlɪk] adj (fig) beißend; (chem) Vitriol–

vituperate [vaɪˈt(j)upəˌret] tr schelten

vivacious [vɪˈveʃəs] adj lebhaft

vivid [ˈvɪvɪd] adj lebhaft

vivi·fy [ˈvɪvɪˌfaɪ] v (pret & pp –fied) tr beleben

vivisection [ˌvɪvɪˈsɛkʃən] s Vivisektion f

vixen [ˈvɪksən] s Füchsin f

viz. abbr nämlich

vizier [vɪˈzɪr] s Vezier m, Wesir m

vocabulary [voˈkæbjəˌlerɪ] s (word range) Wortschatz m; (list) Wörterverzeichnis n

vocal [ˈvokəl] adj stimmlich, Stimm–; (outspoken) redselig

voc'al cord' s Stimmband n

vocalist [ˈvokəlɪst] s Sänger –in mf

vocalize [ˈvokəˌlaɪz] tr (phonet) vokalisieren ‖ intr singen; (phonet) in e–n Vokal verwandelt werden

vocation [voˈkeʃən] s Beruf m; (relig) Berufung f

voca'tional guid'ance [voˈkeʃənəl] s Berufsberatung f

voca'tional school' s Berufsschule f

voca'tional train'ing s Berufsausbildung f

vocative [ˈvɑkətɪv] s Vokativ m

vociferous [voˈsɪfərəs] adj laut

vodka [ˈvɑdkə] s Wodka m

vogue [vog] s (herrschende) Mode f; be in v. Mode sein

voice [vɔɪs] s Stimme f; in a low v. mit leiser Stimme ‖ tr äußern; (phonet) stimmhaft aussprechen

voiced [vɔɪst] adj (phonet) stimmhaft

voiceless [ˈvɔɪslɪs] adj stimmlos

void [vɔɪd] adj leer; (invalid) ungültig ‖ s Leere f ‖ tr für ungültig erklären; (the bowels) entleeren

volatile [ˈvɑlətɪl] adj (explosive) jähzornig; (changeable) unbeständig; (chem) flüchtig

volcanic [vɑlˈkænɪk] adj vulkanisch

volca·no [vɑlˈkeno] s (–noes & –nos) Vulkan m

volition [vəˈlɪʃən] s Wollen n; of one's own v. aus eigenem Antrieb

volley [ˈvɑlɪ] s (of gunfire) Salve f; (of stones) Hagel m; (sport) Flugschlag m

vol'leyball' s Volleyball m

volt [volt] s Volt n

voltage [ˈvoltɪdʒ] s Spannung f

voluble [ˈvɑljəbəl] adj redegewandt

volume [ˈvɑljəm] s (book) Band m; (of a magazine series) Jahrgang m; (of sound) Lautstärke f; (amount) Ausmaß n; (of a container) Rauminhalt m; speak volumes Bände sprechen; v. of sales Umsatz m

vol'ume control' s Lautstärkeregler m

voluminous [vəˈluminəs] adj (writer) produktiv; (of great extent or size) umfangreich

voluntary [ˈvɑlənˌterɪ] adj freiwillig

volunteer [ˌvɑlənˈtɪr] adj Freiwilligen– ‖ s Freiwillige mf ‖ tr freiwillig anbieten ‖ intr (for) sich freiwillig erbieten (für, zu)

voluptuary [vəˈlʌptʃʊˌerɪ] s Wollüstling m

voluptuous [vəˈlʌptʃʊ·əs] adj wollüstig

vomit [ˈvɑmɪt] s Erbrechen n ‖ tr (er)brechen; (smoke) ausstoßen; (fire) speien; (lava) auswerfen ‖ intr sich erbrechen

voodoo [ˈvudu] adj Wudu– ‖ s Wudu m

voracious [vəˈreʃəs] adj gefräßig

voracity [vəˈræsɪtɪ] s Gefräßigkeit f

vor·tex [ˈvɔrtɛks] s (–texes & –tices [tɪˌsiz]) (& fig) Wirbel m

votary [ˈvotərɪ] s Verehrer –in mf

vote [vot] s Stimme f; (act of voting) Abstimmung f; (right to vote) Stimmrecht n; put to a v. zur Abstimmung

bringen || *tr* (*approve of, e.g., money*)
(**for**) bewilligen (für); **v. down** nieder-
stimmen || *intr* stimmen; **v. by accla-
mation** durch Zuruf stimmen; **v. for**
wählen; **v. on** abstimmen über (*acc*)
vote' get'ter [ˌgetər] *s* Wahllokomotive
f
vote' of con'fidence *s* Vertrauensvotum
n
vote' of no' con'fidence *s* Mißvertrau-
ensvotum *n*
voter [ˈvotər] *s* Wähler –in *mf*
vot'ing booth' *s* Wahlzelle *f*
vot'ing machine' *s* Stimmenzählapparat
m
votive [ˈvotɪv] *adj* Votiv–, Weih–
vo'tive of'fering *s* Weihgabe *f*
vouch [vautʃ] *tr* bezeugen || *intr*—**v.
for** bürgen für
voucher [ˈvautʃər] *s* Beleg *m*
vouchsafe' *tr* gewähren

vow [vau] *s* Gelübde *n;* **take a vow of**
geloben || *tr* geloben; (*revenge*)
schwören; **vow to** (*inf*) sich [*dat*]
geloben zu (*inf*)
vowel [ˈvau·əl] *s* Selbstlaut *m,* Vokal
m
voyage [ˈvɔɪ·ɪdʒ] *s* Reise *f;* (*by sea*)
Seereise *f* || *intr* reisen
voyager [ˈvɔɪ·ɪdʒər] *s* Reisende *mf;* (*by
sea*) Seereisende *mf*
V'-shaped' *adj* keilförmig
V'-sign' *s* Siegeszeichen *n*
vulcanize [ˈvʌlkəˌnaɪz] *tr* vulkanisieren
vulgar [ˈvʌlgər] *adj* vulgär
vulgarity [vʌlˈgærɪti] *s* Gemeinheit *f*
Vul'gar Lat'in *s* Vulgärlatein *n*
Vulgate [ˈvʌlget] *s* Vulgata *f*
vulnerable [ˈvʌlnərəbəl] *adj* verwundbar; (*position*) ungeschützt; (fig) an-
greifbar; **v. to** anfällig für
vulture [ˈvʌltʃər] *s* Geier *m*

W

W, w [ˈdʌbəlˌju] *s* dreiundzwanzigster
Buchstabe des englischen Alphabets
wad [wɑd] *s* (*of cotton*) Bausch *m;* (*of
money*) Bündel *n;* (*of papers*) Stoß
m; (*of tobacco*) Priem *m*
waddle [ˈwɑdəl] *s* Watscheln *n* || *intr*
watscheln
wade [wed] *intr* waten; **w. into** (fig)
anpacken; **w. through** (fig) sich mühsam durcharbeiten durch
wafer [ˈwefər] *s* Oblate *f*
waffle [ˈwɑfəl] *s* Waffel *f*
waf'fle i'ron *s* Waffeleisen *n*
waft [wæft], [wɑft] *tr & intr* wehen
wag [wæg] *s* (*nod*) Nicken *n;* (*shake*)
Schütteln *n;* (*of the tail*) Wedeln *n;*
(*mischievous person*) Schalk *m* || *v*
(*pret & pp* **wagged;** *ger* **wagging**) *tr*
(*the tail*) wedeln mit; (*nod*) nicken
mit; (*shake*) schütteln || *intr* (*said
of a tail*) wedeln; (*said of tongues*)
nicht still sein
wage [wedʒ] *adj* Lohn– || *s* Lohn *m;*
wages Lohn *m* || *tr* (*war*) führen
wage' cut' *s* Lohnabbau *m*
wage' freeze' *s* Lohnstopp *m*
wager [ˈwedʒər] *s* Wette *f;* **lay a w.**
e–e Wette eingehen || *tr & intr* wet-
ten
waggish [ˈwægɪʃ] *adj* schalkhaft
wagon [ˈwægən] *s* Wagen *m*
wag'on load' *s* Wagenladung *f*
waif [wef] *s* (*child*) verwahrlostes Kind
n; (*animal*) verwahrlostes Tier *n*
wail [wel] *s* Wehklage *f* || *intr* (**over**)
wehklagen (über *acc*)
wain·scot [ˈwenskət] *s* Täfelung *f* || *v*
(*pret & pp* **–scot[t]ed;** *ger* **–scot-
[t]ing**) *tr* täfeln
waist [west] *s* Taille *f;* **strip to the w.**
den Oberkörper freimachen
waist'-deep' *adj* bis an die Hüften
(reichend)

waist'line' *s* Taille *f;* **watch one's w.**
auf die schlanke Linie achten
wait [wet] *s* Warten *n;* **an hour's w.**
e–e Stunde Wartezeit || *intr* warten;
that can w. das hat Zeit; **w. for** (*a
person*) warten auf (*acc*); (*e.g., an
answer*) abwarten; **w. on** bedienen;
w. up for aufbleiben und warten auf
(*acc*)
wait'-and-see' **pol'icy** *s* Politik *f* des
Abwartens
waiter [ˈwetər] *s* Kellner *m;* **w.!** Herr
Ober!
wait'ing line' *s* Schlange *f*
wait'ing list' *s* Warteliste *f*
wait'ing room' *s* Warteraum *m;* (*e.g.,
in a railroad station*) Wartesaal *m*
waitress [ˈwetrɪs] *s* Kellnerin *f*
waive [wev] *tr* verzichten auf (*acc*)
waiver [ˈwevər] *s* Verzicht *m*
wake [wek] *s* (*at a funeral*) Totenwache
f; (naut) Kielwasser *n;* **in the w. of**
im Gefolge (*genit*) || *v* (*pret* **waked &
woke** [wok];* *pp* **waked**) *tr* wecken;
w. up aufwecken || *intr* erwachen;
w. up aufwachen; **w. up to** (fig) bewußt werden (*genit*)
wakeful [ˈwekfəl] *adj* wachsam
waken [ˈwekən] *tr* (auf)wecken || *intr*
erwachen
walk [wɔk] *s* Spaziergang *m;* (*gait*)
Gang *m;* (*path*) Spazierweg *m;* **a five-
minute w. to** fünf Minuten zu Fuß
zu; **from all walks of life** aus allen
Ständen; **go for a w.** spazierengehen;
take for a w. spazierenführen || *tr* (*a
dog*) spazierenführen; (*a person*) begleiten; (*a horse*) führen; (*the streets*)
ablaufen || *intr* (zu Fuß) gehen, lau-
fen; **w. off with** klauen; **w. out on**
sitzenlassen; **w. up to** zugehen auf
(*acc*)
walk'-away' *s* (coll) leichter Sieg *m*

walker ['wɔkər] s Fußgänger –in mf
walkie-talkie ['wɔki'tɔki] s Sprechfunk-
gerät n
walk'-in' adj (closet) begehbar
walk'ing pa'pers spl Laufpaß m
walk'ing shoes' spl Straßenschuhe pl
walk'ing stick' s Spazierstock m
walk'-on' s (theat) Statist –in mf
walk'out' s Ausstand m
walk'-o'ver s (sport) leichter Sieg m
walk'-up' s Mietwohnung f ohne Fahrstuhl
wall [wɔl] s Mauer f; (between rooms)
Wand f || tr—w. up vermauern
wall' brack'et s Konsole f
wall' clock' s Wanduhr f
wallet ['wɑlɪt] s Brieftasche f
wall'flow'er s (coll) Wandblümchen n
wall' map' s Wandkarte f
wallop ['wɑləp] s Puff m; **have a w.**
Schlagkraft haben || tr verprügeln;
(defeat) schlagen
wal'loping adj (sl) mordsgroß
wallow ['wɑlo] intr sich wälzen; **w. in**
(fig) schwelgen in (dat)
wall'pa'per s Tapete f || tr tapezieren
walnut ['wɔlnət] s Walnuß f; (wood)
Walnußholz n; (tree) Walnußbaum m
walrus ['wɔlrəs] s Walroß n
waltz [wɔlts] s Walzer m || intr Walzer
tanzen
wan [wɑn] adj (wanner; wannest)
bleich; (smile) schwach, matt
wand [wɑnd] s Stab m; (in magic)
Zauberstab m
wander ['wɑndər] intr wandern; (from
a subject) abschweifen
wanderer ['wɑndərər] s Wanderer –in
mf
wan'derlust' s Wanderlust f
wane [wen] s—**be on the w.** abnehmen
|| intr abnehmen
wangle ['wæŋgəl] tr sich [dat] er-
schwindeln
want [wɔnt] s Bedürfnis n; **for w. of**
mangels (genit) || tr wollen; **wanted**
(sought, desired) gesucht
want' ad' s Kleinanzeige f
want'ing adj—**be w. in** ermangeln
(genit)
war [wɔr] s Krieg m; **at war** im Kriege;
go to war with e-n Krieg beginnen
gegen; **make war on** Krieg führen
gegen || v (pret & pp **warred; ger
warring**) intr kämpfen
warble ['wɑrbəl] s Trillern n || intr
trillern
war' bond' s Kriegsanleihe f
war' cry' s Schlachtruf m
ward [wɔrd] s (in a hospital) Station
f; (of a city) Bezirk m; (person
under protection) Schützling m; (person under guardianship) Mündel n;
(guardianship) Vormundschaft f ||
tr—**w. off** abwehren
warden ['wɔrdən] s Gefängnisdirektor
m
ward'robe' s Garderobe f
ward'room' s (nav) Offiziersmesse f
ware [wɛr] s Ware f
ware'house' s Lagerhaus n, Warenlager
n

ware'house'man s (–men) Lagerist m
war'fare' s Kriegsführung f, Krieg m
war' foot'ing s Kriegsbereitschaft f
war'head' s Gefechtskopf m
war'-horse' s (coll) alter Kämpe m
war'like' adj kriegerisch
war' lord' s Kriegsherr m
warm [wɔrm] adj warm; (friends) in-
tim || tr wärmen; **w. up** aufwärmen ||
intr—**w. up** warm werden; (sport)
in Form kommen
warm'-blood'ed adj warmblütig
warm'front' s Warmfront f
warm'-heart'ed adj warmherzig
warmonger ['wɔr,mʌŋgər] s Kriegs-
hetzer –in mf
warmth [wɔrmθ] s Wärme f
warm'-up' s (sport) Lockerungsübun-
gen pl
warn [wɔrn] tr (against) warnen (vor
dat)
warn'ing s Warnung f; **let this be a w.
to you** lassen Sie sich das zur Warnung dienen
warn'ing shot' s Warnschuß m
war' of attri'tion s Zermürbungskrieg
m
warp [wɔrp] s (of a board) Verziehen
n || tr (wood) verziehen; **w. s.o.'s
mind** j–n verschroben machen || intr
sich verziehen
war'path' s Kriegspfad m
warped adj (wood) verzogen; (mind,
opinion) verschroben
war'plane' s Kampfflugzeug n
warrant ['wɔrənt] s (justification)
Rechtfertigung f; (authorization)
Berechtigung f; **w. for arrest** Haft-
befehl m || tr (justify) rechtfertigen;
(guarantee) garantieren
war'rant of'ficer s (mil) Stabsfeldwebel
m; (nav) Deckoffizier m
warranty ['wɔrənti] s Gewährleistung f
war'ranty serv'ice s Kundendienst m
warren ['wɔrən] s Kaninchengehege n
war'ring adj kriegsführend
warrior ['wɔrɪ·ər] s Krieger m
Warsaw ['wɔrsɔ] s Warschau n
war'ship' s Kriegsschiff n
wart [wɔrt] s Warze f
war'time' adj Kriegs– || s Kriegszeit f
war'-torn' adj vom Krieg verwüstet
wary ['wɛri] adj vorsichtig
war' zone' s Kriegsgebiet n
wash [wɔʃ] adj Wasch– || s Wäsche f;
(aer) Luftstrudel m; (paint) dünner
Farbüberzug m; **do the w.** die
Wäsche waschen || tr waschen;
(metal) schlämmen; (paint) tuschen;
(phot) wässern; **w. ashore** anschwem-
men; **w. away** wegspülen; **w. off** ab-
waschen; **w. out** auswaschen; (a
bridge) wegreißen; **w. up** aufwaschen
|| intr waschen; **w. ashore** ans Land
spülen
washable ['wɔʃəbəl] adj waschbar
wash'-and-wear' adj bügelfrei
wash'ba'sin s Waschbecken n
wash'bas'ket s Wäschekorb m
wash'board' s Waschbrett n
wash'bowl' s Waschbecken n
wash'cloth' s Waschlappen m

wash'day' s Waschtag m

washed'-out' adj verwaschen; (tired) schlapp

washer ['wɔʃər] s Waschmaschine f; (of rubber) Dichtungsring m; (of metal) Unterlegscheibe f

washed'-up' adj (coll) erledigt

wash'er·wom'an ·s (-wom'en) Waschfrau f

wash'ing s Waschen n; (clothes) Wäsche f

wash'ing machine' s Waschmaschine f

wash'out' s Auswaschung f; (failure) Pleite f; (person who fails) Versager –in mf

wash'rag' s Waschlappen m

wash'room' s Waschraum m

wash'stand' s Waschtisch m

wash'tub' s Waschtrog m

wasp [wɑsp] s Wespe f

wasp' waist' s Wespentaille f

waste [west] adj (superfluous) überflüssig; (land) öde ‖ s (of material goods, time, energy) Verschwendung f; (waste material) Müll m; (wilderness) Wildnis f; go to w. vergeudet werden ‖ tr verschwenden, vergeuden ‖ intr—w. away verfallen

waste'bas'ket s Papierkorb m

wasteful ['westfəl] adj verschwenderisch

waste'land' s Ödland n

waste'pa'per s Makulatur f

waste'pipe' s Abflußrohr n

waste'pro'duct s Abfallprodukt n

wastrel ['westrəl] s Verschwender –in mf

watch [wɑtʃ] s Uhr f; (lookout) Wache f; be on the w. for acht haben auf (acc) ‖ tr (observe) beobachten; (guard) bewachen; (oversee) aufpassen auf (acc); w. how I do it passen Sie auf, wie ich es mache; w. your step! Vorsicht, Stufe! ‖ intr (keep guard) wachen; (observe) zuschauen; w. for abwarten; w. over überwachen; w. out! Vorsicht!; w. out for ausschauen nach; (some danger) sich hüten vor (dat); w. out for oneself sich vorsehen

watch'band' s Uhrarmband n

watch'case' s Uhrgehäuse n

watch' crys'tal s Uhrglas n

watch'dog' s Wachhund m

watch'dog commit'tee s Überwachungsausschuß m

watchful ['wɑtʃfəl] adj wachsam

watchfulness ['wɑtʃfəlnɪs] s Wachsamkeit f

watch'mak'er s Uhrmacher –in mf

watch'man s (-men) Wächter m

watch' pock'et s Uhrtasche f

watch' strap' s Uhrarmband n

watch'tow'er s Wachtturm m

watch'word' s Kennwort n, Parole f

water ['wɔtər] s Wasser n; (body of water) Gewässer n; pass w. Wasser lassen ‖ tr (e.g., flowers) begießen; (fields) bewässern; (animals) tränken; (the garden, streets) sprengen; w. down (& fig) verwässern ‖ intr (said of the eyes) tränen; my mouth

waters das Wasser läuft mir im Mund zusammen

wa'ter boy' s Wasserträger m

wa'ter clos'et s Wasserklosett n

wa'tercol'or s (paint) Aquarellfarbe f; (painting) Aquarell n

wa'tercourse' s Wasserlauf m

wa'tercress' s Brunnenkresse f

wa'terfall' s Wasserfall m

wa'terfront' s Hafenviertel n

wa'ter heat'er s Warmwasserbereiter m

wa'tering can' s Wasserkanne f

wa'tering place' s (for cattle) Tränke f; (for tourists) Badeort m

wa'ter lev'el s Wasserstand m

wa'terlogged' adj vollgesogen

wa'ter main' s Wasserleitung f

wa'termark' s Wasserzeichen n

wa'ter mat'tress s Wasserbett n

wa'termel'on s Wassermelone f

wa'ter me'ter s Wasserzähler m

wa'ter pipe' s Wasserrohr n

wa'ter po'lo s Wasserball m

wa'ter pow'er s Wasserkraft f

wa'terproof' adj wasserdicht ‖ tr imprägnieren

wa'ter-repel'lent adj wasserabstoßend

wa'tershed' s Wasserscheide f

wa'ter-ski' intr wasserschifahren

wa'terspout' s (orifice) Wasserspeier m; (pipe) Ablaufrohr n

wa'ter supply' s Wasserversorgung f

wa'ter ta'ble s Grundwasserspiegel m

wa'ter tank' s Wasserbehälter m

wa'tertight' adj wasserdicht; (fig) eindeutig

wa'ter wag'on s—be on the w. Abstinenzler sein

wa'terway' s Wasserstraße f

wa'ter wheel' s (for raising water) Schöpfwerk n; (water-driven) Wasserrad n

wa'ter wings' spl Schwimmkissen n

wa'terworks' s Wasserwerk n

watery ['wɔtəri] adj wäss(e)rig

watt [wɑt] s Watt n

wattage ['wɑtɪdʒ] s Wattleistung f

wattles ['wɑtəlz] spl Flechtwerk s

watt'me'ter s Wattmeter m

wave [wev] s (fig, meteor, mil, phys, rad) Welle f; w. of the hand Wink m mit der Hand ‖ tr (a hat, flag) schwenken; (a hand, handkerchief) winken mit; (hair) wellen; w. one's hands about mit den Händen herumfuchteln; w. s.o. away j–n abwinken ‖ intr (said of a flag) wehen; (said of grain) wogen; (with the hand) winken; w. to zuwinken (dat)

wave'length' s Wellenlänge f

waver ['wevər] intr schweben, wanken

wavy ['wevi] adj wellenförmig; w. line Wellenlinie f

wax [wæks] adj Wachs– ‖ s Wachs n ‖ tr (the floor) bohnern; (skis) wachsen ‖ intr werden; (said of the moon) zunehmen; wax and wane zu– und abnehmen

wax' muse'um s Wachsfigurenkabinett n

wax' pa'per s Wachspapier n

way [we] adv weit; way ahead weit

voraus ‖ *s* Weg *m;* (*manner*) Art *f;* (*means*) Mittel *n;* (*condition*) Verfassung *f;* (*direction*) Richtung *f;* **across the way** gegenüber; **a long way from** weit weg von; **a long way off** weit weg; **by the way** übrigens; **by way of** über (*acc*); **by way of comparison** vergleichsweise; **get s.th. out of the way** etw aus dem Wege schaffen; **get under way** in Gang kommen; **go all the way** aufs Ganze gehen; **go one's own way** aus der Reihe tanzen; **have a way with** s.o. mit j–m umzugehen verstehen; **have in the way of** (*merchandise*) haben an (*dat*); **have it both ways** es sich [*dat*] aussuchen können; **have one's own way** seinen Willen durchsetzen; **I'm on my way!** ich komme schon!; **in a way** gewissermaßen; **in no way** keineswegs; **in the way** im Weg; **in this way** auf diese Weise; **in what way** in welcher Hinsicht; **make one's way through the crowd** sich [*dat*] e–n Weg durch die Menge bahnen; **one way or another** irgendwie; **on the way** unterwegs; **on the way out** (fig) im Begriff unmodern zu werden; **see one's way clear** bereit sein; **that way** auf diese Weise; (*in that direction*) in jener Richtung; **the way it looks** voraussichtlich; **way back** Rückweg *m;* **way here** Herweg *m;* **way out** Ausgang *m;* (fig) Ausweg *m;* **way there** Hinweg *m*

wayfarer ['we‚ferər] *s* Wanderer *m*

way'lay' *v* (*pret & pp* **–laid**) *tr* auflauern (*dat*)

way' of life' *s* Lebensweise *f*

way' of think'ing *s* Denkweise *f*

ways' and means' *spl* Mittel und Wege *pl*

way'side' *adj* an der Straße gelegen ‖ *s* Wegrand *m;* **fall by the w.** dem Untergang anheimfallen

wayward ['wewərd] *adj* ungeraten

we [wi] *pers pron* wir

weak [wik] *adj* schwach

weaken ['wikən] *tr* (ab)schwächen ‖ *intr* schwach werden

weakling ['wiklɪŋ] *s* Schwächling *m*

weak'-mind'ed *adj* willenlos

weakness ['wiknɪs] *s* (& fig) Schwäche *f*

weak' spot' *s* schwache Stelle *f*

weal [wil] *s* Strieme *f,* Striemen *m*

wealth [wɛlθ] *s* (**of**) Reichtum *m* (an *dat*)

wealthy ['wɛlθi] *adj* wohlhabend

wean [win] *tr* (**from**) entwöhnen (*genit*)

weapon ['wɛpən] *s* Waffe *f*

weaponry ['wɛpənri] *s* Bewaffnung *f*

wear [wɛr] *s* (*use*) Gebrauch *m;* (*durability*) Haltbarkeit *f;* (*clothing*) Kleidung *f;* (*wearing down*) Verschleiß *m* ‖ *v* (*pret* **wore** [wor]; *pp* **worn** [worn]) *tr* tragen; **w. down** (*a heel*) abtreten; (*a person*) zermürben; **w. out** abnützen; (*tires*) abfahren; (*a person*) erschöpfen; **w. the pants in the family** die Hosen anhaben ‖ *intr* sich tragen; **w. off** sich abtragen; **w.**

out sich abnützen; **w. thin** (*said of clothes*) fadenscheinig werden; (*said of patience*) zu Ende gehen

wearable ['wɛrəbəl] *adj* tragbar

wear' and tear' [ter] *s* Verschleiß *m;* **takes a lot of w.** strapazierfähig sein

weariness ['wɪrɪnɪs] *s* Müdigkeit *f*

wearisome ['wɪrɪsəm] *adj* mühsam

wea·ry ['wɪri] *adj* müde ‖ *v* (*pret & pp* **–ried**) *tr* ermüden ‖ *intr* (**of**) müde werden (*genit*)

weasel ['wizəl] *s* Wiesel *n* ‖ *intr*—**w. out of** sich herauswinden aus

weather ['wɛðər] *s* Wetter *n;* **be under the w.** unpäßlich sein; **w. permitting** bei günstiger Witterung ‖ *tr* dem Wetter aussetzen; (*the storm*) (fig) überstehen ‖ *intr* verwittern

weath'erbeat'en *adj* verwittert

weath'er bu'reau *s* Wetterdienst *m*

weath'er condi'tions *spl* Wetterverhältnisse *pl*

weath'er fore'cast *s* Wettervoraussage *f*

weath'erman' *s* (**–men'**) Wetteransager *m*

weath'er report' *s* Wetterbericht *m*

weath'erstrip'ping *s* Dichtungsstreifen *pl*

weath'er vane' *s* (& fig) Wetterfahne *f*

weave [wiv] *s* Webart *f* ‖ *v* (*pret* **wove** [wov] & **weaved;** *pp* **woven** ['wovən]) *tr* weben; (*a rug*) wirken; (*a basket*) flechten; (*a wreath*) winden; **w. one's way through traffic** sich durch den Verkehr schlängeln ‖ *intr* weben

weaver ['wivər] *s* Weber –in *mf*

web [wɛb] *s* (*of a spider*) Spinngewebe *n;* (*of ducks*) Schwimmhaut *f;* **web of lies** Lügengewebe *n*

web'-foot'ed *adj* schwimmfüßig

wed [wɛd] *v* (*pret & pp* **wed** & **wedded;** *ger* **wedding**) *tr & intr* heiraten

wed'ding *adj* (*cake, present, day, reception*) Hochzeits–; (*ring*) Trau– ‖ *s* Hochzeit *f;* (*ceremony*) Trauung *f*

wedge [wɛdʒ] *s* Keil *m* ‖ *tr*—**w. in** einkeilen

wed'lock' *s* Ehestand *m;* **out of w.** unehelich

Wednesday ['wɛnzde] *s* Mittwoch *m;* **on W.** am Mittwoch

wee [wi] *adj* winzig; **a wee bit** ein klein wenig

weed [wid] *s* Unkraut *n;* (*marijuana*) (sl) Marihuana *n;* (*cigarette*) (sl) Zigarette *f;* **pull weeds** jäten ‖ *tr* jäten; **w. out** (fig) aussondern

weed' kill'er *s* Unkrautvertilgungsmittel *n*

week [wik] *s* Woche *f;* **a w. from today** heute in e–r Woche; **a w. ago today** heute vor acht Tagen; **for weeks** wochenlang

week'day' *s* Wochentag *m*

week'end' *s* Wochenende *n*

weekender ['wik‚ɛndər] *s* Wochenendausflügler –in *mf*

weekly ['wikli] *adj* wöchentlich; (*wages*) Wochen– ‖ *s* Wochenblatt *n*

weep [wip] *v* (*pret & pp* **wept** [wɛpt]) *tr & intr* weinen

weep'ing wil'low *s* Trauerweide *f*
weevil ['wivəl] *s* Rüsselkäfer *m*
weft [wɛft] *s* (tex) Schußfaden *m*
weigh [we] *tr* wiegen; (*ponder*) wägen; (*anchor*) lichten || *intr* wiegen; **w. heavily on** schwer lasten auf (*dat*)
weight [wet] *s* Gewicht *n;* (*burden*) Last *f;* (*influence*) Einfluß *m;* (*importance*) Bedeutung *f;* **carry great w.** sehr ins Gewicht fallen; **lift weights** Gewichte heben; **pull one's w.** das Seine tun; **throw one's w. about** sich breitmachen
weightless ['wetlɪs] *adj* schwerelos
weightlessness ['wetlɪsnɪs] *s* Schwerelosigkeit *f*
weighty ['weti] *adj* (& fig) gewichtig
weird [wɪrd] *adj* unheimlich
weir·do ['wɪrdo] *s* (−dos) (sl) Kauz *m*
welcome ['wɛlkəm] *adj* willkommen; (*news*) erfreulich; **you're w.!** bitte sehr!; **you're w. to** (*inf*) es steht Ihnen frei zu (*inf*) || *s* Empfang *m,* Willkomm *m* || *tr* empfangen; (*an opportunity*) mit Freude begrüßen || *interj* (**to**) willkommen! (**in** *dat*)
weld [wɛld] *s* Schweißnaht *n* || *tr & intr* schweißen
welder ['wɛldər] *s* Schweißer −in *mf*
weld'ing *s* Schweißung *f,* Schweißarbeit *f*
welfare ['wɛlˌfɛr] *s* Wohlfahrt *f*
wel'fare work'er *s* Wohlfahrtspfleger −in *mf*
well [wɛl] *adj* gesund; **all is w.** alles ist in Ordnung; **feel w.** sich wohl fühlen || *adv* gut, wohl; **as w.** ebenso; **as w. as** so gut wie; (*in addition to*) sowohl ... als auch; **he is doing w.** es geht ihm gut; **his company is doing w.** seine Firma geht gut; **leave w. enough alone** es gut sein lassen; **w. on in years** schon bejahrt; **w. on the way** mitten auf dem Wege; (fig) auf dem besten Wege; **w. over** weit über || *s* Brunnen *m;* (*hole*) Bohrloch *n;* (*source*) Quelle *f* || *intr—* **w. up** hervorquellen || *interj* na!; (*in surprise*) nanu!
well'-behaved' *adj* artig
well'-be'ing *s* Wohlergehen *n*
well'born' *adj* aus guter Familie
wellbred ['wɛl'brɛd] *adj* wohlerzogen
well'-deserved' *adj* wohlverdient
well'-disposed' *adj* (**toward**) wohlgesinnt (*dat*)
well-done ['wɛl'dʌn] *adj* (culin) durchgebraten || *interj* gut gemacht!
well'-dressed' *adj* gut angezogen
well'-found'ed *adj* wohlbegründet
well'-groomed' *adj* gut gepflegt
well'-heeled' *adj* (coll) steinreich
well'-informed' *adj* wohlunterrichtet
well'-inten'tioned *adj* wohlmeinend
well-kept ['wɛl'kɛpt] *adj* gut gepflegt; (*secret*) gut gehütet
well'-known' *adj* wohlbekannt
well'-mean'ing *adj* wohlmeinend
well'-nigh' *adv* fast
well'-off' *adj* wohlhabend, vermögend
well'-preserved' *adj* gut erhalten
well-read ['wɛl'rɛd] *adj* belesen

well'-spent' *adj* (*money*) gut verwendet; (*time*) gut verbracht
well'spring' *s* Brunnquell *m*
well'-thought'-of' *adj* angesehen
well'-timed' *adj* wohl berechnet
well-to-do ['wɛltə'du] *adj* wohlhabend
well-wisher ['wɛl'wɪʃər] *s* Gratulant −in *mf*
well'-worn' *adj* (*clothes*) abgetragen; (*phrase, subject*) abgedroschen
Welsh [wɛlʃ] *adj* walisisch || *s* Walisisch *n;* **the W.** die Waliser *pl* || welsh *intr*—**welsh on** (*a promise*) brechen
Welsh' rab'bit or rare'bit ['rɛrbɪt] *s* geröstete Käseschnitte *f*
welt [wɛlt] *s* Striemen *m*
welter ['wɛltər] *s* Durcheinander *n* || *intr* sich wälzen
wel'terweight' *s* Weltergewichtler *m*
we'lterweight divi'sion *s* Weltergewicht *n*
wench [wɛntʃ] *s* Dirne *f,* Weibsbild *n*
wend [wɛnd] *tr*—**w. one's way** seinen Weg nehmen
werewolf ['wɛrˌwʌlf] *s* Werwolf *m*
west [wɛst] *adj* westlich || *adv* nach Westen || *s* Westen *m*
western ['wɛstərn] *adj* westlich || *s* (cin) Wildwestfilm *m*
West' Ger'many *s* Westdeutschland *n*
West' In'dies, the ['ɪndiz] *spl* Westindien *n*
Westphalia [ˌwɛst'felɪ·ə] *s* Westfalen *n*
westward ['wɛstwərd] *adv* westwärts
wet [wɛt] *adj* (**wetter; wettest**) naß; **all wet** (coll) auf dem Holzwege || *v* (*pret & pp* **wet & wetted**; *ger* **wetting**) *tr* naß machen
wet' blan'ket *s* (fig) Miesepeter *m*
wet' nurse' *s* Amme *f*
whack [wæk] *s* (coll) Klaps *m* || *tr* (coll) klapsen
whale [wel] *s* Wal(fisch) *m;* **have a w. of a time** sich großartig unterhalten
whaler ['welər] *s* Walfänger *m*
wharf [wɔrf] *s* (**wharves** [wɔrvz]) Kaianlage *f*
what [wɑt] *interr adj* welcher, was für ein || *interr pron* was; **so w.?** na und?; **w. about me?** und was geschieht mit mir?; **w. if** was geschieht, wenn; **w. is more** außerdem; **w. next?** was noch?; **w. of it?** was ist da schon dabei?; **what's new?** was gibt es Neues? **what's that to you?** was geht Sie das an? || *interj* was für ein
whatev'er *adj* welch ... auch immer; **no ... w.** überhaupt kein || *pron* was auch immer; **w. I have** alles, was ich habe; **w. you please** was Sie wollen
what'not' *s*—**and w.** und was weiß ich noch (alles)
what's-his-name' *s* (coll) Dingsda *m*
wheal [wil] *s* Pustel *f;* (*welt*) Striemen *m*
wheat [wit] *s* Weizen *m*
wheedle ['hwidəl] *tr*—**w. s.o. into** (*ger*) j-n beschwatzen zu (*inf*); **w. s.th. out of s.o.** j-m etw abschwatzen

wheel [wil] *s* Rad *n;* **at the w.** (aut) am Steuer ‖ *tr* fahren ‖ *intr* sich drehen; **w. around** sich umdrehen

wheelbarrow ['wil‚bæro] *s* Schubkarre *f*

wheel'chair' *s* Krankenfahrstuhl *m*

wheeler-dealer ['wilər'dilər] *s* Drahtzieher –in *mf*

wheeze [wiz] *s* Schnaufen *n* ‖ *intr* schnaufen

whelp [wɛlp] *s* Welpe *m* ‖ *tr* werfen

when [wɛn] *adv* wann ‖ *conj* (*once in the past*) als; (*whenever; at a future time*) wenn

whence [wɛns] *adv & conj* woher

whenev'er *conj* wenn, wann immer

where [wɛr] *adv & conj* wo; (*whereto*) wohin; **from w.** woher

whereabouts ['wɛrə‚bauts] *adv* wo ungefähr ‖ *s & spl* Verbleib *m*

whereas' *conj* während, wohingegen

whereby' *conj* wodurch

where'fore' *adv & conj* weshalb

wherefrom' *adv* woher

wherein' *adv & conj* worin

whereof' *adv & conj* wovon

whereto' *adv* wohin

where'upon' *adv* worauf, wonach

wherever [wɛr'ɛvər] *conj* wo auch

wherewith' *adv* womit

wherewithal ['wɛrwɪð‚ɔl] *s* Geldmittel *pl*

whet [wɛt] *v* (*pret & pp* **whetted;** *ger* **whetting**) *tr* wetzen, schleifen; (*the appetite*) anregen

whether ['wɛðər] *conj* ob

whet'stone' *s* Wetzstein *m*, Schleifstein *m*

whew [hwju] *interj* hui!; ui!

which [wɪtʃ] *interr adj* welcher ‖ *interr pron* welcher ‖ *rel pron* der, welcher

whichev'er *rel adj & rel pron* welcher

whiff [wɪf] *s* Geruch *m*, Nasevoll *f*

while [waɪl] *s* Weile *f* ‖ *conj* während ‖ *tr*—**w. away** sich [dat] vertreiben

whim [wɪm] *s* Laune *f*, Grille *f*

whimper ['wɪmpər] *s* Wimmern *n* ‖ *tr & intr* wimmern

whimsical ['wɪmzɪkəl] *adj* schrullig

whine [waɪn] *s* Wimmern *n;* (*of a siren, engine, storm*) Heulen *n* ‖ *intr* wimmern; heulen

whin·ny ['wɪni] *s* Wiehern *n* ‖ *v* (*pret & pp* –**nied**) *intr* wiehern

whip [wɪp] *s* Peitsche *f* ‖ *v* (*pret & pp* **whipped;** *ger* **whipping**) *tr* peitschen; (*egg whites*) zu Schaum schlagen; (*defeat*) schlagen; **w. out** blitzschnell ziehen; **w. up** (*a meal*) hervorzaubern; (*enthusiasm*) erregen

whip'lash' *s* Peitschenhieb *m;* (fig) Peitschenhiebeffekt *n*

whipped' cream' *s* Schlagsahne *f*

whipper-snapper ['wɪpər‚snæpər] *s* Frechdachs *m*

whip'ping *s* Prügel *pl*

whip'ping boy' *s* Prügelknabe *m*

whip'ping post' *s* Schandpfahl *m*

whir [wʌr] *s* Schnurren *n* ‖ *v* (*pret & pp* **whirred;** *ger* **whirring**) *intr* schnurren

whirl [wʌrl] *s* Wirbel *m;* **give s.th. a w.** (coll) etw ausprobieren ‖ *tr* wirbeln ‖ *intr* wirbeln; **my head is whirling** mir ist schwindlig

whirl'pool' *s* Strudel *m*, Wirbel *m*

whirl'wind' *s* Wirbelwind *m*

whirlybird ['wʌrli‚bʌrd] *s* (coll) Hubschrauber *m*

whisk [wɪsk] *s* Wedel *m;* (culin) Schneebesen *m* ‖ *tr* wischen; **w. away** (fig) eilends mitnehmen; **w. off** wegfegen

whisk' broom' *s* Kleiderbesen *m*

whiskers ['wɪskərz] *spl* Bart *m;* (*on the cheeks*) Backenbart *m;* (*of a cat*) Barthaare *pl*

whiskey ['wɪski] *s* Whisky *m*

whisper ['wɪspər] *s* Flüsterton *m* ‖ *tr & intr* flüstern

whistle ['wɪsəl] *s* (*sound*) Pfiff *m;* (*device*) Trillerpfeife *f;* **wet one's w.** sich [dat] die Nase begießen ‖ *tr* pfeifen ‖ *intr* pfeifen; (*said of the wind, bullet*) sausen; **w. for** (coll) vergeblich warten auf (*acc*)

whit [wɪt] *s*—**not care a w. about** sich keinen Deut kümmern um

white [waɪt] *adj* weiß; **w. as a sheet** kreidebleich ‖ *s* Weiß *n;* (*of the eye*) Weiße *f*

white'caps' *spl* Schaumkronen *pl*

white'-col'lar work'er *s* Angestellte *mf*

white'fish' *s* Weißfisch *m*

white'-haired' *adj* weißhaarig

white'-hot' *adj* weißglühend

white' lie' *s* Notlüge *f*

white' meat' *s* weißes Fleisch *n*

whiten ['waɪtən] *tr* weiß machen ‖ *intr* weiß werden

whiteness ['waɪtnɪs] *s* Weiße *f*

white' slav'ery *s* Mädchenhandel *m*

white' tie' *s* Frackschleife *f;* (formal) Frack *m*

white'wash' *s* Tünche *f;* (fig) Beschönigung *f* ‖ *tr* tünchen; (fig) beschönigen

whither ['wɪðər] *adv* wohin

whitish ['waɪtɪʃ] *adj* weißlich

whittle ['wɪtəl] *tr* schnitzeln; **w. away** (or **down**) verringern ‖ *intr*—**w. away** at herumschnitzeln an (*dat*); (fig) verringern

whiz(z) [wɪz] *s* Zischen *n;* (fig) Kanone *f* ‖ *v* (*pret & pp* **whizzed;** *ger* **whizzing**) *intr* zischen; **w. by** flitzen

who [hu] *interr pron* wer; **who the devil** wer zum Teufel ‖ *rel pron* der; **he who** wer

whoa [wo] *interj* halt!

whoev'er *rel pron* wer, wer auch immer

whole [hol] *adj* ganz ‖ *s* Ganze *n;* **as a w.** im großen und ganzen

whole'-heart'ed *adj* ernsthaft

whole' note' *s* (mus) ganze Note *f*

whole' rest' *s* (mus) ganze Pause *f*

whole'sale' *adj* Massen–; (com) Großhandels– ‖ *adv* en gros ‖ *s* Großhandel *m* ‖ *tr* en gros verkaufen ‖ *intr* im großen handeln

wholesaler ['hol‚selər] *s* Großhändler –in *mf*

wholesome ['holsəm] *adj* gesund; (*food*) zuträglich

whole'-wheat' bread' *s* Vollkornbrot *n*

wholly ['holi] *adv* ganz, völlig

whom [hum] *interr pron* wen; **to w.** wem || *rel pron* den, welchen; **to w.** dem, welchem

whomev'er *rel pron* wen auch immer; **to w.** wem auch immer

whoop [hup], [hwup] *s* Ausruf *m* || *tr—w.* **it up** Radau machen

whoop'ing cough' *s* Keuchhusten *m*

whopper ['wɑpər] *s* Mordsding *n;* (*lie*) (coll) faustdicke Lüge *f*

whop'ping *adj* (coll) enorm, Riesen–

whore [hor] *s* Hure *f* || *intr—w.* **around** huren

whose [huz] *interr pron* wessen || *rel pron* dessen

why [waɪ] *adv* warum; **that's why** deswegen; **why, there you are!** da sind Sie ja!; **why, yes!** aber ja! || *s* Warum *n;* **the whys and the wherefores** das Warum und Weshalb

wick [wɪk] *s* Docht *m*

wicked ['wɪkɪd] *adj* (*evil*) böse; (*roguish*) boshaft; (*vicious*) bösartig; (*unpleasant*) ekelhaft; (*cold, pain, storm, wound*) (coll) schlimm; (*fantastic*) (coll) großartig

wicker ['wɪkər] *adj* (*basket, chair*) Weiden– || *s* (*wickerwork*) Flechtwerk *n*

wide [waɪd] *adj* breit; (*selection*) reich || *adv* weit

wide'-an'gle lens' *s* Weitwinkelobjektiv *n*

wide'-awake' *adj* hellwach

wide'-eyed' *adj* mit weit aufgerissenen Augen; (*innocence*) naiv

widely ['waɪdli] *adv* weit

widen ['waɪdən] *tr* ausweiten, verbreiten || *intr* sich ausweiten

wide'-o'pen *adj* weit geöffnet

wide' screen' *s* (cin) Breitleinwand *f*

wide'spread' *adj* weitverbreitet; (*damage*) weitgehend

widow ['wɪdo] *s* Witwe *f*

widower ['wɪdo·ər] *s* Witwer *m*

wid'owhood' *s* Witwenstand *m*

width [wɪdθ] *s* Breite *f;* **in w.** breit

wield [wild] *tr* (*a weapon*) führen; (*power, influence*) ausüben

wife [waɪf] *s* (**wives** [waɪvz]) Frau *f*

wig [wɪg] *s* Perücke *f*

wiggle ['wɪgəl] *s* Wackeln *n* || *tr* wackeln mit

wigwag ['wɪg‚wæg] *s* Winksignal *n*

wigwam ['wɪgwɑm] *s* Wigwam *m* & *n*

wild [waɪld] *adj* wild; **w. about** scharf auf (*acc*); **go w.** verwildern; **grow w.** (*become neglected*) verwildern; **make s.o. w.** (coll) j–n rasend machen || *adv—grow w.* (*grow in the wild*) wild wachsen; **run w.** verwildern

wild' boar' *s* Wildschwein *n*

wild' card' *s* wilde Karte *f*

wild'cat' *s* Wildkatze *f*

wilderness ['wɪldərnɪs] *s* Wildnis *f*

wild'fire' *s—like w.* wie Lauffeuer

wild' flow'er *s* Feldblume *f*

wild'-goose' chase' *s—go on a w.* sich [*dat*] vergeblich Mühe machen

wild'life' *s* Wild *n*

wild' oats' spl—sow one's w. sich [*dat*] die Hörner abstoßen

wile [waɪl] *s* List *f* || *tr—w.* **away** sich [*dat*] vertreiben

will [wɪl] *s* Wille(n) *m;* (jur) Testament *n;* **at w.** nach Belieben || *tr* (*bequeath*) vermachen || *v* (*pret &* *cond* **would** [wʊd]) *aux* werden

willful ['wɪlfəl] *adj* absichtlich; (*stubborn*) eigensinnig

William ['wɪljəm] *s* Wilhelm *m*

will'ing *adj* bereitwillig; **be w. to** (*inf*) bereit sein zu (*inf*)

willingly ['wɪlɪŋli] *adv* gern

willingness ['wɪlɪŋnɪs] *s* Bereitwilligkeit *f*

will-o'-the-wisp ['wɪləðə'wɪsp] *s* (& fig) Irrlicht *n*

willow ['wɪlo] *s* Weide *f*

willowy ['wɪlo·i] *adj* biegsam

will' pow'er *s* Willenskraft *f*

willy-nilly ['wɪli'nɪli] *adv* wohl oder übel

wilt [wɪlt] *tr* verwelken lassen || *intr* verwelken

wilt'ed *adj* welk

wily ['waɪli] *adj* schlau, listig

wimple ['wɪmpəl] *s* Kinntuch *n*

win [wɪn] *s* Gewinn *m;* (sport) Sieg *m* || *v* (*pret & pp* **won** [wʌn]; *ger* **winning**) *tr* gewinnen; **win over to one's side** auf seine Seite ziehen || *intr* gewinnen, siegen

wince [wɪns] *s* Zucken *n* || *intr* zucken

winch [wɪntʃ] *s* (*windlass*) Winde *f;* (*handle*) Kurbel *f;* (min, naut) Haspel *f & m*

wind [wɪnd] *s* Wind *m;* **break w.** e–n Darmwind lassen; **get w. of** Wind bekommen von; **take the w. out of s.o.'s sails** j–m den Wind aus den Segeln nehmen; **there is s.th. in the w.** es liegt etw in der Luft || [waɪnd] *v* (*pret & pp* **wound** [waund]) *tr* wickeln, winden; (*a timepiece*) aufziehen; **w. up** aufwickeln; (*affairs*) abwickeln; (*a speech*) abschließen || *intr* (*said of a river, road*) sich winden; **w. around** (*said of a plant*) sich ranken um

windbag ['wɪnd‚bæg] *s* (coll) Schaumschläger –in *mf*

windbreak ['wɪnd‚brek] *s* Windschutz *m*

windbreaker ['wɪnd‚brekər] *s* Windjacke *f*

winded ['wɪndɪd] *adj* außer Atem, atemlos

windfall ['wɪnd‚fɔl] *s* (*fallen fruit*) Fallobst *n;* (fig) Glücksfall *m*

wind'ing road' ['waɪndɪŋ] *s* Serpentinenstraße *f;* (public sign) kurvenreiche Straße *f*

wind'ing sheet' ['waɪndɪŋ] *s* Leichentuch *n*

wind' in'strument [wɪnd] *s* Blasinstrument *n*

windlass ['wɪndləs] *s* Winde *f*

windmill ['wɪnd‚mɪl] *s* Windmühle *f*

window ['wɪndo] s Fenster n; (of a ticket office) Schalter m; (for display) Schaufenster n
win'dow display' s Schaufensterauslage f
win'dow dress'er s Schaufensterdekorateur –in mf
win'dow dress'ing s Schaufensterdekoration f
win'dow en'velope s Fensterumschlag m
win'dow frame' s Fensterrahmen m
win'dowpane' s Fensterscheibe f
win'dow screen' s Fliegengitter n
win'dow shade' s Rollvorhang m, Rollo n
win'dow-shop' v (pret & pp –shopped; ger –shopping) intr e-n Schaufensterbummel machen
win'dow shut'ter s Fensterladen m
win'dow sill' s Fensterbrett n
windpipe ['wɪnd,paɪp] s Luftröhre f
windshield ['wɪnd,ʃild] s Windschutzscheibe f
wind'shield wash'er s Scheibenwäscher m
wind'shield wip'er s Scheibenwischer m
windsock ['wɪnd,sak] s Windsack m
windstorm ['wɪnd,stɔrm] s Sturm m
wind' tun'nel [wɪnd] s Windkanal m
wind-up ['waɪnd,ʌp] s (of affairs) Abwicklung f; (of a speech) Schluß m
windward ['wɪndwərd] adj (side) Wind– || adv windwärts || s Windseite f; turn to w. anluven
windy ['wɪndi] adj windig; (speech) weitschweifig; (person) redselig
wine [waɪn] s Wein m || tr mit Wein bewirten
wine' cel'lar s Weinkeller m
wine'glass' s Weinglas n
winegrower ['waɪn,gro.ər] s Weinbauer –in mf
wine'grow'ing s Weinbau m
wine' list' s Weinkarte f
wine' press' s Weinpresse f
winery ['waɪnəri] s Weinkellerei f
wine'skin' s Weinschlauch m
wing [wɪŋ] s (of a bird, building, party) Flügel m; (unit of three squadrons) Geschwader n; (theat) Kulisse f || tr (shoot) in den Flügel treffen; w. one' way dahinfliegen
wing' chair' s Ohrensessel m
wing' nut' s Flügelmutter f
wing'spread' s Spannweite f
wink [wɪŋk] s Augenwink m; quick as a w. im Nu || intr blinzeln; w. at zublinzeln (dat); (overlook) ein Auge zudrücken bei (dat)
winner ['wɪnər] s Gewinner –in mf, Sieger –in mf; (e.g., winning ticket) Treffer m
win'ning adj (e.g., smile) gewinnend; (sport) siegreich || **winnings** spl Gewinn m
winsome ['wɪnsəm] adj reizend
winter ['wɪntər] s Winter m || intr überwintern
winterize ['wɪntə,raɪz] tr winterfest machen

wintry ['wɪntri] adj winterlich; (fig) frostig
wipe [waɪp] tr wischen; w. clean abwischen; w. out auswischen; (e.g., a debt) tilgen; (destroy) vernichten; (fin) ruinieren; w. up aufwischen
wire [waɪr] s Draht m; (telg) Telegramm n; get in under the w. es gerade noch schaffen || tr mit Draht versehen; (a house) (elec) elektrische Leitungen legen in (dat); (a message) drahten; (a person) telegraphieren (dat)
wire' cut'ter s Drahtschere f
wire'draw' v (pret –drew; pp –drawn) tr drahtziehen
wire' entan'glement s Drahtverhau m
wire' gauge' s Drahtlehre f
wire'-haired' adj drahthaarig
wireless ['waɪrlɪs] adj drahtlos
wire' nail' s Drahtnagel m
Wire'pho'to s (–tos) (trademark) Bildtelegramm n
wire' record'er s Drahttonaufnahmegerät n
wire'tap' s Abhören n || v (pret & pp –tapped; ger –tapping) tr abhören
wir'ing s Leitungen pl; do the w. die elektrischen Leitungen legen
wiry ['waɪri] adj drahtig
wisdom ['wɪzdəm] s Weisheit f
wis'dom tooth' s Weisheitszahn m
wise [waɪz] adj (person, decision) klug; (impertinent) naseweis; be w. to sich [dat] klar werden über (acc); put s.o. w. to j-n einweihen in (acc) || s–in no w. keineswegs || intr—w. up endlich mal vernünftig werden
wise'a'cre s Neunmalkluge mf
wise'crack' s schnippische Bemerkung f
wise' guy' s (sl) Naseweis m
wisely ['waɪzli] adv wohlweislich
wish [wɪʃ] s Wunsch m || tr wünschen || intr—w. for sich [dat] wünschen
wish'bone' s Gabelbein n
wish'ful think'ing ['wɪʃfəl] s ein frommer Wunsch m
wishy-washy ['wɪʃi,waʃi] adj charakterlos; be w. ein Waschlappen sein
wisp [wɪsp] s (of hair) Strähne f
wistful ['wɪstfəl] adj versonnen
wit [wɪt] s Geist m; (person) geistreicher Mensch m; be at one's wit's end sich [dat] keinen Rat mehr wissen; keep one's wits about one e-n klaren Kopf behalten; live by one's wits sich durchschlagen
witch [wɪtʃ] s Hexe f
witch'craft' s Hexerei f
witch' doc'tor s Medizinmann m
witch' ha'zel s Zaubernuß f; (ointment) Präperat n aus Zaubernuß
witch' hunt' s Hexenjagd f
with [wɪð], [wɪθ] prep mit (dat); (at the house of) bei (dat); (because of) vor (dat), e.g., green w. envy grün vor Neid; (despite) trotz (genit); not be w. it nicht bei der Sache sein
with'draw' v (pret –drew; pp –drawn) tr zurückziehen; (money) abheben || intr sich zurückziehen

withdrawal [wɪð'drɔ·əl] *s* Zurückziehung *f;* (*retraction*) Zurücknahme *f;* (*from a bank*) Abhebung *f;* (mil) Rückzug *m*

withdraw'al slip' *s* Abhebungsformular *n*

wither ['wɪðər] *intr* verwelken

with·hold' *v* (*pret & pp* **–held**) *tr* (*pay*) einbehalten; (*information*) (*from*) vorenthalten (*dat*)

withhold'ing tax' *s* einbehaltene Steuer *f*

within' *adv* drin(nen); **from w.** von innen ‖ *prep* (*time*) binnen (*dat*), innerhalb von (*dat*); (*place*) innerhalb (*genit*); **w. walking distance** in Gehweite

without' *adv* draußen ‖ *prep* ohne (*acc*); **w.** (*ger*) ohne zu (*inf*), ohne daß; **w. reason** ohne allen Anlaß

with·stand' *v* (*pret & pp* **–stood**) *tr* widerstehen (*dat*)

witness ['wɪtnɪs] *s* Zeuge *m*, Zeugin *f;* (*evidence*) Zeugnis *n;* **bear w. to** Zeugnis ablegen von; **in w. whereof** zum Zeugnis dessen; **w. for the defense** Entlastungszeuge *m;* **w. for the prosecution** Belastungszeuge *m* ‖ *tr* (*an event*) anwesend sein bei; (*an accident, crime*) Augenzeuge sein (*genit*); (*e.g., a contract, will*) als Zeuge unterschreiben

wit'ness stand' *s* Zeugenstand *m*

witticism ['wɪtɪ,sɪzəm] *s* Witzelei *f*

wittingly ['wɪtɪŋli] *adv* wissentlich

witty ['wɪti] *adj* geistreich, witzig

wizard ['wɪzərd] *s* Hexenmeister *m*

wizardry ['wɪzərdri] *s* (& fig) Hexerei *f*

wizend ['wɪzənd] *adj* runzelig

wobble ['wɑbəl] *intr* wackeln

wobbly ['wɑbli] *adj* wackelig

woe [wo] *s* Weh *n* ‖ *interj*—**woe is me!** weh mir!

woebegone ['wobɪ,gɔn] *adj* jammervoll

woeful ['wofəl] *adj* jammervoll

wolf [wʊlf] *s* (**wolves** [wʊlvz]) Wolf *m;* (coll) Schürzenjäger *m;* **cry w.** blinden Alarm schlagen; **keep the w. from the door** sich über Wasser halten ‖ *tr*—**w. down** verschlingen

wolf'pack' *s* Wolfsrudel *n;* (nav) U-bootrudel *n*

wolfram ['wʊlfrəm] *s* (chem) Wolfram *n;* (mineral) Wolframit *n*

woman ['wʊmən] *s* (**women** ['wɪmən]) Frau *f*

wom'an doc'tor *s* Ärztin *f*

wom'anhood' *s* Frauen *pl;* **reach w.** e–e Frau werden

womanish ['wʊmənɪʃ] *adj* weibisch

wom'ankind' *s* Frauen *pl*

womanly ['wʊmənli] *adj* fraulich

womb [wʊm] *s* Mutterleib *m*

wom'enfolk' *spl* Weibsvolk *n*

wom'en's dou'bles *spl* (tennis) Damendoppelspiel *n*

wom'en's sin'gles *spl* (tennis) Dameneinzelspiel *n*

wonder ['wʌndər] *s* Wunder *n* ‖ *intr* (*be surprised*) sich wundern; (*ask*

oneself) sich fragen; (*reflect*) überlegen; **wonder at** sich verwundern über (*acc*)

wonderful ['wʌndərfəl] *adj* wunderbar

won'derland' *s* Wunderland *n*

won'der work'er *s* Wundertäter –in *mf*

wont [wʌnt], [wɔnt] *adj*—**be w. to** (*inf*) pflegen zu (*inf*) ‖ *s* Gepflogenheit *f*

wont'ed *adj* gewöhnlich, üblich

woo [wu] *tr* den Hof machen (*dat*)

wood [wʊd] *s* Holz *n;* **out of the woods** (fig) über den Berg; **woods** Wald *m*

wood' al'cohol *s* Methylalkohol *m*

woodbine ['wʊd,baɪn] *s* Geißblatt *n;* (*Virginia creeper*) wilder Wein *m*

wood' carv'ing *s* Holzschnitzerei *f*

wood'chuck' *s* Murmeltier *n*

wood'cock' *s* Holzschnepfe *f*

wood'cut' *s* (*block*) Holzplatte *f;* (*print*) Holzschnitt *m*

wood'cut'ter *s* Holzfäller *m*

wood'ed *adj* bewaldet

wooden ['wʊdən] *adj* (& fig) hölzern

wood' engrav'ing *s* Holzschnitt *m*

wood'en leg' *s* Stelzbein *n*

wood'en shoe' *s* Holzschuh *m*

woodland ['wʊdlənd] *adj* Wald– ‖ *s* Waldland *n*

wood'man *s* (**–men**) Holzhauer *m*

woodpecker ['wʊd,pɛkər] *s* Specht *m*

wood' pi'geon *s* Ringeltaube *f*

wood'pile' *s* Holzhaufen *m*

wood'pulp' *s* Holzfaserstoff *m*

wood' screw' *s* Holzschraube *f*

wood'shed' *s* Holzschuppen *m*

woods'man *s* (**–men**) Förster *m;* (*lumberman*) Holzhauer *m*

wood'winds' *spl* Holzblasinstrumente *pl*

wood'work' *s* Holzarbeit *f;* (*structure in wood*) Gebälk *n*

wood'work'er *s* Holzarbeiter –in *mf*

wood'worm' *s* (ent) Holzwurm *m*

woody ['wʊdi] *adj* waldig; (*woodlike*) holzig

wooer ['wu·ər] *s* Verehrer *m*

woof [wuf] *s* (*of a dog*) unterdrücktes Bellen *n;* (tex) Gewebe *n*

woofer ['wufər] *s* (rad) Tieftöner *m*

wool [wʊl] *adj* wollen ‖ *s* Wolle *f*

woolen ['wʊlən] *adj* wollen, Woll– ‖ **woolens** *spl* Wollwaren *pl*

woolly ['wʊli] *adj* wollig; (*e.g., thinking*) verschwommen

woozy ['wuzi] *adj* benebelt

word [wʌrd] *s* Wort *n;* **be as good as one's w.** zu seinem Wort stehen; **by w. of mouth** mündlich; **get w. from** Nachricht haben von; **give one's w.** sein Wort geben; **have a w. with** ein ernstes Wort sprechen mit; **have words** e–n Wortwechsel haben; **in a w.** mit e–m Wort; **in other words** mit anderen Worten; **in so many words** ausdrücklich; **leave w.** Bescheid hinterlassen; **not another w.!** kein Wort mehr!; **not a w. of truth in it** kein wahres Wort daran; **put in a good w. for s.o.** ein gutes Wort für j–n einlegen; **put into words** in

Worte kleiden; **put words in s.o.'s mouth** j-m Worte in den Mund legen; **send w. to s.o.** j-n benachrichtigen; **take s.o.'s w. for it** j-n beim Wort nehmen; **w. for w.** Wort für Wort ‖ *tr* formulieren

word'-for-word' *adj* wörtlich

word'ing *s* Formulierung *f*

word' of hon'or *s* Ehrenwort *n;* **w.!** auf mein Wort!

word' or'der *s* Wortfolge *f*

wordy ['wʌrdi] *adj* wortreich

work [wʌrk] *s* Arbeit *f; (production, book)* Werk *n;* **be in the works** (coll) im Gang sein; **get to w.** sich an die Arbeit machen; *(travel to work)* zum Arbeitsplatz kommen; **give s.o. the works** (coll) j-n fertigmachen; **have one's w. cut out** zu tun haben; **it took a lot of w. to** *(inf)* es hat viel Arbeit gekostet zu *(inf);* **make short w. of** kurzen Prozeß machen mit; **out of w.** arbeitslos; **works** (horol) Uhrwerk *n* ‖ *tr (a machine)* bedienen; *(a pedal)* treten; *(a mine)* abbauen; *(the soil)* bearbeiten; *(metal)* treiben; *(dough)* kneten; *(wonders)* wirken; **w. in** einarbeiten; **w. off** *(a debt)* abarbeiten; **w. oneself to death** sich totarbeiten; **w. one's way up** sich hocharbeiten; **w. out** *(a solution)* ausarbeiten; *(a problem)* lösen; **w. to death** abhetzen; **w. up an appetite** sich *[dat]* Appetit machen ‖ *intr* arbeiten; *(function)* funktionieren; *(succeed)* klappen; **w. against** wirken gegen; **w. away at** losarbeiten auf *(acc);* **w. at** *(a trade)* ausüben; **w. both ways** für beide Fälle gelten; **w. loose** sich lockern; **w. on** *(a person)* bearbeiten; *(a patient, car)* arbeiten an *(dat);* **w. out** (sport) trainieren; **w. out well** gut ausgehen

workable ['wʌrkəbəl] *adj* brauchbar; *(plan)* durchführbar

work'bench' *s* Werkbank *f*

work'book' *s* Übungsheft *n*

work' camp' *s* Arbeitslager *n*

work'day' *s* Arbeitstag *m*

work' detail' *s* (mil) Arbeitskommando *n*

worked'-up' *adj* erregt; **get s.o. w.** j-n erregen; **get w.** sich erregen

worker ['wʌrkər] *s* Arbeiter –in *mf*

work' force' *s* Belegschaft *f*

work'horse' *s* Arbeitspferd *n*

work'ing day' *s* Arbeitstag *m*

work'ing girl' *s* Arbeiterin *f*

work'ing hours' *spl* Arbeitsstunden *pl*

work'ingman' *s* (–men') Arbeiter *m*

work'ing or'der *s*—**in w.** betriebsfähig

work'ingwom'an *s* (–wom'en) Arbeiterin *f; (professionally)* berufstätige Frau *f*

work'man *s* (–men) Arbeiter *m*

work'manship' *s* Ausführung *f*

work'men's compensa'tion insur'ance *s* Arbeiterunfallversicherung *f*

work' of art' *s* Kunstwerk *n*

work'out' *s* Training *n*

work' per'mit *s* Arbeitsgenehmigung *f*

work'room' *s* Arbeitszimmer *n*

work' sche'dule *s* Dienstplan *m*

work'shop' *s* Werkstatt *f*

work' stop'page *s* Arbeitseinstellung *f*

world [wʌrld] *adj* Welt– ‖ *s* Welt *f;* **a w. of** groß; **from all over the w.** aus aller Herren Ländern; **not for all the w.** nicht um die Welt; **see the w.** in der Welt herumkommen; **they are worlds apart** es liegen Welten zwischen den beiden; **think the w. of** große Stücke halten auf *(acc);* **who (where) in the w.** wer (wo) in aller Welt

world' affairs' *spl* internationale Angelegenheiten *pl*

world'-fa'mous *adj* weltberühmt

worldly ['wʌrldli] *adj (goods, pleasures)* irdisch; *(person)* weltlich; *(wisdom)* Welt–

world'ly-wise' *adj* weltklug

world's' fair' *s* Weltausstellung *f*

world'-shak'ing *adj* weltbewegend

world'-wide' *adj* weltweit

worm [wʌrm] *s* Wurm *m* ‖ *tr*—**w. one's way** sich schlängeln; **w. secrets out of s.o.** j-m die Würmer aus der Nase ziehen

worm-eaten ['wʌrm,itən] *adj* (& fig) wurmstichig

wormy ['wʌrmi] *adj* wurmig

worn [worn] *adj (clothes)* getragen; *(tires)* abgenutzt; *(wearied)* müde

worn'-out' *adj (clothes)* abgetragen; *(tires)* abgenutzt; *(exhausted)* erschöpft

worrisome ['wʌrɪsəm] *adj (causing worry)* beunruhigend; *(inclined to worry)* sorgenvoll

wor·ry ['wʌri] *s* Sorge *f; (source of worry)* Ärger *m* ‖ *v (pret & pp* –ried) *tr* beunruhigen; **be worried** besorgt sein ‖ *intr* **(about)** sich *[dat]* Sorgen machen (um); **don't w.!** keine Sorge!

worse [wʌrs] *comp adj* schlechter, schlimmer; **be w. off** schlimmer daran sein; **he's none the w. for it** es hat ihm nichts geschadet; **what's w.** was noch schlimmer ist

worsen ['wʌrsən] *tr* verschlimmern ‖ *intr* sich verschlimmern

wor·ship ['wʌrʃɪp] *s* Anbetung *f; (services)* Gottesdienst *m* ‖ *v (pret & pp* –ship[p]ed; *ger* –ship[p]ing) *tr* (& fig) anbeten ‖ *intr* seine Andacht verrichten

worship(p)er ['wʌrʃɪpər] *s* Anbeter –in *mf; (in church)* Andächtige *mf*

worst [wʌrst] *super adj* schlimmste ‖ *super adv* am schlimmsten ‖ *s* Schlimmste *n;* **at the w.** schlimmstenfalls; **get the w. of** den kürzeren ziehen bei; **if w. comes to w.** wenn alle Stricke reißen; **the w. is yet to come** das dicke Ende kommt noch ‖ *tr* schlagen

worsted ['wʊstɪd] *adj* Kammgarn–

worth [wʌrθ] *adj* wert; **it is w.** (ger) es lohnt sich zu *(inf);* **it is w. the trouble** es ist der Mühe wert; **ten dollars' w. of meat** für zehn Dollar Fleisch; **w. seeing** sehenswert ‖ *s* Wert *m*

worthless ['wʌrθlɪs] *adj* wertlos; (*person*) nichtsnutzig
worth'while' *adj* lohnend
worthy ['wʌrði] *adj* (**of**) würdig (*genit*)
would [wʊd] *aux* used to express 1) indirect statements, e.g., **he said he w. come** er sagte, er würde kommen; 2) the present conditional, e.g., **he w. do it if he could** er würde es tun, wenn er könnte; 3) past conditional, e.g., **he w. have paid, if he had had the money** er würde gezahlt haben, wenn er das Geld gehabt hätte; 4) habitual action in the past, e.g., **he w. always buy the morning paper** er kaufte immer das Morgenblatt; 5) polite requests, e.g., **w. you please pass me the butter?** würden Sie mir bitte die Butter reichen; 6) a wish, e.g., **w. that I had never seen it** wenn ich es nur nie gesehen hätte!; **w. rather** möchte lieber, e.g., **I w. rather go on foot** ich möchte lieber zu Fuß gehen
would'-be' *adj* angeblich, Möchtegern—
wound [wund] *s* Wunde *f* ‖ *tr* verwunden
wound'ed *adj* verwundet ‖ **the w.** *spl* die Verwundeten *pl*
wow [wau] *s* (coll) Bombenerfolg *m* ‖ *tr* (coll) erstaunen ‖ *interj* nanu!
wrack [ræk] *s*—**go to w. and ruin** untergehen, in Brüche gehen
wraith [reθ] *s* (*apparition*) Erscheinung *f*; (*spirit*) Geist *m*
wrangle ['ræŋgəl] *s* Streit *m* ‖ *intr* streiten
wrap [ræp] *s* Überwurf *m* ‖ *v* (*pret & pp* **wrapped; ger wrapping**) *tr* wikkeln; (*a package*) einpacken; **be wrapped up in** (e.g., *thoughts*) versunken sein in (*dat*); **wrapped in darkness** in Dunkelheit gehüllt; **w. up** (*a deal*) abwickeln
wrapper ['ræpər] *s* Verpackung *f*; (*for mailing newspapers*) Streifband *n*
wrap'ping *s* Verpackung *f*
wrap'ping pa'per *s* Packpapier *n*
wrath [ræθ] *s* Zorn *m*, Wut *f*
wrathful ['ræθfəl] *adj* zornig, wütend
wreak [rik] *tr* (*vengeance*) üben; **w. havoc** schlimm hausen
wreath [riθ] *s* (**wreaths** [riðz]) Kranz *m*; **w. of smoke** Rauchfahne *f*
wreathe [rið] *tr* bekränzen, umwinden
wreck [rɛk] *s* (*of a car or train*) Unglück *n*; (*wrecked ship, car, person*) Wrack *n* ‖ *tr* (e.g., *a car*) zertrümmern; (*a building*) in Trümmer legen; (*a marriage*) zerrütten; (fig) zum Scheitern bringen; **be wrecked** (fig & naut) scheitern
wreckage ['rɛkɪdʒ] *s* Wrackgut *n*; (*of an accident*) Trümmer *pl*
wrecker ['rɛkər] *s* Abschleppwagen *m*
wren [rɛn] *s* (orn) Zaunkönig *m*
wrench [rɛntʃ] *s* (*tool*) Schraubenschlüssel *m*; (*of a muscle*) Verrenkung *f* ‖ *tr* verrenken
wrest [rɛst] *tr* (**from**) entreißen (*dat*)
wrestle ['rɛsəl] *tr* ringen mit ‖ *intr* ringen

wrestler ['rɛslər] *s* Ringer *m*; (*professional wrestler*) Catcher *m*
wrestling ['rɛslɪŋ] *s* Ringen *n*; (*professional wrestling*) Catchen *n*
wres'tling match' *s* Ringkampf *m*
wretch [rɛtʃ] *s* armer Kerl *m*; (*vile person*) Schuft *m*
wretched ['rɛtʃɪd] *adj* elend; (*terrible*) scheußlich
wriggle ['rɪgəl] *s* Krümmung *f*; (*of a worm*) schlängelnde Bewegung *f* ‖ *tr* hin- und herbewegen; **w. one's way** sich dahinschlängeln ‖ *intr* sich winden
wring [rɪŋ] *v* (*pret & pp* **wrung** [rʌŋ]) *tr* (*the hands*) ringen; **w. out** (*the wash*) auswinden; **w. s.o.'s neck** j—m den Hals umdrehen
wringer ['rɪŋər] *s* Wringmaschine *f*
wrinkle ['rɪŋkəl] *s* Falte *f*; **new w.** (fig) neuer Kniff *m*; **take out the wrinkles** (fig) den letzten Schliff geben ‖ *tr* falten, runzeln; (*paper, clothes*) zerknittern ‖ *intr* Falten werfen
wrin'kle-proof' *adj* knitterfrei
wrinkly ['rɪŋkli] *adj* faltig, runzelig
wrist [rɪst] *s* Handgelenk *n*
wrist'band' *s* Armband *n*
wrist' watch' *s* Armbanduhr *f*
writ [rɪt] *s* gerichtlicher schriftlicher Befehl *m*
write [raɪt] *v* (*pret* **wrote** [rot]; *pp* **written** ['rɪtən]) *tr* schreiben; (*compose*) verfassen; **it is written** (*in the Bible*) es steht geschrieben; **it is written all over his face** es steht ihm im Gesicht geschrieben; **w. down** aufschreiben; **w. off** abschreiben; **w. out** ausschreiben; (*a check*) ausstellen ‖ *intr* schreiben; **w. for information** Informationen anfordern
write'-off' *s* Abschreibung *f*
writer ['raɪtər] *s* Schreiber –in *mf*; (*author*) Schriftsteller –in *mf*
writ'er's cramp' *s* Schreibkrampf *m*
write'-up' *s* Pressebericht *m*
writhe [raɪð] *intr* (**in**) sich krümmen (*vor dat*)
writ'ing *s* Schreiben *n*; (*handwriting*) Schrift *f*; **in w.** schriftlich; **put in w.** niederschreiben
writ'ing desk' *s* Schreibtisch *m*
writ'ing pad' *s* Schreibblock *m*
writ'ing pa'per *s* Schreibpapier *n*; (*stationery*) Briefpapier *n*
written ['rɪtən] *adj* schriftlich; (*law*) geschrieben; (*language*) Schrift—
wrong [rɔŋ] *adj* (*incorrect*) falsch; (*unjust*) unrecht; **be w.** (*be incorrect*) nicht stimmen; (*be in error*) Unrecht haben; (*said of a situation*) nicht in Ordnung sein; **be. w. with** fehlen (*dat*); **sorry, w. number!** (telp) falsch verbunden! ‖ *s* Unrecht *n*; **be in the w.** im Unrecht sein; **do w.** ein Unrecht begehen; **do w. to s.o.** j—m ein Unrecht zufügen; **get in w. with s.o.** es sich (*dat*) mit j—m verderben ‖ *adv* falsch, unrecht; **go w.** (*morally*) auf Abwege geraten; (*in walking*) sich verirren; (*in reckoning*)

irregehen; (*in driving*) sich verfahren; (*said of plans*) schief gehen
wrongdoer [ˈrɔŋ ˌduˑər] *s* Missetäter –in *mf*

wrong'do'ing *s* Missetat *f*
wrought' i'ron [rɔt] *s* Schmiedeeisen *n*
wrought'-up' *adj* aufgebracht
wry [raɪ] *adj* schief

X

X, x [eks] *s* vierundzwanzigster Buchstabe des englischen Alphabets
xenophobia [ˌzɛnəˈfobɪˑə] *s* Fremdenhaß *m*
Xerox [ˈzɪrɑks] *s* (trademark) Xerographie *f* ‖ **xerox** *tr* ablichten
Xer'ox-cop'y *s* Ablichtung *f*

Xmas [ˈkrɪsməs] *adj* Weihnachts– ‖ *s* Weihnachten *pl*
x'-ray' *adj* Röntgen– ‖ *s* (*picture*) Röntgenbild *n*; **x-rays** Röntgenstrahlen *pl* ‖ *tr* röntgen
x'-ray ther'apy *s* Röntgentherapie *f*
xylophone [ˈzaɪlə ˌfon] *s* Xylophon *n*

Y

Y, y [waɪ] *s* fünfundzwanzigster Buchstabe des englischen Alphabets
yacht [jɑt] *s* Jacht *f*
yacht' club' *s* Jachtklub *m*
yam [jæm] *s* Yamwurzel *f*
yank [jæŋk] *s* Ruck *m*; **Yank** Ami *m* ‖ *tr*—**y. s.th. out of** reißen aus ‖ *intr* —**y. on** heftig ziehen an (*dat*)
Yankee [ˈjæŋki] *s* Yankee *m*
yap [jæp] *s* (*talk*) (sl) Geschwätz *n*; (*mouth*) (sl) Maul *n*; (*bark*) Gekläff *n* ‖ *v* (*pret & pp* **yapped;** *ger* **yapping**) *intr* (*bark*) kläffen; (*talk*) (sl) schwätzen
yard [jɑrd] *s* (*measure*) Yard *n*; (*ground adjoining a building*) Hof *m*; (naut) Rahe *f*; (rr) Rangierbahnhof *m*
yard'arm' *s* (naut) Nock *f & n*
yard' mas'ter *s* (rr) Rangiermeister *m*
yard'stick' *s* Yardmaß *n*; (fig) Maßstab *m*
yarn [jɑrn] *s* (*thread; story*) Garn *n*; **spin yarns** (fig) Garne spinnen
yaw [jɔ] *s* (aer, rok) Schwanken *n*; (naut) Gieren *n* ‖ *intr* (aer, rok) schwanken; (naut) gieren
yawl [jɔl] *s* (naut) Jolle *f*
yawn [jɔn] *s* Gähnen *n* ‖ *intr* gähnen; (*said, e.g., of a gorge*) klaffen
ye [ji] *pers pron* ihr
yea [je] *s* Jastimme *f* ‖ *adv* ja
yeah [je] *adv* ja
year [jɪr] *s* Jahr *n*; **all y. round** das ganze Jahr hindurch; **a y. from today** heute übers Jahr; **for years** seit Jahren; jahrelang; **in years** seit Jahren; **y. in y. out** jahraus jahrein
year'book' *s* Jahrbuch *n*
yearling [ˈjɪrlɪŋ] *s* Jährling *m*
yearly [ˈjɪrli] *adj & adv* jährlich
yearn [jʌrn] *intr*—**y. for** sich sehnen nach; **y. to** (*inf*) sich danach sehnen zu (*inf*)
yearn'ing *s* Sehnsucht *f*

yeast [jist] *s* Hefe *f*
yell [jɛl] *s* Ruf *m*, Aufschrei *m*; (sport) Kampfruf *m* ‖ *tr* (gellend) schreien; **y. one's lungs out** sich tot schreien ‖ *intr* schreien; **y. at** anschreien
yellow [ˈjɛlo] *adj* gelb; (sl) feige ‖ *s* Gelb *n* ‖ *tr* gelb machen ‖ *intr* vergilben
yellowish [ˈjɛloˑɪʃ] *adj* gelblich
yel'lowjack'et *s* Wespe *f*
yel'low jour'nalism *s* Sensationspresse *f*
yel'low streak' *s* Zug *m* von Feigheit
yelp [jɛlp] *s* Gekläff *n* ‖ *intr* kläffen
yen [jen] *s* (*Japanese money*) Yen *m*; (**for**) brennendes Verlangen *n* (nach)
yeo·man [ˈjomən] *s* (**–men**) (nav) Verwaltungsunteroffizier *m*
yeo'man's serv'ice *s* großer Dienst *m*
yes [jes] *adv* ja; **yes, Sir** jawohl ‖ *s* Ja *n*; **say yes to** bejahen
yes' man' *s* Jasager *m*
yesterday [ˈjɛstər ˌde] *adv* gestern; **y. morning** gestern früh ‖ *s* Gestern *n*; **yesterday's** gestrig
yet [jet] *adv* (*still*) noch; (*however*) doch; (*already*) schon; **and yet** trotzdem, dennoch; **as yet** schon; **not yet** noch nicht ‖ *conj* aber
yew [ju] *s* Eibe *f*
Yiddish [ˈjɪdɪʃ] *adj* jiddisch ‖ *s* Jiddisch *n*
yield [jild] *s* Ertrag *m* ‖ *tr* (*profit*) einbringen; (*interest*) tragen; (*crops*) hervorbringen; (*give up*) überlassen ‖ *intr* (**to**) nachgeben (*dat*)
yo-del [ˈjodəl] *s* Jodler *m* ‖ *v* (*pret & pp* **–del[l]ed;** *ger* **–del[l]ing**) *intr* jodeln
yodeler [ˈjodələr] *s* Jodler –in *mf*
yogurt [ˈjogurt] *s* Yoghurt *m & n*
yoke [jok] *s* (*part of harness; burden*) Joch *n*; **pass under the y.** sich in ein Joch fügen; **y. of oxen** Ochsengespann *n* ‖ *tr* ins Joch spannen

yokel [ˈjokəl] s Bauerntölpel m
yolk [jok] s Dotter m & n
yonder [ˈjɑndər] adv dort drüben
yore [jor] s—of y. vormals
you [ju] pers pron du; (plural form) ihr; (polite form) Sie; **to you** dir; (plural form) euch; (polite form) Ihnen; **you of all people!** ausgerechnet Sie! ‖ indef pron man
young [jʌŋ] adj (younger [ˈjʌŋgər]; youngest [ˈjʌŋgɪst]) jung; **y. for one's age** jugendlich für sein Alter ‖ spl (of animals) Jungen pl; **the y.** die Jungen, die Jugend; **with y.** (pregnant) trächtig
young′ la′dy s Fräulein n
young′ man′ s junger Mann m; (boyfriend) Freund m
youngster [ˈjʌŋstər] s Jugendliche mf
your [jur] poss adj dein; (plural form) euer; (polite form) Ihr
yours [jurz] poss pron deiner; (plural form) eurer; (polite form) Ihrer; **y. truly** hochachtungsvoll
your·self [jurˈself] intens pron (–selves [ˈselvz]) selbst, selber ‖ reflex pron dich; (plural form) euch; (polite form) Sich; **to y.** dir; (polite form) Sich; **to yourselves** euch; (polite form) Sich
youth [juθ] s (youths [juθs], [juðz]) (age) Jugend f; (person) Jugendliche mf
youthful [ˈjuθfəl] adj jugendlich
youth′ hos′tel s Jugendherberge f
yowl [jaul] s Gejaule n ‖ tr & intr jaulen
Yugoslav [ˈjugoˈslɑv] adj jugoslawisch ‖ s Jugoslawe m, Jugoslawin f
Yugoslavia [ˈjugoˈslɑvɪ·ə] s Jugoslavien n
yule′ log′ [jul] s Weihnachtsscheit n
yule′tide′ s Weihnachtszeit f

Z

Z, z [zi] s sechsundzwanzigster Buchstabe des englischen Alphabets
zany [ˈzeni] adj närrisch ‖ s Hanswurst m
zeal [zil] s Eifer m
zealot [ˈzelət] s Zelot –in mf
zealous [ˈzeləs] adj eifrig
zebra [ˈzibrə] s Zebra n
zenith [ˈzinɪθ] s Scheitelpunkt m, Zenit m
zephyr [ˈzefər] s Zephir m
zeppelin [ˈzepəlɪn] s Zeppelin m
ze·ro [ˈziro] s (–ros & –roes) Null f ‖ tr—z. **in a rifle** Visier e–s Gewehrs justieren ‖ intr—z. **in on** zielen auf (acc)
ze′ro hour′ s Stunde f Null
zest [zest] s Würze f
Zeus [zus] s Zeus m
zig·zag [ˈzɪgˌzæg] adj Zickzack– ‖ adv im Zickzack ‖ s Zickzack m ‖ (pret & pp –zagged; ger –zagging) intr im Zickzack fahren
zinc [zɪŋk] s Zink n
Zionism [ˈzaɪ·əˌnɪzəm] s Zionismus m
zip [zɪp] s (coll) Schmiß m ‖ v (pret & pp zipped; ger zipping) tr (convey with speed) mit Schwung befördern; (fasten with a zipper) mit e–m Reißverschluß schließen ‖ intr sausen; **zip by** vorbeisausen ‖ interj wuppdich!
zip′ code′ s Postleitzahl f
zipper [ˈzɪpər] s Reißverschluß m
zircon [ˈzʌrkɑn] s Zirkon m
zither [ˈzɪðər] s Zither f
zodiac [ˈzodɪˌæk] s Tierkreis m
zombie [ˈzɔmbi] s (sl) Depp m
zone [zon] s (& geol) Zone f; (postal zone) Postbezirk m; (mil) Bereich m
zoo [zu] s Zoo m, Tiergarten m
zoologic(al) [ˌzo·əˈlɑdʒɪk(əl)] adj zoologisch
zoologist [zoˈɑlədʒɪst] s Zoologe m, Zoologin f
zoology [zoˈɑlədʒi] s Zoologie f
zoom [zum] s lautes Summen n; (aer) Hochreißen n ‖ intr laut summen; **z. up** (aer) hochreißen
zoom′ lens′ s Gummilinse f

METRIC CONVERSIONS

Multiply:	By:	To Obtain:
acres	43,560	sq. ft.
	0.4047	hectares
	0.0015625	sq. mi.
ampere-hours	3600	coulombs
atmospheres	76.0	cm. of mercury
	33.90	ft. of water
	14.70	lbs./sq. in.
British thermal units	1054	joules
	777.5	ft.-lbs.
	252.0	gram calories
	0.0003927	horsepower-hrs.
	0.0002928	kilowatt-hrs.
B.T.U./hr.	0.2928	watts
B.T.U./min.	12.96	ft.-lbs./sec.
	0.02356	horsepower
bushels	3523.8	hectoliters
	2150.42	cu. ins.
	35.238	liters
°C + 17.78	1.8	°F
centimeters	0.3937	inches
cm-grams	980.1	cm.-dynes
chains	66	ft.
circumference	6.2832	radians
cubic centimeters	0.0610	cu. ins.
cu. feet	1728	cu. ins.
	62.43	lbs. of water
	7.481	gals. (liq.)
	0.0283	cu. m.
cu. ft./min.	62.43	lbs. water/min.
cu. ft./sec.	448.831	gals./min.
cu. inches	16.387	cu. cm.
	0.0005787	cu. ft.
cu. meters	264.2	gals. (liq.)
	35.3147	cu. ft.
	1.3079	cu. yds.
cu. yards	27	cu. ft.
	0.765	cu. m.
days	86,400	seconds
degrees/sec.	0.1667	revolutions/min.
°F − 32	0.5556	°C
faradays/sec.	96,500	amperes
feet	30.48	cm.
	0.3048	meters
	0.0001894	mi. (stat.)
	0.0001645	mi. (Brit. naut.)

Multiply:	By:	To Obtain:
ft. of water	62.43	lbs./sq. ft.
	0.4335	lbs./sq. in.
ft./min.	0.5080	cm./sec.
ft./sec.	0.6818	mi./hr.
	0.5921	knots
fluid ounces	29.573	milliliters
furlongs	660	feet
	0.125	mi.
gallons	231	cu. ins.
	8.345	lbs. of water
	8	pts.
	4	qts.
	3.785	liters
	0.003785	cu. m.
gals./min.	8.0208	cu. ft./hr.
grains	0.0648	grams
grams	980.1	dynes
	15.43	grains
	0.0353	oz. (avdp.)
	0.0022	lbs. (avdp.)
hectares	107,600	sq. ft.
	2.47	acres
hectoliters	2.838	bushels
horsepower	33,000	ft.-lbs./min.
	2545	B.T.U./hr.
	745.7	watts
	42.44	B.T.U./min.
	0.7457	kilowatts
inches	25.40	mm.
	2.540	cm.
	0.00001578	mi.
ins. of water	0.03613	lbs./sq. in.
kilograms	980,100	dynes
	2.2046	lbs. (avdp.)
kg. calories	3086	ft.-lbs.
	3.968	B.T.U.
kg. cal./min.	51.43	ft.-lbs./sec.
	0.06972	kilowatts
kilometers	3280.8	ft.
	0.621	mi.
km./hr.	0.621	mi./hr.
	0.5396	knots
kilowatts	737.6	ft.-lbs./sec.
	56.92	B.T.U./min.
	1.341	horsepower
kilowatt-hrs.	2,655,000	ft.-lbs.
	3415	B.T.U.
	1.341	horsepower-hrs.
knots	6080	ft./hr.
	1.151	stat. mi./hr.
	1	(Brit.) naut. mi./hr.
liters	61.02	cu. ins.
	2.113	pts. (liq.)
	1.057	qts. (liq.)
	0.264	gals. (liq.)
	1.816	pts. (dry)
	0.908	qts. (dry)
	0.1135	pecks
	0.0284	bushels

369

Multiply:	By:	To Obtain:
meters	39.37	inches
	3.2808	ft.
	1.0936	yds.
	0.0006215	mi. (stat.)
	0.0005396	mi. (Brit. naut.)
miles		
statute	5280	ft.
	1.609	km.
	0.8624	mi. (Brit. naut.)
nautical (Brit.)	6080	ft.
	1.151	mi. (stat.)
mi./hr.	1.467	ft./sec.
milligrams/liter	1	parts/million
milliliters	0.0338	fluid oz.
millimeters	0.03937	inches
ounces		
avoirdupois	28.349	grams
	0.9115	oz. (troy)
	0.0625	lbs. (avdp.)
troy	31.103	grams
	1.0971	oz. (avdp.)
pecks	8.8096	liters
pints		
liquid	473.2	cu. cm.
	28.875	cu. ins.
	0.473	liters
dry	0.550	liters
pounds		
avoirdupois	444,600	dynes
	453.6	grams
	32.17	poundals
	14.58	oz. (troy)
	1.21	lbs. (troy)
	0.4536	kg.
troy	0.373	kg.
lbs. (avdp.)/sq. in.	70.22	g./sq. cm.
	2.307	ft. of water
quarts		
liquid	57.75	cu. ins.
	32	fluid oz.
	2	pts.
	0.946	liters
dry	67.20	cu. ins.
	1.101	liters
quires	25	sheets
radians	3437.7	minutes
	57.296	degrees
reams	500	sheets
revolutions/min.	6	degrees/sec.
rods	16.5	ft.
	5.5	yds.
	5.029	meters
slugs	32.17	lbs. (mass)
square centimeters	0.155	sq. ins.
sq. feet	0.093	sq. m.
sq. inches	6.451	sq. cm.
sq. kilometers	247.1	acres
	0.3861	sq. mi.

Multiply:	By:	To Obtain:
sq. meters	10.76	sq. ft.
	1.1960	sq. yds.
sq. miles	27,878,400	sq. ft.
	640	acres
	2.5889	sq. km.
sq. yards	0.8361	sq. m.
tons		
long	2240	lbs. (avdp.)
	1.12	short tons
	1.0160	metric tons
metric	2204.6	lbs. (avdp.)
	1000	kg.
	1.1023	short tons
	0.9842	long tons
short	2000	lbs. (avdp.)
	0.9072	metric tons
	0.8929	long tons
watts	3.415	B.T.U./hr.
	0.001341	horsepower
yards	36	inches
	3	ft.
	0.9144	meters
	0.0005682	mi. (stat.)
	0.0004934	mi. (Brit. naut.)

LABELS AND ABBREVIATIONS

BEZEICHNUNGEN DER SACHGEBIETE UND ABKÜRZUNGEN

abbr abbreviation—Abkürzung
acc accusative—Akkusativ
(acct) accounting—Rechnungswesen
adj adjective—Adjektiv
(adm) administration—Verwaltung
adv adverb—Adverb
(aer) aeronautics—Luftfahrt
(agr) agriculture—Landwirtschaft
(alg) algebra—Algebra
(Am) American—amerikanisch
(anat) anatomy—Anatomie
(angl) angling—Angeln
(archeol) archeology—Archäologie
(archit) architecture—Architektur
(arith) arithmetic—Rechnen
art article—Artikel
(arti) artillery—Artillerie
(astr) astronomy—Astronomie
(atom. phys.) Atomic physics—Atomphysik
(Aust) Austrian—österreichisch
(aut) automobile—Automobile
aux auxiliary verb—Hilfsverb
(bact) bacteriology—Bakteriologie
(baseball) Baseball
(basketball) Korbball
(bb) bookbinding—Buchbinderei
(Bib) Biblical—biblisch
(billiards) Billard
(biochem) biochemistry—Biochemie
(biol) biology—Biologie
(bowling) Kegeln
(bot) botany—Botanik
(box) boxing—Boxen
(Brit) British—britisch
(cards) Kartenspiel
(carp) carpentry—Zimmerhandwerk
(checkers) Damespiel

(chem) chemistry—Chemie
(chess) Schachspiel
(cin) cinematography—Kinematographie
(coll) colloquial—umgangssprachlich
(com) commercial—Handels-
comb.fm. combining form—Wortbildungselement
comp comparative—Komparativ
conj conjunction—Konjunktion
(crew) Rudersport
(culin) culinary—kulinarisch
(data proc.) data processing—Datenverarbeitung
dem demonstrative—hinweisend
(dent) dentistry—Zahnheilkunde
(dial) dialectical—dialektisch
(dipl) diplomacy—Diplomatie
(eccl) ecclesiastical—kirchlich
(econ) economics—Wirtschaft
(educ) education—Schulwesen
e–e a(n)—eine
e.g. for example—zum Beispiel
(elec) electricity—Elektrizität
(electron) electronics—Elektronik
e–m to a(n)—einem
e–n a(n)—einen
(eng) engineering—Technik
(ent) entomology—Entomologie
e–r of a(n), to a(n)—einer
e–s of a(n)—eines
etw something—etwas
f feminine noun—Femininum
(fa) fine arts—schöne Künste
fem feminine—weiblich
(fencing) Fechtkunst
(fig) figurative—bildlich
(& fig) literal and figurative—buchstäblich und bildlich
(fin) finance—Finanzwesen
(fb) football, soccer—Fußball
fut future—Zukunft
genit genitive—Genitiv
(geog) geography, Geographie
(geol) geology—Geologie
(geom) geometry—Geometrie
ger gerund—Gerundium
(golf) Golf
(gram) grammar—Grammatik
(gym) gymnastics—Gymnastik
(heral) heraldry—Wappenkunde
(hist) history—Geschichte
(horol) horology—Zeitmessung
(hort) horticulture—Gartenbau
(hum) humorous—scherzhaft
(hunt) hunting—Jagdwesen
(ichth) ichthyology—Ichthyologie

imperf imperfect—Imperfekt
impers impersonal—unpersönlich
ind indicative—Indikativ
indecl indeclinable—undeklinierbar
indef indefinite—unbestimmt
(indust) industry—Industrie
inf infinitive—Infinitiv
(ins) insurance—Versicherungswesen
insep inseparable—untrennbar
intens intensive—verstärkend
interj interjection—Interjektion
interr interrogative—Frage-
intr intransitive—intransitiv
invar invariable—unveränderlich
(iron) ironical—ironisch
j–m to someone—jemandem
j–n someone—jemanden
(journ) journalism—Zeitungswesen
j–s someone's—jemand(e)s
(jur) jurisprudence—Rechtswissenschaft
(libr) library science—Bibliothekswissenschaft
(ling) linguistics—Linguistik
(lit) literary—literarisch
(log) logic—Logik
m masculine noun—Maskulinum
(mach) machinery—Maschinen
(mech) mechanics—Mechanik
(med) medicine—Medizin
(metal) metallurgy—Metallurgie
(meteor) meteorology—Meteorologie
mf masculine or feminine noun according to sex—Maskulinum
    oder Femininum je nach Geschlecht
(mil) military—Militär-
(min) mining—Bergwerkswesen
(mineral) mineralogy—Mineralogie
mod aux modal auxiliary—Modalverb
(mount) mountain climbing—Bergsteigerei
(mus) music—Musik
(myth) mythology—Mythologie
m & f masculine and feminine noun without regard to sex—
    Maskulinum oder Femininum ohne Rücksicht auf Geschlecht
(naut) nautical—nautisch
(nav) navy—Kriegsmarine
neut neuter—sächlich
(obs) obsolete—veraltet
(obstet) obstetrics—Geburtshilfe
(opt) optics—Optik
(orn) ornithology—Ornithologie
(paint) painting—Malerei
(parl) parliamentary—parlamentarisch
(pathol) pathology—Pathologie
(pej) pejorative—pejorativ
pers personal—Personal-

(pharm) pharmacy—Pharmazie
(philos) philosophy—Philosophie
(phonet) phonetics—Phonetik
(phot) photography—Photographie
(phys) physics—Physik
(physiol) physiology—Physiologie
pl plural—Plural
(poet) poetical—dichterisch
(pol) politics—Politik
poss possessive—besitzanzeigend
pp past participal—Partizip Perfekt
pref prefix—Präfix
prep preposition—Präposition
pres present—Gegenwart
pret preterit—Präteritum
pron pronoun—Pronomen
pros prosody—Prosodie
(Prot) Protestant—protestantisch
(psychol) psychology—Psychologie
(public sign) Hinweisschild
(rad) radio—Radio
(radar) Radar
recip reciprocal—wechselseitig
ref reflexive verb—Reflexivverb
reflex reflexive—reflexiv
rel relative—relativ
(relig) religion—Religion
(rhet) rhetoric—Rhetorik
(rok) rocketry—Raketen
(rr) railroad—Eisenbahn
s substantive—Substantiv
(sculp) sculpture—Bildhauerkunst
sep separable—trennbar
(sewing) Näherei
sg singular—Einzahl
(sl) slang—Slang
s.o. someone—jemand
s.o.'s someone's—jemand(e)s
spl substantive plural—pluralisches Substantiv
(sport) sports—Sports
(st. exch.) stock exchange—Börse
subj subjunctive—Konjunktiv
suf suffix—Suffix
super superlative—Superlativ
(surg) surgery—Chirurgie
(surv) surveying—Vermessungswesen
(tech) technical—Fachsprache
(telg) telegraphy—Telegraphie
(telp) telephone—Fernsprechwesen
(telv) television—Fernsehen
(tennis) Tennis
(tex) textiles—Textilien
(theat) theater—Theater

(theol) theology—Theologie
tr transitive—transitiv
(typ) typography—Typographie
usw. and so forth—und so weiter
v verb—Verb
var variant—Variante
(vet) veterinary medicine—Veterinärmedizin
(vulg) vulgar—vulgär
(zool) zoology—Zoologie